1980 Writer's Market

1980 Writer's Market

where to sell what you write

Edited By
William Brohaugh

Assistant Editor
Judith Ann Beraha

Assisted By
Barbara Kuroff

Writer's Digest Books
Cincinnati, Ohio

About this Book

This is the first edition of *Writer's Market* produced on a computerized word processing system recently installed in the Writer's Digest Books editorial offices. Developed by the Quadex Corporation, Boston, the system is designed to store all the material in the book on a magnetic disk, which allows for easy and immediate access to information. Thus we have a master file of the most current markets information available. The market listings are read—and updated—on a video display terminal—much like a TV screen.

The text of the book was set in Times Roman, a type face designed by Stanley Morrison at the turn of the century for the *London Times*. It is a practical "work-horse" type which, because of its legibility, allows us to pack a generous amount of type onto the page, thus keeping *Writer's Market* to a convenient size.

The book is printed on a blue-white shade of Madison Superset, an uncoated groundwood paper, and is adhesive bound and attached to a hard case.

Barron Krody, a Cincinnati freelance artist, created the interior book design using supergraphic letters and numbers to contrast with the text. He chose a two-column layout for the articles in the front of the book and the market section introductions so as to visually separate this material from the market listings.

The book jacket showcases tools of the writing trade that—along with the markets inside—will help you "ring up" those freelance sales on the 1890s brass cash register. The jacket was designed and photographed by Lawrence Zink Inc.

Writer's Market. Copyright© 1979. Published by Writer's Digest Books, 9933 Alliance Rd., Cincinnati, Ohio 45242. Publisher/Editorial Director: Richard Rosenthal. Managing Editor: Douglas Sandhage. Assistant to the Managing Editor: Connie Achabal. Printed and bound in the United States of America.

Library of Congress Catalog Number 31-20772
International Standard Serial Number 0084-2729
International Standard Book Number 0-89879-000-X

Preface

Some people seem to think of writing as some mystical alchemy in which worthless blank paper is transformed into golden words (i.e., something from nothing). Or they think writing results from some happy accident (witness the silly maxim that equates *Hamlet* with an infinite number of monkeys pecking at an infinite number of typewriters). They think writers do nothing more than create.

Writers *do* create, but to describe them simply as creators is to slight them. Writers are observers. They are interpreters, chroniclers, organizers, idea-generators, thinkers. They're workers.

Consolidating so many duties into a single profession isn't easy. That's why we at *Writer's Market* respect writers and writing. The fact that we're writers ourselves doesn't hurt; in fact, it helps us understand writers' problems, needs and skills.

It also helps in compiling *Writer's Market*. It's a product that makes us proud, edited for a profession that makes us proud.

—William Brohaugh, Judith Ann Beraha, Barbara Kuroff

All markets in *Writer's Market* are updated annually to ensure accuracy. Since publication of the 1979 edition, the following important changes have occurred and have been corrected in this 1980 edition:

Address Changes. . .356

Editor Changes. . .493

Changes in Editorial Requirements. . .2,157

In addition, there are 650 listings that appear for the first time in this edition. 791 listings that appeared in the 1979 edition have been deleted from the 1980 book for one of the following reasons: (1) The market no longer accepts freelance material; (2) The market asked to be deleted from the book; (3) The market did not respond to our three or more requests for updated information; (4) The market changed its freelance needs and we felt it no longer was of service to our readers; and (5) The market resulted in our receiving complaints about it and we deleted it.

It is important for the freelance writer to have *Writer's Market 1980,* which contains the most recent market information available. It can result in much time and money saved.

Contents

Opportunities & Services

Glossary

Index

Writers and Writing

Using Your Writer's Market

Writer's Market, like any tool, must be used properly to be effective. This book is more than a compendium of names and addresses; it is a chronicle of information a writer *must* know in order to sell to a particular market. Close examination of the book as a whole and of individual listings is, therefore, essential.

Start by reading the material in the front portion of the book introducing you to the writing field. Here you'll find information on writing query letters, preparing manuscripts, copyright and other legal tips, and the many fascinating and lucrative ways writers can sell their work. These articles discuss the basics of professional writing. Learn those basics, because even the best word-craftsman won't make a sale if he doesn't act professionally in the market.

After reading the introductory material, move on to The Markets section. Listed here are thousands of places that will consider freelance work, ranging from play producers to magazines to book publishers. Markets are categorized according to their type, and, often, according to their subject needs. Almost 180 categories compose the trade journals and consumer publications sections alone; obviously a market exists for almost *any* kind of writing.

Don't limit your marketing to a single category. Editorial needs often overlap, so a writer might make a sale in any of a number of places. An article about a movie star who jogs, for example, could be sold to a general-interest magazine, a sports publication, the city magazine where the star lives, etc. With sufficient rewriting and new information, the same article can be sold to *all* three publications. Because some publications accept previously published work, you can resell the article printed in the general-interest magazine to a sports publication that reprints material, if you still own the rights to the piece. (Try to maintain your rights to anything you sell. See "Stand Up for Your Rights" for more information.)

Letting you know if a particular magazine accepts previously published submissions—and all other needs and requirements of any market—is the purpose of *Writer's Market*. Listings are designed to efficiently relate a buyer's policies, requirements and editorial needs. Each listing is stuffed with information, and is a how-to manual in itself. Consider these samples, taken from the Book Publishers and Periodicals sections:

E.P. DUTTON, 2 Park Ave., New York NY 10016. (212)725-1818. Editor-in-Chief, General Books: Henry Robbins. Editorial Director, Special Books (formerly Sunrise): Constance Schrader. Editor, Juvenile Department: Ann Durell. Editor, Dutton Paperbacks: Cyril Nelson. Editor, Windmill Books: Robert Kraus. Imprints include Dutton Paperbacks, Thomas Congdon Books, Henry Robbins Books, Everyman Library, Windmill Books, Phaidon Books and Unicorn Books. Estab. 1852. Published 137 titles in 1978, 125 in 1979; plans 100 in 1980. Pays variable royalty and advance. Simultaneous and photocopied submissions OK. SASE. Reports in 1 month.
Nonfiction: Americana, animals, biography, business/economics, history, humor, juveniles, music, nature, philosophy, photography, politics, psychology, reference, religion, science, sociology, sports, technical, fine arts, memoirs, belles-lettres translations. Query. Recently published *Star Shots*, by John Engstead (photography/film); *Alan Chadwick's Enchanted Garden*, by Tom Cuthberson (gardening/philosophy); and *Mosquitoes, Malaria and Man*, by Gordon Harrison (science/history).
Fiction: Novels of "permanent literary value," quality paperbacks and juveniles. Adventure, confession, erotica, experimental, fantasy, gothic, historical, humor, mainstream, mystery, religious, romance, suspense and western. Query. Recently published *The World According to Garp*, by John Irving (literary novel); *Fear in a Handful of Dust*, by John Ives (suspense); and *Fair Blows the Wind*, by Louis L'Amour (western).

NUESTRO: THE MAGAZINE FOR LATINOS, 1140 Avenue of the Americas, New York NY 10036. Editor-in-Chief: Charles R. Rivera. Managing Editor: Philip Herrera. 85% freelance written. Monthly magazine; 64 pages. Estab. April 1977. Circ. 190,000. Pays on publication. Buys all rights, but may reassign following publication. Pays 50% kill fee. Byline given. Phone queries OK. Photocopied submissions OK. SASE. Reports in 6 weeks. Free sample copy and writer's guidelines.
Nonfiction: General interest (politics, sports, religion, education, housing, etc.) material related to Latinos living in the US. Query or submit complete ms. Length: 750-3,000 words. Pays $50-500.
Photos: Donna Nicholson, photo editor. State availability of photos with query or ms. Pays $50-100 for 8x10 b&w semigloss prints; $75-150 for 35mm color transparencies. Buys first North American serial rights. Model release "preferred, but it depends on the situation." SASE.
Columns/Departments: Yesterday (articles on events of recent or distant past); Travel; Fashions; Food; Music; and Reviews (books, movies and arts). "All material must relate directly to Latinos." Query or submit complete ms. Length: 500-2,000 words. Pays $35-100/printed page.
Fiction: "Submissions must be in English, of high quality and a Latino slant." No erotica. Query or submit complete ms. Length: 2,000-3,000 words. Pays $100/printed page.

All information in the listings have been provided and approved by the buyer/editor (or a member of his staff), so they are reported precisely as the buyer/editor wanted them stated. Consider each fact carefully before putting anything on paper. The value of some statements—such as preferred word length, required article slant, how to contact the market, preferred subject matter—is obvious. But other facts should be considered, too. The year the publication or firm was established, for example, can tell the writer this: Older publications and firms are usually more stable than newer ones, though the newer ones might be more receptive to new writers because these markets lack the contacts an older one might have. Exceptions do, of course, exist, but this example demonstrates that listings should be *interpreted*, in addition to being carefully read.

If you don't have a certain magazine or area of publishing in mind, glance through the table of contents. Once you find a section that interests you, read that section thoroughly. You may find just the market you want, or an idea may be spawned from an editor's comments.

Don't take wild swings at markets. If you swing an ax at a tree and miss, you can wound yourself. You can wound your freelance career by swinging wildly at a market by submitting *anything* to it, hoping that it *might* sell. Editors make mental notes about freelancers who have submitted material way off the mark, and will remember the name later. We've received letters from a number of editors complaining about freelance writers who don't read market listings properly. (Read "Abusing Your Writer's Market" for one editor's view of freelancers who misuse market listings.) If a listing states that the publication or firm wants queries only, *don't* expect to beat the crowd by sending in a completed manuscript, no matter how extraordinary you might think it is. Violation of the rules stated in listings rarely brings more than a rejection slip—and not even that if the editor asks you to enclose a self-addressed, stamped envelope (SASE) and you haven't.

Information in listings is as current as possible, but editors come and go, companies and publications move, and editorial needs change between the publication date of *Writer's Market* and when you buy it. Drop us a note if you have any new information about a market, because we research, review and update all listings annually. Listings for new markets and changes in others can be found throughout the year in *Writer's Digest*, the monthly magazine for freelancers. If you know of a market not listed in this book, write us and give the market's name and address; we'll solicit it for the next edition.

When looking for a specific market, check the index. A market might not be listed for one of these reasons: 1) It doesn't solicit freelance material. 2) It has gone out of business. 3) It doesn't pay for material (we have, however, included nonpaying listings in the journalism, literary, alternative, poetry and education categories because publication in those magazines could be valuable to a writer). 4) It has failed to verify or update its listing for the 1980 edition. 5) It requests to not be listed. 6) Complaints have been received about it, and it hasn't answered *Writer's Market* inquiries satisfactorily.

Problems occasionally arise in dealings with editors. *Writer's Market* editors will look into any complaints related to these two areas: 1) nonpayment of a promised sum for accepted material (or getting less payment than promised) and 2) an editor/publisher's failure to report on *solicited* material. Promises *must* be made in writing; send us photocopies of the unfulfilled agreements. Enclose

SASE with any correspondence with us. Letters concerning complaints other than those mentioned above will *not* be acknowledged unless the complaint is serious. *No* letters lacking SASE will be acknowledged (postal increases affect editors, too). Letters will be filed and later reviewed when we publish subsequent editions of this book.

If you're just getting started in freelance writing, write us and request our free reprint, "Getting Started in Writing," by Allan Eckert. Preferred manuscript submission procedures, facts on book contracts, a sample of manuscript preparation, and a list of commonly asked questions are covered. Send SASE to Mechanics Editor, *Writer's Market*, 9933 Alliance Rd., Cincinnati 45242. Also geared to beginners is *The Beginning Writer's Answer Book*, published by Writer's Digest Books.

Now you can put paper in your typewriter.

State Abbreviations

Each listing in this book uses the US Postal Service's two letter state abbreviations in the address line. They are as follows:

AK	Alaska	LA	Louisiana	OK	Oklahoma
AL	Alabama	MA	Massachusetts	OR	Oregon
AR	Arkansas	MD	Maryland	PA	Pennsylvania
AZ	Arizona	ME	Maine	PR	Puerto Rico
CA	California	MI	Michigan	RI	Rhode Island
CO	Colorado	MN	Minnesota	SC	South Carolina
CT	Connecticut	MO	Missouri	SD	South Dakota
DC	District of Columbia	MS	Mississippi	TN	Tennessee
DE	Delaware	MT	Montana	TX	Texas
FL	Florida	NC	North Carolina	UT	Utah
GA	Georgia	ND	North Dakota	VA	Virginia
HI	Hawaii	NE	Nebraska	VI	Virgin Islands
IA	Iowa	NH	New Hampshire	VT	Vermont
ID	Idaho	NJ	New Jersey	WA	Washington
IL	Illinois	NM	New Mexico	WI	Wisconsin
IN	Indiana	NV	Nevada	WV	West Virginia
KS	Kansas	NY	New York	WY	Wyoming
KY	Kentucky	OH	Ohio		

Abusing Your Writer's Market

By Joe Zambone

Only about 3% of the hundreds of freelancers I've "met" through the mail over the past few years will ever become a success at the business. The remaining 97% who won't make it have one thing in common—they know how to read a market listing to get an address, but stop there without learning what the particular publication wants to see from freelancers.

My prediction comes from long experience behind an editor's desk. Some time back *Writer's Digest* ran a market listing for a monthly tabloid camping newspaper, which I then edited. The listing stressed that I wanted material about family camping, especially with recreational vehicles (RVs); it instructed writers to send for a free sample copy, and to enclose SASE with all manuscripts; it mentioned that we were willing to read anyone once because we wanted to help beginning freelancers.

Within days of the listing's appearance, a Pandora's Box of material landed on my desk, and my Alka-Seltzer intake rose dramatically. One fact became painfully evident almost immediately: Darned few writers had really read the listing beyond the address and the statement that we'd try anyone once.

For weeks frustrated and unpublished writers crawled out of the woodwork to drop manuscripts in their mailboxes; my sideburns turned gray. While the terrible writers were sending in what had been rejected a dozen times elsewhere, the smart ones sent for the free sample copy. They knew enough to read a publication before hitting it with an article, and some of them sold articles to me. The others? Nope.

Over the following months I kept a tally, just for my own information, as to what was wrong with submissions. If you really want to make it into print, don't duplicate the mistakes I discovered:

Hitting the Wrong Market. Fully 90% of the manuscripts should never have been sent to my publication. One of the first items received was a dissertation on how to win at blackjack by cheating; its companion, by the same writer, was about winning at billiards by cheating. This hardly applies to family camping.

I also received a nice story about how to build a rock garden, one on plant care on your screened porch, a ridiculous story about discouraging smoking in your presence (spray the offender's cigarette with a water pistol!), and a story about how to cheat service station owners out of a few pennies' worth of gas.

By the end of the first week, I had the feeling that no one had even read the market listing requirements, let alone the publication itself. Things got worse. Along came an article on various lovemaking positions in a recreational vehicle—really appropriate for my Southern Baptist readership. That one made the rounds quickly, and was returned with a nasty note from the editor.

Failure to Read the Listing Thoroughly and Entirely. So far I've touched on only the *blatant* failures. Other articles came closer, but still failed. Although the market listing had clearly spelled out the Southeast as our distribution area, dozens of submissions prominently featured other locales, including one about camping Alaska. You can't get much farther away from the Southeast (or from a sale to a publication about the Southeast) than that. An editor doesn't specify something like general location to fill space in a listing, and many writers wasted time writing darned good articles because they didn't realize that.

Several people with personal axes to grind wrote negative articles about RV dealers. I had clearly specified that no "soap box" material was needed. What's more, if any of these writers had read even one copy of the paper, they would have noticed that most of the advertising comes from the RV industry. When you have a publication that's distributed free, you naturally try to please those paying for it: the advertisers. Score several rejects for not paying attention. Moral? *Read* the listing, and the publication, thoroughly.

Although all writers have heard advice to study the publication before submitting, few follow the rule. I received a nicely done piece about saving money by camping in the family car in free rest areas. To publish that story would have amounted to heresy on my part, and would have cost us many advertisers. "The Ads: This is probably the most important reading you'll ever do," says Duane Newcomb in *A Complete Guide to Marketing Magazine Articles* (Writer's Digest Books). "The reason is that advertisers advertise the items in the magazines they think readers will buy. By looking at them, you can begin to get an idea of the reader himself, his income, his religion, what he will think about contemporary issues, and more." To this I add *amen*.

The market listing also mentioned that fiction was OK if it related directly to RVs. What did I get? The first was a story about a little old professor who had a sumptuous meal in a restaurant, then palmed some other fellow's check for far less money. I sent it back right after taking another Alka-Seltzer. It came back two weeks later with a cover letter explaining how the writer believed I should use the story because it revealed human

nature and could apply as well to RVs. I have yet to make the connection here, and I'd bet that the writer has yet to sell a story.

Another chap wrote a neat science fiction story about an extraterrestrial visitation that occurred while someone walked in the woods, but I rejected it because it didn't apply to family camping. If the writer had read the listing well, he would have saved time at his typewriter.

Perhaps 75% of the rejects could have been avoided had the writers paid attention to the market listing, and read a copy of the paper. I can hear the chuckles out there in the crowd now—*he means the other guy, not me, hee, hee, hee*—but all these glaring errors were made by folks who read the market listing. Spending years cultivating skill with the written word, only to lose out at the last minute by faultily reading a market listing, is a shame.

Failure to Note Information About Editorial Style. Plain words spend with us, as was pointed out in the market listing. Yet, I received a classic story written by a husband-wife team of supposedly well-published writers. The manuscript would have been fine for a doctoral dissertation, but for a family camping paper . . . *ugh!* They used 50-cent language. They got a 50-cent rejection letter because they ignored our style requirements.

No SASE. Market listings include the acronym "SASE" for a reason. It means you should enclose a self-addressed, stamped envelope for the return of the submission. Unless you're working with an editor on an assignment, always send SASE with submissions and queries. I have personally thrown out maybe three reams of paper with writing on it because of a missing SASE. Submissions received with postage due are another problem. When a manuscript comes in with one stamp missing, I'll pay for it and figure the writer's scales were off. When it zips in with 39¢ missing, it gets zipped into File 13: my wastebasket. If a writer spends hours at a labor of love, but doesn't care enough about it to put the proper postage on it or to accompany it with SASE, why should I care what happens to it? I don't.

Misspelled, Names. When my name as editor is misspelled, the submission gets an instant rejection without a reading. This isn't being hard or pompous on my part. The articles I use refer to directions, statistics and figures, and when a writer can't even get my name right out of a listing, I can't trust his figures. Instead of checking them all, which takes time, I reject his offering.

Sloppy Submissions. Pay attention not only to the information in the market listings, but to the advice given in other sections of *Writer's Market* as well. For example, pay heed to suggestions presented in the article, "Standard Manuscript Preparation"; it's important. Head down to your local Lincoln dealership and ask to see a $15,000 car with mud all over it. You won't find one. The folks there know enough to clean something up before they try to sell it. Writers should also clean up what they're trying to sell, or risk turning off an editor.

The rest of the rejections are accounted for by people who will never be writers. Lack of talent is something you and I can do nothing about, but if you can write, do yourself a favor and take the time required to read a market listing, and to *study* it. Then read the publication. This is National Save-an-Editor-From-Heartburn Week. Please do your part.

Joe Zambone is an editor/writer whose freelance credits include Writer's Digest *and* Popular Off-Roading.

The Two Faces of Freelancing

By William Brohaugh

Like many writers, I have two spouses. Both have pretty faces, but only one needs its keys cleaned now and again.

I courted my second spouse—my typewriter with its pretty typeface—for more than eight years before I became serious enough about writing to enter into a workable writer-typewriter "marriage" a few years ago. Before then, I wrote when inspiration coaxed me from my lethargy. I wrote to please only myself (and I suspected that anyone—including editors—who didn't share my pleasure suffered from cauliflower cranium). During that period I wrote short stories and plays, which I naively thought made me a *writer*. I wasn't.

I still write to please myself, but I now imagine myself a part of my eventual audience (I also remember that making a sale is one way of pleasing myself). I still grumble about editors with cauliflower (between the) ears. But dependence on inspiration no longer enslaves me, because I learned the importance of discipline and a professional attitude.

No typewriter is so easy to use that it anticipates your intentions and taps out your story without benefit of human touch. Three years ago I was only thinking about establishing a daily writing quota for myself. Three years ago I was a fool. At some pivotal point I evolved into a *writer* when I set a goal of writing 400 words a day. That figure doesn't seem like much; hell, you can almost count 400 words on one hand. Yet, that amount is almost two pages of typewritten copy. It's slightly more than a typeset page in a typical paperback. It's a novel in just 150 days of steady, disciplined work. Now I'm the tortoise, sure to win the race I never won when I depended on inspiration in my hare-brained pre-quota days. I can't totally wave off inspiration—it helped me produce many short stories and plays of which I'm proud. But many of those inspiration-fueled stories took a year and a half from idea to completion. I laugh at that now, because I can complete a discipline-fueled novel in about half the time.

A quota is especially important if, like I do, you hold down a fulltime job. After eight hours as an editor working with a mistress typewriter, I don't eagerly approach my typewriter at home. My quota beckons, however.

What's more, a quota is only a *minimum*. I never write only 400 words. Sometimes I write 404 words. Sometimes 480. Sometimes 2,200.

A quota gives you more than a steadily rising stack of papers. It gives you confidence. Writer's block can't grip you when you sit down to the typewriter knowing you've turned out at least 400 words of good material every day for the past 538 days. Looking back over your output, you'll realize that the 400 inspired words you wrote swiftly and easily yesterday are no better than the 400 you splashed sweat on the day before. Inspired work is no better than other work; you simply like it better when you're writing it.

My quota, of course, probably won't work for you. You might do more; you might do less. If you write poems, plays or movie scripts, a quota based on wordage won't do you much good. You might even find that you and quotas are incompatible. However, the form of discipline is secondary to developing it in the first place.

I discuss quotas in such detail because a quota is one element of the professional attitude a writer must have if he expects to sell regularly. A casual writer sells irregularly, if at all. As a former casual writer, I know.

Discipline and professionalism can be demonstrated in many ways. As I stumbled toward becoming a writer, I learned the importance of neat submissions, polished query letters and careful attention to market needs.

I also learned the importance of that much-maligned quality: ego. Writers must have a healthy ego, lest their insecurities stifle their creativities. My occasionally ailing ego is often cured by the two books written by Fred (the name has been changed to protect innocent me from a libel suit) that I keep on my desk at all times. Whenever I get discouraged or feel insecure, I take a look at Fred's books and remember the unmotivated plots, labored writing and characters that make cardboard look thick; I look at the nice covers and tell myself that some editor liked Fred's work—some editor will love mine. Find yourself a Fred and remember his or her work often. My Fred is one of my best ego-supports.

Memories of Fred taught me that a timid approach to the mailbox is nonsensical. Waylay the mailbox with queries and manuscripts. One freelancer I know keeps 50 queries and manuscripts before editors at all times. That number's a little high for the average writer, but keeping more than a handful of submissions in the mail at all times is wise. The more you submit, the higher the chances of selling. Besides, keeping the mailman busy eliminates anxiety attacks. Send out only one manuscript, and you'll hover around the mailbox, wringing your hands just a little harder every day you receive no word about it. It's like sending your only son to war. Dump a dozen or more in the mail, and you tend to forget about individual manuscripts.

Keep the mailbox busy with not only submissions, but also resubmissions. Don't let a rejection linger on your desk. I discovered that lingering rejections aren't much more pleasant than lingering diseases. You can't pack a disease into an envelope and send it away, but you can a rejected manuscript. Don't brood about rejections like I once did. Simply tell yourself that the editor couldn't use that particular manuscript or idea, and that, like a conscionable salesman, you don't want to sell anyone something he can't use.

That's another thing I learned with some difficulty: Editors are right. Sometimes. A science fiction short story I wrote was rejected by an editor who claimed the story had no plot. I shrugged off the comment and continued submitting the piece. To this date, no sale. Now, a couple of years after writing the story, I realize why. The damn thing has no plot. The rewrite starts the minute after I complete this article.

I say editors are sometimes right because of another science fiction story I wrote and submitted to *Analog*, then the top-paying science fiction magazine. "I regret having to return this story to you," the editor wrote. "I'm currently overstocked with stories on this theme. But I'm sure you'll have no trouble placing this elsewhere." Other editors weren't so sure. I still haven't sold the story, but I guarantee that if I haven't sold it by the time you read this, it will still be in the mail. I believe you should work any story you have faith in until you have exhausted all possible markets.

The same logic applies to ideas. Last year I wrote a short piece on the *Guinness Book of World Records* with a slant on writing records for *Writer's Digest*. Flipping a few pages in *Guinness*, I found some interesting equestrian records, which I covered in a piece sold to *Horse Lover's National Magazine*. Skipping around the record book, I found material that led to sales to *Rider*, *Model Retailer* and *Flower and Garden*. Good ideas can be reworked for different audiences. For example, if you can't sell the magazine parody you wrote, turn it into a novel. Sound ridiculous? Maybe, but that's what *I* did, and I'm pleased with the results.

When you present an idea to an editor, be prepared to back it up with writing. Failing to produce a manuscript after getting a go-ahead is one of the quickest ways to alienate an editor. I've made this mistake only once, but even now I still feel guilty about it. Present the requested material quickly. Speed impresses editors and leads to lasting writer-editor relationships. Last year a producer-director I know approached me about doing a short play to cap off his planned "tuba extravaganza"— three hours of music played by a 150-instrument tuba choir. I accepted the assignment on Friday, finished the rough draft on Saturday, presented the script on Monday. The script was accepted even more quickly than it was written—within the half hour.

One of the reasons acceptance came so quickly (and one of the reasons that I *know* the director will turn to me the next time he needs tailor-made material) is that I gave the producer-director flexibility by supplying the script ahead of schedule. He now had time to make needed changes and work out any flaws. Besides, my quickness in writing the play reassured him that I could be equally quick in making changes.

As it turned out, the director did request changes. He seemed a bit surprised when I didn't balk at the revisions, but instead made them quietly and quickly. I think he expected me to fulfill some *prima donna* playwright stereotype and start screaming some melodramatic nonsense like, "My words are my children; how can you mutilate them!" But, as I mentioned before, editors are sometimes right. In this case, making the changes not only improved the play, but also improved my professional relationship with the director.

When the play went into rehearsals, I felt again the joy of being a freelance writer. Whether done full- or part-time, freelancing is an enthralling, gratifying job. For me, freelancing is the excitement I felt in my freshman year of college when a play I had co-written became my first acceptance (the excitement about that play is rekindled every six months when I receive my royalty statement). It's the satisfaction I felt when a newsletter reprinted one of my favorite puns from a column I write as a freelancer (discussing the dash—called an "em dash" in typography—I wrote, "More than one editor has said, 'I think, therefore I em' "). It's the pride I feel knowing I'm entertaining and informing people, fascinating them with the interesting quote and the pertinent fact. It's the thrill I get when I interview famous people, or not-so-famous people that should be. Most of all, it's the realization that I share all these feelings with thousands of other writers who agree that writing is a wonderful, irresistable vocation.

That's why I say I'm happily married. Twice. When I go home tonight, I'll give one of my spouses a hug, and then start pecking at the other.

I think you'll understand which is which.

The Creative Query Letter

By Art Spikol

Sometimes I think that writers tend to view editors as stereotypically hard-nosed people with short attention spans who react to writing as if it were a laxative: that is, you don't buy it unless you need it. That's partly true—at least, the first two parts of the statement sometimes are. But the last—well, that's what's wrong with stereotypes; since they're based on appearances, they often ignore the human equation.

I proved this once when I was an advertising copywriter. I had to write an ad to motivate a group of doctors to buy a particular product—a teaching aid that could contribute greatly to the understanding of a particular treatment.

I thumbed through a few medical journals and magazines. Every ad, it seemed, featured a photograph of somebody in pain. Or somebody who had just found relief from pain. Or somebody in the process of changing from a person in pain to a person who was absolutely euphoric.

All in all, it was an extremely depressing cluster of ads. In fact, I doubted that doctors could be that different from the rest of us.

So I wrote a funny ad.

The client, normally conservative, went along with me, and the product sold like crazy.

This may sound like a strange beginning for an article about query letters, but it's really quite appropriate. Just as doctors are human beings first and doctors second, so are editors human beings first. And while doctors and editors *do* buy based on their professional needs, that may not always—or ever—be the best way to get their attention and cause them to respond positively.

There are two people inside every editor. The human being is the one that says, *Gee, this sounds like a story I'd like to read* in response to a good query. The professional asks pertinent questions: *Can I afford this? Do I need it? Can I justify buying it?* The professional will occasionally overrule the human being, but not as often as the human being will overrule the professional.

So, it makes sense to write to the human being. This is how the human being in me feels:

He wants an opening sentence strong enough to get him to the next sentence and the next, until he's read the whole letter.

He wants to care about your subject, and you have to make him care.

He should finish your letter wondering about all the answers you *haven't* provided.

He wants to know specifically what he'll be getting—what kinds of information, what point of view. And don't tell him you intend to be objective, because nobody is. He'll settle for *fairness*.

He wants to hear any special reasons why *you* should get the assignment.

He can't tell everything from a letter. If you have samples or clips, send them. If you don't, you'll probably have to offer to write the article on speculation—it'll give him a chance to get used to your work, and it'll get you a foot in the door.

If you have a gut feeling that what you're offering *isn't* quite right for his magazine, you're probably right.

He has purchased manuscripts with misspelled words, poor punctuation and occasional bad grammar, but even if you'd sold him every one he ever bought, you'd still have starved.

He doesn't want to hear your suggestions about how you could improve his magazine or how you could write an article better than so-and-so did it in a recent issue. If you don't like the magazine the way it is, you probably shouldn't be attempting to write for it.

In the nonfiction magazine writing class I teach, I have a few query letters I use as examples of what *not* to do. Each of them does something, or several things, almost guaranteed to discourage any editor. I'm not going to reprint the actual letters here, nor even the actual words (and, because I removed the names long ago, I've long since forgotten who wrote them)—but I am going to keep the examples similar enough so you can see why the "no thanks" letters went out to:

The person who wrote, "Such existences I perceive as the Skid Row life since it is there that one can often locate a vast panorama of emaciated forms immersed in alcohol seeking warmth and smelling like damp shoes," for trying too hard—without punctuation, yet.

The person who wrote, "Would you be interested in an article entitled, 'Star on the Rise'? It's about John Smith, who is one of the most promising politicians, at age 26, that our state has ever seen," because if I want to buy puff pieces, I'll go to a pastry shop or ask John Smith's mother to write the article.

The person who wrote, "I have recently done some research on the soft pretzel, and have found roots in Austrian tradition which relate to it. Knowing of the large number of Austrian immigrants in the Philadelphia area. . . ." because not only am I convinced that the number is smaller than the person thinks, but I'm *very* convinced that the story would be a bore to most readers, Austrian or not.

The person who wrote, "As a third-year journalism student who has never had the opportunity or background that is now available to publish an article, I've been struck with an idea which seeks recognition—namely, fathers and daughters in business with lucrative results. An article of this unprecedented nature would undoubtedly shed new light on the old saying, 'chip off the old block,' " because he sounds like a *freshman* journalism student.

The person who wrote, "The courts seem to circumlocute a policy of laissez faire, whereas Congress is evasive, and parents are inordinate," because I wouldn't want to force readers (or myself) through one paragraph like that, let alone an entire article.

The person who wrote me a hand-written, nearly illegible letter containing a decent story idea, wondering if we could supply someone to keep him company while he did the story, because the research was going to be boring. Don't laugh; it's true.

That's kind of an honor roll of queries that didn't quite make it, but I'm aware that some of the letters are rather extreme and some of these people may actually one day be writers. Their trouble was not knowing how to approach me. They figured that because I was an editor and they were just beginning writers—something of which I'm certain—they had to write something that was literally *beyond themselves* so I'd be impressed.

Meanwhile, I was looking for a simple, straightforward, interesting letter. In fact, let's take a look at what that third-year journalism student could have said:

"The '& son' that appears after the names of so many area businesses are gradually being

Ten Ways to Turn Editors Off

What you say:	What they think:
1. "Have you done a story yet about . . . ."	You should know this before you query. There are ways to find out.
2. "I am writing to give you the opportunity to publish . . ."	How did we get so lucky?
3. "Would you be interested in the truly hilarious (or tragic) story of . . . ."	I don't know if we can survive it.
4. "This is the kind of story you should be doing . . ."	Don't hold your breath.
5. "Just tell me which approach you'd like me to take . . . ."	Just tell us which approach is appropriate.
6. "The author can . . . ."	What're you, an agent?
7. "There would obviously be two sides to the story . . . ."	If it's obvious, isn't it a bit patronizing to tell us about it?
8. "I know I can write this better than so-and-so did for you some time back . . . ."	We'll bet your mother told you so.
9. "If you're not interested, please let me know, since I'm sure I can sell this elsewhere . . . ."	Go to it.
10. "I'll be willing to take a little less than your regular fee to get this published . . . ."	Yes, but we're not willing to pay less, assuming it's worth publishing.

joined by '& daughter.' In fact, there are now about a dozen of father-daughter partnerships in and around Philadelphia—from a dental lab to a trucker to an antique shop. And chances are good that it'll be the wave of the future as more women stop thinking primarily of marriage as a career.

I'd like to take a look at this new phenomenon, find out how these businesses make out both in terms of profitability and peaceful coexistence, and see what happens when I toss out the old sexist standard, 'Hey, hon, is the boss around?' Also: will the logical conclusion be mother-son and mother-daughter businesses?

"I've never been published, so I don't have any clips—but I'll work on spec if you're even mildly interested. I'm pretty good with a camera, too, so I'll send along contact sheets of each pair if you like. . . .

I'd have to say, "Okay." It's not a *great* letter, but it's readable, the language is clear, and I have a pretty solid idea as to what I'll be getting. And there's no risk—which is probably the best incentive for me to read the work of a writer with whom I haven't previously dealt.

That's all there is to it. Good thinking and a 15¢ stamp and you can put your idea in front of just about any editor in the country. The price is right, anyway.

The author of Magazine Writing: The Inside Angle *(Writer's Digest Books), Art Spikol is a former editor of* Philadelphia Magazine.

Standard Manuscript Preparation

Would you walk into a job interview wearing sneakers? Torn T-shirt? Egg yolk from your breakfast clinging to your chin?

No. Nor would you send a manuscript to an editor with wrinkled pages; whole paragraphs scratched out and corrections hastily (and illegibly) jotted in; a rust stain marking the former position of an aged paperclip. Yet, a surprising number of writers tuck such manuscripts into envelopes every day. The number of editors that tuck those manuscripts into the accompanying SASE for quick return to the writer *isn't* surprising.

To belabor a cliche, neatness counts, and what it counts is the extra money that demonstrating a conscientious, careful, *professional* attitude will earn you. This doesn't imply that having a superbly typed, well-scrubbed, perfect manuscript will guarantee a sale. The appearance of your submission is always second in importance to its content. But the appearance of your submission is an editor's first impression of you as a writer. Editors consider sloppy, careless submissions the work of sloppy, careless writers. They reason that a dog-eared, torn manuscript must have gotten into that condition somehow, probably by earning rejection slips from other editors. Previous rejection of a manuscript *shouldn't* prejudice an editor, but often does nonetheless.

The point is that professionalism shows. The writer who *cares* about his work, who cares about the appearance of the work, is a professional.

The base for all professional submissions is provided by your typewriter. Handwritten submissions are tantamount to editorial suicide; most editors refuse to read them. The typewriter needn't be fancy. One that doesn't shred your paper or leave stray ink spots on the manuscript is good enough. Similarly, the type size of the typewriter makes little difference, though *pica* type is larger and slightly easier to read than the other available size: *elite*. The kind of typeface used *does* matter, however. Don't buy a script typewriter; don't buy a radio station typewriter (which types in all capital letters) and consider it a bargain. Unusual typefaces are distracting.

Clean the typewriter keys before tackling a manuscript. Change the ribbon often enough to keep the letters crisp and easy-to-read. Avoid correcting mistakes by typing over them (these are called strike-overs). Use correction paper or fluid (Liquid Paper is a popular product, though others are available) to eliminate errors.

Don't, however, use erasable bond. Sure, two swipes with an eraser and the mistake has vanished, but erasable bond sticks to the fingers and is hard to handle. It also smears when edited on. Likewise, avoid onion skin (which is slightly easier to handle than toilet paper) and colored paper. Unless you're using it for the carbon copy, paper should be white, 8½x11, and of a good bond (between 16- and 20-pound paper is usual).

Thus prepared, type your name (and any desired pseudonym), address, telephone number, and word length of the manuscript onto the first page of the manuscript or on a separate title page. You can use two methods of estimating word length: multiply the number of pages by 250 for a pica typewriter or by 300 for an elite typewriter, or count the words on three "typical" pages and multiply the average by the number of pages in the manuscript. The first page is also the place to type your copyright notification, which consists of a phrase structured like this: c 1980 by I.M. DeWriter. (See "Stand Up for Your Rights" and "Copyrights and (Copy)Wrongs" for details on the use of the copyright notification.)

Center the name of your manuscript about a third of the way down the page in capital letters. Below the title, type your byline as you want it published. The story itself should start three lines below the byline.

Consecutive pages must be identified with your name, a key word from the title and the page number in the upper lefthand corner. If you're preparing a book manuscript, number the pages consecutively, not by chapters.

The number of lines appearing on each page should be uniform, as should the pages' margins. Leave about 1¼ inch at the top of the page, and about an inch on the sides and the bottom.

Always *double-space* your copy, unless the particular market prefers triple-spaced material. Double-space between paragraphs; extra space between paragraphs is distracting. Indenting paragraphs five spaces is enough to set them off. Indent long quotes and other references to be set off from the rest of the text with five extra spaces, but don't single-space them.

Paperclip, don't staple, manuscripts together once they're completed. Avoid plastic binders or other unusual methods of holding a manuscript together.

Unless the manuscript is very short (a couple of pages), use 10x13 mailing envelopes for submissions. Enclose a self-addressed, stamped envelope (SASE) for the manuscript's return (9x12 envelopes that can fit into a 10x13 envelope without being folded are available at stationery stores). Book manuscripts can be mailed in a box that typing paper comes in. Submit the pages loose, without stapling or binding in any way. Clip a self-addressed mailing label and return postage to the first page of the manuscript, along with mailing instructions (4th Class Manuscript Rate, First Class). Mark the box, "Save for return—label and postage enclosed," to assure the use of the box when your manuscript is returned.

You'll probably want to mail the manuscript via First Class, which is faster and more expensive than 4th Class Manuscript Rate. Also, the post office isn't required to return undeliverable 4th class mail to the sender. Clearly mark the rate by which the manuscript is to be delivered on both outside envelope and SASE. If you have enclosed photos, back the submission with cardboard and mark, "Photos, Do Not Bend" on the envelope. Use Certified or Registered mail only when conducting official correspondence (for example, inquiring about a manuscript's whereabouts).

When mailing via First Class, weigh the manuscript with an accurate scale and determine the postage needed. Don't guess. Putting too little postage on a submission irritates editors who have to pay postage due (some refuse and send the submission back unread), and putting too much on is a waste of your money.

Don't affix American postage to SASEs going to Canada or other foreign countries. American postage may delight foreign stamp collectors, but will not be honored by the postal system of the country in question. Affix postage from the particular country you're dealing with, or enclose International Reply Coupons, which can be exchanged for appropriate postage. International Reply Coupons can be purchased at any post office.

The last thing into the envelope is the cover letter, which should be brief and to-the-point. Editors aren't interested in your health or the history of the manuscript unless such information is germane to the submission. The letter should cover your qualifications to write the particular submission, as well as any other pertinent credits. If you're submitting your manuscript as a result of an editor's OK of a query, mention that in your letter or send along a photocopy of the editor's go-ahead.

With a neat, professionally prepared manuscript in the mail representing you to an editor, you can afford to put on your tennis shoes and torn T-shirt. You can type your next manuscript with egg yolk clinging to your chin. Just as long as none of the egg lands on the manuscript; to an editor, that manuscript is you.

Copyrights and (Copy)Wrongs

Despite their reputation as loners, writers often depend on friends for help. US copyright law is one such friend; in fact, it can be one of your best allies.

The copyright law protects your writing and your right to govern how it's used. It unequivocally recognizes the creator of the work as its owner, and grants the creator all the rights, benefits and, yes, *privileges* ownership entails.

In other words, the moment you finish a piece of writing—whether it be short story, article, novel, poem or even paragraph—the law recognizes that you and only you can decide how it's to be used.

This concept is so basic that stating it seems pointless. Yet, we're covering copyright law here for two reasons. First, the law gives writers power in dealing with editors and publishers, and they should understand how to use that power. Second, certain circumstances can complicate and confuse the concept of ownership. Writers must be wary of these circumstances, or risk losing ownership of their work.

Here, then, are answers to commonly asked questions about copyright law:

To what rights am I entitled under copyright law? The law gives you, as creator of your work, the right to print, reprint and copy the work; to sell or distribute copies of the work; to prepare "derivative works"—dramatizations, translations, musical arrangements, novelizations, etc.; to record the work; and to perform or display literary, dramatic or musical works publicly. These rights give you control over how your work is used, and assure you that you receive payment for any use of your work.

If, however, you create the work as a "work-for-hire," you *do not* own any of these rights. The person or company that commissioned the work-for-hire owns the copyright. The work-for-hire agreement will be discussed in more detail later.

When does copyright law take effect, and how long does it last? A piece of writing is copyrighted the moment it is put to paper. Protection lasts for the life of the author plus 50 years, thus allowing your heirs to benefit from your work. For material written by two or more people, protection lasts for the life of the last survivor plus 50 years. The life-plus-50 provision applies if the work was created or registered with the Copyright Office after Jan. 1, 1978, when updated copyright laws took effect. The old law protected works for a 28-year term, and gave the copyright owner the option to renew the copyright for an additional 28 years at the end of that term. Works copyrighted under the old law that are in their second 28-year term automatically receive an additional 19 years of protection (for a total of 75 years). Works in their first term also receive the 19-year extension, but must still be renewed when the first term ends.

If you create a work anonymously or pseudononymously, protection lasts for 100 years after the work's creation, or 75 years after its publication, whichever is shorter. The life-plus-50 coverage takes effect, however, if you reveal your identity to the Copyright Office any time before the original term of protection runs out.

Works created on a for-hire basis are also protected for 100 years after the work's creation or 75 years after its publication, whichever is shorter.

Must I register my work with the Copyright Office to receive protection? No. Your work is copyrighted whether or not you register it, although registration offers certain advantages. For example, you must register the work before you can bring an infringement suit to court. You can register the work *after* an infringement has taken place, and *then* take the suit to court, but registering after the fact removes certain rights from you. You can sue for actual damages (the income or other benefits you lost as a result of the infringement), but you can't sue for statutory damages and you can't recover attorney's fees unless the work has been registered with the Copyright Office *before* the infringement took place. Registering before the infringement also allows you to make a stronger case when bringing the infringement to court.

If you suspect that someone might infringe on your work, register it. If you doubt that an infringement is likely (and infringements are relatively rare), you might save yourself the time and money involved in registering the material.

I have an article that I want to protect fully. How do I register it? Request the proper form from the Copyright Office. Send the completed form, a $10 registration fee, and one copy (if the work is unpublished; two if it's published) of the work to the Register of Copyrights, Library of Congress, Washington, D.C. 20559. You needn't register each work individually. A group of articles can be registered simultaneously (for a single $10 fee) if they meet these requirements: They must be assembled in orderly form (simply placing them in a notebook binder is sufficient); they must bear a single title ("Works by Jon Dough," for example); they must represent the work of one person (or one set of collaborators); and they must be the subject of a single claim to copyright. No limit is placed on the number of works that can be copyrighted in a group.

If my writing is published in a "collective work"—such as a magazine—does the publication handle registration of the work? Only if the publication owns the piece of writing. Although the copyright notice carried by the magazine covers its contents, you yourself must register any writing to which *you* own the rights if you want the additional protection registration provides.

What else should I know about contributing to "collective works"? Collective works are publications with a variety of contributors. Magazines, newspapers, encyclopedias, anthologies, etc., are considered collective works. If you sell something to a collective work, state specifically—*in writing*—what rights you're selling. If you don't, you're automatically selling the nonexclusive right to use the writing in the collective work and in any succeeding issues or revisions of it. For example, a magazine that buys your article without specifying in writing the rights purchased can reuse the article in that magazine—but in no other, not even in another magazine put out by the same publisher—without repaying you. The same is true for other collective works, so always detail *in writing* what rights you're selling before actually making the sale (see "Stand Up for Your Rights" for more information).

When contributing to a collective work, ask that your copyright notice be placed on or near your published manuscript (if you still own the manuscript's rights). Prominent display of your copyright notice on published work has two advantages: It signals to readers and potential reusers of the piece that it belongs to you, and not to the collective work in which it appears; and it allows you to register all published works bearing such notice with the Copyright Office as a group for a single $10 fee. A published work *not* bearing notice indicating you as copyright owner can't be included in a group registration.

Display of copyright notice is especially important when contributing to an uncopyrighted publication—that is, a publication that doesn't display a copyright symbol and doesn't register with the Copyright Office. You risk losing copyright protection on material that appears in an uncopyrighted publication. Also, you have no legal recourse against a person who infringes on something that's published without appropriate copyright notice. That person has been misled by the absence of the copyright notice and can't be held liable for his infringement. Copyright protection remains in force on material published in an uncopyrighted publication without benefit of copyright notice if the notice was left off only a few copies, if you asked (in writing) that the notice be included and the publisher didn't comply, or if you register the work and make a reasonable attempt to place the notice on any copies that haven't been distributed after the omission was discovered.

Official notice of copyright consists of the word "Copyright," the abbreviation "Copr." or the symbol ©; the name of the copyright owner or owners; and the year date of creation (for example, "©1980 by Jon Dough").

Under what circumstances should I place my copyright notice on unpublished works that haven't been registered? Place official copyright notice on the first page of *any* manuscript, a procedure intended not to stop a buyer from stealing your material (editorial piracy is very rare, actually), but to demonstrate to the editor that you understand your rights under copyright law, that you own that particular manuscript, and that you want to retain your ownership after the manuscript is published. Seeing this notice, an editor might be less apt to try to buy all rights from you. Remember, you want to retain

your rights to any writing. For more on this, see "The Copyright War Between Editors & Writers" in the January 1979 issue of *Writer's Digest* magazine.

How do I transfer copyright? Do I want to? A transfer of copyright, like the sale of any property, is simply an exchange of the property for payment. The law stipulates, however, that the transfer of any exclusive rights (and the copyright is the most exclusive of exclusive rights) must be made in writing or isn't valid. Various types of exclusive rights exist; see "Stand Up for Your Rights" for details.

Again, it's best not to sell your copyright. If you do, you lose control over use of the manuscript, and forfeit future income from its use.

What is a "work-for-hire"? This is a work that another party commissions you to do. Two types of for-hire works exist: Work done as a regular employee of a company, and commissioned work that is specifically called a "work-for-hire" in writing at the time of assignment. The phrase "work-for-hire" or something close must be used in the written agreement, though you should watch for similar phrasings. The work-for-hire provision was included in the new copyright law so that no writer could unwittingly sign away his copyright. The phrase "work-for-hire" is a bright red flag warning the writer that the agreement he's about to enter into will result in loss of rights to any material created under the agreement.

Some editors and publishers, however, have perverted the purpose of the work-for-hire provision. Instead of seeing it as a warning flag used to help writers, they've adopted it as a banner with which to herald an attack on writers' rights. They offer work-for-hire agreements when making assignments, and expect writers to sign them routinely.

Avoid work-for-hire agreements. By signing them, you forfeit the potential for additional income from a manuscript. Suppose a magazine assigns you to write a solar energy story as a work-for-hire. A month after the story is published, an anthologist wants to reprint it in a collection covering alternative energy sources. A major television producer, fascinated with the unusual angle and compelling information used in the story, decides to option it for a documentary. A book publisher sees possibilities for a popular nonfiction book in the article. Now, the anthologist is willing to pay a flat $150 fee and a royalty percentage of book sales. The producer offers a four-figure option fee. The book publisher offers another four-figure advance against royalties. You, the author, don't see a penny of it; you don't own the copyright. *But if I write the book, won't I get paid for that?* you ask. Maybe—if the copyright owner gives you permission to prepare a "derivative work," which a book would be.

Granted, this is an extreme example (though it's not impossible). Many articles written as works-for-hire or to which all rights have been sold are never resold, but if you retain the copyright, you might try to resell the article—something you wouldn't do if you forfeited your rights to the piece.

Can I get my rights back if I sell all rights to a manuscript, or if I sell the copyright itself? Yes. You or certain heirs can terminate the transfer of rights 40 years after creation or 35 years after publication of a work by serving written notice to the person to whom you transferred rights within specified time limits. Consult the Copyright Office for the procedural details. This may seem like a long time to wait, but remember that some manuscripts remain popular (and earn royalties and other fees) for much longer than 35 years.

Must all transfers be in writing? Only work-for-hire agreements and transfers of exclusive rights *must* be in

writing. However, getting any agreement in writing before the sale is wise. Beware of other statements about what rights the buyer purchases that may appear on checks, writer's guidelines or magazine mastheads. If the publisher makes such a statement elsewhere, you might insert a phrase like "No statement pertaining to purchase of rights other than the one detailed in this letter—including masthead statements or writer's guidelines—applies to this agreement" into the letter that outlines your rights agreement.

Are ideas copyrightable? No. Nor can information be copyrighted. Only the actual expression of ideas or information can be copyrighted. You can't copyright the idea to do a solar energy story, and you can't copyright information about building solar energy converters. But you can copyright the article that results from that idea and that information.

Where do I go for more information about copyright law? Write or call (not collect) the Copyright Office (Library of Congress, Washington, D.C. 20559, 703/557-8700) for a free Copyright Information Kit. The Copyright Office will answer specific questions, but won't provide legal advice.

For more information about copyright and other law, consult these books: *Law and the Writer*, edited by Kirk Polking and Leonard S. Meranus (Writer's Digest Books); *The Writer's Legal Guide*, by Tad Crawford (Hawthorn Books); and *Law of Mass Communications*, by Harold L. Nelson and Dwight L. Teeter Jr. (Foundation Press).

Stand Up for Your Rights

Never let a manuscript rest.

Submit it and resubmit it until it's sold, and then work at selling it *again*. Any manuscript worthy of printing is worthy of reprinting. Many writers forget that material can be resold, and therefore lose an opportunity to make additional income.

Before you can resell any piece of writing, however, you must own the rights to that piece. If you have sold all rights to an article, for instance, it can be reprinted *without* your permission and without further reimbursement. That's why taking careful stock of what rights you sell is important.

Here are the types of rights buyers most often seek.

First Rights. The author sells the right to use a piece of writing for the first time. The writer can't allow any other use of the article until the purchaser of first rights has used it (the purchaser must use the material within a year, or rights revert back to the author). Once the buyer of first rights has used the material, you can resell it. *First rights* usually implies that you've sold the buyer the right to use the material for one time only, but it's best to state that in writing when selling the article.

Serial Rights. The author sells the right to use a piece of writing in a periodical ("serial" refers to the periodical nature of publications, and doesn't imply "serialization"). This type of right is often combined with others—for example, *first serial rights*, in which the author sells the right to use a piece of writing for the first time in a periodical. If you sell first serial rights, you still own, for example, *first book rights*. You can allow the article to be published in a book without interfering with the other party's claim to first serial rights. Remember, too, that if you sold first serial rights, you retain second serial rights, and can resell the article. Another common type of right purchased is *first North American serial rights*, in which the author sells the right to use a piece of writing for the first time in any periodical located in North America.

One-Time Rights. The author sells the right to use a piece of writing one time. This differs from *first rights* in that selling one-time rights gives the purchaser no guarantee that he will get first shot at publishing the article. *One-time rights* is most often used in regard to photo and graphic material, but can be applied to writing, too.

All Rights. The author sells all rights to a piece of writing, meaning the buyer can use the article however and as many times as he pleases, without further reimbursement offered the writer. Selling all rights is selling, in other words, ownership of the piece. The writer cannot use the piece again in its present form. If you sell all rights, you can get your rights back after 35 years under copyright law. See "Copyrights and (Copy)Wrongs" for more information.

As expected, few writers want to sell everything they own on what they write—unless, of course, the price is right. That's why—because the price usually isn't "that right"—you should avoid selling all rights. Consider that the article you sell once can be sold again and again. Yet, without right to do so, the writer loses that potential income.

Many of the publications listed in *Writer's Market* indicate that they buy all rights but will reassign those rights after the material's publication. The author must request such reassignment after publication.

The term *all rights* can be combined with other types of rights to specify exactly what is being purchased. For example, a magazine might seek *all serial rights*, in which case you can sell the piece to a book publisher, for example, but not to any other magazine.

The same is true when the phrase *exclusive rights* is used. You can sell exclusive rights to an article (synonymous with selling all rights), or you can sell more specific exclusive rights, for example, exclusive serial rights.

If you sign a "work-for-hire" agreement, you have signed away all rights (and the copyright) to the person making the assignment. You can't get your rights back after 35 years if you signed a work-for-hire agreement as you can if you sold all rights, so signing such an agreement is inadvisable.

Note: Rights discussed in this section are loosely referred to as *exclusive rights*, and no exclusive right to your material can be sold unless the transfer is stated specifically in writing.

Reprint Rights. The author sells the right to reprint an already published work. When selling a piece that's already appeared in print, you are offering reprint rights to buyers. Using terms like *first reprint rights* indicates to the buyer that he is the second user of the work and that no third buyer can use it before he does. *Second rights* and other such terms are sometimes used interchangeably with *reprint rights*.

Simultaneous Rights. The author simultaneously sells the right to use a piece of writing to more than one buyer. If you have a general feature story that's suitable for Sunday newspaper supplements, for example, you might sell simultaneous rights to a number of supplements whose circulations don't overlap. Religious magazines also often purchase simultaneous rights. By selling these rights, you have clarified to the buyers that others are using the story. Never sell simultaneous rights unless all parties involved

know you're doing so.

Before submitting material to a market, check its listing in this book to see what rights are purchased. Some buyers are adamant about what rights they'll accept; others will negotiate. In any case, the rights purchased should be stated specifically *in writing* sometime during the course of the sale, either in a letter or in some sort of written agreement. *Note:* If no rights are transferred in writing, and the material is sold for use in a collective work (that is, a work that derives material from a number of contributors), you are authorizing unlimited use of the piece in that work or in subsequent issues or updates of the work. Thus, you can't collect reprint fees if the rights weren't spelled out in advance, in writing. See "Copyrights and (Copy)Wrongs."

Give as much attention to the rights you *haven't* sold as you do to the rights you have sold. Be aware of the rights you retain, with an eye out for additional sales. If you sold exclusive North American rights to an article, for instance, you are free to sell the article in Europe. If you sold all serial rights to a short story, you can resell it to "nonserial" markets such as book publishers and film companies.

Whatever rights you sell or don't sell, make sure all parties involved in any sale understand the terms of the sale. Clarify what is being sold, for how long, and with what stipulations *before* any actual sale, and do it in writing. Don't restrict yourself to the terms we've defined here; if you must, take some space in a letter to outline specifically what you're relinquishing and what you're not. Communication, coupled with these guidelines and some common sense, will preclude harangues with buyers over rights.

Fair Pay for Freelancers

Writers deserve better.

Freelance writers are a boon to magazine publishing, saving publishers the expense of hiring a salaried writer and paying him fringe benefits. Yet this very economic usefulness is slowly cutting the freelance throat.

That's right: freelancers are being penalized for being useful. Consider the editor who, in 1970, paid $300 for a 3,000-word nonfiction piece. Chances are the same editor, himself earning more than he did in 1970, now pays $300 for a piece of equal length. With inflation working against him, the freelancer actually earns less for the article than he did nearly ten years ago. No pay raise in the space of a decade.

Writer's Market recently compared the 1970 pay rates of selected magazines with present rates, and discovered that several major women's magazines, for instance, now pay the same rates as they did in 1970. Some publications examined in the comparison had upped their rates, of course, but one magazine had actually cut payments, and another now pays just a penny a word more than they did in (we looked it up) *1940*.

One of the reasons pay for freelancers doesn't keep up with the rest of the economy is that writers are too often satisfied to accept, without question or negotiation, an editor's offer. Writers are either too ecstatic over making a sale or too afraid to offend an editor to think about bargaining. Granted, the average writer doesn't have a forceful bargaining position; if you are too stubborn in your demands, the editor will turn to another writer who's eager for a shot at publication. You build bargaining power by developing credentials, ability and reliability.

The only bargaining power available to new writers, therefore, is the option to accept or reject an assignment. Sometimes, quite honestly, accepting an assignment costs the writer more than he's being paid. Before accepting any project, consider carefully what it will cost you and weigh that against what the assignment is worth to you.

First consider how long it will take you to complete the project, and convert that into an hourly figure. Remember to add in research time, time spent soliciting the assignment, and potential rewriting time. Then consider some of the hidden costs of completing the assignment:

Supplies. Pencils, paper, postage, photocopies, typewriter ribbons—all cost money.

Transportation. Figure in time spent driving to and from interviews, as well as the cost of gas (which has *not* stayed the same in the past 10 years).

Depreciation of your equipment. Every time you use your typewriter, it takes one more step toward breakdown. Typewriters must be cleaned, too.

Insurance. You undoubtedly spend a certain amount of your income on insuring yourself.

Overhead. Whether you're a fulltime freelancer with a downtown office or a part-timer with an office in your home, you spend money heating, lighting, and paying rent for your work space.

Other considerations include the rights the editor wants to buy from you. You shouldn't sell all rights, but if you do, you should receive a much higher fee than you would if you sold only one-time rights. (See "Stand Up for Your Rights" for more information about rights.)

Consider, too, your own value to the editor. Are you reliable? Do you meet deadlines? If so, you have added value to the harried editor who couldn't force some of his writers to meet a deadline if he used a gun, and he should be willing to pay a little extra for your reliability.

Times occur, however, when you'll be willing to accept "low" payment. For instance, you might accept low-paying assignments to build your list of credits and, therefore, build your bargaining power when the next assignment comes up. When writer Robert Bahr accepted an assignment from *Human Behavior*, he considered the offered fee too low, but took the assignment anyway. "The loss was a promotional expense which I can afford a couple of times a year," he reports in "Getting Tough," an article he published in the April 1979 *Writer's Digest*. He considered the prestige value of a *Human Behavior* byline worth the loss he incurred. (The April 1979 *Writer's Digest* is a special "getting tough with editors" issue. Recommended reading, the issue can be ordered for $1.50 at 9933 Alliance Rd., Cincinnati 45242).

If you think payment offered for an article isn't enough, ask for more. Writers are too often afraid to negotiate. Don't be. Writer Florence H. Wright wasn't afraid to negotiate when an editor asked for all rights on an article she submitted. She didn't want to sell all rights because she wanted to use the article as a part of a book-length manuscript later, so she asked the editor if she could negotiate. The editor agreed to buy only first rights, reduced the fee from $75 to $60 (a nominal reduction, considering the value of the rights Wright retained), and bought the piece.

In this case, negotiation amounted to little more than a polite assertion of rights. Wright discovered that, as the old saw so appropriately points out, there's no harm in asking.

Other things writers should ask for include:

A definite assignment. Writing time is more efficiently applied to articles an editor has approved. Writing on speculation—that is, without a commitment from an editor to use the completed manuscript—is akin to wearing a blindfold while playing darts. Assignments usually aren't given to unestablished writers, who may be forced to write on spec until they have the bargaining power to command assignments, but that doesn't mean you can't ask.

A kill fee. This is a fee paid to you if an editor can't use an article you wrote *on assignment* for that magazine. Kill fees usually range from 20% to 33% of the original agreed purchase price. Some editors pay the full price for an article, even if he doesn't publish it. Only 27.5% of the editors questioned in a recent *Writer's Market* survey indicated that they pay a kill fee on assigned articles. Many of the 68.9% of those who pay no kill fee said they don't pay them because they don't make assignments. A full 3.6%—*nearly four editors out of every hundred*—had never even heard of a kill fee and didn't know what the term meant.

Payment on acceptance. In the above-mentioned "getting tough with editors" issue, writer J. David Truby uses this analogy: "You just bought a hefty new riding mower to trim your author's acres, but since you won't use it until June, you tell the clerk you won't pay for it until you use the machine. Want to wager how far that gimmick would go?" Like the clerk, you deserve payment when the product is purchased.

Reimbursement for expenses. Long-distance phone calls and transportation costs (and even film for your camera) are expenses that the magazine, not you, should absorb. "There's no reason even a new writer shouldn't mention expenses," says

Grace Weinstein, president of the American Society of Journalists and Authors (ASJA).

Higher fees the next time around. Most magazines have a range of fees. They offer fees at the lower end of that range to writers they haven't worked with before, and the fees go up once the writers prove their reliability. You should be paid more for the second article you do for a magazine than for the first.

Request these politely and in a businesslike manner. The worst the editor can do is say "No." If he does, you can then determine if the work is so important to you that you can't move on to the next market—and that is your decision to make. If he says, "Yes," then you've won a victory for yourself and for your freelance colleagues.

How Much Should You Charge?

By Kirk Polking

When you are approached by a local business or national organization for a special writing/editing job, how do you determine the "right" fee to charge?

You can contact writers or friends in a related business that has employed freelancers to get an idea of what's been paid for similar jobs. Otherwise, you must set a fee based on two considerations: how much you think your time is worth, and how much you think the client is willing or can afford to pay for the job.

Most freelancers, however, forget to figure overhead costs into their fees. A writer's "overhead work" is work not attributable to specific jobs, according to Bill Palmer of the Associated Business Writers of America. "For every four hours of interview, writing or travel, one hour or more goes into queries, negotiations, correspondence, phoning, bookkeeping, tax work, planning, purchasing, mailing, filing and maintenance. Publishing houses use secretaries, typists, clerks and bookkeepers for such work and their wages are charged to editorial budgets." The freelancer can charge these costs to no one but himself. In addition, most businesses figure a minimum of 20% over an employee's salary to be paid in fringe benefits: social security, unemployment insurance, paid vacations, hospitalization, retirement funds, etc. Freelance writers have no such fringes unless they pay for them directly. If you're serious about freelancing, quote a fee that includes a 20-25% markup for these overhead expenses.

One way to calculate your "hourly billing rate" is to figure out what you think an annual salary might be for the same type of work done by a staff person. Dividing that by 2,000 (approximately 40 hours per week for 50 weeks) will give you an hourly rate. For more about what should be considered when determining fees, see "Fair Pay for Freelancers."

Listed below are fees charged for certain jobs, as reported to us by freelance writers. Keep in mind that the rates paid by advertising agencies, businesses, retail stores and other consistent users of freelancers vary from city to city, so rates reported here can serve only as rough guidelines.

The list can also be used to locate freelance work you hadn't thought about before. Check this list against jobs in your local community to determine the freelance markets available in your own backyard.

Advertising Copywriting. Ad agencies need part-time help in rush seasons, but you might also contact small merchants who can't afford an agency. Fees range from $10 to $25 an hour. Some freelancers charge a package price, which might be just $25 for writing a press release or a small ad, on up to several hundred dollars for a more complex assignment.

Book Publishing. Jobs for freelancers include:

Book manuscript/copy-editing. $6-15/hour and up; occasionally, 75¢/page.

Indexing a book. $5-15/hour, or a flat fee.

Paperback cover or book jacket copy. $40-75.

Proofreading. 30-40¢/page; $4-10 an hour.

Preparing a reader's report on a book manuscript. $10 for a half-page summary of the book; half-page recommendation.

Manuscript ghost writing, rewriting and

content editing $350/day and up; $8-20/hour and up; or a flat fee.

Research. $5-10/hour.

Writing as-told-to books. Author gets full advance and 50% royalties; subject gets 50% royalties.

Writing a biography for a sponsor. $500-3,000, plus expenses.

Translation work. $25-50/thousand words minimum.

Business-Related Jobs. On the local level, these can range from copywriting ads for small retailers to writing annual reports and anniversary booklets for local manufacturers. On the national level, major corporations hire top writers and pay top rates. Some freelance rates for both regional and national jobs here include:

Announcement folders. $25-350, flat fee.

Annual reports $10-30/hour for brief report with some economic information and explanation of figures; $40-50/hour and up for a report that must meet Securities and Exchange Commission (SEC) standards, reports that use legal language, etc.

Booklets (writing and editing). $500-1,000, flat fee.

Business films. 10% of production cost of films up to $30,000; $150/day or $20/hour where percentage not applicable.

Catalogs or brochures for business. $60-75/printed page; more if many tables or charts must be reworked for readability and consistency.

Commercial reports for business, insurance companies, credit agencies and market research firms. $1.85-5/report.

Company newsletters and in-house publications. $100-400 for 2-4 pages.

Consultation. $75-100/hour.

Editing text for business brochures and publications. $20-35/hour.

Ghostwriting business speeches in major markets. $2,750, flat fee.

Industrial and business brochures

(consultation, research and writing). $3,500, flat fee.

Industrial films. $500-1,200 for a 10-minute reel; 5-12% of the production cost of films that cost the producers $750-1,000/release minute.

Industrial promotions. $7.50-40/hour.

Industrial slide-films. 14% of gross production cost.

Industrial writing. $25-30/hour, including conference interview and writing time; long distance travel time and expenses billed separately.

In-house publications (writing and editing). $200-500 for a 2- to 4-page publication; $500-1,000/issue for editing (with some writing) a 16- to 32-page publication.

Miscellaneous business writing. $25-50/hour.

New product releases. $300-500 plus expenses.

Newspaper ads for small businesses. $25 for a small, one-column ad, or $3.50/hour and up.

Public relations for conventions. $500-5,000, flat fee.

Retail business newsletters. $200 for writing, photography, layout and printing supervision of 4-page publications.

Sales letter, business or industrial. $150 for one or two pages.

Shopping mall promotion. 15% of promotion budget for the mall.

Technical typing. $1-1.50/page.

Technical typing masters for reproduction. $3/hour for rough setup, then $2-4/page or $5-6/hour.

Technical translation. $2.75-3.95/150 words.

Technical writing. $10-15/hour.

Travel folder. $100 flat fee.

Education-Related Jobs. If you're a teacher *and* a writer, you have two skills to sell. Projects include:

Audio cassette scripts. $120 for 20 minutes.

Educational filmstrips. $1,200 flat fee.

Education films. $200 for one reel (11 minutes of film); $1,000-1,500 for

30 minutes.

Educational grant proposals.
$50-125/day, plus expenses.

Programmed instruction materials.
Writing: $1,000-3,000/hour of programmed training provided. Consulting/editorial work: $25/hour;
$200/day minimum, plus expenses.

School public relations. $3.50-10/hour.

Slide presentation for an educational institution. $1,000 flat fee.

Teaching creative writing, part-time.
$15-30/hour of instruction.

Teaching high school journalism, part-time. Percentage of regular teacher's salary.

Teaching home-bound students.
$5/hour.

Magazine and Newspaper Work:

Editing a group of religious publications. $200-500/month.

Local criticism of art, music, drama.
Free tickets, plus $5-15 (or a per-word fee).

Magazine stringing. 20¢-$1/word, based on circulation. Daily rate:
$200, plus expenses. Weekly rate:
$750, plus expenses.

Newspaper column (local). 80¢/column inch up to $20/column.

Newspaper stringing.
50¢-$2.50/column inch; up to
$4-5/column inch for some national publications.

Regional magazine correspondent.
$5-15/hour, plus expenses.

Reviews of art, drama or music for national magazines. $25-50;
$20-50/column for newspapers;
$100-200 in Sunday supplements.

Trade journal articles, ghostwritten under someone else's byline.
$250-400.

Photo/Film Jobs. Those writers who are also photographers or who want to work with another freelancer can seek extra checks for projects like these:

Audiovisual scripts. $1,000-1,500 advance against 5-10% royalty for 5-10 script/visual units.

Photo-brochures. $700-15,000 flat fee.

Slide-film, single image photo. $75 flat fee.

TV filmed news and features. $15/film clip.

TV news film still photo. $3-6, flat fee.

TV news story. $16-25, flat fee.

Other ideas:

Associations—writing miscellaneous projects. $10-25/hour, or on a per-project basis.

Comedy writing for night club entertainers. Gags only: $5-7.
Routines: $100-300/minute. Some new comics try to get 5-minute routines for $100-150, but some comics may pay $1,500 for a 5-minute bit from a top writer.

Ghostwriting a novel rewrite. $1,000 (based on $10/hour for about 100 hours work.

Ghostwriting political speeches.
$10-20/hour.

Record album cover copy. $100-200, flat fee.

Syndicated newspaper column, self-promoted. $2 each for weeklies;
$5-25/week for dailies, based on circulation.

If you know of substantial differences in local rates for any of these jobs—or if you'd like to tell us about other freelance opportunities with which you have personal experience—please drop a line to Kirk Polking, Jobs for Writers, in care of *Writer's Market*, 9933 Alliance Rd., Cincinnati 45242. Your comments will help other freelancers in future editions.

A long-time freelance veteran, Kirk Polking is director of the Writer's Digest School.

Markets

Audiovisual

Audiovisuals involve the marriage of the two most powerful communications tools available—words and pictures.

You are concerned with the audio—the words. You supply the thousand words a picture might be worth, yet can't replace. In short, audiovisual producers need you.

"The audiovisual field is wide open for good freelance writers," says Bernie Michaels, president of MBM Productions in Dallas. "Most AV houses use freelance writers/producers extensively." Some producers don't agree with Michaels' appraisal of the field's openness, but the overwhelming majority of those recently surveyed by *Writer's Market* are optimistic about opportunities available to the talented, persistent writer.

The audiovisual industry offers a variety of fascinating opportunities to writers, because it has so many facets. Filmstrips, multimedia kits, educational films, feature films for entertainment, videotape—all are produced by the firms listed in this section. "If, by the audiovisual field, we include local television commercials, educational and institutional films and other nonentertainment aspects of the visual media, the field is quite open and expanding rapidly," says Richard Staley, director of product development for Schick Sunn Classic Pictures. What's more, "New technology—videodiscs, cable television, TV superstations, etc.—may have an impact on opportunities that is unmeasurable at this time."

Staley's comments reflect a general optimism expressed by many AV producers about the health and future of the audiovisual industry. One producer estimates that one segment of the field—industrial audiovisuals—is growing by 20-25% per year. As a whole, "The field has never been healthier," says Sid Glenar, president of Maxfilms.

Just as the AV field comprises many products, it comprises many audiences. Audiovisuals are used by schools, government, business and industry, advertising agencies, libraries, publishers and organizations. These organizations use AV materials to teach and to disseminate information, whether the teaching takes the form of classroom instruction, vocational training, product demonstration, skill training or public education.

Audiovisuals are also an entertainment medium trying to reach mass audiences. Movies such as *Alien* and TV programs such as *M*A*S*H* are, after all, audiovisuals.

Producers of audiovisuals fall into two categories: the independent producer, and the audiovisual arms of corporations or companies. The "dependent" audiovisual production departments far outnumber the independents, yet these production departments tend to be self-contained, producing all material internally. The real opportunities for the freelancer, therefore, lie with the independents.

Independent AV firms usually specialize in one form or another, concentrating on educational materials, sales training materials, entertainment, etc. The greatest opportunities currently lie in audiovisuals for business and industry. "More and more industries are finding this [AV] a practical way of training and motivating employees," says Bernie Michaels. Another producer, K.L. Rubel of Kapco Communications, predicts that the surging demand for business audiovisuals will have a positive effect on the AV field as a whole. "The entire field will open up more in the next two years due to the increased demand for software [the words and the pictures, as opposed to *hardware*—the AV machinery] for business and industry," he says. Technical and medical AV materials also offer opportunities, and "more activity seems to be developing in AV production in the health sciences," says Richard J. Sternberg, vice president of Professional Research.

Less opportunity is available in the field of educational audiovisuals, a field that has been "slow," as one producer termed it. Budget cutbacks continue to plague schools, and AV materials are often viewed as a luxury that can be cut out first.

Competition is felt most in entertainment audiovisuals. "Prime-time television and theatrical feature film writing remains a narrow specialty, and is as difficult to crack as ever," says Richard Staley. Breaking into this branch of AV writing usually requires a West Coast location and association with an agent.

Television and theatrical films aside, most AV producers will want to see a query letter or a resume from you before they see anything else. They want evidence that you can perform a job quickly and correctly. That's why sample scripts you've written should accompany the query. Few want to see an outline/synopsis of your project before seeing an initial query, and almost no producers will review completed scripts. Producers are primarily concerned about your ability to produce what they want; thus the emphasis on queries. "Provide us with information on your availability, fields of interest, background and credits for our writer file," says Paul J. Fournier, president of Film Communication. In the query letter, outline your strengths, your interests, the potential market for the project you suggest, and any other qualifications you have that enables you to handle an assignment (e.g., teaching experience if you're proposing an educational audiovisual).

If you have no credits, spend some time writing a short sample in proper script format and submit it with your query. Script formats are covered in "Audiovisual Writing: A World Beyond Words" in the July 1977 *Writer's Digest* (available in your library, or for $1.50 from *WD*, 9933 Alliance Rd., Cincinnati 45242). In your query letter, ask to arrange an interview with the producer so you can discuss your work in person. The audiovisual field is one of many in which personal contact is important.

The submission procedure is summed up well by Bob Kalsey of Bravura Films: "Be very patient, send a sample of your best work that is appropriate, be very patient, ask to meet one of the producers, be very patient."

Additional names and addresses of audiovisual producers can be found in *Audiovisual Market Place* (R.R. Bowker), available in most libraries.

A/V CONCEPTS CORP., 30 Montauk Blvd., Oakdale NY 11769. (516)587-7229. Editor: Sharon Diane Orlan. Estab. 1968. Produces material for el-hi language arts students, both those on grade level and in remedial situations. Query. SASE. Reports on outline in 10 days; on final scripts in 1 month. Buys all rights. Catalog for SASE.

Needs: "Authors must receive a set of our specifications before submitting material. Manuscripts must be written using our lists of vocabulary words, and must meet readability formula requirements provided by us. Length of manuscript and subjects will vary according to grade level for which material is prepared. Basically, we want articles and stories that will motivate people to read. Authors must be highly creative and highly disciplined." No "history lessons, moral teachings, etc. We no not want 'preaching' types of materials." Pays $75.

Tips: "If possible, contact the editor or editorial department by phone and 'meet' the company through 'personal' contact."

ADVERTISING AND DESIGN SERVICES, 1701 S. Prospect, Champaign IL 61820. (217)356-3600. Vice President: Linda Westbrook. Estab. 1970. Produces material for business and general audiences. Buys 50 scripts/year. Submit resume. SASE. Reports in 1 week. Buys all rights.

Needs: Scripts for multi-image presentations that use up to 15 projectors. Produces charts, silent and sound filmstrips, models, 8mm and 16mm films, multimedia kits, overhead transparencies, tapes and cassettes, and slides. Pays according to Writers Guild standards.

AERO PRODUCTS RESEARCH, INC., 11201 Hindry Ave., Los Angeles CA 90045. (213)641-7242. Contact: J. Parr. Produces material for pilot training and schools (private and public schools from K through college). SASE.

Needs: Aviation/aeroscience/aerospace education material and "developing and editing both technical and nontechnical material. Charts, silent filmstrips, models, multimeda kits, overhead transparencies, phonograph records, prerecorded tapes and cassettes, slides and study prints. Royalty arrangements are handled on an individual project basis. Writers should have flight instructor and ground school instructor experience."

DOM ALBI ASSOCIATES, INC., 40 E. 34th St., New York NY 10016. (212)6790979. President: Dom Albi. Estab. 1972. Produces material for corporate and government audiences. Buys 20-30 scripts/year. Query or submit resume. Buys all rights.

Needs: Produces charts, 8mm and 16mm film loops, sound filmstrips, models, 16mm films, multimedia kits, overhead transparencies, tapes and cassettes, and slides. Payment negotiable.

ALLEGRO FILM PRODUCTIONS, INC., 201 W. 52nd St., New York NY 10019. President: Mr. J. Forman. Produces for the general and school markets. Buys 3-20 scripts/year. Submit resume. Buys all rights.

Needs: Science films for education, films for industry and government, and documentaries. Produces 16mm and 35mm films. Pays $1,000-1,500.

ANCO/BOSTON, INC., 441 Stiart St., Boston MA 02116. (617)267-9700. Director, Instructional Systems: R. Hoyt. Estab. 1959. Produces for the industrial and business communities. Submit resume. SASE. Reports in 1 week. Buys all rights.

Needs: "Often technical or business-oriented material on specific subjects for specific customized needs." Produces charts, sound filmstrips, multimedia kits, overhead transparencies and cassettes and slides. Pays by outright purchase price of $400-800.

KEN ANDERSON FILMS, Box 618 Winona Lake IN 46590. (219)267-5774. President: Ken Anderson. Produces material for church-related libraries with evangelical bias; films for all ages, with particular interest in children and teenagers. Prefers true stories; rarely purchases fiction, but will consider for the younger ages. No objections to previously published material. Buys motion picture rights. Free catalog. "We cannot guarantee consideration for material unless a brief one-page story synopsis is included. Other than that, writers may send rough material, a collection of anecdotes, published material, a book or whatever form the material may be in as long as it's good film material. We like to maintain a very warm attitude toward writers and will try to give careful consideration either to queries or to full-blown material. We only produce 4-6 films/year, so our quantity needs are limited." Produces sound filmstrips, films, and tapes and cassettes.

Needs: Religious material only. "We are constantly looking for good material that is positively Christian and relates realistically to today's lifestyle." Pays "as low as $100 for basic story idea, which the author could then market elsewhere. But general payment runs more between

$250-1,000, depending upon story quality and adaptability for audiovisual production."

ANIMATION ARTS ASSOCIATES, INC., 2225 Spring Garden St., Philadelphia PA 19130. (215)563-2520. Contact: Harry E. Ziegler Jr. For "government, industry, engineers, doctors, scientists, dentists, general public, military." Send "resume of credits for motion picture and filmstrip productions. The writer should have scriptwriting credits for training, sales, promotion, public relations." SASE.
Business: Produces 3½-minute, 8mm and 16mm film loops; 16mm and 35mm films (ranging from 5-40 minutes); 2¼x2¼ or 4x5 slides; and teaching machine programs for training, sales, industry and public relations. Fee arrangements dependent on client's budget.
Tips: "Send us a resume listing writing and directing credits for motion pictures and sound/slide programs."

HAL MARC ARDEN AND CO., Executive Offices, 240 Central Park S., New York NY 10019. President: Hal Marc Arden. "Writer must have experience in writing for motion pictures. Scripts are not solicited, but we welcome resumes." Query. SASE.
Needs: "We specialize in sponsored production only: documentary, educational, public service." Produces silent and sound filmstrips, 16mm films, multimedia kits, phonograph records, prerecorded tapes and cassettes, and slides. "No royalties. Fee negotiated."

AVCOM CORP., 8 Front St., Salem MA 01970. Executive Producer: George Guanci. Estab. 1975. Produces material from government and industrial audiences. Buys 50 scripts from 5 writers/year. Submit resume. SASE. Reports in 1 month. Not copyrighted. Free catalog.
Needs: Produces super 8mm film loops, sound filmstrips, 8mm and 16mm films, multimedia kits, overhead transparencies, slides and teaching machine programs. "We look for professional attitude, desire for success, concern for quality, clarity and conciseness." Pays according to Writers Guild standards.
Tips: "Send a resume, and follow it up with an attempt to obtain an appointment."

BACHNER PRODUCTIONS, INC., 45 W. 45th St., New York NY 10036. (212)354-8760. Produces 16mm and 35mm films; videotape programs; and 2-inch, 1-inch, and ¾-inch cassettes. Not copyrighted. Does not accept unsolicited material. Prospective writer usually must have experience in subject related to proposed film, and needs knowledge of videotape or film requirements. Sometimes will use good writer without specialized experience and then supply all necessary research. SASE.
Needs: Produces training and sales films and documentaries. Subject matter and style depend on client requirements. "Sometimes clients supply outlines and research from which our writers work. We usually pay Writers Guild scale, depending on usage and what is supplied by us. Price varies with assignments."

BARR FILMS, 3490 E. Foothill Blvd., Pasadena CA 91107. "Produces material for all age levels; grades K through college level as well as in the public library market to the same age span and adult audience. We also have interest in materials aimed at business and industry training programs." Catalog $1. Query. "We will assign projects to qualified writers. We require previous experience in film writing and want to see samples of films previously written and completed for sale in the market." SASE.
Needs: "We produce and distribute 16mm films in all curriculum and subject areas. We prefer a semi-dramatic form of script with a moral or informational point. Avoid excess verbiage—we produce films, not books. The length of our films is 10-20 minutes. We will also consider pure informational subjects with voice over narration. Fees are entirely negotiable, but we normally pay approximately in the area of $500 per script. We will accept film treatments and/or completed visual and dialog scripts. Please inquire prior to sending your materials to us."
Tips: "Meet the producer; share previous films; talk film; and be available."

BLACKSIDE, INC., 145 Dartmouth St., Boston MA 02116. President: Henry Hampton. Estab. 1968. Produces material for "all types" of audiences. "Query only. No scripts are accepted unless they're requested." Buys all rights.
Needs: Produces silent and sound filmstrips, kinescopes, 16mm and 35mm films, multimedia kits, overhead transparencies, phonograph records, tapes and cassettes, slide sets, and teaching machine programs.

BOARD OF JEWISH EDUCATION OF NEW YORK, 426 W. 58th St., New York NY 10019. (212)245-8200. Associate in media and Curriculum Materials Development: Yaakov Reshef. Produces material for Jewish schools, youth groups, temples and synagogues; for audience

from kindergarten to old age. Buys 12-15 scripts/year. Submit outline/synopsis or resume. SASE. Reports in 2-3 months. Buys first rights or all rights.
Needs: General, educational and informational. "Generally, length is up to 20-25 minutes maximum; most material geared to 10-12 years old and up. Jewish background needed." Produces sound filmstrips, 16mm films, tapes and cassettes, and slide sets. Pays 10-15% royalty or $300 up/outright purchase.

LEE BOWDEN PRODUCTIONS, 243 State St., Schenectady NY 12305. (518)374-4388. Director/Producer: Lee Bowden. Estab. 1972. Produces material for TV commercial audiences, and sales and informational film screenings. "We purchase 16 scripts annually, with our need increasing." Query with samples or submit resume. SASE. Reports in 6 weeks. Buys first rights. Catalog for SASE.
Needs: Scripts for 10- to 30-minute programs for audiences ranging from educational, business and consumer groups to nonprofit organizations. "At least half of the material is of a humorous nature, or is otherwise informative and thought-provoking. We seek imagination, motivation, experience, and the ability to not laugh when hearing the word 'Schenectady.' Obviously, Schenectady is not a landmark to most people. While our market primarily encompasses the Northeast, our requirements span a spectrum of subjects. With expansion in the future, we need access to a pool of freelance writers experienced in producing film scripts that are creative and practical." Produces 16mm films, multimedia kits and slide sets. Pays $30-80/minute of finished film.

ROBERT J. BRADY CO., Routes 197 & 450, Bowie MD 20715. Contact: Director, Product Development. Produces material for professionals and paraprofessionals in medical, allied health, nursing, emergency medicine, fire service, vocational and business fields. Buys all rights. Free catalog. "We are always eager to develop new writers who can blend both book skills and audiovisual skills. Since most of our writing needs would be commissioned, all submissions should be in the form of resumes, sample materials, and client and title lists." Query. Produces sound filmstrips, films, overhead transparencies, audio tapes and cassettes, 35mm slides, and books and manuals.
Needs: Educational (35mm sound/slide programs, 35mm sound filmstrips—instructional); subject areas: business (training, skills, general); medicine (allied health, nursing, emergency medicine); and fire service training. Pays $400-1,200/script.
Tips: "Send a resume with samples of writing ability and grasp of subject."

BRAVURA FILMS, INC., 680 Beach St., #373, San Francisco CA 94109. Producers: Bob Kalsey, John Armstrong. Estab. 1969. "We produce sponsored films only—for public relations, sales promotion, technical, and television specials." Submit resume and a complete script as a sample—"all work would be on assignment. No reports until an assignment is available, though we will respond with encouragement or discouragement if we think the work is good or 'otherwise.'" Work is assigned on a work-for-hire basis.
Needs: "We produce sponsored films for businesses. They may be technical, motivational, educational or promotional, and subject areas are virtually unlimited. We are big on energy, agriculture and selling. The writer should be in the vicinity of San Francisco, or should be readily available. Don't telephone, and don't expect an appointment unless *we* initiate it; we're just too busy making movies. Don't send dramas you wrote in school, only scripts for our kind of films. We look for clarity of expression, minimum use of words, maximum use of images, strong research ability, the ability to handle complicated ideas, the ability to get along with clients, and the ability to meet deadlines. The writer should be eager about the subject area. Scripts must be *practical*. The writer should understand the difficulties of production, and preferably should have experience in the real world of films." Produces 16mm films. Payment is negotiated before the assignment, and depends on the budget, the difficulty of the assignment and the legwork involved.

CAMBRIDGE FILM CORP., 123 Thorndike St., Cambridge MA 02141. Producer: Richard MacLeod. Estab. 1973. Produces material for general theatrical and TV audiences. "Films range from G-rated children's pictures to R-rated sex and action." Buys "not more than four feature-length scripts per year. However, we are currently working on putting together packages that could best be called long shorts, i.e., 3-4 films totaling 90- to 100-minutes." Query, query with samples, submit outline/synopsis, or submit completed script. "We are not interested in receiving resumes." SASE. Reports in 2-6 weeks. Usually buys film and TV rights.
Needs: "All our releases are 35mm films. However, we've done several from 16mm blow-ups. We don't employ writers; all scripts are freelanced. The easiest approach is with a short synopsis, plus a cover indicating the highlights and the major selling features (the sales

handles, as it were) of the film as the author sees it."

CENTURY MEDIA, INC., 155 N. Dean St., Englewood NJ 07631. (201)568-5525. President: Jeffrey Berger. Estab. 1976. Produces material for business, industrial and consumer audiences. Query with samples, submit completed script, or submit resume. SASE. Reports in 6 weeks. Buys first rights.
Needs: "We hire writers to 'custom' write sales presentations, films, filmstrips and multimedia on a nonproprietary, contractual basis." Produces sound filmstrips, 16mm films, and tapes and cassettes. Pays according to Writers Guild standards.

THE CHAMBA ORGANIZATION, Box 1231, Hollywood CA 90028. President: St. Clair Bourne. Produces material for "the new hip, activist-oriented audience; the general audience (PG), and in the educational film market, we aim at high school and adult audiences, especially the so-called 'minority' audiences. Assignments are given solely based upon our reaction to submitted material. The material is the credential." Query. SASE.
Needs: "I concentrate primarily on feature film projects. However, I am always interested in a unique feature-length documentary film project. We prefer submission of film treatments first. Then, if the idea interests us, we then negotiate the writing of the script." Payment negotiable according to Writers Guild standards.

CINE/DESIGN FILMS, INC., 255 Washington St., Denver CO 80203. (303)777-4222. Producer/Director: Jon Husband. Produces educational material for general, sales training and theatrical audiences. Buys 10-15 scripts/year. Query with samples; "original ideas are encouraged." SASE. Reports in 3-4 weeks. Rights purchased vary.
Needs: "Motion picture outlines in the theatrical, documentary, sales or educational areas. We are seeking theatrical scripts in the low-budget area that are possible to produce for under $1,000,000. We seek flexibility and personalities who can work well with our clients. Produces 16mm and 35mm films. Pays $75-150/screen minute on 16mm productions. Theatrical scripts negotiable according to budget.
Tips: "Understand the economic needs of film production today."

CINEMAGRAPHICS, 101 Trowbridge St., Cambridge MA 02140. Producer: Jim Herzig. Estab. 1970. Produces material for educational markets, industry and TV. Buys 3 scripts/year. Query with samples. SASE. Reporting time varies. "We hire writers on a per-project basis."
Needs: "Our needs vary. We frequently need educational, fundraising or sales material, usually 15 to 20 minutes in length. We look for elegance, clarity, and the ability to focus on the specific needs of *our* clients." Produces 16mm and 35mm films. Pays on a per-assignment basis.

CINEMAKERS, INC., 200 W. 57th St., New York NY 10019. President: Ed Schultz. Estab. 1965. "We produce corporate sponsored audiovisuals for use in education, communication and persuasion with all kinds of audiences." Submit resume and sample of professionally produced film, filmstrip or slide show. SASE. Reports in 4 weeks. Buys all rights.
Needs: "We want to build a list of New York City freelancers who know how to write movies, videotapes, slide shows, filmstrips, teachers' guides, activity sheets and multimedia kits for use in education, training, public relations, employee relations, sales promotions, and fund raising, on topics varying from 'sewing patterns' to 'cancer in children' to 'behavorial approaches to environments.' We like easy-going, nondidactic scripts that encourage audiences to think and discover for themselves." Produces super 8mm film loops; silent and sound filmstrips; 8mm, 16mm and 35mm films; videotapes; multimedia kits; phonograph records; tapes and cassettes; and slide sets. Pays $25-2,000.

CINETUDES FILM PRODUCTIONS, LTD., 377 Broadway, New York NY 10013. (212)966-4600. Director: Neal Marshad. Estab. 1970. Produces material for TV, schools, government and corporations. Works with 20 writers/year. Query with samples or submit resume. SASE. Reports in 2 weeks. Buys all rights.
Needs: Scripts about the arts, sociological history, technical information and education. Length: 30 minutes to 1 hour. "We look for the willingness to listen, and past experience in visual writing." Produces 16mm and 35mm films and videotape. Pays by outright purchase, or pays daily rates.

DOUGLAS CLARK ASSOCIATES, INC., 18 W. Court, Sausalito CA 94965. President: Douglas E. Clark. Estab. 1966. Produces material for general audiences. Works with 25 writers/year. Submit completed script. SASE. Reports in 4 weeks. Buys all rights or first rights.
Needs: Scripts for feature films for general theatrical release, and for educational/documentary

films. Produces 16mm and 35mm films. Pays according to Writers Guild Standards.

COCHRAN FILM PRODUCTIONS, INC., 110 Tiburon Blvd., Mill Valley CA 94941. (415)388-2371. President: Ted Cochran. Estab. 1971. Produces material for educational, medical and general TV audiences. Buys 3 scripts/year. Query. SASE. Reports in 2 weeks. Buys all rights or first rights.
Needs: Nontheatrical, travel, industrial and medical scripts, and specials for TV/cable. "We seek enthusiasm, a working knowledge of specific subjects, experience in the technical field, and experience with writing nontheatrical films." Produces 16mm films. Pays according to Writers Guild standards.

COLEMAN FILM ENTERPRISES, INC., 9101 Barton, Overland Park KS 66214. Vice President, Production: Maurice Prather. Estab. 1967. Produces material for the junior and senior high and college levels. "We also produce material for technical-minded adults. We purchase 15-25 scripts annually, and work with 3-5 writers (each writer usually does a series of 3-5)." Query with samples or submit resume. "We are *not* looking for script ideas, but would like to see some sample educational script pages by the writer." SASE. Reports in 3-4 weeks. Buys all rights.
Needs: "We produce educational filmstrips and films mainly for use in junior and senior high school, mostly in vocational education areas. We also produce the same type of material for the junior college level, and for use in technical training situations in industry. All of our scripts are written to specific requirements outlined to us by our clients, so we *do not* need script ideas. We need writers who can research a given area and create a script to meet given parameters. Writers with experience in education and/or vocational education are most interesting to us. A writer who has knowledge of the subject area is usually desirable over one not too well-informed in the subject. Good educational credentials are very helpful." Produces sound filmstrips, 16mm films, tapes and cassettes, slides and videotapes. Pays by outright purchase of 5-10% of the project's budget.

COMART ANIFORMS, INC., 122 E. 42nd St., New York NY 10017. Producer: Richard Gottlieb. Estab. 1969. Produces material for a variety of audiences, including internal sales forces, trainees, industrial plant workers, and people attending international exhibits. Buys 20-30 scripts/year. Query with samples or submit resume. SASE. Reports in 6 weeks. Not copyrighted.
Needs: "AV needs depend entirely upon the clients. They can include business, technical, general or educational. We look for visual sense, clarity, economy, speed, flexibility, and an understanding of the differing requirements of various media." Produces sound filmstrips, 16mm films, multimedia kits, tapes and cassettes, slides and videotapes. Pays by outright purchase of $750-3,000.

COMMAND PRODUCTIONS, 99 Lafayette Ave., White Plains NY 10603. Executive Producer: G. Stromberg. Estab. 1973. Produces material for business clients. Works with 3-4 writers/year. Submit resume. SASE. Buys all rights.
Needs: Technical and nontechnical business presentations and customized training programs. Produces sound filmstrips, multimedia kits, overhead transparencies, slides, booklets and brochures. Pays by outright purchase.

COMPASS FILMS, 683 Vance Ave., Franklin Lakes NJ 07417. Executive Producer: Robert Whittaker. Estab. 1964. Produces material for educational, industrial and general adult audiences. Works with 4 writers/year. Query with samples or submit resume. SASE. Reports in 3 weeks. Buys all rights.
Needs: Scripts for 10- to 30-minute business films, and general documentary and theatrical feature films. "We would like to consider theatrical stories for possible use for feature films. We also would like to review writers to develop existing film treatments and ideas with strong dialog." Produces 16mm and 35mm films. Pays according to Writers Guild standards.

COMPRENETICS, INC., 5821 Uplander Way, Culver City CA 90230. (213)204-2080. President: Ira Englander. Estab. 1967. "Target audience varies. In the health care field it goes from entry level health workers with minimal academic background to continuing education programs for physicians and health professions. In manpower training, from entry level to top supervisors; in the cultural area, all levels." Buys approximately 10-20 scripts/year. Query with samples or submit resume. SASE. Reports in 1 month. Buys all rights.
Needs: "Films are generally 10 to 20 minutes in length and tend to have a dramatic framework. They are often programmed with response frames included. Subject topics include

all educational areas with emphasis on health and medical films, manpower and management training and multi-cultural education. Our staff normally does subject matter research and content review which is provided for the writer who is then required to provide us with an outline or film treatment for review. Due to the extensive review procedures, writers are frequently required to modify through three or four drafts before final approval." Produces sound filmstrips, 16mm films, and tapes and cassettes. Pays $1,000-2,500.

CONCORDIA PUBLISHING HOUSE, Product Development Division, 3558 S. Jefferson Ave., St. Louis MO 63118. (314)664-7000. Produces religious material for preschool through adult audiences, for institutional and home use. "Writer must have demonstrated skills in writing produceable material for print and the audio and visual fields. Competence in the content area is necessary. Initial query is preferred in view of existing production commitments and necessity to maintain a satisfactory product mix. Do not send completed manuscripts or multiple submissions." SASE. Free catalog.
Needs: Manuscripts and scripts for educational and religious subjects. "The content areas relate to the requirements of religious and moral guidance instruction. The emphasis may be curricular, quasi-curricular or enriching." Produces books, silent and sound filmstrips, 16mm films, multimedia kits, overhead transparencies, phonograph records, tapes and cassettes, 35mm slides and study prints. "Writing fees are negotiated in consideration of such factors as type of production, configuration, complexity of assignment, research required, field tests and production deadlines."
Tips: "Send a prospectus of project to be evaluated as to produceability, market, etc."

DAVID C. COOK PUBLISHING CO., 850 N. Grove Ave., Elgin IL 60120. Editor: Anne Blischke. Estab. 1876. Produces material for preschool, K-3. Buys 3 scripts/year. Query with samples or submit outline. SASE. Reports in 2 weeks. Buys all rights. Free catalog.
Needs: Education (various topics with pictures and stories for children; manual for teachers). Pays $35-60/print.
Tips: "Send a resume and samples of work that have been accepted by other publishers in the same field. No textbook materials, negative subjects, poetry or 1,000-word stories."

THOMAS CRAVEN FILM CORP., 316 E. 53rd St., New York NY 10022. (212)688-1585. President: Thomas Craven. Vice President: Willis Briley. Estab. 1952. "We produce government films, industrial films, a few TV spots, and some general-interest films. We buy up to 10 scripts a year, although we sometimes buy far fewer (e.g., one or two)." Query, query with samples, submit outline/synopsis or submit resume. "The shorter, the better." No completed scripts; "we have no one to thoroughly read and consider them." SASE. "We are a small company. We report as soon as is reasonably possible, given our level of business and the people available to read material." Material is not usually copyrighted. "There are occasional exceptions, of course. No generalizations are possible. We don't have a catalog, per se, but we will respond promptly to specific information requests."
Needs: Scripts for industrial films, government films, and public service and fundraising spots. Produces 16mm and 35mm films and videotape cassettes. "Though we make occasional forays into multimedia kits, tapes and cassettes, and slide sets, 16mm and 35mm film production is our main business. We look for the ability to visualize the scripts being shot, the ability to present educational material in an entertaining manner, the ability to come up with new approaches to old material, and the ability to work under pressure. Payment is completely dependent on the film budget. The amount is negotiated with writers."

CREATIVE PRODUCTIONS, INC., 200 Main St., Orange NJ 07050. (212)290-9075. Contact: Gus Nichols, Bill Griffing. Estab. 1953. Produces material for industrial, business and medical clients. Query. SASE. Buys all rights.
Needs: "We can use staff writers/associate producers with AV experience. We may consider help from time to time on a project basis. The writer must have the ability to create visual sequences as well as narrative. Flexibility is a must; treatments might be technical, humorous, etc." Produces sound filmstrips, 16mm films, slides and multi-image shows. Pays salary to writers added to the staff; a negotiable fee to freelancers.

CREATIVE VISUALS, Division of Gamco Industries, Inc., Box 1911, Big Spring TX 79720. (915)267-6327. Vice President, Research and Development: Judith Rickey. Free catalog and author's guidelines. "Provide a list of your educational degrees and majors. Explain your teaching experience, including subjects taught, grades taught, and the number of years you have taught. Please describe any writing experience, and, if possible, include a sample of your published educational material currently on the market. We ask for this information because

we have found that our best authors are usually experienced classroom teachers who are writing in their subject area. Once we have information about your background, we will ask you for the subject and titles of your proposed series." Produces sound filmstrips, overhead transparencies, cassettes, study prints, posters, games and reproduceable books.
Needs: Education (grades K-12, all subjects areas). Payment by royalty; usually 7-10% of net sales.

DEFENSE PRODUCTS CO., Audiovisual Div., 645 Azalea Dr., Rockville MD 20850. (301)279-0808. Manager: Harry A. Carragher. Estab. 1958. Produces material for industrial and public relations clients and the general public. Buys 4 scripts/year. Submit outline/synopsis, submit complete ms, or query with resume. Does not return unsolicited submissions. Reports in 2 weeks. Buys first rights. Free catalog.
Needs: Sample treatments in business, technical and general material; also exhibit design and fabrication. Produces sound filmstrips; 16mm films; multimedia kits; and slide sets. Pays 5% royalty; or by outright purchase of $100 minimum.

DOCUMENT ASSOCIATES, INC., 211 E. 43rd St., New York NY 10017. (212)682-0730. Contact: Mary Ann Hobel. Estab. 1971. Produces material for TV, educational, corporate and theatrical audiences. Query with samples or submit outline/synopsis. SASE. Reports "as soon as possible." Free catalog.
Needs: "We are looking for feature film material." Produces 16mm and 35mm films, and tapes and cassettes. Payment varies; may pay royalty or by outright purchase.

MARK DRUCK PRODUCTIONS, 300 E. 40th St., New York NY 10016. Produces audiovisuals for "mostly industrial audiences or women's groups." Produces 16mm films, multimedia kits and videotape industrials. Subjects: retail items, drugs, travel, industrial products, etc. Material is sometimes copyrighted. "The whole production belongs to the client. No unsolicited scripts; only resumes, lists of credits, etc. The freelance writer must have some expertise in the subject, and in writing AV scripts." SASE.
General: Pays $500/reel minimum. "Writer will be expected to produce outline, treatment and shooting script."

DYNACOM COMMUNICATIONS INTERNATIONAL, Box 702, Snowdon Station, Montreal, Quebec, Canada H3X 3X8. (514)342-5200. Director: David P. Leonard. Estab. 1969. Produces material for industrial and business management training and development and exhibits (entertainment, PR, motivation). Buys 12 10- to 20-minute scripts/year. Submit resume. SAE and International Reply Coupons. Reports in 2-4 weeks. Buys all rights. Brochure/presentation $4.
Needs: Business (sales and marketing presentations); industry (technical and nontechnical training programs in motivation, management, etc.); education (learning modules for elementary and high school and college); and general (exhibit audiovisuals for museums, conferences, meetings). Produces charts, dioramas, super 8mm and 16mm films, color television videocassettes, multimedia kits, overhead transparencies, phonograph records, tapes and cassettes, slide sets, and teaching machine programs. Pays in outright purchase "based on length and complexity of project, and the research required."

ECHO FILM PRODUCTIONS, 3105 W. State St., Boise ID 83703. (208)336-0349. Producer: Norman Nelson. Estab. 1972. Produces material for "local TV audiences, national TV audiences concerned with the environment, national and worldwide audiences concerned with sports and action film documentaries." Buys 2-6 scripts/year. Query. SASE. Reports in 1 week. Buys all rights.
Needs: Material for action sports documentaries, wildlife documentaries, short dramas, and promotional films. Avoid "overwriting and flowery wording." Produces 16mm films. Pays $500-2,000.

EDUCATIONAL COMMUNICATIONS, INC., Box 56, Wayne PA 19087. (215)688-2002. President: Dr. Philip Minter. Estab. 1969. Produces material for trainees in all types of industry. Buys approximately 25 scripts/year. Query with samples or submit resume. SASE. Reports in 2 weeks. Buys all rights. Free catalog.
Needs: Scripts on engineering and biomedical topics. Produces sound filmstrips, 16mm films, tapes and cassettes, and slide sets. Pays $1,000-2,500.

EDUCATIONAL DIMENSIONS GROUP, Box 126, Stamford CT 06904. Managing Editor: Gregory A. Byrnes. Produces material for K-12 levels. Query. Catalog $1.

Needs: 40-80 frames geared to proper grade level; all educational disciplines. Produces sound filmstrips, video, multimedia kits and 2¼x2¼ slides. Pays $100 minimum for consultation. Script writing fees vary.

EDUCATIONAL FILMSTRIPS, 1401 19th St., Huntsville TX 77340. (713)295-5767. Vice President: George H. Russell. Estab. 1953. Produces filmstrips for schools, junior high to university level. Submit complete script "with original slides in Kodak Carousel tray or original camera ready art." SASE. Reports "as soon as possible." Buys all rights. Free catalog.
Needs: Educational and technical. Produces silent and sound filmstrips. Pays 10% royalty or by outright purchase price of $100-500, per strip.

EDUCATIONAL IMAGES, Box 367, Lyons Falls NY 13368. (315)348-8211. Executive Director: Dr. Charles R. Belinky. Produces material for schools, K-college and graduate school, public libraries, parks, nature centers, etc. Buys all AV rights. Free catalog. "We are looking for complete AV programs. This requires high quality, factual text and pictures." Query. Produces silent and sound filmstrips; multimedia kits; and slide sets.
Needs: Science and education. Slide sets and filmstrips. Pays $150 minimum or percentage royalties.

EDUCATIONAL RESEARCH, INC., 1768 Willow Point, Shreveport LA 71119. (318)635-2111. President: Dr. James W. Stockard Jr. Estab. 1970. Produces material for schools (grades K-12) and adult education programs. "Most scripts are prepared internally; however, we have about 8 outside authors on royalty now." Query with samples. SASE. Reports in 2-4 weeks. Buys all rights. Catalog for SASE.
Needs: "Educational programs that can be produced in a lesson card/cassette tape format. The printed portion may be workbook or lesson cards. Reading aids, math aids, and special education aids are especially interesting. We market to schools through an extensive dealer network." Produces cassette tapes with accompanying visuals (lesson cards/workbooks). Pays in royalties or by outright purchase price "according to the amount of work needed at this end. Determined by agreement with author."

EFFECTIVE COMMUNICATION ARTS, INC., 47 W. 57th St., New York NY 10019. (212)688-6225. Vice President: W.J. Comcowich. Estab. 1965. Produces material for the general public; and sales training, medical education and science students. Buys 30 scripts/year. Submit resume. Buys all rights.
Needs: "Primarily 10- to 30-minute films on science, medicine and technology. Also need 3- to 5-minute films on product promotion. A writer must have the ability to 'translate' technical material, and a good visual sense." Produces sound filmstrips, models, 16mm films, multimedia kits, tapes and cassettes, slides, and allied print materials. Pays by negotiation based on the project's budget.

EMC CORP., 180 E. 6th St., St. Paul MN 55101. Book Editor: Connie McMillan. Editor-in-Chief: Northrop Dawson Jr. Produces material for children and teenagers in the primary grades through high school. Buys world rights. catalog for SASE. "The writer, via submitted sample, must show the capability to write appropriately for the medium." Query. Produces sound filmstrips, multimedia kits, and tapes and cassettes.
Needs: "No standard requirements, due to the nature of educational materials publishing." Payment varies.
For '80: "Math materials, consumer education, special education (as related to language arts and math especially), low vocabularly but high interest fiction and nonfiction for problem readers at secondary grade levels."

MOREY ENGLE PRODUCTIONS, 2085 S. Hudson St., Denver CO 80222. (303)758-4436. Script Supervisor: Ronn Spargur. Estab. 1952. Produces material for management personnel, trainees, and the general public. Works with 2 writers/year. Query with samples. SASE. Reports in 2 weeks. Buys all rights.
Needs: "Scripts will be contracted and written to our specifications." Seeks "imaginative, articulate" writers. Produces film loops, silent and sound filmstrips, and 16mm and 35mm films. Pays $800-5,000.
Tips: "Check for information on work coming up to see if you're qualified for any freelance work on projects."

ENT/GATE FILMS, INC., 200 Chicago St., Buffalo NY 14204. (716)856-3220. Executive Vice President: Paul G. Ent. Estab. 1972. Produces material for sales, marketing and general

consumer audiences. Buys $30,000 worth of scripts/year. Query with samples. SASE. Reports in 3 weeks. Buys all rights.
Needs: Material for product sales and general public information. Produces sound filmstrips and films. Payment negotiable.

FAMILY FILMS, 14622 Lanark St., Panorama City CA 91402. Director of Product Development: Paul R. Kidd. Produces 16mm films and sound filmstrips for interdenominational church market for all age levels from preschool through adult. Query. Free catalog.
Needs: "The majority of the projects are assigned and developed to our specifications. Writers may submit their credentials and experience. Some experience in writing film and filmstrip scripts is desired. Teaching credentials or experience are valuable for our school materials. An active involvement in a mainstream church is desirable." "Motion pictures vary from 10 minutes to 30-40 minutes. Filmstrips are about 50-60 frames with running time of 7-10 minutes. The emphasis is on the application of Christian values to everyday living and person-to-person relationships. No royalty arrangements. Outright payment depends on project and available budget. As an example, our usual filmstrip project requires four scripts, for which we pay $200-250 each; motion picture scripts through final draft, $1,500-2,000."

FGH, INC., 6400 Westpark, #400, Houston TX 77057. (713)781-9676. President: Lars Giertz. Estab. 1969. Produces material for local and regional television, corporate investors, and employees of large corporations. Buys 2-3 scripts/year. Submit resume or submit treatment. SASE. Reports in 3 weeks. Buys all rights.
Needs: Corporate image, sales and marketing scripts. "We prefer fast-paced material, and are not opposed to humor. The emphasis is on entertainment. The most important quality is the writer's information-gathering abilities. I need writers I can safely send alone to the client once the deal is made."
Tips: "With us, neatness *does* count."

FILM COMMUNICATION, INC., Outer Winthrop Rd., Hallowell ME 04347. (207)623-9466. President: Paul J. Fournier. Estab. 1970. Produces material for schools, medical and industrial associations, the general TV-viewing public, etc. Buys 10-12 scripts from 4-5 writers/year. Query with samples or submit resume. "Do not send completed scripts; we are not currently producing on speculation." SASE. Reports in 1 month. Rights purchased are negotiable.
Needs: Scripts are written "usually on assignment for specific client needs in the medical, business, educational and general fields. We look for writing skill, reliability in meeting deadlines, and accuracy of information." Produces sound filmstrips, 16mm films, multimedia kits, tapes and cassettes, and slide sets. Pays $400-1,000.
Tips: "Provide us with info on your availability, fields of interest, background and credits for our writer file."

FILM COMMUNICATORS, 11136 Weddington St., North Hollywood CA 91601. Production Administrator: Pat Davies. Estab. 1967. Produces material on fire science, police science, fire education for children, and emergency medical care training for fire service, law enforcement, industrial and educational audiences. Buys 1-3 scripts/year. Submit resume of related writing experience to the production department. "Resumes are retained in our files. We do not solicit writing samples as a first contact. If a resume is of interest, we may initiate a request for samples." Buys all rights.
Needs: "Writers must be based in Los Angeles, since we require consultations on our premises. Our educational films and other AV programs are all slanted towards the various safety markets—fire prevention, fire survival, fire education, emergency medical care, law enforcement, industrial safety. All films are high in dramatic content. They are hard-core training with a high entertainment value, as well. They are generally 15-25 minutes long. The writer must be very heavily into research. Total accuracy in fire/medical procedures is extremely critical. We frequently go into the fourth or fifth drafts of a script before arriving at a final shooting script. We look for originality, the ability to take a dry, technical, demanding subject and turn it into an entertaining script. Basically, we look for writers who are also all-around filmmakers, i.e., they are also able to direct and edit film." Produces sound filmstrips, 16mm films, tapes, cassettes, and slide sets. Pays by outright purchase.

FRANCISCAN COMMUNICATIONS CENTER, 1229 S. Santee St., Los Angeles CA 90015. Associate Producer: Corinne Hart. Estab. 1946. Produces material for the educational and religious market. Buys approximately 6-15 scripts/year. Query with samples, or submit outline/synopsis or completed script. SASE. Reports in 1 month. Buys all rights. Free catalog.

Needs: 10- to 15-minute dramatic scripts, with good story and well-developed characters. "Themes in value areas: personal worth, faith, problem areas for youth, caring and concern, and social responsibility. Avoid sterotyped characters representing a point of view or single dimension. Be upbeat without being simplistic; insight without didacaticism. The majority of our films are oriented toward a junior high and high school audience. However, we are always on the look out for the really good story that appeals to a wide range of people." We are also looking for 5- to 7-minute scripts for children ages 4-7. Produces sound filmstrips and 16mm films. Pays $150 maximum for story ideas; $700 for completed script.

JOEL FRIED PRODUCTIONS, INC., Box 61, Simsbury CT 06070. President: Joel Fried. Executive Producer: Wendy Rappaport. Production Coordinator: Donna Carey. Production Assistant: Jennie Kellogg. "We produce filmstrips that are aimed at the high school/college market." Query; "tell us what your idea is, and why you can write on this particular subject." SASE. Buys all rights.
Needs: "Vocational education is very important to us. You should be familiar with the market and what subjects are of interest to today's students. We are open to any good idea." Subjects include vocational education and academics, including high school chemistry, physics and biology, horticulture and home management. Produces sound filmstrips, multimedia kits, and tapes and cassettes. Pays about $300-450/program.

FRIEDENTAG PHOTOGRAPHICS, 356 Grape St., Denver CO 80220. (303)333-7086. Contact: Harvey Friedentag. Estab. 1957. Produces training and information material for commercial, industrial and governmental audiences. Buys 24 scripts from 22 writers each year. Submit outline/synopsis or submit completed script. "We often work with writers to produce audiovisuals or films." SASE. Reports in 4 weeks. Not copyrighted.
Needs: "We need good ideas for training and information for business productions, either ordered or submitted on speculation. We're looking for someone qualified and easy to get along with, who can communicate. *Deadlines are a must.*" Produces silent and sound filmstrips, kinescopes, 16mm films, overhead transparencies, slide sets, study prints, videotapes and videocassettes. Pays by outright purchase; assignments are determined "based on bids from the writer, or by "50% speculation on unordered projects."

GALLERYWEST, LTD., 630 Oakwood Ave., West Hartford CT 06110. (203)246-7231. Director: Paul Gregory. Estab. 1973. Produces material for consumer and corporate/industrial audiences. Buys 8 scripts/year. Query. SASE. Reports in 1 month. Rights purchased vary. Free catalog.
Needs: "GalleryWest is a producer of industrial films and TV commercials, and our audiovisual material needs vary with each job." Produces 16mm and 35mm films, tapes and cassettes, and slide sets. Pays by outright purchase.

GENERAL EDUCATIONAL MEDIA, INC., 350 Northern Blvd., Great Neck NY 11021. (516)829-5333. President: David Engler. Estab. 1973. Produces for schools, colleges, business and industry, and general adult audiences. Buys 30-40 scripts/year from 5-6 writers. Query with samples. SASE. Reports in 3 weeks. Buys all rights.
Needs: Typical length, 12- to 15-minute scripts; subjects, style and format variable. Produces sound filmstrips; multimedia kits; tapes and cassettes; slides; and teaching machine programs. Pays $200-500.

GOLDSHOLL ASSOCIATES, 420 Frontage Rd., Northfield IL 60093. (312)446-8300. President: M. Goldsholl. Query. Buys all rights.
Needs: Scripts for industrial PR films. Also interested in original screenplays, and short stories to be made into screenplays. "Describe your material before sending it. Do not send 'fantasy' scripts!" Produces sound filmstrips, 16mm and 35mm films, multimedia kits, tapes and cassettes, and 35mm slide sets. Pays 5-10% of budget.

GRAND CENTRAL PICTURES, INC., 12 E. 46th St., New York NY 10017. (212)687-4312. Vice President: Robert Aurech. Estab. 1977. Produces material for a "mass theatrical audience, those moviegoers 18-34 years of age." Buys 5 scripts/year. Query with samples, submit completed script, or submit resume. SASE. Reports in 2 months. Buys all rights or first rights.
Needs: "Feature-length film scripts, treatments, synopses based on concepts developed by Grand Central Pictures, writers' concepts, and adaptations of existing properties." Length: scripts, 100-135 pages; treatments, 15-30 pages; synopses, 1-6 pages. "We look for a professional approach to deadlines." Produces 35mm films. Pays $1,000-10,000; pays according to Writers Guild standards.

GARY GRIFFIN PRODUCTIONS, 12667 Memorial Dr., Houston TX 77024. (713)465-9017. Estab. 1975. Produces material for general audiences. Buys half of material used from outside writers. Submit outline/synopsis or submit resume. SASE. Reports in 2 weeks. Buys all rights. **Needs:** "We offer a broad entertainment package and can profide our clients with any of the services required, from concept to finished product. We prefer general-interest topics, but we also have many clients that require technical, medical, industrial, etc., material. We look for the ability to work in a flexible range, creative and innovative ideologies, and an amiable personality." Produces 16mm and 35mm films, TV commercials, videotape specials, commerical and TV pilots. Pays $100-75,000; pays according to Writers Guild standards.

HANDEL FILM CORP., 8730 Sunset Blvd., West Hollywood CA 90069. Contact: Peter Mertens. Produces material for a variety of audiences, depending on the film. Query. SASE. Buys all rights.
Needs: Material for educational and documentary films in science, history and other areas. Produces 16mm films. Payment negotiable.

HAYES SCHOOL PUBLISHING CO., INC., 321 Pennwood Ave., Wilkinsburg PA 15221. (412)371-2373. 2nd Vice President: Clair N. Hayes III. Produces material for school teachers, principals, elementary and junior high school students. Buys all rights. Catalog for SASE. Query. Produces charts, workbooks, teachers handbooks, posters, bulletin board material, and liquid duplicating books.
Needs: Education material only ("we will consider all types of material suitable for use in elementary schools"). Pays $25 minimum.

HESTER & ASSOCIATES, INC., 11422 Hines Blvd., Dallas TX 75229. (214)241-4859. President: Stew Hester. Produces material for school population—kindergarten through post-graduate students. Query. "We would prefer an outline of the idea; then we can respond if there is a relevance to our needs." Produces 8mm film loops, sound filmstrips, multimedia kits, tapes and cassettes, 35mm slides, and workbooks (with and without tapes). Buys "exclusive or nonexclusive" rights. Free catalog.
Needs: Education ("our major efforts at present are sales to schools—usually workbooks and activity books in math, art and science"). Pays 5-15% royalty.

IDEAL SCHOOL SUPPLY CO., Div. of Westinghouse Learning Corp., 11000 S. Lavergne Ave., Oak Lawn IL 60453. (312)425-0800. Manager, Product Development: Barbara Stiles. Estab. 1898. Produces material for primary, elementary and high school students. "The majority of our product line comes from outside sources, most of them practicing classroom teachers. The audiovisual materials have come from qualified educators or writers experienced in educational materials." Query with samples, submit outline/synopsis, or send resume. SASE. Reports in 3 months. Buys all rights. Free catalog.
Needs: "Style, format and length vary, according to grade level and subject matter of program. We are saturated in the career area, but would be interested in reviewing programs in language arts, reading, math for all grade levels K-12, and science for elementary levels." Produces charts, models, books, printed material, multimedia kits, tapes and cassettes, and study prints. Pays in royalties; "individual should contact company for information."
Tips: "Prepare a product idea by stating the objectives of the material and providing detailed instructions and uses of the product for review purposes."

IMARC CORP., Box H, Newtown Square PA 19073. (215)356-2000. President: Bob Barry. Estab. 1977. Produces material for management, sales people; customers; and trainees. "In the past 8 months we have worked with 7 writers and produced 16 audiovisual projects." Submit resume. SASE. Reports in 1 week. Buys all rights, or material is not copyrighted.
Needs: "We are very broad-based—from speech writing to full-length industrial films, brochures, technical writing, presentation formats, training and learning manuals and audiovisual projects, etc. We cover all fields, e.g., chemical, services, telephone, insurance, banks, manufacturers, etc." Produces charts, dioramas, film loops, silent and sound filmstrips, models, 16mm and 35mm films, phonograph records, tapes and cassettes, and slide sets. Pays $300-4,000/project.

IMPERIAL INTERNATIONAL LEARNING CORP., Box 548, Kankakee IL 60901. Director of Product Development: Anthony Iacuzzi. Educational AV publisher producing a variety of instructional aids for grades K through high school. Draws mainly from freelance sources on an assignment basis. Seeks authors skilled in writing sound filmstrips, cassette tape and multimedia programs. "Writers should submit a query letter which includes background and

professional writing experience." Reports in 6 weeks.
Needs: Reading and math are main areas of concentration. Pays fee within 30 days after acceptance of ms. Contract provided.
Tips: "Offer concrete evidence that specific needs and requirements of the company would be met."

IN-PERSPECTIVE COMMUNICATIONS, INC., 205 Lexington Ave., New York NY 10016. (212)889-2111. President: Sheppald Kerman. Estab. 1974. Produces material for corporate communications and industrial audiences. "Writers are hired for speeches, modules, new product intros, etc." Submit resume and sample scripts. SASE. Reports in 2-3 weeks. Buys all rights.
Needs: Scripts for educational, business, technical and general topics. "We look for experience." Produces charts, dioramas, film loops, silent and sound filmstrips, 16mm films, and song lyrics. Payment negotiable.

INSGROUP, INC., 16052 Beach Blvd., Huntington Beach CA 92647. Produces material for industrial, military (both enlisted men and officers), public schools (K-graduate level), police, nurses, and public administrators. Criteria for writers are determined on a project by project basis. Query with resume; be prepared to submit copies of previous efforts. SASE.
Needs: General material. Produces charts, silent and sound filmstrips, multimedia kits, overhead transparencies, tapes and cassettes, 35mm slides, study prints, teaching machine programs, and videotapes. "Insgroup develops objective-based validated audiovisual instructional programs both for commercial customers and for publication by Insgroup. These programs cover the entire range of subject areas, styles, formats, etc. Most writing is on a fee basis. Royalties, when given, are 5-8%."

INSTAR PRODUCTIONS, INC., 145 W. 55th St., New York NY 10019. Executives in Charge: John Gentile and Anthony Gentile. Estab. 1976. Produces material for the general movie-going public. Buys 3-4 completed screenplays/year. Query with completed script and synopsis. SASE. Reports in 2 months. Buys all rights.
Needs: "Intelligent feature film screenplays only—comedy, horror, action-thrillers. We look for the utmost professionalism." Produces 35mm films. Pays according to Writers Guild standards.

INSTRUCTOR CURRICULUM MATERIALS, 7 Bank St., Dansville NY 14437. (716)335-2221. Editorial Director: Margie H. Richmond. "US and Canadian school supervisors, principals, and teachers purchase items in our line for instructional purposes." Buys all rights. Writer should have "experience in preparing materials for elementary students, including suitable teaching guides to accompany them, and demonstrate knowledge of the appropriate subject areas, or demonstrable ability for accurate and efficient research and documentation. Please query. SASE. Free catalog.
Needs: "Elementary curriculum enrichment—all subject areas. Display material, copy and illustration should match interest and reading skills of children in grades for which material is intended. Production is limited to printed matter: posters, charts, duplicating masters, resource handbooks, teaching guides." Length: 6,000-12,000 words. "Standard contract, but fees vary considerably, depending on type of project."

INTERGROUP PRODUCTIONS, INC., 300 E. 59th St., New York NY 10022. (212)832-8169. Executive Producer: Rudolf Gartzman. Estab. 1971. Produces material for industry; theatrical release feature films; TV specials and documentaries; and dramatic nonfiction and fiction. Buys 12-15 scripts/year. Query with samples. SASE. Reports in 4-6 weeks. Buys all rights.
Needs: Industrial films and slide/sound productions; general sales, technical and promotional material; and sales training material. Produces 16mm and 35mm films, and slide sets. Pays $1,200-1,700 for 15-minute script with 1 draft and 3 rewrites; "individual company standard contract for industrial material; Writers Guild standards for film."

INTER-AMERICAN PRODUCTIONS, 630 9th Ave., Suite 908, New York NY 10036. Vice President/Director: Joe Schulman. Estab. 1976. Produces material for all audiences. Submit completed script. SASE. Reports in 3 weeks. Buys all rights or first rights.
Needs: "Our prime interest is in films for theatrical and/or TV use; however, we're always open to any interesting possibilities. We seek professionalism." Produces 16mm and 35mm films, phonograph records, tapes and cassettes, and slide sets. Pays according to Writers Guild standards.

JEAN-GUY JACQUE ET COMPAGNIE, 633 N. La Brea Ave., Los Angeles CA 90036. (213)936-7177. Owner: J.G. Jacque. Estab. 1971. Produces TV commercials. Query with samples. SASE. Reports in in 2-3 weeks. Buys all rights.
Needs: Produces 16mm and 35mm films. Pays according to Writers Guild standards.

JALOR PRODUCTIONS, INC., 119 W. 57th St., New York NY 10019. President: Paul L. Jacobson. Estab. 1962. Produces material for theatrical film, industrial film and television audiences. Submit outline/synopsis or submit resume. SASE. Reports in 4 weeks. Buys theatrical, TV and other film rights.
Needs: Produces 35mm films. Pays according to Writers Guild standards.

KAPCO COMMUNICATIONS, 5221 N. Elston Ave., Chicago IL 60630. (312)545-2544. President: K.L. Rubel. Produces material for general and business management audiences. "Most of our material comes from freelancers. Query to find out our specific needs, or about projects in the making. Do not submit stories or outlines; we want to see script ideas and finished scripts." Phone queries OK. SASE. Reports in 3 weeks. Buys all rights. Free writer's guidelines.
Needs: General interest, humorous (10-20 minutes), interview (related to business management), new product, technical, and travel (about the US, with visual appeal) subjects, and education subjects for students. Produces videotapes. Pays $100-750.

KEN-DEL PRODUCTIONS, INC., 111 Valley Rd., Richardson Park, Wilmington DE 19804. (302)655-7488. President: Ed Kennedy. Produces material for "elementary, junior high, high school, and college level, as well as interested organizations and companies." Query. SASE.
Needs: "Topics of the present (technology, cities, traffic, transit, pollution, ecology, health, water, race, genetics, consumerism, fashions, communications, education, population control, waste, future sources of food, undeveloped sources of living, food, health, etc.); topics of the future; and how-to series (everything for the housewife, farmer, banker or mechanic, on music, art, sports, reading, science, love, repair, sleep—on any subject)." Produces sound filmstrips; 8mm, 16mm, and 35mm films; 16mm film loops; phonograph records; prerecorded tapes and cassettes; slides.

KEY FILMS, 812 N. Highland, Hollywood CA 90038. (213)464-3303. President: Tod Jonson. Estab. 1974. Produces material for theatrical audiences. Buys 6 scripts/year. Submit outline/synopsis. SASE. Reports in 2 weeks. Buys all rights.
Needs: Full-length films rated PG, R and X. Produces 35mm films. Pays $1,000-3,500.

KNOWLEDGE TREE GROUP, INC., 12 E. 69th St., New York NY 10021. (212)737-0578. President/Editorial Director: H. Nabourney. Estab. 1967. Produces for the elhi and college market. Works with 10-15 writers/year. Query with samples or submit resumé. SASE. Reports in 3 weeks. Buys all rights. Catalog for SASE.
Needs: Elhi and college material in various subject areas: language arts, social studies, science, math, etc. Produces charts, sound filmstrips, 16mm films, multimedia kits, tapes and cassettes, and study prints. Pays 5-10% royalty, or by outright purchase.

LANSFORD PUBLISHING CO., Box 8711, San Jose CA 95155. (408)287-3105. Editor: Mary Chatton. Estab. 1968. Produces material for college, adult, industrial and business audiences. Buys 10-30 scripts/year. Query. SASE. Reports in 1 month. Buys all rights. Free catalog.
Needs: "Our chief sales area is in the fields of management, communication, psychology, and social problems. Produces multimedia kits; overhead transparencies (10-20 visuals plus booklet); tapes and cassettes (2-6 one-hour tapes/set); and slides (20 or more slides). Pays royalty.

WILLIAM V. LEVINE ASSOCIATES, INC., 18 E. 48th St., New York NY 10017. (212)751-1880. President: William V. Levine. Estab. 1967. Presentations for business and industry. Buys 1-2 scripts/month. Submit resume. SASE. Reports in 3 weeks. Buys all rights.
Needs: Business-related scripts on assignment for specific clients for use at sales meetings or for desk-top presentations. Also uses theme-setting and inspirational scripts with inherent messages of business interest. Produces charts, sound filmstrips, films, multimedia kits, tapes and cassettes, and slide sets. Pays $250-1,500.

LORI PRODUCTIONS, INC., 6430 Sunset Blvd., Hollywood CA 90028. (213)466-7567. Vice President, Administration: Emmy Cresciman. Estab. 1961. Produces material for industrial clients. Buys 5-10 scripts/year. Submit resume. SASE. Reports in 2-3 weeks. Buys all rights.

Needs: "We produce industrial films (sales, corporate image, training, safety), which generally run from six to twenty minutes in length." Seeks writers with a "clean, concise writing style; a familiarity with film production; and experience with industrial films." Produces silent and sound filmstrips, 16mm films, multimedia kits, tapes and cassettes, and slide sets. Pays by outright purchase of $500-2,000.

MAGNETIX CORP., 770 W. Bay St., Winter Garden FL 32787. (305)656-4494. President: John Lory. Produces material for the general public. "Personal contact must be made due to wide variety of very specific scripts we require." Buys all rights.
Needs: Produces tapes and cassettes: 20- to 30-minute audio programs with sound effects written to be sold to general public as a souvenir with some educational value. "Writers must have the ability to dramatize our subjects using sound effects, etc." Pays $300 minimum.

MAHAN & ASSOCIATES, INC., 1122 N. Grant, Odessa TX 79761. (915)332-1132. President: Richard L. Mahan. Estab. 1971. Produces material for business and professional audiences in the oil and gas industry and the medical profession. Buys 6 scripts/year. Query with samples or submit resume. SASE. Reports in 2 weeks. Buys all rights or first rights.
Needs: "We do a variety of work. We look for knowledge of the subject, on-time completion, and properly spelled words." Pays by outright purchase; pays according to Writers Guild standards.

ED MARZOLA & ASSOCIATES, 8831 Sunset Blvd., Suite 408, Hollywood CA 90069. (213)652-7481. Vice President/Creative Director: William Case. Estab. 1970. Produces material for educational and industrial audiences. Query with samples or submit resume. SASE. Reports in 10 days. Buys all rights.
Needs: "We now produce shows for the grammar school levels; also feature-length films for theatrical release." Produces sound filmstrips; 16mm and 35mm films; and videotaped presentations. Pays by outright purchase; "We negotiate each case individually." Pays according to Writers Guild standards.

MAXFILMS, INC. 2525 Hyperion Ave., Los Angeles CA 90027. (213)662-3285. Vice President: Sid Glenar. Estab. 1971. Produces material for audiences "from primary grade-school children to graduate students in our educational film division, and to all business and technical people in our industrial division. We also produce TV films and documentaries. The amount of material we use varies greatly from year to year, but on the average, perhaps 10-20 scripts are bought each year, with an additional 5-10 story ideas for TV films or documentaries." Query or submit outline/synopsis. SASE. Reports in 3 weeks. Rights purchased vary.
Needs: "The primary criterion is that the subject matter have entertainment as well as educational value. This does not preclude straight educational-informational scripts, but they must be entertainingly presented. All our productions are of low to moderate budgets, and therefore should not involve expensive locations, personalities, etc. Filmed animation is one of our primary areas of production." Produces 16mm and 35mm films and multimedia kits. Payment varies according to rights purchased.
Tips: "Develop skills at visualization as well as verbalization and utilize imagination to its fullest extent. Good ideas are always in demand."

MBM PRODUCTIONS, INC., 1909 Abrams Rd., Dallas TX 75214. (214)823-7130. President: Bernie Michaels. Estab. 1974. Produces material for business and industrial accounts and their clients/customers. Buys 20-40 scripts/year. Query; "our scripts are custom-written for our clients, as are our AV programs. We do not buy scripts on speculation." Not copyrighted.
Needs: "Our audiovisuals are custom-designed for our clients. We look for the ability to analyze the client's needs and audience needs, the ability to take criticism and respond to the client's requests for revisions objectively, the ability to think in visual as well as literal terms, and the ability to write in a conversational matter for audiovisual programs. We seek careful researchers (careful listeners)." Produces super 8mm film loops, sound filmstrips, 8mm and 16mm films, multimedia kits, tapes and cassettes, slide sets, teaching machine programs and videotapes. Pays $500-2,500, depending on the complexity of the job.

MEDIA-FOUR PRODUCTIONS, 6519 Fountain Ave., Hollywood CA 90028. (213)466-2266. Producer: Charles Finance. Estab. 1973. Produces material for television, school and lay audiences. Buys 4 scripts/year. Query with samples or submit resume. "Submit only materials that show talent for imaginative visual treatment of subject matter."SASE. Reports in 4 weeks. Buys all rights.

Needs: "Primarily treatments and complete shooting scripts on subjects dealing with science and technology. We seek imagination in your approach to scientific topics." Produces 16mm films. Payment, by outright purchase, is negotiated according to the script length and complexity.

MEDIAMAKERS, INC., 1443 11th St., Los Osos CA 93402. Media Public Relations Specialist: Patty Hodgin. Produces audiovisual materials geared to specific grade/acceptance levels: junior high school, high school, continuation school, college, trade/technical institutions, and health care service groups—all subjects considered. "Also, printed materials of interest to specialist bookstores, resource centers, libraries and direct-mail book clubs—how-to, self-help and back-to-the-earth subjects. Assignments considered/selected on basis of our reaction to synopsis of script; then, script/shooting script (split column form), production suggestions and teaching outline. Writer must be qualified in AV formats, with a clear understanding of age/grade level. Writing fees negotiated; relative to type of production, complexity of project, research required, production timelines and quality of material. Authors with established reputations whose name helps sell product net larger fee/percentage." SASE.
Needs: Multimedia kits, sound filmstrips, film loops, 35mm slide sets, comic format books and vocational education skillbooks. "Our filmstrips are fast-paced and average 50-75 frames with a 10- to 15-minute screen time. Well-planned series programs with 2, 3, 4 or 6 lessons always create quite a stir with us because their potential marketability."
Tips: "We have a genuine interest in producing either a series of filmstrips or animated featurettes in the woodcraft trades from a vocational perspective. Much material already exists in this area that offers only a basic skill approach; what's needed is an amplification into particular woodcraft skills/trades, We want to keep the pace fast, but not by sacrificing the basic instructional quality—the 'lessons' should progress well and knit together, yet still be able to stand on their own as a single unit. An excellent opportunity exists for 'that' writer with a special flare for creatively interlacing instructional depth with that unique sensitivity that not only holds students' interests, but wins awards."

ARTHUR MERIWETHER, INC., Box 457, Downers Grove IL 60515. Produces material for elementary and high school students. "Prior professional experience is required. Query. Background as an educator is often helpful." SASE. Catalog 75¢.
Needs: Educational material. "We prefer items applying to language arts, English, speech and drama studies to be used as a supplement to regular curriculum materials." Filmstrips (silent and sound), films, multimedia kits, and prerecorded tapes and cassettes. Games for learning also considered. "We will also consider filmstrip scripts that deal with subjects of contemporary religious interest for elementary and high school religious education groups. Liberal approach preferred. Professional quality only. Scripts purchased outright, or by royalty arrangement." Also needed are business-oriented mss or scripts on marketing and staff training. Pays 5% royalty.

MODE-ART PICTURES, INC., 3075 W. Liberty Ave., Pittsburgh PA 15216. (412)343-8700. Chairman: James L. Baker. Produces material for "all" audiences. Buys 5-10 scripts/year, but "each year is different." Query; "we write by contract." SASE. Reports in 3 weeks. Buys all rights. Free catalog.
Needs: Produces sound filmstrips, 16mm and 35mm films, slide sets, and teaching machine programs. "We seek writers who are flexible and willing to work. Good writers in our field are hard to find." Pays $1,000-5,000.

DOUG MOODY MYSTIC SOUND STUDIO'S MYSTIC MUSIC CENTER, 6277 Selma Ave., Hollywood CA 90028. For home entertainment, all ages. Works to be produced on phonograph albums and audiovisual records. "We are looking for works capable of being performed within one hour can be nonvisual. Can rely on sound effects to replace visual effects. Think about the medium!" Payment depending upon royalties to artists and musical copyright royalties. Buys phonograph and audiovisual rights. Query with synopsis. SASE.

TOM MORRIS, INC., 621 Devon Ave., Park Ridge IL 60068. (312)825-7182. President: Tom Morris. Buys 6-8 scripts/year. Query with samples or submit resumé. SASE. Reports in 2 weeks. Buys all rights.
Needs: Industrial, religious, teaching and training materials. Produces charts, silent and sound filmstrips, 16mm films, multimedia kits, tapes and cassettes, and slide sets. "Every job is custom; no set payment."

MOSS COMMUNICATIONS, INC., Suite 6A, 160 E. 38th St., New York NY 10016.

President: Jack Moss. Estab. 1966. Produces material for corporate audiences. Query or submit resume. Buys all rights.

Needs: "We would like to have a file of available writers of scripts for slidefilms, videotapes and films. We look for business-oriented writers who use good narration, good dialog and a creative approach." Produces super 8mm film loops, sound filmstrips, 16mm films, tapes and cassettes, slide sets, videotape, printed materials and leaders' guides. Payment, by outright purchase, is negotiable.

MOTIVATION MEDIA, INC., 110 River Rd., Des Plaines IL 60016. (312)297-4740. Executive Producer: Frank Stedronsky. Estab. 1969. Produces material for salespeople, customers, corporate/industrial employees and distributors. Query with samples. SASE. Reports in 3-4 weeks. Buys all rights.

Needs: Material for all audiovisual media—particularly marketing-oriented (sales training, sales promotional, sales motivational) material. Produces sound filmstrips, 16mm films, multimedia sales meeting programs, tapes and cassettes and slide sets. Pays $150-5,000.

MRC FILMS, Div. McLaughlin Research Corp., 71 W. 23rd St., New York NY 10010. Executive Producer: Larry Mollot. "Audience varies with subject matter, which is wide and diverse." Writer "should have an ability to visualize concepts and to express ideas clearly in words. Experience in motion picture or filmstrip script writing is desirable. Write us, giving some idea of background. Submit samples of writing. Wait for reply. We will always reply, one way or another. We are looking for new talent. No unsolicited material accepted. Work upon assignment only." Query. SASE.

Needs: "Industrial, documentary, educational, and television films. Also, public relations, teaching, and motivational filmstrips. Some subjects are highly technical in the fields of aerospace and electronics. Others are on personal relationships, selling techniques, ecology, etc. A writer with an imaginative visual sense is important." Produces silent and sound filmstrips, 16mm films, video programs, and tapes and cassettes. "Fee depends on nature and length of job. Typical fees: $500-1,000 for script for 10-minute film; $1,000-1,400 for script for 20-minute film; $1,200-2,000 for script for 30-minute film. Produces material for narration writing only, the range is $200-500 for a 10-minute film; $400-800 for a 20-minute film; $500-1,000 for a 30-minute film. Produces material for script writing services by the day, fee is $60-100 per day. All fees may be higher on specific projects with higher budgets."

MULTI-MEDIA PRODUCTIONS, INC., Box 5097, Stanford CA 94305. Assistant Program Director: Mark Vining. Estab. 1967. Produces material for elementary (grades 4-6) and secondary (grades 9-12) school students. Buys 24 scripts/year. Query or submit outline/synopsis. SASE. Reports in 3 weeks. Buys all rights. Free catalog.

Needs: "Material suitable for general high school and elementary school social studies curriculums: history, biography, sociology, psychology, anthropology, archeology and economics. Style should be straightforward, lively and objective." Approximate specifications: 50 frames, 10 minutes/program part; 2 sentences and one visual per frame; 1- or 2-part programs. Writer supplies script, slides for filmstrip, and teachers manual (as per our format). Royalties are paid quarterly, based on 12½% of return on each program sold.

Tips: "Submit creative ideas for filmstrip programs covering major curriculum topics as well as treating areas that larger companies will not touch because of the fear of not making enough profit through mass sales."

HENRY NASON PRODUCTIONS, INC., 250 W. 57th St., New York NY 10019. President: Henry Nason. Estab. 1972. Produces custom audiovisual presentations for corporate clients. Query with samples or contact for personal interview. SASE. Reports in 1 month. Buys all rights.

Needs: "Usually 10- to 15-minute scripts on corporate subjects, such as sales, marketing, employee benefits, products, systems, etc. Usually freestanding audiovisual modules. The style should be clear and relaxed, well-researched and organized. Writers must live in the New York City area." Produces filmstrips, multimedia material, tapes and cassettes, and slide sets. Pays "an average of 10% of the production budget."

NEBRASKA EDUCATIONAL TELEVISION COUNCIL FOR HIGHER EDUCATION, Box 83111, Lincoln NE 68501. (402)472-3611. Senior Producer—ITV: Darrell Wheaton. Produces material for educational/instructional television programs for college students for use in college classrooms. Query.

Needs: "Only persons experienced in preparing material for college level instructional film need inquire. Copies of previous materials must be available for consideration. We need full scripts in production format including all dialog and production suggestions, typed in a split column form, preferably. Requirements are specifically tailored to the particular lesson under development; the organization prepares material in most areas of study." Produces 16mm films, tapes and cassettes, and videotapes. Pays $50-2,000.

NORTHWOODS STUDIO, 12605 NE 2nd St., Bellevue WA 98005. (206)454-9470. Owner: Ron Arnold. Produces material for industrial audiences ranging from technical experts to the general public. Buys 2-3 scripts/year. Query. SASE. Reports in 2 weeks. Buys the rights requested by the client for whom Northwoods is producing the material.
Needs: "Scripts deal with specific industry/environment conflicts, giving a balanced view with a slightly pro-industry bias. Most work deals with forest-related subjects. Technical knowledge and a legislative background are essential. We use interviews with experts extensively. Our scripts require an ability to explain technical subjects to a general audience and to still keep the overall issues or field in mind. Writers must be able to deal with the emotional tensions of environmental/industry conflicts without taking sides. We look for the ability to research in depth, the ability to find relationships between seemingly disparate ideas and to give the audience the feeling of discovery and wonder in highly technical subjects. Those without a first-hand knowledge of the subject will not be considered. We have two rules: Heed *Elements of Style* and know the subject. Tyros need not apply." Length: 20 minutes. Produces sound filmstrips, 16mm films and slide sets. Pays according to Writers Guild standards.

NYSTROM, 3333 Elston Ave., Chicago IL 60618. Produces material for school audiences (kindergarten through 12th grade). Required credentials depend on topics and subject matter and approach desired. Query. SASE. Free catalog.
Needs: Educational material on social studies, earth and life sciences, career education, reading, language arts and mathematics. Produces charts, sound filmstrips, models, multimedia kits, overhead transparencies and realia. Payment varies with circumstances.

OUR SUNDAY VISITOR, INC., Audiovisual Dept., 200 Noll Plaza, Huntington IN 46750. Audiovisual Manager: Richard D. Hawthorne. Produces material for students (kindergarten through 12th grade), adult religious education groups, and teacher trainees. Query. SASE. Free catalog.
Needs: "We are looking for well-developed, detailed proposals. Complete programs are also considered. Programs should display an up-to-date audiovisual technique and cohesiveness. Broadly speaking, material should deal with religious education, including liturgy and daily Christian living, as well as structured catechesis. It must not conflict with sound Catholic doctrine, and should reflect modern trends in education. Word lengths may vary." Produces charts, sound filmstrips, overhead transparencies, phonograph records, tapes and cassettes, and multimedia kits. "Work-for-hire and royalty arrangements possible."

OUTDOOR PICTURES, Box 277, Anacortes WA 98221. (206)293-3200. Contact: Ernest S. Booth. "We would like to find qualified persons to design filmstrips, take the original photos or prepare the artwork, write the scripts and submit to us the entire package ready to produce. We make the internegative master then return the originals to you. We copyright all such materials, but allow you the right to sell any of the originals to others on a one-time basis."
Needs: "We are interested in all subjects that schools will buy. You should look at audiovisual catalogs and examine existing filmstrips, and work closely with one or more teachers in the grade level where your material would be used. We pay 10% royalty on the retail price of the production. Before you begin, write us for a set of guidelines and a free catalog of our filmstrips."

PACE FILMS, INC., 411 E. 53rd St., New York NY 10022. Contact: Mr. R. Vanderbes. Produces material for "TV and theatrical audiences in the US and worldwide." Writing assignments are handled through agencies, but independent queries or submissions are considered. SASE. Buys all rights.
Needs: "Feature films for TV and theaters." Pays according to Writers Guild of America standards.

PARAMOUNT COMMUNICATIONS, A Subsidiary of Paramount Pictures Corp., 5451 Marathon St., Hollywood CA 90038. Produces material for general audiences. Free catalog. Query. SASE.
Education: 16mm films and filmstrips. "Because we are distributors as well as producers of educational films and filmstrips, much of our activity concerns post-production work on films and filmstrips acquired and the marketing of these. For media that we produce, scripts are

usually written on assignment script writers known to us; educational films have special requirements to meet curriculum needs. Therefore, the opportunity for freelance writers here is limited. However, if a writer has information on an unusual subject which could be of interest it wouldn't hurt to query us. We consider films suitable for schools, business and industry, adult, health and vocational groups.

PENTACLE PRODUCTIONS, INC., 1408 W. 50th Terrace, Kansas City MO 64112. (816)931-2119. President: John Altman. Produces theatrical and made-for-TV films. "We buy or option 15-20 scripts and/or synopses per year." Submit outline/synopsis, submit completed script, or submit resume. SASE. Reports in 3 weeks. Buys all rights.
Needs: Theatrical motion picture properties. Produces 35mm feature films. Pays according to Writers Guild standards, and "varies greatly."

THE PERFECTION FORM CO., 8350 Hickman Rd., Des Moines IA 50322. Editor-in-Chief: Wayne F. DeMouth. Produces original manuscripts, sound filmstrips, cassette programs and learning packages for use in secondary language arts and social studies education. Reports in 30 days. Write for catalog.
Manuscripts: Prefers manuscripts of approximately 30,000-40,000 words—novelle written for young adult audiences ages 12-18. Fiction only. Pays on publication. Buys all rights. Content should be appropriate for average young people. Adventure stories, humor, school problems, personal conflict and choice, sports, family, courage and endurance. "No heavy moral overtones."
Tips: "Writers should study our products carefully before trying to submit their material."

PERPETUAL MOTION PICTURES, INC., 11 E. 44th St., New York NY 10017. (212)953-9110. Contact: Story Editor. Estab. 1968. Produces material for general, industrial, programming and sports audiences. Query with samples. SASE. Reports "rapidly." Buys all rights.
Needs: "We seek intelligence, and the ability to understand the requirements of specific jobs." Produces 16mm and 35mm films, videotape and TV programs. Payment varies.

PHOTOCOM PRODUCTIONS, Box 3135, Pismo Beach CA 93449. Creative Services Director: Brenda L. Pattison. Estab. 1970. Produces material for schools, junior high to university level. Query with samples or submit outline/synopsis. SASE. Reports in 2-3 weeks. Buys all rights. Free guidelines.
Needs: "We're most interested in how-to-do-its in vocational areas that can be used in high school shop classes or adult education classes. Material that we've been buying is 60-70 frames long." Produces sound filmstrips, multimedia kits, cassettes, and slide sets. Pays 10-15% royalty or $200 minimum/script.

PHOTO/GRAPHICS, 1125 E. Orange Ave., Monrovia CA 91016. (213)359-9414. Owner: Gary Moore. Estab. 1963. Produces educational material. Query and follow up with a personal call, or submit outline/synopsis. SASE. Reports in 3 weeks. Rights purchased vary.
Needs: "Educational material of an unusual nature with a slight theatrical slant. I am practically a one-man show and prefer to work with flexible people." Produces film loops, silent and sound filmstrips, 16mm and 35mm films, and slide sets. Pays royalty.

PHOTO-SYNTHESIS, INC., 440 Lincoln, Denver CO 80203. (303)744-1414. Head Copywriter: Sherry White. Estab. 1973. Produces material for internal and external industrial and corporate audiences. Query with samples, submit outline/synopsis, or submit resume. SASE. Reports in 2 weeks. Rights purchased vary.
Needs: Material about business ("with a motivational, educational, or thought-provoking slant on current issues"), communications, and technology and its impact. "We look for the ability to think and organize visually. Writers should understand practical business uses and applications." Produces multimedia kits; slide sets; and multi-image, multiscreen corparate cinema. Payment varies, but pays according to Writers Guild standards; may pay royalty or by outright purchase.

PIX PRODUCTIONS, 3843 S. Main St., Santa Ana California 92707. (714)957-1749. Executive Producer: M.D. Wertenberger Jr. Produces material for sales, public relations, business & industry training and school audiences. Buys 40-100 scripts/year—half are original, half are rewrite assignments. Query with samples or submit resume. SASE. Reports in 3 weeks. Buys all rights or first rights.
Needs: "All material is done on specific assignment. We look for previous filmstrip or film

experiences, and the ability to give a subject a new twist or a different viewpoint than the usual or obvious." Produces silent and sound filmstrips, multimedia kits, tapes and cassettes, and slide shows. Pays variable royalty, or by outright purchase of $250-2,000.

PLAYETTE CORP., 301 E. Shore Rd., Great Neck NY 11023. Contact: Sidney A. Evans. Produces material for "all school levels, teachers, and libraries." Writer must have "a complete and thorough knowledge of the subject with practical applied usage. Material must have been classroom-tested before submission." Query. SASE. No phone calls.
Education and Foreign Languages: Requirements "depend on subject selected." Produces charts, silent filmstrips, sound filmstrips, multimedia kits, overhead transparencies, records, tapes and cassettes, slides, study prints, and foreign language training aids and games. "Financial arrangements expected with inquiry."

PRODUCERS GROUP, LTD., 1 IBM Plaza, Suite 2519, Chicago IL 60611. (312)467-1830. Produces material for general audiences. "There is very little point in submitting scripts unless we have a specific project in hand. First, we get the assignment; then we go into creative work. We're not the best market for freelance submissions. Unsolicited mss are wasteful, inappropriate. If the writer has proven record, we match the project to the writer's skills and expertise. We originate most of our own creative material here. We prefer any writer to have at least a B.A., or equivalent experience. Must have a record in AV writing, and hopefully, production. We require a clean shooting script, with all visuals completely designated." Query. SASE.
Needs: Film loops and sound filmstrips, 16mm films, and multimedia kits. Business-oriented multimedia shows, educational films, and talk demonstrations. Editorial requirements vary according to assignments. Usually aim toward higher levels of educational background for business communications; aim toward specific age groups for educational films, as required. Usual lengths are 10-20 minutes. Fees negotiable. No royalty arrangements. Straight buyout.

PROFESSIONAL RESEARCH, INC., 12960 Coral Tree Place, Los Angeles CA 90066. Vice President: Richard J. Sternberg, M.D. Produces material for medical/surgical/dental/health care institutional patients, doctors, nurses, allied health professionals. "Looking for writers with experience in development of educational media for health care markets. Only require a few writers each year who must have familiarity with biological and medical/dental sciences, as well as have experience in AV writing." Query. Produces 16mm films, multimedia kits and videotapes.
Needs: Medicine (patient education films: live action and animation, lay language, 20 minutes or less; continuing education: content and format adapted to meet subject and audience needs). Pays $350 minimum (first draft)—$1,500 (completed script maximum).

Q-ED PRODUCTIONS, INC., Box 4029, Thousand Oaks CA 91359. Vice President, Marketing: Dave Anderson. Produces material for grade levels K-12. Buys all rights. Free catalog. "We are interested in reviewing completed filmstrip packages (4-6 filmstrips in a set) for distribution on royalty basis, or outright buy. Knowledge of the field and experience as a writer of filmstrips for education required. Also, demonstrated ability in research required. We look for the new approach. Unique ways of imparting information so that children will want to learn more and on their own. Definitely not interested in didactic, mundane approaches to learning." Query. SASE.
Education: Grade levels K-12. Interested in core curriculum materials. Historically strong in values. Materials should be inquiry-oriented, open-ended, strong objectives (cognitive, affective, psycho-motor). Royalties open on original materials. Fees range from $450 for a 10-minute filmstrip.

RHYTHMS PRODUCTIONS, Whitney Bldg., Box 34485, Los Angeles CA 90034. Contact: R.S. White. "Our audience is generally educational, with current projects in early childhood." Query. "We need to know a writer's background and credits and to see samples of his work." SASE for response to queries.
Education: Books, sound filmstrips, 16mm films, multimedia kits, phonograph records, tapes and cassettes, and study prints. "Our firm specializes in creative productions, so though content is basic to the productions, a creative and imaginative approach is necessary."

RIDDLE VIDEO AND FILM PRODUCTIONS, INC., 507 5th Ave., New York NY 10017. (212)697-5895. President/Executive Producer: William Riddle. Produces material for "general public, young and old alike. Also for theater distribution." Free writer's guidelines. Writer "must be experienced and well-qualified in the subject in order to handle work assignments satisfactorily. We must see a sample of his or her work." Query. SASE for response to queries. Reports in 2 months.

General: "Story boards and scripts are needed." Produces 8mm, 16mm and 35mm film loops; silent filmstrips; sound filmstrips; kinescopes; models; 8mm, 16mm and 35mm films; multimedia kits; tapes and cassettes; slides; study prints; videotape productions. Pays "standard going rates, with bonus on super work performed."

RMI MEDIA PRODUCTIONS, INC., 120 W. 72nd St., Kansas City MO 64114. (816)561-2284. President: David L. Little. Estab. 1964. Produces material for schools (grades K-12), colleges, and adults (business and industry). Query with samples or submit resume. SASE. Reports in 3 weeks. Buys all rights. Free catalog.

Needs: Vocational, technical and general training. Produces sound filmstrips and slide sets. Pays "negotiable" outright purchase price.

DICK ROBERTS FILM CO., INC., 48 W. 10th St., New York NY 10011. President: Dick Roberts. Estab. 1964. Produces material for public and children's audiences. Buys $10,000 worth of material/year. Submit outline/synopsis. SASE. Reports in 3 months. Not copyrighted.

Needs: "Short motion picture subjects, preferably without words (for foreign markets)." Produces 16mm films. Pays royalty.

ROSEWORLD ENTERTAINMENT, 9000 Sunset Blvd., Suite 1020, Los Angeles CA 90069. (213)273-5573. President: Jack Rose. Estab. 1973. Produces material for general audiences. Buys 5 scripts/year. Submit completed script. SASE. Reports in 2 weeks. Buys all rights.

Needs: General feature film material. Produces 35mm films. Pays by outright purchase.

SAVE THE CHILDREN, 48 Wilton Rd., Westport CT 06880. (203)226-7272. Producer: Joseph Loya. Generally buys all rights, "but it depends on project. We use work only written for specific assignments." Produces 16mm films, tapes and cassettes, 2¼x2¼ slides and posters and displays.

Needs: General (radio and TV); and education (high school, college and adult). Pays $250-500 minimum/assignment.

ELLIOT SCHICK PRODUCTIONS, 2175 Castilian Dr., Los Angeles CA 90068. (213)874-2722. President: Elliot Schick. Estab. 1960. Produces theatrical features and "long-form television." Works with 10 writers/year, but this figure "varies from year to year." Submit outline/synopsis or submit completed script. SASE. Reports in 6 weeks.

Needs: Produces feature-length 35mm films. Payment is negotiable.

SCHICK SUNN CLASSIC PICTURES, 556 E. 200 S., Salt Lake City UT 84102. Director, Product Acquisition: Richard Staley. Estab. 1969. Produces G-rated family films and primetime television. Reports in 4 weeks. Buys all rights.

Needs: We really seek ideas—we have our own staff of sceenwriters to write scripts. We want to know what creative non-industry writers are interested in, subjects that we hope will appeal to a large audience of widely varying ages now pretty much ignored by Hollywood. Because we emphasize family films there are obvious limits to what is acceptable to us: properties emphasizing sex, violence, vulgar language generally do not meet our requirements. But G films need not be pap. Nor are we looking for Disney-type films—our audiences tend to be older than Disney's; parents bring their children to Sunn films, not the other way around. We are very interested in themes the major studios will not cover. Themes with religious overtones (*In Search of Noah's Ark* or *Beyond and Back*) but of wide general interest have worked well for us. Another genre we have done successfully is the unexplained or mysterious phenomena docu-drama (*The Lincoln Conspiracy* or *The Bermuda Triangle*). Sunn's early successes were with outdoor action-adventures (*The Life and Times of Grizzly Adams*) although our interest has largely shifted from this feature film genre. We do not wish to be limited to these categories, however, and thus encourage ideas on any subject that will appeal to parents and their children. Minimum payment for a feature film idea is $1,000. Minimum payment for a television idea is $500. If we buy an idea (concept) from a writer, we will research. Under the above conditions, separate payment for a writer's services as a consultant, researcher or technical adviser is possible. On the approach writers should take in submitting material to us: please make a postcard request for our submissions package. Be sure to specify whether you are submitting a feature film or television concept. Concepts must be limited to 500 words or they will be returned unread, as will all unsolicited materials. We will only accept material accompanied by our own unrevised standard agreements. If you specify that you have a full screenplay, we will send you appropriate forms, but please include a short (500 words maximum) treatment. We prefer that screenplays be submitted only by recognized literary agents. With just 500 words to work with a writer should imagine he or she is doing a 60-second radio commercial—i.e., advance the plot along simply or quickly, present as much visual imagery and as many exciting elements as space will allow.

Tips: "Learn as much about Sunn Classic Pictures as possible and tailor story ideas (concepts) accordingly—essentially what any good freelancer does anyway. We get a tremendous number of submissions that simply do not indicate any real awareness of our needs. We still do best with subjects the *National Enquirer*, for example, might capitalize on. Since we have a staff of professional screenwriters and receive many projects from established agents it is very unlikely that we are going to buy nonprofessional scripts. Getting such a specialized, difficult job done quickly and effectively leaves little time to bring along new talent. But through our concept review process a writer at least has a chance to get his foot in our door simply with an idea, something Hollywood rejects."

SEVEN OAKS PRODUCTIONS, 9145 Sligo Creek Pkwy., Silver Spring MD 20901. (301)587-0030. Production Manager: M. Marlow. Estab. 1957. Produces material for students, civic and professional groups, and PTA chapters. Buys 30 scripts from 10 writers/year. Query with samples, submit outline/synopsis or submit completed script. SASE. Reports in 8 weeks. Buys all rights or first rights, but rights purchased are negotiable.
Needs: Educational, medical, safety and general entertainment material. "We look for clarity in style, imagination with the ability to get information across and accomplish objectives, the ability to meet deadlines and to dig if necessary to get sufficient information to make the script better than another on the same subject. Writers should know the film format." Produces 16mm films, multimedia kits, phonograph records, tapes and cassettes, and slide sets. Payment negotiable according to project.

AVI SHULMAN & SONS, 19 Grove St., Monsey NY 10952. Contact: Avi Shulman. Estab. 1967. Produces material for Jewish and general educational audiences. Buys 5 scripts/year. Query with samples. SASE. Reports in 3 weeks. Buys all rights.
Needs: Educational, religious and general material. Produces silent and sound filmstrips, multimedia kits, tapes and cassettes, and slide sets. Pays royalty or by outright purchase.

SKYLINE FILMS, INC., 160 E. 38th St., New York NY 10016. (212)430-1668. Vice President: David Saperstein. Estab. 1963. Produces material for television, industrial and educational clients. Buys 12 scripts/year. Query, submit outline/synopsis, or submit completed script. SASE. Reports in 4 weeks. Buys options on material.
Needs: "Our needs are general." Produces sound filmstrips, 16mm and 35mm films, tapes and cassettes, and videotape. Pays in royalties or by outright purchase.

SOUND CONCEPTS, INC., 30 Hazel Terrace, Woodbridge CT 06525. (203)397-1363. President: James Lush. Executive Vice President: Jeffrey Hedquist. Estab. 1968. Produces material for industrial customers, employees, students and the general public. Buys 7 scripts/year. Submit resume. SASE. Reports in 1 month. Buys all rights.
Needs: Educational, religious, business, technical, medical and general radio and TV scripts and storyboards. "Our productions are so varied that we would be interested in the credentials of a writer. Then, as projects come up, we will discuss them on an individual basis, and at that time look at or listen to previous work. We seek flexibility, experience, willingness to get involved, the ability to communicate, and, sometimes, geographic proximity." Produces 8mm and 16mm film loops, sound filmstrips, 16mm films, phonograph records, tapes and cassettes, and slide sets. Pays $200-20,000.

SOUTH CAROLINA EDUCATIONAL TELEVISION NETWORK, Drawer L, Columbia SC 29250. (803)758-7261. Assistant Director, Professional Organizations/Program Development: Ms. Mickey Rogers. Estab. 1960. Produces material for the general public; training and career development for business and industry; college courses; and on-going adult education in fields of medicine, dentistry and technical education. Query or submit resume. SASE. Reports in 2 weeks. Buys all rights.
Needs: "The Division of Continuing Education works in all media. Since, as a state agency, we work with other state agencies of varying needs, style, format, length, etc. are determined for each individual project." Produces kinescopes, 16mm films, multimedia kits, overhead transparencies, tapes and cassettes, slides, videotape and live in-studio television productions, also related printed materials for training programs. Payment "depends on funding governed by South Carolina state law guidelines."

Tips: Submit resume and if possible come in for an interview and bring in samples of previous work.

SPENCER PRODUCTIONS, INC., 507 5th Ave., New York NY 10017. (212)697-5895. Contact: Bruce Spencer. Produces material for high school students, college students, and adults. Occasionally uses freelance writers with considerable talent. Query. SASE.
Satire: 16mm films, prerecorded tapes and cassettes. Satirical material only. Pay is negotiable.

SPOKEN LANGUAGE SERVICES, INC., Box 783, Ithaca NY 14850. (607)257-0500. President: J.M. Cowan. Estab. 1972. Produces material for "any and all foreign language beginners in 30+ languages." Produces 6 new books/year. Submit resume. SASE. Reports in 2 weeks. Buys all rights. Free catalog.
Needs: Produces tapes and cassettes. Pays in outright purchase price "depending on time put in."

SPOTTSWOOD STUDIOS, 2524 Old Shell Rd., Box 7061, Mobile AL 36607. (205)478-9387. Co-owner: M.W. Spottswood. Estab. 1952. "We normally work for sponsors (not always) who seek public attention." Query with samples. SASE. Reports in 2 weeks. Buys all rights.
Needs: Business; religious; and general. Produces 16mm films and 8mm loops; sound filmstrips; and slide sets. Pays in outright purchase price.

AL STAHL ANIMATED, 1600 Broadway, New York NY 10019. (212)265-2942. President: Al Stahl. Estab. 1950. Produces industrial, sales promotion, educational and television commercial material. Query. SASE. Buys first rights. Free catalog.
Needs: "We specialize in making movies from slides, and in converting slide shows and multimedia (three or more screens) into a one-screen movie." Produces 8mm and 16mm films, and multimedia kits. Pays by outright purchase.

SUNTREE PRODUCTIONS, LTD., 220 E. 23rd St., New York NY 10010. (212)686-4111. President: D.W. Funt. Estab. 1974. Produces material for commercial, industrial and educational audiences. "We bought 16 scripts last year from six writers." Submit resume; we will call writers with interesting resumes when projects are available." Buys all rights.
Needs: "We are contract producers. Our needs vary from big-budget multimedia shows to educational filmstrips. We look for speed, accuracy, flexibility, wit and intelligence." Produces charts, sound filmstrips, multimedia shows, tapes and cassettes, and slide sets. "Payment varies according to the project and the writer's experience."

SUPER 8 FILMS BY SUTHERLAND, 28 Smith Terrace, Staten Island NY 10304. (212)447-3908. General Manager: Don Sutherland. Estab. 1975. "Ours are made-for-hire films that serve specific functions for our clients, usually firms or institutions that benefit from expedient, low-cost motion picture communication. Sales demos, personnel training, fundraising and sociological documentations are typical. Nearly all our scripts are created in-house, on assignment from clients; however, possible expansion into the videocassette field may broaden future requirements." Query. SASE. Reports "as soon as possible." Rights purchased depend on the application of the completed production.
Needs: "There is a possibility of our entering the home-distribution videocassette market. We may do so through materials that represent nonmainstream points of view in dramatic programming. Thus our bad guys may be good, our good guys bad, our sexy stuff more erotic than hamburger; but hamburger is what we may make of assorted sacred cows. We think that most sacred cows, whether traditional or 'now,' comprise a lot of bull. We tend to favor themes and concepts that encourage optimism and people's pride in themselves. Activism and self-determination are values we like to hold as ideals; self-pity, though generally fashionable these days, will not find its way into any catalog we produce. We subscribe to the philosophy that people of various races, religions, sexes and sexual inclinations are different from one another, and that such differences should be played to the hilt. We look for the ability and willingness to do as promised." Produces super 8mm films. Payment is negotiable.

TALCO PRODUCTIONS, 279 E. 44th St., New York NY 10017. (212)697-4015. President: Alan Lawrence. Produces for TV and film programming for schools, foundations, industrial organizations and associations. Buys all rights. "We maintain a file of writers and call on those with experience in the general category. We do not select unsolicited ms. We prefer to receive a writer's resume—listing credits. If his experience merits, we will be in touch when a project seems right." Produces sound filmstrips, films, videotapes, phonograph records, tapes and cassettes, and slide sets.

Needs: General (client-oriented productions to meet specific needs); education (peripheral market); business (public relations, documentaries, industrial); foreign language (we sometimes dub shows completed for clients for a specific market). Payment runs $500 and up; usually Writers Guild minimums apply.

TELSTAR PRODUCTIONS, INC., 366 N. Prior Ave., St. Paul MN 55104. Program Consultant: Dr. Victor Kerns. Produces video material for adult, college-level audience, in industry and continuing education. Buys video recording rights. Query. Produces instructional videotapes not intended for broadcast.
Needs: Education (curricular materials for small group or independent study); business (training and development material); and medicine (paramedical topics). Pays $100 plus royalties.

BOB THOMAS PRODUCTIONS, Box 1787, Wayne NJ 07470. (201)696-7500. President: Robert G. Thomas. Buys all rights. "Send material with introductory letter explaining ideas. Submit outline or rough draft for motion picture or business matter. If possible, we will contact the writer for further discussion." SASE.
Business, Education, and General: "We produce 3 types of material for 3 types of audiences: 8mm film loops in sports and pre-teen areas (educational); 8mm and 16mm films for business (educational, distributed by agencies); 35mm films for entertainment for a general audience (theater type). General subject matter may be of any style, any length. Produces material for the future, 35mm theatrical shorts for distribution." Payment "depends on agreements between both parties. On 8mm and 16mm matter, one fee arrangement. On 35mm shorts, percentage or fee."

FRANCIS THOMPSON, INC., 231 E. 51st St., New York NY 10022. Vice President: Byron McKinney. Estab. 1957. Produces material for varied audiences. Query with samples. SASE.
Needs: "Sophisticated material." Produces films. Pays by outright purchase.

TROLL ASSOCIATES, 320 Rt. 17, Mahwah NJ 07430. (201)529-4000. Contact: M. Schecter. Estab. 1968. Produces material for elementary and high school students. Buys approximately 200 scripts/year. Query or submit outline/synopsis. SASE. Reports in 2-3 weeks. Buys all rights. Free catalog.
Needs: Produces film loops, silent and sound filmstrips, multimedia kits, tapes and cassettes, and books. Pays royalty or by outright purchase.

UNIVERSAL TRAINING SYSTEMS CO., 3201 Old Glenview Rd., Wilmette IL 60091. (312)251-8700. Creative Director: Paul W. Jensen. Estab. 1968. Produces complete training programs for business and industry. "We work with 10-12 freelance writers on a fairly steady basis." Submit resume. SASE. Reports in 2-4 weeks. Buys all rights.
Needs: "We produce custom training programs in a variety of media. Subject areas include sales training, management development, technical skills, data entry and word processing, and customer service. Experience in training and/or subject matter expertise are almost essential. We do not use 'pure creative' writers for freelance assignments. Potential new sources may be asked to complete a brief test assignment for which no fee is paid." Produces workshops, self-instructional programs, sound filmstrips, motion pictures, videotapes, audio cassettes, manuals, texts, study guides, workbooks, etc. Pays $300-3,000.
Tips: Submit a letter and resume, with a description of the projects and request the company's application for freelance assignments. After returning the completed application be prepared to submit typewritten manuscript of requested samples of work."

VIDEO FILMS, INC., 2211 E. Jefferson Ave., Detroit MI 48207. (313)393-0800. President: Clifford Hanna. Produces material for industrial audiences. Submit resume. SASE.
Needs: Industrial and commercial market material. Produces filmstrips, 8mm and 16mm films, prerecorded tapes and cassettes, and slide sets. Payment negotiable.

VIDEOCOM, INC., 502 Sprague St., Dedham MA 02026. (617)329-4080. Executive Vice President: W.S. Taylor. Vice president of production and creative services: L.A. Lessard. Estab. 1970. Produces materials for broadcast, industrial and educational audiences. Buys 25 scripts/year. Query with samples. Buys all rights.
Needs: "Scripts and copy for broadcast and industrial clients ranging from commercials to marketing and training programs and printed materials. We look for originality in the ability to understand problems and in the design of a solution." Produces videotape (all formats), motion pictures, slide presentations and printed materials. Pays by outright purchase.

NORMAN VIRAG PRODUCTIONS, 3415 N. East St., US 27, Lansing MI 48906. (517)374-8193. Owner: Norman J. Virag. Estab. 1977. Produces material for general audiences. Buys 6 scripts/year. Query with samples. SASE. Reports in 2 weeks. Buys all rights. Free catalog.
Needs: "We are an audiovisual production company experienced in producing and directing 16mm films, sound filmstrips and slide shows, multimedia presentations, videotapes, radio and television spots, pamphlets, brochures and live shows in the areas of public relations, sales, training, industry and education. We look for an understanding of the material and the ability to translate that understanding into script form." Pays $500-1,500, or pays 10% of budget royalty.

VISUAL EDUCATION CORP., Box 2321, Princeton NJ 08540. Vice President: William J. West. Estab. 1969. Produces material for elementary and high schools. Submit resumé and samples. Submissions will not be returned; "we like to keep a file of freelancers on whom we can call." Reports in 1 month. Buys all rights.
Needs: "Most of our audiovisual work is in filmstrips of about 80 frames (10 minutes). Topics range from language arts to social studies and home economics. Most use a combination of live-action photography and artwork." Produces sound filmstrips, films, teacher's guides and student activity material, multimedia kits, and tapes and cassettes. Pays $250 minimum.

VISUAL HORIZONS, 208 Westfall Rd., Rochester NY 14620. (716)442-3600. President: Stanley Feingold. Estab. 1972. Produces material for general audiences. Buys 20 programs/year. Query with samples. SASE. Reports in 5 months. Buys all rights. Free catalog.
Needs: Business, medical and general subjects. Produces silent and sound filmstrips, multimedia kits and slide sets. Payment negotiable.

VOCATIONAL EDUCATION PRODUCTIONS, California Polytechnic State University, San Luis Obispo CA 93407. (805)546-2623. Production Supervisor: Rick Smith. Query. SASE.
Needs: Produces sound filmstrips, multimedia kits, tapes and cassettes, and 35mm slide sets. "We usually furnish script development pages for the typing of final drafts, just to make it easier to work with the script. Our productions deal almost exclusively with agricultural subjects. Since we sell around the world, we cannot focus on a limited regional topic. Total length of our filmstrips is about 10 minutes, or 50-70 frames. Avoid talking down to the viewer. Technical accuracy is an absolute must." Pays $200/script for a series of 3-6; $400-600 for a single script.

JERRY WARNER & ASSOCIATES, 8455 Fountain Ave., # 309, Los Angeles CA 90069. Produces material for business, government, school and television audiences. Copyright depending on client situation. "We buy full rights to writers' works for sponsored films. Writer must be a professional screenwriter or within the discipline of the special area of subject matter. Do not submit single copy material. Have the material registered for datemark, or Writers Guild protection. We accept no responsibility of unsolicited manuscripts." Will answer inquiries within the boundaries of production interest. SASE.
Needs: Scripts on business and general topics. Produces sound filmstrips; multimedia kits; tapes and cassettes; sponsored business and government films; and training, public information, public relations, sales promotion, educational and report films. Royalties are paid on proprietary films that writers take equity in rather than full fee, participations. "We read concepts for educational and documentary films and properties for feature films, but do not solicit scripts as a general rule. Fees vary and depend upon individual client or agency. We frequently pay from $75-100 per day for research periods and from $650-2,000 per reel of script. The wide variance is indicative of how each project has different scope and must be approached on the basis of talent requirement."

WILMAC RECORDS, TAPES AND FILMSTRIPS, 301 East Shore Rd., Great Neck NY 11023. Production Supervisor: Leah D. Evans. Estab. 1950. Produces foreign language-related products. Buys 10 projects/year. Submit resume. SASE. Reports in 4 weeks. Buys all rights.
Needs: Foreign language. Produces charts, silent and sound filmstrips, multimedia kits, overhead transparencies, phonograph records, tapes and cassettes, relia, slides, and study prints. Pays no royalties; "negotiation only per project."

WREN ASSOCIATES, INC., 145 Witherspoon St., Princeton NJ 08540. (609)924-8085. President: Karl Faller. Estab. 1972. Produces material for corporate personnel and sales audiences. Buys 35-40 scripts/year. Query or submit resume. Not copyrighted.
Needs: Business, sales, public relations and training scripts. "We look for experience in our

field." Produces sound filmstrips, 16mm films, tapes and cassettes, slide sets and videotapes. Pays $500-6,000.

YASNY PRODUCTIONS, 8282 Sunset Blvd., Los Angeles CA 90046. (213)654-6306. Executive Story Editor: Muriel Seligman. Estab. 1972. Produces material for theatrical audiences. "Our *new* program will expect to do 10 films in the next three years." Submit outline/synopsis, submit completed script or submit resume. "The submitted material must have a Writers Guild of America number." SASE. Reports in "about one month at most; we try to report as soon as possible." Buys movie and TV rights.

Needs: "We're making feature films to appeal to as broad an audience as possible with budgets of up to $2 million. So, our main interest is in stories with characters of interest (as opposed to special effects, etc.). We are interested in encouraging minority and handicapped writers—as well as 'mainstream' writers. We look for an understanding of what a motion picture script is. We seek good use of dialog and a strong story sense." Produces feature-length films, with an eye for foreign and television use. Payment is negotiable, but is in accordance with Writers Guild standards.

Book Publishers

The book publishing industry has "never been healthier," says Alan Turner, editorial director of the Chilton Book Company. "The really professional writer probably has more opportunities today than ever before."

Charles Adams with Dell Publishing echoes Turner's optimism, saying the book industry is "expanding and eager to develop new writers."

Other editors are more cautious when evaluating a writer's chances in today's book market. Paper shortages, concentration on mass-market titles, mergers of large publishing houses, rising postage costs—all are cited as promoting an industry-wide atmosphere of caution that works against writers.

Yet, more and more books are being published. Therefore, more and more writers are being published. "Publishers' lists keep getting larger, increasing the marketplace for writers," says Michael Seidman, editorial director of Charter Books.

What's more, David Wright of Coward, McCann & Geoghegan sums up many editors' beliefs when he says, "It should be pointed out that editors are eager to publish novels of quality, and that, even in today's sales-oriented atmosphere, novels of true merit *will* get published, somewhere. It's a matter of finding a sympathetic editor (best done by first finding a sympathetic agent)." Wright's comments can also apply to nonfiction.

Finding a sympathetic reader involves research, knowledge of the marketplace, and a feel for trends in not only what's being published, but also what's being read.

Begin your research by touring a few bookstores. Check what's displayed prominently; note what's collecting dust in the back. Study bestseller lists. (*Publishers Weekly*, a trade magazine available in most libraries, publishes such lists, as well as detailed information on what's being published and by whom. Add it to your reading list.) Consider not only the subjects covered in popular books, but also how the subjects were treated. For example, are heavily illustrated books popular this year? Books written in the first person? Books quoting authorities as opposed to books written by authorities?

This research isn't intended to provide ideas, subjects and treatments to copy. Instead, it gives you a handle on your competition. Mimicry sometimes works, but original subjects—or original treatments of standard subjects—sell more books than what might be termed "creative plagiarism."

Note trends (which are different from fads), and try to respond to them. Some trends observed in book publishing over the last year include:

● More specialization. "Specialization is the new strength of publishing today, whether it be in an academic field or gothic,"says John Luckman, editorial director of GBC press. "A house that thoroughly understands its subject and its audience can produce a better-for-the-consumer, more-profitable-for-the-publisher title." Crestline Publishing's editorial director, George Dammann, concurs, adding that business seems good for small, specialized publishers. "For competent writers," he says, "highly specialized fields appear to hold good promise—though financial rewards might be lower than in the broader markets."

● Religious books remain an important part of the market. "The religious book field is healthier today than it was 10 years ago," says Anne Geoghegan, book editorial director of Our Sunday Visitor. "New writers—who write well and who have something worth reading to write about—have unlimited opportunity."

● University presses are making forays into general trade subjects. "University presses will be looking for scholarly books of wider than academic interest: biography, history, criticism and the like that will appeal to wider (though not necessarily mass) audiences," says Paul Rohmann, director of the Kent State University Press. "Specialized monographs will probably be fewer or appear in different formats: microform, publishing-on-demand and the like." For coverage of the university press scene, see "Send Your Book Manuscripts to College" in the November 1978 *Writer's Digest* (available at the library or for $1.50 from *WD*, 9933 Alliance Rd., Cincinnati 45242).

● Though the number of nonfiction titles published overwhelms the number of fiction titles, interest remains high in genre fiction and well-plotted mainstream novels. "We do quite well with vicarious adventure for both men and women," says David Harris of Belmont-Tower Books. "This means war, adventure and westerns for men, and action romances for women. We don't anticipate any change in the need for such books, but we're very interested in seeing anything that would fill it in new ways, as the only constant in readers' taste is that it changes." Genre, Harris says, isn't as important as it once was. "Although there normally are trends in the book market, at present we seem to be between them. Historical romances are fading, but nothing has come forward to replace them. For that reason, it is easier now for a book to succeed simply because it is good, without having to be tied in to a particular theme or format." Cynthia Kirk of Thomas Y. Crowell observes that "good, solid novels, with strong plots and convincing characterizations, that are well-written and thoughtful (like *Garp, Final Payments* and *Thorn Birds* seem to do well in hardcover."

This, by no means, reflects a dissolution of genre fiction. "Category publishing (mysteries, science fiction, westerns) are holding their own and should continue to do so, perhaps even providing the basis for the big sellers in a couple of years," says Charter's Michael Seidman. Don't, however, try to conquer one of the category markets if you're not familiar with it. Seidman finds it "upsetting" that some writers "think that just because they've read a mystery they can write a mystery."

a Budget cuts for schools and libraries are affecting juvenile material. "The institutional market is weaker than a few years ago, and publishers are trying for more bookstore sales," says James Giblin, editor-in-chief of Clarion Books. This means that children's books are becoming more like adult trade books, he says. Another trend noted in children's books is that "the 'heavy realism' is fading," says Independence Press's Margaret Baldwin. "But what next? That's the question. Whoever comes up with the answer will have it made."

Once you've selected a topic, consult *Books in Print* to see what's currently on the market covering that subject. "Take a hard-nosed look at what else is available on the same subject for the same audience, and try to convince, first of all yourself, then the prospective publisher, that what I have written is sufficiently different *and better* to warrant publication," advises Marlin VanEldern, editor-in-chief of William B. Eerdmans Publishing Company.

The next step, says VanEldern, is to find the likeliest publisher for the proposal. More research is required. "Too many writers who submit material to us have not done their homework," says Crowell's Cynthia Kirk. "Research into a house's publishing history and practices should be the first step in getting a manuscript published. Trying to pair the right book with the right house with the right editor (whenever possible) saves a great deal of time, effort and money all around."

Start the research by studying the following listings, which include the essentials for choosing the right publisher. Many publishers prefer to be queried or sent an outline/synopsis of the proposal and a few sample chapters. When using the latter method, type a succinct one- or two-page synopsis of your book, attach it to the first two chapters and one other that is well-written, and include an outline of the whole work. Only in cases where a publisher's listing states that complete manuscripts are considered should you send one (see "Submitting Your Work" for more information on submissions).

Put your best into the proposal. The first page should captivate the reader, and the rest should hold him through to the end. "We are looking for writers who can grab the reader just as a TV show does," says Dr. Robert Bender, editorial director of Fearon/Pitman Publishers. "Like it or not, publishers are competing with TV programming." Seidman says, "If you're going after the category market, grab the reader. Start with some action.

Make the submission neat and concise. Everything you do to polish the manuscript and give it a professional look helps. "There are certain qualities that will tip our decision on a marginal book one way or the other," says David Harris. "We like accuracy of detail and grammar. Good typing without extensive corrections by hand will make a book easier to read—and easier to like." Michael Seidman adds, "I hate it when everything's misspelled. That's just sloppy."

Also study the company's book catalog, which is an informative chronicle of the company's focus and interests. Libraries and major bookstores often carry catalogs, and many publishers are willing to send interested writers a catalog (either free, for SASE, or for some small charge).

In many cases, having an agent helps, not only in getting your manuscript to the right editor, but also in negotiating a contract, reselling the book, etc. (For more on agents, see the introduction to the Authors' Agents section.)

When that letter of acceptance reaches you, celebrate—but don't let the euphoria carry you away. You still have work to do. A contract will be offered you; scrutinize it. Take it to a lawyer for further scrutiny. Know what each clause of the contract means before you sign it. Unpublished writers don't have much bargaining power, but you should know enough about contracts that you can recognize a bad one should you be offered one. Don't sign a contract you're unhappy with.

Publishers sometimes offer an *advance* against royalties; that is, money paid when the manuscript is accepted that is later charged against the author's profits. Advances vary greatly, depending on who you are, who your publisher is, what you've written, and how well the book is expected to sell. Advances can range from $100 allowances for typing fees to hundreds of thousands of dollars for major multiple book contracts. A few publishers may pay a flat fee for the manuscript, avoiding royalties.

Hardbound trade books (those sold in bookstores) usually earn a minimum royalty arrangement of 10% on the first 5,000-10,000 copies sold, 12½% on the next several thousand, and 15% thereafter. The percentage is based on the retail price of the book. For paperback originals, standard royalty is 4% on the first 150,000 copies and 6% thereafter.

If that letter of acceptance *doesn't* reach you, and your book has made all the rounds it (and you) can take, but you still consider it worth publishing, you might want to turn to a subsidy publisher. Also called a "vanity press," a subsidy publisher will publish your book only if you pay for it. He expects to profit from the venture, regardless of how well the book sells. Many subsidy publishers lack the resources for promoting and selling that a standard publisher has; therefore, your chances for turning a profit are slim at best.

Be cautious of subsidy book contracts. Make sure it covers the number of copies to be printed (and bound), the type of paper to be used, how it will be bound, the extent of marketing and promotion, and who will pay "hidden costs." Generally, subsidy publishing is a costly venture. Write to *Writer's Digest* (and enclose SASE) for a copy of the free reprint, "Does it Pay to Pay to Have it Published?" Another route is to publish the book yourself; consult the August 1978 *WD* for an exploration of that route.

Continue submissions to standard publishers. "If you think you've got a story to tell, if you think you can entertain—because the primary purpose of a book is to entertain—keep slugging away," says Charter's Michael Seidman. "Don't give up." Editors want good material, *need* good material. Seidman recalls the day Victor Canning submitted a manuscript called *The Crimson Chalice*: He told his secretary to hold all calls so he wouldn't be interrupted. Seventy-five pages from the end, he instructed the secretary to put through *all* calls; he was enjoying the book so much that he hoped interruptions would delay his finishing it. "I'm waiting for the next one to do that to me."

---

*Asterisk preceeding a listing indicates that individual subsidy publishing (where author pays part or all of publishing costs) is also available. Those firms that specialize in total subsidy publishing are listed at the end of the book publishers' section.

ABBEY PRESS, St. Meinrad IN 47577. (812)357-6677. Editor: John T. Bettin. Publishes original and reprint paperbacks. Published 10 titles in 1978; plans 16 in 1979, 18 in 1980. Royalty schedule and advances variable. Send query with outline and sample chapter. Reports in 3 weeks. SASE.
Nonfiction: "Primarily books aimed at married and family life enrichment." Recently published *Christian Reflections on Human Sexuality*, edited by David M. Thomas, Ph.D.; *When Your Child Needs a Hug*, by Larry Losoncy; and *When Your Son/Daughter Plans for the Future*, by Thomas D. Bachhuber.

ABC-CLIO, INC., 2040 A.P.S., Santa Barbara CA 93103. (805)963-4221. Associate Editor: Paulette Wamego. Editor: Shelly Lowenkopf. Publishes hardcover originals (95%) and paperback reprints (5%). Published 15 titles in 1978; plans 17 in 1979, 22 in 1980. Pays 10-12% royalty; no advance. Photocopied submissions OK. Reports in 6-8 weeks. SASE. Free book catalog.
Nonfiction: Guides, reference books, bibliographies in the field of history and political science (specifically in ethnic studies, war/peace issues, comparative and international politics, library science—acquisition guides, collection guides for the reference librarian, or for the el-hi market). Mss on comparative politics should be forwarded directly to the series editor, Prof. Peter H. Merkl; bibliographies on war/peace issues may be forwarded to Prof. Richard D. Burns. Query or submit outline/synopsis and sample chapters. Recently published *The Asian in North America*, by S. Lyman; *Articles on Women Writers*, by N.L. Schwartz; and *The Korean Diaspora*, by Hyung-chan Kim.

ABINGDON PRESS, 201 8th Ave. S., Nashville TN 37202. (615)749-6403. Editorial Director: Ronald P. Patterson. Managing Editor: Robert Hill Jr. Professional Resources: Paul M. Pettit. Senior Editor, Reference Resources. Editor of Academic Resources: Pierce S. Ellis Jr. Editor of Children Resources: Ernestine Calhoun. Editor of Special Projects: Jean Hager. Published 80 titles last year. Pays royalty. Write for ms preparation guide. Reports in 1 month. SASE.
Nonfiction, Juveniles and Textbooks: Religious, children's and general interest books, college texts. Length: 32-200 pages. Query.

ACADEMIC PRESS, INC., 111 5th Ave., New York NY 10003. (212)741-6836. Editorial Vice President: E.V. Cohen. Royalty varies. Published 400 titles in 1978; plans 420 in 1979, 420 in 1980. Free book catalog. Reports in 1 month. SASE.
Science: Specializes in scientific, technical and medical works. Textbooks and reference works only in natural, behavioral-social sciences at college and research levels. Submit outline, preface and sample chapter.

ACCENT BOOKS, a division of Accent-B/P Publications, 12100 W. 6th Ave., Box 15337, Denver CO 80215. (303)988-5300. Executive Editor: Mrs. Violet T. Pearson. Publishes evangelical Christian paperbacks.
Nonfiction: Biography, health, how-to, recreation, self-help, sports, marriage and family, other contemporary subjects, written in easy-to-read style containing Christian message and offering help to people in troubled specific areas. All mss considered must appeal to the contemporary reading public while maintaining Christian standards. Recently published *Train Up a Child—and Be Glad You Did*, by Harold J. Sala (child-rearing from a Biblical viewpoint); *Your Marriage Needs Three Love Affairs*, by John Allan Lavender (marriage and family life); *By Death or Divorce . . . It Hurts to Lose*, by Amy Ross Young (self-help for partnerless people); *Diary of a Jogging Housewife*, by Shirley Cook (physical fitness).

Fiction: All fiction must be developed out of a contemporary, conservative Christian point of view, presenting Jesus Christ or Biblical teachings as ultimate solution to contemporary problems. No children's stories, science fiction or Biblical novels. Recently published *Be Thou Pleased to Dwell With Me*, by William D. Rodgers; *All This, and Mrs. Calucci Too!*, by Alan Cliburn. Query. Submit outline/synopsis and sample chapters or submit complete ms. Enclose return postage. Reports in 4-8 weeks. Free author's information sheet.

ACE BOOKS, Editorial Department, 360 Park Ave. S., New York NY 10010. Publishes paperback originals and reprints. "Terms vary; usually on royalty basis." Published more than 200 titles last year. Fiction only. Query with detailed outline. "Do not send completed manuscripts." Reports in 4-8 weeks. SASE.
Fiction: Romantic suspense, western, science fiction and women's fiction. Length: 75,000-140,000 words. Recently published *The Magic Goes Away*, by Larry Niven; and *Dangerous Obsession*, by Natasha Peters.

ADDISON-WESLEY PUBLISHING CO., INC., Children's Book Division, Jacob Way, Reading MA 01867. Children's Book Editor: Mary K. Harmon. Publishes hardcover originals and trade paperbacks. Pays royalty. Simultaneous and photocopied submissions OK. SASE. Reports in 3-4 weeks.
Nonfiction: The arts, sciences, the environment, biography and picture books for grades K-12. Submit complete ms.
Fiction: Science ficton, mystery, adventure, picture books, folk tales and poetry. No adult fiction. Submit complete ms. Recently published *Meet Guguze*, by S. Vangheli (Russian folk tale); and *Sara and the Door*, by V.A. Jensen (picture book).

ADDISON-WESLEY PUBLISHING CO., INC., General Books Division, Jacob Way, Reading MA 01867. Editor-in-Chief: Ann Dilworth. Adult Trade Editor: Dorothy Coover. Estab. 1942. Publishes hardcover and paperback originals. Published 30 titles in 1978. Pays royalty. Simultaneous and photocopied submissions OK. SASE. Reports in 3-4 weeks. Free book catalog.
Nonfiction: Biography, business/economics, health, how-to, juveniles, nature, politics, psychology, recreation, religion, science, self-help, sociology and sports. "Also needs books on 'tools for living' related to finance, everyday law, health, education, and parenting by people well-known and respected in their field. No cookbooks or books on transactional analysis." Submit outline/synopsis and sample chapters. Recently published *Shyness: What It Is, What to Do About It*, by Philip Zimbardo (self-help); *Psychic Side of Sports*, by Michael Murphy and Rhea White; and *Take Care of Yourself: A Consumer's Guide to Medical Care*, by Dr. James Fries and Dr. Donald Vichery.

AERO PUBLISHERS, INC., 329 W. Aviation Rd., Fallbrook CA 92028. (714)728-8456. Editorial Director: Ernest J. Gentle. Publishes hardcover and paperback originals. Published 15 titles in 1978; plans 20 in 1979, 25 in 1980. "Our book publishing has increased 25-40% each year for the last 5 years." 10% royalty; no advance. Simultaneous and photocopied submissions OK. Reports in 1-3 months. SASE. Free catalog.
Nonfiction: "Manuscripts submitted must be restricted to the fields of aviation and space—and should be of a technical or nontechnical nature. Manuscripts should be 50,000-100,000 words in length and well illustrated." No personal biographies. Submit outline/synopsis and sample chapters. Recently published *The Interrogator*, by Toliver; *Space Shuttle: America's Wings to the Future*, by M. Kaplan; and *Boeing 727 Scrapbook* by Ken and Terry Morgan.

ALASKA NORTHWEST PUBLISHING CO., Box 4-EEE, Anchorage AK 99509. Managing Editor: Marty Loken. Publishes hardcover and paperback originals. "Contracts vary, depending upon how much editing is necessary. Everybody gets 10% of gross, which averages around 8% because direct mail retail sales are high. Pros may get a flat fee in addition, to increase the percentage. Advances may be paid when the manuscript is completed." Free book catalog. "Rejections are made promptly, unless we have 3 or 4 possibilities in the same general field and it's a matter of which one gets the decision. That could take 3 months." Send queries and unsolicited mss to the Book Editor. Enclose return postage.
Nonfiction: "Alaska, northern British Columbia, Yukon and Northwest territories are subject areas. Emphasis on life in the last frontier, history, outdoor subjects such as hunting and fishing. Writer must be familiar with the North first-hand. We listen to any ideas. For example, we recently did a book of woodprints." Art, nature, history, sports, hobbies, recreation, pets, and travel. Length: open.

*ALBA HOUSE, 2187 Victory Blvd., Staten Island, New York NY 10314. (212)761-0047. Editor-in-Chief: Anthony L. Chenevey. Publishes hardcover and paperback originals (90%) and reprints (10%). Specializes in religious books. Pays 10% royalty. Subsidy publishes 5% of books. Subsidy publishing is offered "if the author is able to promote the sale of a thousand copies of a book which we would not venture on our own." Published 16 titles in 1978; plans 16 in 1979, 16 in 1980. Query. State availability of photos/illustrations. Simultaneous and photocopied submissions OK. Reports in 2-4 weeks. SASE. Free book catalog.
Nonfiction: Publishes philosophy, psychology, religious, sociology, textbooks and Biblical books. Recently published *Thirsting for the Lord*, by C. Stuhlmueller; *Elements of Philosophy*, by W. A. Wallace; and *Proclaimed from the Rooftops*, by M. Mahning.

ALLEN PUBLISHING CO., 5711 Graves Ave., Encino CA 91316. Published 3 titles in 1978; plans 3 in 1979, 6-10 in 1980. 10% royalty; no advance. Simultaneous and photocopied submissions OK. Reports in 2-4 weeks. SASE.
Nonfiction: "Self-help material, 25,000-50,000 words, aimed at opportunity seekers, wealth-builders, or people seeking self-fulfillment. Material must be original and authoritative, not rehashed from other sources. Most of what we market is sold via mail order in softcover book form. No home fix-it, hobby hints, health or 'cure' books, or 'faith' stories, poetry or fiction." One-page author guidelines available for SASE. "Query or send sample chapter and table of contents, rather than complete ms. New writers welcome!"

ALLYN AND BACON, INC., 470 Atlantic Ave., Boston MA 02210. Editors: John D. Roberts (college texts), P. Parsons (el-hi texts), John Gilman (professional books). Publishes hardcover and paperback originals. Published 200 titles last year. "Our contracts are competitive within the standard industry framework of royalties." Rarely offers an advance. Reports in 1-3 months. SASE.
Nonfiction: "We are primarily a textbook, technical and professional book publisher. Authoritative works of quality. No fiction or poetry." Will consider business, medicine, music, reference, scientific, self-help and how-to, sociology, sports and hobbies, technical mss and other course related texts. Letter should accompany ms with author information, ms prospectus, etc. Query or submit complete ms.

ALMAR PRESS, 4105 Marietta Dr., Binghamton NY 13903. Editor-in-Chief: A.N. Weiner. Managing Editor: M.F. Weiner. Publishes hardcover and paperback originals and reprints. Published 3 titles in 1978; plans 4 in 1979, 6 in 1980. 10-12½-15% royalty; no advance. Simultaneous (if so indicated) and photocopied submissions OK. Reports in 1 month. SASE. Catalog for SASE.
Nonfiction: "Publishes business, technical, and consumer books and reports. These main subjects include general business, financial, travel, career, technology, personal help, hobbies, general medical, general legal, and how-to. *Almar Reports* are business and technology subjects published for management use and prepared in 8½x11 and book format. Publications are printed and bound in soft covers as required. Reprint publications represent a new aspect of our business." Submit outline/synopsis and sample chapters. Recently published *How to Buy, Install, and Maintain Your Own Telephone Equipment*, by J. LaCarrubba and L. Zimmer; and *How to Reduce Business Losses From Employee Theft and Customer Fraud* (Almar Report).

AMERICAN ASTRONAUTICAL SOCIETY (Univelt, Inc., Publisher), Box 28130, San Diego CA 92128. (714)746-4005. Editorial Director: H. Jacobs. Publishes hardcover originals. Published 7 titles in 1978; plans 8 in 1979, 8 in 1980. 10% royalty; no advance. Simultaneous and photocopied submissions OK. Reports in 4 weeks. SASE. Free book catalog.
Nonfiction: Proceedings or monographs in the field of astronautics, including applications of aerospace technology to Earth's problems. Submit outline/synopsis and sample chapters. Recently published *Export of Aerospace Technology*, edited by Carl H. Tross; *Two Hundred Years of Flight in America*, edited by Eugene M. Emme; and *The Future United States Space Program*, edited by Richard S. Johnston.

AMERICAN CATHOLIC PRESS, 1223 Rossell Ave., Oak Park IL 60302. (312)339-4646. Editorial Director: Father Michael Gilligan. Publishes hardcover originals (90%) and hardcover and paperback reprints (10%). Published 3 titles in 1978; plans 4 in 1979, 2 in 1980. "Most of our sales are by direct mail, although we do work through retail outlets." Pays by outright purchase of $25-100; no advance. Simultaneous and photocopied submissions OK. Reports in 2 months. SASE. Free book catalog.
Nonfiction: "We publish books on the Roman Catholic Liturgy, for the most part books on

religious music and educational books and pamphlets. We also publish religious songs for church use, including Psalms as well as choral and instrumental arrangements. We are very interested in new music, meant for use in church services. Books, or even pamphlets, on the Roman Catholic Mass are especially welcome. We have no interest in secular topics at all, and are not interested in religious poetry of any kind." Query. Recently published *The Role of Music in the New Roman Liturgy*, by W. Herring (educational); *Noise in our Solemn Assemblies*, by R. Keifer (educational); and *Song Leader's Handbook*, by W. Callahan (music).

AMERICAN CLASSICAL COLLEGE PRESS, Box 4526, Albuquerque NM 87196. Editor-in-Chief: Leslie Dean. Pays a flat sum plus royalties of 10-15%. Published 27 titles last year. Query. SASE.
Nonfiction: Publishes history, biography, scientific phenomena, politics, psychology and philosophy books. Also economics, Wall Street and the stock market. Mss should be short, to the point, informative, and practical. Length: 20,000-40,000 words. Publishes The Science of Man Research Books series.

AMERICAN UNIVERSAL ARTFORMS CORP., Box 2242, Austin TX 78768. Editor-in-Chief: R.H. Dromgoole. Hardcover and paperback originals. Pays 10% (of net invoice) royalty. Possibility of advance "depends on many factors." Send sample print if photos and/or artwork are to accompany ms. Simultaneous submissions OK (if so advised); photocopied submissions OK. Reports in 2-4 weeks. SASE. Book catalog for SASE.
Nonfiction: Publishes textbooks (bilingual educational material, K-12; Spanish/English); books on hobbies; how-to; humor; politics; poetry and juveniles. Submit complete ms.

AMPHOTO, American Photographic Book Publishing Co., Inc., 750 Zeckendorf Blvd., Garden City NY 11530. (516)248-2233. Editor-in-Chief: Herb Taylor. Managing Editor: Cora Marquez. Publishes hardcover and paperback originals. Published 35 titles in 1978; plans 40 in 1979, 50 in 1980. Pays 4-15% royalty, or by outright purchase; offers variable advance. Simultaneous and photocopied submissions OK. Reports in 1 month. SASE. Free book catalog.
Nonfiction: "Photography only. We cover all aspects of photography—technical and how-to. Few portfolios or picture books." Submit outline/synopsis, sample chapters and sample photos. Recently published *Professional Fashion Photography*, by Robert Farber (how-to); *The Fine 35mm Portrait*, by Jack Manning (portraiture with a small camera); and *The Encyclopedia of Practical Photography* (14 volumes of photography A to Z.)
Tips: "Consult the photo magazines for book ideas."

ANDERSON PUBLISHING CO., 602 Main St., Suite 501, Cincinnati OH 45201. (513)421-4393. Editorial Director: Jean Martin. Publishes hardcover and paperback originals (98%) and reprints (2%). Published 13 titles in 1978; plans 14-20 in 1979, 14-20 in 1980. Pays 12-15% royalty; "advance in selected cases." Simultaneous and photocopied submissions OK. Reports in 6 weeks. SASE. Free book catalog.
Nonfiction: Criminal justice, law, and law-related books and texts and social studies. Query or submit outline/synopsis and sample chapters along with vitae. Recently published *The Invisible Justice System: Discretion and the Law*, by B.M. Atkins/M.R. Pogrebin; *Constitutional Law for Police*, by J.C. Klotter/J.R. Kanovitz; and *Consumer Protection: Text and Materials*, by D.P. Rothschild/D.W. Carroll.

AND/OR PRESS, Box 2246, Berkeley CA 94702. Executive Editor: Peter Beren. Paperback originals (90%); hardcover and paperback reprints (10%). Specializes in "nonfiction works with youth market interest. We function as an alternative information resource." Pays 5-10% royalty; advance of 10% of first print run. Published 12 titles in 1978; plans 15 in 1979, 25 in 1980. Reports in 2 weeks to 3 months. SASE. Queries only. Book catalog $1.
Nonfiction: Publishes appropriate technology, human potential, the future, health and nutrition, travel, human potential, and psycho-pharmacology books. Also alternative lifestyles. Query. Recently published *Cosmic Trigger*, by R.A. Wilson; *Daily Planet Almanac*, by T. Reim; and *Holistic Health Hand Book*, edited by Berkeley Holistic Health Center.
Special Needs: Planning a series on health, sex and old age.

ANGLICAN BOOK CENTRE, 600 Jarvis St., Toronto, Ontario, Canada M4Y 2J6. (416)924-9192. Editorial Director: Robert Maclennan. Publishes hardcover and paperback originals (90%) and reprints (10%). Published 12 titles in 1978; plans 12 in 1979. Pays 7½% royalty; no advance. Simultaneous and photocopied submissions OK. Reports in 6 weeks. SAE and International Reply Coupons.

Nonfiction: Religion—theology, self-help, Bible study, and popular theology; also social action books. Query. Recently published *Do This*, by Gordon Baker; *The Gift of Courage*, by James Wilkes; and *For All Seasons*, by Herbert O. Driscoll.

ANTONSON PUBLISHING CO., 12165 97th Ave., Surrey, British Columbia, Canada V3V 2C8. (604)584-9922. Editor-in-Chief: Richard Antonson. Editor: Dale Flexman. Editors of Canadian Frontier Annual: Brian Antonson, Gordon Stewart. Publishes hardcover and paperback originals. Pays 8-10% royalty; no advance. Published 6 titles in 1978; plans 4 in 1979, 3 in 1980. State availability of photos and/or illustrations to accompany ms. Simultaneous and photocopied submissions OK. Reports in 2-4 weeks. SAE and International Reply Coupons. Free book catalog.
Nonfiction: Publishes Canadiana; how-to (guide books); politics (Canadian perspective); history (Canadian emphasis); nature and wildlife; recreation and conservation; and travel. "We are developing a strong line of outdoor-oriented books both in the story form and in the guidebook area. Titles vary in length from 60,000 to 100,000 words. In addition, we are planning more titles on regional and national history."

THE AQUARIAN PUBLISHING CO. (LONDON) LTD., Denington Estate, Wellingborough, Northamptonshire NN8 2RQ England. Editor-in-Chief: J.R. Hardaker. Hardcover and paperback originals. Pays 8-10% royalty. Photocopied submissions OK. SAE and International Reply Coupons. Reports in 2-4 weeks. Free book catalog.
Nonfiction: Publishes books on astrology, magic, witchcraft, palmistry and other occult subjects. Length: 15,000-60,000 words.

THE AQUILA PUBLISHING CO., LTD., P.O. Box 1, Portree, Isle of Skye, Scotland IV51 9BT. Editor-in-Chief: J.C.R. Green. Publishes hardcover and paperback originals (99%); paperback reprints and pamphlets (1%). Pays 10% royalty. If ms is to be illustrated, state availability of prints and send photocopies. Simultaneous submissions OK (if informed); photocopied submissions OK. Reporting time varies with workload. SAE and International Reply Coupons. Free book catalog.
Nonfiction: Publishes books on art, biographies, business; cookbooks, cooking and foods, erotica, hobbies, how-to, humor, music, nature, philosophy, photography, poetry, recreation and self-help. Also publishes translations from any language and work with a Scottish/Celtic bias. Query. Recently published *Cantata Underorion*, by E. Milne (poetry); and *The Lamplighter*, by A. Buttigigg/The President of Malta.
Fiction: Erotica, experimental, fantasy, humorous, mystery, suspense and science fiction. Query. Work with a Scottish/Celtic bias. Recently published *In Search of Jasper McDoom*, by S. Wade.
Special Needs: "New series of pamphlet/paperbacks of critical essays on American writers and writing; the ecology, humor, etc."

ARCHER EDITIONS PRESS, Box 562, Danbury CT 06810. Editorial Director: Wanda Hicks. Publishes hardcover and paperback originals (60%) and paperback reprints (40%). Pays 15% royalty; occasionally offers $250-750 advance. Published 2 titles in 1978; plans 3 in 1979, 3-5 in 1980. Simultaneous and photocopied submissions OK. Reports in 2-3 months. SASE. Free book catalog.
Nonfiction: "We are interested in books that could go to the academic and public library market in the fields of history, literature and art. We would especially like biographies in this field." Query. Recently published *Miracle of the Wilderness*, by O. Faulk/B. Jones (history); *Noa Noa*, by P. Gauguin (art/biography reprint); and *Thomas Francis Meagher*, by W.F. Lyons (Civil War reprint).

ARCHITECTURAL BOOK PUBLISHING CO., INC., 10 E. 40th St., New York NY 10016. (212)689-5400. Editor: Walter Frese. Royalty is percentage of retail price. Prefers queries, outlines and sample chapters. Reports in 2 weeks. Enclose return postage.
Architecture and Industrial Arts: Publishes architecture, decoration, and reference books on city planning and industrial arts. Also interested in history, biography, and science of architecture and decoration.

ARCO PUBLISHING, INC., 219 Park Ave. S., New York NY 10003. Editor-in-Chief: David Goodnough. Medical Editor: Don Simmons. Hardcover and paperback originals (30%) and reprints (70%). Pays 10-12½-15% royalty. Advance averages $1,000. Published 150 titles in 1978; plans 130-160 in 1979. Simultaneous and legible photocopied submissions OK. Reports in 4-6 weeks. SASE (manuscripts and materials submitted without postage will not be automatically returned). Book catalog for 50¢ for postage and handling.

Nonfiction (in order of preference): Publishes hobbies (crafts and collecting); pets (practical and specific); self-help (medical, mental, career guidance, economic); career guidance; medicine and psychiatry (technical and authoritative); test preparation and study guides; travel (informative—not "My Trip to . . ."); sports (but not the usual stories about baseball, football, etc.); specialized cookbooks in health food and nutrition areas; how-to; medical review books; military history; reference. Query or submit outline/synopsis and sample chapters.

ARK BOOKS, 3049 Columbus Ave. S., Minneapolis MN 55407. Editoral Director: Al Palmquist. Editor-in-Chief: Joyce Hovelsrud. Publishes paperback originals. Pays 5-10% royalty; no advance. Published 5 titles in 1978; plans 8 in 1979. Simultaneous and photocopied submissions OK. SASE. Reports in 6 weeks. Free book catalog.

Nonfiction: "We're a new religious market looking for manuscripts which present tangible solutions to problems faced by the individual in society today and which address current issues as they can be related to the Bible. Material must be scripturally sound. We don't want watered down or surface religion. We believe in a life-changing, dynamic gospel and are interested in material with impact." Query or submit complete ms. Recently published *The Bible Said It Would Happen*, by Paul R. Olson (how to discern God's voice and test spiritual leaders); *How to Live with an Alcoholic and Win*, by Jim and Cyndy Hunt (employing the principles of Alcoholics Victorious); and *Gift of Years*, by Margonet Wyatt and Lucy Woodward (inspirational meditations for the elderly).

ARKHAM HOUSE PUBLISHERS, INC., Sauk City WI 53583. Editor: James Turner. Publishes hardcover originals and reprints; fiction only, no poetry. Published 3 titles in 1978; plans 5 in 1979, 5 in 1980. Pays 10% royalty; advances negotiable. Send query/synopsis first accompanied by return postabe; complete manuscripts considered by invitation only. Reports in 4-6 weeks. Catalog send on request.

Fiction: "Arkham House is a fantasy imprint, specializing in supernatural horror and weird literature. Mss should be well-written, preferably on original fantastic themes, with particular attention to atmosphere and style. No occult, psychological or humorous fiction." Query. Recently published *Born to Exile*, by Phyllis Eisenstein (fantasy novel) and *The Princess of All Lands*, by Russell Kirk (weird tales).

*ARLINGTON HOUSE PUBLISHERS, 165 Huguenot St., New Rochelle NY 10801. President: Thomas J. Sullivan. Senior Editors: Richard Bishirjian, Karl T. Pflock, Kathleen Williams. Publishes hardcover originals (80%) and reprints (20%). Published 28 titles in 1978; plans 35 in 1979. Subsidy publishes 5-10% of titles. "If we feel the book is valuable but will not pay its way commercially we will entertain an offer for subsidy publishing. This happens rarely with us, because we believe that most books can make their way commercially if they are worth publishing." Pays 10-15% royalty; offers advance. Simultaneous and photocopied submissions OK. SASE. Reports in 3-4 weeks. Free book catalog.

Nonfiction: Biography, business/economics, health, history, politics, reverence, religion, self-help, investing, films, TV and entertainment. No devotional/inspirational religious books or memoirs. Query, submit outline/synopsis and sample chapters, or submit complete ms. Recently published *Dr. Taylor's Self-Help Medical Guide*, by Robert B. Taylor, MD (self-help, health); *The Power of the Positive Woman*, by Phyllis Schlafly (politics/social issues); and *Who's Who in Hollywood, 1900-1976*, by David Ragan (films).

ARTISTS & WRITERS PUBLICATIONS, Drawer 668, San Rafael CA 94902. (415)456-1213. Editor-in-Chief: Owen S. Haddock. Publishes paperback originals. Specializes in how-to cookbooks. Pays 5% minimum royalty; no advance. Reports in 2-4 months. SASE.

Nonfiction: Publishes business, cookbooks, cooking and foods, hobbies, how-to, law, scientific and self-help books. "Will examine closely any book outlines which could be used as premium-promotion books for private companies. We prefer all submissions to be in outline/synopsis form, not requiring return, plus a brief resume of the author." State availability of photos/illustrations. Prefers photocopied submissions. Recently published *Ghirardelli Original Chocolate Cookbook*, by P. Larsen; and *The New T-Fal French Cookbook*, by M. Pendergast.

*ASHLEY BOOKS, INC., 223 Main St., Port Washington NY 11050. (516)883-2221. Editorial Director: Simeon Paget. Senior Editor: Albert Young. Publishes hardcover originals. Published 40 titles in 1978; plans 55 in 1979, 55 in 1980. Subsidy publishes 2% of books based on "no definite criteria. It depends upon the subject matter." May on occasion offer writers a cooperative publishing contract. 10-12½-15% royalty; advance "depends on the property and the agent." Simultaneous and photocopied submissions OK. Reports in 6 weeks. SASE. Book catalog for SASE.

Nonfiction: "We seek books like *The Surgical Beauty Racket*, by Dr. Kendall Moore and Sally Thompson, which discusses the pitfalls of cosmetic surgery and the danger to the consumer; *How to Recover From a Stroke and Make a Successful Comeback*, by Clarence Longenecker, a former stroke victim who wrote a Baedeker of how to get well; and *Soul Talk: How to Rejuvenate Your Life Style*, by James Jacobson, which inspires one to live fully while alive. Natural food and gourmet cookbooks are always welcome. We don't do any craft books. We habitually seek consumer material on medical topics plus explicit medical undercover vehicles and medical self-help books." Submit complete ms.

Fiction: "We seek mainstream fiction that fulfills a responsibility to the quality of life; ideas that are not repressed but breathe integrity and uphold the dignity of what human life should be about. For instance, *The Nuclear Catastrophe*, by Bett Pohnka and Barbara Griffin; *The Hospital Plot* (a racial theme); *Project Lambda* (a gay book which recreates the *Holocaust*). We want books that penetrate the consciousness of the reader and awaken some sentiment, be it anger, passion, excitement, sadness or happiness; books that clamor to be talked about and remain in the mind of the reader long after they have been put aside. Books that pertain to the changing values of life today and have appeal for a large audience. Books for people who would rather read than watch TV whether they are reading for recreation, relaxation, or just because the topic turns them on. Give them warmth or give them hate, give them fear or give them love, but write about something that will make them feel honest emotion." No juvenile or pornographic material. Recently published *Among the Carnivores*, by D. Curzon (gay mainstream fiction); *The Hospital Plot*, by C. Pugh; and *The Nuclear Catastrophe*, by B. Pohnka/B.C. Griffin.

ASI PUBLISHERS, INC., 127 Madison Ave., New York NY 10016. Editor-in-Chief: Henry Weingarten. Publishes hardcover and paperback originals and reprints. Offers 7½-10% royalty; advance varies. Published 7 titles in 1978; plans 10 in 1979, 10 in 1980. Book catalog for SASE. Will consider photocopied submissions. Query. Submit outline and sample chapters. Mss should be typed, double-spaced. Enclose return postage. Reports in 1-3 months.

Nonfiction: "We specialize in guides to balancing inner space, e.g., acupuncture, astrology, yoga, etc. Our editors are themselves specialists in the areas published. We will accept technical material with limited sales potential." Medical editor: Barbara Somerfield. Astrology editor: H. Weingarten. Recently published *Synastry*, by R. Davison (astrology); *Complete Method of Prediction*, by R. DeLuce (astrology); and *The Day with Yoga*, by E. Haith.

*ASSOCIATED BOOKSELLERS, 147 McKinley Ave., Bridgeport CT 06606. (212)366-5494. Editor-in-Chief: Alex M. Yudkin. Hardcover and paperback originals. Pays 10% royalty; advance averages $500. Subsidy publishes 25% of books. Subsidy publishing is offered "if the marketing potential is limited." Query. Simultaneous and photocopied submissions OK. Reports in 2-4 weeks. SASE. Book catalog for SASE.

Nonfiction: Publishes how-to, hobbies, recreation, self-help, and sports books. Recent Titles: *Key to Judo*; *Ketsugo*; and *Kashi-No-Bo*.

ASSOCIATED PUBLISHERS, INC., 1015 Howard Ave., Box 1032, San Mateo CA 94403. Editor: Ivan Kapetanovic. Publishes paperback originals. "Offer standard minimum book contract, but there could be special cases, different from this arrangement. We have not made a practice of giving advances." Published 5 titles in 1978; plans 15 in 1979, 20 in 1980. Will consider photocopied submissions. Submit outline and sample chapters, or submit complete ms. Reports in 30 days. Enclose return postage.

Education: "In addition to bibliographies, which we develop and publish ourselves, we are interested in all kinds of guidance materials. We would especially consider publication of books and pamphlets suitable for high school students, in the field of guidance, including occupational information, college entrance and orientation, and personal and social problems. We are less concerned with a single title than a group of related titles or a series of publications which may be developed over a period of time. We would like a series of career materials which can be produced and sold inexpensively for junior and senior high school students, with or without tape and/or filmstrip materials correlated with them. We would like materials relating to the *Dictionary of Occupational Titles* for student use; a first-class student study guide or a series for different levels to and including college freshmen; a series of pamphlets on occupations. Individually and/or in groups. The vocabulary level usually should be that of average students in the seventh to tenth grades. We are planning a series of occupational pamphlets, a filing system on American colleges. Someone knowledgeable in labor statistics, employment problems, etc., could do the first one; someone familiar with materials on college entrance could do the latter. Definitely not interested in poetry, fiction, and pseudo-scientific material. Books published in following categories: Economics, Linquistics, Dictionaries, Cooking and Nutrition, History, Self-help and How-to, Sociology, and Guidance. No strict length requirements."

ATHENEUM PUBLISHERS, 122 E. 42nd St., New York NY 10017. Editor-in-Chief: Herman Gollob. Published 56 titles in 1978; plans 58 in 1979. Simultaneous and photocopied submissions OK. Reports in 6 weeks. Enclose return postage.
Nonfiction: General trade material dealing with politics, psychology, popular health, cookbooks, sports, biographies and general interest. Length: 40,000 words minimum. Query or submit outline/synopsis and a sample chapter. Recently published *The Best Years*, by J. Goulde (historical/personal); *The Night Watch*, by D.A. Phillips (about a 25-year-long experience in the CIA); and *The Hunting Hypothesis*, by R. Ardrey (anthropology).
Fiction: "All types." Length: 40,000 words minimum. Query or submit outline/synopsis and a sample chapter. Recently published *Shogun*, by J. Clavell (popular fiction); *Feast of Snakes*, by H. Crews (Southern gothic); and *An American Romance*, by J. Casey (love story).

ATHENEUM PUBLISHERS, INC., Juvenile Department, 122 E. 42nd St., New York NY 10017. Editor: Jean Karl. Publishes hardcover originals and paperback reprints. Published 56 titles in 1978; plans 58 in 1979. Reports in 6 weeks. SASE.
Nonfiction: Juvenile books for ages 3-16. Picture books for ages 3-8. "We have no special needs; we publish whatever comes in that interests us. No bad animal fantasy but fantasy and science fiction of many varieties." Special science fiction list. Submit complete ms.

ATHENEUM PUBLISHERS, INC., College Department, 122 E. 42nd St., New York NY 10017. College Dept. Editor: Mrs. E. Soschin. Estab. 1959. Publishes paperback reprints. Published 12 titles in 1978; plans 15 in 1979, 15 in 1980. Free book catalog.
Nonfiction: "We will not seek to acquire books, relying on our own backlist for our paperback list at least for the next several seasons."

ATLANTIC MONTHLY PRESS, 8 Arlington St., Boston MA 02116. (617)536-9500. Director: Peter Davison; Associate Director: Upton Birnie Brady. Children's Book Editor: Melanie Kroupa. Published 38 titles in 1978. "Advance and royalties depend on the nature of the book, the stature of the author, and the subject matter." Enclose return postage.
General Fiction, Nonfiction and Juveniles: Publishes, in association with Little, Brown and Company, fiction, general nonfiction, juveniles, biography, autobiography, science, philosophy, the arts, belles lettres, history, world affairs and poetry. Length: 70,000-200,000 words. Query letters welcomed. Mss preferred, but outlines and chapters are acceptable. Recently published *Eskimos, Chicanos, Indians*, by R. Coles; *Bel Ria*, by S. Burnford, and *Dear Me*, by P. Ustinov (autobiography).

THE ATLANTIC MONTHLY PRESS, Children's Books, 8 Arlington St., Boston MA 02116. (617)536-9500. Editor of Children's Books: Melanie Kroupa. Publishes hardcover and paperback originals. Published 13 titles in 1978; plans 13 in 1979, 13-15 in 1980. Pays 10% minimum royalty; offers $2,000-2,500 average advance. Photocopied submissions OK. SASE. Reports in 1 month. Book catalog for SASE.
Nonfiction: Books for children and young adults. Subjects include animals, art, biography, history, hobbies, how-to, humor, juveniles, music, nature, photography, poetry, psychology, recreation, science and sports, including picture books, and "books for young adults that approach a subject with imagination and enthusiasm, that stimulate a fresh vision, and have substance, logical organization, accuracy." Submit outline/synopsis and sample chapters. Recently published *Next Year in Jerusalem*, by Robert Goldston (short history of Zionism for readers 12 and older); *Inside Animals*, by Dr. Gale Cooper (picture-book introduction to comparative anatomy and how animals function for children 8-12).
Fiction: Adventure, fantasy, historical, humor, mainstream, mystery, romance, science fiction, suspense, picture books, and "books for young adults which show superior story-telling with strong characterizations and convincing action and plot development." Submit complete ms. Recently published *The Deadly Mandrake*, by Larry Callen ("down-to-earth humor with suspense"); *Humbug Mountain*, by Sid Fleischman (tall-tale humor); *The Biggest Christmas Tree on Earth*, by Fernando Krahn (wordless picture-book fantasy); and *Words By Heart*, by Ouida Sebestyen.

AUGSBURG PUBLISHING HOUSE, 426 S. 5th St., Minneapolis MN 55415. (612)332-4561.

Director, Book Department: Roland Seboldt. Publishes hardcover and paperback originals (95%) and paperback back reprints (5%). Published 44 titles in 1978; plans 45 in 1979, 45 in 1980. Pays 10-15% royalty. Advance negotiable. Simultaneous and photocopied submissions OK. Reports in 6 weeks. SASE.

Nonfiction: Health, psychology, religion, self-help and textbooks. "We are looking for manuscripts that apply scientific knowledge and Christian faith to the needs of people as individuals, in groups and in society." Query or submit outline/synopsis and a sample chapter or submit complete ms. Recent titles *Sex, Love, or Infatuation*, by Ray Short (personal self-help); *Why Am I Shy?*, by Norman Rohrer and S. Philip Sutherland; and *The Critical Moment*, by Margaret Wold.

Fiction: "We are looking for good religious fiction with a Christian theme for the young readers age 8-11." Submit complete ms.

*AUTO BOOK PRESS, 1511 Grand Ave., San Marcos CA 92069. (714)744-2567. Editorial Director: William Carroll. Publishes hardcover and paperback originals. Publishes 3 titles/year. Subsidy publishes 25% of books based on "author's exposure in the field." Pays 15% royalty; offers variable advance. Simultaneous and photocopied submissions OK. Reports in 2 weeks. SASE. Free book catalog.

Nonfiction: Automotive material only: technical or definitive how-to. Query. Recently published *Brief History of San Marcos*, by Carroll (area history); *Honda Civic Guide*, by Carroll; and *How to Sell*, by Woodward (sales hints).

AUTUMN PRESS, INC., 25 Dwight St., Brookline MA 02146. (617)738-5680. President/Editor-in-Chief: M. Nahum Stiskin. Publishes hardcover and paperback originals and paperback reprints. Published 8 titles in 1978; plans 10 in 1979. Distributed by Random House, Inc. Standard royalty; sometimes offers a small advance. Simultaneous and photocopied submissions OK. Reports in 1-3 months. SASE. Free book catalog.

Nonfiction: "We are interested in books on holistic health, natural foods cooking, alternative lifestyles, psychology and growth, philosophy and religion, Eastern and Western thought, ecology, and environmental concerns. No poetry. Submit outline/synopsis and sample chapters. Recently published *Nuclear Madness*, by Helen Caldicott; *The Book of Honey*, by Claude Francis and Fernande Gontier; *Yoga for Couples*, by James Lewis; *The Temple in Man*, by R. A. Schwaller de Lubicz; and *The Vegetarians*, by Rynn Berry Jr.

Fiction: "We may be interested in fiction that reflects the above themes, as well as children's books that reflect these same themes."

AVALON BOOKS, Thomas Bouregy & Co., Inc., 22 E. 60th St., New York NY 10022. Editor: Rita Brenig. "We like the writers to focus on the plot, drama, and characters, not the background." Publishes hardcover originals. Published 60 titles in 1978; plans 60 in 1979, 60 in 1980. Pays $300 advance which is applied against sales of the first 3,000 copies of the book. SASE. Reports in 12 weeks. Free book list for SASE.

Fiction: "We want well-plotted, fast-moving light romances, romance-mysteries, gothics, westerns, and nurse-romance books of about 50,000 words." Query or submit outline/synopsis or submit complete ms. SASE. Recent titles: *Trouble at Crossed Forks*, By B.A. Collier (western); *A Dream House for Nurse Rhonda*, by Berta LaVan Barker (nurse-romance); and *No Time for Love*, by Kay Richardson (romance).

*AVI PUBLISHING CO., 250 Post Rd. E., Box 831, Westport CT 06880. (203)266-0738. Editor-in-Chief: Norman W. Desrosier, PhD. Hardcover and paperback originals. Specializes in publication of books in the fields of food science and technology, food service, nutrition, health, agriculture and engineering. Pays 10% royalty on the first 1,000 copies sold; $500 average advance (paid only on typing and art bills). Subsidy publishes 2% of titles (by professional organizations) based on "quality of work; subject matter within the areas of food, nutrition and health, endorsed by appropriate professional organizations in the area of our specialty." Published 50 titles in 1978, 55 in 1979; will do 62 in 1979. Reports in 2-4 weeks. SASE. Free book catalog.

Nonfiction: Publishes books on foods, agriculture, nutrition and health, scientific, technical, textbooks and reference works. Query or "submit a 300-word summary, a preface, a table of contents, estimated number of pages in manuscript, when to be completed and a biographical sketch."

Recent Titles: *Alcohol and the Diet*, by D.A. Roe (health); *Vegetable Growing Handbook*, by W.E. Splittstoesser (agriculture); *Candy Technology*, by J. Alkonis (food technology).

AVIATION BOOK CO., 555 W. Glenoaks Blvd., Box 4187, Glendale CA 91202.

(213)240-1771. Editor: Walter P. Winner. Publishes hardcover and paperback originals and reprints. Published 7 titles in 1978; plans 6 in 1979. No advance. Free book catalog. Query with outline. Reports in 2 months. Enclose return postage.

Nonfiction: Aviation books, primarily of a technical nature and pertaining to pilot training. Young adult level and up. Also aeronautical history. Recently published *Airmen's Information Manual*, by Winner (pilot training); *Their Eyes on the Skies*, by Martin Cole (aeronautics history); and *"Upside-Down" Pangborn*, by Cleveland (aeronautics history).

AVON BOOKS, 959 8th Ave., New York NY 10019. Editor-in-Chief: Walter Meade. Executive Editor: Susan Moldow. Publishes paperback originals (40%) and paperback reprints (60%). Published 380 titles in 1978; plans 380 in 1979, 380 in 1980. Pay and advance are negotiable. Simultaneous and photocopied submissions OK. SASE. Reports in 6 weeks. Free book catalog for SASE.

Nonfiction: Animals, biography, business/economics, cookbooks/cooking, health, history, hobbies, how-to, humor, juveniles, music, nature, philosophy, phtography, poetry, politics, psychology, recreation, reference, religion, science, self-help, sociology, and sports.

Fiction: Adventure, fantasy, gothic, historical, mainstream, mystery, religious, romance, science fiction, suspense, and western. Submit outline/synopsis and sample chapters.

AZTEX CORP., 1126 N. 6th Ave., Tucson AZ 85705. (608)882-4656. Publishes hardcover and paperback originals. Published 12 titles in 1978; 12 in 1979. Pays 15% royalty; offers $250 advance. SASE. Reports in 3 months. Free catalog.

Nonfiction: "We specialize in transportation subjects, how-to and history of automobiles, trucks, fire engines, sailboats, powerboats, motorcycles and motor sports. We also use material on railroading. We are open to new approches in cookbooks and regional histories related to American Indians." Submit outline/synopsis and sample chapters or complete ms. Recently published *Night Sailing*; *Jaguar-Motor Racing Manufacturers* (history); and *The Instant Navigation*, by Bud Kane (how-to).

Fiction: "We would like historical fiction that would complement our nonfiction themes." Submit outline/synopsis and sample chapters or submit complete ms. Recently published *Council Fires*, by Bruce Calhoun (historical novel on the American Indian).

*BADGER CREEK PRESS, Box 728, Galt CA 95632. Editor-in-Chief: James Singer. Managing Editor: Peggy Flynn. Paperback originals. Specializes in how-to (including cookbooks) pamphlets, up to 32 pages, and technical health/medicine texts. Flat rate of up to $100 for pamphlets; 15% for technicals. Subsidy publishes small percentage of books. "Each subsidy is usually not paid by the author, but by his/her sponsor (university, foundation, etc.)." Photocopied submissions OK. Reports in 1-2 weeks. SASE.

Nonfiction: Publishes (in order of preference) how-to; cookbooks, cooking and foods; self-help; books on small farms; reference, medicine and psychiatry; and technical books. Query. "We do not read unsolicited mss. We send style sheet with go-ahead."

Recent Title: *Rug Tufting—How to Make Your Own Rugs*, by S. Lambert (how-to).

BALE BOOKS, Box 2727, New Orleans LA 70176. Editor-in-Chief: Don Bale Jr. Publishes hardcover and paperback originals and reprints. Offers standard 10-12½-15% royalty contract; "no advances." Sometimes purchases mss outright for $500. Published 12 titles in 1978; plans 6-12 in 1979, 6-12 in 1980. "Most books are sold through publicity and ads in the coin newspapers." Book catalog for SASE. Will consider photocopied submissions. "Send ms by registered or certified mail. Be sure copy of ms is retained." Reports usually within several months. SASE.

Nonfiction and Fiction: "Our specialty is coin and stock market investment books; especially coin investment books and coin price guides. We are open to any new ideas in the area of numismatics. The writer should write for a teenage through adult level. Lead the reader by the hand like a teacher, building chapter by chapter. Our books sometimes have a light, humorous treatment, but not necessarily."

BALLANTINE BOOKS, Division of Random House, 201 E. 50th St., New York NY 10022. Publishes trade and mass market paperback originals and reprints. Royalty contract varies. Published 350 titles last year; about 25% were originals.

General: General fiction and nonfiction, science fiction and fantasy. "Currently, Ballantine is interested in across-the-board fiction, including good mysteries, westerns, suspense novels and thrillers, and historical novels and contemporary fiction geared to both men and women. We're not interested in poetry, old-fashioned first-person gothics and books exclusively for children or young adults; books under 60,000 words are too short for consideration. We do very few biographies, and very little on the occult or psychic phenomena. We are not interested in collections of short stories, or books that depend largely on photographs. Since we are a mass market house, books which have a heavy regional flavor would be inappropriate for our list, and we also do not publish cookbooks or puzzle books."

Tips: "Science fiction and fantasy should be sent to Judy-Lynn Del Rey, editor-in-chief of Del Rey Books at Ballantine. Proposals for trade books, poster books, calendars, etc., should be directed to Ward Mohrfield, Editor of Trade Books. All else to Editorial Department.

BANTAM BOOKS, INC., 666 5th Ave., New York NY 10019. (212)765-6500. Editor-in-Chief: Marc Jaffe. Associate Editorial Director: Allan Barnard. Publishes hardcover and paperback reprints (75%) and paperback originals (25%). Publishes approximately 375 titles/year. Royalty and advance vary. Reports in 4 weeks. SASE. Free book catalog.

Nonfiction: "We no longer accept unsolicited manuscripts. Material will be returned unread unless sent at our request. Please query as appropriate: Grace Bechtold, Executive Editor (religious and health books); Toni Burbank, Executive Editor, School & College Books (nonfiction); Jean Highland, Senior Editor (political science); and Linda Price, Senior Editor (cookbooks). Recently published *Montgomery Clift*, by P. Bosworth; *The Amityville Horror*, by J. Anson; and *Coming Into the Country*, by J. McPhee.

Fiction: "We no longer accept unsolicited manuscripts, and material will be returned unread. Please query as appropriate: Linda Price, Senior Editor (romances, historicals, general women's fiction); Sydney Weinberg, Editor (science fiction and fantasy); and Roger Cooper, Senior Editor (young adult fiction). Recently published *The Holcroft Covenant*, by R. Ludlum; *Firefox*, by C. Thomas; and *Flesh and Blood*, by P. Hamill.

BANYAN BOOKS, INC., Box 431160, Miami FL 33143. (305)665-6011. Director: Ellen Edelen. Publishes hardcover and paperback originals (90%) and reprints (10%). Published 7 titles in 1978; plans 5-8 in 1979. Specializes in Florida regional and natural history books. Pays 10% royalty; no advance. Subsidy publishes 10% of books; "worthwhile books that fill a gap in the market, but whose sales potential is limited." Send prints if illustrations are to be used with ms. Photocopied submissions OK. Reports in 1 month. SASE. Free book catalog.

Nonfiction: Publishes regional history and books on nature and horticulture. Submission of outline/synopsis, sample chapters preferred, but will accept queries. Recently published *Nature Guide to Florida*; *Florida by Paddle and Pack*; *Balustrades and Gingerbread*; and *Key West's Handcrafted Homes and Buildings.*

BARLENMIR HOUSE PUBLISHERS, 413 City Island Ave., New York NY 10064. Editor-in-Chief: Barry L. Mirenburg. Managing Editor: Leonard Steffan. Publishes hardcover and paperback originals. Pays 10-12½-15% royalty; varying advance. Submit outline/synopsis and sample chapters. State availability of photos and/or illustrations to accompany ms. Simultaneous (if informed) and photocopied submissions OK. Reports in 2-4 weeks; "sometimes sooner." SASE.

Nonfiction: Publishes Americana, art, biography, business; cookbooks, cooking and foods, economics, history, hobbies, how-to, humor, law; medicine and psychiatry, multimedia material, music, nature, philosophy, photography, poetry, politics, psychology, recreation, reference, scientific, self-help, sociology, sports, technical textbooks and travel books. "No adherence to specific schools of writing, age, or ethnic group. Acceptance based solely on original and quality work."

Recent Titles: *UFO, The Eye and The Camera*, by A. Vance (nonfiction); and *The Painterly Poets*, by F. Moramarco (nonfiction).

A.S. BARNES AND CO., INC., Cranbury NJ 08512. (609)655-0190. Editors: Barbara Tieger, Maureen O'Connor Geruth. Publishes hardcover and paperback originals and reprints; occasionally publishes translations and anthologies. Contract negotiable: "each contract considered on its own merits." Advance varies, depending on author's previous works and nature of book. Published 90 titles in 1978; plans 100 in 1979, 120 in 1980. Will send a catalog to a writer on request. Query. Reports "as soon as possible." Enclose return postage.

Nonfiction: "General nonfiction with special emphasis on cinema, antiques, sports, and crafts." Recently published *The Complete Encyclopedia of Television Programs*, by Vincent Terrace; *The International Antiques Market*, by Marjorie Luecke; and *The New York Elevated*, by Robert C. Reed.

BARRE PUBLISHERS, Valley Rd., Barre MA 01005. Publisher: Jane West. Publishes hardcover and paperback originals. Offers standard minimum book contract. Published 10 titles last year. Free book catalog. Photocopied submissions OK. Submit outline and sample chapters or complete ms. Reports in 4 weeks. SASE.

Nonfiction: "We specialize in books on fine craftsmanship and design. History, Americana, art, photography, travel, cooking and foods, nature, recreation and pets. No length requirements; no restrictions for style, outlook, or structure. Our emphasis on quality of manufacture sets our books apart from the average publications. Particularly interested in art and folk art." Recently published *The Log Cabin, Scarecrows, Running the Rivers of North America* and *Pamper Your Possessions.*

BARRON'S EDUCATIONAL SERIES, INC., 113 Crossways Park Dr., New York NY 11797. Publishes hardcover and paperback originals. Pays royalty. Simultaneous and photocopied submissions OK. Reports in 3 months. SASE. Free book catalog.

Nonfiction: Adult education, art, cookbooks, foreign language, review books, sports, test preparation materials and textbooks. Query or submit outline/synopsis and a sample chapter. Recently published *Jimmy Who?,* by Leslie Wheeler (social studies); *Maeread Corrigan/Betty Williams,* by Richard Deutsch (social studies); and *Lenotre's Desserts and Pastries,* by Gaston Lenotre (cookbook).

BEACON PRESS, 25 Beacon St., Boston MA 02108. (617)742-2110. Director/Editor-in-Chief: MaryAnn Lash. Publishes hardcover originals (50%) and paperback reprints (50%). Published 30 hardcover titles in 1978; plans 14 in 1979. Pays 7½% royalty on paperback; 10% on hardbound; advance averages $3,000. Photocopied submissions OK. Reports in 6-8 weeks. SASE. Free book catalog.

Nonfiction: General nonfiction, religion, world affairs, social studies, history, psychology, art, literature, and philosophy. Query. Recently published *Gyn/Ecology, The Metaethics of Radical Feminism,* by Mary Daly (feminist philosophy); *Healing at Home: A Guide to Health Care for Children,* by Mary Howell; *The North Will Rise Again: Pensions, Power & Politics in the 1980's,* by Jeremy Rifkin and Randy Barber (comtemporary politics).

BEAU LAC PUBLISHERS, Box 248, Chuluota FL 32766. Publishes hardcover and paperback originals. SASE.

Nonfiction: "Military subjects. Specialist in the social side of service life." Query. Recently published *The Officer's Family Social Guide,* by M.P. Gross; and *Military Weddings and the Military Ball,* by M.P. Gross.

BELMONT TOWER BOOKS/LEISURE BOOKS, Nordon Publishing, Inc., 2 Park Ave., New York NY 10016. (212)679-7707. Editorial Director: Milburn Smith. Estab. 1970. Publishes paperback originals (70%) and reprints (30%). Published 97 titles in 1978, 96 in 1979, plans 96 in 1980. Pays 4-8% royalty or $500-1,500 for outright purchase; average advance $1,750. Simultaneous and photocopied submissions OK. SASE. Reports in 6 weeks. Book catalog for SASE.

Nonfiction: History, humor, self-help, and sports. "We publish very little nonfiction, but what we do publish must be timely and popularly oriented with a core of solid information. We do not want to see manuscripts on crafts, technical or texts." Query or submit outline/synopsis and sample chapters. Recently published *Beyond the Body,* by Sandra Gibson (occult); *Sex Without Anxiety,* by Nathan Shiff (self-help); and *Zane Grey,* by Frank Gruber (biography).

Fiction: Adventure, erotica (soft-core), fantasy, historical, humor, mainstream, mystery, romance, science fiction, suspense, western, and war. "Of the books we publish each year, most are category novels, so we have a continual need for category fiction of nearly all sorts. We are also interested in seeing general novels of a popular nature. We do not want any juvenile or gothic manuscripts." Query or submit outline/synopsis and sample chapters. Recently published *This Fiery Promise,* by Joan VanEvery Frost (historical romance); *Alien Perspective,* by David Houston (science fiction); *The Rig,* by Ronald Wilcox (general fiction); and *The Free and the Brave,* by John Cornwell (war novel).

CHARLES A. BENNETT CO., INC., 809 W. Detweiller Dr., Peoria IL 61615. (309)691-4454. Editor-in-Chief: Michael Kenny. Publishes hardcover and paperback originals. Specializes in textbooks and related materials. Pays 10% royalty for textbooks, "less for supplements"; no advance. Published 25 titles in 1978; plans 25 in 1979, 25 in 1980. Query "with a sample chapter that represents much of the book; not a general introduction if the ms is mostly specific 'how-to' instructions." Send prints if photos/illustrations are to accompany the book. Photocopied submissions OK. Reports in 2-4 weeks. SASE. Free book catalog.

Nonfiction: Publishes textbooks and related items for home economics, industrial education, and art programs in schools, junior high and above. Recently published *Discovering Food,* by

H. Kowtaluk; *Consumer Skills*, by I. Oppenheim; and *Basic Woodworking*, by Feirer.

BERKLEY PUBLISHING CORP., 200 Madison Ave., New York NY 10016. Editor-in-Chief: Caroline Fireside. Managing Editor: Mark Hurst. Pays 6% royalty to 150,000 copies; 8% thereafter; usually offers advance. Publishes about 180 titles/year. Simultaneous and photocopied submissions OK. Reports in 1-2 months. SASE.
Nonfiction: Biography, hobbies, how-to, pets, psychology (popular), and self-help. "We publish mainly reprints of hardcovers; sometimes we buy the book as a paperback and arrange for hardcover publication." Submit through agent only. State availability of photos or illustrations.
Fiction: Fantasy, historical, mainstream, mystery, romance, science fiction, suspense and western. Submit through agent only.
Recent Titles: *Children of Dune*, by Frank Herbert (science fiction); *The Last Convertible*, by A. Myrer (fiction); and *A Time for Truth*, by William E. Simon.

THE BETA BOOK CO., Trade Division, 2801 Camino Del Rio S., San Diego CA 92108. Vice President Editorial and Marketing: Dr. Jean-Louis Brindamour. Senior Editor: W. James DeSaegher. Editor: Janet L. Tronstad. Estab. 1975. Publishes paperback originals (95%) and reprints (5%). Published 18 titles in 1978; plans 48 in 1979, 60 in 1980. Pays 5-10% royalty; no advance. Photocopied submissions OK. SASE. Reports in 2-3 months. Free book catalog.
Nonfiction: Americana, animals, biography, health, history, hobbies, how-to, humor, juveniles, music, nature, philosophy, poetry, politics, psychology, recreation, religion, science, self-help, sports and textbooks. "Needs are only established by manuscripts received. Quality and content of manuscripts are considered." Submit outline/synopsis and sample chapters. Recently published *Transcendental Misconceptions*, by R.D. Scott (self-help/expose); *The Together Experience*, by Len Sperry (marriage and family/self-help); and *Superman for a Total Woman*, by Gerald H. Twombly (marriage/self-help/male mystique).
Fiction: Adventure, fantasy, gothic, historical, humor, mystery, religious, romance, science fiction, suspense and western. "We accept no manuscripts with profanity or elicit sex scenes." Submit outline/synopsis and sample chapters. Recently published *A Place Called Empty*, by Mary Lieber (romance/adventure); *Lolly*, by Kelly Segraves (romance/fictionalized biography); and *The Other Mrs. Wyngate*, by Ann Long (romance/adventure/gothic).

BETHANY FELLOWSHIP, INC., 6820 Auto Club Rd., Minneapolis MN 55438. (612)944-2121. Editor-in-Chief: Alec Brooks. Managing Editor: Carol Johnson. Publishes hardcover and paperback originals (75%) and paperback reprints (25%). Pays 10% royalty on hardcover and original trade paperbacks; 6% on original mass market books; no advance. Published 40 titles in 1978; plans 45 in 1979, 50 in 1980. Simultaneous and photocopied submissions OK. Reports in 1-2 months. Free book catalog.
Nonfiction: Publishes biography (evangelical Christian), nature, religious (evangelical charismatic) and self-help books. Query. Recently published *My Magnificient Machine*, by Coleman; *Especially for Wives*, by Campian; and *The Music Machine*, by Wright.
Fiction: Well-written stories with a Christian message. Submit outline and 2-3 sample chapters.

BETHANY PRESS, Book Division of Christian Board of Publication, Box 179, St. Louis MO 63166. (314)371-6900. Editor-in-Chief: Sherman R. Hanson. Publishes hardcover and paperback originals. Published 11 titles in 1978; plans 14 in 1979, 12-15 in 1980. Pays 17% royalty. Query. Reports in 30 days. Enclose return postage.
Nonfiction: Books dealing with Christian experience, church life, devotions, programming, Christian education, Bible reading and interpretation. "Writer should offer clear prose, readable by lay persons, speaking to their concerns as Christians and churchmen or churchwomen." Recently published *Experiment in Liberty*, by R.E. Osborn; *Reading the Bible With Understanding*, by J. Trefzger; *How to Raise the Level of Giving In Your Church*, by John McGinty; and *The Church Is a Who*, by Bernice Hogan.

BETTER HOMES AND GARDENS BOOKS, 1716 Locust St., Des Moines IA 50336. Editor: Gerald Knox. Publishes hardcover originals and reprints. Published 18 titles in 1978; plans 18 in 1979, 20 in 1980. "Ordinarily we pay an outright fee for work (amount depending on the scope of the assignment). If the book is the work of one author, we sometimes offer royalties in addition to the fee." Prefers outlines and sample chapters, but will accept complete ms. Will consider photocopied submissions. Reports in 6 weeks. Enclose return postage.
Home Service: "We publish nonfiction in many family and home service categories, including gardening, decorating and remodeling, sewing and crafts, money management, entertaining, handyman's topics, cooking and nutrition, and other subjects of home service value. Emphasis

is on how-to and on stimulating people to action. We require concise, factual writing. Audience is primarily husbands and wives with home and family as their main center of interest. Style should be informative and lively with a straightforward approach. Stress the positive. Emphasis is entirely on reader service. We approach the general audience with a confident air, instilling in them a desire and the motivation to accomplish things. Food book areas that we have already dealt with in detail are currently overworked by writers submitting to us. We rely heavily on a staff of home economist editors for food books. We are interested in non-food books that can serve mail order and book club requirements (to sell at least for $8.95 and up) as well as trade. Rarely is our first printing of a book less than 100,000 copies. Publisher recommends careful study of specific *Better Homes and Gardens* book titles before submitting material.

*BINFORD & MORT, PUBLISHERS, 2536 SE 11th Ave., Portland OR 97202. (503)238-9666. Editor-in-Chief: L.K. Phillips. President: Thomas Binford. Publishes hardcover and paperback originals (80%) and reprints (20%). Pays 10% royalty; advance (to established authors) varies. Occasionally does some subsidy publishing, "when ms merits it, but it does not fit into our type of publishing." Publishes about 24 titles annually. Reports in 2-4 months. SASE. Free book catalog.
Nonfiction: Publishes books about the Pacific Northwest, mainly in the historical field. Also Americana, art, biography; cookbooks, cooking and foods; history, nature, photography, recreation, reference, sports, and travel. Query. Recently published *Diving for Northwest Relics*, by James S. White; *Ancient Modocs of California and Oregon*, by Carrol Howe; and *Frontier Politics: Alaska's James Wickersham*, by Evangeline Atwood.
Fiction: Publishes historical and western books. Must be strongly laced with historical background.

JOHN F. BLAIR, PUBLISHER, 1406 Plaza Dr., Winston-Salem NC 27103. (919)768-1374. Editor-in-Chief: John F. Blair. Publishes hardcover originals; occasionally paperbacks and reprints. Royalty to be negotiated. Published 8 titles in 1978; plans 10 in 1979. Free book catalog. Submit complete ms. "Authors are urged to inquire if they have not received an answer within 6 weeks." SASE.
General Fiction, Nonfiction, and Juveniles: In juveniles, preference given to books for ages 10 through 14 and up; in history and biography, preference given to books having some bearing on the southeastern United States. Very little poetry. No length limits for juveniles. Other mss may be 140 pages or more. Recently published *Outer Banks Mysteries and Seaside Stories* (folklore); *Pier Fishing in North Carolina* (nonfiction); *The Gallows Lord* (poetry); *None to Comfort Me* (fiction); and *Serpent Treasure* (nonfiction).

THE BOBBS-MERRILL EDUCATIONAL PUBLISHING CO., 4300 W. 62nd St., Indianapolis IN 46268. (317)298-5400. Editorial Director: Thomas D. Wittenberg. Published 50 titles in 1978; plans 75 in 1979, 100 in 1980. "Queries are acceptable, but do not send complete manuscripts." SASE.
Nonfiction: "We are interested in the following disciplines: business education, business administration, humanities, vocational and technical books."

THE BOBBS-MERRILL CO., INC., 4 W. 58th St., New York NY 10019. Editor-in-Chief: Eugene Rachlis. Publishes hardcover originals. Pays standard 10-12½-15% royalty; advances vary, depending on author's reputation and nature of book. Published 50 titles in 1978; plans 35 in 1979, 30 in 1980. Query. No unsolicited mss. Reports in 4-6 weeks. Enclose return postage.
General Fiction and Nonfiction: Little fiction; emphasis on nonfiction: publishes American and foreign novels, history, travel, crafts, biography/autobiography, current events, business. No poetry.

BOOKCRAFT, INC., 1848 W. 2300 South, Salt Lake City UT 84119. Editor: H. George Bickerstaff. Publishes (mainly hardcover) originals and reprints. Pays standard 10-12½-15% royalty; "we rarely make an advance on a new author." Published 20 titles in 1978; plans 24 in 1979, 25 in 1980. Will send a catalog and a copy of information for authors to a writer on request. Query. Will consider photocopied submissions. "Include contents page with ms." Reports in about 2 months. Enclose return postage.
Nonfiction: "We publish for members of The Church of Jesus Christ of Latter-Day Saints (Mormons). Our books are directly related to the faith and practices of that church. We will be glad to review such mss, but mss having merely a general religious appeal are not acceptable. Ideal book lengths range from about 64 pages to 200 or so, depending on subject, presentation,

and age level. We look for a fresh approach—rehashes of well-known concepts or doctrines not acceptable. Mss should be anecdotal unless truly scholarly or on a specialized subject. Outlook must be positive. We do not publish anti-Mormon works. We almost never publish poetry. Recently published *The Windwalker*, by Blaine Yorgoson (fiction); *Born of the Spirit*, by Richard Packhome (nonfiction); and *Take Time to Smell the Dandelions*, by Karla Erickson (raising children).

Teen and Young Adult: "We publish short and moderate length books for Mormon youth, about ages 14 to 19, mostly nonfiction. Must reflect LDS principles without being 'preachy'; must be motivational. 18,000-25,000 words is about the length, though we would accept good longer mss. This is a tough area to write in, and the mortality rate for such mss is high." Recently published *Wonderful Me*, by Verna Johnson (nonfiction).

BOOKS FOR BUSINESS, INC., 1100 17th St., NW., Washington DC 20036. (202)466-2372. Publishes hardcover and paperback originals (80%) and reprints. Specializes in high-priced books on business or international trade. "Looking for a unique content area geard to business and/or the entrepreneur. New and different concepts are welcomed. Usually royalties start at 10%; sometimes 5% for anthologies, but this is not a fixed rule." No advance. Send contact sheets for selection of illustrations. Simultaneous and photocopied submissions OK. Reports in 1-2 months. Book catalog for SASE.

Recent Titles: *How the IRS Selects Individual Tax Returns for Audit*; *How to Develop and Manage a Successful Condominium*; and *Tax Shelters for You That Work for the experts*.

BOOKWORM PUBLISHING CO., Box 3037, Ontario CA 91761. Editor-in-Chief: Maisic Meier. Publishes paperback originals and reprints. Published 2 titles in 1978; plays 4 in 1979, 6 in 1980. "We publish limited library hardback editions." Offers royalty of 5% of net publisher revenues. "Author receives 33% of all auxiliary revenues, e.g., translations, serial, TV rights, etc. We hold all copyrights ourselves in most cases." Advances paid only to previously established authors. Average advance is $500. "We rely on aggressive nontrade promotion to special outlets in addition to regular trade distribution channels, e.g., nurseries for garden books, worm farms for books on vermiculture. Books lending themselves to this additional thrust have an extra edge in our consideration." Query. First-time authors should submit complete ms. Established authors should submit outline and sample chapters. Will consider simultaneous and photocopied submissions. Typed, double-spaced ms essential. "If photos or drawings, send some samples of artist's or photographer's work." Enclose return postage if submitting complete ms on initial contact. Include phone number. Reports usually within 10 days.

Nonfiction: Any subject area related to natural or social ecology. Primary interests are agriculture, horticulture (gardening), waste management, self-sufficiency and organic living. Prefers practical "how-to-do-it" treatment. Mss may range from 7,500 to 30,000 words. "We seek mss from authors having authentic qualifications as 'authorities' in their subject areas, but qualification may be by experience as well as academic training." Interested in "needed" books either covering subjects relatively rare in existing literature or taking an unusual approach to conventional subject matter. Marketability of book is prime consideration. "We dislike issuing books which must compete in too crowded a field." See *The Elements of Style*. "We demand clear, concise and effective use of English, appropriate to subject and intended audience. Technical terms, if used, should be defined in text on initial appearance and/or in accompanying glossary. We publish for the average person, and wish even our books for specialists to be understandable to the neophyte. We're more interested in creating books of lasting value to readers than in following current trends or fads." Abstract philosophy, poetry, fiction are "just not in our fields." Recently published *The Real Roy Rogers*, by W. Roper.

Textbooks: Publishes social science texts for the elementary-high school market, emphasizing traditional values.

Business and Professional: Publishes business and "organization management."

BOREALIS PRESS, LTD., 9 Ashburn Dr., Ottawa, Ontario, Canada K2E 6N4. Editorial Director: Frank Tierney. Senior Editor: Glenn Clever. Publishes hardcover and paperback originals. Published 25 titles in 1978; plans 30 in 1989, 25 in 1980. Pays 10% royalty; no advance. Reports in 8 weeks. SAE and International Reply Coupons. Book catalog $1.

Nonfiction: "Only material Canadian in content." Query. Recently published *Seventy Years of Service: A History of the Royal Canadian Army Medical Corps*, by Col. G.W.L. Nicholson.

Fiction: "Only material Canadian in content." Query. Recently published *Song and Silence*, by D. Madott.

THE BORGO PRESS, Box 2845, San Bernardino CA 92406. (714)884-5813. Editor-in-Chief:

R. Reginald. Publishes paperback originals. Published 12 titles in 1978; plans 13 in 1979, 14 in 1980. "About 60% of our line consists of The Milford Series: Popular Writers of Today, critical studies on modern popular writers, particularly science fiction writers." Royalty: "4% of gross, with a 6% escalator; 6-8% for second books, if the first has sold well." No advance. "At least a third of our sales are to the library market." Reports in 1-2 months. SASE. Free book catalog.
Nonfiction: Publishes literary critiques. Submit outline/synopsis and sample chapters. "We appreciate people who've looked at our books before submitting proposals; all of the books in our author series, for example, are based around a certain format that we prefer using." Recently published *Kurt Vonnegut: The Gospel from Outer Space*, by C. Mayo (literary critique); and *The Clockwork Universe of Anthony Burgess*, by R. Mathews.
Fiction: Fantasy and science fiction. "We only publish fiction by established authors (those with previous book credits)." Query. Recently published *Hasan*, by P. Anthony; *A Usual Lunacy*, by D.G. Compton; *Sir Henry*, by Robert Nathan; and *The Quest of Excalibur*, by L. Wibberley.

THOMAS BOUREGY AND CO., INC., 22 E. 60th St., New York NY 10022. Editor: Rita Brenig. Offers advance on publication date. Published 60 titles in 1979. Reports in 10 weeks. SASE.
Fiction: Romances, nurse/romances, westerns and gothic novels for teenagers and young adults. Avoid sensationalist elements. Query. Length: about 50,000 words. Also publishes Airmont Classics Series. Recently published *No Time for Love*, by Kay Richardson (romance); *Ridge of Fear*, by Georgia M. Shewmake (gothic); and *Trouble at Crossed Forks*, by B.A. Collier (western).

R.R. BOWKER CO., 1180 Avenue of the Americas, New York NY 10036. (212)764-5100. Executive Editor, Book Division: Judith S. Garodnick. Managing Editor, Directories: Olga S. Weber. Pays negotiable royalty. Reports in 4-6 weeks. Enclose return postage.
Nonfiction: Publishes books for the book trade and library field, reference books and bibliographies. Query; "send in a very thoroughly developed proposal with a table of contents, representative chapters, and analysis of the competition to my idea."

BOWLING GREEN UNIVERSITY POPULAR PRESS, Popular Culture Center, Bowling Green State University, Bowling Green OH 43403. Editors: Ray B. Browne, Pat Browne. Publishes hardcover and paperback originals. Offers variable royalty; no advance. Published 15 titles last year. Free book catalog. SASE.
Nonfiction: "Popular culture books generally. We print for the academic community interested in popular culture and popular media." Interested in nonfiction mss on "science fiction, folklore, black culture, popular literature, detective fiction and westerns." Will consider any book-length mss. "No multiple submissions." Submit complete ms. Recently published *Bret Harte, Literary Critic*, by Patrick Morrow; and *Watteau's Shepherds: The Detective Novel in Britain, 1914-1940*, by LeRoy Panek.

BOWMAR/NOBLE PUBLISHING, INC., 4563 Colorado Blvd., Los Angeles CA 90039. (213)247-8995. Editor-in-Chief: Mel Cebulash. Managing Editor: Dolly Hassinbiller. Publishes hardcover and paperback originals (80%) and reprints (20%). Specializes in El-hi educational books. Royalties or flat fees are negotiable; "there is no average advance amount, and we don't always give advances." Published 42 titles in 1978. "We sell directly to the schools; we have very few titles in bookstores." Submit complete ms. Photocopied submissions OK. Reports in 1-3 months. SASE. Book catalog for SASE.
Nonfiction: Publishes textbooks, biography, business, history, juveniles and sports books.
Fiction: Publishes adventure, mystery, science fiction "and anything else that might be of interest to kids 8-16." Especially interested in easy reading books.

BRADBURY PRESS, INC., 2 Overhill Rd., Scarsdale NY 10583. (914)472-5100. Editor-in-Chief: Richard Jackson. Publishes hardcover originals. Published 12 titles in 1978, plans 18 in 1979, 18 in 1980. "We're distributed by E.P. Dutton." Pays 10% royalty or 5% to author, 5% to artist; advance averages $1,000. Photocopied submissions OK. Reports in 3 months. SASE. Book catalog for 28¢.
Fiction: Contemporary fiction: adventure, science fiction, and humor. Also "stories about real kids; special interest in realistic dialogue." No fantasy or religious material. Recently published *Starring Sally J. Freedman as Herself*, by J. Blume; *The Girl Who Loved Wild Horses* (1979 Caldecott Medal), by P. Goble; and *The Slave Dancer*, by P. Fox.

BRANDEN PRESS, INC., 221 Columbus Ave., Boston MA 02116 (617)267-7471.

Editor-in-Chief: Edmund R. Brown. Publishes hardcover and paperback originals (70%) and reprints (30%). Pays 10% royalty up to 5,000 copies; 15% thereafter. "We offer an advance only on important books and cannot give an average amount. We publish some books for which the authors furnish a partial subsidy, or have grants." Publishes about 50 titles annually. Photos and/or illustrations are generally discussed with the author after ms is received. Photocopied submissions OK. Reports in 2-4 weeks. SASE. Free book catalog.

Nonfiction: "We publish books of all sorts and kinds and are willing to consider any ms, but are not interested in fiction." Query.

Recent Titles: *Fundamentals of Applied Industrial Management*, by J. Glasser (educational); *They Too Made America Great*, by A. Caso (biographical); *House Plants That Really Grow*, by E.S. Parcher (handbook); and *Travel At Its Best!*, by A. Schwartz.

GEORGE BRAZILLER, INC., 1 Park Ave., New York NY 10016. Offers standard 10-12½-15% royalty contract. Advance varies, depending on author's reputation and nature of book. No unsolicited mss. Reports in 6 weeks. Enclose return postage.

General Fiction and Nonfiction: Publishes fiction and nonfiction; literature, art, philosophy, history, science. Query.

BRASCH AND BRASCH, PUBLISHERS, INC., 220A W. 'B' St., Ontario CA 91762. (714)986-3631. Editorial Director: Walter M. Brasch, Ph.D. Publishes hardcover and paperback originals. Published 3 titles in 1978, plans 5-6 in 1979; 7-8 in 1980. "We have full and complete marketing plans developed for every book; the nature of the book determines the means of primary marketing. But, we are aggressive in promotion of works. It is only when we get creative in our marketing that everyone benefits." Pays 10-12½-15% royalty. Simultaneous and photocopied submissions OK. Reports in 2 weeks on queries, 4 weeks on sample chapters, 2 months on complete mss. SASE. Book catalog for SASE. "Send *only* query; we will advise if we wish to see full ms."

Nonfiction: "We are especially interested in books written by journalists on topics involving society and the role of the person in society. In this aspect, we are open to many kinds of manuscripts. The writings of Lafcadio Hearn, Mark Twain, Tom Wolfe, Jimmy Breslin, John Hershey, and others who view the American scene are guidelines on topics. The ms should reflect careful research, and should be exceptionally well-written. Within this scope, there is a wide latitude of topics. No cookbooks, how-to books, crafts, sports or religious." Query or submit outline/synopsis and sample chapters. Recently published *The Baja Feeling*, by Ben Hunter (travel-adventure); and *They Was Just Niggers*, by Michael W. Fedo.

Fiction: "We will publish at least one science fiction title per year, and at least one novel. The science fiction book *must* reflect society through a thorough comprehension of the human process of interaction. We are *not* interested in science fantasy, but in science fiction as a means to understanding the present, and the human condition. Our novels must have well-developed plots that also reflect deep studies of the human condition, as seen through individuals in the novel. We are not interested in novels that 'go nowhere' or are merely stream-of-consciousness attempts to explain what probably can't be explained anyway. We would also like to see fiction that deals with Jewish themes. Our fiction must have a certain 'power' within it; a power to influence and make readers think." No westerns, mysteries, gothics or romances. Recently published *Time Span*, by B. Diamond (science fiction).

BREVET PRESS, INC., 519 W. 10th St., Box 1404, Sioux Falls SD 57101. Editor-in-Chief: Donald P. Mackintosh. Managing Editor: Peter E. Reid. Publishes hardcover and paperback originals (67%) and reprints (33%). Published 4 titles in 1978; plans 4 in 1979, 6 in 1980. Specializes in business management, history, place names, historical marker series. Pays 5% royalty; advance averages $1,000. Query; "after query, detailed instructions will follow if we are interested." Send copies if photos/illustrations are to accompany ms. Simultaneous and photocopied submissions OK. Reports in 1-2 months. SASE. Free book catalog.

Nonfiction: Publishes Americana (A. Melton, editor); business (D.P. Mackintosh, editor); history (B. Mackintosh, editor); and technical books (Peter Reid, editor). Recently published *Illinois Historical Markers and Sites* (nonfiction historical series); and *Challenge*, by R. Karolevitz (history).

Fiction: Publishes historical books (T.E. Kakonis, editor). Recently published *The Thresher*, by H. Krause (historical fiction).

BRICK HOUSE PUBLISHING CO., 3 Main St., Andouver MA 01810 (617)475-9568. Publisher: Jack D. Howell. Publishes hardcover and paperback originals. Published 3 titles in 1978; plans 8 in 1979, 10 in 1980. Pays 7-10% royalty; "negotiable" advance. Photocopied submissions OK. Reports in 4 weeks. SASE. Free book catalog.

Nonfiction: Trade paperbacks generally in the $6-12 range. Alternative sources of energy material; "and would like to diversify into other how-to and alternative lifestyle books. We will consider any quality nonfiction trade material." Recently published *The Solar Home Book*, by B. Anderson/M. Riordan; and *New Inventions In Low-Cost Solar Heating*, by W. Shurcliff.

*BRIGHAM YOUNG UNIVERSITY PRESS, University Press Bldg, Provo Utah 84602. Director: Ernest L. Olson. Managing Editor: John Drayton. Publishes hardcover and paperback originals (85%) and reprints (15%). Published 25 titles in 1978; plans 25 in 1979, 25 in 1980. "We subsidy publish 15% of our books. If a book has scholarly merit but little potential for repaying the cost of publication, we encourage the author to seek a subsidy from an institution or foundation." Royalties are based on estimated market potential, ranging 0-15%; no advance. Reports in 3-6 weeks. SASE. Free book catalog.
Nonfiction: Scholarly nonfiction, textbooks, and high-level popularizations. "We are interested in high-quality work from any discipline, but we focus mainly on Western regional studies, elementary education, outdoor recreation, and the social sciences, especially anthropological studies dealing with the American Indian. No length preferences. Query. Recently published *Utah's History*, edited by Richard D. Polletal; *School Can Wait*, by Raymond S. Moore; and *Kayaks Down The Nile*, by John Goddard.
Fiction and Poetry: "We publish an average of one book of poetry or short stories annually. We have not published a novel. We do not publish children's or juvenile literature."

BROADMAN PRESS, 127 9th Ave. N., Nashville TN 37234. Editorial Director: Thomas L. Clark. Estab. 1891. Publishes hardcover and paperback originals (85%) and reprints (15%). Published 108 titles in 1978; plans 105 in 1979, 105 in 1980. Pays 5-10% royalty; no advance. Photocopied submissions OK "only if they're sharp and clear." SASE. Reports in 2 months.
Nonfiction: Religion. "We are open to some freelance submissions in the children's and inspirational areas. Materials in both areas must be suited for a conservative Protestant readership. No poetry, biography, sermons, or anything outside the area of Protestant religion." Query, submit outline/synopsis and sample chapters, or submit complete ms. Recently published *A Philosopher's Way: Essays and Address of D. Elton Trueblook*, edited by Elizabeth Newby (essays on Christian life and beliefs); *How Churches Grow in an Urban Environment*, by Frances M. DuBose (church growth); and *Exploring the Christian Way*, by Vernon O. Elmore (Bible study).
Fiction: Religious. "We publish almost no fiction—less than one title per year. For our occasional publication we want not only a very good story, but also one that sets forth Christian values. Nothing that lacks a positive Christian emphasis; nothing that fails to sustain reader interest." Submit complete ms.
Tips: "Bible study is very good for us, but our publishing is largely restricted in this area to works that we enlist on the basis of specific quthor qualifications."

WILLIAM C. BROWN CO., PUBLISHERS, 2460 Kerper Blvd., Dubuque IA 52001. Executive Director of Product Development: Raymond C. Deveaux. Royalties vary. Enclose return postage.
Nonfiction: College textbooks. Query.

BUCKNELL UNIVERSITY PRESS, Lewisburg PA 17837. (717)524-3674. Director: Mills F. Edgerton Jr. Associate Director: Cynthia Fell. Publishes hardcover originals. Publishes 15 titles/year. Pays 10% royalty; no advance. Photocopied submissions OK. Reports in 3 months, "sooner if rejected." SASE. Free book catalog.
Nonfiction: Scholarly books, especially in the humanities and social sciences. No highly technical scientific or mathematical manuscripts, textbooks, general readership books, fiction or poetry. "We publish only scholarly books written by and for the academic professional." Query; "we prefer to begin with a letter of inquiry, but once we have expressed an interest in a particular proposal, we require a complete and finished manuscript." Recently published *Cosmic Satire in the Contemporary Novel*, by J. Tilton; *The Later Philosophy of Schelling*, by R. Brown; and *H.G. Wells & Modern Science Fiction*, by D. Suvin/R. Philmus.

BUSINESS WEEK, McGraw-Hill Publications, Inc., 1221 Avenue of the Americas, 40th Floor, New York NY 10020. Editorial Director: Lincoln Platt. Editorial Director: Sue Cymes. Publishes hardcover and paperback originals (90%) and reprints (10%). Published 4 titles in 1978; plans 6 in 1979. "Financial arrangements are made individually." Simultaneous and photocopied submissions OK. Reports in 3 weeks. SASE. Book catalog from McGraw-Hill, Inc.
Nonfiction: "*Business Week* is interested in manuscripts which appeal to the business man and

woman. Mss should contribute to knowledge in a professional way. An emphasis on 'personal' business as well as strictly financial and business books. Submit outline/synopsis and sample chapters. Recently published *Executive Health: How to Live Without Stress*, by P. Goldberg (health and well-being, zeroing in on the role corporations can play to advance the health of their executives).

*C.S.S. PUBLISHING CO., 628 S. Main St., Lima OH 45804. (419)227-1818. Editor-in-Chief: Wesley T. Runk. Managing Editor: Mary Lou Buyakie. Publishes paperback originals. Specializes in religious books. Pays 4-10% royalty; no advance. Subsidy publishes 5% of books. Subsidy publishing is offered "to all whose mss we reject, but we do not offer marketing for any ms outside our categories." Published 60 titles in 1978; plans 60 in 1979, 60 in 1980. Markets by direct mail and bookstores. Simultaneous submissions OK. Reports in 2-4 months. SASE. Free book catalog.
Nonfiction: "We publish titles geared to helping members of the clergy and lay leaders of all denominations in the work of their parishes. Our titles are practical helps to these leaders; worship resources, sermon books, dramas for church use, stewardship and evangelism materials, youth programming materials, Bible study guides, children's sermon stories, pastoral care resources, and multimedia sermons and stories. Generally, the more creative and contemporary the ms is, the more likely we are to offer a contract. Length may vary from a 12-page drama to a 150-page book of sermons. Clarity and creativity should be the first consideration. Send a complete manuscript of practical—not theoretical—field-tested programs for churches." Recently published *Holy Ballyhoo*, by O. Arnold (church public relations); *Wings of the Spirit*, by J. Weekley (worship); and *When Jesus Exaggerated*, by H. Sheets (sermons).

CAMARO PUBLISHING CO., Box 90430, Los Angeles CA 90009. (213)837-7500. Editor-in-Chief: Garth W. Bishop. Publishes hardcover and paperback originals. "Every contract is different. Many books are bought outright." Published 5 titles last year. Query. SASE.
Nonfiction: Books on travel, food, wine and health. Recently published *Mother-to-Mother Baby Care Book*, by Sills and Henry.

CAMBRIDGE UNIVERSITY PRESS, 32 E. 57th St., New York NY 10022. Editor-in-Chief: Walter Lippincott. Publishes hardcover and paperback originals. Pays 10% royalty; 6% on paperbacks; no advance. Query. Reports in 2 weeks to 6 months. Enclose return postage.
Nonfiction and Textbooks: Anthropology, economics, psychology, upper-level textbooks, academic trade, scholarly monographs, biography, history, music. Looking for academic excellence in all work submitted. Department Editors: Ken Werner (science); Steven Fraser (economics, economic history, American history, social and political theory); Susan Milmoe (psychology); Jane Majeski (humanities).

CAMELOT BOOKS, Division of Avon Books, 959 8th Ave., New York NY 10019. (212)262-7454. Senior Editor: Jean Feiwel. Publishes paperback originals (25%) and reprints (75%). Published 24 titles in 1978; 36 in 1979, plans 36 in 1980. Pays 6-10% royalty; offers $1,500 minimum advance. Simultaneous and photocopied submissions OK. SASE. Reports in 6 weeks. Free book catalog.
Nonfiction: Animals, biography, health, history, how-to, humor, and self-help. Query or submit outline/synopsis and sample chapters. Recently published *The Picture Life of Stevie Wonder*, by Audrey Edwards and Garry Wahl (biography); *Winners in Gymnastics*, by Frank Ubky (biography); and *Winners on the Tennis Court*, by Gluckman (biography).
Fiction: Adventure, fantasy, humor, mainstream, mystery, science fiction, picture books and suspense. Query or submit outline/synopsis and sample chapters. Recently published *Maria Cooney and the Comic Circus*, by Jerome Beatty (science fiction/humor); *Summerdog*, by Thom Roberts; and *The Velveteen Rabbit*, by Margery Williams (picture book/reprint).

CANADIAN MUSEUMS ASSOCIATION, 331 Cooper St., Suite 400, Ottawa, Ontario, Canada K2P 0G5. (613)233-5653. Editorial Director: John Vollmer. Senior Editor: Gary Sirois. Publishes hardcover and paperback originals. Published 5 titles in 1978. Pays 10% royalty; no advance. Simultaneous submissions OK. Reports in 2-3 months. SASE. Free book catalog.
Nonfiction: Must be related to the museum and art gallery field, primarily Canadian. Museology, museography, care of collections, security, environmental control, museum architecture, exhibition care and design, cataloguing and registration, conservation methods, glossaries of terminology, staff training, extension and educational services, and technical skills. "Serious material only. Primarily concerned with the Canadian scene, with a view to the

international market." Submit outline/synopsis and sample chapters. Consult Chicago *Manual of Style.* Recently published *Handbook for the Travelling Exhibitionist,* by V. Dickenson/B. Tyler; *Fellows Lecture,* by E. Turner; and *Cataloguing Military Uniforms,* by D. Ross/R. Chartrand.

CAPRA PRESS, 631 State St., Santa Barbara CA 93101. Editor-in-Chief: Noel Young. Publishes hardcover and paperback originals. Specializes in documentary lifestyle books, and biographies (no fiction). Pays 8% royalty; advance averages $1,000. Published 15 titles in 1978. State availability of photos and/or illustrations to accompany ms. Simultaneous submissions OK "if we are told where else it has been sent." Reports in 2-4 weeks. SASE. Book catalog for SASE.
Nonfiction: Publishes western contemporary nonfiction (30,000 words); biography (30,000 words); how-to; and nature books. Submit outline/synopsis and sample chapters. Recently published *Guns, Gold and Caravans,* by R. Easton (biography); *Sweat,* by M. Aalund (health/history); and *The Toilet Papers,* by S. VanderRyn.

CAREER PRESS, Division of Singer Communications, 1500 Cardinal Dr., Little Falls NJ 07424. (201)256-4712. Chief Editor: Don Bolander. Publishes hardcover and paperback originals. Publishes 10-20 titles/year. Pays in royalties, or more often, in outright purchase, "which varies with size and complexity of project." No advance. Simultaneous and photocopied submissions OK. SASE. Reports in 2-4 weeks. Free book catalog.
Nonfiction: "Primarily self-study education materials or programs, or how-to-do-it books (i.e., photography, locksmithing, dress design, interior decoration, and similar subjects). Also reading programs for children and adults." Query or submit complete ms. Recently published *The Dr. Bruno Furst Memory Course; Automotive Locksmithing Handbook;* and *The Encyclopedia of Photography.*

CAREER PUBLISHING, INC., Box 5486, Orange CA 92667. (714)997-0130. Senior Editor: S. Michele McFadden. Publishes paperback originals. Published 19 titles in 1978; plans 24 in 1979, 28 in 1980. Pays 10% royalty; no advance. Simultaneous (if so informed with names of others to whom submissions have been sent) and photocopied submissions OK. Reports in 1-2 months. SASE. Book catalog 25¢.
Nonfiction: "Textbooks should provide core upon which class curriculum can be based: textbook, workbook or kit with 'hands-on' activities and exercises, and teacher's guide. Should incorporate modern and effective teaching techniques. Should lead to a job objective. We also publish support materials for existing courses, and are open to unique, marketable ideas with schools in mind. Reading level should be controlled appropriately—usually 8th-9th grade equivalent for vocational school and community college level courses. Any sign of sexism or racism will disqualify the work. No career awareness masquerading as career training." Submit outline/synopsis and sample chapters or complete ms. Recently published *Medical Office Management,* by G.E. Bonito (allied health textbook); *Medical Sound-Alikes,* by L. Rowe; and *Growing Pains,* by A. Frigone (juvenile self-help).

CARLTON HOUSE, 91 Station St. Ajax, Ontario, Canada L1S 3H2. (416)683-3800. Editorial Director: Roger Carlton. Publishes hardcover originals. Published 3 titles in 1978, 5 in 1979. Pays 10% royalty; advance varies. Simultaneous and photocopied submissions OK. SAE and International Reply Coupons. Reports in 3 weeks. Free book catalog.
Nonfiction and Fiction: "We are interested in children's books in particular."

CAROLINE HOUSE PUBLISHERS, INC., Box 738, Ottawa IL 61350. Editorial Director: Jameson Campaigne Jr. Senior Editor: Richard W. Wheeler. Publishes originals (85%) and reprints (15%) and distributes for about other publishers. Published 50 titles in 1979. Pays 6-15% royalty; outright purchase averages $2,500. Advance averages $2,000. Simultaneous and photocopied submissions OK. Reports in 2 months. SASE. Book catalog for SASE.
Nonfiction: Racquet sports, how-to, guides and biographies (of major subjects). No autobiographies or "nostrum-peddling." Query; all unsolicited mss are returned unopened. Recently published *Watch the Ball, Bend Your Knees, That'll Be $20 Please,* by E. Collins (tennis instruction); *The Great American Beer Book,* by J. Robertson; *Cooper Rollow's Bears 1977 Football Book,* by C. Rollow (sports); and *Successful Community Fundraising,* by S. Petersen. No fiction. Query; all unsolicited mss are returned unopened. "We prefer detailed precis with query." Recently republished *Anatomy of a Murder,* by R. Traver (suspense reprint); and *Kids Say the Darndest Things,* by Art Linkletter (humor).

CARSTENS PUBLICATIONS, INC., Hobby Book Division, Box 700, Newton NJ 07860.

(201)383-3355. Publisher: Harold H. Carstens. Estab. 1933. Publishes paperback originals. Published 6 titles in 1978, 8 in 1979; plans 10 in 1980. Pays 10% royalty; average advance. SASE. Book catalog for SASE.

Nonfiction: Model railroading, toy trains, model aviation, railroads and model hobbies. "We have scheduled or planned titles on several railroads as well as model railroad and model airplane books. Authors must know their field intimately since our readers are active modelers. Our railroad books presently are primarily photographic essays on specific railroads." Query. Recently published *The Final Years of the NYO & W*, by John Krause and Ed Crist; *Long Island Rail Road*, by John Krause and F. Kramer; *Design Handbook for Model RR*, by Paul Mallery; *Model Plan Building A to Z*, by Don McGovern; and *Complete Layout Plans 2nd Edition*, by Hal Carstens.

CATHOLIC TRUTH SOCIETY, 38/40 Eccleston Square, London, England SW1V 1PD. (01)834-4392. Editorial Director: David Murphy. Publishes hardcover and paperback originals (70%) and reprints (30%). Published 40 in 1978; plans 50 in 1979, 60 in 1980. Pays in outright purchase of $50-400; no advance. Simultaneous and photocopied submissions OK. Reports in 4 weeks. SASE. Free book catalog.

Nonfiction: Books dealing with how to solve problems in personal relationships, parenthood, teen-age, widowhood, sickness and death, especially drawing on Christian and Catholic tradition for inspiration; simple accounts of points of interest in Catholic faith, for non-Catholic readership; and books of prayer and devotion. Query, submit outline/synopsis and sample chapters, or submit complete ms. Recently published *Nuclear Energy— A Christian—Christian Concern*, by S. Triolo (pamphlet to draw attention to moral and ecological danger); *The Charismatic Prayer Meeting*, by A.D. Parry, O.S.B. (an account of features of this new movement); and *Margaret Clitherow*, by P. Caraman, S.J. (illustrated biography of a 16th-Century martyr).

CATHOLIC UNIVERSITY OF AMERICA PRESS, 620 Michigan Ave. NE, Washington DC 20064. (202)635-5052. Manager: Miss Marian E. Goode. Published 4 titles in 1978; plans 5 in 1979, 5 in 1980. Pays 10% royalty. Query with sample chapter plus outline of entire work, along with curriculum vita and list of previous publications. Reports in 2 months. Enclose return postage.

Nonfiction: Publishes history, biography, languages and literature, philosophy, religion, church-state relations, social studies. Length: 100,000-500,000 words. Recently published *Walter George Smith*, by T.A. Bryson; *Christian Sacrifice*, by R.J. Daly; *Events, Reference and Logical Form*, by R.M. Martin and *Cajetan Responds: A Reader in Reformation Controversy*, by Jared Wicks, S.J.

THE CAXTON PRINTERS, LTD., Box 700, Caldwell ID 83605. Publisher: Gordon Gipson. Pays 10% royalty; advance is negotiable. Published 7 titles in 1978; plans 6-8 in 1979, 10 in 1980. Free catalog, available on request. Query, before submitting ms. Reports in 6-8 weeks. Enclose return postage.

Americana and Politics: Publishes adult books of nonfiction, Western Americana or occasionally of conservative political nature. No fiction or scientific mss. Length: 40,000 words minimum.

CBI PUBLISHING CO., INC. 51 Sleeper St., Boston MA 02210. (617)426-2224. Editorial Director: Norman A. Stanton. Estab. 1971. Publishes hardcover and paperback originals. Published 42 titles in 1978, 56 in 1979; plans 65 in 1980. Pays 10-15% royalty; $500-1,000 advance. Simultaneous and photocopied submissions OK. SASE. Reports in 2 weeks. Free book catalog.

Nonfiction: Business/economics, cookbooks/cooking, health, reference, technical, textbooks, and travel. "We would like to see more professional and reference in foodservice, management training, consumer cookbooks, health care planning and management, textbooks in hospitality, and business computer service." Submit outline/synopsis and sample chapters. Recently published *Travel Your Taste*, by Kraft Kitchens (professsional foodservice); *Procurement Management*, by Raymond Corey (reference/management); and *No-Nonsense Nutrition*, by J. Heslin (consumer nutrition).

CELESTIAL ARTS, 231 Adrian Rd., Millbrae CA 94030. Editor-in-Chief: David Morris. Publishes paperback originals (95%) and reprints (5%). Published 20 titles in 1978; plans 20 in 1979, 25 in 1980. Pays royalty; offers "small advance." Simultaneous and photocopied submissions OK. SASE. Reports in 6-8 weeks. Book catalog for SASE.

Nonfiction: Biography, cookbooks/cooking, health, poetry, psychology, recreation, self-help, and sports. Query or submit outline/synopsis and sample chapters. Recently published *Your Many Faces*, by Virginia Satir (psychology/self-help); *San Francisco: Creation of a City*, by Tom Moulin (history in photographs); and *Don't Hit Him, He's Dead*, by John McDonough with Paul Owens (memories of an NFL official).

Fiction: "We will consider fiction, but we have published very few fiction titles and have no plans to develop fiction list."

*CENTURY HOUSE, INC., Watkins Glen NY 14891. Editor: John C. Freeman. Published 7 titles in 1978; plans 10 in 1980. Pays standard royalty contract. Preservation Press, related to Century House, does some subsidy publishing. "Preservation Press will report on such publication costs and related distribution problems if such requests accompany mss." SASE.

Americana and Hobbies: Publishes Americana and books on American decorative arts: history, historical biography, American arts, books on antiques and other collector subjects; hobby handbooks. Pictorial preferred.

Recent Titles: *Cavalcade of Dolls: A Source Book for Collectors*, by Ruth S. Freeman (hobbies); *Matchcovers: A Guide to Collecting*, by E. Rancier (hobbies); and *Wish You Were Here: Centennial Guide to Postcard Collecting*, by Dr. L. Freeman (hobbies).

CHARIOT BOOKS, David C. Cook Co., 850 N. Grove, Elgin IL 60120. (312)741-2400. Childrens Editor: Janet Hoover Thoma. Publishes hardcover and paperback originals and paperback reprints. Published 18 titles in 1978; plans 39 in 1979, 52 in 1980. Pays 6-15% royalty. Photocopied submissions OK. "We prefer a 2- to 4-page synopsis and first four chapters. SASE. Reports in 1-2 months. Free book catalog.

Fiction and Nonfiction: "Our company is interested in good Christian literature for young people. We want books with a spiritual dimension that is an integral and inevitable part of the story. They must be entertaining—a good story for the sake of a good story—but they must have a theme that conveys some truth about the Christian faith. Our average reader comes from a home in which a high value is placed on church and on Christianity. However, we do not want preachy books in which the characters are super-evangelists. We want to see faith portrayed as part of daily living. We look for plots in which there is spiritual as well as an external conflict, and where the characters resolve those conflicts throught faith in God. In nonfiction we want stories of outstanding Christians, written for young people. We are paraticularly interested in books for the middle-age reader ages 10 to 14." Submit outline/synopsis and sample chapters. Recently published *The Crooked Gate*, by Marilyn Cram Donahue (adventure); *Canal Boy*, by Karin Clafdford Farley (historical adventure); and *River of Fire*, by Bettie Wilson Story (adventure).

CHARTER BOOKS, 360 Park Ave. S., New York NY 10010 (212)481-5000. Editorial Director: Michael Seidman. Associate Editor: Pat Crain. Publishes paperback originals (50%) and reprints (50%). Published 72 titles in 1978; plans 85 in 1979, 96 in 1980. Pays royalty; adverage advance $3,000 on most titles; some series are purchased outright. Simultaneous and photocopied submissions OK. Reports in 4 weeks. SASE. Catalog for SASE.

Fiction: "Our fiction is generally male-oriented—mysteries, suspense, adventure, espionage, etc. We are in the market for series with a continuing character, and for epic/saga type stories. While we have no objection to scenes of a sexual nature, we are more in the 'R' range than the 'X' so no *Hustler*-type submissions. Query or submit outline/synopsis and sample chapters or submit complete ms. Submit "chapters that show best development of the character and with examples of both dialogue and narrative styles." Recently published *Deceit and Deadly Lies*, by Frank Bandy (suspense); *Casca: The Eternal Mercenary*, by Barry Sadler (adventure series); and *By Blood Alone*, by Bernhardt Hurwood (occult/suspense). "We also publish Victor Canning, some Donald E. Westlake and Nick Carter series. We do not want gothics, romances, short stories or novellas."

CHARTER HOUSE PUBLISHERS, INC., 2121 Belcourt Ave., Nashville TN 37212. (615)297-4615. Editorial Director: Denise Jones. Senior Editor: Carolyn Aylor. Publishes hardcover and paperback reprints (50%). Published 28 titles in 1978; plans 14 in 1979, 20 in 1980. Pays 10-15% royalty; advance averages $500-1,500. Simultaneous and photocopied submissions OK. Reports in 3 months. SASE.

Nonfiction: "Style and treatment would vary with topics, but basically we use a popular, easy-reading, direct style—always keeping the reader in mind." Publishes how-to; cookbooks; self-help and travel. No religious material. Query or submit outline/synopsis and sample chapters. Recently published *Culinary Classics*, by Gloria Olson; *The Golden Age of B Movies*, by Doug McClelland; and *Transition to Nowhere*, by William T. Liu.

Fiction: Adventure. science fiction, mysteries and juvenile material. Query. Recently published *The Venture*, by Jack Cummings; *Mirrors of the Apocalypse*, by Donald L. Moore; *Encounters With Aliens*, by George Earley; and *The Wise Owl of the Ballet*, by Albert Gallegos.

THE CHATHAM PRESS, a subsidiary of Devin-Adair, 143 Sound Beach Ave., Old Greenwich CT 06310. Editor: Devin A. Garrity. Publishes hardcover and paperback originals, reprints, and anthologies. "Standard book contract does not always apply if the book is heavily illustrated. Average advance is low." Published 7 titles in 1978; 10 in 1979. Will send a catalog to a writer on request. Send query with outline and sample chapter. Reports in 2 weeks. SASE.
General Nonfiction, The arts, and history and biography. Publishes mostly "regional history and natural history, involving almost all regions of the US. all illustrated, with emphasis on conservation and outdoor recreation, photographic works, and the arts." Recently published *Skiing Colorado*, *The Soft-Hackled Fly*, *Green Fun*, *Seasons of the Salt Marsh* and *An Age of Flowers*.

CHILDRENS PRESS, 1224 W. Van Buren St., Chicago IL 60607. (312)666-4200. Editor-in-Chief: Joan Downing. Offers outright purchase or small advance against royalty. Published 80 titles in 1978. Reports in 3-6 weeks. SASE.
Juveniles: Publishes fiction and nonfiction for supplementary use in elementary and secondary schools; easy picture books for early childhood and beginning readers; high-interest, easy reading material. Specific categories include careers, social studies, fine art, plays, and special education. Length: 50-10,000 words. For picture books, needs are very broad. They should be geared from pre-school to grade 3. Length: 50-1,000 words. Send outline with sample chapters; complete ms for picture books. Do not send finished artwork with ms. Recently published *Scariest Night in Troll Forest*, by Torgersen; *Mystery Music in the Night*, by Witter; *Collecting Toy Trains*, by McComas and Tuohy; and *Hockey is Our Game*, by Gemme.

THE CHILD'S WORLD, INC., Box 681, Elgin IL 60120. Editor: Sylvia Tester. Editorial Director: Jane Buerger. Estab. 1968. Publishes hardcover originals and paperback reprints. Published 30 titles in 1978, 35 in 1979; plans 35 in 1980. Pays $300-350 maximum for outright purchase; no advance. Simultaneous submissions OK. SASE. Reports in 1-3 months. Book catalog for SASE.
Nonfiction: Animals, art, biography, health, juveniles, nature, science and sports. "We publish books for children in nursery school, kindergarten, and grades 1-3, sometimes grades 4 and 5. Subjects are school-curriculum related. All our books are 32 pages, ranging from a word or sentence per page to several paragraphs per page. Since our books are *not* textbooks, we look for particularly appealing ways to present knowledge to young children. We are also looking for series ideas or for books that fit into series we already have." Submit complete ms. Recently published *Why Does the Tiger Have Stripes?*, by Jane Davis (simple introduction to concept of protective coloration in animals); *My "S" Sound Box*, by Jane Belk Moncure (book stressing the use of the beginning consonant "s"); and *Birds, Baboons, and Barefoot Bears*, by Jane Belk Moncure (creative dramatics book in which children imitate actions of animals).
Fiction: Historical, mystery and science fiction. "We might be interested in some simple fiction stories for young children, involving home or school situations. We have published some very simple mysteries aimed at young children and might want to do more. Mostly, though, our books are factual. We do not want any manuscripts for adults or teenagers." Submit complete ms. Recently published *Thomas James the Sound and Friends*, by Dorothy Fay Richards (books about entering first grade); *That Big Bruno*, by Sylvia Root Tester (book about a boy who is afraid of a big dog); and *Something for Sara—A Book About Money*, by Sandra Ziegler (a fictional frame work is used to teach beginning concepts about the value of coins in relation to each other).

CHILTON BOOK CO., Chilton Way, Radnor PA 19089. Editorial Director: Alan F. Turner. Estab. 1955. Publishes hardcover originals. Published 65 titles in 1978; plans 65 in 1979, 65 in 1980. Pays royalty; average advance. Simultaneous and photocopied submissions OK. SASE. Reports in 3 weeks.
Nonfiction: Business/economics, health, hobbies, how-to, recreation, self-help, and technical. "We only want to see any manuscripts with informational value." Query or submit outline/synopsis and sample chapters. Recently published *Do I Really Need a Lawyer?*; *Divorced Dads*; *Mail Order*; *Starting Up—Making It Pay*; *The Retirement Daybook*; and *Stained Glass Magic*.

CHOSEN BOOKS, Lincoln VA 22078. (703)338-4131. Executive Director: Leonard E.

LeSourd. Managing Editor: Richard Schneider. Hardcover and paperback originals. Published 5 titles in 1978; 6 in 1979. Pays 10-12½-15% royalty; advance averages $1,000. Simultaneous submissions OK. SASE. Free book catalog for SASE.

Religion: Seeks out significant developments in the Christian world to present in dramatic book form. Wants quality books that are highly interesting as well as spiritually enriching. Length: 40,000-60,000 words. Prefers complete ms but will consider outline and sample chapters. Recently published *The Seven Last Years*, by Balizet; *Harold E. Hughes, The Man From Ida Grove*, by Hughes; and *The Comeback*, by Robinson.

Tips: "Write a book that grips the reader in the first pages and then holds them through all chapters. Give the reader a 'you are there feeling'."

CHRISTIAN HERALD BOOKS, 40 Overlook Dr., Chappaqua NY 10514. (914)769-9000. Editorial Director: Mr. Leslie H. Sjobbe. Publishes hardcover originals. Published 12 titles in 1978; 14 in 1979 and 20 in 1980. Emphasizes Christian themes. Pays 10% royalty; advance negotiable. State availability of photos and/or illustrations to accompany ms. Simultaneous and photocopied submissions OK. Reports in 2-3 months. SASE. Book catalog for SASE.

Nonfiction: Publishes Christian evangelical books. Query or submit outline/synopsis and sample chapters. Recently published *Free To Be Single*; *Born Again But Still Wet Behind the Ears*; and *Walk With the King Today*.

CHRONICLE BOOKS, 870 Market St., San Francisco CA 94102. Editor-in-Chief: R.C. Schuettge. Senior Editor: Jane Vandenburgh. Estab. 1971. Publishes hardcover and paperback originals. Published 14 titles in 1978, 16 in 1979. Pays 6-15% royalty; $1,500 advance. Simultaneous and photocopied submissions OK. SASE. Reports in 3 weeks. Free book catalog.

Nonfiction: Art, biography, how-to, nature, photography, recreation, sports and travel. "We are particularly interested in manuscripts that deal with biography, travel, leisure activities, and sports; and in photographs/manuscripts dealing with architecture, popular fine art, and contemporary lifestyles. We do not want any science fiction, drama or poetry." Query or submit outline/synopsis and sample chapters. Recently published *To Save a Whale*, by Robert Hunter and Rex Weyler (current events/ecology); *Woven Works*, by John and Susan Hamamura (art: the visual history of weaving); and *MsAdventures*, by Gail Rubin Berney (travel guide for single women).

CITADEL PRESS, 120 Enterprise Ave., Secaucus NJ 07094. (212)736-0007. Editorial Director: Allan J. Wilson. Publishes hardcover originals and paperback reprints. Published 48 titles in 1978; 42 in 1979. Pays 10% royalty on hardcover, 5-7% on paperback; advance averages $1,000. Simultaneous and photocopied submissions OK. Reports in 2 months. SASE.

Nonfiction: Biography, film, psychology, humor and history. Query. Recently published *Moe Howard and the Three Stooges*, by M. Howard (filmography); *The Great American Amusement Parks*, by G. Kyriazi (Americana); and *Documentary History of the Negro People in the U.S.*, by H. Aptheker (history).

CLARION BOOKS, Juvenile Division, Seabury Press, 815 2nd Ave. New York NY 10017. (212)557-0500. Editor-in-Chief: James C. Giblin. Estab. 1965. Publishes hardcover originals. Published 20 juvenile titles in 1978; plans 20 in 1979; 20-25 in 1980. Pays 10-12½% royalty; $750-1,500 advance, depending on whether project is a picture book or a longer work for older children. Photocopied submissions OK. SASE. Reports in 6-8 weeks. Free book catalog.

Nonfiction: Americana, biography, history, humor and nature. Query. Recently published *Superpuppy*, by D. Manus and Jill Pinkwater (puppy care) and *Suicide and Young People*, by Arnold Madison.

Fiction: Adventure, fantasy, humor, mystery, science fiction and suspense. "We would like to see more humorous contemporary stories that young people of 8-12 or 10-14 can identify with readily." Query on ms of more than 30 pages. Recently published *And You Give Me a Pain, Elaine*, by Stella Pevsner (teenage story); *Foster Child*, by Marrion Dane Bauer (contemporary drama); and *Alone in Wolf Hollow*, by Dana Brookins (mystery).

CLARKE, IRWIN & CO., LTD., 791 St. Clair Ave., W., Toronto, Ontario, Canada M6C 1B8. Publishes hardcover and paperback originals (90%) and reprints (10%). Specializes in Canadian subjects. Royalty schedule varies; minimum of 10%. Publishes about 20 titles a year. Submit outline/synopsis and sample chapters or complete ms. Must be typed double-spaced. "Don't send only copy." Send samples of prints for illustration. Photocopied submissions OK. Reports in 1-2 months. SASE.

Nonfiction: Publishes juveniles and books on Canadiana, art, biography, history, how-to, music, nature, poetry, politics, recreation, self-help, sports, textbooks, travel. Recently

published *Old Women At Play*, by A. Wiseman (autobiography); *Ski Free*, by Greg Athans (how-to on free style skiing); and *Ask Me Why*, by J. Hoyle and G. Robertson (juvenile).
Fiction: Publishes juveniles, adventure, historical, humorous, and mainstream books. Recently published *The Wars*, by T. Findley; *Parade on an Empty Street*, by M. Gane; and *Hold Fast*, by L. Major.

COBBLESMITH, Box 191, RFD 1, Freeport ME 04032. Editor-in-Chief: Gene H. Boyington. Publishes hardcover and paperback originals (90%); hardcover and paperback reprints (10%). Pays 8½% royalty; no advance. Simultaneous and photocopied submissions OK. SASE. Query. *"Unsolicited mss are often treated as though only a little better than unsolicited third class mail."* Reports in 2-4 months. Free book catalog.
Nonfiction: Americana and art topics (especially New England and antiques); law (popular, self-help); cookbooks, cooking and foods; gardening; psychology (applied—not theory); how-to (home and homestead crafts); philosophy (educational and new developments); sociology (applied—not theory); material on alternative life styles; nature, travel (offbeat guide books); and self-help.
Recent Titles: *Wood Cook's Cookbook*, by S.D. Haskell (cooking); *Practical Hooked Rugs*, by S.H. Rex (how-to, crafts); and *Do Your Own Divorce in North Carolina*, by M.H. McGee (self-help/law).

COLES PUBLISHING CO., LTD., 90 Ronson Dr., Rexdale, Ontario, Canada M9W 1C1. (416)249-9121. Vice President/Editorial Director: Jeffrey Cole. Publishes hardcover and paperback originals (10%) and reprints (90%). Published 300 titles in 1978; 350 in 1979. "We are a subsidiary company of 'Coles, the Book People,' a chain of 150 bookstores throughout North America." Pays by outright purchase of $500-2,500; advance averages $500. Simultaneous and photocopied submissions OK. Reports in 2-3 weeks. SAE and International Reply Coupons.
Nonfiction: "We publish in the following areas: language, science, math, pet care, gardening, cookbooks, medicine and health, occult, business, reference, technical and do-it-yourself, crafts and hobbies, antiques, games, and sports." No philosophy, religion, history or biography. Submit outline/synopsis and sample chapters. Recently published *Guide to Canadian Business Law*, by T. Rocchi; *The Ed Allen Exercise Book*, by E. Allen; and *Landlord/Tenant Law in Ontario*, by P. Brace.

COLLECTOR BOOKS, Box 3009, Paducah KY 42001. Editor-in-Chief: Steve Quertermous. Publishes hardcover and paperback originals. Pays 5% royalty of retail; no advance. Published 25-30 titles in 1978; plans 25-30 in 1979, 25-30 in 1980. Send prints or transparencies if illustrations are to accompany ms. SASE. Reports in 2-4 weeks. Free book catalog.
Nonfiction: "We only publish books on antiques and collectibles. We require our authors to be very knowledgeable in their respective fields and have access to a large representative sampling of the particular subject concerned." Query. Recently published *Collector's Encyclopedia of Depression Glass*, by G. Florence; and *Madame Alexander Collector Dolls*, by P. Smith.

COLLIER MACMILLAN CANADA, LTD., 1125 B Leslie St., Don Mills, Ontario, Canada. Published both originals and reprints in hardcover and paperback. Advance varies, depending on author's reputation and nature of book. Published 35 titles last year. Reports in 6 weeks. SAE and International Reply Coupons.
General Nonfiction: "Topical subjects of special interest to Canadians." Query.
Textbooks: Mathematics, language arts, and reading: mainly texts conforming to Canadian curricular requirements. Also resource books, either paperback or pamphlet for senior elementary and high schools. Length: open.

COLORADO ASSOCIATED UNIVERSITY PRESS, University of Colorado, 1424 15th St., Boulder CO 80309. (303)492-7191. Editor: Frederick Rinehart. Publishes hardcover and paperback originals. Published 9 titles in 1978; 9 in 1979. Offers standard 10-12½-15% royalty contract; "no advances." Free book catalog. Will consider photocopied submissions "if not sent simultaneously to another publisher." Query. Reports in 3 months. Enclose return postage.
Nonfiction: "Scholarly and regional." Length: 250-500 ms pages. Recently published *Coronal Holds*, by Zinnor (scholarly); and *Along the Ramparts of the Tetons*, by Betts.

*COLUMBIA PUBLISHING CO., INC., Frenchtown NJ 08825. (201)996-2141. Editorial Director: Bernard Rabb. Publishes hardcover originals. Published 6 titles in 1978; 6 in 1979. Pays 10% royalty; average advance. Subsidy publishes 10% of books. "Subsidy publishing is offered if we feel the book to be worthy to have our name on it." Simultaneous and photocopied submissions OK. Reports in 2 months. SASE.

Nonfiction: Biography, theater, film, dance, classical music, political science, business, recreation, and nature/ecology. "We do not want fad books, religious titles, sex guides, photography books, or academic books not applicable to a lay audience." Submit complete ms. Recently published *Back to Nature in Canoes*, by Esslen (canoe guide); *Saving The Great Swamp*, by Cavanaugh (ecology); and *Conductors on Conducting*, by Jacobson (classical music).

Fiction: Quality novels, plays and filmscripts. "We do not want any poetry." Submit complete ms. Recently published *Golcz*, by Herrick.

COLUMBIA UNIVERSITY PRESS, 562 W. 113th St., New York NY 10025. (212)678-6777. Editor-in-Chief: John D. Moore. Publishes hardcover and paperback originals. Royalty contract to be negotiated. Query. SASE.

Nonfiction: "General interest nonfiction of scholarly value."

Scholarly: Books in the fields of literature, philosophy, fine arts, Oriental studies, history, social sciences, science, law. Recently published *The Creation of Tomorrow: Fifty Years of Magazine Science Fiction*, by P. Carter; and *Christopher Isherwood: Myth and Anti-myth*, by P. Piazza.

COMMONERS' PUBLISHING, 432 Rideau St., Ottawa, Ontario, Canada K1N 5Z1. (613)233-4997 Editorial Director: Glenn Cheriton. Senior Editors: Lucille Shaw, Dianne Desaulniers. Publishes hardcover and paperback originals. Published 4 titles in 1978; 6 in 1979 and plans 6 in 1980. Royalties paid yearly based on 10% of sales, list. Photocopied submissions OK. "We do not like simultaneous submissions." Reports in 2-4 months. SAE and International Reply Coupons. Book catalog for SASE.

Nonfiction: Self-help, alternative lifestyles and crafts books. Submit complete ms. Recently published *Ottawa Valley Peoples' Yellow Pages*, by Nichiels, Brecks, et. al. (guidebook); and *Apple II*, by Cheriton (historical).

Fiction: Canadian short stories, plays and fiction; also full-length novels with Canadian themes, locations, and authors; and Canadian poetry. Submit complete ms. Recently published *Stations*, by P. White (poetry); *Hard Road*, by G. Forbes (humor); and *The Buffalo Trails*, by E.L. Frame (novel).

COMPUTER SCIENCE PRESS, INC., 9125 Fall River Lane, Potomac MD 20854. (301)299-2040. Editorial Director: Arthur D. Friedman. Publishes hardcover originals. Published 6 titles in 1978, 6 in 1979. Pays in royalties; no advance. Simultaneous and photocopied submissions OK. Reports in 3 weeks. SASE. Free book catalog.

Nonfiction: "Technical books in all aspects of computer science and computer engineering. Both text and reference books. Will also consider public appeal 'trade' books in computer science." Query or submit complete ms. "We prefer 3 copies of manuscripts." Recently published *Fundamentals of Computer Algorithms*, by Horowitz/Sahni (college text); and *Computer Aided Design of Digital Systems, Volume III*, by W. van Cleemput (reference bibliography).

CONCORDIA PUBLISHING HOUSE, 3558 S. Jefferson Ave., St. Louis MO 63118. Pays royalty on retail price; outright purchase in some cases. Free book catalog. Submit outline and sample chapter for nonfiction; complete ms for fiction. Reports in 3 months. Enclose return postage.

Religion, Juveniles, and Fiction: Publishes Protestant, general religious, theological books and periodicals; music works, juvenile picture and beginner books and adult fiction. "As a religious publisher, we look for mss that deal with Bible stories, Bible history, Christian missions; and mss that deal with ways that readers can apply Christian beliefs and principles to daily living. Any ms that deals specifically with theology and/or doctrine should conform to the tenets of the Lutheran Church-Missouri Synod. We suggest that, if authors have any doubt about their submissions in light of what kind of mss we want, they first correspond with us." Recently published *Theology of Concord*, by Preus; and *The Wanderers*, by Rimland.

CONTINUUM BOOKS, Adult (General) Division, Seabury Press, 815 2nd Ave., New York NY 10017. (212)557-0500. Editor: Justus G. Lawler. Estab. 1951. Publishes hardcover originals and paperback reprints. Published 15 titles in 1978, 15 in 1979; plans 15 in 1980. Pays 10-15% royalty; $1,500 advance. Photocopied submissions OK. SASE. Reports in 6-8 weeks. Free book catalog.

Nonfiction: Americana, biography, humor, psychology and sociology. "We also are looking for self-help books." Query. Recently published *Growing Up Handicapped*, by Evelyn Ayrault (self-help).

DAVID C. COOK PUBLISHING CO., 850 N. Grove, Elgin IL 60120. (312)741-2400. Book Division Manager: Robert Murphy. Managing Editor: Janet Thoma. Publishes hardcover and paperback originals (99%) and paperback reprints (1%). Published 30 titles in 1978; 30 in 1979, plans 40 in 1980. Pays 6-15% royalty; $1,000 advance. Simultaneous and photocopied submissions OK. SASE. Reports in 1-2 months.
Nonfiction: Religious. Submit outline/synopsis and sample chapters. Recently published *The Man Who Keeps Going to Jail*, by John Erwin (autobiography); *How to Grow a Young Reader*, by John and Kay Lindskoog (parent education); and *For the Love of My Daughter*, by Mary Ellen Ton (narrative).
Fiction: Religious. Submit outline/synopsis and sample chapters. Recently published *The Kiowa*, by Elgin Groseclose (historical) and *Ararat*, by Elgin Groseclose (epic).

CORDOVAN CORP., 5314 Bingle Rd., Houston TX 77018. (713)688-8811. Editor-in-Chief: Bob Gray. Published hardcover and paperback originals and reprints under the Cordovan Press, Horseman Books and Fisherman Books imprints. Offers standard minimum book contract of 10-12½-15%. Published 8 titles in 1978, 5 in 1979; and plans 6 in 1980. Marketed heavily by direct mail and through various consumer and trade periodicals. Will consider photocopied submissions. Query or submit outline and sample chapters. Reports in 1 month. Enclose return postage.
Nonfiction: Cordovan Press, a trade book division, seeks books on Texas history for the history buff interested in Texana. Horseman Books are practical, how-to books on horse training, grooming, feeding, showing, riding, etc., either by experts in the field or as told to a writer by an expert. "Fisherman Books are how-to, where-to, when-to books on fishing in Texas and/or the Southwest. Author must be noted expert on fishing, or be retelling what a noted expert told him. The emphasis is on plain language in all of these lines. Short sentences. Make the verbs sing the song. Pungent quotes. Don't try to snow the readers; they are too sharp and already know most of the score in all areas. Use humor when it isn't forced." Length: 150 ms pages. Recently published *Rick Clunn's Championship Bass Fishing Techniques*, by R. Clunn; *Eyes of Texas Travel Guide*, by R. Miller; and *The Cowgirls*, by J.G. Roach (Americana).

CORNELL MARITIME PRESS, INC., Box 456, Centreville MD 21617. Publisher: George Rinehart. Publishes hardcover and quality paperbacks, both originals and reprints. Published 8 titles in 1978, 10 in 1979; plans 15 in 1980. Payment is negotiable under special circumstances, but usually standard royalty; 10% for first 5,000 copies, 12½% for second 5,000 copies, 15% on all additional. Revised editions revert to original royalty schedule. Subsidy publishing is done only in conjunction with universities. Published 10 titles last year. Free book catalog. Send queries first, accompanied by writing samples and outlines of book ideas. Reports in 2-4 weeks. Enclose return postage.
Marine: Nonfiction relating to marine subjects, highly technical; manuals; how-to books on any maritime subject. Tidewater Publishers imprint publishes books on leather-craft, model building, regional history, folklore and wildlife of the Chesapeake Bay and the Delmarva Peninsula. Recently published *Tanker Operations: A Handbook for the Ship's Officer*; and *The Deep Sea Diver: Yesterday, Today and Tomorrow*.

R.D. CORTINA CO., INC., 136 W. 52nd St., New York NY 10019. General Editor: MacDonald Brown. Pays on a fee or a royalty basis. Published 27 titles last year. "Do not send unsolicited mss; send outline and sample chapter." Reports in 2 months or less.
Textbooks: Publishes language teaching textbooks for self-study and school; also publishes language teaching phonograph records and tapes. Materials of special ESL interest. Word length varies.

COURIER OF MAINE BOOKS, 1 Park Dr., Rockland ME 04841. (207)549-4401. Director: William E. Dennen. Publishes hardcover and paperback originals (80%) and paperback reprints (20%). Specializes in books about Maine only. Pays 10% royalty; "low" advance. Marketing is limited to people and institutions interested in Maine. Submit outline/synopsis and sample chapters. State availability of illustrations and photos. Simultaneous ("if we know about it") and photocopied submissions OK. Reports in 2-4 weeks. SASE. Free book catalog.
Nonfiction: Publishes art, biography, cookbooks, cooking and foods, economics, history, hobbies, how-to, humor, juveniles, nature, poetry, politics, recreation, reference, sociology and travel books. All mss must pertain to Maine. Recently published *All-Maine All-Poultry*, edited

by Shibles and Rogers (cookbook); *Tombstones and Paving Blocks*, by Grindle (history); and *Nature I Loved*, by Geagan.
Fiction: Adventure, historical, humorous, mainstream and mystery books.

COWARD, McCANN & GEOGHEGAN, INC., 200 Madison Ave., New York NY 10016. (212)765-8900. President/Publisher: John J. Geoghegan. Vice President/Editor-in-Chief: Patricia B. Soliman. Estab. 1928. Publishes hardcover originals. "We publish about 60 adult titles a year." Pays 10-15% royalty; offers $5,000 average advance on first book. Simultaneous and photocopied submissions OK. SASE. Reports in 4 weeks. Free book catalog.
Nonfiction: Animals, biography, health, history, how-to, juveniles, nature, politics, psychology, recreation, science, self-help, sociology and sports. "We are looking for nonfiction books on topics of current and/or lasting popular interest, for general, not specialized audiences. Our scope is broad; our needs are for quality manuscripts marketable in the hardcover arena. We do not want manuscripts in specialized or technical fields that require extensive design and art work that lead to high cover prices." Query. Recently published *The Rise of Theodore Roosevelt*, by Edmund Morris (biography); *Strangers Among Us: Enlightened Beings From a World to Come*, by Ruth Montgomery; *The Flying White House*, by J. Horst and Col. Ralph Albertazzi (popular history of Air Force One and the Presidency); and *The Fall of Shanghai*, by Noel Barber.
Fiction: Adventure, historical, humor, mainstream, mystery, occult, romance and suspense. "We also want historicals, family sagas, espionage thrillers, and novels for and about contemporary women. We also want gothics and mysteries, although the market for these is not as strong as it once was. We do not want science fiction, fantasy or experimental novels." Submit complete ms. Recently published *Ghost Story*, by Peter Straub (occult novel in the tradition of Hawthorne and James); *Shadow of the Wolf*, by James Barwick (WWII espionage); *The Cutting Edge*, by Penelope Gilliatt (novel about a love triangle); and *The Mating Dance*, by Rona Randall (historical romance).

COWARD, McCANN & GEOGHEGAN, Books for Boys and Girls, 200 Madison Ave., New York NY 10016. (212)576-8900. Editor-in-Chief, Books for Boys and Girls: Refna Wilkin. Pays royalties on juvenile. Advances are competitive. Query. Enclose return postage.
Juveniles: "Our publishing program is small and selective but we will consider fiction and nonfiction for ages 4 and up."

CRAFTSMAN BOOK CO. OF AMERICA, 542 Stevens Ave., Solana Beach CA 92075. (714)755-0161. Editor-in-Chief: Gary Moselle. Publishes paperback originals. Royalty of 12½-15% of gross revenues, regardless of quantity sold. Published 8 titles in 1978; plans 8 in 1979; 8 in 1980. "About 75% of our sales are directly to the consumer and since royalties are based on gross revenues, the author's share is maximized." Will send free catalog to writer on request. Will consider photocopied submissions. Submit outline and sample chapters. Reports in 2 weeks. Enclose return postage.
Technical: "We publish technical books and are aggressively looking for manuscripts related to construction, building trades, civil engineering, construction cost estimating and construction management. Our books are written as practical reference for professionals in the construction field and each should be written to answer practical questions and solve typical problems. Emphasis is on charts, graphs, illustrations, displays and tables of information. We don't want to see reprints of magazine articles and isolated essays which do not have the breadth or scope to warrant." Recently published *Plumbers Handbook*, by Howard Massey; and *Excavation and Grading Handbook*, by Nick Capachi.

CRAIN BOOKS, 740 Rush St., Chicago IL 60611. Editor-in-Chief: Melvin J. Brisk. Publishes hardcover and paperback originals. Published 6 titles in 1978; 9 in 1979. Pays 10% royalty, "although this varies, depending on the book, its potential and the market"; makes an advance only under exceptional circumstances. Send contact sheet if photos/illustrations are to accompany ms. Simultaneous and photocopied submissions OK, "but will rarely receive priority status as compared to the exclusive submission." Reports in 2-4 months. SASE. Free book catalog.
Nonfiction: Publishes business books for the advertising and marketing professional and student, including the academic market. "We're interested in mss that have a definite communications theme, and we usually work on assignment unless the author is a professional or academician. No rehashes. We want innovative ideas that will appeal to business types looking for improvement." Recently published *100 Best Sales Promotions of 1977/78*, by W. Robinson (promotion); and *Successful Direct Marketing Methods*, by Bob Stone (direct marketing).

CRANE, RUSSAK & CO., INC., 3 E. 44th St., New York NY 10017. Editor-in-Chief: Ben Russak. Publishes scientific journals and scientific and scholarly books. Published 26 titles (15 journals) in 1978, 22 (17 journals) in 1979; plans 20 (journals) in 1980.
Technical and Reference: "We publish scientific and scholarly works at the graduate and reference level: postgraduate textbooks and reference books for scholars and research workers. Our publications also appeal to members of professional societies. "Please do not submit material. Our publishing program is full for the next two years."

CREATIVE BOOK CO., Box 214998, Sacramento CA 95821. (916)489-4390. Editor-in-Chief: Sol H. Marshall. Estab. 1966. Publishes paperback originals (90%) and reprints (10%). Published 15 titles in 1978, 20 in 1979; plans 20 in 1980. Pays $50-200 in outright purchase. Simultaneous and photocopied submissions OK. SASE. Reports in 2 weeks. Book catalog for SASE.
Nonfiction: Cookbooks/cooking. "We would like to see manuscripts on professional self-improvement/development for people in education and community services. Public relations and promotion in education and community service. We do not want to see how-to in crafts, how to teach specific subjects, and how to lead specific activities in recreation." Query or submit outline/synopsis and sample chapters or submit complete ms. Recently published *How to Conduct a Gold Rush Carnival*, by John J. Lesjack (fund-raising); *Publicize It With Pictures*, by Ken Waters (publicity photography); *How To Be Your Own Publisher and Get Your Book Into Print*, by Paul Thompson (publishing); *How To Publicize Your Self-Publishing Book*, by Herman Blackey (publishing/publicity); and *Public Relations Basics for Community Organizations*, by Sol H. Marshall.

CRESCENDO PUBLISHING, 200 Park Ave. S., New York NY 10003. Publishes hardcover and paperback originals and reprints. Offers standard 10-12½-15% royalty contract. "Advances are rare; sometimes made when we seek out an author." Published 20 titles last year. Free book catalog. Will look at queries or completed mss. SASE. Address submissions to Gerald Krimm. Reports in 4 weeks.
Music: Trade and textbooks in music. Length: open.

CRESCENT PUBLICATIONS, INC., 5410 Wilshire Blvd., #400, Los Angeles CA 90036. Editor-in-Chief: Joseph Lawrence. Publishes hardcover and paperback originals. Offers royalty contract "on the basis of the ms published." Does 75% subsidy publishing. Free book catalog. Will consider simultaneous submissions. Submit complete ms for fiction and nonfiction. Mss must be typed, double-spaced, on one side of paper only. Reports in 2 weeks. Enclose return postage.
Fiction, Nonfiction, Juveniles and Poetry: Publishes general trade books which are sold to book publishers and book distributors. Length: open. Also interested in Americana, politics, self-help and how-to, sports, hobbies, recreation and pets. "All subjects." Recently published *Where To, America?*, by James T. Triplett (Americana); *The Claudia Sanders Dinner House of Shelbyville, Kentucky, Cookbook*, by Cherry Settle, Tommy Settle and Edward G. Klemm Jr.; and *By Bread Alone—The Story of A-4685*, by Mel Mermelstein (first person story by a man who was incarcerated in a concentration camp).

CRESTWOOD HOUSE, INC., Box 3427, Mankato MN 56001. (507)388-1616. Editorial Director: Karyne Jacobsen. Publishes hardcover originals. Published 14 titles in 1978; 29 in 1979. "All fees are negotiated based upon subject matter, length of publication, and additional work furnished." Occasionally offers advance. Simultaneous and photocopied submissions OK. Reports will be furnished. SASE.
Nonfiction: "Crestwood House publishes high-interest, low-vocabulary books for children with a reading level of grades 2-5. Our books are always published in series which have related subject matter (probably 5-10 titles per series). We do current topics on sports, recreation, and other topics of high interest to children and young adults. Books are generally between 32-48 pages, and always include a generous number of photographs." Submit complete ms.
Fiction: Same basic requirements as nonfiction. Science fiction; adventure; and sports. No material on "bears, ducks, frogs, etc."

CROSSROAD BOOKS, Adult (religious) Division, Seabury Press, 815 2nd Ave., New York NY 10017. (212)557-0500. Editor: William H. Gentz. Estab. 1952. Publishes hardcover originals. Published 100 titles in 1978, 80 in 1979; plans 80-90 in 1980. Pays 10-15% royalty; $1,500 advance. Photocopied submissions OK. SASE. Reports in 6-8 weeks. Free book catalog.

THOMAS Y. CROWELL, Adult Trade Dept., 521 5th Ave., New York NY 10017. Publisher: Edward Burlingame. Senior Editors: Hugh Rawson, Patrick Barrett and Arnold Dolin. Estab. 1834. Publishes hardcover originals (90%) and paperback reprints (10%). Published 55 titles in 1978, 55 in 1979 and plans 55 in 1980. Pays 7½-15% royalty; average advance. Agented and solicited submissions only. Book catalog for SASE.
Nonfiction: Americana, animals, art, biography, business/economics, health, history, hobbies, how-to, juveniles, music, nature, photography, politics, psychology, recreation, reference, science, self-help, sociology, sports, textbooks, and travel. "We no longer accept manuscripts for publication under the following imprints: Minerva, Apollo, Abelard-Schuman, John Day, Chandler and Intext." Recently published *Photography in America*, by William Welling; *Pulling Your Own Strings*, by Wayne Dyer (self-help); *Fragments of Isabella*, by Isabella Leitner (memoir); and *Feminist Quotations*, by Carol McPhee and Ann Fitzgerald.
Fiction: Adventure, historical, mainstream, mystery, and suspense. "We publish very few novels and have a very small fiction back list." Submit outline/synopsis and sample chapters. Recently published *Haakon*, by C.I. Griffin (homosexual novel); *Silence in Eden*, by Jerry Allan Potter (sex, religion, violence); and *The Murder of Lawrence of Arabia*, by Matthew Eden (historical thriller).

THOMAS Y. CROWELL, 10 E. 53rd St., New York NY 10022. Send trade submissions to Acquisitions Editor; reference book submissions to Patrick Barrett; Children's book submissions to Patrick Allen. Offers standard soyalty contract. Published 230 titles last year. Query. Reports in 1-2 months. SASE.
Nonfiction, Juveniles, and Textbooks: "Trade and reference books, children's books, and college and secondary school reference books. Interested in general books of an informational nature."

THOMAS Y. CROWELL JUNIOR BOOKS, 10 E. 53rd St., New York NY 10021. (212)593-7011. Editorial Director: Patricia Allen. Submit manuscripts to Patricia Allen. Publishes hardcover originals. Published 50 titles in 1978; 45 in 1979; plans 45 in 1980. Pays standard royalties. Photocopied submissions OK. SASE. Reports in 6-8 weeks. Free book catalog for self-addressed label.
Nonfiction: Science and history. Submit outline/synopsis and sample chapters or submit complete ms. Recently published *Disease Detectives*, by Berger; *Woman Against Slavery*, by Scott (biography); and *Native American Testimony*, by Nabokoy.
Fiction: "All kinds for all ages. Submit outline/synopsis and sample chapters or submit complete ms. Recently published *Bridge to Terabithia* and *Great Gilly Hopkins*, by Paterson (fiction); *Wheels*, by Barton (picture book); and *Conouista!*, by Bulla.

CROWN PUBLISHERS, INC., 1 Park Ave., New York NY 10016. (212)532-9200. Imprints include Clarkson N. Potter, Barre, Harmony and Julian Press. Editor-in-Chief: Herbert Michelman. Estab. 1936. Publishes hardcover and paperback originals. Published 250 titles in 1978, 250 in 1979; plans 250 in 1980. Pays royalty; average advance. Simultaneous and photocopied submissions OK. SASE. Reports in 6 weeks. Free book catalog.
Nonfiction: Americana, animals, art, biography, cookbooks/cooking, health, history, hobbies, how-to, humor, juveniles, music, nature, philosophy, photography, politics, psychology, recreation, reference, science, self-help, and sports. "We want well-written books on marketable subjects. We do not want texts books, technical or poetry." Query or submit outline/synopsis and sample chapters. Recently published *Cambridge Energy of Astronomy*, by Simon Meritou (science); *The Kitchen Book*, by Terrence Cowran (home directory); and *Inside Cuba Today*, by Fred Ward (contemporary history).
Fiction: Experimental, historical, humor, mainstream, mystery and suspense. Query or submit outline/synopsis and sample chapters. Recently published *Scruples*, by Judith Krantz (commercial fiction); *The Dancing Floor*, by Michael M. MacNamara (contemporary Irish novel); and *The Fabricator*, by Hollis Hodges (humor).

CROWN PUBLISHERS, INC., Children's Book Department, 1 Park Ave., New York NY 10016. (212)532-9200. Imprints include Clarkson Potter Inc., and Harmony Books. Director Children's Book Department: Norma Jean Sawicki. Publishes hardcover originals. Published 20 titles in 1978, 22 in 1979; plans 22-30 in 1980. Pays 10% royalty on books for older children. Royalty for books for younger readers is divided between the writer and illustrator; advance depends on the submission. SASE. Reports in 6-8 weeks. Book catalog for SASE.
Nonfiction: Animals, biography, humor, history, nature and science. Query. Recently published *Books: From Writer to Reader*, by Howard Greenfeld; *Small Worlds Close Up*, by

Lisa Grillone and Joseph Gennaro (science); and *Weird and Wacky Inventions*, by Jim Murphy.
Fiction: Adventure, experimental, fantasy, historical, humor and mystery. "We would like to publish more fiction especially humorous contemporary fiction for ages 8-10 and 12 up." Submit outline/synopsis and sample chapters or submit complete ms. SASE must be included with all submissions. Recently published *Exit From Home*, by Anita Heyman; *In Face of Danger*, by Mara Kay; and *Tell Me No Lies*, by Hila Colman.

THE CUMBERLAND PRESS, INC., Box 296, Freeport ME 04032. (207)865-6045. Editor: Mary Louise Morris. Pays 10% royalty; no advance. SASE.
Nonfiction: "We are interested in nonfiction only—books that have a regional interest or specialized subject matter (if the writer is an authority), or how-to-do-it books." Query.

*CYRCO PRESS, INC., PUBLISHERS, 342 Madison Ave., New York NY 10017. (212)682-8410. Editorial Director: Benjamin Rosenzweig. Senior Editor: George Schwab. Publishes hardcover originals. Published 15 titles in 1978; 15 in 1979. "Our books are distributed to the trade by the Bobbs-Merrill Co., and distributed in the UK and Europe by Eurospan Ltd." Subsidy publishes 1-2% of books. "We do not accept subsidies from authors. Any subsidy we have accepted has been from either a university or a nonprofit organization in the form of a co-publishing venture." Pays 10% royalty; no advance. Simultaneous and photocopied submissions OK. Reports in 3-4 weeks. SASE. Free book catalog.
Nonfiction: Politics, history, journals and biography. Query. Submit introduction, table of contents, and 1-2 sample chapters. Follow Chicago *Manual of Style*. Recently published *The Politics of Defeat: America's Decline in the Middle East*, by J. Churba (political analysis); *Detente in Historical Perspective*, by G. Schwab (politics); and *The European Left*, by B. Brown (politics).

DARTNELL CORP., 4660 N. Ravenswood Ave., Chicago IL 60640. (312)561-4000. Editorial Director: John Steinbrink. Publishes manuals, reports, hardcovers. Royalties: sliding scale. Published 6 titles last year. Send outline and sample chapter. Reports in 4 weeks. SASE.
Business: Interested in new material on business skills and techniques in management, supervision, administration, advertising sales, etc. Recently published *Executive Compensation*, by J. Steinbrink (general business); *How to Participate Profitably in Trade Shows*, by R. Konikow (sales); and *How to Conduct Better Meetings*, by Kirkpatrick (business).

DAVID & CHARLES (PUBLISHERS), LTD., Brunel House, Forde Rd., Newton Abbot, Devon, England. Publishes hardcover and paperback originals. Published 140 titles in 1978; 140 in 1979. Pays 10% royalty; advance "varies." Simultaneous and photocopied submissions OK. Reports in 2-3 weeks. SASE. Free book catalog.
Nonfiction: "General wide-interest 'trade' nonfiction, including lavishly illustrated and produced books: how-to books, country, outdoor, sports, natural history, hobbies, topics, history, business, travel and the arts. Treatment must vary according to the subject, market, etc., so early consultation is urged." Query or submit outline/synopsis and sample chapters. Recently published *Shell Book of Rural Britain*, by K. Mossman (country); *Lover's Companion*, by E.J. Howard (anthology); and *House Plants in Colour*, by R. Herwig (practical).

DAVIS PUBLICATIONS, INC., 50 Portland St., Worcester MA 01608. Published 10 titles last year. Write for copy of guidelines for authors. Submit complete ms. Enclose return postage.
Art and Reference: Publishes art and craft books. "Keep in mind the reader for whom the book is written. For example, if a book is written for the teacher, avoid shifting from addressing the teacher to addressing the student. Include illustrations with text. All illustrations should be collated separately from the text, but keyed to the text. Photos should be good quality original prints. Well-selected illustrations can explain, amplify, and enhance the text. It is desirable for the author's selection of illustrations to include some extras. These may be marked 'optional.' The author should not attempt to lay out specific pages. Poorly selected illustrations or too many competing illustrations in a short space can mar a book. For instance, if you are planning a 125-150 page book and you have over 300 photos (more than 2 photos per page, average), you probably have too many." Recently published *The Art of Sketching*, by Porter (how-to); *Painting with Oils*, by Sheaks (how-to); and *Drawing Handbook*, by Purser (text).

DAW BOOKS, INC., 1301 Avenue of the Americas, New York NY 10019. Editor: Donald A. Wollheim. Estab. 1971. Publishes paperback originals (80%) and reprints (20%). Published 62 titles in 1978, 62 in 1979; plans 62 in 1980. Pays 6% royalty; $2,000 advance and up.

Simultaneous and photocopied submissions OK. SASE. Reports in 6 weeks. Free book catalog.
Fiction: "We are interested in novels only. We are not seeking collections of short stories or ideas for anthologies. We do not want any nonfiction manuscripts." Submit complete ms. Recently published *Yurth Burden*, by Andre Norton (science fiction); *Stormqueen!*, by Marion Zimmer Bradley; and *Interstellar Empire*, by John Brunner.

DELACORTE PRESS, 245 E. 47th St., New York NY 10017. (212)832-7300. Imprints include Seymour Lawrence and Eleanor Friede. Editorial Director: Ross Claiborne. Publishes hardcover originals. Published 50 titles in 1978, 70 in 1979; plans 70 in 1980. Pays 10-12½-15% royalty; average advance. Simultaneous and photocopied submissions OK. SASE. Reports in 4-6 weeks.
Fiction and General Nonfiction: Query or submit outline or brief proposal. Complete ms accepted only through an agent otherwise returned unopened. Recently published *My Mother My Self*, by Nancy Friday (women's psychology); *The Admirel's Daughter*, by Victoria Fydorova; *Class Reunion*, by Rona Jaffe (contemporary fiction); *Evergreen*, by Beva Plain (family saga); and *Going After Cacciato*, by Tim O'Brien (national book award for fiction 1979).

DELL PUBLISHING CO., INC., 1 Dag Hammarskjold Plaza, New York NY 10017. Imprints include Dell, Delacorte Press, Delta Books, Yearling and Laurel. Managing Editor: Charles Adams. Publishes hardcover and paperback originals and reprints. Publishes 416 titles/year. Pays standard royalty; offers advance. Simultaneous and photocopied submissions OK. SASE. Reports in 3 months.
Nonfiction: Philosophy, biography, history, religion, science and the arts. Query; unsolicited mss are returned unopened.
Fiction:"On fiction queries, we would like to know what sort of book the author has written or proposes to write—whether straight novel, romance-suspense, mystery, historical or gothic. A paragraph further describing the story would also be helpful. Manuscripts that arrive without a preceding query answered in the affirmative by a member of our staff will have to be returned unread."

DELTA BOOKS, Division of Dell Publishing Co., 1 Dag Hammarskjold Plaza, New York NY 10017. (212)832-7300. Editorial Director: Christopher J. Kuppicg. Publishes trade paperbacks originals and reprints. Published 40 titles in 1979; plans 40 in 1980. Pays 6-7½% royalty; average advance. Simultaneous and photocopied submissions OK. SASE. Reports in 5-6 weeks. Book catalog for SASE.
Nonfiction: Americana, consciousness cookbooks/cooking, health, how-to, humor, music, new age photography, politics, psychology, recreation, reference, science, self-help, sociology, and sports. "We would like to see books of The New Age, popular music, social history, popular psychology, social criticism and annalysis, and women's studies. We also publish oversized, heavily illustrated books in many subjects which lend themselves to this format. We do not want to see biography, philosophy, academic books, textbooks, juveniles, or poetry books." Query or submit outline/synopsis and sample chapters. Recently published *The Future of China*, by Ross Terrill (report on China today, and its prospects after Mao); *Out of This World: American Space Photography*, by Paul Dickson (collection of NASA space shots, including many of Earth); *Jazz Rock Fusion: The People-The Music*, by Julie Coryell and Laura Friedman (interviews with 58 jazz-rock musicans, including photos of each).
Fiction: Experimental, fantasy and humor. "We are looking for original, innovative and contemporary novels." Submit through an agent. Recently published *Who Is Teddy Villanova?*, by Thomas Berger; *Slapstick*, by Kurt Vonnegut; and *Dreaming of Babylon*, by Richard Brautigan.

*DELTA DESIGN GROUP, 518 Central Ave., Box 112, Greenville MS 38701. (601)335-6148. Editor-in-Chief: Noel Workman. Publishes hardcover and paperback originals. Pays 10-12½-15% royalty; no advance. 25% of books are subsidy published. Send contact sheet to accompany ms. Simultaneous submissions OK, "but tell us what is really going on". Photocopied submissions OK. Reports in 2-4 weeks. SASE.
Nonfiction: Publishes Americana, cookbooks, cooking and foods, history, multimedia material, travel and regional architectural subject (lower Mississippi Valley) books. "Our market is the lower Mississippi Valley (Louisiana, Mississippi, Arkansas, Tennessee, Missouri) and we edit for this audience." No autobiographies. Recently published *Son of a Seacook Cookbook*, by K. Tolliver; *75 Years in Leland*, by N. Workman (history); *A Mississippi Architectural Handbook*, by W. Lack (architecture); and *Please Listen to Me*, by A. Wood (poetry).

T.S. DENISON & CO., INC., 5100 W. 82nd St., Minneapolis MN 55437. Editor-in-Chief: W.E. Rosenfelt. Publishes hardcover and paperback originals. Published 20 titles in 1978; 20 in 1979 and plans 20-80 in 1980. Specializes in educational publishing, textbooks, supplemental textbooks, and teacher aid materials. Royalty varies, usually $80-100 per 1,000 copies sold; 10% on occasion; no advance. Send prints if photos are to accompany ms. Photocopied submissions OK. Reports in 2-4 weeks. SASE. Book catalog for SASE.
Nonfiction: Publishes textbooks and teaching aid books. Query. Recently published *How To Make Bulletin Board Designs*, by Barnes (teaching aid); and *Getting To Know You Through Art*, by Kenny (art activity book).

*DENLINGER'S PUBLISHERS, LTD., Box 76, Fairfax VA 22030. (703)631-1501. Publisher: W.W. Denlinger. Editor: R. Annabel Rathman. Publishes hardcover and paperback originals (90%) and reprints (10%). Published 20 titles in 1978; 30 in 1979. "Will consider highly specialized books with limited market on a partial or fully subsidized basis. We have been successful in returning to the author his investment. Our plan is not the usual plan of subsidy publishing. Only books of worthwhile material which we would add to our list would be considered." 10½% royalty or negotiable outright purchase; no advance. Simultaneous and photocopied submissions OK. Reports in 6 weeks. SASE. Free book catalog.
Nonfiction: Southern historical material. "Will consider other kinds."

THE DEVIN-ADAIR CO., INC., Subsidiary: The Chatham Press, 143 Sound Beach Ave., Old Greenwich CT 06870. (203)637-4531. Editor-in-Chief: Devin A. Garrity. Managing Editor: Florence Norton. Publishes hardcover and paperback originals (90%) and reprints (10%). Royalty on sliding scale, 7-12½%; advance averages $100-3,500. Published 8 titles in 1978; 10 in 1979; plans 12 in 1980. Send prints to illustrate ms. Simultaneous submissions OK. SASE. Free book catalog.
Nonfiction: Publishes Americana, art, biography, business, how-to, politics, cookbooks, history, medicine, nature, economics, sports and travel books. Query or submit outline/synopsis and sample chapters. Recently published *Life's Second Half*, by J. Ellison (popular psychology); and *Rambles M. Ireland*, by M. Begley.

*DHARMA PUBLISHING, 2425 Hillside Ave., Berkeley CA 94704. Editorial Director: Tarthang Tulku. Managing Editor: Merrill 'Peterson. Estab. 1964. Publishes hardcover and paperback originals (90%) and paperback reprints (10%). Published 10 titles in 1978, 10 in 1979; plans 12 in 1980. Pays 5-7% royalty; no advance. Subsidy publishes 5% of books. SASE. Reports in 1-2 months. Free book catalog.
Nonfiction: Art (Tibetan and other Buddhist); biography (Buddhist); history (Asia and Buddhism); philosophy (Buddhist); photography (Buddhist); psychology (Buddhist); religion (Buddhism); and self-help. "We want translations of Buddhist texts from Tibetan or Sanskrit. Please no original discussions of Buddhist topics." Query. Recently published *Life and Liberation of Padmasambhava*, by Yeshe Tsogyal (biography); *Time, Space, and Knowledge*, by Tarthang Tulkv (philosophy/religion); and *Ancient Images of Tibet*, by LiGotami Govinda (photography).

THE DIAL PRESS, 1 Dag Hammarskjold Plaza, New York NY 10017. (212)832-7300. Publishes hardcover and paperback originals. Published 60 titles in 1978; 70 in 1979. Pays 10-12½-15% royalty. Simultaneous and photocopied submissions OK. Reports in 4 weeks. SASE. Free book catalog.
Nonfiction: "All general trade nonfiction is of interest." Submit outline/synopsis and sample chapters.
Fiction: All general adult categories. Submit outline/synopsis and sample chapters.

THE DIETZ PRESS, INC., 109 E. Cary St., Richmond VA 23219. Editor: August Dietz III. SASE.
Nonfiction: Biography, historical and cookbooks (with a Virginia slant). No poetry. Query, stating the subject and briefly outlining the material. Length: 40,000-50,000 words.

DILLON PRESS, INC., 500 S. 3rd St., Minneapolis MN 55415. (612)336-2691. Editorial Director: Uva Dillon. Senior Editor: Linda Kusserow. Publishes hardcover originals. Published 14 titles in 1978; 18 in 1979; plans 20-25 in 1980. Pays royalty or by outright purchase. Contract to be negotiated. Submit complete ms or outline and sample chapters. Reports in 6 weeks. SASE. Book catalog for SASE.
Nonfiction: "We are actively seeking manuscripts for both the juvenile, educational and adult trade markets. American Indians, contemporary biographies, new craft ideas, environmental

action, ethnic heritage and women are some areas of interest for juvenile books. Travel, true-life adventure, outdoor sports, heritage, and popular history are adult trade specialties. We prefer complete ms." Recently published *Tall Grass and Trouble, A Story of Environmental Action*, by Ann Sigford (juvenile, environment); *Fair Winds and Far Places*, by Zane Mann (adult travel adventure); *Contributions of Women: Theater*, by A. Dillon and C. Bix (juvenile, women biography); *Little Turtle, The Story of an American Indian*, by M. Cunningham (juvenile, Indian biography); *Of Scottish Ways*, by E. Begley (adult heritage); and *Catching Fish*, by C. Meyers and A. Lindner (adult, outdoor sports).

DILITHIUM PRESS, 30 NW 23rd Place, Portland OR 97210. (503)243-1158. Editorial Director: Merl Miller. Estab. 1977. Publishes paperback originals. Published 12 titles in 1978, 15 in 1979; plans 20 in 1980. Pays 5-25% royalty; average advance. Photocopied submissions OK. SASE. Reports in 2 months. Free book catalog.
Nonfiction: Textbooks and books about small computers. "We are looking for manuscripts in the field of microcomputers. Topics should be geared to general information, hardcover and software." Query.

DIMENSION BOOKS, INC., Box 811, Denville NJ 07834. (201)627-4334. Contact: Thomas P. Coffey. Regular royalty schedule; advance is negotiable. Book catalog for SASE. Query. Reports in 1 week on requested mss. SASE.
General Nonfiction: Publishes general nonfiction including religion, principally Roman Catholic. Also psychology and music. Length: 40,000 words minimum. Recently published *Looking for Jesus*, by A. van Kaam; *Called By Name*, by P. van Breemen; and *Jesus, Set Me Free!*, by G. Maloney.

DOANE AGRICULTURAL SERVICE, INC, 8900 Manchester Road, St. Louis MO 63144. (314)968-1000. Editor: Tom Corey. Publishes hardcover and paperback originals. Pays 8% of the gross sales. "Policy on advances has been quite liberal to authoritative authors." Submit outline/synopsis and sample chapter. Reports in 1-2 months. SASE.
Nonfiction: "Publishes books written for farmers and ranchers and others involved in agriculture. Most titles are guides, handbooks, references or how-to books. Other works directed at our specific audience may also be considered."
Recent Titles: *The Brass Tacks of Animal Health*, by Blakely/King; and *Estate Planning for Farmers*, by J.W. Looney.

DODD, MEAD & CO., 79 Madison Ave., New York NY 10016. (212)685-6464. Executive Editor: Allen T. Klots. Royalty basis: 10-15%. Advances vary, depending on the sales potential of the book. A contract for nonfiction books is offered on the basis of a query, a suggested outline and a sample chapter. Write for permission before sending mss. Published 150 titles last year. Adult fiction, history, philosophy, the arts, and religion should be addressed to Editorial Department. Reports in 1 month. SASE.
General Fiction and Nonfiction: Publishes book-length mss. Length: 70,000-100,000 words. Fiction and nonfiction of high quality, mysteries and romantic novels of suspense, biography, popular science, travel, yachting, music and other arts. Very rarely buys photographs or poetry.
Juveniles: Length: 1,500-75,000 words. Children's Books Editor: Mrs. Joe Ann Daly.

THE DONNING COMPANY/PUBLISHERS, INC., 5041 Admiral Wright Rd., Virginia Beach VA 23510. Editorial Director: Robert S. Friedman. Publishes hardcover and paperback originals. Published 18 titles in 1978, 22 in 1979; plans 25 in 1980. Pays 10-12½-15% royalty on hardcover titles; 8-10-12% royalty on paperback; advance "negotiable." Simultaneous (if so informed) and photocopied submissions OK. Reports in 12 weeks. SASE. Book catalog for SASE.
Nonfiction: Wants material for 3 series: 1) Portraits of American Cities Series (pictorial histories of American cities with 300 illustrations, primarily photographs, with fully descriptive captions and historical overview text of approximately 10,000 words. "The intent is to capture the character of a community in transition, from earliest known settlers to the present. Author need not be a professional historian, but must have close ties to the community and cooperation of local historians and private and public photo archives); 2) Regional Specialty Books (specialty, regional cookbooks, popular history and art collections); and 3) Unilaw Library imprint (Editor: Robert Friedman. Religious, inspirational, metaphysical subjects and themes). Query or submit complete ms. Recently published *Alexandria (VA): A Pictorial History*, by K.G. Harvey/R. Stansfield; *Virginia Supernatural Tales*, by H. Tucker; and *Frank Kelly Freas: Art of Science Fiction*, by F. Kelly Freas.
Fiction: Starblaze Editions imprint. Editors: Kelly and Polly Freas.

DORISON HOUSE PUBLISHERS, 69-12 223rd St., Bayside NY 11364. (212)224-0672. Editorial Director: Trudy Settel. Senior Editor: Marilyn Kostick. Publishes hardcover and paperback originals. Published 11 titles in 1978; 11 in 1979. Pays $3,000-3,500 by outright purchase; average advance of $1,000. "We do not use unsolicited manuscripts. Ours are custom books prepared for businesses and assignments are initiated by us."
Nonfiction: How-to, cookbooks, sports, travel, fitness/health, diet, gardening, and crafts. "We want our books to be designed to meet the needs of specific businesses." Query. Recently published *About the House*, by Joyce Lynn (new ideas for easy management from Bissell); *Mini Meals in Minutes*, by June Roth (fast cooking with hamburger makers and small deep fryers from Hamilton Beach); and *Sterno Guide to the Outdoors*, by Ken Anderson (book of family camping, backpacking, fishing, outdoor cookery and safety tips). .

DOUBLEDAY & CO., INC., 245 Park Ave., New York NY 10017. (212)553-4561. Managing Editor: Pyke Johnson Jr. Publishes hardcover and paperback originals; publishes paperback reprints under Anchor, Dolphin and Image imprints. Offers standard 10-12½-15% royalty contract. Advance varies. Reports in 1 month. Published 596 titles in 1978; 550 in 1979; plans 550 in 1980. Special submission requirements outlined below. Query with outline and sample chapters for both fiction and nonfiction. "Your letter of inquiry should be addressed to the Editorial Department. The letter may be as short as one page, but no longer than six pages (double-spaced). The first sentence should tell us whether your book is a novel, a biography, a mystery, or whatever. The first paragraph should give us an idea of what your book is about. This description should be clear and straightforward. If your book is a novel, please give us an engaging summary of the plot and background, and a quick sketch of the major characters. If you have already been published, give us details at the end of your letter. You should also tell us of any credentials or experience that particularly qualify you to write your book. For a nonfiction book, it will be helpful to you to consult the *Subject Guide to Books in Print* (available in most libraries) so that you are aware of other books on the same or similar subjects as your own, and can tell us how your book differs from them. Finally, letters of inquiry should be inviting and typed with a good ribbon. If we ask to see your ms, it should be submitted double-spaced on white paper. You should retain a carbon copy, since we cannot assume responsibility for loss or damage to mss. Sufficient postage, in the form of loose stamps, should accompany your submission to insure the return of your ms in the event it is not accepted for publication."
Nonfiction and Fiction: "Doubleday has a policy concerning the handling of manuscripts. We return unopened and unread all complete manuscripts, accompanied by a form telling how we would like submissions made. However, in 2 areas, we will accept complete manuscripts: Mysteries and science fiction. These mss should be addressed to the appropriate editor (for example, Science Fiction Editor) and not just to Doubleday. We have a moratorium on poetry publishing and are not accepting mss."

DOUBLEDAY CANADA, LTD., 105 Bond St., Toronto, Ontario, Canada M5B 1Y3. (416)366-7891. Editorial Director: Betty Jane Corson. Publishes hardcover originals. Published 15 titles in 1978, 15 in 1979; plans 15 in 1980. Pays in royalties; advance "varies." Simultaneous and photocopied submissions OK. Reports in 2 months. SAE and International Reply Coupons. Free book catalog.
Nonfiction: General interest. "We do not specialize, but the major part of our list consists of biography, popular history, and subjects of contemporary interest. Our main concern is to publish books of particular interest to the Canadian market, although our books are published in the US as well. We will consider any nonfiction proposal." Query, submit outline/synopsis and sample chapters, or submit complete ms. Recently published *The Royal Winnipeg Ballet: The First Forty Years*, by Max Wyman (dance history); *Lester Pearson and the Dream of Unity*, by Peter Stursberg (oral history); and *Love Affair With a Cougar*, by Lyn Hancock (nature/autobiography).
Fiction: "No particular preferences as to style or genre. We publish both 'literary' and 'commercial' books. Once again, we are most interested in fiction with a Canadian angle (author, setting, subject). Of course, we hope they have North American potential as well." Query or submit complete ms. Recently published *The Musk Ox Passion*, by T. York; and *Murder By Microphone*, by John Keeves.

DOUGLAS & McINTYRE, 1875 Welch St., North Vancouver, British Columbia, Canada V7P 1B7. (604)986-4311. Editor-in-Chief: J.J. Douglas. Managing Editor: Marilyn Sacks. Publishes hardcover and paperback originals (90%) and reprints (10%). Published 15 titles in 1978; 15 in 1979; plans 15 in 1980. Pays 10% royalty; $500 average advance. State availabilty of photos

and/or illustrations. Query or send complete ms. Reports in 1-2 months. SAE with International Reply Coupons. Free book catalog.
Nonfiction: Publishes reference books and books on Canadian history, nature, hobbies, recreation and sports, how-to, hobbies, cookbooks, cooking and foods, pets, self-help, music and art books.

DRAKE PAPERBACK, Imprint of Sterling Publishing Co., 2 Park Ave., New York NY 10016. (212)532-7106. Publisher: Charles Nurnberg. Publishes hardcover and paperback originals (75%) and reprints (25%). Published 40 titles in 1978, 25 in 1979; plans 25 in 1980. Pays 10% royalty; offers $1,000 average advance. Simultaneous and photocopied submissions OK. Reports in 4-6 weeks. SASE. Book catalog for SASE.
Nonfiction: Americana, biography, business, foods, economics, history, hobbies, how-to, humor, law, medicine, nature, pets, photography, psychology, recreation, reference, self-help, sports, technical and woodworking. No inspirational or religious books. Query or submit outline/synopsis and sample chapters. Recently published *How To Build Shaker Furniture*, by T. Moser (woodworking); *Jackie: The Price of the Pedestal*, by L. Guthrie and *Dancers on Dancing*, by C. Lyle (stage and screen).

DRAMA BOOK SPECIALISTS (PUBLISHERS), 150 W. 52nd St., New York NY 10019. (212)582-1475. Contact: Ralph Pine. Publishes hardcover and paperback originals. Pays 10% royalty; advance varies. Published 25 titles in 1978, 25 in 1979; plans 25 in 1980. Reports in 4-8 weeks. SASE.
Nonfiction: "Theatrical history, texts, technical books and books dealing with the performing arts." Query; no complete mss.

DUQUESNE UNIVERSITY PRESS, Pittsburgh PA 15219. (412)434-6610. Pays 10% royalty; no advance. Query. Reports in 8 weeks. Enclose return postage.
Nonfiction: Scholarly books on philosophy and philology and psychology. Length: open. Recently published *Man and Technology*, by E.G. Ballard (philosophical); *Kierkegaard's Psychology*, by K. Nordentoft (psychological); and *Schizophrenia*, by A. De Waelhens (philosophical/psychological).

E.P. DUTTON, 2 Park Ave., New York NY 10016. (212)725-1818. Editor-in-Chief, General Books: Henry Robbins. Editorial Director, Special Books (formerly Sunrise): Constance Schrader. Editor, Juvenile Department: Ann Durell. Editor, Dutton Paperbacks: Cyril Nelson. Editor, Windmill Books: Robert Kraus. Imprints include Dutton Paperbacks, Thomas Congdon Books, Henry Robbins Books, Everyman Library, Windmill Books, Phaidon Books and Unicorn Books. Estab. 1852. Published 137 titles in 1978, 125 in 1979; plans 100 in 1980. Pays variable royalty and advance. Simultaneous and photocopied submissions OK. SASE. Reports in 1 month.
Nonfiction: Americana, animals, biography, business/economics, history, humor, juveniles, music, nature, philosophy, photography, politics, psychology, reference, religion, science, sociology, sports, technical, fine arts, memoirs, belles-lettres translations. Query. Recently published *Star Shots*, by John Engstead (photography/film); *Alan Chadwick's Enchanted Garden*, by Tom Cuthberson (gardening/philosophy); and *Mosquitoes, Malaria and Man*, by Gordon Harrison (science/history).
Fiction: Novels of "permanent literary value," quality paperbacks and juveniles. Adventure, confession, erotica, experimental, fantasy, gothic, historical, humor, mainstream, mystery, religious, romance, suspense and western. Query. Recently published *The World According to Garp*, by John Irving (literary novel); *Fear in a Handful of Dust*, by John Ives (suspense); and *Fair Blows the Wind*, by Louis L'Amour (western).

THE EAST WOODS PRESS (Trade name of Fast & McMillan Publishers, Inc.), 820 E. Blvd., Charlotte NC 28203. Editorial Director: Sally Hill McMillan. Publishes hardcover and paperback originals. Published 5 titles in 1978; 10 in 1979; plans 12 in 1980. Pays 10% royalty. Reports in 2-4 weeks. SASE. Book catalog for SASE.
Nonfiction: "We are strictly interested in travel and the outdoors. Regional guidebooks are our specialty: hiking, fishing, skiing, etc., but anything on travel and outdoors will be considered." Submit outline/synopsis and sample chapters. "A list on competitive books should be submitted, along with specific reasons why this manuscript should be published. Also, maps and art should be supplied by the author." Recently published *Hosteling USA—The Official American Youth Hostels Handbook*; *The New England Guest House Book*, by Corinne Ross; and *Backcountry Cooking*, by J. Wayne Fears.

EDITS PUBLISHERS, Box 7234, San Diego CA 92107. (714)488-1666. Editorial Director: Robert R. Knapp. Publishes hardcover and paperback originals. Published 6 titles in 1978; 10 in 1979. Royalty "varies"; no advance. Photocopied submissions OK. Reports in 1-2 months. SASE. Book catalog for SASE.
Nonfiction: "Edits publishes scientific and text books in social sciences, particularly counseling and guidance, psychology, statistics and education." Query. Recently published *Actualizing Therapy*, by E. Shostrom (therapy text); *Naked Therapist*, by S. Kopp; and *Handbook in Research and Evaluation*, by S. Isaac.

EDUCATIONAL CHALLENGES, INC., 1608 20th St. NW, Washington DC 20009. (202)483-1255. Editor: Diane Willard. Published 10 titles in 1978; 10 in 1979. Pays by outright purchase; sometimes an advance. Simultaneous and photocopied submissions OK. SASE. Reports in 1 month. Writer's guidelines for SASE.
Nonfiction: "We use nonfiction writers for specific projects by assignment only. Resumes and writing samples are kept on file for future consideration on a project to project basis." Query.
Fiction: Humor, romance, sports, science fiction and twilight zone. "We are interested in stories with a wide range of contemporary settings and problems. Selections based on intergenerational conflicts and peer-group pressures will be considered." Length: 700-3,000 words. Submit outline/synopsis and sample chapters. Recently published *The Christie Caper*, by David Bantz and George Kressley; and *Phantom Cycle*, by Jeanne M. Schinto.

EDUCATIONAL INSIGHTS, 20435 S. Tillman Ave., Carson CA 90746. Vice President of Development: E. Sidley. Pays by outright purchase. Simultaneous and photocopied submissions OK. SASE. Reports in 1 month. Submit outline/synopsis and sample chapters. Catalog and writer's guidelines for SASE.
Nonfiction and Fiction: "We want supplementary educational materials with knowledge of teaching skills and strategies and the ability to adapt and rewrite to specific reading levels for specific learning objectives." Recently published *Short Stories Around the World*, and *Charlie*.

WILLIAM B. EERDMANS PUBLISHING CO., Christian University Press, 255 Jefferson Ave. SE, Grand Rapids MI 49503. (616)459-4591. Editor: Marlin J. Van Elderen. Estab. 1911. Publishes hardcover and paperback originals (80%) and reprints (20%). Published 55 titles in 1978; 60 in 1979; plans 60 in 1980. Pays 7½-10% royalty; no advance. Simultaneous and photocopied submissions OK. SASE. Reports in 3 weeks for queries and 4 months for ms. Free book catalog.
Nonfiction: History, philosophy, psychology, reference, religion, sociology and textbooks. "Approximately 80% of our publications are religious—specifically Protestant and largely of the more academic or theological (as opposed to devotional, inspirational or celebrity-conversion type of book) variety. Our history and 'social studies' titles aim, similarly at an academic audience; many of them are 'documentary' histories. We prefer writers take the time to notice if we have published anything at all in the same category as their manuscript before sending it to us." Query. Recently published *The Ethnic Frontier*, by Peter Jones and Melvin Holli (anthology of essays pertaining to diverse ethnic groups in Chicago); *Paul: Apostle of the Heart Set Free*, by F.F. Bruce (study of the life and thought of the apostle); and *Christ and the Media*, by Malcolm Muggeridge (essays on the influence of television).

*EFFECTIVE LEARNING, INC., 7 N. MacQuesten Pkwy, Mt. Vernon NY 10550. (914)664-7944. Editor: John Vance. Publishes hardcover and paperback originals (95%) and reprints (5%). Subsidy publishes 2% of books. Simultaneous submissions OK. Query. SASE. Reports in 1-2 months. Free book catalog.
Nonfiction: Americana, biography, business, cookbooks, cooking and food, economics, history, hobbies, how-to, multimedia material, nature, philosophy, politics, reference, religious, scientific, self-help, sociology, technical, textbooks and travel. "All manuscripts should be sent to the editorial review committee. Recently published *The Middle East: Imperatives & Choices*, by Alon Ben-Meir (politics).

ELSEVIER/NELSON BOOKS, 2 Park Ave., New York NY 10016. (212)725-1818. Editor-in-Chief: Gloria Mosesson. Hardcover originals. Published 50 titles in 1978; plans 50 in 1979 and 50 in 1980. 7½% royalty; advance offered. State availability of photos and/or illustrations. Photocopied submissions OK. Reports in 2-4 months. SASE. Book catalog for SASE.
Nonfiction: Publishes Americana art, biography, business, history, hobbies, how-to, humor, juveniles, nature, politics, psychology, recreation, reference, scientific, self-help and sports books. Query or submit outline/synopsis and sample chapters.

Fiction: Publishes adventure, experimental, fantasy, historical, humorous, mainstream, mystery, science fiction, suspense and western books. Submit complete ms.

EMC CORP., 180 E. 6th St., St. Paul MN 55101. Editorial Director: Northrop Dawson Jr. Senior Editor: Constance Van Brunt McMillan. Publishes hardcover and paperback originals (90%) and reprints (10%). Publishes 32 titles in 1978. "We publish for the school (educational) market only, in limited runs as compared to trade publishers. Writers should not have expectations of huge quantity sales." Contract and advance "open to negotiation." Reports in 4 weeks. Free book catalog.

Nonfiction: "Topics of interest to juvenile readers: sports; the media; popular entertainers; outdoor life and activity (wild animals, outdoor sports such as cross-country skiing, ballooning, etc.); "the unexplained" (supernatural, esp, etc.); unusual occupations; and biographies of achievers surmounting great odds. No how-to, religious, or travel material." Query: "send one or more samples of previously published work." Recently published *Arthur Ashe: Alone in the Crowd*, by L. Jacobs (sports biography); *Animals Around Us*, by J. Becker (wildlife/science enrichment); and *Hispanic Heroes of the U.S.A.*, by W. Wheelock (biography).

Fiction: Juvenile fiction: mystery; "the unexplained"; young detectives; stories focussing on non-stereotyped, active, aggressive girls; adventure stories involving young people; sports fiction involving juvenile athletes, both male and female; outdoor and wildlife adventure involving juveniles; realistic stories of juveniles overcoming handicaps; science fiction geared to juveniles; and stories involving animals. No religious material. Query, "send one or more samples of previously published work. After we have indicated interest in initial query, submit outline and sample chapters." Recently published *Time of Danger, Time of Courage*, by G. Gray; *No Such Things . . . ?*, by B. Hunting (series of supernatural stories); and *Sea Wolf Mysteries*, by R. Wise (outdoor mystery).

EMERSON BOOKS, INC., Reynolds Lane, Buchanan NY 10511. (914)739-3506. Managing Editor: Barry Feiden. Publishes hardcover originals (80%) and reprints (20%). Published 6 titles in 1978; 5 in 1979. Photocopied submissions OK. Reports in 3 months. SASE.

Nonfiction: Hobbies, how-to, recreation, self-help. Query. Recently published *Collecting and Identifying Old Clocks*, by Harris (antiques); and *Principles of Collage*, by French (crafts).

ENSLOW PUBLISHERS, Box 301, Short Hills NJ 07078. (201)379-6308. Editor: Ridley Enslow. Estab. 1976. Publshes hardcover and paperback originals. Published 12 titles in 1978; 12 in 1979; plans 15 in 1980. Pays 10-15% royalty; $500-5,000 advance. Photocopied submissions OK. SASE. Reports in 2 weeks. Free book catalog.

Nonfiction: Business/economics, health, hobbies, how-to, juveniles, philosophy, psychology, recreation, reference, science, self-help, sociology, sports and technical. Query. Recently published *Ice Ages*, by John Imbrie (science); *Eggshell Ego*, by Beata Bishop (sociology-masculinity); and *Scream Quietly or the Neighbors Will Hear*, by Erin Pizzey (social issue: wife battering).

Fiction: Mainstream and science fiction. Query. Recently published *Callahan's Crosstime Saloon*, by Spider Robinson (science fiction); and *Let Me Alone*, by Anna Kavan (feminist).

ENTELEK, Ward-Whidden House/The Hill, Portsmouth NH 03801. Editor-in-Chief: Albert E. Hickey. Publishes paperback originals. Offers royalty contract of 5% trade; 10% textbook. No advance. Published 8 titles last year. Will send free catalog to writer on request. Will consider photocopied and simultaneous submissions. Submit outline and sample chapters or submit complete ms. Reports in 1 week. Enclose return postage.

Nonfiction and Business: Publishes computer, calculator, math, business and how-to books. "We seek books that have not been undertaken by other publishers." Would like to see material for career guides. Length: 3,000 words minimum. Recently published *Genetic With the Computer*.

ENTERPRISE PUBLISHING CO., INC., 1300 Market St., Wilmington DE 19801. (302)575-0440. Publisher: T.N. Peterson. Editor: Beverly H. Kirby. Publishes hardcover and paperback originals. Published 3 titles in 1978; 10 in 1979; plans 20 in 1980. Advance averages $1,000. Simultaneous and photocopied submissions OK, but "let us know." Reports in 1 month. SASE. Catalog for SASE.

Nonfiction: "Subjects of interest to the small business owner/entrepreneur. Self-help topics on business, including starting and managing a small enterprise, advertising, marketing, raising capital and public relations." Business/economics, health, legal self-help and how-to. Query; all unsolicited mss are returned unopened. Recently published *Total Glow: Dr. Rona's Unbeatable Health Program*, by Luanne Rona, M.D. (holistic health); *Writing Part-Time—For*

Fun and Money, by Jack Clinton McLarn; and *How to Form Your Own Professional Corporation*, by Ted Nicholas (self-help).

EPM PUBLICATIONS, INC., 1003 Turkey Run Road, McLean VA 22101. Editor: Evelyn P. Metzger. Publishes hardcover and paperback originals. Published 5 titles in 1978; 5 in 1979; plans 7 in 1980. Pays 10% (hardcover) and 6% (paperback) royalty; sometimes an advance. Simultaneous and photocopied submissions OK. Reports in 4 weeks. SASE. Catalog for SASE.
Nonfiction: "We are open to almost any topic that people would be willing to spend money to read about. We want good, well-written manuscripts that will appeal to the public. We do not want to see any obscene or libelous material, textbooks, short children's books, poetry, regional books about other regions, short stories, essays, research papers or anything illiterate." Query. "If we ask to see sample chapters and an outline or the entire manuscript, we expect it to be neatly typed, doubled-spaced with wide margins, and SASE accompanying it." Recently published *The Foxes' Union*, by James J. Kilpatrick (regional reminiscences); *Your Natural Gifts*, by Margaret Broadley (apititudes); and *Catching Freshwater Striped Bass*, by Pete Elkins (how-to).
Fiction: "We're open to fiction, but it would really have to be a blockbuster of a manuscript for us to risk publishing it. We have not published any so far."

*PAUL S. ERIKSSON, PUBLISHER, Battell Bldg., Middlebury VT 05753. (802)388-7303. President: Paul S. Eriksson. Estab. 1960. Publishes hardcover and paperback trade originals (99%) and paperback trade reprints (1%). Published 7 titles in 1978; 10 in 1979; plans 10 in 1980. Pays 10-15% royalty; advance offered if necessary. Subsidy publishes 5% of books. "We have to like the book and probably the author." Photocopied submissions OK. SASE. Reports in 3 weeks. Free book catalog.
Nonfiction: Americana, animals, art, biorgaphy, business/economics, cookbooks/cooking/foods, health, history, hobbies, how-to, humor, juveniles, music, nature, philosophy, photography, politics, psychology, recreation, self-help, sociology, sports and travel. Submit outline/synopsis and sample chapters. Recently published *Three Alexander Calders*, by Margaret Calder Hayes (a family memoir); *The Jewish-Low Cholesterol Cookbook*, by Roberta Leviton (cookbook); *Steinbeck and Couici*, by Thomas Fensch; and *William O. Douglas*, by Edwin P. Noyt.
Fiction: Mainstream. Submit outline/synopsis and sample chapters. Recently published *The Silkies*, by Charlotte Koplinka (novel of the Shetlands).

EVANS AND CO., INC., 216 E. 49 St., New York NY 10017. Editor-in-Chief: Herbert M. Katz. Publishes hardcover originals. Royalty schedule to be negotiated. Publishes 30 titles/year. Will consider photocopied submissions. "No mss should be sent unsolicited. A letter of inquiry is essential." Reports in 6-8 weeks. SASE.
General Fiction and Nonfiction: "We publish a general trade list of adult fiction and nonfiction, cookbooks and semi-reference works. The emphasis is on selectivity since we publish only 30 titles a year. Our fiction list represents an attempt to combine quality with commercial potential. Our most successful nonfiction titles have been related to the behavioral sciences. No limitation on subject. A writer should clearly indicate what his book is all about; frequently the task the writer performs least well. His credentials, although important, mean less than his ability to convince this company that he understands his subject and that he has the ability to communicate a message worth hearing." Recently published *Women Who Wait* and *The Marriage Premise*.

FAIRCHILD BOOKS & VISUALS, Book Division, 7 E. 12th St., New York NY 10003. Manager: E.B. Cold. Publishes hardcover and paperback originals. Offers standard minimum book contract; no advance. Pays 10% of net sales distributed twice annually. Published 12 titles last year. Photocopied submissions OK. Free book catalog. Query, giving subject matter and brief outline. Enclose return postage.
Business and Textbooks: Publishes business books and textbooks relating to fashion, electronics, marketing, retailing, career education, advertising, home economics, and management. Length: open. Recently published *Fashion Production Terms*, by Gioello; and *Fashion Advertising and Promotion*, by Winters/Goodman.

FAR EASTERN RESEARCH AND PUBLICATIONS CENTER, Box 31151, Washington DC 20031. Contact: Editor-in-Chief. Publishes hardcover and paperback originals and reprints. Pays standard royalties, or by outright purchase. Enclose "enough postage to cover registered mail for return of submissions."
Nonfiction: Reference materials on the Far East, especially on the Chinese, Japanese and

Korean people. All lengths. Submit outline/synopsis and sample chapter, and table of contents, if possible.

FARNSWORTH PUBLISHING CO., INC., 78 Randall Ave., Rockville Centre NY 11570. (516)536-8400. President: Lee Rosler. Publishes hardcover originals. "Standard royalty applies, but 5% is payable on mail order sales." Published 18 titles in 1978; 20 in 1979; plans 20 in 1980. Free book catalog. Reports in 3-6 weeks. SASE.
General Nonfiction, Business and Professional: "Our books generally fall into 2 categories: books that appeal to executives, lawyers, accountants and life underwriters (subject matter may cover selling techniques, estate planning, taxation, money management, etc.); and books that appeal to the general population and are marketable by direct mail and mail order, in addition to bookstore sales." Recently published *Complete Book of Walking*, by Raymond Dreyfoek; *No More Mr. Nice Guy*, by Earl Epstein; *Where There's a Will*, by Robert Mendin; and *Global Employment Guide*, by James Powell.

FARRAR, STRAUS AND GIROUX, INC., 19 Union Square West, New York NY 10003. Editor: Sandra Jordan. Publishes hardcover and paperback originals. Published 22 titles in 1978; 24 in 1979; plans 24 in 1980. Pays royalty; advance. Photocopied submissions OK. SASE. Reports in 2 months. Catalog for SASE.
Nonfiction: History, humor, juveniles, philosophy, psychology and sociology. "We are only interested in nonfiction for the 7-12 age group unless the book is specifically keyed to young adult readers—no biography or nature books of a general nature for that age group." Submit outline/synopsis and sample chapters. Recently published *Gay: What you Should Know About Homosexuality*, by Martin Hunt and Jovem Portugal and *After The Revolution*, by Jason and Ettegale Laure.
Fiction: Adventure, fantasy, historical, humor, mainstream, mystery, romance, science fiction, suspense and western. "We particulary want to see contemprary fiction for 7-10 and 10 and up age group." Submit outline/synopsis and sample chapters. Recently published *A Swiftly Tilting Planet*, by Madeleine L. Engle; *A Fine, Soft Day*, by James Forman and *Toby Lived Here*, by Wilma Wolitzer.

FAWCETT BOOKS GROUPS, CBS Publications, Consumer Division, 1515 Broadway, New York NY 10036. Fawcett Books Groups consists of three imprints. Fawcett Gold Medal (generally paperback originals); contact Maureen Baron, (212)975-7673. Fawcett Crest (generally reprints) and Fawcett Popular Library (originals and reprints); contact Eileen Freed, (212)975-7693.

F.W. FAXON CO., INC., 15 Southwest Park, Westwood MA 02090. (617)329-3350. Publisher: Albert H. Davis Jr. Editor-in-Chief: Beverly D. Heinle. Publishes hardcover originals. Published 10 titles in 1978; 10 in 1979; plans 10 in 1980. Offers 10% of sales net price for each book sold, payable at the end of each fiscal year. No advance. Books are marketed through advertising, mail campaigns, book reviews, and library conventions. Will send catalog to writer on request. Mss must be original copy, double-spaced, and must be accompanied by a copy. They should contain reference material useful to library users throughout the world. Query. Reports in 2 months. SASE.
Reference: "We publish library reference books. These are primarily indexes but we would also consider bibliographies and other material useful to library users. Develop proposals for reference works in subject areas where there is a need for organized access to a body of information. Such reference works should be of particular value to libraries (school, college, university and public)." Recently published *Public Relations*; *The Edward L. Bernayses*; and *The American Scene: A Bibliography*, by Keith A. Larson.

FEARON/PITMAN PUBLISHERS, INC., 6 Davis Dr., Belmont CA 94002. Editorial Director: Dr. Robert G. Bander. Published 30 titles in 1978; plans 30 in 1979, 40 in 1980. Photocopied submissions OK. SASE. Query or Submit outline/synopsis and sample chapters. Reports in 1 month. Free book catalog.
Nonfiction: "We don't want to see material for the general trade market—our books are sold to elementary, secondary and adult basic education schools. Query.
Fiction: "We are looking for easy-to-read fiction written to a vocabulary scale we provide and suitable for the junior high school through adult basic education market. We are not looking for juvenile fiction, but prefer the major characters to be adults in adult situations. Sex role stereotyping is taboo." Recently published *Galaxy 5 Space Pack*, by Leo P. Kelley (adult science fiction series, including teacher's guide, cassette tapes, and 6 books, written at a 3rd grade reading level); and *Typing in Plain English*, by Ann Hamill (basic typwriting instruction

for the high school or adult student at the 6th grade level).

FREDERICK FELL PUBLISHERS, INC., 386 Park Ave., S., New York NY 10016. (212)685-9017. Editor-in-Chief: Frederick V. Fell. Publishes hardcover and paperback originals (85%) and reprints (15%). Pays 10% royalty. Published 24 titles in 1978; 30 in 1979, plans 30 in 1980. Query. Send sample prints or contact sheet if photos/illustrations are to accompany ms. Simultaneous and photocopied submissions OK. Reports in 3-5 weeks. SASE. Free book catalog.
Nonfiction: Publishes Americana, business, hobbies, how-to, law, medicine and psychiatry, pets, photography, psychology, recreation, reference, self-help and sports books. Recently published *Complete Guide to Eye Care, Eyeglasses, & Contact Lenses*, by Drs. Zinn/Soloman (medical self-help); and *Ken Rosewall on Tennis*, by K. Rosewall (sports).
Special Needs: Pet Lovers Library; Home Medical Library.

THE FEMINIST PRESS, Box 334, Old Westbury NY 11568. (516)997-7660. Publishes paperback and hardcover originals and historical reprints. Published 7 titles in 1978; plans 10 in 1979 and 10 in 1980. Pays 6½% royalty; no advance. Simultaneous and photocopied submissions OK. Reports in 2 months. Query or submit outline/synopsis and sample chapters.
Adult Books: Elisabeth Phillips, Editor. Feminist books for a general trade and women's studies audience. "We publish biographies, reprints of lost feminist literature, women's history, bibliographies, educational materials, general nonfiction. No material without a feminist viewpoint. No contemporary adult fiction, drama, or poetry." Recently published *The Maimie Papers*, by Rosen and Davidson (historical letters); *Changing Learning/Changing Lives*, by Gates, Klaw and Steinberg (curriculum materials); *Rights and Wrongs*, by Nicholas, Price and Rubin (nonfiction); *Women Working*, by Hoffman and Howe (literary anthology); *Black Foremothers*, by Sterling (biography); and *Out of the Bleachers*, by S. Twin (sports anthology).
Children's Books: Jeanne Bracken and Sharon Wigutoff, editors. "We publish juvenile fiction and biographies. No picture books." Recently published *Tatterhood and Other Tales*, by E. Phelps (folklore); and *The Lilith Summer*, by H. Irwin.
Tips: "Submit a proposal for an important feminist work that is sophisticated in its analysis, yet popular in its writing style. Both historical and contemporary subjects will be considered. We are especially interested in works that appeal to both a trade audience and a women's studies classroom market."

FFORBEZ ENTERPRISES, LTD., Box 35340, Station E, Vancouver, British Columbia, Canada V6M 4G6. (604)872-7325. Editor-in-Chief: P.W. Zebroff. Managing Editor: James Wright. Publishes paperback originals. Specializes in how-to and health-oriented books. Pays 10% royalty; no advance. Published 5 titles in 1978; plans 10 in 1979, 15 in 1980. Markets books through health and book stores. Send at least 1 copy of illustration and 1 print. Simultaneous submissions OK if exclusive to Canada. Photocopied submissions OK. Reports in 2-4 weeks. SAE and International Reply Coupons. Free book catalog.
Nonfiction: Publishes cookbooks dealing with nutritious foods, how-to, multimedia material, nature, recreation, self-help, sports and health. Submit outline/synopsis, sample chapters and table of contents. Recently published *Surgery: Yes or No*, by N. Rogers (health); *Get Your Back Up*, by Kareen Zebroff (health); and *Kid, Kids, Kids, and British Columbia*, by D. Wood, B. Campbell and Lyndon Grove.

*FIDES/CLARETIAN, Box F, Notre Dame IN 46556. Editor: James F. Burns. Publishes originals and reprints. Published 4 titles in 1978; plans 8-10 in 1979, 10-12 in 1980. Pays 8-10% royalty; no advance. Publishes about 1 subsidy book a year. Free book catalog. Send outline and sample chapter. Reports in 6 weeks. Enclose return postage.
Religion: Publishes religious books (Christian and ecumenical) and general nonfiction with theological, spiritual, pastoral implications. The new look in religion and religious education, and the attitude of freedom and personal responsibility. Length: 20,000 words minimum. Recently published *A New Look at the Sacraments*, by W.J. Bausch (pastoral theology); *A Call to Action*, by F. Manning; and *How to Pray Always Without Always Praying*, by S. Fittipaldi (spirituality).

*THE FILER PRESS, Box 5, Palmer Lake CO 80133. (303)481-2523. Editorial Director: Gilbert L. Campbell. Senior Editor: Lollie W. Campbell. Publishes hardcover and paperback originals (50%) and reprints (50%). Publishes 8 titles/year. Subsidy publishes less than 10% of titles/year. "These are usually family histories in short runs, although subjects have ranged from preaching, ranching, history debunking, to a study of UFOs. If we feel we can market a book profitably for us and the author, and it is a good book and the author feels he needs it published, we will consider it." Pays 10% royalty; no advance. Simultaneous and photocopied submissions OK. Reports in 2-3 weeks. SASE. Book catalog for SASE.

Nonfiction: "Cookbooks must apppeal to westerners, campers, and tourists. We have one on game cookery, one on pancakes, one on camp cooking, one on Southwestern Indian recipes. In prep is one on Mexican cooking for the Anglo bride (our daughter is one!). Also Western legends, and other Western Americana, as we are quite regional. We must stay at or near our 64-page limit, as most booklets are sold softbound, saddle stitched. We have done some verse, but prefer light verse of Western interest. Our morgue of antique wood engravings is used extensively, so books with a Victorian feel fit in best. Western Americana on our list includes Indians, explorations, lawmen, and bandits. We have Butch Cassidy, Pat Garrett, and will add Jim Reavis, The Bogus Baron of Arizona, one of America's more successful swindlers. Family histories and very local history have not done well for us. Writers must remember we are small, publish few books, and they must be things that a tourist will buy to take home, although we are in many Eastern bookstores." Query; "it is much cheaper to send a query and SASE than to send the manuscript to us cold." Recently published *What Am I Doing Here?*, by Wanden Kane; *Navajo Native Dyes*, by Nonobah Bryan; *Sketchbook of Colorado Ghost Towns*, by Hugh Riker; and *Papago & Pina Indians of Arizona*, by Ruth Underhill.

Fiction: "Practically all our fiction has been reprinted from 19th century authors, a distinguished group who never ask for an up-to-date royalty statement! Our poetry is evenly divided between old and new. I suppose if something very short and imaginative should come along on the 19th-Century West, we might do it, but. . . ." Query.

FITZHENRY & WHITESIDE, LTD., 150 Lesmill Rd., Don Mills, Ontario, Canada. Editor-in-Chief: Robert Read. Publishes hardcover and paperback originals and reprints. Chiefly educational materials. Royalty contract varies; advance negotiable. Published 40 titles in 1978; plans 40 in 1979, 50 in 1980. Photocopied submissions OK. Reports in 1-3 months. Enclose return postage.

General Nonfiction, Drama and Poetry: "Especially interested in topics of interest to Canadians, and by Canadians." Biography, business, history, medicine and psychiatry, nature and politics. Submit outline and sample chapters. Length: open. Recently published *The Mind of Norman Bethune*, by R. Stewart; *Gabriel Dumont*, by G. Woodcock; and *Member of the Legislature*, by Morton Shulman.

Textbooks: Elementary and secondary school textbooks, audiovisual materials in social studies and language arts and science. Submit outline and sample chapters.

FLEET PRESS CORP., 160 5th Ave., New York NY 10010. (212)243-6100. Editor: Susan Nueckel. Publishes hardcover and paperback originals and reprints. Royalty schedule and advance "varies." Published 17 titles in 1978; plans 15 in 1979. Free book catalog. Reports in 6 weeks. Enclose return postage with ms.

General Nonfiction: "History, biography, arts, religion, general nonfiction, sports." Length: 45,000 words. Query with outline; no unsolicited mss.

Juveniles: Nonfiction only. Stress on social studies and minority subjects; for ages 8-15. Length: 25,000 words. Query with outline; no unsolicited mss.

FODOR'S MODERN GUIDES, 2 Park Ave., New York NY 10016. (212)340-9800. Editorial Director: Robert C. Fisher. Senior Editor: Leslie Brown. Publishes hardcover and paperback originals. Published 53 titles in 1978. Pays $50 minimum outright purchase; 10-20% advance. Simultaneous and photocopied submissions OK. Reports in 1-3 months. SASE. Book catalog for SASE.

Nonfiction: "We publish only travel guidebooks in these two general formats: guides to individual countries, cities, areas or continents (e.g. Europe, New England, Paris, Germany); and guides for special interest travel (e.g. railways, Old West, etc.). No material unrelated to travel. Query, submit outline/synopsis and sample chapters, or complete ms. Recently published *China*, by J. Summerfield; *Worldwide Adventure Guide*; and *Budget Europe '79*.

FOLLETT PUBLISHING CO., General Books Division, 1010 W. Washington Blvd., Chicago IL 60607. (312)666-5858. Estab. 1873. Editorial Director: Elaine Goldberg. Publishes hardcover and paperback originals. Published 140 titles in 1978; 100 in 1979; plans 100 in 1980. Pays 7½-10% royalty; advance. Simultaneous and photocopied submissions OK. SASE. Reports in 2 weeks. Free book catalog.

Nonfiction: Reference books, jobs and careers, personal skills and self-development, leisure activities, recreation, sports, textbooks. "We do not want autobiography or mystic religious cults material." Query. Recently published *The Woman's Dress for Success Book*, by John T.

Molloy; *Backpacking, Sixth Edition*, by Robert C. Rethmel, and *The Triumph of Age*, by Dorothy C. Finkelhor.

FOLLETT PUBLISHING CO., Children's Book Dept., 420 Lexington Ave., Suite 2603, New York NY 10017. Chicago Office: 1010 W. Washington Blvd., Chicago IL 60607. (312)666-5858. Department Editorial Director: Ellen Rudin. Publishes hardcover originals and some paperback reprints. Pays negotiable royalty and advance. "Photocopied manuscripts are OK, but simultaneous submissions are not accepted." Reports in 4-6 weeks. SASE. Book catalog for SASE (use Chicago address).
Nonfiction: "We are interested in quality nonfiction of all kinds with strong, direct appeal to children from preschool to teens. Subjects and themes not often covered in books for children are especially welcome." Query, submit outline/synopsis and sample chapters, or submit complete ms.
Fiction: "We are interested in quality fiction of all kinds, without regard to genre, if well-written and well characterized. We publish picture books for the youngest children, storybooks, poetry and novels for both middle grades and teenagers." Submit complete ms.

FORDHAM UNIVERSITY PRESS, University Box L, Bronx NY 10458. (212)933-2233, ext. 366. Director: H.G. Fletcher. Published 5 titles in 1978; plans 10 in 1979, 8 in 1980. Pays royalty. Photocopied submissions OK. SASE. Reports in 1 week. Free book catalog.
Nonfiction: humanities. "We would like the writer to use the *MLA Style Sheet*, latest edition. We do not want dissertations or fiction material."

FORTRESS PRESS, 2900 Queen Lane, Philadelphia PA 19129. (215)848-6800. Editorial Director: William G. Rusch. Publishes hardcover and paperback originals. Published 47 titles in 1978; plans 52 in 1979, 50 in 1980. Specializes in general religion for laity and clergy; academic texts and monographs in theology (all areas). Pays 7% royalty on paperbacks; 10% on hardcover; modest advance. Mss must follow *Chicago Manual of Style* (17th edition). Photocopied submissions OK. Reports in 90 days. SASE. Free book catalog.
Nonfiction: Publishes philosophy, religious and self-help books. Query. No religious poetry or fiction. Recently published *Karl Barth*, by E. Busch (biography); *Paul and Palestinian Judaism*, by E.P. Sanders; and *Tradition and Theology in the Old Testament*, edited by D. Knight (essays).

FOUR CORNERS PRESS, 232 Washington St., Hanover MA 02339. Editor-in-Chief: Carl W. Lindsay. Publishes paperback originals. "We buy all material outright. No byline. Payment will vary from a minimum of $25 for simple reports to well over $500 for acceptable book-length material." Published 25 titles, reports and booklets last year. Published material is sold by mail order to the public, or sold to a business and sent to their customers or prospects as if it were published by them. "Do *not* ask for samples, etc. They have no bearing on what we expect from a new submission." Query. Reports in 2 weeks. SASE.
Nonfiction: Americana, business, humor, politics, reference, self-help, how-to and technical. "We are always on the lookout for material that can be sold by mail or syndicated." Publishes reports, short books. Most material published in report form, 8½x11 pages, offset printed, stapled rather than bound. Longer material published as saddle-stitched or softcover booklet. "Material must be useful, well-researched and, we hope, unique. This is not a market for off-the-cuff writing. Usually the writer must have some specialized knowledge or be able to do good research." Audience is specialized, but material should also be of interest to a cross-section of professional, business and personal people. Mss must be practical and useful. No preconceived notions. "Household hints are a drug on the market for us. We use no poetry but keep getting it."

FRANCISCAN HERALD PRESS, 1434 W. 51st St., Chicago IL 60609. (312)254-4455. Editor: The Rev. Mark Hegener O.F.M. Senior Editor: Marion A. Habig. Inprints include Synthesis Booklets and Herald Biblical Booklets. Estab. 1921. Publishes hardcover and paperback originals (90%) and reprints (10%). Published 52 titles in 1978; plans 75 in 1979. Pays 8-12% royalty; offers $200-1,000 advance. Photocopied submissions OK. SASE. Reports in 2 weeks. Free book catalog.
Nonfiction: Biography, history, philosophy, psychology and religion. Query or Submit outline/synopsis and sample chapters. Recently published *Ethics*, by Von Hildebrand (philosophby); *Human Existence*, by William E. May (bioethics); *Introduction to Franciscan Literature of the Middle Ages*, by John V. Fleming (literary evaluation); and *Christian Humanism*, by Thomas Molnar (philosophy).

GAMBLER'S BOOK CLUB, GBC Press, Box 4115, Las Vegas NV 89106. (702)382-7555. Editorial Director: John Luckman. Publishes hardcover and paperback originals (67%) and reprints (33%). Published 18 titles in 1978; plans 18 in 1979, 20 in 1980. Pays 10% royalty; advance averages $300. Photocopied submissions OK. Reports in 1 month. SASE. Book catalog for SASE.

Nonfiction: 20,000-word mss pertaining to gambling or to games on which people wager money. Submit complete ms. Recently published *Professional Blackjack*, by S. Wong; *Poker Poker*, by P. Dangel; and *Average Purse Tables*, by H. Mahl.

GARDEN WAY PUBLISHING, Charlotte VT 05445. (802)425-2171. Editor: Roger Griffith. Publishes hardcover and paperback originals. Offers a flat fee arrangement varying with book's scope, or royalty, which usually pays author 6% of book's retail price. Advances are negotiable, but usually range from $1,500 to $2,000. "We stress continued promotion of titles and sales over many years. None of our titles has yet gone out of print." Emphasizes direct mail sales, plus sales to bookstores through salesmen. Book catalog for SASE. Photocopied submissions OK. Enclose return postage.

Nonfiction: Books on gardening, cooking, animal husbandry, homesteading and energy conservation. Emphasis should be on how-to. Length requirements are flexible. "The writer should remember the reader will buy his book to learn to do something, so that all information to accomplish this must be given. We are publishing specifically for the person who is concerned about natural resources and a deteriorating life style and wants to do something about it." Would like to see energy books with emphasis on what the individual can do. Query. Recently published *Woodstone Cookery*, by J. Cooper; and *Harnessing Water Power for Home Energy*, by D. McGuigan.

*GENEALOGICAL PUBLISHING CO., INC., 111 Water St., Baltimore MD 21202. (301)837-8271. Editor-in-Chief: Michael H. Tepper, Ph.D. Publishes hardcover originals and reprints. Offers straight 10% royalty. Does about 10% subsidy publishing. Published 85 titles in 1978; plans 90 in 1979, 90-100 in 1980. Will consider photocopied submissions. Prefers query first, but will look at outline and sample chapter or complete ms. Reports "immediately." Enclose SAE and return postage.

Reference, Textbooks and History: "Our requirements are unusual, so we usually treat each author and his subject in a way particularly appropriate to his special skills and subject matter. Guidelines are flexible and generous, though it is expected that an author will consult with us in depth. Most, though not all, of our original publications are offset from camera-ready typescript. Since most genealogical reference works are compilations of vital records and similar data, tabular formats are common. We hope to receive more ms material in the area of census indexes, specifically indexes to statewide censuses. We also anticipate mss documenting the Revolutionary War service of large numbers of early Americans. We would like to have an on-going Revolutionary War genealogy project." Family history compendia, basic methodology in genealogy, and advanced local history (for example, county histories, particularly those containing genealogy); heraldry: dictionaries and glossaries of the art and science, armorials of families entitled to bear coat armor, manuals and craftbooks describing heraldic painting, etc. Recently published *Index to the 1820 Census of Virginia* , by J. Felldin; *Heraldic Design*, by H. Child; and *Researcher's Guide to American Genealogy*, by V. Greenwood (textbook).

GINN AND CO., 191 Spring St., Lexington MA 02173. Publisher: Dr. James R. Squire. Royalty schedule: from 10% of net on a secondary book to 4% on elementary materials. Published 450 titles last year. Sample chapters, complete or partially complete mss will be considered. Reports in 2 to 6 weeks. Enclose return postage.

Textbooks: Publishers of textbooks and instructional materials for elementary and secondary schools.

GLENMARK PUBLISHING CO., 5041 Byrne Rd., Oregon WI 53575. Editorial Director: Glenn Schaeffer. Senior Editor: Mike Pearlman. Publishes paperback originals. Published 6 titles in 1978; plans 10 in 1979. Buys mss outright, or pays royalties "based on audited sales." SASE.

Nonfiction: "We deal in mail order books that have mass appeal. Our specialty is books on making money or success including such topics as real estate, stock market, starting a business, easy way to riches and so on. However we will seriously consider books that strike a nerve in the public such as on astrology, ESP, mysticism and so on. The bigger, the more exciting the idea, the better we like it." Query. Recently published *The Best Things in Life Are Free*, by G.

Shay (how to get just about anything free); and *Foolproof Theory for Making a Fortune in the Stock Market*, by G. Shay.

THE GLOBE PEQUOT PRESS, INC., Old Chester Rd., Chester CT 06412. (203)526-9571. Publications Director: Linda Kennedy. Publishes hardcover and paperback originals (95%) and paperback reprints (5%). Published 17 titles in 1978; plans 23 in 1979. Pays 10% royalty; advance offered, "but usually just for specific expenses." Simultaneous and photocopied submissions OK. Submit sample chapters, table of contents and one-page precis of manuscript. Reports in 2 weeks. SASE. Free book catalog.
Nonfiction: Publishes history, biography, special interest and how-to books. Special field is New England guide books, short walks series, New England historical sidelights, railways, maritime and New England arts and crafts, including antiques and architecture. Interested in Connecticut history and the arts. "For book trade and elementary and high school markets." Length: open. Recently published *Only in New England*, by J.C. Hill; *Short Walks Maine Coast*, by H. & H. Sadlier; and *25 Bird Walks in Connecticut*, by N. Proctor.

GOLDEN WEST BOOKS, Box 8136, San Marino CA 91108. (213)283-3446. Editor-in-Chief: Donald Duke. Managing Editor: Jeff Dunning. Publishes hardcover and paperback originals. Published 8 titles in 1978; plans 7 in 1979. Pays 10% royalty contract; no advance. Simultaneous and photocopied submissions OK. Reports in 2-4 weeks. SASE. Free book catalog.
Nonfiction: Publishes western Americana and transportation Americana. Query or submit complete ms. "Illustrations and photographs will be examined if we like ms." Recently published *Grand Central . . . World's Greatest Railway Terminal*, by W. Middleton; and *Mount Lowe Railway*, by C. Seims.

GRAPHIC ARTS CENTER PUBLISHING CO., 2000 NW Wilson St., Portland OR 97209. (503)224-7777. Executive Vice-President: Charles H. Belding. Publishes hardcover originals. Published 6 titles in 1978; will do 6 in 1979. Pays outright purchase averaging $3,000 (less for paperbacks); no advance. Simultaneous and photocopied submissions OK. Reports in 3 weeks. SASE. Free book catalog.
Nonfiction: "All titles are pictorials with text. Text usually runs separately from the pictorial treatment. State and regional book series are published under the imprint name (D.B.A.) Belding. Several theme series of pictorial books have also been begun and length and style are more flexible." Query. Recently published *New York*, by L. Atwill; *California II*, by D. Pike; and *Georgia*, by C. Wharton.

GRAY'S PUBLISHING LTD., Box 2160, Sidney, BC, Canada V8L 3S6. (604)656-4454. Editor: Maralyn Horsdal. Publishes hardcover and paperback originals. Offers standard royalty contract. Published 5 titles in 1978; plans 8 in 1979 and 6-8 in 1980. Free book catalog. Query with outline. Reports in 6-10 weeks. SAE and International Reply Coupons.
Nonfiction: Wants "nonfiction, Canadiana," especially Pacific Northwest. Biography, natural history, history, Indian culture, nautical. Length: 60,000-120,000 words. Recently published *The Man for a New Country*, by D.R. Williams (biography); *Fifty Dollar Bride*, by J. Carpenter (biography); and *Pere Murray and the Hounds*, by J. Gorman (biography).
Fiction: "We are beginning to accept fiction with a Pacific Northwest interest."

GREAT OUTDOORS PUBLISHING CO., 4747 28th St. N., St. Petersburg FL 33714. (813)522-3453. Editor-in-Chief: Charles Allyn. Publishes paperback originals. Offers royalty of 5% of retail price. No advance. Published 8 titles last year. Will send free catalog to writer on request. Will consider photocopied submissions and simultaneous submissions. Query for nonfiction. Reports in 1 month. Enclose return postage.
Nonfiction: Books of regional interest. Fishing, gardening, shelling in Florida. Also publishes some cookbooks of Southern emphasis. Should be straightforward, how-to style with consideration for the hobbyist or sportsman who needs the basic facts without flowery phrasing. "No other publisher is geared to the tourist market in Florida. Our books are low-cost and especially suited to their market." Would like to see more shell books with illustrations. No personal narratives. Department editors: Joyce Allyn, cooking, nature, recreation; Charles Allyn, self-help and how-to. Length: cooking, 9,000-17,000 words; nature, 52,000-90,000 words; self-help, how-to, sports, hobbies, recreation and pets, 9,000-17,000 words.

GREEN TREE PUBLISHING CO., LTD., 95 Grinity St., Toronto, Ontario, Canada M5A 3C7. (416)869-3321. Editor-in-Chief: W.H.P. Parr. Publishes hardcover and paperback originals. Pays 10% royalty; advance "depends on how badly we want the book. We've paid up to $3,500 and in many cases just a lunch." Published 15 titles in 1978; plans 15 in 1979 and 15-20 in 1980. Simultaneous submissions OK "if we're given a date by which we must respond and given the book if we offer the best deal." Reports in 1-2 months. SAE and International Reply Coupons.

Nonfiction: Publishes business; economics; history; hobbies; how-to; humor; juveniles (adventure); politics; psychology (self-help type); reference; self-help; sociology; and textbooks. "We are a Canadian firm and publish for our market. In the craft and self-help line, there is no border. We are big on trains and welcome just about anything. No more poetry please." Query.

Special needs: Hobby/craft books. "Technical, simple and cheap to carry out."

WARREN H. GREEN, INC., 8356 Olive Blvd., St. Louis MO 63132. Editor: Warren H. Green. Publishes hardcover originals. Offers "10-20% sliding scale of royalties based on quantity distributed. All books are short run, highly specialized, with no advance." About 5% of books are subsidy published. Published 51 titles in 1978; plans 63 in 1979 and 75 in 1980. "37% of total marketing is overseas." Will send a catalog to a writer on request. Will consider photocopied submissions. Submit outline and sample chapters. "Publisher requires 300- to 500-word statement of scope, plan, and purpose of book, together with curriculum vitae of author." Reports in 60-90 days.

Medical and Scientific: "Specialty monographs for practicing physicians and medical researchers. Books of 160 pages upward. Illustrated as required by subject. Medical books are non-textbook type, usually specialties within specialties, and no general books for a given specialty. For example, separate books on each facet of radiology, and not one complete book on radiology. Authors must be authorities in their chosen fields and accepted as such by their peers. Books should be designed for all doctors in English-speaking world engaged in full or part-time activity discussed in book. We would like to increase publications in the fields of radiology, anesthesiology, pathology, psychiatry, surgery and orthopedic surgery, obstetrics and gynecology, and speech and hearing. Recently published *Nursing Care for Myocardial Infarction*, by M. Rubin (nursing); and *Ultrasonography*, by Brown (radiology).

Education: "Reference books for elementary and secondary school teachers. Authors must be authorities in their fields. No textbooks."

THE STEPHEN GREENE PRESS, Box 1000, Brattleboro VT 05301. (802)257-7757. Editorial Director: Castle Freeman Jr. Publishes hardcover and paperback originals (99%); hardcover and paperback reprints (1%). Royalty "variable; advances are small." "Ask for our list of submission requirements with your query. Refer to Chicago *Manual of Style, Elements of Style, Words into Type.*" Send contact sheet or prints to illustrate ms. Photocopied submissions OK. Reports in 2-3 months. SASE. Book catalog for SASE.

Nonfiction: Americana; biography; cookbooks, cooking and foods; history; how-to (self-reliance); nature and environment; recreation; self-help; sports (outdoor and horse); popular technology; and regional (New England). Recently published *Dowsing for Everyone*, by Howells (how-to); and *Cross-Country Skiing Today*, by Caldwell (outdoor sports).

GREENLEAF CLASSICS, INC., Box 20194, San Diego CA 92120. Editorial Director: Douglas Saito. Managing Editor: James Koelmel. Estab. 1961. Publishes paperback originals. Specializes in adult erotic fiction. Publishes 360 titles/year. Pays by outright purchase price on acceptance. Photocopied submissions OK. Reports in 2-4 weeks. SASE. Writer's guidelines for SASE.

Fiction: Erotic novels. "All stories must have a sexual theme. They must be mainstream novels dealing with the serious problems of everyday people. All plots are structured so that characters must get involved in erotic situations. Write from the female viewpoint. Request our guidelines before beginning any project for us." Preferred length: 35,000 words. Submit complete ms.

GREENWICH PRESS, 335 Bleecker St., New York NY 10014. Editor: Anton Hardt. Publishes hardcover originals and reprints. Query. Enclose return postage.

Nonfiction: "Books only on the subject of antiques and possibly allied fields."

GREGG DIVISION, McGraw-Hill Book Co., 1221 Avenue of the Americas, New York NY 10020. Vice President and General Manager: Charles B. Harrington. Publishes hardcover and paperback originals. "Contracts negotiable; no advances." Query. "We accept very few unsolicited mss." Reports in 1-2 months. Enclose return postage with query.

Textbooks: "Textbooks and related instructional materials for the career education market."

Publishes books on typewriting, office education, shorthand, accounting and data processing, distribution and marketing, agriculture, trade and industrial education, health and consumer education and adult/continuing education. Recently published *Preparing for a Home Economics Career*, by Jacoby (career educaton); *Modern Business English*, by Wittenberg and Voiles (business education; and *The Auto Book*, by Crouse (technical education).

GROSSETT AND DUNLAP, INC., (including Tempo Teenage Paperbacks and Universal Library), 51 Madison Ave., New York NY 10010. (212)689-9200. Editor-in-Chief: Robert Markel. Publishes hardcover and paperback originals and reprints, as well as a "very few" translations, and anthologies "on occasion." Royalty and advance terms generally vary. Published "close to 400" titles last year. Will send a catalog to a writer on request. Send query letter, outline, or sample chapter only; do not send complete ms. "We do not accept unsolicited manuscripts." Reports in 3-5 weeks. SASE.
General Fiction: "Very seldom—usually only via literary agent."
General Nonfiction and Reference: "No limits—anything and everything that would interest the 'average' American reader: sports, health, ecology, etc." Interested in history, science, religion, biography, the arts, and literature. Favors writers with strong experience and good credits.
Juveniles and Teen: Editor-in-Chief, Children's Picture Books: Doris Duenewald.

GROVE PRESS. 196 W. Houston St., New York NY 10014. Editoral Director: Barney Rosset. Senior Editor: Kent Carroll. Imprints include Evergreen and Black Cat books. Publishes hardcover and papberback originals and paperback reprints. Publishes 35 titles/year. Pays standard royalty; advance. Photocopied submissions OK. SASE. Reports in 3-6 weeks. Free book catalog.
Nonfiction: "We have published investigative works on important issues, Eastern religion and philosophy, transactional analysis psychology books, biographies, consumer information manuals and digests. We do not want cookbooks, how-to, crafts or children's literature." Query or Submit outline/synopsis and sample chapters. Recently published *Terror or Love? The Personal Account of a West German Urban Guerrilla*, by Michael Baumann (biography/political science); *New Age Training for Fitness and Health*, by Dyveke Spino (health); *Give Sorrow Words: Maryse Holder's Letters From Mexico* (literary journal); and *Kicking It: The New Way to Stop Smoking Permanently*, by David Gelsinger (consumer information/psychology).
Fiction: "We are looking for high quality fiction and drama." Submit outline/synopsis and sample chapters. Recently published *Gates of Fire*, by Elwyn Chamberlain (India in 1970s); *The Woods*, by David Mamet (off-Broadway play); *Mulligan Stew*, by Gilbert Sorrentino (novel); *The Intimacy*, by August Coppola (first novel); and *American Hurrah and Other Plays*, by Jean-Claude van Itallie (collection of plays).

GROUPWORK TODAY, INC., Box 258, South Plainfield NJ 07080. Editor-in-Chief: Harry E. Moore Jr. Publishes hardcover and paperback originals. Published 2 titles in 1978; plans 8 in 1979, 8 in 1980. Offers $100 advance against royalties on receipt of contract; 10% of gross receipts from sale of book. "If a book is of special value, we will pay 10% of gross earnings on first 1,000 copies and 15% thereafter." Average advance is $100. Books are marketed by direct mail to Groupwork Agency executives and professionals (YMCA, YWCA, Scouts, Salvation Army, colleges, directors of organized camps, and libraries.) Will send catalog to a writer for SASE with 28¢ in stamps. "Also will answer specific questions from an author considering us as a publisher." Will not consider simultaneous submissions. Submit outline and sample chapters for nonfiction. Reports in 6-8 weeks. Enclose return postage.
Nonfiction: "We are publishers of books and materials for professionals and volunteers who work with people in groups. Some of our materials are also suited to the needs of professionals who work with individuals. Groupwork agency management, finance, program development and personnel development are among the subjects of interest to us. Writers must be thoroughly familiar with 'people work' and have fresh insights to offer. New writers are most welcome here. Lengths are open but usually run 30,000-50,000 words." Readers are mainly social agency administrators and professional staff members. Groupwork materials are also read by volunteers serving in the social agencies. Mss are judged by experienced professionals in social agencies. The company is advised on policy direction by a council of advisors from national agencies and colleges across the nation. "We also are publishing our 'Seminar' series to deal with the most important problems with which social work agencies must deal today."

GUIDANCE CENTRE, Faculty of Education, University of Toronto, 1000 Yonge St., Toronto, Ontario, Canada M4W 2K8. (416)978-3210. Editorial Director: S.J. Totton. Senior Editor: Hazel Ross. Publishes hardcover and paperback originals. Published 20 titles in 1978. Pays in royalties. Reports in 1 month. Submissions returned "only if Canadian postage is sent." Free book catalog.

Nonfiction: "The Guidance Centre is interested in publications related to career planning and guidance and in measurement and evaluation. Also general education. No manuscripts which have confined their references and illustrations to United States material." Submit complete ms. Consult Chicago *Manual of Style*. Recently published *Saturday's Stepchildren*, by S. Shack; and *Population and Canada*, by M. Barrett/C. Taylor.

*GULF PUBLISHING CO., Box 2608, Houston TX 77001. (713)529-4301. Editor-in-Chief: C.A. Umbach Jr. Senior Editor: B.J. Lowe. Publishes hardcover originals. Pays 10% royalty; advance averages $300-2,000. Published 36 titles in 1978; plans 48 in 1979, 45-50 in 1980. Subsidy publishes 1-2 titles a year. Simultaneous and photocopied submissions OK. Reports in 1-2 months. SASE. Free book catalog.

Nonfiction: Business, reference, regional trade, regional gardening, scientific and self-help.

H.P. BOOKS, Box 5367, Tucson AZ 85703. Senior Editor: Jonathan Latimer. Publishes hardcover and paperback originals. Specializes in how-to books in several fields, all photo-illustrated. Pays royalty; advance negotiable. Publishes 12 titles/year. Simultaneous and photocopied submissions OK. Reports in 2-4 weeks. SASE. Free book catalog.

Nonfiction: Cookbooks, cooking and foods; hobbies; how-to; leisure activities; photography; automotive; recreation; self-help; and technical books. All books are 160 pages minimum; "word count varies with the format." Query and state number and type of illustrations available. Recently published *Chocolate Cookery*, by Mable Hoffman; *Nikon Cameras*, by Carl Shipman; *Western Home Landscaping*, by Ken Smith; and *How to Rebuild Your Small-Block Ford*, by Tom Monroe.

HAMMOND, INC., 515 Valley St., Maplewood NJ 07040. (201)763-6000. Acquisitions Editor: Dana L. Hammond. Hardcover and paperback originals. "Books are negotiated from flat fee for outright purchase to advances against standard royalties, depending on subject." Published 25 titles in 1978; plans 25 in 1979. Submit outline/synopsis and sample chapters. State availability of photos/illustrations. Simultanous submissions OK. Reports in 2-4 weeks. SASE. Book catalog for SASE.

Nonfiction: Publishes Americana, art, business, cookbooks, cooking and foods, history, hobbies, how-to, humor, nature, photography, recreation, reference, sports and travel books.

Recent Titles: *Discover Brunch*, by R. MacPherson (cookbook); *Living Longer*, by A. and D. Geller; and *Gomer's Budget Travel Directory*, by Gomer Lewis.

HANCOCK HOUSE PUBLISHERS, INC./BOOKS AMERICA. 12008 1st Ave. S., Seattle WA 98168. (206)243-1500. Published 6 titles in 1978; plans 14 in 1979.

Nonfiction: Publishes Americana, natural history guides, anthropology and do-it-yourself books.

HANCOCK HOUSE PUBLISHERS LTD., 3215 Island View Rd., Saanichton, British Columbia, Canada V05 1M0. Editor-in-Chief: David Hancock. Managing Editor: Robert Sward. Hardcover and paperback originals (97%) and reprints (3%). Pays 10% royalty; $100 minimum advance. Published 25 titles in 1978; plans 22 in 1979, 25 in 1980. State availability of photos and/or illustrations to accompany ms. Reports in 1-2 months. SAE and International Reply Coupons. Free book catalog.

Nonfiction: Publishes (in order of preference): nature, history, biography, reference, Americana (Canadian), cookbooks, cooking and foods, hobbies, how-to, juveniles, photography, recreation, self-help, sport and travel books. Query. Recently published *British Columbia: Our Land*, by P. St. Pierre; and *Our UFO Visitors*, by J. Magor.

HARCOURT BRACE JOVANOVICH, 757 3rd Ave., New York NY 10017. Director of Trade Books Department: Carol Hill. Publishes hardcover and paperback originals and reprints. SASE.

Adult Trade Hardcovers: "We regret that all unsolicited mss for hardcover trade publication must be returned unread. Only mss submitted by agents or recommended to us by advisors or actively solicited by us will be considered. However, we will consider queries or brief proposals."

Adult Trade Paperbacks: Editor-in-Chief: John Ferrone. Publishes original and reprint trade paperbacks under the Harvest imprint, including illustrated material, reprints of literary works, and novelty art, crafts and photography.

HARCOURT BRACE JOVANOVICH, INC., Juvenile Trade Division, 757 3rd Ave., New York NY 10017. (212)888-3947. Editorial Director: Barbara Lucas. Managing Editor: Anna Bier. Associate Editor: Nancy Rockwell. Assistant Editor: Sandra Kitain. Publishes hardcover and paperback originals. Published 30 titles in 1978; plans 40 in 1979, 45 in 1980. Pays 8-10% royalty; offers $1,500 average advance. Simultaneous (if indicated) and photocopied submissions OK. SASE. Reports in 2 months. Free catalog.
Nonfiction: "Easy-reading" nonfiction for juveniles. "Before submitting your manuscript, write to the Children's Book Editor and describe it briefly. Give its approximate word length and the age group for which it is planned." *Who's Running Your Life: A Look at Young People's Rights*, by Archer; *Mysteries of Nature*, by Caras; and *How to Play Power Tennis With Ease*, by Huse.
Fiction: Material for young adults and young people in the middle grades. Query. Recently published *The Clown of God*, by de Paola; *A Special Gift*, by Simon; and *The Island of the Grass King*, by Willard.

HARLEQUIN BOOKS, LTD., 220 Duncan Mill Rd., Don Mills, Ontario, Canada M3B 3J5. (416)445-5860. Editorial Director: George Glay. Senior Editor: Alice Johnson. Vice President, Publishing: Fred Kerner. Imprints include Harlequin Romances and Harlequin Presents. Estab. 1949. Publishes paperback originals. Published 191 titles in 1978; plans 240 in 1979, 288 in 1980. Pays royalty; offers advance. Photocopied submissions OK. SAE and International Reply Coupons. Reports in 3 months.
Fiction: "The usual Harlequin romance. Read many before trying to write one." Submit outline/synopsis and sample chapters.
Tips: "While the rewards are great if you hit, the odds against you are high as only approximately one manuscript in a thousand is accepted for publication."

HARPER & ROW PUBLISHERS, INC., 10 E. 53rd St., New York NY 10022. (212)593-7000. Vice President/Editor-in-Chief: M.S. Wyeth Jr. Editorial Coordinator: Peggy Jeanes. Imprints include T.Y. Crowell (521 5th Ave., New York NY 10017), Basic Books, Barnes & Noble, J.B. Lippincott Co. (521 5th Ave., New York NY 10017), and Harper & Row—San Francisco. Estab. 1817. Publishes hardcover and paperback originals, and paperback reprints. Publishes 400 titles/year. Pays 10-15% royalty; "the advance ranges from $3,000 to five and sometimes six figures. Simultaneous and photocopied submissions OK. SASE. Reports in 8-12 weeks.
Nonfiction: Americana, animals, art, biography, business/economics, cookbooks, cooking and foods, health, history, hobbies, how-to, humor, juveniles, music, nature, philosophy, photography, poetry, politics, psychology, recreation, reference, religion, science, self-help, sociology, sports, textbooks and travel. "No technical books." Submit outline/synopsis and sample chapters or submit complete ms. Recently published *In Search of History*, by Theodore H. White (memoir); *Feelings: Our Vital Signs*, by Willard Gaylin (psychology); and *White Nights: The Story of a Prisoner in Russia*, by Menachem Begin (autobiography).
Fiction: Adventure, fantasy, gothic, historical, mainstream, mystery, romance, science fiction, suspense, western and literary. "We look for a strong story line and exceptional literary talent. No self-indulgent, autobiographical fiction." Submit outline/synopsis and sample chapters or submit complete ms. Recently published *Six of One*, by Rita Mae Brown (mainstream); *Trial Run*, by Dick Francis (suspense); *Incandescence*, by Craig Nova (literary); *The Thorn Birds*, by Colleen McCullough (mainstream); *The Azanian Assignment*, by Iain Finlay (adventure/suspense); and *Blue in Chicago*, by Bette Howland (literary).

HART PUBLISHING CO., INC., 12 E. 12th St., New York NY 10003. (212)260-2430. Hardcover and paperback originals. Royalty of 5% of list price for paperbacks and hardcovers. Advance averages $1,500. Published 50 titles in 1979. Reports in 2-3 weeks. SASE.
Nonfiction: Publishes only nonfiction books on cooking, education, hobbies, how-to, psychology, recreation, reference, self-help and sociology. Query, submit outline and sample chapter or submit complete ms.
Special Needs: "We need crossword puzzles with reproducible art, quizzes, puzzles and original word games. We pay anywhere from $5-20 per piece, depending on length and merit. Payment is made immediately upon acceptance. All material must be accompanied by SASE. Replies will be made within 2 weeks."

HARVARD UNIVERSITY PRESS, 79 Garden St., Cambridge MA 02138. (617)495-2600. Director: Arthur J. Rosenthal. Editor-in-Chief: Maud Wilcox. Publishes hardcover and paperback originals and reprints. Published 116 titles in 1978; plans 120 in 1979, 120 in 1980. Free book catalog.

Fiction: "The Harvard Program in the Short Novel constitutes our sole work in fiction. Manuscripts of any previously unpublished short novel in the English language may be submitted at any time. Length: 25,000-60,000 words. An outright grant of $1,000 is made on acceptance. Program brochure available on request. Send completed mss to general editor William Goodman."

HARVEY HOUSE PUBLISHERS. 20 Waterside Plaza, New York NY 10010. Publisher: L.F. Reeves. Managing Editor: Larry Bograd. Publishes hardcover originals. Published 20 titles in 1979. Pays 5% minimum royalty; advance "depends on the manuscript." Simultaneous (if so informed) and photocopied submissions OK. Reports in 3 weeks. SASE. Book catalog for SASE.

Nonfiction: Juvenile leisure-time activity books. "We have successful books on skateboards, minicycles, hang gliding, etc. Our biography series "Star People" covers athletes; we have books on Dorothy Hamill, Tracy Austin, Janet Guthrie, Reggie Jackson and people in the news. Also occasional science books." No religious, self-help, strictly adult textbooks or travel books. Query.

Fiction: "We publish only a couple of novels a year. Recently, we have opted toward realistic fiction about contemporary problems—e.g., foster children, American Indians, etc. We are always looking for good picture books." No science fiction, romances, fantasy, talking animal stories or rehashed fairy tales. Query.

HASTINGS HOUSE PUBLISHERS, INC., 10 E. 40th St., New York NY 10016. (212)689-5400. Editor: Walter Frese. Hardcover and paperback originals (80%) and reprints (20%). 10% minimum royalty. Reports in 1-2 weeks. SASE. Free book catalog.

Nonfiction: Publishes Americana, biography; cookbooks, cooking and foods; history, humor, juveniles, photography, recreation, sports and travel. Query or submit outline/synopsis and sample chapters. Recently published *Food Processor Magic*, by Hemingway/DeLima (cooking); *Inside ABC-American Broadcasting Company's Rise to Power* by Sterling/Quinlan; *Martha's Vineyard in Color* by Lazarus/Vuillevmier (travel).

HAWTHORN BOOKS, INC., 260 Madison Ave., New York NY 10016. (212)725-7740. Executive Editor: Joan B. Nagy. Estab. 1952. Publishes hardcover and quality paperback originals and paperback reprints. Published 100 titles in 1978, 110 in 1979; plans 120 in 1980. Pays advance; royalty. Photocopied submissions OK. SASE. Reports in 3 weeks. Free book catalog.

Nonfiction: Biography, business/economics, cookbooks/cooking/food, health, history, how-to, politics, psychology, recreation, reference, self-help and sports. Query.

HAYDEN BOOK CO., INC., 50 Essex St., Rochelle Park NY 07662. (201)843-0550. Editorial Director: William Cook. Publishes hardcover and paperback originals. Published 60 titles in 1978; plans 60 in 1979, 60 in 1980. 12% royalty; offers "minimal" advance. Simultaneous (if so identified) and photocopied submissions OK. Reports in 6 weeks. SASE. Free book catalog.

Technical: Publishes technician-level and engineering texts and references in many subject areas (emphasis on electronics and computer science); text and references for hotel, restaurant and institution management and other personnel (emphasis on management, food service).

Textbooks: Texts and references for senior high schools, technical institutes and community colleges in English (literature and composition), computer sciences, mathematics and other subject areas.

HEALTH PROFESSION PUBLISHING, McGraw-Hill Book Co., 1221 Avenue of the Americas, New York NY 10020. General Manager: Patrick A. Clifford. Pays on royalty basis. SASE.

Textbooks: Publishes textbooks, major reference books and continuing education materials in the fields of medicine, dentistry, nursing and allied health.

D.C. HEATH & CO., 125 Spring St., Lexington MA 02173. (617)862-6650. Editor-in-Chief: Robert Runck. Economics and Math Editor: Robert Macek. History & Political Science Editor: Ann Knight. Science Editor: Stanley Galek. Biology & Psychology Editor: Harvey Panzis. Modern Languages Editor: Mario Hurtado. English Editor: Holt Johnson. General Manager, College Division: John Harney. Lexington Books: Michael McCarroll. Publishes hardcover and paperback textbooks and professional reference books. Published 187 titles in 1978; plans 189 in 1979, 183 in 1980. Offers standard royalty rates for textbooks. Free book catalog. Query. Reports in 4 weeks. "Final revised mss accepted are published within 1 year." SASE.

Textbooks: "Texts at the college level in sociology, psychology, history, political science, chemistry, math, physical science, economics, education, modern language and English." Length varies.

HELIOS PUBLISHING CO., INC., 150 W. 28th St., New York NY 10001.

HENDRICKS HOUSE, INC., 488 Greenwich St., New York NY 10013. (212)966-1765. Editorial Office: Putney VT 05346. Editor: Walter Hendricks. Publishes hardcover originals and hardcover and paperback reprints. Published 5 titles in 1978; plans 5 in 1979. Free book catalog. Photocopied submissions OK. Submit complete ms. Reports in 1 month. SASE.
Nonfiction: "Mainly educational." Publishes Americana, biography, history, philosophy, reference and textbooks.

*HERALD PRESS, Mennonite Publishing House, 616 Walnut Ave., Scottdale PA 15683. (412)887-8500. Book Editor: Paul M. Schrock. Estab. 1908. Publishes hardcover and paperback originals and reprints. Published 30 titles in 1978, 30 in 1979; plans 30 in 1980. Two or 3 titles a year are subsidized by church organizations. "Subsidy is accepted only for only for books sponsored by an official board or committee of the Mennonite Church to meet discriminating needs when a book is not otherwise economically feasible." Pays 10-15% royalty; no advance. Photocopied submissions OK. SASE. Catalog 50¢. Reports in 3 weeks.
Nonfiction: Biography (religious); cookbooks; history (church); how-to; juveniles; psychology (religion); reference (Mennonite); religion; self-help (Christian); sociology (of religion); and textbooks (Christian). Query. Recently published *Living in Christian Community*, by Art Gish (religious); *How-To-Write Your Memories*, by Katie Funk Wiebe (how-to); and *Making Decisions: A Guide for Couples*, by David R. Leaman (self-help).
Fiction: Adventure (juvenile); historical and religious. Query. Recently published *Mystery of the Lost Treasure*, by Ruth Nulton Moore (juvenile); *Michael Faraday, Father of Electronics*, by Charles Ludwig (historical); and *Caught in the Crossfire*, by Levi O. Keidel (religious).

*HERITAGE BOOKS, INC., 3602 Maureen, Bowie MD 20715. (301)464-1159. Editorial Director: Laird C. Towle. Publishes hardcover and paperback originals (20%) and reprints (80%). Published 7 titles in 1978; plans 8 in 1979, 8 in 1980. Co-publishes 20% of titles. "Quality of the book is of prime importance; next is its relevance to our fields of interest. Our co-publishers is done in collaboration with individuals, groups or organizations. We normally expect to participate extensively in the marketing of the book." 10% royalty; occasional advance. Simultaneous and photocopied submissions OK. Reports in 1 month. SASE. Free book catalog.
Nonfiction: "We particularly desire nonfiction titles dealing with history and genealogy including how-to and reference works, as well as conventional histories and genealogies. The titles should be either of national interest or restricted to New England. Other subject matter will be considered provided that it is of either national or New England interest. We prefer writers to query, submit an outline/synopsis, or submit a complete ms, in that order, depending on the stage the writer has reached in the preparation of his work." Recently published *Genealogical Periodical Annual Index, Vol. 15*, by Towle; *The History of Exeter, N.H.*, by Bell; and *The Architectural Heritage of the Merrimack*, by Howells.
For '80: "Our primary interest at the present time is in the development of a series of medically oriented books for the lay person. We are always interested in offering royalty contracts for good patient-oriented mss."

HERMAN PUBLISHING, 45 Newbury St., Boston MA 02116. Editor: M.J. Philips. Publishes hardcover and paperback originals. Published 20 in 1979; plans 18 in 1979, 20 in 1980. "Standard 10% royalty (7% on paperbacks) up to break-even point; higher beyond." Advance varies, depending on author's reputation and nature of book. Will send copy of current catalog on request. Send query, outline and sample chapter to C.A. Herman. Reports in 2 months, "longer if jammed up." SASE.
Nonfiction: Business, technical and general nonfiction; reference, science, hi-fi, music, antiques, gardening, cooking, the arts, health, self-improvement, psychology, travel, regional, religion, history, biography, ships, audio, acoustics, electronics, radio, TV, architecture, communications arts, engineering and technology, food service and home economics, health care and management, manufacturing and marketing. "It might be worth noting that we also perform a unique service. We will market to the book trade (and elsewhere possibly), books that may have been privately published by the author or by a small publisher. Naturally, we must first see a sample copy and be satisfied that we can market it." Writing must be factual and authoritative. No length limits.

HOLIDAY HOUSE, 18 E. 53rd St., New York NY 10022. (212)688-0085. Editorial Director: Margery Cuyler. Publishes hardcover originals. Published 27 titles in 1978; plans 30 1979. Pays in royalties; offers variable advance. Photocopied submissions OK. Reports in 2 months. SASE. Free book catalog.

Nonfiction and Fiction: General fiction and nonfiction for young readers—pre-school through high school. Submit outline/synopsis and sample chapters or complete ms. "No certified, insured or registered mail accepted."

HOLT, RINEHART & WINSTON OF CANADA, LTD., 55 Horner Ave., Toronto, Ontario Canada M8Z 4X6. (416)255-4491. School Editorial Director: Joan Smith. College Acquisitions Editor: Joe McKeon. Publishes hardcover and paperback text originals. Published 40 titles in 1978; plans 20 in 1979, 40 in 1980. Royalty varies according to type of book; pays $200-500 for anthologies. No advance. Simultaneous and photocopied submissions OK. Reports in 1-3 months. SAE and International Reply Coupons. Free book catalog.

Nonfiction: Education texts. Query. Recently published *Essentials of Canadian Managerial Finance*, by Weston, Brigham, Halpem (college finance text); *Inside, Outside*, by Jack Booth (elementary language arts text).

Fiction: "Interested in fiction with realistic Canadian background." No science fiction or romances. Query.

HORIZON PRESS, 156 5th Ave., New York NY 10010. Royalty schedule standard scale from 10% to 15%. Published 80 titles in 1978. Free book catalog. Prefers complete ms. Reports in 6 weeks. SASE.

Nonfiction: History, literature, science, biography, the arts, general. Length: 40,000 words and up. Recently published *The Encyclopedia of Jazz in the Seventies*, by L. Feather; *Understanding Human Nature*, by J.K. Feibleman; and *Witnessing: The Seventies*, by S. Bernard.

Fiction: Recently published *A Kingdom*, by James Hanley and *The Wish Sonata*, by James Hanley.

HOUGHTON MIFFLIN CO., 2 Park St., Boston MA 02107. (617)725-5000. Editor-in-Chief: Austin G. Olney. Managing Editor: David B. Harris. Hardcover and paperback originals (95%) and paperback reprints (5%). Royalty of 7½% for paperbacks; 10-15% on sliding scale for standard fiction and nonfiction; advance varies widely. Published 148 titles in 1978; plans 150 in 1979, 150 in 1980. Simultaneous submissions and photocopied submissions OK. Reports in 4 weeks. SASE. Free book catalog.

Nonfiction: Americana, animals, biography, cookbooks/cooking/food, health, history, how-to, juveniles, poetry, politics, psychology and self-help. Query. Recently published *The Bunker*, by James P. O'Donnell (history); *Travels With Henry*, By Richard Valeriani (politics); and *Taking Chances*, by Robert T. Lewis (psychology).

Fiction: Historical, mainstream, mystery and suspence. Query. Recently published *Gulliver House*, by John Leggett (mainstream); *Special Effects*, by Harriet Frank Jr. (mainstream); and *The Maine Massacre*, by Janwillem van de Wetering (suspense).

HOUSE OF ANANSI PRESS, LTD., 35 Britain St., Toronto, Ontario, Canada M5A 1R7. (416)363-5444. Editorial Director: James Polk. Managing Editor: Ann Wall. Hardcover and paperback originals 99% and paperback (out-of-print important Canadiana) reprints 1%. Royalty "varies, depending whether we publish the book first in hardcover or paperback or both; not less than 8%;" advance averages $500. "but we also participate in the author subsidy plan of the Ontario Arts Council, and through them can offer up to $3,000." Query, submit outline/synopsis and sample chapters or complete ms. "We're flexible, but prefer for nonfiction to have a pretty good idea of what we're going to get. Don't send photos or illustrations with first submission. Tell us about them and if we are interested in the writing, we'll talk about those later." Photocopies submissions OK. Reports in 1-2 months. SASE. Free book catalog. Publishes Canadian authors only.

Nonfiction: Publishes biography; history; law; medicine and psychiatry; music; philosophy; poetry; politics; pyschology; and sociology books. "we have no length requirement. A book should be as long as it has to be to cover its topic adequetely, and no longer. the slant should be toward the general reader with some university education. We like well-researched but not heavy or over-footnoted books." Recently published *Six Journeys: A Canadian Pattern*, by C. Taylor (biographies); and *George Grant in Process: Essays on Conversations*, edited by L. Schmidt.

Fiction: Publishes experimental books. Recently published *The Rosedale Hoax*, by R. Wyatt and *The Garden of Delights*, by R. Carrier.

CARL HUNGNESS PUBLISHING, Box 24308, Speedway IN 46224. (317)244-4792. Editorial Director: Carl Hungness. Senior Editor: John Mahoney. Publishes hardcover and paperback originals. Published 4 titles in 1977, 5 in 1978; plans 7 in 1979. Pays "negotiable" outright purchase; advance averages $500. Reports in 3 weeks. SASE. Free book catalog.
Nonfiction: Stories relating to professional automobile racing. No sports car racing or drag racing material. Query. Recently published *Indianapolis 500 Yearbook*, by C. Hungness and others (historical); and *The Mighty Midgets*, by J.C. Fox (historical).

HURTIG PUBLISHERS, 10560 105th St., Edmonton, Alberta, Canada T5H 2W7. (403)426-2359. Editor-in-Chief: Sarah Reid. Hardcover and paperback originals (80%) and reprints (20%). 10% royalty on first 7,000 copies; 12% on next 1,000; 15% thereafter. Advance averages $500-1,000. State availablity of photos and/or illustrations to accompany ms. Photocopied submissions OK. Reports in 1-2 months. SASE. Free book catalog.
Nonfiction: Publishes biographies of well-known Canadians; cookbooks, cooking and foods; Canadian history; humor; nature; topical Canadian politics; reference (Canadian); and material about native Canadians. No reminiscences. Query or submit outline/synopsis and sample chapters; or submit complete ms. Recently published *Great Canadian Animal Stories*, edited by M. Whitaker (juvenile anthology); *Mountains of Canada*, by R. Morse (photography); *Faces From History*, by G. Woodcock (history and photographs); *Joy of Hockey*, by E. Nicol and D. More (humor); *Life among the Qallunaat*, by M. Freeman (autobiography).

*HWONG PUBLISHING CO., 10353 Los Alamitos Blvd. Los Alamitos CA 90720. Editor-in-Chief: Hilmi Ibrahim. Managing Editor: Ann Kilbride. Specializes in college textbooks, minorities literature, and Chinese publications. Textbook areas: social sciences, history, humanities, business, and science. Some fiction, biographies and other subjects published on a subsidy basis. Submit complete manuscript. Include any prints of photos and/or illustrations. Simultaneous photocopied submissions OK. Reports in 2-4 weeks. SASE. Publishes paperback originals and some hardcover. Recently published: *American Ethnics and Minorities* (textbook). *The Complete Book on Disco and Ballroom Dancing*, and *The Complete Travel Guide to China*.

*IDEAL WORLD PUBLISHING CO., Box 1237-EG, Melbourne FL 32935. New Idea Publishing Co. is a division of Ideal World Publishing Co. Editor: Harold Pallatz. Publishes hardcover and paperback originals and reprints. Offers subsidy publication of "difficult-to-place" manuscripts. "If the book looks like it might sell, but we are not certain of exact demand, then, instead of outright rejection, we will try subsidy. Costs vary between $50-100 for very simple booklets, depending upon number of pages, copies, text, etc." Published 5 titles in 1978; plans 5 in 1979, 25 in 1980. Will consider photocopied submissions. Query. Reports in 2-4 weeks. *"No material will be returned unless SASE is attached."*
Health: "Natural approaches to good health through nutrition, herbs, vegetarianism, vitamins, unusual medical approaches for specific ailments, particularly from authorities in the field. Any style is acceptable, but it must hold the reader's attention and make for fairly smooth nonintensive (no brain taxation) requirements. Ideas should be in a simple, easygoing pace."

IDEALS PUBLISHING CORP., 11315 Watertown Plank Rd., Milwaukee WI 53226. Editorial Director: James A. Kuse. Estab. 1944. Publishes hardcover and paperback originals, and greeting booklets. Published 68 titles in 1978; plans 78 in 1979. Pays on royalty basis. "Good" photocopied submissions OK. SASE. Reports in 4-6 weeks. Sample copy on request.
Poetry: Seasonal and suitable for all types of greetings.
Nonfiction: Juvenile, cookbooks and religious or inspirational.
Photography: 4x5 or 8x10 transparencies; include consignment sheet.

INDEPENDENCE PRESS, Drawer HH, 3225 S. Noland Rd., Independence MO 64055. (816)252-5010. Editorial Director: Margaret Baldwin. Publishes hardcover and paperback originals (50%) and paperback reprints (50%). Publishes 5 titles/year. Pays 10-12½-15% royalty; advance averages $200. Simultaneous and photocopied submissions OK. Reports in 2 months. SASE. Book catalog 50¢.
Nonfiction: "Very interested in books with strictly local themes and settings. Kansas City history, Independence history, Missouri history, well-known local figures or sports personalities; local outlaws such as Jesse and Frank James, Quantrill, the Youngers; books on political figures such as Tom Pendergast, etc. All material should be well-researched, preferably by experts in the field. Material should be geared to the general reading public." Submit outline/synopsis and sample chapters *only*, along with a brief biographical sketch of

author. Recently published *Independence, Missouri,* by B. Foerster, Ph.D.; and *Images of Greatness,* by D. Melton.

Fiction: "Fiction for young people including books of local themes either historical or current." Science fiction; adventure; mystery; for young people (no sex, clean language, little violence); westerns, and sports. "We like action stories with girls for central characters. No storybooks for grades pre-school through 3rd grade will be accepted. We do not publish in this field any longer." Query or submit outline/synopsis and sample chapters. Recently published *The Green Recruit,* by Gary Paulsen; and *The Ghost Boy of El Toro,* by Ida Chittum.

INDIANA UNIVERSITY PRESS, 10th & Morton Sts., Bloomington IN 47401. (812)337-4203. Director: John Gallman. Publishes hardcover and paperback originals (75%) and paperback reprints (25%). Published 72 titles in 1978; plans 75 in 1979. Pays 10% royalty; occasional advance. Photocopied submissions OK. Reports in 2 months. SASE. Free book catalog.

Nonfiction: Scholarly books on humanities, history, philosophy, translations, semiotics, public policy, film, music, linguistics, social sciences, regional materials and serious nonfiction for the general reader. Query or submit outline/synopsis and sample chapters. "Queries should include as much descriptive material as is necessary to convey scope and market appeal to us." Recently published *A Theory of Semiotics,* by U. Eco; *Shakespeare on Film,* by J. Jorgens (film/literature criticism); and *How Animals Communicate,* edited by T. Sebeok.

Fiction: "Only translations of fiction are published." Query or submit outline/synopsis and sample chapters.

*INSTITUTE FOR THE STUDY OF HUMAN ISSUES. (ISHI Publications). 3401 Market St., Suite 252, Philadelphia PA 19104. (215)387-9002. Director of Publications: Betty C. Jutkowitz. Managing Editor: Douglas C. Gordon. Publishes hardcover and paperback originals (85%) and hardcover reprints (15%). Published 20 titles in 1978; plans 20 in 1979, 25 in 1980. Subsidy publishes 10% of books. "Some of our books are partly subsidized by grants from other institutions, but we never ask money from an author. When financial support for a particular book (or series of books) is necessary, we seek funding from appropriate institutions." Pays 10-12½% royalty; no advance. Photocopied submissions OK. Reports in 3 months. SASE. Free book catalog.

Nonfiction: Books on political science, history, anthropology, folklore, sociology, narcotics and macro-economics, suitable for scholars in these fields. Submit outline/synopsis and sample chapters. Recently published *Essays in Understanding Latin America,* by K.H. Silvert (political science); *Origins of the State,* edited by R. Cohen and E.R. Service (anthropology); and *Red Years/Black Years: A Political History of Spanish Anarchism, 1911-1937,* by R.W. Kern (history).

*INTERMEDIA PRESS, Box 3294, Vancouver, British Columbia, Canada V6B 3X9. (604)681-3592. Editors-in-Chief: Henry Rappaport; Edwin Varney. Hardcover and paperback originals. Published 12 titles in 978; plans 10 in 1979 and in 1980. Pays 7% royalty; occasionally offers advance. Query, or submit outline/synopsis and sample chapters or complete ms. State availability of photos and/or illustrations. Reports in 2-4 months. SASE. Book catalog $1.

Nonfiction: Karl Bergman, Managing Editor. Publishes art (avant-garde, personal); cookbooks, cooking and foods; erotica (in a literary context); humor (absurdist); juveniles; multimedia material; poetry; recreation; sports; textbooks; and travel books. Recently published *The Coffee Lover's Handbook,* by Cathy Ford and Dona Sturmanis; and *New West Coast,* edited by F. Candelaria (poetry anthology).

Fiction: Dona Sturmanis, Managing Editor. Publishes erotica; experimental; fantasy; historical (with a Canadian content); humorous; mainstream; and science fiction books. Recently published *The Immigrant,* by G. Szohner; *Stories for Late Night Drinkers,* by M. Tremblay; and *16 Ways to Skin a Cat,* by G. Seanto.

Special Needs: "We are especially interested in juvenile and trade books. Anthologies of poetry and fiction also."

INTERNATIONAL MARINE PUBLISHING CO., 21 Elm St., Camden ME 04843. Managing Editor: Kathleen Brandes. Editor: Bruce White. Publishes primarily hardcover originals and reprints. Published 13 titles in 1978; plans 15 in 1979, 16 in 1980. "Standard royalties, with advances." Free book catalog. "Material in all stages welcome. Query invited, but not necessary." Reports in 6 weeks. Enclose return postage.

Marine Nonfiction: "Marine nonfiction only—but a wide range of subjects within that category: fishing, boatbuilding, boat design, yachting, sea ecology and conservation, maritime history, true sea adventure, etc. —anything to do with boats, lakes, rivers, seas, and the people who do things on them, commercially or for pleasure. No word length requirements. Pictorial books with short texts are as welcome as 60,000-word mss." Recently published *The Charter Game*, by R. Norgrove (boat chartering); and *Building the St. Pierre Dory*, by M. White (boatbuilding).

INTERNATIONAL SELF-COUNSEL PRESS, LTD., 306 W. 25th St., North Vancouver, British Columbia, Canada V7N 2G1. (604)986-3366. Editorial Director: Jack James. Legal Editor: Heather Fayers. Publishes paperback originals. Published 35-40 titles in 1978; will do 35-40 in 1979. Pays 10% royalty; no advance. Simultaneous and photocopied submissions OK. Reports in 2 weeks. SASE. Free book catalog.
Nonfiction: "Books only on law and business for the layperson (how-to)." Submit outline/synopsis and sample chapters. Follow Chicago *Manual of Style*. Recently published *You and the Police*, by R. Stoll; *Divorce Guide for Oregon*, by K. Lamar; and *Our Accountant's Guide for Small Business*, by C.G. Cornish.

INTERNATIONAL WEALTH SUCCESS, Box 186, Merrick NY 11566. (516)766-5850. Editor: Tyler G. Hicks. Published 6 titles in 1978; plans 8 in 1979, 10 in 1980. Pays 10% royalty. Usual advance is $1,000, but this varies, depending on author's reputation and nature of book. Will consider photocopied submissions. Query. Reports in 4 weeks. enlose return postage.
Self-Help and How-to: "Techniques, methods, sources for building wealth. Highly personal, how-to-do-it with plenty of case histories. Books are aimed at the wealth builder and are highly sympathetic to his and her problems." Financing, business success, venture capital, etc. Length 60,000-70,000 words.
Tips: "Concentrate on practical, hands-on books showing people how to build wealth today, starting with very little cash. Most of the manuscripts we get today assume that everyone has money to invest in gold, rare coins, stocks, etc. This is not so! There are millions who haven't made it yet. This is *our* audience, an audience that can build great wealth for a writer who tells these people what to do, where to do it and how to do it. Forget theories; concentrate on the day-to-day business of making money from one's own business and you've got it made!"

THE INTERSTATE PRINTERS AND PUBLISHERS, INC., 19-27 N. Jackson St., Danville IL 61832. (217)446-0500. Editor-in-Chief: R. L. Guin. Managing Editor: Ronald McDaniel. Hardcover and paperback originals. Published 60 titles in 1978; plans 50-60 in 1979, 50-60 in 1980. Usual royalty is 10% of wholesale price; no advance. Publishes about 60 titles/year. Markets books by mail and exhibits to all elementary, junior/middle and high schools in the US. Reports in 1-2 months. SASE. Free book catalog.
Nonfiction: Publishes textbooks; agriculture; special education; trade and industrial; home economics; athletics; career education; outdoor education; school law; marriage counseling; and learning disabilities books. Query or submit outline/synopsis and sample chapters. Recently published *Modern Agricultural Mechanics*, by T.J. Wakeman; and *Animal Science*, by M.E. Ensminger.

INTERVARSITY PRESS, Box F, Downers Grove IL 60515. (312)964-5700. Editorial Director: James W. Sire. Publishes hardcover and paperback originals. Published 42 titles in 1978; plans 45 in 1979. Pays 10% royalty; advance averages $500. Photocopied submissions OK. Reports in 16 weeks. SASE. Free book catalog.
Nonfiction: "InterVarsity Press publishes books geared to the presentation of Biblical Christianity in its various relations to personal life, art, literature, sociology, psychology, philosphy, history and so forth. Though we are primarily publishers of trade books, we are cognizant of the textbook market at the college, university and seminary level within the general religious field. The audience for which the books are published is composed primarily of university students and graduates; stylistic treatment varies from topic to topic and from fairly simplified popularizations for college freshmen to extremely scholarly works primarily designed to be read by scholars." Query or submit outline/synopsis and sample chapters. Recently published *Fire in the Fireplace: Contemporary Charismatic Renewal*, by C. Hummel (theology); *Rich Christians in an Age of Hunger*, by R. Sider (practical theology); and *Developing a Christian Mind*, by N. Barcus (humanities).

*IOWA STATE UNIVERSITY PRESS. S. State Ave., Ames IA 50010. (515)294-5280. Director: Merritt Bailey. Managing Editor: Rowena Malone. Hardcover and paperback originals. Pays 10-12½-15% royalty; no advance. Subsidy publishes 10-50% of titles, based on potential of book and contribution to scholarship. Published 40 titles in 1978; plans 35 in 1979, 35 in 1980. Send b&w glossy prints to illustrate ms. Simultaneous submissions OK, if advised;

photocopied submissions OK if accompanied by an explanation. Reports in 2-4 months. SASE. Free book catalog.

Nonfiction: Publishes biography, history, recreation, reference, scientific technical, textbooks and Iowana books. Submit outline/synopsis and sample chapters; must be double-spaced throughout. Recently published *Physics of Stereo/Quad Sound,* by J.G. Traylor (audio reference); *Those Radio Commentators,* by I.E. Fang (biography); and *Family Afoot,* by E. Young (travel).

JANUS BOOK PUBLISHERS, 3541 Investment Bldg., Suite 5, Hayward CA 94545. (415)785-9625. Vice President: Charles Kahn. Published 8 titles in 1978; plans 12 in 1979. Pays 4-10% royalty or outright purchase; average advance. Query or submit outline/synopsis and sample chapters. SASE. Reports in 3 weeks. Free book catalog.

Nonfiction: "We publish work texts written at a 2.5 reading level for young adults with limited reading ability." Recently published *Reading a Newspaper,* by Larned and Randall; and *Getting Around Cities and Towns,* by Roderman.

JOHNS HOPKINS UNIVERSITY PRESS, Baltimore MD 21218. Editorial Director: Andrea Richter. Publishes mostly clothbound originals and paperback reprints; some paperback originals. Published 97 titles in 1978; plans 95 in 1979, 95 in 1980. Payment varies; contract negotiated with author. Reports in 2 months. SASE.

Nonfiction: Publishes scholarly books and journals, biomedical sciences, history, literary theory and criticism, wildlife biology and management, psychology, political science, regional material, and economics. Query. Length: 50,000 words minimum.

Fiction: Occasional fiction by invitation only.

JONATHAN DAVID PUBLISHERS, 68-22 Eliot Ave., Middle Village NY 11379. (212)456-8611. Editor-in-Chief: Alfred J. Kolatch. Publishes hardcover and paperback originals. Published 25 titles in 1978; plans 28 in 1979. Pays 10-15% royalty, or by outright purchase of $1,000-3,000; offers $2,500 average advance. Reports in 3 weeks. SASE. Free catalog.

Nonfiction: Adult nonfiction books for a general audience. Americana, cookbooks, cooking and foods, how-to, recreation, reference, self-help and sports. "We are open to any worthwhile manuscript. Query. Recently published *Completely Cheese,* by Anita May Pearl (food); *The Lilt of the Irish,* by Henry Spalding (folklore and humor); and *The Football Handbook,* by Sam DeLuca (sports).

JOSSEY-BASS, INC., PUBLISHERS, 433 California St., San Francisco CA 94104. (415)433-1740. Editorial Director: Allen Jossey-Bass. Senior Editors: J.B. Hefferlin, Higher Education; William E. Henry, Social and Behavioral Science. Publishes hardcover originals. Published 75 titles in 1978; plans 75 in 1979, 75-100 in 1980. Pays 10-15% royalty; no advance. Simultaneous (if so informed) and photocopied submissions OK. Reports in 4 weeks. SASE. Free book catalog.

Nonfiction: Professional, scholarly books for senior administrators, faculty, researchers, graduate students, and professionals in private practice. Research-based books developed for practical application. "We do not want undergraduate texts or collections of previously published materials." Submit outline/synopsis and sample chapters. Recently published *Problem-Solving Therapy,* by J. Haley (social and behavioral science); *The Open University,* by W. Perry (higher education series); and *Handbook of Institutional Advancement,* edited by A.W. Rowland.

JOVE PUBLICATIONS, 757 3rd Ave., New York NY 10017. Editor: Diana Levine. Publishes paperback originals and reprints. Published 180 titles in 1978; plans 200 in 1979, 200 in 1980. Pays 6-12% royalty; offers advance. Simultaneous and photocopied submissions OK. SASE. Reports in 1-2 months.

Nonfiction: Health, humor, psychology, religion and self-help. Submit mss through an agent. Recently published *Mommie Dearest,* by Christina Crawford (biography).

Fiction: Adventure, erotica, fantasy, historical, mystery, science fiction, suspense and western. Submit mss through agent. Recently published *Give of Golden Hair,* by Leslie Deane; *The Women's Room,* by Marlyn French; and John Jakes's bicentennial series *The Bastard, The Lawless, Furies* and *The Rebels* (historical saga).

JUDSON PRESS, Valley Forge PA 19481. (215)768-2116. Managing Editor: Harold L. Twiss. Publishes hardcover and paperback originals. Generally 10% royalty on first 7,500 copies; 12½% on next 7,500; 15% above 15,000. "Payment of an advance depends on author's

reputation and nature of book." Published 39 titles in 1978; plans 40 in 1979, 40 in 1980. Free book catalog. Query with outline and sample chapter. Reports in 3 months. Enclose return postage.
Religion: Adult religious nonfiction of 30,000-200,000 words. Recently published *Friends, Partners, and Lovers*, by Warren Molton; *Pastoral Counseling in Work Crises*, by H.H. Rightor; and *Memo to a Weary Sunday School Teacher*, by D.S. McCarthy.

WILLIAM KAUFMANN, INC., 1 1st St., Los Altos CA 94022. Editor-in-Chief: William Kaufmann. Hardcover and paperback originals (90%) and reprints (10%). "Generally offers standard minimum book contract of 10-12½-15% but special requirements of book may call for lower royalties"; no advance. Published 10 titles in 1978; plans 12 in 1979, 15 in 1978. State availability of photos and/or illustrations to accompany ms. Simultaneous and photocopied submissions OK. Reports in 1-2 months. SASE. Free book catalog.
Nonfiction: "We specialize in not being specialized; we look primarily for originality and quality." Publishes Americana; art; biography; business; economics; history; how-to; humor; medicine and psychiatry; nature; psychology; recreation; scientific; sports; and textbooks. Does not want to see cookbooks, novels, poetry, inspirational/religious and erotica. Query. Recently published *Chicken Soup and Other Medical Matters* by S. Harris; and *Authors by Profession*, by Victor Bonham-Carter.

KEATS PUBLISHING, INC., 36 Grove St., Box 876, New Canaan CT 06840. Editor: Ms. An Keats. Publishes hardcover and paperback originals and reprints, and two magazines on health and nutrition. Offers standard 10-12½-15% royalty contract. Advance varies. Free book catalog. Query with outline and sample chapter. Reports in 2 months. Enclose return postage.
Nonfiction: "Natural health, special interest; industry-subsidy. Also, mss with promotion and premium potential. In natural health, anything having to do with the current interest in ecology, natural health cookbooks, diet books, organic gardening, etc." Length: open.
Religion: "Largely in the conservative Protestant field."

J.J. KELLER & ASSOCIATES, INC., 145 W. Wisconsin Ave., Neenah WI 54956. (414)722-2848. President: John J. Keller. Publishes paperback originals. Payment by arrangement. Published 7 titles in 1978. Query. SASE.
Technical and Reference: "Working guides, handbooks and pamphlets covering the regulatory requirements for the motor carrier industry at both the federal and individual state levels. Technical and consumer publications pertaining to the International System of Units (Metric system of measurement)." Contact must be made in advance to determine applicability of subject matter and method of presentation. Recently published *National Backhaul Guide* (source directory); *Hazardous Materials Shipments* (reference); and *Multi-Day Logging* (reference).

KENT STATE UNIVERSITY PRESS, Kent State University, Kent OH 44242. (216)672-7913. Director: Paul H. Rohmann. Publishes hardcover originals. Standard minimum book contract; rarely offers advance. Published 12 titles in 1978. Free book catalog. "Always write a letter of inquiry before submitting mss. We can publish only a limited number of titles each year and can frequently tell in advance whether or not we would be interested in a particular ms. This practice saves both our time and that of the author, not to mention postage costs." Reports in 10 weeks. Enclose return postage.
Nonfiction: Especially interested in "scholarly works in history of high quality, particularly any titles of regional interest for Ohio. Also will consider scholarly biographies, social sciences, scientific research, the arts, and general nonfiction." Recently published *The Cistercians: Ideals and Reality*, by L.J. Lekai; *The Swastika Outside Germany*, by D.M. McKale; and *The Mapping of Ohio*, by T.H. Smith.

KIRKLEY PRESS, INC., Box 200, Timonium MD 21093. Editor: Walter Kirkley. Publishes paperback 16-page booklets. "We buy mss outright and pay upon acceptance. Payment (total) varies between $200 and $300, depending on subject and strength with which written. Sample of our material sent on request." Send complete ms. "We try to answer in 2 weeks." Enclose return postage.
Business: "We publish small booklets which are sold to businesses for distribution to the employee. They attempt to stimulate or motivate the employee to improve work habits. Basically they are pep talks for the employee. We need writers who are so close to the problems of present-day employee attitudes that they can take one of those problems and write about it in a warm, human, understanding, personal style and language that will appeal to the

employee and which the employer will find to his advantage to distribute to the employees." Length: 2,400-2,600 words.

B. KLEIN PUBLICATIONS, Box 8503, Coral Springs FL 33065. (305)752-1708. Editor-in-Chief: Bernard Klein. Hardcover and paperback originals. Specializes in directories, annuals, who's who type of books; bibliography, business opportunity, reference books. Published 7 titles in 1978; plans 7-10 in 1979, 7-10 in 1980. Pays 10% royalty, "but we're negotiable." Advance "depends on many factors." Markets books by direct mail and mail order. Simultaneous and photocopied submissions OK. Reports in 1-2 weeks. SASE. Catalog for SASE.

Nonfiction: Business, hobbies, how-to, reference, self-help, directories and bibliographies. Query or submit outline/synopsis and sample chapters or complete ms.

Current Titles: *Reference Encyclopedia of the American Indian*; *Your Business, Your Son and You*, by J. McQuaig (nonfiction); *Guide to American Directories*; and *Mail Order Business Directory*.

ALFRED A. KNOPF, INC., 201 E. 50th St., New York NY 10028. (212)751-2600. Senior Editor: Ashbel Green. Children's Book Editor: Ms. Pat Ross. Publishes hardcover and paperback originals (90%) and paperback reprints (10%). Publishes 123 titles in 1978; plans 135 in 1979. Royalties and advance "vary." Simultaneous (if so informed) and photocopied submissions OK. Reports in 2-4 weeks. Book catalog for SASE.

Nonfiction: Book-length nonfiction, including books of scholarly merit on special subjects. Preferred length: 40,000-150,000 words. "A good nonfiction writer should be able to follow the latest scholarship in any field of human knowledge, and fill in the abstractions of scholarship for the benefit of the general reader by means of good, concrete, sensory reporting." Query. Recently published *The Powers That Be*, by D. Halbertstam (public affairs); *Your Baby and Child*, by Penelope Beach (child care); and *The Shaping of a Behaviorist*, by B.F. Skinner (autobiography).

Fiction: Publishes book-length fiction of literary merit by known or unknown writers. Length: 30,000-150,000 words. Submit complete ms. Recently published *SS/6B*, by Len Deighton; *The Dog of the South*, by Charles Portis; and *Book of Days*, by Mary Robison.

JOHN KNOX PRESS, 341 Ponce de Leon Ave. NE, Atlanta GA 30308. (404)873-1531. Director: Richard A. Ray. Estab. 1865. Publishes hardcover and paperback originals and paperback reprints. Published 28 titles in 1978; plans 36 in 1979, 36 in 1980. Pays royalty; no advance. Photocopied submissions OK. SASE. Free book catalog.

Nonfiction: "We publish books dealing with Biblical studies, Christian faith and life, family relationships, Christian education, and the relationship of faith to history and culture." Query or submit outline/synopsis and sample chapters. Recently published *When In Doubt, Hug Em: How to Develop a Caring Church*, by Cecil B. Murphey; *Empowered: Living Experiences With God*, by Bowdon; *These Things Are Written: An Introduction to the Religious Ideas of the Bible*, by Efird; *The Asundered: Biblical Teachings of Divorce and Remarriage*, by Kysar; and *Bio-Babel: Can We Survive the New Biology*, by Utke.

KODANSHA INTERNATIONAL, LTD., 2-12-21 Otowa, Bunkyo-Ku, Tokyo 112, Japan. Hardcover originals and a limited number of paperback originals. Pays 3-8% royalty, either against sales or printing; determined case by case. Advance varies. Published 26 titles in 1978; plans 28 in 1979; 30 in 1980. Markets trade books through Harper & Row, by direct mail to Asian studies specialists. State availability of prints or transparencies to illustrate ms. Photocopied submissions OK. SAE and International Reply Coupons. Reports in 2-4 months. Free book catalog from 10 E. 53 St., New York NY 10022.

Nonfiction: "Books about Japan and the Far East of interest to American general readers or specialists. Translations of Japanese classics in all fields. Books on arts and crafts of highest quality." Oriental arts and crafts of the world, especially ceramics. Books on Oriental cooking; on economics related to Japan and Asia; how-to on arts and crafts and Oriental martial arts. Biography, philosophy, photography, politics, psychology, comparative religion, reference and sociology. Query. "We especially welcome innovative approaches to arts and crafts subjects. Currently, we are actively soliciting translations of previously untranslated modern Japanese fiction and classics of modern Japanese political science and sociology."

Recent Titles: *Introducing Japan*, by D. Richie and E. O. Reischauer; *The Voices and Hands of Bunraku*, by B. Adachi (dramatic arts); and *Washi: The World of Japanese Paper*, by S. Hughes (crafts).

LAKEWOOD BOOKS, 4 Park Ave., New York NY 10016. Editorial Director: Donald Wigal.

2

Publishes 96- and 64-page paperback originals. Published 38 titles in 1978; plans 38 in 1979, 38 in 1980. Pays 1% royalty per copy; about 50,000 copies of each title are printed; average advance. Simultaneous and photocopied submissions OK. SASE. Reports in 4-6 weeks.
Nonfiction: "Our books are apparently bought by women who have families, or are attracted to a rather middle-of-the-road life style. Our titles are mainly self-help (exercise, diet) and informational. We avoid controversial topics."
Tips: "Consider the competition and see what seems to be working. Find a slightly new approach and blend the tried and true with the innovative."

LAW-ARTS PUBLISHERS, 453 Greenwich St., New York NY 10013. Editorial Director: Joseph Taubman. Publishes hardcover and paperback originals (90%) and paperback reprints (10%). Published 7-10 titles in 1978; plans 10 in 1979. Pays 10% royalty; no advance. Simultaneous and photocopied submissions OK. Reports in 1 month. SASE. Free book catalog.
Nonfiction: Legal-related, in-depth textbooks; books on creative work, audiovisual techniques, management, publicity, etc. No photography books. Submit outline/synopsis and sample chapters. Recently published *Performing Arts Management and Law*, by J. Taubman; and *Professional Sports and the Law*, by L. Sobel.

SEYMOUR LAWRENCE, INC., 90 Beacon St., Boston MA 02108. Publisher: Seymour Lawrence. Editor: Merloyd Ludington Lawrence. Publishes hardcover and paperback originals. Seymour Lawrence books are published in association with the Delacorte Press. Royalty schedule: 10% to 5,000 copies; 12½% to 10,000; 15% thereafter on adult hardcover books; 10% on children's books. Published 18 titles in 1978; plans 16 in 1979. Send outline and sample chapters. SASE.
Nonfiction: Child care and development and behavioral science books for the general reader; no textbooks.
Fiction: Adult fiction. Recent titles include *Slapstick* (Vonnegut).
Special Needs: Radcliffe Series of biographies of women.

LEAVES OF GRASS PRESS, INC., Box 129 Bolinas CA 94924. Editorial Director: Stephen Gerstman. Publishes hardcover and paperback originals and reprints. Published 3 titles in 1978; plans 10 in 1979. Pays 10% royalty; 1,000 advance. Simultaneous and photocopied submissions OK. Reports in 4 weeks. SASE. Free book catalog.
Nonfiction: New age orientation, spiritual, how-to, current cultural phenomena, native American and pre-Colombian mysticism. psychic subjects, Jewish spirituality, consciousness expansion, and contemporary art and music themes. Query or submit outline/synopsis and sample chapters. Recently published *The Primo Plant: Growing Sinsemilla Marijuana*, by Mountain Girl (manual); *Secret of the Andes*, by Brother Phillip (occult speculation); and *Fragments of a Future Scroll*, by Reb Zalman Schachter (Jewish spirituality).

LEBHAR-FRIEDMAN, 425 Park Ave., New York NY 10022. (212)371-9400. Executive Editor: Barbara Miller. Senior Editor: Linda Marks. Publishes hardcover and paperback originals (100%). Published 15 titles in 1978; plans 15 in 1979, 22 in 1980. Pays royalty; average advance. Photocopied submissions OK. Reports in 4-8 weeks. SASE. Book catalog for SASE.
Nonfiction: "Most of our books published are for the retail business field (food service and supermarket). Our market is directed at both the retailer, administrator, and the college and junior college student wishing to enter the field and needing a good hard look at the facts and how-to's of the business. We are not interested in the generalist approach but with specifics that will be of importance to the business person." Submit outline/synopsis and sample chapters. Recently published *Food Service Management and Control*, by C. Villano; *Store Planning and Design*, by A. Novak; and *Retail Personnel Management*, by R. Glaser.

LES FEMMES PUBLISHING, 231 Adrian Rd., Millbrae CA 94030. Editor: Joycelyn Moulton. Publishes paperback originals. Offers standard royalty payment schedule. Nationwide distribution, plus distribution to most English-speaking countries. Free book catalog. Will consider photocopied submissions. Query and submit outline and sample chapters. Must be typed, double-spaced. Reports in 6 weeks. Enclose return postage.
Nonfiction and Fiction: Publishes "all subjects of interest to contemporary women, especially those conveying educational or self-help benefits." Needs material for the Everywoman's Guide Series. Must be concise, packed with information, presenting guides on subjects of interest to women. Would also like to see material about women in sports, menopause, biographies of famous women. Submit mss about the arts, sociology, sports, hobbies, and special interest material, such as health and history.

LESTER AND ORPEN DENNYS, LTD., PUBLISHERS, 42 Charles St. E., 8th Floor, Toronto, Ontario M4Y 1T4, Canada. (416)961-1812. President:Malcolm Lester. Vice President: Louise Dennys. Publishes hardcover and paperback originals. Offers standard minimum book contract of 10-12½-15%. Published 8 titles in 1978; plans 8 in 1979, 12 in 1980. Free book catalog. Will consider photocopied submissions. Query with outline and one sample chapter showing style and treatment. Submit complete ms only if writer has been published before. Reports in 6 weeks. SAE and International Reply Coupons.

General Fiction and Nonfiction: "Our basic philosophy of publishing only carefully selected books is stronger than ever; each and every title reflects a uniqueness in concept, careful and imaginative editing and design, and powerful and creative promotion." Publishes adult trade fiction, biography, sociology, economics and philosophy. Recently published *The Ion Effect*, by F. Soyka/A. Edmonds (health); *Five Lives of Ben Hecht*, by D. Fetherling (biography); *Stokowski*, by P. Robinson (biography); *The Trial of Adolf Hitler*, by Philipe Van Rindt (fiction); and *The Bass Saxophone*, by Joseph Sevorecky (fiction).

LIBERTY FUND, INC., 7440 N. Shadeland, Indianapolis IN 46250. (317)842-0880. Director of Publications: David Franke. Publishes hardcover and paperback originals (25%) and reprints (75%). Published 12 titles in 1978; plans 15 in 1979, 20 in 1980. Pays in royalties or outright purchase; usually no advance. Simultaneous and photocopied submissions OK. Reports in 4 weeks. SASE. Free book catalog.

Nonfiction: "Liberty Fund is a foundation established to encourage study of the ideal of a society of free and responsible individuals. Under the Liberty Press imprint we publish academic-level books on political, economic and social philosophy, written from a perspective that values individual liberty. No works written on a popular level; no political activism and no fiction." Query. "Very few of our titles are published as a result of unsolicited submissions. Authors, therefore, should take care *not* to submit a ms initially, but just a letter and outline." Recently published *Adam Smith: The Man and His Works*, by E.G. West (biography); *Essays on Individuality*, edited by F. Morley (collection); and *The Roots of Capitalism*, by J. Chamberlain (history).

LIBERTY PUBLISHING CO., INC., 50 Scott Adam Rd. Cockeysville MD 21030. (301)667-6680. Editorial Director: Lucien Rhodes. Publishes paperback originals. Published 4 titles in 1978; plans 6-7 in 1979, 5-6 in 1980. Pays 10-15% royalty; small advance. Simultaneous and photocopied submissions OK. SASE. Free book catalog.

Nonfiction: Business/economics, health, how-to, humor, juveniles, photography, recreation, self-help and sports. "We want clear, jargon-free discussion and in-depth coverage in any of the areas noted above. In either humor or juvenile fields, we look for an important and durable second appeal above and beyond the story or angle. We do not want fad-riding or me-too material." Submit outline/synopsis and sample chapters or submit complete ms. Recently published *Understanding Wall Street*, by Jeffrey Little and Lucien Rhodes (business/reference); *Learn to Type*, by Robert Flanders (business/self-help); and *Everything You Should Know About Pension Plans*, by Leo and Fay Young (business/reference/how-to).

*LIBRA PUBLISHERS, INC., 391 Willets Rd., Box 165, Roslyn Heights NY 11577. (516)484-4950. Publishes hardcover and paperback originals. Specializes in the behavioral sciences. Published 12 titles in 1978; plans 15 in 1979, 18 in 1980. 10-15% royalty; no advance. Subsidy publishes a small percentage of books (those which have obvious marketing problems or are too specialized). Simultaneous and photocopied submissions OK. Reports in 1-2 weeks. SASE. Free book catalog.

and Fiction: Mss in all subject areas will be given consideration, but main interest is in the behavioral sciences. Submit outline/synopsis and sample chapters. Recently published *Emotional Aspects of Heart Disease*, by H. Giest, Ph.D.; *The Counseling Process: A Cognitive Behavioral Approach*, by J. Lembo, Ph.D.

LIBRARIES UNLIMITED, INC., Box 263, Littleton CO 80160. (303)770-1220. Editor-in-Chief: Bohdan S. Wynar. Publishes hardcover and paperback originals (95%) and hardcover reprints (5%). Specializes in library science and reference books. 10%; advance averages $500. Published 35 titles in 1978. Marketed by direct mail to 20,000 libraries in this country and abroad. Query or submit outline/synopsis and sample chapters. All prospective authors are required to fill out an author questionnaire. Query if photos/illustrations are to accompany ms. Reports in 2-4 months. SASE. Free book catalog.

Nonfiction: Publishes reference and library science text books. Recently published *Library Management*, by R.D. Stueart and J. T. Eastlick (textbook); and *The Islamic Near East and*

North Africa: An Annotated Guide to Books in English for Non-Specialists, by D. W. Littlefield (reference).

LIGHT BOOKS. Box 425, Marlton NJ 08053. Publisher: Paul Castle. Editor: Marion Sande. Estab. 1974. Publishes hardcover and paperback originals. Published 3 titles in 1978; plans 5 in 1979, 12 in 1980. Pays 10-15% royalty; advance. Simultaneous and photocopied submissions OK. SASE. Reports in 4 weeks.
Nonfiction: Photography. "We are always interested in good mss on technique and/or business of photography. We especially want mss on *marketing* one's photography as art or home decor. We don't want mss on art criticism of photography, collections of art photos, basic photo teaching books, or anything other thatn books on the technique and/or business of photography. Query. If the idea is good, we'll ask for outline/synopsis and sample chapters." Recently Published *$54,000 a Year in Spare Time Wedding Photography*, by Feltner; *Promotional Portrait Photography*, by Castle; and *Money Making Ideas for Portrait Studios*, by Abel.

LIGUORI PUBLICATIONS. 1 Liguori Dr., Liguori, MO 63057. (314)464-2500. Editor-in-Chief: Christopher Farrell. Managing Editor: Roger Marchand. Publishes paperback originals. Specializes in religion-oriented materials. Published 16 titles in 1978; plans 18 in 1979, 20 in 1980. Pays 8% royalty; no advance. Query or submit outline/synopsis and sample chapters. State availability of photos and/or illustrations. Photocopied submissions OK. Reports in 2-4 months. SASE. Free book catalog.
Nonfiction: Publishes (in order of preference) religious; self-help; juvenile (with religious tone or approach); and how-to (self-help, not mechanical) books. Recently published *Discovering the Bible*, by J. Tickle; and *I'm Not an Alcoholic Because . . .*, by R. Reilly, D.O.

*LION BOOKS. 111 E. 39th St., New York NY 10016. Editorial Director: Harriet Ross. Publishes originals (80%) and reprints (20%). Published 20 titles in 1978. Pays 7-12% royalty, or pays $500-7,500 outright purchase price; advance varies. Photocopied submissions OK. Reports in 4 weeks. SASE.
Nonfiction: Biography (in all areas, especially political); African and Arabian tales; black historical nonfiction; and sports (how-to on gymnastics, swimming, riding). Query or submit complete ms. Recently published *Vince Lombardi*, by Klein; *Sports Injuries of Young Athletes*, by Schavi; *Black Heroes*, by Lindquist; and *Phillip Wheatley, Slave*, by Marlyn Jenken.

J.B. LIPPINCOTT CO., (General Division), E. Washington Square, Philadelphia PA 19105. General Adult Book Editor: Edward L. Burlingame. Publishes hardcover and paperback originals and reprints. Standard royalty schedule. Published 161 titles last year. Free book catalog. Reports in 3 to 4 weeks. Query. SASE.
General: Publishes general nonfiction; also history, biography, nature, sports, the arts, adult fiction. Submit outline/synopsis and sample chapters.

J.B. LIPPINCOTT JUNIOR BOOKS, 10 East 53rd St., New York NY 10022. Editorial Director: Patricia Allen. Senior Editor: Dinah Stevenson. Submit all manuscripts to Dinah Stevenson. Publishes trade books for kindergarten through high school. Standard royalty schedule. Reports in 8-10 weeks. Free book catalog.
Fiction and Nonfiction: For children of all ages. Particularly interested in social sciences and self-help. Recently published *Queen Of Hearts*, by Cleavers and *Jonah*, by Brodsky.

LITTLE, BROWN AND CO., INC., 34 Beacon St., Boston MA 02106. Editorial Director: Robert Emmett Ginna Jr. Publishes hardcover and paperback originals and paperback reprints. Publishes 105 titles/year. "Royalty and advance agreements vary from book to book and are discussed with the author at the time an offer is made." Simultaneous (if so notified) and photocopied submissions OK. Reports in 6-8 weeks for queries/proposals. SASE. Free book catalog.
Nonfiction: "Some how-to books, select and distinctive cookbooks, biographies, history, science and sports." Query or submit outline/synopsis and sample chapters. Recently published *Male Sexuality: A Guide to Sexual Fulfillment*, by B. Zilbergeld, Ph.D.; *The People Shapers*, by V. Packard; *American Caesar: Douglas MacArthur 1880-1964*, by William Manchester; and *Crockett's Indoor Garden*, by James Underwood Crockett.
Fiction: Contemporary popular fiction as well as fiction of literary distinction; some mysteries, suspense novels and adventure novels. "We are not particularly active in the fields of science fiction or gothic romances. Our poetry list is extremely limited; those collections of poems that we do publish are usually the work of poets who have gained recognition through publication

in literary reviews and various periodicals." Query or submit outline/synopsis and sample chapters. Recently published *War and Remembrance*, by Herman Wouk and *Motal Friends*, by James Carroll.

LOGOS INTERNATIONAL, 201 Church St., Plainfield NJ 07060. (201)754-0745. Editorial Director: Viola Malachuk. Publishes hardcover and paperback originals (95%) and paperback reprints (5%). Published 45 titles in 1978; plans 45 in 1979, 45-50 in 1980. Pays 10% royalty; advance offered "on a limited basis." Reports in 2 months. SASE. Book catalog for postage.
Nonfiction: "Logos books are primarily written to propagate and inform the charismatic movement within the Christian church. They are typically evangelical in flavor; many authors are Roman Catholic; some are Messianic Jews. Frequently the books are the stories or the testimonies of leaders in the charismatic movement; how they came to receive the Baptism of the Holy Spirit and experience the gifts of the Holy Spirit, like speaking in tongues, miracles, prophecy, etc. The first Logos book was a warning against spiritualism, seances and the occult. The first bestseller was *Run, Baby, Run*, the story of a converted teenage gang leader, Nicky Cruz. The author must be a serious Christian who regards the Bible as authoritative; any attempt to approach this material apart from personal involvement will likely be judged unsuccessful. Especially interested in popular treatments of biblical prophecy, serious trends in discipleship, teaching for children, and biography testimony." Length: 25,000-500,000 words. Submit outline/synopsis and sample chapters. Recently published *Child of Satan, Child of God*, by S. Atkins/B. Slosser (biography); *Let My People Grow*, by M. Harper (teaching on church structure); and *Eldridge Cleaver: Reborn*, by J. Oliver (biography).

*LONE STAR PUBLISHERS, INC., Box 9774, Austin TX 78766. (512)255-2333. Editorial Director: A.J. Lerager. Publishes hardcover and paperback originals. Published 6 titles in 1978; plans 5 in 1979. Subsidy publishes approximately 1 title/year based on "the subject matter, the author's reputation, the potential market, the capital investment, etc." Pays 12½-15% royalty; no advance. Simultaneous and photocopied submissions OK. Reports in 3 weeks. SASE. Free book catalog.
Nonfiction: College textbooks; how-to; cookbooks; self-help and sports. No poetry. Query. Recently published *The Texas Press Women's Cookbook*, by D. Hunt, K. Pill and B. Field (cookbook); *Poverty, Manpower, & Social Security*, by P. Brinker and J. Klos (college text); *Multidimensional Marketing*, by T. Anderson, et. al. (college text); *Texas Real Estate Law*, by Nelson (reference and college text); and *Business Policy and Strategy: Selected Readings*, by G. Gray (college text).

LOTHROP, LEE & SHEPARD (a division of William Morrow Company), 105 Madison Ave., New York NY 10016. (212)889-3050. Editor-in-Chief: Dorothy Briley. Hardcover original children's books only. Royalty and advance vary according to type of book. Published 54 titles in 1978; plans 45 in 1979, 45 in 1980. State availability of photos and/or illustrations to accompany ms. Photocopied submissions OK, but originals preferred. Reports in 4-6 weeks. SASE. Free book catalog.
Juveniles: Publishes biography, hobbies, and sports books. Submit outline/synopsis and sample chapters for nonfiction. Juvenile fiction emphasis on contemporary novels, but also includes adventure, fantasy, historical, humorous, mystery, science fiction and suspense. Submit complete ms for fiction. Recently published *Warton and Morton*, by R.E. Erickson (fantasy) and *Harvey the Beer Can King*, by J. Gibson.
Special Needs: "Fun-To-Read series includes both fiction and nonfiction in the easy reader format.

LOUISIANA STATE UNIVERSITY PRESS, Baton Rouge LA 70803. (504)388-2071. Editor: Beverly Jarrett. Director: L.E. Phillabaum. Published 44 titles in 1978; plans 60 in 1979, 60 in 1980. Pays royalty; no advance. Photocopied submissions OK. SASE. Reports in 2 weeks (queries); 1-6 months (mss). Free book catalog.
Nonfiction: "We would like to have mss on humanities and social sciences, with special emphasis on Southern history and literature; Southern studies; French studies; Latin-American studies; translations from French, Spanish, and Portuguese; music, especially jazz." Query. Recently published *Blanco*, by Allen Wier; and *Lightning Joe: An Autobiography*, by J. Lawton Collins.

LOYOLA UNIVERSITY PRESS, 3441 N. Ashland, Chicago IL 60657. (312)281-1818. Director: the Rev. Horrigan. Assistant Director: Mary FitzGerald. Published 8 titles in 1978; plans 10 in 1979. Pays 10% royalty; no advance. Simultaneous and photocopied submissions OK. SASE. Reports in 1 month.

Nonfiction: History and religion. Query. Recently published *Reading of the Wreck*, by Milward; and *Abortion: Development of Catholic Perspective*, by Connery.

McCLELLAND AND STEWART, LTD., 25 Hollinger Rd., Toronto, Ontario, Canada M4B 3G2. Editor-in-Chief: J.G. McClelland. Publishes hardcover and paperback originals. Offers sliding scale of royalty on copies sold. Advance varies. Free book catalog. Submit outline and sample chapters for nonfiction. Submit complete ms for fiction. Reports in 6 weeks, average. SAE and International Reply Coupons.
Nonfiction, Poetry and Fiction: Publishes "Canadian fiction and poetry. Nonfiction in the humanities and social sciences, with emphasis on Canadian concerns. Coffee-table books on art, architecture, sculpture and Canadian history." Will also consider general adult trade fiction, biography, history, nature, photography, politics, sociology, textbooks.

McCORMICK-MATHERS PUBLISHING CO., 135 W. 50th St., New York NY 10020. Executive Vice-President: Anthony J. Quaglia. Publishes paperback originals. Contract negotiated by flat fee. Published 119 titles last year. Will send catalog to writer on request. Will consider photocopied submissions. Submit outline and sample chapters. Reports as soon as possible. Enclose return postage.
Textbooks and Fiction: El-hi textbooks and action fiction within the el-hi age level from short stories to novellas; rural, suburban, city and inner city subject matter; school situations, inter-peer relationships, inter-family situations. Prefers third-person narrative without flashbacks. Value based in outlook, with strong emphasis on ethical good over ethical evil. "Our books are geared primarily to students with reading difficulties who have not profited from traditional reading instructions. We rewrite submitted material."

MARGARET K. McELDERRY BOOKS, Atheneum Publishers, Inc., 122 E. 42nd St., New York NY 10017. Editor: Margaret K. McElderry. Publishes hardcover originals. Reports in 6 weeks. SASE.
Nonfiction and Fiction: Quality material for preschoolers to 18-year-olds.

McGRAW-HILL BOOK CO., 1221 Avenue of the Americas, New York NY 10020. Hardcover and paperback originals, reprints, translations and anthologies. Pays 10-12½-15% royalty. Submit outline and sample chapter; unsolicited mss rarely accepted. Reports in 3 weeks. SASE.
General Trade Division: "McGraw-Hill Trade Division is no longer assessing unsolicited ms. Rising costs have made it uneconomic for us to employ skilled editors to read all manuscripts without consideration of the company's area of interest or the chances of achieving success on publication. All mss not sought by McGraw-Hill will be returned unopened to the sender via 4th-class manuscript rate, regardless of the postal rate selected by the sender."
Professional and Reference: Publishes books for engineers, scientists and business people who need information on the professional level. Some of these books also find use in college and technical institute courses. This division also publishes multi-volume encyclopedias (which are usually staff-prepared using work from outside contributors who are specialists in their fields) and one-volume encyclopedias prepared by experts in a given field. The professional books are usually written by graduate engineers or scientists or business people (such as accountants, lawyers, stockbrokers, etc.) Authors of the professional books are expected to be highly qualified in their fields. Such qualifications are the result of education and experience in the field; these qualifications are prerequisite for authorship. The multi-volume encyclopedias rarely accept contributions from freelancers because the above education and experience qualifications are also necessary. Single-volume encyclopedias are usually prepared by subject specialists; again freelancers are seldom used unless they have the necessary experience and educational background. Technical and Scientific Book Editor: Tyler G. Hicks; Multi/volume Encyclopedia Editor: Sybill Parker; Single-volume Encyclopedia Editor: Robert A. Rosenbaum; Business Editor: William Sabin; Architecture Editor: Jeremy Robinson; Handbook Editor: Harold B. Crawford.
College Textbooks: The College Division publishes textbooks. The writer must know the college curriculum and course structure. Also publishes scientific texts and reference books in business, economics, engineering, social sciences, physical sciences, mathematics, medicine and nursing. Material should be scientifically and factually accurate. Most, but not all, books should be designed for existing courses offered in various disciplines of study. Books should have superior presentations and be more up-to-date than existing textbooks. Department Publishers: Patrick Clifford, J.L. Farnsworth.
High School and Vocational Textbooks: The Gregg Division publishes instructional materials in two main areas, business and office education (accounting, data processing, business

communication, business law, business mathematics and machines, management and supervision, secretarial and clerical, records management, shorthand, typing) and career and vocational education (career development, marketing and distribution, public and personal services, applied arts and sciences, technical and industrial education, consumer education, health occupations, and agribusiness). Materials must be accurate, with clearly stated objectives, and should reflect a structuring of technical and interpersonal skills which mesh with both career clustering and course content. A. J. Lemaster, Editor-in-Chief, Shorthand. E. E. Byers, Editor-in-Chief, Business Management and Office Education; D. Cripps, Editor-in-Chief, Accounting, Computing and Data Processing; P. Voiles, Editor-in-Chief, Typing, Communications and Record Management; D. E. Hepler, Editor-in-Chief, Trade and Technical Education.

DAVID McKAY CO., INC., 2 Park Ave., New York NY 10016. Editor: James Louttit. Estab. 1895. Publishes hardcover and paperback originals (90%) and hardcover reprints (10%). Published 200 titles in 1978, 200 in 1979; plans 200 in 1980. Pays royalty; average advance. Photocopied submissions OK. SASE. Reports in 4 weeks.
Nonfiction: Cookbooks/cooking, health, hobbies, how-to, juveniles, sports, travel, nautical, chess, and outdoors. Query or submit complete ms. Recently published *The Midwestern Jr. League Cookbook*, edited by Anne Schanne; *Book of Close-Up Magic*, by Bill Severn; and The Authentic American John Boat, by Larry Dablemont.

RAND McNALLY & CO., Adult Division, Box 7600, Chicago IL 60657. Editor: Stephen P. Sutton. Estab. 1856. Publishes hardcover and paperback originals and paperback reprints. Pays royalty; advance varies. Photocopied submissions OK. SASE. Reports in 6-8 weeks. Free book catalog.
Nonfiction: Americana, travel, natural history, history, personal adventure, self-help and some sports. "We do not want any personal travel stories unless they're unique." Query. Recently published *Arizona*, by David Muench/Barry Goldwater (photographic book); *The Official Soccer Book of the United States Soccer Federation*, by Walter Chyzowych (sports); and *Backroads of Colorado*, by Boyd Norton (travel/adventure).

RAND McNALLY & CO., Juvenile Division, Box 7600, Chicago IL 60657. Trade Editor: Dorothy Haas. Mass Market Editor: Roselyn Bergman. Estab. 1856. Publishes hardcover and paperback originals and paperback reprints. Pays royalty, or by outright purchase for trade books; by outright purchase for mass market books; advance varies. Photocopied submissions OK. SASE. Reports in 6-8 weeks. Free book catalog.
Nonfiction: Americana, animals, history, how-to, juveniles, recreation, self-help, sports and travel. "We are interested in natural science, humor, preschool subjects, subjects of broad interest, all of which should lend themselves well to illustration. We do not want any ABC's, counting books, holiday stories, poetry and biographies." Submit outline/synopsis and sample chapters. Recently published *Album of Reptiles*, by Tome McGowen (scientific, readable, ages 8-12); and *Lost Treasures of America*, by Arnold Madison (stories and clues to ancient treasures).
Fiction: "We use preschool books of broad national and wide personal appeal. Humor for the 8- to 12-year olds and facts presented in an interesting way." Submit complete ms. Recently published *A Time to Keep*, by Tasha Tudor (the holidays in another lifestyle); and *Silly Dinosaurs* (collection, large picturebook, nonsense stories).

MACMILLAN OF CANADA, 70 Bond St., Toronto, Ontario, Canada M5B 1X3. Editorial Director: Douglas M. Gibson. Senior Editor: Jan Walter. Publishes hardcover originals and paperback reprints. Published 30 titles in 1977, 34 in 1978. 10% royalty. Sample chapters and outlines preferred form of submission. Reports in 6 weeks. SAE and International Reply Coupons. Book catalog for SAE and International Reply Coupons.
Nonfiction: "We publish Canadian books of all kinds. Biography; history; art; current affairs; how-to; and juveniles. Particularly looking for good topical nonfiction." Textbook/Educational Editor: Carl Heimrich, Scientific/College Editor: Virgil Duff. Query. Recently published *Trudeau*, by George Radwanski (biography); *The Other Side of Hugh MacLennan* (essays); *In Search of Your Roots*, by Angus Baxter (how-to); and *Greetings from Canada*, by A. Anderson and B. Tomlinson (postcard collection).
Fiction: Query. Recently published *Who Do You Think You Are?*, by Alice Murro; *The Invention of the World*, by J. Hodgins; and *The Eagle and the Raven*, by Pauline Gedge.

MACMILLAN PUBLISHING CO., INC., 866 3rd Ave., New York NY 10022. Publishes hardcover and paperback originals and reprints. Published 111 titles in 1978; plans 128 in

1979; 145 in 1980. Will consider photocopied submissions. Send query letter before sending ms. Address all mss except juveniles to Trade Editorial Department; children's books to Children's Book Department. Enclose return postage.
Fiction and Nonfiction: Publishes adult fiction and nonfiction. Length: 75,000 words minimum.
Juveniles: Children's books.

MACRAE SMITH CO., Rts. 54 and Old 147, Turbotville PA 17772. Pays 10% royalty. Published 12 titles in 1978; plans 36 in 1979, 48 in 1980. Send outline and sample chapters or complete ms and letter reviewing relevant background and experience of author. Address mss to Larry Sieg. Reports in 4-6 weeks. Enclose return postage.
General: "Adult trade books, fiction and nonfiction. Current issues and topical concerns, adventure, mysteries and gothics, history and science, biography."
Juveniles: For nonfiction books, interested in "biographies, history of world cultures, impact of the sciences on human affairs, cultural anthropology, scientific and medical discoveries, ecology, current social concerns and theory, peace research, international cooperation and world order, controversial issues, sports. Future-oriented subjects. For all ages, but prefer 8 to 12 and junior and senior high school." Also buys adventure stories, mysteries, history and science, biography, and girls' fiction. Length: 40,000-60,000 words.

MAJOR BOOKS, 21335 Roscoe Blvd., Canoga Park CA 91304. (213)999-4100. Editor-in-Chief: Harold Straubing. Managing Editor: John Mitchell. Estab. 1974. Publishes paperback originals (90%) and reprints (10%). Published 58 titles in 1978, 65 in 1979; plans 75 in 1980. Pays 4-6% royalty; average advance. SASE. Reports in 1-2 months. Book catalog for SASE.
Nonfiction: History (World War II). "We want strong biographies and new angles on World War II. Untold stories with drama and action, photographs if available." Submit outline/synopsis and sample chapters Recently published *Don't Die on My Shift*, by William F. Sayers (personal experience of a hospital patient); *Wake Island*, by Gen. J.P. Devereux (experience on war-torn Wake Island); and *Vince Lombardi: His Life and Times*, by Robert Wells (biography of one of football greats).
Fiction: Science fiction, western, and historical romance. "We are looking for westerns, science fiction, science fantasy and fast-paced adventure. Stories should be set in solid backgrounds. Romance and historical romance should have solid emotional impact. No erotica, please." Submit outline/synopsis and sample chapters Recently published *Gunfire at Purgatory Gate*, by M. Ryerson (western); *The Sandcats of Rhyl*, by Robert E. Vardeman (science fiction); and *Born for Love*, by Ursula Bloom (romance).

MANOR BOOKS, INC., 432 Park Ave., S., New York NY 10016. (212)686-9100. Editor-in-Chief: Larry Patterson. Assistant Editor: Lucille Koppelman. Publishes paperback originals and some reprints. Published more than 260 titles in 1978; plans 250 in 1979; 250 in 1980. "Submit one-page queries or complete mss, each accompanied by a one-page outline and a one-page biography including publishing credits, education and fields of specialization. No partials. Multiple submissions OK if you tell us." Reports in 6 weeks. No telephone queries. SASE. Writer's guidelines for SASE. "We are mass market publishers and a writer who wishes to place work with us must write to the popular market. This includes westerns, crime novels, science fiction and fantasy, romances, nurse novels, occult and other commercial books. We are also receptive to nonfiction with mass market appeal. We don't like off-trail books and literary experimentation is not for us. We are working for a family audience and a decent and pleasant good read is what we want."
Tips: "This house is receptive to the new writer and to regional writers with regional themes from outside the New York area."

*MANYLAND BOOKS, INC., 84-39 90th St., Woodhaven NY 11421. Editor-in-Chief: Stepas Zobarskas. Publishes hardcover and paperback originals. Pays 5-10-12½-15% royalty; offers $250-500 average advance. About 25% of books are subsidy published. Published 4 titles last year. Photocopied submissions OK. Submit complete ms. Reports in 6-8 weeks. Enclose return postage with ms.
Fiction, Nonfiction, Poetry, and Juveniles: "Manyland is concerned primarily with the literature of the lesser known countries. It has already published a score of novels, collections of short stories, folk tales, juvenile books, works of poetry, essays, and historical studies. Most of the publications have more than local interest. Their content and value transcend natural boundaries. They have universal appeal. We are interested in both new and established

writers. We will consider any subject as long as it is well-written. No length requirements. We are especially interested in memoirs, biographies, anthologies." Recently published *From Common Clay*, by Adalberto Joel Acosta (novel of Mexican life).

*MEDCO BOOKS, 1640 S. La Cienega Blvd., Los Angeles CA 90035. Editor-in-Chief: Gil Porter. Hardcover and paperback originals. Specializes "primarily in sex, health, wealth topics, popular medicine such as dealing with diabetes, weight, arthritis, etc." Pays $500-1,500 for outright purchase; advance averages ⅓-½ on contract, balance on acceptance. Subsidy publishes 1% of books. Subsidy publishing offered "if writer has a viable means of selling his book himself, such as personality with media access, etc. We charge our cost plus about 20% for each step of production as a working average." Query. Send prints if photos are to accompany ms. Simultaneous submissions OK. Reports in 1-2 weeks. SASE.
Nonfiction: Publishes erotica, how-to, medicine and psychiatry, and self-help.

MEDICAL EXAMINATION PUBLISHING CO., INC., 969 Stewart Ave., Garden City NY 11530. Royalty schedule is negotiable. Free catalog. Submit outline. Reports in 1 month.
Medical: Medical texts and medical review books; monographs and training material for the medical and paramedical professions.

MED-PSYCH DIVISION, 3695 G.N. 126th St., Brookfield WI 53005. (414)781-1430. Editorial Director: Patricia Wick. Publishes hardcover and paperback originals. Published 2 titles in 1978, 4 in 1979; plans 4 in 1980. Pays 7% royalty; no advance. Simultaneous and photocopied submissions OK. SASE. Reports in 2 months. Book catalog $1.
Nonfiction: Health, how-to psychology, and self-help."We would like to see more para-psychology, folk medicine and counseling material. We do not want any text books." Query. Recently published *Elements of Contemporary Counseling*, by Liebman (how-to psychology counseling); and *What is Love and How to Find It*, by Liebman (self-help and/or counseling hand book).

*MEMPHIS STATE UNIVERSITY PRESS, Memphis State University, Memphis TN 38152. (901)454-2752. Editor-in-Chief: Odie B. Faulk. Publishes hardcover and paperback originals. Pays 10% "unless an exceptional book. Each contract is subject to negotiation. We prefer not to offer an advance." Does about 10% subsidy publishing. "We don't ask a subsidy from the author and do not make subsidy contracts with authors. We do make an effort to obtain outside (other than university) money to assist books which have an identifiable source of public support; associations, commissions, museums and galleries, and the like." Free book catalog and writer's guidelines. Will consider photocopied submissions. Query. Reports in 3-6 months. SASE.
General Nonfiction: Americana Editor: Odie B. Faulk. "We publish scholarly nonfiction, books in the humanities, social sciences, and regional material. Interested in nonfiction material within the Mississippi River Valley, Tennessee history, and regional folklore." Recently published *Lincoln and the Economics of the American Dream*, by Gabor S. Boritt; *A Painter's Psalm*, by Redding S. Sugg Jr.; and *I Called Him Babe: Elvis Presley's Nurse Remembers*, by Marian J. Cocke.

ARTHUR MERIWETHER, INC., Box 457, 921 Curtiss St., Downers Grove IL 60515. Editor-in-Chief: Arthur L. Zapel Jr. Publishes paperback originals on how-to subjects relating to youth activities or communication arts. Published 5 titles in 1978; plans 7 in 1979, 10 in 1980. Payment by royalty arrangement. Marketed by direct mail. Book catalog 50¢. Editorial guidelines also available. Query. "Do not send ms until after query response from us." Reports in 1 month. Enclose return postage.
Education: Mss for educational use in schools and churches. Mss for business and staff training on subjects related to business communications and advertising. Religious, self-help, how-to, sociology, and humor books are also published.
Drama: Plays on the same subjects as above.

CHARLES E. MERRILL PUBLISHING CO., a Bell & Howell Co., 1300 Alum Creek Dr., Columbus OH 43216. Publishes hardcover and paperback originals. "Royalties and contract terms vary with the nature of the material. They are very competitive within each market area. Some projects are handled on an outright purchases basis." Publishes approximately 200 titles per year. Submit outline/synopsis and sample chapters. Reports in 4-12 weeks. Will accept simultaneous submissions if notified. SASE.
Education Division: Editor: Ann Turpie. Publishes texts, workbooks, instructional tapes, overhead projection transparencies and programmed materials for elementary and high

schools in all subject areas, primarily language arts and literature, mathematics, science and social studies (no juvenile stories or novels).

College Division: Executive Editor, Education and Special Education: Tom Hutchinson; Executive Editor, Business, Mathematics, Science and Technology: Greg Spatz. Publishes texts and multimedia programs in college areas which include Education and Special Education, Business and Economics, Math and Science, and Technology.

General Trade Division: Editorial Manager: Gwen Hiles. A newly formed division publishing general interest adult and juvenile fiction and nonfiction and children's picture books. "We are looking for quality works with large market appeal. We are particularly interested in self-improvement and how-to books." If submitted by agent or recommended by reviewer, we will at times consider adult and juvenile fiction of literary quality. "No short stories or religious books."

JULIAN MESSNER (Simon & Schuster Division of Gulf & Western Corp.), 1230 Avenue of the Americas, New York NY 10020. Senior editor for elementary grades: Ms. Lee M. Hoffman. Editor for junior and senior high school: Jane Steltenpohl. Hardcover originals. Published 48 titles in 1978; plans 35 in 1979, 35 in 1980. Royalty varies. Advance averages $1,500. State availability of photos and/or illustrations to accompany ms. "Propose book ideas to start with. If the editor is interested, we will ask for detailed outline and sample chapters." Reports in 2-3 months. SASE. Free book catalog.

Juveniles: Nonfiction books only for young people. Recently published *The Evil that Men Do*, by A.P. Rubin; *Driving Your Bike Safely*, by C.J. Naden; and *Is There a Loch Ness Monster?*, by G.S. Snyder.

MIT PRESS, 28 Carleton St., Cambridge MA 02142. (617)253-1624. Acquisition Coordinator: Arthur Kaplan. Published 95 titles in 1978; plans 105 in 1979, 120 in 1980. Pays 20% royalty; $500-1,000 advance. SASE. Reports in 4-6 weeks Free book catalog.

Nonfiction: Computer science/artificial intelligence, civil engineering/transportation, nutrition, neuroscience, work and quality of life, public policy, history, linguistics/psychology/philosophy, architecture, design, film, visual communication, economics, management, business, international affairs, physics, math, biochemistry, history of science and technology, urban planning and energy studies. "Our books must reflect a certain level of technological sophistication. We do not want fiction, poetry, literary criticism, education, pure philosophy, European history before 1920, belles-lettres, drama, personal philosophies and children's books." Submit outline/synopsis and sample chapters. Recently published *A Sense of the Future*, by Bronowski (technology and society); and *10,000 Working Days*, by Robert Schrank (work).

*MODERN BOOKS AND CRAFTS, INC., Box 38, Greens Farms CT 06436. Editor-in-Chief: Robert Paul. Publishes paperback originals and hardcover reprints. Pays 10% royalty; no advance. Subsidy publishes a small percentage of books. "We do this only if author is unknown in the field." Photocopied submissions OK. Reports in 1-2 weeks. SASE.

Nonfiction: Publishes erotica, hobbies, and psychology books. Also books on antiques.

Recent Titles: *Collector's Handbook to Marks on Porcelain and Pottery*, edited by E. Paul and A. Petersen; *Dictionary of American Painters, Sculptors and Engravers*, by M. Fielding.

MONITOR BOOK CO., INC., 195 S. Beverly Dr., Beverly Hills CA 90212. (213)271-5558. Editor-in-Chief: Alan F. Pater. Hardcover originals. Pays 10% minimum royalty or by outright purchase, depending on circumstances; no advance. Send prints if photos and/or illustrations are to accompany ms. Reports in 2-4 months. SASE. Book catalog for SASE.

Nonfiction: Americana, biographies (only of well-known personalities); law and reference books.Recently published *What They Said in 1978: The Yearbook of Spoken Opinion* (current quotations); *Anthology of Magazine Verse for 1979*; and *United States Battleships: A History of America's Greatest Fighting Fleet*.

MONTANA COUNCIL FOR INDIAN EDUCATION, 1810 3rd Ave., N., Billings MT 59101. Editor: Hap Gilliland. Publishes paperback originals. Published 5-10 titles in 1978; plans 5-10 in 1979. Pays 1½¢/word for short stories on acceptance, 10% royalty for book length; no advance. Simultaneous and photocopied submissions OK. Reports in 1-2 months. "All mss must be evaluated by an Indian Editorial Committee before we can publish. We immediately acknowledge the receipt of a ms, but the committee meets randomly, every month or two." SASE. Free book catalog.

Nonfiction: "We will consider material on any Indian-related subject (e.g., anything on Indian life and culture, past or present, fiction, biography, how-to-do-it, etc. All material must be culturally accurate). We stress that most of our books are paperback, of 32-50 pages in length. That usually means that we need from 16-35 pages of text per book (double-spaced, typed) because our books are heavily illustrated. Mss can be submitted in book or story length. Most of our books are compilations of two or more stories." Submit complete ms. Include illustrations if available. Recently published *Indian Canoeing*, by P. Pulling (how-to); *Chief Joseph's Own Story*, by Chief Joseph; and *A History of the Cheyenne People*, by T. Weist (history).

Fiction: Specialized fiction aimed mainly at young readers who read below the level of their class. Must be fast-moving to hold interest. "We prefer Indian authors because Indian students can more easily relate to stories written by Indians, but we will consider anything that does accurately portray the Indian way of life, culture, values, etc. We will also consider adult-level material. Again, we stress cultural accuracy. No stereotyped cowboy-Indian type stories. We encourage legends, folk tales and fiction stories." Submit complete ms. Recently published *In the Beginning*, by E. Clark; *The Heritage*, by Armstrong/Lee/Hildreth; and *Cheyenne Short Stories*, compiled by W. Leman.

MOODY PRESS, 820 N. LaSalle St., Chicago IL 60610. (312)329-4337. Director: Robert Flood. Managing Editor: Beverly Grimm. Publishes hardcover and paperback originals (90%) and reprints (10%). Published 80 titles in 1978, 75 in 1979; plans 75 for 1980. Pays 5-10% royalty; occasional advance. Simultaneous and photocopied submissions not encouraged. SASE. Reports in 1-3 months.

Nonfiction: Reglious. "We publish books that are definitely Christian in content. Christian education, Christian living, inspirational, theology, missions and missionaries, pastors' helps. Conservative theological position. Clothbound between 45,000 and 60,000 words." Submit outline/synopsis and sample chapters Recently published *My Searching Heart*, by Crying Wind; *Living with Cancer*, by Mary Beth Moster; *Hearts of Iron, Feet of Clay*, by Gary Inrig; and *The Theology of John*, by W. Robert Cook.

Fiction: Religious. "We do not encourage Biblical fiction but will accept historical and contemporary fiction." Submit complete ms. Recently published *Rusticus*, by Lonnie Mings (historical and *The Secret at Pheasant Cottage*, by Patricia M. St. John (juvenile mystery).

*MOREHOUSE-BARLOW CO., INC., 78 Danbury Rd., Wilton CT 06897. Editor-in-Chief: Margaret L. Sheriff. Publishes paperback originals (75%) and reprints (25%). Published 25 titles in 1978; plans 29 in 1979. Subsidy publishes "at most, one book per year. Author must come highly recommended. We do not encourage subsidy publishing." Pays 10% royalty; advance varies. Simultaneous and photocopied submissions OK. SASE. Reports in 2 months. Free book catalog.

Nonfiction: Religious books, education, arts & crafts, books on prayer, healing, spirituality; how-to books on church-related subjects, worship aids; books on all aspects of the Christian life. No novels, biographies or autobiographies of an inspirational nature. Submit outline/synopsis and sample chapters. Recently published *The Real Prayer Book*, by William Sydnor. *Companion of Prayer for Daily Living*, by Massey H. Shepherd Jr., *Searching for God*, by Basil Cardinal Hume; and *Fairs and Festivals*, by Kerry Dexter.

MORGAN & MORGAN, INC., 145 Palisade St., Dobbs Ferry NY 10522. Editor-in-Chief: Douglas O. Morgan. Publishes hardcover and paperback originals and reprints. Pays 10% royalty; no advance. Published 15 titles last year. Free book catalog. Submit outline and sample chapters. Reports in 2 months." SASE.

Photography: Books on all phases of photography. "We want to see an outline on what the book is about; various chapter headings; and how this material will be covered in various chapters. Would like one chapter in its entirety so that we could better grasp the method of approach in writing and also would like to have writer's reasons why he feels this book would have a good sale potential. We feel that our books go into greater detail on the particular subject and reasons why the book is relevant to the person looking for help in that field. We're looking for mss dealing with the how-to side of photography aimed at the amateur market and the more serious amateur photographer." Length depends on book.

WILLIAM MORROW AND CO., 105 Madison Ave., New York NY 10016. Editor-in-Chief: Hillel Black. Payment is on standard royalty basis. Published 301 titles in 1978. Query on all books. No unsolicited mss. Address to specific department. Reports in 6-8 weeks. SASE.

General Trade: Publishes fiction, nonfiction, history, biography, arts, religion, poetry, how-to books and cookbooks. Length: 50,000-100,000 words. Recently published *The Book of Lists*, by Wallace/Wallace/Wallechinsky; *Bloodline*, by S. Sheldon (mystery/romance); and *Proteus* by Morris West.

Juveniles: Juvenile Editor: Connie C. Epstein.

MOTORBOOKS INTERNATIONAL, INC., Box 2, Osceola WI 54020. (715)294-3345. Editor-in-Chief: William F. Kosfeld. Hardcover and paperback originals. Specializes in automotive literature. Escalating royalty begins at "10% retail on each copy; 10% gross where books sold at unusually large discount such as foreign rights sales. Advance depends on reputation of author and the work being considered." Published 5 titles in 1978; plans 7 in 1979, 6 in 1980. Also markets books through mail order subsidiary. State availability of photos and/or illustrations and include a few photocopied samples. Photocopied submissions OK. Reports in 1-3 months. SASE. Free book catalog.
Nonfiction: Publishes automotive and truck literature written for serious enthusiasts (histories, biographies, photographic works). Prefers not to see anything on "narrow" topics more suitable for magazine articles. Recently published *The Art and Science of Grand Prix Driving*, by N. Lauda; *American Trucking*, by Robert Roll; and *Hudson: The Post War Years*, by R.M. Langworth.

MOTT MEDIA, Box 236, 305 Caroline, Milford MI 48042. Editor: Diane Zimmerman. Hardcover and paperback originals (90%) and paperback reprints (10%). Specializes in religious books, including trade and textbooks. Pays 7% base royalty with sliding scale for mass sales; usually offers advance, "varies with experience." Query or submit outline/synopsis and sample chapters. Photocopied submissions OK. Reports in 2-4 months. SASE. Free book catalog.
Nonfiction: Publishes Americana (religious slant); biography (for juveniles on famous Christians, adventure-filled; for adults on Christian people, scholarly, new slant for marketing); how-to (for pastors, Christian laymen); juvenile (biographies, 30,000-40,000 words); politics (conservative, Christian approach); religious (conservative Christian); self-help (religious); and textbooks (all levels from a Christian perspective, all subject fields). No preschool materials or early elementary stories. Main emphasis of all mss must be religious. Recently published *By Their Blood*, by James Hefley (missions); *Proverbs*, by G. Santa (commentary)/and *Holy Days: Holidays*, by J. Ritchie and V. Niggemeyer (juvenile).

*MOUNTAIN PRESS PUBLISHING CO., 279 W. Front, Missoula MT 59801. Publisher: David P. Flaccus. Hardcover and paperback originals (90%) and reprints (10%). Royalty of 12% of net amount received; no advance. Subsidy publishes less than 5% of books. "Top-quality work in very limited market only." Published 8 titles in 1978; plans 10 in 1979, 15 in 1980. State availability of photos and/or illustrations to accompany ms. Simultaneous submissions OK. Reports in 2-4 weeks. SASE. Free book catalog.
Nonfiction: Publishes history (Western Americana); hobbies, how-to (angling, hunting); medicine and psychiatry (coronary care and critical care); nature (geology, habitat and conservation); outdoor recreation (backpacking, fishing, etc.); technical (wood design and technology); and textbooks. Recently published *Roadside Geology of Oregon*, by Alt/Hyndman.

MUDBORN PRESS, 209 W. De la Guerra, Santa Barbara CA 93101. Poetry Editor: Judyl Mudfoot. Fiction Editor: Sasha Newborn. Publishes hardcover and paperback originals. Royalty schedule varies with project. Published 6 titles in 1978. Query with sample or project outline. Will consider photocopied submissions. Reports in 6 weeks. SASE.
Translation: Publishes prose and poetry. "Presently we have two translation series: *Inklings* are bilingual poetry chapbooks (24-32 pages, letterpress) from uncommon languages. *Rockbottom Specials* (120-160 pages, offset) are contemporary literary language/culture anthologies. Occasional larger works also."
Fiction: Autobiographical.
Poetry: Contemporary.

MULTIMEDIA PUBLISHING CORP. (affiliates: Steinerbooks, Rudolf Steiner Publications, Biograf Books), 72 5th Ave., New York 10011. Editor: Paul M. Allen. Publishes paperback originals and reprints. Published 16 titles in 1978; plans 12 in 1979, 12 in 1980. Pays 5-7% royalty; advance averages $1,000. Free book catalog. Query with outline and sample chapters for nonfiction. Will consider photocopied submissions. Reports in 2 months. SASE.
Nonfiction: "Spiritual sciences, occult, philosophical, metaphysical, ESP. These are for our Steiner books division only. Scholarly and serious nonfiction. How-to-do or make books using our patented format of Biograf Books. Examples: origami, breadbaking, calendar." Department Editor, Multimedia Materials and Self-Help: Beatrice Garber; Department Editor, Philosophy and Spiritual Sciences: Gene Gollogly.

MUSEUM OF NEW MEXICO PRESS, Box 2087, Santa Fe NM 87503. (505)827-2352. Editor-in-Chief: Richard L. Polese. Director and Acquisitions Editor: James Mafchir. Hardcover and paperback originals (90%) and reprints (10%). Published 4 titles in 1978, 4 in 1979; plans 6 in 1980. Royalty of 10% of list after first 1,000 copies; no advance. Prints preferred for illustrations; transparencies best for color. Sources of photos or illustrations should be indicated for each. Simultaneous and photocopied submissions OK. Submit complete mss. addressed to James Mafchir, Publisher. Mss should be typed double-spaced, follow Chicago *Manual of Style* and *Words Into Type*, and be accompanied by information about the author's credentials and professional position. Reports in 1-2 months. SASE. Free book catalog.
Nonfiction: "We publish both popular and scholarly books in anthropology, history, fine and folk arts; geography, natural history, the Americas and the Southwest; regional cookbooks; some children's and foreign language books." Art, biography (regional and Southwest); hobbies, how-to, music, nature, photography, reference, scientific, technical and travel. Recently published *Rogue*, by Thomas Caperton; *Medicinal Plants of the Mountain West*, by Michael Moore; and *Spanish Textile Tradition*, by the Museum of International Folk Art.
Fiction: Historical, and other regional (New Mexico/Southwest) fiction. Recently published *Riders to Cibola*, by N. Zollinger.

THE NAIAD PRESS, INC., 7800 Westside Dr., Weatherby Lake MO 64152. (816)741-2283. Editorial Director: Barbara Grier. Publishes paperback originals. Published 2 titles in 1978; plans 4 in 1979, 4 in 1980. Pays 50% royalty; no advance. Reports in 6 weeks. SASE. Book catalog for SASE.
Fiction: "We publish lesbian fiction, preferably lesbian/feminist fiction. We are not impressed with the 'oh woe' school and prefer realistic (i.e., happy) novels." Query. Recently published *Love Image*, by V. Taylor; *A Woman Appeared to Me*, by R. Vivien; and *Berrigan*, by G. Lox.

THE NATIONAL GALLERY OF CANADA, Publications Division, Ottawa, Ontario, Canada K1A 0M8. (613)995-6526. Head: Peter L. Smith. Senior Editors: Jean-Claude Champenois, Julia Findlay. Publishes hardcover and paperback originals. Published 23 titles in 1978; plans 22 in 1979 and 25 in 1980. Pays in outright purchase of $1,500-2,500; advance averages $700. Photocopied submissions OK. Reports in 3 months. SASE. Free book catalog.
Nonfiction: "In general, we are exclusively interested in mss on art, particularly Canadian art, and must, by the way, publish them in English and French. Exhibition catalogs are commissioned, but we are open to mss for the various series, monographic and otherwise, that we publish. All mss should be directed to our Editorial Coordinator, who doubles as an editor. Since we publish translations into French, authors have access to French Canada and the rest of Francophonie. Also, because we are a national institution, authors have the attention of European as well as American markets." Query. Recently published *Twenty-Five African Sculptures*, by Jacqueline Fry (exhibition catalog); *The Works of Joseph Legare 1795-1855*, by John R. Porter (catalog raisonne); *A Tribute To Paul Klee 1879-1940*, by David Burnett (exhibition catalog); *Van Dyck: Suffer Little Children To Come*, by Ellis Waterhouse and *Marc-Aurele de Foy Suzor-Cote: Winter Landscape*, by Jean-Rene Ostiguy.

NATIONAL TEXTBOOK CO., 8259 Niles Center Rd., Skokie IL 60076. Editorial Director: Leonard I. Fiddle. Mss purchased on either royalty or buy-out basis. Published 60 titles in 1978; plans 60 in 1979, 60 in 1980. Free book catalog and writer's guidelines. Send sample chapter. Reports in 6-8 weeks. Enclose return postage.
Textbooks: Major emphasis being given to language arts area, especially secondary level material. Emphasis is on true orientation materials which give an accurate description of a field, its requirements and opportunities, all of which should be written for a 9th-10th grade reading level. Donna A. Drews, Language Arts Editor. Also interested in elementary education material: supplementary, enrichment, and professional materials in reading, writing, and social studies. Faith Wolfe, Elementary Education Editor.

NATUREGRAPH PUBLISHERS, INC., Box 1075, Happy Camp CA 96039. (916)493-5353. Editor: David L. Moore. Quality trade books. "We offer 10% of wholesale; 12½% after 10,000 copies are sold. Please state what photographs are available in query; send ms only upon request." Photocopied submissions OK. Reports in 1-2 months. SASE. Free book catalog.
Nonfiction: General natural history and the American Wildlife Series); history (Indian lore, ethnographic studies on native Americans); how-to (in our subject areas); land and gardening; seashore life; cookbooks, cooking and foods (modern nutritional knowledge for the layman); hobbies (nature- or science-related); spiritual and religious (Baha'i and new thought); and the varied pursuits of harmonious living. Follow *Chicago Manual of Style*. "All material must be

well-grounded. Author must be professional, but in good command of his/her English. Some of our books are used by teachers, particularly for natural science courses and anthropology (special studies)." Recently published *Fieldbook of Pacific Northwest Sea Creatures*, by McLachlan and Ayres; *Answers to Your Questions About Sharks*, by Scharp; *The Big Missouri Winter Count*, by Cheney; and *The Death of the Prophet*, by Leen.

NAVAL INSTITUTE PRESS, Annapolis MD 21402. Editor: Richard R. Hobbs. Editorial Director: Thomas F. Epley. Published 23 titles in 1978; 25 in 1979. Pays 14-18-21% royalty based on net sales; no advance. Simultaneous and photocopied submissions OK. SASE. Reports in 2 weeks (queries); 2-4 weeks (others). Free catalog.
Nonfiction: "We are interested in naval and maritime subjects: navigation, naval history, biographies of naval leaders and naval aviation. Query. Recently published *Double-Edged Secrets*, by W. J. Holmes (nonficton) and *Dutton's Navigation & Piloting*, by E.S. Maloney (text/reference).

NAZARENE PUBLISHING HOUSE, Box 527, Kansas City MO 64141. Trade name: Beacon Hill Press of Kansas City. Editor: J. Fred Parker. Publishes hardcover and paperback originals and reprints. Offers "standard contract (sometimes flat rate purchase). Advance on royalty is paid on first 1,000 copies at publication date. Pays 10% on first 5,000 copies and 12% on subsequent copies at the end of each calendar year." Published 61 titles in 1978; plans 65 in 1979, 60 in 1980. Query. Follow *Chicago Manual of Style*. Address all mss to Book Editor. Reports in 2-5 months. "Book Committee meets quarterly to select, from the mss which they have been reading in the interim, those which will be published." Query. SASE.
General Fiction and Juvenile Fiction: "Must have religious content germane to plot not artificially tacked on. At the same time not preachy or moralistic." Publishes 1 adult fiction and 1 juvenile a year. "Currently a moratorium on adult fiction."
Nonfiction: "Basically religious, (inspirational, devotional, Bible study, beliefs) but of wide scope from college textbook level to juvenile. Doctrinally must conform to the evangelical, Wesleyan tradition. Conservative view of Bible. Personal religious experience. We want the accent on victorious life, definitely upbeat. Social action themes must have spiritual base and motivation. Popular style books should be under 128 pages." Interested in business and professional books on church administration, Sunday school, etc. Textbooks are "almost exclusively done on assignment. Send query first." Length: 10,000-30,000 words. Recently published *God, Man, and Salvation*, by W.T. Purkiser, R. Taylor and W. Taylor (Biblical theology); *Get Ready to Grow*, by P.R. Orjala (church growth); and *How to Live with Less Tension*, by P.E. Spray.

NELLEN PUBLISHING CO., INC., 386 Park Ave., S., New York NY 10016. (212)679-0937. Editorial Director: Nancy W. Dunn. Senior Editor: M.F. Valentine. Publishes hardcover and paperback originals. Published 10 titles in 1978; plans 10 in 1979, 10 in 1980. Pays 10-12½-15% royalty; no advance. Photocopied submissions OK. Reports in 2-4 weeks. SASE. Free book catalog.
Nonfiction: "We are seeking titles of interest to both trade and scholarly markets. Our emphasis is on the trade. If a book is addressed tro the scholarly or technical market we may ask the author to rewrite with the larger market in mind. Our subject areas are wide: history, politics, economics, health, crime, self-help, management, the arts, etc. We are especially interested in Americana books on names (like our Smith book) and genealogy. Submit outline/synopsis and sample chapters. "With a clear synopsis of the book we appreciate knowing something about the author. We prefer authors with published works to their credit. If not books, at least magazine or journal articles."
Fiction: "We will consider all types of novel. Submit outline/synopsis and sample chapters. Recently published *The Book of Smith*, by Elsdon C. Smith (fact book); *Managing Change*, by John Flaherty (management); and *Living With Epilepsy*, by Margaret Sullivan (self-help). Forthcoming titles include *On a Field of Black*, by Gerald Tomlinson (suspense); and *The Great Founding Clans of America, by Avery Kolb (genealogy, popular history).

THOMAS NELSON PUBLISHERS, 407 7th Ave. S., Nashville TN 37203. (615)244-3733. Imprint include Sceptre Books. Editor: Lawrence M. Stone. Estab. 1798. Publishes hardcover and paperback originals (95%) and hardcover reprints (5%). Published 100 titles in 1978; plans 60 in 1979, 65 in 1980. Pays royalty or by outright purchase; sometimes an advance. Photocopied submissions OK. SASE. Reports in 6-8 weeks. Book catalog for SASE.
Nonfiction: Americana, cookbooks/cooking, juveniles, reference, and religion (must be orthodox in theology). Recently published *Beyond Death's Door*, by Maurice Rawlings (religious); *Parents' Magazine Cookbook*, by Rita Molter (cookbook); and *Promised Land*, by

Gordon Westmore, Abba Eban and Leon Uris (gift book/art book).

NELSON-HALL PUBLISHERS, 111 N. Canal St., Chicago IL 60606. (312)922-0856. Editorial Director: Harold Wise, Ph.D. Estab. 1909. Publishes hardcover and paperback originals. Published 84 titles in 1978, plans 100 in 1979, 110 in 1980. Pays 15% royalty; average advance. Photocopied submissions OK. SASE. Reports in 1 month. Free book catalog.
Nonfiction: Americana, biography, business/economics, cookbooks/cooking, health, history, hobbies, how-to, music, philosophy, photography, politics, psychology, recreation, reference, religion, science, self-help, sociology, sports, technical, and textbooks. "We do not want essays, opinions, speculations, memoirs or armchair ruminations." Query. Recently published *Stonehenge*, by Stover and Kraig (anthropology); *Parallel Play for Parents*, by Dinkin and Urbont (health); and *Home Pool Safety*, by Jacobs and Brent (sport).

NEW AMERICAN LIBRARY, 1301 Avenue of the Americas, New York NY 10021. (212)956-3800. Imprints include Signet, Mentor, Classic, Plume and Meridian. Publisher: Elaine Geiger Koster. Editor-in-Chief: Diana Levine. Executive Editors: Angela Rinaldi, Bill Contradi. Publishes hardcover and paperback originals and hardcover reprints. Publishes 350 titles/year. Royalty is "variable;" offers "substantial" advance. Simultaneous and photocopied submissions OK. Reports in 2 months. SASE. Free book catalog.
Nonfiction: "We will consider all nonfiction sent—educational, mystic, self-help, inspirational, topical, etc. Submit outline/synopsis and sample chapters. Recently published *Born to Win*, by James and Jongeward; *Hazards of Being Male*, by Herb Goldberg; and *Male Mid-Life Crisis*, by Nancy Mayer.
Fiction: "We will consider all fiction. We publish romance sagas, gothics, romances, science fiction, contemporary, suspense, thrillers, family sagas, etc." Submit outline/synopsis and sample chapters. Recently published *How to Save Your Own Life*, by Erica Jong; *I Judas*, by Taylor Caldwell; and *Kramer vs Kramer*, by Arney Corman.

NEW HAMPSHIRE PUBLISHING CO., 9 Orange St., Somersworth NH 03878. (603)692-3727. Editor: Catherine J. Baker. Estab. 1968. Publishes hardcover and paperback originals (90%) and hardcover reprints (10%). Published 11 titles in 1978; plans 13 in 1979 and 15 in 1980. Pays 5-10% royalty; advance varies. Simultaneous and photocopied submissions OK. Query. SASE. Reports in 4-8 weeks. Free book catalog.
Nonfiction: Health (related to outdoor sports only); history (New England reprints only); how-to (related to outdoors recreation only); nature; recreation; sports and travel (guides to Northeastern areas only). "We do not want to see anything that is not related in some way to those areas we have mentioned." Query or submit outline/synopsis and sample chapters along with resume or author biographical information. Recently published *Fifty Hikes in Central Pennsylvania*, by Tom Thwaites (outdoor recreation guidebook); *20 Bicycle Tours in Vermont*, by John S. Freidin; *Dan Doan's Fitness Program for Hikers and Cross-Country Skiers*, by Dan Doan (outdoor recreation/health); and *25 Ski Tours in Connecticut*, by Stan Wass.

NEWCASTLE PUBLISHING CO., INC., 13419 Saticoy, North Hollywood CA 91605. (213)873-3191. Editor-in-Chief: Alfred Saunders. Publishes paperback originals (20%) and reprints (80%). Published 8 titles in 1978; plans 9 in 1979 and 12 in 1980. Pays 5% royalty; no advance. Send prints or copies of items to illustrate ms. Simultaneous and photocopied submissions OK. Reports in 2-4 months. SASE. Free book catalog.
Nonfiction: Publishes how-to, diet, multimedia material, popular psychology, reference, self-help, sociology, inspirational, books on the occult, mythology and physical fitness. Submit outline/synopsis and sample chapters or complete ms. Alfred Saunders and Daryl Jacoby, editors.
Fiction: Fantasy, mystery and science fiction and mythology. Submit outline/synopsis and sample chapters. Doug Menville, editor.

NEW LEAF PRESS, INC., Box 1045, Harrison AR 72061. Editor-in-Chief: Cliff Dudley. Hardcover and paperback originals. Specializes in charismatic books. Pays 10% royalty on first 10,000 copies, paid once a year; no advance. Send photos and illustrations to accompany ms. Simultaneous and photocopied submissions OK. SASE. Reports in 30-60 days. Free book catalog.
Nonfiction: Biography; self-help. Charismatic books; life stories; how-to live the Christian life. Length: 100-400 pages. Submit complete ms. B. Springer, editor.
Recent Titles: *The C. M. Ward Story*, by D. Wead (biography); *Christian Catechism*, by E. B. Gentile (curriculum for non-Christians).

NEW READERS PRESS, Publishing division of Laubach Literacy International, Box 131, Syracuse NY 13210. Editorial Director: Caroline Blakely. Assistant Editorial Director: Kay Koschnick. Publishes paperback originals. Published 17 titles in 1978; plans 27 in 1979, 21 in 1980. "Most of our sales are to public education systems, including adult basic education programs, with some sales to volunteer literacy programs, private human-services agencies, prisons, and libraries with outreach programs for poor readers." Pays in royalties or by outright purchase. "Rate varies according to type of publication and length of ms." Advance is "different in each case, but does not exceed projected royalty for first year." Photocopied submissions OK. Reports in 2 months. SASE. Free book catalog.

Nonfiction: "Our audience is adults and older teenagers with limited reading skills (6th grade level and below). We publish coping skills materials that are of immediate practical value to our readers in such areas as consumer education, career education, health, family life, parenting skills, self-awareness, life-span development (adolescence through old age), legal rights, community resources, and adapting to US culture (for functionally illiterate English-as-a-second-language students). We are particularly interested in mss written at the 3rd-4th grade level or below. Mss must be not only easy to read but also adult in tone and concepts, and sensitive to the needs and circumstances of low-income adults. We also publish basic education materials in reading and writing, math, and English-as-a-second-language for double illiterates. Our *basic* programs are usually commissioned by us, but we would consider submissions of materials in areas like reading comprehension, composition, and practical math or materials for specialized audiences of nonreaders, such as the learning disabled or speakers of nonstandard dialects. We prefer proposals for a cluster of related titles; we are interested in isolated titles only if they could fit in existing clusters. We are not interested in biography, poetry, or anything at all written for children." Recently published *Learning Games for Infants and Toddlers*, by Dr. J.R. Lally/Dr. I.J. Gordon (handbook); *Settlers in America*, by B.W. Lowrie/W. Stein (text); and *It's on the Map*, by P.K. Waelder (workbook).

Fiction: "We're looking for original, realistic fiction written for adults, but written at a 3rd-grade reading level. We want well-developed believable characters in realistic situations. We want mss of approximately 10,000 words that can be published as short novels. We are not interested in genres like adventure, mystery, science fiction, gothic romances or any other kinds of formula fiction that develop plot at the expense of characterization. We do not want simplified versions of already published works." Query.

NEW REVIEW BOOKS, Box 31, Station E, Toronto, Ontario, Canada M6H 4E1. (416)536-5083. Editorial Director: Dr. Oleh S. Pidhainy. Senior Editor: Dr. Alexander S. Pidhainy. Publishes hardcover and paperback originals. Published 10 titles in 1978-1979. 10% royalty to 2,000 copies, 15% thereafter; no advance. Photocopied submissions OK. Reports in 3 months. SAE and International Reply Coupons. Free book catalog.

Nonfiction: Academic works in bibliography, archeology, history, literature, international relations, sociology, politics and etc., in regard to Eastern Europe/Soviet Union and northern Asia. No propaganda or improperly researched works. Interested primarily in academic monographs (revised dissertations will be considered). Consult Chicago *Manual of Style*. Submit outline/synopsis and sample chapters.

NEW VIEWPOINTS, division of Franklin Watts, 730 5th Ave., New York NY 10019. Executive Editor: Will Davison. Publishes hardcover and paperback originals. Specializes in college textbooks. Standard royalty, "depending on the author's reputation, subject matter and work involved." Published 8 titles in 1978; plans 12 in 1979, 16 in 1980. Query. Follow MLA *Style Sheet, Words into Type,* or Chicago *Manual of Style*. Simultaneous ("if so advised") and photocopied submissions OK. Reports "immediately on queries; about 2 months on mss." Free book catalog.

Nonfiction: Publishes textbooks on history, political science and sociology. Length: 300 book pages (100,000 words). Publishes textbooks for colleges, junior and community colleges, continuing education, and upper levels of high school. Recently published *Police and the Community*, by Robert Clark; *Post-Affluent America: The Social Economy of the Future*, by Gary Gappert; and *History: A Workbook of Skill Development*, by Conal Furay and Michael J. Salevouris.

NEWBURY HOUSE PUBLISHERS, INC., 54 Warehouse Lane, Rowley MA 01969, Editor-in-Chief: R.H. Ingram. Publishes hardcover and paperback originals (75%) and reprints (25%). Pays 5-10% royalty. Pays $500 maximum advance against royalties "in special cases." Published 20 titles in 1978; plans 25-30 in 1979. State availability of photos and/or illustrations to accompany ms. Photocopied and simultaneous submissions OK. Reports in 1-2 months. SASE. Free book catalog.

Nonfiction: "Any topic of motivating intererst to students (adult and near-adult) of English as a second/foreign language." Query.

Fiction: "These materials are intended for students of English as a second language; wanted are materials created especially for the purpose, or simplified and abridged versions of already published materials. Avoid topics that may give offense to persons overseas and topics that are dated or provincial."

NICHOLS PUBLISHING CO., Box 96, New York NY 10024. Editorial Director: W.G. Nichols. Publishes hardcover originals. Published 15 titles in 1978; plans 20 in 1979, 25 in 1980. Simultaneous and photocopied submissions OK. Reports in 6 weeks. SASE. Book catalog for SASE.

Nonfiction: Professional/academic materials in architecture, business, education, library science, international affairs, marine reference, and energy topics. Query. Recently published *Resource Management at the International Level*, by O. Young; *International Dictionary of Education*, by G.T. Page, et. al.; and *Marinas: A Working Guide to Their Development and Design*, by D. Adie.

NORTHERN ILLINOIS UNIVERSITY PRESS, DeKalb IL 60115. (815)753-1826. Director: R.T. Congdon. Published 8 titles in 1978; 10 in 1979. Pays 10-15% royalty; $250 advance offered. SASE. Free catalog.

Nonfiction: "We are interested in history, literary criticism and regional studies. We do not want a collection of previously published articles, essays, etc., nor do we want unsolicited poetry." Query with outline/synopsis and sample chapters. Recently published *Diary of a Common Soldier*, by Bray and Bushnell and *Hentland II, Poet of the Midwest*, by Lucien Stoyk.

NORTHLAND PRESS, Box N, Flagstaff AZ 86002. (602)774-5251. Hardcover and paperback originals (95%) and reprints (5%). Advance varies. Published 10 titles 12 in 1978; plans 20 in 1979, 20 in 1980. Transparencies and contact sheet required for photos and/or illustrations to accompany ms. Simultaneous and photocopied submissions OK. Reports in 6-8 weeks. SASE. Free book catalog.

Nonfiction: Publishes Western Americana, Southwestern natural history and fine photography with a Western orientation. Query. "Submit a proposal including an outline of the book, a sample chapter, the introduction or preface and sample illustrations. Include an inventory of items sent."

NORTHWOODS PRESS, INC., Rt. 1, Meadows of Dan VA 24120. (703)953-2388. Editor-in-Chief: Robert W. Olmsted. Publishes hardcover and paperback originals and reprints. 10-12½-15% royalty; "we are just beginning to offer an advance for local histories or biographies 'set' at $300." Published 16 titles in 1978; plans 30 in 1979, 40-50 in 1980. Simultaneous submissions OK. SASE. Book catalog for SASE.

Nonfiction: Americana; biography; cookbooks, cooking and foods; erotica; local history; hobbies; how-to; juvenile; nature; poetry; politics; recreation; self-help; sports; textbooks; and travel. Submit complete ms. Recently published *Trails Through the Northwoods: A History of the Bigfork Trail*, by Nauratil (local history); *Grandpa and the Red Haired Black Giants*, by Menkin (juvenile); and *Shadows on Cassiopeia*, by Olmsted (fantasy/poetry).

Fiction: Adventure; erotica; fantasy; historical; mainstream; and western. Submit complete ms or request author's guide.

W.W. NORTON CO., INC., 500 5th Ave., New York NY 10036. (212)354-5500. Managing Editor: Sterling Lawrence. Pays 10-12½-15% royalty; advance varies. Published 301 titles in 1978; plans 300 in 1979, 300 in 1980. Photocopied and simultaneous submissions OK. Submit outline and/or sample chapters for fiction and nonfiction. Return of material not guaranteed without SASE. Reports in 4 weeks.

Nonfiction, Fiction and Poetry: "General, adult fiction and nonfiction of all kinds on nearly all subjects and of the highest quality possible within the limits of each particular book." Last year there were 58 book club rights sales; 20 mass paperback reprint sales; "innumerable serializations, second serial, syndication, translations, etc."

NOYES DATA CORP. (including Noyes Press), Noyes Bldg., Park Ridge NJ 07656. Publishes hardcover originals. Published 50 titles in 1978; plans 60 in 1979, 70 in 1980. Pays 10% royalty; advance varies, depending on author's reputation and nature of book. Free book catalog. Query Editorial Department. Reports in 1-2 weeks. Enclose return postage.

Nonfiction: "Art, classical studies, archeology, history, mental health, and other nonfiction. Material directed to the intelligent adult and the academic market."

Technical: Publishes practical industrial processing science; technical, economic books pertaining to chemistry, chemical engineering, food and biology, primarily those of interest to the business executive; books relating to international finance. Length: 50,000-250,000 words.

OCCUPATIONAL AWARENESS, Box 948, Los Alamitos CA 90720. Editor-in-Chief: Edith Ericksen. Publishes educational originals. Offers standard minimum book contract; advance varies. Photocopied submissions OK. Submit outline and sample chapters for books and textbooks. Reports in 1 month. SASE.
Nonfiction: Materials should relate to students, careers, personnel, teachers, counselors and administrators. "We are an educational publishing company, relating occupations to curriculum."

OCEANA PUBLICATIONS, INC., 75 Main St., Dobbs Ferry NY 10522. (914)693-1394. Acquisitions Editor: Mel Hecker. Estab. 1945. Publishes hardcover originals. Published 150 titles in 1978; 160 in 1979; plans 175 in 1980. Pays 10% royalty; no advance. Simultaneous and photocopied submissions OK. SASE. Reports in 6 weeks. Free book catalog.
Nonfiction: Business/economics, politics and reference. "We are mostly concerned with international and comparative Law and most especially with reference books in this area." Submit outline/synopsis. Recently published *Government Regulation of Business Ethics*, by Y. Kugel and N. Cohen (reference); *Law of Separation and Divorce*, by P. Callahan (legal almanac for laymen); and *The International Law of Development*, by A. P. Mutharika (reference).

ODDO PUBLISHING, INC., Box 68, Beauregard Blvd., Fayetteville GA 30214. (404)461-7627. Managing Editor: Genevieve Oddo. Publishes hardcover and paperback originals. Scripts are usually purchased outright. "We judge all scripts independently." Royalty considered for special scripts only. Will send free catalog to writer on request. Send complete ms, typed clearly. Reports in 3-4 months. SASE.
Juveniles and Textbooks: Publishes language arts, workbooks in math, writing (English), photophonics, science (space and oceanography), and social studies for schools, libraries, and trade. Interested in children's supplementary readers in the areas of language arts, math, science, social studies, etc. "Texts run from 1,500 to 5,000 words. Presently searching for mss carrying the positive mental attitude theme—how to improve oneself, without preaching. Ecology, space, oceanography, and pollution are subjects of interest. Books on patriotism. Ms must be easy to read, general, and not set to outdated themes. It must lend itself to full color illustration. No stories of grandmother long ago. No love angle, permissive language, or immoral words or statements." Recently published *Little Indians' ABC*, by F.H. Lucero; *Uncle Sam and the Flag*, by L. Mountain; and *Cotton Carta*, by G. Worsham.

OHIO STATE UNIVERSITY PRESS, 2070 Neil Ave., Columbus OH 43210. (614)422-6930. Director: Weldon A. Kefauver. Pays on royalty basis. Published 14 titles last year; plans 24 in 1979. Query letter preferred with outline and sample chapters. Reports in 2 months. Ms held longer with author's permission. Enclose return postage.
Nonfiction: Publishes history, biography, science, philosophy, the arts, political science, law, literature, economics, education, sociology, anthropology, geography, and general scholarly nonfiction. No length limitations.

*OHIO UNIVERSITY PRESS, Scott Quad, Ohio University, Athens OH 45701. (614)594-5505. Director: Patricia Elisar. Managing Editor: Holly Panich. Publishes hardcover and paperback originals (97%) and reprints (3%). Published 27 titles in 1978; plans 30 in 1979, 35 in 1980. Subsidy publishes 6% of titles, based on projected market. Pays in royalties starting at 1,500 copies. No advance. Photocopied submissions OK. Reports in 3-5 months. SASE. Free book catalog.
Nonfiction: "General scholarly nonfiction with particular emphasis on 19th century literary criticism. Also history, social sciences, philosophy, and regional works. We do not publish in the hard sciences." Query or submit complete ms. Recently published *Hitler's War and the Germans*, by M. Steinert; *Dimity Convictions: The American Woman in The Nineteenth Century*, by B. Welter; and *Nietzsche's Gift*, by H. Alderman.

THE OLD ARMY PRESS, 1513 Welch, Ft. Collins CO 80521. (303)484-5535. Editor-in-Chief: Michael J. Koury. Hardcover and paperback originals (90%) and reprints (10%). Specializes in Western Americana. Pays 10% royalty; no advance. State availability of photos and/or illustrations to accompany ms. Simultaneous and photocopied submissions OK. SASE. Free book catalog.

Nonfiction: Publishes Americana (60,000 words or less); history (60,000 words or less). Query. Recently published *Washington's Eyes*, by B. Loescher; *Legend Into History*, by C. Kuhlman (western Americana); and *Dust to Dust*, by J. Gaddy.

101 PRODUCTIONS, 834 Mission St., San Francisco CA 94103. (415)495-6040. Editor-in-Chief: Jacqueline Killeen. Publishes paperback originals. Offers standard minimum book contract. Published 9 titles in 1978; plans 11 in 1979. Free book catalog. Will consider photocopied submissions. Query. No unsolicited mss will be read. SASE.
General Nonfiction: All nonfiction, mostly how-to: cookbooks, the home, gardening, outdoors, travel, sports, hobbies, recreation and crafts. Heavy emphasis on graphics and illustrations. Most books are 192 pages.
Recent Titles: *Secrets of Salt Free Cooking*, by Jeanne Jones; and *Best Restaurants Chicago*, by Sherman Kaplan.

OPEN COURT PUBLISHING CO., Box 599, LaSalle IL 61301. Publisher: M. Blouke Carus. General Manager: Howard R. Webber. Editor: Thomas G. Anderson. Published 5 titles in 1978; plans 4 in 1979 and 10 in 1980. Royalty contracts negotiable for each book. Query. Reports in 6 to 8 weeks. Enclose return postage.
Nonfiction: Philosophy, psychology, mathematics, comparative religion, education, chemistry, orientalia and related scholarly topics. "This is a publishing house run as an intellectual enterprise, to reflect the concerns of its staff and as a service to the world of learning."
Recent Titles: *Albert Einstein Autobiographical Notes*, by Paul Schilpp, editor and translator (philosophy and science); *Philosophy of Jean-Paul Sartre*, by Paul Schilpp (philosophy); *Trial and Error and the Idea of Progress*, by Madsen Pirie (philosophy); *Oxidation of Organic Compounds by Permanganate Ion and Hexavalent Chromium*, by David G. Lee (chemistry); and *Manganese Compounds as Oxidizing Agents in Organic Chemistry*, by Diether Arndt (chemistry).

OPTIMUM PUBLISHING CO., LTD., 245 rue St-Jacques, Montreal, Quebec, Canada H2Y 1M6. (514)282-2491. Managing Director and Editor-in-Chief: Michael S. Baxendale. Hardcover and paperback originals and reprints. 10% royalty. Published 20 titles in 1978; plans 20 in 1979 and approximately 25 in 1980. Publishes in both official Canadian languages (English and French). Query or submit outline/synopsis and sample chapters. Photocopied submissions OK. Reports in 2-4 weeks. SAE and International Reply Coupons.
Nonfiction: Biography; cookbooks, cooking and foods; gardening; history; natural history; how-to; health; nature; crafts; photography; art; self-help; crime; sports; and travel books.
Recent Titles: *The Murderers' Who's Who*, by Gaute and Odell (crime); *The Life of the Harp Seal*, by F. Breummer; and *Illustrated Encyclopedia of House Plants*, by Jud Arnold (gardening).

ORBIS BOOKS, Maryknoll NY 10545. (914)941-7590. Editor: Philip Scharper. Publishes paperback originals. Published 23 titles in 1978; plans 27 in 1979 and 27 in 1980. 10-12½-15% royalty; advance averages $1,000. Query with outline, sample chapters, and prospectus. Reports in 4 to 6 weeks. Enclose return postage.
Nonfiction: "Religious developments in Asia, Africa, and Latin America. Christian missions. Justice and peace. Christianity and world religions." Recently published *The Liberation of Theology*, by J.L. Segundo (theology); *In Search of the Beyond*, by C. Carretto (inspiration); and *The Gospel of Peace and Justice*, by J. Gremillion.

OREGON STATE UNIVERSITY PRESS, 101 Waldo Hall, Corvallis OR 97331. (503)754-3166. Hardcover and paperback originals. Published 5 titles in 1978; plans 8 in 1979. "Very seldom pay royalties." No advance. Submit contact sheet of photos and/or illustrations to accompany ms. Reports in 2-4 months. SASE. Free book catalog for SASE.
Nonfiction: Publishes Americana; biography; economics; history; nature; philosophy; energy and recreation; reference; scientific (biological sciences only); technical (energy); and American literary criticism books. Emphasis on Pacific or Northwestern topics. Submit outline/synopsis and sample chapters. Recently published *The Marine Plant Biomass of the Pacific Northwest Coast*, edited by R. Krauss (biological science); and *The Fiction of Bernard Malamud*, edited by Astro/Benson.

OUR SUNDAY VISITOR, INC., Noll Plaza, Huntington IL 46750. (219)356-8400. Book Editorial Director: Anne Geoghegan. Publishes hardcover and paperback original and reprints. 10% royalty of price received; advance averages $250. Published 50 titles in 1978,

plans 50 in 1979, 50 in 1980. Send prints of photos with ms. Reports in 2 weeks on queries; 1-2 months on mss. SASE. Free book catalog.
Nonfiction: Publishes books of religious connection and value. Biography, history, how-to, philosophy, psychology, reference, religious, textbooks, and travel. Submit outline/synopsis and sample chapters. Recently published *Streets*, by Margart Budenz (autobiography); *Cartoons Catholic*, by Jean Chaolot and Frank Sheed (meditation); and four juveniles.

OXMOOR HOUSE (a division of The Progressive Farmer Co.), Box 2262, Birmingham AL 35202. Director: Don Logan. Editor: John Love. Publishes hardcover and paperback originals. Pays on royalty basis or fee. Published 13 titles in 1978; plans 12 in 1979, 13 in 1980. Submit outline and sample chapter. Reports in 1 month. SASE.
General Nonfiction: "Publishes books of general interest to Southern readers—cookbooks, garden books; books on crafts, sewing, photography, art, outdoors, antiques and how-to topics. Recently published *The Art of Food*; *Folklore, for the Time of Your Life*; and *Rugs*.

P. A. R., INC., Abbott Park Place, Providence RI 02903. (401)331-0130. President: Barry M. Smith. Hardcover and paperback originals. Specializes in textbooks for business schools, junior or community colleges, and adult continuing education programs. Pays 10% royalty. Markets through fall and winter workshops throughout the country with special seminars that are periodically held by authors and sales staff. State availability of photos or illustrations to furnish at a later date. Simultaneous submissions OK. Reports in 2-4 months. SASE. Free book catalog.
Nonfiction: K. L. Short, Department Editor. Business, economics, law, politics, psychology, sociology, technical, textbooks.
Recent Titles: *Library of Adult Basic Educations*; *The Person You Are* (personal development); *Concepts of Business* (management); and *Principles of Marketing* (management).

PACIFIC BOOKS, PUBLISHERS, Box 558, Palo Alto CA 94302. (415)856-0550. Editor: Henry Ponleithner. Royalty schedule varies with book. No advance. Published 6 titles in 1978; plans 8 in 1979, 10 in 1980. Will send catalog on request. Send complete ms. Reports "promptly." SASE.
Nonfiction: General interest, professional, technical and scholarly nonfiction trade books. Specialties include western Americana and Hawaiiana. Recently published *Chinatown's Angry Angel: The Story of Donaldina Cameron*, by Martin (biography); and *For Health's Sake: A Critical Analysis of Medical Care in the United States*, by Grossman (history).
Textbooks and Reference: Text and reference books; high school and college.

PADRE PRODUCTIONS, Box 1275, San Luis Obispo CA 93406. Editor-in-Chief: Lachlan P. MacDonald. Publishes hardcover and paperback originals (90%) and reprints (10%). Pays 6% minimum royalty; advance ranges from $200-1,000. Published 2 titles in 1978; plans 8 in 1979 and 12 in 1980. State availability of photos and/or illustrations or include contact sheet or stat. Simultaneous submissions OK. Reports in 2-4 weeks. SASE. Book catalog for SASE.
Nonfiction: Publishes Americana (antiques); art; collectibles; cookbooks; history (local California); hobbies; how-to; nature (with illustrations); photography; poetry (about collectibles); psychology; recreation; reference; self-help; and travel books. Query or submit outline and sample chapters. "Ample packaging; type all material; don't send slides unless asked." Recently published *An Uncommon Guide to San Luis Obispo County California*, by Lee, et. al. (travel guide); and *Where the Highway Ends*, by G. Hamilton (local history).
Fiction: Publishes (in order of preference): adventure, fantasy, experimental, mainstream, and suspense books. "Also full-length narratives for the 10-14 year group, especially adventure with either strong contemporary situations or exceptional fantasy. Submit complete ms.

PAGURIAN PRESS LTD., Suite 1106, 335 Bay St., Toronto, Ontario, Canada M5H 2R3. Editor-in-Chief: Christopher Ondaatje. Publishes paperback and hardcover originals and reprints. Offers negotiable royalty contract. Advance negotiable. Published 37 titles in 1978; plans 25 in 1979. Free book catalog. Will consider photocopied submissions. Submit 2-page outline; synopsis or chapter headings and contents. Reports "immediately." SAE and International Reply Coupons.
Nonfiction: Publishes general interest trade books. Would like to see outdoor topics, sports, instruction. Will consider Americana, biography, cookbooks and cooking, economics, erotic, history, reference, self-help and how-to, sports, travel. Length: 40,000-70,000 words. Recently published *The Last of the Artic*, by W. Kurelek; *The Agatha Christie Mystery* , by D. Murdoch (biography); and *Wilderness Living*, by B. Berglund (outdoor).

PALADIN PRESS, Box 1307, Boulder CO 80306. (303)443-7250. President/Publisher: Peder C. Lund. General Manager: Timothy J. Leifield. Publishes hardcover and paperback originals (50%) and paperback reprints (50%). Published 14 titles in 1978; plans 18 in 1979, 22 in 1980. Pays 10-12-15% royalty. Simultaneous and photocopied submissions OK. Reports in 1 month. SASE. Free book catalog.
Nonfiction: "Paladin Press primarily publishes original manuscripts on military science, weaponry, self-defense, survival, police science, guerrilla warfare and fieldcraft. Survival and how-to manuscripts, as well as pictorial histories, are given priority. Manuals on building weapons, when technically accurate and cleanly presented, are encouraged. If applicable, send sample photographs and line drawings with outline and sample chapters." Query or submit outline/synopsis and sample chapters. Recently published *War Story*, by Jim Morris; *To Keep and Bear Arms*, by Bill R. Davidson; and *Home Workshops Guns for Defense and Resistance, Volume II*, by B. Holmes.

PANTHEON BOOKS, Division of Random House, Inc., 201 E. 50th St., New York NY 10022. Managing Editor: Kathleen Steed. Published more than 60 titles last year. Address queries to Nan Graham, Adult Editorial Department (15th Floor). Enclose return postage.
Fiction: Publishes fewer than 5 novels each year, primarily mysteries. Query. Recently published *Herland*, by Charlotte Perkins Gilman; and *Naples 44*, by Norman Lewis.
Nonfiction: Books mostly by academic authors. Emphasis on Asia, international politics, radical social theory, history, medicine, and law. Query.
Juveniles: Publishes some juveniles. Address queries to Juvenile Editorial Department (6th floor).

PARENTS MAGAZINE PRESS, A division of Parents Magazine Enterprises, Inc., 52 Vanderbilt Ave., New York NY 10017. (212)661-9080. Editor-in-Chief: Barbara Francis. Publishes hardcover originals and paperback reprints. Published 20 titles in 1978, 20 in 1979; plans 28 in 1980. Pays royalty or outright purchase for the right to use the work in our own "Read Aloud" book club only; advance averages. Photocopied submissions OK. SASE. Reports in 6-8 weeks. Free book catalog.
Nonfiction: "We are not considering any new nonfiction in the near future." Recently published *The Boy Who Dreamed of Rockets*, by Robert Quackenbush (for grades 1-4).
Fiction: "We will continue publishing quality picture books and are expanding our list to include middle group and teenage fiction, also humorous easy readers that would make either 32- or 40-page books with self-ends; illustrations in full color. Submit complete ms. Recently published *Sand Cake*, by Frank Asch; *Sam Sunday and the Strange Disappearance of Chester Cats*, by Robyn Supraner and Robert Tallon; *The Young Performing Horse*, by John Yeoman and Quentin Blake; and *We Came A Marching-1-2-3*, by Mildred Hobzek and William Pene du Bois.

PARKER PUBLISHING CO., West Nyack NY 10994. Publishes hardcover originals and paperback reprints. Pays 10% royalty; 5% mail order and book clubs. Published 60 titles in 1978; plans 80 in 1979. Will send catalog on request. Reports in 3-5 weeks.
Nonfiction: Publishes practical, self-help, how-to books. Subject areas include popular health, letterwriting, money opportunities, occult/inspiration, secretarial, selling, personal and business self-improvement, money opportunities. Length: 65,000 words. Recently published *Miracle Healing Foods*, by Adams; and *Speakers on the Spot*, by Bernhard.

PAULIST PRESS, 1865 Broadway, New York NY 10023. (212)265-4028. Imprints include Newman Books, Deus Books, and Exploration Books. Editorial Director: Kevin A. Lynch. Managing Editor: Donald Brophy. Publishes hardcover and paperback originals (90%) and paperback reprints (10%). Published 110 titles in 1978; plans 120 in 1979. Pays royalty; sometimes an advance. Photocopied submissions OK. SASE. Reports in 4 weeks.
Nonfictions: Philosophy, religion, self-help, and textbooks (religious subject). "We would like to see theology (Catholic and ecumenical Christian), popular spirituality, liturgy, and religious education texts." Submit outline/synopsis and sample chapters Recently published *Healing Life's Hurts*, by Dennis and Matthew Linn (spirituality); *Jesus the Christ*, by Walter Kasper (theology); and *Human Sexuality*, by Anthony Kosnik (moral theology).

PAY DAY PRESS, 8208 E. Vista Dr., Scottsdale AZ 85253. (602)994-1724. Editorial Director: David L. Markstein. Publishes paperback originals. Plans 4-5 titles in 1979. Pays 8% royalty on mail order books, 10-12½-15% on trade books; no advance. Simultaneous and photocopied submissions OK. Reports in 2 months. SASE.
Nonfiction: "Anything that can make the reader's life easier or richer, or that assist him to

avoid pain. Anything a wide audience will take to, which will aid that audience and make it richer or happier." Query or submit outline/synopsis and sample chapters. Recently published *Guide to Much Bigger Investment Income; Secrets of a Successful Race Handicapper;* and *Bugging—Are Your Phones Tapped?.*

PEACE PRESS, INC., 3828 Willat Ave., Culver City CA 90230. President: Bob Zaugh. Publishes paperback originals and reprints. Specializes in how-to, health, appropriate technology and self-help books. Pays 5% royalty; no advance. Published 8 titles in 1978; plans 8 in 1979, 10 in 1980. Submit outline/synopsis and sample chapters. State availability of photos and/or illustrations. Simultaneous and photocopied submissions OK. Reports in 2-3 months. SASE.
Nonfiction: Publishes how-to; self-help; religious; cookbooks; ecology; and health. Recently published *The Intelligence Agents and Neuropolitics,* by T. Leary (future history); *The Solar Cook Book,* by B. and D. Halacy; *Doomsday Has Been Cancelled,* by J. Peter Vajk; and *The Apartment Vegetarian Cookbook,* by Lindsay Miller.

PELICAN PUBLISHING CO., INC., 630 Burmaster St., Gretna LA 70053. (504)368-1175. Imprints include Pelican Publishing House, Paddlewheel Publications, Dixie Press, Hope Publications, Friends of the Cabildo, Sam Mims, Jackson Square Press, and Mississippi Library Association. Editor-in-Chief: James Calhoun. Managing Editor: Jayne Ramsey. Publishes hardcover and paperback originals (90%) and reprints (10%). Published 26 titles in 1978; plans 30 titles in 1979, 31 in 1980. Pays 10-15% royalty; "sometimes" offering $2,000 advance. Photocopied submissions preferred. SASE if manuscript is to be returned. Reports in 3 months. Book catalog for SASE.
Nonfiction: Art; cookbooks/cooking; self-help (especially motivational); inspirational and travel (guidebooks). Submit outline/synopsis and sample chapters Recently published *Communicate Effectively,* by Arnold Nick Carter (motivational, how-to); *Confessions of a Happy Christian,* by Zig Ziglar (inspirational, motivational); and *The Maverick Guide to Australia,* guidebook.
Fiction: Adventure and suspense. "We only publish one title per year." Query. Recently published *The Catalyst,* by Nelda Gavlin (suspense).

THE PENNSYLVANIA STATE UNIVERSITY PRESS, 215 Wagner Bldg., University Park PA 16802. (814)865-1327. Editor-in-Chief: Jack Pickering. Hardcover and paperback originals. Specializes in books of scholarly value, and/or regional interest. Published 30 titles in 1978; plans 35 in 1979, 40 in 1980. Pays 10% royalty; no advance. Maintains own distribution company in England which serves the British Empire, Europe, etc. Submit outline/synopsis and sample chapters or complete ms. Send prints if photos/illustrations are to accompany ms. Simultaneous and photocopied submissions OK. Reports in 2-4 months. SASE. Free book catalog.
Nonfiction: Publishes art, biography, business, economics, history, hobbies, medicine and psychiatry, multimedia material, music, nature, philosophy, politics, psychology, recreation, reference, religious, scientific, sociology, technical, textbooks, women's studies, black studies and agriculture books.
Special Needs: Keystone Books (a paperback series concentrating on topics of special interest to those living in the mid-Atlantic states.) Recently published *Seaweeds of the East Coast.*

PEREGRINE SMITH, INC., 1877 E. Gentile St., Layton UT 84041. (801)376-9800. Editorial Director: Richard A. Firmage. Publishes hardcover and paperback originals (50%) and reprints (50%). Published 7 titles in 1978; plans 10 in 1979, 10 in 1980. Pays 10% royalty; no advance. Photocopied submissions OK. Reports in 3 months. SASE. Book catalog 26¢.
Nonfiction: "Western American history, American architecture, art history, arts and crafts (including how-to) and fine arts. We consider biographical, historical, descriptive and analytical studies in all of the above. Much emphasis is also placed on pictorial content. Many of our books are used as university texts." Query or submit outline/synopsis and sample chapters. Consult Chicago *Manual of Style.* Recently published *Greene & Greene: Architecture as a Fine Art,* by R. Makinson; *Bernard Maybeck: Artisan, Architect, Artist,* by K. Cardwell; and *The Diary of a Writer,* by Feodor Dostoevsky.
Fiction: "We have mainly published reprints or anthologies of American writers; but are very interested in expanding in the areas of serious fiction: novels, short stories, drama and poetry. This will include reprints of important work as well as new material." Query or submit outline/synopsis and sample chapters. Recently published *Wild Animals I Have Known,* by E. Thompson Seton (short stories); *The Valley of the Moon,* by J. London; and *Okies,* by G. Haslem.

Tips: "Write seriously. If fiction, no potboilers, bestseller movie tie-in type hype books. We like Pynchon and Gaddis. If nonfiction, only serious, well-researched critical, historical or craft-related topics. No self-help books."

THE PERFECTION FORM CO., 8350 Hickman Rd., Suite 15, Des Moines IO 50322. (515)278-0133. Senior Editor: Wayne F. DeMouth. Estab. 1926. Publishes paperback originals. Published 10 titles in 1978; plans 15 in 1979, 25 in 1980. Pays $200-850 outright purchase; no advance. Simultaneous and photocopied submissions OK. SASE. Reports in 1 month. Free book catalog.
Fiction: Adventure, humor and mainstream. "Original manuscripts of approximately 30,000-40,000 words written for young adult audiences ages 12-18. Content should be appropriate for average young people. We do not want stories with heavy moral overtones, offensive language, sex, etc." Submit complete ms. Recently published *The Ghost Boy, The Vandal* and *An Alien Spring,* by Anne Schraff (young adult).

S.G. PHILLIPS, INC., 305 W. 86th St., New York NY 10024. (212)787-4405. Editor: Sidney Phillips. Publishes hardcover originals. "Graduated royalty schedule varies where artists or collaborators share in preparation." Published 3 titles in 1978; plans 3 in 1979. Will send a catalog to a writer on request. "Query; no unsolicited mss." Reports in 30-60 days. SASE.
General and Juveniles: "Fiction and nonfiction for children and young adults. Particular interests—contemporary fiction, mysteries, adventure, science fiction; nonfiction: biography, politics, urban problems, international affairs, anthropology, archaeology, geography. Length depends on age group."

THE PICKWICK PRESS, 5001 Baum Blvd., Pittsburgh PA 15213. Editorial Director: Dikran Y. Hadidian. Publishes paperback originals and reprints. Published 9 titles in 1978; plans 8 in 1979, 5 in 1980. Pays 8-10% royalty; no advance. Photocopied submissions OK. Reports in 2 months. SASE. Free book catalog.
Nonfiction: Religious and scholarly mss in Biblical archeology, Biblical studies, church history and theology. Also reprints of outstanding out-of-print titles and original texts and translations. No popular religious material. Query. Consult *MLA Style Sheet* or Turabian's *A Manual for Writers.* Recently published *Crux Imperatorum Philosophies,* by R.G. Heath; *Manipulated Man,* by C. Robert; and *The Emergence of Contemporary Judaism,* by P. Sigal.

PILOT BOOKS, 347 5th Ave., New York NY 10016. (212)685-0736. Publishes paperback originals. Offers standard royalty contract. Usual advance is $250, but this varies, depending on author's reputation and nature of book. Published 24 titles in 1978; plans 30 in 1979, 30 in 1980. Send outline. Reports in 4 weeks. Enclose return postage.
General Nonfiction, Reference, and Business: "Publishes financial, business, travel, career, personal guides and training manuals. Directories and books on moneymaking opportunities." Wants "clear, concise treatment of subject matter." Length: 8,000-30,000 words. Recently published *The Where-To-Sell-It Directory,* by Margaret Boyd and Sue Scott-Martin; and *Avoiding Travel Rip-Offs,* by Harold Gluck.

PINNACLE BOOKS, 1 Century Plaza, Century City CA 90067. Editor: Andrew Ettinger. Publishes paperback originals and reprints. "Contracts and terms are standard and primarily competitive." Published 160 titles in 1978; plans 160 in 1979, 160 in 1980. Catalog and requirements memo for SASE. "Will no longer accept unsolicited mss. Most books are assigned to known writers or developed through established agents. However, an intelligent, literate and descriptive letter of query will often be given serious consideration." SASE.
General: "Books range from general nonfiction to commercial trade fiction in most popular categories. Pinnacle's list is aimed for wide popular appeal, with fast-moving, highly compelling escape reading, adventure, espionage, historical intrigue and romance, science fiction, western, popular sociological issues, topical nonfiction."
Tips: "Become familiar with our list of published books, and follow our instructions. It is a difficult market—paperbacks—with publishers competing for rack space. Watch what sells best and follow the trends as closely as possible. Study the original books that work as well as the reprints. Good, persuasive query letters are the best and fastest tools you have to get an editor's attention. The idea, or angle is vital . . . then we trust the author has or can complete the manuscript."

PIPER PUBLISHING, INC., 400 Butler Square Bldg., Minneapolis MN 55403. President: Paul C. Piper. Editorial Director: John M. Sullivan Jr. Publishes hardcover and paperback originals and reprints. Published 10 titles in 1978; plans 12 in 1979, 15 in 1980. Pays royalty

and advance. Simultaneous and photocopied submissions OK. SASE. Reports in 6 weeks.
Nonfiction: Americana, art, biography, business/economics, cookbooks/cooking/foods, health, history, hobbies, how-to, humor, photography, politics, psychology, restaurant guides, sports and travel. Submit outline/synopsis and sample chapters. Recently published *Out of Bounds, An Anecdotal History of Notre Dame Football*, by Bonifer and Weaver (history/sports); *Almost to the Presidency, Two American Politicans*, by Eisele (biography/history/political science); and *Wine Diet Cookbook*, by Chase and Dr. Lucia (cookbook/wine/food).
Fiction: Erotica, humor, mainstream, mystery and science fiction. Submit outline/synopsis and sample chapters. Recently published *Women! From Mars*, by Langley (science fiction).

PLATT & MUNK PUBLISHERS, division of Grosset & Dunlap, 51 Madison Ave., New York NY 10010. Editor-in-Chief: Nancy Hall. Publishes hardcover and paperback originals. Published 40 titles in 1978, 25 in 1979; plans 40 in 1980. Pays $1.000-3.500 in outright purchase; no advance. Simultaneous and photocopied submissions OK. SASE. Reports in 5 weeks.
Nonfiction: Juvenile. "We want picturebook manuscripts describing how the world works—demystification of machinery and natural processes, and animal nonfiction." Submit complete ms. Recently published *More Easy Answers*, by Joyce Richards; *Dinosaurs!*, by Anthony Rao; and *Sharks and Whales*, by Burton Albert.
Fiction: Fantasy. "We want original picturebook manscripts for children ages 3-7." Submit complete ms. Recently published *Not Counting Monsters*, by Ross (counting book); *Little Brown Bear*, by Upham (storybook); and *Tasha Tudor's Bedtime Book*, by Klimo (storybook).

PLAYBOY PRESS, Division of Playboy Enterprises, Inc., 919 Michigan Ave., Chicago IL 60611. New York office: 747 3rd Ave., New York NY 10017. (212)688-3030. Editorial Director (hardcover): Charles Sopkin; Editorial Director (softcover): Robert Gleason. Publishes hardcover and paperback originals and reprints. Royalty contract to be negotiated. Published 91 titles last year. Query. SASE.
General: Fiction and nonfiction slanted to the adult male who reads *Playboy* magazine.

PLENUM PUBLISHING CORP., 227 W. 17th St., New York NY 10011. Imprints: Da Capo Press, Consultants Bureau, IFI/Plenum Data Corporation, Plenum Press, Plenum Medical Book Company, Plenum Rosetta. Publishes hardcover and paperback reprints. Offers standard minimum contract of 7½-10%. Query B. Friedland/Da Capo and H. Evans for Plenum. SASE.
Nonfiction: Scientific, medical and technical books including the social and behavioral sciences, physics, engineering and mathematics. Da Capo division publishes art, music, photography, dance and film.

POCKET BOOKS, 1230 Avenue of the Americas, New York NY 10020. Paperback originals and reprints. Published 300 titles last year. Reports in one month. Submit through agent only. Enclose return postage.
General: History, biography, philosophy, inspirational, general nonfiction and adult fiction (mysteries, science fiction, gothics, westerns). Reference books.

POET GALLERY PRESS, 224 W. 29th St., New York NY 10001. Editor: E.J. Pavlos. Publishes paperback originals. Pays standard 10-12½-15% royalty contract. Published 4 titles last year. Submit complete ms only. Enclose return postage with ms.
General: "We are a small specialty house, and we place our emphasis on publishing the works of young Americans currently living in Europe. We are interested in creative writing rather than commercial writing. We publish for writers who live overseas, who write and live, who produce writings from the self. Our books might turn out to be commercial, but that is a secondary consideration. We expect to emphasize poetry; however, our list will be concerned with all aspects of literature: the novel, plays, and cinema, as well as criticism. We urge that authors recognize our imposed restrictions; we can not, and do not wish at this time to compete with major publishing companies." Recently published *Sarah*, by Gamela; and *Iris Elegy*, by Hakim.

POLARIS PRESS, 16540 Camellia Terrace, Los Gatos CA 95030. (408)356-7795. Editor: Edward W. Ludwig. Paperback originals. Specializes in el-hi books with appeal to general juvenile public. Published 1 title in 1978; plans 2 in 1979, 3 in 1980. Pays 10% royalty; advance averages $100-300. Send contact sheets or prints if photos and/or illustrations are to accompany ms. Simultaneous and photocopied submissions OK. Reports in 1-2 weeks. SASE. Free book catalog.
Fiction: Publishes some fantasy and science fiction "Please, *no* mss which require extensive

(and expensive) use of color in inner pages." Query. Recently published *A Mexican American Coloring Book*, by Rascon; and *The California Story: A Coloring Book*, by Bernal.
Tips: "Query to determine immediate needs, which are usually specialized. There is little chance that a nonsolicited manuscript will be accepted spontaneously."

PORTER SARGENT PUBLISHERS, INC., 11 Beacon St., Boston MA 02108. (617)523-1670. Publishes hardcover and paperback originals, reprints, translations and anthologies. Published 2 titles in 1978; plans 5 in 1979, 5 in 1980. "Each contract is dealt with on an individual basis with the author." Free book catalog. Send query with brief description, table of contents, sample chapter and information regarding author's background. Enclose return postage.
Reference, Special Education, and Academic Nonfiction: "Handbooks Series and Special Education Series offer standard, definitive reference works in private education and writings and texts in special education. The Extending Horizons Series is an outspoken, unconventional series which presents topics of importance in contemporary affairs, viewpoints rarely offered to the reading public, methods and modes of social change, and the framework of alternative structures for the expansion of human awareness and well-being." This series is particularly, although not exclusively, directed to the college adoption market." Contact Christopher Leonesio for Special Education Books; J. Kathryn Sargent for EHB Books.

G. HOWARD POTEET, INC., Box 217, Cedar Grove NJ 07009. Publishes paperback originals. Published 5 titles in 1978; plans 6 in 1979, 7 in 1980. Pays 10% royalty; no advance. Simultaneous submissions OK. Reports in 1-2 weeks. SASE. Book catalog for SASE.
Nonfiction: How-to books in the areas of business, hobbies, multimedia material; photography; technical material and textbooks. Query or submit outline/synopsis and sample chapters. Recently published *Between the Lines in the Mail Order Game*, by Matt Dol.
Tips: "Try to speak to the reader as clearly, simply and directly as possible on an interesting topic supplying precise information."

CLARKSON N. POTTER, INC., 1 Park Ave., New York NY 10016. (212)532-9200. Vice President/Publisher: Jane West. Senior Editor: Carol Southern. Publishes hardcover and paperback originals. Pays 10% royalty on hardcover; 5% on paperback, varying escalations; advance depends on type of book and reputation or experience of author. Published 20 titles in 1978; plans 28 in 1979, approximately 40 in 1980. Samples of prints may be included with outline. Photocopied submissions OK. Reports in 2-4 weeks. SASE. Free book catalog.
Fiction: Quality and commercial.
Nonfiction: Publishes Americana, art, biography, cookbooks, cooking and foods, decorating, history, how-to, humor, nature, photography, politics, self-help and annotated literature. "Mss must be cleanly typed on 8½x11 bond; double-spaced. Chicago *Manual of Style* is preferred." Query or submit outline/synopsis and sample chapters. Recently published *High Tech*, by Joan Kron and Suzanne Slesin (decorating); *Werner Erhard*, by W. W. Bartley III (biography); *O Thou Improper Thou Uncommon Now*, by Willard R. Espy (humor/etymology); and *The Annotated Shakespeare*, by A. L. Rowse (literature).

*A.R. PRAGARE CO., INC., 3695G N. 126th St., Brookfield WI 53005. (414)781-1430. Publisher: Robert W. Pradt. Publishes hardcover and paperback originals and reprints. Specializes in firearms, hunting, and other topics of interest in this area. Published 5 titles in 1978; plans 10 in 1979, 20 in 1980. Pays 7-10% royalty; no advance. Subsidy publishes a varying percentage of books through Pine Mountain Press, a division of the corporation. "Author must be previously published with good sales record and have some knowledge of publishing (marketing) and the financing to start a publishing venture." Markets books by mail order through gun and hunting magazines. Submit outline/synopsis and sample chapters. "No onion skin paper." Send prints to illustrate ms. Reports in 1-2 months. SASE.
Nonfiction: Publishes Americana; cookbooks; cooking and foods; history; humor; recreation; sports (limited to our area); technical (in field of guns); biographies and children's books. Recently published *Book of the Garand*, by Hatcher; and *What is Love and Where to Find It*, by Liebman.
Fiction: Publishes adventure, humorous and western fiction books.
Special Needs: Guns, hunting, related adventure and historical books for Leather Stocking division.

PRECEDENT PUBLISHING, INC., 520 N. Michigan Ave., Chicago IL 60611. (312)828-0420. Editorial Director: Louis A. Knafla. Senior Editor: Henry Cohen. Publishes hardcover and paperback originals. Plans to publish 2-3 titles in 1979. Pays 10% royalty; advance averages $400. Reports in 2 weeks-1 month. SASE. Free book catalog.

Nonfiction: Scholarly books: history and historical methodology, Afro-American life, philosophy and science. Query, including outline of chapters, synopsis of book, maximum number of words projected and tentative date of ms. Recently published *Envelopes of Sound*, by Grele (oral history); nd *Introduction to Thoroughbred Handicapping*,(multi-disciplinary); *Perception, Theory, Commitment*, by Brown (philosophy/science) and *US Diplomatic Codes*, by Weber (history).

PRENTICE-HALL, Juvenile Division, Englewood Cliffs NJ 07632. Manuscripts Editor: Rose Lopez. Publishes hardcover and paperback originals (90%) and paperback reprints (10%). Published 42 titles in 1978, 50 in 1979; plans 50 in 1980. Pays royalty; average advance. SASE. Reports in 2 weeks. Book catalog for SASE.
Nonfiction: Americana (8-12 in short chapters), biography (7-10 of outlaws, magicians and other characters), business/economics (7-10 and 9-12), health (teenage problems by MDs only), history (any unusual approaches), humor (no jokes or riddles but funny fiction), music (keen interest in basic approaches, no biographies), politics (7-10 and 8-12), sociology (8-12), and sports (6-9). Query. Recently published *A Kids Guide to the Economy*, by Riedel; *Museum People*, by Thomson; and *Grains*, by Brown.
Fiction: Gothic, humor, mainstream and mystery. Submit outline/synopsis and sample chapters Recently published *Haunted House*, by Hughes (bubblegum gothic); *Go Ask Alice* (documentary); and *Flat On My Face*, by First (8-12 sports humor).

PRENTICE-HALL, INC., Trade Division, Englewood Cliffs NJ 07632. Editor-in-Chief: John Grayson Kirk. Publishes hardcover and paperback originals and reprints. Free book catalog. Submit outlines and sample chapters for nonfiction; submit complete ms for fiction. Will consider photocopied submissions. "Always keep 1 or more copies on hand in case original submission is lost in the mail." Reports in 4-6 weeks. SASE.
General: "All types of fiction and trade nonfiction, save poetry, drama and westerns. Average acceptable length: 80,000 words. The writer should submit his work professionally and be prepared to participate to the extent required in the book's promotion." Publishes adult trade mainstream fiction, Americana, art, biography, business, history, humor, medicine and psychiatry, music, nature, philosophy, politics, reference, religion, science, self-help and how-to, sports, hobbies and recreation.

PRENTICE-HALL OF CANADA, LTD., 1870 Birchmont Rd., Scarborough, Ontario, Canada M1P 2J7. (416)293-3621. Editor-in-Chief: G.B. Halpin. Trade Editor: Janice Whitford. Publishes hardcover and paperback originals (90%) and reprints (10%). Published 40 titles in 1978; plans 50 in 1979. Pays 10-12½-15% royalty; advance "is determined by publication." Simultaneous and photocopied submissions OK. Reports in 4-6 weeks. SAE and International Reply Coupons. Free book catalog.
Nonfiction: Publishes art, biography, history, hobbies, how-to, humor, nature, photography, politics, recreation, references, self-help, sports and technical. Submit outline and "3-4 representative sample chapters along with brief author biography including previous publishing experience, if any." Recently published *The Art of Glen Loates*, by Loates/Duval (art); *Complete Guide to Total Fitness*, by Percival/Taylor (how-to/reference); and *The OK Way to Slim: Weight Control Through Transactional Analysis*, by Laverty (self-help).

THE PRESERVATION PRESS, National Trust for Historic Preservation, 1785 Massachusetts Ave. NW, Washington DC 20036. Publishes nonfiction books and periodicals on historic preservation (saving and reusing the "built environment"). Books are almost entirely commissioned by the publishers. Subject matter encompasses architecture and architectural history, neighborhood preservation, regional planning, preservation law, building restoration and rural area conservation. No local history. Query. Recently published *Built to Last: A Handbook on Recycling Old Buildings*, *What Style Is It?*; and *Old and New Architecture: Design Relationships*.

PRESS PACIFICA, Box 47, Kailua HI 96734. Publisher: Jane Wilkins Pultz. Publishes hardcover and paperback originals (50%) and reprints (50%). Published 6 titles in 1979. Pays 10% royalty "with escalations"; advance averages $100. Simultaneous and photocopied ("if on good white paper and very readable") submissions OK. Reports in 4 weeks-3 months. SASE. Book catalog for 50¢.
Nonfiction: History (especially women and Hawaii); Hawaiiana; women (history, biography, anthologies, feminist theory); self-help; and how-to. "We are open to new authors who have expertise in their field." No technical or supernatural material. Submit outline/synopsis and sample chapters. Recently published *Loom and Spindle*, by H.H. Robinson (women's

history/autobiography); *I Like Poems and Poems Like Me*, edited by P. Pagliaro; and *Job Searching in Hawaii*, by A. Lim.

PRICE/STERN/SLOAN INC., PUBLISHERS, 410 N. La Cienega Blvd., Los Angeles CA 90048. Imprints include Cliff House Books, Serendipity Books and Laughter Library. Executive Editor: L.L. Sloan. Publishes paperback trade originals. Published 50 titles in 1978 and 50 in 1979. Pays royalty or by outright purchase; no advance. Simultaneous and photocopied submissions OK. SASE. Reports in 2-3 months. Book catalog for SASE.
Nonfiction: Humor; self-help; and satire (limited). Submit outline/synopsis and sample chapters. Recently published *How to Flatten Your Stomach*, by J. Everroad (how-to); *Murphy's Law*, by A. Bloch (collection of humor); *Legal Guide to Mother Goose*, by D. Sandburg; and *The Excuse Book*, by M. Jacobs (original humor).

*PRINCETON BOOK CO., PUBLISHERS, 20 Nassau St., Princeton NJ 08540. (609)924-2244. Editorial Director: Charles Woodford. Publishes hardcover and paperback originals (70%) and reprints (30%). Published 5 titles in 1978; plans 6 in 1979. Subsidy publishes 10% of titles, based on "the marketability of the book and the expense of producing it." Pays 10% royalty; no advance. Simultaneous and photocopied submissions OK. Reports in 6 weeks. SASE. Free book catalog.
Nonfiction: Professional books and college textbooks on education, physical education, dance, psychology, sociology, physical therapy and recreation. No "books that have a strictly trade market." Submit outline/synopsis and sample chapters. Recently published *Making it Till Friday: A Guide to Successful Classroom Management*, by Long/Frye (college textbook); *Motor Development: Issues and Applications*, by Ridenour (professional book); and *The Dance Technique of Doris Humphrey and Its Creative Potential*, by Stodelle (text).

PRUETT PUBLISHING CO., 3235 Prairie Ave., Boulder CO 80301. Managing Editor: Gerald Keenan. Published 24 titles in 1978; plans 26 in 1979. Royalty contract is "dependent on the price we receive from sales." No advance. "Most books that we publish are aimed at special interest groups. As a small publisher, we feel most comfortable in dealing with a segment of the market that is very clearly identifiable, and one we know we can reach with our resources." Free catalog on request. Mss must conform to the Chicago *Manual of Style*. Legible photocopies acceptable. Query. Reports in 2-4 weeks. SASE.
General Adult Nonfiction and Textbooks: Pictorial railroad histories; outdoor activities related to the Intermountain West; some Western Americana. Textbooks with a regional (Intermountain) aspect for pre-school through college level. Also, special education, with emphasis on student-oriented workbooks. Does not want to see anything with the personal reminiscence angle or biographical studies of little-known personalities. "Like most small publishers, we try to emphasize quality from start to finish, because, for the most part, our titles are going to a specialized market that is very quality conscious. We also feel that one of our strong points is the personal involvement ('touch') so often absent in a much larger organization." Recently published *Montana: Images of the Past*, by K. Ross Toole/William Farr (pictorial history); and *The Circus Moves by Rail*, by Parkinson/Fox.

PSG PUBLISHING CO., INC., 545 Great Rd., Littleton MA 01460. (617)486-8971. President/Editor-in-Chief: Frank Paparello. Managing Editor: Sarah Jeffries. Hardcover and paperback originals. Specializes in publishing medical and dental books for the professional and graduate student market. Pays 10% royalty; no advance. Send prints of photos to accompany ms. Simultaneous submissions OK. Reports in 2-4 weeks. SASE. Free book catalog.
Nonfiction: Sarah Jeffries, Department Editor. Publishes scientific books and ones on medicine and psychiatry. Query or submit complete ms. Recently published *Reproductive Development of the Female*, by Montagu; *Clinical Psychopharmacology*, by J. Bernstein (drug reference); *Suicide*, by Hankoff and Einsidler; and *Bone Tumors*, by Jaffe.

PULSE-FINGER PRESS, Box 16697, Philadelphia PA 19139. Editor-in-Chief: Orion Roche. Publishes hardcover and paperback originals. Published 7 titles in 1978; plans 8 in 1979 and not more than 10 in 1980. Offers standard minimum book contract; less for poetry. Advance varies, depending on quality. "Not less than $100 for poetry; or $500 for fiction." Query. No unsolicited mss. Reports in 3 months. "SASE must accompany inquiries, or they will not be acknowledged."
Fiction and Poetry: "We're interested in subjects of general concern with a focus on fiction and poetry. All types considered; tend to the *contemporary-cum-avant-garde*. No length requirements. Our only stipulation is quality, as we see it." Recently published *Bronchitis*

Caper, by DeAria; *The Circular Seesaw*, by Finkel; *Disco Candy and Other Stories*, by L. C. Phillips; and *Loan Mower*, by Vanzetti Stine.
Tips: "Concentrate on fiction, poetry and drama of the highest quality. We are not interested in how-to books or the contemporary versions of commercial success. We are not interested in fiction which is a disguised form of 'fact.' We want prose which is vivid but not overblown; poetry which is dramatic and daring in terms of image and metaphor."

PURDUE UNIVERSITY PRESS, South Campus Courts, D., West Lafayette IN 47907. (317)749-6083. Director: William J. Whalen. Managing Editor: Verna Emery. Publishes hardcover and paperback originals. Specializes in scholarly books from all areas of academic endeavor. Pays 10% royalty on list price; no advance. Published 7-8 titles in 1978. Photocopied submissions OK "if author will verify that it does not mean simultaneous submission elsewhere." Reports in 2-4 months. SASE. Free book catalog.
Nonfiction: Publishes agriculture, Americana, art (but no color plates), biography, communication, engineering, history, nature, philosophy, poetry, political science, psychology, reference, religious, scientific, sociology, technical, and literary criticism. "Works of scholarship only." Recently published *Mark Twain Speaks for Himself*, edited by Paul Fatout; *Rhetoric, Philosophy, and Literature*, by Don M. Burks; and *In Quest in Crisis: Emperor Joseph I and the Habsburg Monarch*, by Charles W. Ingrao. "As a university press, we are interested only in works of academic merit which display creative research and scholarship."

G.P. PUTNAM'S SONS, 200 Madison Ave., New York NY 10016. (212)576-8900. Editor-in-Chief: Phyllis Grann. Juvenile Editor-in-Chief: Charles Mercer. Publishes hardcover and paperback originals. "Payment is on standard royalty basis." Free book catalog. "Well-known authors may submit outline and sample chapter." Unsolicited mss not accepted. Reports on queries in 1 week. SASE.
Nonfiction, Fiction and Juveniles: Nonfiction in history, biography, exploration, etc. Publishes juvenile fiction and nonfiction. "Adult mss must be a bare minimum of 60,000 words; juveniles vary in length, of course, depending upon whether they are young adult or picture book texts."

QUEENSTON HOUSE PUBLISHING, LTD., 102 Queenston St., Winnipeg, Manitoba, Canada R3N 0W5. 9204)489-6862. Editorial Director: Joan Parr. Publishes hardcover and paperback originals. Published 10 titles in 1978; plans 10 in 1979, 10 in 1980. Pays 10% royalty; no advance. Photocopied submissions OK. Reports in 3-6 months. SASE. Book catalog for SASE.
Nonfiction: Autobiography; biography; history; and political issues. Query. Recently published *Ed Schreyer: A Social Democrat in Power*, edited by P. Beaulieu; *Political Warriors*, by L. Stinson (history); and *Paper Tomahawks*, by J. Burke (expose).
Fiction: "We are not interested in fiction of a strictly sensational nature, i.e., sex, disaster. A lot depends on the quality of writing, so we will look at query letters on about any subject." Query. Recently published *Corner Stone*, by B. Kaplan; *A Small Informal Dance*, by H. Levi; and *Wanna Fight, Kid?*, by C. Duncan.

QUICK FOX (formerly *Links Books*), 33 W. 60th St., New York NY 10023. Editor-in-Chief: Jim Charlton. Managing Editor: Jeanette Mall. Publishes paperback originals. Published 40 titles in 1978; will do 50 in 1979. Pays 7% royalty; advance varies. Simultaneous and photocopied submissions OK. Reports in 1 month. SASE. Free book catalog.
Nonfiction: "We publish general interest books in a special way—contemporary culture and society; practical and instructional books; and photography and art books." Query or submit outline/synopsis and sample chapters. Recently published *Good Lives*, by Wise/Weiss (home design); *Art Deco Internationale*, by Brown/Weinstein (design); and *Paul Simon* (photo/song collection).

RAND McNALLY, Trade and Education Division, Box 7600, Chicago IL 60680. Variable royalty and advance schedule. Trade books payment on royalty basis or outright; mass market juveniles outright. Reports in 6 to 8 weeks. Enclose return postage.
General Nonfiction: Adult manuscripts should be sent to Stephen P. Sutton, Editor, Adult Books, Trade Division, but query first on the subjects of Americana, travel, natural history, personal adventure or self-help. Contracts are sometimes offered on the basis of outline and sample chapter.
Trade Juveniles: Dorothy Haas, Editor. Picture books ages 3-8; fiction and nonfiction ages 8-12; special interest books (no fiction) for young adults. Send picture book manuscripts for review. Query on longer manuscripts.
Mass Market Juveniles: Roselyn Bergman, Editor. Picture book scripts, six years and under;

Jr. Elf Books, Elf Books, activity formats. Realistic stories, fantasy, early learning material; not to exceed 600 words and must present varied illustration possibilities.

Textbooks: Education Division publishes books, equipment, other printed materials, and maps for elementary, high schools and colleges in restricted fields. Query Executive Editor, Education Division.

RANDOM HOUSE, INC., 201 E. 50th St., New York NY 10022. Also publishes Vintage Books. Publishes hardcover and paperback originals and reprints. Payment as per standard minimum book contracts. Query. SASE.

Fiction and Nonfiction: Publishes fiction and nonfiction of the "highest standards."

Poetry: Some poetry volumes.

RANDOM HOUSE, INC., Juvenile Division. 201 E. 50th St., New York NY 10022. (212)751-2600. Managing Editor: Elma Otto. Publishes hardcover and paperback originals (95%) and reprints (5%). Published 89 titles in 1978, 80 in 1979. Pays royalty; average advance depending on book. Simultaneous and photocopied submissions OK. SASE. Reports in 6 weeks. Free book catalog for SASE.

Nonfiction: "We are interested in almost all topics, except material for senior-high ages. No mss on cookbooks, how-to, poetry, plays, religion, textbooks and curriculum-oriented materials." Query or submit outline/synopsis and sample chapters or submit complete ms.

Fiction: "We want good stories for pre-school through junior-high." Submit complete ms.

RED DUST, INC., 218 E. 81st St., New York NY 10028. Editor: Joanna Gunderson. Publishes hardcover and paperback originals and translations. Specializes in quality work by new writers. Books printed either simultaneously in hard and paper covers or in hardcover alone, in editions of 1,000 copies. Pays 10-12-15% royalty; offers $300 average advance. Catalog for 15¢ stamp. Will consider photocopied submissions. "Authors should not submit photos or artwork with mss." Query preferred. Submit sample of no more than 10 pages. Reports in 2 months. SASE.

Fiction: Novels and short stories.

Nonfiction and Poetry: Scholarly, art, art history, film and poetry.

REGAL BOOKS, Division of Gospel Light Publications, 110 W. Broadway, Glendale CA 91204. (213)247-2330. Senior Editor: Donald E. Pugh. Estab. 1933. Publishes hardcover and paperback originals and paperback reprints. Published 40 titles in 1978; plans 50 in 1980. Pays 6-14% royalty on paperback titles, 10% for curriculum books. Photocopied submissions OK. Reports in 2-6 weeks. SASE. Free book catalog.

Nonfiction: Missions (gift books); Bible studies (Old and New Testament); Christian living; counseling (self-help; the future); contemporary concerns (biographies); evangelism (church growth); marriage and family; youth; children's books; handcrafts; communication resources; teaching enrichment resources; Bible commentary for Laymen Series; and material for the International Center for Learning. Query or submit outline/synopsis and sample chapters. Recently published *Autobiography of God*, by Lloyd John Ogilve (Parables of Jesus); *Be a Leader People Follow*, by David L. Hocking; and *Your Spiritual Gifts Can Help Your Church Grow*, by C. Peter Wagner (leadership growth).

THE REGENTS PRESS OF KANSAS, (formerly The University Press of Kansas), 366 Watson Library, Lawrence KS 66045. (913)864-4154. Managing Editor: John Langley. Hardcover and paperback originals. Published 17 titles in 1978; plans 16 in 1979, 18 in 1980. "No royalty until manufacturing costs are recovered." No advance. Markets books by direct mail, chiefly to libraries and scholars. "State availability of illustrations if they add significantly to the ms." Photocopied submissions OK. Reports in 4-6 months. SASE. Free book catalog.

Nonfiction: Publishes biography, history, literary criticism, politics, regional subjects, and scholarly nonfiction books. "No dissertations." Query. Recently published *The Korean War: A 25-Year Perspective*, edited by Francis H. Heller (history); *The Crystal Cage: Adventures of the Imagination in the Fiction of Henry James*, by Daniel J. Schneider (literary criticism); and *Philosophical Scepticism and Ordinary Language Analysis*, by Garrett L. Vander Veer (philosophy).

REGENTS PUBLISHING CO., INC., 2 Park Ave., New York NY 10016. Published 28 titles last year. Prefers queries, outlines, sample chapters. Reports in 3 to 4 weeks. Enclose return postage.

Textbooks: Publishes foreign language texts, multimedia packages and English books for the foreign-born.

*RESOURCE PUBLICATIONS, Box 444, Saratoga CA 95070. Editorial Director: William Burns. Publishes paperback originals. Published 2 titles in 1978; plans 6 in 1979, 6 in 1980. Has subsidy published 1 title; "if the author can present and defend a personal publicity effort, and the work is in our field, we will consider it." Pays 8% royalty; no advance. Photocopied submissions (with written assurance that work is not being submitted simultaneously) OK. Reports in 2 months. SASE.
Nonfiction: "We look for creative source books for the religious education, worship and religious art fields. How-to books, especially for contemporary religious art forms, are of particular interest (dance, mime, drama, choral reading, singing, music, musicianship, bannermaking, statuary, or any visual art form). No heavy theoretical, philosophical, or theological tomes. Nothing utterly unrelated or unrelatable to the religious market as described above." Query or submit outline/synopsis and sample chapters. Recently published *The Music Locator*, by Cunningham (index of published religious music).
Fiction: "Light works providing examples of good expression through the religious art forms. Any collected short works in the areas of drama, dance, song, stories, anecdotes or good visual art. Long poems or illustrated light novels which entertain while teaching a life value which could be useful in religious education or to the religious market at large." Query or submit outline/synopsis and sample chapters. Recently published *Pilgrim's Road*, by M. Wood (collected songs); *Picture the Dawning*, by P.F. Page (songs); and *We Believe*, by G. Collopy (assorted notepapers).
Tips: "Prepare a clear outline of the work and an ambitious schedule of public appearances to help make it known and present both as a proposal to the publisher. With our company a work that can be serialized or systematically excerpted in our periodicals is always given special attention."

RESTON PUBLISHING CO. (subsidiary of Prentice-Hall), 11480 Sunset Hills Rd., Reston VA 22090. President: Matthew I. Fox. Publishes hardcover originals. Offers standard minimum book contract of 10-12-15%; advance varies. Published 85 titles last year. Free catalog on request. Will consider photocopied submissions. Submit outline and sample chapters. Reports immediately. Enclose return postage.
Textbooks: "Primarily for the junior college and vocational/technical school market. Professionally oriented books for in-service practitioners and professionals. All material should be written to appeal to these markets in style and subject. We are able to attract the best experts in all phases of academic and professional life to write our books. But we are always seeking new material in all areas of publishing; any area that is represented by courses at any post-secondary level."

FLEMING H. REVELL CO., Central Ave., Old Tappan NJ 07675. Imprints include Power Books and Spire. Editorial Director: Ernest Owen. Managing Editor: A. Curtiss. Estab. 1897. Publishes hardcover and paperback originals and reprints. Publishes 60 titles/year. Pays royalty; sometimes an advance. Simultaneous and photocopied submissions OK. SASE. Reports in 2 months. Book catalog for SASE.
Nonfiction: Religion and inspirational. "All books must appeal to Protestant-evangelical readers." Query. Recently published *Hear the Children Crying*, by Dale Evans Rogers; *Father Ten Boom*, by Corrie Ten Boom; and *Sipping Saints*, by David Wilkerson.

REYMONT ASSOCIATES, 29 Reymont Ave., Rye NY 10580. Editor-in-Chief: D.J. Scherer. Managing Editor: Felicia Scherer. Paperback originals. Pays 10-12-15% royalty; no advance. Submit outline/synopsis and sample chapters. Simultaneous and photocopied submissions OK. Reports in 2-4 weeks. SASE. Book catalog for SASE.
Nonfiction: Publishes business; how-to; self-help; and unique directories. "Aim for 7,500-10,000 words." Recently published *'Til Business Do Us Part*, by Dr. E. Jerry Walker.

ROBERTSON/MERRELL, Box 5307A, Whitney Towers, Hamden CT 06518. Editorial Director: D. Trevor Michaels. Senior Editor: J.D. Roberts. Publishes hardcover and paperback originals (20%) and reprints (80%). Published 25 titles in 1978; plans 100 in 1979. Pays 10-15% royalty; no advance. SASE. Reports in 1-3 months.
Nonfiction: Business and management, medical, personnel, photographic presentations and general topics. Recently published *Cardiac Emergencies*, by D.T. Michaels (supplemental medical text); *Operational Management*, by Roberts and Michaels (business management reference manual); *Personnel Management and Management Aspects*, multi-authored.

RICHARDS ROSEN PRESS, 29 E. 21st St., New York NY 10010. (212)777-3017. Editor: Ruth C. Rosen. Estab. 1950. Publishes hardcover originals. Pays royalty; no advance.

Simultaneous and photocopied submissions OK. SASE. Reports in 3-4 weeks. Free book catalog.

Nonfiction: Arts, health, history, hobbies, psychology, science, self-help, sociology and sports. "Our books are geared to the young adult audience whom we reach via school and public libraries. Most of the books we publish are related to guidance-career and personal adjustment. We also publish material on the theater, science and women, as well as journalism for schools. Interested in supplementary material for enrichment of school curriculum." Query. Recently published *Coping With School Age Motherhood*, by Walsworth and Bradley (teenage pregnancy); *Your Future in Creative Careers*, by Fixman (how-to find jobs in this area—preparations, etc.); and *Gilbert and Sullivan Lexicon*, by Benford (terms in Gilbert and Sullivan made clear for American audience).

ROUTLEDGE & KEGAN PAUL, LTD., 9 Park St., Boston MA 02108. Publishes hardcover and paperback originals and reprints. Pays standard 10-12½-15% royalty contract "on clothbound editions, if the books are not part of a series"; usual advance is $250-2,500. Published 175 titles in 1978; plans 185 in 1979, 200 in 1980. Query with outline and sample chapters. Submit complete ms "only after going through outline and sample chapters step." Reports in 2-3 months. Enclose check for return postage.

Nonfiction: "Academic, reference, and scholarly levels: English and European literary criticism, drama and theater, social sciences, philosophy and logic, psychology, parapsychology, oriental religions, mysticism, history, political science and education. Our books generally form a reputable series under the general editorship of distinguished academics in their fields. The approach should be similar to the styles adopted by Cambridge University Press, Harvard University Press and others." Interested in material for the International Library of Sociology. Length: 30,000-250,000 words.

RUTGERS UNIVERSITY PRESS, 30 College Ave., New Brunswick NJ 08903. Published 18 titles in 1978; plans 20 in 1979, 22 in 1980. Free book catalog. Final decision depends on time required to secure competent professional reading reports. Enclose return postage.

Nonfiction: Scholarly books in history, literary criticism, anthropology, sociology, political science, biography and criminal justice. Regional nonfiction must deal with mid-Atlantic region with emphasis on New Jersey. Query. Length: 60,000 words minimum. Recently published *Alcuin and Beowulf: An Eighth-Century View*, by Bolton; and *Sir Philip Sidney: Rebellion in Arcadia*, by McCoy.

WILLIAM H. SADLIER, INC., 11 Park Place, New York NY 10007. Vice President/Director of Product Development: Eileen Anderson. Pays 6% royalty contract for elementary textbooks; 8% for high school textbooks. Submit outline and sample chapters to Product Development. Reports "as soon as possible." SASE.

Textbooks: Elementary and secondary textbooks. Whole or significant part of school market should be identified, competition studied, proposal developed and submitted with representative sample. Interested in language ars and social studies, economics, history, politics, religion and sociology.

ST. ANTHONY MESSENGER PRESS, 1615 Republic St., Cincinnati OH 45210. Editor-in-Chief: The Rev. Jeremy Harrington, O.F.M. Publishes paperback originals. Published 6 titles in 1978; plans 8 in 1979, 10 in 1980. Pays 6-8% royalty; offers $500 average advance. Books are sold in bulk to groups (study clubs, high school or college classes). Will send free catalog to writer on request. Will consider photocopied submissions if they are not simultaneous submissions to other publishers. Query or submit outline and sample chapters. Enclose return postage.

Religion: "We try to reach the Catholic market with topics near the heart of the ordinary Catholic's belief. We want to offer insight and inspiration and thus give people support in living a Christian life in a pluralistic society. We are not interested in an academic or abstract approach. Our emphasis is on the popular writing with examples, specifics, color amd anecdotes." Length: 25,000-40,000 words. Recently published *Learning to Live Again*, by Judith Tate; and *Beyond the Kitchen Sink*, by Robin Worthington.

ST. MARTIN'S PRESS, 175 5th Ave., New York NY 10010. Published 350 titles last year. SASE. Reports "promptly."

General: Publishes general fiction and nonfiction; major interest in adult fiction and nonfiction, history, self-help, political science, popular science, biography, scholarly, popular reference, etc. "No children's books." Query. Recently published *The Fan Pavilions*, by M.M. Kaye.

Textbooks: College textbooks. Query.

SCHENKMAN PUBLISHING CO., INC., 3 Mt. Auburn Place, Cambridge MA 02138. (617)492-4952. Editor-in-Chief: Alfred S. Schenkman. Publishes hardcover and paperback originals. Specializes in textbooks. Published 30 titles in 1978; plans 40 in 1979, 50 in 1980. Royalty varies, but averages 10%. "In some cases, no royalties are paid on first 2,000 copies sold." No advance. State availability of photos and/or illustrations. Simultaneous and photocopied submissions OK. Reports in 1-2 months. SASE. Free book catalog.
Nonfiction: Publishes economics, history, psychology, sociology and textbooks. Query.
Recent Titles: *A Spectre Is Haunting America*, by Harold Freeman; and *Health Care Services in China*, by Rhoda Sun.

SCHIRMER BOOKS, Macmillan Publishing Co., Inc., 866 3rd Ave., New York NY 10022. Editor-in-Chief: Ken Stuart. Publishes hardcover and paperback originals (90%) and paperback reprints (10%). Pays in royalties; small advance. Published 20 books in 1978; plans 20 in 1979, 20 in 1980. Submit photos and/or illustrations "if central to the book, not if decorative or tangential." Photocopied and simultaneous submissions OK. Reports in 1-2 months. SASE. Book catalog for SASE.
Nonfiction: Published how-to, music, self-help and textbooks. Submit outline/synopsis and sample chapters. Recently published *Beethoven*, by M. Solomon (biography); and *Baker's Biographical Dictionary of Musicians*, by Nicolas Slanimsky (reference).

SCHOLIUM INTERNATIONAL, INC., 130-30 31st Ave., Flushing NY 11354. Editor-in-Chief: Arthur L. Candido. Publishes hardcover and paperback orignals. Published 5 titles in 1978; plans 8 in 1979. Standard minimum book contract of 12%. Free book catalog. Will consider photocopied submissions. Query. Reports in 2 weeks. SASE.
Science and Technology: Subjects include cryogenics, electronics, aviation, medicine, physics, etc. "We also publish books in other areas whenever it is felt the manuscript has good sales and reception potential. Contact us prior to sending ms, outlining subject, number of pages and other pertinent information which would enable us to make a decision as to whether we would want to review the manuscript."

CHARLES SCRIBNER'S SONS, 597 5th Ave., New York NY 10017. Director of Publishing: Jacek K. Galazka. Publishes hardcover originals and hardcover and paperback reprints. Published 300 titles last year. "Our contract terms, royalties and advances vary, depending on the nature of the project." Prefers photocopied submissions. Reports in 1-2 months. Enclose return postage.
General: Publishes adult fiction and nonfiction, practical books, garden books, reference sets, cookbooks, history and science. Query. Adult Trade Editors: Laurie Graham, Charles Scribner III, Wendy Rieder, Susanne Kirk, Dwight Allen.

CHARLES SCRIBNER'S SONS, Children's Books Department, 597 5th Ave., New York NY 10017. (212)486-4035. Editorial Director, Children's Books: Lee Anna Deadrick. Senior Editor, Children's Books: Clare Costello. Estab. 1846. Publishes hardcover originals and paperback reprints. Published 35 titles in 1978; plans 35 in 1979, 35 in 1980. Pays royalty; offers advance. Photocopied submissions OK. SASE. Free book catalog.
Nonfiction: Animals, art, biography, health, hobbies, humor, nature, photography, recreation, science and sports. Query.
Fiction: Adventure, fantasy, historical, humor, mainstream, mystery, science fiction and suspense. Submit outline/synopsis and sample chapters.

THE SEABURY PRESS, 815 2nd Ave., New York NY 10017. (212)557-0500. Imprints include Crossroad Books, Clarion Books and Continuum Books. Estab. 1952. Publishes hardcover originals (85%) and paperback (adult only) reprints (15%). Published 100 titles in 1978; plans 80 in 1979, 80-90 in 1980. Pays 10-15% royalty; offers $1,500 advance. Photocopied submissions OK. SASE. Reports in 6-8 weeks. Free book catalog.
Nonfiction: Americana, animals, biography, juveniles, philosophy, politics, psychology, reference, religion, self-help and sociology. Query. Recently published *Growing Up Handicapped*, by Evelyn Ayrault (self-help); *Brother to a Dragonfly*, by Will Campbell (memoir); *Superpuppy*, by D. Manus and Jull Pinkwater; and *Suicide and Young People*, by Arnold Madigor (juvenile).

'76 PRESS, Box 2686, Seal Beach CA 90740. (213)596-3491. Editor-in-Chief: Wallis W. Wood. Publishes hardcover and paperback originals. Published 3 titles in 1978; plans 4 in 1979, 4 in

1980. Pays 5% royalty; offers $2,500 average advance. Simultaneous and photocopied submissions OK. SASE. Free book catalog.

Nonfiction: "Economics, politics and international relations written from conservative, anti-big government perspective. Information on author's credentials on subject matter is very important." Submit outline/synopsis and sample chapters. State availability of photos and/or illustrations. Recently published *The War on Gold*, by A. C. Sutton; *Confrontation*, by M. Spring; *The Rockefeller File*, by G. Allen; and *Tax Target: Washington*, by G. Allen.

ANDREWS AND McMEEL, INC., 6700 Squibb Rd., Mission KS 66202. Editor-in-Chief: James F. Andrews. Managing Editor: Donna Martin. Publishes hardcover and paperback originals. Publishes 30 titles annually. Pays standard royalties; offers negotiable advance. Simultaneous submissions OK, but "the letter should indicate if the submission is simultaneous"; photocopied submissions OK. SASE. Reports in 1-2 months. Book catalog on request.

Nonfiction: Biography, cooking and foods, health, history, how-to, humor, philosophy, politics, psychology, religion, self-help, sociology, sports and travel. Query. Recently published *Saga of a Wayward Sailor*, by Tristan Jones (true adventure); *A Catch of Anti-Letters*, by Thomas Merton and Robert Lax (religious); and *Formula Book 3*, by Ed Nigh and Stark Research Associates (how-to).

Fiction: Adventure, mainstream and suspense. Submit complete ms. Recently published *The Rosary Murders*, by William X. Kienzle; and *At Button's*.

SHOAL CREEK PUBLISHERS, INC., Box 9737, Austin TX 78766. (512)451-7545. Senior Editor: Judith Timberg. Publishes hardcover originals (90%) and reprints (10%). Published 6 titles in 1978; plans 8 in 1979, 9 in 1980. Pays 10% royalty; no advance. Simultaneous and potocopied submissions OK. Reports "as soon as practical." SASE. Free books catalog.

Nonfiction: Historical, biographical and children's books. Submit outline/snyopsis and sample chapters. Recently published *Hondo, My Father*, by Becky Crouch Patterson (biographical memoir); and *Indianola, The Mother of Western Texas*, by Brownson Malsch (history).

Fiction: Some fiction (historical novels).

Tips: "Since this is a small company where one person does everything, it helps to be an editor and proofreader as well as a writer. Take at least one course in book editing."

THE SHOE STRING PRESS, (Archon Books, Linnet Books), 995 Sherman Ave., Hamden CT 06514. (203)248-6307. President: Mrs. Frances T. Rutter. Published 60 books in 1978; plans 65 in 1979, 70 in 1980. Royalty of net; no advance. Reports in 4-6 weeks. Enclose return postage.

Nonfiction: Publishes scholarly books: history, biography, literary criticism, reference, geography, bibliogaphy, military history, information science, library science, education and general adult nonfiction. Preferred length: 40,000-130,000 words, though there is no set limit. Query with table of contents and sample chapters.

SIGNPOST BOOKS, 8912 192nd SW, Edmonds WA 98020. Editor-in-Chief: Cliff Cameron. Publishes paperback originals. Offers standard minimum book contract of 10%. Free book catalog. Query. Reports in 3 weeks. SASE.

Nonfiction: "Books on outdoor subjects emphasizing self-propelled activity such as hiking, canoeing and bicycling. Also books of general interest to Northwesterners. History, natural science, related to the Pacific Northwest. Books should have strong environmenal material for a general audience, where applicable." Recently published *Trails of the Sawtooth and White Clouds*, by Margaret Fuller; *The Bicycle: A Commuting Alternative*, by Fred Wolfe; and *Canoeing the Boundary Waters*, by Marion Stresau.

SILVER BURDETT, Subsidiary of Scott, Foresman Co., 250 James St., Morristown NJ 07960. Editor-in-Chief: Barbara Howell. Publishes hardcover and paperback originals. Published 180 titles in 1978; plans 180 in 1979, 150 in 1980. "Textbook rates only, el-hi range." Query. SASE.

Education: Produces educational materials for preschoolers, elementary and high school students and professional publications for teachers. Among materials produced: textbooks, teachers' materials, other print and nonprint classroom materials including educational games, manipulatives and audiovisual aids (silent and sound 16mm films and filmstrips, records, multimedia kits, overhead transparencies, tapes, etc.). Assigns projects to qualified writers on occasion. Writer must have understanding of school market and school learning materials.

SILVERMINE PUBLISHERS, INC., Comstock Hill, Silvermine, Norwalk CT 06850. President: Marilyn Z. Atkin. Free book catalog. Query. SASE.

Nonfiction: Publishes general nonfiction, biogaphy and books dealing with fine arts and architecture. "We are not interested in name authors, but insist on good writing. Our books are designed to last (that is, they are not 1-season phenomena). Thus, a typical book over a period of 3-5 years may earn $3,000-6,000 royalties. It is our opinion that books that are solid text, unillustrated, are not salable avy longer unless they are news or topical (which we are not interested in), fiction by established writers (which we are not interested in), or books on special subjects."

SIMON & SCHUSTER, Trade Books Division, 1230 6th Ave., New York NY 10020. Editor-in-Chief: Michael Korda. Administrative Editor: Daniel Johnson. "If we accept a book for publication, business arrangements are worked out with the author or his agent and a contract is drawn up. The specific terms vary according to the type of book and other considerations. Royalty rates are more or less standard among publishers. Special arrangements are made for anthologies, translations and projects involving editorial research services." Published over 200 titles in 1978. Free book catalog. "All unsolicited mss will be returned unread. Only mss submitted by agents or recommended to us by friends or actively solicited by us will be considered. Our requirements are as follows: All mss submitted for consideration should be marked to the attention of the editorial department. Mystery novels should be so labeled in order that they may be sent to the proper editors without delay. It usually takes at least three weeks for the author to be notified of a decision—often longer. Sufficient postage for return by first-class registered mail, or instructions for return by express collect, in case of rejection, should be included. Mss must be typewritten, double-spaced, on one side of the sheet only. We suggest margins of about one inch all around and the standard 8"x11" typewriter paper." Prefers complete mss.
General: "Simon and Schuster publishes books of adult fiction, history, biography, science, philosophy, the arts and religion, running 50,000 words or more. Our program does not, however, include school textbooks, extremely technical or highly specialized works, or, as a general rule, plays. Exception have been made, of course, for extraordinary mss of great distinction or significance." Recently published *Sideshow*, by William Showcross (history/current affairs); *The Second Ring of Power*, by C. Castaneda (anthropology); and *White Album*, by Joan Gidion.

CHARLES B. SLACK, INC., 6900 Grove Rd., Thorofare NJ 08086. (212)285-9777. Editor-in-Chief: Kenton T. Finch. Managing Editors: Kaye Coraluzzo, Ken Senerth, Peg Carnine. Book Editor: Pamela Wight. Assistant Managing Editors: Pamela Ballinger, Judy Faulkner. Editorial Assistants: Linda Breyan, Kathy Dunn, Giny Miller, Frank Malinowski. Publishes hardcover and paperback originals (90%) and reprints (10%). Specializes in medical and health education texts. Pays 10% (of net proceeds) royalty; advances are discouraged. Published 9 titles in 1978; plans 10 in 1979, 9-10 in 1980. State availability of photos and/or illustrations to accompany ms. Simultaneous submissions OK. Reports in 1-2 months. SASE. Free book pamphlet for SASE.
Nonfiction: Publishes medicine and psychiatry, psychology, scientific and textbooks. Query, submit outline/synopsis and sample chapters, or submit complete ms. All queries, outlines and mss should be sent to the attention of Kenton T. Finc. Recently published *The Mature Years: A Geriatric Occupational Therapy Text*, by S.C. Lewis and *Human Advocacy and PL 94-142: The Educator's Roles*, by L.F. Buscaglia and E. Williams.
How to Break In: "We specialize in publications for the allied health and educational fields, consequently a strong English background with a broad medical knowledge is necessary. As more publishers realize the need for specialization, the writer today should direct his education to complement the publishing industry to increase his chances of marketing his skills."

SLEEPY HOLLOW RESTORATIONS, INC., 150 White Plains Rd., Tarrytown NY 10591. (914)631-8200. Editor-in-Chief: Saverio Procario. Managing Editor: Bruce D. MacPhail. Publishing hardcover and paperack originals (85%) and hardcover reprints (15%). Pays 5-10% (net) royalty; no advance. Published 5 titles in 1978. State availability of photos and/or illustrations to accompany ms. Simultaneous and potocopied submissions OK. Reports in 1-2 months. SASE. Free book catalog.
Nonfiction: Publishes Americana; art (American decorative arts); biography; cookbooks; cooking and foods (regional, historical); history (especially American, New York state and colonial through modern times); technical (17th- to 19th-Century technology); travel (regional and New York state); American literature and literary criticism (especially 10th-Century). Query, addressing it to the Managing Editor. Recently published *Life Along the Hudson*, by A. Keller (regional history); *Van Cortlandt Family Papers*, edited by J. Judd (American history);

A Century of Commentary on the Works of Washington Irving, edited by A. Myers (American literary criticism).

THE SMITH, 5 Beekman St., New York NY 10038. Publishes hardcover and paperback originals. The Smith is now owned by the Generalist Association, Inc., a nonprofit organization, which gives to writers awards averaging $500 for book projects. Published 8 titles in 1978; plans 12 in 1979. Free book catalog. Send query first for nonfiction; sample chapter preferred for fiction. Reports in six weeks. SASE.
Nonfiction and Fiction: "Original fiction—no specific schools or categories; for nonfiction, the more controversial, the better." Editor of Adult Fiction: Harry Smith. Nonfiction Editor: Sidney Bernard.

SOCCER ASSOCIATES, Box 634, New Rochelle NY 10802. Editor: Jeff Miller. Published 75 titles in 1978; plans 200 in 1979, 125 in 1980. Send finished book to Milton Miller. SASE.
Nonfiction: Publishes sports, recreation, leisure time and hobby books under Sport Shelf and Leisure Time Books imprints. Most titles are British and Australian although they do have a special service for authors who publish their own books and desire national and international distribution, promotion and publicity.

SOUNDVIEW BOOKS, 100 Heights Rd., Darien CT 06820. (203)655-4918. Editorial Director: Harold Longman. Publishes hardcover and paperback originals. Published 4 in 1979; plans 8 titles in 1980. Pays 10% royalty; advance averages $1,000 minimum. Simultaneous and photcopied submissions OK. Reports in 4 weeks. SASE.
Nonfiction: "Books on self-help and self-improvement, or perhaps more accurately, self-development. Books can be inspirational in nature, or they can deal with current concerns which are of general interest. The books can be practical. For example, a book on how to avoid heart attacks. If anything this specific were chosen, it should be sympathetically written, and provocative rather than preachy. We are new. This does not mean that we are publishers of last resort and should be the recipients of everything that everybody else has turned down. Although we can't promise stellar advances, we'll probably give the author a better break than most because we understand advertising and promotion, as most publishers do not—and we will push any book we publish. But we're fussy. We happen to like good writing."

SOUTHERN ILLINOIS UNIVERSITY PRESS, Box 3697, Carbondale IL 62901. (618)453-2281. Acting Director: Walter Kent. Published 47 titles in 1978; plans 50 in 1979. Pays 10-12.5% royalty; offers advance. Simultaneous and photocopied submissions OK. SASE. Reports in 1 week. Free book catalog.
Nonfiction: "We are interested in social sciences and contemporry affairs material. No dissertations or collections of previously published articles." Query. Recently published *Delilah*, by Marcus Goodrich, and *Peru: A Short History*, by David Werlich.

SOUTHERN METHODIST UNIVERSITY PRESS, Dallas TX 75275. (214)692-2263. Director: Allen Maxwell; Associate Director and Editor: Margaret L. Hartley. Published 3 titles in 1978; plans 6 in 1979, 9 in 1980. Payment is on royalty basis: 10% of list up to 2,500 copies; 12% for 2,500-5,000 copies; 15% thereafter; no advance. Free book catalog. Appreciates query letters, outlines and sample chapters. Reports "tend to be slow for promising mss requiring ouside reading by authorities." Enclose return postage.
Nonfiction: Regional and scholarly nonfiction. History, Americana, economics, banking, literature and anthropology. Length: open. Recently published *Dallas Yesterday*, by S. Acheson (regional history); *New Perspectives for Bank Directors*, edited by R. B. Johnson; and *The Well-Tempered Lyre: Songs and Verse of the Temperance Movement*, by G.W. Ewing.

SOUTHERN PUBLISHING ASSOCIATION, Box 59, Nashville TN 37202. (615)889-8000. Editor-in-Chief: Richard W. Coffen. Publishes hardcover and paperback originals. Specializes in religiously oriented books. Published 40 titles in 1978; plans 45 in 1970, 40 in 1980. Pays 5-10% royalty; advance averages $100. Simultaneous and photocopied submissions OK. SASE. Reports in 2-4 months. Free book catalog.
Nonfiction: Juveniles (religiously oriented only; 20,000-60,000 words; 128 pages average); Nature (128 pages average); and religious (20,000-60,000 words; 128 pages average). Query or submit outline; synopsis and sample chapters. Recently published *Mindy*, by J. Strong; *No Forty-Hour Week*, by G. Down; and *How to Handle Competition*, by M. Moore.
Tips: "Familiarize yourself with Adventist theology because Southern Publishing Association is owned and operated by the Seventh-day Adventist Church."

STACKPOLE BOOKS, Box 1831, Harrisburg PA 17105. (717)234-5091. Editorial Director: Neil McAleer. Publishes hardcover and paperback originals (90%) and reprints (10%). Specializes in true suspense, outdoor activity, craft, early Americana, music, the future, space and space colonization. Published 35 titles in 1978; plans 35 in 1979, 40 in 1980. Pays 15% royalty of net recepts. Advance averages $1,000. Query and include author's credentials. Send prints if photos/illustrations are to accompany ms. Simultaneous ("no more than to 2 other publishers") and photocopied submissions OK. Reports in 4 weeks. SASE. Free book catalog.
Nonfiction: Publishes true suspense, Americana, how-to, outdoors, psychology, self-help, travel-adventure, future, space activities and energy books.

STANDARD PUBLISHING, 8121 Hamilton Ave., Cincinnati OH 45231. (513)931-4050. Publishes hardcover and paperback originals (85%) and reprints (15%). Specializes in religious books. Published 40 titles in 1978; plans 50 in 1979. Pays 10% maximum royalty. Advance averages $200-1,500. Query or submit outline/synopsis and sample chapter. Reports in 1-2 months. SASE.
Nonfiction: Publishes how-to; crafts (to be used in Christian education); juveniles; reference; Christian education; quiz; puzzle and religious books. All mss must pertain to religon. Recently published *Check Your Lifestyle*, by K. Staton; *Things Happen When Women Care*, by M. Frost; and *Christian Mothers Reveal Their Joys and Sorrows*, by R. Elwood.
Fiction: Publishes religious, devotional books. Recently published *Soaring*, by R. Elwood.

STANFORD UNIVERSITY PRESS, Stanford CA 94305. (415)323-9471. Contact: Editor. Published 36 titles in 1978; plans 29 in 1979, 40 in 1980. Pays 10-15% royalty; "rarely" offers advance. Photocopied submissions OK. SASE. Reports in 2 weeks. Free book catalog.
Nonfiction: Books on European history, the history of China and Japan, anthropology, psychology, taxonomy, literature and Latin American studies. Query. Recently published *Reconciling Man With the Environment*, by Ashby; and *The Development of the Modern State*, by Poggi (sociology).

*STATE HISTORICAL SOCIETY OF WISCONSIN, 816 State St., Madison WI 53706. (608)262-9604. Editorial Director: Paul H. Hass. Senior Editor: William C. Marten. Publishes hardcover and paperback originals (75%) and hardcover reprints (25%). Published 2 titles in 1978; plans 2 in 1979. Subsidy published 66% of titles based on "an educated guess on the availability of a subsidy from some source and the strength of the market for the title." Pays 10% royalty; no advance. Photocopied submissions OK. Reports in 8 weeks. SASE. Free book catalog.
Nonfiction: "Research and interpretation in history of the American Middle West—broadly construed as the Mississippi Valley. Must be thoroughly documented but on topics of sufficient interest to attract the layman as well as the scholar. 150,000-200,000 words of text, exclusive of footnotes and other back matter. No extremely narrowly focused monographs on non-Wisconsin subjects." Recently published *The Old Northwest in the American Revolution: An Anthology*, by D. C. Skaggs; *At Home: Domestic Life in the Post-Centennial Era, 1876-1920*, by G. Talbot; and *The History of Wisconsin, Volume 2: The Civil War Era*, by R. N. Current.

STEIN AND DAY, Scarborough House, Briarcliff Manor NY 10510. Published 105 titles in 1978; plans 100 in 1979, 100 in 1980. Offers standard royalty contract. No unsolicited mss without querying first. Nonfiction, send outline or summary and sample chapter; fiction, send first chapter only. *Must* furnish SASE.
General: Publishes general adult fiction and nonfiction books; no juveniles or college. All types of nonfiction except technical. Quality fiction. Length: 65,000 words. Recently published *Warsaw Diary of Adam Czerniakow*, edited by Raul Hilberg, Stanislaw Staron and Joseph Kermisz; *Secrets*, by F. Lee Bailey; and *Party of the Year*, by John Crosby.

STONE WALL PRESS, INC., 5 Byron St., Boston MA 02108. Senior Editor: Henry Wheelwright. Publishes hardcover and paperback originals. Published 3 titles in 1978; plans 4 in 1979, 4 in 1980. Pays 7% royalty on paperback books, 10% on hardcover; no advance. Simultaneous and photocopied submissions OK. Reports in 2 weeks. SASE. Free book catalog.
Nonfiction: Regional (Northeastern USA) and national outdoors books on specific subjects. Complete treatment is generally required—how-to, where-to, anecdotes, humor, ecology, etc. Photos/drawings to be included with the text. Query. Recently published *Movin' On: Equipment and Techniques for Winter Hikers*, by H. Roberts; *Wild Preserves: Illustrated Recipes for over 100 Natural Jams and Jellies*, by J. Freitus; and *The Northeastern Outdoors: A Field and Travel Guide*, by S. Berman.

STRAWBERRY HILL PRESS, 616 44th Ave., San Francisco CA 94121. President: Jean-Louis Brindamour, PH.d. Senior Editors: Orly Kelly, Diane Sipes. Publishes paperback originals. Published 12 titles in 1978; plans 12 in 1979 , 12 in 1980. "We are a small house, proud of what we do, and intending to stay relatively small (that does not mean that we will do a less-than-professional job in marketing our books, however). The author-publisher relationship is vital, from the moment the contract is signed until there are no more books to sell, and we operate on that premise. We do no hardcovers, and, for the moment at least, our format is limited strictly to 6x9 quality paperbacks, prices between $3.95-7.95. We never print fewer than 5,000 copies in a first printing, with reprintings also never falling below that same figure. Our books are distributed to the trade by Stackpole Books." Pays 10-20% royalty; no advance. Photocopied submissions OK. Reports in 2-3 weeks. SASE. Book catalog for SASE.
Nonfiction: Self-help; inspiration (not religion); cookbooks; health and nutrition; aging; diet; popular philosopy; metaphysics; alternative life styles; third world; minority histories; oral history and popular medicine. No religion, sports, craft books, photography or fine art material. Submit outline/synopsis and sample chapters. Recently published *Sounds From Josephine's Kitchen*, by Josephine Araldo; *The Book of Internal Exercises*, by Dr. Stephen T. Chang with Rick Miller; and *Mirror of the Body*, by Anna Kaye and Don C. Matchan.

STRUCTURES PUBLISHING CO., Box 423, Farmington MI 48024. General Manager: George Williams. Publishes hardcover and paperback originals. Published 10 titles in 1978; plans 9 in 1979, 10 in 1980. Offers standard 10-12% royalty contract. Advance varies, depending on author's reputation and nature of book. Will send a catalog to a writer on request. Submit outline and sample chapters. Photocopied submissions OK. Reports in 4-6 weeks. Enclose return postage.
Technical and How-To: Books related to building. Wants to expand Successful Series which includes books published both for professionals and homeowners in paperback and hardcover. Will consider structure, construction, building and decorating-related topics. "Manuscripts are commissioned, usually. Book layout and design expertise of interest."

*SUN PUBLISHING CO., Box 4383, Albuquerque NM 87106. (505)255-6550. Editor-in-Chief: Skip Whitson. Publishes hardcover and paperback originals (40%) and reprints (60%). Pays 8% royalty; no advance. Will subsidy publish "if we think the book is good enough and if we have the money to do it, we'll publish it on our own; otherwise, the author will have to put up the money." Query or submit outline/snyopsis and table of contents. Send photocopies if photos/illustrations are to accompany ms. Simultaneous and photocopied submissions OK. Reports in 2-4 months. SASE. Book list for SASE.
Nonfiction: Publishes Americana, art, biography, cookbooks, cooking and foods, history, how-to, politics, scientific, self-help, metaphysical, Oriental and new age books. "40- 200-page lengths are preferred." Recently published *Science and Art of Hot Air Ballooning*, by Dichtl/Jackson (science/sports); and *Meditation for Healing*, by J. F. Stone (metaphysical).
Fiction: Publishes science fiction books.
Special Needs: "The Sun Historical Series is looking for short, illustrated manuscripts on various US cities and regions."

THE SUNSTONE PRESS, Box 2321, Santa Fe NM 87501. (505)988-4418. Editor-in-Chief: James C. Smith Jr. Publishes paperback originals; "sometimes hardcover originals." Published 6 titles in 1970; plans 6 in 1979, 6 in 1980. Free book catalog. Query. Reports in 2 months. Enclose return postage.
Nonfiction: How-to series craft books. Books on the history of the Southwest; poetry. Length: open. Recently published *Woody Plants of the Southeast*, by S. Lamb; *Tamotzu in Haiku*, by H. Kimbro; and *Dichos: Sayings from the Spanish*, by C. Aranda (proverbs).

THE SWALLOW PRESS, INC., 811 W. Junior Terrace, Chicago IL 60613. (312)781-2760. Senior Editor: Donna Ippolito. Estab. 1945. Publishes hardcover and paperbacks (95%) and reprints (5%). Published 10 titles in 1978. Pays 10% royalty; advance varies. Photocopied submissions OK. SASE. Reports in 3 months Book catalog for SASE.
Nonfiction: Biography (Western); cookbooks/cooking; history (Western); nature; poetry; politics; recreation; reference (literary); self-help; travel; Western Americana and books on Chicago; particularly unusual guide books; restaurant guides; etc. "We do not want to see books on religion, sports, juvenile, technical or artbooks." Query or submit outline/synopsis and sample chapters. SASE. Recently published *The Creative Journal: The Art of Finding Yourself*, by Lucia Capacchione (finding your inner feelings and using over 50 exercises in journal-keeping for discovering one's inner treasures); *Guide to the Wyoming Mountains and*

Wilderness Areas, by Orrin and Lorraine Bonney; and *Collage of Dreams: The Writings of Anais Nin*, by Sharon Spencer.
Fiction: "We're interested in quality fiction, not genre fiction. No unsolicited fiction manuscripts considered." Query or submit outline/synopsis and sample chapters. SASE. Recently published *There Must Be More to Love Than Death*, by Charles Newman; *The Beach Umbrella*, by Cyrus Colter; and *Cities of the Interior*, by Anais Nin.

SWEET PINE PRESS, 715 N. 4th Ave., Yakima WA 98901. Editorial Director: R.A. Swanson. Publishes paperback originals (100%). Published 5 titles in 1978; 5 in 1979. Pays 40% royalty; no advance. Simultaneous and photocopied submissions OK. Reports in 3 weeks. SASE.
Fiction: Poetry or prose poems. Query or submit complete ms.

*SYMMES SYSTEMS, Box 8101, Atlanta GA 30306. Editor-in-Chief: E.C. Symmes. Publishes hardcover and paperback originals. Pays 10% royalty. "Contracts are usually written for the individual title and may have different terms." No advance. Does 40% subsidy publishing. Will consider photocopied and simultaneous submissions. Acknowledges receipt in 10 days; evaluation within 1 month. Query. SASE.
Nonfiction and Nature: "Our books have mostly been in the art of bonsai (miniature trees). We are publishing quality information for laypersons (hobbyists). Most of the titles introduce information that is totally new for the hobbyist." Clear and concise writing style. Text must be topical, showing state-of-the-art and suggestions on how to stay on top. All books so far have been illustrated with photos and/or drawings. Would like to see more material on bonsai, photography, collecting photographica, and other horticultural subjects. Length: open.

SYRACUSE UNIVERSITY PRESS, 1011 E. Water St., Syracuse NY 13210. (315)423-2596. Director/Editor: Arpena Mesrobian. Published 18 titles in 1979; plans 20 in 1979. Pays royalties. Simultaneous and photocopied submissions OK "only if we are informed." SASE. Reports in 2 weeks on queries; "longer on submissions." Free book catalog.
Nonfiction: "The best opportunities for freelance writers are in our regional program. A catalog is available. We have published books by people with limited formal education, but they were thoroughly acquainted with their subjects, and they wrote simply and directly about them. No vague descriptions or assumptions that a reference to a name (in the case of a biography) or place is sufficient information. The author must make a case for the importance of his subject." Query. Recently published *Adirondack Fishing in the 1930's*, by Vincent Engles (collection of fishing stories); and *Canal Boatman*, by Richard Garrity (semiautobiographical reminiscences of growing up on the Erie Canal).

TAB BOOKS, Sylvester Court, East Norwalk CT 06855. (203)866-5450. Editorial Director: Dorothy M. Greenberg. Senior Editors: Aircraft Series, Joe Christy; Sports Car Series, Dic Van der Feen. Publishes hardcover and paperback originals and reprints. Published 24 titles in 1978; 24 in 1979. Pays 10% royalty; advance averages $700. Photocopied submissions OK. Reports in 3-4 weeks. SASE. Free book catalog.
Nonfiction: Modern Sports Car Series: marque cars, sports, how-to collecting and restoration of antique, classic, milestone and special interest cars. Also vans, trucks and leisure vehicles; Modern Aircraft Series: all subjects on single and twin-engine planes of interest to private pilots; individual planes, sports, do-it-yourself, restoration, passing flight tests, etc. Submit outline/synopsis and sample chapters. Recently published *The New Mercedes Benz Guide*, by J. Oldham; and *Precision Aerobatics*, by H.D. Ettinger.

TAFT CORP., 1000 Vermont Ave. NW, Washington DC 20005. (800)424-9477, (202)347-0788. Editor-in-Chief: James Hickey. Published 11 titles in 1978; plans 13 in 1979, 11 in 1980. Publishes paperback originals. Specializes in books directed toward nonprofit industry. Pays 9% royalty on first 3,000 copies, 11% on next 2,000, 14% over 5,000; advance of $250-500. State availability of photos and/or illustrations to accompany ms "and whether right to use has already been obtained." Simultaneous and photocopied submissions OK. Reports in 1-2 months. SASE. Free book catalog.
Nonfiction: Publishes how-to and technical books and monthly newsletters on subjects and trends in philanthopy. "All dealing with fund raising and other elements of the nonprofit industry. Query or submit outline/synopsis and sample chapters. Recently published *Taft Corporate Foundation Directory*, by J. Brodsky; *Nonprofits' Handbook on Lobbying*, by J. Grupehoff/J. Murphy; *Trustees of Wealth: A Biographical Directory of Private Foundation and*

Corporate Foundation Officers, by J. Hickey; and *Prospecting: Searching Out the Philantropic Dollar*, by E. Koochoo.

TALON BOOKS, LTD., 201/1019 E. Cordova, Vancouver, British Columbia, Canada V6A 1M8. (604)255-5915. Editors: David Robinson (fiction), Peter Hay (drama), Karl Siegler (poetry). Publishes paperback originals and reprints. Published 19 titles in 1978; plans 16 in 1979, 16 in 1980. Royalty. Simultaneous and photocopied submissions OK. No unsolicited mss; query. Reports in 3-6 months. SASE. Free book catalog.
Nonfiction: "Occasionally publishes nonfiction (local history and georgraphy, 'whole earth' and about native peoples). Recently launched a new series of children's drama scripts and a book about the growth of theater for young audiences."
Fiction: Publishes Howard O'Hagan, Jane Rule, George Ryga, Audrey Thomas) and poetry by Canadian and American poets (Bill Bissett, Georg Bowering, Ed Dorn, Barry Gifford, Duncan McNaughton, bp Nichol, Fred Wah and Phyllis Webb among others)."
Drama: "Talon Books is the major publisher of plays in Canada (Michael Cook, David Fennario, James Reaney, Georg Ryga, Beverley Simons, Michel Tremblay among others) and is now expanding to include American and international drama with the acquisiton of works by Israel Horovitz, David Rudkin and Sam Shepard (for Canada).

TAMARACK PRESS, Box 5650, Madison WI 53705. (608)238-5564. Editorial Director: Jill Weber Dean. Publishes hardcover and paperback originals (75%) and reprints (25%). Published 4 titles in 1978; plans 5 in 1979, 4-5 in 1980. Pays 15% royalty on net cash receipts, "if the author supplies all materials needed for book." Advance averages $500. Photocopied submissions OK if not simultaneous. Reports in 2 week on queries, 2 months on outline/synopsis and sample chapters. SASE. Author/illustrator quidelines.
Nonfiction: "We are seeking adult nonfiction books that deal in a positive way with the world of nature and the state of Wisconsin. Within the Wisconsin category, we are willing to review a broad range of subjects and approaches, but we do not want religious, academic or technical titles. No book should deal with an area smaller than the entire state, though titles dealing with Wisconsin and neighboring states are welcome. We reach a general audience, but one that's well-educated and environmentally minded. Within the 'world of nature' category, we want titles of broad national appeal, focusing on nature and the environment." Query. Recently published *Easy Going: Madison and Dane County*, by S. Rath (travel guide); *Barns of Wisconsin*, by J. Apps ("all you ever wanted to know about . . ."); *A Sand County Almanac Illustrated*, by A. Leopold; *Wisconsin*, by Jill Dean (the essence of Wisconsin in words and photos); *Yarns of Wisconsin*, by Sue McCoy, Jill Dean and Maggie Dewey (a collection of anecdotes about life in Wisconsin before and after 1900); and *Wisconsin Country Cookbook and Journal*, by Edward Harris Heth (reprint of original *Wonderful World of Cooking*).

TAPE 'N TEXT, Williamsville Publishing Co., Box 237, Williamsville NY 14221. Editor-in-Chief: William R. Parks. Publishes printed text closely coordinated with narration on cassette tape and home computer software. Offers royalty contract of 10% minimum. Published 12 tape 'n text titles last year and 8 home computer programs. Marketing currently through direct mail to schools, libraries, retail stores and through distributors. Photocopied submissions OK. Query. Reports in 6 weeks. SASE.
Education and Training: "The kind of tape 'n text material we want from prospective authors is either a narration on tape with printed text which is very closely coordinated, *or* taped lectures or talks. We are now in English, computer science, mathematics and home and hobby computing, both software and instruction. We must have inquiries first before writers or programmers send in their material. We also request that writers consider that their educational background and experience are important factors. Authors should examine the existing Tape 'n Text titles and computer software so that they can follow our format for their development of material. It is important that the writer and/or programmer establish what his target audience is, i.e., level: elementary school, junior high school, high school, junior college, university, or the general trade market." Current titles include *Basic English Language Usage*, by Dr. G.H. Poteet; *Programming in Basic*, by W.R. Parks; and *Home Computer Software* (Apple-Z), by John H. Barnes.

J.P. TARCHER, INC., 9110 Sunset Blvd., Los Angeles CA 90069. (213)273-3274. Editor-in-Chief: Victoria Pasternack. Publishes hardcover and trade paperback originals. Pays 10-12½-15% royalty; advance averages $5,000-7,500. Published 12 titles in 1978; plans 22 in 1979, 25 in 1980. State availability of photos and/or illustrations to accompany ms. Simultaneous and photocopies submission OK. Reports in 3-5 weeks. SASE. Free book catalog.

Fiction and Nonfiction: Publishes popular psychology, sociology, health and fitness, popular medicine, cookbooks, cooking and foods. Submit outline/synopsis and sample chapters. Recently published *Getting Well Again*, by O. Carl Simonton, MD; *The Woman's Headache Relief Book*, by June Biermann and Barbara Toohey; *Mother Care*, by Lyn DelliQuadri and Kati Breckenridge; and *The Art of Buffet Entertaining*, by Diana and Paul von Welanetz.

TEACHERS COLLEGE PRESS, 1234 Amsterdam Ave., New York NY 10027. (212)678-3929. Senior Editor: Mary L. Allison. Publishes hardcover and paperback originals (90%) and reprints (10%). Royalty varies; "very rarely" offers advance. Published 20 titles in 1978; plans 22 in 1979, 26 in 1980. Reports in 3-6 months. SASE. Free book catalog.
Nonfiction: "This university press concentrates on books in the field of education in the broadest sense from early childhood to higher education: good classroom practices, teacher training, special education, innovative trends and issues, administration and supervision, film, continuing and adult education, all areas of the curriculum, comparative education, guidance and counselling and the politics, economics, philosophy, sociology and history of education. The press also issues classroom materials for students at all levels, with a strong emphasis on reading and writing." Submit outline/synopsis and sample chapters. Recently published *Families and Communities as Educators*, edited by Hope Jensen Leichter.

TEMPLE UNIVERSITY PRESS, Broad and Oxford Sts., Philadelphia PA 19122. (215)787-8787. Editor-in-Chief: Kenneth Arnold. Published 23 titles in 1978; plans 30 in 1979. Pays royalty. Photocopied submissions OK. SASE. Reports in 4 weeks. Free book catalog.
Nonfiction: American history, public policy and regional (Philadelphia area). "All books should be scholarly. Authors are generally connected with a university. No memoirs, fiction or poetry." Uses University of Chicago *Manual of Style*. Query. Recently published *Social Darwinism*, by Robert Bannister; *American Studies*; and *Corporal Punishment in American Education* (public policy).

TEMPO BOOKS, A Division of Grosset and Dunlop, 360 Park Ave. S., New York NY 10010. Editor: Ms. Robin Landon.(212)889-9800. Editorial Assistant: Wendy Wallace. Estab. 1898. Publishes hardcover and paperback originals. Published 106 titles in 1978; plans 111 in 1979. Pays 6-7% royalty or $500 minimum for outright purchase; average advance. Simultaneous and photocopied submissions OK. SASE. Reports in 3 weeks. Free book catalog.
Nonfiction: Biography, humor and sports. Submit outline/synopsis and sample chapters Recently published *Haunted House Handbook*, by D. Scott Rogo; *Santa Claus Jokes and Riddles*, by Phil Hirsch; and *Bill Adler's All-Time Great Classic Letters From Camp*, by Bill Adler.
Fiction: Adventure, fantasy, mystery, romance, science fiction and suspense. "We would like to see more young adult fiction dealing with today's contemporary world." Submit outline/synopsis and sample chapters Recently published *No Laughing Matter*, by Joan L. Oppenheimer; *One Step Apart*, by Joan L. Oppenheimer; and *The Lottery Rose*, by Irene Hunt.

TEN SPEED PRESS, Box 7123, Berkeley CA 94707. Editor: P. Wood. Publishes hardcover and paperback originals and reprints. Offers royalty of 10% of list price; 12½% after 100,000 copies are sold. Published 8 titles in 1978; plans 12 titles in 1979, 12 in 1980. Will send catalog to writer on request. Submit outline and sample chapters for nonfiction. Reports in 1 month. Enclose return postage.
Nonfiction: Americana, book trade, cookbooks, cooking and foods, history, humor, law, nature, self-help, how-to, sports, hobbies, recreation and pets and travel. Publishes mostly trade paperbacks. Subjects range from bicycle books to William Blake's illustrations. No set requirements. Some recipe books and career development books. Recently published *The Three Boxes of Life*, by Bolles; *Mousewood Cookbook*, by Katzen; and *Mail Order Moonlighting*, by Hoge.

TEXAS A&M UNIVERSITY PRESS, Drawer C, College Station TX 77843. (713)845-1436. Director: Lloyd G. Lyman. Assistant to the Director: Gayla Christiansen. Published 18 titles in 1978; plans 20 in 1979, 20 in 1980. Pays in royalties; no advance. Photocopied submissions OK. SASE. Reports in 1 week (queries); 1 month (submissions). Free book catalog.
Nonfiction: History, natural history, economics, agriculture and regional studies. "We do not want fiction and poetry." Query. Recently published *The Natural World of the Texas Big Thachet*, by Blair P. Homan (pictorial natural history); and *The Shadow of Pearl Harbor*, by Martin V. Melori (history).

TEXAS WESTERN PRESS, The University of Texas at El Paso, El Paso TX 79968. (915)747-5688. Director: E.H. Antone. Publishes hardcover and paperback originals. Published 6 titles in 1978; plans 9 in 1979, 7 in 1980."We are a university press, not a commercial house; therefore, payment is in books and prestige more than money. Most of our books are sold to libraries, not to the general reading public." Published 10 titles last year. Will send a catalog to a writer on request. Query. Will consider photocopied submissions. Follow "MLA Style Sheet." Reports in 1 to 3 months. Enclose return postage.
Nonfiction: "Scholarly books. Historic accounts of the Southwest (west Texas, southern New Mexico, and northern Mexico). Some literary works, occasional scientific titles. Our Southwestern Studies use mss of 20,000 words. Our hardback books range from 30,000 words up. The writer should use good exposition in his work. Most of our work requires documentation. We favor a scholarly, but not overly pedantic, style. We specialize in superior book design." Recently published *The Paradox of Pancho Villa,* by H. Braddy; and *Border Patrol,* by Clifford A. Perkins.

A. THOMAS & CO., LTD., Denington Estate, Wellingborough, Northamptonshire England NN8 2RQ. Editor-in-Chief: J.R. Hardaker. Publishes hardcover and paperback originals and reprints. Specializes in inspirational, practical psychology and self-improvement material. Pays 8-10% royalty. Photocopied submissions OK. SAE and International Reply Coupons. Reports in 2-4 weeks. Free book catalog.
Nonfiction: Publishes books on how-to methods, psychology and self-help. Submit outline/synopsis and sample chapters.

THORSONS PUBLISHERS, LTD. Denington Estate, Wellington, Northamptonshire NN8 2RQ England. Editor-in-Chief: J.R. Hardaker. Publishes hardcover and paperback originals and reprints. Specializes in health books, psychology, self-improvement, hypnotism, self-sufficiency; alternative medicine and business success books. 5-10% royalty. Photocopied submissions OK. SAE and International Reply Coupons. Reports in 2-4 weeks. Free book catalog.
Nonfiction: Business; cookbooks, cooking and foods; philosophy, psychology, self-help themes. Submit outline/synopsis and sample chapters.

THREE CONTINENTS PRESS, 1346 Connecticut Ave. NW, Washington DC 20036. Editor-in-Chief: Donald E. Herdeck. Publishes hardcover and paperback originals (90%) and reprints (10%). Pays 10% royalty; advance "only on delivery of complete ms which is found acceptable; usually $150." Query. Prefers photocopied submissions. State availability of photos/illustrations. Simultaneous submissions OK. Reports in 1-2 months. SASE. Free book catalog.
Nonfiction and Fiction: Specializes in African and Caribbean literature and criticism, third world literature and history. Scholarly, well-prepared mss; creative writing. Fiction, poetry, criticism, history and translations of creative writing. "We search for books which will make clear the complexity and value of African literature and culture, including bilingual texts (African language/English translations) of previously unpublished authors from less well-known areas of Africa. We are always interested in genuine contributions to understanding African and Caribbean culture." Length: 50,000 words. Recently published *Fire: Six Writers from Angola, Mozambique, and Cape Verde,* by D. Bwuness; and *Bozambo's Revenge,* by B. Juminer.

TIDEWATER PUBLISHERS, Box 456, Centreville MD 21617. Editor: George Rinehart. An imprint of Cornell Maritime Press, Inc. Publishes hardcover and paperback originals and reprints. Offers standard 10-12½-15% royalty contract. SASE. Reports in 2-3 weeks. Free book catalog.
Nonfiction: "General nonfiction on Maryland and the Delmarva Peninsula." Query with outline and sample chapters. Recently published *Pioneer Decoy Carvers,* by the Berkeys.

TIMBER PRESS, 30 NW 23rd Place, Portland OR 97210. (503)243-1158. Editor: Richard Abel. Assistant Publisher: Sherre Wegner. Estab. 1976. Publishes hardcover and paperback originals. Published 11 titles in 1978; plans 10 in 1979, 10 in 1980. Pays 10-20% royalty; "sometimes" offers advance. Photocopied submissions OK. SASE. Reports in 2 months. Free book catalog.
Nonfiction: Americana, art, arts and crafts, how-to, nature, travel in the Northwest, forestry, horticulture and Indian studies. Query or submit outline/synopsis and sample chapters. Recently published *Japanese Maples,* by J.D. Vertrees (horticulture); *Without a Thorn,* by

Stuart Mechlin and Ellen Bonanno (horticulture); and *The Mud Pie Dilemma*, by John Nance (arts and crafts).

TIME-LIFE BOOKS INC., 777 Duke St., Alexandria VA 22314. (703)960-5000. Managing Editor: Jerry Korn. Publishes hardcover originals. Published 42 titles in 1978; plans 40 in 1979, 40 in 1980. "We have no minimum or maximum fee because our needs vary tremendously. Advance, as such, is not offered. Author is paid as he completes part of contracted work." Books are almost entirely staff-generated and staff-produced, and distribution is primarily through mail order sale. Query to the Director of Planning. SASE.
Nonfiction: "General interest books. Most books tend to be heavily illustrated (by staff), with text written by assigned authors. We very rarely accept mss or book ideas submitted from outside our staff." Length: open. Recently published *The End and the Myth* (Old West Series); *San Francisco* (Great Cities Series); and *The Whalers* (The Seafarers Series).

TIMES BOOKS. The New York Times Book Co., Inc., 3 Park Ave., New York NY 10016. (212)725-2050. Vice President and Editorial Director: Edward T. Chase. Senior Editor: Roger Jellinek. Estab. 1969. Publishes hardcover and paperback originals (75%) and reprints (25%). Published 80 titles/year. Pays royalty; average advance. Simultaneous and photocopied submissions OK. SASE. Reports in 2-3 weeks. Free book catalog.
Nonfiction: Americana, animals, art, biography, business/economics, cookbooks/cooking, health, history, hobbies, how-to, humor, juveniles, music, nature, philosophy, photography, politics, psychology, recreation, reference, religion, science, self-help, sociology, sports and travel. "We do not want technical, textbook or portry manuscripts." Query or submit outline/synopsis and sample chapters. Recently published *The Ends of Power*, by H.R. Haldeman with Joseph MiMona ('Insider' Watergate); *Lifeboats to Ararat*, by Sheldon Campbell (zoos/conservation); and *Yankee From Georgia*, by William Miller (analysis/Jimmy Carter).
Fiction: Adventure, confession, erotica, experimental, fantasy, gothic, historical, humor, mainstream, mystery, religious, romance, science fiction, suspense and western. Query or submit outline/synopsis and sample chapters. Recently published *Compromising Positions*, by Susan Isaacs (sophisticated mystery); *Mixed Blessings*, by Marian Cockrell (romance); and *Sigmet Active*, by Thomas Page (suspense).

TIMES MIRROR MAGAZINES, INC., BOOK DIVISION. (Subsidiary of Times Mirror Co.) 380 Madison Ave., New York NY 10017. Publishing books in the Popular Science and Outdoor Life fields. Editor: John W. Sill. Royalties and advance according to size and type of book. Wants outlines, sample chapters, author information. Enclose return postage.
Nonfiction: Publishes books in Popular Science field: energy saving, home renovation, repair and improvement, workshop, hand and power tools, automobile how-to. In the Outdoor Life field: wildlife, especially big game and deer; fishing, camping, firearms. Small books to 35,000 words; large books to 150,000 words.

THE TOUCHSTONE PRESS. Box 81, Beaverton OR 97005. (503)648-8081. Editor-in-Chief: Thomas K. Worcester. Publishes paperback originals. Specializes in field guide books. Royalty of 10% of retail price; seldom offers an advance. Published 5 titles in 1978, plans 4 in 1979, 4-6 in 1980. Photocopied submissions OK. Reports in 1-2 months. SASE. Free book catalog. No fiction or poetry.
Nonfiction: Cookbooks, cooking and foods; history, hobbies, how-to, recreation, sports and travel books. "Must be within the range of our outdoor styles." Query. Recently published *Indian Heaven Back Country*, by M. Hansen (trail guide/history); *I Know You're Hurt, but There's Nothing to Bandage*, by D.D. Fisher, MD (self-help); and *Central Oregon Hiking Tours*, by D. Lowe and R. Lowe.

TOWER PUBLICATIONS, INC., 2 Park Ave., New York NY 10016. (212)679-7707. Editorial Director: Milburn Smith. Estab. 1960. Publishes paperback originals (75%) and reprints (25%). Published 205 titles in 1978; plans 210 in 1979, 210 in 1980. Pays 4-6% royalty on originals; buys reprints outright for $500-1,500. Offers $1,500 average advance. Simultaneous submissions OK, but "we must be told"; photocopied submissions OK. SASE; "without SASE, we do not return the manuscript." Book catalog for SASE.
Nonfiction: History of World War II, self-help, sports, crime and sex. "Our nonfiction program is very limited. Some World War II battle stories and Some self-help are all we do regularly. We're willing to consider something that's particularly timely or especially interesting. Any really strong and popular idea is worth a query letter. No personalities or crafts manuscripts." Query.

Fiction: Adventure, modern softcore erotica, fantasy, historical, mainstream, mystery, science fiction, suspense, western and war. "Most of what we publish is category fiction. We do not publish juvenile fiction, confessions, category romances, or (at least in the present market) gothics." Query.

Tips: "We happen to be very open to first novels, since we try to build up a long-term relationship with an author. We feel that, as a small publishing house, we are an ideal market for the first-time novelist who might not even be considered by a larger house, particularly if he is not represented by an agent. We prefer receiving outline or synopsis and sample chapters to entire manuscripts, and typescript must be legible and double-spaced."

TRANSACTION BOOKS, Rutgers University, New Brunswick NJ 08903. (201)932-2280. Book Division Director: Kerry V. Donnelly. Publishes hardcover and paperback originals (65%) and reprints (35%). Specializes in scholarly social science books. Published 60 titles in 1978; plans 60 in 1979. Royalty "depends almost entirely on individual contract, we've gone anywhere from 2-15%." No advance. Photocopied submissions OK "if they are perfectly clear." Reports in 2-4 months. SASE. Free book catalog.

Nonfiction: Americana, art, biography, economics, history, law, medicine and psychiatry, music, philosophy, photography, politics, psychology, reference, scientific, sociology, technical and textbooks. "All must be scholarly social science or related." Query or submit outline/synopsis and sample chapters. "Send introduction or first chapter and conclusion or last chapter. Use Chicago *Manual of Style*." State availability of photos/illustrations and send one photocopied example. Recently published *Yankee Family*, by J.R. McGovern (social history); *Basic Human Needs*, by J. McHale and M.C. McHale (Third World public policy); and *Who Really Rules? New Haven and Community Power Reexamined*, by G.W. Domhoff.

TRANS-ANGLO BOOKS, Box 38, Corona del Mar CA 92625. Editorial Director: Spencer Crump. Pays 5-10% royalty. Published 3 titles in 1978; plans 4 in 1979, 4 in 1980. Reports in 3-4 weeks. Enclose return postage. Free book list on request.

Nonfiction: Americana, Western Americana and railroad books. Also planning to enter the college text field. "We are not interested in family histories or local history that lacks national appeal." Most books are 8½x11 hardcover with many photos supplementing a good text of 5,000-15,000 words. Query. Recently published *Rail Car Builders*; *Matches, Flumes and Rails* (railroadiana); and *California's Spanish Missions* (Western Americana).

TREACLE PRESS, 437 Springtown Rd., New Paltz NY 12561. Editor: Bruce McPherson. Imprints include Documentext. Publishes hardcover and paperback originals. Published 3 titles in 1978; plans 9 in 1979, 10 in 1980. Pays 6-10% royalty, "plus a percentage of the edition in copies." Simultaneous and photocopied submissions OK. SASE. Reports in 3 weeks to 3 months.

Fiction: "Treacle Press publishes novels, short fiction, and literary criticism of innovative and expressive character. Since 1976 we have been issuing short fiction in a new format, the Treacle Story Series, presenting single or related short works as autonymous quality paperbacks that are collected into clothbound library volumes. The stories are accompanied by original drawings specially commissioned. In 1980 we will issue an anthology of original short fiction, which we intend to make an annual event. We are only interested in serious fiction, with particular emphasis on experimental works. A high percentage of the books published under the Treacle Press imprint are books of poetry. The interest here is in *books*—rather than collections—of poetry, resulting in our tendency to favor long poems, poem cycles, and other extended or open forms, including translations. We are interested in stylistic innovations marked by transumptive or transformative vision. Documentext is a new imprint, specifically for the publication of unique works presenting and detailing seminal artists and art movements of the past 20 years. We are interested in untraditional monographs and artist self-documentation." Query. Recently published *Smithsburg*, by Michael Brondoli (short fiction); *The Sex Token*, by James Shreeve (short fiction); *The Book of Persephone*, by Robert Kelly (poetry); and *More Than Meat Joy*, by Carolee Schneemann (performance art).

TREASURE CHEST PUBLICATIONS, Box 5250, Tucson AZ 85703. (602)623-9558. Contact: Sterling Mahan. Publishes paperback originals. Published 2 titles in 1978; plans 4 in 1979, 4 in 1980. Pays 5% minimum royalty; advance "depends on the situation." Simultaneous and photocopied submissions OK. Reports in 6 weeks. SASE. Free book catalog.

Nonfiction: "We specialize in books concerning the lifestyle, culture, history and arts of the Southwest, and especially would like to see related works. We are particularly interested in manuscripts by and/or about Native Americans, and works about Native American artists. Also art, history, biography, and photography with a Southwestern theme. Recently published

Indian Jewelry Making, by O. Branson; and *Wild Brothers of the Indians*, by A. Wesche.

TREND HOUSE, Box 2350, Tampa FL 33601. (813)247-5411. Publisher: Harris Mullen. Editor: Walker Roberts. Publishes hardcover and paperback originals (90%) and reprints (10%). Specializes in books on Florida and the South—all categories. Pays 10% royalty; no advance. Books are marketed through *Florida Trend* and *The South* magazines. Photocopied submissions OK. Reports in 2-4 weeks. SASE. Free book catalog.
Nonfiction: Business, economics, history, law, politics, reference, textbooks and travel. "All books pertain to Florida and Southern US." Query. State availability of photos and/or illustrations. Recently published *300 Most Abused Drugs*, by E. Bludworth (police handbook); *The Power Structure*, by L. Butcher (Florida business); *All About Wills for Florida Residents*, by R. Richards (legal information).

*TRIUMPH PUBLISHING CO., Box 292, Altadena CA 91001. (213)797-0075. Editor-in-Chief: William Dankenbring. Hardcover and paperback originals. Pays 5% royalty; no advance. Subsidy publishes 10% of books; "depends on the ms." Published 3 titles in 1978. State availability of photos and/or artwork to accompany ms. Simultaneous and photocopied submissions OK. Reports in 1-2 months. SASE. Free book catalog.
Nonfiction: Americana (inspirational); business (how-to); history (Biblical); nature (creation); psychology and scientific books (for laymen); religious and self-help. Recently published *Golden Prince*, by Ramsay (juvenile); *Ascent to Greatness*, by McNair (Americana); and *Last Days*, by Dankenbring (religious).

TROUBADOR PRESS, 385 Fremont St., San Francisco CA 94105. (415)397-3716. Publisher: Malcolm K. Whyte. Manuscript Submissions: Dennis Zaborowski. Publishes hardcover and paperback originals. Published 12 titles in 1978; plans 14 in 1979. Pays 4-12% royalty; advance averages $500-1,000. Simultaneous and photocopied submissions OK. Reports in 1 month. SASE. Book catalog for SASE.
Nonfiction: "Troubador Press publishes project, activity, entertainment, art, game, nature, craft and cookbooks. All titles feature original art and exceptional graphics. Primarily nonfiction. Current series include creative cut-outs; in-depth, readable cookbooks; 3-D mazes and other puzzle books; color and story books; how-to-draw and other art and entertainment books. Interested in expanding on themes of 75 current titles. We like books which have the potential to develop into series." Query or submit outline/synopsis and sample chapters. Recently published *How to Draw Prehistoric Monsters*, by L. Evans; *Stereo Views*, by Arthur Chandle and Wayne Pope (a book of 3-D photos with viewing glasses); and *Giants & Gnomes Coloring Album*, by Lana Slaton.

CHARLES E. TUTTLE CO., INC., Publishers & Booksellers, Drawer F, 26-30 S. Main St., Rutland VT 05701. Publishes originals and reprints. Pays $250 against 10% royalty; advance varies. Published 21 titles in 1978. Book catalog 25¢. Send complete mss or queries accompanied by outlines or sample chapters to Charles E. Tuttle Co., Inc., Suido 1—Chome, 2-6, Bunkyo-Ku, Tokyo, Japan, where the editorial and printing offices are located. Reports in 4-6 weeks. SASE.
Nonfiction: Specializes in publishing books about Oriental art and culture as well as history, literature, cookery, sport and children's books which relate to Asia, Hawaiian Islands, Australia and the Pacific areas. Also interested in Americana, especially antique collecting, architecture, genealogy and Canadiana. No travel, sociological or topical works even when in subject field. No poetry and fiction except that of Oriental theme. Normal book length only.

TWAYNE PUBLISHERS, A division of G.K. Hall & Co., 70 Lincoln St., Boston MA 02111. (617)423-3990. Editor: Caroline L. Birdsall. Payment is on royalty basis. Published 126 titles in 1978; plans 129 in 1979, 135 in 1980. Query. Reports in 5 weeks. Enclose return postage.
Nonfiction: Publishes scholarly books in series. Literary criticism, biography, history of immigration, film and theater studies, scholarly annuals and critical editions.
Recent Titles: *Kurt Vonnegut Jr.*, by S. Schatt; *Alexander Solzhenitsyn*, by A. Kodjak; *Francis Ford Coppola*, by R. Johnson; *Studies in the American Renaissance 1978* (annual collection of bibliographical, biographical and critical essays); and *America's Immigrant Women*, by C. Neidle.

TYNDALE HOUSE PUBLISHERS, INC., 336 Gunderson Dr., Wheaton IL 60187. (312)668-8300. Managing Editor: Virginia Muir. Editor-in-Chief and Acquisitions: Wendell Hawley. Publishes hardcover and trade paperback originals (90%) and hardcover and mass paperback reprints (10%). Published 60 titles in 1978; plans 100 in 1979, 110 in 1980. Pays 10%

royalty; negotiable advance. Simultaneous queries OK; prefers photocopied submissions. Reports in 6 weeks. SASE. Free book catalog.

Nonfiction: Religious books only: personal experience, family living, marriage, Bible studies and commentaries, books for children, Christian living, devotional, inspirational, church and social issues, Bible prophecy, missions, theology and doctrine, counseling and Christian psychology, Christian apologetics and church history. Submit table of contents, chapter summary, preface, first two chapters and one later chapter. Recently published *Revelation Unfolded*, by Dr. Jack B. Scott (theology and doctrine); and *F.B. Meyer Bible Commentary*, by F.B. Meyer (devotional).

Fiction: Bible and contemporary novels, children's books for juniors and junior high, religious and allegory. Submit outline/synopsis and sample chapters. Recently published *Checkpoint*, by Rod Huron; and *The Mystery of Five Finger Island*, by Jan Pierson.

UNITED SYNAGOGUE BOOK SERVICE, 155 5th Ave., New York NY 10010. (212)533-7800. Publishes hardcover and paperback originals. Published 5 titles in 1978; plans 5 in 1979. Pays 10% royalty; no advance. Free book catalog. Send query, outline, sample chapter first. Address juveniles and history to Dr. Morton Siegel; biography, philosophy and adult religion to Rabbi Marvin Wiener. "Address general inquiries to George L. Levine, Director." Reports in 1-8 weeks. SASE.

Religion: Publishes religious books only: textbooks, readers, Hebrew Language books, history, picture books. No length requirements.

Recent Title: *The Jewish Experience, Book II*, by F. Hyman (history).

UNITY PRESS, 113 New St., Santa Cruz CA 95060. (408)427-2020. Publisher: Craig Caughlan. Publishes paperback originals. Pays standard royalty; prefers to put advance money into promotion." Published 6 titles in 1978; plans 2 in 1979, 12 in 1980. Simultaneous and photocopied submissions OK. Reports in 6 weeks. SASE. Free book catalog.

Nonfiction: "Our editorial direction could be defined as follows: books that bring an individual to a better understanding of self and environs. Prefer books that are on the leading edge of the social sciences and human behavior. With each submission, author should state in 50 words or less the purpose of his book, and what makes it better than others that are available on similar subjects." Query or submit outline/synopsis and sample chapters.

Fiction: "Our editorial direction includes fiction as well. Would like to see books on futurism." No poetry, mysteries, or romances. Query or submit outline/synopsis and sample chapters.

UNIVELT, INC., Box 28130, San Diego CA 92128. (714)746-4005. Editorial Director: H. Jacobs. Publishes hardcover originals. Published 12 titles in 1978; plans 10 in 1979. Pays 10% royalty; no advance. Simultaneous and photocopied submissions OK. Reports in 4 weeks. SASE. Free book catalog.

Nonfiction: Publishes in the field of aerospace, especially astronautics, and technical communications, but including application of aerospace technology to Earth's problems. Submit outline/synopsis and sample chapters. Recently published *Satellite Communications in the Next Decade*, by L. Jaffe; and *200 Years of Flight in America*, by E.M. Emme.

*UNIVERSE BOOKS, 381 Park Ave. S., New York NY 10016. (212)685-7400. Editorial Director: Louis Barron. Estab. 1956. Publishes hardcover and paperback originals (95%) and reprints (5%). Published 60 titles in 1978; plans 60 in 1979, 60 in 1980. Pays 10-15% royalty on hardbound books. "On a few extra-illustrated art books we may pay a smaller royalty." Offers $1,000-4,000 average advance. Subsidy publishes 5% of books; "if a book makes a genuine contribution to knowledge but is a commercial risk, we might perhaps accept a subsidy from a foundation or other organization, but not directly from the author." Simultaneous and photocopied submissions OK. SASE. Reports in 2 weeks. Book catalog for SASE.

Nonfiction: Animals, art, history, nature, performing arts, politics, reference and science. Universe also pays secondary attention to biography, cooking and foods, health, how-to and psychology. Also uses "discussions of specific animal, bird or plant species; social histories of specific types of artifacts or social institutions; art histories of specific types of artifacts or symbols. We publish books in the following categories: antiques, crafts and collectibles, art, architecture and design, history and biography, life, physical and agricultural sciences, the performing arts, social sciences (especially books on survival, appropriate technology, and the limits to growth). We do not publish fiction, poetry, criticism or belles lettres." Submit outline/synopsis and sample chapters. Recently published *Footprints on the Planet: A Search for an Environmental Ethic*, by Robert Cahn; *Possum Living: How to Live Well Without a Job and With Almost No Money*, by Dolly Freed; *Plantcraft: A Guide to the Everyday Use of Wild Plants*, by Richard Mabey; and *Hawks and Owls of North America*, by Donald S. Heintzelman.

UNIVERSITY ASSOCIATES, INC., 7596 Eads Ave., La Jolla CA 92037. (714)454-8821. President: J. William Pfeiffer. Vice-President/Editor-in-Chief: John E. Jones. Publishes paperback originals (65%) and reprints (35%). Specializes in practical materials for human relations trainers, consultants, etc. Pays 10-15% royalty; no advance. Markets books by direct mail. Simultaneous submissions OK. SASE. Reports in 2-4 months. Free book catalog.
Nonfiction: Marion Mettler, Department Editor. Publishes (in order of preference) human relations training and group-oriented material; management education and community relations and personal growth; business; psychology and sociology. No materials for grammar school or high school classroom teachers. Use *American Psychological Association Style Manual.* Query. Send prints or completed art or rough sketches to accompany ms. Recently published *The 1979 Annual Handbook for Group Facilitators*, by J.E. Jones and J.W. Pfeiffer; *The Consulting Process in Action*, by R. Lippitt and G. Lippitt; and *Sociotechnical Systems: A Sourcebook*, edited by W. Pasmore and J.J. Sherwood.

UNIVERSITY OF ALABAMA PRESS, Box 2877, University AL 35486. Director: Malcom MacDonald. Assistant director: John P. Defaunt. Publishes hardcover originals. Published 28 titles last year. "Maximum royalty is 12½%; no advances made." Photocopied submissions OK. Enclose return postage. Free book catalog.
Nonfiction: Biography, business, economics, history, music, philosophy, politics, religion and sociology. Considers upon merit almost any subject of scholarly interest, but specializes in linguistics and philology, political science and public administration, literary criticism and biography, philosophy, and history. Also interested in biology, ecology, medicine, and agriculture. Submit outline/synopsis and sample chapters.

UNIVERSITY OF ARIZONA PRESS, Box 3398, Tucson AZ 85722. (602)626-1441. Director: Marshall Townsend. Publishes hardcover and paperback originals and reprints. "Contracts are individually negotiated, but as a 'scholarly publishing house' operating primarily on informational works, does not pay any advances. Also, royalty starting point may be after sale of first 1,000 copies, by virtue of the nature of the publishing program." Published 18 titles in 1978; plans 25-30 in 1979, 25-30 in 1980. Marketing methods "are based on 'what is considered best for the book,' giving individual treatment to the marketing of each book, rather than a generalized formula." Free catalog and editorial guidelines. Will consider photocopied submissions if ms is not undergoing consideration at another publishing house. "Must have this assurance." Query and submit outline and sample chapters. Reports on material within 90 days. SASE.
Nonfiction: "Significant works of a regional nature about Arizona, the Southwest and Mexico; and books of merit in subject matter fields strongly identified with the universities in Arizona; i.e., anthropology, arid lands studies, Asian studies, Southwest Indians, Mexico, etc. Each ms should expect to provide its own answer to the question, "Why should this come out of Arizona?" The answer would be that either the work was something that ought to be made a matter of record as a service to Arizona and the Southwest, or that it was presenting valuable information in a subject matter field with which the Arizona institutions hold strong identification. The University of Arizona Press strongly endorses 'the target reader' concept under which it encourages each author to write for only *one* reader, then leave it up to the publisher to reach the thousands—as contrasted with the author's trying to write for the thousands and not 'hitting home' with anyone. The press believes this approach helps the author come to a consistent level of subject matter presentation. The press also insists upon complete departure of 'time-dating' words such as 'now,' 'recently,' and insists that the author consider how the presentation will read three years hence." Americana, art, biography, business, history, nature, scientific, technical. Length: "what the topic warrants and demands." No "personal diary types of Western Americana, mainly directed only toward family interest, rather than broad general interest." Recently published *Mexican Folk Tales*, by A.J. Campos; and *Ethnic Medicine in the Southwest*, edited by E.H. Spicec.

UNIVERSITY OF CALIFORNIA PRESS, 60 Powell Library, Los Angeles CA 90024. Director: James H. Clark. Assistant Director: Stanley Holwitz. New York Office, Room 513, 50 E. 42nd St., New York NY 10017. London Office IBEG, Ltd., 2-4 Brook St., London W1Y 1AA, England. Publishes hardcover and paperback originals and reprints. "On books likely to do more than return their costs, a standard royalty contract beginning at 10% is paid; on paperbacks it is less." Published 175 titles last year. Queries are always advisable, accompanied by outlines or sample material. Address to either Berkeley or Los Angeles address. Reports vary, depending on the subject. Enclose return postage.
Nonfiction: "It should be clear that most of our publications are hardcover nonfiction written

by scholars." Publishes scholarly books including art, literary studies, social sciences, natural sciences and some high-level popularizations. No length preferences.
Fiction and Poetry: Publishes fiction and poetry only in translation, usually in bilingual editions.

UNIVERSITY OF ILLINOIS PRESS, Box 5081, Station A, Champaign IL 61820. Publishes hardcover and paperback originals (95%) and paperback reprints (5%). Published 47 titles in 1978; plans 50 in 1979, 50 in 1980. "Royalty varies greatly; from zero on small edition scholarly books to sliding scale beginning at 15% of net income." Rarely offers advance. State availability of photos and/or illustrations to accompany ms. Simultaneous (in some cases) and photocopied submissions OK. SASE. Reports in 1-2 months. Free book catalog.
Nonfiction: "Particular emphasis on American studies in history, literature, music, and other areas of specialization including anthropology, communications, urban and regional planning, and Western Americana." Query or submit complete ms. Recently published *Four Men, Four Women, and Neighbors: An Oral History of Contemporary Cuba*, by O. Lewis, et al (anthropology).
Fiction: "We publish four collections of short stories, each collection by a single author, each year in the Illinois Short Fiction series. Should be the kind of stories published in literary journals and quality magazines. Queries to fiction editor." Recently published *One More River*, by L. Goldberg (short stories).

*UNIVERSITY OF IOWA PRESS, Graphic Services Bldg., Iowa City IA 52242. (319)353-3181. Editor: Art Pflughaupt. Publishes hardcover and paperback originals. Published 7 titles in 1978; plans 6 in 1979, 7 in 1980. Pays 10% royalty. Subsidy publishes 5% of books. Subsidy publishing is offered "if a scholarly institution will advance a subsidy to support publication of a worthwhile book. We market mostly by direct mailing of fliers to groups with special interests in our titles." Query or submit outline/synopsis and sample chapters. University of Chicago *Manual of Style*. State availability of photos/illustrations. Photocopied submissions OK. Reports in 2-4 months. SASE. Free book catalog.
Nonfiction: Publishes art; economics; history; music; philosophy; reference; and scientific books. "We do not publish children's books. We do not publish any poetry or short fiction except the Iowa Translation Series and the Iowa School of Letters Award for short fiction." Recently published *Russian Poetry: The Modern Periods*, edited by John Glad and Daniel Weissbort; and *The Information Process: World News Reporting to the 20th Century*, by R. Desmond.

*UNIVERSITY OF MASSACHUSETTS PRESS, Box 429, Amherst MA 01002. (413)545-2217. Editorial Director: Leone Stein. Senior Editor: Richard Martin. Publishes hardcover and paperback originals (95%) and reprints (5%). Published 20 titles in 1978; plans 22 in 1979, 24 in 1980. "Royalties depend on character of book; if offered, generally at 10% of list price. Advance, if offered, averages $250." Subsidy publishes 10% of books; "Press specifies subsidy requirement on basis on estimated edition loss." No author subsidies accepted. Simultaneous (if advised) and photocopied submissions OK. Preliminary report in 1-2 months. SASE. Free book catalog.
Nonfiction: Publishes art, biography, criticism, history, nature studies, philosophy, poetry, politics, psychology, scientific and sociology. Submit outline/synopsis and sample chapters. Recently published *Our Fiery Trial: Abraham Lincoln, John Brown, and the Civil War Era*, by Stephen B. Oakes (history); *Design: Purpose, Form and Meaning*, by John F. Pile (art/design); and *Claude Levi-Strauss: Social Psychotherapy and the Collective Unconscious*, by Thomas Shalvey (sociology/psychology).

UNIVERSITY OF MISSOURI PRESS, 107 Swallow Hall, Columbia MO 65211. (314)882-7641. Director: Edward D. King. Managing Editor: Susan E. Kelpe. Publishes hardcover and paperback originals. Published 23 titles in 1978; plans 22 in 1979, 25 in 1980. Pays 10% royalty; no advance. Photocopied submissions OK. Reports in 3 months. SASE. Free book catalog.
Nonfiction: "Scholarly publisher interested in history, literary criticism, political science, social science, music, art, art history, and original poetry." Also regional books about Missouri and the Midwest. "We do not publish very much in mathematics or hard sciences." Query or submit outline/synopsis and sample chapters. Consult Chicago *Manual of Style*. Recently published *Infinite Jest: Wit and Humor in Italian Renaissance Art*, by Paul Barolsky; *The Fierce Embrace: A Study of Contemporary American Poetry*, by Charles Molesworth (literary criticism); and *F.R. Leavis*, by R. Boyers (literary criticism).
Fiction: "Will not be reading fiction manuscripts again until February, 1981. We publish

original short fiction in Breakthrough Series, not to exceed 35,000 words. May be short story collection or novella. We also publish poetry and drama in the same series. No limitations on subject matter." Query. Recently published *Dowry*, by Janet Beeler and *Van Gogh Field and Other Stories*, by William Kittredge.

UNIVERSITY OF NEBRASKA PRESS, 901 N. 17th St., Lincoln NE 68588. Editor-in-Chief: Virginia Faulkner. Publishes hardcover and paperback originals (60%) and hardcover and paperback reprints (40%). Specializes in scholarly nonfiction (particularly literary); some regional books; reprints of western Americana; natural history. Royalty is usually graduated from 10% for original books; no advance. Published 31 titles in 1978; plans 30 in 1979, 30 in 1980. SASE. Reports in 2-4 months. Free book catalog.
Nonfiction: Publishes Americana, biography, history, medicine, psychiatry, nature, photography, psychology, sports, literature, agriculture and American Indian themes. Query. Recently published *Anatomies of Egotism: A Reading of the Last Novels of H.G. Wells*, by R. Bloom (literature); *Oglala Religion*, by W.K. Powers (American Indian); *North American Game Birds of Upland and Shoreline*, by P.A. Johnsgard (nature).

THE UNIVERSITY OF NORTH CAROLINA PRESS, Box 2288, Chapel Hill NC 27514. (919)933-2105. Editor-in-Chief: Malcolm Call. Publishes hardcover and paperback originals. Specializes in scholarly books and regional trade books. Royalty schedule "varies greatly. Depends on nature of ms and its marketability; zero to 15% of retail price." No advance. Published 29 titles in 1978; plans 51 in 1979, 55 in 1980. "As a university press, we do not have the resources for mass marketing books." Send prints to illustrate ms only if they are a major part of the book. Photocopied submissions OK. Reports in 2-5 weeks. SASE. Free book catalog.
Nonfiction: "Our major fields are American and European history." Also scholarly books on Americana, classics, biography, political science, philosophy, psychology and sociology. History books on art, law and music. Books on nature, particularly on the Southeast; literary studies. Submit outline/synopsis and sample chapters. Must follow University of Chicago *Manual of Style*. Recently published *The Development of American Citizenship, 1609-1870*, by J. Kettner (American history); *Catullus: A Critical Edition*, by D.F.S. Thomson (classics); *The National Archives*, by D. McCoy (history); *Oral History*, by J. Hoopes (history); and *A History of the Oratorio*, 2 volumes, by H. Smither (music).

UNIVERSITY OF NOTRE DAME PRESS, Notre Dame IN 46556. Editor: Ann Rice. Publishes hardcover and paperback originals and paperback reprints. Pays 10-12½-15% royalty; no advance. Published 28 titles in 1978. Free book catalog. Will consider photocopied submissions. Query. Reports in 2-3 months. SASE.
Nonfiction: "Scholarly books, serious nonfiction of general interest; book-length only. Especially in the areas of philosophy; theology; history; sociology; English literature (Middle English period, and modern literature criticism in the area of relation of literature and theology); government; international relations; and Mexican-American studies. Recently published *Anamnesis*, by E. Voegelin; *Four Hassidic Masters*, by E. Wiesel; and *Varieties of Interpretation*, by J. Mazzeo.

*UNIVERSITY OF OKLAHOMA PRESS, 1005 Asp Ave., Norman OK 73019. (405)325-5111. Editor-in-Chief: Luther Wilson. Publishes hardcover and paperback originals (85%); and reprints (15%). Royalty ranges from zero to 15% "depending on market viability of project"; no advance. Subsidy publishes 5% of books. "If a book has scholarly merit, but is destined to lose money, we seek a subsidy." Submit sample photos or 8x10 glossy prints. Simultaneous and photocopied submissions OK. Reports in 2-4 months. SASE. Book catalog for SASE.
Nonfiction: Publishes Americana and art (western and Indian); biographies of major western and Indian figures; history; hobbies; how-to; music; nature; politics; reference; sociology; technical; textbooks; archeology (Mesoamerican); classics; and anthropology books. Query. Recently published *Maya Ruins of Mexico in Color*, by Ferguson/Royce; *Propertius*, by Richardson (scholarly); and *The Indian Tipi*, by Laubin/Laubin.

*UNIVERSITY OF PENNSYLVANIA PRESS, 3933 Walnut St., Philadelphia PA 19104. (215)243-6261. Director: Robert Erwin. Hardcover and paperback originals (90%) and reprints (10%). Pays 10% royalty on first 5,000 copies sold; 12½% on next 5,000 copies sold; 15% thereafter; no advance. Subsidy publishes 10% of books. Subsidy publishing is determined by: evaluation obtained by the press from outside specialists; work approved by Press Editorial Committee; subsidy approved by funding organization. Published 20 books in 1978. State availability of photos and/or illustrations to accompany ms, with copies of illustrations.

Photocopied submissions OK. Reports in 1-3 months. SASE. Free book catalog.
Nonfiction: Publishes Americana; biography; business (especially management); economics; history; law; medicine and psychiatry; philosophy; politics; psychology; reference; scientific; sociological; technical; folklore and folk life books. "Serious books that serve the scholar and the professional." Follow the Chicago *Manual of Style.* Query with outline and sample chapter addressed to the director. Recently published *Triumph of Evolution: American Scientists and the Heredity-Environment Controversy 1900-1941,* by Hamilton Cravens (history); and *Daily Life in the World of Charlemagne,* by Pierre Riche, translated by JoAnn McNamara (history).

UNIVERSITY OF PITTSBURGH PRESS. 127 N. Bellefield Ave., Pittsburgh PA 15260. (412)624-4110. Director: Frederick A. Hetzel. Senior Editor: Louise Craft. Publishes hardcover and paperback originals. Published 30 titles in 1978; plans 30 in 1979, 30 in 1980. Pays 12½% royalty on hardcover, 8% on paperback; no advance. Photocopied submissions OK. Reports in 1-4 months. SASE. Free book catalog.
Nonfiction: Scholarly nonfiction. No textbooks or general nonfiction of an unscholarly nature. Submit outline/synopsis and sample chapters. Recently published *Fragile Families, Troubled Children: The Aftermath of Infant Trauma,* by E. Elmer; *The Overthrow of Allende & the Politics of Chile, 1964-1976,* by P.E. Sigmund; and *Ruins & Empire: The Evolution of a Theme in Augustan & Romantic Literature,* by L. Gold.

UNIVERSITY OF PUERTO RICO PRESS (UPRED). Box X, UPR Station, Rio Piedras PR 00931. Director: Dr. Carmelo Delgado-Cintron. Published 25 titles in 1978; plans 40 in 1979. Pays 10% royalty. Photocopied submissions OK. SASE. Reports in 1-3 months. Free catalog.
Nonfiction:. Special interests are Puerto Rican topics and literature and studies relevant to the Caribbean and Latin America. Recently published *Amphibians and Reptiles of Puerto Rico,* by Juan A. Rivero; *El Mar de Puerto Rico (Puerto Rico's Seas),* by J.A. Suarez-Caabro; and *El Sistema Judicial de Puerto Rico (The Judical System of Puerto Rico),* by J. Trias-Monge.

UNIVERSITY OF SOUTH CAROLINA PRESS, Columbia SC 29208. (803)777-5243. Director: Robert T. King. Published 15 titles in 1978; plans 15 in 1979, 15 in 1980. "Royalties vary from book to book"; offers $250 average advance. Photocopied submissions OK. SASE. Reports in 1 month. Free catalog.
Nonfiction: Regional studies, European and American history, social work, philosophy and economics. "We don't publish manuscripts of less than 30,000 words. Research your subject thoroughly. No fiction, poetry or political polemics." Query. Recently published *Of Books and Men,* by Louis B. Wright; and *The Chinese Economy,* by Jan S. Prybyla (economics).

THE UNIVERSITY OF TENNESSEE PRESS, 293 Communications Bldg., Knoxville TN 37916. Contact: Acquisitions Editor. Published 20 titles in 1978; plans 25 in 1979. Pays royalty. Photocopied submissions OK. SASE. Reports in 1 week on queries; "in 1 month on submissions we have encouraged." Free catalog and writer's guidelines.
Nonfiction: American history, political science, literary criticism, anthropology, folklore and regional studies. Prefers "scholarly treatment and a readable style. Authors usually have PhDs. No fiction, poetry or plays." Submit outline/synopsis and sample chapters. Recently published *Intellectual Life in the Colonial South,* by Richard Beale Davis (reference); and *Wilderness Calling . . . 1750-1900,* by Nicholas Perkins Hardeman (Americana).

UNIVERSITY OF TEXAS PRESS, Box 7819, Austin TX 78712. Executive Editor: Barbara L. Burnham. Published 50 titles in 1978; plans 55 in 1979. Pays royalty; occasionally offers advance. Photocopied submissions OK. SASE. Reports in 6-8 weeks. Free catalog and writer's guidelines.
Nonfiction: General scholarly subjects: human social science, economics, anthropology, archeology, political science, psychology, linguistics, photography and comparative literature. Also uses specialty titles related to the Southwest, national trade titles, regional trade titles and studies in the sciences and humanities. "No popular psychology or popular books." Query or submit outline/synopsis and sample chapters. Recently published *The Book of Merlyn,* by T.H. White (general trade book); and *On Broadway,* text by William and Jane Stott and photography by Fred Sehl (theater).

*UNIVERSITY OF THE TREES PRESS, Box 644, Boulder Creek CA 95006. (408)338-3855. Editorial Director: Dr. D. Rozman. Senior Editor: Ann Ray, Ph.D. Publishes hardcover and paperback originals (85%) and reprints (15%). Published 10 titles in 1978; plans 5 in 1979. Will consider subsidy publishing: "have done none so far, but we are open to works of great originality. Originality of work must be high even if the market for the work may be only a few

key people. Pays 10% royalty; no advance. Simultaneous and photocopied submissions OK. Reports in 4 weeks. SASE. Book catalog 25¢.
Nonfiction: "All our books relate to consciousness research or scientific approach to spiritual objects. We are interested in original research into dowsing, ESP, brain development, evolution of forms, breath control, yoga, mental phenomena or meditation techniques. Also research into light and energies; original spiritual guides or manuals; and education for children by new classroom techniques." Recently published *Nuclear Evolution: Discovery of the Rainbow Body*, by C. Hills, *Energy, Matter and Form*, by Bearne/Smith/Allen; and *Journey into Light*, by A. Ray.

UNIVERSITY OF UTAH PRESS, University of Utah, University Services Bldg., Salt Lake City UT 84112. (801)581-6771. Director: Norma B. Mikkelsen. Publishes hardcover and paperback originals and reprints. Pays 10% royalty on first 2,000 copies sold; 12% on 2,001 to 4,000 copies sold; 15% thereafter. No advance. Published 10 titles last year. Free book catalog. Query with outline and sample chapter. Reports in 6-8 months. SASE.
Nonfiction: Scholarly books on history, philosophy, religion, anthropology, the arts, poetry and general nonfiction. Author should specify page length in query. Recently published *The Zunis of Cibola*, by C.G. Crampton; *Country to City*, by E. Norbeck; and *The English Spenserians*, by W.B. Hunter Jr.

UNIVERSITY OF WISCONSIN PRESS, 114 N. Murray St., Madison WI 53715. (608)262-4928 (telex: 265452). Director: Thompson Webb. Editor: Irving E. Rockwood. Publishes hardcover and paperback originals, reprints and translations. Pays standard royalties; no advance. Published 32 titles in 1978. Send complete ms. Follow Modern Language Association Style Sheet. Reports in 3 months. Enclose return postage with ms.
Nonfiction: Publishes general nonfiction based on scholarly research. Recently published *The American Jeremiad*, by Sacvan Bercovithch; *The Crisis of Chinese Consciousness*, by Lin Yu-sheng and *Madness and Sexual Politics in the Feminist Novel*, by Barbara Hill Rigney.

UNIVERSITY PRESS OF AMERICA, 4710 Auth Place SE, Washington DC 20023. (301)899-9600. Editorial Director: James E. Lyons. Publishes paperback originals (95%) and reprints (5%). Published 250 titles in 1978; plans 300 in 1979, 350 in 1980. Pays 10% royalty; no advance. Simultaneous and phQocopied submissions OK. Reports in 6 weeks. SASE. Free book catalog.
Nonfiction: Scholarly monographs, college, and graduate level textbooks in history, political science, African studies, Black studies, philosophy, religion, sociology and education. No juvenile or el-hi material. Submit outline. Recently published *African Society, Culture, and Politics*, edited by C. Mojekwu; *The Weimar in Crisis: Cuno's Germany*, by A. Cornebise; and *Thirteen Thinkers: An Introduction to Philosophy*, by G. Kreyche.

UNIVERSITY PRESS OF KENTUCKY, 102 Lafferty Hall, Lexington KY 40506. (606)258-2951. Director: Kenneth Cherry. Editor-in-Chief: Jerome Crouch. Managing Editor: Evalin F. Douglas. Hardcover originals (95%); paperback reprints (5%). Pays 10% royalty after first 1,000 copies; no advance. State availability of photos and/or artwork to accompany ms. "Author is ultimately responsible for submitting all artwork in camera-ready form." Reports in 2-4 months. SASE. Free book catalog.
Nonfiction: Publishes (in order of preference): history, sociology, literary criticism and history, sociology, politics, anthropology, law, philosophy; medical history and nature. "All mss must receive an endorsement (secured by the press) from a scholar in the appropriate area of learning and must be approved by an editorial board before final acceptance." Query or submit outline/synopsis with sample chapters. Recently published *Finley Peter Dunne & Mr. Dooley: The Chicago Years*, by Charles F. Danning (American studies); *Bomber Pilot: A Memoir of World War 11*, by Philip Ardery; and *The Hatfields & The McCoys*, by Otis K. Rice.

*UNIVERSITY PRESS OF VIRGINIA, Box 3608, University Station, Charlottesville VA 22903. (804)924-3468. Editor-in-Chief: Walker Cowen. Publishes hardcover and paperback originals (95%) and reprints (5%). Published 45 titles in 1978; plans 45 in 1979, 1980. Royalty depends on the market for the book; sometimes none is made. "We subsidy publish 40% of our books, based on cost vs. probable market." Photocopied submissions OK. Returns rejected material within a week. Reports on acceptances in 1-2 months. SASE. Free catalog.
Nonfiction: Publishes Americana, business, history, law; medicine and psychiatry; politics, reference, scientific, bibliography, and decorative arts books. "Write a letter to the director, describing content of manuscript, plus length. Also specify if maps, tables, illustrations, etc., are included. Please, no educational or sociological or psychological manuscripts." Recently

published *The Immigrant in Industrial America*, by R.L. Ehrlich; and *The New Humanism*, by J.D. Hoeveler Jr.

URIZEN BOOKS, INC., 66 W. Broadway, New York NY 10007. Editor-in-Chief: Michael Roloff. Publishes paperback and hardcover originals. Offers standard minimum book contract of 10-12½-15%. Average advance is $3,000. Book catalog $1. Will consider photocopied submissions. Query for nonfiction. Reports in 6 weeks. Enclose return postage.
Fiction, Nonfiction, Drama, Poetry: Sociology, philosophy, history of industrialization, history of economics, communication theory, "first-class fiction." High caliber writing necessary.
Recent Titles: *Detour*, by Michael Brodsky; *Blue of Noon*, by Georges Bataille (fiction); and *The Civilizing Process*, by Norbert Elias (nonfiction).

VANGUARD PRESS, INC., 424 Madison Ave., New York NY 10017. Editor-in-Chief: Mrs. Bernice S. Woll. Estab. 1926. Publishes hardcover originals and reprints. Published 25 titles in 1978; plans 20 in 1979. Pays 7½-15% royalty, or by outright purchase; pays variable advance. Simultaneous and photocopied submissions OK. SASE. Reports in 3-4 weeks. Free book catalog.
Nonfiction: Animals; art; biography (especially of musicians, artists and political figures); business (management, making money, how-to); cookbooks (gourmet and diet books); cooking and foods; history (scholarly, but written with flare); hobbies (crafts, especially sewing); how-to; humor; juveniles (folk stories, nature and art topics); music (no scores, but anything pertaining to the field—also, jazz); nature (ecology and nature adventure); philosophy; poetry; politics (current issues); psychology; religion in literature and society (no tracts); current sociology studies; sports; travel; juvenile science; and literary criticism. "No textbooks, reference books or technical material." Query or submit outline/synopsis and sample chapters. Recently published *Solti: The Art of the Conductor Series*, by Paul Robinson (musical biography); *Babyselling: The Scandal of Black Market Adoption*, by Nancy C. Baker (sociology); and *Turning the Tables on Las Vegas*, by Ian Anderson (behavior).
Fiction: Believable adventure, experimental, humor, mystery, modern suspense and "good literature." No confessions, erotica or gothics. Query or submit outline/synopsis and sample chapters. Recently published *Son of the Morning*, by Joyce Carol Oates (modern literary fiction); *The Good Leviathan*, by Pierre Boulle (modern suspense); and *Bishop as Pawn: A Father Dowling Mystery*, by Ralph McInerny (modern mystery).

*VESTA PUBLICATIONS, LTD., Box 1641, Cornwall, Ontario, Canada K6H 5V6. (613)932-2135. Editor-in-Chief: Stephen Gill. Paperback and hardcover originals. 10% minimum royalty. Subsidy publishes 5% of books. "We ask a writer to subsidize a part of the cost of printing; normally, it is 50%. We do so when we find that the book does not have a wide market, as in the case of university theses and the author's first collection of poems. The writer gets 50 free copies and 10% royalty on paperback editions." No advance. Published 19 titles in 1978; plans 17 in 1979 and 30 in 1980. State availabiliy of photos and/or illustrations to accompany ms. Simultaneous submissions OK if so informed. Photocopied submissions OK. Reports in 1-4 weeks. SAE and International Reply Coupons. Free book catalog.
Nonfiction: Publishes Americana, art, biography, cookbooks, cooking and foods; history, philosophy, poetry, politics, reference, religious. Query or submit complete ms. "Query letters and mss should be accompanied by synopsis of the book and biographical notes." Recently published *Immigrant*, by S. Gill (a novel) and *Under the Spell of India*, by Olga Dey.

VICTOR BOOKS, Box 1825, Wheaton IL 60187. (312)668-6000. Editorial Director: James R. Adair. Managing Editor: Jennifer Greene. Paperback originals. Pays 7½-10% royalty; occasionally offers an advance. Prefers outline/synopsis and sample chapters, but queries are acceptable. Reports in 1-2 months. SASE. Free book catalog.
Nonfiction: Only religious themes. "Writers must know the evangelical market well and their material should have substance. Many of our books are by ministers, Bible teachers, and seminar speakers. We are looking for freelancers who can furnish ideas and find experts to team up to put together good books." Recently published *How to Say No to a Stubborn Habit*, by E. Lutzer; and *Lord, Change Me!*, by E. Christenson.

THE VIKING PRESS, INC., PUBLISHERS, 625 Madison Ave., New York NY 10022. Royalties paid on all books. Published over 200 titles last year. Juvenile mss should be addressed to Viking Junior Books. Adult mss should be addressed to the Viking Press. Studio mss should be addressed to Viking Studio Books. Reports in 4 to 6 weeks. Enclose return postage with ms.

General: Publishes adult and Studio books (art, photography, etc.). Also publishes Viking Portable Library and Viking Critical Library.
Juveniles: Publishes juvenile books.

VISAGE PRESS, INC., 2333 N. Vernon St., Arlington VA 22207. (703)525-9622. Editor-in-Chief: Emilio C. Viano. Managing Editor: Sherry Icenhower. Hardcover and paperback originals. "At this time, interested in particular in how-to books and books about sports, particularly written by and for women athletes." Pays 10% royalty on first 5,000 hardcover; 12% next 5,000; 14% thereafter. Paperback royalty depends on the run. "Average advance is $1,000, generally given upon receipt of acceptable ms; rarely given on basis of outline alone. For scholarly works, please follow the style of the American Sociological Review (see their *Notice to Contributors*), or send for style sheet." Published 5 titles in 1978; plans 8 in 1979 and 10 in 1980. Send contact sheets (if available) or prints to illustrate ms. Pictures must always be captioned and accompanied by proper releases. Photocopied submissions OK. Reports in 1-2 months. SASE. Book catalog for SASE.
Nonfiction: Publishes business; cookbooks, cooking and foods (regional cuisine and Mid-Atlantic and Southern states); hobbies, medicine and psychiatry (particularly about emergencies, crisis, rape, child abuse, other victimizations, prevention of victimization); pets (a consumer guide to pet books; "gourmet" foods for pets); psychology (particularly in the area of the rapist, sex offender and victims repeatedly victimized); recreation (soccer, in particular); religious (books about the coming millenium sought); sports (for the woman athlete in particular); and sexuality "after 50." Query or submit outline/synopsis and sample chapters.
Special Needs: "A series on skiing of the travel book variety, telling people where to go, what to expect in terms of facilities, schools, lifts, accommodations, etc. Also books on soccer."

VULCAN BOOKS, Division of Trinity-One, Inc., Box 25616, Seattle WA 98125. Publisher: Michael H. Gaven. Publishes hardcover and paperback originals and reprints. Offers standard minimum book contract. "Advances offered only in special cases." Published 14 titles in 1979. "Our books are marketed by all major occult distributors and we sell them to practically every store in America dealing with our subject matter." Submit outline and sample chapters for nonfiction; complete ms for fiction. Reports in 4-8 weeks. SASE.
Nonfiction: "We are expanding into all areas of truth, even a bit into fiction. We are still committed to our original field of astrology, and are especially searching for books on astrometerology, astrocartography, astropyschology. We will accept religious books that are nondenominational, truly nondenominational, that will appeal to people of all the world. Books that cover the new mutation of mankind into a global consciousness are welcomed. We are at the end of an age where we must group together to survive to fight those who think that freedom only belongs to a few. Books on these subjects, without fire and brimstone preaching are needed. Recently published *Gifts of the Crystal Skull, The Dorland Discoveries* and *Is It True What They Say About Edgar Cayce?*.

WALKER AND CO., 720 5th Ave., New York NY 10019. Editor-in-Chief: Richard Winslow. Managing Editor: Andrea Curley. Hardcover and paperback originals (90%) and reprints (10%). Pays 10-12-15% royalty or by outright purchase; advance averages $1,000-2,500 "but could be higher or lower." Publishes 80 titles annually. Query or submit outline/synopsis and sample chapters. Submit samples of photos/illustrations to accompany ms. Photocopied submissions OK. SASE. Free book catalog.
Nonfiction: Publishes Americana; art; biography; business; cookbooks, cooking and foods; histories; hobbies; how-to; juveniles; medicine and psychiatry; multimedia material; music; nature; pets; psychology; recreation; reference; religious; self-help; sports; travel; and gardening books. Recently published *The New York Philharmonic Guide to the Symphony*, by E. Downs (music nonfiction); *The Santa Claus Book*, by Jones (nonfiction); and *Collapsing Universe*, by Isaac Asimov (nonfiction).
Fiction: Mystery; science fiction; suspense; gothics; and regency books.

FREDERICK WARNE & CO., INC., 101 5th Ave., New York NY 10003. Editor, Books for Young People: Meredith J. Charpentier. Publishes juvenile hardcover originals. Offers 10% royalty contract. Published 10 titles in 1978; plans 15 in 1979, and 20 in 1980. Minimum advance is $500. Will consider photocopied submissions. Submit outline and sample chapters for nonfiction. Submit complete ms for fiction. Reports in 10 weeks. "Ms will not be considered unless accompanied by a correct-size SASE."
Juveniles: Hardcover trade books for children and young adults. Picture books (age 4-7), fiction and nonfiction for the middle reader (age 7-12) and young adults (ages 11 and up). Mss must combine a high-interest level with fine writing. Prefers to see fewer picture books and

more submissions for 8- to 12-year-olds. Recently published *Halk-a-Ball-of-Kenki*, by Verna Aardema; *My Island Grandma*, by Kathryn Lasky; *April Spell*, by Joanne Hoppe; *Alicia Alonao: The Story of a Ballerina*, by Beatrice Siegel; and *Benjamin's Perfect Solution*, by Beth Weiner Woldin.

WATSON-GUPTILL PUBLICATIONS, 1515 Broadway, New York NY 10036. Imprints include Whitney Library of Design. Publishes originals. Pays 10-12½-15% royalty; usual advance is $1,000, but average varies, depending on author's reputation and nature of book. Published 57 titles in 1978; plans 73 in 1979 and 70 in 1980. Address queries (followed by outlines and sample chapters) to Marcia Melnick, Editorial Director. Reports on queries within 10 days. Enclose return postage.
Art: Publishes art instruction books. Interested only in how-to books in any field of painting, crafts, graphic design, etc. Length: open.

FRANKLIN WATTS, INC., 730 5th Ave., New York, NY 10019. Vice President/Editorial Director: Jeanne Vestal. Royalty schedule varies according to the type of book. Usual advance for a series title is $1,000. Single title varies according to reputation of author and type of book. Published 135 titles in 1978; plans 125 in 1979, 120 in 1980. Current catalog available on request. Query. Prefers complete manuscript on fiction. Reports in approximately six weeks. Enclose return postage.
Juveniles: Publishes quality juveniles for pre-school through senior-high youths. Especially interested in humorous novels and science fiction for children ages 9-12. Also looking for high interest/low reading level fiction, adult nonfiction, and contemporary teenage fiction. No historical fiction, please. Would suggest that writers check catalog before submitting nonfiction ideas. Recent titles include: *Mob, Inc.*; *Metric Puzzles* and *Vampires.*

WAYNE STATE UNIVERSITY PRESS, 5959 Woodward Ave., Detroit MI 48202. (313)577-4601. Editor-in-Chief: B.M. Goldman. Managing Editor: J. Owen. Publishes hardcover and paperback originals. "Standard royalty schedule"; no advance. Published 30 titles in 1978; plans 30 in 1979, 30 in 1980. Reports in 1-6 months. SASE. Free book catalog.
Nonfiction: Publishes Americana, biography, economics, history, law, medicine and psychiatry, music, philosophy, politics, psychology, religious, and sociology books. Query or submit outline/synopsis and sample chapters. "Do not send photos unless requested, or send photocopies." Recently published *Theodore Dreiser: A Selection of Uncollected Prose,* by D. Pizer (literature); and *Latin via Ovid: a First Course,* by Goldman/Nyenhuis.

WEBSTER DIVISION, McGraw-Hill Book Co., 1221 Avenue of the Americas, New York NY 10020. General Manager: Lawrence A. Walsh. Royalties vary. "Our royalty schedules are those of the industry, and advances are not commonly given." Photocopied submissions OK. Reports in 2-4 weeks. SASE.
Textbooks: Publishes school books, films, equipment and systems for elementary and secondary schools. Juveniles, social studies, science, language arts, foreign languages, the arts, mathematics. "Material is generally part of a series, system, or program done in connection with other writers, teachers, testing experts, et. al. Material must be matched to the psychological age level, with reading achievement and other educational prerequisites in mind. Interested in a Basic Reading program, a Career Education program, a Guidance program, a Health program, and a Special Education program for the elementary schools."

WESLEYAN UNIVERSITY PRESS, 55 High St., Middletown CT 06457. Associate Editor: Joan Bothell. Published 20 titles in 1978; plans 20 in 1979, 20 in 1980. "Payment varies with the author." Photocopied submissions OK, but no multiple submissions. SASE. Reports in 3-4 weeks. Free catalog.
Nonfiction: Scholarly material in American studies (especially regional studies), maritime history, dance, theater (especially the physical theater) and the philosophy of history. Query. "I want to see no unsolicited manuscripts." Recently published *The Theater of Donald Oenslager,* by Donald Oenslager (theatrical design); and *Anthropology Toward History: Culture and Work in a 19th-Century Maine Town,* by Richard Horowitz (American Studies).

WESTERN ISLANDS, 395 Concord Ave., Belmont MA 02178. Managing Editor: C.O. Mann. Publishes hardcover and paperback originals (75%) and reprints (25%). Published 3 titles in 1978. Pays 10% royalty on hardcover, 5% on paperback; no advance. Simultaneous and photocopied submissions OK. Reports in 2 months. SASE. Book catalog for SASE.
Nonfiction: "We are interested in conservative books on current events: economics, politics, contemporary history, etc. We are not interested in biographies, autobiographies (unless by a

famous conservative), fiction, poetry, etc. Anti-communist books, if not overly autobiographical, are welcome." Query or submit complete ms. Recently published *To Covet Honor*, by H. Alexander; *F.D.N.Y.*, by G. Johnson; and *The Siecus Circle*, by C. Chambers.

WESTERN PRODUCER PRAIRIE BOOKS, Box 2500, Saskatoon, Saskatchewan, Canada S7K 2C4. Manager: Rob Sanders. Publishes hardcover and paperback originals (95%) and reprints (5%). Specializes in nonfiction historical works set in Western Canada by Western Canadian authors. Pays 10% (of list price) royalty. Published 12 titles in 1978; plans 15 in 1978 and 19 in 1980. Submit contact sheets or prints if illustrations are to accompany ms. Simultaneous submissions OK. Reports in 2-4 months. SAE and International Reply Coupons. Free book catalog.
Nonfiction: Publishes history, nature, photography, biography, reference, agriculture, economics, politics and cookbooks. Submit outline, synopsis and sample chapters. Recently published *Uphill All the Way*, by E. Jaques (autobiography); *Out West*, by R. Phillips; and *Cornerstone Colony*, by G. MacEwan.

WESTERN PUBLISHING CO., INC., Juvenile Picture/Storybook Department, 1220 Mound Ave., Racine WI 53404. Imprints include Golden and Whitman. Editorial Director: Mel Benstead. Juvenile Fiction Editor: William H. Larson. Picture/Storybooks Editors Cecily R. Hogan and Donna Kelly. Publishes hardcover and paperbacks originals (25%) and reprints (75%). Publishes 200/titles year. Buys by outright purchase; no advance. Simultaneous and photocopied submissions OK. SASE. Reports in 6-8 weeks. Book catalog for SASE.
Nonfiction: Animals, humor, juveniles and nature."While most of our manuscripts are done on an assignment basis, we are always pleased to review an unsolicited manuscript written by an author who has created an entirely *new* story or who has found a successful, novel way to handle a tired and true subject. Picturebooks, intended for ages 3-6, should be from 200-800 words. These books are planned to be read to children, but the vocabulary should be simple enough for easy understanding and for young readers who wish to do the reading themselves. Books in our young picturebook lines include Little Golden Books, Whitman Tell-a-Tale Books, Golden Shape Books, Big Golden Books, and Golden Play and Learn Books." Query or submit outline/synopsis and sample chapters or submit complete ms. Recently published *Facts and Quizzes*, by Eileen Daly, et. al. (family funtime); *Multiply and Divide*, by Joanne Wylie (Whitman help-yourself workbook); and *All Kinds of Animals*, by Adelaide Holl (Golden Readiness Workbook).
Fiction: Adventure, humor, mystery, science fiction and picturebooks for children. "We are going to do 6 Trixie Belden books this year." Query or submit outline/synopsis and sample chapters. Recently published *Where Will All The Animals Go?*, by Sharon Holaves (Little Golden Book); *Gypsy and Nimblefoot*, by Sharon Wagner (Golden Fiction); and *Tee-Bo, The Persnickety Prowler*, by Mary Burg Whitcomb (Golden Fiction).

WESTERNLORE PRESS, Box 4304, 126 LaPorte, Suite F, Arcadia CA 91006. Editor: Lynn R. Bailey. Publishes 6-12 titles/year. Pays standard royalties "except in special cases." Query. Reports in 60 days. Enclose return postage with query.
Americana: Publishes Western Americana of a scholarly and semi-scholarly nature: anthropology, archeology, historic sites, restoration, and ethnohistory pertaining to the greater American West. Republication of rare and out-of-print books. Length: 25,000-100,000 words.

THE WESTMINSTER PRESS, Department CBE, 925 Chestnut St., Philadelphia PA 19107. (215)928-2700. Children's Book Editor: Barbara S. Bates. Publishes hardcover originals. Published 17 titles in 1978; plans 18 in 1979, 18 in 1980. Royalty and advance "vary with author's experience and credentials, and the amount of illustration needed." Photocopied submissions OK if not simultaneous. Reports in 3 months. SASE. Book catalog for SASE.
Nonfiction: Juvenile only, for readers 8-12. Career; consumer education; ecology and nature; science and math; social studies; recreation and how-to; and sports and hobbies. Query or submit outline/synopsis and sample chapters. Recently published *Five! How Do They Fight It?*, by Anabel Dean (social studies/career); and *Who Do You Think You Are?*, by S. Hilton (hobby/social studies resource).
Fiction: Juvenile only, for ages 8-12. Adventure; humor; mystery; family; science fiction; and suspense. No picture books or stories in verse. Submit outline/synopsis and sample chapters. Recently published *Never Mind Murder*, by F. Wosmek (mystery); *I Gotta Be Free*, by R. Hallman (suspense); and *Getting Rid of Roger*, by Ellen Matthews.

*WESTVIEW PRESS, 5500 Central Ave., Boulder CO 80301. (303)444-3541. Publisher: F.A. Praeger. Associate Publisher/Editorial Director: Lynne Rienner. Hardcover and paperback originals (90%), lecture notes, reference books, and paperbook texts (10%). Specializes in scholarly monographs or conference reports with strong emphasis on applied science, both social and natural. Zero to 10% royalty, depending on marketing. Accepts subsidies for a small number of books, "but only in the case of first class scholarly material for a limited market when books need to be priced low, or when the manuscripts have unusual difficulties such as Chinese or Sanscrit characters; the usual quality standards of a top-flight university press apply, and subsidies must be furnished by institutions, not by individuals." Published 200 titles in 1978. Markets books mainly by direct mail. State availability of photos and/or illustrations to accompany manuscript. Reports in 1-4 months. SASE. Free book catalog.

Nonfiction: Public policy, energy, natural resources, international economics and business, international relations, area studies, geography, science and technology policy, agriculture, sociology, anthropology and reference. Query and submit sample chapters. Use University of Chicago *Manual of Style.*"Unsolicited manuscripts receive low priority; inquire before submitting projects."

WHITAKER HOUSE, Pittsburgh and Colfax Sts., Springdale PA 15144. (412)274-4440. Editorial Assistant: Carol Thomas. Paperback originals (80%) and reprints (20%). "We publish only Christian books, especially dealing with charismatic Christianity. Royalty of a straight percentage (6%) of the cover price of the book. Advance is made only under certain circumstances. Publishes about 5 titles annually. "We market books in Christian book stores and in rack-jobbing locations such as supermarkets and drug stores." Looking for "teaching testimonies"; typed, double-spaced, about 200 pages in length. Send prints to illustrate ms. Simultaneous and photocopied submissions OK. Reports in about 2-4 weeks. SASE. Free book catalog.

Nonfiction: Publishes biography or autobiography (testimony of spirit-filled Christians; 60,000 words); how-to ("how to move on in your Christian walk"; 60,000 words); religious ("don't want heavy theology"; 60,000 words). "Testimonies of drug addicts or ex-convicts are somewhat overworked. Please note that we call our books 'teaching testimonies' because they give the author's life experiences as well as solid Christian teaching." Recently published *Forgiven*, by Myrle Morris (autobiography); and *Life in a New Dimension*, by Don Double (how-to).

WHITMORE PUBLISHING CO., 35 Cricket Terrace, Ardmore PA 19003. Contact: Linda S. Peacock. Offers "standard royalty contract, profit-sharing contract, or outright purchase." Published 10 titles last year. Reports in 2-3 weeks. Send queries and sample chapters or poems. SASE.

General Nonfiction and Poetry: "Books that will provide the reader with insight and techniques to manage his or her life more effectively. Interests include education, nutrition, community life, philosophy, self-improvement, family study and planning, career planning; explanations of significant science and technology not broadly understood." Recently published *Isorbics: A Better Way to Fitness*, by Ueseldinger with Richards; and *Total Health Tennis: A Lifestyle Approach*, by Wilson

THE WHITSTON PUBLISHING CO., Box 958, Troy NY 12181. (518)283-4363. Editorial Director: Stephen Goode. Publishes hardcover originals. Published 22 titles in 1978; plans 30 in 1979, 40 in 1980. Pays 10-12-15% royalty; no advance. Simultaneous and photocopied submissions OK. Reports in 10-14 weeks. SASE. Free book catalog.

Nonfiction: "We publish scholarly and critical books in the arts, humanities and social sciences. We also publish reference books, bibliographies, indexes and checklists. We do not want author bibliographies in general unless they are unusual and unusually scholarly. We are, however, much interested in catalogs and inventories of library collections of individuals, such as the Robert Graves collection at Southern Illinois, etc." Query or submit complete ms. Recently published *Two Faces of Ionesco (A Collection of 15 Essays by and about Ionesco)*, edited by R. Lamont/M. Friedman.

WILDERNESS PRESS, 2440 Bancroft Way, Berkeley CA 94704. (415)843-8080. Editorial Director: Thomas Winnett. Publishes paperback originals. Published 9 titles in 1978; plans 5 in 1979, 8 in 1980. Pays 8-10% royalty; advance averages $200. Simultaneous and photocopied submissions OK. Reports in 2 weeks. SASE. Book catalog for SASE.

Nonfiction: "We publish books about the outdoors. Most of our books are trail guides for hikers and backpackers, but we also publish how-to books about the outdoors and perhaps will publish personal adventures. The manuscript must be accurate. The author must research an area thoroughly in person. If he is writing a trail guide, he must walk all the trails in the area his book is about. The outlook must be strongly conservationist. The style must be appropriate for a highly literate audience." Query, submit outline/synopsis and sample chapters, or submit complete ms. Recently published *Pacific Crest Trail*, by Schaffer et. al. (trail guide); *Huckleberry Country*, by Thompson/Thompson (wild food plant guide); and *Waxing for Cross-Country Skiing*, by Brady/Skjemstad (how-to manual).

JOHN WILEY & SONS, INC., 605 3rd Ave., New York NY 10016. (212)867-9800. Publishes hardcover and paperback originals. Pays 15% (of net receipts) royalty. Follow MLA Style Sheet. Simultaneous and photocopied submissions OK. Reports in 6 months. SASE. Free book catalog.
Nonfiction: Publishes college textbooks, professional reference titles and journals in engineering, social science, business, life sciences, politics, medicine and psychology. Query or submit outline/synopsis and sample chapters. Recently published *Craft of Power*, by Siu; *My Body, My Health*, by Stewart; and *Real Estate Investment Strategy*, by Seldin and Swesnick.

WILLAMETTE MANAGEMENT ASSOCIATES, INC., 534 SW 3rd Ave., Portland OR 97204. (503)224-6004. Query Editor: Dixie L. Sims. Publishes paperback and hardcover originals. Pays 10-15% royalty of net; advance varies. "We will consider photocopies, but would like to know the track record of a copied manuscript. (Turned down texts are no problem—if they fit our needs)." Query with outline and sample chapters or completed ms. Reports in 1 month. No report without SASE.
Business: Interested in business investment books. "They should be technical and of current interest (timing) as well as of good long-range material. We deal with publicly held securities and topics relating to the value of closely held businesses. We are not interested in coins, collectibles, options or nonequity investments."

WILSHIRE BOOK CO., 12015 Sherman Rd., North Hollywood CA 91605. (213)875-1711. Editorial Director: Melvin Powers. Publishes paperback originals (50%) and reprints (50%). Publishes 50 titles in 1978; plans 50 in 1979, 50 in 1980. Pays 5% minimum royalty; "advance varies with nature of the book." Simultaneous and photocopied submissions OK. SASE. Reports in 2 weeks. Catalog for SASE.
Nonfiction: Calligraphy, health, hobbies, how-to, psychology, recreation, self-help and sports. "We are always looking for self-help and psychological books, such as *Psycho-Cybernetics and Guide to Rational Living*. We need manuscripts teaching calligraphy. We publish 70 horse books and need books dealing with instruction and teaching circus tricks." Query. "All that I need is the concept of the book to determine if the project is viable. I welcome phone calls to discuss manuscripts with authors." Recently published *Exuberance*, by Dr. Paul Kurtz (psychological self-help); *Healing Power of Natural Foods*, by May Bethel (health); *Racquetball Made Easy*, by Steve Lubarsky and Jack Scagnetti (sports); *Reflexology*, by Dr. Maybelle Segal (health); *Winning at Poker*, by John Archer (gambling); and *You & Your Pony*, by Pepper Mainwaring Healey (sports).

WINCHESTER PRESS, Box 1260, Tulsa OK 74101. (981)835-3161. Managing Editor: Robert Elman. Vice President/General Manager: Don Karecki. Publishes hardcover originals. Pays 10-12½-15% royalty; offers $1,500 average advance. Published 30 titles in 1978. "Submit sample photos and some idea of total number projected for final book." Simultaneous and photocopied submissions OK. Reports in 3 months. SASE. Free book catalog.
Nonfiction: Main interest is in outdoor sports, crafts and related subjects. Publishes cookbooks, cooking and foods (if related to their field); how-to (sports and sporting equipment); pets (hunting dogs and horses); recreation (outdoor), sports (hunting, fishing, etc.); and technical (firearms). Submit outline/synopsis and sample chapters. Recently published *American Shotgun Design and Performance*, by L.R. Wallack; and *Wildlife Watcher's Handbook*, by F.T. Hanenkrat.

WINSTON PRESS, INC., CBS Educational Publishing, 430 Oak Grove, Minneapolis MN 55403. (612)871-7000. Imprints include Winston House (backlist audiovisual). Editorial Director: John G. Welshons. Publishes hardcover and paperback originals (90%) and reprints (10%). Publishes 45 titles/year. Pays 10-12½-15% royalty; advance varies. Photocopied submissions OK. SASE. Reports in 2 months. Book catalog for SASE.
Nonfiction: "Religion and human development: most titles are done on request. Curriculum materials for preschool through adult education. Specialized and general trade books, gift and photography books. Also, audiovisual material." Query or submit outline/synopsis. Recently published *Self-Esteem: A Family Affair*, by Jean Illsley Clarke (trade book on parenting); *Breaking the Cycle of Child Abuse*, by Christine Comstock Herbruck; *Permanent Love*, by Edward E. Ford and Steven Englund; *A Spirituality Named Compassion and the Healing of the*

Global Village and *Humpty Dumpty and Us*, by Matthew Fox; and *The Christmas Pageant*, by Tomie de Paola (children's storybook).

*ALAN WOFSY FINE ARTS, 150 Green St., San Francisco CA 94111. Publishes hardcover and paperback originals (75%) and hardcover reprints (25%). Specializes in art reference books, specifically catalogs of graphic artists; bibliographies related to fine presses and the art of the book; original, illustrated books. Payment usually made on a flat fee basis, which begins at $200. Subsidy publishes 15% of books "where a very high quality of reproduction is necessary for a very limited market, and we feel the book should be published." No advance. Publishes 6 titles annually. SASE. Reports in 2-4 weeks. Free book catalog.
Nonfiction: Publishes reference books on art and photography. Query.

WOODBRIDGE PRESS PUBLISHING CO., Box 6189, Santa Barbara CA 93111. Editor-in-Chief: Howard B. Weeks. Publishes hardcover and paperback originals. Standard royalty contract. Rarely gives an advance. Published 8 titles in 1977. Will consider photocopied submissions. Query. Returns rejected material as soon as possible. Reports on material accepted for publication in 3 months. Enclose return postage with query.
General Nonfiction: "How-to books on personal health and well-being. Should offer the reader valuable new information or insights on anything from recreation to diet to mental health that will enable him to achieve greater personal fulfillment, with emphasis on that goal. Should minimize broad philosophy and maximize specific, useful information." Length: Books range from 96 to 300 pages. Also publishes cookbooks and gardening books. Recent titles include *The Oats, Peas, Beans and Barley Cookbook* (Cottrell), *More Food From Your Garden* (Mittleider) and *Butterflies in My Stomach* (Taylor).

THE WRITER, INC., 8 Arlington St., Boston MA 02116. Editor: Sylvia K. Burack. Publishes hardcover originals. Standard royalty schedule. Advance varies. Published 5 titles last year. Catalog on request. Query. Reports in three weeks. Enclose return postage.
Nonfiction: Books on writing for writers. Length: open.

WRITER'S DIGEST BOOKS, 9933 Alliance Rd., Cincinnati OH 45242. (513)984-0717. Senior Book Editor: Carol Cartaino. Assistant Book Editors: Barbara O'Brien, Howard Wells. Publishes hardcover originals. Trade publisher for books about writing, art, crafts, songwriting and photography. Pays 10% royalty; offers $3,000 average advance. Published 10 titles in 1979 (not counting "market books" like *Writer's Market*); plans 10-12 titles in 1980. Simultaneous (if so advised) and photocopied submissions OK. Reports in 3 months. Enclose return postage. Book catalog for SASE.
Nonfiction: "How-to, reference and other books about writing, photography, art and crafts. We're seeking up-to-date, instructional treatments by authors who can write from successful experience, not merely hold forth. Style should be well-researched, yet lively and anecdotal." Query or submit outline/synopsis. "Be prepared to explain how the proposed book differs from existing books on the subject." Recently published *Magazine Writing: The Inside Angle*, by Art Spikol; *Successful Outdoor Writing*, by Jack Samson; *Writing the Novel: From Plot to Print*, by Lawrence Block; and *Sell Copy*, by Webster Kuswa.

YALE UNIVERSITY PRESS, 92A Yale Station, New Haven CT 06520. Editor-in-Chief: Edward Tripp. Executive Editor: Jane Isay. Publishes hardcover and paperback originals (96%) and reprints (4%). Published 90 in 1978; plans 90 in 1979. Pays 5-10% royalty; no advance. Photocopied submissions OK. Reports in 2-3 months. SASE. Book catalog for SASE.
Nonfiction: Works of original scholarship in the humanities, social sciences and hard sciences. No fiction, cookbooks or popular nonfiction. Query or submit outline/synopsis and sample chapters. Recently published *Caught in the Web of Words*, by K.M.E. Murray; *Democracy in Plural Societies*, by A. Lijphart (political science); and *The Rise of American Philosophy*, by Kublick.

Subsidy Book Publishers

The following listings are for book publishing companies who are totally subsidy publishers, meaning they do no standard trade publishing, and will publish a work only if the author is willing to underwrite the entire amount of the venture. This can be costly, and may run into thousands of dollars, usually returning less than 25% of the initial investment.

Read any literature or contracts carefully and thoroughly, being sure that all conditions of the venture (binding, editing, promotion, number of copies to be printed, etc.) are spelled out specifically.

For more information on subsidy publishing, write to us asking for the reprint "Does It Pay to Pay to Have It Published?" Address to *Payin' For It Editor,* 9933 Alliance Rd., Cincinnati OH 45242. SASE.

Dorrance & Company, Cricket Terrace Center, Ardmore PA 19003.

Exposition Press, 900 S. Oyster Bay Rd., Hicksville NY 11801.

Mojave Books, 7040 Darby Ave., Reseda CA 91335.

Vantage Press, 516 W. 34th St., New York NY 10001.

William-Frederick Press, 55 E. 86th St., New York NY 10028.

Company Publications

Company and in-house publications are those magazines, newspapers, newsletters and tabloids that are sponsored by a particular company to inform employees, customers and interested parties of the company's activities. Basically, six kinds of company publications exist: employee magazines published to keep employees abreast of company policy and the goings-on of their co-workers; customer magazines edited to remind customers of the desirability of owning or using that company's products or services; stockholder or corporate magazines put out for the shareholder to inform him of financial or policy matters; sales magazines telling the company's field representatives how to better push their wares; dealer magazines published to maintain open channels of communication between manufacturer and independent dealers; and technical service magazines sponsored by companies to which technical data is important in the use and application of products. A single company may publish any or all of these types, enlarging their need for well-written information regarding their products, employees and services.

The trick to successful (meaning selling) writing in the field is the word *company*. These magazines are published as a service to the sponsor, whether in an internal publication (which is a controlled circulation magazine distributed only among the employees of a company) or in an external publication (published for the public relations benefits to the company and circulated among the customers and users of that company's products or services). These publications vary in emphasis, some giving more space to company product-related information, and others highlighting the interesting activities or unique doings of company personnel. Manuscripts lacking a strong company tie-in, or derogatory material about the company or its goods are worthless to company publication editors.

Article ideas for company publications are as numerous as the number of companies that publish magazines. Stay alert for new businesses or unique applications of company's products in your own home town. "The best way to get story ideas," says Tod Watts, editor of *Caterpillar World*, "is to stop in at a local Cat dealer and ask about big sales, projects, events, etc."

Quite often, an out-of-the-ordinary use of a company's product is the way to a sure sale. Due to the limited nature of the publication, and the fact that editors have run stories on the use of their company's goods in all the conventional ways, an article about some merchant in your town who uses products in an offbeat manner will catch the editor's eye.

Showing recreational and other benefits of a product can also lead to sales. *Cat's Pride,* publication of the Arctic Cat snowmobile company, wants to "convey the fun, excitement and fellowship that is part of owning and operating a snowmobile," says managing editor Adele Malott. "The lifesaving capabilities of the sleds during blizzards or medical emergencies are an extra benefit."

Photos are a must for most company publications. Shoot photos that prominently display the company's product. Show off the product in a manner which compliments its qualities.

Company publications aren't the "puffy" magazines they were years ago. Editors seek articles that do more than praise the merits of their companies. They want well-developed, lively pieces that inform the reader about aspects of the firm other than his own job. Writing for these publications can be profitable and rewarding. The freelancer who can turn in polished copy to these busy editors may find himself more often than not on the company's payroll. "A good freelancer is worth his/her weight in gold to an editor," says Tod Watts.

AMERICAN GENERAL JOURNAL, American General Life Insurance Co., Box 1931, Houston TX 77001. Editor-in-Chief: Richard H. Cutrer. 30% freelance written. Emphasizes life and health insurance for a "very articulate, conservative, family-oriented audience, age 30-50, interested in hunting, fishing, golf and people." Monthly magazine; 24 pages. Estab. 1964. Circ. 1,500. Pays on publication. Byline given. Submit seasonal/holiday material 2 months in advance of issue date. SASE. Reports in 4 weeks. Free sample copy and writer's guidelines.
Nonfiction: "Mostly sales-oriented material." Exposé (impact of life and health insurance on US and world economy); how-to ("sell life insurance, avoid call reluctance, deal with rejection, find prospects, use spare time wisely"); general interest ("any well-written, interesting article—especially behavior-related—on life and health insurance"); historical ("how and why life and health insurance got started, when, what course it has taken or will take") and profile ("we will assign a feature story on one of our agents in a specific region"). No material on products or great salespeople. Buys 12 mss/year. Query with clips of published work and a 100-word biography. Length: 1,000-3,000 words. Pays 5¢/word.
Photos: State availability of photos. Pays $10-20/8x10 b&w glossy with border.

AMERICAN YOUTH MAGAZINE, Ceco Publishing Co., Campbell-Ewald Bldg., 7th Floor, 30400 Van Dyke, Warren MI 48093. Editor: Al Lee. Emphasizes free enterprise, driver safety, career opportunities, celebrities in entertainment and sports for high school seniors. Magazine published 4 times during school year; 36 pages. Circ. 1,000,000. Buys all rights. Previously published work OK. SASE. Reports in 3 weeks.
Nonfiction: General interest (celebrities who appeal to 17 to 18-year-olds); how-to (drive safely, find a job, select a career, start a small business); inspirational (17 to 18-year-olds performing positive achievements in a career or art field); interview (with teen celebrities and driving pros); profile (of celebrities) and career information. Articles should not be geared to youths. "Our readers are young adults looking ahead, not backwards, at college or careers." Buys 5-6 mss/issue. Query with clips of published work. Length: 1,500-3,000 words. Pays $350-1,000.
Photos: B&w contact sheets or negatives, or color transparencies. Payment is negotiated with story. Captions and model releases required.

ASHLAND NOW, Ashland Oil, Inc., Box 391, Ashland KY 41101. (606)329-3780. Editor: Melinda Hamilton. 80% freelance written. Emphasizes industry issues, stockholder communications and general interest material for an audience of employees, shareholders, opinion makers and community leaders. Quarterly magazine; 24 pages. Estab. May 1977. Circ. 100,000. Pays on acceptance. Buys all rights. Phone queries OK. Previously published submissions OK. Reports in 2 weeks.

BANKOH, Bank of Hawaii, Box 2900, Honolulu HI 96846. (808)537-8380. Editor: Catherine K. Enomoto. For bank employees. Quarterly magazine; 24 pages. Estab. 1945. Circ. 2,600. Pays on publication. Not copyrighted. Simultaneous, photocopied and previously published submissions OK. SASE. Reports in 2 weeks. Free sample copy.
Nonfiction: Company news, new product and general interest. No articles about specific products. Company tie-in essential. Buys 1-2 mss/year. Length: 500-1,500 words. Query. Pays $25-100.
Photos: Uses b&w glossy prints.

BAROID NEWS BULLETIN, Box 1675, Houston TX 77001. Editor-in-Chief: Marvin L. Brown. Editorial Assistant: Virginia Myers. 50% freelance written. Emphasizes the petroleum industry for a cross-section of ages, education and interests, although most readers are employed by the energy industries. Quarterly magazine; 36 pages. Estab. 1948. Circ. 20,000. Pays on acceptance. Buys first North American serial rights. Byline given. Submit seasonal/holiday material 1 year in advance. SASE. Reports in 3 weeks. Free sample copy and writer's guidelines.
Nonfiction: General interest and historical. Buys 12 mss/year. Submit complete ms. Length: 1,000-3,000 words. Pays 8-10¢/word.
Photos: "Photos may be used in the publication, or as reference for illustration art." Submit b&w prints. Offers no additional payment for photos accepted with ms. Captions preferred. Buys first North American serial rights.

BARTER COMMUNIQUE, Full Circle Marketing Corp., Box 2527, Sarasota FL 33578. (813)349-3300. Editor-in-Chief: Robert J. Murely. Emphasizes bartering for radio and TV station owners, cable TV, newspaper and magazine publishers and select travel and advertising agency presidents. Semiannual tabloid; 48 pages. Estab. 1975. Circ. 30,000. Pays on

publication. Rights purchased vary with author and material. Phone queries OK. Simultaneous, photocopied and previously published submissions OK. SASE. Reports in 4 weeks. Free sample copy and writer's guidelines.
Nonfiction: Articles on "barter" (trading products, goods and services), primarily travel and advertising. Length: 1,000 words. "Would like to see travel mss on southeast US and the Bahamas, and unique articles on media of all kinds. Include photos where applicable." Pays $30-50.

THE BLOUNT BANNER, Blount Brothers Corp., 4520 Executive Park Dr., Box 4577, Montgomery AL 36116. (205)277-8860. Editor-in-Chief: Victor R. McLean. Associate Editor: George E. Norris Jr. Emphasizes construction and engineering for a business and professional audience that includes company employees. Bimonthly magazine; 20-24 pages. Estab. 1958. Circ. 5,000. Pays on publication. Buys all rights. Byline given. Phone queries OK. Photocopied submissions OK. Reports in 3 weeks. Free sample copy; mention *Writer's Market* in request.
Nonfiction: Articles on company projects and photo features on project sites and company projects. Query. Length: 1,500-2,500 words. Pays $50-250.
Photos: "All features in our publication require photographic coverage." State availability of photos. Pays $5-50/5x7 b&w glossy print; $25-125/35mm color transparency. Captions required. Buys all rights. Model release required.
How To Break In: "Writers interested in doing work for our publication should simply write the editor and include a brief summary of experience. Most freelance work is on assignment."

BRISTOL-MYERS NEW YORK, 345 Park Ave., New York NY 10022. (212)644-3956. Editor: Chris Arrington. Emphasizes consumer and pharmaceutical products for employees. Monthly magazine. Estab. 1971. Circ. 2,000. Pays on publication. Buys first rights. Simultaneous and photocopied submissions OK. SASE. Reports in 3 weeks. Free sample copy.
Nonfiction: Company news, employee news, humor, job safety, new products, photo features and profiles. "Company tie-in essential." Buys less than 1 ms/issue. Query. Length: 350-750 words. Pays $100-300.

BUCKEYE MONITOR, Buckeye Pipe Line Co., 201 King of Prussia Rd., Radnor PA 19087. Editor: Stephen D. Hibbs. Emphasizes petroleum transportation for "blue-collar and technical employees and retirees—many living in rural areas." Bimonthly magazine. Estab. 1976. Circ. 1,500. Pays on acceptance. Not copyrighted. SASE. Reports in 3 weeks. Free sample copy and writer's guidelines.
Nonfiction: Company news; employee news; interview (limited to employees and retirees); personal experience (limited to employees and retirees); profile (limited to employees and retirees); and job safety (also off-the-job safety). Company tie-in essential. Buys 12 mss/year. Query with clips of published work. Length: 600-1,200 words. Pays $300-500.

BUSINESS ON WHEELS, Box 13208, Phoenix AZ 85002. (602)264-1579. Editor: Frederick H. Kling. "External house organ of Goodyear Tire and Rubber Company for distribution to owners and operators of truck fleets, both common carrier trucking systems and trucks used in connection with businesses of various types." Quarterly. Not copyrighted. Pays 25% kill fee. Byline given. Pays on acceptance. "Stories on assignment only. We like to choose our own subjects for case history stories." Query. SASE.
Nonfiction and Photos: "Freelance writers and photographers (especially writer-photographer teams or individuals) are invited to send in their qualifications for assignment of articles on truck-fleet operators in their territory. Pays from $250-300, plus expenses, for complete editorial-photographic coverage, additional for color, if used."

CAL-TAX NEWS, 921 11th St., Suite 800, Sacramento CA 95814. (916)441-0490. Editor: Ralph Juvinall. Emphasizes state and local government expenditures in California for corporate tax managers, local government officials, local taxpayer organizations and California media outlets. Bimonthly newsletter. Estab. 1959. Circ. 5,500. Pays on acceptance. Not copyrighted. Simultaneous, photocopied and previously published submissions OK. SASE. Reports in 1 week. Free sample copy.
Nonfiction: "Scholarly essays related to public expenditure control." Buys 2-3 mss/year. Query or submit complete ms. Length: 500-2,000 words. Pays $50-250.

CATERPILLAR WORLD, Caterpillar Tractor Co., 100 NE Adams AB1D, Peoria IL 61629. (309)675-4724. Editor-in-Chief: Tod Watts. 25-40% freelance written. Emphasizes "anything of interest about Caterpillar people, plants, or products. The magazine is distributed to 100,000 Caterpillar people and friends worldwide. It's printed in French, English and Portuguese."

Reader's ages, interests and education vary all over the map." Quarterly magazine; 32 pages. Estab. 1963. Circ. 100,000. Pays on acceptance. Buys one-time rights in 3 languages. Pays 50% kill fee and expenses; "however, we've never had to pay it." Byline given. Phone queries OK. "We rarely use seasonal or holiday material. All material has at least a 3-month lag time." Simultaneous and previously published submissions OK. First submission is usually on speculation. "It's unfortunate, but our experience has shown we need to establish a 'track-record' with freelance writers before we assign articles." Reports in 4 weeks. Free sample copy and writer's guidelines.

Nonfiction: "Everything must have a Caterpillar tie. It doesn't have to be strong, but it has to be there." How-to (buy one piece of equipment and become a millionaire, etc.); general interest (anything that may be of interest to Cat people worldwide); humor (it's hard to find something humorous yet interesting to an international audience; we'd like to see it, however); interview (with any appropriate person: contractor, operator, legislator, etc.); new product (large projects using Cat equipment; must have human interest); personal experience (would be interesting to hear from an equipment operator/writer); photo feature (on anything of interest to Cat people; should feature people as well as product); and profile (of Cat equipment users, etc.). "We don't want anything that has not been read and approved by the subjects of the article. Their written approval is a must." Buys 10 mss/year. Query. Length: "Whatever the story is worth." Pays $200 minimum.

Photos: "The only articles we accept without photos are those obviously illustrated by artwork." State availability of photos. Pays $25 minimum for b&w photos; $50 minimum for color. Submit contact sheets or negatives. Captions required; "at least who is in the pix and what they're doing." Model release required.

How To Break In: "Best way to get story ideas is to stop in at local Cat dealers and ask about big sales, events, etc."

CAT'S PRIDE, The Webb Co., 1999 Shepard Rd., St. Paul MN 55116. (612)647-7383. Editor: Don Picard. Managing Editor: Adele Malott. Emphasizes snowmobiling for people who like to ice fish, camp and attend snowmobile races and rallys. "We want to convey the fun, excitement and fellowship that is part of owning and operating a snowmobile. The lifesaving capabilities of the sleds during blizzards or medical emergencies are an extra benefit. A writer communicating knowledge of the snowmobiler's world through unique people or adventures would fit this magazine's target." Magazine published 4 times/year; 36 pages. Estab. 1978. Circ. 25,000. Pays on publication. Simultaneous submissions OK. SASE. Reports in 2 months. Free sample copy.

Nonfiction: Profile (of owners of Arctic Cat snowmobiles, who use their sleds in interesting ways); travel (via snowmobile); personal experience (with Arctic Cat snowmobiles); and photo feature (outstanding snow scenes of places where snowmobiles can travel). Buys 4-6 mss/issue. Query. Length: 1,200-2,000 words. Pays $150 minimum.

Photos: State availability of photos or send photos with ms. Pays $25 minimum for b&w 8x10 glossy prints and $75 minimum for 35mm or larger color transparencies; $250 for cover or center spread. Captions preferred; model releases required. Buys one-time rights.

CHANNELS MAGAZINE, Northwestern Bell Telephone Co., 100 S. 19th St., Omaha NE 68102. Editor: G.T. Metcalf. For top-level executives in Iowa, Minnesota, Nebraska, and North and South Dakota. Quarterly magazine. Estab. 1966. Circ. 47,000. Pays on acceptance. Buys all rights, but may reassign following publication. No byline. SASE. Reports in 1 month.

Nonfiction: Wants mss designed to keep executives up to date on new developments and techniques in business communications such as WATS, data transmission, time-shared computers, industrial television. Also uses occasional general interest features on sports, hobbies, personalities, events and points of interest in the five states covered. "Writing must be good and it must be tight." Length: 500-1,500 words. Query. Pays $150 minimum.

CIBA-GEIGY JOURNAL, 4002 Basel, Switzerland. Editor: Stanley Hubbard. For "employees of Ciba-Geigy, together with 'opinion leaders,' customers, educational institutions, etc., in most English-speaking countries." Estab. 1971. Circ. 27,000. Rights purchased vary with author and material; may buy all rights, but will reassign rights to author after publication. Pays 20% kill fee. Byline given. Buys 4 to 6 mss a year. Pays on publication. Will send a sample copy to a writer on request. Will consider photocopied submissions. Submit seasonal material 5 months in advance. Reports in 4 weeks. Query.

Nonfiction and Photos: "Popularized scientific and technical presentations, international cooperation subjects, regional and historical contributions related to group activities, human interest with product or operational tie-in. The approach should be literate; no writing down. The internationalism of our company is the basic determining factor—we are interpreting from continent to continent rather than talking to a homogeneous, neatly defined readership." Buys company-related informational articles, think pieces, photo features, and technical articles. Length: 500-3,000 words. Pays $100 minimum. Photos purchased with mss; captions required. Pays $10.

CIRCUIT, The Horace Mann Insurance Co., 1 Horace Mann Plaza, Springfield IL 62715. Editor: Brad Whitworth. For the home office and claims office personnel of personal lines insurance company specializing in the teacher market. Weekly newspaper. Estab. 1964. Circ. 1,200. Pays on publication. Buys all rights. Byline given. Simultaneous, photocopied and previously published submissions OK. SASE. Reports in 3 weeks. Free sample copy and writer's guidelines.
Nonfiction: Company news, employee news, historical (insurance industry), interview, new product (insurance developments in industry) and profile. "We do not want articles on humor, travel, personal opinion and job safety." Company tie-in preferred. Buys 5-7 mss/year. Query. Length: 500-1,000 words. Pays $15-100.

THE COMPASS, Mobil Sales and Supply Corp., 150 E. 42nd St., New York NY 10017. Editor-in-Chief: R. Gordon MacKenzie. 60% freelance written. Emphasizes marine or maritime activities for the major international shipowners and ship operators. Quarterly magazine; 40 pages. Estab. 1920. Circ. 20,000. Pays on acceptance. Buys one-time rights. Byline given. Simultaneous, photocopied and previously published submissions OK. SASE. Reports in 2 weeks. Free sample copy.
Nonfiction: Marine material only. General interest; humor; historical; nostalgia; new product; personal experience; and technical. No travelogues. Buys 20 mss/year. Query or submit complete ms. Length: 2,000-4,000 words. Pays $125-250.
Photos: Purchased with accompanying ms. Submit 5x7 or larger b&w prints or 35mm color transparencies. No additional payment for photos accepted with ms. Captions preferred. Buys one-time rights. Model release required.

CORRESPONDENT, Aid Association for Lutherans, Appleton WI 54919. (414)734-5721. Editor: Jim C. Hoyer. Emphasizes fraternal insurance for Lutherans and their families. Quarterly magazine. Estab. 1902. Circ. 750,000. Pays on publication. Buys one-time rights. Simultaneous and photocopied submissions OK. SASE. Reports in 1 month. Free sample copy.
Nonfiction: Profiles of Lutherans doing unusual jobs. Company tie-in essential. Buys 2-3 mss/year. Query. Length: 500-1,500 words. Pays 10¢/word.
Photos: Pays $5 for b&w glossy prints; $10 for color prints or slides.

CORVETTE NEWS, 2-129 General Motors Bldg., Detroit MI 48202. For Corvette owners worldwide. Bimonthly. Circ. 265,000. Buys all rights. Pays on acceptance. Free sample copy and editorial guidelines. Query. SASE.
Nonfiction and Photos: "Articles must be of interest to this audience. Subjects considered include: (1) Technical articles dealing with engines, paint, body work, suspension, parts searches, etc. (2) Competition, 'Vettes vs. 'Vettes, or 'Vettes vs. others. (3) Profiles of Corvette owners/drivers. (4) General interest articles, such as the unusual history of a particular early model Corvette, and perhaps its restoration; one owner's do-it-yourself engine repair procedures, maintenance procedures; Corvettes in unusual service; hobbies involving Corvettes; sports involving Corvettes. (5) Road hunts. (6) Special Corvette events such as races, drags, rallies, concourse, gymkhanas, slaloms. (7) Corvette club activities." Length: 800-2,400 words. Pays $50-$500, including photos illustrating article. Color transparencies or b&w negatives required. Pays additional fee of $35 for cover shot which is selected from photos furnished with article used in that issue.

CREDITHRIFTALK, CREDITHRIFT Financial, Box 59, Evansville IN 47701. (812)464-6638. Editor-in-Chief: Gregory E. Thomas. Emphasizes consumer finance. All readers are employees of CREDITHRIFT Financial or one of its financial or insurance subsidiaries, age range 18-65, with most in the 25-45 bracket. Most are high school graduates with one year of college, interested in company advancement. Monthly magazine; 12-16 pages. Estab. December 1937. Circ. 3,000. Pays on acceptance. Not copyrighted. Pays 100% kill fee. Byline given only if requested. Phone queries OK. Submit seasonal/holiday material 3 months in advance of issue date. Simultaneous, photocopied and previously published submissions OK. Reports in 2 weeks. Free sample copy.
Nonfiction: Interview (must be with company employee; subject need not be limited to consumer finance and could center on employee's personal experience, hobby, volunteer work, etc.); personal opinion; photo feature (employee engaged in a unique activity); profile

(employee); and finance industry trends. Query., Length: 800-3,000 words. Pays $35 minimum. **Photos:** State availability of photos. Pays $5 minimum for b&w photos; submit contact sheet. Captions preferred. Buys one-time rights. Model release required "in some cases where a non-employee is included in the photo."

THE ENERGY PEOPLE, PSE&G, 80 Park Place, Newark NJ 07101. (201)430-5989. Editor: Eugene Murphy. For employees. Quarterly magazine. Estab. 1972. Circ. 19,000. Pays on acceptance. Not copyrighted. Simultaneous, photocopied and previously published submissions OK. SASE. Reports in 3 weeks. Free sample copy.
Nonfiction: Company news, employee news and humor (industry-related). Company tie-in preferred. Buys 3 mss/year. Query with clips of published work. Pays $75-200.

EUA SPECTRUM, EUA Service Corp., Box 212, Lincoln RI 02865. (401)333-1400. Editor: Jerry Campbell. Monthly. Circ. 2,500. Pays on publication. Not copyrighted. Submit seasonal or holiday material 2 months in advance. SASE. Reports monthly.
Nonfiction: How-to articles, humor, think pieces, new product coverage, photo, and travel and safety articles. Length: open. Pays $10-50.
Photos: No additional payment for b&w glossy prints purchased with mss.

THE ENTHUSIAST, 3700 W. Juneau, Milwaukee WI 53208. (414)342-4680. Editor: Bob Klein. 50% freelance written. Published by Harley-Davidson Motor Co., Inc. for "motorcycle riders of all ages, education, and professions." Estab. 1916. Circ. 150,000. Quarterly magazine. Not copyrighted. Pays on publication. Will send a sample copy to a writer on request. Write for copy of guidelines for writers. Will consider photocopied submissions. Submit seasonal material 2 months in advance. Reports in 8 weeks. Query or submit complete ms. SASE.
Nonfiction and Photos: "Stories on motorcycling—humor, technical, racing, touring, adventures, competitive events. All articles should feature Harley-Davidson products and not mention competitive products. We do not want stories concerning sex, violence, or anything harmful to the image of motorcycling. We use travel stories featuring Harley-Davidson motorcycles, which must be illustrated with good quality photos of the motorcycle and travelers with scenic background taken on the trip. Also needed are stories of off-road usage, e.g., scrambles, racing, trail riding, or any other unusual usage." Informational articles, how-to's, personal experience articles, interviews, profiles, inspirational pieces, humor, historical articles, photo features, travel articles, and technical articles. Length: 3,000 words. Pays 5¢ "per published word, or as previously agreed upon." Photos purchased with mss and without mss; captions optional. Uses "quality b&w or color 35mm transparencies or larger." Pays $7.50 to $25.
Fiction: "Good short stories with the image of clean motorcycling fun. No black leather jacket emphasis." Buys adventure and humorous stories. Length: 3,000 words maximum. Pays 5¢/published word, "or as previously agreed upon."
Fillers: Short humor. Length: open. Pays $15.

EQUIFAX NEWS, Box 4081, Atlanta GA 30302. Editor: H.A. McQuade. Associate Editor: Roger Allen. For management employees of most American corporations, especially insurance companies. This includes Canada and Mexico. Pass-along readership involves submanagement and nonmanagement people in these firms. Quarterly. Circ. 90,000. Pays on acceptance. SASE. Reports in 2 weeks. Sample copy on request.
Nonfiction: "Insurance-related articles, new trends, challenges, and problems facing underwriters, actuaries, claim men, executives, and agents; articles of general interest in a wide range of subject—the quality of life, ecology, drug- and alcohol-related subjects, safe driving, law enforcement, and insurance-related Americana; inspirational articles to help managers and executives do their jobs better. Write with our audience in mind. Only articles of the highest quality will be considered. Especially interested in material written by insurance underwriters, insurance executives, college instructors and professors on previously unpublished or updated facets of our area of interest. More than 90% of our readers are customers of Equifax, Inc. or its various affiliates, and they expect to see articles that help them know and understand the business information business." Buys inspriational articles, think pieces about insurance industry's need for business information service, etc. Buys 3-5 mss/year. Query. Length: 1,000-2,000 words. Pays 1-2¢/word depending on quality and importance of material, but not less than $25.
Photos: Pays $5-15 for b&w 5x7 or 8x10 glossy prints purchased with mss.

FAMILY MAGAZINE, General Mills, 9200 Wayzata Blvd., Minneapolis MN 55440. Editorial Director: Syl Jones. Emphasizes plant and subsidiary company activities for employees of the corporation at every level from the president to workers in the plant. Quarterly magazine; 24

pages. Estab. 1977. Circ. 40,000. Pays on acceptance. Buys all rights. Byline given unless "an article has been rewritten so completely that it is no longer the writer's work or the subject matter is purely factual and the personal interplay of author and audience is a hinderance to the enjoyment of the piece." Submit seasonal/holiday material 6 months in advance of issue date. Photocopied and previously published submissions OK. "We do not accept unsolicited manuscripts without prior query." SASE. Reports in 6 weeks. Free sample copy.

Nonfiction: General interest; humor; historical; new product; and technical (for Progress Thru Research column). Query. Length: 2,500 words maximum. Pays $50-250.

Photos: State availability of photos. Pays $10-50 for 8x10 b&w glossy prints. Captions required. Buys all rights. Model release required.

THE FLYING A, Aeroquip Corp., 300 S. East Ave., Jackson MI 49203. (517)787-8121. Editor-in-Chief: Wayne D. Thomas. 10% freelance written. Emphasizes Aeroquip customers and products. Quarterly magazine; 24 pages. Estab. 1949. Circ. 32,000. Pays on acceptance. Buys all rights. Phone queries OK. Simultaneous submissions OK. SASE. Reports in 1 month. Free sample copy; mention *Writer's Market* in request.

Nonfiction: General interest (feature stories with emphasis on free enterprise, business-related articles); interview (by assignment only); and human interest. Buys 1 ms/issue. Query. Length: 1-4 printed pages. Pays $100 minimum.

Photos: "Photos are generally by specific assignment only."

Fillers: Human interest, business-related. Pays $50.

FRIENDS MAGAZINE, Ceco Publishing Co., 30400 Van Dyke Blvd., Warren MI 48093. (313)575-9400. Managing Editor: Bill Gray. "The only common bond our audience shares is they own Chevrolets. Monthly magazine; 32 pages. Estab. 1937. Circ. 2,000,000. Pays on acceptance. Buys all rights. Phone queries OK. Submit seasonal/holiday material 6 months in advance. Simultaneous and photocopied submissions OK. SASE. Reports in 4 weeks. Free sample copy and writer's guidelines.

Nonfiction: General interest (lifestyle); historical (when story has contemporary parallel); how-to (service features for families, especially financial topics); humor (any subject); travel; and photo feature (strong photo essays that say something about American lifestyle, especially focusing on family life). "We're looking for freelancers who can spot lifestyle trends in their areas that have potential national impact. We're looking for fresh ideas and different ways of telling familiar stories."

Photos: State availability of photos. Pays $50 for b&w contact sheets and $75 for 35mm color transparencies. Captions and model releases required.

HOSPITAL FORUM, 830 Market St., San Francisco CA 94102. (415)421-8720. Editor: James Keough. For hospital administrators and top-level management in hospitals. Magazine published 7 times/year. Estab. 1957. Circ. 11,000. Pays on publication. Buys all rights. Simultaneous and photocopied submissions OK. SASE. Reports in 1 month. Free writer's guidelines.

Nonfiction: How-to (development and improvements in the hospital system in the West); interview; and technical (hospital administration ideas and practical working information). Buys 6 mss/year. Send complete ms. Length: 2,000-3,500 words.

Photos: "Photos and graphics are helpful." Uses b&w 5x7 or 8x10 glossy prints.

HNG MAGAZINE, Houston Natural Gas, Box 1188, Houston TX 77001. (713)654-6449. Editor: Ms. Mica McCutchen. Emphasizes the energy industry—oil, gas, coal, industrial gases and river commerce—for employees. Bimonthly magazine. Estab. 1969. Circ. 7,500. Pays on acceptance. Buys all rights. Simultaneous and photocopied submissions OK. SASE. Reports in 1 month. Free sample copy and writer's guidelines.

Nonfiction: Historical (on locations of subsidiaries); personal opinion; technical; and new forms of energy. "Material must be issue-oriented or about subjects relevant to the industry." Company tie-in preferred. Buys 4 mss/year. Query with clips of published work. Pays $300.

Photos: "We use freelance photographers exclusively."

INDUSTRIAL PROGRESS, Box 13208, Phoenix AZ 85002. (602)264-1579. Editor: Frederick H. Kling. External house organ of Goodyear Tire and Rubber Company, for "executives, management, and professional men (designers, engineers, etc.) in all types of industry." Quarterly. Not copyrighted. Pays 25% kill fee. Byline given. Pays on acceptance. SASE.

Nonfiction and Photos: Male-interest features: hobbies, sports, novelty, mechanical, do-it-yourself, personalities, adventure, industrial case histories and roundup stores—methods, techniques, etc. Must be strongly photographic. Some color features used. Pays from $25-50 for a single photo caption item to $200 for full-length features (up to 1,000 words) with 4 or 5 b&w photos; up to $300 for full-length color features.

INLAND, The Magazine of the Middle West, Inland Steel Co., 30 W. Monroe St., Chicago IL 60603. (312)346-0300. Managing Editor: Sheldon A. Mix. 25% freelance written. Emphasizes steel products, services and company personnel. Quarterly magazine; 24 pages. Estab. 1953. Circ. 12,000. Pays on acceptance. Buys one-time rights. Kill fee: "We have always paid the full fee on articles that have been killed." Byline given. Submit seasonal/holiday material at least a year in advance. Simultaneous submissions OK. SASE. Reports in 6-8 weeks. Free sample copy.
Nonfiction: Articles, essays, humorous commentaries and pictorial essays. "We encourage individuality. Half of each issue deals with staff-written steel subjects; half with widely ranging nonsteel matter. Articles and essays related somehow to the Midwest (basically Illinois, Wisconsin, Minnesota, Michigan, Missouri, Iowa, Indiana and Ohio) in such subject areas as history, folklore, sports, humor, the seasons, current scene generally; nostalgia and reminiscence if well done and appeal is broad enough. But subject is less important than treatment. We like perceptive, thoughtful writing, and fresh ideas and approaches. Please don't send slight, rehashed historical pieces or any articles of purely local interest." Personal experience, profile, humor, historical, think articles, personal opinion and photo essays. Length: 1,200-5,000 words. Pays $300-500; less for extremely short pieces.
Photos: Purchased with or without mss. Captions required. "Payment for pictorial essay same as for text feature."

IOWA REC NEWS, Box AP, Des Moines IA 50302. (515)244-6297. Editor: Thomas P. Graves. Emphasizes rural energy issues for residents of rural Iowa. Monthly magazine. Estab. 1948. Circ. 142,000. Pays on publication. Not copyrighted. Simultaneous, photocopied and previously published submissions OK. SASE. Reports in 2 weeks.
Nonfiction: General interest; historical; humor; nostalgia (farm); and photo feature. "We especially need rural history and articles about rural life with an Iowa, or at least a Midwestern, slant." Buys 2 mss/issue. Send complete ms. Pays $25-125.

THE LENNOX NEWS, Lennox Industries, Inc., Box 400450, Dallas TX 75240. Editor: Howard A. Olson II. Emphasizes heating and air conditioning for Lennox dealers, architects, and mechanical and consulting engineers in the US, Canada and overseas. Bimonthly tabloid. Estab. 1946. Circ. 15,000. Pays on acceptance. Not copyrighted. Byline not given. Photocopied submissions OK. Reports in 1 week. Free sample copy and writer's guidelines.
Nonfiction: Company news, employee news, historical (related to Lennox or Lennox products), and personal experience (testimonials for Lennox products by users). Also needs "Interesting and unique applications of Lennox residential, commercial or solar equipment. Topics related to the heating and air conditioning industry, e.g., energy, housing, operating a small business, and solar power." Company tie-in preferred. Query. Length: 500-1,500 words. Pays $25 minimum.
Photos: "We require photos for most stories. Negatives with contact prints will be accepted (b&w or color, depending on the story)."

LLOYD'S LISTENING POST, Box 5867, Rockford IL 61125. (815)399-6970. Editor: David M. Mathieu. For persons age 50 and over. Publication of Lloyd Hearing Aid Corp. Tabloid; 8-12 pages. Estab. 1972. Quarterly. Circ. 200,000. Not copyrighted. Buys 25 mss/year. Pays on acceptance. Free sample copy. Will consider photocopied and simultaneous submissions. Reports in 2 weeks. Submit only complete ms. SASE.
Nonfiction and Photos: Uses "self-help; inspirational; stories on active and happy people; solutions to senior citizens' problems; nostalgia; travel; profile; how-to; and informational. Keep material positive—and short. We use short features and wide variety of subjects in each issue." Would like to see mss on social security problems; travel (places and costs); "handyman" ideas around the home; relationships between old and young; profiles of active senior citizens. Length: 500-1,500 words. Pays 3-5¢/word. Photos used with accompanying ms with no additional payment. Captions required.

MARATHON WORLD, Marathon Oil Co., 539 S. Main St., Findlay OH 45840. (419)422-2121. Editor-in-Chief: Robert Ostermann. 20% freelance written. Emphasizes petroleum/energy; for shareholders, educators, legislators, government officials, libraries, community leaders, students and employees. Quarterly magazine; 28 pages. Estab. 1964. Circ. 72,000. Pays on acceptance. Buys first North American serial rights. Pays 20% kill fee. Byline given on contents page, not with article. Photocopied submissions OK. SASE. Reports in 3 weeks. Free sample copy and writer's guidelines.

Nonfiction: Informational; interview and photo feature. Buys 2-3 mss/issue. Query. Length: 800-2,500 words. Pays $400-1,200.

Photos: Photos purchased with accompanying ms or on assignment. Pay negotiable for b&w and color photos. Total purchase price for a ms includes payment for photos.

How To Break In: "Because of the special nature of the *World* as a corporate external publication and the special limits imposed on content, the best approach is through initial query."

MONTGOMERY WARD AUTO CLUB NEWS, Montgomery Ward Auto Club, 1400 W. Greenleaf Ave., Chicago IL 60626. Editor: Michael J. Connelly. Associate Editor: Linda Tritz. Emphasizes travel, automotive, recreational vehicles (RVs) and camping for middle-income readers, 25-65 years old. Bimonthly magazine; 36 pages. Estab. 1974. Circ. 1,200,000. Pays on acceptance. Buys first North American serial rights. Reports in 1 month. Free sample copy and writer's guidelines to published writers.

Nonfiction: How-to, informational, historical, humor, interview, nostalgia, profile, travel, photo feature and semi-technical. Buys 6 mss/issue. Query with published samples. Length: 600-1,800 words. Pays about 15¢/word.

Photos: Pays $25 for b&w and $50 minimum for color. Captions required; model releases preferred.

MORE BUSINESS, 69-12 223 St., Bayside, New York NY 11364. (212)224-0672. Editor: Trudy Settel. "We sell publications material to business for consumer use (incentives, communicaton, public relations)—look for book ideas and manuscripts." Monthly magazine. Estab. 1950. Circ. 10,000. Pays on acceptance. Buys all rights. SASE. Reports in 1 month. Free writer's guidelines.

Nonfiction: General interest, how-to, vocational techniques, nostalgia, photo feature, profile and travel. Buys 10-20 mss/year. Query. Pays $3,000-4,000 for book mss.

PGW NEWS, Philadelphia Gas Co., 1800 N. 9th St., Philadelphia PA 19122. (215)796-1260. Editor-in-Chief: William B. Hall, III. Emphasizes gas utility; for employees, retirees, their families, suppliers, other utility editors in US and abroad. Monthly magazine; 24 pages. Estab. 1928. Circ. 5,000. Pays on acceptance. Buys one-time rights. Submit seasonal/holiday material 3-4 months in advance, preferrably relating to Greater Philadelphia or Pennsylvania—New Jersey regions. SASE. Reports in 1-2 months. Free sample copy.

Nonfiction: How-to (being a better employee); informational; inspirational (from a job approach). Send complete ms. Length: 1,000-2,000 words. Pays $25 minimum.

THE PILOT'S LOG, New England Mutual Life Insurance Co., 501 Boylston St., Boston MA 02117. Editor: Dennis Driscoll. Emphasizes advanced techniques in selling life insurance for fulltime agents countrywide. Magazine published 6 times/year. Estab. 1915. Circ. 5,000. Pays on acceptance. Buys all rights. Photocopied submissions OK. Simultaneous and previously published submissions may be considered, depending on material. SASE. Reports "as soon as possible." Request free sample copy from Edna Canter.

Nonfiction: How-to, interview, new product, personal experience and profile. "All must relate to expert ideas on life insurance selling or to the psychology of selling—and should be our agents." Company tie-in essential. Buys 1-2 mss/year. Query with clips of published work. Pays $50/article. Photos help sell the ms.

PORT OF BALTIMORE MAGAZINE, The World Trade Center Baltimore, Baltimore MD 21202. (301)383-5718. Editor: Connie Young. Emphases maritime industry for freight forwarders, customhouse brokers, shippers and port service industries. "This publication's slant is the advantages and capabilities of the port of Baltimore." Monthly magazine. Estab. 1921. Circ. 12,000. Pays on acceptance or publication. Not copyrighted. Reports in 1 month. Free sample copy and writer's guidelines.

Nonfiction: Company news (on firms involved in maritime industry); historical (maritime facets of the port of Baltimore); job safety; vocational techniques; new product (maritime-related products); profile (on companies involved in maritime industry); and technical. Company tie-in essential. Buys 4 mss/year. Query. Length: "depends on topic—will advise." Pays $50.

Photos: B&w for inside of magazine; color for cover. Payment negotiable.

THE PRESS, The Greater Buffalo Press, Inc., 302 Grote St., Buffalo NY 14207. Managing Editor: Janet Tober. For advertising people. Bimonthly tabloid; 8 pages. Estab. 1976. Circ.

3,000. Pays on acceptance. Buys all rights. Submit seasonal/holiday material 2 months in advance. Photocopied submissions and previously published submissions OK. SASE. Reports in 2 weeks. Sample copy 50¢; free writer's guidelines.

Nonfiction: General interest (of interest to advertising people in the newspaper, ad agency and retailing fields); interview (of people in retailing, newpaper field, business, sports, etc.); and travel (suggest "if interesting to our readers"). Buys 4-6 mss/issue. Query. Length: 1,000-2,500 words. Pays $100-200.

Photos: State availability of photos. Uses negatives or prints. Offers no additonal payment for photos accepted with ms. Captions optional. Photos are usually returned after publication.

Fillers: Buys a few short humor pieces.

THE RED DEVIL, Wm. Underwood Co., 1 Red Devil Lane, Westwood MA 02090. Editor: Eleanor Monahan. 25% freelance written. Emphasizes food products and history of food. Published 3 time/year magazine; 16 pages. Estab. 1968. Circ. 3,700. Pays on acceptance. Buys one-time rights. Byline given. Submit seasonal/holiday material 3 months in advance of issue date. Photocopied and previously published submissions OK. SASE. Reports in 3 weeks.

Nonfiction: General interest; historical; humor; new product; and technical. "All articles must be related to food." Buys 2 mss/issue. Query. Length: 725-2,000 words. Pays $50-150.

Photos: State availability of photos with query. Pays $5-10 for b&w contact sheets. Captions preferred. Buys one-time rights. Model release required.

ROSEBURG WOODSMAN, Roseburg Lumber Co., 1220 SW Morrison St., Portland OR 97205. (503)227-3693. Editor: Rodger Dwight. 25% freelance written. For wholesale and retail lumber dealers and other buyers of forest products, such as furniture manufacturers and paper products companies. Monthly magazine; 8 pages. Publishes a special Christmas issue. Estab. 1955. Circ. 10,000. Buys all rights, but will reassign rights to author after publication. No byline given. Buys approximately 20 mss/year. Pays on publication. Free sample copy and writer's guidelines. No photocopied or simultaneous submissions. Submit seasonal material 3 months in advance. Reports in 1 week. Query or submit complete mss.

Nonfiction and Photos: Features on the "residential, commercial and industrial applications of wood products, such as lumber, plywood, prefinished wall paneling, and flakeboard—vinyl-laminated and printed." Informational, how-to, interview, profile, new products, technical and merchandising techniques articles. Length: 500-1,000 words. Pays 10¢/word. Pays $10/b&w glossy prints purchased with mss, 8x10. Pays $25-50/color transparency or print.

ROWAN GRAPEVINE, Rowan Companies, Inc., 1900 Post Oak Tower, 5051 Westheimer, Houston TX 77056. (713)621-7800. Editor: Susan L. Hedding. For workers on drilling rigs, pilots of rotor/fixed wing craft, mechanics for aircraft and administrative personnel. Quarterly magazine. Estab. 1948. Circ. 3,500. Pays on publication. Not copyrighted. SASE. Reports in 2 weeks. Free sample copy.

Nonfiction: General interest (public service such as health and finance); job safety; technical (on petroleum/aviation); and travel (southeast Asia, Scotland, the Middle East and Latin America). Buys 2 mss/year. Query. Length: 750-1,500 words. Pays $50-150.

RURALITE, Box 557, Forest Grove OR 97116. (503)357-2105. Editor: Ken Dollinger. For primarily rural families, served by consumer-owned electric utilities in Washington, Oregon, Idaho, Nevada and Alaska. Estab. 1954. Monthly. Circ. 175,000. Buys first North American rights only. Byline given. Pays on acceptance. Submit seasonal material at least three months in advance. Query. SASE.

Nonfiction and Photos: Primarily human-interest stories about rural or small-town folk, preferably living in areas (Northwest states and Alaska) served by Rural Electric Cooperatives; emphasis on self-reliance, overcoming of obstacles, cooperative effort, unusual or interesting avocations, hobbies or histories, public spirit or service, humor, inspirational. Will also consider how-to, advice for rural folk, little-known and interesting Northwest history, people or events. "Looking specifically for energy (sources, use, conservation) slant and items relating to rural electric cooperative."Good art or pix required (b/w negatives with proofsheets). Length 500-1,500 words. Pays $5-$70, depending upon length, quality, appropriateness and interest, number and quality of pix.

THE SERVICE BULLETIN, H.M. Gousha Co., Box 6227, San Jose CA 95150. (408)296-1060. Editor: Ken Layne. For service station/garage mechanics and oil company marketing and technical people. Monthly magazine. Estab. 1929. Circ. 20,000. Pays on publication. Buys first

rights. Photocopied and previously published submissions OK. Reports in 2 weeks. Free sample copy and writer's guidelines.
Nonfiction: Automotive technical articles only. Buys 5 mss/year. Query. Length: 500-1,000 words. Pays $100.
Photos: "Photos or illustrations are nice, but query first."

SEVENTY SIX MAGAZINE, Box 7600, Los Angeles CA 90051. Editor: Karen Saunders. For employees, politicians, retirees and community leaders. Publication of Union Oil Company. Estab. 1920. Bimonthly. Circ. 38,000. Not copyrighted. No byline given. Buys 2-3 mss/year. Pays on acceptance. Free sample copy and writer's guidelines. Reports "as soon as possible." SASE.
Nonfiction and Photos: "Articles about the petroleum industry, Union Oil Company, or Union Oil's employees or retirees. No articles about service stations or dealers. The history of oil or the unusual uses of petroleum are good subjects for freelancers." No straight news. People-oriented. Does not want to see travel features or cartoons. Buys informational, profile, humor, historical mss. Pays 10¢/word minimum. Photos purchased with ms with extra payment. 8x10 b&w; 35mm color transparencies. Captions required.

SMALL WORLD, Volkswagen of America, 818 Sylvan Ave., Englewood Cliffs NJ 07632. Editor: Burton Unger. For "Volkswagen owners in the United States." Magazine; 24 pages. Circ. 300,000. 5 times/year. Buys all rights. Byline given. Buys about 20 mss/year. Pays on acceptance. Free writer's guidelines. Reports in 6 weeks. "If you have a long feature possibility in mind, please query first. Though queries should be no longer than 2 pages, they ought to include a working title, a short, general summary of the article, and an outline of the specific points to be covered. Where possible, please include a sample of the photography available. We strongly advise writers to read at least 2 past issues before working on a story." SASE.
Nonfiction and Photos: "Interesting stories on people using Volkswagens; useful owner modifications of the vehicle; travel pieces with the emphasis on people, not places; Volkswagenmania stories, personality pieces, inspirational and true adventure articles. VW arts and crafts, etc. The style should be light. All stories must have a VW tie-in, preferably with a new generation VW model, i.e., Rabbit, Scirocco or Dasher. Our approach is subtle, however, and we try to avoid obvious product puffery, since *Small World* is not an advertising medium. We prefer a first-person, people-oriented handling. Length: 1,500 words maximum; shorter pieces, some as short as 450 words, often receive closer attention." Pays $100 per printed page for photographs and text; otherwise, a portion of that amount, depending on the space allotted. Most stories go 2 pages; some run 3 or 4. Photos purchased with ms; captions required. "We prefer color transparencies, 35mm or larger. All photos should carry the photographer's name and address. If the photographer is not the author, both names should appear on the first page of the text. Where possible, we would like a selection of at least 40 transparencies. It is recommended that at least one show the principal character or author; another, all or a recognizable portion of a VW in the locale of the story. Quality photography can often sell a story that might be otherwise rejected. Every picture should be identified or explained." Model releases required. Pays $250 maximum for cover photo.
Fillers: "Short, humorous anecdotes about Volkswagens." Pays $15.

SPERRY NEW HOLLAND PUBLIC RELATIONS NEWSFEATURES, New Holland PA 17557. (717)354-1274. Contact: Don Collins, Press Relations Supervisor. "Prepared for distribution to newspapers and farm publications to be used free. Also used in our own publications." Special Thanksgiving, Christmas and July 4 issues. Estab. 1895. Buys all rights. Buys 40 mss/year. Pays on acceptance. Write for editorial guidelines. Will consider photocopied submissions. Submit seasonal material 4 months in advance. Reports in 2 weeks. Query. SASE.
Nonfiction and Photos: "We send releases on how-to; getting the most out of; new twists in old practices; good management practices; work and time saving tips; safety tips—as these topics apply to farming and ranching. Most subjects will be owners of Sperry New Holland agricultural machinery. Give us an outline of a story of interest to a farm magazine editor. Tell us about the operation and the farmer and equipment involved. Always looking for good freelancers we can contact with our own leads and get coverage." This publication contains newsfeature articles for farm publications and newspapers. Circulation is to various farm publications. "We discuss rates before assignment is made. We usually pay expenses involved in gathering articles. Payment for unsolicited materials, that are accepted depends on quality and value to us. We're fair, but want only good materials that don't require a lot of rework." Buys informational mss on new farming practices, profiles of good farmers who use Sperry

New Holland equipment, spot news, successful business operations of farms and Sperry New Holland dealers, and new product applications. Photos purchased with ms with extra payment, without ms, or on assignment. Captions required. Uses "good cover shots in which our equipment appears" and agricultural photos. Payment: "no set figure for photos. If they are good we'll pay a fair price." Size: 8x10 for b&w; any size color transparencies.

SPERRY UNIVAC NEWS, Box 500, Blue Bell PA 19424. (215)542-4215. Editor: Pete Sigmund. Emphasizes computers for "all US employees of Sperry Univac." Monthly newspaper. Estab. 1960. Circ. 40,000. Buys all rights. Photocopied submissions OK. Reports in 1 week.
Nonfiction: Company news, employee news, general interest, and how-to. Company tie-in preferred. Query. Pay negotiable.

THE STERN VIEW, Mercury Marine, MerCruiser Div., 1939 Pioneer Rd., Fond du Lac WI 54935. Editor: Brian Callaghan. Emphasizes "all aspects of operating a boat dealership; finance, service, advertising and promotion, personnel, etc." Quarterly magazine; 8 pages. Estab. 1977. Circ. 5,000. Pays on acceptance. Buys all rights. Submit seasonal/holiday material 3 months in advance. Simultaneous submissions and previously published submissions OK. SASE. Reports in 6 weeks. Free sample copy and writer's guidelines.
Nonfiction: How-to (concentrate on business aspects of operating a profitable boat dealership); interview (with successful dealers who have a unique perspective); and technical (aspects of unique, money-saving and reliable marine engine servicing). All material should be written for the "stern drive" boat market. Buys 1-2 mss/issue. Query or submit complete ms. Length: 500-1,500 words. Pays $100-250.

SUN MAGAZINE, Sun Co., 1608 Walnut St., Philadelphia PA 19103. For "local, state and national government officials; community leaders; news and financial communicators; educators, shareholders, customers, and employees of Sun Company." Estab. 1923. Published four times/year. Circ. 140,000. Not copyrighted. Byline given. Buys 1-2 mss/year. "Most are staff-written." Pays on acceptance. Free sample copy. Reports in 3-6 weeks. Query.
Nonfiction: "Articles only. Subject matter should be related to Sun Company, oil industry or national energy situation. Articles should be directed toward a general audience. Style: magazine feature. Approach: nontechnical. Travel themes are currently being overworked." Buys informational articles, interviews, profiles, historical articles, think pieces, coverage of successful business operations. Length: 1,000-3,000 words.
Photos: Purchased on assignment; captions optional. "We do not buy photos on spec."

SUNSHINE SERVICE NEWS, Florida Power & Light Co., Box 529100. (305)552-3891. Editor: Jay Osborne. For the electrical utility industry. Monthly employee newspaper. Estab. 1936. Circ. 12,000. Pays on publication. Not copyrighted. Reports in 1 week. Free sample copy.
Nonfiction: Company news, employee news, general interest, historical, how-to, humor and job safety. Company tie-in preferred. Query. Pays $25-100.

TIME BREAK, GeoSpace Corp., Box 36374, Houston TX 77036. (713)666-1611. Editor: Lee C. Dominey. 2-5% freelance written. "The purpose of *Time Break* is to inform 'friends and customers' about all products and applications plus trends and items of interest in the geophysical field. It includes technical and semitechnical articles." Semiannual magazine; 20 pages. Estab. 1962. Circ. 4,000. Pays on acceptance. Buys all rights, but may reassign following publication. Byline given. Submit seasonal/holiday material 3 months in advance of issue date. Simultaneous and previously published submissions OK. SASE. Reports in 4 weeks. Free sample copy; mention *Writer's Market* in request.
Nonfiction: "All articles need to be related to seismic explorations." General interest (to people engaged in seismic exploration); historical; interview; and nostalgia. Query. Length: 500-5,000 words. Pays $50-250.
Photos: "Hopefully, *all* articles in the magazine have photos." State availability of photos with query. Pays $10-50 for b&w photos. Captions preferred. Buys all rights, but may reassign following publication. Model release required.

VICKERS VOICE, Box 2240, Wichita KS 67201. (316)267-0311. Editor: Derald Linn. For employees of Vickers Petroleum Corp. Quarterly magazine; 24 pages. Estab. 1956. Quarterly. Circ. 2,000. Not copyrighted. Pays 100% kill fee. Byline given. Pays on publication. Free sample copy. Query or submit complete ms. SASE.
Nonfiction and Photos: Articles about activities of the company, its parent company, and its subsidiaries. Articles showing, by example, how a service station owner or manager can make

more money from an existing outlet; travel articles. Length: 500-1,000 words. Pays $100-150. Photos purchased with or without mss or on assignment. Captions required. Pays $10 for 8x10 b&w glossy prints.

WDS FORUM, Writer's Digest School, 9933 Alliance Rd., Cincinnati OH 45242. (513)984-0717. Editor: Kirk Polking. Emphasizes writing techniques and marketing for students of seven courses in fiction and nonfiction writing offered by Writer's Digest School. Bimonthly magazine; 16 pages. Estab. 1971. Pays on acceptance. Buys all rights, but may reassign following publication. Pays 25% kill fee. Byline given. Phone queries OK. Submit seasonal/holiday material 3 months in advance of issue date. Simultaneous, photocopied and previously published submissions OK. SASE. Reports in 3 weeks. Free sample copy.
Nonfiction: How-to (write or market short stories, articles, novels for young people, etc.); and interviews (with well-known authors of short stories, novels and books). Buys 10 mss/year. Query. Length: 500-1,500 words. Pays $10-30.
Photos: Pays $2-5 for 8x10 b&w prints. Captions required. Buys all rights, but may reassign following publication.

Consumer Publications

Small magazines, large magazines—they need freelance writers.

The small: "We feel freelancers are *vital* to smaller, growing publications like ourselves who must limit staff writing positions for the sake of variety," says Becky Brown of *American Pie*, a humor tabloid. "Contributors who take the time to submit work *geared properly* to our readers are invaluable to us."

The large: "Editors really can't do without freelance writers," says Ceri Hadda of *Family Circle Great Ideas*, a *Family Circle* publication. "Since there is too much going on today to have the staff editors, writers and reporters keep up with everything, they do need help."

The key to selling to magazines is summed up by Becky Brown's comment about gearing your material to the magazine you're approaching. Tailoring your material to specific magazines is essential because of the continuity of style and format editors try to maintain. "We try to keep the tone of the publication consistent: If a submission seems to fit the editorial mood that we have tried to develop, it is more likely to be accepted," says David A. Drucker, editor of *Complete Buyer's Guide to Stereo/Hi-Fi Equipment*. The editor is ultimately "concerned with the quality of the article and the role it plays in his publication," says Joseph Daffron, editor of *Science and Mechanics*.

Daffron puts his recommendation that you know the publication to which you're submitting strongly when he says, "For Christ's sake, study the magazine you're aiming at." Daffron says he often gets queries from writers who read enough about the magazine to pick up the name and address, but doesn't read the magazine itself. "It's rather preposterous, but it happens regularly." Read the publication and "try to get inside the editor's head and see what he's thinking," Daffron says.

Try to get inside the reader's head, too. Predict what will interest the reader, and then cater to that interest. This sometimes involves close contact with readers. For example, "you can't write to teens if you have no contact with teens," says Sherry Morris, editor of *Glad!* "Keep up with trends, styles and changes; let your writing reflect this."

It also involves close contact with the subject about which you're writing. Many editors recommend that writers specialize. "Freelancers should become specialists in a particular area and keep up with all the latest trends in the field," says Ceri Hadda. "Freelancer who have a strong background in a specific area can bring a new point of view and excitement to a publication." Writers who specialize are also more able to become visible in that particular field, says Grace Weinstein, president of the American Society of Journalists and Authors (ASJA). Specialists can develop a reputation more quickly than other writers.

Yet, a writer needn't be a specialist to succeed. The trend of writers becoming specialists was, over the past couple of years, a response to the trend of magazines becoming more specialized. That latter trend has leveled off; specialized magazines continue to pop up, but general interest publications, heralded by the reemergence of *Look* and *Life*, are returning. City and regional magazines, which are really nothing more than general interest magazines with localized coverage, are booming.

Other trends noticed over the past year include the adherence of the publishing industry to fads. Skateboarding is waning; skateboarding magazines are dying. Racquetball is the new rages, as are the racquetball magazines.

Religious publications remain stable. Genre magazines (such as science fiction magazines) are also holding their own. Nonfiction still seems to be the stock in trade of magazines, though interest in fiction is increasing slowly.

Magazine editors expect to receive submissions in one of two forms: a query letter or a complete manuscript. Before sending *anything* to a publication, consult its listing in the pages that follow to see which format the editor prefers. If a query is requested, write a knowledgeable, cleanly typed, one-page letter outlining your article idea. "Write sound query letters with a factual presentation of what will appear in the article, approximate length, whether illustrative material will be available," says Rita Witherwax, editor of *Aloha, The Magazine of Hawaii*. If the editor is interested, he'll reply, often with ideas for slanting the story to the publication's audience. Including clippings of some of your published work is sometimes helpful, though Daffron admits that samples can mislead an editor. "In certain areas you can't tell how much the editor put in and how much the writer put in" in terms of writing and organization.

If the listing instructs you to submit a complete manuscript (as is usually the case for fiction and poetry), package your article neatly. "An author's respect for his own manuscript is an indication to us of his seriousness," says Charles C. Ryan, editor of *Galileo* science fiction magazine. "A clean, well-typed manuscript with adequate envelope and return postage makes an immediate good first impression."

Give as much thought to your cover letter as you do your manuscript. "A good *descriptive* cover letter with your finished manuscript and photos guarantees faster response from us," says Patti Crane, editor-in-chief of *Reach* magazine. Eleanor Sullivan, editor of *Alfred Hitchcock's Mystery Magazine*, adds that covering letters should be polite and businesslike. Too many writers try to be funny in cover letters in order to attract attention, she says, adding that they succeed only in gaining negative attention because they end up sounding juvenile.

Sullivan also recommends that writers not ask the editor where the manuscript should be sent next if that particular magazine can't use it. The editor rarely has time to respond to such queries, and, besides, "It's still up to the writer to know the field," says Sullivan.

The rest of the submission package should be as complete as possible. Include photos, captions, artwork, and anything else pertinent to the story. Marcia Spires, editor of Davis Publications' Home Plans Group, is one editor that likes a complete package. For example, "Imagine you're the editor having to write the captions," she says. "I want writers who make my life easy. I have 22 issues a year to get out." If Spires receives a submission that's incomplete or that needs a lot of work, it is placed in a sort of "hold" stack on her desk. Most submissions that are routed to the hold stack never see publication.

A complete package also means an error-free, well-typed manuscript. Read over your manuscript before submitting it to catch any misspellings or other errors. Gail Hayden, managing editor of the Home Plans Group, notes that "I myself won't send somebody something I haven't read at least twice."

Most important of all, however, is the quality of the writing and of the information in your manuscript. Research all articles carefully. One of the biggest mistakes writers make, says Spires, is "They don't know about knowledge"; that is, they don't know how to research an article, and they don't keep files of other articles published on the subject.

Make certain the article can stand by itself. "It's English Composition 101," says Andrew Carra, associate publisher and editor of *Camping Journal* and *Backpacking Journal*. "You have to have a beginning, middle and end." Carra says that although information can sometimes sell a poorly written article, a clear, concise style (*and* the ability to develop a style suitable to the magazine) is important. "If it takes half a day to take a good piece and turn it into an excellent piece, it's worth it," he says. "But if it takes three days to turn a bad piece into a good piece, it's not worth it."

With all this in mind, you're ready to begin submitting. When waiting to hear from a publication on the outcome of a query or article, allow a few more weeks than stated in the listing as a reporting time. Editors *are* busy—constantly. Once you've allowed the editor the allotted time (and a bit more), however, drop a gentile reminder in the mail, asking for a progress report.

For the latest marketing tips and information, including reports of new markets, read *Writer's Digest* magazine.

WD has four columns—The Markets, N.Y. Newsletter, L.A. Report and Market Update—designed to keep you up-to-date on the changing publications scene. *The Writer* also reports market information, though it is much less detailed than coverage in *Writer's Digest*. *WD* also includes features on marketing, and coverage of trends.

Alternative

Publications in this section offer writers a forum for expressing anti-establishment or minority ideas and views that wouldn't necessarily be published in the commercial or "establishment" press. Included are a number of "free press" publications that do not pay except in contributor's copies. Writers should be aware that some of these publications remain at one address for a limited time or prove unbusinesslike in their reporting on, or returning of, submissions. However, the writer will also find a number of well-established, well-paying markets in this list.

THE ADVOCATE, Liberation Publications, Inc., 1 Peninsula Place, Bldg. 1730, Suite 225, San Mateo CA 94402. Editor-in-Chief: Robert I. McQueen. For gay men and women, age 21-40; middle-class, college-educated, urban. Biweekly tabloid; 80 pages. Estab. 1968. Circ. 65,000. Pays on publication. Rights purchased vary with author and material. Byline given. SASE. Reports in 6 weeks.
Nonfiction: "Basically, the emphasis is on the dignity and joy of the gay lifestyle." News articles, interviews, lifestyle features. "Major interest in interviews or sketches of gay people whose names can be used." Informational, personal experience, profile, humor, historical, photo feature, spot news, new product. Query. Length: open.
Photos: "Payment for b&w photos purchased without ms or on assignment depends on size of the reproduction."

APPLEWOOD JOURNAL, The Applewood Group, Box 1781, San Francisco CA 94101. (415)668-6691. Publisher/Editor: Mr. Kim Huegel. "Our philosophy is directed toward taking charge of one's life, rural living, the joys of nature, the honest-to-god enjoyment that comes with independence." Bimonthly magazine; 72 pages. Estab. 1979. Circ. 35,000. Pays on acceptance or publication. Buys first rights. Pays 10-20% kill fee. Byline given. Phone queries OK. Submit seasonal/holiday material 4-6 months in advance. Photocopied and previously published submissions OK. SASE. Reports in 3-4 weeks. Sample copy $1.50; free writers guidelines.
Nonfiction: Accurate and concise reportage on government energy and conservation policy, seminars, conventions and expos, movers and shakers, the ins and outs of why something did or didn't happen, exposes, major new national and international rural/New Age, personal growth and consciousness happenings/trends—"good solid make-em-laugh, make-em-cry reporting, a la Jimmy Breslin/Hunter Thompson." General interest (intelligent reflections on life, especially country life); historical ("old timey tales around the fireplace"); how-to (appropriate technology, gardening, energy, self-sufficiency, home business, construction, shelter, organic lifestyles, cooking); humor (subtle, country-oriented, new age humor); interview (including national and international environmentalists, ecologists, authors, futurists, space); nostalgia (about the good old days, and why they worked, *a la* Randy Newman, New England tales, and more); profile (on activists in environment, lifestyles, Erhard, Cousteau, Ehrlich, Fuller, Berry, *et al.*); travel (rural living in other countries); new product (organic products, convenience product, old timey useful product, nonplastic products, useful products for self-sufficiency); personal experience (business experience, successful experience in the country, for the reader to use); photo feature (pastoral, bucolic, intense dirty city scenes, beautiful country life, hot tubs, more); and technical (energy systems, farming, etc.). Interested in "clever, simple ideas that are practical." Buys 6-8 mss/issue. Send complete ms, but query for longer pieces. Provide accurate word count on completed ms. Length: 500-4,000 words. Pays $20-300.

Photos: "All how-to articles must be accompanied by photos or drawings. We need good visuals, and will show preference to the article that is submitted with same. If you can't provide photos, indicate with words your visual treatment of the article." Payment varies on 3x5 or 8x10 b&w prints and 8x10 glossy color prints and 8x10 transparencies. Offers no additional payment for photos accepted with ms. Buys one-time and reprint rights.

Columns/Departments: Applecore (environmental news, latest on pesticide poisonings, food additives, FDA news, with a positive slant to the organic); Planting Tips (simple, helpful tips for planting various growing crops); Friends ("lists of groups and individuals that we feel need publicity"); Book Reviews (the latest in appropriate technology, slants on gardening); Interviews (regular feature with environmentalists and conservationists, scientists); Working at Home (a regular column on self-employment); Energy (the latest in applicable solar, wind, wood, methane, etc., energy); and "additional columns. Ask." Buys 4 mss/issue. Send complete ms. Length: 1,000-2,500 words. Pays $20-100. Open to suggestions for new columns and departments.

Fiction: Fantasy (futurist pieces on the quality of life, as near to reality as fiction can be—including space pieces, lifestyle pieces); humorous (on city and country life and money); science fiction (futurist pieces, space, polluted earth, chemical futures, impersonalized earth); and western (tales of the West, including the modern West). Buys 1 ms/issue. Send complete ms. Length: 750-5,000 words. Pays $20-250.

Poetry: Avant-garde, free verse, haiku, light verse and traditional. No "excessively, ponderously, obviously negative poetry. We are looking for open and introspective poetry that celebrates life, especially nature, freedom and independence." Buys 2 poems/issue. Submit approximately 4 at one time (depends on length). Length: 6-60 lines. Pays $10-25.

Fillers: Clippings, jokes, anecdotes, short humor, newsbreaks, puzzles for kids and adults and intriguing, simple games. Buys 6-8/issue. Length: 100-400 words. Pays $10-25.

How to Break In: "Read our writers guidelines, distill same. Then, if you're good enough, forget everything you read. We are seriously looking for terrific material, and the guidelines are for the average writer. Don't be afraid to send us something that is very different, with a different slant; you name it. You must obtain a copy of the magazine to understand our drift. We currently excerpt a great deal due to below-average material that has been submitted by freelancers."

BERKELEY BARB, International News Keyus, Inc., Box 1247, Berkeley, CA 94701. (415)849-1040. Editor-in-Chief: Mark Powelson. Alternative biweekly newspaper. Audience ranges from college age to upper 40s, well-educated, interested in leftist politics, avant-garde art, sex, drugs and the counter-culture. Estab. 1965. Circ. 40,000. Pays on publication. Buys all rights, but may reassign following publication. Phone queries OK. Submit seasonal/holiday material 6 weeks in advance. Simultaneous and photocopied submissions OK. SASE. Reports in 6 weeks. Free sample copy and writer's guideline.

Nonfiction: Exposé (mainly political, but must be hard-hitting, well substantiated, investigative journalism); historical (San Francisco Bay area historical sketches only); interview (with leftist, political leaders, avant-garde artists and other counter-culture figures; write in prose narrative, not Q&A form); photo feature; and profile (of individuals, groups or movements which are leftist, avant-garde or part of the counter-culture). Buys 5 mss/issue. Send complete ms. Length: 500-1,400 words. Pays 3-5¢/word.

Photos: Waren Sharpe, Photo Editor. Photos purchased with or without accompanying ms. Captions required. Pays $10-50 for b&w photos. Send prints and contact sheet.

Columns/Departments: Warren Sharpe, Columns/Departments Editor. Alternatives (lifestyles, energy, scams); Off-The-Wall (uncommon people, events, enterprises); Reviews (unsung heroes/heroines, innovators, writers). Buys 10 mss/year. Query. Length: 300-800 words. Pays 3¢/word.

BERKELEY MONTHLY, 2275 Shattuck Ave., Berkeley CA 94704. (415)848-7900. Publishers/Editors: Tom and Karen Klaber. Editorial Director: Mark Osaki. 60% freelance written. "Stresses variety, from practical subjects to the esoteric." Monthly tabloid; 72 pages. Estab. November 1970. Circ. 65,000. Pays on publication. Buys all rights, but may reassign following publication. Pays 25% kill fee. Byline given. Phone queries OK. Submit seasonal/holiday material 2-3 months in advance of issue dtae, "depending on subject matter and/or topical importance." Simultaneous and photocopied submissions OK. SASE. Reports in 1-2 weeks. Sample copy 50¢ and writer's guidelines 50¢ with SASE; mention *Writer's Market* in request.

Nonfiction: Eclectic general interest (human interest articles which provoke a sense of wonder); how-to (arts, science); humor (wry, ironic—topnotch only); interview (figures in arts, music, literature, science, philosophy, zen, and alternative health); personal experience (paramount interest only); photo feature (willing to consider ideas); technical (science or new technology made interesting and accesible); and travel (multileveled articles, no travelogues or scenic jaunts). No politics, topical news, conventional religious tracts, sports or opinion material. Buys 4-6 mss/issue. Query or submit complete ms. Length: 1,000-2,500 words. Pays $1.50/column inch minimum.

Photos: "Manuscripts with accompanying illustrations—if the article needs them—naturally stand a better chance of acceptance. Usually we provide some kind of art work for each article." Pays $5 minimum for 5x7 glossy or semiglossy print. Submit contact sheets. Captions required. Buys one-time rights.

Fiction: Erotica; humorous; and mainstream. No romance, religious, suspense, etc. Buys 1-2 mss/issue. Length: 2,000 words maximum. Pays $25 minimum.

Poetry: Avant-garde; free verse; and traditional. No "religious, political or first attempts." Buys 1-2/issue. Limit submissions to batches of 5. Length: 60 lines maximum. Pays $15 minimum.

BLACK MARIA, 815 W. Wrightwood, Chicago IL 60614. (312)929-4883. Collective editorship. Mostly for women interested in redefining women's position in society and in the family. Magazine; 64 pages. Estab. 1971. Published 3-4 times/year. Circ. 1,000. Rights acquired vary with author and material. Byline given. May acquire all rights, with the possibility of reassigning rights to author after publication, or second serial (reprint) rights. Uses about 40 mss/year. Pays in contributor's copies and a subscription. Sample copy $1.50. Will consider photocopied submissions, but would prefer the original. Will consider simultaneous submissions. Reports in 1 month. Query or submit complete ms. SASE.

Nonfiction and Photos: "Articles must be written by women. Subjects include those pertinent to women. Articles which are pro-woman and define her as active, intelligent; a complete human being. We prefer a more subtle approach than political rhetoric. We do not want immediate, newsy articles about specific events. We prefer more general, nontransitory themes for articles." B&w photos (2x3 or 8x10) used with mss.

Fiction and Poetry: "Writer should use understatement in stories; gutsy and to the point." Experimental, mainstream, science fiction, fantasy, humorous and historical fiction. Traditional forms of poetry, free verse, light verse and avant-garde forms. Submit at least 3 poems, no more than 10. Length: 4-75 lines.

BLUEBOY MAGAZINE, Blueboy Inc. of Florida, 6969 NW 69th St., Miami FL 33166. (305)940-0155. Editor: Bruce Fitzgerald. "*Blueboy* magazine is edited for gay men. Divergent viewpoints are expressed in both feature articles and fiction examining the values and behavior patterns characteristic of the gay lifestyle. *Blueboy* also emphasizes cultural and political trends of national importance, frequently profiling the people who set them. The magazine regularly covers performers and places of entertainment, travel, health and grooming, fashion, environmental design and new consumer products. Male nudes are showcased monthly in illustrative and/or photographic portfolios." Monthly magazine; 98 pages. Estab. 1974. Circ. 175,000. Pays on publication. Buys first North American serial rights. Pays 50% kill fee. Byline given. Submit seasonal/holiday material 4-5 months in advance. SASE. Reports in 4-6 weeks. Free writer's guidelines. Minimum three months lead time on all editorial material.

Nonfiction: Exposé, general interest, historical, how-to, humor, interview, new product, nostalgia, personal experience, personal opinion, photo feature, profile and travel. "*Blueboy* articles and fiction generally have a gay slant. Interviews or investigative reports, however, might be political or cultural in content without being gay-oriented." Buys 10-12 mss/issue. Query or send complete ms. Length: 2,000-5,000 words. Pays $200-500.

Photos: Offers some additional payment for photos accepted with ms. Model releases required. Buys all rights.

Fiction: Confession, erotica, experimental, fantasy and humorous. Buys 2 mss/issue. Send complete ms. Length: 2,000-5,000 words. Pays $200-500.

THE BOSTON PHOENIX, 100 Massachusetts Ave., Boston MA 02115. (617)536-5390. Editor: Robert J. Sales. 40% freelance written. For 18-40 age group, educated middle-class and post-counterculture. Weekly alternative newspaper; 124 pages. Circ. 125,000. Buys all rights. Pays at least 50% kill fee. Byline given. Pays on publication. Sample copy $2. Photocopied submissions OK. Reports in 2-6 weeks. Query letter preferable to ms. SASE. No fiction or poetry. Sections are: News (investigative, issues, some international affairs, features, think pieces and profiles), Lifestyle (features, service pieces, consumer-oriented tips, medical, food, mental health, some humor if topical, etc.), Arts (reviews, essays, interviews), Supplements (coverage of specific areas, e.g., stereo, skiing, automotive, education, apartments with local angle). Query Section Editor. "Liveliness, accuracy and great literacy are absolutely required." Pays 4¢/word and up.

COMMUNITY, 343 S. Dearborn St., Room 317, Chicago IL 60604. (312)939-3347. Editor: Albert Schorsch. For teachers, religious students and movement types (high school age up) interested in social change through nonviolent action. Quarterly magazine; 32 pages. Estab. 1942. Circ. 1,000. Acquires all rights, but will reassign rights to author after publication. Byline given. Uses about 40 mss/year. Pays in contributor's copies. Sample copy $1. Will consider clear photocopied submissions. Occasionally considers simultaneous submissions. Reports in 6-8 weeks. Query. SASE.

Nonfiction and Photos: "All types of material concerning tt e reconciliation and liberation of peoples and how to achieve such through scripturally-based nonviolence. Our approach is from the viewpoint of the Catholic left. We like to publish material extracted from personal experience whether theoretical or practical, also transcripts of talks and interviews. No term paper types. We also use book reviews and photo essays." Length: 2,400 words. 8x10 glossy or matte photos are used with mss.

Poetry: Johnny Baranski, poetry editor. Nothing trite. Traditional forms. Blank verse, free verse, avant-garde forms and haiku. Length: 3-30 lines.

COSMOPOLITAN CONTACT, Pantheon Press, Box 1566, Fontana CA 92335. Editor-in-Chief: Romulus Rexner. Managing Editor: Nina Norvid. Assistant Editor: Irene Anders. "It is the publication's object to have as universal appeal as possible—students, graduates and others interested in international affairs, cooperation, contacts, travel, friendships, trade, exchanges, self-improvement and widening of mental horizons through multicultural interaction. This polyglot publication has worldwide distribution and participation, including the Communist countries. As a result of listing in *Writer's Market*, more and better literary material is being contributed and more space will be allocated to literary material relevant to the philosophy and objectives of Planetary Legion for Peace (PLP) and Planetary Universalism." Irregularly published 3 or 4 times a year. Magazine; 32 pages. Estab. 1962. Circ. 1,500. Pays on publication in copies. Byline given. Simultaneous, photocopied and previously published submissions OK. SASE. Reports in 6 weeks. Sample copy $1.

Nonfiction: Exposé (should concentrate on government, education, etc.); how-to; informational; inspiration; personal experience; personal opinion; and travel. Submit complete ms. Maximum 500 words. "Material designed to promote across all frontiers bonds of spiritual unity, intellectual understanding and sincere friendship among people by means of correspondence, meetings, publishing activities, tapes, records, exchange of hospitality, books, periodicals in various languages, hobbies and other contacts."

Poetry: Haiku and traditional. Length: Maximum 40 lines.

Rejects: "We are not interested in any contribution containing vulgar language, extreme, intolerant, pro-Soviet or anti-American opinions."

DOING MORE WITH LESS, Box 682-W, Franklin MI 48025. (313)645-1174). Editor: Bill Griffin. Practical guide to living environmentally in the city or suburbs. Stresses the power of the individual to make changes. Emphasizes an optimistic view of the future. Bimonthly magazine; 24-32 pages. Estab. January 1977. Circ. 2,000. Pays on publication. Buys all rights. Phone queries OK. Submit seasonal/holiday material 3-4 months in advance. Previously published submissions OK. SASE. Reports in 6 weeks. Sample copy $1; writer's guidelines $1.

Nonfiction: How-to (on ways to conserve in home or apartment); interview (with authorities or average citizens active in alternative urban living); news (of what individuals are doing around the country to make their jobs or home lives more ecologically sound). "As a practical guide to environmental living, we do not cover environmental politics nor report about environmental disasters." Buys 30 mss/year. Query or send complete ms. Pays 1¢/word.

EARTH'S DAUGHTERS, Box 41, Station H, Buffalo NY 14214. Collective editorship. 75-90% freelance written. For women and men interested in literature and feminism. Estab. 1971. Publication schedule varies from 2-4 times a year. Circ. 1,000. Acquires first North American serial rights. Reverts to author after publication. Byline given. Pays in contributor's copies. Sample copy $1.50. Will consider clear photocopied submissions and clear carbons. Reports in 10 weeks. Submit complete ms. SASE.

Editorial Statement: "Our subject is the experience and creative expression of women. We require a high level of technical skill and artistic intensity; although we work from a left-feminist political position, we are concerned with creative expression rather than propaganda. On *rare* occasions we publish feminist work by men." Pays in copies only.

Fiction: Feminist fiction of any and all modes. Length: 2,500 words maximum.
Poetry: All modern, contemporary, avant-garde forms. Length: 6 pages maximum.

EAST WEST JOURNAL, East West Journal, Inc., 233 Harvard St., Brookline MA 02146. (617)738-1760. Editor: Sherman Goldman. Emphasizes alternative living for "people of all ages seeking to live harmoniously in a world of change." Monthly magazine; 90 pages. Estab. 1971. Circ. 50,000. Pays on publication. Buys one-time rights. Byline given. Phone queries OK. Submit seasonal/holiday material 5 months in advance. Simultaneous, photocopied and previously published submissions OK. SASE. Reports in 4 weeks. Free sample copy.
Nonfiction: Exposé (petro-chemical industry: fertilizers, pesticides, food additives, preservatives, pharmacology); Buys 6 mss/year. Query. Length: 500-10,000 words. Pays 3-8¢/word.
Photos: Send photos with ms. Offers no additional payment for photos accepted with accompanying ms; Pays $15-40 for b&w prints; $15-175 for 35mm color transparencies (cover only). Captions preferred; model release required.
Columns/Departments: Body, Food, Healing, Restaurant Reviews (natural foods, vegetarian) and Spirit. Buys 6 mss/year. Submit complete ms. Length: 1,500-1,000 words. Pays 3-5¢/word. Open to suggestions for new columns/departments.
Fillers: Jokes, gags, anecdotes, puzzles and short humor. "All fillers must relate to to food, health and the Orient."

FARMSTEAD MAGAZINE, Box 111, Freedom ME 04941. (207)382-6200. Eidtor-in-Chief: George Frangoulis. 95% freelance written. Emphasizes gardening, small farming, homesteading and self-sufficiency. Bimonthly magazine; 96 pages. Estab. 1974. Circ. 75,000. Pays on publication. Buys first serial and reprint rights. Phone queries OK. Submit seasonal/holiday material 3 months in advance of issue date. SASE. Reports in 3 months. Free sample copy and writer's guidelines.
Nonfiction: General interest (related to rural living, gardening and farm life); how-to (gardening, farming, construction, conservation, wildlife livestock, crafts, and rural living); interview (with interesting and/or inspirational people involved with agriculture, farm life or self-sufficiency); new product (reviews of new books); nostalgia (of rural living; farm life self-sufficiency); and occasionally travel (agriculture in other lands). Buys 60 mss/year. Submit complete ms. Length: 1,000-5,000 words maximum. Pays $50-250.
Photos: State availability of photos with ms. Pays $5 for each 5x7 b&w print used. Buys all rights.

FOCUS: A JOURNAL FOR LESBIANS, Daughters of Bilitis, 1151 Massachusetts Ave., Cambridge MA 02138. A literary journal for lesbians of all ages and interests. Monthly magazine; 20 pages. Estab. 1970. Circ. 350. Pays in contributor's copies. Obtains all rights. Byline given. Submit seasonal/holiday material 3 months in advance of issue date. Simultaneous and photocopied submissions OK. SASE. Reports in 3 months. Sample copy $1.35.
Nonfiction: Historical; humor; informational; interview; personal experience; personal opinion; profile and book reviews (includes monthly D.O.B. calendar). Send complete ms. Length: 2,500 maximum words.
Fiction: Relating to magazine theme. Confession; erotica; fantasy; historical; humorous; romance; and science fiction. Send complete ms. Length: 2,500 words maximum.
Poetry: Avant-garde; free verse; haiku; light verse; and traditional. Length: 2,500 words maximum.
Fillers: Clippings, jokes, gags, anecdotes, newsbreaks, short humor, graphics, cartoons and drawings. Send fillers. Length: 200 words maximum.

FREE FOR ALL, Better World Educational Corp., Box 962, Madison WI 53701. (608)255-2798. Editor: Michael Kaufman. 50% freelance written. For the student community—university students; people with high political commitments; liberal readers; and craftspeople/artists. Biweekly tabloid; 16 pages. Estab. March 1973. Circ. 11,000. Byline given. Pays on publication. Phone queries OK. Simultaneous, photocopied and previously published submissions OK. SASE. Reports in 2 month. Sample copy 35¢.
Nonfiction: Exposé; general interest; humor; inspirational (socialist-feminist perspective culture, news, economy); interview (prominent movement personalities); and photo feature. "We do not want to see any racist, sexist, homophobic or anti-labor articles." Buys 20/year. Send complete ms. Length: 50-750 words. Pays $1-10.
Photos: State availability of photos with ms or send photos with ms. Offers no additional

payment with photos accepted with accompanying ms; pays $1-5 for b&w prints. Buys one-time rights. Captions preferred.

Columns/Departments: Culture (reviews, news releases, socio-political angles); education; minorities and national/international. Buys 20/year. Query. Length: 50-500 words. Pays $1-10. Open to suggestions for new columns/departments.

GAY COMMUNITY NEWS, Gay Community News, Inc., 22 Bromfield St., Boston MA 02108. (617)426-4469. Editor: Richard Burns. Emphasizes gay rights for men and women of all ages and backgrounds. Weekly newspaper; 20 pages. Estab. June 1972. Buys all rights. Byline given. Phone queries OK. Photocopied and previously published submissions OK. SASE. Reports in 2 weeks. Sample copy 50¢; free writer's guidelines.

Nonfiction: Exposé (on gay politics); general interest (on gay lifestyle); historical (on gay history); humor (cartoons and columns); interview (with authors and elected officals); personal opinion (our Speaking Out column); profile (on prominent gays) and travel (on gay life in other countries). Query.

Photos: State availability of photos. Uses 5x7 b&w prints. Buys one-time rights.

HARROWSMITH MAGAZINE, Camden House Publishing, Ltd., Camden East, Ontario, Canada K0K 1J0. (613)378-6661. Editor-in-Chief: James M. Lawrence. 90% freelance written. "For those interested in country life, nonchemical gardening, solar and wind energy, folk arts, small-stock husbandry, owner-builder architecture and alternative styles of life." Publishes 8 issues/year; 150 pages. Estab. 1976. Circ. 100,000. Pays on acceptance. Buys first North American serial rights. Pays 50% kill fee. Byline given. Submit seasonal/holiday material 6 months in advance of issue date. SASE. Reports in 3 weeks. Sample copy $1; free writer's guidelines.

Nonfiction: Exposé; how-to; general interest; humor; interview; photo feature; and profile. "We are always in need of quality gardening articles geared to northern conditions. No articles whose style feigns 'folksiness.' " Buys 15 mss/issue. Query. Length: 500-4,000 words. Pays $75-500.

Photos: State availability of photos with query. Pays $25 for 8x10 glossy b&w prints; $50 for 35mm or larger color transparencies. Captions required. Buys all rights, but may reassign following publication.

How To Break In: "We have standards of excellence as high as any publication in the country. However we are by no means a closed market. Most of our material comes from unknown writers. We welcome and give thorough consideration to all freelance submissions."

HIGH TIMES, Trans-High Corp., Box 386, Cooper Station, New York NY 10003. (212)481-0120. Editor: Shelley Levitt. For persons under 35 interested in lifestyle changes, cultural trends, personal freedom, sex and drugs. Monthly magazine; 124 pages. Estab. 1974. Circ. 400,000. Pays on acceptance. Buys all rights or second serial (reprint) rights or first North American serial rights. Submit seasonal/holiday material 5 months in advance. SASE. Reports in 6-8 weeks. Sample copy $1.75.

Nonfiction: Exposé (on political, government or biographical behind the scenes); general interest (political or cultural activities); historical (cultural, literary, dope history, political movements); how-to (that aid the enhancement of one's lifestyle); interview (of writers, scientists, musicians, entertainers and public figures); new product (on dope-related or lifestyle enhancing); nostalgia (dope—related); opinion (only from public figures); photo feature (on dope- or travel-related topics); profile, technical (explorations of technological breakthroughs related to personal lifestyle); travel (guides to places of interest to a young hip audience). "We want no material on 'my drug bust'." Buys 4 ms/issue. Query with clips of published work. Length: 2,500-3,500 words. Pays $400-750.

Photos: Send photos with ms. Pays $150-250 for 8x10 glossy print per page; and $350-450 for 35mm color transparencies per page. Captions preferred; model releases required. Buys one-time rights.

Columns/Departments: Books (contemporary reviews); Flash (new products); Media (how it works and new media events of interest); Records (contemporary reviews); Sex (tales of erotic sensual adventures); and Sports (new trends). Buys 3 columns/issue. Query. Length: 500-750 words. Pays $150-250.

Fillers: Newsbreaks. Buys 10/issue. Length: 100-300 words. Pays $25-75.

INTEGRITY FORUM, Box 891, Oak Park IL 60303. (312)386-1470. Editor: David R. Williams. For "gay Episcopalians and friends. About one-fourth of our readers are clergy, many of them gay themselves, and others of them trying thereby to become more informed of our basically gay point of view. We also have many non-Christian gays seeking to be informed of our Christian witness. We have now developed chapters in over 35 cities, meeting regularly for eucharist and other programs." Newsletter; 12 pages. Estab. 1974. 6 times a year. Circ. 1,200. Rights acquired vary with author and material. Byline given. Usually acquires all rights, but may reassign rights to author after publication. Uses 15 to 20 mss/year. Pays in contributor's copies. Will send sample copy to writer for $1. Will consider photocopied submissions. Will consider simultaneous submissions only if other distribution is explained. Reports in 2 weeks. Query or submit complete ms. SASE.

Nonfiction: "Personal experience items, particularly with a Christian (but not sentimental) focus, and particularly with the poignancy to be forceful about the truth of the gay experience. We like materials that discuss gay sexuality in the broader context of human sexuality." Length 25-1,000 words.

Poetry and Fillers: Traditional forms of poetry, blank verse, free verse, avant-garde forms, haiku. Length 2-25 lines. Newsbreaks, clippings, jokes, gags, anecdotes, short humor used as fillers. Length: 1-10 lines.

JIM'S JOURNAL, Box 3563, Bloomington IL 61701. Editor: James E. Kurtz. 50% freelance written. For young adult to middle-age readers. All professions. Interested in controversial themes. Estab. 1962. Monthly. Circ. 5,000. Not copyrighted. Pays 25% kill fee. Byline given. Payment in contributor's copies. Will not consider photocopied submissions. Reports in 3 to 5 weeks. Query or submit complete ms. SASE.

Nonfiction and Photos: Controversial, underground material, sociology, philosophy, current events, religion, men's liberation, sex. "We honestly invite stimulating material. We want well-written material and we favor the new writer. Be bold, speak out with confidence; no punches pulled. All subjects are carefully read." Informational, personal experience, inspirational, think pieces, personal opinion, expose. Length: 2,500 words maximum. 5x7 or 8x10 b&w photos used with accompanying mss. Captions required.

Fiction: Experimental, mainstream, adventure, erotica, humor, confession, condensed novels. Length: 3,000 words maximum.

THE LESBIAN TIDE, 8706 Cadillac, Los Angeles CA 90034. (213)839-7254. Collective editorship. Managing Editor: Jeanne Cordova. For lesbian feminists of any age, educational level, interest, or political viewpoint. Bimonthly magazine; 40 pages. Estab. 1971. Circ. 10,000. Not copyrighted. Pays 50% kill fee. Byline given. Uses about 50 mss/year. Sample copy $1.50. Will consider photocopied and simultaneous submissions. Reports in 60 days. Submit complete ms. SASE.

Nonfiction and Photos: News regarding lesbian organizations, conferences, social alternatives, "zaps," etc.; civil rights, historical/political analyses; book, film, and music reviews; interviews, profiles, instructional pieces. "Writers must be women writing for a readership of feminist lesbians of any political orientation. We will not consider material written by men." Will consider articles on "lesbian child custody cases, job and credit discrimination against women, armed services discharge battles, abuse of women in prison, and general oppression of lesbians and other feminists by the legal power structure and short stories, fiction and interviews on same topics." Length: 250-1,500 words. Pays $10. B&w photos (any size) used with or without mss or on assignment.

Fiction and Fillers: Stories of interest to lesbians and other feminists; all types, except religious fiction. Length: 250-1,500 words. Short humor (100-200 words), jokes, gags, anecdotes, clippings, newsbreaks used as fillers.

THE MOTHER EARTH NEWS, Box 70, Hendersonville NC 28739. (704)692-4256. Editor-in-Chief: Jane Shuttleworth. Emphasizes "back-to-the-land self-sufficiency for the growing number of individuals who seek a more rational self-directed way of life." Bimonthly magazine; 180 pages. Estab. 1970. Circ. 650,000. Pays on acceptance. Buys all rights, but will reassign following publication. Byline given. Submit seasonal/holiday material 3-4 months in advance. Simultaneous, photocopied and previously published submissions OK. SASE. Reports in 2-3 months. Free sample copy and writer's guidelines.

Nonfiction: How-to ("*Mother* is always looking for good, well-documented home business pieces and reports on alternative energy systems as well as low cost—$100 and up—housing stories and seasonal cooking and gardening articles") and profile (250- to 400-word thumbnail biographies of "doers" are always welcome). Buys 150-200 mss/year. Query. Length: 300-3,000 words. Pays $40-500.

Photos: Purchased with accompanying ms. Captions and credits required. Send prints or transparencies. Uses 8x10 b&w glossies; any size color transparencies. Include type of film, speed and lighting used. Total purchase price for ms includes payment for photos.

Columns/Departments: "Contributions to Mother's Down-Home Country Lore; and Successful Swaps are rewarded by a one-year subscription; Bootstrap Business pays a two-year subscription; Profiles and Newsworthies." Length: 100-500 words. Pays $25-50. Open to suggestions for new columns/departments.

Fillers: Short how-to's on any subject normally covered by the magazine. Query. Length: 150-300 words. Pays $7.50-25.

How To Break In: "Probably the best way is to send a tightly written, short (1,000 words), illustrated (with color slides) piece on a slightly offbeat facet of gardening, cooking or country living. It's important that the writer get all the pertinent facts together, organize them logically, and present them in a fun-to-read fashion. It's also important that the ms be accompanied by top-notch photos, which is why, as a matter of policy, we reimburse authors for the cost of hiring professional photographers."

NATURAL LIFE MAGAZINE, Natural Dynamics, Inc., Box 444, Oakville, Ontario, Canada L6J 5A8. Editor-in-Chief: Wendy Priesnitz. 75% freelance written. Emphasizes "new age and ecology matters for a readership (both rural and urban) interested in natural foods, alternate energy, do-it-yourself-projects and self-sufficiency. Bimonthly magazine; 80 pages. Estab. November 1976. Circ. 50,000. Pays on acceptance. Buys all rights, but may reassign following publication. Byline given. Submit seasonal/holiday material 2-3 months in advance. Previously published submissions OK. SASE. Reports in 3 weeks. Free sample copy and writer's guidelines; mention *Writer's Market* in request.

Nonfiction: How-to (on becoming self-sufficient, e.g., organic gardening, vegetarian cooking, homestead carpentry, useful crafts, etc.); interview (ecology-oriented, new age personalities/natural healers, alternate energy people); personal experience (with homesteading, self-sufficient lifestyle); and technical (solar and wind energy). Buys 30 mss/year. Query with clips of published work. Length: 2,000 words maximum. Pays $10-75.

Photos: State availability of photos with query. "Our readers want to see how everything is done, or built, etc." Offers no additional payment for photos accepted with ms. Uses b&w prints mainly. Captions preferred. Buys all rights, but may reassign following publication.

Columns/Departments: Book Reviews. Buys 6-7 mss/year. Query. Length: 600 words maximum. Pays $10-25.

NORTH COUNTRY ANVIL, Anvil Press, Box 37, Millville MN 55957. Editor-in-Chief: Jack Miller. Emphasizes alternatives, lifestyles, back-to-the-soil movements, and social justice. For a "Midwestern audience interested in subject matter, distributed among all ages, but 25-40 age group most predominant." Bimonthly magazine; 40-44 pages. Estab. 1972. Circ. 2,200. Pays in copies. Acquires all rights, but may reassign following publication. Byline given. Submit seasonal or holiday material 6-9 months in advance. Simultaneous and photocopied submissions OK. SASE. Reports in 12 weeks. Sample copy $1.

Nonfiction: Exposé (mistreatment and triumphs of minorities), historical (populist and land reform movements); how-to (gardening, alternative sources of energy, small-scale farming), humor and informational (lifestyles). Uses 20 mss/issue. Length: 3,000 words maximum.

Poetry: Mara and Ray Smith, Poetry Editors. Uses all kinds. Uses 20 poems/issue. Pays in copies.

How To Break In: "Start by being well-informed on the subject matter, then present it in clear, concise fashion. We want our writers to touch all the bases without dying on them. We're always on the lookout for people-oriented articles, particularly when the people involved are accomplishing something worthwhile in spite of the 'establishment,' and not because of it."

PRAIRIE SUN, Box 876, Peoria IL 61652. (309)673-6624. Editor-in-Chief: Bill Knight. 10-20% freelance written. For music listeners who are also interested in films, books and general entertainment. Weekly tabloid; 16 pages. Estab. 1972. Circ. 35,000. Pays on publication. Buys all rights, but may reassign following publication. Byline given. Phone queries OK. Simultaneous, photocopied and previously published submissions OK. SASE. Reports in 3 weeks. Sample copy 50¢.

Nonfiction: Exposé (government and corporate interests); how-to (back to nature; gardening; living with less; alternative energy systems); interview (especially cultural and entertainment personalities); and profile (music personalities). Buys 20 mss/year. Query. Length: 400-1,000 words. Pays $15-40.

SAN FRANCISCO BAY GUARDIAN, 2700 19th St., San Francisco CA 94110. (415)824-7660. Editor: Bruce Brugmann. 25% freelance written. For "a young liberal to radical, well-educated audience." Estab. 1966. Weekly. Circ. 35,000. Buys all rights, but will reassign them to author after publication. Byline given. Buys 200 mss/year. Pays on publication. Will consider photocopied submissions. Query for nonfiction with sample of published pieces. SASE.

Nonfiction and Photos: Department Editors: Louis Dunn (photos) and Michael E. Miller (articles). Publishes "investigative reporting, features, analysis and interpretation, how-to and consumer reviews, and stories must have a Bay Area angle." Freelance material should have a "public interest advocacy journalism approach (on the side of the little guy who gets pushed around by large institutions). More interested in hard investigative pieces. Fewer stories about isolated suffering welfare mothers and other mistreated individuals; should be put in context (with facts) of groups and classes. We would like to see articles on how to survive in the city—in San Francisco." Reviews of 800 to 1,500 words pay $25 minimum; short articles of 1,500 to 2,500 words pay $35 minimum; long articles of over 2,500 words pay $50 minimum. Photos purchased with or without mss. B&w full negative prints, on 8x10 paper. Pays $15 per published photo, $40 minimum photo essay.

How To Break In: "Work with our volunteer projects in investigative reporting. We teach the techniques and send interns out to do investigative research. Submit applications at start of each term."

THE SECOND WAVE, Box 344, Cambridge A., Cambridge MA 02139. (617)491-1071. Editors: Women's Editorial Collective. For women concerned with issues of feminism. Quarterly magazine; 52 pages. Estab. 1971. Circ. 5,000. Acquires first serial rights. Byline given. Uses 20 mss/year. Pays in contributor's copies. Sample copy $1.50. Photocopies OK. Reports in 1 to 3 months. Query or submit complete ms. SASE.

Nonfiction and Photos: All material must be related to the theme of women's liberation. "She (the writer) should write only on issues involving women's struggle for liberation, or women's relationships with other women. We do not want work glorifying men, marriage, traditional women's roles, etc. Would like to see articles on feminism outside the big cities and in other countries; new issues being dealt with by women, etc." Informational, personal experience, interview, historical and think articles. Length: varies. Line drawings and b&w photos are used with or without accompanying mss. Captions optional.

Fiction and Poetry: Must relate to feminist themes. Experimental, mainstream, science fiction, fantasy. Free verse.

SIPAPU, Route 1, Box 216, Winters CA 95694. Editor: Noel Peattie. For "libraries, editors and collectors interested in Third World studies, the counterculture and the underground press." Estab. 1970. Semi-annually. Circ. 500. Buys all rights, but will reassign rights to author after publication (on request). Byline given. Pays on publication. Sample copy $2. Will consider photocopied submissions. Reports in 3 weeks. Query. SASE.

Nonfiction: "Primarily book reviews, interviews, descriptions of special libraries and counterculture magazines and underground papers. We are an underground 'paper' about underground 'papers.' We are interested in personalities publishing dissent, counterculture and Third World material. Informal, clear and cool. We are not interested in blazing manifestos, but rather a concise, honest description of some phase of dissent publishing, or some library collecting in this field, that the writer knows about from the inside." Personal experience, interview, successful library operations. Pays 4¢/word.

THE UNSPEAKABLE VISIONS OF THE INDIVIDUAL, Inc., Box 439, California PA 15419. Editors-in-Chief: Arthur Winfield Knight, Kit Knight. For "an adult audience, generally college-educated (or substantial self-education) with an interest in Beat (generation) writing." Annual magazine/book; 176 pages. Estab. 1971. Circ. 2,000. Payment (if made) on acceptance. Acquires first North American serial rights. Reports in 2 months. Sample copy $2.

Nonfiction: Interviews (with Beat writers), personal experience, photo feature. Uses 20 mss/year. Query or submit complete ms. Length: 300-15,000 words. Pays 2 copies, "sometimes a small cash payment, i.e., $10."

Photos: Used with or without ms or on assignment. Captions required. Send prints. Pays 2 copies to $10 for 8x10 glossies.

Fiction: Uses 10 mss/year. Submit complete ms. Length: Pays 2 copies to $10.

Poetry: Avant-garde, Free verse, traditional. Uses 15/year. Limit submissions to batches of 10. Length: 100 lines maximum. Pays 2 copies to $10.

VILLAGE VOICE, 80 University Plaza, New York NY 10003. Editor-in-Chief: David Schneiderman. Emphasizes arts and politics. Weekly tabloid; 125 pages. Estab. 1956. Circ. 150,000. Pays on acceptance. Buys all rights. SASE. Reports in 3 weeks.

Nonfiction: Exposé, how-to, informational, historical, humor, interview, nostalgia, personal opinion, profile, personal experience, photo feature. Query. Length: 2,000 words maximum. Pays $150 minimum for features.

WOMEN: A JOURNAL OF LIBERATION, 3028 Greenmount Ave., Baltimore MD 21218. (301)235-5245. Collective editorship. For women; specifically feminists. Quarterly magazine; 64 pages. Estab. 1969. Circ. 20,000. Payment in contributor's copies. Acquires all rights. Byline given. Phone queries OK. Simultaneous and photocopied submissions OK. SASE. Reports in 4-5 months. Sample copy $1.25.

Nonfiction: "All articles should be related to upcoming themes and reflect nonsexist and, hopefully, a socialist/feminist approach." Uses 60 mss/year. Submit complete ms. Length: 1,000-3,000 words.

Photos: Photos used with or without mss or on assignment. Uses 5x7 or larger b&w.

Graphics: Drawings, cartoons or paintings 11x14 or smaller b&w.

Columns/Departments: Uses reviews of feminist press books about women.

Fiction: Adventure, experimental, fantasy, historical, humorous, mainstream, mystery, suspense and science fiction. Uses 6 or more/year. Length: 4,000-5,000 words.

Poetry: Avant-garde and traditional forms; free verse, blank verse, haiku and light verse. Submit complete ms. Length: open.

WOMEN'S RIGHTS LAW REPORTER, 15 Washington St., Newark NJ 07102. (201)648-5320. Legal journal emphasizing law and feminism for lawyers, students and feminists. Quarterly magazine; 64-80 pages. Estab. 1971. Circ. 2,000. No payment. Acquires all rights. Submit seasonal/holiday material 3-4 months in advance. SASE. Reports in 2 months. Sample copy $4.00.

Nonfiction: Historical and legal articles. Query or submit complete ms. Length: 20-100 pages plus footnotes.

WOODSMOKE: Burnt Fork Publishing Co., Box 62, Stevensville MT 59870. Editor: Richard Jamison. Emphasizes survival and self-sufficiency for people 18-40 years old with an outdoor interest. Quarterly magazine; 68 pages. Estab. 1977-78. Circ. 1500. Pays on publication. Buys one-time rights. Byline given. Submit seasonal/holiday material 2 months in advance. Photocopied and previously published submissions OK. SASE. Reports in 4 weeks. Free sample copy.

Nonfiction: Historical (on pioneer and Indian historical trips and hardships); how-to (on self-sufficiency theme, cooking, homestead etc.) and personal experience (how-to and interesting experiences in the outdoors, true survival experiences). "We do not want any *researched* articles on edible plants or herbal medicines. Actual experiences OK." Buys 12-14 mss/year. Query or send complete ms. Length: 500-3,500 words. Pays 2¢/word.

Photos: State availability of photos with ms. Offers no additional payment for photos accepted with ms. Uses b&w prints. Captions preferred.

Columns/Departments: Wild and Free (wild edible plants and herbs); Recipe Box (natural and outdoor recipes); Survival Journal (true life survival experiences); Who's Who (people with expertise in survival education or outdoor experience); and Woodsmoke Humor (cartoons with outdoor slant). Buys 6 columns/year. Send complete ms. Length: 500-1,000 words. Pays 2¢/word.

Poetry: Light Verse and traditional. "We have not published poetry but are open to verse that will fit our outdoor, homestead format." Submit in batches of 3. Pays $3 each.

Fillers: Jokes, gags, anecdotes, short humor and outdoor recipes. Buys 2/issue. Length: 50-100 words.

Animal

These publications deal with pets, racing and show horses, and other pleasure animals. Magazines about animals bred and raised for food are classified in Farm Publications.

AMERICAN HUMANE MAGAZINE, Coyle Publications, 2 Park Central, Suite 740,1515 Arapahoe St., Denver CO 80202. (303)534-8843. Editor-in-Chief: William N. Vaile. Associate Editor: Alan D. Miller. 80-90% freelance written. For "persons interested in the care and protection of animals, children and adults. Readers are professionals in veterinary medicine, animal welfare and control, social service, education, law and medicine, as well as the pet-owning public." Monthly magazine; 48 pages. Estab. 1913. Circ. 15,000. Pays on publication. Buys all rights, but may reassign following publication. Phone queries OK. Submit seasonal/holiday material at least 4 months in advance of issue date. Photocopied and previously published submissions OK. SASE. Reports in 8 weeks. Sample copy 50¢; free writer's guidelines.

Nonfiction: How-to (concentrate on animal care and/or animal shelter operation); general interest (concentrate on animals, animal protection, and child or adult protection and welfare); humor; historical (relating to humane movement—animals or child protection); inspirational (relating to humane concerns); interview (prominent or acknowledged authority in animal/child/adult protection); personal experience (relating to *very* unusual experiences); photo feature (concentrate on newsworthy events relating to animals); and profile (prominent or acknowledged authority). No overly sentimental, mushy animal stories; no editorializing. Buys 180 mss/year. Query or submit complete ms. Length: 500-2,000 words. Pays $25 minimum.

Photos: Pays $15 minimum for 8x10 b&w glossy prints. Captions preferred. Buys all rights, but may reassign following publication. Model release preferred.

Columns/Departments: Update (breaking news on animal protection and welfare legislation, same for children); Point/Counterpoint (issue forum with photos related to humane aims and movement); and Profiles. Submit complete ms. Length: open. Pays $10 minimum. Open to suggestions for new columns/departments.

Fiction: "We will consider nearly all types of fiction relating to animals." Adventure, fantasy, historical, humorous, mystery, suspense, mainstream and western. No overly sentimental material or flagrant editorialization. Buys 12 mss/year. Submit complete ms. Length: 500-1,500 words. Pays $25.

Fillers: Clippings and short humor. "All must relate to humane movement." Length: open. Pays $10 minimum.

ANIMAL KINGDOM, New York Zoological Park, Bronx NY 10460. (212)220-5121. Editor: Eugene J. Walter Jr. For individuals interested in wildlife, zoos, aquariums and members of zoological societies. Bimonthly. Buys first North American serial rights. Usually pays 25% kill fee but it varies according to length, amount of work involved, etc. Byline given. Pays on acceptance. Reports in 2-3 months. SASE.

Nonfiction and Photos: Wildlife articles dealing with animal natural history, conservation, behavior. No pets, domestic animals, or botany. Articles should be scientifically well-grounded, but written for a general audience, not scientific journal readers. No poetry, cartoons or fillers. Length: 1,500-14,000 words. Pays $100-500 (rarely, average is $350-400). Payment for photos purchased with mss is negotiable.

How To Break In: "It helps to be a working scientist dealing directly with animals in the wild. Or a scientist working in a zoo such as the staff members here at the New York Zoological Society. Most of the authors who send us unsolicited mss are nonscientists who are doing their research in libraries. They're simply working from scientific literature and writing it up for popular consumption. There are a fair number of others who are backyard naturalists, so to speak, and while their observations may be personal, they are not well grounded scientifically. It has nothing to do with whether or not they are good or bad writers. In fact, some of our authors are not especially good writers, but they are able to provide us with fresh, original material and new insights into animal behavior and biology. That sort of thing is impossible from someone who is working from books. Hence, I cannot be too encouraging to anyone who lacks field experience."

ANIMAL LOVERS MAGAZINE, Box 918, New Providence NJ 07974. (201)665-0812. Editor: Anita Coffelt. 50% freelance written. Emphasizes animals and pets for readership of animal lovers, pet owners, veterinarians, school/public libraries and universities. Quarterly magazine; 24 pages. Estab. 1969. Circ. 4,000. Pays on acceptance. Buys all rights, but will reassign rights to author following publication. Byline given. Seasonal/holiday material must be submitted 3 months in advance. Photocopied submissions OK. SASE. Reports in 6 weeks. Sample copy $1; writer's guidelines with SASE.

Nonfiction: How-to (building a cat-proof bird cage, etc.); humor (between pet and owner; two pets, etc.); informational, personal experience; personal opinion (on euthanasia, veterinarian fees, cruelty, hunting, etc.) and profile (animal lovers who have gone to extraordinary lengths to help animals). Buys 60 mss/year. Submit complete ms. Length: 300-600 words. Pays 1¢/published word; $3-6/article.

Photos: Purchased with or without accompanying ms. Captions required. Send b&w or color prints. Pays $2 maximum for b&w or color.

Fiction: Humor. Buys 5 mss/year. Length: 300-600 words. Pays 1¢/word; $3-6/ms. Send complete ms.

Fillers: Short Humor (brief incidents involving animals). Buys 5-10/year. Length: 75-200 words. Pays 1¢/word; $1-2, maximum.

Rejects: "Poetry, cartoons, puzzles, articles or stories which depict cats stalking their prey; gory details about dying animals; stories which contain profanity or sexual overtones. No inconsequential accounts of pets, manuscripts that are 1,000 words, clippings or foreign markets."

ANIMALS. MSPCA, 350 S. Huntington Ave., Boston MA 02130. Editor: Susan Burns. 50% freelance written. For members of the MSPCA. Bimonthly magazine; 40 pages. Estab. 1868. Circ. 30,000. Pays on publication. Buys all rights, but may reassign to author following publication. Photocopied and previously published submissions OK. Reports in 2 weeks. Sample copy $1.25 with 8½x11 SASE; writer's guidelines for SASE.
Nonfiction and Photos: Uses practical articles on animal care and articles on humane/animal protection issues. Nonsentimental approach. Length: 300-3,000 words. Pays 2¢/word. Photos purchased with accompanying ms with extra payment, without accompanying ms or on assignment. Captions required. Payment: $5 for b&w; $7.50 for color. Size: 5x7 minimum for b&w; color transparencies. Pays $5-$10.

APPALOOSA NEWS, Box 8403, Moscow ID 83843. (208)882-5578. Emphasizes Appaloosa horses for Appaloosa owners and breeders, and people interested in horses. Monthly magazine; 186 pages. Estab. 1950. Circ. 29,000. Buys all rights, but may reassign rights to author following publication. Byline given. Seasonal/holiday material should be submitted 90 days in advance. SASE. Reports in 2 weeks. Free sample copy.
Nonfiction: How-to (horse-related articles); historical (history of Appaloosas); humor (cartoons); informational; interview (horse-related persons—trainer, owner, racer, etc.); personal opinion ("we have a forum"); photo feature; profile (must be authentic); and technical. Submit complete ms. Pays $35-125, however, "most are gratis by owners."
Photos: Purchased with accompanying manuscript for article, without accompanying manuscript for cover. Captions are required. Send prints or transparencies. 8x10 or 5x7 b&w glossy prints or color transparencies for cover. No additional payment for photos accepted with accompanying ms, total purchase price for ms includes payment for photos.
Columns/Departments: For regional reports for appaloosa horse club, horse shows or sales. Send complete ms. No payment.

CAT FANCY, Fancy Publications, Inc., Box 4030, San Clemente CA 92672. (714)498-1600. Editor: Linda Lewis. 90% freelance written. For men and women of all ages interested in all phases of cat ownership. Bimonthly magazine; 40 pages. Estab. 1967. Circ. 55,000. Pays after publication. Buys all rights, but may reassign following publication. Byline given. Submit seasonal/holiday material 4 months in advance. SASE. Reports in 3 months. Sample copy $1.25; free writer's guidelines.
Nonfiction: Historical; how-to; humor; informational; personal experience; photo feature; and technical. Buys 5 mss/issue. Send complete ms. Length: 500-3,500 words. Pays 3¢/word.
Photos: Photos purchased with or without accompanying ms. Pays $7.50 minimum for 8x10 b&w glossy prints; $50-100 for 35mm or 2¼x2¼ color transparencies. Send prints and transparencies. Model release required.
Fiction: Adventure; fantasy; historical; and humorous. Buys 1 ms/issue. Send complete ms. Length: 500-5,000 words. Pays 3¢/word.
Poetry: Avant-garde, free verse, haiku, light verse and traditional. Buys 4 poems/issue. Length: 5-50 lines. Pays $10.
Fillers: Short humor. Buys 10 fillers/year. Length: 100-500 words. Pays 3¢/word.

CATS MAGAZINE, Box 4106, Pittsburgh PA 15202. Editor: Jean Amelia Laux. For men and women of all ages; cat enthusiasts, vets and geneticists. Monthly magazine. Estab. 1945. Circ. 50,000. Buys first North American serial rights and Japanese first rights. Byline given. Buys 50 mss/year. Pays on publication. Free sample copy. Submit seasonal Christmas material 4-6 months in advance. Reports in 6 weeks. SASE.
Nonfiction and Photos: "Cat health, cat breed articles, articles on the cat in art, literature, history, human culture, cats in the news. Cat pets of popular personalities. In general how cats and cat people are contributing to our society. We're more serious, more scientific, but we do like an occasional light or humorous article portraying cats and humans, however, as they really are. No talking cats! Would like to see something on psychological benefits of cat ownership; how do cat-owning families differ from others?" Length: 800-2,500 words. Pays $15-$75. Photos purchased with or without accompanying ms. Captions optional. Pays $10 minimum for 4x5 or larger b&w photos; $100 minimum for color. Prefers 2¼x2¼ minimum, but can use 35mm (transparencies only). "We use color for cover only. Prefer cats as part of scenes rather than stiff portraits."
Fiction and Poetry: Science fiction, fantasy and humorous fiction; cat themes only. Length:

800-2,500 words. Pays $15-$100. Poetry in traditional forms, blank or free verse, avant-garde forms and some light verse; cat themes only. Length: 4-64 lines. Pays 30¢/line.

DOG FANCY, Fancy Publications, Inc., Box 4030, San Clemente CA 92672. (714)498-1600. Editor: Linda Lewis. For men and women of all ages interested in all phases of dog ownership. Bimonthly magazine; 40 pages. Estab. 1969. Circ. 40,000. Pays after publication. Buys all rights, but may reassign following publication. Byline given. Submit seasonal/holiday material 4 months in advance. Sample copy $1.25; free writer's guidelines. SASE.
Nonfiction: Historical, how-to, humor, informational, interview, personal experience, photo feature, profile and technical. Buys 5 mss/issue. Length: 500-3,500 words. Pays 3¢/word.
Photos: Photos purchased with or without accompanying ms. Pays $7.50 minimum for 8x10 b&w glossy prints; $50-100 for 35mm or 2¼x2¼ color transparencies. Send prints and transparencies. Model release required.
Fiction: Adventure, fantasy, historical and humorous. Buys 5 mss/year. Send complete ms. Length: 500-5,000 words. Pays 3¢/word.
Fillers: "Need short, punchy photo fillers and timely news items." Buys 10 fillers/year. Length: 100-500 words. Pays 3¢/word.

THE EQUESTRIAN IMAGE, Image Publications and Promotions, Rt. 5, Fenwick, Ontario, Canada L0S 1C0. (416)892-2222. Editor-in-Chief: Pat Mellen. Emphasizes the equine world; from novice to professional, all breeds from pony to draft, all facets from breeding to clipping. Monthly magazine; 56 pages. Estab. 1973. Circ. 6,500. Pays on publication. Buys one-time rights. Submit seasonal/holiday material 1 month in advance. Simultaneous, photocopied and previously published submissions OK. SAE and International Reply Coupons. Reports in 6 weeks. Free sample copy.
Nonfiction: "All topics open to writers." Buys 6-12 mss/year. Send complete ms. Pays 40¢/column inch.
Photos: Photos purchased with accompanying ms or on assignment. Captions required. Pays $2 minimum for b&w and color photos. Send prints.
Fiction: Historical and humorous. Buys 6-12 mss/year. Send complete ms. Pays 40¢/column inch.
Fillers: Jokes, gags, anecdotes, puzzles and short humor. Buys 6-12 mss/year. Pays $3.

FAMILY PET, Box 22964, Tampa FL 33622. Editor-in-Chief: M. Linda Sabella. 25% freelance written. Emphasizes pets and pet owners in Florida. "Our readers are all ages; many show pets, most have more than one pet, and most are in Florida." Quarterly magazine; 16-24 pages. Estab. 1971. Circ. 3,000. Pays on publication. Buys one-time rights. SASE. Reports in 1-2 months. Free sample copy and writer's guidelines.
Nonfiction: Historical (especially breed histories); how-to (training and grooming hints); humor (or living with pets); informational; personal experience; photo feature; and travel (with pets). Buys 1-2 mss/issue. Send complete ms. Length: 500-1,000 words. Pays $5-20.
Photos: Photos purchased with or without accompanying ms. Captions required. Pays $3-5 for 5x7 b&w glossy prints. Send prints. Total purchase price for ms includes payment for photos.
Columns/Departments: New Books (reviews of recent issues in pet field). Send complete ms. Length: 200-400 words. Pays $3-5. Open to suggestions for new columns/departments.
Poetry: Light verse, prefers rhyme. Buys 1/issue. Length: 25 lines maximum. Pays $3-5.
Fillers: Jokes, gags, anecdotes, puzzles and short humor. Buys 4-5 fillers/year. Length: 100-400 words. Pays $2-5.

HORSE AND HORSEMAN, Box HH, Capistrano Beach CA 92624. Editor: Mark Thiffault. 75% freelance written. For owners of pleasure horses; predominantly female with main interest in show/pleasure riding. Monthly magazine; 74 pages. Estab. 1973. Circ. 96,000. Buys all rights, but will reassign rights to author after publication. Byline given. Buys 40-50 mss/year. Pays on acceptance. Sample copy $1.25 and writer's guidelines free with SASE. Submit special material (horse and tack care; veterinary medicine pieces in winter and spring issues) 3 months in advance. Reports in 1 month. Query or submit complete ms. SASE.
Nonfiction and Photos: Training tips, do-it-yourself pieces, grooming and feeding, stable management, tack maintenance, sports, personalities, rodeo and general horse-related features. Emphasis must be on informing, rather than merely entertaining. Aimed primarily at the beginner, but with information for experienced horsemen. Subject matter must have thorough, in-depth appraisal. Interested in more English (hunter/jumper) riding/training copy, plus pieces on driving horses and special horse areas like Tennessee Walkers and other gaited breeds. More factual breed histories. Uses informational, how-to, personal experience, interview, profile, humor, historical, nostalgia, successful business operations, technical articles.

Length: 2,500 words average. Pays $75-$200. B&w photos (4x5 and larger) purchased with or without mss. Pays $4-$10 when purchased without ms. Uses original color transparencies (35mm and larger). No duplicates. Pays $100 for cover use. Payment for inside editorial color is negotiated.

HORSE ILLUSTRATED, Box A, Lake Elsinore CA 92330. (714)674-1404. Editor-in-Chief: Richard Gibson. 80% freelance written. Bimonthly magazine; 68 pages. Estab. August 1977. Circ. 102,000. Pays on publication. Buys second serial (reprint) rights and first North American serial rights. Byline given. Submit seasonal material 3 months in advance of issue date. Previously published submissions OK. SASE. Reports in 8 weeks. Sample copy $1; free writer's guidelines; mention *Writer's Market* in request.
Nonfiction: Exposé; general interest (anything as long as it concerns the horse); historical (how horses were treated and their accomplishments); how-to (better ways to feed and groom horses and success in show ring or on event course); inspirational (success stories); interview (usually with show judges and trainers—tips on improving); new product (consumer information); nostalgia (movie cowboys and old cowboys in general); photo feature (as long as there is considerable caption material); profile (riders, judges, horses); technical (explaining things to readers); and travel (good places for trail riding). Buys 120 mss/year. Query. Length: 1,000-1,500 words. Pays 5¢/word.
Photos: State availability of photos with query. Offers no additional payment for 5x7 or 8x10 b&w glossy prints. Captions preferred. Buys all rights, but may reassign following publication.
Columns/Departments: I Learned About Horses From. Buys 4 mss/issue. Query. Length: 100-500 words. Pays 5¢/word. Open to suggestions for new columns/departments.
Fiction: "Would be interested if we receive well-written, interesting material." Length: 1,000-2,500 words. Submit complete ms. Pays 5¢/word.
Fillers: Cartoons. Pays $10 for each cartoon used.

HORSE LOVER'S NATIONAL MAGAZINE, Box 3003, Menlo Park CA 94025. (415)328-7182. Managing Editor: Nanette Meek. Emphasizes horses and horse owners. Monthly magazine; 72 pages. Estab. 1936. Circ. 96,000. Pays on publication. Buys first North American serial rights. Byline given. Query first; do not send complete ms. Phone queries OK. Submit seasonal/holiday material 6 months in advance. No photocopied and previously published submissions. SASE. Reports in 6 weeks. Sample copy $1.50; free writer's guidelines.
Nonfiction: Lunette Antonor, associate editor. Practical, authoritative, well-illustrated instructional articles; high quality general horse interest features; knowledgeable health care and stable management articles; interviews with top horse people; no "personal experience" stories. Buys 100 mss/year. Query. Length: 1,000-3,000 words. Pays 5-10¢/word.
Photos: Photos purchased with or without accompanying ms or on assignment. Captions required. Pays $7.50 for b&w, $12 for inside color, $100-200 for cover. Prefers b&w prints at least 5x7, color transparencies or prints at least 5x7.
Fiction: Adventure, historical, humorous, mainstream, mystery, suspense and western. Buys 1 ms/issue. Send query. Length: 1,000-2,000 words. Pays 5¢/word.

HORSE, OF COURSE, Derbyshire Publishing Co., Temple NH 03084. (603)654-6126. Editor-in-Chief: R.A. Greene. 80% freelance written. For novice, backyard horsemen. Monthly magazine; 84 pages. Estab. 1972. Circ. 120,000. Pays on publication. Buys all rights. Submit seasonal/holiday material 6 months in advance. SASE. Reports in 3 weeks. Sample copy $1.50; free writer's guidelines.
Nonfiction: How-to (about all aspects of horsemanship, horse care and horse owning); historical (on breeds, famous horse-related people, etc., would be particularly salable if you include some tips on riding and horse care); interview (with trainers, riders giving their methods); and photo feature (profiles, personalities). Buys 50-60 mss/year. Submit complete ms. Length: 800-2,000 words. Pays $50-200.
Photos: Purchased with accompanying ms. Captions required. Submit prints. Pays minimum $5 for 4x5 or larger b&w glossy prints; pays $50-100 for 35mm or 8x10 glossy color prints (for cover). Model release required.

HORSE PLAY, 443 N. Frederick Ave., Gaithersburg MD 20760. (301)840-1866. Editor-in-Chief: Susanne Sauer. Managing Editor: Cordelia Doucet. 50% freelance written. Emphasizes horses and horse sports for a readership interested in horses, especially people who show, event and hunt. Monthly magazine; 48 pages. Estab. 1975. Circ. 20,234. Pays on publication. Buys first North American serial rights. Pays negotiable kill fee. Byline given. Phone queries OK. Submit seasonal/holiday material 3 months in advance. SASE. Reports in 6 weeks. Sample copy $1.50; free writer's guidelines.

Nonfiction: Expose; how-to (various aspects of horsemanship, course designing, stable management, putting on horse shows, etc.); humor; interview; photo feature; profile; and technical. Buys 40 mss/year. Length: 1,000-3,000 words. Pays $35-75.
Photos: Margaret Thomas, Photo Editor. Purchased on assignment. Captions required. Query or send contact sheet, prints or transparencies. Pays $5 for 8x10 b&w glossy prints; $50 maximum for color transparencies.
Columns/Departments: Book Reviews, Roundup, and News Releases. Pays $10.

HORSE WOMEN, Rich Publishing, Inc., 41919 Moreno, Temecula CA 92390. Editor: Ray Rich. Emphasizes western and English riding for those interested in taking better care of their horse and improving their riding. Annual magazine; 120 pages. Estab. September 1978. Pays on publication. Buys all rights. Pays 100% kill fee. Byline given. Phone queries OK. Submit seasonal/holiday material 3 months in advance. SASE. Reports in 3-4 weeks. Sample copy $2.95; free writer's guidelines.
Nonfiction: How-to (anything relating to western and English riding, jumping, barrel racing, etc.); humor; interview (with well-known professional trainers); new product (want new product releases, description of the product and b&w photo, featuring the latest in Western and English tack and clothing) and photo feature (preferably foaling). Buys 10-15 mss/issue. Query or send complete ms. Length: 1,000-1,500 words. Pays $40-50/printed page depending on quality and number of photos.
Photos: Send photos with ms. Offers no additional payment for 5x7 or 8x10 b&w glossy prints. Captions preferred.

HORSEMAN, 5314 Bingle Rd., Houston TX 77092. (713)688-8811. Editor: Tad Mizwa. For people who own and ride horses for pleasure and competition. Majority own western stock horses and compete in western type horse shows as a hobby or business. Monthly. Estab. 1954. Circ. 160,000. Rights purchased vary with author and material. Buys all rights, first North American serial rights, or second serial (reprint) rights. Byline given unless excessive editing must be done. Pays on publication. Free sample copy and writer's guidelines. Submit seasonal material 4 months in advance. Reports in 3 weeks. Query. SASE.
Nonfiction, Photos: "How-to articles on horsemanship, training, grooming, exhibiting, nutrition, horsekeeping, mare care and reproduction, horse health and history dealing with horses. We really like articles from professional trainers, or articles about their methods written by freelancers. The approach is to educate and inform readers as to how they can ride, train, keep and enjoy their horses more." Length: 1,000-2,500 words. Pays to 7¢/word. Photos purchased with accompanying ms. Captions required; also purchased on assignment. Pays $8 minimum for b&w 5x7 or 8x10 prints; 35mm or 120 negatives. Pays $25 for inside color. Prefers transparencies. Pays $100 for covers; all rights.

HORSEMEN'S YANKEE PEDLAR NEWSPAPER, Wilbraham MA 01095. (413)589-9088. Editor-in-Chief: Beverly Foisy. "All-breed monthly newspaper for horse enthusiasts of all ages and incomes, from one-horse owners to large commercial stables." Monthly newspaper; 116 pages. Estab. 1962. Circ. 12,500. Pays on publication. Buys all rights for one year. Submit seasonal/holiday material 2-3 months in advance of issue date. SASE. Reports in 4 weeks. Sample copy $1.
Nonfiction: How-to, humor, educational, interview, and some fiction about horses and the people involved with them. Buys 50-60 mss/year. Submit complete ms or outline. Length: 1,500-2,500 words. Pays $50-100, including photos.
Photos: Purchased with ms. Captions required. Buys 1 cover photo/month; pays $10. Submit b&w prints.
Columns/Departments: Area news column. Buys 85-95/year. Length: 1,200-1,400 words. Pays 75¢/column inch. Query.

HUNTING DOG MAGAZINE, 9714 Montgomery Rd., Cincinnati OH 45242. (513)891-0060. Editor-in-Chief: George R. Quigley. Emphasizes sporting dogs. Monthly magazine; 56 pages. Estab. 1965. Circ. 31,000. Pays on publication. Buys all rights but may reassign following publication. Byline given. Phone queries OK. Submit seasonal/holiday material 5-6 months in advance. Photocopied submissions OK. Reports in 3-4 weeks. Free sample copy and writer's guidelines.
Nonfiction: How-to (training dogs, hunting with dogs, building dog-related equipment), informational, interview (with well-known outdoor and dog-related persons), personal opinion (by the experts), profile, new product, photo feature, technical (guns, dog-related items). Buys 175-200 mss/year. Query or submit complete ms. Length: 1,500-2,200 words. Pays 3¢/word minimum.

Photos: Purchased with or without accompanying ms. Captions required. Send contact sheet, prints or transparencies. Pays $5 minimum for 8x10 b&w glossy prints; $50 for 35mm or 2¼" transparencies (for cover).
Fillers: "Short (200-700 words) pieces about hunting dogs or new uses for equipment." Buys 100 mss/year. Submit complete ms. Pays 3¢/word.

PAINT HORSE JOURNAL, American Paint Horse Association, Box 18519, Fort Worth TX 76118. (817(439-3400. Editor: Byron Travis. For people who raise, breed and show paint horses. Monthly magazine; 150 pages. Estab. 1965. Circ. 10,000. Pays on acceptance. Buys all rights. Pays 50% kill fee. Byline given. Phone queries OK. Submit seasonal/holiday material 2-3 months in advance. Photocopied and previously published submissions OK. SASE. Reports in 1 month. Free sample copy and writer's guidelines.
Nonfiction: General interest (personality pieces on well known owners of paints, western artists); historical (paint horses in the past—particular horses and the breed in general); how-to (training and showing horses); new product (western clothes, tack, saddles, all types of products for horsemen); and photo feature (paint horses). Buys 2-3 mss/issue. Send complete ms. Pays $50-250.
Photos: Send photos with ms. Offers no additional payment for photos accepted with accompanying ms. Uses 4x5 or larger b&w glossy prints; 4x5 color transparencies. Captions preferred. Buys all rights.

PETS OF THE WORLD, Marin Publishing Co., 1325 Chestnut St., San Francisco CA 94123. Editor: Dorothy Wilson. Emphasizes pets and people with an interest in every kind of animal. Monthly magazine; 64 pages. Estab. June 1978. Circ. 112,000. Pays on publication. Buys one-time rights. Submit seasonal/holiday material 4 months in advance. Simultaneous and photocopied submissions OK. SASE. Reports in 2-4 weeks. Free sample copy and writer's guidelines.
Nonficton: Expose (animal abuse, etc.); general interest (on animals and the way they figure in our lives); historical; humor; interview (with celebrities about animals); new product; nostalgia (animals in other times); personal experience; personal opinion (on controversial subjects); photo feature; and travel. "We do not want to see articles on how-to groom, feed, breed or show animals." Buys 12-14 mss/issue. Query. Length: 1,200-1,500 words. Pays 7½¢/word.
Photos: Ted Cabarga, photo editor. State availability of photos or send photos with ms. Pays $15 for b&w prints; $25-100 for color transparencies. Captions preferred; model releases required.
Columns/Departments: Animal Tales (brief, interesting fillers about pet animals) and Nostalgia (pets in other times). Send complete ms. Length: 150-600 words. Pays 7½¢/word. Open to suggestions for new columns/departments.
Fillers: Anecdotes and newsbreaks. Pays 7½¢/word.

PRACTICAL HORSEMEN, The Pennsylvania Horse, Inc., 225 S. Church St., West Chester PA 19380. Editor-in Chief: Pamela Goold. For knowledgeable horsemen interested in breeding, raising and training thoroughbred and thoroughbred-type horses for show, eventing, dressage, racing or hunting, and pleasure riding. Monthly magazine; 88-96 pages. Estab. 1973. Circ. 32,000. Pays on publication. Buys all rights. Simultaneous and photocopied submissions OK, but will not use any submission unless withdrawn from other publishers. SASE. Reports in 2 months. Free sample copy and writer's guidelines.
Nonfiction: How-to interviews with top professional horsemen in the hunter/jumper field; veterinary and stable management articles; photo features; and step-by-step ideas for barn building, grooming, trimming, and feeding and management tips. Buys 3-4/issue. Query with sample of writing or complete ms. Length: open. Pays $150.
Photos: Purchased on assignment. Captions required. Query. Pays $7.50 minimum for b&w glossy prints (5x7 minimum size); $50 maximum for 35mm or 2¼x2¼ color transparencies for covers.

THE QUARTER HORSE JOURNAL, Box 9105, Amarillo TX 79105. (806)376-4811. Editor-in-Chief: Audie Rackley. Official publication of the American Quarter Horse Association. Monthly magazine; 612 pages. Estab. 1948. Circ. 72,000. Pays on acceptance. Buys all rights or first rights. Phone queries OK. Submit seasonal/holiday material 2 months in advance. SASE. Reports in 2 weeks. Free sample copy and writer's guidelines.
Nonfiction: Historical ("those that retain our western heritage"); how-to (fitting, grooming, showing, clipping, or anything that relates to owning, showing, or breeding); informational (educational clinics, current news); interview (feature-type stories—must be about established people who have made a contribution to the business); new product; personal opinion; and

technical (medical updates, new surgery procedures, etc.). Buys 15 mss/year. Length: 800-2,500 words. Pays $40-100.

Photos: Purchased with accompanying ms. Captions required. Send prints or transparencies. Uses 5x7 or 8x10 b&w glossy prints; 2¼x2¼ or 3x5 color transparencies. Offers no additional payment for photos accepted with accompanying ms.

THE QUARTER HORSE OF THE PACIFIC COAST, Pacific Coast Quarter Horse Assn., Box 254822, Gate 12 Cal Expo, Sacramento CA 95825. Editor-in-Chief: Jill L. Scopinich. 90% freelance written. Emphasizes quarter horses for owners, breeders and trainers on the West Coast. Monthly magazine; 150 pages. Estab. 1945. Circ. 8,200. Pays on publication. Buys all rights or first North American serial rights. Pays 50% kill fee. Byline given. Simultaneous submissions OK. SASE. Reports in 4 weeks. Sample copy $1.

Nonfiction: How-to; informational; interview; personal experience; photo feature; and profile. Buys 2 mss/issue. Send complete ms. Length: 500-3,000 words. Pays $50-150.

Photos: Photos purchased with or without accompanying ms. Captions required. Pays $3-5 for 8x10 b&w glossy prints. Model release required.

Columns/Departments: Of Course, A Horse; Racing Room; and The Stable Pharmacy. Buys 3 mss/issue. Send complete ms. Length: 500-2,000 words. Pays $50-100.

Fiction: Humorous and western. Buys 6 mss/year. Send complete ms. Length: 500-3,000 words. Pays $50-150.

TODAY'S ANIMAL HEALTH, Animal Health Foundation, 1905 Sunnycrest Dr., Fullerton CA 92635. Editor-in-Chief: Richard Glassberg, D.V.M. Managing Editor: Jane Wright. 100% freelance written. Emphasizes animal health, nutrition and care for people who own animals. Bimonthly magazine; 32-40 pages. Estab. 1970. Circ. 35,000. Pays on publication. Buys all rights. Submit seasonal/holiday material 6 months in advance of issue date. Simultaneous, photocopied and previously published submissions OK. SASE. Reports in 2 months. Sample copy $1; writer's guidelines for SASE; mention *Writer's Market* in request, to Mr. Harry Maiden, 8338 Rosemead, Pico Rivera CA 90660.

Nonfiction: Exposé, how-to, general interest, interview, photo feature, profile and technical. Buys 6/issue. Submit complete ms. Length 250-2,000 words. Pays $5-25.

Photos: D.M. Diem, photo editor. Submit photo material with accompanying ms. Pays $5-25 for 8x10 b&w glossy prints and $5-25 for 5x7 color prints. Caption preferred. Buys all rights, but may reassign following publication.

TROPICAL FISH HOBBYIST, 211 W. Sylvania Ave., Neptune City NJ 17753. Editor: Marshall Ostrow. 75% freelance written. For tropical fish keepers. Monthly magazine; 100 pages. Estab. 1952. Circ. 40,000. Rights purchased vary with author and material. Usually buys all rights. Byline given. Buys 50 mss/year. Pays on acceptance. Sample copy $1. No photocopied or simultaneous submissions. Query or submit complete ms. SASE.

Nonfiction and Photos: "Don't submit material unless you're an experienced keeper of tropical fishes and know what you're talking about. Offer specific advice about caring for and breeding tropicals, and about related topics. Study the publication before submitting." Informal style preferred. Can use personality profiles of successful aquarium hobbyists, but query first on these.

THE WESTERN HORSEMAN, Box 7980, Colorado Springs CO 80933. Editor: Dan Bergen. Emphasizes western horsemanship. Monthly magazine. Estab. 1936. Circ. 187,000. Pays on acceptance. Buys one-time rights. Byline given. Submit seasonal/holiday material 3 months in advance. SASE. Reports in 2-3 weeks. Sample copy $1.25.

Nonfiction: How-to (horse training, care of horses, tips, etc.); and informational (on rodeos, ranch life, historical articles of the West emphasizing horses). Buys 15-20/issue. Submit complete ms. Pays $35-85; "sometimes higher by special arrangement."

Photos: Send photos with ms. Offers no additional payment for photos. Uses 5x7 or 8x10 b&w glossy prints. Captions required.

THE ZOOGOER, Friends of the National Zoo, c/o The National Zoo, Washington DC 20008. Editor: Mary W. Matthews. Bimonthly magazine; 24 pages. Estab. 1970. Circ. 13,000. Pays on publication. Byline given only if article is written by a member of *ZooGoer* editorial staff. Makes assignments on a work-for-hire basis. Short and to-the-point phone queries OK. Submit seasonal/holiday material 3 months in advance. Previously published work OK. SASE. Reports in 3-4 weeks. Free sample copy and writer's guidelines.

Nonfiction: General interest and historical material related to wildlife, natural history, zoology, wild life conservation or to the activities, history, or interests of the National Zoological Park;

interview and profile (with staff members of the National Zoo or well-known people whose activities are of interest to the zoo-going audience); personal experience.

Columns/Departments: ZooNews (news of the National Zoo); FONZNews (news of the Friends of the National Zoo); and BookNews (reviews of books on appropriate zoological topics). Length: 1,500 words maximum. Pays 10¢/published word. Open to suggestions for new columns/departments.

Fiction: "We don't as a general rule use fiction or poetry—but only because we don't see any that is good and appropriate to the interests of a zoo-going audience. Our doors are open to any piece that fits both descriptions" No anthropomorphism of animals. Pays 10¢/word.

Poetry: Free verse, haiku, light verse and traditional. Must be on animal or zoo theme. See fiction comment. Payment negotiable.

Fillers: "Gee-whiz" facts about wild animals. Pays 10¢/word.

Art

THE AMERICAN ART JOURNAL, Kennedy Galleries, Inc., and Israel Sack, Inc., 40 W. 57th St., 5th Floor, New York NY 10019. (212)541-9600. Editor-in-Chief: Jane Van N. Turano. Scholarly magazine of American art history of the 17th, 18th, 19th and 20th Centuries, including painting, sculpture, architecture, decorative arts, etc., for people with a serious interest in American art, and who are already knowledgeable about the subject. Readers are scholars, curators, collectors, students of American art, or persons who have a strong interest in Americana. Quarterly magazine; 96 pages. Estab. 1969. Circ. 2,000. Pays on acceptance. Buys all rights, but may reassign following publication. Byline given. Photocopied submissions OK. SASE. Reports in 2 months. Sample copy $6.

Nonfiction: "All articles are historical in the sense that they are all about some phase or aspect of American art history." Buys 25-30 mss/year. Submit complete ms "with good cover letter." Length: 2,500-8,000 words. Pays $250-300.

Photos: Purchased with accompanying ms. Captions required. Uses b&w only. Offers no additional payment for photos accepted with accompanying ms.

How To Break In: "Actually, our range of interest is quite broad. Any topic within our time frame is acceptable if it is well-researched, well-written, and illustrated. Whenever possible, all mss must be accompanied by b&w photographs which have been integrated into the text by the use of numbers."

Rejects: No how-to articles or reviews of exhibitions. No book reviews or opinion pieces. No human interest approaches to artists' lives.

AMERICAN GRAPHICS, Box 363W, Salisbury CT 06068. Editor: Tryntje Van Ness Seymour. 75% freelance written. Emphasizes fine art prints for members of mail order print club. Quarterly bulletin; 24 pages. Estab. 1978. Pays on acceptance. Buys first or second serial (reprint) rights. Simultaneous, photocopied, and previously published submissions OK. SASE. Reports in 4 weeks. Free sample copy.

Nonfiction: How-to articles on printmaking, care of prints, framing, etc; and interviews and profiles of prominent American printmakers, print collectors, museum print curators and master printers. No art criticism articles. Buys 8-12 mss/year. Query or submit complete ms. Length: 1,000-2,500 words. Pays $50-150.

Photos: "Illustrated articles are preferred in all cases." Pays $5-25 for 5x7 or 8x10 b&w glossy prints. Captions required. Buys one-time rights.

ART NEWS, 122 E. 42nd St. New York NY 10017. Editor: Milton Esterow. For persons interested in art. Monthly. Circ. 67,000. Query. SASE.

Nonfiction: "I'm buying in-depth profiles of people in the art world—artists, curators, dealers. And investigative pieces, including some on antiques. The format is very flexible to cover personalities, trends, a single painting." Wants "humanized" art coverage. Length: 800 words; "some major pieces as long as 8,000 words." Pays $75-300.

ARTS MAGAZINE, 23 E. 26th St., New York NY 10010. (212)685-8500. Editor: Richard Martin. A journal of contemporary art, art criticism, analysis and history, particularly for artists, scholars, museum officials, art teachers and students, and collectors. Estab. 1926. Monthly, except July and August. Circ. 28,500. Buys all rights. Pays on publication. Query. SASE.

Nonfiction and Photos: Art criticism, analysis and history. Topical reference to museum or gallery exhibition preferred. Length: 1,500-2,500 words. Pays $100, with opportunity for negotiation. B&w glossies or color transparencies customarily supplied by related museums or galleries.

ARTS MANAGEMENT, 408 W. 57th St., New York NY 10019. (212)245-3850. Editor: A.H. Reiss. 5% freelance written. For cultural institutions. Published five times/year. Circ. 6,000. Buys all rights. Byline given. Pays on publication. Mostly staff-written. Query. Reports in "several weeks." SASE.
Nonfiction: Short articles, 400-900 words, tightly written, expository, explaining how art administrators solved problems in publicity, fund raising, and general administration; actual case histories emphasizing the how-to. Also short articles on the economics and sociology of the arts and important trends in the nonprofit cultural field. Must be fact-filled, well-organized and without rhetoric. Payment is 2-4¢/word. No photographs or pictures.

THE CULTURAL POST, National Endowment for the Arts, 2401 E St. NW., Washington DC 20506. Editor: George Clack. The official newspaper of the Arts Endowment, a federal agency that gives grants to nonprofit cultural institutions and individual artists. Bimonthly newspaper. Buys all rights, but may reassign following publication. Pay 10% kill fee. Byline given. Reports in 1 month. SASE.
Nonfiction: "Interested in carefully researched articles on the financial or administrative side of Arts Endowment grantees, examinations of important trends or problems in various art fields, and reports on arts activities at the state and community level." Buys 20 mss/year. Query. Length: 1,000-3,000 words. Pays $300-500, including photos.

DESIGN FOR ARTS IN EDUCATION MAGAZINE, Box 1463, Indianapolis IN 46206. Editor/Publisher: Mary Alice Simpson. "For teachers, art specialists, and administrators who work with children in education." Bimonthly magazine. Estab. 1898. Pays on publication. Buys all rights. Byline given. SASE. Reports in 8-10 weeks. Sample copy $1. Editorial guidelines for SASE.
Nonfiction: "We use articles that help to promote the following program objectives in schools: enhance instruction in basic studies with interdisciplinary arts-related activities; provide innovative staff development programs based on existing district curriculum; develop and maintain ongoing arts programs that integrate community resources with district curriculum; assist in development of aural, oral, visual and nonverbal communication skills; provide experiences in a variety of arts forms in order to assist in the development of realistic self-concepts through creative processes; and strengthen and expand existing arts programs." Submit complete ms. Length: 1,000-1,500 words. Pays approximately 3¢/word.

FUNNYWORLD, THE MAGAZINE OF ANIMATION & COMIC ART, Box 1633, New York NY 10001. Editor: Michael Barrier. Publisher: Mark Lilien. For animation and comic art collectors and others in the field. Quarterly magazine; 56 pages. Estab. 1966. Circ. 7,000. Pays on publication. Buys all rights. Photocopied and previously published work OK. SASE. Reports in 1 month. Sample copy $3.50.
Nonfiction: Historical (history of animation and its creators; history of comic books, characters and creators); interview (with creators of comics and animated cartoons); and reviews (of materials in this field). Buys 4 mss/issue. Query. Pays $20 minimum.
Photos: "Photos of creators, film stills, comic strips and art used extensively." State availability of photos. Pay varies for 8x10 b&w and color glossy prints. Offers no additional payment for photos accepted with ms. Captions preferred.

GLASS, Box 23383, Portland OR 97223. For artists working in blown glass, stained glass, conceptual glass, collectors, museum curators, gallery and shop owners, art critics, high school and college students in the arts and the general public. Bimonthly magazine; 64 pages. Estab. 1973. Circ. 7,000. Pays on publication. Buys all rights, but may reassign after publication. Byline given. Simultaneous, photocopied and previously published submissions OK. SASE. Reports in 4 weeks. Sample copy $4.
Nonfiction: "We want articles of a general nature treating the arts and crafts in the US and abroad; psychology of art; urban artist. We'll gladly look at anything dealing with the arts and crafts, especially contemporary glass in the US. We confine our main interest to contemporary glass arts, and to subjects touching thereon, viz., the energy crisis. Art-oriented themes. Pays $25-350.
Photos: No additional payment made for 8x10 b&w glossy prints used with mss. Captions required.

NEWORLD: THE MULTI-CULTURAL MAGAZINE OF THE ARTS, Inner City Cultural

Center, 1308 S. New Hampshire Blvd., Los Angeles CA 90006. (213)387-1161. Editor-in-Chief: Fred Beauford. Managing Editor: Jan Alexander-Leitz. 75% freelance written. Bimonthly magazine; 60 pages. Estab. September 1974. Circ. 15,000. Pays on publication. Buys all rights, but may reassign following publication. Pays $25 kill fee. Byline given. Phone queries OK. Submit seasonal/holiday material 4 months in advance of issue date. Photocopied submissions OK. SASE. Reports in 3 weeks. Sample copy $1.25.

Nonfiction: "Only articles related to dance, theater, photography, visual arts, music and poetry." How-to; general interest; historical; interview; personal opinion; photo feature; and profile. Buys 3 mss/issue. Submit complete ms. Length: open. Pays $50-75.

Photos: State availability of photos with ms. Submit contact sheets. Pays $5-10/b&w photo. Captions and model release required. Buys one-time rights.

Poetry: Avant-garde; free verse; light verse; and traditional. Buys 7/issue. Limit submissions to batches of 3. Length: 42 lines maximum. No payment.

NEW YORK ARTS JOURNAL, Manhattan Arts Review, Inc., 560 Riverside Dr., New York NY 10027. (212)663-2245. Editor-in-Chief: Richard Burgin. Emphasizes the arts: fiction, poetry, book reviews, music and visual arts. Bimonthly tabloid; 44 pages. Estab. 1975. Circ. 25,000. Buys one-time rights. Phone queries only. Sample copy $1.

Nonfiction: Historical, informational, interview, photo feature and profile. "We publish full-page portfolios of photos which stand on their own, not necessarily as illustration." Buys 3-6 mss/issue. Send complete ms. Pays $3/page.

THE ORIGINAL ART REPORT, Box 1641, Chicago IL 60690. Editor and Publisher: Frank Salantrie. Emphasizes "visual art conditions for visual artists, art museum presidents and trustees, collectors of fine art, art educators, and interested citizens." Monthly newsletter; 6-8 pages. Estab. 1967. Circ. 1,000. Pays on publication. Buys all rights. SASE. Reports in 2 weeks. Sample copy $1.

Nonfiction: Expose (art galleries, government agencies ripping off artists, or ignoring them), historical (perspective pieces relating to now), humor (whenever possible), informational (material that is unavailable in other art publications), inspirational (acts and ideas of courage), interview (with artists, other experts; serious material), personal opinion, technical (brief items to recall traditional methods of producing art), travel (places in the world where artists are welcome and honored) philosophical, economic, aesthetic, and artistic. Query or submit complete ms. Length: 1,000 words maximum. Pays 1¢/word.

Columns/Departments: WOW (Worth One Wow), Worth Repeating, and Worth Repeating Again. "Basically, these are reprint items with introduction to give context and source, including complete name and address of publication. Looking for insightful, succinct commentary." Submit complete ms. Length: 500 words. Pays ½¢/word.

TODAY'S ART, 6 E. 43rd St., New York NY 10017. Editor: George A. Magnan. For "artists (professional and amateur), art teachers, and museums." Monthly. Circulation: 86,000. Buys first rights. Byline given. Pays on publication. Query. SASE.

Nonfiction and Photos: "Only items referring to art and how-to articles in all fields of art with b&w and some color illustrations. Articles should be easy to follow. Most articles we receive are not sufficiently detailed and a lot have to be rewritten to make them more informative." Length: 500 to 1,000 words. Pays $25-50.

How To Break In: "There are many technical and esthetic possibilities in art. If a writer discusses these, in the context of 'how-to' methods presented in an instructive, easily comprehensible manner, we are glad to consider the article. But we don't want art history stories or philosophizing about art, and we do not wish to promote unknown artists."

WESTART, Box 1396, Auburn CA 95603. (916)885-3242. Editor-in-Chief: Jean L. Couzens. Emphasizes art for practicing artists and artist/craftsmen; students of art and art patrons. Semimonthly tabloid; 20 pages. Estab. 1962. Circ. 7,500. Pays on publication. Buys all rights, but may reassign following publication. Byline given. Phone queries OK. Photocopied submissions OK. Sample copy 50¢; free writer's guidelines.

Nonfiction: Informational; photo feature; and profile. No hobbies. Buys 6-8 mss/year. Query or submit complete ms. Length: 700-800 words. Pays 30¢/column inch.

Photos: Purchased with or without accompanying ms. Send b&w prints. Pays 30¢/column inch.

Association, Club, and Fraternal

The following publications exist to publicize—to members, friends, and institutions—the ideals, objectives, projects, and activities of the sponsoring club or organization. Club-financed magazines that carry material not directly related to the group's activities (for example, *Manage* magazine in the Management and Supervision Trade Journals) are classified by their subject matter in the Consumer and Trade Journals sections of this book.

THE AMERICAN LEGION MAGAZINE. Box 1055, Indianapolis IN 46206. (317)635-8411. 75% freelance written. Monthly. Circ. 2.6 million. Reports on most submissions promptly; borderline decisions take time. Buys first North American serial rights. Byline given. Pays on acceptance. Include phone number with ms. SASE.
Nonfiction: Most articles written on order. Some over transom. Writers may query for subject interest. Subjects include national and international affairs, American history, reader self-interest, great military campaigns and battles, major aspects of American life, vignettes of servicemen, veterans and their families, etc. Length: maximum of 20 double-spaced typewritten pages. Pay varies widely with length and worth of work. Research assignments for some skilled reporters. Proven pros only.
Photos: Chiefly on assignment. "Some over-transom stories or photos click."
Poetry and Humor: Limited market for short, light verse, and short, humorous anecdotes, epigrams, jokes, etc. No serious verse. Taboos: old or reprinted material; bad taste; amateurish work. Short humorous verse: $4.50 per line, minimum $10. Epigrams: $10. Anecdotes: $20.

CALIFORNIA HIGHWAY PATROLMAN. California Association of Highway Patrolmen, 2030 V St., Sacramento CA 95818. (916)452-6751. Editor: Richard York. Monthly magazine; 100 plus pages. Estab. 1937. Circ. 17,000. Pays on publication. Buys all rights, but may reassign following publication. SASE. Reports in 2 months. Free sample copy.
Nonfiction: Publishes articles on transportation safety and driver education. "Topics can include autos, boats, bicycles, motorcycles, snowmobiles, recreational vehicles and pedestrian safety. We are also in the market for travel pieces and articles on early California. We are *not* a technical journal for teachers and traffic safety experts, but rather a general interest publication geared toward the layman. Please note that we are not 120 color transparencies. Captions and model releases required.
Photos: "Illustrated articles always receive preference." Pays $2.50/b&w photo.

D.A.C. NEWS. Detroit Athletic Club, 241 Madison Ave., Detroit MI 48226. Editor: John H. Worthington. For business and professional men. Much of the magazine is devoted to member activities, including social events and athletic activities at the club. Magazine published 9 times/year. Pays after publication. Buys first rights. Byline given. SASE. Reports in 4 weeks. Sample copy for 9x12 SASE.
Nonfiction: General interest articles, usually male-oriented, about sports (pro football, baseball, squash, golf, skiing and tennis); travel (to exclusive resorts and offbeat places); drama; personalities; health (jogging, tennis elbow, coronary caution); and some humor, if extremely well-done. Some nostalgia (football greats, big band era are best examples). "We do not want any fiction, verse or fillers, but would like to see articles on eccentric millionaires, sunken treasure, the world's biggest yacht, old English pubs, Arab money and where it's going, the economy, football's greatest game, and differences in bourbon whiskey." Buys 1 ms/issue. Send complete ms. Length: 750-3,000 words. Pays $50-250.
Photos: Send photos with ms. Offers no additional payment for photos accepted with mss.

THE ELKS MAGAZINE. 425 W. Diversey, Chicago IL 60614. Managing Editor: Donald Stahl. 80% freelance written. Emphasizes general interest with family appeal. Monthly magazine; 56 pages. Estab. 1922. Circ. 1,600,000. Pays on acceptance. Buys first North American serial rights. Submit seasonal/holiday material 4-6 months in advance. SASE. Reports in 4-6 weeks. Free sample copy and writer's guidelines.
Nonfiction: Expose; historical (no textbook stuff); informational; and new product (like smoke detectors, etc.). Buys 3-4 mss/issue. Query letter a must. Length: 2,000-3,500. Pays $150-550.
Photos: Purchased with or without accompanying manuscript (for cover). Captions required. Query with b&w photos or send transparencies. Uses 8x10 or 5x7 b&w glossies and 35mm or 2¼x2¼ color transparencies (for cover). Pays $250 minimum for color (cover). Total purchase price for ms includes payment for photos.

Fiction: "Rarely used." Buys 1-2 mss/year. Submit complete ms. Length: 1,500-2,500 words. Pays $150 minimum.

How To Break In: "A freelancer desiring to break in would do best to think in terms of nonfiction. Since we continue to offer sample copies and guidelines for the asking there is no excuse for being unfamilar with TEM. A submission, following a query letter, would do the best to include several b&w prints, if the lead piece lends itself to illustration, and a short cover letter. It's not wise to try to sneak through by implying the submission is in answer to a go ahead. If we didn't ask to see it, we'll know. Family appeal is the watchword."

THE KIWANIS MAGAZINE, 101 E. Erie St., Chicago IL 60611. Executive Editor: David B. Williams. 90% of feature articles are freelance written. For business and professional men. Published 10 times/year. Buys first North American serial rights. Pays 20-40% kill fee. Byline given. Pays on acceptance. Free sample copy. Query. Reports in 4 weeks. SASE.
Nonfiction and Photos: Articles about social and civic betterment, business, education, religion, domestic affairs, etc. Emphasis on objectivity, intelligent analysis and thorough research of contemporary problems. Concise writing, absence of cliches, and impartial presentation of controversy required. Length: 1,500-3,000 words. Pays $300-600. "No fiction, personal essays, fillers or verse of any kind. A light or humorous approach welcomed where subject is appropriate and all other requirements are observed. Detailed queries can save work and submission time. We often accept photos submitted with mss, but we do not pay extra for them; they are considered part of the price of the ms. Our rate for a ms with good photos is higher than for one without."

LEADER, The Order of United Commercial Travelers of America, Box 159019, 632 N. Park St., Columbus OH 43215. (614)228-3276. Editor-in-Chief: James R. Eggert. 5% freelance written. Emphasizes fraternalism for its officers and active membership. Magazine published 8 times/year; 32 pages. Estab. 1976. Circ. 25,000. Pays on publication. Buys all rights, but may reassign following publication. Byline given. Submit seasonal/holiday material 3 months in advance of issue date. SASE. Reports in 1 week. Free sample copy and writer's guidelines; mention *Writer's Market* in request.
Nonfiction: General interest; how-to; humor; interview; and profile. Buys 1 ms/issue. Submit complete ms. Length: 500-3,000 words. Pays 1½¢/word.
Photos: State availability of photos with ms. Pays $5 for 5x7 b&w glossy prints. Captions preferred. Buys all rights. Model release required.
Fiction: Humorous. Buys 2 mss/year. Submit complete ms. Length: 500-1,500 words. Pays 1½¢/word.

THE LION, 300 22nd St., Oak Brook IL 60570. (312)986-1700. Editor-in-Chief: Roy Schaetzel. Senior Editor: Robert Kleinfelder. Emphasizes service club organization for Lions Club members and their families. Monthly magazine; 48 pages. Estab. 1918. Circ. 670,000. Pays on acceptance. Buys all rights. Byline given. Phone queries OK. Submit seasonal/holiday material 4 months in advance. Photocopied submissions OK. SASE. Reports in 2 weeks. Free sample copy and writer's guideline.
Nonfiction: Humor; informational (stories of interest to civic-minded men); and photo feature (must be of a Lions club service project). Buys 4 mss/issue. Query. Length: 500-2,200. Pays $50-400.
Photos: Purchased with or without accompanying ms or on assignment. Captions required. Query for photos. B&w glossies at least 5x7. Total purchase price for ms includes payment for photos.

THE LOOKOUT, Seaman's Church Institute, 15 State St., New York NY 10004. (212)269-2710. Editor: Carlyle Windley. 30% freelance written. "Basic purpose is to engender and sustain interest in the work of the institute and to encourage monetary gifts in support of its philanthropic work among seamen." Bimonthly except May and December when monthly. Magazine; 20 pages. Estab. 1909. Buys first North American serial rights. Byline given. Pays on publication. Free sample copy. Query. Reports in 1 month. SASE.
Nonfiction: Emphasis is on the merchant marine; not Navy, pleasure yachting, power boats, commercial or pleasure fishing. Buys freelance marine-oriented articles on the old and new, oddities, adventure, factual accounts, unexplained phenomena. Length: 200-1,000 words. Pays $40 maximum, depending on quality, length, etc.
Photos: Buys vertical format b&w (no color) cover photo on sea-related subjects. Pays $20;

lesser amounts for miscellaneous photos used elsewhere in the magazine.

Poetry: Buys small amount of short verse; seafaring-related but not about the sea per se and the cliches about spume, spray, sparkle, etc. Pays $5.

NATIONAL 4-H NEWS, 150 N. Wacker Dr., Chicago IL 60606. (312)782-5021, ext. 44. Editor: Bonnie B. Sarkett. For "young to middle-aged adults and older teens (mostly women) who lead 4-H clubs; most with high school, many with college education, whose primary reason for reading us is their interest in working with kids in informal youth education projects, ranging from aerospace to swimming, and almost anything in between." Monthly. Circ. 90,000. Buys first serial or one-time rights. Buys about 25 mss/year. Pays on acceptance. Free sample copy and writer's guidelines. Query. "We are very specialized, and unless a writer has been published in our magazine before, he more than likely doesn't have a clue to what we can use. When query comes about a specific topic, we often can suggest angles that make it usable." Submit seasonal material 6 months to 1 year in advance. Reports in 4 weeks. SASE.
Nonfiction: "Education and child psychology from authorities, written in light, easy-to-read fashion with specific suggestions how the layman can apply them in volunteer work with youth; how-to-do-it pieces about genuinely new and interesting crafts of any kind. This is our primary need now but articles must be fresh in style and ideas, and tell how to make something worthwhile ... almost anything that tells about kids having fun and learning outside the classroom, including how they became interested, most effective programs, etc., always with enough detail and examples, so reader can repeat project or program with his or her group, merely by reading the article. Speak directly to our reader (you) without preaching. Tell him in a conversational text how he might work better with kids to help them have fun and learn at the same time. Use lots of genuine examples (although names and dates are not important) to illustrate points. Use contractions when applicable. Write in a concise, interesting way—our readers have other jobs and not a lot of time to spend with us. Will not print stories on 'How this 4-H club made good' or about state or county fair winners. Reasons for rejection of freelance submissions include: failure of the writer to query first; failure of the writer to study back issues; and mss submitted on subjects we've just covered in depth." Length: 3-8 pages, typewritten, doublespaced. Payment up to $100, depending on quality and accompanying photos or illustrations.
Photos: "Photos must be genuinely candid, of excellent technical quality and preferably shot 'available light' or in that style; must show young people or adults and young people having fun learning something. How-to photos or drawings must supplement instructional texts. Photos do not necessarily have to include people. Photos are usually purchased with accompanying ms, with no additional payment. Captions required. If we use an excellent single photo, we generally pay $25 and up."

PERSPECTIVE, Pioneer Girls, Inc., Box 788, Wheaton IL 60187. (312)293-1600. Editor: Julie Smith. 40% freelance written. "All subscribers are volunteer leaders of clubs for girls in grades 1-12. Clubs are sponsored by evangelical, conservative churches throughout North America." Quarterly magazine; 32 pages. Estab. 1964. Circ. 20,000. Pays on acceptance. Buys first North American serial rights. Submit seasonal/holiday material 9 months in advance. Simultaneous submissions OK. SASE. Reports in 3 weeks. Sample copy $1; writer's guidelines for SASE.
Nonfiction: Lorabeth Norton, Articles Editor. How-to (projects for girls' clubs, crafts, cooking service), informational (relationships, human development, mission education, outdoor activities), inspirational (Bible studies, women leading girls), interview (Christian education leaders), personal experience (women working with girls). Buys 4-12 mss/year. Byline given. Query. Length: 200-1,500 words. Pays $5-40.
Columns/Departments: Lorabeth Norton, Column/Department Editor. Storehouse (craft, game, activity, outdoor activity suggestions—all related to girls' club projects for any age between grades 1-12). Buys 8-10 mss/year. Submit complete ms. Length: 150-250 words. Pays $5.
Fiction: Julie Smith, Fiction Editor. Humorous (women leading girls' clubs), religious (Christian education—message inherent, not tacked on). Buys 1-2 mss/year. Query. Length: 1,000-2,000 words. Pays $20-40.
How To Break In: "Submit articles directly related to club work, practical in nature, i.e., ideas for leader training in communication, Bible knowledge, teaching skills. They must have practical application. We want substance—not ephemeral ideas."

PLANNING, 1313 E. 60th St., Chicago IL 60637. (312)947-2108. Editor: Sylvia Lewis. Publication of the American Planning Association. For urban planners, public officials, and citizens active in community groups. Magazine; 48 pages. Estab. 1972. Published monthly. Circ. 20,000. Buys first serial rights. Byline given. Buys about 50 mss/year. Pays on publication.

Free sample copy and writer's guidelines. Photocopied submissions OK. Reports in 1 month. Query. SASE.

Nonfiction and Photos: Articles on architecture, environment, energy, housing, health care, planning, historic preservation, land use, transportation, urban renewal, neighborhood conservation and zoning. "Articles should be written in magazine feature style. Topics should be current and stress issues, not personalities, though quotes should be used. We are national and international in perspective and are interested in stories from all parts of the country and the world." Length: 100-1,200 words for news; 1,200-3,000 for features; 300-800 words for book reviews. Pays $25 for book reviews; $50 for news articles, and $125 for features. B&w (8x11) glossies purchased on assignment. Pays $15 minimum. Buys color slides for covers; pays $125.

PORTS O' CALL, Box 530, Santa Rosa CA 95402. (707)542-0898. Editor: William A. Breniman. Newsbook of the Society of Wireless Pioneers. Society members are mostly early-day wireless "brass-pounders" who sent code signals from ships or manned shore stations handling wireless or radio traffic. Twice yearly. Not copyrighted. Pays on acceptance. Editorial deadlines are May 15 and October 15. Reports on submissions "at once." SASE.

Nonfiction: Articles about early-day wireless as used in ship-shore and high power operation. Early-day ships, records, etc. "Writers should remember that our members have gone to sea for years and would be critical of material that is not authentic. We are not interested in any aspect of ham radio. We are interested in authentic articles dealing with ships (since about 1910)." Oddities about the sea and weather as it affects shipping. Query. Length: 500-2,000 words. Pays 1¢/word.

Photos: Department Editor: Dexter S. Bartlett. Purchased with mss. Unusual shots of sea or ships. Wireless pioneers. Prefers b&w, "4x5 would be the most preferable size but it really doesn't make too much difference as long as the photos are sharp and the subject interests us." Fine if veloxed, but not necessary. Payment ranges from $2.50 to $10 "according to our appraisal of our interest." Ship photos of various nations, including postcard size, if clear, 25¢ to $1 each.

Poetry: Ships, marine slant (not military), shipping, weather, wireless. No restrictions. Pays $1 or $2.50 each.

THE ROTARIAN, 1600 Ridge Ave., Evanston IL 60201. (312)328-0100. Editor: Willmon L. White. 50% freelance written. For Rotarian business and professional men and their families; for schools, libraries, hospitals, etc. Monthly. Circ. 458,000. Usually buys all rights. Pays on acceptance. Free sample copy and editorial fact sheet. Query preferred. Reports in 2-4 weeks. SASE.

Nonfiction: "The field for freelance articles is in the general interest category. These run the gamut from inspirational guidelines for daily living to such weighty concerns as world hunger, peace, and preservation of environment. Recent articles have dealt with international illiteracy, salary, energy, dehumanization of the elderly, and worldwide drug abuse and prevention. Articles should appeal to an international audience and should in some way help Rotarians help other people. An article may increase a reader's understanding of world affairs, thereby making him a better world citizen. It may educate him in civic matters, thus helping him improve his town. It may help him to become a better employer, or a better human being. We are interested in articles on unusual Rotary club projects or really unusual Rotarians. We carry debates and symposiums, but we are careful to show more than one point of view. We present arguments for effective politics and business ethics, but avoid expose and muckraking. Controversy is welcome if it gets our readers to think but does not offend ethnic or religious groups. In short, the rationale of the organization is one of hope and encouragement and belief in the power of individuals talking and working together." Length: 2,000 words maximum. Payment varies.

Photos: Purchased with mss or with captions only. Prefers 2¼x2¼ or larger color transparencies, but also uses 35mm. B&w singles and photo essays. Vertical shots preferred to horizontal. Scenes of international interest. Color cover.

Poetry and Fillers: "Currently overstocked on serious poetry, but will look at short, light verse." Pays $2 a line. Pays $10 for brief poems. "We occasionally buy short humor pieces."

THE TOASTMASTER, 2200 N. Grand Ave., Box 10400, Santa Ana CA 92711. (714)542-6793. Editor-in-Chief: Sherry Angel. Emphasizes communication and leadership techniques; self-improvement. For members of Toastmasters International, Inc. Monthly magazine; 32 pages. Estab. 1932. Circ. 68,000. Pays on acceptance. Buys all rights, but may reassign following publication. Byline given. Photocopied submissions and previously published work

OK. SASE. Reports in 2 weeks. Free sample copy and writer's guidelines.
Nonfiction: How-to (improve speaking, listening, thinking skills; on leadership or management techniques, meeting planning, etc., with realistic examples), humor (on leadership, communications or management techniques), interviews (with communications or management experts offering advice that members can directly apply to their self-improvement efforts; should contain "how to" information). Buys 20-30 mss/year. Query. Length: 1,500-3,000 words. Pays $25-150.
Photos: Purchased with or without ms. Query. Pays $10-50 for 5x7 or 8x10 b&w glossies; $35-75 for color transparencies. No additional payment for those used with ms.
How To Break In: "By studying our magazine and sending us (after a query) material that is related. Since we get a number of articles from our members on 'how to build a speech,' freelancers should concentrate on more specific subjects such as body language, time management, etc. We're a nonprofit organization, so if they're looking to get rich on one article, they can probably forget it. But we do provide a good place for the inexperienced freelancer to get published."

V.F.W. MAGAZINE, Broadway at 34th St., Kansas City MO 64111. (816)561-3420. Editor: James K. Anderson. 30-50% freelance written. For members of the Veterans of Foreign Wars, men who served overseas, and their families. They range in age from the 20s to veterans of World War I and the Spanish-American War. Interests range from sports to national politics. Monthly magazine; 48 pages. Estab. 1913. Circ. 1,900,000. Buys all rights. Buys 40 mss/year. Pays on acceptance. Sample copy 50¢; free writer's guidelines. Seasonal material should be submitted 3 months in advance. Query. SASE. Reports in 1 week.
Nonfiction and Photos: "Nonfiction articles on sports, personalities and history. Special emphasis within a subject, special outlook related to veterans. The Veterans of Foreign Wars organization is geared to the man who has served overseas, a distinction that other veterans organizations do not make." Buys informational, how-to, personal experience, interview, profile, historical, think articles, and travel articles. Length: 1,000-1,500 words. Pays 5-10¢/word. B&w and color photos purchased with accompanying ms. Captions required. Pays $5 each.

Astrology and Psychic

The following publications regard astrology, psychic phenomena, ESP experiences, and related subjects as sciences or as objects of serious scientific research. Semireligious, occult, mysticism, and supernatural publications are classified in the Alternative category.

AMERICAN ASTROLOGY, Clancy Publications, Inc., 2505 N. Alvernon Way, Tucson AZ 85712. (602)327-3476. Editor: Joanne S. Clancy. 50% freelance written. For all ages, all walks of life. Monthly magazine; 116 pages. Estab. 1933. Circ. 265,000. Buys all rights. Buys 50-75 mss/year. Pays on publication. Free writer's guidelines. Reports in 4 weeks. Submit complete ms. SASE.
Nonfiction: Astrological material, often combined with astronomy. More interested in presenting results of research material and data based on time of birth, instead of special Sun-sign readings. Source of birth data must be included. Length: 3,500 words. "Payment is made according to the astrological knowledge and expertise of the writer."
Tips: Clancy Publications also publishes a 158-page yearbook, *American Astrology Digest*. Articles of about 3,500 words based on astrology that concern environment, sports, vocation, health, etc., will be given prompt consideration for the yearbook.

ASTROLOGY GUIDE, Sterling's Magazines, Inc., 355 Lexington Ave., New York NY 10017. (212)391-1400, ext. 21. Editor: Marsha Kaplan. "For a special interest audience involved in astrology on all levels, from the merely curious to the serious student and practitioner." Bimonthly magazine; 96 (6½x9½) pages. Estab. 1937. Circ. 55,000. Buys all rights. Buys 30 mss/year, mostly assigned. Pays on acceptance. Submit seasonal (Christmas, vacation-time, etc.) and special (major astrological events) material 5-6 months in advance. Reports in 8-12 weeks minimum. Query or submit complete ms. SASE.
Nonfiction: "Mostly astrological articles: Sun-sign, mundane, speculative or research. Slightly more technical for advanced readers, but prefer intelligent popular approach. Emphasis is on use of astrology for self-betterment in the reader's life. Very interested in buying articles on timely themes in these fields. We are more interested in featuring new ideas and new writers than in repeating what has been done in the past. We are attempting to develop a more

personal, intimate approach." Sun-sign articles on the traditional themes (health, money, love) should refer (at least in preparation) to other aspects of the birth chart, and should be written by a practicing astrologer, or serious student. Length: 2,000-3,500 words, but will accept shorter articles. Also uses book reviews and will consider new ideas for new departments. Pays 3¢/word minimum.

Fillers: Short humor and material on astrological experiences and insights are used as fillers. Length: 750 words maximum. Pays 3¢/word.

ASTROLOGY NOW, Llewellyn Publications, Box 43383, St. Paul MN 55164. Editor: Noel Tyl. Emphasizes modern astrology. Bimonthly magazine; 65 pages. Estab. 1975. Circ. 7,000. Pays 30 days after publication. Buys all rights. Submit seasonal/holiday material 6 months in advance. Photocopied and previously published submissions OK. SASE. Reports in 6 months. Free sample copy and writer's guidelines.

Nonfiction: How-to, inspirational, interview, new product, personal experience, photo feature, profile and technical. Buys 4 mss/issue. Query. Length: 2,000-5,000. Pays 2¢/word.

Photos: State availability of photos. Buys b&w and color contact sheets; pay varies. Model releases required.

Columns/Departments: Book Reviews, Editoral, Interviews, Research and Speaking out for Astrology. Buys 2 columns/issue. Query. Length: 500-2,500 words. Pays 2¢/word.

BEYOND REALITY MAGAZINE, 303 W. 42nd St., New York NY 10036. (212)265-1676. Editor: Harry Belil. 75% freelance written. Primarily for university students interested in astronomy, archeology, astrology, the occult (the whole range), UFOs, ESP, spiritualism, parapsychology, exploring the unknown. Bimonthly magazine; 64 pages. Estab. 1971. Circ. 83,000. Buys all rights. Buys 30-35 mss/year. Pays on publication. Sample copy $1; writer's guidelines for SASE. Photocopied submissions OK. Query or submit complete ms. SASE.

Nonfiction and Photos: Interested in articles covering the range of their readers' interests, as well as any new discoveries in parapsychology. How-to, interview, inspirational, historical, think pieces, spot news. Length: 1,000-2,000 words. Pays 3¢/word maximum, or "whatever the editor feels such a feature warrants." No additional payment for b&w photos used with mss.

Fillers: "We pay $1 for clippings used."

How To Break In: "Show me some pieces you've written and if I like your style, I'll provide you with the subjects to write on. Also looking for current ideas from the campuses, so student writers should give us a try." Lack of research documentation, or re-hashing old material will bring a rejection here.

DAILY PLANETARY GUIDE, Llewellyn Publications, Box 43383, St. Paul MN. (612)291-1970. Editor: Carl Weschcke. Emphazies astrology. Annual book; 300 pages. Estab. 1977. Circ. 20,000. Pays 30 days after publication. Buys all rights. Phone queries OK. Photocopied submissions OK. SASE. Reports in 6 months. Free sample copy and writer's guidelines.

Nonfiction: How-to and technical.

Photos: State availability of photos with ms. Buys b&w and color contact sheets. Pay varies.

FATE, Clark Publishing Co., 500 Hyacinth Place, Highland Park IL 60035. Editor: Mary Margaret Fuller. 70% freelance written. Monthly. Buys all rights; occasionally North American serial rights only. Byline given. Pays on publication. Query. Reports in 4-8 weeks. SASE.

Nonfiction and Fillers: Personal psychic experiences, 300-500 words. Pays $10. New frontiers of science, and ancient civilizations, 2,000-3,000 words; also parapsychology, occultism, witchcraft, magic, spiritual healing miracles, flying saucers, etc. Must include complete authenticating details. Prefers interesting accounts of single events rather than roundups. "We very frequently accept manuscripts from new writers; the majority are individuals' first-person accounts of their own psychic experience. We do need to have all details, where, when, why, who and what, included for complete documentation." Pays minimum of 3¢/word. Fillers should be fully authenticated. Length: 100-300 words.

Photos: Buys good glossy photos with mss or with captions only. Pays $5-10.

GNOSTICA, Llewellyn Publications, Box 43383, St. Paul MN 55164. (612)291-1970. Editor: C.L.Weschcke. *Gnostica* is "A guide to the techniques of esoteric knowledge for the Aquarian Age." Bimonthly magazine; 96 pages. Estab. 1970. Circ. 7,000. Pays 30 days after publication. Buys all rights. Byline given. Phone queries OK. Photocopied submissions OK. SASE. Reports in 6 months. Free sample copy and writer' guidelines.

Nonfiction: How-to, interview, personal experience, photo feature, profile and technical. Buys 11 mss/issue. Query. Length: 2,000-10,000 words. Pays 2¢/word.

Photos: Buys b&w and color contact sheets. Pays varies. Captions and model releases required.
Columns/Departments: Book Reviews, News of the Occult and Astrology, Occult Contacts, Parapsychology and Research Projects. Buys 3 columns/issue. Query. Length: 1,000-2,000 words. Pays 2¢/word. Open to suggestions for new columns/departments.

THE HEFLEY PSYCHIC REPORT, U.S. Research, Inc., Box 7242, Burbank CA 91510. (213)841-2733. Editor-in-Chief: Carl D. Hefley. Executive Editor: Richard De A'Morelli. Emphasizes psychic phenomena for a mass readership interested in the occult, psychic happenings, science, UFOs and witchcraft. Bimonthly magazine; 56-64 pages. Estab. 1977. Pays on publication. Buys first North American rights and the right to reprint material in *The Hefley Psychic Report*; all other rights automatically revert to author on publication. Byline given. Submit seasonal/holiday material 2 months in advance of issue date. Photocopied and previously published material "of good quality" OK. SASE. Free sample copy and writer's guidelines.
Nonfiction: Expose; historical; how-to (develop psychic skills, etc.); informational; interview; true psychic experiences; personal opinion (brief); photo feature; profile; and technical, slanted to a mass market audience. Buys 150-200 mss/year. Query. Length: 100-1,500 words. Pays $10-350.
Photos: State availability of photos with query. "Photos will really help sell the author's work here, as we are a very visual-oriented magazine." Pays $5-25 for 3¼x3¼ or larger glossy b&w prints. Captions required. Model release required.
Columns/Departments: Not presently in the market for new columns or departments. Fillers, clippings and newsbreaks $1-10. Buys 3-5/issue. SASE must be enclosed for return.

HOROSCOPE, 1 Dag Hammarskjold Plaza, 245 E. 47th St., New York NY 10017. Editor-in-Chief: Julia A. Wagner. Monthly magazine; 126 pages. Estab. 1939. Circ. 240,000. Buys all rights. Buys 300 mss/year. Pays on acceptance. Free sample copy and writer's guidelines. All submissions must be accompanied by a carbon copy. Submit project forecast material at least 6 months in advance. Reports in 2 months. Query or submit complete ms. SASE.
Nonfiction: Articles on astrology only. "Love, family, money, employment, and health are our most popular subjects. Must appeal to general readers with some knowledge of astrology. Articles dealing with prevailing conditions are always considered. We will not accept any articles related to witchcraft." Informational, how-to, profile, inspirational. Length: 3,000-3,500 words. Pays 6¢/word.
Fillers: On astrology only. Length: 50-150 words. Submissions must consist of a minimum of 10 fillers. Pays 6¢/word.

HOROSCOPE GUIDE, 350 Madison Ave., Cresskill NJ 07626. (201)568-0500. Editor: Jim Hendryx. For persons interested in astrology as it touches their daily lives; all ages. Estab. 1967. Monthly. Circ. 60,000. Buys all rights, but may reassign rights to author after publication "for noncompetitive use. Byline given. That is, for book publication, but never for magazine resale." Buys 40 mss/year. Pays on acceptance. Sample copy for $1. Will consider photocopied submissions. Submit seasonal material 5 months in advance. Submit complete ms. SASE.
Nonfiction, Poetry and Fillers: No textbook-type material. Wants anything of good interest to the average astrology buff, preferably not so technical as to require more than basic knowledge of birth sign by reader. Mss should be light, readable, entertaining and sometimes humorous. Not as detailed and technical as other astrology magazines, "with the astro-writer doing the interpreting without long-winded reference to his methods at every juncture. We are less reverent of astrological red tape." Does not want to see a teacher's type of approach to the subject. Wants mss about man-woman relationships, preferably in entertaining and humorous fashion. Length: 900-4,000 words. Pays 1½-2¢/word. Buys traditional forms of poetry. Length: 4-16 lines. Pays $2-$8.
How To Break In: "Best way to break in with us is with some lively Sun-sign type piece involving some area of man-woman relationships—love, sex, marriage, divorce, differing views on money, religion, child-raising, in-laws, vacations, politics, life styles, or whatever."

MOON SIGN BOOK, Box 43383, St. Paul MN 55164. (612)291-1970. Editor: Carl Weschcke. For "persons from all walks of life with interests in gardening, natural living and astrology." Annual Book; 460 pages. Estab. 1906. Annual. Circ. 125,000. Buys all rights. Byline given. Pays on publication. Phone queries OK. Photocopied and previously published submissions OK. SASE. Reports in 6 months.
Nonfiction: How-to and photo features. "We can use material in natural medicine, healing, and living in intelligent cooperation with nature. We are a yearly publication dealing with

farming, gardening, yearly forecasts for all types of activities, with informative articles on astrology. We try to be educational as well as practical." Buys 5-10 mss/iussue. Query. Length: 3,000-10,000 words. Pays 3¢/word.

Photos: State availabiltiy of photos with ms. Buys b&w and color contact sheets. Pay varies. Captions and model releases required.

How To Break In: "The *Moon Sign Book* is a farming and gardening almanac emphasizing astronomical effects on planting, growing, harvesting and using crops to maximum advantage. Since a good portion of the book is taken up with tables and in-house material, we have room for only a few outside articles. Those articles should have something to do with either astrology or gardening (we are also interested in herbs, herbal remedies). Since most freelancers are not astrologers I would suggest that they concentrate on the many aspects of organic gardening or possibly how-to-do features that relate in some way to farming and gardening. Short articles on the occult phenomena (enhancing growth psychically), are also good possibilities for the beginning writer. We are continually looking for astrologers capable of writing Sun sign predictions for *Moon Sign Book*. Also astrological predictions for weather, stock and commodity markets, news and political developments, etc. We generally stick with one, but we find that quality depends on a variety, and would like to find a few more writers to back us up."

NEW REALITIES, 680 Beach St., Suite 408, San Francisco CA 94109. (415)776-2600. Editor: James Bolen. 20% freelance written. For general public interested in holistic approach to living and being—body, mind, and spirit—and straightforward, entertaining material on parapsychology, consciousness research, and the frontiers of human potential and the mind. Bimonthly. Buys all rights. Pays on publication. Reports in 4-6 weeks. Query. SASE.
Nonfiction and Photos: "Documented articles on mental, physical andspiritual holistic dimensions of man. Balanced reporting, no editorializing. No personal experiences as such. Accept profiles of leaders in the field. Must have documented evidence about holistic leaders, healers, researchers. Short bibliography for further reading." Length: 3,000-4,000 words. Pays $75-250.

QUEST, North American UFO Organization, Box 2485, Cedar Rapids IA 52406. Editor-in-Chief: Kevin D. Randle. Emphasizes unusual phenomena. Bimonthly magazine; 45-60 pages. Estab. 1975. Circ. 100,000. Pays on acceptance. Buys all rights, but may reassign following publication. Phone queries OK. Simultaneous and photocopied submissions OK. SASE. Reports in 2 weeks.
Nonfiction: "Exposes should show how good UFO cases have been 'edited' so the public gets only one side, either pro or con. We are interested in articles showing how information in the field differs from the public belief. All facts must be verified. Interviews, personal opinion, photo features." Length: 3,000-12,000 words. Pays $150-500.

SADIC MAGAZINE, Box 2026, North Hollywood CA 91602. (213)762-6995. Editor-in-Chief: S.E. Adlai. Managing Editor: T.L. Adlai. 35% freelance written. Monthly magazine; 41 pages. Estab. 1976. Circ. 35,000. Pays on acceptance. Buys all rights. Byline given. Simultaneous submissions OK. SASE. Reports in 3 months. Sample copy $2.
Nonfiction: "We only publish articles and research materials relating to astrology, ESP and related subjects." General interest; historical; inspirational; interview; profile; and technical. Buys 3 mss/year. Query. Length: 200-600 words. Pays 10-25¢/word.

Automotive and Motorcycle

Publications listed in this section are concerned with the maintenance, operation, performance, racing, and judging of automobiles and motorcycles. Publications that treat vehicles as a means of transportation or shelter instead of as a hobby or sport are classified in the Travel, Camping, and Trailer category. Journals for teamsters, service station operators, and auto dealers will be found in the Auto and Truck classification of the Trade Journals section.

AMERICAN MOTORCYCLIST, American Motorcyclist Association, Box 141, Westerville OH 43081. (614)891-2425. Editor: Bill Amick. For "enthusiastic motorcyclists, investing considerable time and money in the sport." Monthly magazine; 48-64 pages. Estab. 1974. Circ. 126,000. Pays on publication. Rights purchased vary with author and material. Pays 25-50% kill fee. Byline given. Phone queries OK. Submit seasonal/holiday material 3 months in advance. SASE. Reports in 4 weeks. Free sample copy.

Nonfiction: How-to (different and/or unusual ways to use a motorcycle or have fun on one), historical (the heritage of motorcycling, particularly as it relates to the AMA), interviews (with interesting personalities in the world of motorcycling), photo feature (quality work on any aspect of motorcycling), technical (well-researched articles on safe riding techniques). Buys 10-20 mss/year. Query. Length: 500 words minimum. Pays $2/published column inch.
Photos: Greg Harrison, Art Director. Purchased with or without accompanying ms, or on assignment. Captions required. Query. Pays $15 minimum per photo published.

AUTOMOBILE QUARTERLY, 221 Nassau St., Princeton NJ 08540. (609)924-7555. Editor-in-Chief: Beverly Rae Kimes. Senior Editor: Start Grayson. Emphasizes automobiles and automobile history. Quarterly hardbound magazine; 112 pages. Estab. 1962. Circ. 40,000. Pays on acceptance. Buys all rights. Pays expenses as kill fee. Byline given. SASE. Reports in 3 weeks. Sample copy $8.95.
Nonfiction: Authoritative articles relating to the automobile and automobile history. Historical, humor, interview and nostalgia. Buys 5 mss/issue. Query. Length: 2,000-10,000 words. Pays $200-600.
Photos: Purchased on assignment. Captions required. Query. Uses 8x10 b&w glossy prints and 4x5 color transparencies. "Payment varies with assignment and is negotiated prior to assignment."
Tips: "Familiarity with the magazine a *must*."

AUTOWEEK, Real Resources Group, Inc., Box A, Reno NV 89506. Editor: Reed Flickinger. Emphasizes automobile racing and the auto industry, domestic and international. Weekly tabloid; 40 pages. Estab. 1955. Circ. 150,000. Pays on publication. Buys first-time rights or by agreement with author. SASE. Reports in 2-4 weeks. Free sample copy.
Nonfiction: Informational (group-based vs. assembly line system; does Volvo/Kalmar plant really work?, etc.); historical (the first Indy race, first successful Ferrari, first European assembly line, etc.); nostalgia ("we'd have room for 2-3/month if we had them on tap"). Technical articles on radical design changes. News reports on auto racing. "Any literate auto racing enthusiast can offer articles to *AutoWeek*. If the beginner is at a local race and he sees no *AW* reporter around, he might try covering the event himself. If he's going to a big race, he should query first since we undoubtedly already have it covered. A number of stringers got started just that way. Industry stories may range from General Motors to consumerists. In either case, remember we're not the auto section in a family paper." Length: 2,000 words maximum. Query. Pays $3/column inch.
Photos: Purchased with or without mss, or on assignment. "Photo rates by arrangement."
Fillers: Clippings ("rewrite clips and enclose"); newsbreaks. Buys 3/issue. Send fillers in. Length: 50-500 words. Pays $3/column inch.

BMW JOURNAL, A. Christ Zeitschriftenverlag GmbH, Pettenkoferstrasse 22, 8000 Munich 2, W. Germany. (089)53.59.11. USA editorial office: 2540 Bonito Way, Laguna Beach CA 92651. Editor: Ron Wakefield. Editor-in-Chief: Udo Wust. An automobile customer magazine for owners and enthusiasts of BMW automobiles; upper income audience; generally, people with active life styles and an eye for the unusual. Bimonthly magazine; 52 pages. Estab. 1962. Circ 50,000. Pays on publication. Buys all rights, but may reassign following publication. Phone queries OK. SASE. Reports in 4 weeks.
Nonfiction: Historical (having to do with places or with history of automobiles if related to BMW); informational; nostalgia, photo features; profiles (of interesting BMW owners); travel (by automobile, BMW in photos). Buys 3-5/issue. Query. Length: 500-1,500 words. Pays $75-150/printed page.
Photos: Used with or without ms, or on assignment. Captions required. Query. No additional payment for 5x7 b&w glossy prints or 35mm minimum (larger preferred) color transparencies. Model release required. Need not relate to publication's subject matter; can encompass a broad range of life style themes.
Fiction: Adventure, experimental, historical, mystery, science fiction, suspense. Buys 1 ms/issue. Query. Length: 500-1,500 words. Pays $75-150/printed page.
How To Break In: "Author must know the magazine, available at local BMW dealers. Articles must be submitted with excellent photos, captioned."

CAR AND DRIVER, 2002 Hogback Rd., Ann Arbor MI 48104. (313)994-0055. Editor/Publisher: David E. Davis Jr. For auto enthusiasts; college-educated, professional, median 26-28 years of age. Monthly magazine; 100 pages. Estab. 1957. Circ. 730,000. Rights purchased vary with author and material. Buys all rights, but may reassign rights to author after publication, or first North American serial rights. Buys 10-12 unsolicited mss/year. Pays on acceptance. No photocopied or simultaneous submissions. Submit seasonal material 4 months in advance. Query and include samples of previous work. Reports in 2 months. SASE. **Nonfiction and Photos:** Nonanecdotal articles about the more sophisticated treatment of autos and motor racing. Exciting, interesting cars. Automotive road tests, informational articles on cars and equipment; some satire and humor. Personalities, past and present, in the automotive industry and automotive sports. "Treat readers as intellectual equals. Emphasis on people as well as hardware." Informational, how-to, humor, historical, think articles, and nostalgia. Length: 750-2,000 words. Pays $200-$1,000. B&w photos purchased with accompanying mss with no additional payment. Also buys book reviews for book review department, and mini-features for FYI department. Length: about 500 words. Pays $50-150.

How To Break In: "It is best to start off with an interesting query and to stay away from nuts-and-bolts stuff since that will be handled in-house or by an acknowledged expert. Probably the very best way for a new writer to break in with us is with a personal, reasonably hip approach which shows a real intimacy with what we are trying to do. A while back, for instance, we ran a freelance piece on automobiles in Russia, which was the product of an interesting query. We are not like other automotive magazines inasmuch as we try to publish material that could just as well appear in the general magazines. We're not interested in antique cars or hot rods. To us the Ford Mustang is infinitely more important than a 1932 Ruxton wicker-seat five-passenger touring car. Good writing and unique angles are the key."

CAR COLLECTOR/CAR CLASSICS, Classic Publishing, Inc., 5430 Jimmy Carter Blvd., Suite 108, Norcross GA 30093. Editor: Donald R. Peterson. For people interested in all facets of classic, milestone, antique, special interest and sports cars. Maclots, models, restoration, license plates and memorabilia. Monthly magazine; 70 pages. Estab. January 1978. Circ. 55,000. Pays on publication. Byline given "by author's request only." Submit seasonal/holiday material 3-4 months in advance. Photocopied submissions OK. SASE. Reports in 2 months. Free sample copy and writer's guidelines.

Nonfiction: General interest, historical, how-to, humor, inspirational, interview, nostalgia, personal opinion, profile, photo feature, technical and travel. Buys 25-50 mss/year. Query with clips of published work. Length: 300-3,000 words. Pays 5¢/word.

Photo: State availability of photos with ms. Offers no additional payment for photos with accompanying mss. Uses b&w glossy prints; color glossy prints and transparencies. Buys one-time rights. Captions and model releases required.

Columns/Departments: "Rarely add a new columnist but we are open to suggestions." Buys 36/year. Query with clips of published work. Length: 400-600 words. Pays 5¢/word.

Fiction: "We buy very little fiction, but would not exclude a well-written fiction piece directed to our market."

CAR CRAFT, Petersen Publishing Co., 8490 Sunset Blvd., Los Angeles CA 90069. (213)657-5100, ext. 345. Editor: Rick Voegelin. For men and women, 18-34, automotive-oriented. Monthly magazine; 124 pages. Estab. 1953. Circ. 300,000. Buys all rights. Buys 12 mss/year. Pays on acceptance. Query. SASE.

Nonfiction and Photos: Photo Department Editor: Charlie Hayward. Drag racing articles, technical car features, how-to articles, and general car features. Interview, profile, and photo features. Length: open. Pays $100-125/page. Photos are purchased with or without accompanying ms. Captions optional. 8x10 b&w glossy; 35mm or 2¼x2¼ color transparencies. Pays $12.50 for b&w photos; $100 minimum (one page) color.

CARS MAGAZINE, Arden Communications, Inc., Box 99, Amawalk NY 10501. (914)962-7570. Publisher: John McCluskey. Emphasizes automotive high performance: factory muscle cars, hot street machines, drag race cars, and racing. For enthusiasts from early teens through thirties, some older; assume fair technical knowledge of cars. Monthly magazine; 82 pages. Estab. 1957. Circ. 80,000. Pays on publication. Buys one-time or all rights. Byline given. Phone queries OK. SASE. Reports in 3 months. Sample copy $1.50.

Nonfiction: How-to (budget hop-ups, speed tricks, suspension modification, customizing, repair, body work, or race car building); informational and new product offerings; high-performance or automotive humor; interviews and profiles (of prominent people in drag racing or automotive field); historical and nostalgia (looking back on hot rods, muscle cars of the '50s and '60s); technical (drivetrain and suspension subjects); and some drag race coverage. Buys 12 mss/issue. Submit complete ms. Length: 500-3,000 words. Pays $100-500.

Photos: Pays $25/b&w photo (if separate from article package), 8x10 glossy prints preferred; $50/color photos (35mm or larger transparencies). Model release required.

THE CLASSIC CAR, Box 3013, Orange CA 92665. Editor: William S. Snyder. For the classic car enthusiast, highly specialized in his interest. Uses writing with a "good nonfiction prose style. More interested in clear, factual writing than a lot of 'flash.' " The publication has a "finer focus than general automotive magazines. The reader is extremely knowledgeable to begin with. Accuracy is of utmost importance." Quarterly. Circ. 5,000. Buys first rights. Buys 4-8 mss/year. Pays on publication. Query. Reports in 7-10 days. SASE.

Nonfiction and Photos: Wants "historical articles on various makes and models of classic cars (high quality cars of 1925-1948 vintage), restoration how-to articles, interviews, and profiles." Length: 500-5,000 words. Pays $25-$100. 8x10 b&w glossy photos, 4x5 color transparencies. Preferred with captions only. Pays $1-$5 for b&w; $5-$25 for color.

CORVETTE FEVER, Michael Lee Associates, Box 6317, Toledo OH 43514. (419)893-5544. Editor: Mike Doolin. Monthly magazine; 68-84 pages. Estab. October 1978. Circ. 36,000. Pays on publication. Buys all rights. Byline given "if we pre-arrange it." Phone queries OK. Submit seasonal/holiday material 2 months in advance. Photocopied submissions OK. SASE. Reports in 4 weeks. Sample copy 75¢; free writer's guidelines.

Nonfiction: Expose (on Corvette crime, the inside story of how, why, by whom); general interest (event coverage, personal experience,); historical (special or unusual Corvette historical topics); how-to (technical and mechanical articles, photo's are a must); humor (special section Schlick Shift is devoted to Corvette-related humor); interview (with important Corvette persons, race drivers, technical persons, club officials, etc.); new product (new Corvette-related items); nostalgia (relating to early Corvette car and development); personal experiences (related to Corvette car use and esperiences); profile (prominent and well-known Corvette personalities wanted for interviews and articles); photo feature (centerspread in color of Corvette and Vetternote; photo essays on renovation, customizing and show cars); technical (any aspect of Corvette improvement or custom articles); and travel (relating to Corvette use and adventure). Buys 7-10 mss/issue. Query or send complete ms. Length: 500-3,000 words. Pays $40-300.

Photos: Send photos with ms. Pays $5-25 for 5x7 b&w glossy prints; $10-50 for color contact sheets and transparencies. Captions preferred; model release required.

Columns/Departments: Innovative Ideas, In Print, Model Shop, Pit Stop, Schlick Shift and Tech Vette. Buys 5 mss/issue. Send complete ms. Length: 300-800 words. Pays $24-200.

Fiction: "Any type of articles as long as it is related to the Corvette." Buys 1-2 mss/issue. Query or send complete ms. Length: 500-2,500 words. Pays $40-200.

Fillers: Clippings, jokes, gags, anecdotes, short humor and newsbreaks. Buys 2-3/issue. Length: 25-150 words. Pays $2.50-15.

CYCLE NEWS, WEST, 2201 Cherry Ave., Box 498, Long Beach CA 90801. (213)427-7433. Managing Editor: Charles Morey. Publisher: Sharon Clayton. Emphasizes motorcycle recreation for motorcycle racers and recreationists west of Mississippi River. Weekly tabloid; 48 pages. Estab. 1963. Circ. 60,000. Pays on 15th of month for work published in issues cover-dated the previous month. Buys all rights, but may reassign rights to author following publication. SASE. Reports in 4 weeks. Free writer's guidelines.

Nonfiction: Expose; how-to; historical; humor; informational; interview (racers); personal experience (racing, nonracing with a point); personal opinion (land use, emission control, etc.); photo feature; profile (personality profiles); technical; and travel (off-road trips, "bikepacking"). Buys 1,000 mss/year. Submit complete ms. Pays $1/column inch.

Photos: Purchased with or without accompanying manuscript. Captions required. Submit contact sheet, prints, negatives or transparencies. Pays $5 minimum for 5x7 or 8x10 glossy prints; $10 minimum for 35mm slides or 2¼x2¼ color transparencies. Model release required. No additional payment for photos accepted with accompanying ms.

CYCLE TIMES, Multi-Media Publications, 222 W. Adams St., Suite 312, Chicago IL 60606. (312)236-5550. Editor: Mark Schmidlin. For "experienced motorcyclists, early teens and up, race and performance-bike oriented." Semimonthly tabloid (26 issues/year); 32 pages (winter), 56 (summer). Estab. April 1975. Circ. 110,000. Pays on publication. Buys all rights. Byline given. Photocopied submissions OK. SASE. Reports in 4 weeks. Sample copy $1; free writer's guidelines.

Nonfiction: General interest; historical (query first); how-to (motorcycle maintenance, performance modifications, repairs); informational (race coverage, event reports); interviews; personal opinion (no first motorcycle rides, no crash/death stories); technical (query first); and travel (touring). "We do not want fillers, poetry, clippings or chopper/custom articles." Buys 20 mss/issue. Submit complete ms. Length: 1,000-3,000 words. Pays $1/column inch.

Photos: Send photos with ms. Pays $2.50-5 for 5x7 b&w glossy prints; $10-15 for 35mm color transparencies. Captions required.
How To Break In: "Start covering the races anywhere in the US. Include usable photos and a sufficient re-cap of the day's events. All of us started this way. Once we know who you are, you'll get all the work you can handle."

CYCLE WORLD, 1499 Monrovia Ave., Newport Beach CA 92663. Editor: Allan Girdler. For active motorcyclists, "young, affluent, educated, very perceptive." Subject matter includes "road tests (staff-written), features on special bikes, customs, racers, racing events; technical and how-to features involving mechanical modifications." Monthly. Circ. 300,000. Buys all rights, but will reassign rights to author after publication. Buys 200-300 mss/year from freelancers. Pays on publication. Sample copy $1; free writer's guidelines. Submit seasonal material 2½ months in advance. Reports in 4-6 weeks. Query. SASE.
Nonfiction: Buys informative, well-researched, technical, theory and how-to articles; interviews; profiles; humor; and historical pieces. Taboos include articles about "wives learning to ride; 'my first motorcycle.'" Length: 800-5,000 words. Pays $75-100/published page. Columns include Competition, which contains short, local racing stories with photos. Column length: 300-400 words. Pays $75-100/published page.
Photos: Purchased with or without ms, or on assignment. Captions optional. Pays $50 for 1-page; $25-35 for a half page. 8x10 b&w glossy prints, 35mm color transparencies.
Fiction: Humorous stories. No racing fiction or "rhapsodic poetry." Length: 1,500-3,000 words. Pays $75 minimum/published page.

DIESEL MOTORIST, Box 335, Fort Lee NJ 07024. 10% freelance written. Magazine of the Diesel Automobile Association for a "largely professional readership—engineers, auto industry executive, diesel automobile owners, RV and light truck owners, with an interest in diesel travel, economics, technical trends, etc." Quarterly magazine; 32 pages. Estab. 1977. Circ. 13,000. Pays on publication. Buys all rights, but may reassign following publication. Byline given. Submit seasonal/holiday material 4-6 months in advance of issue date. Photocopied submissions OK. SASE. Reports in 6 weeks.
Nonfiction: Exposé (regulatory agencies of governments, EPA, etc.); how-to (diesel auto information); general interest (energy, economics); historical (related to automobile industry, etc.); new product (automotive and inventions); photo feature (new autos, events, etc.); profile (on assignment only); technical (automotive, particularly diesel, also petroleum, energy); and travel (vehicle). Buys 1-2 mss/issue. Query with outline of new work and clips of published work. Length: 600-1,500 words. Pays $25-100.
Photos: Pays $5-25 for 5x7 glossy prints. State availability of photos with query.
Fiction: Will consider queries for adventure and historical fiction. Pays $25-100.

DIRT BIKE MAGAZINE, Box 317, Encino CA 91436. Editor: Rick Sieman. For dirt bike riders. Magazine; 84 (8x10) pages. Estab. 1971. Monthly. Circ. 175,000. Buys all rights. Buys 18 mss/year. Will consider photocopied submissions. Submit special material 3 months in advance. Query. SASE.
Nonfiction and Photos: Competition reports outside of southern California of national interest. Light, humorous style, but accurate facts. Informational, how-to, expose, spot news, technical. Length: 1,000 to 8,000 words. Pays $40/page, b&w. Photos are used in special Crash & Burn and Photo Album issues. Also purchased with or without ms, or on assignment. Pays $10 for 8x10 b&w glossy prints; $25 to $50 for 35mm (or larger) transparencies upon publication.

DUNE BUGGIES & HOT VWS, Wright Publishing Co., Inc., Box 2260, Costa Mesa CA 92626. Editor: Tom Chambers. Monthly magazine; 100 pages. Estab. 1967. Circ. 50,000. Pays on publication. Buys one-time rights. Submit seasonal or holiday material 3 months in advance. SASE. Free sample copy.
Nonfiction: Technical how-to and informational articles. Buys 6-8 mss/issue. Submit complete ms. Length: 500-2,000 words. Pays $50/published page.
Photos: Purchased with ms. Captions required. Send contact sheet. Pays $10 maximum for 8x10 b&w glossy prints; $10 minimum for color negs or slides.
Rejects: First-person articles.

EASYRIDERS MAGAZINE, Entertainment for Adult Bikers, Box 52, Malibu CA 90265. (213)889-8701. Editor: Lou Kimzey. For "adult men—men who own, or desire to own, expensive custom motorcycles. The individualist—a rugged guy who enjoys riding a chopper and all the good times derived from it." Monthly. Circ. 385,000. Buys all rights. Buys 26-36 mss/year. Pays on acceptance. Will send a sample copy to a writer for 25¢. Reports in 2-3 weeks. SASE.

Nonfiction, Fiction, and Fillers: Department Editor: Louis Bosque. "Masculine, candid material of interest to men. Must be bike-oriented, but can be anything of interest to any rugged man. It is suggested that everyone read a copy before submitting—it's not *Boy's Life*. Light, easy, conversational writing style wanted, like men would speak to each other without women being around. Gut level, friendly, man-to-man. Should be bike-oriented or of interest to a man who rides a motorcycle. *Easyriders* is entirely different from all other motorcycle magazines in that it stresses the lifestyle and good times surrounding the owning of a motorcycle—it's aimed at the rider and is nontechnical, while the others are nuts and bolts. Not interested in overly technical motorcycle articles. We carry no articles that preach or talk down to the reader, or attempt to tell them what they should or shouldn't do." Buys personal experience, interviews, especially humor, expose (of Big brother, big government, red, white and blue, motorcycle-oriented) articles. Length: 1,000-3,000 words. Pays 10¢/word minimum, depending on length and use in magazine. "It's the subject matter and how well it's done—not length, that determines amount paid." Risque jokes, fillers, short humor. Length: open. Pays on acceptance.

Photos: Department Editor: Pete Chiodo. B&w glossy prints, 35mm color, 2¼x2¼ color transparencies purchased with mss. "We are only interested in *exclusive* photos of exclusive bikes that have never been published in, or photographed by, a national motorcycle or chopper publication. Bikes should be approved by editorial board before going to expense of shooting. Submit sample photos—Polaroids will do. Send enough samples for editorial board to get good idea of the bike's quality, originality, workmanship, interesting features, coloring." Payment is $50 to $250 for cover, $75-$250 for centerspread, $20 for b&w and $35 for color for "In the Wind," $25 up for arty, unusual shots, and $100 to $350 for a complete feature.

Fiction: "Gut level language okay. Any sex scenes, not to be too graphic in detail. Dope may be implied, but not graphically detailed. Must be biker male-oriented, but doesn't have to dwell on that fact. Only interested in hard-hitting, rugged fiction." Length: 2,000-3,500 words. Pays 10¢/word minimum, depending on quality, length and use in magazine.

How To Break In: "There is no mystery about breaking into our publications (*Iron Horse*), as long as the material is aimed directly at our macho, intelligent, male audience. We suggest that the writer read the requirements indicated above and seriously study a current copy of the magazine before submitting material."

4x4's, AND OFF ROAD VEHICLES, E-Go Enterprises, Inc., Box 1084, Reseda CA 91335. (213)782-2502. Editor: Regis Moore. Emphasizes off-road vehicles and related activities. Monthly magazine; 84 pages. Estab. 1976. Circ. 135,000. Pays on publication. Buys all rights, but may reassign following publication. Byline given. Phone queries OK. Submit seasonal/holiday material 4 months in advance. SASE. Reports in 2 weeks. Free sample copy and writer's guidelines.

Nonfiction: Expose (on government bills and such related to off roaders); how-to; informational; technical and travel (off-road areas). Buys 5-7 mss/issue. Query or send complete ms. Length: 1,500-3,000 words. Pays $35/published page.

Photos: Photos purchased with accompanying ms. Captions required. Uses 8x10 b&w photos and 35mm or 2¼x2¼ color transparencies. Send prints and transparencies. Total purchase price for ms includes payment for photos.

Columns/Departments: Willie's Work Bench (budget mechanical tips). Buys 3-4/issue. Query or send complete ms. Length: 400-1,000 words. Pays $25-50. Action photos near disaster pays $25.

Fillers: Short humor and cartoons. All off-road related. Buys 2/issue. Length: 50-200 words. Pays $5-10.

FOUR WHEELER MAGAZINE, 2126 Vanowen St., Canoga Park CA 91303. (213)992-4777. Editor/Publisher: Bill Sanders. Senior Editor: Dennis Adler. Emphasizes four-wheel-drive vehicles. Monthly magazine; 108 pages. Estab. 1956. Circ. 170,000. Pays on publication. Buys all rights. Phone queries OK. Submit seasonal/holiday material at least 4 months in advance. SASE. Reports in 6-12 months. Free sample copy and writer's guidelines.

Nonfiction: Historical (4-wheeling in ghost towns), how-to, interview (4WD industry), new product, profile (prominent 4WD enthusiast), technical and travel. Query or send complete ms. Length: 5-6 pages. Pays $50-250.

Fillers: Newsbreaks and 4WD outings.

HOT ROD, 8490 Sunset Blvd., Los Angeles CA 90069. (213)657-5100. Editor: Lee Kelley. For readers 10 to 60 years old with automotive high performance, street rod, truck and van, drag racing and street machine interest. Monthly magazine; 120 pages. Estab. 1948. Circ. 830,000. Buys all rights. Buys 30 mss per year. Byline given. Pays on acceptance. Free sample copy and editorial guidelines. No photocopied or simultaneous submissions. Submit seasonal material 3-4 months in advance. Reports on accepted and rejected material "as soon as possible." SASE.

Nonfiction and Photos: Wants how-to, interview, profile, photo, new product and technical pieces. Length: 2-12 ms pages. Pays $125-150/per printed page. Photos purchased with or without accompanying ms and on assignment. Photos purchased without accompanying mss sometimes receive no additional payment. Captions required. Pays $15 for b&w prints and $25 minimum for color.

How To Break In: "Freelance approach should be tailored for specific type and subject matter writer is dealing with. If it is of a basic automotive technical nature, then story slant and info should be aimed at the backyard enthusiasts. If the story is dealing with a specific personality, then it must include a major portion of human interest type of material. What we do is attempt to entertain while educating and offer exceptional dollar value."

KEEPIN' TRACK OF CORVETTES, Box 5445, Reno NV 89513. (702)972-3444. Editor: Frank Kodl. For Corvette owners and enthusiasts. Monthly magazine; 68-84 pages. Estab. 1976. Circ. 58,000. Pays on publication. Buys all rights. Byline given. Submit seasonal/holiday material 2-3 months in advance. Photocopied and previously published submissions OK. SASE. Reports in 3-4 weeks. Free sample copy and writer's guidelines.

Nonfiction: Expose (telling of Corvette problems with parts, etc.); historical (any and all aspects of Corvette developments); how-to (restorations, engine work, suspension, race, swapmeets); humor; informational; interview (query); nostalgia; personal experience; personal opinion; photo feature; profile (query); technical; and travel. Buys 4-5 mss/issue. Query or submit complete ms. Pays $50-200.

Photos: Send photo with ms. Pays $10-35 for b&w contact sheets or negatives; $10-50 for 35mm color transparencies; offers no additional payment for photos with accompanying ms.

MOTOCROSS ACTION MAGAZINE, 16200 Ventura Blvd., Encino CA 91436. (213)981-2317. Editor: Dick Miller. For "primarily young and male, average age 12 to 30, though an increasing number of females is noticed. Education varies considerably. They are interested in off-road racing motorcycles, as either a profession or a hobby." Monthly magazine; 72 pages. Estab. 1973. Circ. 85,000. Buys all rights but may reassign them to author after publication. Buys 20-25 mss/year. Pays on publication. Sample copy $1; free writer's guidelines. Will consider photocopied but no simultaneous submissions. Reports in 1-6 months. Query. SASE.

Nonfiction and Photos: Wants "articles on important national and international motocross events, interviews with top professionals, technical pieces, and in-depth investigative reporting. Short stories and/or poetry will be greeted with a heartfelt yawn. It's best to obtain a copy of the magazine and read recent stories. Stories should be brief and to the point, though flair is appreciated. Top photography is a must." No blatant hero worship. For the coming year, Miller also wants to see articles on "the evolution of motocross from a backyard to a big time, multi-million dollar sport and business." Takes informational, how-to, profile, humor and photo pieces. Length: 500-2,000 words. Pays $25-$200. Photos purchased with accompanying ms with extra payment and on assignment. Captions optional. Pays $8-$10 for b&w, 8x10 glossy prints. $25-$50 for 35mm or 2¼x2¼ color slides.

MOTOR TREND, 8490 Sunset Blvd., Los Angeles CA 90069. (213)657-5100. Editor: John Dianna. For automotive enthusiasts and general interest consumers. Monthly. Circ. 750,000. Buys all rights, except by negotiation. "Fact-filled query suggested for all freelancers." Reports in 30 days. SASE.

Nonfiction: Automotive and related subjects that have national appeal. Emphasis on money-saving ideas for the motorist, high-performance and economy modifications, news tips on new products, pickups, RVs, long-term automotive projects. Packed with facts.

Photos: Buys photos, particularly of prototype cars and assorted automotive matter. 8x10 b&w glossy prints or 35mm and 2¼x2¼ transparencies. Pays $25 minimum for b&w.

Fillers: Automotive newsbreaks. Any length.

MOTORCYCLIST MAGAZINE, Petersen Publishing, 8490 Sunset Blvd., Los Angeles CA 90069. Editor-in-Chief: Dale Boller. Emphasizes motorcycles for motorcycle enthusiasts. Monthly magazine; 100 pages. Estab. 1912. Circ. 150,000. Pays on publication. Buys all rights. Byline given. Submit seasonal/holiday material 90 days in advance. SASE. Reports in 1 month. Free writer's guidelines.

Nonfiction: How-to, humor, informational, interview, new product, photo feature, profile and technical. Buys 12 mss/year. Query. Length: 500-2,000 words. Pays $100/published page.

NORTHEAST VAN, 4x4 & PICKUP, Box 2180, Waterbury CT 06722. (203)755-0158. Editor: John Florian. Estab. 1975. Readers are people interested in trucking and off-roading in the Northeast. Ages vary, though most are in early twenties to late thirties, in the process of customizing a vehicle, or a member of a club. Tabloid newspaper; 32-plus pages. Seasonal features considered. Monthly. Not copyrighted. Pays 20% kill fee. Byline given "by request only." Expects to buy 3 or 4 mss/issue. Pays on publication. Free sample copy and writer's guidelines. Submit seasonal material 3 months in advance. Reports in 2 weeks. Query. SASE.
Nonfiction and Photos: "We publish 'how-to' articles about customizing vans and trucks, features about what others in the Northeast have done to their vehicles, and other features of interest to readers, like truck-ins, club news, maintenance/safety advice. We are open to all ideas. Material should be snappy and easy-reading, yet without a load of cliches." Wants informational, how-to, personal experience, humor, and travel articles. Length: 800-2,000 words. Pays $20-80; $80 maximum with b&w photos. "Good photos are very important to complement any article, though manuscripts will be considered without them." For photos alone, pay is $10 for each b&w 8x10.

PICKUP, VAN & 4WD MAGAZINE, CBS Consumer Publishing, 1499 Monrovia Ave., Newport Beach CA 92663. (714)646-4451. Associate Publisher/Editor: Don E. Brown. Managing Editor: Jon Thompson. For off-road vehicle enthusiasts. Monthly magazine; 104 pages. Estab. 1972. Circ. 250,000. Pays on publication. Buys all rights. Pays kill fee "depending on assignment." Byline given. Submit seasonal/holiday material 3-4 months in advance. Photocopied submissions OK. SASE. Reports 1-2 months. Free writer's guidelines.
Nonfiction: How-to (modifications to light duty trucks, such as extra seats, tool storage, etc.), historical, nostalgia (old restored trucks and 4-wheel drives), technical and travel (4-wheel drive travel only, must show vehicle being used). Buys 4-5 mss/issue. Submit complete ms. Length: 1,000-3,000 words. Pays $75/published page.
Photos: Purchased with accompanying manuscript or on assignment. Captions required. Query for photos. Pays $12.50-75 for 8x10 b&w glossy prints; $25-75 for 35mm or 2¼x2¼ color transparencies; offers no additional payment for photos accepted with ms. Model release required.

RACING CARS, Carl Hungness & Associates, Box 24308, Speedway IN 46224. Editor-in-Chief: John Mahoney. For automobile racing fans; 30-50; blue collar. Quarterly magazine; 64 pages. Estab. 1977. Circ. 5,000. Pays on publication. Buys first North American serial rights. Byline given. Submit seasonal/holiday material two months in advance. SASE. Reports in 3 weeks.
Nonfiction: Historical (on racing in general, race cars, speedways, etc.); humor (anything to do with racing); informational (on racing personalities, profiles or specific enterprises); interviews (major racing personality; hard-hitting; not restricted to questions on racing subjects); nostalgia (old races, drivers, mechanics, cars, etc.); profiles (any racing personalities of national interest). "Remember, we cover only oval racing in America and personalities, cars, tracks associated with it. No road racing, please." Buys 24 mss/year. Query. Length: 2,000-5,000. Pays $50-100.
Photos: Purchased with or without mss or on assignment. Captions required. Send contact sheet, prints or transparencies. Pays $5-15 for 5x7 or 8x10 b&w glossy prints; $25 minimum for color transparencies, any size.

RIDER, 23945 Craftsman Rd., Calabasas CA 91302. Editor: Bill Estes. For owners and prospective buyers of motorcycles to be used for touring, sport riding, and commuting. Bimonthly magazine; 100-120 pages. Estab. 1974. Buys all rights. Pays on acceptance. Sample copy $1; free writer's guidelines. Submit seasonal material 3 months in advance. Photocopied submissions OK. Query. Reports in 1 month. SASE.
Nonfiction and Photos: Articles directly related to motorcycle touring, camping, commuting and sport riding including travel, human interest, safety, novelty, do-it-yourself and technical. "Articles which portray the unique thrill of motorcycling." Should be written in clean, contemporary style aimed at a sharp, knowledgeable reader. Buys informational, how-to, personal experience, profile, historical, nostalgia, personal opinion, travel and technical. Length is flexible. Pays $150-300. Photos purchased with ms with no additional payment. Captions required. "Quality photographs are critical. Graphics are emphasized in *Rider*, and we must have photos with good visual impact."

ROAD & TRACK, 1499 Monrovia Avenue, Newport Beach CA 92663. Editor: John Dinkel. For knowledgeable car enthusiasts. Monthly magazine. Buys all rights, but may be reassigned to author after publication. Query. Reports in 6 weeks. SASE.

Nonfiction: "The editor welcomes freelance material, but if the writer is not thoroughly familiar with the kind of material used in the magazine, he is wasting both his time and the magazine's time. *Road & Track* material is highly specialized and that old car story in the files has no chance of being accepted. More serious, comprehensive and in-depth treatment of particular areas of automotive interest." Payment is minimum 12¢/word but often reaches 20¢/word or more depending upon subject covered and qualifications and experience of author.

ROAD KING MAGAZINE, 233 E. Erie, Chicago IL 60611. (312)664-2959. Editor-in-Chief: Mary Anthony. Managing Editor: Mary Anthony. 20% freelance written. Truck driver leisure reading publication. Quarterly: 48 pages. Estab. 1963. Circ. 200,122. Pays on acceptance. Buys one-time rights. Byline given "always on fiction—if requested on nonfiction—copyright mentioned only if requested." Submit seasonal/holiday material 3 months in advance of issue date. Simultaneous and photocopied submissions OK. Send 41¢ in stamps with a 7x10 SASE. Reports in 3 months. Free sample copy; mention *Writer's Market* in request.

Nonfiction: Trucker slant or general interest; humor; and photo feature. No articles on violence or sex. Buys 8 mss/year. Submit complete ms. Length: 500-2,500 words. Pays $50-100.

Photos: Submit photos with accompanying ms. No additional payment for b&w contact sheets or 2¼x2¼ color transparencies. Captions preferred. Buys one-time rights. Writer must have obtained photo release and release for right to use name and quote.

Fiction: Adventure, historical, humorous, mystery, suspense and western. Especially about truckers. No stories on sex and violence. Buys 4 mss/year. Submit complete ms. Length: 2,500 words maximum. Pays $100.

Poetry: Light verse and traditional. No avant-garde poetry. Buys 2 poems/year. Submit 1 poem/batch. Length: 250 words. Pays $50-100.

Fillers: Jokes, gags, anecdotes and short humor. Buys 20-25/year. Length: 50-500 words. Pays $5-100.

ROAD RIDER, Box 678, South Laguna CA 92677. Editor-in-Chief: Roger Hull. Managing Editor: R.L. Carpenter. Emphasizes touring on motorcycles. Monthly magazine; 96 pages. Estab. 1969. Circ. 35,000. Pays on acceptance. Buys all rights. Submit seasonal/holiday material 4 months in advance. "We schedule seasonal material 1 year in advance." SASE. Reports in 2-3 weeks. Sample copy $1.50; free writer's guidelines.

Nonfiction: "We will consider any articles providing they have of sound base so far as motorcycling knowledge is concerned. Must be cycle-oriented. On expose we need documentation. How-to's usually are of technical nature and require experience. We would love to see more humorous cycle experience type of material. Cycling personalities are also big here. We try to do three or four historical pieces per year. All evaluation/testing pieces are done in house. Travel pieces need good photos; same thing is true on historical or nostalgia material." Buys 48 mss/year. Query or send complete ms. Length: 300-2,000 words. Pays $100-150.

Photos: Send photos with ms. Offers no additional payment for photos with accompanying ms. Uses 5x7 b&w glossy prints; 2x3 color transparencies. Captions and model releases required.

Fiction: "We are open for good, motorcycling fiction which is slanted at a family-type audience. No erotica." Buys 1 ms/year. Send complete ms. Length: 300-2,000 words. Pays $100-150.

Poetry: "We use very little poetry." Buys 3-4/year. Pays $10-15.

How To Break In: "We are an enthusiast publication—as such, it is virtually impossible to sell here unless the writer is also an enthusiast and actively involved in the sport. A good, well-written, brief item dealing with a motorcycle trip, accompanied by top quality b&w photos receives prime time editorial attention. We are always on the lookout for good material from eastern seaboard or Midwest. Best way to hit this market is to request sample and study same prior to submitting. Most of our contributors are Road Rider People. If you are unsure as to what "Road Rider People" refers, you will propably not be able to sell to this magazine."

Rejects: We continue to be overstocked on following: beginner articles (all ages, sexes, etc.), Journal-format travel articles (not welcome), travel articles from southwestern US.

ROAD TEST, Road Test Publishing, Inc., 1440 W. Walnut St., Compton CA 90220. (213)822-1077. Publishers: Bill Quinn and Frank Kirmss. Emphasizes in-depth road test of domestic and foreign cars. Monthly magazine; 72 pages. Estab. 1964. Circ. 80,000. Pays on publication. Buys first North American serial rights. Submit seasonal/holiday material 3

months in advance. SASE. Reports in 3 weeks. Free sample copy.
Nonfiction: How-to (make cars more reliable, responsive, economical, etc.); humor; informational; interview (racing or industry); nostalgia (old car stuff) and profile. Buys 3-4 mss/issue. Query. Length: 1,500-3,000 words. Pays $250-500.
Photos: Purchased with accompanying manuscript. Captions required. Query for photos. B&w 35mm/2¼x2¼ proof sheets and negatives; 35mm kodachrome color. Model release required.

SOUTHERN RV, Intra-South Publications, 6637 Superior Ave., Sarasota FL 33581. (813)921-5687. Editor-in-Chief: George J. Haborak. Emphasizes recreational vehicles and the outdoors for "generally middle-class, middle-aged folks who use recreational vehicles as a way of escaping the daily ratrace." Monthly tabloid; 72 pages. Estab. June 1976. Circ. 30,000. Pays 30 days after publication. Buys all rights, but may reassign following publication. Submit seasonal/holiday material 2 months in advance of issue date. Simltaneous (but not to another publication in the Southeast), photocopied and previously published submissions OK. SASE. Reports in 2 weeks. Free sample copy; mention *Writer's Market* in request.
Nonfiction: General interest (anything related in some way to the great southeastern outdoors scene, fishing, camping, but not hunting); how-to (get the most out of a camping trip, cook camp meals, do something 'outdoorsy' and do it easily); historical (short articles on historical areas of the south are welcome); humor (any tidbit of humor related to camping out or using an RV); personal experience (camping experiences not based on specific locales); photo feature (on the southeast—any area); technical (semi-technical how-to-fix-it articles would fit well occasionally); and travel (any travel experience relating to the southeast and RV's). Buys 6 mss/issue. Submit complete ms. Length: 800-2,000 words. Pays $15-25.
Photos: "We like graphically exciting layouts. They lend credence to the stories we publish." State availability of photos with query. Offers no additional payment for photos accepted with ms, "they just make for a better article and better chances of being published." Uses 3x5 glossy b&w prints. Captions required. Buys all rights, but may reassign following publication.
Fiction: "We would consider humorous fiction as long as it is tied into the outdoors scene in some way." Query. Length: 800-1,500 words. Pays $10-20.

SPORT TRUCKING, (formerly *1001 Truck and Van Ideas Magazine*), Argus Publishers Corp., 12301 Wilshire Blvd., Los Angeles CA 90025. (213)820-3601. Editor-in-Chief: Peter Dupre. 40% freelance written. Emphasizes use of trucks, RVs, vans and mini-trucks for drivers who use, modify, customize and 'go fun truckin' with these vehicles. Monthly magazine; 96 pages. Estab. 1975. Circ. 200,000. Pays either on acceptance or publication. Phone queries OK. Submit seasonal/holiday material 3 months in advance. SASE. Reports in 2 weeks. Free writer's guidelines.
Nonfiction: How-to (on building interiors for custom vans and pickups, engine swaps, suspension work, etc.); informational; interview, new product, photo feature (for Van Idea Notebook and Tricks for Trucks); technical (step-by-step) and travel (tie in with type of vehicle). "No copy without photos, and no 'look, world, here's my very own custom van I built and captured on my polaroid for you' articles." Buys 6-7 mss/issue. Query. Length: 1,500 maximum. Pays $50-75/page.
Photos: Steve Reyes, Photo Editor. Photos purchased with or without accompanying ms or on assignment. Captions required. Pays $10-25 for 5x7 minimum b&w glossy prints; $25-75 for 2¼x2¼ or 35mm color transparencies. Total purchase price for ms includes payment for photos. Model release required.

STOCK CAR RACING MAGAZINE, 67 Peach Orchard Rd., Burlington MA 01803. Editor: Dick Berggren. For stock car racing fans and competitors. Monthly magazine; 84 pages. Estab. 1966. Circ. 120,000. Pays on publication. Buys all rights. Byline given. SASE. Reports in 2-6 weeks.
Nonfiction: "Uses primarily nonfiction on stock car drivers, cars, and races. We are looking for Canadian and California people. We are interested in the story behind the story in stock car and sprint car racing. Technical articles are also sought." Query. Buys 75 mss/year. Length: 100-6,000 words. Pays $10-175.
Photos: State availability of photos Pays $15 for 8x10 b&w photos; $50-150 for 35mm or larger color transparencies. Captions required.

STREET RODDER MAGAZINE, TRM Publications, Inc., 2145 W. La Palma, Anaheim CA 92801. Editorial Director: Bud Lang. For the automotive enthusiast with an interest in street-driven, modified old cars. Monthly magazine; 76 pages. Estab. 1972. Circ. 105,000. Buys all rights, but will reassign rights to author after publication. Buys 25-35 mss/year. Pays on acceptance. Sample copy $1.50; free writer's guidelines. No photocopied or simultaneous submissions. Reports in 1 month. Query or submit complete ms. SASE.

Nonfiction and Photos: "We need coverage of events and cars that we can't get to. Street rod events (rod runs); how-to technical articles; features on individual street rods. We don't need features on local (Southern California) street rods, events or shops. We stress a straightforward style; accurate and complete details; easy to understand (though not 'simple') technical material. Need good, clear, complete and well-photographed technical and how-to articles on pertinent street rod modifications or conversions. We very seldom accept a story without photos." Length: 250-1500 words. Pays $35 minimum. Average payment for 2-page feature with 5x7 or 8x10 b&w photos: $100.

SUPER STOCK AND DRAG ILLUSTRATED, Lopez Publications, 205 S. Whiting St., Suite 502, Alexandria VA 22304. Editor: Mike Towell. For "mostly blue-collar males between 12-35 years old; high performance, drag racing oriented." Monthly magazine; 80 pages. Estab. 1964. Circ. 140,000. Pays on publication. Buys all rights, but may reassign following publication. Byline given. Simultaneous and photocopied submissions OK. SASE. Reports in 2-6 weeks. Sample copy $1.50.

Nonfiction: Interview (with prominent drag racers); profile (on local or national drag cars); photo features (on drag racing cars or racing events); and technical. Buys 120 mss/year. Query or submit complete ms. Length: 500-5,000 words. Pays $50-250.

Photos: Purchased with accompanying ms. Captions required. Submit prints or transparencies. Pays $10 for 8x10 b&w glossy prints; $50-150 for 35mm color transparencies.

Fiction: Adventure, humorous. Must be drag racing oriented. Submit complete ms. Length: 500-5,000 words. Pays $50-250.

VAN LIFE AND FAMILY TRUCKING, Trailer Life Publishing Co., 23901 Agoura Rd., Agoura CA 91301. (213)991-4980. Editorial Director: Alice Robison. Managing Editor: Bob Howells. Emphasizes recreational trucking for young family men and women right on through to older retired folks who enjoy using their vans, trucks, four-wheel drive vehicles and campers in a recreational context. Monthly magazine; 100 pages. Estab. April 1978. Pays on publication. Buys all rights. Phone queries OK. Submit seasonal/holiday material 5 months in advance. Photocopied submissions OK. SASE. Reports in 4 weeks. Sample copy $1.50; free writer's guidelines.

Nonfiction: General interest (on travel pieces concentrating on areas or journeys ideal for vans/trucks); how-to (do simple, detailed, low-cost modifications to vans, trucks or campers with b&w photos, captions, and/or drawings); and personality pieces (on van/truck hobbies, details on interesting conversions, product evaluations, examinations of recreational trucking issues).

VAN, PICKUP AND OFF-ROAD WORLD MAGAZINE, Hi-Torque Publications, Inc., 16200 Ventura Blvd., Encino CA 91436. Editor-in-Chief: Chris Hosford. Managing Editor: Rik Paul. 15% freelance written. Emphasizes custom vans, trucks and off-road vehicles for enthusiasts. Monthly magazine; 76 pages. Estab. 1973. Circ. 75,000. Pays on publication. Buys all rights. Byline given. Submit seasonal/holiday material 4 months in advance. Photocopied submissions OK. SASE. Reports in 3 weeks. Sample copy $1.50; free writer's guidelines.

Nonfiction: Feature vans: (photo features with brief description); how-to (interior/exterior customizing and engine/mechanical with emphasise on economy); and photo feature (b&w, color with short article on custom vans, trucks or off-road vehicles in action). Buys 30-50 mss/year. Query. Length: 200-1,000 words. Pays $40 maximum/page.

Photos: Purchased with or without accompanying manuscript or on assignment. Captions required. Submit contact sheet or transparencies. Pays $5-10 for 8x10 b&w glossy prints; $10-25 for 35mm or 2¼x2¼ color transparencies. Total purchase price for ms includes payment for photos. Model release required.

Aviation

Publications in this section aim at professional and private pilots, and at aviation enthusiasts in general. Magazines intended for passengers of commercial airlines are grouped in a separate In-Flight category. Technical aviation and space journals, and publications for airport operators, aircraft dealers and other aviation businessmen are listed under Aviation and Space in the Trade Journals section.

AIR LINE PILOT, 1625 Massachussetts Ave. NW, Washington DC 20036. (202)797-4176. Editor-in-Chief: C.V. Glines. Production Engineer: Anne Kelleher. Emphasizes commercial aviation. Monthly magazine; 56 pages. Estab. 1931. Circ. 43,000. Pays on acceptance. Buys all rights, but may reassign following publication. Submit seasonal material 4 months in advance. SASE. Reports in 4 weeks. Free sample copy and writer's guidelines.
Nonfiction: Historical (aviation/personal or equipment, aviation firsts); informational (aviation safety, related equipment or aircraft aids); interview (aviation personality); nostalgia (aviation history); photo feature; profile (airline pilots; must be ALPA members); and technical. Buys 25 mss/year. Query. Length: 1,000-2,500 words. Pays $100-300.
Photos: Purchased with or without accompanying ms. Captions required. Query. Pays $10-25 for 8x10 b&w glossy prints; $20-250 for 35mm or 2¼x2¼ color transparencies.
How To Break In: "Unless a writer is experienced in aviation, he is more likely to score with a pilot profile or aviation historical piece."

THE AOPA PILOT, 7315 Wisconsin Ave., Washington DC 20014. (301)654-0500. Editor: Edward G. Tripp. For plane owners, pilots, and the complete spectrum of the general aviation industry. Official magazine of the Aircraft Owners and Pilots Association. Monthly. Circ. 225,000. Pays on acceptance. Reports in 2 months. SASE.
Nonfiction: Factual articles up to 2,500 words that will inform, educate and entertain flying enthusiasts ranging from the student to the seasoned professional pilot. These pieces should be generously illustrated with good quality photos, diagrams or sketches. Quality and accuracy essential. Topics covered include maintenance, how-to features, reports on new or unusual aircraft or aeronautical equipment, places to fly (travel), governmental policies (local, state or federal) relating to general aviation. Additional features on weather in relation to flying, legal aspects of aviation, flight education, pilot fitness, aviation history and aero clubs are used occasionally. Short features of 100-300 words written around a single photograph, and strong photo features. Pays $400 maximum.
Photos: Pays $25 minimum for each photo or sketch used. Exceptionally good cover color transparencies also purchased.

AVIATION MAGAZINE (formerly *Great Lakes Aircraft Bulletin*, *North Atlantic Aircraft Bulletin*, and *Southern Aviation Times*), Data Publications, Box 186, Brookfield CT 06804. (203)789-5802. Editor: Robert S. Dorr. Published in 3 regional editions: Great Lakes, North Atlantic, and Southern. For further details, see listing for *Flightline Times*.

AVIATION QUARTERLY, Box 606, Plano TX 75074. Publisher: Brad Bierman. Editor: David Hadeler. For the serious aviation enthusiast, interested in the history of aviation. Quarterly; hardbound volume with four-color illustrations. Estab. 1975. Circ. 7,000. Buys all rights. Pays 50% kill fee. Byline given "only if commissioned." Pays on acceptance. Phone queries OK. Submit seasonal/holiday material 4-5 months in advance. Simultaneous, photocopied and previously published submissions OK. SASE. Reports in 2-4 weeks. Sample copy $10; free writer's guidelines.
Nonfiction: Historical (on any historical aspect of aviation—past, present or future); interview (with aviation pioneers, those connected with aviation's history); nostalgia (on any aviation-oriented piece); personal experience (on any historical piece); photo feature (especially photo essays on any of the classic airplanes); and profile (on any aviation/history-oriented piece). "All our articles must be well-written and well-documented with historical photos. Articles supported by fewer than a dozen photographs have little chance of making it." Buys 20 mss/year. Query or send complete ms. Length: 1,500-10,000 words. Pays $100-600.
Photos: Send photos with ms. Buys any size b&w or 2x3 and 4x5 color transparencies. Payment for all photography work varies, and is negotiated. Captions preferred.

AVIATION TRAVEL, Box 606, Piano TX 75074. Editor: David A. Hadeler. For owners of business and private aircraft who are interested in fishing, hunting, boating, photography, golf, sightseeing, beaches, resorts, outdoor and other sports. Buys all rights. Buys about 30-50 mss/year. Pays on acceptance. Sample copy $2. Will consider photocopied submissions. Submit seasonal material 3 to 4 months in advance. Query or submit complete ms. Reports in 2 months. SASE.
Nonfiction and Photos: "Short travel articles—where to go, what to see and do. We may feature a general area or special activity, event, or resort which must be accessible by private or business plane. The US, Canada, Mexico and the Bahamas are preferred. Airport and flight info are helpful, but not required. The style should be light and nontechnical. Stories must be

short, informational, and specific enough to be helpful to the traveler. Destinations must be emphasized, rather than flight. Dates, admission, what to take, etc., increase the value of a story. We're the only travel-oriented aviation magazine, featuring places and events accessible by general aviation. We're interested in fly-in wilderness, fishing, hunting, golfing and camping stories at specific locations. Each issue features items of particular interest during the period immediately following." Buys informational articles, how-to's, personal experience articles, humor, historical articles, photo features, travel pieces and technical articles. Length: 200-1,200 words. Pay "varies: about 5¢ per word, depending on subject and quality." Photos purchased with or without mss; captions required. Pay "$5 and up, depending on photo, for b&w glossy prints 5x7 and larger." Pays $5 and up, "depending on photo and use for transparencies only."

EXXON AIR WORLD, Exxon International Co., Division of Exxon Corp., 115 Spring Valley Rd., Ossining NY 10562. Editor: Warren H. Goodman. 40% freelance written. For worldwide audience of technical and semitechnical aviation readers. Quarterly. Byline given. Pays on publication. Query. Reports "quickly." SASE.
Nonfiction and Photos: Uses articles on aviation in action, worldwide; especially the offbeat aviation operation; technical articles. "No military subjects." Style should be "unsensational, good 'international' English, informative accurate." Length 300-2,000 words. Must be accompanied with quality good photos. Pays about 10¢/word. Photos must be of interesting subjects, using "striking composition," and adequately captioned. Pays $10 minimum for photos.

FLIGHTLINE TIMES, Data Publications, Box 186, Brookfield CT 06804. (203)743-7721. Editor: Mark M. Lacagnina. Emphasizes national issues and broad interest features from within the aviation community of pilots, student pilots, airplane owners, controllers, aviation specialists, etc. Weekly tabloid; 16 pages. Estab. 1974. Pays on publication. Buys all rights. Byline given. Phone queries OK. Submit seasonal/holiday material 1 month in advance. Photocopied submissions OK. SASE. Reports in 4 weeks.
Nonfiction: Exposes (on government and industry as their decisions affect the lives of aviation people); how-to (e.g., how to fly in certain tricky conditions, such as wind shear); informational; interviews (with outstanding, important and unusual people in aviation); travel (about the features—resorts, museums, vacation spots, etc.—of places to fly.) "Our outlook is not as formal as most publications. We would rather have the material in hand to look at than to answer queries and talk about writing. We have been stung too many times by people who like to promise, but don't come across with the story. On the other hand, we provide special help and advice for nonwriters when they show they have a commitment to fair, quick and accurate aviation reporting." Buys 10 mss/issue. Length: 800 words maximum. Pays $1/column inch (maximum $10) for news stories; $20 for features at least 15 column inches long.
Photos: Purchased with or without mss. Captions required. Pays $2.50-5 for b&w or color prints.
Columns/Departments: Restaurant reviews. Buys 1/issue. Send complete ms. Length: 400-800 words. Pays $20. Open to suggestions for new columns/departments.

FLYING, Ziff-Davis Publishing Co., 1 Park Ave., New York NY 10016. (212)725-3799. Editor-in-Chief: Richard L. Collins. Editorial Coordinator: Melissa Gray. 5% freelance written. For private or commercial pilots involved with, or interested in, the use of general-aviation aircraft (not airline or military) for business and pleasure. Monthly magazine; 128 pages. Estab. 1927. Circ. 398,892. Pay on acceptance. Buys all rights and first North American serial rights. Phone queries OK. Submit seasonal/holiday material 4 months in advance of issue date. SASE. Reports in 3 weeks.
Nonfiction: How-to (piloting and other aviation techniques, including a monthly series of personal experiences, "I Learned About Flying From That"); personal experience ("I Learned About Flying From That" department); and technical (aviation-related). No articles on "My Trip" travel accounts, or historical features. Buys about 12 mss/year. Submit complete ms. Length: 750-3,500 words. Pays $50-1,000.

GENERAL AVIATION NEWS, Box 1094, Snyder TX 79549. (915)573-6318. Editor-in-Chief: M. Gene Dow. 20% freelance written. Biweekly tabloid; 40 pages. Estab. 1949. Circ. 30,000. Pays on publication. Buys all rights. Byline given "only on features and short features, not on straight news stories." Phone queries OK. Submit seasonal/holiday material 1 month in advance of issue date. Photocopied submissions OK. SASE. Reports in 4 weeks. Sample copy 50¢; writer's guidelines for return postage.
Nonfiction: General interest (aviation subjects that would be of interest to nationwide, not

regional, audience; historical (on general aviation history, not including "War Birds"); how-to (fly better or move safely or how to use any type aviation equipment); inspirational (successful aviation businesses, pilots and airport operations); interview (well-known pilots); new product (new aviation projects); nostalgia (pioneer pilot and aircraft); personal experience (flying experiences); photo feature (unique aviation subjects); profile (aviation businessman); and technical (aviation, equipment or pilot techniques). No articles on commercial or military airplanes. Buys 50 mss/year. Submit complete ms. Length: 2,000 words. Pays $25/1,000 words.
Photos: Send photo material with accompanying ms. Pays $3-5 for 4x5 b&w or color prints. Captions required. Buys all rights.

PLANE & PILOT MAGAZINE, Werner & Werner Corp., 606 Wilshire, Suite 100, Santa Monica CA 90401. (213)451-1423. Editorial Director: Steve Werner. 75% freelance written. Emphasizes all aspects of general aviation. Monthly magazine; 80 pages. Estab. 1965. Circ. 75,000. Pays on publication. Buys all rights. Phone queries OK. Submit seasonal/holiday material 6 months in advance. SASE. Reports in 3 months. Sample copy $1.50.
Nonfiction: How-to articles (emergency procedures); informational (proficiency); humor (strongly encouraged); personal experience (regular features on "Flight I'll Never Forget"). Buys 150 mss/year. Query. Length: 1,000-2,200 words. Pays $50-250.
Photos: Purchased with mss; no additional payment. Only uses 8x10 b&w. Prefers 2¼x2¼ or larger slides, but will consider 35mm. Query.

PRIVATE PILOT, Macro/Comm Corp., Box 4030, San Clemente CA 92672. (714)498-1600. Editor: Dennis Shattuck. 60% freelance written. For owner/pilots of private aircraft, for student pilots and others aspiring to attain additional ratings and experience. Estab. 1955. Circ. 100,000. Buys first North American serial rights. Buys about 30-60 mss/year. Pays after publication. Sample copy $2; writer's guidelines for SASE. Will consider photocopied submissions if guaranteed original. No simultaneous submissions. Reports in 30 days. Query. SASE.
Nonfiction and Photos: Material on techniques of flying, developments in aviation, product and specific airplane test reports, travel by aircraft, development and use of airports. All must be related to general aviation field. "Freelancer must know the subject about which he is writing; use good grammar; know the publication for which he's writing; remember that we try to relate to the middle segment of the business/pleasure flying public. We see too many 'first flight' type of articles. Our market is more sophisticated than that. Most writers do not do enough research on their subject. Would like to see more material on business-related flying, more on people involved in flying." Length: 1,000-4,000 words. Pays $25-$200. Material is also used in the following columns: Business Flying, Homebuilt/Experimental Aircraft, Pilot's Logbook. Length: 1,000 words. Pays $50-$100. 8x10 b&w glossy prints purchased with mss or on assignment. Pays $15. Color transparencies of any size are used for the cover. Pays $100.

WINGS MAGAZINE, (formerly *Canadian Wings*), Corvus Publishing Group, Ltd., 203-2003 McKnight Blvd., Calgary, Alberta, Canada T2E 6L2. (403)277-2337. Editor-in-Chief: Wayne D. Ralph. Emphasizes aviation: private, commercial and military. The audience ranges from age 15-70 and are predominently people employed in aviation or with a hobbyist's interest in the field. Monthly magazine; 52 pages. Estab. 1958. Circ. 8,500. Pays on publication. Buys all rights, but may reassign following publication. Phone queries OK. SASE. Sample copy $1.50.
Nonfiction: Historical (mainly Canadian history); how-to (technical); informational (technical aviation); interview (Canadian personalities in aviation circles); new product, photo feature; profile (Canadian individuals); technical; travel (flying-related); aircraft handling tests and technical evaluation on new products. Query. Length: 500-2,000 words. Pays $50-200.
Photos: Purchased with or without accompanying ms. Captions required. Query for photos. Pays $5-20 for 5x7 b&w glossy prints; $25-50 for 35mm color transparencies. Total purchase price for ms includes payment for photos. Buys one-time rights.

Black

General interest publications for blacks are listed in this category. Additional markets for black-oriented material are in the following sections: Business and Finance Publications; Confession Publications; Juvenile Publications; Literary and Little Publications; Poetry Publica-tions; Politics and World Affairs Publications; Sport and Outdoor Publications; Teen and Young Adult Publications; Theater, Movie, TV and Entertainment Publications; Play Publishers; Book Publishers; Greeting Card Publishers; and Syndicates.

BLACK FORUM MAGAZINE, Box 1090, Bronx NY 10451. Editor-in-Chief: Julia Coaxum. Managing Editor: Horace Mungin. 50% freelance written. For unpublished black writers interested in literary subjects. Semiannual magazine; 48 pages. Estab. 1975. Circ. 2,000. Pays on publication. Buys first North American serial rights. Byline given. Photocopied submissions OK. SASE. Reports in 1-2 months. Sample copy $1.25; free writer's guidelines.

Nonfiction: Informational; interview (with black writers, artists, etc.); and profile. Buys 2 mss/issue. Submit complete ms. Length: 750-1,000 words. Pays $15 minimum.

Photos: Reginald Ward, Photo Editor. Purchased on assignment. Query for photos.

Columns/Departments: Movie, book, theater and dance reviews. Submit complete ms. Open to suggestions for new columns/departments; address to Horace Mungin.

Fiction: Fred Richardson, Fiction Editors. Adventure, experimental, historical, humorous and suspense. Buys 2 mss/issue. Submit complete ms. Length: 500-750 words. Pays $15 maximum.

Poetry: Revish Windham, Zandra Holmes, Poetry Editors. Avant-garde, free verse, light verse and traditional. Limit submissions to batches of 5. Length: maximum 20 lines. Pays in copies of magazine.

Fillers: Puzzles (subject should deal with black history).

How To Break In: "All material will be personally read by the editor of each department. Comments and notations will accompany all returned material. We ask that freelancers read and note our comments and continue to send in material."

CORE, 1916-38 Park Ave., New York NY 10037. (212)694-9300. Editor: Doris Innis. Publication of the Congress of Racial Equality. Estab. 1970. Bimonthly. Circ. 30,000. Rights acquired vary with author and material. Uses about 60 freelance articles/year. "Most of our articles are donated." Free sample copy. Will consider photocopied submissions. Submit seasonal/holiday material at least 2 months in advance. Query. Reports in 6 months. SASE.

Nonfiction and Photos: "Articles about or related to the black movement, black people's oppression, projected or attempted solutions. Also profiles of Black Movement people. Interviews. Health, food, books, sports. Also interested in travel, fashion, movies or African affairs. The writer's style and emphasis is up to him. We like variety. Of course, it helps if his outlook is black nationalist, but it's not mandatory. We try to make black nationalism (a little understood concept) digestible for the common man as well as the intellectual. Most articles are donated." Length: 500-5,000 words. Pays $25 for b&w photos on assignment. Captions optional.

Fiction: Should relate to magazine's theme. Length: 500-5,000 words. "Most are donated."

Poetry and Fillers: Free verse and avant-garde forms. Length: open. Short humor and anecdotes. Length: 500-1,500 words. "Most are donated."

THE CRISIS, 1790 Broadway, New York NY 10019. (212)245-2100. Editor: Warren Marr II. 80% freelance written. Official publication of the NAACP. "Our audience includes government officials, schools and libraries, representative of the leadership group in the black community across the nation, and persons involved in the broad area of human relations." Estab. 1910. Monthly (June/July, August/September issues are combined). Circ. 114,000. Acquires all rights. Byline given. "In most situations, upon request, we will grant permission to reprint provided proper credit is included." Uses 50 freelance mss a year. "Our payment to writers at this time is in contributor's copies only." Submit complete ms. Reports on material within a month. SASE.

Nonfiction: "Articles dealing with civil rights and general welfare of Negroes and other minorities." Informational, interview, profile, historical, think pieces, exposes. Length: 3,000 words maximum.

Fiction: Short stories with a constructive racial theme.

Poetry: Traditional forms, blank verse and free verse. Should relate to magazine's theme. Length: 40 lines maximum.

How To Break In: 'What we don't get and would appreciate is material dealing with blacks in the arts and sciences. And that means all the arts —performing, graphic, etc. We haven't had any material on blacks in the classical music area, for instance. When dealing with other minorities, stick to material that is applicable across the board—to minorities in general. For example, how does the struggle of a Puerto Rican writer relate to the struggle of all third world writers?"

EBONY MAGAZINE, 820 S. Michigan Ave., Chicago IL 60605. Editor: John H. Johnson. Managing Editor: Charles L. Sanders. For black readers of the US, Africa, and the Caribbean. Monthly. Circ. 1,300,000. Buys all rights. Buys about 20 mss/year. Pays on publication. Submit seasonal material 2 months in advance. Query. Usually reports in less than 30 days, but this varies. SASE.

Nonfiction: Achievement and human interest stories about, or of concern to, black readers. Photo essays, interviews, think pieces, profiles, humor, inspirational and historical pieces are bought. Length: 2,500 words minimum. Pays $150 minimum.

Photos: Purchased with mss, and with captions only. Buys 8x10 glossy prints, color transparencies, 35mm color. Submit negatives and contact sheets when possible. Photo stories. Pays $150 minimum.

ESSENCE, 1500 Broadway, New York NY 10036. (212)730-4260. Editor-in-Chief: Marcia Ann Gillespie. Editor: Daryl R. Alexander. Managing Editor: Teadra Allen. 70% freelance written. Emphasizes black women. Monthly magazine; 150 pages. Estab. May 1970. Circ. 600,000. Pays on acceptance. Makes assignments on work-for-hire basis. 3-month lead time. Pays 25% kill fee. Byline given. Submit seasonal/holiday material 6 months in advance of issue date. SASE. Reports in 6-8 weeks. Sample copy $1; free writer's guidelines.

Nonfiction: Exposé; general interest; historical; how-to; humor; interview; personal experience; arts; financial; business-career; health; education; diet; nutrition; personal opinion; profile; and travel. Buys 200 mss/year. Query. Length: 1,500-6,000 words. Pays $200-850.

Photos: Ron Albrecht, art director. State availability of photos with query. Pays $50-300 for b&w contact sheets; $100-600 for color transparencies. Captions and model release required.

Columns/Departments: Daryl Alexander. Entertainment; Health; Travel; and Work. Query. Length: 1,500-2,000 words. Pays $100 minimum.

Fiction: Adventure; experimental; fantasy; humorous; romance; and condensed and serialized novels. Buys 33 mss/year. Submit complete ms. Length: 1,500 words. Pays $200 minimum.

JET, 820 S. Michigan Ave., Chicago IL 60605. Executive Editor: Robert E. Johnson. For black readers interested in current news and trends. Weekly. Circ. 750,000. Pays 100% kill fee. No byline. Study magazine before submitting. SASE.

Nonfiction and Photos: Articles on topics of current, timely interest to black readers. News items and features: religion, education, African affairs, civil rights, politics and entertainment. Buys informational articles, interviews, profiles, spot news, photo pieces and personal experience articles. Length: varies. Payment negotiated.

MISS BLACK AMERICA MAGAZINE, 24 W. Chelten Ave., Phildelphia PA 19144. Executive Editor: Norman Hayes. Service magazine for black women between the ages of 18 and 34. Quarterly magazine; 48 pages. Estab. 1969. Circ. 125,000. Pays on publication. Buys all rights. SASE. Reports in 1 month. Sample copy and writer's guidelines $1.

Nonfiction: Profiles of young black women who have made significant achievements in the arts, entertainment, business or professions; how-to articles on fashions, beauty, careers, human relationships, money management, or any area of interest to young women. Submit complete ms. Length: 1,500-2,500 words. Pays $25.

Photos: Purchased with accompanying ms only. Pays $15/8x10 b&w print. Model release required.

SEPIA, 1220 Harding St., Ft. Worth TX 76102. Editor: A.S. "Doc" Young. For "black readers of all age groups and interests." Monthly. Circ. 160,000. Buys all rights. Buys about 75 mss/year. Pays on acceptance. Will send a sample copy to a writer for $1. Will consider photocopied submissions. Submit seasonal material 3 months in advance. Reports in 1 month. Query. SASE.

Nonfiction and Photos: "We are in the market for well-written, provocative, factual articles on the role of black Americans in all phases of American life. We look for a good writing style, no different from any popularly written publication. We are constantly in need of articles with current news value, but strictly projected for future publication. In this respect, we specifically look for queries on events that will be in the news when our magazine reaches its readers. Articles may be on interesting personalities, entertainers, sports figures, human interest or controversial topics. We will consider any subject if it has good reader appeal for a black audience. It cannot be overemphasized that contributors should study recent issues for general content and style." Buys interviews, profiles, historical articles, exposes, coverage of successful business operations, photo essays. Length: 3,000 words. Pays $200-$250. Photos are required with mss. B&w glossy prints, color transparencies.

SOUL NEWSMAGAZINE, Soul Publications, Inc., 8271 Melrose Ave., Suite 208. Los Angeles CA 90046. (213)653-7775. Editor: Regina Jones. Managing Editor: Leonard Pitts. *Soul* is a national entertainment newsmagazine geared to keep one aware of what is happening on the Black entertainment scene. Biweekly tabloid; 24 pages. Estab. April 1966. Circ. 175,000. Pays on acceptance. Buys one-time rights. Pays 20% kill fee. Byline given. Phone queries OK. Submit seasonal/holiday material 3 months in advance. SASE. Reports in 1 month. Free sample copy.

Nonfiction: Interview, new product (album reviews) and photo feature. Buys 120 mss/year. Query or send clips of previously published work. Length: 1,000-2,250 words. Pays $25-150.

Photos: State availability of photos. Pays $5-20 for 8x10 b&w matt prints; $25-50 for 35mm color transparencies. Captions preferred; model releases required.

Business and Finance

National and regional publications of general interest to businessmen are listed here. Those in the National grouping cover national business trends, and include some material on the general theory and practice of business and financial management. Those in the Regional grouping report on the business climates of specific regions.

Magazines that use material on national business trends and the general theory and practice of business and financial management, but which have a technical or professional slant, are classified in the Trade Journals section, under the Business Management, Finance, Industrial Management, or Management and Supervision categories.

BARRON'S NATIONAL BUSINESS AND FINANCIAL WEEKLY, 22 Cortlandt St., New York NY 10007. (212)285-5245. Editor: Robert M. Bleiberg. For business and investment people. Weekly. Free sample copy. Buys all rights. Pays on publication. SASE.

Nonfiction: Articles about various industries with investment point of view; shorter articles on particular companies, their past performance and future prospects as related to industry trends for "News and Views" column. "Must be suitable for our specialized readership." Length: 2,000 words or more. Pays $200 to $500 for articles; $100 and up for News and Views material. Articles considered on speculation only.

How To Break In: "News and Views might be a good way, but the key thing to remember here is these pieces must be fully researched and thoroughly documented."

BUSINESS WEEK, 1221 Avenue of the Americas, New York NY 10020. Does not solicit freelance material.

BUSINESS WORLD MAGAZINE, Advertising World Specialty House Corp., 35 King St. N., Waterloo, Ontario, Canada N2J 3Z6. (519)886-5370. Editor: Ron Mason. Managing Editor: D.H. Peters. "Our audience consists of such people as the local and regional retailer, franchisers, manufacturers, distributors, sales people from every industry, people from the service industry, auto and farm equipment dealers, lawyers, accountants and other professionals." Magazine published every 6 weeks; 64 pages. Estab. 1977. Circ. 32,000. Pays on publication. Buys all rights and makes assignments on a work-for-hire basis. Pays negotiable kill fee. Byline given. Phone queries OK. Submit seasonal/holiday material 2 months in advance. Photocopied and previously published submissions OK. SAE and International Reply Coupons. Reports in 2 weeks. Free sample copy and writer's guidelines. Deadline: 15th of each month.

Nonfiction: General interest, historical, how-to, inspirational, personal opinion and profile—all must relate to business. Also wants expose, interview, travel, new product, personal experience and photo feature. "We are seeking articles that outline new innovative methods of marketing. We are also seeking articles which reflect a broad realm of interest areas: media, fashion, dining, travel, office, financial and building themes. We welcome feature articles reflecting both the national and local scene, new products, turn-around, and, more importantly, the entrepeneurial success story." Buys 8 mss/issue. Query with clips of published work or submit complete ms. Length: 200-4,000 words. Pays $25-125. Higher rates negotiable depending on quality, depth and length.

Photos: State availability of photos. Pays $15-50 for b&w contact sheets and 2¼x2¼ color transparencies. Captions and model release required.

Columns/Departments: Opinion: An opinion concerning anything in the business market place. Buys 1 ms/issue. Send complete ms or query with clips from published work. Length: 200-600 words. Pays $25 maximum.

Fillers: Jokes, anecdotes, short humor and cartoons. Buys 5/issue. Length: 50-200 words. Pays $5.

COMMODITY JOURNAL, American Association of Commodity Traders, 10 Park St., Concord NH 03001. Editor: Arthur N. Economou. For investors interested in commodity trading based on cash forward and option markets, alternative energy sources and foreign currencies. Bimonthly tabloid: 24 pages. Estab. September 1965. Circ. 105,000. Pays on publication. Buys all rights. Byline given. Written queries OK. Photocopied and previously published submissions OK. SASE. Reports in 1 month. Free sample copy and writer's guidelines.
Nonfiction: Technical (alternative energy sources; commodity and foreign currency, trading, investing and hedging; commodity markets and foreign currency trends; written intelligible for general public). "We are not interested in articles concerning the conventional futures market, except insofar as the spot or cash-based markets privide a better alternative." Buys 4 mss/issue. Query. Length: 1,000-2,500 words. Pays 5¢/word.

DOLLARS & SENSE, National Taxpayers Union, 325 Pennsylvania Ave. SE, Washington DC 20003. Editor-in-Chief: Adrian Day. 10% freelance written. Emphasizes taxes and government spending for a diverse readership. Monthly newspaper; 8-12 pages. Estab. 1970. Circ. 90,000. Pays on publication. Buys all rights. Submit seasonal/holiday material 1 month in advance. Previously published submissions OK. SASE. Free sample copy and writer's guidelines.
Nonfiction: Expose dealing with wasteful government spending and excessive regulation of the economy. Buys 10 mss/year. Query. Length: 500-1,500 words. Pays $15-100. "We look for original material on subjects overlooked by the national press and other political magazines. Probably the best approach is to take a little-known area of government mismanagement and examine it closely. The articles we like most are those that examine a federal program that is not only poorly managed and wasteful, but also self-defeating, hurting the very people it is designed to help. We are also interested in the long term harm done by different kinds of taxation. Articles on IRS harassment and abuses are always needed and welcome. We have no use for financial or investment advice or broad philosophical pieces."

DUN'S REVIEW, Dun & Bradstreet Publications Corp., 666 5th Ave., New York NY 10019. (212)489-2200. Editor: Clem Morgello. Emphasizes business, management and finances for a readership "concentrated among senior executives of those companies that have a net worth of $1 million or more." Monthly magazine; 90-140 pages. Estab. 1893. Circ. 260,000. Pays on acceptance. Buys all rights. Submit seasonal/holiday material 3 months in advance. Photocopied submissions OK. Reports in 1 month. Sample copy $1.50.
Nonfiction: Exposé (business and government), historical (business; i.e., law or case history), management (new trends, composition), finance and accounting, informational (business and government), interview (assigned only), personal opinion (submitted to The Forum, opinion from high-ranked sources), and profile (companies, turnarounds, etc). Buys 12 mss/year. Query. Length: 1,500-3,000 words. Pays $200 minimum.
Photos: Gene Landino, Art Director. Purchased with accompanying ms. Query. Pays $75 for b&w photos; $150 for color.
Columns/Departments: Footnote (historical or important issues impacting business world), Spotlight, Forum, and The Economy (by invitation only). Buys 1 ms/issue. Query. Length: 1,000-1,500 words. Pays $200.

THE EXECUTIVE FEMALE DIGEST, NAFE Publishing Co., 160 E. 56th St., 2nd Floor, New York NY 10022. (212)371-8086. Editor: Karin Abarbanel. Associate Editor: Susan Strecker. Emphasizes "upbeat and useful career and financial information for the upwardly mobile female." Bimonthly magazine; 60 pages. Estab. 1978. Circ. 35,000. Byline given. Pays on publication. Submit seasonal/holiday material 6 months in advance. Simultaneous and photocopied submissions OK. SASE. Reports in 3 months. Sample copy $1.50; free writer's guidelines.
Nonfiction: Profile (of successful working women and the story of their careers) and technical (stories of women entrepreneurs, and career advancement and financial planning for women). "Articles on any aspect of career advancement and financial planning for women are welcomed." Sample topics: investment, coping with inflation, money-saving ideas, financial planning, business communication, and career goal setting and advancement. No negative or radical "women's lib" material. Buys 1-2 mss/issue. Query. Length: 800-1,500 words. Pays $50 minimum.
Columns/Departments: Profiles (interviews with successful women in a wide range of fields); Entrepreneur's Corner (successful female business owners with unique ideas); Horizons (career

planning personal and professional goal-setting); and $$$ and You (specific financial issues, social security, tax planning). Buys 1-2/issue. Query. Length: 800-1,200 words. Pays $50 minimum.

FINANCE, The Magazine of Money & Business, 25 W. 39th St., New York NY 10018. (212)221-7900. Publisher/Editor: James C. Burke. 50% freelance written. For senior executives and decision-makers in the business and financial communities. Magazine; 48 pages. Estab. 1941. Circ. 30,000. Pays on publication. Buys all rights. Phone queries OK. Submit seasonal/holiday material 6 weeks in advance of issue date. Simultaneous and photocopied submissions OK. SASE. Reports in 3 months. Free sample copy and writer's guidelines.
Nonfiction: Survey articles of banking and corporate fincance trends. Interviews and profiles with high ranking business and financial executives. "No nuts-and-bolts or lower/middle management-related how-to articles." Query. Length: 1,000-5,000 words. Pays $100-500.
Photos: State availability of photos with query. Pays $10 for 5x7 glossy b&w prints; $10 for color transparencies. Captions preferred. Buys all rights, but may reassign following publication.
Columns/Departments: Buys 3 mss/year. Query. Length: 1,000-2,000 words. Pays $100. Open to suggestions for new columns/departments.

FORBES, 60 5th Ave., New York NY 10011. "We do not buy freelance material." But, on occasion, when a writer of some standing (or whose work is at least known to them) is going abroad or into an area where they don't have regular staff or bureau coverage, they have given assignments or sometimes helped on travel expenses. Pays negotiable kill fee. Byline usually given, "but we reserve the right to omit the byline, as most of our articles are not bylined."

FORTUNE, 1271 Avenue of the Americas, New York NY 10020. Staff-written, but they do buy a few freelance articles (by Irwin Ross, for example) and pay well for them.

MBA MAGAZINE, 730 3rd Ave., New York NY 10017. (212)557-9240. Editor-in-Chief: Ann Meadow. Emphasizes business management and managerial careers. Monthly magazine; 80 pages. Estab. 1966. Circ. 200,000. Pays on the tenth of the month of publication. Buys all rights. Byline given. Submit seasonal/holiday material 4 months in advance. Simultaneous and photocopied submissions OK. SASE. Reports in 3 months. Sample copy $1.25.
Nonfiction: Expose (of business and government); how-to (business management and career planning); interview (business and government executives); profile; new product (for management market, e.g., calculators, computers); photo feature (business or economic); and technical (management science). Buys 5 mss/issue. Submit outline. Length: 500-2,000 words. Pays 10¢/word.
Photos: Cathy Cacchione, Art Director. Purchased on assignment. Captions required. Query. Pays $25-50 per b&w photo; $75-100 for color. Model release required. Will make appointments to see portfolios.

MONEY, Time-Life Bldg., Rockefeller Center, New York NY 10020. Managing Editor: William Simon Rukeyser. "For the middle to upper middle income, sophisticated, well-educated reader. We picture our readers as neither insiders or idiots." Estab. 1972. No freelance material.

Regional

ALASKA CONSTRUCTION & OIL MAGAZINE, 109 W. Mercer St., C#19081, Seattle WA 98119. Executive Editor: Roscoe E. Laing. Associate Editor: Christine A. Laing. For management level personnel in construction/oil/timber/mining. Monthly magazine; 70 pages. Estab. 1959. Circ. 9,500. Pays on publication. Buys first North American serial rights. Submit seasonal/special interest material 3-4 months in advance. Previously published work OK. SASE. Reports in 2 weeks. Sample copy $1. Free writer's guidelines.
Nonfiction: "Only informational articles on the fields we cover." Buys 10-15/year. Query. Length: 500-2,000 words. Pays $1.50/column inch.
Photos: Purchased with mss. Pays $10-25/5x7 or 8x10 b&w glossy prints; $25-50/color positives of any size.

ATLANTA BUSINESS CHRONICLE, 1750 Century Circle, Atlanta GA 30345. (404)325-2442. Editor: Mike Weingart. Emphasizes Atlanta business for upper-income executives. Weekly tabloid; 24 pages. Estab. June 1978. Circ. 10000. Pays on publication. Buys all rights. Phone queries OK. Submit seasonal/holiday material 2 months in advance. SASE. Reports in 1 month. Sample copy $1; free writer's guidelines.
Nonfiction: Expose, how-to, humor and photo feature. "All articles should relate to business in

Atlanta." Buys 2 mss/issue. Query. Length: 1,000-2,500 words. Pays $2.50/column inch.
Photos: State availability of photos. Pays $10 for 8x10 glossy b&w prints. Captions and model releases required.
Columns/Departments: Comparison shopping, Car repairs, Executive Lifestyle, Gourmet and Profile. Buys 155 columns/year. Query. Length: 750-2,500 words. Pays $2.50/column inch.

AUSTIN MAGAZINE, Austin Chamber of Commerce, Box 1967, Austin TX 78767. Editor: Hal Susskind. A business and community magazine dedicated to telling the story of Austin and its people to Chamber of Commerce members and the community. Magazine published monthly by the Chamber; 64-96 pages. Estab. 1960. Circ. 7,500. Not copyrighted. Pays kill fee. Byline given "except if the story has to be conpletely rewritten, the author would be given credit for his imput but he may not be given a byline." Sample copy for $1. Will consider original mss only. Reports in 1 month. SASE.
Nonfiction and Photos: Articles should deal with interesting businesses or organizations around town with emphasis on the Austin community and Chamber of Commerce members. Articles are also accepted on Austin's entertainment scene. Length: 1,000 to 2,000 words. Pays 2½¢/word. B&w photos are purchased with mss.

B.C. BUSINESS MAGAZINE, 101-1256 W. Pender St., Vancouver, British Columbia, Canada V6E 2S8. (604)685-2376. Editor-in-Chief: J. R. Martin. Managing Editor: Kent MacKay. 20% freelance written. Emphasizes British Columbian business. Monthly magazine; 96 pages. Estab. May 1973. Circ. 23,000. Pays on publication. Buys all rights. Phone queries OK. Simultaneous and photocopied submissions OK. Reports in 2 weeks. Sample copy $1.50.
Nonfiction: Interview (B.C. business people); profile (B.C. business people); and general business (in B.C.). No items unrelated to business in British Columbia and no how-to business articles. Buys 6 mss/issue. Query. Length: 500-2,500 words. Pays $50-500.
Photos: No additional payment for 5x7 or 8x11 b&w prints. Captions required.

CANADIAN BUSINESS, CB Media, Ltd., 59 Front St., E., Toronto, Ontario, Canada. (416)364-4266. Editor-in-Chief: Alexander Ross. Managing Editor: Peggy Wente. 80% freelance written. Emphasizes general business. Monthly magazine; 150 pages. Estab. 1919. Circ. 70,000. Pays on acceptance. Buys first North American serial rights. Pays 50% kill fee. Byline given. Submit seasonal/holiday material 3 months in advance of issue date. Photocopied submissions OK. SASE. Reports in 1 month. Sample copy $2.
Nonfiction: How-to. Buys 6 mss/issue. Query. Length: 500-5,000 words. Pays $150-1,000.

CARIBBEAN BUSINESS NEWS, 1255 Yonge St., Toronto, Ontario, Canada M4T 1W6. (416)925-1086. Managing Editor: Colin Rickards. 3% freelance written. Emphasizes business and financial news affecting the entire Caribbean area for upper- and middle-echelon business/managment people worldwide. Monthly tabloid; 16-20 pages. Estab. October 1969. Circ. 32,000. Pays on publication. Buys all rights, but may reassign following publication. Byline given "but there might be a circumstance, at our discretion, where a byline would not be given." Phone queries OK. Photocopied and previously published submissions OK. SASE. Reports in 2 weeks. Free sample copy and writer's guidelines; mention *Writer's Market* in request.
Nonfiction: General interest, interview and business/financial articles on Caribbean topics. No travel u aterial. Buys 8 mss/year. Query. Length: 500-1,000 words. Pays $50-250.
Photos: Pays $25 minimum for 5x7 or 8x10 b&w prints. Captions required.

COLUMBUS BUSINESS FORUM, Columbus Area Chamber of Commerce, Box 1527, Columbus OH 43216. Managing Editor: Peggy Maize Olson. Emphasizes business and civic news and trends in the Columbus area. Monthly magazine; 48 pages. Circ. 4,900. Pays on acceptance. Buys all rights. Phone queries OK. Submit seasonal/holiday material 4-6 months in advance. Photocopied submissions OK. SASE. Reports in 1 month. Sample copy $1.50.
Nonfiction: Expose (business and government); general interest (business, civic trends); historical (local history); how-to (business success or problem solving); interview (business or civic leaders, local or regional); new product (business-related); nostalgia (by-gone business trends); personal experience (business-related); and personal opinion (management consulting). Buys 2-3/mss issue. Send complete ms or clips of published work. Length: 250-700 words. Pays $25 minimum.
Columns/Departments: "We don't currently carry columns or departments but would be interested in starting some." Query. Length: 250 words minimum. Pays $25 minimum.

COMMERCE MAGAZINE, 130 S. Michigan Ave., Chicago IL 60603. (312)786-0111. Editor:

Gordon A. Moon II. For top businessmen and industrial leaders in greater Chicago area. Also sent to chairmen of and presidents of *Fortune* 1,000 firms throughout United States. Monthly magazine; varies from 100 to 400 pages, (8¼x11¼). Estab. 1904. Circ. 12,000. Buys all rights, but will reassign rights to author after publication. Buys 30-40 mss/year. Pays on acceptance. Will send sample copy to writer for $1. Query. SASE.
Nonfiction: Business articles and pieces of general interest to top business executives. "We select our freelancers and assign topics. Many of our writers are from local newspapers. Considerable freelance material is used but almost exclusively on assignment from Chicago area specialists within a particular business sector." Pays 4-8¢/word.

CONNECTICUT BUSINESS TIMES, Connecticut Business Times, Inc., 544 Tolland St., East Hartford CT 06108. (203)289-9341. Managing Editor: Stan Jaskiewicz. Emphasizes business in Connecticut for executives and blue- and white-collar workers. Monthly tabloid; 24 pages. Estab. July 1978. Circ. 20,000. Pays on publication. Buys all rights. Byline given. Phone queries OK. Submit seasonal/holiday material 2 months in advance. Simultaneous submissions OK. SASE. Reports in 2 weeks. Free sample copy.
Nonfiction: Expose, general interest material, historical material, how-to items, interviews and profiles, new product descriptions, photo features, technical articles, and pieces about travel in Connecticut. "All articles must have a connection with business. No short-straight news clips." Buys 10 mss/issue. Query. Pays $1./colunm inch.
Columns/Departments: New Product. Buys 3 columns/issue. Send complete ms. Pays $1/inch. Open to suggestions for new columns/departments.

THE EXECUTIVE OF ORANGE COUNTY, THE EXECUTIVE OF LOS ANGELES, 3931 MacArthur Blvd., Suite 200, Newport Beach CA 92660. (714)752-8885. Editor: Thomas M. Self. For executives and professionals in Orange County and Los Angeles. Monthly magazine. Pays on publication. Buys first rights. Pays 50% kill fee. Byline given. Previously published submissions OK. SASE. Reports in 5 weeks. Sample copy $1.50; SASE for writer's guidelines.
Nonfiction: "Stories about executives, entrepreneurs and professionals, and stories and service articles of interest to them." Buys 6 mss/issue. Query. Length: 1,000-3,500 words. Pays $100-250.
Photos: State availability of photos or send photos with ms. Pays $200/day on assignment for b&w 8x10 glossy prints. Buys first and reprint rights. Captions and model releases required.

FINANCIAL POST, Maclean-Hunter, Ltd., 481 University Ave., Toronto, Ontario, Canada M5W 1A7. Editor: Neville J. Nankivell. Executive Editor: Dalton S. Robertson. News Editor: Michael Fox. 10% freelance written. Emphasizes Canadian business, investment/finance and public affairs. Weekly newspaper; 36-48 pages. Estab. 1907. Circ. 184,000. Pays on publication. Buys one-time rights. Pays 100% kill fee. Byline given. Reports in 2-3 weeks. Sample copy 75¢.
Nonfiction: Useful news and information for executives, managers and investors in Canada. Buys 3 mss/issue. Query. Length: 700-800 words. Pays 10-15¢/word.
Photos: State availability of photos with query. Pays $15-50 for 8x10 b&w glossy prints. Captions required. Buys one-time rights.

HOUSTON BUSINESS JOURNAL, Cordovan Corp., 5314 Bingle Rd., Houston TX 77092. (713)688-8811. Editor: Mike Weingart. Emphasizes Houston business. Weekly tabloid; 40-64 pages. Estab. 1971. Circ. 20,000. Pays on publication. Buys all rights. Byline given. Phone queries OK ("but prefer mail"). Submit seasonal/holiday material 2 months in advance. SASE. Reports in 1 month. Sample copy $1.
Nonfiction: Exposé (business, if documented), How-to (finance, business, management, lifestyle), informational (money-making), interview (local business topics), nostalgia (possible, if business), profile (local business executives), personal experience and photo feature. Buys 3 mss/issue. Length: 500-2,000. Pays $2.50/column inch.
Photos: State availability of photos or send photos with ms. Pays $10 for b&w prints. Buys all rights. Captions required.
Columns/Departments: Automotive Review, Profile and Restaurants. Query. Pays $2.50. Open to suggestions for new columns/departments.

INDIANA BUSINESS AND INDUSTRY, 1100 Waterway Blvd., Indianapolis IN 46202. (317)634-1100. Publisher: Nancy Purdy. Monthly magazine. Pays on publication. Rights negotiable. Simultaneous and previously published submissions OK. SASE. Reports in 3 weeks. Free sample copy.
Nonfiction: "All articles must relate to business industry." Buys 2-3 mss/issue. Query or send complete ms or send clips of published work. Pay negotiable.

Photos: State availability of photos. Pay negotiable for b&w or color photos. Captions and model releases required.

NEAR EAST BUSINESS, 386 Park Ave. S., New York NY 10016. Editor: John Townsend. US Editor: Martha Downing. Monthly magazine; 60-80 pages. For business and government leaders (English-speaking) in the Middle East. Estab. 1976. Circ. 17,000. Buys first serial rights. Buys 3-4 mss/year. Pays on publication. Free sample copy. Will consider photocopied submissions. Reports in 1 month. SASE.
Nonfiction: Stories and news items relating to business, industry, markets, management in the Middle East, Iran and Turkey. Length: 1,000-2,000 words. Pays average of $175.

NEW JERSEY BUSINESS, Hotel Robert Treat, 50 Park Place, Newark NJ 07102. (201)623-8359. Editor: James Prior. Emphasizes business in the *State* of New Jersey. Monthly magazine. Pays on acceptance. Buys all rights. Simultaneous and previously published work OK. SASE. Reports in 3 weeks. Sample copy $1; SASE for writer's guidelines.
Nonfiction: "All freelance articles are upon assignment, however, they deal with business and industry either directly or more infrequently, indirectly pertaining to New Jersey." Buys 6 mss/year. Query or send clips of published work. Pays $150-200.
Photos: Send photos with ms. Captions preferred.

NORTHWEST INVESTMENT REVIEW, 534 SW 3rd Ave., Portland OR 97204. (503)224-6004. Editor-in-Chief: Shannon P. Pratt. For investors and corporate leaders who pay $150 a year to read about the 300-plus Northwestern publicly held corporations covered by this publication. Newsletter; 8-20 pages. Estab. 1971. Semimonthly. Pays on publication. Will send sample packet of newsletters to writer for $2.50. No photocopied or simultaneous submissions. Reports in 2-4 weeks. Query to Gregory A. Gilbert. SASE.
Nonfiction: "We need top regional articles, appealing to investors." Corporate profiles, personnel changes, industry surveys. "If well researched in our field, we will consider freelance work; ideally, from business page writers, individuals with finance/security backgrounds." Length: 500-2,500 words. "With query first, we would quote what the piece would be worth to us. Many are done for a fee. No set minimum."

THE SOUTH MAGAZINE, Trend Publications, Inc., Box 2350, Tampa FL 33601. Editor: Roy B. Bain. Emphasizes the Southern business community and climate. Monthly magazine; 64-96 pages. Estab. January 1974. Circ. 50,000. Pays on acceptance. Buys first North American serial rights. SASE. Reports in 6 weeks. Sample copy $1; free writer's guidelines.
Nonfiction: No articles on how-to. Buys 8 mss/issue. Query. Length: 300-1,800 words. Pays $45-300.
Photos: State availability of photos with query. No additional payment for 5x7 b&w glossy prints or 35mm color transparencies. Captions required. Buys one-time rights. Model release preferred.

TIDEWATER VIRGINIAN, Box 327, Norfolk VA 23501. Editor: Marilyn Goldman. 90% freelance written. Published by Tidewater Chamber of Commerce. Monthly magazine; 84 pages. Circ. 72,000. Byline given. Buys 60 mss/year. Pays on publication. Sample copy for $1, plus mailing charges. Will consider photocopied and simultaneous submissions. Reports in 2-3 weeks. Query or submit complete ms. SASE.
Nonfiction: Articles dealing with business and industry in Virginia, primarily the surrounding area of southeastern Virginia (Tidewater area). Profiles, successful business operations, new product, merchandising techniques, business book reviews. Length: 500-2,500 words. Pays $25-125.

CB Radio

CANADIAN TRANSCEIVER, Walgram Publishing Ltd., 75 The Donway West, Suite 1009, Don Mills, Ontario, Canada M3C 2E9. (416)444-1188. Editor-in-Chief: J.R. Graham. Managing Editor: Robert Arculli. 80% freelance written. Emphasizes CB, ham, and commercial 2-way radio and automotive sound. Monthly magazine; 64 pages. Estab. 1975. Circ. 22,000. Pays on publication. Buys all rights. Phone queries OK. Submit seasonal/holiday material 3 months in advance of issue date. Photocopied submissions OK. SAE and International Reply Coupons. Reports in 6-8 weeks. Free sample copy; mention *Writer's Market* in request.

Nonfiction: How-to (building electronic items, installing 2-way radios and antennas, etc.); and technical (electronics and specifically 2-way radio). Buys 60 mss/year. Query. Length: 500-1,500 words. Pays 6-10¢/word.

Photos: State availability of photos with query. Pays $5 for 3x4 b&w glossy prints; $25-50 for 2¼x2¼ color transparencies. Captions required. Buys all rights, but may reassign following publication. Model release required.

CB MAGAZINE, 531 N. Ann Arbor, Oklahoma City OK 73127. Editor: Leo G. Sands Technical Editor: Gordon West. New York City. Managing Editor: William B. Roberts. All: (405)947-6113 Oklahoma City. For operators of citizens band 2-way radio for personal and business communications. Estab. 1961. Monthly. Circ. 180,000. Pays on publication. Buys all rights. Byline given "except if there is major rewriting or additional research required." Free sample copy. SASE.

Nonfiction: Case histories of use of citizens band radio in disaster, crime or public service. Semitechnical articles about equipment installation, operation and repair. Interested in true-life stories where CB radio was used to render public service. Uses informational, how-to, personal experience; expose and technical. Buys 4 mss/issue. Query. Length: 500-1,500 words. Payment varies.

Photos: Send photos with ms. Offers no additional payment for photos accepted with ms. Uses b&w prints.

CB TIMES, Charlton Publications, Inc., The Charlton Bldg., Derby CT 06418. (203)735-3381. Editor-in-Chief: John E. Bartimole. 80% freelance written. For anyone involved in CBing. Bimonthly magazine; 64 pages. Estab. 1976. Circ. 150,000. Pays on publication. Buys all rights. Byline given. Phone queries OK. Submit seasonal/holiday material 4 months in advance. SASE. Reports in 2 weeks. Sample copy 50¢.

Nonfiction: "We want any type of article which would interest CBers. In other words, nothing to do with CBs is out of bounds. In fact, some of our most popular articles have been extremely offbeat. We pride selves on being the only CB magazine which devotes itself primarily to the 'human' side of CB. So, we're interested in humor, expose, information—just about anything—as long as it has a shred of CB in it." Buys 8-10 mss/issue. Query or submit complete ms. Length: 1,000-11,000 words. Pays $25 minimum.

Photos: B&w (8½x11 glossy prints) and color (2¼x2¼ or 35mm) purchased with or without mss. Captions required. "If someone's thinking about submitting a color transparency for a cover, he might be better off querying, but we'll look at unsolicited cover shots, too." Pays $5 minimum for b&w; $25 minimum for color.

Fiction: "We pioneered the field in CB fiction—and we're always looking for fiction pieces dealing with CB and its people. We'll look at any type of fiction dealing with CB." Buys 1 ms/issue. Query or submit complete ms. Length: 1,000 words minimum. Pays $50 minimum.

Fillers: Clippings, jokes, gags, anecdotes, newsbreaks, short humor. "This is a new area for us. We're giving it a try, experimentally." Send complete ms. Length: 500 words maximum. Pays $5 minimum.

How To Break In: "Just write the best you can on any subject dealing with CB. We'll look at everything. We feel every manuscript deserves an equal shot. Everyone started out as an 'unknown' writer once—we're always looking for fresh new talent. We are currently in need of freelance material, and we sincerely hope that need never diminishes. Freelancers will be a constant source of new ideas for us. We ask freelancers to remember one thing, and this keys our whole editorial philosophy: We emphasize the 'human' side of CB. CBers are people who are interested in other people, in communicating. That's what keys our contents, good buddies!"

Rejects: Super-technical articles and unprofessional looking mss. "Neatness does count!"

CQ: THE RADIO AMATEUR'S JOURNAL, Cowan Publishing Corp., 14 Vanderventer Ave., Port Washington NY 11050. (516)883-6200. Technical Editor: Irwin S. Schwartz. For the amateur radio community. Monthly journal. Estab. 1945. Circ. 100,000. Pays on publication. Buys first rights. Phone queries OK. Submit seasonal/holiday material 3 months in advance. Photocopied submissions OK. SASE. Reports in 2-3 weeks. Free sample copy.

Current Needs: "We are interested in articles that address all technical levels of amateur radio. Included would be basic material for newcomers and intermediate and advanced material for oldtimers. Articles may be of a theoretical, practical or anecdotal nature. They can be general interest pieces for all amateurs or they can focus in on specific topics. We would like historical articles, material on new developments, articles on projects you can do in a weekend, and pieces on long-range projects taking a month or so to complete." Length: 6-10 typewritten pages. Pays $35/published page.

Child Care and Parental Guidance

The following publications are concerned with child care and parental guidance. Other categories that include markets that buy items about child care for special columns and features are: Confession, Religious, and Women's in Consumer Publications; Education Journals in Trade Journals.

AMERICAN BABY MAGAZINE, 575 Lexington Ave., New York NY 10022. (212)752-0775. Editor-in-Chief: Judith Nolte. 50% freelance written. Emphasizes how-to and medical information for the expectant and new parents. Monthly magazine; 60 pages. Estab. 1938. Circ. 1,000,000. Pays on publication. Buys one-time rights. Byline given. Phone queries OK. Submit seasonal/holiday material 4-5 months in advance of issue date. Simultaneous, photocopied, and previously published submissions OK. SASE. Reports in 3-4 weeks. Free sample copy and writer's guidelines; mention *Writer's Market* in request.
Nonfiction: How-to (on pregnancy and child-related subjects); interview (with medical authority on some subject of interest to expectant and new parents); new product; personal experience; personal opinion; and profile (well-known figure in child care). No breast-feeding or natural childbirth experiences. Buys 5 mss/issue. Submit complete ms. Length: 500-2,000 words. Pays $50-250.
Photos: Editor: Jeanne Dzienciol. State availability of photos with query or ms. Pays $50-200 for 8x10 b&w glossy prints; and $100-300 for 35mm color transparencies. Buys one-time rights. Model release required.
Fillers: Newsbreaks. Buys 5 mss/year. Length: 25-200 words. Pays $25-75.

BABY CARE, 52 Vanderbilt Ave., New York NY 10017. Editor: Evelyn A. Podsiadlo. For "mothers of babies from birth through the first year." Quarterly. Circ. 500,000. Buys all rights. Pays 100% kill fee. Byline given. Pays on acceptance. Free sample copy and writer's guidelines. Submit seasonal material 5-6 months in advance. Reports in 1-4 weeks. SASE.
Nonfiction: Feature articles "include basic infant care (bathing, feeding, common illness, safety); emotional and physical development; how-to; effect of new baby on family relations; seasonal topics (travel, summer or winter care). Shorter features with a humorous, narrative or reflective approach. Articles can be first-person accounts by mothers and fathers, but prefer medical subject to be written by MDs and RNs or writer who can work well with doctors." Worthy material is used to aid mothers of the very young child. Buys informational, how-to, personal experience, inspirational, humor, nostalgia and travel. Length: 1,000-1,800 words. Pays $50-$125; and slightly higher to professionals such as MDs. Regular columns include Family Corner, short anecdotes about life with the new baby. Pays $10 on publication.
Poetry: Uses poetry occasionally; all forms. Length: 4-24 lines. Pays $5-$10. Should relate to subject matter.

BABY TALK, 66 E. 34th St., New York NY 10016. Editor: Patricia Irons. For new and expectant mothers interested in articles on child development and baby care. Monthly. Estab. 1934. Circ. 750,000. Buys first North American serial rights. Byline given "unless a short article is combined with another on the same subject (author would be told in advance)." Pays on acceptance. Submit complete ms. SASE.
Nonfiction and Photos: "Articles on all phases of baby care. Also true, unpublished accounts of pregnancy, life with baby or young children. Informational, how-to and personal experiences. Pays $20 minimum. B&w and color photos are sometimes purchased with or without ms. Payment varies.

EXCEPTIONAL PARENT, Room 600, Statler Office Bldg., 20 Providence St., Boston MA 02116. (617)482-0480. Editor-in-chief: Dr. Maxwell J. Schleifer; Editor: Dr. Stanley D. Klein; Associate Editor: Robert F. Boucher. Magazine provides practical information for parents and professionals concerned with the care of children with disabilities (physical disabilities, emotional problems, mental retardation, learning disabilities, perceptual disabilities, deafness, blindness, chronic illness, etc.). Estab. 1971. Bimonthly. Circ. 20,000. Buys all rights. Buys about 20 mss/year. Pays on publication. Sample copy for $2.50; writer's guidelines for SASE. Send query with outline. Reports in 6 months. SASE.
Nonfiction and Photos: "The general intent of the magazine is to provide practical information for the parents and professionals concerned with the care of children with disabilities. We print articles covering every conceivable subject within this area, including legal issues, tax and economic information, recreation programs, adaptive aids, parent groups, personal experience and instructional advice, etc. This is a consumer publication within a very specialized market.

Articles should be comprehensible for the layperson. Articles within special areas are checked by an advisory board in the medical and allied professions. There is no other magazine of this type." Length: 2,500-3,000 words maximum. Pays $25/printed page. Flat fee for professionals: $25. Photos accompanied by signed releases are of interest.

EXPECTING, 52 Vanderbilt Ave., New York NY 10017. Editor: Evelyn A. Podsiadlo. Issued quarterly for expectant mothers. Circ. 1,000,000. Buys all rights. Pays 100% kill fee. Byline given. Pays on acceptance. Reports in 2-4 weeks. Free writer's guidelines. SASE.
Nonfiction: Prenatal development, layette and nursery planning, budgeting, health, fashion, husband-wife relationships, naming the baby, minor discomforts, childbirth, expectant fathers, working while pregnant, etc. Length: 800-1,600 words. Pays $50-$125 for feature articles, somewhat more for specialists.
Fillers: Short humor and interesting or unusual happenings during pregnancy or at the hospital; maximum 100 words, $10 on publication; submissions to "Happenings" are not returned.
Poetry: Occasionally buys subject-related poetry; all forms. Length: 4-24 lines. Pays $5-10.

HOME LIFE, Sunday School Board, 127 9th Ave., N., Nashville TN 37234. (615)251-2271. Editor-in-Chief: George W. Knight. Emphasizes Christian family life. For married adults of all ages, but especially newlyweds and middle-aged marrieds. Monthly magazine; 64 pages. Estab. 1947. Circ. 800,000. Pays on acceptance. Buys all rights. Byline given. Phone queries OK, but written queries preferred. Submit seasonal/holiday material 9-10 months in advance. SASE. Reports in 6 weeks. Free sample copy and writer's guidelines.
Nonfiction: How-to (good articles on marriage and child care); informational (about some current family-related issue of national significance such as "Television and the Christian Family" or "Whatever Happened to Good Nutrition?"); personal experience (informed articles by people who have solved family problems in healthy, constructive ways). Buys 10 mss/month. Submit complete ms. Length: 1,200-2,400 words. Pays $45-85.
Fiction: "Our fiction should be family-related and should show a strong moral about how families face and solve problems constructively." Buys 12 mss/year. Submit complete ms. Length: 1,600-2,400 words. Pays $40-70.
How To Break In: "Study the magazine to see our unique slant on Christian family life. We prefer a life-centered case study approach, rather than theoretical essays on family life."

MOTHERS' MANUAL MAGAZINE, 441 Lexington Ave., New York NY 10017. Editor-in-Chief: Beth Waterfall. Emphasizes pregnancy and parenting. Bimonthly magazine; 60-72 pages. Estab. 1964. Circ. 900,000. Pays on publication. Buys all rights. Pays 50% kill fee. Byline given, "unless work is extensively rewritten." SASE required. Reports in 6 weeks. Sample copy 75¢.
Nonfiction: Well-researched, and well documented how-to, humor, informational, inspirational, interview, personal experience and personal opinion stories. Read the magazine before submitting complete ms. Length: 500-2,000 words. Pays 2-5¢/published word; $10-500/article.
Poetry: Lyn Roessler, Poetry Editor. Free Verse, light verse and traditional. "We are looking for good humor; short, crisp poetry, upbeat, fun poetry as well as narrative. Buys 72/year. Pays 50¢/line; $3-30.

PARENT'S CHOICE, Parent's Choice Foundation, Box 185, Waban MA 02168. (617)332-1298. Editor: Diana Huss Green. Emphasizes reviews of children's media, designed to alert parents to trends and events in books, TV, records, films, toys and educational issues. Bimonthly magazine; 16 pages. Estab. September 1978. Pays on publication. Buys all rights. Phone queries OK. SASE. Reports in 1 month. Sample copy $1; writer's guidelines 25¢.
Nonfiction: General interest (to parents interested in uses of the media); how-to (use books, films, TV, tops, games and records); humor; essays (on social and political issues related to media); interview (with writers of fiction for young adutls and children, and directors, producers of films and TV); personal experience; photo feature (of parents and children, grandparents and children) and profile. Buys 10 mss/issue. Query. Length: 500-1,500 words. Pays 10¢/word.
Photos: State availability of photos. Offers no additional payment for photos accompanying ms. Uses b&w prints. Captions preferred.
Columns/Departments: A Parent's Essay, Choice Books and Full Platter. Send complete ms. Length: 200-1,000 words.

PARENTS MAGAZINE, 52 Vanderbilt Ave., New York NY 10017. Editor: Elizabeth Crow.

Monthly. Circ. 1,500,000. Usually buys first North American serial rights; sometimes buys all rights. Pays $50-150 kill fee. Byline given "except for 'Parents Report' or 'Parents in the News' or short items for which we pay only $50-60 and purchase all rights." Pays on acceptance. Reports in approximately 3 weeks. Query; enclose outline and sample opening. SASE.

Nonfiction: "We are interested in well-documented articles on the problems and success of preschool, school-age, and adolescent children—and their parents; good, practical guides to the routines of baby care; articles which offer professional insights into family and marriage relationships; reports of new trends and significant research findings in education and in mental and physical health; articles encouraging informed citizen action on matters of social concern. We prefer a warm, colloquial style of writing, one which avoids the extremes of either slang or technical jargon. Anecdotes and examples should be used to illustrate points which can then be summed up by straight exposition." Length: 2,500 words maximum. Payment varies; pays $300 minimum.

Fillers: Anecdotes for "Parents Exchange," illustrative of parental problem-solving with children and teenagers. Pays $20 on publication.

YOUR BABY (service section of *Modern Romances* magazine), *Modern Romances*, Macfadden Women's Group, 215 Lexington Ave., New York NY 10016. Editor: Jean Sharbel. Buys all rights. Byline given. Pays on publication. Reports in 12-16 weeks. SASE.

Nonfiction: Uses warmly written, genuinely helpful articles of interest to mothers of children from birth to three years of age, dealing authoritatively with pregnancy problems, child health, child care and training. Editors recommend you study this market before trying to write for it. Length: up to 1,000 words. Pays $100 maximum.

City

ALOHA THE MAGAZINE OF HAWAII, 2003 Kalia Rd., Honolulu HI 96815. Editor: Rita Witherwax. Bimonthly magazine. Pays on publication. Buys all rights. Byline given. SASE. Reports in 6 weeks. Sample copy $2.50.

Nonfiction: Arts, business, historical, interviews, profiles, sports, travel and some fiction. "All articles must have a Hawaii-related theme." Buys 12 mss/issue. Query or send clips of published work. Length: 1,500-4,000 words. Pays 10¢/word.

Photos: State availability of photos or send photos with ms. Pays $25 for 8x10 b&w glossy prints; $50 for color transparencies, $150 for covers. Buys first rights. Captions and model releases are required.

ATLANTIC CITY MAGAZINE, Menus International, Inc., 101 S. Swarthmore Ave., Ventnor NJ 08406. Editor: Donna Andersen. For residents and tourists, as well as people interested in investing in Atlantic City. Bimonthly magazine; 140 pages. Estab. 1977. Circ. 60,000. Pays on publication. Buys one-time rights. Byline given. Submit seasonal/holiday material 2 months in advance. Simultaneous and photocopied submissions OK. SASE. Reports in 4 weeks. Sample copy $2.

Nonfiction: Expose, general interest, how-to, entertainment, interview, photo feature and profile. "Articles should be related to the South Jersey shore area in general and Atlantic City in particular. We will especially need city-related profiles, trend pieces and investigative articles. No confession articles." Buys 28 mss/year. Query and/or send clips of previously published work. Length: 1,000-5,000 words. Pays $25-250.

Photos: State availability of photos. Buys 8x10 b&w prints and 2¼x2¼ color transparencies. Pay varies. Captions preferred.

Columns/Departments: Art, Business, Environment, Sports and Real Estate. Buys 12 columns/year. Query and/or send clips of published work. Length; 1,000-3,000 words. Pays $25-250.

ATLANTA MAGAZINE, 6285 BarField Rd., Atlanta GA 30328. (404)393-2920. Editor: Larry Kent Woods. Emphasizes general consumer interest for metro Atlanta with some circulation in the state. Monthly magazine. Pays on acceptance. Buys all rights. Pays 10% kill fee. Byline given. SASE. Reports in 6-8 weeks. Sample copy $3.

Nonfiction: "The majority of articles in any issue must relate to metro Atlanta. Statewide, regional and national articles are acceptable." Query. Length: 2,000-4,000 words. Pays $200 minimum.

Photos: State availability of photos. Buys 8x10 b&w prints or 35mm color transparencies; pay varies. Captions preferred.

Columns/Departments: Art (reviews and comments); Books (reviews); Consumer (advice); Cuisine (cooking); Around Town (brief items describing metro events, oddities and personalities); Metro (community coverage); Money (investment advice); People (short profile); Records (reviews); Restaurants (reviews); The Funnies (brief humor); Sports; Theatre (general comment); and Travel (in-country and out). Query. Length: 250-1,200 words. Pays $20-125.

AVENUE M, 920 N. Michigan Ave., Suite 503, Chicago IL 60611. (312)787-9415. Editor: Art Desmond. 85% freelance written. Emphasizes news and features around the Magnificent Mile in Chicago for all ages. Monthly magazine; 36-48 pages. Estab. 1975. Circ. 15,000. Pays on publication. Buys all rights, but may reassign to author following publication. Phone queries OK. Photocopied and previously published submissions OK. SASE. Reports in 3 weeks. Sample copy $1.
Nonfiction: Historical, humor, informational, inspirational, interview, nostalgia, personal experience, personal opinion, photo feature, profile and travel. Buys 80 mss/year. Query. Length: 500-750 words. Pays $25-50.
Photos: Purchased with accompanying ms. Captions required. Offers no additional payment for photos accepted with accompanying ms. Total purchase price for ms includes payment for photos.

BALTIMORE MAGAZINE, 131 E. Redwood St., Baltimore MD 21202. (301)752-1300. Editor: Stan Heuisler. Managing Editor: Jane Crystal. Monthly magazine; 150 pages. Circ. 40,000. Pays on publication. Buys all rights. Pays 33⅓% kill fee, except for first-time writer. Byline given. Phone queries OK. Submit seasonal/holiday material 2-3 months in advance. Photocopied submissions OK. SASE. Reports in 6 weeks. Sample copy $2; free writer's guidelines.
Nonfiction: Expose, how-to, interview, profile and travel. "We do not want to see any soft, non-local features." Buys 15 mss/issue. Send complete ms or clips of published work. Length: 1,000-7,000 words. Pays $50-350.
Photos: State availability of photos with ms. Uses b&w glossy prints. Captions preferred.
Columns/Departments: Hot Stuff (local news tips); and Tips & Touts (local unsual retail opportunities). Query. Open to suggestions for new columns/departments.

BOSTON MAGAZINE, Municipal Publications, 1050 Park Square Bldg., Boston MA 02116. (617)357-4000. Editor-in-Chief: Terry Catchpole. For young, upscale readers; vast majority are professionals, college-educated and affluent. Monthly magazine; 160 pages. Estab. 1910 as a Chamber of Commerce publication, becoming an independent publication in 1971. Pays on acceptance. Buys all rights, but may reassign following publication. Pays 25% kill fee. Byline given unless article has to be rewritten by a staff member. Submit seasonal/holiday material 3 months in advance. Simultaneous and photocopied submissions OK. SASE. Reports in 2 weeks.
Nonfiction: Exposé (subject matter varies); profiles (of Bostonians; sometimes, New Englanders); travel (usually only in New England or eastern Canada); personal experience. Buys about 40 mss/year. Query. Length: 1,000-10,000 words. Pays $100-500.
Photos: Sam Savage, Design Director. B&w and color purchased on assignment only. Query. Specifications vary. Pays $25-150 for b&w; payment for color (used on cover only) averages $275.
Fillers: E. J. Kahn III, Department Editor. Newsbreaks. Short items of interest about Boston personalities, institutions or phenomena. Buys about 5 per issue. Send fillers in. Length: 100-500 words. Pays $15-25.
How To Break In: "If we are unfamiliar with a writer's work, we want to see clips that are representative of his/her style and range of interest and expertise. Remember, we consider ourselves in the entertainment business, so the emphasis here is on compelling, entertaining writing. The one thing that this or any other magazine can never afford to do is bore the reader."

BFLO. (formerly *Buffalo Fan*), Box 294, Buffalo NY 14240. (716)885-1500. Editor: Richard Hirsch. 80% freelance written. The city magazine of Buffalo and Western New York. Magazine; 64 pages. Estab. 1974. Buys all rights. Pays 50% kill fee. Byline given. Pays on acceptance. Photocopied submissions OK. SASE. Reports in 1 week. Sample copy $1.
Nonfiction: "Features on subjects of interest to those who live in Buffalo or western New York state." Informational; personal experience; profiles; humor; historical; "think" pieces; and nostalgia. Buys 40 mss/year. Query. Length: 1,000-2,000 words. Pays up to $125.
Photos: B&w and color photos purchased with or without accompanying ms, or on assignment. Pay varies, but pays $10 minimum for b&w; $25 for color.

BUFFALO SPREE MAGAZINE, Box 38, Buffalo NY 14226. (716)839-3405. Editor: Johanna V. Shotell. For "a highly literate readership." Estab. 1967. Quarterly. Circ. 20,000. Buys first serial rights. Buys 15-20 mss/year. SASE.
Nonfiction and Fiction: Department Editor: Gary Goss. "Intellectually stimulating prose exploring contemporary social, philosophical and artistic concerns. We are not a political magazine. Matters of interest to western New York make up a significant part of what we print." Length: 3,000 words maximum. Pays $75 for a lead article. "We print fiction, but it must be brilliant." Length: 3,000 words maximum. Pays approximately $75.
Poetry: Department Editor: Janet Goldenberg. "Serious, modern poetry of nature and of man's relationship with nature interests us, provided it is of the highest quality." Pays approximately $15.

CHARLOTTE MAGAZINE, Box 240843, Charlotte NC 28224. (704)588-2120. Editor: Clarice Warren. Emphasizes articles on local people and local places. Bimonthly magazine. Pays on publication. Buys first rights. SASE. Reports in 3 weeks. Free sample copy.
Nonfiction: Departments: lifestyles (alternative and typical); business (spotlight successful, interesting business and people); town talk (short, local articles of interest); theater, arts.
Fillers: Local people (spotlighted); travel pieces (anything from listing Carolina Islands, Grand Strand to Africa and Belgium); Sports. Listings: Restaurants; antique (shops); specialty (shops); and the Last Word (editorial comments). Buys 12 mss/issue. Query. Length: 1,200-2,400 words. Pays $25-75.
Photos: State availability of photos. Buys b&w and color prints; pay negotiable. Captions preferred; model releases required.
Columns/Departments: "Will consider all type of articles." Buys 6 columns/issue. Query. Length: 1,200 words maximum. Pays $75.

CHICAGO MAGAZINE, 500 N. Michigan Ave., Chicago IL 60611. Editor-in-Chief: Allen H. Kelson. Editor: John Fink. 80% freelance written. For an audience which is "95% from Chicago area; 90% college-trained; upper income; overriding interests in the arts, dining, good life in the city. Most are in 30 to 50 age bracket and well-read and articulate. Generally liberal inclination." Monthly. Circ. 180,000. Buys first rights. Buys about 50 mss/year. Pays on acceptance. Free sample copy and writer's guidelines. Submit seasonal material 3 months in advance. Reports in 2 weeks. Query. SASE.
Nonfiction and Photos: "On themes relating to the quality of life in Chicago; "past, present, future." Writers should have "a general awareness that the readers will be concerned, influential native Chicagoans reading what the writer has to say about their city. We generally publish material too comprehensive for daily newspapers or of too specialized interest for them." Buys personal experience and think pieces, interviews, profiles, humor, spot news, historical articles, travel, and exposés. Length: 1,000-6,000 words. Pays $100-$750. Photos purchased with mss. Uses b&w glossy prints, 35mm color transparencies, or color prints.
Fiction: Mainstream, fantasy, and humorous fiction. Preferably with Chicago orientation. No word length limits, but "no novels, please." Pays $250-500.

CHICAGO READER, Box 11101, Chicago IL 60611. (312)828-0350. Editor: Robert A. Roth. "The *Reader* is distributed free in Chicago's lakefront neighborhoods. Generally speaking, these are Chicago's best educated, most affluent neighborhoods—and they have an unusually high concentration of young adults." Weekly tabloid; 100 pages. Estab. 1971. Circ. 96,000. Pays "by 15th of month following publication." Buys all rights. Byline given. Phone queries OK. Photocopied submissions OK. SASE. Reports in 12 months.
Nonfiction: "We want magazine features on Chicago topics. Will also consider reviews." Buys 500 mss/year. Submit complete ms. Length: "whatever's appropriate to the story." Pays $25-350.
Photos: By assignment only.
Columns/Departments: By assignment only.

THE CINCINNATI MAGAZINE, Greater Cincinnati Chamber of Commerce, 120 W. 5th St., Cincinnati OH 45202. (513)721-3300. Editor-in-Chief: Laura Pulfer. Emphasizes Cincinnati living. Monthly magazine; 88-120 pages. Estab. 1967. Circ. 25,534. Pays on acceptance. Buys all rights, but may reassign following publication. Pays 33% kill fee. Byline given. Submit seasonal/holiday material 2 months in advance. Simultaneous, photocopied and previously published submissions OK. SASE. Reports in 3 weeks.
Nonfiction: How-to; informational; interview; photo feature; profile; and travel. Buys 3-4 mss/issue. Query. Length: 2,000-4,000 words. Pays $200-400.

Photos: Laurie Peterson, Art Director. Photos purchased on assignment only. Model release required.
Columns/Departments: Travel; How-To; Sports and Consumer Tips. Buys 6 mss/issue. Query. Length: 750-1,500 words. Pays $75-150.

CLEVELAND MAGAZINE, 1621 Euclid Ave., Cleveland OH 44115. Editor-in-Chief: Michael D. Roberts. 10-15% freelance written. Emphasizes local news and information. Monthly magazine; 190 pages. Estab. April 1972. Circ. 55,000. Pays on publication. Buys all rights. Phone queries OK. Submit seasonal/holiday material 2 months in advance of issue date. Photocopied submissions OK. SASE. Reports in 2 months. Sample copy $1.50.
Nonfiction: Exposé (local government, business, politics, banking, etc.); general interest; historical (local or statewide); interview; photo feature; and profile. Buys 15-20 mss/year. Query. Length: 5,000 words maximum. Pays $50-700.

COLUMBUS MONTHLY, 171 E. Livingston Ave., Columbus OH 43215. (614)464-4567. Associate Editor: Lenore E. Brown. Emphasizes subjects of general interest primarily to Columbus and Central Ohio. Monthly magazine. Pays on publication. Buys all rights. Byline given. SASE. Reports in 1 month. Sample copy $2.25.
Nonfiction: "We want general articles as long as they pertain to Columbus area." Buys 6 mss/issue. Query. Length: 100-4,500 words. Pays $15-400.
Photos: State availability of photos. Pay varies for b&w or color prints. Model releases required.
Columns/Departments: Art, Business, Food and Drink, Movies, Politics, Sports and Theatre. Buys 2-3 columns/issue. Query. Length: 1,000-2,000 words. Pays $100-175.

D MAGAZINE, Dallas Southwest Media Corp., 1925 San Jacinto, Dallas TX 75201. Editor-in-Chief: Wick Allison. Managing Editor: Wade Leftwich. 40% freelance written. For readers in the Dallas-Fort Worth area; primarily the middle to upper income group. Monthly magazine; 198 pages. Estab. 1974. Circ. 60,000. Pays on publication. Buys all rights. Pays 50% kill fee. Byline given. Submit seasonal/holiday material 3 months in advance. Photocopied submissions OK. SASE. Reports in 1 month. Sample copy $2.
Nonfiction: Informational; political; profile; travel; and business. Buys 2-3 mss/issue. Query. Length: 750-4,000 words. Pays $50-400.
Photos: Photos purchased with accompanying ms or on assignment. Pays $25-150 for 8x10 b&w glossy prints; $50-150 for color transparencies. Model release required.
Columns/Departments: Previews (arts, entertainment, books, movies, and concert reviews); Up Front (business and gossip); Dining (reviews); and Windfalls (special products and services). "All pieces must relate to Dallas and the Fort Worth area." Open to suggestions for new columns/departments.

DALLAS MAGAZINE, Dallas Chamber of Commerce, 1507 Pacific Ave., Dallas TX 75201. (214)651-1020. Editor: Susan L. Sanders. Emphasizes business and other topics of interest to Dallas business people. Monthly magazine; 72 pages. Estab. 1922. Circ. 15,000. Pays on acceptance. Buys all rights. Pays 100% kill fee "but kill fee is not offered on stories where quality is poor or editor's directions are not followed." Byline given. Submit seasonal/holiday material 3 months in advance. Photocopied submissions OK. SASE. Reports in 4 weeks. Sample copy $1.25.
Nonfiction: General interest (of interest to successful work-oriented men and women); historical (only on Dallas); humor (rarely accepted, but will use exceptional articles); interview (of Dallas executive or Dallas resident in an important government job or the like); profile (same as interview); and business features. "We do not want stories that underestimate our readers. Controversies involving technique or practices, not people, can be acceptable." Buys 3-5/mss issue. Query. Length: 2,500-4,000 words. Pays $100-350.
Photos: State availability of photos. Pays $75-200 for 8x10 b&w glossy prints; $75-200 for color transparencies. Captions required.
Columns/Departments: Book Review (business or nonfiction; biography) and Civic Affairs (short seasonal features on civic events). Query. Length: 1,000-1,500 words. Pays $50-150.
Fillers: Cartoons (business-oriented). Buys 3/issue. Pays $15.

DENVER MONTHLY, 1763 Williams, Denver CO 80218. (303)399-5931. Publisher: John W. Hoffman. Associate Editor: Michael H. Rudeen. Assistant Editor: Will Keener. For an urban, sophisticated, well-educated audience interested in community events, sports and entertainment. Monthly magazine; 96 pages. Estab. 1972. Circ. 25,000. Pays on acceptance.

Buys all rights. Pays 20% kill fee. Byline given except for very short articles or ones requiring extensive rewrite. Submit seasonal/holiday material 4 months in advance of issue date. Photocopied submissions OK. SASE. Reports in 2-8 weeks.

Nonfiction: Expose (anything that is a "genuine scoop"); informational (Denver and Colorado residents); and interviews and profiles (famous Coloradians). Buys 45 mss/year. Query. Length: 800-1,500 words. "Payment varies depending on story quality, length, and author. Base rates range from $50 to $200."

Photos: B&w and color transparencies used with mss or by assignment. Payment negotiable. Query.

HONOLULU, 828 Fort Street Mall, Suite 400, Honolulu HI 96813. (808)524-7400. Editor: David Pellegrin. Emphasizes life in Hawaii. Monthly magazine. Pays on publication. SASE. Reports in 8 weeks. Sample copy $1.50.

Nonfiction: *"Locally produced* articles on problems, lifestyles, history and personalities of the 50th state." Buys 4 mss/issue. Query or send clips of published work. Length: 1,000-5,000 words. Pays $50-350.

Photos: State availability of photos. Pays $10-25 for b&w glossy prints or contact sheets plus negatives; $10-50 for color transparencies. Buys one-time rights. Captions required.

Columns/Departments: Travel. Buys 1 ms/issue. Query. Length: 800-1,500 words. Pays $50-75.

HOUSTON, Houston Chamber of Commerce, 1100 Milam Bldg., 25th Floor, Houston TX 77002. Editor: Richard Stanley. Assistant Editors: Barbara Stokes, and Jennifer Lawrence. Emphasizes the Houston business community. The median reader is 48 years old, a college graduate in a top management position with an income of $54,700. Monthly magazine; 64-90 pages. Estab. 1930. Circ. 15,000. Pays on acceptance or publication. Buys all rights. Pays 100% kill fee. Byline given. Prefers mail queries. Photocopied submissions OK but must be neat. Reports in a few weeks.

Nonfiction: Informational (on economy, businesses, people, etc.); historical (on Houston); interview; profile (business people); and travel (include economy and business attitudes of destinations). Query. Pays $30-500.

INDIANAPOLIS, 320 N. Meridian, Indianapolis IN 46204. (317)635-4747. Editor: Pegg Kennedy. Emphasizes any Indianapolis-related problems/features or regional related topics. Monthly magazine; 56 pages. Estab. August 1962. Circ. 7,000. Pays on publication. Buys first North American serial rights. Pays 30-50% kill fee. Byline given. Written queries only. Submit seasonal/holiday material 3 months in advance. Simultaneous, photocopied and previously published submissions OK. SASE. Reports in 4 weeks. Sample copy $1.25; free writer's guidelines.

Nonfiction: Expose (interested, but have no specifics; "we're interested in any Indianapolis-related topic including government and education"); historical (Indianapolis-related only); how-to (buying tips); humor ("broad-category for us"); inspirational (not generally but will read submitted ms); interview (Indianapolis-related person, native sons and daughters); nostalgia (Indianapolis-related); personal experience (Indianapolis-related); photo feature (human interest, Indianapolis-related); profile (Indianapolis-related); and travel (within a day's drive of Indianapolis). "We only want articles with Indianapolis ties, no subjects outside of our region. We aren't very interested in broad-based, national topics either." Buys 3-5 mss/issue. Query with clips of published work. Length: 500-3,500 words. Pays $50-125.

Photos: State availability of photos. Pays $5-25 for b&w contact sheets; $5-35 for color transparencies. Buys one-time rights. Captions preferred.

Fiction: Fantasy, experimental, humorous, mainstream and science fiction. "We haven't used much fiction in the past but we are open for some, depending on quality and content." Send complete ms. Length: 500-2,500 words. Pays $35-80.

JACKSON, THE MISSISSIPPI MAGAZINE, Jackson Magazine, Inc., Box 16847, 1 LeFlure's Square, Jackson MS 39206. (601)366-6496. Editor/Publisher: Herb Phillips. Emphasizes Mississippi tie-ins for readers of refined interests, middle- to upper-income, and well-educated. Monthly magazine; 88 pages. Estab. 1977. Circ. 22,000. Buys one-time rights. Submit seasonal/holiday material 3 months in advance. Simultaneous submissions (if not submitted to a publication in the mid-South; photocopied submissions OK. SASE. Reports in 2 weeks. Sample copy $1; free writer's guidelines.

Nonfiction: Expose (of government, education, energy, etc.); general interest, historical; how-to (general); humor; inspirational; interview; nostalgia; profile; travel; new product; and photo feature. Buys 10 mss/issue. Query. Length: 150-2,000 words. Pays $10-150.

Photos: State availability of photos with ms. Pays $10-75/5x7 or 8x10 b&w glossy print (reviews contact sheets); and $15-100/color photo (reviews contact sheets). Model release required.

Fillers: Anecdotes, which "must have a Mississippi or Southern linkage." Pays $5-15.

JACKSONVILLE MAGAZINE, Drawer 329, Jacksonville FL 32201. (904)396-0100. For civic-minded, concerned community types. Estab. 1963. Bimonthly. Circ. 8,000. Buys all rights. Buys 20-25 mss/year. Pays on publication. Query. Submit seasonal material 3-6 months in advance. Reports in 3 weeks. SASE.

Nonfiction and Photos: Buys historical, photo and business articles. Length: usually 1,500-3,000 words. Pays $50-$150. "We accept b&w glossies, good contrast; color transparencies." Pays $15 minimum for b&w; color terms to be arranged.

KANSAS CITY MAGAZINE, Box 2298, Shawnee Mission KS 66201. (913)384-0770. Editor-in-Chief: Floyd E. Sageser. Managing Editor: Norman Rowland. 85% freelance written. Emphasizes Kansas City lifestyle and business. Monthly magazine; 68 pages. Estab. January 1976. Circ. 16,000. Pays on publication. Buys all rights, but may reassign following publication. Byline given. Phone queries OK. Submit seasonal/holiday material 3 months in advance of issue date. SASE. Simultaneous, photocopied and previously published submissions OK. Reports in 3 weeks. Sample copy $1.25.

Nonfiction: All material must relate to Kansas City areas, activities or personalities. Exposé; historical; interview; nostalgia; photo feature; and profile. Buys 4 mss/issue. Query. Length: 800-2,500 words. Pays 5¢/word.

Photos: Submit photo material with accompanying query. Pays $5-10 for 5x7 or 8x10 b&w glossy prints and $25-50 for color transparencies. Captions required. Buys all rights, but may reassign following publication.

Columns/Departments: Art; Books; indoor gardening; movies; and travel. Buys 5/issue. Query. Length: 400-1,500 words. Pays 5¢/word. Open to suggestions for new columns/departments.

LOS ANGELES MAGAZINE, 1888 Century Park E., Los Angeles CA 90067. Editor: Geoff Miller. Monthly. Buys first North American serial rights. Pays 50% kill fee. Byline given except for short "Peoplescape" personality profiles. Query. SASE.

Nonfiction: Uses articles on how best to live (i.e., the quality of life) in the "changing, growing, diverse Los Angeles urban-suburban area; ideas, people, and occasionally places. Writer must have an understanding of contemporary living and doing in Southern California; material must appeal to an upper-income, better-educated group of people. Fields of interest include urban problems, pleasures, personalities and cultural opportunities, leisure and trends, candid interviews of topical interest; the arts. Solid research and reportage required. No essays." Length: 1,000-3,000 words. Also uses some topical satire and humor. Pays 10¢/word minimum.

Photos: Most photos assigned to local photographers. Ocassionally buys photographs with mss. B&w should be 8x10. Pays $25-50 for single article photos.

LOUISVILLE TODAY, 1031 S. 4th St., Louisville KY 40203. (502)5892170. Publisher: John Yarmuth. Editor: Elizabeth Bibb. Emphasizes features, news analysis and service pieces related to Louisville, for an upper-middle-class audience. Monthly city magazine. Pays on publication. Buys first publication rights. "We will help author resell article but we split the profit 50-50." Simultaneous and previously published submissions OK. Reports in 1 week. SASE.

Nonfiction: Features on local personalities, news analysis of local issues and how-to service pieces. Query with clips of published work or submit complete ms. Length: 1,500-3,000 words. Pays $150-300.

Photos: Send photos with ms. Pays $25-200 for b&w contact sheet with negatives and Kodachrome 25 or 64 color slides. Captions preferred; model release required.

Columns/Departments: Going Places (travel pieces); Tale End (short humorous articles about anything); Sports Page; Book marks (short book reviews); and Left Bank (arts and leisure in Louisville). Buys 4/issue. Length: 750-1,000 words. Pays $75-150.

MADISON MAGAZINE, Box 1604, Madison WI 53701. Editor: James Selk. For business, civic and social leaders of Madison. Magazine; 40-56 pages. Estab. 1958. Monthly. Circ. 15,000. Buys all rights, but may reassign rights to author after publication. Buys 10-15 mss/year. Pays on publication. Sample copy $2. Reports on material accepted for publication 10 days after publication. Returns rejected material immediately. Query. SASE.

Nonfiction and Photos: "Subjects of interest to the business, civic and social leaders in the

Madison metropolitan area. We regularly review one aspect each of the business, arts, sports, society, fashion and travel scene. We like humor as well as serious material, as long as it relates to Madison or Madisonians." Length: 350-1,250 words. Pays $10-100. No additional payment for b&w photos used with mss. Pays $5 to $10 for b&w, $25 for color, when purchased without mss. Captions required.

MEMPHIS, Towery Press, 1535 E. Brooks Rd., Memphis TN 38116. (901)345-8000. Executive Editor: Ed Weathers. Estab. April 1976. Circ. 20,000. Pays on publication. Buys all rights. Pays $35 kill fee. Byline given. Phone queries OK. Simultaneous, photocopied and previously published submissions OK. SASE. Reports in 3 weeks. Sample copy $1.50
Nonfiction: Expose, general interest, historical, how-to, humor, interview and profiles. "Virtually all our material has strong Memphis connections." Buys 2 mss/issue. Query or submit complete ms or clips of published work. Length: 1,500-5,000 words. Pays 5¢/published word.

MIAMI MAGAZINE, Box 340008, Miami FL 33134. (305)856-5011. Editor: Ron Sachs. For affluent, involved citizens of south Florida; generally well educated. Monthly magazine. Estab. 1975. Circ. 25,000. Rights purchased vary with author and material. Usually buys first publication rights. Buys about 200 mss/year. Pays on publication. Sample copy $1.50. Reports in 60 days. Query or submit complete ms. SASE.
Nonfiction: Investigative pieces on the area; thorough, general features; exciting, in-depth writing. Informational, how-to, personal experience, interview, profile, humor and expose. Strong local angle. Length: 3,000 words maximum. Pays $85-250. Departments: Film, business, books, art and travel. Length: 1,500 words maximum. Payment ranges from $50-75.

MILWAUKEE IMPRESSIONS, Spectrumedia Communicatons/The Marcus Corp., 212 W. Wisconsin Ave., Milwaukee WI 53203. (414)272-6020. Editor-in-Chief: Bruce Olson. Associate Editor: Judie Kommrusch. "For Milwaukee's up-scale individual. Its readers are in the 25-50 age bracket, well-educated, articulate, affluent and interested in all aspects of contemporary living, especially in what is being said and done in their city. Regular features keep readers up-to-date on quality restaurants, entertainment, chic boutiques, civic issues, book and film reviews, financial reports, cultural news and travel. Material published is too comprehensive for daily newspapers or of too specialized interest for them." Monthly magazine; 60 pages. Estab. 1977. Circ. 30,000. 80% freelance written. Pays on publication. Buys first exclusive rights. Phone queries OK. Submit seasonal/holiday material 3 months in advance. Simultaneous, photocopied and previously published submissions OK. Reports in 45 days. Free sample and writer's guidelines available.
Nonfiction: Expose; general and current interest; profile and interview (of local interest); personal opinion; travel; and how-to. Buys 6 mss/issue. Submit complete ms or query with clips of published work. Length: feature of 2,400 word minimum; fillers of 600 words minimum. Payment is negotiable.

MONTHLY DETROIT MAGAZINE, Detroit Magazine Inc., 1404 Commonwealth Bldg., Detroit MI 48226. (313)962-2350. Editor: Gary W. Diedrichs. Emphasizes metro Detroit for an audience of city and suburban residents. Monthly magazine; 136 pages. Estab. 1978. Circ. 40,000. Pays on publication. Buys first North American serial rights. Pays 25% kill fee. Byline given. Phone queries OK. Submit seasonal/holiday material 3 months in advance. SASE. Reports in 1 month. Sample copy $2.25; free writer's guidelines.
Nonfiction: Expose, how-to and nostalgia on any metro Detroit subject; and profiles of important metro Detroiters or ex-Detroiters. Query with clips of published work. Buys 10 mss/issue. Length: 200-5,000 words. Pays $50-500 or 10¢/published word for feature articles.

MPLS. ST. PAUL MAGAZINE, 512 Nicollet Mall, Suite 615, Minneapolis MN 55402. (612)339-7571. Editor-in-Chief: Brian Anderson. 90% freelance written. For "professional people of middle-upper income levels, college educated, interested in the arts, dining, and the good life of Minnesota." Monthly magazine; 125 pages. Estab. 1971. Circ. 32,000. Pays on publication. Buys all rights, but may reassign following publication. Pays 25% maximum kill fee. Byline given except for extremely short pieces and stories that require considerable rewriting. Submit seasonal/holiday material 4 months in advance of issue date. Photocopied submissions OK. SASE. Reports in 3 weeks.
Nonfiction: Expose; how-to; informational; historical; humor; interview; profile; and photo feature. "We can use any of these as long as they are related to Minneapolis-St. Paul." Query. Length: 300-3,000 words. Pays $20-300.

Photos: Maureen Ryan, Art Director. Purchased on assignment. Query. Pays $25-100 for b&w; $25-175 for color.

NASHVILLE! PlusMedia, Inc., 1 Vantage Way, Suite 238, Nashville TN 37228. (615)259-4600. Editor-in-Chief: C. Turney Stevens Jr. For affluent families who live in Nashville/middle Tennessee; business people, professionals in management positions." Monthly magazine; 120 pages. Estab. 1973. Circ. 23,000. Usually pays 30% kill fee. Byline given. Pays on publication. Phone queries OK. Submit seasonal/holiday material 4-5 months in advance. Simultaneous and photocopied submissions OK. SASE. Reports in 6-8 weeks. Sample copy $1.50; free writer's guidelines.
Nonfiction: Wayne Gurley, Managing Editor. Expose (politics, government); how-to (hobbies, gardening, recreational activities); historical (local only); interview; nostalgia; profile; travel; and business. Buys 80 mss/year. Query. Length: 2,000-4,000 words. Pays $100-250.
Photos: Don Milstead, Art Director. Purchased with or without accompanying ms or on assignment. Captions required. Query. Pays $5.50-15 for 5x7 or 8x10 b&w prints; $12.50-25 for 35mm or 2¼x2¼ color transparencies. Model release required.
Columns/Departments: Politics, Consumer's Notebook, People, Science, Medicine, After Hours (entertainment, recreation). Buys 36 mss/year. Query. Length: 1,500-2,500 words. Pays $75-125. Open to suggestions for new columns or departments.

NEW HAVEN INFO MAGAZINE, Box 2017, 53 Orange St., New Haven CT 06521. (203)562-5413. Editor: Sol D. Chain. For those interested in art, music, theater, recreational activities, etc. Monthly magazine; 64 pages. Estab. 1952. Circ. 5,000. Not copyrighted. Byline given. Buys 20 mss/year. Pays on publication. Sample copy 50¢. Will consider photocopied and simultaneous submissions. Reports in 1 month. Query. SASE.
Nonfiction: "Most of our material is on assignment. We publish articles dealing with New Haven area events and people." Personal experience, interview, profile, historical, nostalgia. Length: 350-700 words. Pays $10/page (about 350 words).

NEW ORLEANS MAGAZINE, Flambeaux Publishing Co., 6666 Morrison Rd., New Orleans LA 70126. (504)246-2700. Editor: Don Lee Keith. 50% freelance written. Monthly magazine; 125 pages. Estab. October 1966. Circ. 60,000. Pays on publication. Buys all rights, but may reassign following publication. Pays 50% kill fee. Byline given. Submit seasonal/holiday material 2 months in advance of issue date. Previously published submissions OK. SASE. Reports in 3 weeks.
Nonfiction: General interest; interview; and profile. Buys 6 mss/issue. Query or submit complete ms. Length: 1,200-3,000 words. Pays $100-500.
Photos: Craig Bloodworth, art director. State availability of photos with query or ms. Offers no additional payment for b&w photos accepted with accompanying ms. Captions required. Buys one-time rights. Model release required.

NEW YORK MAGAZINE, New York Magazine Co., 755 2nd Ave., New York NY 10017. (212)986-4600. Editor-in-Chief: Joe Armstrong. Managing Editor: Laurie Jones. Emphasizes the New York metropolitan area. Weekly magazine. Pays on acceptance. Submit seasonal/holiday material 2 months in advance. Photocopied submissions OK. SASE. Reports in 4-5 weeks. Sample copy $1.
Nonfiction: Expose, general interest, how-to, interview, profile, travel, new product, personal experience and photo feature. Query. Pays $300-1,000.

NEW YORK AFFAIRS, 419 Park Ave. S., New York NY 10016. (212)689-1240. Editor-in-Chief: Dick Netzer. Emphasizes urban problems. "Readers tend to be academics, public officials, corporation presidents and intellectual types." Quarterly magazine; 128 pages. Estab. 1973. Circ. 5,000. Pays on publication. Buys all rights, but may reassign following publication. Phone queries OK. Photocopied submissions OK. SASE. Reports in 4 weeks. Sample copy $3; free writer's guidelines.
Nonfiction: Michael Winkleman, Articles Editor. Expose; interview (figures who are key to urban policymaking); and personal opinion. Buys 8 mss/year. Query. Length: 3,000-7,500 words. Pays $50-200. "We also have a section for short articles (250-3,000 words) called 'Side Streets' in which we run much that is good about cities—humor especially. Most of our authors are academics whom we don't pay. For those whom we can't afford to pay, which includes most articles and Side Streets, we pay in copies of the magazine."
Columns/Departments: Book reviews. "We don't pay reviewers. They just get to keep the book." Uses 30 pages/year. Query.
How To Break In: "We are looking for hard-hitting, well-written articles on general urban

problems. We especially like articles that take the unconventional approach—that transit fares should be raised, or that the cost of welfare should *not* be picked up by the federal government."

OMAHA MAGAZINE, Omaha, The City Magazine, Inc., 1517 Harney St., Omaha NE 68102. (402)342-8365. Executive Editor: Michael O. Klug. Managing Editor: Julie M. Salem. Emphasizes Omaha people, events and urban issues for "upper-income (or those who aspire to be), educated Omahans; those who vote and who have the money to spend on entertainment, recreation, etc. The target age is 30-50, but we get all ages." Monthly magazine; 56 pages. Estab. 1976. Circ. 10,000. Pays on publication. Buys first North American serial rights. Byline given. Phone queries OK. Submit seasonal/holiday material 3 months in advance. Simultaneous, photocopied and previously published submissions OK. SASE. Reports in 6 months. Sample copy $1; writer's guidelines free.
Nonfiction: Expose (about local issues); general interest (local or native sons in these categories: entertainment, leisure, lifestyle, people, city, consumer, food, drink, politics, business, finanace); historical (on assignment only—usually about Omaha); how-to (throw a party, cure boredom, improve quality of life—any topic, but should have specific local application); humor (most articles should strive to be an entertainment vehicle in themselves); profile (of famous or controversial Omahans); travel (the February travel section has a Nov. 1 deadline); and photo feature (local). Buys 5-10 mss/issue. Query with clips of published work. Length: 800-4,000 words. Pays $20-150, usually $50/feature.
Photos: State availability of photos or send samples with ms. Pays $20-150 for b&w contact sheets and negatives, and for color transparencies. Captions required. Buys one-time rights.

PHILADELPHIA MAGAZINE, 1500 Walnut St., Philadelphia PA 19102. Editor: Alan Halpern. 35-50% freelance written. For sophisticated middle- and upper-income people in the Greater Philadelphia/South Jersey area. Monthly magazine. Estab. 1908. Circ. 130,000. Buys all rights. Pays 33% kill fee. Byline given. Buys 100 mss/year. Pays on publication, or within 2 months. Free writer's guidelines for SASE. Reports in 4 weeks. Queries and mss should be sent to Polly Hurst, Managing Editor. SASE.
Nonfiction and Photos: "Articles should have a Philadelphia focus, but should avoid Philadelphia stereotypes—we've seen them all. Life styles, city survival, profiles of interesting people, business stories, music, the arts, sports, local politics, stressing the topical or unusual. No puff pieces. We're in the 'new journalism' tradition—exposes, fast-moving, first-person accounts—and we're a steady award winner, so quality and professionalism count. We offer lots of latitude for style, but before you make like Norman Mailer, make sure you have something to say." Length: 1,000-7,000 words. Pays $75-500. Photos occasionally purchased with mss at additional payment of $35-150.

PHOENIX MAGAZINE, 4707 N. 12th St., Phoenix AZ 85014. (602)248-8900. Editor: Manya Winsted. 75% freelance written. For professional, general audience. Monthly magazine. Estab. 1966. Circ. 60,000. Buys all rights, but will reassign rights to author after publication. Pays 50-75% kill fee. Byline given except for regular columns. Buys 60 mss/year. Pays on publication. Sample copy $1. February issue: Real Estate; March issue: Arizona Lifestyle; August issue: Annual Phoenix Progress Report; June issue: Salute to Summer. Submit special issue material 3 months in advance. Reports in 1 month. Query or submit complete ms. SASE.
Nonfiction and Photos: Predominantly features on some aspect of Phoenix life; urban affairs, arts, life style, etc. Subject should be locally oriented. Informational, how-to, interview, profile, historical, photo, successful local business operations. Length: 1,000-3,000 words. Payment is negotiable. Photos are purchased with ms with no additional payment, or on assignment.

PITTSBURGH MAGAZINE, Metropolitan Pittsburgh Public Broadcasting, Inc., 4802 5th Ave., Pittsburgh PA 15213. (412)622-1360. Editor-in-Chief: Herb Stein. "The magazine is purchased on newsstands and by subscription and is given to those who contribute $20 or more a year to public TV in western Pennsylvania." Monthly magazine; 100 pages. Estab. 1970. Circ. 60,000. Pays on publication. Buys all rights, but may reassign following publication. Pays 33% kill fee. Byline given. Phone queries OK. Submit seasonal/holiday material 6 months in advance. SASE. Reports in 6 weeks. Sample copy $1.50; free writer's guidelines.
Nonfiction: Expose, historical, how-to, humor, informational, inspirational, interview, nostalgia, personal experience, personal opinion, profile and travel. Buys 6 mss/issue. Query or send complete ms. Length: 2,500 words. Pays $50-250.
Photos: Purchased with accompanying ms or on assignment. Captions required. Uses b&w and color. Query for photos. Model release required.

Columns/Departments: Travel; humor; nostalgia. "All must relate to Pittsburgh or western Pennsylvania."

THE PITTSBURGHER MAGAZINE, The Express House, Station Square, Pittsburgh PA 15219. (412)281-9716. Editor: Vince Gagetta. Emphasizes people, places, events and news of Pittsburgh and southwestern Pennsylvania. Monthly magazine. Buys magazine and newspaper rights. Pays negotiable kill fee. Byline given. Simultaneous submissions OK. SASE. Reports in 3-4 weeks. Sample copy $1.
Nonfiction: "We feature articles on people, places and events in the Pittsburgh/southwestern Pennsylvania area. We also run stories with statewide emphasis if the focus is on this part of the state. The range of subject matter is broad: politics, historical pieces, current events, crime stories, personality pieces, in-depth interviews with area business/political/educational leaders and stories dealing with economics, business and educational themes." Buys 1-2 mss/issue. Query. Length: 900-3,500 words. Pay is negotiable.

RICHMOND MAGAZINE, 701 E. Franklin, Suite 1100 Richmond VA 23219. Editor-in-Chief: Deborah Woodward. 90% freelance written. For anyone interested in Richmond affairs. Monthly magazine; 128 pages. Estab. November 1977. Circ. 17,000. Pays on publication. Buys first North American serial rights. Pays 10% kill fee. Byline given. Phone queries OK. Submit seasonal/holiday material 3 months in advance of issue date. SASE. Reports in 5 weeks. Sample copy $1.25.
Nonfiction: "All articles must be of immediate interest and concern to Richmonders. Exposé (only by experienced professionals); guides; how-to; humor; general interest (some); interview; personal opinion (by recognized local figures); profile (only extremely unique state and local people); and historical. "No reviews or first person stories." Buys 40 mss/year. Query. Length: 1,500-3,500 words. Pays $100-300.
Fillers: Local newsbreaks and short humor. Buys 2-3 fillers/issue. Length: 50-500 words. Pays $10-25.

SACRAMENTO MAGAZINE, 2620 La Mesa Way, Sacamento CA 95825. (916)482-3700. Associate Editor: Carol Gage. Emphasizes local politics, human interest material and consumer items for readers in the higher income brackets. Monthly magazine. Pays on publication. Buys North American rights. Previously published work OK. Phone queries OK. Reports in 2 weeks. SASE. Writer's guidelines for SASE.
Nonfiction: Local politics (profiles); travel; consumer (health, education or shopping); fashion; and general interest. Buys 6 mss/issue. Query or submit complete ms. Length: 1,000 words mininum. Pays $100 minimum.
Photos: State availability of photos. Pays $10 for 8x10 b&w prints or color transparencies. Captions preferred.
Columns/Departments: Gardening and Theater/Arts/Movies/Media. Pays $75 minimum.

ST. JOSEPH MAGAZINE, 1901 Clay St., St. Joseph MO 64501. (816)233-8930. Editor: Karl Stout. Associate Editor: Deb H. Sparks. Emphasizes and promotes the city of St. Joseph. Monthly magazine; 48 pages. Estab. 1977. Circ. 10,000. Pays on publication. Buys all rights. Phone queries OK. Submit seasonal/holiday material 6 months in advance. Photocopied and previously published submissions OK. SASE. Reports in 6 weeks. Sample copy $1.40.
Nonfiction: Expose (of local government, business, education and finance); general interest (related to community pride); profile; humor; interview; nostalgia; travel; and photo feature. Buys 60 mss/year. Query. Length: 1,500-2,000 words. Pays $15-100.
Photos: Send photos with ms. Pays $10/8x10 b&w glossy print; $10-30/8x10 color glossy print or 2¼x2¼ transparency; offers no addtional payment for photos accepted with ms. Captions preferred; model release required.
Columns/Departments: Movies, Books, Wine, Music, Bridge and Calendar. Buys 72/year. Query. Length: 800-1,000 words. Pays $20-35. Open to suggestions for new columns/departments.
Fiction: Experimental, humorous and mainstream. Buys 2 mss/year (1 at Christmas). Send complete ms. Length: 1,500-2,500 words. Pays $25-100.
Poetry: Avant-garde, free verse and haiku. No rhymed poetry. "We use photography with our poetry." Buys 10 poems/year. Submit no more than 3 at one time. Length: 4-16 lines. Pays $10.

ST. LOUIS, 7110 Oakland Ave., St. Louis MO 63117. (314)781-8787. Editor: Greg Holzhauer. For "those interested in the St. Louis area, recreation issues, etc." Estab. 1969. Monthly. Circ. 35,000. Buys all rights, but will reassign rights to author after publication; buys second serial (reprint) rights. Buys 60/mss year. Pays on publication. Photocopied submissions OK. Submit seasonal material 4 months in advance. Reports on material in 1 month. Query or submit complete ms. SASE.

Nonfiction and Photos: "Articles on the city of St. Louis, metro area, arts, recreation, media, law, education, politics, timely issues, urban problems/solutions, environment, etc., generally related to St. Louis area. Looking for informative writing of high quality, consistent in style and timely in topic." Informational, how-to, personal experience, interview, profile, humor, historical, think pieces, expose, nostalgia, personal opinion, travel. Length: 1,000 to 5,000 words. Pays $250-1,000 for 8x10 b&w glossy prints purchased on assignment. "Shooting fee plus $25 minimum print used. All color on individual basis."

SAN ANTONIO MAGAZINE, Greater San Antonio Chamber of Commerce, Box 1628, San Antonio TX 78296. (512)227-8181. Editor: Ann Brawn. 50% freelance written. Emphasizes business and quality of life articles about San Antonio. Monthly magazine; 88 pages. Pays on publication. Buys all rights, but may reassign following publication. Phone queries OK. Photocopied submissions OK. SASE. Reports in 1 month. Free sample copy and writer's guidelines.

Nonfiction: "The magazine's purpose is to inform, educate and entertain readers about the quality of life in San Antonio. We're looking for community and business articles and to inform the business community of current trends." Informational; historical; humor; nostalgia; personal opinion; profiles (personality profiles of people who are interesting, colorful and quotable—must be a San Antonian or have ties to the city); personnel management; business tips; business trends; and photo features. Buys 65 mss/year. Query or send complete ms. Length: 800-3,000 words. Pays $50-300.

Photos: Purchased with mss or on assignment. Captions required. Query. Pays $10-25 for 8x10 b&w glossy prints. Prefers to pay according to the number of photos used in an article, a bulk rate.

How To Break In: "The best way is to be a resident of San Antonio and, therefore, able to write on assignment or to query the editor personally. Again, we are looking for material which is related to the city of San Antonio, its people, and the business community. We consider all possible angles and tie-ins."

SAN DIEGO MAGAZINE, Box 81809, San Diego CA 92138. (714)222-0325. Editor-in-Chief: Edwin F. Self. 65% freelance written. Emphasizes San Diego. Monthly magazine; 250 pages. Estab. 1948. Circ. 35,000. Pays on publication. Buys all rights, but may reassign following publication. Pays negotiable kill fee. Byline given. Submit seasonal/holiday material 3 months in advance of issue date. Simultaneous and photocopied submissions OK. SASE. Reports in 2 months. Sample copy $3.

Nonfiction: Exposé (serious, documented); general interest (to San Diego region); historical (San Diego region); interview (with notable San Diegans); nostalgia; photo essay; profile; service guides; and travel. Buys 7 mss/issue. Query with clips of published work, or submit complete ms. Length: 3,000 words. Pays $300 maximum.

Photos: State availability of photos with query. Pays $7.50-45 for b&w contact sheets or 8x10 glossy prints; $25-100 for color transparencies. Captions required. Buys all rights. Model release required.

SAVANNAH MAGAZINE, Earl Stock Productions, Inc., Box 23647, Savannah GA 31405. (912)925-5428. Editor Ilse Earl. "As with other city magazines, our readers fall into a general profile: 25-65 (age); among city's more affluent, better educated residents with more leisuretime hobbies; professional, business occupations." Bimonthly magazine; 48 pages. Estab. 1970. Circ. 3,000. Pays on publication. Buys all rights. Phone queries OK. Submit seasonal/holiday material 4 months in advance. Simultaneous (depending on location of other submissions) and previously published (if pertinent) submissions OK. SASE. Reports in 2 weeks. Free sample copy.

Nonfiction: Expose, general interest; historical; how-to (need not be Savannah-oriented for such markets as automobile repair, etc.); humor (not necessarily Savannah-oriented); interview (national figures); nostalgia, travel; and photo feature (Savannah and southeast Georgia given priority). All articles, except those specifically outlined above, should be aimed at Savannah. Buys 6-8 mss/issue. Inquire by phone for suitability of article, then follow up if requested. Pays $25.

Photos: State availability of photos. Uses b&w inside; pays $10-25 for cover (35mm color transparencies). Offers no additional payment for photos accepted with ms. Captions required.

Columns/Departments: Gardening (local aspects). Buys 4/issue. Query. Pays $25. Open to suggestions for new columns/departments.

SEATTLE BUSINESS MAGAZINE. Seattle Chamber of Commerce, 215 Columbia St., Seattle WA 98104. (206)447-7266. Editor-in-Chief: Ed Sullivan. Emphasizes regional socio-economic affairs. For business and government · leaders, civic leaders, regional businessmen, educators, opinion makers, and the general public. Monthly magazine; 56 pages. Estab. 1966. Circ. 6,300. Pays on publication. Buys all rights, but may reassign following publication. Submit seasonal/holiday material 2 months in advance. Previously published submissions OK. SASE. Reports in 2 weeks. Free sample copy.
Nonfiction: Informational (socio-economic affairs) and technical. Buys 1-2 mss/issue. Query. Length: 500-2,500 words. Pays $50-300.
Photos: Purchased with accompanying ms or on assignment. Captions required. Pays $50-100 for b&w photos. Total purchase price for ms includes payment for photos. Model release required.
How To Break In: "The freelancer must be able to write—and have a basic awareness of and sympathy for—the interests and problems of the business community as these relate to the community at large."

SPOKANE MAGAZINE. Box 520, Spokane WA 99210. (509)838-2012. Co-publisher/Editor: Judith Laddon. Editor-in-Chief: Lawrence Shook. 90% freelance written. "*Spokane Magazine* is designed as an editorial vehicle for exploring the color, vitality and quality of life in Spokane and the Northwest." Monthly magazine; 72 pages. Estab. May 1977. Circ. 10,000. Pays on publication. Buys one-time rights. Pays 50% kill fee. Byline given. Submit seasonal/holiday material 4 months in advance of issue date. Photocopied submissions OK. SASE. Reports in 8 weeks. Sample copy $1.25; free writer's guidelines.
Nonfiction: "Regular coverage includes politics, the environment, business, the economy, energy, education, agriculture, the arts, medicine, law, architecture, followup or unique angles on news stories with a distinct Northwest identity, the gamut of sports and recreation, profiles of interesting people whose lifestyles reflect the Northwest way of life, travel throughout the West, and fact pieces on subjects of interest to Northwesterners. Humor is always welcome." Buys 5 mss/issue. Query. Length: 500-3,000 words. Pays $50/1,000 words.
Photos: State availability of photos with query. Pays $10 for 8x10 b&w glossy prints; $35-50 for 2¼x2¼ color transparencies. Captions preferred. Buys one-time rights.

SPOTLIGHT ON HARRISON, Meadow Publications Inc., 74 Fairway Ave., Rye NY 10580. (914)967-8619. Editor: Susan Meadow. "The articles we write have to be Westchester-oriented to sophisticated and fairly affluent residents of lower Westchester and Greenwich, Connecticut in the $30,000 range." Monthly magazine; 68 pages. Estab. 1977. Circ. 40,000. Pays on publication. Buys all rights. Phone queries OK. Submit seasonal/holiday material 5 months in advance. SASE. Reports in 4 weeks. Free sample copy.
Nonfiction: General interest, historical, how-to, humor and inspirational. "We are especially interested in articles concerning Harrison." Pays $25.
Poetry: Free verse and light verse. Buys 3 poems/year. Submit no more than 6 at one time. Length: 16 lines minimum. Pays $25.

SPOTLIGHT ON MAMARONECK, Meadow Publications, Inc., 74 Fairway Ave., Rye NY 10580. (914)967-8619. Editor: Susan Meadow. "The articles we write have to be Westchester-oriented to sophisticated and fairly affluent residents of lower Westchester and Greenwich, Connecticut in the $20,000-30,000 range. Monthly magazine; 68 pages. Estab. 1977. Circ. 40,000. Pays on publication. Buys all rights. Phone queries OK. Submit seasonal/holiday material 5 months in advance. SASE. Reports in 4 weeks. Free sample copy.
Nonfiction: General interest, historical, how-to, humor and inspirational. "We are especially interested in articles concerning Mamaroneck." Pays $25.
Poetry: Free verse and light verse. Buys 3 poems/year. Submit no more than 6 at one time. Length: 16 lines minimum. Pays $25.

SPOTLIGHT ON RYE, Meadow Publicaions, Inc., 74 Fairway Ave., Rye NY 10580. (914)967-8619. Editor: Susan Meadow. "The articles we write have to be Westchester-oriented to sophisticated and fairly affluent residents of lower Westchester and Greenwich, Connecticut in the $20,000-30,000 range. Monthly magazine; 68 pages. Estab. 1977. Circ. 40,000. Pays on publication. Buys all rights. Phone queries OK. Submit seasonal/holiday material 5 months in advance. SASE. Reports in 4 weeks. Free sample copy.
Nonfiction: General interest, historical, how-to humor and "We are especially interested in articles concerning Rye." Pays $25.

Poetry: Free verse and light verse. Buys 3 poems/year. Submit no more than 6 at one time. Lenght: 16 lines minimum. Pays $25.

TORONTO LIFE, 59 Front St. E., Toronto, Ontario, Canada M5E 1B3. (416)364-3333. Editor Don Obe. Emphasizes pop sociology, local issues and service features for upper-income, well-educated and, for the most part, young Torontonians. Monthly magazine. Pays on acceptance. Buys first North American rights. Pays 50% kill fee. Byline given. Phone queries OK. Reports in 3 weeks. SAE and International Reply Coupons. Sample copy $1.25
Nonfiction: Uses most all types articles. Buys 17 mss/issue. Query with clips of published work. Length: 1,000-5,000 words. Pays $250-800.
Photos: State availability of photos. Uses good color transparencies and clear, crisp black b&w prints. They seldom used submitted photos. Captions and model release required
Columns/Departments: "We run about five columns an issue. They are all freelanced, though most are from regular contributors. They are mostly local in concern and cover politics, money, relationships, art, movies and sports." Buys issue. Length: 900-2,000 words. Pays $250-400.

TULSA MAGAZINE, Box 1620, Tulsa OK 74101. (918)582-6576. Editor: Larry Silvey. Audience is primarily medium- to upper-income-level Tulsans. Monthly. Circulation: 6,000. Byline given. Pays on acceptance. Sample copy $1. Deadlines are at least 6 weeks prior to publication date, which is normally on the first Thursday of each month. Reports immediately. Query. SASE.
Nonfiction and Photos: Articles must revolve around people or how subject affects people and must have a Tulsa area slant. Style desired is informal and lively. Length: 1,000 to 4,000 words. Payment is negotiable, $50-100, depending on length and research. Photos usually taken by staff or on assignment. May be purchased with mss.

THE WASHINGTONIAN MAGAZINE, 1828 L St. NW, Washington DC 20036. Editor: John A. Limpert. For active, affluent, well-educated audience. Monthly magazine; 250 pages. Estab. 1965. Circ. 95,000. Buys first rights. Buys 75 mss/year. Pays on publication. Simultaneous and photocopied submissions OK. Reports in 4-6 weeks. Query or submit complete ms. SASE.
Nonfiction and Photos: "*The Washingtonian* is written for Washingtonians. The subject matter is anything we feel might interest people interested in the mind and manners of the city. The style, as Wolcott Gibbs said, should be the author's—if he is an author, and if he has a style. The only thing we ask is thoughtfulness and that no subject be treated too reverently. Audience is literate. We assume considerable sophistication about the city, and a sense of humor." Buys how-to, personal experience, interviews, profiles, humor, coverage of successful business operations, think pieces and exposes. Length: 1,000-7,000 words; average feature, 3,000 words. Pays 10¢ a word. Photos rarely purchased with mss.
Fiction and Poetry: Department Editor: Howard Means; Both must be Washington-oriented. No limitations on length. Pays 10¢/word for fiction. Payment for poetry is negotiable.

WINDSOR PUBLICATIONS, 21220 Erwin St., Woodland Hills CA 91365. Editorial/Photographic Director: Glenn R. Kopp. Senior Publications Editor: Rita Johnson. Editor, History Book Division: Don Spring. "We publish pictorial civic publications, business diectories, relocation and travelguides and handbooks for chambers of commerce, boards of realtors, etc. Our audience is anyone considering relocating and/or visiting another part of the country, and our publications document in pictures and words every aspect of a city or area. We also publish hardcover illustrated city history books. Writers, photographers and photo/journalists work on assignment only, after having demonstrated ability through samples. Publications are annual or biennial, vary in size and are titled with the name of a city. Circulation is controlled. Writers and writer/photographers with strong interview, reporting and travel writing experience are especially sought." Queries, stating writing and/or photography experience and including tearsheets, are welcome. Reports in 1-2 weeks. SASE. Sample copy, writer's and photographer's guidelines sent on request.
Nonfiction: "All mss assigned. Unsolicited manuscripts and/or photos not wanted." Buys 150-200/year. Length: 3,000-10,000 words. Pays $500-2,400 on acceptance for all rights. City history book mss average 35,000-50,000 words; fees vary.
Photos: Photography for each publication usually assigned to photographer or photo/journalist on per-day rate plus expenses. Also purchase stock, speculative and existing photos on one-time use basis if they pertain to future publications. 35mm and large color transparencies, b&w contact sheets and negatives or b&w prints (5x7 to 8x10) are acceptable; no color prints. Complete captions required. Photo guidelines, sample copy and upcoming photo needs will be sent in response to all queries. SASE.

College, University, and Alumni

The following publications are intended for students, graduates, and friends of the particular institution involved. Publications for college students in general are found in the Teen and Young Adult category.

ALCALDE, Box 7278, Austin TX 78712. (512)476-6271. Editor-in-Chief: Paula J. Hilbert. 50% freelance written. Bimonthly magazine; 58 pages. Estab. 1913. Circ. 37,000. Pays on acceptance. Buys all rights. Submit seasonal/holiday material 5 months in advance of issue date. SASE. Reports in 2 weeks. Free sample copy and writer's guidelines; mention *Writer's Market* in request.
Nonfiction: General interest; historical (University of Texas, research, and faculty profile); humor (humorous University of Texas incidents or profiles that include background data); interviews (University of Texas subjects); nostalgia (University of Texas traditions); profile (faculty or alumni); and technical (University of Texas research on a subject or product). "We do not want subjects lacking taste or quality or not connected with the University of Texas." Buys 30 mss/year. Query. Length: 1,000-1,800 words. Pays 4¢/word.

DePAUW UNIVERSITY ALUMNUS MAGAZINE, Greencastle IN 46135. (317)653-9721, ext. 480. Editor-in-Chief: Patrick Aikman. Managing Editor: Greg Rice. 25% freelance written. Emphasizes alumni activities and institutional developments. Quarterly magazine; 40 pages. Estab. 1926. Circ. 23,500. Pays on publication. Buys all rights. Submit seasonal/holiday material 3 months in advance of issue date. SASE. Reports in 3 weeks. Sample copy $1.
Nonfiction: General interest; historical; humor; inspirational; interview; nostalgia; personal experience; personal opinion; photo feature; and profile. Buys 2 mss/issue. Query with clips of published work. Length: 1,000-4,000 words. Pays $50-150.
Photos: State availability of photos with query. Pays $5-25 for b&w 8x10 prints or contact sheets; $2-25 for 35mm color transparencies. Captions required. Buys all rights.

MISSISSIPPI STATE UNIVERSITY ALUMNUS, Mississippi State University, Alumni Association, Editorial Office, Box 4930, Mississippi State MS 39762. (601)325-5872. Editor-in-Chief: Lin H. Wright. Emphasizes articles about Mississippi State graduates and former students. For well-educated and affluent audience. Quarterly magazine; 32 pages. Estab. 1921. Circ. 15,508. Pays on publication. Buys one-time rights. Pays 25% kill fee. Byline given. Phone queries OK. Submit seasonal/holiday material 3 months in advance. Simultaneous, photocopied and previously published submissions OK. SASE. Reports in 1 month. Free sample copy.
Nonfiction: Historical, humor (with strong MSU flavor; nothing risque), informational, inspirational, interview (with MSU grads), nostalgia (early days at MSU), personal experience, profile and travel (by MSU grads, but must be of wide interest). Buys 2-3 mss/year ("but welcome more submissions.") Send complete ms. Length: 500-2,500 words. Pays $10-25 (including photos, if used).
Photos: Photos purchased with accompanying ms. Captions required. No additional payment for photos accepted with accompanying ms. Uses 8x10 b&w photos.
Columns/Departments: Statesmen, "a section of the *Alumnus* that features briefs about alumni achievements and professional or business advancement. We do not use engagements, marriages or births. There is no payment for Statemen briefs."
How To Break In: "We welcome articles about MSU grads in interesting occupations and have used stories on off-shore drillers, miners, horse trainers, etc. We also want profiles on prominent MSU alumni and have carried pieces on Senator John C. Stennis, comedian Jerry Clower and baseball manager, Alex Grammas."

Confession

The confession market has come a long way since the old hide-under-the-mattress days, upgrading itself to "family counselor" status. Yet, editors still invent titles that often make even a veteran confession writer blush. Such titles are usually come-ons.

Another concern among freelancers is the cheaper looking appearance of even the best confession magazines. Those magazines that used to be slick are apparently caught in the paper crunch, using part pulp and part coated stock. What's ahead if the paper shortage continues? Will a cheapened appearance cost the reader and writer the respect the markets have gained in recent years? This is unlikely since readers are becoming used to this stock in other publications, as well.

See the August 1979 issue of *Writer's Digest* for a look at the current state of the confession magazines.

Marketing Tip: Confession magazines may use psychic phenomena and supernatural stories, even though some use them very rarely. These stories should not be in the realm of fantasy; they must be plausible. Male-narrator or humorous stories might be another type they'll consider. Suspense crime yarns are always well received if the confessional tone is preserved. Courtroom stories and mental health problems are usually sure sales. It might be wise to query the confession editor first about these out-of-the ordinary stories.

BRONZE THRILLS, 1220 Harding St., Ft. Worth TX 76102. Editor: Mrs. Edna K. Turner. Monthly magazine; 82 pages. Estab. 1957. Circ. 80,000. Buys all rights. Buys 60 mss/year. Pays on acceptance. Sample copy 50¢; free writer's guidelines. Reports in 90 days. Submit complete ms. SASE.
Fiction: All material must relate to blacks. Romance or confession; black-oriented. Particularly interested in occult themes or those concerned with UFOs or mental illness. Does not want to see anything dealing with pregnancy, venereal disease, virginal girls getting pregnant after "first mistake" or old woman/young man love affairs unless the story has an unusual angle. Length: 4,000-6,000 words. Pays $30.
Photos: B&w and color photos are purchased on assignment. 8x10 b&w glossy prints. 2¼x2¼ or 4x5 color transparencies. Pays $35 for b&w; $50 for color.

INTIMATE ROMANCES, Rolat Publishing Corp., 667 Madison Ave., New York NY 10021. Editorial Director: Cara Sherman. Requirements same as *True Secrets*.

INTIMATE SECRETS, Rolat Publishing Corp., 667 Madison Ave., New York NY 10021. Editorial Director: Cara Sherman. Requirements same as *True Secrets*.

INTIMATE STORY, 2 Park Ave., New York NY 10016. Editor: Janet Wandel. 95% freelance written. For women; 14-70 years old; small minority of readership composed of men; blue-collar. Monthly magazine; 74 pages. Estab. 1948. Circ. 170,000. Buys all rights. No byline. Buys about 100 mss/year. Pays on acceptance. Rarely sends sample copies. No photocopied or simultaneous submissions. Submit seasonal material 6 months in advance. Reports in 2 months. SASE.
Fiction: "Sex-oriented and human interest stories; all types of fictional confession stories. Always first person; always enough dialogue. Our stories are within the realm of the believable." Does not want to see anything with the theme of hopelessness. No depressing situations. All titles are house-generated. Length: 2,000-7,000 words. Pays 3¢/word; $160 maximum.

LOPEZ ROMANCE GROUP: REAL ROMANCES, REAL STORY, REAL STORY SPECIAL, NEW GIRL CONFESSIONS, 23 W. 26th St., New York NY 10010. (212)689-3933. Editor: Ardis Sandel. For housewives, teenagers, and working women. Monthly magazines; 64 pages. Buys all rights. Byline given. Buys about 350 mss/year. Pays on publication. Sample copy 75¢. Reports in 6-8 weeks. Submit seasonal or holiday material 6 months in advance. Submissions addressed to individual publications in this listing will be considered by all of the publications. SASE.
Nonfiction and Fiction: "First-person confession stories and service articles on sex, decorating, arts and crafts, fashions, homemaking, beauty, cooking, children, etc. Stories must be well-plotted, have realistic situations, motivation and characterization." Writer should read several issues for style and approach. Strong emphasis on realism. No racial stories. "Sexy passages and dialogue are okay if integral part of the story." Mss should feature a different twist or angle to make the story usable. Lengths from short-shorts to 7,500 words maximum. Pays $150 maximum, depending on length.

MODERN ROMANCES, Macfadden Women's Group, Inc., 215 Lexington Ave., New York NY 10016. Editor: Jean Sharbel. 100% freelance written. For blue-collar, family oriented women, 18-35 years old. Monthly magazine; 80 pages. Estab. 1929. Circ. 200,000. Pays on publication. Buys all rights. Byline given. Submit seasonal/holiday material 4 months in advance of issue date. SASE. Reports in 12-16 weeks.

Nonfiction: General interest; how-to (homemaking subjects); humor; inspirational; and personal experience. Submit complete ms. Length: 200-1,500 words. Pay "depends on merit."

Fiction: "Confession stories with reader identification and a strong emotional tone. No third person material" Buys 14 mss/issue. Submit complete ms. Length: 1,500-8,500 words. Pays 5¢/word.

Poetry: "Light, romantic poetry, to 24 lines." Buys 36/year. Pay "depends on merit."

NEW GIRL CONFESSIONS, 23 W. 26th St., New York NY 10010. See Lopez Romance Group.

PERSONAL ROMANCES, Ideal Publishing Corp., 2 Park Ave., New York NY 10016. Editor: Ilene Dube. Monthly. Buys all rights. No byline. Pays on publication. Reports on submissions in 8-10 weeks. SASE. "Query letter not necessary."

Fiction: First-person stories told in strong up-to-date terms by young marrieds, singles, and teens revealing their emotional, sexual, and family conflicts and their search to resolve personal problems. Blue-collar, white collar group identification. "We are interested in fresh ideas, and occasionally buy supernatural and macabre stories if they fit in with the confession format, and have plausible explanations." Length: 2,000-6,000 words. Top pay is up to $160, based on 3¢/word.

REAL CONFESSIONS, MODERN LOVE CONFESSIONS, Sterling Library, Inc., 261 5th Ave., New York NY 10016. Editor: Susan Silverman. 50% freelance written. For female readers from teenage on up. Monthly. Circ. 300,000. Buys all rights. Pays on publication. No photocopied or simultaneous submissions. Submit seasonal material 5 months in advance. Reports in 1 month. Submit only complete ms. SASE.

Fiction: "Current sexual themes; quantity of description, although it should not be too explicit." Payment: "In the area of 3¢/word."

REAL ROMANCES, 23 W. 26th St., New York NY 10010. See Lopez Romance Group.

REAL STORY, 23 W. 26th St., New York 10010. See Lopez Romance Group.

SECRETS, Macfadden Women's Group, 215 Lexington Ave., New York NY 10016. (212)983-5644. Editor: Jean Press Silberg. For blue-collar family women, ages 18-35. Monthly magazine; 80 pages. Estab. 1936. Buys all rights. Buys about 150 mss/year. Pays on publication. No photocopied or simultaneous submissions. Submit seasonal material 4-5 months in advance. Submit only complete ms. Reports in 6 weeks. SASE..

Nonfiction, Fiction and Poetry: Wants realistically told, strongly plotted stories of romantic nature; self-help or inspirational fillers. Length: 300-1,000 words for nonfiction; 1,500-7,500 words for full-length mss. Occasional 10,000-worders. Pays 3¢/word for confession mss. Greatest need: 2,000-5,000 words. Also buys light, romantic verse. Length: 24 lines maximum.

TRUE CONFESSIONS, Macfadden Women's Group, 215 Lexington Ave., New York NY 10016. Editor: Barbara J. Brett. For high-school-educated blue-collar women, teens through maturity. Monthly magazine. Estab. 1922. Circ. 350,000. Buys all rights. Byline given. Pays on publication. No photocopied or simultaneous submissions. Submit seasonal material at least 5 or 6 months in advance. Reports in 8-12 weeks. Submit complete ms. SASE.

Stories, Articles, and Fillers: Timely, exciting, emotional first-person stories on the problems that face today's young women. The narrators should be sympathetic, and the situations they find themselves in should be intriguing, yet realistic. Every story should have a strong romantic interest and a high moral tone, and every plot should reach an exciting climax. Careful study of a current issue is suggested. Length: 2,000-7,000 words; 5,000 word stories preferred; also book-lengths of 10,000-12,000 words. Pays 5¢/word. Also, articles, regular features, and short fillers.

Poetry: Romantic poetry, free verse and traditional, of interest to women. Limit submissions to batches of 4. Pays $10 minimum.

TRUE EXPERIENCE, Macfadden Women's Group, 215 Lexington Ave.; New York NY 10016. Editor: Lydia E. Paglio. For young marrieds, blue-collar, high school education. Interests: children, home, arts, crafts, family and self-fulfillment. Monthly magazine; 80 pages. Estab. 1925. Circ. 225,000. Buys all rights. Byline given. Buys about 150 mss/year. Pays on publication. "Study the magazine for style and editorial content." No photocopied or simultaneous submissions. Submit seasonal material for holiday issues 5 months in advance. Reports in 3 months. Submit complete ms. SASE.

Fiction and Nonfiction: Stories on life situations, e.g., death, love and sickness. Romance and confession, first-person narratives with strong identification for readers. Articles on health, self-help or child care. "Remember that we are more contemporary. We deal more with women's self-awareness, and consciousness of their roles in society." Length: 250-1,000 words for nonfiction; 1,000-7,500 words for fiction. Pays 3¢/word.

Poetry: Only traditional forms. Length: 4-20 lines. Payment varies.

TRUE LIFE SECRETS, Charlton Publications, Charlton Bldg., Derby CT 06418. (203)735-3381. Editor-in-Chief: John E. Bartimole. 90% freelance written. Bimonthly magazine; 64 pages. Estab. 1960. Circ. 150,000. Pays on publication. Buys all rights, but may reassign following publication. Byline given "only if requested." Phone queries OK. Submit seasonal/holiday material 6 months in advance of issue date. Photocopied submissions OK. SASE. Reports in 4-8 weeks. Sample copy and writer's guidelines for SASE; mention *Writer's Market* in request.

Nonfiction: How-to (sex-aids, guide to sex, and anything of interest to women). Buys 1 ms/issue. Query or submit complete ms. Length: 1,000-2,500 words. Pays $75-150.

Fiction: Confession. "We welcome manuscripts on a racier theme than most confession magazines. We welcome the new writer and anticipate our needs to remain high for the next several issues." Buys 6-7 mss/issue. Submit complete ms. Length: 3,000-10,000 words. Pays $75 minimum.

TRUE LOVE, Macfadden Women's Group, 215 Lexington Ave., New York NY 10016. Editor: Lois E. Wilcken. For young, blue-collar women. Monthly magazine; 80 pages. Estab. 1924. Circ. 225,000. Buys all rights. Byline given. Buys about 150 mss a year. Pays on publication. Submit seasonal material (Christmas, Easter, Thanksgiving Day, Mother's Day, Father's Day, Valentine's Day) at least 6 months in advance. Reports in 12-16 weeks. Submit complete ms. SASE

Fiction: Confessions, true love stories; problems and solutions. Avoid graphic sex. Stories dealing with reality, current problems, everyday events, with emphasis on emotional impact. Length: 1,500-8,000 words. Pays 3¢/word.

Nonfiction: Informational and how-to articles. Length: 250-800 words. Pays 3¢/word minimum.

TRUE ROMANCE, Macfadden Women's Group, 205 E. 42nd St., New York NY 10017. (212)983-5644. Editor: Susan Weiner. "Our readership ranges from teenagers to senior citizens. The majority are high school educated, married, have young children and also work outside the home. They are concerned with contemporary social issues, yet they are deeply committed to their husbands and children. They have high moral values and place great emphasis on love and romance." Monthly magazine; 80 pages. Estab. 1923. Circ. 225,000. Pays on publication. Buys all rights. Submit seasonal/holiday material at least 5 months in advance. SASE. Reports in 3 months.

Nonfiction: How-to and informational. Submit complete ms. Length: 300-1,000 words. Pays 3¢/word, special rates for short features and articles.

Fiction: Confession. Buys 13 stories/issue. Submit complete ms. Length: 2,000-7,500. Pays 3¢/word; slightly higher flat rate for short-shorts.

Poetry: Light verse and traditional. Buys 30/year. Length: 4-20 lines. Pays $10 minimum.

How To Break In: "The freelance writer is needed and welcomed. A timely, well-written story that is told by a sympathetic narrator who sees the central problem through to a satisfying resolution is all that is needed to 'break into' *True Romance.*"

TRUE SECRETS, Rolat Publishing Corp., 667 Madison Ave., New York NY 10021. Editorial Director: Cara Sherman. For women between the ages 15-35. Magazine. Circ. 170,000. Pays on acceptance. Buys all rights. Submissions addressed to *True Secrets* are also considered for publication for *Intimate Romances,* and *Intimate Secrets.* Reports in 4-6 weeks. Free writer's guidelines.

Nonfiction: "Though we do not purchase much nonfiction, if the subject is of interest, relevance, and handled appropriately for our readership, we'll consider it." Length: 3,000-5,000 words. Pays $125-150.

Fiction: "We look primarily for tender love stories, touching baby stories, and stories dealing with identifiable marital problems, particularly sexual. We are interested in realistic teen stories, and, on occasion, male-narrated stories and tales with occult and gothic overtones. Stories should be written in the first-person. They should deal with a romantic or emotional problem that is identifiable and realistically portrays how the narrator copes with her conflict and resolves it. We reject stories based on hackneyed themes and outdated attitudes. In our contemporary society, stories condemming premarital sexual experience, abortion, and those that preach chastity, etc., are unsuitable for our needs." Length: 1,500-7,000 words. Pays $75-150.

How To Break In: Avoid the "sin-suffer-repent" syndrome. Tailor your needs to suit a young, rural audience who, though unsophisticated, no longer live by Puritanical values. Buy a copy of one of our books and study it. Don't think that all confessions are the same. They're not."

TRUE STORY, Macfadden Women's Group, 215 Lexington Ave., New York NY 10016. Editor: Helen Vincent. 80% freelance written. For young married, blue-collar women, 20-35; high school education; increasingly broad interests; home-oriented, but increasingly looking beyond the home for personal fulfillment. Monthly magazine; 104 pages. Estab. 1919. Circ. 1,700,000. Buys all rights. Byline given "on nonfiction only." Buys about 125 full-length mss/year. Pays on publication. No photocopied or simultaneous submissions. Submit seasonal material 4 months in advance. Make notation on envelope that it is seasonal material. Query for nonfiction. Submit only complete mss for fiction. Reports in 2-3 months. SASE.

Nonfiction, Fiction and Fillers: "First-person stories covering all aspects of women's interest: love, marriage, family life, careers, social problems, etc. Nonfiction would further explore same areas. The best direction a new writer can be given is to carefully study several issues of the magazine; then submit a fresh, exciting, well-written story. We have no taboos. It's the handling that makes the difference between a rejection and an acceptance." How-to, personal experience, inspirational. Length: 1,000-2,500 words. Pays 5-10¢ or more/word. Also seeks material for Women are Wonderful column. Length: 1,500 words maximum. Pays 5¢/word. Pays a flat rate for column or departments, announced in the magazine. Query Art Director, Gus Gazzola, about all possible photo submissions. Length: 1,500-8,000 words. Pays 5¢/word; $100 minimum. Regular departments—New Faces and Children's Corner—bring $5/item.

Consumer Service and Business Opportunity

Magazines in this classification are edited for individuals who don't necessarily have a lot of money, but who want maximum return on what they do have—either in goods purchased or in earnings from investment in a small business of their own. Publications for business executives are listed under Business and Finance. Those on how to run specific businesses are classified in Trade, Technical and Professional Journals.

BUYWAYS, 1000 Sunset Ridge Rd., Northbrook IL 60062. (312)777-7000. For members of National Association of Consumers and Travelers (NACT). Association members are middle-income high school graduates. They joined their association to save money on a variety of products (for example, new cars, motels, group travel, car rental, appliances, etc.). Quarterly magazine; 16-24 pages. Estab. 1972. Circ. 60,000. Buys first North American serial rights. Byline given. Buys 12-16 mss/year. Pays on acceptance. Will consider photocopied and simultaneous submissions. Query. Reports in 6 weeks. SASE.

Nonfiction and Photos: "Consumer-oriented articles on how to save, how to buy wisely (money and management); some travel articles (domestic and foreign). Emphasis on wise buying for home and travel. Looking for well-researched articles. Informational, how-to, personal experience, interview, profile, humor, historical, photo, travel, successful business operations, and new product articles. Length: 500-2,500 words. Pays 10-20¢/word.

CANADIAN CONSUMER, Consumers' Association of Canada, 200 1st Ave., Ottawa, Ontario, Canada K1S 5J3. (613)238-4840. Editor: David Shaw. 40% freelance written. Emphasizes consumer information for a "very broad readership." Bimonthly magazine; 48-56 pages. Estab. 1963. Circ. 145,000. Pays on publication. Buys all rights. Phone queries OK. Simultaneous and photocopied submissions OK. SASE. Reports in 1 month. Free sample copy.

Nonfiction: "Anything of specific interest to consumers." Expose and how-to. Buys 18 mss/year. Submit complete ms. Length: 1,200-2,700 words. Pays $50.

Photos: State availability of photos with ms. Pays $10-25 for 8½x11 b&w glossy prints; $10-25 for 35mm color transparencies. Captions preferred. Buys all rights.

CA$H NEWSLETTER, Box 1999, Brooksville FL 33512. Editor-in-Chief: G. Douglas Hafely Jr. Managing Editor: K.R. Baker. Emphasizes "making, saving and investing money." Monthly newsletter; 8 pages. Estab. 1976. Pays on acceptance. Buys all rights. Usually no bylines unless requested on outstanding articles. Regular contributors are listed as "contributing editors." Submit seasonal/holiday material 2 months in advance. Simultaneous and photocopied submissions OK. SASE. Reports in 2 weeks. Sample copy 50¢.

Nonfiction: Small businesses (ones the average person could start with little or no capital, preferably from home); expose (rags to riches, how the little guy got started and made it big; need full details on how); humor (pertaining to making and saving money); how-to (make, save, keep, use and invest money; how to get services, information and goods free); informational (ways for anyone to succeed); inspirational (hope for the small man); interview (with successful people who started small); new product (hot items for resale, new items of interest to mass audience, how to buy and save); personal experience (if from small to successful); technical (on interesting new ways to invest; market projections and contacts); and travel (any inexpensive and/or unusual vacations). Buys 2-10 mss/issue. Submit complete ms. Length: 100-1,000 words. "Omit puffery and flowery phrases; write in telegraphese, short and to the point." Pays $2-10.

Photos: Purchased with or without accompanying ms. Captions required. Send prints. Pays $2-5 for 4x5 b&w glossy prints. No additional payment for photos accepted with accompanying ms.

Fillers: Clippings and newsbreaks. Buys 1-10/issue. Length: 5-50 words. Pays 50¢-$2.

CONSUMER REPORTS, 256 Washington St., Mt. Vernon NY 10550. Editor: Irwin Landau. Staff-written.

CONSUMERS DIGEST MAGAZINE, Consumer Digest, Inc., 5705 N Lincoln Ave., Chicago IL 60659. (312)275-3590. Editor: Larry Teeman. Emphasizes anything of consumer business interests. Monthly magazine; 64 pages. Estab. 1961. Circ. 600,000. Pays on publication. Buys all rights. Phone queries OK. Submit seasonal/holiday material 3 months in advance. SASE. Reports in 4 weeks. Free writer's guidelines.

Nonfiction: Expose; general interest (on advice to consumers and consumer buying products, service, health, business, investments, insurance and money management); how-to; news product and travel. Buys 10 mss/issue. Query. Length: 2,500-3,500 words. Pays 15¢/word.

CONSUMERS' RESEARCH MAGAZINE, Washington NJ 07882. Editor: F.J. Schlink. 5% freelance written. Monthly. Byline given "except when the article as written requires extensive editing, improvement, amplification, which may occur when a nontechnical person writes in a field where engineering or physical science knowledge is essential." Limited amount of freelance material used. Query. SASE.

Nonfiction and Photos: Articles of practical interest to consumers concerned with tests and expert judgment of goods and services they buy. Must be accurate and, well-supported by chemical, engineering, scientific, medical, or other expert or professional knowledge of subject. Pays approximately 2¢/word. Buys b&w glossy prints with mss only. Pays $5 minimum. "Photos are accepted only if they are clearly relevant to the article being published."

CURRENT CONSUMER, Curriculum Innovations, Inc., 501 Lake Forest Ave., Highwood IL 60040. (312)432-2700. Editor: Jan Farrington. 10% freelance written. Emphasizes consumer education. For junior and senior high school students at approximately 9th grade reading level. Teacher's edition aimed at home economics, business, economics and consumer education teachers. Monthly during the school year (Sept-May). Magazine; 32 pages. Estab. 1976. Circ. 65,000. Pays on publication. Buys all rights. Submit seasonal/holiday material 4 months in advance. Simultaneous submissions OK. SASE. Reports in 2 weeks.

Nonfiction: "Our editorial philosophy is to educate young people toward becoming effective and aware consumers. We do not take an advocacy stance or endorse singular viewpoints. Material submitted for our consideration must correspond to this philosophy." How-to (on ways to becoming a more effective and confident consumer); informational (on anything a junior or senior high school student should know as a future consumer); interview; profile (of a consumer who has a valuable story to tell or lesson to teach); new product (that offers unique alternatives or advantages to the consumer); personal experience and photo feature. Buys 9 mss/year. Query. Length: 750-3,000 words.

Columns/Departments: Marketplace (guide to buying goods and services—no product listing or rating), Money Management, Consumer Law, Teacher's Edition (activities for teachers). Buys 5-10/year. Query. Length: 750-1,000 words. Pays $50-75 for short features. Open to suggestions for new columns or departments.

ECONOMIC FACTS, The National Research Bureau, Inc., 424 N. 3rd St., Burlington IA 52601. Editor-in-Chief: Nicholas Pasqual. 95% freelance written. For industrial workers of all ages. Published 3 times/year. Magazine; 16 pages. Estab. 1970. Circ. 30,000. Pays on publication. Buys all rights, but may reassign following publication. Byline given. Submit seasonal/holiday material 3-4 months in advance of issue date. Previously published submissions OK. SASE. Reports in 1 week. Free sample copy and writer's guidelines; mention *Writer's Market* in request.

Nonfiction: Barbara Boeding, articles editor. General interest (private enterprise, government data, graphs, taxes and health care). Buys 2-3 mss/issue. Query with outline of article. Length: 400-600 words. Pays $20 minimum.

FDA CONSUMER, 5600 Fishers Lane, Rockville MD 20857. (301)443-3220. Editor: Roger W. Miller. 10% freelance written. For "all consumers of products regulated by the Food and Drug Administration." A federal government publication. Monthly magazine, 40 pages. Estab. 1967. December/January and July/August issues combined. Circ. 20,000. Not copyrighted. Pays 50% kill fee. Byline given. "All purchases automatically become part of public domain." Buys 4-5 freelance mss a year. Pays on publication. Query. "We cannot be responsible for any work by writer not agreed upon by prior contract." SASE.

Nonfiction and Photos: "Articles of an educational nature concerning purchase and use of FDA regulated products and specific FDA programs and actions to protect the consumer's health and pocketbook. Authoritative and official agency viewpoints emanating from agency policy and actions in administrating the Food, Drug and Cosmetic Act and a number of other statutes. All articles subject to clearance by the appropriate FDA experts as well as the editor. The magazine speaks for the federal government only. Articles based on facts and FDA policy only. We cannot consider any unsolicited material. All articles based on prior arrangement by contract. The nature and subject matter and clearances required are so exacting that it is difficult to get an article produced by a writer working outside the Washington DC metropolitan area." Length: average, 2,000 words. Pays $750. B&w photos are purchased on assignment only.

ENTREPRENEUR MAGAZINE, 631 Wilshire Blvd., Suite 200, Santa Monica CA 90401. Editor-in-Chief: Chase Revel. Managing Editor: John Hiatt. 10% freelance written. For a readership looking for highly profitable opportunities in small businesses, as owners, investors or franchisees. Monthly magazine; 100 pages. Estab. 1972. Circ. 50,000. Pays on acceptance. Buys all rights. Byline given. Submit seasonal/holiday material 2 months in advance of issue date. Photocopied submissions OK. SASE. Reports in 4 weeks. Sample copy $1; free writer's guidelines.

Nonfiction: How-to (in-depth start-up details on 'hot' business opportunities like skateboard parks or computer stores). Buys 12 mss/year. Query with clips of published work. Length: 3,500-5,000 words. Pays $300-750 for features; $100 for featurettes.

Photos: "We need good b&w glossy prints to illustrate articles." Offers no additional payment for photos accepted with ms. Uses 8x10 b&w glossy prints or standard transparencies. Captions preferred. Buys all rights. Model release required.

Columns/Departments: New Products; New Ideas; Promo Gimmicks; and Frauds. Query. Length: 200-500 words. Pays $25-50.

INFO: A WORLD OF $ENSE, Consumer Services, Inc., Box 123, Lyndhurst NJ 07071. (201)661-0700. Editor: Jordan Goodman. Emphasizes consumer affairs. Monthly newspaper insert; 32 pages. Estab. 1978. Pays on publication. Buys all rights. Phone queries OK. Submit seasonal/holiday material 3 months in advance. Simultaneous submissions OK. SASE. Reports in 2 weeks.

Nonfiction: How-to (do-it-yourself tips around the home, car, kitchen); new product (explaining new products consumers will see in the home, how to use and buy them); travel (tips on how to travel); and articles explaining new laws or regulations affecting consumers. "No articles on personal experiences, religion, nostalgia, profiles, interviews, personal opinions or humor." Buys 3 mss/issue. Send complete ms. Length: 500-1,700 words. Pays $30/half page and $60/full page.

Photos: Send photos with ms. Pays $25 for 9x6 b&w glossy prints. Buys one-time rights.

Columns/Departments: Health, Food, Travel, Leisure, Cars, Money Management, Women, Retirement, Shopping, Family Advice, Teen Scene, Home, Do-it-Yourself, Energy, and Apartment Living. Buys 24/issue. Send complete ms. Length: 500-700 words. Pays $25.

MONEYTREE NEWSLETTER, Task Bldg., Kerrville TX 78028. Editor: Marshall Sideman. Pays on acceptance. Send #10 SASE and $1 for sample copy to the attention of M. Sideman.

Fillers: "Items dealing with money. How to invest it, make it grow rapidly, how to get big savings—these have the best chance of acceptance. Our readers want to get rich, or if wealthy already, stay rich." Also uses capsule articles on health, self-help, vocational training, practical science, money-making opportunities, etc. Also capsulized write-ups about free publications, product samples, items of value, etc. All submissions must be documented by author. Length: 10 to 60 words. Pays $5.

NEW VENTURES, Observer Publishing Co., 4822 MacArthur Blvd., Washington DC 20016. (202)337-4211. Editor: George Spencer. Managing Editor: Barry Crickmer. "Our readers are entrepreneurs and professionals interested in small business investment possibilities. They prefer opportunities in the under-$100,000 range. Areas of greatest interest: businesses suitable for absentee owners, real estate services, new products and technology, sources of capital." Biweekly newsletter; 8 pages. Estab. 1978. Circ. 4,000. Pays on acceptance. Buys all rights. No byline given. Phone queries OK. Photocopied submissions OK. SASE. Reports in 2 weeks. Free sample copy and writer's guidelines.
Nonfiction: Expose (of frauds preying on small business owner or potential owner); how-to (make money on a new small business product or service); interview (with successful inventor/entrepreneur in new small business field); and new product (suitable for manufacture/sale by small business). "A well-written article with these characteristics has an excellent chance of acceptance: new, profitable small-business idea (or new twist on old idea); analysis of the success of pioneers in field, with return-on investment figures; step-by-step instructions on how to enter the business, with breakdowns of construction/production/operating costs; tips on marketing, potential problems; a human-interest lead that draws the reader into the text." No material dealing with securities or commodities trading or rewritten promotional material from manufacturers/franchisors. Buys 1-2 mss/issue. Send complete ms. Length: 500-5,000 words. Pays 15¢/word.
Photos: "We consider photos only if visual element is essential to reader comprehension." State availability of photos.

SUBURBAN SHOPPER, Box 208, East Millstone NJ 08873. (201)873-2156. Editor-in-Chief: Kevin K. Kopec. 100% freelance written. For convenience shoppers, working women who are interested in savings and unusual gagets/home items. Quarterly tabloid; 24 pages. Estab. February 1978. Pays on publication. Buys one-time rights. Phone queries OK. Submit seasonal/holiday material 1 month in advance of issue date. Simultaneous, photocopied, and previously published submissions OK. SASE. Reports in 3 weeks. Sample copy $1.25; free writer's guidelines; mention *Writer's Market* in request.
Nonfiction: General interest (any aspect of mail order shopping-buying tips, etc.); and new product (mail order product reviews). Buys 5 mss/issue. Submit complete ms. Length: 500-1,000 words. Pays $5-10.

SUPERMARKET SHOPPER, American Coupon Club, Inc., Box 1149, Great Neck NY 11023. President: Martin Sloane. Managing Editor: Ruth Brooks. Emphasizes smart supermarket shopping and the use of cents-off coupons and refund offers for "a wide audience of supermarket shoppers who want to save money. The editorial slant is definitely consumer-oriented." Monthly; 36 pages. Estab. 1978. Circ. 10,000. Pays on publication. Buys all rights. Byline given. Simultaneous, photocopied and previously published submissions OK. SASE. Reports in 2-4 weeks. Free sample copy; writers guidelines for SASE.
Nonfiction: General interest; expose (of supermarket operations, management, coupon misredemption); how-to (save money at the supermarket, tips, dollar stretchers; etc.); humor; interview (of top management, food manufacturers or supermarkets); new product (food, household products); and personal experience (couponing and refunding). Buys 2-3 mss/issue. Send complete ms. Length: 750-2,500 words. Pays 5¢/published word.
Fiction: "We have not used fiction, but we might be interested if the events are in context of supermarket shopping." Query. Length: 750-2,500 words. Pays 5¢/published word.
Fillers: Jokes, short humor and newsbreaks. Buys 1-2/issue. Length: 50-200 words. Pays $5-10.

Detective and Crime

Publications listed in this section provide markets for nonfiction accounts of true crimes. Markets for criminal fiction (mysteries) are listed in Mystery Publications.

DETECTIVE CASES, Detective Files Group, 1440 St. Catherine St. W., Montreal, Quebec, Canada H3G 1S2. Editor-in-Chief: Dominick A. Merle. Art Director: Art Ball. Bimonthly magazine; 72 pages. See *Detective Files*.

DETECTIVE DRAGNET, Detective Files Group, 1440 St. Catherine St. W., Montreal, Quebec, Canada H3G 1S2. Editor-in-Chief: Dominick A. Merle. Art Director: Art Ball. Bimonthly magazine; 72 pages. See *Detective Files*.

DETECTIVE FILES, Detective Files Group, 1440 St. Catherine St. W., Montreal, Quebec, Canada H3G 1S2. Editor-in-Chief: Dominick A. Merle. Art Director: Art Ball. Bimonthly magazine; 72 pages. Pays on acceptance. Buys all rights. Submit seasonal/holiday material 4 months in advance. Photocopied submissions OK. SASE. Reports in 4 weeks. Free sample copy and writer's guidelines.
Nonfiction: True crime stories. "Do a thorough job; don't double-sell (sell an article to more than one market), and deliver and you can have a steady market. Neatness, clarity and pace will help you make the sale." Query. Length: 3,500-6,000 words. Pays $175-250.
Photos: Purchased with accompanying ms; no additional payment. B&w only. Model release required.

FRONT PAGE DETECTIVE, INSIDE DETECTIVE, Official Detective Group, R.G.H. Publishing Corp. 235 Park Ave. S., New York NY 10003. Editor-in-Chief: Albert P. Govoni. Editor: Diana Lurvey.
Nonfiction: The focus of these two publications is similar to the others in the Official Detective Group, but concentrates less on pre-trial stories. Byline given. For further details, see *Official Detective*.

HEADQUARTERS DETECTIVE, Detective Files Group, 1440 St. Catherine St. W., Montreal, Quebec, Canada H3G 1S2. Editor-in-Chief: Dominick A. Merle. Art Director: Art Ball. Bimonthly magazine; 72 pages. See *Detective Files*.

MASTER DETECTIVE, Official Detective Group, R.G.H. Publishing Corp., 235 Park Ave. S., New York NY 10003. Editor-in-Chief: Albert P. Govoni. Managing Editor: Walter Jackson. Monthly. Estab. 1929. Circ. 350,000; Buys 9-10 mss/issue. See *Official Detective*.

OFFICIAL DETECTIVE, Official Detective Group, R.G.H. Publishing Corp., 235 Park Ave. S., New York NY 10003. Editor-in-Chief: Albert P. Govoni. Manager Editor: Walter Jackson. "For detective story or police buffs whose tastes run to *true*, rather than fictional crime/mysteries." Monthly magazine; 80 pages. Estab. 1930. Circ. 500,000. Pays on acceptance. Buys all rights. Byline given. Phone queries OK. Buys 11-12 mss/issue. SASE. Reports in 2 weeks.
Nonfiction: "Only *fact* detective stories. We are actively trying to develop new writers, and we'll work closely with those who show promise and can take the discipline required by our material. It's not difficult to write, but it demands meticulous attention to facts, truth, clarity, detail. Queries are essential with us, but I'd say the quickest rejection goes to the writer who sends in a story on a case that should never have been written for us because it lacks the most important ingredient, namely solid, superlative detective work. We also dislike pieces with multiple defendants, unless all have been convicted." Buys 150 mss/year. Query. Length: 4,500-6,500 words. Pays $200-400.
Photos: Purchased with accompanying mss. Captions required. Send prints for inside use; transparencies for covers. Pays $12.50 minimum for b&w glossy prints, 4x5 minimum. Pays $200 minimum for 2¼x2¼ or 35mm transparencies. Model release required for color photos used on cover.

STARTLING DETECTIVE, Detective Files Group, 1440 St. Catherine St. W., Montreal, Quebec, Canada H3G 1S2. Editor-in-Chief: Dominick A. Merle. Art Director: Art Ball. Bimonthly magazine; 72 pages. See *Detective Files*.

TRUE DETECTIVE, Official Detective Group, R.G.H. Publishing Corp., 235 Park Ave., S., New York NY 10003. Editor-in-Chief: Albert P. Govoni. Managing Editor: Walter Jackson. Monthly. Estab. 1924. Circ. 500,000. Buys 11-12 mss/issue. Byline given. See *Official Detective*.

TRUE POLICE CASES, Detective Files Group, 1440 St. Catherine St. W., Montreal, Quebec, Canada H3G 1S2. Editor-in-Chief: Dominick A. Merle. Art Director: Art Ball. Bimonthly magazine; 72 pages. See *Detective Files*.

Education

Magazines here cover education for parents and the general public. Journals for professional educators and teachers are included in the Education category are included in the Trade Journals section. Because of their value to educators and parents, nonpaying markets are included in this section.

AMERICAN EDUCATION, U.S. Office of Education, 400 Maryland Ave. SW, Washington DC 20202. (202)245-8907. Editor: William A. Horn. Managing Editor: Gertrue Mitchell. Presents successful education programs with some federal involvement for readership of education and others with special interest in the field. Monthly magazine; 36-42 pages. Estab. 1965. Circ. 40,000. Pays on acceptance. Buys all rights. Pays $100-150 kill fee. Byline given. Submit seasonal/holiday material 4 months in advance. Photocopied submissions OK. SASE. Reports in 2-3 weeks. Free sample copy and writer's guidelines.
Nonfiction: Informational (successful projects or programs with federal involvement). Buys 30 mss/year. Query. Length: average 2,500 words. Pays $350 and up, depending on quality.
Photos: Alyce Jackson, Photo Editor. Purchased with accompanying manuscript. Submit b&w glossy photos and contact sheet. Pays $15 minimum.

AMERICAN TEACHER, 11 Dupont Circle NW, Washington DC 20036. (202)797-4430. Editor: Linda Chavez. For "members of the American Federation of Teachers, AFL-CIO, and other classroom teachers." Monthly except July and August. Buys first North American serial rights; will buy simultaneous rights. Pays on publication. Free sample copy. Reports in 4 months. SASE.
Nonfiction and Photos: "We want material directly concerned with our primary interests: educational innovation, academic freedom, the teacher union movement, better schools and educational methods, legislation concerning teachers, etc." Query. Pays $25-$70. Photos purchased with and without mss; captions required. "Stock photos of classroom scenes." Subjects must be in range of subject interest. No specific size. Pays $15.

CANADIAN CHILDREN'S MAGAZINE, 4150 Bracken Ave., Victoria, British Columbia, Canada, V8X 3N8. (604)479-6906. Editor-in-Chief: Evelyn Samuel. "This magazine is geared toward children 6-12 years old in Canada or interested in Canadian materials." Quarterly magazine; 48 pages. Estab. 1976. Circ. 25,000. Byline given. Pays in copies. Acquires one-time rights. Phone queries OK. Submit seasonal/holiday material 6 months in advance. Photocopied submissions OK. SASE. Reports in 1 month. Sample copy $1.25; free writer's guidelines.
Nonfiction: How-to (always with a Canadian slant—ethnic, Indian or regional), historical (Canadian material only), and informational (current Canadian contributions, inventions, etc). Uses 25 mss/issue. Query. Length: 500-1,500 words. Pays in copies.
Fiction: Uses 2 mss/year. Query. Length: 500-1,500 words. Pays in copies.

CAREER WORLD, Curriculum Innovations, Inc., 501 Lake Forest Ave., Highwood IL 60040. (312)432-2700. Editor: Bonnie Bekken. 80% freelance written. Emphasizes career education for junior and senior high school students at approximately 9th grade reading level. Teacher's edition aimed at guidance and career education personnel. Monthly (September-May) magazine; 32 pages. Estab. 1972. Circ. 130,000. Pays on publication. Buys all rights. Byline given. Submit seasonal/holiday material 4 months in advance. SASE. Reports in 2 weeks.
Nonfiction: How-to, informational, interview, profile and photo feature. Buys 9 mss/year. Query. Length: 750-3,000 words. Pays 4¢/word minimum.
Columns/Departments: Lifestyle (worker profile), Offbeat Job (unusual occupation), New Careers. Buys 9/year. Query. Length: 300-1,500 words. Pays 4¢/word and up. Open to suggestions for new columns or departments.

CHANGE MAGAZINE, Council on Learning, Inc., NBW Tower, New Rochelle, NY 10801. Editor-in-Chief: George W. Bonham. Emphasizes higher learning/higher education. *"Change* is an opinion magazine broadly concerned with academic matters, social issues, and subject matter of intellectual interest." Monthly magazine; 64 pages. Estab. 1969. Circ. 20,000. Pays on acceptance. Buys all rights. Pays 33% kill fee. Byline given. Simultaneous and photocopied submissions OK. SASE. Reports in 6 weeks. Sample copy $1.
Nonfiction: Joyce Bermel, Articles Editor. Informational; interview; personal opinion; and profile. Buys 150 mss/year. Length: 1,200-10,000 words. Pays $100-300.
Columns/Departments: Cullen Murphy, Column, Department Editor. Book Reviews (reviews

of books on education, social issues, intellectual interests), Community Colleges (reports on community colleges and their programs and problems), Media (broad-based pieces on all forms of media, educational and others). Buys 2/issue. Query. Length: 1,600-2,000 words. Pays $100-150. Open to suggestions for new columns and departments.

DAY CARE AND EARLY EDUCATION, 72 5th Ave., New York NY 10011. Contact: Editor. 40% freelance written. For day care professionals—teachers, paraprofessionals, administrators, family day care providers and parents. Quarterly magazine; 64 pages. Estab. 1973. Circ. 20,000. Pays on publication. Buys all rights, or "will make arrangements with authors." Pays 33% kill fee. Byline given. Submit seasonal/holiday material 6 months in advance of issue date. Photocopied submissions OK. SASE. Reports in 2 months. Free sample copy and writer's guidelines.
Nonfiction: How-to (activity ideas, staff training, administrative ideas); interview (on research or innovations in day care or educational programs); photo feature; and travel (child care in other countries). No "highly technical, jargon-filled research." Buys 5 mss/issue. Query. Length: 1,000-3,000 words. Pays $35-150.
Photos: State availabilty of photos with query. No additional payment for 8x10 glossy b&w photos accepted with ms. Captions preferred. Buys all rights.
Fiction: "We discourage fiction submissions unless *unusual*. Must be for young children. Very little published. We prefer that there be non-stereotyped situations and characters, teaching a useful lesson." Buys 2 mss/year. Submit complete ms. Length: 1,000-2,000 words. Pays $35-75.

THE EDUCATIONAL ABC OF INDUSTRY RESOURCE BOOK, 2212-11th St., Niagara Falls NY 14305. Publisher: Terence J. Hughes. Managing Editor: Neil MacVicar. 20% freelance written. For students aged 12-16 and teachers of grades 7-10. Annual magazine; 36 pages. Estab. 1957. Circ. 2,800,000. Pays on publication. Buys first North American serial rights. Byline given. Reports in 10 weeks. Free sample copy; mention *Writer's Market* in request.
Nonfiction: Neil MacVicar, Managing Editor. "Articles are educational in nature and must be aimed at students 12-16. Articles must be informative, concise, documented and interesting. Do not send complete ms. We require a pre-statement on the article and teaching questions, photo suggestions, project bibliography, and class discussion questions. All articles should lead to resources. We are interested in articles from educators that can be understood. No Jargon." How-to; historical; interview; personal experience (from students only); profile; and travel. Buys 2 mss/issue. Length: 3,000-5,000 words. Query. Pays $300-500.
Columns/Departments: Careers; Sports; Communications; Social Science; Science; and Coming Across. Query. Length: 1,000-3,000 words. Pays $250-300. Open to suggestions for new columns/departments.

Food and Drink

Magazines classified here aim at individuals who are interested in and appreciate fine wines and fine foods.

Journals aimed at food processors, manufacturers, and retailers will be found in the Trade Journals.

BON APPETIT, Knapp Communications, 5900 Wilshire Blvd., Los Angeles CA 90036. Editor-in-Chief: Paige Rense. Managing Editor: Marilou Vaughan. 90% freelance written. Emphasizes food, cooking and wine "for affluent young, active men and women, interested in the good things of life." Monthly magazine; 120 pages. Circ. 1 million. Pays on acceptance. Rights purchased vary. Submit seasonal/holiday material 6 months in advance of issue date. Photocopied and previously published submissions OK. SASE. Reports in 6 weeks.
Nonfiction: Arline Inge, articles editor. How-to cook, and food articles with recipes. No historical food pieces. Query. Length: 2,000 words. Pay varies.

DINING IN & OUT, Kraft & Kraft, 39 Garner Road, Stow MA 01775. Editor: Eric Kraft. Emphasizes entertaining and dining. Monthly magazine; 48 pages. Estab. September 1978. Circ. 6,600. Pays on publication. Buys all rights. Pays 10% kill fee. Byline given. Submit seasonal/holiday material 2 months in advance. Photocopied submissions OK. SASE. Reports in 6 weeks. Sample copy 50¢; free writer's guidelines.
Nonfiction: General interest (on nutrition, ethnic foods and food in literature); historical (on origins of dishes, introductions of foods to America, dining out in the past, antique recipes, methods of cooking and changing tastes in food); how-to (on cooking tips, preserving food, recipes, shopping, entertaining, menu planning and diet); humor (on restaurant experiences,

food faddism and food snobbery); interview (on chefs, nutritionists and cookbook authors); nostalgia (on dining experiences of the past, family dinners and old food fads); profile (on chefs, nutritionists and cookbook authors); new product (on kitchen equipment and gadgets); personal experience (in restaurants, or as a host or hostess); and photo feature (on kitchens and kitchen design for homes and apartments). "We do not want elitist articles or foreign travel articles." Buys 3 mss/issue. Query. Length: 500-2,500 words, but prefers 1,000-1,500 words. Pays $10-25.

Photos: State availability of photos or send photo with ms. Offers no additional payment for photos accepted with ms; uses b&w contact sheets. Model release is required.

Fiction: Humorous (must be related to food in some way.) Buys 1 mss/issue. Send complete ms. Length: 500-1,000 words. Pays $10.

Fillers: Cartoons. Buys 2/issue. Pays $10.

FINE DINING (formerly *Dining Out*), Roth-Connell Publications, Inc., 168 SE 1st St., Suite 801, Miami FL 33131. Editor: Sean O'Connell. Emphasizes restaurant dining and gourmet cuisine. Bimonthly magazine; 68 pages. Estab. 1975. Circ. 31,000. Pays on publication. Buys all rights. Byline given. Submit seasonal/holiday material 3 months in advance. Photocopied submissions OK. SASE. Reports in 2 months. Sample copy $2.25.

Nonfiction: Historical, interview, nostalgia, and travel. Buys 6 mss/issue. Query with clips of published work. Length: 1,800-2,500 words. Pays $150.

Photos: Send photos with ms. Offers no additional payment for photos accepted with ms. Captions preferred.

GOURMET, 777 3rd Ave., New York NY 10017. Managing Editor: Miss Gail Zweigenthal. For moneyed, educated, traveled, food-wise men and women. Monthly. Purchases copyright, but grants book reprint rights with credit. Pays on acceptance. Suggests a study of several issues to understand type of material required. Reports in 2 months. Query. "We prefer published writers, so if you haven't written for us before, you should enclose some samples of previous work." SASE.

Nonfiction: Uses articles on subjects related to food and wine—travel, adventure, reminiscence, fishing and hunting experiences. Prefers personal experiences to researched material. Recipes included as necessary. Not interested in nutrition, dieting, penny-saving or bizarre foods, or in interviews with chefs or food experts, or in reports of food contests, festivals or wine tastings. Buys recipes only as part of an article with interesting material to introduce them and make them appealing. "Gourmet Holidays" written by staff contributors only. The same is true for material including specific hotel or restaurant recommendations. Sophisticated, light, nontechnical. Length: 2,500-3,000 words. Current needs include American regional pieces (no restaurants). Pays $650 minimum.

Poetry and Verse: Light, sophisticated with food or drink slant. Pays $50 minimum.

How To Break In: "Personal reminiscences are the easiest way to break in, since we always use staff writers when recommending hotels or restaurants. Our biggest problem with freelancers is that they are not familiar with our style or that they fail to treat their material with enough sophistication or depth. We don't want pieces which sound like press releases or which simply describe what's there. We like to really cover a subject and literary value is important. We'd very much like to see more regional American material. It seems to be much easier to get people traipsing around Europe."

WINE WORLD MAGAZINE, 15101 Keswick St., Van Nuys CA 91405. (213)785-6050. Editor-Publisher: Dee Sindt. For the wine-loving public (adults of all ages) who wish to learn more about wine. Bimonthly magazine; 48 pages. Estab. 1971. Buys first North American serial rights. Buys about 72 mss/year. Pays on publication. Free sample copy and writer's guidelines. No photocopied submissions. Will consider simultaneous submissions, "if spelled out." Reports in 30 days. Query. SASE.

Nonfiction: "Wine-oriented material written with an in-depth knowledge of the subject, designed to meet the needs of the novice and connoisseur alike. Wine technology advancements, wine history, profiles of vintners the world over. Educational articles only. No first-person accounts. Must be objective, informative reporting on economic trends, new technological developments in vinification, vine hybridizing, and vineyard care. New wineries and new marketing trends. We restrict our editorial content to wine, and wine-oriented material. No restaurant or food articles accepted. No more basic wine information. No articles from instant wine experts. Authors must be qualified in this highly technical field." Length: 750-2,000 words. Pays $50-100.

WOMEN'S CIRCLE HOME COOKING, Box 1952, Brooksville FL 33512. Editor: Barbara

Hall Pedersen. For women (and some men) of all ages who really enjoy cooking. "Our readers collect and exchange recipes. They are neither food faddists nor gourmets, but practical women and men trying to serve attractive and nutritious meals. Many work full time, and most are on limited budgets." Monthly magazine; 72 pages. Circ. 225,000. Pays on acceptance. Buys all rights. Submit seasonal/holiday material 6 months in advance. SASE. Reports in 2-8 weeks. Sample copy for large SASE.

Nonfiction: Expose, historical, how-to, informational, inspirational, nostalgia, photo feature and travel. "We like a little humor with our food, for the sake of the digestion. Keep articles light. Stress economy and efficiency. Remember that at least half our readers must cook after working a full-time job. Draw on personal experience to write an informative article on some aspect of cooking. We're a reader participation magazine. We don't go in for fad diets, or strange combinations of food which claim to cure anything." Buys 50 mss/year. Query. Length: 50-1,000 words. Pays 2-5¢/word.

Photos: State availability of photos. Pays $5 for 4x5 b&w sharp glossy prints; $35 for 4x5 color prints.

Fiction: Humorous fiction, related to cooking and foods. Length: 1,200 words maximum. Pays 2-5¢/word.

Poetry: Light verse related to cooking and foods. Length: 30/lines. Pays $5/verse.

Fillers: Short humorous fillers. Length: 100 words. Pays 2-5¢/word.

Original Recipes: For Slow Pot Cooking column. Pays $2/each, if printed.

General Interest

Publications classified here are edited for national, general audiences and carry articles on any subject of interest to a broad spectrum of people. Other markets for general interest material will be found in the Black, In-Flight, Men's, Newspapers and Weekly Magazine Sections, Regional, City magazine, and Women's classifications in the Consumer section. Some company publications cover general-interest topics.

THE ATLANTIC MONTHLY, 8 Arlington St., Boston MA 02116. (617)536-9500. Editor-in-Chief: Robert Manning. For a professional, academic audience interested in politics, arts and general culture. Monthly magazine; 100 pages. Estab. 1857. Circ. 325,000. Pays on acceptance. Buys first North American serial rights. Pays negotiable kill fee. Byline given. Phone queries OK. Submit seasonal/holiday material 3-5 months in advance. Simultaneous and photocopied submissions OK. SASE. Reports in 2-6 weeks. Sample copy $1.50.

Nonfiction: General interest, historical, humor, interview, nostalgia, personal experience, personal opinion, profile and travel. Query with clips of published work or send complete ms. Length: 1,000-6,000 words. Pays $100 minimum/published page.

Fiction: Mainstream. Buys 2 mss/issue. Send complete ms. Length: 2,000-6,000 words. Pays $100/page.

Poetry: Avant-garde, free verse, light verse and traditional. "No concrete or haiku poetry." Buys 2-3 poems/issue. Submit in batches of 8. Length: 100 lines maximum. Pays $2/line.

BANCLUB DIGEST, Banclub Association, 1100 Kermit Dr., Suite 206, Nashville TN 37217. Associate Editor: Owen Taylor. Emphasizes trends in small towns and cities; shows how small town Americans are overcoming problems, improving living conditions, etc.; re-enforces the idea that small towns are good places in which to live. Published 3 times/year; 48 pages. Estab. 1974. Circ. 1.9 million. Pays on acceptance. Buys all rights. Phone queries OK. Submit seasonal/holiday material 5 months in advance. SASE. Reports on queries in 3 weeks; 2 weeks for manuscripts. Sample copy 50¢; writer's guidelines for SASE.

Nonfiction: General interest (travel to out-of-the-way places; anything of interest to small-town folks); how-to (holiday projects; gardening, home-craft); humor (light, short; non-offensive); interview (famous people who live in small towns); photo feature (small town); profile (famous people who live in small towns); travel (American places); and some health. Buys 5 mss/issue. Query. Length: 800-1,500 words. Pays $125-400.

Photos: State availability of photos. Pays $25-50 for b&w contact sheets; $50-125 for 35mm or 120 color transparencies. Captions and model releases required.

BLACKWOOD'S MAGAZINE, William Blackwood & Sons, Ltd., 32 Thistle St., Edinburgh EH2 1HA, Scotland. (031)225-3411. Editor: David Fletcher. 80% freelance written. Monthly magazine; 96 pages. Estab. 1817. Circ. 8,500. Pays on publication. Buys first British serial rights. Phone queries OK. Submit seasonal/holiday material 3 months in advance. SAE and

International Reply Coupons. Reports in 1 week. Sample copy $1.50 (International postal coupons); free writer's guidelines.

Nonfiction: Historical; nostalgia; personal experience; personal opinion; and travel. "Would-be contributors should first study the magazine." Buys 50 mss/year. Submit complete typescript. Length: 1,500-5,000 words.

Fiction: Adventure; historical; humorous; mainstream; mystery; and religious. Buys 50 mss/year. Submit complete typescript. Length: 2,500-5,000 words.

Poetry: Traditional forms. Buys 12/year. Length: 14-69 lines.

How To Break In: "*Blackwood's* is one of the world's oldest monthlies and we are always keen to see work by US and Canadian writers. "Writers must, first of all, have studied the magazine and remember that material must not have appeared in print before submission to us."

CAPPER'S WEEKLY, Stauffer Communications, Inc., 616 Jefferson St., Topeka KS 66607. (913)295-1108. Editor: Dorothy Harvey. Emphasizes home and family. Biweekly tabloid; 24-36 pages. Estab. 1879. Circ. 420,000. Pays for poetry and cartoons on acceptance; articles on publication. Buys first North American serial rights. Byline given. Submit seasonal/holiday material 2 months in advance. SASE. Reports in 2-3 weeks, 6-8 months for serialized novels. Sample copy 35¢.

Nonfiction: Historical (local museums, etc.), inspirational, nostalgia, travel (local slants) and people stories (accomplishments, collections, etc.). Buys 2-3 mss/issue. Submit complete ms. Length: 700 words maximum. Pays $1/inch.

Photos: Purchased with accompanying ms. Submit prints. Pays $5 for 8x10 b&w glossy prints. Total purchase price for ms includes payment for photos.

Columns/Departments: Heart of the Home (homemakers' letters, hints), Hometown Heartbeat (descriptive). Submit complete ms. Length: 500 words maximum. Pays $2-10.

Fiction: Novel-length mystery and romance mss. Buys 2-3 mss/year. Query. Pays $200.

Poetry: Free verse, haiku, light verse, traditional. Buys 7-8/issue. Limit submissions to batches of 5-6. Length: 4-16 lines. Pays $3-5.

CARTE BLANCHE, 3460 Wilshire Blvd., Los Angeles CA 90010. (213)480-3328. Editor: Margaret M. Volpe. For affluent professional people and their families; highly educated, well-read, well-traveled; interested in fine food and drink. Bimonthly magazine; 84-96 pages. Estab. 1964. Circ. 750,000. Pays on acceptance. Buys one-time reproduction rights. Byline given. Submit seasonal/holiday material 5-6 months in advance. Photocopied submissions OK. SASE. Reports in 4 weeks. Sample copy and writer's guidelines for SASE.

Nonfiction: "We publish articles relating to our travel, dining and entertaining format. Photos are very important. Food stories should have expository text, recipes and photos. Some articles on crafts, hobbies, sports, art, or personality profiles (no film stars). We occasionally give assignments." Buys 12-20 mss/year. Query or submit complete ms. Length: 2,000-3,000 words. Pays $300-400.

Photos: Purchased with or without accompanying ms. Captions preferred. Send list of stock photos. Uses any size b&w prints or color transparencies from 35mm and larger.

COMMENTARY, 165 East 56th St., New York NY 10022. Editor: Norman Podhoretz. Monthly magazine, 96 pages. Estab. 1945. Circ. 60,000. Buys all rights. Byline given. "All of our material is done freelance, though much of it is commissioned." Pays on publication. Query, or submit complete ms. Reports in 4 weeks. SASE.

Nonfiction and Fiction: Nonfiction Editor: Brenda Brown. Fiction Editor: Marion Magid. Thoughtful essays on political, social and cultural themes; general, as well as with special Jewish content. Informational, historical and think articles. Length: 3,000 to 7,000 words. Pays approximately $75/printed page. Uses some mainstream fiction. Length: flexible.

THE CONTINENTAL MAGAZINE, Ford Motor Co., Box 1509-B, Dearborn MI 48121. Editor: Robert M. Hodesh. For mature, well-to-do people. Quarterly magazine; 24 pages. Estab. 1960. Circ. 875,000. Pays on acceptance. Buys first North American serial rights. Pays 100% kill fee. Byline given. SASE. Reports in 3 weeks. Free sample copy.

Nonfiction: How-to on spending money and time on culture, sports, travel and liesure. Buys 6 mss/issue. Query. Length: 1,000-1,500 words. Pays $350-500.

EASY LIVING MAGAZINE, The Webb Co., 1999 Shepard Rd., St. Paul MN 55116. (612)647-7304. Executive Editor: Don Picard. Editor: Adele Renee Malott. 75% freelance written. "The publication's editorial goal is to inform and entertain the readers, with emphasis on the former." Emphasizes profiles, lifestyles, family activities, consumer and food articles and international travel; for an audience between 45 and 75; fairly high income. Distributed by Creative Marketing Enterprises, Inc. Quarterly magazine; 36 pages. Estab. 1974. Circ. 250,000. Pays on acceptance. Buys one-time rights and nonexclusive reprint rights. Submit seasonal/holiday material 1 year in advance. Simultaneous and photocopied submissions OK. SASE. Reports on queries in 3 weeks; on mss in 6 weeks. Free sample copy and writer's guidelines.

Nonfiction: Informational (about popular activities, new trends), profile (of unknown), and travel (international, Europe, Caribbean, Mexico, Far East, and Hawaii only). Query. Length: 1,000-2,500 words. Pays $100-400.

Photos: Photos purchased with or without accompanying ms (but only to illustrate ms already purchased). Pays $50 for 8x10 b&w glossies; $100 minimum for color photos; $250 for color cover photos. 35mm acceptable. Captions required; model release preferred, but in some circumstances may be dispensed with."

EASY TIMES MAGAZINE, Fantasma Productions, Inc. of Florida, 1675 Palm Beach Lakes Blvd., Suite 902, Forum III, West Palm Beach FL 33401. (305)686-6387. Editor: Michael Berlyn. Associate Editor: Debi Cooper. Emphasizes general interest features for a young adult readership interested in the entertainment media, sports, health, travel and clothes. Monthly magazine. Estab. April 1974. Circ. 62,500. Pays on publication. Buys simultaneous rights, second serial (reprint) rights or first North American serial rights. Byline given. Submit seasonal/holiday material 4 months in advance. Simultaneous, photocopied and previously published submissions OK. SASE. Reports in 6 weeks. Sample copy 9x12 SASE with 40¢; writer's guidelines for #10 SASE.

Nonfiction: General interest (music, sports, latest fads); how-to (make money, save money or get credit); interview (researched and highly informative interviews/profiles with famous youns adults); profile (of young adults across the nation who are doing exciting things—changing laws, leading people, living new lifestyles—in all the fields of science, medicine, law and the arts); and travel (true accounts with story angle—Bahamas, the Keys, Southeastern United States). Buys 36 mss/year. Query or submit complete ms. Length: 400-1,250 words. Pays $25-40.

Photos: "Each feature is illustrated in some way. Sending photos along makes our job easier." Submit photo material with accompanying ms. Pays $5-10 for 8x10 b&w prints. Captions preferred; model releases required. Buys all rights. Cover photos: pays $25-50/per 35mm color slide.

How To Break In: "Keep the writing concise and light, with a strong identification for the young adult. Keep an 'up' attitude and entertain as well as inform. Articles that contain personal experiences as well as informative reading are great. Don't have to overdose with factual writing, but give the readers enough meat to chew on."

FORD TIMES, Ford Motor Co., Box 1509-B, Dearborn MI 48121. Managing Editor: Richard L. Routh. "Family magazine designed to attract all ages." Monthly magazine. Circ. 1,700,000. Buys first serial rights. Pays 50% kill fee. Byline given. Buys about 125 mss/year. Pays on acceptance. Free sample copy and writer's guidelines. Query. Submit seasonal material 6 months in advance. Reports in 2-4 weeks. SASE.

Nonfiction and Photos: "Almost anything relating to American life, both past and present, that is in good taste and leans toward the cheerful and optimistic. Topics include motor travel, sports, fashion, where and what to eat along the road, vacation ideas, reminiscences, big cities and small towns, the arts, Americana, and the outdoors. We strive to be colorful, lively and engaging. We are particularly attracted to material that presents humor, anecdote, first-person discourse, intelligent observation and, in all cases, superior writing. We are committed to originality and try as much as possible to avoid subjects that have appeared in other publications and in our own. However, a fresh point of view and/or exceptional literary ability with respect to an old subject will be welcomed." Length: 1,500 words maximum. Pays $250 minimum for full-length articles. "Speculative submission of good quality color transparencies and b&w photos with mss is welcomed. We want bright, lively photos showing people. We need publicity releases for people whose identity is readily apparent in photos. Writers may send snapshots, postcards, brochures, etc., if they wish."

GOOD READING, Henry F. Henrichs Publications, Litchfield IL 62056. (217)324-2322. Editor: Diane M. Dudley. 75% freelance written. Monthly magazine. Estab. 1964. Circ. 12,000. Buys 100-125 mss/year. Buys first North American serial rights. Pays on acceptance. SASE.

Nonfiction and Photos: Accurate articles on current or factual subjects, adventure or important places. Material based on incidents related to business or personal experiences that reveal the elements of success in human relationships. Humorous material welcome. Uses some quizzes and 400-word youth fiction. All published material is wholesome and noncontroversial.

Length: 500-1,000 words. Pays $20-60. Short filler length: 200-500 words. Pays $10-20. Good-quality b&w glossy prints illustrating an article are desirable and should be submitted with the article.
Poetry: Do not pay for poetry, but publish 4-5/month. Prefer pleasantly rhythmic humorous or uplifting material of 4-16 lines.

GOODSTAY, Hart, Inc., 22 Throckmorton St., Freehold NJ 07728. (201)780-4278. Publisher/Editor: S. Harvey Price. Executive Editor: Arthur S. Schreiber. Features human interest for patients in hospitals (adults only). "We want to help them 'escape' their present environment. Tell them how to buffer the time between discharge and return to normal routine." Bimonthly magazine; 40 pages. Circ. 100,000. Byline given. Pays on acceptance. Makes assignments on a work-for-hire basis. Phone queries OK. Submit seasonal/holiday material 3 months in advance. Simultaneous, photocopied and previously published submissions OK. SASE. Reports in 2 weeks. Free sample copy and writer's guidelines.
Nonfiction: General interest (hobbies, second careers, interesting careers, educational opportunities); how-to (understand everyday activity: weather forecasting, hobbies); travel; and photo feature. "No discussion of diseases or disorders." Buys 6 mss/issue. Send complete ms. Length: 250-1,500 words. Pays $50-150.
Photos: State availability of photos or send photos with ms. B&w not encouraged; uses 35mm or 4x5 color transparencies. Offers no additional payment for photos accepted with ms. Captions preferred; model release required. Buys one-time rights.
Columns/Departments: Away (travel for one week or less), and Living Plants (how to care for seasonal plants, flowers in patient's room). Buys 2 mss/issue. Query. Length: 250-1,500 words. Pays $50-150.

GREEN'S MAGAZINE, Box 313, Detroit MI 48231. Editor: David Green. 100% freelance written. For a general audience; "the more sentient, literate levels." Quarterly magazine; 100 pages. Estab. 1972. Circ. 1,000. Buys first North American serial rights. Byline given. Buys 48 mss/year. Pays on publication. Sample copy $2.00. Reports in 8 weeks. Submit complete ms. SASE.
Fiction: Mainstream, suspense, humorous, must have a realistic range in conflict areas. Slice of life situations enriched with deep characterization and more than superficial conflict. Avoid housewife, student, businessmen problems that remain "so what" in solution. Open on themes as long as writers recognize the family nature of the magazine. Length: 1,000-3,000 words. Pays $15-$25.
Poetry: Haiku, blank verse, free verse. Length: about 36 to 40 lines. Pays $2 to $3.

GRIT, 208 W. 3rd St., Williamsport PA 17701. (717)326-1771. Editor: Terry L. Ziegler. For "residents of all ages in small-town and rural America who are interested in people and generally take a positive view of life." Tabloid newspaper; 44 pages. Estab. 1882. Weekly. Circ. 1,300,000. Buys first serial rights and second serial (reprint) rights. Byline given. Buys 800-1,000 mss/year. Pays on acceptance for freelance material; on publication for reader participation feature material. Free sample copy and writer's guidelines. Reports in 2-4 weeks. Query or submit complete ms. SASE.
Nonfiction and Photos: Feature Editor: Kenneth D. Loss. Wants mss demonstrating the power of free enterprise as a desirable and vital aspect of life in the US, with emphasis on specific examples. Mss should show "value of honesty, thrift, hard work and generosity as keys to better living." Also wants patriotic stories which have an immediate tie-in with a patriotic holiday. Avoid sermonizing, but mss should be interesting and accurate so that readers may be inspired. Also mss about men, women and teenagers involved in unusual occupations, hobbies or significant personal adventures. "*Grit* seeks to present the positive aspect of things. When others point out the impending darkness, *Grit* emphasizes the beautiful sunset or approaching rest before another day." No mss promoting alcoholic beverages, immoral behavior, narcotics, unpatriotic acts. Wants good Easter, Christmas and holiday material. Mss should show some person or group involved in an unusual and/or uplifting way. "We lean heavily toward human interest, whatever the subject. Writing should be simple and down-to-earth." Length: 300-800 words. Pays 5¢/word for first or exclusive rights; 2¢/word for second or reprint rights. Photos purchased with or without ms. Captions required. Size: prefers 8x10 for b&w, but will consider 5x7; transparencies only for color. Pays $10 for b&w photos accompanying ms; $35 for accompanying color transparencies.
Fiction and Poetry: Department Editor: Mrs. Fran Noll. Buys only reprint material for fiction. Western, romance. Pays 2¢/word. Buys traditional forms of poetry and light verse. Length: 32 lines maximum. Pays $4 for 4 lines and under, plus 25¢/line for each additional line.

HARPER'S MAGAZINE, 2 Park Ave., Room 1809, New York NY 10016. (212)481-5220. Editor: Lewis H. Lapham. 90% freelance written. For well-educated, socially concerned, widely read men and women and college students who are active in community and political affairs. Monthly. Circ. 300,000. Rights purchased vary with author and material. Buys approximately 12 non-agented, non-commissioned, non-book-excerpted mss/year. Pays negotiable kill fee. Byline given. Pays on acceptance. Sample copy $1.50. Will look only at material submitted through agents or which is the result of a query. Reports in 2-3 weeks. SASE.
Nonfiction: "For writers working with agents or who will query first only, our requirements are: Public affairs, literary, international and local reporting, humor." Also buys exposes, think pieces and profiles. Length: 1,500-6,000 words. Pays $250-$1,500.
Photos: Art Director: Sheila Wolfe. Occasionally purchased with mss; others by assignment. Pays $35-$400.
Fiction: On contemporary life and its problems. Also buys humorous stories. Length: 1,000-5,000 words. Pays $300-$500.
Poetry: 60 lines and under. Pays $2/line.

KNOWLEDGE, Research Services Corp., 5280 Trail Lake Dr., Drawer 16489. Ft.Worth TX 76133. (817)292-4272. Editor: Dr. O.A. Battista. For lay and professional audiences of all occupations. Quarterly magazine; 60 pages. Estab. 1976. Circ. 1000. Pays on publication. Buys all rights. Byline given. Submit seasonal/holiday material 6 months in advance. SASE. Reports in 2 weeks. Sample copy $2.
Nonfiction: Informational—original new knowledge. Buys 4 mss/issue. Query. Length: 1,500 words maximum. Pays $100 minimum.

MACLEAN'S, 481 University Ave., Toronto, Ontario, Canada M5W 1A7. (416)596-5328. Editor: Peter C. Newman. For news oriented-audience. Weekly newsmagazine; 90 pages. Circ. 700,000. Buys first North American serial rights. Pays on acceptance. Will send free sample copy to writer on request. Will consider photocopied submissions. "Query with 200- or 300-word outline before sending any material." Reports in 2 weeks. SAE and International Reply Coupons.
Nonfiction: "We have the conventional newsmagazine departments (science, medicine, law, art, music, etc.) with slightly more featurish treatment than other newsmagazines. We usually have 3 middle-of-the-book features on politics, entertainment, etc. We buy short features, but book reviews and columns are done by staffers or retainer freelancers. Freelancers should write for a free copy of the magazine and study the approach." Length: 400-3,500 words. Pays $300-$1,000.

MIDNIGHT/GLOBE, 200 Railroad Ave., Greenwich CT 06830. Chief Articles Editor: Paul Dougherty. "For everyone in the family over 18. *Midnight/Globe* readers are the same people you meet on the street, and in supermarket lines, average hard-working Americans who prefer easily digested tabloid news." Weekly national tabloid newspaper. Estab. 1954. Circ. 2,000,000. Buys more than 1,000 mss/year. Pays negotiable kill fee. Byline given. Pays on acceptance. "Writers should advise us of specializations on any submission so that we may contact them if special issue or feature is planned." Submit special material 2 months in advance. Reports in 1 week. SASE.
Nonfiction, Photos and Fillers: Photo Department Editor: Vin Alabiso. "Sex and violence are taboo. We want upbeat human interest material, of interest to a national audience. Stories where fate plays a major role are always good. Always interested in features on well-known personalities, offbeat people, places, events and activities. Current issue is best guide. Stories are best that don't grow stale quickly. No padding. Grab the reader in the first line or paragraph. Tell the story, make the point and get out with a nice, snappy ending. Don't dazzle us with your footwork. Just tell the story. And we are always happy to bring a new freelancer or stringer into our fold. No cliques here. If you've got talent, and the right material—you're in. Remember—we are serving a family audience. All material must be in good taste. If it's been written up in a major newspaper or magazine, we already know about it." Buys informational, how-to, personal experience, interview, profile, inspirational, humor, historical, expose, nostalgia, photo, spot news, and new product articles. Length: 1,000 words maximum; average 500-800 words. Pays $50-$300 (special rates for "blockbuster" material). Photos are purchased with or without ms, and on assignment. Captions are required. Pays $50 minimum for 8x10 b&w glossy prints. "Competitive payment on exclusives." Buys puzzles, quizzes, and short humor.
How To Break In: "*Midnight/Globe* is constantly looking for human interest subject material from throughout the United States and much of the best comes from America's smaller cities and villages, not necessarily from the larger urban areas. Therefore, we are likely to be more

responsive to an article from a new writer than many other publications. This, of course, is equally true of photographs. A major mistake of new writers is that they have failed to determine the type and style of our content and in the ever-changing tabloid field, this is a most important consideration. It is also wise to keep in mind that what is of interest to you or to the people in your area may not be of equal interest to a national readership. Determine the limits of interest first. And, importantly, the material you send us must be such that it won't be 'stale' by the time it reaches the readers."

MODERN PEOPLE, Aladdin Dist., 11058 W. Addison St., Franklin Park IL 60131. Managing Editor: Diane Dean. Emphasizes celebrities, consumer affairs and offbeat stories for white lower- and middle-class, blue collar, non-college educated people with religious, patriotic, conservative background. Weekly tabloid; 40 pages. Estab. 1969. Circ. 200,000. Pays on acceptance. Buys all rights. Byline given. Submit seasonal/holiday material 6-8 weeks in advance. Photocopied submissions OK. SASE. Reports in 2 weeks. Free sample copy and writer's guidelines.
Nonfiction: Expose (consumer ripoffs); how-to (get rich, save money, be healthy, etc.); interviews (celebrities); photo feature (offbeat subjects). Buys 10 mss/issue. Query. Length: 150-500 words. Pays $10-150.
Photos: Photos purchased with accompanying ms. Pays $5-15 for 8½x11 b&w glossy prints; $25-200 for 8x5.5-pica color slides or transparencies. Total purchase price for ms includes payment for photos. Model release required.
Columns/Departments: Psychic Prediction, TV Soap Operas, Celebrity Gossip and Dieting. Buys 2 mss/issue. Query. Length: 15-300 words. Pays $25-50. Open to suggestions for new columns/departments.

NATIONAL ENQUIRER, Lantana FL 33464. Executive Editor: Tom Kuncl. Weekly tabloid. Circ. 6,000,000. Pays on publication. Buys first North American serial rights. Pays negotiable kill fee. No byline. Query. "Story idea must be accepted first. We're no longer accepting unsolicited mss and all spec material will be returned unread." SASE.
Nonfiction and Photos: Any subject appealing to a mass audience. Requires fresh slant on topical news stories, waste of taxpayers' money by government, the entire field of the occult, how-to articles, rags to riches success stories, medical firsts, scientific breakthroughs, human drama, adventure and personality profiles. "The best way to understanding our requirements is to study the paper." Pays $325-500 for most completed features, plus separate lead fees; more with photos. "Payments in excess of $1,000 are not unusual; we will pay more for really top, circulation-boosting blockbusters." Uses single or series b&w photos that must be attention-grabbing. Wide range; anything from animal photos to great action photos. "We'll bid against any other magazine for once-in-lifetime pictures."

NATIONAL EXAMINER, Box 711, Rouses Point NY 12979. (514)866-7744. Editor-in-Chief: John Elder. For a contemporary, upbeat audience. Weekly color tabloid. Pays on publication. Buys first North American serial rights. Phone queries OK. SASE.
Nonfiction: Informational, how-to, personal experience, interview, profile, inspirational, humor, historical, expose, nostalgia, photo feature, spot news and new product. Especially interested in pieces on ghosts, psychics and astrology. Query.
Photos: Purchased with or without accompanying ms. "Celebrities, off-beat shots, humorous and spot news photos always in demand." Send prints or transparencies.

NATIONAL GEOGRAPHIC MAGAZINE, 17th and M Sts. NW, Washington DC 20036. Senior Assistant Editor: James Cerruti. Editor: Gilbert M. Grosvenor. For members of the National Geographic Society. Monthly. Circ. 9,325,000. Buys first publication rights with warranty to use the material in National Geographic Society copyrighted publications. Pays 50% kill fee. Byline given. Buys 40-50 mss/year. Pays on acceptance. Sample copy $1.25. Reports in 2-4 weeks. Query. Writers should study several recent issues of *National Geographic* and send for leaflets "Writing for National Geographic" and "National Geographic Photo Requirements." SASE.
Nonfiction and Photos: "First-person narratives, making it easy for the reader to share the author's experience and observations. Writing should include plenty of human-interest incident, authentic direct quotation, and a bit of humor where appropriate. Accuracy is fundamental. Contemporary problems such as those of pollution and ecology are treated on a

tactual basis. The magazine is especially seeking short American place pieces with a strong regional 'people' flavor. The use of many clear, sharp color photographs in all articles makes lengthy word descriptions unnecessary. Potential writers need not be concerned about submitting photos. These are handled by professional photographers. Historical background, in most cases, should be kept to the minimum needed for understanding the present." Length: 8,000 words maximum for major articles. Shorts of 2,000-4,000 words "are always needed." Pays $3,000-6,000 (and, in some cases, more) for acceptable articles; from $300/page for color transparencies. A paragraph on an article idea should be submitted to James Cerruti, Senior Assistant Editor. Please do not phone. If the idea is appealing, he will ask for a one- or two-page outline for further consideration. Photographers are advised to submit a generous selection of photographs with brief, descriptive captions to Mary G. Smith, Assistant Editor. **How To Break In:** "Send 4 or 5 one-paragraph ideas. If any are promising, author will be asked for a one- to two-page outline. Read the latest issues to see what we want."

THE NEW YORKER, 25 W. 43rd St., New York NY 10036. Editor: William Shawn. Weekly. Reports in two weeks. Pays on acceptance. SASE.
Nonfiction, Fiction and Fillers: Single factual pieces run from 3,000-10,000 words. Long fact pieces are usually staff-written. So is "Talk of the Town," although ideas for this department are bought. Pays good rates. Uses fiction, both serious and light, from 1,000-6,000 words. About 90% of the fillers come from contributors with or without taglines (extra pay if the tagline is used).

PEOPLE ON PARADE, Meridian Publishing Co., 1720 Washington Blvd., Box 2315, Ogden UT 84404. (801)394-9446. Senior Editor: Dick Harris. Editor: Valerie Sagers. For employees, stockholders, customers and clients of 2,000 business and industrial firms. Monthly magazine; 28 pages. Estab. 1976. Circ. 450,000. Pays on acceptance. Buys one-time rights. Byline given. Submit seasonal/holiday material 9 months in advance. SASE. Reports in 3-4 weeks. Sample copy 35¢; free writer's guidelines.
Nonfiction: Valerie Sagers, articles editor. "*POP* focuses on people—active, interesting, exciting, busy people; personality profiles on people succeeding, achieving, doing things." Humorous, informational, inspirational. "We want material from all regions of the country and about all types of people. Big-name writers are fine, but we know there is a lot of talent among the little knowns, and we encourage them to submit their ideas. We read everything that comes in, but writers will save their time and ours by writing a good, tantalizing query. *POP* has a strong family-community orientation. Without being maudlin or pious, we cherish the work ethic, personal courage and dedication to the American dream. So we look for material that reflects positively on the man/woman who succeeds through diligence, resourcefulness and imagination, or finds fulfillment through service to community or country. Tell us about people whose lives and accomplishments inspire and encourage others. We like humor and nostalgia. We want tight writing, with lively quotes and anecdotes. Pictures should be fresh, sharp, unposed, showing action, involvement." Buys 10 mss/issue. Length: 400-1,000 words. Pays 10¢/word.
Photos: Purchased with or without mss or on assignment. Captions required. Pays $20 for 8x10 b&w glossy; $25 for 35mm, 2¼x2¼ or 4x5 color used inside; up to $400 for cover color. Model release required.
Fillers: "We welcome fillers and shorts with a humorous touch, featuring interesting, successful, busy people." Buys 1-2/issue. Length: 200-300 words. Pays 10¢/word.
How To Break In: "*People on Parade* has started a celebrity cooking section. We'd like to feature a celebrity each month with his/her favorite foods or recipes, meal planning, dieting tips, etc. Length should be 500-600 words, and we'd need at least one photo of the celebrity in the kitchen, dinning, etc.—preferably a color transparency. B&w glossy prints will work. Pay 10¢/word, $25 for a color photo, $20 for b&w. We pay on acceptance. Everything comes to us on spec."

PEOPLE WEEKLY, Time, Inc., Time & Life Bldg., Rockefeller Center, New York NY 10020. Editor: Richard B. Stolley. For a general audience. Estab. 1974. Weekly. Circ. 2,300,000. Rights purchased vary with author and material. Usually buys first North American serial rights with right to syndicate, splitting net proceeds with author 50/50. Pays on acceptance. Query. SASE.
Nonfiction and Photos: "Nearly all material is staff-produced, but we do consider specific story

suggestions (not manuscripts) from freelancers. Every story must have a strong personality focus. Payment varies from $125 for Lookouts to $1,000 for Bios. Photo payment is $200/page for b&w, minimum $75. Prefer minimum size of 8x10 from original negatives."

POOR RICHARD, The Poor Richard Co., Independence Square, Philadelphia PA 19105. Editor: John Gilpin. "This is a renewal of the famous *Poor Richard's* Almanac, with three updated supplements 'to provide useful reference information and observances of remarkable events'." Annual magazine with quarterly updates; 1,056 pages. Estab. December 1732. Circ. 1,000,000. Pays on publication. Buys all rights. Phone queries OK. Simultaneous, photocopied and previously published submissions OK. SASE. Reports in 2 weeks. Free sample copy and writer's guidelines.
Nonfiction: Expose (on government powers and current events); general interest (current events); historical; inspirational; interview; new product; nostalgia, photo feature; profile; and travel. Buys 150 mss/year. Apply for accreditation by company. Pays $1,500-5,000.
Photos: Send photos with ms. Pays $1,500-5,000 for b&w glossy prints or contact sheets; $1,500-5,000 for glossy color contact sheets or prints; offers no additional payment for photos with ms. Captions and model releases are required.
Columns/Departments: Agricultural Economics Analysis, Art Review, Book Review, Movie Review, and Music Review. Send complete ms. Pays $1,500-5,000.
Fillers: Newsbreaks and crossword puzzles. Pays $1,500-5,000.

QUEST/79, 1133 Avenue of the Americas, New York NY 10036. Editor-in-Chief: Robert Shnayerson. Managing Editor: Molly McKaughan. Emphasizes "the pursuit of human excellence for an educated, intelligent audience, interested in the positive side of things; in human potential, in sciences, the arts, good writing, design and photography. We have no connection with the feminist magazine, *Quest*." 10 issues/year; 112 pages. Estab. 1977. Circ. 300,000. Pays on acceptance. Buys all rights. Pays negotiable kill fee. Byline given. Submit seasonal/holiday material 4 months in advance. Photocopied submissions OK. Free writer's guidelines.
Nonfiction: Humor (short pieces deflating or satirizing world views or "good" things), interviews (with fascinating individuals in government, the arts, business, science), personal experience (adventures, unusual experiences), profiles (of risk taking people, great craftsmen, adventurers), reviews (books, products, thoughts, places, etc.), and technical (new inventions, applications of science). Query. Length: 500-5,000 words. Pays $600-2,500. Does *not* accept unsolicited fiction.
Columns/Departments: Book Reviews (William Plummer, editor).

READER'S DIGEST, Pleasantville NY 10570. Monthly. Buys all rights to original mss. "Items intended for a particular feature should be directed to the editor in charge of that feature, although the contribution may later be referred to another section of the magazine as seeming more suitable. Manuscripts cannot be acknowledged, and will be returned—usually within eight or ten weeks—only when return postage accompanies them." Pays $250-500 kill fee. Byline given.
Nonfiction: "*Reader's Digest* is interested in receiving First Person articles. An article for the First Person series must be a previously unpublished narrative of an unusual personal experience. It may be dramatic, inspirational or humorous, but it must have a quality of narrative and interest comparable to stories published in this series. Pays $3,500 on acceptance. Address: First Person Editor. Base rate for *general* articles is $2,600 for first sale."
Fillers: "Life in These United States contributions must be true, unpublished stories from one's own experience, revelatory of adult human nature, and providing appealing or humorous sidelights on the American scene. Maximum length: 300 words. Address Life in U.S. Editor. Payment rate on publication: $300. True and unpublished stories are also solicited for Humor in Uniform, Campus Comedy and All in a Day's Work. Maximum length: 300 words. Payment rate on publication: $300. Address Humor in Uniform, Campus Comedy or All in a Day's Work Editor. Toward More Picturesque Speech: The first contributor of each item used in this department is paid $35. Contributions should be dated, and the sources must be given. Address: Picturesque Speech Editor. For items used in Laughter, the Best Medicine, Personal Glimpses, Quotable Quotes, and elsewhere in the magazine, payment is made at the following rates: to the *first* contributor of each item from a published source, $35. For original material, $15 per *Digest* two-column line, with a minimum payment of $35. Address: Excerpts Editor."

READERS NUTSHELL, Box 9820, Fort Worth TX 76107. Editor: Elinor Musick Hubbard. 75% freelance written. Emphasizes safety and insurance. Bimonthly magazine; 16 pages. Pays on acceptance. Buys first North American serial rights. Byline given. Submit seasonal/holiday material 8 months in advance of issue date. Simultaneous and previously published submissions OK. SASE. Reports in 1 month.
Nonfiction: General interest, how-to and humor. No articles on drinking or sex. Buys 3 mss/issue. Submit complete ms. Length: 500-1,000 words. Pays 5¢/accepted word.
Photos: State availability of photos with ms or submit with accompanying ms. Pays $5 for 5x7 b&w glossy prints. Model release required.

REALITES, Realites USA Publications, Ltd., 132 Welsh Rd., Horsham PA 19044. (215)657-4600. Editor: James L. Forsht. Monthly magazine; 90 pages. Estab. October 1978. Pays 33% kill fee. Byline given "at author's request." Pays on acceptance. Submit seasonal/holiday material 6 months in advance. SASE.
Nonfiction: International travel and discovery, the Arts, cultural topics—religion, sociology, psychology, science). "No Americana. Query with clips of published. Length: 1,000-4,000 words. Pays $300-1,200.
Columns/Departments: Buying Property, Collecting, Dining, Entertaining, General Exotica, Investing, Living, Shopping and Travel. Query with clips of published work.

THE SATURDAY EVENING POST, The Curtis Publishing Co., 1100 Waterway Blvd., Indianapolis, IN 46202. (317)634-1100. Editor-in-Chief: Cory Ser Vaas M.D. Associated Editor/Publisher: Fredrick Birmingham. For general readership. Magazine published 9 times/year; 144 pages. Estab. 1728. Circ. 535,000. Pays on publication. Buys all rights. Phone queries OK. Simultaneous and photocopied submissions OK. SASE. Reports in 1 month. Sample copy $1; free writer's guidelines for SASE.
Nonfiction: Ms. Holly Miller, Nonfiction Editor. Historical (especially nostalgia and Americana); how-to (health, general living); humor; informational (people; celebrities and ordinary but interesting personalities); inspirational (for religious columns); interview; nostalgia; personal experience (especially travel, yachting, etc.); personal opinion; photo feature; profile (especially government figures); travel and small magazine "pick-ups." Buys 5 mss/issue. Query. Length: 1,500-3,000 words. Pays $100-1,000.
Photos: Janet Kioski, photo editor. Photos purchased with or without accompanying ms. Pays $25 minimum for b&w photos; $50 minimum for color photos. Total purchase price for ms includes payment for photos. Model release required.
Columns/Departments: Editorials ($100 each); Food ($150-450); Medical Mailbox ($50-250); Religion Column ($100-250) and Travel ($150-450).
Fiction: Sam Walton, fiction editor. Adventure; fantasy; humorous; mainstream; mystery; romance; science fiction; suspense; western; and condensed novels. Buys 5 mss/issue. Query. Length: 1,500-3,000 words. Pays $150-750.
Poetry: John D. Craton, poetry editor. Free verse, light verse and traditional. Buys 1 poem/issue. Pays $15-150.
Fillers: Ms. Louise Fortson, fillers editor. Jokes, gags, anecdotes, cartoons, postscripts and short humor. Buys 1 filler/issue. Length: 500-1,000 words. Pays $10-100.
How To Break In: "Interested in topics related to science, government, the arts, personalities with inspirational careers and humor. We read unsolicited material."

SATURDAY NIGHT, New Leaf Publications, Ltd., 69 Front St. E., Toronto, Ontario, Canada M5E 1R3. (416)362-5907. Editor: Robert Fulford. Managing Editor: Bernadette Sulgit. 70% freelance written. Emphasizes "politics, business/economics, lifestyles and literary topics for readers 18 and up, with most ranging in age between 18-49; well-educated, with a high percentage in managerial/professional occupations." Published 10 times/year. Magazine; 88 pages. Estab. 1887. Circ. 100,000. Pays on acceptance. Buys first North American serial rights in French and English. Phone queries OK. Submit seasonal/holiday material 4 months in advance of issue date. Photocopied submissions OK. SAE and International Reply Coupons. Reports in 4 weeks. Sample copy $1.25.
Nonfiction: General interest (Canadian government, business, the arts, lifestyles); interview (in-depth profiles of interest to Canadians); and profile. Buys 4 mss/issue. Query. Length: 1,500-3,500 words. Pays $400-1,100.
Fiction: "High quality writing by new or established writers. No restrictions on theme but should appeal to a fairly sophisticated audience who do not read literary journals. Buys 10 mss/year. Submit complete ms. Length: 2,500-4,000 words. Pays $1,100 maximum.

SATURDAY REVIEW, 1290 Avenue of the Americas, New York NY 10019. Editor: Carl

Tucker. Managing Editor: Susan Heath. "A review of ideas, the arts, and the human condition for above average educated audience. Biweekly magazine; 64 pages. Estab. 1924. Circ. 550,000. Usually pays on publication. Buys first North American serial rights. Pays 30% kill fee. Byline given. Photocopied submissions OK. SASE. Reports in 3-4 weeks. Free writer's guidelines.
Nonfiction: Expose (government, education, science); informational (analytical pieces on national or international affairs, sciences, education, and the arts); interview; and profile. Buys 100 mss/year. Query. Length: 2,500 words maximum. Pays $200/page.

SIGNATURE, The Diners' Club Magazine, 880 3rd Ave., New York NY 10016. Managing Editor: Peter Andrews. For Diners' Club members—"businessmen, urban, affluent, traveled, and young." Monthly. Circ. 800,000. Buys first rights. Buys 75 mss/year. Pays on acceptance. Write for copy of guidelines for writers. Submit seasonal material, including seasonal sports subjects, at least 3 months in advance. Returns rejected material in 2 weeks. Query. SASE.
Nonfiction: "Articles aimed at the immediate areas of interest of our readers—in travel, social issues, personalities, sports, entertainment, food and drink, business, humor. *Signature* runs 5 to 8 nonfiction articles an issue, all by freelancers. Subjects covered in past issues of *Signature* include profiles of Norman Lear and Pete Rose. Articles on secretarial crisis, Wall Street reform, British TV invasion, natural foods dispute and small town U.S.A. restoration. Travel pieces require a *raison d'etre,* a well-defined approach and angle. Eschew destination or traditional travel piece. Feature articles run 2,500 words maximum. Also buy shorter 1,500-word pieces which are a slice of some travel experience and usually written in very personal style. These pay $450 and up. It's important that writer be familiar with our magazine."
Photos: "Picture stories or support are usually assigned to photographers we have worked with in the past. We rarely ask a writer to handle the photography also. But if he has photos of his subject, we will consider them for use." Pays $50 minimum/photo; $200/page.

THE STAR, 730 3rd Ave., New York NY 10017. (212)557-9200. Editor: Ian Rae. Deputy Editor: John Canning. Editorial Manager: Peter Faris. 25-40% freelance written. "For every family; all the family—kids, teenagers, young parents and grandparents." Weekly tabloid; 48 pages. Estab. February 1974. Circ. 3,400,000. Pays on publication. Buys all rights, but may reassign following publication, second serial (reprint) rights, and first North American serial rights. Pays negotiable kill fee. Byline given. Submit seasonal/holiday material 2-3 months in advance of issue date. SASE. Free sample copy and writer's guidelines.
Nonfiction: Leslie Hinton, News Editor. Expose (government waste, consumer, education, anything affecting family) general interest (human interest, consumerism, informational, family and women's interest); how-to (psychological, practical on all subjects affecting readers); inspirational (off-beat personal experience, religious, and psychic); interview (celebrity or human interest); new product (but not from commercial interests); personal experience (adventure, human drama, etc.); photo feature; profile (celebrity or national figure); travel (how to cheaply); health; medical; and diet. Buys 50 mss/issue. Query or submit complete ms. Length: 500-2,000 words. Pays $50-1,000.
Photos: State availability of photos with query or ms. Pays $25-100 for 8x10 b&w glossy prints, contact sheets or negatives; $125-1,000 for 35mm color transparencies. Captions required. Buys one-time, or all rights, but may reassign following publication.
Fillers: Statistical-informational. Length: 50-400 words. Pays $15-40.

SUNSHINE MAGAZINE, Henry F. Henrichs Publications, Litchfield IL 62056. (217)324-2322. Editor: Diane M. Dudley. 75% freelance written. For general audience of all ages. Monthly magazine. Estab. 1924. Circ. 80,000. Buys 125-150 mss/year. Buys first North American serial rights. Pays on acceptance. Sample copy 50¢; free writer's guidelines. Complimentary copy sent to included authors on publication. Submit seasonal material 6 months in advance. Reports in 1-2 months. Ms without SASE not returned. No query necessary.
Nonfiction: "We accept some short articles, but they must be especially interesting or inspirational. *Sunshine Magazine* is not a religious publication, and purely religious material is rarely used. We desire carefully written features about persons or events that have real human interest—that give a 'lift'." Length: 100-300 words. Pays $10-50. Special feature: My Most Extraordinary Experience—Yes, It Happened to Me. Must be in first person, deal with a very unusual or surprising situation and have a positive approach. Length: 350-600 words. Payment: $25.
Fiction: "Stories must be wholesome, well-written, with clearly defined plots. There should be a purpose for each story, but any moral or lesson should be well-concealed in the plot development. Humorous stories are welcome. Avoid trite plots that do not hold the reader's

interest. A surprising climax is most desirable. Material should be uplifting, and noncontroversial." Length: 400 to 1,250 words. Youth story: 400-700 words. Pays $20-100.
Poetry: Buy one poem for special feature each month. Payment: $15. Use several other poems each month but do no purchase these. Prefer pleasantly rhythmic, humorous or uplifting material. Length: 4-16 lines.
Fillers: 100-200 words. Payment: $10.

TODAY'S PROFESSIONALS MAGAZINE, Today's Professionals, Inc. (Widmaier & Goss), 3030 W. 6th St., Suite 110, Los Angeles CA 90020. (213)386-7470. Editor: Rose Goss. Emphasizes how to articles, success articles, controversy and ways of doing things better. Monthly magazine; 40 pages. Estab. September 1978. Circ. 18,000. Pays on publication. Buys all rights. Submit seasonal/holiday material 2 months in advance. Simultaneous, photocopied and previously published submissions OK. SASE. Reports in 1 month. Sample copy $1.25; free writer's guidelines.
Nonfiction: Expose (concerning major topics of our times, covering controversy on that topic and giving a very wide view of it); general interest ("definately general interest—things that the regular guy could read and really have gotten something from the article or news piece"); historical ("we are open for histories of different professionals of our times and the effects they have upon our world now"); how-to (this in form of "interview" mostly and could be article form—also how to be successful in different professions); humor (satires about specific issues of our times and short stories we are now excepting with humor in them); inspirational ("this will give our public a good area to look forward to read"); interview; new product; personal experience; personal opinion; photo feature; profile; technical; and travel. "We do not want sex articles." Query with clips of published work. Buys 5 mss/issue. Length: 2,500 words "or whatever is arranged." Pays 1¢/word.
Photos: State availability of photos. Pays $3 for b&w contact sheets; $4 for color negatives. Captions are required.
Columns/Departments: Book reviews; Health bulletin and People section. Query with clips of published work. Length: 300 words. Pays $5. Open to suggestions for new columns/departments.
Fiction: Adventures, humorous, mainstream, mystery, religious and science fiction. "We do not want anything impertinent to professionals." Query with clips of published work. Buys 10 mss/issue. Length: 2,500 words. Pays $25.
Fillers: Anecdotes, cartoons, gags, jokes and short humor. Buys 1-2/issues. Pays $5 if published.

TOWN AND COUNTRY, 717 5th Ave., New York NY 10022. Managing Editor: Jean Barkhorn. For upper-income Americans. Monthly. Not a large market for freelancers. Always query first. SASE.
Nonfiction: Department Editors: Richard Kagan, Frank Zachary. "We're always trying to find ideas that can be developed into good articles that will make appealing cover lines." Wants provocative and controversial pieces. Length: 1,500-2,000 words. Pays $300. Also buys shorter pieces for which pay varies.

VISION MAGAZINE, Vision Magazine, Inc., 2333 Camino del Rio South, Suite 360, San Diego CA 92108. Editor: Jack Grobstein. Emphasizes affluent lifestyle. Monthly magazine; 112 pages. Estab. November 1978. Circ. 200,000. Pays on publication. Buys all rights, simultaneous rights, second serial (reprint) rights and one-time rights. Byline given. Submit seasonal/holiday material 5 months in advance. Simultaneous, photocopied and previously published submissions OK. SASE. Reports in 1 month. Sample copy $4; free writer's guidelines.
Nonfiction: Expose (on government, game industry, health care, crime, religion); general interest (if relating to an upwardly mobile lifestyle); how-to (preparation of gourmet foods—photographs required); humor (travel experiences, cooking *sexual*, lifestyle); inspirational (the psychic); interview (celebrity—television, movies, government, recording); new product (if geared to the consumer); and travel. Buys 10 mss/issue. Query or send clips of published work. Length: 1,500-6,000 words. Pays $50-1,500.
Photos: Send photos with ms. Pays $25 for 4x5 b&w glossy prints and $50 for 35mm color transparencies. Buys all rights. Captions preferred; model releases required.
Columns/Departments: New Sounds (music—generally known or upcoming groups or individuals); Shaplier Vision (health, personal care, personal grooming, body care); Travel and Book Reviews. Buys 4/issue. Query or send clips of published work. Length: 1,500-2,500 words. Pays $75/page.
Fiction: Erotica (heterosexual; bi-sexual); humorous; mystery (Edgar Allan Poe-ish); religious

(psychic); science fiction (emphasis on the possible); suspense; condensed and serialized novels. Query or send clips of previously published work. Length: 4,500-7,000 words. Pays $100-500.

Poetry: Avant-garde. Buys 5 poems/year. Submit in batches of 10. Length 30-150 lines. Pays $25-100.

Fillers: Short humor. Buys 5/issue. Length: 250-500 words. Pays $25-100.

Health

ACCENT ON LIVING, Box 700, Bloomington IL 61701. (309)378-2961. Editor: Raymond C. Cheever. For physically disabled persons and rehabilitation professionals. Quarterly magazine, 128 pages. Estab. 1956. Circ. 18,000. Buys all rights. Byline given but "sometimes the article is digested to one paragraph in our photo section, news section or other column. Sometimes the article is combined with a great deal of other research. In those cases, bylines are not always possible." Buys 20-40 mss/year. Pays on publication. Sample copy $1; free writer's guidelines. Will consider photocopied submissions. Reports in 2 weeks. SASE.

Nonfiction: Articles about seriously disabled people who have overcome great obstacles and are pursuing regular vocational goals. Home business ideas with facts and figures on how someone confined to their home can run a business and make an average income. Especially interested in new technical aids, assistive devices, devised by an individual or available commercially, such as: bathroom and toilet aids and appliances, clothes and aids for dressing and undressing, aids for eating and drinking, as would be helpful to individuals with limited physical mobility. Intelligent discussion articles concerning the public image of and acceptance or non-acceptance of the physically disabled in normal living situations. Articles reporting on lawsuits, demonstrations or protests by handicapped individuals or consumer groups to gain equal rights and opportunities. Length: 200-750 words. Pays $5-100.

Photos: B&w photos purchased with accompanying ms. Captions required. Pays $5-25.

ARISE, American Research Foundation in Special Education, 55 W. Park Ave., New Haven CT 06511. Editor: Eric Sandahl. For "all persons concerned with the welfare and advancement of the mentally and physically handicapped." Monthly magazine; 40-48 pages. Estab. September 1977. Pays on publication. Buys all rights, but may reassign following publication. Submit seasonal/holiday material 3 months in advance of issue date. Previously published submissions OK "depending on the medium in which previously published." SASE. Reports in 2 weeks. Free sample copy and writer's guidelines.

Nonfiction: Informational; inspirational (if not too "shmaltzy"); interview; personal experience; photo feature; and profile. Buys 6-8 articles/issue. Submit complete ms. Length: 1,000 words minimum. Pays 5¢/word for up to 1,000 words; payment thereafter negotiable.

Photos: Submit photo material with accompanying ms. Pays $10-25 for 5x7 or 8x10 b&w glossy prints. Model release required.

How To Break In: "Send us a straightforward, crisp, simply written manuscript dealing with a mentally or physically handicapped person or group. Manuscripts that show concrete gains made in behalf of a handicapped person or group, or that pinpoint obstacles to such gains, will have priority."

BESTWAYS MAGAZINE, Box 2028, Carson City NV 89701. Editor/Publisher: Barbara Bassett. Emphasizes health and nutrition. Monthly magazine; 120 pages. Estab. 1973. Circ. 125,000. Pays on publication. Buys all rights, but may reassign following publication. Byline given. Submit seasonal/holiday material 6 months in advance of issue date. SASE. Reports in 6 weeks. Sample copy and writer's guidelines for SASE; mention *Writer's Market* in request.

Nonfiction: General interest (nutrition, preventive medicine, vitamins and minerals); how-to (natural cosmetics, diet and exercise); personal experience; profile (natural life style); and technical (vitamins, minerals and nutrition). "No direct or implied endorsements of refined flours, grains or sugar, tobacco, alcohol, caffeine, drugs or patent medicines." Buys 6 mss/issue. Query. Length: 2,500 words. Pays $50.

Photos: State availability of photos with query. Pays $5 for 4x5 b&w glossy prints; $15 for 2¼x2¼ color transparencies. Captions preferred. Buys all rights, but may reassign following publication. Model release required.

BODY FORUM MAGAZINE, Cosvetic Laboratories, Box 80883, Atlanta GA 30305. Editor: Louis Rinaldi. Emphasizes "health and beauty from standpoint of nutrition for an audience mid 20s to 60s with 50% below 38. Education level high school to post-grad. Average income $16,000." Monthly magazine; 54 pages. Estab. 1976. Circ. 2.2 million. Pays on acceptance.

Buys all rights. "We only assign articles to qualified PhDs and MDs or DOs. Interested professionals can send queries." Free sample copy.

Nonfiction: Expose, how-to, informational, interview and technical. Length: 1,500-1,800 words. Pays $200-500; "specialist articles at negotiated rates."

THE CRITICAL LIST MAGAZINE, 44 Wellington St. E., Suite 403, Toronto, Canada M5E 1C8. (416)363-3657. Editor-in-Chief: Jerry Green, M.D. Quarterly magazine. Estab. 1975. Pays on acceptance. Usually buys first North American serial rights. Sample copy and writer's guidelines on request.

Nonfiction: Areas of consumer education and preventive medicine, essentially Canadian in content or information and research that is universal in appeal. Query. Length: 1,500-3,000 words. Pays $200-400 depending on originality and quality.

Photos: $25/photo for general use; increased rates for cover or center photo.

Poetry and Fillers: 7-20¢/word.

FAMILY HEALTH, 149 5th Ave., New York NY 10010. Editor: Dalma Heyn. For health-minded young men and women. Magazine; 66 pages. Estab. 1969. Monthly. Circ. 800,000. Rights purchased vary with author and material. May buy all rights but may reassign rights to author after publication; or first North American serial rights. Pays 20% kill fee. Byline given. Buys most of their articles from freelance writers. Pays within 8 weeks of acceptance. Will send sample copy to writer for $1. No photocopied or simultaneous submissions. Reports in 6 weeks. Query for fresh, new approaches; strongly angled. Submit complete ms for first-person articles. SASE.

Nonfiction: Articles on all aspects of health mental, emotional and physical; advocacy articles; and medical breakthroughs. No "all about" articles (for example, "All About Mental Health"). Informational, how-to, personal experience, interview, profile, think articles, expose; book reviews. Length: 500-3,000 words. Pays $350-750.

HEALTH REVIEW, St.Vincent Hospital, Box1221, Green Bay WI 54305. Editor: Thomas M. Plantenberg. Emphasizes consumer-oriented health information. Quarterly magazine; 24 pages. Estab. 1976. Circ. 6,000. Pays on acceptance. Buys all rights. Phone queries OK. Submit seasonal/holiday material 6 months in advance. Photocopied and previously published submissions OK. Reports in 4-6 weeks. Free sample copy and writer's guidelines.

Nonfiction: General interest; how-to; interview (with medical/health-related person); new product (medical only) and personal experience. "We are particularly interested in personal experience with St. Vincent Hospital. We do not want to see articles on pro-abortion or pro-birth-control." Buys 2 mss/issue. Query. Length: 3,500 words maximum. Pays $75 maximum.

Fillers: Clippings, jokes, gags, anecdotes, newsbreaks, short humor and political/editorial cartoons (hospital-oriented). Length: 50-200 words. Pays $10.

HEALTHWAYS MAGAZINE, 2200 Grand Ave., Des Moines IA 50312. Editor: Tracy Mullen. 75% freelance written. Emphasizes chiropractic and good health. Bimonthly magazine, 50 pages. Estab. 1946. Circ. 96,000. Pays on publication. Buys one-time rights. Byline given. Submit seasonal/holiday material 6 months in advance of issue date. Simultaneous submissions OK. SASE. Reports in 3 weeks. Free sample copy and writer's guidelines.

Nonfiction: General interest and humor, articles on chiropractic, nutrition, environment and exercise. Buys 30 mss/year. Query or submit complete ms. length: 400-1,200 words. Pays $10-75.

Photos: State availability of photos with query or ms. Pays $2.50-25 for 8x10 b&w glossy prints and $15-50 for 35mm color transparencies. Captions required. Buys one-time rights. Model release required.

Poetry: Light verse. "No long, maudlin stuff." Buys 8 mss/issue. Length: 4-10 lines. Pays $1-5.

HEALTH SCIENCE, The American Natural Hygiene Society, Inc., 1920 Irving Park Rd., Chicago IL 60613. (312)929-7420. Editor: Allan J. Smith. Emphasizes the importance of one's habits and one's environment to one's health. Monthly magazine; 28 pages. Estab. April 1978. Circ. 5,000. Pays on publication. Buys second serial (reprint) rights, first North American serial rights and one-time rights. Pays 25% kill fee. Byline given. Phone queries OK. Submit seasonal/holiday material 4 months in advance. Simultaneous, photocopied and previously published submissions OK. SASE. Reports in 2 months. Free sample copy and writer's guidelines.

Nonfiction: "We particularly encourage how-to articles on such subjects as avoiding air, noise and food pollution, stress, radiation, etc.; living more healthfully on the job; relaxing; and making the home environment more healthful. We would like to see articles relating health to sound, light, climate, architecture, geography and interpersonal relationships. We are also interested in explanation and application of new discoveries in physiology, anatomy and biochemistry; reports of remarkable examples of the endurance and resiliency of the human organism; ideas and inspiration for conquering addictions and other habits; suggestions for organizing life so that it is more efficient, creative and satisfying; safety recommendations and advice for first aid. We do not want articles pertaining to religion or the occult." Buys 6 mss/issue. Send complete ms. Length: 1,200-3,600 words. Pays $20-100.

Photos: Send photos with ms. Pays $3-10 for negatives and 5x7 b&w glossy prints. Captions and model releases are required.

Columns/Departments: Buys 6/issue. Query with clips of published work. Length: 750-2,500 words. Pays $15-50.

Fillers: Newsbreaks and short humor. Buys 6/issue. Length: 100-600 words. Pays $5-15.

LET'S LIVE MAGAZINE, Oxford Industries, Inc., 444 N. Larchmont Blvd., Los Angeles CA 90004. (213)469-3901. Managing Editor: William Koester. Associate Publisher: Peggy MacDonald. Emphasizes nutrition. Monthly magazine; 160 pages. Estab. 1933. Circ. 140,000. Pays on publication. Buys all rights. Byline given unless "it is a pen name and author fails to furnish legal name; vast amount of editing is required (byline is then shared with the editors of *Let's Live*); it is an interview by assignment in which 'questioner' is *LL* (*Let's Live*)." Submit seasonal/holiday material 2 months in advance. SASE. Reports in 3 weeks for queries; 6 weeks for mss. Sample copy $1.50; free writer's guidelines.

Nonfiction: Expose (of misleading claims for benefits of drug products or food in treatment of physical disorders); general interest (effects of vitamins, minerals and nutrients in improvement of health or afflictions); historical (documentation of experiments or treatment establishing value of nutrients as boon to health); how-to (acquire strength and vitality, improve health of children and prepare tasty health food meals); inspirational (first-person accounts of triumph over disease through substitution of natural foods and nutritional supplements for drugs and surgery); interview (benefits of research and/or case studies in establishing prevention as key to good health); new product (120-180 words plus 5x7 or 8x10 b&w glossy of product); personal experience (my story feature in conquering poor health); personal opinion (views of orthomolecular doctors or their patients on value of health foods toward maintaining good health); profile (background and/or medical history of preventive medicine MDs or PhDs in advancement of nutrition); and health food recipes ($5 on publication). "We do not want kookie first-person accounts of experiences with drugs or junk foods, faddist healers or unorthodox treatments." Buys 10-14 mss/issue. Query with clips of published work. Length: 750-2,000 words. Pays $50-250.

Photos: State availability of photos with ms. Pays $17.50-35 for 8x10 b&w glossy prints; $35-60 for 8x10 color prints and 35mm color transparencies. $150 for good cover shot. Captions and model releases required.

Columns/Departments: My Story and Interviews. Buys 1-2/issue. Query. Length: 450-250. Pays $50-250.

Fillers: Anecdotes (200-300 words on rewarding encounter with person in nutrition field that influenced writer's views on nutrition). Pays $15.

LIFE AND HEALTH, 6856 Eastern Ave. NW, Washington DC 20012. Acting Editor: Joyce McClintock. Estab. 1884. Monthly. Circ. 100,000. Buys all rights. Byline given. Buys 100-150 mss/year. Pays on acceptance. Sample copy 50¢; free writer's guidelines. Submit seasonal health articles 6 months in advance. Reports on material within 2-3 months. SASE.

Nonfiction, Photos, and Poetry: General subject matter consists of "short, concise articles that simply and clearly present a concept in the field of health. Emphasis on prevention; faddism avoided." Approach should be a "simple, interesting style for laymen. Readability important. Medical jargon avoided. Material should be reliable and include latest findings. We are perhaps more conservative than other magazines in our field. Not seeking sensationalism." Buys informational, interview, some humor. "Greatest single problem is returning articles for proper and thorough documentation. References to other lay journals not acceptable." Length: 1,500 words maximum. Pays $50-150. Purchases photos with mss. 5x7 or larger b&w glossy prints. Color photos usually by staff. Buys some health-related poetry.

LISTEN MAGAZINE, 6830 Laurel St. NW, Washington DC 20012. (202)723-0800. Editor: Francis A. Soper. 75% freelance written. Primarily for teens. "*Listen* is used in many high school curriculum classes, in addition to use by professionals; medical personnel, counselors, law enforcement officers, educators, youth workers, etc." Monthly magazine, 28 pages. Estab. 1948. Circ. 200,000. Buys all rights. Byline given. Buys 100-200 mss/year. Pays on acceptance. Free sample copy and writer's guidelines. Reports in 4 weeks. Query. SASE.

Nonfiction: Specializes in preventive angle, presenting positive alternatives to various drug dependencies. Especially interested in youth-slanted articles or personality interviews encouraging nonalcoholic and nondrug ways of life. Teenage point of view is good. Popularized medical, legal and educational articles. "We don't want typical alcoholic story/skid-row bum, AA stories." Length: 500-1,500 words. Pays 2-5¢/word.

Photos: Purchased with accompanying ms. Captions required. Pays $5-15 per b&w print (5x7, but 8x10 preferred).

Poetry and Fillers: Blank verse and free verse only. Some inspirational poetry; short poems preferred. Word square/general puzzles are also considered. Pays up to $5 for poetry. Payment for fillers varies according to length and quality. Pays $15 for puzzles.

How To Break In: "Personal stories are good, especially if they have a unique angle. Other authoritative articles need a fresh approach."

MUSCLE MAGAZINE INTERNATIONAL, Unit 1, 270 Rutherford Rd. S., Brampton, Ontario, Canada L6W 3K7. Editor: Robert Kennedy. 80% freelance written. For 16- to 30-year-old men interested in physical fitness and overall body improvement. Bimonthly magazine; 84 pages. Estab. 1974. Circ. 120,000. Buys all rights. Byline given. Buys 80 mss/year. Pays on acceptance. Sample copy $2. Reports in 2 weeks. Submit complete ms. SAE and International Reply Coupons.

Nonfiction and Photos: Articles on ideal physical proportions and importance of protein in the diet. Should be helpful and instructional and appeal to young men who want to live life in a vigorous and healthy style. "We do not go in for huge, vein-choked muscles and do not want to see any articles on attaining huge muscle size. We would like to see articles for the physical culturist or an article on fitness testing." Informational, how-to, personal experience, interview, profile, inspirational, humor, historical, expose, nostalgia, personal opinion, photo, spot news, new product, merchandising technique articles. Length: 1,200-1,600 words. Pays 6¢/word. Columns purchasing material include Nutrition Talk (eating ideas for top results) and Shaping Up (improving fitness and stamina). Length: 1,300 words. Pays 6¢/word. B&w and color photos are purchased with or without ms. Pays $8 for 8x10 glossy exercise photos; $16 for 8x10 b&w posing shots. Pays $100 for color cover and $25 for color used inside magazine.

Fillers: Newsbreaks, clippings, puzzles, jokes, short humor. Length: open. Pays $5, minimum.

How To Break In: "Best way to break in is to seek out the muscle-building 'stars' and do in-depth interviews with biography in mind. Picture support essential."

WEIGHT WATCHERS MAGAZINE, 149 5th Ave., New York NY 10011. (212)475-5400. Editor: Bernadette Carr. For middle-class females, mostly married, with children. Monthly magazine; 64 pages. Estab. 1968. Circ. 830,000. Buys all rights. Buys 3-5 mss/month. Pays on acceptance. Sample copy $1.25. No photocopied or simultaneous submissions. Submit seasonal material 5 months in advance. Reports in 4 weeks. SASE.

Nonfiction: "Subject matter should be related to weight control, although we are not interested in diet pieces. We are interested in developing medical and psychological pieces related to weight; humor. No fiction. Fashion, beauty, exercises and recipes are all handled on staff." Length: 3,000 words maximum. Pay varies, usually $300-600.

WELL-BEING MAGAZINE, Box 1829, Santa Cruz CA 95061. (408)425-5411. Editor: Barbara Salat. Reports on "do-it-yourself" health care techniques for readers interested in change for the better, for the individual and the planet. Monthly magazine; 64 pages. Estab. 1975. Circ. 30,000. Pays on publication. Pays 25% kill fee. Byline given. Phone queries OK. Submit seasonal/holiday material 4 month in advance. Photocopied and previously published submissions OK. Reports in 1-2 months. Sample copy $1; free writer's guidelines.

Nonfiction: Reports on various health care techniques, alternative and traditional. Subjects include diet, massage, herbs, exercise, life styles, gardening, recycling, alternative energy, wild foods, wholistic medicine, home birth, etc. How-to (use solar energy, recycling methods, garden naturally, conserve, improve health); informational (effects of common foods, drugs, additives, flavorings, colorings); interviews (with folks who live natural, positive, healthy, active lives; doctors, midwives, inventors); nostalgia (living on the land, homesteading); personal experience (home remedies, home birth, new herbal uses); profiles (natural life style personalities); and technical (how to build inexpensive solar devices, composters, etc., for the home). Buys 6-8/issue. Length: 500-5,000 words. Pays $15-200.

Photos: Purchased with or without mss, or on assignment. Query. Pays $10/published page. Send 8x10 b&w glossy prints. Color slides by arrangement.

History

AMERICAN HERITAGE, 10 Rockefeller Plaza, New York NY 10020. Editor: Geoffrey C. Ward. Estab. 1954. Bimonthly. Circ. 145,000. Buys all rights. Pays 33% kill fee. Byline given. Buys 20 uncommissioned mss/year. Pays on acceptance. Before submitting, "check our five-and ten-year indexes to see whether we have already treated the subject." Submit seasonal material 12 months in advance. Returns rejected material in 1 month. Acknowledges acceptance of material in 1 month, or sooner. Query. SASE.
Nonfiction: Wants "historical articles intended for intelligent lay readers rather than professional historians." Emphasis is on authenticity, accuracy and verve. Style should stress "readability and accuracy." Length: 4,000-5,000 words.
Fillers: "We occasionally buy shorts and fillers that deal with American history."
How To Break In: "Our needs are such that the criteria for a young, promising writer are unfortunately no different than those for an old hand. Nevertheless, we have over the years published quite a few 'firsts' from young writers whose historical knowledge, research methods and writing skills meet our standards from the start. Everything depends on the quality of the material. We don't really care whether the author is 20 and unknown, or 80 and famous."

AMERICAN HISTORY ILLUSTRATED, Box 1831, Harrisburg PA 17105. (717)234-5091. Editor: William C. Davis. Aimed at general public with an interest in sound, well-researched history. Monthly except March and September. Buys all rights. Byline given. Pays on acceptance. Sample copy $1.50; free writer's guidelines. "Do not bind the manuscript or put it in a folder or such. Simply paperclip it. We prefer a ribbon copy, not a carbon or photocopy. No multiple submissions, please. It is best to consult several back issues before submitting any material, in order to see what we have already covered and to get an idea of our editorial preferences. Please include informal annotations and a reading list of materials used in preparing the article." Reports in two weeks. Query. SASE.
Nonfiction: US history from prehistoric times to the 1960s. Topics include biographic, military, social, cultural and political. Also covers the US in relation to the rest of the world, as in World Wars I and II. Style should be readable and entertaining, but not glib or casual. Slant generally up to the author. No shallow research or extensive quotation. Length: 2,500-5,000 words. Pays $50-350.
Photos: Occasionally buys 8x10 glossy prints with mss; welcomes suggestions for illustrations. Address to Frederic Ray, Art Director.

THE AMERICAN WEST, 20380 Town Center Lane, Suite 160, Cupertino CA 95014. Managing Editor: Pamela Herr. Editor: Ed Holm. Published by the Buffalo Bill Historical Center, Cody WY. Emphasizes western American history. Sponsored by the Western History Association. Bimonthly magazine; 64 pages. Estab. 1964. Circ. 22,000. Pays within 30-45 days of acceptance. Buys first North American periodical rights, plus anthology rights. Pays 33⅓% kill fee. Byline given. Submit seasonal/holiday material 6 months in advance. Photocopied submissions OK. SASE. Reports in 6-8 weeks. Free sample copy and writer's guidelines.
Nonfiction: Historical (carefully researched, accurate, lively articles having some direct relationship to western American history) and photo feature (essays relating to some specific historical theme). Buys 5 mss/issue. Length: 2,000-5,000 words. Pays $150 minimum.
Photos: Purchased with or without accompanying ms. Captions required. Query. Pays minimum.
How To Break In: "We publish a relatively small number of articles, emphasizing careful research (preferably based on primary sources) and historical accuracy. The articles should be written with a general audience in mind and should be lively in tone. Most accepted mss fall into the following subject areas: biography (noteworthy men and women figuring in the western American heritage); historical narrative; personal experience (reminiscences having some relation to the western heritage); and 'living history' (articles on museums, historical sites, historical reenactments, or other events). Geographic area is limited to the United States west of the Mississippi River."

ART AND ARCHAEOLOGY NEWSLETTER, 243 East 39 St., New York NY 10016. Editor: Otto F. Reiss. 5% freelance written. For people interested in archeology; educated laymen, educators, some professional archeologists. Quarterly newsletter, 20 pages. Estab. 1965. Circ. 1,500. Buys all rights, but will reassign rights to author after publication; buys second serial (reprint) rights. Buys 1-2 mss/year. Pays on publication. Will send sample copy to writer for $1.50 in 15¢ stamps. Will consider photocopied or simultaneous submissions. Reports in 2 weeks. Query. SASE.

Nonfiction: "Ancient history, archeology, new discoveries, new conclusions, new theories. Our approach is similar to the way *Time Magazine* would treat archeology or ancient history in its science section. A lighter tone, less rigidly academic. Don't avoid mystery, glamour, eroticism. Primarily interested in Old World antiquity. No travel articles a la *Holiday*. Definitely not interested in Indian arrowheads, Indian pots, kivas, etc." Length: 400-2,500 words. Pays $20.
Photos: Purchased with accompanying ms with no additional payment. Purchased also without ms for $7.50 minimum for b&w. Information (data) required for all b&w photos. No color. Will write own captions.
How To Break In: "Spend five years reading books about archeology and ancient history so that you become something of an expert on the subject. Be prepared to give precise sources, with page and paragraph, for factual statements. Some freelance writers, pretending to submit nonfiction, invent their material. Altogether, dealing with freelance people in this field is more trouble than it is worth. But hope blooms eternal. Perhaps there's another enthusiast who sneaked his way into an Alexander's Tomb."

CANADA WEST, Box 3399, Langley, British Columbia, Canada V3A 4R7. (604)534-8222. Editor-in-Chief: T.W. Paterson. 75% freelance written. Emphasizes pioneer history, primarily of Alberta, British Columbia and the Yukon. Quarterly magazine; 40 pages. Estab. 1969. Circ. 5,000. Pays on publication. Buys First North American serial rights. Phone queries OK. Previously published submissions OK. SASE. Reports in 2 months. Free sample copy and writer's guidelines.
Nonfiction: How-to (related to gold panning and dredging); historical (pioneers, shipwrecks, massacres, battles, exploration, logging, Indians and railroads). Buys 28 mss/year. Submit complete ms. Length: 2,000-3,500. Pays 2¢/word.
Photos: All mss must include photos or other artwork. Submit photos with ms. Pays $5 maximum for 5x7 or larger b&w glossy prints. Captions preferred. "Photographs are kept for future reference with the right to re-use. However, we do not forbid other uses, generally, as these are historical prints from archives."
Columns/Departments: Open to suggestions for new columns/departments.

CHICAGO HISTORY, Chicago Historical Society, Clark St. at North Ave., Chicago IL 60614. (312)642-4600. Editor-in-Chief: Fannia Weingartner. 30% freelance written. Emphasizes history for history scholars, buffs and academics. Quarterly magazine; 64 pages. Estab. 1970. Circ. 6,500. Pays on acceptance. Buys all rights (but may reassign following publication), second serial (reprint) rights and one-time rights. Byline given. Ribbon copy preferred. SASE. Reports in 2 months. Sample copy $1; free writer's guidelines.
Nonfiction: Historical (of Chicago and the Old Northwest). "Articles should be well researched, analytical, informative, and directed at a popular audience, but one with a special interest in history." Buys 6 mss/issue. Query. Length: 4,500 words maximum. Pays $75-250.

CIVIL WAR TIMES ILLUSTRATED, Box 1831, Harrisburg PA 17105. (717)234-5091. Editor: William C. Davis. Magazine published monthly except March and September. Estab. 1958. Circ. 100,000. Pays on acceptance. Buys all rights, first rights or one-time rights, or makes assignments on a work-for-hire basis. Submit seasonal/holiday material 10-12 months in advance. SASE. Reports in 2 weeks on queries; in 1-2 months on mss. Sample copy $1.50; free writer's guidelines.
Nonfiction: Profile, photo feature, and Civil War historical material. "Positively no fiction or poetry." Buys 20 mss/year. Length: 500-4,000 words. Query. Pays $25-300.
Photos: Frederic Ray, art director. State availability. Pays $5-25 for 8x10 b&w glossy prints or 4x5 color transparencies.

EL PALACIO, QUARTERLY JOURNAL OF THE MUSEUM OF NEW MEXICO, Museum of New Mexico Press, Box 2087, Santa Fe NM 87503. (505)827-2352. Editor-in-Chief: Richard L. Polese. Emphasizes anthropology, history, folk and fine arts, natural history and geography. Quarterly magazine; 48 pages. Estab. 1913. Circ. 2,500. Pays on publication. Buys all rights, but may reassign following publication. Byline given. Phone queries OK. Submit seasonal/holiday material 9-12 months in advance. Photocopied submissions OK. SASE. Reports in 2-6 weeks. Sample copy $2; free writer's guidelines.
Nonfiction: Historical (on Southwest; technical approach OK); how-to (folk art and craft, emphasis on the authentic); informational (more in the fields of geography and natural history); photo feature; technical; and travel (especially if related to the history of the Southwest). Buys 5 ms/issue. Send complete ms. Length: 1,750-5,000 words. Pays $50 minimum.
Photos: Photos purchased with or without accompanying ms or on assignment. Captions

required. Pays "on contract" for 5x7 (or larger) b&w photos and 5x7 or 8½x11 prints or 35mm color transparencies. Send prints and transparencies. Total purchase price for ms includes payment for photos.

Columns/Departments: The Museum's World, Photo Essay, Books (reviews of interest to *El Palacio* readers). Open to suggestions for new columns/departments.

How To Break In: "*El Palacio* magazine offers a unique opportunity for writers with technical ability to have their work reach publication and be seen by influential professionals as well as avidly interested lay readers. The magazine is highly regarded in its field.

FAMILY HERITAGE, Folk History Press, Inc., Box 1809, New York NY 11231. (212)643-9061. Editor: Scott McDade. Emphasizes family history, folklore, local history and genealogy. Bimonthly magazine; 32 pages. Estab. February 1978. Circ. 5,000. Pays on publication. Buys all rights. Pays 50% kill fee. Byline given. Phone queries OK. Submit seasonal/holiday material 6 months in advance. Photocopied and previously published submissions OK. SASE. Reports in 12 weeks (we send confirmation of receipt within 24 hours). Sample copy $1; free writer's guidelines.

Nonfiction: Expose (studies of agencies, persons and trends that threaten the maintenance of historical landmarks, traditions or cultures in the US); folklore (folk beliefs and customs, local tales, language styles and dialects; and any aspect of American folklife); general interest (family and community characters; profiles of interesting ethnic communities. Profiles of families who preserve their heritage in interesting ways); how-to (genealogical and historical research methods; old-time crafts; heritage projects ("build a replica of this 1840 smokehouse"); old recipes "authentic to the writer's family"; photo care and analysis; historical (immigrant life, culture and technological history; old time customs; family life in the "old days"; oral history narratives; migration; "we will consider any ms on subjects relating to social and cultural or technological history if they slant toward community/family/ethnic life"); interview (folklorists, historians, writers, public officials of note, on subject of their contribution to family and community heritage); nostalgia (turn of the century to late '40s life, work; emphasis on change of environment, values); new product ("we are not actively seeking this type of article, but would consider relevant product treatments"); photo feature (of on going family/local traditional folklife; ethnic festival; site study); profile (loving, reflective pieces on the theme of "my most unforgetable relative—" must be of wide interest); technical (photograph, art restoration; antique restoration; architectural renovation); travel (to places of a family origin, site of historical research); and analysis of the historical meaning of any heirloom or artifact, either a how-to or an example of what the writer learned about an ancestor by studying an antique the ancestor owned). Buys 6-12 mss/issue. Send complete ms or clips of published work. Length: 1,000-5,000 words. Pays $50-250.

Photos: Send photos with ms (on queries, photocopies are usually adequate). Pays $5 for 4x5 glossy prints or contact sheets; $15 for color transparencies. Buys one-time rights. Captions required.

Columns/Departments: You Should Know About (historical, genealogical, heritage, ethnic organizations of general interest, which readers can avail themselves of by correspondence or membership); and Favorite Recipes (old family recipes that have been in the family for two or three generations, or were created under special circumstances). Send complete ms. Length: 200-2,000 words. Pays $5-10 ($5 flat fee for recipes).

Fillers: Vignettes of old-time family life: customs, humorous incidents and memorable events. Uses 2-3 issue. Length: 100-400 words. Pays 5¢/word.

FRONTIER TIMES, Western Publications, Inc., Box 3338, Austin TX 78764. Bimonthly. Byline given. See *True West.*

HISTORIC PRESERVATION, National Trust for Historic Preservation, 1785 Massachusetts Ave. NW, Washington DC 20036. Vice President and Editor: Mrs. Terry B. Morton. A benefit of membership in the National Trust for Historic Preservation and for others interested in or involved with historic preservation efforts. Bimonthly magazine; 56 pages. Estab. 1949. Circ. 150,000. Pays on publication. May buy all, second serial (reprint), or one-time rights. Photocopied submissions OK. SASE. Reports in 2-4 weeks. Free sample copy and writer's guidelines.

Nonfiction: "Willing to review queries on subjects directly related to historic preservation, including efforts to save buildings, structures and neighborhoods of historical, architectural and cultural significance. No local history; must relate to sites, objects, buildings and neighborhoods specifically. Most material prepared on a commissioned basis. Writer must be very familiar with our subject matter, which deals with a specialized field, in order to present a unique publication idea." Length: 1,000-2,500 words. Pays $250 maximum.

Photos: Additional payment not usually made for photos purchased with mss. Query or send contact sheet. Pays $10-50 for 8x10 b&w glossy prints purchased without mss or on assignment; $40-70 for color.

JOURNAL OF AMERICAN HISTORY, Ballantine Hall, Indiana University, Bloomington IN 47401. (812)337-3034. Editor: Lewis Perry. For professional historians of all ages. Quarterly journal; 350 pages. Estab. 1907. Circ. 12,500. Buys all rights. Pays on publication. Reports in 10-12 weeks. Submit 2 copies of complete ms. SASE.
Nonfiction: Material dealing with American history; analytical for the audience of professional historians. Length: 5,000-7,500 words. Pays a nomial fee.

JOURNAL OF GENEALOGY, Anderson Publishing Co., Inc., Box 31097, Omaha NE 68131. (402)554-1800. Editor-in-Chief: Robert D. Anderson. Emphasizes genealogy and history. Monthly magazine; 48 pages. Estab. 1976. Circ. 10,000. Pays on publication. Buys all rights, but may reassign following publication. Submit seasonal/holiday material 4 months in advance. Previously published submissions OK. SASE. Reports in 6 weeks. Sample copy $2.50; writer's guidelines for SASE.
Nonfiction: Historical (on places or obscure pioneers, place names, etc); how-to (new or different ways to trace ancestors, new ways to keep notes, or new ways to diagram a pedigree chart); interview (of well-known persons involved in genealogy); new product (about innovations in capturing, storing, indexing and retrieving data—such as computors and microfiche relating to historical or genealogical data); personal experience (must have profound impact on genealogical research); personal opinion (must be in-depth and scholarly dealing with genealogy and/or history); profile; travel (genealogists like to combine a vacation with genealogical research); and scholarly (we need thought provoking articles on the science of genealogy and how it relates to other sciences). Buys 20 mss/year. Query. Length: 750-4,500 words; "longer considered, but need natural breaks for serialization." Pays 2¢/word.
Photos: Purchased with or without accompanying ms or on assignment. Captions required. Query. Pays $5-25 for 8x10 b&w photos. Model release required.
Columns/Departments: Society Station (this column is devoted to helping genealogical and historical societies in their day-to-day activities, e.g., "How to Write a News Release" or "Should We File for Non-Profit Status?"). Query. Length: 750-2,000 words. Pays 2¢/word. Open to suggestions for new columns/departments.
How To Break In: "We want articles that will help the most people find the most genealogy. Always ask yourself, as we do, 'is it meaningful?' We need good articles on researching in foreign countries."

NORTH CAROLINA HISTORICAL REVIEW, Historical Publications Section, Archives and History, 109 E. Jones St., Raleigh NC 27611. (919)733-7442. Editor: Memory F. Mitchell. Emphasizes scholarly historical subjects for historians and others interested in history. Quarterly magazine; 100 pages. Estab. 1924. Circ. 2,200. Buys all rights, but may reassign following publication. Phone queries OK. SASE. Reports in 3 months. Free writer's guidelines.
Nonfiction: Articles relating to North Carolina history in particular, Southern history in general. Topics about which relatively little is known or are new interpretations of familiar subjects. All articles must be based on primary sources and footnoted. Length: 15-25 typed pages. Pays $10/article.

NOVA SCOTIA HISTORICAL QUARTERLY, Box 1102, Halifax, Nova Scotia, Canada B3J 2X1. Editor-in-Chief: William H. McCurdy. 100% freelance written. "For a readership interested in the history of Nova Scotia, Canada." Quarterly magazine; 100 pages. Estab. 1971. Circ. 1000. Pays on publication. Buys one-time right and credit in subsequent publishing. Simultaneous and photocopied submissions OK. SASE ("Canadian stamps please"). Reports in 1 week.
Nonfiction: Historical (factual articles only). "No personal reminicences or previously published mss please." Buys 20 mss/year. Submit complete ms. Length: 2,500-5,000 words. Pays $25-50.

OLD WEST, Quarterly Western Publications, Inc., Box 3338, Austin TX 78764. (512)444-3674. Editor: Pat Wagner. Byline given. See *True West*.

PERSIMMON HILL, 1700 NE 63rd St., Oklahoma City OK 73111. Editor: Dean Krakel. Senior Editor: Sara Dobberteen. For an audience interested in Western art, Western history, ranching and rodeo; historians, artists, ranchers, art galleries, schools, libraries. Publication of the National Cowboy Hall of Fame and Western Heritage Center. Estab. 1970. Quarterly. Circ.

25,000. Buys all rights. Byline given. Buys 12-14 mss/year. Pays on publication. Sample copy $3. Reporting time on mss accepted for publication varies. Returns rejected material immediately. Query. SASE.
Nonfiction and Photos: Historical and contemporary articles on famous Western figures connected with pioneering the American West; Western art; rodeo; cowboys; etc. (or biographies of such people); stories of Western flora and animal life; environmental subjects. Only thoroughly researched and historically authentic material is considered. May have a humorous approach to subject. Not interested in articles that reappraise, or in any way put the West and its personalities in an unfavorable light. Length: 2,000-3,000 words. Pays $150 minimum. B&w glossy prints or color transparencies purchased with or without ms, or on assignment. Pays according to quality and importance for b&w and color. Suggested captions appreciated.

TRUE WEST, Western Publications, Inc., Box 3338, Austin TX 78764. (512)444-3674. Editor: Pat Wagner. Bimonthly magazine. Estab. 1953. Circ. 90,000. Pays on acceptance. Buys first North American serial rights. Byline given. "Magazine is distributed nationally, but if not on the newsstands in a particular location will send sample copy for 75¢. Queries should give proposed length of article, what rights are offered, whether pix are available, and enough information for us to check our file for material covered or on hand. Example: an ageless query, 'Would you like an article on a mountain man?' Without his name, we simply can't say." SASE.
Nonfiction and Photos: "Factual accounts regarding people, places and events of the frontier West (1850-1910). Sources are required. If based on family papers, records, memoirs, etc., reminiscences must be accurate as to dates and events. Please write in third person whenever possible. Family relationship can be stated at end. We strive for stories with an element of action, suspense, heroics and humor, but those about the better-known outlaws, Indians, lawmen and explorers will probably overlap material we have already run. At present we are receiving too much material from the 1920s, '30s and '40s. We regret that many first-hand accounts have to be returned because the happenings are too recent for us. We also receive considerable material which is good local history, but would have limited appeal for a national readership." Length: 750-4,000 words. pays 2¢/word minimum, plus allowances for photos. "We usually buy mss and photos as a package. Photos are returned after publication."

VIKINGSHIP, Leif Ericson Society, Box 301, Chicago IL 60690. (312)761-1888. Editor: W.R. Anderson. 40% freelance written. Emphasizes medieval American history for a readership interested in pre-Columbian American exploration by Norse Vikings. Quarterly newsletter; 10 pages. Estab. 1965. Circ. 1,200. Pays on acceptance. Buys first North American serial rights. Photocopied submissions OK. SASE. Reports in 1 week. Sample copy $1.
Nonfiction: Historical articles on Norse Viking exploration in America from the 10th-14th centuries. "We have no interest in run-of-the-mill rehashes of well-known evidence. Our readers are very sophisticated in the subject." Buys 5-10 mss/year. Submit complete ms. Length: 300-1,000 words. Pays $10 minimum.

VIRGINIA CAVALCADE, Virginia State Library, Richmond VA 23219. Primarily for Virginians and others with an interest in Virginia history. Quarterly magazine; 48 pages. Estab. 1951. Circ. 17,000. Buys all rights. Byline given. Buys 15-20 mss/year. Pays on acceptance. Sample copy $1; free writer's guidelines. Rarely considers simultaneous submissions. Submit seasonal material 15-18 months in advance. Reports in 4 weeks to 1 year. Query. SASE.
Nonfiction and Photos: "We welcome readable and factually accurate articles that are relevant to some phase of Virginia history. Art, architecture, literature, education, business, technology and transportation are all acceptable subjects, as well as political and military affairs. Articles must be based on thorough, scholarly research. We require footnotes but do not publish them. Authors should avoid contemporary political and social topics on which people hold strong and conflicting opinions. Any period from the age of exploration to the mid-20th century, and any geographical section or area of the state may be represented. Must deal with subjects that will appeal to a broad readership, rather than to a very restricted group or locality. Fresh and little known themes are preferred; manuscripts on more familiar subjects will be considered. Articles must be suitable for illustration, although it is not necessary that the author provide the pictures. If the author does have pertinent illustrations or knows their location, the editor appreciates information concerning them." Uses 8x10 b&w glossy prints; color transparencies should be at least 4x5. Length: approximately 3,500 words. Pays $100.

VIRGINIA MAGAZINE OF HISTORY AND BIOGRAPHY, Virginia Historical Society, Box 7311, Richmond VA 23221. Editor: William M.E. Rachal. 95% freelance written. Quarterly for serious students of Virginia history. Usually buys all rights. Byline given. Pays on publication. Reports in 2 months. SASE.

Nonfiction: Carefully researched and documented articles on Virginia history, and well-edited source material relating to Virginia. Must be dignified, lucid and scholarly. Length: 1,500-15,000 words. Appropriate illustrations are used. Pays $2/printed page.

Hobby and Craft

Publications in this section are for collectors, do-it-yourselfers, and craft hobbyists. Publications for electronics and radio hobbyists will be found in the Science classification.

AMERICAN BLADE, Beinfeld Publishing, Inc., 12767 Saticoy St., N. Hollywood CA 91605. (213)982-3700. Editor: Wallace Beinfeld. For knife enthusiasts who want to know as much as possible about quality knives and edge weapons. Bimonthly magazine; 52 pages. Estab. 1972. Circ. 15,000. Pays on publication. Buys all rights. Submit seasonal/holiday material 6 months in advance. Previously published submissions OK. SASE. Reports in 4-6 weeks. Sample copy $1.50; free writer's guidelines.

Nonfiction: Historical (on knives and weapons); how-to; interview (knifmakers); new product; nostalgia; personal experience; photo feature; profile and technical. Buys 6 mss/issue. Query. Length: 1,000-2,000 words. Pays 5¢/word.

Photos: Send photos with ms. Pays $5 for 8x10 b&w glossy prints; $25-75 for 35mm color transparencies. Captions required.

AMERICAN COLLECTOR, Crain Communications, Inc. 740 Rush St., Chicago IL 60611. Editor: Merle Kingman. Managing Editor: John Maloney. 80% freelance written. Emphasizes collecting for antique buffs , collectors of all kinds, dealers, and investors. Monthly tabloid; 48 pages. Estab. 1970. Circ. 100,000. Pays on publication. Buys all rights, but may reassign following publication. Byline given. Submit seasonal/holiday material 3 months in advance of issue date. SASE. Reports in 1 month. Sample copy $1; free writer's guidelines.

Nonfiction: Exposé (fake collectibles and fake antiques); how-to (evaluate, protect an item, tips on finding or buying, and prices); interview; unusual collections and/or collectors; nostalgia; personal experience (related to collecting); and photo feature (related to collecting). Buys 100 mss/year. Submit complete ms. Length: 500-1,200 words. Pays $3/inch.

Photos: Submit photo material with accompanying ms. Pays $5 for 8x10 b&w glossy prints and $10-20 for 2¼x2¼ color transparencies. Captions required. Buys all rights, but may reassign following publication.

AMERICAN CRAFT (formerly *Craft Horizons*), American Craft Council Publishers, 22 W. 55th St., New York NY 10019. Managing Editor: Patricia Dandignac. Bimonthly. Circ. 38,000. Published by American Crafts Council for professional craftspeople, artists, teachers, architects, designers, decorators, collectors, connoisseurs and the consumer public. Pays on publication. Free sample copy. Reports "as soon as possible." Query. SASE.

Nonfiction and Photos: Articles and accompanying photos on the subject of creative work in ceramics, weaving, stitchery, jewelry, metalwork, woodwork, etc. Discussions of the technology, the materials and the ideas of artists throughout the world working in the above media. Length: 1,000 words. Pays $75-100. Accompanying photos should be 8x10 b&w glossy prints. Pays $7.50 per b&w glossy.

THE ANTIQUARIAN, Box 798, Huntington NY 11743. (516)271-8990. Editor-in-Chief: Marguerite Cantine. Managing Editor: Elizabeth Kilpatrick. Emphasizes antiques and 19th-century or earlier art. Monthly magazine; 32-40 pages. Estab. 1974. Circ. 10,000. Pays on publication. Buys all rights, but may reassign following publication. Pays 10% kill fee. Byline given. Submit seasonal/holiday material 3 months in advance of issue date. Photocopied and previously published (if not published in antiques publication) submissions OK. SASE. Reports in 6 weeks. Sample copy for SASE (8½x11, 41¢); mention *Writer's Market* in request.

Nonfiction: How-to (refinish furniture, repair glass, restore old houses, paintings, rebind books, resilver glass, etc.); general interest (relations of buyers and dealers at antique shows/sales, auction reports); historical (data, personal and otherwise, on famous people in the arts and antiques field); interview; photo feature (auctions, must have caption on item including price it sold for); profile (want articles around movie stars and actors who collect antiques, query); and travel (historical sites of interest in New York, New Jersey, Pennsylvania and Deleware). Wants no material on art deco, collectibles, anything made after 1900, cutesy things to

'remake' from antiques, or flea markets and crafts shows. Buys 6 mss/year. Submit complete ms. Length: 200-2,000 words. Pays ½¢/word.
Photos: Pays $.50-1 for 3½x5 glossy b&w prints. Captions required. Buys all rights, but may reassign following publication. Model release required.
Fillers: Newsbreaks. Length: 100-200 words. Pays ½¢/word.
How To Break In: "Don't write an article unless you *love* this field. Antiques belong to a neurotic group. Collecting is a sickness as expensive as gambling, and twice as hard to break, because we are all content in our insanity. Don't write like a textbook. Write as though your were carrying on a nice conversation with your mother. No pretentions. No superiority. Simple, warm, one-to-one, natural, day-to-day, neighbor-over-coffee writing."

ANTIQUE & COLLECTORS MART, 15100 W. Kellogg, Wichita KA 67235. (316)524-5308. Editor: Sandy Bales. Pays on publication. Buys first rights. Photocopied submissions OK. SASE. Reports in 1 month. Free sample copy.
Nonfiction: "We want anything that has to do with antiques, but must be educational and authenticated. No first-party stories. We prefer active current events, market trends, etc. Buys 4-5 mss/issue. Query. Length: 500-2,500 words. Pays $15-35.
Photos: State availability of photos. Pays $5 for 5x7 or 8x10 b&w glossy prints; $10 for 35mm color transparencies.
Columns/Departments: Market trends, Book reviews, Furniture, and Good Glass and China. Query. Open to suggestions for new columns/departments.
Fillers: Anecdotes, newsbreaks, auctions reports, show reports and price reports. Length: 50-200 words. Pays $5.

ANTIQUE & COLLECTOR'S TRADING POST, Deja Vu Publishing, 1956½ Lombard St., San Francisco CA 94123. Editor: Jackie Cohn. Managing Editor: Beverly Frazier. For those interested in antique buying, selling, trading and the serious collector of nostalgia and memorabilia. Monthly magazine; 8-12 pages. Estab. July 1976. Circ. 20,000. Pays on publication. Buys all rights. Byline given. Phone queries OK. Submit seasonal/holiday material 3 months in advance. SASE. Reports in 2 weeks. Free sample copy and writer's guidelines.
Nonfiction: General interest (to collectors, antiques and nostalgia buffs); historical (example—"collecting gold around the mother lode"); how-to (restoring furniture, care of paper collectibles, repairing, refinishing, etc.); interview (with famous collectors, people with unusual collections, etc.); new products (of interest to collectors, also books and book reviews on antiques and collectibles); nostalgia (movies, TV, radio, sports, paper collectibles, sports, dolls, etc.); personal experience (as a collector, dealer); photo feature ("most welcomed! any collecting-related subject"); and travel (example—"the traveling collector"). Buys 3-6 mss/issue. Query. Length: 350-2,000 words. Pays 50¢/column inch.
Photos: Send photos with ms. Pays 50¢/column inch for 8x11 b&w glossy prints. Captions preferred.
Columns/Departments: "We accept book reviews, fillers, crossword puzzles—virtually anything of interest to collectors." Query. Pays 50¢/column inch.

THE ANTIQUE TRADER WEEKLY, Box 1050, Dubuque IA 52001. (319)588-2073. Editor: Kyle D. Husfloen. 75% freelance written. For collectors and dealers in antiques and collectibles. Weekly newspaper; 90-120 pages. Estab. 1957. Circ. 90,000. Buys all rights, but will reassign rights to author after publication. Buys about 200 mss/year. Payment at beginning of month following publication. Free sample copy and writer's guidelines. Will consider photocopied and simultaneous submissions. Submit seasonal material (holidays) 3 to 4 months in advance. Query or submit complete ms. SASE.
Nonfiction and Photos: "We invite authoritative and well-researched articles on all types of antiques and collectors' items. Submissions should include a liberal number of good b&w photos. We also welcome feature cover stories which are accompanied by a good, clear color transparency which illustrates the feature. The feature should also have several b&w photos to illustrate the inside text. A color transparency of 4x5 is desirable for use as cover photo, but a smaller transparency is sometimes acceptable." Pays $5-50 for feature articles; $50-100 for feature cover stories. "We do not pay for brief information on new shops opening or other material printed as service to the antiques hobby."

ANTIQUES JOURNAL, Babka Publishing Co., Box 1046, Dubuque IA 52001. Emphasizes antiques and collecting for "experienced and incipient antiques collectors and dealers age 20-80 interested in learning the background of both the older antiques and the more recent collectible objects." Monthly magazine; 68 pages. Estab. 1946. Circ. 60,000. Pays on acceptance. Buys first North American serial rights. Byline given. Submit seasonal/holiday

material 10 months in advance. SASE. Reports in 2 weeks. Sample copy $1.25.
Nonfiction: Historical; informational; interview (only occasionally); and nostalgia (if related to collectible objects of the 1920s-50s). Buys 100 mss/year. Query. Length: 300-2,000 words. Pays $35-105.
Photos: Photos purchased with accompanying ms. Captions required. Uses 4x5 or 8x10 b&w glossy prints; pays $35-40 for 35mm-4x5 color transparencies (for cover). Total purchase price for ms includes payment for photos (excluding color transparencies for cover). Model release required.

ARMS GAZETTE, Beinfeld Publishing, Inc., 12767 Saticoy St., N. Hollywood CA 91605. (213)982-3700. Editor: Wallace Beinfeld. Emphasizes arms collecting and antique guns, swords, etc. Monthly magazine; 52 pages. Estab. 1971. Circ. 15,000. Pays on publication. Buys all rights. Byline given. Phone queries OK. Submit seasonal/holiday material 6 months in advance. Previously published submissions OK. SASE. Reports in 4-6 weeks. Sample copy $1.25; free writer's guidelines.
Nonficton: Historical, how-to, interview, new product, nostalgia, photo feature, profile and technical. Buys 6 mss/issue. Query or send complete ms. Length: 1,000-2,000 words. Pays 5¢/word.
Photos: Send photos with ms. Pays $5 for 8x10 b&w glossy print; $25-75 for 35mm or larger color transparencies. Detailed captions required.

BOOK BUYER'S GUIDE/MARKETPLACE, Franklin Publishing Co., Box 208, East Millstone NJ 08873. Editor: Kevin K. Kopec. Emphasizes mail order book buying/collecting. Quarterly tabloid; 16 pages. Estab. 1977. Circ. 5,000. Pays on acceptance. Buys all rights. Byline given. Phone queries OK. Submit seasonal/holiday material 1 month in advance. Simultaneous, photocopied and previously published submissions OK. SASE. Reports in 2 weeks. Sample copy $1.25.
Nonfiction: General interest (buying by mail, sources, tips, reviews); how-to (collect, maintain old books); interview (publishers, authors); and new product (book reviews). Buys 5-6 mss/issue. Send complete ms. Length: 200-500 words. Pays 1¢/word-$5.
Fillers: Clippings and newsbreaks. Buys 8-10/issue. Length 50-100 words. Pays 1¢/word.

THE BOOK-MART, Box 481, Pinellas Park FL 33565. Editor/Publisher: David G. MacLean. 60% freelance written. Emphasizes book collecting and the used-book trade. Monthly tabloid; 12-16 pages. Estab. March 1977. Circ. 2,000. Pays on publication. Buys one-time rights. Submit seasonal/holiday material 6 weeks in advance of issue date. Simultaneous, photocopied and previously published submissions OK. SASE. Reports in 4-6 weeks. Sample copy for 28¢ in postage; mention *Writer's Market* in request.
Nonfiction: "Especially need articles of interest to book dealers and collectors containing bibliographical and pricing data." Expose (literary forgeries); general interest (articles about regional authors, expecially those highly collected); historical (about books, authors, publishers, printers, booksellers); how-to (book conservation and restoration techniques, no amateur binding); interview (if in field of interest); nostalgia (articles about paper collectibles, especially those with pricing information); personal experience; and travel (literary landmarks). "No rambling accounts with no specific focus or articles about an unknown poet who has published his/her first book." Buys 2 mss/issue. Query. Length: 1,000-2,500 words. Pays 50¢/column inch.
Photos: State availability of photos with query. Pays $5 minimum for 5x7 or larger b&w glossy or matte finish prints. Buys one-time rights.
Columns/Departments: Books in Review. Query "unless of a timely nature." Pays 50¢/column inch.

CERAMIC SCOPE, 5208 W. Pico Blvd., Los Angeles CA 90019. (213)935-1122. Editor: Mel Fiske. Managing Editor: Karen Kaye. Emphasizes hobby ceramics business. "We have small-business people who are running their shops without too much experience in business or retailing. We require stories that would expand their knowledge." Monthly magazine; 64 pages. Estab. 1964. Circ. 6,300. Pays on acceptance. Buys all rights. Byline given unless it is a round-up story with any number of sources. Phone queries OK. Submit seasonal/holiday material 4-5 months in advance. SASE. Reports in 2 weeks. Sample copy $1; free writer's guidelines.
Nonfiction: Interview, opinion, profile, personal experience, photo feature and "in-depth material on business experiences." No articles on how studio owners started in business. Buys 2 mss/issue. Query with clips of published work. Length: 1,500-3,000 words. Pays $100-150.
Photos: State availability of photos or send photos with ms. Pays $5 for 4x5 or 5x7 b&w glossy

prints; $25-50 for color contact sheets. Captions required.

COLLECTIBLES AND ANTIQUES GAZETTE, 1626-A, Alton Rd., Miami FL 33139. (305)674-8555. Editor-in-Chief: Arthur Brickman. Managing Editor: Nettie Brickman. Emphasizes all collectibles and antiques including rare books. Bimonthly magazine; 36 pages. Estab. 1977. Circ. 5,000. Pays on publication. Buys all rights, but may reassign following publication. Phone queries OK. Submit seasonal/holiday material 3 months in advance of issue date. Simultaneous and photocopied submissions OK. SASE. Reports in 4 weeks. Free sample copy and writer's guidelines.
Nonfiction: Sal Perrine, articles editor. Informational; historical; interview; nostalgia; personal opinion; photo feature; and technical. Buys 100-120 mss/year. Query or submit complete ms. Length: 300-1,500 words. Pays 3¢/word.
Photos: Lee Gottlieb, photo editor. Pays $2 for b&w photos. Captions required.
Fillers: Clippings, newsbreaks and short humor. Pays $1.

COLLECTOR EDITIONS QUARTERLY (formerly *Acquire: The Magazine of Contemporary Collectibles*), 170 5th Ave., New York NY 10010. Editor: R. C. Rowe. For collectors, mostly 30 to 65 in ages in any rural and suburban, affluent and reasonably well educated. Published 5 times a year, quarterly with an annual issue. Estab. 1973. Circ. 90,000. Rights purchased vary with author and material. Buys all rights, but will reassign rights to author after publication; first North American serial rights; first serial rights; second serial (reprint) rights; simultaneous rights. Buys 15-30 mss/year. "First assignments are always done on a speculative basis." Pays on acceptance. Will send sample copy to writer for $1. Will consider photocopied submissions and simultaneous submissions. Query with outline. Reports in 1 month. SASE.
Nonfiction: "Short features about collecting, written in tight, newsy style. We specialize in contemporary (postwar) collectibles. Particularly interested in items affected by scarcity." Informational, how-to, interview, profile, expose, nostalgia. Length: 500-2,500 words. Pays $50-150. Columns cover stamps, cars, porcelains, glass, western art and graphics. Length: 750 words. Pays $75.
Photos: B&w and color photos purchased with accompanying ms with no additional payment. Also purchased without ms and on assignment. Captions are required. "Wants clear, distinct, full-frame image that says something." Pays $10-50.

COLLECTORS NEWS, Box 156, 606 8th St., Grundy Center IA 50638. (319)824-5456. Editor: Mary E. Croker. For dealers in, and collectors of, antiques. Monthly tabloid newspaper; 80-104 pages. Estab. 1960. Circ. 30,000. Buys 60 mss/year. Byline given. Pays on publication. Free sample copy. Submit seasonal material (holidays) 2 months in advance. Reports in 30 days. Query or submit complete ms. SASE.
Nonfiction and Photos: Only factual articles pertaining to some phase of collecting or interesting collections. Informational, profile, nostalgia. Length: 1,200 words minimum; 1,600 words average. Pays 50¢/column inch. No additional payment for b&w photos used with mss. Captions required.

CRAFTS MAGAZINE, PJS Publication, Box 1790, News Plaza, Peoria IL 61656. (309)682-6626. Editor: Joyce Bennett. Assistant Editor: Candace Watson. Monthly magazine; 100 pages. Estab. May 1978. Circ. 200,000. Pays on acceptance. Buys all rights. Phone queries OK. Submit seasonal/holiday material 6 months in advance. Photocopied submissions OK. SASE. Reports in 6 weeks. Free sample copy and writer's guidelines.
Nonfiction: How-to (crafts related to craft store products). Query. Buys 7 mss/issue. Pays $650-250.
Photos: State availability of photos with ms or send photos with accompanying ms. Offers no additional payment for photos accompanying ms. Uses 3x5 or 5x7 b&w glossy prints. Captions preferred; model release required.

CREATIVE CRAFTS, Carsten's Publications, Inc., Box 700, Newton NJ 07860. Editor-in-Chief: Sybil C. Harp. 80-90% freelance written. Emphasizes crafts for the serious adult hobbyist. Bimonthly magazine; 76 pages. Estab. 1967. Circ. 100,000. Pays on publication. Buys all rights. Byline given. Submit seasonal/holiday material 7 months in advance. SASE. Reports in 4 weeks. Mss cannot be considered unless accompanied by photos of completed project. Sample copy $1; free writer's guidelines.
Nonfiction: How-to (step-by-step of specific projects or general techniques; instructions must be clearly written and accompanied by b&w procedural photos and/or drawings). Buys 50-60 mss/year. Query. Length: 1,200 words average. Pays $50/magazine page. No human interest articles.

Photos: Purchased with accompanying ms. "We give $50 maximum allowance for photo expenses."

Columns/Departments: Going Places (articles dealing with annual fairs, craft "villages" or museums of special interest to craft enthusiasts). Buys 1 mss/issue. Query. Length: 1,200 words average. Pays $50/magazine page without advertising; $25/page mixed. Open to suggestions for new columns/departments.

Special Needs: "Articles written by knowledgable craftsmen covering projects that can be done at home. Our need is for quality crafts that offer some challenge to the hobbyist. No scrapcraft."

EARLY AMERICAN LIFE, Early American Society, Box 1831, Harrisburg PA 17105. Editor: Robert G. Miner. Executive Editor: Frances Carnahan. 70% freelance written. For "people who are interested in capturing the warmth and beauty of the 1600 to 1850 period and using it in their homes and lives today. They are interested in arts, crafts, travel, restoration, collecting." Bimonthly magazine; 100 pages. Estab. 1970. Circ. 360,000. Buys all rights. Buys 50 mss/year. Pays on acceptance. Free sample copy and writer' guidelines. Will consider photocopied submissions. Reports in 1 month. Query or submit complete ms. SASE.

Nonfiction and Photos: "Social history (the story of the people, not epic heroes and battles); crafts such as woodworking and needlepoint; travel to historic sites; country inns; antiques and reproductions; refinishing and restoration; architecture and decorating. We try to entertain as we inform, but always attempt to give the reader something he can do. While we're always on the lookout for good pieces on any of our subjects, the 'travel to historic sites' theme is most frequently submitted. Would like to see more how-to-do-it (well-illustrated) on how real people did something great to their homes." Length: 750-3,000 words. Pays $50-400. Pays $10 for 5x7 (and up) b&w photos used with mss; minimum of $25 for color. Prefers 2¼x2¼ and up, but can work from 35mm.

How To Break In: "Get a feeling for 'today's early Americans', the folks who are visiting flea markets, auctions, junkyards, the antiques shops. They are our readers and they hunger for ideas on how to bring the warmth and beauty of early America into their lives. Then, conceive a new approach to satisfying their related interests in arts, crafts, travel to historic sites, and the story of the people of the 1600 to 1850 period. Write to entertain and inform at the same time, and be prepared to help us with illustrations, or sources for them."

GEMS AND MINERALS, Box 687, Mentone CA 92359. (714)794-1173. Editor: Jack R. Cox. Monthly for the amateur gem cutter, jewelry maker, mineral collector and rockhound. Buys first North American serial rights. Byline given. Buys 15-20 mss/year. Pays on publication. Free sample copy and writer's guidelines. Query. Reports in a month. SASE.

Nonfiction and Photos: Material must have how-to slant. No personality stories. Field trips to mineral or gem collecting localities used; must be accurate and give details so they can be found. Instructions on how to cut gems; designs and creations of jewelry. Four to eight typed pages plus illustrations preferred, but do not limit if subject is important. Frequently good articles are serialized if too long for one issue. Pays 50¢ per inch for text and pix as published.

How To Break In: "Because we are a specialty magazine, it is difficult for a writer to prepare a suitable story for us unless he is familiar with the subject matter: jewelry making, gem cutting, mineral collecting and display, and fossil collecting. Our readers want accurate instructions on how to do it and where they can collect gemstones and minerals in the field. The majority of our articles are purchased from freelance writers, but most of them are hobbyists (rockhounds) or have technical knowledge on one of the subjects. Infrequently, a freelancer with no knowledge of the subject interviews an expert (gem cutter, jewelry maker, etc.) and gets what this expert tells him down on paper for a good how-to article. However, the problem here is that if the expert neglects to mention all the steps in his process, the writer does not realize it. Then, there is a delay while we check it out. My best advice to a freelance writer is to send for a sample copy of our magazine and author's specification sheet which will tell him what we need. We are interested in helping new writers and try to answer them personally, giving any pointers that we think will be of value to them. Let us emphasize that our readers want how-to and where-to stories. They are not at all interested in personality sketches about one of their fellow hobbyists."

GOLDMINE, Arena Magazine Co., Emans Rd., LaGrangeville NY 12540. Editor: Rick Whitesell. Emphasizes record collecting and musicology. Monthly magazine; 64 pages. Estab. 1973. Circ. 10,000. Pays on publication. Buys all rights but may return upon request. Byline given. Submit seasonal/holiday material 3 months in advance. Simultaneous and photocopied submissions OK. SASE. Reports in 2-3 weeks. Sample copy $1.50.

Nonfiction: General interest, historical, interview, new product, nostalgia and profile. "All articles should be on anything from 1900 to the present that is on record and is collectible. We do not want to see paraphrased, rehashed versions of other writers—whether in fan magazines, LP liner notes or newspapers. Originality and accuracy are essential ingredients." Buys 75-100 mss/year. Send complete ms. Length: 750 word minimum. Pays $10-25.

Photos: Send photos with ms. Pays $1.50 for 5x7 or 8x10 b&w glossy prints; $1.50 for color prints; offers no additional payment for photos with ms. Captions required.

HOBBY ARTIST NEWS, Rt. 2, Fort Atkinson IA 52144. Editor: Ray Gillem. 10% freelance written. For artists, hobbyists and authors. Bimonthly magazine; 8-12 pages. Estab. 1970. Circ. 300. Not copyrighted. Byline given. Pays on publication. Sample copy 75¢; free writer's guidelines. Reports on material accepted for publication in 2-3 weeks. Submit complete ms. SASE.

Nonfiction: How-to and moneymaking idea type of articles on art, artists, handicrafts, song writing. Should be informative, educational, entertaining, first-person material on actual experiences. "New ways for an artist to make a buck." Length: 300-500 words. Pays ½¢/word.

HOBBY COMPUTER HANDBOOK, Davis Publications, Inc., 380 Lexington Ave., New York NY 10017. (212)557-9100. Associate Publisher/Editor-in-Chief: Julian S. Martin. Managing Editor: Alan Rose. 100% freelance written. Emphasizes home hobby computers and theory. Annual magazine; 112 pages. Estab. 1978. Pays on acceptance. Buys all rights. Pays 100% kill fee. Byline given. Previously published submissions OK. SASE. Reports in 4-6 weeks. Free writer's guidelines; mention *Writer's Market* in request.

Nonfiction: "The nature of the magazine's title limits the manuscript contributions to the subject matter. Aim at the hobbyist who is a beginner, or working with his first computer. Stick to theory articles, how to ideas that are universal to hobby computers and simple project ideas. If you know nothing about hobby computers, have not worked with a hobby computer, don't write to us! You can't fake it in this field." Buys 350 mss/year. Query. Length: 1,000-3,500 words. Pays $150-250.

Photos: State availability of photos with query. Offers no additional payment for b&w negatives with proof sheet. Buys all rights. "In most cases, we give permission for author and/or photographer to use material in other publications after publication date. Authorization given in writing only.

Fillers: Jokes, gags, anecdotes. Buys 3/issue. Pays $20-30.

JOEL SATER'S ANTIQUES & AUCTION NEWS, 225 W. Market St., Marietta PA 17547. (717)426-1956. Managing Editor: Joel Sater. Editor: Denise Murphy. For dealers and buyers of antiques, nostalgics and collectibles; and those who follow antique shows and shops. Biweekly tabloid; 24 pages. Estab. 1967. Circ. 80,000. Pays on publication. Buys all rights. Phone queries OK. Submit seasonal/holiday material 6 weeks to 3 months in advance. Simultaneous (if so notified), photocopied and previously published submissions OK. SASE. Reports in 6 weeks. Free sample copy (must identify *Writer's Market*).

Nonfiction: Historical (related to American artifacts or material culture); how-to (restoring and preserving antiques and collectibles); informational (research on antiques or collectibles; "news about activities in our field"); interview; nostalgia; personal experience; photo feature; profile; and travel. Buys 100-150 mss/year. Query or submit complete ms. Length: 500-2,500 words. Pays $5-25.

Photos: Purchased with or without accompanying ms. Captions required. Send prints. Pays $2-10 for b&w photos. Total purchase price for ms includes payment for photos.

LAPIDARY JOURNAL, Box 80937, San Diego CA 92138. Editor: Pansy D. Kraus. For "all ages interested in the lapidary hobby." Estab. 1947. Monthly. Circ. 61,617. Rights purchased vary with author and material. Buys all rights or first serial rights. Byline given. Pays on publication. Free sample copy and writer's guidelines. Will consider photocopied submissions. Query. SASE.

Nonfiction and Photos: Publishes "articles pertaining to gem cutting, gem collecting and jewelry making for the hobbyist." Buys informational, how-to, personal experience, historical, travel and technical articles. Pays 1¢/word. Buys good contrast b&w photos. Contact editor for color. Payment varies according to size.

LOST TREASURE, 15115 S. 76th E. Ave., Bixby OK 74008. Editor: Michael Rieke. 95% freelance written. For treasure hunting hobbyists, bottle and relic collectors, amateur prospectors and miners. Monthly magazine; 72 pages. Estab. 1969. Circ. 100,000. Buys all rights, but will reassign rights to author after publication. Byline given. Buys 180 mss/year. Pays on acceptance. Free sample copy and writer's guidelines. Will consider photocopied

submissions. No simultaneous submissions. Reports in 3-4 weeks. Submit complete ms. SASE.
Nonfiction and Photos: Articles about lost mines and buried and sunken treasures. Avoid writing about the more famous treasures and lost mines. Length: 100-3,000 words. Pays 3¢/word. Pays $5-40 for b&w glossy prints purchased with mss. Captions required. Pays $75 for color transparencies used on cover; 2¼x2¼ minimum size. "Treasure Nuggets" section uses short articles on publication's theme. Length: 100-250 words. Pays $15.

McCALL'S NEEDLEWORK & CRAFTS MAGAZINE, 230 Park Ave., New York NY 10017. Managing Editor: Margaret Gilman. Quarterly. All rights bought for original needlework and handcraft designs. SASE.
Nonfiction: Accepts the made-up items accompanied by the directions, diagrams and charts for making them. Preliminary photos may be submitted. Variety of payment depends on items sent in. The range of payment could be from a few dollars to a few hundred dollars.

MAINE ANTIQUE DIGEST, Box 358, Waldoboro ME 04572. (207)832-7534. Editor: Samuel Pennington. For collectors and dealers in early Americana, antique furniture (country and formal), marine, redware, folk art, "Shaker things." Tabloid newspaper; 152 pages. Estab. 1973. Monthly. Circ. 16,000. Buys first North American serial rights. Pays 50% kill fee. Byline given. Buys 60 mss/year. Pays on acceptance. Free sample copy. No photocopied or simultaneous submissions. Reports in 1 week. Query or submit complete ms. SASE.
Nonfiction and Photos: Auction and show articles (mostly assigned); on antiques from 1700 to 1875. "We want writers who are very knowledgeable about antiques; writers who can write with feeling and 'tell it like it is' about the antiques business and collecting. We would be particularly interested in articles (chapters or selections) by authors of forthcoming antique books." Length: 1,000 words minimum. Pays $50-100. No additional payment for b&w photos used with mss. Captions required.

MAKE IT WITH LEATHER, Box 1386, Fort Worth TX 76101. (817)335-4161. Editor: Earl F. Warren. Buys all rights. Pays negotiable kill fee for assigned articles. Byline given except for news releases or if ghosted or written on assignment with predetermined no byline. Bimonthly. Estab. 1956. Circ. 60,000. Buys 60 or more mss/year. Pays on publication. Free sample copy and writer's guidelines. Reports in 6-8 weeks. SASE.
Nonfiction and Photos: "How-to-do-it leathercraft stories illustrated with cutting patterns, carving patterns. First-person approach even though article may be ghosted. Story can be for professional or novice. Strong on details; logical progression in steps; easy to follow how-to-do-it." Length: 2,000 words or less suggested. Payment normally starts at $50 plus $10 per illustration. "All articles judged on merit and may range to '$250 plus' per ms. Depends on project and work involved by author." 5x7, or larger, b&w photos of reproduction quality purchased with mss. Captions required. Color of professional quality is used on cover at $50/accepted photo. Ektachrome slides or sheet film stock. Negatives needed with all print film stock. All photos are used to illustrate project on step-by-step basis and finished item. "We can do photos in our studio if product sample is sent. No charge, but no payment for photos to writer. Letting us 'do it our way' does help on some marginal story ideas and mss since we can add such things as artist's sketches or drawings to improve the presentation."
Fillers: "Tips and Hints." Short practical hints for doing leathercraft or protecting tools, new ways of doing things, etc. Length: 100 words maximum. Pays $10 minimum.
How To Break In: "There are plenty of leathercraftsmen around who don't feel qualified to write up a project or who don't have the time to do it. Put their ideas and projects down on paper for them and share the payment. We need plenty of small, quick, easy-to-do ideas; things that we can do in one page are in short supply."

MINIATURE COLLECTOR, Acquire Publishing Co., Inc., 170 5th Ave., New York NY 10010. (212)989-8700. Editor: Peter Dwyer. Semimonthly magazine; 60 pages. Estab. April 1977. Circ. 60,000. Pays 20% kill fee. Byline given. Pays on publication. Submit seasonal/holiday material 4 months in advance. Photocopied and previously published submissions OK. SASE. Reports in 1 month. Sample copy $1.
Nonfiction: How-to (detailed furniture and accessories projects in 1/12th scale with accurate patterns and illustrations); interview (with well-established collectors, museum curators with pictures); new product (very short-caption type pieces—no payment); photo feature (show reports, heavily photographic, with captions stressing pieces and availability of new and unusual pieces); and profile (of collectors with photos). Buys 3-6 mss/issue. Query. Length: 600-1,200 words. Pays $65-175.
Photos: Send photos with ms. Pays $20-100 for 5x7 or 8x10 b&w glossy prints; $30-125 for color transparencies. Buys one-time rights. Captions required.

THE MINIATURE MAGAZINE, Box 700, Newton NJ 07860. (201)383-3355.Editor: Sybil C. Harp. *"The Miniature Magazine* is edited for the miniaturist working in 1"-1' scale dollhouse miniatures." Quarterly magazine. Circ. 40,000. Pays on publication. Buys all rights. Submit seasonal/holiday material 7 months in advance. SASE. Reports in 4 weeks. Sample copy $1; free writer's guidelines.
Nonfiction: "I am in the market for articles dealing with dollhouse construction, furniture making and all types of craft techniques which can be applied to the creation of miniatures. The magazine covers both the crafting and collecting aspects of the hobby, with emphasis upon scale and quality. It does not cover dollhouses as children's playthings, but regards them as a serious, three-dimensional art form."
Photos: Purchased with accompanying ms. "We give $35 maximum allowance for photo expense."
Columns/Departments: Going Places in Lilliput covers places to visit to see fine miniatures. "We desire articles that are written by craftsmen (or collectors) knowledgeable of the hobby."

MINIATURE WORLD, House of White Birches, Inc., Box 337, Seabrook NH 03874. Editor: Karen P. Sherrer. "Our readers are interested in dollhouses and miniature collecting as a hobby. We are looking for articles on dollhouses, interesting miniature collections, amateur and professional miniaturists." Bimonthly magazine: 64 pages. Estab. 1977. Circ. 40,000. Pays on acceptance. Buys all rights. Submit seasonal/holiday material 8-10 months in advance. SASE. Reports in 6-8 weeks. Writer's guidelines for SASE.
Nonfiction: How-to (illustrated with art or b&w photos; miniatures to make); informational (where to buy miniatures, book reviews, miniature makers techniques); historical (famous miniature collections, antique miniatures, etc.); profiles (people who make miniatures or have miniature collections or dollhouses); cover quality transparencies with accompanying article, cartoons, verse and humor. Buys 15-20 mss/issue.

MODEL RAILROADER, 1027 N. 7th St., Milwaukee WI 53233. Editor: Russell G. Larson. For hobbyists interested in scale model railroading. Monthly. Buys exclusive rights. Study publication before submitting material. Reports on submissions within 4 weeks. Query. SASE.
Nonfiction: Wants construction articles on specific model railroad projects (structures, cars, locomotives, scenery, benchwork, etc.). Also photo stories showing model railroads. First-hand knowledge of subject almost always necessary for acceptable slant. Pays base rate of $36/page.
Photos: Buys photos with detailed descriptive captions only. Pays $7.50 and up, depending on size and use. Color: double b&w rate. Full color cover: $112.

99 IC PROJECTS, Davis Publications, Inc., 380 Lexington Ave., New York NY 10017. (212)557-9100. Associate Publisher/Editor-in-Chief: Julian S. Martin. Managing Editor: Alan Rose. 100% freelance written. Emphasizes home hobby projects and theory. Annual magazine; 112 pages. Estab. January 1979. Pays on acceptance. Buys all rights. Pays 100% kill fee. Byline given. Previously published submissions OK. SASE. Reports in 4-6 weeks.
Nonfiction: "We are looking for brief, simple IC construction ideas that authors have assembled and operated. Refer to *101 Electronic Projects* or *99 IC Projects* for style and size." Buys 100 mss/issue. Query. Length: 100-150 words. Pays $25-50/project.
Photos: State availability of photos with query. Offers no additional payment for b&w negatives with proof sheet. Buys all rights. "In most cases, we give permission for author and/or photographer to use material in other publications after publication date. Authorization given in writing only."
Fillers: Jokes, gags, anecdotes. Buys 3/issue. Pays $20-30.

OHIO ANTIQUE REVIEW, Box 538, Worthington OH 43085. (614)885-9757. Editor: James Lowder. (614)885-9757. 60% freelance written. For an antique-oriented readership, "generally well-educated, interested in folk art and other early American items." Monthly tabloid; 76-84 pages. Estab. September 1975. Circ. 10,000. Pays on publication date assigned at time of purchase. Buys first North American serial rights and one-time rights. Byline given. Phone queries OK. Submit seasonal/holiday material 2 months in advance. Simultaneous, photocopied and previously published submissions OK. SASE. Reports in 2 weeks. Free sample copy and writer's guidelines.
Nonfiction: "The articles we desire concern history and production of furniture, pottery, china, and other antiques of the period prior to the 1880s. In some cases, contemporary folk art items are acceptable. We are also interested in reporting on antique shows and auctions with statements on conditions and prices. We do not want articles on contemporary collectibles." Buys 5-8 mss/issue. Query with clips of published work. Length: 200-2,000 words. Pays $25-60.

Photos: State availability of photos with query. Payment included in ms price. Uses 3x5 or 5x7 glossy b&w prints. Captions required.

THE OLD BOTTLE MAGAZINE, Box 243, Bend OR 97701. (503)382-6978. Editor: Shirley Asher. For collectors of old bottles, insulators, relics. Monthly. Circ. 7,000. Buys all rights. Byline given. Buys 35 mss/year. Pays on acceptance. Will send a sample copy to a writer on request. No query required. Reports in 1 month. SASE.
Nonfiction, Photos and Fillers: "We are soliciting factual accounts on specific old bottles, canning jars, insulators and relics." Stories of a general nature on these subjects not wanted. "Interviews of collectors are usually not suitable when written by noncollectors. A knowledge of the subject is imperative. Would highly recommend potential contributors study an issue before making submissions. Articles that tie certain old bottles to a historical background are desired." Length: 250-2,500 words. Pays $20/published page. B&w glossy prints and clippings purchased separately. Pays $5.

OLD CARS NEWSPAPER, Krause Publications, 700 E. State St., Iola WI 54945. (715)445-2214. Editors: Bob Lemke, R.C. Halla. 40% freelance written. "Our readers collect, drive and restore everything from 1899 locomobiles to '76 Cadillac convertibles. They cover all age and income groups." Weekly tabloid; 60 pages. Estab. October 1971. Circ. 95,000. Pays on acceptance. Buys all rights, but may reassign following publication. Byline given. SASE. Reports in 2 months. Sample copy 50¢; mention *Writer's Market* in request.
Nonfiction: Historical (sites related to auto history, interesting oldsters from the automobile past, etc.); how-to (good restoration articles); interview (with important national-level personages in the car hobby); nostalgia (auto-related, and only occasionally); and photo feature (by knowing hobby reporters, definite query). No "local man restores Model T Ford, Local club sponsors parking lot show, or local couple takes trip in Model A" stories. Buys 4 mss/issue. Query. Pays 3¢/word.
Photos: State availability of photos with query. Pays $5 for 5x7 b&w glossy prints. Captions required. Buys all rights, but may reassign following publication.
Columns/Departments: Book reviews (new releases for hobbyists). Buys 1 ms/issue. Query. Pays 3¢/word.
Fillers: Newsbreaks. Buys 50/year. Pays 3¢/word.

PAPERBACK QUARTERLY, 1710 Vincent, Brownwood TX 76801. (915)643-1182. Editor: Billy C. Lee. For paperback collectors. Quarterly magazine; 60 pages. Estab. March 1978. Circ. 145. Pays on publication. Buys all rights. Pays 50% kill fee. Byline given. Phone queries OK. Submit seasonal/holiday material 1 month. Photocopied and previously published submissions OK. SASE Reports in 4 weeks. Sample copy $1.25; free writer's guidelines.
Nonfiction: Historical (notes or articles on paperback publishers, paperback writers, paperback cover artists, and paperback distributors of used, rare or new paperbacks); interview (with paperback cover artists, paperback publishers, or paperback writers of new, used or rare paperbacks); and nostalgia (as related to the paperback industry of the 1940-1960s). Buys 2-3 mss/issue. Send complete ms. Length: 1,000-3,000 words. Pays ½¢/word.
Photos: Send photos with ms. Uses 2x3 or 4x6½ b&w prints; offers no additional payment for photos. Captions required.
Columns/Departments: Notes & Queries (500-word ms concerning a paperback publisher, writer, cover artist or distributor, or any aspect of the paperback industry both current and old) and Paperbacks on Review (250- to 500-word review of a paperback original, never before published in hardback). Send complete ms.

POPULAR HANDICRAFT HOBBIES, Tower Press, Inc., Box 428, Seabrook NH 03874. Editor-in-Chief: Karen P. Sherrer. "Our readers are primarily women interested in crafts and hobbies. Many are looking for projects suitable for sale at church bazaars and fund-raising events. They also like crafts that are easy and inexpensive to do." Bimonthly magazine; 64 pages. Estab. 1966. Circ. 140,000. Pays on acceptance. Buys all rights, but may reassign following publication. Byline given. Submit seasonal/holiday material 8-10 months in advance. SASE. Reports in 6-8 weeks. Writer's guidelines for SASE.
Nonfiction: How-to (illustrated with art and b&w photos; craft projects to make); informational (about new craft projects or techniques); historical (material about collecting as a hobby); humor (craft-related); profile (people who have an interesting hobby or do an unusual craft); new product; and photo feature. Buys 15 mss/issue. Query. Length: 200-1,500 words. Pays 2¢/word.
Photos: Purchased with accompanying ms. Submit prints or transparencies. Pays $5 minimum

for 4x5 or larger b&w glossy prints; $20 minimum for 35mm, 2¼x2¼ or 4x5 color transparencies. Model release required.

QUILTER'S NEWSLETTER MAGAZINE, Box 394, Wheatridge CO 80033. Editor: Bonnie Leman. Estab. 1968. Monthly. Circ. 95,000. Buys first or second North American serial rights. Buys 15 mss/year. Pays on acceptance. Free sample copy. Will consider photocopied submissions. Reports in 3-4 weeks. Submit complete ms. SASE.
Nonfiction, Photos and Fillers: "We are interested in articles, fillers and photos on the subject of quilts and quiltmakers *only*. We are not interested in anything relating to 'Grandma's Scrap Quilts,' but could use material about contemporary quilting." Pays 1½¢/word minimum. Additional payment for photos depends on quality.

RAILROAD MODEL CRAFTSMAN, Box 700, Newton NJ 07860. (201)383-3355. Editor: Tony Koester. 75% freelance written. For "adult model railroad hobbyists, above average, including mature youngsters. All gauges, scales, plus railfanning." Estab. 1933. Monthly. Circ. 97,000. Buys all rights. Buys 50-100 mss/year. Pays on publication. Sample copy $1.25. Submit seasonal material six months in advance. SASE.
Nonfiction and Photos: "How-to model railroad features written by persons who did the work. They have to be good. Glossy photos a must. Drawings where required must be to scale, accurately and completely rendered. Some railroad prototype features if of interest to modelers and with modelers' slant. All of our features and articles are written by active model railroaders familiar with the magazine and its requirements. 'Outsiders' don't have the technical know-how to write for us. Nonmodel railroad writers invariably write up some local hobbyist as 'Joe Doaks has a railroad empire in his basement made all by himself,' treating him as some kind of nut. We do not want the cartoon of little men tying the little girl to model railroad track. We *do* want topnotch how-to model railroading articles." Purchases photos with and without mss. Captions required. Buys sharp 8x10 glossy prints and 35mm transparencies. Minimum payment: $1/column inch of copy ($30/page); $10 for photos ($1/diagonal inch of published b&w photos, $3 for color transparencies); $75 for covers (must tie in with feature material in that issue).
How To Break In: "Frankly, there is virtually no chance of making a sale to us unless the author is a very experienced hobbyist in our field. I doubt that a nonmodel railroad hobbyist has authored a single line of copy for us in the past 40 years, so it's 'hobbyist first, author second' as far as we're concerned. Our material is for the serious hobbyist, not the general public trying to better understand our hobby, as a rule."

ROCK & GEM, Behn-Miller Publishers, Inc., 17337 Ventura Blvd., Encino CA 91316. (213)788-7080. Senior Editor: W.R.C. Shedenhelm. 95% freelance written. For amateur lapidaries and rockhounds. Monthly magazine; 100 pages. Estab. 1971. Circ. 75,000. Rights purchased vary with author and material. May buy first North American serial rights or first serial rights. Byline given. Pays on publication. Sample copy $1.25. Reports in 1 month. Query or submit complete ms. SASE.
Nonfiction and Photos: Knowledgeable articles on rockhounding and lapidary work; step-by-step how-to articles on lapidary and jewelry making. Length: open. Pays $40-50/published page. No additional payment for 8x10 b&w glossy prints used with mss. Color for cover (4x5 transpariencies) is by assignment only.

ROCKHOUND, 15115 S. 76th East Ave., Bixby OK 74008. Editor: Michael Rieke. For gem and mineral hobbyists. Bimonthly magazine; 52 pages. Estab. 1971. Circ. 20,000. Buys all rights, but will reassign rights to author after publication. Byline given. Buys 75-100 mss/year. Pays on acceptance. Free sample copy and writer's guidelines. Will consider photocopied submissions. Reports in 4 weeks. Submit complete ms. SASE.
Nonfiction and Photos: Articles on where and how to find gems and minerals. "We cover where and how to collect gems and minerals as well as the whole lapidary field." Length: 250-3,000 words. Pays 2¢/word. B&w glossy prints of any size purchased with mss. Captions required. Pays $5-10. Pays $5-35 for color transparencies used on cover.
How To Break In: "Write about collecting sites anywhere in the US, except the western states. We receive a glut of mss from the West. We particularly welcome new writers who write about the East, North, South or Midwest. A bit of research on collecting sites (for gems and minerals) in these parts of the country will really sell us. We have just begun to cover the lapidary side of rockhounding so we are encouraging stories in that area."

SCOTT'S MONTHLY STAMP JOURNAL, 3 E. 57th St., New York NY 10022. (212)371-5700. Editor: Ira S. Zweifach. For stamp collectors, from the beginner to the sophisticated philatelist. Monthly magazine; 64 pages. Estab. 1920. Circ. 25,000. Rights purchased vary with author and material. Byline given. Usually buys all rights. Buys 24-36 mss/year. Pays on publication. Submit seasonal or holiday material 3 months in advance. Reports in 4 weeks. Query. SASE.

Nonfiction and Photos: "Stories about *stamps only*. Human interest and historical perspective very important. Must be lively, well-researched articles. Emphasize philatelic detail and human interest at the same time. Stamps capture the time and place of events. An interesting article might be one of a period in a country's stamp history such as 'Sweden, 1800 to 1900' or whatever historical events define as a period. We recently published a story about stamp collecting in the USSR." Length: 500-4,000 words. Pays $50-250. No additional payment is made for b&w photos used with mss.

How To Break In: "*Scott's Monthly Stamp Journal* is undergoing a complete change. Although all material deals with stamps, new writers are invited to seek assignments. It is not necessary to be a stamp collector or a published professional. You must be a good writer, and be willing to do careful research on strong material. Because our emphasis is on lively, interesting articles about stamps, including historical perspectives and human interest slants, we are open to writers who can produce the same. Of course, if you are an experienced philatelist, so much the better. We do *not* want to see finished manuscripts. What we *do* want is this: A query letter with paragraph summaries of suggested articles, followed by a phone call. Because our magazine does require philatelic detail, phone contact throughout the assignment is necessary. Long distance—please call collect."

THE SPINNING WHEEL, Everybodys Press, Inc., Hanover PA 17331. (717)632-3535. Editor: A. Christian Revi. For antique collectors and dealers. 10 times a year. Pays on publication. Buys exclusive rights unless author wishes some reservations. Byline given. SASE.

Nonfiction: Authentic, well-researched material on antiques in any and all collecting areas; home decorating ideas with antiques. Prefers combined scholar-student-amateur appeal. No first-person or family history. Prefers draft or outline first. Requires bibliography with each ms. Quality illustrations. Length: 500-1,500 words. Pays minimum $1/published inch, including pictures.

Photos: Photos and professional line drawings accepted. Photos should be top quality b&w, no smaller than 5x7. If of individual items shown in groups, each should be separated for mechanical expediency. Avoid fancy groupings.

STITCH 'N SEW, Tower Press, Box 338, Chester MA 01011. Editor: Barbara Hall Pedersen. For women of all ages who like to sew. Magazine published every 2 months; 64 pages. Estab. 1968. Circ. 200,000. Buys all rights. Buys 50 mss/year. Byline given. Pays on acceptance. Will send free sample copy to writer on request, if 9x12 SASE is enclosed. For copy of guidelines for writers send letter and SASE. Submit holiday crafts, especially Christmas, 6 months in advance. Query or submit complete ms with SASE. Reports in 2-8 weeks. SASE.

Nonfiction, Photos and Fillers: "Articles on various facets of needlework; knitting, crocheting, garment construction, embroidery, tatting, gift and toy making, decorative items for the home. Our emphasis is on old-fashioned practicality. Our projects appeal to the woman on a tight budget. We like 'scratch' projects that utilize readily available materials that do not cost much. How-to articles must include either a sharp photograph, or drawing or actual sample." Length: 1,500 words maximum. Pays $5-50. B&w and color photos purchased with accompanying ms. Captions required. Pays $35 for 4x5 color transparency used on cover.

TREASURE, Jess Publishing, 16146 Covello St., Van Nuys CA 91406. (213)988-6910. Editor-in-Chief: David Weeks. Managing Editor: Jim Williams. Emphasizes treasure hunting and metal detecting. Monthly magazine; 74 pages. Estab. 1969. Circ. 100,000. Pays on publication. Buys all rights, but may reassign following publication. Byline given. Phone queries OK. Submit seasonal/holiday material 4 months in advance. Previously published submissions OK. SASE. Reports in 1 month. Free writer's guidelines.

Nonfiction: Jim Williams, Articles Editor. How-to (coinshooting and treasure hunting tips); informational and historical (location of lost treasures with emphasis on the lesser-known); interviews (with treasure hunters); profiles (successful treasure hunters and metal detector hobbyists); personal experience (treasure hunting); technical (advice on use of metal detectors and metal detector designs). Buys 6-8 mss/issue. Send complete ms. Length: 300-3,000 words. Pays $15-150. "Our rate of payment varies considerably depending upon the proficiency of the author, the quality of the photographs, the importance of the subject matter, and the amount of useful information given."

Photos: No additional payment for 5x7 or 8x10 b&w glossy prints used with mss. Pays $50 minimum for color transparencies (120 or 2¼x2¼). Color for cover only. Model release required.

THE WORKBASKET, 4251 Pennsylvania, Kansas City MO 64111. Editor: Roma Jean Rice. Issued monthly. Buys first rights. Pays on acceptance. Query. Reports in six weeks. SASE.
Nonfiction and Photos: Uses articles, 400-500 words, that explain how a person or a family has benefited, financially or otherwise, by sewing, needlecraft, etc. Interested in step-by-step directions for making project. Also has a how-to short-stuff section which uses material on hobbies, ideas for pin-money and the like. These are limited to 250 words or under and bring a flat sum of $5. Pays 5¢/word for articles, plus $5-7 for accompanying art. 5x7 or 8x10 pix with mss.

WORKBENCH, 4251 Pennsylvania Ave., Kansas City MO 64111. (816)531-5730. Editor: Jay W. Hedden. 75% freelance written. For woodworkers. Estab. 1946. Circ. 600,000. Pays on publication. Buys all rights, but returns all but first magazine rights on request, after publication. Byline given if requested. Reports in 10-14 days. Query. SASE.
Nonfiction and Photos: "In the last couple of years, we have increased our emphasis on home improvement and home maintenance, and now are getting into alternate energy projects. Ours is a nuts-and-bolts approach, rather than telling how someone has done it. Because most of our readers own their own homes, we stress 'retrofitting' of energy-saving devices, rather than saying they should rush out and buy or build a solar home. Energy conservation is another subject we cover thoroughly; insulation, weatherstripping, making your own storm windows. We still are very strong in woodworking, cabinetmaking and furniture construction. Projects range from simple toys to complicated reproductions of furniture now in museums. We pay a minimum of $150/published page. Shop tips bring $20 maximum with drawing and/or photo. If we pay less than the rate, it's because we have to supply photos, information, drawings or details the contributor has overlooked. Contributors should look over the published story to see what they should include next time. Our editors are skilled woodworkers, do-it-yourselfers and photographers. We have a complete woodworking shop at the office and we use it often to check out construction details of projects submitted to us."

YESTERYEAR, Yesteryear Publications, Box 2, Princeton WI 54968. (414)295-3969. Editor: Michael Jacobi. Managing Editor: Denis Kitchen. For antique dealers and collectors, people interested in collecting just about anything, and nostalgia buffs. Monthly tabloid; 28 pages. Estab. 1974. Circ. 6,000. Pays on publication. Buys one-time rights. Byline given. Submit seasonal/holiday material 3 months in advance. Simultaneous, photocopied and previously published submissions OK. SASE. Reports in 2 weeks for queries; 1 month for mss. Sample copy $1.
Nonfiction: General interest (basically, anything pertaining to antiques, collectible items or nostalgia in general); historical (again, pertaining to the above categories); how-to (refinishing antiques, how to collect); nostalgia; and personal experience. "We do not want opinion articles." Buys 4 mss/issue. Send complete ms. Pays $5-25.
Photos: Send photos with ms. Pays $5 for 5x7 b&w glossy or matte prints; $5 for 5x7 color prints. Captions preferred.
Columns/Departments: "We will consider new column concepts as long as they fit into the general area of antique, collectibles, nostalgia. These can include book reviews." Buys 3/issue. Send complete ms. Pays $5-25.

Home and Garden

APARTMENT LIFE, 750 3rd Ave., New York NY 10017. Editor: Joanna Krotz. For city dwellers. Monthly magazine; 110 pages. Estab. 1968. Circ. 850,000. Buys all rights. Buys 60-100 mss/year. Pays on acceptance. No photocopied or simultaneous submissions. Submit seasonal material 5-6 months in advance. Reports in 2 months. Query. SASE.
Nonfiction and Photos: "Service material specifically for people who live in cities. Thorough, factual, informative articles." Informational, how-to, travel. Length: 300-1,000 words. Pays $250-400. B&w photos and color are purchased only on assignment.

BETTER HOMES AND GARDENS, 1716 Locust St., Des Moines IA 50336. (515)284-9011. Editor: James A. Autry. For "middle-and-up income, homeowning and community-concerned families." Monthly. Circ. 8,000,000. Buys all rights. pays on acceptance. Query preferred. Submit seasonal material 1 year in advance. Mss should be directed to the department where the story line is strongest. SASE.

Nonfiction: "Freelance material is used in areas of travel, health, cars, money management, and home entertainment. Reading the magazine will give the writer the best idea of our style. We do not deal with political subjects or areas not connected with the home, community and family." Pays top rates based on estimated length of published article; $100-2,000. Length: 500-2,000 words.

Photos: Shot under the direction of the editors. Purchased with mss.

How To Break In: "Follow and study the magazine, to see what we do and how we do it. There are no secrets, after all; it's all there on the printed page. Having studied several issues, the writer should come up with one or several ideas that interest him, and, hopefully, us. We consider freelance contributions in the areas of health, education, cars, money matters, home entertainment and travel. The next step is to write a good query letter. It needn't be more than a page in length (for each idea), and should include a good stab at a title, a specific angle, and a couple of paragraphs devoted to the main points of the article. This method is not guaranteed to produce a sale, of course; there is no magic formula. But it's still the best way I know to have an idea considered."

LOG HOUSE MAGAZINE, Box 1205, Prince George, British Columbia, Canada V2L 4V3. Editor-in-Chief: B. Allan Mackie. 40% freelance written. "For a middle- to upper-income audience; well-educated, otherwise all ages and sexes. Everyone needs a home, but these are the people who have the energy, the drive, the intelligence to want to create a superior home with their own hands." Annual magazine; 96 pages. Estab. 1974. Circ. 20,000. Pays on acceptance. Buys one-time rights. Byline given. Annual deadline: August 1. Reports in 1 week.

Nonfiction: Historical (on excellent log construction methods), how-to (do any part/portion of a good solid timber house), informational, humor, inspirational, interview (with a practicing, professional builder, or a factual one on an individual who built a good house), new product (if relevant), personal experience (house building), photo feature (on good log buildings of a permanent residential nature; absolutely no cabins or rotting hulks), and technical (preservatives, tools). Query. Length: 3,000 words maximum. Pays $50 minimum.

Photos: Mary Mackie, Photo Editor. Purchased with accompanying ms. Captions required. Send contact sheet. Pays $3 minimum for 5x7 b&w glossy photos (negatives appreciated); $10 minimum for 2¼x2¼ transparencies.

THE FAMILY FOOD GARDEN, 1999 Shepard Rd., St. Paul MN 55116. (612)647-7478. Managing Editor: Sharon Ross. For food gardeners. Magazine published 10 times/year; 48 pages. Estab. 1973. Circ. 250,000. Buys all rights. Byline given. Buys 60 mss/year. Pays on acceptance. Writer's guidelines for SASE. Sample copy $1. Submit seasonal material 5-6 months in advance. Reports on queries in 2 weeks; reports on submissions in 6 weeks. Query. SASE.

Nonfiction and Photos: "We look for straightforward, practical and technically accurate writing about food growing in the home garden or orchard. We do not cover flower gardening, commerical growing or small farming. Recipe stories are by assignment only. We prefer to buy ms, photographs and illustrations as a package." Length: 500-2,000 words. Pays $50-300 for illustrated articles. Submit large b&w glossies or any size color transparency.

FAMILY HANDYMAN, Webb Co., 1999 Shepard Rd., St. Paul MN 55116. Editor: Gene Schnaser. Emphasizes do-it-yourself—home maintenance, repair and improvement. Publishes 10 issues yearly. Magazine; 100 plus pages. Estab. 1955. Circ. 1,000,000. Pays on acceptance. Buys all rights. Submit seasonal material 6 months in advance. SASE. Reports in 4-6 weeks. Free sample copy and writer's guidelines.

Nonfiction: How-to home, lawn and garden maintenance; repairs; remodeling; and shop projects. Buys 5 mss/issue. Query or send complete ms. Length: 700-1,200 words. Pays $150-1,000 (depends on length, whether color or b&w photos; quality of entire piece).

Photos: Send photos with ms. Uses 5x7 or 8x10 b&w glossy or 35mm or larger color transparencies; photos and ms purchased as package. Captions and model releases required.

FLOWER AND GARDEN MAGAZINE, 4251 Pennsylvania, Kansas City MO 64111. Editor-in-Chief: Rachel Snyder. 20-50% freelance written. For home gardeners. Monthly. Picture magazine. Circ. 500,000. Buys first rights. Byline given. Pays on acceptance. Free writer's guidelines. Query. Reports in 6 weeks. SASE.

Nonfiction: Interested in illustrated articles on how to do certain types of gardening, descriptive articles about individual plants. Flower arranging, landscape design, house plants, patio gardening are other aspects covered. "The approach we stress is practical (how-to-do-it, what-to-do-it-with). We try to stress plain talk, clarity, economy of words. We are published in 3 editions: Northern, Southern, Western. Some editorial matter is purchased just for single

edition use. Most, however, is used in all editions, so it should be tailored for a national audience. Material for a specific edition should be slanted to that audience only." Length: 500-1,500 words. Pays 5¢/word or more, depending on quality and kind of material.
Photos: Buys photos submitted with mss or with captions only. Pays up to $12.50 for 5x7 or 8x10 b&w prints, depending on quality, suitability. Also buys color transparencies, 35mm and larger. Pays $30-125 for these, depending on size and use.
How To Break In: "Prospective author needs good grounding in gardening practice and literature. Then offer well-researched and well-written material appropriate to the experience level of our audience. Illustrations help sell the story."

GARDEN MAGAZINE, The Garden Society, A Division of the New York Botanical Garden, Bronx Park, Bronx NY 10458. Editor: Ingrid Eisenstadter. 30% freelance written. Emphasizes horticulture, environment and botany for a diverse readership, largely college graduates and professionals united by a common interest in plants and the environment. Bimonthly magazine; 44 pages. Estab. March 1977. Circ. 20,000. Buys all rights, but may reassign following publication. Submit seasonal/holiday material 4 months in advance of issue date. Photocopied and previously published submissions OK. SASE. Reports in 2 months. Sample copy $2.
Nonfiction: Ann Botshon, associate editor. "All articles must be of high quality, meticulously researched and botanically accurate." Expose (environmental subjects); how-to (horticultural techniques, must be unusual and verifiable); general interest (plants of interest, botanical information); humor (pertaining to botany and horticulture); Photo feature (pertaining to plants and the environment); and travel (great gardens of the world). Buys 1-2 mss/issue. Query with clips of published work. length: 500-2,500 words. Pays $50-300.
Photos: Ilene Wagner, designer. Pays $35-50 for 5x7 glossy b&w prints; $40-150 for 4x5 or 35mm color transparencies. Captions preferred. Buys one-time rights.

GARDENING MAGAZINE, Scrambling Press, 1 Aldwyn Center, Villanova PA 19085. (215)527-5100. Editor: Peter Tobey. Managing Editor: Edward Claflin. "Emphasis on home gardening and landscape projects. Specific how-to information is a must. Articles are well-illustrated." Bimonthly magazine; 112 pages. Estab. January 1979. Circ. 100,000 (newsstand). Pays on publication. Buys all rights. Byline given unless writer requests otherwise. Phone queries OK. Submit seasonal/holiday material 6 months in advance. Simultaneous and photocopied submissions OK. SASE. Reports in 2-4 weeks. Sample copy $1.75; free writer's guidelines with SASE.
Nonfiction: General interest (arboretums and places to visit); how-to (designs for lawn furniture, special gardens—annuals, perennials, etc, repairing tools, vegetable garden ideas); humor (quirky solutions to garden problems); profile (gardening authority); new product (lawn care equipment and gardening tools); photo feature (preferably high quality 35mm color transparencies); and technical (hybridization, tissue culture, hydroponics, etc.). "We're looking for feature articles. This magazine is about lifestyle as well as gardening, so articles should be written in an informal, confidential style. Take delight in the mundane, from composting to looking at a flower." Buys 5-10 mss/issue. Query with clips of published work. Length: 1,500-3,500 words. Pays 10¢/word.
Photos: Send photos with ms. Pays from $10 for 8x10 b&w prints; from $25 for color transparencies. Captions preferred; model release required. Buys one-time rights.
Columns/Departments: Symptoms & Cures (common garden bugs and blights); Gardening Under Glass (greenhouse column); Gardening Oddities (odd and unusual plants); A Visiting Authority; Regional Perspectives; Fundamentals (plant science); News; Help (gardening tips); A Project (how-to); House Plant (one per issue); and Gardening Under Lights (for the artificial light gardener). Buys 3-5 mss/issue. Query. Length: 1,500-2,000 words. Pays 10¢/word. Open to suggestions for new columns/departments.

GREENLEAVES MAGAZINE, 6240 S. Old State Rt. 37, Bloomington IN 47401. Editor: Mr. Gael L. Cooper. Emphasizes indoor/outdoor gardening. Monthly magazine. Estab. December 1978. Paid circ. over 1,570,000. Pays on publication. Buys all rights. Phone queries OK. Submit seasonal/holiday material 3-4 months in advance. SASE. Reports in 2-3 weeks. Free sample copy and writer's guidelines.
Nonfiction: General interest; historical; how-to (keep plants alive; enjoy flowers, vegetables year round; greenhouse construction; landscaping; plant buying, etc.); interview (with gardeners, stars who have gardens, etc.); new product (on gardening products); personal experience (must be based on sound horticultural practices); personal opinion (on gardening only); photo feature (travel with restructions to horticultural interest; flowers, etc.—many possibilities; heavy use of color); and travel (related to horticultural wonders of the world).

"All articles must deal with indoor/outdoor gardening." Buys 7-8 mss/issue. Send complete ms. Length: 300 words minimum. Pays $25-250.

Photos: State availability of photos or send photos with ms; SASE for return. Pays $15-50 for 8x10 b&w glossy prints; $25-70 for color transparencies. Captions and model releases required.

HOME BUYERS GUIDE, Bryan Publications, Inc., 3355 Via Lido, Newport Beach CA 92660. Editor: Parke E. Bryan. Emphasizes new homes available for homebuyers and homebuilders. Monthly magazine; 112 pages. Estab. 1960. Circ. 115,000. Pays on publication. Buys first North American serial rights. Submit seasonal/holiday material 6 months in advance. Photocopied submissions OK. Previously published work OK, but state where and when it appeared. SASE. Reports in 2 months.

Nonfiction: General interest (taxes, insurance, home safety, mortgages); historical (California only); how-to (beat high prices, build a patio, select wallpaper, set up a tool bench, panel a wall, landscape); interview (with celebrities from sports world and show biz—must have photos of subject in their home); and personal opinion (by experts in a field, e.g., a CPA on taxes). "Gear all material to the California homeowner and consumer. Write in an informative yet entertaining style. Give examples the reader can identify with." Buys 2 mss/issue. Send complete ms. Length: 500-1,500 words. Pays $100-300.

Photos: Send photos with ms. Uses b&w 8x10 glossy prints and 4x5 color transparencies. Offers no additional payment for photos accepted with ms. Captions preferred, model release required. Buys one-time rights.

Columns/Departments: Energy; Taxes; Finance; Landscape; Home Safety; Home Improvement; and Personalizing Your Home (how homeowners have customized development homes). Buys 2 mss/issue. Send complete ms. Length: 500-1,200 words.

HOME, CANADA'S HOUSE & GARDEN (formerly *Home, The Canadian Family Magazine*), Home Information Distributing, Ltd., Box 188, Station D, Scarborough, Ontario, Canada M1R 5B5. (416)759-0215. Managing Editor: Arthur Christopher. 50% freelance written. Emphasizes homes, gardens, cooking and crafts for Canadian homeowners. Quarterly magazine; 64 pages. Estab. 1976. Circ. 40,000I Pays on publication. Buys all rights. Phone queries OK. Submit seasonal/holiday material 4 months in advance. SAE and International Reply Coupons. Reports in 2 months. Free sample copy and writer's guidelines.

Nonfiction: How-to (do-it-yourself projects for the home, crafts, decorating, cooking); new product (of use to the homeowner available in Canada, must be new); and technical (energy-saving techniques, wood, wind, solar energy, written specifically for a Canadian readership). Buys 4-5 mss/issue. Query with clips of published work. Length: 1,500-3,000 words. Pays $25-150.

Photos: State availability of photos with query. Offers no additional payment for photos accepted with ms. Captions preferred. Buys all rights.

HOMEOWNERS HOW TO HANDBOOK, The Make-It, Fix-it Magazine, 380 Madison Ave., New York NY 10017. Editor: Jim Liston. 90% freelance written. A *Popular Science* publication of Times Mirror Magazines. Estab. 1974. Bimonthly. Circ. 400,000. Buys all rights. Pays 50% kill fee. Byline given. Pays on acceptance. Sample copy $1.50; address request to Milton J. Norcross, *Homeowners How To Handbook* Subscription Department. Submit seasonal material 7 months in advance. Reports in 3 weeks. SASE.

Nonfiction and Photos: Wants how-to information based on facts and experience—not theory. "Design ideas shold be original and uncomplicated. They should be directed at young homeowners working with simple tools, and if possible, the kind of project that can be completed on a weekend. All articles should contain a list of necessary materials and tools. Photos are as important as words. B&w preferred. 4x5's are OK, but 8x10's are better." Length: 1,800 words maximum. Pays $150 per published page maximum. No additional payment for b&w photos used with mss.

Fillers: Problem Solvers, a regular filler feature, pays $25 per captioned photo that contains a work-saving hint or solves a problem.

HORTICULTURE, 300 Massachusetts Ave., Boston MA 02115. Editor: Denis G. Meacham. Published by the Massachusetts Horticultural Society. Monthly. "We buy only first North American serial rights to mss; one-time use rights for photos." Byline given. Pays after publication. Query. Reports in 6 weeks. SASE.

Nonfiction and Photos: Uses articles from 500-5,000 words on plant science, practical gardening and the environment. Study publication. Photos: color transparencies and good quality b&w prints, preferably 8x10; "accurately identified."

HOUSE AND GARDEN, The Conde Nast Bldg, 350 Madison Ave., New York NY 10017. Editor-in-Chief: Mary Jane Pool. For homeowners and renters in middle and upper income brackets. Monthly. Circ. 1,136,444. Buys all rights. Pay on acceptance. "Study magazine before querying." Reports immediately. Query and include sample of previous writing. SASE.
Nonfiction and Photos: Subjects of interest to "families concerned with their homes. Nothing for young marrieds specifically." Anything to do with the house or garden and affiliated subjects such as music, art, books, cooking, etc. Length: about 1,500 words. Payment varies. Jerome H. Denner, Managing Editor, is department editor. Photos purchased with mss only.
How To Break In: "This is a very tough market to break into. We very seldom use unsolicited material, but if anything is going to have a chance of making it here, it should be on a news breaking item. It must be something which has not already been covered in the other major magazines. It must have a new slant. Read the magazine closely for style and avoid things we've already done. We get too many freelancers sending us material on subjects for which the crest of wave has already passed. There's no guarantee that providing a short item (say, for Gardener's Notes, which is mostly staff-written) will be an easier way in, but if you understand our needs and provide something that's really good, there's always a chance. It's best to send a query and a sample of previous writing."

HOUSE BEAUTIFUL, The Hearst Corp., 717 5th Ave., New York NY 10022. Editor: Joann Barwick. Executive Editor: Norma Skurka. Emphasizes design, architecture and building. Monthly magazine; 200 pages. Estab. 1896. Circ. 850,000. Pays on acceptance. Pays 25% kill fee. Byline given. Submit seasonal/holiday material 4 months in advance of issue date. SASE. Reports in 5 weeks.
Nonfiction: Carol Cooper Garey, Copy Editor. Historical (landmark buildings and restorations); how-to (kitchen, bath remodeling service); humor; interview; new product; profile; and travel. "No articles on religion." Buys 10 mss/year. Submit complete ms. Length: 300-1,000 words. Pays $150-400.
Photos: State availability of photos with ms. Offers no additional payment for photos.

HOUSTON HOME/GARDEN, Bayland Publishing, Inc., Box 25386, Houston TX 77005. Editor: Carol Sama. Emphasizes shelter. Monthly magazine; 200 pages. Estab. 1974. Circ. 80,000. Pays on publication. Buys all rights. Byline given. Submit seasonal/holiday material 4-6 months in advance. SASE. Reports in 1 month. Sample copy $3.25; free writer's guidelines.
Nonfiction: How-to (home maintenance and repairs); informational (city, tax information) and new product (short description). Needs Houston angle. Buys 20 mss/year. Query. Length: 1,000-2,000 words. Pays $2.50/published inch.
Photos: Photos puchased with accompanying ms. Captions required. Pays $15-20 for 8x10 b&w glossies. Model release required.

ORGANIC GARDENING AND FARMING, Rodale Press Publications, 33 E. Minor St., Emmaus PA 18049. (215)967-5171. Managing Editor: Jeff Cox. For a readership "interested in health and conservation, in growing plants vegetables and fruits without chemicals and in protecting the environment." Monthly magazine; 160-240 pages. Estab. 1942. Circ. 1,200,000. Buys all rights and the right to reuse in other Rodale Press Publications with agreed additional payment. Pays 25% kill fee, "if we agree to one." Byline given. Buys 400-500 mss/year. Pays on publication (actually, on preparation for publication). Free sample copy and writer's guidelines. Reports in 4-6 weeks. Query or submit complete ms. SASE.
Nonfiction, Photos and Fillers: "Factual and informative articles or fillers, especially on backyard gardening and family farming, stressing organic methods. Interested in all crops, soil topics, livestock, indoor gardening, greenhouses; natural foods preparation, storage, etc.; biological pest control; variety breeding, nutrition, recycling, energy conservation; community and club gardening. Strong on specific details, step-by-step how-to, adequate research. Good slant and interesting presentation always help. We do not want to see generalized garden success stories. And some build-it-yourself topics are often repeated. We would like to see material on development, techniques, different approaches to organic methods in producing fruit crops, grains, new and old vegetables; effective composting, soil building, waste recycling, food preparation, and insect control. Emphasis is on interesting, practical information, presented effectively and accurately." Length: 1,200-2,500 words for features. Pays $100-350. B&w and color purchased with mss or on assignment. Enlarged b&w glossy print and/or negative preferred. Pays $15-25. 2¼x2¼ (or larger) color transparencies. Fillers on above topics are also used. Length: 150-500 words. Pays $35-50.

PERFECT HOME MAGAZINE, 427 6th Ave. SE, Cedar Rapids IA 52401. Editor: Donna Nicholas Hahn. For "homeowners or others interested in building or improving their homes."

Estab. 1929. Monthly. Buys all rights. "Only bylined feature is celebrity editorial which is written in first-person format." Pays on acceptance. Study magazine carefully before submitting. No seasonal material used. Submit editorial material at least 6 months in advance. Reports "at once." Free sample copy. Query. SASE.

Nonfiction: "Ours is a nationally syndicated monthly magazine sponsored in local communities by qualified home builders, real estate companies, home financing institutions, and lumber and building supply dealers. We are primarily a photo magazine that creates a desire for an attractive, comfortable home. We need homebuilding, decorating and remodeling features; decorating idea photographs, complete home coverage, and plans on homes." No do-it-yourself features. Length: 1-3 paragraphs. No set price. "Each month we feature one nationally known guest editor on the theme "What Home Means to Me." Check with us before contacting a celebrity since we have had so many of them." Length: 500-1,000 words. Pays $100, including copy, photos, signature, and signed release from individual.

Photos: Purchases photos with articles on home building, decorating and remodeling; also purchases photos of interest to homeowners with captions only. Buys either b&w or color; color 3¼x4¼ up. "We return color; keep b&w unless return is requested as soon as issue has been printed. May hold photos 1 year." Photos must be well-styled and of highest professional quality. No models in pictures. Interested in series (for example, several pictures of gates, bay windows, window treatment, fireplaces, etc.). Pays $35 minimum.

PLANTS ALIVE, 5509 1st Ave. S. Seattle WA 98108. Publisher and Editor: Theodore R. Marston. 88% freelance written. Emphasizes all form of gardening. For an audience extremely interested in gardening (indoors and outdoors). Monthly magazine: 100 pages. Estab. 1972. Circ. 140,000. Pays on publication. Buys all rights, but may reassign following publication. Byline given. Submit seasonal/holiday material at least 3 months in advance. Photocopied submissions OK. SASE. Reports in 4 weeks to 12 months. Free sample copy and writer's guidelines.

Nonfiction: How-to (related to growing plants, building plant equipment, greenhouses); informational (to help readers with all aspects of gardening); histories (of popular flowers, usually combined with useful information); interviews (with leading growers or horticulturists, especially if article includes useful information for readers); travel (pieces on unique and unusual gardens around the world); new product ("will it help our readers or is it a dud?"); and newsworthy, first-person accounts on gardening; capillary watering, plant photography and personality articles (how this person built a greenhouse or an indoor atrium, etc.). Buys 220 mss/year. Query or submit complete ms. Length: 300-2,000 words. Pays 4¢/word.

Photos: Purchased with mss. Pays $10/8x10 b&w glossies; $35/color transparencies (35mm minimum). Model release required.

Columns/Departments: How-to (ideas on building plant stands, light units, greenhouses, planters); Plant Propagation (how to increase plants in general or a specific kind of plant, or by one particular method). Buys 24 mss/year. Query or send complete ms. Pays 4¢/word plus $10 for each drawing or b&w photo used.

How To Break In: "Freelancer should be specific, know subject and be accurate. Article shouldn't be too technical, though. Organize thoughts and present in logical manner. Ideas should be somewhat newsworthy; not something that has appeared in other publications. Leads should be snappy. Copy should be clear with no extra baggage."

POOLIFE, Olin Corp., 120 Long Ridge Rd., Stamford CT 06904. (203)356-3251. Editor: Russell Pendergast. Managing Editor: Eileen Sharkey. For "a broad-based family audience of men, women, and children with the bulk of readers consisting of young adults (18-35) and adults (35-54). Their common bond is ownership of a home swimming pool and a lifestyle that is heavily oriented toward the home, home entertaining, family leisure activities (cooking, gardening, etc.) and backyard sports and games." Semiannual magazine; 40 pages. Estab. 1970. Circ. 725,000. Pays on acceptance. Buys all rights. Byline given. Submit seasonal/holiday material 8 months in advance of issue date. Photocopied and previously published submissions OK. SASE. Reports in 8 weeks. Free sample copy.

Nonfiction: How-to (improve life in and around the pool—landscaping, building, poolside structures, energy saving, decorating, cooking and entertaining); informational (health, safety, swimming); interview (related to poolside living); and photo feature (related to pools). Buys 10-16 mss/year. Query. Length: 550-2,000 words. Pays $200 minimum.

Photos: Offers no additional payment for photos accepted with accompanying ms. Uses all types of color transparencies and 8x10 b&w prints. Captions and model release required.

REAL ESTATE, Box 1689, Cedar Rapids IA 52406. (319)366-1597. Editor: C.K. Parks. 65% freelance written. "A publication sponsored by real estate brokers for distribution to homebuyers, clients, and community leaders." Bimonthly magazine; 16 pages. Special Christmas issue. Estab. 1972. Circ. 80,000. Buys all rights. No byline. Buys 24 mss/year. Pays on acceptance. Free sample copy. Photocopied submissions OK. No simultaneous submissions. Submit seasonal material 4 months in advance. Reports in 30 days. SASE.

Nonfiction and Photos: "The work of freelance writers fits particularly well into this type of publication because we are looking for nontechnical material of interest to the general public." Wants mss about how-to projects that can be done around the home, decorating in the home, and investing in real estate. Prefer articles with b&w photos. Length: 700-1,200 words. Pays $100.

SELECT HOME DESIGNS, 382 W. Broadway, Vancouver, British Columbia, Canada V5Y 1R2. (604)879-4144. Editor: Ralph Westbrook. Publisher: Brian Thorn. 50% freelance written. Emphasizes building, renovation and interior design of single-family homes. Quarterly magazine. Estab. 1948. Circ. 150,000. Pays on acceptancen. Buys all rights, but may reassign following publication. Byline given. Phone queries OK. Submit 60 days in advance of issue date. Simultaneous, photocopied with previously published submissions OK. SASE. Reports in 2 weeks. Free sample copy and writer's guidelines; mention *Writer's Market* in request.

Nonfiction: General interest (explaining new products or innovations in methods relating to home and cottage); how-to (pertaining to home or cottaging); new product (energy sources, interior design products, lighting, etc.); photo feature (furniture, interiors, housing in general); and technical (new products or techniques relative to home or cottage). Buys 4-5 mss/issue. Query. Length: 250-2,000 words. Pays 3-10¢/word.

Photos: Geoffrey Noble, artistic director. "We are a 4-color consumer magazine. We prefer color photography for maximum effect." Pays $2 minimum for 8x10 glossy b&w prints; $5 minimum for 35mm color transparencies. Captions preferred. Buys all rights, but may reassign following publication. Model release required.

Columns/Departments: "We have no established columns or departments, but are open to their establishment on a continuing basis." Query. Length: 250-1,000 words. Pays 3-10¢/word.

SOUTHERN ACCENTS, W.R.C. Smith Publishing Co., 1760 Peachtree Rd. NW, Atlanta GA 30357. (404)874-4462. Editor: James A. Hooton. Managing Editor: Diane Burrell. Emphasizes interior design and gardens of Southern homes for upper middle class and above. Most, but not all, readers live in the South. Read by interior designers and landscape architects "but most are simply people with varied vocations who are interested in interiors, collections, gardens and in the South—her cultural heritage and places of beauty." Quarterly magazine; 144 pages. Estab. 1977. Circ. 45,000. Pays on publication. Buys all rights. Phone queries OK. Submit seasonal/holiday material 3 months in advance. SASE. Reports in 2-3 weeks. Sample copy/$3.50; free writer's guidelines.

Nonfiction: They are interested in: historical "Each issue carries at least one story on the renovation of a Southern home or historical garden. Other subjects of interest would be histories of certain decorative arts, forms—Chinese Export porcelains and American Coin silver are two we have covered in the past. These articles depend less on illustration and can run considerably longer" (than their requested average length); how-to ("these articles should help our readers learn to be more sophisticated collectors, etc., e.g: 'A Primer for the Buyer of English Antique Furniture' "); interview ("a brief, regular feature called 'Inside Decorating' lets an interior designer tell how he or she approached and solved the problems of decorating a particular space"); and photo feature ("the majority of our articles describe the architecture and interior design of a house and simply tell how it got to look that way—text should tell the story and explicitly captions should spell out anything not immediately apparent from the pictures: names of manufacturers of fabrics, furniture, etc., origins of decorative articles. We use lots of pictures"). This publication wants the writer to have some expertise and credentials in the area in which they are writing such as knowledge of period furniture. Buys 2-3 mss/issue. Query with clips of published work. Length: 500-600 words.

Photos: "We need to see photos in order to be able to judge whether or not we would be interested in the story." Rarely uses b&w photos. Payment varies for 4x5 or 2¼x2¼ color transparencies. Captions required.

YOUR HOME, Box 2315, Ogden UT 84403. (801)394-9446. Editor: Helen S. Crane. 30% freelance written. For young marrieds of middle income and better than average education who own their homes and are interested in improving them. Monthly magazine; 16 pages. Estab. 1945. Circ. 650,000. Buys all rights, but may reassign rights to author after publication. Byline given. Buys about 20 mss/year. Pays on acceptance. Free sample copy. Query, with copies of published material. SASE.

Nonfiction and Photos: "Articles on decorating the home, small vignettes on lifestyles past or present. Our emphasis is on articles that can be illustrated effectively. We want short, but pertinent, pieces that give the reader new ideas. Articles must be general in scope and timeless in appeal; short, yet meaty. We don't want to see amateur photos of one's own do-it-yourself project, nor do we want heavy, pedantic tomes on nutrition or any household tips." Length: 400-700 words. Pays $40-70. Pays $15-20 for b&w glossies purchased with mss. Can use 35mm color transparencies, but prefers larger. "Must be sparkling." Pays $25 minimum.

Humor

Publications in this category specialize in humor. Other publications that use humor can be found in nearly every category in this book. Some of these have special needs for major humor pieces; some use humor as fillers; many others are simply interested in material that meets their ordinary fiction or nonfiction requirements but has a humorous slant.

MAD MAGAZINE, 485 Madison Ave., New York NY 10022. Editor: Al Feldstein. Buys all rights. Byline given.
Humor/Satire: "You know you're *almost* a *Mad* writer when: You include a self-addressed, stamped envelope with each submission. You realize we are a visual magazine and we don't print prose, text or first/second/third-person narratives. You don't send us stuff like the above saying, 'I'm sure one of your great artists can do wonders with this.' You first submit a 'premise' for an article, and show us how you're going to treat it with three or four examples, describing the visuals (sketches not necessary). You don't send in 'timely' material, knowing it takes about 6 months between typewriter and on-the-stands. You don't send poems, song parodies, fold-ins, movie and/or TV show satires, Lighter Sides or other standard features. You understand that individual criticism of art or script is impossible due to the enormous amount of submissions we receive. You don't ask for assignments or staff jobs since *Mad* is strictly a freelance operation. You concentrate on new ideas and concepts other than things we've done (and over-done), like 'You Know You're a . . . When . . . .' "

ORBEN'S CURRENT COMEDY, ORBEN'S COMEDY FILLERS, 1200 N. Nash St. Arlington VA 22209. (703)522-3666. Editor: Robert Orben. For "speakers, toastmasters, businessmen, public relations people, communications professionals." Biweekly; monthly. Buys all rights. Pays at the end of the month for material used in issues published that month. "Material should be typed and submitted on standard size paper. Please leave 3 spaces between each item. Unused material will be returned to the writer within a few days if SASE is enclosed. We do not send rejection slips. Please do not send us any material that has been sent to other publications. If SASE is not enclosed, all material will be destroyed after being considered except for items purchased."
Fillers: "We are looking for funny, performable one-liners, short jokes and stories that are related to happenings in the news, fads, trends and topical subjects. The accent is on comedy, not wit. Ask yourself, 'Will this line get a laugh if performed in public?' Material should be written in a conversational style and, if the joke permits it, the inclusion of dialogue is a plus. We are particularly interested in material that can be used by speakers and toastmasters: lines for beginning a speech, ending a speech, acknowledging an introduction, specific occasions, anything that would be of use to a person making a speech. We can use lines to be used at sales meetings, presentations, conventions, seminars and conferences. Short, sharp comment on business trends, fads and events is also desirable. Please do not send us material that's primarily written to be read rather than spoken. We have little use for definitions, epigrams, puns, etc. The submissions must be original. If material is sent to us that we find to be copied or rewritten from some other source, we will no longer consider material from the contributor." Pays $4.

In-Flight

This list consists of publications read by commercial airline passengers. They use general interest freelance material such as travel articles, etc., as well as general interest material on aviation.

AIR CALIFORNIA MAGAZINE, Box 707, South Laguna CA 92677. (714)494-1727. Editor-in-Chief: Michael McFadden. Emphasizes all aspects of California for airline passengers on Air California. Monthly magazine; 128 pages. Estab. 1967. Circ. 350,000. Pays on publication. Buys one-time rights. Submit seasonal/holiday material 3 months in advance. Simultaneous, photocopied and previously published submissions OK. SASE. Reports in 2 months. Sample copy $1.

Nonfiction: Address queries to Cristofer Gross, Managing Editor. Historical; humor; informational (travel); inspirational (if not sentimental); interview (California personalities); nostalgia; photo feature; profile and travel (California or international). Buys 35-40 mss/year. Query. Length: 1,500-5,000 words. Pays $50-150.

Photos: Photos purchased with accompanying ms or on assignment. Captions required. Pays $10-25 for 8x10 b&w photos; $25-50 for 35mm color photos. No additional payment for photos accepted with accompanying ms. Model release required.

ALASKAFEST, Seattle Northwest Publishing Co., 1932 1st Ave., Suite 503, Seattle WA 98101. (206)682-5871. Editor: Denise DiPietro. For travelers on Alaska Airlines. Monthly magazine; 44 pages. Estab. February 1977. Circ. 100,000. Pays on publication. Buys all rights or one-time rights. Byline given. Phone queries OK. Submit seasonal/holiday material 4 months in advance. SASE. Free sample copy and writer's guidelines.

Nonfiction: General interest, historical, humor, interview, nostalgia, personal experience, personal opinion, photo feature, profile and travel. "All articles must relate to the Northwest or Alaska." Buys 4 mss/issue. Query with clips of published work. Length: 500-3,000 words. Pays $25-275.

Photos: State availability of photos with mss or send photos with ms. Pays $5-100 for b&w prints; $20-100 for 35mm color transparencies. Captions preferred.

Fiction: Adventure, historical, humorous and mainstream. "Articles should relate to the Northwest or Alaska."

ALOFT, Wickstrom Publishers, Inc., 2701 S. Bayshore Dr., Suite 501, Miami FL 33133. (305)858-3546. Executive editor: Pat Winkerton. Editor: Karl Wickstrom. 75% freelance written. For National Airlines passengers. General interest with emphasis on subjects of interest to high-income audience having a high educational level. Bimonthly. Rights to be negotiated. Pays on publication. Sample copy 25¢. Will consider photocopied submissions. Reports in 4-6 weeks. SASE.

Nonfiction and Photos: Articles on unusual or little-known places rather than national monuments and commercial attractions. New emphasis on leisure activity of interest to the affluent male. Most issues have at least one piece by or about a known personality. No expose articles. Query. Length: 800-2,000 words. Pays $150 and up for articles. Color transparencies are purchased with mss or captions on travel, sports, adventure. Must be top quality with imaginative approach. Payment negotiated. Photo Editor: Theodore R. Baker.

AMERICAN WAY, 1701 W. Marshall Dr., Grand Prairie TX 75050. The inflight magazine for American Airlines. Monthly magazine. Pays on acceptance. Buys all rights or other rights depending on author and material. Sometimes pays kill fee. Byline given. Submit seasonal/holiday material 7 months in advance. Reports in 4 months. SASE.

Nonfiction: News-oriented rather than travel-oriented. "We seek articles that deal with current issues—thoughtful, stimulating treatment of news events, business, arts, culture, important historical events, business and ecology. Query. "We would like writing samples that show a writer's abilities and scope. These will not be returned." Submit Attn: Articles Editor. Nearly all articles written by a well-established group of freelancers. Length: 1,500-1,750 words for think pieces, interviews, profiles, humor, nostalgia, travel pieces, sports articles and how-to. Pays $200 minimum.

PSA CALIFORNIA MAGAZINE, East/West Network, 5900 Wilshire Blvd., Suite 300, Los Angeles CA 90036. See East/West Network.

CLIPPER, East/West Network, 488 Madison Avenue, New York NY 10022. Editorial Director: Fred R. Smith. See East/West Network.

EAST/WEST NETWORK, INC., 488 Madison Ave., New York NY 10022. Vice President/Editor: Fred R. Smith. Executive Editors: Joseph Poindexter and John Johns. Publishes monthly inflight publications: *California Magazine* (Pacific Southwest Airlines), *Clipper* (Pan American), *Flightime* (editions for Allegheny Airlines, Ozark Airlines and Southern Airlines, Continental 'Continental Airlines'), *Mainliner* (United Airlines), *ReView* (Eastern Airlines) and *Sundancer* (Hughes Airwest). Estab. 1968. Combined Circ. 18 million.

Pays within 60 days of acceptance. Buys all East/West Network Publications: author retains other rights. Pays 50% kill fee. Byline given. SASE. Reports in 1 month.

Nonfiction: "General magazine material aimed at the frequent business (executive) traveler. Topics include sports, money, management, health, and fitness, living (leisure and trends), products, personalities and entertainment. Only 18% of material used in "destination-oriented" material (travel pieces). Fashion pieces are staff-produced. Query. "Brief; and in writing, plus a sample or two of published work." Length: 1,000-2,500 words. Pays $200-500.

Photos: "Most are purchased through agencies."

How To Break In: "Sell us on an idea and then deliver on what you sell."

FLIGHTIME, East/West Network, 488 Madison Ave., New York NY 10022. Editorial Director: Fred R. Smith. See East/West Network.

LATITUDE/20, 532 Cummins St., Honolulu HI 96814. Editor: Jeri Bostwick. For Hawaiian Air passengers; tourists and local people traveling inter-island. Monthly magazine; 48 pages. Estab. 1974. Circ. 2,500,000. Not copyrighted. Byline given. Buys about 30 mss/year. Pays on publication. Sample copy for $1. Will consider photocopied submissions. Query. SASE.

Nonfiction and Photos: Primarily interested in Hawaiiana. Practical information and historical facts. Self-improvement articles. Ethnic stories are always welcome (Japanese, Chinese, Korean, Filipino, Hawaiian, Samoan, Portuguese). No word pictures of swaying palms and scarlet sunsets. Length: 1,000-1,500 words. Pays $50. No additional payment for photos used with mss. Pays $50 for cover photos; model release required.

MAINLINER, East/West Network, 488 Madison Ave., New York NY 10022. Editorial Director: Fred R. Smith. See East/West Network.

NORTHWEST PASSAGES, The Webb Co., 1999 Shepard Rd., St. Paul MN 55116. Editor-in-Chief: Jean Marie Hamilton. Managing Editor: Jim Carney. 80% freelance written. For Northwest Orient Airlines passengers. Monthly magazine. Pays on acceptance. Buys all rights, but may reassign following publication. Buys 61 mss/year. Reports in 2-4 weeks. Query with samples of published work. No complete mss accepted. SASE. Sample copy $1; free writer's guidelines.

Nonfiction: Controversial ("rather than pure expose, but we want to explore both sides of any controversy"); how-to (on business, health, etc.,—no crafts); informational (sports, business trends, modern living, current issues); historical (with current peg); interviews and profiles (on interesting people who are saying things of significance); personal opinion (only from writers with the proper credentials); travel (no broadbrush, what-to-see, where-to-stay pieces); and business management. Length: 1,500-2,200 words. Pays $75-500.

Photos: Purchased with mss and on assignment. Query. Pays $25-75/b&w; $50-100/color; $200/cover shots. For photos purchased with mss, "the package price is negotiated ahead of time." Model release required.

PSA CALIFORNIA MAGAZINE, East/West Network, Inc., 5900 Wilshire Blvd., Suite 300, Los Angeles CA 90036. (213)937-5810. Editor: John Johns. Managing Editor: Covi Reminck. 90% freelance written. Monthly magazine; 160 pages. Pays within 60 days after acceptance. Buys first rights, but may reassign following publication. Pays 25% kill fee. Byline given. Submit seasonal/holiday material 4 months in advance of issue date. Simultaneous and photocopied submissions OK. SASE. Sample copy $1.50.

Nonfiction: Prefers California/West Coast slant. General interest; humor; interview (top-level government, entertainment, sports figures); new product (trends, survey field); profile; and business (with California and West Coast orientation). Buys 10 mss/issue. Query. Length: 500-2,000 words. Pays $150-500.

Photos: Cliff Wynne, Art director. State availability of photos with query. Pays $50-100 for b&w contact sheets or negatives; pays $75-175 for 35mm or 2¼x2¼ color transparencies. Captions required. Buys one-time rights. Model release required.

Columns/Departments: Business Trends. Buys 1 ms/issue. Query. Length: 700-1,500 words. Pays $100-300.

Fiction: Humorous. No esoteric or historic fiction. Buys 3 mss/year. Submit complete ms. Length: 500-1,500 words. Pays $100-200.

Fillers: Short humor. Buys 4/year. length: 500-700 words. Pays $100.

REVIEW, East/West Network, 488 Madison Ave., New York NY 10022. Editorial Director: Fred R. Smith. See East/West Network.

SKY, East/West Network, 488 Madison Ave., New York NY 10022. Editorial Director: Fred R. Smith. See East/West Network.

SOUTHWEST AIRLINES MAGAZINE, Summit Publishing Co., 11824 Radium, San Antonio TX 78216. (512)349-1281. Editor-in-Chief: Al Mogavero. Managing Editor: Dani Presswood. 50% freelance written. "Readership consists primarily of passengers of Southwest Airlines, which serves the major cities of Texas." Monthly magazine; 80 pages. Estab. 1971. Pays on acceptance. Buys first North American serial rights. Submit seasonal/holiday material at least 3 months in advance of issue date. Photocopied and previously published submissions OK. SASE. Reports in 2-4 weeks. Sample copy $1.50.
Nonfiction: "Most articles have a Texas orientation; however, there are some of a general nature with no local connection, for example, "The Psychology of Color." General interest ("these make up the majority of our stories. We're looking for interesting and unusual articles that will hold the reader's attention as he/she flies the airline. Recent example are "Houston's Boy in the Plastic Bubble" and "The Newton Boys: Uvalde's Favorite Bank Robbers."); how-to (e.g., "How to Diet When You're Traveling", "How to Cope with Stress"); interview (question & answer format; subject must be well-known in his/her field); photo feature; profile (subject must be a Texan who has succeeded in his field or line of work); and articles of particular interest to business executives. No personal opinion or experience articles. Buys 50 mss/year. Query or submit complete ms. Length: 1,500-3,000 words. Pays $60-125.
Photos: Franco Cernero, photo editor. State availability of photos with query or ms. Offers no additional payment for photos accepted with accompanying ms. Uses 5x7 or 8x10 b&w glossy prints. Buys one-time rights. Model release required.

SUNDANCER, East/West Network, 5900 Wilshire Blvd., 8th Floor, Los Angeles CA 90036. General interest inflight of Hughes Airwest, published by East/West in combination with *Texas Flyer* magazine for Texas International Airlines. Major features, exclusive of columns and travel stories that are unique to each publication, are common to both books and are slanted to the airlines' overlapping Sunbelt audiences. *Sundancer* monthly readership: 275,000; *Texas Flyer's*: 175,000. Editor: Jonathan P. Miller. Pays on acceptance. Pays negotiable kill fee. Byline given. Topical material should be submitted 4-6 months in advance of the proposed publication date. Query by mail, "not by phone, enclosing published writing samples, preferably magazine or hard news features. Please familiarize yourself with *Sundancer* before querying and include phone number on all correspondence." Reports in 4 weeks. Sample copy $1.50; free writer's guidelines.
Nonfiction: "Regional (lead articles spotlight emerging *Sunbelt* stories—"The Return of the Cattle Rustler"; "The Colorado: The Coming Crunch in Water"; strong reporting a must); business, science and health (keyed to affluent businesspersons who constitute our major inflight audience; stories range from mainstream articles on investment opportunities and coping with being fired, to offbeat spreads on chocolate chip cookie barons and the future of aviation); travel (please, no laundry lists and 'breathtaking' views, just fine writing and story telling and a love of place, people and the histories they embody); profiles (sunbelters in the news or on the rise, be they in the fields of business, the arts, sports or show business); lifestyle (ballooning, panning for gold or building dream castles in the desert; in short, offbeat stuff that's also fun)." Length of major features: 1,500-2,000 words. Pay: $200-400. "Generally speaking, think of *Sundancer* as an informative, entertaining, service publication that just happens to be an inflight. We are not a travel magazine, though we do carry travel stories."
Photos: Purchased with accompanying ms. Query. Pays $50-100 for b&w photos; $75-150 for 35mm and larger color transparencies. "We often buy photos with mss; the package price is negotiated ahead of time." Model releases required. Contact: Art Director, Celest Swayne-Courtney.
Secondary Features: "We also buy short, travel-oriented features (750-1,000 words) for *Sundancer*. Such stories range from a preview of the Portland Rose festival to a business/travel spread on the Utah mines of the Kennicott Copper Company. Payment ranges from $75 (first-time contributors) to $150. Most new *Sundance* writers break in here." Contact: Assistant Editor, Frank Bies. Pays negotiable kill fee. Byline given. See East/West Network.

TWA AMBASSADOR, (for Trans World Airlines), The Webb Co., 1999 Shepard Rd., St. Paul MN 55116. Editor-in-Chief: David Martin. 90% freelance written. "For TWA passengers, top management executives, professional men and women, world travelers; affluent, interested and responsive." Monthly magazine. Estab. 1968. Circ. 321,000. Pays on acceptance. Buys all rights. Pays 25% kill fee. Byline given. Submit seasonal/holiday material 6 months in advance. SASE. Reports in 2-4 weeks. Sample copy $1; free writer's guidelines.

Nonfiction: Controversial (rather than the pure expose; we insist on exploring all sides in any topic); historical (with current peg); how-to (in business subjects, health; no crafts or hobbies); humor (on current topics); informational (sports, business, modern living, current issues, etc.).
Fiction: Personal opinion (from writers with the proper credentials); profile (people who're topical, timely; covered in-depth. Not just what they do, but why they do it); travel (no "where-to-go, what-to-see" pieces) and business management. Buys 72 mss/year. Query. Length: 3,00-4,500 words. Pays $450-700.
Photos: Purchased with accompanying ms. Query. Pays $25-75 for b&w photos; $50-150 for 35mm and larger color transparencies ($250 for cover). "We often buy photos with mss; the package price is negotiated ahead of time." Model release required.
Columns/Departments: American Journal, Sports, Spectrum (Science and technology); Business, Personal Finance, The Arts, Media, Books and The Law. "We buy words pieces and run them as columns, under the appropriate heading." Length: 1,500-2,000 words. Pays $150-200.

VOYAGER, 63 Shrewsbury Lane, Shooters Hill, London, England SE18 3JJ. Editor: Dennis Winston. 80% freelance written. 20% of material from American/Canadian writers. Emphasizes travel for "a reasonably sophisticated audience, middle- to upper-income and intelligence, both sexes, all ages." Quarterly magazine; 36 pages. Estab. 1973. Circ. 25,000. Pays on publication. Buys one-time rights. Byline given unless author requests otherwise. Submit seasonal/holiday material 6 months in advance. Photocopied and previously published submissions OK ("if not previously published in UK"). SAE and International Reply Coupons. Reports in 1 month.
Nonfiction: Humor (real-life travel experiences); informational (articles concerning business and/or holidays in areas with which magazine is concerned); and travel (relevant to area served by magazine). "*Voyager* is the free inflight magazine for passengers of British Midland Airways, which has several domestic routes within the UK, and international routes to France, West Germany, Belgium, Holland and the Republic of Ireland. Our need is for well-informed, entertaining articles about business, tourism, and facets of life in those countries and in others for which those countries are gateways." Buys 6 mss/issue. Submit complete ms. Length: 800-1,500 words maximum. Pays 25-45 pounds.
Photos: Purchased with accompanying ms. Captions required. Submit b&w prints or transparencies. Pays 3-12 pounds for 8x6 b&w glossy prints; 7-20 pounds for color transparencies. Total purchase price for ms includes payment for photos.
How To Break In: "Articles must be informative, specific (e.g., name hotels and restaurants, give prices), not outdated, entertaining. First-person material is welcomed."

WESTERN'S WORLD, 141 El Camino, Beverly Hills CA 90212. (213)273-1990. Editor: Frank M. Hiteshew. Assistant Editor/Art Director: Tom Medsger. Published by Western Airlines for the airline traveler. Estab. 1970. Magazine published 6 times/year. Circ. 250,000. Buys all rights. Pays 50% kill fee. Byline given. Buys 20-25 mss/year. Pays on publication. Photocopied submissions OK. Submit seasonal material 1 year in advance of issue date. Reports in 1-3 months. Query. SASE.
Nonfiction: "Articles should relate to travel, dining, or entertainment in the area served by Western Airlines: Hawaii, Minneapolis/St. Paul, Alaska to Mexico, Miami and between. General interest (nontravel) articles are welcome too, as a change of pace. Compared to other airline magazines, *Western's World* strives for a more editorial approach. It's not as promotional-looking; all articles are bylined articles. Some writers are the top names in the field." Buys photo features and travel articles. Length: 1,000-2,000 words. Pays 10¢/word.
Photos: Department Editor: Tom Medsger. Purchased with or without mss or on assignment; captions required. Uses 8x10 b&w glossy prints, but "rarely." Pays $25. Uses 35mm, 4x5 or larger color transparencies. Pays $25-125; "more for cover, subject to negotiation."
Fiction: Short stories, fantasy and humor. "Rarely printed because we've seen so few good ones. Should relate to the geographic areas served by Western Airlines. No personality profiles." Length: 1,000-2,000 words. Pays 10¢/word.

Jewish

The following publications use material on topics of general interest slanted toward a Jewish readership. Publications using Jewish-oriented religious material are categorized in Religious Publications.

AMERICAN JEWISH TIMES-OUTLOOK, Box 33218, Charlotte NC 28234. (704)372-3296.

Editor: Ronald D. Unger. For Jewish middle and upper class; religious; primarily own their own businesses or corporations; most of the women are club-oriented. Monthly magazine; 48 pages. Special issues for Rosh Hashanah, Hanukkah, Purim and Passover. Circ. 5,000. Not copyrighted. Byline given. Buys 12-15 mss/year. Pays on publication. Free sample copy and writer's guidelines. Will consider photocopied and simultaneous submissions. Submit special holiday material at least 2 months in advance; usually earlier. Query. SASE.

Nonfiction and Photos: Articles primarily dealing with Jewish topics of interest: economic news, Israel, Soviet Jewry, holy days, Jewish personalities, art, music, sports, etc. Book reviews and short features. Articles usually take an analytical, rather than reportive, style. A more condensed style is preferred. Length: 3 typed, double-spaced pages maximum. Pays $25/article. Additional payment for b&w photos used. $10-15/each depending on subject.

Fiction, Poetry and Fillers: Fantasy, humorous, religious and historical fiction. If timely, may be linked to Holy Days. Pays $25. Traditional and avant-garde forms of poetry, blank verse, free verse, haiku. Must relate to publications's theme. Pays $15 minimum. Groups of jokes, gags, anecdotes; and short humor used as fillers. Pays $10 minimum.

THE AMERICAN ZIONIST, Zionist Organization of America, 4 E. 34th St., New York NY 10016. Editor-in-Chief: Elias Cooper. 15% freelance written. Political journal pertaining to Israel, Middle East and Jewish affairs. Monthly magazine; 32 pages. Estab. 1910. Circ. 44,000. Pays "some time after publication." Buys all rights, but may reassign following publication. Byline given. Photocopied submissions OK. SASE.

Nonfiction: Expose, historical, humor, informational, inspirational, interview, nostalgia, profile and travel. Buys 48 mss/year. Length: 2,000-3,000 words. Pays $50-100.

Poetry: "Mainly used as filler material." Buys 4 poems/year. Pays $15.

CANADIAN ZIONIST, 1310 Greene Ave., Montreal, Quebec, Canada H3Z 2B2. Editor-in-Chief: Dr. Leon Kronitz. Associate Editor: Rabbi Sender Shizgal. Assistant Editor: Irene Welik. 40% freelance written. Emphasizes Zionism. Published 7-8 times/year; 40-48 pages. Estab. 1934. Circ. 34,000. Byline given. Pays on publication. Submit seasonal/holiday material 2 months in advance of issue date. Photocopied submissions OK. Reports in 3 weeks. Free sample copy.

Nonfiction: General interest (Jewish or Zionist current events); historical (Jewish or Zionist history); interview (with prominent figures in Israeli politics, art or science); profile (on Israeli political figures); and technical (Zionism, Jewish interest, Middle East politics). No stories on personal experiences or travel to Israel. Buys 10 mss/year. Query with clips of published work. Length: 1,500-2,500. Pays $125 maximum.

Photos: State availability of photos with query. No additional payment for b&w prints.

JEWISH CURRENT EVENTS, 430 Keller Ave., Elmont NY 11003. Editor: S. Deutsch. 25-30% freelance written. For Jewish children and adults; distributed in Jewish schools. Biweekly. Pays on publication. Byline given. No sample copies available. Reports in 1 week. SASE.

Nonfiction: All current event items of Jewish content or interest; news; featurettes; short travel items (non-Israel) relating to Jewish interests or descriptions of Jewish communities or personalities; life in Jewish communities abroad; "prefer items written in news-style format." Length must be short. Pays $10-300, depending on content, illustrations, length and relevance.

Photos: Purchased with mss, if available, but not required. All items of Jewish content or interest. B&w snapshots only. "We prefer small pictures rather than 8x10 or 5x7," for direct contact use not requiring enlargements or reduction of the original print's size." Payment varies.

JEWISH POST AND OPINION, National Jewish Post, Inc., 611 N. Park Ave., Indianapolis IN 46204. (317)634-1307. Editor: Gabriel Cohen. Emphasizes Jewish news. Weekly tabloid. Estab. 1931. Circ. 112,000. Pays on publication.

Nonfiction: "Straight reporting of news involving Jews and human interest stories." Query. Pays 2-4¢/word plus retainer.

MIDSTREAM, 515 Park Ave., New York NY 10022. Editor: Joel Carmichael. Monthly. Circ. 14,000. Buys first rights. Pays 30% kill fee. Byline given. Pays on publication. Reports in 2 weeks. SASE.

Nonfiction and Fiction: "Articles offering a critical interpretation of the past, searching examination of the present, and affording a medium for independent opinion and creative cultural expression. Articles on the political and social scene in Israel, on Jews in Russia and the US; generally it helps to have a Zionist orientation. If you're going abroad, we would like

to see what you might have to report on a Jewish community abroad." Buys historical and think pieces and fiction, primarily of Jewish and related content. Pays 7¢ minimum/word.
How To Break In: "A book review would be the best way to start. Send us a sample review or a clip, let us know your area of interest, suggest books you would like to review."

MOMENT MAGAZINE, 462 Baylston St., Boston MA 02116. (617)536-6252. Editor-in-Chief: Leonard Fein. Emphasizes Jewish affairs. Monthly magazine; 64 pages. Estab. 1975. Circ. 25,000. Pays on publication. Buys all rights. Pays 25% kill fee. Byline given. Phone queries OK. Submit seasonal/holiday material 6 months in advance. Reports in 4 weeks. Sample copy $2.
Nonfiction: Expose, how-to, informational, historical, humor, nostalgia, profile and personal experience. Top literary quality only. Buys 100 mss/year. Query or submit complete ms. Length: 1,000-5,000 words. Pays $50-400.
Fiction: Anne Fishman, fiction editor. "We use only the highest quality fiction. If you wouldn't send it to the *New Yorker,* don't send it to us. Stories must have high Jewish content." Buys 8 mss/year. Submit complete ms. Length: 1,000-5,000 words. Pays $100-400.
How To Break In: "We rarely publish beginners. Best way to break in is to have published in other quality magazines."
Rejects: "We don't want anything sentimental or cliched. We receive far too many mss on the Holocaust. No room for memoirs or family stories."

THE NATIONAL JEWISH MONTHLY, 1640 Rhode Island NW, Washington DC 20036. (202)857-6645. Editor: Charles Fenyvesi. Published by B'nai B'rith. Monthly magazine. Buys North American serial rights. Pays on publication. SASE.
Nonfiction: Articles of interest to the Jewish community: economic, demographic, political, social, biographical. Length: 4,000 words maximum. Pays 10¢/word maximum.

RECONSTRUCTIONIST, 432 Park Ave. S., New York NY 10016. (212)889-9080. Editor: Dr. Ira Eisenstein. A general Jewish religious and cultural magazine. Monthly. Estab. 1935. Circ. 6,000. Buys all rights. Buys 10 mss/year. Pays on publication. Free sample copy. Query. SASE.
Nonfiction: Publishes literary criticism, reports from Israel and other lands where Jews live, and material of educational or communal interest. Also uses interviews and features dealing with leading Jewish personalities. Preferred length is 3,000 words. Pays $15-25.
Fiction and Poetry: Uses a small amount of poetry and fiction as fillers.

SOUTHERN JEWISH WEEKLY, Box 3297, Jacksonville FL 32206. (904)355-3459. Editor: Isadore Moscovitz. 10% freelance written. For a Jewish audience. Estab. 1924. General subject matter is human interest and short stories. Weekly. Circ. 28,500. Pays on acceptance. Not copyrighted. Buys all rights. Submit seasonal/holiday material 1 month in advance. Simultaneous, photocopied and previously published submissions OK. SASE. Reports in 1 week. Free sample copy and writer's guidelines.
Nonfiction: "Any type of articles as long as it is of Southern Jewish interest."Buys 15 mss/year. Length: 250-500 words. Pays $10-100.
Photos: State availability of photos. Pays $5-15 for b&w prints.

WORLD OVER, 426 W. 58th St., New York NY 10019. Editor: Stephen Schaffzin. 50% freelance written. Buys first serial rights. Byline given. Pays on acceptance. Reports in 4-6 weeks. SASE.
Nonfiction, Photos and Fiction: Uses material of Jewish interest, past or present for ages 8-13 and up. Articles up to 1,000 words. Fiction should be Jewish in content. Length: 600-800 words. Pays 10¢/word minimum. Query. B&w glossy prints purchased with mss.

Juvenile

This section of Writer's Market includes publications for children ages 2-12. Magazines for young people 12-25 appear in a separate Teen and Young Adult category.

Most of the following publications are produced by religious groups, and wherever possible, the specific denomination is given. For the writer with a story or article slanted to a specific age group, the sub-index which follows is a quick reference to markets for his story in that age group.

Those editors who are willing to receive simultaneous submissions are indicated. (This is the technique of mailing the same story at the same time to a number of low-paying religious markets of nonoverlapping circulation. In each case, the writer, when making a simultaneous submission, should so advise the editor.) The few mass circulation, nondenominational publications included in this section that have good pay rates are not interested in simultaneous submissions and should not be approached with this technique. Magazines that pay good rates expect, and deserve, the exclusive use of material.

Writers will also note in some of the listings that editors will buy "second rights" to stories. This refers to a story which has been previously published in a magazine and to which the writer has already sold "first rights." Payment is usually less for the re-use of a story than for first-time publication.

Juvenile Publications Classified by Age

Two- to Five-Year Olds: The Beehive, Children's Playmate, Children's Service, The Friend, Highlights for Children, Humpty Dumpty, The Kindergartner, Nursery Days, Odyssey, Our Little Friend, Primary Treasure, Ranger Rick's Nature Magazine, Story Friends, Wee Wisdom.

Six- to Eight-Year-Olds: The Beehive, Children's Playmate, Children's Service, Cricket, Dash, Ebony, The Friend, Highlights for Children, Humpty Dumpty, Jack and Jill, My Devotions, Odyssey, Our Little Friend, Primary Treasure, R-A-D-A-R, Ranger Rick's Nature Magazine, Story Friends, Touch, Trails, Video-Presse, The Vine, Wee Wisdom, Weekly Bible Reader, Wonder Time, The Young Crusader, Young Judaean.

Nine- to Twelve-Year-Olds: Child's Life, Children's Service, Cricket, Crusader Magazine, Dash, Discoveries, Discovery, Ebony, The Friend, Highlights for Children, Jack and Jill, My Devotions, On the Line, R-A-D-A-R, Ranger Rick's Nature Magazine, Story Friends, Touch, Trails, Video-Presse, The Vine, Wee Wisdom, Weekly Bible Reader, The Young Crusader, Young Judaean, Young Musicians.

THE BEEHIVE, 201 8th Ave., S., Nashville TN 37203. Editor: Martha Wagner. Published monthly in weekly format for children in grades 5 and 6 in United Methodist Church schools. Free sample copy. Buys all rights. Byline given. Pays on acceptance. Submit double-spaced copy, 32-character line count. Reports on submissions within three months. SASE.
Nonfiction and Photos: Most articles requested by editor from writers. Subject matter relates to or correlates with church school curriculum and interests of children in grades 4, 5 and 6. Should not be overly moralistic or didactic. May provide information to enrich cultural understanding in religion and in relationships with other people. Also well-written biography, not composed from encyclopedias. Length: 200-800 words. Pays 3¢/word. Photos purchased with mss. B&w glossy prints; color transparencies. Pays $1-25.
Fiction and Poetry: Modern day life, problems. Unusual historical stories; church history. No slang or references to drinking or smoking. Might-have-happened Biblical stories. "Many stories are too long, too unrealistic, or unimagenative." Length: about 700 words. Poetry to 20 lines. Pays 50¢/line.

CHILD LIFE, For Twixt and Teen (now incorporating *Young World*). Saturday Evening Post Co., Youth Publications, 1100 Waterway Blvd., Box 567B, Indianapolis IN 46206. Editor: John D. Craton. For youngsters 9-14. Monthly (except bimonthly issues in June/July and August/September) magazine; 48 pages. Estab. 1921. Pays on publication. Buys all rights. Byline given. Submit seasonal/holiday material 8 months in advance. Photocopied submissions OK. SASE. Reports in 8-10 weeks. Sample copy 50¢; free writer's guidelines.
Nonfiction: How-to (crafts and hobbies); informational (science, nature, wildlife, astronomy and linguistic); historical; biographical; and contemporary. Buys 2-3 mss/issue. Submit complete ms; query not necessary. Length: 1,200 word maximun. Pays 3¢/word. Given word count on ms.
Photos: Purchased with accompanying ms. Captions required. Submit prints or transparencies. Pays $2.50 for b&w glossy prints; $5 for color transparencies. Model release required.
Fiction: Adventure, historical fiction, fantasy, humorous, mystery and science fiction. Buys 3-6 mss/issue. Submit complete ms; query not necessary. Length: 1,200-3,600 words. Pays approximately 3¢/word. Give word count on ms.
How To Break In: "While we often use some of the same authors over and again, we also

encourage new authors to submit their works as we buy on quality and not on name. We are looking for material with substance. Children love a good story as much as anyone and have little appreciation or use for the anemic and languid type of trivia that has taken over to such a large extent our modern children's literature. Our writers should bear in mind the 'betwixt' age group that our periodical attempts to reach, those in that prepubescent stage in which they are more than children but not yet full-fledged teenagers. However, we believe our readers to be of creditable intelligence and encourage authors never to write condescendingly. Authors should realize simply that they are writing for younger people whose only basic attributes that may not yet be fully developed are attention span, vocabulary and understanding of convoluted syntax."

CHILDREN'S PLAYMATE, 1100 Waterway Blvd., Box 567B, Indianapolis IN 46206. (317)634-1100, ext. 296. Editor: Beth Wood Thomas. For children, ages 5-8. Magazine published 10 times/year. Buys all rights. Byline given. Pays on publication. Sample copy 50¢; free writer's guidelines with SASE. No query. "We do not consider resumes and outlines. Reading the whole ms is the only way to give fair consideration. The editors cannot criticize, offer suggestions, or review unsolicited material that is not accepted." Submit seasonal material 8 months in advance. Reports in 8-10 weeks. Sometimes may hold mss for up to 1 year; with author's permission. "Material will not be returned unless accompanied by a self-addressed envelope and sufficient postage."
Fiction: Short stories, not over 600 words for beginning readers. No inanimate, talking objects. Humorous stories, unusual plots. Vocabulary suitable for ages 5-8. Pays about 3¢/word.
Nonfiction: Beginning science, 600 words maximum. Monthly "All about . . ." feature, 300-500 words, may be an interesting presentation on animals, people, events, objects or places. Pays about 3¢/word.
Fillers: Puzzles, dot-to-dots, color-ins, mazes, tricks, games, guessing games, and brain teasers. Payment varies.
Needs: Stories, poems and articles about special holiday, customs and events.

CHILDREN'S SERVICE PROGRAMS, Concordia Publishing House, 3558 S. Jefferson Ave., St. Louis MO 63118. (314)664-7000. Issued annually by The Lutheran Church—Missouri Synod, for children, aged three through eighth grade. Buys all rights. Receipt of children's worship scripts will be acknowledged immediately, but acceptance or rejection may require up to a year. All mss must be typed, double-spaced on 8½x11 paper. SASE. Write for details.
Nonfiction and Drama: "Two Christmas worship service programs for congregational use published yearly. Every script must include usual elements embodied in a worship service. Children lead the worship with adults participating in singing some of the hymns. Youth and adult choir selections optional. Every script must emphasize the Biblical message of the Gospel through which God shares His love and which calls for a joyful response from His people. Services requiring elaborate staging or costumes not accepted." Pays $125, but buys few mss.

CRICKET, Box 100, LaSalle IL 61301. Editor: Marianne Carus. For children ages 6-12. Monthly magazine. Estab. 1973. May buy all rights, first serial rights, or second serial (reprint) rights. Buys about 100 mss/year. Pays on publication. Sample copy $1.50; free writer's guidelines for SASE. Special material should be submitted 9-12 months in advance. "We work 1 year in advance of publication." Reports in 6-8 weeks. Submit complete ms. SASE.
Nonfiction: "We are interested in high-quality material written for children, not down to children." Biography, science, history, foreign culture, informational, humor, travel. Pays 25¢/word maximum.
Fiction: Realistic and historic fiction; fantasy, myth, legend, folk tale. No life-cycle, natural history, or retold folk tales that appear in standard story collections and anthologies. Length: 200-2,000 words. Pays 25¢/word maximum.
Poetry: Traditional forms, light verse, limericks, nonsense rhymes. Length: 100 lines maximum. Pays $3/line maximum.
Fillers: Short humor, puzzles, songs, crafts, recipes. Length: 200 words maximum. Pays 25¢/word maximum.

CRUSADER MAGAZINE, Box 7244, Grand Rapids MI 49510. Editor: David Koetje. For boys, age 9-14. Magazine published 7 times/year; 24 pages, in cartoon format. Estab. 1962. Circ. 12,500. Rights purchased vary with author and material. Byline given. Buys 15 to 20 mss a year. Pays on acceptance. Free sample copy and writer's guidelines. Will consider photocopied and simultaneous submissions. Submit seasonal material (Christmas, Easter) at least 5 months in advance. Reports in 1-2 months. Query or submit complete ms. SASE.
Nonfiction and Photos: Articles about young boys' interests: sports, outdoor activities, bike

riding, science, crafts, etc., and problems. Emphasis is on a Christian perspective, but no simplistic moralisms. Material appropriate to Christmas and Easter. Informational, how-to, personal experience, interview, profile, inspirational, humor. Length: 500-1,500 words. Pays 2-5¢/word. Pays $4-25 for b&w photos purchased with mss.
Fiction and Fillers: "Considerable fiction is used. Fast-moving stories that appeal to a boy's sense of adventure or sense of humor are welcome. Avoid 'preachiness.' Avoid simplistic answers to complicated problems. Avoid long dialog and little action." Length: 500-1,500 words. Pays 2-5¢/word. Uses short humor and any type of puzzles as fillers.

DASH, Box 150, Wheaton IL 60187. Editor: Randall Nulton. 50% freelance written. For boys 8-11 years of age. Most subscribers are in a Christian Service Brigade program. Monthly magazine; 32 pages. Estab. 1972. Circ. 32,000. Rights purchased vary with author and material. Usually buys all rights, but will sometimes reassign rights to author after publication. Buys 5 mss/year. Pays on publication. Submit seasonal material 4 months in advance. Reports in 2 months. Query. SASE
Nonfiction and Photos: "Our emphasis is on boys and how their belief in Jesus Christ works in their everyday life." Uses short articles about boys of this age; problems they encounter. Material on crafts and games. Interview, profile. Length: 1,000-1,500 words. Pays $30-60. Pays $7.50 for 8x10 b&w photos purchased with ms. Captions required.
Fiction: Religious. Length: 1,000-1,500 words. Pays $20-60.

DISCOVERIES, 6401 The Paseo, Kansas City MO 64131. Editor: Mark York. 100% freelance written. For boys and girls 9-12. Weekly. Buys first rights and some second rights. "No comments can be made on rejected material." SASE.
Nonfiction: Articles on Christian faith, biography of Christian leaders, Bible manners and customs, family projects. Should be informal, spicy, and aimed at 4th grade vocabulary. Sharp photos and artwork help sell features. Submit complete ms. Length: 400-800 words. Pays 2¢/word.
Photos: Sometimes buys pix submitted with mss. Buys them with captions only if subject has appeal. Send quality photos, 5x7 or larger.
Fiction: Stories with Christian emphasis on high ideals, wholesome social relationships and activities, right choices, Sabbath observance, church loyalty, goodwill, and missions. Informal style. Submit complete ms. Length: 1,000-1,250 words. Pays 2¢/word.
Poetry: Nature and Christian thoughts or prayers, 4-16 lines. Pays $1 for each 4 lines.

DISCOVERY, Free Methodist Publishing House, 999 College Ave., Winona Lake IN 46590. (219)267-7161. Editor-in-Chief: Vera Bethel. 100% freelance written. For "57% girls, 43% boys, age 9-11; 48% city, 23% small towns." Weekly magazine; 8 pages. Estab. 1929. Circ. 15,000. Pays on acceptance. Rights purchased vary; may buy simultaneous rights, second serial rights or first North American serial rights. Submit seasonal/holiday material 3 months in advance. Simultaneous and previously published submissions OK. Reports in 4 weeks. Free sample copy and writer's guidelines.
Nonfiction: How-to (craft articles, how to train pets, party ideas, how to make gifts); informational (nature articles with pix); historical (short biographies except Lincoln and Washington); and personal experience (my favorite vacation, my pet, my hobby, etc.). Buys 150 mss/year. Submit complete ms. Length: 300-1,000 words. Pays 2¢/word. SASE must be enclosed; no return without it.
Photos: Purchased with accompanying ms. Captions required. Submit prints. Pays $5-10 for 8x10 b&w glossy prints. $2 for snapshots.
Fiction: Adventure, humorous, mystery and religious. Buys 100 mss/year. Submit complete ms. Length: 1,200-2,000 words. Pays 2¢/word. SASE must be enclosed; no return without it.
Poetry: Free verse; haiku; light verse; traditional; devotional; and nature. Buys 100/year. Limit submissions to batches of 5-6. Length: 4-16 lines. Pays 25¢/line.
How To Break In: "Send interview articles with children about their pets, their hobbies, a recent or special vacation—all with pix if possible. Kids like to read about other kids."

EBONY JR!, Johnson Publishing Co., 820 S. Michigan Ave., Chicago IL 60605. (312)786-7722. Managing Editor: Mary C. Lewis. For all children, but geared toward black children, ages 6-12. Monthly magazine (except bimonthly issues in June/July and August/September); 48 pages. Estab. 1973. Circ. 75,000. Pays on acceptance. Buys all rights, second serial (reprint) rights or first North American serial rights. Byline given. Submit seasonal/holiday material 4 months in advance. Previously published work OK. SASE. Acknowledges receipt of material in 3 weeks to 3 months. Sample copy 75¢; free writer's guidelines.

Nonfiction: How-to (make things, gifts and crafts; cooking articles); informational (science experiments or articles explaining how things are made or where things come from); historical (events or people in black history); inspirational (career articles showing children they can become whatever they want); interviews; personal experience (taken from child's point of view); profiles (of black Americans who have done great things—especially need articles on those who have not been recognized). Buys 3/issue. Query or submit complete ms. Length: 500-1,500 words. Pays $75-200.

Photos: Purchased with or without mss. Must be clear photos; no Instamatic prints. Pays $10-15/b&w; $25 maximum/color. Send prints and transparencies. Model release required.

Columns/Departments: Ebony Jr! News uses news of outstanding black children, reviews of books, movies, TV shows, of interest to children. Pays $25-100.

Fiction: Must be believable and include experiences black children can relate to. Adventure, fantasy, historical (stories on black musicians, singers, actors, astronomers, scientists, inventors, writers, politicians, leaders; any historical figures who can give black children positive images). Buys 2 mss/issue. Query or submit complete ms. Length: 300-1,500 words. Pays $75-200.

Poetry: Free verse, haiku, light verse, traditional forms of poetry. Buys 2/issue. Send poems in. No specific limit on number of submissions, but usually purchase no more than two at a time. Length: 5-50 lines; longer for stories in poetry form. Pays $15-100.

Fillers: Jokes, gags, anecdotes, newsbreaks and current events written at a child's level. Brain teasers, word games, crossword puzzles, guessing games, dot-to-dot games; games that are fun, yet educational. Pays $15-85.

THE FRIEND, 50 East North Temple, Salt Lake City UT 84150. Managing Editor: Lucile C. Reading. 75% freelance written. Appeals to children ages 4-12. Publication of the Church of Jesus Christ of Latter-day Saints. Issues feature different countries of the world, their cultures and children. Special issues: Christmas and Easter. Estab. 1970. Monthly. Circ. 200,000. Pays on acceptance. Free sample copy and guidelines for writers. "Submit only complete ms—no queries, please." Submit seasonal material 6 months in advance. SASE.

Nonfiction: Subjects of current interest, science, nature, pets, sports, foreign countries, and things to make and do. Length: 1,000 words maximum. Pays 3¢/word minimum.

Fiction: Seasonal and holiday stories; stories about other countries and their children. Wholesome and optimistic; high motive, plot, and action. Also simple, but suspense-filled mysteries. Character-building stories preferred. Length: 1,200 words maximum. Stories for younger children should not exceed 700 words. Pays 3¢/word minimum.

Poetry: Serious, humorous and holiday. Any form with child appeal. Pays 25¢/line minimum.

How To Break In: "Do you remember how it feels to be a child? Can you write stories that appeal to children ages four to twelve in today's world? We're interested in stories with an international flavor and those that focus on present day problems."

HIGHLIGHTS FOR CHILDREN, 803 Church St., Honesdale PA 18431. Editors: Walter B. Barbe and Caroline C. Myers. For children 2-12. Magazine published 11 times/year. Circ. 1,200,000. Buys all rights. Pays on acceptance. Free writers guidelines. Reports in 2 months. SASE.

Nonfiction: "We prefer factual features, including history and science, written by persons with rich background and mastery in their respective fields. Contributions always welcomed from new writers, especially science teachers, engineers, scientists, historians, etc., who can interpret to children useful, interesting and authentic facts, but not of the bizarre or 'Ripley' type; also writers who have lived abroad and can interpret well the ways of life, especially of children, in other countries, and who don't leave the impression that US ways are always the best. Sports material, biographies, articles about sports of interest to children. Direct, simple style, interesting content, without word embellishment; not rewritten from encyclopedias. State background and qualifications for writing factual articles submitted. Include references or sources of information. Length: 1,000 words maximum. Pays $50 minimum. Also buys original party plans for children 7-12, clearly described in 600-800 words, including drawings or sample of items to be illustrated. Also, novel but tested ideas in arts and crafts, with clear directions and made-up models. Projects must require only free or inexpensive, easy-to-obtain materials. Especially desirable if easy enough for early primary grades and appropriate to special seasons and days. Also, fingerplays with lots of action, easy for very young children to grasp and parents to dramatize, step-by-step, with hands and fingers. Avoid wordiness. Pays minimum $30 for party plans; $10 for arts and crafts ideas; $25 for fingerplays.

Fiction: Unusual, wholesome stories appealing to both girls and boys. Vivid, full of action and word-pictures, easy to illustrate. Seeks stories that the child 8-12 will eagerly read, and the child 2-6 will like to hear when read aloud. "We print no stories just to be read aloud; they must serve this two-fold purpose. We encourage authors not to hold themselves to controlled word lists. We especially need humorous stories, but we also need winter stories, urban stories, horse stories, and especially some mystery stories void of violence, stories introducing characters from different ethnic groups and holiday stories void of Santa Claus and the Easter Bunny. Avoid suggestion of material reward for upward striving. Moral teaching should be subtle. The main character should preferably overcome difficulties and frustrations through her or his own efforts. The story should leave a good moral and emotional residue. War, crime and violence are taboo. Some fanciful stories wanted." Length: 400-1,000 words. Pays 7¢/word minimum.

How To Break In: "We are pleased that many authors of children's literature report that their first published work was in the pages of *Highlights*. It is not our policy to consider fiction on the strength of the reputation of the author. We judge each submission on its own merits. With factual material, however, we do prefer either authorities in their fields or people with first-hand experience. In this manner we can avoid the encyclopedic article that merely restates information readily available elsewhere. A beginning writer should first become familiar with the type of material which *Highlights* publishes. We are most eager for easy stories for very young readers, but realize that this is probably the most difficult kind of writing."

HUMPTY DUMPTY'S MAGAZINE, Parents Magazine Enterprises, Inc., 52 Vanderbilt Ave., New York NY 10017. Editor: Michaela Muntean. For children 3-7. Magazine published monthly except June and August. Estab. 1952. Circ. 1,000,000. Rights purchased vary with author and material. Usually buys all rights. Pays kill fee. Byline given. Buys 25 mss/year. Pays on acceptance. Write for copy of guidelines for writers enclosing self-addressed, stamped envelope. No sample copies. Will consider photocopied submissions. Submit seasonal material 6-8 months in advance. Reports in 2-6 weeks. Submit complete ms. SASE.

Fiction: "Like stories with real-life children, not all suburban types; more urban material. One thing that's always anathema to me is the animated inanimate object. I also dislike cliche pieces about sugar girls with dolls at tea parties. We use old-fashioned stories and folk tales—but real children must be up-to-date. We're cautious about adaptations because we don't want to give our readers something they have seen before." Length: 1,000 words maximum. Pays $50 minimum.

Poetry: Rhyme or free verse. Length: 4-16 lines. Pays $10.

JACK AND JILL, 1100 Waterway Blvd., Box 567B, Indianapolis IN 46206. (317)634-1100. Editor: William Wagner. For children 8-12. Magazine published 10 times/year. Buys all rights. Byline given. Pays on publication. Sample copy 50¢; writer's guidelines for SASE. Submit seasonal material 8 months in advance. Reports in 8 weeks. May hold material seriously being considered for up to 6 months. "Material will not be returned unless accompanied by self-addressed envelope with sufficient postage."

Nonfiction and Photos: "*Jack and Jill's* primary purpose is to encourage children to read for pleasure. The editors are actively interested in material that will inform and instruct the young reader and challenge his intelligence, but it must first of all be enjoyable reading. Submissions should appeal to both boys and girls." Current needs are for "short factual articles concerned with nature, science, sports and other aspects of the child's world. Longer, more detailed features: 'My Father (or My Mother) Is a . . .'; first-person stories of life in other countries; some historical and biographical articles." When appropriate, articles should be accompanied by good 35mm color transparencies or sharp, contrasty b&w glossy prints. Pays approximately 3¢/word. Pays $2.50 for each b&w photo. Pays $5 each for color photo.

Fiction: "May include, but is not limited to, realistic stories, fantasy, adventure—set in the past, present, or future. All stories need plot structure, action and incident. Humor is highly desirable." Length: 500-1,200 words, short stories; 1,200 words/installment, serials of 2 or 3 parts. Pays approximately 3¢/word.

Fillers and Drama: "Short plays, puzzles (including varied kinds of word and crossword puzzles), poems, games, science projects and creative construction projects. Instructions for activities should be clearly and simply written and accompanied by models or diagram sketches. We are also in need of projects for our feature, For Carpenters Only. Projects should be of the type our young readers can construct with little or no help. Be sure to include all necessary information—materials needed, diagrams, etc. Whenever possible, all materials used in projects should be scrap materials that can be readily found around the workshop and home." Payment varies for fillers. Pays approximately 3¢/word for drama.

How To Break In: "We have been accused of using the same authors over and over again, not keeping an open mind when it comes to giving new authors a chance. To some extent, perhaps we do lean a little heavier toward veteran authors. But there is a good reason for this. Authors who have been published in *Jack and Jill* over and over again have shown us that they can write the kind of material we are looking for. They obtain *current* issues of the magazine and *study* them to find out our present needs, and they write in a style that is compatible with our current editorial policies. That is the reason we use them over and over; not because they have a special 'in.' We would reject a story by the world's best known author if it didn't fit our needs. After all, our young readers are more interested in reading a good story than they are in reading a good byline. We are constantly looking for new writers who have told a good story with an interesting slant—a story that is not full of outdated and time-worn expressions. If an author's material meets these requirements, then he stands as good a chance of getting published as anyone."

THE KINDERGARTNER, The United Methodist Publishing House, 201 8th Ave. S., Nashville TN 37202. Editor: Sonia Aguila. 98% freelance written. For children of kindergarten age. Monthly in weekly parts. Magazine; 4 pages/week. Estab. 1964. Circ. 84,000. Pays on acceptance. Buys all rights. Submit seasonal/holiday material 1½ years in advance. SASE. Reports in 4 weeks. Free sample copy and writer's guidelines for SASE.
Nonfiction: How-to (inexpensive craft ideas, simple science discoveries that kindergartners can experiment with, gift ideas, games); informational (about nature, animals, or community services such as doctors, plumbers, etc.); inspirational (prayers and Biblical stories); personal experience (any that would be of interest to a kindergarten age child); and photo feature. Buys 60 mss/year. Query. Length: 250-300 words. Pays 3-4¢/word.
Photos: Purchased with or without accompanying ms. Query. Pays $15-20 for 8x10 glossy b&w photos; $35-45 for 2¼x2¼ color transparencies. Model release required.
Fiction: Adventure; experimental ("in the area of Bible stories there often is not sufficient dialogue or background to make a story. Therefore, we add experiences typical of the historical period—but not necessarily authentic as to the Biblical account. Also, since the child learns by experience, we often use stories about children whose experiences are typical but at the same time fictitious"); humorous; and religious. Buys 60 mss/year. Query. Length: 200-300 words. Pays 3-4¢/word.
Poetry: Free verse and traditional. Buys 60/year. Query. Length: 8-12 lines. Pays 75¢-$1/line.

MY DEVOTIONS, Concordia Publishing House, 3558 S. Jefferson Ave., St. Louis MO 63118. For young Christians, 8-13. Buys little freelance material. Guidelines for #10 SASE. Material is rejected here because of poor writing, lack of logic, and lack of Lutheran theology. Byline given. Pays $10.00/printed devotion.

NURSERY DAYS, The United Methodist Publishing House, 201 8th Ave. S., Nashville TN 37202. Editor-in-Chief: Dr. Ewart Watts. Children's Editor: Leo Kisrow. 100% freelance written. A story paper for children 2-4 years of age, distributed through Sunday school classes of the United Methodist Church and Christian Church. Weekly magazine; 4 pages. Circ. 125,000. Pays on acceptance. Buys all rights. Submit seasonal/holiday material 12 months in advance. SASE. Reports in 1-2 months. Free sample copy and writer's guidelines.
Nonfiction: Doris Willis, Nursery Editor. Informational (Biblical, nature, seasonal); inspirational (Biblical, church, family, prayers, etc.); and personal experience (familiar to children 2-4 years old). Buys 1 ms/issue. Length: 250 words maximum. Pays 4¢/word.
Photos: Dave Dawson, Photo Editor. Purchased without accompanying ms. Send prints or transparencies. Pays $15-30 for 8x10 b&w glossy prints; $25-125 for 35mm color transparencies. Model release required.
Fiction: Religious (Jesus, God, prayer, church, Bible). Buys 1 ms/issue. Submit complete ms. Length: 250 words. Pays 4¢/word.
Poetry: Doris Willis, Nursery Editor. Free verse and light verse. Buys 3-4/issue. Length: 4-12 lines. Pays 50¢/line.

ODYSSEY, AstroMedia Corp., 411 E. Mason St., Milwaukee WI 53202. Editor: Nancy Mack. Emphasizes astronomy and outer space for children of ages 8-12. Monthly magazine; 32 pages. Estab. January 1979. Circ. 18,000. Pays on publication. Buys all or first North American serial rights. Submit seasonal/holiday material 3-4 months in advance. Photocopied and published submissions OK. SASE. Reports in 4-6 weeks. Free sample copy,
Nonfiction: General interest (astronomy, outer space, spacecraft, planets, stars, etc.); how-to (astronomy projects, experiments, etc.); and photo feature (spacecraft, planets, stars, etc.). "We do not want science fiction articles." Buys 2-3 mss/issue. Query with clips of previously published work. Length: 750-2,000 words. Pays $100.
Photos: State availability of photos. Pays $7.50 for 8x10 b&w glossy prints; $10 for any size color transparencies. Buys one-time rights. Captions preferred; model release required.

ON THE LINE, Mennonite Publishing House, 616 Walnut Ave., Scottdale PA 15683.

(412)887-8500. Editor: Helen Alderfer. For children 10-14. Weekly magazine; 8 pages. Estab. 1970. Circ. 17,650. Pays on acceptance. Buys one-time rights. Byline given. Submit seasonal/holiday material 6 months in advance. Simultaneous, photocopied and previously published submissions OK. SASE. Reports in 2 weeks.

Nonfiction: How-to (things to make with easy-to-get materials); and informational (500-word articles on wonders of nature, people who have made outstanding contributions). Buys 25-40 mss/issue. Length: 500-1,200 words. Pays $10-24.

Photos: Photos purchased with or without accompanying ms. Pays $5-25 for 8x10 b&w photos. Total purchase price for ms includes payment for photos.

Columns/Departments: Fiction, adventure, humorous and religious. Buys 25 mss/year. Send complete ms. Length: 800-1,200 words. Pays $15-24.

Poetry: Light verse and religious. Length: 3-12 lines. Pays $5-15.

OUR LITTLE FRIEND, PRIMARY TREASURE, Pacific Press Publishing Association, 1350 Villa St., Mountain View CA 94042. (415)961-2323, ext. 335. Editor: Louis Schutter. Published weekly for youngsters of the Seventh-day Adventist church. *Our Little Friend* is for children ages 2-6; *Primary Treasure*, 7-9. Buys first serial rights (international); or second serial (reprint) rights (international). Byline given. "The payment we make is for one magazine right. In most cases, it is for the first one. But we make payment for second and third rights also." Query on serial-length stories. Will accept simultaneous submissions. "We do not purchase material during June, July and August." SASE.

Nonfiction and Fiction: All stories must be based on fact, written in story form. True to life, character-building stories; written from viewpoint of child and giving emphasis to lessons of life needed for Christian living. True to life is emphasized here more than plot. Nature or science articles, but no fantasy; science must be very simple. All material should be educational or informative and stress moral attitude and religious principle. Honesty, truthfulness, courtesy, health and temperance, along with stories of heroism, adventure, nature and safety are included in the overall planning of the editorial program. *Our Little Friend* uses stories from 700-1,000 words. *Primary Treasure*, 600-1,200 words. Fictionalized Bible stories are not used. Pays 1¢/word.

Photos, Poetry and Fillers: 8x10 glossy prints for cover. "Photo payment: sliding scale according to quality." Juvenile poetry; up to 12 lines. Puzzles.

PRIMARY TREASURE, Pacific Press Publishing Association, 1350 Villa St., Mountain View CA 94042. See *Our Little Friend*.

R-A-D-A-R, 8121 Hamilton Ave., Cincinnati OH 45231. (513)931-4050. Editor: Dana Eynon. 75% freelance written. For children 8-11 in Christian Sunday schools. Weekly. Rights purchased vary with author and material. Buys first serial rights or second serial (reprint) rights. Occasionally overstocked. Pays on acceptance. Will send a sample copy to a writer on request. Submit seasonal material 12 months in advance. Reports in 4-6 weeks. SASE.

Nonfiction: Articles on hobbies and handicrafts, nature (preferably illustrated), famous people, seasonal subjects, etc., written from a Christian viewpoint. Length: 500-1,000 words. Pays 2¢/word maximum.

Fiction: Short stories of heroism, adventure, travel, mystery, animals and biography. True or possible plots stressing clean, wholesome, Christian character-building ideas, but not preachy. Make prayer, church attendance, Christian living a natural part of the story. "We correlate our fiction and other features with a definite Bible lesson." Length: 900-1,200 words; 2,000 words complete length for 2-part stories. Pays 2¢/word maximum.

Fillers: Bible puzzles and quizzes. Pays 2¢/word maximum.

How To Break In: "We give the same consideration to a new writer as we do to regular contributors. We just checked our files, and this past year purchased mss from 35 new writers. We look for Christian character-building stories, filled with action and conversation, based on true-to-life situations; and articles on a wide range of subjects, filled with accurate facts, and written from a Christian viewpoint. Writers may send for list of themes coming up, and submit stories that correlate with the lesson stressed in a particular issue."

Rejects: Talking animal stories, science fiction, Halloween stories, first-person stories from an adult's viewpoint, non-Biblical puzzles, and articles about saints of the opposite, or historical figures with an absence or religious implication.

RANGER RICK'S NATURE MAGAZINE, National Wildlife Federation, 1412 16th St. NW, Washington DC 20036. (202)797-6800. Editorial Director: Trudy D. Farrand. For "children from ages 4-12, with the greatest concentration in the 7-10 age bracket." Monthly. Buys all world rights. Byline given but "ocasionally, on very brief pieces, we will identify author by name at the end. Contributions to regular departments are not usually bylined." Pays on acceptance. Anything written with a specific month in mind should be in our hands at least 10 months before that issue date." Query. SASE.

Nonfiction and Photos: "Articles may be written on any phase of nature, conservation, environmental problems, or natural science. Do not try to humanize wildlife in features. We limit the attributing of human qualities to animals in our regular feature, Ranger Rick and His Friends. The publisher, National Wildlife Federation, discourages wildlife pets." Length: 900 words maximum. Pays from $10-250 depending on length. "Photographs, when used, are paid for separately. It is not necessary that illustrations accompany material."

STORY FRIENDS, Mennonite Publishing House, 616 Walnut Ave., Scottdale PA 15683. (412)887-8500. Editor: Marjorie Waybill. For children 4-9 years of age. Published monthly in weekly parts. Not copyrighted. Byline given. Pays on acceptance. Submit seasonal/holiday material 6 months in advance of issue date. SASE. Free sample copy.

Nonfiction and Fiction: "The over-arching purpose of this publication is to portray Jesus as a friend and helper—a friend who cares about each happy and sad experience in the child's life. Persons who know Jesus have values which affect every area of their lives. Stories of everyday experiences at home, at church, in school or at play can provide models of these values. Of special importance are relationships, patterns of forgiveness, respect, honesty, trust and caring. Prefer short stories that are exciting but plausible, offer a wide variety of settings, acquaint children with a wide range of friends, and mirror the joys, fears, temptations and successes of the readers. Length: 300-800 words. Pays 2½-3¢/word.

Poetry: Traditional and free verse. Length: 3-12 lines. Pays $5.

TOUCH, Box 7244, Grand Rapids MI 49510. Editor: Joanne Ilbrink. 50-60% freelance written. Purpose of publication is to show girls ages 8-15 how God is at work in their lives and in the world around them. Monthly magazine; 24 pages. Estab. 1970. Circ. 14,000. Pays on acceptance. Buys simultaneous, second serial and first North American serial rights. Byline given. Submit seasonal/holiday material 3-5 months in advance. Simultaneous, photocopied or previously published submissions OK. SASE. Reports in 3 weeks. Free sample copy and writer's guidelines.

Nonfiction: How-to (crafts girls can make easily and inexpensively); informational (write for issue themes); humor (needs much more); inspirational (seasonal and holiday); interview; travel; personal experience (avoid the testimony approach) and photo feature (query first). "Because our magazine is published around a monthly theme, requesting the letter we send out twice a year to our established freelancers would be most helpful. We do not want easy solutions or quick character changes from bad to good. No pietistic characters. Constant mention of God is not necessary, if the moral tone of the story is positive. We do not want stories that always have a good ending." Buys 20 mss/year. Submit complete ms. Length: 100-1,000 words. Pays 2¢/word, depending on the amount of editing.

Photos: Purchased with or without ms. Submit 3x5 clear glossy prints. B&w only. Pays $5-25.

Fiction: Adventure (that girls could experience in their home towns or places they might realistically visit); humorous; mystery (believable only); romance (stories that deal with awakening awareness of boys are appreciated); suspense (can be serialized); and religious (nothing preachy). Buys 20 mss/year. Submit complete ms. Length: 300-1,500 words. Pays 2¢/word.

Poetry: Free verse, haiku, light verse and traditional. Buys 10/year. Length: 50 lines maximum. Pays $5 minimum.

Fillers: Puzzles, short humor and cartoons. Buys 6/issue. Pays $2.50-7.

TRAILS, Pioneer Girls, Inc., Box 788, Wheaton IL 60187. Editor: Laura Alden. Assistant Editor: Lorraine Mulligan. Emphasizes Christian education for girls, 6-12, most of whom are enrolled in the Pioneer Girls club program. It is kept general in content so it will appeal to a wider audience. Bimonthly magazine; 32 pages. Estab. 1961. Circ. 23,000. Pays on acceptance. Buys first, second, or simultaneous rights. Byline given. Submit seasonal/holiday material 6 months in advance. SASE. Reports in 4-8 weeks. Sample copy $1.50; free writer's guidelines.

Nonfiction: How-to (crafts and puzzles); humor; informational; inspirational; and biography. Query or submit complete ms. Length: 800-1,500 words. Pays $25-35.

Fiction: Adventure, fantasy, historical, humorous, mainstream, mystery and religious. Buys 6 mss/issue. Query or submit complete ms. Length: 800-1,500 words. Pays $25-40.

Fillers: Jokes, gags, cartoons and short humor. Buys 4/issue. Pays $5-15.

VIDEO-PRESSE, 3965 est, boul. Henri-Bourassa, Montreal, Quebec, Canada H1H 1L1. Editor: Pierre Guimar. For "French Canadian boys and girls of 8 to 15." Monthly. Circ.

45,000. Buys all rights. Buys 20-30 mss/year. Pays on publication. Will send a sample copy to a writer on request. Reports in 2 weeks. SAE and International Reply Coupons.

Nonfiction: "Material with a French-Canadian background. The articles have to be written in French, and must appeal to children aged 8 to 15." Buys how-to, personal experience articles, interviews, profiles, humor, historical articles, photo features and travel pieces. Length: 1,500-3,000 words. Pays 3¢/word.

Photos: B&w glossy prints, color transparencies; with captions only. Pays $9.95.

Fillers: Puzzles, jokes and short humor.

THE VINE, 201 8th Ave. S., Nashville TN 37202. (615)749-6369. Editor: Betty M. Buerki. Publication of The United Methodist Church. For children in grades 3 and 4. Monthly in weekly parts. Buys all rights. Byline given. Pays on acceptance. Free sample copy. Deadlines are 18 months prior to publication date. Reports in 1 month. SASE.

Nonfiction and Photos: Articles about science, nature, animals, customs in other countries, and other subjects of interest to readers. Length: approximately 500 words. Pays 3¢/word. Uses photo features. Prefers 8x10 glossy prints, but also uses transparencies.

Fiction: Historical stories should be true to their setting. Stories which make a point about values should not sound moralistic. Also accepts stories written just for fun. Length: 500-800 words. Writers must know children. Fictionalized Bible stories must be based on careful research. Pays 3¢/word.

Poetry: Accepts light verse or religious verse. Pays 50¢-$1/line.

Fillers: Puzzles, quizzes, and matching games. Pays 3¢ minimum/word. Pays more for clever arrangements. Puzzles, such as crossword, mazes, etc.; pays $4.50-12.50.

WEE WIDSOM, Unity Village MO 64065. Editor: Colleen Zuck. Magazine published 10 times/year. A Christian magazine for boys and girls aged 13 and under dedicated to the truths: that each person is a child of God and that as a child of God each person has an inner source of wisdom, power, love and health from their Father that can be applied in a practical manner to every-day life." Free sample copy, editorial policy on request. Buys first North American serial rights. Byline given. Pays on acceptance. SASE.

Nonfiction: Entertaining nature articles or projects, activities to encourage appreciation of all life. Pays 3¢/word minimum.

Fiction: "Character-building stories that encourage a positive self-image. Although entertaining enough to hold the interest of the older child, they should be readable by the third grader. Characters should be appealing but realistic; plots should be plausible, and all stories should be told in a forthright manner but without preaching. Life itself combines fun and humor with its more serious lessons, and our most interesting and helpful stories do the same thing. Language should be universal, avoiding the Sunday school image." Length: 500-800 words. Pay 3¢/word minimum.

Poetry: Very limited. Pays 50¢/line. Prefers short, seasonal or humorous poems. Also buys rhymed prose for "read alouds" and pays $15 minimum.

Fillers: Pays $3 minimum for puzzles and games.

WEEKLY BIBLE READER, Standard Publishing, 8121 Hamilton Ave., Cincinnati OH 45231. Editor: Barbara Cottrell. For children 6-7 years of age. Quarterly in weekly parts; 4 pages. Estab. 1965. Circ. 95,459. Buys first serial rights. Byline given. Pays on acceptance. Will send free sample copy to writer on request. Write for copy of guidelines for writers. Submit seasonal material 18 months in advance. Reports in 1 month. Query or submit complete ms. SASE.

Nonfiction, Photos and Poetry, and Fillers: Religious-oriented material. Stories with morals, short fiction (150-250 words), fun poems, puzzles and other interesting items. Emphasis is on material that can be read by children themselves. "No fanciful material, superstitions or luck, things that talk, fairies, Easter rabbits, or Santa Claus. We'd like to see material on things children can do to help others; to be pleasing to God, etc." Do not send Bible stories or Buzzy Bee items, as these are staff-written from preplanned outlines. Length for fiction and nonfiction: 300 words maximum. Pays $1-10. B&w photos purchased with or without mss. Pays $10. Light verse. Length: 12 lines maximum. Very simple puzzles for this age group. Pays 50¢-$10.

WONDER TIME, 6401 The Paseo, Kansas City MO 64131. (816)333-7000. Editor: Evelyn Beals. Published weekly by Church of the Nazarene for children ages 6-8. Free sample copy. Buys first rights. Byline given. Pays on acceptance. SASE.

Fiction and Poetry: Buys stories portraying Christian attitudes without being preachy. Uses stories for special days—stories teaching honesty, truthfulness, helpfulness or other important spiritual truths, and avoiding symbolism. "God should be spoken of as our Father who loves and cares for us; Jesus, as our Lord and Savior." Length: 400-650 words. Pays 2¢/word on acceptance. Uses verse which has seasonal or Christian emphasis. Length: 8-12 lines. Pays 25¢/line minimum.

THE YOUNG CRUSADER, 1730 Chicago Ave., Evanston IL 60201. (312)864-1396. Managing Editor: Michael Vitucci. For children ages 6-12. Monthly. Not copyrighted. Pays on publication. Free sample copy. Submit seasonal material 6 months in advance. SASE.
Nonfiction and Fiction: Uses articles on total abstinence, character-building, love of animals, Christian principles and world friendship. Also science stories. Length: 650-800 words. Pays ½¢/word.

YOUNG JUDAEAN, 817 Broadway, New York NY 10003. (212)260-4700. Editor: Barbara Gingold. For Jewish children aged 8-13, and members of Young Judaea. Publication of Hadassah Zionist Youth Commission. All material must be on some Jewish theme. Special issues for Jewish/Israeli holidays, or particular Jewish themes which vary from year to year; for example, Hassidim, Holocaust, etc. Estab. 1916. Monthly (November through June). Circ. 8,000. Buys all rights, but will reassign rights to author after publication; or buys first North American serial rights; buys first serial rights. Byline given. Buys 10-20 mss/year. Payment in contributor's copies or small token payment. Sample copy and annual list of themes for 50¢. Prefers complete ms. Will consider photocopied and simultaneous submissions. Submit seasonal material 4 months in advance. Reports in 3 months. SASE.
Nonfiction and Photos: "Articles about Jewish-American life, Jewish historical and international interest. Israel and Zionist-oriented material. Try to awaken kids' Jewish consciousness by creative approach to Jewish history and religion, ethics and culture, politics and current events. Style can be didactic, but not patronizing." Informational (300-1,000 words), how-to (300-500 words), personal experience, interview, humor, historical, think articles, photo, travel, and reviews (book, theater and movies). Length: 500-1,200 words. Pays $5-25. "Token payments only, due to miniscule budget."
Photos: Photos purchased with accompanying mss. Captions required. 5x7 maximum. B&w preferred. Payment included with fee for article. Illustrations also accepted.
Fiction: Experimental, mainstream, mystery, suspense, adventure, science fiction, fantasy, humorous, religious and historical fiction. Length: 500-1,000 words. Pays $5-25. Must be of specific Jewish interest.
Poetry and Fillers: Traditional forms, blank verse, free verse, avant-garde forms and light verse. Poetry themes must relate to subject matter of magazine. Length: 25-100 lines. Pays $5-15. Newsbreaks, jokes and short humor purchased for $5.
How To Break In: "Think of an aspect of Jewish history/religion/culture which can be handled in a fresh, imaginative way, fictionally or factually. Don't preach; inform and entertain."

YOUNG MUSICIANS, 127 9th Ave. N., Nashville TN 37234. Editor: Jimmy R. Key. 5-10% freelance written. For boys and girls age 9-11, and their leaders in children's choirs in Southern Baptist churches (and some other churches). Monthly magazine; 52 pages. Estab. 1963. Buys all rights. Buys 5-6 mss/year. Pays on acceptance. Free sample copy. No photocopied or simultaneous submissions. Query. SASE.
Nonfiction: "All material is slanted for use with and by children in church choirs. Music study materials related to study units in *The Music Leader*. Ours is a curriculum magazine written almost entirely on assignment." Informational, how-to, historical. Length: 300-900 words. Pays approximately 3¢/word.
Fiction: Child-centered stories related to church music and music in the home. Length: 600-900 words. Pays approximately 2½¢/word.

Literary and "Little"

Many of the publications in this category do not pay except in contributor's copies. Nonpaying markets are included because they offer the writer a vehicle for expression that often can't be found in the commercial press. Many talented American writers found first publication in magazines like these. Writers are reminded that many "littles" remain at one address for a limited time; others are notoriously unbusinesslike in their reporting on or returning of submissions. University-affiliated reviews are conscientious about manuscripts but some of these are also slow in replying to queries or returning submissions.

Magazines that specialize in publishing poetry or poetry criticism are found in the Poetry category. Many "little" publications that offer contributors a forum for expression of minority opinions are classified in the listings for Alternative Publications.

THE AMERICAN BOOK REVIEW, The Writers' Review, Inc., Box 188, New York NY 10003. Editors: Charles Russell and Suzanne Zavrian. For anyone interested in contemporary literature. Bimonthly tabloid; 20 pages. Estab. December 1977. Circ. 9,000. Pays in copies. Buys all rights. Photocopied submissions OK. SASE. Reports in 2 weeks. Free sample copy and writer's guidelines.
Nonfiction: Book Reviews only. Query. Length: 300-1,500 words.

AMERICAN NOTES AND QUERIES, Erasmus Press, 225 Culpepper, Lexington KY 40502. (606)266-1058. Editor: John Cutler. Ten times a year. No payment. Byline given. SASE.
Nonfiction: Historical, artistic, literary, bibliographical, linguistic and folklore matters; scholarly book reviews and reviews of foreign reference books; items of unusual antiquarian interest.

AMERICAN QUARTERLY, Van Pelt Library, University of Pennsylvania, 3420 Walnut St., Philadelphia PA 19104. (215)243-6252. Editor: Dr. Bruce Kuklick. For college professors, teachers, museum directors, researchers, students, college and high school libraries. Readers professionally interested in American studies. Acquires all rights. Byline given. Does not pay. Reports in 2-4 months. SASE and 2 copies of article.
Nonfiction and Photos: Scholarly, interdisciplinary articles on American studies, about 20 pages. Bibliography issue contains bibliographic essays, dissertation listings, American Studies programs. Occasionally uses photos.

THE AMERICAN SCHOLAR, 1811 Q St. NW, Washington DC 20009. (202)265-3808. Editor: Joseph Epstein. "For college-educated, mid-20s and older, rather intellectual in orientation and interests." Quarterly magazine, 144 pages. Estab. 1932. Circ. 32,000. Buys all rights, but will reassign rights to author after publication. Byline given. Buys 20-30 mss/year. Pays on publication. Sample copy $2; free writer's guidelines. Will consider photocopied submissions. No simultaneous submissions. Reports in 3 weeks. Query, with samples, if possible. SASE.
Nonfiction and Poetry: "The aim of the *Scholar* is to fill the gap between the learned journals and the good magazines for a popular audience. We are interested not so much in the definitive analysis as in the lucid and creative exploration of what is going on in the fields of science, art, religion, politics, and national and foreign affairs. Advances in science particularly interest us." Informational, interview, profile, historical, think articles, and book reviews. Length: 3,500-4,000 words. Pays $250 per article and $50 for reviews. Pays $50 for poetry on any theme. Approximately 5 poems published per issue. "We would like to see poetry that develops an image or a thought or event, without the use of a single cliche or contrived archaism. The most hackneyed subject matter is self-conscious love; the most tired verse is iambic pentameter with rhyming endings. The usual length of our poems is 10-12 lines. From 1-4 poems may be submitted at one time; *no more* for a careful reading. We urge prospective contributors to familiarize themselves with the type of poetry we have published by looking at the magazine."

THE ANTIGONISH REVIEW, St. Francis Xavier University, Antigonish, Nova Scotia, Canada B2G 1C0. Editor: R.J. MacSween. For "those with literary interests." Quarterly magazine; 100 pages. Circ. 500. Pays in copies only. Not copyrighted. Photocopied submissions OK. SASE. Reports in 6 weeks. Free sample copy.
Nonfiction: Literary articles of general interest. Submit complete ms.
Fiction: Fantasy; experimental; and mainstream. No erotica. Submit complete ms.
Poetry: Avant-garde and traditional. Uses 30/issue.

ANTIOCH REVIEW, Box 148, Yellow Springs OH 45387. Editor: Robert S. Fogarty. For general, literary and academic audience. Quarterly. Buys all rights. Byline given. Pays on publication. Reports in 4-6 weeks. SASE.
Nonfiction: "Contemporaneous articles in the humanities and social sciences, politics, economics, literature and all areas of broad intellectual concern. Somewhat scholarly, but never pedantic in style, eschewing all professional jargon. Lively, distinctive prose insisted upon." Length: 2,000-8,000 words. Pays $8/published page.
Fiction: No limitations on style or content. Pays $8/published page.
Poetry: No light or inspirational verse. Contributors should be familiar with the magazine before submitting. Rarely uses traditional, or rhymed verse.

APALACHEE QUARTERLY, Box 20106, Tallahassee FL 32304. Collective Editorship. For an artistic/critical audience; 20-60 years of age. Quarterly magazine; 44-60 pages. Estab. 1972. Circ. 400. Acquires all rights. Uses 80 mss/year. Pays in contributor's copies. Sample copy for $1. No simultaneous submissions. Reports in 1-10 weeks. Submit complete ms. SASE.

Nonfiction and Photos: Emphasis is on creative writing, rather than criticism. Uses interviews and reviews of fiction and poetry. Length: 300-3,000 words. B&w photos purchased without ms. Captions optional.

Fiction and Poetry: Short stories, experimental or mainstream. Length: 300-6,000 words. Traditional forms of poetry, blank verse, free verse, avant-garde forms. Length: 3-100 lines.

ARION, University Professors, Boston University, Room 607, 745 Commonwealth Ave., Boston MA 02215. (617)353-4025. Editors-in-Chief: William Arrowsmith and D. S. Carne-Ross. "Journal of humanities and classics for persons interested in literature of the classical periods of Greece and Rome." Estab. 1962. Quarterly journal; 128 pages. Circ. 1,000. No payment. Acquires all rights, but will reassign rights to author after publication. Byline given. Sample copy for $3. Query or submit complete ms. Will consider photocopied submissions. Reports in 3 months. SASE.

Nonfiction: Uses articles on literature, Greece and Rome. The articles printed are in the form of literary essays. "We deal with the classics as literature, rather than philology." Length: 10-40 pages.

THE ARK RIVER REVIEW, c/o A. Sobin, English Department, Wichita State University, Wichita KS 67208. Editors-in-Chief: Jonathan Katz, A.G. Sobin. 100% freelance written. For "the well-educated, college age and above; poets, writers, and the readers of contemporary poetry and fiction." Published 3-4 times a year. Magazine; 52 pages. Estab. 1971. Circ. 1,000. Pays on publication. Buys all rights, but will reassign to author following publication. Byline given. Photocopied submissions OK. Reports in 1-3 weeks. Sample copy $1.50

Fiction: "Conventional fiction stands little chance. We are interested only in highly innovative and sophisticated material. Type and subject matter is far less important to us than the way in which the story is written. We are looking for freshness in approach, style and language. We suggest strongly that you read back issues before submitting." Buys 3 mss/issue. Send complete ms. No length limit (no novels). Pays $40/story and contributor's copies.

Poetry: "Poetry should be substantial, intelligent and serious (this doesn't mean it can't be funny). Any form is OK, though we almost never print rhyming poems." Buys 30/issue. Limit submissions to batches of 5. No length limits. Pays $10/poem.

How To Break In: "Your work should demonstrate to us that you know what has gone on in literature in the last 50 years, and that you're working toward something better."

ART AND LITERARY DIGEST, Summer address: Madoc-Tweed Art Centre, Tweed, Ontario, Canada. Winter address: 1109 N. Betty Lane, Clearwater FL 33515. Editor: Roy Cadwell. "Our readers are the public and former students of the Art and Writing Centre. As an educational publication we welcome new writers who have something to say and want to see their name in print and get paid for it." Quarterly. Estab. 1969. Circ. 1,000. Not copyrighted. Byline given. Pays on publication. Will send sample copy for $1. "Photocopied mss are accepted, but not returned. You may submit elsewhere after 30 days. Original mss must be accompanied by return envelope and unattached postage." SASE.

Nonfiction and Fiction: How-to articles, inspirational, humorous, travel and personality improvement. "Good writing is essential with integrity and knowledge. Ask yourself, 'What have I to say?' Slant toward students and alumni. Our readers want to be informed and, hopefully, learn how to live better." "I was there" type of travel articles are appreciated. Length: 500 words. Pays $5. "We need digests of articles on art, music, poetry and literary subjects." Pays 1¢/word.

Fillers: Ideas and short humor. Length: 500 words maximum. Pays 1¢/word.

Poetry: All types. Free verse, light verse, blank verse, traditional and avant-garde. Length: usually 12 lines, but no limit. Payment in contributor's copies.

ASPECT, 66 Rogers Ave., Somerville MA 02144. Collective Editorship. 90% freelance written. Primarily for people interested in new and experimental, as well as traditional and widely accepted writing. Many readers are themselves involved in the field of writing. Triannual magazine; 100 pages. Estab. 1969. Circ. 1000. Pays in copies. Acquires first North American serial and one-time anthology rights. Photocopied submissions OK. SASE. Reports in 1-3 months. Sample copy $2.00.

Nonfiction: Informational; historical (social, political or literary subjects); humor; interview (with emerging, exciting poets and writers or people involved in alternative literary publishing); personal experience; personal opinion (social, political or literary subjects); photo feature (social, political, literary, historical focus). Buys 6-8 mss/year. Query. Length: 5,000 words maximum. Pays in copies.

Columns/Departments: News & Reviews (short news pieces about the field of alternative literary publishing; magazine and small press manuscript needs; Reviews of little magazines and small press books). Uses 15/issue. Submit complete ms. Length: 400 words for news; 300-1,000 for reviews.

Fiction: Adventure; experimental; historical; humorous; mainstream; and science fiction.

Poetry: Avant-garde; free verse; traditional. Uses 30/issue. Limit submissions to batches of 3-6.

How To Break In: "Subject area is broad, but tends to focus most on literature, and secondly, politics, broadly defined. We are a mature (in growth stage), independent literary magazine that still publishes, almost entirely, work by unknowns. Know what you're doing, and do it very well."

ASPEN ANTHOLOGY, Aspen Leaves, Inc., Box 3185, Aspen CO 81611. (303)925-8750. Editor: J.D. Muller. For poets, short fiction writers, novelists, teachers and literate readers. Biannual magazine; 130 pages. Estab. 1973. Circ. 1,000. Pays in contributor's copies. Acquires all rights, but may reassign following publication. Phone queries OK. SASE. Reports in 4 weeks. Sample copy $3.

Fiction: Address Fiction Editors. Experimental. Uses 2-4 mss/issue. Submit complete ms. Length to 10,000 words. Pays in 2 copies.

Poetry: Address Poetry Editors. Any style. Uses 30-40/issue. No length limit. Pays in 2 copies.

Tips: Selection cycles usually end September 15 and March 15.

BIOGRAPHY: An Interdisciplinary Quarterly, Biographical Research Center and University Press of Hawaii, 2840 Kolowalu St., Honolulu HI 96822. (808)948-8188. Editor: George Simson. Associate Editor: Joseph Kau. Review Editor: Anthony Friedson. Emphasizes biographical studies. Quarterly magazine; 96 pages. Estab. January 1978. Circ. 375. Holds all rights unless negotiated otherwise. Byline given. Phone queries OK. Photocopied submissions OK. SASE. Reports in 3 months. Sample copy $3.50 in US; $4, elsewhere; free writer's guidelines.

Nonfiction: All scholarship: interdisciplinary, historical, psychological, literary, interview, personal experience and profile. Query or send complete ms. Length: 2,500-10,000 words.

Photos: Must be camera-ready. State availability of photos. Offers no additional payment for photos accepted with accompanying ms. Captions required.

Columns/Departments: Yearly index, annual bibliography and communications. Query or send complete ms.

BLACK AMERICAN LITERATURE FORUM, Indiana State University, Parsons Hall 237, Terre Haute IN 47809. (812)232-6311, ext. 2760. Editor-in-Chief: Joe Weixlmann. 90% freelance written. Emphasizes black American literature. Quarterly magazine; 40 pages. Estab. 1967. Circ. 850. Pays in copies. Acquires simultaneous rights. Byline given. Phone queries OK. Submit seasonal/holiday material at least 3 months in advance. Simultaneous and photocopied submissions OK. SASE. Reports in 3 months. Free sample copy and writer's guidelines.

Nonfiction: "We publish scholarly criticism and bibliographies of black American writers, also pedagogical articles and curricular evaluations. We also use poetry by black writers and original graphic work by black artists."

Photos: Sketches and photos used without accompanying ms. Pays $15/graphic work.

BLACK SCHOLAR, Box 908, Sausalito CA 94965. Editor: Robert Allen. Mainly for black professionals, educators, and students. Monthly journal of black studies and research, 64 pages. Estab. 1969. Circ. 20,000. Acquires all rights. Uses about 60 mss per year. Payment in contributor's copies. Free sample copy and writer's guidelines. Will consider photocopied submissions. Will consider simultaneous submissions, "but must be so informed." Reports in 2 months. Query about upcoming topics. SASE.

Nonfiction: "We seek essays discussing issues affecting the black community (education, health, economics, psychology, culture, literature, etc.). Essays should be reasoned and well-documented. Each issue is organized around a specific topic: black education, health, prisons, family, etc., with a variety of viewpoints." Informational, interview, profile, historical, think articles, and book and film reviews. Length: 1,500-7,000 words.

THE BLACK WARRIOR REVIEW, The University of Alabama, Box 2936, University AL 35486. (205)348-7839. Editor-in-Chief: Rodney Simard. Emphasizes fiction and poetry. Semiannual magazine; 128 pages. Estab. 1974. Circ. 1,000. Pays in copies. Acquires all rights, but may reassign following publication. Phone queries OK. Submit seasonal material for fall by Oct. 1; for spring by Feb. 1. SASE. Reports in 2 months. Sample copy $2.50.

Nonfiction: Interview and criticism of contemporary literature. Buys 4 mss/year. Query.
Fiction: Ross White, fiction editor. Experimental and mainstream. "Acceptance depends on quality, not subject matter, genre or treatment." Buys 1-4 mss/issue. Submit complete ms.
Poetry: Leslie Nail, poetry editor. Avant-garde, free verse and traditional. Buys 20/issue.

BLACKBERRY, Box 4757, Albuquerque NM 81796. Editor: Jeanne Shannon. 95% freelance written. For readers interested in literature, especially poetry. Estab. 1975. Quarterly. Circ. 100. Acquires first North American serial rights. Uses about 90 mss a year. No payment, but contributors may buy copies of issues containing their work at reduced rate. Sample copy $2. Photocopied and simultaneous submissions OK. Reports in 2 weeks. SASE.
Nonfiction and Poetry: "We use a few reviews, primarily of poetry books and magazines. How-to articles; i.e., lessons in poetry and fiction writing. Personal experiences of writers in learning their craft. Interviews with writers and poets." Length: 800 words maximum. Traditional and avant-garde forms of poetry; blank verse, free verse and haiku. Length: 30 lines maximum.

BOOK ARTS, The Center for Book Arts, 15 Bleecker St., New York NY 10012. (212)260-6860. Managing Editor: Kathleen Weldon. Emphasizes bookbinding and exploring the arts of the book. Quarterly newsletter; 8 pages. Estab. 1974. Circ. 2,000. Pays in copies. Acquires all rights, but may reassign following publication. Byline given. Submit seasonal/holiday material 3 months in advance. Simultaneous, photocopied and previously published submissions OK. Reports in 2 months. Free sample copy.
Nonfiction: Expose (on banning books in schools, other censorship, etc.); historical (bookburnings, looking at the history of watermarks and any other book experience); interview (with book artists) and technical (e.g., "William Blake's Method of Printing"). Query. Pays in copies.

BOOK FORUM, Hudson River Press, 38 E. 76th St., New York NY 10021. (212)861-8328. Editor-in-Chief: Marshall Hayes. Editorial Director: Marilyn Wood. Emphasizes contemporary literature, the arts and foreign affairs for "intellectually sophisticated and knowledgeable professionals: university-level academics, writers, people in government, and the professions." Quarterly magazine; 192 pages. Estab. 1974. Circ. 5,200. Pays on publication. Buys all rights, but may reassign following publication. Pays 33⅓% kill fee. Byline given. Phone queries OK. Photocopied submissions OK. SASE. Reports in 2 weeks. Sample copy $3.
Nonfiction: "We seek highly literate essays that would appeal to the same readership as, say, the *London Times Literary Supplement* or *Encounter*. Our readers are interested in professionally written, highly literate and informative essays, profiles and reviews in literature, the arts, behavior, and foreign and public affairs. We cannot use material designed for a mass readership, nor for the counter-culture. Think of us as an Eastern establishment, somewhat snobbish literary and public affairs journal and you will have it right." General interest; interview (with select contemporary writers); opinion (some personal essays which exhibit an exceptional level of literary skill and originality of viewpoint); profiles and essays about contemporary writers. Buys 20 mss/year. Query. Length: 1,400-3,000 words. Pays $25-75.

THE CALIFORNIA QUARTERLY, 100 Sproul, University of California, Davis CA 95616. Editor: Elliot Gilbert. 95% freelance written. "Addressed to an audience of educated, literary and general readers, interested in good writing on a variety of subjects, but emphasis is on poetry and fiction." Quarterly. Usually buys first North American serial rights. Reports in 4-6 weeks but the editorial office is closed from July 1 to September 30. SASE.
Fiction and Nonfiction: Department Editor: Diane Johnson. "Short fiction of quality with emphasis on stylistic distinction; contemporary themes, any subject." Experimental, mainstream. Length: 8,000 words. Original, critical articles, interviews and book reviews. Length: 8,000 words maximum. Pays $2/published page.
Poetry: Department Editor: Sandra M. Gilbert. "Original, all types; any subject appropriate for genuine poetic expression; any length suitable to subject." Pays $3/published page.

CANADIAN FICTION MAGAZINE, Box 946, Station F, Toronto, Ontario, Canada M4Y 2N9. Editor-in-Chief: Geoffrey Hancock. 95% freelance written. Emphasizes Canadian fiction, short stories and novel excerpts. Quarterly magazine; 148 pages. Estab. 1971. Circ. 1,800. Pays on publication. Buys first North American serial rights. Byline given. SASE (Canadian stamps). Reports in 4-6 weeks. Sample copy $3.75 (in Canadian funds).
Nonfiction: Interview (must have a definite purpose, both as biography and as a critical tool focusing on problems and techniques) and book reviews (Canadian fiction only). Buys 35 mss/year. Query. Length: 1,000-3,000 words. Pays $10/printed page plus one-year subscription.

Photos: Purchased on assignment. Send prints. Pays $5 for 5x7 b&w glossy prints; $20 for cover. Model release required.
Fiction: "No restrictions on subject matter or theme. We are open to experimental and speculative fiction as well as traditional forms. Style content and form are the author's prerogative. We also publish self-contained sections of novel-in-progress and French-Canadian fiction in translation. Please note that *CFM* is an anthology devoted exclusively to Canadian fiction. We publish only the works of writers and artists residing in Canada and Canadians living abroad."

THE CANADIAN FORUM, 70 The Esplarade, 3rd Floor, Toronto, Ontario, Canada M5E 1R2. Editor-in-Chief: Sam Sulecki. Managing Editor: Susan Glover. Emphasizes Canadian arts, letters, affairs for a highly educated readership interested in and committed to Canadian affairs. Monthly magazine; 36 pages. Estab. 1920. Circ. 10,000. Pays on publication. Buys one-time rights. Pays 50% kill fee. Byline given. SASE. Reports in 1-2 months. Sample copy $1.25
Nonfiction: Canadian political and literary commentary. Must be intellectual. Preferred subjects are research, politics, sociology and art. Length: 2,000-3,000 words.
Poetry: Avant-garde, free verse, haiku, light verse and traditional.
How To Break In: "We accept very little material from the US and are not a 'commercial' market for writers. However, we have published poetry and occasional articles about politics, economics, social analysis, etc., written by Americans."

CANADIAN LITERATURE, University of British Columbia, Vancouver, British Columbia, Canada V6T 1W5. Editor: W.H. New. Quarterly. Circ. 2,500. No fiction, fillers or photos. Not copyrighted. Pays on publication. Query. SAE and International Reply Coupons.
Nonfiction: Articles of high quality on Canadian books and writers only. Articles should be scholarly and readable. Length: 2,000-5,500 words. Pays $5/printed page.

CAROLINA QUARTERLY, Greenlaw Hall, O66-A, University of North Carolina, Chapel Hill NC 27514. (919)933-0244. Editor: Dorothy Combs Hill. 3 issues per year. "*Carolina Quarterly* has first rights to any submission until after publication is copyrighted. Following publication rights may be reassigned to the author. Permission to reprint given at any time on request. Pays on publication. Sample copy $3. Reports in 3-4 months. Submissions should be marked Fiction or Poetry on envelope. SASE or ms will not be returned.
Fiction: "Quality, primary emphasis is on stylistic achievement as well as character development and interesting point of view. A place for both the new writer and the professional. Mainly interested in new writers who demonstrate excellence in both control of material and sophistication of language. We publish a significant number of unsolicited mss." Pays $3/printed page. A contest in fiction and poetry for new writers, with cash prizes and publication, is held annually Septembe 15th to December 1st. Winners appear in spring issue. Only major restriction is that entrant not have published a book-length ms in the field of entry.
Poetry: "Quality; poems must have original subjects or points of view and demonstrate maturity in technique and in use of language. Popular or conventional verse not wanted." Pays $5/poem.
How To Break In: "The writer, first of all, needs experience in writing even if unpublished. We publish only those pieces that show evidence of craft. Second, the writer would benefit from perusal of recent copy of magazine to appreciate the type of thing we publish. After that, it's a matter of quality and editorial taste."

CHELSEA, Box 5880, Grand Central Station, New York NY 10017. Editor: Sonia Raiziss. Acquires first North American serial rights, but returns rights to author on request. Payment in copies. SASE.
Nonfiction, Fiction and Poetry: "Poetry of high quality; short fiction; occasional nonfiction articles, interviews and special issues. Accent on style. Also interested in fresh, contemporary translations."
How To Break In: "Best thing to do: Read several issues of the magazine to get the tone/content, themes, penchants and range of contributions."

CHICAGO REVIEW, University of Chicago, Faculty Exchange Box C, Chicago IL 60637. (312)753-3571. Editors: Michael Gorman and Maggie Hivnor. Readership interested in contemporary literatures and criticisms. Quarterly magazine; 140 pages. Estab. 1946. Circ. 3,000. Pays in copies. Acquires all rights, but may reassign following publication. Photocopied submissions OK. SASE. Reports in 3 months. Sample copy $2.85, plus postage.
Nonfiction: Linda S. Bergman and Ellen Grinde, nonfiction editors. Informational and

interview. "We consider essays on and reviews of contemporary writing and the arts." Submit complete ms. Length: 500-5,000 words.

Fiction: John Morse and Giudi Weiss, fiction editors. Experimental and mainstream. "We welcome the work of younger, less established writers." Uses 3-12/issue. Submit complete ms.

Poetry: Catherine Mouly, Mara Anne Tapp, poetry editors. Avant-garde; free verse; translations; and traditional. Uses 12/year. Limit submissions to batches of 3-5.

CHICAGO SUN-TIMES SHOW/BOOK WEEK, *Chicago Sun-Times*, 401 N. Wabash Ave., Chicago IL 60611. (312)321-2131. Editor: Jean Adelsman. Emphasizes entertainment, arts and books. Weekly newspaper; 10 pages. Circ. 750,000. Pays on publication. Buys all rights. Pays negotiable kill fee, except on speculative articles. Submit seasonal/holiday material at least 2 months in advance. Photocopied and previously published work OK. SASE. Reports in 2 weeks.

Nonfiction: "Articles and essays dealing with all the serious and lively arts—movies, theater (pro, semipro, amateur, foreign), filmmakers, painting, sculpture, music (all fields, from classical to rock—we have regular columnist in these fields). Our Book Week columns have from 5 to 10 reviews, mostly assigned. Material has to be very good because we have our own regular staffers who write almost every week. Writing must be tight. No warmed-over stuff of fan magazine type. No high-schoolish literary themes." Query. Length: 500-800 words. Pays $50-100.

CHILDREN'S LITERATURE, The Children's Literature Foundation, Box 370, Windham Center CT 06280. (203)456-1900. Editor: Francelia Butler. Managing Editor: John C. Wandell. Annual journal; 250-300 pages. Estab. 1972. Circ. 3,500. Pays in reprints. Byline given. Phone queries OK. Submit seasonal/holiday material 1 year in advance. SASE. Reports in 1 month.

Nonfiction: Scholarly or critical essays. Uses 20 mss/issue. Query or send complete ms. Length: 7,500 words.

Photos: State availability of photos. Uses 4x5 or 8x10 b&w glossy prints. Captions and permission to publish required.

Columns/Departments: Book Review Articles (send to David L. Greene, Chairman, English Department, Piedmont College, Demorest GA). Uses 20/year. Query. Length: 3,000 words. Open to suggestions for new columns/department.

CIMARRON REVIEW, Oklahoma State University, Stillwater OK 74074. Editor-in-Chief: Neil J. Hackett. Managing Editor: Jeanne Adams Wray. 100% freelance written. For educated readers, college- and university-oriented. Quarterly magazine, small and humanistic, 72 pages, (6x9). Estab. 1967. Circ. 500. Acquires all rights. Byline given. Payment in contributor's copies. Will send free sample copy to writer on request. Reports in 2 weeks. Submit only complete ms. SASE.

Nonfiction and Fiction: "Poetry, short stories, articles and essays. We wish to publish work of vision and high quality dealing with a wide variety of themes. Occasional theme issues. We are particularly interested in articles and essays on topics of contemporary concern and significance."

COLLAGE, 2444 Moorpark Ave., Suite 214, San Jose CA 95128. (408)279.4224. Editor: Timothy Seidler. Literary Arts Editor: Cheryl Kidder. Monthly tabloid; 24 pages. Estab. May 1977. Circ. 100,000. Phone queries OK. Byline given. Submit seasonal/holiday material 3 months in advance. Simultaneous and photocopied submissions OK. SASE. Reports in 3-5 weeks. Free sample copy.

Nonfiction: Informational; interview; personal opinion; and profile. Uses 24 mss/year. Query or submit complete ms. Length: 1,000-3,500 words. Pays 2¢/word.

Photos: Uses b&w prints. Pays $5 minimum.

Columns/Departments: Movie Reviews; Book Reviews; and Record reviews. Uses 72 mss/year. Submit complete ms. Length: 50-500 words. Pays 2¢/word. Open to suggestions for new columns/departments.

Fiction: Adventure; fantasy; humorous; mainstream; mystery; science fiction; and suspense. Uses 12 mss/year. Submit complete ms. Length: 1,200-3,500 words. Pays 2¢/word.

Poetry: Free verse and avant-garde. Uses 72/year. Submit up to 20 poems. Pays 2¢/word.

THE COLORADO QUARTERLY, Hellems 134C, University of Colorado, Boulder CO 80309. Editor: Walter G. Simon. Quarterly magazine. Estab. 1952. Circ. 850. Buys all rights, "but liberal on returning rights." Byline given. Reports in 3-4 weeks. SASE. Publishes Award Issue each spring; devoted to one author or artist. Carries $1,000 award. Must be able to fill 1 issue. Deadline: December 31. Also publishes bonus issues sponsored by private businesses or

individuals. "These contain materials felt worthy of publication but not in keeping with the format of regular *Quarterly* issues. Payment determined by staff—up to $500. 4-5 issues scheduled this year." Sample copy $2.50; mention *Writer's Market* in request.
Nonfiction: Articles written by experts on any subject for the general educated reader in nontechnical, nonacademic style. Length: 4,000-6,000 words. Pays $50.
Fiction: Interested in all styles. Length: 4,000-6,000 words. Pays $50.
Poetry: Interested in all styles. Pays $20.

CONFRONTATION, Long Island University, 1 University Plaza, Brooklyn NY 11201. (212)834-6170. Editor-in-Chief: Martin Tucker. 90% freelance written. Emphasizes creative writing for a "literate, educated, college-graduate audience." Semiannual magazine; 190 pages. Estab. 1968. Circ. 2,000. Pays on publication. Buys all rights, but will reassign following publication. Pays 50% kill fee. Byline given. Phone queries OK. Simultaneous and photocopied submissions OK. SASE. Reports in 2 months. Sample copy $1.
Nonfiction: "Articles are, basically, commissioned essays on a specific subject." Memoirs wanted. Buys 6 mss/year. Query. Length: 1,000-3,000 words. Pays $10-50.
Fiction: Ken Bernard, Fiction Editor. Fantasy, experimental, humorous, mainstream. Buys 20 mss/year. Submit complete ms. Length: "completely open." Pays $15-75.
Poetry: W. Palmer, Poetry Editor. Avant-garde, free verse, haiku, light verse, traditional. Buys 40/year. Limit submissions to batches of 10. No length requirement. Pays $5-40.

CONNECTICUT FIRESIDE AND REVIEW OF BOOKS, Box 5293, Hamden CT 06518. (203)248-1023. Editor-in-Chief: Albert E. Callan. Emphasizes writing and literary subjects for an intelligent, well-educated readership interested in writing. Quarterly magazine; 120 pages. Estab. 1972. Circ. 1,500. Pays in copies on publication. Acquires first North American serial rights. Byline given. Phone queries OK. Simultaneous, photocopied and previously published submissions OK. Reports in 2 weeks. Sample copy $1.50.
Nonfiction: Historical (have had an article about a Connecticut person, usually literary, in each issue so far); and humor. Uses 4 mss/year. Submit complete ms. Length: 1,000-2,500 words.
Photos: "We would use good art photos if offered, otherwise we take our own. We are interested in anything of artistic nature."
Columns/Departments: L.R. Langley, Reviews Editor. "We have about 20 pages of tradebook reviews/issue. Also 5 pages of small press books and poetry chapbooks." Length: open.
Fiction: Confession; experimental; fantasy; historical; humorous; mystery; and suspense. Uses 16-20/year. Submit complete ms. Length: 1,500-5,000 words.
Poetry: Avant-garde; free verse; haiku; light verse; and traditional. Uses 160/year. Length: 30 lines or less.
How To Break In: "We need articles about Connecticut literary people, or literary people associated with Connecticut in some way, or with New England. Such articles should have a fresh viewpoint, or new information to offer. We also need good serious fiction, nothing commercial."

CONTEMPORARY LITERATURE, Dept. of English, Helen C. White Hall, University of Wisconsin, Madison WI 53706. Editor: L.S. Dembo. Quarterly. "All details should conform to those recommended by the *MLA Style Sheet*." Does not encourage contributions from freelance writers without academic credentials. SASE.
Nonfiction: A scholarly journal which examines various aspects of contemporary literature, from generalizations on current trends and themes, to studies of a writer, his technique, and/or his work, to other specialized treatments or studies in modern literature.

CREAM CITY REVIEW, Department of English, Box 413, University of Wisconsin-Milwaukee, Milwaukee WI 53201. Editor-in-Chief: Debra Kay Vest. 100% freelance written. Emphasizes poetry, fiction, criticism, reviews, graphics and interviews. "We have existed very locally for 4 years, and are now under the auspices of the English Department, and will soon be distributed over a 5-state area of the Midwest. Libraries, universities, high schools, etc., subscribe." Published 3 times/year. Magazine; 65-120 pages. Estab. 1973. Circ. 700 at present. Pays in copies. Obtains all rights, but may reassign following publication. Byline given. Direct each submission to the attention of the appropriate department: Fiction, Poetry, Nonfiction or Art. Submit seasonal/holiday material 1 month in advance of issue date. Photocopied and previously published submissions OK. SASE. Reports in 12-16 weeks. Sample copy $2.00; free writer's guidelines; mention *Writer's Market* in request.
Nonfiction: General interest (of or pertaining to established writers or writing); think pieces; historical; humor; interview (of literary or creative interest); personal opinion (as in book reviews, reviews of readings, etc.); and profile (of writers past and present). "Religious,

patriotic and sentimental things are not for us—our readership is always excited by the newness of what we try to print." Submit complete ms. Length: 3,000 words maximum.

Fiction: Adventure; experimental (as long as there is a discerniable beginning, middle and end); fantasy; historical; humorous; mainstream; suspense; condensed novels; and serialized novels. Uses 5-7 mss/issue. Submit complete ms. Length: 15 pages maximum.

Poetry: All types, from sonnets to prose poems. Uses 90-150/year. Limit submissions to batches of 4.

Art and Graphics: B&w photos, lithographs, cartoons, pencil drawing an cover design if possible. All art should be proportioned for a 6x9 format (to cover one full page).

CREATIVE PITTSBURGH, Box 7346, Pittsbourgh PA 15213. Managing Editor: G. Ulrich Musinsky. Assistant Editors: Michael O'Conner and Joe McFadden. For a readership 18 years old and up, ranging from the general public to the academia. Triannual magazine; 52-72 pages. Estab. 1976. Pays in copies. Buys all rights, but may reassign following publication. SASE. Reports on queries in 2 weeks; complete mss in 6 months. Sample copy $2.75.

Nonfiction, Fiction, and Poetry: "*Creative Pittsburgh* is a journal designed to publish contemporary literature that major literary magazines pass by. The contention of our staff is that major American literary magazines, in an effort to keep up with the times, are overlooking the type of short stories, essays and poetry that coincide with the traditions of the media. We do not limit our publication to new fads in literature or specified styles. Our criteria are open, requiring material of high quality. We believe it takes more than words, trends or styles to be literary. *Creative Pittsburgh* is a magazine that is read." Submit complete ms. Length: 500-6,000 words. Payment in contributor's copies.

CRITIQUE: STUDIES IN MODERN FICTION, Department of English, Georgia Institute of Technology, Atlanta GA 30332. Editor: James Dean Young. For college and university teachers and students. Estab. 1956. Triannual. Circ. 1,500. Acquires all rights. Pays in contributor's copies. Submit complete original ms. Writers should follow the *MLA Style Sheet*. Reports in 4 to 6 months. SASE.

Nonfiction: "Critical essays on writers of contemporary fiction. We prefer essays on writers from any country who are alive and without great reputations. We only rarely publish essays on well-known, established writers such as James, Conrad, Joyce and Faulkner." Uses informational articles and interviews. Length: 4,000-8,000 words.

DARK HORSE, 102 Beacon St., Somerville MA 02143. Editors: Jane Barnes, June Gross. Estab. 1974. Quarterly. Circ. 3,000. Uses about 200 mss/year. Pays in contributor's copies for poetry; modest fee for fiction. Sample copy $1.50. No photocopied or simultaneous submissions. Reports ("frankly, supportively") in 12 weeks. SASE.

Nonfiction and Photos: "We welcome intelligent reviews of poetry and fiction books; of prisoners, gay men and lesbians, minorities, news about literary events in New England; small press publishing. Length: 600-1,200 words. B&w photos and drawings used.

Fiction and Poetry: Experimental and mainstream. No science fiction, fantasy or serialized novels. Length: 8,000 words maximum. "Traditional and avant-garde forms of poetry—no Hallmark card verse or sentimental or sexist doggeral. Fold poems together. Identify each page with name and address."

Tips: "Include a business-sized envelope folded in 3. We highly recommend reading a sample issue before submitting. All correspondents must send SASE. Type all submissions; 1 poem/page. Include bio."

DE KALB LITERARY ARTS JOURNAL, 555 N. Indian Creek Dr., Clarkston GA 30021. (404)292-1520. Editor: William S. Newman. 90% freelance written. For those interested in poetry, fiction and/or art. Quarterly. Magazine; 100 pages. Estab. 1966. Circ. 5,000. Acquires first serial rights. Pays in contributor's copies. Sample copy for $1.75 (cost plus postage). "Look for announcements of special issues." Seeking material for National Poets Issue. Submit complete ms. Reports in 2-3 months. SASE.

Nonfiction, Fiction, Photos and Poetry: Subject matter is unrestricted. "We consider all types of nonfiction and fiction. Our decisions are based on quality of material. Traditional, blank verse, free verse, light verse and avant-garde forms of poetry." B&w photos are used with mss; 8x10 glossy prints preferred.

THE DENVER QUARTERLY, University of Denver, Denver CO 80208. (303)753-2869. Editor-in-Chief: Leland H. Chambers. For an intellectual/university readership. Quarterly magazine; 125-160 pages. Estab. 1965. Circ. 800. Pays on publication. Buys first North American serial rights. Phone queries OK. Photocopied (if explained as not simultaneous) submissions OK. SASE. Reports in 4 weeks. Sample copy $2. "Each issue focuses on a topic of contemporary concern. For example, Winter, 1979: Mexican letters since 1968; future issues: Australian literature, American translators, and the '70s novel. Submissions need not coincide with these topics."

Nonfiction: Historical, humor, personal opinion and profile. Buys 10-12 mss/year. Send complete ms. Pays $5/printed page.

Fiction: Adventure, fantasy, experimental, historical, humorous, mainstream and science fiction. Buys 8-10 mss/year. Send complete ms. Pays $5/printed page.

Poetry: Avant-garde, free verse and traditional. Buys 30 poems/year. Send poems. Pays $10/printed page.

How To Break In: "We decide on the basis of quality only. Prior publication is irrelevant. Promising material, even though rejected, will receive some personal comment from the editor; some material can be revised to meet our standards through such criticism."

DESCANT, Texas Christian University Press, Department of English, TCU, Fort Worth TX 76129. (817)921-7240. Editor-in-Chief: Betsy Feagan Colquitt. Quarterly magazine; 48 pages. Estab. 1956. Circ. 650. Pays in contributor's copies on publication. Acquires first rights. Phone queries OK. Simultaneous and photocopied submissions OK. SASE. Reports in 6 weeks. Sample copy $1.50.

Nonfiction: Informational (articles used are literary criticism, with examination of modern literature as principal concern of the essay). Uses 4 mss/year. Submit complete ms. Length: 3,000-5,000 words.

Fiction: Fantasy, confession, experimental, historical. Uses 10-12 mss/year. Submit complete ms. Length: 2,000-6,000 words.

Poetry: Avant-garde, free verse, traditional. Uses 40/year. Limit submissions to batches of 6. Length: 10-40 lines.

THE DRAMA REVIEW, New York University, 51 W. 4th St., Room 300, New York NY 10012. (212)598-2597. Editor-in-Chief: Michael Kirby. 75% freelance written. Emphasizes avant-garde performance art for professors, students and the general theater and dance-going public as well as professional practitioners in the performing arts. Quarterly magazine; 144 pages. Estab. 1955. Circ. 10,000. Pays on publication. Reassigns rights following publication. Phone queries OK. Submit seasonal/holiday material 4 months in advance. Photocopied and previously published (if published in another language) submissions OK. SASE. Reports in 3 months. Sample copy $4. Free writer's guidelines.

Nonfiction: Terry Helbing, managing editor. Historical (the historical avant-garde in any performance art, translations of previously unpublished plays, etc.) and informational (documentation of a particular performance). Buys 10-20 mss/issue. Query. Pays 1¢/word for translations; 2¢/word for other material.

Photos: Terry Helbing, Managing Editor. Photos purchased with or without accompanying ms or on assignment. Captions required. Pays $10 for b&w photos. No additional payment for photos accepted with accompanying ms.

Rejects: "No criticism in the sense of value judgments—we are not interested in the author's opinions. We are only interested in documentation theory and analysis."

EVENT, Douglas College, Box 2503, New Westminster, British Columbia, Canada V3L 5B2. For "those interested in literature and writing." Biannual magazine; 176-192 pages. Estab. 1970. Circ. 800. Uses 65-75 mss/year. Small payment and contributor's copies. Byline given. Photocopied and simultaneous submissions OK. Reports in 4 months. Submit complete ms. SAE and International Reply Coupons.

Nonfiction, Fiction, Poetry and Drama: "High-quality work." Reviews, essays, the novella, the short story, poetry and drama.

EXPLORATIONS IN ETHNIC STUDIES, National Association of Interdisciplinary Ethnic Studies (NAIES), 101 Main Hall, University of Wisconsin-La Crosse, La Crosse WI 54601. (608)785-8225. Editor: George E. Carter. Emphasizes the study of ethnicity, ethnic groups, intergroup relations, and the cultural life of ethnic minorities. Biannual (January and July) journal; 90 pages. Estab. January 1978. Circ. 300. Phone queries OK. Byline given. Submit seasonal/holiday material 2 months in advance. Simultaneous and photocopied submissions OK. SASE. Reports in 3 weeks (queries); 6 months (mss). Free sample copy.

Nonfiction: Research (involving pursuit of explorations and solutions within the context of oppression as it relates to the human experience). Send complete ms.

Columns/Departments: "Within the field of ethnic/minority studies: book and film reviews, new programs, bibiographies, employment notices, conferences, fellowships, research opportunities, letters to the editor and NAIES news." Query or send complete ms. Length: 1,500 words.

Poetry: "To reflect intent of journal." Submit in batches of 2. Length: 10 words.

THE FAULT, 33513 6th St., Union City CA 94587. (415)487-1383. Editor: Terrence Ames. Emphasizes innovative literature for the small press collector, libraries, anyone interested in experimental and contemporary works of art. Semiannual magazine; 125 pages. Estab. 1971. Circ. 500. Pays in copies. Buys one-time and reprint rights. Byline given. Phone queries OK. Submit seasonal/holiday material 2 months in advance. Photocopied and previously published submissions OK. SASE. Reports in 4 weeks. Sample copy $1.50. Free writer's guidelines.

Photos: Purchased without accompanying manuscript. Send prints.

Fiction: Science fiction, dada, visual, erotica, experimental, fantasy and mainstream. Uses 10 mss/year. Send complete ms. Length: 100-5,000 words.

Poetry: Avant-garde and free verse. Uses 40 poems/year. Limit submissions to batches of 10. Length: 2-100.

Fillers: Collages. Uses 10/year. Length: 1-100 words.

How To Break In: "No need for formula fiction filled with cliches and unimaginative writing; poetry with end rhymes filled with abstractions and archaic ideas; any work that lacks style, invention, originality. Each issue is constructed around a particular theme, subject or style. Send SASE for future guidelines."

FICTION, City College, 138th St. and Convent Ave., New York NY 10031. (212)690-8170. Editor: Mark Mirsky. Published by a cooperative of writers. For individual subscribers of all ages; and college libraries, bookstores and college bookstores. Published 2 times a year. Book; 150-250 pages. Estab. 1972. Circ. 5,000. Acquires all rights, but will reassign rights to author after publication. Byline given. Payment in contributor's copies only. Submit complete ms. Mss not accepted between June 1st and September 15th. Allow 3 months for report, hopefully less." SASE.

Fiction: "We publish only fiction." Length: 15 pages or less.

Photos: Photos purchased without accompanying ms. Photo Editor: Inger Grytting.

FICTION INTERNATIONAL, St. Lawrence University, Canton NY 13617. Editor: Joe David Bellamy. For "readers interested in the best writing by talented writers working in new forms or working in old forms in especially fruitful new ways; readers interested in contemporary literary developments and possibilities." Published annually in the spring—150-300 pages in perfect-bound book format. Pays on publication. Copyrighted; rights revert to author. Reports in 1-3 months. SASE.

Fiction: Study publication. Previous contributors include: Asa Baber, Russell Banks, Jonathan Baumbach, T. Coraghessan Boyle, Rosellen Brown, Jerry Bumpus, David Madden, Joyce Carol Oates, Ronald Sukenick, Gordon Weaver and Robley Wilson Jr. Highly selective. Not an easy market for unsophisticated writers. No length limitations but "rarely use short-shorts or mss over 30 pages." Portions of novels acceptable if self-contained enough for independent publication.

Interviews: Seeking interviews with well-known or innovative fiction writers "able to discuss their ideas and aesthetic predilections intelligently."

Reviews: Review Editor: G. E. Murray. By assignment only. No payment. *Fiction International* also sponsors the annual $1,000 St. Lawrence Award for Fiction for an outstanding first collection of short fiction published in North America and the annual *Fiction International*/St. Lawrence University Writers' Conference, held at the University's conference center at Saranac Lake in the Adirondacks and featuring writers such as Margaret Atwood, Russell Banks, E. L. Doctorow, Gail Godwin, Daniel Halpern, Joyce Carol Oates, Robie Macauley, Charles Simmons and James Tate.

FIRELANDS ARTS REVIEW, Firelands College, Huron OH 44839. Editor: Joel Rudinger. For general educated audience. Annual magazine, 80 pages. Estab. 1972. Circ. 1,000. Acquires first serial rights. Byline given. Uses 50 mss a year. Pays in copies. Will send sample copy to writer for $2.30. Submit only complete ms. Accepts mss from October to March of each year. Reports in 4-8 weeks. SASE.

Fiction: "Any style and approach and subject matter as long as the quality is professional and mature. Length: 3,000 words maximum. Will accept short prose sketches and characterizations sensitive to the human condition. We need stories that display humor and irony."

Photos: 5x7 or 8x10 b&w prints. Will consider any subject or style. Unusual perspective, high contrast, experimental materials are of interest as well as fresh approaches to traditional photography.

Poetry: Any subject, theme, style, length.

FORMS, The Review of Anthropos Theophoros, Box 3379. San Francisco CA 94119. (415)768-4295. Editor-in-Chief: Emily McCormick. 90% freelance written. For adults interested in ideas, especially as related to all forms of art. Quarterly magazine; 50 pages. Estab. 1976. Circ. 200. Pays on publication. Buys one-time rights. Phone queries OK. Submit seasonal/holiday material 2 months in advance of issue date. Simultaneous and photocopied submissions OK. SASE. Reports in 6 weeks. Sample copy $1; mention *Writer's Market* in request.
Nonfiction: Expose, general interest, humor, historical, interview, personal opinion, profile, travel "and music, art, and book reviews of more than topical interest." Buys 5 mss/issue. Submit complete ms. Length: 500-5,000 words. Pays from contributor's copies to $50 maximum.
Fiction: Adventure; experimental; fantasy; humorous; and mainstream. Buys 4 mss/issue. Submit complete ms. Length: 500-5,000 words. Pays in contributor's copies to $50 maximum.
Poetry: Avant-garde, free verse, haiku, light verse and traditional. Buys 6/issue. Limit submissions to batches of 10. Length 4-200 words. Pays in contributor's copies minimum to $25 maximum.

FOUR QUARTERS, LeSalle College, Olney Ave. at 20th St., Philadelphia PA 19141. Editor: John C. Kleis. For college-educated audience with literary interests. Quarterly. Circ. 700. Buys all rights; grants permission to reprint on request. Pays on publication. Sample copy 50¢. Reports in 6-8 weeks. "Do not submit during July and August." SASE.
Nonfiction: "Lively critical articles on particular authors or specific works. Think pieces on history, politics, the arts. Prefer footnotes incorporated. Style must be literate, lively, free of jargon and pedantry." Buys 4 mss/year. Length: 1,500-5,000 words. Pay is $25 maximum.
Fiction: "Technical mastery gets our attention and respect immediately. We admire writers who use the language with precision, economy and imagination. But fine writing for its own sake is unsatisfying unless it can lead the reader to some insight into the complexity of the human condition without falling into heavy-handed didacticism." Buys 10-12 mss/year. Length: 2,000-5,000 words. Pays $25 maximum.
Poetry: "Quality poetry from 8-32 lines. Some shorter ones used as fillers without payment." Buys 30-40/year. Pay is $5 maximum.

GRAFFITI, English Department, Box 418, Lenoir Rhyne College, Hickory NC 28601. Editor: Kermit Turner. For writers, college students, faculty and all persons interested in literature. Semiannual magazine; 44 pages. Estab. 1972. Circ. 250. Acquires first serial rights. Byline given. All rights return to author after publication. Uses 6 to 8 short story mss a year and about 80 poems. Payment in contributor's copies. Sample copy $1. No photocopied or simultaneous submissions. Reports on material accepted for publication in 6 months. Returns rejected material in 4 months. Submit complete ms. SASE.
Fiction: Short stories, experimental and mainstream. Length: 2,000-5,000 words.
Poetry: Traditional forms and free verse. Will consider any length.

THE GREAT LAKES REVIEW, Central Michigan University, Box 122, Anspach Hall, Mt. Pleasant MI 48859. Editors: Martha Brown, Richard Primeau. Mostly for scholars and academics who are interested in Midwest studies. Semi annual magazine, 100 pages. Estab. 1974. Circ. 1,000. "We require no rights outside of copyright." Payment in contributor's copies. Query or submit complete ms. Reports in 6 months. SASE.
Nonfiction, Fiction and Poetry: Scholarly articles, bibliographies and poetry features.

GREAT RIVER REVIEW, 211 W. 7th St., Winona MN 55987. (507)454-1212. Editors: Emilio DeGrazia and Sandra Bennett. Published 2 times/year. Magazine; 150 pages. Estab. November 1977. Pays on publication. Submit seasonal material 3-4 months in advance of issue dates. Photocopied submissions OK. SASE. Reports in 2-4 months. Sample copy $2.75.
Nonfiction: Articles on midwestern authors. Submit complete ms. Pays $20-50.
Fiction: Experimental and mainstream. "We are not interested in most mass-circulation type fiction. We give priority to Minnesota writers but seek work outside the region." Buys 6 mss/issue. Submit complete ms. Length: 2,000-10,000 words. Pays $20-50; $200 award for best fiction each issue.
Poetry: Avant-garde; free verse; and traditional. No newspaper poetry. Buys 30 poems/issue. Limit submissions to batches of 10-15. Pays modest rates for poetry.

HANGING LOOSE, 231 Wyckoff St., Brooklyn NY 11217. Editors: Dick Lourie, Emmett

Jarrett, Ron Schreiber, Robert Hershon. Quarterly. Acquires first serial rights. Payment in copies. Will send sample copy to writer for $1.50. Reports in 2-3 months. SASE.

Poetry and Fiction: Fresh, energetic poems of any length. Excellent quality. Experimental fiction. "Space for fiction very limited."

Tips: "We strongly suggest that writers read the magazine before sending work, to save our time and theirs. Also note that artwork and book mss are by invitation only."

HEIRS MAGAZINE, 657 Mission St., Room 205, San Francisco CA 94105. Editor: Alfred Durand Garcia. Poetry Editor: Ernest J. Oswald. For educators, artists, students, professionals, poets, libraries and public institutions; specifically, people interested in art and literature viewed from a multi-cultural perspective. Quarterly magazine; 80 pages. Estab. 1968. Circ. 2,000. Rights acquired vary with author and material. Pays negotiable kill fee. Byline given. May acquire first North American serial rights, first serial rights, or all rights. Token monetary payment and/or copies. Sample copy $3; free writer's guidelines. Will consider photocopied submissions. No simultaneous submissions. Reports in 6-8 weeks. Submit complete ms. SASE.

Nonfiction and Photos: Art criticism, feature articles on art and artists. Must be written from a humanistic perspective. Book reviews. Reviews of Third World literature and women's literature. B&w photos used with or without mss. "Because of our unique format, we suggest that writers see a sample copy first since we publish major articles in English, Spanish and Chinese." Length: 1,500 words.

Fiction and Poetry: Experimental fiction. Length: 1,500 words. Blank verse, free verse and avant-garde forms of poetry.

THE HUDSON REVIEW, 65 E. 55th St., New York NY 10022. Managing Editor: Helen Handley. Quarterly. Pays on publication. Reports in 6-8 weeks. SASE for return of submissions.

Nonfiction, Fiction and Poetry: Uses "quality fiction up to 10,000 words, articles up to 8,000 words; translations, reviews and poetry." Pays 2½¢/word for prose, and 50¢/line for poetry.

IN A NUTSHELL, Hibiscus Press, Box 22248, Sacramento CA 95822. Editor-in-Chief: Margaret Wensrich. 99% freelance written. Emphasizes poetry and fiction. Quarterly magazine; 24 pages. Estab. 1975. Circ. 5,000. Pays on publication. Buys one-time rights. Submit seasonal/holiday material 6 months in advance. Photocopied submissions OK. SASE. Reports in 4 weeks. Sample copy $2; writer's guidelines for SASE.

Fiction: Adventure, fantasy, confession, experimental, historical, humorous, mystery, romance, suspense, mainstream, science fiction and western. Buys 12 mss/year. Submit complete ms. Length: 1,500-3,500 words. Pays ½¢/word.

Poetry: Joyce Odam, poetry editor. No line or subject limit. Buys 60-80/year. Limit submissions to batches of 4-6. Pays $2 minimum. "We have an annual poetry and short story contest. We give cash and other awards. Send SASE for contest rules and entry form."

INLET, Virginia Wesleyan College, Norfolk VA 23502. Editor: Joseph Harkey. Poetry and fiction for liberally educated readership of all ages. Annual magazine; 30 pages. Estab. 1971. Circ. 700. Pays in copies. Acquires all rights, but will reassign rights to author following publication. Byline given. Photocopied submissions OK. Submissions accepted September 1 to March 15. SASE. Reports in 2 months. Sample copy for 35¢ in postage.

Fiction: Any type that is handled successfully. Especially interested in engaging, well-written short shorts of 600-1,500 words, but will consider mss up to 3,000 words long. Uses 1-4 mss/year.

Poetry: "Anything that is not maudlin will be considered. The only requirement is good writing." Preferred lengths: 2-30 lines, 40-80 lines, or 100-160 lines. "The longer the poem, the better it has to be." Uses 20-40 poems/year. Limit submissions to batches of 5.

INTER-AMERICAN REVIEW OF BIBLIOGRAPHY, Organization of American States, Washington DC 20006. Editor: Elena Castedo-Ellerman. Quarterly magazine; 120-150 pages. Estab. 1951. Circ. 3,000. Pays in subscription to magazine. Byline given. Sample copy $1.50; free writer's guidelines.

Nonfiction: Scholarly material only in the humanities: literature, history, philosophy and related fields. Uses 16 mss/year. Query.

Columns/Departments: Book reviews on serious literature and humanistic studies dealing with the American continent, especially Latin America and the Caribbean. Also News and Notes about cultural news dealing with same. Submit complete ms. Length: 20-30 pages for articles; 2 pages for book reviews; 1 paragraph for news. Pays in copy of book to be reviewed.

THE INTERCOLLEGIATE REVIEW, Intercollegiate Studies Institute, 14 S. Bryn Mawr Ave., Bryn Mawr PA 19010. (215)525-7501. Editor-in-Chief: Robert A. Schadler. Emphasizes intellectual conservatism on cultural, economic, political, literary and philosophical issues. Quarterly magazine; 64 pages. Estab. 1975. Circ. 30,000. Pays on publication. Buys all rights. Byline given. Phone queries OK. SASE. Reports in 6 months. Free sample copy.
Nonfiction: Historical; informational; and personal. Buys 4 mss/issue. Query. Length: 1,000-5,000 words. Pays $50-150.

INTERSTATE, Box 7068, University Station, Austin TX 78712. Editors: Loris Essary and Mark Loeffler. For "anyone interested in creative arts." Quarterly magazine; 108 pages. Estab. 1974. Circ. 500. Acquires all rights, but will reassign rights to author after publication. Payment in contributor's copies. Sample copy $3. Photocopied submissions OK. Reports in 1-3 weeks. "Occasionally longer." No query necessary. SASE.
Nonfiction and Photos: "We actively seek nonfiction in the form of 'creative essays.' Such work is best defined by reference to John Cage, Norman O. Brown and Merleau-Ponty. We accept mss and then fit them to the issues for the year. Frequently, we have holdover." Increasingly emphasis on theater and performance pieces. Photos used with and without mss. Size: open. "Must be b&w glossy prints."
Fiction and Poetry: All forms and subjects open. Length: open. "Piece should be creative in either terms of style or theme. We are interested in seeing all forms of creative material, particularly experimental."

THE IOWA REVIEW, 308 EPB, The University of Iowa, Iowa City IA 52242. (319)353-6048. Editor: David Hamilton. Fiction Editor: Frederick Bush. Poetry Editor: Stanley Plumly. Quarterly magazine; 96-128 pages. Estab. 1970. Buys first rights, but may reassign following publication. Photocopied submissions OK. SASE. Reports in 1 week to 3 months.
Nonfiction, Fiction and Poetry: "We publish essays, stories and poems. We are more interested in essays than in academic criticism and are willing to consider writing that do not fall neatly into one of those categories." Buys 100 mss/year. Query or submit complete ms. Pays $1/line for verse; $10/page for prose.

JAPANOPHILE: Box 223, Okemos MI 48864. Editor: Earl Snodgrass. For literate people who are interested in Japanese culture or in Japan itself. Quarterly magazine. Pays on publication. Buys first North American serial rights. Previously published submissions OK. SASE. Reports in 4 weeks. Sample copy $1.75; free writer's guidelines.
Nonfiction: "We want material on Japanese culture in North America or anywhere in the world, even Japan. We want articles, preferably with pictures about persons engaged in arts of Japanese origin: a Michigan naturalist who is a haiku poet, a potter who learned raku in Japan, a vivid 'I was there' account of a Go tournamant in California. We use some travel articles if exceptionally well-written. It is important to study the magazine." Buys 8 mss/issue. Query or send complete ms. Length: 800-2,000 words. Pays $8-15.
Photos: State availability of photos. Pays $5 for 8x10 b&w glossy prints.
Columns/Departments: "We are looking for columnists to write about cultural activities in Chicago, New York, Los Angeles, San Francisco, Tokyo and Honolulu. That is, one columnist for each city." Query. Length: 600-1,200 words. Pays $7-15.

JOHNSONIAN NEWS LETTER, 610 Philosophy Hall, Columbia University, New York NY 10027. Editor: John H. Middendorf. For scholars, book collectors and all those interested in 18th-century English literature. 4 times a year. No payment. Acknowledgement given. Reports "immediately." SASE.
Nonfiction: Interested in news items, queries, short comments, etc., having to do with 18th-century English literature. Must be written in simple style. Length: maximum 500 words.

THE JOURNAL OF MEXICAN AMERICAN HISTORY, Box 13861-UCSB, Santa Barbara CA 93107. (805)968-5915. Editor-in-Chief: Joseph Peter Navarro. Emphasizes history for specialists in Mexican-American history, including professors, graduate and undergraduate students. Annual magazine; 150-200 pages. Estab. 1970. Circ. 1,500. No payment. Acquires simultaneous rights. Phone queries OK. Submit seasonal/holiday material 6-12 months in advance. Photocopied submissions OK. SASE. Reports in 2 weeks. Sample copy $17.50.
Nonfiction: Historical (Mexican-American history from 1848 to present); interview; personal experience (documented carefully); personal opinion; photo feature (if historical and pertinent). Send complete ms. Length: 1,500-4,500 words. Prize of $100 for best article. Captions required for b&w photos used.

JOURNAL OF MODERN LITERATURE, Temple University, 1241 Humanities Bldg., Philadelphia PA 19122. (215)787-8505. Editor-in-Chief: Maurice Beebe. Managing Editor: Kathleen Quinn. Emphasizes scholarly literature for academics interested in literature of the past 100 years. Quarterly magazine; 160-200 pages. Estab. 1970. Circ. 2,000. Buys all rights, but may reassign rights to author following publication. Phone queries OK. Photocopied submissions OK. SASE. Reports in 8 weeks. Free sample copy.
Nonfiction: Historical (20th-century literature); informational (20th-century literature); and photo feature on art and literature. Buys 30 mss/year. Query or send complete ms. Pays $50-100.
Photos: Purchased only with accompanying nonfiction manuscript. Total purchase price for ms includes payment for photos.

JOURNAL OF THE NORTH AMERICAN WOLF SOCIETY, Box 118, Eatonville WA 98328. Editor: Sandra L. Gray. For audience with interest in "conservation issues and a strong concern for the preservation and promotion of the wolf and its habitat, and other wild canids of North America." Estab. 1975. Quarterly. Circ. 350. Rights acquired vary with author and material. Acquires all rights, but may reassign rights to author after publication; first North American serial rights; or simultaneous rights. Payment in contributor's copies. Will send sample copy to writer for $1. Write for editorial guidelines sheet. Will consider simultaneous and photocopied submissions. Reports in 4-6 weeks. Query not necessary. SASE.
Nonfiction: "Subject matter must be relevant to wolves, or other wild canids such as coyotes, their prey, their habitat, or activities of individuals or groups on their behalf. Our approach is factual and objective. We try to provide space for as many positions as possible in this complex and emotional subject, as long as these positions have their bases in fact and are rationally presented. We generally like to see sources and references though they may not be published with the article." Length: 600-1,800 words. For personal opinion, 300-600 words. For reviews, 150-300 words. Regular columns: "Thinking It Over" and "Views and Reviews."
Fiction: "New section entitled 'Post Scripts.' Creative fiction based in sound ecological fact is desired. Must relate to wild canids. Length: 1,000-1,500 words.
Photos and Fillers: "No specific requirements yet for photos, will negotiate on individual basis." Uses newsbreaks and clippings.

JOURNAL OF POPULAR CULTURE, University Hall, Bowling Green State University, Bowling Green OH 43402. (419)372-2610. Editor: Ray B. Browne. 100% freelance written. For students and adults, interested in popular culture, TV, films, popular literature, sports, music, etc. Quarterly magazine, 192 pages. Estab. 1967. Circ. 3,000. Acquires all rights, but will reassign rights to author after publication. Payment in copies. Sample copy $5. Original copies only. Reports in 3-6 months. SASE.
Nonfiction and Photos: "Critical essays on media, books, poetry, advertising, etc." Informational, interview, historical, think pieces, nostalgia, reviews of books, movies, television. Length: 5,000 words maximum. Pays in contributor's copies (25 reprints). Uses b&w glossy prints.

JOURNALISM MONOGRAPHS, School of Journalism, University of Kentucky, Lexington KY 40506. (606)258-2671. Editor: Bruce H. Westley. For all journalism educators in the US, Canada and the world. Magazine; 30-85 pages. Estab. 1966. Published serially, 1 ms/issue; 4-6 issues/year. Circ. 2,000. "Author grants all rights." Byline given. Uses 4-6 mss/year. No payment. Sample copy $2.50; free guidelines for writers. Will consider photocopied submissions. No simultaneous submissions. Reports on material accepted for publication in 1-6 months. Query or submit complete ms. SASE.
Nonfiction: "Scholarly articles (any methodology) in the field of journalism and mass communications. We do not encourage freelancers without scholarly discipline."

KANSAS QUARTERLY, Dept. of English, Kansas State University, Manhattan KS 66506. (913)532-6716. Editors: Harold W. Schneider, Ben Nyberg, W.R. Moses. For "adults, mostly academics, and people interested in creative writing, literary criticism, Midwestern history, and art." Estab. in 1968. Quarterly. Circ. 1,100. Acquires all rights, but will reassign them to author for republication upon request. Pays in contributor's copies. Sample copy $2.50. Query for nonfiction. "Follow *MLA Style Sheet* and write for a sophisticated audience." Reports in about 2-4 months. SASE.
Nonfiction, Photos, Fiction, and Poetry: Accepts poetry, short stories; art, history and literary criticism on special topics. "We emphasize but do not limit ourselves to the history, culture, and life style of the Mid-Plains region. We do not want children's literature, 'slick' material, or special interest material not in keeping with our special numbers." Accepts historical articles

on "special topics only." Photos should have captions; 4x6 rectangular b&w preferred. Accepts experimental and mainstream fiction. Length: 250-10,000 words. Accepts traditional and avant-garde forms of poetry, blank verse and free verse. Poetry themes open.

KARAMU, English Department, Eastern Illinois University, Charleston IL 61920. (217)345-5013. Editor: Bruce Guernsey. For literate, university-educated audience. Estab. 1967. Annually. Circ. 500. Acquires first North American serial rights. Uses 25 mss/year. Payment in 2 contributor's copies. Sample copy $1.50. Submit complete ms. Reports on poetry, 1-2 weeks; fiction, 1 month. SASE.
Nonfiction: Articles on contemporary literature. Length: open.
Fiction: Experimental, mainstream. Length: 2,000-8,000 words.
Poetry: Traditional forms, free verse and avant-garde. Dept. Editor: Bruce Guensey.

THE LAKE SUPERIOR REVIEW, Box 724, Ironwood MI 49938. Editors: Faye Korpi, Lee Merrill. Emphasizes contemporary poetry and short stories for readership interested in good contemporary literature. Published 2 times a year; 64 pages. Estab. 1970. Circ. 450. Pays on publication in copies. Buys first North American serial rights. Phone queries OK. Reports in 2 weeks to 5 months. Sample copy $2.
Photos: Purchased without accompanying manuscript. Maximum size b&w without reduction 5x8. Artwork is either matched to a piece of writing or presented singly.
Fiction: Adventure, erotica, experimental, fantasy, historical, humorous, mainstream, mystery and science fiction. Uses 7-8 mss/year. Length: 4,000 words maximum.
Poetry: Avant-garde, free verse, haiku, light verse and traditional. Uses 90 poems/year. Limit submissions to batches of 6-8.

L'ESPRIT CREATEUR, Box 222, Lawrence KS 66044. (913)864-3164. Editor: John D. Erickson. Bilingual journal for persons interested in French literature (educators, critics). Quarterly; 95 to 100 pages. Estab. 1961. Circ. 1,250. Acquires all rights, but will reassign rights to author after publication. Uses about 30-35 mss/year. Payment in 5 contributor's copies. Will send sample copy to writer for $2.25. Prefers the *MLA Style Sheet* style. "All issues are devoted to special subjects, though we print book reviews and review articles of critical works that do not correspond to the issue subject. Please note subjects of coming issues, listed in each issue. Submit June 1 for spring issue, May. 1 for summer issue, Feb. 1 for fall issue, and April 1 for winter issue." Reports in 3-6 months. Query ahead or submit complete ms. SASE.
Nonfiction: "Criticism of French literature centered on a particular theme each issue; interviews with French writers or critics that appear irregularly; book reviews of critical works on French literature. Critical studies of whatever methodological persuasion that observe the primacy of the text. We notice a bit too much emphasis on extra-literary matters and a failure to note the special issues scheduled. Interested in new critical practices in France. We prefer articles that are direct and honest, avoid pedantry, respect the integrity of the literary work and have something intelligent to say." Length: about 15 double-spaced typed pages, or 4,500 words.

LETTERS, Mainespring Press, Box 82, Stonington ME 04681. (207)367-2484. Editor-in-Chief: Helen Nash. Publication of the Maine Writers' Workshop. For general literary audience. Quarterly magazine; 4-10 pages. Estab. 1972. Circ. 6,500. Pays on acceptance. Buys all rights. Submit seasonal/holiday material 5 months in advance. Simultaneous and photocopied submissions OK. SASE. Reports in 1 month. Sample copy for SASE.
Nonfiction: "Any subject within moral standards and with quality writing style." Query. Length: 100-500 words. Pays 5¢/word.
Fiction: No pornography, confession, religious or western. Buys 5 mss/year. Query. Pays 5¢/word.
Poetry: G.F. Bush, poetry editor. Light verse, traditional, blank verse, humorous, narrative, avant-garde, free verse and haiku.. Buys 15/year. Length: 30-42 lines. Pays $1/line maximum.

LITERARY REVIEW, Fairleigh Dickinson University, 285 Madison Ave., Madison NJ 07940. (201)377-4050. Editors: Martin Green, Harry Keyishian. For international literary audience, largely libraries, academic readers and other poets and writers. Quarterly magazine; 128 pages. Estab. 1956. Circ. 1,000. Pays in copies. Acquires first North American serial rights. Photocopied submissions OK. Reports in 2-3 months. Sample copy $3.50.
Nonfiction: Literary criticism on contemporary American and world literature; themes, authors and movements aimed at nonspecialist audience. "Review essays of recent books or above topics welcome." Uses 2-3 mss/issue.
Fiction: Experimental or traditional. "We seek literary stories, not slick types." Uses 3-4/issue.

Poetry: Avant-garde, free verse and traditional. Uses 5-10/issue.

LITERARY SKETCHES, Box 711, Williamsburg VA 23185. (804)229-2901. Editor: Mary Lewis Chapman. For readers with literary interests; all ages. Monthly newsletter; 14 pages. Estab. 1961. Circ. 500. Not copyrighted. Byline given. Buys about 12 mss a year. Pays on publication. Sample copy for SASE. Will consider photocopied and simultaneous submissions. Reports in 1 month. Submit complete ms. SASE.
Nonfiction: "We use only interviews of well-known writers and biographical material on past writers. Very informal style; concise. Centennial or bicentennial pieces relating to a writer's birth, death or famous works are usually interesting. Look up births of literary figures and start from there." Length: 1,000 words maximum. Pays ½¢/word.

THE LONDON COLLECTOR, 1005 Bond St., North Manchester IN 46962. (219)982-8750. Editor-in-Chief: Dennis E. Hensley. Managing Editor: Richard Weiderman. 80% freelance written. For students, book collectors, readers, fans and professors who are interested in the career and life of Jack London. Magazine published 3 times/year; 32 pages. Estab. 1968. Circ. 322. Pays in copies. Buys first North American serial rights. Byline given. SASE. Reports in 2 weeks. Sample copy $2.
Nonfiction: Book reviews (any and all reviews of books and monographs written about Jack London); general interest (literary analysis of London's writings); historical (London family history); humor (articles on London's use of humor in his articles, novels and short stories). Buys 12 mss/year. Submit complete ms with clips of published work. Length: 250-1,400 words. Pays 4 copies.
Photos: State availability of photos with ms. Offers no additional payment for 5x7 b&w glossy prints. Captions preferred. Buys one-time rights. Model release required.
Fillers: Clippings and newsbreaks. Buys 7/year. Length: 50-175 words.

MARK TWAIN JOURNAL, Kirkwood MO 63122. Editor: Cyril Clemens. For those interested in American and English literature. Semiannual magazine. Estab. 1936. Not copyrighted. SASE. Sample copy $1. Pays in contributor's copies. Reports in 2 weeks. "Queries welcome."
Nonfiction: Critical and biographical articles dealing with Mark Twain and other American, English and foreign authors.

THE MARKHAM REVIEW, Horrmann Library, Wagner College, Staten Island NY 10301. (212)390-3000. Editor: Joseph W. Slade. For academics; specialists in American culture. Newsletter; 20 pages. Estab. 1968. Quarterly. Circ. 1,000. Rights purchased vary with author and material. Byline given. Usually buys all rights, but may reassign rights to author after publication. Buys 15-20 mss/year. Pays in contributor's copies. Will send free sample copy to writer on request. No photocopied or simultaneous submissions. Reports in 4 weeks. Query or submit complete ms. SASE.
Nonfiction: Interdisciplinary treatments of any aspect of American culture between 1965 and 1940. Scholarly approach following *MLA* style. Does not want articles on Henry James or Ernest Hemingway or other major writers. Would consider material on the history of science and technology. Length: 6,000 words maximum.

THE MASSACHUSETTS REVIEW, Memorial Hall, University of Massachusetts, Amherst MA 01003. Editors: Lee R. Edwards, Mary T. Heath, John Hicks, Robert Tucker. Quarterly. Buys first North American serial rights. Pays on publication. Reports "promptly." SASE. Sample copy $3.00.
Nonfiction: Articles on literary criticism, women, public affairs, art, philosophy, music and dance. Average length: 6,500 words. Pays $50.
Fiction: Short stories or chapters from novels when suitable for independent publication. Pays $50.

MICHIGAN QUARTERLY REVIEW, 3032 Rackham Bldg., University of Michigan, Ann Arbor MI 48109. Editor: Laurence Goldstein. Quarterly. Circ. 2,000. Pays on acceptance. Buys first rights. Reports in 4 weeks for mss submitted in September-May; in summer, 8 weeks. SASE. Sample copy $2.00.
Nonfiction: "*MQR* is open to general articles directed at an intellectual audience. Essays ought to have a personal voice and engage a significant subject. Scholarship must be present as a foundation but we are not interested in specialized essays directed only at professionals in the field. We prefer ruminative essays, written in a fresh style, which reach interesting conclusions. Length: 2,000-5,000 words. Pays $100-175, sometimes more.
Fiction and Poetry: No restrictions on subject matter or language. "We publish about 12 stories

a year and are very selective." Pays $8-10/published page.

THE MIDWEST QUARTERLY, Kansas State College of Pittsburg, Pittsburg KS 66762. (316)231-7000. Editor: V. J. Emmett Jr. 95% freelance written. Published "for an educated adult audience interested in contemporary thought in a variety of scholarly disciplines." Magazine; 100 pages. July issue is all literary analysis. Estab. 1959. Quarterly. Circ. 1,000. Acquires all rights, but may reassign rights to author after publication. Byline given. Uses 24 articles; 48 poems/year. Payment in contributor's copies. Will send free sample copy to writer on request. Will consider photocopied submissions. Submit seasonal material 6-9 months in advance. Reports in 3 months for prose; 6 months for verse. SASE.
Nonfiction and Poetry: "Literary analysis, history, social sciences, art, musicology, natural science in nontechnical language. Write standard literary English without jargon or pedantry. We do not use fiction. Would like to see more history and social science." Length: 3,500-5,000 words. Publishes traditional forms of poetry, blank verse, free verse, avant-garde forms and haiku. Subject: open. Length: 4-200 lines. Poetry Editor: Michael Heffernan.

MISSISSIPPI REVIEW, Center for Writers, University of Southern Mississippi, Southern Station, Box 5144, Hattiesburg MS 39401. (601)266-7189. Editor: Frederick Barthelme. For general literary audiences, including students, libraries and writers. Published 3 times/year; 120 pages. Estab. 1972. Buys all rights, but may reassign following publication. Byline given. Pays in copies. SASE. Reports in 8-10 weeks. No submissions in June or July. Sample copy $2.50.
Fiction: All types considered.
Poetry: All types considered.

MISSISSIPPI VALLEY REVIEW, Department of English, Western Illinois University, Macomb IL 61455. Editor: Forrest Robinson. For persons active in creating, teaching or reading poetry and fiction. Magazine; 64 pages. Estab. 1971. Published twice a year. Circ. 400. "Permission to reprint must be gained from individual authors." Accepts 80-100 mss/year. Payment in 2 contributor's copies, plus a copy of the next 2 issues. Will send sample copy to writer for $1.50 plus postage. Will consider "only excellent" photocopied submissions. Will consider simultaneous submissions only if the author "notifies us immediately upon receipt of an acceptance elsewhere. We try to return mss within 3 months. We do not mind writers asking for progress reports if we are a bit late. Allow for no ms reading during summer." Submit complete ms. SASE.
Fiction and Poetry: Publishes stories and poems. Tries to provide a range and variety of style and subject matter. "*Writer's Market* guidelines for ms submission suggested. We take pride in trying to help those who are breaking in. We publish no articles. We usually solicit our reviews." Fiction Editor: Loren Logsdon. Poetry Editor: John Mann.

MODERN FICTION STUDIES, Dept. of English, Purdue University, West Lafayette IN 47907. (317)493-1684. Editors: William T. Stafford, Margaret Church. For students and academic critics and teachers of modern fiction in all modern languages. Quarterly magazine; 140-160 pages. Estab. 1955. Circ. 4,000. Acquires all rights, but with written stipulated agreement with author permitting him or her to republish anywhere, any time as long as *MFS* is cited, and splitting 50/50 with him reprints by others of his agreed-to-be-reprinted material. Byline given. No payment. Reports in 2-4 months. "Every other issue is a special issue. See current copy for future topics. Submit material any time before announced deadline for special issue." SASE.
Nonfiction: Interested in critical or scholarly articles on American, British, and Continental fiction since 1880. Length: notes, 500-2,500 words; articles, 3,000-7,000 words.

MOUNTAIN REVIEW, Box 660, Whitesburg KY 41858. (606)633-4811. Editor: Betty Edwards. For Appalachians of all ages and backgrounds and others interested in life in the mountains. Quarterly magazine; 48 pages. Estab. 1974. Circ. 2,000. Acquires all rights, but may reassign rights to author after publication. Byline given. Uses about 20 mss/year. No payment. Will send sample copy to writer for $1.50. Will consider photocopied submissions. No simultaneous submissions. Submit seasonal material (spring, summer, fall, winter) 4 months in advance. Reports in 3-6 months. SASE.
Nonfiction and Photos: "We publish articles, preferably by mountain people, about some aspect of life in the mountains; life—not repetitions of old stereotypes. The material we choose deals with Appalachia, but in a fresh (often surprising) way." Personal experience, interview, historical, think pieces, expose, nostalgia, personal opinion articles and reviews of books about

the mountains. Query or submit complete ms. Length: 1,000-3,000 words. B&w glossy prints used with or without mss.
Fiction and Poetry: Open to all writing by Appalachian writers, including, but not limited to, themes that deal with some aspect of mountain life. Traditional and avant-garde forms of poetry, blank verse, free verse, haiku.

MOUNTAIN SUMMER, Glen Antrim, Sewanee TN 37375. (615)598-5795. Coordinating Editor: Don Keck DuPree. For literary, college and university audience. Estab. 1972. Published annually. Circ. 1,000. Acquires all rights, but may reassign rights to author after publication. Uses 12 to 16 mss/year. Pays in contributor's copies. Sample copy $2.50. Will consider photocopied and simultaneous submissions. Reports in 2 to 4 weeks. SASE.
Poetry and Nonfiction: "We publish material which shows an interest in traditional English forms." Likes "good, sound material." Poetry and essays. Preferred submission time: March 15 to July 15. Length for poetry: 4 to 48 lines.

MOVING OUT, Wayne State University, 4866 3rd, Detroit MI 48202. Editors: Margaret Kaminski, Gloria Dyc. Feminist literary and arts journal for college and career women and others interested in women's studies and writing. Magazine; 1 time a year; 100 pages. Estab. 1971. Circ. 800. Pays in contributor's copies. Acquires all rights, but may reassign following publication. Byline given unless writer wants name withheld. Phone queries OK. Simultaneous and photocopied submissions OK. SASE. Reports in 6-12 months. Sample copy $2.00.
Nonfiction: Literary criticism (not too academic in style); reviews of women's books; magazines, records or film reviews of interest to women. Historical (papers on famous women writers, artists, etc.). Interviews and personal experience (diary excerpts). Photo features (portfolios of fine art photography or artwork, graphics, paintings, etc.); uses 1/issue. Query or submit complete ms. Length: about 20 pages.
Fiction: Must be related to women's experience. Also uses novel excerpts. Query or submit complete ms. Length: 20 pages.
Poetry: Free verse, haiku, prose poems, feminist poetry.

MUNDUS ARTIUM, A Journal of International Literature and the Arts, University of Texas at Dallas, Box 688, Richardson TX 75080. Editor: Rainer Schulte. 30-50% freelance written. For all levels "except the scholarly, footnote-starved type." Semiannual magazine; 160 pages. Estab. 1967. Circ. 2,000. Buys all rights, but will reassign rights to author after publication. Buys about 50 mss/year. Pays on publication. Sample copy $3.50. Will consider photocopied submissions. No simultaneous submissions. Reports in 90 days. Submit complete ms. SASE.
Nonfiction and Photos: "In articles, we look for people who are able to talk about our nontraditional, conceptual kind of orientation from a broad, esthetic point of view. We like interdisciplinary emphasis. We don't want scholarly articles, kitsch, or social-political material, or descriptive, representational work." Length: open. Pays $15-100. Only avant-garde photography is acceptable.
Fiction: Experimental and fantasy. Must be nontraditional and conceptual. Length: open. Pays $5/page minimum.
Poetry: Avant-garde forms. Prefers to publish young, outstanding poets from the international and American scene who, as yet, are unrecognized. Pays minimum of $5 per page.
How To Break In: "Since we have a bilingual format, translations of contemporary international poets is a good way. Otherwise, creative work which goes beyond description and regional, national restrictions."

NAMES, American Name Society, State University College, Potsdam NY 13679. Editor: Conrad M. Rothrauff. Emphasizes onomatology (the study of names). Quarterly magazine; 72 pages. Estab. 1953. Circ. 1,000. Submit seasonal/holiday material 6 months in advance. Byline given. SASE. Reports in 8 weeks. Sample copy $1.
Nonfiction: General interest (general or specialized interest, may be very erudite); and historical (general or specialized interest, may be erudite). "We want articles to be scholarly, documented, presenting new facts or old facts with a new interpretation, not before published, in area of name-study. We do not want anything that is nonscholarly; subjectivity per se; genealogies, except when incident to the research of a name and its history. Nothing 'creative' or imaginative. Send complete ms. The journal offers no remuneration whatsoever."

NATCHEZ TRACE LITERARY REVIEW, The Bluff Press, Box 6945, Jackson MS 39212. Editor-in-Chief: Rosalie Daniels. Emphasizes poetry and fiction. For an educated, literary audience. Semiannual magazine; 16-20 pages. Estab. 1976. Circ. 200. Pays on acceptance. Acquires all rights. Byline given. Submit seasonal/holiday material 3 months in advance.

SASE. Reports in 2 months. Sample copy $2; writer's guidelines $2.
Fiction: Experimental. Buys 3 mss/issue. Send complete ms. Length: 3,000-3,500 words. Pays in copies.
Poetry: Avant-garde, free verse, haiku and traditional. Buys 14 poems/issue. Limit submissions to batches of 2. Pays in copies.

NEBULA, 970 Copeland St., North Bay, Ontario, Canada P1B 3E4. (705)472-5127. Editor-in-Chief: Ken Stange. Managing Editor: Ursula Stange. Emphasizes literature for an intellectually sophisticated readership. Semiannual magazine; 88 pages. Estab. 1974. Circ. 750. Pays on publication in copies and grants. Buys first North American serial rights. Byline given. Phone queries OK. SAE and International Reply Coupons. Reports in 5 weeks. Sample copy and writer's guidelines $1.00.
Nonfiction: Interview (with literary figures); and personal opinion (critical essays). Submit complete ms.
Fiction: Erotica; experimental; fantasy; mainstream; and science fiction. Submit complete ms.
Poetry: Quality poetry of all kinds.
How To Break In: "We do thematic issues, the themes announced in preceeding issues, so a would-be contributor is advised to send for a recent sample. Seeing the type of material we publish generally and learning what specific themes we will be exploring in future issues is the best guide to any writer considering our publication."
Rejects: "We are very tired of receiving submissions from the states where the postage affixed to the return envelope is American. Canada is a separate country and has its own postal system. Canadian postage or International Reply Coupons should accompany submissions."

NEW BOSTON REVIEW, 77 Sacramento St., Somerville MA 02143. Editors: Gail Pool, Lorna Condon. For people interested in the arts. Bimonthly magazine; 28-32 pages. Estab. 1975. Circ. 12,000. Acquires all rights, unless author requests otherwise. Byline given. Pays in copies. Photocopied and simultaneous submissions OK. SASE. Reports in 4-6 weeks. Sample copy $1.
Nonfiction, Fiction and Poetry: Critical essays and reviews in all the arts: literature, painting, music, film, theatre, photography, dance. Length: 1,000-3,000 words. Accepts 20 mss/year. Fiction length: 2,000-4,000 words.

NEW INFINITY REVIEW, Box 804, Ironton OH 45638. (614)377-4182. Editor: James R. Pack. Manuscript Editor: Ron Houchin. Art Editor: Leonard Miller. For the lovers of new writing with "pizzazz and verve." Quarterly magazine; 56 pages. Estab. 1969. Circ. 500. Acquires North American serial rights. Pays in copies or gift subscriptions. Free sample copy and writer's guidelines. Photocopied submissions OK "if readable." All submissions should be accompanied by a brief autobiography, stressing the individual and his/her unique personality, and including current activities and publication credits. Reports in 6 weeks. SASE.
Nonfiction and Photos: "Short essays that chronicle new perspectives, the mysterious and fantastic. Subjects can range from the psychic to the sociological." Length: 3,000 words maximum. Accompanying photos or illustrations are welcome.
Fiction: "We seek stories that are mentally exciting and germinal with ideas. Mystery, science fiction and fantasy find an eager eye." Length: 4,000 words maximum.
Poetry: "Send as large a sample as possible (4-20). We try to feature one poet every issue, using 4-8 or more poems. Free verse; experimental; avant-garde; and all poetry approaching the visual are encouraged. What we seek most is clear voice and lots of energy. No length limit."
How To Break In: "We especially need good short fiction, 3-6 pages, that deals with the new and the strange."

NEW ORLEANS REVIEW, Box 195, Loyola University, New Orleans LA 70118. (504)865-2294. Editor: Dawson Gaillard. Managing Editor: Leisa Reinecke Flynn. Emphasizes art and literature "for anyone who likes literature and is interested in current culture." Magazine published 3 times/year. Estab. 1968. Circ. 1,500. Pays on publication. Buys first North American serial rights. Byline given. SASE. Reports in 1 month. Sample copy $2.50; free writer's guidelines.
Nonfiction: Interviews with writers, photographers, film directors, producers and artists. "We are also interested in articles dealing with science and the humanities. These much be directed to an educated lay audience. We are not interested in academic articles." Buys 6 mss/year. Query. Length: 2,000-5,000 words. Pays $25-50.
Fiction: Quality fiction. Buys 9 mss/year. No length restrictions. Submit complete ms. Pays $50 minimum.

Poetry: "All types, as long as it is good." Buys 75 poems/year. Pays $10.

NEW YORK LITERARY FORUM, Box 262, Lenox Hill Station, New York NY 10021. Editor: Jeanine P. Plottel. For teachers, scholars, college students of literature, philosophy, and the humanities and the general reader interested in keeping abreast of current serious, academic literary work. Published 2 times/year. Book format; 322 pages. Estab. 1978. Byline given. SASE. Reports in 6 weeks. Sample copy $7.50; free writer's guidelines.
Nonfiction: Interview (with important writers) and any article about literature. Query. Length: 2,500-3,750 words.
Columns/Departments: Texts and Documents. Buys 2 mss/year. Query. Length 4,000 words maximum.
Fiction: "We have not yet included any fiction, but may do so in our Texts and Documents section. Query. Length 3,500 words maximum.
Poetry: "We do not normally include poetry but are considering doing so in future issues."

NEWSART, 5 Beekman St., New York NY 10038. Editor: Harry Smith. Newspaper. Estab. 1974. Published 2 times a year, as a supplement to *The Smith.* Circ. 5,000. Buys first rights. Byline given. Pays on acceptance. Sample copy $1. Reports in 4 weeks. Query for nonfiction. Submit complete ms for fiction and poetry. SASE.
Nonfiction, Fiction and Poetry: Essays, humor, interviews. Pays $15 minimum for nonfiction. Fiction "should be reasonably short for newspaper format—newsy element helpful." Pays $15 minimum for fiction. Poetry should be short, though occasional longer poems are used. Pays $5 for poetry.
Photos: Purchased with accompanying ms with extra payment. B&w only. "8x10 best but not exclusively used." Pay: open.

NIMROD, University of Tulsa, 600 S. College, Tulsa OK 74104. (918)939-6351. Editor: Francine Ringold. For readers and writers interested in good literature and art. Semiannual magazine; 96 (6x9) pages. Estab. 1955. Circ. 1,000. Acquires all rights but will return rights to author on request. Byline given. Payment in contributor's copies and $5/page when funds are available. Will consider photocopied submissions, but they must be very clear. No simultaneous submissions. Reports in 3 to 6 months. Query or submit complete ms. SASE.
Nonfiction: Interviews and essays. Length: open.
Fiction and Poetry: Experimental and mainstream fiction. Traditional forms of poetry; blank verse, free verse and avant-garde forms. "We are interested in quality and vigor. We often do special issues. Writers should watch for announced themes and/or query."

NIT & WIT LITERARY ARTS MAGAZINE, 1908 W. Oakdale, Chicago IL 60657. (312)248-1183. Publisher: Katheen Cummings. Editor: Leonard J. Dominguez. 100% freelance written. Quarterly magazine; 48 pages. Estab. July 1977. Circ. 5,000. Pays in copies. Rights reassigned following publication. Byline given. Phone queries OK. Simultaneous, photocopied and previously published submissions OK, "but please indicate." SASE. Reports in 6 weeks. Sample copy for $1 postage; mention *Writer's Market* in request.
Nonfiction: "Anything well-written will be considered." Exposé; social commentary and critiques; how-to; general interest; humor; historical; inspirational; interview; nostalgia; personal experience; personal opinion; photo feature; profile; and travel. Uses 12 mss/year. Submit complete ms. Length: 2,000 words maximum.
Photos: Submit photos with accompanying ms. Uses 5x7 or 5x3 b&w glossy prints. Captions preferred; model release required.
Fiction: Adventure; confession; erotica (light erotica is OK); experimental; fantasy; historical; humorous; mainstream; mystery; religious; romance; science fiction; and suspense. Uses 12 mss/year. Length: 2,000 words maximum. Submit complete ms.
Poetry: Avant-garde, free verse, haiku, light verse, traditional and senryu. Uses 60/year.

NITTY-GRITTY, Goldermood Rainbow Publisher, 331 W. Bonneville, Pasco WA 99301. (509)547-5525. Editor-in-Chief: W.R. Wilkins. Each issue has a "tool-theme" subject. Biannual magazine; 100 pages. Estab. 1975. Circ. 3,000. Pays on acceptance. Buys all rights, but may reassign following publication. Pays 100% kill fee. Byline given. Submit seasonal/holiday material 2 months in advance. Potocopied submissions OK. SASE. Reports in 2 months. Sample copy $4; free writer's guidelines.
Nonfiction: Humor; interview; personal experience; personal opinion and profile. Buys 60-70 mss/issue. Send complete ms. Length: 100-3,000 words. Pays $2-15.
Fiction: Adventure; experimental; fantasy; historical; humorous; mainstream; mystery;

romance; science fiction; and suspense. Send complete ms. Length: 1,000-10,000 words. Pays $15 minimum.

Poetry: Free verse. Buys 50 poems/issue. Limit submissions to batches of 4. Length: 100 lines maximum. Pays $2.

Fillers: Clippings, jokes, gags, anecdotes and short humor. Buys 20 fillers/issue. Length: 50-1,000 words. Pays $2-15.

NORTH AMERICAN MENTOR MAGAZINE, 1745 Madison St., Fennimore WI 53809. (608)822-6237. Editors: John Westburg, Mildred Westburg. 95% freelance written. For "largely mature readers, above average in education, most being fairly well-to-do; many being retired persons over 60; college personnel and professional writers or aspirants to being professional." Quarterly. Acquires all rights, but may share rights with author after publication. Byline given. Payment in contributor's copies. Sample copy $2. Photocopied and simultaneous submissions OK. Reports in 1 week to 6 months. SASE.

Nonfiction: "We desire writing in reasonably good taste; traditional is preferable, but emphasis should be on creativity or scholarship. I know of no other of the small magazine genre that is like this one. We make no claim to being avant-garde, but have been accused of being a rear-guard periodical, for we try to follow the general traditions of western civilization (whatever that might be). Would be interested in readable but well-documented articles on anthropology, archeology, American Indians, black or white Africa. Do not want vulgarity or overworked sensationalism. No stuff on riots, protests, drugs, obscenity or treason. We do not want to discourage a writer's experimental efforts. Let the writer send what he thinks best in his best style. Study a current issue first, though." Length: "maximum about 5,000 words."

Photos: "Please make inquiry about photographs in advance. We like to use them if they can be reproduced on multilith offset masters."

Fiction: "Short stories should have a plot, action, significance, and depth of thought, elevating rather than depressing; would be glad to get something on the order of Dickens, Thackeray or Dostoyevsky rather than Malamud, Vidal or Bellow. Sustained wit without sarcasm would be welcome; propaganda pieces unwelcome." Length: 1,000-4,000 words.

Poetry: Accepts traditional, blank and free verse, avant-garde forms and light verse. "Poetry from many cultures." Length: 50 lines maximum.

THE NORTH AMERICAN REVIEW, University of Northern Iowa, Cedar Falls IA 50613. (319)273-2681. Editor: Robley Wilson Jr. Quarterly. Circ. 3,000. Buys all rights for nonfiction and North American serial rights for fiction and poetry. Pays on publication. Sample copy $1. Familiarity with magazine helpful. Reports in 8-10 weeks. Query for nonfiction. SASE.

Nonfiction: No restrictions, but most nonfiction is commissioned by magazine. Rate of payment arranged.

Fiction: No restrictions; highest quality only. Length: open. Pays minimum $10 per page.

Poetry: Department Editor: Peter Cooley. No restrictions; highest quality only. Length: open. Pays 50¢ per line minimum.

NORTHWEST REVIEW, 369 P.L.C., University of Oregon, Eugene OR 97403. (503)686-3957. Editor-in-Chief: Michael Strelow. 85% freelance written. For literate readership. "We have one issue per year with Northwest emphasis, the other two are of general interest to those who follow American/world poetry and fiction." Published 3 times/year; 130 pages. Estab. 1958. Circ. 2,000. Pays on publication in copies. Buys all rights, but will reassign rights to author following publication. Phone queries OK. Submit seasonal/holiday material 6 months in advance. Photocopied submissions OK. SASE. Reports in 6-8 weeks. Sample copy $2.00. Free writer's guidelines.

Photos: Purchased without accompanying manuscript. Send prints. Total price for ms includes payment for photos.

Fiction: Deb Casey, Fiction Editor. All types. Uses 5 mss/issue. Send complete ms.

Poetry: Jay Williams, Poetry Editor. Uses 30-35 poems/issue. Limit submissions to batches of 10-15.

NORTHWOODS JOURNAL, Rt. 1, Meadows of Dan VA 24120. (703)952-2100. Editor-in-Chief: Robert W. Olmsted. Editor: Paul Hodges. 95% freelance written. For writers. Quarterly magazine; 48-60 pages. Estab. 1972. Circ. 500. Pays on acceptance. Buys all rights. Submit seasonal or holiday material 4-6 months in advance. SASE. Reports in 4-6 weeks. Sample copy $1.

Nonfiction: Historical; how-to; humor; informational; nostalgia; personal opinion; profile; technical (as pertains to small press publishing only). Buys 2-3 mss/issue. Submit complete ms. Length: 400-2,400 words. Pays $5-40.

Photos: Purchased with accompanying ms. Captions required. Query. Pays $5-25 for 8x10 b&w photos. Total purchase price for ms includes payment for photos. Model release required.
Columns/Departments: The Shovelman, Merritt Clifton. Reviews (small press and self-published books only). Submit complete ms. Length: 100-1,000 words. Pays $1-4. Open to suggestions for new columns/departments.
Fiction: "Anything that is a bit different." Buys 8-16 mss/year. Submit complete ms. Length: 500-5,000 words. Pays $5-25.
Poetry: Avant-garde; free verse; haiku; and traditional. Buys 80/year. Pays 50¢-$3.

THE OHIO JOURNAL, A Magazine of Literature and the Visual Arts, Department of English, Ohio State University, 164 W. 17th Ave., Columbus OH 43210. Editor: William Allen. Magazine; 3 times a year. Estab. 1972. Circ. 1,250. Pays in contributor's copies. Acquires all rights, but will reassign rights following publication. Byline given. Photocopied and simultaneous submissions OK. SASE. Reports in 6 weeks.
Nonfiction and Photos: Material of interest to an audience knowledgeable of literature and the arts, but not of an academic nature. Interviews and photo essays welcome. No color reproductions.
Fiction and Poetry: Robert Collins, Poetry Editor. No restrictions as to category or type. Maximum length for fiction: 10,000 words.

THE OHIO REVIEW, Ellis Hall, Ohio University, Athens OH 45701. (614)594-5889. Editor: Wayne Dodd. "A balanced, informed engagement of contemporary American letters, special emphasis on poetics." Published 3 times yearly. Estab. 1959. Circ. 1,000. Rights acquired vary with author and material. Acquires all rights or first North American serial rights. Will send sample copy to writer for $2. Submit complete ms. Unsolicited material will be read only September-June. Reports in 6 to 8 weeks. SASE.
Nonfiction, Fiction and Poetry: Buys essays of general intellectual and special literary appeal. Not interested in narrowly focused scholarly articles. Seeks writing that is marked by clarity, liveliness, and perspective. Interested in the best fiction and poetry. Pays minimum $5 a page, plus copies.

OHIOANA QUARTERLY, Ohioana Library Association, 65 S. Front St., 1105 Ohio Departments Bldg., Columbus OH 43215. (614)466-3831. Editor: James Barry. Quarterly magazine; 60 pages. Estab. 1943. Circ. 1,800. No payment. Byline given. Phone queries OK. Reports in 2 weeks.
Nonfiction: "Limited to articles about Ohio authors, musicians or other artists, and current book reviews; or articles by published Ohio authors." Query. Length: 500-3,000 words.

OPINION, Box 3563, Bloomington IL 61701. Editor: Dr. James E. Kurtz. 80% freelance written. For readers from 18 and older; people who have an appetite for invigorating, inspiring, thought-provoking articles. Numerous teachers, clergymen and professional people. Monthly magazine. 16 (8½x11) pages. Estab. 1957. Circ. 3,700. Not copyrighted. Pays 25% kill fee. Byline given. Uses about 38 mss/year. Pays in contributor's copies. Will send sample copy to writer for 30¢. Will consider photocopied submissions and simultaneous submissions. Submit complete ms. Reports in 3 to 5 weeks. SASE.
Nonfiction: "We publish articles dealing with social problems, philosophical themes, theological studies. Our articles are on current subjects but inspirational as well. Controversy but not just for the sake of being 'different.' Our writers believe in what they write. Be yourself. Take a deep subject and make it simple—don't write down to people but lift people up to a higher level of understanding. *Opinion* is down to earth. We carry some in-depth essays but for the most part we present to our readers, articles that hit the nail on the head. We are informal but we adhere to the old principles of good writing. Articles on marriage problems are a bit heavy and we prefer to see more material on philosophy and theology. Common sense philosophy. Particularly we want articles on religious adventure; new trends, new happenings." Informational, personal experience, profile, inspirational, historical, think articles, expose, nostalgia, personal opinion, spot news and new product. Length: 1,500 words maximum.
Photos: Uses 5x7 or 8x10 b&w glossy prints. Captions optional.
Poetry: Traditional forms, free verse and light verse.

PACIFIC PHILOSOPHICAL QUARTERLY (formerly *The Personalist*), School of Philosophy, University of Southern California CA 90007. Editors: John Hospers, Brian Loar and Bas C. van Fraassen. Quarterly. No honorarium. Follow the *MLA Style Sheet*. Put footnotes at end of article. Reports in approximately 4 months. SASE for return of submissions.

Nonfiction: Uses critical articles pertaining only to the field of philosophy.

PAINTBRUSH, Department of English, Northeastern University, Boston MA 02115. (617)437-3693. Editor: B. M. Bennani. For professional and "up-and-coming" writers, college and university groups; teachers. Magazine; 65 pages. Estab. 1974. Semiannually. Circ. 500. Buys all rights, but may reassign rights to author after publication. Byline given. Buys about 50 mss a year. Pays on publication. Will send sample copy to writer for $3. No photocopied or simultaneous submissions. Reports in 2-4 weeks. Query for interviews. SASE.
Nonfiction and Photos: Criticism, nonscholarly articles, translations from any language. Interviews with known writers and poets. Length: 2,000 to 3,000 words. Book reviews of small press publications are always welcome. Length: 500 words maximum. "No soul-searching, back-scratching junk. No book reviews that begin with 'This is a terrific book.' No politically inspired propaganda. Only the best goes." Would like to see work on "popularizing poetry without barbarizing it." Pays $5 per published page. B&w glossy prints (minimum 3x5) are used only with interviews.
Poetry: "All schools are welcome but, please, no four-letter rhymes or jingles." Traditional forms of poetry, blank verse, free verse, prose poems. Short lyrics preferred; 30 lines maximum. Pays $5 per poem per page.

PARABOLA, 150 5th Ave., New York NY 10011. (212)924-0004. Executive Editor: Susan Bergholz. Managing Editor: Lee Ewing. "Audience shares an interest in exploring the wisdom and truth transmitted through myth and the great religious traditions." Quarterly magazine; 136 pages. Estab. 1974. Circ. 14,000. Buys all rights, but will reassign following publication, or reprint rights. Pays 33⅓% kill fee. Byline given. Pays on publication. Photocopied submissions OK. SASE. Reports in 3-5 weeks. Free writer's guidelines.
Nonfiction: "We handle work from a wide range of perspectives—from comparative religion and anthropology to psychology and literary criticism. We seek to use these disciplines in the quest for meaning. Don't be scholarly, don't footnote, don't be dry. We want fresh approaches to timeless subjects. Length: 5,000 words maximum. Buys 30 mss/year. Query. Pays $25-150.
Photos: Purchased with or without accompanying ms. No color. Pays $25.
Fiction: Prefers retellings of traditional stories, legends, myths. Length: 3,000 words maximum. Pays "negotiable rates."

THE PARIS REVIEW, 45-39 171 Place, Flushing NY 11358. Editor: George A. Plimpton. Quarterly. Buys all rights. Pays on publication. Address submissions to proper department. SASE.
Fiction: Study publication. No length limit. Pays up to $150. Makes award of $500 in annual fiction contest.
Poetry: Study publication. Pays $10 to 25 lines; $15 to 50 lines; $25 to 100 lines; $50 thereafter. Poetry mss must be submitted to Jonathan Galassi at 541 E. 72nd St., New York NY 10021.

PERSPECTIVES, English Department, West Virginia University, Morgantown WV 26506. (304)293-5525. Editor: Arthur C. Buck. A column of literature and higher education. Associated with the Charleston *Gazette-Mail State Magazine.* Circ. 110,000. Appears on a space-available basis. Not copyrighted. Byline given. Space for freelance material is strictly limited. Pays after publication. No sample copies available. Reports in 1 month. SASE.
Nonfiction: Short, informal, personal essays on literature and higher education. Interesting, informal style desired. Preference is given to informational or interpretive essays or essays of personal opinion. Pays on the average of 2¼¢ per word. Length: 500-900 words preferred. Longer articles are rarely used. Satire is sometimes used.
Rejects: Seasonal material, formal research or scholarly articles, previously published work, poorly prepared mss, simultaneous submissions.

PIERIAN SPRING, Box 5, Brandon University, Manitoba Canada R7A 6A9. Chief Editor: Dr. Robert W. Brockway. Quarterly (January, April, July, October). Magazine; 50 pages. Estab. 1969. Circ. 300. Pays in copies. $25 prize for best poem and best story; book prizes for second place. Special featured poet section in some issues by invitation. "We are international and do not have a national or regional emphasis. We are primarily interested in quality and effectiveness of submissions rather than the address of the writer." Both beginning and established writers welcome. Submit complete ms. Sample copy and writers' guidelines for $1. All rights revert to author. Byline given. SASE requested but not required (Canadian postage or International Reply Coupons). Reprints seldom accepted; originals preferred.
Fiction: Any type of short story up to 3,000 words.

Poetry: "We are not particularly experimental or avant-garde although we will consider all submissions."

PHOEBE, The George Mason Review, George Mason University, 4400 University Dr., Fairfax VA 22030. Editor: Patty Summers. For the literary community. Quarterly magazine; 64-80 pages. Estab. 1968. Circ. 4,000. Pays in contributor copies on publication. Buys all rights. Byline given. Rights revert to author on publicaiton. SASE. Reports in 2 months. Sample copy $2.
Nonfiction: General interest. Buys 2-3 mss/issue. Send complete ms. Pays in contributor copies.
Photos: General interest. Uses 5-10 b&w 8x10 prints/issue. Pays in contributor copies.
Fiction: Adventure, experimental, fantasy, historical, humorous, mystery, romance, suspense, science fiction, western and serialized novels. "We use only exceptionally well-written material." Buys 6-10 mss/issue. Send complete ms. Length: no limit. Pays in contributor's copies.
Artwork: General interest. Uses 5-10 b&w pieces/issue. Pays in contributor's copies.
Poetry: Avant-garde, free verse, haiku and traditional. Buys 20-30 poems/issue. Length: no limit. Pays in contributor's copies.

PIG IRON MAGAZINE, Pig Iron Press, Box 237, Youngstown OH 44501. (216)744-2258. Editor-in-Chief: Jim Villani. 70% freelance written. Emphasizes literature/art for writers, artist and intelligent lay audience with bias towards social responsibility in the arts. Semiannual magazine; 100 pages. Estab. 1975. Circ. 1,500. Pays on publication. Buys one-time rights. Byline given. Submit seasonal/holiday material 4 months in advance of issue date. Photocopied and previously published submissions OK. SASE. Reports in 3 months. Sample copy $2; free writer's guidelines.
Nonfiction: General interest, interview, personal opinion, profile or alternative lifestyle/systems. Buys 3 mss/year. Query. Length: 8,000 words maximum. Pays $2 minimum.
Photos: Submit photo material with accompanying query. Pays $2 minimum for 5x7 or 8x10 b&w glossy prints. Buys one-time rights.
Columns/Departments: Fascia and Alternative lifestyle/systems. Buys 3 mss/year. Query. Pays $2. minimum.
Fiction: Pam Cook, fiction editor. Fantasy, avant-garde, experimental and science fiction. Buys 4 mss/issue. Submit complete ms. Length: 8,000 words maximum. Pays $2 minimum.
Poetry: Terry Murcko, poetry editor. Avant-garde, and free verse. Buys 25/issue. Submit in batches of 10 or less. Length: open. Pays $2 minimum.

PLOUGHSHARES, Box 529, Dept. M, Cambridge MA 02139. Editor: DeWitt Henry. For "readers of serious contemporary literature; students, educators, adult public." Quarterly magazine; 188 pages. Estab. 1971. Circ. 3,000. Rights purchased vary with author and material. Usually buys all rights, but may reassign rights to author after publication; or may buy first North American serial rights. Buys 50-100 mss per year. Pays on publication. Sample copy $3.50. Photocopied submissions OK. No simultaneous submissions. Reports in 3 months. SASE.
Nonfiction, Poetry and Fiction: "Highest quality poetry, fiction, criticism." Interview and literary essays. Length: 5,000 words maximum. Pays $50. Reviews (assigned). Length: 500 words maximum. Pays $15. Fiction. Experimental and mainstream. Length: 300-6,000 words. Pays $5-50. Poetry. Buys traditional forms, blank verse, free verse, avant-garde forms. Length: open. Pays $10/poem.

POTPOURRI INTERNATIONAL., Box 533-WM, Exton PA 19341. Editor-in-Chief: Elizabeth M. Downing. Managing Editor: Lenny Fields. 100% freelance written. "Devoted to the advancement of authors; read primarily by other writers, editors, and publishers." Semiannual book; 100 pages. Estab. 1975. Byline given. Submit seasonal/holiday material 6 months in advance of issue date. Photocopied and previously published (if so stated) submissions OK. SASE. Reports in 2-4 months. Sample copy $6.50; free writer's guidelines for SASE; mention *Writer's Market* in request. Accepting poetry only.

PRAIRIE SCHOONER, Andrews Hall, University of Nebraska, Lincoln NE 68588. Editor: Bernice Slote. Quarterly. Usually acquires all rights, unless author specifies first serial rights only. Small payment, depending on grants, plus copies of the magazine, offprints and prizes. Reports usually in 1-2 months. SASE.
Nonfiction: Uses 1 or 2 articles per issue. Subjects of literary or general interest. Seldom prints extremely academic articles. Length: 5,000 words maximum.

Fiction: Uses several stories per issue.
Poetry: Uses 20-30 poems in each issue. These may be on any subject, in any style. Occasional long poems are used, but the preference is for the shorter length. High quality necessary.

PRISM INTERNATIONAL, Department of Creative Writing, University of British Columbia, Vancouver, British Columbia, Canada V6T 1W5. Editor-in-Chief: Peter Crowell. Managing Editor: Leonard Turton. Emphasizes contemporary literature, including translations. For university and public libraries, and private subscribers. Semiannual magazine; 200 pages. Estab. 1959. Circ. 1,000. Pays on publication. Buys first North American serial rights. Photocopied submissions OK. SAE and International Reply Coupons. Reports in 10 weeks. Sample copy $4.
Fiction: Experimental and traditional. Buys 12 mss/issue. Send complete ms. Length: 5,000 words maximum. Pays $5/printed page.
Poetry: Avant-garde and traditional. Buys 60 poems/issue. Limit submissions to batches of 6. Pays $5/printed page.

PULP, c/o Sage, 720 Greenwich St., New York NY 10014. Editor: Howard Sage. For writers and any persons interested in quality fiction, poetry, art. Quarterly tabloid; 16 pages. Estab. 1975. Circ. 2,000. Acquires all rights, but will reassign rights to author after publication. Payment in contributor's copies. Sample copy $1, check payable to Howard Sage. Will consider photocopied submissions. No simultaneous submissions. Reports in 1 month. Submit complete ms. SASE.
Fiction and Poetry: "Fiction topics of human relations (especially intercultural relations). Quality fiction is especially needed and welcome. Translations of poetry and fiction welcome. Submit clear, publishable copy of original with translation. Brief biography should accompany all submissions." Experimental fiction and serialized novels. Length: open. "Poems on all topics as long as subject is well handled and control is deft." Traditional and avant-garde forms; free verse. Length: open.

PULP: FICTION & POETRY, Box 243, Narragansett RI 02882. Editor: Robert E. Moore. Fiction Editor: Thomas R. Rankin. Poetry Editor: Pat Leitch. For a general, educated readership. Quarterly magazine. Estab. 1975. Circ. 600. Acquires all rights; reassigns on publication. Pays in contributor's copies. Photocopied submissions OK. SASE. Reports in 6-12 weeks.
Fiction: Mainstream, mystery, suspense, adventure, fantasy, science fiction and "shades between." Serialized novels and continuing sagas considered. Length: 15,000 words maximum. Submit complete ms.
Poetry: All forms. Limit submissions to batches of 5. Uses 6-16/issue. "We're interested in all 'pulp' forms—those of today and 5 years from now."

REVISTA/REVIEW INTERAMERICANA, G.Box 3255, San Juan, Puerto Rico 00936. (809)763-9622. Editor: John Zebrowski. For "mostly college graduates and people with higher degrees." Publication of the Inter American University of Puerto Rico. Estab. 1971. Quarterly. Circ. 2,000. Acquires all rights, "but will pay 50% of money received if reprinted or quoted." Byline given. Uses about 75 mss/year. Payment in reprints (25) mailed to author. Free sample copy. Query or submit complete ms. Will consider photocopied submissions. No simultaneous submissions. Submit seasonal material at least 3 months in advance. Reports in 3 months. SASE.
Nonfiction: "Articles on the level of educated laymen; bilingual. Also book reviews. Multidisciplinary with preference to Puerto Rican and Caribbean and Latin American themes from multidisciplinary approach." Length: maximum 10,000 words.
Photos: B&w glossy prints, 4x5 minimum. Captions required. No color.
Fiction and Poetry: "Bilingual; Spanish or English." Experimental, fantasy, humorous and historical fiction. Blank verse, free verse, experimental, traditional and avant-garde forms of poetry.

ROCKBOTTOM, Mudborn Press, 209 W. De la Guerra, Santa Barbara CA 93101. Editor: Sasha Newborn. Managing Editor: Judyl Mudfoot. Emphasizes contemporary literature, American and foreign. "Our bias is strongly toward the personal autobiographical, direct, intimate. Our readers are adult, literate but not necessarily from college, male and female." Quarterly magazine; 120 pages. Estab. 1976. Circ. 500. Pays on acceptance. Buys first rights. Byline given. Photocopied submissions OK. SASE. Reports on queries in 2 weeks; on mss in 2 months. Sample copy $3.

Fiction: Experimental; condensed novels (autobiographical); mainstream; and translations from any language. "We are looking for direct writing, autobiographical pieces, journals, letters, conversations that aren't properly called 'fiction' but would be classed as literature rather than 'nonfiction.' We're after a revitalizing literature that's spilled out of the old modes of writing but doesn't have a name yet." Buys 4 mss/issue. Send complete ms. Length: 10-20,000 words. Pays $1 minimum; 1¢ maximum/word.

ROMANCE PHILOLOGY, University of California, Berkeley CA 94720. Editor: Yakov Malkiel, Department of Linguistics. For college and university professors, including graduate students. Quarterly magazine, 120 pages. Estab. 1947. Circ. 1,250. No payment. Write for copy of editorial guidelines for writers. Query. Reports in 6 weeks. SASE.
Nonfiction: "Scholarly articles, notes, review articles, book reviews, briefer reviews, editorial comments, necrologies and technical essays. Examine very carefully some of the recent issues." General linguistics, theory of literature, historical grammar; dialectology, textual criticism applied to older Romance materials.

THE ROMANTIST, F. Marion Crawford Memorial Society, Saracinesca House, 3610 Meadowbrook Ave., Nashville TN 37205. (615)292-9695 or 292-2918. Editor: John C. Moran. Associate Editors: Don Herron and Steve Eng. Emphasizes modern Romanticism; especially fantastic literature and art. Annual magazine. Estab. 1977. Circ. 300. Buys all rights. Byline given. Photocopied and previously published submissions OK. SASE. Reports in 4 weeks. Free writer's guidelines.
Nonfiction: General interest (Romanticism, fantasy, weird, horror); interview (with authors writing in the Romantic tradition, mainly fantasy and horror); nostalgia (about authors); personal opinion (about authors); and profile (about authors). "We do not want unrestrained, emotional articles or cliche-ridden, overly academic articles." Uses 5-10 mss/issue.
Columns/Departments: Lost Crawfordiana (reprints undiscovered or forgotten items by and about Francis Marion Crawford). Query.
Poetry: Free verse and traditional. "We much prefer rhymed and metered poems, no experimental or concrete verse." Uses 10-15/issue.

RUSSIAN LITERATURE TRIQUARTERLY, 2901 Heatherway, Ann Arbor MI 48104. (313)971-2367. Editors: Carl R. and Ellendea Proffer. For "readers of material related to Russian literature and art." Estab. 1971. 3 times a year. Circ. 1,400. Acquires all rights. Byline given. Uses about 50 mss/year. Except for photographs, payment is made in contributor's copies. Will send sample copy for $5. Query or submit complete ms. Will consider photocopied and simultaneous submissions. Reports on material in 1 to 2 months. SASE.
Nonfiction and Photos: Translations of Russian criticism, bibliographies, parodies, texts and documents from English literature. Critical articles. All in English. Interviews and reviews of Russia-related books. Payment by arrangement for b&w glossy prints or negatives. "Only requirement is relation of some kind to Russian art, literature."

THE RUSSIAN REVIEW, Hoover Institution, Stanford CA 94305. (415)497-2067. Editor: Terence Emmons. Quarterly journal; 128 pages. Estab. 1941. Circ. 1,850. Will consider photocopied submissions. No simultaneous submissions. Reports in 6-8 weeks. Query. SASE.
Nonfiction: A forum for work on Russia past and present. Uses material of high quality in the fields of Russian history, politics and society, literature and the arts. Scholarly reviews. Length: 2,500-7,500 words.

ST. CROIX REVIEW, Religion Society, Inc., Box 244, Stillwater MN 55082. Editor-in-Chief: Angus MacDonald. For an audience from college presidents to students. Bimonthly magazine; 56 pages. Estab. 1968. Circ. 2,000. Pays in copies. Buys all rights. Submit seasonal/holiday material 2 months in advance. Simultaneous, photocopied and previously published submissions OK. SASE. Reports in 2 weeks. Sample copy 50¢.
Nonfiction: "Articles must be germane to today's problems." Scholarly, but not pedantic articles for intelligent and concerned American and foreign audience. Must analyze and evaluate current problems in terms of West European intellectual heritage. Editorial viewpoint is classical liberalism. Length: 5,000 words maximum.

SALT LICK PRESS, Box 1064, Quincy IL 62301. Editor-in-Chief: James Haining. Emphasizes literature. Published irregularly; magazine; 68 pages. Estab. 1969. Circ. 1,500. Pays by arrangement. Photocopied and previously published submissions OK. SASE. Reports in 2 weeks. Sample copy $2.
Nonfiction: Informational and personal opinion. Send complete ms.

Photos: Photos purchased with accompanying ms. Send contact sheet. Total purchase price for ms includes payment for photos.
Fiction: Experimental. Send complete ms.
Poetry: Open to all types. Limit submissions to batches of 4.
Fillers: Query.

SAMISDAT, Box 231, Richford VT 05476. Editor-in-Chief: Merritt Clifton. 85% freelance written. Emphasizes literature, art and aesthetics for an anarcho-libertarian, educated audience "alienated from commercial and academic tastes, yet not aligned with the conventional underground either. Highly demanding, many are themselves well-published writers with a lifelong commitment to alternative and rebel literature." Monthly magazine; 60-80 pages. Estab. 1973. Circ. 500. Byline given. "We handle all submissions as personal correspondence." No carbons or photocopies. Pays in copies on publication. SASE. Reports in 1 month. Sample packet $2.
Nonfiction: Robin Michelle Clifton, Nonfiction Editor. Expose (of commercial publishing practices; corruption in both big and little publishing circles; name names and be accurate); historical (background on little magazine and small pressmanship; contemporary small press criticism within historical context); interview; personal opinion; and profile. Buys 6 mss/year. Send complete ms, "but be familiar with the publication." Length: 1,000-5,000 words.
Fiction: June Kemp, fiction editor. Experimental, fantasy, humorous, mainstream and science fiction. "We do not use mere 'genre' material; give us stories that make us think and rouse our emotions as well as our intellects. No mock Henry James or James Joyce." Uses 50 mss/year. Send complete ms. Length: 500-3,000 words.
Poetry: Avant-garde and free verse. "Read and understand our critical manifesto, *The Pillory Poetics*. We are open to imagism and surrealism, but only so long as the devices make a point and statement beyond themselves." Uses 200 poems/year.

SAN FRANCISCO REVIEW OF BOOKS, 2140 Vallejo St., #10, San Francisco CA 94123. Editor: Ron Nowicki. For a college-educated audience interested in books and publishing. Monthly magazine; 40 pages. Estab. 1975. Circ. 20,000. Acquires all rights, but will reassign rights to author after publication. Byline given. Uses about 180 mss/year. Payment in contributor's copies and subscription. Sample copy $1. No photocopied or simultaneous submissions. Reports on material accepted for publication in 4-6 weeks. Query for nonfiction; submit complete ms for book reviews. SASE.
Nonfiction: Book reviews; articles about authors, books and their themes. "No glib, slick writing. Primarily serious; humor occasionally acceptable. No restrictions on language provided it is germane to the book or article." Interviews, profiles, historical and think articles. Length: 1,000 words maximum for reviews; 2,000 words maximum for articles.

SAN JOSE STUDIES, San Jose State University, San Jose CA 95192. (408)277-3460. Editor: Arlene N. Okerlund. For the educated, literate reader. Academic journal; 112 pages. Estab. 1975. Three times a year; February, May and November. Circ. 500. Acquires first serial rights. Uses about 40 mss/year. Pays in contributor's copies. Sample copy $3.50. Reports in 2-3 months. Submit complete ms. SASE.
Nonfiction and Photos: In-depth, erudite discussions of topics in the arts, humanities, sciences, and social sciences. Review essays of authors. Informational, interview, profile, humor. Photo essays can be free-wheeling. "We need more science articles and more in-depth review essays of significant, but little known, contemporary writers." Recently published articles include previously unpublished letters of William James; "Deriddling Tillie Olsen's Writings," "Of Mice and Marshes" and "The Political Odyssey of George D. Herron." Length: 5,000 words maximum. Payment consists of 2 copies of the journal.
Fiction and Poetry: Experimental, mainstream, fantasy, humorous, mystery and science fiction. Length: 5,000 words maximum. Traditional and avant-garde forms of poetry; blank verse and free verse. Themes and length are open.

SCRIBES MAGAZINE: A LITERARY JOURNAL FOR, BY, AND ABOUT SENIOR CITIZENS, Metropolitan State College, Department of English, Box 32, Denver CO 80204. (303)629-2495. Editor: Robert J. Pugel. Managing Editor: Anne Keane. Biannual magazine; 72 pages. Estab. 1975. Circ. 15,000. Pay on publication in contributor's copies. Buys one-time rights. Phone queries OK. Submit seasonal/holiday material 4 months in advance. Simultaneous, photocopied and previously published submissions OK. SASE. Reports in 1 month. Sample copy $1; free writer's guidelines.
Nonfiction: "We are in the market for any kind of article as long as it is written by a senior

citizen. We also want feature articles, interviews and profiles of seniors." Uses 5-10 mss/issue. Send complete ms.

Photos: Send photos with accompanying mss. Uses 5x7 b&w prints. Captions preferred.

Fiction: "We want all kinds of fiction—if it is written by a senior. We're an award-winning, nonprofit publication, dedicated to providing a showcase for the literary talents of our senior citizen population." Uses 20 mss/year. Send complete ms. Length: 1,000 words.

Poetry: Avant-garde, free verse, haiku, light verse and traditional. Uses 100 poems/year.

Fillers: Clippings, jokes, gags, anecdotes, puzzles and short humor. Uses 5-10/year. Length: 100 words.

SECOND COMING, Box 31249, San Francisco CA 94131. Editor-in-Chief: A.D. Winans. Semiannual magazine; 80-120 pages. Estab. 1972. Circ. 1,000. Pays in copies. Acquires one-time rights. SASE. Reports in 1-4 weeks. Sample copy $2.

Fiction: Experimental (avant-garde) and humorous. Uses 4-6 mss/year. Submit complete ms. Length: 1,000-3,000 words. Pays in copies.

Poetry: Avant-garde, free verse, traditional and surrealism. Uses 160-200/year. Limit submissions to batches of 6. No length requirement. Pays in copies.

Photos: Pays $5 token plus copies for b&w photos.

SEQUOIA, Storke Publications Bldg., Stanford University, Stanford CA 94305. Editor: Ted Gioia. 80% freelance written. "At present *Sequoia* serves the Stanford College community, but is planning to expand to a more widespread audience." Quarterly magazine; 100 pages. Estab. 1956. Circ. 1,200. Pays in copies. Submit seasonal/holiday material 3 months in advance of issue date. SASE. Reports in 4-6 weeks. Sample copy $1.

Nonfiction: Interviews with writers. Uses 1-2 mss/issue. Submit complete ms. Length: 30 pages maximum.

Fiction: Joe Mailander, fiction editor. "The only criterion is quality." Uses 2 mss/issue. Submit complete ms. Length: 30 pages maximum.

Poetry: Avant-garde, free verse, haiku, light verse and traditional. Nothing "trite and conventional." Uses 20/issue. Length: 20 pages maximum.

SEWANEE REVIEW, University of the South, Sewanee TN 37375. (615)598-5931. Editor: George Core. For audience of "variable ages and locations, mostly college-educated and with interest in literature." Quarterly. Circ. 3,800. Buys all rights. Pays on publication. Sample copy $3.25. Returns in 4-8 weeks. SASE.

Nonfiction and Fiction: Short fiction (but not drama); essays of critical nature on literary subjects (especially modern British and American literature); essay-reviews and reviews (books and reviewers selected by the editors). Payment varies: averages $10 per printed page.

Poetry: Selections of 4 to 6 poems preferred. In general, light verse and translations are not acceptable. Maximum payment is 60¢ per line.

THE SHAKESPEARE NEWSLETTER, University of Illinois at Chicago Circle, English Department, Chicago IL 60680. (312)996-3289. Editor: Louis Marder. 20% freelance written. For professors of English, students, and Shakespeare enthusiasts. Published 6 times per academic year. Estab. 1951. Circ. 2,600. Not copyrighted. Payment in contributor's copies. Sample copy $1. Will consider photocopied submissions. No simultaneous submissions. Query or submit complete ms. "Send the conclusions and I will tell you if I want the facts." SASE.

Nonfiction: Solid, original articles. Wants new facts on Shakespeare. Scholarly, yet popular. Articles must show thorough knowledge of the literature on the subject. Length: 1,500 words maximum.

Poetry and Fillers: Occasional poems. No abstract poetry. Shakespeare only; anything that works. Length: 20 lines maximum. Newsbreaks, clippings, jokes and short humor. Length: 75 words or so.

SHAW REVIEW, S-234 Burrowes Bldg., University Park PA 16802. (814)865-4242. Editor: Stanley Weintraub. For scholars and writers and educators interested in Bernard Shaw and his work, his milieu, etc. Published every 4 months. Estab. 1954. Circ. 800. Pays in contributor's copies. Will consider photocopied submissions. Submit complete ms. Reports in 6 weeks. SASE.

Nonfiction: "Articles must pertain to G.B. Shaw, his writing life and environment." Uses informational and historical articles and interviews. Length: open.

SIGNS: JOURNAL OF WOMEN IN CULTURE & SOCIETY, Barnard College, 307 Barnard Hall, New York NY 10027. Editor: Catharine R. Stimpson. For academic and professional women; women and men interested in the study of women. Journal; 196 pages. Estab. 1975. Quarterly. Circ. 7,000. Acquires all rights. Payment in copies and offprints. Write for copy of guidelines for writers. Will consider photocopied submissions. Reports in 2-6 months. SASE. **Nonfiction:** "Scholarly essays exploring women, their roles and culture, their relations with society, etc. We are especially looking for articles with larger theoretical implications." Length: 20-45 typed, double-spaced pages.

THE SMALL POND MAGAZINE OF LITERATURE, 10 Overland Dr., Stratford CT 06497. (203)378-9259. Editor: Napoleon St. Cyr. For some "high school students, the rest college and college grad students who read us in college libraries, or in general the literati." Published 3 times a year. 40 pages. Estab. 1964. Circ. 300. Acquires all rights. Uses about 100 mss/year. Payment in contributor's copies. Sample copy $1.75. Will consider photocopied submissions. No simultaneous submissions. Query or submit complete ms. Reports in 10-30 days. SASE. **Nonfiction, Fiction, and Poetry:** "About ⅔ poetry, the rest is open to any and all subjects, essays, articles, and stories. We've had an uncanny knack for discovering talent which has gone on and risen rapidly in the literary field. We don't want anything on the high school and college drug scene, or fiction based on *Love Story*. Particularly interested in authoritative inside exposes (not rabid yellow journalism) of some aspect of business, government, international affairs, or even the world of literature and performing arts." Nonfiction length: 2,500 words maximum. Experimental, mainstream, fantasy, historical and humorous fiction. Length: 200-2,500 words. Traditional and avant-garde forms of poetry, blank, free and light verse. Length: 100 lines maximum.

SMALL PRESS REVIEW, Box 1056, Paradise CA 95969. Editor: Len Fulton. Associate Editor: Ellen Ferber. For "people interested in small presses and magazines, current trends and data; many libraries." Monthly. Circ. 3,000. Accepts 50-200 mss/year. Pays 100% kill fee. Byline given. Free sample copy. "Query if you're unsure." Reports in 1 to 2 months. SASE. **Nonfiction and Photos:** "News, short reviews, photos, short articles on small magazines and presses. Get the facts and know your mind well enough to build your opinion into the article." Uses how-to's, personal experience articles, interviews, profiles, spot news, historical articles, think pieces, photo pieces, and coverage of merchandising techniques. Length: 100-200 words. Uses b&w glossy photos.

THE SMITH, 5 Beekman St., New York NY 10038. Editor: Harry Smith. 75% freelance written. For writers, professors, librarians, others who are interested in literature as art and revolutionary thought. 2 book-size issues, plus supplements. Book format magazine. Estab. 1964. Circ. 2,500. Buys first North American serial rights and second serial (reprint) rights. Byline given. Buys 150 mss/year. Pays on acceptance. Sample copy $1.50. Query for nonfiction. Submit complete ms for fiction and poetry. Reports in 6-8 weeks. SASE. **Nonfiction:** Department Editor: Sidney Bernard. Speculative essays. No taboos. Length: 2,500 words or less. Payment is "modest," by arrangement. **Fiction and Poetry:** Department Editor (fiction): Raphael Taliaferro. Long stories as well as short-shorts and vignettes of under 2,000 words. Modest payment by arrangement. Pays $5 per short poem. **How to Break In:** "The only thing I can say about the trend in this office in the use of over-the-transom mss is that the best chance lies in poetry and fiction. Newcomers might want to try their hands at topical essays, perhaps with a polemical stroke, on the aesthetics of literature. But query first. I should point out that we prefer the unknown writer to the known."

SOUTH ATLANTIC QUARTERLY, Box 6697, College Station, Durham NC 27708. Editor: Oliver W. Ferguson. For the academic profession. Quarterly. No payment. Proceeds of sale of rights to reprint divided with author. Reports in 6 weeks. SASE. **Nonfiction:** Articles on current affairs, literature, history and historiography, art, education, essays on most anything, economics, etc.—a general magazine. No taboos. Length: 4,500 words maximum.

SOUTH CAROLINA REVIEW, English Dept., Clemson University, Clemson SC 29631. (803)656-3229. Editor: R. Calhoun. Managing Editor: F. Day. Publishes in April and November. Magazine; 72 pages. Estab. 1965. Circ. 500. Pays in copies. Acquires all rights, but may reassign following publication. Phone queries OK. Submit seasonal/holiday material 3 months in advance. Simultaneous and photocopied submissions OK. SASE. Reports in 2 months. Free sample copy. **Nonfiction:** Literary criticism, liteay history and history of ideas. Submit complete ms. Pays in copies.

Fiction: "We have no set types; if it's fiction, we'll look at it." Submit complete ms. **Poetry:** "If it's poetry, we'll look at it."

SOUTH DAKOTA REVIEW, Box 111, University Exchange, Vermillion SD 57069. (605)677-5229. Editor: John R. Milton. For a university audience and the college educated, although reaches others as well. Quarterly. Acquires North American serial rights and reprint rights. Byline given. Pays in contributor's copies. Reports in 4 weeks. SASE.
Nonfiction: Prefers, but does not insist upon, Western American literature and history; especially critical studies of Western writers. Open to anything on literature, history, culture, travel, the arts, but selection depends on patterns and interests of individual numbers within each volume. Contents should be reasonably scholarly, but style should be informal and readable. All well-written mss will be considered. Length: 6,000 words maximum, but at times has used longer.
Fiction: Contemporary Western setting preferred (Great Plains, Rockies, Southwest), but receptive to almost anything that is disciplined and original. Quality is more important than subject or setting. No excessive emotions. Rarely uses hunting, fishing, or adolescent narrator or subject studies. Open to paramyth, Jungian treatments, serious themes. Length: 6,000 words maximum, but has used longer at times.
Poetry: Prefers poetry which is disciplined and controlled, though open to any form (tends to prefer traditional free verse). Any length considered, but prefers 10-30 lines.

THE SOUTHERN REVIEW, Drawer D, University Station, Baton Rouge LA 70893. (504)388-5108. Editors: Donald E. Stanford and Lewis P. Simpson. For academic, professional, literary, intellectual audience. Quarterly. Circ. 3,000. Buys first rights. Byline given. Pays on publication. Will send sample copy to writer for $1.50. No queries. Reports in 2 to 3 months. SASE.
Nonfiction: Essays; careful attention to craftsmanship and technique and to seriousness of subject matter. "Willing to publish experimental writing if it has a valid artistic purpose. Avoid extremism and sensationalism. Essays exhibit thoughtful and sometimes severe awareness of the necessity of literary standards in our time." Emphasis on contemporary literature, especially Southern culture and history. Minimum number of footnotes. Length: 4,000-10,000 words. Pays 3¢/word minimum.
Fiction and Poetry: Short stories of lasting literary merit, with emphasis on style and technique. Length: 4,000-8,000 words. Pays minimum of 3¢/word. Pays $20/page for poetry.

SOUTHWEST REVIEW, Southern Methodist University, Dallas TX 75275. (214)692-2263. Editor: Margaret L. Hartley. For adults and college graduates with literary interests and some interest in the Southwest, but subscribers are from all over America and some foreign countries. Quarterly magazine; 120 pages. Estab. 1915. Circ. 1,200. Buys all rights, but will reassign rights to author after publication. Byline given. Buys 65 mss/year. Pays on publication. Sample copy $1. Query for nonfiction. Submit only complete ms for fiction and poetry. Reports in 3 months. SASE.
Nonfiction and Photos: "Articles, literary criticism, social and political problems, history (especially Southwestern), folklore (especially Southwestern), the arts, etc. Articles should be appropriate for a literary quarterly; no feature stories. Critical articles should consider a writer's whole body of work, not just one book. History should use new primary sources or a new perspective, not syntheses of old material. We're regional but not provincial." Interviews with writers, historical articles, and book reviews of scholarly nonfiction. Length: 1,500-5,000 words. Pays½¢/word. Regular columns are Regional Sketchbook (Southwestern) and Points of View (personal essays). Uses b&w photos for cover and occasional photo essays.
Fiction: No limitations on subject matter for fiction. No experiences of adolescents—that's overworked. Experimental (not too far out), and mainstream fiction. Length: 1,500-5,000 words. Pays ½¢/word. Regular columns are Regional Sketchbook (Southwestern) and Points of View.
fiction and nonfiction pieces published in *SR*.
Poetry: No limitations on subject matter. "We don't care for most religious and nature poetry." Free verse, avant-garde forms (not too far out), and open to all serious forms of poetry. Length: prefers 18 lines or shorter. Pays $5 per poem.

SOU'WESTER, Department of English, Southern Illinois University, Edwardsville IL 62026. Editor: Lloyd Kropp. For "poets, fiction writers, teachers, and anyone else connected with or interested in the small press scene." Magazine; 92 pages. Estab. 1960. Three times a year. Circ. 400. Acquires all rights, but will return rights to author after 6 months, upon request. Uses about 70 mss/year. Payment in contributor's copies. Several prizes are offered yearly for fiction and poetry. Sample copy $1.50. Will consider photocopied submissions. Will

"reluctantly" consider simultaneous submissions. Reports in 4 to 6 weeks except in the summer. "We do not read mss during June, July and August." Submit complete ms. SASE.
Fiction and Poetry: "We publish fiction, poetry and letters. We do not have any particular editorial bias, but we do insist on meaningful, imaginative development and technical proficiency. No doggerel; no old-fashioned magazine fiction aimed at old-fashioned housewives." Experimental, mainstream, fantasy, historical and science fiction. Length: 8,000 words maximum. Traditional and avant-garde forms of poetry; blank verse, free verse, haiku. Length: 80 lines maximum.

SUN AND MOON: A JOURNAL OF LITERATURE AND ART, 4330 Hartwick Rd., #418, College Park MD 20740. (301)864-6921. Editors: Douglas Messerli and Howard N. Fox. For those interested in contemporary issues of literature and art, and experimental works. Publishes 1-3 issues/year. Magazine;150 pages. Estab. 1976. Circ. 500. Buys all rights. Photocopied submissions OK. SASE. Reports in 1-4 weeks. Sample copy $3.50; free writer's guidelines.
Nonfiction: Interview (with art and literary figures) and critical essays on literature and art. "We want only the those mentioned above." Buys 1-2 mss/issue. Query or send complete ms. Length: 15 typed pages maximum. Pays in copies.
Fiction: Experimental (any good experimental fiction); mainstream (if the story is of high quality). "We want only those mentioned above." Buys 3-4 mss/issue. Send complete ms. Pays in copies.
Poetry: Avant-garde and free verse. "No traditional or light verse." Buys 40-50 poems/issue. Pays in copies.

13TH MOON, Box 3, Inwood Station, New York, NY 10034. Editor-in-Chief: Ellen Marie Bissert. Emphasizes quality work by women for a well-read audience. Semiannual magazine; 80-120 pages. Estab. 1973. Pays in copies. Acquires all rights, but will reassign following publication. SASE. Reports in 2 months. Sample copy $2.25 plus 50¢ postage and handling.
Nonfiction: Literary criticism and aesthetics. Query.
Photos: Photos used without accompanying ms. Uses b&w photos. Send prints.
Fiction: Woman-oriented. Open to all styles. "Send complete ms, but study magazine first."
Poetry: Open to all styles.

THOUGHT, The Quarterly of Fordham University, Fordham University Press, Box L, Fordham University, The Bronx NY 10458. Editor: G. Richard Dimler, S.J. Acquires all rights. Byline given. Payment in copies. Reports in a month. SASE.
Nonfiction: A review of culture and idea, *Thought* discusses questions of permanent value and contemporary interest in every field of learning and culture in a scholarly but not excessively technical way. Articles vary from 5,000 to 10,000 words.

TRI-QUARTERLY, Fiction Editor, 1735 Benson Ave., Northwestern University, Evanston IL 60201. (312)492-3490. Editor: Elliott Anderson. 3 times yearly. For an intellectual and literary audience. "Our format is extremely eclectic. The tone and intentions of each issue may vary." Buys first serial rights. Reports on unsolicited mss within 4-6 weeks; solicited mss immediately. Pays on publication. Study publication before submitting mss; enclose SASE.
Fiction and Photos: No length limits. "We are not committed to the short story as the only publishable form of fiction. Frequently excerpts from longer works tell us more about an author and his work." Payment at $10 per page, if possible. Occasionally uses photos.

UNICORN, A Miscellaneous Journal, 345 Harvard St., #3B, Cambridge MA 02138. Editor: Karen S. Rockow. 75% freelance written. Estab. 1967. Mainly for college and graduate school students and faculty. "Well-educated and sophisticated. Not jaded." Published irregularly. Circ. 700. Acquires all rights, but will reassign rights to author after publication. Byline given. Uses 15-25 freelance mss a year. Pays an honorarium only for nonfiction. Submit complete ms. Generally reports in 3-4 weeks, longer over summer. Sample copy $1.50. Will consider photocopied submissions. SASE.
Nonfiction and Photos: "*Unicorn* is a community of writers and readers brought together to share their favorite books and topics. Primarily, we publish essays. These range from personal essays to graceful, scholarly papers directed at a general audience. Areas of greatest interest are folklore, popular culture (especially fantasy literature, detective fiction, children's books) and medieval studies, but we will consider mss on any subject. Scholarly and semischolarly papers may include footnotes (use *MLA* form). The supporting scholarship must be rigorous, but avoid 'intellectualese.' Also have a very offbeat foods column, The Galumphing Gourmet, and publish many reviews, long and short. We are looking for crisp, honest prose and stand

committed against pretentiousness. We pay $5 honorarium for each article and essay accepted." B&w glossy prints, any size. Payment in cost of film plus extra roll and offprints. Optimum length: 2,500-5,000 words; 7,500 words maximum, but will break longer articles and consider series.

UNIVERSITY OF TORONTO QUARTERLY, University of Toronto Press, Toronto, Ontario M5S 1A6. Editor-in-Chief: W.J. Keith. Emphasizes literature and the humanities for the university community. Quarterly magazine; 96 pages. Estab. 1931. Pays on publication. Buys all rights. Byline given. Photocopied submissions OK. SASE. Sample copy $4.50.
Nonfiction: Scholarly articles on the humanities; literary criticism and intellectual discussion. Buys 15 mss/year. Pays $50 maximum.

UNIVERSITY OF WINDSOR REVIEW, Windsor, Ontario, Canada. N9B 3P4 (519)253-4232. Editor: Eugene McNamara. For "the literate layman, the old common reader." Estab. 1965. Biannual. Circ. 300 plus. Acquires first North American serial rights. Accepts 50 mss/year. Sample copy $1.75 plus postage. Follow *MLA Style Sheet*. Reports in 4 to 6 weeks. Enclose SAE and International Reply Coupons.
Nonfiction and Photos: "We publish articles on literature, history, social science, etc. I think we reflect competently the Canadian intellectual scene, and are equally receptive to contributions from outside the country; I think we are good and are trying to get better. We are receiving too many poems, too many short stories. Everybody in the world is writing them. Too many articles on literature itself. Not enough in the other areas: history, etc." Seeks informational articles. Length: about 6,000 words. Pays $25. For photos, please inquire to Evelyn McLean.
Fiction: Department Editor: Alistair MacLeod. Publishes mainstream prose with open attitude toward themes. Length: 2,000-6,000 words. Pays $25.
Poetry: Department Editor: John Ditsky. Accepts traditional forms, blank verse, free verse, and avant-garde forms. No epics. Pays $10.

UNMUZZLED OX, 105 Hudson St., New York NY 10013. (212)431-8829. Editor-in-Chief: Michael Andre. Emphasizes art and poetry. Quarterly magazine; 140 pages. Estab. 1971. Circ. 4,000. Pays on publication. Buys all rights, but may reassign following publication. Photocopied submissions OK. SASE. Reports in 1 month. Sample copy $3.
Nonfiction: Interviews (artists, writers and politicians). Buys 1 ms/issue. Query. Pays $1-50.
Photos: Photos purchased on assignment only. Pays $1-25 for photos. Model release required.
Fiction: Ellen Kahow, Fiction Editor. Experimental. Buys 1 ms/issue. Mostly solicited. Pays $1-50.
Poetry: Avant-garde. Pays $1-25.

VAGABOND, Box 879, Ellensburg WA 98926. Editor: John Bennett. For "libraries, poets, writers, sensitive and free spirits, minority groups, people of all ages, varied education and with an interest in life." Estab. 1966. Quarterly. Circ. 700. Acquires all rights, but will reassign them to author after publication. Uses about 80 mss/year. Pays in contributor's copies. Sample copy $1.50. Query for nonfiction. Reports in 3 to 4 weeks. SASE.
Nonfiction: "I would prefer not to see work that was written with a market in mind. I would like to see material that deals with life and death and all their accoutrements ... joy, laughter, love and hate." Accepts interviews, reviews and personal opinion articles. Length: not more than 5,000 words.
Fiction and Poetry: Publishes genuine experimental, suspense, adventure, erotica, fantasy, humorous fiction. Length: 5,000 words maximum. Traditional and avant-garde forms of poetry; blank verse, free verse and haiku.

THE VILLAGER, 135 Midland Ave., Bronxville NY 10708. (914)337-3252. Editor: Amy Murphy. Publication of the Bronxville Women's Club. For club members and families; professional people and advertisers. Estab. 1929. Monthly, October through June. Circ. 750. Acquires all rights. Uses 40 mss/year. Pays in copies only. Will send sample copy to writer for 50¢. Submit seasonal material (Thanksgiving, Christmas, Easter) 2 months in advance. Submit only complete ms. Reports in 2 weeks. SASE.
Nonfiction, Fiction and Poetry: Short articles about interesting homes, travel, historic, pertinent subjects, sports, etc. Informational, personal experience, inspirational, humor, historical, nostalgia, travel.
Fiction: Mainstream, mystery, suspense, adventure, humorous, romance, and historical fiction. Length: 900-2,500 words.
Poetry: Traditional forms of poetry, blank verse, free verse, avant-garde forms, light verse. Length: 20 lines.

VILTIS (Hope), Box 1226, Denver CO 80201. (303)839-1589. Editor: V.F. Beliajus. For teenagers and adults interested in folk dance, folk customs and folklore; all professions and levels of education. Bimonthly magazine; 40 pages. Estab. 1942. Circ. 2,500. Acquires all rights, but will reassign rights to author after publication on request. No payment. Free sample copy. Query. SASE.
Nonfiction: Uses articles on folklore, legends, customs and nationality backgrounds. Folkish (not too erudite) but informative. Can be any length. Everything must be based on custom, interview, profile, humor, expose reportage. Length: 500-3,500 words.

THE VIRGINIA QUARTERLY REVIEW. 1 W. Range, Charlottesville VA 22903. (804)924-3124. Editor: Staige Blackford. Quarterly. Pays on publication. Reports in 4 weeks. SASE.
Nonfiction: Articles on current problems, economic, historical; literary essays. Length: 3,000-6,000 words. Byline given. Pays $10/345-word page.
Fiction: Good short stories, conventional or experimental. Length: 2,000-7,000 words. Pays $10/350-word page. Prizes offered for best short stories and poems published in a calendar year, beginning in 1978.
Poetry: Generally publishes 10 pages of poetry in each issue. No length or subject restrictions. Pays $1/line.

WALT WHITMAN REVIEW. Business Office: Wayne State University Press, Detroit MI 48202. (313)626-6404. Editorial Office: Journalism Program, Communication Arts Department, Oakland University, Rochester MI 48063. Editors: William White and Charles E. Feinberg. For specialists in American literature. Quarterly. Payment in contributor's copies. Wayne State University Press and author share all rights. Byline given unless author requests otherwise. Reports "in a few days." SASE.
Nonfiction: All articles and book reviews, notes and queries should deal with Walt Whitman and his writings. Length: 500-6,000 words.

WASCANA REVIEW, University of Regina, Saskatchewan, Canada. Editor-in-Chief: W. Howard. Emphasizes literature and the arts for readers interested in serious poetry, fiction and scholarship. Semiannual magazine; 90 pages. Estab. 1966. Circ. 300. Pays on publication. Buys all rights. Photocopied submissions OK. SAE and International Reply Coupons. Reports in 6-8 weeks.
Nonfiction: Literary criticism and scholarship in the field of English, American, Canadian, French or German literature and drama; reviews of current books (2,000-6,000 words). Buys 1-4 mss/issue. Send complete ms. Pays $3-4/page.
Fiction: Quality fiction with an honest, meaningful grasp of human experience. Any form. Buys 5-10 mss/issue. Send complete ms. Length: 2,000-6,000 words. Pays $3/page.
Poetry: Avant-garde, free verse, haiku, light verse and traditional. Buys 10-15 poems/issue. Length: 2-100 lines. Pays $10/page.

WAVES, Room 357 Strong, Founders College, York University, 4700 Keele St., Downsview, Ontario, Canada M4J 1P3. Editor: Bernice Lever. For university and high school English teachers and readers of literary magazines. Magazine published 4 times/year; 80-100 pages. Estab. 1972. Circ. 1,000 plus. Acquires first North American serial rights. Byline given. Payment in contributor's copies. Sample copy $1. Will consider photocopied submissions. No simultaneous submissions. Reports in 3-6 weeks. Submit complete ms. SAE and International Reply Coupons.
Nonfiction and Photos: "Intelligent, thorough, unique, humanitarian material. Good quality; yet wide variety of genres and styles." Uses interviews, essays, literary think pieces and book reviews. Length: 250-7,000 words. B&w photos and graphics are used.
Fiction: Experimental, mainstream, fantasy, humorous and science fiction. Length: 500-5,000 words.
Poetry and Drama: Formal and free verse. Playlets. Length: 2,000 words maximum.

WEBSTER REVIEW, Webster College, Webster Groves MO 63119. (314)432-2657. Editor: Nancy Schapiro. For "academics, students, all persons interested in contemporary international literature." Magazine; 64 pages. Estab. 1974. Quarterly. Circ. 400. Not copyrighted. Byline given. Uses 200 mss/year. Pays in copies. Free sample copy. Will consider photocopied and simultaneous submissions. Reports in 1 month. SASE.
Fiction and Poetry: "Stories, poems, excerpts from novels, essays and English translations of foreign contemporary literature. Subject matter is not important, but quality is. Our emphasis

is on international as well as American contemporary quality writing." No restrictions on length.

WEST COAST WRITER'S CONSPIRACY, 2800 Moraga Dr., Los Angeles CA 90024. Editor-in-Chief: Barbara Hall. Editor: Susan Golant. For writers of all ages and education levels and all persons interested in the West Coast writing scene. Quarterly magazine; 50 pages. Estab. 1977. Circ. 6,000. Pays on publication. Buys first rights. Byline given. SASE. Reports in 3 months. Sample copy $2.50; free writer's guidelines.
Nonfiction: Articles must be slanted for West Coast writing scene. Interviews; profiles; how-to; literary history (especially of West Coast writers and trends); humor (must pertain to writer's life); travel (locales of interest to West Coast writer); literary criticisms; book reviews; personal opinion (pertaining to writing only—must be unique and of the highest quality); etc. Buys 5 mss/issue. Length: 500-3,000. Pays in copy. Query Articles Editor, Randy Hilfman.
Fiction: Robert M. Morris, Fiction Editor. "All types of high quality fiction." Buys 1-5 mss/issue. Send complete ms. Length: 1,500-3,000 words. Pays $25-75.
Poetry: Bayla Winters, Poetry Editor. Avant-garde and contemporary. Focused on "human(e) concerns in which poet's role is one of dynamic participation. Excessive length and obscure posturing are taboo." Buys 10/issue. Pays $10-25.

WESTERN HUMANITIES REVIEW, University of Utah, Salt Lake City UT 84112. (801)581-7438. Editor-in-Chief: Jack Garlington. For educated, university-centered, sophisticated readers. Quarterly magazine; 96 pages. Estab. 1947. Circ. 1,000. Pays on acceptance. Buys all rights, but may reassign following publication. Phone queries OK. Simultaneous and photocopied submissions OK. SASE. Reports in 4 weeks.
Nonfiction: Authoritative, readable, sophisticated articles on literature, art, philosophy, current events, history, religion, anything in the humanities. Interdisciplinary articles encouraged. Departments on film and books.
Fiction: Experimental, fantasy, historical and humorous. Buys 2 mss/issue. Send complete ms. Pays $25-150.
Poetry: Avant-garde; free verse and traditional. "We seek freshness and significance." Buys 5-10 poems/issue. Pays $25-50.

WILLOW SPRINGS MAGAZINE, The Literary Guild at Eastern Washington University, P.U.B. Box 1063, Cheney WA 99004. Editor: Thomas Smith. Emphasizes poetry and prose. Semiannual magazine; 70 pages. Estab. 1977. Circ. 500. Pays on publication. Buys all rights. Phone queries OK. SASE. Reports in 3 weeks. Sample copy $2.50; writer's guidelines for SASE.
Nonfiction: Interview (with a writer or publisher, editor or agent) and personal opinion (should deal with the writing of poetry/prose and new ideas). Send complete ms. Pays $10 maximum/magazine page.
Fiction: "No limitations." Buys 2-5 mss/issue. Send complete ms. Pays $10 maximum/magazine page.
Poetry: Avant-garde, free verse, light verse, haiku and traditional. Buys 20-30 poems/issue. Pays $10 maximum/magazine page.

WIND/LITERARY JOURNAL, R.F.D. 1, Box 809K, Pikeville KY 41501. (606)631-1129. Editor: Quentin R. Howard. For literary people. Magazine; 80 pages. Estab. 1971. Quarterly. Circ. 500. Uses 500 mss/year. Payment in contributor's copies. Sample copy $1.50. No photocopied or simultaneous submissions. Reports in 10-20 days. Submit complete ms. SASE.
Nonfiction, Fiction, Drama and Poetry: Short essays and book reviews (preferably from small presses) are used, as well as short stories and 1-act plays. Blank verse, traditional and avant-garde forms of poetry, free verse, haiku.

WISCONSIN REVIEW, Box 145, Dempsey Hall, University of Wisconsin-Oshkosh, Oshkosh WI 54901. (414)424-2267. Senior Editor: Linda Grabner. Quarterly magazine; 40 pages. Estab. 1966. Circ. 2,000. Acquires first rights but will reassign after publication. Pays in contributor's copies. Sample copy $1.25. Reports in 2-3 months. Submit complete ms. SASE.
Needs: Poetry, prose, art and taped reading (30 minutes) for FM broadcast. "All literary forms welcomed year round. Prose selections up to 5,000 words. Imaginative materials that are experimental should include explanation of writer's intent."

WOMEN ARTISTS NEWS, Midmarch Associates, Box 3304 Grand Central Station, New York NY 10017. Editor-in-Chief: Cynthia Navaretta. For "artists and art historians, museum and gallery personnel, students, teachers, crafts personnel, art critics, writers." Monthly

magazine; 12 pages. Estab. 1975. Circ. 5,000. "Payment based on grant for that purpose from New York State Council on the Arts, $5 or $10, as long as the money lasts." Buys all rights, but may reassign following publication. Byline given. Submit seasonal/holiday material 1-2 months in advance. SASE. Reports in 1 month. SASE for free sample copy.
Nonfiction: Expose; how-to; informational; historical; interview; personal opinion; profile; personal experience; photo feature; and technical. Uses 4-6 mss/issue. Query or submit complete ms. Length: 500-1,000 words.
Photos: Used with or without accompanying ms. Captions required. Query or submit contact sheet or prints. Pays $5 for 5x7 b&w prints when money is available.

WORLD LITERATURE TODAY, 630 Parrington Oval, Room 110, University of Oklahoma, Norman OK 73019. Editor: Ivar Ivask. University of Oklahoma holds all rights to materials published unless otherwise noted. SASE.
Nonfiction: Articles (maximum length 3,000 words) concerned with contemporary literature; book reviews of 200-300 words on new, important, original works of a literary nature in any language. All contributions in English. Pays only in offprints (25) of a major article, plus 3 complimentary copies.

WRITERS FORUM, University of Colorado, Colorado Springs CO 80907. (303)598-3737, ext. 318. Editor: Alex Blackburn. Emphasizes quality fiction and poetry. For people of all ages interested in excellence in creative writing and in contemporary American literature, especially from regions west of the Mississippi. Annual book; 250 pages. Estab. 1974. Circ. 1,000. Authors retain rights. Byline given. Simultaneous, photocopied and previously published submissions OK. "Send 2 copies of all submissions after March 1 and before April 10." SASE. Reports in 3-6 weeks. Sample copy $3.95; free writer's guidelines.
Fiction: Confessions (genuine autobiography); experimental ("any technique that reveals truth of the human heart"); and mainstream (short fiction, novella, coherent excerpt from a novel-in-progress). Buys 12 mss/year. Send complete ms. Length: 1,000-15,000 words. Payment pending national grants.
Poetry: Avant-garde, free verse, and traditional, including poetic drama. Publishes 40/year. Submit in batches of 5. Length: 10-2,000 words. Payment pending national grants.

THE YALE REVIEW, 1902A Yale Station, New Haven CT 06520. Editor: Kai T. Erikson. Managing Editor: Sheila Huddleston. Buys all rights. Pays on publication. SASE.
Nonfiction and Fiction: Authoritative discussions of politics, literature and the arts. Pays $75-100. Buys quality fiction. Length: 3,000-5,000 words. Pays $75-100.

ZVEZDA, University of California, Box 9024, Berkeley CA 94709. Editor-in-Chief: Mark Osaki. Managing Editor: Steven Mikulan. Emphasizes poetry, short fiction and photography. Semiannual magazine; 30-50 pages. Estab. 1976. Circ. 1,000. Pays in copies on publication. Buys one-time rights. Byline given. Submit seasonal/holiday material 2-3 months in advance. Simultaneous submissions OK. SASE. Reports in 3-4 weeks. Sample copy $1, plus postage.
Fiction: Erotica, experimental, humorous, mainstream, and serialized novels. "We do not want adventure, confessions, fantasy, historical, mystery, religious, romance, science fiction, suspense, western or condensed novels." Buys 4-8 mss/year. Send complete ms. Length: 50-1,200 words. Pays $5-20.
Poetry: Free verse and traditional. "Unless your work is of the caliber of Milton, Donne, etc., do not submit religious poetry." Buys 20/issue. Length: 500 words maximum. Pays $5-10.
Photos: Send photos with ms. Pays $5-20 for 5x7 b&w matte prints; $5-20 for color negatives; offers no additional payment for photos with ms. Buys one-time rights.

Men's

ADAM, Publishers Service, Inc., 8060 Melrose Ave., Los Angeles CA 90046. 90% freelance written. For the adult male. General subject: "Human sexuality in contemporary society." Monthly. Circ. 500,000. Buys first North American serial rights. Occasionally overstocked. Pays on publication. Writer's guidelines for SASE. Reports in 3-6 weeks, but occasionally may take longer. SASE.
Nonfiction: "On articles, please query first. We like hard sex articles, but research must be thorough." Length: 2,500 words. Pays $100-200.
Photos: All submissions must contain model release including parent's signature if under 21; fact sheet giving information about the model, place or activity being photographed, including

all information of help in writing a photo story, and SASE. Photo payment varies, depending upon amount of space used by photo set.

AFFAIR, Sunway Periodicals, Inc., 21335 Roscoe Blvd., Canoga Park CA 91304. Editor: Herb Hills. For uninhibited young men from about 21 to 35, with above-average interest in erotic entertainment and improving their sex lives. Bimonthly magazine; 100 pages. Estab. 1975. Circ. 65,000. Buys first North American rights. Buys 75 mss/year. Pays 30-60 days after acceptance. Reports in 3-4 weeks. SASE, or we cannot return mss or answer questions.

Nonfiction and Fiction: "We're looking for things that are warm and enjoyable, not so superslick that they're over the heads of most of our readers. Articles and fiction pieces with sexual and erotic themes. Areas covered are self-help, do-it-yourself or how-to articles; new trends, humor, entertainment (of the reader), all with a strong man-woman orientation. Articles should be helpful to the male reader and give him insights and approaches to better relations with women. Writers with interesting personal experiences should have an edge in this approach. Fiction must have strong, action plots with erotic orientation and activity." Length (for both fiction and nonfiction): 2,500-3,000 words. Query or submit complete ms. Pays $100 minimum.

How To Break In: "Submit an article or a piece of fiction for our consideration, and then suggest several other ideas that could be developed (with our approval) into other submissions."

BEAVER, Reese Publishing Co., Inc., 235 Park Ave., S., New York NY 10003. Editor: Jeff Goodman. 80% freelance written. For men, age 18-34; high school education; interested in sex, cars, scandal in government, etc. Magazine; 80 pages. Monthly. Estab. 1976. Circ. 200,000. Buys first North American serial rights. Byline given. Buys 24 mss/year. Pays on acceptance. Will consider photocopied submissions. Reports in 1 month. SASE.

Nonfiction and Photos: "Articles of interest to our male readers." Informational, personal experience, humor, historical and expose. Query. Length: 2,500 words. Pays $250-500. Spot news (humorous items). Pays $25 maximum. Sets of nudes are purchased without mss. Pays $500 for 35mm kodachrome transpariences.

Fiction: "Short, erotic fiction. The approach should be fresh, explicit and very erotic. It should be a real turn on. We don't want to see anything like the typical fiction run in other men's books." Experimental, adventure, erotica and science fiction. Submit complete ms. Length: 2,500 words. Pay $250-500.

CASINO BUSTOUTS, Sunway Periodicals, 21335 Roscoe Blvd., Canoga Park CA 91304. Editor-in-Chief: Herb Hills. Emphasizes adult male topics, especially as they relate to young women. For the active, sexually motivated male; 21-40. Bimonthly magazine; 100 pages. Estab. 1972. Pays 30-60 days after acceptance. Buys first rights. Submit seasonal/holiday material at least 6 months in advance of issue date. Reports in 4 weeks. Send SASE with all mss and questions.

Fiction: Adventure; erotica; fantasy; confession; experimental; humorous; mystery; suspense; and mainstream. Buys 25 mss/year. Query or submit complete ms. Length: 2,000-3,500 words. Pays $100, "but may pay less for shorter material. Plotted material, please."

Articles: Any subject likely to help young men to be happier, especially sexually. Interviews, self-help, gambling (casino style), how-to, humor (but keep in touch with reality), new trends, personal experiences, travel, getting more for your money (male division). Length: 2,000-2,500 words. Pays $100.

CAVALIER, Suite 209, 316 Aragon Ave., Coral Gables FL 33134. Editor: Douglas Allen. For "young males, 18-29, 80% college graduates, affluent, intelligent, interested in current events, ecology, sports, adventure, travel, clothing, good fiction." Monthly. Circ. 250,000. Buys first rights. Byline given. Buys 35-40 mss/year. Pays on publication or before. See past issues for general approach to take. Submit seasonal material at least 3 months in advance. Reports in 3 weeks. SASE.

Nonfiction and Photos: Personal experience, interviews, humor, think pieces, expose and new product. "Frank—open to dealing with controversial issues." No material on Women's Lib, water sports, hunting, homosexuality or travel, "unless it's something spectacular or special." Query. Length: 2,800-3,500 words. Pays $300 maximum. Photos purchased with mss or with captions. No cheesecake.

Fiction: Department Editor: Nye Willden. Mystery, science fiction, humorous, adventure and contemporary problems. Send complete ms. Length: 2,500-3,500 words. Pays $250 maximum, "higher for special."

How To Break In: "Our greatest interest in in originiality—new ideas, new approaches; no tired, overdone stories—both feature and fiction. We do not deal in sensationalism but in high-quality pieces. Keep in mind the intelligent 18- to 29-year-old male reader."

CHIC MAGAZINE, Larry Flynt Publications, 2029 Century Park E., Suite 3800, Los Angeles CA 90067. Editorial Director: Ben Pesta. For affluent men, 20-35 years old, college-educated and interested in current affairs, luxuries, entertainment, sports, and fashion. Monthly magazine; 104 pages. Estab. 1976. Circ. 450,000. Pays 30 days after acceptance. Buys first North American and anthology rights but may reassign following publication. Pays 20% kill fee. Byline given unless writer requests otherwise. Submit seasonal/holiday material 5-6 months in advance. SASE. Reports in 3-4 weeks.
Nonfiction: Expose (national interest only); how-to (male-oriented consumer interest); humor (parody, satire); informational (entertainment, fashion, food, drink, etc.); interview (personalities in news and entertainment); celebrity profiles; and travel (rarely used, but will consider). Buys 90 mss/year. Query. Length: 750-3,200 words. Pays $500-1,200.
Fiction: Erotic, strongly plotted. Buys 12 mss/year. Send complete ms. Length: 2,500-3,500 words. Pays $500 minimum.
Photos: Bob Elia, Photo Editor. Purchased with or without mss or on assignment. Query or send transparencies. Pay $35-100/8x11 b&w glossies; $50-150/transparency. Model release required.
Columns/Departments: Zbigniew Kindela, Senior Editor in charge of Dope, Sex Life, Close Up (short profiles) columns. Length: 1,500 words. Pays $200. Dan Nussbaum, Associate Editor in charge of Chic Thrills (front of the book shorts; study the publication first). Pays $50-75. Length: 100-300 words.

DUDE, GENT, NUGGET, Suite 209, 316 Aragon Ave., Coral Gables FL 33134. (305)443-2378. Editor: Bruce Arthur. 80% freelance written. "For men 21 to ?; adventure and sex are their interests." Male-oriented subject matter. Published every 2 months. Buys first North American serial rights. Byline given. Buys 100 mss/year. Pays on publication. Submit complete ms. Reports on material in 6-8 weeks. SASE.
Nonfiction and Photos: "Articles that are male-oriented; primarily concerning sex or adventure." Informational, how-to, personal experience, interview, humor, historical, opinion and travel. Length: 1,500-4,000 words. Pays $100-200. Photos purchased with mss.
Fiction: Adventure, erotica, science fiction and humorous. Length: 1,500-3,500 words. Pays $100-200.

ELITE MAGAZINE, 234 Eglington Ave. E., #204, Toronto, Ontario, Canada M4P 1K5. Editor-in-Chief: David Wells. Managing Editor: Christine Curl. Emphasizes male entertainment. Monthly magazine; 100 pages. Estab. 1975. Circ. 500,000. Pays on publication. Buys all rights or First North American serial rights. Pays 25% kill fee. Byline given. Submit seasonal/holiday material 4 months in advance of issue date. Simultaneous and photocopied submissions OK. SASE. Reports in 4 weeks. Sample copy $1; free writer's guidelines.
Nonfiction: Expose; general interest (anything topical); humor (satire); interview (topical personalities); photo feature; and travel. Buys 3 mss/issue. Submit complete ms. Length: 2,000-4,000 words. Pays $100-400.
Fiction: Adventure; erotica; fantasy; and humorous. Buys 12 mss/year. Submit complete ms. Length: 2,500-3,500 words. Pays $150-400.
Photos: Purchased with or without accompanying ms. Send contact sheet or transparencies. Pays $20-100 for standard size b&w photos; $100-400 for 35mm or 2¼x2¼ transparencies. Submit at least 20 transparencies. Offers no additional payment for photos accepted with ms. Model release required.
Columns/Departments: Reviews of film and pop music. Submit complete ms. Length: 500-1,000 words. Pays $50-100. Open to suggestions for new column/departments.
Fiction: Adventure; erotica; fantasy; humorous; and science fiction. Buys 12 mss/year. Length: 1,500-3,000 words. Pays $150-400.
Fillers: Clippings, jokes, gags, anecdotes and newsbreaks. Pays $20-50.

ESCAPADE MAGAZINE, Escapade Corp., 210 E. 35th St., New York NY 10016. Editor-in-Chief: Christopher Watson. 75% freelance written. Emphasizes sophisticated sex. Readers are 18-40, high school educated, interested in sexual entertainment. Monthly magazine; 100 pages. Estab. 1955. Circ. 150,000. Pays 2-3 weeks after scheduling for specific issue. Buys first North American serial rights. Byline given. Submit seasonal/holiday material 6 months in advance. SASE. Reports in 2-3 weeks.
Nonfiction: "Material in keeping with contemporary 'sophisticate' magazine standards; must

be frank in sexual detail without being tasteless (racist, etc.). Expose (of sexual nature); interviews (with sex personalities); and photo features (nudes). Buys about 6 mss/issue. Send complete ms. Length: 2,500-3,500 words. Pays $75-125.

Photos: B&w and color purchased with or without mss. Send contact sheet or transparencies. Pays $10 minimum for b&w contacts; $15-20 for 2¼x2¼ or 35mm color. Model release required. All photos must relate to theme of magazine.

Columns/Departments: Offbeat sex news, sex puzzles (crossword), pieces with reader involvement (sexual). Buys 1-2/issue. Length: 1,000-1,500 words. Pays $35-50. Open for suggestions for new columns or departments.

Fiction: Adventure, erotica, fantasy, confession (all sexual). Buys 2 mss/issue. Send complete ms. Length: 2,500-3,000 words. Pays $100.

ESQUIRE, 2 Park Ave., New York NY 10016. Editor: Phillip Moffitt. Biweekly. Usually buys all rights. Pays on acceptance. Reports in 3 weeks. "We depend chiefly on solicited contributions and material from literary agencies. Unable to accept responsibility for unsolicited material." Query. SASE.

Nonfiction: Articles vary in length, but usually average 3,000 words and rarely run longer than 4,000 words. Articles should be slanted for sophisticated, intelligent readers; however, not highbrow in the restrictive sense. Wide range of subject matter. Rates run roughly between $350 and $1,250, depending on length, quality, etc. Expenses are sometimes allowed, depending on the assignment.

Photos: Art Director, Robert Priest. Accepts both contacts and 11x14 b&w matte prints. Uses 35mm and larger Ektachrome and Kodachrome color transparencies. Buys all rights. Payment depends on how photo is used, but rates are roughly $25 for single b&w; $100-200 for b&w full page; $150 to $350 for full color page. Guarantee on acceptance. Prefers to be queried. Gives assignments and pays some expenses.

Fiction: Rust Hills, Fiction Editor. "Literary excellence is our only criterion, but we accept only solicited contributions and material from literary agents." Length: about 1,000-6,000 words. Payment: $350-1,500.

FLING, 1485 Bayshore Blvd., San Francisco CA 94124. Editor/Publisher: Arv Miller. For male readership, 25-35-years old, college-educated and "hip in the sense that he knows what rings true and what sounds phony." Magazine. Estab. 1957. Bimonthly. Buys first rights (additional payment if reprinted in *Fling* special edition); first or second rights for photos, with additional payment for reprint use. Pays on acceptance. SASE. Sample copy for 70¢ in postage; free writer's guidelines.

Nonfiction: "We want contemporary subjects that have a special interest to men. Areas such as crime, film reviews, sport figures, personality profiles, new sexual activities, foreign travel, pornography, health-diets, making money and sexual news items are currently needed. Style of text should reflect a modern-day, sophisticated approach to prose. No long-winded, scholarly sentences or paragraphs. We want the writer's personal feelings to come through." Quotes and anecdotes important to mss. Also buys humor-fillers, personalities and investigative reporting. Query. Length: 2,500-4,500 words. Pays $125-350 on acceptance.

Fiction: Wants humor or satire only. No straight fiction bought. Current interest ideas, timely spoofs preferred. Filler humor also used. Send complete ms.

GALLERY, Montcalm Publishing Corp., 800 2nd Ave., New York NY 10017. (212)986-9600. Editor: Eric Protter. Executive Editor: F. Joseph Spicler. Managing Editor: Barbara Chonie. Design Director: Derek Burton. "We are similar to *Playboy* and *Penthouse.* Monthly magazine; 128 pages. Estab. 1965. Circ. 700,000. Pays 50% on acceptance,50% on publication. Buys first North American serial rights or will make assignments on a work-for-hire basis. Pays 25% kill fee. Byline given. Submit seasonal/holiday material 6 months in advance. Photocopied submissions OK. SASE. Reports in 3 weeks on queries; in 1 month on mss. Sample copy $2.50.

Nonfiction: Investigative pieces, general interest, how-to, humor, interview, new products and profile. "We do not want to see articles on pornography." Buys 6-8 mss/issue. Query or send complete mss. Length: 1000-6,000 words. Pays $200-1,000. "Special prices negotiated."

Photos: Send photos with accompanying mss. Pay varies for b&w contact sheets or color contact sheets and negatives. Buys one-time rights. Captions preferred; model release required.

Fiction: Adventure, erotica, experimental, humorous, mainstream, mystery and suspense. Buys 1 ms/issue. Send complete ms. Length: 500-3,000 words. Pays $250-750.

GENESIS MAGAZINE, 770 Lexington Ave., New York NY 10021. Editor: Joseph Kelleher. Monthly magazine; 110 pages. Estab. 1973. Circ. 600,000. Query. Reports in 2-3 weeks. SASE.

Nonfiction, Photos and Fiction: "Newsmaking articles, interviews with celebrities—political and entertainment, and erotic photo essays of beautiful women. Remember that we are oriented toward male entertainment. We want top quality first and foremost. Nothing downbeat, depressing or nostalgic."

GENTLEMEN'S QUARTERLY, Conde Nast, 488 Madison Ave., New York NY 10022. Editor-in-Chief: Jack Haber. Managing Editor: Roger C. Sharpe. Emphasizes fashion and service features for men in their late 20s, early 30s, with a large amount of discretionary income. Published 10 times/year. Pays 50% kill fee. Byline given. Pays on publication. Submit seasonal/holiday material 4-6 months in advance. Photocopied submissions OK. SASE. Reports in 3 weeks.
Nonfiction: "Content is mostly geared toward self-help and service areas. Subject should cover physical fitness, grooming, nutrition, psychological matters (different types of therapy, etc.), health, travel, money and investment, business matters—all geared to our audience and filling our format." Buys 6-10 mss/issue. Query with outline of story content. Length: 1,500-2,500 words. Pays $300-450.
Columns/Departments: Aileen Stein, Associate Editor. Looking Good (physical fitness, diet, nutrition and grooming); Money (investments); Lifelines (self-help); Destinations and Adventure (travel); Health; and Living (catchall for various stories that fit magazine format). Buys 5-8/issue. Query with outline of story content. Length: 1,500-2,500 words. Pays $300-400.

HUSTLER MAGAZINE, 2029 Century Park E., Floor 38, Los Angeles CA 90067. (213)556-9200. Executive Editor: Lee Quarnstrom. Monthly magazine; 140 pages. Estab. 1974. Circ. 3 million. Rights purchased vary with author and material. Usually buys all rights, but may reassign rights to author after publication, or buys first world serial rights. Buys 72 mss/year. Pays on acceptance. Write for editorial guidelines. Will consider photocopied submissions (although original is preferred). Reports in 6-8 weeks. Query for nonfiction. Query or submit complete ms for other material. SASE.
Nonfiction, Photos and Fiction: Will consider expose, profiles, interviews. Should be hard-hitting, probing, behind-the-scenes material. "We do not want fluff pieces or PR releases. Avoid overly complex sentence structure. Writing should nonetheless be sophisticated and contemporary, devoid of any pretensions, aggressive and down-to-earth, exhibiting no-nonsense attitude. We deal in a realistic world where people sweat and pick their noses. We mirror the reality of our times." The publication is "sexually explicit but no pornography. No interviews or profiles on porno actors or actresses." Wants expose material, particularly exposes/in political/celebrity/business world. Length: 4,000-5,000 words. Pays $500-1,500. Material also needed for regular columns, "Kinky Korner" and "Sex Practices." Length: 2,000 words for "Korner"; 1,500-2,000 words for "Practices." Pays $100 for "Korner"; $350 for "Practices." Photos used with mss with no additional payment. Size: 35mm Kodachrome. Buys "total exclusive rights." Pays $300/page for color. "Check a recent copy to see our style. Slides should be sent in plastic pages. Soft-focus and diffusion are not acceptable." Considers all good fiction. Length: 4,000-5,000 words. Pays $500-1,000.

OUI MAGAZINE, 8560 Sunset Blvd., Los Angeles CA 90069. (213)652-7870. Editor: Richard Cramer. Senior Editor: Stewart Weiner. For young, well-educated, urban-oriented men. Monthly. Estab. 1972. Circ. 1 million. Buys all rights. Pays 20% kill fee. Byline given. Buys 200 mss/year. Pays on acceptance. Seasonal material for year-end holidays must be submitted 6 months in advance. Reports in 4 weeks. Query. Submit only complete ms for fiction. SASE.
Nonfiction and Photos: "Articles dealing with subjects of national and international interest (including travel) as well as pop culture (including entertainment), sex, sports, service, human behavior. Humor and satire are especially welcome. Most material should be characterized by irreverence, wit, humor." Informational, interview, profile, humor, nostalgia, photo, travel, and spot news. Length: 4,000 words maximum. Pays $750-1,200 for full-length article. Spot news is used for regular column, Openers. Photos (both b&w and color) are purchased without accompanying ms or on assignment. Pays $200-400.
Fiction: Contemporary, experimental, mainstream, mystery, suspense, erotica, fantasy and humorous fiction. Length: 1,500-2,500 words. Pays $750 minimum.

PENTHOUSE, 909 3rd Ave., New York NY 10022. Editorial Director: James Goode. For male (18-34) audience; upper-income bracket, college-educated. Estab. 1965. Monthly. Circ. 5,350,000. Buys all rights. Pays 25% kill fee. Byline given. Buys 70-80 mss/year. Pays on acceptance. Will consider photocopied submissions. Reports in 2-4 weeks. Query. SASE.
Nonfiction: Department Editor: Peter Bloch. Articles on general themes, but not sport- or

family-orientated; money, sex, humor, politics, health, crime, etc. Male viewpoint only. Length: 3,500-5,000 words. General rates: $1,000 minimum.
Fiction: Department Editor: Paul Bresnick. Quality fiction. Experimental; mainstream; mystery; suspense and adventure with erotic flavor; erotica; and science fiction. Length: 3,500-5,000 words. Pays $750 minimum.
Photos: Purchased without mss and on assignment. Pays $200 minimum for b&w; $350 for color. Spec sheet available from Art Director Joe Brooks.

PLAYBOY, 919 N. Michigan, Chicago IL 60611. Editor-Publisher: Hugh M. Hefner; Editorial Director: Arthur Kretchmer. Monthly. Reports in 2 weeks. Buys first rights and others. SASE.
Nonfiction: "Articles should be carefully researched and written with wit and insight; a lucid style is important. Little true adventure or how-to material. Check magazine for subject matter. Pieces on outstanding contemporary men, sports, politics, sociology, business and finance, games, all areas of interest to the urban male." Query. Length: 4,000-6,000 words. On acceptance, pays $2,000 minimum. If a commissioned article does not meet standards, will pay a turn-down price of $400. The *Playboy* interviews run between 8,000 and 15,000 words. After getting an assignment, the freelancer outlines the questions, conducts and edits the interview, and writes the introduction. Pays $2,500 on acceptance. Also, selected shorts pay $750 for 1,000 word essays on contemporary topics; query first. For interviews and selected shorts, contact G. Barry Golson, Executive Editor.
Photos: Gary Cole, Photography Editor, suggests that all photographers interested in contributing make a thorough study of the photography currently appearing in the magazine. Generally all photography is done on assignment. While much of this is assigned to *Playboy's* staff photographers, approximately 50% of the photography is done by freelancers and *Playboy* is in constant search of creative new talent. Qualified freelancers are encouraged to submit samples of their work and ideas. All assignments made on an all rights basis with payments scaled from $600/color page; $300/b&w page; cover, $1,000. Playmate photography for entire project: $6,000. Assignments and submissions handled by Associate Editor: Janice Moses, Chicago; Hollis Wayne, New York; Marilyn Grabowski, Los Angeles. Assignments made on a minimum guarantee basis. Film, processing, and other expenses necessitated by assignment honored.
Fiction: Both light and serious fiction. Entertainment pieces are clever, smoothly written stories. Serious fiction must come up to the best contemporary standards in substance, idea and style. Both, however, should be designed to appeal to the educated, well-informed male reader. General types include comedy, mystery, fantasy, horror, science fiction, adventure, social-realism, "problem" and psychological stories. *Playboy* has serialized novels by Ian Fleming, Vladimir Nabokov, Graham Greene, Michael Crichton and Irwin Shaw. Other fiction contributors include Saul Bellow, John Cheever, Bernard Malamud and Kurt Vonnegut. Fiction lengths are 3,000-6,000 words; short-shorts of 1,000 to 1,500 words are used. Pays $2,000; $1,000 short-short. Rates rise for additional acceptances. Rate for Ribald Classics is $400.
Fillers: Party Jokes are always welcome. Pays $50 each on acceptance. Also interesting items for Playboy After Hours, front section (best check it carefully before submission). The After Hours front section pays anywhere from $50 for humorous or unusual news items (submissions not returned) to $350 for original reportage. Subject matter should be new trends, fads, personalities, cultural developments. Has movie, book, record reviewers but solicits queries for short (1,000 words or less) pieces on art, places, people, trips, adventures, experiences, erotica, television—in short, open-ended. Playboy's Pipeline pay $500 for 900 word how-to's. Ideas for Playboy Potpourri pay $75 on publication. Query.

PLAYERS MAGAZINE, Players International Publications, 8060 Melrose Ave., Los Angeles CA 90046. (213)653-8060. For the black male. Monthly magazine; 94 pages. Estab. 1973. Circ. 400,000. Pays on publication. Buys all rights. Submit seasonal/holiday material 4-6 months in advance. Photocopied submissions OK. SASE. Reports in 3 weeks.
Nonfiction: "*Players* is *Playboy* in basic black." Expose; historical; humor; inspirational; sports; travel; reviews of movies, books and records; profile and interview on assignment. Length: 1,000-5,000 words. Pays 6¢/word. Photos purchased on assignment (pays $25 minimum for b&w; $500 and expenses for 100 shots). Model release required.
Fiction: Adventure; erotica; fantasy; historical (black); humorous; science fiction; and experimental. Length: 1,000-4,000 words. Pays 6¢/word.

RESPONSE MAGAZINE, Can-Am Media, 313 W. 53rd St., New York NY 10019. (212)265-3400. Editor: Warren Tabb. Emphasizes adult relationships that generally include some sex. Monthly; 98 pages. Estab. 1975. Circ. 75,000. Pays on publication. Buys all rights. Byline given unless unwanted. Submit seasonal/holiday material 5 months in advance. SASE. Reports in 3 weeks. Free sample copy and writer's guidelines.

Nonfiction: General interest (marriage and sex); how-to (sexual expertise, regenerate a marriage, have a special affair, etc.); humor (marriage, relationships, sex); current trends in sex; strange and unusual (sexually oriented); nostalgia (sexually oriented); personal experience (sexually oriented); personal opinion (sexually oriented); and warm human interest stories that relate to sexual experiences among adults. Query with short proposal/outline of intentions. Length: 1,000-2,000 words. Pays $75-125.

SAGA, Gambi Publications, Inc., 333 Johnson Ave., Brooklyn NY 11206. (212)456-8600. Editor-in-Chief: David J. Elrich. General interest men's magazine. "We offer an alternative to the many 'skin' magazine across the country in that we give an exciting, contemporary look at America today without the porn. A man's magazine that can be read by the entire family." Monthly magazine; 80 pages. Estab. 1950. Circ. 300,000. Pays on acceptance. Buys first North American serial rights. Byline given. Phone queries OK. Submit seasonal/holiday material 3 months in advance. SASE. Reports in 3-4 weeks. Sample copy $1.25.

Nonfiction: Expose (government); how-to (save money); humor (topical); interview; new product; profile; and travel. Buys 12 mss/issue. Query. Length: 1,500-3,500 words. Pays $250-600.

Photos: Photos purchased with accompanying ms or on assignment. Captions required. Pays $35 minimum for b&w photos; $75 minimum for 35mm color photos. Query for photos. Model release required.

SCREW, Box 432, Old Chelsea Station, New York NY 10011. Managing Editor: Richard Brandes. For a predominantly male, college-educated audience; 21 through mid-40s. Tabloid newspaper; 48 pages. Estab. 1968. Weekly. Circ. 125,000. Buys all rights. Byline given. Buys 150-200 mss/year. Pays on publication. Free sample copy and writer's guidelines. Reports in 2-4 weeks. Submit complete ms for first-person, true confessions. Query on all other material. SASE.

Nonfiction and Photos: "Sexually related news, humor, how-to articles, first-person and true confessions. Frank and explicit treatment of all areas of sex; outrageous and irreverent attitudes combined with hard information, news and consumer reports. Our style is unique. Writers should check several recent issues." Length: 1,000-3,000 words. Pays $100-200. Will also consider material for "Letter From . . .", a consumer-oriented wrapup of commercial sex scene in cities around the country; and "My Scene," a sexual true confession. Length: 1,000-1,200 words. Pays about $40. B&w glossy prints (8x10 or 11x14) purchased with or without mss or on assignment. Pays $10-50.

SWANK, 888 7th Ave., New York NY 10019. Editor-in-Chief: Herman Petras. Managing Editor: Halsey Munson. For urban men, ages 18-40. Monthly magazine; 108 pages. Circ. 350,000. Pays 30 days after acceptance. Buys first North American serial rights or second serial (reprint) rights (for books). Pays 25% kill fee. Byline given unless otherwise requested. Submit seasonal/holiday material 4 months in advance. SASE. Reports in 4 weeks. Sample copy $3.

Nonfiction: Expose (of government, big business and organized crime); how-to (get a raise, find a divorce lawyer, seduce women); humor; interview (must be established names); photo feature (usually nude sets); profile; and travel (with a strong men's slant). Buys 5-6 mss/issue. Length: 3,000 words maximum (except for *very* strong investigative pieces). Pays $400 minimum.

Photos: Norman Oberlander, Art Director. Purchased without accompanying ms. Send transparencies. Pays $800/set for 2¼x2¼ or 35mm color transparencies. Model release required. "The photos we're looking for are female nudes, not your kids, your puppy, your vacation, etc."

Fiction: Humor; erotica; mystery; science fiction; and suspense. Buys 1 mss/issue. Length: 3,000 words. Pays $300 minimum.

How To Break In: "The best way is to read several issues which will give you an idea of what we do. Local events and celebrities that are singular enough to be of national interest are usually good query material. With your query, enclose tearsheets of pieces you've written that are fairly close in style to what you'd like to do for us. Don't just list your credits. We have to know if you can write."

Military

Technical and semitechnical publications for military commanders, personnel and planners, as well as those for military families and civilians interested in Armed Forces activities; are listed here. All of these publications require submissions emphasizing military subjects or aspects of military life.

AIR UNIVERSITY REVIEW, United States Air Force, Air University, Bldg. 1211, Maxwell Air Force Base AL 36112. (205)293-2773. Editor: David R. Mett, Lt. Col., USAF. 95% freelance written. Professional military journal for military supervisory staff and command personnel and top level civilians. Circ. 20,000. Not copyrighted. Byline given. Buys no mss, but gives cash awards on publication. Reports in 6 weeks. Query.
Nonfiction and Photos: "Serves as an open forum for exploratory discussion. Purpose is to present innovative thinking and stimulate dialogue concerning Air Force doctrine, strategy, tactics, and related national defense matters. Footnotes as needed. Prefer the author to be the expert. Reviews of defense-related books. Expository style. B&w glossy photos or charts to supplement articles are desired. Length: 1,500-3,500 words. Cash awards up to $150 unless written by US federal personnel on duty time.

ARMED FORCES JOURNAL, 1414 22nd St. NW, Washington DC 20037. Editor: Benjamin F. Schemmer. For "senior career officers of the US military, defense industry, Congressmen and government officials interested in defense matters, international military and defense industry." Estab. 1863. Monthly. Circ. 20,000. Buys all rights. Buys 25-45 mss/year. Pays on publication. Sample copy $2.75. Photocopied submissions OK. Reports in 2-4 weeks. Submit complete ms. SASE.
Nonfiction: Publishes "national and international defense issues: weapons programs, research, personnel programs, international relations (with emphasis on defense aspect). Also profiles on retired military personnel. We do not want broad overviews of a general subject; more interested in detailed analysis of a specific program or international defense issue. Our readers are decision-makers in defense matters—hence, subject should not be treated too simplistically. Be provocative. We are not afraid to take issue with our own constituency when an independent voice needs to be heard." Buys informational, profile and think pieces. Length: 1,000-3,000 words. Pays $50-100/page.

ARMY MAGAZINE, 2425 Wilson Blvd., Arlington VA 22201. (703)841-4300. Editor-in-Chief: L. James Binder. Managing Editor: Poppy Walker. 80% outside contributions. Emphasizes military interests. Monthly magazine; 72 pages. Estab. 1898. Circ. 119,000. Pays on publication. Buys all rights. Byline given except for back-up research. Submit seasonal/holiday material 3 months in advance of issue date. Photocopied submissions OK. SASE. Free sample copy and writer's guidelines.
Nonfiction: Historical (military and original); humor (military feature-length articles and anecdotes); interview; new product; nostalgia; personal experience; photo feature; profile; and technical. No rehashed history. "We would like to more pieces about interesting military personalities and feature stories about military-civilian relations. We especially want material lending itself to heavy, contributor-supplied photographic treatment." Buys 10 mss/issue. Submit complete ms. Length: 4,000 words. Pays 7-10¢/word.
Photos: Submit photo material with accompanying ms. Pays $15-50 for 8x10 b&w glossy prints; $25-150 for 8x10 color glossy prints or 2¼x2¼ color transparencies, but will accept 35mm. Captions preferred. Buys all rights.
Columns/Departments: Military news; books, comment (*New Yorker*-type "Talk of the Town" items). Buys 8/issue. Submit complete ms. Length: 1,000 words. Pays $30-100. Open to suggestions for new columns/departments.

ARMY RESERVE MAGAZINE, DAAR-PA, The Pentagon, Washington DC 20310. (202)697-2470. Editor: Arthur E. Houre. For Army Reserve members and for civilians interested in the military. Quarterly magazine; 32 pages. Estab. 1954. Circ. 450,000. Not copyrighted. No payment. Credit given. Various prizes are awarded from time to time. Free sample copy. Reports in 6 weeks. Query. SASE.
Nonfiction: "We use news and personality features, consumer information, articles on happenings in world military affairs, weapons, foreign armies, off-duty activities, and happenings in the Army, Army Reserve and ROTC units. And good, amusing military history. We assume the reader knows little about the subject and develop it carefully attempting to find a universal level of interest. Articles are short, to the point, filled with information and often

written tongue in cheek." Length: 1,200-2,500 words.
Fillers: Newsbreaks, anecdotes; short humor. Length: 150-500 words.

ASIA-PACIFIC DEFENSE FORUM, Commander-in-Chief, Pacific Command (US Military), Editor, CINCPAC Staff, Box 13, Camp H. M. Smith HI 96861. (808)477-6128. Executive Editor: Major Fred W. Walker. Editor: Phillip P. Katz. Managing Editor: Lt. Col. Edward C. Kay. For military officers in Pacific and Indian Ocean regions; all services—Army, Navy and Air Force. Secondary audience—government officials, business and industry personnel and academicians concerned with defense issues. "We seek to enhance international professional dialogue on training, force employment, leadership, strategy and tactics, policy matters and international exchange and cooperation." Quarterly magazine; 48 pages. Estab. 1976. Circ. 21,000. Pays on acceptance. Buys simultaneous, second serial (reprint) or one-time rights. Byline given. Phone queries OK. Simultaneous, photocopied and previously published submissions OK. SASE. Reports in 2-3 weeks on queries; in 4-10 weeks on mss. Free sample copy and writer's guidelines.
Nonficton: General interest (strategy and tactics, descriptions of type forces and weapons systems, strategic balance and security issues); historical (occasionally used, if relation to present-day defense issues is apparent); how-to (training, leadership, force employment procedures, organization); interview and personal experience (in terms of developing professional military skills). "We do not want highly technical weapons/equipment descriptions or controversial policy and budget matters, nor do we seek discussion of in-house problem areas. We do not deal with military social life, base activities or PR-type personalities/job descriptions." Buys 1-2 mss/issue. Query or send complete ms. Length: 1,000-4,000 words. Pays $25-100.
Photos: State availability of photos with ms. "We provide nearly all photos; however, will consider good quality photos with mss." Uses 5x7 or 8x10 b&w glossy prints or 35mm color transparencies. Offer no additional payment for photos accompanying mss. Buys one-time rights. Captions required.

INFANTRY, Box 2005, Fort Benning GA 31905. (404)545-2350. Editor: LTC Thomas J. Barham. Published primarily for combat arms officers and noncommissioned officers. Bimonthly magazine; 64 pages. Estab. 1921. Circ. 25,000. Not copyrighted. Pays on publication. Payment cannot be made to US employees. Free sample copy and writer's guidelines. Reports in 30 days.
Nonfiction and Photos: Interested in current information on US military organization, weapons, equipment, tactics and techniques; foreign armies and their equipment; lessons learned from combat experience, both past and present; solutions to problems encountered in the active Army and the Reserve components. Departments include Letters, Features and Forum, Training Notes, Book Reviews. Length of articles: 1,500-3,500 words. Length for Book Reviews: 500-1,000 words. Query. Accepts 75 mss/year.

LADYCOM, Downey Communications, Inc., 1800 M St. NW, Suite 650 S., Washington DC 20036. Editor: Sheila Gibbons. 75% freelance written. For wives of military men who live in the US or overseas. Published eight times a year. Magazine; 64 pages. Estab. 1969. Circ. 400,000. Pays on publication. Buys first North American serial rights. Submit seasonal/holiday material 4 months in advance. SASE. Reports in 2-3 weeks. Sample copy 50¢ and writer's guidelines.
Nonfiction: All articles must have special interest for military wives. How-to (crafts, food), humor, interview, personal experience, personal opinion, profile and travel. Buys 10-12 mss/issue. Query. Length: 800-3,000 words. Pays $35-400/article.
Photos: Purchased with accompanying ms and on assignment. Uses 5x7 or 8x10 b&w glossy prints; 35mm or larger color transparencies; no additional payment for photo with accompanying ms. Captions and model releases are required. Query Claudia Burwell, Design Director.
Columns/Departments: It Seems to Me—"personal experience" pieces by military wives. Pros & Cons—opinion pieces on a controversial topic of interest to military wives. Query. Length: 1,100-1,800 words. Pays $75-175.
Fiction: Mystery, romance and suspense. Buys 6-8 mss/year. Query. Length: 1,500-2,500 words. Pays $100-250.
How To Break In: "Our ideal contributor is a military wife who can write. However, I'm always impressed by a writer who has analyzed the market and can suggest some possible new angles for us."

LEATHERNECK, Box 1775, Quantico VA 22134. (703)640-3171. Editor: Ronald D. Lyons.

Managing Editor: Tom Bartlett. 10% freelance written. Emphasizes all phases of Marine Corps activities. Monthly magazine; 64 pages. Estab. 1917. Circ. 50,000. Pays on acceptance. Buys all rights. Phone queries OK. Submit seasonal/holiday material 3 months in advance of issue date. SASE. Reports in 2 weeks. Free sample copy and writer's guidelines; mention *Writer's Market* in request.

Nonfiction: "All material submitted to *Leatherneck* must pertain to the U.S. Marine Corps and its members." General interest; how-to; humor; historical; interview; nostalgia; personal experience; profile; and travel. No articles on politics, subjects not pertaining to the Marine Corps, and subjects that are not in good taste. Buys 12 mss/year. Query. Length: 1,500-3,000 words. Pays $100 minimum.

Photos: "We like to receive a complete package when we consider a manuscript for publication." State availability of photos with query. No additional payment for 4x5 or 8x10 b&w glossy prints. Captions required. Buys all rights. Model release required.

Fiction: Adventure; historical; and humorous. All material must pertain to the U.S. Marine Corps and its members. Buys 3 mss/year. Query. Length: 1,000-3,000 words. Pays $100 minimum.

Poetry: Free verse; light verse; and traditional. No poetry that does not pertain to the U.S. Marine Corps. Buys 40 mss/year. Length: 12 lines. Pays $10-20.

MARINE CORPS GAZETTE, Marine Corps Association, Box 1775, MCB, Quantico VA 22134. Editor: Lt. Col. Robert W. Smith, U.S.M.C. (Ret.). May issue is aviation-oriented. November issue is historically-oriented. Monthly. Circ. 25,000. Buys all rights. Buys 170-200 mss/year. Pays on publication. Free sample copy and writer's guidelines. Submit seasonal or special material at least 3 months in advance. Query. Reports in 30-60 days. SASE.

Nonfiction: Uses articles up to 5,000 words pertaining to the military profession. Does not want copy advocating political positions. Wants practical articles on military subjects, especially amphibious warfare, close air support and helicopter-borne assault. Also uses any practical article on artillery, communications, leadership, etc. Particularly wanted are articles on relationship of military to civilian government, in-depth coverage of problem areas of the world, foreign military strategy and tactics. Also historical articles about Marines are always needed for the November issue, the anniversary of the Marine Corps. In addition, seeks news stories up to 500 words about US military, particularly Navy/Marine Corps. All offerings are passed on by an editorial board as well as by the editor. Does not want "Sunday supplement" or "gee whiz" material. Pays 3-6¢/word.

Photos: Purchased with mss. Pays $5 each. 8x10 or 5x7 glossy prints preferred.

THE MILITARY ENGINEER, Suite 905, 740 15th St. NW, Washington DC 20005. (202)638-4010. Managing Editor: John J. Kern. 98% freelance written. Bimonthly magazine. Estab. 1919. Circ. 22,000. Pays on publication. Buys all rights. Byline given. Phone queries OK. SASE. Reports in 1 month. Sample copy and writer's guidelines $4.

Nonfiction: Well-written and illustrated semi-technical articles by experts and practitioners of civil and military engineering, constructors, equipment manufacturers, defense contract suppliers and architect/engineers on these subjects and on subjects of military biography and history. "Subject matter should represent a contribution to the fund of knowledge, concern a new project or method, be on R&D in these fields; investigate planning and management techniques or problems in these fields, or be of militarily strategic nature." Buys 80-100 mss/year. Length: 2,000-4,000 words. Query.

Photos: Mss must be accompanied by 6-8 well-captioned photos, maps or illustrations; b&w, generally. Pays approximately $20/page.

MILITARY JOURNAL, International Graphics Corp., 218 Beech St., Bennington VT 05201. (802)447-0313. Publisher/Editor: Ray Merriam. 80% freelance written. Emphasizes military history from 1900 to present time. Quarterly magazine; 56 pages. Estab. 1977. Circ. 3,000. Pays on publication. Buys one-time rights. Byline given. Phone queries OK. Submit seasonal/holiday material 6 months in advance of issue date. Simultaneous and photocopied and previously published submissions OK. SASE. Reports in 2 weeks. Sample copy $2; free writer's guidelines for SASE.

Nonficition: Expose (military subjects-past and present); humor (military-oriented and preferably true experience); historical (military history—battles, personalities, weapons, equipment, uniforms, insignia, unit histories, personal accounts, etc.); interview (with veterans and servicemen); nostalgia and personal experience ("What it was like"-type accounts—in military, home front, etc.); photo feature (anything military); and technical (military weapons, equipment, tactics, etc.). "No fiction or how-to-do-it hobby pieces." Buys 10 mss/issue. Query. Pays 50¢/column inch.

Photos: State availability of photos with query. Pays $2 for any size b&w prints. Captions required. Buys one-time rights.

Columns/Departments: Book Reviews (military history books); Medal of Honor (accounts of winners of award); Military Briefs (unusual, little known facts and oddities); current data on world's military forces and equipment; and Signs of the Times (military signs, illustrations and description). Query. Length: 200-500 words. Pays 50¢/column inch.

Fillers: Clippings, newsbreaks, and short articles. Buys 12 fillers/issue. Length: 250-1,000 words.

MILITARY LIVING, Box 4010, Arlington VA 22204. (703)521-7703. Editor: Ann Crawford. For military personnel and their families. Monthly. Circ. 30,000. Buys first serial rights. "Very few freelance features used last year; mostly staff-written." Pays on publication. Sample copy for 50¢ in coin or stamps. "Slow to report due to small staff and workload." Submit complete ms. SASE.

Nonfiction and Photos: "Articles on military life in greater Washington DC area. We would especially like recreational features in the Washington DC area. We specialize in passing along morale-boosting information about the military installations in the area, with emphasis on the military family—travel pieces about surrounding area, recreation information, etc. We do not want to see depressing pieces, pieces without the military family in mind, personal petty complaints or general information pieces. Prefer 700 words or less, but will consider more for an exceptional feature. We also prefer a finished article rather than a query." Payment is on an honoraium basis, 1-1½¢/word. Photos purchased with mss. 8x10 b&w glossy prints. Payment is $5 for original photos by author.

MILITARY LIVING AND CONSUMER GUIDE'S R&R REPORT, Box 4010, Arlington VA 22204. Publisher: Ann Crawford. For "military consumers worldwide." Bimonthly newsletter. "Please state when sending submission that it is for the *R&R Report Newsletter* so as not to confuse it with our monthly magazine which has different requirements." Buys first rights, but will consider other rights. Pays on publication. Sample copy $1. SASE.

Nonfiction: "We use information on little-known military facilities and privileges, discounts around the world and travel information. Items must be short and concise. Stringers wanted around the world. Payment is on an honorarium basis. 1-1½¢/word."

MILITARY REVIEW, US Army Command and General Staff College, Fort Leavenworth KS 66027. (913)684-5642. Editor-in-Chief: Col. Edward Bradford. Managing Editor: Lt. Ernie Webb. Business Manager: Harry Acker. Emphasizes the military for senior military officers, students and scholars. Monthly magazine; 96 pages. Estab. 1922. Circ. 24,000. Pays on publication. Buys one-time rights. Byline given. Phone queries OK. Photocopied submissions OK. SASE. Reports in 4 weeks. Free sample copy and writer's guidelines.

Nonfiction: Historical, humor, informational, new product, personal opinion and technical. Buys 5-7 mss/issue. Query. Length: 2,000-4,000 words. Pays $10-50.

Photos: Purchased on assignment. Captions required. Send b&w/color prints. Offers no additional payment for photos accepted with accompanying ms. Model release required.

NATIONAL DEFENSE, 819 Union First Bldg., 740 15th St., Washington DC 20005. (202)347-7250. Editor: D. Ballou. For members of industry and U.S. Armed Forces. Publication of the American Defense Preparedness Association. Bimonthly magazine; 96 pages. Estab. 1920. Circ. 34,000. Buys all rights. Pays 100% kill fee. Byline given. Buys 12-18 mss a year. Pays on publication. Sample copy $4; free writer's guidelines. Will consider photocopied submissions. No simultaneous submissions. Reports in 4 weeks. Query or submit complete ms. SASE

Nonfiction: Military-related articles: weapons, systems, management and production. "We emphasize industrial preparedness for defense and prefer a news style, with emphasis on the 'why'." Length: 1,500-2,500 words. Pays $25/published page. Book reviews are sometimes used, but query is required first and no payment is made.

NATIONAL GUARD (formerly the *National Guardsman*), 1 Massachusetts Ave. NW, Washington DC 20001. (202)789-0031. Editor: Bruce Jacobs. 50% freelance written. For offrcers of the Army and Air National Guard. Monthly. Circ. 62,000. Rights negotiable. Byline given. Buys 10-12 mss/year. Pays on publication. Query. SASE.

Nonfiction and Photos: Military policy, strategy, training, equipment, logistics, personnel policies; tactics, combat lessons learned as they pertain to the Army and Air Force (and impact on Army National Guard and Air National Guard). Material must be strictly accurate from a technical standpoint. Does not publish "exposes." Length: 2,000-3,000 words. Payment

($75-300/article) depends on originality, amount of research involved, etc.

OFF DUTY, US: 3303 Harbor Blvd., B-8, Costa Mesa CA 92626; Europe: Eschersheimer Landstrasse 69, D-6 Frankfurt/Main, West Germany; Pacific: 30 D'Aguilar St., Tak Yan Cmcl. Bldg., 8/F., Central, Hong Kong. Editor: Jim Shaw. For "US servicemen and their families, mostly between 18-30 years old. Interested in travel, sport, hi-fi and photography, cars, hobbies." Monthly magazine: 40-104 pages. Estab. 1969. Circ. 390,000 (combined editions). Pays on acceptance. Buys second serial or one time rights. Submit seasonal/holiday material 5-6 month in advance. Photocopied and previously published (if not in conflicting distribution) submissions OK. SASE. Free sample copy and writer's guidelines.

Nonfiction: "We like articles on travel, hobbies, recreation, entertaining, motoring, family activities, the home and budget-saving ideas. Emphasis is on things to do. In travel articles we like anecdotes, lots of description, color and dialog. Our readers are not looking simply to relax in unspoiled scenery. They want to know what to do." Buys 12-15 mss/issue. Query. Length: 500-3,000 words. Pays 7-13¢/word.

Photos: Purchased with accompanying ms. Pays $10-25 for b&w glossy prints; $15-50 for color transparencies, $100 minimum for covers. Captions and model releases required. Photos often decisive in acceptance of article. Rejects: "No fiction, poetry, or war stories." Send submissions and queries regarding European material to West Germany address, attn. Bruce Thorstad, Assistant Editor. All other material should be sent to California or Hong Kong address.

OVERSEAS LIFE, Postfach 29, 6382 Friedrichsdorf 2, West Germany. Editor-in-Chief: Bob Cullen. General entertainment magazine serving American and Canadian military personnel stationed throughout Europe. Specifically directed to males 18-30. Monthly magazine; 80 pages. Estab. 1973. Circ. 82,000. Pays on publication. Buys rights to military communities in Europe. Submit seasonal/holiday material 3 months in advance of issue date. Simultaneous, photocopied and previously published submissions OK. SAE and International Reply Coupons (not US postage). Sample copy for 1 International Reply Coupon.

Nonfiction: "We are a commercial giveaway magazine looking for flashy, sexy, young-male-interest writing and photography. In the past we've bought how-to (travel by bike, van, foot, motorcycle; how to photograph girls, rock stars, traveling subjects); and do-it-yourself-sports (skiing, kayaking, sailing, soccer, tennis). Also need music features—rock, soul, C&W, especially on musicians soon coming to Europe. We're looking for a new kind of travel article: the "in scenes" of Europe written up especially for our young GIs. Should include nightlife, discos, bars, informal eating out, good music scenes rather than fancy restaurants, cathedrals, or museums. Above all, tell our servicemen where the girls are. Buys 80 mss/year. Length: 800-1,500 words. Pays 10¢/word.

Photos: Purchased with accompanying ms. Captions required. Pays $20 for b&w; $35 minimum for color and $150 for covers.

PARAMETERS: JOURNAL OF THE U.S. ARMY WAR COLLEGE, U.S. Army War College, Carlisle Barracks PA 17013. (717)245-4943. Editor: Colonel Lloyd J. Matthews, U.S. Army. 49% freelance written. For military audience (large percentage of graduate-level degrees) interested in national and international security affairs, defense activities and management; also a growing audience among civilian academicians. Quarterly. Circ. 7,000. Not copyrighted. Unless copyrighted, articles may be reprinted. Byline given. Pays on publication. Reports in 2 months.

Nonfiction and Photos: The purpose of *Parameters* is to provide a forum for the expression of mature, professional thought on national and international security affairs, military history, military strategy, military leadership and management, the art and science of land warfare, and other topics of significant and current interest to the U.S. Army and the Department of Defense. Further, it is designed to serve as a vehicle for continuing the education, and thus the professional development, of War College graduates and other military officers and civilians concerned with military affairs. Military implications should be stressed whenever possible. Length: 5,000-7,000 words. B&w glossy prints purchased with mss. Pays $25 minimum; $100 maximum (to include half-tones, artwork, charts, graphs, maps, etc.).

PERIODICAL, Council on Abandoned Military Posts, 4970 N. Camino Antonio, Tucson AZ 85718. Editor-in-Chief: Dan L. Thrapp. 100% freelance written. Emphasizes old and abandoned forts, posts and military installations; military subjects for a professional, knowledgeable readership interested in one-time defense sites or other military installations. Quarterly magazine; 40-64 pages. Estab. 1967. Circ. 1,500. Pays on publication. Buys one-time rights. Simultaneous, photocopied and previously published (if published a long time ago) submissions OK. SASE. Reports in 3 weeks. Sample copy 50¢.

Nonfiction: Historical; personal experience; photo feature; technical (relating to posts, their construction/operation and military matters); and travel. Buys 4-6 mss/issue. Query or send complete ms. Length: 300-4,000 words. Pays minimum $2/page.

Photos: Purchased with or without accompanying ms. Captions required. Query. Glossy, single-weight, b&w up to 8x10. Offers no additional payment for photos accepted with accompanying ms.

THE RETIRED OFFICER MAGAZINE. 201 N. Washington St., Alexandria VA 22314. (703)549-2311. Editor: Colonel Minter L. Wilson Jr., USA-Ret. For "officers of the 7 uniformed services and their families." Estab. 1945. Monthly. Circ. 275,000. May buy all rights or first serial rights. Byline given. Pays on publication. Free sample copy. Will consider photocopied submissions "if clean and fresh." Submit seasonal material (holiday stories in which the Armed Services are depicted) at least 3 months in advance. Reports on material accepted for publication within 6 weeks. Returns rejected material in 4 weeks. Submit complete ms. SASE.

Nonfiction and Photos: History, humor, cultural, second-career opportunities and current affairs. "Currently topical subjects with particular contextual slant to the military; historical events of military significance; features pertinent to a retired military officer's milieu (second career, caveats in the business world; wives' adjusting, leisure, fascinating hobbies). True military experiences (short) are also useful, and we tend to use articles less technical than a single-service publication might publish." Length: 1,000-2,500 words. Pays $25-250. 8x10 b&w photos (normal halftone). Pays $5. Color photos must be suitable for color separation. Pays $25 if reproduced in color; otherwise, same as b&w. Department Editor: Sharon F. Golden.

US NAVAL INSTITUTE PROCEEDINGS. Annapolis MD 21402. (301)268-6110. Editor: Clayton R. Barrow Jr. Managing Editor: Paul Stillwell. Emphasizes sea services (Navy, Marine Corps, Coast Guard) for sea services officers and enlisted personnel, other military services in the US and abroad and civilians interested in naval/maritime affairs. Monthly magazine; 128 pages. Estab. 1873. Circ. 65,000. Pays on acceptance. Buys all rights. Byline given. Phone queries OK, but all material must be submitted on speculation. Submit seasonal/anniversary material at least 6 months in advance. Photocopied submissions OK. SASE. Reports in 2 weeks (queries); 3 months (manuscripts). Free sample copy.

Nonfiction: Historical (based on primary sources, unpublished and/or first-hand experience); humor; informational; nostalgia; personal experience; personal opinion; photo feature; technical; professional notes; and book reviews. Query. Length: 4,000 words maximum. Pays $200-400.

Photos: Purchased with or without accompanying ms or on assignment. Captions required. Query. Pays $15 maximum for b&w 8x10 glossy prints. "We pay $2 for each photo submitted with articles by people other than the photographer."

Columns/Departments: Fred Rainbow, Column/Department Editor. Comment and Discussion (comments 500-700 words on new subjects or ones previously covered in magazine); Professional Notes; Nobody Asked Me, But . . . (700-1,000 words, strong opinion on naval/maritime topic); and Book Reviews. Buys 35 Book Reviews; 35 Professional Notes; 100 Comment and Discussion and 10 NAMB columns a year. Pays $25-50.

Fillers: Miss Nancy B. Smith, Fillers Editor. Anecdotes should be humorous actual occurrences, not previously published. Buys 25 fillers/year. Length: maximum 200 words. Pays $25 flat rate.

How To Break In: "The Comment and Discussion section is our bread and butter. It is a glorified letters to the editor section and exemplifies the concept of the *Proceedings* as a forum. We particularly welcome comments on material published in previous issues of the magazine. This offers the writer of the comment an opportunity to expand the discussion of a particular topic and to bring his own viewpoint into it. This feature does not pay particularly well, but it is an excellent opportunity to get one's work into print."

Miscellaneous

A BETTER LIFE FOR YOU, The National Research Bureau, Inc., 424 N. 3rd St., Burlington IA 52601. (319)752-5415. Editor-in-Chief: N. Pasqual. Editor: M. Cuppy. 95% freelance written. For industrial workers of all ages. Quarterly magazine: 32 pages. Estab. 1956. Circ. 30,000. Pays on publication. Buys all rights. Previously published submissions OK. SASE. Reports in 1 week. Free sample copy and writer's guidelines.

Nonfiction: General interest (steps to better health, on the job attitudes); how-to (perform better on the job, how-to do home repair jobs, and how-to keep up maintenance on a car).

Buys 4-5 mss/issue. Query or send outline. Length: 400-600 words. Pays $20 minimum.

AIR TRAVEL JOURNAL, Airport Publishers Inc., Van Dusen Bldg., Logan International Airport, East Boston MA 02128. Editor: James Calogero. Emphasizes air travel and airline personalities. Weekly tabloid; 16 pages. Estab. 1971. Circ. 30,000. Pays on publication. Buys all rights. Byline given. Submit seasonal/holiday material 1 month in advance. Simultaneous and previously published submissions OK. SASE. Reports in 2 weeks.
Nonfiction: Interview, profile and travel. Buys 20 mss/year. Query. Length: 750 words maximum. Pays $100 maximum.
Photos: State availability of photos with ms. Pays $5 for 8x10 b&w glossy prints.

AMERICAN DANE MAGAZINE, Danish Brotherhood in America, Box 31748, Omaha NE 68131. (402)341-5049. Administrative Editor: Howard Christensen. Submit only material with Danish ethnic flavor. Monthly magazine; 20-28 pages. Estab. 1916. Circ. 11,000. Pays on publication. Buys all rights, but will reassign to author following publication. Submit seasonal/holiday material 4 months in advance (particularly Christmas). Photocopied or previously published submissions OK. SASE. Byline given. Reports in 1 month. Sample copy $1. Free writer's guidelines.
Nonfiction: Historical; humor (satirical, dry wit notoriously Danish); informational (Danish items, Denmark or Danish-American involvements); inspirational (honest inter-relationships); interview; nostalgia; personal experience; photo feature and travel. Buys 20-25 mss/year. Query. Length: 1,500 words maximum. Pays $25.
Photos: Purchased on assignment. Query. Pays $10-25 for b&w. Total purchase price for ms includes payment for photos. Model release required.
Fiction: Danish adventure; historical; humorous; mystery; romance; and suspense. Must have Danish appeal. Buys 12 mss/year. Query. Length: 500-1,500 words. Pays $25.
Poetry: Danish avant-garde, free verse, haiku, light verse and traditional. Buys 6-8 poems/year. Query. Limit submissions to batches of 5. Length: maximum 40 lines. Pays $25-75.
Fillers: Danish clippings, jokes, gags, anecdotes, puzzles (crossword, anagrams etc.) and short humor. Query. Length: 50-300 words.

ANDY WARHOL'S INTERVIEW MAGAZINE, 860 Broadway W., New York NY 10003. (212)533-4700. Editor: Bob Colacello. For those interested in fashion, movies, art and music. Estab. 1970. Monthly. Circ. 82,000. All rights purchased but will negotiate on individual basis. Buys 25 mss/year. Pays on publication. Will send sample copy for $1. Query. SASE.
Nonfiction and Photos: Features exclusive interviews with interesting people in fashion, art, movies, television, music, books, and whatever is happening now. Length: 10,000 words maximum. Pays $25. Prefer 8x10 or larger b&w photos.
How To Break In: "We are interested in interviews with entertainment figures as well as with *entertaining* figures. Usually with famous people with whom I want an interview, I'll assign it to someone I know. So the best way to break in is either with a well-known person to whom you happen to have some kind of access or, more likely, a lesser known *entertaining* person who you can get to yourself. If we like what you do—and I don't know how to describe it; basically what you need is a good interviewing personality rather than writing skill—then I will certainly want to use you in the future and will arrange access for you when it comes to interviewing the more famous types."

ARARAT, The Armenian General Benevolent Union of America, 628 2nd Ave., New York NY 10016. Editor-in-Chief: Leo Hamalian. Emphasizes Armenian life and culture for Americans of Armenian descent and Armenian immigrants. "Most are well-educated; some are Old World." Quarterly magazine; 48 pages. Estab. 1960. Circ. 2,200. Pays on publication. Buys first North American serial rights. Submit seasonal/holiday material at least 3 months in advance. Photocopied and previously published submissions OK. SASE. Reports in 6 weeks. Sample copy $1.50.
Nonfiction: Historical (history of Armenian people, of leaders, etc.); interviews (with prominent or interesting Armenians in any field, but articles are preferred); profile (on subjects relating to Armenian life and culture); personal experience (revealing aspects of typical Armenian life); travel (in Armenia and Armenian communities throughout the world and the US). Buys 3 mss/issue. Query. Length: 1,000-6,000 words. Pays $25-100.
Columns/Departments: Reviews of books by Armenians or relating to Armenians. Buys 6/issue. Query. Pays $20. Open to suggestions for new columns/departments.
Fiction: Any stories dealing with Armenian life in America or in the old country. Religious

stories relating to the Armenian Church. Buys 2 mss/year. Query. Length: 2,000-5,000 words. Pays $35-75.
Poetry: Any verse that is Armenian in theme. Buys 6/issue. Pays $10.
How To Break In: "Read the magazine, and write about the kind of subjects we are obviously interested in, e.g., Kirlian photography, Aram Avakian's films, etc. Remember that we have become almost totally ethnic magazine in subject matter, but we want articles that present the Armenian to the rest of the world in an interesting way."

C.S.P. WORLD NEWS, Editions Stencil, Box 2608, Station D, Ottawa, Ontario, Canada K1P 5W7. Editor-in-Chief: Guy F. Claude Hamel. Emphasizes book reviews. Monthly literary journal; 20 pages. Estab. 1965. Circ. 200,000. Buys all rights. Photocopied submissions OK. SAE and International Reply Coupons. Reports in 2 months. Sample copy $1.
Nonfiction: Publishes on sociology and criminology. Buys 12 mss/year. Send complete ms. Length: 2,600-5,000 words. Pays $1-2/typewritten, double-spaced page. Submit complete ms.
Columns/Departments: Writer's Workshop material. Buys 12 items/year. Send complete ms. Length: 20-50 words. Pays $1-2.
Poetry: Publishes avant-garde forms. Buys 12/year. Submit complete ms; no more than 2 at a time. Length: 6-12 lines. Pays $1.
Fillers: Jokes, gags and anecdotes. Pays $1-2.

CAMPAIGN, Lowry Enterprises, Box 896, Fallbrook CA 92028. Editor: Don Lowry. Emphasizes military history and wargaming. Bimonthly magazine; 48 pages. Estab. 1972. Circ. 2,200. Pays on publication. Buys all rights. Byline given. Photocopied and previously published submissions OK but must be identified as such. SASE. Reports in 3 weeks queries; in 8 weeks on mss. Sample copy $2.25; free writer's guidelines.
Nonfiction: Historical (military); how-to (create a game, play well, design game); interview (with game designer, publisher); new products (reviews); personal experiences (description of game played to illustrate strategy); personal opinion (on game reviews); and photo feature (new games, coventions). Buys 4-6 mss/issue. Query or send complete ms. Pays $6/printed page.
Photos: State availability of photos or send photos with ms. Pays $6/printed page for b&w glossy prints; and color will be printed as b&w. Captions preferred.

CLUB LIVING, Club Living Magazine, Inc., 250 Station Plaza, Hartsdale NY 10530. (212)298-1503, (914)472-9191. Editor: Diana Lyons. For private club members. Monthly magazine; 48 pages. Estab. August 1977. Circ. 52,000. Pays on publication. Buys all rights. Byline given. Submit seasonal/holiday material 2 months in advance. Simultaneous and photocopied submissions OK. SASE. Reports in 2 weeks. Sample copy $1.50; free writer's guidelines.
Nonfiction: New products and travel. "*Club Living* concerns private country and city club members and club life. All features must be geared for clubs—that includes travel at exclusive resorts; profiles on prestigious club members; coverage of sport tournaments and social and charity activities; interviews with club chefs; club architecture and renovations; products that are unique, unusally expensive, etc.; financial columns about clubs." Query with clips of published work. Length: 500-1,500 words. Pays $25-125.
Photos: Send photos with ms. Pays $5-50 for b&w contact sheets and prints; $15-75 for color transparencies; no additional payment for photos with accompanying ms. Buys one-time rights. Captions preferred; model releases required.
Columns/Departments: Dining In (exceptional club dining rooms, cuisine or resort cuisine); Par For The Course (all about golf tournaments, sports people at country clubs); and Pro-Scribed (tennis and golf tips). Buys 2/issue. Query. Length: 1,000-1,500 words. Pays $50-100.
Fillers: Newsbreaks and what's going on at country clubs in the future and sports, and national club policy. Pays $25.

CREDIT NEWSLETTER, Emerson Enterprises, 5775 Mosholu Ave., Riverdale NY 10471. Editor: H. Emerson-Ezekiel. Emphasizes consumer credit. Quarterly newsletter; 4 pages. Estab. July 1978. Circ. 5,000. Pays on publication. Buys all rights. Pays 30-60% kill fee. Byline given except for certain fillers and/or quizzes. Submit seasonal/holiday material 6 months in advance. SASE. Reports in 6-8 weeks. Sample copy $1; writer's guidelines 25¢.
Nonfiction: Expose, general interest, historical, how-to, humor, interview, new product, nostalgia, personal experience, personal opinion, profile, technical and travel. "All articles should provide imaginative treatment on the subject of how consumers who have lost their good credit rating can regain and maintain it. Step-by-step details have the best chance of

being accepted. How-to articles on ironing out differences with credit bureaus and creditors, etc. No sob stories on How-I-Got-Gypped, unless they have a specific point to make that will inform our readers." Buys 24 mss/year. Send complete ms. Length: 1,000 maximum. Pays $5 for fillers and $50 for "finely-crafted writing."

Fillers: Clippings, jokes, gags, anecdotes, newsbreaks and short humor. Buys 10-15/issue. Length: 200 words maximum. Pays $5.

CREATIVE LIVING, 515 Madison Ave., New York NY 10022. (212)752-4530. Editor: Robert H. Spencer. Published by Northwestern Mutual Life. Estab. 1972. Quarterly. Circ. 200,000. Rights purchased vary with author and material. Usually buys all rights but may reassign rights to author after publication. Buys 40-50 mss/year. Occasionally overstocked. Pays on publication. Free sample copy and writer's guidelines. Prefers items not written in first-person. Submit seasonal sports material 6 months in advance. Reports in 2-3 months. Query, with writing sample. SASE.

Nonfiction: "We publish *Creative Living* because we think it helps turn people on to themselves. We think it totally conceivable that people who read articles about others living their lives to the hilt might be motivated to think of themselves in a brighter, more creative light. Writers should bone up a bit on what makes the creative process tick. Get behind the facts. Many people lead creative lives. Importantly, we want to know their philosophical basis for living. Stress individuality and use specific examples. Give advice to the reader for gaining greater self-fulfillment. We try to avoid sex and partisan politics." Length: 600-2,500 words with greater need for short manuscripts. Pays $50-300, sometimes more for complex assignments.

THE DEAF CANADIAN MAGAZINE, Box 1291, Edmonton, Alterta., Canada T5J 2M8. Editor-in-Chief: David Burnett. For "general consumers who are deaf, parents of deaf children/adults, professionals on deafness, teachers, ministers, and government officials." Monthly magazine; 24 pages. Estab. 1972. Circ. 141,000. Pays on publication. "Although the publication is copyrighted, we do not purchase any rights which are reserved to the individual contributor." Byline given. Submit seasonal/holiday material 2 months in advance. Simultaneous, photocopied and previously published submissions OK. *Contributions cannot be acknowledged or returned.* Sample copy $1.

Nonfiction: Expose (education); how-to (skills, jobs, etc.); historical; humor; informational (deafness difficulties); inspirational; interview; new product; personal experience; personal opinion; photo feature (with captions); profile; technical; and travel. "Mss must relate to deafness or the deaf world." Buys 1-10 mss/issue. Submit complete ms. Length: 3,000 words maximum. Pays $20-150. "Articles should be illustrated with at least 4 good b&w photos."

Photos: Purchased with accompanying ms or on assignment. Captions required (not less than 15 words). Query. Pays $20 for 2½x3 (preferably) and 5x7 b&w glossy; $100 for color transparencies used as cover. Total purchase price for ms includes payment for photos.

Columns/Departments: Here and There, Sports and Recreation, Foreign, Cultural Events and Books. Submit complete ms. Length: 1 page maximum. Pays $50-125. Open to suggestions for new columns/departments.

Fiction: Adventure, experimental, historical, humorous, mystery, mainstream, religious, romance, science fiction, suspense, condensed novels and serialized novels. Buys 1-10 mss/issue. Length: 3,000 words maximum. Pays $50-150.

Fillers: Clippings, jokes, gags, anecdotes, newsbreaks, puzzles and short humor. Must be related to deafness or the deaf world. Buys 1-20 mss/issue. Submit complete ms. Length:½ page maximum. Pays $1-50.

DIRECTORS & BOARDS, The Journal of Corporate Action, Information for Industry, Inc., 1621 Brookside Rd., McLean VA 22101. (703)534-7771. Editor-in-Chief: Stanley Foster Reed. Emphasizes corporate decisionmaking at board level. Quarterly magazine; 64 pages. Estab. 1976. Circ. 3,000. Pays 21 days after publication. Buys all rights. Byline given. Photocopied submissions OK (two copies). SASE. Reports in 4-6 weeks. Free sample copy and writer's guidelines to writers who propose specific projects.

Nonfiction: Alexandra Reed, senior editor. "*D&B* article topics usually fall into one of three categories: specific, detailed ideas (generally from seasoned directors) for improving board function, structure or performance; analyses of legal, social or industrial developments in the US or abroad, examined from the perspective of evolving board responsibilities; board considerations of subjects that come before directors for review and/or approval—for example, long-range strategic planning, executive succession and compensation, corporate performance appraisals, compliance audits, shareholder relations, annual reports, disclosure standards, corporate social responsibilities, etc." Buys 20 mss/year. Length: 5,000-15,000 words. Pays

$100-1,000, depending on length of article, amount of research involved, and stature of author.

FAR WEST, Wright Publishing Co., Inc., 2949 Century Plaza, Costa Mesa CA 92626. (714)979-2560. Editor: Scott McMillan. Emphasizes "western fiction for a wide field of interest groups—everything from MDs to ditch diggers. They're mostly conservative, but hard to pin down." Quarterly magazine; 160 pages. Estab. 1978. Circ. 125,000. Pays on publication. Buys all rights. Phone queries OK. Submit seasonal/holiday material 6 months in advance. Previously published submissions OK. SASE. Reports in 10 weeks. Sample copy $1.50; writer's guidelines for SASE.
Fiction: Historical and western. "No avant-garde stuff. Avoid over-violence and explicit sex. Try not to write like Zane Grey." Buys 10 mss/issue. Send complete ms. Length: 1,500-50,000 words. Pays $150-500.

FORWARD, Forward Publishing Co., 5501 W. North Ave., Milwaukee WI 53208. Publisher: Richard A. Miller. Emphasizes free enterprise. Annual magazine; 60-90 pages. Estab. 1969. Circ. 25,000. Pays on publication. Buys second serial (reprint) rights. Phone queries OK. Simultaneous and previously published submissions OK. SASE. Reports in 3-4 months. Sample copy $1.
Nonfiction: General interest and how-to. "Articles should be about the advantages of private business and the free enterprise system. Advantages of living and working in Wisconsin." Send complete ms or query with clips of published work. Payment open.
Photos: Send photos with ms. Uses 4x5 or larger b&w prints; 4x5 color transparencies. Captions and model releases required.

JOURNAL OF GRAPHOANALYSIS, 111 N. Canal St. Chicago IL 60606. Editor: V. Peter Ferrara. For audience interested in self-improvement. Monthly. Buys all rights. Pays negotiable kill fee. Byline given. Pays on acceptance. Reports on submissions in 1 month. SASE
Nonfiction: Self-improvement material helpful for ambitious, alert, mature people. Applied psychology and personality studies, techniques of effective living, etc.; all written from intellectual approach by qualified writers in psychology, counseling and teaching, preferably with degrees. Length: 2,000 words. Pays about 5¢/word.

MASTHEAD, Box 1009, Marblehead MA 01945. Editor-in-Chief: Walter A. Day Jr. "A journal for teaching history with old newspapers" for teachers, genealogists, collectors and people interested in printing, journalism and general history. Tabloid; 9 times/year; 20 pages. Estab. 1977. Circ. 6,000. Pays on publication. Not copyrighted. Byline given. Phone queries OK. Simultaneous, photocopied and previously published submissions OK. SASE. Reports in 2 weeks. Sample copy $1.
Nonfiction: Informational; historical; humor (in historical vein); interviews (with people in history field); nostalgia; profile; travel and personal experience. Length: 500-5,000 words. Query. Pays 1¢/word.
Photos: Used with mss with no additional payment for 5x7 glossy prints. Model release required.
Columns/Departments: Open Forum (letters on developments in printing, journalism and collecting history); The Hidden Side to History (articles tracing the original, firsthand account in a newspaper of an historical event tempered with a current perspective). Length: 100-750 words. Pays 1¢/word. Open to suggestions for new columns/departments.

THE NEW YORK ANTIQUE ALMANAC, The New York Eye Publishing Co., Inc., Box 335, Lawrence NY 11559. (516)371-3300. Editor-in-Chief: Carol Nadel. Emphasizes antiques, art, investments and nostalgia. Tabloid published 10 issues/year; 24 pages. Estab. 1975. Circ. 33,000. Pays on publication. Buys all rights, but may reassign following publication. Byline given. Phone queries OK. Submit seasonal/holiday material "whenever available." Previously published submissions OK but must advise. SASE. Reports in 6 weeks. Free sample copy.
Nonfiction: Expose (fradulent practices), historical (museums, exhibitions, folklore, background of events), how-to (clean, restore, travel, shop, invest), humor (jokes, cartoons, satire), informational, inspirational (essays), interviews (authors, shopkeepers, show managers, appraisers), nostalgia ("The Good Old Days" remembered various ways), personal experience (anything dealing with antiques, art, investments, nostalgia), personal opinion, photo feature (antique shows, art shows, fairs, crafts markets, restorations), profile, technical (repairing, purchasing, restoring), travel (shopping guides and tips) and investment, economics, and financial reviews. Buys 9 mss/issue. Query or submit complete ms. Length: 3,000 words maximum. Pays $15-35. "Expenses for accompanying photos will be reimbursed."

Photos: "Occasionally, we have photo essays (auctions, shows, street fairs, human interest) and pay $3/photo with caption."
Fillers: Personal experiences, commentaries, anecdotes. "Limited only by author's imagination." Buys 45 mss/year. Pays $5-15.

THE NEWS CIRCLE, Box 74637, Los Angeles CA 90004. (213)469-7004. Editor: Joseph Haiek. For Arab Americans. Monthly newspaper; 16 pages. Estab. 1972. Circ. 3,000. Not copyrighted. Byline given. Buys 10-25 mss/year. Pays on publication. Free sample copy. Will consider photocopied and simultaneous submissions. Reports in 1 week. Query with title of proposed article. SASE.
Nonfiction, Photos and Fillers: Wants mss about Middle East issues; mainly business, and economic conditions. Would like to see mss on Mideast business conferences and expos. Length: 400 words maximum. Pays 5-10¢/word. Photos purchased with accompanying ms with extra payment and purchased on assignment. Captions required. Pays $5-10. Also buys newsbreaks and clippings on Mideast business. Pays 8-10¢/word.

NUESTRO: THE MAGAZINE FOR LATINOS, 1140 Avenue of the Americas, New York NY 10036. Editor-in-Chief: Charles R. Rivera. Managing Editor: Philip Herrera. 85% freelance written. Monthly magazine; 64 pages. Estab. April 1977. Circ. 190,000. Pays on publication. Buys all rights, but may reassign following publication. Pays 50% kill fee. Byline given. Phone queries OK. Photocopied submissions OK. SASE. Reports in 6 weeks. Free sample copy and writer's guidelines.
Nonfiction: General interest (politics, sports, religion, education, housing, etc.) material related to Latinos living in US. Query or submit complete ms. Length: 750-3,000 words. Pays $50-500.
Photos: Donna Nicholson, photo editor. State availability of photos with query or ms. Pays $50-100 for 8x10 b&w semi-glossy prints; $75-150 for 35mm color transparencies. Buys first North American serial rights. Model release "preferred, but it depends on the situation." SASE.
Columns/Departments: Yesterday (articles on events of recent or distant past); Travel; Fashions; Food; Music; and Reviews (books, movies and arts). "All material must relate directly to Latinos." Query or submit complete ms. Length: 500-2,000 words. Pays $35-100/printed page.
Fiction: "Submissions must be in English, of high quality and a Latino slant." No erotica. Query or submit complete ms. Length: 2,000-3,000 words. Pays $100/printed page.

PILLOW TALK, 208 E. 43rd St., New York NY 10017. Editorial Director: Jesse James Leaf. 100% freelance written. "For people interested in all areas of human relationships—meetings, dating, arguing, making up, sex (in all aspects). We're a light, fun, but helpful and reliable publication—a counselor, a friend, a shoulder to lean on, and an entertainment." Monthly magazine; 96 pages. Estab. July 1976. Pays on publication. Buys all rights, but may reassign following publication. Pays 25% kill fee but rarely assigns. Byline given unless author requests otherwise. Simultaneous and photocopied submissions OK. SASE. Reports in 1 week. Sample copy $1.75; free writer's guidelines for SASE.
Nonfiction: How-to (romantic and sexual techniques, meeting new people, handling relationships, overcoming emotional hurdles); humor (sexual, romantic); interview (maybe in rare cases); personal experience (sexual/romantic scenarios if they illustrate a specific topic); and medical/technical (lightly done on sex-related health topics). "No out-and-out pornography unless incorporated in our new sexual fantasy department. Should be top-class." Buys 11 mss/issue. Query. Length: 1,000-3,000 words. Pays $80-300.
Photos: State availability of photos with query. Pays $25-50 for b&w; $250 for color covers. Buys all rights, but may reassign following publication. Model release required.
Columns/Departments: Front Entry, unusual and interesting news items. The Centerfold, puzzles; crosswords; games; and anything out of the ordinary. Buys 1 ms/issue. Rear Entry, sexual fantasy. Regular columns on The Gay Life, The Swinging Life and The Kinky Life. Query with clips of published work. Length: 1,250 words. Pays $100. Open to suggestions for new columns/departments.
Fiction: "Only sexual fantasy for our new Rear Entry department." Length: 500 words. Pays $75-100.
Fillers: Clippings and newsbreaks (funny, unusual relating to the broad area of sex). Buys 6 clippings/issue. Pays $5.

POSITIVE LIVING MAGAZINE, Humaneering, Inc., 5705 Stage Rd., Suite 240, Drawer 341227, Memphis TN 38134. (901)372-8178. Editor: Judy L. Heinrich. Emphasizes the virtues of positive attitudes in success. Monthly magazine; 64-80 pages. Estab. November 1977. Circ.

55,000. Pays on publication. Buys first North American rights. Byline given. Phone queries
OK. Submit seasonal/holiday material 3 months in advance. Photocopied and previously
submissions OK. SASE. Reports in 4 weeks. Free sample copy.
Nonfiction: How-to (especially methods for attaining success at work, at home); inspirational
(non-denominational, motivational); Q&A interview (with people exemplifying the
characteristics of positive attitude, preferably "known" personalities such as athletes,
celebrities, etc.); and profile (of people who have made successes of themselves through hard
work and determination). Buys 2 mss/issue. Query. Length: 750-2,500 words. Pays 7½¢/edited
word.
Photos: State availability of photos. Pays $10 minimum for 8x10 b&w glossy prints; $25
(inside) or $100 (cover) minimum for color transparencies. Captions and model releases
required.
Columns/Departments: Tell Us Your Story (personal experience relative to how they overcame
adversities, found success, etc.). Buys 1 column/issue. Send complete ms. Length: 500-1,000
words. Pays $20.
Fillers: Jokes, gags, anecdotes, short humor and motivational/inspirational. Buys 20/year.
Length: 300-500 words. Pays $15. Pays $5 for one- or two-liners.

PRACTICAL KNOWLEDGE, 111 N. Canal St., Chicago IL 60606. Editor: Lee Arnold.
Bimonthly. A self-advancement magazine for active and involved men and women. Buys all
rights, "but we are happy to cooperate with our authors." Pays on acceptance. Reports in 2-3
weeks. SASE.
Nonfiction and Photos: Uses success stories of famous people, past or present; applied
psychology; articles on mental hygiene and personality by qualified writers with proper
degrees to make subject matter authoritative. Also human interest stories with an optimistic
tone. Up to 5,000 words. Photographs and drawings are used when helpful. Pays 5¢/word
minimum; $10 each for illustrations.

REACH MAGAZINE, Stamats Publishing Co., 427 6th Ave., Cedar Rapids IA 52406.
(319)364-6167. Editor: Patti Crane. Emphasizes the life of the non-executive working person.
Bimonthly magazine; 12 pages. Estab. January 1979. Pays on publication. Buys all rights.
Phone queries OK. Submit seasonal/holiday material 3-4 months. Simultaneous and
photocopied submissions OK. SASE. Reports in 4 weeks (queries); 4-6 weeks (mss). Sample
copy for 8½x11 SASE.
Nonfiction: General interest (oriented for combined incomes under $25,000); how-to (home
decorating and maintenance, food, pop psychology, anything of general interest); humor
(stories about working); inspirational (nonreligious human achievement only); interview
(celebrities, interesting plain people. Lots of quotes accompanied by colorful descriptions);
personal experience (anecdotal, positive, and good-humored in nature); personal opinion
("may be a little 'in defense of the middle American working person' but not much like 'being
a good secretary' "); photo features (about working or recreation; profile (details of family
life and working style especially of interest to our readers). "We do not want to see any articles
on government or political issues, no religion or moral controversy and no anti-industry
articles." Buys 6-8 mss/issue. Send complete ms. Length: 250-1,350 words. Pays $25-100.
Photos: State availability of photos with ms. Pays $10-25 for 5x7 or 8x10 b&w glossy prints;
$15-60 for color slides or transparencies. Buys one-time rights. Captions preferred.
Fillers: Anecdotes, short humor, kid's corner material and quotes about working.

READERS REVIEW, The National Research Bureau, Inc., 424 N. 3rd St., Burlington IA
52601. Editor-in-Chief: N. Pasqual. Editor: M. Cuppy. 95% freelance written. "For industrial
workers of all ages." Quarterly magazine; 32 pages. Estab. 1956. Circ. 42,000. Pays on
publication. Buys all rights, but may reassign following publication. Previously published
submissions OK. SASE. Reports in 1 week. Free sample copy and writer's guidelines.
Nonfiction: General interest (steps to better health, attitudes on the job); how-to (perform
better on the job, do home repairs, car maintenance); and travel. Buys 4-5 mss/issue. Query
with outline. Length: 400-600 words. Pays $20 minimum.

REVIEW, Center for Inter-American Relations, 680 Park Ave., New York NY 10021.
(212)249-8950. Editor-in-Chief: Ronald Christ. Emphasizes "views, reviews, interviews, news
on Latin-American literature and arts." Published spring, fall and winter. Magazine; 95 pages.
Estab. 1968. Circ. 2,000. Pays on publication. Buys all rights, but may reassign following
publication. Phone queries OK. Previously published submissions OK (if originally published
in Spanish). Reports in 2 months. Free sample copy.

Nonfiction: Interview, personal opinion, personal experience, literary essays on Latin American authors, art, film. Buys 30 mss/year. Length: 8-14 pages. Pays $35-75.

Fiction: "All types—but has to be by Latin Americans." Buys 3/issue. Query. No length requirement. Pays $50/essay.

Poetry: Uses all types. Buys 3/issue. Limit submissions to batches of 3.

ROSICRUCIAN DIGEST, Rosicrucian Order, AMORC, Rosicrucian Park, San Jose CA 95191. (408)287-9171, ext. 213. Editor-in-Chief: Robin M. Thompson. 50-60% freelance written. Emphasizes mysticism, science and the arts. For "men and women of all ages, many well-educated, and into alternative answers to life's questions." Monthly magazine; 40 pages. Estab. 1916. Circ. 70,000. Pays on acceptance. Buys first rights and rights to reprint. Byline given. Phone queries OK. Submit seasonal or holiday material 5 months in advance. Photocopied and previously published submissions OK. SASE. Reports in 4 weeks. Free sample copy and writer's guidelines.

Nonfiction: How-to (deal with life's problems and opportunities in a positive and constructive manner); informational (new ideas and developments in science, the arts, philosophy and thinking), historical (biographies, historical sketches, human interest), inspirational ("no religion articles—we are looking for articles with a constructive, uplifting outlook; philosophical approach to problem-solving"), interview ("occasionally, but we would definitely have to work with author on this"), philosophy and psychology. Buys 40-50 mss/year. Query. Length: 1,000-1,700 words. Pays 4¢/word for first rights.

Photos: Purchased with accompanying ms. Send prints. Pays $3/8x10 b&w glossy print.

Fillers: Short inspirational or uplifting (not religious) anecdotes or experiences. Buys 6/year. Query. Length: 25-250 words. Pays 2¢/word.

How To Break In: "Be specific about what you want to write about—the subject you want to explore—and be willing to work with editor. Articles should appeal to worldwide circulation".

Rejects: Religious or political material or articles promoting a particular group or system of thought.

SAVING ENERGY, Box 75837 Sanford Station, Los Angeles CA 90075. (213)874-1453. Editor/Publisher: Larry Liebman. 20% freelance written. Emphasizes energy conservation, ideas and case histories aimed at business, industry and commerce. Monthly newsletter; 8 pages. Estab. February 1977. Pays on acceptance. Buys all rights. No byline given. Phone queries OK. SASE. Reports in 2 weeks. Free writer's guidelines.

Nonfiction: "I need good, tightly written case histories on how industry and commerce are saving energy, listing problems and solutions. The item should present an original energy saving idea. Include full name and address of business so readers can contact for follow-up." How-to (conserving energy, what the problem was, how it was resolved, cost, how fast the payback was, etc.); and technical (case histories). Buys 5 mss/issue. Submit complete ms. Length: 200-800 words. Pays $10-25.

SCANDINAVIAN REVIEW, American-Scandinavian Foundation, 127 E. 73rd St., New York NY 10021. (212)879-9779. Editor-in-Chief: Nadia Christensen. "The majority of our readership is over 30, well-educated, and in the middle income bracket. Most similar to readers of *Smithsonian* and *Saturday Review*. Have interest in Scandinavia by birth or education." Quarterly magazine; 96 pages. Estab. 1913. Circ. 7,000. Pays on publication. Buys all rights. Byline given. Submit seasonal/holiday material 9 months in advance. Previously published material (if published abroad) OK. SASE. Reports in 1 month. Sample copy $4. Free writer's guidelines.

Nonfiction: Historical, informational, interview, photo feature and travel. "Modern life and culture in Scandinavia." Buys 35 mss/year. Send complete ms. Length: maximum 2,500 words. Pays $50-100.

Photos: Purchased with accompanying ms. Captions required. Submit prints or transparencies. Prefers sharp, high contrast b&w enlargements. Total purchase price for ms includes payment for photos.

Fiction: Adventure, fantasy and historical. Prefers work translated from the Scandinavian. Buys 8 mss/year. Send complete ms. Length: 2,000 words maximum. Pays $50-100.

Poetry: Translations of contemporary Scandinavian poetry and original poems with a Scandinavian theme. Buys 5-15 poems/year. Pays $10.

SELECTED READING, The National Research Bureau, Inc., 424 N. 3rd St., Burlington IA 52601. Editor-in-Chief: N. Pasqual. Editor: M. Cuppy. 95% freelance written. For industrial workers of all ages. Quarterly magazine; 16 pages. Estab. 1956. Circ. 32,000. Pays on publication. Buys all rights, but may reassign following publication. Submit seasonal material 2

months in advance of issue date. Previously published submissions OK. SASE. Reports in 1 week. Free sample copy and writer's guidelines.
Nonfiction: General interest (economics, health, safety, working relationships); how-to; and travel. Buys 2-3 mss/issue. Query with outline. Length: 400-600 words. Pays $20 minimum.

SMITHSONIAN MAGAZINE, 900 Jefferson Drive, Washington DC 20560. Editor: Edward K. Thompson. For "associate members of the Smithsonian Institution; 85% with college education." Monthly. Circ. 1,500,000. "Our material is automatically copyrighted. In the case of selling off second rights, *Smithsonian* keeps half, gives the rest to writer. Payment for each article to be negotiated depending on our needs and the article's length and excellence." Pays "first half on assignment or tentative acceptance, remainder on scheduling." Submit seasonal material 3 months in advance. Reports "as soon as possible." Query. SASE.
Nonfiction: "Our mandate from the Smithsonian Institution says we are to be interested in the same things which now interest or should interest the Institution: folk and fine arts, history, natural sciences, hard sciences, etc." Length and payment "to be negotiated."
Photos: Purchased with or without ms and on assignment. Captions required. Pays "$300 a color page, $250 b&w."

STEREO, ABC Leisure Magazines, Inc., The Publishing House, State Rd., Great Barrington MA 01230. (413)528-1300. Editor-in-Chief: William Tynan. 10% freelance written. Emphasizes high-quality home audio equipment. Quarterly magazine; 96 pages. Estab. 1960. Circ. 50,000. Pays on acceptance. Buys all rights. Byline given. Phone queries OK. Submit seasonal/holiday material 6 months in advance. Photocopied submissions OK. SASE. Reports in 2 weeks. Free writer's guidelines.
Nonfiction: How-to (technically expert articles dealing with audio equipment); humor; interview (with personalities in audio field) and technical (workings of audio equipment). Buys 1-2 mss/year. Query. Length: 2,000-5,000 words. Pays 8-10¢/word.
How To Break In: "We are interested in the small minority of freelancers who are genuine audio experts with the training and experience that qualifies them to write with real authority. *Stereo* is almost entirely staff-written. At the moment, we buy very few manuscripts. However, we would buy more if material meeting our very high technical standards were available. Because every issue is themed to a specific aspect of audio, and all articles are written on assignment, it is *imperative* that freelancers query us before writing."
Rejects: "We are not interested in record buffs with 'golden ears'."

SUCCESS UNLIMITED, 401 N. Wabash Ave., Chicago IL 60611. Contact: Articles Editor. "Average reader is 25-40, married with 2 children; working in professional, sales or management capacity; college-educated (85%) and has a strong motivation to go into business for himself. Financially, he's doing fine—but he wants to do even better." Monthly magazine; 96-128 pages. Estab. 1954. Circ. 210,000. Pays on acceptance. Rights purchased vary with author and material. Free sample copy and writer's guidelines. SASE.
Nonfiction: "Our publication continues to stress the importance of a positive mental attitude (PMA) in all areas of endeavor." Uses material on self-motivation and the psychology of success; profiles of business leaders and successful (not necessarily wealthy) persons of all types—especially individuals who have overcome adversity to achieve success. How-to articles on entrepreneurship, management techniques, health, moneymaking ideas and investments. Length: 500-2,500 words. Pays 10¢/word, $250 maximum. Query.

SWINGERS WORLD, 8060 Melrose Ave., Los Angeles CA 90046. Editors: Norman Scott, Michael Carey. 90% freelance written. For "swingers and would-be swingers." Estab. 1972. Subject matter must be "swinger-oriented." Bimonthly. Buys first North American serial rights. Pays 20% kill fee. Byline given. Buys 50 mss/year. Pays on publication. Sample copy $2.75; free writer's guidelines. Reports in 3-4 weeks. Query. SASE.
Nonfiction: "Articles must be pro-swinger. Slick. We want new imformation on sex-oriented subjects and products, with an occaisional allied subject acceptable. Even if it is humorous in treatment (which we do like), your research must be thorough." Length: 1,500-3,000 words. Pays $65-150.

TREASURE FOUND, 16146 Covello St., Van Nuys CA 91406. (213)988-6910. Editor: Dave Weeks. Managing Editor: Jim Williams. For "all ages, all levels of education. The magazine appeals to all metal detector users, scuba divers, miners, bottle diggers, coin collectors—in short, anyone interested in treasure, especially treasure that has been found." Quarterly magazine. Byline given. Submit seasonal/holiday material 3 months in advance. Photocopied and previously published submissions OK. SASE. Reports in 6 weeks. Sample copy $1; free writer's guidelines.

Nonfiction: Stories of discovered treasure, illustrated with clear photos, maps or drawings. Submit complete ms. Pays approximately $25/magazine page.

Photos: 35mm or 2¼x2¼ color transparencies for cover photos; subject should be of something found (e.g., someone with a collection of bottles; the bottles effectively arranged; coins found, etc.).

UFO REVIEW, Global Communications, 303 5th Ave., Suite 1306, New York NY 10016. (212)685-4080. Editor: Timothy Beckley. Emphasizes UFOs and space science. Published 8 times/year. Tabloid; 12 pages. Circ. 15,000. Pays on publication. "We syndicate material to European markets and split 50-50 with writer." Phone queries OK. Photocopied submissions OK. SASE. Reports in 3 weeks. Sample copy 50¢.

Nonfiction: Expose (on government secrecy on UFOs). "We also want articles detailing on-the-spot field investigations of UFO landings, contact with UFOs, and UFO abductions. No lights-in-the-sky stories." Buys 1-2 mss//issue. Query. Length: 1,200-2,000 words. Pays $50-75.

Photos: Send photos with ms. Pays $5-10 for 8x10 b&w prints. Captions required.

Fillers: Clippings. Pays $2-5.

VEGETARIAN TIMES, 41 E. 42nd St., New York NY 10017. (212)490-3999. Editor: Paul Barrett Obis Jr. For "nonmeat eaters and people interested in organic food." Monthly magazine; 88 pages. Estab. 1973. Circ. 60,000. Rights purchased vary with author and material. Will buy first serial or simultaneous rights ("always includes right to use article in our books or 'Best of' series"). May pay 20% kill fee. Byline given unless extensive revisions are required or material is incorporated into a larger article. Buys 50 mss/year. Pays on acceptance. Sample copy $1. Will consider photocopied and simultaneous submissions. Submit seasonal material 3 months in advance. Reports in 8 weeks. Query. SASE.

Nonfiction and Photos: Features concise articles related to "vegetarianism (cooking, humanism, pacifism), environment, self-sufficiency, animal welfare and liberation, articles about vegetarian nutrition—all material should be well-documented and researched. It would probably be best to see a sample copy—remember that despite our name, we are beholden to our readers and we do not necessarily care if the health food stores sell more vitamins. We are not in the business of selling health foods. We are strongly pro consumer. We are not interested in personal pet stories or wonder cure-all foods." Informational, how-to, experience, interview, profile, historical, expose, personal opinion, successful health food business operations, and restaurant reviews. Length: 500-3,000 words. Pays 2¢/word minimum. Will also use 500- to 1,000-word items for regular columns. Pays $10-15. Pays $5 total for photos purchased with accompanying ms. No color; b&w ferrotype preferred.

WESTERN & EASTERN TREASURES, People's Publishing, Inc., 1440 W. Walnut St., Box 7030, Compton CA 90224. (213)537-0896. Managing Editor: Ray Krupa. Emphasizes treasure hunting for all ages, entire range in education, coast-to-coast readership. Monthly magazine; 68 pages. Estab. 1966. Circ. 70,000. Pays on publication. Buys all rights, but may reassign rights to author following publication. SASE. Reports in 2-3 weeks. Free sample copy and writer's guidelines.

Nonfiction: How-to (use of equipment, how to look for rocks, gems, prospect for gold, where to look for treasures, rocks, etc., "first-person" experiences). Buys 150 mss/year. Submit complete ms. Length: maximum 1,500 words. Pays 2¢/word maximum.

Photos: Purchased with accompanying ms. Captions required. Submit prints or transparencies. Pays $5 maximum for 3x5 and up b&w glossy prints; $10 maximum for 35mm and up color transparencies. Model release required.

Columns/Departments: Treasures in the Headlines, Look What They Found, Off Road/This & That and Around the Campfire. Buys 50/year. Send complete ms. Length: 800-1,500 words. Pays 2¢/word maximum. Open to suggestions for new columns or departments; address Ray Krupa.

WHAT MAKES PEOPLE SUCCESSFUL, The National Research Bureau, Inc., 424 N. 3rd St., Burlington IA 52601. Editor-in-Chief: N. Pasqual. Editor: M. Cuppy. 95% freelance written. For "industrial workers of all ages." Published quarterly. Magazine; 16 pages. Estab. 1951. Circ. 25,000. Pays on publication. Buys all rights, but may reassign following publication. Submit seasonal material 3-4 months in advance of issue date. Previously published submissions OK. SASE. Reports in 1 week. Free sample copy and writer's guidelines.

Nonfiction: How-to (be successful); general interest (personality, employee morale, guides to successful living, biographies of successful persons, etc.); experience; personal opinion; and travel. Buys 2-3 mss/issue. Query with outline. Length: 400-600 words. Pays $20 minimum.

Music

AUDIO MAGAZINE, 401 N. Broad St., Philadelphia PA 19108. Editor: Gene Pitts. For persons interested in high fidelity components, electronics and music. Monthly magazine; 120 pages. Estab. 1947. Circ. 130,000. Buys all rights. Buys about 15 mss/year. Pays on publication. Free sample copy. Will consider photocopied submissions. No simultaneous submissions. Reports in 6 weeks. Query recommended, but not required. SASE.
Nonfiction and Photos: Articles on hi-fi equipment, design technique, hi-fi history; explanations for buffs and of widely known commercial uses. Pays $35/published page minimum. No additional payment made for photos used with mss.

AUDIOSCENE CANADA, MacLean-Hunter, Ltd., 481 University Ave., Toronto, Ontario, Canada M5W 1A7. (416)595-1811. Editor-in-Chief: Ian G. Masters. 50% freelance written. Emphasizes high fidelity and music. Monthly magazine; 60 pages. Estab. 1964. Circ. 25,000. Pays on publication. Buys all rights, but may reassign following publication. Byline given. Submit seasonal/holiday material 2 months in advance. SASE. Reports in 4 weeks. Free sample copy.
Nonfiction: How-to (must have first-hand technical knowledge); interview; and technical. Buys 6-8 mss/year. Query. Length: 1,500-2,500 words. Pays 10¢/word.
Photos: Wants photos for personality pieces and appropriate artwork for technical material. Pays $15 minimum for 4x5 or 8x10 b&w glossy prints. Captions preferred. Buys all rights. Model release required.

BLUEGRASS UNLIMITED, Box 111, Broad Run VA 22014. (703)361-8992. Editor-in-Chief: Peter V. Kuykendall. Managing Editor: Marion C. Kuykendall. 50% freelance written. Emphasizes old-time traditional country music for musicians and devotees of bluegrass, ages from teens through the elderly. Monthly magazine; 48 pages. Estab. 1966. Circ. 14,000. Pays on publication. Buys all rights, but may reassign to author following publication. Kill fee varies. Byline given. Phone queries OK. Submit seasonal/holiday material 2-3 months in advance. Photocopied and previously published submissions OK. SASE. Reports in 1 month. Free sample copy and writer's guidelines.
Nonfiction: Historical, how-to, humor, informational, interview, nostalgia, personal experience, personal opinion, photo feature, profile and technical. Buys 20-40 mss/year. Query. Length: 500-5,000 words. Pays 3½-4¢/word.
Photos: Purchased with or without accompanying ms. Query for photos. Pays $15-20/page for 5x7 or 8x10 b&w glossy prints, 35mm or 2¼x2¼ color transparencies; $40 for covers.
Columns, Departments: Record and book reviews. Buys 5-10/year. Query. Length: 100-500 words. Pays 3½-4¢/word.
Fiction: Adventure and humorous. Buys 5-7 mss/year. Length: 500-2,500 words. Pays 3½-4¢/word.

BUDDY MAGAZINE, Box 8366, Dallas TX 75205. (214)562-6049. Editor: Stoney Burns. *Buddy* is totally music-oriented, primarily focusing on rock, but also covering pop, country and soul. Monthly magazine. Estab. 1973. Circ. 50,000. Pays on publication. "We share the copyright with the writer for our protection and theirs. They can do anything they want with the copy after publication." Byline given. SASE. Reports in 2 weeks. Free sample copy.
Nonfiction: Personality profiles of and interviews with artists, stories about the music scene (studios, fashions, instruments, etc.), and album reviews. "We need 'Fave Rave' stories on big stars. First priority goes to stories with a Texas angle. No long stories, articles that are overly laudatory, or stories comparing unknown groups with the Beatles or the Rolling Stones." Query or send complete ms. Length: 500-1,000 words. Pays 3¢/word for features; 2¢/word for reviews.
Photos: Send photos with ms. Pays 5-10 for b&w prints.

COMPLETE BUYER'S GUIDE TO STEREO/HI-FI EQUIPMENT, Service Communications, Ltd., 50 Rockefeller Plaza, New York NY 10020. Editor: David A. Drucker. For people interested in buying audio equipment: the demographics are probably similar to the audio equipment purchaser profile. Bimonthly magazine; 160 pages. Estab. 1974. Circ. 75,000. Pays on publication. Buys all rights. Byline given "on request only." Photocopied submissions OK. SASE. Reports in 6 weeks. Free sample copy.

Nonfiction: General interest, how-to, new product and technical. Buys 2-3 mss/issue. Send complete ms. Length: 1,000-3,000. Pays $75-300.

CONTEMPORARY KEYBOARD MAGAZINE, The GPI Corp., Box 615, Saratoga CA 95070. (408)446-3220. Editor: Tom Darter. For those who play piano, organ, synthesizer, accordion, harpsichord, or any other keyboard instrument. All styles of music; all levels of ability. Monthly magazine; 84-92 pages. Estab. 1975. Circ. 54,500. Pays on acceptance. Buys all rights. Byline given. Phone queries OK. Submit seasonal/holiday material 4 months in advance. SASE. Reports in 2 week. Free sample copy and writer's guidelines.
Nonfiction: "We publish articles on a wide variety of topics pertaining to keyboard players and their instruments. In addition to interviews with keyboard artists in all styles of music, we are interested in historical and analytical pieces, how-to articles dealing either with music or with equipment, profiles on well-known instrument makers and their products. In general, anything that amateur and professional keyboardists would find interesting and/or useful." Buys 3-4 mss/issue. Query. Length: 2,000-4,500 words minimum. Pays $70-150.

CORNHUSKER COUNTRY, Box 42, Louisville NE 68037. Editor: Robert Everhart. 50% freelance written. Emphasizes traditional country music. Monthly magazine; 40 pages. Estab. 1976. Circ. 2,000. Pays on acceptance. Buys one-time rights. Byline given. Submit seasonal/holiday material 3 months in advance of issue date. Simultaneous, photocopied and previously published submissions OK. SASE. Reports in 4 weeks. Free sample copy.
Nonfiction: Historical (relating to country music); how-to (play, write, or perform country music); inspirational (on country gospel); interview (with country performers, both traditional and contemporary); nostalgia (pioneer living); personal experience (country music); and travel (in connection with country music contests or festivals). Buys 6 mss/year. Query. Length: 200-2,000 words. Pays $20-50.
Photos: State availability of photos with query. Payment is included in ms price. Uses 5x7 b&w prints. Captions and model release required. Buys one-time rights.
Poetry: Free verse and traditional. Buys 1/issue. Length: 3-15 lines. Limit submissions to batches of 3. Pays in copies.

COUNTRY MUSIC MAGAZINE, KBO Publishers, 475 Park Ave. S., New York NY 10016. Editor-in-Chief: Russell D. Barnard. 80% freelance written. Monthly magazine; 64 pages. Estab. September 1972. Circ 211,000. Pays on publication. Buys all rights, but may reassign following publication. Submit seasonal/holiday material at least 4 months in advance of issue date. Photocopied and previously published (book excerpts) OK. SASE. Reports in 3-4 weeks. Free sample copy and writer's guidelines.
Nonfiction: General interest ("about country music or subjects of interest to a country music audience"); humor (some, but must be taken article by article); historical (about music, items of interest to our audience); interview (country artist, craftsman, etc.); photo feature; profile; and travel. Buys 6-10 mss/issue. Query with clips of published work. Length: 1,500-3,500 words. Pays $250-400.
Photos: Cheh Nam Low, photo editor. State availability of photos with query. Pays $25/b&w photo; $50/35mm color transparency. Captions required. Buys all rights, but may reassign following publication.
Columns/Departments: Record reviews. Buys 5-10/issue. Query. Length: 100-250 words. Pays $25.

COUNTRYSTYLE, 11058 W. Addison, Franklin Park IL 60131. (312)455-7178. Managing Editor: Ray Bachar. Emphasizes country music and country life style. Bimonthly tabloid; 48 pages. Estab. 1976. Circ. 250,000. Pays on acceptance. Buys all rights, but may reassign following publication. Phone queries OK. Submit seasonal/holiday material 3 months in advance. Photocopied submissions and previously published work OK. SASE. Reports in 2 weeks. Sample copy $1. Free writer's guidelines.
Nonfiction: Expose, informational, interview, nostalgia, profile and photo feature. Buys 100 mss/year. Query. Length: 500-2,000 words. Pays minimum of $10 per ms page.
Photos: Purchased with or without ms, or on assignment. Send contact sheet, prints or transparencies. Pays $15-100 for 8x10 b&w glossy prints; $35-250 for color. Prefers 2¼x2¼, but color negatives OK.
Columns/Departments: Country Music. Record Review. Send complete ms. Length: 100-500 words. Pays 5-10¢/word.
Fiction: Western. Buys 10/year. Query. Pays minimum of $10/ms page.
Fillers: Newsbreaks. Buys 40/year. Length: 100-300 words. Pays $5-15.
How To Break In: "With a timely (in the sense that the artist has a hot song on the charts)

feature with good color art. But, no microphones, please."

CREEM, 187 S. Woodward Ave., Suite 211, Birmingham MI 48011. (313)642-8833. Editor: Susan Whitall. Estab. 1969. Buys all rights. Pays on publication. Query. Reports in 6 weeks. SASE.
Nonfiction and Photos: Freelance photos and short articles, mostly music-oriented. "Feature-length stories are mostly staff-written, but we're open for newcomers to break in with short pieces. Please send queries and sample articles to Linda Barber, Submissions Editor. We bill ourselves as America's Only Rock 'n' Roll Magazine." Pays $35 minimum for reviews.

FRETS MAGAZINE, GPI Publications, Box 615, Saratoga CA 95070. (408)446-1105. Editor: Roger H. Siminoff. "For amateur and professional acoustic string music enthusiasts; for players, makers, listeners and fans. Country, jazz, classical blues, pop and rock. For instrumentalists interested in banjo, mandolin, guitar, violin, upright bass, dobro, dulcimer and others." Monthly magazine; 72 pages. Estab. 1979. Circ. open. Pays on acceptance. Buys first rights. Phone queries OK. Submit material 4 months in advance. SASE. Reports in 2 weeks. Free sample copy and writer's guidelines.
Nonfiction: General interest (artist-oriented); historical (instrument making or manufacture); how-to (instrument craft and repair); interview (with artists or historically important individuals); profile (music performer); travel (if in conjunction with music event); photo feature (in conjunction with music event); and technical (instrument making, acoustics, instrument repair). Buys 35 mss/year. Query with clips of published work. Length: 1,000-2,500 words. Pays $75-125. Experimental (instrument design, acoustics). Pays $50-75.
Photos: State availability of photos. Pays $35-50 for b&w prints (reviews contact sheets); $75-100 for 35mm or 2¼x2¼ color transparencies. Additional payment for photos accepted with ms. Captions and model release required. Buys one-time rights.
Columns/Departments: Repair Shop (instrument craft and repair); The Collector (instrument collecting—highlights 1 instrument/month); and *FRETS* Visits (on-location visit to manufacturer). Buys 10 mss/issue. Query. Length: 1,200-1,700 words. Pays $50-75.
Fillers: Newsbreaks and music crossword puzzles. Pays $20-40.

FUGUE, Watts & Johnson Publications, Ltd., York Square, 49 Avenue Rd., Toronto, Ontario, Canada. (416)960-5889. Editor and Publisher: Diane Watts. Basically freelance written. Covers classical music only. Magazine; 64-72 pages. Estab. September 1976. Circ. 25,000 in Canada, US and UK. Pays 30 days after acceptance. Buys all rights, but may reassign following publication. Pays 50% kill fee. Byline given. Phone queries OK. Submit all material 3 months in advance of issue date. SAE and International Reply Coupons. Reports in 3 weeks. Free sample copy; mention *Writer's Market* in request.
Nonfiction: General interest features (profiles of performers, composers, articles on trends and new works); how-to articles (record buying, how to build a Mahler collection, etc.); historical/analytical pieces (feature-length approaches to performers, composers, specific genres or works); interviews (with performers, composers, specific genres or works); reviews (of recordings or books, usually staff-assigned); news reports (short pieces on current events or trends of interest to the classical community); photo features (covering orchestras, artists, tours and premiere performances).
Fiction: Short stories on a musical theme or topic; humor (whimsical or satirical approach to classical music). Buys 6-8 mss/issue. Length: 1,000-3,000 words. Query. Pays $75-200.
Photos: David Campbell, photo editor. State availability of photos with query. Pays $10-50 for 8x10 b&w glossy prints or color transparencies. "Obviously assignments are negotiated at different rates than stock photos." Captions preferred. Buys one-time rights. Model release required.

THE FUGUE, 2951 S. Bayshore Dr., Miami FL 33133. (305)443-5251. Executive Editor: Lawrence Litt. 50% freelance written. Emphasizes classical music, jazz, ballet and opera for a middle- and upper-income readership, well-educated with an interest in higher forms of culture. Monthly magazine; 64 pages. Estab. 1970. Circ. 40,000. Pays on publication. Buys all rights, but may reassign following publication. Pays 20% kill fee. Byline given. Phone queries OK. Submit seasonal/holiday material 3 months in advance of issue date. Simultaneous and previously published submissions OK. SASE. Reports in 3 weeks. Sample copy $1; free writer's guidelines.
Nonfiction: *"The Fugue* is glad to consider manuscripts from anybody at any time on most cultural subjects. Feel free to submit any items or articles you think might be good reading for people who love fine music. We are interested in light, informative articles that hold the reader's attention. If you use a technical term you must define it the first time its used in the

piece. We have a record reviewer, but we're always interested in the possibility of guest reviews. Our point of view is that fine arts is for everyone, not the culturally sophisticated audience. Keep in mind that we are aware of new recordings and are especially interested in tie-in article topics such as crossovers, young new stars, and people who support and promote fine arts music of all types. If we don't accept an article that doesn't mean we won't assign an article to a writer if he or she writes well. Mathematical or technical discourses are not welcome unless they are presented in a breezy, readable style that will hold the interest of the reader of average intelligence." General interest (on music and the arts; travel for music); historical (music history, especially American); and interview (composers, conductors, musicians, artists, producers and important people in the field). No academic or scholastic treatises on music or the arts. "We are a general consumer magazine, and our readers want to enjoy reading about their favorite forms of entertainment." Buys 60 mss/year. Query with clips of published work. Length: 800-2,000 words. Pays $40-150.

Columns/Departments: Record reviews and puzzles and quizes with a musical point of view. Query with clips of published work. Length: 500-750 words. Pays $15-50. Open to suggestions for new columns/departments.

Fillers: Clippings, newsbreaks, puzzles, and short humor. Buys 3-5/issue. Length: 500-1,000 words. Pays $15-50.

GUITAR PLAYER MAGAZINE, Box 615, Saratoga CA 95070. (408)446-1105. Editor: Don Menn. For persons "interested in guitars and guitarists." Magazine published 12 times/year. Circ. 127,800. Buys all rights. Byline given. Buys 60-80 mss/year. Pays on acceptance. Will send a sample copy to a writer on request. Reports in 1 week. Query. SASE.

Nonfiction and Photos: Publishes "wide variety of articles pertaining to guitars and guitarists: interviews, guitar craftsmen profiles, how-to features—anything amateur and professional guitarists would find fascinating and/or helpful. On interviews with 'name' performers, be as technical as possible regarding strings, guitars, techniques, etc. We're not a pop culture magazine, but a music magazine." Also buys features on such subjects as a "guitar museum; the role of the guitar in elementary education, personal reminiscences of past greats, technical gadgets and how to work them, analysis of flamenco, etc." Length: open. Pays $50-200. Photos purchased with mss. B&w glossy prints. Pays $25-35. Buys 35mm color slides. Pays $150 (for cover only). Buys all rights.

HI-FI STEREO BUYERS' GUIDE, 380 Lexington Ave., New York NY 10017. (212)557-9100. Associate Publisher/Editor-in-Chief: Julian S. Martin. Editor: Christine Begole. Bimonthly magazine whose function is to assist the prospective buyer of high fidelity components in their purchase. Writers are advised to obtain a copy of the magazine and examine it carefully for content. Pays 100% kill fee. Byline given. "If you think you can write for us, we suggest you submit to us a precis of the story you would like to write, and await our comments. We pay on 'impulse' before publication." SASE.

Nonfiction: "We run a short jazz column and a comprehensive record-review column on classical music. Also, we have a continuing series on opera which takes about 2 pages in the magazine. We don't plan to increase this coverage, nor do we plan to take on additional freelancers to assist us in this area. We are interested in discovering new authors who are familiar with the buying habits of the audiophile and know the current audio marketplace. Average payment is about $250."

HIGH FIDELITY, The Publishing House, State Road, Great Barrington MA 01230. Editorial Director: Robert Clark. For well-educated, young, affluent readers, interested in home recording and playback systems (all disc and tape formats) and music. Special issues: August, tape; June, speakers; September, new recordings and new equipment; December, year's best recordings. Monthly magazine. Estab. 1951. Circ. 365,000. Buys all rights. Kill fee varies. Byline given. Buys 36-42 mss/year. Pays on acceptance. Will consider photocopied submissions, "if they are legible." Submit seasonal material 5 months in advance. Reports in 1 month. Query or submit complete ms. SASE.

Nonfiction: "Material for feature articles is divided between consumer and semipro audio equipment and music makers. Equipment articles should be backed up with as much technical sophistication as possible and appropriate and readily understandable to the lay reader. Music articles should be slanted toward the classical or popular musician's recording career or recordings of his works or aimed at increasing the reader's understanding of music. Articles are sophisticated, detailed and thoroughly backgrounded." Regular columns include interviews with noted music and recording personalities about their work; and Behind the Scenes, reports of in-progress recording sessions here and abroad. Length: 1,000-3,000 words. Pays $200-500.

Photos: Purchased with accompanying manuscripts. Captions required. 8x10 b&w glossy payment included in ms payment. Color rarely used; inquire first.

HIGH FIDELITY/MUSICAL AMERICA, 130 E. 59th St., New York NY 10022. Editor: Shirley Fleming. Monthly. Estab. 1888. Circ. 25,000. Buys all rights. Pays on publication. SASE.

Nonfiction and Photos: Articles, musical and audio, are generally prepared by acknowledged writers and authorities in the field, but does use freelance material. Length: 3,000 words maximum. Pays $25 minimum. New b&w photos of musical personalities, events, etc.

IMAGINE, Box 2715, Waterbury CT 06720. (203)755-4443. Editor: Gorman Bechard. Managaing Editor: Sandy Skarnulis. Emphasizes popular music, reviews and features. Monthly magazine; 52 pages. Estab. March 1978. Circ. over 10,000. Pays 2 months after publication. Buys second serial (reprint) rights. Phone queries OK. Submit seasonal/holiday material 2 months in advance. Photocopied submissions OK. SASE. Reports in 3 weeks. Free sample copy and writer's guidelines.

Nonfiction: Expose (having to do with music/recording industry only); interview (rock music personalities; new product (stereo or audio only); nostalgia (old time rock 'n roll); opinion (record, concert, book); photo feature (rock groups); and profile (rock music personalities). "We do not want articles laced with biased personal opinion." Buys 10 mss/issue. Query with clips of published work. Length: 150-5,000 words. Pays $5-65. Reviews average $5/each; articles $15 for the first 1,000 words, $10 for each additional 1,000.

Photos: Send photos with accompanying mss. Pays $2.50-10 for 4x5 b&w prints. Buys one-time rights. Captions preferred.

Columns/Departments: Long Players (album reviews, 200-1,000 words); Inside Pages (book reviews, 200 words); and Ticket Returns (rock concert reviews, 200-400 words). Buys 5/issue. Query with clips of published work. Length: 200-1,000 words. Pays $5-10.

Fillers: Newsbreaks (music). Length: 50-100 words. Pays $1-2.50.

INTERNATIONAL MUSICIAN, 1500 Broadway, New York NY 10036. (212)869-1330. Editor: J. Martin Emerson. For professional musicians. Monthly. Byline given. Pays on acceptance. Reporting time varies. Query. SASE.

Nonfiction: Articles on prominent instrumental musicians (classical, jazz, rock or country).

KEYBOARD WORLD, Box 4399, Downey CA 90241. (213)923-0331. Publisher: Bill Worrall. Emphasizes organ, piano and synthesizer music. Monthly magazine; 48-64 pages. Estab. 1972. Circ. 18,000 in US and Canada; 10,000 in Australia; and 7,000 in Continental Europe. Pays on acceptance. Buys all rights, but may reassign following publication. Byline given. Phone queries OK. Submit seasonal/holiday material at least 4 months in advance. Simultaneous and photocopied submissions OK. Previously published work OK, if author owns rights. SASE. Reports in 4 weeks. Sample copy $1.

Nonfiction: Jean Garland, Managing Editor. How-to (playing technique, forming clubs, repairing or building instruments, theory of music, information for teachers); informational (profiles of artists, prominent personalities, news of concerts, conventions); historical (keyboard instrument history, history of composers, songs—but related to the present, restoring old instruments); inspirational (human interest on handicapped, etc., musicians who are nevertheless outstanding); interview (with organ/piano and all keyboard teachers and musicians, and others related to this field); nostalgia (old theater organs, older songs, musicians of the past); opinion (letters to the editor welcomed); profile (of teachers and musicians); new product (reviews of books, records and products); personal experience (human interest about relationships with teachers, musicians, students overcoming difficulties); photo feature (good, clear pix of concerts, etc., especially candid shots, rather than posed); technical (advice on repair and maintenance and tuning of instruments, and on teaching/practice/learning methods). Query. Length: 500-4,000 words. Pays ½-1¢/word.

Photos: David Rivas, Advertising Manager. Purchased with or without mss or on assignment. Captions optional, "but must have names and situation info." Send prints. Pays $2 minimum for b&w and color; $25 for cover use. Model release required.

Fillers: Clippings, jokes, anecdotes, newsbreaks, short humor related to keyboard music. Pays $1 minimum.

How To Break In: "Read *Keyboard World*. Most of our material is contributed free. Therefore, we want something we can't readily get from the experts who write for us. Well-researched and slanted material, especially on pianos and synthesizers, and for children."

THE LAMB, 5518 Chaucer, Houston TX 77005. (713)526-7793. Editor-in-Chief: Michael Point. Emphasizes music for a readership interested in the current shape and future course of contemporary music. Primary readership lies in the 20-30-year-old bracket with some college affiliation (past or present) and a serious interest in music. Monthly tabloid; 28 pages. Estab. 1976. Circ. 30,000. Pays on publication. Buys all rights, but may reassign rights to author following publication. Pays 50% kill fee. Byline given. Phone queries OK. Photocopied (if clean and clear) submissions OK. SASE. Reports in 4 weeks. Sample copy $1.

Nonfiction: Historical, informational, interview, nostalgia, personal opinion, photo feature and profile. "All articles must deal with music, musicians or the music world." Buys 50 mss/year. Query. Length varies. Pays minimum $10.

Photos: Geary Davis, Photo Editor. Purchased with or without accompanying ms or on assignment. Captions required. Pays $5 minimum for 8x10 b&w glossy prints. Send contact sheet or prints. Total purchase price for ms includes payment for photos.

Fiction: Adventure, confession, erotica, experimental, fantasy, historical, humorous and science fiction. Buys 10 mss/year. Query. Pays minimum $10.

Poetry: Nancy McKinney, poetry editor. Avant-garde, free verse, haiku, light verse and traditional. Buys 50 poems/year. Send poems. Pays minimum $5.

How To Break In: *"The Lamb* is not a teen or pop music publication. It deals with "progressive music" of all styles (jazz, rock, classical, etc.) and requires writers able to communicate to an audience of musically informed and interested readers. *The Lamb* is open to all forms of alternative expression dealing with music and invites writers, photographers, etc., to use their creativity when submitting material. Remember that this is a music magazine and, as such, concentrates almost exclusively on the permutations of the music world. Album reviews and performance reviews are customary starting points for new writers."

MODERN DRUMMER, 1000 Clifton Ave., Clifton NJ 07013. (201)340-3004. Editor-in-Chief: Ronald Spagnardi. 70% freelance written. For "student, semi-pro and professional drummers at all ages and levels of playing ability, with varied specialized interests within the field." Bimonthly magazine; 64 pages. Estab. 1975. Circ. 20,000. Pays on publication. Buys all rights. Phone queries OK. Photocopied and previously published submissions OK. SASE. Reports in 6 weeks. Sample copy $1.75; free writer's guidelines.

Nonfiction: How-to, informational, interview, personal opinion, new product, personal experience and technical. "All submissions must appeal to the specialized interests of drummers." Buys 15-20 mss/issue. Query or submit complete ms. Length: 1,500-3,000 words. Pays 5-10¢/word.

Photos: Purchased with accompanying ms. Considers 8x10 b&w and color glossy prints. Submit prints or negatives. Total ms purchase price includes payment for photos.

Columns/Departments: Jazz Drummers Workshop, Rock Perspectives, Rudimental Symposium, Complete Percussionist, Teachers Forum, Drum Soloist, Record, Book and Live Action Review and Shop Talk. "Technical knowledge of area required for all columns." Buys 10-15 mss/issue. Query or submit complete ms. Length: 500-1,500 words. Pays 5-10¢/word. Open to suggestions for new columns and departments.

Fillers: Jokes, gags and anecdotes. Buys 3 fillers/issue. No length requirement. Pays $2-5.

MUSIC CITY NEWS, 1302 Division St., Nashville TN 37203. (615)244-5187. Managing Editor: Lee Rector. Emphasizes country music. Monthly tabloid; 40 pages. Estab. 1963. Circ. 170,000. Buys all rights. Phone queries OK. Submit seasonal or holiday material 2 months in advance. Photocopied submissions OK. SASE. Reports in 8-10 weeks. Free sample copy.

Nonfiction: "We prefer interview type articles with country music personalities, not question/answer but narrative/quote interviews leaning toward the personality telling his own story. We prefer new slants to biographical material." Buys 4-5 mss/issue. Query. Length: 500-1,250 words. Pays $1.50/column inch.

Photos: Purchased on acceptance by assignment. Query. Pays $10 maximum for 8x10 b&w glossy prints.

MUSIC JOURNAL, 149 Hampton Rd., Southampton NY 11968. (516)283-2360. Editor: Mary Cummines. 70% freelance written. Emphasizes serious music for college and conservatory faculty and students, professional and amateur musicians, and music lovers. Monthly magazine. Pays on publication. Submit seasonal/holiday material 4 months in advance of date. Simultaneous and photocopied submissions OK. SASE. Reports in 6 weeks. Sample copy $1.50.

Nonfiction: General interest (composers, performers, music festivals, instruments, new trends, recordings, music business and audio); interview (important figures in the music world); profile (important figures in the music world); technical (new compositions, and new techniques in audio music); and travel (as related to classical music or jazz). Buys 35 mss/year. Query with 3 clips of published work. Length: 1,000-3,000 words. Pays $75-200.

Photos: State availability of photos with query. No additional payment for b&w prints. Buys one-time rights.

MUSIC MAGAZINE, Barrett & Colgrass Inc., 56 The Esplanade, Suite 202, Toronto, Ontario, Canada M5E 1A7. (416)364-5938. Editor: Ulla Colgrass. Emphasizes classical music. Bimonthly magazine; 40 pages. Estab. January 1978. Circ. 11,000. Pays on publication. Buys all rights. Byline given. Phone queries OK. Submit seasonal/holiday material 4 months in advance. Photocopied and previously submissions OK. SAE and International Reply Coupons. Reports in 3 weeks. Free sample copy and writer's guidelines.
Nonfiction: Interview, personal experience, photo feature and profile. "All articles should pertain to classical music and people in that world. We do not want any academic analysis." Query with clips of published work. Length: 1,500-3,500 words. Pays $50-150.
Photos: State availability of photos. Pays $15-25 for 8x10 b&w glossy prints or contact sheets; $100 for color transparencies. Buys one-time rights. Captions required.
Columns/Departments: Notes (describes a personal, unique experience in the world of classical music, open to professional musicians and listeners alike). Buys 1 ms/issue. Query. Length: 800-12,000 words. Pays $50.

OPERA CANADA, 366 Adelaide St. E., Suite 533, Toronto, Ontario Canada M5A 1N4. (416)363-0395. Editor: Ruby Mercer. For readers who are interested in serious music; specifically, opera. Quarterly magazine; 52 pages. Estab. 1960. Circ. 5,000. Not copyrighted. Byline given. Buys 10 mss/year. Pays on publication. Sample copy $2. Will consider photocopied and simultaneous submissions. Reports on material accepted for publication within 1 year. Returns rejected material in 1 month. Query or submit complete ms. SAE and International Reply Coupons.
Nonfiction and Photos: "Because we are Canada's opera magazine, we like to keep 75% of our content Canadian, i.e., by Canadians or about Canadian personalities/events. We prefer informative and/or humorous articles about any aspect of music theater, with an emphasis on opera. The relationship of the actual subject matter to opera can be direct or barely discernible. We accept record reviews (*only* operatic recordings); book reviews (books covering any aspect of music theater) and interviews with major operatic personalities. Please, no reviews of performances. We have staff reviewers." Length (for all articles except reviews of books and records): 350-5,000 words. Pays $25-50. Length for reviews: 50-100 words. Pays $10. No additional payment for photos used with mss. Captions required.

PICKIN' MAGAZINE, North American Publishing Co., 401 N. Broad St., Philadelphia PA 19108. (215)574-9600. Editor-in-Chief: Don Kissil. Managing Editor: Marilyn Kochman. 60-70% freelance written. For people who play, but who also listen and collect records of old-time bluegrass, country, folk, jazz and all of the specialty type musics with a special emphasis on stringed instruments. Monthly magazine; 74-96 pages. Estab. February 1974. Circ. 40,000. Pays on publication. Buys all rights, but may reassign following publication. Byline given. Phone queries OK. Submit seasonal/holiday material 6-8 months in advance of issue date. Photocopied and previously published submissions OK. SASE. Reports in 4-6 weeks. Free sample copy and writer's guidelines; mention *Writer's Market* in request.
Nonfiction: "All related to our kind of music or instruments." General interest; historical; how-to; humor; interview; new product (unusual, not commercial); nostalgia; personal experience (music tablature for pickers, lifestyles and fashions for "down home folk"); personal opinion; photo feature; profile; technical (instrument making); and travel (festivals). No articles of promo pieces on bands or artists. Buys 100 mss/year. Query with clips of published work. Length: 500-5,000 words. Pays 4-10¢/word.
Photos: State availability of photos with query. Pays $5-50 for b&w contact sheets or prints; $10-200 (cover only) for 35mm color transparencies or contact prints. Captions required. Buys all rights, but may reassign following publication. Model release required.
Columns/Departments: Across the Pond (overseas music); Crafts Corner (instrument repair tips); Music Book Reviews (stringed); Music Tablature; Record Reviews; Workbench (on building instruments); and Song Book Reviews. Query. Length: 300-12,000 words. Pays $15-50. Open to suggestions for new columns/departments.
Poetry: "Related to our music only." Avant-garde, free verse, haiku, light verse and traditional. Buys 4/year. Submit in batches of 2. Pays $10-20.
Fillers: Jokes, gags, anecdotes, puzzles, short humor and cartoons related to stringed music. Buys 10/year. Pays $5-25.

ROLLING STONE, 745 5th Ave., New York NY 10022. Editor: Jann S. Wenner. "Seldom accept freelance material. All our work is assigned or done by our staff." Pays 33% kill fee. Byline given.

THE SENSIBLE SOUND, 403 Darwin Dr., Snyder NY 14226. Editor/Publisher: John A. Horan. 50% freelance written. "All readers are high fidelity enthusiasts, and many have a high fidelity industry-related job." Quarterly magazine; 56 pages. Estab. 1976. Circ. 4,650. Pays on acceptance. Buys all rights. Byline given. Simultaneous, photocopied and previously published submissions OK. SASE. Reports in 2 weeks. Sample copy $1; mention *Writer's Market* in request.
Nonfiction: Expose; how-to; general interest; humor; historical; interview (people in hi-fi business, manufacturers or retail); new product (all type of new audio equipment); nostalgia (articles and opinion on older equipment); personal experience (with various types of audio equipment); photo feature (on installation, or how-to tips); profile (of hi-fi equipment) and technical (pertaining to audio). "Subjective evaluations of hi-fi equipment make up 70% of our publication. Will accept 10/issue." Buys 2 mss/issue. Submit outline. Pays $25 maximum.
Columns/Departments: Bits & Pieces (short items of interest to hi-fi hobbyists); Ramblings (do-it-yourself tips on bettering existing systems); Record Reviews (of records which would be of interest to audiophiles). Query. Length: 25-400 words. Pays $5 maximum.
Fillers: Clippings, jokes, gags, anecdotes and newsbreaks. Buys 2/issues. Length: 25-400 words. Pays $10 maximum.

SHEET MUSIC MAGAZINE, Sheet Music Magazine, Inc., 60 Goldens Bridge Rd., Katonah NY 10536. Editor: Edward J. Shanaphy. Emphasizes music and the home musician. Published 9 times/year. Magazine; 60 pages. Estab. 1976. Circ. 150,000. Pays on publication. Buys all rights. Pays 20% kill fee. Byline given. Submit seasonal/holiday material 4 months in advance. Simultaneous and previously published submissions OK. SASE. Reports in 1 month. Sample copy $2.
Nonfiction: General interest, how-to and nostalgia. Buys 3 mss/issue. Send complete ms. Length: 1,000-3,500 words. Pays $50-300.

Mystery

ALFRED HITCHCOCK'S MYSTERY MAGAZINE, Davis Publications, Inc., 380 Lexington Ave., New York NY 10017. Editor: Eleanor Sullivan. Associate Editor: Susan Calderella. Emphasizes mystery fiction. Monthly magazine; 130 pages. Estab. 1956. Circ. 270,000. Pays on acceptance. Buys all rights. Byline given. Submit seasonal/holiday material 7 months in advance. Simultaneous and photocopied submissions OK. SASE. Reports in 6 weeks. Free writer's guidelines.
Fiction: Original and well-written mystery, suspense and crime fiction. No reprints or true crimes. "A 'now' feeling is preferred for every story, both as to plot urgency and today's world. Plausibility counts heavily even in supernatural stories." Length: 1,000-10,000 words. Rates are basically the same as those paid by *Ellery Queen's Mystery Magazine.*
How To Break In: "Think Hitchcock. It's the master's brand of suspense that we want. Avoid gore, profanity and explicit sex."

ELLERY QUEEN'S MYSTERY MAGAZINE, Davis Publications, Inc., 380 Lexington Ave., New York NY 10017. Editor-in-Chief: Ellery Queen. Managing Editor: Eleanor Sullivan. Monthly magazine; 160 pages. Estab. 1941. Circ. 415,000. Pays on acceptance. Buys first North American serial rights. Byline given. Submit seasonal/holiday material 7 months in advance. Simultaneous, photocopied and previously published submissions OK. SASE. Reports in 6 weeks. Free writer's guidelines.
Fiction: "We publish every type of mystery: the suspense story, the psychological study, the deductive puzzle—the gamut of crime and detection from the realistic (including the policeman's lot and stories of police procedure) to the more imaginative (including 'locked rooms' and impossible crimes). We need private-eye stories, but do not want sex, sadism or sensationalism-for-the-sake-of-sensationalism" Buys 13 mss/issue. Length: 6,000 words maximum. Pays 3-8¢/word.
How To Break In: "We have a department of First Stories to encourage writers whose fiction has never before been in print. We publish an average of 24 first stories a year."

MIKE SHAYNE MYSTERY MAGAZINE, Renown Publications, Inc., Box 178, Reseda CA 91335. Monthly magazine; 128 pages. Estab. 1956. Buys magazine serial rights only. Byline given. Submit seasonal/holiday material 4 months in advance. Photocopied submissions OK. SASE. Reports in 2 weeks.

Fiction: Strong, fast-moving mystery stories. Buys 8 mss/issue. Length: 1,000-6,000 words. Pays 1¢/word minimum.
How To Break In: "Study the type of material we use. Know pace of story, type of mystery we buy. Best to send very short material to start, as the new author doesn't handle novelette lengths convincingly."

Nature, Conservation, and Ecology

The magazines classified here are "pure" nature, conservation and ecology publications; that is, they exist to further the study and preservation of nature and do not publish recreational or travel articles except as they relate to conservation or nature. Other markets for this kind of material will be found in the Regional; Sport and Outdoor; and Travel, Camping, and Trailer categories, although the magazines listed there require that nature or conservation articles be slanted to their specialized subject matter and audience.

AMERICAN FORESTS, American Forestry Association, 1319 18th St. NW, Washington DC 20036. (202)467-5810. Editor: Bill Rooney. "We are an organization for the advancement of intelligent management and use of our forests, soil, water, wildlife, and all other natural resources necessary for an environment of high quality and the well-being of all citizens." Monthly magazine; 64 pages. Circ. 80,000. Pays on acceptance. Buys one-time rights. Byline given. Phone queries OK. Submit seasonal/holiday material 5 months in advance. SASE. Reports in 6 weeks. Free sample copy and writer's guidelines.
Nonfiction: General interest, historical, how-to, humor and inspirational. "All articles should emphasize trees, forests, wildlife or land use." Buys 5 mss/issue. Query. Length: 2,000 words. Pays $100-350.
Photos: State availability of photos. Offers no additional payment for photos accompanying mss. Uses 8x10 b&w glossy prints; 35mm color transparencies. Buys one-time rights. Captions required.
Poetry: Free verse, haiku, light verse and traditional. Buys 8-10/year. Submit in batches of 4. Pays $20.

AUDUBON, 950 3rd Avenue, New York NY 10022. "Not soliciting freelance material; practically all articles done on assignment only. We have a backlog of articles from known writers and contributors. Our issues are planned well in advance of publication and follow a theme." Pays negotiable kill fee. Byline given.

ENVIRONMENT, 4000 Albemarle St. NW., Washington DC 20016. Managing Editor: Barbara Ferkiss. For citizens, scientists, business and government executives, teachers, high school and college students interested in environment or effects of technology and science in public affairs. Magazine; 48 pages. Estab. 1958. Magazine published 10 times/year. Circ. 20,000. Buys all rights. Byline given. Pays on publication to professional writers. Sample copy $3. Will consider photocopied submissions. Reports in 6-8 weeks. Query or submit complete ms. SASE.
Nonfiction: Scientific and environmental material; effects of technology on society. Preferred length: 2,500-6,500 words. Pays $100-300, depending on material.

ENVIRONMENTAL ACTION, 1346 Connecticut Ave., Washington DC 20036. Editor: Gail Robinson. 20% freelance written. Emphasizes citizen action and legislative/governmental activity affecting the environment for a well-educated, sophisticated, politically oriented readership. Monthly magazine; 32 pages. Estab. April 1970. Circ. 20,000. Pays on publication. Buys all rights, but may reassign following publication. Pays 20% kill fee. Byline given. Simultaneous (if so identified), photocopied and previously published submissions OK. SASE. Reports in 6 weeks. Free sample copy.
Nonfiction: "All articles must be written for a sophisticated, politically oriented audience, well informed on environmental issues." Expose; general interest; and profile. Buys 15 mss/year. Query. Length: 1,000-2,500 words. Pays $25-225.
Photos: State availability of photos with query. Pays $15-50 for 8x10 b&w glossy prints. Buys all rights, but may reassign following publication.

THE EXPLORER, Cleveland Museum of Natural History, Wade Oval, University Circle, Cleveland OH 44106. (216)231-4600. Editor: Bill Baughman. 50% freelance written. For readers with a strong interest in natural history and science. Estab. 1938. Quarterly. Circ. 32,000. Audience are members of 22 museums and many independent subscribers. Buys one-time rights. Byline given. Payment in contributor's copies. Submit seasonal material 6 months in advance. Reports in 3-4 weeks. SASE.

Nonfiction and Photos: "We are especially concerned with interpreting the natural history and science of North America, but mostly US. We endeavor to give a voice to the natural scientists and naturalists functioning within these geographical boundaries and feel an obligation to make our readers aware of the crucial issues at stake in the world regarding conservation and environmental problems. Now assigning most articles, but will consider articles by scientists, naturalists and experts in nature, ecology, and environmental areas. Writing should have a lively style and be understandable to scientists of all ages. Exploring nature can be exciting. Your writing should reflect and encourage the exploring mind." Length: 1,000-3,000 words. B&w (8x10) photos. Some color transparencies and color prints are used. 35mm Kodachrome color, 2¼x2¼ and 4x5 transparencies are acceptable for inside editorial and cover illustrations. All photos, particularly close-ups of birds and animals, must be needle-sharp. Also interested in b&w photo essays (12 photos maximum) on natural history topics.

INTERNATIONAL WILDLIFE, 225 E. Michigan, Milwaukee WI 53202. Editor: John Strohm. 80% freelance written. For persons interested in natural history, outdoor adventure and the environment. Bimonthly. Buys all rights to text; usually one-time rights to photos and art. Pays on acceptance. Query. "Now assigning most articles but will consider detailed proposals for quality feature material of interest to broad audience." Reports in 2 weeks. SASE.

Nonfiction and Photos: Focus on world wildlife, environmental problems and man's relationship to the natural world as reflected in such issues as population control, pollution, resource utilization, food production, etc. Especially interested in articles on animal behavior and other natural history, little-known places, first-person experiences, timely issues. "Payment varies according to value and use of feature articles, but usually begins at $750. Purchase top-quality color and b&w photos; prefer 'packages' of related photos and text, but single shots of exceptional interest and sequences also considered. Prefer Kodachrome transparencies for color, 8x10 prints for b&w."

JOURNAL OF FRESHWATER, Freshwater Biological Research Foundation, 2500 Shadywood Rd., Box 90, Navarre MN 55392. (612)471-7467. Editor: Richard A. Hughes. 50% freelance written. Emphasizes freshwater/environmental issues. Quarterly magazine; 32 pages. Estab. January 1977. Pays on acceptance. Buys all rights, but may reassign following publication. Byline given. Phone queries OK. Submit seasonal/holiday material 6 months in advance of issue date. SASE. Reports in 4-6 weeks. Sample copy $3; free writer's guidelines.

Nonfiction: "We will consider virtually any material dealing with freshwater environment as long as it is well-written, interesting, etc. We're always looking for new slants and ideas." How-to; general interest; humor; interview; nostalgia; personal opinion; photo feature; profile; and technical. "No 'bumper-sticker' philosophies, please; and no dry encyclopedia-type articles or obviously slanted, unresearched material." Buys 15-20 mss/year. Submit complete ms. Length: "However long it takes—and not a word more." Pays $100-300 (more with photos or art).

Photos: Submit photos with accompanying ms. Payment for photos is included in purchase price of article. Uses 5x7 minimum b&w glossy photos or 35mm, 2¼x2¼ or larger color transparencies. Captions preferred. Buys all rights, but may reassign following publication. Model release required.

Fiction: "We have never purchased any fiction, since we have not received good fiction material. But we're always open to something new." Experimental and humorous. Pays $50-300.

Poetry: Avant-garde; free verse; haiku; light verse; and traditional. Buys 4-6/issue. Limit submissions to batches of 5-10. Pays $20-50.

THE LIVING WILDERNESS, 1901 Pennsylvania Ave. NW., Washington DC 20006. (212)293-2732. Editor: James G. Deane. For members of the Wilderness Society, libraries and educational institutions. Estab. 1935. Circ. 65,000. Quarterly. "There may be a considerable wait for return of unsolicited materials." Pays on publication. SASE. Sample Copy $2; free writer's guidelines.

Nonfiction, Poetry and Photos: Articles on wilderness preservationa and appreciation and on wildlife conservation. Special interest in threats to North American wild areas. Occasional articles on other environmental issues and natural history; occasional nature-oriented essays and high-caliber wilderness-oriented poetry. Some book reviews are assigned. Mss should be of professional quality. Payment depends on character of material. Editors consider only highest quality photographs relevant to the foregoing subjects, usually to illustrate specific articles. Pays $25 minimum for b&w; $75 minimum for color, except when bought in article photo package.

NATIONAL PARKS & CONSERVATION MAGAZINE, 1701 18th St. NW, Washington DC 20009. (202)265-2717. Editor: Eugenia Horstman Connally. For a mature, highly educated audience interested in out-of-doors and environmental matters. Monthly magazine; 32 pages. Estab. 1919. Circ. 43,000. Pays on acceptance. Buys North American serial rights. Submit seasonal/holiday material 4 months in advance. SASE. Reports in 4-6 weeks. Sample copy $2; free writer's guidelines
Nonfiction: Expose (on threats to national parks); general interest (natural parks); historical (natural parks); nostalgia (on the good old days on natural parks); technical (environmental problems, alternative energy); and endangered species of wildlife. "We do not want articles on humor, personal experience, or inspiration nature." Buys 3-4 mss/issue. Query or send complete ms. Length: 1,500-2,000 words. Pays $75-200.
Photos: State availability of photos or send photos with ms. Pays $20-50 for 8x10 b&w glossy prints; $25-75 for 4x5 color transparencies; offers no additional payment for photos accompanying ms. Buys one-time rights. Captions required.

NATIONAL WILDLIFE, 225 E. Michigan Ave., Milwaukee WI 53202. Editor-in-Chief: John Strohm. Emphasizes wildlife. Bimonthly magazine; 52 pages. Estab. 1962. Circ. 900,000. Pays on acceptance. Buys all rights. Submit seasonal/holiday material 6 months in advance. Previously published submissions OK. SASE. Reports in 2 weeks. Free writer's guidelines.
Nonfiction: Mark Wexler, Nonfiction Editor. How-to; humor; informational; interview; personal experience; photo feature and profile. Buys 8 mss/issue. Query. Length: 2,000-3,000 words. Pays $500-1,000.
Photos: Karen Altpeter, Photo Editor. Photos purchased with or without accompanying ms or on assignment. Pays $35-100 for 8x10 b&w glossy prints; $100 minimum for 35mm color Kodachromes.

NATURAL HISTORY, Natural History Magazine Circulation Dept., 79th and Central Park W., New York NY 10024. Editor: Alan Ternes. For "well-educated, ecologically aware audience. Includes many professional people, scientists, scholars." Monthly. Circ. 460,000. "Copyright on text of articles is held by The American Museum of Natural History." Buys 50 mss/year. Kill fee varies. Byline given. Pays on publication. Sample copy $1.50. Submit seasonal material 6 months in advance. Query or submit complete ms. SASE.
Nonfiction: Uses all types of scientific articles except chemistry and physics—emphasis is on the biological sciences and anthropology. Prefers professional scientists as authors. "We always want to see new research findings in almost all the branches of the natural sciences —anthropology, archeology, zoology, ornithology. We find that it is particularly difficult to get something new in herpetology (amphibians and reptiles) or entomology (insects) and we would like to see material in those fields. We lean heavily toward writers who are scientists or professional science writers. High standards of writing and research. Favor an ecological slant in most of our pieces, but do not generally lobby for causes, environmental or other. Writer should have a deep knowledge of his subject. Then submit original ideas either in query or by ms. Should be able to supply high-quality illustrations." Length: 2,000-4,000 words. Pays $300-750, plus additional payment for photos used.
Photos: Uses some 8x10 b&w glossy photographs; pays $100/page maximum. Much color is used; pays $150 for inside and up to $250 for cover. Photos are purchased for one-time use.
How To Break In: "Learn about something in depth before you bother writing about it."

THE NATURALISTS' DIRECTORY AND ALMANAC (INTERNATIONAL), World Natural History Publications, Inc., Box 550, Marlton NJ 08053. (609)654-6500. Editor-in-Chief: Dr. Ross H. Arnett Jr. Emphasizes outdoor natural history recreation. Published every two years; 320 pages, with a supplement every other year. Estab. 1877. Circ. 5,000. Pays on publication. Buys one-time rights. Byline given. Phone queries OK. Submit seasonal or holiday material any time. Photocopied submissions and previously published work OK. Query. SASE. Reports in 2 months. Sample copy $12.95; writer's guidelines for SASE.
Nonfiction: Informational (sources must be documented) and historical articles. "Some suggested subjects are: nature sayings; records such as tallest trees, smallest living organisms; value of minerals; where and what to collect; poisonous plants and animals; state trees, state birds, state fish, state mammals, state insects, etc." Buys 5-10 mss/year by assignment. Length: 50-1,000 words. "Payment generally is not made for articles and/or photographs. Two copies

of the volume will be sent upon publication and permission to reprint, or to sell, is granted upon request. All photographs and mss are returned after publication if requested. We do, upon occasion, send out lists of photographs and/or articles that we desire and will purchase." Pays $10 minimum.

Photos: Purchases with or without mss on assignment or if on want list. Send b&w prints and color prints or transparencies. Pays $5-15 for 5x7 b&w glossy; $10-50 for 35mm, 2¼x2¼ or 2¼x3¼ color transparencies or up to 8x10 color prints with glossy finish. Captions required.

How To Break In: "Material must be technically accurate. Most freelance material is too elementary or is written in newspaper style, and is not acceptable."

Rejects: Humorous or sensational material; hunting and fishing themes.

NEW ENGLAND OUTDOORS, New England Digest, Inc., 803 Statler Bldg., Boston MA 02116. Editor: Mike Ricciuto. Emphasizes natural history, conservation and environment. Monthly magazine; 72 pages. Estab. 1975. Circ. 25,000. Pays on publication. Buys first rights. Submit seasonal/holiday material 3 months in advance. Simultaneous and photocopied submissions OK. SASE. Reports in 3 weeks on queries; in 1-2 months on mss. Sample copy 25¢.

Nonfiction: Expose, how-to, humor, interview, nostalgia, photo feature, profile and travel. "Articles should be related to the outdoors, but no hunting or fishing." Buys 2 mss/issue. Query. Length: 1,500-3,000 words. Pays $75-150.

Photos: State availability of photos with ms. Pays $5-25 for b&w prints; $25-75 for color transparencies. Buys one-time rights.

OCEANS, Fort Mason, San Francisco, CA 94123. Editor-in-Chief: Keith K. Howell. 100% freelance written. For people interested in the sea. Bimonthly magazine; 72 pages. Estab. 1969. Circ. 50,000. Pays on publication. Buys one-time rights. Pays 100% kill fee. Byline given. Submit seasonal/holiday material 4 months in advance. Simultaneous and photocopied submissions OK. SASE. Reports in 8 weeks. Sample copy 50¢. Free writer's guidelines.

Nonfiction: "Want articles on the worldwide realm of salt water; marine life (biology and ecology), oceanography, maritime history, geography, undersea exploration and study, voyages, ships, coastal areas including environmental problems, seaports and shipping, islands, food-fishing and aquaculture (mariculture), peoples of the sea, including anthropological materials. Writer should be simple, direct, factual, very readable (avoid dullness and pedantry, make it lively and interesting but not cute, flip or tongue-in-cheek; avoid purple prose). Careful research, good structuring, no padding. Factual information in good, narrative style. *Oceans* is authoritative, but less technical than *Scientific American*. We do not want articles on scuba; adventuring, travel tend to be overworked. Prefer no sport fishing, boating, surfing, or other purely sport-type matter. Diving okay if serious in purpose, unusual in results or story angle. We want articles on rarely visited islands, ports or shores that have great intrinsic interest, but not treated in purely travelogue style. Can use more on environmental concerns." Length: 1,000-5,000 words. Pays $60/page.

OUTDOOR INDIANA, Room 612, State Office Bldg., Indianapolis IN 46204. (317)633-4332. Editor: Herbert R. Hill. 2% freelance written. For subscribers who seek information regarding programs, projects, services and facilities of the Indiana Department of Natural Resources. Published 10 times/year. Circ. 36,000. Buys first serial rights. Byline given. Pays on publication. Reports in 2-4 weeks. Query. SASE.

Nonfiction and Photos: Informative, concise, illustrative, bright articles on Indiana Department of Natural Resources-related topics only. No fiction, essays or verse. Length: 1,000-2,000 words. Usually pays 2¢/word. Photos of Indiana interest only; purchased with mss or with captions only. B&w photos, 8x10; color transparencies, 2¼x2¼ or larger. Pays $5 for b&w; $25 for color; $50 for color cover.

PACIFIC DISCOVERY, California Academy of Sciences, Golden Gate Park, San Francisco CA 94118. (415)221-5100. Editor: Bruce Finson. 100% freelance written. "A journal of nature and culture around the world, read by scientists, naturalists, teachers, students, and others having a keen interest in knowing the natural world more thoroughly." Estab. 1948. Published bimonthly by the California Academy of Science. Circ. 14,000. Buys first North American serial rights of articles; one-time use of photos. Usually reports within 3 months; publishes accepted articles in 3-6 months. Pays on publication. Query with 100-word summary of projected article for review before preparing finished ms. SASE.

Nonfiction and Photos: "Subjects of articles include behavior and natural history of animals and plants, ecology, anthropology, geology, paleontology, biogeography, taxonomy, and related topics in the natural sciences. Occasional articles are published on the history of natural science, exploration, astronomy and archeology. Types of articles include discussions of individual species or groups of plants and animals that are related to or involved with one another, narratives of scientific expeditions together with detailed discussions of field work and results, reports of biological and geological discoveries and of short-lived phenomena, and explanations of specialized topics in natural science. Authors need not be scientists; however, all articles must be based, at least in part, on firsthand fieldwork." Length: 1,000-3,000 words. Pays $50-150. B&w photos or color slides must accompany all mss or they will not be reviewed. Send 15-30 with each ms. Photos should have both scientific and aesthetic interest, be captioned in a few sentences on a separate caption list keyed to the photos and numbered in story sequence. Some photo stories are used. Pays $10/photo. All slides, negatives, and prints are returned soon after publication.

PACIFIC SEARCH, 222 Dexter Ave. N., Seattle WA 98109. Editor: Eleanor McCarthy. Emphasizes the public stewardship of nature and life in the Pacific Northwest. Monthly magazine (except August and January). Pays on acceptance. Buys first rights. Simultaneous and previously published submissions OK. SASE. Reports in 6 weeks. Free sample copy and writer's guidelines.
Nonfiction: "Topics include nature and wildlife, news events of environmental affairs, places to go, regional history, character profiles, how-to, humor, items that show something unique, zany, paradoxical, or little-known about the Northwest. Editorial material is selected for Pacific Northwest regional interest, clarity, informative value, factual accuracy, thoroughness of research, simplicity of presentation, timeliness and tight writing." Buys 4 mss/issue. Query with clips of published work. Length: 600-3,000 words. Pays 5-10¢/word.
Photos: Send photos with ms. Pays $15 for b&w prints; $30-75 for 35mm color transparencies. Buys one-time rights. Captions preferred.
Columns/Departments: Fishing; Skywatch (astronomy, sky events); Scannings (news items); Making Waves (environmental affairs); Books; Washington DC Report; Trade-Offs (environmental impact; Mushrooms; Who Knows: (questions and answers); and Exploring (places to go). Query.

SAERCH, Social Science and Environmental Research, Box 614, Corte Madera CA 94925. Editor: William Whitney. For professionals in the environmental and sociological fields. Bimonthly magazine; 52 pages. Estab. 1975. Circ. 5,000. Rights purchased vary with author and material. Buys all rights, but may reassign rights to author after publication, first serial rights, or simultaneous rights. Buys 20 mss/year. Pays on acceptance. Sample copy $1. Will consider simultaneous submissions. Reports in 8-10 weeks. Query or submit complete ms. SASE.
Nonfiction, Photos and Fillers: "Our material centers on the subjects of environmental science, impacts on sociological areas, etc. All material should be up-to-date and informative. Our readers are aware of their fields and the need to stay abreast of new developments. The writer's approach and outlook should be problem oriented with stress on solutions to the multi-faceted sciences of today. Nothing trite or generalized. We would like to see more coverage of current debates in the fields of environmental and sociological science. Our recent coverage has included activities of the Sierra Club, as well as specific topics such as shell oil retrieval." Informational, interview, profile, historical, think pieces, expose and technical articles. Length: 2,000-3,500 words. Pays 3-10¢/word. Spot news. Length: 500-750 words. Pays 3-10¢/word. Pays $5-20 for 8x10 b&w glossy prints used with mss. Pays $10-50 for 35mm or larger color transparencies used with mss. Newsbreaks of 500-750 words used as fillers. Same rate of payment as for other material.

SIERRA, The Sierra Club Bulletin, 530 Bush Street, San Francisco CA 94108. (415)981-8634. Editor-in-Chief: Frances Gendlin. Managing Editor: David Gancher. 70% freelance written. Emphasizes conservation and environmental politics for people who are well-educated, activist, outdoor-oriented, and politically well-informed with a dedication to conservation. Magazine published 6 times/year; 72 pages. Estab. 1892. Circ. 183,000. Pays on publication. Buys one-time rights. Byline given. Simultaneous and photocopied submissions OK. SASE. Reports in 6 weeks. Writer's guidelines.
Nonfiction: Expose (well-documented on environmental issues of national importance such as energy, forestry, fisheries, etc.); general interest (well-researched pieces on areas of particular environmental concern); historical (relevant to environmental concerns); how-to (on camping, climbing, outdoor photography, etc.); interview (with very prominent figures in the field); personal experience (by or about children and wilderness); photo feature (photo essays on threatened areas); and technical (on energy sources, wildlife management land-use, solid waste management, etc.). No "My trip to . . . "; or why we must save wildlife/nature articles; no

poetry or general superficial essays on environmentalism and local enviromental issues. Buys 2-3 mss/issue. Query with clips of published work. Length: 800-3,000 words. Pays $200.
Photos: Gerald Klein, production manager. State availability of photos with query letter. Pays $50 maximum for color tranparencies; $100 for cover photos. Buys one-time rights.
Columns/Departments: Book Reviews. Buys 5 mss/year. Length: 800-2,000 words. Query. Open to suggestions for new columns/departments. Submit to Carey Charlesworth, assistant editor.

SNOWY EGRET, 205 S. 9th St., Williamsburg KY 40769. (606)549-0850. Editor: Humphrey A. Olsen. For "persons of at least high school age interested in literary, artistic, philosophical and historical natural history." Semiannual. Circ. less than 500. Buys first North American serial rights. Byline given. Buys 40-50 mss/year. Pays on publication. Sample copy $2. Usually reports in 2 months. SASE.
Nonfiction: Subject matter limited to material related to natural history, especially literary, artistic, philosophical, and historical aspects. Criticism, book reviews, essays, biographies. Pays $2/printed page.
Fiction: "We are interested in considering stories or self-contained portions of novels. All fiction must be natural history or man and nature. The scope is broad enough to include such stories as Hemingway's 'Big Two-Hearted River' and Warren's 'Blackberry Winter.'" Length: 10,000 words maximum. Pays $2/printed page. Send mss and books for review to Dr. William T. Hamilton, Dept. of English, Otterbein College, Westerville OH 43081. "It is preferable to query first."
Poetry: No length limits. Pays $4/printed page, $2 minimum. Send poems and poetry books for review to Dr. Hamilton, Literary Editor, and to West Coast Editor, Gary Elder, 22 Ardith Lane, Alamo CA 94507.

Newspapers and Weekly Magazine Sections

This section includes daily newspapers as well as Saturday and Sunday magazine sections of daily newspapers. They are listed geographically by state headings although some cover wider areas (for example, *Michiana* serves both Michigan and Indiana).

Most of these markets seek submissions about persons, places and things in their specific circulation areas. However, some large city and national newspapers that welcome general interest material from nonlocal writers are also included in this list. Newspapers with specialized subject matter or audiences, like *The Wall Street Journal*, are classified with magazines dealing with the same subject matter or audience.

A few editors report that some correspondents in their area are attracted to small feature items but let big news stories from their communities slip through their fingers. Freelancers, on the other hand, report that some busy newspaper editors return their submissions without even a rejection slip—or in a few cases, fail to return it at all, even when it's accompanied by a stamped, self-addressed envelope. (Because newspaper editors receive many submissions from public relations firms and other individuals who do not expect return of their material, they sometimes automatically toss material they're not interested in publishing. That means a retyping job for the freelancer. It also means you should be wary of sending original photographs which are your only copies.)

Arizona

ARIZONA MAGAZINE, Box 1950, Phoenix AZ 85001. (602)271-8291. Editor: Bud DeWald. For "everyone who reads a Sunday newspaper." Weekly; 60 pages. Estab. 1953. Circ. 400,000. Kill fee varies. Byline given. Buys 250 mss/year. Pays when article is scheduled for publication. For sample copy and guidelines for writers send 50¢. Will consider photocopied submissions. Will consider simultaneous submissions if exclusive regionally. Reports in 2 weeks. Query or submit complete ms. SASE.
Nonfiction and Photos: "General subjects that have an Arizona connection. Should have a bemused, I-don't-believe-it approach. Nothing is that serious. Should have an abundance of quotes and anecdotes. Historical and travel subjects are being overworked. We don't need

someone's therapy." Length: 1,000-3,000 words. Pays $50-250. B&w and color photos purchased with or without mss or on assignment. Pays $10-25 for 8x10 b&w glossy prints; $15-70 for color (35mm or larger).

How To Break In: "Find a good personal subject and write about him so the reader will feel he is with the subject. Describe the subject in anecdotes and let him reveal himself by his quotes."

California

CALIFORNIA TODAY, 750 Ridder Park Dr., San Jose CA 95190. (408)289-5563. Editor: John Parkyn. For a general audience. Weekly rotogravure newspaper-magazine, published with the San Jose Mercury News. Circ. 250,000. Not copyrighted. Byline given. Buys 100 mss a year. Pays on acceptance. Free sample copy. Will consider photocopied and simultaneous submissions, if the simultaneous submission is out of their area. Submit seasonal material (skiing, wine, outdoor living) 3 months in advance. Reports in 4 weeks. Query. SASE.
Nonfiction and Photos: A general newspaper-magazine requiring that most subjects be related to California and interests in that area. Will consider subjects outside California if subject is of broad or national appeal. Length: 1,000-3.500 words. Pays $100-400. Payment varies for b&w and color photos purchased with or without mss. Captions required.

GOOD LIFE MAGAZINE (formerly *Sacramento Weekender*), *Sacramento Union,* 301 Capitol Mall, Sacramento CA 95812. Editor: Jackie Peterson. Weekly. Not copyrighted. Byline given. Buys 12 mss/year. Query. SASE.
Nonfiction and Photos: Home decor, home handiwork and gourmet cookery. Needs color transparencies for illustration. Length: 1,000-1,500 words. Pays $100 for color cover story with at least 3 photos.

THE SACRAMENTO BEE, Box 15779, Sacramento CA 95813. For a general readership; higher-than-average education; higher-than-average interest in politics and government; oriented toward outdoor-activity. Newspaper; 48 pages. Estab. 1857. Daily. Circ. 190,000 daily; 220,000 Sunday. Not copyrighted. Buys 200 mss/year. Pays on publication. Will consider simultaneous submissions if they are not duplicated in Northern California. Reports in 2 weeks. Query or submit complete ms to Features Editor. SASE.
Nonfiction and Photos: Human interest features, news background. Prefers narrative feature style. Does not want to see sophomoric humor. Will consider interviews, profiles, nostalgic and historical articles; expose; personal experience. Length: 100-1,500 words. Pays $20-100. B&w glossy prints and color (negatives) purchased with or without mss. Pays $15-75 for b&w; $25-100 for color. Captions required.

Colorado

BOULDER DAILY CAMERA FOCUS MAGAZINE, Box 591, Boulder CO 80306. (303)442-1202. Editor-in-Chief: Barbara Baumgarten. 50% freelance written. Emphasizes subjects of particular interest to Boulder County residents. Weekly tabloid.; 40 pages. Estab. 1964. Circ. 28,000. Pays on first of month following publication. Buys one-time rights. Byline given. Phone queries OK. Submit seasonal/holiday material 6-8 weeks in advance. Photocopied submissions OK. SASE. Reports in 2 weeks.
Nonfiction: Expose (anything relevant to Boulder County that needs exposing); informational (emphasis on good writing, warmth and impact); historical (pertaining to Boulder County or Colorado in general); interview and profile (stress local angle); photo feature (featuring Boulder County or areas in Colorado and Rocky Mountain West where Boulder County residents are apt to go). Buys 100 mss/year. Query. Length: 700-3,300 words. Pays 30-50¢ a column inch.
Photos: Purchased with or without mss, or on assignment. Captions required. Query. Pays $3-6 for 8x10 b&w glossy prints; $4-8 for 35mm or 2¼x2¼ (or larger) color transparencies.

CONTEMPORARY MAGAZINE, Sunday supplement to *The Denver Post*, 650 15th St., Denver CO 80201. Editor: Joan White. For "young adults to senior citizens (both sexes), aware of today's world." Newspaper format. Buys first rights. Pays on publication. Free sample copy. No query required. "We are being very selective and use a very limited amount of freelance material." Submit seasonal material 3 months in advance. Reporting time varies. SASE.

Nonfiction: "Mostly a family and women's interest magazine." Length of 500-1,500 words. Pays $50-75.

EMPIRE MAGAZINE, *The Denver Post,* Box 1709, Denver CO 80201. (303)297-1687. Editor: Carl Skiff. Weekly. Estab. 1950. Buys 250 mss/year. Buys first rights. Byline given. Pays on acceptance for nonfiction; on publication for photos. Query. SASE.
Nonfiction and Photos: "A rotogravure magazine covering the general scene in our circulation area. We are looking for material of national magazine quality in interest and writing style, but with a strong, regional peg. Our region focuses on Colorado, Wyoming, Utah, New Mexico, western Kansas and Nebraska. We need solidly researched articles about exciting things, personalities and situations. We also need light humor and reminiscences." Length: 2,500 words maximum. Pays about 5¢/word. "Photographs can help sell a story." B&w photos are purchased with ms or as singles or series or as picture stories (500 words). Picture stories use 5-8 photos; query. Pays $50 for color transparencies used for cover; $100 for double spread; $25 for singles (color) used inside; $10 for b&w.

SUN COUNTRY (formerly *Showcase Magazine*), Box 130, Colorado Springs CO 80901. (303)633-3881, ext. 379. Editor: Larry Haise. 90% freelance written. For "the young reader, around 18-35, interested in light features on popular arts, leisure, trends and issues with a state or regional angle." Sunday supplement of the *Colorado Springs Sun*; 16 pages. Estab. 1948. Circ. 25,000. Pays on publication. Phone queries OK. Submit seasonal/holiday material 1 month in advance of issue date. Simultaneous, photocopied and previously published submissions OK. SASE. Reports in 4 weeks. Free sample copy; mention *Writer's Market* in request.
Nonfiction: General interest (emphasis on entertainment and leisure, particularly outdoor recreation, the Pikes Peak region and Colorado); humor; interview; personal experience; profile; developments in Colorado arts; trends in Colorado living; issues; and travel. No governmental exposes. Buys 120 mss/year. Query. Length: 500-2,000 words. Pays $10-100.
Photos: State availability of photos with query. Pays $10 for 8x10 b&w prints or contact sheets; $25 for color transparencies, more for cover shots. Captions required. Buys one-time rights. Model release required.

District of Columbia

PRESERVATION NEWS, National Trust for Historic Preservation, 1785 Massachusetts Ave. NW, Washington DC 20036. Vice President and Editor: Mrs. Terry B. Morton. Organizational publication for members of the National Trust for Historic Preservation. Emphasizes historic preservation. Monthly tabloid newspaper; 12-16 pages. Estab. 1961. Circ. 170,000. Pays on publication. May buy all, second serial (reprint) or one-time rights. Byline given. Photocopied submissions and previously published work OK. SASE. Reports in 6 weeks. Free sample copy and editorial guidelines.
Nonfiction: Carleton Knight, Associate Editor. "Most of our material is prepared in-house, but willing to review queries on subjects directly related to historic preservation, including efforts to save and re-use buildings, structures, and to restore neighborhoods of historical, architectural and cultural significance. Writer must be very familiar with our subject matter, which deals with a specialized field, in order to present a unique publication idea." Length: 750-1,000 words. Buys about 15-18 mss/year. Pays 10¢/word.
Photos: Additional payment not usually made for photos used with mss. Pays $10-25 for 8x10 b&w photos purchased without mss or on assignment. Query or send contact sheet. No conversions from slides.

Florida

THE FLORIDIAN, Box 1211, St. Petersburg FL 33731. Editor: Judy Sedgeman. For middle-income readers with contemporary outlook. Weekly magazine; 24-40 pages. Estab. 1967. Circ. 200,000. Pays on acceptance. Buys first North American serial, second serial or simultaneous rights; exclusive rights within Florida. Simultaneous and photocopied submissions OK. SASE. Free writer's guidelines.
Nonfiction: Incisive articles should focus on Florida. Subject areas include government and politics, consumer issues, business and finance, health, leisure and recreation, food, fashion, interior design, architecture, and profiles of high-interest personalities. "Presentation should be crisp, original, innovative. No once-over-lightly features. Articles must be validated by

substantial research and a high degree of professionalism is expected. Style is as important as substance." Buys 200 mss/year. Length: 1,000-3,000 words. Pays $75-500.

THE TAMPA TRIBUNE, Box 191, Tampa FL 33601. Features Editor: Leland. Hawes. For a general-circulation, newspaper audience. Daily newspaper; 80-160 pages. Estab. 1894. Circ. 175,000-210,000. Not copyrighted, but special stories are copyrighted. Byline given. Buys very limited number of mss (primarily from area freelancers). Pays 2-4 weeks after publication. Will consider photocopied and simultaneous submissions (but not if made to nearby publications). Reports on material accepted for publication within a month. Returns rejected material. Query or submit complete ms. SASE.
Nonfiction and Photos: Articles on travel, human interest, history, news events, profiles, trends, etc. Must have central Florida emphasis or tie-in. Open to any literate style. Personal experience, interview and humor. Length: 150-1,000 words. Pays $25-100. Pays $10-25 for b&w glossy prints purchased with or without ms. Pays $25-50 for color transparencies purchased with or without ms.

Illinois

CHICAGO TRIBUNE MAGAZINE, 435 N. Michigan Ave., Chicago IL 60611. Editor: Robert Goldsborough. "The magazine is largely staff-written, but we do use a limited number of freelance articles. Pays 33% kill fee. Byline given. Query, however." Pays $200 minimum. Length: 1,500-3,000 words.

Indiana

INDIANAPOLIS STAR MAGAZINE, 307 N. Pennsylvania St., Indianapolis IN 46206. Editor-in-Chief: Fred D. Cavinder. 10-15% freelance written. Emphasizes subjects of interest in Indiana. Weekly magazine section of newspaper; 40 pages. Estab. 1947. Circ. 380,000. Pays on publication. Buys one-time rights. Byline given. Phone queries OK. Submit seasonal/holiday material 2 months in advance. Simultaneous and photocopied submissions OK. SASE. Reports in 2 weeks. Free sample copy.
Nonfiction: Informational; historical and interview (Indiana only); profiles (Hoosiers or ex-Hoosiers only); and technical (health/medical developments). "Too many freelancers send us too general material. We are not interested in household hints, consumer tips, oddities, celebrities, etc. We want stories which would be of specific interest to Indiana readers. That is, if the story doesn't include some relationship to Indiana, the subject must be of significant universal interest. An example would be a health breakthrough, major social development, or a new national trend. But our overwhelming topic is Indiana, her people or her former residents." Buys 50 mss/year. Query. Length: 5,000 words maximum. Pays $25-75.
Photos: Purchased with mss. Query or send prints or transparencies. Pays $5-7.50 for 5x7 or larger b&w glossy prints or mattes; $7.50-10 for 35mm or larger color transparencies.

MICHIANA, *The South Bend Tribune*, Colfax at Lafayette, South Bend IN 46626. (219)233-6161. Editor: Bill Sonneborn. 70% freelance written. For "average daily newspaper readers; perhaps a little above average since we have more than a dozen colleges and universities in our area." Weekly; 24 pages. Estab. 1873. Circ. 125,000. May buy first North American serial rights or simultaneous rights providing material offered will be used outside of Indiana and Michigan. Byline given. Buys 200 mss/year. Pays on publication. Will consider photocopied submissions if clearly legible. Submit special material for spring and fall travel sections at least 1 month in advance. Reports in 2 weeks. Submit complete ms. SASE.
Nonfiction and Photos: "Items of general and unusual interest, written in good, clear, simple sentences with logical approach to subject. We like material oriented to the Midwest, especially Indiana, Michigan, Ohio and Illinois." "We avoid all freelance material that supports movements of a political nature. We seldom use first-person humor. We can use some offbeat stuff if it isn't too far out." Length: 800-3,000 words. Payment is $50-60 minimum, with increases as deemed suitable. All mss must be accompanied by illustrations or b&w photos or 35mm or larger color transparencies.

Iowa

DES MOINES SUNDAY REGISTER PICTURE MAGAZINE, *Des Moines Register*, 715

Locust St., Des Moines IA 50304. Editor: Charles J. Nettles. 15% freelance written. For mass newspaper audience, metropolitan and rural. Estab. 1950. Weekly. Circ. 420,000. Buys first rights. Pays $50 maximum kill fee. Byline given. Buys 25 mss/year. Pays on publication. Submit seasonal material 8 weeks in advance. SASE.

Nonfiction and Photos: "Articles heavily concentrated on Iowa, mostly picture stories. Anything interesting in Iowa, or interesting elsewhere with some kind of tie to Iowans." Length: 1,500 words maximum. Material must lend itself to strong photographic presentation. If the idea is good, a photographer will be assigned if writer does not have professional quality photos. Pays $100-200/ms. Photo purchased with or without mss. Captions required. Prefers 8x10 b&w glossy prints. Pays $15 minimum. 35mm or larger transparencies. Pays $50 minimum for cover; $25 for inside use.

Kentucky

THE COURIER-JOURNAL MAGAZINE, 525 W. Broadway, Louisville KY 40203. Publisher: Barry Bingham Jr. Editor: James Pope. 25% freelance written, mostly from regular professional sources. For general readership in Kentucky and Indiana. Weekly magazine; 52 pages. Estab. 1942. Circ. 350,000. Pays on publication. Buys one-time rights. Byline given. Submit seasonal/holiday material 2 months in advance of issue date. Simultaneous, photocopied and previously published submissions OK. SASE. Reports in 4 weeks.

Nonfiction: General interest but some link to Kentucky-Indiana region almost mandatory; humor; photo feature; and profile. Buys 100 mss/year. Query. Length: 1,500-3,000 words. Pays $100-300.

Photos: State availability of photos with query. Pays $15-25 for 10x12 b&w glossy prints and $20-40 for color transparencies. Captions required. Buys one-time rights.

THE VOICE-JEFFERSONIAN, Chenoweth Square, St. Matthews KY 40207. (502)895-5436. Managing Editor: Roger Harris. For middle- and upper-income suburban audience. Family readership, but no taboos. Weekly. "No copyright unless the story is super-special and exclusive to us." SASE.

Nonfiction and Photos: News and Features departments. 300-1,500 words on local (east Jefferson County) subjects. "Manuscripts must have a local angle. Writers persistently ignore this fundamental standard." 5x7 b&w glossy prints. Pays 2¢-$1/inch; $5-15 for photos.

Louisiana

SUNDAY ADVOCATE MAGAZINE, Box 588, Baton Rouge LA 70821. (504)383-1111, ext. 319. Editor: Charles H. Lindsay. Byline given. Pays on publication. SASE.

Nonfiction and Photos: Well-illustrated, short articles; must have local, area or Louisiana angle, in that order of preference. Photos purchased with mss. Rates vary.

Massachusetts

THE CHRISTIAN SCIENCE MONITOR, 1 Norway St., Boston MA 02115. (617)262-2300, ext. 2303. Editor: Earl W. Foell. International newspaper issued daily except Saturdays, Sundays and holidays in North America; weekly international edition. Special issues: travel, winter vacation and international travel, summer vacation, autumn vacation, and others. February and September: fashion. Estab. 1908. Circ. 196,680. Buys all rights. Buys 3,700 mss a year. Pays on acceptance or publication, "depending on department." Submit seasonal material 2 months in advance. Reports in 4 weeks. Submit only complete original ms. SASE.

Nonfiction: Managing Editor, Features: Robert P. Hey. In-depth features and essays. "Style should be bright but not cute, concise but thoroughly researched. Try to humanize news or feature writing so reader identifies with it. Avoid sensationalism, crime and disaster. Accent constructive, solution-oriented treatment of subjects. Feature pages use colorful human interest material usually not exceeding 800 words. Home Forum page buys essays of 400-800 words, and poetry of high quality in a wide variety (traditional, blank and free verse). Pays $20-40. Education, arts, real estate, travel, living, garden, furnishings, consumer, and science pages will consider articles not usually more than 800 words appropriate to respective subjects." Pays $20-100. Some areas covered in travel pages include: Switzerland, Britain, Canada and the Caribbean.

Photos: Department Editor: Gordon Converse. Purchased with or without mss. Captions required. Pays $10-50 depending upon size and where used in paper.

NEW ENGLAND MAGAZINE, *Boston Globe*, Boston MA 02107. Editor-in-Chief: Michael Janeway. 25% freelance written. Weekly magazine; 44 pages. Estab. 1936. Circ. 693,679. Pays on publication. Buys one-time rights. Submit seasonal/holiday material 3 months in advance. Reports in 4 weeks. SASE must be included with ms or queries for return.
Nonfiction: Karen Dobkin, Articles Editor. Expose (variety of issues including political, economic, and scientific); informational; personal essay and humor (limited use, but occasionally published in short columns of 1,000 words); interview; and profile. Buys 65 mss/year. Query. Length: 1,000-3,000 words. Pays $200-500.
Photos: Purchased with accompanying ms or on assignment. Captions required. Send contact sheet. Pays $35-100 for b&w photos; $50-225 for color. Total purchase price for ms includes payment for photos.

SUNDAY MORNING MAGAZINE, *Worcester Sunday Telegram*, 20 Franklin St., Worcester MA 01613. (617)755-4321. Sunday Editor: Robert Z. Nemeth. Charles F. Mansbach. 25% freelance written. Sunday supplement serving a broad cross-section of Central Massachusetts residents; 20 pages. Estab. 1933. Circ. 110,000. Pays on publication. Buys first North American serial rights. Byline given. Phone queries OK. Submit seasonal/holiday material 2 months in advance. SASE. Free sample copy.
Nonfiction: Expose (related to circulation area); informational (should have broad application); personal experience (something unusual); photo feature; and profile. Buys 2 mss/issue. Query. Length: 600-2,400 words. Pays $50-100. "All pieces must have a local angle. Also travel pieces and humor."
Photos: Photos purchased with or without accompanying ms or on assignment. Captions required. Pays $5 for 5x7 b&w glossy prints.
Columns/Departments: City Life ("a brief slice-of-life piece that says something about life in our city; heavy on dialogue and description.") Query. Length: 600-1,200 words. Pays $32-50. Open to suggestions for new columns/departments.

UPCOUNTRY, The Magazine of New England, 33 Eagle St., Pittsfield MA 01201. (413)447-7311. Managing Editor: William H. Tague. For people who are interested in the country and small town life of New England. Estab. 1973. Newsprint magazine published 12 times a year and carried as a monthly supplement by daily newspapers in New England. Circ. 421,000. Buys all rights, but will reassign rights to author after publication. Buys 100-150 mss/year. Pays on acceptance. "Prefer written or telephone query in advance of sending material, although we consider everything received." SASE.
Nonfiction and Photos: "The magazine deals with life in New England as a whole, and country living, in particular; not as a fantasy, but as a reality. We look for articles on specific topics of current interest to our readership. Above all, articles must deal with New England subjects. New England writers strongly preferred. Articles concerned with moving to and living in the country; coping with country living; rural medicine, taxation, political issues affecting country life; gardening, music, art, theater, birdwatching, outdoor sports, restaurants, country inns, restorations, preservation, etc. Articles on how to come to terms with our environment; profiles of noteworthy people, interesting characters, socioeconomic profiles of towns; short (1,200 words maximum) humorous pieces. How-to articles with a New England setting, on subjects relating to country or small town living." Length: 700-3,000 words. Pays $30-150. For b&w photos, payment is $10 each, or per advance arrangements. Pays $90 for color transparencies used or cover only (no inside color).
Poetry: Poetry considered, but sparingly used. Traditional forms preferred. Pays $15 minimum.

Maryland

PERSPECTIVE, *The Baltimore Sun*, 501 N. Calvert St., Baltimore MD 21203. Editor: Richard O'Mara. 50% freelance written. Emphasizes current affairs, national and international politics, social issues, etc. Weekly newspaper section; 3 pages. Estab. 1968. Circ. 300,000. Pays on publication. Buys all rights, but may reassign following publication. Phone queries OK. SASE. Reports in 3-4 weeks. Free sample copy.
Nonfiction: "We are looking for tightly-written articles on current issues, politics, national and international affairs. We run articles similar to those of the *New York Times*, and occasionally an offbeat piece, but never any fiction. We will look at humor pieces, but they must be well executed to make it." Buys 4 mss/issue. Query. Length: 1,000-5,000 words. Pays $125.

Michigan

DETROIT MAGAZINE, *The Detroit Free Press*, 321 Lafayette Blvd., Detroit MI 48231. (313)222-6477. Editor: Elizabeth Rhein. For a general newspaper readership; urban and suburban. Weekly magazine. Estab. 1965. Circ. 714,000. Pays within 6 weeks of publication. Buys first rights. Kill fee varies. Byline given. Reports in 3-4 weeks. SASE. Sample copy for SASE.

Nonfiction: "Seeking quality magazine journalism on subjects of interest to Detroit and Michigan readers: lifestyles and better living, trends, behavior, health and body, business and political intrigue, crime and cops, money, success and failure, sports, fascinating people, arts and entertainment. *Detroit Magazine* is bright and cosmopolitan in tone. Most desired writing style is literate, but casual—the kind you'd like to read—and reporting must be unimpeachable. We also use guides or service pieces." Buys 65-75 mss/year. Query or submit complete ms. Length: 3,500 words maximum. Pays $125-250.

Photos: Purchased with or without accompanying ms. Pays $25 for b&w glossy prints or color transparencies used inside; $100 for color used as cover.

FENTON INDEPENDENT, 112 E. Ellen St., Fenton MI 48430. (313)629-2203. Editor: Robert G. Silbar. Weekly. Newspaper, not a magazine supplement. Buys all rights. Byline given. Query. SASE.

Nonfiction and Photos: News stories, features and photos of local interest. Wants local material on local people, not generalized articles. Appreciates opinion articles on local topics. All material must have local flavor. Pays 25¢/column inch.

Nevada

LAS VEGAS REVIEW-JOURNAL, Donrey Media Group, Inc., Box 70, Las Vegas NV 89101. (702)385-4241. Editor-in-Chief: Don Digilio. Emphasizes stories about Nevada, either a timely or interesting feature or a historical piece. "We accept freelance work only for our Sunday Nevada magazine." Daily newspaper; 64 pages. Circ. 72,000. Pays on publication. Buys all rights, but may reassign following publication. Phone queries OK. Submit seasonal/holiday material 1 month in advance. Photocopied submissions OK. SASE. Reports in 1 month. Free sample copy.

Nonfiction: A.D. Hopkins, nonfiction editor. Historical (on Nevada only); how-to; informational; interview; photo feature (on Nevada only). Send complete ms. Length: 800 words. Pays $30 minimum.

Photos: Rene Germanier, Photo Editor. Photos purchased with accompanying ms. Captions required. Pays $10 minimum for 8x10 b&w glossy prints; $10 minimum for color photos. Send prints and transparencies.

THE NEVADAN, The *Las Vegas Review Journal*, Box 70, Las Vegas NV 89101. (702)385-4241. Editor-in-Chief: A.D. Hopkins. 15% freelance written. For Las Vegas and surrounding small town residents of all ages "who take our Sunday paper—affluent, outdoor-oriented." Weekly tabloid; 28 pages. Estab. 1962. Circ. 83,000. Pays on publication. Buys one-time rights. Byline given. Phone queries OK. Submit seasonal/holiday material 2 months in advance of issue date. Photocopied and previously published submissions OK. SASE. Reports in 3 weeks. Free sample copy and writer's guidelines; mention *Writer's Market* in request.

Nonfiction: General interest (contemporary off-beat features on Nevada's outdoors, mining towns and back country); historical (more of these than anything else, always linked to Nevada, southern Utah, northern Arizona and Death Valley); how-to (on nostalgic arts, e.g., recent article on how to play mumbledy-peg); nostalgia (about small-town life in Nevada mining camps); personal experience (any with strong pioneer Nevada angle, pioneer can be 1948 in some parts of Nevada); and travel (interesting new Nevada destinations). "No articles on history that is based on doubtful sources; no current showbusiness material; no commercial plugs." Buys 52 mss/year. Query. Length: 600-2,400 words. Pays $40.

Photos: State availability of photos with query. Pays $5 for 5x7 or 8x10 b&w glossy prints; $15 for 35 or 120mm color transparencies. Captions required. Buys one-time rights.

New York

FAMILY WEEKLY, 641 Lexington Ave., New York NY 10022. Executive Editor: Arthur Cooper. Managing Editor: Tim Mulligan. 60% freelance written. No longer accepting

unsolicited mss, but will consider queries. SASE.
Fillers: Will consider short jokes and humor items. Pays $10.

LI MAGAZINE, *Newsday*, Pinelawn Ave., Melville NY 11454. (516)454-2063. Managing Editor: Stanley Green. For well-educated, affluent suburban readers. Estab. 1972. Weekly. Circ. 550,000. Buys all rights. Byline given. Pays on publication. Query. SASE.
Nonfiction and Photos: Art Director: Miriam Smith. "Stories must be about Long Island people, places or events." Length: 600-2,500 words. Pays $100-600. B&w contacts and 35mm transparencies purchased on assignment. Pays $100/page maximum for b&w; $200/page maximum for color, including cover.

NEW YORK NEWS MAGAZINE, *New York Daily News*, 220 E. 42nd St., New York NY 10017. Editor: Richard C. Lemon. For general audience. Weekly. Circ. 3 million. Buys first serial rights. Pays 30% kill fee. Byline given. Buys 40 mss/year. Pays on acceptance. Will send free sample copy to a writer on request. Submit seasonal material 2 months in advance. Will consider photocopied submissions. Reports in 4 weeks. Query. "If you have published before, it is best to include a sample clip." SASE.
Nonfiction and Photos: "Interested in all sorts of articles: most interested in human interest stories, articles about people (famous or unknown) and service pieces; least interested in essays and discussion pieces. Continuing need for New York City area subjects. Freelancer should use his own approach news photos always in demand." Send prints or transparencies.
Iousnumber, but they are mostly staff-written." Buys informational, personal experience, interview, profile, humor, nostalgia and photo articles. Length: 600-3,000 words. Pays $50-750. Photos purchased with or without mss. Captions are required. Specifications for b&w glossy prints or jumbo contacts: 8x10. Pays $25 for single, $150 for complete picture story. Color specifications: 2½, 4x5 or 35mm transparency. Pays from $35 for single, $200 for set.
How To Break In: "For new writers, the key thing to remember is to start with a suggestion that grabs us and keep your material within screaming distance of New York City."

THE NEW YORK TIMES, 229 W. 43rd St., New York NY 10036. SASE.
Nonfiction and Photos: *The New York Times Magazine* appears in *The New York Times* on Sunday, and is edited by Edward Klein. "We are looking for fresh, lively and provocative writing on national and international news developments, science, education, family life, social trends and problems, arts and entertainment, personalities, sports, and the changing American scene. Freelance contributions are invited. Articles must be timely. They must be based on specific news items, forthcoming events, or significant anniversaries, or they must reflect trends. Our full-length articles run from 2,500-5,000 words, and for these we pay $850 on acceptance. ($1,000 after two prior acceptances). Our shorter pieces run from 1,500-2,500 words, and for these we pay $500 on acceptance. We pay a basic minimum of $50 for photos." *Travel* section buys "literate, sophisticated, factual articles, evoking the experience of travel with quotes, anecdotes and even-handed reportage. Authors must be personally familiar with subjects about which they write, free to praise or criticize; under no circumstances will we publish articles growing out of trips in any way subsidized by airlines, hotels or other organizations with direct or indirect interest in the subjects. It is best to submit brief, written proposals for stories. All stories are to be submitted on speculation; payment upon publication is approximately 15¢/word; additional $50 for each photo used." *Travel* Editor: Michael Sterne. *Arts and Leisure* section of *The New York Times* appears on Sunday. Wants "to encourage imaginativeness in terms of form and approach—stressing ideas, issues, trends, investigations, symbolic reporting and stories delving deeply into the creative achievements and processes of artists and entertainers—and seeks to break away from old-fashioned gushy, fan magazine stuff." Length: 750-2,000 words. Pays $100-250, depending on length. Pays $50 for photos. *Arts and Leisure* Editor: William H. Honan.
How To Break In: "The Op Ed page is always looking for new material and publishes many people who have never been published before. We want material of universal relevance which people can talk about in a personal way. When writing for the Op Ed page, there is no formula, but the writing itself should have some polish. Don't make the mistake of pontificating on the news. We're not looking for more political columnists. Op Ed length runs about 700 words, and pays about $150."

NEWSDAY, 550 Stewart Ave., Garden City NY 11530. Travel Editor: Steve Schatt. For general readership of Sunday Travel Section. Newspaper. Estab. 1947. Weekly. Circ. 515,000. Buys all rights for the New York area only. Buys 100 mss/year. Pays on publication. Will consider photocopied submissions. Simultaneous submissions considered if others are being made outside of New York area. Reports in 4 weeks. Submit complete ms. SASE.

Nonfiction and Photos: Travel articles with strong focus and theme for the Sunday Travel Section. Emphasis on accuracy, honesty, service, and quality writing to convey mood and flavor. Destination pieces must involve visit or experience that typical traveler can easily duplicate. Skip diaries, "My First Trip Abroad" pieces or compendiums of activities; downplay first-person. Length: 600-1,750 words; prefers 800- to 1,000-word pieces. Pays 10¢/word. Also, regional "weekender" pieces of 700-800 words plus service box, but query first.

PARADE, The Sunday Newspaper Magazine, 733 3rd Ave., New York NY 10017. (212)953-7557. Weekly. Circ. 21 million. Buys first North American serial rights. Pays kill fee. Byline given. Pays on acceptance. Query. SASE.
Nonfiction: "Interested in features that will inform, educate or entertain a mass-circulation domestic audience. Exclusive, news-related articles and photos are required. Subjects may include: well-known personalities, sports, religion, education, community activities, family relations, science and medicine. Articles should be current, factual, authoritative." Length: about 1,500 words. Pays $2,500 maximum.
Photos: "Photos should have visual impact and be well-composed with action-stopping qualities. For the most part, color is used on cover. Transparencies of any size are accepted. Either b&w 8x10 enlargements or contact sheets may be submitted. Accurate caption material must accompany all photos."

Ohio

THE BLADE TOLEDO MAGAZINE, 541 Superior St., Toledo OH 43660. (419)259-6132. Editor: Tom Gearhart. General readership. Weekly magazine; 32 pages. Estab. 1948. Circ. 210,000. Pays on publication. Buys one-time rights. Byline given. Phone queries OK. Submit seasonal/holiday material 6 months in advance. Simultaneous, photocopied and previously published submissions OK. SASE.
Nonfiction: Historical (about northwestern Ohio); informational; interview; personal experience; and photo feature. Buys 1 ms/issue. Query. Length: 600-2,000 words. Pays $35-150.
Photos: Photos purchased with accompanying ms. Captions required. Pays $15-30 for 8x10 b&w glossy prints; $10-45 for 35mm, 2¼x2¼ or 8x10 color glossy prints. Total purchase price for ms includes payment for photos. Model release required.
Tips: "Stories should pertain to our circulation area: Toledo, northwestern Ohio and southern Michigan."

COLUMBUS DISPATCH SUNDAY MAGAZINE, 34 South 3rd St., Columbus OH 43216. (614)461-5250. Editor: Hal Schellkoph. 50% freelance written. Buys one-time rights. Byline given. Payment after publication. SASE.
Nonfiction: "We accept offerings from beginning writers, but they must be professionally written, and a good picture helps." Strong Ohio angle is preferable. Buys singles, photo series and illustrated articles. Length: 1,000-1,500 words. Pays 4¢/word minimum. B&w photos only. Pays $10 maximum/photo.

DAYTON LEISURE, *Dayton Daily News*, 4th and Ludlow Sts., Dayton OH 45401. (513)225-2240. Editor: Jack M. Osler. Sunday supplement. Circ. 225,000. Byline given. Pays on publication. Usually reports in 1 week. SASE.
Nonfiction and Photos: Magazine focuses on leisure-time activities particularly in Ohio—that are interesting and unusual. Emphasis is on photos supplemented by stories. Length: 1,000 words maximum. Photos should be glossy. "*The Daily News* will evaluate articles on their own merits. Likewise with photos. Average payment per article: $30." Payments vary depending on quality of writing.

THE ENQUIRER MAGAZINE, 617 Vine St., Cincinnati OH 45201. (513)721-2700. Editor: Graydon DeCamp. Art Director: Ron Huff. Weekly newspaper supplement; 52 pages. Circ. 290,000. Pays on publication. Free writer's guidelines. Photocopied and simultaneous submissions OK. Submit "dated" material at least 2 months in advance. SASE.
Nonfiction: Local articles, current subjects, issues, trends, personalities, topical material, "think" pieces. Will use some local nostalgia/history. "Will not accept manuscripts about any organization or event written by anyone connected with that organization or event, except in unusual first-person cases." Buys 100 mss/year. Query. Length: 1,500-3,000 words. Pays $50-200.

Photos: Will buy photos with ms; must be of professional quality. Pays $10-50 for 8x10 b&w prints.

Oregon

NORTHWEST MAGAZINE, *The Sunday Oregonian*, 1320 SW Broadway, Portland OR 97201. Editor: Joseph R. Bianco. For a family audience with somewhat higher education level in Oregon than average. Weekly Sunday supplement magazine; 28-40 pages. Estab. 1965. Circ. 400,000. Buys all rights, but will reassign rights to author after publication. Buys 600-650 mss/year. Pays in the closest period to the 15th of the month following publication. No photocopied submissions. Will consider simultaneous submissions. Reports in 2 weeks. Query or submit complete ms. SASE.
Nonfiction and Photos: "Articles of interest to the Northwest. Topical and (sometimes) controversial. Periodically, an issue is devoted to a theme. For example, the theme of 'Outdoors' is how-to. How to do the hockey stop in skiing, how to find a remote hiking ridge, etc. Keep Northwest articles short, topical, and of interest to the Northwest. Ecology, environment and social mores are always subjects of interest. Also, personality profiles of people of interest." Length: 800-1,500 words. Pays $80-100. 8x10 b&w glossy prints are purchased with mss or on assignment. Captions required. Pays $15.

Pennsylvania

THE PITTSBURGH PRESS, 34 Blvd. of Allies, Pittsburgh PA 15230. (412)263-1100. Features Editor: William Allan. For general newspaper readers. Estab. 1920. Publishes 3 weekly magazines. Circ. 700,000. Not copyrighted. Byline given. Buys 25-50 mss/year. Pays on publication. Reports in 2 weeks. Submit complete ms. SASE.
Nonfiction and Photos: Picture-oriented material for the *Roto Magazine*; family type stories for *Family Magazine*. Must be local subjects with good general interest. Informational, how-to, personal experience, profile, inspirational, humor, historical and nostalgia. Pays $25/published page. Some additional payment for b&w photos used with mss.
How To Break In: "Submit good copy."

TODAY MAGAZINE, *Philadelphia Inquirer*, 400 N. Broad St., Philadelphia PA 19101. Editor-in-Chief: David Boldt. Managing Editor: John Lubell. Sunday magazine section for city and suburban readers. Weekly; 42 pages. Circ. 850,000. Pays on publication. Buys first North American serial rights. Submit seasonal/holiday material 3 months in advance of issue date. Photocopied submissions OK. SASE. Reports in 2 months. Free sample copy.
Nonfiction: "Most of our material is written by freelance writers. Articles run from 300-7,000 words. Occasionally we run first-person articles but they are the exception to our general rule of reporting on and analysis of local issues and personalities. Query. Pays $125-500 for writers whose work has been used several times previously.

Rhode Island

SUNDAY JOURNAL MAGAZINE (formerly *Rhode Islander*), *The Providence Journal*, Providence RI 02902. (401)277-7263. Editor: Douglas Riggs. Sunday magazine section. Circ. 215,000. Buys first rights. Pays on publication. Free sample copy. Reports in 2 weeks. Query or submit complete ms. SASE.
Nonfiction and Photos: "Always looking for new writers with real talent. Prefer articles with 'new journalism' flavor (anecdotal, subjective, highly descriptive, thought-provoking, etc.). Strongly oriented toward Rhode Island and southern New England." Pays $50-200. Photos purchased with mss. "Our new weekly feature 'The Black Page' needs opinion pieces, essays, humor, nostalgia, etc., intelligently written and thought-provoking. Length: 1,000 words maximum. Pays $100.
How To Break In: "A phone call or personal visit is better than a query letter. If you have some specific story ideas, you are always welcome. Read the magazine first; sample copies sent on request. Personal contact with writer may mean difference between a rejection slip and a letter suggesting revisions. But if your stuff is really good, we'll buy it if it comes in by pony express. We're always looking for new talent, especially in southern New England."
Rejects: "Light" essays on homey topics, historical narrations unrelieved by anecdotes, commentary on national events, single photographs.

Washington

PANORAMA MAGAZINE, *The Everett Herald,* Box 930, Everett WA 98206. (206)259-5151. Editor: Jeanne Metzger. Weekly magazine section; 20 pages. Estab. 1973. Circ. 60,000. Pays on publication. Buys one-time rights. Byline given. Phone queries OK. Submit seasonal/holiday material 6 weeks in advance. Simultaneous, photocopied and previously published submissions OK. SASE. Reports in 1 month.
Nonfiction: Historical (Pacific Northwest history); humor; interview and profile; nostalgia; personal experience; photo feature; travel; and book reviews. Query or send complete ms. Pays $15-60.
Photos: Pays $35 for good color photos to go with "people" covers. No payment for b&w photos accompanying ms.

SEATTLE TIMES MAGAZINE, Seattle Times Co., Box 70, Seattle WA 98111. (206)464-2283. Editor: Larry Anderson. 40% freelance written. For people 20-80, above average in education and income. Weekly newspaper supplement; 16 pages. Circ. 320,000. Pays on publication. Buys first rights. Pays 20-30% kill fee. Byline given. Submit seasonal/holiday material 2 months in advance. Photocopied and previously published submissions OK. SASE. Reports in 1 week. Free sample copy and writer's guidelines.
Nonfiction: Humor; informational; inspirational; interview; personal experience; and profile. Buys 3 mss/issue. Query or send complete ms. Length: 200-1,500 words. Pays $50-70/page.
Photos: Photos purchased with accompanying ms. Captions required. Pays $10-20 for b&w glossy prints. Query or send prints.

SEATTLE TIMES PICTORIAL, Box 70, Seattle WA 98111. Editor: Tom Stockley. For a general audience, above average in education. Sunday newspaper supplement. Circ. 325,000. Buys first rights. Pays on·publication. Reports in 1 week. SASE.
Nonfiction and Photos: Looking for pictorial essays on regional (Washington, British Columbia) material. Uses b&w photos inside with possible tie-in color (4x5 transparencies) cover. B&w, submit negatives with contact sheets. Text length: 500-1,000 words. Pays $30-50 for text. Pays $125 for color cover; $30/page for b&w. Unused negatives and transparencies returned after publication.

SUNDAY MAGAZINE, *Tacoma News Tribune,* 1950 S. State St., Tacoma WA 98411. (206)597-8671. Editor: Dick Kunkle. 15% freelance written. Sunday supplement. Circ. 100,000. Pays on publication. Byline given. Query. Reports "immediately." SASE.
Nonfiction and Photos: Articles and photos about Pacific Northwest, particularly the Puget Sound area. Historical, biographical, recreational stories. Length: 1,000 words maximum. Pays $50/printed tabloid page, whether pictures, text or both. Also occasionally buys a color cover transparency for $60. Northwest subjects only.

TOTEM TIDINGS MAGAZINE, *The Daily Olympian,* Box 407, Olympia WA 98507. Editor: Louise Wojtech. For newspaper readers. Sunday tabloid; 16 pages. Estab. 1974. Weekly. Circ. 31,000. Not copyrighted. Byline given. Buys 50 mss/year. Pays on publication. Free sample copy to writer on request if postage is included. Write for copy of guidelines for writers. No photocopied or simultaneous submissions. Reports in 30 days. Query. SASE.
Nonfiction and Photos: Washington state-oriented articles, preferably from southwestern part of state. Must be bright and fast-paced material. People, places or things—but no first-person articles. Historical, water-oriented and topical pieces dealing with the immediate area. Informational, how-to, interview, profile, humor, historical, nostalgia and travel (but only in the Northwest). Length: 1,440 words maximum. Pays $20-50. Buys color transparencies or b&w (8x10) prints with mss. Pays $5 for both b&w and color.

West Virginia

STATE MAGAZINE, *Sunday Gazette-Mail,* 1001 Virginia St. E, Charleston WV 25330. Editor: Diane Lytle. 50% freelance written. For family newspaper readers. Weekly newspaper magazine. Estab. 1952. Circ. 110,000. Not copyrighted. Byline given. Buys 150-200 mss/year. Pays on publication. Sample copy for SASE. Will consider photocopied submissions. Simultaneous submissions are considered, if not made to other West Virginia newspapers. Reports in 30-90 days. Query. SASE.
Nonfiction and Photos: Emphasis is on West Virginia material; articles and photo essays. "Simple, lucid, tight writing with a logical organization. Writer must want to catch and hold

readers' attention in a busy, busy world. We do not want to see material that has obviously been rejected by other publications. We're easy to sell, but not that easy." Length: 500-2,500 words. Pays $10-50. Annually publishes a special issue on travel in which articles on enjoyable vacation locales are used. Length: 500-2,000 words. Pays $10-50. B&w photos with good contrast, good composition, and sharp focus purchased with or without ms. Pays $5. Ultra-sharp, bright, 35mm (or up to 4x5) color transparencies purchased with or without ms. Pays $20.

How To Break In: "Always query first. Beginning West Virginia writers have best chance. Our freelance policy is designed to encourage them to write about their home state."

Wisconsin

INSIGHT MAGAZINE, *Milwaukee Journal,* 333 W. State, Milwaukee WI 53201. (414)224-2341. Editor: Mike Moore. Emphasizes general interest reading for a cross-section of Wisconsin and upper Michigan. Weekly magazine; 24-88 pages. Estab. 1969. Circ. 530,000. Pays shortly after publication. Buys one-time rights. Byline given. Submit seasonal/holiday material at least 2 months in advance. SASE. Reports in 1-2 weeks. Free sample copy.
Nonfiction: Humor; profiles; personal experience; provocative essays; and nostalgia. Buys 50 mss/year. Length: 1,000-3,000 words. Pays $50-250.
How To Break In: "Read the magazine and get a feel for its content. Then you might try a personal experience article, a thought-provoking essay or a lively profile. We also need 750-1,000 word fillers—examples of which you'll find in the magazine. Much of our material comes from Wisconsin writers. Generally, we're not a good market for out-of-state writers, although we may buy originals or reprints from time to time from established writers."

MIDWEST ROTO, Rural Gravure Service, Inc., 6501 Mineral Point Rd., Madison WI 53719. Editor-in-Chief: Jerry C. Curren. Managing Editor: Bonnie Currie. Emphasizes "hometown Midwest America. A newspaper supplement which carries human interest articles about the Midwest and Midwest people. Circulates in 150 newspapers." Monthly magazine; 16 pages. Estab. 1936. Circ. 651,000. Pays on publication. Buys simultaneous rights. Submit seasonal/holiday material 6 months in advance. Simultaneous and previously published submissions OK. SASE. Reports in 1 week.
Nonfiction: Historical, humor, interview, nostalgia, photo feature and profile. Mss must relate to Midwest people and places. Buys 4-6/issue. Submit complete ms. Length: 1,000-3,000 words. Pays $50-300.
Photos: Purchased with accompanying ms. Captions required. Send prints. Pays $15-150 for 8x10 b&w glossy prints. Total purchase price for ms includes payment for photos. Model release required.

Canada

THE CANADIAN MAGAZINE, 2180 Yonge, Suite 1702, Toronto, Ontario, Canada M4S 3A2. (416)485-1552. Editor: Ann Rhodes. Buys first North American serial rights. Pays on acceptance. "We only consider mss written with a very strong Canadian slant." Query. SAE and International Reply Coupons.
Nonfiction: Managing Editor: David Cobb. "Looking for articles of interest to Canadians from coast to coast, on Canadian subjects, written in a lively and informative manner with plenty of human interest. Effective use of anecdotes quite frequently provides this human interest; therefore, use an anecdotal approach to the subject. Articles submitted may cover a wide range of topics—human affairs, religion, science, politics, personalities, humor and sport, hobbies, cookery and fashion. Looking for good literary quality. Strongly recommend an outline letter, of 200-300 words, staking out the extent and burden of the article." Length: 800-3,000 words. Pays $400-1,000.

THE ISLANDER MAGAZINE, Sunday supplement of *The Daily Colonist,* Victoria, British Columbia, Canada. (604)383-4111. Editor: Alec Merriman. For "just about everyone who lives on Vancouver Island." Weekly; 16 pages. Estab. 1858. Circ. 50,000. Not copyrighted. Byline given. Buys 400-500 mss/year. Pays on publication. Free sample copy. Reporting time varies "from a week or two to a year, if it is an article we hope to use." Submit complete ms. SASE.
Nonfiction and Photos: "*The Islander* is very personally Pacific Northwest, mainly Vancouver Island, and takes a folksy, homespun, almost chatty outlook. We aim at our local market and don't try to compete with the syndicated magazine sections with articles of wide-ranging

general interest. We use feature articles about people, places and things, with a Pacific Northwest slant, plus a heavy interest in Northwest history. All material must have the Pacific Northwest angle." Length: 500-2,000 words. Pays about $25/magazine page. Prefers 5x7 or 8x10 b&w glossy prints, but sometimes uses snapshots. Pays $5 for photos used with ms; $10.50 for cover use (always a local scene). Captions required.

How To Break In: "*The Islander* leans heavily toward the local slant which is an advantage for Pacific Northwest writers. But, a person from this area who is doing something unique or making a success of living elsewhere always makes an acceptable feature. Travel literature is distributed freely by the yard, so a local and different slant must be sought."

WEEKEND MAGAZINE, The Montreal Standard Limited/Limitee, 390 Bay St., Suite 504, Toronto, Ontario Canada M5H 2Y2. Editor: John Macfarlane. Weekly section of 23 newspapers. Circ. 1,700,000. Buys first North American rights. Buys 100 mss/year. Pays on acceptance. "All mss and photos sent in are done so on a speculative basis only and should be addressed to the Editor or Art Director respectively." Query before submitting material. SAE and International Reply Coupons.

Nonfiction and Photos: "Articles should be about some person, event or activity of interest to Canadians. We don't use travel articles or fillers." Length: 1,500-2,500 words. Pays $400-800. If photos or transparencies are sent in and used in addition to the ms, payment is adjusted accordingly. "Our photographic requirements are for all sizes of color from 35mm up; we prefer color transparencies and b&w prints." Pays from $75-250.

THE WESTERN PRODUCER, Box 2500, Saskatoon, Saskatchewan, Canada. (306)665-3500. Publisher: R.H.D. Phillips. Editor: R.H.D. Phillips. 6% freelance written. Emphasizes Western Canadian agriculture for farm families, children to grandparents. Weekly newspaper; 56 pages. Estab. 1923. Circ. 142,000. Pays on acceptance. Buys first North American serial rights. Byline given. Submit seasonal/holiday material 2 months in advance of issue date. Previously published submissions OK. SASE. Reports in 2 weeks. Free writer's guidelines.

Nonfiction: How-to; general interest; historical (Western Canada); inspirational; nostalgia; personal experience; photo feature and profile. Buys 1,200 mss/year. Submit complete ms. Pays $5-300.

Photos: Submit photos with ms. Pays $5-25 for 5x7 b&w prints. Captions and model release required. Buys one-time rights.

Fiction: Adventure; historical; humorous; mainstream; mystery; religious; romance; suspense; and Western Canadian subjects. Buys 20 mss/year. Length: 1,500 words maximum. Pays $25-100.

Poetry: Traditional. Buys 51/year. Pays $5-15.

Op-Ed Pages

Within the last few years, a new forum for opinion and observation (and freelance opportunity) has emerged—the op-ed page. The op-ed page is that page in a newspaper opposite the editorial page which solicits commentary on any subject concerning its readers.

Here are the requirements for some of the largest and best-known newspapers that solicit material for their op-ed pages. Be sure to check with your own local newspaper to see if it contains an op-ed page, or if it solicits freelance material for use on its editorial page.

THE BALTIMORE NEWS AMERICAN, Box 1795, Baltimore MD 21203. (301)752-1212. Op-Ed Page Editor: William Stump. "We are interested in news backgrounders—even when the subject is not widely known to the public. The topics can have national, state or local focus." Buys 1-2 mss/week. Byline given. Query. SASE. Length: 500-1,500 words. Pays $50-75.

JOURNAL-NEWS, Box 298, Hamilton OH 45012. (513)863-8200. Op-Ed Page Editor: Jim Blout. "We prefer topics treated so they are useful to our readers. Emphasis is on practical information, not literary style. Topics should have state and local focus." Buys 6-7 mss/issue. Query "unless it would delay timely material. Our interest usually can be determined via phone. Copy can be sent via Telecopier (six-minute cycle, phone 863-7988, unattended." Length: "We prefer a series of three 600-word stories to one story of 1,500 words or a series of five 500- 600-word stories to one of 2,000 words." Pays $20-75.

NEW YORK TIMES, 229 W. 43rd St., New York NY 10036. Op-Ed Page Editor: Charlotte

Curtis. Daily. Copyrighted, if requested. Submit complete ms. SASE. "No limit to topics, just something of interest to the public. However, it should be an opinion or commentary. No news reports. We are always looking for new and exciting writers to add to the page." Length: 700 words maximum. Pays $150 maximum.

NEWSDAY, Melville NY 11747. Editorial Page Editor: William C. Sexton. Daily. Copyrighted. SASE. Seeks "opinion on current events, trends, issues—whether national or local government or lifestyle. Must be timely, pertinent, articulate and opinionated. Strong preference for authors within the circulation area, and it's best to consult before you start writing." Byline given. Length: 600-2,000 words. Pays $50-500.

THE OREGONIAN, 1320 SW Broadway, Portland OR 97201. (503)221-8204. Op-Ed Editor: Paul Adams. Daily and Sunday. Copyrighted. Byline given. SASE. "We use commentaries on current topics with issues in the Northwest given priority: energy, environment, politics, outdoors, metropolitan affairs, and so forth. We want opinions, but they must be supported with facts, examples, anecdotes—not just letters to the editor. We get the most of, and use the least of, humorous material, but fantasies in particular get little use." Buys 1 ms/issue. Length: 750 words. Pays $40 average.

THE PLAIN DEALER, 1801 Superior Ave., Cleveland OH 44114. (216)344-4500. Op-Ed Page Editor: Robert T. Stock. "We will use almost anything that hasn't been beaten to death in syndicated columns and feature sections. We want topics with a national, state or local focus. Articles should make a point and provide supporting evidence." Buys 1-2 mss/issue. Byline given. Submit complete ms. Length: 300-900 words. Pays $35-50.

ROANOKE TIMES & WORLD-NEWS, Box 2491, Roanoke VA 24010. (703)981-3220. Op-Ed Page Editor: Robert N. Fishburn. "We use a broad spectrum of mainly political articles. We want topics with a national, state or local (whenever possible) focus." Buys 3/issue. Byline given. Submit complete ms. Length: 500-900 words. Pays "rarely."

THE SAN DIEGO UNION, 350 Camino De La Reina, San Diego CA 92112. Op-Ed Page Editors: Ed Nichols, Ed Fike. "We want topics of concern to readers in our circulation area but subjects do not have to be limited to San Diego. Topics should have a national, state or local focus." Buys 5-10 mss/week. Query or submit complete ms. Length: 500-1,200 words. Byline given. Pays $100 maximum.

THE SCRANTON TIMES-SUNDAY TIMES, Penn Ave. and Spruce St., Scranton PA 18501. (717)348-9113. Op-Ed Page Editor: William T. Cullen Jr. "We want topics on current events and important anniversaries. Topics should have a national, state or local focus." Byline given. Length: 550 words maximum.

THE WASHINGTON STAR, 225 Virginia Ave. SE, Washington DC 20061. (202)484-4227. Comment Page Editor: Bob Berger. "We want articles that present a wide range of ideas and issues about the world and this society in their political, economic and sociological aspects. Articles can have national, regional or local focus." Byline given. Buys 8 mss/week. Submit article. Length: 750-2,000 words.

Photography

CAMERA 35, U.E.M. Publishing, Inc., 150 E. 58th St., New York NY 10022. (212)355-5705. Editor: Willard Clark. "A very special magazine within a vertical field, directed at thinking photographers." Monthly magazine. Estab. 1957. Circ. 115,000. Buys first North American serial rights. Kill fee varies. Byline given. Pays on publication. Query. Reports in 1-3 months. SASE.
Photos: "Photography published in form of portfolios and essays. No taboos for either words or pictures, as long as they fit our needs. To determine needs, study at least 3 recent issues. Good literate writing mandatory." Payment rates negotiable prior to acceptance.

CAMERA USER, Link House Publications, Link House Dingwall Ave., Croydon England CR9 2TA. (01)686-2599. Editor: Rex Hayman. Monthly magazine; 80 pages. Estab. 1972. Circ. 30,000. Pays on publication. Buys all rights or one-time rights. Phone queries OK. Submit seasonal/holiday material 3 months in advance. Simultaneous, photocopied and previously published submissions OK. SASE. Reports in 4 weeks. Free sample copy.

Nonfiction: "We are interested in all types so long as it contains strong reference to photography. There is no limit to the amount of articles we buy, or to payments. Query or submit complete ms.

Photos: Send photos with accompanying mss. Offers no additional payment for photos accompanying mss. Uses 8x10 b&w and color prints. Current page rate $10/b&w photo, $15/color photo. Captions and model releases required.

Columns/Departments: Around & About, Letters and Product News. Send complete ms.

PETERSEN'S PHOTOGRAPHIC MAGAZINE, Petersen Publishing Co., 8490 Sunset Blvd., Los Angeles CA 90069. (213)657-5100. Publisher: Paul R. Farber. Editor: Karen Geller. Emphasizes how-to photography. Monthly magazine; 108 pages. Estab. 1972. Circ. 260,000. Pays on publication. Buys one-time rights. Submit seasonal/holiday material 5 months in advance. Photocopied submissions OK. SASE. Reports in 2 months. Sample copy $2.

Nonfiction: Karen Geller, Editor. How-to. Buys 3 mss/issue. Send story, photos and captions. Pays $60/printed page.

Photos: Gallery Editor. Photos purchased with or without accompanying ms. Pays $25-35 for b&w and color photos. Model release required.

PHOTO INSIGHT, Suite 2, 169-15 Jamaica Ave., Jamaica NY 11432. Managing Editor: Jacqueline Y. Wright. 82% freelance written. Emphasizes up-to-date photography contests. For amateur and professional photographers. Bimonthly newsletter; 12 pages. Estab. 1975. Circ. 2,005. Pays on publication. Buys one-time rights. Submit seasonal or holiday material 3 months in advance. Simultaneous and previously published submissions OK. SASE. Reports in 2 months. Sample copy $1.

Nonfiction: How-to on winning contests, humor, inspirational and new products (related to photography). Buys 6-12 mss/issue. Length: 800-2,000 words. Pays $35 for photo-text package. Captions required. Portfolios accepted for publication based on themes.

Columns/Departments: Gallery Insight (photo show reviews) and In The News (new products or seminars). Buys 2 ms/issue. Query. Length: 100-300 words. Pays $15. Open to suggestions for new columns/departments.

Poetry: Poetry Editor. Traditional. Length: 4-12 lines. Pays $5.

Fillers: Jokes, gags and anecdotes. Pays $5.

PHOTOGRAPHY, Model and Allied Publications, Ltd., 13035 Bridge St., Hemel Hempstead. Herts, England. Editor: John Wade. Monthly magazine; 80 pages. Estab. 1888. Circ. 35,000. Pays on publication. Buys first British serial rights. Phone queries OK. Submit seasonal/holiday material 3 months in advance. Photocopied submissions OK. SASE. Reports in 4 weeks. Writer's guidelines $2.

Nonfiction: How-to (photographic topics); photo feature; and technical. "We do not want picture portfolios." Buys 2-3 mss/issue. Query. Length: 500-3,000 words. Pays 5¢/published word minimum.

Photos: State availability of photos. Offers no additional payment for 8x10 b&w glossy prints or 35mm color transparencies. Buys one-time rights. Captions and model releases required.

PHOTOMETHODS, Ziff-Davis Publishing Co., 1 Park Ave., New York NY 10016. (212)725-3942. Editor-in-Chief: Fred Schmidt. Managing Editor: Richard Cooper. 90% freelance written. Emphasizes photography (still, motion, video) as a tool; most readers are college or technical school graduates, many readers are in science, engineering or education." Monthly magazine; 80 pages. Estab. 1958. Circ. 50,000. Pays on publication. Buys one-time rights. Pays 100% kill fee. Byline given. Phone queries OK. SASE. Reports in 4 weeks. Free sample copy and writer's guidelines; mention *Writer's Market* in request.

Nonfiction: How-to (application stories to help readers in his/her work); interview; personal experience (that will benefit the reader in his/her work); photo feature (rare, but will consider); profile; and technical (always interested in 'popularizing' highly technical applications). No material dealing with amateur photography or snapshooters. Buys 60-70 mss/year. Query. Length: 1,500-3,000 words. Pays $75-300.

Photos: Steven Karl Weininger, art director. State availability of photos with query. Offers no additional payment for photos accepted with ms. Uses 5x7 and up matte-dried or glossy b&w prints and 35mm and up color transparencies. Captions required. Buys one-time rights. Model release required.

Columns/Departments: How We Did It!. Submit complete ms. Length: 1,000-1,500 words. Pays $75 minimum.

PHOTOPHILE, R.M. Gately Publishing Co., Box 2412, Cherry Hill NJ 08034. Editor: R.M.

Gately. For amateur and professional photographers. Quarterly magazine; 32 pages. Estab. 1974. Circ. 5,000. Pays on publication. Buys all rights. Submit seasonal/holiday material 2 months in advance. Photocopied and previously published submissions OK. SASE. Reports in 4 weeks. Sample copy $2.50; free writer's guidelines.

Nonfiction: How-to (photographic); interview (photographic); photo feature (photofolios); and technical (photographic). Buys 8 mss/issue. Send complete ms. Length: 2-4 published pages. Pays $30-100/page.

Photos: Send photos with accompanying ms. Uses 8x10 b&w glossy prints; offers no additional payment for photos accompany ms. Buys one-time rights. Captions and model releases required.

POPULAR PHOTOGRAPHY, 1 Park Ave., New York NY 10016. Editor: Kenneth Poli. "Mostly for advanced hobby photographers; nearly 90% are men." Monthly. Circ. 800,000. Also publishes 6 annuals or one-shots edited by Jim Hughes. "Rights purchased vary occasionally but usually buy one-time." Byline given. Buys 35-50 mss/year, "mostly from technical types already known to us." Pays on acceptance. Submit material 4 months in advance. Reports in 3-4 weeks. Query. SASE.

Nonfiction: This magazine is mainly interested in instructional articles on photography that will help photographers improve their work. This includes all aspects of photography, from theory to camera use and darkroom procedures. Utter familiarity with the subject is a prerequisite to acceptance here. It is best to submit article ideas in outline form since features are set up to fit the magazine's visual policies. "Style should be easily readable but with plenty of factual data when a technique story is involved. We're not quite as 'hardware'-oriented as some magazines. We use many equipment stories, but we often give more space to cultural and aesthetic aspects of the hobby than our competition does." Buys how-to, interviews, profiles, historical articles, new product coverage, photo essays. Length: 500-2,000 words. Pays $125/b&w display page; $200/color page.

Photos: Interested in seeing b&w prints of any type finish that are 8x10 or larger. Also uses any size color transparency. Buys one-time rights except when assigned, then all-time. No additional payment is made except for occasional reuse of color in "annuals." Gives few assignments.

Fillers: Uses featurettes that run from 1-2 columns to 1-pagers which are short how-to-do-its, illustrated possibly by a single picture. Featurette length should be from 500-1,000 words; for the "Photo Tips," fewer than 100 words or whatever is necessary to give all pertinent information. Pays $25-75 for featurettes, depending on use; $25 for illustrated "Photo Tips."

PRACTICAL PHOTOGRAPHY, EMAP National Publications, Ltd., Bretton Ct., Bretton Centre, Peterborough England PE3 8DZ. 0733-264666. Editor: Robert Scott. Emphasizes amateur photography. Monthly magazine; 116 pages. Estab. 1959. Circ. 65,791. Pays on publication. Buys one-time rights. Phone queries OK. Submit seasonal/holiday material 3 months in advance (5 months for color). Photocopied submissions OK. SASE. Reports in 3 weeks.

Nonfiction: how-to (any aspect of photography) and humor (related to photography). Buys 1-2 mss/issue. Send complete ms. Length: 300-3,000 words. Pays 20 pounds minimum/thousand words.

Photos: 8 pounds for 8x10 glossy prints and 35mm color transparencies. Captions preferred; model release required.

PHOTOGRAPHER'S FORUM, 25 Wanapamu, Santa Barbara CA 93101. (805)966-9392. Editor-in-Chief: Glen Serbin. 50% freelance written. Emphasizes college photographic work. Quarterly magazine; 64 pages. Estab. November 1978. Pays on publication. Buys all rights. Byline given. Simultaneous and previously published submissions OK. SASE. Reports in 3 weeks.

Nonfiction: Expose; interview; general interest; and historical. "Articles must deal with some aspect of photography or student photography." Interviews (how one got started, views on the different schools); profile (of schools); and photo feature. "No technical articles." Submit complete ms. Length: 1,000-3,000 words. Pays $40.

Photos: State availability of photos with ms. 5x7 or 8x10 b&w matte prints. Buys one-time rights. Model release is recommended.

Columns/Departments: Book Review; Historical Analysis; Interview; and School Profile. Buys 6 mss/issue. Submit complete ms. Length: 1,000-3,000 words. Pays $35. Open to suggestions for new columns/departments.

UNDERWATER PHOTOGRAPHER, Drawer 608, Dana Point CA 92629. Editor/Publisher:

F.M. Roberts. 25% freelance written. Quarterly magazine; 24 pages. Estab. 1973. Circ. 2,000. Pays on publication. Buys one-time rights. Byline given. Submit seasonal/holiday material 6 months in advance. Simultaneous and photocopied submissions OK. SASE. Reports in 3-4 months. Sample copy $1.50.

Nonfiction: General interest; how-to (building equipment); interview (with well-known underwater photographers); photo feature; technical (on photography); and travel. Buys 3-4 mss/year. Query. Length: 1,000-2,000 words. Pays 1¢/word.

Photos: State availability of photos with query. Pays $5 for 5x7 or 8x10 glossy b&w prints; $5-25 for 35mm or 2¼x2¼ color transparencies. Captions required. Buys one-time rights. Model release required.

Poetry

This category includes publications that exist to discuss and publish poetry. A few newspapers and other special media using poetry are also included. Many publications in the Literary and Little category are also interested in poetry submissions. Various other poetry markets are listed in other categories throughout the Consumer section.

Many of the markets that follow pay in contributor's copies, prizes or some form of remuneration other than money. We have included such markets because there are limited commercial outlets for poetry and these at least offer the poet some visibility.

Poetry manuscripts should have the poet's name and address typed in the upper left-hand corner. Total number of lines in the poem should appear in the upper right-hand corner. Center the title of the poem 8 to 10 lines from the top of the page. The poem should be typed, double-spaced. The poet's name should again appear at the end of the poem. In the case where the poet submits more than one poem to the editor, each poem should always be typed on a separate sheet of paper. Always enclose SASE with poetry submissions.

ADVENTURES IN POETRY MAGAZINE, Box 253, Junction TX 76849. (915)446-2004. Publisher/Editor: Dr. Stella Woodall. Quarterly magazine; 64-72 pages. Estab. 1968. Circ. 500. Byline given. Submit seasonal/holiday material 3 months in advance. Previously published submissions OK. SASE. Reports in 4 weeks. Sample copy $3.

Poetry: Free verse; haiku; light verse; traditional, lyrics and sonnets. Uses about 100 poems/issue. "Only poems that help people live better and happier lives are used. We have prizes for each issue, contest prizes and annual prizes and feature the 'most outstanding poet' using photography, biography and poems in each edition. Each edition is dedicated to poets of a certain state with poems by the president of the state poetry society and by the state Poet Laureate. It is not necessary to be a member of Stella Woodall Poetry Society International to be published but poems by members are given preference and used first. To become a member poets much be recommended by a member and must submit their photograph, biography and a poem for the magazine. Those sending good poems in any category will be recommended."

AMERICAN POETRY LEAGUE MAGAZINE, Box 253, Junction TX 76849. (915)446-2004. Editor-in-Chief: Dr. Stella Woodall. Quarterly magazine. Byline given. See *Adventures in Poetry Magazine.*

ASFA POETRY QUARTERLY, Alabama School of Fine Arts, 820 N. 18th St., Birmingham AL 35203. Editor: Charles Ghigna. For high school and college audience. Poetry quarterly. Estab. 1975. Circ. 1,000. Pays in contributor's copies. Byline given. Submit complete poem and brief biography. SASE.

Poetry: Wants poetry that is "fresh, concise; strong use of imagery." No sentimental lyrics.

BARDIC ECHOES, 1036 Emerald Ave. NE, Grand Rapids MI 49503. (616)454-9120. Editor: Clarence L. Weaver. Quarterly. Byline given. Payment in contributor's copies. Will send sample copy to writer for 75¢. Reports in 1-3 months. Limit submissions to 5 poems. Occasionally overstocked. SASE.

Poetry: Poetry may be on any subject, but in good taste. Varied style. Length: 40 lines maximum including title, byline, and stanzaic spaces (one full page).

BELOIT POETRY JOURNAL, Box 2, Beloit WI 53511. Editors: David Stocking, Marion

Stocking. "Our readers are people of all ages and occupations who are interested in the growing tip of poetry." Quarterly magazine; 40 pages. Estab. 1950. Circ. 1,100. Pays in copies of publication. Acquires all rights, but will reassign following publication. Byline given. Photocopied submissions OK. SASE. Reports in 4 months; "actually most rejections are within a week; four months would be the maximum for a poem under serious consideration." Sample copy $1; free writer's guidelines.

Poetry: Avant-garde; free verse; and traditional. Uses 60/year. Limit submissions to batches of 6. "We publish the best contemporary poetry submitted, without bias as to length, form, school or subject. We are particularly interested in discovering new poets, with strong imagination and intense, accurate language."

BIRTHSTONE MAGAZINE, Box 27394, San Francisco CA 94127. (415)334-4681. Editor-in-Chief: Daniel Brady. Emphasizes poetry, graphics and photography. Usually, quarterly magazine; 16 pages or more. Estab. 1975. Circ. 500. Pays in copies. Reassigns all rights to author after publication. Previously published submissions OK.

Photos: B&w glossy prints, maximum size 7x10. No additional payment for photos accepted with accompanying ms. "We use pen and ink graphics."

Poetry: Avant-garde, free verse, haiku, light verse, traditional, and "anything that we agree is good." Buys 20-25 poems/issue. Limit submissions to batches of 5. Length: 1-48 lines, but "will consider longer if very good."

BITTERROOT, International Poetry Magazine, Blythebourne Station, Box 51, Brooklyn NY 11219. Editor: Menke Katz. Quarterly. Payment in 1 contributor's copy. SASE. Regular letter-sized envelopes. Please notify of change of address.

Poetry: "We need good poetry of all kinds. If we think a poem is very good, we will publish a two-page poem; mostly however, we prefer shorter poems, not longer than one page. We always discourage stereotyped forms which imitate fixed patterns and leave no individual mark. We inspire all poets who seek their own selves in original forms of many moods, in harmony with their poems which may be realistic or fantastic, close to earth and cabalistic." We have two annual contests with awards amounting to $225. December 31 of each year is the deadline for the Kaitz award and the William Kushner award.

BLUE UNICORN, 22 Avon Rd., Kensington CA 94707. Editors: Ruth G. Iodice, B. Jo Kinnick, Harold Witt. "We appeal especially to the discriminating lover of poetry, whatever his/her taste runs to." Published 3 times/year. Magazine; 40-50 pages. Estab. 1977. Circ. 500. Pays in copies on publication. Buys one-time rights. Photocopied submissions OK. SASE. Reports in 3-4 months. Sample copy $2.50.

Poetry: "The main criterion is excellence. We like poems which communicate in a memorable way whatever is deeply felt by the poet—ones which delight with a lasting image, a unique twist of thought, and a haunting music. We don't want the hackneyed, the trite, or the banal." Uses 150 poems/year. Limit submissions to batches of 3-4. Prefers shorter verse; "rarely use poetry over 1 page in length." Pays 1 copy.

THE CAPE ROCK, Southeast Missouri State University Press, English Department, Cape Girardeau MO 63701. (314)651-2151, ext. 278. Editor: R.A. Burns. For libraries and persons interested in poetry. Estab. 1964. Semiannual. Circ. 800. Acquires all rights, but may reassign rights to author after publication. Uses 100 mss/year. Pays in contributor's copies. Sample copy $1; writer's guidelines for SASE. Will consider photocopied submissions. No simultaneous submissions. Reports in 1 to 4 months. SASE.

Poetry: "We publish poetry—any style, subject. Avoid cuteness, sentimentality, didacticism. We have summer and winter issues and try to place poetry in the appropriate issue, but do not offer strictly seasonal issues." Photos acquired with accompanying ms with no additional payment; also used without accompanying ms. B&w only. Length: 70 lines maximum.

CEDAR ROCK, 1121 Madeline, New Braunfels TX 78130. (512)625-6002. Editor-in-Chief: David C. Yates. For "persons with an active interest in poetry." Quarterly tabloid; 24 pages. Estab. 1975. Circ. 800. Pays on acceptance. Buys all rights but may reassign following publication. Byline given. Phone queries OK. Photocopied submissions OK. SASE. Reports in 3 weeks. Sample copy $1.50; free writer's guidelines.

Poetry: Avant-garde, free verse, haiku, light verse and traditional. "No deliberately obscure poems." Buys 200 poems/year. Limit submissions to 6 at one time. Length: 3-75 lines. Pays $2-100.

Fiction: Buys 2/issue. Pays $2-100. Submit to R.S. Gwynn, Dept. of English, Lamar University, Beaumont TX 77710.

CHOOMIA Collections of Contemporary Poetry, Yarrow Press, Box 40322, Tuson AZ 85719. Editor-in-Chief: Jay Barwell. Managing Editor: Ann Guido. Annual magazine; 100 pages. Estab. 1975. Circ. 500. Pays in copies on publication. Acquires all rights, but may reassign following publication. Photocopied submissions OK. SASE. Reports in 1 month. Sample copy $2.50.

Poetry, Fiction and Reviews: "We suggest the writer purchase a sample copy for guideline/interest purposes. Recently we have been soliciting; however, unsolicited mss are considered."

THE CHUNGA REVIEW, The Chunga Press, Box 158, Felch MI 49831. Editor: Mike Felten. Emphasizes poetry for all ages, college-educated and self-educated to a college level. "We hope to help bridge the gap between the cerebral university press and the *Jaws 2* mentality. We want street corner savvy mixed with a literary awareness." Quarterly magazine; 40 pages. Estab. 1978. Circ. 200. Pays on publication. Buys one-time rights. Byline given. Photocopied submissions OK. SASE. Reports in 4-6 weeks. Sample copy $1.

Fiction: Fantasy and experimental "with strong imagery, arranged in some coherent fashion"; humorous (anything well done appealing to the absurd); and mainstream. Buys 4-5 mss/year. Send complete ms. Length: 5,000 word maximum. Pays in contributor copies.

Poetry: Avant-garde, free verse, light verse and traditional. Buys 60 poems/year. Send poems in batches of 6. Length: 4 lines minimum. Pays in contributor copies.

CONNECTIONS MAGAZINE, Bell Hollow Rd., Putnam Valley NY 10579. Editor-in-Chief: Toni Ortner-Zimmerman. Annual magazine; 70 pages. Estab. 1971. Circ. 600. Pays in copies. SASE. Reports in 2 weeks. Sample copy $3.50.

Poetry: Avant-garde, free verse and traditional. Limit submissions to batches of 5. Length: 50 lines maximum.

CREATIVE REVIEW, 1718 S. Garrison, Carthage MO 64836. Editor: Glen Coffield. For hobbyists, educated, retired, handicapped, educators. Quarterly mimeographed magazine; 14 to 18 pages. Estab. 1961. Not copyrighted. Uses 250 poems/year. Payment in contributor's copies. Sample copy 50¢. Reports in 3 months. Submit complete ms; "one poem to a page (8½x11)." SASE.

Poetry: "Poems on creativity, good description, local history, examples of good writing, pictures of life, positive approach, good taste, simple and clear. Good grammar and punctuation, logical structure, understandable to the average reader; interesting beginnings, strong endings, objective imagery, not too abstract. We're perhaps more selective and demanding; more traditional in a knowledgeable sense. We don't want anything risque, no negativism or tearing down, no difficult typographical experiments, no excess verbosity and repetition, no intellectual snobbery or trite sophistication. No personal frustrations. Not especially interested in the topical, except positive suggestions on current problems." Length: 32 lines maximum. "Quality demands are greater the longer the poem."

DRAGONFLY: A QUARTERLY OF HAIKU, 4102 NE 130th Place, Portland OR 97230. Editor-in-Chief: Lorraine Ellis Harr. Quarterly magazine; 68 pages. Estab. 1965. Circ. 500. Cash and book awards. Reassigns rights on request. SASE. Reports in 1 month. Sample copy $2.00; free writer's guidelines.

Nonfiction: 300-word articles on haiku or related matter. "Must be concise and have something to say." Uses 2-3 mss/issue.

Poetry: Mostly haiku. Uses some senryu poetry and oriental forms. Uses 150/issue. Limit submissions to batches of 5.

ENCORE, A Quarterly of Verse and Poetic Arts, 1121 Major Ave. NW, Albuquerque NM 87107. (505)344-5615. Editor: Alice Briley. For "anyone interested in poetry from young people in high school to established poets. Good poetry on any theme." Estab. 1966. Quarterly. Circ. 600. Acquires all rights but will reassign rights to author after publication. Byline given. Uses 300 mss/year. Pays in contributor's copies. Sample copy 50¢. Will consider photocopied submissions "provided the author is free to assign rights to *Encore*. Will require assurance if poem is accepted." Submit seasonal material 6-9 months in advance. Reports on material within a month. Submit complete poetry ms. Query, for short reviews. SASE.

Nonfiction, Poetry and Photos: "Particularly like poetry which illustrates the magazine's theme that poetry is a performing art. Fresh approach greatly desired." Traditional forms, blank verse, free verse, avant-garde and light verse. Limit submissions to batches of 4. Some articles on related subjects. Profiles of poets, poetry reviews, technical verse writing. Length: open, but "very long articles rarely used." Prefer no larger than 5x8 b&w glossy photos with good contrast. Pays in contributor's copies. Also has poetry contests. "My poetry contests have grown considerably. Continuous contests have November 1 and May 1 deadlines. In addition, there are often very good special contests."

THE FREE LANCE, A Magazine of Poetry & Prose, 6005 Grand Ave., Cleveland OH 44104. Editors: Russell Atkins, Casper L. Jordan. For college students, teachers and persons who practice the creative arts. Estab. 1950. Published irregularly. Circ. 600. Pays in contributor's copies. No sample copies. No photocopied or simultaneous submissions. Reports in 6 months. Query for book reviews. SASE.
Nonfiction, Fiction and Poetry: "Largely avant-garde, emphasis on literary techniques and ideas, should be experimental. Book reviews. We are more creative than 'topical,' consequently there are not many themes we would single out." Fiction. Length: 3,000 words maximum. Poetry: mainstream, contemporary and avant-garde forms. "Not in the market for poetry or verse that rhymes, or verse that has a message on social problems, or work that is rigidly traditional in form, etc." Length: open.

GRAVIDA, Box 118, Bayville NY 11709. Editor: Lynne Savitt. Magazine published 3 times a year; 44-60 pages. Estab. 1973. Circ. 1,000. Pays in copies on publication. Acquires all rights, but may reassign following publication. Submit seasonal/holiday material 6 months in advance. Photocopied submissions OK. SASE. Reports in 2 weeks. Sample copy $1.50.
Poetry: Avant-garde, free verse, haiku, light verse and traditional. Uses 120/year. Limit submissions to batches of 5. Pays in 2 copies and a $25 prize for best poem in each issue.

HAPPINESS HOLDING TANK, 1790 Grand River Ave., Okemos MI 48864. Editor: Albert Drake. For "poets of various ages, interests; other editors; students." Triannual magazine; 45 pages, (8½x11). Estab. 1970. Circ. 300-500. All rights revert to author automatically. Byline given. Payment in contributor's copies. Sample copy $1. Reports in 1-3 weeks. Not reading during summer months. Submit complete ms. SASE.
Nonfiction and Poetry: Publishes "poems of various kinds, somewhat eclectic—looking for 'excellence.' Essays and articles on modern poetry. Emphasis on younger but unestablished poets: their work to date. Emphasis on information of various kinds—to make magazine useful. Interested in printing methods of all kinds." Buys informational, how-to, and poetry book reviews. Uses all forms of poetry except light verse. Now doing chapbooks and poetry posters.
Rejects: "What we see repeatedly, and do not want, is a kind of poem which can best be described as a 'beginner's poem.' It's usually entitled 'Reflections' or 'Dust' or 'Spring' and has to do with death, love, etc. These are abstractions and the poet treats them in an abstract way. This kind of poem has to be written, but shouldn't be published."

HIRAM POETRY REVIEW, Box 162, Hiram OH 44234. (216)569-3211. Editors: David Fratus and Carol Donley. Published 2 times a year; magazine, 40 to 60 pages, (6x9). "Since our chief subscribers are libraries in major cities or libraries of colleges and universities, our audience is highly literate and comprises persons who are actively interested in poetry of high quality." Estab. 1967. Circ. 500. Copyrighted. Acquires all rights, but will reassign rights to author upon written request. Byline given. Uses approximately 75 poems a year. Payment in 2 contributor's copies plus one year's subscription. Free sample copy. Reports in 8 weeks. Submit only complete ms. SASE.
Poetry: "All forms of poetry used. No special emphasis required. Length: open, but we have printed few very long poems." Limit submissions to 4-6 to a batch.

HUERFANO, Daran, Inc., 5730 N. Via Elena, Tucson AZ 85718. Editor-in-Chief: Randell Shutt. Semiannual magazine; 40 pages. Estab. 1972. Circ. 250. Pays in copies. Acquires all rights, but may reassign following publication. Photocopied submissions OK. SASE. Reports in 1 month. Sample copy $1. Free writer's guidelines.
Poetry: Vicki Thompson, poetry editor. Free verse, light verse and traditional. Uses 50-60 poems/year. Length: 4-50 lines. "Daran Award of $50 to one of our published poets annually."

LIGHT: A POETRY REVIEW, Box 1105M, Stuyvesant PO, New York NY 10009. Editor-in-Chief: Roberta C. Gould. Annual magazine; 64 pages. Estab. 1973. Circ. 800. Pays in copies. Acquires first North American serial rights. SASE. Reports in 3 months. Sample copy $1.25. Suggest writers read sample issue before contributing. Uses graphics and some 7½x5 b&w photos.
Poetry: Avant-garde, free verse and formal. Uses 40 poems/issue. Limit submissions to batches of 4. Length: 5-40 words.

THE LITTLE MAGAZINE, Box 207, Cathedral Station, New York NY 10025. Managing Editor: Felicity Thoet. Quarterly magazine; 64 pages. Circ. 1,000. Pays in copies. Acquires all rights, but may reassign following publication. Photocopied submissions OK. SASE. Reports in 4-6 weeks. Sample copy $1.50; free writer's guidelines.
Fiction: Uses all types. Uses 12 mss/year.
Poetry: Avant-garde, free verse, light verse and traditional. Uses 75/year. Limit submissions to batches of 10.

THE LITTLE REVIEW, Box 205, Marshall University, Huntington WV 25701. Editor: John McKernan. Biannual. Circ. 1,000. Acquires first rights. No payment. Sample copy $1.25. Reports in 2 months or more. SASE.
Nonfiction and Poetry: "Poetry, translations, critical reviews of contemporary poets, parodies, and satire. We are mainly a poetry magazine."

THE LYRIC, 307 Dunton Dr. SW, Blacksburg VA 24060. Editor: Leslie Mellichamp. Quarterly magazine; 26 pages. Estab. 1921. Circ. 1,000. Pays in prizes only $25-100. Acquires first North American serial rights. Submit seasonal/holiday material 3-6 months in advance. Photocopied submissions OK. SASE.
Poetry: Traditional, preferably rhymed, several light pieces/issue. Uses 45 poems/issue. Limit submissions to batches of 5. Length: 40 lines maximum.

THE MODULARIST REVIEW, Wooden Needle Press, 53-18 68th St., Maspeth NY 11378. Director: R.C. Morse. Annual magazine. Estab. 1972. Circ. 1,000. Pays in contributor's copies. Acquires all rights but reassigns following publication. Byline given. SASE. Reports in 3 months. A $2 submission fee is required to accompany all unsolicited mss. Checks should be made payable to the Wooden Needle Press.
Fiction, Photos, Poetry: "All literary, visual and plastic arts." Length: Short fiction mss preferred, but will consider long poems.

MONTHLY POETRY ANTHOLOGY (formerly *Seven Stars Poetry*), Realities Library, Box 33512, San Diego CA 92103. Editor-in-Chief: Richard A. Soos Jr. Emphasizes poetry/modern literature. "Each monthly issue follows a specific theme. A list of themes available with writer's guidelines." Monthly magazine; 20 pages. Estab. 1975. Circ. 800-1,000. Pays on acceptance. Buys all rights, but may reassign following publication. Photocopied submissions OK. SASE. Reports in 6 weeks. Sample copy $1.50; writer's guidelines for SASE.
Poetry: Avant-garde, free verse, haiku and dada/surreal. Buys 10-20 poems/issue. Limit submissions to batches of 5. Pays $3-10/poem.
Nonfiction: Interviews with any modern poet, or fictional interview with a historic poet. Query. No length requirement. Pays $1/printed page.
Columns/Departments: Reviews on poetry books and TV poetry. Buys 10 mss/issue. Query. No length requirements. Pays 1¢/word. Open to suggestions for new columns, departments.

NEW COLLAGE MAGAZINE, 5700 N. Trail, Sarasota FL 33580. (813)355-7671, ext. 203. Editor: A. McA. Miller. For poetry readers. Magazine; 24 pages minimum. Estab. 1971. Triquarterly. Circ. 2,000. Acquires all rights, but usually reassigns rights to author after publication. Uses 80 poems per year. Token payment or 3 contributor's copies. Sample copy $1, together with editorial guidelines sheet. Will consider photocopied submissions. No simultaneous submissions. Reports in 3 weeks. SASE.
Poetry: "We want poetry as a fresh act of language. No tick-tock effusions about everyday sentiments, please. First, read a sample copy. Then, and only then, send us poems. We especially want strong poems, more in Yeats' vein than in W.C. Williams, but we are open to any poem that sustains clear imagery and expressive voice." Length: 150 lines maximum.

NEW JERSEY POETRY MONTHLY, New Jersey Poetry Monthly Press, Box 824 Saddle Brook NJ 07662. Editor: George W. Cooke. For the general public, libraries and colleges, for the most part aimed at college graduates and poetry workshop circles, where the educational level is high. Monthly magazine; 24 pages. Estab. 1977. Circ. 500. Pays on publication. Buys simultaneous rights. Byline given. Submit seasonal/holiday material 3-4 months in advance. Photocopied submissions OK. SASE. Reports in 2 months. Sample copy $1.50.
Poetry: Avant-garde and free verse. "Most poems should not exceed 24 lines. We will accept any kind of verse form rhymed or not, provided the work is of high literary merit. We are not favorably impressed by obscure poems designed to convey an impression of profundity. We are most sympathetic with new writers and never condemn anyone's work." Buys 24 poems/issue. "We pay 2 copies. We are a little literary magazine and we exist to publish

previously unpublished poets and to encourage creative writing in New Jersey. We make no profit and can not pay for submissions."

NEW WORLDS UNLIMITED, Box 556-WM, Saddle Brook NJ 07662. Editor-in-Chief: Sal St. John Buttaci. Managing Editor: Susan Linda Gerstle. For "professional and aspiring poets of all ages from here and abroad. We've published high school students, college students, graduates, and people from all walks of life who write good poetry." Annual hardcover anthology; 130 pages. Estab. 1974. Circ. 500-700. No payment. Obtains all rights, but may reassign following publication. Photocopied submissions OK. SASE. Reports in 6 months. Writer's guidelines and contest rules for annual poetry contest for SASE.
Poetry: "We want previously unpublished poems rich in imagery, poems that show intelligent treatment of universal themes and reveal the poet's understanding, even limited, of the poetry craft." Avant-garde; free verse; haiku; light verse; and traditional. Uses 400/issue. Limit submissions to batches of 5. Length: 2-14 lines

NORTHERN LIGHT, 605 Fletcher Argue Bldg., University of Manitoba, Winnipeg, Manitoba R3T 2N2. (204)474-8145. Editor-in-Chief: George Anabile. Audience is poets, libraries, professors, teachers and English students. Semiannual magazine; 64 pages. Estab. 1968. Circ. 1,000. Pays in contributor's copies. Buys all rights, but may reassign following publication. Byline given. Phone queries OK. SAE and International Reply Coupons. Reports in 4 weeks. Sample copy $1.50.
Nonfiction: Reviews of recent poetry publications and interviews with poets. Buys 2 mss/issue. Send complete ms. Length: 1,000-1,800 words.
Photos: Photos purchased without accompanying ms. Uses 8x10 b&w photos.
Poetry: Avant-grade, free verse and traditional. Buys 30 poems/issue. Pays in contributor's copies.
How To Break In: "We prefer to publish Canadians, so Americans have to be good."

OUTPOSTS, 72 Burwood Rd., Walton-on-Thames, Surrey KT12 4AL. Editor-in-Chief: Howard Sergeant. Quarterly magazine; 40 pages. Estab. 1944. Circ. 1,500. Pays on publication. Buys first serial rights. Photocopied submissions OK. SAE and International Reply Coupons. Reports in 2 weeks. Sample copy $2.
Nonfiction: Articles on poetry or critical studies of poetry. Buys 4/year. Length: 1,000-2,500 words. Pays about 2 pounds/page.
Poetry: Any type of poetry, but not of epic length. Buys 25-50/issue. Limit submissions to 6. Length: 80 lines maximum. Pays about 2 pounds/page.

PARIS VOICES, 37 rue de la Bucherie, Paris 75005 France. Editor: Ken Timmerman. Publishes 3 issues/year. Reports in 6 weeks. Pays in copies (3). Sample copy $1.
Poetry: "We are interested in prose fiction, poetry, graphics, photos, some translations and reviews. However, will not consider work from outside of Eurpoe unless it is in some way reflecting the subtle alterations on a writer's spirit which results from living in a foreign culture. Stylistically we're open to anything which shows a serious confrontation with craft."

POEM, Box 1247, West Station, Huntsville AL 35807. Editor: Robert L. Welker. For adults; well-educated, interested in good poetry. Published 3 times a year; magazine, 65 pages. Estab. 1967. Circ. 500. Acquires all rights, but will reassign rights to author after publication. Byline given. Uses 200 poems a year. Payment in contributor's copies. Reports in 2 months. Submit complete ms only. SASE.
Poetry: "We use nothing but superior quality poetry. Good taste (no pornography for its own sake) and technical proficiency. We give special attention to young and less well-known poets. Do not like poems about poems, poets, and other works of art." Traditional forms, blank verse, free verse, and avant-garde forms. Length and theme: open.

THE POET, 2314 W. 6th St., Mishawaka IN 46544. (219)255-8606. Editor: Doris Nemeth. For professional people, freelance writers, students, etc. Anthology; 200 pages. Estab. 1963. Twice a year. Circ. 25,000. Acquires first North American serial rights. Pays 10% kill fee. Byline given. Uses about 1,000 mss a year. No payment. Sample copy $4.50. Will consider photocopied and simultaneous submissions. Reports in 4 to 6 weeks. Submit complete ms. SASE.
Poetry and Photos: Wanda Bearden, art editor. "All forms of poetry. No set rules. We read all manuscripts. We prefer not to see religious material." Length: 16 lines maximum. Uses 8x10 (or smaller) b&w glossy prints. Uses 8x11 art.

POETRY, The Modern Poetry Association, 1228 N. Dearborn Pkwy., Chicago IL 60610,

Editor-in-Chief: John F. Nims. Monthly magazine; 64 pages. Estab. 1912. Circ. 8,000. Pays on publication. Buys all rights, but may reassign following publication. Byline given. Submit seasonal/holiday material 9 months in advance. SASE. Reports in 4-6 weeks. Sample copy $2; writer's guidelines for SASE.

Poetry: "We consistently publish the best poetry being written in English. All forms may be acceptable." Buys 500/year. Limit submissions to batches of 6-8. Pays $1/line.

POETRY NEWSLETTER, Department of English, Temple University, Philadelphia PA 19122. (215)787-1778. Editor: Richard O'Connell. For readers of serious poetry. Quarterly newsletter; 20-40 pages. Estab. 1971. Circ. 500 to 1,000. Not copyrighted. Payment in contributor's copies. Will send sample copy to writer for $1. Will consider photocopied submissions. No simultaneous submissions. Reports in 1 to 3 months. Submit complete ms. SASE.

Poetry: "Poetry of high literary quality. No biases. Commercial verse will not be considered. The news is the poetry."

POETRY NORTHWEST MAGAZINE, *The Oregonian*, 1320 SW Broadway, Portland OR 97201. Editor: Penny Avila. Poetry column in Sunday magazine of newspaper. Pays on 15th of month following publication. Buys first newspaper rights which revert to poet after publication. SASE. Reports in 2-3 weeks.

Poetry: "We publish 4 poems/week from many schools and disciplines old and new. Rarely use religious poems. Seek fresh metaphor and imagery in issue and ethic-oriented poems. Welcome the new and experimental, but in good taste." Length: 14-21 lines maximum. Pays $5.

POETRY VIEW, 1125 Valley Rd., Menasha WI 54952. Editor: Dorothy Dalton. Published weekly as half-page in *View*, the magazine section of the *Post-Crescent*. Estab. 1970. Circ. 50,000. Not copyrighted. Buys 250 poems per year. Pays on 10th of month following publication. Prefers original submissions; no photocopies. No simultaneous submissions. Submit seasonal material 2 to 3 months in advance. Reports in 2 to 3 months. SASE with submissions and queries. Tearsheets are sent to out-of-town contributors.

Poetry: Well-written poetry, showing a fresh use of language. No religious poetry or poetry that is overly sentimental. Uses some traditional forms, free verse, and light verse. Length: serious poetry, to 24 lines; light verse, 4 to 8 lines. Pays $3 per poem.

SEVEN, 115 S. Hudson, Oklahoma City OK 73102. Editor: James Neill Northe. Published 4 times a year on an irregular basis. Estab. 1954. Circ. 1,000. Buys all rights. Pays on acceptance. Will send sample copy to writer for $1.25. No photocopied submissions. Will consider simultaneous submissions. Reports on material accepted for publication in 10 days. Returns rejected material immediately. Submit complete ms. SASE.

Poetry: "We strive to present only the most sheerly lyrical, poignant and original material possible. Seven poems and 1 reprint are used in each issue. We prefer the classical sonnet over the variations, accenting adherence to the form. Free verse is acceptable, but not as chopped prose. Good ballads are always acceptable. We like titles, punctuation and capitalization where needed. We like well-written and finely expressed spiritual poems, but they must be spiritual (not religious). We prefer the universal approach, rather than the personal. We want lines that communicate; not rambling, disjointed, chopped prose in or out of rhyme, lacking the rhythm and power of free verse." No restrictions as to form or subject. "We are not interested in chopped pose or conversational prose." Length: open. Pays $5 per poem.

SOUTH AND WEST, 2406 South S St., Fort Smith AZ 72901. Editor: Sue Abbott Boyd. Quarterly. Buys North American serial rights. Pays in contributor's copies. SASE. Reports in 1 month. Sample copy $1.

Nonfiction: Book reviews, scholarly articles on poetry. Length: open.

Fiction: "Will use a timely or experimental short story. Can by on any subject treated with good taste except 'I Love God' themes. We will even consider imaginative God themes, if a new dimension is offered that relates to humanity, the arts, culture and education." Length: 2,000 words maximum.

Poetry: "The purpose of the magazine is to encourage new poets as well as give voice to those already established. Emphasis is on modern poetry, expression of new and young thought. This does not, however, mean prejudice against traditional poetry. All types of poems receive equal consideration. We prefer work that is individualistic, that reflects the personality of the writer. No subject is taboo that is handled in good taste. We prefer freshness to merely skillful execution of form." Length: 37 lines maximum.

SPARROW POVERTY PAMPHLETS (formerly *Sparrow*), Sparrow Press, 103 Waldron St., West Lafayette, IN 47906. Editor-in-Chief: Felix Stefanile. Triannual magazine; 32 pages. Estab. 1954. Circ. 800. Pays on publication. Buys first North American serial rights. "We share anthology rights. Some previously published submissions OK, but major portion of ms should be first-time original." SASE. Reports in 6 weeks. Sample copy $2.
Poetry: "No form bias. Mature, serious work in the modern manner. Poetry must be human and relevant." Buys 20-30 poems/issue, each issue devoted to one poet. Pays $20 plus royalties; 20% after cost.

STAR WEST, Box 731, Sausalito CA 94965. Editor: Leon Spiro. Semiannual newspaper, with mini-supplements. Estab. 1963. Circ. 1,000. Not copyrighted. Byline given. Payment in contributor's copies. Will send sample copy to writer for $1.50. Reports in 2 to 4 weeks. SASE.
Poetry: Traditional, contemporary, avant-garde, light verse, surrealism. "Poetry that's dynamic." Length: 16 lines maximum.

STONE COUNTRY, 20 Lorraine Rd., Madison NJ 07940. (201)377-3727. Editor: Judith Neeld. "For poets who have never been in the closet." Magazine published 3 times a year; 40 pages. Circ. 800. Acquires first North American serial rights. Byline given. Accepts 100-150 poems/year. Payment in contributor's copy plus Phillips Poetry Award ($25) for best poem published in each issue. Sample copy $1.75. Reports in 1 month, "more or less." Query or submit complete ms. "SASE, required, or we will destroy ms."
Poetry and Graphics: Art Editor: Pat McCormick. "We publish poetry, poetry criticism, commentaries, and graphics. No thematic or stylistic limitations, but we are unable to publish long narrative poems in full. All themes must be handled in depth and with a search for language. We must be made to see new!" Free verse, traditional forms, blank verse, avant-garde forms. Length: 40 lines maximum. Limit submissions to 5 poems a time.

TAR RIVER POETRY, East Carolina University, Department of English, Greenville NC 27834. Editor: Peter Makuck. Biannual magazine; 52 pages. Estab. 1960. Circ. 850. Pays in contributor's copies. Copyright reassigned upon request. No fee. SASE. Reports in 6-8 weeks. Sample copy $1.50.
Poetry: Free verse and haiku. "We do not want sentimental or flat-statement poetry." Uses 40 poems/issue. Submit in batches of 6. Length: 50 lines maximum.

VOICES INTERNATIONAL, South and West, Inc., 1115 Gillette Dr., Little Rock AR 72207. Editor-in-Chief: Clovita Rice. Quarterly magazine; 32-40 pages. Pays in copies on publication. Acquires all rights. Submit seasonal/holiday material 1 year in advance. SASE. Reports in 3 weeks. Sample copy $2.00.
Poetry: Free verse. Uses 50-60 poems/issue. Limit submissions to batches of 5. Length: 3-40 lines. Will consider longer ones if good.
How To Break In: "We accept poetry with a new approach, haunting word pictures and significant ideas. Language should be used like watercolors to achieve depth, to highlight one focal point, to be pleasing to the viewer, and to be transparent, leaving space for the reader to project his own view."

WEST COAST POETRY REVIEW, 1335 Dartmouth Dr., Reno NV 89503. Editor-in-Chief: William L. Fox. Emphasizes experimental literature. Semiannual magazine; 80 pages. Estab. 1970. Circ. 750. Pays in copies on publication. Acquires first North American serial rights. Byline given. SASE. Reports in 1 week. Sample copy $5.
Nonfiction: Criticism of experimental poetry only. Query. Uses some fiction.
Poetry: Avant-garde. Uses 50 poems/issue. Limit submissions to batches of 10.

THE WINDLESS ORCHARD, English Department, Indiana-Purdue University, Ft. Wayne IN 46805. Editor: Dr. Robert Novak. For poets and photographers. Estab. 1970. Quarterly. Circ. 300. Acquires all rights, but will reassign rights to author after publication. Payment in contributor's copies. Reports in 3 to 14 weeks. Submit complete ms. SASE.
Poetry and Photos: Avant-garde forms of poetry, free verse and haiku. Use of photos restricted to b&w.

THE WORMWOOD REVIEW, Box 8840, Stockton CA 95204. Editor: Marvin Malone. Quarterly. Circ. 700. Acquires all rights, but will reassign rights to author on request. Pays in copies or cash equivalent. Pays on publication. Will send sample copy to writer for $1.50. Reports in 2-8 weeks. SASE.
Poetry: Modern poetry and prose poems that communicate the temper and depth of the

human scene. All styles and schools from ultra avant-garde to classical; no taboos. Especially interested in prose poems or fables. 3-500 lines.

How To Break In: "Be original. Be yourself. Have something to say. Say it as economically and effectively as possible. Don't be afraid of wit and intelligence."

XANADU, Box 773, Huntington NY 11743. Editors: Beverly Lawn, Coco Gordon. "For an audience interested in reading the best new poetry being written." Magazine; 64 pages. Estab. 1974. Biannually. Circ. 1,000. Acquires all rights, but will reassign rights to author after publication if proper credit line is given. Uses about 90 poems a year. Payment in 2 contributor's copies. Will send sample copy to writer for $2.00. No photocopied or simultaneous submissions. Reports in 3 months. Query for nonfiction. Submit 5-6 poems. SASE.

Poetry, Graphics and Photos: "Our main criteria for poetry are excellence of craft and clarity and force of vision. Only the highest quality contemporary poetry. We like to see at least 5 poems by a contributor at one time. Strongly realized poems rooted in human experience have an edge." B&w photos and line drawings appropriate to size of publication are used without mss.

Politics and World Affairs

Other categories in *Writer's Market* include publications that will also consider articles about politics and world affairs. Some of these categories are Business and Finance, Regional, City magazines, General Interest, and Newspapers and Weekly Magazine Sections.

ADA REPORT, Box 5, Ada MI 49301. Editor: David J. Cullen. Emphasizes the humorous side of government: federal, state and local. Monthly newsletter. Estab. 1978. Circ. 3,500. Pays on publication. Buys all rights. Photocopied submissions OK. SASE. Reports in 2-3 weeks. Free sample copy.

Columns/Departments: Guest Speaker (provides an open forum to speak-out on government spending, The Congress, job safety, environmental protection, regulation, inflation, cost of living, etc.); Flu Report ("will contain examples of how the Washington bureaucratic flu virus is spreading—and showing up in law and rules enacted by state governments and county councils"); Tape Worm ("articles on incredible encounters with governmental red tape"); and Whistle Blower ("stories that will 'blow the whistle' on government excesses or abuses"). Query. Length: 200-500 words. Pays $75-150.

AFRICA REPORT, 833 United Nations Plaza, New York NY 10017. (212)949-5731. Editor: Anthony J. Hughes. 60% freelance written. For US citizens, residents with a special interest in African affairs for professional, business, academic or personal reasons. Not tourist-related. Estab. 1956. Every 2 months. Circ. 10,500. Rights purchased vary with author and material. Usually buys all rights. Negotiable kill fee. Byline given unless otherwise requested. Buys 70 mss/year. Pays on publication. Sample copy for $2.25. Write for editorial guidelines sheet. SASE.

Nonfiction and Photos: Interested in mss on "African political, economic and cultural affairs, especially in relation to US foreign policy and business objectives. Style should be journalistic but not academic or light. Articles should not be polemical or long on rhetoric but may be committed to a strong viewpoint. I do not want tourism articles." Would like to see in-depth topical analyses of lesser known African countries, based on residence or several months stay in the country." Pays $150 for nonfiction. Photos purchased with or without accompanying mss with extra payment. B&w only. Pays $25. Submit 12x8 "half-plate."

AMERICAN MERCURY, Box 1306, Torrance CA 90505. Managing Editor: La Vonne Furr. Quarterly. Write for copy of guidelines for writers. "All mss must be typed, double-spaced, clean, ready for printer, left margin at least 1½ inches. Break up articles with periodic italicized paragraphs and/or subheads. Authors should submit biographical material to aid editor in preparing a suitable introduction." SASE.

Nonfiction: *Mercury's* editorial policy is nonpartisan but generally conservative. "It will stress the positive and hopeful aspects of life and Western tradition through reliable and well-written exposes. Articles on fads, dances, narcotics, crime, entertainers are generally unwanted." Wants Americana, nature briefs, humorous comment on everyday life, politics, science, health; particular emphasis on heroic and patriotic themes; satire. "Precede book reviews with a very brief title, then describe book: Title of book in caps, by (name of author), number of pages, publisher, date of publication." Length: 1,000 words maximum for book reviews; 900-2,000 words for articles. Payment ranges from one-year complimentary subscription to $50 for unsolicited articles.

AMERICAN OPINION MAGAZINE, Belmont MA 02178. Managing Editor: Scott Stanley Jr. "A conservative, anti-communist journal of political affairs." Monthly except August. Circ. 50,000. Buys all rights. Kill fee varies. Byline given. Pays on publication. Sample copy $1.50. SASE.
Nonfiction: Articles on matters of political affairs of a conservative, anti-communist nature. "We favor highly researched, definitive studies of social, economic, political and international problems that are written with verve and originality of style." Length: 3,000-4,000 words. Pays $25/published page.

AMERICAS, Organization of American States, Washington DC 20006. Managing Editor: Flora L. Phelps. 10% freelance written. Official cultural organ of Organization of American States. Audience is persons interested in inter-American relations. Editions published in English, Spanish, Portuguese. Monthly. Circ. 100,000. Buys first publication and reprint rights. Byline given. Pays on publication. Free sample copy. Articles received only on speculation. Include cover letter with writer's background. Reports in two months. Not necessary to enclose SASE.
Nonfiction: Articles of general hemisphere interest on history, art, literature, music, development, travel, etc. Taboos are religious and political themes or articles with non-international slant. Photos required. Length, about 2,000 words. Pays about $100.

THE ASIA MAIL, Potomac-Asia Communications, Inc., Box 1044, Alexandria VA 22313. (703)548-2881. Editor and Publisher: Edward Neilan. Managing Editor: Donna Gays. Executive Editor, West Coast: Charles C. Keely Jr. Emphasizes "American perspectives on Asia and the Pacific" for business executives, opinion leaders, diplomats, scholars, and other Americans who travel, do business or have demonstrated an interest in Asia and Asian affairs. "We are particularly looking for sharp articles, profiles, case studies of US-Asian business." Monthly tabloid; 28 pages. Estab. 1976. Circ. 30,000. Pays on publication. Buys first North American serial rights. SASE. Reports in 4 weeks. Free sample copy and writer's guidelines.
Nonfiction: "The *Asia Mail* will purchase about 4-5 mss from freelance writers each month. The Asia-related articles must show a US interest in an Asian country or Asian interests within the US. The publication is comprehensive in business and scholarly aspects and includes articles of information, nostalgia, personal interest, historic interest, as well as reviews of books, art and theatre." Query. Length: 1,500 words maximum for features; 800 words maximum for reviews. Pays $50-150, "higher by special assignment."

CALIFORNIA JOURNAL, California Center for Research and Education in Government. 1617 10th St., Sacramento CA 95814. (916)444-2840. Editor-in-Chief: Ed Salzman. Managing Editor: Alice Nauman. Emphasizes California politics and government. Monthly magazine; 40 pages. Estab. 1970. Circ. 17,500. Pays on publication. Buys all rights. Byline given. Phone queries OK. SASE. Reports immediately. Free sample copy.
Nonfiction: Profiles and state and local government and political analysis. No outright advocacy pieces. Buys 75 mss/year. Query. Length: 900-6,000 words. Pays $50/printed page.

CONSERVATIVE DIGEST, 7777 Leesburg Pike, Suite 416, Falls Church VA 22043. (703)893-1411. Editor-in-Chief: Brien Benson. 10% freelance written. Monthly magazine; 48 pages. Estab. 1974. Circ. 100,000. Pays on publication. Buys second serial and one-time rights. Pays 20% kill fee. Byline given. SASE. Simultaneous and previously published submissions OK. Reports in 3 weeks. Sample copy $1.75.
Nonfiction: Expose (government); how-to (political ideas); and interview. Buys 1 ms/issue. Submit complete ms. Length: 750-1,200 words. Pays 10¢/word.
Fillers: Susan Fourt, fillers editor. Clippings, bureaucratic blunders, cartoons and newsbreaks. Buys 20 fillers/issue. Pays $15-25.

CURRENT HISTORY, 4225 Main St., Philadelphia PA 19127. Editor: Carol L. Thompson. Monthly. Pays on publication. Reports in 1-2 weeks. Query preferred. "All articles contracted for in advance." SASE.
Nonfiction: Uses articles on current events, chiefly world area studies, stressing their historical, economic, and political background, 3,500-4,000 words in length. Academician contributions almost exclusively. Pays an average of $100.

EUROPE, 2100 M St. NW, 707, Washington DC 20037. Editor: Walter Nicklin. For anyone with a professional or personal interest in Western Europe and European—US relations. Monthly magazine; 60 pages. Estab. 1954. Circ. 40,000. Copyrighted. Buys about 50 mss/year. Pays on acceptance. Free sample copy. Will consider photocopied and simultaneous submissions. Submit seasonal material 3 months in advance. Reports in 4 weeks. Query or submit complete ms. Include resume of author's background and qualifications with query or ms. SASE.
Nonfiction and Photos: Interested in current affairs (with emphasis on economics and politics), the Common Market and Europe's relations with the rest of the world. Publishes occasional cultural pieces, with European angle. High quality writing a must. "Please, no more M.A. theses on European integration. We're looking for European angle in topic current in the US." Length: 250-2,000 words. Average payment is $250. Photos purchased with or without accompanying mss. Also purchased on assignment. Buys b&w and color. Average payment is $25-35 per b&w print, any size; $50 for inside use of color transparencies; $200-300 for color used on cover.

FOREIGN AFFAIRS, 58 E. 68th St., New York NY 10021. (212)734-0400. Editor: William P. Bundy. For academics, businessmen (national and international), government, educational and cultural readers especially interested in international affairs of a political nature. Estab. 1922. Published 5 times a year. Circ. 75,000. Buys all rights. Pays kill fee. Byline given. Buys 45 mss/year. Pays on publication. Will send sample copy to writer for $3.50, post paid. Will consider photocopied submissions. Reports in 2-4 weeks. Submit complete ms. SASE.
Nonfiction: "Articles dealing with international affairs; political, educational, cultural, philosophical and social sciences. Develop an original idea in depth, with a broad basis on topical subjects. Serious, in-depth, developmental articles with international appeal." Length: 2,500-6,000 words. Pays $300.

THE FREEMAN, 30 S. Broadway, Irvington-on-Hudson NY 10533. (914)591-7230. Editor: Paul L. Poirot. 60% freelance written. For "fairly advanced students of liberty and the layman." Monthly. Buys all rights, including reprint rights. Byline given. Buys 44 mss/year. Pays on publication. SASE.
Nonfiction: "We want nonfiction clearly analyzing and explaining various aspects of the free market, private enterprise, limited government philosophy, especially as pertains to conditions in the United States. Though a necessary part of the literature of freedom is the exposure of collectivistic cliches and fallacies, our aim is to emphasize and explain the positive case for individual responsibility and choice in a free economy. Especially important, we believe, is the methodology of freedom; self-improvement, offered to others who are interested. We try to avoid name-calling and personality clashes, and find satire of little use as an educational device. Ours is a scholarly analysis of the principles underlying a free market economy." Length: 3,500 words maximum. Pay is 5¢/word.

THE LIBERTARIAN REVIEW, Libertarian Review, Inc., 1620 Montgomery St., San Francisco CA 94111. Editor: Roy A. Childs Jr. Managing Editor: Jeff Riggenbach. Emphasizes politics and the arts. Monthly magazine; 48 pages. Estab. 1972. Circ. 18,000. Pays on publication. Buys all rights. Submit seasonal/holiday material 2 months in advance. Photocopied submissions OK. SASE. "Queries are encouraged and are reported in 2 weeks; only solicited mss are welcome and are reported on immediately." Sample copy $1.25.
Nonfiction: Expose (of government malfeasance); historical (on background and root causes of social problems—must be related to current events) and interview (with newsmakers and opinion makers, especially those in conflict with the state). "Articles and reviews must emphasize the relevance of libertarian ideas to the issues and events of the day." Buys 35 mss/year. Query. Length: 1,000-4,000 words. Pays $150-250.
Photos: State availability of photos. Pays $5-35/photo. Supply b&w contact sheets and negatives. Buys one-time rights.
Columns/Departments: Book Reviews (literally anything of possible interest to libertarians; stress on relevance of libertarian ideas to almost everything—750-1,500 words); and The Media ("criticism of the news media, especially for its inability to see through government lies"—1,000-2,000 words). Buys 40/year. Query with clips of published work. Pays $50-150.

THE NATION, 333 6th Ave., New York NY 10014. Editor: Victor Navasky. Weekly. Query. SASE.
Nonfiction and Poetry: "We welcome all articles dealing with the social scene, particularly if they examine it with a new point of view or expose conditions the rest of the media overlooks. Poetry is also accepted." Length and payment to be negotiated.

How To Break In: "We are absolutely committed to the idea of getting more material from the boondocks. For instance, a fellow in Denver just sent us a piece we're printing on the firings that are going on at the newspaper there. Right now we're getting stuff at the ratio of about 10 to one from the New York area and I would like to reverse that ratio. If you live somewhere where you think nothing is going on, look again! If you do a piece for us from someplace where we don't have anyone, you could develop into a stringer."

NATIONAL DEVELOPMENT, Intercontinental Publications, Inc., 15 Franklin St., Westport CT 06880. (203)226-7463. Editor-in-Chief: Martin Greenburgh. Emphasizes 3rd world infrastructure. For government officials in 3rd world—technocrats, planners, engineers, ministers. Monthly magazine; 120 pages. Estab. 1960. Circ. 23,000. Pays on acceptance. Buys all rights, but may reassign following publication. Pays 50% kill fee. Byline given. Phone queries OK. Previously published submissions OK. SASE. Reports in 4 weeks. Free sample copy and writer's guidelines.
Nonfiction: How-to (tourism, case studies, government management, planning, telecommunications); informational (agriculture, economics, public works, construction management); interview; photo feature and technical. Buys 6-10 mss/issue. Query. Length: 1,800-5,000 words. Pays $150-250.
Photos: B&w and color. Captions required. Query. Total price for ms includes payment for photos.
Columns/Departments: Managing Maintenance (public works maintenance from managerial viewpoint), Financial Technology (finances as they might affect 3rd world governments). Buys 4 mss/issue. Query. Length: 750-1,500 words. Pays $75-150. Open to suggestions for new columns/departments.

NATIONAL JOURNAL, 1730 M St. NW, Washington DC 20036. (202)857-1400. Editor: Richard Frank. "Very limited need for freelance material because fulltime staff produces virtually all of our material." Pays negotiable kill fee. Byline given.

NATIONAL OPINION POLL MAGAZINE, 30 N. San Pedro Rd., San Rafael CA 94903. (415)472-2950. Editor: Richard Hine. Publisher: Geoffrey Dohrmann. Emphasizes political feature reporting. Quarterly magazine; 64 pages. Estab. January 1978. Circ. 25,000. Pays on publication. Buys one-time rights. Phone queries OK. Submit seasonal/holiday material 2 months in advance. Simultaneous and photocopied submissions OK. SASE. Reports in 6 weeks. Free sample copy and writer's guidelines.
Nonfiction: General interest (personal perspectives on issues—emphasize experiences, feelings, quotes; integrate national opinion poll results and responses to polls in Congress); how-to (participate more fully in governing process, i.e.; how to reach Congressman directly, how to gain access to galleries, etc.); humor (political irony or satire); inspirational ('Portrait in Courage' on political personage); interview (political figures on key issues); nostalgia (background relating to current issue or process); personal experience (in political process); personal opinion (position paper on issue); photo feature (on an issue, political person or the human side of politics); profile (human side of political people). Buys 12-60 mss/year. Query. Length: 300-3,000 words. Pays 7¢/word.
Photos: State availability of photos. Pays $50-200 for 8x10 b&w glossy prints; $50-200 for color transparencies. Captions and model releases required.
Columns/Departments: Perspectives (personal features on political reporting); Great Debate (major cover articles; includes debate on issues by political leaders and/or members of the Poll); Personal View (highly personal look at a political situation); and Poli People (personal sketches on political people). Open to suggestions for new columns/departments. Length: 50-100 words. Pays $10.

NATIONAL REVIEW, 150 E. 35th St., New York NY 10016. (212)679-7330. Editor: Wm. F. Buckley Jr. Issued fortnightly. Buys all rights. Pays 50% kill fee. Byline given. Pays on publication. Will send sample copy. Reports in a month. SASE.
Nonfiction: Kevin Lynch, articles editor. Uses articles, 1,000-3,500 words, on current events and the arts, which would appeal to a politically conservative audience. Pays about 7½¢/word. Inquiries about book reviews, movie, play, TV reviews, or other cultural happenings, or travel should be addressed to Chilton Williamson Jr., 150 E. 35th St., New York NY 10016.
Poetry: Uses only short, satirical poems of a political nature. Should not run over 30 lines.

NEW GUARD, Young Americans for Freedom, Woodland Rd., Sterling VA 22170. (703)450-5162. Editor-in-Chief: Richard F. LaMountain. Emphasizes conservative political ideas for readership of mostly young people with a large number of college students. Age range 14-39. Virtually all are politically conservative with interests in politics, economics, philosophy, current affairs. Mostly students or college graduates. Quarterly magazine; 48 pages. Estab. 1961. Circ. 12,000. Pays on publication. Buys all rights. Byline given. Phone queries OK. Submit seasonal/holiday material 2-3 months in advance. SASE. Reports in 1 month. Free sample copy.

Nonfiction: Expose (government waste, failure, mismanagement, problems with education or media); historical (illustrating political or economic points); humor (satire on current events); interview (politicians, academics, people with conservative viewpoint or something to say to conservatives); personal opinion; and profile. Buys 40 mss/year. Submit complete ms. Length: 3,500 words maximum. Pays $40-100.

Photos: Purchased with accompanying manuscript.

Fiction: Humorous (satire or current events). Buys 5 mss/year. Submit complete ms. Length: 1,800 words maximum. Pays $10-40.

THE NEW REPUBLIC, A Weekly Journal of Opinion, 1220 19th NW, Washington DC 20036. Managing Editor: Michael Kinsley. 50% freelance written. Estab. 1914. Circ. 90,000. Buys all rights. Byline given. Pays on publication. SASE.

Nonfiction: This liberal, intellectual publication uses 1,000- to 1,500-word comments on public affairs and arts. Pays 10¢/published word.

NEWSWEEK, 444 Madison Ave., New York NY 10022. Staff-written. Unsolicited mss accepted for "My Turn," a column of personal opinion. Length: 1,100 words maximum.

OREGON VOTER DIGEST, 108 NW 9th, Portland OR 97209. (503)222-9794. Editor: C. R. Hillyer. For top-echelon of leaders and decisionmakers in private industry and government in Oregon. Magazine; 40 pages. Frequent topical issues; apply for schedule. Estab. 1915. Monthly. Circ. 3,000. Not copyrighted. Pays on publication. Will send sample copy to writer on request. Will consider photocopied and simultaneous submissions. Submit topical issue material 1 month in advance. Reports on material accepted for publication in 1 month. Returns rejected material in 1 week. Query or submit complete ms. SASE.

Nonfiction and Photos: News of business and industry, public affairs, legislation; statewide or affecting Oregon. Land use planning, forest industry, big government, economic trends, political items. "Looking for short political items (in state or affecting Oregon) of an expose or investigative nature. A writer's approach should be traditional, conservative stance, in support of private enterprise, against sprawling bureaucracy of government. Remember that this is not a mass consumer readership." Length: 500 words maximum. Pays 4¢/word minimum. B&w glossy prints purchased with mss. Pays $7 minimum.

PRACTICAL POLITICS, 2225 Spring St., Springfield IL 62704. Editor: Terry Lutes. 80% freelance written. Emphasizes campaign politics for elected officials and their aides, party officials, political consultants, writers, and election officials. Bimonthly magazine; 40 pages. Estab. 1977. Circ. 8,000. Pays on acceptance. Buys first North American serial rights. Submit seasonal/holiday material 3 months in advance of issue date. Simultaneous, photocopied and previously published submissions OK. SASE. Reports in 1 month. Sample copy $1.50; free writer's guidelines.

Nonfiction: How-to (campaigns, media preparation, research); historical (past campaigns); interview (elected officials, candidates, consultants, writers); new product (campaign techniques); personal experience (campaign); personal opinion (electoral change); and photo feature (campaign activity). No partisan or idealigical opinion. Buys 40mss/year. Query. Length: 500-2,000 words. Pays $15-60.

Photos: Pays $5-50 for b&w photos. Buys one-time rights.

Columns/Departments: Donna Vaught, department editor. Book Reviews (on campaign books). Buys 12/year. Query. Length: 500-1,500 words. Pays $15-45. Open to suggestions for new columns/departments.

Fillers: Clippings. Length: 10-60 words. Pays $5-10.

PRESENT TENSE: THE MAGAZINE OF WORLD JEWISH AFFAIRS, 165 E. 56th St., New York NY 10022. (212)751-4000. Editor: Murray Polner. For college-educated, Jewish-oriented audience interested in Jewish life throughout the world. Quarterly magazine; 80 pages. Estab. 1973. Circ. 25,000. Buys all rights, but will reassign rights to author after publication. Byline given. Buys 60 mss/year. Pays on acceptance. Sample copy $2.50. Reports in 6-8 weeks. Query. SASE.

Nonfiction: Quality reportage of contemporary events (a la *Harper's, Atlantic, New Yorker,* etc.) and well-written memoirs. Personal experience, profiles and photo essays. Length: 3,000 words maximum. Pays $100-250.

THE PROGRESSIVE, 408 W. Gorham St., Madison WI 53703. (608)257-4626. Editor: Erwin Knoll. Issued monthly. Buys all rights. Byline given. Pays on publication. Reports in two weeks. Query. SASE.
Nonfiction: Primarily interested in articles which interpret, from a progressive point of view, domestic and world affairs. Occasional lighter features. Length: 3,000 words maximum. Pays $50-200.

REASON MAGAZINE, Box 40105, Santa Barbara CA 93103. (805)963-5993. Editor: Robert Poole Jr. 50% freelance written. For a readership interested in individual liberty, economic freedom, private enterprise alternatives to government services and protection against inflation and depressions. Monthly; 52 pages. Estab. 1968. Circ. 20,000. Rights purchased vary with author and material. May buy all rights; but will sometimes reassign rights to author after publication; first North American serial rights or first serial rights. Pays 75% kill fee. Byline given. Buys 40 mss/year. Pays on publication. Sample copy $1; free guidelines for writers. "Manuscripts must be typed, double- or triple-spaced on one side of the page only. The first page (or a cover sheet) should contain an aggregate word count, the author's name and mailing address, and a brief (100- to 200-word) abstract. A short biographical sketch of the author should also be included." Will consider photocopied submissions. Reports in 3 months. Query. SASE.
Nonfiction and Photos: "*Reason* is a libertarian publication, dealing with social, economic and political problems, and supporting both individual liberty and economic freedom. Articles dealing with the following subject areas are desired: analyses of current issues and problems from a libertarian viewpoint (e.g., education, energy, victimless crimes, regulatory agencies, foreign policy, etc.). Discussions of social change, i.e., strategy and tactics for moving toward a free society. Discussions of the institutions of a free society and how they would deal with important problems. Articles on self-preservation in today's environment (economic, political, cultural). Lessons from the past, both revisionist history and biographical sketches of noteworthy individuals. Case studies of unique examples of the current application of libertarian/free-market principles." Length: 1,500-5,000 words. Book reviews are needed. No additional payment is made for b&w photos. Captions required.

THE SPOKESWOMAN MAGAZINE (formerly *Washington Women's Representative*), 854 National Press Bldg., Washington DC 20045. (202)347-3553. Editor: Mary Blake French. 10-15% freelance written. Emphasizes "legislative, judicial and political actions by and affecting women at federal, state, and local levels for professionals and women activists of all ages and occupations." Monthly magazine; 16-24 pages. Estab. 1970. Circ. 8,000. Pays on publications. Buys all rights, but may reassign following publication. Phone queries OK. Submit seasonal/holiday material 4 weeks in advance of issue date. Simultaneous and photocopied submissions OK. SASE. Reports in 2 weeks. Free sample copy and writer's guidelines; mention *Writer's Market* in request.
Nonfiction: Expose ("we are looking for the inside story on any governmental or political action affecting women; just the facts, no opinion"); general interest (innovative government or political actions; stories on the group or individual who has adopted new strategies to bring about change); interview (occasionally if interpretive); and profile (interpretive). "We do not want personal opinion pieces. Our emphasis is on current news of national interest." Buys 1-2 mss/issue. Query. Length: 750-1,500 words. Payment negotiable.
Columns/Departments: "We currently run a monthly syndicated column by Ellen Goodman and are considering the development of other regular features written by freelancers. Writers must be experts in the fields they write about. We are open to ideas for regular features."

THIS MAGAZINE, Red Maple Publishing Co., Ltd., 70 The Esplanade, 3rd floor, Toronto, Ontario, Canada M5E 1R2. (416)364-2431. Managing Editor: Lorraine Filyer. 40% freelance written. Emphasizes Canadian education, culture and politics for a well-educated readership of teachers, professors, students, radicals, union leaders and community workers. Bimonthly magazine; 48 pages. Estab. 1966. Circ. 6,000. Pays on publication. Buys all rights, but may reassign following publication. Pays 50% kill fee. Byline given. Submit seasonal/holiday material 3 months in advance of issue date. SAE and International Reply Coupons. Reports in 2 months. Free sample copy; mention *Writer's Market* in request.
Nonfiction: Humor (add a bit of it to everything); historical (analysis of political events, labour events, etc.); interview (with people making important contributions to the Canadian experience); personal opinion (on any field: labor, education, culture); photo feature (include

300-500 words); and in-depth analysis on matters relating to the Canadian experience i.e., Canada and the Third World, Canada's economy, etc. Buys 4 mss/issue. Submit complete ms. Length: 2,000-3,500 words. Pays $25-50.

Photos: Submit photos with accompanying ms. Pays $15 for b&w glossy prints. Captions preferred. Buys one-time rights.

Fiction: Adventure; experimental; fantasy; humorous, mystery; science fiction; and suspense. Buys 1 ms/issue. Submit complete ms. Length: 2,000-3,500 words. Pays $25-50.

TIME, Rockefeller Center, New York NY 10010, Staff-written.

US NEWS & WORLD REPORT, 2300 N St. NW, Washington DC 20037. "We are presently not considering unsolicited freelance submissions."

WASHINGTON MONTHLY, 1611 Connecticut Ave. NW, Washington DC 20009. Editor: Charles Peters. For "well-educated people interested in politics and government; well-read." Monthly. Circ. 30,000. Rights purchased depend on author and material. Buys all rights or first rights. Buys 40 mss/year. Pays on publication. Sample copy $2.25. Sometimes does special topical issues. Query or submit complete ms. Tries to report in 2-4 weeks. SASE.

Nonfiction and Photos: Responsible investigative or evaluative reporting about the US government, business, society, the press and politics. Length: "average 2,000-6,000 words." Pays 5-10¢/word. Buys b&w glossy prints.

WORLD POLITICS, Corwin Hall, Princeton NJ 08540. Editors: Cyril E. Black, Gerald Garvey and Henry S. Bienen. Issued quarterly to academic readers in social sciences. Pays on publication. Buys all rights. Reports in 1-6 months. SASE.

Nonfiction: Uses articles based on original scholarly research on international aspects of the social sciences. Mss should be double-spaced throughout (including footnotes), and have wide margins. Footnotes should be placed at the end of article. Length: 3,000-5,000 words. Pays $50.

WORLDVIEW, 170 E. 64th St., New York NY 10021. Phone: (212)8384120. Managing Editor: Susan Woolfson. For "the informed and concerned reader who insists that discussion of public issues must take place within an ethical framework." Monthly. Buys all rights. Pays on publication. Study the magazine and query first.

Nonfiction: Articles on public issues, religion, international affairs, world politics and "moral imperatives." "The editors believe that any analysis of our present cultural and political problems which ignores the moral dimension is at best incomplete—at worst, misleading. *Worldview* focuses on international affairs, puts the discussion in an ethical framework, and relates ethical judgment to specifically religious traditions." Article length: 2,500-5,000 words; "Excursus," 300-1,000 words; Book reviews; 1,000 words. Payment depends on length and use of material.

How To Break In: "Short pieces for the 'Excursus' section must be as well written and have the same degree of ethical orientation as the longer ones, but it is one way to break in. Book reviews are also a possibility. If a writer sends some samples of previous work and a list of the types of literature he is interested in, we might try him out with an assignment, though with the understanding it is on speculation."

Puzzle

This category includes only those publications devoted entirely to puzzles. The writer will find many additional markets for crosswords, brain teasers, acrostics, etc., by reading the *Filler* listings throughout the Consumer, Trade and Company Publications sections of this book. Especially rich in puzzle markets are the Religious, Juvenile, Teen and Young Adult, and General Interest classifications in the Consumer section.

JO-GO CO., Box 1086, Reseda CA 91335. Editor: Joanne Goldstein. General puzzle books for all ages. Bimonthly magazines; 64 pages. Estab. 1975. Circ. 145,000. Pays on publication. Buys all rights. SASE. Free puzzle guidelines.

Puzzles: Crossword, word quests, varieties, fill-ins and other types. Query. Pays $5-10.

OFFICIAL CROSSWORDS, DELL CROSSWORDS, POCKET CROSSWORDS, DELL WORD SEARCH PUZZLES, DELL PENCIL PUZZLES AND WORD GAMES, DELL

CROSSWORD ANNUALS, DELL CROSS WORD PUZZLES, PAPERBACK BOOK SERIES, DELL PUZZLE PUBLICATIONS, 245 E. 47th St., New York NY 10017. Editor: Kathleen Rafferty. For "all ages from 8-80—people whose interests are puzzles, both crosswords and variety features." Buys all rights. SASE.
Puzzles: "We publish puzzles of all kinds, but the market here is limited to those who are able to construct quality pieces which can compete with the real professionals. See our magazines. They are the best guide for our needs. We publish quality puzzles, which are well-conceived and well-edited, with appeal to solvers of all ages and in about every walk of life. We are the world's leading publishers of puzzle publications and are distributed in many countries around the world in addition to the continental US. However, no foreign language puzzles, please! Our market for crosswords and anacrostics is very small, since long-time contributors supply most of the needs in those areas. However, we are always willing to see material of unusual quality, or with a new or original approach. Since most of our publications feature variety puzzles in addition to the usual features, we are especially interested in seeing quizzes, picture features, and new and unusual puzzle features of all kinds. Please do not send us remakes of features we are now using. We are interested only in new ideas. Kriss Krosses are an active market here. However, constructors who wish to enter this field must query us first before submitting any material whatever. Prices vary with the feature, but ours are comparable with the highest in the general puzzle field."

ORIGINAL CROSSWORD, EASY-TIMED CROSSWORD'S, 575 Madison Ave., New York NY 10022. (212)838-7900. Editorial Director: Arthur Goodman. Bimonthly. Buys all rights. Pays on acceptance. Refer to current issue available on newsstand as guide to type of material wanted. Submissions must be accompanied by self-addressed, stamped envelope for return.
Puzzles: Original adult crossword puzzles; sizes 15x15 and 13x13; medium and not hard. Same requirements for diagramless, but 15x15 irregular patterns only. Pays $7-15.

SOLVE A PUZZLE, Armor Publishing Co., 120 E. 56th St., New York NY 10022. Editor: Ann MacHarris. Associate Publisher: H.D. Birns. For "a cross-section of the adult American public from 20-70 years old, with the emphasis on women over 40 years old. The average reader has a high school education." Bimonthly magazine; 64 pages. Estab. 1978. Pays on acceptance. Buys all rights. Submit seasonal/holiday material 5 months in advance. SASE. Reports in 6 weeks. Sample copy 75¢; guidelines free.
Puzzles: Word-find puzzles (also called hidden words, search-a-words, find-a-words). Submit themes and word lists. Plus crosswords and all sorts of variety pubbles. Buys 70-80 word-find puzzles/issue. Queries welcome.

Regional

General interest publications slanted toward residents of and visitors to a particular region are listed below. Because they publish little material that doesn't relate to the area they cover, they represent a limited market for writers who live outside their area. Many buy manuscripts on conservation and the natural wonders of their area; additional markets for such material will be found under the City, Nature, Conservation, and Ecology, and Sport and Outdoor headings.

Publications that report on the business climate of a region are grouped in the regional division of the Business and Finance category. Newspapers and weekly magazine sections, which also buy material of general interest to area residents, are classified separately under that category heading.

ADIRONDACK LIFE, Box 137, Keene NY 12942. Editor-in-Chief: Bernard R. Carman. Emphasizes the Adirondack region of New York State for a readership aged 30-60, whose interests include outdoor activities, history, and natural history directly related to the Adirondacks. Bimonthly magazine; 64 pages. Estab. 1970. Circ. 42,000. Pays on publication. Buys all rights, but may reassign following publication. Pays 20% kill fee. Byline given. Submit seasonal/holiday material 4 months in advance. Previously published book excerpts OK. SASE. Reports in 4 weeks. Sample copy $1; free writer's guidelines.
Nonfiction: Historical (Adirondack relevance only); how-to (should relate to activities and lifestyles of the region, e.g., how to make your own maple syrup); informational (natural history of the region); interview (Adirondack personalities); personal experience; photo feature (Adirondack relevance required); profile; and travel (Adirondacks only). Buys 6-8 mss/issue.

Query. Length: 1,500-3,500 words. Pays $125-225.

Photos: Purchased with or without mss or on assignment. Captions required (Adirondacks locale must be identified). Submit contact sheet or transparencies. Pays $10 for 8x10 glossy, semi-glossy or matte photos; $25-50 for 35mm or larger color transparencies, $100 for covers.

How To Break In: "Start with a good query that tells us what the article offers—its narrative line and, most importantly, its relevance to the Adirondacks. We tolerate all sorts of aberrations at least once. The exception: failure to determine what the magazine is all about. At the risk of being tiresome, let me repeat again: it's all about the Adirondacks, broadly conceived—and not about anything else."

THE ALASKA JOURNAL, Alaska Northwest Publishing Co., Box 4-EEE, Anchorage AK 99509. (907)243-1723. Managing Editor: Marty Loken. 90% freelance written. Quarterly magazine; 96 pages. Estab. 1971. Circ. 10,000. Pays on publication. Buys first North American serial rights. Byline given. SASE. Reports in 4 weeks. Sample copy $1.

Nonfiction: Contemporary affairs and history (Alaska, Northern Canada, Arctic), and articles on Northern art and artists, present and past. Buys 30-36 mss/year. Query. Length: 1,000-6,000 words. Pays on publication; contact editors for rates and details.

Photos: Purchased with accompanying ms. Captions required.

ALASKA MAGAZINE, Box 4-EEE, Anchorage AK 99509. Managing Editor: Marty Loken. 80% freelance written. Monthly magazine. Pays on publication. Buys first North American serial rights. Byline given. SASE.

Nonfiction and Photos: *"Alaska Magazine's* subtitle is 'The Magazine of Life on the Last Frontier,' and, as implied, our interests are broad. We're heavy on sharp color photographs of Alaska and northwestern Canada, buying about 1,000 transparencies each year, and rely heavily on freelance writers. Feature subjects include backpacking, resource management, sport fishing, wildlife encounters, kayaking and canoeing, trapping, cross-country skiing, snowshoeing, hunting, travel in Alaska, commercial fisheries, Native affairs, mining, arts and crafts, mountaineering, bush-country life, profiles of Alaskans, history, town profiles, and wilderness photo essays. Manuscripts may run up to about 4,000 words, but we prefer shorter photo-illustrated pieces in the 1,000- to 2,000-word range. Rates for illustrated material range from $50-400, depending on length."

Photos: "Photos should ideally be Kodachrome slides—no duplicates, please—with attention given to sharpness. One-time rates are $100 for covers, $75 for 2-page spreads, $50 for full-page; and $25 for half-page. We also purchase photos outright for $150, providing a duplicate slide for the contributor's files.

Columns/Departments: "Regular monthly features include full-page color photos, letters, book reviews, personality profiles, bush-living tips, and short factual stories on Alaskan creatures."

ALOHA, THE MAGAZINE OF HAWAII, Coral Publishing Co., Box 3404, Honolulu HI 96813. Editor: Rita Witherwax. For those who have been to Hawaii or those who would like to know more about Hawaii; new places to stay, eat or visit. Bimonthly magazine; 112 pages. Estab. January 1978. Circ. 75,000. Pays on publication. Buys all rights. Byline given. Submit seasonal/holiday material 8 months in advance. Photocopied submissions OK. SASE. Reports in 6 weeks. Sample copy $2.

Nonfiction: Art, business, historical, interview, personal experience, photo feature, profile, sports and travel. "All articles must have a Hawaii-related look. Please no articles on impressions of romantic sunsets or articles aimed at the tourist." Buys 12 mss/issue. Query or send clips of published work. Length: 1,500-4,000 words. Pays 10¢/word.

Photos: State availability of photos. Pays $25 for 8x10 b&w glossy prints; $50 for color transparencies or $150 for covers. Buys exclusive rights. Captions and model releases required.

Fiction: "Any type of story as long as it has a Hawaii-related theme." Buys 1 ms/issue. Send complete ms. Length: 4,000 words maximum. Pays 10¢/word.

Poetry: Free verse, haiku and traditional. Buys 4-6 poems/year. Submit no more than 6. Pays $25.

ARIZONA HIGHWAYS, 2039 W. Lewis Ave., Phoenix AZ 85009. (602)258-6641. Editor: Tom. C. Cooper. "We are drastically overstocked on copy and photos."

BACK HOME IN KENTUCKY, Cockrel Corp., Box 645, Bowling Green KY 42101. (502)781-2249. Editor: Clement Cockrell. To inform and entertain those having roots or interest in the Bluegrass State. Bimonthly magazine; 40 pages. Estab. May 1977. Circ. 10,000. Pays on publication. Buys all rights. Submit seasonal/holiday material 1 month in advance. SASE, Reports in 4 weeks. Sample copy $1.

Nonfiction: Historical (Kentucky events); interviews (famous Kentuckians); new product; nostalgia (Kentucky living); photo features (Kentucky locations and events); and travel. "We consider only articles dealing with Kentucky heritage." Buys 2 mss/issue. Query. Length: 5 typed pages. Pays $10/typed page, doubled spaced.
Photos: Send photos with ms. Pays $5 for 5x7 b&w prints; pay varies for 2¼x2¼ color transparencies. Captions preferred; model releases required.

BAJA CALIFORNIA BULLETIN, J L Publications, Apdo. Postal 127, La Paz, Baja California Sur, Mexico. Co-Editors: Luisa Porter, Jerry Klink. Emphasizes tourism in Baja California. Bimonthly magazine; 32 pages. Estab. 1972. Circ. 10,000. Pays on acceptance. Buys one-time rights. Pays 100% kill fee. Byline given. Submit seasonal/holiday material 4 months in advance of issue date. Previously published submissions OK. SASE. Reports in 4 weeks. Sample copy $1.
Nonfiction: Historical (Pre-Columbian Baja California and Baja Indian lore, mission stories, revolutionary highlights); how-to (and where-to on camping, scuba-diving, shopping for bargains); humor (anything humorous about travel in Baja, but nothing about poverty); informational (towns visited, off-beat areas); interview (with famous person who travels in Baja California, related to his experiences on the peninsula); nostalgia (Baja in earlier times, personal experience only); and photo feature (sports, bullfights, off-road racing, boat racing); and animal and plant life of Baja. Buys 12 mss/year. Submit complete ms. Length: 500-1500 words. Pays $15-35.
Photos: Purchased with accompanying ms, no additional payment. Submit 5x7 or larger b&w prints. Captions optional.

BAJA TIMES, Editorial Playas De Rosarito, S.A., Rosarito Beach Hotel Shopping Center III, Rosarito Beach, Baja California. Editor: Hugo Torres. About travel in Baja for Americans visiting or living in northern Baja California, Mexico. Semimonthly tabloid; 16 pages. Circ. 5,000. Byline given. Pays on acceptance. Makes assignments on a work-for-hire basis. Submit seasonal/holiday material 3 months in advance. Simultaneous, photocopied and previously published submissions OK. Reports in 2-3 weeks. Free sample copy.
Nonfiction: Historical (Baja and the missions); travel (in Baja); and personal experience (while visiting Baja). Buys 2 mss/issue. Send complete ms. Length: 300-700 words. Pays $30-60.
Photos: Send photos with ms. Pays $4-20 for b&w. Captions required. Buys one-time rights.

BEND OF THE RIVER MAGAZINE, Box 239, Perrysburg OH 43551. (419)874-1691. Publishers: Christine Raizk Alexander, Lee Raizk. For readers interested in history, antiques, etc. Monthly magazine; 24 pages. Estab. 1972. Circ. 2,000. Usually buys all rights, but will reassign rights to author after publication. Byline given. Buys 50-60 mss/year. Pays on publication. Sample copy 25¢. No photocopied or simultaneous submissions. Submit seasonal material 2 months in advance; deadline for holiday issue is October 15. Reports in 2 months. Submit complete ms. SASE.
Nonfiction and Photos: "We deal heavily in Ohio history. We are looking for articles about modern day pioneers, doing the unusual. Another prime target is the uplifting feature, spiritual and/or religious sketch or interview. Don't bother sending anything negative; other than that, we can appreciate each writer's style. We'd like to see interviews with historical (Ohio) authorities; travel sketches of little-known but interesting places in Ohio; grass roots farmers; charismatic people. Nostalgic pieces will be considered. Our main interest is to give our readers happy thoughts. We strive for material that says 'yes' to life, past and present." Length: 1,500 words. Pays $5 minimum. Purchases b&w photos with accompanying mss. Pays $1 minimum. Captions required.
How To Break In: "Any Toledo-area, well-researched history will be put on top of the heap! Send us any unusual piece that is either cleverly humorous, divinely inspired or thought provoking. We like articles about historical topics treated in down-to-earth conversational tones."

BLUENOSE MAGAZINE, Box 580, Port Maitland, Nova Scotia, Canada B0W 2V0. (902)649-2789. Editor-in-Chief: Bill Crowell. Managing Editor: Frances Crowell. 75% freelance written. Quarterly magazine; 50 pages. Estab. 1976. Circ. 3,000. Pays on acceptance. Buys first North American serial rights. Submit seasonal/holiday material 6 months in advance of issue date. SASE. Reports in 3 months. Sample copy $1; free writer's guidelines.
Nonfiction: How-to (environmental, gardening, energy alternatives); historical (regional); interview (Bluenose character); new product (regional, craft-related); and nostalgia (regional). Buys 48 mss/year. Query or submit complete ms. Length: 500-1,500 words. Pays 1¢/word.
Photos: "No payment for non-copyrighted work except by arrangement." Pays $2.50-5 for any

size b&w prints. Captions preferred. Buys one-time rights.
Fiction: Historical; humorous; and nostalgia. Buys 4 mss/year. Submit complete ms. Length: 1,500 words maximum. Pays 1¢/word.
Poetry: Free verse; haiku; light verse; and traditional. Buys 16/year. Length: 5-10 lines. Pays $3-7.

BROWARD LIFE, Brenda Publishing Co., 3081 E. Commercial Blvd., Fort Lauderdale FL 33308. (305)491-6350. Editor-in-Chief: Joanne Myers. 50% freelance written. Emphasizes leisure activities in Broward County. Monthly magazine; 72 pages. Estab. 1974. Circ. 15,000. Pays on publication. Buys all rights, but may reassign following publication, or first North American serial rights. Pays 20-25% kill fee. Byline given "except if there is a lot of rewriting or research." Phone queries OK. Submit seasonal/holiday material 1 month in advance. Simultaneous, photocopied and previously published submissions OK. SASE. Reports in 6 weeks. Sample copy for $1.25.
Nonfiction: Expose (must pertain to persons or events in Broward County); how-to (must appeal to high-income lifestyles); interview (Broward County-oriented); profile (Broward County resident); travel; new product; and photo feature. Buys 2 mss/issue. Submit complete ms. Length: 1,000-3,000 words. Pays $25-200. "We will consider students' work for credit only. Writers previously published in other magazines will be given preference."
Photos: Purchased with accompanying ms or on assignment. Pays $5-50 for b&w or 35mm color transparencies. Query or send contact sheet. Model release required.

CALIFORNIA BUSINESS, Box 4360, Burbank CA 91503. (213)843-2121. Editor: Mike Harris. Emphasizes Western business for business executives, businessmen, market analysts, etc. Monthly magazine. Pays on publication. Buys first rights. Pays negotiable kill fee. Byline usually given. Simultaneous submissions OK. SASE. Reports in 4-6 weeks. Sample copy $1; SASE for writer's guidelines.
Nonfiction: "General business pieces both with California/Western states focus. We also do trends for industries, company features and an occasional piece on business men and women who've done something unique or have something to say relating to their field of expertise." Buys 2-3 mss/issue. Query. Length: 1,000-2,000 words. Pays $200-350.
Photos: State availability of photos. Pay negotiable for b&w prints and color transparencies. Casptions and model releases required.

CANADIAN GOLDEN WEST MAGAZINE, Box 3720, Station D., Calgary, Alberta, Canada T2M 4M4. (403)282-9181. Editor: Pat Donaldson. For residents and visitors to Western Canada. Magazine; 40-48 pages. Estab. 1965. Quarterly. Circ. 16,270. Buys first North American serial rights. Buys about 50 mss/year. Pays on acceptance. Will send free sample copy to writer on request. Submit seasonal material 3 months in advance. Reports in 4 weeks. SAE and International Reply Coupons.
Nonfiction and Photos: Uses Canadian writers only. "Emphasis on the history, fine arts, people, places and opinions of western Canada; well-illustrated with b&w photos. No Wild West cowboy and Indian stuff!" Prefers informal, relaxed writing in third-person, but first-person narratives considered if the writer was personally involved in an event of major importance. "Golden Notes" features true anecdotes and original humor. Pays $5-15 for 100-600 words. Indian stories accepted only if they are written by Indians. Would like to see personality profiles on public figures. "The magazine, published 5 times/year, likes to run material that corresponds to the seasons—historical slant appreciated." Length: 1,000-3,000 words. Pays 3-5¢/word. "Regular contributors are paid more, as are writers who have done original historical research." Photos purchased with mss with no additional payment. Captions optional, but some explanation preferred.
Fiction and Fillers: Buys fiction with western Canadian slant. Will consider mystery, suspense, adventure, Western, science fiction and historical. Buys 1 ms/issue. Pays 1-5¢/word. "Average article is paid 3¢/word." Will consider fillers with Canadian slant. Buys crossword and word puzzles, jokes, gags, anecdotes, and short humor. Pays $5-15.

CASCADES EAST, 1230 NE 3rd St., Bend OR 97701. (503)382-0127. Editor: Geoff Hill. 20% freelance written. For "all ages as long as they are interested in outdoor recreation in Central Oregon: fishing, hunting, sight-seeing, hiking, bicycling, mountain climbing, backpacking, rockhounding, skiing, snowmobiling, etc." Quarterly magazine; 48 pages. Estab. May 1976. Circ. 10,000. Pays on publication. Buys all rights, but may reassign following publication. Byline given. Submit seasonal/holiday material 6 months in advance of issue date. SASE. Reports in 4 weeks. Sample copy $1.
Nonfiction: General interest (first-person experiences in outdoor Central Oregon—with photos,

can be dramatic, humorous or factual); historical (for feature, "Little Known Tales from Oregon History," with photos); and personal experience (needed on outdoor subjects: dramatic, humorous or factual). "No articles that are too general, sight-seeing articles that come from a travel folder, or outdoor articles without the first-person approach." Buys 1-2 mss/issue. Query. Length: 1,000-3,000 words. Pays 3-4¢/word.

Photos: "Old photos will greatly enhance chances of selling a historical feature. First-person articles need black and white photos, also." Pays $5-10 for b&w; $15-50 for color transparencies. Captions preferred. Buys one-time rights.

CENTRAL FLORIDA SCENE MAGAZINE, Box 7624, Orlando FL 32854. Editor: Nancy N. Glick. Emphasizes people, local concerns, fashion, dining, entertainment, gardening and sports for Central Floridians. Magazine published 8 times/year. Pays on publication. Buys all rights. Byline given. Previously published work OK. SASE. Reports in 2-3 weeks. Sample copy $1.50.

Nonfiction: Personality features on Central Floridians, national personalities who have a Central Florida tie-in, investigative reporting on a topic of interest to Floridians, financial articles, sports, fashion, and interior decorating. "All articles should have a Central Florida connection." Send complete ms. Length: 1,000-3,000 words. Pays $25-100.

Photos: Send photos with ms; offers additional payment of $5 for b&w glossy prints or color transparencies. Captions preferred. Model releases required.

CHESAPEAKE BAY MAGAZINE, 130 Severn Ave., Annapolis MD 21403. (301)263-2662. Editor: Betty D. Rigoli. 45% freelance written. *"Chesapeake Bay Magazine* is a regional publication for those who enjoy reading about the bay and its tributaries. Our readers are yachtsmen, boating families, fishermen, ecologists—anyone who is part of Chesapeake Bay life." Monthly magazine; 56-64 pages. Estab. 1971. Circ. 16,000. Pays either on acceptance or publication, depending on "type of article, timeliness and need." Buys all or first North American serial rights. Submit seasonal/holiday material 3 months in advance of issue date. Simultaneous (if not to magazines with overlapping circulations) and photocopied submissions OK. SASE. Reports in 1 month. Sample copy $1.25; writer's guidelines for SASE; mention *Writer's Market* in request.

Nonfiction: "All material must be about the Chesapeake Bay area—land or water." How-to (fishing, hunting, and sports pertinent to Chesapeake Bay); general interest; humor (welcomed, but don't send any 'dumb boater' stories where common safety is ignored); historical; interviews (with interesting people who have contributed in some way to Chesapeake Bay life: authors, historians, sailors, oystermen, etc.); nostalgia (accurate, informative and well-paced. No maudlin ramblings about 'the good old days'); personal experience (drawn from experiences in boating situations, adventures, events in our geographical area); photo feature (with accompanying ms); profile (on natives of Chesapeake Bay); technical (relating to boating, hunting, fishing); and Chesapeake Bay Folklore. "We do not want material written by those unfamiliar with the Bay area, or general sea stories. No personal opinions on environmental issues." Buys 3 mss/issue. Query or submit complete ms. Length: 1,000-2,500 words. Pays $45-85.

Photos: Susan Dippel, art director. Submit photo material with ms. Uses 8x10 b&w glossy prints; pays $50 for 35mm, 2¼x2¼ or 4x5 color transparencies used for cover photos; $15/color photos used inside. Captions required. Buys one-time rights with reprint permission. Model release required.

Fiction: "All fiction must deal with the Chesapeake Bay, and be written by persons familiar with some facet of bay life." Adventure; fantasy; historical; humorous; mystery; and suspense. "No general stories with Chesapeake Bay superimposed in an attempt to make a sale." Buys 8 mss/year. Query or submit complete ms. Length:' 1,000-2,500 words. Pays $45-85.

Poetry: Attention: Poetry Editor. Free verse or traditional. "We want well-crafted, serious poetry. Do not send in short, 'inspired' sea-sick poetry or 'sea-widow' poems." Buys 6/year. Limit submissions to batches of 4. Length: 5-30 lines. Pays $10-20.

How To Break In: "We are a regional publication entirely about the Chesapeake Bay and its tributaries. Our readers are true 'Bay' lovers, and look for stories written by others who obviously share this love. We are particularly interested in material from the Lower Bay (Virginia) area and the Upper Bay (Maryland-Delaware) area."

COAST, Box 2448, Myrtle Beach SC 29577. Managing Editor: Karen Dover. For tourists to the Grand Strand. Magazine; 180 pages. Estab. 1955. Weekly. Circ. 17,500. Buys all rights. Byline given "only on feature stories." Buys 5-6 mss/year. Pays on acceptance. Free sample copy. Will consider photocopied and simultaneous submissions. Reports in 60-90 days. Query. SASE.

Nonfiction and Photos: "Timely features dealing with coastal activities and events, and an occasional historical article related to the area. Submit an idea before a manuscript. It should be directly related to this coastal area. No vague, general articles." Emphasis is on informational and historical articles. Length: 800-1,000 words. Pays $25-30. B&w photos purchased with mss. Prefers 5x7. Pays $5-10 for b&w. Buys some color for editorial purposes. Must relate to area. Pays $15-25.

COASTLINE MAGAZINE, Box 914, Culver City CA 90230. Editor/Publisher: Robert M. Benn. For audience in major urban complexes; age 24-48. Quarterly magazine; 64 pages. Estab. 1973. Rights purchased vary with author and material. May buy all rights, with the possibility of reassigning rights to author after publication; first North American serial rights, first serial rights, or second serial (reprint) rights. Pays on publication. Sample copy $2; free writer's guidelines. Photocopied submissions OK. Reports in 3-7 weeks. Query. SASE.
Nonfiction: Department Editor: Stephen Lawrence Berger. Will consider mss about regional lifestyles, investigative articles (municipal to international); socially significant trends in the arts (reviews, columns, events); and expanded print/electronic media-related mss. Establishment, avant-garde approach. Writer should study sample copy and contributor guidelines before submitting. Favors regional artists and writers. "We favor in-depth over gimmick and consider all, not merely a portion of our region." Interested in nonspecific promotion of travel, restaurants and specific city cultural events. Length: 400-6,000 words. Pays $10-600. Length preferred for regular columns: 200-300 words. Pays $45 minimum.
Photos: Contact: Art Director. Purchased with ms with extra payment, without ms, or on assignment. Captions required. B&w only. Pays $5-25. Size: 8x10 b&w glossy prints or very clear 35mm transparencies.
Fiction and Poetry: Poetry Editor: Charles Price. Uses "significant fiction (especially novel excerpts); and major poetry tied in with West Coast slant." Buys experimental, mainstream, erotica, science fiction, humorous, historical, condensed novels and serialized novels. Length: 500-4,000 words. Pays $25 minimum. Buys blank verse, free verse, traditional forms, and avant-garde forms of poetry. Length: 4-50 lines (2 columns wide). Pays $5-$50.

THE COLORADO EXPRESS, Box 18214, Capitol Hill Station, Denver CO 80218. Editor-in-Chief: Karl Kocivar. 80% freelance written. Emphasizes "the outdoors, travel, food, consumer information, crafts, essential living and natural sciences for educated, well-informed people of all ages who *read* rather than skim." Semianual magazine; 96 pages. Estab. 1972. Pays on publication. Buys all rights. Byline given. Submit seasonal/holiday material 6 months in advance of issue date. Simultaneous, photocopied and previously published submissions OK. SASE. Reports in 5-8 weeks. Sample copy $3.50.
Nonfiction: *"The Express* covers a wide range of interest areas. Features might fall under the headings of how-to, personal experience, nostalgia and travel all at once. They are complete to the extent that a reader must rarely feel the need to go elsewhere for more information. But should he feel that need, he can find 'elsewhere' in *the Express.* Each feature is a complete reference and each volume is designed to be kept, read and used. So timely pieces about something that happened last week are not what we're looking for. Nor are straight technical pieces. What we search for is readable, literate (but not literary) writing about almost anything educated, active people who participate in life might enjoy involving themselves with through reading. Our readers are looking for useful information that often isn't readily available through other sources. Features have included glaciers, lightning and winter camping for example; and consumer pieces on banking services and charge cards and how they work. How-to pieces should not be limited to a dozen candlemaking recipes; they should include historical and anecdotal information as well. Travel pieces shouldn't be limited to the ten best hotels in your favorite city." Buys 5 mss/issue. Submit complete ms. Length: 2,500-7,000 words. Payment varies.
Photos: Send photo mnaterial with accompanying ms. Pays $10-50 for 8x10 b&w glossy prints. Captions required. Buys all rights, but may reassign following publication.

COLORADO/MAGAZINE, Titsch Publication, Inc., 1139 Delaware Plaza, Rocky Mountain West, Denver CO 80204. (303)573-1433. Emphasizes the scenic/lifestyle Rocky Mountain West (Colorado, Wyoming, Utah, Montana, Idaho, New Mexico and Arizona only). Bimonthly magazine; 100 pages. Estab. 1965. Circ. 160,000. Pays on publication. Buys all rights (one-time rights for photos). Byline given. Submit seasonal/holiday material 3-6 months in advance. Simultaneous, photocopied and previously published submissions OK. SASE. Reports in 4 weeks. Free sample copy and writer's guidelines.
Nonfiction: How-to (Rocky Mountain flavor); informational (useful 'where-to' lifestyle); personal experience (adventure, sports, recreation); photo feature; and profiles of people who

are fascinating and from the Western states). Buys 2-3 mss/issue. Query or send complete ms. Length: 1,500-2,500 words. Pays 10¢/word.
Photos: Bonnie Macdonald, photo editor. Photos purchased with or without accompanying ms or on assignment. Captions required. Uses b&w and 35mm color photos. Total purchase price for ms includes payment for photos. Model release required. "Want photos with people involved in outdoor activities: camping, climbing, hiking, swimming, kayaking, canoeing, hangliding, ranching, etc."

COMMERCIAL WEST MAGAZINE, Financial Communications, Inc., 5100 Edina Industrial Blvd., Edina MN 55435. (612)835-5853. Editor: Thomas L.Mason. For banking and corporate executives. Weekly magazine; 40 pages. Estab. 1901. Circ. 4,700. Pays on acceptance. Byline given. Phone queries OK. Submit seasonal/holiday material 6 weeks in advance of issue date. Simultaneous and previously published submissions OK. SASE. Reports in 2 weeks. Sample copy $1; free writer's guidelines.
Nonfiction: Expose; general interest; historical; inspirational; interview; personal opinion; profile; technical; financial legislation and corporation profiles. Buys 12 mss/year. Query. Pays $3-5¢/word, 1,200 word maximum.
Photos: State availability of photos with query. Pays $25 for 5x7 b&w prints.

COMMONWEALTH, Virginia State Chamber of Commerce, 611 E. Franklin St., Richmond VA 23219. (804)643-7491. Editor-in-Chief: James S. Wamsley. Emphasizes Virginia. Monthly magazine; 48 pages. Estab. 1934. Circ. 11,000. Pays on publication. Buys all rights, but may reassign following publication. Byline given. Submit seasonal/holiday material 4 months in advance. Photocopied submissions OK. SASE. Reports in 6 weeks. Sample copy $l.
Nonfiction: Informational; historical; humor; interview; nostalgia; profile; travel; and photo feature. Buys 25-30 mss/year. Query or submit complete ms. Length: 1,200-3,000 words. Pays $75-150.
Photos: Purchased with or without accompanying ms or on assignment. Captions required. Query. Pays $5-10 for 8x10 b&w glossy prints; $50 maximum for 35mm color transparencies.
How To Break In: "Very difficult for a non-Virginian, or one not familiar with the magazine. We always need good ideas but find most outside freelancers want to provide subjects which are cliches to our readers."

CONNECTICUT MAGAZINE, 831 Black Rock Turnpike, Fairfield CT 06430. (203)576-1205. Editor: Beth Conover. Monthly magazine. Pays on publication. Buys all rights. Reports in 2 months. Sample copy $1.25.
Nonfiction: "We want only those articles which pertain specifically to Connecticut, with emphasis on service, investigative and consumer articles." Buys 30 mss/year. Query with clips of published work. Pays $50-1,000.
Photos: State availability of photos. Pays $35-75 for b&w slides; $75-200 for color slides. Captions and model releases required.
Columns/Departments: General features, Opinion and Politics. Buys 60 columns/year. Query. Length: 1,000 words minimum. Pays $100-350.

CUE NEW YORK (formerly *Cue Magazine*), 545 Madison Ave., New York NY 10022. (212)371-6900. Editor-in-Chief: Nancy Love. Emphasizes leisure and entertainment for upscale New Yorkers interested in all areas of the arts. Biweekly magazine; 128 pages. Estab. 1935. Circ. 240,000. Pays on publication. Buys first rights. Query. SASE. Reports in 4 weeks.
Nonfiction: Entertainment and service in the New York area. Query. Length: 1,000-2,500.
Photos: Query for photos. Additional payment; b&w/color. Model release required.

DELAWARE TODAY MAGAZINE, 2401 Pennsylvania Ave., Wilmington DE 19806. (302)655-1571. Editor-in-Chief: Leondard A. Quinn. 95% freelance written. Monthly magazine; 68 pages. Estab. 1962. Circ. 8,000. Pays on publication. Buys all rights, but may reassign following publication. Submit seasonal/holiday material 3 months in advance. Photocopied submissions OK. SASE. Reports in 4-6 weeks.
Nonfiction: Expose, historical, informational, inspirational, interview, new product, nostalgia, personal experience, profile, arts/crafts, hobbies and fashion. "The material must always relate to Delaware; it must have substance and holding power. Contemporary articles on social or political issues will be considered as well as consumer, ecological and economic pieces that are bright in style and locally oriented, especially in-depth, well-researched work." Buys 65 mss/year. Query or send complete ms. Length: 500-6,000 words. Pays $15-200.
Photos: Purchased with accompanying manuscript. Captions required. Pays $5-50 for b&w;

$5-50 for color. Query for photos. Total purchase price for ms includes payment for photos. Model release required.

DELAWARE VALLEY BUSINESS MAGAZINE, 611 Delsea Dr., Westville NJ 08093. Editor: Irwin Schier. Emphasizes general business-oriented and quality of life material for people in business. Articles usually require some human interest angles, for anyone in business in the Delaware Valley. Monthly magazine. Pays on publication. Buys first North American serial rights. Previously published submissions OK. SASE. Reports in 2 weeks. Sample copy $1; SASE for writer's guidelines.
Nonfiction: "New trends in business; exclusive reports on subjects relating to the business of the Delaware Valley; health and quality of life articles; once-a-month technical articles of general interest—like 'How to Sell Your Business'; a fresh look or unique prespective on area problems." Buys 5 mss/issue. Query or send clips of published work. Length: 1,500-2,000 words. Pays 3½-4½¢/word.
Photos: State availability of photos or send photos with ms. Pays up to $10 maximum for b&w or color prints. Captions preferred; model releases required.
Columns/Departments: "Depends heavily on freelance material in most departments." Buys 2 pages/issue. Length: 150-1,200 words. Pays 3½-4½¢/word.

DELTA SCENE, Box B-3, Delta State University, Cleveland MS 38733. (601)846-1976. Editor-in-Chief: Dr. Curt Lamar. Managing Editor: Ms. Susie Thomas Ranager. For an art-oriented or history-minded audience wanting more information (other than current events) on the Mississippi Delta region. Quarterly magazine; 32 pages. Estab. 1973. Circ. 700. Pays on publication. Buys one-time rights. Byline given. Submit seasonal/holiday material at least 4 months in advance. Simultaneous, photocopied and previously published submissions OK. SASE. Reports in 4 weeks. Sample copy 50¢.
Nonfiction: "Only local writers should apply." Historical and informational articles; interviews, profiles and travel articles; technical articles (particularly in reference to agriculture). "We have a list of articles available free to anyone requesting a copy." Buys 2-3 mss/issue. Query. Length: 1,000-2,000 words. Pays $5-20.
Photos: Purchased with or without ms, or on assignment. Pays $5-15 for 5x7 b&w glossy prints or any size color transparency.
Fiction: Humorous and mainstream. Buys 1/issue. Submit complete ms. Length: 1,000-2,000 words. Pays $10-20.
Poetry: Traditional forms, free verse and haiku. Buys 1/issue. Submit unlimited number. Pays $5-10.

DOWN EAST MAGAZINE, Camden ME 04843. (207)594-9544. Editor: Davis Thomas. Emphasizes Maine people, places, events and heritage. Monthly magazine; 116 pages. Estab. 1954. Circ. 70,000. Pays on acceptance for text; on publication for photos. Buys first North American serial rights. Pays 15% kill fee. Byline given. Phone queries OK. Submit seasonal/holiday material 6 months in advance. SASE. Reports in 2-3 weeks. Sample copy $1.50; free writer's guidelines if SASE provided.
Nonfiction: Submit to Manuscript Editor. "All material must be directly related to Maine: profiles, biographies, nature, gardening, nautical, travel, recreation, historical, humorous, nostalgic pieces, and photo essays and stories." Length: 600-2,500 words. Pays up to $250, depending on subject and quality.
Photos: Purchases on assignment or with accompanying ms. Each photo or slide must bear photographer's name. Captions required. Pays page rate of $50. Accepts 35mm color transparencies and 8x10 b&w. Also purchases single b&w and color scenics for calendars. Model release required.
Columns/Departments: Short travel (600-1,500 word, tightly written travelogs focusing on small geographic areas of scenic, historical or local interest); I Remember (short personal accounts of some incident in Maine, less than 1,000 words); and It Happened Down East (1- or 2-paragraph, humorous Maine anecdotes). Pay depends on subject and quality.

THE DRUMMER, 250 W. Girard Ave., Philadelphia PA 19123. Editor: Robert Cherry. Tabloid newspaper; 24 pages. Estab. 1967. Weekly. Circ. 60,000. Rights purchased vary with author and material. Usually buys all rights, but will reassign rights to author after publication. Byline given. Buys 50 mss/year. Pays on publication. Free sample copy. Will consider photocopied submissions. No simultaneous submissions. Reports "as soon as possible." Query. SASE.
Nonfiction and Photos: "Articles that, we hope, will either edify or entertain, with a decided emphasis on Philadelphia. This emphasis is most important. We like clarity and brevity and

would prefer not to see think pieces." Interview, profile, humor, expose. Length: 750-1,000 words. Pays $5-30. 8x10 b&w glossy prints purchased with or without ms. Pays $5-10.

ENCHANTMENT MAGAZINE, 614 Don Gaspar Ave., Santa Fe NM 87501. (505)982-4671. Editor: John Whitcomb. 10% freelance written. For diversified audience. Estab. 1950. Monthly. Circ. 71,000. Rights purchased vary with author and material. May buy all rights, with the possibility of returning rights to author after publication, or second serial reprint rights, or simultaneous rights. Byline given. Buys 12-15 mss/year. Pays on publication. Free sample copy. Will consider photocopied and simultaneous submissions. Reports "as soon as possible." SASE.
Nonfiction, Fiction and Photos: Buys historical features about rural New Mexico. Also occasional short stories on wide range of subjects. Length: 600-1,200 words. Pays $15 maximum. Photos purchased with accompanying ms with extra payment. Captions required. Pays $5. B&w only.

FAIRFIELD COUNTY MAGAZINE, County Communications, Inc., Playhouse Square, Box 269, Westport CT 06880. (203)227-0809. Editor-in-Chief: Elizabeth Hill O'Neil. Emphasizes regional material of interest to high-salaried, well-educated readers. Monthly magazine; 64 pages. Estab. 1954. Circ. 26,500. Pays on publication. Buys all rights. Phone queries OK. Submit seasonal/holiday material 3 months in advance. Photocopied submissions OK. SASE. Reports in 2 weeks. Sample copy $1.50.
Nonfiction: How-to, informational, historical, interview, profile and travel. "All articles should relate to readers in the Fairfield Country area which stretches from Greenwich to Danbury and includes Stamford, Bridgeport and surrounding towns." Buys 50 mss/year. Query. Length: 750-2,000 words. Pays $50-200.
Photos: State availability of photos. Pays $10 for b&w 4x6 glossy prints or contact sheets; 35mm color transparencies, $100 for cover only. Captions preferred.
Columns/Departments: Art, Books, Education, Music, Profiles and Sports. Buys 2 columns/issue. Query. Length: 750-1,500 words. Pays $50-100.

FLORIDA KEYS MAGAZINE, Island Communications, Inc., 11399 Overseas Hwy., Marathon FL 33050. (305)743-3721. Editor/Publisher: Bill Beach. 70% freelance written. "Our audience is primarily affluent, early retirees, hard-working, above-average executives and tourist-oriented folks." Quarterly magazine; 60 pages. Estab. 1977. Circ. 7,500. Pays on publication. Buys all rights, but may reassign following publication. Phone queries OK. Submit seasonal/holiday material 3 month in advance of issue date. Simultaneous and previously published (if not in conflicting area) submissions OK. SASE. Reports in 2 weeks. Sample copy 75¢.
Nonfiction: Features and articles on the Keys or similar sub-tropic living. Articles should deal with 'how-to' in this or similar areas with regard to efficient use of water and ecological topics unless specifically geared to Keys life and people. "While our articles are primarily pointed toward the Florida Keys they are not restricted to that content. For example, a how-to article on saving energy in southern California would certainly apply to us. A slice of life, especially with some humor, would do good. The watchword is *quality*. We have people for correcting breeches of the language but we do not want to see a manuscript which needs to be revised as to content." Buys 3-5 mss/issue. Query with clips of published work. "We maintain an open mind as to the length of an article. Keep in mind that the publisher is an old newspaper man. Use as many words as needed to tell the story, but don't use one damn word more than it takes." Pays 3-5¢/word.
Photos: "Photos must be of top quality for reproduction, and applicable to subject of article." State availability of photos with query. Pays $10-75 for b&w photos; $50-100 for 2¼x2¼ color transparencies. Captions preferred. Buys all rights, but may reassign following publication.
Fiction: Adventure; fantasy; historical; humorous (especially); suspense; and serialized novels. Submit complete ms. Length: 1,000-3,000 words. Pays 6¢/word.
Fillers: Short humor. Pays $10.

FOCUS/MIDWEST, 928A N. McKnight, St. Louis MO 63132. (314)991-1698. Editor/Publisher: Charles L. Klotzer. For an educated audience in Illinois, Missouri and the Midwest. Bimonthly magazine; 28-42 pages. Estab. 1962. Circ. 5,000. Buys all rights. Pays on publication. Reports in 4-6 weeks. SASE.
Nonfiction: Controversial articles; main emphasis on Illinois and Missouri. Facts, interpretation, analyses presenting political, social, cultural and literary issues on the local, regional and national scene of direct interest to the reader in or observer of the Midwest. Informational, interview, profile, think pieces. Length: open. Pays minimum of $25.

Poetry: Blank verse and free verse. Length: open. Pays minimum of $10.

FOX RIVER PATRIOT, Fox River Publishing Co., Box 54, Princeton WI 54968. (414)295-6252. Editor: Michael Jacob. For country folks of all ages. Bimonthly tabloid; 36 pages. Estab. 1976. Circ. 17,500. Pays on publication. Buys first North American serial rights and one-time rights. Byline given. Submit seasonal/holiday material 2 months in advance. Simultaneous, photocopied and previously published submissions OK. SASE. Reports in 4 weeks. Sample copy 50¢.
Nonfiction: Expose, general interest, historical, how-to, humor, interview, nostalgia, personal experience, photo feature, profile, and travel. "In general, we are a country-oriented publication—we stress environment, alternative energy technology, alternative building trendfs, farming and gardening, etc.—submissions should be in this general area." Buys 4 mss/issue. Send complete ms. Pays $5-35.
Photos: Send photos with ms. Pays $5 for 5x7 b&w prints; $5 for 5x7 color prints. Captions preferred.

GLIMPSES OF MICRONESIA AND THE WESTERN PACIFIC, Box 3191, Agana, Guam 96910. Editor-in-Chief: Ruth Ann Becker. 90% freelance written. "A regional publication for Micronesia lovers, travel buffs and readers interested in the United States' last frontier. Our audience covers all age levels and is best described as well-educated and fascinated by our part of the world." Quarterly magazine; 80 pages. Estab. 1974. Circ. 15,000. Pays on proof. Buys one-time rights. Pays 10% kill fee. Byline given. Submit seasonal/holiday material 8 months in advance. Previously published work OK. SASE. Reports in 2 weeks. Sample copy $2; free writer's guidelines.
Nonfiction: Expose (well-documented of Micronesian cover-ups; mismanagement of funds, etc.—CIA bugging is recent example); cultural examinations; historical (anything related to Micronesia and the Western Pacific that is lively and factual); interviews; personal experience ("first-person adventure as in our recently published piece about 1,000-mile open-ocean outrigger canoe trip across Micronesia"); photo features ("very photo-oriented magazine—query us on Island or Pacific themes"); profiles (of outstanding Micronesian or Western Pacific individuals—e.g., looking for Lee Marvin's relationship with Micronesia); travel (uses one/issue about areas reachable from Micronesia); scientific/nature history articles (in lay terms). Buys 30 mss/year. Query. Length: 5,000 words maximum. Pays 5¢/word.
Photos: Purchased with or without accompanying ms. Pays minimum of $10 for 8x10 b&w prints or $15 for 4x5 color transparencies or 35mm slides. Pay $200-300 for photo essays; $100 for covers. Captions required. Model release required.
Fiction: Adventure (believable; related to Micronesia); historical ("as long as it's related to our part of the world"). Buys 2 mss/year. "Most fiction is rejected because of poor quality." Submit complete ms. Length: 4,000 words maximum. Pays 10¢/word.
Poetry: "Use very little, but willing to look at Pacific-related themes to be used with photos." Only traditional forms. Pays $10 minimum.
How To Break In: "Writers living in or having first-hand experience with Micronesia and the Western Pacific are scarce. (That's because we *truly* are the United States' last frontier). Therefore, we'll work with a writer on making his manuscript suitable for publishing in *Glimpses*. If a writer has a good idea and is willing to work, we have the time to spare."

GULFSHORE LIFE, Gulfshore Publishing Co., Inc., 1039 5th Ave. N., Naples FL 33940. (813)649-9125. Editor: Merri Pate. For an upper-income audience of varied business and academic backgrounds. Published monthly, November through May. Magazine; 80 pages. Estab. 1970. Circ. 16,000. Buys all rights, with permission in writing to reproduce. Byline given. Buys 10 mss/year. Pays on publication. Will consider photocopied or simultaneous submissions. Submit seasonal material 3 months in advance. Reports in 2 months. Query. SASE.
Nonfiction: "People, sports, homes, boats; pinpointing all features to seasonal residents, year-round residents and visitors of southwest Florida. Travel, fishing and environmental articles are also used. Emphasis on "at home" life styles. Yachting, personality profiles; some historical material. Everything must be localized." Length: 500-1,000 words. Pays 5¢/word.
How To Break In: "Familiarize yourself with the magazine and the location: Naples, Marco Island, Ft. Myers, Ft. Myers Beach, Sanibel-Captiva, Whiskey Creek, Punta Gorda Isles and Port Charlotte."

HAMPTON LIFE, Box 1592, 149 Hampton Rd., Southampton NY 11968. Editor/Publisher: Andrew Boracci. "Focuses on people of The Hamptons who live most of the year from commercial fishing, farming (potatoes), duck breeding and small business. From June through

September nearly one million tourists invade and *Hampton Life* changes to meet their recreational needs: where to go, what to do, how to do it without getting arrested, etc." Monthly magazine. Estab. 1974. Circ. 15,000 (increases during summer tourist season). Pays on publication. Buys all rights. Byline given. Submit seasonal/holiday material 3 months in advance. SASE. Reports in 2-3 weeks. Sample copy $1; free writer's guidelines.

Nonfiction: Profiles, biographies, nature, gardening, restaurants, nautical, travel, recreation, historical, humorous, nostalgic pieces and photo essays and stories. "All material must be directed to either year-round Hamptons readership or summer tourists." Length: 600-2,000 words. Pay varies depending on subject and quality.

Photos: Uses 8x10 b&w prints, or 2¼x2¼, 35mm or 4x5 color transparencies. Captions and model release required.

Columns/Departments: "Staff-produced, but we will listen to theme ideas and may assign."

HIGH COUNTRY, *The Idaho Mountain Record*, Box 494, Council ID 83612. (208)253-4551. Editor-in-Chief: Leo Peurasaari. Monthly tabloid: 32 pages. Estab. 1977. Circ. 3,000. Pays on acceptance. Buys one-time rights. Phone queries OK. Submit seasonal/holiday material 3 months in advance of issue date. Simultaneous, photocopied and previously published submissions OK. SASE. Reports in 4-6 weeks. Sample copy 50¢; free writer's guidelines.

Nonfiction: Historical (we are interested in historical articles pertaining to the Old West with a new slant); how-to ("rural lost arts, 'back-to-Mother Earth-type' skills"); interviews (with local Idaho or well-known figures in the West); and offbeat and unusual inventions and products. Humor always welcome. Articles with photos have best chance. Keep in mind we are a rural magazine appealing to a rural audience. Buys 150 mss/year. Submit complete ms. Length: 400-1,500 words. Pays 5-10¢/word.

Photos: Minimum $10/8x10 b&w glossy. Captions and model release required.

Fiction: Historical, humorous and western. Buys 6 mss/year. Length: 400-1,000 words. Pays 3-10¢/word.

Poetry: Light verse, traditional and western. Buys 20/year. Limit submissions to batches of 3. Pays $2-5.

Fillers: Clippings, jokes, gags, anecdotes, newsbreaks, puzzles, short humor or unusual facts. Buys 60/year. Length: 25-200 words. Pays $2-5.

Column: Always seeking novel column ideas. 500-700 words monthly. Pays $25.

ILLINOIS ISSUES, Sangamon State University, 226 CC, Springfield IL 62708. Publisher: J. Michael Lennon. Editor: Caroline Gherardini. Emphasizes Illinois government and issues for state and local government officials and staff plus citizens and businessmen concerned with Illinois and its government (local government also). Monthly magazine; 36 pages. Estab. 1975. Circ. 6,000. Pays on publication. Buys all rights. SASE. Reports in 4 weeks. Sample copy $1.75; free writer's guidelines.

Nonfiction: How-to (use state services and processes as a citizen); informational (explaining state/local government agency in Illinois, detailing new process initiated by state legislation, city or county ordinance); interview (Illinois government or political leaders) and technical (related to government policy, services with issues stressed, e.g., energy). Buys 5 mss/issue. Query. Length: 800-2,500 words (best chance: 1,200 words). Pays 4-10¢/word.

How To Break In: "Local issues tied to state government in Illinois have a good chance, but writer must research to know state laws, pending legislation and past attempts that relate to the issue."

INLAND SHORES, Inland Shores Land Preservation Foundation, Ltd., 1135 Legion Dr., Elm Grove WI 53122. (414)784-4770. Publisher: Van B. Hooper. Editor: Marilyn Jeppesen. Emphasizes Great Lakes area travel/tourism for an affluent, leisure-oriented audience who take two or more vacation trips each year, and are interested in dining out, entertainment and recreation. Quarterly magazine; 52 pages. Estab. 1977. Circ. 55,000. Pays on publication. Buys second serial (reprint) rights. Byline given. Phone queries OK. Submit seasonal material 6 months in advance. Simultaneous, photocopied and previously published submissions OK if identified as such. SASE. Reports in 4-8 weeks. Sample copy $3; writer's guidelines free. SASE.

Nonfiction: General interest (about scenic or historical places, unusual businesses, architecture, people, etc., within the 8 states and Ontario which border the Great Lakes); historical; nostalgia; travel (interesting places to visit in Great Lakes area); personal experience (hiking, camping, sailing, skiing as it relates to the general interest reader); and photo feature (scenic or historical places in Great Lakes area). Buys 50 mss/year. Query or send complete ms. Length: 1,000-3,000 words. Pays 5¢/edited word.

Photos: Pays $10 for 8x10 glossy b&w prints; $25 for 35mm color transparencies, $50-100 for

4x5 or 8x10 color prints. Captions and model release required. Buys reprint rights.

THE IRON WORKER, Lynchburg Foundry, A Mead Co., Drawer 411, Lynchburg VA 24505. (804)847-1724. Editor-in-Chief: Patrick M. Early. 50% freelance written. Emphasizes Virginia-related history for customers and schools. Quarterly magazine; 28 pages. Estab. 1919. Circ. 9,500. Pays on acceptance. Buys all rights, but may reassign following publication. Byline given. Simultaneous and photocopied submissions OK. SASE. Reports in 6 weeks. Free sample copy and writer's guidelines.
Nonfiction: Historical (Virginia-related). "No dull, badly researched articles without a strong tie to Virginia." Buys 6 mss/year. Query. Length: 3,000-5,000 words. Pays $200-600.

KANSAS!, Kansas Department of Economic Development, 503 Kansas Ave., 6th Floor, Topeka KS 66603. (913)296-3806. Editor: Andrea Glenn. 60% freelance written. Emphasizes Kansas "faces and places for all ages, occupations and interests." Quarterly magazine; 32 pages. Estab. 1965. Circ. 28,000. Pays on acceptance. Buys one-time rights. Byline given. Submit seasonal/holiday material 6 months in advance of issue date. Simultaneous, photocopied and previously published submissions OK. SASE. Reports in 2 months. Free sample copy and writer's guidelines.
Nonfiction: "Material must be Kansas-oriented and well-written." General interest; historical; interview; nostalgia; photo feature; profile; and travel. No exposes. Buys 4 mss/issue. Query. Length: 1,000-2,000 words. Pays $75-125.
Photos: "We are a full-color photo/manuscript publication." State availability of photos with query. Pays $10-25 ("generally included in ms rate") for 35mm color transparencies. Captions required.

KENTUCKY BUSINESS LEDGER, Box 3508, Louisville KY 40201. (502)635-5212. Editor: Judith Berzof. Contributing Editor: Dot Ridings. 60% freelance written. Emphasizes Kentucky business and finance. Monthly tabloid; 32-44 pages. Estab. January 1976. Circ. 11,000. Pays on publication. Buys all rights, but may reassign following publication. Byline given at editor's option. Phone queries OK. Submit seasonal/holiday material 1 month in advance of issue date. Simultaneous, photocopied and previously published submissions OK. SASE. Reports in 2 weeks. Sample copy $1; free writer's guidelines.
Nonfiction: How-to (tips for businesses on exporting, dealing with government, cutting costs, increasing profits); interview (government officials on issues important to Kentucky businessmen); new product (new uses for coal); profile (of Kentucky businessmen); and articles on the meanings of government laws and regulations to Kentucky businesses. Buys 15-20 mss/issue. Query. Length: 1,250 words maximum. Pays $1/inch.
Photos: State availability of photos with query. Pays $5-25 for 8x10 b&w glossy prints; $10-35 for color transparencies.

MAINE LIFE, Sedgwick ME 04676. Editors: Pat and Tom Schroth. For readers of all ages in urban and rural settings. 70% of readers live in Maine; balance are readers in other states who have an interest in Maine. Monthly magazine; 56-80 pages. Estab. 1946. Circ. 25,000. Pays on publication. Buys first rights. Sample copy $1. Photocopied and simultaneous submissions OK. Submit seasonal/holiday material 2 months in advance. Reports in 1 month. SASE.
Nonfiction: Interview, profile, humor, historical, nostalgia and poetry. Buys 110 mss/year. Query. Length: 500-2,000 2,000 words. Pays $5-35.
Photos: B&w photos purchased with accompanying ms. Captions required.

METRO, THE MAGAZINE OF SOUTHEASTERN VIRGINIA, Metro Magazine, Inc., Box 1995, Norfolk VA 23501. (804)622-4122. Editor: William H. Candler. For urban adults interested in lifestyles and important issues in Southeastern Virginia. Monthly magazine; 96 pages. Estab. 1970. Circ. 20,000. Pays on publication. Buys all rights. Pays negotiable kill fee. Byline given. Phone queries OK. Submit seasonal/holiday material 6 months in advance. Photocopied and previously published submissions OK. SASE. Reports in 4-6 weeks. Sample copy $1.79; free writer's guidelines.
Nonfiction: Expose (must be related to Southeastern Virginia issues); general interest; historical (related to people and events of Virginia); how-to (on anything consumer-oriented); humor (particularly related to people and their experiences); interview (prefer interviews with Virginia-related personalities); opinion (on issues pertinent to Southeastern Virginia or issues of general interest); photo; and travel. "We do not want religious articles." Buys 10 mss/issue. Query. Length: 1,000-4,500 words. Pays $75-150.
Photos: State availability of photos. Pays $3 minimum/5x7 b&w glossy print; $5

minimum/color contact sheet; offers no additional payment for photos accompanying ms. Captions preferred; model releases required.

Columns/Departments: Arts/Entertainment; Business; History and Outdoors; Journal; and Travel (prefer inside story on popular or unusual spots any place in the world). Buys 4 columns/issue. Query. Length: 800-1,200 words. Pays $20-100.

Fiction: Adventure, experimental, fantasy, historical, humorous, mainstream, mystery, science fiction, suspense and western. "We have no preferences, as we rarely publish fiction, but we would only use outstanding pieces of fiction relative to the area or by a local author." Buys 1 ms/year. Send complete ms. Length: 1,000-4,000 words. Pays $75-250.

Fillers: Use only area-related items, such as clippings, anecdotes, newsbreaks and short humor. "No cartoons, limericks or humorous ditties, please." Buys 2/issue. Length: 10-250 words. Pays $5-25.

MISSOURI LIFE, 216 E. McCarty., Jefferson City MO 65101. (314)635-7921. Editor: W.R. Nunn. 95% freelance written. For readers whose ages range from the upper twenties to retirees; education varies from high school to PhDs. Occupations range from farmers to professionals, such as doctors, lawyers, engineers, etc. Bimonthly magazine; 56 pages. Estab. 1973. Circ. 33,000. Buys all rights, but will reassign rights to author after publication. Pays 50% kill fee. Byline given. Buys 20 mss/year. Pays on publication. Sample copy $2.50. Will consider photocopied and simultaneous submissions. Submit seasonal material 3 months in advance. Reports on material in 3 weeks. Query or submit complete ms. SASE.

Nonfiction and Photos: "Almost any kind of material if it's about Missouri or Missourians. History, travel, recreation, human interest, personality profiles, business, scenic, folklore. The emphasis is on the approach and quality. Because it is a bimonthly, *Missouri Life* must look for the different angle, the human interest, the long-lasting information and appeal, the timelessness of quality and beauty. Prospective contributors would best be guided by recent issues of *Missouri Life.*" Does not want to see "the stereotyped Ozark hillbilly piece, the travelogue with no feel of the country, the 'social message'." Seasonal material should have a different approach, with a seasonal flavor. "Back issues are the best reference." Length: 1,200-2,500 words. 8x10 b&w glossy prints and color transparencies purchased with mss. Pays $50 for ms with b&w; $75 for mss with color transparencies; more if exceptional.

MONTANA MAGAZINE, Box 5630, Helena MT 59601. (406)443-2842. Publisher: Rick Graetz. For residents of Montana and out-of-state residents with an interest in Montana. Estab. 1970. Bimomthly. Pays on publication. Byline given "on request only." Sample copy $1.25; free writer's guidelines. Will consider photocopied and simultaneous submissions. Reports in 8 weeks. Query. SASE.

Nonfiction and Photos: Articles on life in Montana; history, recreation. "How-to, where and when type articles." Limited usage of material on Glacier and Yellowstone National Park. Prefers articles on less-publicized areas. Informational, profile, think pieces, nostalgia, travel, history. Length varies. Pays $40-75 for short articles with b&w photos; $75-150 for larger articles and accompanying b&w photos. Photo size: 5x7 or 8x10. "We can make b&w photos from color transparencies at a cost of $5 each. This amount would be deducted from the fee for the article."

NEVADA MAGAZINE, Carson City NV 89710. (702)885-5416. Editor-in-Chief: Caroline J. Hadley. Managing Editor: David Moore. 50% freelance written. Bimonthly magazine; 64 pages. Estab. 1936. Circ. 55,000. Pays on publication. Buys first North American serial rights. Byline given. Phone queries OK. Submit seasonal/holiday material 4 months in advance of issue date. SASE. Reports in 2 months. Sample copy $1; free writer's guidelines.

Nonfiction: Nevada topics only. Historical, nostalgia, photo feature, people profile, recreational and travel. "We welcome stories and photos on speculation." Buys 10-15 mss/issue. Submit complete ms. Length: 500-2,500 words. Pays $75-300.

Photos: Send photo material with accompanying ms. Pays $10-50 for 8x10 glossy prints; $15-100 for color transparencies. Captions required and name and address labeled. Buys one-time rights.

NEW ALASKAN, Rt. 1, Box 677, Ketchikan AK 99901. Publisher: R.W. Pickrell. 75% freelance written. For residents of southeast Alaska. Tabloid magazine; 28 pages. Estab. 1964. Monthly. Circ. 15,000. Rights purchased vary with author and material. May buy all rights, but will reassign rights to author after publication; or second serial (reprint) rights. Byline given. Buys 40 mss/year. Pays on publication. Sample copy 50¢. Will consider photocopied submissions. Submit complete ms. SASE.

Nonfiction and Photos: Feature material about southeast Alaska. Emphasis is on full photo or art coverage of subject. Informational, how-to, personal experience, interview, profile, inspirational, humor, historical, nostalgia, personal opinion, travel, successful business operations, new product. Length: 1,000 words minimum. Pays 1½¢/word. B&w photos purchased with or without mss. Minimum size: 5x7. Pays $5 per glossy used. Pays $2.50 per negative (120 size preferred). Negatives are returned. Captions required.

Fiction: Historical fiction related to Alaska. Length: open. Pays 1½¢/word.

THE NEW ENGLAND GUIDE, Stephen W. Winship & Co., Box 1108-2 Steam Mill Ct., Concord NH 03301. (603)224-4231. Editor-in-Chief: Stephen W. Winship. Travel/vacation guide to New England. Annual magazine; 200 pages. Estab. 1958. Circ. 150,000. Pays on publication. Buys one-time rights. Deadline for queries is October 31. Reports in 2-3 weeks. Sample copy $1.90. Free writer's guidelines.

Nonfiction: Historical (New England subjects only, offbeat material preferred—"we didn't run a piece on Paul Revere's ride, but we did on the man who hung the lanterns"); humor (as an essay); informational (personal experience while traveling in New England, or a piece on a New England institution, such as antiquing, auctions, country fairs); nostalgia ("this is tricky going"); and profiles (of little known but unusual people). Buys 6 mss/issue. Query. Length: 400-700 words. Pays $40-100.

Fillers: Anecdotes "one paragraph long, short and sharp history info is preferred. These tend to have a bit of wry humor to them, and that is preferred." Buys 10 mss/year. Length: 20-110 words. Pays $10.

How To Break In: "There is such a vast reservoir of history, legend and folklore on New England that we want the more offbeat variety. We don't pan individuals, groups or hotels. Writing is to a large extent expository and sources are needed."

NEW HAMPSHIRE PROFILES, Profiles Publishing Co., 2 Steam Mill Ct., Concord NH 03301. Associate Editor: Brenda Joziahs. Editor: Arthur Gwynne. Managing Editor: Robert Sullivan. Emphasizes the state of New Hampshire for 30- to 40-year-olds in the middle-income bracket who are relatively active in enjoying sports such as skiing, etc. About a 50-50 in-state vs. out-of-state readership. Magazine published 11 times/year. 72 pages. Estab. 1951. Circ. 20,000. Pays on publication. Buys all rights, "but this may change soon." Submit anecdotes and short humor. Length: 25-150 words. Pays $10-50. SASE. Reports in 2 months. Sample copy $1.25; free writer's guidelines.

Nonfiction: General interest; historical (on little known New Hampshire characters or incidents); humor; interview; nostalgia; opinion; profile; personal experience; photo feature; arts and crafts; and interesting activities. "All should be oriented to New Hampshire; even New England is too broad an area to interest us. Except for opinion and experience pieces, we prefer articles in the third person. No general articles on how pretty the state is." Buys 7-8 mss/issue. Query with clips of published work. Length: 1,500-2,500 words. Pays $100-200.

Photos: Pays $15 for b&w 5x7 or 8x10 glossy prints; $25-50 for 2¼x2¼ or 35mm color transparencies—$150 for cover. Captions preferred; model release required if submitting for cover consideration. Buys one-time rights for color and all rights for b&w.

Columns/Departments: Last Word is a piece that closes the magazine. They want to develop this as a personal essay section on granite state topics. Buys 1 ms/issue. Send complete ms. Length: 750-900 words. Pays $100 minimum. They are open to suggestions for new columns or departments.

Fillers: "We've never used any of this, but we're open for any material."

NEW JERSEY MONTHLY, 1101-I State Rd., Princeton NJ 08540. Editor: Michael Aron. Managing Editor: Daniel Laskin. 70% freelance written. Emphasizes New Jersey interests. Monthly magazine; 100-150 pages. Estab. November 1976. Circ. 105,000. Pays on publication. Buys all rights. Submit seasonal/holiday material 4 months in advance of issue date. SASE. Reports in 6 weeks.

Nonfiction: Expose (government or any institution in New Jersey); general interest (people doing unusual things, in-depth look at situations which define a community); how-to (service pieces must cover entire state; should concentrate on living the "better" life at reasonable cost); interview (people who are living and doing something in New Jersey—something that affects our readers, as opposed to someone who is from New Jersey and hasn't lived here in years); and personal experience (only if it sheds light on something going on in the state). "We're interested in high-quality magazine writing and original thinking." Buys 4-6 mss/issue. Query. Length: 1,500-6,000 words. Pays $250-1,000.

Columns/Departments: Departments run shorter than articles and include sports, media, politics, money and others. "Also have an arts section—800- to 1,200-word pieces on a subject concerning movies, music, art, dance, and theater—no reviews, just pieces that deal with the ongoing arts scene in New Jersey." Buys 3 mss/issue. Query. Length: 1,000-2,000 words. Pays $50-200.

NEW MEXICO MAGAZINE, Bataan Memorial Bldg., Santa Fe NM 87503. (505)827-2642. Editor-in-Chief: Sheila Tryk. Associate Editors: Richard Sandoval, Scottie King. 75% freelance written. Emphasizes the Southwest, especially New Mexico, for a college-educated readership above average income, interested in the Southwest. Monthly magazine; 48-64 pages. Estab. 1923. Circ. 80,000. Pays on acceptance for mss; on publication for photos. Buys first North American serial or one-time rights for photos/compilation. Submit seasonal/holiday material 8 months in advance. SASE. Reports in 10 days to 4 weeks. Sample copy $1.25
Nonfiction: "New Mexico subjects of interest to travelers. Historical, cultural, humorous, nostalgic and informational articles." Buys 5-7 mss/issue. Query. Length: 500-2,000 words. Pays $25-300.
Photos: Purchased with accompanying ms or on assignment. Captions required. Query, or send contact sheet or transparencies. Pays $20-30 for 8x10 b&w glossy prints; $25-50 for 35mm; prefers Kodachrome; (photos in plastic-pocketed viewing sheets). Model release required. SASE.
How To Break In: "Send a superb short (1,000 words) manuscript on a little-known event, aspect of history or place to see in New Mexico. Faulty research will immediately ruin a writer's chances for the future. Good style, good grammar, please!"
Rejects: "No generalized odes to the state or the Southwest. No sentimentalized, paternalistic views of the Indians or of the Hispanos. No glib, gimmicky 'travel brochure' writing."

NEW WEST MAGAZINE, 9665 Wilshire Blvd., Beverly Hills CA 90212. (213)273-7516. Editors: Jon Carroll (Southern California), Rosalie Muller Wright (Northern California). For Californians who want to know how to live the good life in California. Publishes 26 issues/year. Buys first rights. Pays 20% kill fee. Byline given. Simultaneous submissions OK. SASE. Reports in 6 weeks. Sample copy $1.25.
Nonfiction: "Articles should be based on California—how to live well, but also hard indepth features on politics, business, crime, food, restaurants, etc.," Buys 20 mss/issue. Query with clips of published work. Length: 1,200-4,000 words. Pays $250-1,500.
Photos: State availability of photos. "We assign almost all photos." Buys first rights. Captions preferred; model releases required.
Columns/Departments: Art, Architecture, Bay Area Journal, Business, Current Fantasies, Food, Health, Law, Music, Politics, Religion, Restaurants, and Theatre." Buys 10/issue. Send complete ms. Length: 900-1,800 words. Pays $250-500.

NORTH/NORD, Northern Affairs Publications, Ottawa, Ontario Canada K1A 0H4. Editor: Robert F.J. Shannon. For a varied audience, from libraries and educational institutions to businessmen and diplomats, Canadian and international. Special issues on various special subjects in the North. Bimonthly. Estab. 1959. Circ. 19,500. Rights purchased vary with author and material. Buys full rights to publish and permit to be republished. Buys 100 mss/year. Pays on acceptance. Free sample copy and writer's guidelines. Submit seasonal material 4 months in advance. Reports in 6 weeks. Submit only complete original mss.
Nonfiction: "Subjects must pertain to Canada's north or other northern areas of the world such as Alaska and Scandinavia. Topics can include resource development (business, mining, pipeline, construction and oil and gas industries); history (exploration, archeology, fur trade); conservation (wilderness, wildlife, national parks, geology); adventure and human interest stories; the arts (folklore, sculpture, print making, etc.); life in the North (housing, transportation, education, communications, health and welfare, government, entertainments); native peoples (customs, life styles, organizations etc.); features on outstanding personalities of the North as well as northern communities." Length: 750-3,000 words. Pays $50-300.
Photos: Purchased with or without mss. "We use mainly color transparency or print film; some black and white." Pays from $10-50 for single shot; $50 for "Face of the North," a photo feature profile of a northern personality. Pays $100-200 for cover photo and center spread scenic.

NORTHERN VIRGINIAN, 127 Park St., Box 334, Vienna VA 22180. (703)938-0666. "Freelance manuscripts welcomed on speculation. B&w photos as appropriate, with mss enhances publication probability." Reports in 30 days. Free sample copy and writer's guidelines.
Nonfiction: "Particularly interested in historical articles about or related to Northern Virginia."

OHIO MAGAZINE, O Magazine, Inc., Subsidary of Dispatch Printing Co., 40 S. 3rd St.,

Columbus OH 43215. Publisher: Robert Burdock. Associate Publisher/Managing Editor: J. Porter. Emphasizes news and feature material of Ohio for an educated, urban and urbane readership. Monthly magazine; 96-156 pages. Estab. 1977. Circ. 98,776. Pays on publication. Buys all rights, second serial (reprint) rights, or one-time rights. Pays 20% kill fee. Byline given "except on short articles appearing in sections." Submit seasonal/holiday material 2 months in advance. Simultaneous, photocopied and previously published submissions OK. SASE. Reports in 8 weeks. Free writer's guidelines.

Sections: Reporter and People (should be offbeat with solid news interest; 50-250 words, pays $15-50); Short Cuts (on Ohio or Ohio-related products including mail ordering and good or people that perform a service that are particularly amusing or offbeat; 100-300 words, pays $15-20); Ohioguide (pieces on upcoming Ohio events, must be offbeat and worth traveling for; 100-300 words, pays $10-15); Diner's Digest ("we are still looking for writers with extensive restaurant reviewing experience to do 5-10 short reviews each month in specific sections of the state on a specific topic. Fee is on a retainer basis and negotiable"); Money (covering business-related news items, profiles of prominent people in business community, personal finance—all Ohio angle; 300-1,000 words, pays $50-250); Review (covering classical, jazz, rock, blues, bluegrass music; books; performing arts; visual arts; and film; 300-1,000 words, pays $50-250); and Living (embodies dining in, home furnishings, gardening and architecture; 300-1,000 words, pays $50-250). "Send submissions for Reporter People and Ohioguide sections to Michael Castranova, associate editor; Short Cuts, Living and Diner's Digest to Ellen Stein, associate editor; and Money and Review to J. Porter, managing editor.

Columns/Departments: Sports, Politics and Last Word to Michael Castranova; Media to J. Porter; and Travel, Fashion, Wine, Dining Out and Dining In to Ellen Stein. Open to suggestions for new columns/departments.

Features: J. Porter, Managing Editor. 2,000-8,000 words. Pays $250-700. Cover pieces $700-850.

Photojournalism: J. Porter, Managing Editor. Rate negotiable.

ORLANDO-LAND MAGAZINE, Box 2207, Orlando FL 32802. (305)644-3355. Editor-in-Chief: E.L. Prizer. Managing Editor: Carole De Pinto. Emphasizes central Florida information for "a readership made up primarily of people new to Florida—those here as visitors, traveling businessmen, new residents." Monthly magazine; 144 pages. Estab. 1946. Circ. 26,000. Pays on acceptance. Buys all rights, but may reassign following publication; or first North American serial rights. Byline given. Phone queries OK. Submit seasonal/holiday material 2 months in advance. Photocopied and previously published submissions OK. SASE. Reports in 6 weeks. Sample copy $1.25.

Nonfiction: Historical, how-to and informational. "Things involved in living in Florida."

How To Break In: "Always in need of *useful* advice-type material presented as first-person experience. Central Florida subjects only."

PALM BEACH LIFE, Post Office Box 1176, Palm Beach FL 33480. (305)655-5755. Managing Editor: Ava Van de Water. "*Palm Beach Life* caters to a sophisticated, high-income readership and reflects its interests. Readers are affluent . . . usually over 40, well-educated." Special issues on travel (February), the arts (March), yachting (November), and elegant living, interiors, etc. (September). Estab. 1906. Monthly. Circ. 18,000. Buys first North American rights. Pays on acceptance. Will consider photocopied submissions. Submit seasonal material 5 months in advance. Reports in 3 weeks. Query. SASE. Sample copy $1.81.

Nonfiction and Photos: Subject matter involves "articles on fashion, travel, music, art and related fields; subjects that would be of interest to the sophisticated, well-informed reader. We feature color photos, 'but are crying for good b&w.' Buys informational, interview, profile, humor, historical, think, photo and travel articles. Length: 1,000-2,500 words. Pays $100-300. Purchases photos with and without mss, or on assignment. Captions are required. Buys 8x10 b&w glossy prints at $10 each. Also buys 35mm or 2¼x2¼ transparencies and photo stories. Pay is negotiable.

PANORAMA MAGAZINE, Community Communications, 123 S. 3rd St., Rockford IL 61104. (815)964-4373. Editor: Marty Bitter. For the northern Illinois and southern Wisconsin area. Monthly magazine; 24 pages. Estab. April 1978. Circ. 8,000. Pays on publication. Submit seasonal/holiday material 2 months in advance. SASE. Reports in 1 month. Free sample copy and writer's guidelines.

Nonfiction: General interest, historical, humor, interview, nostalgia, photo feature, profile and travel. Query. Pays $20.

Photos: State availability of photos. Pays $10 for 8x10 b&w prints.

Fiction: Adventure, erotica, fantasy, historical, humorous, mainstream and serialized novels. Query. Pays $25.
Poetry: Free verse. Pays $10.

PENINSULA MAGAZINE, 260 Sheridan Ave., Palo Alto CA 94306. (415)327-6666. Editor/Publisher: Lee Oftedahl. "For alert, active and aware individuals who have a strong desire to know what's going on right in their own backyard." Monthly magazine; 66 pages. Estab. 1975. Circ. 15,000. Pays within 30 days of publication. Buys first North American serial rights. Photocopied submissions OK. SASE. Reports in 4 weeks. Free sample copy and writer's guidelines.
Nonfiction: Expose, how-to, informational, humor, profile, interview, new product, personal experience, photo feature and travel. Buys 3 mss/issue. Query or send complete ms. Length: 1,500-3,500 words. Pays 3¢/word.
Photos: Query Linda Longley, art director. Pays $5-10 for b&w 5x7 or 8x10.
Columns/Departments: Profiles—buys 3 mss/issue, 350-500 words. Notable, interesting Peninsula residents, business, professional, civic, artistic. El Camino Real—hard-to-find services and items; 250 words. Profiles; 400 words. Also vignettes, new products and services; 250 words maximum, photo and art. Query or send complete ms. Pays 15¢/word. Open to suggestions for new columns/departments; address to Dennis King or Lee Oftedahl, Publishers.
How To Break In: "All items must strictly and definitely have a real and believable Peninsula angle. We define the Peninsula as running bayside and coastside from the city/county line of San Francisco to and including San Jose."

PENNSYLVANIA ILLUSTRATED, Box 703, 17 S. 19th St., Camp Hill PA 17011. Editor-in-Chief: Pat Minarcin. 50% freelance written. Audience is 25-50 years old, mostly college-educated, interested in self-improvement, civic and state affairs, history. Bimonthly magazine; 68 pages. Estab. 1976. Circ. 110,000. Pays on publication. Buys first North American serial rights. Submit seasonal/holiday material 6 months in advance. Simultaneous, photocopied and previously published submissions not OK. SASE. Reports in 2-3 weeks. Sample copy $1.50; free writer's guidelines.
Nonfiction: Expose; how-to (any general interest subject); informational; humor; business; some historical; profile; travel; new product (made in Pennsylvania); and personal experience (unique). Buys 5-7 mss/issue. Query. Length: 250-5,000 words. Pays $25-650.
Photos: Seldom purchased with or without accompanying ms or on assignment. Captions required. Query. Pays $5-10 for 5x7 b&w glossy prints or semigloss prints; $25-50 for 2¼x2¼ color transparencies.

THE SAN GABRIEL VALLEY MAGAZINE, Miller Books, 409 San Pasqual Dr., Alhambra CA 91801. (213)284-7607. Editor-in-Chief: Joseph Miller. For upper- to middle-income people who dine out often at better restaurants in Los Angeles County. Bimonthly magazine; 52 pages. Estab. 1976. Circ. 3,400. Pays on publication. Buys simultaneous, second serial (reprint) and one-time rights. Phone queries OK. Submit seasonal/holiday material 1 month in advance. Simultaneous, photocopied and previously published submissions OK. SASE. Reports in 2 weeks. Sample copy $1.
Nonfiction: Expose (political); informational (restaurants in the valley); inspirational (success stories and positive thinking); interview (successful people and how they made it); profile (political leaders in the San Gabriel Valley); and travel (places in the valley). Buys 2 mss/issue. Length: 500-10,000 words. Pays 5¢/word.
Columns/Departments: Restaurants, Education, Valley News and Valley Personality. Buys 2 mss/issue. Send complete ms. Length: 500-1,500 words. Pays 5¢/word.
Fiction: Historical (successful people) and western (articles about Los Angeles County). Buys 2 mss/issue. Send complete ms. Length: 500-10,000 words. Pays 5¢/word.
How To Break In: "Send us a good personal success story about a valley or a California personality."

SOUTH BAY MAGAZINE, South Bay Magazine Publications, 205 Avenue 1, Suite 1, Redondo Beach, CA 90277. Editor: Sheridan Crawford. Emphasizes the coastal communities in the southwest region of LA basin: Marinadel Rey South to Long Beach. Bimonthly magazine; 96 pages. Estab. March/Arpil 1978. Circ. 30,000. Pays on publication. Buys first North American serial rights. Submit seasonal/holiday material 3 months in advance. Previously published submissions OK. SASE. Reports in 4 weeks. Sample copy $1.50.
Nonfiction: Social and political issues (referred to as investigative articles on subjects such as ecology, parenting, the economy and real estate); general interest/interview (personalities

residing in our region only, fashion people, the famous artists, athletes, scholars); historical (local harbors); how-to (live the good life, improve your environment, quality of social life, health, mind); humor (slanted toward Southern California living, not freeways or Disneyland); service pieces ("goods and services in our region"); photo feature (preferable on natural features of environment); and travel (adventure in Western US, weekends in Southern California).

Columns/Departments: Billboard (local and Southern California events, mini-reviews of plays, movies, records, books.); Profiles (people with a story; must be local); Sampler ("a melange of special products and services in our region"); and Scanner (interesting/ironic slants on local news). Send complete ms. Length: 50-500 words. Pays 5¢/word.

Poetry: Avant-garde, free verse haiku, light verse, and traditional. "No more mood poems about the ocean." Buys 1 poem/issue. Submit in batches of 5. Length: 25 words minimum. Pays $15-25.

SOUTH CAROLINA MAGAZINE, Box 89, Columbia SC 29202. (803)796-9200. Monthly. Buys all rights. Pays on publication. Reports in about 1 week. Will send free sample copy on request. SASE.

Nonfiction and Photos: Matters of interest to South Carolinians about state history, places, people, education, art, etc. Length: 500-1,000 words. Pays 3¢/word. Photos purchased with mss. Glossy prints, 8x10 or 5x7. Pays $5.

SOUTHERN EXPOSURE, Box 230, Chapel Hill NC 27514. (919)929-2141. Editor: Bob Hall. 70% freelance written. For Southerners interested in "left-liberal" political perspective and the South; all ages; well-educated. Magazine; 100 to 230 pages. Estab. 1973. Quarterly. Circ. 7,500. Buys all rights. Pays 33⅓% kill fee. Byline given. Buys 20 mss/year. Pays on publication. Will consider photocopied and simultaneous submissions. Submit seasonal material 2-3 months in advance. Reports in 1-2 months. "Query is appreciated, but not required." SASE.

Nonfiction and Photos: "Ours is probably the only publication about the South *not* aimed at business or the upper-class people; it appeals to all segments of the population. *And*, it is used as a resource—sold as a magazine and then as a book—so it rarely becomes dated." Needed are investigative articles about the following subjects as related to the South: politics, energy, institutional power from prisons to universities, women, labor, black people and the economy. Informational interview, profile, historical, think articles, expose, opinion and book reviews. Length: 6,000 words maximum. Pays $50-200. "Very rarely purchase photos, as we have a large number of photographers working for us." 8x10 b&w preferred; no color. Payment negotiable.

Fiction and Poetry: "Fiction should concern the South, e.g., black fiction, growing up Southern, etc." Length: 6,000 words maximum. Pays $50-100. All forms of poetry accepted, if they relate to the South, its problems, potential, etc. Length: open. Pays $15-200.

THE STATE, "Down Home in North Carolina," Box 2169, Raleigh NC 27602. Editor: W.B. Wright. Monthly. Buys first rights. Free sample copy. Pays on acceptance. Deadlines 1 month in advance of publication date. SASE.

Nonfiction and Photos: "General articles about places, people, events, history, nostalgia, general interest in North Carolina. Emphasis on travel in North Carolina; (devote features regularly to resorts, travel goals, dining and stopping places)." Will use humor if related to region. Length: average of 1,000-1,200 words. Pays $15-50. B&w photos purchased with mss. Pays average of $3-5.

TAR HEEL: The Magazine of North Carolina, The New East Corp., Box 7286, 1001 E. 4th St., Greenville NC 27834. (919)758-1288. Editor: James E. Wise. "Our magazine maintains a strict policy of being for and about North Carolina—its people, environment, culture and heritage; its nostalgia; and its character." Bimonthly magazine; 80-96 pages. Estab. 1972. Circ. 25,000. Pays on publication. Buys all rights, but may reassign following publication. Pays 25% kill fee. Byline given. Phone queries OK. Submit seasonal/holiday material 3-4 months in advance of issue date. Photocopied and previously published submissions OK. SASE. Reports in 2-3 weeks. Sample copy $1.50 plus 50¢ postage; free writer's guidelines.

Nonfiction: Historical (pertinent to North Carolina history, written in informal, anecdotal style); interview (by assignment); nostalgia (must have strong Carolina flavor and appeal; must be well-written, not maudlin); photo feature; profile; and travel (about North Carolina places, with emphasis on uniqueness, attraction, and atypical features). Buys 30-40 mss/year. Query or submit complete ms. Length: 200-1,500 words. Pays 4¢/published word.

Fiction: Claire Pittman, fiction editor. "Generally, a recognizably Southern, preferably a North Carolina setting is needed." Adventure; historical; humorous; mystery; romance; and

suspense. Buys 5-6 mss/year. Query or submit complete ms. Length: 1,800-2,200 words. Pays 2¢/word.
Poetry: Free verse; haiku; and traditional. Buys 2-3/issue. Length: 1 page maximum. Pays $10.

THE TOWNSHIPS SUN, The Townships Sun, Ltd., Box 28, Lennoxville, Quebec, Canada J1M 1Z3. (891)849-3543. Editor: Charles Bury. For rural English-speaking Quebec residents and those with roots in the eastern townships. Monthly newspaper; 48 pages. Estab. 1973. Circ. 5,000. Pays 2-4 weeks after publication. Buys first rights. Byline given. Phone queries OK. Submit seasonal/holiday material 2 months in advance. Simultaneous, photocopied and previously published submissions OK. SAE and International Reply Coupons. Reports in 6 weeks for queries; 2 months for mss. Sample copy $1.
Nonfiction: Expose (only of eastern townships interests); historical (eastern townships, Quebec and Canada); how-to (agriculture, gardening and handcrafts); humor, interview (local people); nostalgia; personal experience (rural living); profile (local people and Quebec political figures); regional interest (rural living); and travel. "We do not want to see articles on sex, Hollywood gossip, global politics or the usual mass-market general interest articles." Buys 5 mss/issue. Send complete ms. Length: 200-2,500 words. Pays $20-50.
Photos: Send photos with ms. Uses 5x7 b&w matte prints. Offers no additional payment for photos accompanying mss. Buys one-time rights. Captions preferred.
Poetry: Light verse and traditional. Buys 20/year. Pays $2-5.

VERMONT LIFE MAGAZINE, 61 Elm St., Montpelier VT 05602. (802)828-3241. Editor: Brian Vachon. Quarterly magazine; 64 pages. Estab. 1946. Circ. 150,000. Buys first rights. Pays 25% kill fee. Byline given. Buys 80 mss/year. "Query is essential." SASE.
Nonfiction: Wants articles on Vermont, those which portray a typical or, if possible, unique, attractive aspect of the state or its people. Style should be literate, clear and concise. Subtle humor favored. No nature close-ups or ecology stories, no Vermont dialect attempts as in "Ayup," or an outsider's view on visiting Vermont. Word length averages 1,500 words. Payment averages 10-20¢/word.
Photos: Buys photographs with mss and with captions and seasonal photographs alone. Prefers b&w contact sheets to look at first on assigned material. Color submissions must be 4x5 or 35mm transparencies. Buys one-time rights, but often negotiates for re-use rights also. Rates on acceptance; b&w, $10; color, $75 inside, $200 for cover. Gives assignments but not on first trial with photographers. Query.

WESTCHESTER ILLUSTRATED, 16 School St., Yonkers NY 10701. (914)472-2061. Editor-in-Chief: Peter Porco. Emphasizes life in Westchester County, New York, for active, sophisticated, college-educated, 25- to 49-year-old suburbanites living within the New York Metropolitan area. "Interests range from participatory sports to the safety and convenience ofWestchester's highways, from where to get the best cheesecake in the county to what our famous and not-so-famous neightors are up to." Monthly magazine; 80 pages. Estab. 1976. Circ. 37,000. Buys all rights, but may reassign following publication. Submit seasonal/holiday material 3 months in advance of issue date. Simultaneous and photocopied submissions OK. SASE. Reports in 3-5 weeks. Sample copy $1; free writer's guidelines.
Nonfiction: "*Westchester Illustrated's* essential function is to aid survival in Westchester and make life here as pleasant and hassle-free as possible. If we can entertain readers in the process, all the better. We like how-to articles, reports on new developments in county lifestyles, and profiles of local personalities and celebrities. Consumer-oriented articles receive high priority—we're always looking for fresh material that people can use—material with practical value. Other favored topics are participatory sports, home care and home design, local controversy, the arts in Westchester and feature news. We do not want personal opinion, puffery or booster pieces, travel and technical writings and articles not about Westchester County. In general we want lots of personality and color—lively writing, full of anecdotes, quotes and the sounds of smells of a subject. We want to be able to visualize scenes. Stories should demonstrate genuine reporting; we're not interested in stories or essays that read as if they were reported over the telephone." Buys about 60 mss/year. Query or submit complete ms. Length: 800-4,000 words. Pays $50-200.
Photos: Purchased with or without accompanying ms, or on assignment. Detailed captions required. Pays $10-40 for minimum 5x7 b&w glossy or matte prints. Send query and contact sheet. Model release required.
Columns/Departments: Emporium (a shopper's guide and compilation of special buys and bargains in the Westchester area—$10 for 100-150 words); Locals (profiles of prominent

Westchesterites—$25-40 for 500-1,000 words); Scoops (series of shorts in front of book which take a look at interesting, newsworthy, offbeat and humorous goings-on in Westchester—$10-25 for 100-500 words). Query or submit complete ms.

WESTCHESTER MAGAZINE, County Publications, 437 Ward Ave., Mamaruneck NY 10543. (914)698-8203. Editor-in-Chief: Vita Nelson. Emphasizes general interests in Westchester County and the metropolitan area. Monthly magazine; 96 pages. Estab. 1969. Circ. 30,000. Pays on publication. Buys all rights, but may reassign following publication. Submit seasonal/holiday material 3-4 months in advance. Simultaneous, photocopied and previously published (occasionally) submissions OK. SASE. Reports in 5 weeks. Sample copy $1.25.
Nonfiction: Expose; informational (new phenomena, attitudes, new sports, hobbies, current fads); interview; profile; new product; and personal experience (only to make a point on a broader issue). Buys 5 mss/issue. Query. Length: 2,000 words minimum. Pays $75-125.

THE WESTERN RESERVE MAGAZINE, Box 243, Garrettsville OH 44231. (216)527-2030. Editor-in-Chief: Mary Folger. Managing Editor: Betty Clapp. 40% freelance written. Emphasizes historical, where-to-go, what-to-do, crafts and collectibles for Northeastern Ohioians with an interest in the region and all it has to offer an upper middle class readership. Published 8 times/year; 64 pages. Estab. 1973. Circ. 10,000. Pays on publication. Buys all rights, but may reassign following publication.
Nonfiction: Historical (northeastern Ohio); how-to (crafts with history); and humor (if northeastern Ohio historical slant).
How To Break In: "Our goal is to help preserve the heritage of the Western Reserve. We need *good* copy and the ability to produce it is all that's needed to break in. Need both history and contemporary if the contemporary preserves local heritage."

WESTWAYS, Box 2890, Terminal Annex, Los Angeles CA 90051. (213)741-4410. Editorial Chief: Frances Ring. For "fairly affluent, college-educated, mobile and active Southern California families. Average age of head of household is 42. Monthly. Buys first rights. Byline given. Pays on acceptance for mss; on publication for most photos. Reports in 4-6 weeks. Query. SASE.
Nonfiction: "Informative articles, well-researched and written in fresh, literate, honest style." This publication "covers all states west of the Rockies, including Alaska and Hawaii, western Canada and Mexico. We're willing to consider anything that interprets and illuminates the American West—past or present—for the Western American family. Employ imagination in treating subject. Avoid PR hand-out type style and format, and please know at least something about the magazine." Subjects include "travel, history and modern civic, cultural and sociological aspects of the West; camping, fishing, natural science, humor, first-person adventure and experience, nostalgia, profiles, and occasional unusual and offbeat pieces. One article a month on foreign travel." Length: 1,000 to 2,500 words. Pays 10¢/word minimum.
Photos: Buys color and b&w photos with or without mss. Prefers 8x10 b&w glossy prints. Often publishes photo essays. Pays $25 minimum "for each b&w used as illustration;" $25 to $100 per transparency.
Poetry: Publishes 12-15 poems/year. Length: up to 24 lines; "occasionally longer." Pays $25.

WESTWORLD, Box 6680 Vancouver, British Columbia, Canada V6B 4L4. (604)732-1371. Editor-in-Chief: W.J.B. Mayrs. Assistant Editor: Elspeth Woodske. 75% freelance written. Emphasis is mainly on British Columbia, but also on Alberta, Saskatchewan and Manitoba. Bimonthly magazine; 80 pages. Estab. 1975. Circ. 224,000. Pays on publication. Buys first North American serial rights. Phone queries OK. Submit seasonal/holiday material 6-12 months in advance of issue date. Photocopied submissions OK. SAE and International Reply Coupons. Reports in 4-6 weeks. Free sample copy and writer's guidelines.
Nonfiction: General interest (should be oriented to British Columbia or western Canada oriented); historical (on British Columbia); how-to (only rarely; preferably on seasonal subjects); humor; photo feature (rarely; must be western-oriented and must include copy); travel; and informational. No US subjects. Buys 40-50 mss/year. Query or submit complete ms, or submit outline and pictures. Length: 500-2,500 words. Pays $25-250.
Photos: "No articles are used without some visual material." Submit photo material with accompanying query. No additional payment for 5x7 or larger b&w glossy prints and 35mm

color transparencies accepted with ms. Pays $10-100 for color cover photos. Captions required. Buys one-time rights. Model release required.

WINDSOR THIS MONTH MAGAZINE, Box 1029, Station A, Windsor, Ontario, Canada N9A 6P4. (519)256-7162. Managing Editor: Ron Bala. 75% freelance written. "*Windsor This Month* is mailed out in a system of controlled distribution to 18,000 households in the area. The average reader is a university graduate, middle income, and active in leisure areas." Published 12 times/year; magazine; 32-40 pages. Estab. 1974. Circ. 22,000. Pays on publication. Buys first North American serial rights. Phone queries OK. Submit seasonal/holiday material 3-4 months in advance of issue date. SASE. Reports in 4 weeks.
Nonfiction: "Windsor-oriented editorial: issues, answers, interviews, profiles, photo essays, opinion. How-to accepted if applicable to readership. Special inserts: design and decor, gourmet and travel featured periodically through the year. Buys 5 mss/issue. Query. Length: 500-5,000 words. Pays $20-75.
Photos: State availability of photos with query. Pays $10 for first-published and $5 thereafter for b&w prints. Captions preferred. Buys all rights.

WISCONSIN TRAILS, Box 5650, Madison WI 53705. (608)288-5564. Editor: Jill Weber Dean. For readers interested in Wisconsin; its natural beauty, history, personalities and recreation; and the arts. Quarterly magazine; 44 pages. Estab. 1960. Circ. 28,000. Rights purchased vary with author and material. Byline given. Buys 30-40 mss/year. Pays on publication. Free sample copy and writer's guidelines. Will consider photocopied submissions. Submit seasonal material at least 1 year in advance. Reports in 1 month. Query or send outline. SASE.
Nonfiction: "Our articles focus on some aspect of Wisconsin life; an interesting site or event, a person or industry, or history and the arts. We do not use first-person essays (reminiscences are sometimes OK), ecstasies about scenery, or biographies about people who were born in Wisconsin, but made their fortunes elsewhere. No cartoons, crosswords or fillers. Poetry exclusively on assignment." Length: 1,500 to 3,000 words. Pays $50-250, depending on length and quality.
Photos: Purchased without mss or on assignment. Captions preferred. B&w photos usually illustrate a given article. Color is mostly scenic. Pays $10 each for b&w on publication. Pays $50 for inside color; pays $100 for covers and center spreads. Transparencies; 2¼x2¼ or larger are preferred.

THE WITTENBURG DOOR, 861 6th Ave., Suite 411, San Diego CA 92101. (714)234-6454. Editors: Wayne Rice, Mike Yaconelli. For men and women, usually connected with the church. Bimonthly magazine; 36 pages. Estab. 1968. Circ. 9,100. Buys all rights, but may reassign rights to author after publication. Byline given. Buys 12 mss/year. Pays on publication. Free sample copy. Reports in 2 weeks. Query or submit complete ms. SASE.
Nonfiction: Articles on church renewal, the Christian life, book reviews, satire and humor. Length: 2,500 words maximum. Pays $15-$100.

WORCESTER MAGAZINE, 25 West St., Worcester MA 01609. (617)799-0511. Editor: Dan Kaplan. 50% freelance written. Emphasizes the central Massachusetts region. Biweekly tabloid; 48 pages. Estab. October 1976. Circ. 20,000. Pays on acceptance. Buys all rights. Byline given. Submit seasonal/holiday material 2 months in advance of issue date. Simultaneous and photocopied submissions OK. SASE. Reports in 2 weeks. Sample copy $1; free writer's guidelines.
Nonfiction: Expose (area government, corporate); how-to (concerning the area, homes, vacations); interview (local); personal experience; opinion (local); and photo feature. "We leave national and general topics to national and general publications." Buys 30 mss/year. Query with clips of published work. Length: 1,000-3,500 words. Pays $50-125.
Photos: State availability of photos with query. Pays $25-75 for b&w photos. Captions preferred. Buys all rights. Model release required.

YANKEE, Dublin NH 03444. (603)563-8111. Editor-in-Chief: Judson D. Hale. Managing Editor: John Pierce. Emphasizes the New England region. Monthly magazine; 176 pages. Estab. 1935. Circ. 750,000. Pays on acceptance. Buys all, first North American serial or one-time rights. Byline given. Submit seasonal/holiday material at least 4 months in advance.

SASE. Reports in 2-4 weeks. Free sample copy and writer's guidelines.

Nonfiction: Historical (New England history, especially with present-day tie-in); how-to (especially for "Forgotten Arts" series of New England arts, crafts, etc.); humor; interview (especially with New Englanders who have not received a great deal of coverage); nostalgia (personal reminiscence of New England life); photo feature (prefer color, captions essential); profile; travel (to the Northeast only, with specifics on places, prices, etc.); current issues; nature; antiques to look for; food. Buys 50 mss/year. Query. Length: 1,500-3,000 words. Pays $25-500.

Photos: Purchased with accompanying ms or on assignment. (Without accompanying ms for "This New England" feature only; color only). Captions required. Send prints or transparencies. Pays $15 minimum for 8x10 b&w glossy prints. $100/page for 2¼x2¼ or 35mm transparencies; 4x5 for cover or centerspread. Total purchase price for ms includes payment for photos.

Columns/Departments: New England Trip (with specifics on places, prices, etc.); Antiques to Look For (how to find, prices, other specifics); At Home in New England (recipes, gardening, crafts). Buys 10-12 mss/year. Query. Length: 1,000-2,500 words. Pays $150-350.

Fiction: Deborah Stone, fiction editor. "Emphasis is on character development." Buys 12 mss/year. Send complete ms. Length: 2,000-4,000 words. Pays $400-600.

Poetry: Jean Burden, poetry editor. Free verse and modern. Buys 3-4 poems/issue. Send poems. Length: 32 words maximum. Pays $25 for all rights. Annual poetry contest with awards of $150, $100 and $50 for 1st, 2nd and 3rd prizes.

YANKEE MAGAZINE'S GUIDE TO NEW ENGLAND, 581 Boylston St., Boston MA 02116. (617)266-0813. Editor: Sharon Smith. Emphasizes travel and leisure for a readership from New England area and from all states in the union. Biannual magazine; 160-192 pages. Estab. 1971. Circ. 110,000. Pays on acceptance. Buys first North American serial rights. Pays 40% kill fee. Byline given. Submit seasonal/holiday material 6-12 months in advance. Simultaneous and photocopied submissions OK. SASE. Reports in 2 weeks. Sample copy $1.50; free writer's guidelines.

Nonfiction: "Unusual activities, places to stay, restaurants, shops, the arts, annual events, towns or areas to visit. Strict emphasis on travel discoveries within New England. Since the *Guide* is set up on a state-by-state basis, each story must be confined to activities or attractions with a single state. Buys 15-25 mss/issue. Query. Length: 500-2,500 words. Pays $50-300.

Photos: Cynthia Shaw, assistant editor. Purchased with or without accompanying ms or on assignment. Send contact sheet or transparencies plus list of stock photos on file. Pays $10-75 for b&w 8x10 glossy prints; $25-150 for 35mm or 2¼x2¼ color transparencies.

How To Break In: "Send us a letter letting us know where you have been in New England and what ideas you think best fit our publication. Please don't send in suggestions if you have not bothered to obtain a copy of the magazine to see what we are all about! Send a query letter for your ideas, and explain why you think you are qualified to write about a given subject. Include samples. Ask for a copy of our writer's guidelines."

YANKEE MAGAZINE'S GUIDE TO THE STATE OF NEW YORK, 581 Boylston St., Boston MA 02116. (617)266-0813. Editor: Sharon Smith. Emphasizes travel and leisure for a readership from the New York state area. Biannual magazine; 160-192 pages. Estab. 1971. Circ. 110,000. Pays on acceptance. Buys first North American serial rights. Pays 40% kill fee. Byline given. Submit seasonal/holiday material 6-12 months in advance. Simultaneous and photocopied submissions OK. SASE. Reports in 2 weeks. Sample copy $1.50; free writer's guidelines.

Nonfiction: "Unusual activities, places to stay, restaurants, shops, the arts, annual events, towns or areas to visit. Strict emphasis on travel discoveries within New York. Since the *Guide* is set up on a region-by-region basis, each story must be confined to activities or attractions within a single region." Buys 15-20 mss/issue. Query. Length: 500-2,500 words. Pays $50-300.

Photos: Cynthia Shaw, assistant editor. Purchased with or without accompanying ms or on assignment. Send contact sheet or transparencies, plus list of stock photos on file. Pays $10-75 for b&w 8x10 glossy prints; $25-150 for 35mm or 2¼x2¼ color transparencies.

How To Break In: "Send us a letter letting us know where you have been in New York and what ideas you think best fit our publication. Please don't send in suggestions if you have not bothered to obtain a copy of the magazine to see what we are all about! Send a query letter for your ideas, and explain why you think you are qualified to write about a given subject. Include samples. Ask for a copy of our writer's guidelines."

Religious

Educational and inspirational material of interest to church members, workers and leaders) within a denomination or religion is the primary interest of publications in this category. Publications intended to assist lay and professional religious workers in teaching and managing church affairs are classified in Church Administration and Ministry in the Trade Journais section. Religious magazines for children and teenagers will be found in the Juvenile, and Teen and Young Adult classifications. Jewish publications whose main concern is with matters of general Jewish interest (rather than religious interest) are listed in the Jewish Publications category.

A.M.E. REVIEW, 468 Lincoln Dr. NW, Atlanta GA 30318. Editor/Manager: William D. Johnson. For the ministerial majority. Quarterly magazine; 68-70 pages. Estab. 1880. Circ. 6,455. Not copyrighted. Byline given. Pays on publication. Sample copy $1.50. Reports in 60 days. Query or submit complete ms. SASE.
Nonfiction and Photos: Uses material on personal experiences and personal achievements of a religious nature; ministerial profiles, human interest articles, pulpit reviews and book reviews (religious and racial). Length: 2,500 words. Pays 10¢/word. B&w (3x5) photos are purchased with or without accompanying mss. Pays $2.50.
Fiction: Mainstream, fantasy, humorous, religious. Length: open. Pays 8¢/word.
Poetry: Free verse and light verse for the Poets' Corner. Length: open. Pays $5.
Fillers: Short humor with a religious slant. Pays $2/line up to 4 lines.

AMERICA, 106 W. 56th St., New York NY 10019. (212)581-4640. Editor: Joseph A. O'Hare. Published weekly for adult, educated, largely Roman Catholic audience. Usually buys all rights. Byline given. Pays on acceptance. Reports in 2-3 weeks. Write for copy of guidelines for writers. SASE.
Nonfiction and Poetry: "We publish a wide variety of material on politics, economics, ecology, and so forth. We are not a parochial publication, but almost all of our pieces make some moral or religious point. We are not interested in purely informational pieces or personal narratives which are self-contained and have no larger moral interest." Articles on literature, current political and social events. Length: 1,500-2,000 words. Pays $50-75. Poetry length: 10-30 lines. Address to Poetry Editor.

AMERICAN REVIEW OF EASTERN ORTHODOXY, Box 447, Indian Rocks Beach FL 33535. (813)596-0310. Editor: Robert Burns Jr. Principally for clergy, students, seminarians, prominent laity of Eastern Orthodox, Roman Catholic, Episcopal background. Bimonthly religious news magazine; 32 pages. Estab. 1954. Circ. 3,000. Not copyrighted. Buys 6 mss/year. Pays on acceptance. Sample copy $1. Will consider photocopied and simultaneous submissions. Reports "immediately." Submit complete ms. SASE.
Nonfiction and Photos: News, short items of religious topical interest. Eastern Orthodox items principally. American view, rather than old country view. Photos and terse descriptive matter dealing with the subject are necessary. News exposes. Informational, interview, historical and photo articles. Length: 500-2,500 words. Pays $10-25. Photos purchased with ms with no additional payment. Purchased without accompanying ms for $5 minimum. Captions required. Clear b&w glossy prints.

THE ANNALS OF SAINT ANNE DE BEAUPRE, Basilica of St. Anne, Quebec, Canada G0A 3C0. (418)827-4538. Editor-in-Chief: E. Lefebure. Managing Editor: Francois J. Plourde. 60% freelance written. Emphasizes the Catholic faith for the general public, of average education; mostly Catholic; part of the audience is made up of people who came to The Shrine of St. Anne de Beaupre. Monthly magazine; 32 pages. Estab. 1976. Circ. 70,000. Pays on acceptance. Buys first North American serial rights. Phone queries OK. Submit seasonal/holiday material 2 months in advance. SAE and International Reply Coupons. Reports in 3-4 weeks. Free sample copy and writer's guidelines.
Nonfiction: Humor (short pieces on education, family, etc.); inspirational; interview; and personal experience. Buys 10 mss/issue. Query. Length: 700-1,700 words. Pays $25-35.
Photos: Purchased with or without accompanying ms. Submit prints. Pays $5-15 for b&w glossy prints; $25-40 for color transparencies. "We buy very few color photos." Total purchase price for ms includes payment for photos.

Columns/Departments: Query. Length: 700-1,700 words. Pays $25-35. Open to suggestions for new columns/departments.

Fiction: Religious (Catholic faith). Buys 1 ms/issue. Query. Length: 700-1,700 words. Pays $25-35.

Poetry: Light verse. Buys 12 poems/year. Limit submissions to batches of 6. Pays $5 minimum.

Fillers: Jokes, gags, anecdotes and short humor. "We buy few fillers." Pays $5 minimum.

THE ASBURY THEOLOGICAL SEMINARY HERALD, SPO 11, Asbury Theological Seminary, Wilmore KY 40390. For a general Christian audience. Bimonthly magazine; 32 pages. Estab. 1888. Circ. 38,000. Pays on acceptance. Simultaneous and photocopied submissions OK. SASE. Reports in 1 month. Free sample copy.

Nonfiction: G. Alice George, articles editor. "Bible-based material dealing with the Christian life, the work of the church, etc. Inspirational anecdotes, personal experience, interviews, informational articles." Buys 15 mss/year. Submit complete ms. Length: open. Pays $20-35.

ASPIRE, 1819 E. 14th Ave., Denver CO 80218. Editor: Jeanne Pomranka. 50% freelance written. For teens and adults: "those who are looking for a way of life that is practical, logical, spiritual or inspirational." Monthly; 64 pages. Estab. 1914. Circ. 2,900. Buys all rights, but may reassign to author after publication provided credit given *Aspire*. Byline given. Buys 100 mss/year. Pays following publication. Sample copy 20¢ in stamps. Submit seasonal material 6-7 months in advance. Reports in 2 weeks.

Nonfiction: Uses inspirational articles that help to interpret the spiritual meaning of life. Needs are specialized, since this is the organ of the Divine Science teaching. Personal experience, inspirational, think pieces. Also seeks material for God at Work, a department "written in the form of letters to the editor in which the writer describes how God has worked in his life or around him. Teen Talk includes short articles from teenagers to help other teenagers find meaning in life." Length: 100-1,000 words. Pays maximum 1¢/published word.

Fiction: "Anything illustrating spiritual law at work in life." Length: 250-1,000 words. Pays maximum 1¢/published word.

Poetry: Traditional, contemporary, light verse. "We use very little poetry." Length: average 8-16 lines. Pays $1-2/page.

BAPTIST HERALD, 1 S. 210 Summit Ave., Oakbrook Terrace IL 60181. (312)495-2000. Dr. Reinhold J. Kerstan. For "any age from 15 and up, any educational background with mainly religious interests." Estab. 1923. Monthly. Circ. 9,000. Buys all rights. Byline given. Pays on publication. Occasionally overstocked. Free sample copy. Submit seasonal material 3-4 months in advance. SASE.

Nonfiction and Fiction: "We want articles of general religious interest. Seeking articles that are precise, concise, and honest. We hold a rather conservative religious line." Buys personal experience, interviews, inspirational and personal opinion articles. Length: 700-2,000 words. Pays $10 minimum. Buys religious and historical fiction. Length: 700-2,000 words. Pays $10 minimum.

BAPTIST LEADER, Valley Forge PA 19481. (215)768-2158. Editor: Vincie Alessi. For ministers, teachers, and leaders in church schools. Monthly; 64 pages. Buys first rights, but may reassign rights to author after publication. Pays on acceptance. Free sample copy. Deadlines are 8 months prior to date of issue. Reports immediately. SASE.

Nonfiction: Educational topics. How-to articles for local church school teachers. Length: 1,500-2,000 words. Pays $25-$40.

Photos: Church school settings; church, worship, children's and youth activities and adult activities. Purchased with mss. B&w, 8x10; human interest and seasonal themes. Pays $15-20.

BIBLICAL ILLUSTRATOR, The Sunday School Board, 127 9th Ave. N., Nashville TN 37234. Editor: William H. Stephens. For members of Sunday School classes that use the International Sunday School Lessons and other Bible study lessons, and for adults seeking in-depth Biblical information. Quarterly. Circ. 90,000. Buys all rights. Byline given. Rarely purchases freelance material. Pays on acceptance. Submit seasonal material (for Christmas and Easter) 1 year in advance. Reports in 2 weeks. Query. SASE.

Nonfiction and Photo: Journalistic articles and photo stories researched on Biblical subjects, such as archeology and sketches of Biblical personalities. Material must be written for laymen but research quality must be up-to-date and thorough. Should be written in a contemporary, journalistic style. Pays 4¢/word. B&w and color photos purchased with ms or on assignment. Captions required. Pays $7.50-10.

BRIGADE LEADER, Box 150, Wheaton IL 60187. Editor: Paul Heidebrecht. Managing Editor: Randall Nulton. 30% freelance written. For men associated with Christian Service Brigade clubs throughout US and Canada. Quarterly magazine; 32 pages. Buys all rights or second serial (reprint) rights. Buys 4 mss/year. Pays on acceptance. Submit seasonal material 5 months in advance. Photocopied submissions OK. Reports in 2 months. Query. SASE.
Nonfiction and Photos: "Articles about men and things related to them. Relationships in home, church, work. Specifically geared to men with an interest in boys. Besides men dealing with boys' physical, mental, emotional needs—also deals with spiritual needs." Informational, personal experience, inspirational. Length: 900-1,500 words. Pays 3¢ minimum/word. Photos purchased with or without ms. Pays $7.50 for b&w.

CALVINIST-CONTACT, 99 Niagara St., St. Catharines, Ontario, Canada L2R 4L3. (416)682-5614. Editor: Keith Knight. Christian weekly newspaper. No rights purchased. Byline given. SASE.
Nonfiction: "Any material as long as it is suitable for our publication, which has as its aim the practical application of the principles of the Bible as the only true guide in life."

CANADIAN CHURCHMAN, 600 Jarvis St., Toronto, Ontario, Canada M4Y 2J6. Editor: Jerrold F. Hames. 10-15% freelance written. For a general audience; Anglican Church of Canada; adult, with religio-socio emphasis. Monthly tabloid newspaper; 24-28 pages. Estab. 1874. Circ. 280,000. Not copyrighted. Buys 10-12 mss/year. Pays on publication. Will consider photocopied submissions and simultaneous submissions. Query. SAE and International Reply Coupons.
Nonfiction: "Religion, news from churches around the world, social issues, theme editions (native rights, abortion, alcoholism, etc.). Newsy approach; bright features of interest to Canadian churchmen. Prefer rough sketch first; freelance usually on assignment only. Our publication is Anglican-slanted, progressive, heavily socially oriented in presenting topical issues." Informational, interview, spot news. Length: 750-1,200 words. Pays $35-100.

CATHOLIC LIFE, 35750 Moravian Dr., Fraser MI 48026. Editor-in-Chief: Robert C. Bayer. 75% freelance written. Emphasizes foreign missionary activities of the Catholic Church in Burma, India, Bangladesh, the Philippines, Hong Kong, Africa, etc., for middle-aged and older audience with either middle incomes or pensions. High school educated (on the average), conservative in both religion and politics. Monthly (except July or August) magazine; 32 pages. Estab. 1954. Circ. 19,200. Pays on publication. Buys all rights, but may reassign following publication. Byline given. Submit seasonal/holiday material 3-4 months in advance. Simultaneous submissions OK. SASE. Reports in 2 weeks.
Nonfiction: Informational; inspirational (foreign missionary activities of the Catholic Church; experiences, personalities, etc.). Buys 30 mss/year. Query or send complete ms. Length: 1,000-1,500 words. Pays 4¢/word.

CATHOLIC NEAR EAST MAGAZINE, Catholic Near East Welfare Association, 1011 1st Ave., New York NY 10022. (212)826-1480. Editor: Claudia McDonnell. For a general audience with interest in the Near East, particularly its religious and cultural aspects. Quarterly magazine; 24 pages. Estab. 1974. Circ. 163,000. Buys first North American serial rights. Byline given. Buys 16 mss/year. Pays on publication. Free sample copy and writer's guidelines. Photocopied submissions OK if legible. Submit seasonal material (Christmas and Easter in different Near Eastern lands or rites) 6 months in advance. Reports in 3-4 weeks. Query or submit complete ms. SASE.
Nonfiction and Photos: "Cultural, territorial, devotional material on the Near East, its history, peoples and religions (especially the Eastern Rites of the Catholic Church. Style should be simple, factual, concise. Articles must stem from personal acquaintance with subject matter, or through up-to-date research. No preaching or speculations." Length: 800-1,400 words. Pays 10¢/word. "Photographs to accompany ms are always welcome; they should illustrate the people, places, ceremonies, etc., which are described in the article. We prefer color but occasionally use b&w. Pay varies depending on the quality of the photos."

CHICAGO STUDIES, Box 665, Mundelein IL 60060. (312)566-1462. Editor: George J. Dyer. 50% freelance written. For Roman Catholic priests and religious educators. Magazine; published 3 times/year; 112 pages. Estab. 1962. Circ. 10,000. Buys all rights. Buys 30 mss a year. Pays on acceptance. Sample copy $1. Will consider photocopied submissions. Submit complete ms. Reports in 6 weeks. SASE.
Nonfiction: Nontechnical discussion of theological, biblical and ethical topics. Articles aimed

at a nontechnical presentation of the contemporary scholarship in those fields. Length: 3,000-5,000 words. Pays $35-100.

THE CHRISTIAN ATHLETE, Fellowship of Christian Athletes, 8701 Leeds Rd., Kansas City MO 64129. Editor: Skip Stogsdill. Topical format aimed at enabling high school and college athletes and coaches to grow stronger in their Christian faith. Estab. 1959. Bimonthly. Circ. 50,000. Buys first rights only. Byline given. Buys 10 mss/year. Pays on publication. Free sample copy and writer's guidelines, plus a list of topics for the current year. Seasonal material should be submitted 2 months in advance of issue date. Reports in 1 week. SASE.

Nonfiction: "All articles must pivot around the topic and be applicable to Christian high school and college athletes and coaches, male and female. Topics for 1980 include endurance, anger, friendships, church and greed. An article must contain an authentic spiritual emphasis depicting a real flesh and blood faith with a person's warts showing—not a pie-in-the-sky testimony. We like features on both 'name' athletes and the third-string benchwarmer. Profiles and other articles should be accompanied by pictures whenever possible. Photos must relate to the topic at hand. We use little or no poetry. Length: 1,000 words maximum. Pays $25 maximum.

THE CHRISTIAN CENTURY, 407 S. Dearborn St., Chicago IL 60605. (312)427-5380. Editor: James M. Wall. For college-educated, ecumenically minded, progressive church people, both clergy and lay. Weekly magazine; 24-32 pages. Estab. 1884. Circ. 30,000. Pays on publication. Usually buys all rights. Query appreciated, but not essential. SASE. Reports in 3 weeks. Free sample copy.

Nonfiction: "We use articles dealing with social problems, ethical dilemmas, political issues, international affairs, and the arts, as well as with theological and ecclesiastical matters. We focus on concerns that arise at the juncture between church and society, or church and culture." Length: 2,500 words maximum. Payment varies, but averages $20/page.

CHRISTIAN HERALD, 40 Overlook Dr., Chappaqua NY 10514. (914)769-9000. Editor: David E. Kucharsky. 80% freelance written. Emphasizes religious living in family and church. Monthly magazine; 64 pages. Estab. 1878. Circ. 270,000. Pays on acceptance. Buys all rights, but may reassign following publication. Byline given "except when we buy the data and condense it to a short feature." Submit seasonal/holiday material 5-6 months in advance. Photocopied submissions OK. SASE. Sample copy $1.25; free writer's guidelines.

Nonfiction: How-to; informational; inspirational; interview; profile; and evangelical experience. Buys 50-75 mss/year. Query or send complete ms. Length: 1,000-2,500 words. Pays $50 minimum.

Photos: Purchased with or without accompanying ms. Send transparencies. Pays $10 minimum for b&w; $25 minimum for 2¼x2¼ color transparencies.

Poetry: Light verse, traditional, religious and inspirational. Buys 30 poems/year. Length: 4-20 lines. Pays $10 minimum.

CHRISTIAN LIFE MAGAZINE, Gundersen & Schmale, Wheaton IL 60187. Editor-in-Chief: Robert Walker. Executive Editor: Janice Franzen. 75% freelance written. Religious publication. Monthly magazine; 88 pages. Circ. 100,000. Pays on publication. Buys all rights, but may reassign following publication. Submit seasonal/holiday material 8-12 months in advance of issue date. SASE. Free sample copy and writer's guidelines.

Nonfiction: Adventure articles (usually in the first-person, told in narrative style); devotional (include many anecdotes, preferably from the author's own experience); general features (wide variety of subjects, with special programs of unique benefit to the community); inspirational (showing the success of persons, ideas, events and organizations); personality profiles (bright, tightly-written articles on what Christian are thinking); short stories (with good characterization and mood); news (with human interest quality dealing with trends); news feature (providing interpretative analysis of person, trend, event and ideas); and trend (should be based on solid research). Pays $175 maximum.

CHRISTIAN LIVING, Mennonite Publishing House, 616 Walnut Ave., Scottdale PA 15683. (412)887-8500. Editor: J. Lorne Peachey. For Christian families. Monthly. Buys first or second rights. Pays on acceptance. Submit complete ms. SASE.

Nonfiction and Photos: Articles about Christian family life, parent-child relations, marriage, and family-community relations. Material must address itself to one specific family problem and/or concern and show how that problem/concern may be solved. If about a family activity, it should deal only with one such activity in simple, direct language. All material must relate to the adult members of a family, not the children. Length: 1,000-1,500 words. Pays $70 maximum. Additional payment for b&w photos used with mss.

Fiction and Poetry: Short stories on the same themes as above. Length: 1,000-2,000 words. Poems related to theme. Length: 25 lines. Pays $70 maximum for fiction; $5 minimum for poetry.

CHRISTIANITY & CRISIS, 537 W. 121st St., New York NY 10027. (212)662-5907. Editor: Wayne H. Cowan. For professional clergy and laymen; politically liberal; interested in ecology, good government, minorities and the church. Journal published every 2 weeks; 12-16 pages. Estab. 1941. Circ. 19,000. Rights purchased vary with author and material. Usually buys all rights, but may reassign to author after publication. Buys 5-10 mss a year. Pays on publication. Free sample copy. Will consider photocopied and simultaneous submissions. Reports on material in 3 weeks. SASE.

Nonfiction: "Our articles are written in depth, by well-qualified individuals, most of whom are established figures in their respective fields. We offer comment on contemporary, political and social events occurring in the US and abroad. Articles are factual and of high quality. Anything whimsical, superficial, or politically dogmatic would not be considered." Interested in articles on bio-medical ethics, new community projects; informational articles and book reviews. Length: 500-5,000 words. Pays $25-$50.

How To Break In: "It is difficult for a freelancer to break in here but not impossible. Several authors we now go to on a regular basis came to us unsolicited and we always have a need for fresh material. Book reviews are short (800-1,500 words) and may be a good place to start, but you should query first. Another possibility is Viewpoints which also runs short pieces. Here we depend on people with a lot of expertise in their fields to write concise comments on current problems. If you have some real area of authority, this would be a good section to try."

CHRISTIANITY TODAY, 465 Gundersen Dr., Carol Stream IL 60187. Editor: Kenneth Kantzer. Emphasizes orthodox, evangelical religion. Semimonthly magazine; 55 pages. Estab. 1956. Circ. 175,000. Pays on acceptance. Usually buys all rights, but may reassign following publication. Submit seasonal/holiday material 8 months in advance. SASE. Reports in 4-8 weeks. Free sample copy and writer's guidelines.

Nonfiction: Theological, ethical and historical and informational (not merely inspirational). Buys 4 mss/issue. Query or send complete ms. Length: 1,000-2,000 words. Pays $100 minimum.

Columns/Departments: Ministers' Workshop (practical and specific, not elementary). Buys 12 mss/year. Send complete ms. Length: 900-1,100 words. Pays $75.

THE CHURCH HERALD, 1324 Lake Dr. SE, Grand Rapids MI 49506. Editor: Dr. John Stapert. Publication of the Reformed Church in America. Biweekly magazine; 32 pages. Estab. 1826. Circ. 74,000. Buys all rights, first serial rights, or second serial (reprint) rights. Buys about 60 mss/year. Pays on acceptance. Sample copy 50¢; free writer's guidelines. Will consider photocopied and simultaneous submissions. Submit material for major Christian holidays 2 months in advance. Reports in 4 weeks. Query or submit complete ms. SASE.

Nonfiction and Photos: "We expect all of our articles to be helpful and constructive, even when a point of view is vigorously presented. Articles on subjects such as Christianity and culture, government and politics, forms of worship, the media, ethics and business relations, responsible parenthood, marriage and divorce, death and dying, challenges on the campus, evangelism, church leadership, Christian education, Christian perspectives on current issues, spiritual growth, etc. Length: 400-1,500 words. Articles for children, 750 words. Pays 3¢/word. Photos purchased with or without accompanying ms. Pays $5-15/8x10 b&w glossy.

Fiction, Poetry, and Fillers: Religious fiction. Length: 400-1,500 words. Children's fiction, 750 words. Pays 3¢/word.

Poetry: Length: 30 lines maximum. Pays $5-$15.

CHURCH & STATE, Americans United for Separation of Church and State, 8120 Fenton St., Silver Spring MD 20910. (301)589-3707. Editor: Edd Doerr. 15% freelance written. Emphasizes religious liberty and church-state relations matters. Readership "includes the whole religious spectrum, but is predominantly Protestant and well-educated." Monthly magazine; 24 pages. Estab. 1947. Circ. 85,000. Pays on acceptance. Buys all rights, but may reassign following publication. Simultaneous, photocopied and previously published submissions OK. SASE. Reports in 4 weeks. Free sample copy and writer's guidelines.

Nonfiction: Expose; general interest; historical; and interview. Buys 15 mss/year. Query. Length: 3,000 words maximum. Pays 3¢/word.

Photos: State availability of photos with query. Pays $10 for b&w prints. Captions preferred. Buys one-time rights.

COLUMBIA, Drawer 1670, New Haven CT 06507. Editor: Elmer Von Feldt. For Catholic families; caters particularly to members of the Knights of Columbus. Monthly magazine. Estab. 1920. Circ. 1,250,000. Buys all rights. Buys 50 mss/year. Pays on acceptance. Free sample copy and writer's guidelines. Submit seasonal material 6 months in advance. Reports in 4 weeks. Query or submit complete ms. SASE.

Nonfiction and Photos: Fact articles directed to the Catholic layman and his family and dealing with current events, social problems, Catholic apostolic activities, education, ecumenism, rearing a family, literature, science, arts, sports and leisure. Length: 1,000-3,000 words. Glossy photos (8x10) b&w are required for illustration. Articles without ample illustrative material are not given consideration. Payment ranges from $200-400, including photos. Photo stories are also wanted. Pays $15/photo used and 10¢/word.

Fiction and Humor: Written from a thoroughly Christian viewpoint. Length: 3,000 words maximum. Pays $300 maximum. Humor or satire should be directed to current religious, social or cultural conditions. Pays up to $100 for about 1,000 words.

COMMONWEAL, 232 Madison Ave., New York NY 10016. (212)683-2042. Editor: James O'Gara. Edited by Roman Catholic laymen. 20% freelance written. For college-educated audience. Special book and education issues. Biweekly. Circ. 20,000. Buys 75 mss/year. Pays on acceptance. Free sample copy. Submit seasonal material 2 months in advance. Reports in 3 weeks. "A number of our articles come in over-the-transom. I suggest a newcomer either avoid particularly sensitive areas (say, politics) or let us know something about yourself (your credentials, tearsheets, a paragraph about yourself)." SASE.

Nonfiction: "Articles on timely subjects: politics, literature and religion." Original, brightly written mss on value-oriented themes. Buys think pieces. Length: 1,000-3,000 words. Pays 2¢/word.

Poetry: Department Editor: John Fandel. Contemporary and avant-garde. Length: maximum 150 lines ("long poems very rarely"). Pays $7.50-25.

THE COMPANION OF ST. FRANCIS AND ST. ANTHONY, Conventual Franciscan Friars, Box 535, Postal Station F, Toronto, Ontario, Canada M4Y 2L8. (416)924-6349. Editor-in-Chief: the Rev. Nicholas Weiss. 75% freelance written. Emphasizes religious and human values. Monthly magazine; 32 pages. Estab. 1937. Circ. 7,000. Pays on acceptance. Buys all rights, but may reassign following publication. Phone queries OK. Submit seasonal/holiday material 2 months in advance. SASE. Reports in 3 weeks. Free writer's guidelines.

Nonfiction: Historical; how-to (medical and psychological coping); informational; inspirational; interview; nostalgia; profile; and travel. Buys 6 mss/issue. Send complete ms. Length: 1,200-1,500 words. Pays 4¢/word.

Photos: Photos purchased with accompanying ms. Captions required. Pays $7/5x7 (but all sizes accepted) b&w glossy prints and color photos. Send prints. Total purchase price for ms includes payment for photos.

Fiction: Adventure; humorous; mainstream; and religious. Buys 1 ms/issue. Send complete ms. Length: 1,200-1,500 words. Pays 4¢/word.

How To Break In: "Mss on human interest with photos are given immediate preference."

CONTACT, United Brethren Publishing, 302 Lake St., Box 650, Huntington IN 46750. (219)356-2312. Editor-in-Chief: Stanley Peters. Managing Editor: Steve Dennie. Sunday School weekly; 8 pages. Circ. 7,000. For conservative evangelical Christians, ages 16 and up. Buys simultaneous, second serial (reprint) and first rights. Byline given. Pays on acceptance; 1¢/word for first rights, ¾¢ otherwise. Submit seasonal/holiday material 9 months in advance. Photocopied and previously published submissions OK. SASE. Reports in 4-8 weeks. Buys at least 2 mss/issue. Free sample copy and writer's guidelines upon request.

Nonfiction: Historical; how-to; humor; informational; inspirational; personal experience. Must have religious slant. Length: 1,300 words maximum.

Fiction: All types, but religious slant necessary. Length: 1,300 words maximum.

Poetry: Buys "a few poems, preferably rhyming." Pays 7¢/line.

Fillers: Jokes; gags; puzzles; cartoons. Buys 2/issue. Pays 1¢/word; $2 for puzzles and cartoons.

Photos: Bought normally accompanying manuscript. B&w glossy prints only. Pays $3/8x10 photo; $2, all others.

THE COVENANT COMPANION, 5101 N. Francisco Ave., Chicago IL 60625. (312)784-3000. Editor-in-Chief: James R. Hawkinson. 25% freelance written. Emphasizes Christian life and faith. Semimonthly (monthly issues July and August) magazine; 32 pages. Circ. 28,000. Pays on publication. Buys all rights, but may reassign following publication. Submit

seasonal/holiday material 3 months in advance. Simultaneous, photocopied and previously published submissions OK. SASE. Reports in 2 months. Sample copy 50¢.
Nonfiction: Humor; informational; inspirational (especially evangelical Christian); interviews (Christian leaders and personalities); and personal experience. Buys 15-20 ms/year. Length: 100-110 lines of typewritten material at 70 characters/line (double-spaced). Pays $10-20.

DAILY MEDITATION, Box 2710, San Antonio TX 78299. Editor: Ruth S. Paterson. Quarterly. Rights purchased vary. Byline given.
Nonfiction: Inspirational, self-improvement, nonsectarian religious articles, 600-2,000 words, showing path to greater spiritual growth; new Mayan archeological discoveries. Fillers, to 400 words. Pays ½-1½¢/word for articles. Seasonal material six months in advance. Sample copy sent to writer on receipt of 25¢.
Poetry: Inspirational. Length: 16 lines maximum. Pays 14¢/line.

DECISION MAGAZINE, 1300 Harmon Place, Minneapolis MN 55403. (612)338-0500. Editor: Roger C. Palms. Conservative evangelical monthly publication of the Billy Graham Evangelistic Association. Magazine; 16 pages. Estab. 1960. Circ. 3,000,000. Buys first rights on unsolicited manuscripts. Byline given. Pays on publication. Reports in 2 months. SASE.
Nonfiction: Uses some freelance material; best opportunity is in testimony area (1,800-2,200 words). Also uses short narratives, 400-800 words. "Our function is to present Christ as Savior and Lord to unbelievers and present articles on deeper Christian life and human interest articles on Christian growth for Christian readers. No tangents. Center on Christ in all material."
Poetry: Uses devotional thoughts and short poetry in Quiet Heart column. Positive, Christ-centered.

THE DISCIPLE, Box 179, St. Louis MO 63166. Editor: James L. Merrell. 5-10% freelance written. Published by Christian Board of Publication of the Christian Church (Disciples of Christ). For ministers and church members, both young and older adults. Semimonthly. Circ. 73,500. Buys all rights, but may reassign rights to author after publication, upon request. Pays on publication. Payment for photos made at end of month of acceptance. Sample copy 35¢; free writer's guidelines. Will consider photocopied and simultaneous submissions. Submit seasonal material at least 6 months in advance. Reports in 2 weeks to 3 months. SASE.
Nonfiction: Articles and meditations on religious themes; short pieces, some humorous. Length: 500-800 words. Pays $10-20.
Photos: B&w glossy prints, 8x10. Occasional b&w glossy prints, any size, used to illustrate articles. Pays $10-25. Pays $35 when used for covers. No color.
Poetry: Uses 3-5 poems/issue. Traditional forms, blank verse, free verse and light verse. All lengths. Themes may be seasonal, historical, religious, occasionally humorous. Pays $3-10.

EMPHASIS ON FAITH & LIVING, 336 Dumfries Ave., Kitchener, Ontario, Canada N2H 2G1. Editor: Dr. Everek R. Storms. 25% freelance written. Official organ of the Missionary Church. For church members. Magazine is published twice a month in US but serves the Missionary Church in both the U.S. and Canada. Estab. 1969. Circ. 11,000. Not copyrighted. Buys "only a few" mss/year. Will consider photocopied and simultaneous submissions. Uses a limited amount of seasonal material, submitted 3 months in advance. Reports in 1 month. Submit only complete ms. SAE and International Reply Coupons.
Nonfiction: Religious articles, presenting the truths of the Bible to appeal to today's readers. "We take the Bible literally and historically. It has no errors, myths or contradictions. Articles we publish must have this background. No poetry, please. Especially would like articles covering the workings of the Holy Spirit in today's world." Length: approximately 500 words—"not too long." Pays $5-10.

ENGAGE/SOCIAL ACTION, 100 Maryland Ave. NE, Washington DC 20002. (202)488-5632. Editor: Lee Ranck. 30% freelance written. For "United Methodist clergy and lay people interested in in-depth analysis of social issues, particularly the church's role or involvement in these issues." Estab. 1973. Monthly. Circ. 7,000. Rights purchased vary with author and material. May buy all rights and reassign rights to author after publication. Buys 25 mss/year. Pays on publication. Free sample copy and writer's guidelines. Will consider photocopied submissions, but prefers original. Returns rejected material in 2-3 weeks. Reports on material accepted for publication in several weeks. Query or submit complete ms. SASE.
Nonfiction and Photos: "This is the social action publication of the United Methodist Church published by the denomination's Board of Church and Society of the United Methodist Church. We publish articles relating to current social issues as well as church-related

discussions. We do not publish highly technical articles or poetry. Our publication tries to relate social issues to the church—what the church can do, is doing; why the church should be involved. We only accept articles relating to social issues, e.g., war, draft, peace, race relations, welfare, police/community relations, labor, population problems, drug and alcohol problems. Reviews of books and music should focus on related subjects." Length: 2,000 words maximum. Pays $50.

ETCETERA. 6401 The Paseo, Kansas City MO 64131. (816)333-7000, ext. 277. Editor: Mike Estep. 50% freelance written. Published by the Church of the Nazarene for the 18- to 23-year-old college/university student. Monthly magazine. Circ. 18,000. Pays on acceptance. Buys first rights or second rights. Byline given. Submit seasonal material 6 months in advance. SASE. Free sample copy.
Nonfiction: Articles which speak to students' needs in light of their spiritual pilgrimage. How they cope on a secular campus from a Christian life style. First-person articles have high priority since writers tend to communicate best that which they are in the process of learning themselves. Style should be evangelical. Material should have "sparkle." Wesleyan in doctrine. Buys interviews, profiles, inspirational and think pieces, humor, photo essays. Length: 1,500 words maximum. Pays 2¢/word.
Photos: B&w glossy prints. Pays $5-15. Interested in photo spreads and photo essays.

THE EVANGELICAL BEACON. 1515 E. 66th St., Minneapolis MN 55423. (612)866-3343. Editor: George Keck. 30% freelance written. For Evangelical and conservative Protestant audience. Denominational magazine of the Evangelica Free Church of America. Issued biweekly. Rights purchased vary with author and material. Buys first rights, second serial (reprint) rights, or all rights. Byline given "except when the author requests not to be mentioned or if we feel it best to remain anonymous." Pays on publication. Free sample copy. Reports on submissions in 6-8 weeks. SASE.
Nonfiction and Photos: Devotional material; articles on the church, people and their accomplishments. "Crisp, imaginative, original writing desired—not sermons put on paper." Length: 250-1,800 words. Pays 2¢/word. Prefers 8x10 photos. Pays $5 minimum.
Fiction and Poetry: "Not much fiction used, but will consider if in keeping with aims and needs of magazine." Length: 100-1,500 words. Pays 2¢/word. "In poetry, content is more important than form." Length: open. Pays $2.50 minimum.

EVANGELICAL FRIEND. Box 232, Newberg OR 97132. (503)538-7345. Editor: Jack Willcuts. Managing Editor: Harlow Ankeny. Readership is evangelical Christian families, mainly of the Quaker church denomination. Monthly magazine; 28 pages. Estab. 1967. Circ. 12,000. Pays on publication. Buys all rights, but may reassign following publication. Byline given. Phone queries OK. Submit seasonal/holiday material 3-4 months in advance. Simultaneous, photocopied and previously published submissions OK. SASE. Reports in 4 weeks. Free sample copy and writer's guidelines.
Nonfiction: Historical (church-related); how-to (church growth methods, Christian education ideas, etc.); inspirational (Biblically based); interview; personal experience (spiritual); personal opinion (on various controversial subjects that relate to the church, etc.); photo feature (unusual people doing unusual Christian-related services). Buys 2-3 mss/year. Query. Length: 300-1,800 words. Pays $10-25.
Photos: Purchased on assignment. Send contact sheet. Pays $8-20 for b&w glossy or matte finish photos.

EVANGELIZING TODAY'S CHILD. 6136 W. Roxbury Place, Littleton CO 80123. (303)979-3313. Editor: B. Milton Bryan. For teachers and parents of children ages 6-12. 10-20% freelance written. Bimonthly magazine. Estab. 1942. Circ. 35,000. Pays on publication. Buys all rights. Byline given. Submit seasonal/holiday material 2 months in advance. Photocopied and previously published submissions OK. SASE. Writer's guide for SASE (no stamps).
Nonfiction: Personal experience (childhood experiences of adults). Also, Bible lessons and missionary stories, which clearly present the Gospel and a step in Christian growth. Buys 10-12 mss/year. Query. Length: 2,000-3,000 words. Pays 2¢/word minimum.
Photos: Submissions of photos on speculation accepted. Pays $10-25 for 8x10 b&w glossy prints; $50-150 for 8x10 color prints. "We need photos of children or related subjects. Please include SASE."
Fiction: "We are interested in realistic items which are relevent and valuable in teaching principles of Christian growth. Write for age 8-9 comprehension level." Buys 6 mss/year. Send complete ms. Length: 1,000-1,500 words. Pays $20 minimum.

FAITH AND INSPIRATION, Seraphim Publishing Group, Inc., Editorial Office: 160 5th Ave., New York NY 10010. Editorial Director: Warner Hutchinson. 50% freelance written. Emphasizes religious and secular inspirational material for a family readership. Bimonthly magazine; 128 pages. Estab. January 1978. Circ. 80,000. Pays on publication. Buys all rights. Byline given. Submit seasonal/holiday material 4 months in advance of issue date. Photocopied submissions OK. SASE. Reports in 30 days. Sample copy and writer's guidelines $1.25.

Nonfiction: Inspirational; interview; personal experience (moving articles of inspiration, does not have to be religious); and profile. Buys 20 mss/issue. Submit complete ms. Length: 50-1,200 words. Pays $5-75.

Poems: Light verse and traditional. Buys 3 poems/issue. Limit submissions to batches of 3. Length: 5-20 lines. Pays $5-15.

Fillers: Short humor, religious and inspirational material. Buys 10/issue. Length: 25-100 words. Pays $5-15.

FAMILY LIFE TODAY MAGAZINE, 110 W. Broadway, Glendale CA 91204. (213)247-2330. Editor: Georgiana Walker. Articles Editor: Phyllis Alsdurf. 70% freelance written. Emphasizes "helping families develop a Christian lifestyle." Monthly magazine; 32 pages. Estab. December 1974. Circ. 32,000. Pays on acceptance. Byline given. Submit seasonal/holiday material 9-10 months in advance of issue date. Simultaneous and previously published submissions OK. SASE. Reports in 3 months. Free sample copy and writer's guidelines; mention *Writer's Market* in request.

Nonfiction: How-to (any family-related situation. Does need narrow focus: How to help the "slow-poke" child, etc.); humor (if wholesome and family related); inspirational (especially as it deals with the practicality of biblical principles in terms of everyday life); interview (with person who is recognized authority in area of family life); personal experience ("family personal experience especially when story illustrates a Christian principle—God's help, etc."); and photo feature (family-related). Buys 6 mss/issue. Query. Length: 300-1,500 words. Pays 4-5¢/word for original; 3¢/word for reprints.

Photos: State availability of photos with query. Pays $15-30 for 8x10 b&w glossy prints; $35-85 for 35mm color transparencies. Buys one-time rights. Model release preferred.

FREEINDEED, Freeindeed, Inc., 547 Morris St., Allentown PA 18102. Publisher: Jan Abramsen. Editor: Diane R. Jepsen. For women who desire to be disciples of Jesus. Bimonthly magazine; 32 pages. Estab. March 1978. Circ. 1,100. Pays on publication. Buys one-time rights. Byline given. Submit seasonal/holiday material 6 months in advance. Query. Simultaneous and previously published submissions OK. SASE. Reports in 6 weeks. Sample copy $1.50; free writer's guidelines.

Nonfiction: Personal experience and profile (of women living life deliberately). Buys 4 mss/year. Query. Length: 1,500-2,500 words. Payment is negotiable.

Photos: Send photos with ms. Pays $5-20 for b&w contact sheets; offers no additional payment for photos accepted with accompanying ms.

Fiction: Humorous, religious (dealing with a person's spiritual life) and romance. "We do not want to see shallow, trashy, saccharine stories. No stories that are just explanded tracts." Buys 2 mss/year. Query or send clips of published work. Length: 1,500-3,200 words. Pays $10 minimum.

Poetry: Free verse and haiku. "Again, not the stuff often passed off as inspirational or religious. Generally *not* about the seasons or holidays or sunsets. Buys 2/year. Submit in batches of 5. Pays $5 minimum.

Fillers: Newsbreaks and short humor. Length: 20-250 words. Pays $2.50 minimum.

FRIAR, Butler NJ 07405. Editor: Father Rudolf Harvey. For Catholic families. Estab. 1954. 10 times a year. Not copyrighted. Pays on acceptance. SASE.

Nonfiction: Uses articles and features on current problems or events; profiles of notable individuals; trends in sociology and education. Length: 1,800-3,000 words. Minimum payment of $15.

FRIDAY FORUM (OF THE JEWISH EXPONENT), 226 S. 16th St., Philadelphia PA 19102. (215)893-5745. Editor: Jane Biberman. 95% freelance written. For the Jewish community of Greater Philadelphia. Monthly newspaper supplement. Estab. 1971. Circ. 70,000. Usually buys all rights, but will reassign rights to author after publication. Pays 25% kill fee. Byline given. Buys 40 mss/year. Pays after publication. Free sample copy and writer's guidelines. Will consider photocopied submissions. No simultaneous submissions. Submit special material 6 months in advance. Reports in 2 months. SASE.

Nonfiction and Photos: "We are interested only in articles on Jewish themes, whether they be historical, thought pieces, Jewish travel sites, photographic essays, or any other nonfiction piece on a Jewish theme. Topical themes are appreciated." Length: 6-12 double-spaced pages. Pays $35 minimum.

Poetry: Traditional forms, blank verse, free verse, avant-garde forms, light verse; must relate to a Jewish theme. Length varies. Pays $15 minimum.

GOOD NEWS, The Forum for Scriptual Christianity, Inc., 308 E. Main St., Wilmore KY 40390. (606)858-4661. Editor-in-Chief: Charles W. Keysor. For United Methodist lay people and pastors, primarily middle income; conservative and biblical religious beliefs; broad range of political, social and cultural values. Bimonthly magazine; 88 pages. Estab. 1967. Circ. 15,000. Pays on acceptance. Byline given. Phone queries OK. Submit seasonal/holiday material 6 months in advance. Simultaneous, photocopied and previously published submissions OK. SASE. Reports in 2 months. Sample copy $1; free writer's guidelines.

Nonfiction: Historical (prominent people or churches from the Methodist/Evangelical United Brethren tradition); how-to (to build faith, work in local church); humor (good taste); inspirational (related to Christian faith); personal experience (case histories of God at work in individual lives) and any contemporary issues as they relate to the Christian faith and the United Methodist Church. Buys 36 mss/year. Query. Pays $10-50.

Photos: Photos purchased with accompanying ms or on assignment. Captions required. Uses fine screen b&w glossy prints. Total purchase price for ms includes payment for photos. Payment negotiable.

Columns/Departments: Good News Book Forum. Query. Open to suggestions for new columns/departments.

Fillers: Clippings, jokes, gags, anecdotes, newsbreaks and short humor. Buys 20 fillers/year. Pays $5-10.

GOSPEL CARRIER, Messenger Publishing House, Box 850, Joplin MO 64801. (417)624-7050. Editor-in-Chief: Roy M. Chappell, D.D. Denominational Sunday school take-home paper for adults, ages 20 through retirement. Quarterly publication in weekly parts; 104 pages. Circ. 3,500. Pays quarterly. Buys simultaneous, second serial and one-time rights. Byline given. Submit seasonal/holiday material 1 year in advance. Simultaneous, photocopied and previously published submissions OK. SASE. Reports in 3 months. Sample copy 50¢; free writer's guidelines.

Nonfiction: Historical (related to great events in the history of the church); informational (may explain the meaning of a Bible passage or a Christian concept); inspirational (must make a Christian point); nostalgia (religious significance); and personal experience (Christian concept). Buys 50-80 mss/year. Pays ½¢/word.

Photos: Purchased with accompanying ms. Send prints. Pays $2 for b&w glossy prints.

Fiction: Adventure, historical; romance; and religious. Must have Christian significance. Buys 13-20 mss/issue. Submit complete ms. Length: 800-2,000 words. Pays ½¢/word.

Fillers: Short inspirational incidents from personal experience or the lives of great Christians. Buys 52-80/year. Length: 200-500 words. Pays 6¢/word.

GUIDEPOSTS MAGAZINE, 747 3rd Ave., New York NY 10017. Editorial Director: Arthur Gordon. 40-50% freelance written. "*Guideposts* is an inspirational monthly magazine for all faiths in which men and women from all walks of life tell how they overcame obstacles, rose above failures, met sorrow, learned to master themselves, and became more effective people through the direct application of the religious principles by which they live." Buys all rights. Pays 25% kill fee. Byline given "most of our stories are first-person ghosted articles, so the author would not get a byline unless it was his/her story." SASE.

Nonfiction and Fillers: Articles and features should be written in simple, anecdotal style with an emphasis on human interest. Short features up to approximately 250 words ($10-25) would be considered for such *Guideposts* features as "Fragile Moments," and other short items which appear at the end of major articles. Short mss of approximately 250-750 words ($25-100) would be considered for such features as "Quiet People" and general one-page stories. Full-length mss, 750-1,500 words ($200-300). All mss should be typed, double-spaced and accompanied by a stamped, self-addressed envelope. Inspirational newspaper or magazine clippings often form the basis of articles in *Guideposts*, but it is unable to pay for material of this type and will not return clippings unless the sender specifically asks and encloses postage for return. Annually awards scholarships to high school juniors and seniors in writing contest.

How To Break In: "The freelancer would have the best chance of breaking in by aiming for a 1-page or maybe 2-page article. That would be very short, say 2½ pages of typescript, but in a small magazine such things are very welcome. A sensitively written anecdote that could provide us with an additional title is extremely useful. And they are much easier to just sit down and write than to have to go through the process of preparing a query. They should be warm, well-written, intelligent and upbeat. We like personal narratives that are true and have some universal relevance, but the religious element does not have to be hammered home with a sledge hammer." Address short items to Van Varner.

HIGH ADVENTURE, 1445 Boonville Ave., Springfield MO 65802. (417)862-2781, ext. 1497. Editor: Johnnie Barnes. For boys and men. Estab. 1971. Quarterly; 16 pages. Circ. 35,000. Rights purchased vary with author and material. Buys 10-12 mss/year. Pays on acceptance. Free sample copy and writer's guidelines. Query or submit complete ms. SASE.
Nonfiction, Fiction, Photos and Fillers: Camping articles, nature stories, fiction adventure stories and jokes. Nature study and campcraft articles about 500-600 words. Buys how-to, personal experience, inspirational, humor and historical articles. Pays $10/page. Photos purchased on assignment. Adventure and western fiction wanted. Length: 1,200 words. Puzzles, jokes and short humor used as fillers.

INSIGHT, The Young Calvinist Federation, Box 7244, Grand Rapids MI 49510. (616)241-5616. Editor-in-Chief: the Rev. James C. Lont. Assistant Editor: Tammy Rutgers. For young people, 16-21, Christian backgrounds and well-exposed to the Christian faith. Monthly (except June and August) magazine; 32 pages. Estab. 1921. Circ. 22,000. Pays on publication. Buys simultaneous, second serial (reprint) and first North American serial rights. Byline given. Phone queries OK. Submit seasonal/holiday material 6 months in advance. Simultaneous, photocopied and previously published submissions OK. SASE. Report in 4 weeks. Sample copy and writer's guidelines for 9x12 SASE.
Photos: Photos purchased without accompanying ms or on assignment. Pays $15-25/8x10 b&w glossy prints; $50-150 for 35mm or larger color transparencies. Total purchase price for ms includes payment for photos.
Fiction: Humorous; mainstream; and religious. "I'm looking for short stories that are not preachy but that lead our readers to a better understanding of how their Christian beliefs apply to their daily living. They must do more than entertain—they must make the reader think something in a new light." Buys 1-2 mss/issue. Send complete ms. Length: 1,000-3,000 words. Pays $45-100.
Poetry: Free verse; light verse, haiku and traditional. Buys 10 poems/year. Length: 4-25 lines. Pays $20-25.
Fillers: Youth-oriented cartoons, jokes, gags, anecdotes, puzzles and short humor. Buys 6 fillers/year. Length: 50-300 words. Pays $10-35.

INTERLIT, David C. Cook Foundation, Cook Square, Elgin IL 60120. (312)741-2400, ext. 142. Editor-in-Chief: Gladys J. Peterson. 90% freelance written on assignment. Please study publication and query before submitting mss. Emphasizes Christian communications and journalism for missionaries, broadcasters, publishers, etc. Quarterly newsletters; 20 pages. Estab. 1964. Circ. 9,000. Pays on acceptance. Buys all rights, but may reassign following publication. Photocopied submissions OK. SASE. Reports in 2 weeks. Free sample copy.
Nonfiction: Informational; interview; and photo feature. Buys 7 mss/issue. Length: 500-3,000 words. Pays 2-4¢/word.
Photos: Purchased with accompanying ms or on assignment. Captions required. Query or send prints. Uses b&w. Offers no additional payment for photos accepted with ms.

LIBERTY, A Magazine of Religious Freedom, 6840 Eastern Ave. NW, Washington DC 20012. (202)723-0800, ext. 745. Editor: Roland R. Hegstad. For "responsible citizens interested in community affairs and religious freedom." Bimonthly. Circ. 500,000. Buys first rights. Buys approximately 40 mss/year. Pays on acceptance. Free sample copy and writer's guidelines. Will consider photocopied submissions. Submit seasonal material in our field 6-8 months in advance. Reports in 1-3 weeks. Query not essential, but helpful. SASE.
Nonfiction: "Articles of national and international interest in field of religious liberty church-state relations. Current events affecting above areas (Sunday law problems, parochial aid problems, religious discrimination by state, etc.). Current events are most important; base articles on current events rather than essay form." Buys how-to's, personal experience and think pieces, interviews, profiles in field of religious liberty. Length: maximum 2,500 words. Pays up to $150.
Photos: "To accompany or illustrate articles." Purchased with mss; with captions only. B&w glossy prints, color transparencies. Pays $15-35. Cover photos to $150.

LIGHT AND LIFE, Free Methodist Publishing House, 999 College Ave., Winona Lake IN

46590. Editor: G. Roger Schoenhals. 40% freelance written. Emphasizes evangelical Christianity with Wesleyan slant for a cross-section of adults. Published 20 times yearly. Magazine; 16 pages. Estab. 1867. Circ. 60,000. Pays on publication. Buys all rights, but may reassign following publication. Byline given. Submit seasonal/holiday material 6 months in advance. Previously published submissions OK. SASE. Reports in 6 weeks. Sample copy 50¢; writer's guidelines for SASE.

Nonfiction: "Each issue uses a lead article (warm, positive first-person account of God's help in a time of crisis; 1,500 words); a Christian living article (a fresh, lively, upbeat piece about practical Christian living; 750 words); a Christian growth article (an in-depth, lay-level article on a theme relevant to the maturing Christian; 1,500 words); a discipleship article (a practical how-to piece on some facet of Christian discipleship; 750 words); news feature (a person-centered report of a 'good news' event showing God at work at the local, conference, or denominational level of the Free Methodist Church; 500 words, 2 photographs); and a back page article (contents must be brief and attractive; poem, parable or 400-word article, profound and unforgettable)." Buys 90 mss/year. Submit complete ms. Pays 2¢/word.

Photos: Purchased without accompanying ms. Send prints. Pays $7.50-20.00 for b&w photos. Offers no additional payment for photos accepted with accompanying ms.

LIGUORIAN, Liguori MO 63057. Editor: the Rev. Norman Muckerman. 50% freelance written. For families with Catholic religious convictions. Monthly. Circ. 465,000. Pays 50% kill fee. Byline given "except on short fillers and jokes." Buys 60 mss/year. Pays on acceptance. Submit seasonal material 5-6 months in advance. Reports in 6-8 weeks. SASE.

Nonfiction and Photos: "Pastoral, practical and personal approach to the problems and challenges of people today. No travelogue approach or unresearched ventures into controversial areas." Length: 400-2,000 words. Pays 5-7¢/word. Photos purchased with mss; b&w glossy prints.

LIVING MESSAGE, Box 820, Petrolia, Ontario, N0N 1R0, Canada. Editor: Rita Baker. For "active, concerned Christians, mainly Canadian Anglican." Publication of the Anglican Church of Canada. Estab. 1889. Monthly except July and August. Circ. 14,000. Not copyrighted. Byline given. Pays on publication. Free sample copy. Will consider photocopied submissions. Submit seasonal material 5 months in advance. Reports on material in 4 weeks. Submit complete ms. SAE and International Reply Coupons or Canadian stamps.

Fiction, Nonfiction and Photos: "Short stories and articles which give readers an insight into other lives, promote understanding and stimulate action in areas such as community life, concerns of elderly, handicapped, youth, work with children, Christian education, poverty, the Third World, etc. No sentimentality or moralizing. Readers relate to a warm, personal approach; uncluttered writing. 'Reports' or involved explanatory articles are not wanted. The lead-in must capture the reader's imagination. A feeling of love and optimism is important." Length: up to 2,000 words. Pays $10-25. 8x10 b&w prints (with article). Pays $5. Fiction length: 1,000-1,500 words. Pays $15-25.

LOGOS JOURNAL, Logos International Fellowship, Inc., 201 Church St., Plainfield NJ 07060. (201)754-0745. Executive Editor: William L. Carmichael. Managing Editor: Evelyn P. Marrinan. For a readership interested in charismatic renewal. Bimonthly magazine; 80 pages. Estab. 1971. Circ. 56,000. Pays on publication; on acceptance if assigned. Buys all rights, but may reassign following publication, or first North American serial rights. Submit seasonal/holiday material 3 months in advance of issue date. Photocopied submissions OK. SASE. Reports in 6 weeks. Sample copy $1.50; free writer's guidelines.

Nonfiction: "The *Logos Journal* is an interdenominational magazine which seeks to communicate the renewal, through the Holy Spirit, of individuals and the church. Some of our standing feature sections are: Saints, Church, Family, Health and Spirit. All of these will be brief photographic profiles of people, laymen and clergy, famous or obscure, anyone with a unique ministry to share with others in Christ. In addition we have a feature called Interview, which will highlight a well-known personality sharing details, in dialogue format, of how they live, think and relate the Holy Spirit to their everyday lives." Buys 20-25 mss/year. Length: 800-2,000 words. Pays $75-200.

Photos: Must accompany ms. Pays $15-25 for 2¼x2¼ color transparencies or 5x7 b&w glossy prints.

Columns/Departments: "Desire first-hand reports of charismatic-oriented events/people plus news of spiritual significance." Also column (informed person addressing subject significant to a sizable element in the church). Buys 1/issue. Query. Length: 800-1,000 words.

THE LOOKOUT, 8121 Hamilton Ave., Cincinnati OH 45231. (513)931-4050. Editor: Mark A.

Taylor. 50% freelance written. For the adult and young adult of the Sunday morning Bible school. Weekly. Pays on acceptance. Byline given. Simultaneous submissions OK. SASE. Reports in 6 weeks. Sample copy and writer's guidelines 50¢.

Nonfiction: "Seeks stories about real people or Sunday-school classes; items that shed Biblical light on matters of contemporary controversy; and items that motivate, that lead the reader to ask, 'Why shouldn't I try that?' or 'Why couldn't our Sunday-school class accomplish this?' Should tell how real people are involved for Christ. In choosing topics, *The Lookout* considers timeliness, the church and national calendar, and the ability of the material to fit the above guidelines. Tell us about ideas that are working in your Sunday school and in the lives of its members. Remember to aim at laymen." Submit complete ms. Length: 1,200-1,800 words. Pays 1-3¢/word, occasionally higher.

Fiction: "A short story is printed in most issues; it is usually between 1,200-1,800 words long, and should be as true to life as possible while remaining inspirational and helpful. Use familiar settings and situations."

Fillers: Inspirational or humorous shorts. "About 400-800 words is a good length for these. Relate an incident that illustrates a point without preaching. Pays 1-3¢/word.

Photos: B&w prints, 4x6 or larger. Pays $5-15. Pays $50-125 for color transparencies for covers. Needs photos of people, especially adults in a variety of settings.

THE LUTHERAN, 2900 Queen Lane, Philadelphia PA 19129. (215)848-6800. Editor: Edgar R. Trexler. General interest magazine of the Lutheran Church in America. Twice monthly, except single issues in July and August. Buys first rights. Pays on acceptance. Free sample copy and writer's guidelines. SASE.

Nonfiction: Popularly written material about human concerns with reference to the Christian faith. "We are especially interested in articles in 4 main fields: Christian ideology; personal religious life, social responsibilities; Church at work; human interest stories about people in whom considerable numbers of other people are likely to be interested." Write "primarily to convey information rather than opinions. Every article should be based on a reasonable amount of research or should exploit some source of information not readily available. Most readers are grateful for simplicity of style. Sentences should be straightforward, with a minimum of dependent clauses and prepositional phrases." Length: 500-2,000 words. Pays $75-200.

Photos: Buys pix submitted with mss. Good 8x10 glossy prints. Pays $10-20. Also color for cover use. Pays up to $100.

LUTHERAN FORUM, 155 E. 22nd St., New York NY 10010. (212)254-4640. Editor: Glenn C. Stone. 70% freelance written. For church leadership, clerical and lay. Magazine; 40 pages. Estab. 1967. Quarterly. Circ. 5,400. Rights purchased vary with author and material. Buys all rights, but will sometimes reassign rights to author after publication; first North American serial rights; first serial rights; second serial (reprint) rights; simultaneous rights. Byline given. Buys 12-15 mss/year. Pays on publication. Sample copy 75¢. Will consider photocopied and simultaneous submissions. Reports in 4-6 weeks. Query or submit complete ms. SASE.

Nonfiction: Articles about important issues and developments in the church's institutional life and in its cultural/social setting. Payment varies; $15 minimum. Length: 1,000-3,000 words. Informational, how-to, interview, profile, think articles and expose. Length: 500-3,000 words. Pays $15-50.

Photos: Purchased with mss or with captions only. Prefers 8x10 prints. Uses more vertical than horizontal format. Pays $10 minimum.

THE LUTHERAN JOURNAL, 7317 Cahill Rd., Edina MN 55435. Editor: The Rev. Armin U. Deye. Conservative journal for Lutheran church members, middle age and older. Quarterly magazine; 32 pages. Estab. 1937. Circ. 105,000. Not copyrighted. Byline given. Buys 12-15 mss/year. Pays on publication. Free sample copy. Submit seasonal/holiday material 4 months in advance. Will consider photocopied and simultaneous submissions. Reports in 8 weeks. Submit complete ms. SASE.

Nonfiction and Photos: Inspirational, religious, human interest and historical articles.

Fiction and Poetry: Experimental, mainstream, religious and historical fiction. Must be suitable for church distribution. Length: 2,000 words maximum. Pays 1-1½¢/word. Traditional poetry, blank verse, free verse, related to subject matter.

THE LUTHERAN STANDARD, 426 S. 5th St., Minneapolis MN 55415. (612)332-4561. Editor: The Rev. Lowell G. Almen. 50% freelance written. For families in congregations of the American Lutheran Church. Estab. 1842. Semimonthly. Circ. 565,000. Buys first rights or multiple rights. Byline given. Buys 30-50 mss/year. Pays on acceptance. Free sample copy. Reports in 3 weeks. SASE.

Nonfiction and Photos: Uses human interest, inspirational articles, especially about members of the American Lutheran Church who are practicing their faith in noteworthy ways, or congregations with unusual programs. "Should be written in language clearly understandable to persons with a mid-high school reading ability." Also publishes articles that discuss current social issues and problems (crime, family life, divorce, etc.) in terms of Christian involvement and solutions.

Fiction: "We use almost no fiction but will consider substantive fiction with a positive Christian theme." Tie-in with season of year, such as Christmas, often preferred. Length: limit 1,200 words. Pays 4¢/word.

Poetry: Uses very little poetry. The shorter the better. 20 lines. Pays $10/poem.

LUTHERAN WOMEN, 2900 Queen Lane, Philadelphia PA 19129. Editor: Terry Schutz. 10% freelance written. 10 times yearly. Circ. 40,000. Decides acceptance within two months. Prefers to see mss 6 months ahead of issue, at beginning of planning stage. Can consider up to 3 months before publication. SASE.

Nonfiction: Anything of interest to mothers—young or old, professional or other working women—related to the contemporary expression of Christian faith in daily life, community action, international concerns. Family publication standards. No recipes or housekeeping hints. Length: 1,500-2,000 words. Some shorter pieces accepted. Pays up to $50 for full-length ms and photos.

Photos: Purchased with or without mss. Women; family situations; religious art objects; overseas situations related to church. Should be clear, sharp b&w. No additional payment for those used with mss. Pays $5 for those purchased without mss.

Fiction: Should show deepening of insight; story expressing new understanding in faith; story of human courage, self-giving, building up of community. Not to exceed 2,000 words. Pays $30-40.

Poetry: "Biggest taboo for us is sentimentality. We are limited to family magazine type contributions regarding range of vocabulary, but we don't want almanac-type poetry." No limit on number of lines. Pays $10 minimum/poem.

MARIAN HELPERS BULLETIN, Eden Hill, Stockbridge MA 01262. (413)298-3691. Editor: the Rev. Walter F. Pelcczynski, MIC. 90% freelance written. For average Catholics of varying ages with moderate religious views and general education. Quarterly. Estab. 1947. Circ. 625,000. Not copyrighted. Byline given. Buys 18-24 mss/year. Pays on acceptance. Free sample copy. Reports in 4-8 weeks. Submit seasonal material 6 months in advance. SASE.

Nonfiction and Photos: "Subject matter is of general interest on devotional, spiritual, moral and social topics. Use a positive, practical and optimistic approach, without being sophisticated. We would like to see articles on the Blessed Virgin Mary." Buys informational and inspirational articles. Length: 300-900 words. Pays $25-35. Photos are purchased with or without mss; captions optional. Pays $5-10 for b&w glossies.

MARRIAGE & FAMILY LIVING, St. Meinrad IN 47577. (812)357-8016. Editor: Ila M. Stabile. 75% freelance written. Monthly magazine. Circ. 60,000. Pays on acceptance. Buys first North American serial rights, first book reprint option and control of other reprint rights. Byline given. SASE. Reports in 3-4 weeks. Sample copy 25¢.

Nonfiction: Uses 3 different types of articles: 1) Articles aimed at enriching the husband-wife and parent-child relationship by expanding religious and psychological insights or sensitivity. (Note: Ecumenically Judeo-Christian but in conformity with Roman Catholicism.) Length: 1,000-2,000 words. 2) Informative articles aimed at helping the couple cope, in practical ways, with the problems of modern living. Length: 2,000 words maximum. 3) Personal essays relating amusing and/or heart-warming incidents that point up the human side of marriage and family life. Length: 1,500 words maximum. Pays 5¢/word.

Photos: Bob Weaver, Art Director. B&w glossies (5x7 or larger) and color transparencies or 35mm slides (vertical preferred). Pays $125 for 4-color cover photo; $50 for b&w cover photo; $35 for 2-page spread in contents, $30 for 1 page in contents; $10 minimum. Photos of couples, families and individuals especially desirable. Model releases required.

MARYKNOLL MAGAZINE, Maryknoll NY 10545. Editor: Darryl Hunt. 15% freelance written. Foreign missionary society magazine. Monthly. Pays on acceptance. Byline given. Free sample copy. Query before sending any material. Reports in several weeks. SASE.

Nonfiction: Articles and pictures concerning foreign missions. Articles developing themes such as world hunger, environmental needs, economic and political concerns. Length: 800-1,500 words. Send an outline before submitting material. Pay $50-150.

Photos: "We are a picture/text magazine. All articles must either be accompanied by top-quality photos, or be easily illustrated with photos." Pays $15-25 for b&w; $25-50 for color. Payment is dependent on quality and relevance.

MATURE CATHOLIC, 1100 W. Wells, Milwaukee WI 53233. (414)271-8926. Editor: Carol Mitchell. Emphasizes involvement in all aspects of living—cultural, political, emotional, religious, etc.—for the mature reader. Bimonthly magazine; 24 pages. Estab. 1972. Circ. 6,000. Pays on publication. Byline given. Submit seasonal/holiday material 3 months in advance. Simultaneous, photocopies and previously published submissions OK. SASE. Reports in 3 weeks. Sample copy sent.
Nonfiction: Historical, how-to, humor, personal experience, technical and travel (only exceptional nostalgia).
Fiction: Short stories and cartoons. "Our readers are retired Catholics. Our philosophy is that age is a natural part of living. We frown on labels like 'senior citizens.' We encourage participation in life and mental and spiritual growth." Buys 12 mss/year. Length: 2,000 words maximum. Pays 1¢/word.

MENNONITE BRETHREN HERALD, 159 Henderson Hwy., Winnipeg, Manitoba, R2L 1L4, Canada. Editor: Harold Jantz. Family pulbication. Biweekly. Circ. 10,600. Pays on publication. Not copyrighted. Byline given. Sample copy 40¢. Reports in 1 month. SAE and International Reply Coupons.
Nonfiction and Photos: Articles with a Christian family orientation; youth directed, Christian faith and life, current issues. 1,500 words. Pays $10-30. Photos purchased with mss; pays $5.

MESSAGE, Southern Publishing Association of Seventh-day Adventists, Box 59, Nashville TN 37202. Editor: Louis B. Reynolds. 90% freelance written. International religious journal for people of African heritage. Monthly July-October; bimonthly November-June. Pays on acceptance or publication. Buys all rights. Byline given. SASE. Free sample copy and writer's guidelines.
Nonfiction: Articles on current events; social problems such as divorce, drugs, diet, family, marriage, abortions, etc. "Subjects should be examined in the light of the Holy Scriptures. New approach to doctrinal subjects such as law vs. grace, the Godhead, the birth, death and resurrection of Christ, Second coming, millennium, the Sabbath, immortality, etc. Short, inspirational themes and unusual human interest stories welcome, but most themes and unusual human interest stories welcome, must be creative, original, warm—not the usual run-of-the-mill types. When possible, all articles should be geared to black audience." All references should be fully documented. Length 500-1,500 words. Pays $25 for minor articles; $35 for major.
Poetry: Market is small. Buys about 10 poems/year. Short poetry up to 12 lines. Free verse welcome. Not many nature poems needed. Should tell of divine truths of the Christian experience—struggle and victory and praise. Pays $10 maximum.

THE MESSENGER OF THE SACRED HEART, 833 Broadview Ave., Toronto, Ontario, Canada M4K 2P9. Editor: the Rev. F.J. Power, S.J. 10% freelance written. For "adult Catholics in Canada and the US who are members of the Apostleship of Prayer." Monthly. Circ. 22,000. Buys first rights. Byline given. Buys 12 mss/year. Pays on acceptance. Free sample copy. Submit seasonal material 3 months in advance. Reports in 1 month. SAE and International Reply Coupons.
Nonfiction: Department Editor: Mary Pujolas. "Articles on the Apostleship of Prayer and on all aspects of Christian living." Current events and social problems that have a bearing on Catholic life, family life, Catholic relations with non-Catholics, personal problems, the liturgy, prayer, devotion to the Sacred Heart. Material should be written in a popular, nonpious style. Length: 1,800-2,000 words. Pays 2¢ word.
Fiction: Department Editor: Mary Pujolas. Wants fiction which reflects the lives, problems, preoccupations of reading audience. "Short stories that make their point through plot and characters." Length: 1,800-2,000 words. Pays 2¢/word.

THE MIRACULOUS MEDAL, 475 E. Chelten Ave., Philadelphia PA 19144. Editorial Director: the Rev. Robert P. Cawley, C.M. Quarterly. Buys first North American serial rights. Buys articles only on special assignment. Pays on acceptance. Free sample copy. SASE.
Fiction: Should not be pious or sermon-like. Wants good general fiction—not necessarily religious, but if religion is basic to the story, the writer should be sure of his facts. Only restriction is that subject matter and treatment must not conflict with Catholic teaching and practice. Can use seasonal material. Christmas stories. Length: 2,000 words maximum. Pays 2¢ and up per word. Occasionally uses short-shorts from 750-1,250 words.

Poetry: Maximum of 20 lines, preferably about the Virgin Mary or at least with religious slant. Pays 50¢/line minimum.

MODERN LITURGY. Box 444, Saratoga CA 95070. Editor: William Burns. For artists and musicians, creative individuals who plan group worship services; teachers of religion. Magazine; 32 pages. Estab. 1973. Eight times a year. Circ. 15,000. Buys all rights, but may reassign rights to author after publication. Byline given. Buys 10 mss/year. Pays on publication. Sample copy $2.50; free writer's guidelines. No photocopied or simultaneous submissions. Reports in 6 weeks. Query. SASE.
Nonfiction and Fiction: Articles (historical and theological and practical), example services, liturgical art forms (music, poetry, stories, dances, dramatizations, etc.). Practical, creative ideas and art forms for use in worship and/or religious education classrooms. Length: 750-2,000 words. Pays $5-30.

NEW COVENANT MAGAZINE. Servant Publications, Box 8617, Ann Arbor MI 48107. (313)761-8505. Editor: Bert Ghezzi. Managing Editor: John Blathner. Emphasizes the charismatic renewal of Christian churches. Ecumenical, with a higher percentage of Roman Catholic readers. Monthly magazine; 36 pages. Estab. 1971. Circ. 78,000. Pays on publication. Buys all rights. Photocopied submissions OK. SASE. Reports in 6-8 weeks. Free sample copy.
Nonfiction: Historical; informational (coverage of recent and upcoming events in the charismatic renewal); inspirational; interview and personal experience (life testimonials relating to the charismatic experience). Buys 2-3 mss/year. Query. Length: 1,000-3,000 words. Pays 2½-3½¢/word.
Photos: Photos purchased with or without accompanying ms., or on assignment. Pays $10-35 for 8x10 b&w glossies. Send contact sheet and prints. No additional payment for photos accepted with accompanying ms. Model release required.

THE NEW ERA. 50 E. North Temple, Salt Lake City UT 84150. (801)531-2951. Editor: Brian K. Kelly. 40-60% freelance written. For young people of the Church of Jesus Christ of Latter-Day Saints (Mormon); their church leaders and teachers. Monthly magazine; 51 pages. Estab. 1971. Circ. 160,000. Buys all rights, but will reassign rights to author after publication. Byline given. Buys 100 mss/year. Pays on acceptance. Will send sample copy to writer for 40¢. Will consider simultaneous submissions. Submit seasonal material 6 months to a year in advance. Reports in 30 days. Query preferred. SASE.
Nonfiction and Photos: "Material that shows how the Church of Jesus Christ of Latter-Day Saints is relevant in the lives of young people today. Must capture the excitement of being a young Latter-Day Saint. Special interest in the experiences of young Latter-Day Saints in other countries. No general library research or formula pieces without the *New Era* slant and feel." Uses informational, how-to, personal experience, interview, profile, inspirational, humor, historical, think pieces, travel, spot news. Length: 150-3,000 words. Pays 3-6¢ a word. Also seeks material for the FYI column (For Your Information) which uses news of young Latter-Day Saints around the world. Uses b&w photos and color transparencies with mss. Payment depends on use in magazine, but begins at $10.
Fiction: Experimental, adventure, science fiction and humorous. Must relate to the young Mormon audience. Pays minimum 3¢/word.
Poetry: Traditional forms, blank verse, free verse, avant-garde forms, light verse and all other forms. Must relate to their editorial viewpoint. Pays minimum 25¢/line.

NEW WORLD OUTLOOK. 475 Riverside Dr., Room 1328, New York NY 10027. (212)678-6031. Editor: Arthur J. Moore. For United Methodist lay people; not clergy generally. Monthly magazine; 46 pages. Estab. 1911. Circ. 40,000. Buys all rights, but will reassign to author after publication; buys first North American serial rights. Buys 15-20 mss/year. Pays on publication. Free sample copy and writer's guidelines. Query or submit complete ms. SASE.
Nonfiction: "Articles about the involvement of the church around the world, including the US in outreach and social concerns and Christian witness. Write with good magazine style. Facts, actualities important. Quotes. Relate what Christians are doing to meet problems. Specifics. We have too much on New York and other large urban areas. We need more good journalistic efforts from smaller places in US Articles by freelancers in out-of-the-way places in the US are especially welcome." Length: 1,000-2,000 words. Usually pays $50-150.

NORTH AMERICAN VOICE OF FATIMA. Fatima Shrine, Youngstown NY 14174. Editor: Steven M. Grancini, C.R.S.P. 75% freelance written. For Roman Catholic readership. Circ. 15,000. Not copyrighted. Pays on acceptance. Free sample copy. Reports in 6 weeks. SASE.

Nonfiction, Photos and Fiction: Inspirational, personal experience, historical and think articles. Religious and historical fiction. Length: 700 words. B&w photos purchased with mss. All material must have a religious slant. Pay 1¢/word.

THE OTHER SIDE, Box 12236, Philadelphia PA 19144. Co-Editors: John Alexander, Alfred Krass, Mark Olson. "A magazine of Christian discipleship, radical in tone and outlook, with a definite point of view but open to other opinions." Monthly. Estab. 1965. Circ. 10,000. Pays on publication. Buys first serial, second serial or simultaneous rights. Byline given. SASE. Reports in 1-2 weeks. Sample copy $1. Writer's guidelines available.
Nonfiction: "Articles are not encouraged unless they are highly creative descriptions of personal experiences relative to Christian discipleship amidst current issues of society or interviews or profiles which don't just 'grind an axe' but communicate personality." Length: 250-2,500 words. Pays $25-100.
Photos: "Shots depicting 'the other side' of affluence or the juxtaposition of affluence and poverty are needed." Photo essays on social issues will be considered. Pays $15-25 for b&w photos.
Fiction: "Short pieces of creative writing on hard social issues. A Christian perspective should be clear." Length: 300-2,800 words. Pays $25-50.

OUR FAMILY, Oblate Fathers of St. Mary's Province, Box 249, Battleford, Saskatchewan, Canada S0M 0E0. (306)937-2131, 937-7344. Editor-in-Chief: A.J. Reb Materi, O.M.I. For average family men and women of high school and early college education. Monthly magazine; 36 pages. Estab. 1949. Circ. 14,261. Pays on acceptance. Generally purchases first North American serial rights. Will also buy all rights but may reassign following publication; or simultaneous, second serial (reprint) or one-time rights. Pays 100% kill fee. Byline given. Phone queries OK. Submit seasonal/holiday material 4 months in advance. Simultaneous, photocopied and previously published submissions OK. SASE. Reports in 2-4 weeks. Sample copy 75¢; free writer's guidelines.
Nonfiction: Humor (related to family life or husband/wife relations); inspirational (anything that depicts people responding to adverse conditions with courage, hope and love); personal experience (with religious dimensions); and photo feature (particularly in search of photo essays on human/religious themes and on persons whose lives are an inspiration to others).
Photos: Photos purchased with or without accompanying ms. Pays $20-25 for 5x7 or larger b&w glossy prints and color photos (which are converted into b&w). Total purchase price for ms includes payment for photos. Free photo spec sheet.
Fiction: Humorous and religious. "Anything true to human nature. No moralizing or sentimentality." Buys 1 ms/issue. Send complete ms. Length: 750-3,000 words. Pays 3¢/word minimum for original material. Free fiction requirement guide.
Poetry: Avant-garde; free verse; haiku; light verse; and traditional. Buys 4-10 poems/issue. Length: 3-30 lines. Pays 40-60¢/line.
Fillers: Jokes, gags, anecdotes and short humor. Buys 2-10 fillers/issue.

OUR SUNDAY VISITOR MAGAZINE, Noll Plaza, Huntington IN 46750. (219)356-8400. Executive Editor: Robert Lockwood. For general Catholic audience. Weekly. Circ. 400,000. Buys all rights. Byline given. Buys 80 mss/year. Pays on acceptance. Will send a sample copy to a writer on request. Submit seasonal material 2 months in advance. Reports in 3 weeks. Query. SASE.
Nonfiction: Uses articles on Catholic-related subjects. Should explain Catholic religious beliefs in articles of human interest; articles applying Catholic principles to current problems, Catholic profiles, etc. Payment varies depending on reputation of author, quality of work and amount of research required. Length: 1,000-1,200 words. Minimum payment for major features is $100 and a minimum payment for shorter features is $50-75.
Photos: Purchased with mss; with captions only. B&w glossy prints, color transparencies, 35mm color. Pays $125 for cover photo story, $75 for b&w story; $25 per color photo. $10 per b&w photo.

PARISH FAMILY DIGEST, Our Sunday School Visitor, Inc., 200 Noll Plaza, Huntington IN 46750. (219)356-8400. Editor: Patrick R. Moran. "*Parish Family Digest* is geared to the Catholic family, and to that family as a unit of the parish." Bimonthly magazine; 48 pages. Estab. 1945. Circ. 140,399. Pays on acceptance. Buys all rights on a work-for-hire basis. Byline given. Submit seasonal/holiday material 3 months in advance. Photocopied and previously published submissions OK. SASE. Reports in 1 week for queries; 2 weeks for mss. Free sample copy and writer's guidelines.

Nonfiction: General interest, historical, inspirational, interview, nostalgia (if related to overall Parish involvement); and profile. Send complete ms. Buys 140 mss/year. Length: 1,000 words maximum. Pays $5-50.

Photos: State availability of photos with ms. Pays $10 for 3x5 b&w prints. Buys all rights. Captions preferred and model release required.

Fillers: Anecdotes and short humor. Buys 6/issue. Length: 100 words maximum.

PENTECOSTAL EVANGEL, The General Council of the Assemblies of God, 1445 Boonville, Springfield MO 65802. (417)862-2781. Editor-in-Chief: Robert C. Cunningham. Managing Editor: Richard G. Champion. 33% freelance written. Emphasizes news of the Assemblies of God for members of the Assemblies and other Pentecostal and charismatic Christians. Weekly magazine; 32 pages. Estab. 1913. Circ. 268,000. Pays on publication. Buys first rights, simultaneous, second serial (reprint) or one-time rights. Byline given. Submit seasonal/holiday material 6 months in advance. Simultaneous, photocopied and previously published submissions OK. SASE. Reports in 3 months. Free sample copy and writer's guidelines.

Nonfiction: Informational (articles on home life that convey Christian teachings); inspirational; and personal experience. Buys 8 mss/issue. Send complete ms. Length: 500-2,000 words. Pays 2¢/word maximum.

Photos: Photos purchased without accompanying ms. Pays $7.50-15 for 8x10 b&w glossy prints; $10-35 for 35mm or larger color transparencies. Total purchase price for ms includes payment for photos.

Poetry: Religious and inspirational. Buys 1 poem/issue. Limit submissions to batches of 6. Pays 15-30¢/line.

PENTECOSTAL TESTIMONY, 10 Overlea Blvd., Toronto, Ontario, Canada M4H 1A5. Editor: Joy E. Hansell. Monthly. For church members and general readership. Estab. 1920. Circ. 18,000. Not copyrighted. Pays on publication. Free sample copy. Submit seasonal material at least 3 months in advance. Query. SAE and International Reply Coupons.

Nonfiction: Must be written from Canadian viewpoint. Subjects preferred are contemporary public issues, events on the church calendar (Reformation month, Christmas, Pentecost, etc.) written from conservative theological viewpoint. Pays 1¢/word for originals. Preferred lengths are 800-1,200 words.

Photos: Occasionally buys photographs with mss if they are vital to the article. Also buys b&w photos if they are related to some phase of the main topic of the particular issue. Should be 8x10 b&w prints. Payment is $6-10 for cover photos.

Fiction: Might use youth-slanted fiction. Same theological slant, same lengths, same payment as nonfiction.

PRESBYTERIAN JOURNAL, Southern Presbyterian Journal Co, Inc., Box 3108, Asheville NC 28802. Editor: the Rev. G. Aiken Taylor. Managing Editor: Joel Belz. "Emphasis is Presbyterian, although material appeals to religious conservatives. Highly educated readership." Weekly magazine; 24 pages. Estab. 1942. Circ. 30,000. Pays on publication. Not copyrighted. Submit seasonal/holiday material at least 2 months in advance. Simultaneous and photocopied submissions OK; might consider previously published work. SASE. Reports in 2-6 weeks. Free sample copy.

Nonfiction: General interest (must have a religious slant); how-to (teach Sunday School more effectively—whatever would appeal to readers of religious publications); humor; interview; opinion (does not necessarily have to agree with editorial policy); and personal experience (testimonials welcome). Buys 1-2 mss/issue. Send complete ms. Length: 3,000 word maximum. Pays $20.

Columns/Departments: Under My Palm Tree is directed towards women. No recipes or household hints. Anything else of particular interest to women. Buys 20 mss/year. Send complete ms. Length: 650-1,500 words. Pays $5-25. Open to suggestions for new columns/departments.

PRESBYTERIAN RECORD, 50 Wynford Dr., Don Mills, Ontario, Canada M3C 1J7. (416)444-1111. Editor: the Rev. James Dickey. 40-50% freelance written. For a church-oriented, family audience. Monthly magazine. Estab. 1876. Circ. 89,500. Buys 10 mss/year. Pays on publication. Free sample copy. Submit seasonal material 3 months in advance. Reports on manuscripts accepted for publication in 2 weeks. Returns rejected material in 4 weeks. Query. SAE and Canadian stamps.

Nonfiction and Photos: Material on religious themes. Check a copy of the magazine for style. Also, personal experience, interview, and inspirational material. Length: 800-1,600 words. Pays

$20-50. Pays $5-12 for b&w glossy photos. Captions required. Uses positive color transparencies for the cover. Pays $30-50.

PURPOSE, 616 Walnut Ave., Scottdale PA 15683. Editor: David E. Hostetler. 85% freelance written. "For adults, young and old, general audience with interests as varied as there are persons. My particular readership is interested in seeing Christianity work in tough situations and come out on top." Monthly magazine. Estab. 1968. Circ. 21,500. Buys first serial rights; second serial (reprint) rights; simultaneous rights. Byline given. Buys 200 mss a year. Pays on acceptance. Free sample copy and writer's guidelines. Submit seasonal material 5 months in advance. Will consider photocopied and simultaneous submissions. Reports in 6 weeks. Submit complete ms. SASE.

Nonfiction and Photos: Inspirational articles from a Christian perspective. "I want material that goes to the core of human problems—morality on all levels, or lack of it in business, politics, religion, sex and any other area—and shows how Christian answers resolve some of these problems. I don't want glib, sweety-sweet, or civil religion pieces. I want critical stuff that's upbeat. *Purpose* is a story paper and as such wants truth to be conveyed either through quality fiction or through articles that use the best fiction techniques to make them come alive. Our magazine has an accent on Christian discipleship. Basically, this means we think our readers take Christianity seriously and we do not accept a compartmentalized expression of faith. Christianity is to be applied to all of life and we expect our material to show this. We're getting too much self-centered material. By that, I mean many writers see religion as a way of getting their needs met with very little concern for how the other fellow may be affected by their selfishness. I would like to see articles on how people are intelligently and effectively working at some of the great human problems such as overpopulation, food shortages, international understanding, etc., motivated by their faith." Length: 200-1,200 words. Pays 1-3¢/word. Photos purchased with ms. Captions optional. Pays $5-35 for b&w, depending on quality. Normal range is $7.50-15. Must be sharp enough for reproduction; prefers prints in all cases. Can use color for halftones at the same rate of payment.

Fiction, Poetry and Fillers: Humorous, religious and historical fiction related to the theme of magazine. "Should not be moralistic." Traditional poetry, blank verse, free verse and light verse. Length: 3-12 lines. Pays 25-75¢/line. Jokes, short humor, and items up to 400 words. Pays 1¢ minimum/word.

How To Break In: "We are a good market for new writers who combine Christian perceptions with craftsmanship. We are looking for articles which show Christianity slugging it out where people hurt but we want the stories told and presented professionally. Good photographs help place material with us."

REVIEW FOR RELIGIOUS, 3601 Lindell Blvd., Room 428, St. Louis MO 63108. (314)535-3048. Editor: Daniel F. X. Meenan, S.J. 100% freelance written. Bimonthly. For Roman Catholic religious men and women. Pays on publication. Byline given. Reports in about 8 weeks. SASE.

Nonfiction: Articles on ascetical, liturgical and canonical matters. Length: 2,000-8,000 words. Pays $6/page.

ST. ANTHONY MESSENGER, 1615 Republic St., Cincinnati OH 45210. Editor-in-Chief: Jeremy Harrington. For a national readership of Catholic families, most of them have children in grade school, high school or college. Monthly magazine; 59 pages. Estab. 1893. Circ. 305,000. Pays on acceptance. Buys first North American serial rights. Byline given. Submit seasonal/holiday material 4 months in advance. SASE. Free sample copy and writer's guidelines.

Nonfiction: How-to (on psychological and spiritual growth; family problems); humor; informational; inspirational; interview; personal experience (if pertinent to our purpose); personal opinion (limited use; writer must have special qualifications for topic); profile. Buys 12 mss/year. Length: 1,500-3,500 words. Pays 7¢/word.

Fiction: Mainstream and religious. Buys 12 mss/year. Query. Length: 2,000-3,500 words. Pays 7¢/word.

How To Break In: "The freelancer should ask why his/her proposed article would be appropriate for us, rather than for *Redbook* or *Saturday Review*. We treat human problems of all kinds, but from a religious perspective."

ST. JOSEPH'S MESSENGER & ADVOCATE OF THE BLIND, Sisters of St. Joseph of Peace, St. Joseph's Home, Box 288, Jersey City NJ 07303. Editor-in-Chief: Sister Ursula Maphet. 50% freelance written. Quarterly magazine; 30 pages. Estab. 1900. Circ. 65,000. Pays on acceptance. Buys all rights, but may reassign following publication. Submit seasonal/holiday material 3 months in advance (no Christmas issue). Simultaneous and previously published submissions OK. Reports in 3 weeks. Free sample copy and writer's guidelines.

Nonfiction: Humor; inspirational; nostalgia; personal opinion; and personal experience. Buys 24 mss/year. Submit complete ms. Length: 300-1,500 words. Pays $3-15.

Fiction: "Fiction is our most needed area." Romance; suspense; mainstream; and religious. Buys 30 mss/year. Submit complete ms. Length: 600-1,600 words. Pays $6-25.

Poetry: Light verse, traditional. Buys 25/year. Limit submissions to batches of 10. Length: 50-300 words. Pays $5-20.

Fillers: Jokes, gags, anecdotes. Buys 30/year. Length: 25-150 words. Pays $5-10.

SANDAL PRINTS, 1820 Mt. Elliott, Detroit MI 48207. Editor: William La Forte. For people who are interested in the work of the Capuchins. Estab. 1952. Circ. 8,000. Not copyrighted. Pays on acceptance. Free sample copy. Reports in 1 week. Query. SASE.

Nonfiction and Photos: Material on the contemporary apostolates and life style of Capuchins (especially in the Midwest). "We do not use any general religious material; no topical subjects or themes accepted." Length: 2,500 words. Pays $25-50. Pays $5/b&w photo.

How To Break In: "Write about actually living Capuchins and their work. Query before writing the first word."

SCOPE, 426 S. 5th St., Minneapolis MN 55415. (612)332-4561, ext. 397. Editor: Dr. Lily M. Gyldenvand. 30% freelance written. For women of the American Lutheran Church. Monthly. Circ. 325,000. Buys first rights. Byline given. Buys 200-300 mss/year. Occasionally overstocked. Pays on acceptance. Free sample copy. Submit seasonal material 4-5 months in advance. Reports in 2-3 weeks. SASE.

Nonfiction and Photos: "The magazine's primary purpose is to be an educational tool in that it transmits the monthly Bible study material which individual women use in preparation for their group meetings. It contains articles for inspiration and growth, as well as information about the mission and concerns of the church, and material that is geared to seasonal emphasis. We are interested in articles that relate to monthly Bible study subject. We also want articles that tell how faith has affected, or can influence, the lives of women or their families. But we do not want preachy articles. We are interested in any subject that touches the home. The possibilities are limitless for good, sharp, stimulating and creative articles." Length: 700-1,000 words. Pays $10-50. Buys 3x5 or 8x10 b&w photos with mss or with captions only. Pays $7-10.

Poetry and Fillers: "We can use interesting, brief, pithy, significant or clever filler items, but we use very little poetry and are very selective." Pays $5-15.

How To Break In: "Examine a copy of *Scope* and submit a well-written manuscript that fits the obvious slant and audience."

SEEK, Standard Publishing, 8121 Hamilton Ave., Cincinnati OH 45231. (513)931-4050, ext. 187. Editor: R.W. Baynes. 60% freelance written. For young and middle-aged adults who attend church and Bible classes. Sunday School paper; 12 pages. Estab. 1970. Quarterly, in weekly issues. Circ. 60,000. Rights purchased vary with author and material. Byline given. Prefers first serial rights. Buys 100-150 mss/year. Pays on acceptance. Free sample copy and writer's guidelines. Submit seasonal (Christmas, Easter, New Year's) material 9-12 months in advance. Reports in 30-60 days. Query or submit complete ms. SASE.

Nonfiction and Photos: "We look for articles that are warm, inspirational, devotional, of personal or human interest; that deal with controversial matters, timely issues of religious, ethical or moral nature, or first-person testimonies, true-to-life happenings, vignettes, emotional situations or problems; communication problems, and examples of answered prayer. Article must deliver its point in a convincing manner, but not be patronizing or preachy. Must appeal to either men or women. Must be alive, vibrant, sparkling and have a title that demands the article be read. We will purchase a few articles that deal with faith or trials of blacks or other racial groups. Always need stories of families, marriages, problems on campus, and life testimonies." Length: 400-1,200 words. Pays 1½-2¢/word. B&w photos purchased with or without mss. Pays $7.50 minimum for good 8x10 glossy prints.

Fiction: Religious fiction and religiously slanted historical and humorous fiction. Length: 400-1,200 words. Pays 1½-2¢/word.

THE SIGN, Union City NJ 07087. (201)867-6400. Editor: the Rev. Patrick McDonough, C.P. 60% freelance written. Magazine; 56 pages. 10 issues/year. Buys all rights. Free sample copy. Reports in 3 weeks. SASE.

Nonfiction and Photos: Prime emphasis on religious material: prayer, sacraments, Christian

family life, religious education, liturgy, social action—especially "personal testimony" genre. Length: 3500 words maximum. Pays $75-300. Uses photos and artwork submitted with articles.
Fiction: Uses, at most, 1 story/month. Length: 3500 words maximum. Pays $200-300.

SISTERS TODAY, The Liturgical Press, St. John's Abbey, Collegeville MN 56321. Editor-in-Chief: Sister Mary Anthony Wagner, O.S.B. Associate Editor: Sister Barbara Ann Mayer, O.S.B. 90% freelance written. For religious women of the Roman Catholic Church, primarily. Monthly magazine; 72 pages. Estab. 1929. Circ. 18,000. Pays on publication. Buys all rights, but may reassign following publication. Byline given "by request." Submit seasonal/holiday material 4 months in advance. SASE. Reports in 1 month. Free sample copy.
Nonfiction: How-to (pray, live in a religious community, exercise faith, hope, charity etc.); informational; and inspirational. Also articles concerning religious renewal, community life, worship and the role of Sisters in the world today. Buys 6 mss/issue. Query. Length: 500-3,000 words. Pays $5/printed page.
Poetry: Free verse; haiku; light verse; and traditional. Buys 3 poems/issue. Limit submissions to batches of 4. Pays $10.

SOCIAL JUSTICE REVIEW, 3835 Westminister Place, St. Louis MO 63108. (314)371-1653. Editor: Harvey J. Johnson. Issued bimonthly. Not copyrighted; "however special articles within the magazine may be copyrighted, or an occasional special issue has been copyrighted due to author's request." Query. SASE.
Nonfiction: Wants scholarly articles on society's economic, religious, social, intellectual and political problems with the aim of bringing Catholic social thinking to bear upon these problems. 2,000-4,000 words. Pays about 2¢/word; $6/column.

SPIRITUAL LIFE, 2131 Lincoln Rd. NE, Washington DC 20002. (202)832-6622. Editor: the Rev. Christopher Latimer, O.C.D. 80% freelance written. "Largely Catholic, well-educated, serious readers. High percentage are priests and religious, but also some laymen. A few are non-Catholic or non-Christian." Quarterly. Circ. 17,000. Buys first rights. Buys 20 mss/year. Pays on acceptance. Free sample copy and writer's guidelines. "Brief autobiographical information (present occupation, past occupations, books and articles published, etc.) should accompany article. Follow *A Manual of Style* (University of Chicago)." Reports in 2 weeks. SASE.
Nonfiction: Serious articles of contemporary spirituality. Quality articles · about man's encounter with God in the present-day world. Language of articles should be college-level. Technical terminology, if used, should be clearly explained. Material should be presented in a positive manner. Sentimental articles or those dealing with specific devotional practices not accepted. "*Spiritual Life* tries to avoid the 'popular,' sentimental approach to religion and to concentrate on a more intellectual approach. We do not want first-person accounts of spiritual experiences (visions, revelations, etc.) nor sentimental treatments of religious devotions." Buys inspirational and think pieces. No fiction or poetry. Length: 3,000-5,000 words. Pays $50 minimum. "Five contributor's copies are sent to author on publication of article." Book reviews should be sent to Brother Edward O'Donnell, O.C.D., Carmelite Monastery, Box 189, Waverly NY 14892.

SPIRITUALITY TODAY, Aquinas Institute of Theology, 2570 Asbury, Dubuque IA 52001. (319)556-7593. Editor: the Rev. Christopher Kiesling O.P. 50% freelance written. "For those interested in a more knowing and intense Christian life in the 20th century." Buys all rights, but right to re-use the material is assigned back without charge if credit line is given to *Spirituality Today*. Byline given. Pays on publication. Query or submit complete ms. SASE.
Nonfiction: "Articles that seriously examine important truths pertinent to the spiritual life, or Christian life, in the context of today's world. Scriptural, biographical, doctrinal, liturgical and ecumenical articles are acceptable." Length: 4,000 words. Pays 1¢/word.

SUNDAY DIGEST, 850 N. Grove Ave., Elgin IL 60120. Editor: Darlene McRoberts. 50% freelance written. Issued weekly for Christian adults. Prefers to buy all rights. Pays on acceptance. Free sample copy and writer's guidelines. Reports in 8 weeks. SASE.
Nonfiction and Photos: Needs articles applying the Christian faith to personal and social problems, articles of family interest and on church subjects, personality profiles, inspirational self-help articles, personal experience articles and anecdotes. Length: 500-1,800 words. "Study our product and our editorial requirements. Have a clear purpose for every article or story—use anecdotes and dialog—support opinions with research." Pays 5¢/word minimum. Currently running a series on Christians in unique secular occupations. Query. Photos purchased only

with mss. Pays about $10 each, depending on quality. Negatives requested; b&w or color. Return of prints cannot be guaranteed.

Fiction: Interested in fiction that is hard-hitting, fast-moving, with a real woven-in, not "tacked on," Christian message. Length: 1,000-1,500 words. Pays 5¢/word minimum.

Poetry: Only occasionally if appropriate to format. Pay 5¢/word minimum.

Fillers: Anecdotes of inspirational value, jokes and short humor; must be appropriate to format and in good taste. Length: up to 500 words. Pays 5¢/word minimum.

THE TEXAS METHODIST/UNITED METHODIST REPORTER, Box 221076, Dallas TX 75222. (214)630-6495. Editor/General Manager: Spurgeon M. Dunnam III. For a national readership of United Methodist pastors and laypersons. Weekly newspaper. Circ. 460,000. Pays on acceptance. Not copyrighted. Byline given. SASE. Free sample copy and writer's guidelines.

Nonfiction: "We welcome short features, approximately 500 words, focused on United Methodist persons, churches or church agencies. Write about a distinctly Christian response to human need or how a person's faith relates to a given situation." Pays 3¢/word.

Photos: Purchased with accompanying ms. "We encourage the submission of good action photos (5x7 or 8x10 b&w glossy prints) of the persons or situations in the article." Pays $10.

Poetry: "Poetry welcome on a religious theme; blank verse or rhyme." Length: 2-20 lines. Pays $2.

Fillers: Crossword, word-find and other puzzles on religious or Biblical themes. Pays $5.

THESE TIMES, Southern Publishing Association, Box 59, Nashville TN 37202. (615)889-8000. Editor: Kenneth J. Holland. For the general public; adult. Monthly magazine; 36 pages. Estab. 1891. Circ. 207,000. Rights purchased vary with author and material. May buy first North American serial rights, second serial (reprint) rights or simultaneous rights. Pays 33⅓% kill fee. Byline given. Buys 50 mss/year. Pays on acceptance. Free sample copy and writer's guidelines. Will consider photocopied and simultaneous submissions. Submit seasonal material 6 months in advance. Reports in 2 weeks. Query. SASE.

Nonfiction and Photos: Material on the relevance of Christianity and everyday life; inspirational articles. How-to; home and family problems; health; drugs, alcohol, gambling, abortion, Bible doctrine. Marriage; divorce; country living or city living. "We like the narrative style. Find a person who has solved a problem. Then, tell how he did it." Length: 250-2,500 words. Pays 6-10¢/word. B&w and color photos are purchased with or without ms, or on assignment. Pays $20-25 for b&w; $75-150 for color.

TODAY'S CHRISTIAN PARENT, 8121 Hamilton Ave., Cincinnati OH 45231. (513)931-4050. Editor: Mrs. Mildred Mast. Quarterly. Rights purchased vary with author and material. Buys first North American serial rights and first serial rights. Pays on acceptance. Free sample copy. Reports on submissions within 6 weeks. SASE.

Nonfiction: Devotional, inspirational and informational articles for the family. Also articles concerning the problems and pleasures of parents, grandparents and the entire family, and Christian child training. Length: 600-1,200 words. Also can use some handcraft and activity ideas; short items on Christian living; and fillers—serious or humorous. Very little poetry. Study magazine before submitting. Pays 1½¢/word minimum.

How To Break In: "Write about familiar family situations in a refreshingly different way, so that help and inspiration shine through the problems and pleasures of parenthood."

"TRUTH ON FIRE!" The Bible Holiness Movement, Box 223, Station A, Vancouver, British Columbia, Canada V6C 2M3. (604)683-1833. Editor-in-Chief: Wesley H. Wakefield. 20% freelance written. Emphasizes Evangelism and Bible teachings. Bimonthly magazine; 60 pages. Estab. 1949. Circ. 5,000. Pays on acceptance. Buys all rights, but may reassign following publication. Byline given unless author request otherwise. Simultaneous, photocopied and previously published submissions OK. SASE. Reports in 4 weeks. Free sample copy and writer's guidelines.

Nonfiction: "Evangelical articles; articles dealing with social reforms (pacifism, civil rights, religious liberty); expose (present-day slavery, cancer, tobacco, etc.), first-person testimonies of Christian experience; doctrinal articles from Wesleyan interpretation. Must observe our evangelical taboos. Nothing favoring use of tobacco, alcohol, attendance at dances or theaters; nothing in favor of abortion, divorce or remarriage; no hip or slang. Also, we do not accept Calvinistic religious or right-wing political material. Would like to see material on Christian pacifism, anti-semitism, present-day slavery, marijuana research, religious issues in Ireland, and religious articles." Length: 300-2,500 words. Pays $5-35.

Photos: Photos purchased with or without accompanying ms. Pays $5-15 for 5x7 b&w photos.

"Subjects should conform to our mores of dress (no jewelry, no makeup, no long-haired men, no mini-skirts, etc.).
Fillers: Newsbreaks, quotes. Length: 30-100 words. Pays $1-2.50.

THE UNITED CHURCH OBSERVER, 85 St. Clair Ave. E., Toronto 7, Ontario, Canada. (416)925-5931. Interim Editor: Patricia Clarke. For families in The United Church of Canada. Monthly. Pays on publication. Byline given. Sample copy 50¢. Reports in 1 month. Query. SAE and International Reply Coupons.
Nonfiction: Wants general interest articles on all subjects of interest to church people. Material must have some church connection. Well-researched articles on developments in religion. Also deal in international affairs. Bright, journalistic style is necessary. Length: 1,500-2,500 words. Thorough knowledge of the subject, authority and topnotch writing are sought. Pays $100 minimum.
Photos: Buys photographs with mss and occasional picture stories. Use both b&w and color; b&w should be 8x10; color, prefers 4x5 transparencies but can work from 2¼x2¼ or 35mm. Payment varies.

UNITED EVANGELICAL ACTION, Box 28, Wheaton, IL 60187. (312)665-0500. Editor: Harold Smith. 5% freelance written. For evangelical pastors and church leaders, including denominational executives. Quarterly magazine; 44 pages. Estab. 1942. Circ. 9,000. Pays on publication. Buys all rights. Phone queries OK. SASE. Reports in 4 weeks. Free sample copy and writer's guidelines.
Nonfiction: Anita Moreland, Managing Editor. Informational (new trends in evangelical denominations or missions or on practical help to local churches and pastors). Buys 3-4 mss/year. Query. Length: 1,500-2,500 words. Pays 2-5¢/word.

UNITY MAGAZINE, Unity Village MO 64065. Editor: Thomas E. Witherspoon. Publication of Unity School of Christianity. Magazine; 66 pages. Estab. 1889. Monthly. Circ. 350,000. Buys first serial rights. Buys 200 mss/year. Pays on acceptance. Free sample copy and writer's guidelines. No photocopied or simultaneous submissions. Submit seasonal material 6-8 months in advance. Reports in 4 weeks. Submit complete ms. SASE.
Nonfiction and Photos: "Inspirational articles, metaphysical in nature, about individuals who are using Christian principles in their living." Personal experience and interview. Length: 3,000 words maximum. Pays minimum of 2¢/word. 4x5 or 8x10 color transparencies purchased without mss. Pays $75-100.
Poetry: Traditional forms, blank verse and free verse. Pays 50¢-$1/line.

UNIVERSAL MAGAZINE, Box 1537, Palm Desert CA 92260. Editor-in-Chief: the Rev. Paul von Johl. 50% freelance written. Emphasizes family unity. Quarterly magazine; 12 pages. Estab. 1975. Pays on acceptance and publication. Not copyrighted. "We buy for one-time use only. We will include copyright listing for previously copyrighted work at request." Submit seasonal/holiday material 6 months in advance of issue date. Previously published work OK. SASE. Reports in 3 weeks. Sample copy and writer's guidelines 15¢ each.
Nonfiction: How-to (as it relates to the family); inspirational (without sounding religious); new product (for better family living in relationships to the family); and family unity and help for family togetherness. No political articles. Buys 1 ms/issue. Submit complete ms. Length: 500-1,500 words. Pays $2.50-20.
Photos: Submit photo material with accompanying ms. No additional payment for photos. Captions preferred. Buys one-time rights. Model release required.
Columns/Departments: Bookshelf (reviews for books, tape clubs, "spiritual" and other publications of general interest); For Better Human Relationship ("stories should be just what the title implies"). Buys 1 ms/issue. Submit complete ms. Length: 500-2,500 words. Pays $2.50-20. Open to suggestions for new columns/departments.
Fiction: Humorous. Submit complete ms. Length: 250-1,000 words. Pays $3-8.
Poetry: Any style as long as it is "clean." Submit in batches of 3. Length: 4-20 lines. Pays $1 or 15¢/line.

VERONA MISSIONS, 8108 Beechmont Ave., Cincinnati OH 45230. (513)231-8910. Editor: William Jansen, FSCJ. Associate Editor: Jo Anne Moser Gibbons. For those interested in Third World topics and foreign mission efforts of the Verona Fathers and Sisters. Bimonthly; 36 pages. Estab. 1950. Circ. over 45,000. Buys all rights (but will reassign rights after publication); first rights; or second serial (reprint) rights. Byline given. Pays on publication. Will send sample copy to writer on request. Reports in 4-6 weeks. Send to Jo Anne Gibbons. SASE.

Nonfiction: Background information, human interest articles, interviews, profiles, personal experience articles, and photo features on the developing countries of Africa and Latin America. Should be written knowledgeably, in a popular, conversational style, and reflect a positive outlook on efforts in social and religious fields. Informational, personal experience, interview, inspirational, travel articles. Length: 250-1,000 words, shorter features; 3,000 words maximum, major articles. Pays $25/minimum. "We treat Third World subjects sympathetically and multi-dimensionally, and always in a Christian context."

Photos: B&w (5x7 minimum) photos and color transparencies purchased with ms or on assignment. Captions required. Payment to be agreed upon with the photographer/writer, but begins at $10.

VISTA, Wesleyan Publishing House, Box 2000, Marion IN 46952. Address submissions to Editor of Sunday School Magazines. Publication of the Wesleyan Church. For adults. Weekly. Circ. 63,000. Not copyrighted. "Along with mss for first use, we also accept simultaneous submissions, second rights, and reprint rights. It is the writer's obligation to secure clearance from the original publisher for any reprint rights." Pays on acceptance. Byline given. Free sample copy. Editorial deadlines are 9 months in advance of publication. Reports in 6 weeks. SASE.

Nonfiction and Poetry: Devotional, biographical, and informational articles with inspirational, religious, moral or educational values. Favorable toward emphasis on: "New Testament standard of living as applied to our day; soul-winning (evangelism); proper Sunday observance; Christian youth in action; Christian education in the home, the church and the college; good will to others; worldwide missions; clean living, high ideals, and temperance; wholesome social relationships. Disapprove of liquor, tobacco, theaters, dancing. Mss are judged on the basis of human interest, ability to hold reader's attention, vivid characterizations, thoughtful analysis of problems, vital character message, expressive English, correct punctuation, proper diction. Know where you are going and get there." Length: 500-1,500 words. Pays 2¢/word for quality material. Also uses verse. Length: 4-16 lines. Pays 25¢/line.

Photos: Purchased with mss. 5x7 or 8x10 b&w glossy prints portraying action, seasonal emphasis or scenic value. Various reader age-groups should be considered. Pays $1-2.50 depending on use.

Fiction: Stories should have definite Christian emphasis and character-building values, without being preachy. Setting, plot and action should be realistic. Length: 1,500-2,500 words; also short-shorts and vignettes. Pays 2¢/word for quality material.

THE WAR CRY, The Official Organ of the Salvation Army, 120-130 W. 14th St., New York NY 10011. (212)691-8780. Editor: Lt. Col. Ralph I. Miller. 5% freelance written. For "persons with evangelical Christian background; members and friends of the Salvation Army; the 'man in the street'." Weekly. Circ. 275,000. Buys first rights. Buys 100 mss/year. Pays on acceptance. Free sample copy. Submit seasonal material for Christmas and Easter issues at any time. "Christmas and Easter issues are 4-color. Rate of payment for material used in these issues is considerably higher than for weekly issue material." Reports in 2 months. SASE.

Nonfiction: Inspirational and informational articles with a strong evangelical Christian slant, but not preachy. Prefers an anecdotal lead. In addition to general articles, needs articles slanted toward most of the holidays, including Mother's Day, Father's Day, Columbus Day, Washington's and Lincoln's birthdays, etc. Length: approximately 1,000 words. Pays $15-35.

Photos: Occasionally buys pix submitted with mss, but seldom with captions only. B&w glossy prints. Pays $5-20.

Fiction: Prefers complete-in-one-issue stories. "Stories should run 1,500-2,000 words and have a strong Christian slant. May have Salvation Army background, but this is not necessary and may be detrimental if not authentic. Can have modern or Biblical setting, but must not run contrary to Scriptural account. Principal Bible characters ordinarily should not be protagonists." Pays 2¢/word.

Poetry: Religious or nature poems. Uses very little poetry "except on Christmas and Easter themes." Length: 4-24 lines. Pays $2.50-15.

Fillers: Inspirational and informative items with a strong Christian slant. 1-2¢/word.

WORLD ENCOUNTER, 2900 Queen Lane, Philadelphia PA 19129. (215)438-6360, ext. 373. Editor: the Rev. William A. Dudde. For persons who have more than average interest in, and understanding of, overseas missions and current human social concerns in other parts of the world. Quarterly magazine; 32 pages. Estab. 1963. Circ. 8,000. Buys all rights, but will reassign rights to author after publication. Pays 35% kill fee. Byline given. Buys 10 mss/year. Pays on publication. Free sample copy. Will consider photocopied, and simultaneous submissions, if information is supplied on other markets being approached. Reports in 1 month. Query or submit complete ms. SASE.

Nonfiction and Photos: "This is a religious and educational publication using human interest features and think pieces related to the Christian world mission and world community. Race relations in southern Africa; human rights struggles with tyrannical regimes; social and political ferment in Latin America; resurgence of Oriental religions. Simple travelogues are not useful to us. Prospective writers should inquire as to the countries and topics of particular interest to our constituents. Material must be written in a popular style but the content must be more than superficial. It must be theologically, sociologically and anthropologically sound. We try to maintain a balance between gospel proclamation and concern for human and social development. We focus on what is happening in Lutheran groups. Our standards of content quality and writing are very high." Length: 500-1,800 words. Pays $25-150. B&w photos are purchased with or without accompanying mss or on assignment. Pays $10-20. Captions required.

How To Break In: "Contact Lutheran missionaries in some overseas country and work out an article treatment with them. Or simply write the editor, outlining your background and areas of international knowledge and interest, asking at what points they converge with our magazine's interests."

Retirement

DYNAMIC YEARS, 215 Long Beach Blvd., Long Beach CA 90801. Executive Editor: James Wiggins. Managing Editor: Carol Powers. "*Dynamic Years* is the official publication of Action for Independent Maturity (AIM). AIM members are the 45-65 age bracket, pre-retirees." Estab. 1966. Bimonthly. Circ. 230,000. Rights purchased vary with author and material. Buys all rights or first serial rights. Pays negotiable kill fee. Byline given. Buys 100 mss a year. Pays on acceptance. Will send a free sample copy to a writer on request. Submit seasonal material 6 months in advance. Reports in 2 weeks. Query or submit complete ms. "Submit only 1 ms at a time." SASE.

Nonfiction: General subject matter is "health for middle years, pre-retirement planning, second careers, personal adjustment, well-developed hobbies, 'people in action' with useful activities, exciting use of leisure, financial preparation for retirement. We like the 'you' approach, nonpreachy, use of lively examples. We try to slant everything toward our age group. We do not want pieces about individuals long retired. Prefer not seeing poetry, fiction or inspirational preachments." Buys how-to, personal experience, profile, humor and travel articles. Length: 1,000-2,000 words. Pays up to $350 minimum per article.

Photos: State availablity of photos with ms. Photos purchased with and without mss for covers. Captions required. Pays $25 minimum for professional quality b&w photos (5x7, 8x10). Pays $100 minimum for professional quality color photos (35mm or 2¼x2¼ transparencies).

50 PLUS (formerly *Retirement Living*), 850 3rd Ave., New York NY 10022. (212)593-2100. Editor-in-Chief: Roy Hemming. Executive Editor: Meg Whitcomb. "A service-oriented publication (no nostalgia) for pre-retirees (age 50 up) and retirees (age 65 and up). Readers are alert, active, forward-looking, interested in all aspects of meaningful living in the middle and later years." Monthly. Buys all rights. Pays kill fee. Byline given. Buys 35-100 mss/year. Pays on acceptance. Will send a sample copy for $1 and 18¢ postage. Write for copy of guidelines for writers (enclose SASE). Submit seasonal and holiday material 6 months in advance. Reports in 6-8 weeks. Queries preferred, but will look at complete ms. No phone inquiries. "Manuscripts must be accompanied by SASE; otherwise not returned."

Nonfiction and Photos: "We like factual articles with a strong service value or how-to with names and sources for reader follow-up. Personal experiences, humor, income ideas, money management, unusual hobbies, self-fulfillment, celebrity interviews, food, fashion and controversial issues." Unusual travel stories, directly relevant to older people, only. Length: 500-1,500 words. Pays $50-250 an article; $20-25 for short spot news, anecdotes and personality items. "We reserve all rights to edit and rewrite to our style and space requirements. Photos and color slides must be of professional quality." Pays $35 minimum.

How To Break In: "Profile a dynamic person in your community whose recent retirement activities or retirement plans are unusual and could prove meaningful or instructive to another person."

MATURE LIVING, The Sunday School Board of the Southern Baptist Convention, 127 9th Ave. N., Nashville, TN 37234. (615)251-2274. Assistant Editor: Zada Malugen. A Christian magazine for retired or about-to-be-retired senior adults. Monthly magazine; 52 pages. Estab.

1977. Pays on acceptance. Buys all rights, but may reassign following publication. Byline given. Submit seasonal/holiday material 12 months in advance. SASE. Reports in 2-6 weeks. Free sample copy and writer's guidelines.

Nonfiction: How-to (easy, inexpensive craft articles made from easily obtained materials), informational (safety, consumer fraud, labor-saving and money-saving for senior adults), inspirational (short paragraphs with subject matter appealing to elders), interviews, nostalgia, personal experience, profile and travel. Buys 7-8 mss/issue. Send complete ms. Length: 400-1,400 words; prefers articles of 875 words. Pays $14-49.

Photos: Some photos purchased with accompanying ms. Pays about $5 for any size b&w glossy prints. Model release required.

Fiction: Everyday living, humor and religious. "Must have suspense and character interaction." Buys 1 ms/issue. Send complete ms. Length: 875-1,400 words. Pays 3½¢/word.

Fillers: Short humor, religious or grandparent/grandchild episodes. Length: 125 words. Pays $5.

How To Break In: "We want warmth. Presentations don't have to be moralistic or religious, but must reflect Christian standards. Use case histories and examples. Don't write down to target audience. Speak *to* senior adults on issues that interest them. They like inspirational, good-samaritan, and nostalgia articles. We'll buy some light humor and some travel. We continually need medium-length character studies of unusual people—especially those who have triumphed over adverse circumstances."

MATURE YEARS, 201 8th Ave., S., Nashville TN 37202. Editor: Daisy D. Warren. 55% freelance written. For retired persons and those facing retirement; persons seeking help on how to handle problems and privileges of retirement. Estab. 1954. Quarterly. Rights purchased vary with author and material; usually buys all rights. No byline. Buys 50 mss/year. Pays on acceptance. Write for copy of guidelines for writers. Submit seasonal material 1 year in advance. Reports in 6 weeks. Submit complete ms. SASE.

Nonfiction, Fiction and Photos: "*Mature Years* is different from the secular press in that we like material with Christian and church orientation. Usually we prefer materials that have a happy, healthy outlook regarding aging, although advocacy (for older adults) articles are at times used. Each issue is developed on a specific theme and the majority of theme-related articles are solicited. However, many freelance materials are used. Articles dealing with all aspects of pre-retirement and retirement living. Short stories and leisure-time hobbies related to specific seasons. Examples of how older persons, organizations, and institutions are helping others. Writing should be of interest to older adults, with Christian emphasis, though not preachy and moralizing. No poking fun or mushy, sentimental articles. We treat retirement from the religious viewpoint. How-to, humor and travel also considered." Length for nonfiction: 1,200-2,000 words. 8x10 b&w glossy prints purchased with ms or on assignment. "We buy fiction for adults. Humor is preferred. Please, no children's stories and no stories about depressed situations of older adults." Length: 1,000-2,000 words. Payment varies.

MODERN MATURITY, American Association of Retired Persons, 215 Long Beach Blvd., Long Beach CA 90801. Editor-in-Chief: Hubert C. Pryor. Managing Editor: Ian Ledgerwood. 75% freelance written. For readership over 55 years of age. Bimonthly magazine; 72 pages. Circ. 10 million. Pays on acceptance. Buys all rights. Pays 50% kill fee. Byline given. Submit seasonal/holiday material 6 months in advance. Photocopied submissions OK. SASE. Reports in 2 weeks. Free sample copy and writer's guidelines.

Nonfiction: Historical; how-to; humor; informational; inspirational; interview; new product; nostalgia; personal experience; personal opinion; photo feature; profile; and travel. Query or send complete ms. Length: 1,000-2,000 words. Pays $200-750.

Photos: Photos purchased with or without accompanying ms. Pays $25 minimum for 8x12 b&w glossy prints, "much more for color slides or prints."

Fiction: Buys some fiction, but must be suitable for older readers. Buys 2-3 mss/year. Send complete ms. Length: 1,000-2,000 words. Pays $300 minimum.

Poetry: All types. Length: 40 lines maximum. Pays $10-50.

Fillers: Clippings, jokes, gags, anecdotes, newsbreaks, puzzles (find-the-word, not crossword) and short humor. Length: 200-500 words. Pays $10 minimum.

NEW ENGLAND SENIOR CITIZEN/SENIOR AMERICAN NEWS, Prime National Publishing Corp., 470 Boston Post Rd., Weston MA 02193. Editor-in-Chief: Ira Alterman. 50% freelance written. For men and women aged 60 and over who are interested in travel, finances, retirement life styles, special legislation, nostalgia, etc. Monthly newspaper; 24-32 pages. Estab. 1970. Circ. 60,000. Pays on publication. Buys all rights. Pays 100% kill fee. Byline given.

Submit seasonal/holiday material 2-3 month in advance. Previously published material OK. SASE. Reports in 4-6 weeks. Sample copy 50¢.
Nonfiction: General interest, how-to (anything dealing with retirement years); inspirational; historical; humor; interview; nostalgia; profile; travel; personal experience; photo features; and articles about medicine relating to gerontology. Buys 3-6 mss/issue. Submit complete ms. Length: 500-1,500 words. Pays $25-50.
Photos: Purchased with or without ms. or on assignment. Captions required. Submit prints. Pays $5-15 for 5x7 or 8x10 b&w glossy prints. Captions and model releases required.
Columns/Departments: Humor. Buys 1/issue. Submit complete ms. Length: 500-1,000 words. Pays $25-50. Open to suggestions for new columns and departments.
Fiction: Adventure, historical, humorous, mystery, romance, suspense and religious. Buys 1 ms/issue. Submit complete ms. Length: 500-1,500 words. Pays $15-25.
How To Break In: "Remember that companionship is the theme we seek to pursue. Clean, typed, top-quality copy aimed at satisfying that need would be of great interest."

NRTA JOURNAL, 215 Long Beach Blvd., Long Beach CA 90801. (213)432-5781. Editor: Hubert Pryor. 75% freelance written. Publication of the National Retired Teachers Association. For retired teachers. Bimonthly. Buys all rights. Pays 50% kill fee. Byline given. Pays on acceptance. Free sample copy. Reports in 4 weeks. SASE.
Nonfiction and Fiction: Service pieces for the retired teacher relating to income, health, hobbies, living; Americana, nostalgia, reminiscence, personality pieces, inspirational articles, current trends. "Also in market for pieces on cultural leaders, cultural subjects and Christmas and other holiday material." Buys fiction occasionally. Length: 1,000-2,000 words for nonfiction; 1,000-2,000 words maximum for fiction. Pays $100-500.
Photos: "Special consideration for picture stories, photographic portfolios, etc." Pays $25 and up each; much more for color and covers.
Fillers: Puzzles, jokes, short humor. Pays $10 and up.

SENIOR EXCHANGE, Woodall Publishing Co., 500 Hyacinth Place, Highland Park IL 60035. (312)433-4550. Editor: James D. Saul. Emphasizes the interests of retired and pre-retired persons, 55 years old and over. "They like coverage on golf, fishing, travel, moneysaving deals, stories of accomplishment by seniors, legal rights and privileges of seniors, exposes about myths concerning aging, recreation vehicle campgrounds other seniors have enjoyed, physical fitness, health care, seniors and sex, retirement communities, singles activities, crafts, hobbies, vacations, book reviews on senior citizen concerns and seniors who choose to keep working." Bimonthly tabloid; 8 pages. Estab. 1977. Circ. 10,000. Pays on acceptance. Buys all rights. Phone queries OK. Submit seasonal/holiday material 3 months in advance. Previously published work OK if accompanied by written permission from copyright owner. SASE. Send label and 25¢ for sample copy.
Nonfiction: Expose (of myths about aging or discrimination against seniors); how-to (crafts, hobbies and other activities for seniors); humor (at the expense of those who would put down seniors); inspirational (accomplishments by seniors); interview (of seniors who do interesting things, or who perform useful services); profile (of outstanding seniors); travel (especially recreation vehicle travel or low-cost travel); personal experience (if useful in retirement planning or living); and photo feature. Buys 3 mss/issue. Query. Length: 250-1,500 words. Pays $25-125, "depending on merit."
Photos: State availability of photos with query or send photos with ms. Uses b&w 8x10 glossy prints. Does not yet print color, but has used color prints for b&w reproduction. Offers no additional payment for photos accepted with ms. Captions required. Buys all rights.
Columns/Departments: Book reviews of books about senior citizens. Buys 7/year. Query. Length: 250-500 words. Pays $25-100. Open to suggestions for new columns/departments.

Science

Publications classified here aim at laymen interested in technical and scientific developments and discoveries, applied science, and technical or scientific hobbies. Journals for professional scientists, engineers, repairmen, etc., will be found in Trade Journals.

ASTRONOMY, AstroMedia Corp., 411 E. Mason St., 6th Floor, Milwaukee WI 53202. (414)276-2689. Editor: Richard Berry. Emphasizes the science of astronomy. Monthly magazine; 80 pages. Estab. 1973. Circ. 77,000. Pays on publication. Reports in 6-8 weeks. Sample copy $2; free writer's guidelines.

Nonfiction: How-to (build a telescope; grind a mirror); informational (latest research; what you can observe using a specific type or size of equipment, etc.). "We do not accept articles on UFOs, astrology or religion." Buys 40-50/year. Submit complete ms. Length: 1,500-3,000 words. Pays 3-7¢/word.

Photos: Purchased with or without mss, or on assignment. B&w and color. Send prints and transparencies. Pays $7.50-10/b&w; $10 minimum for color.

Columns/Departments: Astro News and Astronomy Reviews (books). Buys 20-30/year. Query. Length: 150-500 words. Pays $1.25-1.75/typeset line. Open to suggestions for new columns/departments.

BYTE MAGAZINE, 70 Main St., Peterborough NH 03458. (603)924-7217. Editor-in-Chief: Raymond G.A. Gote. 90% freelance written. Emphasizes personal computers for college-educated users of computers. Monthly magazine; 280 pages. Estab. September 1975. Circ. 160,000. Pays on acceptance. Buys all rights. Photocopied submissions OK. SASE. Reports in 3 months. Sample copy $2.75; writer's guidelines for SASE, plus 26¢.

Nonfiction: How-to (technical information about computers) and technical. Buys 240 mss/year. Submit complete ms. Length: 20,000 words maximum. Pays $50/typeset magazine page maximum.

How To Break In: "The best way for a writer to break into our publication is by totally immersing himself in computer techniques and reading the magazine for 2-3 months since we publish almost exclusively technical information written for personal computer users."

CB YEARBOOK, 380 Lexington Ave., New York NY 10017. (212)557-9100. Associate Publisher & Editor-in-Chief: Julian S. Martin. For anyone getting started in electronics as a hobby. Annual magazine; 112 pages. Estab. 1968. Circ. 200,000. Buys all rights. Pays 100% kill fee. Byline given. Pays on acceptance. Reports in 2-3 weeks. Query. SASE.

Nonfiction: "We like new and exciting ideas. No padding; straight from the hip writing. Factual, with no puff. There will be a need for good stories on Citizens' Band Radio. Use our current issue as a style manual. Ask the question, is my next writing effort suitable for the issue I hold now?" How-to, personal experience, think pieces and technical articles. Length: open. Pays $100-250.

ELECTRONICS HOBBYIST, 380 Lexington Ave., New York NY 10017. (212)557-9100. Associate Publisher & Editor-in-Chief: Julian S. Martin. 100% freelance written. For "guys who like to build electronic projects from simple one-transistor jobs to complex digital clocks." Magazine; 112 pages. Estab. 1964. Semi-annually. Circ. 145,000. Buys all rights. Pays 100% kill fee. Byline given. Buys 60 mss/year. Pays on acceptance. No photocopied or simultaneous submissions. Reports in 2-3 weeks. Query. SASE.

Nonfiction: Construction projects only. "Write a letter to us telling details of proposed project." Length: open. Pays $100-250.

ELECTRONICS TODAY INTERNATIONAL, Unit 6, 25 Overlea Blvd., Toronto, Ontario, Canada M4H 1B1. (416)423-3262. Editor: Steve Braidwood. 40% freelance written. Emphasizes audio, electronics and personal computing for a wide-ranging readership, both professionals and hobbyists. Monthly magazine; 76 pages. Estab. February 1977. Circ. 27,000. Pays on publication. Buys all rights. Byline given. Phone queries OK. Submit seasonal/holiday material 4 months in advance of issue date. Photocopied submissions OK. SAE and International Reply Coupons. Reports in 4 weeks. Sample copy $2; free writer's guidelines.

Nonfiction: How-to (technical articles in electronics field); humor (if relevant to electronics); new product (if using new electronic techniques); and technical (on new developments, research, etc.). Buys 3-4 mss/issue. Query. Length: 600-3,500 words. pays $15-30.

Photos: "Ideally we like to publish 2 photos or diagrams per 1,000 words of copy." State availability of photo material with query. Offers no additional payment for photos accepted with accompanying ms. Captions required. Buys all rights.

Fillers: Puzzles (mathematical). Buys 10/year. Length: 50-250 words. Pays $6-10.

ELEMENTARY ELECTRONICS, Davis Publications, 380 Lexington Ave., New York NY 10017. (212)557-9100. Associate Publisher & Editor-in-Chief: Julian S. Martin. For electronics hobbyists, amateur radio operators, shortwave listeners, CB radio operators and computer hobbyists. Bimonthly magazine; 100 pages. Estab. 1950. Circ. 250,000. Buys all rights. Pays 100% kill fee. Byline given. Pays on acceptance. No photocopied or simultaneous submissions. SASE. Reports in 2 weeks. Free sample copy and writer's quidelines.

Nonfiction: "Construction articles are most needed; also, theory and feature articles related to hobby electronics." How-to and technical articles. "The writer should read our book and

decide whether he can be of service to us; and then send us a precis of the story he wishes to submit." Buys 15 mss/issue. Query. Length: 1,000-5,000 words. Pays $100 minimum.
Photos: No additional payment for photos used with mss.
How To Break In: "I would make three suggestions. First, how-to pieces are always winners. The same goes for construction projects. But they must be to fulfill some need, not just for the sake of selling an article. Finally, installation stories are very good—something that you buy and where the installation takes some degree of know-how that can be illustrated with step-by-step photos. The author will have to take the photos as he does the job. Theory pieces are tougher—you have to really know us and sense our needs and the sorts of things our readers want to learn about. Feeling and timing are key. We are about 98% freelance and most of our material originates in queries. Please read the magazine first!"

FREY SCIENTIFIC COMPANY CATALOG, 905 Hickory Lane, Mansfield OH 44905. Published annually. Buys all rights. Buys 70-100 rhymes/year. Pays "on acceptance, between October 1 and January 1. Rhymes that arrive after the latter date are held and paid for about November 1, the start of our next publication season." SASE.
Poetry: "We use humorous quatrains and limericks in our annual school science materials catalog, which is sent to every high school and college in the US. Each rhyme—limerick, quatrain, or couplet—is matched as best as possible to the appropriate section of our catalog. Rhymes pertaining to physics are included in the physics section, biology in the biology section, chemistry in the chemistry section, earth science to earth science, etc." Interested in buying material from writers "who can combine, in a single rhyme, our requirements of proper rhyme construction, distinct scientific reference, and humor. Generally, we will waive any of the three requirements if the rhyme is strong in the other two." Pays $5/rhyme.

MECHANIX ILLUSTRATED, 1515 Broadway, New York NY 10036. (212)975-4111. Editor: Robert G. Beason. Recreation Editor: Bill D. Miller. Home and Shop Editor: Burt Murphy. Managing Editor: Paul M. Eckstein. Special issues include boating (spring), new cars (October). Monthly magazine; 106 pages. Buys all rights except for picture sets. Pays kill fee. Byline given. Pays on acceptance. Send SASE for copy of guidelines for writers. Reports "promptly." Query. SASE.
Nonfiction: Feature articles about science, inventions, novel boats, planes, cars, electronics, recreational vehicles, weapons, health, money management, alternative energy, unusual occupations, usually with mechanical or scientific peg, but not too technical. Length: 1,500 words. Pays $400 minimum. Also uses home workshop projects, kinks, etc., for Home and Shop section. Pays $75-500, and higher in exceptional circumstances. "We offer a varied market for all types of do-it-yourself material, ranging from simple tips on easier ways to do things to major construction projects. Boatbuilding, furniture construction, painting, photography, electronics, gardening, astronomy, concrete and masonry work or any type of building construction or repair are just a few of the subjects that interest." Pays minimum of $15 for a tip submitted on a post card without an illustration. Pays $20-25 for an illustrated and captioned tip.
Photos: Photos should accompany mss. Pays $400 and up for transparencies of interesting mechanical or scientific subjects accepted for cover; prefers 4x5, but 2¼x2¼ square is acceptable. Inside color: $300 for 1 page, $500 for 2, $700 for 3, etc. Pays $35 for single (b&w) feature photos involving new developments, etc., in the field, Home and Shop tips illustrated with 1 photo, $25. Captions are required. B&w picture sets, up to $350. Requires model releases.
Fillers: Pays $75 for half-page fillers.
How To Break In: "If you're planning some kind of home improvement and can write, you might consider doing a piece on it for us. Good how-to articles on home improvement are always difficult to come by. Aside from that, no particular part of the book is easier to break into than another because we simply don't care whether you've been around or been published here before. We don't care who you are or whether you have any credentials—we're in the market for good journalism and if it's convincing, we buy it."

MODERN ELECTRONICS MAGAZINE, Cowan Publishing Corp., 14 Vanderventer Ave., Port Washington NY 11050. (516)883-6200. Editor: Mort Waters. Emphasizes all kinds of electronics for the hobbyist. Monthly magazine; 80 pages. Estab. February 1978. Circ. 225,000. Pays of acceptance if on assignment; pays on publication if unsolicited. Buys all rights. Submit seasonal/holiday material 4 months in advance. Photocopied and previously published submissions OK. SASE. Reports in 4 weeks. Sample copy $1; writer's guidelines for SASE.
Nonfiction: New products and technical. "Articles about electronics. General interest articles about technical aspects of electronics explained in near-layman's terms. Need carefully drawn

schematics (accurate, that is; not pretty, we redraw here but must have the author do properly in the first place)." Buys 10-20 mss/issue. Query. Length: 1,000-4,000 words. Pays $300 maximum (more if cover photo involved).

Photos: State availability of photos. Offers no additional payment for 4x5 or larger b&w glossy prints; 4x5 color transparencies. Captions and model releases required.

Fillers: Puzzles (word games with electronic terms). Length: 300 words maximum. Pays $5-20.

ON COMPUTING MAGAZINE, 70 Main St., Peterborough, NH 03458. (603)924-7217. Editor: Christopher P. Morgan. 60% freelance written. Emphasizes personal computers and its particularly directed at beginners and professional people such as educators, attorneys, doctors and so on. Monthly magazine; 116 pages. Estab. May 1979. Circ. 28,000. Pays on acceptance. Buys all rights. Photocopied submissions OK. SASE. Reports in 3 months. Sample copy $2.75; writer's guidelines for SASE.

Nonfiction: "Articles should contain information about buying personal computers plus reviews of computers and other material related to personal computers. Buys 80 mss/year. Submit complete ms. Length: 20,000 words maximum. Pays Pays $60/page.

How to Break In: "Visit personal computer stores or read any of the books on the market pertaining to personal computers. *On Computing Magazine* will be similar to *Byte Magazine* in some ways but will be at a lower technical level, designed for the mass market. The ideal *On Computing Magazine* article is one which popularizes personal computer concepts without talking down to the reader. Articles should be free of computer jargon as much as possible."

PERSONAL COMPUTING, 1050 Commonwealth Ave., Boston MA 02215. (617)232-5470. Editor-in-Chief: Harold G. Buchbinder. Managing Editor: Don Wood. 90% freelance written. Emphasizes small business, office, home and school computing. Monthly magazine; 116 pages. Estab. 1977. Circ. 35,000. Pays on publication. Buys all rights. Byline given. Phone queries OK. Submit seasonal/holiday material 3-4 months in advance of issue date. Photocopied submissions OK, but state if material is not multiple submission. SASE. Sample copy $3; free writer's guidelines; mention *Writer's Market* in request.

Nonfiction: Comparison pieces, product reviews and evaluations; general interest (related to micro computers); historical (original pieces concerning computer history); how-to (program and use computers; especially articles with programs our readers can use in business, office, home and school); humor (fiction relating to computers and personal stories concerning computers); interview (with prominent figures in the field); new product (review, but not puff piece, must be objective); nostalgia (only if related to computing or in the form of fiction about computing); computer chess and computer bridge; personal experience (someone who has worked with a specific system and has learned something readers can benefit from); personal opinion (editorials, or opinion of someone in field); photo feature (only if accompanied by article); profile (of prominent person in field); and technical (program writing, debugging; especially good are applications for business, education, or home use). No articles on product hype, personal experiences that don't pass anything on to the reader, games that have been published in similar form already, and puzzles. Buys 10 mss/issue. Query but complete ms preferred. Length: 1,000 words minimum. Pays $20/printed page minimum.

Photos: State availability of photos with query or ms. Offers no additional payment for b&w or color pictures. Captions preferred. Buys all rights.

Columns/Departments: Editorials (on any topic in the field); Future Computing (a detailed look at one or more aspects of what's going on in the field and what's projected); PC Interview (of prominent figures in the field); Random Access (unusual applications, goings on, or stories about computers); Computer Chess (and other games) and What's Coming Up (product reviews, comments on, criticism of, and comparison). Query but complete ms preferred. Length: 500 words minimum. Pays $20/printed page; Random Access pieces are paid anywhere from $5-25. Re-written press releases are not acceptable.

Fiction: "Fiction should relate to computers—especially micro computers. Science fiction showing computer uses in the future also acceptable." Buys 1 ms/issue. Submit complete ms. Length: 750 words minimum. Pays $20/printed page.

POPULAR ELECTRONICS, 1 Park Ave., New York NY 10016. (212)725-3566. Editor: Arthur P. Salsberg. 80% freelance written. For electronics experimenters, hi-fi enthusiasts, computer hobbyists, CB'ers, hams. Monthly. Estab. 1954. Circ. 415,000. Buys all rights. Pays 50% kill fee. Byline given. Buys about 100 mss/year. Pays on acceptance. Write for copy of guidelines for writers. No photocopied or simultaneous submissions. Reports in 2-4 weeks. Query. SASE.

Nonfiction and Photos: "State-of-the-art reports, tutorial articles, construction projects, etc. The writer must know what he's talking about and not depend on 'hand-out' literature from a few manufacturers or research laboratories. The writer must always bear in mind that the reader has some knowledge of electronics." Informational, how-to, and technical articles. Length: 500-3,000 words. Pays $70-125/published page with photo illustration, rough diagrams. B&w glossy prints preferred.

Fillers: Electronics circuits quizzes, circuit and bench tips. Length: 100-1,000 words. Pays $10-80.

POPULAR MECHANICS, 224 W. 57th St., New York NY 10019. (212)262-4815. Editor: John A. Linkletter. Executive Editor: Robin Nelson. Managing Editor: Arthur Maher. Home and Shop Editor: Harry Wicks. Magazine; 200 pages. Monthly. Circ. 1,671,216. Buys all rights. Byline given. Pays "promptly." Query. SASE.

Nonfiction: "Our principal subjects are automotive (new cars, car maintenance) and how-to (woodworking, metalworking, home improvement and home maintenance). In addition, we use features on new technology, sports, electronics, photography and hi-fi." Exciting male interest articles with strong science, exploration and adventure emphasis. Looking for reporting on new and unusual developments. The writer should be specific about what makes it new, different, better, cheaper, etc. "We are always looking for fresh ideas in home maintenance, shop technique and crafts for project pieces used in the back part of the book. The front of the book uses articles in technology and general science, but writers in that area should have background in science." Length: 300-2,000 words. Pays $300-600 and up.

Photos: Dramatic photos are most important, and they should show people and things in action. Occasionally buys picture stories with short text block and picture captions. The photos must tell the story without much explanation. Topnotch photos are a must with Craft Section articles. Can also use remodeling of homes, rooms and outdoor structures. Pays $25 minimum.

Fillers: How-to articles on craft projects and shop work well-illustrated with photos and drawings. The writer must provide the drawings, diagrams, cutaways, and/or photos that would be appropriate to the piece. Finished drawings suitable for publication are not necessary; rough but accurate pencil drawings are adequate for artist's copy. Pays $15.

POPULAR SCIENCE MONTHLY, 380 Madison Ave., New York NY 10017. Editor: Hubert P. Luckett. For the well-educated adult male, interested in science, technology, new products. Monthly magazine; 200 pages. Estab. 1872. Circ. 1,800,000. Buys all rights. Pays negotiable kill fee. Byline given. Buys several hundred mss a year. Pays on acceptance. Free guidelines for writers. No photocopied or simultaneous submissions. Submit seasonal material 3 to 4 months in advance. Reports in 2 to 3 weeks. Query. SASE.

Nonfiction and Photos: "*Popular Science Monthly* is devoted to exploring (and explaining) to a nontechnical but knowledgeable readership the technical world around us. We are a 'thing'-oriented publication: things that fly or travel down a turnpike, or go on or under the sea, or cut wood, or reproduce music, or build buildings, or make pictures, or mow lawns. We are especially focused on the new, the ingenious and the useful. We are consumer-oriented and are interested in any product that adds to a man's enjoyment of his home, yard, car, boat, workshop, outdoor recreation. Some of our 'articles' are only a picture and caption long. Some are a page long. Some occupy 4 or more pages. Contributors should be as alert to the possibility of selling us pictures and short features as they are to major articles. Freelancers should study the magazine to see what we want and avoid irrelevant submissions." Length: 2,000 words maximum. Pays a minimum of about $150 a published page. Prefers 8x10 b&w glossy prints. Pays $20.

Fillers: Uses shortcuts and tips for homeowners, home craftsmen, car owners, mechanics and machinists.

How To Break In: "Probably the easiest way to break in here is by covering a news story in science and technology that we haven't heard about yet. We need people to be acting as bird-dogs for us out there and we are willing to give the most leeway on these performances. What impresses us the most in a freelance piece—when we're thinking about uncovering a good contributor for the future—is the kind of illustrations the writer supplies. Too many of them kiss off the problem of illustrations. Nothing impresses us more than knowing that the writer can take or acquire good photos to accompany his piece. We probably buy the most freelance material in the do-it-yourself and home improvement areas."

PROGRAMMERS SOFTWARE EXCHANGE, 2110 N. 2nd Street, Cabot AR 72023. (501)843-6037. Editor: Linda Brown. Emphasizes personally owned computers. Quarterly magazine; 32 pages. Estab. 1977. Circ. 3,000. Pays on acceptance. Buys all rights. Pays 25% kill fee. Byline given. Phone queries OK. Submit seasonal/holiday material 1 months in advance. Simultaneous, photocopied and previously published submissions OK. SASE. Reports in 2 weeks. Free sample copy and writer's guidelines.

Nonfiction: Expose (computer crime); general interest (game programs); historical; how-to (program computers); humor; inspirational; nostalgia; personal opinion; profile; and travel. "All articles must be related to personal computers in various uses and configurations." Buys 2 mss/issue. Send complete ms. Length: 100-600 words. Pays 15¢/word.
Photos: State availability of photos. Pays $10-50 for b&w contact sheets; $10-50 for color contact sheets; offers no additional payment for photos with accompanying mss. Buys one-time rights. Captions preferred.
Columns/Departments: Why Not Do It In Software. Send complete ms. Length: 100-600 words. Pays 15¢/word.
Fiction: Adventure, erotica, fantasy, experimental, historical, humorous and mainstream. "All articles must be slanted to computer use by people." Send complete ms. Length: 200-600 words. Pays $30-90.
Poetry: Free verse, haiku, light verse and traditional. Submit in batches of 10. Length: 5-20 lines. Pays $10-50.
Fillers: Clippings, jokes, gags, anecdotes and puzzles. Buys 5/issue. Length: 10-100 words. Pays $5-20.

RADIO-ELECTRONICS, 200 Park Ave. S., New York NY 10003. (212)777-6400. Editorial Director: Larry Steckler. Managing Editor: Art Kleiman. For electronics professionals and hobbyists. Monthly. Circ. 175,000. Buys all rights. Byline given "by request only." Pays on acceptance. Submit seasonal/holiday material 6-8 months in advance. SASE. Reports in 2-4 weeks. Send for "Guide to Writing."
Nonfiction: Interesting technical stories on electronics, TV and radio, written from viewpoint of the electronics professional, serious experimenter, or layman with technical interests. Construction (how-to-build-it) articles used heavily. Unique projects bring top dollars. Cost of project limited only by what item will do. Emphasis on "how it works, and why." Much of material illustrated with schematic diagrams and pictures provided by author. Also high interest in how-to articles. Length: 1,000-2,500 words. Pays about $50-500.
Photos: State availability of photos. Offers no additional payment for b&w prints or 35mm color transparencies. Model releases required.
Columns/Departments: Pays $50-200/column.
Fillers: Pays $15-35.
How To Break In: "The simplest way to come in would be with a short article on some specific construction project. Queries aren't necessary; just send the article, 5 or 6 typewritten pages."

SCIENCE DIGEST, Hearst Magazines Division, Hearst Corp., 224 W. 57th St., New York NY 10019. (212)262-4161. Editor-in-Chief: Daniel E. Button. Emphasizes sciences and technologies for all ages with a scientific bent. Monthly magazine; 100 pages. Estab. 1937. Circ. 160,000. Pays on acceptance. Buys all rights. Pays kill fee. Byline given. Submit seasonal/holiday material 3 months in advance. Simultaneous and previously published submissions OK. Reports in 1 month.
Nonfiction: Informational (authentic, timely information in all areas of science); interview (with outstanding authorities in various fields of science); photo feature (usually single photos with adequate cutlines); profile; and technical (not overly so). Buys 30 mss/year. Query. Length: 750-1,500 words. Pays $50-500.
Photos: Purchased with or without accompanying ms or on assignment. Captions required. Query. Pays $25-100 for 8x10 b&w photos; $50-300 for color. Total purchase price for ms includes payment for photos. Model release required.
Fillers: Anecdotal or nostalgic. Query. Length: 50-250 words. Pays $25-50.

SCIENCE & MECHANICS, Davis Publications, 380 Lexington Ave., New York NY 10017. Editor-in-Chief: Joseph Daffron. Managing Editor: Anthony Assenza. Published 3 times/year. Magazine; 122 pages. Estab. 1937. Pays on acceptance. Buys all rights. Submit seasonal/holiday material 5 months in advance of issue date. SASE. Reports in 2 weeks.
Nonfiction: How-to (wood, mechanical, electronic and outdoor projects; home fix-up and repair); general interest (science, mechanics, technology, energy saving); and technical (what's new, inventions, electronics, science, technology, automotive and mechanical). Buys 6-8 mss/issue. Query. Length: 2,500-4,000 words. Pays $200 minimum.
Photos: "Technical and how-to material must be illustrated; would like to see drawings and diagrams, if applicable." State availability of photos with query. Captions preferred.

SCIENCE NEWS, Science Service, Inc., 1719 N St. NW, Washington DC 20036. Editor-in-Chief: Robert Trotter. For scientists and science-oriented laymen. Weekly magazine; 16 pages. Estab. 1922. Circ. 175,000. Pays on acceptance. Buys all rights. SASE.

Nonfiction: Profile and technical news. Buys 4 mss/year. Query or send complete ms. Pays $75-200. "We are primarily staff-written for two reasons: Freelancers should study the magazine to see what we want and avoid irrelevant submissions." Length: 2,000 words maximum. Pays a minimum of about $150 a published page. Prefers 8x10 b&w glossy prints. Pays $75-200. "We are primarily staff-written for two reasons: (1) Being a weekly newsmagazine, we work very close to deadline. Communications and coordination are crucial. Everyone must note what we've previously reported on the same subject and then add what's new. (2) Quality control. We have really gotten burned in the past by freelance articles that were factually inaccurate. We are occasionally in the market for prepublication excerpts from books, especially those involving a thoughtful, humanistic approach toward science, by noted scientists of established reputaton; but again this is seldom."

How To Break In: "Acceptance occurs when the writer is either covering a newsworthy scientific meeting that for some reason we have no reporter at, or has a topical news-feature articles (1,500-1,800 words) on a specific science topic that we haven't already covered. For them to work for us, the writer must be very familiar with *Science News* (suitable for scientists and the scientifically interested lay public) and for the subjects we already cover thoroughly. These include, generally, physics, astronomy, the space sciences and medical sciences. Articles must have both news and science value."

SCIENTIFIC AMERICAN, 415 Madison Ave., New York NY 10017. Articles by professional scientists only.

73 MAGAZINE, Peterborough NH 03458. (603)924-3873. Publisher: Wayne Green. For amateur radio operators and experimenters. Monthly. Buys all rights. Pays on acceptance. Reports on submissions within a few weeks. Query. SASE.
Nonfiction and Photos: Articles on anything of interest to radio amateurs, experimenters and computer hobbyists—construction projects. Pays $40-50/page. Photos purchased with ms.

TECHNOLOGY REVIEW, Alumni Association of the Massachusetts Institute of Technology, Room 10-1040, Massachusetts Institute of Technology, Cambridge MA 02139. Editor-in-Chief: John I. Mattill. Managing Editor: Steven J. Marcus. 10% freelance written. Emphasizes technology and its implications. Published 8 times/year. Magazine; 88 pages. Estab. 1899. Circ. 65,000. Pays on publication. Buys all rights, but may reassign following publication. Phone queries OK. Submit seasonal/holiday material 6 months in advance of issue date. Simultaneous and photocopied submissions OK. SASE. Reports in 4-6 weeks. Sample copy $2.50.
Nonfiction: General interest; interview; photo feature; and technical. Buys 3-5 mss/year. Query. Length: 1,000-10,000 words. Pays $75-300.
Columns/Departments: Book Reviews; Trend of Affairs; Society; Technology and Science; and Prospects (guest column). Also special reports on other appropriate subjects. Buys 1 ms/issue.

Science Fiction, Speculative Fiction, and Fantasy

ANALOG SCIENCE FICTION & SCIENCE FACT, 350 Madison Ave., New York NY 10017. Editor: Dr. Stanley Schmidt. 100% freelance written. For general future-minded audience. Monthly. Buys all English serial rights. Byline given. Pays on acceptance. Reports in 3-4 weeks. SASE.
Fiction: Stories of the future told for adults interested in science and technology; central theme usually interaction of strong characters with science or technology-based problems. Send complete ms on short fiction; query about serials. Length: 3,000-60,000 words. Pays 3-4¢/word for novelettes and novels; 5¢/word for shorts under 7,500 words.
Nonfiction: Illustrated technical articles. Query. Length: 5,000 words. Pays 5¢/word.
Photos: Buys photos with mss only. Pays $5.

ASIMOV'S SF ADVENTURE MAGAZINE, Box 13116, Philadelphia PA 19101. (215)382-5415. Editor: George Scithers. Managing Editor: Shawna McCarthy. "This is basically similiar to that of *Isaac Asimov's Science Fiction Magazine*." Quarterly magazine; 112 pages. Estab. 1978. Circ. 60,000. Pays on acceptance. Buys first North American serial rights and foreign serial rights. Byline given. Photocopied submissions OK. SASE. Reports in 2 weeks. Sample copy $2; writer's guidelines for SASE.
Fiction: Science fiction. "We do not want to see anything but science fiction." Buys 5 mss/issue. Send complete ms. Pays 3-5¢/word.

ISAAC ASIMOV'S SCIENCE FICTION MAGAZINE, Davis Publications, Inc., Box 13116, Philadelphia PA 19101. (215)382-5415. Editor-in-Chief: George H. Scithers. 95% freelance written. Emphasizes science fiction. Monthly magazine; 192 pages. Estab. 1976. Circ. 100,000. Pays on acceptance. Buys first North American serial rights and foreign serial rights. Photocopied submissions OK. SASE. Reports in 2-3 weeks. Writer's guidelines for SASE.
Fiction: Science fiction only. "At first, each story must stand on its own; but as the magazine progresses, we want to see continuing use of memorable characters and backgrounds." Buys 12 mss/issue. Submit complete ms. Length: 100-12,500 words. Pays 3-5¢/word.

ETERNITY SCIENCE FICTION, Box 510, Clemson SC 29631. Editors: Henry L. Vogel, Stephen Gregg. Quarterly magazine; 90 pages. Estab. 1979. Pays on acceptance. Buys first North American serial rights. Byline given. Simultaneous and photocopied submissions OK. SASE. Reports in 4 weeks.
Nonfiction: Science fiction. Buys 3 mss/issue. Query. Length: 2,000-6,000 words. Pays 1¢/word.
Fiction: Science. "We do not want any Adam and Eve stories, no deals with the devil. Any fantasy submissions should be more than run-of-the mill. We are not interested in *Star Trek* or *Star Wars* imitations. Otherwise, most any type of science fiction or fantasy is welcome." Buys 8 mss/issue. Send complete ms. Length: 1,000-20,000 words. Pays 1¢/word.

GALILEO: Magazine of Science & Fiction, Avenue Victor Hugo, Inc., 339 Newbury St., Boston MA 02115. (617)266-7834. Editor: Charles C. Ryan. Bimonthly magazine; 96 pages. Estab. September 1976. Circ. 100,000. Pays 1 month before publication. Buys first world serial rights. Byline given. Phone queries OK. Submit seasonal/holiday material 6-8 months in advance. Photocopied submissions OK. SASE. Reports in 4-8 weeks. Sample copy $1.95.
Nonfiction: Interview and technical. "We are interested in articles which examine in clear, easy-to-understand, but eloquent language the theoretical limits of science. Also articles which examine future developments as well as interviews with top science fiction authors or top scientists." Buys 3-4 mss/issue. Query with SASE. Length: 2,000-4,000 words.
Columns/Departments: Book and Movie Reviews. Query with SASE. Buys 5/issue. Length 350-500 words. Pays $10-25.
Fiction: Science fiction and serialized novels. Buys 30-42 mss/year. Send complete ms. Length: 1,500-20,000 words. Pays 3-10¢/word.
Poetry: Avant-garde, free verse, haiku, light verse and traditional. "Poems must be about science or science fiction in nature." Buys 1/issue. Pays 3-10¢/word.
Fillers: Jokes, gags, anecdotes and cartoons of science or science fiction. Pays 3¢/word to flat payment for cartoons $25-50.

STARWIND, The Starwind Press, Box 3346, Columbus OH 43210. Editor: Elbert Lindsey Jr. 70-80% freelance written. For a college-educated audience (18-35) interested in science fiction and fantasy. Magazine; 50-60 pages. Estab. 1973. Twice a year (fall and spring). Circ. 2,500. Rights purchased vary with author and material. May buy first North American serial rights or second serial (reprint) rights. Buys about 25 mss/year. Pays on publication. Sample copy $2; free writer's guidelines. Will consider photocopied submissions. No simultaneous submissions. Reports in 6-8 weeks. Submit complete ms. SASE.
Nonfiction: "Interested in analyses of works of well-known science fiction authors and genres in sf and fantasy, or interviews with sf authors or publishers. Reviews of sf books. Also interested in articles dealing with current developments or research in space exploration or colonization, artifical intelligence, genetics, bioengineering, or other subjects. Emphasis should be on extrapolations which are of interest to readers of science fiction." Length: 4,000-20,000 words. Pays ½¢/word.
Fiction: "Both hard and soft science fiction, including extrapolative and speculative stories. "We will consider science fantasy, dark fantasy, sword and sorcery and occult material only if it is both original in content and competent in execution. We are looking for interesting, imaginative story-telling. We like to showcase the work of new authors and welcome stylistic experimentation." Length: 10,000 words maximum. Pays ½-1½¢/word.

TESSERACT SCIENCE FICTION, 134 Windward Dr., Schaumburg IL 60194. (312)843-1319. Editors: Kevin MacAnn, Cory Graberson. 80% freelance written. Emphasizes science fiction and fantasy. Magazine published 2 times/year; 100 pages. Estab. 1977. Circ. 1,000. Pays on publication. Buys first North American serial rights. Phone queries OK. Photocopied submissions OK. SASE. Reports in 2 months. Free writer's guidelines.
Fiction: Fantasy (a limited amount will be considered only, also science fantasy); and science fiction (prefer "hard core" science fiction, but will consider all types). Buys 10 mss/year.

Submit complete ms. Length 15,000 words maximum. Pays ½¢/word.

WEIRDBOOK, Box 35, Amherst Branch, Buffalo NY 14226. Editor-in-Chief: W. Paul Ganley. Emphasizes weird fantasy (swords and sorcery, supernatural horror, pure fantasy) for educated, mature readers of all ages a readership teen-age and up. Semiannual magazine; 64 pages. Estab. 1968. Circ. 900. Pays on publication. Buys first North American serial rights and right to reprint as part of entire issue. Photocopied submissions OK. SASE. "Best time to submit is in December or May if quick response is desired." Sample copy $2.50; writer's guidelines for SASE.
Fiction: Adventure (with weird elements); experimental (maybe, if in fantasy or horror area). Buys 6 mss/year. Submit complete ms. Length: 20,000 words maximum. Pays ¼¢/word minimum.

WHISPERS, Box 904, Chapel Hill NC 27514. Editor: Dr. Stuart David Schiff. 100% freelance written. For intelligent adults with an interest in literate horror, terror, fantasy, and heroic fantasy. Many readers collect first edition books and the like in these fields. Magazine; 64 pages. Estab. 1973. An approximate bimonthly schedule. Circ. 3,000. Buys first North American serial rights only. Buys 15-20 mss/year. Pays half of fee on acceptance; balance on publication. Will consider photocopied submissions. No simultaneous submissions. Reports in 3 months. Submit complete ms. SASE.
Fiction: Stories of fantasy, terror, horror and heroic fantasy. No scien science fiction. No rocket ships, futuristic societies, bug-eyed monsters or the like. Authors whose work is most related to their needs include H. P. Lovecraft, Lord Dunsany, Edgar Allan Poe, Algernon Blackwood, Robert Bloch, Fritz Leiber, Ray Bradbury and Clark Ashton Smith. Length: 500-8,000 words. Pays 1¢/word.

Social Science

IMPACT OF SCIENCE ON SOCIETY, Unesco, 7 place de Fontenoy, 75700 Paris, France. (1)577-16-10. Editor: J. G. Richardson. Emphasizes science-society interactions as well as science and technology for development. Quarterly journal; 96 pages. Estab. 1950. Published in 5 languages. Pays on acceptance. Buys all rights, but may reassign following publication. Photocopied submissions OK. SASE. Reports in 2 weeks. Free sample copy.
Nonfiction: "Would like to see manuscripts dealing with the man-forest interface, military research and development, human vision (the eye), fresh water management, physics and chemistry of the atmosphere." Informational; interview; how-to; profiles; and think pieces. Prefers not to see mystical explanations for natural phenomena or utopian solutions to problems of world development. Length: 4,500 words, illustrated. Pays $250 maximum.

PARAPSYCHOLOGY REVIEW, 29 W. 57th St., New York NY 10019. (212)751-5940. Editor: Betty Shapin. Emphasizes psychic research, parapsychology, research and experiments pertaining to extrasensory perception. For the scientific community, academic community, lay audience with special interest in psychical research and the paranormal. Estab. 1953. Bimonthly. Circ. 2,500. Buys all rights, but will reassign to author following publication. Byline given. Buys 40-50 mss/year. Pays on acceptance. Sample copy $1. Reports in 1-2 weeks. Query or submit complete ms. SASE.
Nonfiction: Articles, news items, book reviews in this general subject area. Must approach psychical research in scientific, experimental fashion. Length: 500-3,000 words. Pays $50 minimum.

PERSONAL GROWTH, Box 1254, Berkeley CA 94701. (415)548-1004. Editor: James Elliott. For psychologists and well-informed laypeople. Monthly magazine; 24 pages. Estab. 1964. Circ. 5,000. Buys all rights. Pays 100% kill fee. Byline given. Buys 6 mss/year. Pays on acceptance. Sample copy to writer for 2 first class postage stamps; free writer's guidelines. Will consider photocopies and simultaneous submissions. Reports in 4-6 weeks. Query. SASE. Interested only in reports of new therapies and growth methods (provided a critique is included). Writers should send for and read guidelines before submitting manuscripts. Length: 200-3,000 words. Pays $15-200.

PSYCHOLOGY TODAY, 1 Park Ave., New York NY 10016. (212)725-3900. For social scientists and intelligent laymen concerned with society and individual behavior. Monthly. Buys all rights. Pays 10% kill fee. Byline given. Each ms will be edited by staff and returned to author prior to publication for comments and approval. Author should retain a copy. Reports in 1 month. Address all queries to Articles Editor. SASE.

Nonfiction: Most mss are written by scholars in various fields. Primary purpose is to provide the nonspecialist with accurate and readable information about society and behavior. Technical and specialized vocabularies should be avoided except in cases where familiar expressions cannot serve as adequate equivalents. Technical expressions, when necessary, should be defined carefully for the nonexpert. References to technical literature should not be cited within article, but 10 to 12 general readings should be listed at end. Suggested length: 3,000 words. Payment is $500.

THE SINGLE PARENT, Parents Without Partners, Inc., 7910 Woodmont Ave., Washington DC 20014. (301)654-8850. Editor-in-Chief: Barbara C. Chase. Emphasizes marriage, family, divorce, widowhood and children. Distributed to members of Parents Without Partners, plus libraries, universities, psychologists, psychiatrists, etc. Magazine, published 10 times/year; 48 pages. Estab. 1965. Circ. 171,000. Pays on publication. Rights purchased vary. Phone queries OK. Submit seasonal/holiday material 3 months in advance of issue date. Simultaneous, photocopied and previously published submissions OK. SASE. Reports in 6-8 weeks. Free sample copy and writer's guidelines.
Nonfiction: Informational (parenting, career development, money management, day care); interview (with professionals in the field, with people who have successfully survived the trauma of divorce); personal experience (adjustment to living alone, to widowhood, to divorce from both the parental and child's point of view); how-to (raise children alone, travel, take up a new career, home/auto fix-up). Buys 4-5 mss/issue. Query. Length: 1,000-6,000 words. Pays $25-50.
Photos: Purchased with accompanying ms. Query. Pays $10-50 for any size b&w glossies. Model release required.
Rejects: "No first-hand accounts of bitter legal battles with former spouses. No poetry or general interest material."

SEXOLOGY (formerly *Together*), 313 W. 53rd St., New York NY 10019., Editor: Barbara Schrank. For a lay readership. Monthly magazine; 80 pages. Estab. 1933. Circ. 100,000. Pays on acceptance. Buys all rights, first serial rights or second serial (reprint) rights. SASE. Reports in 4 weeks.
Nonfiction: "We are seeking articles to bring to the public authoritative and frank information that will help them integrate their sexual natures with the rest of their lives. Themes must be solidly educational or informative and, at the same time, entertaining. Our editorial aim is to provide helpful, accurate guidance and advice. We eschew sensationalism, but any solid attempt to bring information to our public is reviewed. We regularly cover how-to themes with specific advice on promoting compatability, including sexual acts. We seek anatomic articles (medical) about sexuality, psychology, the elderly, singles, new scientific breakthroughs, sociological/philosophical perspectives, other cultures, customs (in sex and relationship) and modern appraisals of the relationship/sex theme." Query with outline. Length: 2,500-3,000 words. Pays $200 minimum.

TRANSACTION/SOCIETY, Rutgers University, New Brunswick NJ 08903. (201)932-2280, ext. 83. Editor: Irving Louis Horowitz. For social scientists (policymakers with training in sociology, political issues and economics). Estab. 1963. Every 2 months. Circ. 55,000. Buys all rights, but may reassign rights to author after publication. Byline given. Pays on publication. Free sample copy and writer's guidelines. Will consider photocopied submissions. No simultaneous submissions. Reports in 4 weeks. Query. SASE.
Nonfiction and Photos: Articles Editor: Barry Lipinski. Photo Editor: Joan DuFault. "Articles of wide interest in areas of specific interest to the social science community. Must have an awareness of problems and issues in education, population and urbanization that are not widely reported. Articles on overpopulation, terrorism, international organizations." Payment for articles is made only if done on assignment. *No payment for unsolicited articles.* Pays $200 for photographic essays done on assignment.

VICTIMOLOGY: An International Journal, Box 39045, Washington DC 20016. Editor-in-Chief: Emilio C. Viano. "We are the only magazine specifically focusing on the victim, on the dynamics of victimization; for social scientists, criminal justice professionals and practitioners, social workers and volunteer and professional groups engaged in prevention of victimization and in offering assistance to victims of rape, spouse abuse, child abuse, natural disasters, etc." Quarterly magazine. Estab. 1976. Circ. 2,500. Pays on publication. Buys all rights. Byline given. SASE. Reports in 6-8 weeks. Sample copy $5; free writer's guidelines.
Nonfiction: Expose, historical, how-to, informational, interview, personal experience, profile, research and technical. Buys 10 mss/issue. Query. Length: 500-5,000 words. Pays $5-100.

Photos: Purchased with accompanying ms. Captions required. Send contact sheet. Pays $15-50 for 5x7 or 8x10 b&w glossies.
Poetry: Avant-garde; free verse; light verse; and traditional. Length: 30 lines maximum. Pays $10-25.
How To Break In: "Focus on what is being researched and discovered on the victim, the victim-offender relationship, treatment of the offender, the bystander-witness, preventive measures, and what is being done in the areas of service to the victims of rape, spouse abuse, neglect and occupational and environmental hazards and the elderly."

Sport and Outdoor

The publications listed in this category are intended for active sportsmen, sports fans, or both. They buy material on how to practice and enjoy both team and individual sports, material on conservation of streams and forests, and articles reporting on and analyzing professional sports.

Writers will note that several editors mention that they do not wish to see "Me 'n Joe" stories. These are detailed accounts of one hunting/fishing trip taken by the author and a buddy—starting with the friends' awakening at dawn and ending with their return home, "tired but happy."

For the convenience of writers who specialize in one or two areas of sport and outdoor writing, the publications are subcategorized by the sport or subject matter they emphasize. Publications in related categories (for example, Hunting and Fishing; Archery and Bowhunting) often buy similar material (in this case articles on bow and arrow hunting).

Consequently, writers should read through this entire Sport and Outdoor category to become familiar with the subcategories and note the ones that contain markets for their own type of writing.

Publications concerned with horse breeding, hunting dogs or the use of other animals in sport are classified in the Animal category. Publications dealing with automobile or motorcycle racing will be found in the Automotive and Motorcycle category. Outdoor publications that exist to further the preservation of nature, placing only secondary emphasis on preserving nature as a setting for sport, are listed in the Nature, Conservation, and Ecology category. Newspapers and Magazine Sections, as well as Regional and City magazines, are frequently interested in conservation or sports material with a local angle. Camping publications are classified in the Travel, Camping and Trailer category.

Archery and Bowhunting

ARCHERY WORLD, 225 E. Michigan, Milwaukee WI 53202. Editor: Glenn Helgeland. 30-50% freelance written. For "archers of average education, hunters and target archers, experts to beginners." Subject matter is the "entire scope of archery—hunting, bowfishing, indoor target, outdoor target, field." Bimonthly. Circ. 98,000. Buys first serial rights. Buys 30-35 mss/year. Pays on publication. Will send a free sample copy to a writer on request. Tries to report in 2 weeks. Query. SASE.
Nonfiction: "Get a free sample and study it. Try, in ms, to entertain archer and show him how to enjoy his sport more and be better at it." Wants how-to, semitechnical, and hunting where-to and how-to articles. "Looking for more good technical stories and short how-to pieces." Also uses profiles and some humor. Length: 1,000-2,200 words. Payment is $50-150.
Photos: B&w glossies purchased with mss and with captions. "Like to see proofsheets and negatives with submitted stories. We make own cropping and enlargements." Color transparencies purchased for front cover only. Will look at color prints "if that's the only photo available." Pays $5 minimum for b&w; $50 minimum for color.

BOW AND ARROW, Box HH/34249 Camino Capistrano, Capistrano Beach CA 92624. Managing Editor: Cheri Elliott. 75% freelance written. For archery competitors and bowhunters. Bimonthly. Buys all rights, "but will relinquish all but first American serial rights on written request of author." Byline given. Pays on acceptance. Free sample copy. Reports on submissions in 6 weeks. Author must have some knowledge of archery terms. SASE.
Nonfiction: Articles: bowhunting, major archery tournaments, techniques used by champs,

how to make your own tackle, and off-trail hunting tales. Likes a touch of humor in articles. Also uses one technical article per issue. Submit complete ms. Length: 1,500-2,500 words. Pays $50-200.

Photos: Purchased as package with mss; 5x7 minimum or submit contacts with negatives (returned to photographer). Pays $75-100 for cover chromes, 35mm or larger.

BOWHUNTER MAGAZINE, 3808 S. Calhoun St., Fort Wayne IN 46807. (219)744-1373 or 432-5772. Editor: M. R. James. For "readers of all ages, background and experience. All share two common passions—hunting with the bow and arrow and a love of the great outdoors." Bimonthly magazine; 80 pages. Estab. 1971. Circ. 105,000. Buys all rights, but may reassign rights to author after publication. Byline given "only be an author's request." Buys 55 mss/year. Pays on acceptance. Will send sample copy to writer on request. Write for copy of guidelines for writers. No photocopied or simultaneous submissions. "We publish a special deer hunting issue each August. Submit seasonal material 6-8 months in advance." Reports in 4-6 weeks. Query or submit complete ms. SASE.

Nonfiction, Photos and Fillers: "Our articles are written for, by and about bowhunters and we ask that they inform as well as entertain. Most material deals with big or small game bowhunting (how-to, where to go, etc.), but we do use some technical material and personality pieces. We do not attempt to cover all aspects of archery—only bowhunting. Anyone hoping to sell to us must have a thorough knowledge of bowhunting. Next, they must have either an interesting story to relate or a fresh approach to a common subject. We would like to see more material on what is being done to combat the anti-hunting sentiment in this country." Informational, how-to, personal experience, interview, profile, humor, historical, think articles, expose, nostalgia, personal opinion, spot news, new product and technical articles. Length: 200-5,000 words. Pays $25-200. Photos purchased with accompanying ms or without ms. Captions optional. Pays $10-25 for 5x7 or 8x10 b&w prints; $50 minimum for 35mm or 2¼x2¼ color. Also purchases newsbreaks of 50-500 words for $5-25.

How To Break In: "The answer is simple if you know bowhunting and have some interesting, informative experiences or tips to share. Keep the reader in mind. Anticipate questions and answer them in the article. Weave information into the storyline (e.g., costs involved, services of guide or outfitter, hunting season dates, equipment preferred and why, tips on items to bring, etc.) and, if at all possible, study back issues of the magazine. We have no set formula, really, but most articles are first-person narratives and most published material will contain the elements mentioned above."

Basketball

BASKETBALL WEEKLY, 17820 E. Warren, Detroit MI 48224. (313)881-9554. Publisher: Roger Stanton. Editor: Larry Donald. 19 issues during season, September-May. Circ. 45,000. Buys all rights. Pays on publication. Sample copy for SASE. Reports in 2 weeks. SASE.

Nonfiction, Photos and Fillers: Current stories on teams and personalities in college and pro basketball. Length: 800-1,000 words. Payment is $30-50. 8x10 b&w glossy photos purchased with mss. Also uses newsbreaks.

HOOP, Professional Sports Publications, 600 3rd Ave., New York NY 10016. (212)697-1460. Vice President: Pamela L. Blawie. 32-page color insert that is bound into the local magazines of each of the NBA teams. Buys all rights, but will reassign rights to author after publication, if author so requests. "For the most part, assignments are being made to newspapermen and columnists on the pro basketball beat around the country. Features are subject to NBA approval." Sample copy $1.50. Reports in 1 week. SASE.

Nonfiction: Features on NBA players, officials, personalities connected with league. Length: 800-1,000 words. Pays $50.

How To Break In: "The best way for a freelancer to break in is to aim something for the local team section. That can be anything from articles about the players or about their wives to unusual off-court activities. The best way to handle this is to send material directly to the PR person for the local team. They have to approve anything that we do on that particular team and if they like it, they forward it to me. They're always looking for new material—otherwise they have to crank it all out themselves."

Bicycling

BICYCLING, Rodale Press, Inc., 33 E. Minor St., Emmaus PA 18049. Editor: James C. McCullagh. Monthly magazine: 80 pages. Circ. 114,000. Pays on publication. Buys all rights. Pays negotiable kill fee. Byline given. Submit seasonal/holiday material 5 months in advance. SASE. Free sample copy and writer's guidelines.

Nonfiction: How-to (on all phases of bicycle touring, bike repair, maintenance, commuting, riding technique, nutrition for cyclists, conditioning); travel (bicycling must be central here); review—query). "We are strictly a bicycling magazine. We seek readable, clear, well-informed pieces. W` rarely run articles that are pure humor or inspiration but a little of either might flavor even our most technical pieces." Buys 5 mss/issue. Query. Length: 2,500 words maximum. Pays $25-300.

Photos: State availability of photos with query letter or send photo material with ms. Pays $10-15 for b&w negatives and $15-30 for color transparencies. Pays $200 for color cover photo. Offers no additional payment for photos accepted with ms. Captions preferred; model release required.

Fillers: Anecdotes. Buys 1-2/issue. Length: 150-200 words. Pays $15-25.

BIKE WORLD, Box 366, Mountain View CA 94040. Editor: Kevin Shafer. For bicyclists aged 5-80 interested in training, technical subjects, sophisticated touring stories at the nonbeginner level. Bimonthly magazine; 76 pages. Estab. 1972. Circ. 30,000. Byline given. Buys 100 mss/year. Pays on publication. Free sample copy. Submit seasonal material (winter, summer and spring tours; training in winter; riding the rollers, etc.) 2 months in advance. Reports "immediately." Query or submit complete ms. SASE.

Nonfiction and Photos: Technical and touring material; physiology and race topics. "All material must be at a level beyond the beginning 'how-to'." Must be tightly written and avoid the "joys of cycling" approach. Tour stories should make the reader feel he would have a good time. Avoid chronological accounts of events that don't involve the reader. "We are more into athletics than ecology or 'romantic bikeology'." Does not want to see material on "how I bought my first 10-speed, or the Rutabaga Canners annual road race, or a peanut butter and flat tire account of a tour to Michigan's world famous glacial moraines." Would like to see material on tours that turn others on without trying to; technical articles that people can use. How to train and tour, etc. Anything of interest to cyclists who enjoy the sport. Length: open. Pays $30-60/published page; more if quality deserves it. B&w photos are purchased with or without accompanying mss or on assignment. Pays $5-25 for 5x7 or larger. Must have snappy contrast and be in focus. Captions required. Pays $50-100 for color slides used for cover. Ektachrome-X or K-II with intensity of action, mood, scenery, etc.

Fillers: News bits, technical tips. Length: 25-300 words. Pays $5-10.

Boating

AMERICAN BOATING ILLUSTRATED, Recreation Publications, Inc., 2019 Clement Ave., Alameda CA 94501. (415)865-7500. Managing Editor: Douglas Molitor. 75% freelance written. Emphasizes how-to and technical articles for an audience of boat owners who do their own work aboard; ages 20-65 with above average incomes and education. Monthly; 80 pages. Estab. January 1977. Circ. 36,000. Pays on publication. Buys all rights. Pays 60% kill fee. Byline given. Submit seasonal/holiday material 3-5 months in advance. Photocopied and previously published submissions OK. SASE. Reports in 1 month. Sample copy $2; free writer's guidelines.

Nonfiction: How-to (all manner of onboard how-to, covering cruising, fishing, electronics, sail rig and sails, onboard safety, engine repairs and installations, galley, navigation and hull and deck repairs); new product (under Gear Section, all manner of new marine products and unusual items); consumer information pieces on marine associations and technical (articles on products, installation and use). "No first-hand accounts and no salt spray in the sunset. Nothing by novice yachtsmen." Buys 100 mss/year. Query. Length: 100-2,500 words. Pays $1.60/column inch.

Photos: "Format calls for articles with numerous illustrations/photos." Pays $5 minimum for 5x7 glossies; $10 minimum for 35mm color transparencies. Captions required. Buys all rights. Model release required "if appropriate."

Columns/Departments: Handyman (short onboard how-to projects) and Ideas from Readers (a better way to do something from personal experience). Buys 12 mss/issue. Submit complete ms. Length: 100-500 words.

How To Break In: "For the boatman who's done anything aboard—building, fixing, installations, cruising, fishing—there is a wealth of personal how-to experience for *Boating Illustrated*. Write a nuts and bolts how-to piece, spelling out first a typical problem then offering a concise, step-by-step solution. The Handyman section is a great spot for short ideas."

BAY & DELTA YACHTSMAN, Recreation Publications, 2019 Clement Ave., Alameda CA 94501. (415)865-7500. Editor: Glenda Carroll. 50% freelance written. Emphasizes recreational boating for small boat owners and recreational yachtsmen in northern California. Monthly tabloid newspaper; 90 pages. Estab. 1965. Circ. 17,000. Pays on publication. Buys all rights. Byline given. Phone queries OK. Submit seasonal/holiday material 2 months in advance.

Photocopied submissions OK. SASE. Reports in 1 month. Free writer's guidelines.

Nonfiction: Historical (nautical history of northern California); how-to (modifications, equipment, supplies, rigging etc., aboard both power and sailboats); humor (no disaster or boating ineptitude pieces); informational (government legislation as it relates to recreational boating); interview; new product; nostalgia; personal experience ("How I learned about boating from this" type of approach); personal opinion; photo feature (to accompany copy); profile; and travel. Buys 10-15 mss/issue. Query. Length: 750-2,000 words. Pays $1/column inch.

Photos: Photos purchased with accompanying ms. Captions required. Pays $5 for b&w glossy or matte finish photos. Total purchase price for ms includes payment for photos.

Fiction: Adventure (sea stories, travel—must relate to San Francisco Bay region); fantasy; historical; humorous; and mystery. Buys 2 mss/year. Query. Length: 500-1,750 words. Pays $1/column inch.

How To Break In: "Think of our market area: the waterways of northern California and how, why, when and where the boatman would use those waters. Think about unusual onboard application of ideas (power and sail), special cruising tips, etc. "We're very interested in local boating interviews—both the famous and unknown." Write for a knowledgeable boating public."

BOATING, 1 Park Ave., New York NY 10016. (212)725-3972. Editor: Richard L. Rath. For powerboat enthusiasts—informed boatmen, not beginners. Publishes special Boat Show issue in January; Fall show issue in September; New York National Boat Show issue in December; annual maintenance issue in April. Monthly. Circ. 200,000. Buys first periodical rights. Buys 100 mss/year. Pays on acceptance. Submit seasonal material 6-8 months in advance. Reports in 2 months. Query. SASE.

Nonfiction: Uses articles about cruises in powerboats with b&w or color photos, that offer more than usual interest; how-to pieces illustrated with good b&w photos or drawings; piloting articles, seamanship, etc.; new developments in boating; profiles of well-known boating people. "Don't talk down to the reader. Use little fantasy, emphasize the practical aspects of the subject." Length: 300-3,000 words. Pays $25-500, and varies according to subject and writer's skill. Regular department "Able Seaman" uses expertise on boat operation and handling; about 1,100-1,500 words; pays $150-300.

Photos: 8x10 b&w preferred. Interested in photos of happenings of interest to a national boating audience. Pays $20-25 each. Also buys color transparencies for both cover and interior use, 35mm slides or larger preferred. Pays $100-300 for one-time use, "but not for anything that has previously appeared in a boating publication."

Fillers: Uses short items pertaining to boating that have an unusual quality of historical interest, timeliness, or instruction. Pays $50-100.

How To Break In: "From a time-invested standpoint, it would make sense for the beginning writer to try a short filler subject for us, rather than to go for the jackpot. Unless, of course, he has a great story or article that will sell itself. Acceptability of a piece for our magazine hinges at least as much on the quality of the writing as it does on the subject matter. One man will take a trip around the world and produce bilge water for a manuscript; another, like E.B. White, will row across Central Park Lake and make it a great adventure in the human experience. There's no substitute for talent."

CANOE MAGAZINE, Voyager Publications Inc., 131 E. Murray St., Fort Wayne IN 46803. Editor: John Viehman. For an audience ranging from weekend canoe-camper to Olympic caliber flatwater/whitewater racing, marathon, poling, sailing, wilderness tripping types. Six times/year; 72 pages. Estab. 1973. Circ. 80,000. Buys all rights, but may reassign rights to author after publication. Pays 25% kill fee. Byline given. Buys 50 mss/year. Pays on acceptance. Free sample copy and writer's guidelines for 9x12 SASE. Reports in 60 days. Query or submit complete ms. SASE.

Nonfiction and Photos: "We publish a variety of canoeing and kayaking articles, striving for a balanced mix of stories to reflect all interests in this outdoor activity, recreational or competitive. Also interested in any articles dealing with conservation issues which may adversely affect the sport. Writing should be readable rather than academic; clever rather than endlessly descriptive. Diary type first-person style not desirable. A good, provocative lead is considered a prime ingredient. We want stories about canoeing/kayaking activities in the 50 states and Canada with which canoeists/kayakers of average ability can identify. Also interested in articles discussing safety aspects or instructional items. Occasional call for outdoor photography feature as relates to water accessible subjects. Length: 2,000 words maximum. Pays $25-175. Will consider relevant book reviews (pay $25 on publication); length, 200-500 words.

THE CHESAPEAKE BOATMAN, Whitney Publications, 222 Severn Ave., Annapolis MD 21403. (301)268-7717. Editor: Mike Roberts. Associate Editor: Laura Oliver. Emphasizes boats and boating on Chesapeake Bay. Monthly magazine; 72 pages. Estab. June 1978. Estab. Circulation 25,000. Pays on publication. Buys all rights unless otherwise stipulated. Byline given. Phone queries OK. Submit seasonal/holiday material 3 months in advance. Photocopied and previously published submissions OK. SASE. Reports in 4 weeks. Sample copy $1.25; free writer's guidelines. Address submissions to Laura Oliver.

Nonfiction: How-to (related to sailing, power boating techniques, maintenance); humor (experiences had while boating); interview (of boating personalities); new products; nostalgia; personal experience (while boating on Chesapeake Bay or tributaries); opinion; photo feature; profile; technical; and travel. Buys 15 mss/issue. Query. Feature Length: 1,000-2,000 words. Pays $75-100.

Photos: State availability of photos. Pays $10 for b&w contact sheets and negatives. Buys one-time rights. Byline given. Full identification of subjects required.

Columns/Departments: Electronics, Fishing and Maintenance, Book Reviews, and Waterfront Restaurant Reviews. Send complete ms. Length: 600-700 words. Pays $25-35.

Fiction: Adventure, historical, mystery and suspense. "All fiction must deal in some way with the subject of boating." Send complete ms. Length: 1,000-2,000 words. Pays $75.

CRUISING WORLD, Box 452, Newport RI 02840. (401)847-1588. Editor: Murray Davis. 75% freelance written. For all those who cruise under sail. Monthly magazine; 180 pages. Estab. 1974. Circ. 82,000. Rights purchased vary with author and material. May buy first North American serial rights or first serial rights. Pays on publication. Reports in about 8 weeks. Submit complete ms. SASE.

Nonfiction and Photos: "We are interested in seeing informative articles on the technical and enjoyable aspects of cruising under sail. Also subjects of general interest to seafarers." Length: 500-3,500 words. Pays $50 minimum. B&w prints (5x7) and color transparencies purchased with accompanying ms.

INTERNATIONAL YACHTSMAN, Hixson Industries, Inc., 4519 Admiralty Way, #206, Marina del Rey CA 90291. (213)822-9555. Editor-in-Chief: Lee Anderson. "*International Yachtsman* is designed and written as a shelf companion for other fine volumes of pictorial and literary excellence. It is edited for worldwide circulation and appeals to yachting enthusiasts, sail and motorboat owners and nonboaters with a venturesome sea spirit and an appreciation of superior waterscape photography." Quarterly magazine; 72 pages. Estab. June 1977. Circ. 20,000. Pays on acceptance. Buys one-time world rights. Byline given. Phone queries OK, "but story approval is made only after submission." Simultaneous, photocopied and previously published submissions OK. Reports in 4 weeks. Sample copy "free, on approval of query"; free writer's guidelines.

Nonfiction: "Articles of interest to us must relate to one of 9 major department headings which remain constant from issue to issue. These are: On Board (pictorial tours through the interiors of the world's great yachts); Hideaways (revealing explorations into little-known and intriguing resorts, harbors, and anchorages); Personality (true-life scrapbook biographies of outstanding yachtsmen and their exceptional experiences afloat); Heritage (photographically creative treatments of yachts or other watercraft of yesteryear); Artisans (reports of talented yacht craftsmen or hobbyists, including their work in painting, sculpture, model-building or design); Galley Gourmet (appetizing collections of practical recipes for the galley chef); Locale (a yachtsman's photo-guide through unusual cruising areas, highlighting their best seasons, accommodations and points of interest); Fashions Afloat (the latest nautical styles captured in and about exotic waterfronts) Classic Cruises (descriptive photo-logs of rare and daring adventures on the seven seas); and Celebrity Yachtsmen (an inside look at glamorous vessels owned and operated by skippers in the public spotlight). Because *International Yachtsman* caters to a global market, all articles must be of an international nature. Any subject photographed within the continental United States will be accepted only if it commands worldwide interest as a truly unique feature in and of itself. We are not interested in technical articles, how-to features on boating equipment and techniques, or stories dealing with racing events, new products, industry news items or any other subject of a timely nature." Buys 28 mss/year. Query with clips of published work. Length: 1,000-3,000 words. Pays $100-500.

Photos: "We are a pictorial quarterly and selection of features is based primarily on photographic excellence. With the exception of cover shots, single photos cannot be considered for publication unless they are incorporated into a complete layout." Pays $50-150 for 35mm or larger color transparencies.

LAKELAND BOATING, Box 745, 320 Springbrook, Adrian MI 49221. (517)265-8680.

Managing Editor: Robert B. Tuttle. Emphasizes pleasure boating, both power and sail boats. Monthly magazine. Pays on publication. Buys first publication, with one reprint rights. Previously published submissions OK. SASE. Reports in 3-4 weeks. Sample copy 50¢; free writer's guidelines.

Nonfiction: "We use one 'Cruise' story per issue. These are personal experience stories of power and sailboat cruises on freshwater lakes or rivers. We like these about 1,500 words with photographs. Usable stories without picture will most likely be rejected. We like details as to how someone else might make such a cruise, not just 'disasters' and close calls. We can use technical articles on sailing, maintenance, boating lakes and rivers. If you plan on writing a 'pre' story on events such as Mackinaw races, and other freshwater events, please query beforehand and advise us what you are thinking. We do not often make assignments, and we do not make cash advances on 'speculation.' We do not use fiction or poetry. We use about two cartoons per issue, and have a modest supply on hand." Buys 6 mss/issue. Query or send complete ms. Length: 1,000-2,000 words. Pays $50 minimum.

Photos: Send photos with ms. Pays $10 for b&w prints; $10 for color prints. "Transparencies are acceptable, but are only necessary if we plan to do color illustration of material." Buys first rights with rights to one reprint. Captions preferred.

Columns/Departments: Buys 5-8 mss/issue. Length: 500-1,000 words. Pay negotiated.

MOTORBOAT MAGAZINE, 38 Commercial Wharf, Boston MA 02110. (617)723-5800. Editor: Martin Luray. For powerboat owners and devotees. Estab. 1973. Monthly. Buys all rights. Buys 50 mss/year. Pays on acceptance. Free sample copy and writer's guidelines. Photocopied submissions OK. Reports in 4 weeks. "Queries are welcome, but the editor reserves the right to withhold his final decision until the completed article has been reviewed." SASE.

Nonfiction and Photos: "We are the only magazine devoted purely to motorboating and we use informative, educational articles that instruct the reader without treating him as a novice. Subject matter may cover any aspect of motorboating including profiles, technical stories, maintenance, sportfishing, cruising and seamanship. Houseboat articles with the emphasis on in-land cruising are welcome, as well as big boat cruising stories and articles dealing with mechanical subjects (engines). But, no sailing, please." Length: 2,500 words maximum. Pays $150-500. 8x10 b&w glossy prints purchased with mss. Color (35mm or larger) used on cover. Pays $300-400 for color used on cover.

PLEASURE BOATING MAGAZINE, Wet Set Publishing, Inc., 1995 NE 150th St., North Miami FL 33181. (305)945-7403. Editor: Tom Henschel. Managing Editor: Jean Lang. For high-income persons interested in all types of Southern boating and fishing. Monthly tabloid; 40-48 pages. Estab. 1970. Circ. 45,000. Pays on publication. Buys all rights. Phone queries OK. Submit seasonal/holiday material 3 months in advance. SASE. Reports in 2 weeks. Free sample copy.

Nonfiction: "Anything dealing with boating and fishing on a how-to, technical, first-person or humorous basis." Buys 6-8 mss/issue. Send complete ms. Length: 500-2,000 words. Pays 5-10¢/word.

Photos: Send photos with ms. Pay is open for b&w contact sheets or 2¼x2¼. Buys all rights. Captions and model releases required.

SAIL, 38 Commercial Wharf, Boston MA 02110. (617)227-0888. Editor: Keith Taylor. For audience that is "strictly sailors, average age 35, better than average education." Special issues: "Cruising issues, fitting-out issues, special race issues (e.g., America's Cup), boat show issues." Monthly magazine. Pays on publication. Buys first North American serial rights. Submit seasonal or special material at least 3 months in advance. Reports in 4-6 weeks. SASE. Free sample copy.

Nonfiction: Want "articles on sailing: technical, techniques and feature stories." Interested in how-to, personal experience, profiles, historical, new products and photo articles. "Generally emphasize the excitement of sail and the human, personal aspect." Buys 200 mss/year. Length: 1,500-3,000 words. Pays $100-500.

Photos: State availability of photos. Offers no additional payment for photos. Uses b&w glossy prints or color transparencies. Pays $350 if photo is used on the cover.

SAILING MAGAZINE, 125 E. Main St., Port Washington WI 53074. (414)284-2626. Editor: William F. Schanen III. For readers mostly between ages of 35 and 44, some professionals. About 75% of them own their own sailboat. Monthly magazine; 64 pages. Estab. 1966. Circ. 25,000. Not copyrighted. Buys 12 mss/year. Pays on publication. Write for copy of guidelines for writers. Photocopied and simultaneous submissions OK. Reports in 1 month. Query or submit complete ms. SASE.

Nonfiction and Photos: Micca Leffingwell Hutchins, managing editor. "Experiences of sailing, whether curising, racing or learning. We require no special style. We're devoted exclusively to sailing and sailboat enthusiasts, and particularly interested in articles about the trend toward cruising in the sailing world." Informational, personal experience, profile, historical, travel and book reviews. Length: open. Payment negotable. B&w photos purchased with or without accompanying ms. Captions required. Pays $10 for each 8x10 b&w glossy used; also flat fee for series.

SEA, CBS Publications, 1499 Monrovia Ave., Newport Beach CA 92663. (714)646-4451. Editor-in-Chief: Chris Caswell. Editor: Harry Monahan. 60% freelance written. Emphasizes recreational boating. Monthly magazine; 130 pages. Estab. 1884. Circ. 191,000. Pays on acceptance. Buys first North American serial rights. Submit seasonal/holiday material 6 months in advance of issue date. SASE. Reports in 5 weeks. Free sample copy and writer's guidelines.

Nonfiction: How-to (improvements to basic boat gear or procedures/techniques which will improve boat use or maintenance); interview (boating personality with a viewpoint of interest to other boat-owners); personal experience (involving use of boat, an experience profitable to other boat-owners); and travel (where-to and how-to go by boat). Buys 20 mss/issue. Query. Length: 3,000 words. Pays 10¢/word.

Photos: "Format of magazine requires illustrations for 90% of articles used; if we can't find suitable illustration material, the story is useless." State availability of photos with query or submit photo material with ms. Pays $20-25 for 8x10 b&w glossy contact sheets and negatives and $75-300 for 35mm color transparencies. Captions preferred. Buys one-time rights. Model release required.

SOUTHERN BOATING MAGAZINE, Southern Boating & Yachting, Inc., 615 SE 2nd Ave., Miami FL 33130. (305)856-7946. Editor: Skip Allen. Monthly magazine; 75 pages. Estab. 1971. Circ. 25,000. Pays on publication. Buys all rights. Byline given. Phone queries OK. Submit seasonal/holiday material 2 months in advance. Photocopied submissions OK. SASE. Reports in 3 weeks.

Nonfiction: Historical, how-to, personal experience and travel. "All articles should be related to yachting. We do want technical articles." Buys 4 mss/issue. Send complete ms. Length: 2,000-5,000 words. Pays $25-50.

Photos: State availability of photos or send photos with ms. Pays $5 for any size b&w or 35mm color transparencies. Captions and model releases required.

SPYGLASS, Spyglass Catalog Co., 2415 Mariner Square Dr., Alameda CA 94501. (415)769-8410. Managing Editor: Dick Moore. 10% freelance written. Emphasizes all aspects of sailing. "For sailors of all ages interested in the perfection of the activity, the betterment of the sailboat, the best available gear and how to apply it." Annual magazine; 400 pages. Estab. 1973. Circ. 25,000. Pays on publication. Buys first North American serial rights. Phone queries OK. Submit material at least 4 months prior to year's end. Previously published submissions OK. SASE. Reports in 1 month. Sample copy $3.

Nonfiction: Historical (old salts, old boats, old seaports); how-to (any build-it-yourself, repair-it-yourself, remodel-it-yourself or rig-it-yourself hints on any facet of sailing); informational (on sailing technique, new developments in construction of the sailboat, navigation, racing or cruising); interview (or profile on noted naval architects, boatbuilders, racing or cruising personalities); personal experience (anything that is educational or has some hard lessons to be learned. No travelogues, but better ways to cruise); photo essays (emphasizing innovative apparatus utilizing stock equipment or custom set-ups); and technical (any aspect of sails, boat construction, electronics and racing tactics). Buys 20 mss/year. Query. Length: 750-3,500 words. Pays 7½¢/word.

Photos: Photos purchased without accompanying ms. Captions required, except for full-page filler photos which should be either action or aesthetic shots. Pays $15 for b&w and color photos. Total purchase price for ms includes payment for photos.

How To Break In: "First, include a basic outline with the query. Too often a proposed subject melds into an overworked area of sailing. Because it's an annual, each piece must 'last' all year. We have a keen interest in the practical 'how-to' pieces. Also, we are a West Coast-based publication with a national readership and need more input from the Great Lakes, Gulf Coast and Eastern boating scene."

TRAILER BOATS MAGAZINE, Poole Publications, Inc., 1440 W. Walnut, Compton CA

90220. (213)537-1037. Editor: Ralph Poole. Managing Editor: Jim Youngs. Emphasizes legally trailerable boats and related aspects. Monthly magazine (Nov./Dec. issue combined); 80 pages. Estab. 1971. Circ. 80,000. Pays on publication. Buys all rights. Byline given. Phone queries OK. Submit seasonal/holiday material 3 months in advance. SASE. Reports in 4 weeks. Free sample copy; writer's guidelines.

Nonfiction: General interest (trailer boating activities); historical (places, events, boats); how-to (repair boats, install installation, etc.); humor (almost any subject); nostalgia (same as historical); personal experience; photo feature; profile; technical; and travel (boating travel on water or highways). Buys 4 mss/issue. Query or send complete ms. Length: 500-3,000 words. Pays $50 minimum.

Photos: Send photos with ms. Pays $7.50-30 for 5x7 or 8x10 b&w glossy prints; $10-100 for 35mm color transparencies. Captions required.

Columns/Departments: Boaters Bookshelf (boating book reviews); Over the Transom (funny or strange boating photos); and Patent Pending (an invention with drawings). Buys 2/issue. Query. Length: 100-500 words. Pays $15. Open to suggestions for new columns/departments.

Fiction: Adventure, experimental, historical, humorous and suspense. "We do not use too many fiction stories but we will consider them if they fit the general editorial guidelines." Query or send complete ms. Length: 500-1,500 words. Pays $50 minimum.

Fillers: Jokes, gags, anecdotes, puzzles and short humor. Buys 5/year. Length: 100 words. Pays $10.

WATERWAY GUIDE, Box 1486, Annapolis MD 21404. (301)268-9546. Assistant Editor: Jerri Anne Hopkins. A pleasure-boater's cruising guide to the Intracoastal Waterway and related East Coast waters. Annual magazine.

Nonfiction: "We occasionally have a need for a special, short article on some particular aspect of pleasure cruising—such as living aboard, sailing vs powerboating, having children or pets on board—or a particular stretch of coast—a port off the beaten track, conditions peculiar to a certain area, a pleasant weekend cruise and so on." Query.

Photos: State availability of photos. "We have a need for good photographs, taken from the water, of ports, inlets and points of interest."

WOODENBOAT, Box 78, Brooklin ME 04616. Editor-in-Chief: Jonathan Wilson. Readership is composed mainly of owners, builders and designers of wooden boats. Bimonthly magazine; 120 pages. Estab. 1974. Circ. 25,000. Pays on publication. Buys first North American serial rights. Pays 50% kill fee. Byline given "except if the material published were substantially revised and enlarged." Photocopied and previously published submissions OK. SASE. Reports in 2 months. Sample copy $2.50; writer's guidelines for SASE.

Nonfiction: Historical (detailed evolution of boat types of famous designers or builders of wooden boats); how-to (repair, restore, build or maintain wooden boats); informational (technical detail on repairs/restoration/construction); new product (documented by facts or statistics on performance of product); opinion (backed up by experience and experimentation in boat building, restoring, maintaining, etc.); photo feature (with in-depth captioning and identification of boats); and technical (on adhesives and other boat-building products and materials, or on particular phases of repair or boat construction). Buys 85 mss/year. Submit complete ms. Length: 1,200-3,500 words. Pays 5-10¢/word.

Photos: Purchased with or without (only occasionally) accompanying ms. Captions required. Send prints, negatives or transparencies. Pays $10 for 8x10 high contrast B&w glossy prints; $15 minimum for color transparencies.

Columns/Departments: "Tidings" (seeking news on developments and contemporary trends of wooden boat construction); and Book Reviews (on wooden boats and related subjects). Buys 1 ms/issue. Length: 300-800 words. Pays 5-10¢/word.

How To Break In: "Because we are bimonthly, and issues are scheduled well in advance, freelancers should bear in mind that if their material is accepted, it will inevitably be some time before publication can be arranged. We seek innovative and informative ideas in freelancers' manuscripts, and the degree to which research and careful attention has been paid in compiling an article must be apparent. We're not looking for scholarly treatises, rather detailed and thought-out material reflecting imagination and interest in the subject."

YACHTING, Yachting Publishing Corp., 1 Park Ave., New York NY 10016. Editor: Wolcott Gibbs Jr. For yachtsmen interested in powerboats and sailboats. Monthly. Circ. 150,000. Buys North American serial rights. Reports in 3 weeks. SASE.

Nonfiction and Photos: Nuts-and-bolts articles on all phases of yachting; good technical pieces on motors, electronics, and sailing gear. Length: 2,500 words maximum. Article should be accompanied by 6-8 photos. Pays $25 each for b&w photos, "more for color when used." Will accept a story without photos, if story is outstanding.

YACHT RACING/CRUISING MAGAZINE, North American Publishing Co., Box 902, 23 Leroy Ave., Darien CT 06820. Editor: Major Hall. Managing Editor: Timothy H. Cole. Magazine published 10/year; 108 pages. Estab. 1977. Circ. 50,000. Pays on publication. Buys First North American serial rights. Pays 33% kill fee. Byline given. SASE. Reports in 2 months. Sample copy $1.50.
Nonfiction: How-to for racing/cruising sailors, personal experience, photo feature, profile and travel. Buys 10 ms/issue. Query. Length: 1,000-2,500 words. Pays $100 minimum.

Bowling and Billiards

BILLIARDS DIGEST, National Bowlers Journal, Inc., 875 N. Michigan Ave., Suite 3734, Chicago IL 60611. (312)266-7179. Editor-in-Chief: Larry Breckenridge. 25% freelance written. Emphasizes billiards/pool for "readers who are accomplished players and hard core fans—also a trade readership." Bimonthly magazine; 48-70 pages. Estab. September 1978. Circ. 7,000. Pays on publication. Buys all rights, but may reassign following publication. Byline given. Phone queries OK. Submit seasonal/holiday material 2 months in advance of issue date. Simultaneous, photocopied and previously published submissions OK. SASE. Reports in 2 weeks. Sample copy $1; free writer's guidelines.
Nonfiction: General interest (tournament results, features on top players); historical (features on greats of the game); how-to (how to improve your game, your billiard room, billiards table maintenance); humor (anecdotes, any humorous feature dealing with billiards); interview (former and current stars, industry leaders); new product (any new product dealing with billiards, short 'blip' or feature); and profile (former and current stars—prefer current stars). No basic news stories. "We want features that provide in-depth material, including anecdotes, atmosphere and facts." Buys 3 mss/issue. Query. Length: 1,000-1,500 words. Pays $40-75.
Photos: State availability of photos with query. Pays $5-25 for 8x10 b&w glossy prints; $5-25 for 35mm or 2¼x2¼ color transparencies. Captions preferred. Buys all rights.

BOWLERS JOURNAL, 875 N. Michigan, Chicago IL 60611. (312)266-7171. Editor-in-Chief: Mort Luby. Managing Editor: Jim Dressel. 30% freelance written. Emphasizes bowling. Monthly magazine; 100 pages. Estab. 1913. Circ. 18,000. Pays on publication. Buys all rights. Phone queries OK. Submit seasonal/holiday material 2 months in advance of issue date. Photocopied submissions OK. SASE. Reports in 2 weeks. Sample copy $1.
Nonfiction: General interest (stories on top pros); historical (stories of old-time bowlers or bowling alleys); interview (top pros, men and women); and profile (top pros). Buys 2 mss/issue. Query. Length: 1,200-3,500 words. Pays $50-150.
Photos: State availability of photos with query. Pays $5-15 for 8x10 b&w prints; and $5-20 for 35mm or 2¼x2¼ color transparencies. Buys one-time rights.

BOWLING, 5301 S. 76th St., Greendale WI 53129. (414)421-6400, ext. 230. Editor: David DeLorenzo. Official publication of the American Bowling Congress. Monthly. Estab. 1934. Rights purchased vary with author and material. Usually buys all rights. Byline given. Pays on publication. Reports in 30 days. SASE.
Nonfiction and Photos: "This is a specialized field and the average writer attempting the subject of bowling should be well-informed. However, anyone is free to submit material for approval." Wants articles about unusual ABC leagues and tournaments, personalities, etc., featuring male bowlers. Length: 500-1,200 words. Pays $25-100 per article; $10-15 per photo.
How To Break In: "Submit feature material on bowlers, generally amateurs competing in local leagues, or special events involving the game of bowling. Should have connection with ABC membership."

JUNIOR BOWLER, 5301 S. 76th St., Greendale WI 53129. (414)421-4700. Official publication of American Junior Bowling Congress. Editor: Jean Yeager. 30% freelance written. For boys and girls ages 21 and under. Estab. 1946 as *Prep Pin Patter*; in 1964 as *Junior Bowler*. Monthly, November through April. Circ. 89,000. Buys all rights. Byline given "except if it were necessary to do extensive rewriting." Pays on publication. Reports in 10 days. Query. SASE.
Nonfiction and Photos: Subject matter of articles must be based on tenpin bowling and activities connected with American Junior Bowling Congress only. Audience includes youngsters down to 6 years of age, but material should feature the teenage group. Length: 500-800 words. Accompanying photos or art preferred. Pays $30-100/article. Photos should be 8x10 b&w glossy prints related to subject matter. Pays $5 minimum.

How To Break In: "We are primarily looking for feature stories on a specific person or activity. Stories about a specific person generally should center around the outstanding bowling achievements of that person in an AJBC sanctioned league or tournament. Articles on special leagues for high average bowlers, physically or mentally handicapped bowlers, etc. should focus on the unique quality of the league, *Junior Bowler* also carries articles on AJBC sanctioned tournaments, but these should be more than just a list of the winners and their scores. Again, the unique feature of the tournament should be emphasized."

THE WOMAN BOWLER, 5301 S. 76th St., Greendale WI 53129. (414)421-9000. Editor: Chris Igler. Emphasizes bowling for women bowlers, ages 8-90. Monthly (except for combined May/June, July/August issues) magazine; 48 pages. Estab. 1936. Circ. 135,000. Pays on acceptance. Buys all rights. Byline given "except on occasion, when freelance article is used as part of a regular magazine department. When this occurs, it is discussed first with the author." Phone queries OK. Submit seasonal/holiday material 2 months in advance. Photocopied and previously published submissions OK. SASE. Reports in 1 month. Free sample copy and writer's guidelines.
Nonfiction: Historical (about bowling and of national significance); interview; profile; and spot news. Buys 25 mss/year. Query. Length: 1,500 words maximum (unless by special assignment). Pays $15-50.
Photos: Purchased with accompanying ms. Identification required. Query. Pays $5-10 for b&w glossy prints. Model release required.

Football

ALL SOUTH CAROLINA FOOTBALL ANNUAL, Box 3, Columbia SC 29202. (803)796-9200. Editor: Mike Monroe. Associate Editor: Dennis Nichols. Issued annually, August 1. Buys first rights. Pays on publication. Deadline for material each year is 10 weeks preceding publication date. Query. SASE.
Nonfiction and Photos: Material must be about South Carolina high school and college football teams, players and coaches. Pays 3¢ minimum a word. Buys photos with ms. Captions required. 5x7 or 8x10 b&w glossy prints; 4x5 or 35mm color transparencies. Uses color on cover only. Pays $5 minimum for b&w; $10 minimum for color.

FOOTBALL NEWS, 17820 E. Warren, Detroit MI 48224. Editor: Roger Stanton. 25% freelance written. For avid grid fans. Weekly tabloid published during football season; 24 pages. Estab. 1939. Circ. 100,000. Not copyrighted. Pays 50% kill fee. Byline given. Buys 12 to 15 mss a year. Pays on publication. Will send sample copy to writer for 25¢. Reports in 1 month. Query. SASE.
Nonfiction: Articles on players, officials, coaches, past and present, with fresh approach. Highly informative, concise, positive approach. Interested in profiles of former punt, pass and kick players who have made the pros. Interview, profile, historical, think articles, and exposes. Length: 800-1,000 words. Pays $35-75/ms.

Gambling

GAMBLING TIMES MAGAZINE, 839 Highland Ave., Hollywood CA 90038. (213)466-5261. Editor: Len Miller. 25% freelance written. Monthly magazine; 100 pages. Estab. February 1977. Circ. 100,000. Pays on publication. Buys first North American serial rights. Byline given. Submit seasonal/holiday material 3-6 months in advance of issue date. Photocopied and previously published submissions OK. SASE. Reports in 1 month. Free writer's guidelines; mention *Writer's Market* in request.
Nonfiction: How-to (related to gambling systems, betting methods, etc.); humor; photo feature (race tracks, jai alai, casinos); and travel (gambling spas and resort areas). "Also interested in articles on gambling personalities, the history of gambling, and local gambling activities around the United States and the world." Buys 100 mss/year. Query. Length: open. Pays $50-150.
Fiction: "We only use gambling-related material." Buys 12 mss/year. Submit complete ms. Pays $50-150.
Fillers: Gambling types only. Jokes, gags, anecdotes and short humor. Buys 12/issue. Pays $5-25.

THE PLAYERS' NEWSLETTER, 1019 Beacon St., Boston MA 02146. Editor-in-Chief: S.D. Bort. For consumers and sports fans of billiards, pool and all other sports. Monthly newsletter; 8 pages. Pays on publication. Buys simultaneous rights. Submit seasonal/holiday material 4 months in advance of issue date. Simultaneous and previously published submissions OK. SASE. Reports in 1-2 months.

Nonfiction: Expose; how-to; humor; informational; new product; and photo feature. Buys 6 mss/issue. Submit complete ms. Pays $20-750.

Photos: All photos are OK to send. Pays $20-200 for b&w prints; $20-350 for color. Model release required.

Fiction: Erotica; fantasy; and science fiction. Buys 25 mss/year. Submit complete ms. Pays $20-750.

Fillers: Clippings and newsbreaks. Submit fillers. Length: 15-150 words. Pays $5-50.

General Sports Interest

AAU NEWS. Amateur Athletic Union of the United States, AAU House, 3400 W. 86th St., Indianapolis IN 46268. (317)297-2900. Editor: Martin E. Weiss. Associate Editor: Pete Cava. Emphasizes amateur sports. Monthly magazine; 20-24 pages. Estab. 1925. Circ. 16,000. Pays on publication. Buys one-time rights. Pays 100% kill fee. Sometimes give bylines; "Etcetera section profiles are not bylined, but assigned sports news articles are." SASE. Reports in 2 weeks. Free sample copy.

Nonfiction: "General subject matter is profiles of top amateur athletes and athletic volunteer or leaders. Reports on AAU championships, previews of coming seasons, etc." Buys interviews, profiles, photo features, sport book review and spot news articles. Length: 1,000 words maximum. Pays $10-50.

Photos: Photo purchased with or without accompanying ms or on-assignment. Captions required. Pays $5-25 for 8½x11 b&w glossy prints; $10-25 for any size color transparencies. No additional payment for photos accepted with accompanying ms. Model release required.

How To Break in: "By staying within the framework of AAU sports: Basketball, baton twirling, bobsledding, boxing, diving, gymnastics, handball, horseshoe pitching, judo, karate, luge, powerlifting, physique, swimming, synchronized swimming, taekwondo, track and field, volleyball, water polo, weightlifting, wrestling and trampoline and tumbling; also AAU Junior Olympics and all matters pertaining to Olympic development in AAU sports."

BC OUTDOORS, Special Interest Publications Division, Maclean-Hunter, Ltd., 202, 1132 Hamilton St., Vancouver, British Columbia, Canada V6B 2S2. (604)687-1581. Editor: Donald Stainsby. Emphasizes any outdoors activity which is not an organized sport. "We're interested in family recreation." Monthly magazine. Estab. late 1940s. Circ. 35,000. Usually pays on acceptance. Buys first rights or first North American serial rights. Phone queries OK. Submit seasonal/holiday material 3 months in advance. Previously published work "occasionally" OK. SAE and International Reply Coupons. Reports in 1-3 weeks. Free sample copy and writer's guidelines.

Nonfiction: General interest (about British Columbia outdoors); historical (about British Columbia and the Yukon only); how-to (canoe, choose your RV, plant a wild-flower garden, catch a rainbow trout in British Columbia, build a cabin, photograph mountain goats, find British Columbia jade, save the environment, etc.); interview (with British Colubmia people involved in outdoors or environment and others involved in British Columbia affairs); profile; travel (in British Columbia and the Yukon); new product (for outdoors activities); personal experience; photo feature; and technical. Buys 6 mss/issue. Query or send complete ms. Length: 1,000-2,500 words, but maximum is usually 2,000. Pays 7½¢/word minimum.

Photos: "We want photos for every story." Send photos with ms. Pays $15 for b&w 8x10 glossy prints; and $15-75 for color slides or prints (not silk). Captions and model release required. Buys one-time rights except for covers; purchase includes further possible use or reproduction for promotional purposes anywhere by SIP-Maclean-Hunter, Ltd.

Columns/Departments: Buys very few. Length: 800 words maximum. Pays 7½¢/word. Open to suggestions for new columns/departments.

MARIAH/OUTSIDE, Mariah Publication Corp., 3401 W. Division St., Chicago IL 60651. (312)342-7777. Emphasizes outdoor activities. Bimonthly magazine; 112 pages. Estab. February 1976. Circ. 200,000. Pays part on acceptance and part on publication. Buys all rights, assignments for hire basis, first rights and first North American serial rights. Submit seasonal/holiday material 4 months in advance. SASE. Reports in 2 weeks (queries); 4 weeks (ms). Sample copy $2; free writer's guidelines.

Nonfiction: Expose (environmental/political and consumer outdoor equipment); general interest (as pertains to the outdoors); historical (profiles of early pioneers and expeditions); how-to (photography, equipment, techniques used in outdoor sports); humor (as pertains to outdoor activities); profiles (leaders and major figures associated with sports, politics, ecology of the outdoors); new product (hardware/software, reviews of performance of products used in camping, packpacking, outdoor sports, etc.); personal experience (major and minor expeditions and adventures); photo feature (outdoor photography); profile (profiles of early pioneers and expeditions, also modern pioneer profiles); technical (of outdoor equipment); and travel (to exotic regions and cultures rarely visited). Buys 40 mss/year. Query with clips of published work. Length: 1,000-4,000 words. Pays $250-1,000.

Photos: Send photos with ms. Pays $50-200 for 35mm color transparencies. Buys one-time rights. Captions required.

Columns/Departments: Dispatches (news items); Cache (off beat products, satire, humor); Equipage (articles on broad categories of outdoor equipment); Hardware/Software (short equipment reviews, slant to new innovative products, must include evaluation); and Natural Acts (natural sciences); Reviews (books, movies, records). Buys 3-4/issue. Query with clips of published work. Length: 200-1,500 words. Pays $150-400.

Fiction: Adventure, fantasy and humorous. Buys 1-2 mss/year. Query with clips of published work. Length: 1,000-4,000 words. Pays $250-1,000.

OUTDOOR CANADA MAGAZINE, 953A Eglinton Ave. E., Toronto, Ontario, Canada M4G 4B5. (416)429-5550. Editor-in-Chief: Sheila Kaighin. 50% freelance written. Emphasizes noncompetitive outdoor recreation. Published 7 times/year; magazine; 64-96 pages. Estab. December 1972. Circ. 53,345. Pays on publication. Buys all rights, but may reassign following publication. Submit seasonal/holiday material 5-6 months in advance of issue date. Byline given. Photocopied submissions OK. SASE. Reports in 4 weeks. Sample copy $1; writer's guidelines, 50¢; mention *Writer's Market* in request.

Nonfiction: Esposé (only as it pertains to the outdoors, e.g. wildlife management); and how-to (in-depth, thorough pieces on how to select equipment for various subjects, or improve techniques only as it relates to outdoor subjects covered). Buys 35-40 mss/year. Submit complete ms. Length: 1,000-3,500 words. Pays $75-150. $250 for cover story—e.g., when one of the author's color transparencies is used as the cover to lead into his story.

Photos: Submit photo material with accompanying ms. Pays $5-30 for 8x10 b&w glossy prints and $50 for 35mm color transparencies; $150/cover. Captions preferred. Buys all rights. Model release required.

Fillers: Outdoor tips. Buys 7/year. Length: 350-500 words. Pays $25.

REFEREE, Referee Enterprises, Inc., Box 161, Franksville WI 53126. (414)632-8855. Editor-in-Chief: Barry Mano. For well-educated, mostly 26- to 50-year-old male sports officials. Monthly magazine; 56 pages. Estab. 1976. Circ. 40,000. Pays either on acceptance or publication. Buys all rights. Submit seasonal/holiday material 4 months in advance. Photocopied and previously published submissions OK. SASE. Reports in 4 weeks. Free sample copy.

Nonfiction: How-to, informational, humor, interview, profile, personal experience, photo feature and technical. Buys 54 mss/year. Query. Length: 700-3,000 words. Pays 4¢/word up to a maximum of $100. "No general sports articles."

Photos: Tom Hammill, managing editor. Purchased with or without accompanying ms or on assignment. Captions required. Send contact sheet, prints, negatives or transparencies. Pays $15 for each b&w used; $25 for each color used; $75-100 for cover.

Columns/Departments: Arena (bios); Library (book reviews); and Guest Editorial (controversial topics). Buys 24 mss/year. Query. Length: 200-1,000 words. Pays 4¢/word up to $50 maximum for Library. Arena and Guest Editorials pay no fee, but full author credit is given.

Fillers: Tom Hammill, managing editor. Jokes, gags, anecdotes, puzzles and sport shorts. Query. Length: 50-200 words. Pays 4¢/word in most cases; others offer only author credit lines.

SOUTHWEST SPORTS, 107 Girard SE, Albuquerque NM 87106. (505)265-8478. Editor: Wally Pobst. Associate Editor. Rodeo Events: Robert P. Everett. 75% freelance written. "The only publication located in the heart of the Southwestern US covering major indoor and outdoor events and key personalities. Emphasizes regional sports, recreation and physical fitness of prime interest to large masses of active people including, but not limited to, participants, spectators, promoters, developers and coaches." Monthly magazine: 56 pages. Estab. 1978. Circ. 30,000. Pays on publication. Buys all rights, but may reassign following publication; or second serial rights. Byline given. Submit seasonal/holiday material 4 months in advance of issue date. Photocopied and previously published (in different region) submissions OK. SASE. Reports in 4-6 weeks. Sample copy $1.00; free writer's guidelines; mention *Writer's Market* in request.

Nonfiction: Competitive sports (key events, all types); rodeo and horse-related activities; horse racing; outdoors (all types, including hunting, fishing, camping and backpacking and conservation); how-to (something unique, not trite advice column); general interest; humor; inspirational; interviews (stars or other athletes with something to say, coaches); new product (sports equipment, recreational travel); personal experience; opinion (how to improve sports or recreational facilities); photo feature; profile; and travel (Southwest recreational). "We use very little material that does not fit our *regional* approach." Buys 5-10 mss/issue. Query on major projects; submit complete ms on short articles. Length: 500-5,000 words. Pays $25-200.
Photos: Submit photo material with accompanying query or ms. Pays $10-100 for 5x7 or 8x10 b&w glossy prints; $10-150 for 5x7 or 8x10 matte color prints or 2¼x2¼ transparencies. Captions and model release required. Buys all rights, but may reassign following publication.
Columns/Department: Book reviews (sports and Southwest); editor's page (opinion or sidelights); equipment (evaluation of sports, travel and equipment); profiles (200 words of sports achievements); and schools (sports programs and facilities at Southwest colleges). Submit complete ms. Length: 200-1,000 words. Pays $10-50. Open for suggestions for new columns/departments.

SPORTING NEWS. 1212 N. Lindbergh Blvd., St. Louis MO 63132. "We do not actively solicit freelance material."

SPORTS ILLUSTRATED. Time & Life Bldg., Rockefeller Center, New York NY 10020. Articles Editor: Robert W. Creamer. Primarily staff-written, with small but steady amount of outside material. Weekly. Reports in 2-3 weeks. Pays on acceptance. Buys all North American rights or first North American publication rights. Pay varies for kill fee. Byline given "except for Scorecard department." SASE.
Nonfiction: "Material falls into two general categories: regional (text that runs in editorial space accompanying regional advertising pages) and national text. Runs a great deal of regional advertising and, as a result, considerable text in that section of the magazine. Regional text does not have a geographical connotation; it can be any sort of short feature (450-2,000 words): Shopwalk, Footloose, Viewpoint (1,000 words and under); As I Did It, As I See It and As I Saw It (1,200-2,000 words), but it must deal with some aspect of sports. National text (1,500-6,000 words) also must have a clear sporting connection; should be major personality, personal reminiscence, knowing look into a significant aspect of a sporting subject, but national text should be written for broad appeal, so that readers without special knowledge will appreciate the piece." Pays $300-500 for regional pieces, $1,000 maximum for national text. Smaller payments are made for material used in special sections or departments.
Photos: "Do not care to see photos or artwork until story is purchased."
How To Break In: "Regional text is the best section for a newcomer. National text is difficult as many of the national sections are staff-written."

THE SPORTS JOURNAL. B4-416 Meridian Rd. SE, Calgary, Alberta, Canada T2A 1X2. (403)273-5141. Editor-in-Chief: Barry A. Whetstone. 80% freelance written. Monthly tabloid; 32 pages. Estab. May 1976. Circ. 30,000. Pays on publication. Buys all rights. Byline given. Phone queries OK. Submit seasonal/holiday material 1 month in advance of issue date. Simultaneous, photocopied and previously published submissions OK. SASE. Reports in 1 month. Free sample copy and writer's guidelines; mention *Writer's Market* in request.
Nonfiction: General interest; interview (sports figures); nostalgia (sports history); personal opinion (on sports-related topics); and profile. Buys 15-25 mss/issue. Submit complete ms. Length: 200-600 words. Pays $10-75.
Photos: "We do not pay extra for photos accompanying mss, but the ms stands a much better chance for publication if photos are included." Submit photos with ms. Uses b&w prints. Buys one-time rights.
Columns/Departments: "We cover all major sports; coverage can be by league, team, or invidual players." Submit complete ms. Length: 200-600 words. Pays $10-75.

SPORTSHELF NEWS. Box 634, New Rochelle NY 10802. Editor: Irma Ganz. For "all ages interested in sports." Estab. 1949. Bimonthly. Circ. 150,000. Handles only assignments.
Nonfiction: Subject matter is exclusively sports and how-to articles.

WOMEN'S SPORTS MAGAZINE. Women's Sports Publications, Inc., 314 Town & Country Village, Palo Alto CA 94301. Editor: Margaret Roach. Emphasizes women's sports, fitness and health. Monthly magazine; 72 pages. Estab. January 1979. Circ. 50,000. Pays on publication. Buys all rights. Submit seasonal/holiday material 2 months in advance. SASE. Reports in 2 weeks (queries): 1 month (ms). Sample copy $2.00; SASE for writer's guidelines.

Nonfiction: Expose, general interest, how-to, humor, interview, new product, nostalgia, personal experience, personal opinion, profile and travel. "All articles should pertain to women's sports, fitness and health. All must be of national interest" Buys 10 mss/issue. Query with clips of published work. Length: 600-6,000 words. Pays $50 minimum.

Photos: State availability of photos. Pays about $10 for b&w prints; about $10 for 35mm color transparencies. Buys one-time rights.

Columns/Departments: Buys 3/issue. Query with clips of published work. Length: 500-1,500 words. Pays $50 minimum.

Fillers: Clippings, anecdotes, short humor, newsbreaks and puzzles. Length: 25-250 words. Pays $5-15.

Golf

CAROLINA GOLFER, Box 3, Columbia SC 29202. (803)796-9200. Editor: Sydney L. Wise. Associate Editor: Larry Booker. Bimonthly. Buys first rights. Pays on publication. Free sample copy. Reports in 3-8 weeks. SASE.

Nonfiction and Photos: Articles on golf and golfers, clubs, courses, tournaments, only in the Carolinas. Stories on the various courses should be done "in the manner that would give the reader a basic idea of what each course is like." Length: 1,200-1,500 words. Pays according to quality of ms; 3¢ minimum/word. Buys photos with mss. 5x7 or 8x10 b&w glossy prints. Color should be 4x5 or 35mm transparencies. Pays $5 minimum for b&w; $25 for color transparencies used for cover.

COUNTRY CLUB GOLFER, 2171 Campus Dr., Irvine CA 92715. (714)752-6474. Editor: Edward F. Pazdur. For private country club members and club golfers; professional, affluent, college-educated. Monthly magazine; 64 pages. Estab. May 1972. Circ. 70,000. Pays on publication. Buys all rights. *Country Club Golfer* is no longer in the market for freelance contributors. Our material is staff-produced. We are, however, in the market for golf-oriented poems on the humorous side."

Poetry: Humorous golf poems. Buys 4/issue. Submit in batches of 12. Length: 6-12 lines. Pays $10.

GOLF DIGEST, 495 Westport Ave., Norwalk CT 06856. (203)847-5811. Editor: Nick Seitz. 10% freelance written. Emphasizes golfing. Monthly magazine; 130 pages. Estab. 1950. Circ. 960,000. Pays on publication. Buys all rights. Pays kill fee. Byline given. Phone queries OK. Submit seasonal/holiday material 4 months in advance. Photocopied submissions OK. SASE. Reports in 4-6 weeks. Free writer's guidelines.

Nonfiction: Expose, how-to, informational, historical, humor, inspirational, interview, nostalgia, personal opinion, profile, travel, new product, personal experience, photo feature and technical; "all on playing and otherwise enjoying the game of golf." Query. Length: 1,000-2,500 words. Pays 20¢/edited word minimum.

Photos: Pete Libby, art editor. Purchased without accompanying ms. Pays $10-150 for 5x7 or 8x10 b&w prints; $25-300 for 35mm color transparencies. Model release required.

Poetry: Lois Haines, poetry editor. Light verse. Buys 1-2/issue. Length: 4-8 lines. Pays $10-25.

Fillers: Lois Haines, fillers editor. Jokes, gags, anecdotes. Buys 1-2/issue. Length: 2-6 lines. Pays $10-25.

GOLF JOURNAL, United States Golf Association, Far Hills NJ 07931. (201)234-2300. Editor: Robert Sommers. For golfers of all ages and both sexes. Official publication of the U.S. Golf Association. Magazine; 32 pages. Estab. 1948. 8 times/year. Circ. 70,000. Buys all rights. Pays 10% kill fee. Byline given. Buys 30 mss/year. Pays on acceptance. Free sample copy. No photocopied or simultaneous submissions. Reports in 2 weeks. Query. SASE.

Nonfiction and Photos: "As the official publication of the United States Golf Association, our magazine is strong on decisions on the Rules of Golf, USGA Championships, history of the game, and on service articles directed to the club golfer. All facets of golf, its history, courses, and clubs. Instruction. Humor." Length: 500-2,000 words. Pays $400 maximum. Pays $15 minimum for b&w photos. Captions required.

GOLF MAGAZINE, Times Mirror Magazines, Inc., 380 Madison Ave., New York NY 10017. (212)687-3000. Executive Editor: George Peper. 20% freelance written. Emphasizes golf for males, ages 15-80, college-educated, professionals. Monthly magazine; 150 pages. Circ. 750,000. Pays on acceptance. Buys all rights. Byline given. Submit seasonal/holiday material 4 months in advance. Photocopied submissions OK. SASE. Reports in 4 weeks. Sample copy $1.25.

Nonfiction: How-to (improve game, instructional tips); informational (news in golf); humor; profile (people in golf); travel (golf courses, resorts); new product (golf equipment, apparel, teaching aids); and photo feature (great moments in golf; must be special. Most photography on assignment only). Buys 4-6 mss/year. Query. Length: 1,200-2,500 words. Pays $350-500.

Photos: Purchased with accompanying ms or on assignment. Captions required. Query. Pays $50 for 8½x11 glossy prints (with contact sheet and negatives); $50 minimum for 3x5 color prints. Total purchase price for ms includes payment for photos. Model release required.

Columns/Departments: Golf Reports (interesting golf events, feats, etc.). Buys 4-6 mss/year. Query. Length: 250 words maximum. Pays $35. Open to suggestions for new columns/departments.

Fiction: Humorous, mystery. Must be golf-related. Buys 2-4 mss/year. Query. Length: 1,200-2,000 words. Pays $350-500.

Fillers: Short humor. Length: 20-35 words. Pays $5-10.

How To Break In: "Best chance is to aim for a light piece which is not too long and is focused on a personality. Anything very technical that would require a consummate knowledge of golf, we would rather assign ourselves. But if you are successful with something light and not too long, we might use you for something heavier later. Probably the best way to break in would be by our Golf Reports section in which we run short items on interesting golf feats, events and so forth. If you send us something like that, about an important event in your area, it is an easy way for us to get acquainted."

GOLF SCORE, Werner Book Corp., 606 Wilshire Blvd., Santa Monica CA 90401. Publisher: Donald Werner. Editor: Steve Werner. For "golfers from their mid-teens to seniors who are avid enthusiasts. They play at least once a week and often travel to participate in the sport." Monthly, nine times/year. Magazine; 68 pages. Estab. 1977. Circ. 82,000. Pays on publication. Buys first North American serial rights. Pays 100% kill fee. Byline given. Phone queries OK. Submit seasonal/holiday material 3 months in advance. Simultaneous submissions OK. SASE. Reports in 2 weeks.

Nonfiction: How-to instruction; historical; humor; interview; nostalgia; profile; travel; new products; photo feature; and technical. Don't send "how-to articles that are not written by established professionals or authorities. When this is not the case, the article should at least quote such authorities." Buys 64 mss/year. Query or submit complete ms. Length: 1,500-2,000 words. Pays $100-300.

Photos: Purchased with or without accompanying ms or on assignment. Captions required. Pays $10-50 for 8x10 b&w glossy prints; $50-150 for 35mm, 2¼x2¼ or 4x5 transparencies. Model release required.

Guns

THE AMERICAN SHOTGUNNER, Box 3351, Reno NV 89505. Editor: Bob Thruston. Monthly tabloid; 48 pages. Estab. 1973. Circ. 183,000. Buys all rights. Buys 24-50 mss/year. Pays on publication. Free sample copy and writer's guidelines. Submit special material (hunting) 3-4 months in advance. Report on material accepted for publication in 30 days. Returns rejected material. Submit complete ms. SASE.

Nonfiction and Photo: All aspects of shotgunning trap and skeet shooting and hunting, reloading, shooting clothing and shooting equipment. Emphasis is on the how-to and instructional approach. "We give the sportsman actual material that will help him to improve his game, fill his limit, or build that duck blind, etc. Hunting articles are used in all issues, year round." Length: open. Pays $75-250. No additional payment for photos used with mss. "We also purchase professional cover material. Send transparencies (originals)."

BLACK POWDER TIMES, Box 842, Mount Vernon WA 98273. (206)424-3881. Editor: Fred Holder. 25-30% freelance written. For people interested in shooting and collecting black powder guns, primarily of the muzzle-loading variety. Tabloid newspaper; 20 pages. Estab. 1974. Monthly. Not copyrighted. Byline given. Pays on publication. Sample copy 75¢. Will consider photocopied and simultaneous submissions. Reports in 2-4 weeks. Query. SASE.

Nonfiction: Articles on gunsmiths who make black powder guns, on shoots, on muzzle-loading gun clubs, on guns of the black powder vintage, and anything related to the sport of black powder shooting and hunting. Emphasis is on good writing and reporting. As an example of recently published material, see "Spring Rendezvous at Camus Meadows" and "Bad Luck Flintlock Hunt." Informational, how-to, personal experience, interview, profile, historical articles and book reviews. Length: 500-2,000 words. Pays 2¢/word.

GUN WEEK, Amos Press, Box 150, 911 Vandemark Rd., Sidney OH 45365. (513)492-4141. Editor-in-Chief: James C. Schneider. Emphasizes gun hobby; sports, collecting and news. Weekly newspaper; 28 pages. Estab. 1966. Circ. 50,000. Pays on publication. Buys first North American serial rights. Phone queries OK. Submit seasonal/holiday material 6 weeks in advance. Simultaneous and photocopied submissions OK. SASE. Reports in 6 weeks. Free sample copy and writer's guidelines.

Nonfiction: Historical (history of firearms or how they affected an historical event); how-to (dealing with firearms, construction, care, etc.); informational (hunting, firearms, legislative news on the West Coast); interview (gun-related persons, heads of college shooting programs, etc.); new product (firearms, ammunition, cleaners, gun-related products, hunting accessories); photo feature (conservation interests); profile (hunters, gun buffs, legislators, conservationists, etc.); technical. Buys 500 mss/year. Query or send complete ms. Length: 125-3,000 words. Pays 50¢/column inch.

Photos: Purchased with or without accompanying ms. Captions required. Send contact sheet, prints and/or slides. Pays $3 minimum for 5x7 or 8x10 b&w glossy prints; $5 minimum for 35mm color slides. (50¢/column inch with manuscript). Total purchase price for ms includes payment for photos. Model release required.

Columns/Departments: Buys 150-300 mss/year. Query or submit complete ms. Length: 500-1,500 words. Pays $20-35. Open to suggstions from freelancers for new columns/departments; address to James C. Schneider. "Our freelance writers are writing under one designated column, 'Muzzle Loader'—Don Davis, etc. We are looking for possible columnists in firearms collecting, history, hunting and conservation."

Fillers: Clippings, jokes, gags, anecdotes, facts. Send fillers. Length: 25-100 words.

GUN WORLD, Box HH, 34249 Camino Capistrano, Capistrano Beach CA 92624. Editorial Director: Jack Lewis. 50% freelance written. For ages that "range from mid-20s to mid-60s; many professional types who are interested in relaxation of hunting and shooting." Estab. 1960. Monthly. Circ. 129,000. Buys all rights but will reassign to author after publication. Byline given. Buys 50 mss/year. Pays on acceptance. Copy of editorial requirements for SASE. Submit seasonal material 4 months in advance. Reports in 6 weeks, perhaps longer. SASE.

Nonfiction and Photos: General subject matter consists of "well-rounded articles—not by amateurs—on shooting techniques, with anecdotes; hunting stories with tips and knowledge integrated. No poems or fiction. We like broad humor in our articles, so long as it does not reflect upon firearms safety. Most arms magazines are pretty deadly and we feel shooting can be fun. Too much material aimed at pro-gun people. Most of this is staff-written and most shooters don't have to be told of their rights under the Constitution. We want articles on new development; off-track inventions, novel military uses of arms; police armament and training techniques; do-it-yourself projects in this field." Buys informational, how-to, personal experience and nostalgia articles. Pays $250 maximum. Purchases photos with mss and caption required. Wants 5x7 b&w.

GUNS & AMMO MAGAZINE. Petersen Publishing Co., 8490 Sunset Blvd., Los Angeles CA 90069. Editor-in-Chief: Howard E. French. Managing Editor: E.G. Bell. Emphasizes the firearms field. Monthly magazine; 108 pages. Estab. 1958. Circ. 450,000. Pays on publication. Buys all rights. Submit seasonal/holiday material 4 months in advance. SASE. Reports in 1 month. Free writer's guidelines.

Nonfiction: Informational and technical. Buys 7-10 mss/issue. Send complete ms. Length: 1,200-3,000 words. Pays $125-350.

Photos: Purchased with accompanying ms. Captions required. Uses 8x10 b&w glossy prints. Total purchase price for ms includes payment for photos. Model release required.

GUNS MAGAZINE. 591 Camino de la Reina, San Diego CA 92108. (714)297-5352. Editor: J. Rakusan. Estab. 1955. Monthly for firearms enthusiasts. Circ. 135,000. Buys all rights. Buys 100-150 mss/year. Pays on publication. Will send free sample copy to a writer on request. Reports in 2-3 weeks. SASE.

Nonfiction and Photos: Test reports on new firearms; how-to on gunsmithing, reloading; round-up articles on firearms types. Historical pieces. Does not want to see anything about "John and I went hunting" or rewrites of a general nature or controversy for the sake of controversy, without new illumination. Length: 1,000-2,500 words. Pays $75-175. Major emphasis is on good photos. No additional payment for b&w glossy prints purchased with mss. Pays $50-$100 for color; 2¼x2¼ minimum.

THE RIFLE MAGAZINE. Box 3030, Prescott AZ 86301. (602)445-7814. Editor: Ken Howell. 50% freelance written. Bimonthly. For advanced rifle enthusiasts. Pays on publication. Buys

North American serial rights. Reports in 30 days. SASE.

Nonfiction and Photos: Articles must be fresh and of a quality and style to enlighten rather than entertain knowledgeable gun enthusiasts. Subject matter must be technical and supported by appropriate research. "We are interested in seeing new bylines and new ideas, but if a writer doesn't have a solid knowledge of firearms and ballistics, he's wasting his time and ours to submit." Length: 1,500-3,000 words. Pays $75-200. Photos should accompany ms. Buys ms and photos as a package.

SHOOTING TIMES, News Plaza, Peoria IL 61601. Executive Editor: Alex Bartimo. "The average *Shooting Times* reader is 29 years old. He has an above average education and income. He is probably a semiskilled or skilled or professional worker who has an avid interest in firearms and the shooting sports." Special reloading issue in February; handgun issue in March. Monthly. Circ. 195,000. Buys all rights. Buys 85-90 mss/year. Pays on acceptance. Free sample copy and writer's guidelines. Submit seasonal or special material 4-5 months in advance. Reports in 4-5 weeks. Query. SASE.

Nonfiction and Photos: "Presents a well-balanced content ranging from nontechnical through semitechnical to technical stories covering major shooting sports activities—handguns, rifles, shotguns, cartridge reloading, muzzle loading, gunsmithing, how-to's and hunting, with a major emphasis on handguns. Hunting stories must be 'gunny' with the firearm(s) and ammunition dominating the story and serving as the means to an end. Articles may run from 1,000-2,000 words and must be accompanied by 10-12 b&w glossy prints, 8x10, including 1 or 2 'lead' pictures." Pays $175-375.

Horse Racing

AMERICAN TURF MONTHLY, 505 8th Ave., New York NY 10018. Editor: Howard Rowe. 50% freelance written. For "horse-racing bettors." Buys 50-100 mss/year. Byline given. Pays before publication. SASE.

Nonfiction: "Articles, systems and material treating thoroughbred horse racing." Approach should be "how to successfully wager on racing. It is the only publication in the country devoted exclusively to the horse bettor. We have a staff capable of covering every facet aside from system articles." Length: 1,500-3,000 words. Pays $40 minimum, with 30 day workouts, $50 minimum.

THE BACKSTRETCH, 19363 James Couzens Hwy., Detroit MI 48235. (313)342-6144. Editor: Ruth LeGrove. For thoroughbred horse trainers, owners, breeders, farm managers, track personnel, jockeys, grooms and racing fans which span the age range from very young to very old. Publication of United Thoroughbred Trainers of America, Inc. Quarterly magazine; 100 pages. Estab. 1962. Circ. 25,000.

Nonfiction: *Backstretch* contains mostly general information. Articles deal with biographical material on trainers, owners, jockeys, horses and their careers on and off the track, historical track articles, etc. Unless writer's material is related to thoroughbreds and thoroughbred racing, it should not be submitted. Articles accepted on speculation basis—payment made after material is used. If not suitable; articles are returned immediately. Articles that do not require printing by a specified date are preferred. No special length requirement and amount paid depends on material. Advisable to include photos if possible. Articles should be original copies and should state whether presented to any other magazine, or whether previously printed in any other magazine. Submit complete ms. SASE. Sample copy $1. We do not buy crossword puzzles, cartoons, newspaper clippings, fiction or poetry."

HUB RAIL, Hub Rail, Inc., 6076 Busch Blvd., Suite 3, Columbus OH 43229. (614)846-0770. Editor: Larry Evans. Emphasizes harness horse racing or breeding. Quarterly magazine; 120 pages. Estab. 1973. Circ. 10,000. Pays on publication. Buys all rights. Phone queries OK. Submit seasonal/holiday material 3 months in advance. Simultaneous and photocopied submissions OK. SASE. Reports in 4 weeks. Free sample copy and writer's guidelines.

Nonfiction: General interest, historical, humor and nostalgia. "Articles should pertain to harness racing." Buys 10 mss/year. Send clips of published work. Length: 1,000-5,000 words. Pays $50-200.

Fiction: "We use short stories pertaining to harness racing and we also use condensed novels in serialized form." Buys 2 mss/year. Send clips of published work. Length: 3,000-30,000 words. Pays $50-200.

TURF & SPORT DIGEST, 511 Oakland Ave., Baltimore MD 21212. Editor-in-Chief: Allen Mitzel Jr. For an audience composed of thoroughbred horseracing fans. Bimonthly magazine;

80 pages. Estab. 1924. Circ. 40,000. Buys all rights, but may reassign following publication. Phone queries OK. Submit seasonal/holiday material 3 months in advance. Photocopied submissions and previously published work OK. SASE. Reports in 3 weeks. Free sample copy.
Nonfiction: Historical, humor, informational and personal experience articles on racing; interviews and profiles (racing personalities). Buys 4 mss/issue. Query. Length: 300-3,000 words. Pays $60-220.
Photos: Purchased with or without mss. Send contact sheet. Pays $15-25/b&w, $100/color.

Hunting and Fishing

AMERICAN FIELD, 222 W. Adams St., Chicago IL 60606. Editor: William F. Brown. Weekly. Buys first publication rights. Pays on acceptance. Free sample copy. Reports in 10 days. SASE.
Nonfiction and Photos: Always interested in factual articles on breeding, rearing, development and training of hunting dogs, how-to material written to appeal to upland bird hunters, sporting dog owners, field trialers, etc. Also wants stories and articles about hunting trips in quest of upland game birds. Length: 1,000-2,500 words. Pays $50-200. Uses photos submitted with manuscripts if they are suitable; also photos submitted with captions only. Pays $5 minimum for b&w.
Fillers: Infrequently uses some 100- to 250-word fillers. Pays $5 minimum.

THE AMERICAN HUNTER, 1600 Rhode Island Ave. NW, Washington DC 20036. Managing Editor: Earl Shelsby. 90% freelance written. For sport hunters who are members of the National Rifle Association; all ages, all political persuasions, all economic levels. Estab. 1973. Circ. over 160,000. Buys first North American serial rights "and the right to reprint our presentation." Byline given. Pays on acceptance. Free sample copy and writer's guidelines. Reports in 1-3 weeks. SASE.
Nonfiction: "Factual material on all phases of sport hunting and game animals and their habitats. Good angles and depth writing are essential. You have to *know* to write successfully here." Not interested in material on fishermen, campers or ecology buffs. Buys 200 mss/year. Query or submit complete ms. Length: 1,000-2,000 words. Pays $25-400.
Photos: No additional payment made for photos used with mss. Pays $10-25 for b&w photos purchased without accompanying mss. Pays $40-200 for color.

THE AMERICAN RIFLEMAN, 1600 Rhode Island Ave. NW, Washington DC 20036. Editor: Ken Warner. Monthly. Official journal of National Rifle Association of America. Buys first North American serial rights, including publication in this magazine, or any of the official publications of the National Rifle Association. Residuary rights will be returned after publication upon request of the author. Pays on acceptance. Free sample copy and writers' guidelines. Reports in 1-4 weeks. SASE.
Nonfiction: Factual articles on hunting, target shooting, shotgunning, conservation, firearms repairs and oddities accepted from qualified freelancers. No semifictional or "me and Joe" type of yarns, but articles should be informative and interesting. No anything that "winks" at lawbreaking, or delineates practices that are inimical to the best interests of gun ownership, shooting, or good citizenship. Articles should run from one to four magazine pages. Pays about $100-600.
Photos: Full-color transparencies for possible use on cover and inside. Photo articles that run one to two magazine pages. Pays $35 minimum for inside photo; $100 minimum for cover; payment for groups of photos is negotiable.

ANGLER, Box 12155, Oakland CA 94604. Managing Editor: Dan Blanton. 50% freelance written. Fishing magazine for western US. Bimonthly magazine; 84 pages. Estab. 1974. Circ. 15,000. Pays on acceptance. Buys one-time rights. Byline given. Submit seasonal/holiday material 4 months in advance of issue date. Photocopied submissions OK. SASE. Reports in 2 weeks. Sample copy $2.50; SASE for free writer's guidelines.
Nonfiction: How-to; humor; inspirational; and travel. Buys 24 mss/year. Query. Length: 1,000-3,000 words. Pays $125-250.
Fiction: Buys 3 mss/year. Query. Length: 1,000-2,500 words. Pays $35-100.

THE ANGLER AND HUNTER IN ONTARIO, Ontario Outdoors Publishing, Ltd., Box 1541, Peterborough, Ontario, Canada K9J 7H7. (705)743-3891. Editor-in-Chief: Jack Davis. 75% freelance written. Emphasizes outdoor activities in Ontario. Monthly magazine; 32 pages. Estab. 1975. Circ. 21,000. Pays on publication. Buys all rights, but may reassign following publication. Byline given. Submit seasonal/holiday material 2 months in advance of issue date.

Previously published submissions OK. SASE. Reports in 3 weeks. Sample copy for 33¢ postage; free writer's guidelines.
Nonfiction: Expose (pollution or factors affecting the environment of people in Ontario); how-to (new angles or techniques of interest to the outdoorsman); general interest (articles of interest to Ontario hunters and anglers); historical; new product; personal experience (of unusual outdoor interest). No material "that is objectionable to family readership." Buys 8-10 mss/issue. Query with clips of previously published work. Length: 1,500-2,500 words. Pays $25-100.
How To Break In: "How-to-do-its with a new angle suitable for angler, hunter, or camper. All material should have a 'where-to-go, how-to-do-it' content."

THE CAROLINA SPORTSMAN, Wing Publications, Inc., Box 9248, Charlotte NC 28299. Editor-in-Chief: Sidney Wise. Managing Editor: Lawrence Booher. 80% freelance written. Emphasizes outdoor activities. Bimonthly magazine; 32 pages. Estab. 1962. Circ. 4,000. Pays on publication. Buys all rights, but may reassign following publication. Phone queries OK (803-796-9200). Submit seasonal/holiday material 3 months in advance of issue date. Simultaneous, photocopied and previously published submissions OK. SASE. Reports in 3 weeks. Sample copy for "minimal cost"; free writer's guidelines; mention *Writer's Market* in request.
Nonfiction: Exposé (related to outdoors matters); general interest (relating to outdoors); how-to (particularly hunting, fishing and camping); humor; historical; nostalgia; new product (related to outdoors); personal experience; photo feature (related to outdoors); profile; and travel (should be written so they will be of interest to people in North and South Carolina). "We do not want to see extremely general encyclopedia entries." Buys 30 mss/year. Submit complete ms. Length: 2,000 words. Pays 3-7¢/word.
Photos: Submit photo material with accompanying ms. Pays $5-25 for 5x7 b&w glossy prints and $5-25 for any size color transparencies. Captions preferred. Buys all rights, but may reassign following publication.
Columns/Departments: "We use a Wildlife Afield column which deals with hunting and fishing with no particular slant." Buys 1 ms/issue. Submit complete ms. Length: 500-1,500 words. Pays 3-7¢/word. Open to suggestions for new columns/departments.
Fiction: Adventure (related to outdoors—fast-moving dialogue); confession (related to outdoors); historical; humorous; mainstream (related to outdoors); mystery (related to outdoors "Bigfoot" type things); and suspense (related to outdoors). "No stories in which nothing of significance happens." Buys 1 ms/issue. Submit complete ms. Length: 2,500 words maximum. Pays 3-7¢/word.
Poetry: Free verse; haiku; light verse; and traditional. Would like to see poetry related to outdoors. Pays 3-7¢/word.
Fillers: Jokes, gags, anecdotes; newsbreaks and short humor. Buys 3/issue. Length: 200 words. Pays 3-7¢/word.

FIELD AND STREAM, 1515 Broadway, New York NY 10036. Editor: Jack Samson. 30% freelance written. Monthly. Buys all rights. Byline given. Reports in 4 weeks. Query. SASE.
Nonfiction and Photos: "This is a broad-based outdoor service magazine. Editorial content ranges from very basic how-to stories that tell either in pictures or words how an outdoor technique is done or a device is made. Articles of penetrating depth about national conservation, game management, resource management, and recreation development problems. Hunting, fishing, camping, backpacking, nature, outdoor, photography, equipment, wild game and fish recipes, and other activities allied to the itdoors. The 'me and Joe' story is about dead, with minor exceptions. Both where-to and how-to articles should be well-illustrated." Prefers color to b&w. Submit outline first with photos. Length, 2,500 words. Payment varies depending on the name of the author, quality of work, importance of the article. Pays 18¢/word minimum. Usually buys photos with mss. When purchased separately, pays $150 minimum for color. Buys all rights to photos.
Fillers: Buys "how it's done" fillers of 150-500 words. Must be unusual or helpful subjects. Pays $250.

FISHING AND HUNTING NEWS, Outdoor Empire Publishing Co., Inc., 511 Eastlake Ave. E., Box C-19000, Seattle WA 98109. (206)624-3845. Managing Editor: Vence Malernee. Executive Editor: Stan Jones. Emphasizes fishing and hunting. Weekly tabloid; 12-28 pages. Estab. 1944. Circ. 135,000. Pays on acceptance. Buys all rights, but may reassign following publication. Submit seasonal/holiday material 3 months in advance. Photocopied submissions OK. Free sample copy and writer's guidelines.
Nonfiction: How-to (fish and hunt successfully, things that make outdoor jaunts more

enjoyable/productive); photo feature (successful fishing/hunting in the western US); informational. Buys 70 or more mss/year. Query. Length: 100-1,000 words. Pays $10 minimum.
Photos: Purchased with or without accompanying ms. Captions required. Submit prints or transparencies. Pays $5 minimum for 8x10 b&w glossy prints; $10 minimum for 35mm or2¼x2¼color transparencies.

FISHING WORLD, 51 Atlantic Ave., Floral Park NY 11001. Editor: Keith Gardner. Bimonthly. Circ. 265,000. Buys first North American serial rights. Byline given. Pays on acceptance. Free sample copy. Photocopied submissions OK. Reports in 2 weeks. Query. SASE.
Nonfiction and Photos: "Feature articles range from 1,000-2,000 words with the shorter preferred. A good selection of color transparencies and b&w glossy prints should accompany each submission. Subject matter can range from a hot fishing site to tackle and techniques, from tips on taking individual species to a story on one lake or an entire region, either freshwater or salt. However, how-to is definitely preferred over where-to, and a strong biological/scientific slant is best of all. Where-to articles, especially if they describe foreign fishing, should be accompanied by sidebars covering how to make reservations and arrange transportation, how to get there, where to stay. Angling methods should be developed in clear detail, with accurate and useful information about tackle and boats. Depending on article length, suitability of photographs and other factors, payment is up to $250 for feature articles accompanied by suitable photography. Color transparencies selected for cover use pay an additional $250. B&w or unillustrated featurettes are also considered. These can be on anything remotely connected with fishing. Length 1,000 words. Pays $25-100 depending on length and photos. Detailed queries accompanied by photos are preferred. Cover shots are purchased separately, rather than selected from those accompanying mss. The editor favors drama rather than serenity in selecting cover shots."

FLY FISHERMAN MAGAZINE, Ziff-Davis Publishing Co., Dorset VT 05251. (802)867-5951. Editor: Donald D. Zahner. Published 7 times/year; 116 pages. Estab. 1969. Circ. 110,000. Pays on publication. Buys first North American magazine rights and one-time periodical rights. Phone queries OK. Submit seasonal/holiday material 6 months in advance. SASE. Reports in 3 weeks. Free sample copy and writer's guidelines.
Nonfiction: How-to or where-to-go, new product, personal experience, photo feature, profile, technical and travel. Buys 10-12 mss/issue. Query or submit complete ms. Length: 100-3,000 words. Pays $35-400.
Photos: Send photos with ms. Pays $15-60 for 8x10 b&w glossy prints; $25-75 for 35mm, 2¼x2¼, 4x5 color transparencies; $100 maximum for cover. Buys one-time rights. Captions preferred.
Columns/Departments: Casting About (where-to-go shorts); Fly Fisherman's Bookshelf (book reviews); Fly-Tier's Bench (technical how-to); and Rod Rack (technical how-to). Buys 5/issue. Query or submit complete ms. Length: 100-1,500 words. Pays $35-200.
Fiction: Adventure, fantasy, humorous and suspense. "We do not want any erotic material." Query or submit complete ms. Length: 1,000-3,000 words. Pays $100-400.
Fillers: Mini-articles (technical or nontechnical). Buys 5/issue. Length: 100-300 words. Pays $35-100.

THE FLYFISHER, 390 Bella Vista, San Francisco CA 94127. (415)586-8332. Editor: Michael Fong. "*The Flyfisher* is the official publication of the Federation of Flyfishermen, a nonprofit organization of member clubs and individuals in the US, Canada, United Kingdom, France, New Zealand, Chile and other nations. It serves an audience of sophisticated anglers." Quarterly magazine; 48 pages. Estab. 1968. Circ. 8,000. Pays on acceptance for solicited material. Buys first North American serial rights. Byline given. Submit seasonal/holiday material 120 days in advance of issue date. SASE. Reports in 4 weeks. Sample copy $1.50, available from 519 Main St., El Segundo CA 90245; writer's guidelines for SASE.
Nonfiction: How-to (fly fishing techniques, fly tying, tackle, etc.); general interest (any type including where to go, conservation); historical (places, people, events that have significance to fly fishing); inspirational (looking for articles dealing with Federation clubs on conservation projects); interview (articles of famous fly fishermen, fly tyers, teachers, etc.); nostalgia (articles of reminiscences on flies, fishing personalities, equipment and places); photo feature (preferably a combination of 35mm slides and b&w prints about places and seasons); technical (about techniques of fly fishing in salt and fresh waters). "Our readers are pretty sophisticated fly fishermen and articles too basic or not innovative do not appeal to us." Buys 8-10

mss/issue. Query. Length: 1,500-3,500 words. Pays $50-175.
Photos: Pays $15-25 for 8x10 b&w glossy prints; $40-100 for 35mm or larger color transparencies. Captions required. Buys one-time rights. Prefers a selection of transparencies and glossies when illustrating with a manuscript, which are purchased as a package.
Fiction: Adventure; confession; fantasy; historical; humorous; and suspense. Buys 2 mss/issue. Query. Length: 1,500-2,500 words. Pays $50-125.

FUR-FISH-GAME, 2878 E. Main, Columbus OH 43209. Editor: A. R. Harding. For outdoorsmen of all ages, interested in fishing, hunting, camping, woodcraft, trapping. Magazine; 64 pages. Estab. 1925. Monthly. Circ. 190,000. Byline given. Buys 150 mss/year. Pays on acceptance. Sample copy 60¢; free writer's guidelines. No simultaneous submissions. Reports in 4 weeks. Submit complete ms. SASE.
Nonfiction and Photos: Articles on outdoor-related subjects. Articles on hunting, fishing, trapping, camping, boating, conservation. Must be down-to-earth, informative and instructive. Informational, how-to, personal experience, inspirational, historical, nostalgia, personal opinion, travel, new product, technical. Length: 2,000-3,000 words. Pays $50-75. Also buys shorter articles for Gun Rack, Fishing, Dog and Trapping departments. Length: 1,000-2,000 words. Pays $20-35. No additional payment for 8x10 b&w glossy prints used with ms.

GRAY'S SPORTING JOURNAL, 1330 Beacon St., Brookline MA 02146. Editor/Publisher: Ed Gray. Managing Editor: Reed Austin. 95% freelance written. Emphasizes hunting, fishing and conservation for sportsmen. Published 7 times/year. Magazine; 98 pages. Estab. November 1975. Circ. 60,000. Buys First North American serial rights. Byline given. Phone queries OK. Submit seasonal material 4 months in advance of issue date. SASE. Reports in 3 months. Sample copy $4; writer's guidelines for SASE.
Nonfiction: Reed Austin, managing editor. Articles on hunting and fishing experiences. Humor; historical; personal experience; opinion; and photo feature. Buys 10/issue. Submit complete ms. Length: 500-5,000 words. Pays $500-1000. "Please inquire about delayed payment schedule."
Photos: Submit photo material with accompanying ms. Pays $50-300 for any size color transparencies. Captions preferred. Buys one-time rights.
Fiction: Reed Austin, managing editor. Adventure (mostly thoughtful and low-key); and humor. Submit complete ms. Length: 500-5,000 words. Pays $500-1000.
Poetry: Free verse; light verse; and traditional. Buys 1/issue. Submit in batches of 5. Pays $50-75.

ILLINOIS WILDLIFE, Box 116-13005 S. Western Ave., Blue Island IL 60406. (312)388-3995. Editor: Ace Extrom. 35% freelance written. For conservationists and sportsmen. "Tabloid newspaper utilizing newspaper format instead of magazine-type articles." Monthly. Circ. 35,000. Buys one-time rights. Byline given. Pays on acceptance. Will send a sample copy to a writer for 50¢. Reports in 2 weeks. SASE.
Nonfiction and Photos: Want "material aimed at conserving and restoring our natural resources." How-to, humor, photo articles. Length: "maximum 2,000 words, prefer 1,000-word articles." Pays 1½¢/word. B&w glossy prints. Prefers 8x10. Pays $7.50.

MARYLAND CONSERVATIONIST, Tawes State Office Bldg., C-2, Annapolis MD 21401. Editor: Raymond Krasnick. 95% freelance written. For "outdoorsmen, between 10-100 years of age." Bimonthly. Circ. 8,000. Not copyrighted. Buys 20-30 mss/year. Pays on publication. Free sample copy. Reports in 30 days. Query. SASE.
Nonfiction: "Subjects dealing strictly with the outdoor life in Maryland. Nontechnical in content and in the first- or third-person in style." How-to, personal experience, humor, photo, travel articles. Overstocked with material on pollution and Maryland ecology. Length: 1,000-1,500 words. Pays 5¢/word.
Photos: 8x10 b&w glossy prints purchased with mss. Pays $15/photo, $35/slide used with article, $10/b&w photo appearing in photo essay. Color transparencies and 35mm color purchased for covers. Pays $50.

MICHIGAN OUT-OF-DOORS, Box 30235, Lansing MI 48909. (517)371-1041. Editor: Kenneth S. Lowe. 50% freelance written. Emphasizes outdoor recreation, especially hunting and fishing; conservation; environmental affairs. Monthly magazine; 116 pages. Estab. 1947. Circ. 110,000. Pays on publication. Buys first North American serial rights. Byline given. Phone queries OK. Submit seasonal/holiday material 6 months in advance. Photocopied and previously published (if so indicated) submissions OK. SASE. Reports in 1 month. Sample copy 50¢; free writer's guidelines.

Nonfiction: Expose, historical, how-to, informational, interview, nostalgia, personal experience, personal opinion, photo feature and profile. "Stories *must* have a Michigan slant unless they treat a subject of universal interest to our readers." Buys 8 mss/issue. Send complete ms. Length: 1,000-3,000 words. Pays $5-100.
Photos: Purchased with or without accompanying ms. Pays $10 minimum for any size b&w glossy prints; $50 maximum for color (for cover). Offers no additional payment for photos accepted with accompanying ms. Buys one-time rights. Captions preferred.

MID WEST OUTDOORS, Mid West Outdoors, Ltd., 111 Shore Drive, Hinsdale (Burr Ridge) IL 60521. (312)887-7722. Editor: Gene Laulunen. Emphasizes fishing, hunting, camping and boating. Monthly tabloid; 80 pages. Estab. November 1967. Circ. 87,000. Pays on publication. Buys simultaneous rights. Byline given. Submit seasonal material 2 months in advance. Simultaneous, Photocopied and previously published submissions OK. SASE. Reports in 3 weeks. Sample copy $1; free writer's guidelines.
Nonfiction: How-to (fishing, hunting, camping in the Midwest) and where-to-go (fishing, hunting, camping within 500 miles of Chicago). "We do not want to see any articles on 'my first fishing, hunting or camping experiences'." Buys 20/mss issue. Sent complete ms. Length: 1,000-1,500 words. Pays $15-25.
Photos: Offers no additional payment for photos accompany ms; uses b&w prints. Buys all rights. Captions required.
Columns/Departments: Archery, Camping, Dogs, Fishing and Hunting. "We would like to have a Wisconsin Outdoor column." Open to suggestions for columns/departments. Buys 8/issue. Send complete ms. Pays $20.
Fillers: Clippings, jokes, gags and anecdotes. Buys 2/issue.

ONTARIO OUT OF DOORS, 11 King St. W., Toronto, Ontario, Canada M5H 1A3. (416)361-0434. Editor-in-Chief: Burton J. Myers. 75% freelance written. Emphasizes hunting, fishing, camping, and conservation. Monthly magazine; 72 pages. Estab. 1968. Circ. 23,000. Pays on acceptance. Buys all rights, but may reassign following publication. Phone queries OK. Submit seasonal/holiday material 3 months in advance of issue date. Photocopied submissions OK. Reports in 6 weeks. Free sample copy and writer's guidelines; mention *Writer's Market* in request.
Nonfiction: Exposé (conservation practices); how-to (improve your fishing and hunting skills); humor; photo feature (on wildlife); travel (where to find good fishing and hunting); and any news on Ontario. "Avoid 'Me and Joe' articles." Buys 240 mss/year. Query. Length: 150-3,500 words. Pays $15-200.
Photos: Submit photo material with accompanying query. No additional payment for b&w contact sheets and 35mm color transparencies. "Should a photo be used on the cover, an additional payment of $150-200 is made."
Fillers: Outdoor tips. Buys 48 mss/year. Length: 20-50 words. Pays $10.

THE OREGON ANGLER, Box 337, Boring OR 97009. Publisher/Editor: Pete Heley. 50% freelance written. Emphasizes fishing in the Northwest and Oregon. Quarterly magazine; 48 pages. Estab. May 1977. Circ. 3,500. Pays on acceptance. Buys first North American serial rights. Phone queries OK. Submit seasonal/holiday material at least 2 months in advance of issue date. Simultaneous, photocopied and previously published submissions OK. SASE. Reports in 3 weeks. Sample copy $1; free writer's guidelines.
Nonfiction: Expose (must concern Northwest angling and/or anglers); how-to (on fishing); humor (concerning fishing); historical (fishing); interview (1/issue on noted angler); new product (fishing product articles always considered); personal experience; personal opinion (must be backed up by research and concern Northwest angling in some way); profile (noted angler or conservationist); technical (on building fishing products); and travel (fishing spots). Buys 18-30 mss/year. Query or submit complete ms. Length: 800-3,000 words. Pays $20-100.
Columns/Departments: Buys 18 mss/year. Query with clips of previously published work. Length: 800-2,000 words. Pays $10-30.
Fiction: Humorous stories concerning fishing. Buys 1 mss/year. Submit complete ms. Length: 1,200-2,000 words. Pays $30 minimum.
Fillers: Jokes, gags, anecdotes and newsbreaks. Length: 200-1,000 words. Pays $10-30.

OUTDOOR LIFE, 380 Madison Ave., New York NY 10017. Editor: Lamar Underwood. For the active sportsman and his family, interested in fishing and hunting and closely related subjects, such as camping, boating and conservation. Buys first North American serial rights. Pays on acceptance. Query. SASE.
Nonfiction and Photos: "What we publish is your best guide to the kinds of material we seek.

Whatever the subject, you must present it in a way that is interesting and honest. In addition to regular feature material, we are also interested in combinations of photos and text for self-contained 1-, 2-, or 4-page spreads. Do you have something to offer the reader that will help him or her? Just exactly how do you think it will help? How would you present it? Material should provide nuts and bolts information so that readers can do likewise. We are interested in articles in which the author is actually a reporter interviewing and gathering information from expert sportsmen. We also like spectacular personal adventure and ordeal pieces and we will even assign a staff man to help with the writing if the story really interests us." B&w photos should be professional quality 8x10 glossy prints. Color photos should be original positive transparencies and 35mm or larger. Comprehensive captions are required. Pays $500-1,000 for 3,000 words, depending on quality, photos and timeliness.

How To Break In: "We are the only magazine of the big three outdoor sports publications with regional sections and that's probably the best in for a writer who is new to us. Check the magazine for one of the 5 regional editors who would be responsible for material from your area and suggest an item to him. Our regional news pieces cover things from hunting and fishing news to conservation topics to new record fish to the new head of a wildlife agency. You have an advantage if you can provide us with quality photos to accompany the story. These pieces range from 300-1,000 words. Another opportunity for writers is the magazine's food page. These articles include a short introduction about the subject species, perhaps an anecdote, and from three to five *tested* recipes. Articles on preparation (smoking, freezing, etc.) of fish and game will also be considered." Pays $50 for 2-4 double-spaced manuscript pages and photos.

THE OUTDOOR PRESS, N. 2012 Ruby St., Spokane WA 99207. (509)328-9392. Editor: Fred Peterson. 10% freelance written. For sportsmen: hunters, fishermen, RV enthusiasts. Weekly tabloid newspaper; 16 pages. Estab. 1966. Circ. 6,000. Usually buys first North American serial rights. Buys 63 mss/year. Pays on acceptance. Will send sample copy to writer for 25¢. Will consider photocopied and simultaneous submissions. Submit seasonal material 2 months in advance. Reports in 2 weeks. Query or submit complete ms. SASE.
Nonfiction and Photos: How-to stories; technical in detail. Would like to see material on crabs, clams, salmon, fly fishing. Does not want anything on ecology. Length: 750-1,000 words. Pays $20-50. B&w photos (5x7 or larger) purchased with or without ms, or on assignment. Pays $10-20. Captions required.

OUTDOORS TODAY, Box 6852, St. Louis MO 63130. Editor: Ronald Olvera. For outdoorsmen: hunters, fishermen, campers, boaters. Weekly newspaper tabloid; 12-24 pages. Estab. 1970. Circ. 90,000. Buys all rights, but will reassign rights to author after publication. Pays 100% kill fee. Byline given. Buys over 200 mss/year. Pays on 10th of month following publication. Free sample copy. Will consider photocopied and simultaneous submissions. Submit seasonal material 30 days in advance. Reports 60 days. Query or submit complete ms. SASE.
Nonfiction and Photos: Outdoor-oriented material dealing with the midwestern United States. Emphasis on area news, i.e., opening of deer season in Missouri; pheasant season roundups by state, etc. Informational, how-to, personal experience, interview, profile, inspirational, humor, historical, think pieces, expose, nostalgia, opinion, lake features, photo and travel features. Length: 500-750 words. Pays $15-100. No additional payment for first photo used with mss. Additional payment for other photos used.

PENNSYLVANIA GAME NEWS, Box 1567, Harrisburg PA 17120. (717)787-3745. Editor-in-Chief: Bob Bell. 85% freelance written. Emphasizes hunting in Pennsylvania. Monthly magazine; 64 pages. Estab. 1929. Circ. 210,000. Pays on acceptance. Buys all rights, but may reassign following publication. Byline given. Phone queries OK. Submit seasonal/holiday material 6 months in advance. Photocopied submissions OK. SASE. Reports in 1 month. Free sample copy and writer's guidelines.
Nonfiction: Historical, how-to, informational, personal experience, photo feature and technical. "Must be related to outdoors in Pennsylvania." Buys 4-8 mss/issue. Query. Length: 2,500 words maximum. Pays $250 maximum.
Photos: Purchased with accompanying ms. Pays $5-20 for 8x10 b&w glossy prints. Model release required.

PENNSYLVANIA'S OUTDOOR PEOPLE, 610 Beatty Rd., Monroeville PA 15146. (412)243-3335. News Editor: Sher Kudranski. Emphasizes hunting, fishing, camping, boating and conservation in Pennsylvania. Monthly magazine. Pays on publication. Buys one-time rights. Byline given. Simultaneous and previously published submissions OK. SASE. Reports in 2-3 weeks. Sample copy 75¢.

Nonfiction: How-to and where-to articles on hunting, fishing, camping and boating. Buys 2-3 mss/issue. Submit outline/synopsis and sample chapters or query. Length: 1,300-1,600 words. Pays $50-100.

Photos: Offers no additional payment for photos accepted with ms; uses 5x7 b&w prints. Captions and model releases are required.

Columns/Departments: How-to do hunting, fishing, boating and camping. Buys 8-10 mss/issue. Length: 750-900 words. Pays $30-50.

PETERSEN'S HUNTING, Petersen Publishing Co., 8490 Sunset Blvd., Los Angeles CA 90069. (213)657-5100. Editor-in-Chief: Gary Sitton. Emphasizes sport hunting. Monthly magazine; 84 pages. Estab. 1973. Circ. 200,000. Pays on acceptance. Buys all rights. Submit seasonal/holiday material 6 months in advance. SASE. Reports in 2 months. Sample copy $1.25. Free writer's guidelines.

Nonfiction: How-to (how to be a better hunter, how to make hunting-related items), personal experience (use a hunting trip as an anecdote to illustrate how-to contents). Buys 3 mss/issue. Query. Length: 1,500-2,500 words. Pays $200-300.

Photos: Photos purchased with or without accompanying ms. Captions required. Pays $15 minimum for 8x10 b&w glossy prints; $50-150 for 2¼x2¼ or 35mm color transparencies. Total purchase price for ms includes payment for photos. Model release required.

SALT WATER SPORTSMAN, 10 High St., Boston MA 02110. (617)426-4074. Editor-in-Chief: Frank Woolner. Managing Editor: Rip Cunningham. 85% freelance written. Emphasizes saltwater fishing. Monthly magazine; 120 pages. Estab. 1937. Circ. 115,000. Pays on acceptance. Buys first North American serial rights. Pays 100% kill fee. Byline given. Phone queries OK. Photocopied submissions OK. SASE. Reports in 4 weeks. Free sample copy and writer's guidelines.

Nonfiction: How-to, personal experience, technical and travel (to fishing areas). Buys 8 mss/issue. Query. Length: 2,200-2,500 words. Pays 5¢/word.

Photos: Purchased with or without accompanying ms. Captions required. Uses 5x7 or 8x10 b&w prints. Pays $200 minimum for 35mm, 2¼x2¼ or 8x10 color transparencies for cover. Offers additional payment for photos accepted with accompanying ms.

SOUTH CAROLINA WILDLIFE, Box 167, Dutch Plaza, Bldg. D, Columbia SC 29202. (803)758-6291. Editor: John Culler. Managing Editor: John Davis. For South Carolinians interested in hunting, fishing, the outdoors. Bimonthly magazine; 64 pages. Estab. 1953. Circ. 85,000. Not copyrighted. Pays 10¢/word kill fee. Byline given. Buys 20-30 mss/year. Pays on acceptance. Free sample copy. Reports in two weeks. Submit complete ms. SASE.

Nonfiction and Photos: Articles on outdoor South Carolina with an emphasis on preserving and protecting our natural resources. Length: 1,000-3,000 words. Pays 10¢/word. Pays $35 for b&w glossy prints purchased with or without ms, or on assignment. Pays $75 for color.

SOUTHERN ANGLER'S GUIDE, SOUTHERN HUNTER'S GUIDE, Box 2188, Hot Springs AR 71901. Editor: Don J. Fuelsch. Covers the Southern scene on hunting and fishing completely. Buys all rights. Byline given. Issued annually. Query. SASE.

Nonfiction: Hunting, fishing, boating, camping articles. Articles that have been thoroughly researched. Condensed in digest style. Complete how-to rundown on tricks and techniques used in taking various species of fresh and saltwater fish and game found in the Southern states. Interested in new and talented writers with thorough knowledge of their subject. Not interested in first-person or "me and Joe" pieces. Length is flexible. 750 and 1,800 words preferred, although may run as high as 3,000 words. Pays 5-30¢/word.

Photos: Buys photographs with mss or with captions only. Fishing or hunting subjects in Southern setting. No Rocky Mountain backgrounds. B&w only—5x7 or 8x10 glossy prints.

SPORTS AFIELD, 250 W. 55th St., New York NY 10019. Editor: Tom Paugh. For people of all ages whose interests are centered around the out-of-doors (hunting and fishing) and related subjects. Monthly magazine. Estab. 1887. Circ. 600,000. Buys first North American serial rights. Byline given. Pays on acceptance. "Our magazine is seasonal and material submitted should be in accordance. Fishing in spring and summer; hunting in the fall; camping in summer and fall." Submit seasonal material 6 months in advance. Reports in 30 days. Query or submit complete ms. SASE.

Nonfiction and Photo: "Informative how-to articles, and dramatic personal experiences with good photos on hunting, fishing, camping, boating and related subjects such as conservation and travel. Use informative approach. More how-to, more information, less 'true-life' adventure. General hunting/fishing yarns are overworked. Our readers are interested in becoming more proficient at their sport. We want first-class writing and reporting." Buys how-to, personal experience, interview, nostalgia and travel. Length: 500-2,000 words. Pays $600 or more, depending on length and quality. Photos purchased with or without ms. Pays $25 minimum for 8x10 b&w glossy prints. Pays $50 minimum for2 ¼x2¼ or larger transparencies; 35mm acceptable.

Fillers: Mainly how-to-do-it tips on outdoor topics. Length: self-contained 1 or 2 pages. Payment depends on length. Regular column, Almanac, pays $10 and up depending on length, for newsworthy, unusual or how-to nature items.

THE TEXAS FISHERMAN, Voice of the Lone Star Angler, Cordovan Corp., 5314 Bingle Road, Houston TX 77092. Editor: Marvin Spivey. For freshwater and saltwater fishermen in Texas. Monthly tabloid; 40-56 pages. Estab. 1973. Circ. 100,000. Rights purchased vary with author and material. Byline given. Usually buys second serial (reprint) rights. Buys 6-8 mss/month. Pays on publication. Free sample copy and writer's guidelines. Will consider simultaneous submissions. Reports in 4 weeks. Query. SASE.
Nonfiction and Photos: General how-to, where-to, features on all phases of fishing in Texas. Strong slant on informative pieces. Strong writing. Good saltwater stories (Texas only). Length: 2,000-3,000 words, prefers 2,500. Pays $35-150, depending on length and quality of writing and photos. Mss must include 8-10 good action b&w photos or illustrations.

TURKEY CALL, Wild Turkey Bldg., Box 467, Edgefield SC 29824. (803)637-3106. Editor: Gene Smith. 30% freelance written. An educational publication for the wild turkey enthusiast. Bimonthly magazine; 24-40 pages. Estab. 1973. Circ. 31,000. Buys one-time rights. Byline given. Buys 20 mss/year. Pays on publication. Free sample copy when supplies permit. Reports in 3 weeks. Query or submit complete ms. SASE.
Nonfiction and Photos: "Feature articles dealing with the history, management, restoration, harvesting techniques and distribution of the American wild turkey. These stories must consist of accurate information and must appeal to the dyed-in-the-wool turkey hunter, as well as management personnel and the general public. While there are exceptions, we find the management-slanted article particularly well-suited to us." Length: 1,200-1,500 words. Pays $50 minimum; $250-275 for illustrated feature. "Seeking how-to and where-to-go articles, along with 'how the wild turkey became re-established' articles of most any length, with specific information and practical hints for success in harvest and management of the wild turkey. We use color transparencies for the cover. We want action photos submitted with feature articles; mainly b&w. For color, we prefer transparencies. We can use 35mm slides. We prefer 8x10 b&w glossy prints for inside illustrations, but will settle for smaller prints if they are of good quality. For contacts, we must have the negatives and contact prints. We want action shots, not the typical 'dead turkey' photos. We are allergic to posed photos. Photos on how-to should make the techniques clear." Pays $10 minimum for b&w gloss.

VIRGINIA WILDLIFE, Box 11104, Richmond VA 23230. (804)257-1000. Editor: Harry L. Gillam. 70% freelance written. For sportsmen and outdoor enthusiasts. Pays on acceptance. Buys first North American serial rights. Byline given. Free sample copy. SASE.
Nonfiction: Uses factual outdoor stories, especially those set in Virginia. "Currently need boating subjects, women and youth in the outdoors, wildlife and nature in urban areas. Always need good fishing and hunting stories—not of the 'Me and Joe' genre, however. Slant should be to enjoy the outdoors and what you can do to improve it. Material must be applicable to Virginia, sound from a scientific basis, accurate and easily readable." Length: prefers approximately 1,200 words. Pays 3-4¢/word.
Photos: Buys photos with mss; "and good photos anytime." Prefers color transparencies, but also has limited need for 8x10 glossy b&w prints. Pays $5-7.50/b&w photo; $7-15 for color.

WASHINGTON FISHING HOLES, Snohomish Publishing Co., Inc., 114 Avenue C, Snohomish WA 98290. (206)568-4121. Editors: Milt Keizer, Terry Sheely, John Thomas. 15-25% freelance written. For anglers from 8-80, whether beginner or expert, interested in the where-to and how-to of Washington fishing. Magazine published every two months; 64 pages. Estab. 1974. Circ. 4,500. Pays on publication. Buys first North American serial rights. Submit material 30 days in advance. SASE. Reports in 3 weeks. Free sample copy and writer's guidelines.
Nonfiction: How-to (angling only); informational (how-to). Buys 8-12 mss/year. Query. Length: 800-1,200 words. Pays $25-60.
Photos: Purchased with accompanying ms. Captions required. Send prints. Buys 5x7 b&w

glossy prints or 35mm color transparencies with article. Offers no additional payment for photos accepted with accompanying ms. Model release required.

Fillers: How-to (only). Buys 4-6 fillers/year. Query. Length: 250-300 words. Pays $10 maximum.

For '80: "Would like to see some pieces on striped bass, shad fishing at mouth of Columbia River and Olympic Peninsula steelheading."

WESTERN SPORTSMAN (formerly *Fish and Game Sportsman*), Box 737, Regina, Saskatchewan, Canada S4P 3A8. (306)523-8384. Editor: J.B. (Red) Wilkinson. 90% freelance written. For fishermen, hunters, campers and others interested in outdoor recreation. "Please note that our coverage area is Alberta and Saskatchewan." Quarterly magazine; 64-112 pages. Estab. 1968. Circ. 17,000. Rights purchased vary with author and material. May buy first North American serial rights or second serial (reprint) rights. Byline given. Pays on publication. Sample copy $1.25; free writer's guidelines. "We try to include as much information on all subjects in each edition. Therefore, we usually publish fishing articles in our winter magazine along with a variety of winter stories. If material is dated, we would like to receive articles 4 months in advance of our publication date." Will consider photocopied submissions. Reports in 4 weeks. SAE and International Reply Coupons.

Nonfiction: "It is necessary that all articles can identify with our coverage area of Alberta and Saskatchewan. We are interested in mss from writers who have experienced an interesting fishing, hunting, camping or other outdoor experience. We also publish how-to and other informational pieces as long as they can relate to our coverage area. Too many writers submit material to us which quite frankly we don't believe. We call these puff stories and generally after reading the first page or two they are returned to the writers without further reading. Our editors are experienced people who have spent many hours afield fishing, hunting, camping etc., and we simply cannot accept information which borders on the ridiculous. The record fish does not jump two feet out of the water with a brilliant sunset backdrop, two-pound test line, one-hour battle, a hole in the boat, tumbling waterfalls, all in the first paragraph. We are more interested in articles which tell about the average guy living on beans, guiding his own boat, stalking his game and generally doing his own thing in our part of western Canada than a story describing a well-to-do outdoorsman traveling by motorhome, staying at an expensive lodge with guides doing everything for him except landing the fish, or shooting the big game animal. The articles that are submitted to us need to be prepared in a knowledgeable way and include more information than the actual fish catch or animal or bird kill. The story should discuss the terrain, the people involved on the trip, the water or weather conditions, the costs, the planning that went into the trip, the equipment and other data closely associated with the particular event in a factual manner. We like to see exciting writing, but leave out the gloss and nonsense. We are very short of camping articles and how-to pieces on snowmobiling, including mechanical information. We generally have sufficient fishing and hunting data but we're always looking for new writers. I would be very interested in hearing from writers who are experienced campers and snowmobilers." Buys 80 mss/year. Submit complete ms. Length: 1,500-3,000 words. Pays $40-175.

Photos: Photos purchased with ms with no additional payment. Also purchased without ms. Pays $7-10/5x7 or 8x10 b&w print; $100-150/35mm or larger transparency.

WESTERN OUTDOORS, 3197-E Airport Loop, Costa Mesa CA 92626. (714)546-4360. Editor-in-Chief: Burt Twilegar. Emphasizes hunting, fishing, camping, boating for 11 Western states only. Monthly magazine; 88 pages. Estab. 1960. Circ. 150,000. Pays on publication. Buys one-time rights. Phone queries OK. Submit seasonal/holiday material 4-6 months in advance. Photocopied submissions OK. SASE. Reports in 4-6 weeks. Sample copy $1; free writer's guidelines.

Nonfiction: How-to (catch more fish, bag more game, improve equipment, etc.); informational; photo feature; and technical. Buys 130 mss/year. Query or send complete ms. Length: 1,000-1,500 words maximum. Pays $100-200.

Photos: Purchased with accompanying ms. Captions required. Uses 8x10 b&w glossy prints; prefers Kodachrome II 35mm. Send prints and/or transparencies. Offers no additional payment for photos accepted with accompanying ms.

WISCONSIN SPORTSMAN, Box 1307 Oshkosh WI 54901. Editor: Tom Petrie. 30% freelance written. Emphasizes Wisconsin fishing, hunting, and outdoors. Bimonthly magazine; 64-72 pages. Estab. 1972. Circ. 50,000. Pays on publication. Buys all rights, but may reassign after publication. Submit seasonal/holiday material 5 months in advance of issue date. Previously published submissions OK. SASE. Reports in 2-3 weeks.

Nonfiction: Historical (Wisconsin state history); how-to (fishing/hunting-oriented, with photos or illustrations if applicable); photo feature (color transparencies on Wisconsin wildlife or touring); and travel (with pix). No 'why-I-hunt' or 'what the outdoors means to me' style articles. Buys 28 mss/year. Query or submit complete ms. Length: 300-2,000 words. Pays $25-300.

Photos: Submit photos with query or ms. Offers no additional payment for photos accepted with ms. Uses 8x10 glossy b&w prints and 35mm color transparencies. Captions preferred. Buys all rights.

Martial Arts

BLACK BELT. Rainbow Publications, Inc., 1845 W. Empire, Burbank CA 91504. (213)843-4444. Publisher: Han Kim. Emphasizes martial arts for both practitioner and layman. Monthly magazine; 72 pages. Estab. 1961. Circ. 75,000. Pays on publication. Buys all rights. Submit seasonal/holiday material 6 months in advance. Simultaneous and photocopied submissions OK. SASE. Reports in 4 weeks. Free sample copy.

Nonfiction: Expose, how-to, informational, interview, new product, personal experience, profile, technical and travel. Buys 6 mss/issue. Query or send complete ms. Length: 100-1,000 words. Pays 4-10¢/word.

Photos: Purchased with or without accompanying ms. Captions required. Send transparencies. Pays $4-7 for 5x7 or 8x10 b&w or color transparencies. Total purchase price for ms includes payment for photos. Model release required.

Fiction: Historical. Buys 1 ms/issue. Query. Pays $35-100.

Fillers: Send fillers. Pays $5 minimum.

KARATE ILLUSTRATED. Rainbow Publications, Inc., 1845 W. Empire Ave., Burbank CA 91504. (213)843-4444. Publisher: Han Kim. Emphsizes karate and kung fu. Monthly magazine; 64 pages. Estab. 1969. Circ. 67,000. Pays on publication. Buys all rights. Submit seasonal/holiday material 6 months in advance. Simultaneous and photocopied submissions OK. SASE. Reports in 4-6 weeks. Free sample copy.

Nonfiction: Expose, historical, how-to, informational, interview, new product, personal experience, personal opinion, photo feature, profile, technical and travel. Buys 6 mss/issue. Query or submit complete ms. Pays $35-150.

Photos: Purchased with or without accompanying ms. Submit 5x7 or 8x10 b&w or color photos. Total purchase price for ms inctudes payment for photos.

Columns/Departments: Reader's Photo Contest and Calendar. Query. Pays $5-25. Open to suggestions for new columns/departments.

Fiction: Historical. Query. Pays $35-150.

Fillers: Newsbreaks. Query. Pays $5.

OFFICIAL KARATE. 351 W. 54th St., New York NY 10019. Editor: Al Weiss. For karatemen or those interested in the martial arts. Estab. 1968. Monthly. Circ. 100,000. Rights purchased vary with author and material; generally, first publication rights. Pays 50% kill fee. Byline given. Buys 60-70 mss/year. Pays on publication. Free sample copy. Will consider photocopied submissions. Reports in 1 month. Query or submit complete ms. SASE.

Nonfiction and Photos: "Biographical material on leading and upcoming karateka, tournament coverage, controversial subjects on the art ('Does Karate Teach Hate?', 'Should the Government Control Karate?', etc.) We cover the 'little man' in the arts rather than devote all space to established leaders or champions; people and happenings in out-of-the-way areas along with our regular material." Informational, how-to, interview, profile, spot news. Length: 1,000-3,000 words. Pays $50-150. B&w contacts or prints. Pays $5.

Miscellaneous

BACKPACKER. 65 Adams St., Bedford Hills NY 10507. Editor: Ms. Dawn de Boer. 80% freelance written. Emphasizes backpacking, wilderness skiing, nature photography for backpackers and wilderness enthusiasts. Bimonthly magazine; 100 pages. Estab. 1973. Circ. 120,000. Pays on acceptance. Buys all rights, but may reassign following publication. Submit seasonal/holiday material 1 year in advance. SASE. Reports in 4 weeks. Sample copy $2.75; writer's guidelines for SASE.

Nonfiction: "We especially need articles on backpacking trips in the US, with photos." Buys 5 mss/issue. Query. Length: 2,000-5,000 words. Pays $150-1,00. "Depends on number of photos and length. Average pay is $500 for complete package."

Photos: Purchased only with accompanying ms. Captions required. Query. Model release usually required.

Tips: "We are looking for cartoons (pays $35-75) and poetry (short poems about hiking and backpacking).

How To Break In: "We receive over 5,000 freelance submissions a year. Many of them are rejected because the author is not familiar with *Backpacker* magazine. Generalized articles just don't work here; our readers are terribly sophisticated backpackers and can spot writing by someone who does not intimately know his subject within ten seconds. Articles on trips must have an angle, as well as where you went, what you took, when you ate, etc."

BACKPACKING JOURNAL, Davis Publications, 380 Lexington Ave., New York NY 10017. Editor-in-Chief: Andrew J. Carra. Managing Editor: Lee Schreiber. 80-90% freelance written. Emphasizes hiking and backpacking. Quarterly magazine; 96 pages. Estab. 1975. Circ. 45,000. Pays on acceptance. Buys all rights, but may reassign following publication. Byline given. Submit seasonal/holiday material 4-6 months in advance. SASE. Reports in 2 months. Sample copy $1.60. Free writer's guidelines.
Nonfiction: Exposé (government, parks service, trail organizations); historical (biographies of conservationists, etc.); how-to; humor; informational; interview; new product; personal experience; personal opinion; profile; technical; travel; and equipment. Buys 12-15 mss/issue. Length: 500-3,000 words. Pays $50-250.
Photos: Purchased with or without accompanying ms. Query or send transparencies. Uses 8x10 b&w glossy prints or 35mm transparencies. Pays $200-250 for cover. Offers no additional payment for photos accepted with accompanying ms.
Columns/Departments: Opinion. Buys 2 mss/issue. Query. Length: 1,000-2,000 words. Pays $150-200.
Fillers: Jokes, gags, anecdotes, newsbreaks and short humor. Query. Length: 100-500 words. Pays $25-50.

CANADIAN RODEO NEWS, Box 99, Station T, Calgary, Alberta, Canada T2H 2G7. (403)243-7359. Editor: Mary Burgoyne. Emphasizes Canadian professional rodeo. Semimonthly tabloid; 12 pages. Estab. 1964. Circ. 4,000. Byline given. Pays on publication. Phone queries OK. Submit seasonal/holiday material 1 month in advance. Simultaneous, photocopied and previously published submissions OK. Reports in 2 weeks. Free sample copy.
Nonfiction: Historical, how-to, interview, personal opinion, photo feature and profile. "Articles must be aimed at Canadian professional rodeo, past and present." Buys 10-20 mss/year. Send complete ms. Length: 500-2,000 words. Pays $1/column inch maximum.
Photos: State availability of photos. Pays $2.50 for 8x10 b&w prints.

GEORGIA SPORTSMAN MAGAZINE, Box 741, Marietta GA 30061. Editor: David Morris. Emphasizes hunting and fishing and outdoor recreational opportunities in Georgia. Monthly magazine; 64 pages. Estab. 1976. Circ. 37,000. Pays on publication. Byline given. Phone queries OK. Submit seasonal/holiday material 4 months in advance. Simultaneous, "very legible" photocopied and previously published submissions OK. Source must be identified for previously published work. SASE. Reports in 4 weeks. Sample copy $1.50; free writer's guidelines.
Nonfiction: Exposé; how-to; informational; historical (acceptable on a very small scale); humor; interviews with fishermen or hunters known statewide; nostalgia (antique weapons such as percussion guns); and articles concerning major legislation and environmental issues affecting Georgia. Length 1,500-2,000 words. Pays $120 maximum.
Photos: B&w and color purchased with or without mss or on assignment. Pays $100 for cover use.
Fillers: Newsbreaks (explanation of source must accompany them) and illustrations. "We are always in the market for illustrations depicting outdoor scenes. Send samples." Newsbreak length: 500 words average. Pays 7½¢/word minimum.

HANG GLIDING, United States Hang Gliding Association, Box 66306, Los Angeles CA 90066. (213)390-3065. Editor: Gilbert Dodgen. Monthly magazine; 72 pages. Estab. May 1972. Circ. 35,000. Buys all rights. Phone queries OK. Submit seasonal/holiday material 6 weeks in advance. Simultaneous, photocopied and previously published submissions OK. SASE. Reports in 2 months. Free sample copy.
Nonfiction: Expose, general interest, historical, how-to, humor, inspirational, interview, nostalgia, new product, experience, personal opinion, photo feature, profile, technical and travel. Buys 1-2 mss/issue. Query with clips of published work or send complete ms. Length: 2-3 typed pages. Pays $25 maximum.
Photos: State availability of photos or send photos with ms. Pays $3.50 for b&w slides. Buys one-time rights. Captions and model releases required.

Fiction: Adventure, fantasy, experimental, historical, humorous, mystery and suspense. "We prefer short, to-the-point articles. We do not want anything other than articles about hang gliding." Query with clips of published work or send complete ms. Pays $15-25.
Poetry: "Anything that pertains to hang gliding. Submit in batches of 4 or 5. Length: 25 lines maximum. No pay.
Fillers: Clippings, jokes, gags, anecdotes, newsbreaks, short humor, comic strips, photos and letters to the editor.

HANDBALL, United States Handball Association, 4101 Dempster St., Skokie IL 60076. (312)673-4000. Editor-in-Chief: Terry Muck. 25% freelance written. For active handball players from 15-70. Bimonthly magazine; 80 pages. Estab. 1951. Circ. 15,000. Pays on publication. Buys all rights, but may reassign following publication. Phone queries OK. Submit seasonal material 2 months in advance. SASE. Reports in 2 months.
Nonfiction: How-to (instructional); historical (I remember so and so); humor (funny experiences with handball); and personal opinion (handball improvement). "Our biggest demand is for instructional articles, with first-person types second." Buys 1-3 mss/issue. Send complete ms. Length: 1,000-2,000 words. Pays $100-200.
Photos: Purchased without accompanying ms. Captions required. Send prints. Pays $10-50 for any size b&w glossy prints. Total purchase price for ms includes payment for photos. No additional payment for photos accepted without accompanying ms.

HOCKEY ILLUSTRATED, 333 Johnson Ave., Brooklyn NY 11206. Editor: Randy O'Neill. For young men and women interested in hockey. Estab. 1960. Published 6 times a year. Circ. 150,000. Buys all rights, but will reassign rights to author after publication. Byline given. Buys 65 mss/year. Pays on acceptance. Submit seasonal material 3 months in advance. Query. SASE.
Nonfiction and Photos: Player profiles, in-depth interviews, humor, informational, historical, expose. Length: 2,000-2,200 words. Pays $100-150. Color: pays $150 for cover; $50-75 for inside use for 35mm.

MARATHONER, World Publications, Inc., Box 366, Mountain View CA 94042. (415)965-8777. Managing Editor: Jim Carr. Senior Editor: Bob Wischnia. Quarterly magazine; 120-128 pages. Estab. 1978. Circ. 40,000. Pays on publication. Buys all rights. Byline given. Phone queries OK. SASE. Reports in 1 month. Sample copy $2.50.
Nonfiction: General interest (marathoners and unusual marathoning events); historical; how-to (run better marathons); humor; inspirational; interview; nostalgia; photo features (not just running but convey emotions); and profile (show motivation more than the time and training involved). "We do not want any first marathon stories." Buys 5-8 mss/issue. Query with clips of published work. Pays $25-50.
Photos: State availability of photos or send photos with ms. Pay negotiable for 8x10 b&w contact sheets, negatives or glossy prints; 35mm color transparencies. Buys one-time rights.

MOUNTAIN STATES RECREATION, Mountain States Ski Association, 1670 York St., Denver CO 80206. (308)399-5066. Managing Editor: Gary Markovitz. Emphasizes outdoor recreation (skiing in winter, other activities year round). Monthly magazine; 24 pages. Estab. June 1978. Circ. 45,000. Pays on publication. Buys all rights. Pays 25% kill fee. Byline given "except if extensive editing/rewriting is necessary." Phone queries OK. Submit seasonal or holiday material 2-3 months in advance. SASE. Reports in 4 weeks. Sample copy 50¢; free writer's guidelines.
Nonfiction: General interest to outdoor enthusiasts (inside story of what is going on in an activity); how-to; interviews; unique experiences; new product. Buys 6-8 mss/issue. Query. Length: 500-2,000 words. Pays $25-75.
Fiction: "We're open, but it must deal with recreation in some form."
Photos: Send photos with ms. Pays $10-20 for b&w prints; $35-50 for color slides. Captions preferred; model release required. Photo essays accepted, price to be negotiated.

NATIONAL RACQUETBALL, United States Racquetball Association, 4101 Dempster, Skokie IL 60076. Editor: Charles S. Leve. Managing Editor: Carol Brusslan. For racquetball players of all ages. Monthly magazine; 88 pages. Estab. 1973. Circ. 50,000. Pays on publication. Buys all rights. Byline given. Submit seasonal/holiday material 2-3 months in advance. SASE. Reports in 2 months. Sample copy $1.50.
Nonfiction: How-to (play better racquetball or train for racquetball); interview (with players or others connected with racquetball business); opinion (usually used in letters but sometimes fullblown opinion features on a phases of the game); photo feature (on any subject

mentioned); profile (short pieces with photos on women players interesting in other ways or on older players); health (as it relates to recquetball players—food, rest, eye protection, etc.); and fashion. Buys 4 mss/issue. Query with clips of published work. Length: 500-2,500 words. Pays $25-200.

Photos: State availability of photos or send photos with ms. Offers no additional payment for photos accompanying ms. Uses b&w prints or color transparencies. Buys one-time rights. Captions and model releases required.

Fiction: Adventure, humorous, mystery, romance, science fiction and suspense. "Whatever an inventive mind can do with racquetball. Buys 3 mss/year. Send complete ms. Pays $25-200.

Poetry: Light verse. Buys 1/year. Pays $10-25.

Fillers: Puzzles. Buys 2/year. Pays $10-25.

ON THE RUN, World Publishing, Inc., 1400 Sterlin Rd., Mountain View CA 94042. (415)965-8777. Editor/Publisher: Bob Anderson. Managing Editor: Paul Perry. Emphasizes running. Semimonthly tabloid; 64 pages. Estab. 1978. Circ. 45,000. Pays on publication. Buys first world serial rights. Phone queries OK. Submit seasonal/holiday material 2 months in advance. Simultaneous, photocopied and previously published submissions OK. SASE. Reports in 2 weeks. Free sample copy.

Nonfiction: Expose, general interest, historical, humor, inspirational, interview, new product, personal experience, photo feature, profile and technical. Buys 20 mss/issue. Query with clips of published work. Length: 500-10,000 words. Pays $25-1,000.

Photos: Send photos with ms. Pays $15-20 for b&w contact sheets or negatives. Buys one-time rights. Captions and model releases required.

Fillers: Short humor. Buys 20/issue. Length: 100 words. Pays $10.

PADDLE WORLD, 37 Quade St., Glens Falls NY 12801. Editor: Marilyn Nason. 50% freelance written. For amateur platform and paddle tennis players. Magazine; 36 or more pages. Estab. 1975. Published 6 times/year. Circ. 15,000. Buys all rights. Buys 5 mss/year. Pays on publication. Sample copy $1.25. Reports in 8-10 weeks. Query, briefly stating credentials. SASE.

Nonfiction: Articles on interesting installations, tournaments, "names" who play platform or paddle tennis for fun. Length: open. Pays $1/printed page minimum.

PRORODEO SPORTS NEWS (formerly *Rodeo Sports News*), 101 Prorodeo Dr., Colorado Springs CO 80919. Publisher: Ken Stemler. Editor: Bill Crawford. For avid rodeo fans and professional rodeo cowboys. Biweekly tabloid newspaper; 16-40 pages. Annual edition published in January. Estab. 1952. Pays 25% kill fee. Byline given "except on hard news, obits, births and one-paragraph items of interest." Pays within 10 days of acceptance. Reports in 2 weeks. SASE. Sample copy $1.

Nonfiction: "All material published in *PSN* must relate directly to our 9,000 members and permit holders (apprentice prorodeo cowboys), and to the 600-620 PRCA-approved rodeos held annually in the US and Canada. We do not use material about amateur, high school, junior college, or so-called team rodeo. All material must be accurate and attributable; no 'informed sources' or 'highly placed officials.' No movie-type treatments with more emphasis on events outside the arena than inside; PRCA contestants are professional athletes who compete in a physically demanding sport—80-100 rodeos a year—and when not competing are usually traveling long distances enroute to a rodeo. They do not abuse their bodies and talents by the incessant drinking, womanizing, brawling, etc., depicted in most movies. Avoid overusing dialect, the countrified bit; most of our members and readers are family men who met their wives in college. Features must have a focus." Query or submit complete ms. Length: 500-2,500 words. Pays $1.35/column inch.

Photos: "B&w 8x10 glossy prints only, rodeo action and human interest, including behind-the-chutes pix. Color: uses one color photo an issue. Pays $5 for b&w; $25 minimum for color."

RACQUET, 342 Madison Ave., New York NY 10017. Editors: H.K. Pickens. Bimonthly magazine. Reports in 3 weeks.

Nonfiction: "We want articles from across the country but advise writers against localizing topics. We want writers who can come up with interesting, off-beat ideas for us. We are not interested in instructionals." Query or send complete ms. Length: 1,000-2,000 words. Pays $150 minimum.

RACQUETBALL, Towery Publishing Co., Inc., Box 16566, 1535 E. Brooks Rd., Memphis TN

38116. (901)345-8000. Editor: Larry Conley. For the amateur racquetball player. Monthly magazine; 52 pages. Estab. 1971. Circ. 35,000. Pays on publication. Buys all rights. Byline given. Submit seasonal/holiday material 2 months in advance. Photocopied submissions OK. SASE. Reports in 3 weeks. Sample copy $1.
Nonfiction: General interest (an unusual court club, a look at racquetball training camps, new developments in racquetball, etc.); how-to (improve your backhand, return serves, play a lefthander, make lob shots, etc.); profile (of interesting people in racquetball—a top amateur player, a racquetball association official, etc.); new product (racquetball-related); and personal experience (directly related to racquetball, preferably with some relevance to other players. Buys 5 mss/issue. Query with clips of published work. Length: 2,000-4,000 words. Pays 3½¢/word.

THE RUNNER, 1 Park Ave., New York NY 10016. Editor-in-Chief: Marc Blume. Emphasizes the world of running in the broadest scope with its main thrust in jogging, roadrunning and marathoning. Monthly magazine. Estab. 1978. Circ. 115,000. Pays on acceptance. Buys first North American serial rights. Pays 20% kill fee. Byline given. Submit seasonal/holiday material 3 months in advance. SASE. Reports in 2-3 weeks. Free sample copy.
Nonfiction: Profiles, body science, historical, event coverage, training, lifestyle, sports medicine, phenomena and humor. Buys 5-6 mss/issue. Query with clips of published work. Length: 1,500 words and up. Pays $250 and up, usually $500 or so for 3,000 words.
Photos: State availability of photos. Pay is negotiable for b&w contact sheets and 35mm color transparencies. Buys one-time rights. Captions required.
Columns/Departments: Reviews (books, film etc.); people; statistical listings; humor; food; medicine; and training. Regular columnists used. Buys 3-4/issue. Length: 900-1,200 words. Pays $150 and up.
Warmups: Short news items and whimsical items. Length: 100-400 words. Pays $25-50.

RUNNER'S WORLD MAGAZINE, World Publications, Box 366, Mountain View CA 94040. (415)965-8777. Managing Editor: Richard Benyo. 70% freelance written. Emphasizes the sport of running, primarily long distance running; for avid runners, coaches, equipment manufacturers and salesmen, race promoters, etc. Monthly magazine; 168 pages. Estab. 1966. Circ. 475,000. Pays on publication. Buys all rights, but may reassign following publication. Pays 25-45% kill fee. Byline given. Submit seasonal/holiday material 3-4 months in advance. Previously published submissions OK. SASE. Reports in 2-4 weeks. Free sample copy and writer's guidelines.
Nonfiction: Exposé; historical (where-are-they-now articles, primarily); how-to (improving one's own running and health); humor; informational; inspirational; interview; opinion (featured in column "Runner's Forum"); technical and profile. Buys 8 mss/issue. Query. Length: 1,000-5,000 words. Pays $25-500.
Photos: Photos purchased with or without accompanying ms or on assignment. Pays $15-25 for 5x7 or 8x10 b&w glossy prints; $50-100 for 35mm or 2¼x2¼ color transparencies. Query and send photos. Total purchase price for ms includes payment for photos.
Columns/Departments: Runner's Forum (1,000 words maximum). Buys 6 mss/issue. Pays $25/ms.

RUNNING TIMES, Running Times, Inc., 12808 Occoquan Rd., Woodbridge VA 22192. (703)550-7799. Editor: Edward Ayres. Emphasizes running, jogging, holistic health and fitness. Monthly magazine; 72 pages. Estab. January 1977. Circ. 100,000. Pays on publication. Buys all rights. Byline given. Submit seasonal/holiday material 3 months in advance. Simultaneous and photocopied submissions OK. SASE. Reports in 1 month. Sample copy $1.75.
Nonfiction: How-to (training techniques, racing techniques, self-treatment of injuries, etc.); humor; interview; photo feature; profile; and technical (written for a general readership). "We do not want opinions or ideas which are not backed up by solid research." Buys 1-2 mss/issue. Query or send complete ms. Length: 500-2,500 words. Pays $25-400.
Photos: State availability of photos. Pays $5-25 for 5x7 or 8x10 b&w glossy prints; $30-200 for color transparencies. Captions preferred.
Fiction: Adventure, erotica, fantasy and humorous. "Subjects must involve runners or running." Buys 4 mss/year. Send complete ms or clips of published work. Length: 700-2,500 words. Pays $50-200.

SAN DIEGO RACQUET REPORT, 1510 Fayette St., El Cajon CA 92020. (714)562-2242. Editor: Joseph Ditler. Monthly tabloid; 12-16 pages. Estab. February 1976. Circ. 12,000. Pays on publication. Buys one-time rights. Phone queries OK. Submit seasonal/holiday material 1 month in advance. SASE. Reports in 2 weeks. Sample copy for SASE.

Nonfiction and Fiction: General interest to San Diego readers. Tournaments, personalities, profiles, new court openings, how-to articles, opinion, photos, short fiction, funny photo of month etc. "We cover tennis, racquetball and will eventually cover all racquet sports (jai alai, squash, badminton and table tennis). Will pay $20 for feature articles (200-1,000 words), $5-10 for photos (b&w only), slightly less for fillers and more for larger manuscripts. Our appeal is to San Diego readers primarily and we use photos to reach our audience. Please identify all photos with captions and numbers."

SIGNPOST MAGAZINE, 16812 36th Ave. W., Lynnwood WA 98036. Publisher: Louise B. Marshall. Editor: Ann M. Stagg. About hiking, backpacking and similar outdoor activities, mostly from a Pacific Northwest viewpoint. Monthly. Estab. 1966. Will consider any rights offered by author. Buys 12 mss/year. Pays on publication. Sample copy $1. Will consider photocopied submissions. Reports in 3 weeks. Query or submit complete ms. SASE.
Nonfiction and Photos: "Most material is donated by subscribers or is staff-written. Payment for purchased material is low, but a good way to break into print or spread a particular point of view."

SKATEBOARDER MAGAZINE, Surfer Publiciations, Box 1028, Dana Point CA 92629. (714)496-5922. Editor: Brian Gillogly. Emphasizes skateboarding. Monthly magazine; 100 pages. Estab. 1965. Circ. 150,000. Pays on publication. Submit seasonal/holiday material 3-4 months in advance. SASE. Reports in 2 months. Free sample copy.
Nonfiction: Expose, general interest, historical, how-to, humor, inspirational, interview, new product, nostalgia, personal experience, personal opinion, photo feature, profile, technical and travel. "Anything submitted must relate to skateboarding." Buys 3 mss/issue. Send complete ms. Length: 300-1,000 words. Payment rates available on request.
Photos: Send photos with ms. Pays $10-100 for 5x7 or 8x10 b&w contact sheets, negatives or glossy prints; $20-300 for 35mm color transparencies. Buys one-time rights. Model release required.
Fiction: Adventure, fantasy, experimental, historical, humorous and science fiction. Buys 2 mss/year. Send complete ms. Length: 300-1,000 words. Payment rates available on request.
Poetry: "Any type of poetry as long as it relates to skating." Buys 5/year. Payment rates available upon request.

SLO PITCH MAGAZINE, Slo Pitch Magazine, Inc., 7120 Hayvenhurst Ave., Suite 213, Van Nuys CA 91406. (213)988-0879. Editor: Jim Dunlap. Managing Editor: Ron Rubenstein. Emphasizes amateur slow pitch softball. Monthly magazine; 96 pages. Estab. 1978. Circ. 50,000. Pays on publication. Buys all rights. Byline given "only on author's request." Phone queries OK. Submit seasonal/holiday material 1-2 months in advance. Photocopied submissions OK. Reports in 2 weeks. Free sample copy.
Nonfiction: How-to (tips on softball skills); humor (related to slow pitch softball); interview and profile. Buys 2-3 mss/issue. Send complete ms. Length: 1,500-5,000 words. Pays $75-125.
Photos: State availability of photos or send photos with ms. Pays $10-50 for 8x10 b&w glossy prints; $15-50 for 35mm color transparencies. Buys all rights. Captions preferred.
Fiction: Humorous. Send complete ms. Length: 1,500-5,000 words. Pays $75-125.

SOUTHERN OUTDOORS MAGAZINE, B.A.S.S. Publications, Number 1 Bell Rd., Montgomery AL 36117. (205)277-3940. Editor: Dave Ellison. Emphasizes a broad range of Southern outdoor activities, including hunting, fishing, boating, travel, water skiing, diving, conservation, controversy, camping, canoeing, RVs, dogs, sailing, backpacking, hiking, powerboat racing, wildlife photography, various community outdoor events or projects, and occasionally offbeat topics such as snuff dipping, tobacco spitting, turtle racing, etc. Published 8 times/year; 80-96 pages. Estab. 1940. Circ. 200,000. Pays on acceptance. Buys all rights. Submit seasonal/holiday material 6 months in advance. SASE. Reports in 4 weeks. Writers should be thoroughly familiar with "To Know Us Is To Sell To Us," a comprehensive, free writers'/photographers' manual available from *Southern Outdoors.*
Nonfiction: Must have obvious, legitimate Southern outdoors slant. Subjects can vary widely. All submissions must be compatible with guidelines; seldom are first-person stories purchased. Article should inform and entertain. Buys 100+/manuscripts a year. Query. Length: up to 3,500 words with sidebars and photos. Pays $200-700.
Photos: Purchased with or without accompanying ms. Captions required. Pays $10 minimum for 8x10 b&w glossy prints or 35mm color transparencies and larger. Offers no additional payment for photos accepted with accompanying ms, unless cover is obtained, then additional payment, on publication, of $150-300 is remitted.

Fillers: 25-1,500 words on outdoor topics, especially how-to and travel in the outdoors. Payment $20-300.
Fiction: Nostalgia, Humor: Length: 500-2,000 words. Payment: $75-400.

STRENGTH & HEALTH MAGAZINE, S&H Publishing Co., Inc., Box 1707, York PA 17405. (717)848-1541. Editor-in-Chief: Bob Hoffman. Managing Editor: John Grimek. 35% freelance written. Emphasizes Olympic weightlifting and weight training. Bimonthly magazine; 74 pages. Estab. 1932. Circ. 100,000. Pays -200 words. Pays $10-25.
   wsbreaks and short humor. Buys 2/issue. LengtSubmit seasonal/holiday material 4-5 months in advance. SASE. Reports in 2 months. Free sample copy.
Nonfiction: Bob Karpinski, Articles Editor. How-to (physical fitness routines); interview (sports figures); and profile. Buys 15 mss/year. Submit complete ms. Length: 1,500-3,000 words. Pays $50-100.
Photos: Melanie Wolpert, Photo Editor. Purchased with accompanying ms. Captions required. Query. Pays $5-10 for b&w glossy or matte finish; $50-100 for 2¼x2¼ color transparencies (for cover). Model release preferred.
Columns/Departments: Robert Denis, Department Editor. Barbells on Campus (weight training program of college or university; captioned photos required, at least one photo of prominent building or feature of campus); In the Spotlight (profile of a championship-caliber weightlifter, training photos as well as "behind the scenes" shots). Buys 1-2/issue. Submit complete ms. Length: 1,500-2,500 words. Pays $50-100.

THE WORLD OF RODEO AND WESTERN HERITAGE, Rodeo Construction Agency, Box 660, Billings MT 59103. Editor-in-Chief: Leslie Stanley. "We reach all of these facets of rodeo: Professional, all-girls rodeo, little britches, college, and high school rodeo, Canadian rodeo, and oldtimers rodeo. Audience age: 17-60." 12 times/year. Tabloid; 40-80 pages. Estab. 1977. Circ. 20,000. Buys all rights. Byline given. Phone queries OK. Previously published submissions OK. SASE. Free sample copy and writers' guidelines.
Nonfiction: Expose (personality); historical (oldtimers and famous rodeo animals); humor (pertaining to cowboys); informational (reports on current rodeo events); interview (with controversy or strong message); photo feature (emphasis on quality rodeo action and/or drama); profile (short in-depth sketch of person or persons); Buys 15/issue. Query or submit complete ms. Length: 500-2,000 words. Pays $15-100.
Photos: B&w purchased with or without mss. Captions required. Send prints. Pays $5/8x10 b&w glossy with good contrast; $35-50/2¼x2¼, 35mm or 8x10 matte or glossy with good color balance.

Skiing and Snow Sports

CANADIAN SKATER, Canadian Figure Skating Association, 333 River Rd., Ottawa, Ontario, Canada K1L 8B9. (416)746-5953. Editor: Teresa C. Moore. 60% freelance written. "*Canadian Skater* appeals to skaters and skating fans of all ages—children, teenagers and adults who skate for fun; coaches, skating officials and parents. Published 4 times/year during winter. Magazine; 52 pages. Estab. 1974. Circ. 12,000. Pays on publication. Buys first North American serial rights or one-time rights. Byline given. Phone queries OK. Submit seasonal/holiday material 2½ months in advance. Simultaneous and photocopied submissions OK. SAE and International Reply Coupons. Reports in 2-3 months. Free sample copy and writer's guidelines.
Nonfiction: "Articles dealing with Canada and the world's best amateur figure skaters, and the amateur figure skating scene in general." How-to (produce skating carnivals, raise funds, administer a skating club); general interest; humor; historical (Canadian figure skating); interview (top world and Canadian skaters, skating personalities actively involved in the amateur skating world); nostalgia; personal experience; personal opinion; photo feature; profile (special club activities); technical (figure skating skills) and competition reports or evaluations. No articles concentrating on professional rather than amateur skaters. Buys 5-8 mss/issue. Query. Length: 500-2,500 words. Pays $2/printed inch.
Photos: "We do not have photographers on staff, and sometimes find it difficult to obtain the photos we wish." Pays $5-25 for 8x10 b&w glossy prints; $15-40 for color prints and $25-50 for cover (2¼x2¼ color transparencies). Captions required. Buys one-time rights. Model release required.
Columns/Departments: Former Canadian Champions; You and Your Instructor; Carnival Productions; Clubs in Canada (special activities); and Book Reviews. Buys 4/issue. Query with clips of published work. Length: 500-1,500 words. Pays $20-50.
Fiction: "Fiction relating to figure skating, especially children's stories." Adventure; fantasy;

historical; and humorous. Buys 1/issue. Query with clips of published work. Length: 500-2,500. Pays $20-50.

Poetry: Free verse; light verse; traditional; and children's poetry. "All poetry must relate to skating." Buys 1/issue. Pays $15-30.

Fillers: Anecdotes, newsbreaks and short humor. Buys 6/issue. Length: 75-150 words. Pays $10-15.

How To Break In: "We depend on freelancers and so are always on the lookout for new contributors, especially in the Western and Atlantic provinces. We appreciate seeing samples of previously published work when inquiries are made."

HOSPICE, 22 High St., Brattleboro VT 05301. (802)257-7113. Editor: Jack Soper. 50% freelance written. Emphasizes Nordic skiing. Tabloid; published 4 times/year. Estab. 1977. Circ. 5,300. Pays on acceptance. Buys all rights, but may reassign following publication. Phone queries OK. Submit seasonal/holiday material 1 month in advance of issue date. Simultaneous, photocopied, and previously published submissions OK. SASE. Reports in 1 week. Free sample copy; mention *Writer's Market* in request.

Nonfiction: Articles on Nordic skiing. Buys 5 mss/issue. Submit complete ms. Pays $30, negotiable.

Photos: State availability of photos with ms. Pays $30/5x7 b&w glossy prints, negotiable.

NORDIC SKIING, Nordic Skiing, Inc., Box 106, West Brattleboro VT 05301. (802)254-9080. Editor: Barbara Brewster. Emphasizes cross country skiing. Monthly (September-March) magazine; 80 pages. Estab. 1976. Circ. 25,000. Pays on publication. Buys first North American serial rights. Pays 40% kill fee. Byline given. Submit seasonal/holiday material 6-9 months in advance. SASE. Reports in 3 weeks (queries); 4 weeks (mss). Sample copy $1.

Nonfiction: Expose (of legislative action affecting federal land use relating to cross country skiing); general interest (vacation areas or places to ski complete with description of facilities); how-to (technique articles on cross country skiing accepted only from qualified people in the field); humor (related to cross country skiing experiences or training); photo feature and travel. Buys 3 mss/issue. Query with clips of published work. Length: 900-3,000 words. Pays $50-200.

Photos: State avaliability of photos with ms. Pays $10-25/8x10 b&w glossy print; $25-150/35mm color transparency. Buys first-time rights. Captions preferred.

Columns/Departments: Trail Smackers (recipes for food for day or overnight ski tours) and Helpful Hints (any information that might be helpful or useful to a cross country skier). Buys 2-3/issue. Send complete ms. Length: 50-200 words. Pays $5.

NORTHWEST SKIER, 903 NE 45th St., Seattle WA 98105. (206)634-3620. Publisher: Ian F. Brown. Biweekly. Circ. 15,000. Not copyrighted. Byline given. Pays on publication. Will send sample copy to writer for 50¢. Reports "immediately." SASE.

Nonfiction: Well-written articles of interest to winter sports participants in the Pacific Northwest and Western Canada, or pieces of a general scope which would interest all of the winter sporting public. Character studies, unusual incidents, slants and perspectives. Must be authoritative, readable and convincingly thorough. Humor accepted. "Politics are open, along 'speaking out' lines. If you're contemplating a European trip or one to some other unusual recreation area, you might query to see what current needs are. When submitting article, consider pictures to supplement your text." Length: 250 words minimum. Pays $10 minimum/article.

Photos: Purchased both with mss and with captions only. Wants strong graphics of winter sports scene. Doesn't want posed shots. 8x10 glossy prints. Pays $2 minimum/photo.

Fiction: Uses very little and use depends on quality and uniqueness. Will use humorous fiction and short-shorts. Length: 250 words. Pays $1/column inch.

POWDER MAGAZINE, Surfer Publications, Box 1028, Dana Point CA 92629. (714)496-5733. Managing Editor: Neil Stebbins. Magazine published 8 times/year; 132 pages. Estab. 1972. Circ. 100,000. Pays on publication. Buys first North American serial rights. Byline given. Phone queries OK. Submit seasonal/holiday material 3 months in advance. Simultaneous, photocopied, and previously published submissions OK. SASE. Reports "as soon as possible." Sample copy 50¢; free writers' guidelines.

Nonfiction: Expose (inside insights into personalities, organizations, their motives and actions); how-to (emphasize advanced skiing techniques); informational (preferably personality-oriented or illustrated by adventures); historical (only if the work has personality interest to supplement facts and dates); humor ("satire, fiction, whatever, but must be in good taste"); inspirational (not religious, but philosophic or psychologically stimulating concept articles will be considered); interviews (with unknown personalities or local characters as well as ski celebrities); opinion (guest editorials are a regular feature); travel ("as long as it's not dry, stuffy, bored or typically informative"); new product (short news release items will be considered if products are exceptional); photo features (high quality slides and b&w will be accepted); and technical articles (only if interesting for an expert audience). Buys 5-10/issue. Query or submit complete ms. Length: 500-3,000 words. Pays 10¢/word.

Photos: Purchased with or without ms or on assignment. Query or send contact sheets and negatives or transparencies. Pays $50 for full-page b&w and $80 for full-page 35mm slides or large format transparencies. Covers and centerfolds earn $250.

Fiction: "Our fiction requirements correspond to our nonfiction standards in terms of our emphasis on originality, style, interest and applicability to our format and involvement with skiing." Buys 4/year. Query or submit complete ms. Length: 250-3,000 words. Pays 10¢/word.

Fillers: Cartoons, news items, personality briefs, good poetry and short humor articles will be considered. Query or send complete ms. Pays 10¢/word.

SKATING, United States Figure Skating Association, Sears Crescent, Suite 500, City Hall Plaza, Boston MA 02108. (617)723-2290. Editor-in-Chief: Gregory R. Smith. Managing Editor: Roy Winder. Monthly magazine; 64 pages. Estab. 1923. Circ. 31,000. Pays on publication. Buys all rights. Byline given "only if requested." Phone queries OK. Submit seasonal/holiday material 3 months in advance. Photocopied and previously published submissions OK. SASE. Reports in 1 month. Sample copy and writer's guidelines for SASE.

Nonfiction: Historical; how-to (photograph skaters, train, exercise); humor; informational; interview; new product; personal experience; personal opinion; photo feature; profile (background and interests of national-caliber skaters); technical; and competition reports. Buys 4 mss/issue. Query or send complete ms. Length: 500-1,000 words. Pays $50.

Photos: Karen Gourley Lehman, Photo Editor. Photos purchased with or without accompanying ms. Pays $15 for 8x10 or 5x7 b&w glossy prints and color slides. Query.

Columns/Departments: European Letter (skating news from Europe); Ice Abroad (competition results and report from outside the US); Book Reviews; People; Club News (what individual clubs are doing) and Music column (what's new and used for music for skating). Buys 4 ms/issue. Query or send complete ms. Length: 100-500 words. Pays $35. Open to suggestions for new columns/departments.

Fillers: Newsbreaks, puzzles (skating-related) and short humor. Buys 2 fillers/issue. Query. Length: 50-250 words. Pays $25.

SKI, 380 Madison Ave., New York NY 10017. (212)687-3000. Editor: Richard Needham. 15% freelance written. 7 times/year, September through spring. Buys first-time rights in most cases. Pays 50% kill fee. Byline given "except when report is incorporated in 'Ski Life' department." Pays on publication. Reports in 1 month. SASE.

Nonfiction: Prefers articles of general interest to skiers, travel, adventure, how-to, budget savers, unusual people, places or events that reader can identify with. Must be authoritative, knowledgeably written, in easy, informative language and have a professional flair. Cater to middle to upper income bracket readers who are college graduates, wide travelers. Length: 1,500-2,000 words. Pays $100-250.

Fiction: "We do not publish fiction."

Photos: Buys photos submitted with manuscripts and with captions only. Good action shots in color for covers. Pays minimum $150. B&w photos. Pays $25 each; minimum $150 for photo stories. (Query on these.) Color shots. Pays $50 each; $100/page.

How To Break In: "We also publish *Guide to Cross Country Skiing*, for which we need individual text and photo stories on cross-country ski touring and centers. We're looking for 1,000-2,000 words on a particular tour and it's an excellent way for us to get acquainted with new writers. Could lead to assignments for *Ski*. Photos are essential. Another possibility is our monthly column, Ski People, which runs 300-400-word items on unusual people who ski and have made some contribution to the sport. For another column, Personal Adventure, we welcome 2,000- to 2,500-word 'It Happened to Me' stories of unique (humorous, near disaster, etc.) experiences on skis. Payment is $100."

SKI AMERICA, Ski America Enterprise, Inc., 8 Bank Row, Box 1140, Pittsfield MA 01201. (413)442-6953. Editor: Barry Hollister. Managing Editor: Jim Hollister. Published 4 times/year. Tabloid; 32-64 pages. Estab. 1973. Circ. 300,000. Pays on publication. Buys one-time rights or makes assignments on work-for-hire basis. Pays 25-50% kill fee. Byline given. Phone queries OK. Submit seasonal/holiday material 1 month in advance. SASE. Reports in 1 month. Free sample copy.

Nonfiction: General interest, humor, new product, photo feature and travel. Buys 4 mss/issue. Query. Length: 1,000-1,500 words.

Photos: State availability of photos. Pays $10-125/8x10 b&w print; $50-250/35mm color transparency. Captions preferred.
Fiction: Adventure and humorous. Query. Length: 1,000-1,500 words. Pays $75-250.

SKIERS DIRECTORY, Ski Earth Publications, Inc., 38 Commercial Wharf, Boston MA 02110. Editor-in-Chief: Neil R. Goldhirsh. Managing Editor: Myra Lieber. Emphasizes skiing for travelers. For male and female traveling skiers age 20-50. Annual magazine; 340 pages. Estab. 1973. Circ. 120,000. Pays on publication. Buys all rights, but may reassign following publication. Byline given. Photocopied submissions encouraged. SASE. Reports in 4 weeks. Free editorial guidelines.
Nonfiction: General interest articles for traveling skiers. How to do anything regarding skiing (how to take a ski vacation; how to repair your skis, etc.) Informational articles on skiing resorts, races. Personality interviews. Travel and personal experience articles on new places to see and explore. Query or submit complete ms. Length: 1,500 words minimum. Pays $250-400.
Photos: No additional payment for b&w and color used with mss. Model release required.

SKIING MAGAZINE, Ziff-Davis Publishing Co., 1 Park Ave., New York NY 10016. Editor-in-Chief: Alfred H. Greenberg. Managing Editor: Robert Morrow. Published 7 times/year (September-March). Magazine; 175 pages. Estab. 1949. Circ. 475,000. Pays on acceptance. Buys all rights. Pays 30% kill fee. Byline given. Submit seasonal/holiday material 3 months in advance. SASE. Sample copy $1.
Nonfiction: "This magazine is in the market for any material of interest to skiers. Material must appeal to and please the confirmed skier. Much of the copy is staff-prepared, but many freelance features are purchased provided the writing is fast-paced, concise and knowledgeable." Buys 10 mss/year. Submit complete ms. Length: 1,500-3,000 words. Pays 10¢/word.
Photos: Rick Fiola, Art Director. Purchased with or without accompanying ms or on assignment. Send contact sheet or transparencies. Pays $100/full page for 8x10 b&w glossy or matte photos; $125 minimum/full page for 35mm kodachrome transparencies. Total purchase price for ms includes payment for photos. Model release required.

SNOTRACK, Market Communications, Inc., 225 E. Michigan Ave., Milwaukee WI 53202. (414)276-6600. Editor-in-Chief: Cynthia Swanson. 20-25% freelance written. Snowmobiling magazine for North American enthusiasts. Published 6 times yearly (September-April); 56 pages. Estab. 1971. Circ. 100,000. Pays on publication. Buys one-time rights. Byline given. Phone queries OK. Submit seasonal/holiday material 60-90 days in advance. SASE. Reports in 2-3 weeks. Free sample copy and writer's guidelines.
Nonfiction: Travel-related (great places to snowmobile; unique snowmobile adventures or events); photo feature (on snowmobiling activities); how-to (for average consumer and high performance readers); and interviews with interesting or prominent personalities who snowmobile. Buys 2-3/issue. Query. Length: 1,500-3,000 words. Pays $50-150.
Photos: Purchased with or without accompanying ms or on assignment. Captions required. Send contact sheet and negatives. Pays $15-25 for 8x10 b&w glossy prints; $50-100 for 35mm or larger color transparencies.
Fillers: Unique human interest. 100-300 words. Pays $5-10.

SNOW GOER, The Webb Co., 1999 Shepard Rd., St. Paul MN 55116. (612)647-7269. Editor: Jerry Bassett. For snowmobilers. Published monthly September through January. Magazine, 60-104 pages. Estab. 1968. Circ. 2,300,000. Buys all rights. Byline given. Pays on acceptance. Submit special issue material 6-9 months in advance. Reports in 1 month. Query or submit complete ms. SASE.
Nonfiction and Photos: Features on snowmobiling with strong secondary story angle, such as ice fishing, mountain climbing, snow camping, conservation, rescue. Also uses about 25% mechanical how-to stories, plus features relating to man out-of-doors in winter. ' "Me and Joe' articles have to be unique for this audience." Buys 2-3 mss/issue. Length: 5,000 words maximum. Pays $100-200.
Photos: State availability of photos with ms. Pays $5-25 for 5x7 or 8x10 b&w glossy contact sheets; $15-50 for 35mm color transparencies. Offers no additional payment for photos with accompanying ms. Buys all rights. Captions preferred.

SNOWMOBILE NEWS, Multi-Media Publications, Inc., 222 W. Adams St., Chicago IL 60606. (312)236-5550. Managing Editor: Paul Hertzberg. Emphasizes snowmobiling. Published 6 times yearly (Sept.-Feb.). Tabloid; 40-56 pages. Estab. 1972. Circ. 45,000. Pays on publication. Buys all rights, but may reassign to author following publication. Phone queries

OK. Submit seasonal/holiday material 2 months in advance. Free sample copy.
Nonfiction: How-to (technical features on repairing snowmobiles), humor (winter-related), travel (snowmobile travel features in the Midwest). Buys 15 mss/year. Submit complete ms. Length: 1,000-5,000 words. Pay $1/column inch.

SNOWMOBILE WEST, 521 Park Ave., Box 981, Idaho Falls ID 83401. Editor: Darryl Harris. 50% freelance written. For recreational snowmobile riders and owners of all ages. Magazine; 48 pages. Estab. 1974. Published five issues each winter. Circ. 50,000. Buys first North American serial rights. Pays kill fee if previously negotiated at time of assignment. Byline given on substantive articles of two pages or more. Buys 10 mss/year. Pays on publication. Free sample copy and writer's guidelines. Reports in 2 months. Articles for one season are generlly photogaphed and written the previous season. Query. SASE.
Nonfiction and Photos: Articles about snowtrail riding in the Western US; issues affecting snowmobilers; and maps of trail areas with good color photos and b&w. Pays 3¢/word; $5/b&w; $10/color. B&w should be 5x7 or 8x10 glossy print; color should be 35mm transparencies or larger, furnished with mss. With a story of 1,000 words, typically a selection of 5 b&w and 5 color photos should accompany. Longer stories in proportion. Length: 500-2,000 words.

Soccer

SOCCER AMERICA, Box 23704, Oakland CA 94623. (415)549-1414. Editor-in-Chief: Ms. Lynn Berling. For a wide range of soccer enthuiasts. Weekly magazine; 40 pages. Estab. 1971. Circ. 6,000. Pays on publication. Buys all rights, but may reassign following publication. Byline given. Submit seasonal/holiday material 14 days in advance. SASE. Reports in 1 month. Free sample copy and writer's guidelines.
Nonfiction: Expose (why a pro franchise isn't working right, etc.); historical; how-to; informational (news features); inspirational; interview; photo feature; profile; and technical. Buys 1-2 mss/issue. Query. Length: 200-2,000 words. Pays 50¢/inch minimum.
Photos: Photos purchased with or without accompanying ms or on assignment. Captions required. Pays $5-15 for 5x7 or larger b&w glossy prints. Query. Total purchase price for ms includes payment for photos.
Columns/Departments: Book Reviews. Buys 25 mss/year. Send complete ms. Length: 200-1,000 words. Pays 1¢/word. Open to suggestions for new columns/departments.

SOCCER WORLD, Box 366, Mountain View CA 94042. (415)965-8777. Editor: Kevin Shafer. For US soccer enthusiasts, including players, coaches, and referees. Predominantly high school players and adult coaches. Bimonthly magazine; 80 pages. Estab. 1974. Buys all rights, but will reassign rights to author after publication. Byline given. Free sample copy and writer's guidelines. Will consider photocopied submissions. Reports in 2 months. Query. SASE.
Nonfiction and Photos: "Articles are primarily of the how-to variety, but usually include a personality feature with each issue. The foremost consideration is always practical value, i.e., Can a player, coach, or referee improve his performance through the information presented? We are interested in anything on soccer skills and techniques." Length: 1,000 words. Pays $20-25/published page. Pays $5-25 for 5x7 (or larger) b&w glossy prints; snappy contrast. Pays a minimum of $50 for 35mm (or larger) color transparencies for cover use. "Must be high impact and vertical format."

Tennis

TENNIS, 495 Westport Ave., Norwalk CT 06856. Publisher: Howard R. Gill Jr. Editor: Shepherd Campbell. For persons who play tennis and want to play it better. Monthly magazine. Estab. 1965. Circ. 440,000. Buys all rights. Byline given. Pays on publication. SASE.
Nonfiction and Photos: Emphasis on instructional and reader service articles, but also seeks lively, well-researched features on personalities and other aspects of the game, as well as humor. Query. Length varies. Pays $100 minimum/article, considerably more for major features. $15-50/8x10 b&w glossy or color transparency.

TENNIS USA, Contact CBS Publishing Co., 1515 Broadway, New York NY 10017. Publisher: Bruce Gray.

TENNIS WEEK, Tennis News, Inc., 120 E. 56th St., New York NY 10022. (212)355-3611. Publisher and Founder: Eugene L. Scott. Managing Editor: Alan Klein. Weekly newspaper; 16-24 pages. Estab. May 1974. Circ. 25,000. Byline given. Pays on acceptance. Photocopied

submissions OK. SASE. Reports in 2 weeks. Sample copy 50¢.
Nonfiction: "Articles should concentrate on players lives off the court." Buys 100 mss/year. Send complete ms. Pays $25-100.
Photos: Send photos with ms. Pays $10/8x10 b&w glossy print.

Water Sports

DIVER. Seagraphic Publications, Ltd., Boaters Village, 1601 Granville St., Vancouver, British Columbia V6Z 2B3. (604)689-8688. Editor-in-Chief: Peter Vassilopoulos. Associate Editor: Neil McDaniel. 45% freelance written. Emphasizes scuba diving, ocean science and technology (commercial and military diving) for a well-educated, outdoor-oriented readership. Published 8 times/year. Magazine; 56 pages. Estab. March 1975. Circ. 20,000. Payment "follows publication." Buys first North American serial rights. Byline given. Phone queries OK. Submit seasonal/holiday material 3 months in advance of issue date. SASE. Reports in 6 weeks.
Nonfiction: How-to (underwater activities such as photography, etc.); general interest (underwater oriented); humor; historical (shipwrecks, treasure artifacts, archeological); interview (underwater personalities in all spheres—military, sports, scientific or commercial); personal experience (related to diving); photo feature (marine life); technical (related to oceanography, commercial/military diving, etc.); and travel (dive resorts). No subjective product reports. Buys 25 mss/year. Submit complete ms. Length: 800-2,000 words. Pays 5¢/word.
Photos: "Features are mostly those describing dive sites, experiences, etc. Photo features are reserved more as specials, while almost all articles must be well illustrated." Submit photo material with accompanying ms. Pays $5 minimum for 5x7 or 8x10 glossy or matte finish b&w prints; $10 minimum for 35mm color transparencies. Captions required. Buys one-time rights.
Columns/Departments: Book reviews. Submit complete ms. Length: 200 words maximum. Pays to $25. Open to suggestions for new columns/departments.
Fillers: Clippings, jokes, gags, anecdotes, newsbreaks and short humor. Buys 3-4/year. Length: 50-150 words. Pays $5.

SKIN DIVER. 8490 Sunset Blvd., Los Angeles CA 90069. (213)657-5100. Editor/Publisher: Paul J. Tzimoulis. Circ. 166,000. Buys only one-time rights. Byline given. Pays on publication. Acknowledges material immediately. All model releases and author's grant must be submitted with mss. Manuscripts reviewed are either returned to the author or tentatively scheduled for future issue. Time for review varies. Mss considered "accepted" when published; all material held on "tentatively scheduled" basis subject to change or rejection up to time of printing. Submit complete ms. SASE.
Nonfiction and Photos: Stories and articles directly related to skin diving activities, equipment or personalities. Features and articles equally divided into following categories: adventure, equipment, underwater photography, wrecks, treasure, spearfishing, undersea science, travel, marine life, boating, do-it-yourself, technique and archeology. Length: 1,000-2,000 words, well illustrated by photos; b&w at ratio of 3:1 to color. Pays $50/printed page. Photos purchased with mss; b&w 8x10 glossy prints; color 35mm, 2¼x2¼ or 4x5 transparencies; do not submit color prints or negatives. All photos must be captioned and marked with name and address. Pays $50/published page for inside photos; with name and address. Pays $50/published page for inside photos; $200/cover photos.

SPORT DIVER MAGAZINE. Ziff-Davis Publishing Co., 444 Brickell Ave., Suite 250, Miami FL 33131. (305)358-0517. Editor: Steve Blount. Managing Editor: Kathy Bentley. Emphasizes scuba diving. Quarterly magazine; 150 pages. Estab. 1977. Circ. 50,000. Pays on acceptance. Buys one-time international rights. Pays 30% kill fee. Byline given except for filler material. Phone queries OK. Submit seasonal/holiday material 1 year in advance. Simultaneous and photocopied submissions OK. SASE. Reports in 6 weeks. Free sample copy and writer's guidelines.
Nonfiction: Exposé (violation of marine protection laws, significant environmental threats); historical (historic divers/diving operations); how-to (prepare for, successfully execute dive; modify equipment for specialty dives); interview (fascinating ocean-related personalities, divers or scientists); photo feature (gallery of personal underwater photographs. Also how-to underwater photo technique); sea technology (ocean-related scientific development); underwater archeology; diving craft (boats and boating); and travel (to specific diving destinations. Query). Buys 80 mss/year. Query. Length: 1,200-3,000 words. Pays $50-650.
Photos: State availability of photos with ms. Pays $25-150 for b&w prints; $25-150 for 35mm, 4x5 or 2¼x2¼ color transparencies. Buys one-time rights. Captions and model releases required.
Columns/Departments: Letter From (literate piece dealing with diving in an unusual area);

Instructor Notes (underwater education); Physical Conditioning (getting into and staying in shape to dive); and Working Diver (life/job of someone who derives income from diving). Buys 10/year. Query. Length: 1,200-2,500 words. Pays $50-350.
Fillers: Clippings, newsbreaks and short humor. Buys 50/year. Length: 100-500 words. Pays $10-25.

SPRAY, THE WATER SKIING MAGAZINE. Spray Publications, 500 St. Andrews Blvd., Suite 224, Winter Park FL 52792. (305)671-0655. Editor: George Shetter. Managing Editor: Harvey McLead. Published 8 times/year. Magazine; 96 pages. Estab. March 1977. Circ. 70,000. Pays on publication. Buys all rights. Byline given. Phone queries OK. Submit seasonal/holiday material 4 months in advance. SASE. Reports in 2 weeks. Free sample copy and writer's guidelines.
Nonfiction: General interest, historical, how-to, humor, inspirational, interview, new products, nostalgia, personal experience, photo feature, profile, technical and travel. "All articles must relate to water skiing. Buys 2 mss/issue. Query. Length: 500-2,000 words. Pays $35-100.
Photos: Send photos with ms. Pays 25-50 for b&w contact sheets and negatives; $35-100 35mm color transparencies. Offers no additional payment for photos accompanying ms. Buys all rights. Captions and model releases required.
Fiction: Humorous. Buys 2 mss/issue. Query. Pays $35-100.
Poetry: Free verse and traditional. Buys 1/issue. Length: 10-50 words. Pays $25-100.
Fillers: Jokes, gags, anecdotes, newsbreaks and short humor. Buys 2/issue. Length: 50-200 words. Pays $10-25.

SURFER. Box 1028, Dana Point CA 92629. (714)496-5922. Editor: Jim Kempton. For late teens and young adults. Slant is toward the contemporary, fast-moving and hard core enthusiasts in the sport of surfing. Monthly. Rights purchased vary with author and material. Pays on publication. Sample copy $1. Reports on submissions in 2 weeks. SASE.
Nonfiction: "We use anything about surfing if interesting and authoritative. Must be written from an expert's viewpoint. We're looking for good comprehensive articles on any surfing spot—especially surfing in faraway foreign lands." Length: open. Pays 5-10¢/word.
Photos: Buys photos with mss or with captions only. Likes 8x10 glossy b&w proofsheets with negatives. Also uses expert color 35mm and 2¼x2¼ slides carefully wrapped. Pays $10-40/b&w; $25-125/35mm transparency.

SWIMMING WORLD. 1130 Florence Ave., Inglewood CA 90301. (213)641-2727. Editor: Robert Ingram. 2% freelance written. For "competitors (10-24), plus their coaches, parents, and those who are involved in the enjoyment of the sport." Estab. 1959. Monthly. Circ. 40,000. Buys all rights, but may reassign rights to author after publication. Byline given. Buys 10-12 mss/year. Pays on publication. Reports in 1-2 months. Query. SASE.
Nonfiction: Articles of interest to competitive swimmers, divers and water poloists, their parents and coaches. Can deal with diet, body conditioning or medicine, as applicable to competitive swimming. Nutrition and stroke and diving techniques. Psychology and profiles of athletes. Must be authoritative. Does not want results of competitions. Length: 1,500 words maximum. Pays $50 maximum.
Photos: Photos purchased with mss. Does not pay extra for photos with mss. 8x10 b&w only. Also photos with captions. Pays $2-3.

UNDERCURRENT. Box 1658, Sausalito CA 94965. (415)332-3684. Editor-in-Chief: Ben Davison. Managing Editor: Ben Davison. 20-50% freelance written. Emphasizes scuba diving. Monthly newsletter; 10 pages. Estab. August 1975. Circ. 11,200. Pays on publication. Buys all rights, but may reassign following publication. Pays $50 kill fee. Byline given. Submit seasonal/holiday material 2-3 months in advance of issue date. Simultaneous (if to other than diving publisher), photocopied and previously published submissions OK. SASE. Reports in 2-4 weeks. Free sample copy and writer's guidelines; mention *Writer's Market* in request.
Nonfiction: Equipment evaluation; how-to; general interest; new product; and travel. Buys 2 mss/issue. Query. Length: 2,000 words maximum. Pays $50-200.
Fillers: Buys clippings and newsbreaks. Buys 20/year. Length: 25-500 words. Pays $5-25.

THE WATER SKIER. Box 191, Winter Haven FL 33880. (813)324-4341. Editor: Thomas C. Hardman. 15% freelance written. Published 7 times/year. Circ. 21,000. Buys North American serial rights only. Byline given. Buys limited amount of freelance material. Pays on acceptance. Free sample copy. Reports on submissions within 10 days. SASE.
Nonfiction and Photos: Occasionally buys exceptionally offbeat, unusual text/photo features on the sport of water skiing. Pays $35 minimum.

Teen and Young Adult

The publications in this category are for young people aged 12 to 26. Publications aimed at 2- to 12-year-olds are classified in the Juvenile category.

ACCENT ON YOUTH, United Methodist Publishing House, 201 8th Ave. S, Nashville TN 37202. Editor: Margaret Barnhart. "For young people 12-14 years of age—planned within the Christian perspective to nurture the early teen in all facets of life: physical, mental emotional and spiritual, keeping in mind the current needs and interests of this age group." Quarterly magazine; 48 pages. Estab. September 1968. Circ. 43,000. Pays on acceptance. Buys simultaneous, second serial (reprint), first North American serial and one-time rights (primarily all serial rights, but will consider others on request). Byline given. Submit seasonal/holiday material 12 months in advance. SASE. Simultaneous submissions OK. Reports in 2-3 months. Free sample copy and writer's guidelines.
Nonfiction: Historical (should be something interesting to teens); how-to (things junior high young people can do or make); humor (slanted to early teens-in good taste, nothing off-color); inspirational (nonpreachy Christian material); interview, experience, personal opinion, photo feature, profile and travel. Send complete ms. Length: 1,200 words. Pays 3¢/word.
Photos: Send photos with ms. Payment negotiable, maximum $25 for 8x10 b&w prints; $50-100 for color transparencies. Buys one-time rights. Captions preferred; model release requested.
Fiction: Adventure, historical, humorous, mystery, religious, science fiction and suspense. Buys 2 mss/issue. Send complete ms. Length: 1,500-2,500 words. Pays 3¢/word.
Poetry: Free verse, light verse and traditional. Buys 1-2/issue. Pays 50¢/line.
Fillers: Puzzles, short humor and cartoons. Pays 3¢/word.

ALIVE!, Christian Board of Publication, Box 179, St. Louis MO 63166. Editor: Jerry O'Malley. "We especially appreciate submissions of useable quality from 12-15 year olds. Those in this age range should include their age with the submission. We appreciate use of humor that early adolescents would appreciate. Please keep the age group in mind." Sample copy 30¢.
Nonfiction: "Articles should concern interesting youth, church youth groups, projects and activities. There is little chance of our taking an article not accompanied by at least 3-4 captioned b&w photos." Length: 800-1,000 words. Pays 2¢/word; photos $3-5.
Fiction: "Give us fiction concerning characters in the *Alive!* readers' age group (12-15), dealing with problems and situations peculiar to that group." Length: 1,000-1,200 words. Pays 2¢/word. Uses 6-10 photos features/issue. Pays $5 maximum for photos.
Photos: Send photos with ms. Submit in batches. Pays $7-10 for b&w prints.
Poetry: Length: 20 lines maxium. Pays 25¢/line.
Fillers: Cartoons ($8); puzzles, riddles, tongue twisters and daffy definitions. Pays $7-10.

AMERICAN NEWSPAPER CARRIER, American Newspaper Boy Press, 915 Carolina Ave. NW, Winston-Salem NC 27101. Editor: Charles F. Moester. 10% freelance written. Buys all rights. Pays on acceptance. Will send list of requirements on request. Reports in 10 days. SASE.
Fiction: Uses a limited amount of short fiction, 1,500-2,000 words. "It is preferable, but not required, that the stories be written around newspaper carrier characters. Before writing this type of fiction for this market, the author should consult a newspaper circulation manager and learn something of the system under which the independent 'little merchant' route carriers operate generally the country over. Stories featuring carrier contests, prize awards, etc., are not acceptable. Humor and mystery are good. Stories are bought with the understanding that *American Newspaper Carrier* has the privilege of reprinting and supplying the material to other newspaper carrier publications in the US, and such permission should accompany all mss submitted." Pays $15 minimum.

THE BLACK COLLEGIAN, 3217 Martin Luther King Jr. Blvd., New Orleans LA 70125. (504)522-2372. Editor: Kalamu Ya Salaam. 40% freelance written. For black college students and recent graduates with an interest in black cultural awareness, sports, fashion, news, personlities, history, trends, current events and job opportunities. Published bimonthly during school year; 148 pages. Estab. 1970. Circ. 245,000. Rights purchased usually first North American serial rights. Byline given. Buys 25 mss/year. Pays on publication. Will send free sample copy to writer on request. Write for copy of guidelines for writers. Will consider photocopied and simultaneous submissions. Submit special material three months in advance of issue date (Careers in Health, Sept.; Black History, Nov.; Engineering and Travel/Summer Programs, Jan. 1980; Science and Jobs, March 1980; Women and Entertainment, May 1980). Returns rejected material in 1½ months. Query. SASE.

Nonfiction and Photos: Material on careers, sports, fashion, black history, news analysis. Articles on problems and opportunities confronting black college students and recent graduates. Informational, personal experience, profile, inspirational, humor, think pieces, travel. Length: 500-4500 words. Pays $10-250. B&w photos or color transparencies purchased with or without mss. 5x7 *and* 8x10 preferred. Pays $10/b&w; $25/color.

BOYS' LIFE, Boy Scouts of America, National Headquarters, North Brunswick NJ 08902. "We are shifting emphasis to staff-written material. Fiction will be drawn from present inventory." Not presently considering freelance submissions.

BREAD, 6401 The Paseo, Kansas City MO 64131. Editor: Debbie Salter. "Teens' magazine with a point of view that attempts to mold as well as reflect the junior and senior high school Christian teen, sponsored by the youth organization of the Church of the Nazarene." Monthly. Pays on acceptance. Accepts simultaneous submissions. Buys all rights, but will reassign rights to author after publication. Also accepts second rights. Byline given. Free sample copy and editorial specifications sheet. Reports in 6 weeks. SASE.

Nonfiction: Helpful articles in the area of developing the Christian life; first-person, "this is how I did it" stories about Christian witness. Length: up to 1,500 words. Articles must be theologically acceptable and make the reader want to turn over the page to continue reading. Should not be morbid or contain excessive moralizing. Looking for fresh approach to basic themes. The writer should identify himself with the situation but not use the pronoun "I" to do it. Also go easy on "you" (unless the second approach is desired). The moral or application should not be too obvious. Also needs articles dealing with doctrinal subjects, written for the young reader. Pays 2¢/word minimum. Works 6 months ahead of publication.

Photos: 8x10 b&w glossy prints of teens in action. Payment is $6 and up. Also considers photo spreads and essays. Uses 1 color transparency/month for cover.

Fiction: "Adventure, school, and church-oriented. No sermonizing." Length: 1,500 words maximum. Pays 2¢/word minimum.

CAMPUS AMBASSADOR MAGAZINE (CAM), 1445 Boonville Ave., Springfield MO 65802. Editor: Dave Gable. For students on secular campuses only. Published by Christ's Ambassadors Department, Assemblies of God. Published 6 times/year (October, November, January through April); magazine, 16 pages. Circ. 12,000. Buys all rights, but will reassign rights to author after publication. Buys 6 mss/year. Pays on acceptance or on publication. "It varies according to type of material." Will send free sample copy to writer on request. Submit Christmas and Easter material 6 months in advance. Will consider photocopied submissions. Reports in several weeks. SASE.

Nonfiction: College-age slanted, religious nonfiction on personal evangelism, missions, Bible doctrines, Christianity and the sciences, devotional material. 400-1,200 words. Pays 2½-3½¢/word.

Photos: Purchased with mss. Prefers 5x7 b&w glossy. Payment varies according to quality and use.

Poetry: Must have spiritual significance and collegiate relevance. Very little used. Length: 50 lines maximum. Pays 20¢/line.

CAMPUS LIFE MAGAZINE, Youth For Christ International, Box 419, Wheaton IL 60187. Senior Editor: Steve Lawhead. Associate Editor: Gregg Lewis. Editorial Administrator: Becky Petersen. 10% freelance written. For a readership of young adults, high school and college age, interested in photography, music, bicycling, cars and sports. Monthly magazine; 100 pages. Estab. 1946. Circ. 220,000. Pays on publication. Buys one-time rights. Pays 75% kill fee. Byline given. Submit seasonal/holiday material 4 months in advance of issue date. Simultaneous, photocopied and previously published submissions OK. SASE. Reports in 2 week. Sample copy $1.50; writer's guidelines for SASE.

Nonfiction: How-to; humor; personal experience; photo feature; and travel. Buys 3 mss/year. Submit complete ms. Length: 1,000-3,000 words. Pays $125-175.

Photos: Steve Lawhead, photo editor. Pays $25/8x10 b&w glossy print; $50/color transparency; $125/cover photo. Buys one-time rights.

Poetry: Steve Lawhead, poetry editor. Free verse. No "rhyming, sing-songy poetry." Buys 2/year. Pays $25-50.

CHRISTIAN ADVENTURER, Messenger Publishing House, Box 850, Joplin MO 64801. (417)624-7050. Editor-in-Chief: Roy M. Chappell, D.D. Managing Editor: Mrs. Marthel Wilson. A denominational Sunday school take-home paper for teens, 13-19. Quarterly; 104 pages. Circ. 3,500. Pays quarterly. Buys simultaneous, second serial (reprint) or one-time rights. Byline given. Submit seasonal/holiday material 1 year in advance. Photocopied and previously published submissions OK. SASE. Reports in 4-6 weeks. Sample copy 50¢. Free writer's guidelines with sample copy.

Nonfiction: Historical (related to great events in the history of the church); informational (explaining the meaning of a Bible passage or a Christian concept); inspirational; nostalgia; and personal experience. Buys 13-20 mss/issue. Send complete ms. Length: 500-1,000 words. Pays ½¢/word.

Photos: Photos purchased with accompanying ms. Pays $2 for any size b&w glossy prints.

Fiction: Adventure; historical; religious and romance. Buys 13-20 mss/issue. Length: 800-2,000 words. Pays ½¢/word.

Fillers: Puzzles (must be Bible-based and require no art). Buys 13-20 fillers/issue. Length: 200-500 words. Pays ½¢/word.

CHRISTIAN LIVING FOR SENIOR HIGHS, David C. Cook Publishing Co., 850 N. Grove, Elgin IL 60120. (312)741-2400. Editor: C. Lawrence Brook. "A take-home paper used in senior high Sunday school classes. We encourage Christian teens to write to us." Quarterly magazine; 4 pages. Estab. 1895. Pays on acceptance. Buys all rights. Byline given. Phone queries OK. Reports in 3-5 weeks. SASE. Free sample copy and writer's guidelines.

Nonfiction: How-to (Sunday school youth projects), historical (with religious base), humor (from Christian perspective), inspirational and personality (nonpreachy), personal teen experience (Christian), poetry written by teens and photo feature (Christian subject). Buys 6 mss/issue. Submit complete ms. Length: 1,200-1,800 words. Pays $60-75; $30 for short pieces.

Fiction: Adventure (with religious theme), historical (with Christian perspective), humorous, mystery and religious. Buys 2 mss/issue. Submit complete ms. Length: 1,200-1,800 words. Pays $60-75. "No preachy experiences."

Photos: Nora Gubbins-Kawa, Photo Editor. Photos purchased with or without accompanying ms or on assignment. Send contact sheet, prints or transparencies. Pays $20-35 for 8½x11 b&w photos; $50 minimum for color transparencies.

CIRCLE K MAGAZINE, 101 E. Erie St., Chicago IL 60611. Executive Editor: Greg Stanman. "Our readership consists almost entirely of college students interested in the concept of voluntary service. They are politically and socially aware and have a wide range of interests." Published 5 times/year. Magazine; 16 pages. Estab. 1967. Circ. 13,000. Pays on acceptance. Normally buys first North American serial rights. Byline given "except on nonfiction, which we do in house." Submit seasonal/holiday material 2 months in advance. SASE. Reports in 4 weeks. Free sample copy and writer's guidelines.

Nonfiction: Informational (general interest articles on any area pertinent to concerned college students); interview (notables in the fields of sports, entertainment, politics); and travel (from a student's angle; how to budget, what to take, where to go, etc.). Buys 10-12 mss/year. Query or submit complete ms. Length: 1,500-2,500 words. Pays $100-150.

Photos: Purchased with accompanying ms. Captions required. Query. Total purchase price for ms includes payment for photos.

CO-ED, Scholastic Magazines, Inc., 50 W. 44th St., New York NY 10036. For girls and boys ages 13-18. Monthly. Buys all rights. Pays on acceptance. Free sample copy. Query. SASE.

Fiction: "Stories dealing with problems of contemporary teenagers. (We prefer stories about older teenagers, 16, 17, 18 years old.) Emphasis on personal growth of one or more characters as they confront problems with friendships, dating, family, social prejudice. Suggested themes: finding identity, reconciling reality and fantasy, making appropriate life decisions. Although we do *not* want stories with a preachy, moralistic treatment, we do look for themes that can be a starting point for class discussion, since our magazine is used as a teaching tool in home economics classrooms. Try for well-rounded characters and strong, logical plots. Avoid stereotyped characters and cliched, fluffy romances. If girls with conventional 'feminine' interests are portrayed, they should nonetheless be interesting, active and realistic people. Humor, sports and adventure stories in colorful local or foreign settings." Length: 3,000 words maximum. Pays $300 maximum.

EVANGEL, Free Methodist Publishing House, 999 College Ave., Winona Lake IN 46590. (219)267-7161. Editor: Vera Bethel. 100% freelance written. Audience is 65% female, 35% male; married, 25-31 years old, mostly city dwellers, high school graduates, mostly nonprofessional. Weekly magazine; 8 pages. Estab. 1897. Circ. 35,000. Pays on acceptance. Buys simultaneous, second serial (reprint) or one-time rights. Submit seasonal/holiday material 3 months in advance. Simultaneous and previously published submissons OK. SASE. Reports in 4 weeks. Free sample copy and write's guidelines.
Nonfiction: Interview (with ordinary person who is doing something extraordinary in his community, in service to others); profile (of missionary or one from similar service profession who is contributing significantly to society); personal experience (finding a solution to a problem common to man; coping with handicapped child, for instance, or with a neighborhood problem. Story of how God-given strength or insight saved a situation). Buys 100 mss/year. Submit complete ms. Length: 300-1,000 words. Pays 2¢/word.
Photos: Purchased with accompanying ms. Captions required. Send prints. Pays $5-10 for 8x10 b&w glossy prints; $2 for snapshots.
Fiction: Religious themes dealing with contemporary issues dealt with from a Christian frame of reference. Story must "go somewhere." Buys 50 mss/year. Submit complete ms. Length: 1,200-1,800 words. Pays 2¢/word. SASE required.
Poetry: Free verse, haiku, light verse, traditional, religious. Buys 50/year. Limit submissions to batches of 5-6. Length: 4-24 lines. Pays 35¢/line. SASE required.
How To Break In: "Seasonal material will get a second look (won't be rejected so easily) because we get so little."

EXPLORING, Boy Scouts of America, Rt. 130, North Brunswick NJ 08902. Editor-in Chief: Robert Hood. Executive Editor: Annette Stec. For "ages 14 to 21. High school, some college age. Members of co-ed BSA Exploring program. Interests are education, colleges, careers, music, sports, cars, fashions, food, camping, backpacking." Published every 2 months. Buys first North American serial rights or first serial rights. Buys about 40 mss/year. Pays on acceptance. Free sample copy for large SASE. Reports in 2 weeks. Query. SASE.
Nonfiction and Photos: Interested in material slanted toward the interests of their audience. "We feature young adults involved in the BSA Exploring program. Write *for* young adults, not at them. Keep articles exciting and informational. Support opinions with quotes from experts. We prefer not to see anything on hang gliding or the martial arts." Personal experience, interviews and profiles. Length: 250-750 words. Pays $150-500. B&w and color photos purchased with mss or on assignment.

FACE-TO-FACE, 201 8th Ave. S., Nashville TN 37202. (615)749-6219. Editor: Eddie L. Robinson. For United Methodist young people, ages 15-18 inclusive. Published by the Curriculum Resources Committee of the General Board of Discipleship of The United Methodist Church. Quarterly magazine; 48 pages. Estab. 1968. Circ. 30,000. Rights purchased vary with author and matrial. Buys first North American serial rights or simultaneous rights. Byline given. Buys about 8 mss/year. Pays on acceptance. Submit Christmas, Easter and summertime material 8-9 months in advance. Reports in 1-2 months. Query. SASE.
Nonfiction: "Our purpose is to speak to young person's concerns about their faith, their purpose in life, their personal relationships, goals, and feelings. Articles and features (with photos) should be subjects of major interest and concern to high school young people. These include home and family life, school, extracurricular activities, vocation, etc. Satires, lampoons, related to the themes of an issue are also used." Length: 2,500 words maximum. Pays 3¢/word.
Photos: Uses 8x10 b&w glossy prints with high impact and good contrast. Pays $15 for one-time use of b&w. "We buy stock photos and those especially taken to illustrate articles."
Fiction: Must deal with major problems and concerns of older teens—such as finding one's own identity, dealing with family and peer-group pressures, and so forth. No straight moral fiction or stories,with pat answers or easy solutions used. Story must fit themes of issue. No serials. Length: 2,500-3,000 words. Pays 3¢/word.
Poetry: Related to the theme of an issue. Free verse, blank verse, traditional and avant-garde

forms. Length: 10-150 lines. Pays 25¢/line.

FREEWAY, Scripture Press, Box 513, Glen Ellyn IL 60137. Publication Editor: R. Michael Sigler. For "Christian high school and college Sunday School class kids." Estab. 1943. Weekly. Circ. 70,000. Buys all rights, "but passes along reprint fees to author, when material is picked up after publication." Buys 100 mss/year. Pays kill fee. Byline given. Free sample copy and writer's guidelines. No photocopied submissions. Reports on material accepted for publication in 4-6 weeks. Returns rejected material in 2-3 weeks. Query or submit complete ms. SASE.
Nonfiction and Photos: "Mostly person-centered nonfiction with photos. Subject must have had specific encounter with Christ. Direct tie-in to faith in Christ. No simply religious or moral stories; subjects must be specifically Christ-centered. Christian message must be woven naturally into a good, true, dramatic, human interest story. Current interest is in sports, social problems (teen alcoholism) and battles by Christians against grief, tragedy, danger, etc." Thought articles on Biblical themes. Length: 500-1,500 words. Pays $25-120. Pays $3-25 for 5x7 and 8x10 b&w photos.
Fiction: Same themes, lengths and rate of payment as nonfiction.

GROUP, Thom Schultz Publications, Box 481, Loveland CO 80537. (303)669-3836. Editor-in-Chief: Thom Schultz. 60% freelance written. For members and leaders of high-school-age Christian youth groups; average age 16. Magazine published 8 times/year; 48 pages. Estab. 1974. Circ. 30,000. Pays on publication. Buys all rights, but may reassign following publication. Byline given. Phone queries OK. Submit seasonal/holiday material 5 months in advance. Simultaneous, photocopied and previously published submissions OK. SASE. Reports in 3-4 weeks. Sample copy $1; writer's guidelines for SASE.
Nonfiction: How-to (fund-raising, membership-building, worship, games, discussions, activities, crowd breakers, simulation games); informational; (drama, worship, service projects); inspirational (issues facing young people today); interview and photo feature (group activities). Buys 3 mss/issue. Query. Length: 500-3,000 words. Pays $15-100.
Photos: Photos purchased with or without accompanying ms or on assignment. Captions required. Pays $15 minimum for 8x10 b&w glossy prints, $30 minimum for 35mm color transparencies.
Columns/Departments: Try This One (short ideas for games; crowd breakers, discussions, worships, fund raisers, service projects, etc.). Buys 6 mss/issue. Send complete ms. Length: 500 words maximum. Pays $10. Open to suggestions for new columns/departments.
For '80: Special Easter, Thanksgiving and Christmas issues and college issues.

GUIDE, 6856 Eastern Ave., Washington DC 20012. (202)723-3700. Editor: Lowell Litten. 90% freelance written. A Seventh-day Adventist journal for junior youth and early teens. Weekly magazine; 32 pages. Estab. 1953. Circ. 60,000. Buys first serial rights. Byline given. Buys about 500 mss/year. Pays on acceptance. Reports in 1 month. SASE.
Nonfiction and Poetry: Wants articles and stories of character-building and spiritual value. All stories must be true and include dialogue. Should emphasize the positive aspects of living—faithfulness, obedience to parents, perseverance, kindness, gratitude, courtesy, etc. "We do not use stories of hunting, fishing, trapping or spiritualism." Length: 1,500-2,500 words. Pays 2-3¢/word. Also buys serialized true stories. Length: 10 chapters. Buys traditional forms of poetry; also some free verse. Length: 4-16 lines. Pays 50¢-$1/line.

HI-CALL, Gospel Publishing House, 1445 Boonville Ave., Springfield MO 65802. (417)862-2781, ext. 1207. Editor-in-Chief: Dr. Charles W. Ford. Youth Editor: Joe Webb. Sunday school take-home paper for church-oriented teenagers, 12-17. Weekly magazine; 8 pages. Estab. 1954. Circ. 160,000. Pays on acceptance. Buys all rights but may reassign following publication, simultaneous or second serial (reprint) rights. Submit seasonal/holiday material 12 months in advance. SASE. Simultaneous and previously published submissions OK. SASE. Reports in 3 weeks. Free sample copy and writer's guidelines.
Nonfiction: Historical; humor; informational; inspirational; and personal experience. "All pieces should stress Christian principles for everyday living." Buys 125-150 mss/year. Send complete ms. Length: 500-1,000 words. Pays 1-2¢/word.
Photos: Photos purchased with or without accompanying ms. Pays $5/8x10 b&w glossy print; $20-35/35mm or 4x5 color transparency.
Fiction: Adventure (strong Biblical emphasis, but not preachy); humorous; mystery; religious; romance; suspense; and western. Buys 130 mss/year. Send complete ms. Length: 1,200-1,800 words. Pays 1-2¢/word.

HIS, 5206 Main St., Downers Grove IL 60515. (312)964-5700. Editor: Linda Doll. Issued monthly from October-June for collegiate students, faculty, administrators and graduate students belonging to the evangelical Christian church. Buys first rights. Pays on acceptance. Reports in 3 months. SASE.

Nonfiction and Fiction: "Articles dealing with practical aspects of Christian living on campus, relating contemporary issues to Biblical principles. Should show relationships between Christianity and various fields of study, Christian doctrine, or missions." Length: up to 1,500 words. Pays $25-50.

Poetry: Pays $10-15.

IN TOUCH, Wesleyan Publishing House, Box 2000, Marion IN 46952. For teens, ages 13-18. Weekly. Special issues for all religious and national holidays. Not copyrighted. Byline given. Pays on acceptance. Submit holiday/seasonal material 9 months in advance. SASE. Reports in 6 weeks. Free sample copy.

Nonfiction: Features of youth involvement in religious and social activity; true life incidents and articles on Christian growth. Avoid implied approval of liquor, tobacco, theaters, and dancing. Length: 1500-1800 words. Pays 2¢/word.

Fiction: Stories with definite Christian emphasis and character-building values, without being preachy. Mystery stories. Setting, plot and action should be realistic. Length: 1,200 words minimum. Pays 2¢/word.

Photos: Purchased with accompanying ms, portraying action or the teenage world, or with seasonal emphasis. Pays $1-10 for 5x7 or 8x11 b&w glossy prints.

Poetry: Religious and/or seasonal, expressing action and imagery. Length: 4-16 lines. Pays 25¢/line.

KEYNOTER MAGAZINE, 101 E. Erie St., Chicago IL 60611. (312)943-2300, ext. 226. Executive Editor: John A. Mars. 50% freelance written. An organizational publication of Key Club International. For a high school audience, male and female, 15 to 18, members of Key Club, a Kiwanis International sponsored youth organization; service-oriented. Published 7 times/year; magazine, 16 pages. Circ. 90,000. Not copyrighted. Buys about 10 mss/year. Pays on acceptance. Free sample copy. Prompt reports on material accepted for publication. Returns rejected material in about a month. Query. SASE.

Nonfiction and Photos: "Topical material directed to mature, service-oriented young men and women. We publish articles on current social concerns and entertaining, though not juvenile, articles. Most of our readers are intelligent and leaders in their communities and schools. Articles should be timely and informative, without talking down to the reader. We also use features on concern areas (aging, consumer protection, etc.). All material should be applicable to all geographic areas covered by our magazine. Keep in mind that our audience is Canadian as well as American. We don't take political or religious stands, so nothing in that area, unless it is strictly informational." Length: 1,200-2,500 words. Pays $75 minimum. Additional payment is not usually made for b&w photos used with mss. Payment for those purchased on assignment varies with use and quality.

LIGHT 'n' HEAVY, 1445 Boonville Ave., Springfield MO 65802. Editor: Carol A. Ball. Official publication of the Assemblies of God Youth Department. Slanted to high school teens. Purpose is to provide news of the Pentecostal youth scene, to inspire to Christlike living and to be used as a witnessing tool. Buys some first rights, but interested in multiple submissions, second rights and other reprints. Pays on acceptance. Will send a free sample copy to a writer on request. Reports in 6 weeks. SASE.

Nonfiction, Photos and Poetry: Photo features, interviews, biographical features, reports on outstanding Christian youth, some fiction and poems, news, motivational articles, seasonal material (4 months prior to special day) and personal experiences. "Avoid cliches, unexplained theological terms, sermonizing, and 'talking down' to youth." Length of articles: 300-1,200 words. Payment is 1½¢/word minimum; poetry is 20¢/line minimum. B&w photos: $25/cover, $15/inside editorial use.

LIVE, 1445 Boonville Ave., Springfield MO 65802. (417)862-2781. Editor: Kenneth D. Barney. 100% freelance written. For adults in Assemblies of God Sunday Schools. Weekly. Circ. 225,000. Not copyrighted. Buys about 100 mss/year. Pays on acceptance. Free sample copy and writer's guidelines. Submit seasonal material 10 months in advance. Reports on material within 6 weeks. SASE.

Nonfiction and Photos: "Articles with reader appeal, emphasizing some phase of Christian living, presented in a down-to-earth manner. Biography or missionary material using fiction techniques. Historical, scientific or nature material with a spiritual lesson. Be accurate in detail and factual material. Writing for Christian publications is a ministry. The spiritual emphasis must be an integral part of your material." Length: 1,000 words maximum. Pays 1-2¢/word, according to the value of the material and the amount of editorial work necessary. Color photos or slides purchased with mss, or on assignment. Pay open.

Fiction: "Present believable characters working out their problems according to Bible principles; in other words, present Christianity in action, without being preachy. We use very few serials, but we will consider 4- to 6-part stories if each part conforms to average word length for short stories. Each part must contain a spiritual emphasis and have enough suspense to carry the reader's interest from one week to the next. Stories should be true to life, but not what we would feel is bad to set before the reader as a pattern for living. Stories should not put parents, teachers, ministers or other Christian workers in a bad light. Setting, plot and action should be realistic, with strong motivation. Characterize so that the people will live in your story. Construct your plot carefully so that each incident moves naturally and sensibly toward crisis and conclusion. An element of conflict is necessary in fiction. Short stories should be written from one viewpoint only. We do no accept fiction based on incidents in the Bible." Length: 1,200-2,000 words. Pays 1-2¢/word.

Poetry: Buys traditional, free and blank verse. Length: 12-20 lines. "Please do not send large numbers of poems at one time." Pays 20¢/line.

Fillers: Brief, purposeful, usually containing an anecdote, and always with a strong evangelical emphasis.

LOOKING AHEAD, 850 N. Grove, Elgin IL 60120. (312)741-2400. Editor: Kristine Miller Tomasik. For junior high school age students who attend Sunday School. Special Christmas, Easter and Thanksgiving issues. Estab. 1895. Weekly. Buys all rights, but may reassign rights to author after publication. Byline given. Buys 50-75 mss/year. Pays on acceptance. Free sample copy and writer's guidelines. Rarely considers photocopied or simultaneous submissions. Submit seasonal material 1 year in advance. Reports in 1½ to 2 months. Query for nonfiction with statement of writer's qualifications. Submit only complete ms for fiction and poetry. SASE.

Nonfiction, Fiction and Photos: Photo Editor: Christine Pearson. Wants "very short stories (1,500-1,800 words); articles reporting on teen involvement in church/community projects; special how-to mss on earning money, dealing with difficult situations and emotional needs of the age level." All mss should present a Christian approach to life. "Because it is used as part of a dated Sunday school curriculum, articles follow a weekly theme." Pays $60 for nonfiction. Length for fiction: 1,200-1,500 words. Pays $60 for fiction. Photos purchased with or without ms or on assignment. Captions optional. Pays $20 for b&w 8x10 glossy prints. Pays $50 for color transparencies. Color photos rarely used.

THE MODERN WOODMEN, 1701 1st Ave., Rock Island IL 61201. (309)786-6481. Editor: Robert E. Frank. For members of Modern Woodmen of America, a fraternal insurance society. Bimonthly magazine; 24 pages. Estab. 1883. Circ. 325,000. Not copyrighted. Pays on acceptance. Free sample copy and writer's guidelines. Photocopied and simultaneous submissions OK. Reports in 3-4 weeks. SASE.

Nonfiction: "Nonfiction may be either for children or adults. Fiction should be slanted toward children up to age 16. Our audience is broad and diverse. We want clear, educational, inspirational articles for children and young people. We don't want religious material, teen romances, teen adventure stories." Buys informational, how-to, historical, and technical articles. Submit complete ms. Length: 1,500-2,000 words. Pays $35.

Photos: B&w photos purchased with ms. Captions optional. Prefers vertical, b&w glossy photos for cover use. Payment varies with quality and need.

Fiction: Mainstream and historical fiction. Length: 1,500-2,500 words. Pays $35. No poetry.

PROBE, Baptist Brotherhood Commission, 1548 Poplar Ave., Memphis TN 38104. (901)272-2461. Editor-in-Chief: Mike Davis. 5% freelance written. For "boys age 12-17 who are members of a missions organization in Southern Baptist churches." Monthly magazine; 32 pages. Estab. 1970. Circ. 45,000. Not copyrighted. Byline given. Pays on acceptance. Buys one-time rights. Phone queries OK. Submit seasonal/holiday material 6 months in advance. Simultaneous submissions OK. SASE. Reports in 1 month. Free sample copy and writer's guidelines.

Nonfiction: How-to (crafts, hobbies); informational (youth, religious especially); inspirational (personalities); personal experience (any first-person by teenagers—especially religious); photo feature (sports, teen subjects). Buys 12 mss/year. Submit complete ms. Length: 500-1,500 words. Pays 3¢/word.

Photos: Purchased with accompanying ms or on assignment. Captions required. Query. Pays $10 for 8x10 b&w glossy prints.

REFLECTION, Pioneer Girls, Inc., Box 788, Wheaton IL 60187. Editor: Laura Alden. Assistant Editor: Lorraine Mulligan. 50% freelance written. Emphasizes Christian education with subjects related to today's girl in today's world. Bimonthly magazine; 32 pages. Estab. 1961. Circ. 12,000. Pays on acceptance. Buys first, second or simultaneous rights. Byline given. Submit seasonal/holiday material 6 months in advance. Simultaneous and previously published submissions OK. SASE. Reports in 4-8 weeks. Sample copy and writer's guidelines $1.50
Nonfiction: How-to (crafts geared especially to teenage girls); humor; inspirational; interview; and personal experience. Buys 6 mss/issue. Length: 800-1,500 words. Pays $20-35.
Fiction: Adventure; fantasy; historical; humorous; mystery; religious; romance; and suspense. Length: 900-1,500 words. Pays $20-35.
Fillers: Jokes, gags, anecdotes, puzzles, short homor. Buys 12/year. Submit complete ms. Pays $5-15.

SCHOLASTIC SCOPE, Scholastic Magazines, Inc., 50 W. 44th St., New York NY 10036. Editor: Katherine Robinson. Circ. 1,100,000. Buys all rights. Byline given. Issued weekly. 4-6th grade reading level; 15-18 age level. Reports in 4-6 weeks. SASE.
Nonfiction and Photos: Articles with photos about teenagers who have accomplished something against great odds, overcome obstacles, performed heroically, or simply done something out of the ordinary. Prefers articles about people outside New York area. Length: 400-1,200 words. Pays $125 and up.
Fiction and Drama: Problems of contemporary teenagers (drugs, prejudice, runaways, failure in school, family problems, etc.); relationships between people (inter-racial, adult-teenage, employer-employee, etc.) in family, job, and school situations. Strive for directness, realism, and action, perhaps carried through dialogue rather than exposition. Try for depth of characterization in at least one character. Avoid too many coincidences and random happenings. Although action stories are wanted, it's not a market for crime fiction. Looking for material about American Indian, Chicano, Mexican-American, Puerto Rican, and black experiences, among others. Occasionally uses mysteries and science fiction. Length: 400-1,200 words. Uses plays up to 3,000 words. Pays $150 minimum.

SEVENTEEN, 850 3rd Ave., New York NY 10022. Executive Editor: Ray Robinson. Monthly. Circ. 1,500,000. Buys all rights for nonfiction, features and poetry. Buys first rights on fiction. Pays 25% kill fee. Byline given. Pays on acceptance. SASE.
Nonfiction and Photos: Articles and features of general interest to young women who are concerned with the development of their own lives and the problems of the world around them; strong emphasis on topicality and helpfulness. Send brief outline and query, summing up basic idea of article. Also like to receive articles and features on speculation. Length: 2,000-3,000 words. Pays $50-500 for articles written by teenagers but more to established adult freelancers. Articles are commissioned after outlines are submitted and approved. Fees for commissioned articles generally range from $350-1,350. Photos usually by assignment only. Tamara Schneider, Art Director.
Fiction: Phyllis Schneider, Fiction Editor. Top-quality stories featuring teenagers—the problems, concerns and preoccupations of adolescence, which will have recognition and identification value for readers. Does not want "typical teenage" stories, but high literary quality. Avoid oversophisticated material; unhappy endings acceptable if emotional impact is sufficient. Humorous stories that do not condescend to or caricature young people are welcome. Best lengths are 2,500-3,000 words. "We publish a novelette every July (not to exceed 30 doubled-spaced manuscript pages)—sometimes with a suspenseful plot." Pays $50-500. Conducts an annual short story contest.
Poetry: By teenagers only. Pays $5-25. Submissions are nonreturnable unless accompanied by SASE.
How To Break In: "The best way for beginning teenage writers to crack the *Seventeen* lineup is for them to contribute suggestions and short pieces to the Free-For-All column, a literary format which lends itself to just about every kind of writing: profiles, puzzles, essays, exposes, reportage, and book reviews."

SEVENTEEN "MINI-MAG," Triangle Communications, 850 3rd Ave., New York NY 10022. Editor: Midge Turk Richardson. Editor: Linda Konner. 50% freelance written. For 13-19 year-old girls. Monthly section; 8 pages. Estab. April 1975. Pays on acceptance. Buys all rights.

Byline given. Submit seasonal/holiday material 3-4 months in advance of issue date. SASE. Reports in 3-4 weeks.

Nonfiction: How-to features (past articles having included fixing bikes, decorating straw hats, coping with gym class, etc.); general interest (teen problems, interfaith dating, holiday loneliness, new findings on love); humor; interview ("17-Second Interviews" with someone of interest to teens; just send background info—staff does interviews by phone); new trends ("Hot Lines"—quick news items under 300 words); career; health; and quizzes. No personal opinion, essays, fiction, poetry, or anything not related to teen-age girls. Buys 8 mss/issue. Query. Length: 750 words for lead pieces; under 300 words for "Hot Lines;" 450-550 for other articles. Pays $25-150.

STRAIGHT (Formerly *Now, For Today's Young Teens*), Standard Publishing Co., 8121 Hamilton Ave., Cincinnati OH 45231. (513)931-4050. Editor: Kathleen Anderson. Freelance written. "Teens, age 12-19, from Christian backgrounds generally receive this publication in their Sunday school classes or through subscriptions." Weekly (published quarterly) magazine; 16 pages. Estab. 1951. Pays on acceptance. Buys all rights, or second serial (reprint) rights. Byline given. Submit seasonal/holiday material 1 year in advance. Reports in 3-6 weeks. Free sample copy; writer's guidelines with SASE. Include Social Security number on ms. SASE.

Nonfiction: Religious-oriented topics, general interest, humor, inspirational, interview (religious leaders, Christian teens, athletes); personal experience. "We want articles that promote Christian ethics and ideals. Submit complete ms. Length: 800-1,100 words. Pays 2¢/word.

Fiction: Adventure, historical, humorous, religious and suspense. "All fiction should have some message for the modern Christian teen." Fiction should deal with all subjects in a forthright manner, without being preachy and without talking down to teens. No tasteless manuscripts that promote anything adverse to Bible's teachings. Submit complete ms. Length: 1,000-1,400 words. Pays 2¢/word; less for reprints.

Photos: Submit photos with ms. Pays $10-20 for 8x10 b&w glossy prints. Captions required; model release should be available. Buys one-time rights.

TEEN MAGAZINE, 8490 Sunset Blvd., Hollywood CA 90069. Editor: Roxanne Camron. For teenage girls. Monthly magazine; 100 pages. Estab. 1957. Circ. 900,000. Buys all rights. Predominantly staff-written. Freelance purchases are limited. Reports in 6-8 weeks. SASE.

Fiction: Feature Editor: Judi Marks. Stories up to 3,500 words dealing specifically with teenagers and contemporary teen issues. More fiction on emerging alternatives for young women. Experimental, suspense, humorous, and romance. Length: 2,000-3,000 words. Pays $100-150.

TEENS TODAY, Church of the Nazarene, 6401 The Paseo, Kansas City MO 64131. (816)333-7000. Managing Editor: John L. Denney. 80% freelance written. For senior high teens, ages 15-18 attending Church of the Nazarene Sunday school. Weekly magazine; 16 pages. Circ. 67,000. Pays on acceptance. Buys all rights, but may reassign following publication. Byline given. Submit seasonal/holiday material 10 months in advance. Simultaneous, photocopied and previously published submissions OK. SASE. Reports in 6-8 weeks. Free sample copy and writer's guidelines.

Nonfiction: How-to (mature and be a better person in Christian life); humor (cartoons); personal experience; and photo feature. Buys 1 ms/issue. Send complete ms. Length: 500-1,500 words. Pays $10-30.

Photos: Photos purchased with or without accompanying ms or on assignment. Pays $10-25 for 8x10 b&w glossy prints; $15-50 (sometimes $100) for 8x10 color glossy prints or any size transparencies. Additional payment for photos accepted with accompanying ms. Model release required.

Columns/Departments: Responsible To Be Whole (helping teens be well-rounded persons, build self-worth); Direction (specific instructions gained from a passage of scripture); Last Word (the everyday life of teens—350 words maximum); and Review (review of contemporary youth reading). Send complete ms. Length: 350-1,000 words. Pays 2¢/word. Open to suggestions for new columns/departments.

Fiction: Adventure (if Christian principles are apparent); humorous; religious; and romance (keep it clean). Buys 1 ms/issue. Send complete ms. Length: 1,500-2,500 words. Pays 2¢/word.

Poetry: Free verse; haiku; light verse; and traditional. Buys 15 poems/year. Pays 20-25¢/line.

Fillers: Puzzles (religious). Buys 15 fillers/year. Pays $5-10.

TIGER BEAT MAGAZINE, 7060 Hollywood Blvd., #800, Hollywood CA 90028. (213)467-3111. Editoral Director: Sharon Lee. Editor: Kathy Kirkland. For young teenage girls and subteens. Median age: 13. Monthly magazine; 100 pages. Estab. 1960. Circ. 700,000. Buys all rights. Buys 10 mss/year. Pays on acceptance. Free sample copy. Query. SASE.

Nonfiction and Photos: Stories about young entertainers; their lives, what they do, their interests. Quality writing expected, but must be written with the 12-16 age group in mind. Length: depends on feature. Pays $50-100. Pays $15 for b&w photos used with mss: captions optional. $50 for color used inside; $75 for cover. 35mm slides preferred.

How To Break In: "We're mostly staff-written; a freelancer's best bet is to come up with something original and exclusive that the staff couldn't do or get."

VENTURE MAGAZINE, Box 150, Wheaton IL 60187. Managing Editor: Randall Nulton. 50% freelance written. Publication of Christian Service Brigade. For young men 12-18 years of age. Most participate in a Christian Service Brigade program. Monthly magazine. Estab. 1959. Circ. 22,000. Rights purchased vary with author and material. Buys all rights, but will sometimes reassign rights to author after publication. Buys 2-4 mss/year. Pays on publication. Sample copy for $1. Submit seasonal material 6-7 months in advance. Reports in 6 weeks. Query. SASE.

Nonfiction and Photos: "Family-based articles from boys' perspective; family problems, possible solutions. Assigned articles deal with specific monthly themes decided by the editorial staff. All material has an emphasis on boys in a Christian setting." Length: 400-1,200 words. Pays $25-75. No additional payment is made for 8x10 b&w photos used with mss. Pays $15 for those purchased on assignment.

Fiction: "Some religious-oriented fiction dealing with religious-related experiences or purposes. No far-out plots or trite themes and settings. Length: 800-1,500 words. Pays $25-75.

VISIONS, Our Sunday Visitor, Noll Plaza, Huntington IN 46750. (219)356-8400. Editor: Marianna McLoughlin. For Catholic junior high school students of above average intelligence. Magazine, published 26 times during the school year; 8 pages. Estab. 1974. Circ. 48,000. Buys all rights, but may reassign following publication. Byline given. Pays on publication. SASE. Free sample copy. Reports in 3 weeks.

Nonfiction and Fiction: "I will be happy to read manuscripts that will appeal to the junior high level. We avoid overly pious pieces. Fiction and nonfiction are acceptable with lengths from 500-750 words, but can be longer if the topic so warrants. Subject matter should relate to the young Catholic Christian's life directly or indirectly." Pays $35-75.

WIND, The Wesleyan Church, Box 2000, Marion IN 46952. (317)674-3301, ext. 146. Editor: Robert E. Black. 10% freelance written. For teen readers. Monthly magazine; 16 pages. Circ. 7,000. Buys first rights or second (serial) reprint rights. Byline given. Buys 5-10 mss/year. Pays on publication. Will send free sample copy to writer on request. Write for copy of guidelines for writers. Will consider photocopied and simultaneous submissions. Submit seasonal material at least 3 months in advance. Reports in 10-14 days. Query or submit complete ms. SASE.

Nonfiction: "Our publication attempts to promote Bible study, personal piety and aggressive evangelism. We attempt to appeal not only to youth within the church, but also to unchurched youth. We publish short, inspirational articles, full-length articles and features. Themes may include spiritual life, personal problems or areas of concern; personality and character development, relationships with others; moral issues such as drugs, etc.; seasonal, historical and informative articles." Length: 1,000 words maximum. Pays 2¢/word for first rights; 1¢/word for second rights.

Fiction: Religious short stories. "We do not use a great amount of fiction, but will occasionally print a piece that fits a theme. Please, no 'easy way out' endings. Be realistic. Even problems that are solved can leave a scar. Sometimes a problem is never solved, but is for the purpose of teaching a lesson. Be honest." Length: 1,000 words maximum. Pays 2¢/word for first rights; 1¢/word for second rights.

Poetry: Related to theme. Pays 25¢/line.

WORKING FOR BOYS, Box A, Danvers MA 01923. Editor: Brother Alphonsus Dwyer, C.F.X. 37% freelance written. For junior high, parents, grandparents (the latter because the magazine goes back to 1884). Quarterly magazine; 28 pages. Estab. 1884. Circ. 20,000. Not copyrighted. Buys 50 mss/year. Pays on acceptance. Free sample copy. Submit special material (Christmas, Easter, sports, vacation time) 6 months in advance. Reports in 1 week. Submit only complete ms. Address all mss to the Associate Editor, Brother Alois, CFX, St. John's High School, Main St., Shrewsbury MA 01545. SASE.

Nonfiction and Photos: "Conservative, not necessarily religious, articles. Seasonal mostly (Christmas, Easter, etc.). Cheerful, successful outlook suitable for early teenagers. Maybe we are on the 'square' side, favoring the traditional regarding youth manners: generosity to others, respect for older people, patriotism, etc. Animal articles and tales are numerous, but an occasional good dog or horse story is okay. We like to cover seasonal sports." Buys informational, how-to, personal experience, historical and travel. Length: 500-1,000 words. Pays 3¢/word. 6x6 b&w glossy prints purchased with ms for $10 each.

Fiction: Mainstream, adventure, religious, and historical fiction. Theme: open. Length: 500-1,000 words. Pays 3¢/word.

YOUNG AMBASSADOR, The Good News Broadcasting Association, Inc., Box 82808. Lincoln NE 68501. (402)474-4567. Editor-in-Chief: Melvin A. Jones. Managing Editor: Robert H. Sink. Emphasizes Christian living for church-oriented teens, 12-15. Monthly magazine; 52 pages. Estab. 1946. Circ. 80,000. Buys second serial (reprint) and first North American serial rights. Byline given. Phone queries OK. Submit seasonal/holiday material at least 6 months in advance. Previously published submissions OK. SASE. Reports in 4 weeks. Free sample copy and writer's guidelines.

Nonfiction: How-to (church youth group activities); interview; personal experience; photo features; a few inspirational and informational features on spiritual topics. Buys 3-4 mss/issue. Query or send complete ms. Length: 500-1,800 words. Pays 3¢/word. "Material that covers social, spiritual and emotional needs of teenagers. Interviews with teens who are demonstrating their faith in Christ in some unusual way. Biographical articles about teens who have overcome obstacles in their lives."

Fiction: "Must be about teens in everyday contemporary situations. Not interested in historical fiction or any fiction without a spiritual lesson." Buys 45 mss/year. Query or send complete ms. Length: 500-2,000 words. Pays 3¢/word. "Stories of interest to early teenagers with strong, well-developed plot and a definite spiritual tone. Prefer not to see 'preachy' stories. Seasonal stories needed. Should have a realistic, contemporary setting and offer scriptual answers to the problems teens are facing."

Fillers: "Accepted exclusively from teens." Jokes and puzzles. Send complete mss. Pays 3¢/word for puzzles.

YOUNG ATHLETE, Box 513, Edmonds WA 98020. (206)774-3589. Editor-in-Chief: Dan Zadra. Managing Editor: Jan Gray. 75% freelance written. Emphasizes youth and amateur sports, recreation and health, ages 10-20. "Also, large peripheral readership of coaches, physical education teachers and athletic directors who work with these athletes." Bimonthly magazine; 64 pages. Estab. 1975. Circ. 200,000. Pays on publication. Buys all rights, but may reassign following publication. Submit seasonal/holiday material 3½ months in advance. Simultaneous, photocopied and previously published submissions OK. SASE. Reports in 5 weeks. Sample copy $1.25; free writer's guidelines. SASE.

Nonfiction: "Interested in any sports-related ms that enlightens, encourages, instructs, challenges or inspires young readers, without preaching or talking down. We cover every sport possible—from marbles to football—from sandlot to the Olympic Games. Want personality features. Length: 250 words for inspirational mss about boys and girls who have achieved in sports at the local level; 800-1,200 words for mss giving insights into the aspirations, philosophies and training techniques of well-known 'Olympic class' amateur athletes; 1,000-1,500 words for mss giving nostalgic glimpses into the early lives, development and eventual rise to fame of today's great professional athletes. Personality features should be liberally spiced with recent quotes from the athlete. How-to mss should be loaded with accurate details. Interested in interpretive articles on new trends in youth or amateur sports; laudatory reports of new and worthwhile sports programs, leagues or organizations for youth." Buys 50 mss/year. Query. Pays $25-200.

Photos: Bob Honey, Photo Editor. Photos purchased with or without accompanying ms. Captions required. Pays $5-15 for b&w photos; $25 minimum for color photos. Query.

How To Break In: "Writing style should be lively, fast-paced, directly involving and easy to understand. Avoid hero worship, cynicism or 'winning at any cost' philosophy. Our posture: Winning is fine, but participation, personal growth, health, fun and fair play for everyone are what it's all about."

YOUNG MISS, 52 Vanderbilt Ave., New York NY 10017. Editor: Rubie Saunders. 75-80% freelance written. Monthly, except June and August, for girls 10 to 14. Buys all rights. Pays 10-25% kill fee. Byline given. Pays on acceptance. Editorial requirement sheet for SASE. Query on nonfiction. Reports on submissions in 3-4 weeks. All mss must be typed, double-spaced. SASE.

Nonfiction: No food, fashion or beauty articles are wanted, but practically everything else goes. Hobbies, unusual projects, self-improvement (getting along with parents, brothers, etc.); how-to articles on all possible subjects. Length: about 1,500 words. Pays $50 minimum. Do not submit illustrations. Rough sketches may accompany a how-to article.

Fiction: "All fiction should be aimed at girls 10-14, with the emphasis on the late 12- to 14-year olds. Stories may be set in any locale or time—urban, western, foreign, past, contemporary or future. Boys may be involved, even in a romantic way, as long as it is tastefully done. Mystery and adventure stories are also welcomed. Stories of today are particularly desirable. Especially interested in fiction with an urban setting dealing with the *real* problems today's young teens face. Overstocked on stories about middle-income, small-town girls who seem to have no problems greater than getting a date for a school dance or adjusting to a new neighborhood." Length: 2,000-2,300 words. Pays $50 minimum.

Fillers: Crossword puzzles and short quizzes on general information and personality subjects. Pays $10-25. Occasionally uses how-to fillers; currently overstocked on these.

YOUNG WORLD, now incorporated into *Child Life*. See *Child Life* under juvenile section.

YOUTH IN ACTION, Free Methodist Church, 901 College Ave., Winona Lake IN 46590. (219)267-7656. Executive Editor: David Markell. For junior high and high school youth. Monthly magazine; 32 pages. Estab. 1956. Circ. 4,000. Pays on publication. Buys one-time rights. Byline given. Phone queries OK. Simultaneous, photocopied and previously published submissions OK. SASE. Reports in 4 weeks. Free sample copy and writers' guidelines.

Nonfiction: How-to (subjects dealing with religious themes such as prayer, Bible study, etc.); humor (any subject relevant to teens); inspirational (anything of a religious nature); interviews ("with people who are in situations that would relate to our themes"); personal experience (which would illustrate a spiritual truth); personal opinion and photo features (on issues and subjects that relate to our theme); profiles; (well-known people, especially teenagers who have become Christians). Buys 10-12/year. Send complete ms. Length: 500-2,000 words. Pays 2¢/word.

Photos: Purchased with or without ms or on assignment. Send 8½x11 prints. Pays $15-25/b&w; $25-50/color.

Fiction: Humorous subjects that relate to teenage interests. Religious themes "along our denominational standards." Buys 5/year. Send complete ms. Length: 500-2,000 words. Pays 2¢/word.

Poetry: Avant-garde and traditional forms; free verse, haiku, light verse. Buys 10/year. Pays $7 minimum.

Theater, Movie, TV, and Entertainment

For those publications whose emphasis is on music and musicians, see the section on Music Publications. Nonpaying markets for similar material are listed in the Literary and "Little" Publications category.

ADAM FILM WORLD, 8060 Melrose Ave., Los Angeles CA 90046. (213)653-8060. Editor: Edward S. Sullivan. For fans of X- and R-rated movies. Bimonthly magazine; 96 pages. Estab. 1966. Circ. 250,000. Buys first North American serial rights. Buys about 18 mss/year. Pays on publication. Will send sample copy to writer for $1.50. No photocopied or simultaneous submissions. Reports on mss accepted for publication in 1-2 months. Returns rejected material in 2 weeks. Query. SASE.

Nonfiction and Photos: "All copy is slanted for fans of X and R movies and can be critical of this or that picture, but not critical of the genre itself. Our main emphasis is on pictorial layouts, rather than text; layouts of stills from erotic pictures. Any article must have possibilities for illustration. We go very strong in the erotic direction, but *no* hard-core stills. We see too many fictional interviews with a fictitious porno star, and too many fantasy suggestions for erotic film plots. No think pieces wanted. We would consider articles on the continuing erotization of legitimate films from major studios, and the increasing legitimization of X and R films from the minors." Length: 1,000-3,000 words. Pays $80-210. Most photos are bought on assignment from regular photographers with studio contacts, but a few 8x10 b&w's are purchased from freelancers for use as illustrations. Pays minimum of $10/photo.

AFTER DARK, 1180 Avenue of the Americas, New York NY 10036. (212)921-9300. Editor: William Como. For an audience "20-55 years old." Monthly. Circ. 360,000. Buys first rights. Buys about 30 mss/year. Pays on publication. Sample copy $2. Submit seasonal material 4 months in advance. Reports in 3-4 weeks. Query, including copies of previously published work. SASE.

Nonfiction and Photos: Articles on "every area of entertainment—films, TV, theater, nightclubs, books, records." Length: 2,500-3,000 words. Pays $150. Photos with captions only. B&w glossy prints, color transparencies. Pays $20-50.

How To Break In: "The best way to crack *After Dark* is by doing a piece on some new trend in the entertainment world. We have people in most of the important cities, but we rely on freelancers to send us material from out-of-the-way places where new things are developing. Some of our contributing editors started out that way. Query."

AFTERNOON TV, Roband Publications, 2 Park Ave., Suite 910, New York NY 10016. Editor: Katherine Keskey. Eight times a year. For soap opera viewers. Pays 10% kill fee. Byline given.

Nonfiction and Photos: Interviews with afternoon TV stars. Pays $100 for six-page story and $15 each for photos. "Daytime TV is a very specialized market. We're only interested in in-depth, intelligent and well-written interviews with daytime actors on any of the 13 soap operas in New York and Los Angeles. We're looking for good writers who can do bright personality profiles with new angles or thoughtful, informed feature pieces on soap operas and daytime TV in general. New writers considered on spec only."

AMERICAN FILM, American Film Institute, Kennedy Center, Washington DC 20566. (202)833-9300. Editor: Hollis Alpert. 80% freelance written. For film professionals, students, teachers, film enthusiasts culturally oriented reader. Monthly magazine; 80 pages. Estab. 1975. Circ. 100,000. Buys First North American serial rights. Pays kill fee. Byline given. Buys 20-30 mss/year. Pays on acceptance. Sample copy $1. Will consider photocopied submissions. Submit seasonal material 3 months in advance. Reports in 1-2 weeks. Query. SASE.

Nonfiction: In-depth articles on film and television-related subjects. "Our articles require expertise and first-rate writing ability." Buys informational, profile, historical and "think" pieces. No film reviews. Length: 2,000-3,000 words. Pays $250-600.

AMERICAN SQUAREDANCE, Box 788, Sandusky OH 44870. Editors-in-Chief: Stan and Cathie Burdick. 50% freelance written. Emphasizes squaredancing. Monthly magazine; 100 pages. Estab. 1945. Circ. 15,000. Pays on publication. Buys all rights. Byline given. Submit seasonal/holiday material 3-4 months in advance. SASE. Reports in 1 week. Free sample copy.

Nonfiction: How-to; informational; historical; humor; inspirational; interview; nostalgia; personal opinion; profile; travel; personal experience; photo feature; and technical. All articles must have dance theme. Buys 18 mss/year. Submit complete ms. Length: 1,000-2,500 words. Pays $10-25.

Photos: Purchased with accompanying ms. Captions required. B&w glossy prints. Pays $2-10.

Fiction: Fantasy; historical; humorous; romance; suspense; science fiction; and western. Must have dance theme. Buys 6 mss/year. Length: 1,500-2,500 words. Pays $10-30.

Poetry: Haiku, light verse, traditional. Must be on a dance theme. Buys 6 poems/year. Limit submissions to 3 at a time. Pays $5-10.

Fillers: Crossword and word puzzles with dance theme. Buys 4/year. Pays $5.

BLACK STARS, Johnson Publishing Co., Inc., 820 S. Michigan Ave., Chicago IL 60605. (312)786-7668. Managing Editor: Ariel Perry Strong. 20% freelance written. Emphasizes entertainment. Monthly magazine; 74 pages. Estab. 1971. Circ. 350,000. Pays on publication. Buys all rights, but may reassign following publication. Seasonal/holiday material should be submitted 3 months in advance. SASE. Reports in 3 weeks. Sample copy $1-2; free writer's guidelines.

Nonfiction: Personal experience and photo feature. "Only articles on black entertainers." Buys 600 mss/year. Query. Length: 3,000 words maximum. Pays $100-200.

Photos: Purchases 8x10 b&w or transparencies. Query, submit prints or transparencies.

CANADIAN THEATRE REVIEW, 4700 Keele St., Downsview, Ontario, Canada M3J 1P3. (416)667-3768. Editor-in-Chief: Don Rubin. Business Manager: Lynn McFadgen. 80% freelance written. Emphasizes theater for academics and professionals. Quarterly magazine; 144 pages. Estab. 1974. Circ. 5,000. Pays on publication. Buys one-time rights. Pays 50% kill fee. Byline given. SAE and International Reply Coupons. Reports in 10-12 weeks. Sample copy $3.

Nonfiction: Historical (theater in Canada); interview (internationally known theater figures); and photo feature (theater worldwide). Buys 40 mss/year. Length: 1,500-5,000 words. Query or submit complete ms. Pays $15/published page.

Photos: State availability of photos with query or mss.

CINEFANTASTIQUE, Box 270, Oak Park IL 60303. (312)383-5631. Publisher/Editor:

Frederick S. Clarke. Managing Editor: Jeffrey Frentzen. For persons interested in horror, fantasy and science fiction films. Magazine; 48 pages; double issues: 96 pages. Estab. 1970. Quarterly. Circ. 25,000. Rights purchased are all magazine rights in all languages. Pays on publication. Photocopied submissions OK. Reports in 4 weeks. SASE.
Nonfiction: "We're interested in articles, interviews and reviews which concern horror, fantasy and science fiction films." Pays 15¢/line, 30-40 spaces.

DANCE MAGAZINE, 10 Columbus Circle, New York NY 10019. (212)399-2400. Editor: William Como. Monthly. For the dance profession and members of the public interested in the art of dance. Buys all rights. Pays on publication. Sample copy $2. Query. SASE.
Nonfiction: Personalities, knowledgeable comment, news. Length: 2,500-3,000 words. Pays $77-100.
Photos: Purchased with articles or with captions only. Pays $5-15.
How To Break In: "Do a piece about a local company that's not too well known but growing; or a particular school that is doing well which we may not have heard about; or a local dancer who you feel will be gaining national recognition. Query."

DANCE SCOPE, American Dance Guild, 152 W. 42nd St., New York NY 10036. Editor-in-Chief: Richard Lorber. 95% freelance written. Emphasizes dance and related performing/visual/musical arts. For performers, university teachers and students, general public audiences, other artists, arts administrators, critics, historians. Quarterly magazine; 80 pages. Estab. 1965. Circ. 7,000. Pays on publication. Buys all rights. Submit seasonal or holiday material 6 months in advance. Photocopied submissions OK. SASE. Reports in 1 month. Sample copy $2.50.
Nonfiction: Informational (contemporary developments, trends, ideas); historical (synthesis of ideas, not narrowly academic); inspirational (documentation and think pieces); interviews (with commentary, intros, etc.); personal experience (with broad relevance). Buys 12 mss/year. Query. Length: 1,500-3,000 words. Pays $25-50.
Photos: No additional payment for b&w glossy prints used with mss. Captions required. Query. Model release required.

DRAMATICS MAGAZINE, International Thespian Society, 3368 Central Pkwy, Cincinnati OH 45225. (513)559-1996. Editor-in-Chief: S. Ezra Goldstein. 25-30% freelance written. For theater arts students, teachers and others interested in theater arts education. Magazine published bimonthly in September, November, January, March and May; 48 pages. Estab. 1929. Circ. 50,000. Pays on acceptance. Buys first North American serial rights. Byline given. Phone queries OK. Submit seasonal/holiday material 3 months in advance. Simultaneous, photocopied and previously published submissions OK. SASE. Reports in 3 weeks. Sample copy $1; free writer's guidelines.
Nonfiction: Historical; how-to (technical theater); informational; interview; photo feature; profile; and technical. Buys 30 mss/year. Submit complete ms. Length: 2,500 words minimum. Pays $25-100.
Photos: Purchased with accompanying ms. Uses b&w photos. Query. Total purchase price for ms includes payment for photos.
Columns/Departments: Technicalities (theater how-to articles); Tag Line (editorials on some phase of the theater) and Promptbook (entertainment arts news relevant to an educational magazine). Buys 15 mss/year. Send complete ms. Length: 250-1,000 words. Pays $30-60.
Fiction: Drama (one-act plays). Buys 5 mss/year. Send complete ms. Pays $50-150.

DRAMATIKA, 429 Hope St., Tarpon Springs FL 33589. Editors: John and Andrea Pyros. Magazine; 40 pages. For persons interested in the theater arts. Estab. 1968. Published 2 times/year. Circ. 500-1,000. Buys all rights. Pays on publication. Sample copy $2. Query. SASE. Reports in 1 month. SASE.
Drama and Photos: Wants "performable pieces—plays, songs, scripts, etc." Will consider plays on various and open themes. Length: 20 pages maximum. Pays about $25/piece; $5-10 for smaller pieces. B&w photos purchased with ms with extra payment. Captions required. Pays $5. Size: 8x11.

E W TV GUIDE, Box 614, Corte Madera CA 94925. (415)924-5311. Editor-in-Chief: William Whitney. Emphasizes television programming and stars. Distributed to television audiences through local trade media. Weekly tabloid; 16-24 pages. Estab. 1971. Circ. 50,000. Pays on publication. Buys one-time rights. Byline given. Submit seasonal or holiday material 3 months in advance. Simultaneous, photocopied and previously published submissions OK. SASE. Reports in 2-4 weeks. Sample copy 25¢.

Nonfiction: Carol Williams, Nonfiction Editor. Expose, informational, humor, interview, photo feature and profile. Buys 5-6 mss/issue. Send complete ms. Length: 500-2,000 words. Pays 2-10¢/word.

Photos: Photos purchased with or without accompanying ms or on assignment. Pays $2-5 for 5x7 b&w glossy prints. Total purchase price for ms includes payment for photos. Model release required.

Fillers: Clippings, jokes, gags, anecdotes, puzzles. Buys 2-5 fillers/issue. Submit complete ms. Length: 200-500 words. Pays $5-15.

FILM QUARTERLY, University of California Press, Berkeley CA 94720. (415)642-6333. Editor: Ernest Callenbach. 100% freelance written. Issued quarterly. Buys all rights. Byline given. Pays on publication. Query. SASE.

Nonfiction: Articles on style and structure in films, articles analyzing the work of important directors, historical articles on development of the film as art, reviews of current films and detailed analyses of classics, book reviews of film books. Length: 6,000 words maximum. Must be familiar with the past and present of the art; must be competently, although not necessarily breezily, written; must deal with important problems of the art. Payment is about 1½¢/word.

HI FI BUYER'S REVIEW, 149 Hampton Rd., Box 1592, Southampton NY 11968. (516)283-2360. Editor: Mary A. Cummings. For the hi-fi enthusiast. Publication of Hampton International Communications, Inc. FM Music Program Guide, Inc. Magazine; 64 pages. Estab. 1978. Monthly. Circ. 60,000. Buys all rights. Byline given. Buys about 36 mss/year. Pays on publication. No photocopied or simultaneous submissions. Reports in 6 months. SASE.

Nonfiction and Photos: Publishes hi-fidelity information, equipment stories and laboratory reports. Length: informational, 1,200-2,500 words; manufacturer profile, 800-1,200 words. Pays $25-125. Photos purchased with ms with no additional payment. Captions optional.

MOVIE LIFE, Ideal Publishing Co., 2 Park Ave., New York NY 10016. Editor: Carol Tormey. "Basically, for women interested in the behind the scenes and events in the lives of entertainment stars." Estab. 1938: Monthly. Circ. 225,000. Buys all rights. Buys 150 mss/year. Pays on publication. No photocopied or simultaneous submissions. Reports in 3-6 weeks. Query. SASE.

Nonfiction and Photos: Feature articles on well-known movie, music and television personalities with older, retired stars as well as upcoming people. Interviews. Length: 1,500-2,000 words. Pays $125-200. 8x10 b&w photos purchased with accompanying mss for $25, or without extra payment, depending on the article and photos.

How To Break In: "Let's suppose Brando comes to town. Check with the local paper to find out who is handling publicity for him. Then see if you can arrange an interview. Also, please get a letter from the press person acknowledging that such an interview actually took place. I'm afraid to say, we sometimes get accounts of meetings which never happened, so we do have to check. You should read our magazine and become familiar with the style. We like first-person accounts and can help out with the style if the facts are good. "We prefer interviews that focus on what the person is really about behind the public image." And don't overlook doing some library research for some interesting background on your subjects."

MOVIE MIRROR, MODERN SCREEN, TV PICTURE LIFE, PHOTO SCREEN, 355 Lexington Ave., New York NY 10017. Editor of *Movie Mirror:* Joan Goldstein. Editor of *TV Picture Life:* Fran Levine. Editor of *Photo Screen:* Marsha Daly. Editor of *Modern Screen:* Joan Goldstein. Monthlies. Buys 8-10 mss/month. Pays on acceptance. Submit complete ms. Reports promptly. SASE.

Nonfiction: "The most desired sort of story is the fresh and strongly angled, dramatically told article about the private life of a leading motion picture or television star. Categories of stories popular with readers (they've changed little over the years): romantic love, weddings, married life, babies, parent/child relationships, religion, health, extra-marital affairs, divorces, dangerous moments survived, feuds. The major difference in fan mag writing then and now is the increased frankness permissible in today's articles. When many stars talk forthrightly about living together without marriage, bearing children out of wedlock, personal sexual inclinations, etc., fan magazine editors have little choice but to go along with contemporary trends. The object, no matter the category of article, is to tell the reader something she did not already know about a favorite performer, preferably something dramatic, provocative, personal. Our readers are female (over 90% of them), youngish (under 45), and often are wives or daughters of bluecollar workers. It is our purpose to bring a bit of vicarious excitement and glamour to these readers whose own lives may not be abundantly supplied with same. Stars they want to read about now are stars of the top 10 TV shows; e.g., Charlie's Angels, Robin Williams and

John Travolta. While most of our manuscripts are written by top magazine and newspaper writers in Hollywood and New York, we have an open-door policy. Writers are strongly advised to read copies of the magazine before making submissions, we insist on a particular type of style of writing. Any writer able to meet our specific editorial needs will get a 'read' here. Until we know your work, however, we would have to see completed manuscripts rather than outlines. Writers outside the two show biz meccas might keep in mind that we are particularly interested in hometown stories on contemporary celebrities. Average length for articles is 2,000 words. Pay starts at $75, going considerably higher for genuine scoops."

MOVIE STARS, Ideal Publishing Co., 2 Park Ave., New York NY 10016. Editor: Ronnie Blum. For anyone from their teens to their sixties who's interested in the lives of top TV and screen personalities. Estab. 1935. Buys all rights. Buys 100 mss/year. Pays on publication. Query. SASE.
Nonfiction and Photos: General subject matter consists of "human interest articles on movies and television personalities." Pays $125/5-6 page article. Pays $25/b&w photo.
How To Break In: "Submit an interview with a secondary character on a popular TV series, or a featured actor in several films, whose face has become known to the public. It is best if you query first, presenting your interview idea and including some personal information about yourself—a resume and some previously published material, for example"

NEW YORK THEATRE REVIEW, 55 W. 42 St., #1218, New York NY 10036. (212)221-6078. Editor: Ira J. Bilowit. Associate Editor: Debbi Wasserman. Emphasizes theater only. 10 issue/year magazine; 52 pages. Estab. November 1977. Circ. 20,000. Pays on publication. Buys all rights. Photocopied submissions OK. SASE. Reports in 6 months. Sample copy for $2.00.
Nonfiction: Interview, nostalgia, photo feature, profile and technical. "We consider only articles which relate to the theater and which enlighten the reader on theater techniques, the work of theater personalities or the theater process." "We do not want humor, personality or personal experiences of unknowns." Query with clips of published work. Buys 2 mss/issue. Length: 750-3,000 words. Pays $25/magazine page.
Photos: State availability of photos. Uses b&w prints. Offers no additional payment for photos accepted with ms. Captions are required.
Columns/Departments: Theater nostalgia, pictures stories of new plays and people who make theater. Query with clips of published work. Buys 1/issue. Length: 700 words. Pays $25. Open to suggestions for new columns/department.

PERFORMING ARTS IN CANADA, Box 517, Station F, Toronto, Ontario, Canada M4Y 1T4. (416)921-2601. Editor: Billyann Balay. Linda Kelley. 50% freelance written. For professional performers and general readers with an interest in Canadian theater, dance and music. Quarterly magazine. Circ. 66,000. Pays 2 weeks following publication. Buys first rights. Pays 30-50% kill fee. Byline given. Reports in 3-6 weeks. SAE and International Reply Coupons. Sample copy 50¢.
Nonfiction: "Lively, stimulating, well-researched articles on Canadian performing artists or group." Buys 35-45 mss/year. Query. Length: 1,500-2,000 words. Pays $100-150.

PERFORMING ARTS MAGAZINE, Performing Arts, Inc., 2100 Travis, Suite 1204, Houston TX 77002. (713)659-4555. Publisher: Carter Rochelle. Editor: Scott Heumann. Managing Editor: David Kaplan. Emphasizes music, dance and theater. Monthly magazine; 60 pages. Estab. September 1977. Circ. 58-84,000. Pays on publication. Buys all rights. Byline given. Submit seasonal/holiday material 3 months in advance. Simultaneous, photocopied and previously published submissions OK. SASE. Reports in 4 weeks. Sample copy 50¢; writer's guidelines for SASE.
Nonfiction: General interest ("need features on music, dance and theater that are informative and aimed at a well-read audience; local slant preferred but not required"); historical (same as general interest); humor (short features related to the performing arts); interview (must be relevant to events in Houston and Texas); and travel (prefer performing arts slant). "We do not want reviews, opinion pieces, didactic or highly technical pieces of specialized interest." Buys 1-2 mss/issue. Send complete ms or query with clips of published work. Length: 500-1,500 words. Pays 10¢/word; 5¢/word if extensive editing is required.
Photos: State availability of photos or send photos with ms. Pays $50 (3 or more photos) for 8x10 b&w glossy prints. Buys one-time rights. Model release required.
Columns/Departments: Andante (travel—bimonthly, performing arts slant) and Repast Perfect (recipes—pays in free subscription only). Query. Length: 600-800 words. Pays 10¢/word.

PHOTO SCREEN, Sterling's Magazines, Inc., 355 Lexington Ave., New York NY 10017.

(212)391-1400. Editor: Marsha Daly. 50-60% freelance written. Emphasizes TV and movie news of star personalities. Bimonthly magazine; 75 pages. Estab. 1960. Circ. 300,000. Pays on publication. Buys all rights. SASE. Reports in 6 weeks.

Nonfiction: Exposes (on stars' lives); informational (on Hollywood life); interviews (with stars); photo features (on stars' personal lives). Buys 5-6 mss/month. Length: 1,500 words. Query. Pays $75-200.

Photos: Roger Glazer, department editor. Purchased without ms; mostly on speculation. Pays $25-35 for 8x10 b&w (glossy or matte); $50 minimum for color. Chromes only; 35mm or 2¼x2¼.

PLAYBILL MAGAZINE, 151 E. 50th, New York NY 10022. Monthly; free to theatergoers. Buys first and second US magazine rights. Pays 25% kill fee. Byline given. SASE.

Nonfiction: "The major emphasis is on current theater and theater people. On occasion, buys humor or travel pieces if offbeat. Wants sophisticated, informative prose that makes judgments and shows style. Uses unusual interviews, although most of these are staff-written. Style should be worldly and literate without being pretentious or arch; runs closer to *Harper's* or *New Yorker* than to *Partisan Review*. Wants interesting information, adult analysis, written in a genuine, personal style. Humor is also welcome. Between 1,000 and 2,500 words for articles." Pays $100-400.

How To Break In: "We're difficult to break into and most of our pieces are assigned. We don't take any theater pieces relating to theater outside New York. We also have short features on boutiquing, fashions, men's wear, women's wear. The best way for a newcomer to break in is with a short humorous or satirical piece or some special piece of reporting on the Broadway theater—no more than 700-1,000 words. A number of people have come in that way and some of them have subsequently received assignments from us."

PRE-VUE, Box 31255, Billings MT 59107. Editor-Publisher: Virginia Hansen. "We are the cable-TV guide for southern and western Montana; our audience is as diverse as people who subscribe to cable TV." Weekly magazine; 32-40 pages. Estab. 1969. Circ. 15,000. Not copyrighted. Byline given. Pays on publication. Reports in 8 weeks. Query. SASE.

Nonfiction and Photos: "Subject matter is general, but must relate in some way to television or our reading area (Montana). We would like articles to have a beginning, middle and end; in other words, popular magazine style, heavy on the hooker lead." Informational, how-to, interview, profile, humor, historical, travel, TV reviews. Feature length: 500-800 words. Pays minimum of 2¢/word. 8x10 (sometimes smaller) b&w photos purchased with mss or on assignment. Pays $3-6. Captions required. Department Editor: Virginia Hansen.

Poetry: Traditional forms; haiku; and light verse. Buys 20/year. Length: 2-8 lines. Pays $2.

Fillers: Short humor, local history and oddities. Buys 12/year. Length: 50-200 words. Pays minimum of 2¢/word.

PROLOG, 104 N. St. Mary, Dallas TX 75204. (214)827-7734. Editor: Mike Firth. 10% freelance written. For "playwrights and teachers of playwriting." Quarterly newsletter; 8 pages. Estab. 1973. Circ. 200. Not copyrighted. Buys 8 mss/year. Pays on acceptance; "may hold pending final approval." Sample copy $1. Will consider photocopied and simultaneous submissions. Reports in "over 3 months." SASE.

Nonfiction: Wants "articles and anecdotes about writing, sales and production of play scripts. Style should be direct to reader (as opposed to third-person observational)." Does not want to see general attacks on theater, personal problems, problems without solutions, or general interest. Pays ½¢/word.

SUPER-8 FILMAKER, PMS Publishing Co., 609 Mission St., San Francisco CA 94105. Editor-in-Chief: Bruce Anderson. 90% freelance written. Emphasizes filmmaking in super-8 for amateur and professional filmmakers, students and teachers of film. Magazine (8 times a year); 66 pages. Estab. 1973. Circ. 46,000. Pays on publication. Buys all rights. Submit seasonal/holiday material 8 months in advance. SASE. Reports in 1 month. Sample copy $1.25; free writer's guidelines.

Nonfiction: How-to; informational; and technical (dealing with filmmaking only). Buys 5 mss/issue. Query. Length: 2,000-3,000 words.

How To Break In: "We are a consumer publication, not a trade publication. Articles written for *Super-8 Filmaker* should contain technical information, but they should not be written in technical terminology. All technical terms and concepts should be defined simply and concisely."

TAKE ONE, Box 1778, Station B, Montreal, Quebec, Canada H3B 3L3. (514)843-7733. Editor:

Phyllis Platt. Publisher: Irving Greeburg. 90% freelance written. For anyone interested in films in modern society. Not a fan magazine. Bimonthly. Circ. 35,000. Buys about 150 mss/year. Buys first North American serial rights. Pays on publication. Free sample copy. Reports in 3 weeks. Query. SAE and International Reply Coupons.

Nonfiction and Photos: Interviews, articles, photo stories, reviews. Anything having to do with film, TV and videography. Articles on directors, actors, etc. On new or classic films, on aspects of the industry, current or historical, on aesthetic developments. Anything of interest in this broad area of the communication arts. No taboos at all. Style should be lively, informed and opinionated rather than "newspaperese." Length: 700-5,000 words; 1,000 words maximum, reviews. Pays about 5¢/word. Prefers photos with mss. Events, people in film and/or TV. 8x10 b&w glossy.

How To Break In: "Most writers who have been published in our magazine started out by sending us a review, interview or article on some subject (a film, a filmmaker) about which they cared passionately and (more often than not) had—as a result of that caring—a particular degree of expertise. Often they just happened to be in the right place at the right time (where a film was being made, where a filmmaker was making a public appearance or near where one lived)."

TV AND MOVIE SCREEN, 355 Lexington Ave., New York NY 10017. (212)391-1400. Editorial Director: William Condie. Editor: Fran Levine. Magazine; 74 pages. Bimonthly. Rights purchased vary with author and material. Usually buys all rights. Pays negotiable kill fee. Byline given. Pays on publication. Query. SASE.

Nonfiction and Photos: Celebrity interviews, profiles and angles that are provocative, enticing and truthful. Length: 1,000-1,500 words. Pays $100 minimum. Photos of celebrities purchased without ms or on assignment. Pays $10 minimum.

TV GUIDE, Radnor PA 19088. Executive Editor: Roger Youman. Weekly. Study publication. Query (with outline) to Andrew Mills, Assistant Managing Editor. SASE.

Nonfiction: Wants offbeat articles about TV people and shows. This magazine is not interested in fan material. Also wants stories on the newest trends of television, but they must be written in layman's language. Length: 200-2,000 words.

Photos: Uses professional high-quality photos, normally shot on assignment, by photographers chosen by *TV Guide*. Prefers color. Pays $150 day rate against page rates—$250 for 2 pages or less.

TV STAR PARADE, 2 Park Ave., New York NY 10016. (212)683-4200, ext. 6. Editor: Jan Musacchio. For "males and females of all ages interested in private lives of TV and movie stars." Monthly. Circ. 400,000. Buys all rights. Pays on publication. Submit seasonal material 2 months in advance. Reports in 2-3 weeks. Query required with basic outline of proposed feature. SASE.

Nonfiction and Photos: General subject matter consists of interviews, "backstage stories," romance, etc. Approach should be a "chatty style with special attention to dialog, quotes from the stars. We like to use as many real interviews as possible. We never publish made-up quotes or interviews. We do not want angles that have been dredged up time and again just to fill space. Interested in timely material." Buys informational, personal experience, interviews, profile, nostalgia, photo articles. "I would appreciate new ideas for columns." Length: 1,000-1,500 words. Pays $100-150. Photos are purchased without mss and on assignment. Captions are optional. Wants candid b&w. Pays $25/photo on publication.

TV TIME AND CHANNEL, Cable Communications Media, Inc., Box 2108, Lehigh Valley PA 18001. (215)865-6600. Production Manager: Sam Guncler. For television and other entertainment forms. Weekly magazine; 44 pages. Estab. 1965. Pays on publication. Buys all rights. Byline given "when requested." Phone queries OK. Submit seasonal/holiday material one month in advance. Simultaneous, photocopied and previously published submissions OK. SASE. Reports in 2 weeks. Sample copy for 50¢.

Nonfiction: Exposé (entertainment world and behind-the-scenes); general interest (TV related); how-to (things a TV watcher would like to know); humor; interviews (stars, producers and directors); photo feature; and personal opinion. "We do not want fan material." Pays 2-7¢/word.

Photos: Uses 8x10 b&w prints. Offers no additional payment for photos accepted with ms. Captions preferred.

WAVE, Side One Productions, 8311 Avenue K, Brooklyn NY 11236. Editor: Americo Figliolini. Emphasizes films, soundtracks and novelizations. Published every 6/weeks.

Magazine; 40 pages. Estab. December 1978. Circ. 10,000. Pays on publication. Buys all rights. Byline given. Simultaneous and previously published work OK. SASE. Reports in 4 weeks. Sample copy $2; SASE for writer's guidelines.

Nonfiction: Expose (on the happenings in the industry, no gossip); interview (top movie stars, recording artists, composers, on directors, writers and distributors); photo feature (photo essays with copy on upcoming films); profile (on new directors, writers, composers and producers); and previews. Buys 4-15 mss/issue. Query or send complete ms. Length: 500-4,000 words. Pays 1-2¢/word.

Photos: Send photos with ms. Pays $5-10 for b&w prints. Offers no additional payment for photos accompanying ms. Captions and model releases required.

Columns/Departments: Words (review of novelizations of films); Sounds (reviews of film soundtracks); and Frame (reviews of currently released foreign films). Buys 10-25 mss/issue. Query or send complete ms. Length: 300-1,000 words. Pays $10-30.

Fillers: Clippings, newsbreaks and anecdotes which happen during productions. Buys 1-5/issue. Length: 100-300 words. Pays $5-10.

Travel, Camping, and Trailer

Publications in this category tell campers and tourists where to go, where to stay, how to get there, how to camp or how to select a good vehicle for travel or shelter. Publications that buy how-to camping and travel material with a conservation angle are listed in the Nature, Conservation and Ecology classification. Newspapers and Weekly Magazine Sections, as well as Regional Publications, are frequently interested in travel and camping material with a local angle. Hunting and fishing and outdoor publications that buy camping how-to material will be found in the Sport and Outdoor category. Publications dealing with automobiles or other vehicles maintained for sport or as a hobby will be found in the Automotive and Motorcycle category. Many publications in the In-Flight category are also in the market for travel articles and photos.

ACCENT, 1720 Washington Blvd., Box 2315, Ogden UT 84404. Editor: Valerie Sagers. 75-90% freelance written. Travel-oriented. Estab. 1968. Monthly. Circ. 600,000. "*Accent* is sold to business and industrial firms coast-to-coast who distribute it with appropriate inserts as their house magazines." Buys first rights. Buys 120-140 mss/year, 200-300 photos/year. Pays on acceptance. Sample copy, 35¢ for postage. Free guidelines with SASE. Query with SASE.

Nonfiction and Photos: "We want travel articles—places to go, advice to travelers, new ways to travel, money-saving tips, new resorts, famous travelers, and humor. Stories and photos are often purchased as a package. Captions required. Feature article length: 500-1000 words. Payment: 10¢/word, $20/b&w photo, $25/color transparency, more for color covers.

Tips: "Please remember we work 9 months in advance, and submit seasonal material accordingly."

ADVENTURE TRAVEL, 444 NE Ravenna Blvd., Seattle WA 98115. (206)527-1621. Editor-in-Chief: Robert Citron. Editor: Barbara Sleeper. Managing Editor: Knute Berger. 95% freelance written. For 25-60 year-old active adventure travelers; well-educated, experienced, interested in conservation. Monthly magazine; 104 pages. Estab. June 1978. Circ. 150,000. Pays on publication. Buys first North American serial rights. Pays 10% kill fee. Byline given. Submit seasonal material 6 months in advance of issue date. Previously published submissions OK. SASE. Reports in 4 weeks. Free sample copy and writer's guidelines for large SASE; mention *Writer's Market* in request.

Nonfiction: Accounts of adventure trips open to members of the public, worldwide, including everything the reader needs to know to plan a similar experience; how-to (articles on travel tips for adventure travelers, photography, equipment use, expedition preparation, etc.); conservation (stories on adventure and conservation, including environmentally-concerned stories on wildlife viewing, endangered species; visiting remote places and peoples, etc.); interview (with noted, controversial, articulate people in adventure today); new travel books and maps; personal experience (first-person accounts of adventure trip experiences); photo feature (people participating in adventurous activities); profile (of interesting adventurers). "No articles on hunting and fishing, non-adventure travel (i.e., tours); or sexist or non-environmental material." Buys 4-5 mss/issue. Query. Length: 1,000-3,000 words. Pays $200-2,000.

Photos: Carrie Seglin, photo coordinator. *"Adventure Travel* uses top-quality color photography. We are always on the lookout for unique, exciting pictures of people participating in outdoor adventure trips. We choose manuscripts frequently on the basis of the photos." Pays $50-500 for 35mm or larger format color transparencies; originals only. Captions and model release required. Buys one-time rights.
Columns/Departments: Gear; Reading; News; and Photography. Buys 2-3/issue. Query. Length: 800-1,500 words. Pays $150-300.

AWAY, 888 Worcester St., Wellesley MA 02181. (617)237-5200. Editor: Gerard J. Gagnon. For "members of the ALA Auto & Travel Club, interested in their autos and in travel. Ages range from approximately 20 to 65. They live primarily in New England." Slanted to seasons. Quarterly. Circ. 220,000. Buys first serial rights. Pays on acceptance. Free sample copy. Submit seasonal material 6 months in advance. Reports "as soon as possible." Although a query is not mandatory, it may be advisable for many articles. SASE.
Photos: Articles on "travel, tourist attractions, safety, history, etc., preferably with a New England angle. Also, car care tips and related subjects." Would like a "positive feel to all pieces, but not the chamber of commerce approach." Buys both general seasonal travel and specific travel articles, for example, travel-related articles (photo hints, etc.); outdoor activities; for example, gravestone rubbing, snow sculpturing; historical articles linked to places to visit; humor with a point, photo essays. "Would like to see more nonseasonally oriented material. Most material now submitted seems suitable only for our summer issue. Avoid pieces on hunting and about New England's most publicized attractions, such as Old Sturbridge Village and Mystic Seaport." Length: 800-1,500 words. "preferably 1,000-1,200." Pays approximately 10¢/word. Photos purchased with mss; with captions only. B&w glossies. Pays $5-10/b&w photo, payment on publication based upon which photos are used. Not buying color at this time.

CAMPING JOURNAL, Davis Publications, 380 Lexington Ave., New York NY 10017. (212)557-9100. Editor-in-Chief: Andrew J. Carra. Managing Editor: Lee Schreiber. 75% freelance written. Emphasizes outdoor recreation. Published 8 times/year. Magazine; 64 pages. Estab. 1962. Circ. 300,000. Pays on acceptance. Buys all rights, but may assign following publication. Byline given. Submit seasonal/holiday material 4-6 months in advance of issue date. Photocopied submissions OK. SASE. Reports in 6 weeks. Sample copy $1; free writer's guidelines.
Nonfiction: General interest (travel); how-to (equipment); humor (personal experience); new product; personal experience; photo feature; and travel. Buys 100 mss/year. Query. Length: 1,500-3,500 words. Pays $100-300.
Photos: John McCorry, photo editor. State availability of photos with query. No additional payment for 8x10 b&w glossy prints and 2¼x2¼ or 35mm color transparencies. Pays $200-250 for cover photos. Captions preferred. Buys all rights, but may reassign after publication. Model release required.
Columns/Departments: Equiptips (concerning hiking and backpacking equipment) and Focal Points (concerning camera equipment). Buys 1/issue. Query. Length: 1,000-2,000 words. Pays $150-150. Open to suggestions for new columns/departments.
Fillers: Buys 1/issue. Length: 500-1,000 words. Pays $50-150.

DESERT MAGAZINE, Box 1318, Palm Desert CA 92260. (714)346-8144. Editor: William Knyvett. 100% freelance written. Emphasizes Southwest travel and history. For recreation-minded families—middle class income, RV owners, bikers and backpackers. Monthly magazine; 48 pages. Estab. 1937. Circ. 40,000. Pays on publication. Buys first North American serial rights. Submit seasonal or holiday material 6 months in advance. SASE. Reports in 4 weeks. Free sample copy and writer's guidelines.
Nonfiction: Historical, informational, personal experience, travel. Buys 8 articles/issue. Query. Length: 500-2,500 words. Pays $20-100.
Photos: Photos purchased with or without accompanying ms. Captions required. Pays $5 for 8x10 b&w glossy prints; $25/inside color photos; $35/4x5 color cover photos. "2¼x2¼ preferred over 35mm."

DISCOVERY MAGAZINE, Allstate Plaza, Northbrook IL 60062. Editor: Alan Rosenthal. 75% freelance written. For motor club members; mobile familes with above-average income. "All issues pegged to season." Estab. 1961. Quarterly. Circ. 940,000. Buys first North American serial rights. Buys 40 mss/year. Pays on acceptance. Free sample copy and writer's guidelines. Submit seasonal material 8-12 months in advance. Reports in 3 weeks. Query. SASE.
Nonfiction and Photos: "Primarily travel subjects. Also automotive and safety. First-person

narrative approach for most travel articles. Short pieces on restaurants must include recipes from the establishment." Travel articles and photos often are purchased as a package. Rates depend on how the photos are used. Color transparencies (35mm or larger) are preferred. Photos should show people doing things; captions required. Send transparencies by registered mail, with plenty of cardboard protection. Buys one-time rights for photography. Color photos are returned after use. Length: 1,000-2,500 words. "Rates vary, depending on type of article, ranging from $200-400 for full-length features." Photos purchased with accompanying mss; captions required. Photos also purchased on assignment.

Fillers: True, humorous travel anecdotes. Length: 50-150 words. Pays $10.

FAMILY MOTOR COACHING, 8291 Clough Pike, Cincinnati OH 45244. (513)474-3622. Editor: Pamela Gramke. Managing Editor: Dave Ginter. 75% freelance written. Emphasizes travel with motor home, and motor home modifications. Monthly magazine; 130 pages. Estab. February 1964. Circ. 22,000. Pays on acceptance. Buys all rights, but may reassign following publication. Byline given. Phone queries OK. Submit seasonal/holiday material 3 months in advance of issue date. SASE. Reports in 2 months. Sample copy $2; free writer's guidelines.
Nonfiction: General interest (motorhome travel and cooking on the road); historical (various areas of country accessible by motor coach); how-to (modify motor coach with added and changing features); nostalgia; and travel. Buys 3 mss/issue. Query. Length: 1,500 words minimum. Pays $50-200.
Photos: State availability of photos with query. No additional payment for b&w contact sheet(s); 35mm or 2¼x2¼ color transparencies. Captions preferred. Buys first rights.

HANDBOOK AND DIRECTORY FOR CAMPERS, 1999 Shepard Rd., St. Paul MN 55116. (612)647-7290. Editor: Don Picard. 100% freelance written. For families whose members range in age from infancy to past retirement, and whose leisure interests are aimed primarily at outdoor recreation and travel with recreational vehicles providing the means to enjoyment of this new life style. Estab. 1971. Annual. Circ. 1,500,000. Buys one-time rights and non-exclusive reprint rights. Buys 6-12 mss/year. Pays on acceptance. Free sample copy and writer's guidelines. Will consider photocopied submissions. Reports in 30 days. Query. SASE.
Nonfiction: "General articles on how to enjoy camping more or do it more efficiently. How-to articles are OK. First-person articles and stories about personal experiences are not acceptable. We try to emphasize that camping is not only fun in itself, but is the means to all kinds of peripheral activities not normally available to the average family." Informational, how-to. Length: 700-1,500 words. Pays $75-250.
Photos: State availability of photos with ms. Captions optional. Uses 35mm and larger; mostly b&w. Pays $200/cover; $50 each for inside use.

JOURNAL OF CHRISTIAN CAMPING, Christian Camping International, Box 400, Somonauk IL 60552. Editor: Bob Kerstetter. Emphasizes the broad scope of organized camping with emphasis on Christian camping. Bimonthly magazine; 32 pages. Estab. 1968. Circ. 4,000. Pays on acceptance. Buys all rights. Pays 25% kill fee. Byline given. Simultaneous, photocopied and previously published submissions OK. SASE. Reports in 4 weeks. Sample copy $1.50; writer's guidelines for SASE.
Nonfiction: General interest (trends in organized camping in general and Christian camping in particular); how-to (anything involved with organized camping from repairing refrigerators, to motivating staff, to programming, to record keeping, to camper follow-up); inspirational (limited use, but might be interested in practical applications of Scriptural principles to everyday situations in camping, no preaching); interview (with movers and shakers in camping and Christian camping in particular, submit a list of basic questions first); and opinion (write a letter to the editor). Buys 18-24 mss/year. Query. Length: 600-3,000 words. Pays $25-150.
Photos: Send photos with ms. Pays $7.50/5x7 b&w contact sheets or prints; price negotiable for 35mm color transparencies. Buys all rights. Captions required.

LEISUREGUIDE, 1515 NW 167th St., Miami FL 33169. Editor-in-Chief: Andrew Delaplaine. 75% freelance written. An in-room hotel guide book emphasizing information for travelers in Chicago, Louisville, Philadelphia, Boston, Houston, the Florida Gold Coast (Palm Beach to Miami), and South Carolina's Grand Strand (Myrtle Beach). Annual hardcover magazine; 84-150 pages. Estab. 1971. Circ. 222,000. Pays on publication. Buys all rights, but may reassign following publication. Byline given. Submit seasonal/holiday material 3 months in advance. Photocopied and previously published submissions OK. SASE. Reports in 2 weeks. Sample copy $2.
Nonfiction: Informational (of interest to sophisticated transients in our cities); historical (of

interest to our transient reader—usually of light, humorous vein"); travel (articles concentrated on the cities in which we publish); photo feature (must be color of very high quality and concentrate on some aspect of interest to the cities served). Buys 28 mss/year. Query. Length: 1,000-3,500 words. Pays $100-500.

Photos: Purchased without mss or on assignment. Query. "A good shot can come from any locale, but be appropriate (because of its general nature) to any of our editions." Pays $10-75 for b&w; $20-125 for color.

Rejects: "We almost never accept the general 'traveler' article to be found in publications such as inflight magazines. Our articles must relate specifically to the areas we serve and tell the readers something about these areas."

THE LUFKIN LINE, Lufkin Industries, Inc., Box 849, Lufkin TX 75901. Editor: Miss Virginia R. Allen. For men in oil and commercial and marine gear industries; readers mostly degreed engineers. Each issue devoted to different areas where division offices located; that is, West Coast, Canada, Mid-Continent, Rocky Mountain, Texas, Gulf Coast, International. Estab. 1924. Quarterly. Circ. 12,000. Not copyrighted. Buys 4-8 mss/year. Pays on acceptance. Free sample copy and writer's guidelines. Submit seasonal material 4 months in advance. Reports in 1 month. Query. SASE.

Nonfiction and Photos: "Travel articles. Subjects dealing with US and Canada, and (rarely) foreign travel subjects. Product articles staff-written. Length: 1,000-1,200 words. Pays $75/ms with illustrating photos. Color transparencies or prints of seasonal subjects are purchased for front cover; pays $50. Illustrations for travel articles may be color prints or transparencies (no smaller than 2¼x2¼). No b&w photos are purchased. Color photos for travel articles may be secured from state tourist or development commissions.

CAMPERWAYS (formerly *Midlantic Camping Trails*), 335 Edgewood Dr., Box 162, Ambler, PA 19002. (215)643-1988. Editor-in-Chief: Charles E. Myers. 60% freelance written. Emphasis on recreation vehicle camping and travel. Monthly (except Dec. and Feb.) tabloid; 36 pages. Estab. 1978. Circ. 40,000. Pays on publication. Buys simultaneous, second serial (reprint) or regional rights. Byline given. Submit seasonal/holiday material 3-4 months in advance. Simultaneous, photocopied and previously published submissions OK. SASE. Reports in 1 month. Free sample copy and writer's guidelines.

Nonfiction: Historical (when tied in with camping trip to historical attraction or area); how-to (selection, care, maintenance of RVs, accessories and camping equipment); humor; personal experience; and travel (camping destinations within 200 miles of Philadelphia-D.C. metro corridor). Buys 75 mss/year. Query. Length: 800-1,500 words. Pays $40-75.

Photos: Photos purchased with accompanying ms. Captions required. Uses 5x7 or 8x10 b&w glossy prints. Total purchase price for ms includes payment for photos.

Columns/Departments: Camp Cookery (ideas for cooking in RV galleys and over campfires. Should include recipes). Buys 10 mss/year. Query. Length: 500-1,000 words. Pays $25-50.

How To Break In: "Articles should focus on single attraction or activity or on closely clustered attractions within reach on the same weekend camping trip rather than on types of attractions or activities in general. We're looking for little-known or offbeat items. Emphasize positive aspects of camping: fun, economy, etc."

THE MIDWEST MOTORIST, The Auto Club of Missouri, 201 Progress Pkwy., Maryland Heights MO 63043. (314)576-7350. Editor: Martin Quigley. Associate Editors: Carolyn Callison, Tim Sitek. For the motoring public. Bimonthly magazine; 32 pages. Circ. 295,000. Pays on acceptance or publication depending on the situation. Not copyrighted. Pays kill fee as agreed. Byline given. Submit seasonal/holiday material 3-4 months in advance. Simultaneous, photocopied and previously published submissions OK. SASE. Reports in 2 months. Free sample copy and writer's guidelines.

Nonfiction: General interest; historical (of Midwest regional interest); humor (motoring slant); interview, profile, travel and photo feature. Buys 3 mss/issue. Query. Length: 1,000-1,800 words. Pays $50-200.

Photos: Send photos with ms. Uses b&w contact sheets or prints and color transparencies for cover. Offers no additional payment for photos accepted with ms. Captions preferred.

MINNESOTA AAA MOTORIST, Minnesota State Automobile Association, 7 Travelers Trail, Burnsville MN 55337. (612)890-2500. Contact: Editor. Bimonthly magazine; 32 pages. Estab. 1914. Circ. 270,000. "We will consider all rights." Pays on acceptance. Sample copy and writer's guidelines for SASE. Reports in 3 weeks.

Nonfiction: General interest (auto-related or Minnesota-related); historical (Minnesota-related); how-to (automobile-related); personal experience (travel-related); photo feature

(Minnesota or travel); technical (automobile-related); and travel (international and domestic). Query. Length: 500-1,200 words. Pays $85-200.
Photos: State availability of photos or send photos with ms. Pays $10-20 for 5x7 b&w glossy prints; $15-150 for 35mm color transparencies. Captions preferred; model release required.

MOBILE LIVING, Box 1418, Sarasota FL 33578. Editor: Frances Neel. Bimonthly. Buys first rights. Byline given. Pays on publication. Free sample copy. Reports in 1 month. SASE.
Nonfiction: Articles on recreational vehicle experiences and travel via recreational vehicles. In travel articles, include names of parks to stay at while seeing the sights, etc. Hobbies involving recreational vehicles and how-to-do-it articles that apply to a general audience also wanted. Length: 1,500 words maximum. Pays 1¢/word.
Photos: With captions and illustrating articles. B&w glossy prints only. Returned after use. Pays $3 each.

THE MOBILE TRAVELLER IN ONTARIO, Box 1509, Peterborough, Ontario, Canada K9J 7H7. Editor-in-Chief: Steve Bronson. 5% freelance written. For users of recreational vehicles, trailers, motorhomes, campers, etc. Published 10 times/year. Magazine; 32 pages. Estab. 1975. Circ. 24,000. Pays on publication. Buys first North American serial rights. Byline given. Submit seasonal/holiday material 1 month in advance of issue date. SAE and International Reply Coupons. Reports in 2 weeks.
Nonfiction: How-to (haul, repair, buy, or build recreational vehicles); general interest (of interest to campers); historical (camping); interview (with RV manufacturers and associated products); new product (in camping); and technical (on RV products). Buys 20 mss/year. Query. Length: 500-1,500 words. Pays $35-100.
Photos: No additional payment for photos accepted with accompanying ms. Uses b&w prints. Captions preferred. Buys all rights, but may reassign following publication.
Columns/Departments: The Frying Pan (outdoor cooking); and Humour (outdoor and recreational vehicle owners with pix if possible). Buys 10 mss/year. Query. Length: 250-1,000 words. Pays $25-100. Open to suggestions for new columns/departments.

MOTOR NEWS/MICHIGAN LIVING, Automobile Club of Michigan, Auto Club Dr., Dearborn, MI 48126. (313)336-1504. Editor-in-Chief: Len Barnes. 50% freelance written. Emphasizes travel and auto use. Monthly magazine; 48 pages. Estab. 1922. Circ. 800,000. Pays on acceptance. Buys first North American serial rights. Pays 100% kill fee. Byline given. Submit seasonal/holiday material 3 months in advance. SASE. Reports in 4-6 weeks. Buys 120 mss/year. Free sample copy and writer's guidelines.
Nonfiction: Marcia Danner, Managing Editor. Travel articles on US and Canadian topics. Send complete ms. Length: 800-2,000 words. Pays $75-220.
Photos: Photos purchased with accompanying ms. Captions required. Pays $25-150 for color transparencies; total purchase price for ms includes payment for b&w photos.
How To Break In: "In addition to descriptions of things to see and do, articles should contain accurate, current information on costs the traveler would encounter on his trip. Items such as lodging, meal and entertainment expenses should be included, not in the form of a balance sheet but as an integral part of the piece. We want the sounds, sights, tastes, smells of a place or experience some one will feel he has been there and knows if he wants to go back."

MOTORHOME LIFE, Trailer Life Publishing Co., Inc., 29901 Agoura Rd., Agoura CA 91301. (213)991-4980. Managing Editor: Rand Christensen. For owners and prospective buyers of motorhomes. Estab. 1962. Published 9 times/year. Circ. 125,000. Buys all rights. Byline given. Buys 50 mss/year. Pays on publication. Sample copy $1; free writer's guidelines. Submit seasonal material 3 months in advance. Reports in 1 month. SASE.
Nonfiction and Photos: "Articles which tell the owner of a self-propelled RV about interesting places to travel and interesting things to do. Human interest and variety articles sought as well. All material must be tailored specifically for our audiences." Information, personal experience, humor, historical, opinion, travel, new product and technical articles. Length: 2,500 words maximum. Pays $75-200. Photos purchased with accompanying ms with no additional payment.

NATIONAL MOTORIST, National Automobile Club, 1 Market Plaza, #300, San Francisco CA 94105. (415)777-4000. Editor: Jim Donaldson. 75% freelance written. Emphasizes motor travel in the West. Bimonthly magazine; 32 pages. Estab. 1924. Circ. 300,000. Pays on acceptance for article, layout stage for pix. Buys first publication rights. Byline given. Submit seasonal/holiday material 3 months in advance. Reports in 1 week. Free sample copy.
Nonfiction: How-to (care for car, travel by car, participate in outdoor sports and hobbies);

historical (interesting history and significant historical personalities behind places and areas readers might visit); humor (occasionally buys a story treating something in motoring from a humorous angle); profile (of someone with unusual skills or engaged in some interesting and unusual art, hobby or craft); and travel (interesting places and areas to visit in the 11 western states). Buys 5-8 mss/issue. Query. Length: around 1,100 words." Pays 10¢/word and up.
Photos: Purchased with accompanying ms. Captions optional, "but must have caption info for pix." Send prints or transparencies. Pays $20 and up for 8x10 b&w glossy prints; $30 and up for 35mm, 2¼x2¼ or 4x5 color transparencies. Model release required.

NORTHEAST OUTDOORS, Box 21801, Waterbury CT 06722. (203)755-0158. Editor: John Florian. 70% freelance written. Monthly. Circ. 20,000. Buys all rights. Pays 20% kill fee. Byline given "by request only." Pays on publication. Free sample copy. "Queries are not required, but are useful for our planning and to avoid possible duplication of subject matter. If you have any questions, contact the editor." Deadlines are on the 1st of the month preceding publication. Reports in 15-30 days. SASE.
Nonfiction and Photos: Interested in articles and photos that pertain to outdoor activities in the Northeast. Recreational vehicle tips and campgrounds are prime topics, along with first-person travel experiences in the Northeast while camping. "While the primary focus is on camping, we carry some related articles on outdoor topics like skiing, nature, hiking, fishing, canoeing, etc. In each issue we publish a 'Favorite Trip' experience, submitted by a reader, relating to a favorite camping experience, usually in the Northeast. Payment for this is $20 and writing quality need not be professional. Another reader feature is My Favorite Campground. Payment is $10. Our pay rate is flexible, but generally runs from $30-40 for features without photos, and up to $80 for features accompanied by 2 or more photos. Features should be from 300-1,000 words. Premium rates are paid on the basis of quality, not length. For photos alone we pay $10 for each 8x10 b&w print we use."

OHIO MOTORIST, Box 6150, Cleveland OH 44101. Editor: A. K. Murway Jr. 10-15% freelance written. For AAA members in 8 northeast Ohio counties. Estab. 1909. Monthly. Circ. 260,000. Buys one-time publication rights. Byline given. Buys 30 mss/year. Pays on acceptance. Free sample copy. Submit seasonal material 2 months prior to season. Reports in 2 weeks. Submit complete ms. SASE.
Nonfiction and Photos: "Travel, including foreign; automotive, highways, etc.; motoring laws and safety. No particular approach beyond brevity and newspaper journalistic treatment. Articles for travel seasons." Length: 2,000 words maximum. Pays $50-200/article including b&w photos. $125-250 for articals with color photos, transparencies any size. 8x10 b&w photos preferred. Purchased with accompanying mss. Captions required. Ohioanna is major needs.
Poetry: Humorous verse. Length: 4-6 lines. Pays $8-15

MARIAH/OUTSIDE MAGAZINE, 3401 Division St., Chicago IL 60651. (312)32-7777. Editor-in-Chief: Lawrence J. Burke. Managing Ediitor: John Rasmus. Emphasizes travel and the outdoors. Monthly magazine. Estab. 1976. Pays on publication. Rights purchased "vary." Reports in 1 month. SASE. Free writer's guidelines.
Nonfiction: Query with clips of published work.

PACIFIC BOATING ALMANAC, Box Q, Ventura CA 93001. (805)644-6043. Publisher/Editor: William Berssen. For "Western boat owners." Estab. 1965. Published in 3 editions to cover the Pacific Coastal area. Circ. 30,000. Buys all rights. Buys 12 mss/year. Pays on publication. Sample copy $5.95. Submit seasonal material 3 to 6 months in advance. Reports in 4 weeks. Query. SASE.
Nonfiction and Photos: "This is a cruising guide, published annually in 3 editions, covering all of the navigable waters in the Pacific coast. Though we are almost entirely staff-produced, we would be interested in well-written articles on cruising and trailer-boating along the Pacific coast and in the navigable lakes and rivers of the western states from Baja, California to Alaska inclusive." Pays $50 minimum. Pays $10 for 8x10 b&w glossy prints.

TRAILER BOATS MAGAZINE, Poole Publications, Inc., 1440 W. Walnut, Compton CA 90220. (213)537-1037. Editor-in-Chief: Ralph Poole. Managing Editor: Jim Youngs. 40% freelance written. Emphasizes trailerable-size boats and related activities. Monthly magazine; 80 pages. Estab. 1971. Circ. 80,000. Pays on publication. Buys all rights, but may reassign following publication. Byline given. Submit seasonal/holiday material 3 months in advance of issue date. SASE. Reports in 2-4 weeks. Free sample copy and writer's guidelines; mention *Writer's Market* in request.
Nonfiction: How-to (boat, motor and trailer maintenance, helpful and labor saving tips,

finishing, etc.); general interest; humor; historical; interview; nostalgia; personal experience; photo feature; technical; and travel. Buys 6-8 mss/issue. Query. Length: 500-2,000 words. Pays $50 minimum.

Photos: Pays $7-50 for 8x10 b&w glossy prints; $15-100 for 35mm or 2¼x2¼ color transparencies. Captions preferred. Buys all rights, but may reassign following publication.

Columns/Departments: Mini-Cruise (travel type featuring a cruise to a place for a day or weekend, telling how to get there, where to stay, what to do, activities, etc.); Over the Transom (photos only, showing humorous or wierd situations in the boating world). Buys 2-4 mss/issue. Query. Length: 300-500 words. Pays $75 minimum. Open to suggestions for new columns or departments.

Fiction: Adventure; historical; humorous; and science fiction. Buys sporadically." Query. Length: 200-1,500 words. Pays $50 minimum.

TRANSITIONS, 18 Hulst Rd., Amherst MA 01002. (413)256-0373. Editor: Bill Gertz. 64 Morton St., New York NY 10014. (212)929-3482. Emphasizes student travel. Quarterly tabloid; 16 pages. Estab. May 1977. Circ. 4,000. Pays on publication. Rights revert to writer. Pays 50% kill fee. Byline given. Phone queries OK. SASE. Reports in 4 weeks. Sample copy $1; free writer's guidelines.

Nonfiction: How-to (find courses, inexpensive lodging and travel); interview (information on specific areas and people); personal experience (evaluation of courses, study tours, economy travel); and travel (what to see and do in specific areas of the world, new learning and travel ideas). Buys 8 mss/issue. Query. Length: 500-1,500 words. Pays $10-75.

Photos: Send photos with ms. Pays $5-15 for 8x10 b&w glossy prints; $5-15 for 35mm color transparencies. Offers no additional payment for photos accompanying ms. Buys one-time rights. Captions required.

Columns/Departments: Study Abroad (evaluation of courses or programs); Travel Abroad (new ideas for offbeat independent travel); and Work Abroad (how to find it and what to expect). Buys 8/issue. Send complete ms. Length: 1,000 words maximum. Pays $20-75.

Fillers: Newsbreaks (having to do with travel, particularly offbeat educational travel). Buys 2/issue. Length: 100 words maximum. Pays $5-20.

THE TRAVEL ADVISOR, Box 716, Bronxville NY 10708. Editor-in-Chief: Hal E. Gieseking. 55% freelance written. Monthly newsletter; 12 pages. Estab. March 1976. Owned by *Travel/Holiday* magazine. Circ. 80,000. Pays on publication. Buys all rights. Pays kill fee sometimes; depends on work done. Byline given on destination reports but not on short travel items. SASE. Reports in 4 weeks. Free sample copy and writer's guidelines. No photos used.

Nonfiction: "Send us short, *very candid* items based on the writer's own travel experience—*not* written first-person. Example: a baggage rip-off in Rome; a great new restaurant in Tokyo (with prices)." Expose (candid look at the travel industry); and how-to (good, inside information on how travelers can avoid problems, save money, etc.). "No typical travel articles that extol the setting sun." Buys 100 mss/year. Submit complete ms. Length: 20-150 words. Pays $20/item. Also buys candid destination reports. Length: 2,500 words. Query. Pays $250 maximum.

TRAVEL AND LEISURE, 1350 Avenue of the Americas, New York NY 10019. (212)586-5050. Editor-in-Chief: Pamela Fiori. 80% freelance written. Monthly. Circ. 925,000. Buys first North American serial rights. Pays 25% kill fee. Byline given unless material is assigned as research. Pays on acceptance. Reports in 1 week. Query. SASE.

Nonfiction and Photos: Uses articles on travel and vacation places, food, wine, shopping, sports. Most articles are assigned. Length: 2,000-3,000 words. Pays $750-2,000.

Photos: Makes assignments to photographers. Pays expenses.

How To Break In: "New writers might try to get something in one of our regional editions (East, West, South and Midwest). They don't pay as much as our national articles ($300-500), but it is a good way to start. We have a great need for these pieces and they run be no more than 800-1,200 words. Regionals cover any number of possibilities from rafting a river in a certain state to unusual new attractions."

TRAVEL/HOLIDAY MAGAZINE, Travel Magazine, Inc., 51 Atlantic Ave., Floral Park NY 11001. (516)352-9700. Editor: Barbara Lotz. Associate Editor: Stephen A. Maguire. For the active traveler with time and money to travel several times a year. Monthly magazine; 100 pages. Estab. 1901. Circ. 800,000. Pays on acceptance. Buys first North American serial rights. Byline given. Phone queries OK. Submit seasonal/holiday material 6 months in advance. Simultaneous and photocopied submissions OK. SASE. Reports in 3 weeks. Free sample copy and writer's guidelines.

Nonfiction: Interested in any travel-related item. Buys 120 mss/year. Query. Length: 1,500-2,500 words. Pays $200 minimum.
Photos: Pays $15 minimum for b&w 5x7 or larger prints; and $35 for 35mm or larger color transparencies. Offers no additional payment for photos accepted with ms. Captions required. Buys one-time rights.

TRAVEL SMART, Communications House, Inc., Dobbs Ferry NY 10522. (914)693-4208. Editor: H.J. Teison. 60% freelance written. Emphasizes "budget/smart, good value travel." Monthly mewsletter; 10 pages. Estab. April 1976. Pays on publication. Buys all rights. Photocopied submissions OK. SASE. Reports in 3-4 weeks. Free sample copy; mention *Writer's Market* in request.
Nonfiction: Exposé (travel rip-offs); how-to (traveling smart); and travel. Query. Length: 200-1,000 words. Pays $10-150.

TRAVELER MAGAZINE (Wisconsin AAA) (formerly *Wisconsin AAA Motor News*), 433 W. Washington Ave., Madison WI 53703. (608)257-0711. Editor: Hugh P. (Mickey) McLinden. 30% freelance written. Aimed at an audience of domestic and foreign motorist-travelers. Monthly magazine. Pays on publication. Buys all rights. Reports "immediately." SASE.
Nonfiction and Photos: Domestic and foreign travel; motoring, safety, highways, new motoring products. Length: 1,000 words maximum. Pays $50 minimum. Photos purchased with ms or with captions only. B&w and color. Pays $15 minimum.

TRAVELIN' VANS, Box 1084, Reseda CA 91423. (213)782-2502. Editor: Jim Matthews. 40-50% freelance written. For van owners and their families. Magazine; 80 pages. Estab. 1976. Monthly. Circ. 80,000. Buys all rights, but may reassign rights to author after publication. Buys 25-35 mss/year. Pays on publication. Free sample copy and editorial guidelines. Submit seasonal material 3 months in advance. Reports in 2 weeks. Query. SASE.
Nonfiction and Photos: Wants mss about methods of customizing; feature articles on outstanding vans, minis, pickups and micro-mini motor homes; coverage of "van happenings"—allies, charity activities, special purpose vans and related subjects. Wants how-to and semi-technical mss. "Keep in mind our audience at all times. Generally thought of as a youth group, they are becoming older and very solid reliable citizens who spend hours and countless dollars making their vans unique and comfortable." No travel articles unless specifically related to van camping. "Never, never any emphasis on antisocial behavior." Would like to see mss on major van events in areas far from Southern California. Buys informational, how-to, profile, fiction and nostalgia. Length: 1,200-2,000 words. Pays $35/page in finished book. "Approximately 50% photos." Photos purchased with ms with no additional payment. Captions required. B&w primarily; color of outstanding vans.

TRAVELORE REPORT, 225 S. 15th St., Philadelphia PA 19102. Editor: Ted Barkus. For affluent travelers; businessmen, retirees, well-educated; interested in specific tips, tours, and bargain opportunities in travel. Monthly newsletter; 4 pages. Estab. 1972. Buys all rights, but will reassign rights to author after publication. Buys 25-50 mss/year. Pays on publication. Sample copy $1. Submit seasonal material 2 months in advance.
Nonfiction and Fillers: "Brief insights (25-200 words) with facts, prices, names of hotels and restaurants, etc., on offbeat subjects of interest to people going places. What to do, what not to do. Supply information. We will rewrite if acceptable. We're candid—we tell it like it is with no sugar coating. Avoid telling us about places in United States or abroad without specific recommendations (hotel name, costs, rip-offs, why, how long, etc.)." Pays $5.

WOODALL'S TRAILER & RV TRAVEL, 500 Hyacinth Place, Highland Park IL 60035. (312)433-4550. Editor: Kirk Landers. 50% freelance written. For recreational vehicle owners and enthusiasts whose interests include travel-camping in North America, and buying, maintaining and customizing their vehicles. Magazine; 125 pages. Estab. 1936. Monthly. Circ. 300,000. Rights purchased vary with author and material. Usually buys all rights, but may reassign rights to author after publication. Pays 25-50% kill fee, depending on the assignment. Byline given "except material purchased for our annual *RV Buyer's Guide*, because of format." Buys about 50 mss/year. Pays on acceptance. Free sample copy and writer's guidelines. No photocopied or simultaneous submissions. Submit seasonal material 4-6 months in advance. Reports in 4 weeks. Query or submit complete ms. SASE.
Nonfiction and Photos: "Travel guides and narratives providing comprehensive views of great camping areas. Also, humor, profiles (especially of those who live and work on the road); recipe and menu ideas; money-saving tips; vehicle maintenance and improvement; insurance, equipment, etc. Our greatest joy is a thoroughly researched article in which facts, figures,

quotes and conclusions are presented in clear, concise prose, and in a logical sequence. We avoid material that is slanted exclusively to the raw beginner. Would consider winter camping ideas; pieces on rainy day recreation for families; RV decorating and improvements; new travel destination ideas (including the offbeat)." Length: 1,000-3,000 words. Pays $150-300; more on assignment. Seasonal photo essays are used when good color is available. B&w and color purchased with or without mss. Pays $25 minimum for b&w; $50 minimum for color. Captions required.

How To Break In: "A background in this special interest field is a must; so is a familiarity with our editorial style and format. The ripest subject areas are probably general interest material, profiles, nostalgia and humor."

WORLD TRAVELING, Midwest News Service, Inc., 30943 Club House Lane, Farmington Hills MI 48018. Editor: Theresa Mitan. Bimonthly magazine; 48 pages. Estab. September 1978. Circ. 2,000. Pays on publication. Buys all rights. Byline given. Submit seasonal/holiday material 6 months in advance. Simultaneous submissions OK. SASE. Reports in 2 weeks. Sample copy $1.25.

Nonfiction: General interest, how-to (on any travel experience that might help other travelers); humor; photo feature and travel. Buys 6 mss/issue. Send complete ms. Length: 1,000 words. Pays $100 for 1,000 words.

Photos: Send photos with ms. Pays $10 for b&w prints; $10 for color transparencies. Buys one-time rights.

Columns/Departments: Good Restaurant Guide and Question and Answers about travel. Query or send complete ms. Length: 500 words.

Fillers: Jokes, gags, anecdotes and short humor. Pays 10¢/word.

Union

ALLIED INDUSTRIAL WORKER, Allied Industrial Workers Union, AFL-CIO, 3520 W. Oklahoma Ave., Milwaukee WI 53215. (414)645-9500. Associate Editor: Ken Germanson. Assistant Editor: Anne Bingham. Emphasizes blue-collar issues. Monthly tabloid; 12 pages. Circ. 100,000. Pays on acceptance. Buys rights on a work-for-hire basis. Phone queries OK. Submit seasonal/holiday material 3 months in advance. Simultaneous, photocopied and previously published submissions OK. SASE. Reports in 2 weeks. Free sample copy.

Nonfiction: General interest (no highbrow); historical (labor history of locals); how-to (out of the ordinary home hobby); interview (labor members leisure activities); new products; and photo feature (workers in shops). Buys 1 ms/issue. Query. Pays $25 minimum.

Photos: State availability of photos. Pays $20 for 8x10 b&w glossy prints. Buys one-time rights. Captions required.

OCAW UNION NEWS, Box 2812, Denver CO 80201. (303)893-0811. Editor: Jerry Archuleta. Official publication of Oil, Chemical and Atomic Workers International Union. For union members. Monthly tabloid newspaper; 12 pages. Estab. 1944. Circ. 180,000. Not copyrighted. Byline given. Pays on acceptance. Free sample copy. Reports in 30 days. Query. SASE.

Nonfiction and Photos: Labor union materials, political subjects and consumer interest articles, slanted toward workers and consumers, with liberal political view. Interview, profile, think pieces and exposes. Most material is done on assignment. Length: 1,500-1,800 words. Pays $50-75. No additional payment is made for 8x10 b&w glossy photos used with mss. Captions required.

UTU NEWS, United Transportation Union, 14600 Detroit Ave., Cleveland, OH 44107. (216)228-9400. Editor-in-Chief: Jim Turner. For members of the union (250,000) working in the crafts of engineer, conductor, firemen and brakemen on North American railroads. Weekly newspaper; 4 pages. (Also one monthly tabloid; 8 pages). Estab. 1969. Pays on publication. Buys photos only. Buys all rights. Phone queries OK. Reports "at once."

Photos: Current news shots of railroad or bus accidents, especially when employees are killed or injured. Captions required. Pays $15 minimum for any size b&w glossy prints.

Women's

The publications listed in this category specialize in material of interest to women. Other publications that occasionally use material slanted to women's interests can be found in the following categories: Alternative, Child Care and Parental Guidance; Confession, Education, Food and Drink; Hobby and Craft; Home and Garden; Religious, and Sport and Outdoor publications.

BRANCHING OUT, New Woman's Magazine Society, Box 4098, Edmonton, Alberta, Canada T6E 4T1. (403)433-4021. Editor-in Chief: Sharon Batt. For Canadian women. "The majority are women with a variety of interests (art, literary, political, feminist); 25-50 years of age." Bimonthly magazine; 48 pages. Estab. 1973. Circ. 4,000. Pays on publication. Buys first North American serial rights. Byline given. Photocopied submissions OK. SAE and International Reply Coupons. Sample copy $1.25; free writer's guidelines.
Nonfiction and Photos: "Unsolicited manuscripts from Canadian women only." Photo features with 4-5 photographs in a series. Buys 60-70/year. Query. Length: 500-3,500 words. Pays $5-15. B&w photos purchased with or without mss. Query. Pays $5-15.
Columns/Departments: Material for all columns and features should take a feminist point of view. Book reviews and columns on law and films. Query. Length: 300-1,500 words. Pays $5-15.
Fiction: "High-quality fiction by Canadian women. Experimental and mainstream. Fiction must be good, not sentimental, tightly constructed, high-quality writing." Submit complete ms. Length: 1,000-5,000 words. Same rate of payment as nonfiction.
Poetry: Avant-garde, free verse, haiku. Buys 3-4/issue. Limit submissions to batches of 8. Pays $5-15.

BRIDE'S, Conde Nast Bldg., 350 Madison Ave., New York NY 10017. (212)880-8533. Editor-in-Chief: Barbara D. Tober. For the first- or second-time bride in her early twenties, her family and friends, the groom and his family. Magazine published 6 times/year. Estab. 1934. Circ. 300,000. Buys all rights. Pays 15% kill fee, depending on circumstances. Byline given. Buys 30 mss/year. Pays on acceptance. Free writer's guidelines. Reports in 8 weeks. Query or submit complete ms. Address mss to Copy and Features Department.
Nonfiction: "We want warm, personal articles, optimistic in tone, with help offered in a clear, specific way. All issues should be handled within the context of marriage. How-to features on all aspects of marriage: communications, in-laws, careers, money, sex; informational articles on the realities of marriage, the changing roles of men and women, the kinds of troubles in engagement that are likely to become big issues in marriage; and first-person narratives or stories from couples or marriage authorities that illustrate marital problems and solutions to men and women both." Length: 1,800-3,000 words. Pays $200-550.
How To Break In: "Send us a well-written article that is both easy to read and offers real help for the bride as she adjusts to her new role. No features on wedding and reception planning, home furnishings, cooking, fashion, beauty, travel—these are all staff-written. For examples of the kinds of features we want, study any issue; read articles listed in table of contents under Planning for Marriage."

CAROLINA WOMAN, Carolina Woman, Inc., 1409 East Blvd., Suite 105, Charlotte NC 28203. (704)373-0784. Editor: Barbara Gammon. Bimonthly magazine; 56 pages. Estab. 1978. Circ. 20,000. Pays on publication. Buys one-time rights. Phone queries OK. Submit seasonal/holiday material 2 months in advance. Photocopied submissions OK. SASE. Reports in 1 month. Free sample copy and writer's guidelines.
Nonfiction: General interest (women in business, transferring from city to city, divorce, separation, marriage, etc.); how-to (move ahead in business, start a new business, deal with problems); how-to; humor; inspirational (overcoming problems that affect women age 30-50); interview (of interesting women in either North or South Carolina); opinion (women's experiences); profile (see interview); personal experience; and photo feature. "All of our material comes from women's own stories about how they have grown both personally and professionally. All stories must have upbeat endings. Love, marriage, family, God (though not bordering on fanaticism). Definitely not women's lib or anti-male." Buys 25 mss/issue. Send complete ms. Length: 500-1,500 words. Pays $25.
Poetry: Free verse, light verse and traditional. "No avant-garde. No psychic, far-out verse. We prefer it be simple but relevant to women's experiences." Buys 15 poems/issue. Pays $10-25.

CHATELAINE, 481 University Ave., Toronto, Canada M5W 1A7. Editor-in-Chief: Mildred Istona. General interest magazine for Canadian women, from age 20 up. Monthly magazine. Estab. 1928. Circ. over 1 million. Pays on acceptance. Buys first World serial rights. Pays negotiable kill fee. Byline given. Free writer's guidelines.
Nonfiction: Betty Lee, articles editor. How-to; general interest; interview; personal experience; profile; and travel. Length: 2,000-3,600 words. Pays $600 minimum.
Fiction: Barbara West, fiction editor. Confession; humorous; mainstream; romance; and condensed novels. No short shorts. Length: 3,000-4,000 words. Pays $400 minimum.

COLORADO WOMAN MAGAZINE, The Colorado Woman Digest Corp., 1572 Race St.,

Denver CO 80206. (303)393-0840. Editor: Judy Bucher. For all women in the Rocky Mountain area. Bimonthly magazine; 80 pages. Estab. February 1976. Circ. 10,000. Pays on publication. Byline given. Phone queries OK. Submit seasonal/holiday material 3-4 months in advance. Simultaneous, photocopied and previously published submissions OK. SASE. Reports in 1 month. Sample copy $1.25.

Nonfiction: General interest, historical, how-to, humor, interview, nostalgia, experience, personal opinion, photo feature, profile and travel. Buys 5-8 mss/issue. Send complete ms. Length: 200-1,500 words. Pays 3¢/published word.

Fiction: "We want fiction articles that relate to women—up-to-date concerns." Buys 2 mss/year. Send complete ms. Length: 300-1,000 words. Pays 3¢/published word.

Poetry: Buys 10-20/year. Pays $5.

COMMUNITY WOMAN, Box 8234, Anaheim CA 92802. 92802. (714)997-9660. Editor-in-Chief: Cheryl Pruett. Managing Editor: Colleen A. Huber. 75% freelance written. For women, 20-80 years-old, interested in home, children, business, personal care, and continuing education (formal and informal). "Our readers are predominately college-trained graduates." Monthly tabloid; 16 pages. Estab. 1977. Circ. 15,000. Pays on publication. Not copyrighted. Byline given. Phone queries OK. Submit seasonal/holiday material 2 months in advance of issue date. Photocopied and previously published submissions OK. SASE. Reports in 2 months. Free sample copy and writer's guidelines; mention *Writer's Market* in request.

Nonfiction: Exposé (consumer frauds or shabby practices, how red tape affects prices, etc.); general interest (successful individual and women's organizations, not women's liberation); historical (women who have shaped history: inventors, writers, politicians, etc.); how-to (saving, decorating, carpentry, painting, establishing a home business); humor (funny situations developed out of home life); inspirational (overcoming obstacles of women); new product (especially if it makes women's role easier). "No put-downs of men or women's liberation material." Buys 60-100 mss/year. Query or submit complete ms. Length: 100-1,000 words. Pays $5-15.

Photos: Pays $2.50-10 for b&w prints. Captions and model release required.

COSMOPOLITAN, 224 W. 57th St., New York NY 10019. Editor: Helen Gurley Brown. Managing Editor: Guy Flatley. For career women, ages 18 to 34. Monthly. Circ. 2,500,000. Buys all rights. Pays on acceptance. Not interested in receiving unsolicited manuscripts. Most material is assigned to established, known professional writers who sell regularly to top national markets, or is commissioned through literary agents.

Nonfiction and Photos: Not interested in unsolicited manuscripts; for agents and top professional writers, requirements are as follows: "We want pieces that tell an attractive, 18- to 34-year-old, intelligent, good-citizen girl how to have a more rewarding life—'how-to' pieces, self-improvement pieces 'as well as articles which deal with more serious matters. We'd be interested in articles on careers, part-time jobs, diets, food, fashion, men, the entertainment world, emotions, money, medicine and psychology, and fabulous characters." Uses some first-person stories. Logical, interesting, authoritative writing is a must, as is a feminist consciousness. Length: 1,200-1,500 words; 3,000-4,000 words. Pays $200-500 for short pieces, $1,000-1,750 for longer articles. Photos purchased on assignment only.

Fiction: Department Editor: Harris Dienstfrey. Not interested in unsolicited manuscripts; for agents and top professional writers, requirements are as follows: "Good plotting and excellent writing are important. We want short stories dealing with adult subject matter which would interest a sophisticated audience, primarily female, 18-34. We prefer serious quality fiction or light tongue-in-cheek stories on any subject, done in good taste. We love stories dealing with contemporary man-woman relationships. Short-shorts are okay but we prefer them to have snap or 'trick' endings. The formula story, the soap opera, skimpy mood pieces or character sketches are not for us." Length: short-shorts, 1,500-3,000 words; short stories, 4,000-6,000 words; condensed novels and novel excerpts. "We also use murder or suspense stories of about 25,000-30,000 words dealing with the upper class stratum of American living. A foreign background is acceptable, but the chief characters should be American." Has published the work of Agatha Christie, Joyce Carol Oates, Evan Hunter, and other established writers. Pays about $1,000 and up for short stories and novel excerpts, $4,500 and up for condensed novels.

FAMILY CIRCLE GREAT IDEAS, Family Circle Magazine, 488 Madison Ave., New York NY 10022. (212)593-8181. Editor: Marie T. Walsh. Managing Editor: Susan Kiely Tierney. Emphasizes how to: decorating, fashion and crafts. Bimonthly magazine; 128 pages. Estab. January 1975. Circ. 1,000,000. Pays on publication. Buys all rights. Submit seasonal/holiday material 9 months in advance. Reports in 4 weeks. Sample copy $1.75.

Nonfiction: How-to (fashion, decorating, crafts, food and beauty) and new product (for home and family). Buys 2 mss/issue. Query. Length: 500-1,500 words. Pays $150-350.

FAMILY CIRCLE MAGAZINE, 488 Madison Ave., New York NY 10022. (212)593-8000. Editor: Arthur Hettich. 60% freelance written. For women/homemakers. Published 17 times/year. Usually buys all rights. Pays 25% kill fee. Byline given. Pays on acceptance. Reports in 6-8 weeks. Query. "We like to see a strong query on unique or problem-solving aspects of family life, and are especially interested in writers who have a solid background in the areas they suggest." SASE.
Nonfiction: Women's interest subjects such as family and social relationships, children, humor, physical and mental health, leisure-time activities, self-improvement, popular culture, travel. Service articles. For travel, interested mainly in local material, no far-flung foreign or extensive travel. "We look for human stories, told in terms of people. We like them to be down-to-earth and unacademic." Length: 1,000-2,500 words. Pays $250-2,500.
Fiction: Occasionally uses fiction related to women. Buys short stories, short-shorts, vignettes. Length: 2,000-2,500 words. Payment negotiable. Minimum payment for full-length story is $500.

FARM WIFE NEWS, 733 N. Van Buren, Milwaukee WI 53202. (414)272-5410. Managing Editor: Judy Borowski. For farm and ranch women of all ages; nationwide. Estab. 1970. Circ. 240,000. Byline given. Buys 400 mss/year. Pays on publication. Sample copy $1; free writer's guidelines. Submit seasonal material 4-6 months in advance. Reports in 4-6 weeks. Query or submit complete ms. SASE.
Nonfiction and Photos: "We are always looking for good freelance material. Our prime consideration is that it is farm-oriented, focusing on a farm woman or a subject that would appeal especially to her." Uses a wide variety of material: daily life, sewing, gardening, decorating, outstanding farm women, etc. Topic should always be approached from a rural woman's point of view. Informational, how-to, personal experience, interview, profile, inspirational, humor, think pieces, nostalgia, opinion, successful sideline business operations from farm and/or ranches. Length: 1,000 words maximum. Departments and columns which also use material are: A Day in Our Lives, Besides Farming, Farm Woman on the Go, Country Crafts, Sewing and Needlecraft, Gardening, Decorating, I Remember When, Farm Nature Stories. Pays $20-100. B&w photos are purchased with or without accompanying mss. Color slides and transparencies are also used. They look for scenic color photos and shots of farm wives at work and at play which show the life on the farm. Captions required. Payment depends on use, but begins at $10 for b&w photos; at $25 for color slides or transparencies.
Fiction: Mainstream, humorous. Themes should relate to subject matter. Length: 1,000 words maximum. Pays $40-75.
Fillers: Word puzzles and short humor. Pays $15-30.

GLAMOUR, 350 Madison ave., New York NY 10017. (212)692-5500. Editor-in-Chief: Ruth Whitney. Features Editor: Wenda Wardell Morrone. For women, 18-35-years old. Circ. 1.7 million; 6.5 million readers. SASE. Pays on acceptance. Pays 20% kill fee. Byline given. Reports in 3-5 weeks.
Nonfiction: "Editorial approach is 'how-to' with articles that are relevant in the areas of careers, health, psychology, interpersonal relationships, etc. Fashion, beauty, decorating and travel are all staff-written. Buys 10-12 mss/issue. Query. Short articles (1,500-2,000 words) pay $500-750; longer mss (2,500-3,000 words) pay $850 and up.

GOOD HOUSEKEEPING, Hearst Corp., 959 8th Ave., New York NY 10019. Editor-in-Chief: John Mack Carter. Executive Editor: Mina Mulvey. Managing Editor: Mary Fiore. Mass women's magazine. Monthly; 250 pages. Estab. 1885. Circ. 5,000,000. Pays on acceptance. Rights very with author and material. Pays 25% kill fee. Byline given. Submit seasonal/holiday material 6-8 months in advance. SASE. Reports "as soon as possible." Sample copy $1.25.
Nonfiction: Jean Block, articles editor. Exposé; how-to-informational; inspirational; interviews; nostalgia; personal experience; profiles. Buys 8-10 mss/issue. Query. Length: 1,000-5,000 words. Pays $500-5,000.
Photos: Herbert Bleiweiss, Art Director. Photos purchased on assignment mostly. Some short photo features with captions. Pays $50-250 for b&w; $50-350 for color photos. Query. Model release required.
Departments: Light Housekeeping & Fillers, edited by Karen Stray. Humorous short-short prose and verse. Jokes, gags, anecdotes. Pays $25-100. The Better Way, edited by Bob Liles. Ideas and in-depth research. Query. Pays 25-35. "Only outstanding material has a chance here."

Fiction: Naome Lewis, Fiction Editor. Romance; mainstream; suspense; condensed novels and serialized novels. Buys 3 mss/issue. Send complete mss. Length: 1,000 words (short-shorts); 10,000 words (novels); average 4,000 words. Pays $1,000 minimum.

Poetry: Leonhard Dowty, Poetry Editor. Light verse and traditional. Buys 3 poems/issue. Pays $25 minimum.

Cartoon Editor: Pat McBride. Pays $150.

Regional Editor: Jean McGuire. Local interest pieces; some travel. Pays $250-350.

GRADUATE WOMAN (formerly *AAUW Journal*), 2401 Virginia Ave. NW., Washington DC 20037. (202)785-7727. Publication of American Association of University Women. Editor: Patricia Jenkins. For women of all ages who have at least a bachelor's degree. Published 6 times/year. Circ. 190,000. Byline given. Pays on acceptance. Sample copy $1. SASE.

Nonfiction and Photos: "Material used is usually related to broad themes with which AAUW is concerned, including the Equal Rights Amendment, laws and public policies affecting women, education, community issues, cultural affairs and international relations. Special concentration next two years on family and on managing resources. Emphasis is on women and their efforts to improve society. Articles must be thoroughly researched, well thought through, and competently written. We pay extra for high-quality photos related to the article (including some color)." Pays "generally $150 maximum."

HADASSAH MAGAZINE, 50 W. 58th St., New York NY 10022. Editorial Director: Helen G. Lusterman. Executive Editor: Jesse Zel Lurie. For members of Hadassah. Monthly, except combined issues (June-July and August-September). Circ. 360,000. Buys US publication rights. Pays on publication. Reports in 6 weeks. SASE.

Nonfiction: Primarily concerned with Israel, the American Jewish community and American civic affairs. Length: 1,500-3,000 words. Pays $200-350.

Photos: "We buy photos only to illustrate articles, with the exception of outstanding color from Israel which we use on our covers. We pay $100 and up for a suitable color photo."

Fiction: Short stories with strong plots and positive Jewish values. Length: 3,000 words maximum. Pays $300 and up.

HARLEQUIN, 220 Duncan Mill Road, Don Mills, Ontario, Canada M3B 3J5 Editor: Beth McGregor. "Not accepting material at present."

HARPER'S BAZAAR, 717 5th Ave., New York NY 10022. Editor-in-Chief: Anthony Mazzola. For "women, late 20s and above, middle income and above, sophisticated and aware, with at least 2 years of college. Most combine families, professions, travel, often more than one home. They are active and concerned over what's happening in the arts, their communities, the world." Monthly. Rights purchased vary with author and material. May buy first North American serial rights. SASE.

Nonfiction and Photos: "We publish whatever is important to an intelligent, modern woman. Fashion questions plus beauty and health—how the changing world affects her family and herself; how she can affect it; how others are trying to do so; changing life pattern and so forth. Query us first."

HERS, I.P.C. Magazines Ltd., King's Reach Tower, Stamford St., London SE1 9LS, England. Editor-in-Chief: Jack McDavid. 80% freelance written. For British readers; young, married women, low-income, interested in self-identification through first-person real-life stories. Buys 15-20 mss/year from American/Canadian writers. Monthly magazine; 64 pages. Estab. 1965. Circ. 150,000. Pays on acceptance. Buys all rights. Byline given. Submit seasonal/holiday materal 4 months in advance. SAE and International Reply Coupons. Reports in 6 weeks. Free sample copy and writer's guidelines.

Photos: Josephine Gange, art editor. Uses 35mm or 2¼x2¼ color transparencies. Model release required.

Fiction: Rosalind Davies, assistant editor. Confessions. Buys 12 mss/issue. Send complete ms. Length: 1,500-5,000 words. Pays $10-15.

LADIES' HOME JOURNAL, Charter Corp., 641 Lexington Ave., New York NY 10022. Editor: Lenore Hershey. Senior Editor: Jan Goodwin. Monthly magazine; 200 pages. Pays on publication. Simultaneous and photocopied submissions OK. "We have in the last year initiated the policy of only accepting manuscripts that are submitted to us through literary agents." Submit seasonal/holiday material 6 months in advance. SASE. Rpeorts in 6 weeks. Free writer's guidelines.

Nonfiction: Exposé, general interest and profile. "No personal essays and memories or travel

pieces." Buys 3 mss/issue. Query. Length: 2,000 words minimum. Pays $500 minimum.
Fiction: "We are sorry to announce a new policy under which we will no longer consider short stories sent through the mail. We do not have facilities that permit proper handling. Please do not send in manuscripts as we will be unable to return them."
Poetry: Light verse and traditional. Buys 30-50/year. Submit in batches of 6. Length: 8-15 lines. Pays $5/line.

LADY'S CIRCLE MAGAZINE, Lopez Publications, Inc., 23 W. 26th St., New York NY 10010. Features Editor: Fran Carpentier-Covello. Service Editor: Barbara Jacksier. For homemakers. Monthly. Buys all rights. Pays 50% kill fee. Byline given. Pays on publication. Reporting time varies from 1 week to 3 months. Query, with brief outline. SASE.
Nonfiction and Photos: Particularly likes first-person or as-told-to pieces about health and doing good. Also how homemakers and mothers make money at home. Hobbies and crafts. Also articles on baby care, home management, gardening, as well as problems of the homemaker. Also, stories of people who have overcome illnesses or handicaps. Articles must be written on specific subjects and must be thoroughly researched and based on sound authority. Length: 2,500 words. Pays $125 and up. Pays $15 for good b&w photos accompanying articles.

McCALL'S, 230 Park Ave., New York NY 10017. Editor: Robert Stein. "Study recent issues." Monthly. Circ. 6,500,000. Pays on acceptance. Pays 20% kill fee. Byline given. Reports in 4-6 weeks. SASE.
Nonfiction: Department Editor: Helen Markel. No subject of wide public or personal interest is out of bounds for *McCall's* so long as it is appropriately treated. The editors are seeking meaningful stories of personal experience. They are on the lookout for new research that will provide the basis for penetrating articles on the ethical, physical, material and social problems concerning readers. They are most receptive to humor. *McCall's* buys 200-300 articles/year, many in the 1,000- to 1,500-word length. Miss Lisel Eisenheimer is Editor of Nonfiction Books from which *McCall's* frequently publishes excerpts. These are on subjects of interest to women: biography, memoirs, reportage, etc. Address queries for Right Now column to Janet Chan. Subjects can be education, medicine, social and community affairs (new ideas and trends), problems being solved in new ways, ecology, women doing interesting things, women's liberation, any timely subject. Short pieces with a news or service angle. Length: 300-500 words. Payment is up to $300. The magazine is not in the market for new columns. Almost all features on food, household equipment and management, fashion, beauty, building and decorating are staff-written. Query. "All manuscripts must be submitted on speculation and *McCall's* accepts no responsibility for unsolicited manuscripts."
Fiction: Department Editor: Helen DelMonte. "Again the editors would remind writers of the contemporary woman's taste and intelligence. Most of all, fiction can awaken a reader's sense of identity, deepen her understanding of herself and others, refresh her with a laugh at herself, etc. *McCall's* looks for stories which will have meaning for an adult reader of some literary sensitivity. *McCall's* principal interest is in short stories; but fiction of all lengths is considered." Length: about 4,000 words. Length for short-shorts: about 2,000 words. Payment begins at $1,250.
How To Break In: "Your best bet is our monthly newsletter section, Right Now. It's an 8-page section and we buy a lot of freelance material for it, much of that from beginning writers. Some people have gone on from Right Now to do feature material for us."

McCALL'S WORKING MOTHER MAGAZINE, McCall's Publishing Co., 230 Park Ave., New York NY 10017. (212)551-9500. Editor: Vivian Cadden. Managing Editor: Mary McLaughlin. For the working mothers in this country whose problems and concerns are determined by the fact that they have children under 18 living at home. Bimonthly magazine; 104-108 pages. Estab. October 1978. Circ. 200,000. Pays on acceptance. Buys all rights. Pays 20% kill fee. Byline given. Submit seasonal/holiday material 6-8 months in advance. Simultaneous and photocopied submissions OK. SASE. Reports in 6-8 weeks. Sample copy $1.50.
Nonfiction: How-to (save time, find a day care center, balance job and housework, find time for yourself) and humor (anything that may be amusing to the working mother). "Don't just go out and find some mother who holds a job, and describe how she runs her home, manages her children and feels fulfilled. Find a unique angle." Buys 9-10 mss/issue. Query. Length: 750-2,000 words. Pays $300-500.
Columns/Departments: Take Care of Yourself (health) and What's In Your Lunchbox (readers ideas for midday meals). Uses 2-3/issue. Query.
Fiction: "We are interested in fiction if the right piece comes along, but we're still more

interested in nonfiction pieces."

Poetry: Light verse and traditional. Uses 1-2/year.

MADEMOISELLE, 350 Madison Ave., New York NY 10017. Editor-in-Chief: Edith Raymond Locke. 60% freelance written. Directed to college-educated women 18-34. Circ. 1,000,000. Reports in 3-4 weeks. Buys first North American serial rights. Pays on acceptance. Prefers written query plus samples of work, published or unpublished. SASE.

Nonfiction: May Cantwell, Senior Editor, Features. Particular concentration on articles of interest to the intelligent young woman that concern the arts, education, careers, travel, current sociological and political problems. Articles should be well-researched and of good quality. Prefers not to receive profile articles of individuals or personal reminiscences. Length: "Opinion" essay column, 1,300 words; articles, 1,500-6,000 words. Pays $300 for "Opinion" essay column; article $100 minimum.

Photos: Department Editor: Susan Niles. Commissioned work assigned according to needs. Photos of fashion, beauty, travel; career and college shots of intrest to accompany articles. Payment ranges from no-charge to an agreed rate of payment per shot, job series, or page rate. Buys all rights. Pays on publication for photos.

Fiction: Department Editor: Mary Elizabeth McNichols. High-quality fiction by both name writers and unknowns. Length: 1,500-3,000 words. Pays $300 minimum. Uses short-shorts on occasion. "We are particularly interested in encouraging young talent, and with this aim in mind, we conduct a college fiction contest each year, open to men and women undergraduates. A $500 prize is awarded for each of the two winning stories which are published in our August issue. However, our encouragement of unknown talent is not limited to college students or youth. We are not interested in formula stories, and subject matter need not be confined to a specific age or theme." Annually awards 2 prizes for short stories.

Poetry: Department: Mary Elizabeth McNichols. Must be of very high literary quality, under 65 lines. Pays $25 minimum. Annually awards 2 prizes for poetry.

MODERN BRIDE, 1 Park Ave., New York NY 10016. Executive Editor: Cele G. Lalli. Bimonthly. Buys first periodical publishing rights. Byline given. Pays on acceptance. Reports in 2 weeks. SASE.

Nonfiction: Uses articles of interest to brides-to-be. "We prefer articles on etiquette, marriage and planning a home. Travel is staff-written or specially assigned. We edit everything, but don't rewrite without permission." Length: about 2,000 words. Payment is about $200 minimum.

Poetry: Occasionally buys poetry pertaining to love and marriage. Pays $15-25 for average short poem.

MS. MAGAZINE, 370 Lexington Ave., New York NY 10017. (212)725-2666. Editor-in-Chief and Publisher: Patricia Carbine. Editor: Gloria Steinem. For "women predominantly; varying ages, backgrounds, but committed to exploring new life styles and changes in their roles and society." Estab. 1972. Monthly. Circ. over 500,000. Rights purchased vary with author and material. Pays on acceptance. Will consider photocopied submissions. Submit seasonal material at least 3 months in advance. Reports in 5-6 weeks. Query for nonfiction only, "with ideas and outline, and include samples of previous work." Address to Query Editor. Submit complete ms for fiction. SASE.

Nonfiction: "Articles, features on the arts, women's minds, women's bodies that relate to exploring new life styles for women and changes in their roles and society. We are a how-to magazine—how a woman may gain control of her life. We are hoping to change the status quo so that women can live their lives as unique people unrestricted by society rules, we reject downputting editorializing or insensitive advertising. We would like more input on what women are doing politically in their communities." Buys informational articles, how-to's, personal experience essays, interviews, profiles, humor, historical articles, exposes, opinion pieces, photo essays, coverage of business, and art, book, and film reviews. Length varies. Pays $100 mimimum. Send to Manuscript Editor.

Photos: Purchased with mss, without mss, or on assignment. Payment "depends on usage." Address to Art Department.

Fiction, Poetry and Fillers: Personal experiece, fantasy, humorous, historical, condensed novels and serialized novels. Address to Fiction Editor. Traditional forms, blank verse, free verse, avant-garde forms and light verse, relating to magazine subject matter. Address to Poetry Editor. "We accept nonfiction filler length material only for the Gazette section of the magazine; news from all over." Length: filler length to 3,000 words maximum. Pays to $500.

How To Break In: "The Gazette section which features short news items is the easiest way to get published here, and are especially receptive to regional material from New York but much has to be rejected because of space limitations and lack of professional standards. We use a lot of material from all over the country on politics, the women's movement, human interest features. It is possible to move from the Gazette to do other work for *Ms.*"

NATIONAL BUSINESS WOMAN, 2012 Massachusetts Ave. NW, Washington DC 20036. (202)293-1100. Editor: Louise G. Wheeler. For "all mature, educated, employed women." Estab. 1919. 10 times a year. Buys all rights and second serial rights. Byline given. Buys 10-12 mss/year. Pays on acceptance. Sample copy $1. Will consider photocopied submissions. Reports in 6 weeks. SASE.
Nonfiction: "Originality preferred. Written specifically for members of the National Federation of Business and Professional Women's Clubs, Inc. No fiction or poems." Buys informational, biographical, and articles of current interest to business and professional women. Length: 1,000-1,200 words. Pays $10-35.

REDBOOK MAGAZINE, 230 Park Ave., New York NY 10017. (212)983-3200. Executive Editor: William A. Robbins. Monthly magazine; 200 pages. Estab. May 1903. Circ. 4,450,000. Rights purchased vary with author and material. Reports in 4 weeks. Pays on acceptance. SASE.
Nonfiction: Silvia Koner, articles editor. Articles relevant to the magazine's readers, who are young women in the 18- to 34-year-old group. Also interested in submissions for "Young Mother's Story." "We are interested in stories offering practical and useful information you would like to share with others on how you, as a mother and a wife, are dealing with the changing problems of marriage and family life, such as the management of outside employment, housework, time, money, the home and children. Stories also may deal with how you, as a concerned citizen or consumer, handled a problem in your community. For each 1,000-2,000 words accepted for publication, we pay $500. Mss accompanied by a large, stamped, self-addressed envelope, must be signed, and mailed to: Young Mother's Story, c/o *Redbook Magazine*. Length: articles, 3,000-3,500 words; short articles, 2,000-2,500 words.
Fiction: Eileen Schnurr, fiction editor. Uses a great variety of types of fiction, with contemporary stories appealing especially to women. Short stories of 3,500-5,000 words are always needed. Also short-shorts of 1,400-1,600 words. Payment begins at $850 for short-shorts; $1,000 for short stories.
How To Break In: "It is very difficult to break into the nonfiction section, although Young Mothers, which publishes short personal experience pieces (1,000-1,500 words), does depend on freelancers. The situation for fiction is quite different. We buy about a third of our stories from writers whose stories come in from the cold in the mail or from writers who were originally found in our unsolicited mail. We buy about 50 stories a year. This is clearly the way to break into *Redbook*. Many of the stories we're proudest of—the fresh material that gives *Redbook* its distinctiveness—are from people we've discovered in the mail. So when we open those brown envelopes it is with a great deal of hope."

SPHERE MAGAZINE, 500 N. Michigan Ave., Chicago IL 60611. Editor: Joan Leonard. Monthly. Study several issues of the publication and query first. SASE. Unsolicited mss not accepted.

SUNDAY WOMAN, The Hearst Corp., 959 8th Ave., New York NY 10019. Editor: Richard Kaplan. Executive Editor: Marcia Cohen. Weekly magazine-tabloid; 24 pages. Estab. August 1978. Circ. 500,000. Pays on acceptance. Buys second serial (reprint) rights and first North American serial rights. Previously published work OK. SASE. Reports in 4 weeks.
Nonfiction: Exposé, how-to, interview, personal experience and profile (show-business, expecially TV and movies). "We do not want any articles that are not of specific interest to women." Query. Length: 1,500-3,000 words. Pays $250-1,000.

VOGUE, 350 Madison Ave., New York NY 10017. Editor: Grace Mirabella. Issued monthly. For highly intelligent women. Query. SASE.
Nonfiction: Feature Editor: Leo Lerman. Uses articles and ideas for features, 1,000-1,500 words. Fashion articles are staff-written. Material must be of high literary quality, contain good information. Pays $300 and up, on acceptance. Byline given.

WOMEN'S CIRCLE, Box 428, Seabrook NH 03874. Editor: Marjorie Pearl. For women of all ages. Monthly magazine; 72 pages. Buys all rights. Byline given. Buys 200 mss/year. Pays on acceptance. Sample copy 75¢. Submit seasonal material 7 months in advance. Reports in 1 to 3 months. Query or submit complete ms. SASE.
Nonfiction: How-to articles on hobbies, handicrafts, etc. Also food, recipes, needlework, dolls,

home, family and children. Informational approach. Needs Christmas crafts for Christmas annual. Length: open. Pays 3¢/word.

W, *Women's Wear Daily,* 7 E. 12th St., New York NY 10003. Completely staff-written newspaper.

WOMAN LOCALLY MAGAZINE, 97 Columbia St., Albany NY 12210. (518)465-8508. Editor: Cheryl Funbeck. Managing Editor: Cathy Cholakis. Monthly magazine; 48 pages. Estab. 1978. Circ. 2,000. Pays no later than publication of next issue. Buys all rights. Byline given. Submit material 2 months in advance. Simultaneous and photocopied submissions OK. **Nonfiction:** Buys 10 mss/issue. Query. Length: 300-1,500 words. Pays $5-50.
Photos: Send photos with ms. Pays 5-15 for b&w prints; model release required.
Columns/Departments: Clinic, Creative Expressions, Job Forum, Sports and Women in Focus. Query. "Mostly consignment with publisher."

WOMAN'S DAY, 1515 Broadway, New York NY 10036. Editor: Geraldine Rhoads. 15 issues/year. Circ. over 8,000,000. Buys first and second North American serial rights. Pays negotiable kill fee. Byline given. Pays on acceptance. Reports in 2 weeks on queries; longer on mss. Submit detailed queries first to Rebecca Greer, Articles Editor. SASE.
Nonfiction: Uses articles on all subjects of interest to women—marriage, family life, child rearing, education, homemaking, money management, travel, family health, and leisure activities. Also interested in fresh, dramatic narratives of women's lives and concerns. Length: 500-3,000 words, depending on material. Payment varies depending on length, whether it's for regional or national use, etc.
Fiction: Department Editor: Eileen Herbert Jordan. Uses little fiction; high-quality, genuine human interest romance and humor, in lengths between 1,500 and 3,000 words. Payment varies. "We pay any writer's established rate, however."
Fillers: Brief (500 words maximum), factual articles on contemporary life, community projects, unusual activities are used—condensed, sprightly, and unbylined—in "It's All in a Woman's Day" section. "Neighbors" column also pays $25 for each letter and $5 for each brief practical suggestion on homemaking or child rearing. Address to the editor of the appropriate section.

WOMEN IN BUSINESS, Box 8728, Kansas City MO 64114. (816)361-6621. Editor: Sharon K. Tiley. 25% freelance written. For working women in all fields and at all levels; largely middle-aged women in traditional "women's" fields. Monthly (combined issues in March/April, July/August, and October/November) magazine; 28 pages. Estab. 1949. Circ. 105,000. Pays on acceptance. Buys all rights, but may reassign following publication. Phone queries OK. Submit seasonal/holiday material 3 months in advance of issue date. SASE. Reports in 2 months. Free sample copy and writer's guidelines.
Nonfiction: General interest; how-to; historical; new product; technical. No interviews or profiles of individuals. Articles should be slanted toward the working women. Buys 9 mss/year. Query or submit complete ms. Length: 1,000-2,000 words. Pays $50-150.
Photos: State availability of photos with query or submit with accompanying ms. Pays $25-60 for 8x10 b&w glossy contact sheets; $75 cover color transparencies. Captions preferred. Buys all rights, but may reassign following publication. Model release required.
Columns/Departments: Books Briefly (short reviews); Business Communications (letters, speeches and memos); Personal Business (financial); The Management Woman (tips); and Your Personality (pop psychology). Buys 9/year. Query. Length: 500-1,200 words. Pays $35-50.

WORKING WOMAN, Hal Publications, Inc., 600 Madison Ave., New York NY 10022. Editor: Kate Rand Lloyd. Executive Editor: Gay Bryant. Monthly magazine; 96 pages. Estab. November 1976. Circ. 300,000. Pays on publication. Buys all rights. Pays 20% kill fee. Byline given. Submit seasonal/holiday material 6 months in advance. SASE. Reports in 5-6 weeks. Sample copy $1.50; free writer's guidelines.
Nonfiction: How-to (career strategies, managing personal life/work life, etc.); humor (related to work and work situations); interview (with women in various career areas, experts in various fields); and profile (use rarely). "We want subjects that have special application to working women or are of particular interest to them." Buys 6 mss/issue. Query with clips of published work or send complete ms. Length: 1,500-2,500 words. Pays $300-500.
Photos: State availability of photos with ms.
Columns/Departments: Consumer Advice, Mind & Body, Money Talks, Education, Traveling Ease and Working Your Way Up. "All columns/departments are geared to specific problems/pluses of working women." Buys 5/issue. Query with clips of published work. Length: 850-1,200 words. Pays $200-350.

Gag

Cartoonists, even those that usually write their own material, turn to freelance gagwriters for additional material. A cartoonist wants to use the funniest material available, and isn't embarrassed if a freelancer's gag is funnier than one of his own. Beyond being a source of extra material, freelancers also provide variety and freshness.

You don't sell gags to a cartoonist *per se*; in effect, you become the cartoonist's partner. Both of you share the payment when a cartoon based on your gag is sold; neither gets paid if the cartoon doesn't sell. (Some cartoonists buy gags outright, though this practice is rare.) Unsold gags are eventually returned to the writer, but cartoons are often circulated for years before the cartoonist gives up on them.

Submit gags on 3x5 cards, one per card. Include an identification number in the upper left-hand corner, and type your name and address on the back of the card. Submitting between 10 and 20 gags at one time is standard.

A rough sketch of the proposed cartoon on the card often helps the cartoonist—and the writer. Using sketches, even if you use simple stick figures, can help you "develop a more visual gag style," says cartoonist Dav Holle.

Submit nothing before studying the cartoonist's work in particular, and cartoons in general. "*Closely* study all the published gags you can with the question in mind, 'Why did they pay money for this?' " says cartoonist Frank Sematones.

That may sound like a lot of work to put into a piece of writing you can submit on a 3x5 card, but cartoonists often complain about the casual gagwriter who doesn't pay enough attention to the craft and discipline of writing comedy material. Cartoonist James Estes advises, "Work at it. *Hard. Fulltime.* And take being funny very seriously. Ninety percent of the gagwriters are hobbyists, and they are *not* funny." Pros recommend that you write daily, polish material continuously, and submit material. regularly. In cartoonist Reamer Keller's words, "Glue yourself to a chair eight house a day—and never give up."

For more information on gagwriting, read *The Cartoonist's and Gag Writer's Handbook*, by Jack Markow (Writer's Digest Books).

RAE AVENA, 36 Winslow Rd., Trumbull CT 06611. Cartoonist since 1965. Likes to see all types of gags. Has sold to *National Enquirer*, *New York Times*, and Pyramid Publications (paperbacks). "Gagwriters should send around 12 gags. Keep descriptions short." Pays 25% commission. Returns rejected material "as soon as possible." SASE.

DOROTHY BOND ENTERPRISES, 2450 N. Washtenaw Ave., Chicago IL 60647. "Been in the cartooning industry since 1944, and have successfully hit all bases. Have sold panels and comic strips to top syndicates and single cartoons to publications in almost every field. When we receive your gag, it is carefully reviewed and, if we think it's salable, it is drawn up at once and sent on its quick way to a wide list of top cartoon buyers. If we reject your gag, it is returned to you within three days. Unsold, retained gags are returned to you within three months. We are happy to see all gags, with the exception of pornography, cannibal, monkey or elephant gags. Any common topic with a new, funny slant sells quickly. Also, more women should enter the gagwriting field because many top magazines welcome submissions with a woman's funny viewpoint. And cartoons *should* be funny since they are meant to amuse and entertain. Bitterness and cruelty should be left out. Be professional and type your gags on 3x5 cards with your name and address on the back, and always enclose SASE. We send you 30% of the sale check the same day we receive it. Please, no clips or rubber bands, or letters with your submissions. We do your accepted submissions as expertly and as cleverly as anyone can. We want to sell them as badly as you do. Trust us, and good luck to us both."

BILL BOYNANSKY, Apt. 13/20, Ansonia Hotel, 2109 Broadway, New York NY 10023.

(212)787-2520. Estab. 1936. Buys over 200 gags/year; sold 328 last year. Submit 15-20 gags at one time. Pays "25% for regular, 35% for captionless; all others—regular payment." Reports in 3 days to 2 months. SASE.

Needs: General, male, female, sexy, girlie, family, children's, adventure, medical. "Prefer to see captionless gag ideas on all subject matters, but no beginners; only those who know their business. I prefer to deal with cartoonists by letter or phone because it saves me time. However, I will respect and consider all mail replies."

ASHLEIGH BRILLIANT, 117 W. Valerio St.. Santa Barbara CA 93101. Estab. 1967. Sells to newspapers. Buys about 50 gags/year; sold about 315 cartoons last year. Has sold to the Chicago Tribune-New York Times News Syndicate. Reports in 2 weeks. Pays $10.

Needs: "My work is so different from that of any other cartoonist that it must be carefully studied before any gags are submitted. Any interested writer not completely familiar with my work should first send $1 for my catalog of 1,000 examples. Otherwise, their time and mine will be wasted."

JOE BUSCIGLIO, 420 W. North Bay, Tampa FL 33603. Cartoonist since 1941. General and family gags only. No sex. Pays 25% commission on sale. Buys 11 gags/year; sold 14 cartoons last year. Currently selling to newspapers, trade journals, and house organs; also "ad" type art and some editorial panels. No returns.

ARTEMAS COLE, Box 408, La Puente CA 91747. Estab. 1974. Buys 30-50 gags/year for use in national magazines (medical, girlie, etc.). Has sold to *National Enquirer*, *Good Housekeeping*, *Boys Life*, etc. Submit gags on 3x5 slips; 10-20/batch. Reports in 1-2 weeks. Pays 30% plus "bonus payment of 50% for every tenth sale." SASE.

Needs: "Basically any general or family gags that are funny and fresh. Humor through children especially. Will look at girlie material, adult attitudes, and humor with sex. Business and home repair gags sought. I do *not* want to see raunchy sex or children engaged in sex with adults. These items are my taboos. I do not find anything funny with child molester humor. I make this statement emphatically because I've received a lot of this type of material lately."

COMEDY UNLIMITED, Suite 625, Jack Tar Office Bldg., 1255 Post St., San Francisco CA 94109. Contact: Jim Curtis. Buys over 2,000 gags/year. "We are always looking for fresh, new premise ideas for unique and creative standup comedy monologues, as well as clever and original sight gags, and crazy pieces of business. We also buy original one-liners tailored especially for any of the following: comedians, public speakers, singers, magicians, or jugglers. Since we build everything from night club acts to humorous corporate speeches, it would be advisable not to submit any material until you have sent an SASE and request our current projects list to find out exactly what we're most interested in buying during any given quarter. Keep in mind we are exclusively concerned with material intended for oral presentation." If SASE is not enclosed with submission, all material will be destroyed after being considered, except items purchased. Pays $1-3/line, on acceptance, and "considerably" more for zany, new premise ideas and sight gags. Reports in 2 weeks.

CREATIVE CARTOON SERVICE, 3109 W. Schubert Ave., Chicago IL 60647. Contact: Peter Vaszilson. Cartoonist since 1965. "Creative Cartoon Service is an art brokerage service, arranging for sale of artwork between cartoonists, gagwriters and publishers. Please inquire before submitting your work to us." SASE.

THOMAS W. DAVIE, 1407 S. Tyler, Tacoma WA 98405. Cartoonist since 1960. Buys 100 gags/year; sold 175 cartoons last year. Has sold to *Medical Economics*, *Sports Afield*, King Features, *Chevron USA*, *Rotarian*, *Saturday Evening Post*, *Ladies' Home Journal*, *Playgirl* and *Boys' Life*. Gags should be typed on 3x5 slips. Prefers batches of 5-25. Pays 25% commission. Reports in 1 month. SASE.

Needs: General gags, medicals, mild girlies, sports (hunting and fishing), business and travel gags.

LEE DeGROOT, Box 115, Ambler PA 19002. Estab. 1956. Now interested in receiving studio greeting card ideas only. "I draw up each idea in color before submitting to greeting card publishers. Therefore, giving the editors a chance to visualize the idea as it would appear when printed . . . and thus increasing enormously the chances of selling the idea. Writer's percentage is 25% of selling price."

GEORGE DOLE, Box 3168, Sarasota FL 33578. Estab. 1952. Buys 60% of gags/year; sold over

200 cartoons last year. Has sold to *Playboy, Parade, Penthouse*. Submit 12 gags at one time. Pays 25% commission. Reports in 1 week. SASE.
Needs: General, male, female, sexy, girlie, family, children's, sports, medical. Must be sophisticated, funny, etc., and submitted on standard index cards.

GERALD DYES, 7207 Norka Dr., Jacksonville FL 32210. Estab. 1969. Buys about 4 gags/year; sold 150 cartoons last year. Has sold to *National Enquirer, Saturday Evening Post, Ebony, Medical Economics, True Treasure* and *Cartoon Carnival*. Send 10-20 gags at one time. SASE. Pays 25% commission.
Needs: Family, general, medical and light girlie material. No hard-core sex. "If I believe that the gag has merits, I will push hard for all top markets—I may push the gag for six months to two years. I'll be glad to look at any subject that is wholesome; although I do 98% of my own material, I'll be glad to help any new gag writer, if I can.

JAMES ESTES, 1103 Callahan, Amarillo TX 79106. "Primarily interested in seeing good, funny material of a general nature. Always interested in a good strip idea. Most themes are acceptable, but the usual taboos apply. Submit on 3x5 cards or paper, 10-20 gags/submission; clear, concise ideas set down without excessive wordiness. Wholesome, family, general material wanted. I don't do sexy or girlie cartoons at all and it's a waste of gagwriters' postage to send that type gag." Buys about 50 gags/year; sold more than 500 last year. Has been selling cartoons for 9 years. Currently selling to *Changing Times, Wall Street Journal, Reader's Digest, Medical Economics, Boys' Life, National Enquirer, Kiwanis, TV Guide, New Woman,* King Features, McNaught Syndicate, *American Legion, Good Housekeeping* and *Dynamic Years,* including several farm magazines, horse and western magazines. Usually returns rejected material in 2-3 days. Pays 25%. SASE.

DON ERIK GJERTSEN, 338 N. Forest Ave., Rockville Centre NY 11570. Estab. 1967. Held 97 gags last year; sold 87 cartoons last year. Has sold to *Gallery, Science Digest, Genesis, Writer's Digest, Skiing,* etc. Submit gags on 3x5 file cards "typed or neatly written with gagwriter's name and address on the back"; 20/batch. Reports in 1-2 weeks. Pays 25% for gags with captions; 30% for captionless. SASE.
Needs: "Girlie" (but not gross); general; sports and outdoors; business; technology; medical; science; and historical. No gross sex; "the higher paying markets don't want it, and the publications that do don't pay enough for the cartoonist, much less a gagwriter."

RANDY HALL, 1121 N. Tulane, Liberal KS 67901. (316)624-2431. Cartoonist since 1974. Buys 300 gags/year; sold 500 cartoons last year. Has sold to *New Woman, American Legion, VFW Magazine, Medical Times, Modern Medicine, Channels, Wallace's Farmer, Farmer/Stockman, Christian Century, Instructor, Massachusetts Teacher* and King Features. Submit 10-25 gags at one time. Pays 25% commission. Returns rejects the same day received, but "keeps gags going forever if there's a chance of selling them." SASE.
Needs: General, male, female, sexy, girlie, family, industrial, professional, children's, sports, medical, farm, religious, antique, education. "Must be original. I see far too much plagiarism. If it's not original, don't send it. Be consistent and don't send me 25th-round rejects. I like to get first looks occasionally, too."

CHARLES HENDRICK JR., Old Fort Ave., Kennebunkport ME 04046. (207)967-4412. Estab. 1942. Buys several gags/year; sold 50-60 cartoons last year. Sells to local markets. Submit 10 gags at a time. Pays 50% of commission. Reports in 10-30 days. SASE.
Needs: General family, trade (hotel, motel, general, travel, vacationers). Safe travel ideas—any vehicle. Gags must be clean; no lewd sex.

DAVID R. HOWELL, Box 170, Porterville CA 93258. (209)781-5885. Estab. 1974. Buys about 130 gags/year; sold about 400 last year. Has sold to *Writer's Digest, New Woman, Modern Medicine, Mechanix Illustrated, Popular Electronics* and the other electronic newsstand magazines and computer slants, *Ag World* and the other farm magazines, the horse magazines, dental magazines, business magazines, general markets, and many technical journals. Submit 6-10 gags at one time. Pays 25-30% commission. Returns rejected gags same day as received. SASE.
Needs: Medical (fresh and topical), dental, electronic, farm, business, family, teenager, current slants and auto mechanics. "I am now the resident cartoonist at *Industrial Launderer,* so if any gagwriters know this particular slant (not the regular drycleaning slant), send some along. I will always look at any to be slanted toward a particular technical journal market."

LARRY (KAZ) KATZMAN, 101 Central Park W., Apt. 4B, New York NY 10023. (212)724-7862. Estab. 1949. Purchased over 100 gags last year. Has sold to *Modern Medicine* and *Medical Economics*. Submit 12-15 gags at one time. Pays 25% commission. Reports in 1 week. SASE.
Needs: "I use only medical (doctor, nurse, hospital) gags; no others." Must be submitted on numbered, separate slips.

JEFF KEATE, 1322 Ensenada Dr., Orlando FL 32807. Cartoonist since 1936. Buys 193 gags/year; sold about 500 cartoons last year. Has sold all of the major publications over the past 30 years. Currently doing syndicated newspaper cartoon panels for Field Newspaper Syndicate. Pays 25% commission. Holds unsold gags for "approximately 2 years unless gagwriter requests gag back sooner." Returns rejected material "immediately." SASE.
Needs: General situation and timely gags, sports gags (all sports in season) for "Time Out" sports panel. "Be funny. No puns. No oldies. No old hat situations."

STEVE KELL, 733 Waimea Dr., El Cajon CA 92021. (714)440-5749. Estab. 1966. Buys 53 gags/year; sold 150 cartoons last year. Has sold to *Playgirl*, *Penthouse*, *Esquire*, etc. Submit gags in batches of 10-15. Reports in 1 week. Pays 25%. SASE.
Needs: "All fresh and surprising slants accepted. I'll also buy gags for syndicated comic strip *The Captain and Mandy*—slant towards airline travel."

REAMER KELLER, Box 3557, Lantana FL 33462. (305)582-2436. Estab. 1940. Buys 225 gags/year; sold 30 cartoons last year. Has sold to *Cosmopolitian*, *Medical Economics*, *National Enquirer*, etc. Submit gags in batches of 20-30. Reports in 2 weeks. Pays 25%. SASE.
Needs: "Action, short captions and captionless." General; medical; hospital; girly; "timely stuff, homey."

MILO KINN, 1413 SW Cambridge St., Seattle WA 98106. Cartoonist since 1942. Has sold to *Medical Economics*, *Modern Medicine*, *Farm Wife News*, *Private Practice*, *Wallace's Farmer*, etc. Pays 25% commission. SASE.
Needs: Medical gags, male slant, girlie, captionless, adventure and family gags. Sells trade journal, farm, medical, office and general cartoons.

LO LINKERT, 1333 Vivian Place, Port Coquitlam, British Columbia, Canada V3C 2T9. Cartoonist since 1957. Has sold to most major markets. Prefers batches of 10-15 gags. Pays 25% commission; $50 for greeting card ideas. Returns rejected material in 1 week. Enclose SAE and 15¢ US postage.
Needs: Clean, general, male, medical, family, office, outdoors gags; captionless ideas; greeting card ideas. "Make sure your stuff is funny. No spreads." Wants "action gags—not two people saying something funny."

ART McCOURT, 3819 Dismount, Dallas TX 75211. (214)339-6865. Estab. 1952. Purchased 300 gags last year. Has sold to *Arizona Republic*, *Wallace's Farmer*, *Independent Banker*, *National Enquirer*, *Changing Times*, *American Legion*, *Mechanix Illustrated* and King Features. Submit 10-15 gags at one time. Pays 25% commission. Reports in 1 week. SASE.
Needs: "Something unique and up-to-date." No "crowds, TV, mothers-in-law or desert islands."

MASTERS AGENCY, Box 427, Capitola CA 95010. Editorial Director: George Crenshaw. Buying cartoon roughs and gags ("sketched only, no typers") for the following syndicated features: Belvedere, syndicated by Field Newspaper Syndicate; a dog panel. Pays $10/gag. Holy Acrimony, syndicated by Field Newspaper Syndicate; husband-wife, pre-marriage and post-marriage material needed. Single panel; pays $10-15/gag. Cartoon Quarterly, syndicated by Master's Agency; general material. Single panel cartoons, needed quarterly; pays $15/cartoon. Proofs furnished upon request to qualified persons only. Send samples or indicate your credits.

BILL MAUL, 328 St. Dunstan Way, Winter Park FL 32792. Estab. 1970. Sells to men's and women's publications and general interest magazines. Has sold to *Better Homes & Gardens*, *Playgirl*, *TV Guide*, *Family Circle*, etc. Submit gags on 3x5 cards or paper, 10-15 in a batch. Reports in 1 week. Pays 25%; "raises to 30% after a successful collaboration period." SASE.
Needs: "Will consider all topics, but the writer should concentrate on general, family-type gags. Topics such as TV, current events and trends warrant special consideration. Sight gags are always desirable."

HAROLD B. MONEY ("HALM"), 1206 Dover Ave., Wilmington DE 19805. (302)994-0272. Estab. 1950. Holds 400 gags/year; sold 260 cartoons last year. Has sold to *Nugget, Dude, Gent, Beaver* and *Hustler*. Submit "brief, concise, neatly-typed gags;" 10-15/batch. Reports in 3-4 days. Pays 25% on sales to $15; 30% thereafter. SASE.
Needs: "Strictly girlie slant gags with a fresh viewpoint on what is essentially a limited human activity, and 'punchy' gaglines. No general or trade journal gags. No orgy scenes, VD gags, flashers, bride and groom, or multi-panel ideas."

RAY MORIN, 140 Hamilton Ave., Meriden CT 06450. (203)237-4500. Estab. 1959. Buys 5 gags/year; sold 75-80 cartoons last year. Has sold to *Boys' Life, Wall Street Journal*, McNaught Syndicate and King Features. Submit 7-10 gags at one time. Pays 25% commission. Holds gags "indefinitely," trying to redraw the cartoon from a different angle. SASE.
Needs: General, family, children's, medical and business. "I do 95% of my own gags, but am willing to look."

MICHAEL J. ("SKI") PELLOWSKI, Box 726, Bound Brook NJ 08805. Estab. 1973. Buys 5-15 gags/year; sold 50-100 cartoons last year. Has sold to *Sick* magazine, *Trucking, Cracked, Trash, Parody, Playboy, Pub, Gem, Crazy* and most men's magazines. Submit gag slips or gags typed on a page with triple spacing. Pays $1-5 outright purchase. SASE.
Needs: Panel-to-panel material for publication in illustrated humor magazines and comic books. Sells jokes, gags, and one-liners to well known stand up comedians. Buys performable comedy material for outright fee and polishes same for sale. Will look at anything that can be performed in night clubs or on TV. "I use few if any cartoon ideas. I will always look at jokes, gags, one-liners, panel to panel pieces of 1-3 pages for illustrated humor publications. I need original gags. My need is for material for comedians not for speakers or DJs. I am not a monthly comedy service. I build comedy routines and rework good one-liners."

IRV PHILLIPS, 2807 E. Sylvia St., Phoenix AZ 85032. Pays 25% commission; $10 minimum on syndication. SASE.
Needs: General, pantomime and word gags. Submit on 3x5 cards.

ANDREW PRESLAR, 133 N. 5th St., La Puente CA 91744. Estab. 1975. Buys 100 gags/year for use in general magazines and trade journals. Has sold to *Life Association News, Dental Survey* and *Western Horseman*. Submit gags on 3x5 slips of paper; 10/batch. Reports in 2-3 weeks. Pays 25%. SASE.
Needs: "Sophisticated generals, general family, new woman, dental and some office gags."

DOM RINALDO, 29 Bay, 20 St., Brooklyn NY 11214. Estab. 1960. Buys 30 gags/year; sold 40 cartoon last year. Has sold to *Cavalier, Oui, Saturday Evening Post, Hustler*, etc. Submit gags on 3x5 cards, numbered or coded. "Keep gag brief." Reports immediately. Pays 25%. SASE.
Needs: "Girlie," family and trade. No golf gags, or making fun of religion.

LEE RUBIN, 9 Murray Ave., Port Washington NY 11050. Buys 20 gags/year; sold 41 cartoons last year. Interested in gags concerning eyesight, eyeglasses and optometrists. Submit maximum of 25 gags at a time. Pays 40% commission. Reports in 1 month. May hold gags for 2 months. SASE.

FRANK ("DEAC") SEMATONES, 5226 Mt. Alifan Dr., San Diego CA 92111. (714)279-7178. Estab. 1950. Sold 500 cartoons last year. Has sold to *National Enquirer* and male and girlie magazines. Pays 25% commission. Reports "immediately, but will keep unsold gags going forever unless return is requested." SASE.
Needs: Male, sexy, girlie. Must be new, fresh and funny. "I need a gagwriter to collaborate on new developing comic strip *Spondulics* (two printers in the Polish mint)—federal reserve notes vs. dollars payable in silver, inflation, declining dollar, etc."

JOSEPH SERRANO, Box 42, Gloucester MA 01930. Cartoonist since 1950. Seasonal and social comment preferred. Has sold to most major and middle markets. Pays 25% commission. SASE.

E.G. SHIPLEY, 4725 Homesdale Ave., Baltimore MD 21206. Estab. 1977. Sells to trade journals and general magazines. Sold 9 cartoons last year. Has sold to *Industry Mart, Computerworld, Tooling and Production, Industrial Machinery News, Automatic Machining*, etc. Submit gags typed on 3x5 cards; 15-20 to a batch. May hold unsold gags indefinitely. Pays 30%.

Needs: Needs general, computer, office and machine shop gags. "I am doing mostly trade journal cartoons." No medical gags.

JOHN W. SIDE, 335 Wells St., Darlington WI 53530. Cartoonist since 1940. Interested in "small-town, local happening gags with a general slant." Pays 25% commission. Will send a sample cartoon to a gagwriter for $1. Returns rejected material "immediately." SASE.

SCOTT SMITH, 170 Madison Ave., Danville KY 40422. (606)236-9390. Estab. 1962. Buys 260 gags/year; sold over 500 cartoon last year. Has sold to *Independent Banker, Saturday Evening Post, New Woman* and *Changing Times*. Submit gags on 3x5 cards; 10-15/batch. Reports "immediately." Pays 25%. SASE.
Needs: "General topics suitable for *National Enquirer, Saturday Evening Post*, etc.

JOHN STINGER, Box 202, New Hope PA 18938. Cartoonist since 1967. Interested in general, family and general business gags. Interested in business-type gags first. Would like to see more captionless sight gags. Currently doing a syndicated panel on business, for which funny ideas are needed. Has sold to *Argosy, True, Industry Week* and other major markets. "Index cards are fine, but please keep short." Pays 25% commission; "more to top writers." Bought about 50 gags last year. Can hold unsold gags for as long as a year. SASE.

BOB THAVES, Box 67, Manhattan Beach CA 90266. Cartoonist for more than 20 years. Pays 25% commission. Returns rejected material in 1-2 weeks. May hold unsold gags indefinitely. SASE.
Needs: Gags "dealing with anything except raw sex. Also buy gags for syndicated (daily and Sunday) panel, *Frank & Ernest*. I prefer offbeat gags (no standard, domestic scenes) for that, although almost any general gag will do."

MARVIN TOWNSEND, 631 W. 88th St., Kansas City MO 64114. Fulltime cartoonist for over 30 years. Buys 12 gags/year; sold about 450 cartoons last year. Interested in gags with a trade journal or business slant. Such as office executives, professional engineers, plant managers, doctors, etc. "Religious and children gags also welcome. Captioned or captionless. No general gags wanted. Don't waste postage sending general gags or worn-out material." Sells to trade and business publications and church and school magazines. Prefers batches of 12 gags. Pays 25% commission. SASE.

BARDULF UELAND, Halstad MN 56548. Estab. 1969. Has sold to *Parade, Legion, New Woman*, King Features, McNaught Syndicate. Submit 12-15 gags at one time. Pays 25% commission. Reports in 1-3 days, but holds unsold gags indefinitely unless return is requested. SASE.
Needs: General, family, medical and farm gags. No sex.

ART WINBURG, 21 McKinley Ave., Jamestown NY 14701. Cartoonist since 1936. Has sold to *National Star, VFW Magazine, Physician's Management, American Legion, Modern Medicine, New Woman* and *Highlights for Children*. Pays 25% commission. Returns rejected material "usually within a week, sometimes same day as received." Will return unsold gags "on request. Always a possibility of eventually selling a cartoon." SASE.
Needs: All types of gags; general, family, trade and professional journals, adventure, sports, medical, children's magazines. Gagwriter should "use variety, be original, and avoid old cliches." Would prefer not to see gags about "smoke signals, flying carpets, moon men, harems, or cannibals with some person in cooking pot."

ANDY WYATT, 10960 SW 174th Terrace, Miami FL 33157. (305)233-9418. Cartoonist since 1960. Buys several dozen gags/year; sold several hundred cartoons last year. Pays 25% commission. Returns rejected material in "1-2 weeks if I definitely can't use; sometimes longer if I feel there's a possibility." May hold unsold gags "until I sell, unless a writer specifies he wants gags back at a certain time." SASE.
Needs: General, topical, family, and business. "I like visual gags, but any good gag is OK."

Greeting Card Publishers

The greeting card field is "very healthy and ever expanding," says Vivian Greene, president of Vivian Greene, Inc. Richard Myles of Rust Craft Greeting Cards says the greetings industry is "as good as ever—perhaps even better, with many promotional ideas emerging, and books and calendars now among the greeting card offerings." The industry-wide healthiness is good news for writers; a representative of one firm notes that he's "heavily dependent upon writers." With good reason. A great drawing or photo attracts the buyer to the card, but the message *sells* it. "The gag is more important than the drawing," notes one greeting card editor.

Greeting card publishers usually specialize in certain types of cards, and many companies use distinctive styles. In fact, one publisher notes that the field is growing even more specialized. This specialization forces writers to study the products of any publishers they're interested in. "Most outside freelance writers are not aware of the style and type of copy required," laments George F. Stanley, editor of Vagabond Creations. "So, in 99% of the submissions, there is no way the writer's particular style can ever tie in with that of a specific company." The advice of one publisher to "get acquainted with our greeting cards and try to fit in" seems simplistic; yet it summarizes comments from a variety of publishers.

A stop at your local card shop will give you a good idea of what's currently selling. Ask the shop owner what's popular. Visiting the shop might also lead you to additional markets for your ideas. Many greeting card publishers issue a regularly revised "current needs list"; check with individual publishers to see if such a list is available. *Greetings Magazine* (Mackay Publishing Corp., 95 Madison Ave., New York City 10016) lists addresses of greeting card publishers, and the National Association of Greeting Card Publishers (170 Mason St., Greenwich, Connecticut) has a membership roster available to writers. Consulting *The Greeting Card Writer's Handbook*, edited by H. Joseph Chadwick (Writer's Digest Books), is also wise.

To submit conventional greeting card material, type or neatly print your verses on either 4x6 or 3x5 slips of paper or file cards. For humorous or studio card ideas, either fold sheets of paper into card dummies about the size and shape of an actual card, or use file cards. For ideas that use attachments, try to get the actual attachment and put it on your dummy; if you can't, suggest the attachment. For mechanical card ideas, you must make a workable mechanical dummy. Most companies will pay more for attachment and mechanical card ideas.

Neatly print or type your idea on the dummy as it would appear on the finished card. Type your name and address on the back of each dummy or card, along with an identification number (which helps both you and the editor in keeping records). Always maintain records of where and when ideas were submitted; use a file card for each idea.

Submit 10-15 ideas at a time (this constitutes a "batch"). Keep the file cards for each batch together until rejected ideas are returned.

Listings below cover publishers' requirements for verse, gags and other product ideas. Artwork requirements are also covered when a company is interested in a complete package of art and idea. You'll encounter these terms when using listings:

Contemporary card: upbeat greeting; studio card belonging to the present time; always rectangular in shape.
Conventional card: general card; formal or sentimental, usually verse or simple one-line prose.
Current needs list: see *market letter.*
Cute card: informal, gentle humor; slightly soft feminine-type card in

which the text is closely tied to the illustration.

Everyday card: for occasions occurring every day of the year, such as birthdays and anniversaries.

Humorous card: card in which the sentiment is expressed humorously; text may be either verse or prose, but usually verse; illustrations usually tied closely to the text, and much of the humor is derived from the illustration itself; often illustrated with animals.

Informal card: see *cute card.*

Inspirational card: slightly more poetic and religious-oriented card within the conventional card line; purpose is to inspire, and is usually poetical and almost Biblical in nature.

Juvenile card: designed to be sent to children up to about age 12; text is usually written keeping in mind that an adult will send the card

Market letter: current needs list; list of categories and themes of ideas and kinds of cards an editor currently needs; some companies publish monthly market letters; others only when the need arises.

Mechanical: card that contains action of some kind.

Novelty: refers to ideas that fall outside realm of greeting cards, but sent for the same occasion as greeting cards; usually boxed differently and sold at prices different from standard greeting card prices.

Other product lines: booklets, books, bumper stickers, buttons, calendars, figurines, games, invitations and announcements, mottos, note papers, placemats, plaques, post cards, posters, puzzles, slogans, stationery and wallhangings.

Pop-up: a mechanical action in which a form protrudes from the inside of the card when the card is opened.

Promotions: usually a series or group of cards (although not confined to cards) that have a common feature and are given special sales promotion.

Punch-outs: sections of a card, usually in juvenile cards, that are perforated so they can be easily removed.

Risque card: one that jokes about sex.

Seasonal card: published for the several special days that are observed during the year, such as Christmas, Easter, graduation and Halloween.

Sensitivity card: beautiful, sensitive, personal greeting.

Soft line: gentle, "me-to-you message" in greeting form.

Studio: contemporary cards using short, punchy gags in keeping with current trends in humor; always rectangular in shape; often irreverent.

Topical: ideas or cards discussing current subjects.

Visual gags: a gag in which most, if not all, the humor depends upon the drawing or series of drawings used in the card; similar to captionless cartoons.

AMBERLEY GREETING CARD CO., Box 37902, Cincinnati OH 45222. (513)242-6630. Editor: Ralph Crown. Buys all rights. Send for list of current needs. Submit ideas on regular 3x5 cards. "We always take a closer look if artwork (a rough sketch on a separate sheet of paper that shows how the card would appear) is submitted with the gag. It gives us a better idea of what the writer has in mind." No conventional cards. Reports in 3-4 weeks. May hold ideas for approximately 2 weeks. SASE.

Humorous, Studio and Promotions: Buys all kinds of studio and humorous everyday cards, "including odd captions such as promotion, apology, etc. Birthday studio is still the best selling caption. We never get enough. We look for belly laugh humor, not cute. All types of risque are accepted. No ideas with attachments. We prefer short and snappy ideas. The shorter gags seem to sell best. We are in special need of get well and hospital studio." Would prefer not to see Easter, Mother's Day, and Father's Day ideas. Buys 200 items/year. Pays $25. Occasionally buys promotion ideas. Payment negotiable, "depending entirely upon our need, the quantity, and work involved."

Other Product Lines: Promotions, plaques, mottoes, post cards, buttons, and bumper stickers. "Humor is what we look for in other product lines." Pays $25 for mottoes and bumper stickers.

AMERICAN GREETINGS CORP., 10500 American Rd., Cleveland OH 44144. Buys all rights. Pays on acceptance. "Always research the card racks before submitting ideas. Like to see total card-line concepts as well as individual card ideas." Query. Does not acept unsolicited material. Reports in 4 weeks. SASE.

Conventional: Considers holiday material, but chances are always better with everyday occasions. No limits on the type of material used, as long as it's of professional quality, and salable. Most sales made are by copy which captures some fundamental aspect of people-to-people sentiment. Verse or prose; any length. Query should be directed to Editor, General Editorial.

Soft Touch: " 'Conversational' is the word to describe our style here. We are looking for sincere and simple (but not trite) ways to say 'Happy Birthday', 'Get better soon', 'I love you" and 'I'm glad we're friends'. We look at any idea, any time, and are in the market for the captions mentioned above." Direct query to Soft Touch Editor.

Humorous: "Our humorous line ranges from whimsical compliments to zap-em punch lines. Besides the usual birthday, get well and friendship directions, we're in the market for family captions, especially mother, father, brother, sister, daughter and son. We don't buy *much* here, but we're always interested in new and original approaches." Send query to Humor Editor.

Studio: "We're looking for funny and fresh material—try for the unexpected inside line. We look at anything, any time—birthdays, get well, friendship, holiday." Query should be addressed to Studio Editor.

Juvenile: "Our juvenile cards range from baby's first birthday to young adult. We don't buy many freelance verses, but we are always interested in concept directions in the things-to-do or novelty areas." Query should be directed to the Juvenile Editor.

Other Product Lines: Calendars, books and promotional concepts.

BARKER GREETING CARD CO., Rust Craft Park, Dedham MA 02026. Humor Director: Bill Bridgeman. Submissions should be typed or neatly printed on separate 3x5 cards or folded paper. Name, address and a code number should be on back of each idea submitted. SASE must accompany each batch. Artwork on ideas is not necessary. Reports in 1-3 weeks. Buys all rights. Pays on acceptance. Send SASE for *Market Letter*.

Needs: Studio card ideas for all everyday and seasonal captions; special need for card ideas involving the use of mechanicals and attachments. Specific needs are detailed in their periodic *Market Letter*. Seasonal needs include Christmas, Hanukkah, Valentine's Day, St. Patrick's Day, Mother's Day, Father's Day, graduation, Halloween and Thanksgiving. Everyday captions are birthday, friendship and get well. "All verse should be as concise as possible." Promotions, mottoes, etc., may be submitted at any time.

Payment: Humorous and studio, $25 minimum.

BRILLIANT ENTERPRISES, 117 W. Valerio St., Santa Barbara CA 93101. Editor: Ashleigh Brilliant. Buys all rights. Will send a catalog and sample set for $1. Submit seasonal material any time. "Submit words and art in black on 5½x3½ horizontal, thin white paper. Regular bond okay, but no card or cardboard." Does not want to see "topical references, subjects limited to American culture, or puns." Reports "usually in 10 days." SASE.

Other Product Lines: Post cards. "All our cards are everyday cards in the sense that they are not intended only for specific seasons, holidays, or occasions." Messages should be "of a highly original nature, emphasizing subtlety, simplicity, insight, wit, profundity, beauty, and felicity of expression. Accompanying art should be in the nature of oblique commentary or decoration rather than direct illustration. Messages should be of universal appeal, capable of being appreciated by all types of people and of being easily translated into other languages. Since our line of cards is highly unconventional, it is essential that freelancers study it before submitting." Limit of 17 words/card. Buys 150 items/year. Pays $25 for "complete ready-to-print word and picture design."

BUTTERNUT CARDS, INC., 103 Hillside Rd., Montague MA 01351. (413)863-2556. Art Director: Claudia Diperi. Estab. 1977. Submit samples; 1- to 8-line verse; 3-6/batch. Submit seasonal/holiday material 6 months in advance. SASE. Reports in 3 weeks. Buys all rights. Pays on acceptance.

Needs: "Our company has developed a line of cards and stationery around quality pen and ink drawings and silkscreens of country and outdoor themes. We are looking for quality verse that is consistent with those themes." Uses inspirational, soft line, conventional, sensitivity and nostalgia. Also interested in material for calendars. No religious themes. Buys 50 items/year. Pays $10-25/idea.

CREATIVE PAPERS, INC., c/o Yankee, Inc., Dublin NH 03444. Art Director: Susann Rogers. "Send photocopies that we can keep, simply because we do not have the time to write to each individual that submits work. If work is submitted to be returned, include a cover note and SASE." Reports in 4 weeks. Buys all reproduction rights to the concept of existing art, or reproduction rights for a specified product, or the original art and exclusive reproduction rights. Pays on acceptance. Free information sheet and registration form available for request with SASE.

Needs: "We are looking for a fresh approach to copy ideas—clever, sophisticated. We are interested in verse and *good* poetry that expresses popular sentiments, and 1- and 2-line copy and card ideas." Especially interested in material for Christmas, Valentine's Day, get well, Easter, birthday, love, sorry, thank you, congratulations, thinking of you, best wishes and invitations. Seasonal/holiday material must be submitted a year in advance. "We prefer simple verse rather than long, melodramatic verses—copy that is intelligent, sensitive and thoughtful."

Payment: Soft line, sensitivity, humorous, conventional, inspirational, informal, juvenile, invitations, announcements; payment negotiated.

CUSTOM CARD OF CANADA, LTD., 1239 Adanac St., Vancouver, British Columbia, Canada V6A 2C8. (604)253-4444. Editor: E. Bluett. Estab. 1964. Submit ideas on 3x5 cards or small mock-ups in batches of ten. Reports in 3-6 weeks. Buys world rights. Pays on acceptance. Current needs list for SAE and International Reply Coupon.

Needs: All types, both risque and nonrisque. "The shorter, the better." Birthday, belated birthday, get well, anniversary, thank you, congratulations, miss you, new job, etc. Seasonal ideas needed for Christmas by March; Valentine's Day (September); graduation (December); Mother's Day and Father's Day (December).

Payment: Studio, etc., $50 minimum.

THE DRAWING BOARD, INC., 256 Regal Row, Dallas TX 75221. (214)637-0390. Editorial Director: Jimmie Fitzgerald. Estab. 1956. Submit ideas on 3x5 cards, typed, with name and address on each card; 20/batch. SASE. Reports in 2 weeks. Buys 200 items/year. Pays on acceptance.

Needs: Announcements; conventional; humorous; informal; inspirational; everyday; seasonal; invitations; juvenile; and studio cards. No 'blue' or sex humor. Pays $30-50.

Other Product Lines: Calendars. Pays $200-600.

THE EVERGREEN PRESS, Box 4971, Walnut Creek CA 94596. (415)825-7850. Editor: Malcolm Nielsen. Buys all rights. Pays on publication. Write for specifications sheet. Submit Christmas material any time. "Initial offering may be in the rough. Will not publish risque or 'cute' art." Reports in 2 weeks. SASE.

Conventional, Inspirational, and Studio: Interested in submissions from artists. Publishes everyday cards in a "very specialized series using verse from Shakespeare, for example. Our major line is Christmas. We avoid the Christmas cliches and attempt to publish offbeat type of art. For Christmas cards, we do not want Santa Claus, Christmas trees, wreaths, poodle dogs or kittens. We don't want sentimental, coy or cloying types of art. For everyday greeting cards we are interested in series of cards with a common theme. We are not interested in single designs with no relation to each other. We can use either finished art which we will separate or can use the artist's separations. Our studio lines are a complete series with a central theme for the series. We do not try to compete in the broad studio line, but only with specialized series. We do not purchase verse alone, but only complete card ideas, including verse and art." Payment for art on "royalty basis, depending on the form in which it is submitted."

Other Product Lines: Bookplates, note papers, invitations, children's books, stationery. Payment negotiated.

D. FORER AND CO., 511 E. 72 St., New York NY 10021. Editor: Barbara Schaffer. Buys all rights. Pays on acceptance. Sometimes holds material up to 3 weeks. SASE.

Informal and Humorous: Anniversary, thank you, new home, birthday, get well, engagement, and general cards. A hint of sophistication. Cute humor. "We read all occasions all year round; Valentine, Christmas, Father's Day, Mother's Day. We prefer 3- to 4-line verse. Buys 100 items/year. Pays $20 for verse, $50 for humorous ideas."

FRAN MAR GREETING CARDS, LTD., Box 1057, Mt. Vernon NY 10550. (914)664-5060. President: Stan Cohen. Estab. 1958. Buys 100-300 items/year. Submit ideas in small batches (no more than 15 in a batch) on 3x5 sheets or cards. SASE. Reports in 1-2 weeks. Buys all rights. Pays on the 15th of the month following acceptance.

Needs: Soft line; invitations; and studio cards. "We are currently in need of risque, birthday, friendship, anniversary and get well card ideas. Copy should be short and have a punch." No juvenile or seasonal material.

Other Product Lines: Promotions (pays $15-50); and plaques (pays $15). "We currently need stationery and pad ideas (with or without captions, humorous or functional); novelty ideas in the paper area; and tote and accessory bag captions."

FREEDOM GREETING CARD CO., INC., 409½ Canal's End Rd., Bristol PA 19007. (215)785-4042. President: Jerome Wolk. Estab. 1969. Buys 200 ideas/year. Query. Limit submissions to batches of 12. Submit seasonal/holiday material 1 year in advance. SASE. Reports in 4-6 weeks. Buys all rights. Pays on acceptance. Needs list for SASE.
Needs: Announcements; conventional; humorous; inspirational; invitations; juvenile; sensitivity; and Spanish. Pays $1/line.

GIBSON GREETING CARDS, INC., 2100 Section Rd., Cincinnati OH 45237. Submit ideas on file cards, 10-15 at one time. SASE. Address materials to editor of appropriate line: seasonal, everyday, studio, humorous, juvenile, cute products. Reports in 2-3 weeks. Buys all rights. Pays on acceptance. Writer's guidelines sheet for SASE.
Needs: Humorous, studio, conventional, everyday and seasonal, cute and juvenile. "For humorous and studio, we look for short, original, punchy, funny, sendable, contemporary ideas. We can't use attachments or very tricky hand folds, but are always interested in clever use of a simple fold. We look for a different idea and/or an original way of expressing the usual sentiments. Prose, or rhymed verse. We'd like to see more good, fresh, humorous material—short, clever ideas with good illustration possibilities for an unexpected ending inside. Also, good conventional rhymed verse, both everyday and seasonal, a fresh approach, with good rhyme and meter, and contemporary wording with different rhyming words. We do not purchase inspirational material; we use Helen Steiner Rice's material for our inspirational line. However, we do purchase religious verse and prose for the major sending situations and seasons. We can't use poetry, except as it ties in with a direct message and greeting card category. Send ideas for all the usual seasons; Christmas and Valentine's Day are the largest, followed by Mother's and Father's Day, and Easter. Need various family categories and combination relatives for all of these (except, no family categories for studio). We work about 1½ years ahead of season. Need everyday cards for general and family birthdays; wedding anniversaries, sympathy and illness. We'd like to see more combinations of material; rhymed verse plus prose; quotes with prose or rhymed verse, etc. Most conventional verse runs 4 to 8 lines, but can run to 16 or even 20, for a special 'page-2'."
Payment: Humorous, $25-50; studio, $50; and conventional prose, $20.

VIVIAN GREENE, INC., 15240 NW 60th Ave., Miami Lakes FL 33014. President: Vivian Greene. Buys all rights. SASE. Buys 200 items/year. Pays on acceptance.
Needs: Only humorous, whimsical comic cards.
Payment: Humorous/studio, $25-150.
Other Product Lines: Gift books, $100-300. Greeting books, $75-300.

HALLMARK CARDS., INC., Contemporary Design Department, 25th and McGee, Kansas City MO 64141. Editor, Contemporary & Humorous: Nancy Saulsbury. Estab. 1910. Submit ideas either on card mock-ups or 3x5 cards; 10-20/batch. SASE. Reports in 2-3 weeks. Buys all rights. Pays on acceptance; "must have writer's Social Security number in order to pay." Market list for SASE.
Needs: Humorous and Studio cards. Pays $55 maximum. "Will pay $40 for an idea needing major or complete change in editorial content."

KALAN, INC., 7002 Woodbine Ave., Philadelphia PA 19151. President: M. Kalan. SASE. Reports in 1 week. Pays on acceptance.
Needs: Ideas for good humor studios and adult (X-rated) studios; primarily birthday. Short verse preferred.
Payment: Humorous, $10-20.
Other Product Lines: Posters (humorous, clever), $10-20.

ALFRED MAINZER, INC., 27-08 40th Ave., Long Island City NY 11101. (212)392-4200. Editor: Arwed Baenisch. Buys all rights. SASE.
Conventional, Inspirational, Informal and Juvenile: All types of cards and ideas. Traditional material. All seasonals and occasionals wanted. Payment for card ideas negotiated on individual basis only.

MARK I, 1733 W. Irving Park Rd., Chicago IL 60613. Editor: Alex H. Cohen. Buys all rights. Reports in 2 weeks. SASE.
Sensitivity, Humorous, Studio, Invitations and Announcements: "The verse should fit the cards;

humorous for the studio cards; sensitive for the 'tenderness' line. Also interested in Christmas, (both sensitivity and studio) and Valentine's Day (sensitivity only), Mother's Day and Father's Day (studio and sensitivity), graduation (studio), Halloween and St. Patrick's Day (studio). Verse should be short and direct, typewritten on one side of 3x5 card." Length: 3-4 lines. Pays $35 for studio ideas; $35 for sensitivity ideas; and $125-150 for photographs.
Other Product Lines: Wall plaques and poster verse.

MILLER DESIGNS, INC., 9 Ackerman Ave., Emerson NJ 07630. Editor: Whitney McDermot. Buys all rights. Submit seasonal ideas any time. Reports in 3 to 4 weeks. SASE.
Soft Line, Humorous, Conventional, Informal and Juvenile: Birthday, anniversary, get well, friendship, bon voyage, birth, as well as ideas for invitations and announcements. Mechanicals if possible, whimsical ideas, clever, witty, and humorous. Also buys Christmas, Easter, Valentine's Day and Mother's Day. Prefers 1 line for front of card and no more than 2 lines for the inside. Pay is open.

NORCROSS, INC., 950 Airport Rd., West Chester PA 19380. (215)436-8000. Art Services Manager: Nancy Lee Fuller. Submit ideas on 3x5 cards with writer's name on each card and SASE. Reports in 3 weeks. Buys all rights. Pays on acceptance. Current needs list available on request.
Needs: Conventional verse and prose in any category (up to 8 lines). All types of humor for all occasions (prose and verse) with or without mechanicals. Risque is OK, short of X-rated type. Especially interested in general, relative and love prose and humorous verse (relative and all-occasion). Ideas for all seasonals also sought. Seasonal schedule available on request. No juvenile or X-rated material.
Payment: Regular verse, $3/line; short prose, $12 minimum; studio/humor, $25/idea minimum.

PANACHE PAPETERIE PRODUCTS, Bank Village, New Ipswich NH 03071. Director of Product: Lew Fifield. For the sophisticated professional, 25-40 years old. Uses seasonal and everyday material. Buys all rights. Photocopied submissions OK. "Material will not be returned unless a SASE is included." Reports on queries in 2 weeks, on mss in 1 month. Free sample copy and writer's guidelines.
Needs: Avant-garde, haiku and light verse poetry in the traditional (not sugary, super sentimental) card text. Submit no more than 12 poems at one time. Length: 5-10 lines. Pays $25-50.
Tips: Textual postcards is the area most open to freelancers.

PAPER M'SHEA, 4640 SW 75th Ave., Miami FL 33155. President: Robert Shea. Query with samples. Reports in 4-6 weeks. Buys all rights. Pays on publication.
Needs: "Looking for strong new graphic ideas for invitations, notes and announcements. Special interest in juvenile designs for ages 3-8.
Payment: Invitations, announcements, $25.

RED FARM STUDIO, 334 Pleasant St., Pawtucket RI 02860. Art Director/Editor: Sondra L. Davidonis. Estab. 1948. Send 6-12 submissions at one time. Submit on 3x5 index cards. SASE. Reports in 1-2 weeks. Pays on acceptance. Pay varies.
Needs: Material for announcements, humorous, inspirational, conventional, informal, sensitivity, Mother's Day, Father's Day, Easter and Christmas (relative or general). Pay varies.
Other Product Lines: Coloring books, paintables, placemats, gift wrap and note paper. Does not want to see studio-type or related subjects.

RUNNING STUDIO, INC., 1020 Park St., Paso Robles CA 93446. (805)238-2232. Editor: Judi Gorham. Submit ideas on 3x5 cards. SASE. Reports in 2 weeks. Buys all rights. Buys 70 items/year. Pays on acceptance.
Needs: Captions and sentiments for two quality card lines: A contemporary, studio line and a more formal, elegant line. "We're looking for humorous, catchy and lighthearted captions for all everyday occasions to go with cute and whimsical art, all in good taste. These should be clever and can be punchy, but not sarcastic or heavy gags. No Christmas. Our second line of pretty and elegant designs need soft, meaningful and more sincere type sentiments. Sensitive, traditional expressions in everyday language for all card sending occasions plus Easter, Valentine, graduation, Mother's Day and Father's Day."

RUST CRAFT GREETING CARDS, INC., Rust Craft Park, Dedham MA 02026. (617)329-6000. Editorial and Creative Planning Director: Richard E. Myles. Submit ideas on individual coded cards (one for each sentiment). Submit around 20 at a time to save postage costs. SASE. Reports in 2-3 weeks. Buys all rights. Buys 200-300 items/year. Pays on acceptance.

Needs: "New material needed most for masculine relations and double relatives, but will purchase material for any title if it is fresh and original, and usable by our market. We're trying to use more imagery in our line, as well as more additional copy for value at higher prices." Also needs ideas for all major seasons (Christmas, Easter, etc.). Particularly need good material for Father's Day and graduation. "Send ideas all year long. Freelancers should request our market letter to find out upcoming needs for particular seasons, however. We buy ideas for any season at any time, if they are good ones." No humorous and studio ideas. Rejects short prose unless it is distinctive and expresses an idea that is original. Also rejects highly traditional verse that sounds like copy already on the greeting card racks. Verse length: No longer than 24 lines. Juvenile material: 12 lines.

Payment: Sensitivity, $10-25; conventional and inspirational, $15-40; informal, $15-30; juvenile $15-40; invitations and announcements, $10-25. Usable quotations (must be in public domain), $5-10; negotiable rates for promotional ideas and copy.

Other Product Lines: Mottoes, $15-30; posters, $15-45; calendars, $30-50. "Generally shorter material preferred. Need material which is cute and light in tone, but inspirational in message. Copy that suggests a design is also good. Can be verse or prose, and we do use some very long inspirational copy.

STRAND ENTERPRISES, 1809½ N. Orangethorpe Park, Anaheim CA 90630. (714)871-4744. President: S. S. Waltzman. SASE. Reports in 2 weeks. Buys all rights. Pays on acceptance.

Needs: Notecards that express one's feelings about love and friendship, philosophical and inspirational; on marriage, children, human relationships, nature and faith in short, poetic form (not too deep), prose or statement. Length: 16 lines maximum.

Payment: Soft line, sensitivity, humorous, inspirational, $5-15.

Other Product Lines: Seeking ideas for humorous posters. Pays $15-25.

VAGABOND CREATIONS, 2560 Lance Dr., Dayton OH 45409. Editor: George F. Stanley Jr. Buys all rights. Submit seasonal material any time; "we try to plan ahead a great deal in advance." Submit on 3x5 cards. "We don't want artwork—only ideas." Reports in same week usually. May hold ideas 3 or 4 days. SASE for return of submissions.

Soft Line and Studio: Publishes contemporary cards. Studio verse only; no slams, puns or reference to age or aging. Emphasis should be placed on a strong surprise inside punch line instead of one that is predictable. Also prefers good use of double entendre. "Mildly risque." Purchases copy for Christmas, Valentine's and graduation. "The current style of the new 'Sophisticates' greeting card line is graphics only on the front with a short tie-in punch line on the inside of the card. General rather than specific subject matter." Buys 120 items/year. Pays $10 "for beginners; up to $15 for regular contributors."

Other Product Lines: Interested in receiving copy for mottoes and humorous buttons. "On buttons we like double-entendre expressions—preferably short. We don't want the protest button or a specific person named. We pay $10 for each button idea." Mottoes should be written in the first-person about situations at the job, about the job, confusion, modest bragging, drinking habits, etc. Pays $10 for mottoes.

Play Producers

The theater is "growing strong and tall," says ElizaBeth King, literary manager of Actors Theatre of Louisville. "In the past five years, producers in New York *and* the regions developed programs specifically designed to discover new playwrights. Why? Money earmarked for special programs was made available by the foundations, and audiences carefully nurtured on the historical and contemporary classics have developed a theater loyalty."

Like King, many producers are happy about the current state of theater and the opportunities for playwrights. They cite competitions, awards, grants, showcases and workshop productions—not to mention the increasing number of plays produced every year—as contributing to expanding playwrights' outlets. "At the moment, there are an unprecedented number of production opportunities for new plays," says David Patt, script editor of Earplay, which produces radio dramas.

Still, competition from established and unestablished playwrights alike can make breaking in "a long and tedious path," as one producer describes it. "Unknown playwrights are difficult for us to book," says Drexel H. Riley, director of the Repertory Theater of America. "It is difficult enough to sell a 'known' show and playwright."

Charles Stillwell of the Waterloo Community Playhouse echoes the thought: "I believe getting new plays produced, let alone to Broadway, is difficult today—but it's not impossible. The playwrights need more help and support, but the best plays usually get done somehow."

Theater *is* competitive, but drive, persistence and (as Stillwell pointed out) *talent* will earn you your break.

Another ingredient of success is a full understanding of theater and its conventions. "See and *do* as much theater as possible," advises one director. Involvement with a local community theater or drama group will give you a useful background in theatrical limitations, practicalities and *potentials*. Moreover, you might meet someone who will produce one of your works. Many producers would rather work with a playwright familiar to them, one who can write specifically to their needs and staging requirements, one who is readily accessible if changes must be made in the script. "For playwrights who can tailor their work to the specific needs of a professional theater like Stage South, there is significant potential," says Stage South's Tim Beall. This doesn't imply that living near the theater is a prerequisite to getting a script accepted (though some theaters ask the playwright to come to the theater while the play is rehearsed)—it simply points up that the more you can match the play with the producer, the better are your chances.

Submit your play to as many theaters as possible, but don't "shotgun" the script to anyone with a mailbox. Instead, take careful aim at as many theaters compatible with your work as you can find. Multiple submissions in theater are condoned and sometimes encouraged. Some producers hold a script for months before deciding to accept or rejected it; multiple submissions allow you to present your script many directors, wasting no time if one or two dally in making a decision. Besides, a play's acceptance by more than one theater presents no conflict, unless the groups work in the same region, or if both want to present the premiere production of the play. Multiple productions (either simultaneously or at different times) of a play is standard; in fact, play publishers depend on multiple productions of their material for their income.

Once your play has been produced, consider submitting it to a play publisher. For a 50% commission, a publisher will handle all marketing of your play, leaving you time to write new material. See the Play Publishers section for details.

Listed below are markets ranging from small, amateur companies to Broadway and off-Broadway producers. Nonpaying theater workshops are included because the experience and exposure offered by these outlets can give playwrights exposure and a chance at commercial production.

Carefully study the requirements of each market before submitting. Note limitations in cast size, scenery, etc. In general, keep the script simple in terms of production requirements (though you should leave room in the script for elaborate production should the director/producer want to add it). Many of these groups are touring companies that appreciate small casts and easy-to-transport scenery.

Most groups listed here concentrate on straight plays (as opposed to musicals). Ironically, one producer noted that a new playwright has a better chance getting a musical produced than getting a drama on the stage. Consult *Songwriter's Market* (Writer's Digest Books) for more specifics on play producers and publishers that solicit musicals.

Most producers want to see completed scripts, but a few will ask that you write them a letter describing your work and yourself before you submit the play itself. If submitting a musical, include a cassette tape demonstrating the songs. Some producers ask, however, that you not send the cassette until they've had a chance to review the "book"—that is, the playscript proper.

Whether you write musicals or straight plays, you can be confident that producers will give your work a careful reading. Everyone wants to produce the best possible work from the best playwrights. John Maynard Jr. of Louisiana's Otrabanda Company sums up why when he asks, "Isn't theater only as healthy as its playwrights?"

ACADEMY FESTIVAL THEATRE, Box 88, Lake Forest IL 60045. Artistic Director: Mr. Vivian Mathalon. Plays will be performed by a professional company from June through mid-September. Audience: well-educated, intelligent. 3-act plays considered. Pays 6% for new scripts. Asks for "certain vested rights." SASE. Reports in 2-4 months. Produces 1-2 plays/year.

ALLEY THEATRE, 615 Texas Ave., Houston TX 77002. A resident professional theater; large stage seating 798; arena stage seating 296.
Needs: "Good plays, with no length restrictions. No musicals." Royalty arrangements vary. Send complete script. SASE. Reports in 6-12 weeks. Produces 6-8 plays/year.

THE AMERICAN REPERTORY THEATRE OF CINCINNATI, 2319 Clifton Ave., Cincinnati OH 45219. (513)241-2376. Artreach Director: Kathryn Schultz Miller. Estab. 1976. Produces 3 musicals and 7 nonmusicals a year; 5 are originals. "The American Repertory Theatre of Cincinnati is a professional children's theater. We have two divisions: a resident 'dinner theater' for children called Peanut Butter Theatre and a program that tours short plays to schools called Artreach. For Peanut Butter Theatre we choose plays for an audience of children aged 5-12. For Artreach we choose one play for pre-schools, two plays for elementary schools and one play for high schools." Query, submit complete ms, or call to discuss work in progress. Reports on Artreach by mid-April and Peanut Butter Theatre by first part of May. Buys exclusive rights to premiere. Artreach pays $3-5/performance for approximately 75 performances/year. Peanut Butter Theatre pays $20/performance, 6 performances per show. Submissions with SASE will be returned, however, they would like to keep them on file.
Needs: "New and innovative scripts for young people adaptable to dinner theater (peanut butter sandwich lunch) for children. For the tour we like plays with educational interest such as Appalachian culture and African myths. We are interested in seeing anything with audience participation or scripts that promote intimacy between actors and audience." Tour scripts must not exceed 45 minutes running time and must require only four actors, minimal costumes and set. They prefer plays for both divisions to be adaptable to being staged in the round or three-quarter round.

AMERICAN STAGE FESTIVAL, Box 225, Milford NH 03055. Artistic Director: Harold Defelice. Plays performed at summer festival (professional equity company) for audience of all

ages, interests, education and sophistication levels. Query with synopsis. Produces 15 musicals (10%) and nonmusicals (90%) a year (6 are mainstage and 9 are children's productions); 40% are originals. Pays 5% standard royalty; "sometimes an additional stipend to playwright if Festival wishes to retain some continuing rights to the script." SASE. Reports in 1 month.
Needs: "The Festival can do comedies, musicals and dramas. However, the most frequent problems come from plays not fitting into the resident acting company system (all men, all young, all black, for examples) and/or that are bolder in language and action than a general mixed audience will accept. We emphasize plays that move; long and philosophical discussion-oriented plays are generally not done. Festival plays are chosen to present scale and opportunities for scenic and costume projects far beyond the 'summer theater' type of play." Length: 2-3 acts.

BARTER THEATRE, Main St., Abingdon VA 24210. Producer: Rex Partington.
Needs: "Good plays, particularly comedies." Two or three acts, preferably, but will consider good quality plays of shorter length. Pays 5% royalties. Send complete script. SASE.

BERKSHIRE THEATRE FESTIVAL, INC., E. Main St., Stockbridge MA 01262. Artistic Director: Josephine R. Abady. Estab. 1928. Submit complete ms. Reports in 4-6 months. Rights purchased "depend on the level of production given." Produces 10-26 plays a year (6 are mainstage and 10-20 are second spaces); originals vary season to season. Pays in royalties for full production, in fees for reading. SASE.
Needs: "The Berkshire Theatre Festival tends to concentrate on plays that illuminate or describe the American experience, either fictive or factual."

THE BOLTON HILL DINNER THEATRE, 1111 Park Ave., Baltimore MD 21201. Manager: A.L. Dorsett. Professional dinner theater. Public audience, middle-aged, who prefer comedy. No more than 5 characters in cast. Uses 3-act comedy and revue material. Payment negotiable. Rarely copyrights plays. Send complete script SASE. Produces 10 plays a year.

GERT BUNCHEZ AND ASSOCIATES, INC., 7730 Carondelet, St. Louis MO 63105. President: Gert Bunchez. "We feel that the time is propitious for the return of stories to radio. It is our feeling that it is not necessary to 'bring back' old programs, and that there certainly should be contemporary talent to write mystery, detective, suspense, children's stories, soap operas, etc. We syndicate radio properties to clients and stations. Requirements are plays with sustaining lead characters, 5 minutes to 30 minutes in length, suitable for radio reproduction. Disclaimer letter must accompany scripts. Produces nonmusicals only, according to need; majority are originals. Rates from $100 per script if acceptable for radio production and actually produced." SASE.

CASA MANANA MUSICALS, INC., 3101 W. Lancaster, Box 9054, Fort Worth TX 76107. (817)332-9319. Producer/General Manager: Bud Franks. Estab. 1958. Produces 12 plays/year. "All performances are staged at Casa Manana Theatre." Query. Reports in 2 months. Produces Summer Musicals (uses Equity people only), Theatre for Youth and new plays. Theater-in-the-round or proscenium.
Needs: Scripts suitable for family productions.

EUGENE S. CASASSA, Ashby West Rd., Fitchburg MA 01420. (617)342-6592. Director: Eugene S. Casassa. Estab. 1963. Produces 8 plays/year. Submit complete ms. Reports in 2 months. Buys one week's production rights. Pays $100-150/week. SASE. Produces a very wide range of plays in a small theater and limited budget.

THE CHANGING SCENE THEATER, 1527½ Champa St., Denver CO 80202. Director: Alfred Brooks. Year-round productions in theater space. Cast may be made up of both professional and amateur actors. For public audience; age varies, but mostly youthful, and interested in taking a chance on new and/or experimental works. No limit to subject matter or story themes. Emphasis is on the innovative. "Also, we require that the playwright be present for at least one performance of his work, if not for the entire rehearsal period. We have a small stage area, but are able to convert to round, semi-round or environmental. Prefer to do plays with limited sets and props." 1-act, 2-act and 3-act. Produces 8-10 nonmusicals a year; all are originals. "We do not pay royalties, or sign contracts with playwrights. We function on a performance share basis of payment. Our theater seats 76; the first 38 seats go to the theater, the balance is divided among the participants in the production. The performance share process is based on the entire production run, and not determined by individual performances."

We do not copyright our plays." Send complete script. SASE. Reporting time varies; usually several months.

CHELSEA THEATER CENTER, 407 W. 43rd St., New York NY 10036. Artistic Director: Robert Kalfin. Looking for full-length plays "that stretch the bounds of the theater in form and content. No limitation as to size of cast or physical production." Pays $500 for a 6-month option for an off-Broadway production." Works 10 months in advance. No unsolicited ms. Essential to submit advance synopsis. SASE.

ALFRED CHRISTIE, 405 E. 54th St., New York NY 10022. "The theater is a summer stock theater and many of the people in the audience are on vacation, most are over age 30." Professional cast. Two-act or three-act plays. "We would like funny situations, contemporary farces or light comedies. Scripts that are sensational in theme, that can compete with today's frank and modern films are also possible. We like a well-written play with interesting switches or avant-garde scripts that are based on reality and make sense. We would expect the author to copyright the play but if the show moves on to other theaters or Broadway or to a film, etc., we would like a small percentage of the action. We want no family situation shows, no period plays involving many period costumes. We prefer small-cast, single-set shows, but if a script is good we would do a larger cast and multiple set production." Produces 5-13 musicals (2-3) and nonmusicals (5-10) a year; 1-2 are originals, if possible. Payment varies. A percentage or a flat fee is possible. "Does the author want to come and work with the people and on the play?" Send synopsis or complete script. "We like scripts by March of each year because we must arrange publicity, hire actors, etc." SASE.

THE CLEVELAND PLAY HOUSE, Box 1989, Cleveland OH 44106. Contact: Robert Snook, New Scripts Department. Plays performed in professional LORT theater for the general public. Submit complete script. Produces 8 musicals (12%) and nonmusicals (88%) a year; 25% are originals. Buys stock rights, and sometimes first class options. Payment varies. SASE. Reports in 6 months.
Needs: "No restrictions. Vulgarity and gratuitous fads are not held in much esteem." Length: 3 acts.

CREEDE REPERTORY THEATRE, Box 269, Creede CO 81130. (303)658-2540. Managing Director: Neal R. Fenter. Estab. 1966. Produces 6 plays/year. "Plays are produced each summer in repertory in the Creede Opera House; production dates are mid-June through Labor day. The Creede Repertory Theatre is a non-Equity professional theater." Submit complete ms. Reports in 3 months. Buys performance rights only; "except for plays written under the auspices of the Creede Theatre." Pays 15-25% royalty or $15-30/performance. SASE.
Needs: "The Creede Theatre produces plays from a number of different genres, including musicals, modern comedies, absurdist plays, mysteries, period comedies and dramas, modern dramas, original and published children's plays, one-act plays. No complicated technical pieces, or plays that require large casts; also, because of the nature of the audiences that attend our plays, no plays with required nudity or excessive vulgarity can be produced." Cast size: 6 men, 5 women.

CRESSON LAKE PLAYHOUSE, Box 368, Spangler PA 15775. Artistic Director: Kenny Resinski. Estab. 1976. Produces 1 original play/year; performed in 200-seat summer barn theater for 13 performances. Submit query and synopsis. Reports in 1 month. Pays $50/performance. SASE.
Needs: "Original works dealing with occupations, trades, or professions or life styles, that would relate to a rural mountainous area. Minimal set, minimal number of men, maximal number of women." No Broadway comedies.

THE CRICKET THEATRE, 528 Hennepin Ave., Minneapolis MN 55403. (612)379-1411. Administrative Assistant: Betsy Husting. Estab. 1971. Audiences consist of adults and students. Submit complete ms. "Must include SASE." Reports in 6 months. Buys production rights for selected dates. Produces 14-15 musicals (14%) and nonmusicals (86%) a year; 64% are originals. Produces plays by living American playwrights only. One-act plays considered for Works in Progress season only.
Needs: "There are no content or form restrictions for scripts of the main season. For Works-in-Progress, any kind of a script is welcomed provided there is a spark of a good play in it. Works-in-Progress productions are seminars, readings and staged readings depending on the availability of the playwright. The focus is on the text and not the fully staged, polished performance as with the main season. All Works-in-Progress playwrights are brought to

Minneapolis to join in the play's rehearsal and revision process. Works-in-Progress cannot use plays currently under option or that have had full professional productions. Such plays will be considered only for the main season." No children's plays or large Broadway-type musicals. Cast limit: 14.

JEAN DALRYMPLE, 130 W. 56th St., New York NY 10019. Producer: Jean Dalrymple. Plays performed on Broadway, off-Broadway, showcase or summer theaters for the general public. Produces 1 play/year. Submit through agent only. Royalty as per Dramatists Guild contract. SASE. Reports in 2-4 weeks.
Needs: "Comedy or suspenseful drama. 2-3 acts at most; regular play format. No pornography."

EARPLAY, Vilas Communication Hall, 821 University Ave., Madison WI 53706. Produces radio dramas for National Public Radio Stations in the United States; jointly sponsored by the National Public Radio and WHA Radio/University of Wisconsin Extension. Scripts are accepted throughout the year with primary interest in plays demonstrating strong character treatment and clear and compelling plot lines. All work that makes creative use of the medium will be considered. Because of broadcast schedules, the 1-hour play is best suited for production. Produces 26 musicals (1%) and nonmusicals (99%) a year; all are originals. Payment: $2,000 for 60 minutes, first rights; $1,000 for 60 minutes, previously performed. Not interested in drama aimed at children, religious drama, educational/instructional material. Send SASE for writers' fact sheet to obtain complete submission details. Reports in 2-3 months. SASE.

EAST CAROLINA PLAYHOUSE, East Carolina University, Greenville NC 27834. Plays will be performed at the University Theatre, for the general public. All types and lengths of plays considered. Not copyrighted. Send complete script only. Reports usually in 6-8 weeks. SASE.

DAVID EASTWOOD, Box 266, Lake George NY 12845. Plays will be for professional casts in summer theater. Audience: public, tourists. Would like to see "Neil Simon-type comedies." Send synopsis. No drama. Maximum of 8 characters; 2 sets. Will consider 3-act plays; 2½ hours in length. Produces 4 plays/year; musicals (25%) and straight plays (75%); 10% originals. Payment flexible. Not copyrighted. Query with synopsis. SASE.

ENTERTAINMENT UNLIMITED (formerly Doug Jensen-Jensen Enterprises), 444 Ruxton Ave., Manitou Springs CO 80829. (303)685-5104. Secretary: Sharon Rose. Estab. 1960. Produces 3 musicals (50%) and nonmusicals (50%) a year; 50% are originals. Plays are performed at the Iron Springs Chateau Dinner Theatre for summer tourist audiences. Submit complete ms. Reports in 2 months. Buys exclusive rights. Pays $200-300. SASE.
Needs: "We produce only old-fashioned comedy 'mellerdramas' with western themes around 1890; approximately 1½ hours long; song parodies, sight gags, dancing, satire, puns and exaggerated gestures included. Plays are performed as a parody of old Victorian dramas. Audience participation is encouraged. There's nothing serious about our shows—they verge on being zany. Themes of mining towns and the Civil War are also welcome. Fast-paced action that is relatively simple."

ZELDA FICHANDLER, c/o Arena Stage, 6th and M Sts. SW, Washington DC 20024. Wants original plays preferably (but not necessarily) submitted through agents. "Plays with relevance to the human situation—which cover a multitude of dramatic approaches—are welcome here." Produces 12 musicals (15%) and nonmusicals (85%) a year; 50% are originals. Pays 5% of gross. Reports in 6 months. SASE.

FOLGER THEATRE GROUP, 201 E. Capitol St., Washington DC 20003. Produced in professional theater, AEA LORT Contract, for general public. All kinds of plays. "Since we produce 2 Shakespeare productions a season, we would rather not read Shakespearean adaptations or treatments." No limitations in cast, props; stage is small but flexible. Any length play. Produces 5 nonmusicals a year; 40% are originals. Payment negotiable. Send complete script or submit through agent. SASE. Reports "as soon as possible, usually 8-10 weeks."

GALWAY PRODUCTIONS, c/o New Jersey Shakespeare Festival, Madison NJ 07940. Director: Paul Barry. Looks for controversial plays on any subject. Pays standard Dramatists Guild royalty percentage. All scripts must be free and clear of subsidiary rights commitments. No musicals or one-acts. Submit synopsis or full-length play. SASE.

GEORGETOWN PRODUCTIONS, 7 Park Ave., New York NY 10016. Producers: Gerald Van De Vorst and David Singer. Estab. 1972. Produces 1-2 plays/year, off-Broadway, for a general audience. Query or submit complete ms. Reports in 3 weeks. Buys 1-year option. Pays 5-10% royalty; offers $500 advance. SASE.
Needs: Small-cast comedies, musicals and dramas. "Any and all" approaches on contemporary topics considered.

HARWICH JUNIOR THEATRE, Box 168, West Harwich MA 02671. President: Marguerite Donovan. Plays performed in summer theater with semi-professional and amateur casts for children. Produces 4 plays/year. Query with synopsis. Pays $10-15/performance. SASE. Reports in 1 year.
Needs: "We produce plays for children; adventure stories and fairy tales." Length: 2 or 3 acts; 1½ hours maximum.

HONOLULU THEATRE FOR YOUTH, Box 3257, Honolulu HI 96801. Produces plays of "1 hour without intermission. Plays are produced in Honolulu in various theater buildings and throughout Hawaii. Casts are professional with a complement of actors from the community; adult actors, with children as needed. Plays are produced for school children, preschool through high school, individual plays directed to specific age groups; also public performances." Interested in new plays, plays about Pacific countries, Pacific legends, Asian legends and Asian history. Plays must have strong character with whom young people can identify, with stress on action rather than exposition, but not at the expense of reality. Plays should be reasonably simple technically and use primarily adult characters. Elaborate musicals requiring large orchestras are not recommended. Casts up to 15, preferably. Technical requirements should be reasonably simple, as sets have to be built at one place and trucked to the theater." Produces 5 nonmusicals a year; 20-30% are originals. "We produce no musicals but we do commission original music." Royalty fee is based on number of performances. Query with synopsis only. Reports in 1-2 months. SASE.

WILLIAM E. HUNT, 801 West End Ave., New York NY 10025. Interested in reading scripts for stock production, off-Broadway and even Broadway production. "Small cast, youth-oriented, meaningful, technically adventuresome; serious, funny, far-out. Must be about people first, ideas second. No political or social tracts." Pays royalties on production. Off-Broadway, 5%; on Broadway, 5%, 7½% and 10%, based on gross. Reports in "a few weeks." SASE.

THE INNER CITY CULTURAL CENTER, 1308 S. New Hampshire Ave., Los Angeles CA 90006. (213)387-1161. Director/Readers Theatre Program: Gene Boland. Estab. 1967. Produces 4-6 plays/year, plus Readers Theatre (monthly). Produced in professional West Coast theater under Equity's 99-seat waiver. Query with synopsis. Reports in 4 weeks. "We request nonreturnable manuscripts."
Needs: "Primarily those plays by or about ethnic minorities (Asians, blacks, Hispanics and Native Americans)."

IRON SPRINGS CHATEAU, c/o Robert Kelly, 813 Duclo, Manitou Springs CO 80820. Professional cast will perform plays at a summer theater, for a general audience. "Old-fashioned, western, comedy melodramas only. Song parodies and sight gags may be included." Cast limitation of 6-7. Drops preferred to sets or flats. Looking for 2-3 act plays only; 40-50 minutes in length. Produces 3 musicals a year. "Rate of payment is $20 to $25 per performance." Send complete script only. SASE. Reports in 1 week.

JON JORY, Producing Director, Actors Theatre of Louisville, 316 W. Main St., Louisville KY 40202. Actors Theatre of Louisville is a resident professional theater operating under a L.O.R.T. contract for a 35-week season from September to June. Subscription audience of 18,000 from extremely diverse backgrounds. "Plays with a strong story line and a basically positive life view. We are not interested in situation comedies or 'absurdists' work. We are particularly interested in new musicals and small-cast straight plays. No more than 12 to 15 actors. There are two theaters, one a 640-seat thrust and one seating 200. Multiple-set shows are impossible here." Produces 19 plays a year; 50% are originals. Payment is negotiated. Submit mss to Elizabeth King, literary manager. SASE. Reports in 4 months.

LORETTO-HILTON REPERTORY THEATRE, 130 Edgar Rd., St. Louis MO 63119. Regional repertory theater, professional equity company, for general public. Plays vary in themes. Interested in any play suitable for a subscription audience of over 17,000. Also seeking small-cast, single-set plays for small experimental theater. No one-acts. Produces 8 nonmusicals a year; 25% are originals. Royalty payments negotiable. Send complete script. SASE. Reports in 4 months.

THE MAC-HAYDN THEATRE, INC., Box 204, Chatham NY 12037. (518)392-9292 (summer). Producers: Lynne Haydn, Linda MacNish. Estab. 1969. Produces 6-15 plays/year. "This is a resort area, and our audiences include rural residents and summer residents from the metropolitan New York City and Albany areas who demand professional quality productions. Submit complete ms; we can only consider a complete script and written score, and would prefer that at least a piano tape be included of the score." Reports in 2 months. Buys exclusive rights to stage production. Pays $25-100/performance. SASE.
Needs: "We are interested in musicals which are wholesome family entertainment; these should be full-length musicals, although we might consider one-act musicals in the future. There is no limitation as to topic, so long as the object is to entertain. We will consider original material as well as adaptations, but any adaptations of copyright material must include proper clearances. We are most interested in legitimate music for trained voices; no rock or fad music. We are looking for scripts which have a story to tell, and which build to a climax; no vignettes, slice of life or character study. We prefer a fast pace and good emotional content, and the score should extend the action, not cause it to stop. We are not interested in political muck-raking or controversy unless it has high entertainment value, and we will not consider obscenity, nudity or bad writing."

MAGIC THEATRE, INC., Bldg. 314, Fort Mason, San Francisco CA 94123. (415)441-8001. General Director: John Lion. Dramaturg: Martin Esslin. Script Reader: Suresa D. Galbraith. "Oldest experimental theater in California, established in 1967." For public audience, generally college-educated. General cross-section of the area with an interest in alternative theater. Plays produced in the Off-Broadway manner. Cast is part Equity, part non-Equity. Produces 10 plays/year. Submit complete ms. SASE.
Needs: "The director of the Magic Theatre's concept leans toward the Surrealist movement in the arts. The playwright should have an approach to his writing with a specific intellectual concept in mind or specific theme of social relevance. We don't want to see scripts that would be television or 'B' movies-oriented. 1- or 2-act plays considered. We pay 5% of gross; $100 advance."

MANHATTAN THEATRE CLUB, Stephen Pascal, Associate Artistic Director, 321 E. 73 St., New York NY 10021. A three-theater performing arts complex classified as Off-Broadway, using professional actors. "We have a large, diversified audience which includes a large number of season subscribers. We want plays about contemporary problems and people. No special requirements. No verse plays or historical dramas or large musicals. Very heavy set shows or multiple detailed sets are out. We prefer shows with casts not more than 15. No skits, but any other length is fine." Payment is negotiable. Query with synopsis. SASE. Reports in 6 months. Produces 20 plays/year.

CHRISTIAN H. MOE, Theater Department, Southern Illinois University, Carbondale IL 62901. Plays will be performed in a university theater (either a 580-seat theater or an experimental theater which can seat 100 to 150). Cast will be non-Equity. Audience is a public one drawn from a university community with disparate interests. Largest percentage is a student and faculty audience. Student age range is roughly from 16 to 25. Also a children's theater audience ranging from pre-school to 13 years. "Submissions are restricted to children's theater plays. We prefer dramas with small casts, not exceeding a running time of 50 minutes. A limited budget prohibits lavish set or property demands." Produces 12+ musicals (20%) and nonmusicals (80%) a year; 10% are originals. Normally pays $15/performance. Special arrangements are made for plays that tour. Query with synopsis. SASE. Reports in 3 months.

NASHVILLE ACADEMY THEATRE, Box 100047, Nashville TN 37210. (615)254-6020. Production Manager: Ken Lambert. Estab. 1931. Produces both amateur and professional productions in a studio situation and in a 696-seat theater. The age groups they play for are: Kindergarten through 4th grade, 5th grade through 8th, and 9th grade to adult. "We are considered a family theater. Although we select plays for different age groups, we feel that any age should enjoy any play we do on some level. In the past we have produced murder mysteries, Shakespeare, plays of the supernatural, fairy tales, *The Mikado*, dance-drama, musical comedy, serious drama, chamber theater, contemporary children's drama—almost anything you can think of." Reports in 1 month. Produces 6 musicals (15%) and nonmusicals

(85%) a year; 15% are originals. Buys exclusive performance rights for middle Tennessee, one year prior to and during their production. Pays $10-35/performance. SASE.
Needs: "We prefer a variety of styles and genres. Length is usually limited to one hour. We are interested in quality new scripts of the old fairy tales for our younger audiences. There is no limit on topics. Interested in musicals also." Wants a richness of language and mood in their productions. no intermissions. Fluid and fast moving. Must have at least some literary merit. No or little obscenity. Cast size: 5-20 players. No limits in staging.

NEW PLAYERS COMPANY, INC., 100 E. Madison St., Baltimore MD 21202. (301)837-6071. Producer: Ray Hamby. Estab. 1953. "Nonprofessional productions for general community audiences presented in our 70-seat studio theater in downtown Baltimore, with tour performances in the immediate geographic vicinity." Submit complete ms. Reports in 2 weeks. Produces 5 musicals (1) and nonmusicals (4) a year; all are originals. Buys rights for specified run of play only (usually 9 performances in theater and 3-4 outside bookings). Pays $50/production. SASE.
Needs: Comedies, dramas, musicals. Open to any type of content, but are not very interested in avant-garde treatment. Prefer small casts (4-8). Simple staging—stylized cube units for set pieces against a black cyc. Sometimes use hand props, other times pantomime them. Authors are welcome at rehearsals and/or performances with the strict contractual understanding that the author will not participate in the direction/production, except through conferences with director and/or producer. No script changes are made without the author's approval.

THE NEW PLAYWRIGHTS' THEATRE OF WASHINGTON, 1742 Church St. NW, Washington DC 20036. (202)232-1122. Producing Director: Harry M. Bagdasian. Literary Manager: Robert Shulte. Estab. 1972. Produces 7 musicals (30%) and straight plays (70%) and 21 readings/year. "Plays are produced in professional productions for general Washington audiences." Submit complete ms, "typed to form, suitably bound." Reports in 3-4 months. "Rights purchased and financial arrangements are individually negotiated." SASE.
Needs: "All styles, traditional to experimental, straight plays to musicals and music-dramas, revues and cabaret shows, one-acts and full-lengths. Plays must ultimately have an affirmative point-of-view. No plays that have had major, full-scale, professional productions, or that have been published." Cast: "no restrictions." Staging: "We have an adaptable playing space."

NORTH LIGHT REPERTORY, 927 Noyes St., Evanston IL 60201. (312)869-7732. Assistant to Producing Director: Lisa Wilson. Estab. 1974. "We are a LORT theater using professional artistic personnel with a season that runs from October through June, located just outside Chicago with a subscription audience. We are committed to producing new plays of high quality rather than pure entertainment or more commercial fare. Audience is college age and over, broad range of socio-economic and religious backgrounds." Query with synopsis or submit complete ms. Reports in 2 months. Produces 5 nonmusicals a year; 50-75% are originals. Rights purchased vary. Pays 4% minimum royalty. SASE.
Needs: "New plays of high quality. Plays may vary in genre and topic. We are most interested in contemporary rather than classic material. Full-length and of a cast size of 10 or less. Though accessibility is an issue, we rate substance as a higher concern for our audience."

OLD LOG THEATER, Box 250, Excelsior MN 55331. Producer: Don Stolz. Produces 2-act and 3-act plays for "a professional cast. Public audiences, usually adult. Interested in contemporary comedies. Small number of sets. Cast not too large." Produces about 14 plays/year. Payment by Dramatists Guild agreement. Send complete script. SASE.

OPERA VARIETY THEATER, 3944 Balboa St., San Francisco CA 94121. Director: Violette M. Dale. Plays to be performed by professional and amateur casts for a public audience; all ages, generally families; upper educational level. Submit complete script. Produces 2-3 musicals (50% or more) and nonmusicals (1-2) a year; all are originals. "Everyone (cast, author, technical people, publicity, etc.) receives equal percentage." SASE. Reports in 6 months.
Needs: "Prefer musicals (but must have singable, tuneful material; arranged, ready to cast). Plays or music on most any theme that conservative audiences would enjoy. Must have substantial, believable plot and good characterizations. Must be simple to produce; fairly small cast, easy setting, etc. (small backstage area limits cast, props, staging, etc.). Emphasis is on entertainment rather than social reform." Length: 1, 2 or 3 acts. "No vulgarity in language or action; no wordy preaching."

OTRABANDA COMPANY, Box 2659, New Orleans LA 70176. (504)566-7729. Managing

Director: John Maynard Jr. Estab. 1971. "Professional productions for touring to universities, and in residence in New Orleans. Audience is primarily adult. We also do an annual production for rural audiences along the Mississippi River; this production is suitable for all ages, and uses a great deal of comedy and popular style." Submit query letter and synopsis. Reports in 6 weeks. Produces 2-3 musicals (50%) and nonmusicals (50%) a year; 75% are originals. Buys exclusive performing rights for 15 months. Pays 5-7½% royalty. SASE.
Needs: "One style should be serious drama for adults, covering any topic of interest to the writer. Play should be 1-1½ hours in length, and suitable for highly physical theatrical techniques; i.e., open to moments of choreography with the actors. The second style is popular theater, using elements of satire, music, vaudeville and circus. Play must have comedy. Cast size is usually limited to 10. The company often performs and tours with small sets, preferring to stress the use of props of all sizes. Playwrights must be capable of rehearsing the play in conjunction with actors and director; changes in script will result out of collaborative work over a 1-2 month period.

OTTERBEIN COLLEGE THEATRE, Westerville OH 43081. Contact: Dr. Charles W. Dodrill. Plays will be performed by the Otterbein College Theatre cast, with a professional guest actor; also summer theater. For a central-Ohio public. No radical plays. Should be 3-act plays. Reports in 6 weeks. Produces 11 plays/year. Send synopsis or complete ms. SASE.

PALISADES THEATRE COMPANY, Box 19717, St. Petersburg FL 33733. (813)1609. Dramaturg: Lach Adair. Estab. 1974. Produces 4-6 plays/year. "Palisades Theatre Company is a professional touring theater for children touring the East Coast. We have offices in Washington DC and St. Petersburg." Query or submit complete ms. Reports in 3 months. "Rights are negotiated on an individual basis with the author." Pays $8 minimum/performance. SASE.
Needs: "We are interested primarily in plays for children, less than one hour in length. We are also interested in adult material. We prefer plays for small casts, but will consider each play on its own merits. Ideally, we would like plays and musicals 30-50 minutes long written for two men and two women, or one man and one woman."

JOSEPH PAPP PRODUCER, New York Shakespeare Festival, 425 Lafayette St., New York NY 10003. (212)677-1750. Gail Merrifield, Director of Play Development. Interested in full-length plays and musical works. No restrictions as to style, historical period, traditional or experimental forms, etc. New works produced on 7 stages at the Public Theater. Produces about 30 musicals and nonmusicals a year; 98% are originals. Standard option and production agreements. Reports in 6 weeks. SASE.

PETERBOROUGH PLAYERS, Box 1, Peterborough NH 03458. Artistic Director: Charles Morey. Estab. 1933. Professional summer theater (Equity). Query with synopsis or submit complete ms. "Submissions will be accepted September-February of the year. Mss should be submitted during that period to Charles Morey, Peterborough Players, 718 W. 171st St., #51, New York NY 10032. Produces 5 nonmusicals a year; 20% are originals. Buys single production rights only (10 performances). Pays $500 minimum. SASE.
Needs: "Interested in all types of material. Quality is the only guideline."

THE PLAYWRIGHTS' LAB, 2010 Minnehaha, Minneapolis MN 55404. "Plays given readings and professional workshops. A staff of 6 playwrights-in-residence reads and critiques plays. Produces 12-18 musicals (10%) and nonmusicals (90%) a year; all are originals. Written critiques are given for $2.50. Reports in 6 months. SASE. The lab has operated for more than 8 years and in that time has produced some 90 plays by more than 50 playwrights."

REPERTORY THEATER OF AMERICA/ALPHA-OMEGA PLAYERS, Box 1296, Rockport TX 78382. Director: Drexel H. Riley. Plays performed on the college and country club circuit (professional national tour); also local churches and civic groups. For a private audience, college age and over; majority are college graduates; wide range of geographic and religious backgrounds and tastes. Query with synopsis. Send no scripts until requested. Scripts not requested will be returned to sender unread. Produces 3-4 musicals (50%) and nonmusicals (50%) a year; 25% are originals. Pays $10-20/performance; averages approximately 100 performances per play per year. SASE. Reports in 3 weeks.
Needs: "Comedies that are fast-paced and adaptable to a dinner theater setting. Adaptations of works by well-known American authors, especially short stories." Length: 2-acts; total running time 1½ hours. No plays with casts larger than 4 (2 men, 2 women). Limited sound facilities, minimum props. "No guerrilla theater, obscenity, intellectualizing or bad writing."

ROANOKE ISLAND HISTORICAL ASSOCIATION, Box 40, Manteo NC 27954. (919)473-2127. Assistant General Manager: Rock Kershaw. Estab. 1937. Produces 6 plays/year; "audience ranges widely from children to families to senior citizens." Query with synopsis. Reports in 2 weeks. Buys production rights. Pays $10-30/performance. SASE. **Needs:** Children's fantasy; musicals; dance producitons; comedies; light opera; and heavy drama. Scripts should be submitted by May 15th.

ST. CLEMENTS, 423 W. 46th St., New York NY 10036. Plays will be produced at St. Clement's, an off-off Broadway theater; all productions are fully professional for public performances. 1-act, 2-act or 3-act plays. "Our productions are presented under the terms of the Equity Showcase Code. There are no royalties. It is a showcase for the playwrights." Send complete script or submit through agent. SASE. Reports in 3-6 months. Produces 5-6 major plays a year and 10-12 readings.

ST. NICHOLAS THEATER, 2851 N. Halsted St., Chicago IL 60657. "Plays are done mainstage plus works in progress children's theater." Submit complete ms. Reports in 6 months. Produces 12-15 musicals (15%) and nonmusicals (85%) a year; 75% are originals. "Royalty information cannot be published." SASE. **Needs:** One-act and full-length plays, children's theater, and musicals. "Must be original, previously unproduced plays. Prefer small casts (6-10)."

SCORPIO RISING THEATRE FOUNDATION, 426 N. Hoover St., Los Angeles CA 90004. Contact: Louise Newmark. For an audience of selected theater buffs. "Scorpio Rising Theatre is a repertory theater dedicated to the works of new playwrights, and winner of Los Angeles Drama Critics' Circle Award. Looking for all kinds of plays, but prefer contemporary themes. We don't want any situation comedies or Broadway type musicals. Simple cast, props, stage, etc. 1-act, 2-act, 3-act, but open to all." Also interested in developmental work with playwrights-in-residence. Buys amateur performance rights. Produces 8-12 musicals (50%) and nonmusicals (50%); 80-90% are originals. Payment to be negotiated. Send complete script. Reports in 1-2 months. SASE.

SCRANTON THEATRE LIBRE, INC., 512-514 Brooks Bldg., Scranton PA 18503. Executive Director: John J. White. Plays performed by semiprofessional casts for the general public. Submit synopsis or complete script. Produces 5 musicals (15%) and nonmusicals (85%) a year; all are originals. Pays 5% royalty. SASE. Reports in 3 months. **Needs:** "Only original scripts of any kind; any format."

SEATTLE REPERTORY THEATRE, Box B, Queen Anne Station, Seattle WA 98109. Plays will be produced on either main stage, or in second theater, with professional casts in both cases. The second house performs younger, more avant-garde and special interest plays. Audience for main stage is middle class; high percentage of college graduates; ages ranging from teens to advanced middle age. Plays for second house, particularly, will involve novel forms of stage, experiments in style; particular interest in works that explore new ways to use language. In main house, more conventional plays with themes related to present time. Almost any format is acceptable providing the writing is of high quality. No limitations in cast. Produces 6 plays on mainstage plus plays-in-progress on second stage. Payment depends on the plays. "When negotiating a new script, we retain a financial interest in subsequent productions of the play for a specified period of time." Send synopsis, with a dozen or so pages of script to give feeling of style, etc. SASE. Reports in about 3 months.

LORAINE SLADE, General Manager, Virginia Museum Theatre, Boulevard and Grove Ave., Richmond VA 23221. For public, well-educated, conservative, adventurous audiences. Professional repertory theater. Looking for biography, experimental styles. Standard format of presentation. Light comedies, musicals. 2-act and 3-act plays considered. Payment is negotiable. For a premiere, theater requires share in future income. Produces one new script/year. Send complete script. Reports in 3-5 months. SASE.

STAGE SOUTH, 829 Richland St., Columbia SC 29201. Assistant Director of Development: Tim Beall. Estab. 1973. Produces 2 plays/year. "Stage South, the state theater of South Carolina and a program of the South Carolina Arts Commission, is a professional, regional touring operation. At present, its season consists of an educational, theater-for-youth production in the fall—generally an original, commissioned script celebrating the history and folklore indigenous to the stage; and a community tour in the spring. Stage South productions are intended to appeal to a wide range of the South Carolina population." Query or submit

complete ms with vita or resume. Reports in 2 months. Rights are negotiable. Pays $300-1,000; "payment varies, depending on the reputation and experience of the playwright." SASE.
Needs: "Plays submitted to Stage South should be suitable for touring to urban and rural communities in South Carolina. We are especially interested in material that speaks to the history and cultural uniqueness of the state. Generally, all plays submitted to Stage South are read and evaluated. Scripts submitted should specify reasonable, tourable sets and should ordinarily require no more than ten actors. We are especially favorable to realistic, convincing characters that command sympathy or identification from the audience. We are open to experimental approaches, formats or structures in this regard."

CHARLES STILWILL, Managing Director, Community Playhouse, Box 433, Waterloo IA 50704. (319)235-0367. Plays performed at Waterloo Community Playhouse with a volunteer cast. "We have 5,606 season members. Average attendance at main stage shows is 5,663; at studio shows 2,247. We try to fit the play to the theater. We do a wide variety of plays. Looking for good plays with more roles for women than men. Our public isn't going to accept nudity, too much sex, too much strong language. We don't have enough black actors to do all-black shows. We have done plays with as few as 3 characters, and as many as 56." Produces 9 musicals (1) and nonmusicals (8) a year; 14% originals. "On the main stage we usually pay between $300 and $500. In our studio we usually pay between $50 and $300." Send synopsis or complete script. SASE. "Reports negatively within 6 months, but acceptance takes longer because they try to fit a wanted script into the balanced season."

JOE SUTHERIN, c/o St. Bart's Playhouse, 109 E. 50th St., New York NY 10022. Plays will be produced at St. Bart's Playhouse, a 350-seat community theater. "I am also looking for material to produce in other (professional) situations." For public/commercial "sophisticated" audience. Looking for revue, comedy material, or writer who likes to do same. No material that relies heavily on sex, four-letter words, etc., to make it viable. Produces 4-6 musicals (2) and nonmusicals (2-4) a year; originals, one every 2-3 years. Payment varies. Copyright negotiable. Send synopsis or complete script. SASE. Reports in "3 months if I'm not snowed under."

SYRACUSE STAGE, 820 E. Genesee St., Syracuse NY 13210. (315)423-4008. Playreader: June Potash. Estab. 1974. A professional regional theater; uses Equity performers, professional directors and designers. Audience is from the Syracuse community. Reports in 2-6 weeks. Produces 6 musicals (1) and nonmusicals (5) a year; 1 is original. Negotiates rights with playwright and/or agent. Pays royalties. SASE.
Needs: "Finished new American plays (one or two per season—the remainder of the plays, four or five, are from the standard international repetoire.) We are looking for anything that is *good*, preferably with a cast of fewer than 15. We are less interested in musicals than in dramas (including comedies), but consider small-scale musicals upon occasion. We are looking for plays that will have importance, not merely clever or gimmicky ideas, and we are open to every kind of form." No elaborate sets (makes exceptions for exceptional scripts). "Our standards are very high. We hope to be able to attract the attention of New York critics and upon occasion take our new American productions to Broadway or off-Broadway. We read everything with care but reject 99% of it."

THEATRE AMERICANA, Box 245, Altadena CA 91001. Contact: Playreading Committee. In operation for 43 seasons. For public general audience. Local theater. Showcase for unknowns in all phases of theater. Awards for best director, set designer, actors, as well as best play. Looking for plays with quality and originality. Selections not made on the basis of any set structure, but if new forms are used, they must work successfully from an audience viewpoint. 2-act or 3-act plays, 1½-2 hours playing time. Not interested in trite material; pornography for shock value unacceptable. Modern verbiage in a valid characterization not censored. Musicals should include piano arrangements. Plays with a Christmas theme or setting are welcomed. No royalties can be paid, but the 4 original plays produced each year are eligible to compete for the $300 C. Brooks Fry Award. Authors copyright own plays. Send complete script only. Reporting time is "very slow. Read year-round. Play finalists retained until April 1, when 4 are selected for next season's production." SASE.

THEATRE EXPRESS, 4615 Baum Blvd., Pittsburgh PA 15213. (412)621-5454. General Manager Caren Harder. Estab. 1975. Produces 5 plays/year. "Professional tour and residency in Pittsburgh. Well-educated liberal audience. Large college, university market." Submit complete ms. Reports in 2½ weeks. Buys all rights on premiere productions and 5% of all future productions. Pays $10-35/performance. SASE. Needs plays for cast of 7-8. Has limited production elements when touring.

THEATRE OF WESTERN SPRINGS, Box 29, Western Springs IL 60558. (213)246-4043. Artistic Director: Ted Kehoe. Produces 7 adult and 2 children's plays a year; 10% nonmusicals. Plays are performed in community theater, main stage or workshops. Submit complete ms. SASE.

THEATRE RAPPORT, 8128 Gould Ave., Hollywood CA 90040. Artistic Director: Crane Jackson. Equity company. Produces plays of 1, 2 and 3 acts. Produces gutsy, relevant plays on highly artistic level and true subjects. No unjustified homosexuality, nudity or profanity; realistic acceptable. For a sophisticated, educated, non-fad, conservative (although venturesome) audience looking for something new and different. Not avant-garde, but a strong point of view is an asset. Approach must be unique. All plays must be West Coast premieres. Pays 20% of gross. Send complete script. Response if interested. All mss read, but *none are returned*. Produces 6 plays a year.

UNIVERSITY AND FESTIVAL THEATRE, John R. Bayless, Business Manager, 137 Arts Bldg., The Pennsylvania State University, University Park PA 16802. (814)863-0381. For general audience 6-60 years of age. Produced at either the Pavilion or the Playhouse Theatres located at University Park. University Theatre is an educational program; the Festival Theatre is an Equity/student theater program offered during the summer. Any kind of play is considered. Usually does not copyright plays. For a straight play, pays $35-50/performance. Produces 6 plays/year. Send complete script. Reports in 1 month. SASE.

UNIVERSITY OF MINNESOTA DEPARTMENT OF THEATRE, Marshall Performing Arts Center, Deluth MN 55812. (218)726-8562. Department Head: Rick Graves. Estab. 1851. Plays are performed in the theater of the Marshall Arts Performing Center; audience is about 50% students and 50% community adults. Submit query and synopsis. Reports in 1 month. Produces 12-20 musicals (25%) and nonmusicals (75%) a year; originals vary each year. Buys "the right to perform the script for a single engagement. Pays $25-50/performance and occasionally fees to bring the playwright on campus during rehearsals." SASE.
Needs: "The department is committed to the development of young playwrights whose works have not attracted wide commercial attention." Opera; dance; "and all types of drama and musical theater."

YALE REPERTORY THEATRE, Literary Manager, 222 York St., New Haven CT 06520. Resident professional theater. For University-oriented audience, but with appeal to a larger community. No limitations of age or special interests, but emphasis on an audience with serious perceptual intelligence, receptive to experiment and innovation. No limitations on subject matter or theme, but not interested in Broadway-type plays, conventional musicals, domestic dramas, etc. "We are generally limited to what the imagination can summon up on a small thrust stage with no flies and little wing space. Full-evening works preferred." Produces 7 musicals (10%) and nonmusicals (90%) a year; 20% are originals. Offers standard LORT author contract. Copyright remains with author. "We retain limited residual rights and a small percentage of author's proceeds on subsequent sales of the work." Send complete script. SASE. Reports in about 6 months.

Play Publishers

A successful play needn't be successful only once. Play publishers exist with the specific intent of making a play available to anyone who wants to produce it, so it can be continuously successful—and profitable.

Publishers handle everything from Broadway plays to children's theater to skits for schools. Some publishers handle all these types; others specialize to a certain degree.

Publishers cater primarily to amateur groups—community theaters, schools, etc.—though professional groups like regional theaters and dinner theaters are also served. The "nonprofessional" theater, therefore, is probably the most open to playwrights. Children's theater, for instance, is growing (see the August 1979 issue of *Writer's Digest*—available for $1.50 from 9933 Alliance Rd., Cincinnati 45242—for a report on writing for children's theater). "Demand for plays by public schools is as great as ever," says J.V. Heuer, president of Heuer Publishing Company. Shubert Fendrich of Pioneer Drama Service adds that the health of the educational theater field is "excellent."

Publishers handle plays on a royalty basis. That is, they charge a set rate for production of your play, and share the proceeds with you. A 50-50 split is standard. In general, you also receive 10% of the cover price for each playbook (that is, printed copy of the play) that's sold to directors and actors.

Publishers prefer to receive submissions that have already demonstrated their potential for success. Trying to get your play produced by a local group is therefore advisable. "If you get it produced first, the publication is just gravy," says Lawrence Harbison, assistant editor of the Samuel French publishing company. Production of the play can be valuable by helping you see flaws in your script. It also allows you to see the potentials and limitations of the theater. One of the limitations you should keep in mind is rising production costs, which forces producers to seek scripts with small casts and limited scenery. See the Play Producers section, which precedes this section, for a full discussion of the advantages of play production, and how you go about getting your play produced.

When submitting your script to a publisher, include reviews of the play. Always include a list of characters at the front of the script; the number of characters often affects the suitability of the play. If characters can be doubled (that is, if one actor can play two characters), explain specifically how it can be done. Don't say, "doubling is possible" when you can say, "the bishop also plays the pawn and the king."

Before submitting, study the specific submission policies of each publisher in the following listings. Write to the publisher and ask for a copy of its current catalog so you can determine the publisher's major thrust. Order a few playbooks and study not only the content of the plays, but also the script preparation format.

Publishers want material that is more than just good; they want material that's current. Lawrence Harbison prefers to work with "people who know what's current," because "we want tomorrow's trends." Be aware of trends, but don't try to follow them too closely. "The best plays we find are not the ones that imitate the trends, but the ones that try to set their own trends," says Harbison.

Publishers will work with promising scripts, sometimes even asking for rewrites if they see potential. Yet, don't expect a detailed critique of your script; "We're not teachers of playwrighting," says Harbison.

If your script is good, however, a publisher will read it carefully, and perhaps add it to his list. If he doesn't, don't get discouraged. Keep at it. "It takes time to develop a reputation and it takes time to develop a play," says Harbison. "If you don't have any time, don't write for the theater." But if you have the time and the talent, │ opportunities—and publishers—await you.

THE ANCHORAGE PRESS, INC., Box 8067, New Orleans LA 70182. (504)283-8868. Editor: Mr. Orlin Corey. Publishes 5-8 plays/year. Query with synopsis, or submit complete ms "with proof of production by someone *other* than the playwright—reviews, programs, etc." Pays 10% royalty on retail playbook sales; 50% production royalty. Buys publication rights for the playbook, including anthology and translation rights; and amateur and professional rights for the stage, television, cinema and radio. Reports in 1 week on queries, in 30-45 days on unsolicited mss, and 2-3 weeks on solicited mss. Free catalog.
Needs: "Adaptations of beloved classics of the world; original plays inclusive of children in their appeal and development (*not* exclusive of adult interest, of course); musicals concerned with either of the above; and any material that honors the child as intelligent, caring, questioning, searching, trusting, hoping. No plays that are essentially cabaret in feeling—that is, utilizing a children's story for purposes of travesty, ridicule or adult-only implications; such plays may be excellent for cabaret, where audiences have an established frame of reference, but when aimed at children, they insult, ignore, underestimate and overlook the child's world—a world of wonder, of new possibilities, of models. Our chief admonishment is that 'theater for children is not different from adult, only better' (Stanislavski). He was obviously not speaking of what is ordinarily written or produced. He was speaking of the ideal. By 'better' he really meant, among other matters, that theater for young audiences is inclusive (it includes the adult, too, who, after all, is—or better be—a child within his adultness), whereas adult theater is essential exclusive—dealing with problems of maturity that children may perceive but are unlikely to fully grasp: anxieties, competition, social and political issues, sex, age. Too many authors underestimate the child. Too many write beneath their own ability when they write for children. Fine playwrights neither underestimate nor write down." Length: 1 hour minimum; prefers "full-length (that is, 90-120 minutes); with options for cutting by producers who desire a shorter length."

AT RISE: MAGAZINE, 9838 Jersey Ave., Santa Fe Springs CA 90670. Editor-in-Chief: Stella Hardy. Managing Editor: Howard D. Hunter. 75-85% freelance written. "For all ages interested in excellent original one-act plays. Cater most specifically to high school, college, and community theater." Quarterly magazine; 90 pages. Estab. January 1977. Circ. 200. Pays on publication. Buys publication and amateur performance rights. Photocopied submissions OK. SASE. Reports in 6-10 weeks. Sample copy $1; free writer's guidelines.
Fiction: "One-act plays only. We are interested in anything well-written." Buys 16 plays/year. Submit complete ms. Length: 15-45 minutes. Pays $25, "plus standard royalty contract for amateur performances."

BAKER'S PLAY PUBLISHING CO., 100 Chauncy St., Boston MA 02111. Editor: John B. Welch. Plays performed by amateur groups, high schools, children's theater, churches and community theater groups. Submit complete script. Publishes 18-25 straight plays; all originals. Pay varies; outright purchase price to split in production fees. Pays $75 for 1-act plays that need work. SASE. Reports in 2-3 months.
Needs: "One-acts (specifically for competition use). Quality children's theater scripts. Chancel drama for easy staging—voice plays ideal. Long plays only if they have a marketable theme. Include as much stage direction in the script as possible." Emphasis on large female cast desired.

CONTEMPORARY DRAMA SERVICE, Box 457, Downers Grove IL 60515. Editor: Arthur Zapel. Plays performed in churches and school classrooms with amateur performers for age level high school to adult. Publishes 25-30 plays/year; (5%) musicals and (95%) straight plays; 85% originals. Submit synopsis or complete script. Usually buys all rights. Pays 10% royalty up to an agreed maximum. Will negotiate for complete rights. SASE. Reports in 1 month.
Needs: "In the church field we are looking for chancel drama for presentation at various holidays: Thanksgiving, Mother's Day, Christmas, Easter, etc. School drama materials can be reader's theater adaptations, drama rehearsal scripts, simple dialogues and short action plays. We like a free and easy style. Nothing formal. Short sentences and fast pace. Humor also welcomed where possible." Length: 1-act, skits or short games. Casts not to exceed 9 players.

DODD, MEAD & CO., 79 Madison Ave., New York NY 10016. Executive Editor: Allen T. Klots. "We're only interested in playwrights after professional production, who promise to contribute to the literature of the theater." Royalty negotiated. Buys book rights only. Reports in about 4 weeks. SASE.

THE DRAMATIC PUBLISHING CO., 4150 N. Milwaukee Ave., Chicago IL 60641. (312)545-2062. Estab. 1885. Produces about 40 new titles/year. Submit complete ms. Reports in 4-6 weeks. Buys amateur and stock theatrical rights. Pays royalty or by outright purchase. SASE. No limitations in cast, props, staging, etc.

ELDRIDGE PUBLISHING CO., Drawer 209, Franklin OH 45005. (513)746-6531. Editor/General Manager: Kay Myerly. Plays performed in high schools and churches; some professional—but most are amateur productions. Publishes plays for all age groups. Publishes 15-20 plays/year; (2%) musicals; 100% originals. Send synopsis or complete script. Buys all rights "unless the author wishes to retain some rights." Pays $75-100 for 1-act plays; $350 for 3-acts. SASE. Reports in 60-90 days.
Needs: "We are looking for good straight comedies which will appeal to high and junior-high age groups. We do not publish anything which can be suggestive. Most of our plays are published with a hanging indentation—2 ems. All stage, scenery and costume plots must be included." Length: 1-acts from 25-30 minutes; 2-acts of around 2 hours; and skits of 10-15 minutes.

SAMUEL FRENCH, INC., 25 W. 45th St., New York NY 10036. "We publish 10-15 manuscripts a year from freelancers. In addition to publishing plays, we also act as agents in the placement of plays for Broadway, Off-Broadway, regional, stock and dinner theater productions. Publishes 75 plays/year; (10%) musicals and (65%) straight plays; 15% originals. Pays on royalty basis. Submit complete ms (bound). Reports in 10 weeks. SASE.
Needs: "Willing at all times to read manuscripts of plays, screenplays and TV pilots. No verse plays, motion picture scenarios or huge-cast plays."

HEUER PUBLISHING CO., 233 Dows Bldg., Box 248, Cedar Rapids IA 52406. Publishes 15-20 plays/year. Amateur productions for schools and church groups. Audience consists of junior and senior high school students and some intermediate groups. Need 1- and 3-act plays. Prefers comedy, farce, mystery and mystery/comedy. Uses 1-act plays suitable for contest work (strong drama). "We suggest potential authors write for our brochure on types of plays." No sex, controversial subjects or family scenes. Prefers 1 simple setting and noncostume plays. Current need is for plays with a large number of characters (16-20). One-act plays should be 30-35 minutes long; 3-act, 90-105 minutes. Most mss purchased outright, with price depending on quality. Minimum of $500 usually. Copyrighted, however, contract stipulates amateur rights only, so author retains professional rights to TV, radio, etc. Query with synopsis only. SASE. Reports in 1 week to 10 days.

LILLENAS PUBLISHING CO., Box 527, Kansas City MO 64141. (816)931-1900. Program Materials Editor: Evelyn Stenbock. Estab. 1924. Publishes 5-6 plays/year, plus skits, readings, recitations and other program material for Sunday school and church use. Submit complete ms. Reports in 3-4 weeks. Buys first rights. No simultaneous submissions; prefers original, rather than photocopies. Pays $2-3 for smaller pieces; up to $10-20 for an average play. SASE.
Needs: "Skits, readings and recitations can be any length, varying from the simple 4-line rhyme and 5-minute skit to a lengthy poem or 45-minute play. The main thing to keep in mind is that our plays and programs are published almost exclusively for presentation to church congregations, so the content, as it relates ot the old-time gospel concept, is most important. We have no use for secular plays, and coarse talk, cursing, or sexually suggestive material won't be considered." Keep cast, props and staging simple. "We receive a lot of seasonal material, so it would be wise to try contemporary Christian plays and skits (possibly recitations) on general subjects."

NATIONAL PUBLISHERS, LTD., 1310 Chardonnay, Houston TX 77077. Editor: S. Bazelides. Estab. 1978. Publishes 10-20 plays/year. Submit complete ms. Buys publishing rights. Pays negotiable royalties. Reports in 3 weeks. SASE.
Needs: Comedies and dramas geared to student audiences and adaptations of great work or plays on subjects of general interest are best. "A catalog of plays is sent to the schools around the United States. We would prefer one-act or three-act plays. We will produce some one-person dramatic works for drama contests. The author needs to keep in mind the student audience that the play should be geared to. Most schools prefer one stage setting."

NEW PLAYS, INC., Box 273, Rowayton CT 06853. Publisher: Patricia Whitton. Estab. 1964.

Publishes 2-4 plays/year. "We are publishers of children's plays; for colleges, high schools, community theater groups, junior leagues, summer camps, etc." Query with synopsis. Reports in 1-2 months. Buys "exclusive rights to publish acting scripts and act as agent for productions—but the author remains the owner of the script." Pays 50% of performance royalties; "we charge our customers a royalty of $35 for the first performance and $25 for each subsequent performance. The author gets one-half of this."

Needs: "Generally, plays of approximately 45 minutes up to 1½ hours long, for teenagers and adults to perform for children. No plays for children to perform, such as assembly skits. We're looking for originality in form or content. We don't want adaptations of material that has already been done a great deal such as Rumplestiltskin and Sleeping Beauty. Plays have to have been successfully produced by at least one organization before being published."

PERFORMANCE PUBLISHING CO., 978 N. McLean Blvd., Elgin IL 60120. Editor: Virginia Butler. "We publish one-, two- and three-act plays and musicals suitable for stock, summer college, high school and childrens' theater. We're looking for comedies, mysteries, dramas, farces, etc. with modern dialogue and theme. Plays for and about high school students are usually the most remunerative and we publish 50% high school, 15% childrens' theater and 35% for the balance of the market. The new writer is advised to obtain experience by limiting himself to one-acts until he has been published. We offer a standard royalty contract. Plays are usually copyrighted in the name of the author and we acquire all publication and stage rights. First-class professional, radio, film and TV rights remain the author's property." Publishes 40 plays/year; (10%) musicals and (90%) straight plays. Authors should retain a copy of any script mailed. No insured, certified or registered scripts accepted. SASE. Reports in 3 months.

PIONEER DRAMA SERVICE, 2171 S. Colorado Blvd., Box 22555, Denver CO 80222. (303)759-4297. Publisher: Shubert Fendrich. Plays are performed by high school, junior high and adult groups, colleges, and recreation programs for audiences of all ages. Publishes 15 plays/year; (40%) musicals and (60%) straight plays. Submit synopsis or complete script. Buys all rights. Pays "usually 10% royalty on copy sales; 50% of production royalty and 50% of subsidiary rights with some limitations on first-time writers." SASE. Reports in 30-60 days.

Needs: "We are looking for adaptations of great works in the public domain or plays on subjects of current interest. We use the standard 1-act and 3-act format, 2-act musicals, melodrama in all lengths and plays for children's theater (plays to be done by adult actors for children). Length: 1-acts of 15-30 minutes; 2-act musicals and 3-act comedies from 90 minutes to 2 hours; and children's theater of 1 hour. "We do not want plays with predominantly male casts, or highly experimental works. Plays should be mature without being obscene or profane."

PLAYS, The Drama Magazine for Young People, 8 Arlington St., Boston MA 02116. Editor: Sylvia K. Burack. Publishes approximately 90 1-act plays each season. Interested in buying good plays to be performed by young people of all age groups—junior and senior high, middle grades, lower grades. In addition to comedies, farces, melodramas, skits, mysteries and dramas, can use plays for holidays and other special occasions, such as Book Week. Adaptations of classic stories and fables; historical plays; plays about other lands; puppet plays; plays for all-girl or all-boy casts; folk and fairy tales; creative dramatics; plays dramatizing factual information and on such concepts as good government, importance of voting, involvement and participation as citizens; and plays for conservation, ecology or human rights programs are needed. Prefers one scene; when more than one is necessary, changes should be simple. Mss should follow the general style of *Plays*. Stage directions should not be typed in capital letters or underlined. Every play ms should include a list of characters; an indication of time; a description of setting; an "At Rise," describing what is taking place on stage as curtain rises; production notes, indicating the number of characters and the playing time, describing the costumes, properties, setting and special lighting effects, if any. No incorrect grammar or dialect. Characters with physical defects or speech impediments should not be included. Desired lengths for mss are: Junior and Senior high—20 to 25 double spaced ms pages (25 to 30 minutes playing time). Middle Grades—12 to 15 pages (25 to 20 minutes playing time). Lower Grades—6 to 10 pages (8 to 15 minutes playing time). Pays "good rates on acceptance." Reports in 3-4 weeks. SASE. "Manuscript specification sheet sent on request."

READ MAGAZINE, 245 Long Hill Rd., Middletown CT 06457. (203)347-7251. Editor: Edwin A. Hoey. 10% freelance written. For high school students. Biweekly magazine; 32 pages. Estab. 1951. Circ. 796,305. Rights purchased vary with author and material. May buy second serial (reprint) rights or all rights. Byline given. Buys 20 mss/year. Pays on acceptance. Free sample copy and writer's guidelines. Will consider photocopied submissions. No simultaneous submissions. Reports in 4-5 weeks. Submit complete ms. SASE.

Drama and Fiction: First emphasis is on plays; second on fiction with suspense, adventure, or teenage identification themes. "No preachy material. Plays should have 12 to 15 parts and not require complicated stage directions, for they'll be used mainly for reading aloud in class. Remember that we try to be educational as well as entertaining." No kid detective stories or plays. No obscenity. Pays $50 minimum.

Syndicates

"We can't get enough good material, but have ready cash for that which meets our needs."

As this comment from Joseph Arkin of the Arkin Magazine Syndicate demonstrates, syndicates hunger for well-written, carefully prepared material that matches their needs. Syndicates sell editorial copy (columns, feature articles, news, puzzles and cartoons) for a commission. The author receives from 40 to 60 percent of the gross proceeds, though some syndicates pay the writer a salary and others buy material outright. The syndicate's percentage covers costs of promotion, mailing, staff, etc. Writers of top syndicated columns can earn more than $50,000 a year, though most syndicated writers can't expect to see anything near that figure. Still, "For those writers with talent, [writing syndicated material] is still a good way to make a living," says Donald Whitacre of Curious Facts Features.

The hunger for material doesn't mean a syndicate will buy anything that floats in through the mail. Their narrowly defined needs force them to maintain exacting standards when reviewing material. Moreover, many syndicates—like Curious Facts and the Hollywood Inside Syndicate—deal with specialized topics.

Syndicates vary widely in not only what they cover, but also how they cover it. Most handle feature material, a practice that will continue. The "emphasis in newspapers to present more feature material in place of hard news will mean better opportunities for writers with syndicates," says Mike LeFan of LeFan Features. Newspapers are a major outlet for syndicated material, though supplying "hard news" is usually left to the wire services—*unless* the syndicate specializes in information not usually covered by conventional news services. Her Say is one such syndicate, and editor Marlene Edmunds advises her writers to "keep an eye on the major news of the country, and look for holes in the news."

Because newspapers are syndicates' primary customers, you must employ a terse "newspaper style," even when writing features. This means "plenty of quotes and short, terse sentences," according to one syndicate editor. Another advises writers to "write brightly, briefly, concisely," and warns against "long, hard-to-read articles." In his list of things he *doesn't* want to see, Joseph Arkin includes "college 'papers' or 'reports' not written in article style."

Study acceptable syndicate style by reading as many examples of syndicated work as you can. A bundle of syndicated material is delivered to most writers every morning or evening: the newspaper. Read syndicated features and columns, paying careful attention to style, length, the audience they are apparently aimed at, and what syndicates handled them. Carefully note the subjects covered in the material, especially in regular columns. Take care to not duplicate an already existing column; create something fresh. Don't even consider doing an astrology column, for instance—every syndicate interested in carrying one probably already has one. And one syndicate editor notes that he's sick of receiving Erma Bombeck imitations.

Consult the following listings for the topic and form of submissions preferred by various syndicates. Some deal with regular features, some with article series, some with individual features. Listings also cover the syndicate's outlets. Most, as mentioned above, sell to newspapers, but many also sell to magazines, and to radio stations that use syndicated material as "brights"—that is, lively, interesting facts and anecdotes. For more information about the titles of columns and features handled by particular syndicates, consult *Editor and Publisher Syndicate Directory* (850 3rd Ave., New York City 10022).

Most syndicate editors prefer that you query them with about six sample columns or features. Enclose a self-addressed, stamped envelope with all queries and submissions.

Some writers self-syndicate their material, earning 100% of the income, but also bearing the expense of soliciting clients, reproducing and mailing the features, billing, etc. See "How to Syndicate Your Own Column" in *The Creative Writer* (Writer's Digest Books).

AMERICAN FEATURES SYNDICATE, 964 3rd Ave., New York NY 10022. Editor: Robert Behren. Copyrights material. Will consider photocopied submissions. Reporting time "varies." Query. SASE.
Nonfiction: Travel and true adventure. Buys single features and article series. Does not contract for columns. Length: 1,000-5,000 words. Pays $100-$750. Usual outlets are newspapers and regional magazines, including some trade publications.

AP NEWSFEATURES, 50 Rockefeller Plaza, New York NY 10020. Assistant General Manager: Dan Perkes. SASE.
Nonfiction and Photos: Buys article series or column ideas "dealing with areas of science, social issues that can be expanded into book form. Do not usually buy single features." Length: 600-1,000 words. Pays $25 minimum.

ARKIN MAGAZINE SYNDICATE, 761 NE 180th St., North Miami Beach FL 33162. Editor: Joseph Arkin. "We regularly purchase articles from several freelancers, most of whom belong to ABWA, for syndication in trade and professional magazines." Submit complete ms. SASE. Reports in 3 weeks. Buys all North American magazine and newspaper rights.
Needs: Magazine articles (nonfiction; 800-1,800 words, directly related to business problems common to several—not just one—business firms, in different types of businesses); and photos (purchased with written material). "We are in dire need of the 'how-to' business article." Will not consider article series. Pays 3-10¢/word; $5-10 for photos; "actually, line drawings are preferred instead of photos." Pays on accepance.
Tips: "Study a representative group of trade magazines to learn style, needs and other facets of the field."

AUTHENTICATED NEWS INTERNATIONAL, ANI, 29 Katonah Ave., Katonah NY 10536. (914)232-7727. Editor: Sidney Polinsky. Syndication and Features Editor: Helga Brink. Supplies material to national magazines, newspapers, and house organs in the United States and important countries abroad. Buys exclusive and non-exclusive rights. Reports in 3 months. SASE.
Nonfiction and Photos: Can use photo material in the following areas: hard news, photo features, ecology and the environment, science, medical, industry, education, human interest, the arts, city planning, and pertinent photo material from abroad. 750 words maximum. Prefers 8x10 b&w glossy prints, color transparencies (4x5, 2¼x2¼ or 35mm color). Where necessary, model releases required. Pays 50% royalty.

BUDDY BASCH FEATURE SYNDICATE, 771 West End Ave., New York NY 10025. Publisher: Buddy Basch. Buys all rights. Will consider photocopied submissions. Reports in 1 week to 10 days. SASE.
Nonfiction, Humor, Photos and Fillers: News items, nonfiction, humor, photos, fillers, puzzles, and columns and features on travel and entertainment. "Mostly staff-written at present. Query."
Tips: "Come up with something really unique. Most writers have the same old hackneyed ideas (*they* think are original) which no one can use. Just because someone in the family or a friend said, 'What a great idea,' doesn't make it so."

CANADIAN SCENE, Suite 305, 2 College St., Toronto, Ontario, Canada M5G 1K3. Editor: Miss Ruth Gordon. Query. Submit seasonal material 3 months in advance. Reports in 1 week. Pays on acceptance. SAE and International Reply Coupons.
Nonfiction: "Canadian Scene is a voluntary information service. Its purpose is to provide written material to democratic, foreign language publications in Canada. The material is chosen with a view to directing readers to an understanding of Canadian political affairs, foreign relations, social customs, industrial progress, culture, history and institutions. In a 700-word article, the writer can submit almost any subject on Canada, providing it leaves the newcomer with a better knowledge of Canada. It should be written in a simple, tightly knit, straightforward style." Length: 500-1,000 words. Pays 3¢/word.

CHICAGO TRIBUNE-NEW YORK NEWS SYNDICATE, INC., 220 E. 42nd St., New York NY 10017. Editor: Don Michel. Supplies material to Sunday supplements and newspapers in North America and abroad. Buys worldwide rights, where possible; must have North American rights to be interested. Submit at least 6 samples of any submission for continuing feature. SASE.
Columns and Puzzles: No fiction. Material must be extremely well-written and must not be a copy of something now being marketed to newspapers. Length varies, though columns should generally be 500 words or less. Pay varies, depending on market; usually 50-50 split of net after production on contractual material.

COLLEGE PRESS SERVICE, 1140 Delaware St., Denver CO 80204. (303)388-1608. Editor: Bill Soon. Estab. 1965. "We work with about 10-15 freelancers a year." SASE. Reports in 2-4 weeks. Not copyrighted.
Needs: Magazine and newspaper features; newspaper columns; news items; and fillers. Query. Pays 3¢/word.

COLUMBIA FEATURES, INC., 36 W. 44 St., New York NY 10036. Associate editor: Helen M. Staunton. Buys all rights and world rights for all media. Will consider photocopied submissions. Submit complete ms. Pays on a regular monthly basis for continuing column or contract. Reports in 2-4 weeks. SASE.
Humor and Puzzles: Cartoons, comic strips, puzzles and columns on a continuing basis. Features for special sections: family, home, women's, Sunday supplements. No single features, except series of 6-12 parts, about 750-1,000 words/article. Lengths vary according to features. Columns: 500-750 words. Pays 50% usually.

COMMUNITY AND SUBURBAN PRESS SERVICE, 100 E. Main St., Frankfort KY 40601. Managing Editor: Mike Bennett. Buys second serial (reprint) rights. Pays on acceptance. SASE.
Humor and Photos: Cartoons, gag panels, human interest photos. 8x10 glossy photos purchased without features. Captions required. Pays $15 per cartoon or photo.

COMMUNITY FEATURES, 870 Market St., Suite 920, San Francisco CA 94102. Editor: Tamar Wise. Estab. 1976. Works with 100 writers. Syndicates material to newspapers. Submit complete ms. SASE. Reports in 6-7 weeks. Buys all rights or second serial rights. Writer's guidelines for SASE and 50¢.
Nonfiction, Photos and Columns: "We need features on women, children and youth, education, senior affairs, science, technology, the environment, ethnic and religious communities, consumer protection, medicine and health. Our readers are concerned with family, community and society issues and want to read how people in other parts of the country deal with problems like their own." Buys single features and article series of 500-1,500 words. Pays 50% of net sales or a flat rate of 5-10¢/word. For b&w 8x10 glossy prints with full range of greys, pays $10-50.

CONTEMPORARY FEATURES SYNDICATE, INC., Box 1258, Jackson TN 38301. Editor: Lloyd Russell. Buys several dozen mss/year for syndication to newspapers (columns) and magazines (single features). Submit complete ms and credits. SASE. Photocopied submissions OK "if not submitted elsewhere also." Reports in 6-8 weeks, sometimes longer. Buys all rights.
Needs: News items (not looking for hard news, but rather the story behind the news); fiction (occasional short story, but no longer fiction); fillers (no rehash of the history book; entertain and inform; usually handled on consignment); and photos (purchased with or without written material or on assignment. Captions required). "We believe our product is a line of 'human interest' features and we want to read about people and their relationships." Article series considered if "there is a story too long to be easily and completely told in one article. Have something to say rather than just lots of words." Pays 50% commission on sales; minimum guarantee of $25 for full-length features to magazines; photos bring $5 minimum. Usually pays on acceptance.
Tips: "Do research into the story behind the headlines, then write and submit. Be professional. Be patient. And be realistic. Quality material is a must. Selling *any* material takes time to get the top dollar and the best treatment. No one should expect to get rich or famous overnight. It's all summed up in the abused term, 'hard work.' That's what it is all about, and that's what it takes."

CREATIVE COMMUNICATIONS, Division of Creative Enterprises, Box 450, Centreville VA 22020. Editor: Sylvia Manolatos. Buys material for syndication to weekly newspapers. Submit complete ms. Prefers photocopied submissions. Buys all rights, first rights or second serial (reprint) rights. SASE.

Needs: Weekly columns of current interest: self-improvement, politics, health, nutrition, ecology, child development and consumer interest. Prefers columns of 500 words or less. Pays 50% of price of item sold, on purchase of the article by a newspaper or periodical.

CRUX NEWS SERVICE, Shickshinny PA 18655. Editor: Thourot Pichel. Does not copyright material. Buys "very few" features a year from freelancers. Will consider photocopied submissions. SASE.

Nonfiction: "History and political only." Buys single features. Does not buy article series or columns. Pays "nominal standard."

CURIOUS FACTS FEATURES, 449 Glenview Dr., Lebanon OH 45036. Editor: Donald Whitacre. Buys all rights. Pays on publication. Reports in 2 weeks. SASE.

Nonfiction: Uses "oddities" of all types including strange animals, strange laws, people, firsts, etc. Length: 50-100 words. Pays $10-15.

Tips: "Be sure that all oddities, strange laws, etc. are verified and not already copyrighted."

DIDATO ASSOCIATES, 280 Madison Ave., New York NY 10016. Rights purchased vary with author and material. Will consider photocopied submissions. Query or submit complete ms. Pays on acceptance or on publication. Reports "immediately." SASE.

Nonfiction: Quizzes which have a behavior science or psychology angle. Must have solid research references by behavior scientists or related professionals. Single feature examples: your clothes tell your personality; study reveals sex attitudes of teenagers; depression linked up with job blahs; terrorists are suicidal personalities, survey shows. Length: 500-2,000 words. Pays negotiable rates. Especially needs news-related story ideas and leads in outline form of about 100 words; also with one or more research references. Pays $50 for leads and psychology quizzes.

EDITORIAL CONSULTANT SERVICE, Box 524 West Hempstead NY 11552. Editorial Director: Arthur A. Ingoglia. Estab. 1965. "We work with 75 writers in the US and Canada." Syndicates material to newspapers, magazines and radio stations. Query. SASE. Reports in 3-4 weeks. Buys all rights. Writer's guidelines for SASE.

Needs: Magazine and newspaper columns and features; news items; and radio broadcast material. Prefers carefully documented material with automotive slant. Also considers trade features. Will consider article series. Author's percentage varies; usually averages 50%. Additional payment for 8x10 b&w and color photos accepted with ms. Currently syndicates *Let's Talk About Your Car*, by R. Hite; *Book Talk*, by L. Stevens; and *Car World*, by A. Ingoglia.

FACING SOUTH, Box 230, Chapel Hill NC 27514. (919)929-2141. Co-Editors: Chris Mayfield, Kathleen Zobel. Buys 52 columns/year for syndication to newspapers. Query or submit complete ms. SASE. Reports in 5 weeks. Buys all rights.

Needs: "700 to 750-word columns focusing on a Southern individual, allowing that person to tell a story. We need portraits of activists, innovators and artists. Each week a different writer does a column, although we will use more than one column by the same writer—just spread them over several months." Pays $50. "Writers must send for our guidelines before attempting a column." No payment for photos; "we just need some kind of a snapshot that our artist can use to do an illustration."

FIELD NEWSPAPER SYNDICATE, 1703 Kaiser Ave., Irving CA 92714. President/Chief Executive Officer: Richard Sherry. Estab. 1925. Syndicates material to newspapers. Submit "examples of work with explanatory letter." SASE. Reports in 1-2 months. Rights purchased vary. Free writer's guidelines.

Needs: Newspapers columns (should be 500-800 words in length and should appeal to a wide audience. Subject matter should not be too specialized because syndicates sell columns to newspapers all over the US and Canada). "Occasionally we use four-part series (approximately 5,000 words) covering a wide variety of subjects." Currently syndicates *Ann Landers*, by Ann Landers; *At Wit's End*, by Erma Bombeck; and *Washington Insight*, by Joseph Kraft.

GLOBAL COMMUNICATIONS, 303 5th Ave., Suite 1306, New York NY 10016. President: Timothy Green Beckley. "We supply material to publications in the US and overseas." Rights purchased vary with author and material. Usually buys second serial (reprint) rights or simultaneous rights. Buys 600 features/year. Will consider photocopied submissions. Send complete ms. Reports in 2 weeks. SASE.

Nonfiction, Fiction and Fillers: "Our interests are varied and include almost every area. Short fiction doesn't move very well. We go in for straight reporting and investigative pieces." Writing should be colorful, to the point, good news angle. "In addition to original material for US and foreign syndication, we are always looking for previously published pieces which the writer owns foreign rights to. Our material goes to publications in about 13 foreign countries. Our standard commission is 33% on all sales. However, sometimes we do purchase outright. Writers should send tearsheets and a letter stating they have rights to sell outside the US from original publisher." Currently, best markets include celebrity interviews and profiles, true psychic/UFO pieces (must be well-researched), adult fiction and nonfiction, human interest and, in general, "anything that is a bit unusual. We do not buy continuing columns." Sometimes will purchase material outright for $35-500, but 95% of material is handled on a commission basis. Mainly buys adult (sex) fiction; also adventure, western, erotica, science fiction, religious. Length: 2,000-5,000 words. Buys fillers: jokes, gags, anecdotes, short humor. Pays $5-25. Buys all rights. No poetry. "We try to give help and advice when possible and are always looking for 'newcomers' to work with. We have about a dozen stringers who send us stories constantly. Always room for more."

Photos: Photos purchased with accompanying ms with no additional payment. Or purchased with or without ms with extra payment. Captions required. Pays $15 minimum for b&w (8x10) and $25 minimum for color slides.

Columns: "Psychic Celebrities" and "Saucers and Celebrities." Materials for these columns are purchased outright. Payment: $50. Buys all rights. No byline.

DAVE GOODWIN & ASSOCIATES, P.O. Drawer 54-6661, Surfside FL 33154. Editor: Dave Goodwin. Rights purchased vary with author and material. May buy first rights or second serial (reprint) rights. Will handle copyrighted material. Buys 25 features/year. Query or submit complete ms. Reports in 3 weeks. SASE.

Nonfiction: "Money-saving information for consumers: how to save on home expenses; auto, medical, drug, insurance, boat, business items, etc." Buys article series on brief, practical, down-to-earth items for consumer use or knowledge. Rarely buys single features. Currently handling "Insurance for Consumers." Length: 300-5,000 words. Pays 50% on publication.

HARRIS & ASSOCIATES PUBLISHING DIVISION, 247 South 800 East, Logan UT 84321. (801)753-3587. President: Dick Harris. Rights purchased vary with author and material. May buy all rights or first rights. Does not purchase many mss per year because "material must be in our special style." Pays on acceptance. Send sample or representative material. Reports in 1 month. SASE.

Nonfiction, Photos and Humor: Material on driver safety and accident prevention. Humor for modern women (not women's lib); humor for sports page. "We like to look at anything in our special interest areas. Golf and tennis are our specialties. We'll also look at cartoons in these areas. Will buy or contract for syndication. Everything must be short, terse, with humorous approach." Action, unposed, 8x10 b&w photos are purchased without features or on assignment. Captions are required. Pays 10¢ minimum/word and $15 minimum/photo.

Tips: "Submit *good* photos or art with text."

HER SAY, 950 Howard St., San Francisco CA 94103. (415)956-3555. Editor/Publisher: Marlene Edmunds. Editors: Shelly Buck, Ann Milner, Marcia Bauman. Estab. May 1977. Buys 110 items/year for use in radio, magazines and newspapers. Query; submissions will not be returned. Reports in 3 weeks. Material is not copyrighted. Writer's guidelines for SASE.

Needs: "Her Say is a national women's weekly news service, going out to a number of radio news outlets and publications around the country, in Canada and in Europe. We are looking for input from researchers, writers and reporters from everywhere to help us keep posted on events concerning women. We would like items which can be rewritten to 75- to 250-word stories for both print and radio outlets. Keep an eye on the major news of the country and look for the holes in the news. Current status of legislation, socio-political research on, by, or for women, humorous items, new breakthroughs in medicine, scientific studies, and Third World news—these are the types of stories we would like to see." Pays $10/item.

HOLLYWOOD INSIDE SYNDICATE, Box 49957, Los Angeles CA 90049. Editor: John Austin. Purchases mss for syndication to newspapers in San Francisco, Philadelphia, Detroit, Montreal, London and Sydney. Query or submit complete ms. SASE. Reports in 4-6 weeks. Buys first rights or second serial (reprint) rights.

Needs: News items (column items concerning entertainment (motion picture) personalities and jet setters for syndicated column; 750-800 words). Also considers series of 1,500-word articles; "suggest descriptive query first." Pay negotiable. Pays on acceptance "but this is also negotiable because of delays in world market acceptance."

Tips: "Study the entertainment pages of Sunday (and daily) newspapers to see the type of specialized material we deal in. Perhaps we are different from other syndicates, but we deal with celebrities and particularly not 'I' journalism such as when 'I spoke to Cloris Leachman.' Many freelancers submit material from the 'dinner theater' and summer stock circuit of 'gossip type' items from what they have observed about the 'stars' or featured players in these productions—how they act offstage, who they romance, etc. We use this material."

INTERNATIONAL EDITORIAL SERVICE/NEWSWEEK, INC., 444 Madison Ave., New York NY 10022. Vice President: R.J. Melvin. Offers on speculation to listing of Newsweek worldwide associates first rights or second serial (reprint) rights. Offers 50-100 features, over 1,000 photos and graphics a year. Will consider photocopied submissions. Query. Reports in 3 months. SASE.

Nonfiction and Photos: News items, backgrounders, personalities in the news. News-related features suitable for international syndication. Prefers 900-1,200 words for features. Pays 50% on publication. Photos purchased with features. Pays $25-75 for b&w if purchased separately.

INTERPRESS OF LONDON AND NEW YORK, 400 Madison Ave., New York NY 10017. (212)832-2539. Editor: Jeffrey Blyth. Buys British and European rights mostly, but can handle world rights. Will consider photocopied submissions. Query or submit complete ms. Pays on publication, or agreement of sale. Reports "immediately or as soon as practicable." SASE.

Nonfiction and Photos: "Unusual stories and photos for British and European press. Picture stories, for example, on such 'Americana' as a five-year-old evangelist; the 800-pound 'con-man,' the nude-male calendar; tallest girl in the world; interviews with pop celebrities such as Yoko Ono, Bob Dylan, Sen. Kennedy, Margaret Trudeau, Priscilla Presley, Cheryl Tiegs, Liza Minelli; cult subjects such as voodoo, college fads, anything amusing or offbeat. Extracts from books such as Earl Wilson's *Show Business Laid Bare*, inside-Hollywood type series ('Secrets of the Stuntmen,' 'My Life with Racquel Welch'). Real life adventure dramas ('Three Months in an Open Boat,' 'The Air Crash Cannibals of the Andes'). No length limits—short or long, but not too long. Payment varies; depending on whether material is original, or world rights. Pay top rates, up to several thousand dollars, for exclusive material. Photos purchased with or without features. Captions required. Standard size prints, suitable for radioing if necessary. Pay $50-100, but no limit on exclusive material."

KEISTER ADVERTISING SERVICE, Strasburg VA 22657. Editor: G. Walton Lindsay. Buys 25-30 mss/year for syndication to newspapers. Query with samples/credits. SASE. Reports in 1-2 months. Buys all rights.

Needs: "Our copy is limited to about 150 words and deals with human-interest illustrations that lead casually but persuasively into a plea for church membership and attendance. Style should compete with rest of newspaper and not be of a 'preachy' sermonette-like nature." Photos purchased without features; captions required. Pays $15-20/item. Pays on acceptance.

KING FEATURES SYNDICATE, INC., 235 E. 45th St., New York NY 10017. (212)682-5600. Executive Editor: Allan Priaulx. Estab. 1920. "We have about 55 regular text features, and add one to five new features annually." Syndicates material to newspapers. Submit "brief cover letter with samples of feature proposals." SASE. Reports in 2-3 weeks. Buys all rights.

Needs: Newspaper features and columns. Will consider article series. Pays "revenue commission percentage."

Tips: "Be brief, thoughtful and offer some evidence that the feature proposal is viable."

KNOWLEDGE NEWS & FEATURES SYNDICATE, Kenilworth IL 60043. (312)256-0059. Executive Editor: Dr. Whitt N. Schultz. Rights purchased vary with author and material. Usually buys all rights. Will consider photocopied submissions. Query. Reports in 10 days. SASE.

Business Features, Photos and Nonfiction: News items; humor; fillers; business, knowledge and education articles; "success stories." Buys article series. May buy single features. Will contract for columns for syndication. Length: 1,000 minimum for features; 500 minimum for columns. Payment negotiable. Photos purchased with features and also on assignment. Captions required. Buys 8x10 glossy photos. Payment negotiable.

Tips: "Clear, crisp, concise, urgent writing—easy to read—open—spotlight success, inspiration; positive news features."

MIKE LeFAN FEATURES. 1802 S. 13th, Temple TX 76501. Editor: Mike LeFan. Estab. 1974. Buys "about 50 items annually. Much of the outside material used is submitted by readers of my features, but I'm quite willing to pay for suitable pieces from freelancers. My syndicated features appear in magazines, and in daily and weekly newspapers." Submit complete ms; 1 item to a page. SASE. Reports in 3 weeks. Material is not copyrighted.
Needs: Fillers (practical, usable items on how people can get more for their money, up to 250 words). "An acceptable filler tells the average man or woman how to get more for their money on food, utilities, travel, clothing, auto, household needs, entertainment, or any other area of daily life, but the ideas must be practical and useful. There are no bylines as such, but items will be credited within the text of a particular column to identify the writer." Pays $2/filler. Currently syndicates *More For Your Money* (a weekly column) and *More For Your Money Fillers* to a readership of about 400,000.
Tips: "I do not want to see general household tips. All the items must relate to column's theme—more for your money."

MEDIA WEST, E. 302-26th, Spokane WA 99203. (509)624-7290. President: George Cole. Estab. 1974. "On the average, I will purchase 1-2 features a week for use in newspapers, newsletters and radio programs." Submit complete ms; for broadcast material, submit tape. SASE. Reports in 3 weeks. Buys first North American serial rights. Writer's guidelines $1.
Needs: Newspaper features (prefers lively style); news items (200-800 words); fillers; and radio broadcast material (prefers interviews or produced features, 1-10 minutes in length). Also interested in longer how-to material and information about job markets, media, trends, life styles. "My radio 'Magazine' series can use book reviews, film reviews, interviews, and features for a general audience." Pays minimum guarantee $10; "will go higher if work so merits." Pays $7-20 for 5x7 or 8x10 b&w glossy photos. Currently syndicates *Careers Today, Media Report,* and *Survival Guide.*

NATIONAL CATHOLIC NEWS SERVICE, 1312 Massachusetts Ave. NW, Washington DC 20005. Editor: Richard W. Daw. "We are served by a number of stringers as well as freelancers. We provide a daily service and have a fairly constant market. Inquiries are welcomed, but they should be both brief and precise. Too many inquiries are coy and/or vague. Will consider photocopied submissions." Pays on publication. Reports in 4-5 weeks. SASE.
Nonfiction: Short news and feature items of religious or social interest, particularly items with a Catholic thrust. Buys single features and article series. Feature examples: FCC plagued by letters about non-existent petition from atheist; clown tours America as God's Good Humor Man; bishop lives in house heated 20 degrees cooler than White House. Series examples: Moral implications and religious involvement in capital punishment issue; Catholic schools and integration. Contracts for columns: "This is a highly competitive market and we are extremely selective. Our columns range from labor concerns to the liturgy." Length for single features: 800 words maximum. Article series: maximum of 3 parts, about 700 words each. Columns: open in length; generally, the shorter the better. Generally pays 5¢/word maximum for news and feature copy. Buys book reviews at 3¢/word for 500 words maximum. Does not buy *unsolicited* reviews, but welcomes queries. We market primarily to more than 100 Catholic weekly newspapers. We also serve foreign Catholic agencies and US Catholic/weekly newspapers."
Photos: Purchased with or without features. "Captions helpful but not required. News and feature photos of interest to Catholic periodicals. Also other religions, family, humor and seasonal. No churches, travel, scenes, animals or flowers. We buy 1,000 photos a year." Pays $20/b&w 8x10. SASE. Samples must accompany queries for assignment. Pay negotiable.

NEW YORK TIMES SYNDICATION SALES CORP., 200 Park Ave., New York NY 10017. (212)972-1070. Acquistions Editor of Special Features: Carlos J. Sandoval. Estab. 1970. Syndicates "about one book or feature per week primarily in newspapers." Also included in foreign newspapers and magazines. "If the feature is not long, like a 2,500-word one-shot, send the complete manuscript. If longer, send one part first." SASE. Prefers world rights but often buys North American second serial rights; for books, "first, second or both" rights.
Needs: Wants magazine and newspaper features; magazine and newspaper columns; and book series. "Medical subjects are good, exclusive interviews with personalities (especially if they are those who don't normally give interviews), how-tos, biographies of stars, and education." Recently ran the Margaret Trudeau memoirs. "Don't send anything fancy, cute or tricky. The field is pretty wide open, but use facts not widely disseminated—news pegs are always good ideas. We recently received a piece about the Amish, but there was no news peg. It was a *National Geographic* kind of story and I didn't think it would sell so we didn't use it."

Advances are rare. After production costs are taken, the syndication usually offers the author a 50-50 split of the profit. Total purchase price includes payment for photos. "If you don't have to include photos, don't."

NEWS FLASH INTERNATIONAL, INC., 508 Atlanta Ave., North Massapequa NY 11758. Editor: Jackson B. Pokress. Supplies material to Observer newspapers and Champion sports publications. "Contact editor prior to submission to allow for space if article is newsworthy." Photocopied submissions OK. Pays on publication. SASE.
Nonfiction: "We have been supplying a 'ready-for-camera' sports page (tabloid size) complete with column and current sports photos on a weekly basis to many newspapers on Long Island as well as pictures and written material to publications in England and Canada. Payment for assignments is based on the article. It may vary. Payments vary from $20 for a feature of 800 words. Our sports stories feature in-depth reporting as well as book reviews on this subject. We are always in the market for good photos, sharp and clear, action photos of boxing, football and baseball. We cover all major league ball parks during the baseball and football seasons. We are accredited to the Mets, Yanks, Jets and Giants. During the winter we cover basketball and hockey and all sports events at the Nassau Coliseum."
Photos: Purchased on assignment; captions required. Uses "good quality 8x10 b&w glossy prints; good choice of angles and lenses." Pays $7.50 minimum for b&w photos.
Tips: "Submit articles, which are fresh in their approach, on a regular basis. Articles should have a hard-hitting approach and plenty of quotes and short, terse sentences."

NEWSPAPER ENTERPRISE ASSOCIATION, INC., 200 Park Ave., New York NY 10017. (212)557-5870. Executive Editor: David Hendin. Estab. 1902. Syndicates material to newspapers. Query or submit complete ms. SASE. Reports in 3 weeks. Buys all rights.
Needs: Newspaper columns and features, fillers and comics. Will consider article series. Pays varies according to purchase. Photos should accompany all submissions; no additional payment.

NEWS WORLD SYNDICATE, 401 5th Ave., New York NY 10016. (212)532-8300. Editor: Julie Phillips. Estab. 1977. "We have purchased 9 columns this year and as the syndicate grows, we will buy more columns and feature articles"; for use in daily and weekly newspapers. Query with clips of published work. Submissions will not be returned; "they will be filed for future consideration. This way the writer always has a chance with us." Reports in 4-6 weeks. Buys first North American and Philippine serial rights.
Needs: Newspaper features (will consider all types, 900 words maximum); newspaper columns (all types, 900 words maximum); and fiction (1,500 words maximum; submit to Julie Phillips). Will consider article series of 5-6 parts, 900 words/part. Pays 50% author's percentage. Currently syndicates *Pop, Rock and Soul*, by Irwin Stambler (popular music), *Tony Brown's Journal* (commentary); and *Spin Off*, by Harold Fuller (jazz music).

NORTH AMERICAN NEWSPAPER ALLIANCE, 200 Park Ave., New York NY 10017. Executive Editor: Sidney Goldberg. Editor: Sheldon Engelmayer. Supplies material to leading US and Canadian newspapers, also to South America, Europe, Asia and Africa. Rights purchased vary with author and material. May buy all rights, first rights, or second serial (reprint) rights. Pays "on distribution to clients." Query or submit complete ms. Reports in 2 weeks. SASE.
Nonfiction and Photos: In the market for background, interpretive and news features. Life style trends, national issues that affect individuals and neighborhoods. The news element must be strong and purchases are generally made only from experienced, working newspapermen. Wants timely news features of national interest that do not duplicate press association coverage but add to it, interpret it, etc. Wants first-class nonfiction suitable for feature development. The story must be aimed at newspapers, must be self-explanatory, factual and well-condensed. It must add measurably to the public's information or understanding of the subject, or be genuinely entertaining. Broad general interest is the key to success here. Length: 300-800 words. Rarely buys columns. Looking for good 1-shots and good series of 2-7 articles. Where opinions are given, the author should advise, for publication, his qualifications to comment on specialized subjects. The news must be exclusive to be considered at all. Length: 800 words maximum. Rate varies depending on length and news value. Minimum rate $25, but will go considerably higher for promotable copy. Buys 8x10 glossy photos when needed to illustrate story; pays $5-10.

NUMISMATIC INFORMATION SERVICE, Rossway Rd., Rt. 4, Box 232, Pleasant Valley

NY 12569. Editor: Barbara White. Estab. 1961. Buys 5 features/year. Query. SASE. Reports in 1-2 weeks. Buys all rights.
Needs: Newspaper columns (anything related to numismatics and philately, particularly the technical aspects of the avocations); news items (relative to the world of coin and stamp collecting); and fillers (on individual coins or stamps, or the various aspects of the hobbies). No fiction. Pays $5/500 word article; 50¢ additional payment for b&w photos accepted with ms.

OCEANIC PRESS SERVICE, Box 4158, North Hollywood CA 91607. Editor: John Taylor. Buys from 12-15 writers annually, "using their published work" for use in magazines, newspapers or books. Query with clips of published work. SASE. Reports in 3 weeks. Buys all rights, or second serial (reprint) rights. Writer's guidelines $1.
Needs: "We like authors and cartoonists, but, for our mutual benefit, they must fit into our editorial policies. The following list will give an idea of the kind of materials we want: interviews or profiles (world figures only); recipes, with color transparencies or b&w pictures; home building and home decoration features with photos; hairstyle features with photos; published cartoons and cartoon books; interviews with movie and TV stars with photos; current books to be sold for translation to foreign markets: mysteries, biographies, westerns, science fiction, romance, psychological and gothic novels; features on family relations, sex, gambling, heroism, and ecology; features on water sports, with color transparencies; and newspaper columns with illustrations. We are always happy to obtain reprint rights, especially book excerpts or serializations. Payment is outright or on a 50/50 basis. We take care of foreign language translations."

PUNGENT PRAYER, 404 E. Elm, West Frankfort IL 62896. (618)937-2898. Editor: Phil E. Pierce. Estab. 1969. Buys 52 items/year for use in secular newspapers. Query with clips of published work or submit complete ms. SASE. Reports in 2 weeks. "Writers may choose to control copyright or not." Samples and writer's guidelines and samples for #10 SASE.
Needs: "*Pungent Prayer* is a weekly feature syndicated to a few secular newspapers. We buy stories of answered prayer and colorful prayers aimed toward the interests of nonchurchmen and, once or twice only each year, an inspiring poem about prayer. Our maximum is 300 words or 37 lines (of 51 spaces each). We are *not interested* in general religious items nor ordinary prayer. We're shifting our emphasis to use fewer prayers and more stories of answered prayers. Submissions (poetry or prose) should carry human interest—family or personal problems, social concerns pathos, candor, joy or especially humor. The prayers of children and youth frequently qualify. We welcome special day and holiday prayers (poetry seems to fit here). Pays $2-8.

THE REGISTER AND TRIBUNE SYNDICATE, INC., 715 Locust St., Des Moines IA 50304. President: Dennis R. Allen. Buys material for syndication in newspapers. Submit complete ms. SASE. Photocopied submissions preferred. Reports in 6 weeks. Buys all rights.
Needs: News items (nonfiction); and photos (purchased with written material). Buys article series "from 500-700 words on current topics such as the metric system, motorcycles, self-improvement programs, seasonal series for Christmas and Easter. Pays in royalties. Pays on publication.

RELIGIOUS NEWS SERVICE, 43 W. 57th St., New York NY 10019. Editor-in-Chief: Lillian R. Block. Managing Editor: Gerald Renner. Supplies material to "secular press, religious press of all denominations, radio and TV stations." SASE.
Nonfiction and Photos: "Good news stories on important newsworthy developments. Religious news." Will buy single features "if they have news pegs. Most of our article series are produced by our own staff." Length: 200-1,000 words. Pays 2¢/word. Photos purchased with and without features and on assignment; captions required. Uses b&w glossy prints, preferably 8x10. Pays $5 minimum.

SAWYER PRESS, Syndication Dept., Box 46-578, Los Angeles CA 90046. Editor: E. Mattlen. Buys all rights. Buys 100 cartoons/year. Will consider photocopied submissions. Submit complete cartoons only. Reports in 3-4 weeks. SASE.
Needs: Articles/columns on how-to topics such as photography and other crafts. Seeking material on "self-sufficiency": starting own business, country living, construction of dwellings, etc. Length: 500-1,000 words. Query with sample. SASE.
Cartoons: Editorial cartoons suitable for college newspapers. Sophisticated social commentary. Royalty or outright purchase; varies with quality of material. Also looking for Barbarella/John Wiley Stanton type of illustrating and cartoon strips, b&w and color.

BP SINGER FEATURES, INC., 3164 W. Tyler Ave., Anaheim CA 92801. (714)527-5650. Acting President: Eldon Maynard. Estab. 1940. Syndicates to newspapers, magazines, and book publishers. Query with clips of published work. SASE. Reports in 3 weeks. Buys all rights, or domestic and foreign reprint rights. Writer's guidelines $1.
Needs: Magazine and newspaper features with international interest; fiction slanted to women readers; and fillers (juvenile puzzles, games, and how-to's). Will consider article series if previously published. Pays 50% author's commission. Pays $25-50 for 8x10 b&w photos or 120mm or 4x5 color transparencies. Currently syndicates *Solv-A-Crime*, by A.C. Gordon (mystery series); and *Celebrities Speak*, by J. Finletter (interviews). Serializes books (romance, western, mysteries, war, historical romance, doctor-nurse books). Published books only.

SOCCER ASSOCIATES, Box 634, New Rochelle NY 10802. Managing Director: Irma Ganz Miller. Estab. 1947. Query. SASE. Reports in 2 weeks. Buys all rights.
Needs: Newspaper features. Payment "varies with assignment." Currently syndicates *Soccer Shots; Book Reviews*; and *New Products*.

TEENAGE CORNER, INC., 70-540 Gardenia Ct., Rancho Mirage CA 92270. President: David J. Lavin. Estab. 1959. Buys 122 items/year for use in newspapers. Submit complete ms. Reports in 1 week. Material is not copyrighted.
Needs: 500-word newspaper features. Pays $25.

TRANS-WORLD NEWS SERVICE, INC., Box 2801, Washington DC 20013. (202)638-5568. President/Managing Editor: Robert F. Hurleigh. Executive Vice President: Claud D. Fleet. Estab. 1924. "We purchase or market 8,000-10,000 articles a year internationally." Query with clips of published work. SASE. Reports in 4-6 weeks. Buys all rights. Writer's guidelines for SASE.
Needs: Newspaper features (400-750 words, prefers balanced articles); newspaper columns (400-800 words; most any subject with continuity); fillers (10-60 words; any suitable subject); radio broadcast material (recorded programs for syndication or scripts 2-30 minutes in length). Buys one-shot features on science, travel, women's material or collectibles. Article series not to exceed 6 in series, average 450-800 words on political, historical, consumer expose, etc. Pays 50% commission or $25-200. Pays $10-100 for 5x7 or larger b&w glossy photos accepted with ms. Currently syndicates *The Handicapped*, by M. Becker (health); *Miracle of Faith*, by G. Katz (religion); and *International Dateline*, by W. Halterman.

UNITED FEATURE SYNDICATE, 200 Park Ave., New York NY 10017. Managing Editor: Sidney Goldberg. Supplies material to newspapers throughout the world. Will handle copyrighted material. Buys 25-50 series/year, preferably 3-7 articles (world rights preferred). Buys first and/or second rights to book serializations. Query with outline. Reports in 3 weeks. SASE.
Nonfiction, Comic Strips and Puzzles: News, features, series, columns, comic strips, puzzles. Current columnists include Jack Anderson, Marquis Childs, Henry Taylor, Virginia Payette, Barbara Gibbons. Comic strips include *Peanuts, Nancy, Tarzan*. Rates negotiable for one-shot purchases. Standard syndication contracts are offered for columns and comic strips.

UNITED PRESS INTERNATIONAL (UPI), 220 E. 42nd St., New York NY 10017. Editor-in-Chief: H.L. Stevenson. "We seldom, if ever, accept material outside our own ranks."

U.S. NEWS SERVICE, 777 National Press Bldg., Washington DC 20045. Bureau Chief: Walter Fisk. Buys all rights. May handle copyrighted material. May not return rejected material. SASE.
Nonfiction, Humor, Fiction, Photos, Fillers and Poetry: Buys singlefeatures and column ideas. Length varies. Payment varies. 8x10 single-weight glossy prints purchased with features, without features, and on assignment. Captions required.

UNIVERSAL PRESS SYNDICATE, 6700 Squibb Rd., Mission KS 66202. Editor: James F. Andrews. Buys syndication rights. Reports normally in 4 weeks. SASE.
Nonfiction: Looking for features—columns for daily and weekly newspapers. "Any material suitable for syndication in daily newspapers." Currently handling *Doonesbury* by G.B. Trudeau, Garry Wills column, etc. Payment varies according to contract.

UNIVERSAL TRADE PRESS SYNDICATE, 85 South St., New York NY 10038. Editor: Paul Gruberg. Buys first trade paper rights only. Query. SASE.
Nonfiction: Buys art features in all fields; fine art merchandising at the retail level; features on

galleries, museums, artists. Length: 1,250 words. Pays 65%.

WILLIAMS NEWSPAPER FEATURES SYNDICATE, INC., Box 8005, Charlottesville VA 22906. (804)293-4709. Vice President/Art Director: Jean S. Lindsay. Estab. 1939. Buys 52 features/year for use in newspapers. Query. SASE. Reports in 2 weeks. Buys all rights.
Needs: Newspaper features and religious advertising copy suitable for illustration. Pays $25. Pays $25 for photos purchased with accompanying ms; "must be suitable for 4-5 column reproduction in newspapers." Currently syndicates *You in the Church; The Church in You.*

WILSON FEATURES. Box 369, Marysville OH 43040. President: Rick Wilson. Estab. October 1974. Buys approximately 50-100 cartoons, fillers, editorial features and informational columns for use in newspapers and magazines. Query with clips of published work. SASE. Reports in 2-3 weeks. Buys second serial (reprint) rights.
Needs: Newspaper features columns, and fillers. Pays 50% author's percentage. Currently syndicates *Tornado*, by Rick Wilson (informational cartoon strip); Editorial cartoons by Ken Fischer; *Doc Doodle*, by Ross Bunch (children's strip); and *From the Kitchen Shelf*, by Doris Smith (cooking column).

WOMEN'S NEWS SERVICE, 200 Park Ave., New York NY 10017. Editor: Sidney Goldberg. Buys 300 features/year for syndication for newspapers. Query or submit complete ms. SASE. Reports in 3 weeks. Buys all rights, first rights, or second serial (reprint) rights.
Needs: News items (news features, backgrounders, sidebars to events in the news of interest to women's and lifestyles pages; best length is 400-600 words); fiction (outline of plot and description of characters, with one sample chapter); fillers (news-pegged fillers preferred, 100-150 words; of interest to women's and lifestyle pages) and photos (purchased with written material; captions required). Considers "series of 3-6 articles, 700 words or so each. Series should be pegged on news event or a trend, unless service-oriented." Pays $150 minimum for series; $25 minimum for one-shots "higher depending on importance or interest;" $5-15 for fillers. Photos bring $5-15 for b&w glossy prints.
Tips: "Put your headline material in your lead, keep your stories short; avoid folksy essays, type accurately with plenty of space for editing. If we like your one-shots and use them frequently, we'll be open to a percentage arrangement."

WORLD-WIDE NEWS BUREAU, 309 Varick St., Jersey City NJ 07302. Editor: Arejas Vitkauskas. SASE.
Nonfiction: "Our multiple writeups (separate, and in our weekly columns), start in greater New York publications, then go simultaneously all over the US and all over the world where English is printed. News from authors, literary agents or publishers on books planned, ready or published. Anything from poetry and children's books, to space technology textbooks. We cover over eighty different trade fields."

ZODIAC NEWS SERVICE, 950 Howard St., San Francisco CA 94103. (415)956-3555. Editor: Jon Newhall. Estab. 1972. "We purchase about 1,000 pieces of material from a loose network of 100+ stringers in the United States and Canada, for radio use mainly, with a few magazines, newspapers, and TV stations." Submissions returned "if specifically requested. We usually assume SASEs are for payment, not return of submissions, so please note otherwise." Buys first North American serial rights; "we want exclusive rights for 48 hours." Writer's guidelines for SASE.
Needs: "We are a reliable source of up-to-date news which is often ignored, overlooked or misinterpreted by the major wire services. Our clients are primarily radio stations, ranging from progressive FM and college radio outlets to top-40 and all-news formats. Although we are based in San Francisco, our coverage is international, and so, we are looking for stringers worldwide. If you have story leads, ideas or news items that can be reported in a radio format (i.e., within the frustrating confines of 200 words) please telephone or mail them to our San Francisco office. We pay $10 for each story lead or item used. Most of our successful stringers receive regular payments by spotting ZNS-type items, which are often overlooked by the major wire services in daily or weekly publications."
Tips: "Scan all the newspapers, magazines and other publications at your disposal, clipping out and sending to ZNS all items that might conceivably be of interest. The greater the number of submissions, the more likely that at least some will be accepted."

Trade, Technical, and Professional Journal

"Freelancers are very important because they can provide much broader coverage than could a centrally based editor," says Paul Krantz, supervisory editor of *Sales Manager's Bulletin*. "Often, they can bring fresh insights to shopworn ideas. Freelancers who submit regularly and professionally are an editor's dream."

A professional submission to a trade journal means a solid, accurate, in-depth approach to writing. Although some trade publications are probably too specialized for the general writer, others are open to the freelancer who can grasp a subject quickly, and write clearly and tightly. Most trade journals appeal to one of three audiences: *retailers*, who are interested in unusual store displays, successful sales campaigns, and other ways of making money or managing businesses efficiently; *manufacturers*, who want stories on solving industry problems, equipment reports, and other such coverage; and *professionals and industry experts*, interested in technical and other developments. Whatever its audience, the trade journal has one purpose: to help its reader to do his job better. "Readers buy our magazine ($7.50 per issue) for profit, not pleasure," says John T. Hiatt, managing editor of *Entrepreneur Magazine*.

For solid tips on approaching magazines in general, consult the introduction to the Consumer Publications section, but remember that writing for trade publications demands more specialization than does writing for consumer magazines. "We are looking for writers experienced in publishing who can write of the field *authoritatively*," says George Trinkaus, editor of *BooksWest Magazine*. Jay Kruzo, editor of *Collision*, puts it succinctly when he says, "Know your subject matter ten times over before putting it on paper. You cannot communicate what you don't know or don't understand."

Of course, a nonspecialist writer who does careful research can sell to these magazines. In fact, such a writer can often take technical material and communicate it in layman's terms, avoiding the jargon a specialist might fall into. Articles for *Entrepreneur* "must have an authoritative tone, yet be written in everyday language for the average reader," says John Hiatt. Paul Krantz notes that well-researched material can open the door at *Sales Manager's Bulletin*: "One of the easiest ways to start is with a 'round-up' article (here's what 12 sales executives have to say about. . .). Get names and numbers from industrial directories at your local library.

Remember that any editor's ultimate need is a publishable manuscript, no matter who submits it. "We are extremely receptive to all writers who display professionalism," says Mary Sprouse, a managing editor with *West Coast Writer's Conspiracy*. "Anyone who meets our market requirements, types his manuscripts and is literate will be given a chance to prove himself. We do not care if a writer is previously unpublished as long as he does a good, professional job for us."

One way of proving you can do a good, professional job is by regularly submitting short, informative items. "As a freelancer myself, I started by writing to certain magazines and offering my services as a stringer, and it paid off," says Carol Saus Goldsmith, editor of *LandMarc*. "Prove yourself to the editor by tracking down news items or info the magazine needs for another story. Then, after the editor sees you are reliable and really seem interested in doing a good job for the magazine, he may trust you to do a larger story."

Reliability is important to editors. "I am always amazed at the number of people who claim they wish to write, but don't follow through," says Paul Krantz. "For every 100 guideline sheets I send out, perhaps five queries will be returned. For every five queries accepted, only one or two articles will be submitted. I don't think most beginners realize that freelance writing—any kind of writing—is hard work—harder in many ways than ditchdigging or selling insurance or just about anything else. Freelancing means running your own business; unless you are willing it invest a good deal of time and energy, your business is going to fail."

Freelancing to trade journals also means helping magazine readers run *their* businesses. Minding the other guy's business can be good business for you.

Accounting

CGA MAGAZINE, #700-535 Thurlow St., Vancouver, British Columbia, Canada V6E 3L2. (604)681-3538. 25% freelance written. For accountants and financial managers. Magazine published 9 times/year; 44 pages. Circ. 25,000. Pays on acceptance. Buys one-time rights. Byline given. Phone queries OK. Simultaneous and photocopied submissions OK. SASE. Reports in 2-4 weeks. Free sample copy and writer's guidelines.
Nonfiction: "Accounting and financial subjects of interest to highly qualified professional accountants as opposed to accountants in public practice. All submissions must be relevant to Canadian accounting. All material must be of top professional quality, but at the same time written simply and interestingly." How-to; humor; informational; personal experience; personal opinion; and technical. Buys 36 mss/year. Query. Length: 1,500-2,000 words. Pays $100-500.
Photos: State availability of photos with query. Offers no additional payment for 8x10 b&w glossy prints.

Advertising and Marketing

Trade journals for professional advertising executives, copywriters and marketing men are listed in this category. Those whose main interests are the advertising and marketing of specific products (such as Groceries or Office Equipment and Supplies) are classified under individual product categories.

AD TECHNIQUES, ADA Publishing Co., 19 W. 44th St., New York NY 10036. (212)354-0450. Managing Editor: Elaine Louie. 10% freelance written. For advertising executives. Monthly magazine; 50 pages. Estab. 1965. Circ. 4,500. Pays on acceptance. Not copyrighted. Reports in 1 month. Sample copy $1.
Nonfiction: Articles on advertising techniques. Buys 10 mss/year. Query. Pays $25-50.

ADVERTISING AGE, 740 N. Rush, Chicago IL 60611. Managing Editor: L.E. Doherty. Currently staff-produced. "New in 1979: A weekly section devoted to one topic (i.e., marketing in Southern California; agribusiness/advertising; TV syndication trends). Much of this material is done freelance—on assignment only." Pays kill fee "based on hours spent plus expenses." Byline given "except short articles or contributions to a roundup."

AMERICAN DEMOGRAPHICS, American Demographics, Inc., Box 68, Ithaca NY 13840. (607)273-6343. Editor: Bryant Robey. For private businessmen, market researchers, media and communications people, public policymakers and those in academic world. Monthly magazine; 48 pages. Estab. 1979. Circ. 2,200. Pays on publication. Copyrighted. Buys all rights. Phone queries OK. Submit seasonal/holiday material 5-6 months in advance. Simultaneous, photocopied and previously published submissions OK. SASE. Reports on queries 1 month; on mss in 2 months. Include self-addressed, stamped postcard for return word that ms arrived safely. Sample copy $3; free writer's guidelines.
Nonfiction: General Interest (on demographic trends, profile of business using demographic data); how-to (on the use of demographic techniques, understand projections, data, apply demography to business and planning); humor (about demographers).
Columns/Departments:"We are writing departments in-house now, but would consider contributors—writers with ideas should call (607)273-6343, those with book review suggestions (607)277-4878.
Fillers: Clippings, anecdotes and newsbreaks. Length: 200-1,000 words. Pays$5-25.

ART DIRECTION, Advertising Trade Publications, Inc., 19 W. 44th St., New York NY 10036. (212)354-0450. Managing Editor: Alexis Gelber. 15% freelance written. Emphasizes advertising

design for art directors of ad agencies (corporate, in-plant, editorial, freelance, etc.). Monthly magazine; 100 pages. Estab. 1949. Circ. 12,000. Pays on publication. Buys one-time rights. SASE. Reports in 3 months. Sample copy $1.75.
Nonfiction: How-to articles on advertising campaigns. Pays $25 minimum.

THE COUNSELOR MAGAZINE, Advertising Specialty Institute, NBS Bldg., 2nd and Clearview Ave., Trevose PA 19047. (215)355-5800. Editor: James L. Trichon. For executives, both distributors and suppliers, in the industry. Monthly magazine; 250 pages. Estab. 1951. Circ. 5,000. Pays on publication. Buys first rights. Submit seasonal/holiday material 3 months in advance. Simultaneous, photocopied and previously published submissions OK. Reports in one month. Free writer's guidelines.
Nonfiction: Expose (of government and financial); how-to (get promotions); interview (with executives and government figures); profile (of executives); travel (business and technical industry material only). Buys 100 mss/year. Length: 1,000 minimum. Query. Pays $75-150.
Photos: State availability of photos. B&w photos only. Prefers contact sheet(s) and 8x10 prints. Offers no additional payment for photos accepted with ms. Captions and model releases required. Buys one-time rights.
Columns/Departments: "We need a sales column." Buys 5 mss/issue. Query with clips of published work. Length: 600-1,000 words. Pays $35-75. Open to suggestions for new columns or departments.
Fillers: Short humor. Buys 5 mss/issue. Length 25-75 words. Pays $5.

INCENTIVE MARKETING, Bill Communications, Inc., 633 3rd Ave., New York NY 10017. (212)986-4800. Editor-in-Chief: Murray Elman. For buyers of merchandise used in motivational promotions. Monthly magazine; 200 pages. Estab. 1905. Circ. 37,000. Pays on acceptance. Buys all rights, but may reassign following publication. No byline. SASE. Reports in 2 weeks. Free sample copy and writer's guidelines.
Nonfiction: Informational, case histories. Buys 60-75 mss/year. Query. Length: 1,500 words minimum. Pays $85-125.

MAC/WESTERN ADVERTISING, 6565 Sunset Blvd., Los Angeles CA 90028. Editor: Lee Kerry. For "people involved in advertising: media, agencies, and client organizations as well as affiliated businesses." Weekly. Buys all rights. Pays on acceptance. Reports in 1 month. Query. SASE.
Nonfiction and Photos: "Advertising in the West. Not particularly interested in success stories. We want articles by experts in advertising, marketing, communications." Length: 1,000-1,750 words. Pays $100. Photos purchased with mss.

PROFESSIONAL SALESMAN'S LETTER, Januz Marketing Communications, Inc., 1370 Longwood Rd., Lake Forest IL 60045. President: L.R. Januz. Emphasizes professional selling techniques for "professional salesmen in industry, finance, automobiles, travel, etc.—our subscriber is the sales manager who buys bulk copies for his salesmen." Semimonthly newsletter; 4 pages. Estab. 1978. Circ. 3,000. Pays on publication. Buys all rights. "No submissions will be returned—will be held for permanent consideraton. If the item is not used (and paid for) within one year the writer can probably figure we won't use it." Sample copy $1.
Nonfiction: Interview ("must be actual stories by a salesman/writer of how he/she sold the big one or cracked the difficult account"). The only thing we want are one- and two-paragraph (if it is over two paragraphs long we cannot use it) articles about how a salesman successfully dosed a sale, or a selling technique that has resulted in selling. We have no use for any other material and will not read or return it." Buys 3-4 mss/issue. Send complete ms; doesn't answer queries. Length: 1-3 paragraphs. Pays $5-10.

SALES & MARKETING MANAGEMENT IN CANADA, Ingmar Communications, Ltd., 416 Moore Ave., Suite 303, Toronto, Ontario, Canada M4G 1C9. (416)424-4441. Editor/Publisher: B.M. (Bob) Gosschalk. For sales and marketing and other business executives responsible for the sale and marketing of their products and services. Magazine published 16 times/year. Estab. 1918. Circ. 45,000. Buys all rights. Buys the occasional outstanding article on selling and marketing; domestic and international. Pays on publication. Will send free sample copy to writer on request. Reports in 2 weeks. Query. SASE
Nonfiction: "Articles on the sales and marketing operations of companies, concerning the evaluation of markets for products and services; the planning, packaging, advertising, promotion, distribution and servicing of them, and the management and training of the sales force." Informational, how-to, personal experience, interview, profile, humor, think pieces, expose, spot news, successful business operations, new product, merchandising techniques.

technical. Length: 500-1,800 words. Payment negotiable.

VISUAL MERCHANDISING, S.T. Publications, 407 Gilbert Ave., Cincinnati OH 45202.
Editor: J. R. Swormstedt. Emphasizes store design and display. Monthly magazine; 72 pages.
Circ. 9,500. Pays on publication. Submit seasonal or holiday material 8 months in advance.
Simultaneous, photocopied and previously published submissions OK. SASE. Reports in 1
month.
Nonfiction: Expose, how-to (display), informational (store design, construction, merchandise
display), interview (display directors and shop owners), nostalgia (store architecture, display,
etc.), profile (new and remodeled stores), new product, photo feature (window display),
technical (store lighting, carpet, wallcoverings, fixtures). Buys 24 mss/year. Query or submit
complete ms. Length: 500-2,000 words. Pays $100-150.
Photos: Purchased with or without accompanying ms or on assignment. Pays $5 for 5x7 b&w
glossy prints. Submit contact sheet. Seeks photos or general subjects on lighting, planning,
design and merchandising.
How To Break In: "Be fashion and design conscious and reflect that in the article. Submit
finished mss with photos always. Look for stories on department store display directors
(profiles, methods, views on the industry, sales promotions and new store design or remodels)."

ZIP MAGAZINE, North American Publishing, 545 Madison Ave., New York NY 10011.
(212)371-7800. Editor: Ray Lewis. Emphasizes direct mail/mailing systems for mail-oriented
professionals in business, industry and direct marketing. A typical article published recently
was on word processing—how mass-produced letters are being individualized effectively and
inexpensively. Some ideas they would be interested in are "Future of Communications in
General" and articles dealing with mail handling/processing. Interested in freelance stories on
equipment and methods used to mail, process mail, transfer names onto and out of computers,
labeling and packaging. Monthly magazine; 88 pages. Estab. 1977. Circ. 37,500. Pays on
publication in some cases, acceptance in others. Rights purchased varies. Phone queries OK.
Simultaneous, photocopied and previously published submissions OK. Reports in 2 weeks.
Free sample copy.
Nonfiction: Expose (on government mail operations); general interest (about magazine
circulation or direct-mail stories); how-to: (improve mailroom operation, direct-marketing case
histories); interview, profile and photo features should be about mail-oriented executives and
professionals. "We are not interested in personal opinion or experience articles." Buys 4
mss/issue. Query or send complete ms. Length: 500-1,000 words. Pays $50-200.
Photos: State availability of photos or send with ms. Accepts only b&w photos and prefers
contact sheet and 4x5 glossy prints. Pays $20-100. Captions preferred. Buys one-time rights.
Fillers: Cartoons.

Agricultural Equipment and Supplies

FARM SUPPLIER, Watt Publishing Co., Sandstone Bldg., Mount Morris IL 61054.
(815)734-4171. Editor-in-Chief: Ray Bates. For retail farm supply dealers and managers over
the US. Monthly magazine; 64 pages. Estab. 1927. Circ. 20,000. Pays on acceptance. Buys all
rights in competitive farm supply fields. Byline given. Phone queries OK. Submit seasonal
material 2 months in advance. OK. SASE. Reports in 2 weeks.
Nonfiction: How-to; informational; interview; new product; and photo feature. "Articles
emphasizing product news, how new product developments have been profitably re-sold, or
successfully used." Buys 20 mss/year. Query. Length: 300-1,500 words. Pays $20-100. "Longer
articles must include photos, charts, etc."
Photos: Purchased with accompanying ms. Submit 5x7 or 8x10 b&w prints; 35mm or larger
color transparencies. Total purchase price for ms includes payment for photos.

Architecture

Architects and city planners whose primary concern is the design of buildings and
urban environments are the target audience for the journals in this category. Those
that emphasize choice of materials, structural details, and methods of constructing
buildings are classified in the Construction and Contracting category.

INLAND ARCHITECT, 727 S. Dearborn St. #900, Chicago IL 60605. Managing Editor: J.
Kiriazis. For architects, planners, engineers, people interested in architecture (buffs) or urban
affairs. Monthly magazine; 36 pages. Estab. 1957. Not copyrighted. Buys 24 mss/year. Pays on

publication. Will send sample copy to writer for $1.50. Will consider simultaneous submissions. Two triple-spaced copies of each submission are required. Reports in 1 month. Query. SASE.
Nonfiction and Photos: "Articles cover appraisal of distinguished buildings, profiles of individual architects and firms, historic buildings and preservation, related education, architectural philosophy, interior design and furnishing, building technology, architectural education, economics of the architectural field, and the business operation of an architect's office. In addition, periodic articles concern such urban matters as city planning, housing, transportation, population shifts, and ecology. The emphasis is regional (Chicago and Illinois) with occasional forays into the greater Midwest. Approach should be one of serious criticism and investigative journalism in journalistic style." Length: flexible, but is usually 1,000-2,500 words. Pays $50-$100. B&w glossy photos are purchased with mss; no additional payment. Captions (and identifications) required.

PROGRESSIVE ARCHITECTURE, 600 Summer St., Stamford CT 06904. Editor: John M. Dixon. Monthly. Buys first-time rights for use in architectural press. Pays on publication. SASE.
Nonfiction and Photos: "Articles of technical professional interest devoted to architecture and community design and illustrated by photographs and architectural drawings. Also use technical articles, which are prepared by technical authorities and would be beyond the scope of the lay writer. Practically all the material is professional, and most of it is prepared by writers in the field who are approached by the magazine for material." Pays $50-250. Buys one-time reproduction rights to b&w and color photos.

Auto and Truck

The journals below aim at automobile and truck dealers, repairmen, or fleet operators. Publications for highway planners and traffic control experts are classified in the Government and Public Service category. Journals for traffic managers and transportation experts (who route goods across the continent) will be found in the Transportation category.

AUTO LAUNDRY NEWS, Columbia Communications, 370 Lexington Ave., New York NY 10017. (212)532-9290. Editor-in-Chief: J.R. Peterson. For sophisticated carwash operators. Monthly magazine; 52 pages. Estab. 1925. Circ. 18,000. Pays on publication. Buys all rights. Phone queries OK. Submit seasonal/holiday material 60 days in advance. Photocopied and previously published submission OK. SASE. Reports in 4 weeks. Free sample copy.
Nonfiction: How-to; historical; humor, informational; new prodict; nostalgia; personal experience; technical; interviews; photo features; and profiles. Buys 40 mss/year. Query. Length: 1,500-3,000 words. Pays $75-175.

AUTOMOTIVE BOOSTER OF CALIFORNIA, Box 765, LaCanada CA 91011. (213)790-6554. Editor: Don McAnally. 3% freelance written. For members of Automotive Booster clubs, automotive warehouse distributors and automotive parts jobbers in California. Estab. 1967. Monthly. Circ. 4,000. Not copyrighted. Byline given. Pays on publication. Submit complete ms. SASE.
Nonfiction and Photos: Will look at short articles and pictures about successes of automotive parts outlets in California. Also can use personnel assignments for automotive parts people in California. Pays $1/column inch (about 2¢/word); $5 for b&w photos used with mss.

AUTOMOTIVE NEWS, 965 E. Jefferson Ave., Detroit MI 48207. Editor: Robert M. Lienert. For management people in auto making and auto dealing. Weekly. Estab. 1925. Circ. 60,000. Buys all rights. Pays on acceptance. Free sample copy. Query. SASE.
Nonfiction and Photos: News material valuable to the auto trade. "Current and complete familiarity with the field is essential, so we don't use much freelance material. Articles must be accurate with the emphasis on the how rather than the what." Pays $3/inch of type (about 50 words). Photos are purchased with mss.

AUTOMOTIVE REBUILDER MAGAZINE, Babcox Publications, Inc., 11 S. Forge St. Akron OH 44304. (216)535-6117. Editor-in-Chief: Andrew J. Doherty. Managing Editor: Katie Champion. Emphasizes the automotive and heavy duty mechanical/parts rebuilding industry and jobber machine shops. Monthly magazine; 108 pages. Estab. 1964. Circ. 17,000. Pays on publication. Buys all rights. Phone queries OK. Submit seasonal/holiday material 6 weeks in advance of issue date. Simultaneous, photocopied and previously published submissions OK.

SASE. Reports in 2 weeks. Free sample copy.
Nonfiction: How-to (technical writing); humor ("we particularly like humor—must be relevant to rebuilders"); historical (historical automotive); inspirational (concentrate on how a rebuilder overcomes disaster or personal handicap); interview (concentrate on growth or success stories); nostalgia (only if it applies to rebuilding); personal experience (experiences with rebuilding); opinion (comment on legislation affecting rebuilders); photo feature ("on machine shops—try to get people in photos, we want photo journalism, not photo illustration"); profile (about individual rebuilder; perhaps the small rebuilder); technical ("you must know what you're talking about—rebuilders don't just fall off Christmas trees"); and articles on regulation at the state and local levels (conservation of resources, air and water pollution). Buys 8 mss/year. Query. Length: 500-1,500 words. Pays 4-6¢/word.
Columns/Departments: People (profile or close-up of industry figures welcome); Tech Notes (this entails technical how-to writing); New Product ("we generally do this ourselves"); and The Forum Guest (opinions on current events relevant to rebuilders). Buys 1 ms/year. Query. Length: 200-1,500 words. Pays 4-6¢/word. Open to suggestions for new columns/departments.

THE BATTERY MAN, Independent Battery Manufacturers Association, Inc., 100 Larchwood Dr., Largo FL 33540. (813)586-1409. Editor-in-Chief: Dan A. Noe. Emphasizes SLI battery manufacture, applications, new developments. For battery manufacturers and retailers (garage owners, servicemen, fleet owners, etc.). Monthly magazine; 28 pages. Estab. 1921. Circ. 7,000. Pays on acceptance. Buys all rights. Byline given. Submit seasonal/holiday material 2 months in advance. Simultaneous, photocopied and previously published submissions OK. SASE. Reports in 2 weeks. Free sample copy.
Nonfiction: Technical articles. Submit complete ms. Length: 1,200-1,500 words. Pays $70-90.

BRAKE & FRONT END SERVICE, 11 S. Forge St., Akron OH 44304. (216)535-6117. Editor: Jeffrey S. Davis. 5-10% freelance written. For owners of automotive repair shops engaged in brake, wheel, suspension, chassis and frame repair, including: specialty shops; general repair shops; new car and truck dealers; gas stations; mass merchandisers and tire stores. Monthly magazine; 68 pages. Estab. 1931. Circ. 28,000. Pays on publication. Buys all rights. Byline given. SASE. Reports "immediately." Sample copy and editorial schedule $2.
Nonfiction and Photos: Specialty shops taking on new ideas using new merchandising techniques; growth of business, volume; reasons for growth and success. Expansions, and unusual brake shops." Query. Length: about 800-1,200 words. Pays 7-9¢/word. Pays $5 for b&w glossy prints purchased with mss.

CANADIAN AUTOMOTIVE TRADE MAGAZINE, MacLean-Hunter, Ltd., 481 University Ave., Toronto, Ontario, Canada M5W 1A7. (416)596-5784. Editor-in-Chief: Edward Belitsky. 30% freelance written. Emphasizes the automotive aftermarket and for mechanics, service station and garage operators, new car dealers and parts jobbers. Monthly magazine; 60 pages. Estab. 1919. Circ. 31,000. Pays on acceptance. Buys all rights, but may reassign following publication. Byline given. Phone queries OK. Submit seasonal/holiday material 2 months in advance. Photocopied submissions OK. SAE and International Reply Coupons. Reports in 2 months.
Nonfiction: Informational; new product; technical; interviews; and profiles. "We can use business articles every month from the 4 corners of Canada. Service articles can come from anywhere." Buys 3 mss/issue. Length: 600-1,400 words. Pays $60-200.
Photos: Purchased with accompanying ms. Captions required. Send contact sheet and/or transparencies. Pays $5-20 for 4x5 b&w prints or 35mm color transparencies. Model release required.

CANADIAN DRIVER/OWNER, 481 University Ave., Toronto, Ontario, Canada M5W 1A7. (416)595-1811. Editor: Simon Hally. 50% freelance written. For owner/operators of heavy-duty trucks in Canada. Bimonthly magazine; 48 pages. Estab. 1972. Circ. 27,000. Usually buys first rights. Offers negotiable kill fee. Byline given. Buys 30-40 mss/year. Pays on acceptance. Free sample copy. Reports in 1-2 weeks. Query or submit complete ms. SAE and International Reply Coupons.
Nonfiction and Photos: Articles on trucks, truck components, maintenance and repair, profiles of independent truckers, small business management, CB radio, legal aspects of trucking, country music, etc. Informal, light style. Special emphasis on the Canadian independent trucking scene since the publication is aimed exclusively at Canadian owner-operators, as opposed to company drivers, truck fleets or US truckers. Material on brokers' contracts and new federal (Canadian) highway vehicle legislation would be of interest. Length: 500-1,200 words except for how-to material which usually runs 200-1,200 words. Pays 10-15¢/word. B&w

photos purchased with or without mss, or on assignment. Pays according to quality. Captions required.

THE CHEK-CHART SERVICE BULLETIN, Box 6227, San Jose CA 95150. Editor-in-Chief: Ken Layne. Managing Editor: Gordon Clark. 20% freelance written. Emphasizes trade news and how-to articles on automobile service for professional mechanics. Monthly newsletter; 8 pages. Estab. 1929. Circ. 20,000. Pays on acceptance. Buys all rights. No byline. Submit seasonal/holiday material 3-4 months in advance of issue date. SASE. Reports in 2 weeks. Free sample copy and writer's guidelines; mention *Writer's Market* in request.
Nonfiction: "The *Service Bulletin* is a trade newsletter, *not* a consumer magazine. How-to articles and service trade news for professional auto mechanics, also articles on merchandising automobile service. No 'do-it-yourself' articles." Buys 1-2 mss/issue. Query. Length: 700-1,100 words. Pays $75-125.
Photos: State availability of photos with query. Offers no additional payment for photos accepted with ms. Uses 8x10 b&w glossy photos. Captions and model release required. Buys all rights.

COLLISION, Info-Quest, Inc., Box 2627, Farmingham MA 01701. Editor: Jay Kruza. For auto body repairmen and managers, and tow truck operators. Magazine published every 6 weeks; 52 pages. Estab. 1977. Pays on publication. Buys all rights. Submit seasonal/holiday material 4 months in advance. Simultaneous, photocopied and previously published submissions OK. SASE. Reports in 2-3 weeks. Sample copy $1; free writer's guidelines.
Nonfiction: Expose (limited usage on insurance fraud or misrepresentation in auto claims); how-to (fix a dent or a frame, repair plastics, run your business better); personal experience (regarding automotive success or failure). Query before submitting interview, opinion or technical articles. "Journalism of newsworthy material in local areas pertaining to auto body is of interest." Buys 20 articles/year. Length: 100-1,500 words. Pays $15-100.
Photos: "Our readers work with their hands and are more likely to be stopped by photo with story. Send photos with ms. Pays $7.50/first, $5/each additional with $50 maximum for 3x5 or 5x7 b&w prints; $7.50/first, $5/each additional for color. Captions preferred. Model release required.
Columns/Departments: Personalities in Auto Body Repair Shops and Association News. Buys 10/year. Query. Length: 50-500 words. Pays $15-35.

COMMERCIAL CAR JOURNAL, Chilton Way, Radnor PA 19089. Editor: James D. Winsor. Monthly. Buys all rights. Pays on acceptance. "Query with article outline." SASE.
Nonfiction: "Articles and photo features dealing with management, maintenance, and operating phases of truck and bus fleet operations. Material must be somewhat specialized and deal with a specific phase of the operation." Length: open. Pays $50-$150.
Photos: "Occasionally use separate photos with captions." Pays $10-25.

FLEET MAINTENANCE & SPECIFYING, 7300 N. Cicero, Lincolnwood IL 60646. (312)588-7300. Editor: Tom Gelinas. For those directly responsible for specification, purchase, repair and maintenance of on-road vehicles of 10,000 GVW or more. Monthly magazine. Estab. 1974. Circ. 50,000. Buys all rights. No byline. Pays on publication. Free sample copy. Photocopied submissions OK. Reports "as soon as possible." SASE.
Nonfiction and Photos: Articles on troubleshooting repair and maintenance of trucks. Articles on fleets and their maintenance programs; management technique stories. "Our publication is technically oriented. Our only interest is in generally superior work." No product-oriented job stories, but will consider industry reports or articles on safety. Length: 2,000-5,000 words. Pays $25/printed page minimum, without photos. Pays extra for 4-color transparencies. No additional payment is made for large format transparencies used with articles.

GO WEST MAGAZINE, 1240 Bayshore Hwy., Burlington CA 94010. Editor-in-Chief: Bill Fitzgerald. Managing Editor: James Sterling. 15% freelance written. Emphasizes truck transport. Monthly magazine; 80 pages. Estab. 1941. Circ. 51,000. Pays on acceptance. Buys all rights. Pays full kill fee. Byline given except "series using same format, but different locations and subjects." Phone queries OK. Submit seasonal/holiday material 6 months in advance of issue date. SASE. Reports in 2 weeks. Free sample copy; mention *Writer's Market* in request.
Nonfiction: Esposé; general interest; historical; how-to; humor; interview; and new product. Buys 2 mss/issue. Query. Length: 500-3,500 words. Pays $200-600.
Photos: State availability of photos with query. Pays $5-15 for b&w photos; $100 for 2¼x2¼ color transparencies. Captions required. Buys all rights.

JOBBER NEWS, Wedham Publications, Ltd., 109 Vanderhoof Ave., Toronto, Ontario, Canada M4G 2J2. (416)425-9021. Editor-in-Chief: Sam Dixon. Emphasizes auto parts merchandising and management for owners and managers of automotive wholesaling establishments, warehouse distributors, and engine rebuilding shops in Canada. Monthly magazine; 58 pages. Estab. 1932. Circ. 8,000. Pays on acceptance. Buys all rights. Pays 100% kill fee. Byline given. Phone queries OK. Submit seasonal/holiday material 2 months in advance. Simultaneous, photocopied and previously published submissions OK. SASE. Reports in 2 weeks. Free sample copy and writer's guidelines.
Nonfiction: How-to articles. Must have authentic Canadian application. Query. Length: 2,000-3,000 words. Pays $50-125.

JOBBER/RETAILER, Bill Communications, Box 5417, Akron OH 44313. Editor: Sarah Frankson. 10% freelance written. "Readership is the automotive parts jobber who has entered the world of retailing to the automotive do-it-yourselfer and also wholesales to dealer trade. Editorial slant is merchandising/marketing with news secondary." Monthly tabloid; 56 pages. Estab. April 1977. Circ. 31,000. Pays on publication. Buys all rights, but may reassign after publication. Submit seasonal/holiday material 1-2 months in advance of issue date. Simultaneous, photocopied and previously published submissions in noncompetitive publications OK. SASE. Free sample copy and writer's guidelines; mention *Writer's Market* in request.
Nonfiction: How-to (merchandising do-it-yourself auto parts, store layout and design, transforming traditional jobber facilities to retail operations as well); interview (of jobber/retailers who have done an excellent job in retail merchandising or a particular item or product line); and technical (on do-it-yourself repairs). Submit complete ms. Length: 2,500 words maximum. Pays $125-175.

JOBBER TOPICS, 7300 N. Cicero Ave., Lincolnwood IL 60646. (312)588-7300. Articles Editor: Jack Creighton. For automotive parts and supplies wholesalers. Monthly. Buys all rights. No byline. Pays on acceptance. Query with outline. SASE.
Nonfiction and Photos: Most material is staff-written. "Articles with unusual or outstanding automotive jobber procedures, with special emphasis on sales and merchandising; any phase of distribution. Especially interested in merchandising practices and machine shop operation." Length: 2,000 words maximum. Pays based on quality and timeliness of feature. 5x7 or 8x10 b&w glossies or 4-color transparencies purchased with mss.

MAGIC CIRCLE, c/o Aitkin-Kynett, 4 Penn Center, Philadelphia PA 19102. For the automobile mechanic in his own shop, in the service station, fleet garage, repair shop or new car dealership. Company publication of the Dana Corporation. Magazine; 20 pages. Estab. 1955. Quarterly. Circ. 80,000. Buys all rights, but will reassign rights to author after publication. Buys 2-3 mss/year. Pays on acceptance. "A free sample copy will be sent only if a viable query is sent at the same time." Will consider photocopied submissions and may consider simultaneous submissions. Reports in 2 weeks. Query. SASE.
Nonfiction and Photos: "Articles on anything that will make the mechanic a better, more efficient, more profitable mechanic and businessman. We need a light style, but with plenty of detail on techniques and methods." Informational, how-to, travel, successful business operations, merchandising techniques, technical articles. Length: 500-2,000 words. Pays $150 maximum. B&w and color photos are purchased with or without ms. Captions required. Pays $25 for b&w 8x10 glossy prints; $50 for 2¼x2¼ or 35mm color.

MERCHANDISER, Amoco Oil Co., Box 6110-A, Chicago IL 60680. Editor: Robert P. Satkoski. For Amoco service station dealers, jobbers. Quarterly. Circ. 30,000. Buys all rights, but will reassign after publication. Buys 3-4 mss/year. Pays on publication. Query. SASE.
Nonfiction and Photos: Short, to-the-point, success stories and how-to stories that will trigger creative thinking by the reader. Storylines are most often in the merchandising, motivational and educational areas. Length: 750 words maximum. Payment varies, with minimum of $100. Uses b&w and color photos.

MODERN BULK TRANSPORTER, 4801 Montgomery Lane, Washington DC 20014. (301)654-8802. Editor: John L. Conley. 10% freelance written. For "management of companies operating tank motor vehicles which transport liquid or dry bulk commodities." Monthly. Buys first rights. Byline given at author's request. Pays on acceptance. Will consider photocopied submissions, but "we're prejudiced against them." SASE.
Nonfiction and Photos: "Articles covering the tank truck industry; stories concerning a successful for-hire tank truck company, or stories about use of tank trucks for unusual

commodities. We especially seek articles on successful operation of tank trucks by oil jobbers or other so-called 'private carriers' who transport their own products. Approach should be about specific tank truck problems solved, unusual methods of operations, spectacular growth of a company, tank truck management techniques, or other subjects of special interest. Articles should speak to management of companies operating tank trucks, *in their terms*, not to truck drivers. Simple description of routine operations not acceptable." Length: 1,000-3,000 words, "preferably accompanied by pictures." Pays minimum 6¢/word. Pays minimum $30/published page "for general articles exclusive in trucking field only (such as maintenance and mechanical subjects)." Pays $25 minimum for reporter assignments—producing fact sheet for rewrite. Pays $7 for 8x10 or 5x7 glossy prints purchased with exclusive features.

MODERN TIRE DEALER, Box 5417, 77 N. Miller Rd., Akron OH 44313. (216)867-4401. Editor: Stephen LaFerre. For independent tire dealers. Published 18 times annually. Buys all rights. Photocopied submissions OK. Query. Reports in 1 month. SASE.
Nonfiction, Photos, and Fillers: "How TBA dealers sell tires, batteries and allied services, such as brakes, wheel alignment, shocks, mufflers. The emphasis is on merchandising. We prefer the writer to zero in on some specific area of interest; avoid shotgun approach." Length: 1,500 words. Pays $50-100. 8x10, 4x5, 5x7 b&w glossy prints purchased with mss. Pays $5. Buys 300-word fillers. Pays $5-10.

MOTHER TRUCKER NEWS, MTN, Inc., Box 6391, San Bernardino CA 92412. (714)686-7201. Editor: Bud Feldkamp. For professional truck drivers. "Our readers are on the road from 5-7 days a week, sometimes up to several months at a time. They are generally conservative and literally keep the country moving. We look for articles, fillers and other materials that are entertaining, informative and fun." Monthly tabloid; 32 pages. Estab. 1977. Circ. 17,500. Pays on publication. Buys one-time rights. Pays 25% kill fee. Byline given. Phone queries OK. Submit seasonal/holiday material 3 months in advance. Simultaneous, photocopied and previously published submissions OK. SASE. Reports in 2 weeks. Free sample copy and writer's guidelines.
Nonfiction: General interest (on medical news, health, etc.); historical (on trucking or trucking companies); humor (on any subject these readers can relate to); nostalgia (what trucking was like in the old days, travel in yesteryear, etc.); profile (on individuals of note in trucking, transportation, or government regulatory agencies); travel (interesting spots for short stops around the US). "The offbeat appeals to them but they aren't easily fooled by shuck." Buys 80 articles/year. Query or send complete ms. Pays 4¢/word.
Photos: State availability of photos or send photos with ms. Pays $5 for b&w 8x10 glossy prints and $10 for color transparencies. Captions and model releases required.
Columns/Departments: Channel Selector—how to better use CBs, amplifiers, etc. Buys 1/issue. Send complete ms. Length: 250-1,500 words. Pays 4¢/word.
Fiction: Adventure."Any subject with heavy action and heroic figures." Humorous. "Any topic which would draw the interest of our readers." Buys 1 ms/issue. Query. Length: 1,200-2,500 words. Pays 4¢/word.
Fillers: Jokes and short humor. Length: 50-500 words. Pays 4¢/word.

MOTOR MAGAZINE, Hearst Corp., 224 W. 57th St., New York NY 10019. (212)262-8616. Editor: Joe Oldham. Emphasizes auto repair. "Readers are professional auto repairmen or people who own auto repair facilities." Monthly magazine; 80-90 pages. Estab. 1903. Circ. 135,000. Pays on acceptance. Buys all rights. Pays 100% kill fee. Byline given. SASE. Reports in 1 month. Free sample copy.
Nonfiction: How-to. "Writers should be able to relate their own hands-on experience to handling specific repair and technical articles." Buys 6 mss/issue. Query. Length: 1,000-2,000 words. Pays $150-300.
Photos: "Photos and/or rough artwork must accompany how-to articles." State availability of photos. Uses 5x7 glossy prints. Offers no additional payment for photos accepted with ms. Captions and model releases required.

MUFFLER DIGEST, 1036 S. Glenstone, Springfield MO 65804. (417)866-3917. Editor: J.M. Ryan. For professional installers and manufacturers of exhaust systems and exhaust system components. Monthly magazine; 60-80 pages. Estab. 1976. Circ. 10,000. Pays on acceptance. Buys all rights, but may reassign following publication. Byline given. Simultaneous and photocopied submissions OK. SASE. Reports in 1 week.
Nonfiction: How-to; humor (in the muffler field); informational; interview (good interviews with shop owners); and profile (industry people). "We're not interested in 'How I Got Ripped

Off at. . . . ' types of features." Buys 6-10 mss/year. Submit complete ms. Length: 1,000-1,500 words. Pays 3-5¢/word.

Photos: Purchased with accompanying ms. Captions required. Query. Pays $5 for b&w photos.

Columns/Departments: How-To column (could be a shop-talk type of article). Query. Length: 500 words. Pays 3-5¢/word.

How To Break In: "We are covering the professional exhaust system installer in the US, Mexico and Canada. When we talk about professional we are talking about muffler specialty shops—Midas, Tuffy and other franchise chain operators as well as independents. We are not interested in service stations, Sears, Wards, etc. We would prefer to see more stories on successful independent installers; how they got started, what special tricks have they picked up, what is their most successful merchandising tool, etc."

NTDRA DEALER NEWS, 1343 L St. NW, Washington DC 20005. Editor: C.D. "Tony" Hylton III. 1-2% freelance written. For tire dealers and retreaders. Publication of the National Tire Dealers & Retreaders Association. Biweekly magazine. Estab. 1935. Circ. 7,500. Occasionally copyrighted, depending on content. Byline given. Buys 10-15 mss/year. Will send free sample copy on request. Wil consider photocopied and simultaneous submissions. Reports "immediately." Query. SASE.

Nonfiction: Articles relating to retailing and marketing, with special emphasis on the tire dealer, retreader and small businessman in general. "Industry news, business aids, new products. Dealer and consumer comments regarding this industry. Most articles received are of too general interest." Uses informational, technical, how-to, interview, think pieces and material on successful business operations and merchandising techniques. Pays $150-200.

O AND A MARKETING NEWS, Box 765, LaCanada CA 91011. (213)790-6554. Editor: Don McAnally. 5% freelance written. For "service station dealers, garagemen, TBA (tires, batteries, accessories) people, oil company marketing management." Bimonthly. Circ. 15,000. Not copyrighted. Pays on publication. Reports in 1 week. SASE.

Nonfiction and Photos: "Straight news material; management, service and merchandising applications; emphasis on news about or affecting markets and marketers within the publication's geographic area of the 11 western states. No restrictions on style or slant. We could use straight news of our industry from some western cities, notably Las Vegas, Reno and Salt Lake City." Query. Length: maximum 1,000 words. Pays $1.25/column inch (about 2½¢/word). Photos purchased with or without mss; captions required. Pays $5.

OHIO TRUCK TIMES, Mezzanine Floor, Neil House Hotel, Columbus OH 43215. Editor: David F. Bartosic. Publication of the Ohio Trucking Association. Quarterly. Buys material for exclusive publication only. Pays on publication. Free sample copy. Reports in 30 days. SASE.

Nonfiction: Modern developments in truck transportation, particularly as they apply to Ohio industry and truck operators. Submit complete mss. Length: 1,500 words. Pay negotiable.

Photos: With mss or with captions only. Transportation subjects. Pay negotiable.

OPEN ROAD, 1015 Florence St., Fort Worth TX 76102. Editor: Chris Lackey. For "professional over-the-road truck drivers of America." Monthly. Buys North American serial rights. Byline given. Pays on publication. Will send a sample copy to a writer on request. Query. Reports in 2-4 weeks. SASE.

Nonfiction and Photos: "Pieces on truck drivers—articles about new model heavy trucks and equipment, acts of heroism, humor, unusual events, special driving articles, advice to other drivers, drivers who do good jobs in community life or civic work, etc." Recently sponsored two special events: selection of an outstanding woman trucker, "Queen of the Road," for 1979; and Truck Drivers Country Music Awards Competition, a national poll among professional truck drivers, picked outstanding artists in 10 country music categories. Length: "prefer 1,000 to 1,500 words, usually." Pays "about 7¢ a word." 5x7 or 8x10 b&w glossies purchased with mss. Pays $5 to $10, depending on quality and newsworthiness, "more for covers."

OWNER OPERATOR MAGAZINE, Chilton Co., 1 Chilton Way, Radnor PA 19089. (215)687-8200. Executive Editor: Brant Clark. Managing Editor: Leon E. Witconis. 20% freelance written. For one-truck owner/operators. Bimonthly magazine; 160 pages. Estab. 1970. Circ. 100,000. Pays on publication. Buys all rights, but may reassign following publication. Submit seasonal/holiday material 6 months in advance of issue date. Previously published submissions OK. SASE. Reports in 3 weeks. Sample copy $1.50.

Nonfiction: Exposé (government, unions, trucking companies, brokers, trucking associations); historical (trucking industry); how-to (perform maintenance, repairs or fix-up on heavy duty trucks); humor; interview (top trucking officials or unusual occupations in trucking); personal experience (only from truckers); photo feature (occupational, with pix); profile; and technical (truck). Buys 3-4 mss/issue. Submit complete ms or query with clips of published work. Length: 600 words maximum. Pays $50-300.

Photos: Submit photos with accompanying ms. Payment included in ms price. Uses 8x10 b&w prints. Buys all rights, but may reassign following publication. Model release required.

Columns/Departments: Chatterbox (interviews with owner/operators at truck stops with pix). Buys 6/year. Query. Length: 300-450 words. Pays $150-250.

REFRIGERATED TRANSPORTER, 1602 Harold St., Houston TX 77006. (713)523-8124. 5% freelance written. Monthly. Not copyrighted. Byline given "except articles which must be extensively rewritten by our staff." Pays on publication. Reports in 1 month. SASE.

Nonfiction and Photos: "Articles on fleet management and maintenance of vehicles, especially the refrigerated van and the refrigerating unit; shop tips; loading or handling systems, especially for frozen or refrigerated cargo; new equipment specifications; conversions of equipment for better handling or more efficient operations. Prefer articles with illustrations obtained from fleets operating refrigerated trucks or trailers." Pays minimum $45/page or $2/inch.

Fillers: Buys newspaper clippings. "Do not rewrite."

SERVICE STATION AND GARAGE MANAGEMENT, 109 Vanderhoof Ave., Suite 101, Toronto, Ontario M4G 2J2, Canada. Editor: Gene Lethbridge. For "service station operators and garagemen in Canada only." Estab. 1956. Monthly. Circ. 26,000. Buys first Canadian serial rights. Buys 1-2 articles/year. Pays on acceptance. Sample copy for 50¢. Query. Reports in 2 days. SAE and International Reply Coupons.

Nonfiction and Photos: "Articles on service station operators in Canada only; those who are doing top merchandising jobs. Also on specific phases of service station doings: brakes, tune-up, lubrication, etc. Solid business facts and figures; information must have human interest angles. Interested in controversial legislation, trade problems, sales and service promotions, technical data, personnel activities and changes. No general, long-winded material. The approach must be Canadian. The writer must know the trade and must provide facts and figures useful and helpful to readers. The style should be easy, simple, and friendly—not stilted." Length: 1,000 words. Pays 4-5¢/word average, "depending on the topic and the author's status." Photos purchased with mss and without mss "if different or novel"; captions required. Pays $5 for 5x7 or 8x10 b&w glossies.

SOUTHERN AUTOMOTIVE JOURNAL, 1760 Peachtree Rd. NW, Atlanta GA 30357. (404)874-4462. Editor: Mike Witter. For automotive jobbers, repairshops, warehouse distributors, new car and truck dealers, retail chain repair outlets. Monthly. Buys all rights. Pays 50% kill fee. Byline given. Pays on acceptance. Query. Reports in 1 week. SASE.

Nonfiction and Photos: Wants personal interviews with Southern jobbers, wholesalers, machine shops etc. on unique methods or solutions of cutting costs, sales promoting, managerial problems. Human interest features dealing with the Southern aftermarket. Length: Optional. Pays $50-200.

Photos: Purchased with mss or with captions. Looking for automotive human interest photos. Pays $5-25.

SOUTHERN MOTOR CARGO, Box 4169, Memphis TN 38104. Editor: William H. Raiford. For "trucking management and maintenance personnel of private, contract, and for-hire carriers in 16 Southern states (Alabama, Arkansas, Delaware, Florida, Georgia, Kentucky, Louisiana, Maryland, Mississippi, North Carolina, Oklahoma, South Carolina, Tennessee, Texas, Virginia and West Virginia) and the District of Columbia." Special issues include "ATA Convention," October; "Transportation Graduate Directory," December; "Mid-America Truck Show," February. Monthly. Circ. 40,000. Buys first rights within circulation area. Pays on publication. Free sample copy. Reports "usually in 3 weeks." SASE.

Nonfiction: "How a Southern trucker builds a better mousetrap. Factual newspaper style with punch in lead. Don't get flowery. No success stories. Pick one item, e.g., tire maintenance, billing procedure, etc., and show how such-and-such carrier has developed or modified it to better fit his organization. Bring in problems solved by the way he adapted this or that and what way he plans to better his present layout. Find a segment of the business that has been altered or modified due to economics or new information, such as 'due to information gathered by a new IBM process, it has been discovered that an XYZ transmission needs overhauling every 60,000 miles instead of every 35,000 miles, thereby resulting in savings of $$$ over the normal life of this transmission.' Or, 'by incorporating a new method of record keeping, claims on damaged freight have been expedited with a resultant savings in time and money.'

Compare the old method with the new, itemize savings, and get quotes from personnel involved. Articles must be built around an outstanding phase of the operation and must be documented and approved by the firm's management prior to publication." Length: 1,500-3,500 words. Pays 4¢/word minimum for "feature material."
Photos: Purchased with cutlines; glossy prints. Pays $5.

SPECIALTY & CUSTOM DEALER. Babcox Publications, 11 S. Forge St., Akron OH 44304. (216)535-6117. Editor/Publisher: Gary Gardner. "Audience is primarily jobbers and retailers of specialty automotive parts and accessories. Average reader has been in business for 10 years, and is store owner or manager. Educational background varies, with most readers in the high school graduate with some college category." Monthly magazine; 56 pages. Estab. 1965. Circ. 20,000. Pays on publication. Buys all rights. Submit seasonal or holiday material 90 days in advance. SASE. Reports in 6 weeks. Sample copy $1.50.
Nonfiction: Publishes informational (business techniques), interview, new product, profile and technical articles. "No hyperbolic accounts of business or those that read like public relations releases. No broad generalizations concerning a 'great product' without technical data behind the information. Lack of detail concerning business operations." Buys 24 mss/year. Query. Length: 1,000-2,000 words. Pays $50-100.
How To Break In: "For the most part, an understanding of automotive products and business practices is essential. Features on a specific retailer, his merchandising techniques and unique business methods are most often used. Such a feature might include inventory control, display methods, lines carried, handling obsolete products, etc."

TIRE REVIEW. 11 S. Forge St., Akron OH 44304. (216)535-6117. Editor: William Whitney. For "independent tire dealers and retreaders, company stores, tire company executives, some oil company executives." Monthly. Circulation: 34,000. Buys first rights. Buys 6-7 mss/year. Pays on publication. Free sample copy. Query. Reports in 1 week. SASE.
Nonfiction and Photos: "Tire industry news, including new product news, research and marketing trends, legislative news, features on independent tire dealers and retreaders, news of trade shows and conventions, tire and related accessory merchandising tips. All articles should be straightforward, concise, information-packed, and not slanted toward any particular manufacturer or brand name. Must have something to do with tires or the tire industry, particularly independent dealers doing brake and front-end and tune-up services." Length: "no limitations." Pays 4-5¢/word. B&w glossies purchased with and without mss. Pays "$5 a photo with story, $8.50 for photos used alone."

TODAY'S TRANSPORT INTERNATIONAL/TRANSPORTE MODERNO. International Publications, Inc., 15 Franklin St., Westport CT 06880. (203)226-7463. Editor: Martin Greenburgh. 100% freelance written. Emphasizes "fleet operations and materials handling for vehicle fleet operators and materials handling executives in 150 developing countries in Africa, Asia, Middle East and Latin America." Bimonthly magazine; 48-72 pages. Estab. 1953. Circ. 39,000. Pays on acceptance. Buys all rights, but may reassign following publication. Pays negotiable kill fee. Byline given. Phone queries OK. Previously published submissions OK. SASE. Free sample copy and writer's guidelines.
Nonfiction: How-to (run a fleet, specify equipment, etc.); informational (fleet operations, new technologies); interview (with fleet executives discussing problem-solving); photo feature (fleets and materials handling); and technical (vehicle/bus/truck systems, fork lifts, materials handling) articles. Buys 24-30 mss/year. Query. Length: 1,500-3,000 words. Pays $150-200. No articles about US or developed countries without direct relevance to the 3rd world.
Photos: Purchased with accompanying ms. Captions required. Query. Pays $50 bonus for illustrations.
Columns/Departments: Materials Handling (tips and methods for materials handling personnel.) Buys 1 ms/issue. Query. Length: 750-1,500 words. Pays $75-100. Open to suggestions for new columns or departments.
How To Break In: "Articles must be written for readers in the 3rd world. Avoid US-oriented approach. Our readers are administrators and executives—address them."

TOW-AGE. Info-Quest, Inc., Box M, Franklin MA 02038. Editor: J. Kruza. For readers who run their own service business. Published every 6 weeks. Circ. 12,000. Buys all rights, but may reassign to author after publication. Buys about 12 mss/year. Pays on acceptance. Sample copy $1; free writer's guidelines. Photocopied and simultaneous submissions OK. Reports in 1-4 weeks. SASE.
Nonfiction and Photos: Articles on business, legal and technical information for the towing industry. "Light reading material; short, with punch." Informational, how-to, personal

experience, interview, profile. Query or submit complete ms. Length: 200-800 words. Pays $20-50. Spot news and successful business operations. Length: 100-500 words. Technical articles. Length: 100-1,000 words. Regular columns sometimes use material of 400 words. Pays $40. Up to 8x10 b&w photos purchased with or without mss, or on assignment. Pays $7.50 for first photo; $5 for each additional photo in series.

WARD'S AUTO WORLD, 28 W. Adams, Detroit MI 48226. (313)962-4433. Editor-in-Chief: David C. Smith. Executive Editor: Albert E. Fleming. Managing Editor: Erwin Maus III. 10% freelance written. For top and middle management in all phases of auto industry. Monthly magazine; 72 pages. Estab. 1965. Circ. 60,000. Pays on publication. Buys all rights. Pay varies for kill fee. Byline given. Phone queries OK. Submit seasonal/holiday material 1 month in advance of issue date. SASE. Reports in 2 weeks. Free sample copy and writer's guidelines.
Nonfiction: Exposé; general interest; historical; humor; interview; new product; nostalgia; personal experience; photo feature; and technical. Few consumer-type articles. Buys 12 mss/year. Query. Length: 2,000-4,000 words. Pay $200-600.
Photos: Submit photo material with query. Pay varies for 8x10 b&w prints or color transparencies. Captions required. Buys all rights.

WAREHOUSE DISTRIBUTION, 7300 N. Cicero Ave., Lincolnwood, Chicago IL 60646. (312)588-7300. Editor: Syd Cowan. For "businessmen in the auto parts distribution field who are doing above one million dollars business per year." Published 10 times/year. Circ. 27,000. Buys all rights. Pays on publication. Most material is staff-written. Reports "within a reasonable amount of time." SASE.
Nonfiction and Photos: "Business management subjects, limited to the automotive parts distribution field." Query. Length: 1,500-2,000 words. Pays 4-10¢ a word, "based on value to industry and the quality of the article." Photos purchased with and without mss; captions required. Wants "sharp 5x7 prints." Pays maximum $6.

WAREHOUSE DISTRIBUTOR NEWS, 11 S. Forge St., Akron OH 44304. Editor: John B. Stoner. 10% freelance written. For warehouse distributors and redistributing jobbers of automotive parts and accessories, tools and equipment and supplies (all upper-management personnel). Magazine; 60 pages. Estab. 1967. Monthly. Circ. 14,000. Rights purchased vary with author and material. May buy all rights or simultaneous rights. Byline given. Buys 12 mss/year. Pays on publication. Sample copy $2. Photocopied and simultaneous submissions OK. Reports "at once." SASE.
Nonfiction and Photos: Automotive aftermarket distribution management articles and those on general management, success stories, etc., of interest to the industry. Articles on manufacturers and their distributors. Must be aftermarket-oriented. Each issue centers around a theme, such as rebuilt parts issue, import issue, materials handling issue, etc. Schedule changes yearly based on developments in the industry. No freelance material on materials handling or product information. Would be interested in merchandising articles; those on EDP startup, and interviews with prominent industry figures. Query. Length: open. Pays 5-9¢/word. B&w (5x7) photos purchased with or without ms. Captions required.

Aviation and Space

In this category are journals for aviation businessmen and airport operators and technical aviation and space journals. Publications for professional and private pilots are classified with the Aviation magazines in the Consumer Publications section.

THE AG-PILOT NEWS MAGAZINE, Tel-N-Ad Co., Box 25, Milton-Freewater OR 97862. (509)525-4131. Editor: Tom J. Wood. Managing Editor: Pat Anderson. Emphasizes aerial agricultural application (crop dusting). "This is intended to be a fun-to-read, nontechnical, humorous and sometimes serious publication for the pilot and operator. They are our primary target. We will enlarge our field in the future, to near related areas." Monthly (except January and February) magazine; 20 pages. Estab. 1978. Circ. 5,400. Pays on acceptance. Buys all rights. Byline given unless writer requested holding name. Phone queries OK. Simultaneous, photocopied and previously (if not very recent) submissions OK. SASE. Reports in 1 week. Sample copy $1; free writer's guidelines.
Nonfiction: Expose (of EPA, OSHA, FAA or any government function concerned with the industry); general interest; historical; interview (of well-known aviation person); nostalgia; opinion; new product; personal experience; and photo feature. "If we receive an article in any area we have solicited, it is quite possible this person could stay on our staff indefinitely, on a

monthly basis. The international input is what we need. Industry-related material is a must." Send complete ms. Length: 300-1,500 words. Pays $20-50 (5-20¢/word).

Photos: "We would like one b&w 5x7 (or smaller) with the manuscript, if applicable—but it will not hurt, nor help, the chance of utilization." No color. Offers no additional payment for photos accepted with ms. Captions preferred, model release required.

Columns/Departments: International (of prime interest, as they need to cultivate this area—aviation/crop dusting-related); Embryo Birdman (should be written, or appear to be written, by a first-year spray pilot); The Chopper Hopper (by anyone in the helicopter industry—not necessarily related to agriculture); BioGraphical Interview Type (of well-known person in aviation-related position, but not necessarily agricultural aviation-related); and Catchin' The Corner (written by a person obviously skilled in the crop dusting field of experience or other interest capturing material related to the industry). Send complete ms. Length: 700-1,500 words. Pays $20-50. Open to suggestions for new columns/departments.

Poetry: Interested in all types of poetry. Buys 1/issue. Submit no more than 5 at one time. Pays $20-40.

Fillers: Short jokes, short humor and industry-related newsbreaks. Length: 10-100 words. Pays $5-20.

EXXON AIR WORLD, Exxon International Co., 115 Spring Valley Rd., Ossining NY 10562. Editor: Warren H. Goodman. Emphasizes commercial aviation for officials in all branches of the aviation industry in 55 countries. Quarterly magazine; 32 pages. Estab. 1938. Circ. 10,000. Pays as soon as layout is prepared and number of words and number of pictures used in known. Buys one-time rights. Photocopied submissions OK. Reports in 2 weeks. Free sample copy and writer's guidelines.

Nonfiction: Historical; profile (on major airlines); technical (on developments in aircraft or engine design, avionics, navigation, fuels and lubricants, or airport design); general interest (on scheduled airlines and other commercial aviation, corporate aviation, private flying, aviation sports, exhibits and shows, aviation schools and training organizations.) "*Air World* seeks articles that portray the industry in a positive way, emphasizing the progress, accomplishments and benefits of aviation." Buys 3-5 mss/issue. Query. Length: 1,000-4,000. Pays 10¢/word.

Photos: "We do not use any manuscripts without good selection of photos, usually b&w." State availability of photos. Pays $10/per photo used for 5x7 or 8x10 b&w glossy prints and will look at contact sheets if large selection is available. Color photos should be 35mm slides or larger transparencies. Rates for color are not yet set and are negotiable. Captions required.

INTERLINE REPORTER, 2 W. 46th St., New York NY 10036. (212)575-9000. Editor: Eric Friedheim. For airline employees. Buys first serial rights. Query. SASE.

Nonfiction and Photos: Wants nontechnical articles on airline activities; stories should be slanted to the sales, reservations and counter personnel. Articles on offbeat airlines and, most of all, on airline employees—those who lead an adventurous life, have a unique hobby, or have acted above and beyond the call of duty. Personality stories showing how a job has been well done are particularly welcome. Length: up to 1,200 words. Pays $50-75 for articles with photographic illustrations.

INTERNATIONAL AVIATION MECHANICS JOURNAL, 211 S. 4th St., Basin WY 82410. (307)568-2413. Editor: Will Triol. For governmentally licensed airframe and powerplant mechanics involved in maintaining general aviation airplanes. Monthly magazine; 72 pages. Estab. 1970. Circ. 12,500. Buys all rights, but may reassign rights to author after publication. Pays within 30 days of publication. Free sample copy. Photocopied submissions OK. Reports in 30 days. SASE.

Nonfiction and Photos: Technical articles on aircraft maintenance procedures and articles helping the mechanics to be more efficient and productive. All material should be written from the point of view of an aircraft mechanic, helping him solve common field problems. Buys 30-40 mss/year. Query or submit complete ms. Informational (length: 500-2,000 words. Pays $25-100); how to (length: 100-500 words. Pays $25); photo articles (length: 50-100 words. Pays $20); and technical (length: 500-4,000 words. Pays $25-150).

Baking

BAKING INDUSTRIES JOURNAL, Maclaren Publishers, Ltd., Box 109, Davis House, 69-77 High St., Croydon, CR9 1QH, England. (01)688-7788. Editor: Chris Whitehorn. Up to 40% freelance written. For the large-scale bakery industry. Monthly magazine; 36 pages. Circ.

1,500. SAE and International Reply Coupons. Sample copy $1.
Nonfiction: Features on baking and allied subjects. Length: 1,000-3,000 words. Submit complete ms. Pays $80/1,000 words.
Photos: B&w glossies used with mss. Captions required. Query.

PACIFIC BAKERS NEWS, Route 2, Belfair WA 98528. (206)275-6421. Publisher: Leo Livingston. 50% freelance written. Business newsletter for commercial bakeries in the western states. Monthly. Pays on publication. No byline given; only news items are published in paragraph form. "We don't require SASE."
Fillers: Uses bakery business reports and news about bakers. Buys only brief "boiled-down news items about bakers and bakeries operating only in Alaska, Hawaii, Pacific Coast and Rocky Mountain states. Welcome clippings. Need monthly news reports and clippings about the baking industry and the donut business. "We don't use how-to and think pieces or feature articles." Length: 10-200 words. Pays 4¢/word for clips and news.
How To Break In: "Send brief news reports or clippings on spot business news about bakers and bakeries in California, Arizona, Nevada, New Mexico, Colorado, Utah, Wyoming, Montana, Idaho, Oregon, Washington, Alaska and Hawaii."

Beverages and Bottling

The following journals are for manufacturers, distributors, retailers of soft drinks and alcoholic beverages. Publications for bar and tavern operators and managers of restaurants are classified in the Hotels, Motels, Clubs, Resorts and Restaurants category.

BEVERAGE WORLD, 150 Great Neck Rd., Great Neck NY 11021. Editor: Richard V. Howard. (516)829-9210. Monthly magazine; 75 pages. Estab. 1882. Monthly. Buys all rights. Pays on publication. Buys 12 mss/year. Free sample copy. Reports in 1 month. SASE.
Nonfiction and Photos: "Articles on any subject pertaining to manufacturers of carbonated and noncarbonated soft drinks, wine or beer. Emphasis should be on sales, distribution, merchandising, advertising and promotion. Historical articles and 'how-to dissertations' are not desired; no shorts, fillers or rewritten newspaper clippings." Most mss rejected because the writers usually don't have a "thorough understanding of what they're writing about. Pieces often shallow and too generalized." Should be written in crisp, clear style. Pays $35/printed page (about 1,200 words). "Illustrations should be supplied where possible." Pays $5 for each photo used.

MARYLAND-WASHINGTON BEVERAGE JOURNAL, 2 W. 25th St., Baltimore MD 21218. (301)235-1716. Editor: Anna A. Pumphrey. For retailers in the alcohol beverage industry in Maryland, Washington and Delaware. Monthly magazine; 210 pages. Estab. 1938. Circ. 12,300. Not copyrighted. Buys 5 mss/year. Pays on publication. Sample copy $1. Simultaneous submissions OK. Submit seasonal material (for December holiday sales) 3 months in advance. Reports "promptly." SASE.
Nonfiction and Photos: Articles of local interest regarding the beer, wine and liquor industry. Biographical stories on local retailers, stories on bars, package goods, restaurants, etc. Emphasis on innovative trends in the industry; articles to interest and educate Maryland/Washington/Delaware retailers. Merchandising trends; advertising; informational, how-to; interview; profile; successful business operations; merchandising techniques. Query or submit complete ms. Length: 1,000-2,000 words. Pays $15-100. No additional payment for b&w photos used with mss.

MICHIGAN BEVERAGE NEWS, 24681 Northwestern Hwy., Suite 408, Southfield MI 48075. Editor: Larry Stotz. For "owners of bars, taverns, package liquor stores, hotels, and clubs in Michigan." Semimonthly. Buys exclusive rights to publication in Michigan. Byline given. Pays on publication. Free sample copy. Reports "immediately." SASE.
Nonfiction and Photos: "Feature stories with pictures. Unusual attractions and business-building ideas in use by Michigan liquor licensees. Profit tips, success stories, etc., slanted to the trade, not to the general public. Especially interested in working with freelancers in Grand Rapids, Flint, Kalamazoo, Marquette, Saulte Ste. Marie, and Bay City areas." Query. Length: 500-750 words. Pays 75¢/column inch. Buys photos of Michigan licensees engaged in business activities. Pays 75¢/column inch.

MID-CONTINENT BOTTLER, 1900 W. 47th Place, Westwood KS 66205. (913)384-0770.

Publisher: Floyd E. Sageser. 3% freelance written. For "soft drink bottlers in the 20-state Midwestern area." Bimonthly. Not copyrighted. Pays on acceptance. Free sample copy. Reports "immediately." SASE.

Nonfiction and Photos: "Items of specific soft drink bottler interest with special emphasis on sales and merchandising techniques. Feature style desired." Length: 2,000 words. Pays $15-$50. Photos purchased with mss.

SOUTHERN BEVERAGE JOURNAL. Box 561107, Miami, FL 33156. (305)233-7230. Editor-in-Chief: Raymond G. Feldman. 25% freelance written. For owners of package stores, bars and restaurants throughout the South. Monthly magazine; 100 pages. Estab. 1947. Circ. 21,000. Pays on publication. Buys all rights. Submit seasonal/holiday material 4 months in advance of issue date. Reports in 2 months. Free sample copy and writer's guidelines.

Nonfiction: How-to articles on improving business practices, etc. Buys 12 mss/year. Submit complete ms. Pays 4-6¢/word.

Photos: State availability of photos with ms. Pays $5 for b&w or color prints. Captions preferred. Buys all rights.

WINES & VINES. 703 Market St., San Francisco CA 94103. Editor: Philip Hiaring. For everyone concerned with the wine industry including winemakers, wine merchants, suppliers and consumers. Monthly magazine. Estab. 1919. Circ. 5,500. Buy first North American serial rights or simultaneous rights. Pays on acceptance. Free sample copy. Submit special material (brandy, January; vineyard, February; champagne, June; marketing, September; aperitif/dessert wines, November) 3 months in advance. Reports in 2 weeks. SASE.

Nonfiction and Photos: Articles of interest to the trade. "These could be on grapegrowing in unusual areas; new winemaking techniques; wine marketing, retailing, etc." Interview, historical, spot news, merchandising techniques and technical. No stories with a strong consumer orientation as against trade orientation. Author should know the subject matter, i.e., know proper winegrowing/winemaking terminology. Buys 4-5 ms/year. Query. Length: 1,000-2,500 words. Pays $25-$50. Pays $5-$10 for 4x5 or 8x10 b&w photos purchased with mss. Captions required.

Book and Book Store Trade

AB BOOKMAN'S WEEKLY. Box AB, Clifton NJ 07015. (201)772-0020. Editor-in-Chief: Jacob L. Chernofsky. For professional and specialist booksellers, acquisitions and academic librarians, book publishers, book collectors, bibliographers, historians, etc. Weekly magazine; 200 pages. Estab. 1948. Circ. 8,000. Pays on publication. Buys all rights. Byline given. Phone queries OK. Submit seasonal or holiday material 1-2 months in advance. Simultaneous, photocopied and previously published submissions OK. SASE. Reports in 1 month. Sample copy $2.

Nonfiction: How-to (for professional booksellers); historical (related to books or book trade or printing or publishing). Personal experiences, nostalgia, interviews, profiles. Query. Length: 2,500 words minimum. Pays $40 minimum.

Photos: Photos used with mss.

AMERICAN BOOKSELLER. Booksellers Publishing, Inc., 122 E. 42nd St., New York NY 10017. (212)867-9060. Editor: Ann S. Haslam. This publication emphasizes retail bookselling and goes to the 5,700 members of the American Booksellers Association and to more than 2,400 other readers nationwide, most of whom are involved in publishing. Monthly magazine; 40 pages. Estab. 1977. Circ. 8,100. Pays on acceptance. Buys all rights. Pays 25% kill fee. Byline given "except on small news stories." Phone queries OK. Submit seasonal/holiday material 3 months in advance. Simultaneous, photocopied and previously published submissions OK. SASE. Reports in 2 weeks. Include self-addressed, stamped postcard for notification that ms has arrived safely. Sample copy $1.

Nonfiction: General interest (on publishing and bookselling); how-to (run a bookstore, work with publishers); interview (on authors and publishers); and photo feature (on book-related events). Buys 6 mss/issue. Query with clips of published work. Length: 750-2,000. Pays $40-100.

Photos: State availability of photos. Uses b&w 5x7 matte prints and contact sheets. Pays $10-20. Uses 35mm color transparencies. Pays $10-50. Caption and model releases required.

BOOK COLLECTOR'S MARKET. (Incorporating Book Collector), 363 7th Ave., New York, NY 10001. Editor: William Burton. For booksellers and book collectors. Bimonthly magazine;

48 pages. Estab. 1975. Buys all rights. Byline given. Pays on acceptance. Sample copy and writer's guidelines $3.50. Photocopied submissions OK. Reports "almost immediately." SASE.
Nonfiction: "We publish articles about the rare, out-of-print and antiquarian book market. Material must appeal to book collectors and rare book dealers. Emphasis is placed on determining market forces in the trade." Query. Length varies.

CHRISTIAN BOOKSELLER, Gundersen & Schmale Rd., Wheaton IL 60187. (312)653-4200. Editor-in-Chief: Jan Lokay. 50% freelance written. Emphasizes "any products that are found in the religious bookstore." Monthly magazine; 68 pages. Circ. 10,000. Pays on publication. Phone queries OK. Submit seasonal/holiday material 2½ months in advance of issue date. Photocopied and previously published submissions OK. SASE. Reports in 2 weeks. Free Sample copy and writer's guidelines.
Nonfiction: "*Christian Bookseller* is a trade magazine serving religious bookstores. Needs successful business stories—reports of Christian bookstores that are utilizing unique methods of merchandising promotions, have unique departments, etc." Query. Length: 1,500-2,000 words. Pays $60-75.
Photos: "Photos are to accompany successful business stories." State availability of photos with query. Uses 3-4 b&w photos/story.

COLLEGE STORE EXECUTIVE, Box 788, Lynbrook, New York NY 11563. (516)887-1800. Editor: Sandra J. Beckerman. 25% freelance written. Emphasizes merchandising and marketing in the college store market. Publishes 10 issues/year tabloid; 40 pages. Estab. 1970. Circ. 10,000. Pays on publication. Buys all rights. Byline given. Submit seasonal/holiday material 2 months in advance of issue date. Photocopied submissions OK. SASE. Reports in 3 weeks. Sample copy $1; free writer's guidelines; mention *Writer's Market* in request.
Nonfiction: Exposé (on inadequate stores; problems in college market); general interest (to managers); how-to (advertise, manage a store, store profile); inspirational (how to be successful in the college store market); interview (with bookstore managers; personal experience (someone who worked for a publisher selling to bookstores); opinion (from those who know about the market); photo feature (on specific colleges in the country or outside); and technical (how to display products). No articles on the typical college student. Buys 40 mss/year. Query. Length: 1,000 words. Pays $2/column inch.
Photos: State availability of photos with query. Pays $5-10 for any size b&w prints or contact sheets. Captions preferred. Buys all rights.

PUBLISHERS WEEKLY, 1180 Avenue of the Americas, New York NY 10036. (212)764-5153. Editor-in-Chief: Nat Brandt. Weekly. Buys first North American rights only. Pays on publication. Reports "in several weeks." SASE.
Nonfiction and Photos: "We rarely use unsolicited mss because of our highly specialized audience and their professional interests, but we can sometimes use news items about publishers, publishing projects, bookstores and other subjects relating to books." Payment negotiable; generally $50-75/printed page. Photos purchased with and without mss "occasionally."

QUILL & QUIRE, 59 Front St. E., Toronto, Ontario M5E 1B3, Canada. Editor: Susan Walker. 30% freelance written. For professional librarians, writers, booksellers, publishers, educators, media people; anyone interested in Canadian books. Monthly newspaper; 48 pages. Estab. 1935. Circ. 12,000. Buys all rights or second serial (reprint) rights. Buys 120 mss/year. Pays on acceptance. Free sample copy. Reports in 1 week. SAE and International Reply Coupons.
Nonfiction and Photos: Interviews, profiles, commentary. Strong emphasis on information. Subject must be of Canadian interest. Query. Length: 1,000-2,000 words. Pays $100-350. B&w photos purchased with mss. Pays $15.

Brick, Glass, and Ceramics

AMERICAN GLASS REVIEW, Box 2147, Clifton NJ 07015. (201)779-1601. Editor-in-Chief: Donald Doctorow. 20% freelance written. Monthly magazine; 32 pages. Pays on publication. Phone queries OK. Buys all rights. Submit seasonal/holiday material 3 months in advance of issue date. SASE. Reports in 2-3 weeks. Free sample copy; mention *Writer's Market* in request.
Nonfiction: Technical (problems in the glass industry and supply problems). No articles on glass blowers. Buys 2 mss/issue. Query. Length: 1,000-3,000. Pays $40-50.
Photos: State availability of photos with query. No additional payment for b&w contact sheets. Captions preferred. Buys all rights but may reassign following publication.

BRICK AND CLAY RECORD, 5 S. Wabash Ave., Chicago IL 60603. (312)372-6880. Editor: Phil Jeffers. For "the heavy clay products industry." Monthly. Buys all rights. Pays on publication. Query. Reports in 15 days. SASE.
Nonfiction and Photos: "News concerning personnel changes within companies; news concerning new plants for manufacture of brick, clay pipe, refractories, drain tile, face brick, glazed tile, lightweight clay aggregate products and abrasives; news of new products, expansion, new building." Pays 8¢/published line minimum. "Photos paid for only when initially requested by editor."
Fillers: "Items should concern only news of brick, clay pipe, refractory, or clay lightweight aggregate plant operations. If news of personnel, should be only of top-level plant personnel. Not interested in items such as patio, motel, or home construction using brick; of weddings or engagements of clay products people, unless major executives; obituaries, unless of major personnel; items concerning floor or wall tile (only structural tile); of plastics, metal, concrete, bakelite, or similar products; items concerning people not directly involved in clay plant operation." Pays $3 "per published 2- or 3-line brief item." Pays $3 minimum for "full-length published news item, depending on value of item and editor's discretion. Payment is only for items published in the magazine. No items sent in can be returned."

CERAMIC INDUSTRY, 5 S. Wabash, Chicago IL 60603. Editor: J.J. Svec. For the ceramics industry; manufacturers of glass, porcelain, enamel, whitewares and electronic/industrial newer ceramics. Magazine; 50-60 pages. Established in 1923. Monthly. Circulation: 7,500. Buys all rights. Byline given. Buys 10-12 mss/year (on assignment only). Pays on acceptance. Will send free sample copy to writer on request. Reports "immediately." Query. SASE.
Nonfiction and Photos: Semitechnical, informational and how-to material purchased on assignment only. Length: 500-1,500 words. Pays $35/published page. No additional payment for photos used with mss. Captions required.

CERAMIC SCOPE, Box 48643, Los Angeles CA 90048. (213)935-1122. Editor-in-Chief: Mel Fiske. 25% freelance written. For "ceramic hobby business people (many emerging housewives, many retired couples) with a love for ceramics but with meager business education." Monthly magazine; 64 pages. Estab. 1964. Circ. 6,300. Pays on acceptance. Buys all rights. Byline given. Phone queries OK. Submit seasonal/holiday material 3 months in advance of issue date. Simultaneous, photocopied and previously published submissions OK. SASE. Reports in 2 weeks.
Nonfiction: "Articles on how business principles are applied in ceramic hobby shops, and how they work specifically, with in-depth examples. We don't need biographical material, or how the business started in the garage or kitchen." Buys 20-25 mss/year. Query with clips of published work. Length: 1,000-2,500 words. Pays $100-200.
Photos: State availability of photos with query. Pays $5-10 for 5x7 glossy prints; $25-50 for 35mm color transparencies. Buys all rights.

GLASS DIGEST, 110 E. 42nd St., New York NY 10017. (212)685-0768. Editor: Oscar S. Glasberg. Monthly. Buys first rights. Byline given "only industry people—not freelancers." Pays on publication "or before, if ms held too long." Will send a sample copy to a writer on request. Reports "as soon as possible." SASE.
Nonfiction and Photos: "Items about firms in glass distribution, personnel, plants, etc. Stories about outstanding jobs accomplished—volume of flat glass, storefronts, curtainwalls, auto glass, mirrors, windows (metal), glass doors; special uses and values; who installed it. Stories about successful glass/metal distributors, dealers, and glazing contractors—their methods, promotion work done, advertising, results." Length: 1,000-1,500 words. Pays 6¢/word, "usually more. No interest in bottles, glassware, containers, etc., but leaded and stained glass good." B&w photos purchased with mss: "8x10 preferred." Pays $7, "usually more."
How To Break In: "Find a typical dealer case history about a firm operating in such a successful way that its methods can be duplicated by readers everywhere."

Building Interiors

DECOR, The Magazine of Fine Interior Accessories, 408 Olive, St. Louis MO 63102. (314)421-5445. Senior Editor: Loraine Wright O'Malley. For retailers of art, picture framing and decorative interior accessories. Subscribers include gallery directors/owners, custom and do-it-yourself picture framers, accessories shop owners, and managers of picture/accessories departments in department and home furnishings stores. Monthly magazine; 200 pages. Estab. 1880. Circ. 16,000. Pays on acceptance. Buys exclusive rights. Byline given. Simultaneous submissions OK. SASE. Reports in 30 days. Submit seasonal/holiday material 3 months in advance of issue date. Sample copy $1; free writer's guidelines.

Nonfiction and Photos: "How-to articles (how to advertise, how to use display space, how to choose product lines, how to use credit) giving, in essence, new and better ways to show a profit. Most often in the form of single store interviews with a successful store manager. No editorializing by the freelancer, unless he has proper credentials. Our emphasis is on useful material, not merely general interest. How does this businessman keep his customers, get new ones, please the old ones, etc." Query. Length: open. Pays $65-125. No additional payment for 5x7 or 8x10 b&w photos used with mss.

KITCHEN BUSINESS, 1515 Broadway, New York NY 10036. Editor: B. Leslie Hart. For "kitchen cabinet and countertop plants, kitchen and bath planning specialists, and kitchen-bath departments of lumber, plumbing, and appliance businesses." Monthly. Buys all rights. Pays on acceptance. Will consider photocopied submissions. Often overstocked. Reports in 1 month. SASE.

Nonfiction and Photos: "Factual case histories with illustrative photos on effective selling or management methods; picture tours of outstanding kitchen showrooms of about 1,000 words; articles on management methods for kitchen distributorships which handle a full range of kitchen products; 'how-to' shop stories on kitchen cabinet shops or countertop fabricators, or stories on how they adapt to growth problems. Must have a business angle other readers can learn from. Just a description of an operation is not sufficient." Length: "600 words and 2 photos to 2,000 words and 10 photos. Pays $100 and up, on a page basis, as estimated at the time of acceptance." Photos purchased with mss.

How To Break In: "Just go ahead and do it. Select the best-looking kitchen firm in your area, go in and tell the boss you're a writer and want to do a story for *Kitchen Business*, ask him to let you sit down and read an issue or two, interview him on a single how-to-do-it topic, shoot some pictures to illustrate the points in the interview, and take a chance. Include his phone number so I can check with him. If it's good, you'll get paid promptly. If it shows promise, I'll work with you. If it's in between, you might not hear for a while because I hate to send them back if they have any value at all."

PROFESSIONAL DECORATING & COATING ACTION, Painting and Decorating Contractors of America, 7223 Lee Hwy., Falls Church VA 22046. (703)534-1201. Editor/Manager: Heskett K. Darby. Emphasizes professional decorating, painting, wallcovering and sandblasting for painting contractors and their top assistants. Monthly magazine; 48-56 pages. Estab. 1938. Circ. 12,000. Pays on acceptance. Buys all rights, but may reassign following publication. Submit seasonal or holiday material 2 months in advance. SASE. Reports in 3 weeks. Free sample copy.

Nonfiction: Publishes how-to and informational articles. Buys 17-20 mss/year. Query. Length: preferably under 1,000 words. Pays 10¢/word maximum.

Photos: Purchased with accompanying ms. Captions required. Pays $7.50-9.50 for professional quality 8½x11 or 4x5 glossy b&w prints. Model release required.

PROFESSIONAL REMODELING, Harcourt Brace Jovanovich, 43 E. Ohio, Chicago IL 60611. Editor: Norman C. Remich Jr. For professional remodeling contractors engaged in home and light commercial remodeling. Monthly tabloid with magazine format. Estab. 1978. Circ. 30,000. Pays on publication. Buys all rights. Phone queries OK. Submit seasonal/holiday material 3 months in advance. SASE. Reports in 1 month. Free sample copy and writer's guidelines.

Nonfiction: How-to (on remodeling projects from inception to completion); interview and profiles of key industry figures. Query. Pays $100.

Photos: "*PR* is strong on four-color graphics." Prefers 5x7 b&w glossy prints and 4x5 color transparencies. Pays $10. Captions required.

RESIDENTIAL INTERIORS, Billboard Publications, 1515 Broadway, New York NY 10036. (212)764-7530. Editor: Susan S. Szenasy. "Written for the professional designer, i.e., a more visually sophisticated person than most consumers." Readership ages range from 18-60 and are "interior designers doing residential interiors (houses, apartments, model apartments, model rooms, showhouses); manufacturers of home furnishing products; students of design; consumers (middle- and high-income) interested in contemporary interior design." Bimonthly magazine; 150 pages. Estab. 1976. Circ. 41,000. Pays on publication. Buys all rights. Phone queries OK. Submit seasonal/holiday material 3 months in advance. Simultaneous, photocopied and previously published submissions OK. SASE. Reports in 2 months. Free sample copy.

Nonfiction: Historical (restoration of houses, adaptive re-use of buildings); how-to (practical solutions to problems relevant to interior design); humor (about interior design/decoration); interview (with designers and architects); opinion (layman's point of view on why a particular interior does or does not work); profile (of designers at retail, retail stores with interior design departments); photo feature (innovative, avant-garde interior design); technical (solar heating of houses, energy conservation, restoration of fabrics). Buys 3 mss/issue. Query with clips of published work and resume. Pays $300.
Photos: Send photos with ms. Pays $20-30 for b&w contact sheets and color transparencies. Captions required.
Columns/Departments: Art and artists, books, and antiques. Buys 4/issue. Query. Length: 500-1,000 words.

WALLS AND CEILINGS, 14006 Ventura Blvd., Sherman Oaks CA 91423. (213)789-8733. Editor-in-Chief: Robert Welch. Managing Editor: Don Haley. For contractors involved in lathing and plastering, drywall, acoustics, fireproofing, curtain walls, movable partitions and their mechanics; together with manufacturers dealers and architects. Monthly magazine; 32 pages. Estab. February 1938. Circ. 10,000. Pays on publication. Buys first North American serial rights. Byline given. Phone queries OK. Submit seasonal/holiday material 3 months in advance of issue date. SASE. Reports in 3 weeks. Sample copy $1.
Nonfiction: How-to (drywall and plaster construction and business management); and interview. Buys 5 mss/year. Query. Length: 200-1,000 words. Pays $75 maximum.
Photos: State availability of photos with query. Pays $5 for 5x7 b&w prints. Captions required. Buys one-time rights.

Business Management

The publications listed here are aimed at owners of businesses and top level business executives. They cover business trends and general theory and practice of management. Publications that use similar material but have a less technical or professional slant are listed in Business and Finance in the Consumer Publications section. Journals dealing with banking, investment, and financial management are classified in the Finance category in this section.

Publications dealing with lower level management (including supervisors and office managers) will be found in Management and Supervision. Journals for industrial plant managers are listed under Industrial Management, and under the names of specific industries such as Machinery and Metal Trade or Plastics. Publications for office supply store operators will be found with the Office Equipment and Supplies Journals.

ADMINISTRATIVE MANAGEMENT, Geyer-McAllister Publications, 51 Madison Ave., New York NY 10010. Editor-in-Chief: Walter A. Kleinschrod. Managing Editor: Jim N. Bruno. 33% freelance written. Emphasizes office systems and their management. Monthly magazine; 120 pages. Estab. 1939. Circ. 53,000. Pays on publication. Buys all rights. Byline given. Photocopied submissions OK. Reports in 8 weeks. Sample copy $1.75; free writer's guidelines.
Nonfiction: Exposé (what's wrong with certain management theories or office products); general interest (business operations); and how-to (run an efficient office operation of some kind).
Photos: State availability of photos with query or submit photo material with accompany query. Possible additional payment for b&w prints or contact sheets or color contact sheets. Captions preferred. Buys one-time rights.

CURRENT MANAGEMENT, Bureau of Business Practice, 24 Rope Ferry Rd., Waterford CT 06386. Supervisory Editor: Barbara Kelsey. The publication is aimed at upper and top level executives who manage white-collar personnel. It deals primarily with the latest techniques in management and current business trends. The emphasis is on how other companies might benefit from or initiate a certain program, approach a specific problem, or improve productivity and morale—with concrete suggestions for doing so. We're interested in any and all types of business and industry where white-collar management problems are faced—hospitals, banks, insurance companies, public utilities, etc." Monthly newsletter; 8 pages. Estab. 1978. Buys all rights. Phone queries OK. Submit seasonal/holiday material 6

months in advance. Photocopied submissions OK. SASE. Reports in 2 weeks. Free sample copy and writer's guidelines.
Nonfiction: Interview (the individual in charge of the program or with authority over the area involved.) Buys 5-6 articles/issue. Length: 400-1,600 words. Query. Pays 10¢/word after editing.

EXECUTIVE REVIEW, 224 S. Michigan Ave., Chicago IL 60604. (312)922-4083. Editor-in-Chief: Harold Sabes. 15% freelance written. For management of small and middle-class companies, middle management in larger companies and enterprises. Monthly magazine; 32 pages. Estab. 1955. Circ. 25,000. Pays on publication. Buys one-time or second rights. Byline given. Submit seasonal/holiday material 6 months in advance of issue date. Simultaneous, photocopied and previously published submissions OK. SASE. Reports in 4 weeks. Free sample copy and writer's guidelines; mention *Writer's Market* in request.
Nonfiction: How-to (of interest to businessmen in the operation of their companies, and ideas that can be adapted and successfully used by others); interview; personal experience (business); profile; and travel. Buys 7 mss/issue. Submit complete ms. Length: 1,000-1,500 words. Pays $15-50.

HARVARD BUSINESS REVIEW, Soldiers Field, Boston MA 02163. (617)495-6800. Editor: Ralph F. Lewis. For top management in US industry, and in Japan and Western Europe; younger managers who aspire to top management responsibilities; policymaking executives in government, policymakers in noncommercial organizations, and professional people interested in the viewpoint of business management. Published 6 times/year. Buys all rights. Byline given. Pays on publication. Reports in 2-6 weeks. SASE.
Nonfiction: Articles on business trends, techniques and problems. "*Harvard Business Review* seeks to inform executives about what is taking place in management, but it also wants to challenge them and stretch their thinking about the policies they make, how they make them, and how they administer them. It does this by presenting articles that provide in-depth analyses of issues and problems in management and, wherever possible, guidelines for thinking out and working toward resolutions of these issues and problems." Length: 3,000-6,000 words. Pays $500.

MANAGING, Graduate School of Business, University of Pittsburgh, 1917 Cathedral of Learning, Pittsburgh PA 15260. (412)624-6416. Editor-in-Chief: Karen Burgio Hoy. Editor: Rebecca R. Schorin. Art Director: Barbara V. Dinsmore. Emphasizes business and management issues. Many of the readers are Graduate School of Business alumni; others are upper- and middle-level managers and executives in the city, tri-state region and country. Magazine published three times/year (January, May and September); 32 pages. Estab. 1979. Circ. 5,000. Pays on acceptance. Buys all rights. Submit seasonal/holiday material 3 months in advance. Photocopied submissions OK; previously published submissions OK, but not for full-length features. SASE. Reports in 1 month. Free sample copy and writer's guidelines.
Nonfiction: Profile (on corporate executive to give full picture of man and his work) and business- or management-oriented features that stem from a regional base, but the story should have national impact. Buys 3-4 mss/issue. Length: 1,500-3,000 words. Query. Pays $100-300.
Photos: State availability of photos. Pays $10-40 for b&w contact sheets.
Columns/Departments: Your Turn (a column on personal views toward a business or management issue written with a background in the area). Buys 1/issue. Send complete ms. Length: 500-800 words. Pays $20-50. Brief Cases (short synopses of interesting managerial topics with humorous twist). Length: 50-100 words. Pays $10.
Fillers: Clippings, jokes, gags, anecdotes and short humor. Length: 25-150 words. Pays $10-50.

MARKETING COMMUNICATIONS, United Business Publications, Inc., 475 Park Ave. S., New York NY 10016. Editor-in-Chief: Ronnie Telzer. 70% freelance written. Emphasizes marketing and promotion. Monthly magazine; 90 pages. Estab: 1976. Circ: 27,000. Pays on publication. Buys all rights, but may reassign (with credit to *MC*) following publication. Byline given. Submit seasonal or holiday material 2-3 months in advance. Photocopied submissions OK (if exclusive). Reports in 2 months. Sample copy $1.50; free writer's guidelines.
Nonfiction: "The preferred format for feature articles is the case history approach to solving marketing problems. Critical evaluations of market planning, premium and incentive programs, point-of-purchase displays, direct mail campaigns, dealer/distributor meetings, media advertising, and sales promotion tools and techniques are particularly relevant." How-to (develop successful product campaigns); informational (marketing case histories); opinion (guest editorials by marketing executives); profiles (on a given industry, e.g., tobacco, razors,

food); technical articles (technology updates on a field of interest to marketing people). Buys 3 mss/issue. Length: 750-1,250 words. Pays $75-250.

Photos: Prefers 8x10 b&w glossies with mss, or 2¼x2¼ color transparencies; other formats acceptable. Submit prints and transparencies. Captions required. No additional payment.

MAY TRENDS, 111 S. Washington St., Park Ridge IL 60068. (312)825-8806. Editor: J.J. Coffey Jr. 100% freelance written. For chief executives of businesses, trade associations, government bureaus, Better Business Bureaus, educational institutions, newspapers. Publication of George S. May International Company. Magazine published 3 times/year; 28-30 pages. Established in 1967. Circulation: 10,000. Buys all rights. Byline given. Buys 15-20 mss/year. Pays on acceptance. Will send free sample copy to writer on request. Reports in 1 week. Query or submit complete ms. SASE.

Nonfiction: "We prefer articles dealing with problems of specific industries (manufacturers, wholesalers, retailers, service businesses, small hospitals and nursing homes) where contact has been made with key executives whose comments regarding their problems may be quoted." Avoid material on overworked, labor-management relations. Interested in small supermarket success stories vs. the "giants"; automobile dealers coping with existing dull markets; contractors solving cost-inventory problems. Will consider material on successful business operations and merchandising techniques. Length: 1,500-3,000 words. Pays $100-250.

SMALL BUSINESS MAGAZINE, Small Business Service Bureau, Inc., 544 Main St., Box 1441, Worcester MA 01601. (617)756-3513. Editor: Jeanne Blum Kissane. Emphasizes small businesses with 1-100 employees. "Most readers are self-employed or small business people with fewer than 50 employees. They are interested in surviving and improving their businesses." Bimonthly magazine; 40 pages. Estab. 1976. Circ. 18,000. Pays on acceptance. Byline given. Buys all rights, but usually reassigns following publication. SASE. Reports in 6-8 weeks. Free sample copy.

Nonfiction: How-to (business-related, bookkeeping, retail display, direct mail, advertising, etc.); informational (about using government resources, new programs, loan sources, legislation, etc.); interview (legislators and regulators with ties to small business); personal experience (short pieces on how you improved your business—e.g., "How I Foiled Bad Check Passers"; buys 25-30 mss/year. Query. Length: 1200-2500 words. Pays $75-200.

Photos: Photos purchased with accompanying ms. Prefers contact sheets and negatives but will accept b&w glossy prints. Total purchase price for a ms. includes payment for photos. Captions required.

Columns/Departments: Consultus (how-to, especially on technical and legal subjects). Buys 1 ms/issue. Query. Length: 900-2000 words. Pays $75-125. Open to suggestions for new columns or departments (except on taxes).

Profiles: Of especially successful or unusual small businesses and how they got that way. 900-1500 words. Pays $70-90. Photos of subject required. Buys 2 ms/issue.

How To Break In: "We are looking for people to contribute regularly and grow with us."

SMALL BUSINESS NEWSLETTER, 7514 N. 53rd St., Milwaukee WI 53223. Editor/Publisher: Don Ristow. For small-business owners and managers. Monthly newsletter; 4 pages. Estab. 1977. Circ. 500. Pays on publication. Buys one-time rights. Submit seasonal/holiday material 1 month in advance of issue date. Simultaneous, photocopied and previously published submissions OK. SASE. Reports in 1 month. Sample copy and writer's guidelines for $1.

Nonfiction: General interest; how-to (cut taxes, improve management, advertise/promote, etc.); inspirational; new product (for small business use); and technical (taxes, administration, other small-business interests). Submit complete ms. Pays $10-100.

Fillers: Jokes, gags and anecdotes (related to tax or business). Pays $5.

Church Administration and Ministry

CHILDREN'S CHURCH: THE LEADER'S GUIDE, 1445 Boonville Ave., Springfield MO 65807. Editor: James E. Erdmann. Assistant Editor: Diana B. Ansley. "For teachers of primary-age children in a children's church, extended session story hour or Bible club setting." Quarterly magazine. Estab. 1975. Circ. 6,500. Pays on acceptance. Buys one-time rights or first North American serial rights. Phone queries OK. Submit seasonal/holiday material 12-15 months in advance. Previously published submissions OK "if you tell us." Reports in 6 weeks. SASE. Free sample copy and writer's guidelines.

Nonfiction: How-to ("Get Seven Helpers Out of an Old Sock," worship through music, etc.); inspirational; and practical help for the teacher. The spiritual must be an integral part of your

material and articles should reflect actual experience or observations related to working with 6- to 8-year-olds. Buys 12 mss/year. Submit complete ms. Length: 500-1,200 words. Pays $8-20.
Photos: Purchased with mss about handcrafted items. Offers no additional payment for photos accepted with ms.
Fiction: Most religious stories done on assignment. Buys 13 mss/issue. Query. Length: 2,000-2,200 words.

THE CHRISTIAN MINISTRY, 407 S. Dearborn St., Chicago IL 60605. (312)427-5380. Editorial Director: James M. Wall. 10% freelance written. For the professional clergy (primarily liberal Protestant). Bimonthly magazine; 40 pages. Estab. 1925. Circ. 12,000. Buys all rights. Buys 50 mss/year. Pays on publication. Free sample copy. Reports in 2 weeks. SASE.
Nonfiction: "We want articles by clergy-theologians who know the clergy audience. We are interested in articles on local church problems and in helpful how-to as well as "think" pieces. Query. Length: 1,200-1,800 words. Pay varies, $10/page minimum.

CHURCH ADMINISTRATION, 127 9th Ave. N., Nashville TN 37234. (615)251-2060. Editor: George Clark. 75% freelance written. For Southern Baptist pastors, staff and volunteer church leaders. Monthly. Buys all rights. Byline given. Will also consider second rights. Uses limited amount of freelance material. Pays on acceptance. Free sample copy and writer's guidelines. SASE.
Nonfiction and Photos: "How-to-do-it articles dealing with church administration, including church programming, organizing, and staffing, administrative skills, church financing, church food services, church facilities, communication, pastoral ministries and community needs." Length: 750-1,500 words. Pays 2½¢/word. Pays $7.50-10 for 8x10 b&w glossies purchased with mss.
How To Break In: "A beginning writer should first be acquainted with organization and policy of Baptist churches and with the administrative needs of Southern Baptist churches. He should perhaps interview one or several SBC pastors or staff members, find out how they are handling a certain administrative problem such as 'enlisting volunteer workers' or 'sharing the administrative load with church staff or volunteer workers.' I suggest writers compile an article showing how *several* different administrators (or churches) handled the problem, perhaps giving meaningful quotes. Submit the completed manuscript, typed 54 characters to the line, for consideration."

CHURCH MANAGEMENT-THE CLERGY JOURNAL, 4119 Terrace Lane, Hopkins MN 55343. (612)933-6712. Editor: Manfred Holck Jr. 80% freelance written. For professional clergy and church business administrators. Monthly (except June and December) magazine; 38 pages. Estab. 1924. Circ. 12,000. Pays on publication. Buys all rights, but may reassign following publication. Pays 50% kill fee. Byline given. Submit seasonal/holiday material 6 months in advance of issue date. Photocopied submissions OK. SASE. Reports in 6 weeks. Sample copy $1.25.
Nonfiction: How-to (be a more effective minister or administrator); and inspirational (seasonal sermons). No poetry or personal experiences. Buys 5 mss/issue. Submit complete ms. Length: 1,000-1,500 words. Pays $10-25.

CHURCH TRAINING, 127 9th Ave. N., Nashville TN 37234. (615)251-2843. Publisher: The Sunday School Board of the Southern Baptist Convention. Editor: Richard B. Sims. For all workers and leaders in the Church Training program of the Southern Baptist Convention. Established in 1926. Monthly. Circulation: 40,000. Buys all rights. Byline given. Buys 25 mss/year. Pays on acceptance. Will send sample copy to writer on request. Write for copy of guidelines for writers. No photocopied or simultaneous submissions. Reports in 6 weeks. Query with rough outline. SASE.
Nonfiction: "Articles that pertain to leadership training in the church. Success stories that pertain to Church Training. Associational articles. Informational, how-to's that pertain to Church Training." Length: 500-1,500 words. Pays 3½¢/word.

THE EDGE on Christian Education, Nazarene Publishing House, 6401 The Paseo, Kansas City MO 64131. Editor: Melton Wienecke. Assistant Editor: Nina Beegle. Emphasizes Christian/religious education for Sunday school teachers, pastors, Sunday school superintendents, supervisors and workers. Quarterly magazine; 48 pages. Estab. 1973. Circ. 40,000. Pays on acceptance. Buys all rights, second serial (reprint) rights, or one-time rights. Byline given. Submit seasonal/holiday material 12 months in advance. Simultaneous, photocopied and previously published submissions OK. SASE. Reports 10-12 weeks. Free sample copy and writer's guidelines.

Nonfiction: Publishes how-to, humor, informational, inspirational, new product, personal experience and technical articles; interviews, profiles of trends, photo features, and articles on philosophy of Christian education. Length: 1,500 words maximum. Buys 80-100 mss/year. Pays 2¢/word.
Photos: B&w and color purchased with or without mss, or on assignment. Send prints and transparencies. Pays $20 maximum b&w. Include your asking price with submissions.
Fiction: Considered if it is short and deals with a problem in the field. Length: 1,000 words maximum. Pays 2¢/word.
Poetry: Publishes light verse or poetry in traditional forms. Buys 10 a year. Submit complete ms. Pays 25¢/line, $2 minimum.

EMMANUEL, 194 E. 76th St., New York NY 10021. (212)861-1076. Editor: the Rev. Paul J. Bernier, S.S.S. Monthly. For the Catholic clergy. Estab. 1895. Circ. 15,000. Rights to be arranged with author. Buys 5-6 mss/year. Pays on publication. Will consider photocopied submissions. Submit seasonal material 3-4 months in advance. Reports in 5 weeks. SASE.
Nonfiction: Articles of Catholic (especially priestly) spirituality; can be biographical, historical or critical. Articles on Eucharistic theology, and those which provide a solid scriptural and/or theological foundation for priestly spirituality (prayer, applied spirituality, etc.). Aims at providing today's priest and involved Catholics with an adequate theology and philosophy of ministry in today's church. Length: 1,500-3,000 words. Usually pays $50.

ENDURING WORD ADULT TEACHER, 6401 The Paseo, Kansas City MO 64131. (816)333-7000. Editor: John B. Nielson. 10% freelance written. For teachers of adults. Quarterly. Buys first and second rights; will accept simultaneous submissions. Pays on acceptance. Will consider photocopied submissions. Reports in 6 weeks. SASE.
Nonfiction: "Articles of interest to teachers of adults and articles relevant to the Enduring Word Series Sunday school lesson outline." Length: 1,300 words maximum. Pays minimum $30/1,000 words.
Photos: Purchased with captions only. Pays minimum $5; 4-color up to $100.
Poetry: Inspirational, seasonal or lesson-related poetry. Length: 24 lines maximum. Pays minimum 25¢/line.

KEY TO CHRISTIAN EDUCATION, Standard Publishing, 8121 Hamilton Ave., Cincinnati OH 45231. (513)931-4050. Editor-in-Chief: Virginia Beddow. 50% freelance written. For "church leaders of all ages; Sunday school teachers and superintendents; ministers; Christian education professors; youth workers." Quarterly magazine; 48 pages. Estab. 1962. Circ. 65,000. Pays on acceptance. Buys first North American serial rights. Byline given. Phone queries OK. Submit seasonal/holiday material 15 months in advance. Photocopied and previously published submissions OK. SASE. Reports in 4 weeks. Free sample copy and writer's guidelines.
Nonfiction: How-to (programs and projects for Christian education); informational; interview; opinion; and personal experience. Buys 10 mss/issue. Query or submit complete ms. Length: 700-2,000 words. Pays $20-50.
Photos: Purchased with or without accompanying ms. Submit prints. Pays $5-25 for any size glossy finish b&w prints. Total price for ms includes payment for photos. Model release required.
Fillers: Purchases short ideas on "this is how we did it" articles. Buys 10 mss/issue. Submit complete ms. Length: 50-250 words. Pays $5-10.

PASTORAL LIFE, Society of St. Paul, Route 224, Canfield OH 44406. Editor: Victor L. Viberti, S.S.P. For priests and those interested in pastoral ministry. Magazine; 64 pages. Monthly. Circulation: 8,800. Buys first rights. Byline given. Pays on acceptance. Will send sample copy to writer on request. "Queries appreciated before submitting mss. New contributors are expected to accompany their material with a few lines of personal data." Reports in 7-10 days. SASE.
Nonfiction: "Professional review, principally designed to focus attention on current problems, needs, issues and all important activities related to all phases of pastoral work and life. Avoids merely academic treatments on abstract and too controversial subjects." Length: 2,000-3,400 words. Pays 3¢/word minimum.

THE SERRAN, Serra International, 22 W. Monroe St., Chicago IL 60603. (312)782-2163. Editor: Ray Prost. 20% freelance written. Emphasizes Catholic priestly and religious vocations for a readership 90% of whom are affluent Catholic laymen and 10% clergymen (bishops, priests). Bimonthly magazine; 16-24 pages. Estab. 1944. Circ. 15,000. Pays on publication. Buys all rights; "the message of our apostolate is spread frequently by the reprinting in the publications of our affiliates and other organizations of material from the *Serran*." Submit seasonal/holiday material 3 months in advance of issue date. Simultaneous and photocopied submissions OK. SASE. Reports in 4 weeks. Sample copy 50¢.

Nonfiction: "Articles should be altruistic and in keeping with our purposes: fostering and preserving Catholic priestly and religious vocations, and assisting our members to fulfill their own Christian vocations to service." Inspirational (religious, priests, nuns, etc.); interview (occasionally on assignment); and photo feature (occasionally, if in keeping with objectives of our apostolate). Buys 6 mss/year. Length: 250-1,800 words. Pays $20-100.

Photo: Pays $5-10 for glossy b&w prints; $2-5 for glossy color prints. "We prefer b&w square photos or horizontal or verticals based on multiples of a square (but not essential)." Captions preferred "for information, subject to editing." Buys all rights. Model release required.

SUCCESS, Box 15337, Denver CO 80215. Editor: Edith Quinlan. 90% freelance written. Quarterly magazine. Byline given. Reports in 2-3 weeks. SASE. Free sample copy and writer's guidelines.

Nonfiction: "Articles should be from 500-2,000 words in length, and should provide ideas helpful to workers in Christian education. We are more interested in receiving articles from people who know Christian education, or workers who have accomplished something worthwhile in Sunday school and youth work, than from experienced writers who do not have such background. A combination of both, however, is ideal. Articles may be of a general nature, or be slanted to specific age groups, such as preschool, elementary, youth and adult." Pays 3¢/word.

SUNDAY SCHOOL COUNSELOR, General Council of the Assemblies of God, 1445 Boonville Ave., Springfield MO 65802. (417)862-2781, ext. 433. Editor: Sylvia Lee. "Our audience consists of local church school teachers and administrators. These are people who, by and large, have not been professionally trained for their positions but are rather volunteer workers. Most would have not more than a high school education." Monthly magazine; 32 pages. Estab. 1939. Circ. 45,000. Pays on acceptance. Buys all rights, but may reassign following publication; or simultaneous rights. Byline given. Submit seasonal/holiday material 9 months in advance. Simultaneous and previously published submissions OK. SASE. Reports in 4-6 weeks. Free sample copy and writer's guidelines.

Nonfiction: How-to (Sunday school teaching, crafts, discipline in the Sunday school, building student-teacher relationships); inspirational (on the teaching ministry); and personal experience (as related to teaching ministry or how a Sunday school teacher handled a particular situation). Buys 70 mss/year. Submit complete ms. Length: 400-1,000 words. Pays 1-3¢/word.

Photos: Purchased with accompanying ms or on assignment. Send prints or transparencies. Pays $5-8 for 5x7 b&w photos; $10-70 for 2¼x2¼ color transparencies. Model release required.

How To Break In: "A freelancer can break into our publication by submitting a first-person account of a Sunday school experience. This must be actual, and contain a new slant or insight on an old topic. We are a good freelance market providing the person has taken time to study our publication first and to see our needs and slant."

YOUR CHURCH, Religious Publishing Co., 198 Allendale Rd., King of Prussia PA 19406. Editor: Phyllis Mather Rice. Production & Design Director: Norman Lock. 30% freelance written. Bimonthly magazine; 56 pages. Estab. 1955. Circ. 188,000. Pays on publication. Buys all rights. Pays 50% kill fee. Byline given "if the author was directly employed by an advertiser in the magazine and that the article was an inhouse article." Photocopied submissions OK. SASE. Reports in 2-3 months.

Nonfiction: "Articles for pastors, informative and cogently related to some aspect of being a pastor (counseling, personal finance, administration, building, etc.)." Buys 15-20 mss/year. Length: 5-15 typewritten pages. Pays $5/page, not to exceed $75.

THE YOUTH LEADER, 1445 Boonville Ave., Springfield MO 65802. Editor: Glen Ellard. For "ministers of youth (Christian)." Evangelical Christianity and Christian activism. Special issues at Christmas and Easter. Estab. 1944. Monthly. Circ. 5,000. Buys all rights, but will reassign rights to author after publication. Byline given. Buys first North American serial rights, second serial (reprint) rights and simultaneous rights. Buys 20-30 mss/year. Pays on acceptance. Free sample copy. Photocopied submissions OK. Submit seasonal material 4 months in advance. Reports in 6 weeks. SASE.

Nonfiction: "How-to" articles (e.g., "How to Evangelize Youth Through Music," "How to Study the Bible for Personal Application," "How to Use the Media for the Christian

Message"); skits and role-plays; Bible raps, original choruses, Bible verses set to music, ideas for youth services, socials and fund raising; interviews with successful youth leaders. Avoid cliches (especially religious ones); educational philosophy; centered on youths (or students) instead of adults (or teachers); relational approach instead of preaching. Submit complete ms. Length: 500-2,500 words. Pays 2½-3½¢/word.

Clothing and Knit Goods

APPAREL INDUSTRY MAGAZINE, 6226 Vineland Ave., North Hollywood CA (213)766-5291. Executive Editor: Carolyn Pressler. For executive management in apparel companies with interests in equipment, government intervention in the garment industry; finance, management and training in industry. Monthly magazine; 70-100 pages. Estab. 1946. Circ. 16,000. Not copyrighted. Byline given. Buys 40-50 mss/year. Pays on publication. Sample copy $1. Will consider legible photocopied submissions. Reports in 3-4 weeks. Query. SASE.
Nonfiction and Photos: Articles dealing with equipment, training, finance; state and federal government, consumer interests, etc., related to the industry. "Use concise, precise language that is easy to read and understand. In other words, because the subjects are technical, keep the language comprehensible. No general articles on finance and management. Material must be precisely related to the apparel industry." Informational, interview, profile, successful business operations, technical articles. Length: 500-1,000 words. No additional payment for b&w photos.

BODY FASHIONS/INTIMATE APPARAL, Harcourt Brace Jovanovich Publications, 757 3rd Ave., New York NY 10017. Editor-in-Chief: Rena Epsten. Emphasizes information about men's and women's hosiery and underwear; women's undergarments, lingerie, sleepwear, robes, hosiery, leisurewear. For merchandise managers and buyers of store products, manufacturers and suppliers to the trade. Monthly tabloid insert, plus 7 regional market issues called *Market Maker*; 24 pages minimum. Estab. 1913. Circ: 13,500. Pays on publication. Buys all rights. Phone queries OK. Submit seasonal/holiday material 2 months in advance. Previously published submissions OK. SASE. Reports in 4 weeks. Free sample copy.
Columns/Departments: New Image (discussions of renovations of *Body Fashions/Intimate Apparel* department); Creative Retailing (deals with successful retail promotions); Ad Ideas (descriptions of successful advertising campaigns). Buys 1 feature/issue. Query. Length: 500-2,500 words. Pays 15¢/word. Open to suggestions for new columns and departments.
Photos: B&w (5x7) photos purchased without mss. Captions required. Send contact sheet, prints or negatives. Pays $5-25. Model release required.

MEN'S WEAR, Fairchild Publications, 7 E. 12th St., New York NY 10003. Editor: Jack Shea. Emphasizes men's and boy's apparel for retailers. Semimonthly magazine; 46 pages. Estab. 1896. Circ. 26,700. Pays on acceptance. Buys all rights. SASE. Reports in 3 weeks. Free sample copy.
Nonfiction: In-depth analysis (pertaining to men's wear industry companies or issues), how-to (on making men's wear retailing more profitable, sales promotions, advertising, displays). Buys 2-3 mss/year. Query. Length: Flexible, from 1,000 words. Pays $100-200.

TACK 'N TOGS MERCHANDISING, Box 67, Minneapolis MN 55440. For "retailers of products for horse and rider and Western and English fashion apparel." Estab. 1970. Monthly. Circ. 16,000. Rights purchased vary with author and material; may buy all rights. Byline given "except on simultaneous submissions, or non-exclusive articles that may appear in slightly edited form in other publications." Buys 5-10 mss/year. Pays on acceptance. Will send a sample copy to a writer on request. Write for copy of guidelines for writers. Query. SASE.
Nonfiction and Photos: "Case histories, trends of industry." Buys informational articles, how-to's, interviews, profiles, coverage of successful business operations, and articles on merchandising techniques. Length: open. Pays "up to $100." B&w glossies and color transparencies purchased with mss.

TEENS & BOYS, 71 W. 35th St., New York NY 10001. Editor: Ellye Bloom. 20% freelance written. For retailers, manufacturers, resident buying offices in male apparel trade. Monthly magazine; 75-100 pages. Estab. 1919. Circ. 8,200. Pays on publication. Buys one-time rights. Byline given unless heavy rewrite is required. Submit seasonal/holiday material 6 months in advance. SASE. Free writer's guidelines; mention *Writer's Market* in request.
Nonfiction: "*Teens & Boys* is edited for retailers of apparel for boys and male teenage students, aged 4-18. It forecasts style trends, reports on retail merchandising, stock control, promotion, display, new products and industry news. All factual, carefully researched, pertinent articles

presented in a lively style will be considered." Buys 2 mss/issue. Query. Length: 1,000-2,000 words. Pays $30-150.

Photos: State availability of photos with query. Pays $7.50-10 for contact sheets, negatives or 5x7 b&w glossy prints. Captions required. Buys one-time rights.

WESTERN OUTFITTER, 5314 Bingle Rd., Houston TX 77092. (713)688-8811. Editor: Mary House Mizwa. For "owners and managers of retail stores in all 50 states and Canada. These stores sell clothing for riders and equipment for horses, both Western and English style. Monthly. Buys all rights. Pays on publication. Query. SASE.

Nonfiction: Method stories: "in-depth treatment of subjects each merchant wrestles with daily. We want stories that first describe the problem, then give details on methods used in eliminating the problem. Be factual and specific." Subjects include merchandising, promotion, customer contact, accounting and finance, store operation, merchandise handling and personnel. "To merit feature coverage, this merchant has to be a winner. It is the uniqueness of the winner's operation that will benefit other store owners who read this magazine." Length: 1,000-1,500 words for full-length feature; 500-600 words for featurette. Pays 6¢/published word for shortcut featurettes; 6¢/published word for full-length feature and featurettes. Send us copies of stories you have done for other trade magazines. Send us queries based on visits to Western dealers in your territory."

Photos: "Excellent photos make excellent copy much better. Plan photos that bring to life the key points in your text. Avoid shots of store fixtures without people. Submit photos in glossy finish, in 8x10 size or smaller. Sharp focus is a must." Captions required. "Cover photos: We will pay $40 for a 2¼x2¼ color transparency if used for a cover. Your 35mm shots are fine for interior b&w art." Pays $6/photo used with ms. Also uses "single photos, or pairs of photos that show display ideas, tricks, promotional devices that are different and that bring more business." Pays $10.

WESTERN WEAR AND EQUIPMENT MAGAZINE, Bell Publishing, 2403 Champa, Denver CO 80205. (303)572-1777. Editor: Alan Bell. Managing Editor: Marlene Leak. For "western wear and equipment retailers, manufacturers and distributors. The magazine features retailing practices such as marketing, merchandising, display techniques, buying and selling, etc. Every issue carries feature stories on western wear and equipment stores throughout the US and occasionally foreign stores." Monthly magazine; 50 pages. Estab. 1959. Circ. 13,000. Pays on publication. Not copyrighted. Byline, given unless extensive rewriting is required. Phone queries OK. Submit seasonal/holiday material 3 months in advance. Simultaneous (to noncompeting publications), photocopied and previously published submissions OK. SASE. Reports in 3 weeks. Free sample copy and writer's guidelines.

Nonfiction: Expose (of government as related to industry or people in industry); general interest (pertaining to western lifestyle); interview (with western store owners or western personalities); new product (of interest to western clothing or tack retailers—send photo); and photo feature (on western lifestyle or western retailing operation). Buys 2 mss/issue. Query with outline. Length: 1,500-3,000 words. Pays $25-100.

Photos: "We buy photos with manuscripts. Occasionally we purchase photos that illustrate a unique display or store with only a cutline." State availability of photos. Pays $10-35 for b&w contact sheets; $15-40 for color contact sheets (higher for cover photo). Captions preferred.

Columns/Departments: "We accept freelance material for a profile column. The material should feature the operations of a western wear or equipment retailers. We prefer accompanying photos."

Coin-Operated Machines

AMERICAN COIN-OP, 500 N. Dearborn St., Chicago IL 60610. (312)337-7700. Editor: Ben Russell. For owners of coin-operated laundry and drycleaning stores. Monthly magazine; 48 pages. Estab. 1960. Circ. 22,000. Rights purchased vary with author and material but are exclusive to the field. No byline. Buys 25 mss/year. Pays two weeks prior to publication. Free sample copy. Reports as soon as possible; usually in 2 weeks. SASE.

Nonfiction and Photos: "We emphasize store operation, management and use features on industry topics: utility use and conservation, maintenance, store management, customer service and advertising. A case study should emphasize how the store operator accomplished whatever he did—in a way that the reader can apply in his own operation. Mss should have no-nonsense, businesslike approach. Uses informational, how-to, interview, profile, think pieces, spot news, successful business operations articles. Length: 500-3,000 words. Pays 4¢/word minimum. Pays $5 minimum for 8x10 b&w glossy photos purchased with mss. (Contact sheets with negatives preferred.) Must be clear and have good contrast.

Fillers: Newsbreaks, clippings. Length: open. Pays 3¢/word; $3 minimum.

How To Break In: "Query about subjects of current interest. Be observant of coin-operated laundries—how they are designed and equipped; how they serve customers; how (if) they advertise and promote their services. Even one-sentence query reports themselves are sometimes bought and published. Most general articles turned down because they are not aimed well enough at audience. Most case histories turned down because of lack of practical purpose (nothing new or worth reporting)."

COINAMATIC AGE. 259 Broadway., New York NY 10007. (213)349-3754. Editor: C.F. Lee. For operators/owners of coin-operated laundries; dry cleaners. Bimonthly. Buys all rights. Pays on publication. "Queries get same-day attention."

Nonfiction and Photos: "We are currently considering articles on coin-operated laundries, and/or in combination with drycleaners. Slant should focus on the unusual, but at the same time should stress possible adaptation by other coinamat operators. Particular interest at this time centers on energy conservation methods. We are interested in promotional and advertising techniques; reasons for expansion or additional locations; attached sidelines such as carwashes and other businesses; Main Street vs. shopping center operations; successes in dealing with permanent press garment laundering and cleaning; ironing services; and, primarily, financial success, personal satisfaction, or any other motivation that the owner derives from his business. Give the story punch, details, and applicability to the reader. Include a list of specifications, detailing the number of units (washers, dryers, etc.), the different pound-loads of each machine and the make and model numbers of all these, as well as any vending machines, changemakers, etc. Three action photos (preferably a minimum of 6) must accompany each article. At this time, we are especially interested in combined laundry-cleaning articles. Submitted photos must include an exterior shot of the installation and interior shots showing customers. Where possible, a photo of the owner at work is also desired. If you have a far-out slant, query first." Pays 3-4¢/word, depending on need to rewrite. Length: 1,200-2,000 words. No "plugola" for manufacturers' products. Photos purchased with mss. Pays $12 for 3 photos and $6 for each additional photo.

PLAY METER MAGAZINE. Skybird Publishing Co., Inc., Box 24170. New Orleans LA 70184. Publisher and Editor: Ralph C. Lally. Managing Editor: David Pierson. 25% freelance written. Trade publication for owners/operators of coin-operated amusement machine companies, e.g., pinball machines, video games, arcade pieces, jukeboxes, etc. Monthly magazine; 70 pages. Estab. December 1974. Circ. 5,400. Pays on publication. Buys all rights. Byline given. Submit seasonal/holiday material 2 months in advance of issue date. Photocopied and previously published submissions OK. SASE. Reports in 2 months. Free sample copy and writer's guidelines.

Nonfiction: General interest (seldom used, but usually this area focuses on a successful operator, operation or manufacturer; include "trade secrets"); how-to (get better locations for machines, promote tournaments, evaluate profitability of route, etc.); interview (with industry leaders); new product (if practical for industry, not interested in vending machines); and photo features (with some copy). "No 'puff' or 'plug' pieces about new manufacturers. Our readers want to read about how they can make more money from their machines, how they can get better tax breaks, commissions, etc. Also no stories about *playing* pinball. Our readers don't play the game per se; they buy the machines and make money from them." Buys 1-2 mss/issue. Submit complete ms. Length: 300-2,500 words. Pays $25-150.

Photos: "The photography should depict some action, not a 'stand 'em up-shoot 'em down' group shot." Pays $10 minimum for 5x7 or 8x10 b&w prints; $10 for color negatives or contact sheets. Captions preferred. Buys all rights, but may reassign after publication.

VENDING TIMES. 211 E. 43rd St., New York NY 10017. Editor: Arthur E. Yohalem. For operators of vending machines. Monthly. Circ. 13,500. Buys all rights. Pays on publication. Query: "we will discuss the story requirements with the writer in detail." SASE.

Nonfiction and Photos: Feature articles and news stories about vending operations; practical and important aspects of the business. "We are always willing to pay for good material. Primary interest is photo fillers." Pays $10/photo.

Confectionery and Snack Foods

CANDY AND SNACK INDUSTRY. 777 3rd Ave., New York NY 10017. (212)838-7778. Editor: Myron Lench. For confectionery and snack manufacturers. Monthly. Buys all rights. Reports in 2 weeks. SASE.

Nonfiction: "Feature articles of interest to large-scale candy, cookie, cracker, and other snack manufacturers that deal with activities in the fields of production, packaging (including package design), merchandising; financial news (sales figures, profits, earnings), advertising campaigns in all media, and promotional methods used to increase the sale or distribution of candy and snacks." Length: 1,000-1,250 words. Pays 5¢/word; "special rates on assignments." **Photos:** "Good quality glossies with complete and accurate captions, in sizes not smaller than 5x7." Pays $5. Color covers.
Fillers: "Short news stories about the trade and anything related to candy and snacks." Pays 5¢/word; $1 for clippings.

CANDY MARKETER, 777 3rd Ave., New York NY 10017. (212)838-7778. Editor/Publisher: Mike Lench. For owners and executives of wholesale and retail businesses. Monthly magazine. Estab. 1967. Circ. 14,000. Buys all rights. Byline given. Buys 20 mss/year. Pays on acceptance. Free sample copy. Photocopied submissions OK. Submit seasonal material at least 6 months in advance. Reports in 2 weeks. SASE.
Nonfiction: News and features on the candy trade. "Describe operation, interview candy buyer or merchandise manager; quote liberally. More interested in mass operations, than in unusual little shops." Informational, how-to, interview, profile, spot news, successful business operations, merchandising techniques. Annual issues on Halloween merchandising, Christmas merchandising and Easter merchandising are published in May, June and November (respectively). Length: 1,000-2,500 words. Pays 5¢/word.
Photos: 5x7 or 8½x11 b&w photos and color transparencies or prints purchased with or without mss. Captions required. Pays $5 for b&w; $15 for color.
Fillers: Pays $1 for each clipping used.

Construction and Contracting

Journals aimed at architects and city planners will be found in the Architecture category. Those for specialists in the interior aspects of consruction are listed under Building Interiors.

ABC AMERICAN ROOFER AND BUILDING IMPROVEMENT CONTRACTOR, Shelter Publications, Inc., 915 Burlington St., Downers Grove IL 60515. (312)964-6200. Editor-in-Chief: J.C. Gudas. For roofing industry contractors. Monthly magazine; 20-32 pages. Estab. 1911. Circ. 28,800. Pays on publication. Buys all rights. Byline given. Submit seasonal/holiday material 4 months in advance. SASE. Reports in 1 week. Free sample copy.
Nonfiction: Publishes how-to (apply various kinds of material on roofs, preferably unusual kinds of data), historical, humor (if original), interview, photo feature (unusual types of roofing), profile (on industry men), and technical. "No generalized industry articles; no women-in-industry stories unless the job is the important part of the article." Buys 5 mss/year. Query. Length: 1,500 words maximum. Pays $10-50. Editorial schedule available.
Photos: Purchased with accompanying ms. Captions required. Pays $5-25 for b&w glossy prints. Query or submit prints.
How To Break In: "Mss must pertain to our industry. Be concise and brief. Spaced-out wordings are not tolerated—articles must be well condensed, yet carry all the pertinent facts."

BATIMENT, 625 President Kennedy Ave., Montreal 111, Quebec, Canada. (514)845-5141. Editor: Marc Castro. Published in French for contractors and architects. Estab. 1927. Monthly. Circulation: 6,000. Rights purchased vary with author and material. Buys 25 mss/year. Pays on acceptance. Will send a sample copy to a writer on request. Write for copy of guidelines for writers. SAE and International Reply Coupons.
Nonfiction: "Articles on new techniques in construction and subjects of interest to builders. Interested in residential, apartment, office, commercial and industrial buildings—not in public works. Generally, articles written in English are rejected." Length: 500-1,000 words, Pays $75-100.

CALIFORNIA BUILDER & ENGINEER, 4110 Transport St., Palo Alto CA 94303. Editor: Cole N. Danehower. "For contractors, engineers, machinery distributors for the construction industry, and civic officials concerned with public works. Our coverage is limited to California, Hawaii, western Arizona and western Nevada." Published twice a month. Estab. 1894. Circ. 12,500. Pays on publication. Not copyrighted. SASE.
Nonfiction: "We are particularly interested in knowledgeable articles on nonconstruction issues that affect the large and small contractor in our region. For example, accounting for the

contractor, labor issues, pending legislation or ecology. These articles must be written with rigid accuracy, often requiring specialized knowledge. We are also interested in job stories from Hawaii on heavy public construction. We are not interested in residential construction. Field experience and in-depth knowledge of the industry are essential in writing for us." Query. Length: 1,500-2,200 words.

CONSTRUCTION EQUIPMENT OPERATION AND MAINTENANCE, Box 1689, Cedar Rapids IA 52406. (319)366-1597. Editor: C.K. Parks. 15% freelance written. For users of heavy construction equipment. Bimonthly. Buys all rights. Pays on acceptance. Query. Reports in 1 month. SASE.
Nonfiction and Photos: "Articles on selection, use, operation, or maintenance of construction equipment; articles and features on the construction industry in general; job safety articles." Length: 1,000-2,000 words. Also buys a limited number of job stories with photos, and feature articles on individual contractors in certain areas of US and Canada. Length varies. Pays $50-200.

CONSTRUCTIONEER, 1 Bond St., Chatham NJ 07928. Editor: Ken Hanan. 10% freelance written. For contractors, distributors, material producers, public works officials, consulting engineers, etc. Estab. 1945. Biweekly. Circ. 18,000. Buys all rights. Byline given "only on rare occasions. Our general policy is 'no byline for either staff-written or supplied material.'" Buys 10 mss/year. Pays on acceptance. Sample copy $1; free writer's guidelines. Photocopied submissions OK. Submit seasonal material 2 months in advance. Reports in 1-2 months. SASE.
Nonfiction: Construction job stories; new methods studies. Detailed job studies of methods and equipment used; oriented around geographical area of New York, New Jersey, Pennsylvania and Delaware. Winter snow and ice removal and control; winter construction methods. Current themes: public works; profiles, conservation. Query. Length: 1,500-1,800 words. Pays $100-200.
Photos: B&w photos purchased with or without accompanying ms or on assignment. Pays $5-8.

CONSTRUCTOR MAGAZINE, 1957 E St. NW, Washington DC 20006. Editor: Diane B. Snow. Publication of the Associated General Contractors of America for "men and women in the age range of approximately 25-70 (predominantly 40s and 50s), 50% with a college education. Most own or are officers in their own corporations." Estab. 1902. Monthly. Circ. 27,500. Buys all rights, but will reassign after publication. Buys 30 mss/year. Pays on publication. Query or submit complete ms. Reports in 30 days. SASE.
Nonfiction: "Feature material dealing with labor, legal, technical and professional material pertinent to the construction industry and corporate business. We deal only with the management aspect of the construction industry." Buys informational articles, interviews, think pieces, exposes, photo features, coverage of successful business operations, and technical articles. Length: "no minimum or maximum; subject much more important than length." Pays $50-300.

CONSTRUCTION SPECIFIER, 1150 17th St. NW, Washington, DC 20036. Editor: Donald L. Day. 100% freelance written. Professional society magazine for architects, engineers, specification writers and contractors. Monthly. Circ. 11,400. Buys one-time North American serial rights. Pays on publication. Free sample copy. Deadline: 60 days preceding publication on the 10th of each month. Reports in 2-3 weeks. SASE. Model releases, author copyright transferral requested.
Nonfiction and photos: "Articles on selection and specification of products, materials, equipment and methods used in construction projects, specifications as related to construction design, plus legal and contractual subjects." Query. Length: approximately 10 mss. pp., double-spaced. Pays $250-400, plus art. Photos critical to consideration for publication; line art, sketches, diagrams, charts and graphs also desired. Full color transparencies may be used. $5/line illustration; $10/photo; $15/transparency published. 8x10 glossies, 3¼ slides preferred.

DIXIE CONTRACTOR, Box 280, Decatur GA 30031. (404)377-2683. Editor: Russell K. Paul. 20% freelance written. For contractors, public officials, architects, engineers, and construction equipment manufacturers and dealers. Biweekly magazine; 125 pages. Estab. 1926. Circ. 9,000. Pays on publication. Buys all rights. Phone queries OK. Submit seasonal/holiday material 2 months in advance of issue date. Photocopied submissions OK. SASE. Reports in 2 weeks. Free sample copy.
Nonfiction: How-to (articles on new construction techniques and innovations); and interview (with government officials influencing construction, or prominent contractors). Buys 7 mss/year. Query or submit complete ms. Length: 1,500-2,000 words. Pays $25 minimum.

Photo: State availability of photos with query or ms. Captions and model release required. Buys all rights.
Columns/Departments: Labor-Management Relations in Construction. Buys 26 mss/year. Submit complete ms. Length: 1,000-1,500 words. Pays $25 minimum.

ENGINEERING AND CONTRACT RECORD, 1450 Don Mills Road, Don Mills, Ontario, Canada M3B 2X7. (416)445-6641. Editor: Nick Hancock. For contractors in engineered construction and aggregate producers. Estab. 1889. Monthly. Circ. 18,000. Buys first and second Canadian rights. Pays on publication. Free sample copy. Reports in 2 weeks. SAE and International Reply Coupons.
Nonfiction: "Job stories. How to build a project quicker, cheaper, better through innovations and unusual methods. Articles on construction methods, technology, equipment, maintenance and management innovations. Management articles. Stories are limited to Canadian projects only." Buys 12-15 mss/year. Query. Length: 1,000-1,500 words. Pays 13¢/printed word.
Photos: B&w 8x10 glossy prints purchased with mss. Pays $5/photo.

FARM BUILDING NEWS, 733 N. Van Buren, Milwaukee, WI 53202. Managing Editor: Don Peach. For farm structure builders and suppliers. 6 times a year. Buys all rights. Pays on acceptance. Will send a free sample copy on request. Query. Deadlines are at least 4 weeks in advance of publication date; prefers 6-8 weeks. Reports "immediately." SASE.
Nonfiction and Photos: Features on farm builders and spot news. "Study magazine before submitting." Length: 600-1,000 words. Pays $150-200. Buys color and b&w photos with ms.

FENCE INDUSTRY, 6285 Barfield Rd., Atlanta GA 30328. (404)393-2920. Editor: Bill Coker. For retailers of fencing materials. Monthly magazine; 54-80 pages. Estab. 1958. Circ. 13,000. Buys all rights. Buys 25-35 mss/year. Pays on publication. Free sample copy. Reports in 3 months. Query or submit complete ms. SASE.
Nonfiction and Photos: Case histories, as well as articles on fencing for highways, pools, farms, playgrounds, homes, industries. Surveys, and management and sales reports. Interview, profile, historical, successful business operations, and articles on merchandising techniques. Length: open. Pays 5¢/word. Pays $10 for 8x10 b&w photos purchased with mss. Captions required.

MID-WEST CONTRACTOR, Box 766, Kansas City MO 64141. (816)842-2902. Editor: Gilbert Mulley. Buys all rights. Pays on acceptance. Query. SASE.
Nonfiction and Photos: "Limited market for articles relating to large construction contracts in the Midwest only—Iowa, Nebraska, Kansas and Missouri. Such articles would relate to better methods of building various phases of large contracts, ranging anywhere from material distribution to labor relations. Also interested in articles on outstanding construction personalities in territory." Query. Length: open. Pays $50 minimum. Photos purchased with and without mss. Captions required. Pays $5 minimum.

MODERN STEEL CONSTRUCTION, American Institute of Steel Construction, The Wrigley Bldg., 400 N. Michigan Ave., 8th Floor, Chicago IL 60611. Editor: Mary Anne Stockwell. 10% freelance written. For architects, engineers and builders. Quarterly. Not copyrighted. Pays on acceptance. Query. SASE.
Nonfiction and Photos: "Articles with pictures and diagrams, of new steel-framed buildings and bridges. Must show new and imaginative uses of structural steel for buildings and bridges; new designs, new developments." Length: "1 and 2 pages." Pays $100 maximum. Photos purchased with mss.

WORLD CONSTRUCTION, 666 5th Ave., New York NY 10019. (212)489-4652. Editor: Henry Mozdzer. 10-20% freelance written. For "English-speaking engineers, contractors, and government officials everywhere except the US and Canada." Monthly. Buys all rights. Byline given unless "the article is less than one page long." Pays on publication. Free sample copy. Query. Reports in 1 month. SASE.
Nonfiction: "How-to articles that stress how contractors can do their jobs faster, better or more economically. Articles are rejected when they tell only what was constructed, but not how it was constructed and why it was constructed in that way." Length: 1,000-6,000 words. Pays $75/magazine page, or 4 typed ms pages.
Photos: Photos purchased with mss; uses 4x5 or larger b&w glossy prints.

Dairy Products

DAIRY SCOPE, 756 Kansas St., San Francisco CA 94107. Editor: Mary Matheson. 50%

freelance written. Bimonthly magazine; 16 pages. Estab. 1901. Circ. 1,500. Pays on publication. Buys one-time rights. Photocopied submissions OK. SASE. Reports in 4 weeks. Free sample copy and writer's guidelines.

Nonfiction: How-to (new or interesting techniques in dairy processing); general interest (to the westren dairy processing industry); historical (western dairy industry); and technical (western dairy processing). Buys 24 mss/year. Query. Length: 100-2,000 words. Pays $2.50/column inch.

Photos: State availability of photos in query. Pays $5-25 for 8x10 b&w glossy prints, contact sheets and negatives. Captions preferred. Buys one-time rights. Model release required.

Fillers: Clippings. Pays $2.

Data Processing

COMPUTER DEALER, Gordon Publications, Inc., 20 Community Place, Morristown NJ 07960. (201)267-6040. Editor: Jeffrey B. Walden. Sales and marketing of computer products and services for dealers, software producers, systems houses, consultants, consumer electronics outlets and business equipment dealers. Monthly magazine; 48-64 pages. Estab. 1978. Circ. 8,500. Pays on publication. Buys all rights. Phone queries OK. Submit seasonal/holiday material 6 months in advance. Previously published submissions OK. SASE. Reports in 1 month. Free sample copy.

Nonfiction: How-to (sell, market, etc.); interview (with computer notables or/and where market information is revealed); and articles on capital formation, etc. Writers "must have a knowledge of marketing and the computer industry, and the ability to ferret information or restate information known in other fields in a usable, interesting and particularly applicable way to those persons engaged in selling machines at the forefront of human knowledge." Buys 3-6 mss/issue. Query. Length: 800-4,000 words. Pays $50 minimum/page; 8¢/word maximum.

Photos: "Photos (artwork) provide and spark greater reader interest, and are most times necessary to explicate text." Send photos with ms. Uses b&w 8½x11 glossy prints or 3x5 color transparencies. Offers no additional payment for photos accepted with ms. Captions and model releases required.

Columns/Departments: "Columns are solicited by editor. If writers have suggestions, please query."

COMPUTER RETAILING, W.R.C. Smith Publishing, 1760 Peachtree Rd., Atlanta GA 30357. (404)874-4462. Editor: Mike Witter. Emphasizes retailing microcomputers. Monthly tabloid; 40 pages. Estab. 1977. Circ. 4,416. Pays on acceptance. Buys first rights. Pays 50% kill fee. Byline given. Phone queries OK. Submit seasonal/holiday material 2 months in advance. SASE. Reports in 2 weeks. Free sample copy and writer's guidelines.

Nonfiction: How-to (succeed on a microcomputer business); interview (person in microcomputer industry); personal opinion and photo feature. Buys 2-3 mss/issue. Query. Length: 2,000 words maximum. Pays $50-150.

Photos: State availability of photos with ms. Pays $5-25 for 8x10 b&w prints; $15-40 for color transparencies. Buys one-time rights. Captions required.

COMPUTER DECISIONS, 50 Essex St., Rochelle Park NJ 07662. Editor: Mel Mandell. 10% freelance written. For computer-involved managers in industry, government, finance, academia, etc. "Audience is well-educated, sophisticated and highly paid." Estab. 1969. Monthly. Circ. 110,000. Buys first serial rights. Pays 30% kill fee. Byline given. Pays on acceptance. Free sample copy to writer "who has a good background." Photocopied submissions OK. Reports in 4 weeks. SASE.

Nonfiction: "Mainly serious articles about technology, business practice. Interviews. Informational, technical, think pieces, spot news. News pieces about computers and their use. Articles should be clear and not stylized. Assertions should be well-supported by facts. We are business-oriented, witty, more interested in the unusual story, somewhat less technical than most. We'll run a good article with a computer peg even if it's not entirely about computers. Business analysis done by people with good backgrounds." Buys 12-24 mss/year. Length: 300-1,000 words for news; 1,000-5,000 words for features. Pays 3-10¢/word.

COMPUTER DESIGN, 11 Goldsmith St., Littleton MA 01460. Editor: John A. Camuso. 35% freelance written. For digital electronic design engineers. Monthly. Buys all rights or simultaneous rights. Pays on publication. Byline given. Free sample copy. Reports in 4-8 weeks. SASE.

Nonfiction: Engineering articles on the design and application of digital circuits, equipment and systems used in computing, data processing, control and communications. Query. Pays $30-40/page.

COMPUTERWORLD, 797 Washington St., Newton MA 02160. Editor: E. Drake Lundell Jr. 10% freelance written. For management-level computer users, chiefly in the business community, but also in government and education. Estab. 1967. Weekly. Circ. 93,000. Buys all rights, but may reassign rights to author after publication. Pays negotiable kill fee; "we have to initiate the assignment in order to pay a kill fee." Pays on publication. Free sample copy, if request is accompanied by story idea or specific query; free writer's guidelines. Photocopied submissions OK, if exclusive for stated period. Submit special issue material 2 months in advance. Reports in 2-4 weeks. SASE.

Nonfiction: Articles on problems in using computers; educating computer people; trends in the industry; new, innovative, interesting uses of computers. "We stress impact on users and need a practical approach. What does a development mean for other computer users? Most important facts first, then in decreasing order of significance. We would be interested in material on factory automation and other areas of computer usage that will impact society in general, and not just businesses. We prefer *not* to see executive appointments or financial results. We occasionally accept innovative material that is oriented to unique seasonal or geographical issues." Buys 100 mss/year. Query. Length: 250-1,200 words. Pays 10¢/word.

Photos: B&w (5x7) glossy prints purchased with ms or on assignment. Captions required. Pays $5-10.

Fillers: Newsbreaks and clippings. Length: 50-250 words. Pays 10¢/word.

CREATIVE COMPUTING, Box 789-M, Morristown NJ 07960. Publisher: David Ahl. Editor: John Craig. Managing Editor: Burchenal Green. Emphasizes the use of computers in homes and schools for students, faculty, hobbyists, everyone interested in the effects of computers on society and the use of computers in school, at home or at work. Monthly magazine; 144 pages. Estab. 1974. Circ. 75,000. Pays on acceptance. Buys all rights, but may reassign after publication. Pays 20% kill fee. Byline given. Submit seasonal/holiday material at least 4 months in advance. SASE. Reports in 4-5 weeks. Sample copy $2.

Nonfiction: How-to (building a computer at home, personal computer applications and software); informational (computer careers; simulations on computers; problem-solving techniques; use in a particluar institution or discipline such as medicine, education, music, animation, space exploration, business or home use); historical articles (history of computers, or of a certain discipline, like computers and animation); interviews (with personalities in the hobbyist field, old-timers in the computer industry or someone doing innovative work); personal experience (first-person accounts of using hardware or software are actively sought); and technical (programs, games and simulations with printouts). Buys 300 mss/year. Length: 500-3,000 words. Pays $10-300.

Photos: Usually purchased with mss, with no additional payment, but sometimes pays $3-50 for b&w glossy prints or $10-150 for any size color.

Columns/Departments: Compendium uses interesting, short articles about crazy, silly, unfortunate or interesting uses of computers (some human interest) about use in menu planning, pole vaulting, exploring, mistakes in computer programming, etc. Length: 50-500 words. Pays $5-30. Pays in copy of publication for book reviews (all books on computer use). Complete Computer Catalog accepts only press releases on new products.

Fiction: Humorous fiction, mysteries and science fiction. "Fiction must be specifically related to robots or computers. Interesting stories that show how computers can benefit society are sought. Writers must keep in mind that people program computers and should program them for people's benefit. Stories dealing with new field of computers in the home are also sought." Buys 30 mss/year. Submit complete ms. Length: 500-3,000 words. Pays $15-400.

Poetry: Avant-garde, free verse, haiku, light verse, traditional forms and computer-generated poetry. Buys 30/year. Pays $10-100.

Fillers: Jokes, gags, anecdotes, puzzles, short humor. Buys 20/year. Pays $3-25.

THE DATA ENTRY MANAGEMENT ASSOCIATION NEWSLETTER, The Data Entry Management Association, Inc., 230 Cedar Heights Rd., Stamford CT 06905. (203)322-1166. Editor: Norman Bodek. Emphasizes data processing and data entry. Aimed at managers and supervisors of data entry installations who are interested in people, management, equipment, career growth opportunities and training. Monthly newsletter; 8 pages. Estab. 1976. Circ. 1,000. Pays on acceptance. Buys all rights. Byline given. Phone queries OK. Submit seasonal/holiday material 2 months in advance. Simultaneous, photocopied and previously published submissions OK. Reports in 1 month. Free sample copy.

Nonfiction: General interest; how-to (manage people, get more from your profession, get more from people, train); inspirational (motivational); interview (people in data entry); personal opinion (about equipment, future); new product (data entry methods); personal experience (with equipment or people in the profession); photo feature (data entry people and

equipment); technical (data entry-computer industry). They need articles that will help data processing people become better managers and aid them in becoming more professional. Buys 4 mss/issue. Send complete ms. Length: 600-2,500 words. Pays 5-9¢/word.
Photos: Send photos with ms. Prefers b&w prints. Pays $10-25. Buys one-time rights.
Fillers: Jokes and short humor. Buys 3/issue. Length: 60 words maximum. Pays $25.

JOURNAL OF SYSTEMS MANAGEMENT, 24587 Bagley Road, Cleveland OH 44138. (216)243-6900. Publisher: James Andrews. 100% freelance written. For systems and procedures and management people. Monthly. Buys all serial rights. Byline given. Pays on publication. Free sample copy. Reports "as soon as possible." SASE.
Nonfiction: Articles on case histories, projects on systems, forms control, administrative practices and computer operations. Query. Length: 3,000-5,000 words. Pays $25 maximum.

Dental

CAL MAGAZINE, 3737 W. 127th St., Chicago IL 60658. Editor: M.E. Yukich. For dentists, dental assistants and dental technicians. Estab. 1935. Monthly. Circ. 50,000. Buys all rights, but will reassign to author after publication. Pays on acceptance. Will send free sample copy on request. Submit complete ms only. Reports in 6 weeks. SASE.
Nonfiction and Photos: Articles pertaining to or about dentists and dentistry; accomplishments of dentists in other fields. History, art, humor, adventure, unusual achievements, successful business operations, new products, merchandising techniques and technical. Length: 1,500-2,000 words. Pays $25-100. B&w photos only, 8x10 or 5x7 glossy, purchased with mss or captions only. Pays $25-50.
Fiction: "Related in some way to dentistry." Length: 1,500-2,000 words. Pays $25-100.
Poetry and Fillers: Light verse. "Related to dentistry." Puzzles, short humor. Pays $3 minimum.

CONTACTS, Box 407, North Chatham NY 12132. Editor: Joseph Strack. For laboratory owners, managers, and dental technician staffs. Estab. 1938. Bimonthly. Circ. 1,200. Pays on acceptance. Byline given. Free sample copy. Reports in 1-2 weeks. SASE.
Nonfiction and Photos: Writer should know the dental laboratory field or have good contacts there to provide technical articles, how-to, and successful business operation articles. Query. Length: 1,500 words maximum. Pays 3-5¢/word. Willing to receive suggestions for columns and departments for material of 400-800 words. Payment for these negotiable.

DENTAL ECONOMICS, Box 1260, Tulsa OK 74101. Editor: Pat Muchmore. 60% freelance written. Emphasizes "practice management for dentists." Monthly magazine; 90 pages. Estab. 1911. Circ. 103,000. Pays on acceptance. Buys all rights, but may reassign following publication. Pays 25% kill fee. Byline given. "Ocasionally no byline is given when it's an article combining talents of several authors, but credit is always acknowledged." Submit seasonal/holiday material 6 months in advance of issue date. SASE. Reports in 4 weeks. Free sample copy and writer's guidelines.
Nonfiction: Exposé (closed panels, NHI); how-to (hire personnel, bookkeeping, improve production); humor (in-office type); investments (all kinds); interview (doctors in the news, health officials); personal experience (of dentists, but only if related to business side of practice); profile (a few on doctors who made dramatic lifestyle changes); and travel (only if dentist is involved). Buys 120 mss/year. Query or submit complete ms. Length: 600-3,500 words. Pays $50-500.
Photos: State availability of photos with query or submit photos with ms. Pays $10 minimum for 8x10 glossy photos; $25 minimum for 35mm color transparencies. Captions and model release required. Buys all North American rights.
Columns/Departments: Viewpoint (issues of dentistry are aired here). Buys 1 ms/issue. Submit complete ms. Length: 600-1,500 words. Open to suggestions for new columns/departments.

DENTAL MANAGEMENT, Harcourt Brace Jovanovich, 757 3rd Ave., New York NY 10017. Editor: M.J. Goldberg. 25% freelance written. "*Dental Management* is the national business publication for dentists." Monthly magazine; 100 pages. Estab. January 1961. Circ. 100,000. Pays on acceptance. Buys all rights, but may reassign following publication. Pays 50% kill fee. Byline given. Submit seasonal/holiday material 4 months in advance of issue date. Photocopied and simultaneous submissions OK. SASE. Reports in 2 weeks. Free writer's guidelines.
Nonfiction: "The editorial aim of *Dental Management* is to help the dentist to build a bigger, more successful practice, to help him conserve and invest his money, and to help him keep

posted on the economic, legal and sociological changes that affect him." Exposé; general interest; how-to; and interview. Buys 2-4 mss/issue. Query. Length: 1,000-2,500 words. Pays 10-15¢/word.

PROOFS, The Magazine of Dental Sales, Box 1260, Tulsa OK 74101. (918)835-3161. Publisher: Joe Bessette. Monthly. Pays on publication. Byline given. Will send free sample copy on request. Query. Reports in 1 week. SASE.
Nonfiction: Uses short articles, chiefly on selling to dentists. Must have understanding of dental trade industry, and problems of marketing and selling to dentists and dental laboratories. Pays about $75.

TIC MAGAZINE, Box 407, North Chatham NY 12132. (518)766-3047. Editor: Joseph Strack. For dentists, dental assistants, and oral hygienists. Monthly. Buys first publication rights in the dental field. Byline given. Pays on acceptance. Reports in 2 weeks. SASE.
Nonfiction: Uses articles (with illustrations, if possible) as follows: 1. Lead feature: Dealing with major developments in dentistry of direct, vital interest to all dentists. 2. How-to-do-it pieces: Ways and means of building dental practices, improving professional techniques, managing patients, increasing office efficiency, etc. 3. Special articles: Ways and means of improving dentist-laboratory relations for mutual advantage, of developing auxiliary dental personnel into an efficient office team, of helping the individual dentist to play a more effective role in alleviating the burden of dental needs in the nation and in his community, etc. 4. General articles: Concerning any phase of dentistry or dentistry-related subjects of high interest to the average dentist. "Especially interested in profile pieces (with b&w photographs) on dentists who have achieved recognition/success in nondental fields—business, art, sport or whatever. Query. Interesting, well-written pieces a sure bet." Query. Length: 800-3,200 words. Pays 4¢ minimum/word.
Photos: Photo stories: 4-10 pictures of interesting developments and novel ideas in dentistry. B&w only. Pays $10 minimum/photo.
How To Break In: "We can use fillers of about 300 words or so. They should be pieces of substance on just anything of interest to dentists. A psychoanalyst broke in with us recently with pieces relating to interpretations of patients' problems and attitudes in dentistry. Another writer just broke in with a profile of a dentist working with an Indian tribe."

Department Store, Variety, and Dry Goods

MILITARY MARKET, Army Times Publishing Co., 475 School St. SW, Washington DC 20024. (202)554-7180. Editor-in-Chief: Bruce Covill. For store managers, headquarters personnel, Pentagon decision-makers, Congressional types, wholesalers to the military, manufacturers. Monthly magazine; 56 pages. Estab. 1954. Circ. 13,500. Pays on acceptance. Buys all rights, but may reassign following publication. Byline given. Phone queries OK. Submit seasonal or holiday material 4 months in advance. SASE. Reports in 2 months. Free sample copy.
Nonfiction: Publishes how-to articles (directed toward improving management techniques or store operations); humor (funny aspects of the business); informational (implementation of policies and directions); interviews (notables in the field); technical (store operations). Buys 1 ms/year. Length: 1,000-4,000 words. Query. Pays $75-300.

SEW BUSINESS, 666 5th Ave., New York NY 10019. Editor: Cristina Holmes. For retailers of home-sewing and needle-work merchandise. Monthly. Circ. 14,000. Not copyrighted. Pays on publication. Free sample copy. Reports in 1 month. SASE.
Nonfiction and Photos: Articles on department store or fabric shop operations, including coverage of art needlework, piece goods, patterns, sewing accessories and all other notions. Interviews with buyers—retailers on their department or shop. "Unless they are doing something different or offbeat, something that another retailer could put to good use in his own operation, there is no sense wasting their or your time in doing an interview and story. Best to query editor first to find out if a particular article might be of interest to us." Buys 100 mss/year. Query. Length: 500-1,500 words. Pays $85 minimum. Photos purchased with mss. "Should illustrate important details of the story." Sharp 8x10 b&w glossies. Pays $5.
Fillers: $2.50 for news items less than 100 words. For news item plus photo and caption, pays $7.50.

Drugs, Health Care, and Medical Products

CANADIAN PHARMACEUTICAL JOURNAL, 175 College St., Toronto, Ontario, Canada M5T 1P8. (416)979-2431. Editor: J.E. Knox. 75% freelance written. For pharmacists. Monthly magazine; 40 pages. Estab. 1868. Circ. 13,540. Pays on publication. Buys all rights, but may reassign following publication. Phone queries OK. SAE and International Reply Coupons. Reports in 1 month. Free sample copy and writer's guidelines.
Nonfiction: Publishes exposes (pharmacy practice, education and legislation); how-to (pharmacy business operations); historical (pharmacy practice, legislation, education); interviews with and profiles on pharmacy figures. Buys 2-4 mss/year. Length: 1,000-3,000 words. Query. Payment is contingent on value; usually 8¢/word.
Photos: B&w (5x7) glossies and color transparencies purchased with mss. Captions required. Payment by arrangement. Model release required.

DRUG SURVIVAL NEWS, Do It Now Foundation/Institute for Chemical Survival, Box 5115, Phoenix AZ 85010. 0797. Managing Editor: Dario McDarby. For directors and workers in drug abuse and alcoholism field; schools, counselors, nurses, state and local mental health agencies and military involved with drug and alcohol programs; and those concerned with the problems of drug and alcohol abuse. Bimonthly tabloid newspaper; 16 pages. Estab. 1976. Circ. 10,000. Buys all rights and retains the option of publishing later as a pamphlet or part of a collection. Pays variable kill fee. Byline given. Pays on publication. Photocopied submissions OK. Simultaneous submissions are considered only if you provide the name of publication to which other submission was sent. SASE. Reports in 1 month. Free sample copy.
Nonfiction: Research, news and articles about the effects of various chemicals, and in-depth articles about prominent programs and the people who run them. Writers should have experience with these subjects, either professionally or subjectively (as a former user, etc.—but not prejudiced against the topics beforehand). Also needs stories on over-the-counter drugs. No marijuana stories or articles by ex-addicts or alcoholics describing their lives. Informational, interview, profile, historical, opinion, photo features, book reviews, successful program operations, new product and technical. Query. Length: 100-2,000 words. Pays $5-50.
Photos: Pays $5-10 for b&w photos purchased with ms or on assignment. Captions required.
Fillers: Drug-related newsbreaks, jokes, gags and anecdotes. Length: 100-300 words. Pays $5-10.

DRUG TOPICS, 680 Kinderkamack Rd., Oradell NJ 07649. (201)262-3030. Editor: Barbara Johnson. Executive Editor: Ralph M. Thurlow. For retail drug stores and wholesalers, manufacturers. Semimonthly. Circ. over 70,000. Buys all rights. Pay varies for kill fee. Byline given "only for features." Pays on acceptance. SASE.
Nonfiction: News of local, regional, state pharmaceutical associations, legislation affecting operation of drug stores, news of pharmacists and store managers in civic and professional activities, etc. Query on drug store success stories which deal with displays, advertising, promotions, selling techniques. Query. Length: 1,500 words maximum. Pays $5 and up for leads, $25 and up for short articles, $100-300 for feature articles, "depending on length and depth."
Photos: May buy photos submitted with mss. May buy news photos with captions only. Pays $10-20.

NARD JOURNAL, The National Association of Retail Druggists, 1750 K St. NW, Washington DC 20006. (202)347-7495. Editor: Robert A. Malone. For the independent pharmacist, aimed at improving his competitive position in the marketplace. Monthly magazine; 48 pages. Estab. 1902. Circ. 24,000. Payment is included in membership. Buys all rights. Phone queries OK. Submit seasonal/holiday material 6 months in advance. Photocopied submissions OK. Reports in 2-4 weeks. Free sample copy and writer's guidelines.
Nonfiction: How-to (solve small business problems); interview (with pharmaceutical industry and regulatory personages); and profile (industry and regulatory personages and successful pharmacists). Buy 12 mss/year. Query. Length 750-1,000 words. Pays $150/printed page.
Fillers: Cartoons and newsbreaks.
Photos: "Photos are welcome if they help clarify material in the article. Don't send merely to pad the package. For space reasons articles should be capable of standing alone, if convenient." State availability of photos with query. Pays $5-25 for 5x7 b&w glossy prints; $25-35 for 35mm color transparencies. Captions and model release required. Buys all rights, but may reassign following publication.

PATIENT AID DIGEST, 2009 Morris Ave., Union NJ 07083. (201)687-8282. Editor: Laurie N. Cassak. For pharmacists, home health care managers and manufacturers of patient aid products. Estab. 1970. Bimonthly. Circ. 11,000. Buys all rights. Pays on publication. Free sample copy and writer's guidelines. Photocopied and simultaneous submissions OK. Reports in 8 weeks. SASE.

Nonfiction and Photos: "Articles about existing home health care centers or opportunities for proprietors; human interest stories that deal with health care; helpful hints for the pharmacist. It is essential to understand your reading audience. Articles must be informative, but not extremely technical." Buys informational, how-to, interview, photo articles. Query. Length: 1,000-1,500 words. Pays 5¢/word. Photos purchased with accompanying ms with no additional payment. Captions optional.

WHOLESALE DRUGS, 1111 E. 54th St., Indianapolis IN 46220. Editor: William F. Funkhouser. Bimonthly. Buys first rights. Query. SASE.

Nonfiction and Photos: Wants features on presidents and salesmen of Full Line Wholesale Drug Houses throughout the country. No set style, but subject matter should tell about both the man and his company—history, type of operation, etc. Pays $50 for text and pictures.

Education

Professional educators, teachers, coaches and school personnel—as well as other people involved with training and education—read the journals classified here. Publications for parents or the general public interested in education-related topics are listed under Education in the Consumer Publications section.

THE AMERICAN SCHOOL BOARD JOURNAL, National School Boards Association, 1055 Thomas Jefferson St. NW, Washington DC 20007. (202)337-7666. Editor-in-Chief: James Betchkal. Emphasizes public school administration and policymaking. For elected members of public boards of education throught the US and Canada, and high level administrators of same. Monthly magazine; 64 pages. Estab. 1891. Circ. 50,000. Pays on acceptance. Buys all rights. Phone queries OK. Submit seasonal/holiday material 4-6 months in advance. Photocopied submissions OK. SASE. Reports in 3 weeks. Free sample copy.

Nonfiction: Publishes how-to articles (solutions to problems of public school operation including political problems); interviews with notable figures in public education. Buys 20 mss/year. Query. Length: 400-2,000 words. Payment varies, "but never less than $100."

Photos: B&w glossies (any size) and color purchased on assignment. Captions required. Pays $10-50. Model release required.

AMERICAN SCHOOL & UNIVERSITY, North American Publishing Co., 401 N. Broad St., Philadelphia PA 19108. Editor-in-Chief: Rita Robison. Emphasizes "facilities and business office matters of schools, colleges, and universities (no curriculum, etc)." For "administrators such as superintendents of buildings and grounds, business officials, school superintendents, college vice-presidents of operations, etc." Monthly magazine; 70-120 pages. Estab. 1928. Circ. 41,000. Pays on publication. Buys all rights, but may reassign following publication. Pays negotiable kill fee. Reports in 3-6 weeks.

Nonfiction: Photo feature (new or renovated buildings, with architectural/engineering description), technical (energy conservation measures, solar energy applications, business practices that save money). "We prefer the 'this was the problem and this is how it was solved' approach." Buys 3-4 mss/year. Query. Length: 500-1,800 words. Pays $25/page minimum.

Photos: Used with accompanying ms for no additional payment. Submit 8x10 b&w glossies or 4x5 color transparencies.

ARTS & ACTIVITIES, 591 Camino de la Reina, San Diego CA 92108. (714)297-5352. Editor-in-Chief: Dr. Leven C. Leatherbury. 90% freelance written. Emphasizes art education. Monthly (except July and August) magazine; 72 pages. Estab. 1937. Circ. 30,000. Pays on publication. Buys all rights, but may reassign following publication. Phone queries OK. Submit seasonal/holiday material 3 months in advance of issue date. Reports in 3 weeks. Free sample copy and writer's guidelines.

Nonfiction: How-to (describing specific lessons and projects which have proved successful); and articles on art history and art education. Buys 10-13 mss/issue. Submit complete ms. Length: 500 words average. Pays $20-80.

Photos: Submit photo material with accompanying ms. No additional payment for 5x7 b&w

glossy prints or color transparencies. Captions preferred. Buys all rights, but may reassign following publication.

THE ARTS IN EDUCATION, 501 N. Virginia Ave., Winter Park FL 32789. Editor-in-Chief: Joan L. Wahl. 50% freelance written. Emphasizes art, craft, music, dance and theater for school teachers in elementary and junior high grades, workshop teachers, scout leaders, and professors in education course studies in elementary education. Monthly magazine; 36 pages. Estab. November 1977. Pays on publication. Buys all rights, but may reassign following publication. Submit seasonal/holiday material 2 months in advance of issue date. Photocopied submissions OK. SASE. Reports in 2 weeks. Sample copy $1.75; writer's guidelines for SASE; mention *Writer's Market* in request.

Nonfiction: How-to (geared toward classroom teacher on visual arts and performing arts); profile (on a professional artist only). Buys 6 mss/issue. Query. Length: 500-1,000 words. Pays 2¢/word.

Photos: State availability of photos with query. Pays $1-5 for 3½x5 or 5x7 b&w prints. Captions required. Buys all rights, but may reassign after publication. Release required.

Fiction: Adventure (plays for children with "goodness and righteousness reigning over all"); fantasy (plays for children grades 3-9); humorous (plays only); mystery (plays only); and science fiction (plays only). Buys 10 mss/year. Query. Length: 8-30 minutes, playing time. Pays $10-15.

CATECHIST, Peter Li, Inc., 2451 E. River Rd., Dayton OH 45439. Editor: Patricia Fischer. Emphasizes religious education for professional and volunteer religious educators working in Catholic schools. Monthly (September-May) magazine; 40 pages. Estab. 1966. Circ. 82,000. Pays on publication. Buys all rights. Submit seasonal or holiday material 3 months in advance. SASE. Reports in 1 month. Sample copy $1; free writer's guidelines.

Nonfiction: Publishes how-to articles (methods for teaching a particular topic or concept); informational (theology and church-related subjects, insights into current trends and developments); personal experience (in the religious classroom). Length: 1,500 words maximum. Buys 45 mss/year. Query. Pays $30-75.

Photos: B&w (8x10) glossies purchased without mss. Send contact sheet. Pays $15-25.

How To Break In: "By writing articles that would be of practical use for the teacher of religion or an article that results from personal experience and expertise in the field."

CHILDREN'S HOUSE, Box 111, Caldwell NJ 07006. Editor: Kenneth Edelson. 75% freelance written. For teachers and parents of young children. Magazine; 32 pages. Estab. 1966. Every 2 months. Circulation: 50,000. Buys all rights. Buys 20-30 mss/year. Pays on publication. Sample copy for $1.25; free writer's guidelines. Will consider photocopied submissions. Reports in 3-6 months. Query or submit complete ms. SASE.

Nonfiction and Photos: Department Editor: Margery Mossman. Articles on education, Montessori, learning disabilities, atypical children, innovative schools and methods; new medical, psychological experiments. "We're not afraid to tackle controversial topics such as sex education, etc., but we don't want to see personal or family histories. No 'why-Johnny-can't-read' articles." Informational, how-to, profile, think articles. Length: 1,200 to 2,000 words. Pays 2¢/word, and up "conditionally." 5x7 or 7x9 b&w glossies purchased on assignment. Pays $5 minimum.

COMMUNITY COLLEGE FRONTIERS, Sangamon State University, Shepherd Rd., Springfield IL 62708. Editor-in-Chief: J. Richard Johnston. 80-85% freelance written. For all persons interested in two-year post-secondary educational institutions, especially faculty, administrators, trustees and students in public community colleges. Quarterly magazine; 56 pages. Estab. 1972. Circ. 5,000. Pays in contributor's copies. Acquires all rights, but will reassign following publication. Phone queries OK. All material should be given minimum of 3 months' lead time. SASE. Reports in 6-8 weeks. Free sample copy and writer's guidelines.

Nonfiction: Publishes historical articles (of community colleges); how-to (college teaching strategies to organize subject material and motivate students); humor (satire on stuffy, pompous educators); informational (analytical reports on college instructional programs); inspirational (individual students/adults; sincerity, handicapped, etc.). Query.

Photos: Uses B&w glossies (8x10) with captions and credit line. Send contact sheet.

Columns/Departments: Say It With Words (stuffy, pretentious, academic language and style; funny errors; play on words, etc.); Marketplace (brief information on special programs, techniques, or ideas). "We are especially interested in informal learning networks for adults, cooperatives, collective, nonprofit enterprises, etc." Length: 300 words maximum. Query with sample lead paragraph.

How To Break In: "Writing fresh viewpoints (critical views are welcome) upon college education in clear, simple language. Personal experience related to important general principles make good material for us."

CURRICULUM REVIEW, Curriculum Advisory Service, 500 S. Clinton St., Chicago IL 60607. (312)939-1333. Editor-in-Chief: Irene M. Goldman. For teachers K-12, curriculum planners, librarians, graduate schools of education. 5 times yearly magazine; 80 pages. Estab. 1961. Circ. 2,000. Pays on publication. Buys all rights, but will reassign following publication. Byline given. Phone queries OK. Photocopied submissions OK. Reports in 6 weeks. Free sample copy and writer's guidelines.
Nonfiction: Charlotte H. Cox, Articles Editor. Informational (on education or curriculum for K-12, current trends, methods, theory). Buys 20 essay mss/year. Query. Length: 1,000-2,000 words. Pays $30-50. Also publishes 300-400 book reviews/year on an assigned basis; classroom text materials in language arts, mathematics, science, social studies. Pays $10-50 a review depending on scope and difficulty of materials. Send educational vita. "We are especially interested in innovative articles by curriculum planners, school superintendents, deans of graduate education, or interdisciplinary specialists on new educational approaches."
For '80: "We will feature competency skills, values education, career education and health education, amoung other topics. Schedule available on request."

EDUCATIONAL STUDIES: A Journal in the Foundations of Education, 331 DeGarmo Hall, Illinois State University, Normal IL 61761. (309)436-5415, ext. 230. Editor-in-Chief: Dr. Joan K. Smith. 85% freelance written. Emphasizes research, reviews and opinions in the foundations of education. Quarterly magazine; 120 pages. Estab. 1970. Circ. 1,500. Pays on publication. Buys all rights, but may reassign following publication. Phone queries OK. Photocopied submissions OK. SASE. Reports in 3 months. Free sample copy and writer's guidelines.
Nonfiction: Historical and informational articles; must relate to the Foundations of Education. Also uses pieces on experimental research. Buys 8-12 mss/year. Submit 3 copies of complete ms. Length: 1,000-3,500 words. Pays $25 maximum, but sometimes no payment is made.
Photos: No additional payment for 8x10 b&w glossies used with mss. Captions required. Send contact sheet or prints. Model release required.
Poetry: Traditional forms, free verse, haiku and light verse. Length: 4-24.

FORECAST FOR HOME ECONOMICS, 50 W. 44th St., New York NY 10036. (212)867-7700. Editor-in-Chief: Gloria S. Spitz. Managing Editor: Renee Maccarrone. 10% freelance written. Monthly (September-June) magazine; 80 pages. Estab. 1954. Circ. 78,000. Pays on publication. Buys all rights. Pays negotiable kill fee. Byline given. Submit seasonal/holiday material 6-8 months in advance of issue date. SASE. Free writer's guidelines.
Nonfiction: Current consumer/home economics-related issues, especially energy, careers, family relations/child development, teaching techniques, health, nutrition, metrics, mainstreaming the handicapped, appealing to both boys and girls in the classroom, money management, housing, crafts, bulletin board and game ideas. Buys 3 mss/issue. Query. Length: 1,000-3,000 words. Pays $25 minimum.
Photos: State availability of photos with query. No additional payment for b&w glossy prints. Captions required. Model release required.

HOSPITAL/HEALTH CARE TRAINING MEDIA PROFILES, Olympic Media Information, 71 W. 23rd St., New York NY 10010. (212)675-4500. Publisher: Walt Carroll. 100% freelance written. For hospital education departments, nursing schools, schools of allied health, paramedical training units, colleges, community colleges, local health organizations. Serial, in loose-leaf format, published every 2 months. Established in 1974. Circulation: 1,000 plus. Buys all rights. Buys 240 mss/year. Pays on publication. Will send free sample copy to writer on request. "Send resume of your experience to introduce yourself." Reports in 1 month. Query. SASE.
Nonfiction: "Reviews of all kinds of audiovisual media. We are the only existing review publication devoted to evaluation of audiovisual aids for hospital and health training. We have a highly specialized, definite format that must be followed in all cases. Samples should be seen by all means. Our writers should first have a background in health sciences, secondly, some experience with audiovisuals; and third, follow our format precisely. Besides basic biological sciences, we are interested in materials for nursing education, in-service education, continuing education, personnel training, patient education, patient care, medical problems. Contact us and send a resume of your experience in writing for hospital, science, health fields. We will assign audiovisual aids to qualified writers and send them these to review for us. Unsolicited mss not welcome." Pays $10/review.

ILLINOIS SCHOOLS JOURNAL, Chicago State University, 95th St. at King Dr., Chicago IL 60628. Editor: Virginia McDavid, Department of English, Room E-356. Primarily for teachers and professional educators. Quarterly magazine; 64-80 pages. Estab. 1906. Circ. 7,000. Acquires all rights, but will reassign rights to author after publication. Pays in contributor's copies. Free sample copy and writer's guidelines. Photocopied submissions OK. No simultaneous submissions. Reports in 3 months. SASE.

Nonfiction: Educational subject matter. Concentrate on practical aspects of education. Submit complete ms. Length: 2,000-3,000 words.

INDUSTRIAL EDUCATION, 77 Bedford St., Stamford CT 06901. For administrators and instructors in elementary, secondary, and post-secondary education in industrial arts, vocational, industrial and technical education. Monthly, except July and August and combined May-June issue. Buys all rights. Pays on acceptance. Free writer's guidelines. Reports in 5 weeks. SASE.

Nonfiction and Photos: "Articles dealing with the broad aspects of industrial arts, vocational, and technical education as it is taught in our junior and senior high schools, vocational and technical high schools, and junior colleges. We're interested in analytical articles in relation to such areas as curriculum planning, teacher training, teaching methods, supervision, professional standards, industrial arts or vocational education, industrial practice, relationship of industrial education to industry at the various educational levels, current problems, trends, etc. How-to-do, how-to-teach, how-to-make articles of a very practical nature that will assist the instructor in the laboratory at every level of industrial education. Typical are the 'activities' articles in every instructional area. Also typical is the article which demonstrates to the teacher a new or improved way of doing something or of teaching something or how to utilize special teaching aids or equipment to full advantage—activities which help the teacher do a better job of introducing the industrial world of work to the student." Photos or rough drawings generally necessary. Pays $30/magazine page minimum.

Fillers: Short hints on some aspect of shop management or teaching techniques. Length: 25-250 words.

INSTRUCTOR MAGAZINE, 757 3rd Ave., New York NY 10017. Editor-in-Chief: Leanna Landsmann. Administrative Editor: Rosemary Alexander. 30% freelance written. Emphasizes elementary education. Monthly magazine; 180 pages Estab. 1889. Circ. 275,000. Pays on acceptance. Buys all rights, but may reassign following publication. Phone queries OK. Submit seasonal/holiday material 6 months in advance of issue date. Photocopied submissions OK. SASE. Reports in 6 weeks. Free sample copy and writer's guidelines; mention *Writer's Market* in request.

Nonfiction: How-to articles on elementary classroom practice—practical suggestions as well as project reports. Buys 10-15 mss/year. Query. Length: 750-2,500 words. Pays $10-500.

JGE: The Journal of General Education, Penn State University Press, 215 Wagner Bldg., University Park PA 16802. Editors-in-Chief: Caroline and Robert Eckhardt. 99% freelance written. Emphasizes general education, for teachers of undergraduates in colleges and universities. Quarterly magazine; 104 pages. Estab. 1946. Circ. 1,450. Acquires all rights, but may reassign following publication. Byline given. SASE. Reports in 4 weeks. Free sample copy and writer's guidelines.

Nonfiction: How-to (teaching specific topics), informational (new ideas, fresh approaches, findings). Uses 30 mss/year. Query. Length: No limits. Pays in 25 offprints of the article.

JOURNAL OF ENGLISH TEACHING TECHNIQUES, University of Michigan, Flint MI 48503. (313)767-4000. Editor: Dr. F.K. Bartz. For public school English teachers, English professors in colleges and universities. Estab. 1968. Quarterly. Circ. 500. Acquires all rights. Pays in contributor's copies. Sample copy $1. Reports in 6 weeks. SASE.

Nonfiction: Articles on the teaching of English; book reviews; short features; bibliographies; exercises; and anything of interest to English teachers. All material must follow the *MLA Style Sheet*. Query or submit complete ms.

JOURNAL OF READING, THE READING TEACHER, International Reading Association, 800 Barksdale Rd., Box 8139, Newark DE 19711. (302)731-1600. Editor-in-Chief: Dr. Janet R. Binkley. 90% freelance written. For teachers, reading specialists, or other school personnel; college and university faculty, independent researchers. Monthly (October-May) magazines; 132 pages *(The Reading Teacher)*; 96 pages *(Journal of Reading)*. Estab: 1948 *(The Reading Teacher)*; 1957 *(Journal of Reading)*. No payment. Phone queries OK. Photocopied submissions OK. SASE. Reports in 3 months. Sample copy $3.50.

Nonfiction: Publishes articles that deal with reading, teaching reading, learning to read; about children or adults. Theory, techniques, research, mental processes, history, humor; current events in reading education, etc. Articles about learners through grade 6 go to *The Reading Teacher*; articles about secondary and adult learners, go to *Journal of Reading.* Length: 100-3,000 words. Submit complete ms.
Photos: "We have no budget for photos, but are delighted to use reading-related photos (b&w) when donated. Can pay $15 for those suitable for *Journal of Reading* covers."
Columns/Departments: Tips on effective teaching techniques for Interchange *(The Reading Teacher)* and Open to Suggestion *(Journal of Reading).*
Poetry: "We don't buy poetry, but would gladly publish more than is contributed at present." Avant-garde, free verse, haiku, light verse and traditional forms acceptable.

LEARNING, The Magazine for Creative Teaching, 530 University Ave., Palo Alto CA 94301. Editor: Morton Malkofsky. 45% freelance written. Emphasizes elementary and junior high school education topics. Monthly during school year. Magazine; 150 pages. Estab. 1972. Circ. 225,000. Pays on acceptance. Buys all rights, but may reassign following publication. Submit seasonal/holiday material 6 months in advance of issue date. Photocopied submissions OK. SASE. Reports in 2 months. Writer's guidelines sent upon request.
Nonfiction: "We publish manuscripts that describe innovative teaching strategies or probe controversial and significant social/political issues related to the professional and classroom interest of preschool to 8th grade teachers." How-to (classroom mangement, specific lessons or units or activities for children—all at the elementary and junior high level, and hints for teaching math and science); interview (with teachers who are in unusual or innovative teaching situations); new product; personal experience (from teachers in elementary and junior high school); and profile (with teachers who are in unusual or innovative teaching situations). Strong interest in articles that deal with discipline, gifted and talented (regular classroom), motivation and working with parents. Buys 6 mss/issue. Query. Length: 1,000-3,500 words. Pays $100-350.
Photos: State availablity of photos with query. Offers no additional payment for 8x10 b&w glossy prints or 35mm color transparencies. Captions preferred. Buys all rights, but may reassign following publication. Model release required.

THE LIVING LIGHT, 1312 Massachusetts Ave. NW, Washington DC 20005. An interdisciplinary review for "professionals in the field of religious education, primarily Roman Catholics." Estab. 1964. Quarterly. Buys all rights but will reassign rights to author after publication. Pays on publication. Sample copy $3.50. Reports in 30-60 days. SASE.
Nonfiction: Articles that "present development and trends, report on research and encourage critical thinking in the field of religious education and pastoral action. Academic approach." Buys 4 mss/year. Submit complete ms. Length: 2,000-5,000 words. Pays $40-100.

THE MANITOBA TEACHER, 191 Harcourt St., Winnipeg, Manitoba, Canada R3J 3H2. (204)888-7961. Editor: Mrs. Miep van Raalte. 25% freelance written. No payment. For teachers in the public schools of Manitoba. Published 10 times/year. Tabloid; 8-12 pages. Estab. 1919. Circ. 17,300. Byline given. Phone queries OK. Submit seasonal/holiday material 3 months in advance of issue date. Photocopied and previously published submissions OK. SAE and International Reply Coupons. Reports in 4 weeks. Free sample copy and writer's guidelines.
Nonfiction: How-to (teach a particular subject, introduce new programs or approaches, etc.); humor (related to education in Manitoba); interview (dealing with education); opinion (issues pertaining to education in Manitoba); profile (of special interest to teachers in Manitoba); personal experience (classroom experiences); and photo feature (educational event). No lengthly scholarly essays. Submit complete ms. Length: 200-1,500 words.
Photos: State availability of photos with ms. Uses any size glossy b&w or color prints.
Columns/Departments: Reaction, Readers Write, News Briefs, President's Message, and General Secretary Comments. Submit complete ms. Length: 300-800 words. Open to suggestions for new columns/departments.

MEDIA & METHODS, 401 N. Broad St., Philadelphia PA 19108. Editor: Anthony Prete. For English and social studies teachers who have an abiding interest in humanistic and media-oriented education, plus a core of librarians, media specialists, filmmakers; the cutting edge of educational innovators. Magazine; 56-64 (8½x11) pages. Estab. 1964. Monthly (September through May). Circ. 50,000. Normally buys all rights. About half of each issue is freelance material. Pays on publication. Free writer's guidelines to qualified writers. Will consider photocopied submissions. Reports in 2-4 months. Submit complete ms or query. SASE.

Nonfiction: "We are looking for the middle school, high school or college educator who has something vital and interesting to say. Subjects include practical how-to articles with broad applicability to our readers, and innovative, challenging, conceptual-type stories that deal with educational change. Our style is breezy and conversational, occasionally offbeat. We make a concentrated effort to be nonsexist; mss filled with 'he,' 'him' and 'mankind' (when the gender is unspecified) will pose unnecessary barriers to acceptance. We are a trade journal with a particular subject emphasis (media-oriented English and social studies), philosophical bent (humanistic, personal), and interest area (the practical and innovative)." Length: 2,500 words maximum. Pays $15-$100.

MOMENTUM. National Catholic Educational Association, 1 Dupont Circle, Suite 350, Washington DC 20036. (202)293-5954. Editor: Carl Balcerak. For Catholic administrators and teachers, some parents and students, in all levels of education (preschool, elementary, secondary, higher). Quarterly magazine; 56-64 pages. Estab. 1970. Circ. 14,500. Buys all rights. Buys 28-36 mss/year. Pays on publication. Free sample copy. Will consider photocopied and simultaneous submissions. Submit special issue material 3 months in advance. Query. Reports in 4 weeks. SASE.
Nonfiction and Photos: "Articles concerned with educational philosophy, psychology, methodology, innovative programs, teacher training, etc. Catholic-oriented material. Book reviews on educational-religious topics. Innovative educational programs; financial and public relations programs, management systems applicable to nonpublic schools. No pious ruminations on pseudoreligious ideas. Also, avoid general topics, such as what's right (wrong) with Catholic education. In most cases, a straightforward, journalistic style with emphasis on practical examples is preferred. Some scholarly writing, but little in the way of statistical. All material has Catholic orientation, with emphasis on professionalism; not sentimental or hackneyed treatment of religious topics." Length: 1,500-2,000 words. Pays 2¢/word. Pays $5 for b&w glossy photos purchased with mss. Captions required.

NATIONAL ON-CAMPUS REPORT. 621 N. Sherman Ave., Suite 4, Madison WI 53704. (608)249-2455. Editor: William H. Haight. 15% freelance written. For education administrators, college student leaders, journalists, and directors of youth organizations. Estab. 1972. Monthly. Pays 25% kill fee. Pays on publication. Sample copy and writer's guidelines for SASE. Photocopied submissions OK. Reports in 1 month. SASE.
Nonfiction and Fillers: Short, timely articles relating to events and activities of college students. "No clippings of routine college news, only unusual items of possible national interest." Also buys newsbreaks and clippings related to college students and their activities. "We particularly want items about trends in student media: newspapers, magazines, campus radio, etc." Buys 100 mss/year. Submit complete ms. Length: 25-800 words. Pays 10-12¢/word.

NJEA REVIEW. New Jersey Education Association, 180 W. State St., Box 1211, Trenton NJ 08607. Editor-in-Chief: George Adams. 20% freelance written. For members of the association employed in New Jersey schools; teachers, administrators, etc. Monthly (September-May) magazine; 48-72 pages. Estab. 1922. Circ. 110,000. Pays on acceptance. Buys all rights, but may reassign following publication. Byline given. Previously published submissions OK. SASE. Reports in 1-2 months. Free sample copy and writer's guidelines.
Nonfiction: How-to (classroom ideas), informational (curriculum area), opinion articles (on educational issues) and interviews with "names" in education. Length: 2,500-3,000 words maximum. Buys 15-20 mss/year. Query or submit complete ms. Pays $35 minimum.
Photos: B&w (5x7 or 8x10) glossies purchased with ms. Query. Pays $5 minimum. Model release required.
How To Break In: "Needed are well-researched articles (but no footnotes, please) on new trends in education (such as teaching and curriculum experimentation) and subject area articles. These are especially suitable if they grow directly out of experience in a New Jersey school or college. Human interest stories about people, teaching situations, or education in general also often acceptable."

PHI DELTA KAPPAN. 8th and Union Sts., Bloomington IN 47401. Editor: Stanley Elam. For educators, especially those in leadership positions, such as administrators; mid-40s; all hold BA degrees; one-third hold doctorates. Monthly magazine; 72 pages. Estab. 1915. Circ. 135,000. Buys all rights, but will sometimes reassign rights to author after publication (this varies with the author and material). Pays on publication. Free sample copy. Reports in 1-2 months. SASE.
Nonfiction and Photos: Feature articles on education, emphasizing policy, trends, both sides of issues, controversial developments. Also, informational, how-to, personal experience, interview,

profile, inspirational, humor, think articles, expose. "Our audience is scholarly but hard-headed." Buys 10-15 mss/year. Submit complete ms. Length: 500-3,000 words. Pays $25-$250. "We pay a fee only occasionally, and then it is usually to an author whom *we* seek out. We do welcome inquiries from freelancers, but it is misleading to suggest that we buy very much from them." Pays average photographer's rates for b&w photos purchased with mss, but captions are required. Will purchase photos on assignment. Sizes: 8x10 or 5x7 preferred.

SCHOOL ARTS MAGAZINE, 72 Printers Bldg., Worcester MA 01608. Editor: David W. Baker. Services arts and craft education profession, K-12, higher education and museum eduction programs. Monthly, except June, July and August. Will send a sample copy to a writer on request. Pays on publication. Reports in 90 days. SASE.
Nonfiction and Photos: Articles, with photos, on art and craft activities in schools. Length: 1,000 words. Payment is negotiable but begins at $25.

SCHOOL SHOP, 416 Longshore Dr., Ann Arbor MI 48107. Editor: Lawrence W. Prakken. For "industrial and technical education personnel." Special issue in April deals with varying topics for which mss are solicited. Monthly. Circ. 45,000. Buys all rights. Pays on publication. Query: "direct or indirect connection with the field of industrial and/or technical education preferred." Submit mss to Howard Kahn, Managing Editor. Submit seasonal material 3 months in advance. Reports in 6 weeks. SASE.
Nonfiction and Photos: Uses articles pertinent to the various teaching areas in industrial education (woodwork, electronics, drafting, machine shop, graphic arts, computer training, etc.). "Outlook should be on innovation in educational programs, processes, or projects which directly apply to the industrial-technical education area." Buys how-to's, personal experience and think pieces, interviews, humor, coverage of new products and cartoons. Length: 500-2,000 words. Pays $15-50. B&w photos purchased with ms.

SCIENCE ACTIVITIES, Room 504, 4000 Albermarle St. NW, Washington DC 20016. (202)362-6445. Publisher: Cornelius W. Vahle Jr. Editor: Jane Powers Weldon. For science teachers (high school, junior high school, elementary and college). Quarterly magazine; 48 pages. Estab. 1969. Circ. 3,000. Pays on publication. Sample copy for $3.50. Reports in 90 days. SASE.
Nonfiction and Photos: "Articles on creative science projects for the classroom, including experiments, explorations, and projects in every phase of the biological, physical and behavioral sciences." Buys 50 mss/year. Length: 1,500-3,000 words. Pays $10/printed page. Photos purchased with ms; no additional payment. Captions required.

SCIENCE AND CHILDREN, National Science Teachers Association, 1742 Connecticut Ave. NW, Washington DC 20009. (202)265-4150. Editor-in-Chief: Phyllis Marcuccio. 70% freelance written. Emphasizes elementary school science for teachers and educational personnel of all levels, kindergarten through college. Monthly (8 issues during academic year) magazine; 48 pages. Estab. 1963. Circ. 18,000. No payment except for subscription. Phone queries OK. Submit seasonal/holiday material 6-8 months in advance. Photocopied submissions OK. SASE. Reports in 2-3 months. Free sample copy and writer's guidelines.
Nonfiction: How-to (science projects and activities for elementary students); informational (relating to science or elementary science programs); inspirational (relating to children and science); personal experience (with an aspect of elementary school science); photo feature (relating to science); research on science education. Submit complete ms. Length: 1,500 words maximum.
Photos: Used with mss. Send prints. Prefers 8x10 b&w glossies. Model release required.
Columns, Departments: Research in Education. Current research, in particular, related to science at the elementary level. Send complete ms. Length: 1,200-1,500 words.
Rejects: "Material that would not be appropriate for elementary school level. The magazine is read by teachers. It is not a children's audience. However, the teachers look for material they can use in the classroom or material that would be relevant to them."

SIGHTLINES, Educational Film Library Association, Inc., 43 W. 61st St., New York NY 10023. (212)246-4533. Editor: Nadine Covert. 80% freelance written. Emphasizes the nontheatrical film world for librarians in university and public libraries, independent filmmakers, film teachers on the high school and college level, film programmers in the community, university, religious organizations, film curators in museums. Quarterly magazine; 44 pages. Estab. 1967. Circ. 3,000. Pays on publication. Buys all rights, but may reassign following publication. Byline given. Phone queries OK. SASE. Reports in 2 months. Free sample copy.

Nonfiction: Informational (on the production, distribution and programming of nontheatrical films), interview (with filmmakers who work in 16mm, video; who make documentary, avant-garde, children's, and personal films), new product, and personal opinion (for regular Freedom To View column). Buys 4 mss/issue. Query. Length: 4,000-6,000 words. Pay 2½¢/word.

Photos: Purchased with accompanying ms. Captions required. Offers no additional payment for photos accepted with accompanying ms. Model release required.

Columns/Departments: Who's Who in Filmmaking (interview or profile of filmmaker or video artist who works in the nontheatrical field); Book Reviews (reviews of serious film, media, and/or library-related books); Members Reports (open to those library or museum personnel, film teachers, who are members of the Educational Film Library Association and who have creative ideas for programming films or media in institutions, have solved censorship porblems, or other nuts-and-bolts thoughts on using film/media in libraries/schools). Buys 1-3 mss/issue. Query. Pays 2½¢/word. Open to suggestions for new columns or departments.

SPECIAL EDUCATION: FORWARD TRENDS. 12 Hollycroft Ave., London NW3 7QL, England. Editor: Margaret Peter. Quarterly. Estab: 1974. Circ: 6,500. Pays token fee for commissioned articles. SAE and International Reply Coupons.

Nonfiction: Articles on the education of all types of handicapped children. "The aim of this journal of the National Council for Special Education is to provide articles on special education and handicapped children that will keep readers informed of practical and theoretical developments not only in education but in the many other aspects of the education and welfare of the handicapped. While we hope that articles will lead students and others to further related reading, their main function is to give readers an adequate introduction to a topic which they may not have an opportunity to pursue further. References should therefore be selective and mainly easily accessible ones. It is important, therefore, that articles of a more technical nature (e.g., psychology, medical, research reviews) should, whenever possible, avoid unnecessary technicalities or ensure that necessary technical terms or expressions are made clear to nonspecialists by the context or by the provision of brief additional explanations or examples." Length: 750-3,750 words. Payment by arrangement for commissioned articles only.

TEACHER, Macmillan Professional Magazines, 77 Bedford St., Stamford CT 06901. (203)357-7714. Editor-in-Chief: Joan S. Baranski. Emphasizes education at the elementary school level. Monthly magazine; 150 pages. Estab. 1883. Circ. 250,000. Pays on acceptance. Buys all rights, but may reassign following publication. Submit seasonal/holiday material 6 months in advance. Photocopied submissions OK. SASE, Reports in 3 months. Free sample copy and writer's guidelines.

Nonfiction: Jeanette Moss, articles editor. "In evaluating potential articles for *Teacher*, we try to keep one thought uppermost in mind: Can an elementary school teacher gain some practical help from this material? We're most interested in the article that says, 'Here's how I did it and it works.' We want teachers talking to teachers as peers who understand and face similar problems. We are not interested in material that is basically theoretical or in the form of a research paper or a textbook-style unit. If you want to describe a successful project or unit, put it into article form." Publishes interviews, personal experience and personal opinion articles; trends in education, newsworthy programs and techniques, short teaching tips. Length: 1,000-1,500 words. Buys 15 mss/issue. Query.

Photos: Vincent Ceci, department editor. B&w and color used with mss. Query. Model release required.

TODAY'S CATHOLIC TEACHER, 2451 E. River Rd., Dayton OH 45439. (513)294-5785. Editor-in-Chief: Ruth A. Matheny. 25% freelance written. For administrators, teachers, parents concerned with Catholic schools, both parochial and CCD. Estab. 1967. Circ. 65,000. Pays on publication. Buys all rights, but may reassign following publication. Byline given. Phone queries OK. Submit seasonal/holiday material 3 months in advance of issue date. SASE. Sample copy $1; free writer's guidelines; mention *Writer's Market* in request.

Nonfiction: How-to (based on experience, particularly in Catholic situations, philosophy with practical applications); inspirational (tribute to teacher); interview (of practicing educators, educational leaders); personal experience (classroom happenings); and profile (of educational leader). Buys 40-50 mss/year. Submit complete ms. Length: 800-2,000 words. Pays $15-75.

Photos: State availability of photos with ms. Offers no additional payment for 8x10 b&w glossy prints. Captions preferred. Buys all rights, but may reassign following publication. Model release required.

TODAY'S EDUCATION, National Education Association, 1201 16th St. NW., Washington

DC 20036. (202)833-5442. Editor-in-Chief: Walter A. Graves. For elementary, secondary and higher education teachers. Quarterly magazine; 96 pages. Estab. 1913. Circ. 1,800,000. Pays on acceptance. Buys all rights, but may reassign following publication. Phone queries OK. Submit seasonal/holiday material 3 months in advance of issue date. SASE. Reports in 4 weeks. Free writer's guidelines.

Nonfiction: How-to (teach); interview (teachers); and nostalgia (early schools and teachers). Buys 5 mss/year. Submit complete ms. Length: 1,600-3,200 words. Pays $200-1,000 "to recognized freelance writers."

Photos: Submit photo material with accompanying ms. Pays $50 for 8x10 b&w glossy prints; $150 for 35mm color transparencies. Buys one-time rights. Model release required.

TRAINING FILM PROFILES, Olympic Media Information, 71 W. 23rd St., New York NY 10010. (212)675-4500. Editor: Walt Carroll. For colleges, community colleges, libraries, training directors, manpower specialists, education and training services, career development centers, audiovisual specialists, administrators. Serial in looseleaf format, published every 2 months. Estab. 1967. Circ. 1,000. Buys all rights. No byline. Pays on publication. "Send resume of your experience to introduce yourself." Reports in 2 months. SASE.

Nonfiction: "Reviews of instructional films, filmstrips, videotapes and cassettes, sound-slide programs and the like. We have a highly specialized, rigid format that must be followed without exception. Ask us for sample *Profiles* to see what we mean. Besides job training areas, we are also interested in the areas of values and personal self-development, upward mobility in the world of work, social change, futuristics, management training, problem solving, and adult education." Buys 200-240 mss/year. Query. Pays $5-15/review.

Electricity

Publications classified here aim at electrical engineers, electrical contractors, and others who build, design, and maintain systems connecting and supplying homes, businesses, and industries with power. Journals dealing with generating and supplying power to users will be found in the Power and Power Plants category. Publications for appliance servicemen and dealers will be found in the Home Furnishings classification.

CEDA CURRENT, Kerrwil Publications, Ltd., 20 Holly St., Suite 201, Toronto, Ontario, Canada M4S 2E8. (416)487-3461. Editor-in-Chief: Bryan S. Rogers. 25% freelance written. For "marketing and operating personnel in electrical maintenance and construction as well as distributors." Bimonthly magazine; 20 tabloid pages. Estab. 1969. Circ. 13,000. Pays on acceptance. Buys first North American serial rights. Pays 10% kill fee. Byline given. Phone queries OK. Submit seasonal/holiday material 4 months in advance of issue date. Previously published submissions "sometimes considered." SAE and International Reply Coupons. Reports in 2 weeks. Free sample copy; mention *Writer's Market* in request.

Nonfiction: Canadian content only. How-to (problem solving, wiring, electrical construction and maintenance); general interest (to the electrical industry); interview (with electrical distributors and maintenance men); new product ("from manufacturers—we don't pay for news releases"); and technical. Query. Length: 500-1,500 words. Pays 5-10¢/word.

Photos: State availability of photos with query. Pays $5 for b&w photos; "negotiable" payment for color transparencies. Captions required. Buys one-time rights.

ELECTRICAL APPARATUS, Barks Publications, Inc., 400 N. Michigan Ave., Chicago IL 60611. (312)321-9440. Editorial Director: Elsie Dickson. 10-15% freelance written. Emphasizes industrial electrical maintenance and repair. Monthly magazine; 60 pages. Estab: 1948. Circ: 15,000. Pays on acceptance. Buys all rights, but may reassign following publication. Phone queries OK. Submit seasonal/holiday material 3 months in advance. SASE. Reports in 2 weeks. Sample copy $1.50.

Nonfiction: Publishes how-to, informational and technical articles. Buys 1-2/issue. Length: 1,000-2,000 words. Query. Pays $50-200.

Photos: B&w glossies (5x7 or 8x10) purchased with mss or on assignment. Query. Pays $10-25.

ELECTRICAL CONTRACTOR, 7315 Wisconsin Ave., Washington DC 20014. (301)657-3110. Editor: Larry C. Osius. 10% freelance written. For electrical contractors. Monthly. Buys first rights, reprint rights, or simultaneous rights. Byline given. Will send free sample copy on request. Usually reports in 1 month. SASE.

Nonfiction and Photos: Installation articles showing informative application of new techniques and products. Slant is product and method contributing to better, faster, more economical construction process. Query. Length: "1 column to 4 pages." Pays $65/printed page, including photos and illustrative material. Photos should be sharp, reproducible glossies, 5x7 and up.

ELECTRICAL CONTRACTOR & MAINTENANCE SUPERVISOR, 481 University Ave., Toronto, Ontario, M5W 1A7, Canada. Editor: Richard Willingham. For "men who either run their own businesses or are in fairly responsible management positions. They range from university graduates to those with public school education only." Estab. 1952. Monthly. Circ. 13,400. Rights purchased vary with author and material. "Depending on author's wish, payment is either on acceptance or on publication." Free sample copy. SAE and International Reply Coupons.

Nonfiction and Photos: "Articles that have some relation to electrical contracting or maintenance and related business management. The writer should include as much information as possible pertaining to the electrical field. We're not interested in articles that are too general and philosophical. Don't belabor the obvious, particularly on better business management. We're interested in coverage of labor difficulties, informational articles, how-to's, profiles, coverage of successful business operations, new product pieces, and technical articles." Length: "no minimum or maximum." Pays "8¢ a published word or 6¢ a word on submitted mss, unless other arrangements are made." Photos purchased with mss or on assignment; captions optional. Pays "$7 for the first print and $2 for each subsequent print, plus photographer's expenses."

Electronics and Communication

Listed here are publications for electronics engineers, radio and TV broadcasting managers, electronic equipment operators, and builders of electronic communication systems and equipment, including stereos, television sets, and radio-TV broadcasting systems. Journals for professional announcers or communicators will be found under Journalism; those for electronic appliance retailers will be found in Home Furnishings; publications on computer design and data processing systems will be found in Data Processing. Publications for electronics enthusiasts or stereo hobbyists will be found in Hobby and Craft or in Music in the Consumer Publications section.

BROADCAST ENGINEERING, Box 12901, Overland Park KS 66212. Editor: Bill Rhodes. For "owners, managers, and top technical people at AM, FM, TV stations, cable TV operators, educational and industrial TV and business communications, as well as recording studios." Estab. 1959. Monthly. Circ. 34,000. Buys all rights. Buys 50 mss/year. Pays on acceptance; "for a series, we pay for each part on publication." Free sample copy and writer's guidelines. Reports in 2 weeks. SASE.

Nonfiction: Wants technical features dealing with design, installation, modification, and maintenance of radio and TV broadcast equipment; interested in features of interest to communications engineers and technicians as well as broadcast management, and features on self-designed and constructed equipment for use in broadcast and communications field. "We use a technical, but not textbook, style. Our publication is mostly how-to, and it operates as a forum. We reject material that is far too general, not on target, or not backed by evidence of proof. Our Station-to-Station column provides a forum for equipment improvement and build-it-yourself tips. We pay up to $30. We're especially interested in articles on recording studios and improving facilities and techniques." Query. Length: 1,500-2,000 words for features. Pays $75-200.

Photos: Photos purchased with or without mss; captions required. Pays $5-10 for b&w prints; $10-35 for 2¼x2¼ or larger color transparencies.

BROADCAST EQUIPMENT TODAY, Diversified Publications, Ltd., Box 423, Station J, Toronto, Ontario, Canada M4J 4Y8. (416)463-5304. Editor-in-Chief: Doug Loney. 50% freelance written. Emphasizes broadcast engineering. Bimonthly magazine; 64 pages. Estab. 1975. Circ. 5,000. Pays on publication. Buys all rights. Byline given. Phone queries OK. Photocopied and previously published submissions OK. SAE and International Reply Coupons. Free writer's guidelines.

Nonfiction: Technical articles on developments in broadcast engineering, especially pertaining to Canada. Query. Length: 500-1,5000 words. Pays $50-150.

Photos: Purchased with accompanying ms. Captions required. Query for b&w or color. Total purchase price for a ms includes payment for photos.

BROADCAST MANAGEMENT/ENGINEERING, 295 Madison Ave., New York NY 10017. (212)685-5320. Editor: D. Hawthorne. 5% freelance written. For general managers, chief engineers and program directors of radio and TV stations. Estab. 1964. Monthly. Circ. 30,000. Buys all rights, but will reassign rights to author after publication. Byline given unless "article is used as backup for staff-written piece, which happens rarely." Buys 7-12 mss/year. Pays on publication. Reports in 4 weeks. Query. SASE.
Nonfiction: Articles on cost-saving ideas; use of equipment, new programming ideas for serving the public. "We're interested in the profile or program sound of competitive stations in a martket." Length: 1,200-3,000 words. Pays $25-100.

BROADCAST PROGRAMMING & PRODUCTION, Box 2449, Hollywood CA 90028. (213)467-1111. Editor: D. Keith Larkin. 30% freelance written. Emphasizes radio and television broadcasting. Bimonthly magazine: 72 pages. Estab. 1975. Circ. 16,000. Pays on publication. Buys all rights. Phone queries OK. Photocopied submissions OK. SASE. Reports in 1 month. Sample copy $2; mention *Writer's Market* in request.
Nonfiction: How-to (articles on radio/TV programming, production and engineering); interview (with important figures in broadcast field); profile (on the production of network or syndicated TV shows); and technical (radio and TV programming production and engineering). No articles on publicity items. Buys 12 mss/year. Query. Length: 2,000-5,000 words. Pays $100-250.

BROADCASTER, 7 Labatt Ave., Toronto, Ontario, Canada M5A 3P2. (416)363-6111. Editor: Barbara Byers. For the Canadian "communications industry—radio, television, cable, ETV, advertisers and their agencies." Estab. 1942. Monthly. Circ. 8,100. Buys all rights, but may reassign rights after publication. Byline given. Buys 50-60 mss/year. Pays on publication. Writers should submit outlines; sample issue will be sent for style. Photocopied and simultaneous submissions OK. Returns rejected material "as soon as possible." SAE and International Reply Coupons.
Nonfiction: "Technical and general articles about the broadcasting industry, almost exclusively Canadian. Length: 1,000-2,000 words. Pays $75-300.
Photos: Rarely purchased.

COMMUNICATIONS NEWS, 124 S. 1st St., Geneva IL 60134. (312)232-1400. Editor: Bruce Howat. 5% freelance written. For managers of communications systems including telephone companies, CATV systems, broadcasting stations and private systems. Estab. 1964. Monthly. Circ. 40,000. Buys all rights. Pays on publication. Free sample copy. Photocopied submissions OK. Reports in 4 weeks. SASE.
Nonfiction: Case histories of problem-solving for communications systems. Factual reporting about new communicatons products, systems and techniques. Must be terse, factual, helpful. Informational news and how-to articles; think pieces. Buys 3-10 mss/year. Query or submit complete ms. Length: 1,600 words maximum. Pays 3¢/word.
Photos: Department Editor: Don Wiley. Purchased with accompanying ms with no additional payment or without accompanying ms. Captions optional. Pays $10 for b&w glossy prints.

ELECTRONIC BUYERS' NEWS, 333 East Shore Rd., Manhasset NY 11030. (516)829-5880. Editor: James Moran. The purchasing publication for the electronics industry. Newspaper; 64 pages. Estab. 1972. Circ. 35,000. Pays on publication. Usually buys first rights. Byline given. SASE. Reports in 2-3 months. Rejected material not returned unless requested. Free sample copy.
Nonfiction: "Each issue features a specific theme or electronic component. Articles are usually accepted from companies involved with that component. Other stories are accepted occasionally from authors knowledgeable in that field." All material is aimed directly at the purchasing profession. Length: open. Pays $100 minimum.

ELECTRONIC PACKAGING AND PRODUCTION, Kiver Publications, 222 W. Adams St., Chicago IL 60606. (312)263-4866. Editor: Donald J. Levinthal. Managing Editor: Howard W. Markstein. 40% freelance written. Emphasizes electronic equipment fabrication for engineering and production personnel, including product testing. Monthly magazine; 150 pages. Estab. 1961. Circ. 27,000. Pays on publication. Buys all rights, but may reassign following publication. Pays 25% kill fee. Byline given. Phone queries OK. Photocopied submissions OK. SASE. Reports in 3 weeks. Free sample copy and writer's guideline.
Nonfiction: How-to (innovative packaging, production or technique); interview (newsy features about technological trends in electronics); and technical (articles pertaining to the electronic packaging, production and testing of electronic systems, hybrids and

semiconductors). "No single-product-oriented articles of a commercial sales-pitch nature." Buys 40 mss/year. Query or submit complete ms. Length: 1,000-2,500 words. Pays $30-150.
Photos: State availability of photos with query or submit photos with ms. Offers no additional payment for 4x5 or larger b&w or color prints. Captions preferred. Buys all rights, but may reassign following publication.

ELECTRONIC TECHNICIAN/DEALER, 43 E. Ohio, Chicago IL 60611. (312)467-0670. Editor: Richard Lay. For owners, managers, technician employees of consumer electronic sales and/or service firms. Magazine; 72 pages. Estab. 1953. Monthly. Circ. 70,000. Buys all rights. Pays on acceptance. Free sample copy and writer's guidelines. Simultaneous submissions OK. Reports "immediately." SASE.
Nonfiction and Photos: Feature articles of a practical nature about consumer electronic technology and servicing techniques; business profiles and/or business management. No generalization; must have concise, practical orientation; a specific approach. No business management articles which are too general and superficial. Informational, how-to, interview, profile, technical articles and those on successful business operations. Buys 36 mss/year. Query or submit complete ms. Length: 1,200-2,500 words. Pays $100-175. No additional payment for b&w photos purchased with mss. Captions required.

ELECTRONICS, 1221 Avenue of the Americas, New York NY 10019. Editor: Kemp Anderson. 10-15% freelance written. Biweekly. Buys all rights. Byline given. Reports in 2 weeks. SASE.
Nonfiction: Uses copy about research, development, design and production of electronic devices and management of electronic manufacturing firms; articles on "descriptions of new circuit systems, components, design techniques, how specific electronic engineering problems were solved; interesting applications of electronics; step-by-step, how-to design articles; monographs, charts, tables for solution of repetitive design problems." Query. Length: 1,000-3,500 words. Pays $30/printed page.

ELECTRONICS JOURNAL, 213 Fernwood Dr., Aurora IL 60538. (312)897-4000. Publisher: William C. Sands Jr. Managing Editor: Ron Stewart. 15-18% freelance written. "Readers are electronic engineers, technicians, buyers or sales personnel." Monthly newspaper; 40 pages. Estab. February 1976. Circ. 31,000. Pays on publication. Buys all rights. Pays 5-25% kill fee. Phone queries OK. Submit seasonal/holiday material 3 months in advance of issue date. Photocopied and previously published submissions OK. SASE. Reports in 1 month. Free sample copy.
Nonfiction: Expose (especially dealing with buyers who are 'on the take'); general interest (any unique application of electronics); historical (dealing with the fathers of electricity electronics, Tesla, Edison, etc.); how-to (dealing with microcomputers); humor (dealing with manufacturer's reps or industrial distributors); interview (with a CEO of an electronics firm); personal experience (limited to CEOs and award winners); photo features (for big shows, new systems, etc.); profile (CEOs or award winners); technical ("state of the art"). No opinion pieces. Buys 1-2 mss/issue. Query or submit complete ms. Length: 600-1,200 words. Pays $25-100.
Photos: "We are dedicated to illustrated articles especially in those which deal with important people in electronics." Offers no additional payment for photos accepted with ms. Uses 5x7 glossy b&w prints and 3x5 color prints. Captions preferred. Buys all rights, but may reassign after publication. Model releases required.
Columns/Departments: Book Reviews (of books published in last 120 days); Lest We Forget (any historical or nostalgia piece about pioneers of electronics); and Around the Great Lakes (any article of commercial use of electronics in Ohio, Illinois, Indiana, Michigan and Wisconsin). Query or submit complete ms. Length: 200 words. Pays $25.
Fillers: Clippings, jokes, gags, anecdotes, newsbreaks, puzzles and short humor. "Any items that deal with electronics in industry." Buys 5-10/issue. Length: 25-100 words. Pays $5-20.
How To Break In: "We are genuinely interested in any articles about the leaders in our field, and are eager to receive articles about the history of specific components such as resistors, capacitors, transformers, power supplies, microcomputers and microprocessors. We do not pay as much as some of the large publications, but we are still growing. We do pay promptly and we advise the writer as soon as we know if we will use the piece or not."

JOB LEADS, Media Service Group, 1680-CP Vine St., Hollywood CA 90028. Editor: Tim Baskerville. For job seekers in the media field and managers and personnel executives of media companies, particularly radio and TV stations. Weekly newsletter; 4 pages. Estab. 1973. Pays on acceptance. Buys all rights. Simultaneous, photocopied and previously published submissions OK. SASE. Reports in 2-6 weeks. Free sample copy.

Nonfiction: "Our weekly newsletter is staff-written. However, we do buy special reports and articles for supplements and premiums. Titles recently purchased: 'Broadcaster's Guide to Resume Preparation' and 'Broadcaster's Legal Handbook of Hiring Practices.' We are open to just about any length, as the format for each project varies. Writers without expertise in a technical or narrow area are discouraged from proposing an idea in that area. For that reason, for example, an attorney who is also a freelance writer got the assignment for the legal handbook mentioned above. We will also consider distributing self-published booklets or reports in our subject area. Send sample for review." How-to (get a job, prepare an audition tape, handle a job interview); and technical (technical and legal guidelines for employers and subjects of interest to broadcasting executives). Buys 6 mss/year. Query for articles over 1,500 words; submit complete ms for mss under 1,500 words. Length: 750 words minimum. Pays $50-500, depending on length and complexity.

MICROELECTRONICS JOURNAL, Mackintosh Publications, Ltd., Box 28, Mackintosh House, Napier Rd., Luton, England LU1 5DB. 0582-417438. Publications Director: Philip Rathkey. For electronics engineers engaged in research design, production, applications, sales in commercial or government organizations, academics (teaching, research) and higher degree students. "Writer must be active in the microelectronics industry (including academics or higher degree students) and have either an original observation to make or be able to inform/update readers on the state-of-the-art in a specialty area, or on the activities of an organization." Bimonthly magazine; 48 pages. Estab. 1967. Circ. 1,500. Pays on publication. Buys all rights. Phone queries OK. Submit seasonal/holiday material 3 months in advance. Photocopied submissions OK. Accepts previously published work only if first English translation of foreign language paper. Reports in 3 weeks to US. Free sample copy and writer's guidelines.

Nonfiction: Expose (technical critique of manufacturers' products, of government, commercial, trade); general interest (state-of-the-art technical/marketing articles); how-to (on new designs, applications, production, materials, technology/techniques); interview (of eminent captain of industry or government politician); nostalgia (concerning how microelectronics companies got started or techniques were invented); personal opinion (on any relevant technical/commercial subject); profile (of company research activities, university research activities); new product (assessment and and evidence of product's importance); photo feature (must include write-up explaining its technical/commercial significance); technical (On integrated circuit technology and systems, memories, microprocessors, optoelectronics, infra-red, hybrid integrated circuits, microwave solid-state devices, CCD and SAW techniques, semiconductor materials and chemicals, semiconductor production equipment and processing tecniques, and automatic test techniques and equipment). Buys 10-30 mss/year. Query or submit complete ms. Length: 4,000-6,000 words. Pays $50/published page including diagrams, photos, etc.

Photos: Prefers b&w 6½x4½ prints unless color is technically essential. Offers no additional payment for photos accepted with ms. Captions required.

Columns/Departments: Book reviews. Buys 1 page/issue. Query. Length: 350-1,000 words. Pays $25.

MICROWAVES, 50 Essex St., Rochelle Park NJ 07662. (201)843-0550. Editor: Stacy V. Bearse. 50% freelance written. Emphasizes microwave electronics. "Qualified recipients are those individuals actively engaged in microwave research, design, development, production, and application engineering, engineering management, administration or purchasing departments in organizations and facilities where application and use of devices, systems and techniques involve frequencies from VHF through visible light." Monthly magazine; 100 pages. Estab. March 1962. Circ. 40,217. Pays on publication. Buys all rights. Phone queries OK. Photocopied submissions OK. SASE. Reports in 4 weeks. Free sample copy and writer's guidelines; mention *Writer's Market* in request.

Nonfiction: "Interested in material on research and development in microwave technology and economic news that affects the industry." How-to (microwave design); new product; opinion; and technical. Buys 60 mss/year. Query. Pays $25-30/published page.

Fillers: Newsbreaks. Pays $10 (minimum).

MILITARY ELECTRONICS/COUNTERMEASURES, Hamilton-Burr Publishing Co., 2065 Martin Ave., Suite 104, Santa Clara CA 95050. (408)985-2280. Editor: Murry Shohat. 30% freelance written. Emphasizes military electronics. Systems for military and industry engineers and program managers in electronics. Monthly magazine; 64 pages. Estab. 1975. Circ. 30,000. Pays on publication. Buys all rights. Byline given "except where publishing the byline compromises the writer's ability to secure source material or 'blows cover'." Submit

seasonal/holiday material 60 days in advance of issue date. SASE. Reports in 2 months. Sample copy free.
Nonfiction: Exposé (very few, nondestructive, military-related); new product (systems); and technical. Buys 10 mss/year. Query with outline. Length: 1,500-3,500 words. Pays 10¢/word and up.
Photos: State availability of photos with query. Uses 5x7 b&w glossy prints. Offers no additional payment for photos accepted with ms. Captions required. Buys all rights, but may reassign following publication.

MONITOR, Alpha Epsilon Rho, c/o CBS-FM National Sales, 630 N McClung Ct., Chicago IL 60611. (312)944-6000. Editor: Tom Matheson. 90% freelance written. For members of the National Honorary Broadcasting Society and members of the broadcast industry. Quarterly magazine; 32 pages. Estab. 1943. Circ. 3,000. Pays on publication. Buys one-time rights. Simultaneous, photocopied and previously published submissions OK. SASE. Reports in 3 weeks. Free sample copy and writer's guidelines; mention *Writer's Market* in request.
Nonfiction: Expose (related to broadcasting); how-to; general interest; historical (development, growth, etc.); humor (true-life incidents, reflections, etc.); interview; new product (broadcast technology); nostalgia (within reason); personal experience; opinion; photo feature (related to a certain program or treatment of an issue); profile (broadcasters); and technical ("interesting articles of this nature are hard to find"). Submit complete ms. Length: 200-2,000 words. Pays: $0-200.
Photos: State availability of photos with ms. Pays $10 maximum for b&w prints. Buys one-time rights. Model release required.
Columns/Departments: Book Reviews. Query. Length: 200-2,000 words. Pays $100 maximum. Open to suggestions for new columns/departments.
Fiction: Fantasy (industry-related, but of a 'what-if?' nature); and humorous (fiction treatment of factual situations). Buys 2 mss/issue. Submit complete ms. Length: 200-2,000 words. Pays $50 maximum.
Poetry: Industry-related poems. Buys 1/issue. Pays $25 maximum.
Fillers: Short humor (industry-related). Buys 5/issue. Length: 10-50 words. Pays $5 maximum.

RADIO-TV EDITORIAL JOURNAL, Foundation for American Communications, 1629 K Street NW, Washington DC 20006. (202)659-0668. Editor-in-Chief: George Mair. For editorial writers, news directors, and general managers of radio and television stations. Monthly magazine; 32 pages. Estab. 1976. Circ. 10,600. Pays on publication. Buys all rights. Phone queries OK. Submit seasonal/holiday material 2 months in advance. Simultaneous, photocopied and previously published submissions OK. SASE. Reports in 1 month.
Nonfiction: Informational (political and social issues), personal opinion. Buys 12 mss/year. Query. Length: 1,000-2,000 words. Pays $25.

RECORDING ENGINEER/PRODUCER, Box 2449, Hollywood CA 90028. (213)467-1111. Editor: Martin Gallay. 100% freelance written. Emphasizes recording technology and concert sound for "all levels of professionals with the recording industry as well as high-level amateur recording interests." Bimonthly magazine; 100-108 pages. Estab. 1970. Circ. 10,500. Pays on publication. Buys first publication rights. Photocopied submissions OK. SASE. Reports in 4 weeks. Sample copy $1.50.
Nonfiction: Interview (known engineering and producing personalities from the recording industry); new product (as related to technological advances within the recording and concert sound industry); and technical (recording and concert sound information, both technical and semi-technical). Buys 6 mss/issue. Query. Pays $100-250.

SATELLITE COMMUNICATIONS, Cardiff Publishing Corp., 3900 S. Wadsworth Blvd., Denver CO 80235. (303)988-4670. Editor: Delbert D. Smith. Emphasizes satellite communications industry. Readership includes broadcasters, industry personnel, cable television operators, government, educators and medical personnel. Monthly magazine; 60 pages. Estab. 1977. Circ. 12,500. Pays on publication. Buys all rights. Byline given. Phone queries OK. SASE. Reports in 3 weeks. Free sample copy.
Nonfiction: Interviews (of industry figures); technical features; systems descriptions and application articles; marketing articles; descriptions of satellite experiments; demonstrations and articles on new products. Buys 5-10 mss/year. Query. Length: 750-2,500. Pays $50/published page.
Photos: Prefers b&w 5x7 glossy prints. Offers no additional payment for photos accepted with ms.

TELEPHONY MAGAZINE, 55 E. Jackson Blvd., Chicago IL 60604. Editor: Leo Anderson. 5% freelance written. For people employed by telephone operating companies. Weekly. Buys all rights. Pays on publication. SASE.
Nonfiction: Technical or management articles describing a new or better way of doing something at a telephone company. "Feature articles range from highly technical state-of-the-art presentations to down-to-earth case studies. Case-history articles should cover a new or particularly efficient way of handling a specific job at a specific telephone company." Query. Length: 1,500 words. Generally pays $30/published magazine page.

TELEVISION INTERNATIONAL MAGAZINE, Box 2430, Hollywood CA 90028. (213)876-2219. Editor: Al Preiss. For management/creative members of the TV industry. Estab. 1956. Every 2 months. Circ. 8,000 (USA); 4,000 (foreign). Rights purchased vary with author and material. Pays on publication. Will send sample copy to writer for $2. Will consider photocopied submissions. Reports in 30 days. Query. SASE.
Nonfiction and Photos: Articles on all aspects of TV programming. "This is not a house organ for the industry. We invite articles critical of TV." Pays $150-350. Column material of 600-800 words. Pays $75. Will consider suggestions for new columns and departments. Pays $25 for b&w photos purchased with mss; $35 for color transparencies.

VIDEO SYSTEMS, Box 12901, Overland Park KS 66212. (913)888-4664. Editor/Publisher: George Laughead. 80% freelance written. For qualified persons engaged in various applications of closed-circuit communications who have operating responsibilities and purchasing authority for equipment and software in the video systems field. Monthly magazine; 60 pages. Estab. November 1975. Circ. 16,000. Pays on acceptance. Buys one-time rights. Submit seasonal/holiday material 2 months in advance of issue date. Photocopied submissions OK. SASE. Reports in 2 months. Free sample copy and writer's guidelines.
Nonfiction: General interest (about professional video); how-to (use professional video equipment); historical (on professional video); new product; and technical. Buys 3 mss/issue. Submit complete ms. Length: 1,000-3,000 words. Pays $125.
Photos: State availability of photos with ms. Pay varies for 8x10 b&w glossy prints; $100 maximum for 35mm color transparencies. Model release required.

Engineering and Technology

Publications for electrical engineers are classified under Electricity; journals for electronics engineers are classified with the Electronics and Communications publications.

CANADIAN CONSULTING ENGINEER, 1450 Don Mills Rd., Don Mills, Ontario, M3B 2X7, Canada. Managing Editor: Russell B. Noble. 80% freelance written. For private engineering consultants. Buys exclusive rights preferably; occasionally exclusive to field or country. Pays on publication. Reports in 15 days. SAE and International Reply Coupons.
Nonfiction: "We serve our readers with articles on how to start, maintain, develop and expand private engineering consultancies. Emphasis is on this management aspect. We are not a how-to magazine. We don't tell our readers how to design a bridge, a high rise, a power station or a sewage plant. Paradoxically, we are interested if the bridge falls down, for engineers are vitally interested in Errors and Omissions claims (much like journalists are about libel suits). We have articles on income tax, legal problems associated with consulting engineering, public relations and interviews with political figures. When we write about subjects like pollution, we write from a conceptual point of view; e.g., how the environmental situation will affect their practices. But because our readers are also concerned citizens, we include material that might interest them from a social, or educational point of view. The word to remember is *conceptual* (new concepts or interesting variations of old ones)." Usually pays $50-175, but this depends on length and extent of research required.

DETROIT ENGINEER, 25875 Jefferson, St. Clair Shores MI 48081. Editor: Jack Grenard. "Our readers are mostly management-level engineers in automotive, construction, medical, technical and educational jobs. Our slant is to show the engineer and scientist as a world hero." Monthly magazine. Estab. 1924. Circ. 7,000. Pays on acceptance. Buys first North American serial rights. Simultaneous, photocopied and previously published submissions OK. SASE. Reports in 3 weeks. Sample copy $1.25.
Nonfiction: General interest (technical background or basis); humor (occasionally, on automotive subjects); and technical (on the *Scientific American* level). Buys 6 mss/year. Query

or submit conplete ms. Length: 1,500 words maximum. Pays $20-200.

ELECTRO-OPTICAL SYSTEMS DESIGN MAGAZINE, Room 900, 222 W. Adams St., Chicago IL 60606. (312)263-4866. Editor: Richard Cunningham. Monthly. Circ. 26,000. Buys all rights. Byline given unless anonymity requested. Pays on publication. Will send a sample copy to a writer on request. Write for copy of guidelines for writers. Will consider cassette submissions. Query. Editorial deadlines are on the 25th of the 2nd month preceding publication. SASE.

Nonfiction and Photos: Articles and photos on lasers, laser systems and optical systems aimed at electro-optical scientists and engineers. "Each article should serve a reader's need by either stimulating ideas, increasing technical competence, improving design capabilities in the following areas: natural light and radiation sources, artificial light and radiation sources, light modulators, optical components, image detectors, energy detectors, information displays, image processing, information storage and processing, system and subsystem testing, materials, support equipment, and other related areas." Rejects flighty prose, material not written for readership, and irrelevant material. Pays $30/page. Submit 8x10 b&w glossies with ms.

LIGHTING DESIGN & APPLICATION, 345 E. 47th St., New York NY 10017. (212)644-7922. Editor: Chuck Beardsley. 25% freelance written. For "lighting designers, architects, consulting engineers, and lighting engineers." Estab. 1971. Monthly. Circ. 13,500. Rights purchased vary with author and material. Pays 100% kill fee. Byline given. Buys 20 mss/year. Pays on acceptance. Query. SASE.

Nonfiction: "Lighting application, techniques, and trends in all areas, indoors and out. Our publication is the chief source of practical illumination information. Interviews with lighting designers stand a better chance of acceptance than do 'how-to' articles on plant lighting or installation stories. Folksy accounts of home relighting are not wanted." Buys informational and think articles. Length: 500-2,000 words. Pays $150.

PARKING MAGAZINE, National Parking Association, Inc., 1101 17th St. NW., Washington DC 20036. (202)296-4336. Editor-in-Chief: Norene Dann Martin. Associate Editor: Kevin Leary. 10% freelance written. "The bulk of our readers are owners/operators of commercial, off-street parking facilities in major metropolitan areas. The remainder is made up of architects, engineers, city officals, planners, retailers, contractors and service equipment suppliers." Quarterly magazine; 60 pages. Estab. 1951. Circ. 5,500. Pays on acceptance. Buys one-time rights. Phone queries OK. Submit seasonal/holiday material 3 months in advance of issue date. Simultaneous, photocopied and previously published submissions OK. Reports in 1 week. Free sample copy and writer's guidelines; mention *Writer's Market* in request.

Nonfiction: General interest (pieces on revitalization of central business districts have a high current priority); how-to (new construction, design, equipment or operational techniques); historical (could deal with some aspect of history of parking, including piece on historic garage, etc.); new product (parking-related equipment); photo feature (range of facilities in a particular city); and travel (parking in other countries). "No general, nebulous pieces or ones not dealing with most current trends in the industry." Query. Length: 1,000-5,000 words. Pays $50-150, or negotiable.

Photos: State availability of photos with query. Pays $5-15 for 8x10 b&w glossy prints and $10-25 for 2¼x2¼ or larger color transparencies. Captions preferred. Buys one-time rights. Model release required.

Columns/Departments: Open to suggestions for new columns/departments.

Farm

Today's farmer is a businessman in bib-overalls with a six-figure investment in producing foodstuffs for the country and the world. Today's farm magazines reflect this, and the successful farm freelance writer is the person who grasps this fact and turns his attention to the business end of farming. "We need management articles," says Dick Hanson, editor of *Successful Farming*. "We don't need nostalgic treatises or ax-grinding material. Our readers are interested in dollars and cents, profit and loss."

Do you need to be a farmer to write about farming? The general consensus is yes, and no, depending on just what you're writing about. For more technical articles, most editors feel that you should have a farm background (and not just summer visits to Aunt Rhodie's farm, either) or some technical farm education. But there are plenty of writing opportunities for the general freelancer, too. Easier stories to undertake for farm publications include straight reporting of agricultural events; meetings of national agricultural organizations; or coverage of agricultural legislation. Other ideas might be articles on rural living, rural health care or transportation in small towns.

Always a commandment in any kind of writing, but possibly even more so in the farm field, is the tenet *"Study Thy Market."* The following listings for farm publications are broken down into seven categories, each specializing in a different aspect of farm publishing: crops and soil management; dairy farming; general interest farming and rural life (both national and local); livestock; miscellaneous; and poultry.

The best bet for a freelancer without much farming background is probably the general interest, family-oriented magazines. These are sort of the *Saturday Evening Posts* of the farm set. The other six categories are more specialized, dealing in only one aspect of farm production. If you do choose to try a specialized magazine, heed this advice from Richard Krumme, managing editor of *Successful Farming:* "The writer must know what he's talking about. If he doesn't, it's terribly easy to look foolish in the trade [farming] business when you're dealing with readers who are specialists."

Where should a writer go for information about farming specialities? Go to a land-grant university; there's one in every state. According to Krumme, "there's a wealth of information there, from a variety of sources. He [the writer] could start with the information branch that each land-grant university has. They have literally thousands, probably millions, of publications about current agriculture. An assortment of these would give him the fastest and best background in a short period of time that he could get anywhere." Also try farming seminars or the county extension offices.

As you can see, there's no room for hayseeds in the farm writing field. But for the freelance writer who is willing to plow in and study, there's a good chance he'll find himself in the middle of a cash crop.

Crops and Soil Management

AVOCADO GROWER MAGAZINE, Rancher Publications, Box 415, Vista CA 92083. (714)758-4743. Editor: Mark Affleck. Emphasizes avocado and subtropical fruit for professionals (doctors, pilots). Monthly magazine; 64 pages. Estab. 1977. Circ. 8,000. Pays on publication. Buys all rights. Pays 50% kill fee. Byline given. Phone queries OK. Submit seasonal/holiday material at least 1 months in advance. Simultaneous, photocopied and previously published submissions OK. SASE. Reports in 2-3 weeks. Sample copy $1.50.
Nonfiction: General interest (relative to avocado industry); historical (on avocado industry); how-to (grow avocados, jojoba or kiwi—any interesting cultural aspects); humor (short pieces of agricultural nature); interview (with avocado industry leader); new product (briefs only). They are open to suggestions for photo features. Buys 2-3 mss/issue. Query with clips of published work or submit complete ms. Pays $1-2/column inch.
Photos: "If it can be said more explicitly with photos, use them to supplement the manuscript." State availability of photos. Pays $3-4.50 for 4x5 b&w prints or 4x5 or standard color prints. Captions preferred, model releases required for minors.

CROPS AND SOILS MAGAZINE, American Society of Agronomy, 677 S. Segoe Rd., Madison WI 53711. Editor: William R. Luellen. Emphasizes practical results of scientific research in agriculture, especially crop and soil science, for "the modern farmer and his advisors, i.e., innovative farmers and seedgrowers, extension personnel, private consultants, agribusiness executives and salesmen." Monthly October-March, bimonthly through summer; 32 pages. Estab. 1948. Circ. 24,000. Byline given. Pays on publication. Submit seasonal/holiday material 4 months in advance. SASE. Reports in 4-6 weeks. Free sample copy and writer's guidelines.
Nonfiction: Technical (factual information regarding any or all agricultural procedures, new and/or better ways to farm). "Most of our articles are written by the scientist who actually makes the discovery. A freelance article approved in writing by the scientist stands the best

chance of being accepted." Buys 1 ms/year. Query. Length: 500-2,000 words. Pays $15-45.
Photos: Uses b&w 8x10 glossy prints. Pays $15-35. Buys one-time rights.
Fillers: Cartoons. Buys 60-70/year. Pays $7.50/cartoon on acceptance. Reports in 1 week.

THE FLUE CURED TOBACCO FARMER, 559 Jones Franklin Rd., Suite 150, Raleigh NC 27606. Editor: Chris Bickers. For farmers who produce 5 or more acres of flue cured tobacco. Magazine; 40 pages. Estab. 1964. Published 8 times/year. Circ. 42,000. Buys all rights, but will reassign rights to author after publication. Buys 24 mss/year. Pays on acceptance. Reports in 30 days. Query. SASE.
Nonfiction and Photos: Production and industry-related articles. Emphasis is on a knowledge of the industry and the ability to write specifically for it. All material must be in-depth and be up to date on all industry activities. Informational, how-to, personal experience, interview, profile, opinion, successful business operations. Length: 500-1,500 words for features; 100 words or less for short items. Pays "competitive rates." B&w illustrations desirable with features. Color illustration purchased only occasionally.

THE PEANUT FARMER, 559 Jones Franklin Rd., Suite 150, Raleigh NC 27606. Editor: Chris Bickers. For peanut farmers with 15 or more acres of peanuts. Magazine; 32 pages. Estab. 1965. Published 8 times/year. Circ. 29,000. Buys all rights, but will reassign rights to author after publication. Pays on acceptance. Reports in 30 days. Query. SASE.
Nonfiction and Photos: Production and industry-related articles. Must be in-depth and up to date on all industry activities. Informational, how-to, personal experience, interview, profile, opinion, successful business operations. Length: 500-1,500 words for features; 100 words or less for short items. Pays "competitive rates." B&w illustrations desirable with features. Color illustration purchased only occasionally.

POTATO GROWER OF IDAHO, Harris Publishing, Inc., Box 981, Idaho Falls ID 83401. (208)522-5187. Editor/Publisher: Darryl W. Harris. 25% freelance written. Emphasizes material slanted to the potato grower and the business of farming related to this subject—packing, shipping, processing, research, etc. Monthly magazine; 32-56 pages. Estab. 1972. Circ. 17,000. Pays on publication. Buys all rights, but may reassign following publication. Byline given. Phone queries OK. Submit seasonal/holiday material 6 weeks in advance. Photocopied submissions and previously published work OK. SASE. Reports in 1 month. Free sample copy and editorial guidelines.
Nonfiction: Expose (facts, not fiction or opinion, pertaining to the subject); how-to (do the job better, cheaper, faster, etc.); informational articles; interviews ("can use one of these a month, but must come from state of Idaho since this is a regional publication, though serving the nation, tells the nation 'how Idaho grows potatoes'"); all types of new product articles pertaining to the subject; photo features (story can be mostly photos, but must have sufficient outlines to carry technical information); technical articles (all aspects of the industry of growing, storage, processing, packing and research of potatoes in general, but must relate to the Idaho potato industry). Buys 24 mss/year. Query. Length: 750 words minimum. Pays 3¢/word.
Photos: B&w glossies (any size) purchased with mss or on assignment; use of color limited. Captions required. Query if photos are not to be accompanied by ms. Pays $5 minimum; $25 for color used on cover. Model release required.
How To Break In: "Choose one vital, but small, aspect of the industry; research that subject, slant it to fit the readership and/or goals of the magazine. All articles on research must have valid source for foundation. Material must be general in nature about the subject or specific in nature about Idaho potato growers. Write a query letter, noting what you have in mind for an article; be specific."

REDWOOD RANCHER, 756 Kansas St., San Francisco CA 94107. (415)824-1563. Editor: Sally Taylor. 50% freelance written. For grape growers, and other California north coast ranchers. Magazine; 48 pages. Special issues: Vintage (September); Viticulture (February). Established in 1945. Bimonthly. Circulation: 7,000. Buys 20-35 mss/year. Byline given "at writer's request." Pays on publication. Free sample copy (to writers "in our area"). Photocopied and simultaneous submissions OK. Submit special issue material at least 2 months in advance. Reports in 2-4 weeks. Query. SASE.
Nonfiction and Photos: "All material must be locally oriented." Technical articles on viticulturists, and country people. "Down-to-earth, humorous, with technical savvy." Articles on pest control, carbonic maceration, pruning, chemical control, new equipment. Informational, personal opinion, how-to, interview, profile, exposes run from 100-3,000 words. Pays $15-300. Pays $10-150 for historical articles of 100-2,000 words. Pays $10-50 for spot

news, articles on successful business operations, new products, merchandising techniques; technical. Length: 25-200 words. 8x10 b&w glossies and color (separations preferred) purchased with mss or on assignment. Pays $7.50 for b&w; $25 for cover.

SOYBEAN DIGEST, Box 27300, St. Louis MO 63144. (314)432-1600. Editor/General Manager: Grant Mangold. 75% freelance written. Emphasizes soybean production and marketing. Monthly magazine; 40 pages. Estab. 1940. Circ. 110,000. Pays on acceptance. Buys all rights, but may reassign following publication. Byline given. Phone queries OK. Submit seasonal material 2 months in advance of issue date. Photocopied submissions OK. Reports in 3 weeks. Sample copy 50¢; mention *Writer's Market* in request.
Nonfiction: How-to (soybean production and marketing); and new product (soybean production and marketing). Buys 100 mss/year. Query or submit complete ms. Length: 1,000-2,000 words. Pays $50-225.
Photos: State availability of photos with query. Pays $5-35 for 5x7 b&w prints and $50-100 for 35mm color transparencies and up to $250 for covers. Captions preferred. Buys all rights, but may reassign following publication.

THE SUGAR BEET, The Almalgamated Sugar Co., Box 1520, Ogden UT 84402. (801)399-3431. Editor-in-Chief: Dake Hicks. "Primarily for beet growers in Idaho, Oregon and Utah. Also goes to research personnel, agricultural companies, local bankers, equipment dealers, etc., and other beet sugar companies." Quarterly magazine; 24 pages. Estab. 1937. Circ. 4,500. Pays on publication. Not copyrighted. Byline given. Phone queries OK. Submit seasonal/holiday material 3-6 months in advance. Previously published submissions OK, "if timely and appropriate." Reports in 2 weeks. Free sample copy and writer's guidelines.
Nonfiction: How-to, informational, interview, personal experience, technical. Buys 3-4 mss/year. Query. Length: 500-2,000 words. Pays $50-100.
Photos: Purchased with accompanying ms. Captions required. No additional payment for photos accepted with ms. Send 5x7 b&w glossies. Query. Model release required.

Dairy Farming

Publications for dairymen are classified here. Publications for farmers who raise animals for meat, wool, or hides are included in the Livestock category. Other magazines that buy material on dairy herds will be found in the General Interest Farming and Rural Life classification. Journals for dairy products retailers will be found under Dairy Products.

DAIRY GOAT JOURNAL, Box 1808, Scottsdale AR 85252. Editor: Kent Leach. 40% freelance written. Monthly for breeders and raisers of dairy goats. Generally buys exclusive rights. Pays on acceptance. Free sample copy. Reports in 10 days. Query. SASE.
Nonfiction and Photos: Uses articles, items, and photos that deal with dairy goats, and the people who raise them. Goat dairies and shows. How-to articles up to 1,000 words. Pays 7¢/word. Also buys 5x7 or 8x10 b&w photos for $1-15.

DAIRY HERD MANAGEMENT, Miller Publishing Co., Box 67, Minneapolis MN 55440. (612)374-5200. Editorial Director: George Ashfield. 50% freelance written. Emphasizes dairy farming. Monthly magazine; 60 pages. Estab. 1963. Circ. 55,000. Pays on acceptance. Buys all rights, but may reassign following publication. Submit seasonal/holiday material 2 months in advance. Photocopied and previously published submissions OK. SASE. Reports in 3-6 weeks. Free sample copy and writer's guidelines.
Nonfiction: How-to, informational, technical. Buys 12-15 mss/year. Query. Length: 1,000-3,000 words. Pays $75-200. "Articles should concentrate on useful management information. Be specific rather than general."

THE DAIRYMAN, Box 819, Corona CA 91720. Editor: Dolores Davis Mullings. For large herd dairy farmers. Monthly. Buys reprint rights. Pays on publication. Free sample copy. Reports in 3 weeks. SASE.
Nonfiction and Photos: Uses articles on anything related to dairy farming, preferably anything new and different or substantially unique in operation, for US subjects. Acceptance of foreign dairy farming stories based on potential interest of readers. Pays $2/printed inch. Buys photos with or without mss. Pays $10 each.

DAIRYMEN'S DIGEST (Southern Region Edition), Box 809, Arlington TX 76010. Editor: Phil Porter. For commercial dairy farmers and their families, throughout the central US, with interests in dairy production and marketing. Magazine; 32 pages. Estab. 1969. Monthly. Circ. 9,000. Not copyrighted. Byline given. Buys 34 mss/year. Pays on publication. Will send free sample copy to writer on request. Reports in 3 weeks. SASE.

Nonfiction and Photos: Emphasis on dairy production and marketing. Buys articles of general interest to farm families, especially dairy-oriented. Seeks unusual accomplishments and satisfactions resulting from determination and persistence. Must be positive and credible. Needs newsbreaks, fresh ideas, profile, personal experience articles. Buys some historical, inspirational or nostalgia. Also articles of interest to farm wives. Length: 50-1,500 words. Pay varies from $10-125, plus additional amount for photos, depending on quality.

General Interest Farming and Rural Life

The publications listed here aim at farm families or farmers in general and contain material on sophisticated agricultural and business techniques. Magazines that specialize in the raising of crops will be found in the Crops and Soil Management classification; publications exclusively for dairymen are included under Dairy Farming; publications that deal exclusively with livestock raising are classified in the Livestock category; magazines for poultry farmers are grouped under the Poultry classification. Magazines that aim at farm suppliers are grouped under Agricultural Equipment and Supplies.

AGWAY COOPERATOR, Box 1333, Syracuse NY 13201. (315)477-6488. Editor: James E. Hurley. For farmers. Monthly. Pays on acceptance. Usually reports in 1 week. SASE.
Nonfiction: Should deal with topics of farm or rural interest in the northeastern US. Length: 1,200 words maximum. Pays $75, usually including photos.
Photos: Pays $10 for photos purchased singly.

AG WORLD, 20 N. Kent St., St. Paul MN 55102. (612)225-6211. Managing Editor: Rudolf Schnasse. Emphasizes economic and social aspects of agriculture. Bimonthly; 32 pages. Estab. 1975. Circ. 5,000. Pays on publication. Buys all rights, but may reassign following publication. Phone queries OK. Simultaneous, photocopied, and previously published submissions OK. SASE. Reports in 4 weeks. Sample copy $1.
Nonfiction: Expose, informational and opinion articles; interviews and profiles. Submit complete ms. Length: 750-3,000 words.

CA HIGHLIGHTS, Communicating for Agriculture, 108 N. Mill, Fergus Falls MN 56537. (218)739-2511. Editor: Jeff Smedsrud. Emphasizes rural lifestyle for farmers and small-town agribusiness people. "Our organization seeks to promote positive aspects of rural life and recognize outstanding, innovative achievements." Monthly tabloid; 12-16 pages. Circ. 21,000. Pays on publication. Buys first rights. Byline given. Phone queries OK. Submit seasonal/holiday material 3 months in advance. Simultaneous submissions OK. SASE. Reports in 2-3 weeks. Free sample copy and writer's guidelines.
Nonfiction: Opinion related to preserving rural lifestyle, and general interest articles. Buys 8 mss/year. Query. Length: 500-4,000. Pays $15-125.

THE COUNTRY GENTLEMAN, 1100 Waterway Blvd., Indianapolis IN 46202. Editor & Associate Publisher: Bruce Kinnaird. Emphasizes country living. Quarterly magazine; 120 pages. Circ. 250,000. Pays on publication. Usually buys all rights, first rights or second serial (reprint) rights. Pays 33% kill fee. Byline given. Photocopied submissions OK. SASE. Reports in about 4 weeks. Sample copy $1.
Nonfiction: Articles and stories geared to the country life. We look for how-to's, but also publish articles on personalities, outdoor sports, travel, food and humor. Every issue contains at least one conservation-oriented article, dealing with either wildlife or natural resources. Recent articles have covered home cheese-making, outdoor photography, fly fishing, solar energy travel in Norway, and interviews with country music personalities. Length: 2,500 words maximum. Pays $75-300.
Photos: "We buy color photographs and illustrations having to do with rural life in America and abroad." Pays $25-75.
Fiction: Mainstream, mystery, adventure, western and humorous stories. Length: 2,000 words maximum. Pays $75-200.

FARM JOURNAL, Washington Square, Philadelphia PA 19105. Editor: Lane Palmer. 15% freelance written. Many separate editions for different parts of the US. Material bought for one or more editions depending upon where it fits. Buys all rights. Byline given "except when article is too short or too heavily written to justify one." Payment made on acceptance and is the same regardless of editions in which the piece is used. SASE.

Nonfiction: Timeliness and seasonableness are very important. Material must be highly practical and should be helpful to as many farmers as possible. Farmers' experiences should apply to one or more of these 8 basic commodities: corn, wheat, milo, soybeans, cotton, dairy, beef and hogs. Technical material must be accurate. Query. Pays $25 minimum.

Photos: Much in demand either separately or with short how-to material in picture stories and as illustrations for articles. Warm human interest pix for covers—activities on modern farms. For inside use, shots of homemade and handy ideas to get work done easier and faster, farm news photos, and pictures of farm people with interesting hobbies. In b&w, 8x10 glossies are preferred; color submissions should be 2¼x2¼ for the cover, and 35mm for inside use. Pays $50 and up for b&w shot; $75 and up for color.

THE FURROW, Deere & Co., John Deere Rd., Moline IL 61265. Executive Editor: Ralph E. Reynolds. 10% freelance written. For commercial farmers and ranchers. Magazine; 8 times/year; 40 pages. Estab. 1895. Circ. 1.1 million. Buys all rights, but may reassign following publication. Submit seasonal/holiday material at least 6 months in advance. SASE. Reports in 2 weeks. Free sample copy and writer's guidelines.

Nonfiction: George R. Sollenberger, North American Editor. "We want articles describing new developments in the production and marketing of crops and livestock. These could be classified as how-to, informational and technical, but all must have a news angle. All articles should include some interviews, but we rarely use straight interviews. We publish articles describing farmers' personal experiences with new practices. We occasionally use photo features related to agriculture, as well as occasional guest editorials on the Commentary page." Buys 10-15 mss/year. Submit complete ms. Length: 600-1,500 words. Pays $150-450.

Photos: Wayne Burkart, Art Editor. Original color transparencies (no copies) or color negatives of any size used only with mss. Captions required. Send negatives or transparencies with ms. No additional payment.

THE NATIONAL FUTURE FARMER, Box 15130, Alexandria VA 22309. (703)360-3600. Editor-in-Chief: Wilson W. Carnes. For members of the Future Farmers of America who are students of vocational agriculture in high school, ranging in age from 14-21; major interest in careers in agriculture/agribusiness and other youth interest subjects. Bimonthly magazine; 52 pages. Estab. 1952. Circ. 528,656. Pays on acceptance. Buys all rights, but may reassign following publication. Byline given. Submit seasonal/holiday material 3-4 months in advance. SASE. Usually reports in 2 weeks. Free sample copy and writer's guidelines.

Nonfiction: How-to for youth (outdoor-type such as camping, hunting, fishing); informational (getting money for college, farming; other help for youth). Informational, personal experience and interviews are used only if FFA members or former members are involved. Buys 2-3 mss/issue. Query or send complete ms. Length: 1,200 words maximum. Pays 2½-6¢/word.

Photos: Purchased with mss (5x7 or 8x10 b&w glossies; 35mm or larger color transparencies). Pays $5-7.50 for b&w; $25-35 for inside color; $100 for cover.

How To Break In: "Find an FFA member who has done something truly outstanding that will motivate and inspire others, or provide helpful information for a career in farming, ranching or agribusiness."

REPORT ON FARMING, Free Press, 300 Carlton St., Winnipeg, Manitoba, Canada R3C 3C1. (204)269-9331. Managing Editor: Leo Quigley. For "upper-income, progressive farmers." Monthly tabloid. Estab. 1872. Circ. 150,000. Pays on acceptance. Buys one-time rights. Phone queries OK. Submit seasonal/holiday material 8 weeks in advance. Simultaneous, photocopied and previously published submissions OK. SAE and International Reply Coupons. Reports in 4 weeks. Free sample copy.

Nonfiction: "Will look at ideas for agricultural news features. Most, however, will be done by assignments." Submit complete ms. Length: 1,500 words maximum. Pays 8¢/word.

Photos: Purchased with accompanying ms. Captions required. Pays $5-20 for b&w prints.

SUCCESSFUL FARMING, 1716 Locust St., Des Moines IA 50336. (515)284-2693. Editor: Dick Hanson. 30% freelance written. For top farmers. Estab. 1902. 13 times/year. Circ. 750,000. Buys all rights. Pays on acceptance. Reports in 4-6 weeks. Query. SASE.

Nonfiction: Semi-technical articles on the aspects of farming with emphasis on how to apply this information to one's own farm. "Most of our material is too limited and unfamiliar for freelance writers—except for the few who specialize in agriculture, have a farm background and a modern agricultural education." Length: about 1,500 words maximum. Pays "competitive rates."

Photos: Ralph Figg, Art Director, prefers 8x10 b&w glossies to contacts; color should be 2¼x2¼, 4x5 or 8x10. Buys exclusive rights and pays $20 for b&w, more for color. Assignments are given, and sometimes a guarantee, provided the editors can be sure the photography will be acceptable. Pays for meals, phone, lodging.

Local

AGROLOGIST, Agricultural Institute of Canada, 151 Slater St., Suite 907, Ottawa, Ontario, Canada K1P 5H4. Managing Editor: W.E. Henderson. For professionals in agriculture: scientists, researchers, economists, teachers, extension workers; most are members of the Agricultural Institute of Canada. Quarterly magazine; 40 pages. Estab. 1934. Circ. 6,500. Not copyrighted. Buys 1-2 mss/year. Pays on acceptance; occasionally in contributor's copies. Free sample copy. Simultaneous submissions OK, if so identified. Reports in 1-2 weeks. Query or submit complete ms. SAE and International Reply Coupons.

Nonfiction and Photos: Articles on subjects of interest to a wide range of disciplines within agriculture, such as results and applications of new research, economic implications, international agricultural trends, overviews, transportation, education, marketing, etc. Highly technical and specialized material presented as much as possible in layman's language. Main interest is not in new facts, but in the interpretation and implication of facts and situations. "We don't publish 'as is' technical papers (such as those prepared for symposia) or scientific journal material. But we will look at it. If the information is of interest, we could suggest how it might be rewritten for our use. We are particularly interested in articles that highlight how some action of agriculture is affecting nonagriculture areas; e.g., ecology topics, food crisis, etc." Length: 500-2,500 words. Most articles are not paid for; those that are average $100 for 1,500 words. No additional payment for b&w photos used with mss. Pays $5-15 for 8x10 b&w glossies purchased without mss or on assignment.

BUCKEYE FARM NEWS, Ohio Farm Bureau Federation, Box 479, Columbus OH 43216. (614)225-8906. Editor-in-Chief: S.C. Cashman. Emphasizes agricultural policy. Monthly magazine; 53 pages. Estab. 1922. Circ. 85,000. Pays on acceptance. Buys all rights, but may reassign following publication. Byline given. Phone queries OK. Submit holiday/seasonal material 3 months in advance. Simultaneous, photocopied and previously published submissions OK. SASE. Reports in 3 weeks. Free sample copy.

Nonfiction: Exposes (of government, agriculture); humor (light pieces about farm life); informational (but no nuts-and-bolts farming); inspirational ("as long as they're not too heavy"); opinion; and interview. Buys 20 mss/year. Query. Length: 500-2,000 words. Pays $25-100.

Photos: B&w and color purchased with mss or on assignment. Captions required. Send prints and transparencies. Pays $5-10 for b&w.

Poetry: Traditional forms and light verse. Buys 12/year. Limit submissions to batches of 3. Pays $10-25.

Fillers: Buys about 6 newsbreaks/year. Length: 100-250 words. Pays $10-25.

CAROLINA COOPERATOR, 125 E. Davie, Raleigh NC 27601. (919)828-4411. Editor: Robert J. Wachs. For Carolina farmers. Monthly. Buys all rights. Byline given. Not many freelance articles bought. Pays on publication. Free sample copy. Reports "as soon as possible." SASE.

Nonfiction: Interested only in material related to Carolina agriculture, rural living and farmer co-ops. Newsy features on successful or unusual farmers and their methods, with the intent to entertain or inform. Length: 1,200 words maximum. Payment is $35-50/published page.

COUNTRY WORLD, Box 1770, Tulsa OK 74102. (918)583-2161, ext. 230. Editor: Herb Karner. For a rural, urban, and suburban readership. Monthly. Buys first serial rights. Pays on publication. Query. SASE.

Nonfiction and Photos: Wants farm and ranch success stories; also suburban living, homemaking, youth, 4-H, and F.F.A. Effective photo illustrations necessary. Preferred length: 700-800 words. Pays $7.50 a column, sometimes more for exceptional copy. Photos purchased with mss and occasionally with captions only. Prefers b&w glossies, at least 5x7.

THE DAKOTA FARMER, Box 1950, Aberdeen SD 57401. (605)225-5170, ext. 30. Editor: Russ Oviatt. 10% freelance written. "We write for farm and ranch families in North and South Dakota. Special purebred beef issue in late summer; material deadline is late June. Rights purchased: flexible. Byline given. Pays on publication. Free sample copy. Submit seasonal/holiday material 3-4 months in advance. Query. SASE. Payment based on sliding scale.

Nonfiction: Production agriculture (Dakota-oriented). Crafts, kitchen ideas and recipes, how-to's, home furnishing and decoration. "We do not want poetry." Length: 750-1,000 words or more if the subject warrants. "Controversial issues are usually staff-handled, but feel free to query."

FARM & COUNTRY, Agricultural Publishing Co., Ltd., 10 St. Mary St., Toronto, Ontario, Canada M4Y 1P9. (416)924-6209. Editor-in-Chief: John Phillips. Managing Editor: Corinne Jefferey. 35% freelance written. Emphasizes farm news, business, and management. Semimonthly tabloid; 40 pages. Estab. 1936. Circ. 84,000. Pays on publication. Buys all rights, but may reassign following publication. Phone queries OK. Submit seasonal/holiday material 6 weeks in advance of issue date. Simultaneous photocopied and previously published submissions OK. SAE and International Reply Coupons. Reports in 4 weeks. Free sample copy and writer's guidelines; send request to News Editor.

Nonfiction: Exposé (government, education, corporate domination); general interest (what's new in farming); how-to (farm application); new product; photo feature; and technical. No 'folksy' material. Buys 10 mss/issue. Query with clips of published work. Length: 200-750 words. Pays $3-5/column inch.

Photos: "We use lots of pix." Pays $10-20 for 5x7 glossy b&w prints. Captions required. Buys one-time rights.

FARMFUTURES, 225 E. Michigan, Milwaukee WI 53202. (414)276-6600. Editor: Royal Fraedrich. For high-income farmers. Monthly magazine; 50-100 pages. Estab. 1973. Circ. 110,000. Buys all rights. Byline given "when it contributes to reader understanding of who is saying what and why, etc." Pays on publication. Free sample copy. Reports in 30 days. Query. SASE.

Nonfiction and Photos: "Ours is the only national farm magazine devoted exclusively to marketing and the financial management side of farming. We are looking for case histories of successful use of commodity futures markets by farm operators. Major articles deal with marketing and financial strategies of high income farmers. Major commodity interests include corn, cattle, hogs, soybeans, wheat, cotton and other grains. Market material must be current; thus, must be written within 2-3 weeks of publication." Interviews, profiles, personal experience and successful business operation articles pertaining to agricultural commodity markets. Length: 1,000-2,000 words. Pays $50-250. No additional payment for b&w photos used with mss.

FLORIDA GROWER & RANCHER, 559 Jones Franklin Rd., Suite 150, Raleigh NC 27606. Editor: Chris Bickers. For citrus grove managers and production managers; vegetable growers and managers. Monthly magazine; 24 pages. Estab. 1912. Circ. 14,100. Buys all rights, but will reassign rights to author after publication. Pays on acceptance. Reports in 30 days. Query. SASE.

Nonfiction and Photos: Articles on production and industry-related topics. In-depth and up to date. Writer must know the market and write specifically for it. Informational, how-to, personal experience, interview, profile, opinion, successful business operations. Length: 500-1,500 words for features; 100 words or less for short items. Pays "competitive rates." B&w illustrations dsirable with features. Color illustrations purchased only occasionally.

MICHIGAN FARMER, 3303 W. Saginaw St., Lansing MI 48901. (517)321-9393. Editor: Richard Lehnert. 10-20% freelance written. Semimonthly. Buys first North American rights. Byline given "except for short news items." Pays on acceptance. Reports in 1 month. Query. SASE.

Nonfiction: Uses articles of interest and value to Michigan farmers, which discuss Michigan agriculture and the people involved in it. Also articles for home section about Michigan farm housewives and what they are doing. Although articles are technical, lucid easy-to-understand writing is desired. Length depends on topic." Rates are 2¢/word minimum; special stories bring higher rates.

Photos: Buys some b&w singles; also a few color transparencies, for cover use. Pays $5-10 for each for b&w, depending on quality. Pays $60 for selected cover transparencies of identifiable Michigan farm or rural scenes.

MONTANA RURAL ELECTRIC NEWS, Montana Associated Utilities, Inc., Box 1641, Great Falls MT 59403. (406)454-1412. Managing Editor: Martin L. Erickson. Emphasizes rural life. For farmers, ranchers and rural dwellers. Monthly magazine; 32 pages. Estab. 1951. Circ.

46,000. Pays on publication. Buys one-time rights. Phone queries OK. Simultaneous photocopied, and previously published submissions OK. SASE. Reports in 3 weeks.
Nonfiction: How-to, informational, historical, humor, inspirational, nostalgic and travel articles; interviews and photo features. Query. Length: 500-2,000 words. Pays $15 minimum.
Photos: Purchased with mss or on assignment. Captions required. Query. Pays $10 minimum for 8x10 (or 5x7 minimum) b&w glossies. Model release required.

NEBRASKA FARMER, Box 81208, Lincoln NE 68501. (402)489-9331. Editor-in-Chief: Robert L. Bishop. Managing Editor: Dave Howe. 5% freelance written. For "9 out of 10 Nebraska farmers." Semimonthly magazine; 80 pages. Estab. 1859. Circ. 80,000. Pays on acceptance. Buys all rights, but may reassign following publication. Byline given. Phone queries OK. Submit seasonal/holiday material 6 months in advance of issue date. SASE. Reports in 2 weeks.
Nonfiction: How-to and new product articles of interest to Nebraska farmers. No human interest material. Buys 10-12 mss/year. Query. Length: 500-2,500 words. Pays $25-150.
Photos: State availability of photos with query. Pays $5-15 for b&w prints; $25-50 for color transparencies. Captions and model release required. Buys one-time rights.

THE OHIO FARMER, 1350 W. 5th Ave., Columbus OH 43212. (614)486-9637. Editor: Andrew Stevens. For Ohio farmers and their families. Biweekly magazine; 50 pages. Estab. 1848. Circ. 103,000. Usually buys all rights, but may reassign rights to author after publication. Buys 15-20 mss/year. Pays on publication. Sample copy $1; free writer's guidelines. Will consider photocopied submissions. Reports in 2 weeks. Submit complete ms. SASE.
Nonfiction and Photos: Technical and on-the-farm stories. Buys informational, how-to, personal experience. Length: 600-700 words. Pays $15. Photos purchased with ms with no additional payment, or without ms. Pays $5-25 for b&w; $35-100 for color. Size: 4x5 for b&w glossies; transparencies or 8x10 prints for color.

PENNSYLVANIA FARMER, Harvest Publishing, Box 3665, Harrisburg PA 17105. (717)761-6050. Editor: Robert Williams. Published for professional farmers in Pennsylvania, Maryland, New Jersey, West Virginia and Delaware. Biweekly magazine; 44 pages. Estab. 1877. Circ. 80,000. Pays on publication. Buys exclusive rights for circulation area. Phone queries OK. Submit seasonal/holiday material 2 months in advance. Simultaneous submissions and photocopied submissions OK. SASE. Reports in 1 week. Sample copy 40¢. Writer's guidelines with SASE.
Nonfiction: How-to, new product, photo feature and technical. "We require submissions to be based on farms in our circulation area and be aimed at the innovative commercial farmer." Buys 25 articles/year. Length: 1,500 maximum. Query. Pays $1/printed column inch.
Photos: State availability of photos. Pays $5 for b&w 5x7 glossy prints and $5-75 for any size color transparencies. Captions preferred. Buys one-time rights.

WALLACES FARMER, 1912 Grand Ave., Des Moines IA 50305. (515)243-6181. Editor: Monte N. Sesker. For Iowa farmers and their families. Semimonthly. Buys Midwest states rights (Nebraska, Minnesota, Wisconsin, Illinois, Missouri, South Dakota and Iowa). Pays on acceptance. Reports in 2 weeks. SASE.
Nonfiction and Photos: Occasional short feature articles about Iowa farming accompanied by photos. Length: 500-750 words. Pays about $50. Photos purchased with or without mss. Should be taken on Iowa farms. Pays $7-15 for 5x7 b&w; $50-100 for 4x5, 2¼x2¼ color transparencies. See recent issue covers for examples.

WYOMING RURAL ELECTRIC NEWS, 340 West B St., Casper WY 82601. (307)234-6152. Editor: Jim McAllister. For rural farmers and ranchers. Monthly magazine; 20 pages. Estab. 1954. Cir. 21,000. Not copyrighted. Byline given. Buys 12 mss/year. Pays on publication. Free sample copy. Will consider photocopied and simultaneous submissions. Submit seasonal material 2 months in advance. Reports "immediately." SASE.
Nonfiction, Photos and Fiction: Wants "feature material, historical pieces about the West, things of interest to Wyoming's rural people." Buys informational, humor, historical, nostalgia and photo mss. Length for nonfiction and fiction: 1,200-1,500 words. Pays $10-25. Photos purchased with accompanying ms with no additional payment, or purchased without ms. Captions required. Pays $25 for cover photos. B&w preferred. Buys experimental, western, humorous and historical fiction. Pays $25.

Livestock

Publications in this section are for farmers who raise cattle, sheep or hogs for meat, wool or hides. Publications for farmers who raise other animals are listed in the Miscellaneous category; also many magazines in the General Interest Farming and Rural Interest classification buy material on raising livestock. Magazines for dairymen are included under Dairy Farming. Publications dealing with raising horses, pets or other pleasure animals will be found under Animal in the Consumer Publications section.

AMERICAN HEREFORD JOURNAL, 715 Hereford Dr., Kansas City MO 64105. Editor: Bob Day. Monthly. Buys first North American serial rights. Pays on publication. Reports in 30 days. Query. SASE.
Nonfiction and Photos: Breeding, feeding, and marketing of purebred and commercial Herefords, with accent on well-substantiated facts; success-type story of a Hereford cattleman and how he did it. Length: 1,000-1,500 words. Pays average of 2½-3¢/word. Buys 5x7 b&w glossy photos for use with articles. Pays $3 each.

BEEF, The Webb Co., 1999 Shepard Rd., St. Paul MN 55116. (612)647-7374. Editor-in-Chief: Paul D. Andre. Managing Editor: William D. Fleming. 5% freelance written. For readers who have the same basic interest—making a living feeding cattle or running a cow herd. Monthly magazine; 40 pages minimum. Estab. 1964. Circ. 95,000. Pays on acceptance. Buys one-time rights. Byline given. Phone queries OK. Submit seasonal material 3 months in advance. SASE. Reports in 6-8 weeks. Free sample copy and writer's guidelines.
Nonfiction: How-to and informational articles on doing a better job of producing feeding cattle, market building, managing, and animal health practices. Buys 8-10 mss/year. Query. Length: 500-2,000 words. Pays $25-200.
Photos: B&w glossies (8x10) and color transparencies (35mm or 2¼x2¼) purchased with or without mss. Captions required. Query or send contact sheet or transparencies. Pays $10-50 for b&w; $25-100 for color. Model release required.
How To Break In: "Be completely knowledgeable about cattle feeding and cowherd operations. Know what makes a story. We want specifics, not a general roundup of an operation. Pick one angle and develop it fully."

THE CATTLEMAN MAGAZINE, Texas & Southwestern Cattle Raisers Association, 410 E. Weatherford, Ft. Worth TX 76102. (817)332-7155. Editor-in-Chief: Paul W. Horn. Emphasizes beef cattle production and feeding. "Readership consists of commercial cattlemen, purebred seedstock producers, cattle feeders, horsemen in the Southwest." Monthly magazine; 200 pages. Estab. 1914. Circ. 27,000. Pays on acceptance. Buys all rights but may reassign following publication. Submit seasonal/holiday material 3 months in advance. SASE. Reports in 3 weeks. Free sample copy and writer's guidelines.
Nonfiction: Need informative, entertaining feature articles on specific commercial ranch operations, cattle breeding and feeding, range and pasture management, profit tips. Will take a few historical western lore pieces. Must be well-documented. No first-person narratives or fiction. Buys 36 articles/year. Query. Length open. Pays $25-200. No articles pertaining to areas outside of Southwestern US.
Photos: Photos purchased with or without accompanying ms. Captions required. Pays $10-25 for 8x10 b&w glossies; $25-100 for color photos. Total purchase price for ms includes payment for photos. Model release required.

CATTLEMEN, The Beef Magazine, Public Press, 1760 Ellice Ave., Winnipeg, Manitoba R3H 0B6 Canada. (204)774-1861. Editor-in-Chief: Harold Dodds. 10% freelance written. For beef producers. Monthly magazine; 50 pages. Estab. 1938. Circ. 40,000. Pays on publication. Buys all rights. Phone queries OK. Submit seasonal/holiday material 3 months in advance. Reports in 2 weeks. Free sample copy and writer's guidelines.
Nonfiction: Industry articles, particularly those on raising and feeding beef in Canada. Also how-to and success stories with good management slant. Writer must be informed. Uses an occasional historical item. Pays up to $150 for industry and historical articles, more for special assignments.
Photos: Canadian shots only, purchased with mss and for cover. B&w and color for cover. Pays up to $10 for b&w; up to $75 for color.

FEEDLOT MANAGEMENT, Box 67, Minneapolis MN 55440. Editorial Director: George

Ashfield. 50% freelance written. For agribusinessmen who feed cattle and/or sheep for slaughter. Special issues include waste management (April) and feeder cattle (September). Monthly. Circ. 20,000. Not copyrighted. Pays on acceptance. Free sample copy. Reports in 1-5 weeks. Query. SASE.

Nonfiction: Wants detailed, thorough material related to cattle or lamb feeding and related subject areas—waste management, nutrition, marketing and processing, feeding, animal health. "Write for a copy of the magazine. Writers should know something about the industry in order to get the information that's important. We can accept highly technical articles, but there's no room for simple cursory articles. Feature articles on feedlots should include photos." No length restriction. Pays $30-200.

Photos and Fillers: 8x10 and 5x7 b&w glossies purchased with mss and with captions only. Pays 50¢/inch for newsbreaks and clippings.

Miscellaneous

GLEANINGS IN BEE CULTURE, 623 W. Liberty St., Medina OH 44256. Editor: Lawrence R. Goltz. For beekeepers. Monthly. Buys first North American serial rights. Pays on publication. Reports in 15-90 days. SASE.

Nonfiction and Photos: Interested in articles giving new ideas on managing bees. Also uses success stories about commercial beekeepers. Length: 3,000 words maximum. Pays $23/published page. Sharp b&w photos pertaining to honeybees purchased with mss. Can be any size, prints or enlargements, but 4x5 or larger preferred. Pays $3-5 a picture.

How To Break In: "Do an interview story on commercial beekeepers who are cooperative enough to furnish accurate, factual information on their operations."

GRAIN & FEED REVIEW, IGFA Services, Inc., 320 Shops Bldg., Des Moines IA 50309. (515)283-0431. Editor: Randy S. Allman. Emphasizes the grain and feed industry for agribusiness management, mostly 40-60 years old. Magazine published 10 times/year; 40 pages. Estab. 1939. Pays on publication. Not copyrighted. Buys one-time rights. Byline given. Phone queries OK. Submit seasonal/holiday material 2 months in advance. Simultaneous submissions OK. Reports in 2 weeks. Free sample copy and writer's guidelines.

Nonfiction: How-to (in management). Wants general interest, interview, profile and photo feature articles on agribusiness. Buys 10 mss/year. Query. Length: 200-1,000 words. Pays $40.

Photos: Interview and profile pieces stand a better chance for publication if accompanied by photos. State availability of photos. Pays $5 for b&w 8x10 glossy prints and $40 for 4x5 color transparencies; offers no additional payment for photos accepted with ms. Captions preferred.

THE SUGAR PRODUCER, Harris Publishing, Inc., 520 Park, Box 981, Idaho Falls ID 83401. (208)522-5187. Editor/Publisher: Darryl W. Harris. 25% freelance written. Emphasizes the growing, storage, use and by-products of the sugar beet. Magazine published 7 times a year; 32 pages. Estab. 1975. Circ. 21,000. Pays on publication. Buys all rights, but may reassign following publication. Byline given. Phone queries OK. Photocopied submissions and previously published work OK. SASE. Reports in 30 days. Free sample copy and writer's guidelines.

Nonfiction: "This is a trade magazine, not a farm magazine. It deals with the business of growing sugar beets, and the related industry. All articles must tell the grower how he can do his job better, or at least be of interest to him, such as historical, because he is vitally interested in the process of growing sugar beets, and the industries related to this." Expose (pertaining to the sugar industry or the beet grower); how-to (all aspects of growing, storing and marketing the sugar beet); interview; profile; personal experience; technical (material source must accompany story—research and data must be from an accepted research institution). Query or send complete ms. Length: 750-2,000 words. Pays 3¢/word.

Photos: Purchased with mss. Captions required. Pays $5 for any convenient size b&w; $10 for color print or slide; $25 for color shot used on cover. Model release required.

Poultry

The publications listed here specialize in material on poultry farming. Other publications that buy material on poultry will be found in the General Interest Farming and Rural Life classification.

CANADA POULTRYMAN, 605 Royal Avenue, New Westminster, British Columbia, Canada V3M 1J4. Editor: Fred W. Beeson. For poultry producers and those servicing this industry. Magazine; 56 pages. Estab. 1912. Monthly. Circ. 12,000. Buys all rights. Pays on publication.

Will send free sample copy to writer on request. Submit seasonal material 2 months in advance. Reports in 1 month. Submit complete ms. Enclose S.A.E. and International reply Coupons.

Nonfiction and Photos: Canadian market facts, management material, pieces on persons in the industry. Length: 200-2,000 words. Pays 4-5¢ a word. Photos (up to 5x7) purchased with mss for $3. Captions required.

INDUSTRIA AVICOLA (Poultry Industry), Watt Publishing Co., Mt. Morris IL 61054. (910)642-2891. Editor: Robert T. Tuten. 15-20% freelance written. For "poultry producers (minimum 1,000 hens and/or 20,000 broilers annually and/or 1,000 turkeys annually) who have direct affiliation with the poultry industry in Latin America." Circ. 12,000. Buys all rights. Pays on acceptance. Free sample copy. "Prefer mss written in English." Reports in 10 days. Query. SASE.

Nonfiction and Photos: Specialized publication "for poultry businessmen of Latin America. Printed only in Spanish. Emphasis is to aid in production, processing, and marketing of poultry meat and eggs. Keep readers abreast of developments in research, breeding, disease control, housing, equipment, marketing production and business management. Analytical and trend articles concerning the poultry industry in Latin countries are given preference." Length: up to 1,000-1,500 words. Pays $40-130 depending on content and quality. Photos are purchased with mss. No size requirements.

Finance

The magazines listed below deal with banking, investment, and financial management. Magazines that use similar material but have a less technical or professional slant are listed in the Consumer Publications under Business and Finance.

ABA BANKING JOURNAL (formerly *Banking, Journal of the American Bankers Association*), 350 Broadway, New York NY 10013. (212)966-7700. Editor: Harry L. Waddall. Managing Editor: William Streeter. Executive Editor: Joe W. Kizzia. 15-20% freelance written. Monthly magazine; 150 pages. Estab. July 1908. Circ. 41,000. Pays on publication. Buys all rights. Phone queries OK. Photocopied submissions OK. SASE. Reports in 4-6 weeks. Sample copy sent to writer "only if a manuscript is commissioned."

Nonfiction: How-to; new product; and articles dealing with banking. Buys 24-36 mss/year. Query. Average length: 2,000 words. Pays $100/magazine page, including headlines, photos and artwork.

Photos: State availability of photos with query. Uses 8x10 b&w glossy prints and 35mm color transparencies. Buys one-time rights.

BANK SYSTEMS & EQUIPMENT, 1515 Broadway, New York NY 10036. Editor: Joan Prevete Hyman. For bank and savings and loan association operations executives. Monthly. Circ. 22,000. Buys all rights. Byline given. Pays on publication. Query for style sheet and specific article assignment. Mss should be triple-spaced on one side of paper only with wide margin at left-hand side of the page. SASE.

Nonfiction: Third-person case history articles and interviews as well as material related to systems, operations and automation. Charts, systems diagrams, artist's renderings of new buildings, etc., may accompany ms and must be suitable for reproduction. Prefers one color only. Length: open. Pays $75 for first published page, $45 for second page, and $40 for succeeding pages.

Photos: 5x7 or 8x10 single-weight glossies. Candids of persons interviewed, views of bank, bank's data center, etc. Captions required. "We do not pay extra for photos."

BURROUGHS CLEARING HOUSE, Box 418, Detroit MI 48232. (313)972-7936. Managing Editor: Norman E. Douglas. For bank and financial officers. Monthly. Buys all publication rights. Byline given. Pays on acceptance. Free sample copy. Query on articles longer than 1,800 words. SASE.

Nonfiction: Uses reports on what banks and other financial institutions are doing; emphasize usable ideas. "We reject an article if we question its authenticity." Length: 1,000-2,000 words; also uses shorter news items. Pays 10¢/word. Additional payment of $5 for usable illustrations.

Photos: Should be 8x10 glossy b&w. Also buys pix with captions only. Pays $5.

THE CANADIAN BANKER & ICB REVIEW, The Canadian Bankers' Association, Box 282,

T-D Centre, Toronto, Ontario Canada M5K 1K2. Editor: Brian O'Brien. 90% freelance written. Emphasizes banking in Canada. Bimonthly magazine; 72 pages. Estab. 1893. Circ. 45,000. Buys first North American serial rights. Byline given. SAE and Internationhal Reply Coupons. Reports in 1 month.
Nonfiction: Informational articles on international banking and economics; interviews, nostalgic and opinion articles; book reviews. Query. Length: 750-2,000 words. Pays $100-250. "Freelancer should be an authority on the subject. Most contributors are bankers, economists and university professors."

COMMODITIES MAGAZINE, 219 Parkade, Cedar Falls IA 50613. (319)677-6341. Publisher: Merrill Oster. Editor: Darrell Jobman. For private, individual futures traders, brokers, exchange members, agribusinessmen; agricultural banks; anyone with an interest in commodities. Monthly magazine; 48-64 pages. Estab. 1971. Circ. 50,000. Buys all rights, but will reassign rights to author after publication. Byline given. Pays on publication. Free sample copy. Photocopied submissions OK. Reports in 1 month. Query or submit complete ms. SASE.
Nonfiction and Photos: Articles analyzing specific commodity futures trading strategies; fundamental and technical analysis of individual commodities and markets; interviews, book reviews, "success" stories; news items. Material on new legislation affecting commodities, trading, any new trading strategy ("results must be able to be substantiated"); personalities. No "homespun" rules for trading and simplistic approaches to the commodities market. Treatment is always in-depth and broad. Informational, how-to, interview, profile, technical. "Articles should be written for a reader who has traded commodities for one year or more; should not talk down or hypothesize. Relatively complex material is acceptable." Buys 30-40 mss/year. Length: No maximum or minimum; 2,500 words optimum. Pays 12¢/word. Pays $15-50 for glossy print b&w photos. Captions required.

COMMODITY JOURNAL, The American Association of Commodity Traders, 10 Park St., Concord NH 03301. Editor-in-Chief: Arthur N. Economou. "Mainly for members of the American Association of Commodity Traders and the general investing public, the journal serves an educational function, because of its design as a clearinghouse for exchanges of ideas and opinions." Bimonthly tabloid. Estab. 1965. Circ. 105,000. Pays on publication. Buys all rights. Simultaneous submissions OK. SASE. Reports in 1 month.
Nonfiction: "Only feature articles dealing with commodities; preferably of a technical nature. We are interested in fresh material concerning alternatives to the commodity futures industry operant in the US today. Special emphasis should be given the spot and forward selling methods and markets. Rather than assigning specific articles, we prefer to consider the ideas of interested writers." Length: 2,500 words maximum. Pays 5-10¢/word. Query.

FLORIDA BANKER, Box 6847, Orlando FL 32803. Editor: William P. Seaparke. 20% freelance written. Monthly magazine; 52 pages. Estab. September 1974. Circ. 5,300. Pays on publication. Buys all rights. Pays 50% kill fee. Byline given. SASE. Reports in 8 weeks.
Nonfiction: General interest (business-oriented); historical (on banking); how-to (anything in banking industry or trade); inspirational (occasionally, must deal with banking); interview; nostalgia; photo feature; profile; technical; and travel. Buys 2-3 mss/issue. Query. Length: 600-8,000 words. Payment varies.
Photos: State availability of photos with query. Pays $10-100 for 5x7 b&w glossy prints; $20-200 for 35mm color transparencies. Captions and model release required. Buys all rights, but may reassign following publication.
Columns/Departments: Inspiration; Interviews; and Potpourri. Query. Length: 600-2,000 words. Pays $20 minimum. Open to suggestions for new columns/departments.

MERGERS & ACQUISITIONS, 1621 Brookside Rd., McLean VA 22101. Editor: Stanley Foster Reed. For presidents and other high corporate personnel, financiers, buyers, stockbrokers, accountants and related professionals. Quarterly. Buys all rights. Byline given. Pays 21 days after publication. Will send a free sample copy to a writer on request. Query with outline. Include 50-word autobiography with mss. SASE.
Nonfiction: "Articles on merger and acquisition techniques (taxes, SEC regulations, anti-trust, etc.) or surveys and roundups emphasizing analysis and description of trends and implications thereof. Articles should contain 20-60 facts/1,000 words (names, dates, places, companies, etc.). We reject articles that are badly researched. We can fix bad writing but not bad research. Accurate research is a must and footnote references should be incorporated into text. Avoid 'Company A, Company B' terminology." Length: maximum 10,000-15,000 words. Pays $100-150/1,000 printed words for articles by professional freelance writers; 200 reprints for articles by professional business persons, such as lawyers and investment analysts.

Fishing

CANADIAN FISHERMAN AND OCEAN SCIENCE, 27 Centrale St., LaSalle, Quebec, Canada, H8R 2J1. (514)457-3250. Editor: Wayne Paterson. Byline given. Pays on publication. Free sample copy. Reports in 1 month. SAE and International Reply Coupons.
Nonfiction: Articles describing new developments in commercial fisheries and oceanography. Will also consider sketches and controversial articles about Canadian fisheries and oceanological developments. Style should be strictly factual and easy to read. Length: up to 1,000 words. Pays 5-8¢/word.
Photos: Buys photos with mss and with captions only. Pays $5 and up.

MAINE COMMERCIAL FISHERIES, Box 37, Stonington ME 04681. (207)367-5590. Managing Editor: Bill Donnell. 33% freelance written. Emphasizes commercial fisheries. Monthly newspaper; 24 pages. Estab. 1973. Circ. 3,200. Pays on publication. Byline given. SASE. Reports in 2 weeks. Sample copy $1.
Nonfiction: "Material strictly limited to coverage of commercial fishing, technical and general; occasional environment, business, etc., articles as they relate to commercial fishing." Query. Pays $50-75.

NATIONAL FISHERMAN, Diversified Communications, 21 Elm St., Camden ME 04843. (207)236-4342. Editor-in-Chief: David R. Getchell. Managing Editor: James W. Fullilove. 65% freelance written. For amateur and professional boatbuilders, commercial fishermen, armchair sailors, bureaucrats and politicians. Monthly tabloid; 120 pages. Estab. 1946. Circ. 63,000. Pays in month of acceptance. Buys one-time rights. Pays negotiable kill fee. Byline given. Phone queries OK. Submit seasonal/holiday material 3 months in advance of issue date. Photocopied submissions OK. SASE. Reports in 4 weeks. Free sample copy and writer's guidelines; mention *Writer's Market* in request.
Nonfiction: Exposé; how-to; general interest; humor; historical, inspirational; interview; new product; nostalgia, personal experience; opinion; photo feature; profile; and technical. No articles about sailboat racing, cruising and sportfishing. Buys 40/issue. Submit complete ms. Length: 100-3,500 words. Pays $10 minimum and $125-250 maximum.
Photos: State availability of photos with ms. Pays $5-15 for 5x7 or 8x10 b&w prints. Buys one-time rights.
Columns/Departments: Boatyard news (photos with captions of new boats, commercial fishboats favored); fishing highlights (short articles on catches); marine book review and seafood recipes. Buys 5/issue. Submit complete ms. Length: 50-1,000 words. Pays $10 or 2.5¢/word minimum, whichever is more. Open to suggestions for new columns/departments.

Florists, Nurserymen, and Landscaping

FLORIST, Florist's Transworld Delivery Association, 29200 Northwestern Hwy., Box 2227, Southfield MI 48037. (313)355-9300. Editor-in-Chief: William P. Golden. Managing Editor: Bill Gubbins. 5% freelance written. For retail florists, floriculture growers, wholesalers, researchers and teachers. Monthly magazine; 96 pages. Estab. 1967. Circ. 24,000. Pays on acceptance. Buys one-time rights. Pays 10-25% kill fee. Byline given "unless the story needs a substantial rewrite." Phone queries OK. Submit seasonal/holiday material 3-4 months in advance of issue date. Simultaneous, photocopied and previously published submissions OK. SASE. Reports in 1 month.
Nonfiction: How-to (more profitably run a retail flower shop, grow and maintain better-quality flowers, etc.); general interest (to floriculture and retail floristry); and technical (on flower and plant growing, breeding, etc.). Buys 10-12 mss/year. Query with clips of published work. Length: 1,200-3,000 words. Pays 6¢/word.
Photos: "We do not like to run stories without photos." State availability of photos with query. Pays $10-25 for 5x7 b&w photos or color transparencies. Buys one-time rights.

FLOWER NEWS, 549 W. Randolph St., Chicago IL 60606. (312)236-8648. Managing Editor: Jean Onerheim. For retail, wholesale florists, floral suppliers, supply jobbers, growers. Weekly newspaper; 40 pages. Estab. 1947. Circ. 13,060. Pays on acceptance. Not copyrighted. Byline given. Submit seasonal/holiday material at least 2 months in advance. Photocopied and previously published submissions OK. SASE. Reports "immediately." Free sample copy.
Nonfiction: How-to articles (increase business, set up a new shop, etc.; anything floral-related without being an individual shop story); informational (general articles of interest to industry); and technical (grower stories related to industry, but not individual grower stories). Submit

complete ms. Length: 3-5 typed pages. Pays $10.
Photos: "We do not buy individual pictures. They may be enclosed with ms at regular ms rate (b&w only)."

TELEFLORIST, 2400 Compton Blvd., Redondo Beach CA 90278. Editor: Karen Charest. Official publication of Teleflora, Inc., for retail florist subscribers to Teleflora's flowers-by-wire service. Positioned as "The Magazine of Professional Flower Shop Management." Monthly. Circ. 17,500. Buys one-time rights in floral trade magazine field. Byline given unless "article is not thorough enough but portions are included in another article." Most articles are staff-written. Pays on publication. Reports in 3 weeks. SASE.
Nonfiction and Photos: Articles dealing with buying and selling profitably, merchandising of product, management, designing, shop remodeling, display techniques, etc. Also, allied interests such as floral wholesalers, growers, tradespeople, gift markets, etc. All articles must be thoroughly researched and professionally relevant. Any florist mentioned must be a Teleflorist. Length: 1,000-3,000 words. Pays 8¢/published word. Photos purchased with mss or with captions only. 8x10 b&w glossies preferred. Captions required. Pays $7.50.

WEEDS TREES & TURF, Harvest Publishing Co., 9800 Detroit Ave., Cleveland OH 44102. Editor: Bruce Shank. For "turf managers, parks, superintendents of golf courses, airports, schools, landscape architects, landscape contractors and sod farmers." Monthly magazine; 72 pages. Estab. 1964. Circ. 45,000. Pays on publication. Buys all rights. Submit seasonal/holiday material 4 months in advance. Photocopied submissions OK. SASE. Reports in 6 weeks. Free sample copy.
Nonfiction: Publishes how-to, informational and technical articles. Buys 24 mss/year. Query or submit complete ms. Length: 750-2,000 words. Pays $50-150.

Food Products, Processing, and Service

In this list are journals for food wholesalers, processors, warehousers, caterers, institutional managers, and suppliers of grocery store equipment. Publications for grocery store operators are classified under Groceries. Journals for food vending machine operators will be found under Coin-Operated Machines.

FAST SERVICE, Harcourt Brace Jovanovich, Inc., 757 3rd Ave., New York NY 10017. (212)888-4324. Editor: David Wolk. Estab. 1940. Monthly. Circ. 50,800. Buys all rights. Pays 50% kill fee. No byline. Pays on acceptance. Reports in 2 weeks. Query. SASE.
Nonfiction and Photos: Articles on operations and case histories of all phases of fast service restaurant operations. Length: 1,500-2,000 words. Pays 10-15¢/word. B&w photos (5x7 or 8x10) purchased with mss or with captions only. Color transparencies used for cover and for feature article illustration. Fee is negotiated for all color photography. Prefers 2¼x2¼ transparencies, but will accept 35mm work if of high quality.

KITCHEN PLANNING, 757 3rd Ave., New York NY 10017. Editor: Thomas Farr. Buys all rights. Pays on acceptance. Query. SASE.
Nonfiction and Photos: How-to, in-depth articles on designing commercial and institutional kitchens—installations based on actual experience of specific operation—with quotes, facts, figures. Length: 1,000-1,500 words. Kitchen floor plans must accompany ms. B&w glossies purchased with ms. Pays 7-10¢/word. Pays $5 for each photo.

MEAT PLANT MAGAZINE, 9701 Gravois Ave., St. Louis MO 63123. (314)638-4050. Editor: Tony Nolan. For meat processors, locker plant operators, freezer provisioners, portion control packers, meat dealers, and food service (food plan) operators. Bimonthly. Pays on acceptance. Reports in 2 weeks. SASE for return of submissions.
Nonfiction, Photos, and Fillers: Buys feature-length articles and shorter subjects pertinent to the field. Length: 1,000 words for features. Pays 1½¢/word. Pays $3.50 for photos.

QUICK FROZEN FOODS, Harcourt & Brace Jovanovich, 757 3rd Ave., New York NY 10017. (212)888-3300. Editor-in-Chief: Sam Martin. Managing Editor: Richard Hodgens. 5-10% freelance written. For executives of processing plants, distributors, warehouses, transport companies, retailers and food-service operators involved in frozen foods. Monthly magazine; 100 pages. Estab. August 1938. Circ. 25,000. Pays on acceptance. Buys all rights, but may reassign following publication. Pays kill fee up to full amount if reasons for kill are not fault of author. Byline given unless it is work-for-hire or ghostwriting. Submit seasonal/holiday

material 3 months in advance of issue date. SASE. Reports in 1 week. Free sample copy; mention *Writer's Market* in request.
Nonfiction: Interview; new product; photo feature; profile; and technical. Buys 12 mss/year. Query or submit complete ms. Length: 1,500-3,000 words. Pays 3¢/word. "For special circumstances will offer flat rate for package which may be higher than word rate."
Photo: State availability of photos with query or ms. Pays $5 for 4x5 b&w smooth prints. Captions required. Buys all rights, but may reassign following publication.

SNACK FOOD, HBJ Publications, Inc., 1 E. 1st St., Duluth MN 55802. (218)727-8511. Editor-in-Chief: Jerry L. Hess. 10-15% freelance written. For manufacturers and distributors of snack foods. Monthly magazine; 60 pages. Estab. 1912. Circ. 10,000. Pays on acceptance. Buys all rights, but may reassign following publication. No byline. Phone queries OK. Photocopied submissions OK. SASE. Reports in 2-3 weeks. Free sample copy and writer's guidelines.
Nonfiction: Informational, interview, new product, nostalgia, photo feature, profile and technical articles. "We use a variety of mini news-features and personality sketches. We are looking for regional correspondents who will be able to move quickly on leads furnished as well as develop articles on their own. A directory of processors in their areas will be furnished upon making working agreement." Length: 300-600 words for mini features; 1,000-1,500 words for longer features. Pays $50-300.
Photos: Purchased with accompanying ms. Captions required. Pays $15 for 5x7 b&w photos; $15-50 for 4x5 color transparencies. Total purchase price for a ms includes payment for photos.

THE WISCONSIN RESTAURATEUR, M/S Publishing, 122 W. Washington, Madison WI 53703. (603)251-3663. Editor: Jan La Rue. Emphasizes restaurant industry for restaurateurs, hospitals, institutions, food service students, etc. Monthly magazine; 32 pages. Circ. 2,800. Pays on acceptance. Buys all rights or one-time rights. Pays 10% kill fee. Byline given. Phone queries OK. Submit seasonal/holiday material 2-3 months in advance. Previously published work OK. SASE. Reports in 2 weeks. Free sample copy and writer's guidelines.
Nonfiction: Interested in expose, general interest, historical, how-to, humor, inspirational, interview, nostalgia, opinion, profile, travel, new product, personal experience, photo feature and technical articles pertaining to restaurant industry. Buys 1 ms/issue. Query. Length: 700-1,500 words. Pays $10-20.
Photos: Fiction and how-to article mss stand a better chance for publication if photo is submitted. State availability of photos. Pays $15 for b&w 8x10 glossy prints. Model releases required, captions are not.
Columns/Departments: Spotlight column provides restaurant member profiles. Buys 6/year. Query. Length: 500-1,500 words. Pays $5-10.
Fiction: Likes experimental, historical and humorous stories related to food service only. Buys 1 ms/year. Query. Length: 1,000-3,000. Pays $10-20.
Poetry: Uses all types of poetry, but must have food service as subject. Buys 2/year. No more than 5 submissions at one time. Length: 10-50 lines. Pays $5-10.
Fillers: Uses clippings, jokes, gags, anecdotes, newsbreaks, puzzles and short humor. Buys 6/year. Length: 50-500 words. Pays $2-10.

Gas

BUTANE-PROPANE NEWS, Box 1419, Arcadia CA 91006. (213)357-2168. Editor-Publisher: William W. Clark. 15% freelance written. For LP-gas distributor dealers with bulk storage plants, LP bottled gas dealers and manufacturers of appliances and equipment. Monthly. Buys all rights. Byline given. Pays on publication. Free sample copy. Query. Reports in 1 week. SASE.
Nonfiction: Articles on advertising and promotional programs; plant design, marketing operating techniques and policies; management problems; new, unusual or large usages of LP-gas; how LP-gas marketers are coping with the energy crisis. Completeness of coverage, reporting in depth, emphasis on the why and the how are musts. "Brevity essential but particular angles should be covered pretty thoroughly." Pays $60/magazine page. "We also publish *The Weekly Propane Newsletter*, which is a market for newsclippings on propane, butane, and other energy-related matters." Will send clipping tips on request.
Photos: Purchased with mss. 8x10 desired but not required; can work from negatives. Pays $6.
Fillers: Clippings and newsbreaks pertinent to LPG industry. Clippings regarding competitive fuels (electricity, oil) with relationship that would have impact on LPG industry. Pays $6 minimum for each clipping used.

GAS DIGEST, Box 35819, Houston TX 77035. (713)723-7456. Editor: Ken Kridner. 50%

freelance written. For operating personnel of the gas industry. Monthly magazine; 50 pages. Estab. 1975. Circ. 9,000. Rights may be retained by the author. Pays on publication. Sample copy for $2; free writer's guidelines. Will consider photocopied submissions. "Submitted material must be accompanied by statement that author is associated with *Writer's Market*." Reports in 10 days. Query. SASE.

Nonfiction and Photos: Applications stories; new developments. All material must be operations oriented and meaningful to one working in the gas industry. How-to, interviews, technical articles. Length: 500-1,000 words. Pays 2½¢/word minimum. B&w photos purchased with mss or on assignment. Pays $5 minimum.

LP-GAS, 1 E. 1st St., Duluth MN 55802. Editor: Zane Chastain. For liquified petroleum gas (propane, 'bottled gas') marketers. Monthly. Buys all rights. Pays $50 kill fee. No byline. Pays on acceptance. Query. SASE.

Nonfiction: Uses dealer and LP-gas utilization articles, how-to features on selling, delivery, service, etc. Tersely written, illustrated by photo or line for documentation. Length: maximum 1,500 words. Pays 5¢/word.

Photos: Pix with mss or captions only; not less than 2¼x2¼. Pays $5-7.

SOONER LPG TIMES, 2910 N. Walnut, Suite 114-A, Oklahoma City OK 73105. (405)525-9386 Editor: John E. Orr. 33% freelance written. For "dealers and suppliers of LP-gas and their employees." Monthly. Not copyrighted. Byline given. Pays on publication. Reports in 3 weeks. SASE.

Nonfiction: "Articles relating to the LP-gas industry, safety, small business practices, and economics; anything of interest to small businessmen." Length: 1,000-2,000 words. Pays $10-15.

Government and Public Service

Below are journals for individuals who provide governmental services, either in the employ of local, state, or national governments or of franchised utilities. Included are journals for city managers, politicians, civil servants, firemen, policemen, public administrators, urban transit managers, utilities managers, etc.

Publications that emphasize the architectural and building side of city planning and development are classified in Architecture. Publications for lawyers are found in the Law category. Journals for teachers and administrators in the schools are found in Education. Publications for private citizens interested in politics, government, and public affairs are classified with the Politics and World Affairs magazines in the Consumer Publications section.

THE CRIMINOLOGIST, Box No. 18, Bognor, Regis, Sussex, UK· P022 7AA. For professionals and students interested in public affairs, criminology, forensic science, the law, penology, etc. Not on sale to the general public. Quarterly. Query. SAE and International Reply Coupons. Sample copy $3.

Nonfiction: Considers articles of very high standards, authoritatively written and factually sound, informative and sober, and not in a popular or sensational style. All material must have attached list of references or sources (title of source, author or editor, town of publication, date and, if a periodical, page number, issue number, and volume). Articles from police officials, experts, etc., are welcomed. Length: 2,000-3,000 words.

Photos: Purchased with mss. Payment negotiable.

FIRE CHIEF MAGAZINE, 625 N. Michigan Ave., Chicago IL 60611. (312)642-9862. Editor: William Randleman. 25% freelance written. For chiefs of volunteer and paid fire departments. Buys all rights. Pays on publication. Reports in 10 days. SASE.

Nonfiction: Wants articles on fire department administration, training or fire-fighting operations. Will accept case histories of major fires, extinguished by either volunteer or paid departments, detailing exactly how the fire department fought the fire and the lessons learned from the experience. "Prefer feature articles to be bylined by a fire chief or other fire service authority." Writing must be simple, clear and detailed, preferably conversational in style. Pays $1-1.50/column inch.

Photos: Used with mss or with captions only. 4x5 or larger; Polaroid or other small prints of individuals or small subjects accepted. Pays up to $35 for acceptable color photos. Pays nothing for public domain photos, up to $5 for exclusives, $1 for mug shots.

FIRE ENGINEERING, 666 5th Ave., New York NY 10019. Editor: James F. Casey. For commissioners, chiefs and senior officers of the paid, volunteer, industrial and military fire departments and brigades. Buys first serial rights. Byline given. Pays on publication. Reports in 3 weeks. SASE.
Nonfiction and Photos: Wants articles on fire suppression, fire prevention, and any other subject that relates to fire service. Length: 750-1,500 words. Pays 3¢/word minimum. Good photos with captions always in demand. Particular need for color photos for cover; small print or slide satisfactory for submission, but must always be a vertical or capable of being cropped to vertical. Transparency required if accepted. Pays $100 for color shots used on cover, $15 and up for b&w shots.

FIREHOUSE MAGAZINE, 515 Madison Ave., New York NY 10022. (212)935-4550. Editor-in-Chief: Dennis Smith. 75% freelance written. For volunteer firefighters, as well as paid firefighters and their families. Monthly magazine; 72 pages. Estab. 1976. Circ. 100,000. Pays on publication. Buys all rights, but may reassign following publication. Submit seasonal or holiday material 4 months in advance. Photocopied submissions OK. SASE. Reports in 6 weeks. Sample copy $1.50. Free writer's guidelines.
Nonfiction: How-to (firefighting); informational (family activities); historical (great fires); profiles (achieving firefighters); new product; personal experience (firefighting); photo features (recent fires); technical (fire science and medicine); and stories on recent large and unusual fires or disasters involving firefighters. Buys 120 mss/year. Query. Length: 1,000-2,000 words. Pays 10¢/word.
Photos: Purchased with or without ms, or on assignment. Captions required. Query. Pays $10-25 for 8x10 glossy prints or color transparencies.

FOREIGN SERVICE JOURNAL, 2101 E St., NW, Washington DC 20037. (202)338-4045. Editor: Shirley R. Newhall. For Foreign Service officers and others interested in foreign affairs and related subjects. Monthly. Buys first North American rights. Byline given. Pays on publication. SASE.
Nonfiction: Uses articles on "international relations, internal problems of the State Department and Foreign Service, informative material on other nations. Much of our material is contributed by those working in the fields we reach. Informed outside contributions are welcomed, however." Query. Length: 2,500-4,000 words. Pays 2-6¢/word.

GOVERNMENTAL PURCHASING, White Eagle, Inc., Box 8307, Trenton NJ 08650. (609)448-7560. Editor: Isabelle Selikoff. Emphasizes government procurement for purchasing agents and other government administrators, some attorneys and elected officials. Bimonthly magazine; 38 pages. Estab. 1978. Circ. 10,000. Pays on publication. Buys first North American serial rights. Byline given. Query. Submit seasonal/holiday material 6 months in advance. Simultaneous submissions OK. SASE.
Nonfiction: Exposé (graft on part of salespeople dealing with government, etc.); how-to (about anything a government agency might purchase); humor (as it pertains to government); interview (profiles of purchasing agents); personal experience (of a purchasing agent); technical (specification development for government purchases). "Articles must reflect sympathetic understanding of problems related to government purchasing. No derogatory articles that attack government." Also needs articles on case studies of good government purchasing programs, use of computers in government purchasing, Life Cycle Costing, energy conservation and energy management programs in use in the government. Buys 2 mss/issue. Query with clips of published work. Length: 2,400-3,600 words. Pays $100 maximum.
Columns/Departments: Kaleidoscope (humor related to purchasing); and Books (review of new books of interest to government purchasing agents). Buys 1/issue. Query. Length: 750 words maximum. Pays $50 maximum. Open to suggestions for new columns/departments.

MODERN GOVERNMENT (SERVICIOS PUBLICOS), Box 5017, Westport CT 06880. (203)226-7463. Editor: Martin Greenburgh. For government officials, private contractors and executives of public utilities and corporations in Latin America and Spain (Spanish) and Asia, Australasia, Africa, the Middle East and the Caribbean (English). 9 times/year. Circ. 50,000. Buys international rights. Pays on acceptance. Free sample copy. Query. Reports in 2 weeks. SASE.
Nonfiction and Photos: All material should interest government officials in developing nations. Strong angle on infrastructure development, public works, public transportation, public health and environmental sanitation, administrative skills, etc. Avoid strict US orientation. Publications go only overseas. Articles are bought in English and translated into Spanish. Length: 1,500-3,500 words. Pays $200; for article with photos: $250.

PASSENGER TRANSPORT, 1100 17th St. NW, Washington DC 20036. Editor: Albert Engelken. Published by the American Public Transit Association for those in urban mass transportation. Pays on publication. Very little material bought. SASE.
Nonfiction: Uses short, concise articles which can be documented on urban mass transportation. Latest news only. No airline, steamship, intercity bus or railroad news. Pays 40¢/column inch.
Photos: Sometimes buys photographs with mss and with captions only, but standards are high. 8x10's preferred. No color.

PLANNING, American Planning Association, 1313 E. 60th St., Chicago IL 60637. (312)947-2100. Editor: Sylvia Lewis. Emphasizes urban planning for adult, college-educated readers who are university faculty or students; or regional and urban planners in city, state or federal agencies or in private business. Published monthly; 48 pages. Estab. 1972. Circ. 20,000. Pays on publication. Buys all rights or second serial rights. Byline given. Phone queries OK. Submit seasonal/holiday material 2 months in advance. Photocopied and previously published submissions OK. SASE. Reports in 1 month. Free sample copy and writer's guidelines.
Nonfiction: Exposé (on government or business, but on topics related to planning, housing, land use, zoning); general interest (trend stories on cities, land use, government); historical (historic preservation); how-to (successful government or citizen efforts in planning, innovations, concepts that have been applied); interview (with well-known people in planning government); profile (only of famous or extraordinary people in our field); photo feature; technical (detailed articles on the nitty-gritty of planning, zoning, transportation but no footnotes or mathematical models). Also needs news stories up to 1,200 words. "It's best to query with a fairly detailed, one-page letter. We'll consider any article that's well-written and relevant to our audience. Articles have a better chance if they are timely and related to planning and land use, and if they appeal to a national audience. All articles should be written in magazine feature style." Buys 3 features, 2 news stories and 2 book reviews/issue. Length: 800-2,500 words. Pays $50-125.
Photos: "We prefer that authors supply their own photos, but we sometimes take our own or arrange for them in other ways." State availability of photos. Pays $15-125 for 8x10 matte or glossy prints and $125 for color covers (35mm transparencies). Captions preferred. Buys one-time rights.
Columns/Departments: Planners Library (book reviews). Books assigned by Tom Gorton. Buys 2 reviews/issue. Query. Length: 800-1,000 words. Pays $25.

POLICE PRODUCT NEWS, Dyna Graphics, Inc., 6200 Yarrow Dr., Carlsbad CA 92008. Editor: John Atkinson. For all law enforcement personnel. Monthly magazine; 72-88 pages. Estab. 1976. Circ. 50,000. Pays on publication. Buys all rights. Byline given. Submit seasonal/holiday material 2 months in advance. SASE. Reports in 2 weeks. Sample copy/$2, free writer's guidelines.
Nonfiction: Expose, historical, how-to, humor interview, profile (of police departments around the country); new product (testing/evaluation/opinion); and technical. "All material must be related to law enforcement in some way and no stories about law enforcement personnel being killed." Buys 4-5 mss/year. Send complete ms. Length: 1,000-4,000 words. Pays $75-400.
Photos: State availability of photos or send photos with ms. Pays $10-25 for b&w 8x10 glossy prints and $25-50 for 2¼x2¼ color transparencies; offers no additional payment for photos accepted with ms. Model release required.
Ficton: Wants law enforcement-related adventure, fantasy, historical, humorous (especially interested in this type), mystery, suspense and science fiction. Buys 1 ms/issue. Send complete ms. Length: 1,000-4,000. Pays $75-400.

POLICE TIMES MAGAZINE, 1100 NE 125th St., North Miami FL 33161. (305)891-1700. Editor: Donald Anderson. 90% freelance written. For "law enforcement officers: federal, state, county, local and private security." Monthly. Circ. 87,000. Buys all rights. Buys 10-20 mss/year. Pays on publication. Sample copy for 50¢ postage. Reports "at once." SASE.
Nonfiction and Photos: Interested in articles about local police departments all over the nation. In particular, short articles about what the police department is doing, any unusual arrests made, acts of valor of officers in the performance of duties, etc. Also articles on any police subject from prisons to reserve police. "We prefer newspaper style. Short and to the point. Photos and drawings are a big help." Length: 300-1,200 words. Pays $5-15—up to $25 in some cases based on 1¢/word. Uses b&w Polaroid and 8x10 b&w glossy prints, "if of particular value." Pays $5-15 for each photo used.

PUBLIC UTILITIES FORTNIGHTLY, Suite 500, 1828 L St. NW, Washington DC 20036.

Editor-in-Chief: Neil H. Duffy. For utility executives, regulatory commissions, lawyers, etc. Semimonthly. Pays on publication. "Study our publication." Reports in 3 weeks. SASE. **Nonfiction:** Length: 2,000-3,000 words. Pays $25-200.

RESERVE LAW, Box 17807, San Antonio TX 78217. Editor: Otto Vehle. 20% freelance written. Publication of Reserve Law Officers Association of America. For sheriffs, chiefs of police, other law enforcement officials and their reserve components. Estab. 1969. Bimonthly. Circ. "over 10,000." Not copyrighted. Byline given. Pays on publication. Photocopied submissions OK. SASE. Free sample copy.
Nonfiction: "Articles describing police reserve and sheriff reserve organizations and their activities should be informative and interesting. Style should be simple, straightforward, and with a touch of humor when appropriate. We need current features on outstanding contemporary lawmen, both regular officers and reserves. We are still hoping to attract freelance writers who have some law enforcement orientation as it actually is, not based upon experiences gained from watching TV. Yet, highly technical writing is not sought. Reserve Law Officers are businessmen and women who generally have incomes considerably above that of the average law officer and who find great satisfaction in donating their time to a law enforcement agency. These few hours per month they donate might possibly produce some excitement and adrenalin flow, but such occasions are rare since most police work is rather dull and monotonous. Therefore, articles submitted to us should contain some thrills, excitement, danger (much like a story submitted to a fishing magazine would place the reader in the big game fishing chair as the line spins off the reel)." Submit complete ms. Length: 500-2,000 words.
Photos: "In most cases, the manuscript should be accompanied by high-contrast 8x10 b&w action photos, properly identified and captioned." Pays $10 minimum; plus $5 for first photo and $2.50 for additional photos used in same article.
Columns/Departments: Ichthus (a chaplain's column dealing with Christian law officers—100-500 words); Law-Haw (humorous anecdotes about police work—40-60 words); Fundamentals (basic how-to's of law enforcement—100-500 words). Pays contributor's copies minimum, $50 maximum.
Fiction: "Fictionalized accounts of true police cases involving reserve officers will be accepted if they meet our needs." Length: 200-800 words. Pays $50 maximum.
Fillers: Jokes and short humor "of the law enforcement type." Length: 20-80 words. Pays $10 maximum.

ROLL CALL, 201 Massachusetts Ave. NE, Washington DC 20002. (202)546-3080. Editor: Sidney Yudain. For US Congressmen, political buffs, editors and TV commentators. Weekly newspaper. Estab. 1955. Circ. 9,000. Buys first North American serial rights. Byline given. Pays on acceptance. Photocopied and simultaneous submissions OK. Reports in 1 week. Query or submit complete ms. SASE.
Nonfiction and Photos: Profiles, humor, historical and nostalgic articles. "Political satire material must measure up to the work of the noted satirists we usually publish." Buys 10 mss/year. Length: 500-2,000 words. Pays $5-25. No additional payment for b&w photos used with articles.
Poetry and Fillers: Light verse related to subject matter. Puzzles on a Congressional or political theme and short humor on political topics are used as fillers. Pays $2 minimum.

SEARCH AND RESCUE MAGAZINE, Box 153, Montrose CA 91020. (213)248-3057. Publisher: Dennis Kelley. For volunteer and paid professionals involved in search and rescue. Estab. 1973. Quarterly. Circ. 30,000. Buys all rights, but will reassign rights to author after publication. Pays on publication. Sample copy for $3.50. Reports in 2 months. SASE.
Fiction, Nonfiction and Photos: All material must be related to search and rescue work. Particularly likes photo essays. Buys 40 mss/year. Query or submit complete ms. Pays $25-100. No additional payment for b&w photos used with mss. Captions required.

STATE LEGISLATURES, National Conference of State Legislatures, 1405 Curtis St., 23rd Floor, Denver CO 80202. (303)623-6600. Editor: Steve Millard. Associate Editor: Dan Pilcher. Emphasizes current issues facing state legislatures for legislators, legislative staff members, corporate executives, political scientists, the press, lobbyists and interested observers of state politics and government. "Readers are politically aware and involved." Magazine published 10 times/year; 32 pages. Pays on acceptance. Buys all rights. Byline given. Phone queries OK. SASE. Reports in 1 month. Free sample copy.
Nonfiction: "We're interested in original reporting on the responses of states (particularly state legislatures) to current problems, e.g., tax reform, health care, women's rights, consumer

protection, etc. We also look for articles on federal actions that affect the states. We're open to a limited number of interviews, but these are always assigned to writers who are thoroughly familiar with the magazine and its audience." Query preferred, but will consider complete ms. Pays $200-350, depending on length.

Columns/Departments: Closeup (profile of a state legislature or report on current issue within a particular state) and Taking the Floor (expression of opinion on an issue of particular interest to states). Query. Length: Closeup, 1,500-2,000 words; Taking the Floor, 1,000-1,500 words. Pays $100-200.

TODAY'S FIREMAN, Box 594, Kansas City MO 64141. (816)474-3495. Editor: Donald Mack. For persons involved in and interested in fire service. Quarterly magazine. Estab. 1960. Circ. 10,000. Pays on acceptance or publication. Sample copy for $2. Photocopied and simultaneous submissions OK. Reports in 1 month. SASE.

Nonfiction, Photos and Fillers: Approach should be expository with research. Interested in psychological and philosophical aspects of current problems. Buys informational, interview, humor, nostalgia, new product, merchandising techniques and technical articles (length: 50-1,500 words; pays $7.50-20); historical (length: 500-2,500 words; pays $10-20); expose (length: 500 words; pays $7.50-20). Buys 6 mss/year. Query. Would like to see humorous articles with photos. Occasionally buys material for 2 regional editions, covering the Eastern US and Western US. Writers may also submit suggestions for new columns or departments. Photos purchased with accompanying mss with no additional payment. Also purchased without mss. Pays $3 for b&w glossies. Captions required. Puzzles, jokes, gags, short humor. Pays $2-10.

VIRGINIA MUNICIPAL REVIEW, Review Publishing Co., Inc., 6 E. Main St., Richmond VA 23219. (804)648-1561. Executive Editor: Joseph Dawes Appleton. Publisher: Richard L. Walker. Emphasizes governmental subjects: federal, state, city, town and county. Monthly magazine; 16 pages. Estab. 1921. Circ. 2,585. Pays on publication. Buys all rights. Submit seasonal/holiday material 2 months in advance. Photocopied submissions OK. SASE. Free sample copy and writer's guidelines.

Nonfiction and Photos: Articles on governmental subjects. Well-researched, informative; current problems. Length: 1,000 words maximum. Pays 5¢/word. No additional payment made for b&w photos used with mss.

WESTERN FIRE JOURNAL, 9072 E. Artesia Blvd., Suite 7, Bellflower CA 90706. (213)866-1664. Managing Editor: David K. McKnight. 8% freelance written, "but only because we receive just 8% freelance material. The more we receive, the more we will use." For fire chiefs of paid and volunteer departments in metropolitan and small communities located in the 11 Western states. Also read by other fire department officers and personnel. Monthly magazine; 56 pages. Estab. 1956. Circ. 4,600. Pays on publication. Buys one-time rights. Offers negotiable kill fee to writers "we know." Byline given, "even in some cases where a writer, unfamiliar with the fire service, comes up with a dynamite idea but only compiles the information for us and does not write the actual article." Phone queries OK. Simultaneous and photocopied submissions OK. SASE. Reports in 2 weeks. Sample copy $1; free writer's guidelines; mention *Writer's Market* in request.

Nonfiction: How-to (develop or build a new piece of fire protection equipment or facility); interview (leaders recognized in fire protection with something constructive to say); and technical (new ideas in fire protection techniques, training and prevention). Topics must concern *Western* fire service activities. No articles on a fire fighter's day. Buys 20 mss/year. Query. Pays $1.50-1.75/inch.

Photos: State availability of photos with query. Pays $4-10 for 8x10 b&w dull prints or $10-25 for 35mm color transparencies. Captions preferred. Buys one-time rights.

Groceries

The journals that follow are for owners and operators of retail food stores. Journals for food wholesalers, packers, warehousers and caterers are classified with the Food Products, Processing and Service journals. Publications for food vending machine operators are found in the Coin-Operated Machines category.

A.G. NEWS AND A.G. NEWSLETTER, 5151 Bannock St., Denver CO 80217. (303)534-1155. Editor-in-Chief: Colleen M. Kirk. 5% freelance written. Emphasizes grocery and food distribution for a readership interested in both wholesale retail operations and development.

Monthly tabloid: 12 pages. Estab. 1949. Circ. 3,000. Byline given. Pays on publication. Phone queries OK. Submit seasonal/holiday material 2 months in advance of issue date. Simultaneous, photocopied and previously published submissions OK. SASE. Free sample copy and writer's guidelines; mention *Writer's Market* in request.

Nonfiction: General interest (trends in the grocery industry, outlook for future of independent grocer); how-to (grocery market operations, personnel, security, management, energy conservation and equipment use); new product (effect on market success in other parts of the country). Buys 2-3 mss/year. Query. Length: 500-2,000 words. Pays $100.

Photos: State availability of photos with query. Pays $25 for 5x7 b&w contact sheet and glossy prints. Captions required.

Columns/Departments: Energy conservation; legislation/consumer news; meat/produce/general merchandise; retail service management; and security. Buys 1-2 mss/year. Query with clips of published work. Length: 100-500 words. Pays $50 minimum.

Fillers: Jokes gags, anecdotes, newsbreaks and short humor. Length: 25-100 words. Pays $25 minimum.

FOODSMAN, 1001 E. Main St., Richmond VA 23219. (804)644-0731. Editor: Brian F. Daly. 10% freelance written. For food retailers, wholesalers, distributors. Monthly magazine; 22-34 pages. Estab. 1939. Circ. 7,000. Not copyrighted. Pays 20% kill fee. Byline given. Pays on publication. Will send free sample copy to writer on request. Query. "Queries handled immediately." SASE.

Nonfiction and Photos: "Consumer articles; anything of interest to food people. From attitude surveys, operational studies, general interest articles or photo layouts on store design. Emphasis is on Virginia and helpful ideas to be implemented by either food retailers, wholesalers or distributors." Informational, interviews with government officials, profiles, think pieces, training reviews, spot news, successful business operations, new product, merchandising techniques. Length: open. Pays 5¢/word.

IGA GROCERGRAM, 5725 E. River Rd., Chicago IL 60631. (312)693-4520. Editor-in-Chief: Marianne Beaudoin. Associate Editor: Pam Cheuvront. 5% freelance written. For "largely independent supermarket owners, managers and department heads, *not* concentrated in metropolitan areas." Monthly magazine; 36 pages. Estab. 1926. Circ. 10,000. Pays on acceptance. Buys all rights. Phone queries OK. Submit seasonal/holiday material 4 months in advance of issue date. SASE. Reports in 2 months. Sample copy $1.

Nonfiction: General interest (about supermarket industry/operations); how-to; interview; and photo feature (operations, displays, unusual sales, IGA stores only). Buys 5 mss/year. Query. Length: "As long as is necessary to tell the story." Pays $50 minimum.

Photos: "We seldom publish a manuscript without photos." State availability of photos with query. Payment for photos is included in ms price. Uses 5x7 glossy b&w prints or color transparencies. Captions preferred. Buys all rights.

PENNSYLVANIA GROCER, 3701 N. Broad St., Philadelphia PA 19140. (215)228-0808. Editor: John McNelis. For grocers, their families and employees, store managers; food people in general. Monthly magazine; 16 pages. Estab. 1913. Circ. 3,500. Byline given. Pays on publication. Sample copy 75¢. Reports in 30 days. SASE.

Nonfiction and Photos: Articles on food subjects in retail food outlets; mainly local, in Pennsylvania and surrounding areas. Informational, interviews, profiles, historical, successful business operations, new product, merchandising technique and technical articles. Buys 10-15 mss/year. Query or submit complete ms. Length: 500-900 words. Pays $25. Pays $25 maximum for minimum of 2 b&w photos purchased with ms.

PROGRESSIVE GROCER, 708 3rd Ave., New York NY 10017. (212)490-1000. Editor: Edgar B. Walzer. For supermarket operators, managers, buyers; executives in the grocery business. Monthly magazine; 150 pages. Estab. 1922. Circ. 90,000. May buy all rights, but will reassign rights to author after publication; first North American serial rights; first serial rights; second serial (reprint) rights; or simultaneous rights. Pays on acceptance. Photocopied and simultaneous submissions OK. Submit seasonal merchandising material (spring, summer, fall, holiday) 3 months in advance. Reports in 2-3 weeks. SASE.

Nonfiction and Photos: Department Editor: Mary Ann Linsen. Articles on supermarket merchandising; success stories; consumer relations pieces; promotional campaigns; personal pieces about people in the business. How grocers manage to relate and communicate with consumers via smart programs that really work. Tight, direct, informal, colorful writing needed. Does not want to see anything about quaint little "mom and pop" stores or "run of mill" stores with nothing more than half-hearted gourmet sections. Buys 20 mss/year. Query.

Length: open. Pays 5¢/word minimum. Pays $15 minimum for b&w glossies; $25 for color. Captions required.

TELEFOOD MAGAZINE, Davies Publishing Co., 136 Shore Dr., Hinsdale IL 60521. (312)325-2930. Contact: National sales manager. Emphasizes only specialty and gourmet foods for retailers, gourmet shops and delicatessens, manufacturers/distributors, food brokers, media and advertisers. Monthly magazine; 70-80 pages. Estab. 1935. Circ. 12,000. Pays on publication. Buys all rights, but may reassign following publication. Byline given. Phone queries OK. Submit seasonal or holiday material 2-3 months in advance. Photocopied submissions and previously published work OK. SASE. Reports in 1-3 weeks. Free sample copy and writer's guidelines.
Nonfiction: "Our needs are for articles on issue themes as determined by demands of readership; for interviews and coverage of gourmet and specialty food shops, business, manufacturers, distributors, large delicatessen operations including those within major supermarket chains or department stores. Prefer contributions from various geographical areas particularly the West and Southwest." Can be in the form of informational articles or interviews. Buys 1-2/issue. Length: 500-2,000 words. Query. "We must approve subject covered." Pays $50 minimum.
Photos: B&w glossies must accompany articles; 5x7 or 8x10. Captions required. Query and send contact sheet. Additional payment.

Grooming Products and Services

HAIRSTYLIST, Allied Publications, Inc., Box 9820, Fort Lauderdale FL 33307. Associate Editor: B. P. Robinson. Buys North American serial rights only. Byline given. Pays on acceptance. Query not necessary. Reports in 2-4 weeks. SASE.
Nonfiction and Photos: Wants "articles of general interest to the professional beautician." Interested in how-to's, interviews and profiles. Length: 500-1,000 words. Payment is 5¢/word. Pays $5 for b&w glossy photos of hairstyles.
Fillers: Cartoons. Pays $5.

PROFESSIONAL MEN'S HAIRSTYLIST, 100 Park Ave., New York NY 10017. Editor: Jody Byrne d'Honau. For "men and women serving the men's hairstyling and barbering profession." Monthly. Circ. 65,000. Rights purchased vary with author and material. Pays on publication. Free sample copy and writer's guidelines. Submit seasonal/holiday material 2 months in advance of issue date. SASE.
Nonfiction and Photos: "Matter only related to the hairstyling profession. Material should be technical—written from the viewpoint of professionals. Currently overworked are articles on female barbers or hairstylists and unisex salons. We're interested in articles on new trends in men's hairstyling." Buys informational articles, how-to's, interviews, coverage of successful business operations, salon management, articles on merchandising techniques, and technical articles. Buys 10-12 mss/year. Query. Length: 750-2,500 words. Pays $25-50. 8x10 b&w glossies purchased with mss and on assignment. Pays $25.

WOMAN BEAUTIFUL, Allied Publications, Inc., Box 9820, Fort Worth TX 76107. Associate Editor: Barbara Robinson. For "students at beauty schools and people who go to beauty salons." Buys North American serial rights. Pays on acceptance. Reports in 4 weeks. SASE.
Nonfiction and Photos: "Articles on hairstyling, beauty, and fashion." Length: 500-1,000 words. Pays 5¢/accepted word. Pays $5 for cartoons.

Hardware

In this classification are journals for general hardware wholesalers and retailers, locksmiths, and retailers of miscellaneous special hardware items. Journals specializing in the retailing of hardware for a certain trade, such as plumbing or automotive supplies, are classified with the other publications for that trade.

DOORS AND HARDWARE, 1815 N. Fort Myer Dr., Suite 412, Arlington VA 22209. (703)527-2060. Executive Editor: Richard M. Hornaday. CAE. Managing Editor: Patricia Duricka. All freelance written. "Readership includes manufacturers, distributors, and special consultants in the wholesale builders hardware trade, plus architects and related engineers/designers in the industry." Monthly magazine; 48 pages. Estab. 1936. Circ 9,000. Pays on publication. Buys all rights, but may reassign following publication. Byline given on request. Phone queries OK. Submit seasonal/holiday material 3 months in advance of issue date. Photocopied and previously published (if in another field) submissions OK. SASE. Reports in 8 weeks. Free sample copy and writer's guidelines; mention *Writer's Market* in request.

Nonfiction: General interest; historical; how-to (management techniques); interview; new product; photo feature; profile and technical. Buys 3-5 mss/year. Query. Length: 4,000-12,000 words. Pays $25 minimum.

Photos: "We try to be highly graphically oriented, and believe illustrations, if well done and appropriate, add to the magazine as well as to the article itself." State availability of photos with query. Pays $5 for b&w photos; "negotiable" payment for color. Captions and model release required. Buys all rights, but may reassign following publication.

How To Break In: "Despite the technical nature of the industry, we welcome queries. We shall be pleased to direct writers to responsible individuals in their geographic region who can give them a good idea of the concerns and background of this type of material."

HARDWARE AGE, Chilton Co., Chilton Way, Radnor PA 19089. (215)687-8200. Editor-in-Chief: Jon Kinslow. Editor: Jay Holtzman. 5% freelance written. Emphasizes retailing, distribution and merchandising of hardware and building materials. Monthly magazine; 180 pages. Estab. 1855. Circ. 56,000. Buys first North American serial rights. No byline. Submit seasonal/holiday material 3 months in advance of issue date. Simultaneous, photocopied and previously published submissions OK, if exclusive in the field. SASE. Reports in 1-2 months. Free sample copy and writer's guidelines; mention *Writer's Market* in request.

Nonfiction: Wendy Kaplan, managing editor. How-to (more profitably run a hardware store or a department within a store. "We particularly want stories on local hardware stores and home improvement centers, with photos. Stories should concentrate on one particular aspect of how the retailer in question has been successful); and technical (possibly will accept stories on retail accounting or inventory management by qualified writers). Buys 1-2 mss/issue. Submit complete ms. Length: 500-2,000 words. Pays $25-75.

Photos: "We like store features with b&w or color photos. Usually use b&w for small freelance features." Send photos with ms. Pays $10 for 4x5 glossy b&w prints; $15 for color contact sheets or transparencies. Captions preferred. Buys one-time rights.

Columns/Departments: Focus on Law and Money Savers. Query or submit complete ms. Length: 1,000-1,250 words. Pays $35. Open to suggestions for new columns/departments.

Fillers: "Would like a *good* hard crossword puzzle related to hardware." Pays $25-50.

HARDWARE MERCHANDISING, MacLean-Hunter Co., Ltd., 481 University Ave., Toronto, Ontario, Canada M5W 1A7. (416)596-5797. Editor-in-Chief: William Kennedy. 25% freelance written. For hardware retailers, followed by home center and building supply operators in Canada. Magazine published 10 issues/year; hardware show guide rates as 11th issue; averages 35 pages. Estab. 1889. Circ. 10,500. Pays on publication. Buys all rights. Phone queries OK. SASE. Reports in 1 month. Free sample copy and writer's guidelines; mention *Writer's Market* in request.

Nonfiction: How-to; interview; new product; market reports; photo feature (stores); and profile (retailers). Buys 12 mss/year. Query. Pays $100/magazine page.

Photos: State availability of photos with query. Pays $10 for b&w contact sheets. Captions required. Buys all rights. Byline given. Model release required.

NORTHERN HARDWARE TRADE, 5901 Brooklyn Blvd., Suite 112, Minneapolis MN 55429. (612)533-0066. Editor: Edward Gonzales. 1% freelance written. For "owners, managers of hardware and discount stores and lumber yards and home centers; hardware, sporting good, wholesalers." Estab. 1890. Monthly. Circ. 16,500. Not copyrighted. Pays on publication. Submit seasonal material 3 months in advance of issue date. SASE.

Nonfiction and Photos: "Case histories on successful retail stores." Buys how-to's and articles on successful business operations. Query or submit complete ms. Pays 4¢/word. B&w photos purchased with mss. Pays $5.

Home Furnishings and Appliances

APPLIANCE SERVICE NEWS, 110 W. Saint Charles Rd., Lombard IL 60148. Editor: William Wingstedt. For professional service people whose main interest is repairing major and portable household appliances. Their jobs consists of either service shop owner, service manager or service technician. Monthly "newspaper style" publication; 24 pages. Estab. 1950.

Circ. 41,000. Buys all rights. Byline given. Buys about 2 mss/issue. Pays on publication. Sample copy 75¢; free writer's guidelines. Will consider simultaneous submissions. Reports in about 1 month. SASE.

Nonfiction and Photos: James Hodl, associate editor. "Our main interest is in technical articles about appliances and their repair. We also consider articles on the business of running a successful service agency. Material should be written in a straightforward, easy-to-understand style. It should be crisp and interesting, with a high informational content. Our main interest is in the major and portable appliance repair field. We are not interested in retail sales." Query. Length: open. Pays 5-7¢/word. Pays $10 for b&w photos used with ms. Captions required.

BEDDER NEWS, The International Newspaper for the Waterbed Industry, 1102 Main St., Lewiston ID 83501. (208)746-9888. Publisher: Kenny Wayne. 15% freelance written. Emphasizes the waterbed industry for waterbed retailers, distributors, and manufacturers, including furniture stores and decorators. Monthly tabloid; 24 pages. Pays on publication. Buys all rights, but may reassign following publication. Byline given "except for stock or standard articles." Phone queries OK. Submit seasonal or holiday material 3 months in advance. SASE. Reports in 4 weeks. Sample copy $1.

Nonfiction: Medical stories related to waterbeds, interviews with people in the waterbed industry, material on old types or use of waterbeds, new product, photo feature and technical. Buys about 25 mss/year. Length: 500-1,500 words. Submit complete ms.

Photos: B&w glossies (5x7) purchased with ms or on assignment. Captions required. Send prints.

Fillers: Clippings, jokes, cartoons and anecdotes related to waterbeds. Pays $1-5.

CHINA GLASS & TABLEWARE, Ebel-Doctorow Publications, Inc., Box 2147, Clifton NJ 07015. (201)779-1600. Editor-in-Chief: Susan Grisham. 30% freelance written. Monthly magazine; 40 pages. Pays on publication. Buys all rights. Byline given. Phone queries OK. Submit seasonal/holiday material 3 months in advance of issue date. SASE. Reports in 2-3 weeks. Free sample copy and writer's guidelines; mention *Writer's Market* in request.

Nonfiction: Technical (on the business aspects of retailing china, glassware and flatware). No articles on how-to or gift shops. Buys 2-3 mss/issue. Query. Length: 1,000-3,000 words. Pays $40-50/page.

Photos: State availability of photos with query. No additional payment for b&w contact sheets or color contact sheets. Captions required. Buys one-time rights.

Fillers: Clippings. Buys 2/issue. Pays $3-5.

COMPETITIVEDGE, 405 Merchandise Mart, Chicago IL 60654. (312)527-3070. Editor: Peggy Heaton. For top management of stores specializing in all home furnishings products. Monthly magazine; 80-100 pages. Estab. 1923. Circ. 15,000. Buys all rights. Buys 2-3 mss/year. Pays on publication. Free sample copy. Reports "immediately." Query. SASE.

Nonfiction and Photos: Articles on managing, merchandising, operating the home furnishings store in all facets from advertising to warehousing. Concise and very factual reporting of new developments or activities within the retail store with explanation of why and how something was accomplished, and results or benefits. "We largely present 'success' stories that give ideas the reader might want to adapt to his own inidividual operation." Interested in material on special services to consumers, internal cost-cutting measures, traffic-building efforts; how the small store competes with the giants; unusual display techniques or interesting store architecture. No straight publicity or "puff" articles about store owners or their operations, with no news value or interest to others on a national basis, or articles that are too general with no specific point. Length: 800-2,000 words. Pays 4½¢/word. 5x7 b&w glossy photos are purchased with or without mss, or on assignment. Pays $5.

FLOORING MAGAZINE, 757 3rd Ave., New York NY 10017. Editor: Michael Korsonsky. 10% freelance written. For floor covering retailers, wholesalers, floor covering specifiers, architects, etc. Monthly. Circulation: 20,000. Buys all rights. No byline. Buys 10-12 mss/year. Pays on acceptance. Free sample copy. Query. Reports in 2-4 weeks. SASE.

Nonfiction and Photos: "Merchandising articles, new industry developments, unusual installations of floor coverings, etc. Conversational approach; snappy, interesting leads; plenty of quotes." Informational, how-to, interview, successful business operations, merchandising techniques, technical. Length: 1,500-1,800 words. Pays 10¢/word. 5x7 or 8x10 b&w photos. Pays $5. Color transparencies (when specified). Pays $10. Captions required.

FURNITURE & FURNISHINGS, 380 Wellington St. W., Toronto, Ontario, Canada M5V 1E3. Editor: Henry Wittenberg. For an audience that includes all associated with making and selling furniture, floorcoverings and fabrics, as well as suppliers in the trade; lamps and accessories manufacturers and dealers; decorators and designers; domestic and contract readers (not consumers). Monthly magazine; 40-150 pages. Estab. 1910. Circ. 11,500. Buys first Canadian serial rights. Buys 20 mss/year. Pays on publication. Free sample copy. Will not consider photocopied submissions if they have been made to other Canadian media. Submit special material for Market Previews and Product Reports 1 month in advance. Reports in 1 month. Query. SAE and International Reply Coupons.

Nonfiction and Photos: "The magazine is not news-oriented. Rather, it is more feature-oriented, covering various subjects in depth. Very much a merchandising magazine for home furnishings retailers in Canada. We publish merchandising and retailer success stories; product trends; management articles; promotion/advertising programs. Styles, designs, color trends. Emphasis is on how-to—what retailers can learn from what others are doing. Writing is tight, semi-aggressive, and interesting. We'd like to see feature reports analyzing the retail situation in various cities and towns in Canada; who are the top retailers in each center and why; or personality profiles of people in this industry. We do not want US or foreign-oriented articles unless they report on trends in styles, designs, colors and materials used in furniture, floorcoverings, fabrics appearing in major trade shows in the US and Europe with photos showing examples of these trends. Must be aimed at Canadian readers." Length: 500-2,000 words. Pays $100 or more, "depending on length and use of real examples." Pays $10 for b&w photos purchased with mss. Captions required.

GIFTS + TABLEWARE, 1515 Broadway, New York NY 10036. (212)764-7317. Editor: Christiane Michaels. For "merchants (department store buyers, specialty shop owners) engaged in the resale of giftwares, china and glass, decorative accessories." Monthly. Circ. 36,000. Buys all rights. Byline given "be request only." Pays on acceptance. Will send a sample copy to a writer on request. Query or submit complete ms. Will consider photocopied submissions. SASE.

Nonfiction: "Retail store success stories. Describe a single merchandising gimmick. We are a magazine format—glossy stock. Descriptions of store interiors are less important than a sales performance unless display is outstanding. We're interested in articles on aggressive selling tactics. We cannot use material written for the consumer." Buys coverage of successful business operations and merchandising techniques. Length: 750 words maximum.

Photos: Purchased with and without mss and on assignment; captions required. "Individuals are to be identified."

GIFTS & DECORATIVE ACCESSORIES, 51 Madison Ave., New York NY 10010. (212)689-4411. Editor-in-Chief: Phyllis Sweed. Managing Editor: Douglas Gilbert-Neiss. 10% freelance written. Published primarily for quality gift retailers. Monthly magazine; 250 pages. Estab. 1907. Circ. 32,000. Pays on publication. No byline. Buys all rights. Submit seasonal/holiday material 6 months in advance of issue date. Photocopied submissions OK. SASE. Reports "as soon as possible." Free writer's guidelines.

Nonfiction: "Merchandising how-to stories of quality stores—how they have solved a particular merchandising problem, or successfully displayed or promoted a particularly difficult area." Nothing about discount stores or mass merchants. Buys 12 mss/year. Query or submit complete ms. Length: 500-1,500 words. Pays $25-100.

Photos: "Photos should illustrate merchandising points made in a story." Pays $5-7.50 for 5x7 glossy b&w prints; $7.50-15 for 4x5 color transparencies or color slides. Captions required. Buys all rights, but may reassign following publication.

HOME LIGHTING & ACCESSORIES, Box 2147, Clifton NJ 07015. (201)779-1600. Editor-in-Chief: Herb Ballinger. 35% freelance written. For lighting stores/departments. Monthly magazine; 80 pages. Estab. 1923. Circ. 7,000. Pays on publication. Buys all rights, but may reassign following publication. Phone queries OK. Submit seasonal/holiday material 6 months in advance of issue date. SASE. Free sample copy.

Nonfiction: How-to (run your lighting store/department, including all retail topics); interview (with lighting retailers); personal experience (as a businessperson involved with lighting); opinion (about business approaches and marketing); profile (of a successful lighting retailer/lamp buyer); and technical (concerning lighting or lighting design). Buys 30 mss/year. Query. Pays $50/page.

Photos: State availability of photos with query. Offers no additional payment for 5x7 or 8x10 b&w glossy prints. Pays additional $75 for 35mm color transparencies used on cover. Captions required. Buys all rights, but may reassign following publication.

LINENS, DOMESTICS AND BATH PRODUCTS, 370 Lexington Ave., New York NY

10017. (212)532-9290. Editor: Alyson Fendel. For department stores, mass merchandisers, specialty stores and bath boutiques. Published 6 times/year. Buys all rights. Pays on publication. Reports in 4-6 weeks. SASE.
Nonfiction and Photos: Merchandising articles that educate the buyer on sales and fashion trends, promotions, industry news, styles; in-depth articles with photos on retail stores/departments for bath accessories, linens and sheets, tablecloths, napkins and place mats, towels, and comforters. Especially focusing on interesting promotions and creative displays within these departments. Length: 700-1,500 words. Pays 10¢/word. Photos purchased with mss. For b&w glossies, pays $6.

MART MAGAZINE, Berkshire Common, Pittsfield MA 01201. (413)499-2550. Editor-in-Chief: Cathy Ciccolella. Managing Editor: Ken Lilienthal. 20% freelance written. For retailers (independent dealers, buyers for department and discount stores, etc.) of major appliances, consumer electronics and electric housewares. Monthly magazine; 75 pages. Estab. 1953. Circ. 45,000. Pays on acceptance. Buys all rights, but may reassign following publication. Byline given. SASE. Reports in 2 weeks. Free sample copy and writer's guidelines.
Nonfiction: "We are edited for all retailers of these products: independent appliance-TV dealers, department stores, audio specialists, discount chains, catalog showrooms, drug chains, hardware stores and buying offices. We want articles about stores large and small, well-known or unknown. The question we ask about every articles is: 'How does this help the guy in the store?' One natural story is how a dealer solved some problem. The problem could be almost anything: financial management, direct mail, radio or TV advertising, salesmanship, etc. We want stories about manufacturers as long as they are directed to retailers." Buys 3-5 mss/issue. Query. Length: 200-2,500 words. Pays $35-500.
Photos: "We do not run any stories that are all text." Pays $15 minimum for b&w contact sheets or negatives; $50 minimum for 2¼x2¼ color transparencies. Captions required. Buys all rights, but may reassign following publication.

RETAILER AND MARKETING NEWS, Box 57194, Dallas TX 75207. (214)528-5910. Editor: Michael J. Anderson. For "retail dealers and wholesalers in appliances, television and furniture." Monthly. Circ. 10,000. Free sample copy. Photocopied submissions OK. SASE.
Nonfiction: "How a retail dealer can make more profit" is the approach. Wants "sales promotion ideas, advertising, sales tips, business builders and the like, localized to the Southwest and particularly to north Texas." Submit complete ms. Length: 100-900 words. Pays $30-50.

Hospitals, Nursing and Nursing Homes

In this section are journals for nurses; medical and nonmedical nursing home, clinical and hospital staffs; and laboratory technicians and managers. Journals for physicians in private practice or that publish technical material on new discoveries in medicine will be found in the Medical category.

HOSPITAL FORUM, Association of Western Hospitals, 830 Market St., San Francisco CA 94102. (415)421-8720. Editor: James Keough. Emphasizes hospital administration. Magazine published 7 times/year; 32-56 pages. Estab. 1959. Circ. 10,000. Buys full rights. Byline given. Phone queries OK. SASE. Reports in 2 months. Free guidelines for writers.
Nonfiction: Publishes informational and how-to articles on hospitals. Length: 2,000-3,000 words. Pays $75-2,000. Query.

HOSPITAL PROGRESS, The Catholic Hospital Association, 1438 S. Grand Blvd., St. Louis MO 63104. (314)773-0646. Editor: Robert S. Stephens. For hospital and nursing home administrators, trustees and department heads. Monthly magazine; 100 pages. Estab. 1920. Circ. 15,000. Buys all rights. Byline given. Phone queries OK. SASE. Photocopied submissions OK. SASE. Reports in 3 months. Free guidelines for writers.
Nonfiction: Publishes how-to, and informational articles and interviews with government and hospital leaders. Must be in-depth (not superficial) reports of hospital administration. Buys 5 mss a year. Length: 1,000-2,000 words. Query. Pays $1/column inch.

HOSPITAL SUPERVISOR'S BULLETIN, Bureau of Business Practice, 24 Rope Ferry Rd., Waterford CT 06386. Editor: Gara Eastman. For hospital supervisors. Semimonthly newsletter; 8 pages. Estab. 1968. Circ. 8,000. Pays on acceptance. Buys all rights. No byline. Submit seasonal/holiday material 6 months in advance. Photocopied submissions OK. SASE.

Reports in 4 weeks. Free sample copy and writer's guidelines.
Nonfiction: Publishes interviews with hospital department heads. "You should ask supervisors to pinpoint current problems in supervision, tell how they are trying to solve these problems and what results they're getting—backed up by real examples from daily life." Also publishes articles on people problems and good methods of management. People problems include the areas of training, planning, evaluating, counseling, discipline, motivation, supervising the undereducated, getting along with the medical staff, etc., with emphasis on good methods of management. "We prefer 4- to 6-page typewritten articles, based on interviews." Pays 10¢/word after editing.

JOURNAL OF PRACTICAL NURSING, 122 E. 42nd St., New York NY 10017. (212)682-3400. Editorial Director: Freda Baron Friedman. Editor: Eve Hammerschmidt. 75% freelance written. For practical vocational nurses, practical nurse educators, registered nurses, hospital and nursing home administrators, and other allied health professionals. Monthly magazine; 42-48 pages. Estab. 1950. Circ. 40,000. Pays on publication. Buys all rights, but may reassign following publication. Submit seasonal/holiday material 3 months in advance of issue date. Reports in 4-6 weeks. Free sample copy and writer's guidelines; mention *Writer's Market* in request.
Nonfiction: General interest (to LPNs); historical (relating to nursing, medicine); how-to (care for patients and their needs); humor (if relevant); inspirational (if relevant); interview (with relevant people); personal experience (of LPN in health situations); opinion (on issues of relevance to LPNs); photo feature (of innovative practical nursing programs); profile (of interest and newsworthy); and technical. Buys 36 mss/year. Query. Length: 700-2,100 words. Pays $10-100.
Photos: State availability of photos with query. No additional payment for photos purchased with accompanying ms. Buys b&w contact sheets or glossy prints. Captions preferred. Buys one-time rights. Model release required.
Columns/Departments: Books. Query. Length: 400-1,000 words. Open to suggestions for new columns/departments.
Fillers: Crossword puzzles and short humor. Buys 8/year. Pays $5-15.

NURSING JOB NEWS, Prime National Publishing Corp., 470 Boston Post Rd., Weston MA 02193. Editor: Ira Alterman. Emphasizes nursing employment for a readership of generally younger nurses interested in new job opportunities, travel and new nursing opportunities. "We are quite eager to receive manuscripts from good writers all over the country who can deal with the helpful aspects of nursing all over the country. We serve the interests of nurses and nursing students, some of whom have never made a move." Monthly tabloid newspaper; 24-72 pages. Estab. 1975. Circ. 40,000. Pays on publication. Buys all rights. Byline given. Submit seasonal/holiday material 1-3 months in advance. Previously published work OK. SASE. Reports in 4-6 weeks. Sample copy $1.
Nonfiction: General interest; how-to; interview (with nurses, students); opinion; profile; travel; personal experience; photo feature; and employment. Buys 1-5 mss/issue. Send complete ms. Length: 500-1,500 words. Pays $25 minimum.
Photos: Pays $5-15 each b&w 5x7 or 8x10 glossy print. Captions and model releases required.
Columns/Departments: Open to suggestions for new columns or departments.

PROFESSIONAL MEDICAL ASSISTANT, 1 E. Wacker Dr., Chicago IL 60601. Editor: Susan S. Croy. "About 95% of our subscribers belong to the American Association of Medical Assistants. They are professional people employed by a doctor of medicine." Estab. 1957. Bimonthly. Circ. 21,000. Rights purchased vary with author and material. Byline given. Pays on publication. Free sample copy. Photocopied submissions OK. Reports in 1 month. SASE.
Nonfiction and Photos: "Articles dealing with clinical and administrative procedures in a physician's office. Request our publication to study for the style we require." Buys informational articles and how-to's. Buys 2 mss/year. Submit complete ms. Length: 500-2,500 words. Pays $15-50.
Fillers: Crosswords for allied health personnel, find the word, or "word-search" puzzles. Pays $8.50.

RN, 680 Kinderkamack Rd., Oradell NJ 07649. (201)262-3030. Editor: David W. Sifton. For registered nurses, mostly hospital-based but also in physicians' offices, public health, schools, industry. Monthly magazine; 120 pages. Estab. 1937. Circ. 275,000. Buys all rights. Pays 25% kill fee. Byline given. Pays on publication. Free sample copy and writer's guidelines. Reports in 6-8 weeks. SASE.
Nonfiction: "If you are a nurse who writes, we would like to see your work. Editorial content:

diseases, clinical techniques, surgery, therapy, research equipment, drugs, etc. These should be thoroughly researched and sources cited. Personal anecdotes, experiences, observations based on your relations with doctors, hospitals, patients and nursing colleagues. Our style is simple, direct, not preachy. Do include examples, case histories that relate the reader to her own nursing experience. Talk mostly about people, rather than things. Dashes of humor or insight are always welcome. Include photos where feasible." Buys 20-30 mss/year. Query or submit complete ms. Length: 8-10 double-spaced, typewritten pages. Payment varies.

Hotels, Motels, Clubs, Resorts, Restaurants

Journals that emphasize retailing for bar and beverage operators are classified in the Beverages and Bottling category. For publications slanted to food wholesalers, processors, and caterers, see Food Products, Processing and Service.

BARTENDER, Bartender Publishing Corp., Box 493, Springfield NJ 07018. (201)379-3112. Editor: Raymond P. Foley. Managing Editor: Michael Cammarano. Emphasizes liquor and bartending for bartenders, tavern owners and owners of restaurants with liquor licenses. Monthly magazine; 50 pages. Estab. June 1979. Circ. 10,000. Pays on publication. Buys all rights. Pays 33⅓% kill fee. Byline given. Phone queries OK. Submit seasonal/holiday material 3 months in advance. Simultaneous, photocopied, and previously published submissions OK. SASE. Reports in 1 month. Free sample copy.
Nonfiction: General interest, historical, how-to, humor, interview (with famous ex-bartenders); new product, nostalgia, personal experience, opinion, photo feature, profile, travel and bar sports. Send complete ms. Length: 500-1,000 words.
Photos: Send photos with ms. Pays $7.50-50 for 8x10 b&w glossy prints; $10-75 for 8x10 color glossy prints. Caption preferred and model release required.
Columns/Departments: Bar of the Month, Bartender of the Month, Drink of the Month, Bar Sports, Quiz, Wine Cellers of the Month, One For The Road (travel); Photo Essays and Legal Bar. Buys 9/issue. Query. Length: 200-1,000 words. Pays $50-500.
Fiction: Adventure, experimental, fantasy, historical, humorous, mystery, science fiction, suspence and condensed novels. Buys 1 ms/issue. Send complete ms. Length: 1,000-3,000 words. Pays $200-500.
Fillers: Clippings, cartoons, jokes, gags, anecdotes, short humor, newsbreaks and anything relating to bartending. Length: 25-100 words. Pays $5-50.

THE CANADIAN INN BUSINESS (formerly *Resort & Motel Magazine*), Page Publications, Ltd., 380 Wellington St. W., Toronto, Ontario, Canada M5V 1E3. (416)366-4608. Publisher: Gwen P. Dempsey. For resort owners and managers; hotels, motels, etc. Bimonthly tabloid; 16-32 pages. Estab. 1962. Circ. 10,700. Buys one-time rights. Pays on publication. Free sample copy. Reports in 6 weeks. SAE and International Reply Coupons.
Nonfiction: Informational, technical and how-to articles. Canadian content required. Interviews; articles on travel, successful business operations, new products and merchandising techniques. Length: open. Pays 5¢/word.

EXECUTIVE HOUSEKEEPER, North American Publishing Co., 401 N. Broad St., Philadelphia PA 19108. (215)574-9600. Editor: Kay Blumenthal. 80% freelance written. Emphasizes institutional (hospital, hotel, school) housekeeping management. "Most readers have received certification in their field and/or recieved training through continuing education courses. Interested in how to manage their departments effectively." Monthly magazine; 56 pages. Circ. 9,000. Pays on publication. Buys all rights. Byline given. Submit seasonal/holiday material 2 months in advance of issue date. SASE. Reports in 2 months. Free sample copy and writer's guidelines; mention *Writer's Market* in request.
Nonfiction: General interest (mostly management-related topics about running the housekeeping department, improving communication with employees and administration, training, etc.); how-to (maintenance in institutional housekeeping departments); humor (humorous treatments of experiences relating to the executive housekeeper's job—anecdotal); interview; personal experience; opinion (on topics such as contract cleaning); profile (of executive housekeepers); and technical (proper use of chemical supplies and equipment, infection control, carpet maintenance). Buys 3 mss/issue. Submit complete ms. Length: 1,000-2,000 words. Pays $75-125.

INNKEEPING WORLD, Motel Services, Inc., Box 1123, Gainesville FL 32602. Editor/Publisher: C.W. Nolte. 50% freelance written. Emphasizes the lodging industry and travel. Bimonthly newsletter; 8 pages. Estab. 1975. Circ. 2,000. Pays on acceptance. Buys one-time rights. No byline. Submit seasonal/holiday material 1 month in advance of issue date. Simultaneous and previously published submissions OK. SASE. Reports in 4 weeks. Free sample copy.

Nonfiction: How-to (increase business, cut expenses, treat guests and anything that would help hotel/motel managers); and travel (statistics). Buys 2 mss/issue. Query. Length: 100-500 words. Pays 10¢/word.

Columns/Departments: Advertising/Promotion; Cutting expenses; Increasing business; Energy; Labor incentives/relations; and news, trends and ideas (for fillers). Buys 2/issue. Length: 50-500 words. Pays 10¢/word.

KANSAS RESTAURANT MAGAZINE, 359 S. Hydraulic St., Wichita KS 67211. (316)267-8383. Editor: Neal D. Whitaker. For food service operators. Special issues: Christmas, October Convention, Who's Who in Kansas Food Service, Beef Month, Dairy Month, Wheat Month. Monthly. Circ. 1,400. Not copyrighted. Pays on publication. Sample copy 50¢. Reports "immediately." SASE.

Nonfiction and Photos: Articles on food and food service. Length: 1,000 words maximum. Pays $10. Photos purchased with ms.

LODGING AND FOOD SERVICE NEWS, 131 Clarendon St., Boston MA 02116. Managing Editor: Mrs. Susan G. Holaday. For managers and executives of hotels, motels, restaurants, fast food operations, contract feeders, country clubs, etc. Estab. 1925. Every 2 weeks. Circ. 8,000. Not copyrighted. Byline rarely given. Pays on publication. Will send sample copy to writer on request. Submit seasonal material 6 months in advance. Reports in 1 month. Query. SASE.

Nonfiction and Photos: News relating to hotels, restaurants, etc. Travel and tourism trends. Features on unusual operations. Stories on new chains and expansions. Must have hard-breaking news orientation. Stories on food service promotions for the holidays and summer merchandising news. Length: 16-80 double-spaced lines. Pays $25 minimum. Pays $5 for 8x10 b&w glossies used with mss.

MANAGING THE LEISURE FACILITY, Billboard Publications, Inc., Box 24970, Nashville TN 37202. (615)741-8100. Editor: Tom Powell. Emphasizes operational aspects of amusement/recreation facilities for management and department heads. Bimonthly magazine; 36 pages. Estab. 1977. Circ. 17,000. Pays upon determination of payment based on typeset galleys. Buys all rights, but may reassign following publication. Phone queries OK. Simultaneous, photocopied and previously published submissions OK. SASE. Reports in 2 weeks. Free sample copy and writer's guidelines.

Nonfiction: How-to; informational; photo feature; and technical. "The writing style is straightforward, based on plain language and logical grammatical construction. Unjustified contractions and breeziness are contrary to our dignified approach. The same inhibition would apply to superlatives and hyperbole." Buys 6 mss/issue. Query or submit complete ms, "but query is a time-saver for original work." Length: 250-2,500 words. Pays $20-250.

Photos: State availability of photos with query. Pays $3-5 for 5x7 or 8x10 b&w glossy prints or color transparencies.

MOTOR INN JOURNAL, Box 769, Temple TX 76501. (817)778-5115. Editor: Walter T. Proctor. For owners and managers of motels, motor inns and resorts in the US. Monthly magazine; 42-100 pages. Estab. 1937. Circ. 29,000. Buys all rights. Buys 15 mss/year. Byline given. Pays on acceptance. Free sample copy and writer's guidelines. Simultaneous submissions OK. Submit seasonal (holiday) material 2 months in advance. Reports in 10 days. Query. SASE.

Nonfiction and Photos: Factual articles designed to help owners/managers to be more effective, and to become more profitable operators of such properties. How-to articles on profitable holiday promotions. "We stress less emphasis on big hotels; more on medium-sized to large motels and motor inns and resorts. We don't want general articles on community relations, or how to be a better manager, etc." Length: "4-6 pages, double-spaced." Pays $10/double-spaced, typed page. B&w photos (5x7 or 8x10) and top-quality color transparencies purchased with mss. Pays $5 for b&w; $10 for color.

NATION'S RESTAURANT NEWS, 425 Park Ave., New York NY 10022. Editor: Charles Bernstein. "National business newspaper for food service chains and independents." Biweekly newspaper. Circ. 52,000. Pays on acceptance.

Nonfiction: "News and newsfeatures, in-depth analyses of specific new types of restaurants,

mergers and acquisitions, new appointments, commodity reports, personalities. Problem: Most business press stories are mere rehashes of consumer pieces. We must have business insight. Sometimes a freelancer can provide us with enough peripheral material that we'll buy the idea, then assign it to staff writers for further digging." Length: 500 words maximum. Pays $5-75. **Photos:** B&w glossies purchased with mss and captions only. Pays $10 minimum.
How To Break In: "Send most wanted material, such as personality profiles, business-oriented restaurant news articles, but no how-to stories."

RESORT MANAGEMENT, Box 4169, Memphis TN 38104. (901)276-5424. Editor: Allen J. Fagans. 40% freelance written. For "the owners and/or managing executives of America's largest luxury vacation resorts." Monthly. Buys first rights only. Byline sometimes given. Pays on publication. Sample copy for SASE. Query. "Editorial deadline is the 1st of the previous month; e.g., January material must be received by December 1." Reports in 10 days. SASE.
Nonfiction and Photos: "This is not a travel or tourist publication. It is a 'how-to-do-it' or 'how-it-was-done' business journal. Descriptive background of any sort used to illustrate the subject matter must be held to a minimum. Our material helps managers attract, house, feed and provide entertainment for guests and their friends, and bring them back again and again. Any facet of the resort operation could be of interest: guest activities, remodeling, advertising and promotion, maintenance, food, landscaping, kitchen, personnel, furnishings, etc. We do not want to see material related to any facet of commercial hotels, motels, motor courts, fishing and hunting camps, housekeeping or other facilities serving transients. Material submitted must be accurate, to the point, and supported by facts and costs, plus pertinent examples illustrating the subject discussed." Length: 800-1,000 words. Pays 60¢/inch for a 20-em column; 40¢/inch for a 13-em column. "Photos of the resort and of its manager, and the subject(s) being discussed are a must." Pays $5/photo.
Fillers: Uses clippings related to resorts and resort area organizations only. Promotions: president, general manager, resident manager (including changes from one resort to another). Resort Obituaries: president, owner, general manager. Resort Construction: changes, additions, new facilities, etc. New Resorts: planned or under construction. Changes in resort ownership. Resort News: factual news concerning specific resorts, resort areas, state tourism development. No clippings about city hotels, roadside motels, motor inns or chain (franchise) operations. Clippings must be pasted on individual sheets of paper, and addressed to Clipping Editor. Your complete mailing address (typed or printed) must be included, as well as the name of the newspaper or magazine and date of issue. Do not send advertisements or pictures. Clippings will not be returned unless a self-addressed envelope and sufficient postage is enclosed. Pays $1/clipping.

Industrial Management

The journals that follow are for industrial plant managers, executives, distributors, and buyers; some industrial management journals are also listed under the names of specific industries, such as Machinery and Metal Trade. Publications for industrial supervisors are listed in Management and Supervision.

COMPRESSED AIR, 253 E. Washington Ave., Washington NJ 07882. Managing Editor: S.M. Parkhill. 5% freelance written. Emphasizes "the application of pneumatics for middle and upper management personnel in all industries." Monthly magazine; 48 pages. Estab. 1896. Circ. 150,000. Pays on publication. Buys all rights. Submit seasonal/holiday material 6 months in advance of issue date. SASE. Reports in 4-6 weeks. Free sample copy and writer's guidelines; mention *Writer's Market* in request.
Nonfiction: "Articles must be reviewed by experts in the field." How-to (save costs with air power); and historical (engineering). Buys 5 mss/year. Query. Pays $60/published page.
Photos: State availability of photos in query. Payment for 8x10 glossy b&w photos is included in total purchase price. Captions required. Buys all rights.

ENERGY NEWS, Energy Publications—division of Harcourt Brace Jovanovich, Box 1589, Dallas TX 75221. (214)748-4403. Managing Editor: Gregory Martin. 5% freelance written. Emphasizes natural gas production, transmission, distribution, regulation and projects for executives or managers of energy, supply and financial companies or the government; particularly utilities. Biweekly newsletter; 4 pages. Estab. 1970. Circ. 500. Pays on publication. Buys all rights. Phone queries OK. Simultaneous and photocopied submissions OK. SASE. Reports in 4 weeks. Free sample copy and writer's guidelines.
Nonfiction: Interviews with energy industry or government leaders keyed to recent news and

technical articles on natural gas projects, trends, prices or new technologies. "Can't use anything not related to natural gas or utilities." Buys 1-2 mss/issue. Length: 250 words maximum. Pays 15¢/word.

ENERGY WEEK, Energy Publications—division of Harcourt Brace Jovanovich, Box 1589, Dallas TX 75221. (214)748-4403. Managing Editor: Gregory Martin. 5% freelance written. Emphasizes energy production, transmission, regulation, prices, etc., for executives or management of energy supply or financial companies or the government. Biweekly newsletter; 4 pages. Estab. 1973. Circ. 500. Pays on publication. Buys all rights. Phone queries OK. Simultaneous and photocopied submissions OK. SASE. Reports in 4 weeks. Free sample copy and writer's guidelines.
Nonfiction: Interview (with energy industry trend-setters, should be keyed to recent news); and technical (new energy technologies, feasibility, costs, or technical features). "No stories dealing with the surface rather than the inner core of energy developments. Our readers are aware of news related to energy; they want to know *why* and how *they* are affected." Buys 1-2 mss/issue. Submit complete ms. Length: 250 words maximum. Pays 15¢/word.

HANDLING AND SHIPPING MANAGEMENT, 1111 Chester Ave., Cleveland OH 44114. (216)696-7000. Editor: H.G. Becker Jr. 10-20% freelance written. For operating executives with physical distribution responsibilities in transportation, material handling, warehousing, packaging, and shipping. Monthly. Buys all rights. Byline given unless article requires substantial editing or previous arrangements made. Pays on publication. "Query with 50-word description of proposed article." SASE.
Nonfiction and Photos: Material on aspects of physical distribution management, with economic emphasis. Informational and successful business operations material. Writer must know the field and the publications in it. Not for amateurs and generalists. Length: 1,500-3,000 words. Pays $30/published page minimum. Additional payment is made for b&w photos used with mss, but they must be sharp, for good reproduction. No prints from copy negatives. Any size. Color used may be prints or transparencies.

INDUSTRIAL DISTRIBUTION, 2 Park Ave., New York NY 10016. (212)573-8100. Editor: George J. Berkwitt. Monthly. Buys all rights. Byline given if author is an expert in his field. Will consider cassette submissions. SASE.
Nonfiction: "Articles aimed at making industrial distributor management, sales and other personnel aware of trends, developments and problems and solutions in their segment of industry. Articles accepted range widely; may cover legislation, sales training, administration, Washington, marketing techniques, case histories, profiles on industry leaders, abstracted speeches—any area that is timely and pertinent and provides readers with interesting informative data. Use either roundups or bylined pieces." Length: 900 words minimum. Pays "flat fee based on value; usually $100/published page."

INDUSTRIAL DISTRIBUTOR NEWS, 1 West Olney Ave., Philadelphia PA 19120. Managing Editor: Jerry Steinbrink. For industrial distributors, industrial equipment wholesalers, business managers and industrial salesmen. Estab. 1959. Monthly. Circ. 32,000. Free sample copy. Reports on material within 6 weeks. "Freelancers would do well to query before testing the waters of distribution without guidance." SASE. Byline given.
Nonfiction and Photos: "Feature material must be tailored to industrial marketing and demonstrate an understanding of the problems of distribution. Case studies or interviews should cite specifics, quote liberally and be written for an audience of top managers." Length: 1,000-3,000 words. B&w 8x10 only.

INDUSTRY WEEK, Penton/IPC, Inc., 1111 Chester Ave., Cleveland OH 44114, (216)696-7000. Editor-in-Chief: Stanley Modic. 5-10% freelance written. Emphasizes manufacturing and related industries for top or middle management (administrating, production, engineering, finance, purchasing or marketing) throughout industry. Biweekly magazine; 120 pages. Estab. 1882. Circ. 260,000. Pays on publication. Buys all rights. Byline given depending on length of article. Phone queries OK. Submit seasonal or holiday material 3 months in advance. Simultaneous and photocopied submissions OK. Previously published work OK. SASE. Reports in 4 weeks. Sample copy $2.
Nonfiction: How-to and informational articles (should deal with areas of interest to manager audience, e.g., developing managerial skills or managing effectively). Length: 1,000-4,000 words. Buys 15-20/year. Query. Pays $60/published page. No product news or clippings.
Photos: Jacqueline Kuhn, art director. B&w and color purchased with ms or on assignment. Query. Pays $35 minimum. Model release required.

THE PHILADELPHIA PURCHASOR, 1518 Walnut St., Suite 610, Philadelphia PA 19102. Editor-in-Chief: Howard B. Armstrong Jr. 35% freelance written. For buyers of industrial supplies and equipment, including the materials of manufacture, as well as the maintenance, repair and operating items; and for buyers of office equipment and supplies for banks and other industries. Monthly magazine; 65 pages. Estab. 1926. Circ. 4,000. Not copyrighted. Pays on acceptance. Free sample copy and writer's guidelines. Photocopied and simultaneous submissions OK. Reports in 1 month. SASE.
Nonfiction and Photos: "We use articles on industrial, service and institutional purchasing—*not* consumer. We also use business articles of the kind that would interest purchasing personnel. Ours is a regional magazine covering the middle Atlantic area, and if material takes this into account, it is more effective." Buys 25-35 mss/year. Query or submit complete ms. Length: 900-1,200 words. Pays minimum of $15. No additional payment for b&w photos used with mss.

PLANT MANAGEMENT & ENGINEERING, MacLean Hunter, 481 University Ave., Toronto, Ontario, Canada M5W 1A7. Editor: William Roebuck. 20% freelance written. For Canadian plant managers and engineers. Monthly magazine; 70 pages. Estab. 1940. Circ. 21,000. Pays on acceptance. Buys first Canadian rights. Phone queries OK. SAE and International Reply Coupons. Reports in 2-3 weeks. Free sample copy.
Nonfiction: How-to, technical and management technique articles. Must have Canadian slant. Query. Pays 10¢/word minimum.
Photos: State availability of photos with query. Pays $25-50 for b&w prints; $50-100 for 2¼x2¼ color transparencies. Captions preferred. Buys one-time rights.

PRODUCTION ENGINEERING, Penton Plaza, Cleveland OH 44114. (216)696-7000. Editor-in-Chief: Larry Boulden. Executive Editor: John McRainey. 20% freelance written. For "men and women in production engineering—the engineers who plan, design and improve manufacturing operations." Monthly magazine; 100 pages. Estab. 1954. Circ. 95,000. Pays on publication. Buys all rights, but may reassign following publication. Byline given "unless, by prior arrangement, an author contributed a segment of a broader article, he might not be bylined." Phone queries OK. Photocopied submissions OK, if exclusive. SASE. Reports in 2 weeks. Free sample copy and writer's guidelines.
Nonfiction: How-to (engineering, data for engineers); personal experience (from *very* senior production or manufacturing engineers only); and technical (technical news or how-to). "We're interested in solid, hard-hitting technical articles on the gut issues of manufacturing. Not case histories, but no-fat treatments of manufacturing concepts, innovative manufacturing methods, and state-of-the-art procedures. Our readers also enjoy articles that detail a variety of practical solutions to some specific, everyday manufacturing headache." Buys 2 mss/issue. Query. Length: 800-3,000 words. Pays $25-150.
Photos: "Sell me the manuscript, then we'll talk about photos."

PURCHASING, 221 Columbus Ave., Boston MA 02116. Editorial Director: Robert Haavind. For purchasing specialists, primarily in manufacturing industries. Semimonthly. Circ. 87,000. Buys all rights. Buys 20 mss/year. Pays on publication. Free sample copy. Submit seasonal material 3 months in advance. Reports in 10 days. Query. SASE.
Nonfiction: Some news items (on price shifts, purchasing problems, etc.) from stringers. Features on better purchasing methods (with real examples), on evaluating or specifying. Items must be generalized and objective. Back up topics with good data, examples, charts, etc. No product pitches. Particularly interested in contract writing, negotiating techniques. Informational, how-to and spot news. Length: 500-1,500 words. Pays $50-250.

PURCHASING EXECUTIVE'S BULLETIN, Bureau of Business Practice, 24 Rope Ferry Rd., Waterford CT 06386. (203)442-4365. Editor: Claire Sherman. Managing Editor: Wayne Muller. For purchasing managers and purchasing agents. Semimonthly newsletter; 4 pages. Estab. 1969. Circ. 5,500. Pays on acceptance. Buys all rights. Submit seasonal/holiday material 3 months in advance. Reports in 2 weeks. Free sample copy and writer's guidelines.
Nonfiction: How-to (better cope with problems confronting purchasing executives) and direct interviews detailing how purchasing has overcome problems and found better ways of handling departments. No derogatory material about a company; no writer's opinions. Buys 2-3 mss/issue. Query. Length: 750-1,000 words.

THE WASHINGTON PURCHASER, Box 9038, Seattle WA 98109. Associate Editor: Christine Laing. 10% freelance written. For readers who are responsible for purchasing for commercial, government and industrial firms. Monthly magazine; 40-84 pages. Estab. 1925. Circ. 2,500. Buys first North American serial rights. Pays on publication. Will send sample copy to writer on request. Reports in 1-4 weeks. Query. SASE.

Nonfiction: Articles on techniques for buying, from office supplies to heavy industrial materials and general business and economic trends. "Use of freelance material is limited and writers must follow typical rules of style, remembering that readers want concise material that must benefit them in their jobs as buyers of various commodities." Informational, how-to, interview, new product, merchandising techniques, technical articles. Pays $10-25.

Insurance

BUSINESS INSURANCE, 740 N. Rush Street, Chicago IL 60611. Editor: Susan Alt. For "corporate risk managers, insurance brokers and agents, insurance company executives. Interested in insurance, safety, security, consumerism, employee benefits." Special issues on safety, pensions, health and life benefits, international insurance. Biweekly during 1979; weekly, beginning 1980. Circ. 36,000. Buys all rights. Pays negotiable kill fee. Byline given. Buys 75-100 mss/year. Pays on publication. Submit seasonal or special material 2 months in advance. Reports in 2 weeks. Query. SASE.

Nonfiction: "We publish material on corporate insurance and employee benefit programs and related subjects. We take everything from the buyers' point of view, rather than that of the insurance company, broker or consultant who is selling something. Items on insurance companies, insurance brokers, property/liability insurance, union contract (benefit) settlements, group life/health/medical plans, of interest—provided the *commercial* insurance or benefits angle is clear. Special emphasis on corporate risk management and employee benefits administration requires that freelancers discuss with us their proposed articles. Length is subject to discussion with contributor." Pays $5/column inch or negotiated fee.

EQUIFAX NEWS, Box 4081, Atlanta GA 30302. (404)885-8000. Editor: H.A. McQuade. For "management employees of most American corporations, especially insurance companies. This includes Canada and Mexico. Pass-along readership involves submanagement and nonmanagement people in these firms. Distributed by Equifax, Inc." Quarterly. Circ. 89,000. Copyrighted; "we allow customer publications free reprint privileges. Author free to negotiate fee independently, however." Buys 3-5 mss/year. Byline given. Pays on acceptance. Will send a sample copy to a writer on request. Query: "present idea in paragraph outline form. Accepted queries should result in authors' submitting double-spaced copy, typed 35 characters to the line, 25 lines to the page." Reports in 2-3 weeks. SASE.

Nonfiction and Photos: "Insurance-related articles—new trends, challenges and problems facing underwriters, actuaries, claim men, executives and agents; articles of general interest in a wide range of subjects—the quality of life, ecology, drug and alcohol-related subjects, safe driving, law enforcement, and insurance-related Americana; inspirational articles to help managers and executives do their jobs better. Write with our audience in mind. Only articles of the highest quality will be considered. Especially interested in material written by insurance underwriters, executives, college instructors, and college professors on previously unpublished or updated facets of our area of interest. More than 90% of our readers are customers of Equifax, Inc., or its various affiliates, and they expect to see articles that help them know and understand the business information business." Buys inspirational articles, think pieces about insurance industry needs for business information services, etc. Length: 1,000-2,000 words. Pays 1-2¢/word, "depending on quality and importance of material, but not less than $25." B&w glossies relating to theme of article purchased with mss; 5x7 or 8x10. Pays $5-15.

LINES MAGAZINE, Reliance Insurance Co., 4 Penn Center, Philadelphia PA 19103. Editor: Beverly Braun. 80% freelance written. Emphasizes insurance and business for "middle-aged, college-educated business people interested in business trends and opinion." Quarterly magazine; 20 pages. Estab. 1977. Circ. 9,000. Pays on acceptance. Not copyrighted. Submit seasonal/holiday material 2 months in advance of issue date. SASE. Reports in 2 weeks. Free sample copy; mention *Writer's Market* in request.

Nonfiction: Exposé (anything insurance related, directly or indirectly); general interest (could be dealing with medical, natural disasters, environment, etc.); interview (with prominent business leaders who might forecast of offer opinion on insurance industry-related matters); nostalgia (insurance, old fire companies); personal experience (interesting and extremely unusual claims); technical (insurance, property/casualty or life). Buys 20 mss/year. Query. Length: 1,500 words minimum.

Fillers: Newsbreaks. Buys 5/issue. Length: 50 words.

Jewelry

AMERICAN HOROLOGIST & JEWELER, 2403 Champa St., Denver CO 80205. (303)572-1777. Managing Editor: Jayne L. Barrick. 30% freelance written. Emphasizes watch/clock-making and jewelry. Monthly magazine; 68 pages. Estab. January 1936. Circ. 13,100. Pays on publication. Phone queries OK. Buys all rights, but may reassign following publication. Byline given. Submit seasonal/holiday material 3 months in advance of issue date. Previously published submissions OK. SASE. Reports in 2-3 weeks. Free sample copy and writer's guidelines.

Nonfiction: How-to (repair articles for watch, clock, jewelry trades, and how-to merchandise, make profits); new product (pertaining to industry and of an unusual nature); photo feature (antique clocks, watches); and technical (repair of jewelry or watches). Buys 10 mss/year. Query or submit complete ms. Length: 1,000-6,000 words. Pays $10-150.

Photos: Submit photo material with accompanying query or ms. No additional payment for b&w glossy prints. Captions preferred. Buys all rights, but may reassign following publication. Model release required.

Columns/Departments: Buys 6/issue. Query. Pays $50. Open to suggestions for new columns/departments.

AMERICAN JEWELRY MANUFACTURER, 340 Howard Bldg., 155 Westminster St., Providence RI 02903. (401)274-3840. Editor: Steffan Aletti. For manufacturers of supplies and tools for the jewelry industry; their representatives, wholesalers and agencies. Estab. 1956. Monthly. Circ. 5,000. Buys all rights (with exceptions). Pays negotiable kill fee. Byline given. Buys 2-5 mss/year. Free sample copy and writer's guidelines. Will consider photocopied submissions. Submit seasonal material 3 months in advance. Reports in 1 month. Query. SASE.

Nonfiction and Photos: "Topical articles on manufacturing; company stories; economics (e.g., rising gold prices). Story must inform or educate the manufacturer. Occasional special issues on timely topics, e.g., gold; occasional issues on specific processes in casting and plating. We reject material that is not specifically pointed at our industry; e.g., articles geared to jewelry retailing, not the manufacturers." Informational, how-to, interview, profile, historical, expose, successful business operations, new product, merchandising techniques, technical. Length: open. Payment "usually around $25." B&w photos purchased with ms. 5x7 minimum.

THE DIAMOND REGISTRY BULLETIN, 30 W. 47th St., New York NY 10036. Editor-in-Chief: Joseph Schlussel. 15% freelance written. Monthly newsletter. Pays on publication. Buys all rights, but may reassign following publication. Submit seasonal/holiday material 1 month in advance of issue date. Simultaneous and previously published submissions OK. SASE. Reports in 3 weeks. Sample copy $5.

Nonfiction: Prevention advice (on crimes against jewelers); how-to (ways to increase sales in diamonds, improve security, etc.); and interview (of interest to diamond dealers or jewelers). Submit complete ms. Length: 50-500 words. Pays $10-150.

JEWELER'S CIRCULAR-KEYSTONE, Chilton Co., Radnor PA 19089. Editor: George Holmes. For retail jewelers. Monthly. Circ. 30,000. Buys all rights. Pays on publication. SASE.

Nonfiction: Wants "how-to articles, case history approach, which specify how a given jeweler solved a specific problem. No general stories, no stories without a jeweler's name in it, no stories not about a specific jeweler and his business." Buys 10-12 mss/year. Length: 1,000-2,000 words.

MODERN JEWELER, 15 W. 10th St., Kansas City MO 64105. Executive Editor: Bill Allison. Managing Editor: Dorothy Boicourt. For retail jewelers and watchmakers. Monthly. Pays on acceptance. Will send sample copy only if query interests the editor. Reports in 30 days. SASE.

Nonfiction and Photos: "Articles with 3-4 photos about retail jewelers—specific jewelers, with names and addresses, and how they have overcome certain business problems, moved merchandise, increased store traffic, etc. Must contain idea adaptable to other jewelry operations; 'how-to' slant. Informal, story-telling slant with human interest. We are not interested in articles about how manufacturing jewelers design and make one-of-a-kind jewelry pieces. Our readers are interested in retail selling techniques, not manufacturing processes. Photos must include people (not just store shots) and should help tell the story. We reject poor photography and articles written as local newspaper features, rather than for a business publication." Pays average $100-150 for article and photos.

THE NORTHWESTERN JEWELER, Washington and Main Sts., Albert Lea MN 56007. Publisher: John R. Hayek. Monthly. Not copyrighted. Pays on publication. SASE.
Nonfiction and Photos: Uses news stories about jewelers in the Northwest and Upper Midwest and feature news stories about the same group. Also buys retail jeweler "success" stories with the how-to angle played up, and occasionally a technical story on jewelry or watchmaking. Pictures increase publication chances. Pays 1¢/published word. Pays $2.50/photo.

PACIFIC GOLDSMITH, 41 Sutter St., San Francisco CA 94104. (415)986-4323. Editor: Robert B. Frier. For jewelers and watchmakers. Monthly magazine; 80-90 pages. Estab. 1903. Circ. 6,000. Not copyrighted. Pays on acceptance. Byline given. Sample copy $1.50. Submit seasonal (merchandising) material 4 months in advance. Reports in 1 week. SASE.
Nonfiction and Photos: "Our main interest is in how Western jewelers can do a better selling job. We use how-to-do-it merchandising articles, showing dealers how to sell more jewelry store items to more people, at a greater profit. Seasonal merchandising articles are always welcome, if acceptable." Buys 12 mss/year. Query or submit complete ms. Length: 1,500-2,000 words. Pays 2¢/word. Pays $5 for b&w photos used with mss; 3x5 minimum. Captions required.

SOUTHERN JEWELER, 75 3rd St. NW, Atlanta GA 30308. (404)881-6442. Editor: Charles Fram. For southern retail jewelers and watchmakers. Monthly. Circ. 4,400. Not copyrighted. Pays on publication. Submit seasonal material 2 months in advance. SASE.
Nonfiction: Articles related to Southern retail jewelers regarding advertising, management, and merchandising. Buys spot news about Southern jewelers and coverage of successful business operations. Prefers *not* to see material concerning jewelers outside the 14 Southern states. Length: open. Pays 1¢/word. $1/clipping.
Photos: Buys b&w glossies. Pays $4.

Journalism

Because many writers are familiar with the journals of the writing profession and might want to submit to them, those that do not pay for contributions are identified in this list. Writers wishing to contribute material to these publications should query about requirements before submitting work.

THE CALIFORNIA PUBLISHER, 1127 11th St., Suite 1040, Sacramento CA 95814. (916)443-5991. Editor: Harvi Callaham. No pay.

CANADIAN AUTHOR & BOOKMAN, Canadian Authors' Association, Box 120, Niagara-on-the-Lake, Ontario, Canada L0S 1J0. (416)468-7391. Editor: Duncan S. Pollock. 75% freelance written. "For writers—all ages, all levels of experience." Quarterly magazine; 48 pages. Estab. 1921. Circ. 5,000. Pays on publication. Buys first North American serial rights. Pays 50% kill fee. Byline given. Phone queries OK. Submit seasonal/holiday material 1 year in advance of issue date. Simultaneous, photocopied and previously published submissions OK. SASE. Reports in 2 months. Free sample copy and writer's guidelines.
Nonfiction: How-to (on writing, selling; the specifics of the different genres—what they are and how to write them); informational (the writing scene—who's who and what's what); interview (on writers, mainly leading ones, but also those with a story that can help others write and sell more often); and opinion. Buys 40 mss/year. Query. Length: open. Pays 1¢/word and up.
Photos: "We're after an interesting looking magazine and graphics are a decided help." State availability of photos with query. Offers no additional payment for b&w photos accepted with ms. Buys one-time rights.
Poetry: "High quality only. Major poets publish with us—others need to be as good." Buys 50 poems/year. Pays $2-5.
Fillers: Short, snappy verse or prose on the writing life. Up to six pieces each issue. Pays $2-5.

THE CATHOLIC JOURNALIST, 119 N. Park Ave., Rockville Center NY 11570. "We are no longer buying freelance material."

COLLEGE PRESS REVIEW, Department of Journalism, University of Mississippi, University MS 38655. (601)232-7146, 232-7147. Editor: John W. Windhauser. For members of the National Council of College Publications staffs, editors and faculty advisors; staff members of student publications, journalism professors and others interested in the student communication media. Estab. 1956. Quarterly. Circ. 1,500. Acquires all rights, but may reassign rights to author after publication. No payment. Sample copy $1.50; free writer's guidelines. Photocopied submissions OK. No simultaneous submissions. Reports in 1-4 months. Query or submit complete ms. SASE.

Nonfiction and Photos: Articles by, about, and of interest to college publication staffs, editors, and faculty advisers. Articles should focus on the editing, advising and production of college newspapers, magazines and yearbooks. "We like to use articles on research and opinion in the student communications media and related areas. We also like to use features on journalism techniques. The writer should write in a readable style. We will accept no manuscripts that read like term papers." Topical subjects of interest include use of new technology on campus publications; case studies of censorship problems at private schools; tips on purchasing new equipment; the advisor's role in revitalizing a dying publication. Length: 3,000 words maximum. B&w glossy photos used with ms. Captions required.

COLUMBIA JOURNALISM REVIEW, 700 Journalism Bldg., Columbia University, New York NY 10027. (212)280-3872. Editor: Robert Karl Manoff. "We welcome queries concerning the media, as well as subjects covered by the media. We emphasize in-depth reporting, critical essays and good writing. All queries are read by editors and we look for coverage of the media that are both thorough and novel. We also publish book reviews and fiction when it illuminates the world of journalism."

EDITOR & PUBLISHER, 575 Lexington Ave., New York NY 10022. (212)752-7050. Editor: Robert U. Brown. For newspaper publishers, editors, executives, employees and others in communications, marketing, advertising, etc. Weekly magazine; 60 pages. Estab. 1884. Circ. 26,000. Pays on publication. Sample copy 75¢. SASE.

Nonfiction: Department Editor: Jerome H. Walker Jr. Uses newspaper business articles and news items; also newspaper personality features and printing technology. Query.

Fillers: "Amusing typographical errors found in newspapers." Pays $2.

FEED/BACK, THE JOURNALISM REPORT AND REVIEW, Journalism Department, San Francisco State University, 1600 Holloway, San Francisco CA 94132. (415)469-2086. Editor: Lynn Ludlow. Executive Editor: Dr. Leonard Sellers. 40-50% freelance written. For the working journalist, the journalism student, the journalism professor and the journalistic layman. Magazine; 60 pages. Estab. 1974. Quarterly. Circ. 1,750. Byline given. Pays in subscriptions and copies. Sample copy $1. Will consider photocopied and simultaneous submissions. Reports in 1 month. Query. SASE.

Nonfiction and Photos: In-depth views of California journalism. Criticism of journalistic trends throughout the country, but with a local angle. Reviews of books concerning journalism. Informational, interview, profile, humor, historical, think pieces, expose, nostalgia, spot news, successful (or unsuccessful) business operations, new product, technical; all must be related to journalism. "Articles must focus on the news media and be of interest to professional journalists—they are our audience. We like articles that examine press performance—strengths and weaknesses; we also like personality articles on offbeat or little-known editors and journalists who escape national attention." Rejects articles that are not documented, or those in which the subject matter is not pertinent or those which show personal prejudice not supported by evidence. Length: 1,000-5,000 words. B&w glossies (8x10 or 11x14) used with or without mss. Pays in subscriptions and/or copies, tearsheets for all material.

FOLIO: The Magazine for Magazine Management, 125 Elm St., Box 697, New Canaan CT 06840. (203)972-0761. Executive Editor: Barbara Love. Managing Editor: James McNally. 5-10% freelance written. Emphasizes magazine management. Monthly magazine. Estab. June 1972. Circ. 9,000. Pays on publication. Photocopied and previously published submissions OK. SASE. Reports in 3 weeks.

Nonfiction: How-to (any aspect of magazine publishing); opinion; and technical articles. Buys 1-2 mss/issue. Query. Length: 1,500-3,000 words.

THE JOURNALISM EDUCATOR, Department of Journalism and Telecommunication, University of Wyoming, Laramie WY 82071. (307)766-3122. Editor: William Roepke. For journalism professors, administrators, and a growing number of news executives in the US and Canada. Published by the Association for Education in Journalism. Founded by the American Society of Journalism Administrators. Quarterly. Byline given. SASE.

Nonfiction: "We do accept some unsolicited manuscripts dealing with our publication's specialized area—problems of administration and teaching in journalism education. Because we receive more articles than we can use from persons working in this field, we do not need to encourage freelance materials, however. A writer, generally, would have to be in journalism/communications teaching or in some media work to have the background to write convincingly about the subjects this publication is interested in. The writer also should become familiar with the content of recent issues of this publication." Maximum length: 2,500 words. Does not pay.

JOURNALISM QUARTERLY, School of Journalism, Ohio University, Athens OH 45701. (614)594-6710. Editor: Guido H. Stempel III. 100% freelance written. For members of the Association for Education in Journalism and other academicians and journalists. Estab. 1923. Quarterly. Usually acquires all rights. Circ. 4,000. Photocopied submissions OK. Free writer's guidelines. Reports in 4-6 months. SASE.
Nonfiction: Research in mass communication. Length: 4,000 words maximum. Submit complete ms "in triplicate." No payment.

MATRIX, Women in Communications, Inc., Box 9561, Austin TX 78766. (512)345-8922. Editor-in-Chief: Ernestine Wheelock. 95% freelance written; "mostly by WICI members and usually without pay." Quarterly magazine; 32 pages. Estab. 1915. Circ. 8,400. Pays on acceptance. Buys all rights, but may reassign following publication. Pays 100% kill fee. Byline given. Photocopied and previously published submissions OK. SASE. Reports in 2 weeks. Sample copy $1.50
Nonfiction: General interest (media, freedom of information, legislation related to communications); how-to (improve graphics, take better photos, write a better story, do investigative reporting, sell ideas, start a magazine or newspaper, improve journalism education, reach decision-making jobs, etc.); personal experience (self-improvement, steps to take to reach management-level jobs); profile (people of interest because of their work in communications); and technical (advancements in print or electronic media). Buys 4-6 mss/year. Query. Length: 1,000-4,000 words. Pays $25-150.
Photos: Offers no additional payment for photos accepted with ms. State availability of photos with query. Use b&w prints. Captions required. Buys one-time rights.

MEDICAL COMMUNICATIONS, 4404 Sherwood Rd., Philadelphia PA 19131. (215)877-1137. Editor: Edith Schwager. For medical libraries, members of the American Medical Writers Association, physicians, journal and magazine editors, medical illustrators and pharmaceutical advertising people. Quarterly, 24- to 32-page digest size magazine. Estab. 1971. Circ. over 2,000. Acquires first North American serial rights. Byline given if requested by the author. Uses 6-8 mss/issue. Pays 3 contributor's copies. Sample copy for $1.25. Submit seasonal or special material 2-3 months in advance. Reports in 6 weeks. Query. SASE.
Nonfiction and Photos: Articles related to any aspect of medical communications. May be either philosophic or how-to with the proviso that it must tell the medical communicator something helpful in his/her profession. "We are more of a journal than a magazine, but like to take a less formal approach in the hope of improving an article's readability across the broad range of AMWA membership." Uses fairly serious, straightforward style. Humor accepted. Footnotes might be required. Does not want to see anything on "how doctors can't communicate with their patients. We know this, and improving the situation is a major purpose of our organization." Length: 1,500-3,000 words. Charts and photos are used with mss, if needed.

MILITARY MEDIA REVIEW, Defense Informational School, Bldg. 400, Fort Benjamin Harrison IN 46216. (317)542-2173. Editor-in-Chief: Mary C. Rothgeb. 100% freelance written. For military and Civil Service employees of the Department of Defense and all military branch services in the fields of information/public affairs, print, broadcast and photojournalism. Quarterly magazine; 32 pages. Estab. 1972. Circ. 1,000. Pays in copies on publication. Not copyrighted. Byline given unless author requests otherwise. Phone queries OK. Submit seasonal/holiday material 5 months in advance of issue date. Simultaneous, photocopied and previously published submissions OK. Reports in 4 weeks. Free sample copy and writer's guidelines; mention *Writer's Market* in request.
Nonfiction: "*Military Media Review* prints how-to articles in the fields of military public affairs, print, broadcast and photojournalism. A sample topic might be 'How to Run a Military Press Center,' or 'How to Design a Post Newspaper,' etc. Occasionally, we run an interview or profile of an outstanding figure in our field. Personal opinion and experience features must be informative. They must relate information our readers will find useful in the field. Photo features and technical articles also must relate to the field." Query or submit complete ms. Length: 1,000-4,000 words.
Photos: State availability of photos with query or submit with ms. Uses 8x10 b&w glossy prints. Model release required.

THE PEN WOMAN MAGAZINE, 1300 17th St. NW, Washington DC 20036. Editor: Wilma W. Burton. For women who are professional writers, artists, composers. Publication of National League of American Pen Women. Magazine; 32-36 pages. Estab. 1920. Published 9 times/year, October through June. Circ. 6,000. Rights purchased vary with author and material. Byline given. Pays on publication. Sample copy for SASE. Photocopied submissions "sometimes" OK. Submit seasonal material 3-4 months in advance. Reports in 6 weeks. SASE.
Nonfiction: "We are overstocked from our own members. Only on occasion do we accept freelance material which must be of unusual appeal in both information and inspiration to our readers." Mss (slanted toward the professional writer, composer and artist) should be 300-1,500 words.
Fiction: Department Editor: Mary Brite, 11405 Farnam Circle, Omaha, Nebraska 68154. "Usually purchase or use reprints from recognized magazines; use some original materials."
Poetry: Department Editor: Donna Dickey Guyer, 1508 SW 22nd Ave., Boynton Beach, Florida 33435. Uses traditional forms, blank verse, experimental forms, free verse, light verse and haiku. "We encourage shorter poems under 36 lines."

PHILATELIC JOURNALIST, Box 150, Clinton Corners NY 12514. (914)266-3150. Editor: Gustav Detjen Jr. For "journalists, writers, columnists in the field of stamp collecting." Estab. 1971. Bimonthly. Circ. 1,000. Not copyrighted. Pays on publication. Free sample copy. Will consider photocopied submissions. Submit seasonal material 2 months in advance. Reports in 2 weeks. Query. SASE.
Nonfiction and Photos: "Articles concerned with the problems of the philatelic journalist, how to publicize and promote stamp collecting, how to improve relations between philatelic writers and publishers and postal administrations. Philatelic journalists, many of them amateurs, are very much interested in receiving greater recognition as journalists. Any criticism should be coupled with suggestions for improvement." Buys profiles and opinion articles. Length: 250-500 words. Pays $15-30. Photos purchased with ms; captions required.

THE QUILL, Magazine for Journalists, 35 E. Wacker Dr., Chicago IL 60601. Editor: Charles Long. Assistant Editor: Helen Raece. 50% freelance written. For newspaper reporters, editors and photographers; television newsmen and women; magazine journalists; freelance writers; journalism educators and students of journalism. Monthly magazine (except for combined July-August issue); 36 pages. Estab. 1912. Circ. 34,000. Pays on publication. Buys all rights. Sometimes pays 50% kill fee. Byline given for all feature articles; Record and Report news sections do not give bylines. Submit seasonal/holiday material 2 months in advance of issue date. SASE. Reports in 3 weeks. Free sample copy and writer's guidelines; mention *Writer's Market* in request.
Nonfiction: Expose (ethical questions related to the practice of journalism and articles dealing with First Amendment questions related to the press); general interest; and opinion ("we have a guest opinion page entitled 'Remark'; of course, we welcome letters to the editor"). Buys 25 mss/year. Query with clips of published work. Length: 200-2,500 words. Pays $25-250.

ST. LOUIS JOURNALISM REVIEW, 928 N. McKnight, St. Louis MO 63132. (314)991-1699. A critique of St. Louis media, print and broadcasting, by working journalists. Bimonthly. Buys all rights. Byline given. SASE.
Nonfiction: "We buy material which analyzes, critically, local (St. Louis area) institutions, personalities, or trends. Payment starts at $20."

WEST COAST WRITER'S CONSPIRACY, 2800 Moraga Dr., Los Angeles CA 90024. Editor-in-Chief: Barbara Hall. Editor: Susan Golant. Emphasizes the West Coast writing scene. Quarterly magazine; 50 pages. Estab. June 1977. Circ. 6,000. Pays on publication. Buys first rights and all rights on interviews only. Submit seasonal/holiday material 6 months in advance. SASE. Reports on queries in 3-4 weeks; 2 months for mss. Sample copy $2.50; free writers' guidelines.
Nonfiction: Exposé (must be in-depth and informative and must relate to writing/publication world); general interest (must be of general interest to West Coast writers, information on conferences, writing programs, prizes, etc.); historical (literary history, expecially of West Coast writers and trends); how-to (craft articles must be unique and informative and marketing tips from pros); humor (must pertain to the writer's life); interview (with West Coast writers and others in the publishing world, must be in-depth and be slanted for writers); personal experience; opinion (must be unique and of the highest quality, pertaining to writing only); travel (locales of interest to West Coast writers); and literary criticism. "We do not want to see whining articles on how a manuscript didn't sell or inspirational articles on how it did." Buys 5

mss/issue. Address query and clips of published work to articles editor. Length: 500-3,000 words. Pays in copies.

Photos: State availability of photos with ms. Offers no additional payment for photos accompanying ms. Uses 8x10 b&w glossy prints. Buys one-time rights.

Columns/Departments: The Writer's Shelf (book reviews of interest to writers; 50-500 words); Bookstore Beat (unique bookstores in Western states, must be accompanied by photos; 100 words); and Critic's Corner (literary criticism by authorities in the field. Must be well-researched, but not obscure. Articles must be general enough that they would be read with interest by a layperson; 3,000 words maximum). Buys 3/issue. Query with clips of published work. Pays in copies.

Fiction: Robert M. Morris, Fiction Editor. Adventure, erotica, experimental fantasy, historical, humorous, mainstream, mystery, romance, science fiction, suspense and western. "We buy fiction of the highest quality and prefer shorter stories. We would especially like to see excellent stories from previously unpublished West Coast writers." Buys 1-5 mss/issue. Send complete ms. Length: 3,000 words maximum. Pays $25-75.

Poetry: Bayla Winters, Poetry Editor. Avant-garde and contemporary poetry. "No sentimental, religious, obscene or sloppy poetry. We want poetry focused on human concerns in which the poet's role is one of dynamic participation as opposed to passive noncommitment. The poet should deal with his/her themes honestly and skillfully. Taboo: excessive length (over 50 lines) and obscure posturing." Buys 3/issue. Pays $10-40.

Fillers: Short humor, newsbreaks, puzzles and light verse about writing. Buys 3/issue. Length: 100 words. Pays in copies.

THE WRITER, 8 Arlington St., Boston MA 02116. Editor: Sylvia K. Burack. Monthly. Pays on acceptance. Uses very little freelance material. SASE.

Nonfiction: Articles of instruction for writers. Length: about 2,000 words. Pays $35 minimum.

WRITER'S DIGEST, 9933 Alliance Rd., Cincinnati OH 45242. (513)984-0717. Editor: John Brady. Emphasizes writing and publishing for writers. Monthly magazine; 60-72 pages. Estab. 1920. Circ. 150,000. Pays on acceptance. Buys first North American serial rights for one-time use only. Pays 20% kill fee. Byline given. Submit seasonal/holiday material 6 months in advance. Photocopied submissions OK. SASE. Reports in 4 weeks. Free sample copy and writer's guidelines.

Nonfiction: "The only tip we can offer is that the writer be current, be alert in spotting the new opportunities for writers and be concise in letting the reader know how to write for that market, and how to market the article once it's written. We like plenty of examples, anecdotes and $$$ in our articles—so other writers can actually see what's been done successfully by the author of a particular piece." General interest (about writing); how-to (writing and marketing techniques that work); humor (short pieces); inspirational; interview (query first on this one); profile; new product; personal experience (marketing and freelancing experiences). Buys 85 mss/year. Query or send complete ms. Length: 500-3,000 words. Pays 10¢/word.

Photos: "If photos are strong and article is weak, we'll ask for a rewrite, and not reject outright. All things being equal, photos do make a difference." State availability of photos or send contact sheet with ms. Pays $25 for b&w contact sheets. Captions preferred.

Columns/Departments: The Writing Life. Buys 6 items/issue. Send complete ms. Length: 50-800 words. Pays 10¢/word.

Poetry: Light verse. Buys 2/issue. Submit poems in batches of 4-6. Length: 2-20 lines. Pays $5-50/poem.

Fillers: Clippings, anecdotes and short humor. Buys 2/issue. Length: 50-200 words. Pays 10¢/word.

WRITER'S YEARBOOK, 9933 Alliance Rd., Cincinnati OH 45242. Editor: John Brady. For writers, writer/photographers and cartoonists. Estab. 1930. Annual. Buys first rights only. Pays 20% kill fee. Byline given. Buys about 20 mss/year. Pays on acceptance. Sample copy $2.50. "Writers should query in spring with ideas for the following year." Will consider *good-quality* photocopied submissions. SASE.

Nonfiction: "I want articles that reflect the current state of writing in America," says editor Brady. "Trends, inside information, money-saving and money-making ideas for the freelance writer. Material on writer's hardware—typewriters, cameras, recorders, etc.—and how they can be used to make writing easier or more lucrative. I'm also interested in the writer's spare time—what she/he does to retreat occasionally from the writing wars; where to refuel and replenish the writing spirit. I also want a big interview (or profile) or two, always with *good* pictures. Articles on writing techniques that are effective today are always welcome." Length: 750-4,500 words. Pays 10¢/word.

Photos: Usually purchased with manuscripts as part of package; b&w only; depending on use, pays $20-50/published photo.

WRITING, Sean Dorman Manuscript Society, 4 Union Place, Fowey, Cornwall, UK PL23 1BY. Editor-in-Chief: Sean Dorman. For writers of all ages and education. Quarterly tabloid; 52 pages. Estab. 1959. Circ. 500. Pays on publication. All rights reserved to the author. No byline. Simultaneous, photocopied and previously published submissions OK. Reports in 1 month. Sample copy $1.
Nonfiction: How-to and informational articles about writing in any form. Buys 4 mss/issue. Length: 300-350 words. Submit complete ms. Pays 2 pounds for double use in linked issues. ("The same articles appear in the spring and summer issues, and in the linked autumn and winter issues.")
Poetry: Traditional forms, free verse and light verse. Buys 4/issue. Submit poems. Pays 2 pounds for double use in a pair of linked issues.

Laundry and Dry Cleaning

Some journals in the Coin-operated Machines category are also in the market for material on laundries and dry cleaning establishments.

AMERICAN DRYCLEANER, 500 N. Dearborn St., Chicago IL 60610. (312)337-7700. Editor: Paul T. Glaman. For professional drycleaners. Monthly. Circ. 30,000. Buys all rights. Pays on publication. Will send free sample copy on request. Reports "promptly." SASE.
Nonfiction and Photos: Articles on merchandising, diversification, sales programs, personnel management, consumer relations, cost cutting, workflow effectiveness, drycleaning methods. "Articles should help the drycleaner build his business with the most efficient utilization of time, money and effort, inform the drycleaner about current developments within and outside the industry that may affect him and his business, introduce the drycleaner to new concepts and applications that may be of use to him, teach the drycleaner the proper methods of his trade. Tight, crisp writing on significant topics imperative. Eliminate everything that has no direct relationship to the article's theme. Select details which add depth and color to the story. Direct quotes are indispensable." Pays 3-5¢/word. Photos purchased with mss; quality 8x10 b&w glossies. Photos should help tell story. No model releases required. Pays $5.

AMERICAN LAUNDRY DIGEST, American Trade Magazines, Inc., 500 N. Dearborn St., Chicago IL 60610. (312)337-7700. Managing Editor: Larry Kai Ebert. 13-26% freelance written. For a professional laundering, linen supply, uniform rental audience. Monthly magazine; 52 pages. Estab. 1936. Circ. 16,000. Pays 2 weeks prior to publication. Buys all rights. Phone queries OK. Photocopied submissions OK. SASE. Reports in 2 weeks. Free sample copy and writer's guidelines.
Nonfiction: How-to articles about how laundrymen have cut costs, increased production, improved safety, gained sales, etc. "Interviews with laundrymen about how they run a successful plant would be welcome." Query. Length: 300-3,000 words. Pays 4¢/word.
Photos: B&w glossies (8x10 preferred; 5x7 acceptable) purchased with mss. Send contact sheet. Pays $5.

INDUSTRIAL LAUNDERER, 1730 M St. NW, Suite 613, Washington DC 20036. (202)296-6744. Editor: James W. Roberts. 15-20% freelance written. For decisionmakers in the industrial laundry industry. Publication of the Institute of Industrial Launderers, Inc. Magazine; 124 pages. Estab. 1949. Monthly. Circ. 2,500. Buys all rights, but will reassign rights (with some exceptions) to author after publication. Buys 15-20 mss/year. Pays on publication. Will send free sample copy to writer on request; limited sample copies available. Write for copy of guidelines for writers. Reports in 1 week. Query. SASE.
Nonfiction and Photos: General interest pieces for the industrial laundry industry; labor news, news from Washington; book reviews on publications of interest to people in this industry. Technical advancements and "people" stories. Informational, personal experience, interview, profile, historical, successful business operations, merchandising techniques. Length: 750 words minimum. Payment negotiable. No additional payment for 8x10 b&w glossies used with ms. Pays $5 minimum for those purchased on assignment. Captions required.

WESTERN CLEANER AND LAUNDERER, Box 722, La Canada CA 91011. (213)247-8595. Editor: Monida Urquhart. 15% freelance written. For owner/managers and key employees of drycleaning, laundry, rug cleaning, drapery, and cleaning plants. Monthly tabloid; 28 pages.

Estab. 1959. Circ. 11,000. Pays on publication. Buys all rights, but may reassign following publication. Phone queries OK. Submit seasonal/holiday material 2 months in advance of issue date. SASE. Reports in 4 weeks. Free sample copy.

Nonfiction: General interest (successful operation of drycleaning or laundry business); how-to (operate a cleaning/laundry plant); new product; and profile. Buys 10-12 mss/year. Query. Length: 400-1,200 words. Pays 5¢/word.

Photos: State availability of photos with query. Pays $4 each for 4x5 b&w glossy prints for number used with story. Captions and model release required. Buys all rights, but may reassign following publication.

Law

BARRISTER, American Bar Association Press, 1155 E. 60th St., Chicago IL 60637. (312)947-4072. Managing Editor: Harvey Rudoff. For young lawyers who are members of the American Bar Association, concerned about practice of law, improvement of the profession and service to the public. Quarterly magazine; 64 pages. Estab. 1974. Circ. 120,000. Pays on acceptance. Buys all rights, but may reassign following publication; or first serial rights or second serial (reprint) rights, or simultaneous rights. Photocopied submissions OK. SASE. Reports in 4-6 weeks. Free sample copy.

Nonfiction: "As a magazine of ideas and opinion, we seek material that will help readers in their inter-related roles of attorney and citizen. Major themes in legal and social affairs. Reference to legal questions in a topic may be helpful; we examine the inter-relationship between law and society. Expository or advocacy articles welcome; position should be defended clearly in good, crisp, journalistic prose." Length: 1,000-3,000 words. Query. Pays $150-400.

Photos: Donna Tashjian, department editor. B&w (8x10) glossies and 35mm color transparencies purchased without accompanying ms. Pays $35 minimum for b&w; $50 minimum for color.

JURIS DOCTOR MAGAZINE FOR THE NEW LAWYER, 730 3rd Ave., New York NY 10017. Editor: Martin Beiser. For "young lawyers, ages 25 to 37." Published 6 times/year. Circ. 160,000. Buys first rights. Pays 25% kill fee. Byline give "unless otherwise requested by author." Pays on publication. Free sample copy. Reports in 5 weeks. SASE.

Nonfiction: Wants articles on the legal profession, as well as travel and leisure items. Writer should show a knowledge of law, but should not be overly technical. Willing to research. "Most articles are muckraking pieces about the profession—the organized bar, law schools, new areas of legal practice. We also run book reviews." Interested in how-to, interviews, and profiles. Buys 30 mss/year. Query. Length: 1,000-3,500 words. Book reviews, 900 words. Pays 10¢/word. $75 for reviews.

Photos: B&w glossies purchased with mss and with captions only. Pays $25.

LAWYER'S NEWSLETTER, 1180 S. Beverly Dr., Los Angeles CA 90035. Editor: Stephan Z. Katzan. 40% freelance written. For attorneys. Bimonthly. Buys all rights. Pays on publication. Free sample copy. Reports in 2 weeks. SASE.

Nonfiction: "Our publication's main purpose is to increase the efficiency of attorneys and of law office operations. We are interested in suggestions and ideas for improvement of office operations as well as articles on legal economics." Length: 2,000 words maximum. Pays $150.

LEGAL ECONOMICS, Box 11418, Columbia SC 29211. Managing Editor/Art Director: Delmar L. Roberts. For the practicing lawyer. Bimonthly magazine; 56-68 pages. Estab. 1975. Circ. 18,000. Rights purchased vary with author and material. Usually buys all rights, but may reassign rights to author after publication for special purposes. Byline given. Pays on publication. Free sample copy and writer's guidelines. Returns rejected material in 90 days, if requested. Query. SASE.

Nonfiction and Photos: "We assist the practicing lawyer in operating and managing his office in an efficient and economical manner by providing relevant articles and editorial matter written in a readable and informative style. Editorial content is intended to aid the lawyer by informing him of management methods that will allow him to provide legal services to his clients in a prompt and efficient manner at reasonable cost. Typical topics of articles include timekeeping systems; malpractice insurance; word processing systems; client/lawyer relations; office equipment; computerized research; professional compensation; information retrieval; and use of paralegals." Pays $50-200. Pays $20 for b&w photos purchased with mss; $15-25 for color.

THE REPORT TO LEGAL MANAGEMENT, Altman & Weil Publications, Inc., Box 472, Ardmore PA 19003. (215)649-4646. Editor: Robert I. Weil. For lawyers and law office managers about the equipment, services, furniture, books, insurance, etc. lawyers purchase. Bimonthly newsletter; 8 pages. Estab. 1975. Pays on publication. Buys all rights. Byline given. Phone queries OK. Previously published submissions OK. SASE. Reports in 4 weeks. Free sample copy.
Nonfiction: How-to (purchase or use insurance, equipment, space, services); new product articles. Buys 3-4 mss/year. Query with clips of published work. Length: 500-2,000 words. Pays $100/printed page.
Photos: State availability of photos. Uses b&w prints. Offers no additional payment for photos accepted with ms.

STUDENT LAWYER, American Bar Association, 1155 E. 60th St., Chicago IL 60637. (312)947-4087. Editor: A.J. Buckingham. Associate Editor: Margaret McCamant. Monthly (during school year) magazine; 60 pages. Estab. 1952. Circ. 40,000. Pays on publication. Buys all rights, but may reassign following publication. Pays negotiable kill fee. Byline given. Submit seasonal/holiday material 2 months in advance of issue date. Photocopied submissions OK. SASE. Reports in 2 weeks. Sample copy $1; free writer's guidelines.
Nonfiction: Expose (government, law, education and business); profiles (prominent persons in law-related fields); opinion (on matters of current legal interest); essays (on legal affairs); interviews and photo features. Buys 8 mss/issue. Query. Length: 3,000-6,000 words. Pays $100-350.
Photos: State availability of photos with query. Pays $35-75 for 8x10 b&w prints; $50-150 for color. Model release required.
Columns/Departments: Briefly (short stories on unusual and interesting developments in the law); Legal Ease (highlighting specific products of interest to law students and attorneys); Legal Fictions (short ironic or humorous pieces); Esq. (brief profiles on people in the law); and Status (news stories on legal education, programs and personalities). Buys 4-8 mss/issue. Length: 50-1,500 words. Pays $25-100.
Fiction: "We buy fiction when it is very good and deals with the issues of law in the contemporary world. No mystery stories accepted." Pays $50-200.
How To Break In: "*Student Lawyer* actively seeks good, new writers. Legal training definitely not essential; writing talent is. The writer should not think we are a law review; we are a features magazine with the law (in the broadest sense) as the common denominator. Past articles concerned gay rights, prison reform, the media, affirmative action and architecture."

Leather Goods

LUGGAGE AND LEATHERGOODS NEWS, G.P. Page Publications, Ltd., 380 Wellington St. W., Toronto, Ontario, Canada M5V 1E3. (416)366-4608. Editor: Jamie Howe. 10-15% freelance written. "The majority of our readers are retailers of luggage, leather goods, handbags, and related products. The remainder are those who supply the luggage retailers with product. 99.9% of all that I buy is of Canadian content." Published 9 times/year. Tabloid; 16 pages. Circ. 4,700. Pays on publication. Buys all rights, but may reassign following publication. Phone queries OK. Submit seasonal/holiday material 3-4 months in advance of issue date. SAE and International Reply Coupons. Reports in 3 weeks. Free sample copy; mention *Writer's Market* in request.
Nonfiction: How-to (more effectively sell luggage and leather goods; articles must be based on the experiences of a retailer); interview (with Canadian industry leaders only); and photo features (open to b&w only). Buys up to 9 mss/year. Query. Length: 500-1,200 words Pays 5¢/word.
Photos: "There's no point in buying an article from a freelancer in another country if I have to go (or send someone) to take photos. Works of art are not necessary—just *good* b&w photos." State availability of photos with query. Pays $5 for 5x7 or 8x10 b&w prints.

Library Science

AMERICAN LIBRARIES, 50 E. Huron St., Chicago IL 60611. (312)944-6780. Editor: Arthur Plotnik. For librarians. "A highly literate audience. They are for the most part practicing professionals with high public contact and involvement interest." 11 times a year. Circ. 38,000. Buys first North American serial rights. Pays negotiable kill fee. Byline given. Will consider photocopied submissions if not being considered elsewhere at time of submission. Submit seasonal material 6 months in advance. Reports in 10 weeks. SASE.

Nonfiction, Photos and Fillers: "Material reflecting the special and current interests of the library profession. Nonlibrarians should browse recent journals in the field, available on request in medium-sized and large libraries everywhere. Topic and/or approach must be fresh, vital, or highly entertaining. Stereotyped stories about old maids, overdue books, fines, etc., are unacceptable. Our first concern is with the American Library Association's activities, and how they relate to the 38,000 reader/members. Tough for an outsider to write on this topic, but not to supplement it with short, offbeat library stories and features. Will look at all good b&w, natural light photos of library situations, and at color transparencies for possible cover use." Pays $15-150 for fillers and articles. Pays $5-50 for b&w photos.
How To Break In: "With a sparkling, 300-word report on a true, offbeat library event, or with an exciting photo and caption."

EMERGENCY LIBRARIAN, 39 Edith Dr., Toronto, Ontario, Canada M4V 1Y9. Co-Editor: Phylis Yoffe. Bimonthly magazine; 24 pages. Estab. October 1973. Circ. 1,300. Pays on publication. Not copyrighted. Photocopied submissions OK. SAE and International Reply Coupons. Reports in 4-6 weeks. Free sample copy.
Nonfiction: Expose (of library practice); how-to (do it better in libraries); interview (with person in alternative librarianship); and profile. Also annotated bibliographies. Buys 3 mss/issue. Query. Length: 1,000-3,500 words. Pays $25.
Columns/Departments: Book Reviews (of small press or Canadian or feminist and socialist books). Query. Length: 250-500 words. Payment consists of book reviewed.

THE HORN BOOK MAGAZINE, 31 St. James Ave., Park Square Bldg., Boston MA 02116. (617)482-5198. Editor-in-Chief: Ethel L. Heins. Assistant Editor: Karen M. Klockner. 50% freelance written. For librarians, teachers, parents, authors, illustrators and publishers. Bimonthly magazine; 100 pages. Estab. 1924. Circ. 24,500. Pays on publication. Phone queries OK. Submit seasonal/holiday material 4 months in advance of issue date. Photocopied submissions OK. SASE. Free sample copy and writer's guidelines.
Nonfiction: All related to children's books. Historical; humor; inspirational; experience; personal opinion; profile; and travel. Query. Pays $20/page.
Poetry: Free verse, haiku, and traditional. Buys 1-6 mss/year. Pays $20.

LIBRARY JOURNAL, 1180 Avenue of the Americas, New York NY 10036. Editor-in-Chief: John N. Berry III. For librarians (academic, public, special). 115-page magazine published every 2 weeks. Estab. 1876. Circ. 40,000. Buys all rights. Buys 50-100 mss/year (mostly from professionals in the field). Pays on publication. Submit complete ms. SASE.
Nonfiction and Photos: "*Library Journal* is a professional magazine for librarians. Freelancers are most often rejected because they submit one of the following types of article: 1) 'A wonderful, warm, concerned, loving librarian who started me on the road to good reading and success'; 'How I became rich, famous, and successful by using my public library'; 'Libraries are the most wonderful and important institutions in our society, because they have all of the knowledge of mankind—praise them.' We need material of greater sophistication, dealing with issues related to the transfer of information, access to it, or related phenomena. (Current hot ones are copyright, censorship, the decline in funding for public institutions, the local politics of libraries, trusteeship, etc.)" Professional articles on criticism, censorship, professional concerns, library activities, historical articles and spot news. Outlook should be from librarian's point of view. Length: 1,500-2,000 words. Pays $50-250. Payment for b&w glossy photos purchased without accompanying mss is $25. Must be at least 5x7. Captions required.

MEDIA: LIBRARY SERVICES JOURNAL, 127 9th Ave. N., Nashville TN 37234. (615)251-2752. Editor: Floyd B. Simpson. For adult leaders in church organizations and people interested in library work (especially church library work). Quarterly magazine; 50 pages. Estab. 1970. Circ. 17,500. Pays on publication. Buys all rights. Byline given. Phone queries OK. Submit seasonal/holiday material 14 months in advance. Previously published submissions OK. SASE. Reports in 1 month. Free sample copy and writer's guidelines.
Nonfiction: "Primarily interested in articles that relate to the development of church libraries in providing media and services to support the total program of a church and in meeting individual needs. We publish personal experience accounts of services provided; promotional ideas, exciting things that have happened as a result of implementing an idea or service; human interest stories that are library-related; media education (teaching and learning with a media mix). Articles should be practical for church library staffs and for teachers and other leaders of the church." Buys 15-20 mss/issue. Query. Pays 3¢/word.

THE PAMPHLETEER MONTHLY, 55 E. 86 St., New York NY 10028. (212)722-7272.

Editor: William Frederick. 20% freelance written. A review source for paper-covered materials; from single-page leaflets to booklets and pamphlets/books up to and beyond 160 pages. For the library trade; buying guide for public school, college, university and special libraries; book review source. Magazine; 48 pages. Estab. 1940. Monthly except July/August. Circ. 6,000. Buys all rights. No byline. Pays on assignment. Query. Send in a resume and clips of previous reviews or published writing.

Nonfiction: Book reviews on assignment only. Length: 50 words, average. Pays $1. (Usually, 50-100 assigned reviews at a time.)

SCHOOL LIBRARY JOURNAL, 1180 Avenue of the Americas, New York NY 10036. Editor: Lillian N. Gerhardt. For librarians in schools and public libraries. Monthly (September-May) magazine; 88 pages. Estab. 1954. Circ. 45,000. Buys all rights. Pays on publication. Reports in 3 months. SASE.

Nonfiction: Articles on library services, local censorship problems, how-to articles on programs that use books or films. Informational, personal experience, interview, expose, successful business operations. "Interested in history articles on the establishment/development of children's and young adult services in schools and public libraries." Buys 6 mss/year. Length: 2,500-3,000 words. Pays $100.

WILSON LIBRARY BULLETIN, 950 University Ave., Bronx NY 10452. (212)588-8400. Editor: Milo Nelson. Associate Editor: Harriet E. Rosenfeld. For professional librarians and those interested in the book and library worlds. Monthly (September-June). Circ. 30,000. Buys North American serial rights only. Pays on publication. Sample copies may be seen on request in most libraries. "Ms must be original copy, double spaced; additional photocopy or carbon is appreciated. Deadlines are a minimum 2 months before publication." Reports in 8-12 weeks. SASE.

Nonfiction: Uses articles "of interest to librarians throughout the nation and around the world. Style must be lively, readable and sophisticated, with appeal to modern professionals; facts must be thoroughly researched. Subjects range from the political to the comic in the world of media and libraries, with an emphasis on the human as well as the technical aspects of any story. No condescension: no library stereotypes." Length: 3,000-6,000 words. Pays about $50-150, "depending on the substance of article and its importance to readers."

How To Break In: "With a first-rate b&w photo and caption information on a library, library service, or librarian that departs completely from all stereotypes and the commonplace. Note: Libraries have changed! You'd better first discover what is now commonplace."

Lumber and Woodworking

B.C. LUMBERMAN MAGAZINE, 2000 W. 12th Ave., Vancouver, British Columbia, Canada, V65 2G2. (403)731-1171. Editor-in-Chief: Len Webster. Managing Editor: Brian Martin. 60% freelance written. Emphasizes forest industry of Canada and US Pacific Northwest. Monthly magazine; 75 pages. Estab. 1916. Circ. 8,500. Pays on acceptance. Buys all rights, but may reassign after publication. Phone queries OK. Submit seasonal/holiday material 2 months in advance of issue date. Reports in 2 weeks. Free sample copy; mention *Writer's Market* in request.

Nonfiction: How-to (technical articles on any aspect of the forest industry); general interest (anything of interest to persons in forest industies in western Canada or US Pacific Northwest); interview (occasionally related to leading forestry personnel); and technical (forestry). Buys 8 mss/issue. Query with clips of published work. Length: 1,500-5,000 words. Pays 9¢/word.

Photos: State availability of photos with query. Pays $5-25 for b&w negatives and $50-80 for 8x10 glossy color prints. Captions required. Buys one-time rights.

CANADIAN FOREST INDUSTRIES, 1450 Don Mills Rd., Don Mills, Ontario, Canada M3B 2X7. Editor: Jim Brown. 25% freelance written. For forest companies, loggers, lumber-plywood-board manufacturers. Estab. 1882. Monthly. Circ. 12,000. Buys first North American serial rights. Byline given. Pays on publication. Free sample copy. Reports in 1 month. SAE and International Reply Coupons.

Nonfiction: Uses "articles concerning industry topics, especially how-to articles that help businessmen in the forest industries. All articles should take the form of detailed reports of new methods, techniques and cost-cutting practices that are being successfully used anywhere in Canada, together with descriptions of new equipment that is improving efficiency and utilization of wood. It is very important that accurate descriptions of machinery (make, model, etc.) be always included and any details of costs, etc., in actual dollars and cents can make the

difference between a below-average article and an exceptional one." Buys 20 mss/year. Query. Length: 1,200-2,500 words. Pays 12¢/word minimum, more with photos.
Photos: Buys photos with mss, sometimes with captions only. Should be 8x10, b&w glossies or negatives.

THE NORTHERN LOGGER & TIMBER PROCESSOR, Box 69, Old Forge NY 13420. (315)369-3078. Editor: George D. Fowler. 10-20% freelance written. Monthly magazine; 48 pages. Estab. 1952. Circ. 7,300. Pays on publication. Buys all rights, but may reassign following publication. Phone queries OK. Submit seasonal/holiday material 3 months in advance of issue date. Previously published submissions OK. SASE. Reports in 4 weeks. Free sample copy; mention *Writer's Market* in request.
Nonfiction: General interest; historical; how-to; interview; new product; and technical. Buys 2-3 mss/year. Query. Length: 1,500-6,000 words. Pays $50-150.
Photos: State availability of photos with query. Pays $5-15 for 5x7 or 8x10 b&w glossy prints; $15-30 for 35mm or larger color transparencies. Captions required. Buys all rights, but may reassign following publication.

PLYWOOD AND PANEL MAGAZINE, Box 567B, Indianapolis IN 46206. (317)634-1100. Co-Publisher: Robert Dixon. For manufacturers and industrial fabricators of plywood, veneer and composite board. Monthly. Buys all rights. Byline given, "but any short industry news item that does not rate full feature treatment would be used at a $5 minimum payment with no byline; this includes clippings from other publications." Pays on publication. SASE.
Nonfiction: "Factual and accurate articles concerning unusual techniques or aspects in the manufacturing or processing of veneer, plywood, particleboard, hardboard; detailing successful and/or unusual marketing techniques for wood panel products; or concerning important or unusual industrial end-uses of these materials in the production of consumer goods." Length: 2,500 words maximum. Pays maximum 5¢/word.
Photos: Of good quality and directly pertinent to editorial needs. Action photos; no catalog shots. No in-plant photos of machinery not operating or not manned in natural fashion. Must be completely captioned; 5x7 b&w or larger preferred. Pays up to $5 per photo.

WOOD & WOOD PRODUCTS, 300 W. Adams St., Chicago IL 60606. Editor-in-Chief: Monte Mace. Managing Editor: Ellen Farnsworth. 10-15% freelance written. For owners and management of sawmills, plywood mills, particleboard mills, wood products such as laminated panels or millwork, and furniture. Monthly magazine; 84 pages. Circ. 30,000. Pays on publication. Buys all rights unless otherwise specified. Pays negotiable kill fee. Byline given. Phone queries OK. Submit seasonal/holiday material 3 months in advance of issue date. Simultaneous, photocopied and previously published submissions OK. SASE. Reports in 2 weeks. Free sample copy and writer's guidelines.
Nonfiction: Exposé (of upcoming government regulations); how-to (increase production, efficiency, and profits); humor (if related to industry in some way); interview (industrial and government leaders); new product (one offering truly new technology, not just a new cap screw); photo feature (how-to, plant story); and technical. No articles on hobbyist woodworking. Buys 15 mss/year. Query. Length: 500-1,500 words. Pays $75 minimum.
Photos: State availability of photos with query. Offers no additional payment for b&w contact sheets or prints; 35mm color transparencies. Captions required. Buys one-time rights.
Columns/Departments: Production Ideas (efficiency tips, how a company solved a problem). Buys 10/year. Query. Length: 500-750 words. Pays $75.

WOOD REVIEW, Publication Development, Inc., Box 23383, Portland OR 97223. (503)620-3917. Editor: Jack Kucera. Emphasizes wood products industry for North American softwood lumber and plywood producers, chief executive officers, production managers, market managers, North American wholesalers of wood products—sales managers and salesmen. Mostly middle-aged, politically conservative men, interested in the outdoors. Weekly newspaper; 8 pages. Estab. 1979. Paid circulation; *First Friday* edition monthly controlled circulation. Pays on publication. Buys all rights. Byline given. Phone queries OK. Advance submission of seasonal/holiday material subject to negotiation. Simultaneous, photocopied and previously published submissions OK. SASE. Reports in 1 week. Free sample copy and writer's guidelines.
Nonfiction: Expose (of government regulation/legislation); general interest (hunting, fishing, camping, logging, sports); historical (history of logging, forestry, wood products production and transportation); how-to (on woodworking); humor (about governmnet regulation and things of general interest, as long as refers to wood industry); interview (of wood products industry key producers, wholesalers, users, association managers and government) nostalgia

(old production, transportation, marketing techniques); opinion (if solicited from key industry person or interested outsider); new product (market segments: softwood lumber, softwood plywood panel, moulding and millwork—major users segments: residential construction, nonresidential construction, mobile home/RV, residential remodeling and furniture cabinets); personal experience (if tied to wood products); photo feature (nostalgia, production); and technical (new techniques in production, warehousing/shipping). Buys 3 mss/issue. Query. Length: 500-1,250 words. Pays 5¢/word.

Photos: Send photos with ms. Pays $10 for b&w and color negatives and. Captions required.
Columns/Departments: Commodities, money supply/finance, construction, government regualtion, transportation, production/new techniques. Buys 3/issue. Query. Length: 500-1,000. Pays 5¢/word. Open to suggestions for new columns/departments.

WOODWORKING & FURNITURE DIGEST, Hitchcock Bldg., Wheaton IL 60187. (312)665-1000. Editor: Richard D. Rea. For industrial manufacturers whose products employ wood as a basic raw material. Monthly. Buys all rights. Pays on publication. Will send free sample copy to serious freelancer on request. Query. Reports in 10 days. Will sometimes hold ms for further evaluation up to 2 months, if it, at first, appears to have possibilities. SASE.
Nonfiction and Photos: "Articles on woodworking and furniture manufacturing with emphasis on management concepts, applications for primary raw materials (including plastics, if involved with wood), technology of remanufacturing methods and machines, and news of broad industry interest. Articles should focus on cost reduction, labor efficiency, product improvement, and profit. No handcraft, do-it-yourself or small custom shopwork. Present theme, or why reader can benefit, in first paragraph. Cover 'feeds and speeds' thoroughly to include operating data and engineering reasons why. Leave reader with something to do or think. Avoid mechanically handled case histories and plant tours that do not include management/engineering reasons. Photos, charts and diagrams which tell what cannot be told in words should be included. We like a balance between technical information and action photos." Length: "no length limit, but stop before you run out of gas!" Pays $35-50/published page. Photos purchased with mss. Good technical quality and perception of subject shown. No posed views. Prefers candid action or tight closeups. Full-color cover photo must be story-related.

Machinery and Metal Trade

ASSEMBLY ENGINEERING, Hitchcock Publishing Co., Wheaton IL 60187. Editor: Robert T. Kelly. 30% freelance written. For design and manufacturing engineers and production personnel concerned with assembly problems in manufacturing plants. Monthly. Buys first publication rights. Pays on publication. Sample copy will be sent on request. "Query on leads or ideas. We report on ms decision as soon as review is completed and provide edited proofs for checking by author, prior to publication." SASE.
Nonfiction and Photos: Wants features on design, engineering and production practices for the assembly of manufactured products. Material should be submitted on "exclusive rights" basis. Subject areas include selection, specification, and application of fasteners, mounting hardware, electrical connectors, wiring, hydraulic and pneumatic fittings, seals and gaskets, adhesives, joining methods (soldering, welding, brazing, etc.) and assembly equipment; specification of fits and tolerances; joint design; design and shop assembly standards; time and motion study (assembly line); quality control in assembly; layout and balancing of assembly lines; assembly tool and jig design; programming assembly line operations; working conditions, incentives, labor costs, and union relations as they relate to assembly line operators; hiring and training of assembly line personnel; supervisory practices for the assembly line. Also looking for news items on assembly-related subjects, and for unique or unusual "ideas" on assembly components, equipment, processes, practices and methods. Requires good quality photos or sketches, usually close-ups of specific details. Pays $30 minimum/published page.

AUTOMATIC MACHINING, 65 Broad St., Rochester NY 14614. (716)454-3763. Editor: Donald E. Wood. For metalworking technical management. Buys all rights. Byline given. Query. SASE.
Nonfiction: "This is not a market for the average freelancer. A personal knowledge of the trade is essential. Articles deal in depth with specific job operations on automatic screw machines, chucking machines, high production metal turning lathes and cold heading machines. Part prints, tooling layouts always required, plus written agreement of source to publish the material. Without personal background in operation of this type of equipment, freelancers are wasting time." Length: "no limit." Pays $20/printed page.

CANADIAN MACHINERY AND METALWORKING, 481 University Ave., Toronto, Ontario, Canada M5W 1A7. (416)595-1811. Editor: J. Davies. Monthly. Buys first Canadian rights. Pays on acceptance. Query. SAE and International Reply Coupons.
Nonfiction: Technical and semitechnical articles dealing with metalworking operations in Canada and in the US, if of particular interest. Accuracy and service appeal to readers is a must. Pays minimum 7¢/word.
Photos: Purchased with mss and with captions only. Pays $5 minimum for b&w features.

CUTTING TOOL ENGINEERING, Box 937, Wheaton IL 60187. (312)653-3210. Editor: N.D. O'Daniell. For metalworking industry executives and engineers concerned with the metal-cutting/metal-removal/abrasive engineering function in metalworking. Bimonthly. Circ. 36,000. Buys all rights. Byline given. Pays on publication. Will send free sample copy on request. Query. SASE.
Nonfiction: "Intelligently written articles on specific applications of all types of metal cutting tools—mills, drills, reamers, etc. Articles must contain all information related to the operation, such as feeds and speeds, materials machined, etc. Should be tersely written, in-depth treatment. In the Annual Diamond/Superabrasive Directory, published in May/June, we cover the use of diamond/superabrasive cutting tools and diamond/superabrasive grinding wheels." Length: 1,000-2,500 words. Pays "$35/published page, or about 5¢/published word."
Photos: Purchased with mss. 8x10 b&w glossies preferred.

FOUNDRY MANAGEMENT AND TECHNOLOGY, Penton Plaza, Cleveland OH 44114. (216)696-7000. Editor: J.C. Miske. Monthly. Byline given. Reports in 2 weeks. SASE.
Nonfiction and Photos: Uses articles describing operating practice in foundries written to interest companies producing metal castings. Length: 3,000 words maximum. Pays $35/printed page. Uses illustrative photographs with article.

INDUSTRIAL MACHINERY NEWS, 29516 Southfield Rd., C.S. #5002, Southfield MI 48037. (313)557-0100. Editor-in-Chief: Lucky D. Slate. Emphasizes metalworking for buyers, specifiers, manufacturing executives, engineers, management, plant managers, production managers, master mechanics, designers and machinery dealers. Monthly tabloid; 200 pages. Estab. 1953. Circ. 100,000. Pays on publication. Buys first North American serial rights. Submit seasonal/holiday material 3 months in advance. Simultaneous, photocopied and previously published submissions OK. SASE. Reports in 3-5 weeks. Sample copy $1.50.
Nonfiction and Photos: Articles on "metal removal, metal forming, assembly, finishing, inspection, application of machine tools, technology, measuring, gauging equipment, small cutting tools, tooling accessories, materials handling in metalworking plants, safety programs. We give our publication a newspaper feel—fast reading with lots of action or human interest photos." Buys how-to's. Pays $25 minimum. Length: open. Photos purchased with mss; captions required. Pays $5 minimum.
Fillers: Newsbreaks, puzzles, jokes, short humor. Pays $5 minimum.
How To Break In: "Stories on old machine tools—how they're holding up and how they're being used."

MODERN MACHINE SHOP, 600 Main St., Cincinnati OH 45202. Editor: Ken Gettelman. Monthly. Byline given. Pays 30 days following acceptance. Query. Reports in 5 days. SASE.
Nonfiction: Uses articles dealing with all phases of metal manufacturing and machine shop work, with photos. Length: 1,500-2,000 words. Pays current market rate.

ORNAMENTAL/MISCELLANEOUS METAL FABRICATOR, Suite 207, 443 E. Paces Ferry Rd. NE, Atlanta GA 30305. Editor: Blanche Blackwell. For fabricators of ornamental and miscellaneous metals who are interested in their businesses and families, their community and nation. Most are owners of small businesses employing an estimated average of 10 persons, usually including family members. Official publication of the National Ornamental and Miscellaneous Metals Association. Magazine published every 2 months; 24 pages. Estab. 1958. Circ. 6,000. Not copyrighted. Byline given. Buys 6 mss/year. Pays on acceptance. Will send free sample copy to writer on request. Will not consider photocopied or simultaneous submissions. Submit seasonal material 2 months in advance. Reports "immediately." Query. SASE.
Nonfiction and Photos: "Our publication deals solely with fabrication of ornamental and miscellaneous metals, a more creative and aesthetic aspect of the metals construction industry. Special emphasis on ornamental and miscellaneous metal trade. How-to articles that will help our readers improve their businesses. Articles on use and history of ornamental metal; on better operation of the business; on technical aspects. News about the association and its

individual members and about 12 chapters affiliated with the national association. Articles on the effects of steel shortage on ornamental metal fabricator and how a typical firm is handling the problem; the search for qualified employees; successful prepaint treatments and finishes." Prefers not to see "character study" articles. Length: 1,000-5,000 words. Pays 3¢/word. B&w glossy photos purchased with accompanying mss. Pays $4.

POWER TRANSMISSION DESIGN, 614 Superior Ave. W., Cleveland OH 44113. (216)696-0300. Editor: Dick Dann. Managing Editor: Les Szabo. 20% freelance written. Emphasizes industrial power transmission systems. Monthly magazine: 96 pages. Estab. 1959. Circ. 50,600. Pays on publication. Buys first-time publication rights and nonexclusive republication rights. Byline given "special agreement with author." Reports in 3 weeks. Free sample copy.
Nonfiction: Articles on design, selection and maintenance of industry power-transmission systems and components. Buys 5 mss/issue. Query. Pays $30/page.

PRODUCTS FINISHING, 600 Main St., Cincinnati OH 45202. Editor: Gerard H. Poll Jr. Monthly. Buys all rights. Byline given "except on press releases from agencies." Pays within 30 days after acceptance. Reports in 1 week. SASE.
Nonfiction: Uses "material devoted to the finishing of metal and plastic products. This includes the cleaning, plating, polishing and painting of metal and plastic products of all kinds. Articles can be technical and must be practical. Technical articles should be on processes and methods. Particular attention given to articles describing novel approaches used by product finishers to control air and water pollution, and finishing techniques that reduce costs." Pays 8¢ minimum/word.
Photos: Wants photographs dealing with finishing methods or processes. Pays $10 minimum for each photo used.

STEEL '79, 1000 16th St. NW, Washington DC 20036. Editor: Jeff Given. For "opinion leaders; all ages and professions." Estab. 1933. Bimonthly. Circ. 90,000. Buys all rights. Buys 4-6 mss/year. Pays on acceptance. Free sample copy. Query. SASE.
Nonfiction and Photos: Articles on the environmental, energy, economics, international trade, new technology aspects of the steel industry. "No product articles." Interviews, think pieces, technical. Length: 50-2,000 words. Pays $25-400. Photos purchased with or without accompanying ms or on assignment. Proofsheets and negatives. Color transparencies. Pays $15-100. Captions required. Freelance articles on assignment only.

33 METAL PRODUCING, McGraw-Hill Bldg., 1221 Avenue of the Americas, New York NY 10020. (212)997-3330. Editor: Joseph L. Mazel. For "operating managers (from turn foreman on up), engineers, metallurgical and chemical specialists, and corporate officials in the steelmaking industry. Work areas for these readers range from blast furnace and coke ovens into and through the steel works and rolling mills. *33's* readers also work in nonferrous industries." Monthly. Buys all rights. Pays on publication. Free sample copy. Query. Reports in 3 weeks. SASE.
Nonfiction: Case histories of primary metals producing equipment in use, such as smelting, blast furnace, steelmaking, rolling. "Broadly speaking, *33 Metal Producing* concentrates its editorial efforts in the areas of technique (what's being done and how it's being done), technology (new developments), and equipment (what's being used). Your article should include a detailed explanation (who, what, why, where and how) and the significance (what it means to operating manager, engineer, or industry) of the techniques, technology or equipment being written about. In addition, your readers will want to know of the problems you experienced during the planning, developing, implementing and operating phases. And, it would be especially beneficial to tell of the steps you took to solve the problems or roadblocks encountered. You should also include all cost data relating to implementation, operation, maintenance, etc., wherever possible. Benefits (cost savings; improved manpower utilization; reduced cycle time; increased quality; etc.) should be cited to gauge the effectiveness of the subject being discussed. The highlight of any article is its illustrative material. This can take the form of photographs, drawings, tables, charts, graphs, etc. Your type of illustration should support and reinforce the text material. It should not just be an added, unrelated item. Each element of illustrative material should be identified and contain a short description of exactly what is being presented. We reject material that lacks in-depth knowledge of the technology on operations involved in metal producing." Pays $50/published page. Minimum 5x7 b&w glossies purchased with mss.

THE WELDING DISTRIBUTOR, 614 Superior Ave. W., Cleveland OH 44113. Executive

Editor: Charles Berka. For wholesale and retail distributors of welding equipment and safety supplies and their sales staffs. Bimonthly. Buys all rights. Byline given. Pays on publication. SASE.

Nonfiction: Management, process/product knowledge, profiles, selling and safety.

Maintenance and Safety

BUILDING SERVICES CONTRACTOR, MacNair-McDorland Co., 101 W. 31st St., New York NY 10001. (212)279-4455. Editor-in-Chief: John Vollmuth. Managing Editor: Joe Thorsen, 10% freelance written. Bimonthly magazine; 60 pages. Estab. 1963. Circ. 6,000. Pays on publication. Buys all rights, but may reassign after publiction. Phone queries OK. Submit seasonal/holiday material 2-3 months in advance of issue date. SASE. Reports in 2 weeks. Free sample copy and writer's guidelines.

Nonfiction: General interest, historical, interview, new product, personal experience, photo feature, profile and technical. Submit complete ms. Length: 800-1,500 words. Pays $90-135.

Photos: Submit photo material with accompanying ms. No additional payment for b&w prints. Buys all rights, but may reassign following publication.

HEAVY DUTY EQUIPMENT MAINTENANCE, 7300 N. Cicero Ave., Lincolnwood IL 60646. (312)588-7300. Editor: Greg Sitek. 10% freelance written. Magazine; 76-110 pages. Estab. 1972. Monthly. Circ. 47,000. Rights purchased vary with author and material. Usually buys all rights, but may reassign rights to author after publication. Buys 12 mss/year. Pays on publication. Free sample copy. No photocopied or simultaneous submissions. Reports in 4 weeks. Query with outline. SASE.

Nonfiction and Photos: "Our focus is on the effective management of equipment through proper selection, careful specification, correct application and efficient maintenance. We use job stories, technical articles, safety features, basics and shop notes. No product stories." Length: 2,000-5,000 words. Pays $25/printed page minimum, without photos. Uses 35mm and 2¼x2¼ or larger color transparencies with mss. Pays $50/printed page when photos are furnished by author.

MAINTENANCE SUPPLIES, 101 W. 31st St., New York NY 10001. (212)279-4455. Editor-in-Chief: John Vollmuth. Managing Editor: Ed Pasternack. 10% freelance written. For distributors of janitorial supplies. Monthly magazine; 100 pages. Estab. 1955. Circ. 11,000. Pays on publication. Buys all rights, but may reassign following publication. Phone queries OK. Submit seasonal/holiday material 2-3 months in advance of issue date. SASE. Reports in 2 weeks. Free sample copy.

Nonfiction: General interest; historical; interview; new product; personal experience; photo feature; profile; and technical. Buys 2 mss/issue. Submit complete ms. Length: 800-1,500 words. Pays $90-135.

Photos: Submit photo material with accompany ms. Offers no additional payment for b&w prints. Buys all rights, but may reassign following publication.

Columns/Departments: New Literature and New Products. Buys 1/issue. Submit complete ms. Length: 500-800 words. Pays $50. Open to suggestions for new columns/departments.

OCCUPATIONAL HAZARDS, 614 Superior Ave. W., Cleveland OH 44113. (216)696-0300. Editor: Peter J. Sheridan. "Distributed by function to middle management officials in industry who have the responsibility for accident prevention, occupational health, plant fire protection, and plant security programs. Job titles on our list include: safety directors, industrial hygienists, fire protection engineers, plant security managers and medical directors." Monthly. Buys first rights in field. Pays on publication. Reports in 30 days. SASE.

Nonfiction: "Articles on industrial health, safety, security and fire protection. Specific facts and figures must be cited. No material on farm, home or traffic safety. All material accepted subject to sharp editing to conform to publisher's distilled writing style. Illustrations preferred but not essential. Work is rejected when story is not targeted to professional concerns of our readers, but rather is addressed to the world at large." Length: 300-2,000 words. Pays 5¢/word minimum.

Photos: Accepts 4x5, 5x7 and 8x10 photos with mss. Pays $10.

THE OSHA COMPLIANCE LETTER, Bureau of Business Practice, 24 Rope Ferry Rd., Waterford CT 06386. Editor: Gail Heller. For "safety directors or persons with safety responsibilities—in all firms covered by job safety and health regulations." Bimonthly newsletter. Pays on acceptance. Buys all rights. Phone queries OK. SASE. Reports in 2 months. Free sample copy and writer's guidelines.

Nonfiction: Interviews revealing ways in which a company complies with job safety/health regulations. Interview safety directors or other supervisors with safety responsibilities. "Get familiar with the field. In the case of safety management, collar friends, neighbors, acquaintances in the field and pump them with questions. Then, at least, you'll be going to interviews with a good idea of the appropriate questions. Direct interviews along specific, topical lines. And when an interviewee lets fall a statement like: 'people who've had accidents are the best people to make suggestions on how to prevent future mishaps'—don't let the comment hang in air. Get at the why and how—not just the what." Buys 2 mss/issue. Query. Length: 1,000-1,300. Pays 1¢/word after editing.

PEST CONTROL MAGAZINE, 9800 Detroit Ave., Cleveland OH 44102. (216)651-5500. Editor: David Schneider. For professional pest control operators and sanitation workers. Monthly magazine; 44 pages. Estab. 1933. Circ. 14,000. Buys all rights. Buys 6 mss/year. Pays on publication. Sample copy $1. Submit seasonal material 2 months in advance. Reports in 30 days. Query or submit complete ms. SASE.
Nonfiction and Photos: Business tips, unique control situations, personal experience articles. Must have trade or business orientation. No general information type of articles desired. "Remember that we are oriented toward the owner-manager more than the serviceman. We might consider something on the view of an outsider to the pest control operator's job, or a report by an outsider after spending a day with a PCO on a route." Length: 4 double-spaced pages. Pays $25 minimum. Regular columns use material oriented to this profession. Length: 8 double-spaced pages. Pays 4¢/word. No additional payment for photos used with mss. Pays $5-25 for 5x7 b&w glossies purchased without mss; $15-50 for 8x10 color or slide.

Management and Supervision

This category includes trade journals for lower level business and industrial managers, including supervisors and office managers. Journals for business executives and owners are classified under Business Management. Those for industrial plant managers are listed in Industrial Management.

AIRPORT SERVICES MANAGEMENT, Lakewood Publications, 731 Hennepin Ave. S., Minneapolis MN 55403. (612)333-0471. Editor: Richard A. Coffey. 20% freelance written. Emphasizes management of airports and airport business. Monthly magazine; 50 pages. Estab. June 1961. Circ. 20,000. Pays on publication. Buys all rights, but may reassign following publication. Byline given. Phone queries OK. Submit seasonal/holiday material 3 months in advance of issue date. Photocopied submissions OK. SASE. Reports in 8 weeks. Free sample copy and writer's guidelines.
Nonfiction: How-to (manage an aviation business or service organization, work with local governments, etc.); interview (with a successful operator); and technical (how to manage maintenance shops, snow removal operations, bird control, security operations). "No flying, no airport nostalgia, or product puff pieces. Just plain 'how-to' story lines, please." Buys 10-12 mss/year. Query. Length: 500-1,500 words. Pays $50/published page.
Photos: State availability of photos with query. Payment for photos is included in total purchase price. Uses 5x7 or 8x10 glossy b&w photos.

THE BUSINESS QUARTERLY, School of Business Administration, University of Western Ontario, London, Ontario N6A 3K7, Canada. (519)679-3222. Editor: Doreen Sanders. For persons in upper and middle management, university education, interested in continuing and updating their management education. Estab. 1933. Quarterly. Circ. 11,500. Buys all rights. Buys 35 mss/year. Pays on publication. Reports in 3 months. Query with brief outline of article. Enclose SAE and International Reply Coupons.
Nonfiction: Articles pertaining to all aspects of management development. Must have depth. "Think" articles and those on successful business operations. Length: 2,000-5,000 words. Pays $100.

CONSTRUCTION FOREMAN'S & SUPERVISOR'S LETTER, Bureau of Business Practice, 24 Rope Ferry Rd., Waterford CT 06386. (203)442-4365. Emphasizes all aspects of construction supervision. Semimonthly newsletter; 4 pages. Estab. 1967. Buys all rights. Phone queries OK. Submit seasonal or holiday material at least 4 months in advance. SASE. Reports in 4-6 weeks. Free sample copy and writer's guidelines.
Nonfiction: Publishes solid interviews with construction managers or supervisors on how to improve a single aspect of the supervisor's job. Buys 100 mss/year. Length: 360-720 words. Pays 7-10¢/word.

Photos: B&w head and shoulders "mug shots" of person interviewed purchased with mss. Send prints. Pays $7.50.

EMPLOYEE RELATIONS BULLETIN, Bureau of Business Practice, 24 Rope Ferry Rd., Waterford CT 06386. Editor: Julia Brandimarti. For personnel, human resources and employee relations managers on the executive level. Semimonthly newsletter; 8 pages. Estab. 1950s. Circ. 3,000. Pays on acceptance. Buys all rights. No byline. Phone queries OK. Submit seasonal/holiday material 6 months in advance. Photocopied submissions OK. SASE. Reports in 2 weeks. Free sample copy and writer's guidelines.
Nonfiction: Interviews about all types of business and industry such as banks, insurance companies, public utilities airlines, consulting firms, etc. Interviewee should be a high level company officer—general manager, president, industrial relations manager, etc. Writer must get signed release from person interviewed showing that article has been read and approved by him/her, before submission. Some subjects for interviews might be management training, communications, compensation, motivation and morale, safety and health, grievance handling, human relations techniques and problems, etc. Buys 3 mss/issue. Query. Length: 700-2,000 words. Pays 10¢/word after editing.

THE FOREMAN'S LETTER, National Foremen's Institute, 24 Rope Ferry Rd., Waterford CT 06386. (203)442-4365. Editor: Frank Berkowitz. For industrial supervisors. Semimonthly. Buys all rights. Pays on acceptance. "Query preferred only if out-of-pocket expenses may be involved." Interested in regular stringers (freelance) on area exclusive basis. SASE.
Nonfiction: Interested primarily in direct in-depth interviews with industrial supervisor in the US and Canada, written in newspaper feature or magazine article style, with concise, uncluttered, non-repetitive prose as an essential. Subject matter would be the interviewee's techniques for managing people, bolstered by illustrations out of the interviewee's own job experiences. Slant would be toward informing readers how their most effective contemporaries function, free of editorial comment. "Our aim is to offer information which, hopefully, readers may apply to their own professional self-improvement." Pays 8¢-10½¢/word "after editing for all rights."
Photos: Buys photos submitted with mss. "Captions needed for identification only." Head and shoulders, any size b&w glossy from 2x3 up. Pays $10.

LE BUREAU, 625 President Kennedy, Montreal, Quebec, Canada, H3A 1K5. (514)845-5141. Editor: Paul Saint-Pierre. For "office executives." Estab. 1965. Published 6 times/year. Circ. 7,500. Buys all rights, but will reassign rights to author after publication. Byline given. Buys about 10 mss/year. Pays on acceptance. Free sample copy. Query or submit complete ms. Submit seasonal material "between 1 and 2 months" in advance of issue date. SAE and International Reply Coupons.
Nonfiction and Photos: "Our publication is published in the French language. We use case histories on new office systems, applications of new equipment, articles on personnel problems. Material should be exclusive and above-average quality." Buys personal experience articles, interviews, think pieces, coverage of successful business operations, and new product articles. Length: 500-1,000 words. Pays $75-100. B&w glossies purchased with mss. Pays $10 each.

MANAGE, 2210 Arbor Blvd., Dayton OH 45439. (513)294-0421. Editor-in-Chief: Douglas E. Shaw. 60% freelance written. For first-line and middle management and scientific/technical managers. Quarterly magazine; 32 pages. Estab. 1925. Circ. 60,000. Pays on acceptance. Buys North American magazine rights with reprint privileges; book rights remain with the author. Phone queries OK. Submit seasonal/holiday material 3 months in advance of issue date. SASE. Reports in 1 month. Free sample copy and writer's guidelines.
Nonfiction: "All material published by *Manage* is in some way management-oriented. Most articles concern one or more of the following categories: communications; cost reduction; economics; executive abilities; health and safety; human relations; job status; labor relations; leadership; motivation and productivity; and professionalism. Articles should be specific and tell the manager how to apply the information to his job immediately. Be sure to include pertinent examples, and back up statements with facts and, where possible charts and illustrations. Manage does not want essays or academic reports, but interesting, well-written and practical articles for and about management." Buys 6 mss/issue. Submit complete ms. Length: 600-2,000 words. Pays 5¢/word.

PERSONNEL ADVISORY BULLETIN, Bureau of Business Practice, 24 Rope Ferry Rd., Waterford CT 06386. (203)442-4365. Editor-in-Chief: C. Starnella. Emphasizes all aspects of personnel management for personnel managers in all types and sizes of companies, both white

collar and industrial. Semimonthly newsletter; 4 pages. Estab. 1973. Pays on acceptance. Buys all rights. Phone queries OK. Submit seasonal/holiday material 4 months in advance of issue date. SASE. Reports in 2 weeks. Free sample copy and writer's guidelines.
Nonfiction: Interviews with personnel managers or human resource executives on topics of current interest in the personnel field. Buys 30 mss/year. Query. Length: 800-1,000 words. Pays 10¢/word after editing.

SALES MANAGER'S BULLETIN, The Bureau of Business Practice, 24 Rope Ferry Rd., Waterford CT 06386. Editor: Jim Cornell. For sales managers and salespeople interested in getting into sales management. Newsletter published twice a month; 8 pages. Estab. 1960. Pays on acceptance. Phone queries from regulars OK. Submit seasonal/holiday material 6 months in advance. Photocopied submissions OK. SASE. Reports in 2 weeks. Free sample copy and writer's guidelines.
Nonfiction: How-to (motivate salespeople, cut costs, create territories, etc.); interview (with working sales managers who use innovative techniques); and technical (marketing stories based on interviews with experts). Break in to this publication by reading their guidelines and sample issue. Follow their directions closely and chances for acceptance go up dramatically. One easy way to start is with an interview article ("Here's what a sales executive has to say about . . ."). Buys 12-24 mss/year. Query. Length: 800-1,500. Pays 8-10¢/word.

SECURITY MANAGEMENT, Bureau of Business Practice, 24 Rope Ferry Rd., Waterford CT 06386. Editor: Ruth Norcia. Emphasizes security for industry. "All material should be slanted toward security directors, preferably industrial, but some white-collar as well." Semimonthly newsletter; 4 pages. Estab. 1960s. Circ. 3,000. Pays on acceptance. Buys all rights. Phone queries OK. Photocopied submissions OK. SASE. Reports in 2 weeks. Free sample copy and writer's guidelines.
Nonfiction: Interview (with security professionals only). "Articles should be tight and specific. They should deal with new security techniques or new twists on old ones. Especially interested in computer security articals. Buys 2 mss/issue. Query. Length: 750-1,000. Pays 10¢/word.

SUPERVISION, 424 N. 3rd St., Burlington IA 52601. Editor-in-Chief: N. Pasqual. Managing Editor: R. Walker. 65% freelance written. For first-line foremen, supervisors and office managers. Monthly magazine; 24 pages. Estab. 1938. Circ. 8,175. Pays on publication. Buys all rights, but may reassign following publication. Previously published submissions OK. SASE. Reports in 3 weeks. Free sample copy and writer's guidelines; mention *Writer's Market* in request.
Nonfiction: How-to (cope with supervisory problems, discipline, absenteeism, safety, productivity, goal setting, etc.); personal experience (unusual success story of foreman or supervisor); and photo feature (will use ms plus 2-3 photos to illustrate it). Buys 7 mss/issue. Query. Length: 800-2,000 words. Pays up to 5¢/word.
Photos: State availaility of photos with query. Pays $5 for b&w glossy prints. Buys all rights, but may reassign following publication.

TRAINING, The Magazine of Human Resources Development, 731 Hennepin Ave., Minneapolis MN 55403. (612)333-0471. Editor: Philip Jones. For persons who train people in business, industry, government and health care. Age 25-65. Magazine; 75 pages. Estab. 1964. Monthly. Circ. 40,000. Rights purchased vary with author and material. Usually buys all rights, but may reassign rights to author after publication; first North American serial rights; first serial rights; or all rights. Pays 20% kill fee. Byline given. Buys 20 mss/year. Pays on acceptance. Will send free sample copy. Write for editorial guidelines sheet. Will consider photocopied submissions. No simultaneous submissions. Reports in 4 weeks. Query. SASE.
Nonfiction and Photos: Articles on management and techniques of employee training. "Material should discuss a specific training problem; why the problem existed; how it was solved, the alternative solutions, etc. Should furnish enough data for readers to make an independent judgment about the appropriateness of the solution to the problem. We want names and specific details on all techniques and processes used." Would like to see "interesting examples of successful traiing and management development programs; articles about why certain types of the above seem to fail; articles about trainers and training directors who have become company presidents or top execs." Most mss should be 200-3,000 words. Informational. Length: 200-2,000 words. Book reviews. Length: 50-1,000 words. Successful business operations. Length: 50-3,000 words. Pays $75/printed page maximum. "In general, we pay more for tightly written articles." No extra payment for photos. No payment for unsolicited material; query only. B&w only. Captions optional.

UTILITY SUPERVISION, Bureau of Business Practice, 24 Rope Ferry Rd., Waterford CT 06386. (203)442-4365. Editor: Peter W. Hawkins. Emphasizes all aspects of utility supervision. Semimonthly newsletter; 4 pages. Estab. 1966. Pays on acceptance. Buys all rights. Phone queries OK. Submit seasonal material 4 months in advance. SASE. Reports in 4-6 weeks. Free sample copy and writer's guidelines.

Nonfiction: Publishes how-to (interview on a single aspect of supervision with utility manager/supervisor concentrating on how reader/supervisor can improve in that area). Buys 100 mss/year. Query. Length: 360-720 words. Pays 6-10¢/word.

Photos: Purchased with accompanying ms. Captions required. Pays $7.50 for b&w prints of "head and shoulders 'mug shot' of person interviewed." Total purchase price for ms includes payment for photos.

How To Break In: "Write solid interview articles on a single aspect of supervision in the utility field. Concentrate on how the reader/supervisor can improve his/her own performance in that area."

Marine Industries and Water Navigation

BOATING BUSINESS, Box 673, Parry Sound, Ontario, Canada P2A 2Z1. (705)732-2095. Editor-in-Chief: Jim Punfield. 35% freelance written. Emphasizes retail marine trade. Quarterly magazine; 32 pages. Estab. September 1976. Circ. 5,400. Pays on acceptance. Not copyrighted. Phone queries OK. Submit seasonal/holiday material 3 months in advance of issue date. Photocopied submissions OK. SAE and International Reply Coupons. Reports in 2 weeks. Free sample copy; mention *Writer's Market* in request.

Nonfiction: How-to (make more profit from your marine dealership, how-to sell more boats, motors, and accessories); inspirational (how one dealer overcame lack of working capital); and interview (successful operations—must be adaptable to Canadian readership). "Articles must either relate to our Canadian readership or be adaptable." Buys 3 mss/issue. Query or send complete ms. Length: 300-800 words. Pays $25-100.

Photos: Submit photo material with accompanying ms. No additional payment for 5x7 or 8x10 glossy b&w prints. Captions preferred. Buys one-time rights.

THE BOATING INDUSTRY, 850 3rd Ave., New York NY 10022. Editor: Charles A. Jones. For "boating retailers and distributors" Estab. 1929. Monthly. Circ. 26,000. Buys all rights, but will reassign rights to author after publication. Byline given. Buys 10-15 mss/year. Pays on publication. "Best practice is to check with editor first on story ideas for go-ahead." Submit seasonal material 3-4 months in advance. Reports in 2 months. SASE.

Nonfiction and Photos: No clippings. Pays 7-10¢/word. B&w glossy photos purchased with mss.

MARINE BUSINESS, 38 Commercial Wharf, Boston MA 02110. (617)227-0888. Editor: Stewart Alsop II. Executive Editor: Tom Kempf. Query and ms sent to the Executive Editor. 50% freelance written. For retailers in the recreational boating business. Monthly magazine; 144 pages. Estab. January 1978. Circ. 28,000. Pays on acceptance. Buys all rights, but reassigns following publication. Pays 50% kill fee. Byline given "except if we have to do extensive additional research and rewrite, and the author was unwilling or unable to do so, we would pay a kill fee, do the work, and publish the article under a different byline." Submit seasonal/holiday material 3 months in advance of issue date. SASE. Reports in 4-6 weeks. Free sample copy and writer's guidelines.

Nonfiction: "We're looking for articles with a direct benefit for marine retailers. These articles explore one unique aspect of a specific store and how the owner solved a problem that other retailers often face. No general profiles, success stories, business history or stock articles. In-depth articles on industry problems are usually staff-written, but don't hesitate to query. Particularly interested in making contact with writers with background in and understanding of the marine business." Buys 50 mss/year. Query. Length: 1,200-3,000 words. Pays $150-500.

Columns/Departments: General Management; Financial Management; Personnel; Service; Marketing; Merchandising; Promotion; Sales Techniques; Taxes & Law; and Marinas. Buys 50 mss/year. Query. Length: 800-1,500 words. Pays $50-200.

Fillers: Ideas for simplifying day-to-day business for "Profitbuilders" or "Charting Your Business Course" departments. Buys 25/year. Length: 25-50 words. Pays $25.

SEAWAY REVIEW, The Journal of the Great Lakes/St. Lawrence Seaway Transportation System, Harbor Island, Maple City Postal Station MI 49664. Senior Editor: Jacques LesStrang. Assistant Editor: Michelle Cortright. 10% freelance written. For "the entire Great Lakes maritime community, executives of companies that ship via the Great Lakes, traffic managers, transportation executives, federal and state government officials and manufacturers of maritime equipment." Quarterly magazine; 100 pages. Estab. 1970. Circ. 14,500. Pays on publication. Buys first North American serial rights. Submit seasonal material 2 months in advance of issue date. Photocopied submissions OK. SASE. Reports in 2 weeks. Sample copy $2.

Nonfiction: "Articles dealing with Great Lakes shipping, shipbuilding, marine technology, economics of 8 states in Seaway region (Michigan, Minnesota, Illinois, Indiana, Ohio, New York, Pennsylvania and Wisconsin), port operation, Seaway's role in economic development, historical articles dealing with Great Lakes shipping, current events dealing with commercial shipping on lakes, etc." Submit complete ms. Length: 1,000-2,000 words. Pay "varies with value of subject amtter and knowledgeability of author, up to $250."

Photos: State availability of photos with query. Pays $10-50 for 8x10 blossy b&w prints; $10-100 for 8x10 glossy color prints. Captions required. Buys one-time rights. Buys "hundreds" of freelance photos each year.

Fillers: Clippings and spot news relating to ports and the Seaway system. Buys 3/issue. Length: 50-500 words. Pays $5-50.

THE WORK BOAT, Box 217, Mandeville LA 70448. (504)6263151. Publisher/Editor: Harry L. Peace. Monthly. Buys first rights. Pays on publication. Query. Reports in 2 weeks. SASE.

Nonfiction: "Articles on waterways, river terminals, barge line operations, work boat construction and design, barges, dredges, tugs. Best bet for freelancers: One-angle article showing in detail how a barge line, tug operator or dredging firm solves a problem of either mechanical or operational nature. This market is semitechnical and rather exacting. Such articles must be specific, containing firm name, location, officials of company, major equipment involved, by name, model, power, capacity and manufacturer; with b&w photos." Length: 1,000-5,000 words. Pays $90 minimum.

Photos: 5x5 or 5x7 b&w; 4x5 color prints only. No additional payment for photos.

Medical

Publications aimed at the private physician, or that publish technical material on new discoveries in medicine, are classified here. Journals for nurses, laboratory technicians, hospital resident physicians, and other medical workers will be found with the Hospitals, Nursing, and Nursing Homes journals. Publications for druggists and drug wholesalers and retailers are grouped with the Drugs, Health Care, and Medical Products journals.

THE AMERICAN CHIROPRACTOR, Box 8015, Erie PA 16505. (814)833-8634. Editor: Randolph A. Byrd. For doctors of chiropractic with 6-8 years of college and graduate school—average age is 42. Interests include travel, leisure activities and sports. Monthly magazine; 96 pages. Estab. 1978. Circ. 30,000. Pays on publication. Buys second serial (reprint) rights and one-time rights. Pays 10% kill fee. Byline given. Phone queries OK. Submit seasonal/holiday material 3 months in advance. Simultaneous, photocopied and previously published submissions OK. SASE. Reports in 6 weeks. Free sample copy.

Nonfiction: General interest (on chiropractic philosophy, financial investments, travel, leisure ideas, nutrition and exercise); historical (concerning the history of chiropractic not already common knowledge, and obscure stories); how-to (lose weight, live longer, maintain health, and nutrition-geared recipes); humor (with educated tone and in good taste); interview (with nutrition experts, chiropractic professionals, legislators concerning current litigations in area: travel (6- to 10-day vacation trips to exotic locales near North America); new product (chiropractic equipment); personal experience (in travel, leisure, investments); photo feature (travel); and technical (chiropractic technique, Roentgenology, office management and research). Articles on nutrition and better health also needed. "Articles must have advertiser marketability! Nutrition articles will sell nutrition company ads for the magazine." Buys 120 mss/year. Query or send complete ms. Length: 500-2,000 words. Pays $50-300.

Photos: "Photos necessary where applicable, i.e., with travel or technical feature material. We prefer color separations, if available." State availability of photos or send photos with ms. Uses b&w negatives or 4x5 or 8x10 glossy prints, 4x5 glossy color prints. Offers no additional payment for photos accepted with ms except by negotiation.

Columns/Departments: Chiropractic News, Travel/Leisure, Investments, Better Health/Nutrition and Chiropractic in lay terms. Send complete ms. Length: 300-1,000 words. Pays $20-200.

Fillers: Jokes, gags, anecdotes, newsbreaks (within profession), crossword puzzles and cartoons. Buys 5/issue. Length: 50-100 words. Pays $5-10.

AMERICAN FAMILY PHYSICIAN, 1740 W. 92nd St., Kansas City MO 64114. (816)333-9700. Publisher: Walter H. Kemp. Monthly. Circ. 126,000. Buys all rights. Pays on publicaion. "Most articles are assigned." Query first. Reports in 2 weeks. SASE.
Nonfiction: Interested only in clinical art items. Length: 2,500 words. Pays $50-250.

AUDECIBEL, Journal of the National Hearing Aid Society, 20361 Middlebelt, Livonia MI 48152. (313)478-2610. Editor: Anthony DiRocco. Managing Editor: Lila R. Johnson. For "otologists, otolaryngologists, hearing aid specialists, educators of the deaf and hard of hearing, clinica audiologists, and others interested in hearing and audiology." Estab. 1951. Quarterly. Circ. 15,000. Buys all rights. Byline given. "Most articles published are from authorities in the field who publish for professional recognition, without fee." Pays on acceptance. Free sample copy and writer's guidelines. Query or submit complete ms. SASE.
Nonfiction and Photos: "Purpose of the magazine is to bring to the otologist, the clinical audiologist, the hearing aid audiologist and others interested in the field authoritative articles and data concerned with current issues, research, techniques, education and new developments in the field of hearing and hearing aids. In general, *Audecibel's* editorial policy emphasizes a professional and technical approach rather than a sales and merchandising approach. Eight types of articles are used: technical articles dealing with hearing aids themselves; technical articles dealing with fitting hearing aids; case histories of unusual fittings; technical articles dealing with sound, acoustics, etc.; psychology of hearing loss; medical and physiological aspects; professional standards and ethics; and current issues in the hearing health care fields. We are not interested in human interest stories, but only in carefully researched and documented material." Length: 200-2,000 words; "will consider longer articles if content is good." Pays 1-2½¢/word. Photos purchased with mss; captions optional. Pays $3-5.

BEHAVIORAL MEDICINE, Magazines for Medicine, Inc., 475 5th Ave., New York NY 10017. (212)889-1050. Editor: Robert McCrie. Emphasizes medical aspects of behavior for MDs in general and family practice, psychiatry and neurology. Monthly magazine; 48 pages. Estab. 1974. Circ. 110,000. Pays on acceptance. Buys second serial (reprint) rights. Pays 10-25% kill fee. Phone queries OK. Simultaneous, photocopied and previously published submissions OK. SASE. Reports in 1 month. Sample copy $2.50; free writer's guidelines.
Nonfiction: Technical pieces; study recent issues. Buys 2-4 mss/issue. Query. Pays $150-500.
Photos: "We have one photo article per issue at least." Uses b&w prints and color transparencies. Offers no additional payment for photos accepted with ms; however, photo articles go for higher rates to established sources. Captions required. Buys one-time rights.

CANADIAN DOCTOR, 310 Victoria Ave., Suite 201, Montreal, Quebec, Canada H3Z 2M9. (514)487-2302. Editor-in-Chief: Peter N. Williamson. Assistant Editor: Linda Scovill. Monthly magazine; 100 pages. Estab. 1935. Circ. 34,000. Pays on acceptance. Buys all rights. Byline given. SAE and International Reply Coupons. Reports in 3 weeks. Free sample copy and writer's guidelines.
Nonfiction: How-to (run a physician's practice efficiently); interview (with Canadian doctor, perhaps those who have moved to US); personal experience (from Canadian doctors); personal opinion (from Canadian doctor about the profession); profile (of Canadian doctor); and travel (only on assignment). Query. Length: 500-2,500 words. Pays $25-150.
Photos: State availability of photos with query. Pays $15 for b&w glossy prints. Captions required. Buys one-time rights. Model release required.

CONTEMPORARY SURGERY, Bobit Publishing, 2500 Artesia Blvd., Redondo Beach CA 90278. Editor: Barbara O'Reilly, M.P.A. Managing Editor: Judi Prow. 10% freelance written. Emphasizes clinical surgery for surgeons-in-practice and surgical residents. Monthly magazine; 128 pages. Estab. 1972. Circ. 40,000. Pays on publication. Buys all rights, but may reassign following publication. Byline given. Photocopied and previously published (if identified) submissions OK. SASE. Reports in 3 weeks.
Nonfiction: Interview; new product (if used by surgeons); profile (medical); technical; and clinical surgery-related topics. Query or submit complete ms. Length: 6,000 words maximum. Pays $50-300.
Photos: Submit photos or illustrations with query or ms. May offer additional payment for photos accepted with ms. Submit b&w or color photos, slides. Model release required.

DRUG THERAPY MEDICAL JOURNAL, Biomedical Information Corp., 919 3rd Ave., New

York NY 10022. (212)758-6104. Editor-in-Chief: Genell Subak-Sharpe. Published in 2 editions: Office edition for practicing physicians; Hospital edition for hospital personnel. Emphasizes drug therapy for physicians in all the clinical specialties as well as internists, residents and attendants in the hospital setting throughout the US. Monthly magazine; 175 pages. Estab. 1970. Circ. 140,000. Pays on publication. Phone queries OK. Submit seasonal or holiday material 4 months in advance. Simultaneous and photocopied submissions OK. Previously published work acceptable as long as reprint rights are clear. SASE. Reports in 1-3 weeks. Free sample copy and editorial guidelines.
Nonfiction: How-to (diagnosis and treatment as clinical entity); informational (use of drugs, new drugs, how a drug works, etc.). Technical and new product articles. Buys 10-15 mss/issue. Query. Length: 1,000 words minimum. Pays $300.
Photos: No additional payment for b&w or color used with mss.

FACETS, American Medical Association Auxiliary, Inc., 535 N. Dearborn St., Chicago IL 60610. (312)751-6166. Managing Editor: Kathleen T. Jordan. For physicians' spouses. Quarterly magazine; 32 pages. Circ. 90,000. Pays on acceptance. Buys all rights, but may reassign following publication. Submit seasonal/holiday material 4 months in advance of issue date. Simultaneous, photocopied and previously published submissions OK. SASE. Reports in 6 weeks. Free sample copy and writer's guidelines.
Nonfiction: All articles must be related to the experiences of physicians' wives. Current health issues; financial topics; physicians' family circumstances and business management. Buys 8 mss/year. Query. Length: 1,000-2,500 words. Pays $250-500.
Photos: State availability of photos with query. Uses 8x10 glossy b&w prints and 2¼x2¼ color transparencies.

LAB WORLD, North American Publishing Co., 401 N. Broad St., Philadelphia PA 19108. (215)574-9600. Editorial Director: A.E. Woolley. 50% freelance written. Emphasizes laboratory medicine for pathologists, lab chiefs, medical technologists, medical technicians and other staff members of laboratories. Monthly magazine; 100 pages. Estab. 1947. Circ. 62,000. Pays on acceptance. Buys first North American serial or one-time rights. Submit seasonal/holiday material 4-6 months in advance of issue date. SASE. Reports in 2 weeks. Sample copy $2.50.
Nonfiction: All articles must pertain to the laboratory field. General interest; humor; inspirational; interview; photo feature; and profile. No technical papers. Buys 20-50 mss/year. Query. Length: 750-7,000 words. Pays $100-300.
Photos: State availability of photos with query. Pays $50-150 for 5x7 or 8x10 b&w semigloss photos; $100-200 for 35mm color transparencies. Captions and model release required. Buys one-time rights.

THE MAYO ALUMNUS, Mayo Foundation, 200 SW 1st St., Rochester MN 55901. (507)284-2511. Editor: David E. Swanson. For physicians, scientists, and medical educators who trained at the Mayo Clinic. Quarterly magazine; 40 pages. Estab. 1965. Circ. 9,000. Pays on acceptance. Buys all rights. Phone queries OK. Submit seasonal/holiday material 6 months in advance of issue date. Previously published submissions OK. SASE. Reports in 2 months. Free sample copy; mention *Writer's Market* in request.
Nonfiction: "We're interested in seeing interviews with members of the Mayo Alumni Association—stories about Mayo-trained doctors/educators/scientists/researchers who are interesting people doing interesting things in medicine, surgery or hobbies of interest, etc." Query with clips of published submissions. Length: 1,000-3,000 words. Pays 15¢/word, first 1,500 words. Maximum payment is $275.
Photos: "We need art and must make arrangements if not provided with the story." Pays $10 for b&w photos. State availability of photos with query. Captions preferred. Buys all rights.

MEDICAL DIMENSIONS, 730 3rd Ave., New York NY 10017. Editor: Decia Fates. Professional but nontechnical publication for medical students and physicians under 40. Journal published 6 times/year. Pays on publication. Buys all rights. Pays 50% kill fee, "but not on unsolicited articles that are accepted for publication and later dropped." Byline given. Photocopied submissions OK; no simultaneous submissions unless noted in cover letter. Reports in 3-8 weeks. Free sample copy.
Nonfiction: Interested in articles on professional trends in practice and medical education, medical politics, career opportunities and profiles of interesting or unorthodox young doctors. Query. Length: 2,000-4,000 words. Pays 10¢/word.

MEDICAL ECONOMICS, 680 Kinderkamack Rd., Oradell NJ 07649. (201)262-3030. Editor-in-Chief: Don L. Berg. Executive Editor: James A. Reynolds. Emphasizes "the business side of medical practice for office-based physicians in private practice." Bimonthly magazine; 200-300 pages. Estab. 1923. Circ. 165,000. Pays on acceptance. Buys all rights, but may reassign following publication. Pays kill fee. Byline given "except when a story is so poorly done that it has to be extensively rewritten or re-researched." Submit seasonal/holiday material 3 months in advance of issue date. Previously published submissions OK. SASE. Reports in 4 weeks. Free sample copy and writer's guidelines.

Nonfiction: "Articles tell the doctor how to manage his practice, his financial affairs, and his dealings with fellow professionals. Major subjects include medicolegal matters, health legislation, investments, fees, hospital problems, taxes, cars and doctor-patient relations. The subject matter is nonmedical, nonclinical and nondiagnostic." Buys 18 mss/year. Query. Length: 1,000-3,000 words. Pays $500-1,500.

Fillers: Jokes, gags, and anecdotes. Buys 100-150/year. Length: 250 words maximum. Pays $30-35.

THE MEDICAL EQUIPMENT CLASSIFIED, Govesco Publications, Box 29268, Minneapolis MN 55429. (612)566-5968. Editor: Rosslyn S. Smith. Emphasizes purchase, use and resale of medical equipment for hospital administrators and department heads, doctors, equipment manufacturers and veterinarians. Monthly magazine; 16-20 pages. Estab. 1978. Circ. 10,000. Pays on acceptance. Buys all rights. Phone queries OK. Submit seasonal/holiday material 3-4 months in advance. Photocopied and previously published submissions OK. SASE. Reports in 2 weeks. Sample copy $2.

Nonfiction: General interest, how-to, interview and technical ("but not to the point of confusion"). Will accept brief articles offering new twist on reducing medical costs. Sample topics: equipment leasing and services contracts. Buys 6 mss/year. Query. Length: 300-2,000 words. Pays $50.

Photos: State availability of photos. Uses b&w prints. Offers no additional payment for photos accepted with ms. Captions preferred, model releases required.

THE MEDICAL POST, 481 University Ave., Toronto, Ontario, Canada M5W 1A7. Editor: Derek Cassels. For the medical profession. Biweekly. Will send sample copy to medical writers only. Buys first North American serial rights. Pays on publication. SAE and International Reply Coupons.

Nonfiction: Uses "newsy, factual reports of medical developments. Must be aimed at professional audience, and not written in 'popular medical' style." Length: 300-800 words. Pays 12¢/word.

Photos: Uses photos with mss or captions only, of medical interest; pays $10 up.

THE NEW PHYSICIAN, 14650 Lee Rd., Chantilly VA 22021. Editor: Todd Dankmyer. 50% freelance written. For medical students, interns and residents. Monthly magazine; 64 pages. Estab. 1952. Circ. 70,000. Buys all rights. Buys 6-12 mss/year. Pays on publication. Free sample copy. Will consider simultaneous submissions. Reports in 4-6 weeks. Query. SASE.

Nonfiction and Photos: "Articles on social, political, economic issues in medicine/medical education. Our readers need more than a superficial, simplistic look into issues that affect them. We want skeptical, accurate, professional contributors to do well-researched, comprehensive reports, and offer new perspectives on health care problems." Not interested in material on "my operation," or encounters with physicians, or personal experiences as physician's patient. Occasionally publishes special topic issues, such as those on death and dying and alternatives in medical training. Informational articles, interviews and exposes are sought. Length: 500-2,500 words. Pays $25-250. Pays $10-25 for b&w photos used with mss. Captions required.

PHYSICIAN'S MANAGEMENT, Harcourt Brace Jovanovich Health Care Publications, 757 3rd Ave., New York NY 10017. (212)888-2938. Editor: Jim Hayes. Emphasizes finances, investments, small office administration, practice management and taxes for physicians in private practice. Monthly magazine; 90 pages. Estab. 1960. Circ. 180,000. Pays on acceptance. Buys all rights, but may reassign following publication. Submit seasonal or holiday material 5 months in advance. SASE. Reports in 2-4 weeks. Sample copy $2; free writer's guidelines.

Nonfiction: *Physician's Management* is a socio-economic publication, not a clinical one." Publishes how-to articles (limited to medical practice management); informational (when relevant to audience); personal experience articles (if written by a physician). Length: 500-3,000 words. Buys 3-5/issue. Query. Pays $50-400.

How To Break In: "Talk to doctors first about their practice, financial interests, and day-to-day nonclinical problems and then query us. Use of an MD byline helps tremendously! Also, the ability to write a concise, well-structured and well-researched magazine article is essential.

Most freelancers think like patients and fail with us. Those who can think like MDs are successful."

PRIVATE PRACTICE, 5100 N. Brookline, Suite 700, Oklahoma City OK 73112. Manuscript Editor: Terri T. Burke. For "medical doctors in private practice." Monthly. Buys first North American serial rights. "If an article is assigned it is paid for in full, used or killed. Byline given "except if it was completely rewritten or a considerable amount of additional material is added to the article." Pays on acceptance. Query. SASE.
Nonfiction and Photos: "Articles that indicate importance of maintaining freedom of medical practice or which detail outside interferences in the practice of medicine, including research, hospital operation, drug manufacture, etc. Straight reporting style. No cliches, no scare words, no flowery phrases to cover up poor reporting. Stories must be actual, factual, precise, correct. Copy should be lively and easy-to-read. Also publish travel, sports, leisure, historical, offbeat, and humorous articles of medical interest." Length: up to 2,500 words. Pays "usual minimum $150." Photos purchased with mss only. B&w glossies, 8x10. Payment "depends on quality, relevancy of material, etc."

SURGICAL BUSINESS, 2009 Morris Ave., Union NJ 07083. Editor: Adrian Comper. For medical/surgical dealers and dealer/salesmen. Monthly magazine; 92 pages. Estab. 1938. Circ. 7,000. Buys exclusive industry rights. Byline given. Buys 5-10 mss/year. Pays on publication. Free sample copy and writer's guidelines. Will consider photocopied and simultaneous submissions. Reports in 3 months. Query or submit complete ms. SASE.
Nonfiction and Photos: "We publish feature-length articles dealing with manufacturers within the industry, as well as domestic and international meeting coverage and general information within the industry. We do not desire promotional material about a company or product. Mss should be objective and to the point." No additional payment for b&w photos used with mss. Length: approximately 2,500 words. Pays 5¢/word.

Mining and Minerals

AMERICAN GOLD NEWS, Box 457, Ione CA 95640. (209)274-2196. Editor: Cecil L. Helms. 25% freelance written. For anyone interested in gold, gold mining, gold companies, gold stocks, gold history, gold coins, the future of gold in our economy. Monthly tabloid newspaper; 20 pages. Estab. 1933. Circ. 3,500. Not copyrighted. Pays 50% kill fee. Byline given. Pays on acceptance. Free sample copy and writer's guidelines. No photocopied or simultaneous submissions. Submit seasonal material (relating to seasonal times in mining country) 2 months in advance. Reports in 2-4 weeks. Query or submit complete ms. SASE.
Nonfiction and Photos: "This is not a literary publication. We want information on any subject pertaining to gold told in the most simple, direct and interesting way. How to build gold mining equipment. History of mines (with pix). History of gold throughout the US. Financial articles on gold philosophy in money matters. Picture stories of mines, mining towns, mining country. Would like to see more histories of mines, from any state. Length: 500-2,000 words. Pays $10-50. B&w photos purchased with or without ms. Must be sharp (if not old historical photos). Pays $2.50-25. Captions required.

COAL AGE, 1221 Avenue of the Americas, New York NY 10020. Editor: Joseph F. Wilkinson. For supervisors, engineers and executives in coal mining. Monthly. Circ. 20,000. Buys all rights. Pays on publication. Query. Reports in 2-3 weeks. SASE.
Nonfiction: Uses some technical (operating type) articles; some how-to pieces on equipment maintenance; management articles. Pays $150/page.

LANDMARC, Mining & Reclamation Council (MARC) of America, 1000 16th St. NW, Suite 700, Washington DC 20036. (202)857-0876. Editor: Carol Saus Goldsmith. Surface coal mining and land reclamation is the subject of this publication aimed at management-level personnel of surface coal mining companies. Monthly magazine; 32 pages. Estab. 1978. Pays on publication. Pays 10% kill fee. Byline given except for brief news updates; author's blurb appears with longer stories. Phone queries OK. Submit seasonal/holiday material 3 months in advance. Simultaneous, photocopied and previously published submissions OK. SASE. Reports in 3-4 weeks. Free sample copy and writer's guidelines.
Nonfiction: Exposé (of government programs and regulations that hamper efficiency and productivity in the industry); interview (with prominent figures or interesting personalities involved with surface coal mining and reclamation); profile (same as interview); new product (innovations in industry products, techniques, research, etc.); photo feature (of successful reclamation efforts or unusual mining operations); technical (reports on any aspects of

subject); and industry news updates. "Keep your eyes open for industry news briefs in your area. If you prove to be a reliable stringer for our news column, you're bound to get assignments." Buys 1-2 mss/issue. Query with clips of published work. Pays 2½¢/word.

Photos: Pays $10 for b&w contact sheets; offers no additional payment for photos accepted with ms. Captions preferred; model release required.

Columns/Departments: Update, new products, LandMarc Interview (with prominent industry or government figure involved with surface mining—Q&A format), and industry news briefs. Buys 2-3 mss/issue. Query with clips of published work. Length: 100-300 words (interview can go as high as 3,000 words). Pays $25 for news items; pay negotiable for longer reports and interviews.

Miscellaneous

AMERICAN CHRISTMAS TREE JOURNAL, 611 E. Wells St., Milwaukee WI 53202, (414)276-6410. Editors: Phil Jones, Mary Garity. Quarterly magazine. Circ. 1,800-2,000. Byline given. Pays on publication. Simultaneous, photocopied and previously published submissions OK. Reports in 1 month. Free sample copy and writer's guidelines.

Nonfiction: How-to, interview, job safety (any farm equipment), vocational techniques, new product (chemicals, equipment, tags, shearing knives and chain saws, etc.), personal experience, profile and technical (foresters, researchers). Query. Length: 2,000 minimum. Pays $50.

AMERICAN FARRIERS' JOURNAL, Drawer 151, Arcadia FL 33821. Editor-in-Chief: Henry Heymering. Emphasizes horseshoeing. Quarterly magazine: 32 pages. Estab. 1975. Circ. 1,500. Pays on publication. Buys all rights. Byline given. Submit seasonal/holiday material 7-9 months in advance of issue date. SASE. Reports in 3 weeks. Free sample copy; mention *Writer's Market* in request.

Nonfiction: Historical (old companies and methods); how-to; informational; interview (with shoers or manufacturers); technical; research findings; and news coverage of contests and competitions. Query. Length: 800-2,000 words. Pays $1/column inch.

Photos: State availability of photos with query. Pays $5-25 for b&w prints.

THE ANTIQUES DEALER, 1115 Clifton Ave., Clifton NJ 07013. Editor: Stella Hall. 90% freelance written. For antiques dealers. Monthly magazine. Estab. 1949. Circ. 7,000. Rights purchased vary with author and material. May buy all rights or first North American rights or exclusive rights in this field. Byline given. Buys 40 mss/year. Pays on publication. Will send free sample copy to writer on request. Will consider photocopied submissions "if clear." SASE.

Nonfiction: "Remember that we are a trade publication and all material must be slanted to the needs and interests of antique dealers. We publish nothing of a too general ("be a good salesman") or too limited (eastern Pennsylvania chairs) nature." Only articles of national interest to dealers; may be tutorial if by authority in one specific field; otherwise of broad general interest to all dealers and news of the international antique trade. Emphasis is currently on heirlooms (50-100 years old), as well as antiques (over 100 years old). Length: no minimum; maximum 2-part article, about 7,000 words; 3,500 words if one-part. Pays $30/page for features; $1.50 for few-sentence obit. Columns cover trade news; anything from a couple of sentences to about 200 words, with photo or two. Usually pays just $1.50 if very short.

Photos: Purchased with or without accompanying mss, or on assignment. Pays $5 per b&w used inside, $10 for covers; no smaller than 5x7 (glossy). Professional quality only; no Polaroids.

Fillers: Suitable for professional dealers; any type of fillers. Length: 300-400 words. Pays approximately $15 for half-page.

APA MONITOR, 1200 17th St. NW, Washington DC 20036. Editor: Pam Moore. Associate Editor: Karen Schaar. For psychologists and other social scientists and professionals interested in behaviorial sciences and mental health area. Monthly newspaper; 40 pages. Estab. 1970. Circ. 61,500. Buys all rights. Pays on publication. Free sample copy. Simultaneous submissions OK.

Nonfiction: News and features articles about issues facing psychology both as a science and a mental health profession; political, social and economic developments in the behavioral science area. Interview, profile, humor, historical, interpretive and think pieces. Buys about 35 mss/year. Query. Length: 300-3,000 words.

BOARDING KENNEL PROPRIETOR, S.A. Faulds & Co., 2785 N. Speer Blvd., Denver CO 80211. Address all correspondence to: Dora Hart, Executive Editor, ABKA, 6440 N. Old

Highway 85/87, Colorado Springs CO 80919. (303)598-7976. For boarding kennel owners, groomers, veterinarians, suppliers, etc. Monthly magazine; 32 pages. Estab. 1977. Circ. 7,500. Pays on publication. Rights negotiable. Byline given. Submit seasonal/holiday material 4 months in advance. Photocopied and previously published submissions OK. SASE. Reports in 4 weeks. Free sample copy and writer's guidelines.
Nonfiction: Interview (of kennel owners, etc.); profile (same as interview); and business (financial, bookkeeping, marketing, personnel, and taxes—related to kennel operations). Buys 3-5 mss/year. Length: 1,500-2,500 words. Send complete ms. Pays $50-125.
Photos: "Need good visuals (photos, graphics, illustrations, etc.) to promote interest in article in magazine." Send photo material with ms. Pays $5 for b&w 3x5 or larger glossy prints; and $10 for 2¼x2¼ and larger color transparencies. Captions preferred; model release required.
Columns/Departments: Interest in this area is in grooming, training (but not how-to on these), pet cemetaries, medical news, and how to add to existing kennel to increase profit, legal problems and problem clients. Buys 3-5 mss/year. Send complete ms. Length: 500-1,000 words. Pays $25-50. Open to suggestions for new columns/departments.

BUILDING ENERGY PROGRESS, Business Communications Co., Inc., 9 Viaduct Rd., Box 2070C, Stamford CT 06906. (203)325-2208. Managing Editor: Gail Greenberg. Bimonthly magazine; 24 pages. Estab. 1978. Pays on publication. Buys all rights. Byline given. Phone queries OK. Reports in 1 month. Free sample copy and writer's guidelines.
Nonfiction: How-to (product application); interview (analysis, state of the art); and profile. Query with clips of published work. Buys 3-4 mss/issue. Length: 1,000-3,000 words.

CANADIAN FUNERAL DIRECTOR, Peter Perry Publishing, Ltd., 1658 Victoria Park Ave., Suite 5, Scarboro, Ontario, Canada M1R 1P7. (416)755-7050. Managing Editor: Peter Perry. 15% freelance written. Emphasizes funeral home operation. Monthly magazine; 60 pages. Estab. 1924. Circ. 1,700. Pays on publication. Buys one-time rights. Byline given. Phone queries OK. Reports in 30-60 days. Simultaneous and photocopied submissions and previously published work OK. SAE and International Reply Coupons. Reports in 3 weeks. Free sample copy.
Nonfiction: Informational, historical, humor, interview, opinion, profile, photo feature, technical. Buys 12 mss/year. Query. Length: 200-1,500 words. Pays $50/1,000 words.
Photos: Purchased with or without ms. Captions required. Query or send contact sheet. Pays $5-10 for 5x7 or 8x10 b&w glossy prints.

CANADIAN RENTAL SERVICE, J. Peter Watkins, Ltd., 49 Queens Dr., Weston, Ontario, Canada M9N 2H3. (416)241-4724. Editor: Naomi Watkins. Emphasizes general rental business. Bimonthly magazine; 44 pages. Estab. 1976. Circ. 2,500. Pays on publication. Buys one-time rights. Phone queries OK. Submit seasonal/holiday material 2 months in advance. Photocopied submissions and previously published work OK. SAE and International Reply Coupons. Reports in 12 weeks. Free sample copy.
Nonfiction: Profiles and technical articles. Buys 1-2 mss/issue. Query. Length: 1,000 words maximum. Pays $50/page minimum.
Photos: Purchased with ms or on assignment. Captions required. Query. Pays $20 minimum for 5x7 b&w glossies. Model release required.
Columns/Departments: Trade News, Association News, Appointments. Query. Length: 1 typewritten page.
Fillers: Clippings, newsbreaks. Buys 1-2/issue. Send complete ms. Pays $10-20.
Rejects: Material related to rental of items not rented by the field involved. Material related to renting in the USA.

C & S (Casket and Sunnyside), 274 Madison Ave., New York NY 10016. (212)685-8310. Editor: Howard Barnard. 10% freelance written. "This magazine is circulated to funeral directors of all ages, more and more who are becoming college-educated." Monthly magazine; 48 pages. Estab. 1871. Circ. 12,000. Pays on publication. Buys all rights. Byline given. Submit seasonal/holiday material 2 months in advance of issue date. SASE. Reports in 2 weeks.
Nonfiction: General interest (stories on mortuaries); historical (articles dealing with embalming, early funeral vehicles and ambulances, etc.); how-to (handle difficult or unusual restorative art or embalming cases); inspirational (public realtions achievements); and "short items or new products in the funeral field." Buys 20 mss/year. Query. Length: 1,500-2,500 words. Pays $75.
Photos: State availability of photos with query. Pays $5 for 5x7 or 8x10 b&w prints. Captions required. Buys all rights.

Fillers: Clippings, obituaries and items concerning various activities of funeral directors. Buys 10-15/issue. Pays $3.

COACHING REVIEW, Coaching Association of Canada, 333 River Rd., Ottawa, Ontario, Canada K1L 8B9. (613)741-0036. Editor: Vic MacKenzie. For volunteer, community and paid coaches, high school and university sports personnel. Bimonthly magazine; 64 pages. Estab. 1977. Circ. 10,000. Pays on acceptance. Buys first North American rights. Pays 50-75% kill fee. Byline given unless author requests otherwise. Phone queries OK. Submit seasonal/holiday material 3 months in advance. Reports in 3 weeks. Free sample copy and writer's guidelines.
Nonfiction: How-to (coach related of a general interest to all sports); humor (in coaching situations); inspirational (coaching success stories); interview (with top successful coaches); and new product (new ideas and ways of coaching). Wants "authoritative original material on coaching topics with a Canadian bias." Does not want sports stories with little or no relevance to coaching. Buys 3 mss/issue. Query with complete ms. Length: 1,500-2,500 words. Pays $50.
Photos: State availability of photos. Pays $5-25 for b&w contact sheets; $15-30 for 35mm color transparencies. Captions required. Buys one-time rights.

COACHING: WOMEN'S ATHLETICS, Intercommunications, Inc., Box 867, Wallingford CT 06492. (203)265-0937. Publisher/Editor: William J. Burgess. For administrators of athletic and/or physical education departments of public, private and parochial junior and senior high schools, preparatory schools, junior colleges and universities. Bimonthly (except July/August) magazine; 90 pages. Estab. 1975. Circ. 10,000. Pays on publication. Buys all rights. Byline given. Phone queries OK. Reports in 2 weeks. Sample copy $4; free writer's guidelines.
Nonfiction: How-to, sports news, personal experience and profile. Buys 100 mss/year. Length: 2,500 words maximum. Pays $100-450.
Photos: Purchased with or without accompanying ms. Captions required. Query. Uses 4x5 or larger b&w glossy prints; 35mm, 2¼x2¼ or 4x5 color transparencies. Pays $200-350 for cover color transparencies.

CONSULTING '79, American Institute of Professional Consultants, American Professional Center, 201 S. Lake Ave., Pasadena CA 91109. (213)796-5700. Editor-in-Chief: W. Marion Carter. Editor: Michael W. Johnson. For professional consultants from various specializations including general business, tax, data processing and marketing. Most are college graduates; 35-54 years old. Interests are in all aspects of the consulting field. Bimonthly magazine; 40 pages. Estab. 1978. Circ. 2,700-3,500. Pays on publication. Buys all rights. Query by phone at their toll-free number: (800)-423-4580; in California: (800)362-7047. Submit seasonal/holiday material 6 months in advance. Simultaneous and previously published submissions OK. Reports in 1 month. Free sample copy and writer's guidelines.
Nonfiction: General interest (general business topics applicable to consultants); how-to (concentrating on marketing and managing a consulting practice—client relations, case studies); interview (with successful consultants); profile (of successful consultants); personal experience (case studies of consultant/client relations); and articles on taxes, finance or other aspects of business. "Articles should be written with the consultant's part of view in mind." Buys 4-6 mss/issue. Send complete ms or query with clips of published work. Length: 1,500-3,500 words. Pays $100 minimum.
Photos: Send photos with ms. Pays $25 for b&w glossy prints. Color photos used for cover only. Limited market. Pays $50-75 for color transparencies. Captions and model release required.
Fillers: "We will consider newsbriefs on subjects pertaining to the field of consulting." Buys 6-8/issue. Length: 50-150 words. Pays $10-25.

DEFENSE TRANSPORTATION JOURNAL, 910 17th St., Suite 301, Washington DC 20006. Publisher/Editor: Gerald W. Collins. For "transportation executives and managers of all ages and military transportation officers. Generally educated with college degree." Estab. 1945. Bimonthly. Circ. 10,000. Rights purchased vary with author and material; may buy all rights, but may reassign rights to author after publication. Byline given. Buys 5-10 mss/year. Pays on acceptance. Free sample copy and writer's guidelines. Submit seasonal material 2-3 months in advance. Reports in 2-3 weeks. SASE.
Nonfiction: "Articles on transportation, distribution, and traffic management in the US and abroad. This publication emphasizes transportation as it relates to defense and emergency requirements." Buys informational and personal experience articles. Length: 2,500-3,000 words, with photos or sketches. Pays $100.

EMERGENCY, Box 159, Carlsbad CA 92008. Managing Editor: Keith Griffiths. 20% freelance written. Emphasizes emergency medical services for anyone involved in emergency services, including ambulance personnel, paramedics, search and rescue personnel, emergency room personnel, law enforcement personnel and firefighters. Monthly magazine; 84 pages. Estab. 1970. Circ. 35,000. Pays on publication. Buys all rights. Pays 15% kill fee. Byline given. Submit seasonal/holiday material 4 months in advance of issue date. SASE. Reports in 2 months. Free sample copy and writer's guidelines.

Nonfiction: How-to (better execute a certain emergency procedure, guidelines for emergency medical techniques). Buys 3 mss/issue. Query. Length: 800-3,000 words. Pays $50-150.

Photos: State availability of photos with query. Pays $15 minimum for 5x7 b&w glossy prints; $10-25 for 35mm color transparencies. Captions required. Buys all rights.

Columns/Departments: News Briefs (short items of interest to emergency personnel); and Funds and Grants (allocated for improvement of emergency care). Buys 10/year. Query. Length: 50-100 words. Pays $1/inch. Open to suggestions for new columns/departments.

THE FIRE FIGHTER'S DIGEST, S.D. Enterprises, 9014 Birchleaf Ave., Downey CA 90241. Editor: S.W. Deeble. Emphasizes fire service and paramedic service. Bimonthly magazine 104 pages. Estab. 1979. Circ. 10,000. Pays on publication. Makes assignments on a work-for-hire basis or buys second serial (reprint) rights or one-time rights. Pays negotiable kill fee. Byline given. Phone queries OK. Submit seasonal/holiday material 2 months in advance. Simultaneous, photocopied and previously published submissions OK. SASE. Reports in 2 weeks. Sample copy $1.50; writer's guidelines $1.

Nonfiction: Expose (of paramedic service); general interest (professional sports and those that firemen take part in); historical (past eras with different departments); humor (funny situations that occur in the fire service); inspirational (fire rescues); interview (with fire chief on fire service subjects); opinion; personal experience; and photo feature. Buys 3 mss/issue. Send complete ms. Length: 400-800 words. Pays $30-100.

Photos: Pays $5-50 for b&w 8x10 or 3x5 prints. Captions required.

Columns/Departments: Books. Need someone to review books which bring the fire service to the public's attention. Length: 800 words.

Poetry: Light Verse. Buys 3 poems/issue. Submit poems in batches of 5. Pays $5-40.

Fillers: Clippings, jokes, gags, anecdotes, short humor and newsbreaks. Buys 21/issue. Length: 100-800. Pays $3-50.

THE GRANTSMANSHIP NEWS, The Grantsmanship Center, 1031 S. Grand Ave., Los Angeles CA 90015. (213)749-4721. Editor: Carol Easton. Managing Editor: Cathleen Collins. Emphasizes funding, philanthropy, grants process and nonprofit management for professionals involved in government or foundation grant making or grant seeking. Bimonthly magazine; 104 pages. Circ. 20,500. Pays on acceptance. Makes assignments on a work-for-hire basis. Pays variable kill fee. Byline given. Simultaneous, photocopied and previously published submissions OK. SASE. Reports in 1 month. Sample copy $2.50.

Nonfiction: Expose, general interest, how-to and interview. "Familiarity with the field is an asset." Buys 2-3 mss/issue. Query with clips of published work. Length: 1,500-10,000 words. Pays 10¢/word minimum.

Photos: State availability of photos. Uses b&w contact sheets and color transparencies. Offers no additional payment for photos accepted with ms. Captions preferred; model release required. Buys all rights.

HOUSEHOLD AND PERSONAL PRODUCTS INDUSTRY, 26 Lake St., Ramsey NJ 07446. Editor: Hamilton C. Carson. 5-10% freelance written. For "manufacturers of soaps, detergents, cosmetics and toiletries, waxes and polishes, insecticides, and aerosols." Estab. 1964. Monthly. Circ. 14,000. Not copyrighted. Buys 3-4 mss/year, "but would buy more if slanted to our needs." Pays on publication. Will send a sample copy to a writer on request. Will consider photocopied submissions. Submit seasonal material 2 months in advance. Query. SASE.

Nonfiction and Photos: "Technical and semitechnical articles on manufacturing, distribution, marketing, new products, plant stories, etc., of the industries served. Some knowledge of the field is essential in writing for us." Buys informational articles, interviews, photo features, spot news, coverage of successful business operations, new product articles, coverage of merchandising techniques, and technical articles. Length: 500-2,000 words. Pays $10-200. 5x7 or 8x10 b&w glossies purchased with mss. Pays $10.

THE INDIAN TRADER, Box 31235, Billings MT 59107. (406)245-0507. Editor-in-Chief: Ms. Jo Smith. 70% freelance written. For traders in the Indian arts, crafts and culture. Monthly tabloid; 72 pages. Estab. 1970. Circ. 10,000. Pays on publication. Buys all rights, but may reassign following publication. Byline given "if the writer requests it and if their reason is valid. We do not byline short advances—mostly the coverage of events, features and lengthy how-to-do articles." Phone queries OK. Submit seasonal/holiday material 2 months in advance. Reports in 3-6 weeks. Free sample copy and writer's guidelines.

Nonfiction: Historical (must be accurately researched and of special interest to collectors of Indian artifacts, traders, or those interested in current American activities); informational (characters of historical interest, their descendants, etc.); interviews (with exceptional Indian craftsmen, collectors, shows, pow-wows, etc.); photo features (coverage of Indian affairs, reservation happenings, etc.); and travel (visits to Indian ruins, trading posts, similar material in areas of the Northwest or Northeast, or Canada). Buys 8-10 mss/issue. Pays 50¢-$1.50/column inch. "This usually works out to about 2-4¢/word, but we do pay by the column inch."

Photos: B&w (8x10) glossies preferred. Purchased with or without mss or on assignment. Captions optional, but information must be included if captionless. Query or send prints. Pays $2-15 when additional payment is made. Total purchase price sometimes includes payment for photos.

Columns/Departments: Buys 1-3 book reviews/issue. Query. Pays 50¢-$1.50/column inch.

INFO FRANCHISE NEWSLETTER, 11 Bond St., St. Catharines, Ontario, Canada L2R 4Z4. (716)754-4669, ext. 5. Editor-in-Chief: E.L. Dixon Jr. Managing Editor: Mrs. D. Hill. Monthly newsletter; 8 pages. Estab. May 1977. Circ. 4,000. Pays on publication. Buys all rights, but may reassign following publication. Byline given. Photocopied submissions OK. SAE and International Reply Coupons. Reports in 4 weeks. Free sample copy.

Nonfiction: "We are particularly interested in receiving articles regarding franchise legislation, franchise litigation, franchise success stories, and new franchises. Both American and Canadian items are of interest. We do not want to receive any information that is not fully documented; or articles which could have appeared in any newspaper or magazine in North America. An author with a legal background, who could comment upon such things as arbitration and franchising, collective bargaining and franchising or class actions and franchising would be of great interest to us." Expose; how-to; informational; interview; profile; new product; personal experience; and technical. Buys 5-10 mss/year. Length: 25-1,000 words. Pays $10-300.

INTERSEARCH, International Terrorist Research Center, Box 26804, El Paso TX 79926. Editor-in-Chief: Frank W. Taggart. Managing Editor: Gavin de Becker. 50% freelance written. For "executives and security directors in business, industry and government concerned about the threat posed by terrorists around the world." Biweekly newsletter; 8 pages. Estab. 1977. Circ. 2,000. Pays on acceptance. Buys all rights, but may reassign following publication. Byline given. Submit seasonal/holiday material 2 months in advance of issue date. Simultaneous, photocopied and previously published submissions OK. SASE. Reports in 2 weeks. Sample copy $1.50.

Nonfiction: Expose (terrorist, subversive or underground groups and organizations); interview (experts in dealing with terrorists); new product (anti-terrorist devices); opinion (best ways to combat terrorism); profile (terrorist groups and organizations); and technical (anti-terrorist devices). Buys 3-5 mss/issue. Query. Length: 500 words maximum. Pays $25 minimum.

JOURNAL OF MICROGRAPHICS, National Micrographics Association, 8719 Colesville Rd., Silver Spring MD 20910. (301)587-8202. Editor. Emphasizes micrographics and related technologies such as facsimile, data processing, word processing and records management. Bimonthly magazine; 48 pages. Estab. 1967. Circ. 9,000. Pays on acceptance. Buys all rights. Byline given. Phone queries OK. Photocopied submission OK. Reports in 4 weeks. Free sample copy and writer's guidelines.

Nonfiction: How-to (applications articles on how organizations interfaced micrographics with other information handling technologies); and technical (new developments in technologies that could interface with micrographics). Query. Length: 6,000 words. Pays $50.

Photos: "In a technical publication like ours, photographs help explain the subject to new readers." Send photos with ms. Wants b&w 5x7 glossy prints. Offers no additional payment for photos accepted with ms. Captions required.

LAWN CARE INDUSTRY, Harvest Publishing Co., 9800 Detroit Ave., Cleveland OH 44102. (216)651-5500. Editor: Bob Earley. 10% freelance written. For lawn care businessmen. Monthly tabloid; 40 pages. Estab. 1977. Circ. 12,000. Pays on acceptance. Buys all rights, but may reassign following publication. Phone queries OK. Submit seasonal/holiday material 3 months in advance of issue date. Simultaneous and photocopied submissions OK. SASE. Reports in 2 weeks. Free sample copy.

Nonfiction: General interest (articles related to small business operation); how-to (running a

lawn care business); interview (with lawn care operator or industry notable); new product (helping to better business practices); and profile (of lawn care businessmen). Buys 3 mss/issue. Query. Length: 500-1,000 words. Pays $50-250.
Photos: State availability of photos with query. Pays $10-100 for 5x7 glossy b&w prints; $50-250 for 35mm color transparencies. Captions required. Buys one-time rights.

MEETINGS & CONVENTIONS, Ziff-Davis Publishing Co., 1 Park Ave., New York NY 10016. Editor-in-Chief: Mel Hosansky. 15% freelance written. For association and corporate executives who plan sales meetings, training meetings, annual conventions, incentive travel trips, and any other kind of off-premises meeting. Monthly magazine; 150 pages. Estab. 1966. Circ. 73,500. Pays on acceptance. Buys all rights. Submit seasonal or holiday material 6 months in advance. Photocopied submissions and previously published work (if not published in a competing publication) OK. SASE. Reports in 1-2 months.
Nonfiction: "Publication is basically how-to. We tell them how to run better meetings; where to hold them, etc. Must be case history, talking about specific meeting." Query. Length: 250-2,000 words. Pays $35-300.
Photos: Purchases 8x10 b&w glossies with mss. Captions required. No additional payment. Query.

MEETINGS & EXPOSITIONS, 22 Pine St., Morristown NJ 07960. (201)538-9470. Editorial Director: William F. Kaiser. Managing Editor: Gale Dopp Curtis. 10% freelance written. Emphasizes meetings, expositions, and incentive travel for "meeting planning" executives in companies and associations. Bimonthly magazine; 48-64 pages. Estab. 1973. Circ. 42,000. Pays on publication. Buys all rights, but may reassign following publication. Byline given. Phone queries OK. Submit seasonal/holiday material 6 months in advance of issue date. Simultaneous submissions OK. SASE. Reports in 2 weeks. Free sample copy and writer's guidelines.
Nonfiction: "*ME*'s editorial philosophy centers on in-depth coverage of the five specific major areas of most importance to meetings, expositions, and incentive travel planners: improving meetings; meeting locations; meetings associations meetings; trade shows and expositions; and incentive travel. In brief, it is *ME*'s editorial philosophy to provide, simple and directly, useful information and a most energetic support for the professional meeting planners who want to hold better meetings, more successful expositions, and more productive incentive travel promotions." Buys 10-12 mss/year. Query. Length: 1,000-3,000 words. Pays $50-150.
Photos: Offers no additional payment for 8x10 or 5x7 b&w glossy prints. Captions preferred. Buys one-time rights.

NATIONAL MALL MONITOR, Suite 500, Arbor Office Center, 1321 US 19 S., Clearwater FL 33516. (813)531-5893. Associate Editor: Barbara D. Engel. 25-40% freelance written. For shopping center industry developers, mall managers, financing institutions, architects, engineers, commercial brokers and retailers. Bimonthly magazine; 64 pages. Estab. 1970. Circ. 15,000. Pays on publication. Buys all rights. Phone queries OK. Submit seasonal/holiday material 4 months in advance of issue date. Photocopied submissions OK. SASE. Reports in 6 weeks. Sample copy $4 plus postage; free writer's guidelines.
Nonfiction: Wants concise, factual, well-written mss that will keep readers informed of the latest happenings within the industry and allied fields. "The pieces should be cleared through the proper channels for accuracy and authenticity and must be written on a free and easy style, similar to consumer magazines." Buys how-to articles (such as the best way to build, renovate or maintain a shopping center). Stories about unusual specialty or theme centers always in demand. "Always looking for articles about noted architects, engineers, designers, as long as they have something to say to the industry that it doesn't already know." No articles on pageants, auto shows, band concerts or local promotional activities. Buys 20 mss/year. Query. Length: 500-2,000 words. Pays 7½¢/word for 1st sale and 10¢/word for each subsequent sale.
Photos: State availability of photos with query. Pays $9 minimum for 5x7 b&w glossy prints and 8x10 glossy color prints or 2¼x2¼ mounted transparencies. Captions required. Buys all rights. Model release required.
Columns/Departments: Spotlights leasing, management and promotion. Query. Length: 800-1,200 words. Pays 7½¢/word for 1st sale and 10¢/word for each subsequent sale. Open to suggestions for new columns/departments.

NON-FOODS MERCHANDISING, Charleson Publishing Co., 124 E. 40th St., New York NY 10024. Editor: Alice Ely. 40% freelance written. For buyers, manufacturers, and distributors of health and beauty aids and general merchandise (non-food) in the supermarket. Monthly tabloid; 75 pages. Estab. 1957. Circ. 19,000. Pays on publication. Buys all rights. Byline given

"except if the story was not anything special or if numerous àrticles by the same author appeared in one issue." Photocopied submissions OK. SASE. Reports in 4 weeks.
Nonfiction: "Reports on aspects of our business." Buys 6 mss/issue. Query. Length: 500-2,000 words. Pays $50-150.

PROBLEMS OF COMMUNISM, International Communication Agency, *Problems of Communism,* PGM/PM, Room 964, 1776 Pennsylvania Ave. NW, Washington DC 20547. (202)632-5119. Editor: Paul A. Smith Jr. For scholars and decisionmakers in all countries of the world with higher education and a serious interest in foreign area studies and international relations. Estab. 1952. Circ. 25,000. Not copyrighted. Pays 20% kill fee. Byline given. Buys 60-70 mss/year. Pays on acceptance. Free sample copy. Photocopied submissions OK. Reports in 3 months.
Nonfiction: "*Problems of Communism* is one of a very few journals devoted to objective, dispassionate discourse on a highly unobjective, passionately debated phenomenon: communism. It is maintained as a forum in which qualified observers can contribute to a clearer understanding of the sources, nature and direction of change in the areas of its interest. It has no special emphasis or outlook and represents no partisan point of view. Standards of style are those appropriate to the field of international scholarship and journalism. We use intellectually rigorous studies of East-West relations, and/or related political, economic, social and strategic trends in the USSR, China and their associated states and movements. Length is usually 5,000 words. Essay reviews of 1,500 words cover new books offering significant information and analysis. Emphasis throughout *Problems of Communism* is on original research, reliability of sources and perceptive insights. We do not publish political statements or other forms of advocacy or apologetics for particular forms of belief." Query or submit complete ms. Pays $500/article; $200/essay reviews.
Photos: Pays $35 for b&w glossy prints.

THE PROFESSIONAL HANDWRITING ANALYST, San Francisco Academy of Handwriting Analysis, 760 Market St., Suite 347, San Francisco CA 94102. (415)397-5246. Editor: Julia Pippin Sellenraad. Emphasizes the psychology of handwriting for a predominately mature adult audience of employers, parents, teachers and educators, counselors and psychologists and people interested in self-improvement. Quarterly newsletter; 16 pages. Estab. 1978. Circ. 3,000. Pays on publication. Buys all rights. Byline given. Submit seasonal/holiday material 6 months in advance. Photocopied submissions and previously published work OK. SASE. Reports in 3 weeks. Sample copy and writer's guidelines $1.
Nonfiction: Exposé (of pseudo-scientific psychological practices); historical (history of psychology); humor (related to psychology and handwriting); interview (of persons in social who have made significant contribution); opinion (views of professional and layman regarding handwriting analysis); profile (of persons in social sciences who have made significant contirbution); travel (only with some special slant pertaining to psychology or education); personal experience (related to handwriting analysis); technical (psychology, and psychology of handwriting. Intellect and intelligence. Lecture preparation and delivery). Also interested in articles on teaching and sales of psychological services. "We are vitally interested in upgrading public opinion of the validity and usefulness of handwriting analysis." Buys 3-4 mss/issue. Query, but will give all "hot" mss full consideration. Length 500-2,000 words. Pays $35.
Columns/Departments: Viewpoint (various aspects of study and practice of psychology, handwriting analysis); Interview (with persons engaged in social sciences, their views, contributions); Psychology (various aspects—especially those relating to study and practice of handwriting analysis); Public Relations (professional modes of conduct to enhance analysts' image); Special Report(s) (anything pertaining to behavioral and social sciences); Digest ("usually a listing of reference works and miscellaneous guides of help to our readers); and Health (nearly any aspect of health information). Buys 4-6 mss/year. Query. Length: 500-2,000 words. Pays $35.
Fiction: Humorous stories only about distortions of psychological practices and ideas. Buys 2 mss/year. Query. Length: 500-1,000 words. Pays $35.
Poetry: "We have not used poetry, but would consider any that are appropriate to our magazine." Length: 2-16 lines. Pays $5-35.
Fillers: Clippings, cartoons and any other material in this category pertinent to content of magazine. Length: 35-100 words. Pays $2.50-7.50.

SANITARY MAINTENANCE, Box 694, Milwaukee WI 53201. (414)271-4105. Editor-in-Chief: Jack Pomrening. Managing Editor: Don Mulligan. 5% freelance written. For distributors of sanitary supplies. Monthly magazine; 110 pages. Estab. 1943. Circ. 11,800. Pays on publication. Buys all rights. Byline given. Photocopied submissions OK. SASE. Free sample copy and writer's guidelines.

Nonfiction: How-to (run a janitorial supply business, hold seminars, etc.); interview (with men in the field); and technical. Buys 3 mss/year. Query. Length: 1,500-3,000 words. Pays $100-150.

Photos: State availability of photos with query. Offers no additional payment for 5x7 b&w glossy prints. Captions preferred. Buys all rights.

SHOPFITTING AND DISPLAY INTERNATIONAL. Link House, Dingwall Ave., Croydon CR9 2TA England. Editor: G. Carroll. Monthly magazine for retailers with purchasing and specifying powers, property and premises managers, architects, designers, shopfitters, display managers, woodworking and metalworking equipment manufacturers, management and executive staffs in all retail trades and in most major commercial organizations which meet the public on their premises. Estab. 1955. Circ. 10,000. Pays on publication. SAE and International Reply Coupons. Query or submit complete ms. Free sample copy.

Nonfiction: News items and features on the fitting-out of shops, departmental stores, restaurants, hotels (public areas only), showrooms, offices, board rooms, bars, night clubs, theaters, banks, building societies; the materials and techniques used; the design brief for interior and exterior; use of subcontractors, cost of job. Pays 30 pounds minimum.

SOLAR ENERGY DIGEST. Box 17776, San Diego CA 92117. Editor: William B. Edmondson. 5-10% freelance written. For manufacturers, scientists, engineers, architects, builders, developers, technicians, energy experts, teachers, inventors, and others interested in solar energy conversion. Newsletter; 12 pages. Estab. 1973. Monthly. Circ. 15,000. Buys all rights, but may reassign rights to author after publication. Pays on publication. Free sample copy for SASE. Reports in 1-3 weeks. SASE.

Nonfiction: Wants mss about new developments in any facet of solar energy conversion, including applications in agriculture, architecture, cooking, distillation, mechanical engines and pumps, photo-electricity, steam generation, flat plate and concentrating collectors, sea thermal plants, furnaces, heat and energy storage, photosynthesis, wind power, wave power, etc. "Assume that the reader knows the fundamentals of the subject and plunge right in without a long introduction. Keep it simple, but not simplistic." No generalized papers on solar energy. "We like to cover a specific new development in each story." Buys 60-75 mss/year. Length: 100-1,000 words. Length for regular columns: 1,000 words maximum. Pays 2-5¢/word.

Fillers: Shorts and news clippings on solar energy. Length: 25-200 words. Pays $1-5.

SOLUTION. 1 Jake Brown Road, Old Bridge NJ 08857. (201)679-4000. Editor: George S. Bahue. 20% freelance written. For persons involved in television servicing; most own their own stores. Also for trade school graduates. Publication of Blonder-Tongue Labs. Estab. 1967. Quarterly. Circ. 30,000. Buys all rights. Buys 6 mss/year. Pays on publication. Free sample copy. Will consider photocopied and simultaneous submissions. Reports in 1 month. SASE.

Nonfiction and Photos: General interest articles on TV and signal distribution, MATV systems, and cable television systems. General knowledge of electronics is a must. Author must be able to talk the language. "Will consider short features." Buys informational, new product and technical articles. Length: 750-1,500 words. Pays $250 minimum. Photos purchased with accompanying mss with no additional payment.

TOBACCO REPORTER. 757 3rd Ave., New York NY 10017. Editor: John Karolefski. For tobacco growers, processors, warehousemen, exporters, importers, manufacturers and distributors of cigars, cigarettes and tobacco products. Monthly. Buys all rights. Pays on publication. SASE.

Nonfiction and Photos: Uses original material on request only. Pays approximately 2½¢/word. Pays $3 for photos purchased with mss.

Fillers: Wants clippings on new tobacco product brands, local tobacco distributors, smoking and health, and the following related to tobacco and tobacco products: job promotions, obituaries, honors, equipment, etc. Pays minimum 25¢/clipping on use only.

WESTERN LANDSCAPING NEWS. William/Lawrence Corp., Box 19531, Irvine CA 92713. (714)979-4720. Editor: Michael J. Snapp. Published for the Western landscaping and nursery industry. Monthly magazine; 64 pages. Estab. 1961. Circ. 17,000. Pays on publication. Buys all rights. Submit seasonal/holiday material 4 months in advance. Photocopied and previously published submissions OK. SASE. Reports in 3 weeks. Free sample copy and writer's guidelines.

Nonfiction: How-to (ideas for the average contractor on design, product selection, planning, irrigation, turf growing, selecting nursery stock, management and marketing, etc.); interview (with respected person in industry in the West or someone promoting or improving the industry); opinion (government regulations; only when author is known and respected in industry); profile (Western landscapers who have unusual qualities); and technical (write in lay terms). "If you're intent on writing for us, interview an expert and let him form the basis of your article." Buys 2 mss/issue. Query. Length: 1,200-3,000 words. Pays $50-150.

Photos: "Ours is basically a visual industry. When we're talking about an interesting landscape design, we'd like to picture it." State availability of photos. Pays $5 for b&w 5x7 or 8x10 prints, and $10-25 for 35mm color transparencies. Captions and model releases required.

Columns/Departments: "In Focus" is a short profile piece on some of the average people in Western landscaping. Query. Length: 1,000-1,500 words. Pays $25-50.

WIRE JOURNAL, Box H, 1570 Boston Post Rd., Guilford CT 06437. Editor: Anita M. Oliva. Associate Editor: Ruth W. Rose. Technical journal for wire and cable manufacturers and for manufacturers of products using wire and cable. Monthly magazine; 120 pages. Estab. 1964. Circ. 10,500. Pays on publication. Buys all rights. Byline given. Photocopied submissions OK. SASE. Reports in 1 month. Sample copy $3.

Nonfiction: Historical (background on wire and cable manufacturers); personal experience (only if from someone in the wire industry); and technical (wiredrawing, stranding, insulating). Query. Length: 1,500 words maximum. Pays $50-100.

Music

THE CANADIAN COMPOSER, Creative Arts Co., #401, 1240 Bay St., Toronto, Ontario, Canada M5R 2A7. (416)925-5138. Editor-in-Chief: Richard Flohil. For "composers of music in Canada; 10% 'serious', the rest involved in various kinds of popular music." Published 10 times/year. Magazine; 48 pages. Estab. 1966. Pays on publication. Buys one-time rights. Phone queries OK. Submit seasonal/holiday material 3 months in advance. Photocopied submissions OK. SASE. Reports in 1 week. Free sample copy.

Nonfiction: Informational, interview and profile. Buys 4 mss/issue. Query. Length: 2,500 words. Pays $90-125.

Photos: Purchased with accompanying ms or on assignment. Captions required. Query or submit contact sheet. Pays $10-20 for 8x10 b&w glossies.

CANADIAN MUSICIAN, Norris Publications, 2453 Yonge St., Suite #3, Toronto, Ontario, Canada M4P 2E8. (416)485-8284. Editor: Jim Norris. For professional and amateur musicians, music students and teachers, music industry people, recording and audio enthusiasts, music enthusiasts. Material must be factral in content, stressing technical and professional aspects of music. Bimonthly magazine; 60 pages. Estab. March 1979. Circ. 25,000. Pays on acceptance. Buys all rights. Phone queries OK. SASE. Reports in 4 weeks. Free sample copy and writer's guidelines.

Nonfiction: How-to (projects for building or repairing musical, audio and recording equipment); interviews or articles (with Canadian music people or of Canadian origin, 2,500-4,000 words); and technical (articles on recording, musical equipment, audio equipment). Buys 4-6 mss/issue. Query. Length: 2,000-5,000 words. Pays $150-300.

Photos: Send photos with ms. Pays $5-25 for 8x10 b&w glossy prints; $25-100 for 2¼ color transparencies. Buys one-time rights.

Columns/Departments: Notes (newsy articles of interest to musicians on any subject, 150-500 words); Profile (on Canadian music people less known or behind the scenes with pictures, 700-800 words); and Captured Live (live reviews of Canadian artists or artists of Canadian origin, with pictures, if possible, 150-300 words). Buys 1-4/issue. Query. Length: 150-800 words. Pays $20-150.

THE MUSICAL NEWSLETTER, 654 Madison Ave., Suite 1703, New York NY 10021. Editor: Patrick J. Smith. For "amateur and professional music lovers who wish to know more about music and be given more specific information." Estab. 1971. Quarterly. Circ. 600. Rights purchased vary with author and material; may buy first serial rights in English or second serial rights. Pays on acceptance. Sample copy $1. Will consider photocopied submissions. Query for nonfiction, "giving a list of subjects of possible interest and outlines, if possible." SASE.

Nonfiction: "Articles on music and the musical scene today. The bulk of articles are on 'classical' music, but we also publish articles on jazz and pop. Articles need not pertain to music directly, such as socio-economic articles on performing entities. As the level of our publication is between the musicological quarterly and the record review magazine, what we want is readable material which contains hard-core information. We stress quality. We are always happy to examine freelance material on any aspect of music, from articles on composers' works to philosophical articles on music or reportorial articles on performing organizations. We discourage reviews of performances and interviews, which we feel are adequately covered elsewhere." Length: 3,000 words maximum. Pays 10¢/word.

OPERA NEWS, 1865 Broadway, New York NY 10023. Editor: Robert Jacobson. For all people interested in opera; opera singers, opera management people, administrative people in opera, opera publicity people, artists' agents; people in the trade and interested laymen. Magazine; 32-72 pages. Estab. 1933. Weekly. (Monthly in summer.) Circ. 101,000. Copyrighted. Pays negotiable kill fee. Byline given. Pays on publication. Will send sample copy to writer for $1.50. Query. SASE.
Nonfiction and Photos: Most articles are commissioned in advance. In summer, uses articles of various interests on opera; in the fall and winter, articles that relate to the weekly broadcasts. Emphasis is on high quality in writing and an intellectual interest in the opera-oriented public. Informational, how-to, personal experience, interview, profile, humor, historical, think pieces, personal opinion; opera reviews. Length: 300 words maximum. Pays 10¢/word for features; 8¢/word for reviews. Pays minimum of $25 for photos purchased on assignment. Captions required.

SOUTHWESTERN MUSICIAN, Box 9908, Houston TX 77013. 20% freelance written. For music teachers. Monthly (August through May). Buys all rights. Pays on acceptance. Reports in 1 month. SASE.
Nonfiction: "Professionally slanted articles of interest to public school music teachers." Pays $25-50.

Oceanography

The journals below are intended primarily for scientists who are studying the ocean. Publications for ocean fishermen will be found under Fishing. Those for persons interested in water and the ocean as a means of travel or shipping are listed with the Marine Industries and Water Navigation journals.

SEA FRONTIERS, 3979 Rickenbacker Causeway, Virginia Key, Miami FL 33149. (305)361-5786. Editor: F.G.W. Smith. 90-95% freelance written. For "members of the International Oceanographic Foundation. For the lay person—anyone with an interest in the sea; professional people for the most part; people in executive positions and students." Estab. 1954. Bimonthly. Circ. 60,000. Buys all rights. Byline given. Buys 20-25 mss/year. Pays on publication. Free sample copy and writer's guidelines. Will consider photocopied submissions "if very clear." Reports on material within 6 weeks. Query. SASE. •
Nonfiction and Photos: "Articles (with illustrations) covering explorations, discoveries or advances in our knowledge of the marine sciences, or describing the activities of oceanographic laboratories or expeditions to any part of the world. Emphasis should be on research and discoveries rather than personalities involved." Length: 500-3,000 words. Pays $20-30/page. 8x10 b&w glossy prints and 35mm (or larger) color transparencies purchased with ms. Pays $50 for color used on front and $25 for the back cover. Pays $15 for color used on inside covers.

Office Equipment and Supplies

GEYER'S DEALER TOPICS, 51 Madison Ave., New York NY 10010. (212)689-4411. Editor: Paul Neuman. For independent office equipment and stationery dealers, and special purchasers for store departments handling stationery and office equipment. Monthly. Buys all rights. Pays kill fee. Byline given "except when there isn't room in a layout." Pays on acceptance. Reports "immediately." SASE.
Nonfiction and Photos: Articles on merchandising and sales promotion; programs of stationery and office equipment dealers. Problem-solving articles related to retailers of office supplies, social stationery items, gifts (if the retailer also handles commercial supplies), office furniture and equipment and office machines. Minimum payment, $50, but quality of article is real determinant. Query. Length: 300-1,000 words. B&w glossies are purchased with accompanying ms with no additional payment.

OFFICE PRODUCTS, Hitchcock Bldg., Wheaton IL 60187. (312)665-1000. Editorial Director:

Robert R. Mueller. For "independent dealers who sell all types of office products—office machines, office furniture and office supplies." Estab. 1904. Monthly. Circ. 25,000. Buys all rights, but will reassign rights to author after publication. Byline given "except on collaborative articles." Pays on acceptance. Article deadlines are the 1st of the third month preceding date of issue. News deadlines are the 1st of each month. Reports in 3-4 weeks. Query on any long articles. SASE.

Nonfiction: "We're interested in anything that will improve an office product dealer's methods of doing business. Some emphasis on selling and promotion, but interested in all phases of dealer operations." Length: "that which tells the story, and no more or less." Pays $25-150 "based on quality of article."

Photos: Purchased with mss.

OFFICE WORLD NEWS, 645 Stewart Ave., Garden City NY 11530. Senior Editor: Eileen McCooey. 5% freelance written. For independent office products dealers. Biweekly tabloid; 24 pages. Estab. 1972. Circ. 16,000. Buys all rights. Pays on publication. Free sample copy. Reports in 2 weeks. Query. SASE.

Nonfiction and Photos: "All freelance material is written on assignment or following queries by our freelance 'stringers.' Our published material consists of news and news-related features. Straight news reporting, with emphasis on the effect on office product dealers. No textbook management articles will be accepted. We try to limit our content to hard news." Length: 100-500 words. Pays 10¢/word. B&w photos are purchased with mss or on assignment. Pays $10 for 5x7 or larger b&w photos.

To Break In: "Will consider any experienced newswriter for stringer assignments, except in New York metropolitan area."

PACIFIC STATIONER, 41 Sutter St., San Francisco CA 94104. Editor: Robert B. Frier. Monthly magazine; 60-70 pages. Estab. 1908. Circ. 5,500. Not copyrighted. Byline given. Buys 12 mss/year. Pays on acceptance. Sample copy $1.50. No photocopied or simultaneous submissions. Submit seasonal (merchandising) material 4 months in advance. Reports in 1 week. Query or submit complete ms. SASE.

Nonfiction and Photos: "Our main interest is in how Western retailers of stationery and office products can do a better selling job. We use how-to-do-it merchandising articles showing dealers how to sell more stationery and office products to more people at a greater profit. Seasonal merchandising articles always welcome, if acceptable." Length: 1,000-1,500 words. Pays 2¢/word. Pays $5 for b&w photos used with mss; 3x5 minimum. Captions required.

SOUTHERN STATIONER AND OFFICE OUTFITTER, 75 3rd St. NW, Atlanta GA 30308. Editor: Earl Lines Jr. For retailers of office products in the Southeast and Southwest. Monthly. Not copyrighted. Pays on publication. Free sample copy. Reports "promptly." SASE.

Nonfiction: Can use articles about retailers in the Southeast and Southwest regarding problems solved concerning store layout, inventory, personnel, etc. "We want articles giving in-depth treatment of a single aspect of a dealer's operation rather than superficial treatment of a number of aspects." Query. Must be approved by subject. Length: 1,000-1,400 words. Pays 2-4¢/word.

Photos: Purchased with mss. Pays $5.

Optical

THE DISPENSING OPTICIAN, Opticians Association of America, 1250 Connecticut Ave. NW, Washington DC 20036. Editor: James M. McCormick. 40% freelance written, but only 20% by paid writers. For dispensing opticians. Published 11 times/year. Magazine; 40-48 pages. Estab. 1950. Circ. 7,500-8,500. Pays "when issue is locked up." Buys all rights, but may reassign following publication. Byline given. Photocopied submissions OK. SASE. "Reports are slow due to clearance by editorial board (up to 60 days)." Will send sample copy to writer "only when we're interested in an article suggestion."

Nonfiction: Publishes informational, how-to, interview, profile, historical, photo feature, successful business operations, merchandising techniques, and technical articles. "All must specifically pertain to or interest the dispensing optician, and profiles and successful business operations must be of Association members." Query. Buys 15-20 mss/year. Length: 400-2,500 words. Pays 9-15¢/word for original work; 4-6¢/word for industry rights to syndicated articles.

Photos: Purchased with or without accompanying ms, or on assignment. Caption material required. Pays $7-50 for 5x7 or 8x10 b&w prints. Query.

N.J. JOURNAL OF OPTOMETRY, Dundee Ave., Box 152, Iselin NJ 08830. (201)283-0418. Editor: Norbert Kastner, O.D. For doctors of optometry practices located in New Jersey. Magazine; 35-40 pages. Estab. 1955. Quarterly. Circ. 1,200. Not copyrighted. Will consider photocopied submissions. Reports in 3 weeks. Query. SASE.
Nonfiction and Photos: Technical articles on eye care, exam techniques, etc.; news reports on eye care, either national or local; practice management articles. "Writer must remember that this is a professional, knowledgeable audience." Length: 1,000-2,000 words. Pays 3¢/word minimum.

Packing, Canning, and Packaging

Journals in this category are for packaging engineers and others concerned with new methods of packing, canning, and packaging foods in general. Other publications that buy similar material will be found under the Food Processing, Products, and Services heading.

MODERN PACKAGING, Morgan Grampian Publishing Corp., 2 Park Ave., New York NY 10016. (212)340-9700. Editor-in-Chief: Gary M. Rekstad. For product manufacturers who package or have contract-packaged their product lines, suppliers of packaging material and equipment. Monthly magazine; 70 pages. Estab. 1927. Circ. 61,000. Pays on publication. Buys all rights. Photocopied submissions OK. SASE. Reports in 6 weeks. Free sample copy. Guidelines for writers (only on technical articles).
Nonfiction: How-to, informational and new product articles. Trend reports, engineering and technical reports. Length: open. Query. Pays $35/printed page.
Photos: B&w and color photos purchased with mss or on assignment. Query, or send contact sheets or prints. Pays $5 minimum. Model release required.

PACKAGE PRINTING, North American Publishing Co., 401 N. Broad St., Philadelphia PA 19108. Editor-in-Chief: Walter Kubilius. Managing Editor: Hennie Marine. 20% freelance written. Emphasizes "any sort of package printing (food, peanuts, candy, etc.) for the plant superintendent or general manager of the company's package printing department." Monthly magazine; 74 pages. Estab. 1970. Circ. 8,000. Pays on acceptance. Buys all rights. Pays 33% kill fee. Byline given. Phone queries OK. Simultaneous and photocopied submissions OK. SASE. Reports in 2 weeks. Sample copy $1.
Nonfiction: "Generally a 'plant' story on the operation of the printing department of a packaging concern. The writer may not know a flexographic machine from a gravure machine or any other, but we expect him to interview the plant manager and get all the technical details. How is the package printed? What is the paper/film/foil used? How many? What kinds? Names and speed of all machines used; number of employees in production; everything relating to the manufacture and printing of any sort of package (look in any supermarket for 1,000 examples of packages." Query. Pays $50/printed page.
Photos: State availability of photos with query. Pays $10 for 5x7 or 8x10 b&w prints. Captions required. Buys all rights, but may reassign following publication.

THE PACKER, Box 1279. Kansas City KS 66117. (913)281-3073. Editor: Paul Campbell. 5% freelance written. For shippers, fruit and vegetable growers, wholesalers, brokers, retailers. Newspaper; 36 pages. Estab. 1893. Weekly. Circ. 16,500. Buys all rights, but may reassign rights to author after publication. Buys about 10 mss/year. Pays on publication. Will send free sample copy to writer on request. Write for copy of guidelines for writers. Will consider simultaneous submissions. Reports in 2 weeks. Returns rejected material in 1 month. Query or submit complete ms. SASE.
Nonfiction: Articles on growing techniques, merchandising, marketing, transportation, refrigeration. Emphasis is on the "what's new" approach in these areas. Length: 1,000 words. Pays $40 minimum.

Paint

Additional journals that buy material on paint, wallpaper, floor covering, and decorating products stores are listed under Building Interiors.

AMERICAN PAINT & COATINGS JOURNAL, American Paint Journal Co., 2911 Washington Ave., St. Louis MO 63103. (314)534-0301. Editor: Fred Schulenberg. 10% freelance written. For the coatings industry (paint, varnish, lacquer, etc.); manufacturers of coatings, suppliers to coatings industry, educational institutions, salesmen. Weekly magazine; 78 pages. Estab. 1916. Circ. 7,300. Pays on publication. Buys all rights. Pays kill fee "depending on the work done." Phone queries OK. Simultaneous and photocopied submissions OK. SASE. Reports in 3 weeks. Free sample copy and writer's guidelines.

Nonfiction: Informational, historical, interview, new product and technical articles and coatings industry news. Buys 2 mss/issue. Query before sending long articles; submit complete ms for short pieces. Length: 75-1,200 words. Pays $5-100.

Photos: B&w (5x7) glossies purchased with or without mss, or on assignment. Query. Pays $3-10.

AMERICAN PAINT AND WALLCOVERINGS DEALER, 2911 Washington Ave., St. Louis MO 63103. (314)534-0301. Editor-in-Chief: Clark Rowley. Assistant Editor: Cathy Hardin. 20% freelance written. Monthly magazine; 60 pages. Estab. 1908. Circ. 33,000. Pays on publication. Buys all rights. Byline given. Phone queries OK. Submit seasonal/holiday material 2 months in advance of issue date. Reports in 2 weeks. Free sample copy and writer's guidelines.

Nonfiction: Informational articles of interest to paint and wallcoverings dealers; usually articles on other successful stores. No articles about name-brand products. Buys 10 mss/year. Submit complete ms. Pays $100-125.

Photos: Submit photos with accompanying ms. Pays $10 for b&w prints; $25 for color transparencies. Captions preferred. Buys one-time rights.

AMERICAN PAINTING CONTRACTOR, American Paint Journal Co., 2911 Washington Ave., St. Louis MO 63103. (314)534-0301. Editor-in-Chief: John L. Cleveland. For painting and decorating contractors, in-plant maintenance painting department heads, architects and paint specifiers. Monthly magazine; 80 pages. Estab. 1923. Circ. 33,000. Buys all rights, but may reassign following publication. Phone queries OK. Submit seasonal/holiday material 2 months in advance. Simultaneous and photocopied submissions OK. SASE. Reports in 3 weeks. Free sample copy and writer's guidelines.

Nonfiction: Historical, how-to, humor, informational, new product, personal experience, opinion and technical articles; interviews, photo features and profiles. Buys 4 mss an issue. "Freelancers should be able to write well and have some understanding of the painting and decorating industry. We do not want general theme articles such as 'How to Get More Work Out of Your Employee' unless they relate to a problem within the painting and decorating industry. Query before submitting copy." Length: 1,000-2,500 words. Pays $75-100.

Photos: B&w and color purchased with mss or on assignment. Captions required. Send contact sheets, prints or transparencies. Pays $15-35.

MODERN PAINT AND COATINGS, Communication Channels, Inc., 6285 Barfield Rd., Atlanta GA 30328. (404)393-2920. Editor: Jan Cameron. For researchers or administrators interested in the development, testing, and application of finishes. Monthly magazine; 80 pages. Estab. 1903. Circ. 15,000. Pays on publication. Buys one-time rights. Phone queries OK. Submit seasonal/holiday material 4 months in advance of issue date. Simultaneous, photocopied and previously published submissions OK. SASE. Reports in 2 weeks. Free sample copy and writer's guidelines.

Nonfiction: Technical (plant stories relating how manufacturer improved operations) and new technology. Buys 2 mss/issue. Submit complete ms. Length: 1,200-3,000 words.

Photos: State availability of photos with ms. Offers no additional payment for 8x10 b&w glossy prints. Captions preferred.

Columns/Departments: Industry News, and other departments. Submit complete ms. Length: 50-300 words.

WESTERN PAINT REVIEW, 2048 Cotner Ave., Los Angeles CA 90025. (213)477-1033. Editor: Larry Dill. For members of the painting and decorating industry, particularly retail paint and decorating center dealers, paint manufacturers and raw materials suppliers. Estab. 1920. Monthly. Circ. 18,000. Buys first North American serial rights. Buys 50-100 mss/year. Pays on publication. Will consider photocopied submissions. Submit seasonal material 2 months in advance. Reports "immediately." Query or send complete ms. SASE.

Nonfiction and Photos: Technical articles, features and profiles on industry leaders in the West. Length: 500-4,000 words. Pays 5-7¢/word minimum. 3x5 minimum b&w glossy photos purchased with ms. Captions required. Pays $5 minimum. Pays $25 minimum for color photos purchased for covers.

Paper

FORET ET PAPIER, 625 President Kennedy Ave., Montreal, Quebec, Canada H3A 1K5. (514)845-5141. Editor: Paul Saint-Pierre, C. Adm. For engineers and technicians engaged in the making of paper. Quarterly magazine; 50 pages. Estab. 1975. Circ. 7,000. Rights purchased vary with author and material. Buys first North American serial rights, second serial (reprint) rights, and simultaneous rights. Buys about 12 mss/year. Pays on acceptance. Will consider photocopied submissions. Reports on mss accepted for publication in 1 week. Returns rejected material in 2 days. SASE.
Nonfiction and Photos: Uses technical articles on papermaking. Buys informational, how-to, personal experience, interview, photo and technical articles. Length: 1,000 words maximum. Pays $25-150. Photos purchased with accompanying ms with extra payment or purchased on assignment. Captions required. Pays $25 for b&w. Color shots must be vertical. Pays $150 maximum for color cover shots.

PAPERBOARD PACKAGING, 777 3rd Ave., New York NY 10017. (212)838-7778. Editor: Joel J. Shulman. For "managers, supervisors, and technical personnel who operate corrugated box manufacturing and folding cartons converting companies and plants." Estab. 1916. Monthly. Circ. 10,000. Buys all rights. Pays on publication. Will send a sample copy to a writer on request. Will consider photocopied submissions. Submit seasonal material 3 months in advance. Query. SASE.
Nonfiction and Photos: "Application articles, installation stories, etc. Contact the editor first to establish the approach desired for the article. Especially interested in packaging systems using composite materials, including paper and other materials." Buys technical articles. Length: open. Pays "$75/printed page (about 1,000 words to a page), including photos. We do not pay for commercially oriented material. We do pay for material if it is not designed to generate business for someone in our field. Will not pay photography costs, but will pay cost of photo reproductions for article."

Petroleum

THE DRILLING CONTRACTOR, International Association of Drilling Contractors, 7400 Harwin Dr., Suite 305, Houston TX 77036. Editor-in-Chief: Ninom Quintrelle. Production Manager: Lillian Martin. 20% freelance written. Emphasizes oilwell drilling for management of drilling contractor firms. Monthly magazine; 100 pages. Estab. 1942. Circ. 16,000. Pays on acceptance. Buys all rights, but may reassign following publication. Pays kill fee. Byline given "if requested by writer." Submit seasonal/holiday material 2 months in advance of issue date. Simultaneous, photocopied and previously published submissions OK. SASE. Reports in 2 weeks. Free sample copy and writer's guidelines.
Nonfiction: Historical (oilfields, drilling); how-to; and drilling articles. Buys 2 mss/issue. Query. Length: 200-2,000 words. Pays $50 minimum.

ENERGY MANAGEMENT REPORT, Box 1589, Dallas TX 75221. (214)748-4403. Editor-in-Chief: Ernestine Adams. Assistant Editors: Julie Fonner, Gregory Martin. 7-10% freelance written. Emphasizes energy for operating management of oil/gas operating companies and supply/service companies. Monthly magazine; 16 pages. Estab. October 1929. Circ. 52,000. Pays on publication. Buys all rights. SASE. Reports in 2 months. Free sample copy; mention *Writer's Market* in request.
Nonfiction: Uses energy briefs and concise analysis of energy situations. "Across-the-board interpretive reporting on current events." Publishes briefs about energy world news, international design and engineering, offshore energy business, environmental action, energy financing, new products (price information on crude oil and gasoline). Pays 10¢/word.

FUELOIL AND OIL HEAT, 200 Commerce Rd., Cedar Grove NJ 07009. (201)239-5800. Feature Editor: M. F. Hundley. For distributors of fueloil, heating and air conditioning equipment dealers. Monthly. Buys first rights. Pays on publication. Reports in 2 weeks. SASE.
Nonfiction: Management articles dealing with fueloil distribution and oilheating equipment selling. Length: up to 2,500 words. Pays $35/printed page.

HUGHES RIGWAY, Hughes Tool Co., Box 2539, Houston TX 77001. Editor-in-Chief: Ken Whanger. For oilfield drilling personnel. Quarterly magazine; 32 pages. Estab. 1963. Circ. 16,000. Pays on acceptance. Buys first North American serial rights. Byline given.

Simultaneous and photocopied submissions OK. SASE. Reports in 1 month. Free sample copy and writer's guidelines.

Nonfiction and Photos: "Character-revealing historical narratives about little-known incidents, heroes, or facts, particularly those which contradict conventional concepts. Also, topical reportorial features about people in oil or drilling. Must be thoroughly documented." Length: 2,000-2,500 words. Pays 10¢/word. Photos purchased with mss.

Fiction: "Top-quality fiction in oilfield settings." Length: 2,000-2,500 words. Pays 10¢/word.

HYDROCARBON PROCESSING, Box 2608, Houston TX 77001. Editor: Frank L. Evans. 95% freelance written by industry authors. For personnel in oil refining, gas and petrochemical processing; or engineering-contractors, including engineering, operation, maintenance and management phases. Special issues: January, Maintenance; April, Natural Gas Processing; September, Refining Processes; November, Petrochemical Processes. Monthly. Buys first publication rights. Write for copy of guidelines for writers. SASE.

Nonfiction: Wants technical manuscripts on engineering and operations in the industry that will help personnel. Also nontechnical articles on management, safety and industrial relations that will help technical men become managers. Length: open, "but do not waste words." Pays about $25/printed page.

How To Break In: "Articles must all pass a rigid evaluation of their reader appeal, accuracy and overall merit. Reader interest determines an article's value. We covet articles that will be of real job value to subscribers. Before writing—ask to see our *Author's Handbook*. You may save time and effort by writing a letter, and outline briefly what you have in mind. If your article will or won't meet our needs, we will tell you promptly."

NATIONAL PETROLEUM NEWS, 1221 Avenue of the Americas, New York NY 10020. (212)997-2361. Editor: William Olcott. For businessmen who make their living in the oil marketing industry, either as company employees or through their own business operations. Monthly magazine; 90 pages. Estab. 1909. Circ. 20,000. Rights purchased vary with author and material. Usually buys all rights. Buys 2 mss/year. Pays on acceptance if done on assignment. Pays on publication for unsolicited material. "The occasional freelance copy we use is done on assignment." Query. SASE.

Nonfiction and Photos: Department Editor: Carolyn Koenig. Material related directly to developments and issues in the oil marketing industry and "how-to" and "what-with" case studies. Informational; successful business operations. Length: 2,000 words maximum. Pays $60/printed page. Payment for b&w photos "depends upon advance understanding."

OCEAN INDUSTRY, Gulf Publishing Co., Box 2608, Houston TX 77001. (713)529-4301. Editor-in-Chief: Donald M. Taylor. Associate Editors: Maretta Tubb, Scott Weeden. Department Editor: Margaret Cashman. 25% freelance written. "Our readers are generally engineers and company executives in companies with business dealings with off-shore petroleum and deepsea mining interests." Monthly magazine; 116 pages. Estab. 1966. Circ. 33,000. Pays on publication. Buys all rights. Pays kill fee "if we assign an article and it is not used, we pay full rate on estimated length." Byline given "except if they have more than one major article per magazine." Phone queries OK. Photocopied and previously published submissions OK. SASE. Reports in 2 months. Free sample copy and writer's guidelines.

Nonfiction: New product (items on new equipment and instruments which can be used offshore); and technical (articles relating to hydrocarbon exploration and development, diving, deepsea mining, oil terminals, and oil and LNG shipping). No oceanographic, fisheries, aquaculture or mariculture material. Buys 120-140 mss/year. Query. Length: 300-1,500 words. Pays $35-50/published page.

Photos: "Technical concepts are easier to understand when illustrated." State availability of photos with query. No additional payment for 5x7 or 8x10 glossy b&w or color prints. Captions required. Buys all rights.

Columns/Departments: New Literature (brochures on company's work); New Equipment; New Instruments; New Business Ventures; Gas & Oil Wrap-up; and New Drilling Rigs. Buys 2-3 mss/issue. Query. Length: 100-500 words. Pays $2/inch.

PETROLEUM INDEPENDENT, 1101 16th St. NW, Washington DC 20036. (202)466-8240. Editor-in-Chief: Robert Gouldy. Associate Editor: Bill Garland. For "college-educated men and women involved in high-risk petroleum ventures. Contrary to popular opinion, they are not all Texans. They live in almost every state. These people are politically motivated. They follow energy legislation closely and involve themselves in lobbying and electoral politics." Bimonthly magazine; 64-88 pages. Estab. 1929. Circ. 13,000. Pays on acceptance. Buys all rights but may reassign following publication. Byline given "except if part of a large report

compiled in-house." Photocopied submissions OK. SASE. Reports in 6 weeks. Sample copy $1.
Nonfiction: "Articles need not be limited to oil and natural gas—but must tie in nicely."
Expose (bureaucratic blunder), informational, historical (energy-related, accurate, with a witty twist), humor (we look for a good humor piece and have found a few), interview (with energy decisionmakers. Center with questions concerning independent petroleum industry. Send edited transcript plus tape), opinion, profile (of Independent Petroleum Association of America members), photo feature. Buys 30 mss/year. Query. SASE. Length: 750-3,000 words. Pays $40-300.
Photos: Purchased with or without accompanying ms or on assignment. Pays $15-75 for b&w and color photos. $200 (for cover only, we are always looking for good oil patch pictures) for 35mm or 2¼x2¼ transparencies. Send contact sheet, prints or transparencies.
Fiction: Experimental, historical, science fiction. Buys 1 ms/issue. Submit complete ms. Length: 750-2,000 words. Pays $40-200.

PIPELINE & GAS JOURNAL, Box 1589, Dallas TX 75221. (214)748-4403. Editor-in-Chief: Dean Hale. 5% freelance written. Emphasizes energy transportation (oil, gas and coal) by pipeline. Monthly magazine; 100 pages. Estab. July 1859. Circ. 25,000. Pays on publication. Buys all rights. Phone queries OK. Photocopied submissions OK. SASE. Reports in 6-10 weeks. Free sample copy.
Nonfiction: Technical. No articles on management. Buys 5-6 mss/year. Query. Length: 800-1,500 words. Pays $35/printed page.
Photos: State availability of photos with query. No additional payment for 8x10 b&w glossy prints and 5x7 or 8x10 color glossy prints. Captions required. Buys all rights, but may reassign following publication. Model release required.

THE REVIEW, 111 St. Clair Ave. W., Toronto, Ontario M5W 1K3, Canada. Editor: Kenneth Bagnell. Bimonthly. Buys all rights. Byline given. Pays on acceptance. Free sample copy. Query. Reports in 1 week. SAE and International Reply Coupons.
Nonfiction: "Subject matter is general. Articles specifically about the oil industry are generally staff-written. Material must be Canadian." Length: 2,500 words maximum. Pays $400 minimum.

Pets

Listed here are publications for professionals in the pet industry: wholesalers, manufacturers, suppliers, retailers, owners of pet specialty stores, pet groomers, aquarium retailers, distributors, manufacturers and those interested in the fish industry.

FROM THE KENNELS, Box 1369, Vancouver WA 98660. (206)696-2971. Editor: J.C. Perkins. Emphasizes material of interest to owners of purebred dogs. Semimonthly newspaper; 16-32 pages. Pays on publication. Not copyrighted. Byline given. Simultaneous, photocopied and previously published submissions OK. SASE. Reports in 2 weeks. Sample copy $1.
Nonfiction: Exposés (of dog show behaviour of individuals). Must be related to the showing of purebred dogs. Query.
Photos: Purchased with accompanying ms. Captions required. Uses b&w only. Query. No additional payment for photos accepted with ms.

PET BUSINESS, Pet Business, Inc., Toadtown, Magalia CA 95954. (916)872-1200. Editor: Robert L. Behme. For the complete pet industry—retailers, groomers, breeders, manufacturers, wholesalers and importers. Monthly tabloid; 30 pages. Estab. 1973. Circ. 18,300. Pays on acceptance. Not copyrighted. Previously published submissions OK. SASE. Reports in 3 weeks. Free sample copy and writer's guidelines.
Nonfiction: General interest (to retailers—what a store is doing, etc.); historical (when there is a reason—death, sale, etc.); how-to (sell more, retailer ideas); humor (cartoons only); interview (with sucessful stores and manufacturers); opinion (with background); photo feature (on occasion). Buys 2-4 mss/issue. "We will consider anything if queried first." Length: 600-1,500 words. Pays $35-250.
Photos: State availability of photos. Pays $5 for 5x7 or larger b&w prints; and $30 for any size color prints. Captions required.
Columns/Departments: "We're interested in ideas that relate to retailing, e.g., dogs, cats, small animals—but it must be on a retail, not hoppy, level." Open to suggestions for new columns/departments. Query. Pays $100.

THE PET DEALER, Howmark Publishing Corp., 225 W. 34th St., New York NY 10001. (212)279-0800. Editor-in-Chief: William G. Reddan. Managing Editor: Peter Dorfman. 15% freelance written. Emphasizes merchandising, marketing and management for owners and managers of pet specialty stores, departments, and dog groomers and their suppliers. Monthly magazine; 80 pages. Estab. 1950. Circ. 10,000. Byline given. Pays on publication. Phone queries OK. Submit seasonal/holiday material 3 months in advance of issue date. SASE. Reports in 1 week. Free sample copy and writer's guidelines.
Nonfiction: How-to (store operations, administration, merchandising, marketing, management, promotion, and purchasing). Buys 2 mss/issue. Length: 1,000-1,200 words. Pays $50-100.
Photos: Submit photo material with ms. No additional payment for 5x7 b&w glossy prints. Captions required. Buys one-time rights. Model release required.
How To Break In: "We're interested in store profiles outside the New York area. Photos are of key importance. Good photos and lots of them can sell an otherwise inadequate piece. The story we can always fix up, but we can't run out and take the photos. The best thing to do is send a sample of your work and some story proposals. Even if your proposals are not that strong, we still might want to use you on one of our own ideas. Articles focus on new techniques in merchandising or promotion."

PETS/SUPPLIES/MARKETING, Harcourt Brace Jovanovich Publications, 1 E. 1st St., Duluth MN 55802. (218)727-8511. Editor/publisher: Paul Setzer. Managing Editor: Barbara Trelevan. For pet retailers (both small, "mom-and-pop" stores and chain franchisers); livestock and pet supply wholesalers, manufacturers of pet products. Monthly magazine; 100 pages. Estab. 1946. Circ. 15,900. Pays on acceptance. Buys all rights. Phone queries OK. Submit seasonal/holiday material 2 months in advance. Photocopied submissions OK. SASE. Reports in 4 weeks. Free sample copy and writer's guidelines.
Nonfiction: How-to (merchandise pet products, display, set up window displays, market pet product line); humor (pertaining to pets and/or their retail sale); interviews (with pet store retailers); opinion (of pet industry members or problems facing the industry); photo features (of successful pet stores or effective merchandising techniques and in-store displays); profiles (of successful retail outlets engaged in the pet trade); technical articles (on more effective pet retailing; e.g., building a central filtration unit, constructing custom aquariums or display areas). Length: 1,000-2,500 words. Buys 5-6 mss/issue. Query. Pays 5-10¢/word.
Photos: Purchased with or without mss or on assignment. "We prefer 5x7 or 8x10 b&w glossies. But we will accept contact sheets and standard print sizes. For color, we prefer 35mm transparencies or 2¼x2¼." Pays $6-7.50 for b&w; $12.50-15 for color.
Columns/Departments: Short, human interest items on the pet trade for Up Front; factual news items on members of the pet industry for Industry News. Buys 3/issue. Submit complete ms. Length: 25-100 words. Pays 5-10¢/word. Suggestions for new columns or departments should be addressed to Paul Setzer.
Fillers: Clippings, jokes, gags, anecdotes, newsbreaks, puzzles, short humor; anything concerned with the pet industry. Buys 3-4/issue. Length: 25-100 words. Pays $10-25.
How To Break In: "Send a letter of introduction and we will send our guidelines for writers and a sample copy of the magazine. After studying each, the freelancer could visit a number of pet stores and if any seem like interesting material for *PSM*, query us. We will check them out through our wholesalers and, if recommended by them, will assign the article to the freelancer. Once we have bought several articles from a writer, we will send the person out on specific assignments."

Photography

AMERICAN CINEMATOGRAPHER, A.S.C. Holding Corp., 1782 N. Orange Dr., Hollywood CA 90028. (213)876-5080. Editor: Herb A. Lightman. Assistant Editor: Three Tyler. Specializes in coverage of 16mm and 35mm motion picture production. For an audience ranging from students to retirees; professional interest or advanced amateurs in cinematography. Monthly magazine; 108 pages. Estab. 1921. Circ. 22,500. Time of payment depends on nature of article. Buys all rights, but may reassign rights after publication. Phone queries OK. Simultaneous and photocopied submissions OK. SASE. Free sample copy.
Nonfiction: How-to articles must be unusual type of treatment, or technique used in filming a production. Interviews with cinematographers. New product pieces on 16mm and 35mm cinematographic items. "The articles we use are primarily those submitted by the photographers of motion pictures. Other material is submitted by the manufacturers of equipment important in our industry. The magazine is technical in nature and the writer must have a background in motion picture photography to be able to write for us." Buys 1 ms per

issue. Query. Length varies with interest. Pays $75-125.
Photos: B&w and color purchased with mss. No additional payment.

BUSINESS SCREEN, 165 W. 46th St., New York NY 10036. For sponsors, producers and users of business, commercial advertising and industrial motion pictures, slidefilms and related audiovisual media. Bimonthly. Buys all rights. ("We could accept an article written for another publication as long as it was not a competing one...if it was printed elsewhere, does not preclude out accepting and using it—we must see it first, and will then make up our minds.") Pays on publication. Query first. Reports in 2 weeks. SASE.
Nonfiction: "Short articles on successful application of these 'tools' in industry and commerce, but only when approved by submission of advance query to publisher's office. Technical articles on film production techniques, with or without illustrations, science film data and interesting featurettes about application or utilization of films in community, industry, etc., also welcomed. Usually, we simply pay $100 flat for an article, 1 page or 2 pages or 3 pages of a magazine sized publication, now called *Back Stage Magazine Supplement With Business Screen*. Sometimes pay $200 flat, usually never more."
Tips: "Material now being eagerly sought...one page outline will be sufficient to tell us if it would be acceptable. Not interested in feature films, radio or records. Not interested in interviews with actors or stars; not interested in theatre or legit. Don't bother us with this stuff! We are interested in interviews with producers/directors/technicians involved in commercials, industrial films, especially those away from major centers of New York, Los Angeles and Chicago."

THE CAMERA CRAFTSMAN, 2000 W. Union Ave., Englewood CO 80110. Editor: Ann McLendon. For camera repair technicians, or people with a specialized interest in photographic equipment. Bimonthly magazine; 32-40 pages. Estab. 1955. Circ. 8,000. Rights purchased vary with author and material. Byline given. Usually buys first rights. Buys about 6 mss a year. Pays on acceptance. Free sample copy. Will consider photocopied and simultaneous submissions. Reporting time varies, but tries to report in 30 days. Query on technical articles. On others, will consider complete mss. SASE.
Nonfiction and Photos: "Technical articles on camera disassembly repair and service; articles of interest to small service businesses (on business management or other appropriate subjects). We do not want superficial or outdated business management articles, many of which are rehashes of publications issued by the Small Business Administration. We are interested in seeing current, problem-solving articles for small businesses. However, our principal interest is in technical articles on photographic equipment; also on related fields, such as optics. We are not interested in reviewing how-to articles on picture taking, or photography as such." Length: 1,000-5,000 words. Pays minimum of 5¢/word. B&w glossies purchased with mss. Captions preferred. Pays minimum of $1.50.

FUNCTIONAL PHOTOGRAPHY, PTN Publishing Corp., 250 Fulton Ave., Hempstead NY 11550. (516)489-1300. Editor: Michael A. Munzer. Emphasizes scientific photography for scientists, engineers and medical professionals who use photography to document their work. Bimonthly magazine; 60 pages. Estab. 1965. Circ. 39,000. Pays on publication. Buys first North American serial rights. Phone queries OK. Submit seasonal/holiday material 2 months in advance. Photocopied submissions OK. Reports in 3 weeks. Free sample copy and writer's guidelines.
Nonfiction: Interview, personal opinion, profile, new products, photo feature and technical. Buys 4-6 mss/issue. Query. Pays $50-350.
Photos: "We must have photos to explain article." Uses 5x7 or 8x10 b&w glossy prints, glossy color prints (any size), and color transparencies. Offers no additional payment for photos accepted with ms. Captions and model releases required. Buys one-time rights.

INDUSTRIAL PHOTOGRAPHY, United Business Publications, Inc., 475 Park Ave. S., New York NY 10016. (212)725-2300. Editor: David A. Silverman. For "the staff industrial photographer and his daily challenges. Our audience ranges from older, conservative, self-educated photographic personnel to younger, college or university educated aggressive individuals. Writers must keep stories simple, regardless." Monthly magazine; 70 pages. Estab. 1951. Circ. 42,000. Pays on publication. Buys first North American serial rights. Byline given. Previously published submissions OK. SASE. Reports in 4-6 weeks. Free sample copy and writer's guidelines.
Nonfiction: How-to (material of value and interest to staff photographic personnel in non-photographic companies or military or government); interview of industrial photographers on staff); profile (of successful in-house depts.); personal experience (applications of

photography in the industrial field); photo feature (as related to how-to); and technical (as related to how-to). "We regularly cover management reform and attitudes, budgeting, related outside activities (and how they may affect the staffer's position within the industry), etc." Buys 10 mss/year. Query. Pays $50-200.

Photos: Photos should be supplied by the subject, not the writer. Uses 4x5 or larger b&w prints, 4x5 or 8x10 glossy color prints and 35mm or larger transparencies. Offers no additional payment for photos accepted with ms. Captions required. Buys one-time rights.

KELLNER'S MONEYGRAM, 1768 Rockville Dr., Baldwin NY 11510. (516)868-3177. Editor: Henry T. Kellner. 100% freelance written. For photographers, art directors, photo editors and anyone interested in selling photos. Monthly newsletter; 8 pages. Estab. 1977. Circ. 2,000. Pays on publication. Buys one-time rights. Byline given. Phone queries OK. Submit seasonal/holiday material 6 months in advance of issue date. Simultaneous and previously published submissions OK. SASE. Reports in 2-3 weeks. Sample copy $1; free writer's guidelines.

Nonfiction: Exposé (unscrupulous editors/agents, buyers who didn't pay); how-to (sell photos, preferably based on first-hand experience); humor (events that occur on assignment); inspirational (how a photographer overcame an obstacle and became successful); interview (famous photographers or editors/art directors who buy photos); nostalgia (old times in photography); personal experience (how I got an assignment, how I contact editors, how I combine writing and photography); and travel (how I made money with vacation photos). Buys 22-23 mss/year. Send complete ms. Length: 300-350 words. Pays 2½-5¢/word.

MILLIMETER MAGAZINE, 12 E. 46th St., New York NY 10017. (212)867-3636. Editor: Alice C. Wolf. 75% freelance written. For personnel in motion picture and television industries, ad agencies, film schools (students), and equipment rental services. Monthly magazine; 150 pages. Estab. 1974. Circ. 17,653. Pays on publication. Buys all rights. Pays 33-50% kill fee. Byline given. Phone queries OK. Submit seasonal/holiday material 6 months in advance of issue date. Photocopied submissions OK. SASE. Reports in 3 weeks. Free sample copy.

Nonfiction: "Production stories that deal with entertainment industries of motion pictures and television programming, including TV commercials. Stories should be somewhat technical, involving equipment used, anecdotal, problems encountered and solved, and deal with nationally known production figures. Also interviews with heads of production of current motion pictures and television personnel. Examples: directors, producers, cinematographers, scriptwriters. No personality pieces on 'stars.' " Buys 8 mss/issue. Query. Length: 1,500-4,000 words. Pays $100 minimum.

THE PHOTOLETTER, PhotoSearch International, Dept. 79, Osceola WI 54020. (715)248-3800. Managing Editor: H.T. White. For professional photographers and serious amateurs interested in publishing their pictures. Newsletter published 2 times/month; 4 pages. Estab. 1976. Circ. 1,576. Pays on acceptance. Buys one-time rights. No byline; "text conforms to a format, authors feed us only details and leave style to our editor." Phone queries OK. Simultaneous, photocopied and previously published submissions OK. SASE. Reports in 2 weeks. Sample copy $1.

Columns/Departments: Current Photos Needed. "Since we pair photographers with picture buyers, we are always seeking up-to-the-minute photo needs of magazines, government agencies, publishers, etc." Buys 10%/issue. Phone first, unless deadline for photos will permit correspondence. Length: 25-100 words.

Fillers: Clippings and inventive ways of selling one's photos. Buys 12/year. Length: 25-100 words. Pays 15-20¢/word.

PHOTOMETHODS, Ziff-Davis Publishing Co., 1 Park Ave., New York NY 10016. (212)725-3942. Editor-in-Chief: Fred Schmidt. For professional, in-plant image-makers (still, film, video, graphic arts, micrographics) and functional photographers. Monthly magazine; 80-96 pages. Estab. 1958. Circ. 50,000. Pays on publication. Buys one-time rights. Pays 100% kill fee. Byline given. Phone queries OK. SASE. Reports in 2 months. Free sample copy and writer's guidelines.

Nonfiction: How-to and photo features (solve problems with image-making techniques: photography, etc.); informational (to help the reader use photography, cinema and video); interviews (with working pros); personal experience (in solving problems with photography, cinema and video); profiles (well-known personalities in imaging); and technical (on photography, cinema and video). Buys 5 mss/issue. Length: 1,500-3,000 words. Pays $75 minimum.

Photos: Steven Karl Weininger, Art Director. B&w photos (8x10 matte or dried glossy) and color (35mm transparencies minimum or 8x10 print) purchased with or without mss, or on assignment. Captions required. Query or submit contact sheet. Pays $35 for b&w; $50 for color. Model release required.

THE PROFESSIONAL PHOTOGRAPHER, PPA Publications and Events, Inc., 1090 Executive Way, Des Plaines IL 60018. (312)298-4680. "Our readers are mostly members of the Professional Photographers of America, Inc., a trade association of portrait, commercial and industrial photographers." Monthly magazine; 116 pages. Estab. 1907. Circ. 29,000. Pays on publication. Buys all rights. Submit seasonal/holiday material 4-5 months in advance. Photocopied submissions OK. SASE. Reports in 1 month. Free sample copy and writer's guidelines.
Nonfiction: General interest (articles about photographers or trends in photography); how-to (business and photographic techniques of interest to professional photographers); interview (with photographers); profile (photographers) and technical. No "business articles that could be applied as easily to grocers or undertakers as to photographers." Buys 3 mss/issue. Query. Length: 500 words minimum. Pays $200 maximum.
Photos: State availability of photos or send them with ms. Uses 8x10 b&w glossy prints and 35mm or larger color transparencies. Offers no additional payment for photos accepted with ms. Captions required.

THE RANGEFINDER, 1312 Lincoln Blvd., Santa Monica CA 90406. (213)451-8506. Editor-in-Chief: Janet Marshall Victor. Associate Editor: Jan Miller. 15% freelance written. Emphasizes professional photography. Monthly magazine; 100 pages. Estab. June 1952. Circ. 44,500. Pays on publication. Buys first North American serial rights. Byline given. Phone queries OK. SASE. Reports in 2 weeks. Sample copy $1.50; free writer's guidelines.
Nonfiction: How-to (solve a photographic problem; such as new techniques in lighting, new poses or setups); interview (success stories); new product (test reports of product in use); and technical (roundup style on equipment in use such as light meters, front projection, large format cameras, etc.). "No biographical articles." Buys 3 mss/issue. Query. Length: 750-2,000 words. Pays $24-36/published page.
Photos: State availability of photos with query. Offers no additional payment for 8x10 b&w glossy prints. Captions preferred. Buys one-time rights. Model release required.

SHOOTING COMMERCIALS MAGAZINE, Shooting Commercials Magazine, Inc., 6407 Moore Dr., Los Angeles CA 90048. (213)936-2138. Editor: Joseph Brosta IV. Associate Editor: Tom Rosa. Emphasizes commercial production for production companies, advertising agencies, equipment houses, clients, animators, actors and sound track composers. Twice monthly magazine; 48 pages. Estab. 1978. Circ. 15,000. Pays on publication. Buys one-time rights. Byline given. Phone queries OK. Photocopied submissions OK. Reports "immediately." Free sample copy and writer's guidelines.
Nonfiction; How-to (how a specific commercial was filmed or videotaped); interview (with ad agency people or production people); profile (of persons involved in production of commercials); new product; personal experience; photo feature; and technical. Also interested in production facility overview by geographic region. "We are limited in space, therefore our articles must be timely, succinct and capture the reader's attention immediately." Buys 6 mss/issue. Query by phone. Length: 700 words preferred, but longer material is accepted if the subject is interesting. Pays $75.
Photos: B&w glossy prints (any size). Offers no additional payment for photos accepted with ms. Captions required.
Columns/Departments: People, Animation & Music, Equipment & Facilities and Industrials and Production Scene. Buys 6 mss/issue. Query by phone.

STUDIO PHOTOGRAPHY, PTN Publishing Corp., 250 Fulton Ave., Hempstead NY 11550. (516)489-1300. Editor: Rick Sammon. Associate Editor: Audrey Perel. 35-40% freelance written. Monthly magazine; 60 pages. Estab. 1964. Circ. 40,000. Pays on publication. Not copyrighted. Submit seasonal/holiday material 3 months in advance of issue date. SASE. Reports in 3 weeks. Free sample copy and writer's guidelines.
Nonfiction: Interview; personal experience; opinion; photo feature; and technical. No travel articles. Buys 2-3 mss/issue. Length: 1,700-3,000 words. Pays $35 minimum/published page.
Photos: State availability of photos with query. Pays $25 minimum for 5x7 b&w prints and color transparencies.
Columns/Departments: Point of View (any aspect of photography dealing with professionals only). Buys 1 ms/issue. Length: 1,700 words minimum. Pays $35 minimum.

TECHNICAL PHOTOGRAPHY, PTN Publishing Corp., 250 Fulton Ave., Hempstead NY 11550. Editor-in-Chief: Michael A. Munzer. 50% freelance written. Publication of the "on-staff (in-house) industrial, military and government still, cinema, video and AV professional who must produce (or know where to get) visuals of all kinds." Monthly magazine; 64 pages. Estab. 1968. Circ. 51,000. Pays on publication. Buys first North American Serial rights. Byline given "except when it needs complete rewrite or when supplied through public relations agency." SASE. Reports in 4 weeks. Free sample copy and writer's guidelines.
Nonfiction: How-to; humor; interview; photo feature; profile (detailed stories about in-house operations); and technical. "All manuscripts must relate to industrial, military or government production of visuals." Buys 75-110 mss/year. Query. Length: "as long as needed to get the information across." Pays $50 minimum/display page.
Photos: Purchased with accompanying ms. Captions required. Query.

Plastics

CANADIAN PLASTICS, 1450 Don Mills Rd., Don Mills, Ontario, Canada. M3B 2X7. (416)445-6641. Managing Editor: Joanne Meithner. For management people in the plastics industry. Monthly. Buys first rights. Pays on publication. Query first. Reports in 4 weeks. SAE and International Reply Coupons.
Nonfiction: Accurate technical writing. Accuracy is more important than style. "We reject some freelance material because of lack of Canadian relevance; we like to publish articles that are meaningful to the reader; something he can use for his benefit as a businessman." Pays 7¢/word.
Photos: Buys photos submitted with ms. Pays $5.
Fillers: Buys newsbreaks. Pays $5 for news items; $15 for longer features.

PLASTICS TECHNOLOGY, 633 3rd Ave., New York NY 10017. (212)986-4800. Editor: Malcolm W. Riley. For plastic processors. Circ. 40,000. Buys all rights. Pays on publication. Will send free sample copy on request. Query. Reports in 2 weeks. SASE.
Nonfiction and Photos: Articles on plastics processing. Length: "no limits." Pays $30-35/published page. Photos and all artwork purchased with ms with no additional payment.

Plumbing, Heating, Air Conditioning, and Refrigeration

Publications for fuel oil dealers who also install heating equipment are classified with the Petroleum journals.

AIR CONDITIONING, HEATING AND REFRIGERATION NEWS, Box 6000, Birmingham MI 48012. (313)642-3600. Editor-in-Chief: Gordon D. Duffy. Managing Editor: John O. Sweet. 20% freelance written. "An industry newspaper that covers both the technology and marketing of air conditioning, heating and refrigeration." Weekly tabloid; 30 pages. Estab. 1926. Circ. 31,000. Pays on publication. Buys all rights, but may reassign following publication. Phone queries OK. Submit seasonal/holiday material 1 month in advance of issue date. Simultaneous and photocopied submissions OK. Reports in 2-3 weeks. Free sample copy.
Nonfiction: How-to (basic business management applied to contracting operations; sophisticated technical problems in heating, air conditioning, and refrigeration); interview (check first); new product (check first); nostalgia; profile; and technical. Buys 2-4 mss/issue. Query. Length: 1,500 words. Pays $1.25-1.70/column inch.
Photos: State availability of photos with query or ms. Pays $10-35 for 5x7 or 8x10 b&w glossy prints. Captions required. Buys all rights, but may reassign following publication.

DOMESTIC ENGINEERING MAGAZINE, Construction Press, 110 N. York Rd., Elmhurst IL 60126. Editor: Stephen J. Shafer. Managing Editor: Donald Michard. Emphasizes plumbing, heating, air conditioning and piping for contractors, and for mechanical contractors in these specialties gives information on management, marketing and merchandising. Monthly magazine; 100 pages. Estab. 1881. Circ. 40,000. Pays on acceptance. Buys all rights, simultaneous rights, or first rights. Simultaneous, photocopied and previously published submissions OK. SASE. Reports in 1 month. Sample copy $2.
Nonfiction: How-to (some technical in industry areas). Expose, interview, profile, personal experience, photo feature and technical articles are written on assignment only and should be about management, marketing and merchandising for plumbing and mechanical contracting businessmen. Buys 12 mss/year. Query. Pays $25 minimum.

Photos: State availability of photos. Pays $10 minimum for b&w prints (reviews contact sheets) and color transparencies.

EXPORT, 386 Park Ave. S., New York NY 10016. Editor: M. Downing. For importers and distributors in 165 countries who handle hardware, air conditioning and refrigeration equipment and related consumer hardlines. Bimonthly magazine; 60-80 pages in English and Spanish editions. Estab. 1877. Circ. 38,500. Buys first serial rights. Byline given. Buys about 10 mss/year. Pays on acceptance. Reports in 1 month. Query. SASE.
Nonfiction: News stories of products and merchandising of air conditioning and refrigeration equipment, hardware and related consumer hardlines. Informational, how-to, interview, profile, successful business operations. Length: 1,000-3,000 words. Pays 10¢/word, maximum.
How To Break In: "One of the best ways to break in here is with a story originating outside the US or Canada. Our major interest is in new products and new developments—but they must be available and valuable to overseas buyers. We also like company profile stories. A key thing we look for in writers is some kind of expertise in our field. Departments and news stories are staff-written."

HEATING/PIPING/AIR CONDITIONING, 2 Illinois Center, Chicago IL 60601. (312)861-0880. Editor: Robert T. Korte. Monthly. Buys all rights. Pays on publication. Query. Reports in 2 weeks. SASE.
Nonfiction: Uses engineering and technical articles covering design, installation, operation, maintenance, etc., of heating, piping and air conditioning systems in industrial plants and large buildings. Length: 3,000-4,000 words maximum. Pays $30/printed page.

HEATING, PLUMBING, AIR CONDITIONING, 1450 Don Mills Rd., Don Mills, Ontario, Canada M3B 2X7. (416)445-6641. Editor: Ronald Shuker. For mechanical contractors; plumbers; warm air heating, refrigeration, ventilation and air conditioning contractors; wholesalers; architects; consulting and mechanical engineers who are in key management or specifying positions in the plumbing, heating, air conditioning and refrigeration industries in Canada. Monthly. Circ. 13,500. Pays on publication. Free sample copy. Reports in 1-2 months. SAE and International Reply Coupons.
Nonfiction and Photos: News, technical, business management and "how-to" articles that will inform, educate and motivate readers who design, manufacture, install, service, maintain or supply all mechanical components and systems in residential, commercial, institutional and industrial installations across Canada. Length: 1,000-1,500 words. Pays 10¢/word. Photos purchased with mss. Prefers 5x7 or 8x10 glossies.

SNIPS MAGAZINE, 407 Mannheim Rd., Bellwood IL 60104. (312)544-3870. Editor: Nick Carter. For sheet metal, warm air heating, ventilating, air conditioning, and roofing contractors. Monthly. Buys all rights. "Write for detailed list of requirements before submitting any work." SASE.
Nonfiction: Material should deal with information about contractors who do sheet metal, warm air heating, air conditioning, ventilation and roofing work; also about successful advertising campaigns conducted by these contractors and the results. Length: "prefers stories to run less than 1,000 words unless on special assignment." Pays 2¢ each for first 500 words, 1¢ each for additional words.
Photos: Pays $2 each for small snapshot pictures, $4 each for usable 8x10 pictures.

Power and Power Plants

Publications in this listing aim at company managers, engineers and others involved in generating and supplying power for businesses, homes and industries. Journals for electrical engineers who design, maintain and install systems connecting users with sources of power are classified under Electricity.

DIESEL & GAS TURBINE PROGRESS, Box 26308, Milwaukee WI 52336. Editor-in-Chief: Bruce W. Wadman. Managing Editor: J. Kane. Associate Editor: Mike Osenga. 5% freelance written. Monthly magazine; 88 pages. Estab. 1935. Circ. 25,000. Pays on publication. Buys all rights. Submit editorial material 6 weeks in advance of issue date. Previously published submissions OK. SASE. Reports in 4 weeks. Sample copy $1.
Nonfiction: "The articles we would consider from freelancers would be technical descriptions of unique diesel or gas turbine engine applications. Including extensive technical descriptions of the installation, the method of operation and maintenance." Buys 20 mss/year. Query and

submit clips of published work. Length: 1,600-2,400 words. Pays $75/page.

Photos: "All stories are illustrated and photos of the engine installation must accompany the text, or it is really of little value." State availability of photos with query. No additional payment for 8x10 b&w glossy prints and 8x10 glossy color prints (cover only). Captions preferred. Buys all rights, but may reassign following publication.

POWER ENGINEERING, 1301 S. Grove Ave., Barrington IL 60010. (312)381-1840. Editor: John Papamarcos. Monthly. Buys first North American serial rights. Byline given. "Must query first." SASE.

Nonfiction and Photos: "We do not encourage freelance writers in general. We do review anything that is sent to us, but will generally accept articles only from people who are involved in the power field in some way and can write to interest engineers and management in the field." Articles on electric power field design, construction, and operation. Length: 500-1,500 words. Pays $80-200, "depending on published length." Uses 8x10 glossies with mss.

PUBLIC POWER, 2600 Virginia Ave. NW, Washington DC 20037. (202)333-9200. Editor: Vic Reinemer. Estab. 1942. Bimonthly. Not copyrighted. Pays variable kill fee. Byline given "depends upon the copy." Pays on publication. Query. SASE.

Nonfiction: News and features on municipal and other local publicly owned electric systems. Payment negotiable.

Printing

AMERICAN INK MAKER, 101 W. 31st St., New York NY 10001. (212)279-4455. Editor-in-Chief: John Vollmuth. 2% freelance written. Monthly magazine; 70 pages. Estab. 1923. Circ. 4,000. Pays on publication. Buys all rights, but may reassign following publication. Phone queries OK. Submit seasonal/holiday material 2 months in advance of issue date. Simultaneous, photocopied and previously published submissions OK. SASE. Reports in 2 weeks. Free sample copy.

Nonfiction: General interest; historical; humor; interview; new product; personal experience; opinion; profile; and technical. Buys 4 mss/year. Submit complete ms. Length: 800-1,500 words. Pays $90-135.

Photos: No additional payment for photos with accompanying ms. Captions preferred. Buys all rights, but may reassign following publication.

AMERICAN PRINTER AND LITHOGRAPHER, 300 W. Adams St., Chicago IL 60606. Editor: Michael Chazin. 60-70% freelance written. For qualified personnel active in any phase of the graphic arts industry. Estab. 1883. Monthly. Circ. 68,000. Buys all rights, unless otherwise specified in writing at time of purchase. Byline given. Pays on publication. Free sample copy. Submit seasonal material 2 months in advance. "Study publication before writing." SASE.

Nonfiction: Management, and technical subjects with illustrations pertinent to the graphic arts industry. Query. Length: 1,500-3,000 words. Pays $50-200.

Photos: Purchased with mss; also news shots of graphic arts occurrences. Uses 5x7 or 8x10 glossy prints. Pays $5-10.

Fillers: Clippings about product installations, plant openings, acquisitions and purchases, business reorganization. Particularly interested in items on newspapers; not interested in personnel announcements. Pays $2-5.

GRAPHIC ARTS MONTHLY, Technical Publishing Co., A Dunn & Bradstreet Co., 666 5th Ave., New York NY 10019. Editor-in-Chief: B.D. Chapman. Managing Editor: Lynne Nicholson. 10% freelance written. For "printers and persons in graphic communications, composition, plate-making, color separations, ink, press room chemicals, etc." Monthly magazine; 170 pages. Estab. 1928. Circ. 80,000. Pays on publication. Buys all rights, but may reassign following publication. Submit seasonal/holiday material 2-3 months in advance of issue date. SASE. Reports in 2 weeks. Free sample copy and writer's guidelines.

Nonfiction: Historical; how-to; interview; new product; photo feature; and technical. "We accept articles directly related to the printing trades. Following criteria to be followed: material should be written objectively, and should stress the savings of cost, enhancement of quality, increased productivity or maximize safety." Query with clips of published work. Length: 1,000-2,500 words. Pays 7-10¢/word.

Photos: State availability of photos with query. Pays $10 for 5x7 or 8x10 b&w prints. Captions for identification. Buys all rights, but may reassign following publication.

WEB NEWSPAPER/MAGAZINE PRODUCTION, North American Publishing Co., 401 N. Broad St., Philadelphia PA 19108. (215)574-9600. Editor-in-Chief: Walter Kubilius. 50% freelance written. For the newspaper industry; production personnel through management to editor and publisher. Bimonthly magazine; 56 pages. Estab. 1972. Circ. 17,500. Pays on publication. Buys all rights. Pays 33% kill fee. Byline given "unless the writer can persuade plant manager to use his name instead, in which case we lean more to accepting and may pay more for the story." Phone queries OK. Photocopied submissions OK. SASE. Reports in 3 weeks.

Nonfiction: Publishes technical news development articles (production case histories) and how-to articles (production techniques). Length: 1,500 words minimum. Query or submit complete ms. Pays $35 minimum.

Photos: B&w and color purchased with or without mss, or on assignment. Captions required. Query or submit contact sheet or prints. No additional payment for those used with mss. Model release required.

PLAN AND PRINT, 10116 Franklin Ave., Franklin Park IL 60131. (312)671-5356. Editor-in-Chief: James C. Vebeck. 50% freelance written. For commercial reproduction companies and in-plant reproduction, printing, drafting and design departments of business and industry. Monthly magazine; 46 pages. Estab. 1928. Circ. 23,000. Pays on publication. Buys all rights. Byline given. Submit seasonal/holiday material 4-6 months in advance of issue date. SASE. Reports in 2 weeks. Free sample and writer's guidelines.

Nonfiction: How-to (how certain problems may have been solved; new methods of doing certain kinds of reproduction and/or design/drafting work); and technical (must relate to industry). Buys 50 mss/year. Query. Length: 250-5,000 words. Pays $25-300.

Photos: State availability of photos with query. Pays $5-10 for 8x10 b&w glossy prints. Captions required. Buys all rights. Model release required.

Columns/Departments: Open to suggestions for new columns/departments.

Poetry: Light verse related to the industry. Buys 6/year. Length: 4-12 lines. Pays $5-10.

Fillers: Puzzles related to the industry. Pays $5-10.

SCREEN PRINTING, 407 Gilbert Ave., Cincinnati OH 45202. (513)421-2050. Editor: Jonathan E. Schiff. For the screen printing industry, including screen printers (commercial, industrial and captive shops), suppliers and manufacturers, ad agencies and allied professions. Monthly magazine; 120 pages. Estab. 1953. Circ. 9,000. Buys all rights, but may reassign rights to author after publication. Byline given. Pays on publication. Free writer's guidelines. Will not consider photocopied submissions. Will consider simultaneous submissions. Reporting time varies. SASE.

Nonfiction and Photos: "Since the screen printing industry covers a broad range of applications and overlaps other fields in the graphic arts, it's necessary that articles be of a significant contribution, preferably to a specific area of screen printing. Subject matter is fairly open, with preference given to articles on administration or technology; trends and developments. We try to give a good sampling of technical articles, business and management articles; articles about unique operations. We also publish special features and issues on important subjects, such as material shortages, new markets and new technology breakthroughs. While most of our material is nitty-gritty, we appreciate a writer who can take an essentially dull subject and encourage the reader to read on through concise, factual, flairful and creative, expressive writing. Interviews are published after consultation with and guidance from the editor." Interested in stories on unique approaches by some shops on how to lick the problems created by the petroleum shortage (the industry relies heavily on petrol products). Length: 1,500-2,000 words. Pays minimum of $125 for major features; minimum of $50 for minor features; minimum of $35 for back of book articles. Cover photos negotiable; b&w or color. Published material becomes the property of the magazine.

SOUTHERN PRINTER, 75 3rd St. NW, Atlanta GA 30308. Editor: Roy Conradi. For commercial printing plant management in 14 Southern states. Estab. 1924. Monthly. Circ. 3,600. Not copyrighted. Byline given. Pays on publication. "Reporting time on submissions varies." SASE.

Nonfiction: Features on commercial printing plants in the South and their personnel. Query. Length: 1,000-1,500 words. Pays 1¢/word.

Photos: Uses b&w photos. Pays $4.

WORLD-WIDE PRINTER, North American Publishing Co., 401 N. Broad St., Philadelphia PA 19108. Editor: Walter Kubilius. Emphasizes printing and printing technology for printers; packagers; and publishers of newspapers, books, magazines, any and all printed matter.

Bimonthly magazine; 110 pages. Estab. 1978. Circ. 15,000. Pays on publication. Buys all rights. Phone queries OK. Submit seasonal/holiday material 2 months in advance. Simultaneous, photocopied and previously published submissions OK. Reports in 3 weeks. Sample copy $2.
Nonfiction: Technical material only. "Knowledge of printing technology is absolutely necessary in the writer, even if the subject is only an interview or plant story." Buys 2-3 mss/issue. Query. Length: 500-2,000 words. Pays $25-150.
Photos: State availability of photos. Pays $5 for b&w 5x7 prints.

Public Relations

PUBLICIST, Public Relations Aids, Inc., 221 Park Ave. S., New York NY 10003. Editor-in-Chief: Lee Levitt. 25% freelance written. Devoted entirely to professional publicity/public relations. For "a controlled circulation of people engaged in publicity on a national or major regional scale." Bimonthly tabloid. Estab. 1976. Circ. 14,000. Pays on acceptance. Pays 100% kill fee. Buys all rights, but may reassign to author following publication. Byline given unless "writers told in response to initial inquiry that material could only be used as part of another article (in which case, of course, he can decide not to submit material); payment also is much lower in such cases too." Submit seasonal/holiday material 6 months in advance. Simultaneous, photocopied and previously published material OK. SASE. Reports in 1 month. Free sample copy and writer's guidelines for self-addressed mailing label plus 40¢ in stamps.
Nonfiction: How-to, informational, humor, interview, nostalgia, profile, personal experience, photo feature and technical. "The subject of every article must be publicity, or organizations or persons engaged in publicity. We cover only national projects." Buys 5 mss/issue. Query. Length: 400-1,500 words. Pays $30-250.
Photos: Purchased with or without accompanying ms or on assignment. Captions required. Uses b&w only. Query. Prefers 8x10 prints. Pays $20-50.
Fiction: Humorous, condensed novels, mainstream, serialized novels. "All fiction must concern publicity people in a realistic professional situation; must exhibit sophisticated comprehension of big time PR practice." Query. Length: 500 words minimum. Pays $50-400.
Fillers: Clippings, jokes, gags, anecdotes, newsbreaks, short humor on professional public relations topics only. Buys 2/issue. Length: 50-400 words. Pays $2-40.
How To Break In: "We are most likely to accept case histories of national publicity projects; the article must include details of the project's cost; you must send documentation of the project. All our articles are in newspaper style: flat, abrupt leads, attributions for all important statements, no editorial comment."

Real Estate

APARTMENT MANAGEMENT NEWSLETTER, Mattco Equities, Inc., 48 W. 21st St., New York NY 10010. Editor: Rivki Beer. 20% freelance written. Emphasizes apartment management. Monthly newsletter; 8 pages. Estab. 1975. Circ. 8,000. Pays on publication. Buys all rights. Byline given. Submit seasonal/holiday material 2 months in advance of issue date. Photocopied submissions OK. SASE. Reports in 8 weeks. Sample copy $2.25.
Nonfiction: How-to (maintenance, occupancy, cost-cutting); informational (taxes, gas, oil, trends affecting apartments) interviews (with successful managers); profiles (successful apartment complexes), new products (snow throwers, rugs, windows, etc.); and technical (for all the foregoing; can include graphs, charts). Query or submit complete ms. Length: 250-1,000 words. Pays $5-10/page.

AREA DEVELOPMENT MAGAZINE, 432 Park Ave. S., New York NY 10016. (212)532-4360. Editor-in-Chief: Albert H. Jaeggin. 50% freelance written. Emphasizes corporate facility planning and site selection. Monthly magazine; 100-130 pages. Estab. 1965. Circ. 32,000. Pays when edited. Buys all rights. Byline given. Photocopied submissions OK. Reports in 1-3 weeks. Free sample copy and writer's guidelines.
Nonfiction: How-to (case histories of companies; experiences in site selection and all other aspects of corporate facility planning); historical (if it deals with corporate facility planning); interview (corporate executives and professional developers); experience (of corporate executives); personal opinion; and photo feature (pictures of new plants, offices and warehouses). Buys 1-5 mss/issue. Query. Pays $50-60/printed page, including illustrations.
Photos: State availability of photos with query. No additional payment for 8x10 or 5x7 b&w glossy prints or color transparencies. Captions preferred. Buys all rights, but may reassign following publication.

COMMUNITY DEVELOPMENT DIGEST, 399 National Press Bldg., Washington DC 20045. (202)638-6113. Various newsletters for government officals and industry executives in housing-community development—housing production; housing market; managing housing; community development programs; neighborhoods and home improvement. Estab. 1961. Pays end of month after publication. SASE if return desired. Sample copy and writer's guidelines for SASE.
Fillers: Uses contributions of newspaper clippings on housing and community development; substantive actions and litigations, that would be of interest to housing and community development professionals beyond immediate area. "We reject material when the territory has already been covered; material not of interest to our needs." Particularly wants regular contributors for multistates, region, or at least a full state, especially state capitals. Normally pays $2.00 for each clipping used.

EMPIRE STATE REALTOR, New York State Association of Realtors, Executive Park Tower, Western Ave. at Fuller Rd., Albany NY 12203. For professional real estate salespeople in New York. Quarterly magazine; 28 pages. Estab. 1977. Circ. 23,000. Pays on publication. Buys all rights, but may reassign following publication. Photocopied submissions OK. SASE. Reports in 6 weeks. Free sample copy.
Nonfiction: "Our readers want information which will help them sell homes. Articles should be specific to that end and may include technical information." How-to (sell a home, must have professional approach); informational (new trends in home selling, mortgage and financial trends); humor (personal experiences while selling or buying a home); and technical (financing a home, office layout). Buys 4 mss/year. Submit complete ms Length: 1,000 words maximum. Pays $25 maximum.

FINANCIAL FREEDOM REPORT, National Institute of Financial Planning, 4751 Holladay Blvd., Salt Lake City UT 84117. (801)272-9633. Editor: Mark O. Haroldsen. Managing Editor: David Mitchell. For "professional and nonprofessional investors, and would-be investors in real estate—real estate brokers, insurance companies, investment planners, truck drivers, housewives, doctors, architects, contractors, etc. The magazine's content is presently expanding to interest and inform the readers about other ways to put their money to work for them." Monthly magazine; 64 pages. Estab. 1976. Circ. 50,000. Pays on publication. Buys all rights. Byline given. Phone queries OK. Simultaneous submissions OK. SASE. Reports in 2 week. Sample copy $3; free writer's guidelines.
Nonfiction: How-to (find real estate bargains, finance property, use of leverage, managing property, developing market trends, goal setting, motivational); and interviews (success stories of those who have relied on own initiative and determination in real estate market or other business endeavors, e.g., Ray Kroc of McDonald's). Buys 9 mss/issue. Query with clips of published work or submit complete ms. Length: 1,500-4,500 words. "If the topic warranted a two- or three-parter, we would consider it." Pays 7-10¢/word.
Photos: Send photos with ms. Uses b&w 8x10 matte prints. Offers no additional payment for photos accepted with ms. Captions required.

PROPERTIES MAGAZINE, 4900 Euclid Ave., Cleveland OH 44103. (216)431-7666. Editor: Gene Bluhm. Monthly. Buys all rights. Pays on publication. Query. SASE.
Nonfiction and Photos: Wants articles of real estate and construction news value. Interested primarily in articles relating to northeastern Ohio. Length: up to 900 words. Buys photographs with mss, 5x7 preferred.

PROPERTY MANAGEMENT JOURNAL (also *Mid Valley News*, El Monte, South El Monte, Rosemead and Baldwin Park), 10922 E. Valley Blvd., El Monte CA 91731. Publisher/Editor: Ben Hegel. For owners and managers of rental property in southern California, realtors and property management firms. Monthly tabloid newspaper. Estab. 1971. Circ. 10,000. Buys first serial rights. Byline given. Buys 5 mss/issue. Pays on acceptance. Sample copy for $1. Reports in 4 weeks. Query or submit complete ms. SASE.
Nonfiction and Photos: How-to articles of vital interest to owners and property managers who control the purchasing of services and products in the rental housing industry. Topics could be on carpet care, painting, draperies, appliance sales and service, electrical and plumbing repair, decorating, swimming pool maintenance, roof repair, laundry services, fire and building safety, etc. Writers should remember that subjects should be applicable to southern California readers—no snowplows or storm window stories. Length: 3 pages, typed, double-spaced. Also uses shorter humorous articles about apartment hunting, resident managers, tenant relations, etc. Length: 1-3 pages, typed, double-spaced. Pays $5-15. Will buy b&w photos, if applicable, at $5 each.

Recreation Park and Campground Management

CAMPING INDUSTRY, 225 E. Michigan, Milwaukee WI 53202. (414)276-6600. Editor: Mike Byrnes. 10% freelance written. Published 8 times/year; magazine; 44 pages. Estab. 1966. Circ. 16,100. Pays after publication. Buys first serial rights. Byline given. Phone queries OK. Submit seasonal/holiday material 3 months in advance of issue date. Simultaneous submissions OK. Reports in 2-3 weeks. Free sample copy and writer's guidelines.
Nonfiction: Selling camping equipment plus dealer stories; interview; new product; photo feature; and technical. No consumer "I went camping stories." Buys 6-8 mss/issue. Query. Length: 1,000-2,500. Pays $75-150 for manuscript and photos.
Photos: Reproduceable b&w photos. Author may submit contact sheet and negatives and magazine will have prints made. Buys one-time rights.

TOURIST ATTRACTIONS AND PARKS, 401 N. Broad St., Suite 904, Philadelphia PA 14108. (201)423-2266. Editor: S. Donat. 10% freelance written. For managers, owners of amusement parks, theme parks, tourist attractions, interested in improving promotion and personnel handling in theme parks and tourist attractions. Biannual magazine; 64 pages. Estab. 1972. Circ. 17,500. Pays between publication and acceptance. Phone queries OK. Buys first North American serial rights. SASE. Reports in 2 weeks. Free sample copy and writer's guidelines.
Nonfiction: How-to; new product (must be new and worthwhile); personal experience (only with a management technique or new type of ride, or of system that improves an amusement park or theme parks operations); technical (a device that does job better or less expensively, a description of a new technique that is successful—a ride or a way to attract visitors). "No articles on travel pieces of scenic wonder or a national or state park." Buys 2 mss/issue. Query. Length: 1,000-3,000 words. Pays 1-2¢/inch.
Photos: State availability of photos with query. Pays $10 for 8x10 b&w glossy with white borders prints. Captions preferred. Buys one-time rights.

WOODALL'S CAMPGROUND MANAGEMENT, 500 Hyacinth Place, Highland Park IL 60035. (312)433-4550. Editor/Associate Publisher: James D. Saul. Audience is the owners and managers of private campgrounds in the US, Canada and Mexico. Monthly tabloid; minimum 24 pages. Estab. 1970. Circ. 16,000. Pays on acceptance. Buys all rights, but may reassign following publication. Pays 25% kill fee. Byline given. Phone queries OK. Submit seasonal/holiday material 2 months in advance. Photocopied (if statement is enclosed stating that material has not been published or accepted elsewhere) and previously published submissions OK. SASE. Reports in 4 weeks. Sample copy 25¢; free writer's guidelines.
Nonfiction: Expose (governmental practices detrimental to private campground industry); how-to (any type that will provide practical, usable information in operation of campgrounds); informational; interview; new product; personal experience (experiences of campground owners/managers); photo feature; and technical. Buys 40-50 mss/year. Query. Length: 500-2,500 words. Pays $50-100.
Photos: Purchased with or without accompanying ms or on assignment. Captions required. Query. Pays $5-10 for 5x7 minimum b&w glossy; $20 minimum for 120mm and larger color transparencies. Offers no additional payment for photos accepted with ms "except for page-1 color transparencies; pays $20 additional whether part of editorial package or not." Model release required.
Fillers: Clippings and newsbreaks. Buys 10-12/year. Length: 50-250 words. Pays $15-25.
How To Break In: "We are seeking freelancers from throughout the country who can provide factual, useful articles pertinent to the private (not tax-supported) campground industry; new ideas that work, success stories, how to solve a problem. Facts and figures must be included."

Secretarial

MODERN SECRETARY, Allied Publications, Drawer 189, Palm Beach FL 33480. Editor: Mary Ellen Green. Monthly magazine; 16 pages. Pays between acceptance and publication. Buys simultaneous rights. Submit seasonal/holiday material 6 months in advance of issue date. Simultaneous, photocopied and previously published submissions OK. SASE. Reports in 2 months. Sample copy $1; writer's guidelines for SASE.
Nonfiction: Office tips for secretaries and picture stories of secretaries of famous personalities. How-to; general interest; humor; historical; interview; new product; nostalgia; personal experience; profile; technical; and travel. Nothing controversial or suggestive. Submit complete ms. Length: 300-1,000 words. Pays 5¢/accepted word.

Photos: Pays $5 for 8½x11 b&w glossy prints. Captions required. Buys simultaneous rights.

TODAY'S SECRETARY, McGraw-Hill, Inc., 1221 Avenue of the Americas, New York NY 10020. (212)997-2166. Editor: Nhora Cortes-Comerer. 75% freelance written. "For a primarily female readership, between 15-21, enrolled in high school, junior college and private business school secretarial programs." Monthly (October-May) magazine 32 pages. Estab. 1898. Circ. 60,000. Pays on publication. Buys all rights. Submit seasonal/holiday material 6 months in advance of issue date. SASE. Reports in 2-3 months. Free sample copy and writer's guidelines; mention *Writer's Market* in request.
Nonfiction: General interest (women's issues, consumer topics); historical (related to business and offices); how-to (crafts, cooking, decorating, office procedures); humor (office situations); interview (interesting secretaries); new prodit (office products and supplies). Buys 32 mss/year. Query with clips of published work. Length: 800-3,000 words. Pays $75-350.
Columns/Departments: Word Teasers (grammatical points); Consumer Wise (consumer information); and Think It Out (secretarial procedure). Buys 24 mss/year. Query. Length: 800-2,000 words. Pays $75-200.
Fillers: Adventure; fantasy; historical; humorous; mystery; suspense; science fiction; and western. No violence, sex or heavy romance. Buys 8 mss/year. Submit complete ms. Length: 800-1,000 words. Pays $75.
How To Break In: 'The best way to break in would be with a short piece of fiction (800 words). Keep in mind that our audience is mostly women, age 16-22, in high school or business school. Also, the stories shouldn't be too heavy—we print them in shorthand as a skill exercise for our readers. Other good freelance possibilities include profiles of secretaries with unusual job responsibilities or in an unusual field, and secretarial procedure stories—tips on filing, making travel arrangements for your boss, etc."

Selling and Merchandising

In this category are journals for salesmen and merchandisers that publish general material on how to sell products successfully. Journals in nearly every other category of this Trade Journal section also buy this kind of material if it is slanted to the specialized product or industry they deal with, such as clothing or petroleum. Publications for professional advertising and marketing men will be found under Advertising and Marketing Journals.

AGENCY SALES MAGAZINE, Box 16878, Irvine CA 92713. (714)752-5231. Editor: Dan Bayless. 60% freelance written. For independent sales representatives and the manufacturers they represent. Publication of Manufacturers' Agents National Association. Magazine; 48-56 pages. Estab. 1950. Monthly. Circ. 13,000. Rights purchased vary with author and material. May buy all rights, with the possibility of reassigning rights to author after publication, or simultaneous rights. Byline given. Buys 36 mss/year. Pays on publication. Free sample copy and writer's guidelines. Will consider photocopied and simultaneous submissions. Reports in 2 months. Query. SASE.
Nonfiction and Photos: Articles on independent sales representatives, the suppliers and customers, and their operations and manufacturers who sell through sales agents. Must be about independent selling from the agent's or manufacturer's point of view. Uses how-to, profile, interview, successful business techniques. "Articles about selling should not be too general—specifics a must." Length: 500-2,500 words. Ideal length is 1,500 words. Pays $50-100. Photos purchased with accompanying ms with extra payment. Captions required. B&w glossies only. Pays $10-15. Size: 3x5, 8x10.

AMERICAN FIREARMS INDUSTRY, American Press Media Association, Inc., 7001 N. Clark St., Chicago IL 60626. Specializes in the sporting arms trade. Monthly magazine; 58 pages. Estab. 1972. Circ. 19,000. Pays on publication. Buys all rights, but may reassign following publication. Submit seasonal/holiday material 60 days in advance. SASE. Reports in 2 weeks. Sample copy, $1.
Nonfiction: John Cahill, Editor. Publishes informational, technical and new product articles. Buys 60 mss/year. Query. Length: 900-1,500 words. Pays $90.
Photos: B&w (8x10) glossies. Mss price includes payment for photos.

ARMY/NAVY STORE AND OUTDOOR MERCHANDISER, 225 W. 34th St., New York NY 10001. (212)279-0800. Editor: Michael Spielman. 15-20% freelance written. For the owners of army/navy surplus and outdoor goods stores. Estab. 1947. Circ. 5,000. Pays 100% kill fee. No byline. Buys 30 mss/year. Pays on publication. SASE. Reports in 1 month. Sample copy $1.50.

Nonfiction and Photos: Articles on the methods stores use to promote items; especially on how Army/Navy items have become fashion items, and the problems attendant to catering to this new customer. Sources of supply, how they promote, including windows, newspapers, etc. "If the guy wants to tell his life story, listen and take notes. Use simple words. Stick to a single subject, if possible. Find out how the man makes money and tell us. The true 'success' story is the most frequently submitted and the most dreadful; yet nothing is of more interest if it is done well. No one truly wishes to tell you how he earns money." Length: open. Pays $50 minimum. "Most articles—especially on stores—must have photos included; minimum 5x7 b&w glossies with captions."

How To Break In: "Am anxious to build our coverage of camping departments. The best material always has a unique—but not forced—slant to most routine store stories."

AUDIO TRADE MERCHANDISING, Maclean-Hunter Ltd., 481 University Ave., Toronto, Ontario, Canada M5W 1A7. (416)596-5000. Editor: Greg Gertz. 40-50% freelance written. For retailers of high-quality audio equipment and operators of stereo stores. Monthly; 40 pages. Estab. 1972. Circ. 6,000. Pays on publication. Buys first North American serial rights. Phone queries OK. Submit seasonal/holiday material 3 months in advance. Previously published submissions OK. SAE and International Reply Coupons. Reports in 3 weeks.

Nonfiction: How-to (run a successful audio retail outlet); profiles (successful dealers); interviews (with top executives in the audio equipment manufacturing industry). Buys 2 mss/issue. Length: 500-2,000 words. Query. "Most freelance material comes to us from regular contributors. Anything else must be either very new, very exciting, or very controversial. Strong Canadian angle required." Pays 10¢/word average.

Photos: Purchased with mss. B&w only. Captions required. Query. Pays $10.

AUTOMOTIVE AGE, Freed-Crown Publishing, 6931 Van Nuys Blvd., Van Nuys CA 92405. (213)873-1320. Editor: Art Spinella. For a primarily male audience with income in the upper middle and upper brackets; sole owners or partners in multi-million dollar businesses. Monthly magazine; 140-150 pages. Estab. 1967. Circ. 47,000. Pays on publication. Buys all rights, but may reassign after publication. Pays 65% kill fee. Byline given. Phone queries OK. Simultaneous submissions OK, if list of other publications receiving same or similar story is furnished. SASE. Reports in 2 weeks. Free sample copy.

Nonfiction: Publishes humorous articles related to retail sales, auto repair, or of general interest to men meeting readers' demographics; informational articles (sales techniques, dealership/retail promotions); interviews (with men in government or industry; auto dealers); nostalgia (automotive- and sales-related); travel (to places where men meeting their demographics would find new and different). "Clean, sophisticated copy that talks to the audience on a professional level." Buys 10 mss/issue. Query. Length: 300-2,000 words. Pays $5/column inch, or $7/hour, plus expenses.

Photos: Pays $25/b&w photo used with articles, columns or departments.

Columns/Departments: Promo Beat (unique auto dealership promotions for new and used car sales, service or parts departments). Buys 12 items/issue. Query. Length: 700-1,000 words. Pays $5/column inch. Open to suggestions for new columns and departments.

Fillers: Buys 15 clippings/issue. Pays $1/clipping or tip leading to a published item.

CAMPGROUND MERCHANDISING, 2101 N. Broad St., Suite 904, Philadelphia PA 19108. Editor: Robert Goodman. For owners and managers of recreation vehicle campgrounds who sell merchandise or equipment to people who vacation in recreation vehicles. Magazine published 4 times a year; 56 pages. Estab. 1972. Circ. 10,000. Buys first North American serial rights. No byline. Buys 5 mss/year. Pays on acceptance. Free sample copy to writer on request. Will not consider photocopied or simultaneous submissions. Submit seasonal material 3 months in advance. Reports in 2 weeks. Query or submit complete ms. SASE.

Nonfiction and Photos: "We specialize in RV campgrounds that resell equipment or merchandise to RV'ers who are visiting the RV campground. We use articles about how to best operate a recreation vehicle campground. The best approach is to interview managers of recreation vehicle campgrounds about their operations. Not interested in RV campgrounds selling, bread, milk, ice cream. Main interest is in their sales of equipment or merchandise wanted only by RV'ers, and how the resale of merchandise and equipment in an RV campground made it profitable." Informational, how-to, personal experience, interview, successful business operations, merchandising techniques. Length: 800-1,500 words. Pays about

4¢/word. Prefers 8x10 b&w glossies, but can use 5x7. Pays $10 for each one used with ms. No color. Captions optional.
Fillers: Clippings are purchased only if about RV parks and newsworthy. Pays 80¢/inch used.

CHAIN STORE AGE, GENERAL MERCHANDISE EDITION, 425 Park Ave., New York NY 10022. Publisher: Paul J. Reuter. Executive Editor: Murray Foreseter. For major chain store executives, field and store management personnel in the general merchandise chain field. Estab. 1925. Monthly. Circ. 33,500. Buys all rights. Purchases of mss are limited to special needs and commitments: "12 columns in fashions (from London), 12-plus pages of government news from Washington." Pays on publication. Will send free sample copy to writer on request. Reports in 2 weeks. Submit complete ms. SASE.
Nonfiction: Retail-related news across a wide band of merchandise categories (housewares, home sewing, toys, stationery, fashionwear, etc.). News about companies, promotions, people-on-the-move. Sharp, to the point, strong on facts. Subjects that are on the tip of chain retailers' minds about their business. How chain retailers are coping with traffic fall-off by tightening productivity screws in day-to-day operations. "We have one definite 'no-no'—sloppy copy that is not proofread." Length: 250-300 words. Pays minimum of $10/page.

CONVENIENCE STORE NEWS, BMT Publications, Inc., 254 W. 31st St., New York NY 10001. (212)594-4120. Associate Editor: David S. Chartock. For convenience-store chain executives, middle-management and owner/operators; franchisors and franchisees; convenience store managers, wholesalers, distributors, service merchandisers, food brokers and manufacturers involved in the food retailing and convenience store business. Semimonthly tabloid; 40 pages. Circ. 38,000. Pays on publication. Buys all rights. Phone queries OK. Query for submission of seasonal/holiday material. Reports on queries in 1-2 weeks. Free sample copy and writer's guidelines.
Nonfiction: General interest, how-to, humor, inspirational, interview, profile and photo feature. Interested in news about convenience stores and chains, their personnel, operations and product mix trends, promotions and legislative activities on all levels of government that affect the operations of these businesses. Buys 20 mss/issue. Query. Pays $2/column inch.
Photos: Send photos with ms. Pays $5 for b&w glossy prints. Polaroid prints acceptable. Captions required.
Columns/Departments: Store Managers Section. Buys 16-20 mss/issue. Query. Length: 6 double-spaced ms pages maximum. Pays $2/column inch.
Fillers: Newsbreaks ("in our industry only"). Length: half page, double-spaced.

GIFTWARE NEWS, 1111 E. Touhy Ave., Des Plaines IL 60018. Editor: Cholm Houghton. For retailers, gift stores, florists, stationers, department stores, jewelry and home furnishings stores. Published 8/year plus an annual *Buyers Guide*; 80 pages. Estab. 1975. Circ. 41,000. Rights purchased vary with author and material. Buys about 24 mss/year. Pays on publication. Sample copy $1.50; free writer's guidelines. Submit seasonal material (related to the gift industry) 2 months in advance. Reports in 1-2 months. Query or submit complete ms. SASE.
Nonfiction and Photos: Trade material. Only informative articles written in a manner applicable to daily business and general knowledge; not mere rhetorical exercises. Articles on store management, security, backgrounds (history) of giftwares, e.g., crystals, silver, (methods, procedures of manufacture); porcelain, etc. Informational, interview, profiles, material on new products and merchandising techniques. Length: 500 words minimum. Pays $40 minimum. Pays $10 minimum for b&w photos used with mss. Captions optional.

HEALTH FOODS BUSINESS, Howmark Publishing Corp., 225 W. 34th St., New York NY 10001. (212)279-0800. Editor-in-Chief: Michael Spielman. 20% freelance written. For owners and managers of health food stores. Monthly magazine; 100 pages. Estab. 1954. Circ. over 5,000. Pays on publication. Buys simultaneous rights, second serial (reprint) rights or first North American serial rights. Pay 100% kill fee "if kill is our fault, otherwise kill fee is negotiable." No byline given unless a technical article by an authority or other special circumstances. Phone queries OK. Simultaneous and photocopied submissions OK if exclusive to their field. Previously published work OK. SASE. Reports in 1 month. Sample copy $2.
Nonfiction: Exposés (government hassling with health food industry); how-to (unique or successful retail operators); informational (how or why a product works; technical aspects must be clear to laymen); historical (natural food use); interviews (must be prominent person in industry or closely related to the health food industry); and photo features (any unusual subject related to the retailer's interests). Buys 2-3 mss/issue. Query for interviews and photo features. Will consider complete ms in other categories. Length: 1,000 words minimum. Pays $25/published page minimum.
Photos: "Most articles must have photos included"; minimum 5x7 b&w glossies. Captions

required. Send prints or contact sheets with negatives. No additional payment.

HOUSEWARES, Harcourt Brace Jovanovich Publications, Inc., 757 Third Ave., New York NY 10017. Editor: Jack BenAry. Emphasizes the retail merchandising of housewares. Published 18 times/year. Tabloid; 50 pages. Estab. 1892. Circ. 12,500. Pays on publication. Buys all rights. Pays 25% kill fee. No bylines generally. SASE. Reports in 3 weeks. Free sample copy.
Nonfiction: Photo features. "Articles without photos are rarely acceptable. We are picture-oriented." Buys 35 mss/year. Query. Length: 1,000-2,500 words. Pays 15¢/word maximum.
Photos: Purchased with accompanying ms. Captions required. Query. Submit 5x7 or 8x10 b&w glossy; transparencies for color. Total price for ms includes payment for photos. Model release required.

KEY NEWSLETTER, Voice Publications, Goreville IL 62939. (618)995-2027. Editor-in-Chief: Bernard Lyons. 5% freelance written; "but would like to see more." Emphasizes direct marketing/mail order, specifically for those using classified columns of national magazines. Monthly newsletter; 4 pages. Estab. 1960. Pays on acceptance. Buys all rights. Submit seasonal/holiday material 2 months in advance of issue date. Photocopied submissions OK. SASE. Reports in 2 weeks. Sample copy $1; mention *Writer's Market* in request.
Nonfiction: Exposé (fraud in mail order/direct marketing); historical (old classified ads); how-to (write classified ads, match markets, increase response to ads); humor (funny classifieds); inspirational (examples of successful classifieds, personal stories of successful mail order through classifieds); interview (with successful mail order/direct market persons using classifieds); new product (if of help to small business); personal experience (summary of test results); profile (successful users of classifieds, written in first person); and technical (math for mail order/direct marketing). Buys 10 mss/year. Submit complete ms. Length: 50-1,500 words. Pays $10-75.

PHOTO MARKETING, 603 Lansing Ave., Jackson MI 49202. Managing Editor: Pamela Weight. For camera store dealers, photofinishers, manufacturers and distributors of photographic equipment. Publication of the Photo Marketing Association, International. Monthly magazine; 62 pages. Estab. 1924. Circ. 15,000. Buys all rights. "Bylines are usually not given unless the writer is a well-known expert in her/his field and thus the name would mean something to our audience." Pays on publication. Reports in 7 days. Query with outline and story line. SASE.
Nonfiction and Photos: Business features dealing with photographic retailing or photofinishing operations, highlighting unique aspects, promotional programs, special problems. Length: 300-500 typewritten lines. Pays 5-7%/word minimum. Pays $10-15/published 5x7 glossy photo.

SALESMAN'S OPPORTUNITY MAGAZINE, 6 N. Michigan Ave., Chicago IL 60602. Managing Editor: Jack Weissman. 30% freelance written. "For anyone who is interested in making money, full or spare time, in selling or in independent business program." Monthly magazine. Estab. 1923. Circ. 180,000. Pays on publication. Buys all rights. Byline given. Submit seasonal/holiday material 6 months in advance of issue date. SASE. Free sample copy and writer's guidelines.
Nonfiction: "We use articles dealing with sales techniques, sales psychology or general self improvement topics." How-to; inspirational; and interview (with successful salespeople who are selling products offered by direct selling firms, especially concerning firms which recruit salespeople through *Salesman's Opportunity Magazine*). Submit complete ms. Length: 250-900 words. Pays $20-35.
Photos: State availability of photos with ms. Offers no additional payment for 8x10 b&w glossy prints. Captions required. Buys all rights. Model release required.

SELLING TODAY, Automotive Service Industry Association, 444 N. Michigan Ave., Chicago IL 60611. Director of Communications: John Corkey. 60% freelance written. Emphasizes selling to automotive service markets by wholesalers/distributors, salesmen and countermen. Bimonthly magazine; 24 pages. Estab. 1959. Circ. 10,000. Pays on acceptance. Buys all rights. Submit seasonal/holiday material 2 months in advance of issue date. Photocopied and previously published submissions OK. SASE. Reports in 2 weeks. Free sample copy; mention *Writer's Market* in request.
Nonfiction: How-to articles on selling in the automotive service industry. Query. Length: 750-3,000 words. Pays $30-100.

SMOKESHOP, BMT Publications, 254 W. 31st St., New York NY 10001. (212)594-4120. Editor: Gerard P. Sullivan. Associate Editor: David Chartock. For owners of high-quality smokeshops who offer personal service and knowledge of products. Monthly magazine; 50 pages. Circ. 3,250. Pays on publication. Buys all rights. Phone queries OK. Submit seasonal/holiday material 6 weeks in advance. SASE. Reports in 2 weeks. Sample copy $1.
Nonfiction: How-to (improve sales through increased traffic; display or any innovative means); humor (if it accomplishes how-to purpose); interview (with shopowners, people with something to offer shopowners); nostalgia (may consider a featurette); profile (of interesting tobacconists); and photo feature. "Don't fall into the trap of writing from a consumer standpoint. We are looking for pieces by experts in display, fixtures, blending, product mix, etc." Buys 3-4 mss/issue. Query with clips of published work. Length: 500-3,500 words. Pays $2/column inch.
Photos: "Good photos make the piece more interesting and the book more attractive." State availability of photos. Pays $5 for b&w glossy prints and color prints. Captions required.
Fillers: Clippings and newsbreaks. Pays $2/column inch.

SPECIALTY SALESMAN MAGAZINE, Communications Channels, Inc., 307 N. Michigan Ave., Chicago IL 60601. (312)726-0743. Editor-in-Chief: Yale A. Katz. Associate Editor: Karen Brodsky. 75% freelance written. For independent businessmen and women who sell door-to-door, store-to-store, office-to-office and by the party plan method as well as through direct mail and telephone solicitation; selling products and services. Monthly magazine; 64 pages. Estab. 1915. Circ. 500,000. Pays on acceptance. Buys all rights. Byline given. Submit seasonal/holiday material 1 month in advance of issue date. SASE. Reports in 3 months. Free sample copy and writer's guidelines.
Nonfiction: How-to (sell better; increase profits); historical (related to the history of various kinds of sales pitches, anecdotes, etc.); humor (cartoon); inspirational (success stories, "rags to riches," type of stories); ith no additional payment.
&inimum. Photos purchased with accompBuys 6 mss/issue. Query or submit complete ms. Length: 500-1,500 words. Pays 3¢/word.
Columns/Departments: Ideas Exchange (generated from our readers). Submit complete ms. Open to suggestions for new columns/departments.
Fillers: Jokes, gags, anecdotes and short humor. Buys 2/issue. Length: 150-500 words. Pays $3/word.

Show People and Amusements

AMUSEMENT BUSINESS, Billboard Publications, Inc., Box 24970, Nashville TN 37202. (615)329-3925. Editor: Tom Powell. Managing Editor: Tim Taggart. Emphasizes the amusement and mass entertainment industry. Weekly tabloid; 24-48 pages. Estab. 1960. Circ. 15,000. Pays on publication. Buys all rights. Byline sometimes given; "it depends on the quality of the individual piece." Phone queries OK. SASE. Submit seasonal/holiday material 2-3 weeks in advance. Reports in 1 month. Free sample copy and writer's guidelines; mention *Writer's Market* in request.
Nonfiction: How-to (case history of successful promotions); interview; new product; and technical (how "new" devices, shows or services work at parks, fairs, auditoriums and conventions). No personality pieces or interviews with stage stars. Buys 500-1,000 mss/year. Query. Length: 400-700 words. Pays $1-2.50/published inch.
Photos: State availability of photos with query. Pays $3-5 for b&w 8x10 glossy prints. Captions required. Buys all rights. Model release required.
Columns/Departments: Auditorium Arenas; Fairs, Fun Parks; Food Concessions; Merchandise; Shopping Centers; Promotion; Shows (carnival and circus); Shopping Centers; Talent; and Tourist Attractions. Query. Length: 25-700 words. Pays $2-2.50/published inch. Open to suggestions for new columns/departments.

BILLBOARD, 9000 Sunset Blvd., Los Angeles CA 90069. Editor-in-Chief/Publisher: Lee Zhito. Managing Editor: Eliot Tiegel. Special Issues Editor: Earl Paige. Sound Business/Studios Editor: Jim McCullaugh. Record Review/Campus Editor: Ed Harrison. Talent Editor: Jean Williams. Marketing News Editor: John Sippel. (All Los Angeles). Radio/TV Editor: Doug Hall. International Editor: Adam White. Publishing Editor: Irv Lichtman. Disco Editor: Radcliffe Joe. (All New York). Country Music Editor: Gerry Wood (Nashville). Classical: Alan Penchansky (Chicago). Weekly. Buys all rights. Pays on publication. SASE.
Nonfiction: "Correspondents are appointed to send in spot amusement news covering

photograph record programming by broadcasters and record merchandising by retail dealers. Concert reviews, interviews with artists; stories on discotheques. We are extremely interested in blank tape, tape playback and record hardware stores." Length: short. Pays 24¢-$1/published inch; $5/published photo. "Special Issues rates are competitive and negotiated, as subjects range into every area of music."

THE HOLLYWOOD REPORTER, Publishers Press, 6715 Sunset Blvd., Hollywood CA 90028. (213)464-7411. Editor: Tichi Wikerson Mies. Managing Editor: Jay Arnold. Emphasizes entertainment industry, film, TV and theater and is interested in everything to do with financial news in these areas. Daily magazine: 25-30 pages. Estab. 1920. Circ: 20,000. Pays on publication. Buys first rights. Submit seasonal/holiday material 3 months in advance. SASE. Reports in 1 month. Sample copy $1; free writer's guidelines.
Nonfiction: Interview, profile, new product and technical. "No sensational material or gossip." Buys 50 mss/year. Query. Length: 50-500 words. Pays $1/column inch up to $300/ms; 50¢/word minimum.
Photos: B&w and color 8x10 glossy prints. Payment is negotiable. Captions and model releases required. Buys first rights.
Fillers: Newsbreaks. Buys 250/year. Length: 50-500 words. Pays 50¢/word minimum up to $300.

PERFORMANCE, 2929 Cullen St., Fort Worth TX 76107. (817)338-9444. Editor: Stephen Fuchs. "Performance publishes tour routing information, updated on a weekly basis. These itineraries, along with box office reports, street news, live performance reviews and industry features are of interest to our readers." Weekly magazine; 59 pages. Circ. 10,000. Buys all rights. Phone queries OK. Submit seasonal/holiday material 2 months in advance. Simultaneous, photocopied and previously published submissions OK. SASE. Reports in 1 month. Sample copy and writer's guidelines $1.
Nonfiction: "This is a trade publication, dealing basically with the ins-and-outs of booking live entertainment. We are interested in adding freelancers from major cities around the US to provide us with 'street news' and spot information on sound lighting, clubs, ticketing, facilities, and college news relevant to live entertainment. Also publish interviews and overviews from time to time." Interviews, opinion and profile.
Photos: State availbility of photos with ms. Pays $1-3 for 8x10 b&w matt prints; $20 for 35mm color transparencies selected for cover use. Captions preferred. Buys all rights.

G-STRING BEAT, Atlanta Enterprises, Box 007, Gays Mills WI 54631. Editor: Rita Atlanta. Emphasizes burlesque and allied fields of entertainment. Quarterly magazine; 48 pages. Estab. 1973. Circ. 12,000. Pays on publication. Buys all rights. SASE. Reports in 2-3 weeks.
Nonfiction: Publishes in-depth, hard-edged profiles of performers. Buys 6-10 mss/year. Submit complete ms. Length: 1,000-2,500 words. Pays $75-150.
Photos: Query. "We have about 5,000 pix on hand and pix must be exceptional for us to buy."
Fiction: John Bane, Department Editor. Publishes mystery, humorous and suspense fiction. "Very little fiction is accepted because freelance writers have a limited 'feel' (no pun intended) of burlesque. The tensions of the business are rarely understood by outsiders. Would say that this is one of the hardest markets to please." Buys 2-3 mss/year. Submit complete ms. Length: 2,500-5,000 words. Pays $100-250.

VARIETY, 154 W. 46th St., New York NY 10036. Does not buy freelance material.

Sport Trade

AMERICAN BICYCLIST AND MOTORCYCLIST, 461 8th Ave., New York NY 10001. (212)563-3430. Editor: Stan Gottlieb. For bicycle sales and service shops. Estab. 1879. Monthly. Circ. 8,188. Buys all rights. "Only staff-written articles are bylined, except under special circumstances." Pays on publication. Reports in 10 days.
Nonfiction: Typical story describes (very specifically) unique traffic-builder or merchandising ideas used with success by an actual dealer. Articles may also deal exclusively with moped sales and service operation within conventional bicycle shop. Emphasis is on showing other dealers how they can follow a similar pattern and increase their business. Articles may also be based entirely on repair shop operation, depicting efficient and profitable service systems and methods. Query. Length: 1,800-2,800 words. Pays 4¢/word, plus "bonus for excellent manuscript."
Photos: Relevant b&w photos illustrating principal points in article purchased with ms 5x7 minimum. No transparencies. Pays $5 per photo.

ARCHERY RETAILER, Market Communications, Inc., 225 E. Michigan, Milwaukee WI 53202. (414)276-6600. Editor: Glenn Helgeland. Emphasizes archery retailing. Magazine published 5 times/year; 54 pages. Estab. 1976. Circ. 11,500. Pays on publication. Buys one-time rights. Byline given. Phone queries OK, "but prefer mail queries." Submit seasonal/holiday material 4 months in advance. SASE. Reports in 3 weeks. Free sample copy and writer's guidelines.
Nonfiction: How-to (better buying, selling, displaying, advertising, etc.); interview; profile. "No stories about dinky shops selling because they love archery but have no idea of profitability." Buys 2-4 mss/issue. Query. Length: 500-2,000 words. Pays $35-125.
Photos: Purchased with or without accompanying ms. Captions required. Pays $10-25 for 8x10 b&w glossies.

BICYCLE DEALER SHOWCASE, Box 19531, Irvine CA 92713. Editor: Steve Ready. For bicycle/moped dealers and industry personnel. Monthly magazine; 70-90 pages. Estab. 1972. Circ. 11,000. Buys all rights. Buys about 12 mss/year. Pays on publication. Free sample copy and writer's guidelines. Submit seasonal material 2 months in advance. Reports in 3-4 weeks. Query or submit complete ms. SASE.
Nonfiction: Articles dealing with marketing bicycle products; financing, better management techniques, current trends, as related to bicycle equipment or selling. Material must be fairly straightforward, with a slant toward economic factors or marketing techniques. Informational, how-to, interview, profile, humor, successful business operations, merchandising techniques, technical. Length: 1,000-1,500 words. Pays $35-50 "or more, depending on the work involved."
Photos: 8x10 b&w glossy prints purchased with mss. Pays $5 minimum/photo.

BICYCLE JOURNAL, 4915 W. Freeway, Box 1570, Fort Worth TX 76101. Publisher: Bill Quinn. Estab. 1947. Monthly. Circ. 7,500. Not copyrighted. Pays on publication. SASE.
Nonfiction and Photos: Stories only about dealers who service what they sell. Stories of a single outstanding feature of a bike store, such as a good display, interior or exterior; sales tip; service tip; unusual sign; advertising or promotion tip; store layout, etc. Photo must be vertical. "One 8x10 photo is sufficient." Length: 200-300 words.

BOWLERS JOURNAL, 875 N. Michigan Ave., Chicago IL 60611. (312)266-7171. Editor-in-Chief: Mort Luby, 30-50% freelance written. For tournament bowlers and billiard players and a trade audience of proprietors, dealers, distributors. Monthly magazine; 90 pages. Estab. 1913. Circ. 17,000. Pays on publication. Buys all rights, but may reassign following publication. Phone queries OK. Submit seasonal/holiday material 1 month in advance of issue date. Simultaneous and photocopied submissions OK. SASE. Reports in 3 weeks.
Nonfiction: Uses illustrated articles about successful bowling and billiard room proprietors who have used unusual promotions to build business, profiles of interesting industry personalities (including bowlers and billiard players), and coverage of major competitive events, both bowling and billiards. "We publish some controversial matter, seek out outspoken personalities. We reject material that is too general; that is, not written for high average bowlers and bowling proprietors who already know basics of playing the game and basics of operating a bowling alley." Length: 1,500-2,500 words. Pays $100.
Photos: B&w (8x10) glossies and color (35mm or 120 or 4x5) transparencies purchased with mss. Captions required. Pays $5-10 for b&w; $15-25 for color.

GOLF BUSINESS, Harvest Publishing Co./Div. of Harcourt Brace Jovanovich, 9800 Detroit Ave., Cleveland OH 44102. (216)651-5500. Editor-in-Chief: David J. Slaybaugh. Emphasizes golf and course management and maintenance. Monthly magazine; 60 pages. Estab. 1927. Circ. 18,000. Pays on publication. Buys all rights. Phone queries OK. Submit seasonal material 4 months in advance. SASE. Reports in 2 months. Free sample copy.
Nonfiction: Expose (may focus on industry problem that would uncover information new and beneficial to business); how-to (find something new that a club or course is doing that can be applied to whole industry); informational (new concepts in club management); interview (with industry or governmental individual involved in business); new product (also interested in new services which are in the news); photo feature (if it demonstrates a new technique in course maintenance operations). Buys 7 mss/year. Query. Length: 1,500-3,000 words. Pays $100-150.
Photos: Used with ms with no additional payment. Query or send contact sheet. B&w glossies, at least 5x7 or color transparencies.

GOLF INDUSTRY, Industry Publishers, Inc., 915 NE 125th St., Suite 2-C, North Miami FL 33161. (305)893-8771. Executive Editor: Michael J. Keighley. Editor: Joan Whaley. Emphasizes the golf industry for country clubs, pro-owned golf shops, real estate developments, municipal courses, military and schools. Bimonthly magazine; 75 pages. Estab. 1975. Circ. 17,000. Pays on publication. Buys all rights. Submit seasonal/holiday material 2-3 months in advance. SASE. Reports "usually in 6-8 weeks." Free sample copy and writer's guidelines.

Nonfiction: Publishes informational articles "dealing with a specific facet of golf club or pro shop operations, e.g., design, merchandising, finances, etc." Buys 20 mss/year. Submit complete ms. Length: 2,500 words minimum. Pays 5¢/word.

How To Break In: "Since we don't make freelance assignments, a query is not particularly important. We would rather have a complete ms which conforms to our policy of general, but informative, articles about one specific facet of the business of golf merchandising, financing, retailing, etc. Well-done mss, if not used immediately, are often held in our files for use in a future issue."

Rejects: "We never publish articles concentrating on one specific manufacturer, or extolling the virtues of one product over another. We seldom feature one club or retail outlet. We don't deal with the game iteself, but with the business end of the game."

GOLF SHOP OPERATIONS, 495 Westport Ave., Norwalk CT 06856. (203)847-5811. Editor: Nick Romano. For golf professionals at public and private courses, resorts and driving ranges. Magazine published 6 times/year; 36 pages. Estab. 1963. Circ. 12,500. Byline given. Pays on publication. Free sample copy. Photocopied submissions OK. Submit seasonal material (for Christmas and other holiday sales, or profiles of successful professionals) 3 months in advance. Reports in 1 month.

Nonfiction: "We emphasize improving the golf professional's knowledge of his profession. Articles should describe how pros are buying, promoting, merchandising and displaying wares in their shops that might be of practical value to fellow professionals. Must be aimed only at the pro audience. We would be interested in seeing material on how certain pros are fighting discount store competition." How-to, profile, successful business operation, merchandising techniques. Buys 8 mss/year. Query. Pays $50-100.

Photos: "Pictures are mandatory with all manuscript submissions." Captions required.

MOTORCYCLE DEALER NEWS, Box 19531, Irvine CA 92713. Editor: Jeff Wetmore. 20% freelance written. For motorcycle dealers and key personnel of the industry. Monthly. Buys first serial rights. Byline given. Pays on publication. Free sample copy and writer's guidelines. Reports in 1 month. SASE.

Nonfiction and Photos: "Looking for articles trat examine problems of dealers and offer a solution. These dealer articles are not a history of the business, but one unique aspect of the store and its attempt to hurdle an obstacle that may aid other dealers in a similar situation. This is not to be a success story, but rather a fresh look at tackling problems within the industry. Tips for dealers on selling merchandise, creating new displays and improving basic business knowledge are also needed. In-depth articles regarding liability insurance, warranty, land usage, noise pollution and advertising. Usually, in-depth articles about current problems are staff-written. However, do not hesitate to query. We do not use articles of a general or unspecific nature. Concrete examples are a must. Photos help sell the article." Query. Length: 750-2,500 words. Pays $75-150. 8x10 b&w glossy photos purchased with mss or with captions only. Modern stores, dealer awards, etc. Pays $10 minimum for photos not accompanied by ms.

POOL & SPA NEWS, Leisure Publications, 3923 W. 6th St., Los Angeles CA 90020. (213)385-3926. Editor-in-Chief: Fay Coupe. 40% freelance written. Emphasizes news of the swimming pool and spa industry for pool builders, pool retail stores and pool service firms. Semimonthly magazine; 56 pages. Estab. 1961. Circ. 10,000. Pays on publication. Buys all rights, but may reassign following publication. Phone queries OK. Photocopied submissions OK. SASE. Reports in 2 weeks.

Nonfiction: Interview, new product, profile, and technical. Length: 500-2,000 words. Pays 5¢/word. Pays $5 per b&w photo used.

RV DEALER MAGAZINE, Hardison Publishing Co., 6229 Northwest Hwy., Chicago IL 60631. (312)774-2525. Emphasizes the entire RV industry including manufacturers, suppliers and dealers. Monthly magazine; 140 pages. Estab. 1950. Circ. 22,500. Pays on publication. Buys all rights. Byline given "except if more than one story by same author appears in one issue." Submit seasonal/holiday material 2 months in advance. Photocopied submissions OK. SASE. Reports in 2 weeks. Free sample copy and writer's guidelines.

Nonfiction: How-to (run a better RV business, on related RV products); humor (cartoons aimed at trade); interview (of dealers, manufacturers and suppliers on how they became

successful); new product (all companies considered); and photo feature (RV store displays). Articles they're interested in seeing this year are: "A portrait of the RV Consumer"—his buying habits, etc., and "Why people don't buy RVs." Buys 2-3 mss/issue. Pays $2/column inch.
Photos: "We prefer illustrating an article. For a manufacturer—his plant and his equipment. For a dealer, we want to see his dealership." Send photos with ms. Pays $7/b&w 5x7 or 8x10 glossy print; and $15-30 (for cover use) for any size (but prefers 2¼x2¼) color transparencies.

RVR, RECREATIONAL VEHICLE RETAILER, 29901 Agoura Rd., Agoura CA 90301. Editorial Director: Alice Robison. 50% freelance written. For men and women of the RV industry, primarily those involved in the sale of trailers, motorhomes, pickup campers, to the public. Also, owners and operators of trailer supply stores, plus manufacturers and executives of the RV industry nationwide and in Canada. Monthly magazine; 100 pages. Estab. 1972. Circ. 28,000. Buys all rights. Pays on publication. Free sample copy and writer's guidelines. Reports in 3 weeks. SASE.
Nonfiction and Photos: "Stories that show trends in the industry; success stories of particular dealerships throughout the country; news stories on new products; accessories (news section); how to sell; how to increase profits, be a better businessman. Interested in broadbased, general interest material of use to all RV retailers, rather than mere trade reporting." Informational, how-to, personal experience, interview, profile, humor, think articles, successful business operations, and merchandising techniques. Buys 100-150 mss/year. Query. Length: 1,000-2,000 words. Pays $100-175. Shorter items for regular columns or departments run 800 words. Pays $50-75. Photos purchased with accompanying ms with no additional payment. Captions required.
Columns/Departments: Dealer/industry items from over the country; newsbreaks. Length: 100-200 words; with photos, if possible. Payment based on length.

THE SHOOTING INDUSTRY, 291 Camino de la Reina, San Diego CA 92108. (714)297-5352. Editor: J. Rakusan. For manufacturers dealers, sales representatives or archery and shooting equipment. Monthly. Buys all rights. Byline given. Pays on publication. Free sample copy. Reports in 2-3 weeks. SASE.
Nonfiction and Photos: Articles that tell "secrets of my success" based on experience of individual gun dealer; articles of advice to help dealers sell more guns and shooting equipment. Also, articles about and of interest to manufacturers and top manufacturers' executives. Buys about 135 mss/year. Query. Length: 3,000 words maximum. Pays $50-150. Photos essential; b&w glossies. Purchased with ms.

SKI BUSINESS, 380 Madison Ave., New York NY 10017. (212) 687-3000. Editor: Seth Masia. Monthly tabloid newspaper; 28 pages. For ski retailers and instructors. Estab. 1960. Circ. 15,000. Pays $75 kill fee. Byline given, except on "press releases and roundup articles containing passages from articles submitted by several writers." Pays on publication. Submit seasonal material 3 weeks in advance. Reports in 1 month. Photocopied submissions OK. Free writer's guidelines and sample copy. SASE.
Nonfiction: Will consider ski shop case studies; mss about unique and succesful merchandising ideas, and ski area equipment rental operations. "All material should be slanted toward usefulness to the ski shop oeprator. Always interested in interviews with successful retailers." Uses round-ups of preseason sales and Christmas buying across the country during September to December. Would like to see reports on what retailers in major markets are doing. Buys about 150 mss/year. Query or submit complete ms. Length: 800-1,500 words. Pays $35-75.
Photos: Photos purchased with accompanying mss. Buys b&w glossy 8x10 photos. Pays $10.

SKIING TRADE NEWS, 1 Park Ave., New York NY 10016. Editor: Carol Feder. For ski shop owners. Annual magazine; 150 pages. Also publishes a tabloid 10 times/year. Estab. 1964. Circ. about 5,000. Buys first North American serial rights. Pays on acceptance. Reports in 1 month. SASE.
Nonfiction: Factual how-to or success articles about buying at the ski trade shows, merchandising ski equipment, keeping control of inventory, etc. Buys 14 mss/year. Query. Length: 2,000 words. Pays 10¢/word.
How To Break In: "Find a ski shop that is a success, one that does something merchandising, etc.) differently and makes money at it. Research the reasons for the shop's success and query."

THE SPORTING GOODS DEALER, 1212 N. Lindbergh Blvd., St. Louis MO 63166. (314)997-7111. Editor: C.C. Johnson Spink. Managing Editor: Gary Goldman. For members of the sporting goods trade; retailers, manufacturers, wholesalers, representatives. Monthly magazine. Estab. 1899. Circ. 16,161. Buys second serial (reprint) rights. Buys about 15 mss/year. Pays on publication. Sample copy $1 (refunded with first mss); free writer's guidelines. Will not consider photocopied or simultaneous submissions. Reports in 2 weeks. Query. SASE.

Nonfiction and Photos: "Articles about specific sporting goods retail stores, their promotions, display techniques, sales ideas, merchandising, timely news of key personnel; expansions, new stores, deaths—all in the sporting goods trade. Specific details on how specific successful sporting goods stores operate. What specific retail sporting goods stores are doing that is new and different. We would also be interested in features dealing with stores doing an outstanding job in retailing of baseball, fishing, golf, tennis, camping, firearms/hunting and allied lines of equipment. Query on these." Successful business operations, merchandising techniques. Does not want to see announcements of doings and engagements. Length: open. Pays $2 per 100 published words. Also looking for material for the following columns: Terse Tales of the Trade (store news); Selling Slants (store promotions); Open for Business (new retail sporting goods stores or sporting goods departments). All material must relate to specific sporting goods stores by name, city, and state; general information is not accepted. Pays minimum of $3.50 for sharp clear b&w photos; size not important. These are purchased with or without mss. Captions optional, but indentification requested.

Fillers: Clippings. These must relate directly to the sporting goods industry. Pays 1-2¢/published word.

SPORTING GOODS TRADE, Page Publications, Ltd., 380 Wellington St. W., Toronto, Ontario, Canada M5V 1E3. (416)366-4608. Editor: Jamie Howe. For sporting goods retailers, manufacturers, wholesalers, jobbers, department and chain stores, camping equipment dealers, bicycle sales and service, etc. Bimonthly magazine; 50-100 pages. Estab. 1972. Circ. 9,200. Free sample copy. Reports in 2 months. SAE and International Reply Coupons.

Nonfiction: Technical and informational articles. Articles on successful business oeprations, new products, merchandising techniques; interviews. Length: open. Pays 4¢/word or $25/published page.

SPORTS MERCHANDISER, W.R.C. Smith Publishing Co., 1760 Peachtree Rd. NW, Atlanta GA 30357. (404)874-4462. Editor: Eugene R. Marnell. For retailers and wholesalers of sporting goods in all categories; independent stores, chains, specialty stores, department store departments. Monthly tabloid; 100 pages. Estab. 1964. Circ. 40,000. Pays on acceptance, buys all rights. Submit seasonal/holiday material 4-6 months in advance. SASE. Reports in 2-4 months. Free sample copy and writer's guidelines.

Nonfiction: "Articles telling how retailers are successful in selling a line of products, successful merchandising programs, and advertising program successes. No articles on business history." Query. Length: 500-1,500 words. Pays $75-175.

Photos: State availability of photos with query. Offers no additional payment for 5x7 or 8x10 b&w prints. Captions required. Buys all rights.

SWIMMING POOL WEEKLY/AGE, Hoffman Publications, Inc., Box 11299, Fort Lauderdale FL 33339. (305)566-8402. Managing Editor: Dave Kaiser. Emphasizes pool industry. Bimonthly tabloid; 36 pages. Estab. 1928. Circ. 16,000. Pays on acceptance. Buys all rights for industry. Phone queries OK. Submit seasonal/holiday material 1 month in advance. SASE. Reports in 2 weeks. Writer's guidelines for SASE.

Nonfiction: Expose (if in industry, company frauds); how-to (stories on installation techniques done with an expert in a given field); interview (with important people within the industry); photo feature (pool construciton or special pool use); technical (should be prepared with expert within the industry). Buys 50-80 mss/year. Query. Length: 1,000 words maximum. Pays $35-50.

Photos: Purchased with or without accompanying ms or on assignment. Captions required. Query or send contact sheet. Pays $5-20 for any size larger than 5x7 b&w photo; $15-25 for any size above 35mm color transparencies.

Columns/Departments: "Short news on personality items always welcome at about $10-15 for 25-100 words."

TENNIS INDUSTRY, Industry Publishers, Inc., 915 NE 125th St., Suite 2-C, North Miami FL 33161. (305)893-8771. Editor: Michael J. Keighley. Emphasizes the tennis industry for teaching pros, pro shop managers, specialty shop managers, country club managers, coaches, athletic directors, etc. Monthly magazine; 200 pages. Estab. 1972. Circ. 19,000. Pays on publication. Buys all rights. Submit seasonal/holiday material 2-3 months in advance. Previously published submissions OK. SASE. Reports "usually in 6-8 weeks." Free sample copy and writer's guidelines.

Nonfiction: Publishes informational articles dealing "with specific facets of the tennis club or pro shop operation, e.g., design, merchandising, finances, etc." Buys 20 mss/year. Submit complete ms. Length: 2,500 words maximum. Pays 5¢/word.

How To Break In: "Since we do not make freelance assignments, a query is not particularly important. We would rather have a complete ms which conforms to our policy of general, but informative articles about one specific facet of the business of tennis merchandising, financing, retailing, etc. Well-done manuscripts if not used immediately, are often held in our files for use in a future issue."

Rejects: "We never publish articles concentrating on one specific manufacturer, or extolling the virtues of one product over another. We seldom feature one club or retail outlet. We don't deal with the game itself, but with the business end of the game."

TENNIS TRADE MAGAZINE, 37 Quade St., Glens Falls NY 12801. Editor: Marilyn Nason. Emphasizes all requet/paddle sports. Monthly magazine; 44 pages. Estab. 1971. Circ. 32,000. Pays on publication. Buys all rights. SASE. Sample copy $1.

Nonfiction: How-to articles related to the tennis/racquet and paddle businesses.

Stone and Quarry Products

CONCRETE, Cement and Concrete Association, 52 Grosvenor Gardens, London SW1 W OAQ. (01)235-6661. Editor: R.J. Barfoot. Emphasizes civil engineering and building and construction. Monthly magazine; 60 pages. Estab. 1969. Circ. 13,000. Pays on publication. Phone queries OK. Submit seasonal/holiday material 6 weeks in advance. Photocopied submissions OK. Free sample copy and writer's guidelines.

Nonfiction: Historical, new product, and technical articles dealing with concrete and allied industries. Buys 12 mss/year. Query or submit complete ms. Length: 1,000-3,000 words. Pays $10-30.

CONCRETE CONSTRUCTION MAGAZINE, 329 Interstate Rd., Addison IL 60101. Editor: William C. Panarese. For general and concrete contractors, architects, engineers, concrete producers, cement manufacturers, distributors and dealers in construction equipment, testing labs. Monthly magazine; 52 pages. Estab. 1956. Circ. 60,000. Buys all rights. "Bylines are used only by prearrangement with the author." Buys 50 mss/year. Pays on acceptance. Free sample copy and writer's guidelines. Photocopied and simultaneous submissions OK. Reports in 1-2 months. Submit complete ms. SASE.

Nonfiction and Photos: "Our magazine has one topic to discuss: cast-in-place (site cast) concrete. Our articles deal with tools, techniques and materials that result in better handling, better placing, and ultimately an improved final product. We are particularly firm about not using proprietary names in any of our articles. Manufacturers and products are never mentioned; only the processes or techniques that might be of help to the concrete contractor, the architect or the engineer dealing with the material. We do use 'bingo cards' that accomplish the purpose of relaying reader interest to manufacturers, but without cluttering up the articles themselves with a lot of name dropping." Does not want to see job stories or promotional material. Length: 3,500 words. Pays 7¢/published word. Pays $10 for b&w glossy photos and color used with mss. Photos are used only as part of a completed ms.

MINE AND QUARRY, Ashire Publishing Ltd., 42 Gray's Inn Rd., London, England WC1X 8LR. Editor: Cyril G. Middup. For senior management at mines and quarries. Monthly magazine; 80 pages. Estab. 1924. Circ. 4,600. Buys all rights. Phone queries OK. Submit seasonal/holiday material 2 months in advance. Simultaneous, photocopied and previously published submissions OK. SAE and International Reply Coupons. Reports in 2 months. Free sample copy and writer's guidelines.

Nonfiction: Technical and new product articles related to the industry. Buys 20 mss/year. Submit complete ms. Length: 200-1,000 words. Pays $10-20.

Photos: B&w glossies and color transparencies purchased with or without mss. Captions required. Send contact sheet, prints or transparencies. Pays $3-6.

STONE IN AMERICA, American Monument Association, 6902 N. High St., Worthington OH 43085. (614)885-2713. Managing Editor: Catherine White. Emphasizes the granite and marble memorial industry for quarriers and manufacturers of memorial stone products in the US and Canada; retail memorial dealers, cemeterians and funeral directors. Monthly magazine; 48 pages. Estab. 1889. Circ. 2,450. Pays on publication. Buys all rights. Phone queries OK. Submit seasonal/holiday material 2 months in advance. Simultaneous, photocopied and previously published submissions OK. SASE. Reports in 2 weeks. Free sample copy and writer's guidelines, but adequate postage must accompany request.

Nonfiction: How-to (setting memorials, carving memorials, selling, managing); historical, informational, inspirational, new product, nostalgia, photo features, profiles, anything of interest to the industry. Technical articles on abrasive technology, diamond technology; tool/machine and product technology. Buys 15 mss/year. Length: 300-5,000 words. Query or submit complete ms.

Photos: Uses b&w glossies (5x7) with or without mss. Send contact sheet or prints. Captions required. No additional payment for those used with mss. Model release required.

Columns/Departments: Buys 50-500 word items for Tool Chest, Films (Business/Technical), Commerative Art Marketing—Sales Techniques, Small Business Management, Stone (Granite & Marble). Buys 15/year. Query or submit complete ms. Open to suggestions for new columns/departments.

Fiction: Adventure, experimental, historical, humorous, mystery, religious, suspense; appropriate to the industry. Length: 1,000-5,000 words.

Poetry: Light verse and epitaphs. Buys 10/year. Limit submissions to batches of 20. Length: 5-65 lines. Pays $5-50.

Textile

AMERICA'S TEXTILES, Box 88, Greenville SC 29602. Editor: Ronald Ussery. For "officials and operating executives of manufacturing corporations and plants in the basic textile yarn and fabric industry." Monthly. Estab. 1878. Circ. 22,000. Not copyrighted. Buys "very few" mss/year. Pays on publication. Sample copy $1; free writer's guidelines "only if background is suitable." Query. "It is extremely difficult for non-textile industry freelancers to write for us." SASE.

Nonfiction: "Technical and business articles about the textile industry." Length: open. Pays $25-50/printed page.

TEXTILE WORLD, 1175 Peachtree St. NE, Atlanta GA 30361. Editor-in-Chief: Laurence A. Christiansen. Monthly. Buys all rights. Pays on acceptance. SASE.

Nonfiction and Photos: Uses articles covering textile management methods, manufacturing and marketing techniques, new equipment, details about new and modernized mills, etc., but avoids elementary, historical, or generally well-known material. Pays $25 minimum/page. Photos purchased with accompanying ms with no additional payment, or purchased on assignment.

Toy, Novelty, and Hobby

MINIATURES DEALER MAGAZINE, Boynton & Associates, Clifton House, Clifton VA 22024. (703)830-1000. Editor: David A. Ritchey. For "retailers in the doll house/miniatures trade. Our readers are generally independent, small store owners who don't have time to read anything that does not pertain specifically to their own problems." Monthly magazine; 60 pages Estab. 1978. Circ. 6,000. Pays on publication. Buys all rights. Byline given. Phone queries OK. Submit seasonal/holiday material 3 months in advance. Photocopied and previously published submissions OK; simultaneous submissions (if submitted to publications in different fields) OK. SASE. Reports in 4-8 weeks. Sample copy $1; free writer's guidelines.

Nonficton: How-to (unique articles—for example, how to finish a dollhouse exterior—are acceptable if they introduce new techniques or ideas; show the retailer how learning this technique will help sell dollhouses); profiles of miniatures stores. Buys 4-6 mss/issue. Query or send complete ms. Pays 5¢/word.

Photos: "Photos must tie in directly with articles." State availability of photos. Pays $5 for each photo used. Prefers 5x2 b&w glossy prints (reviews contact sheets); and $25 for 2¼x2¼ color transparencies. Buys very few color photos. Captions preferred; model release preferred.

MODEL RETAILER MAGAZINE, Clifton House, Clifton VA 22024. (703)830-1000. Editor-in-Chief: David A. Ritchey. 60-70% freelance written. "For hobby store owners—generally well-established small business persons, fairly well educated, and very busy." Monthly magazine; 120 pages. Estab. 1975. Circ. 4,500. Pays on publication. Buys "all rights in our field." Byline given. Phone queries OK. Submit seasonal/holiday material 2-3 months in advance of issue date. Simultaneous, photocopied and previously published submissions OK. SASE. Reports in 4-8 weeks. Sample copy $1.50; free writer's guidelines.

Nonfiction: Hobby store visiting articles; interview (of hobby industry figures); nostalgia (the way things were in the hobby industry); and photo feature (if photos tie in with marketing techniques or hobby store operation, etc.). Buys 5-6 mss/issue. Query. Length: 3,000 words maximum. Pays 5¢/word minimum.
Photos: "Photos that explain the manuscript and are of good quality will help the article, particularly if it concerns business operation." Pays $5 minimum for 3x5 b&w prints. Buys all rights, but may reassign following publication.

PROFITABLE CRAFT MERCHANDISING, PJS Publications, Inc., News Plaza, Box 1790, Peoria IL 61656. (309)682-6626. Editor: Geoffrey Wheeler. Assistant Editor: Marybeth Genis. Emphasizes making and saving money in craft supply retailing for retailers, manufacturers, wholesalers and publishers. Monthly magazine; 128 pages. Estab. 1964. Circ. 23,000. Pays on acceptance. Buys first rights. Byline given. Submit seasonal/holiday material 4-6 months in advance. SASE. Free sample copy and writer's guidelines.
Nonfiction: Profile (on unique or unusual craft stores that are successful); and business articles on how to make and save money, accounting, advertising, store layout, security, classroom instruction, merchandising techniques, etc. Buys 5 mss/issue. Query. Length: 2,500 words maximum. Pays $60-275.
Photos: "If photos can clarify story aspect, they are encouraged. Photos are a must with profiles of craft supply stores." Send photos with ms. Uses b&w 5x7 or 8x10 glossy prints. Offers no additional payment for photos accepted with ms. Captions required.
Fillers: Cartoons. Buys 1/issue. Pays $10.

SOUVENIRS AND NOVELTIES, 401 N. Broad St., Philadelphia PA 19108. Editor: S. Donut. 20% freelance written. For managers and owners of souvenir shops in resorts, parks, museums, and airports. Bimonthly magazine; 88 pages. Estab. 1962. Circ. 11,000. Pays on publication. Buys first North American serial rights. Phone queries OK. Submit seasonal/holiday material 4 months in advance of issue date. Photocopied and previously published submissions OK. SASE. Reports in 2 weeks. Free sample copy and writer's guidelines.
Nonfiction: How-to (operate and improve souvenir shops), interview and profile. "No travel articles on the beauty of an area." Buys 20 mss/year. Query. Length: 1,000-2,000 words. Pays 4-6¢/word.
Photos: State availability of photos with query. Pays $10 for 5x7 or 8x10 glossy prints. Captions preferred. Buys one-time rights.
Fillers: Clippings. Pays 80¢/inch.

THE STAMP WHOLESALER, Box 706, Albany OR 97321. Publisher: Jim Mageuder. 50% freelance written. For small-time independent businessmen; many are part-time and/or retired from other work. Published 24 times/year; 68 pages. Estab. 1936. Circ. 9,000. Buys all rights. Byline given. Buys 40 mss/year. Pays on acceptance. Will send free sample copy to writer on request. Reports in "1 day to 1 year." Submit complete ms. SASE.
Nonfiction: How-to information on how to deal more profitably in postage stamps for collections. Emphasis on merchandising techniques and how to make money. Does not want to see any so-called "humor" items from nonprofessionals. Length: 1,500-2,000 words. Pays 3¢/word minimum.

TOY & HOBBY WORLD, 124 E. 40th St., New York NY 10016. For everyone in the toy and hobby and craft industry from manufacturer to retailer. Magazine. Monthly. Estab. 1961. Circ. 16,500. Not copyrighted. Buys 5 mss/year. Pays on publication. Sample copy 50¢. Will consider photocopied submissions. Returns rejected material when requested. Query. SASE.
Nonfiction and Photos: Merchandising and news. Informational, how-to, new product. Technical articles for manufacturers; features about wholesalers, retailers, chains, department stores, discount houses, etc., concerned with their toy operations. Prefers stories on toy wholesalers or retailers who have unusual success with unusual methods. No "mere histories of run-of-the-mill operators. Use a news style." Length: 1,000-3,000 words. Payment commensurate with quality of material. Buys 8x10 b&w photos with mss and with captions only. Must be glossy on singleweight paper. No color. Pays $6 plus word rate. Prefers captions.

Trailers, Mobile Homes

MOBILE/MANUFACTURED HOME MERCHANDISER, 5225 Old Orchard Rd., Suite 7, Skokie IL 60077. (312)967-0430. Editor/Assistant Publisher: Jim Mack. 5% freelance written. "Primary audience is mobile home retailers—those engaged in selling manufactured housing to the consumer. We also reach housing manufacturers, suppliers to those builders, and other related industry professionals." Monthly magazine; 70 pages. Estab. November 1952. Circ. 20,037. Pays on publication. Buys one-time rights. Submit seasonal/holiday material "at least 6 months in advance of issue date, but this type of material isn't really relevant—writer would need a good slant to fit in this industry with holiday material." Photocopied and previously published submissions OK. SASE. Reports in 3 months. Sample copy $2; free writer's guidelines.

Nonfiction: How-to (sell, merchandise, display, accessorize, promote, advertise, etc.); interview (with retailers detailing how they perform some aspect of sales); photo features (retail story on how he/she does something better—photos illustrate copy explanation, that could be short); and technical (advancements in mobile housing or the products used therein). "No general success stories about mobile home retailers; stories should focus on a specific aspect of business operation." Buys 4-5 mss/year. Query. Pays $35/printed page, including photos.

Photos: "Good photos which illustrate the story are almost mandatory." State availability of photos with query. Uses 5x7 b&w and color prints with borders. Offers no payment for photos accepted with ms. "Will pay $50 for a shot I can use on the cover." Captions required. Buys one-time rights.

TRAILER/BODY BUILDERS, 1602 Harold St., Houston TX 77006. (713)523-8124. Editor: Paul Schenck. 5% freelance written. For the manufacturers and builders of truck trailers, truck bodies, truck tanks, vans, cargo containers, plus the truck equipment distributors. Monthly. Not copyrighted. Pays on publication. Free sample copy. Reports in 30 days. SASE.

Nonfiction: "Material on manufacturers of truck trailers, truck bodies, and school bus bodies; also their sales distributors. These also go under the names of semitrailer manufacturing, custom body builders, trailer sales branch, or truck equipment distributor. No travel trailers, house trailers, mobile homes or tire companies, transmission people or other suppliers, unless it directly affects truck body or truck trailer. Need shop hints and how-to features. Many stories describe how a certain special truck body or truck trailer is built." Length: 900-1,000 words. Pays $2/inch or $50/page.

Photos: Buys photos appropriate to format. Study publication. Pays $10.

Fillers: "New products and newspaper clippings appropriate to format. Do not rewrite clippings." Pays $2/inch or better on news items.

Travel

A.S.U. TRAVEL GUIDE, 1335 Columbus Ave., San Francisco CA 94133. Editor-in-Chief: Ronald Folkenflik. Managing Editor: Pearl Furman. 100% freelance written. All readers are airline employees interested in interline travel benefits and related topics. Quarterly magazine; 288 pages. Estab. 1968. Circ. 30,000. Pays on publication. Buys all rights. Submit seasonal/holiday material 3 months in advance of issue date. Photocopied and previously published submissions OK. SASE. Free sample copy and writer's guidelines; mention *Writer's Market* in request.

Nonfiction: General interest (travel destinations); interview (with airline related personnel); personal experience (travel related); opinion (of destinations); profile (prominent airline industry figures); and travel (destinations with emphasis on interline discounts). Buys 4-5 mss/issue. Query with clips of published work. Length: 1,200-1,500 words. Pays $75-100.

Photos: State availability of photos with query. Pays $25 for 8½x11 b&w finished prints and $75 for 35mm color transparencies. Captions preferred. Buys one-time rights.

ASTA TRAVEL NEWS, 488 Madison Ave., New York NY 10022. Editor-in-Chief: Coleman Lollar. Managing Editor: Kathi Froio. 75% freelance written. Emphasizes travel, tourism and transportation. Monthly magazine; 120 pages. Estab. January 1931. Circ. 19,000. Pays on acceptance. Buys all rights. Submit seasonal/holiday material 3 months in advance of issue date. Simultaneous and photocopied submissions OK. Reports in 4 weeks. Free sample copy.

Nonfiction: How-to; interview; new product; profile; technical; and travel. No first-person personal experience. Buys 75 mss/year. Query. Length: 500-3,000 words. Pays $50-200.

Photos: Submit photo material with accompanying query. No additional payment for b&w prints or color transparencies. Captions required.

THE STAR SERVICE, Sloane Agency Travel Reports, Box 15610, Fort Lauderdale FL 33318. (305)472-8794. Editor: Robert D. Sloane. Editorial manual sold to travel agencies on subscription basis. Buys all rights. Buys about 2,000 reports/year. Pays on publication. "Write for instruction sheet and sample report form. Initial reports sent by a new correspondent will be examined for competence and criticized as necessary upon receipt, but once established, a

correspondent's submissions will not usually be acknowledged until payment is forwarded, which can often be several months, depending on immediate editorial needs." Query. SASE.
Nonfiction: "Objective, critical evaluations of worldwide hotels and cruise ships suitable for North Americans, based on inspections. Forms can be provided to correspondents so no special writing style is required, only perceptiveness, experience and judgment in travel. No commercial gimmick—no advertising or payment for listings in publication is accepted." With query, writer should "outline experience in travel and specific forthcoming travel plans, time available for inspections. Leading travel agents throughout the world subscribe to Star Service. No credit or byline is given correspondents due to delicate subject matter often involving negative criticism of hotels. We would like to emphasize the importance of reports being based on current experience and the importance of reporting on a substantial volume of hotels, not just isolated stops (since staying in hotel is not a requisite) in order that work be profitable for both publisher and writer. Experience in travel writing is desirable." Length: "up to 350 words, if submitted in paragraph form; varies if submitted on printed inspection form." Pays $5 minimum/report used. "Guarantees of acceptance of set numbers of reports may be made on establishment of correspondent's ability and reliability, but always on prior arrangement. Higher rates of payment sometimes arranged, after correspondent's reliability is established."

THE TRAVEL AGENT, 2 W. 46th St., New York NY 10036. Editor: Eric Friedheim. For "travel agencies and travel industry executives." Estab. 1929. Semiweekly. Circ. 26,000. Not copyrighted. Pays on acceptance. Query. Reports "immediately." SASE.
Nonfiction and Photos: Uses trade features slanted to travel agents, sales and marketing people, and executives of transportation companies such as airlines, ship lines, etc. No travelogues such as those appearing in newspapers and consumer publications. Articles should show how agent and carriers can sell more travel to the public. Length: up to 2,000 words. Pays $50-100. Photos purchased with ms.

TRAVELAGE MIDAMERICA, Official Airlines Guide, Inc., A. Dunn & Bradstreet Co., Suite 2416 Prudential Plaza, Chicago IL 60601. (312)861-0432. Editor/Publisher: Martin Deutsch. Managing Editor: Linnea Smith Jessup. 5% freelance written. "For travel agents in the 13 midAmerica states and in Ontario and Manitoba." Biweekly magazine; 30-50 pages. Estab. March 1975. Circ. 13,000. Pays on publication. Buys simultaneous rights. Submit seasonal/holiday material 6 months in advance of issue date. Simultaneous, photocopied and previously published submissions OK. SASE. Reports in 2 weeks. Free sample copy and writer's guidelines.
Nonfiction: "News on destinations, hotels, operators, rates and other developments in the travel business." No general destination stories, especially ones on "do-it-yourself" travel. Buys 8-10 mss/year. Query. Length: 400-1,500 words. Pays $1.50/column inch.
Photos: State availability of photos with query. Pays $1.50/column inch for glossy b&w prints.

TRAVELAGE WEST, Official Airline Guides, Inc., 582 Market St., San Francisco CA 94104. Managing Editor: Donald C. Langley. 5% freelance written. For travel agency sales counselors in the western US and Canada. Weekly magazine; 80 pages. Estab. 1969. Circ. 13,500. Pays on publication. Buys all rights. Pays kill fee. Byline given. Submit seasonal/holiday material 2 months in advance. SASE. Reports in 4 weeks. Free writer's guidelines.
Nonfiction: Travel. Buys 15 mss/year. Query. Length: 1,000 words maximum. Pays $1.50/column inch. "No promotional tones of voice or any hint of do-it-yourself travel."

TRAVELSCENE MAGAZINE, 888 7th Ave., New York NY 10019. Managing Editor: Lesli Korrelman. For three diverse audiences: airline reservationists, travel agents and corporate travel planners. Magazine; 80 pages. Estab. 1965. Monthly. Circ. 110,000. Buys all rights. Buys 30-40 mss/year. Pays on acceptance. Free sample copy. No photocopied or simultaneous submissions. Submit special issue material 5 months in advance. Reports in 2-6 weeks. Query. SASE.
Nonfiction and Photos: "*TravelScene* is the largest circulation magazine in the travel industry and runs articles on important trade issues, destinations, personalities, how-to's and other topics designed to help professional travel planners do a better job and gain a better perspective on their profession." Recently published articles have dealt with the politician/travel agent, women's roles in the airlines, and how tipping can run up the cost of a business meeting. B&w and color photos purchased on assignment. Pays $10-25 for photos; $100 for 2,000 word articles.
How To Break In: "Writer should submit past samples of work, an outline of proposal(s), and include SASE and phone number. Getting a first assignment may not be too difficult, if the

writer can write. We are looking for and need good writers. If stories are submitted, they must be an average of 8-12 pages, double-spaced; 13-15 maximum. Please do not send queries for destination pieces unless you have a specific angle. We have never given an assignment to someone who merely writes, 'I'm going to London. Can I give you something on it?' Also, we rarely buy destination pieces since we can get those articles in exchange for the trips we offer."

Veterinary

MODERN VETERINARY PRACTICE, American Veterinary Publications, Inc., Drawer KK, 300 E. Canon Perdido, Santa Barbara CA 93102. 75% freelance written. For graduate veterinarians. Monthly magazine; 90 pages. Estab. 1920. Circ. 15,500. Pays on publication. Buys all rights, but may reassign following publication. Phone queries OK. Submit seasonal/holiday material 3 months in advance. SASE. Reports in 4 weeks. Sample copy $2.
Nonfiction: How-to articles (clinical medicine, new surgical procedures, business management); informational (business management, education, government projects affecting practicing veterinarians, special veterinary projects); interviews (only on subjects of interest to veterinarians; query first); technical articles (clinical reports, technical advancements in veterinary medicine and surgery). Buys 25-30 mss/year. Submit complete ms, but query first on ideas for pieces other than technical or business articles. Pays $15/page.
Photos: B&w glossies (5x7 or larger) and color transparencies (5x7) used with mss. No additional payment.
How To Break In: "Contact practicing veterinarians or veterinary colleges. Find out what interests the clinician, and what new procedures and ideas might be useful in a veterinary practice. Better yet, collaborate with a veterinarian. Most of our authors are veterinarians or those working with veterinarians in a professional capacity. Knowledge of the interests and problems of practicing veterinarians is essential."

VETERINARY ECONOMICS MAGAZINE, 2728 Euclid Ave., Cleveland OH 44115. Editorial Director: John D. Velardo. For all practicing veterinarians in the US. Monthly. Buys exclusive rights in the field. Pays on publication. SASE.
Nonfiction and Photos: Uses case histories telling about good business practices on the part of veterinarians. Also, articles about financial problems, investments, insurance and similar subjects of particular interest to professional men. "We reject articles with superficial information about a subject instead of carefully researched and specifically directed articles for our field." Pays $20-30/printed page depending on worth. Pays $100 maximum. Photos purchased with ms. Pays $7.50.

VETERINARY MEDICINE/SMALL ANIMAL CLINICIAN, 144 N. Nettleton Ave., Bonner Springs KS 66012. (913)422-5010. Editor-in-Chief: Dr. C.M. Cooper. Managing Editor: Ray Ottinger. 5% freelance written. For graduate veterinarians, student veterinarians, libraries, representatives of drug companies and research personnel. Monthly magazine; 146 pages. Estab. 1905. Circ. 17,500. Pays on publication. Buys first North American serial rights. Byline given. Phone queries OK. Submit seasonal/holiday material 5-6 months in advance of issue date. Previously published submissions OK. SASE. Reports in 2-3 weeks. Free writer's guidelines.
Nonfiction: Accepts only articles dealing with medical case histories, practice management, business, taxes, insurance, investments. Photo feature (new hospital, floor plan, new equipment; remodeled hospital). No "cutesy" stories about animals. Buys 3 mss/issue. Submit complete ms. Length: 1,500-5,000 words. Pays $15-75.
Photos: State availability of photos with ms. Pays $2.50 for 5x7 b&w glossy prints; $2.50 for 4x7 glossy prints or 35mm color transparencies. Captions required. Buys one-time and reprint rights. Model release required.

Water Supply and Sewage Disposal

CLEARWATERS, New York Water Pollution Control Association Inc., Engineering Bldg., Room 112, Manhattan College, Riverdale NY 10471. Editor: Walter P. Saukin. Managing Editor: Robert F. Conway. Emphases water quality management and water pollution control. Quarterly magazine; 40 pages. Estab. 1967. Circ. 4,500. Buys all rights. Byline given. Phone queries OK. Photocopied submissions OK. Reports in 2 weeks. Free sample copy and writer's guidelines.
Nonfiction: How-to, humor, opinion, profile, personal experience and technical. Buys 5 mss/year. Query. Length: 750-4,000 words. Pays $50 maximum.

Photos: State availability of photos. Pays $25 maximum/8x10 b&w print. Buys one-time rights.

GROUND WATER AGE, 135 Addison Ave., Elmhurst IL 60126. (312)833-6540. Editorial Director: Gene Adams. Managing Editor: Pam Smith. 20% freelance written. For water well drilling contractors and water systems specialists. Monthly magazine; 76 pages. Estab. 1965. Circ. 16,000. Pays on acceptance. Buys all rights. Phone queries OK. Submit seasonal/holiday material 4 months in advance of issue date. Photocopied and previously published submissions OK. SASE. Reports in 2 weeks. Free sample copy and writer's guidelines; mention *Writer's Market* in request.

Nonfiction: General interest; historical; how-to; humor; interview; nostalgia; opinion; photo feature; profile; and technical. Buys 18 mss/year. Query or submit complete ms. Length: 3,000 words. Pays 4-8¢/word.

Photos: "State availability of photos with query or submit photos with ms. Pays $5-15 for 4x5 matte b&w prints; $25-75 for 8x10 matte color prints. Captions and model release required. Buys all rights, but may reassign following publication.

SOLID WASTES MANAGEMENT, Communication Channels, Inc., 461 8th Ave., New York NY 10001. (212)239-6200. Editor-in-Chief: Alan Novak. Emphasizes refuse hauling, landfill transfer stations and resource recovery for private haulers, municipal sanitation and consulting engineers. Monthly magazine; 100 pages. Estab. 1958. Circ. 21,000. Pays on acceptance. Buys all rights, but may reassign following publication. Phone queries OK. Submit seasonal or holiday material 3 months in advance. Photocopied submissions OK. SASE. Reports in 4 weeks. Sample copy $1. Free writer's guidelines.

Nonfiction and Photos: Case studies of individual solid wastes companies, landfills, transfer stations, etc. Material must include details on all quantities handled, statistics, equipment used, etc. Informational, how-to, interview, historical, think pieces and technical articles. Length: 1,500 words minimum. Pays $75-150.

Services and Opportunities

Author's Agents/Literary Services

The agent is a literary broker, a middleman who gets your manuscript to the right editor, makes the sale and negotiates the best possible deal. The ideal agent relies on contacts, experience and market savvy to sell your work.

"The writer receives a certain prestige from having an agent," says agent Frieda Fishbein. "Editors know that agents, if they are competent, weed out the hopeless material," thus saving time for the editors. "Material from agents is usually given preference in being read earlier than material that comes in 'cold.'" What's more, some editors refuse to review unsolicited manuscripts that *don't* come from agents; this is especially true in the television and motion picture industries.

If you have an agent, the time you'd normally spend mailing manuscripts, logging submissions and rummaging through market listings can be spent more profitably in writing more material. Agents also eliminate certain business entanglements some writers would rather avoid—principally, contract negotiations—and come out with better deals, besides. "Agents can nearly always obtain better contracts for their clients because they are familiar with terms received in other contracts," says Fishbein.

Agents also work for additional sales of your manuscripts. No good agent will be happy selling your novel to a hardcover publisher, for instance; he'll invest some time in selling it to a paperback house, to a movie producer, to a newspaper syndicate for serialization, to a book club, to a foreign publisher. To do this, the agent exercises connections and business experience the writer probably doesn't have.

To benefit from the agent's expertise and contacts, the writer pays a commission on the sales made by the agent. Standard commission is 10%; thus, an agent who negotiates a $5,000 advance on your novel earns $500 for himself. Most agents charge a 15% or 20% commission on certain types of sales, such as the sale of a book to a foreign publisher, but 10% is the norm for sales within the US. A few agents have jacked the base commission up to 15%, which has raised a few eyebrows (and some ire) around the publishing industry. Most people in the industry (including the Society of Authors' Representatives, the trade organization for agents) believe that a 10% base commission is fair for both author and agent.

Not every writer needs an agent. Some writers find they enjoy business dealings, and can sell without giving up a 10% cut to an agent. Some writers deal primarily in magazine articles and short fiction; agents shy away from short material, which doesn't generate enough capital to make their 10% commission profitable. Like having a spouse, having an agent has advantages and disadvantages that the writer alone can weigh.

Some agents won't consider handling a writer without a "track record" (a history of sales) that proves the writer's ability and salability. A representative of the Richard Huttner Agency recommends that a writer should seek an agent "after having published a number of magazine articles, and having decided it is time to move on to writing books." But other agents consider a good manuscript to be a sufficient track record. The agent's "primary concern is to deal with properties that he believes have commercial value," says an editor at Carter-Bryant & Associates. "Naturally, his job is made simple if he has a prominent name on the manuscript, a name that is presold to the public and to the publishing world. On the other hand, no writer, however successful presently, ever started that way. . . . Our approach is to deal with the book as a commercial property regardless of its author." Check the following listings for policies of individual agents.

When you decide to try to land an agent (or, more accurately, to let an agent land you), approach agents the same way you'd approach editors. After all, many agents are former editors. Some will accept only query letters; others will review entire manuscripts. Others won't review unsolicited material at all. These agents rely on recommendations from publishers, authors and other agents to find new clients.

Use any contact you can in seeking an agent, advises agent Richard Balkin

in his book, *The Writer's Guide to Book Publishing* (a good addition to your library, by the way). Many writers have obtained agents through mutual friends. Ask an editor with whom you have a good working relationship if he will introduce you or recommend you to an agent. Ask published authors who live in your area or belong to your writers' club if they can make recommendations.

Remember, however, that a recommendation is no guarantee of success. You could have a recommendation from the agent's mother and get a rejection if the agent doesn't believe in your work. The work must stand on its own merits.

Some agents charge a reading fee to review your work; though these agents are legitimate, you should approach agents who charge no reading fee first. You'll save money in the short run, and might make more money in the long run. "An agent who's getting paid only from a commission on your work is very interested in selling it," says Grace Weinstein, president of the American Society of Journalists and Authors (ASJA).

Be careful about selecting your agent. He is, after all, your representative to the publishing industry, so you want one who will represent you properly. Some infamous agents are on some publishers' blacklists. For example, "There are some agents I'm *certain* don't read the manuscripts before submitting them," says Michael Seidman, editorial director of Charter Books. That's why you should make a few inquiries into the agent's reputation. Don't worry about offending the agent with such inquiries; with rare exception, only disreputable agents will balk. Remember, your agent is your partner. You should be able to trust him and work closely with him.

In the same way, be careful in signing any contract with an agent. Know what rights he's handling for your material, and check that no charges are made for services other than those you have contracted for (such as editing or marketing fees or charges for criticism). Some agencies legitimately charge for these services (at about the same prices as are charged for reading fees;

sometimes higher for in-depth evaluation), but always take special care to be aware of "hidden" costs or extra charges. The following listings cover the material specific agencies will handle; the commission percentage the agent receives; and fees for reading, evaluating or criticism, if any.

DOMINICK ABEL LITERARY AGENCY, 498 West End Ave., New York NY 10024. (212)877-0710. Estab. 1975. Obtains new clients through recommendations, solicitation, and blind submissions. Will not read unsolicited mss, will read queries and outlines. SASE. Agent receives 10% commission on US sales; 20% on foreign.
Will Handle: Novels, nonfiction books and syndicated material.

DOROTHY ALBERT, 162 W. 54th St., New York NY 10019. Estab: 1959. Obtains new clients through recommendations of editors, educational establishments, contacts in the film industry, and inquiries. Writers should send letter of introduction, description of material, and list of previous submissions, if any. Will not read unsolicited mss; will read unsolicited queries and outlines. SASE. Agent receives 10% on domestic sales; 20% on foreign. No reading fee.
Will Handle: Novels, nonfiction books, motion pictures (completed, no treatments), stage plays (musicals), TV scripts, juvenile and how-to. No poetry, short stories, textbooks, articles, documentaries, or scripts for established episode shows. "We are interested in novels that are well-plotted suspense; quality drama, adult fiction and human relations. The writer should have some foreknowledge of structure and endurance, whether it be motion pictures, television or books."

AMERICAN PLAY CO., INC., 19 W. 44th St. New York NY 10036. (212)686-6333. President: Sheldon Abend. Estab. 1889. Obtains new clients through private referrals and unsolicited submissions. Will read unsolicited mss for a fee of $55-75. "We refund the readers' fee if we license the author's mss." Will read unsolicited outlines and queries. "We waive a reading fee when the writer has been published within the last 7 years." SASE. Agent receives 10% commission on US sales; 20% on foreign.
Will Handle: Novels, nonfiction books, motion pictures, stage plays and TV scripts.
Criticism Services: "We have three readers critiquing the new mss, and make a master composite critique and supply a copy to the writer and the publishing and producing companies."

MARCIA AMSTERDAM, 41 W. 82nd St., New York NY 10024. (212)873-4945. Obtains new clients through client or editor referrals. Will read queries, partials and outlines. SASE. Agent receives 10% on domestic sales; 15% on British; 20% on foreign.
Will Handle: Novels and nonfiction books.
Recent Sales: *The In-Laws*, by David Rogers (Fawcett); *Samantha and the Blue House Mystery*, by Patricia Elmore (Dutton); and *World on a String: The Yo-Yo Book*, by H. Zeiger (contemporary).

ARIZONA LITERARY AGENCY, 1540 W. Campbell Ave., Phoenix AZ 85015. (602)279-9019. Agency Representative: Jenelle Tuttle. Obtains new clients through the referral of past and present clients, and *Writer's Market*. Will read unsolicited queries and outlines, but not mss. SASE. Charges $200 marketing fee. Agent receives 10% commission.
Will Handle: Novels; nonfiction books (psychology, philosophy, parapsychology, all nonfiction books that would have a general interest to readers); and children's books. "Although we do not specifically wish to handle TV scripts or motion picture work, we are still in a negotiating process with a major studio relative to a novel being adapted for a motion picture."
Criticism Services: "Our criticism service is provided automatically with the reading fee, if and when we charge a reading fee. Therefore, criticism services/reading fees are provided to the new writer. This fee ranges from $50 to $100; $100 being charged when the material is of a highly technical nature, 40,000-75,000 words; $50 for fiction, 40,000-50,000 words; $75 for fiction over 50,000 words."

AUTHOR AID ASSOCIATES, 340 E. 52nd St., New York NY 10022. (212)758-4213. Editorial Director: Arthur Orrmont. Estab. 1967. Obtains new clients through word-of-mouth, referrals, listings and advertisements. Will read unsolicited mss for fees (available upon request); will read unsolicited queries and outlines. SASE. Agent receives 10% commission on domestic sales; 20% on foreign.
Will Handle: Magazine articles and fiction, novels, nonfiction books, poetry (collections only),

motion pictures, stage plays, TV scripts and juvenile fiction and nonfiction.
Criticism Services: Will critique all materials. Fees available on request.

AUTHORS' ADVISORY SERVICE, 51 E. 42nd St., New York NY 10017. (212)687-2971. Literary Agent: Marcy Ring. Estab. 1975. Obtains new clients through recommendations, listings in *LMP* and *Writer's Market;* also some direct solicitation. Will read unsolicited mss for $100 (up to 100,000 words). "Reading fee is refundable against commission if work is sold." SASE. Agent receives 10% commission.
Will Handle: Magazine articles and fiction, novels, nonfiction books, poetry, stage plays, and juvenile fiction and nonfiction.
Criticism Services: Will critique material as above. Charges $125 for mss up to 100,000 words, combined rate offered for 2 or more mss on request. "Rule of thumb: $1/page."

AUTHORS' MARKETING SERVICES, INC., 420 Madison Ave., New York NY 10017. (212)751-4699. Director: Kent W. Livingston. Obtains new clients by referrals by publishers and LMP listing. Plans 1-3 sales in 1979. "At this point AMS is more concerned with literary services, and post-publication promotion than selling manuscripts, although we do hope to have some sales in the near future." Will read unsolicited queries and outlines, no fee. SASE. Agent receives 10% commission.
Will Handle: Novels and nonfiction books.
Criticism Services: Will critique works of fiction and nonfiction, particulary book-length works. Fee is $50 for up to 250 page ms; $75 for ms of 250-500 pages. Report consists of 5-page analysis of work submitted.
Recent Sales: *Scenes for Student Actors* by Wyn Handman (Bantam)—did not act as agent but did promotion work after publication; *It's Your Body: A Woman's Guide to Gynecology*, by Niels Lauersen, MD (Grosset)—did not act as agent but worked on book store distribution when problems arose.

THE BALKIN AGENCY, 403 W. 115th St., New York NY 10025. President: Richard Balkin. Estab. 1973. Obtains new clients through recommendations, over-the-transom inquiries, and solicitation. Will not read unsolicited mss; will read unsolicited queries, or outlines and 2 sample chapters. SASE. Made 25 sales in 1978; plans 35 in 1979. Agent receives 10% commission on domestic sales, 20% on foreign.
Will Handle: Magazine articles (only as a service to clients who primarily write books), textbooks (college only), nonfiction books, and professional books (on occasion).
Recent Sales: *Adult Illiteracy in U.S.*, by C. St. John Hunter (McGraw-Hill); *Living With Your Hyperactive Child*, by John Taylor, Ph.D. (Grosset & Dunlap); and *Selling Your House*, by Carolyn Janik (MacMillan).

THE JOSEPH A. BARANSKI LITERARY AGENCY, 214 W. 6th, Suite AA, West Seneca NY 14224. Contact: Dennis A. Baranski at the Midwest office, Box 4527, Topeka KS 66604. Estab. 1972. "Most new authors are obtained through recommendations and referrals. However we are always interested in writers with potential, regardless of their previous track record." Will read unsolicited mss subject to a reading fee of $20 for mss under 10,000 words; $45 for mss over 10,000 words. "This fee will be assessed to writers who have not met a $5,000 sales requirement in the last 18 months." Will read unsolicited queries and outlines. SASE. Agent receives 10% commission on domestic sales; 20% on foreign sales.
Will Handle: Fiction and nonfiction books, stage and screen plays, magazine articles, and short fiction. "Concentrate on submitting professionally prepared material. The basics of proper paper, clear type, and standard ms format are very important in this highly competitive field. Study your specific market with regard to the length of your ms. We deal on an international basis representing over 250 clients on 4 continents. We hope to expand our facilities to handle a maximum of 300 clients by 1981. We will continue an expanded search for new writing talent in the fall of 1979. We are especially interested in works dealing with provocative social and political issues as well as mystery fiction."

BLOOM, BECKETT, LEVY & SHORR, 449 S. Beverly Dr., Beverly Hills CA 90212. (213)553-4850. Estab. 1977; "however, the forerunner of the firm has been in existence for fifteen years." Obtains new clients by recommendations of writers, directors, producers, and studio executives. SASE. Made 350 sales in 1978; plans 350 in 1979. Agent receives 10% commission.
Will Handle: "We will read only completed motion picture screenplays. This may include screenplays for feature films as well as television. We will not read outlines, treatments, or scripts for eposodic or situation comedy television."

Recent Sales: *Night In Old Mexico*, screenplay by William Wittliff (Warner Bros.); *Riley & The General*, a screenplay by David Kinghorn (Universal); and *Theodore*, a novel by David Melton (20th Century Fox).

GEORGES BORCHARDT, INC., 136 E. 57th St., New York NY 10022. (212)753-5785. Estab. 1967. Obtains new clients "mainly through authors already represented by us who refer others." Potential clients "must be highly recommended by someone we know." read unsolicited queries from established writers. Made 175 US book sales in 1978; plans 175-200 in 1979. Agent receives 10% commission.
Will Handle: Magazine articles and fiction, novels, and nonfiction books.
Recent Sales: *The Devil's Alternative*, by Frederick Forsyth (Viking Press); *The Basement*, by Kate Millett (Simon & Schuster); and *The Living End*, by Stanley Elkin (Dutton).

AARON BOWMAN CO., 2813 Willow St., Granite City IL 62040. Chief Agent: Aaron Bowman. Estab: 1972. Obtains new clients through *Writer's Market*. Will read unsolicited mss for a fee of $100. SASE. Made 72 sales in 1978. Agent receives 10% commission.
Will Handle: Novels, textbooks, nonfiction books, short stories, plays, children's books, musical compositions and poetry books. "We are particularly interested in new talent as well as the established writer seeking different representation."
Criticism Services: "We critique all material not submitted to publishers, a service included in the $100 reading/analysis fee required with all mss."

BROOME AGENCY, INC./BROOME LITERARY SERVICE, Box 3649, Sarasota FL 33578. President: Sherwood Broome. Estab. 1957. Obtains new clients "mainly by response to our ads in *Writer's Digest,* plus our listing in *Writer's Market."* Will read unsolicited mss. SASE. Agent receives 10% commission on domestic sales, 15% on Canadian, 20% on foreign.
Will Handle: Magazine articles and fiction, novels, and nonfiction books.
Criticism Services: Will critique short stories, articles, novels, and nonfiction books. Submissions must be in professional format. Charges $30 minimum for short stories and articles (to 5,000 words); $200 minimum for book length mss (to 37,500 words). Rates increase according to length and complexity.
Recent Sales: *Six Who Died Young*, western novel by C.R. Clumpner (Ace Books); *Mail Order: The Easy Money Business*, how-to by J. Frank Brumbaugh (Chilton); and *The Alien*, science fiction by Victor Besan (Fawcett Gold Medal).

JAMES BROWN ASSOCIATES, INC., 25 W. 43rd St., New York NY 10036. (212)840-8272. Estab. 1949. Potential clients "must be professional, not necessarily published." Will read unsolicited queries. SASE. Agent receives 10% commission on domestic sales, 15-20 on British and 20% on translation countries.
 Will Handle: "We handle writers concentrating on books." For writers represented will handle all rights, foreign, performance, etc., and magazine articles and fiction.

SHIRLEY BURKE AGENCY, 370 E. 76th St., B-704, New York NY 10021. (212)861-2309. Estab. 1948. Obtains new clients through recommendations. Potential clients must have published at least one book. Will not read unsolicited mss; will read unsolicited queries. SASE. Agent receives 10% commission.
Will Handle: Magazine fiction, novels, and nonfiction books.
Recent Sales: *Nell Kimball*, by Stephen Lovestreet (Berkley Books); *Storm Watch*, fiction by Stephen lovestreet (Putnam's); and *Temptation*, fiction by Lydia Lancaster (Warner Books).

CHARLES R. BYRNE LITERARY AGENCY, 1133 Avenue of the Americas, 28th Floor, New York NY 10036. (212)221-3145. President: Charles R. Byrne. Estab. 1974. Obtains new clients through recommendations from publishers/editors, other agents, and from present clients. Will read unsolicited mss for a fee "depending on length of mss." Will read unsolicited queries and outlines. SASE. Agent receives 10% commission on domestic sales; 20% on foreign.
Will Handle: Novels, textbooks (a limited number), nonfiction books, young adult novels and nonfiction books.
Recent Sale: *A Private Vendetta,* by R. Grant (Charles Scribner's Sons).

RUTH CANTOR, LITERARY AGENT, 156 5th Ave., New York NY 10010. Estab. 1951. Obtains new clients through recommendations by writers, publishers, editors, and teachers. Potential clients "must be of proven competence as a writer. This means either some publishing record or a recommendation from someone likely to be a competent critic of his work—a teacher of writing, another writer, etc." Will not read unsolicited mss; will read unsolicited queries and outlines. SASE. "Send a letter giving publishing history and writing

experience, plus concise outline of proposed project or of ms you want to send. Do not phone."
Agent receives 10% commission on domestic sales; 20% on foreign.
Will Handle: Novels, nonfiction books and childrens' books.
Recent Sales: *Perky,* by G. Bond (Western); *This Savage Land,* by B. Womack (Fawcett); and
Abigail Scott Dunaway, by D. Morrison (Atheneum).

CARTER-BRYANT & ASSOCIATES, 4424 Apricot Rd., Simi Valley CA 93063. Director:
Randy Harris. Represented 96 clients in 1978. Query with samples. "We specialize in working
closely with unpublished writers under the belief that each ms stands on its own merits." No
poetry. SASE. Agent receives 10% commission.
Will Handle: Mass market hardbacks and paperbacks and periodicals articles.

HY COHEN LITERARY AGENCY, LTD., 111 W. 57th St., New York NY 10019.
(212)757-5237. President: Hy Cohen. Estab. 1975. Obtains new clients through
recommendations. Will read unsolicited mss, queries and outlines. SASE. Agent receives 10%
commission.
Will Handle: Magazine articles and fiction, novels, and nonfiction books.
Recent Sales: *The Seventh Babe,* by J. Charyn (Arbor House); *Earthship and Star Song,* by E.I.
Shedley (Viking Press); and *George's Women,* by Catherine MacArthur (St. Martin's).

COLLIER ASSOCIATES, 280 Madison Ave., New York NY 10016. (212)685-5516. Owner:
Lisa Collier. Associates: Oliver Swan, Leslie Garisto. Estab. 1976. Obtains new clients through
recommendations of existing clients, editors, friends, and through various listings. Will read
unsolicited queries and outlines. SASE. Made 50 sales in 1978; plans 80 in 1979. Agent
receives 10% commission on domestic sales; 15% on British; and 20% on foreign.
Will Handle: Novels and nonfiction books. "Not interested in travel, astrology, occult or
porno."
Recent Sales: *Backstairs at the White House,* by P. Dubov (Bantam); *New Profits From the
Monetary Crisis,* investment advice by H. Browne (Wm. Morrow); and *Down to Earth: The
Complete Directory of Natural Foods,* by T. Riker (Putnam's).

BILL COOPER ASSOCIATES, INC., 16 E. 52nd St., New York NY 10022. (212)758-6491.
Estab. 1963. Obtains new clients through recommendations and personal pursuit. Will read
unsolicited mss. SASE. Marketing fee "subject to submitting source." Made 6 sales in 1978;
plans 5-10 in 1979. Agent receives 10% commission.
Will Handle: Novels, nonfiction books, motion pictures, stage plays and TV scripts (game
shows, situation comedies; only original concepts for series, with fully developed presentation
of theme, characters, and a pilot script).
Recent Sales: *Rocky Marciano,* by E. Skehan (Houghton Mifflin); *A Noble Treason,* by
Richard Hanser (G.P. Putnam's Sons); and *Tumultuous Merriment,* by Heywood Hale Broun.

CREATIVE ENTERPRISES, Box 450, Centreville VA 22020. (703)830-3711. Director: Joyce
Wright. Estab. 1975. Obtains new clients through recommendations of other writers, writers'
organizations and *Writer's Market.* Will read unsolicited queries and outlines. SASE. "Prefer
that new authors send a comprehensive chapter outline, background data on himself, and the
first four chapters of his ms when querying." Agent receives 10% commission.
Will Handle: Novels and nonfiction books. Will also handle magazine articles and fiction,
motion pictures, and TV scripts for clients under contract by agency. Specializes in fiction,
how-to, self-help, and career guidance.
Criticism Services: Will critique novels, self-help books, biographies of historical or literary
figures, and career guidance books. Mss must be neatly typed, double-spaced, with one-inch
margins at top, bottom and sides, author's name in left-hand corner, number in right-hand
corner. Prefers photocopies for editorial comments. Charges $100 flat fee for unsolicited ms
without previous query.
Recent Sales: *The Colchicine Factor* by Robert Boyce (Major Books); *Legend of Shame* by B.
Roche (Dell Publishing); and *Passionate Journey,* by Kathleen Kinney (Simon & Schuster).

CREATIVE WRITERS AGENCY, INC., Box 2280, Satellite Beach FL 32937. (305)773-3622.
President: John C. Roach Jr. Estab. 1971. Obtains new clients through *Writer's Market,*
authors' recommendations, and advertisements. Will read unsolicited mss. SASE. Charges
unpublished authors $300 marketing fee (returnable upon sale of material); no marketing fee
for published authors. Made 6 sales in 1978, plans 6 in 1979. Agent receives 10% commission;
15% for movie rights.
Will Handle: Novels, textbooks, nonfiction books, motion pictures, stage plays and TV scripts.

Specializes in material adaptable to motion pictures.
Criticism Services: Novels, textbooks, nonfiction books. Charges $25 for mss under 25,000 words; $50 over 25,000 words; $100 over 50,000 words.
Recent Sales: *Graze Ovserver's Handbook*, by H. Povenmire (JSB Enterprises, Inc.); and *Hey Ma, The Insurance Man Is Hers!*, by A. Christiano (JSB Enterprises, Inc.).

MARJEL DE LAUER AGENCY, 8961 Sunset Blvd., Los Angeles CA 90069. Obtains new clients through referrals from clients and producers. Made 20 sales in 1978; plans 40 in 1979. "Writers must be published or have motion picture or TV credits. Will not read unsolicited mss; will read queries and outlines. SASE. Agent receives 10% commission.
Will Handle: Novels (will accept unpublished authors—if outline and first 3 chapters are submitted); nonfiction (must see outline and complete mss); motion pictures; and TV scripts.
Recent Sales: *The Spy Who Sat and Waited*, novel by R. Wright Campbell (International Films, Ltd.); *Where Pigeons Go to Die*, novel by R. Wright Campbell (Tony Unger Productions); and *Virgin Kisses*, novel by Gloria Nagy (Michael Douglas, Bigstick Productions).

ANITA DIAMANT: THE WRITERS WORKSHOP, INC., 51 E. 42nd St., New York NY 10017. (212)687-1122. President: Anita Diamant. Estab. 1917. Obtains new clients through recommendations by publishers or other clients. Potential clients must have made some professional sales. Will not read unsolicited mss; will read unsolicited queries. SASE. Made 50 sales in 1978. Agent receives 10% commission. Member S.A.R.
Will Handle: Magazine articles and fiction, novels, nonfiction books, motion pictures, and TV scripts.
Recent Sales: *Blue Collar Jobs For Women*, by Muriel Lederer (E.P. Dutton); *Flowers In The Attic*, by Virginia Cleo Andrews (Pocket Books, Simon & Schuster); and *The Girl Who Had Everything*, by Dorian Leigh and Laura Hober (Doubleday).

ANN ELMO AGENCY, INC., 60 E. 42nd St., New York NY 10017. (212)661-2880. Obtains new clients through writers' queries. Sales average about a book a month. Will read unsolicited manuscripts, queries and outlines at no charge. SASE. Agent receives 10% commission for domestic sales and 20% for foreign sales.
Will Handle: Magazine articles (only strong ideas); magazine fiction (very few short stories); novels, nonfiction books; stage plays; and occasional TV scripts.

PATRICIA FALK FEELEY, INC., AUTHORS' REPRESENTATIVE, 52 Vanderbilt Ave., New York NY 10017. Estab. 1975. Obtains new clients through referrals by clients and editors and by inquiries. Will not read unsolicited mss; will read unsolicited queries and outlines. SASE. Agent receives 10% commission on domestic sales, 15% on British; 20% on foreign.
Will Handle: Novels and nonfiction books.
Recent Sales: *High Barbaree*, by Barbara Annandale (Ballantine); *Promises*, by Charlotee Vale Allen (Condgon/Dutton); *Skin Deep: The Making of a Plastic Surgeon*, by Donald Moynihan and Shirley Hartman (Little and Brown).

BARTHOLD FLES LITERARY AGENCY, 507 5th Ave., New York NY 10017. Contact: Barthold Fles, Vikki Power. Estab. 1933. Obtains new clients through recommendations of clients and editors, scouting tips, and writers' conferences. Will not read unsolicited mss. Made 30 sales in 1978; plans 40-45 in 1979. Agent receives 10% commission on domestic sales; 15% on British; and 20% on foreign.
Will Handle: Novels and nonfiction books. Specializes in intermediate and teenage juveniles; no picture books.
Recent Sales: *The Southeast Conference*, by McCallum (Scribner's); *Felony at Random*, mystery by "Dell Shannon" (Morrow); and *Complete Beginner's Guide to Hi-Fi*, by Lyttle (Doubleday).

FRIEDA FISHBEIN, 353 W. 57th St., New York NY 10019. (212)247-4398. Contact: Frieda Fishbein. Usually obtains clients through other clients' recommendations; will sometimes accept client after they read a ms that seems to be promising. Made 3 sales in 1978; plans 3-4 in 1979. Will read unsolicited mss for $50 for the first 50,000 words and proportionately more for any wordage beyond that amount. Charges $50 for full-length plays and screenplays; $50 for TV scripts no longer than an hour. Sends written report of work. SASE. Agent receives 10% commission.
Will Handle: Magazine articles and fiction as a favor to established clients only; novels (represent writers with genre fiction, but also accept anything that appears to be worthy and

they have some hope of selling; textbooks and nonfiction books (no particular requirements). Will accept a promising script that they believe will sell for motion pictures, stage plays, TV scripts and radio scripts. Does not want poetry, cartoon books, individual short stories or articles.

Recent Sales: *Love, The Sorcerer*, by Ann Lorraine Thompson (Avon Books); *Screaming Eagles*, by Donald Burgett (reprint rights sold to Bantam); and *Tribute*, by Bernard Slade (a play sold to Strassegg-Verlag, a German theater firm).

THE FOLEY AGENCY, 34 E. 38th St., New York NY 10016. (212)686-6930. Estab. 1956. Obtains new clients through recommendations. Will read unsolicited queries. SASE. Agent receives 10% commission.
Will Handle: Novels and nonfiction books.

PEGGY LOIS FRENCH AGENCY, 26051 Birkdale Rd., Sun City CA 92381. (714)679-6325. Estab. 1952. Obtains new clients through referrals and word-of-mouth. Will read unsolicited mss and queries. "Fees for beginners, none for the established professional who has credits with a major publisher or film producer."Agent receives 15% commission.
Will Handle: Juvenile books, science fiction, highly commercial novels, gothics, romantic-suspense and historicals ("must be unusually good and of the best-selling, tempestuous variety). We're looking for straight suspense, including mystery, intrigue, psychological thrillers, horror, contemporary or mainstream novels, including stories based on real-life situations, soap-opera-type melodrama, male adventure, either period or modern. We are one of the few agencies who will develop a writer with talent and work with him through submission, a sale, and the signing of contracts. We will consider magazine fiction of high quality, nonfiction, motion pictures, stage plays and TV scripts."

FULP LITERARY AGENCY, 62 Maple Rd., Amityville NY 11701. (516)842-0972. Agency Representative: M.L. Fulp. Estab. 1976. Will read unsolicited mss, queries or outlines. SASE. Charges $25 marketing fee for all material once client is accepted. Agent receives 10% commission.
Will Handle: Magazine articles and fiction, novels, and nonfiction books. "I like to receive mss from minority writers and females." Recently published *Airborne Ambulance*, magazine article by Jay Fine (*Search and Rescue*); and A Father's Battle, magazine fiction by Quata Merit (*True Confession*).

JAY GARON-BROOKE ASSOCIATES, INC., 415 Central Park W., New York NY 10025. (212)866-3654. President: Jay Garon. Obtains new clients through referrals; "however, we will read and answer query letters wherein material is briefly described." Will not read unsolicited mss; will read queries and outlines. SASE. Agent receives 15% commission, "absorbing all costs; no extra billing to clients."
Will Handle: Novels (general and category fiction suitable for hardcover or paperback publication); textbooks (rarely consider professional and technical material unless there is a clear application to a trade market); nonfiction books (biography, autobiography, self-help and/or improvement, popular history—but generally any nonfiction oriented toward popular appeal or interest); motion pictures (finished screenplays accompanied by treatment only); stage plays and TV scripts (accompanied by treatment).
Recent Sales: *The Restaurant*, novel by Parley J. Cooper (MacMillan); *The Lotteries*, novel by Daoma Winston (William Morrow); and Golden Lotus, novel by Janet Louise Roberts (Warner Books).

MAX GARTENBERG, LITERARY AGENT, 331 Madison Ave., New York NY 10017. (212)661-5270. Estab. 1954. Obtains new clients through referrals and solicitations. Will not read unsolicited mss; will read unsolicited queries. SASE. Agent receives 10% commission.
Will Handle: Novels and nonfiction books.
Recent Sales: *The Sovereign Solution*, by Michael M. McNamara (Crown Publishers); *The Hazardous Road to Rome*, by W.S. Kuniczak (Doubleday & Company); and *Guide to Career Building*, by Richard Germann and Peter Arnold (Harper and Row).

GLORIA GEALE & ASSOCIATES, 9000 Sunset Blvd., Suite 814, Los Angeles CA 90069. (213)657-2125. Contact: Gloria Geale, Lt. Col. Ben Novom. Obtains new clients through recommendations. Made 2 sales in 1978; plans 3 in 1979. Will not read unsolicited mss; will read queries. SASE.
Will Handle: Novels; nonfiction books; motion pictures; and TV scripts.

Recent Sales: *The American Master*, by R. Satriano (Douglas West); and *Mysterious Herbs & Roots*, by Mitzie Keller (Peace Press).

LUCIANNE GOLDBERG LITERARY AGENCY, INC., 255 W. 84th St., New York NY 10024. (212)787-2717. Contact: Lisbeth Mark. Estab. 1974. Obtains new clients through referrals and/or contacts in publishing and journalism. Will read unsolicited mss for $100 up to 100,000 words, if author is previously unpublished. Fee waived if author is accepted for representation. Will read outlines and queries. SASE. Made 42 sales in 1978. Agent receives 10% commission, 20% on dramatic and foreign sales.
Will Handle: Nonfiction and fiction (magazine articles only if author is previously published).
Criticism Services: "$100 reading fee covers an in-depth report on ms, including constructive suggestions for revision and restructuring with an eye to making work a viable product."
Recent Sales: *Defector's Mistress*, autobiography by Judy Chavez and Jack Vitek (Dell); *Cambodia*, novel by Jack Anderson and Bill Pronzini (Doubleday); and *I'm Dancing As Fast As I Can*, autobiography by Barbara Gordon (Harper & Row).

GRAHAM AGENCY, 317 W. 45th St., New York NY 10036. Owner: Earl Graham. Estab. 1971. Obtains new clients through queries and recommendations. "Will accept any playwright whose work I feel is salable, and occasionally will work with a playwright whose initial effort may not be salable, but whom I feel is talented, and whose work I feel merits encouraging." Will read unsolicited queries pertaining to stage plays only. Material submitted without SASE will not be returned. Agent receives 10% commission.
Will Handle: Full-length stage plays only.

SHELLEY GROSS/WORDS UNLIMITED, Box 2415, Hollywood CA 90028. (213)876-8374. Owner: Shelley Gross. Obtains new clients through referrals, personal contact, nominal advertising and writers' clubs. Estimated sales for 1979: 6-8. Will read unsolicited mss and queries. Charges $15 for short stories/articles; $25 for novels and nonfiction (refundable upon sale). SASE. Charges $25 marketing fee. Agent receives 15% commission from new unpublished authors for first sale and 10% commission for published authors by major publisher. Written criticism included with reader's fee.
Will Handle: Magazine articles; magazine fiction (high standards—feminist thrust); novels (feminist, mystery, contemporary, historical romance, occult); nonfiction books (religion, mysticism, relevant topics, psychology); motion pictures; TV scripts (for series or movie of the week by pros or professionally written); and children's books.

HEACOCK LITERARY AGENCY, 1121 Lake St., Venice CA 90291. (213)396-6540. Nonfiction and Ficton: James Heacock. Fiction and Juveniles: Rosalie Heacock. Obtains new clients "from referrals from our present clients, other agents and publishers and *Writer's Market*." Made 3 sales in 1978; plans 15 in 1979. "Will read queries and outlines." SASE. Will read unsolicited ms for fee of $85 for up to 150,000 words. "The fee is waived if the author has been published by a national publisher within two years of submittal of manuscript." Agent receives 10% commission. Authors are paid 10% for domestic sales and 20% for foreign sales.
Will Handle: Novels of all types, including juveniles. Mainstream novels are of special interest, in addition to westerns, historical and family sagas, occult, mystery and romantic suspense, what-if books, fiction and science fiction; nonfiction books including new idea books, occult, how-to, politics, philosophy, biography, ecology, alternate life styles, diet and health, beauty, business, astrology and futurism. "We're looking for fresh ideas." Query with SASE.
Recent Sales: *Tickeoctopus*, by Audrey Wood (Houghton-Mifflin); *Twenty-Four Robbers*, by Audrey and Don Wood (Delacorte); and *Thought Has Wings*, by Carol Bell (New Age Press).

VANCE HALLOWAY AGENCY, Box 518, Pearblossom CA 93553. (714)249-3818 or 327-9653. Agent: Vance Halloway. Estab. 1954. Free reading of unsolicited mss to 60,000 words; will read unsolicited queries and outlines. SASE. Made 11 sales in 1978. Agent's commission "depends on transaction. All contracts are directed to agency and commissions are deducted from advances and royalty payment." Charges marketing fee "only if I cannot foresee an immediate sale."
Will Handle: Novels, nonfiction books and stage plays. "Book properties that are geared for possible series like our Death Merchant, Kung Fu and Murder Master series, contracted to this agency."
Criticism Services: Will criticize commercially slanted material. Submit precis and sample chapters. Fee depends on amount of labor required.
Recent Sales: *Thunderstrike in Syria*, mystery by Rosenberger (Ace Books); *Stitch of the Flesh Needle*, novel by Hutson (New American Library); *Deadly ManHunt*, Mystery by Rosenberger

(Pinnacle Books); *Alaska Conspiracy*, mystery by Rosenberger (Pinnacle Books); *Wrangel Island Mystery*, mystery by Rosenberger (Pinnacle Books); *Untitled*, mystery by Rosenberger (Pinnacle Books); and *Silence Over Sinai*, adventure by Awni (Pyramid).

HEINLE AND HEINLE ENTERPRISES, 29 Lexington Rd., Concord MA 01742. (617)369-4858. Senior Member: Charles A.S. Heinle. Estab. 1973. Obtains new clients through word-of-mouth, *Writer's Market*, activities as resident agents at Cape Code Writer's Conference, and recommendations by clients. "We are less concerned that a writer is unpublished, as long as we believe in the writer and the future." Will not read unsolicited mss; will read unsolicited queries and outlines. SASE. Agent receives 10% commission.
Will Handle: Magazine fiction, novels, textbooks and nonfiction books. "We are most interested in materials with a New England theme, past, present and future, but, of course, good writing is the main consideration. We handle some textbooks in the foreign language area, and some reference materials as bibliographies in selected fields."
Recent Sales: *Everything You Always Wanted to Know About Heating With Wood*, how-to by Michael Harris (Citadel Press); *Bird of Fire*, children's novel by Cecile P. Edwards (Beta Book Co.); *When The White Man Came*, social studies by Cecile P. Edwards (National Educators for Creative Instruction); and *Physicians Assistants*, college text by Judith Greenwood (Technomic Press).

HINTZ LITERARY AGENCY, 2879 N. Grant Blvd., Milwaukee WI 53210. Obtains new clients through "referrals from clients and editors; some from queries." Will not read unsolicited mss; will read outlines and queries. SASE. Agent receives 10% commission.
Will Handle: Novels (adult and juvenile); nonfiction books; and religious fiction and nonfiction.
Recent Sales: *Make Space, Make Symbols*, trade religious by Keith Clark O.F.M. (Ave Maria); *and If I Can't Be Ordained I'll Cookbook*, humor edited by Martin and Sandra Hintz.

RICHARD HUTTNER AGENCY, INC., 330 E. 33rd St., New York NY 10016. Obtains new clients through "referrals, reading recommended manuscripts, literary conferences, people in the news, queries, and *Writer's Market*. We look for publish*able* authors; this does not always mean writers who have many credits. We are selective in the writers we take on, however." Will read unsolicited mss, queries and outlines when accompanied by SASE. Made 50 sales in 1978; plans 100 in 1979. Agent receives 10% commission.
Will Handle: Magazine fiction (for major magazines only, and for our book clients only); novels; TV movies; nonfiction books; motion pictures and syndicated material. "We love family sagas and all types of well-researched nonfiction."
Recent Sales: *The World's Greatest Blackjack Book*, nonfiction by K. Cooper and L. Humble (Doubleday); *Whirlwind*, historic romance by A. York (Pocket); and *The Living Together Kit*, nonfiction by R. Warmer and T. Ihara (Fawcett).

L.H. JOSEPH AND ASSOCIATES, 8344 Melrose Ave., Suite 23, Los Angeles CA 90069. (213)651-2322. Estab. 1954. Licensed artist's managers and signatories to the Writer's Guild of America, West.
Will Handle: Novels, textbooks, nonfiction books (in any field). "Reading fee of $35 required for all ms. SASE. We will critique submissions only if requested." Charges $75. Send check with ms.

IRVING KERNER LITERARY AGENCY, 1216 Pearl St., Boulder CO 80302. (303)447-8112. Contact: Irving Kerner, Agent Attorney. "New clients are obtained primarily through referrals and inquiries. Writers should send letter of introduction, including description of material and previous writing efforts." Will not read unsolicited mss, except completed screenplays. Will read unsolicited queries and outlines. SASE. Standard commission is 10%, however, commission is higher on agency-created projects and a 20% commission is taken on revenues derived from merchandise spin-offs and foreign sales.
Will Handle: Novels; nonfiction books; screen plays; stage plays; and TV scripts.
Criticism Services: "This agency will on occasion supply a writer with a written critique. However, such critiques are supplied at agency discretion. No fees are charged."

VIRGINIA KIDD, WITH JAMES ALLEN AND VALERIE SMITH, LITERARY AGENTS, 538 E. Harford St., Milford PA 18337. (717)296-6205. Estab. 1965. Potential client "must be a published writer; should have earned at least $1,000 (from writing) during the previous year." Will not read unsolicited mss. "I cannot take on *anyone* with no track record. If someone has a special reason for wanting me to handle them, write me a letter explaining why and enclose

SASE. I'm not actively looking for new authors." Kidd's lists are full. Allen and Smith will consider qualitifed writers. Agent receives 10% commission on domestic sales, 15% on dramatic sales, 20% on overseas sales.

Will Handle: Magazine articles and fiction, novels, textbooks, nonfiction books, motion pictures, TV and radio scripts and science fiction.

Recent Sales: *Malafrena*, by Ursula K. Le Guin (Putnam's/Berkley); 3 novels by D. G. Compton (Pocket Books); and *Who Done It?*, by Isaac Asimov & Alice Laurance (Houghton Mifflin).

DANIEL P. KING, LITERARY AGENT, 5125 N. Cumberland Blvd., Whitefish Bay WI 53217. (414)964-2903. Estab. 1974. Obtains new clients through listings in *Writer's Market,* and referrals from clients. Will not read unsolicited mss; will read unsolicited queries. "Reading fee is charged unpublished writers." Made 10 sales in 1978; plans 10 in 1979. Agent receives 10% commission.

Will Handle: Magazine articles and fiction, novels, nonfiction books and syndicated material. "While I handle general material, I specialize in crime literature (fact or fiction)."

BERTHA KLAUSNER INTERNATIONAL LITERARY AGENCY, INC., 71 Park Ave., New York NY 10016. (212)685-2642. President: Bertha Klausner. Estab. 1938. Obtains new clients through recommendation. Will read unsolicited mss; charges reading fees. Will read unsolicited queries and outlines. SASE. Agent receives 10% commission on domestic sales.

Will Handle: Novels, textbooks, nonfiction books, stage plays, and TV and motion picture scripts. "We represent world rights for all subsidiaries and are represented by our own agents throughout the world."

Criticism Services: Will critique novels and plays. Request rate card.

Recent Sales: *David Berkowitz*, biography by Larry Klausner (McGraw-Hill); *Layton Family and Jim Jones*, autobiography by Dr. Thomas Layton (Holt, Rinehart & Winston); and *Vegetable Cookbook*, by Teresa Candler (McGraw-Hill).

LUCY KROLL AGENCY, 390 West End Ave., New York NY 10024. (212)877-0627. Estab. 1954. Obtains new clients through recommendations. Will not read unsolicited mss; will read unsolicited queries and outlines. SASE. Agent receives 10% commission.

Will Handle: Novels, nonfiction books and stage plays.

MICHAEL LARSEN/ELIZABETH POMADA LITERARY AGENTS, 1029 Jones St., San Francisco CA 94109. (415)673-0939. Estab. 1972. Obtains new clients through personal recommendations, *Literary Market Place, Writer's Market,* etc. Will read unsolicited mss for $25 (refundable immediately upon acceptance); no reading charge for published writers. Will read unsolicited queries and outlines. SASE. Agent receives 10% commission on domestic sales; 20% on foreign.

Will Handle: Novels, nonfiction books, motion pictures and TV scripts. "We request a clean copy of the ms, typed double-spaced with pica type on 8½x11 paper; unbound, preferably boxed, with writer's name, address and phone number on the title page."

Recent Sales: *The Kryptonite Kid*, by J. Torchia (Holt); *The Complete Guide to Touch Dancing*, by Karen Lustgarten (Warners); and *Bethany's Sin*, by R. McCammon (Avon).

LENNIGER LITERARY AGENCY, INC., 437 5th Ave., New York NY 10016. Contact: Paul Trevoy. Obtains new clients through recommendations. Made 100 sales in 1977 and 1978. Will read invited mss only, at no charge. SASE. Agent receives 10% commission.

Will Handle: Novels and nonfiction books.

Recent Sales: *Marabelle*, by Tom E. Huff (St. Martin's Press); *Lady Vixen*, by Shirlee Busbee (Avon); and *The Sturbridge Remembrance*, by Amelia French (Warner Books).

LEVY ENTERPRISES, 1570 N. Edgemont, Suite 605, Los Angeles CA 90027. (213)664-2254. President: Ms. Lee K. Levy. Obtains new clients through "referrals, recommendations, and a good query letter showing some strong writing talent." Estab. 1977. Made 2 sales in 1978; plans 6 in 1979. "I will read unsolicited mss for $50 up to 75,000 words; $100 for over 75,000 words. I will read a manuscript for $50 and give a critique. If I decide to take it to market, I require an additional $100 to handle marketing. Should I be successful in marketing the manuscript, the $100 handling fee is charged against my agent's commission. Made 2 sales in 1978; plans 6 in 1979. Agent receives 10% commission.

Will Handle: Magazine articles (only after author has made a sale). "I handle the motion picture rights of the mss I handle, but am willing to read and market a really well-written screenplay, particularly because I'm so close to the motion picture capital. I have two stage plays that are being considered by a small production here in LA." Novels: "Send a short outline of the book, and, if I'm interested in reading it, I'll respond soon." Nonfiction books: "Send a strong query letter describing the property. Then I will ask for an extensive outline, and one or two chapters, following that. No poetry. I am only interested in juvenile fiction, if it is a well plotted, upbeat book length mss for children."

PATRICIA LEWIS, 450 7th Ave., Room 602, New York NY 10001. Owner: Patricia Lewis. Obtains new clients through recommendation. Will not read unsolicited mss. SASE for queries and outlines. Agent receives 10% commission.
Will Handle: Novels and nonfiction books.
Recent Sales: *Valley Village of the Vampire Cat* by Namioka (McKay) for young adults; *Great Game of Soccer* by Liss (Putnam) for young adults; and *Japan* by Namioka (Vanguard).

HILDA LINDLEY LITERARY AGENCY, 128 E. 56th St., New York NY 10022. (212)751-9334. Contact: Hilda Lindley. Obtains new clients through recommendations. Will not read unsolicited mss. SASE for queries and outlines. Agent receives 10% commission.
Will Handle: Magazine articles (as part of book representation); magazine fiction, novels, nonfiction books and motion pictures (stemming from book); and syndicated material (stemming from book).
Recent Sales: *The Man Who Lost The War* (Dial); *The Hawk on the Wind* (Dial); *The Belmont Sting* (Bantam); and *Lullaby* (Harper & Row).

DONALD MacCAMPBELL, INC., 12 E. 41st St., New York NY 10017. (212)683-5580. "Phone queries are preferred but will answer written inquiries that are accompanied by SASE. Made 150 sales in 1978; plans 150 in 1979. Agency works on 10% commission basis."
Will Handle: "Now handling book-length fiction exclusively, with emphasis upon the women's markets."
Recent Sales: *Love's Lone Pilgrimage*, novel by Beverly Byrne (CBS Fawcett); *Golden Fancy*, novel by Patricia Maxwell (CBS Fawcett); and *Canyons of Death*, novel by Susan May (Dell).

CAROL MANN LITERARY AGENCY, 519 E. 87th St., New York NY 10028. (212)879-3034. Contact: Carol Mann. Obtains new clients through "satisfied clients, editors, Author's Guild and Society of Children's Book Writers." Made 48 sales in 1978. Will answer unsolicited queries with SASE. Agent receives 10% commission.
Will Handle: Specializes in children's books and adult nonfiction. Also handles novels (juvenile, young adult and adult).
Recent Sales: *Hocus Pocus Dilemma*, juvenile fiction by Pat Kibbe (Knopf); *Suburbia*, pop culture by McColm/Payne (Doubleday); and *The Dorothy Allison Story*, autobiography by Jacobson/Allison (Jove).
Criticism Services: Charges $25 for mss under 5,000 words; $50 for mss under 25,000 words; and $100 thereafter.

BETTY MARKS, 51 E. 42nd St., New York NY 10017. (212)687-1122. Estab. 1970. Obtains new clients through word-of-mouth recommendations of authors, other agents, editors, and friends. Will read unsolicited mss for $125 up to 100,000 words, if author is previously unpublished. Will read unsolicited queries and outlines. SASE. Made 80 sales in 1978; plans 90 in 1979. Agent receives 10% commission.
Will Handle: Magazine articles and fiction, novels, nonfiction books, poetry, stage plays, TV scripts, juvenile fiction and nonfiction.
Criticism Services: Will critique material as above. Mss must be typed double-spaced, pages unbound, standard professional format. Charges $125 for mss to 100,000 words; $175 for two mss; $250 for three mss; 50¢/page for shorter material ($25 minimum).
Recent Sales: *Rainbows*, by Thom Klika (St. Martin's); *The Complete Medical, Fitness & Health Guide for Men*, by Lawrence Galton (Simon & Schuster); *Eva Evita, The Life and Times of Eva Peron*, by Paul Montgomery (Pocket Books); and *Grand Scam*, by Richard Lopez and Peter Stein (Dial).

HELEN McGRATH, WRITERS' REPRESENTATIVE, 1406 Idaho Court, Concord CA 94521. (415)686-3380. Obtains new clients through referrals and word-of-mouth. Will not read unsolicited mss; will read queries consisting of sample chapter and outlines. Agent receives 10% commission.
Will Handle: Magazine articles and fiction (only if also handling a book for a writer); novels (submit sample chapters); textbooks (submit qualifications); and nonfiction books.

SCOTT MEREDITH LITERARY AGENCY, INC. 845 3rd Ave., New York NY 10022. (212)245-5500. President: Scott Meredith. Estab. 1941. Obtains new clients "through listings such as *Writer's Market*, recommendations by clients, and direct mail advertising. Also, many promising authors are recommended to us by editors, publishers and producers." Will read unsolicited mss, queries and outlines. "We charge a single fee for all services, including readings, criticism, assistance in revision if required, and marketing. The fee is $75 for fiction or articles to 5,000 words; $100 for scripts 5,000-10,000 words; $150 for scripts above 10,000 words; $100 for book mss below 10,000 words; $150 for book mss 10,000-150,000 words; $200 for book mss 150,000-200,000 words; $300 for book mss above 250,000 words; $150 for full-length plays or screenplays; $100 for syndicated packages of 3-6 sample columns." SASE. Made 7,800 sales in 1978; plans 8,000 in 1979. Agent receives 10% on domestic sales, 20% on foreign. "If a writer has sold to a major book publisher in the past year or has begun to make major national magazine or TV sales with some regularity, we drop fees and proceed on a straight commission basis."
Will Handle: "We handle material in all fields except single poems and single cartoons, though we do handle book collections of poetry and cartoons."
Recent Sales: *Broca's Brain*, nonfiction by Dr. Carl Sagan (Random House); *Elegance*, nonfiction by Norman Mailer (Simon & Schuster); and *The Healers*, novel by Gerald Green (G.P. Putnam's Sons).

ROBERT P. MILLS, LTD., 156 E. 52nd St., New York NY 10022. President: Robert P. Mills. Associate: Fred Mills. Estab. 1960. Obtains new clients through recommendations "of someone I know, or if the writer has a respectable publishing history." Will not read unsolicited mss; will read unsolicited queries. SASE. Agent receives 10% commission.
Will Handle: Magazine articles and fiction, novels, nonfiction books, motion pictures, and syndicated material.
Recent Sales: *The Body Language of Sex Power and Aggression,* by J. Fast (M. Evans & Co.); *Twister,* by J. Bickham (Doubleday & Co.); and *Pele's Autobiography,* by Pele, with R.L. Fish (Doubleday & Co.).

HOWARD MOOREPARK, 444 E. 82nd St., New York NY 10028. (212)737-3961. Estab. 1946. Obtains new clients through recommendations. Will read unsolicited mss. SASE. Made 9 sales in 1978; plans 9 in 1979. Agent receives 10% commission.
Will Handle: Novels and nonfiction books.
Recent Titles: *Swan Song*, historical fiction by Violet Ashton (Fawcett); *Land of Leys*, science fiction by L.P. Davies (Doubleday); and *Philosophy of Religion*, nonfiction by N. Smart (Oxford).

MULTIMEDIA PRODUCT DEVELOPMENT, INC., 410 S. Michigan Ave., Room 828, Chicago IL 60605. (312)922-3063. President: Jane Jordan Browne. Estab. 1971. Obtains new clients through recommendations and word-of-mouth. "Multimedia handles only works of professional writers who make their living as authors. The rare exceptions are celebrity autobiographies and the 'new idea' nonfiction book." Will read unsolicited mss for $150; will read unsolicited queries and outlines. SASE. Made 200 sales in 1978; plans 275 in 1979. Agent receives 10% commission on domestic sales; 20% on foreign.
Will Handle: Novels, nonfiction books, motion picture and TV scripts. No poetry, plays, articles or short stories.
Criticism Services: "We will critique all material. Submissions for criticism must be submitted with the fee and SASE. All material must be typed double-spaced." Charges $150 for standard-length novels or nonfiction books; $50 for juvenile books of 50 pages or less; $75 for screenplays; and $50 for teleplays of ½-1 hour. "Although Multimedia provides criticism services, the fees are meant to discourage any nonprofessionals from approaching the agency."
Recent Sales: *The 7th Royale*, by Donald Stanwood (Coward, McCann); *The Art of Scrambling*, by Elwood Chapman (J.P. Tarcher); and *The Prodigy*, by M. Jay Livingston (Maximus Productions).

CHARLES NEIGHBORS, INC., 240 Waverly Plaza, New York NY 10014. (212)924-8296. Estab. 1966. Obtains new clients "mostly through recommendations of existing clients, but also from editors, other agents, and occasionally from *Writer's Market*." Will not read unsolicited mss; will read unsolicited queries and outlines at no charge. SASE. Agent receives 10% commission.
Will Handle: Magazine articles and fiction, novels, nonfiction books and motion pictures.
Recent Sales: *The Grab*, by M. Katzenbach (William Morrow); *The Wolfen*, by W. Strieber (William Morrow); and *Bisbee '17*, by R. Houston (Pantheon).

B.K. NELSON LITERARY AGENCY, 888 7th Ave., New York NY 10019. (212)582-3895. Obtains new clients through inquiries and word of mouth. Made 44 sales in 1978; plans 50 in 1979. Will read unsolicited mss for $60/60,000 words. Will read queries. SASE. Agent receives 10% commission.
Will Handle: Fiction, nonfiction, business books, autobiographies, teleplays and screenplays.
Recent Sales: *Anyone Can Do Business With The Government,* by Herman Holtz (Amacon); *Floors and Doors,* by Barbara WWrenn (Van Nostrand); and *Instant Genius,* by W. Ware Lynch (Sterling).

NICHOLAS LITERARY AGENCY, 161 Madison Ave., New York NY 10016. Owner: Georgia Nicholas. Estab. 1934. Obtains new clients through recommendations. Will not read unsolicited mss; will read unsolicited queries and outlines and published books for reprint. SASE. Charges a one-time marketing fee of $100. Agent receives 10% commission.
Will Handle: Novels, nonfiction books, motion pictures, stage plays, TV and radio scripts.

NORTHEAST LITERARY AGENCY, 69 Broadway, Concord NH 03301. (603)225-9162. Editor: Victor Levine. Estab. 1973. Obtains new clients through listings (*Literary Market Place, Writer's Market*); recommendations from editors, clients; and display advertising. Will read unsolicited mss. SASE. "There is a one-time agency charge of $75, refundable from earned commissions. Depends on writer's credits; if extensive and national in scope, there is no agency charge. The charge, payable with first submission, covers our reading of *all* future mss. Time-frame is deliberately open-ended. We're hopeful it will help writers develop into valued clients; it's good for us as well as them. We promise a sympathetic reading and fast response. In return, we ask that writers don't dump on us soiled and otherwise unmarketworthy mss." Agent receives 10% commission on domestic sales; 20% on foreign.
Will Handle: Magazine articles and fiction, novels, nonfiction books, poetry, motion pictures, TV and radio scripts, and juvenile fiction/nonfiction (including picture book mss). "Particularly interested in juveniles (all kinds) and all genres in popular fiction (Historicals, romances, science fiction, etc.). Be up-front with us. Tell us where you're at in terms of your writing career: what you've done in the past, what you're presently working on; the direction you wish to go. Please be specific. We prefer to see complete mss, but will read partials by arrangement."
Recent Sales: Open Court Publishing Co., Parker Publishing Co., and Tempo Books.

O&K LITERARY CONSULTANTS, At the Meadow of Dan, VA 24120. Manager: Bonnie Link. Obtains new clients through *Writer's Market,* referrals, etc. Will read unsolicited queries, and outlines. SASE. Charges "minimal marketing and/or reading fee." Agent receives 10% commission.
Will Handle: Magazine articles and fiction, novels, nonfiction books, poetry, and all secondary markets connected with novels. "Our specialty is the young and coming writer. After several years of this, the big houses are beginning to look to us for new writers of significant stature. We expect this trend to continue and increase. We are most receptive to new writers and suggest that they query us."
Criticism Services: "Virtually none. Specific help in some cases where a client insists. We simply prefer not to do it, believing it is of little value to the writer."

RAY PEEKNER LITERARY AGENCY (associated with Larry Sterning Literary Agency and Hintz Literary Agency), 2625 N. 36th St., Milwaukee WI 53210. Contact: Ray Puechner. Estab. 1973. Obtains new clients through referrals from clients and editors, some from queries. Will not read unsolicited mss; will read unsolicited queries. SASE. Made 35 sales in 1978; plans 50 in 1979. Agent receives 10% commission.
Will Handle: Novels, nonfiction books, and young adult material.
Recent Sales: *Stamping Ground,* novel by Loren D. Estleman (Doubleday); *The Spitball Gang,* novel by Gary Paulsen (Elsevier/Nelson); and *The Patrimony,* science fiction by Robert Adams (New American Library).

PEMA BROWNE, LTD., 185 E. 85th St., New York NY 10028. (212)369-1925. Treasurer: Perry J. Browne. Obtains new clients through advertising and publishing and people who are in the business. Will read unsolicited mss, queries and outlines at no charge. SASE. Agent receives 15-20% commission.
Will Handle: Magazine articles, novels, textbooks, nonfiction books, motion pictures, TV scripts, syndicated material, children's books and how-to books. They are particularly interested in author-illustrators.
Recent Sales: *Early American Furniture* by Kevin Callahan (Drake Publishing); *The Complete*

Book of Birdhouses and Feeders, by Monica Russo (Drake Publishing); and *Bumble & Stumble* by Kevin Callahan (Western Publishing).

MARJORIE PETERS & PIERRE LONG LITERARY AGENTS, 5744 S. Harper, Chicago IL 60637. (312)752-8377. Estab. 1955. Obtains new clients through recommendations. Will not read unsolicited mss. SASE. Made 6 sales in 1978; plans 6 in 1979. Agent receives 10% commission on domestic sales; 20% on foreign.
Will Handle: Magazine articles and fiction, novels, textbooks, nonfiction books, poetry and stage plays. "Our agency specializes in fiction and serious poetry. We do not handle serious (nonhumorous) sociological/political exposition."
Criticism Services: "Except in the circumstance of 'already established' writers, this agency rarely considers (or handles) mss outside of its two Chicago-area imaginative writing workshops—the North Shore Creative Writers (Winnetka) and the South Side Creative Writers (Chicago).
Recent Sales: *Haakon*, novel by C.F. Griffin (Thomas Y. Crowell); *Easy-Change Ernie*, short story by P.S. Parker (Alfred Hitchcock); and *A Child's Christmas Eve for the World*, short story by M. Beres (Panorama).

ARTHUR PINE ASSOCIATES, INC., 1780 Broadway, New York NY 10019. Vice President: Richard Pine. Obtains new clients through recommendations. Made 100+ sales in 1978 and 1979. "Writers must be professional, and/or have published a book." Does not accept unsolicited mss. Query. SASE. Agent receives 15% commission.
Will Handle: Novels and nonfiction books (all types with mass market appeal).
Recent Sales: *Your Erroneous Zones*, by W.D. Dyer (Funk & Wagnalls); *The Artist*, by N. Garbo (W.W. Norton Co.); and *Tennis Love*, by B.J. King (Macmillan).

THE WALTER PITKIN AGENCY, 11 Oakwood Dr., Weston CT 06883. President: Walter Pitkin. Estab. 1973. Obtains new clients by referral or direct application. Will read unsolicited queries and outlines. "Writers must write an intelligent letter of inquiry and convince us of ability to write marketable material. Inquiry should include some personal background, plus a statement of what it is that the agency would be trying to place. We will solicit the ms if we like the inquiry." SASE. Made 16 sales in 1978. Agent receives 10% commission.
Will Handle: Novels and children's and adult nonfiction books. Also "almost any other material for clients who write books."

SIDNEY E. PORCELAIN AGENCY, Box J, Rocky Hill NJ 08553. (609)924-4080. Authors' Representative: Sidney Porcelain. Associate: Dan Fox. Estab. 1951. Obtains new clients through word-of-mouth and referrals. Will read unsolicited mss, queries and outlines. SASE. Made 29 sales in 1978; plans 35 in 1979. Agent receives 10% commission.
Will Handle: Magazine articles and fiction, novels, nonfiction books and TV scripts.
Recent Sales: *House Sitter*, fiction by Leona C. Karr (Avon Books); *The Judge*, short story by John Foard (ETCetera); and *How to Play the Piano in One Lesson*, how-to booklet by E. Wade (C.O.P.T. Publishing).

PORTER, DIERKS & PORTER-LENT (formerly Porter, Gould & Dierks), 215 W. Ohio St., Chicago IL 60610. (312)527-0626. Estab. 1958. Specialize in nonfiction and juveniles. "Make first contact by mail and include SASE. Detail publishing background and any experience that fits the writer to handle the subject matter." Agent receives standard commission. Reads unsolicited manuscripts for fee. Write for details.
Will Handle: Magazine articles and fiction, novels, textbooks (selectively), nonfiction books, poetry (highly selective), motion pictures, TV scripts (if the writer has credits), and syndicated material. "We are interested in any marketable writing, but do not encourage cookbooks or travel books unless the writer has a national reputation."
Recent Sales: *In the Fullness of Time*, by Carlson (Regnery); *Qeequeg's Odyssey*, by Cultra (Chicago Review Press); and *Norman Mark's Chicago*, by Mark (Chicago Review Press).

PSYCHIATRIC SYNDICATION SERVICE, INC., 22 Greenview Way, Upper Montclair NJ 07043. (201)746-5075. President: Jacqueline Simenauer. Obtains new clients through professional recommendations and advertising. "I only represent psychiatrists and psychologists. Client must either be an M.D. or a Ph.D." Will read unsolicited outlines. SASE. Made 12 sales in 1978; plans 18 in 1979. Agent receives 10% commission.
Will Handle: "I am only interested in nonfiction—psychiatrically oriented books aimed at the trade market, written by psychiatrists or psychologists."
Recent Sales: *Husbands and Wives*, nonfiction by Pietropento/Simenauer (Times Book); *A Natrona de Survey Marriage*, nonfiction by Richard Walzer, MD (Simon & Schuster); and

Children's Dreams, nonfiction by B. Richmond, MD (Dutton).

BARBARA RHODES LITERARY AGENCY, 140 West End Ave., New York NY 10023. (212)580-1300. Owner: Barbara Rhodes. Estab. 1968. Obtains new clients through recommendation or inquiry letters. Will not read unsolicited mss; will read unsolicited queries. SASE. Agent receives 10% commission.
Will Handle: Novels, nonfiction books and stage plays.

RHODES LITERARY AGENCY, 436 Pau St., Suite 6, Honolulu HI 96815. (808)946-9891. Director: Fred C. Pugarelli. Estab. 1971. Obtains new clients through advertising in *Writer's Digest*, referrals, and recommendations. Will read unsolicited mss for $10 (300-1,500 words); $25 (over 1,500 words); fee for material over 5,000 words is by arrangement. Will read unsolicited queries and outlines for $5. SASE. Made 10 sales in 1978; plans 20-40 in 1979. Agent receives 10% commission on domestic sales; 15% on Canadian; 20% on foreign.
Will Handle: Magazine articles and fiction, novels, textbooks, nonfiction books, poetry, motion pictures, stage plays, TV and radio scripts, photos, religious, and juvenile material; cartoons.
Criticism Services: Will critique any material. Charges $10 for up to 1,500 words; $25 for 1,500-5,000 words; $50 over 5,000 words.
Recent Sales: *The Supermen*, short story by Robert Andrea (*Hyacinths and Biscuits Magazine*); *Matteo's Restaurant: One of Best*, article by Sir Alfred Poi (*Waikiki News*); and *Grant Chapman—Great Pieces of Eight*, article by Sir Alfred Poi (*Waikiki News*).

RICHMOND LITERARY AGENCY, Box 57, Staten Island NY 10307. (212)984-3658. Director: Joan Gilbert. Obtains new clients through *LMP*, *Writer's Market*, and other directories and listings. Will read unsolicited mss for $10 handling charge. Will read unsolicited queries and outlines. SASE. Agent receives a 10% commission.
Will Handle: For novels, stage plays, TV scripts and radio scripts send letter, synopsis and author resume; for textbooks send letter, author resume, abstract, table of contents, etc.; for nonfiction books send letter and outline and author resume; and for motion pictures send letter, screen treatment and author resume.
Recent Sales: *Figures of Desire: An Analysis of Surrealist Film*, by Linda L. Williams (University of Illinois Press); "Lost At Sea," by Brandon French (section in anthology *The Classic American Novel & The Movies*); and *Star Without a Name*, by Mihail Sebastian, translated by Hermina Vlasopolos (play).

MINNIE ROGERS LITERARY AGENCY, Box 7895, Stockton CA 95207. (209)478-5671. Obtains new clients through referrals, queries, and announcements in *National Writer's Club Newsletter*. Will read unsolicited mss, queries and outlines. SASE. Charges $20 marketing fee. Agent receives 10% commission.
Will Handle: Textbooks (from basic to college); and nonfiction (how-to books are particularly welcome). No biographies, autobiographies, cookbooks or fiction.

SAN FRANCISCO LITERARY AGENCY, 899 E. Francisco Blvd. E., San Rafael CA 94901. (415)456-7140. Literary Agents: Tom Menkin, Bob Rickard. Obtains new clients through local screenwriting class, word of mouth, publicity releases and advertising in show business magazines. Will read unsolicited mss, queries and outlines at no charge. SASE. Agent receives 10% commission.
Will Handle: Motion pictures (prefer screenplays to story outline); stage plays (from local authors only); and TV scripts—"We prefer movies for TV and new dramatic and sit-com presentations to presenting scripts for established shows. Always state what kind of a presentation you are sending (e.g., 'TV presentation for a 30-minute sit-com series'). Never send us a new sit-com presentation with the pilot script written. We want the premise, the concept and merchandising ideas, if any; and a few story ideas. For dramatic series, a two-hour movie script (110-120 pages) is fine, if it is sent along with the dramatic series presentation."

JACK SCAGNETTI, 5258 Cartwright Ave., North Hollywood CA 91601. Owner: Jack Scagnetti. Obtains new clients through referrals from clients and friends. Represents only published writers of books; if screenplay, must have material previously sold or optioned. Made 4 sales in 1978, 12 in 1979. Will not read unsolicited mss, incomplete fiction or screenplay treatments by unsold writers. Will read unsolicited queries, outlines and screenplays. Fees: $25 for 100 pages; $50 up to 400 pages. SASE. Charges $100 marketing fee. Agent receives 10% commission.
Will Handle: Novels, nonfiction books; motion pictures; TV scripts; and syndicated material.

Criticism Services: Will critique fiction, nonfiction, screenplays and TV plays. Charges $50 minimum for outline with sample chapter of book or screenplay under 25,000 words (100 pages) $4 for each additional 2,500 words (10 pages).
Recent Sales: *Joy of Walking,* by Jack Scagnetti (Wilshire Books); and *Five Simple Steps to Perfect Golf,* by Count Yogi (Cornerstone Library).

JAMES SELIGMANN AGENCY, 280 Madison Ave., New York NY 10016. (212)679-3383. Contact: James F. Seligmann, Nina Seidenfeld. Obtains new clients through recommendation, personal contact, or solicitation. Will not read unsolicited mss; will read unsolicited queries and outlines. SASE. Agent receives 10% commission.
Will Handle: Novels and nonfiction books.
Recent Sales: *Sexual Shakedown: The Sexual Harassment of Women on the Job,* nonfiction by Lin Farley (McGraw-Hill); *Katherine,* historical novel by Antonia Van-Loon (St. Martin's); and *Kelly Among the Nightingales,* mystery novel by J.F. Burke (Dutton).

EVELYN SINGER LITERARY AGENCY, Box 1600, Briarcliff Manor NY 10510. Agent: Evelyn Singer. Estab. 1951. Obtains new clients through recommendations or if writer has earned $10,000 from freelance writing. Will not read unsolicited mss. SASE. Agent receives 10% commission.
Will Handle: Novels, nonfiction books and children's books (no picture books). "I handle all trade book material and arrange subsidiary and foreign rights. Please type (double-spaced) neatly—do not send hand-written queries. Give any literary background pertinent to your material."
Recent Sales: *Best Ride to New York,* novel by Leven (Harper & Row); *Dafydd,* novel by Stephens (Crown); and *Spirit Makes a Man,* nonfiction by Kittler (Doubleday).

ELYSE SOMMER, INC., Box E, 962 Allen Lane, Woodmere, Long Island NY 11598. (516)295-0046. President: Elyse Sommer. Estab. 1952. Obtains new clients through recommendations of authors, editors, and through executives and administrators of various organizations. Will consider carefully detailed queries, with author's background, SASE. Agent receives 10% commission; 15% on children's books.
Will Handle: "I specialize in self-help/improvement, lifestyle books; will handle some novels, but only of highly commercial nature. In response to many requests from authors interested in self-publishing, this agency has developed a consultation service for evaluating and helping to plan all phases of self-publishing projects. Letters and inquiries here should also include SASE."
Recent Sales: *How to Make Money in Antiques* (Houghton-Mifflin); *Time Management Workbook* (Chilton); *Playing Possum* (Universal); Good Time Fitness Series, Working & Living Together (Butterick); and *Women as Friends* (Simon & Schuster).

SOUTHWESTERN LITERARY AGENCY, INC., Box 60784, Oklahoma City OK 73146. (405)232-9887. Business Manager: Hez Downing. Obtains clients "from clients who advise their friends that Oklahoma has an agent." Will read unsolicited mss, queries and outlines at no charge. SASE.
Will Handle: Novels ("that we believe we can sell and on any subject").
Recent Sales: *Fate is the Gleaner* by Woody and Bille Bussey (Ashley Books, Inc.).

PHILIP G. SPITZER LITERARY AGENCY, 111-25 76th Ave., Forest Hills NY 11375. (212)263-7592. Estab. 1969. Obtains new clients through recommendations of editors and clients. "No previous publication necessary, but potential clients must be working on a book." Will read unsolicited queries and outlines. SASE. Made 25 sales in 1978; plans 25 in 1979. Agent receives 10% commission on domestic sales; 15% on British; 20% for foreign language sales.
Will Handle: Novels, nonfiction books, motion pictures. For clients also writing books, will handle magazine articles and fiction. Specializes in general nonfiction; particular interest in sports and politics. "Because I am a one-man office I can take on few new clients. I will often decline projects I think might be salable, and this should not be taken as a reflection on the author or his presentation."
Recent Sales: *The Execution,* novel by Robert Mayer (Viking Penguin); *Being Bernard Berenson,* biography by Meryle Secrest (Holt, Rinehart & Winston); and *The Hoffa Wars,* nonfiction by Dan E. Moldea (Paddington Press).

C.M. STEPHAN JR., 918 State St., Lancaster PA 17603. Estab. 1971. Obtains new clients through advertising and referral. "Writing must display potential or be competitive. Prefers to work with talented newcomers." Will read unsolicited mss for fee of $15 ($1/1000 words for book-length); will read unsolicited queries. SASE. Made 12 sales in 1978; plans 8-10 in 1979. Agent receives 10% commission.

Will Handle: Magazine articles (personality interviews only), magazine fiction, and novels. "Quality writing, self-discipline and the ability to compromise are desirable assets."

Criticism Services: "Agency charges fee to read/evaluate; no other charges are involved."

LARRY STERNIG LITERARY AGENCY, 742 Robertson St., Milwaukee WI 53213. (414)771-7677. Estab. 1953. "I am rarely able to take on new clients; too busy with the pros I now represent." Will not read unsolicited mss. Agent receives 10% commission.

Handles: Magazine articles and fiction, novels and nonfiction books.

Recent Sales: *The Wanting Factor*, fantasy novel by Gene DeWeese (Playboy Press); *The Young Empress*, historical novel by Anne Powers (Pinnacle Books); and *South Wind*, historical novel by Esther Neely (Tower Books).

ELLEN KELLY & ASSOCIATES, 3212 Honeywood Dr., Jacksonville, FL 32211. Estab. 1973. Commissions: 10% on American & Canadian sales, 15% on foreign. Reading fees (refunded from comissions) include evaluation and suggested changes to make ms more salable. SASE.

Will handle: "All writers willing to improve their skills."

GUNTHER STUHLMANN, AUTHOR'S REPRESENTATIVE, Box 276, Becket MA 01223. Contact: Ms. Barbara Ward. Obtains new clients through "personal recommendation from clients, publishers, editors." Will not read unsolicited mss. SASE for queries and outlines. Agent receives 10% commission on domestic and Canadian sales; 15% on British and 20% overseas.

Will Handle: Novels, textbooks and nonfiction books—and motion pictures, stage plays, TV scripts and syndicated material based on established properties.

Recent Sales: *Delta of Venus*, by Anais Nin (Harcourt Brace Jovanovich); *Decision Over Schweinfurt*, by T.M. Coffey (David McKay Co.); and *Khyber—The Story of an Imperial Migraine*, by C. Miller (Macmillan).

TEAL & WATT LITERARY AGENCY, 2036 Vista del Rosa, Fullerton CA 92631. Partners: Patricia Teal, Sandra Watt. Obtains new clients from recommendations of writers and creative writing groups. Estab. 1978. Represents 40 clients. "We will take new writers. They should have some background: writing classes, an academic degree, etc." Will read unsolicited queries, outlines and mss at no charge. SASE. Receives 10-20% commission.

Will Handle: Motion pictures, novels, TV and radio scripts, nonfiction books and syndicated material.

Recent Sales: *Sieglinde* (working title), by Regina Richards (Pinnacle Books).

TWIN PINES LITERARY AGENCY, 123-6 S. Highland Ave., Apt. 4, Ossining NY 10562. (914)941-0848. Executive Director: Martin Lewis. Estab. 1970. Obtains new clients through word-of-mouth. Will read unsolicited queries and outlines. SASE. Charges $75 marketing fee; $50 refundable if ms is not accepted. Agent receives 10% commission.

Will Handle: Magazine articles and fiction, novels, textbooks, nonfiction books, motion pictures, stage plays, and TV scripts. "Interested only in commercially oriented material."

Criticism Services: Will critique any material. Charges $75. Does editing, rewrite, ghost writing, typing and research projects.

AUSTIN WAHL AGENCY, LTD., 332 S. Michigan Ave., Suite 1823, Chicago IL 60604. (312)922-3329. Contact: Thomas Wahl. Estab. 1935. Obtains new clients through recommendation, referrals and solicitation. Will not read unsolicited mss; will read unsolicited queries and outlines. Agent receives 10% on domestic sales; 20% on foreign. "We want professional writers only."

Will Handle: "We do not limit ourselves into categories. We manage the careers of our clients in all areas of their artistry." Magazine articles and fiction, novels (especially those with motion picture potential), textbooks, nonfiction books, technical and reference works, motion pictures, stage plays and TV scripts.

JAMES A. WARREN ASSOCIATES, 7317 Haskell, Suite 108, Van Nuys CA 91406. (213)997-0956. Editors: Joseph August, Alice Hilton, Barbara Thorburn, Maxine Musgrave. Obtains new clients through *Writer's Market*, *LMP*, and word-of-mouth. Made 35 sales in 1978; plans 50-80 in 1979; "does not include articles and other short material." Query; will not read unsolicited mss, but does like to see work from new or undiscovered talent. Charges

reading fees "if not published by a recognized publisher in the last 15 years." SASE. Agent receives 15% on first sale, 10% thereafter.
Will Handle: "This agency handles only book-length fiction and nonfiction, screenplays, television scripts, playscripts, and certain magazine material. We do not handle poetry, inspirational writing, newspaper articles, syndications, short stories or short humor."
Recent Sales: *Kathleen*, by F. Rivers (Jove); *Bentley*, by Marguerite Kloepfer (Major Books); and *The Datax Conspiracy*, by James Galbraith (Douglas-West).
Criticism Services: Will critique book manuscripts ($1.25-1.50/1,000 words); children's and juvenile books ($25 and up); screenplays (query); television scripts ($50 for existing series; $75 for 90-minute specials); and magazine articles (query).

W B AGENCY, INC., merged with Curtis Brown, Ltd., 575 Madison Ave., New York NY 10022.

JOHN E. WEBER/VALERIE WEBER LITERARY AGENTS, Box 911, Lake Geneva WI 53147. Obtains new clients from referrals and queries. Plans 6-7 sales in 1979. Will not read unsolicited mss. Will read unsolicited queries and outlines. SASE. Agent receives 10% commission.
Will Handle: Novels, motion pictures, stage plays and nonfiction books.

WESTCAN LITERARY AGENCY, Box 3535, Station B, Winnipeg, Manitoba, Canada R2W 3R4. (204)956-1214, Telex 07-55459. President: Gary Nerman. Obtains new clients through local advertising and word-of-mouth. Will read unsolicited mss at no charge. SASE. Agent receives 10% commission on novels; 20% on short stories.
Will Handle: Magazine articles (Canadian content only); magazine fiction; novels; nonfiction books; and children's literature. No poetry.

WIESER & WIESER, INC., 60 E. 42nd St., New York NY 10017. (212)867-5454. Principals: George or Olga Wieser. Estab. 1975. Obtains new clients through referrals from publishers and clients. Writers must be published and must be working authors. Will read unsolicited mss for a fee of $100; will read unsolicited outlines. SASE. Made $200,000 worth of sales in 1978; plans $150,000 in 1979. Agent receives 10% commission; 15% for movie rights.
Will Handle: Novels, nonfiction books, motion pictures, and TV scripts.
Criticism Services: General fiction and nonfiction. Mss must be typed double-spaced, and securely bound. "We will evaluate and criticize a complete ms for $100, which will be deducted from our commission if we place the work."
Recent Sales: *Best Little Girl in the World*, fiction by Steve Levenkron (Contemporary Books, Inc. and Warner Books); *Classic Country Inns*, nonfiction by Peter Andrew (Knapp Press & Rinehart & Winston); and *Rainbow Man*, fiction by Ted Pollock (McGraw-Hill).

WILLIAMS/WESLEY/WINANT, 180 E. 79th St., New York NY 10021. President: William A. Winant III. Obtains new clients through listing in *Writer's Market*; *Writer's and Artist's Directory*, London, England; *LMP*; author's recommendations; newsletter to college and university English and film departments. Will read unsolicited mss, queries, outlines and screen treatments at no charge. SASE. Agent receives 10% commission on US sales; 20% foreign.
Will Handle: Novels (adaptable to film); motion pictures (scripts, screen treatments, shooting scripts); stage plays (musical comedies); radio scripts; and syndicated material (open end 15-, 30- and 60-minute dramas).

Contests and Awards

Contests offer a variety of benefits to writers. First, winning awards (particularly the prestigious ones) can increase writer recognition and reputation, making the writer more visible and more attractive to editors.

Second, winning contests and awards can be lucrative. Some contests offer nothing more than plaques or citations as prizes, but many offer substantial sums of money, which sometimes reach into four figures.

Unless otherwise noted, the contests and awards listed here are conducted annually. No contest that charges an entry fee is included. Contests for both published and unpublished work are listed. For update information on contests and awards, check The Markets department in *Writer's Digest* magazine.

Some of the listed contests and awards don't accept entries or nominations directly from writers, and are included because of their national or literary importance. If you feel your work meets the requirements of a competition that accepts entries from publishers only, suggest to your publisher that he enter your material.

Study the following listings carefully, and request any other information the contest director might have available. Always enclose SASE when requesting information, rules or entry blanks, or when conducting *any* correspondence. SASE with actual submissions, as well (though entries are usually aren't returned—see individual listings for each contest's policy).

A.I.P.–U.S. STEEL FOUNDATION SCIENCE WRITING AWARD, Public Information Division, American Institute of Physics, 335 E. 45th St., New York NY 10017. Awards $1,500, a certificate, and a symbolic device to stimulate and recognize distinguished writing that improves public understanding of physics and astronomy. Journalists must be professional writers whose work is aimed at the general public. Write for details and official entry form.

AAAS SOCIO-PSYCHOLOGICAL PRIZE, American Association for the Advancement of Science, 1776 Massachusetts Ave. NW., Washington DC 20036. (202)467-4470. Assistant to the Executive Officer: C. Borras. Estab. 1952. Offered annually.
Purpose: "To recognize a meritorious paper that furthers understanding of the psychological-social-cultural behavior of human beings. The prize is intended to encourage in social inquiry the development and application of the kind of methodology that has proved so fruitful in the natural sciences." Submissions must be unpublished, or published within the last 18 months. Awards $1,000. Deadline for entry: July 1. Rules and entry form for SASE.

AAAS-WESTINGHOUSE SCIENCE WRITING AWARDS, American Association for the Advancement of Science, 1515 Massachusetts Ave. NW., Washington DC 20005. (202)467-4483. Administrator: Grayce A. Finger. Estab. 1947. Annual.
Purpose: To encourage and recognize outstanding writing on the sciences and their engineering and technological application in newspapers and general circulation magazines. Submissions must be previously published between October 1-September 30. Awards $1,000 plus certificate.

AAFP JOURNALISM AWARDS, American Academy of Family Physicians, 1740 W. 92nd St., Kansas City MO 64114. (816)333-9700. Contact: Beth Robertson. Annual. Estab. 1969. Purpose: To recognize the most significant and informative reporting and writing on family practice and health care. Only published submissions are eligible. Award: First prize, $1,000 cash and certificate; second, $500 cash and certificate; and honorable mention. Deadline: Mid-November. Contest rules and entry form for SASE.

ACTF STUDENT PLAYWRITING AWARDS, American College Theatre Festival, John F. Kennedy Center for the Performing Arts, Washington DC 20566. (202)254-3437. The William Morris Agency awards a cash prize of $2,500 and an agency contract to the author of the best student written play produced as part of the annual American College Theatre Festival. Plays must have been produced at a college or university to be eligible.

HERBERT BAXTER ADAMS PRIZE, Committee Chairman, American Historical Association, 400 A St. SE, Washington DC 20003. Awards $300 annually for an author's first or second book in the field of European history.

ADIRONDACK-METROLAND, HARIAN FICTION AWARD, Box 189, Clifton Park NY 12065. Publisher: Harry Barba. Sponsor: Adirondack-Spa Writers & Educators Conference and Harian Creative Press. Annual. Estab. 1976.
Purpose: To encourage the writing and publishing of fiction strong in characterization and plot and written in a functionally suitable style; to encourage writing with a social context (without being "preachy"), quality stories that communicate a moral texture. Writing of resolution is preferred. Unpublished submissions only. Award: first prize, $300; each of two runners-up, $100. "If no manuscript is of sufficient merit, we reserve the right to defer awards. All submitted mss will be considered for publication." Contest rules and entry forms for SASE.

AMATEUR POETRY CONTEST, Poetry Press, Editor, Don Peek, Box 736, Pittsburg TX 75686. Prizes of $100, $50 and $25 will go to top 3 poems. Poems should be between 4 and 16 lines. SASE.

AMATEUR RADIO BITING BUG AWARD, Harter Rd., Morristown NJ 07960. (201)538-3081. Judge: Ray Collins, WA2GBC. Estab. 1976. Annual.
Purpose: For best article about amateur radio published in a US non-amateur radio publication. Articles are judged on how well they attract newcomers to amateur radio. Category I is for articles in national publication; category II is for regional or local publications. Submissions must be previously published. Award Category I: $200 and a plaque; Category II: $100 and a plaque. Deadline for entry: January 31. Rules and entry forms for SASE.

AMERICAN ACADEMY AND INSTITUTE OF ARTS AND LETTERS AWARDS, American Academy and Institute of Arts and Letters, 633 W. 155th St., New York NY 10012. Executive Director: Margaret M. Mills. Annual awards include the Richard and Hinda Rosenthal Award ($3,000 "for that American work of fiction published during the preceding twelve months which, though not a commercial success, is considerable literary achievement"); the Academy Institute Awards ($4,000 awarded to 8 nonmembers to further their creative work).

AMERICAN OSTEOPATHIC ASSOCIATION JOURNALISM AWARDS, 212 E. Ohio St., Chicago IL 60611. (312)944-2713. Director, PR: Robert A. Klobnak. Annual. Estab. 1956.
Purpose: To recognize the growing corps of journalists who report and interpret osteopathic medicine to the scientific community and the general public. Published submissions only. Award: $1,000 for first prize; two additional prizes of $500 each. Deadline: March 1 (for works published from January 1-December 31). Contest rules and entry forms available upon request.

AMERICAN PENAL PRESS CONTEST. Individual awards in writing categories and photography. Sweepstakes awards in 3 categories. "Only prison publications and individual entries published in prison publications are eligible." Sponsored by Southern Illinois University School of Journalism, Carbondale IL 62901. Entries considered between October 1 and September 30. Established in 1964. Write for rules and entry forms.

ANIMAL RIGHTS WRITING AWARD, Helen Jones, Chairman, Reviewing Committee, Society for Animal Rights, Inc., 421 S. State St., Clarks Summit PA 18411. Awards $300 to the author of an exceptionally meritorious published book or article in the field of animal rights.

ANNUAL NARRATIVE AND DRAMATIC POETRY COMPETITION, World Order of Narrative Poets, Box 412, Orinda CA 94563. President: Mr. Lynny L. Prout. Estab. 1975. Offered annually.
Purpose: "To develop a renewed interest in the writing of narrative and dramatic poetry, which has been sadly ignored for many years by clubs, editors and contests.
Requirements: Unpublished submissions only. Awards a minimum of $55 in cash divided in not less than 3 awards, and more if entries deserve same. Deadline: Beginning of September. Rules for SASE.

ANNUAL POETRY CONTEST, New Jersey Institute of Technology, 323 High St., Newark NJ 07102. (201)645-5218. Professor of English: Dr. H. A. Estrin. Estab. 1978. Offered annually. **Purpose:** To encourage young poets to write poetry and to have it eventually published. **Requirements:** Submissions must be unpublished work. Contest open to all elementary, junior high school, senior high school and college students. Winners poetry published in *The Best Student Poetry in New Jersey.* SASE for rules and forms. Deadline: Mid-March.

ASCAP-DEEMS TAYLOR AWARDS, American Society of Composers, Authors And Publishers, 1 Lincoln Plaza, New York NY 10023. (212)595-3050. Director of Public Relations: Karen Sherry. Estab. 1967. Annual.
Purpose: For nonfiction books or articles about music and/or its creators: and to encourage, recognize and reward excellence in nonfiction writing about music and/or its creators. Submissions must be published during the previous year. Awards four $500 prizes for books, four $500 prizes for articles, and plaque to publishers. Deadline for entry: March 1. Submit 4 copies of book and/or articles.

ATLANTIC FIRSTS, 8 Arlington St., Boston MA 02116. (617)536-9500. Continuously. Purpose: First major publication of fiction by an unestablished author. Submissions must be unpublished. Award: Professional fees are paid for the stories, which are published in *The Atlantic.* Prizes of $750 and $250 are awarded for the most distinguished contributions of the preceding period. Rules available for SASE.

AVIATION/SPACE WRITERS ASSOCIATION JOURNALISM AWARDS, Aviation/Space Writers Association, Cliffwood Rd., Chester NJ 07930. Awards $100 and engraved scroll for writing on aviation and space, in 9 categories: newspapers over 200,000 circulation, newspapers under 200,000 circulation, magazines (special interest); magazines (general interest); television (news documentary); radio (news documentary); books (general nonfiction); books (technical/training); still photography. Entries accepted up to January 5 each year for material published or aired previous calendar year. For entry guideline contact William F. Kaiser, Executive Secretary.

BANCROFT PRIZES, Committee, 202 Low, Columbia University, New York NY 10027. Awards 2 prizes of $4,000 for books in American history (including biography) and diplomacy.

GEORGE LOUIS BEER PRIZE, Committee Chairman, American Historical Association, 400 A St. SE, Washington DC 20003. Awards $300 for the best first or second book by a young scholar in the field of European international history since 1895.

MIKE BERGER AWARD, Award Committee, Columbia University, Morningside Hts., New York NY 10027. The award, given to writers whose work best reflects the style of the late Meyer Berger, carries a cash prize of $1,500.

BEST SPORT STORIES AWARDS, 1315 Westport Lane, Sarasota FL 33580. Co-Editor: Edward Ehre. Sponsor: E.P. Dutton & Co., Publisher. Annual. Estab. 1944. Purpose: for best magazine sport story, best coverage sport story and best feature sport story. Published submissions only. Award: $250 for each category. Deadline: December 15. Contest rules and entry forms for SASE.

ALBERT J. BEVERIDGE AWARD, Committee Chairman, American Historical Association, 400 A St. SE, Washington DC 20003. Awards $1,000 for the best book published in English on American history of the US, Canada, and Latin America.

BITTERROOT MAGAZINE POETRY CONTEST. Write Menke Katz, Editor-in-Chief, *Bitterroot,* Blythebourne Station, Box 51, Brooklyn NY 11219. Awards cash prizes for poems of any genre. Annual. Deadline for entry: December 31. "Please send letter size #10 envelope only."

IRMA SIMONTON BLACK AWARD, 610 W. 112th St., New York NY 10025. Contact: Book Award Committee, Publications Division. Sponsor: Bank Street College of Education. Annual. Estab. 1972. Purpose: for excellence of text and graphics in a book for young children published during the preceding calendar year. Published submission only. Award: author and illustrator receive a scroll; winning entry carries an award seal designed by Maurice Sendak. Deadline: January 1 (for works published during the preceding year).

HOWARD W. BLAKESLEE AWARDS, Chairman, Managing Committee, American Heart

Association, 7320 Greenville Ave., Dallas TX 75231. Awards $500 honorarium and a citation to each winning entry, which may be a single article, broadcast, film, or book; a series; or no more than five unrelated pieces. Entries will be judged on the basis of their accuracy and significance, and on the skill and originality with which knowledge concerning the heart and circulatory system and advances in research or in the treatment, care and prevention of cardiovascular disease are translated for the public. Send for official entry blank and more details.

BOLLINGEN PRIZE IN POETRY OF THE YALE UNIVERSITY LIBRARY, Yale University Library, New Haven CT 06520. (203)436-0236. Secretary, Yale Administrative Committee: Donald Gallup. Estab. 1950. Biennial. Awards $5,000 to an American poet whose published book of poetry represents the highest achievement in the field of American poetry.

BOSTON GLOBE-HORN BOOK AWARDS, Stephie Loer, Children's Book Editor, *The Boston Globe*, Boston MA 02107. Awards $200 to a book with outstanding text, $200 to a book with outstanding illustrations and $200 to a book of nonfiction. Up to 3 honor books in each category may be designated by the judges. No textbooks.

BOWLING WRITING COMPETITION, American Bowling Congress, Public Relations, 5301 S. 76th St., Greendale WI 53129. $1,800 in gift certificate prizes divided equally between four divisions—two each in Feature and Editorial. Categories separated by daily newspaper/national publication entrants and bowling publication entrants. Top prize $200 in four divisions for published bowling stories. First through fifth place in each division.

EMIL BROWN FUND PREVENTIVE LAW PRIZE AWARDS, Louis M. Brown, Administrator, University of Southern California Law Center, Los Angeles CA 90007. Awards $1,000 for a praiseworthy leading article or book, and $500 for student work in the field of preventive law published in a law review, bar journal or other professional publication.

RAY BRUNER SCIENCE WRITING FELLOWSHIP, American Public Health Association, 1015 15th St. NW, Washington DC 20005. Managing Editor: Doyne Bailey. Estab. 1971. Offered annually.
Purpose: To promote and reward excellence in the science writing field. It is awarded to an outstanding young health/science/medical journalist with less than two years' fulltime reporting experience in the health field and less than five years experience as a journalist. **Requirements:** Submissions must have been published in the preceding 2 years. Awards travel, lodging and expenses to cover the APHA Annual Meeting, an engraved plaque, and a portable typewriter. Deadline: Mid-September. Rules for SASE.

BULTMAN AWARD, Chairman, Department of Drama, Loyola University, New Orleans LA 70118. Awards $100 for original, unpublished and professionally unproduced plays under one hour in length, written by college students and recommended by teacher of drama or creative writing. Mss must be securely bound and accompanied by SASE, or they will not be returned. Deadline: December 1, annually.

CALIFORNIA LITERATURE MEDAL AWARDS CONTEST, Commonwealth Club of California, 681 Market St., San Francisco CA 94105. (415)362-4903. Executive Director: Michael J. Brassington. Estab. 1931. Offered annually.
Purpose: Awards made to California authors for the finest literature in the following caterogies: fiction, nonfiction, juvenile (young adult), poetry, first, or Californiana (history, society, culture, etc.). Submissions must have been published during the year in which the book is submitted. Awards, gold and silver medals. Entry deadline: January 31. Rules and entry form for SASE.

CANADIAN LIBRARY ASSOCIATION BOOK OF THE YEAR FOR CHILDREN AWARD, Sponsored by the Canadian Library Association, 151 Sparks St., Ottawa, Ontario, Canada K1P 5E3. "The book must have been published in Canada in the previous year and written by a Canadian citizen or on a Canadian subject. Any such work is eligible regardless of format." Deadline: Febuary 1.

CAROLINA QUARTERLY FICTION-POETRY CONTEST, Dorothy Hill, Editor, Greenlaw Hall 066-A, University of North Carolina, Chapel Hill NC 27514. Fiction: Awards $200 first prize, $125 second and $75 third for unpublished manuscripts up to 6,000 words. Poetry: $150 for first, $100 second and $50 third; no limit to length. Entrant may not have published a booklength ms in field of entry. Ms must be postmarked no earlier than September 15th and no later than December 1st. Indicate Fiction or Poetry clearly on outside of envelope.

RUSSELL L. CECIL ARTHRITIS WRITING AWARDS, Arthritis Foundation, 3400 Peachtree Rd. NE, Atlanta GA 30326. (404)266-0795. Communications Specialist: Roy Scott. Estab. 1956. Annual.
Purpose: To recognize and encourage the writing of news stories, articles and radio/TV scripts on the subject of Arthritis. Awards presented in 4 categories: newspaper, magazine, radio and TV. Submissions must be previously published between January 1 and December 31. Deadline for entry January 31. Rules and entry forms for SASE.

CHILDREN'S BOOK AWARD, Child Study Children's Book Committee, Bank Street College, 610 W. 112th St., New York NY 10025. Given to a book for children or young people that deals realistically with problems in their world. The book, published in the past calendar year, must offer an honest and courageous treatment of its theme.

CHILDREN'S SCIENCE BOOK AWARDS, 2 E. 63rd St., New York NY 10021. (212)838-0230. Public Relations Director: Ann E. Collins. Sponsor: The New York Academy of Sciences. Annual. Estab. 1971. Purpose: for the best general or trade books on science for children.
Categories: Younger Category books for children under 7 years; and Older Category books for children between 7 and 14 years. Published submissions only. Award: $250 for each category. Deadline: November 30 (for works published from December 1 to November 30 each year). Contest rules and entry forms for SASE.

CHRISTOPHER AWARDS, 12 E. 48th St., New York NY 10017. Awards Co-ordinator: Peggy Flanagan. Awards bronze medallions for motion pictures (producer, director, writer), network television (producer, director, writer), and books (author, illustrator) to recognize individuals who have used their talents constructively, in the hope that they, and others, will continue to produce high quality works that reflect sound values.

COLLEGIATE POETRY CONTEST, *The Lyric,* 307 Dunton Dr. SW, Blacksburg VA 24060. Editor: Leslie Mellichamp. Annual. Purpose: for the best original and unpublished poem of 32 lines or less, written in traditional form preferably with regular sconsion and rhyme, by US or Canadian undergraduates. Award: 1st prize, $200; 2nd prize, $100; 3rd prize, $50; and a number of honorable mentions at $25 each. Also $100 to the library of the college in which the winner of the first prize is enrolled, provided that library is on the list of subscribers to *The Lyric.* Deadline: June 1. Contest rules and entry forms for SASE.

CONSERVATION NEWS AWARD, Soil Conservation Society of America, 7515 NE Ankeny Rd., Ankeny IA 50021. Awards a pewter plate mounted on a walnut plaque along with an honorarium (amount varies). Usually about $200. Award is given in recognition of outstanding efforts in communicating the story of natural resource conservation through the written word in newspapers or magazines. Entries must be postmarked by no later than Dec. 31. SASE with correspondence.

ALBERT B. COREY PRIZE IN CANADIAN-AMERICAN RELATIONS, Office of the Executive Secretary, American Historical Association, 400 A St. SE, Washington DC 20003. The Canadian Historical Association and American Historical Association jointly award $2,000 for the best book on the history of Canadian-United States relations, or on the history of both countries.

HAROLD C. CRAIN AWARD IN PLAYWRITING, Department of Theatre Arts, San Jose State University, San Jose CA 95192. (408)277-2763. Director of Theater: Howard Burman. Estab. 1976. Offered annually.
Purpose: For original full-length plays of substance regardless of style, subject, and theme. Awards $500 and production of play. Submit entries from September 1 to November 15. Entry form for SASE.

DESIGN FOR LIVING CONTEST, 14531 Stephen St., Nokesville VA 22123. (703)791-3672. Charles A. Mills, Awards Chairman. Sponsor: The March Society. Annual. Estab. 1974. Purpose: awarded to the author of an original essay submitted in response to a social/political question formulated annually by the awards committee. Unpublished submissions only.

Award: 1st prize $100; 2nd prize $25; five honorable mentions, $5 each. Deadline for entry: June 15th. Contest rules and entry forms for SASE.

THE DEVINS AWARD, University of Missouri Press, Columbia MO 65211. For poetry. Write for submission details.

THE DISCOVERY/THE NATION 1980, The Poetry Center, 92nd Street YM-YWHA, 1395 Lexington Ave., New York NY 10028. (212)427-6000, ext. 176. Assistant to the Director: Mary Lisa Burns. Estab. 1975. Offered annually.
Requirements: Open to poets whose work has not yet been published in book form. Book form includes chapbooks and self-published books. Accepts published and unpublished poetry. Submit 10 poems of not more than 500 lines of original poetry in English. Awards: Each of the four winners will receive an honorarium of $50 and will be invited to read at The Poetry Center. Each winner will have one poem, which has never been published, printed in *The Nation* magazine. Deadline for entry: Usually in February, but the exact date varies. SASE for rules.

DOG WRITERS' ASSOCIATION OF AMERICA ANNUAL WRITING COMPETITION, Awards given for excellence in writing about dogs in newspapers, magazines, books, club publications. Separate categories for juniors. Open to all. Details from Sara Futh, Secretary, Kinney Hill Rd., Washington Depot CT 06794. (203)868-2863.

DRAPA (DOROTHY ROSENBERG ANNUAL POETRY AWARD), Religious Arts Guild, affiliate of Unitarian Universalist Association, 25 Beacon, Boston MA 02108. (617)742-2100. Executive Secretary: Barbara M. Hutchins. Estab. 1970. Offered annually.
Purpose: Best poem dealing with "the human spirit."
Requirements: Unpublished submissions only. Deadline: End of March. Rules for SASE.

THE DUBUQUE FINE ARTS SOCIETY NATIONAL ONE-ACT PLAYWRITING CONTEST, 422 Loras Blvd., Dubuque IA 52001. Chairman: Greg Maulson.
Purpose: For the best submitted one-act plays. Entries must be previously unproduced. Awards $100, $75 and $50. Winning plays are performed in a reader's theater format. Entry deadline: December 1. Length: 1 hour reading time. Contest rules and entry form for SASE.

JOHN H. DUNNING PRIZE IN AMERICAN HISTORY, Committee Chairman, American Historical Association, 400 A St. SE, Washington DC 20003. Awards $300 in even-numbered years for an outstanding monograph in manuscript or in print on any subject relating to American history.

DUTTON ANIMAL BOOK AWARD, E. P. Dutton, 2 Park Ave., New York NY 10016. Offers a guaranteed minimum $15,000, as an advance against earnings, for an original book-length manuscript concerning a living creature (only Man and plants are excluded as subjects); fiction or nonfiction. Write for details.

EDUCATION WRITERS AWARD, Ellen A. Morgenstern, Director of Communications, American Association of University Professors, Suite 500, 1 Dupont Circle, Washington DC 20036. Awards a citation to recognize outstanding interpretive reporting of issues in higher education, through newspapers, magazines, radio, television and films. Write for entry details. SASE.

EDUCATOR'S AWARD, Miss LeOra L. Held, Executive Secretary, Delta Kappa Gamma Society International, Box 1589, Austin TX 78767. Awards $1,000 to recognize women and their contribution to education which may influence future directions in the profession. Previously published books may be in the fields of research, philosophy, or any other area of learning which is stimulating and creative. "The book submitted must have been published during the year the award is granted." Deadline: February 1.

EPILEPSY FOUNDATION OF AMERICA JOURNALISM AWARD, 1828 L St. NW, Suite 406, Washington DC 20036. (202)293-2930. Editor, National Spokesman: Ann Scherer. Annual. Estab. 1972. Purpose: for articles which generate better understanding of epilepsy and those who suffer from it. Published submissions only. Award: $500 plus plaque. Deadline: 2nd week in December (for works published from December 1 to November 30). Contest rules and entry forms for SASE.

ERAS REVIEW ART & POETRY CONTEST, Earth Rare Art Society, 511-H Cherrycrest Lane, Charlotte NC 28210. Contest Coordinator: Lori Seifert. Estab. 1975.
Purpose: Awards $25 per issue of *ERAS Review* magazine in the following categories: 1) unpublished poems not to exceed 60 lines; 2) graphics; 3) plays. Entries accepted on continuing basis.

THE EXPLICATOR LITERARY FOUNDATION, INC., 3241 Archdale Rd., Richmond VA 23235. (804)272-6890. Treasurer: J.E. Whitesell. Annual. Estab. 1956. Purpose: encouragement of *explication de texte* in books. Published submissions only. Award: $300 and bronze plaque. Deadline: February 1. Contest rules and entry forms for SASE.

JOHN K. FAIRBANK PRIZE IN EAST ASIAN HISTORY, Committee Chairman, American Historical Association, 400 A St. SE, Washington DC 20003. Awards $300 in odd-numbered years for an outstanding book on the history of China proper, Vietnam, Chinese Central Asia, Manchuria, Mongolia, Korea or Japan, since 1800.

THE FORUM AWARD, Atomic Industrial Forum, Inc., 7101 Wisconsin Ave., Washington DC 20014. Mary Ellen Warren, Contest Coordinator. Annually. Estab. 1967. Conducted to encourage factual news coverage of all aspects of peaceful nuclear applications and to honor significant contributions by the print and electronic news media to public understanding of peaceful uses of nuclear energy. Total of $1,000 in prize money is available in each category (print media and electronic media). Nominees must be professional members of the print or electronic media. Entry must have been available to and intended for the general public.

FREEDOMS FOUNDATION AT VALLEY FORGE AWARDS, Awards Administration, Freedoms Foundation at Valley Forge, Valley Forge PA 19481. Awards honor medal and honor certificates for the most outstanding individual contribution supporting human dignity and American freedom principles in fields of journalism, television and radio. Write for further details.

FRENCH COLONIAL HISTORICAL SOCIETY BOOK AWARD, 611 Ryan Plaza Dr., suite 119, Arlington TX 76011. (817)265-7143. Chairman: Leon B. Blair, Ph.D. Estab. 1974. Offered annually.
Purpose: "For the best book published during the current year, in English or French, on aspects of French colonial history." Awards $500. Entry deadline: December 31. "Publishers nominate and furnish 3 copies to the chairman of the book committee, who in turn submits them to the jury. Writers are welcome to correspond."

FRIENDS OF AMERICAN WRITERS JUVENILE BOOK AWARDS, Chairman for 1978-81: Mrs. John T. Loughlin, 412 N. Prospect, Park Ridge IL 60068. Awards for a book published during current year, with a Midwestern locale or written by a native or resident author of the Midwest. Up to 2 other awards to runners up and on some occasions an award to illustrator. Books submitted by publishers only.

THE GALILEO PRIZE, *Galileo* magazine, 339 Newbury St., Boston MA 02115. Contact: Charles C. Ryan, Editor. Offered annually.
Purpose: "By offering cash prices in addition to our regular payments, we hope to encourage science fiction writers, both new and established, to submit shorter work to *Galileo*. Any previously unpublished science fiction between 2,000 and 5,000 words that is received at *Galileo* is considered for both publication in the magazine and the Galileo Prize. Selection is made in the spring of each year among works received in the previous calendar year. The length requirement was changed at the end of 1978 due to a lack of aceptable entries under the old limit, so the 1978 and 1979 submissions will be judged together in 1980. For 1980 submissions, the competition returns to the one-year rule." Awards $500, $350 and $100.

JOHN GASSNER MEMORIAL PLAYWRITING AWARD, The New England Theatre Conference, Inc., 50 Exchange St., Waltham MA 02154. (617)893-3120. Executive Secretary: Marie L. Philips. Estab. 1967. Offered annually.
Purpose: "To encourage writing and production of new one-act plays." Submissions must be previously unpublished. Awards $200 and $100; "occasionally, one or more honorable mentions." Prize-winning plays are given a script-in-hand performance by selected New England theater groups. Entry deadline: April 15. Contest rules and entry form for SASE.

CHRISTIAN GAUSS AWARD, Phi Beta Kappa, 1811 Q St. NW, Washington DC 20009.

Awards $2,500 for a book of literary criticism or scholarship published in the United States. Books submitted by publishers only.

GAVEL AWARDS, 77 S. Wacker Dr., 6th Floor, Chicago IL 60606. (312)621-9248. Staff Director, Special Events: Dean Tyler Jenks. Sponsor: American Bar Association. Annual. Estab. 1958. Purpose: for outstanding public service by newspaper, television, radio, magazines, motion pictures, theatrical producers, book publishers, wire services and news syndicates in increasing public understanding of the American system of law and justice. Published submissions only. Award: Silver Gavel and certificate of merit. Deadline: for books, Feb. 1; all others, March 1 (for works published from January 1 to December 31, 1979). Contest rules and entry forms for SASE.

GLCA NEW WRITERS AWARDS IN POETRY AND FICTION, Great Lakes Colleges Association, Wabash College, Crawfordsville IN 47933. (317)362-1400, ext. 232. Director: Donald Baker. Estab. 1968. Offered annually.
Purpose: "Competition is for first books in poetry or fiction (either novel or volume of short fiction)." Submissions must have been published the previous year or the current spring season. Awards "recognition, plus invited tour of up to 12 Great Lakes Colleges in Ohio, Indiana and Michigan, with appropriate honoraria from the schools." Entry deadline: February 28. "It should be noted that only publishers may submit entries."

GOETHE HOUSE-P.E.N. TRANSLATION PRIZE, P.E.N. American Center, 47 5th Ave., New York NY 10003. (212)255-1577. Awards $500 for the best translation from the German language into English, published during the calendar year under review.

GREAT AMERICAN PLAY CONTEST, Actors Theatre of Louisville, 316 W. Main St., Louisville KY 40202. (502)584-1265. Literary Manager: ElizaBeth King. Estab. 1976. Offered annually.
Purpose: To promote excellence in playwriting.
Requirements: Those scripts previously submitted to the contest and those having a previous Equity production are ineligible. Equity-waiver or showcase production in permitted. Scripts with 15 or fewer characters preferred. Contestants must be US citizens. Awards $3,000 singly or divided between 2 co-winners. Deadline: March 15th. Contest rules and entry forms for SASE.

GREAT RIVER REVIEW AWARD FOR FICTION, Great River Review, Inc., 211 W. 7th Ave., Winona MN 55987. (507)454-1212. Editor: Emilio De Grazia. Estab. 1978. Offered biennially.
Purpose: "To stimulate the production of quality short fiction."
Requirements: Must be resident of Minnesota, Iowa, Wisconsin, South Dakota or North Dakota. Unpublished work only. Awards $200 to the author of the best piece of fiction published in each issue of *Great River Review*. No entry fee.

GUIDEPOSTS MAGAZINE YOUTH WRITING CONTEST, Guideposts Associates, Inc., 747 3rd Ave., New York NY 10017. Editorial Assistant: Nancy C. Galya. Estab. 1964. Annual.
Purpose: "For high school juniors or seniors or students in equivalent grades overseas. For the best first-person story telling about a true memorable or moving experience they have had." Submissions should be unpublished. Awards: 1st prize, $4,000 scholarship; 2nd prize, $3,500 scholarship; 3rd prize, $3,000 scholarship; 4th prize, $2,500 scholarship; 5th prize, $2,000 scholarship; and 6th through 10th, $1,000 scholarship. Deadline for entry: November 25. Rules and entry forms for SASE.

GUSTO & DRIFTWOOD EAST POETRY CONTEST, Gusto Press, 2960 Philip Ave., Bronx NY 10465. Editor/Publisher: M. Karl Kulikowski. Estab. 1978. Offered annually.
Purpose: To publish a 40-page book of poetry for each 1st prize winner of best poem published in *Gusto* and *Driftwood East*. Categories are: a poem 70 lines or under and a haiku/senryu contest in *Gusto*; and a poem 20 lines or under in *Driftwood East*.
Requirements: Poetry unpublished elsewhere. Awards three 40 page books of poetry, 2 prizes of $15 each, 3rd prize is $10, and 5 honorable mentions and awards in all 3 categories. Rules for SASE.

JOHN HANCOCK AWARDS FOR EXCELLENCE IN BUSINESS AND FINANCIAL JOURNALISM, John Hancock Mutual Life Insurance Co., T-54 John Hancock Pl. Box 111,

Boston MA 02117. (617)421-2270. Special Projects Administrator: Miss Jean Canton. Estab. 1967. Annual.

Purpose: "To foster increased public knowledge of, and interest in, business and finance; to recognize editorial contributions to a better understanding of personal money management; to clarify the significance of political and social developments as they relate to the nation's economy; and to stimulate discussion and thought by bringing together, in an academic environment, newsmakers, reporters, faculty and students." Categories: syndicated and news service writers; writers for national magazines of general interest; writers for financial-business newspapers and magazines; writers for newspapers with circulation above 300,000; writers of newspapers with circulation 100,000 to 300,000; and writers for newspapers with circulation under 100,000. Submissions must be previously published from January 1 to December 31. Award $2,000 plus AFE medallion and expenses to presentations program. Deadline: January 31. Rules and entry forms for SASE.

CLARENCE H. HARING PRIZE, Committee Chairman, American Historical Association, 400 A St. SE, Washington DC 20003. Awards $500 every five years to the Latin American who, in the opinion of the committee, has published the most outstanding book on Latin-American history during the preceding 5 years. Next awarded in 1981.

HEALTH JOURNALISM AWARD, American Chiropractic Association, 2200 Grand Ave., Des Moines IA 50312. (515)243-1121. Executive Secretary/Public Affairs: Joann Ozimek. Estab. 1976. Offered annually.

Purpose: "To motivate the public to practice good health habits and keep it informed of health care advancements; to honor journalists who write and produce superior material; and to stimulate journalists to be free-thinkers and to encourage them to increase the depth and scope of their health writing."

Requirements: Works published or produced between January 1 and December 31 of each year are eligible for entry in that year's competition for categories of newspapers; consumer magazines; television; radio; and trade, professional or special interest publications and audiovisuals. Awards $200 to winner in each category and the ACA Distinguished Journalism Award. Special recognition plaques to runners-up. Deadline: Beginning of March.

ERNEST HEMINGWAY FOUNDATION AWARD, P.E.N. American Center, 47 5th Ave., New York NY 10003. Awards $6,000 for the best first-published book of fiction, either novel or short story collection, in the English language by an American author, published by an established publishing house. Children's books are not eligible. Deadline: December 31.

SIDNEY HILLMAN PRIZE AWARD, Sidney Hillman Foundation, Inc., 15 Union Square, New York NY 10003. Awards $750 annually for outstanding published contributions in nonfiction, radio and television dealing with themes relating to the ideals which Sidney Hillman held throughout his life. Such themes would include the protection of individual civil liberties, improved race relations, strengthened labor movement, advancement of social welfare, economic security, greater world understanding and related problems. Deadline: January 15.

HAROLD HIRSCH PERPETUAL TROPHY FOR OUTSTANDING SKI WRITING, United States Ski Association, 1726 Champa St., Suite 300, Denver CO 80202. (303)825-9183. Executive Office Manager: Evelyn R. Masbruch. Estab. 1963. Offered annually.

Purpose: To promote outstanding ski writing. Entrants are judged on editorial effect of the material on the reading public, initiative by the writer in gathering material, excellence in writing, technical knowledge and variety of coverage.

Requirements: Open to all qualified ski writers. Awards a silver-plated antique typewriter and permanent individual memento. Deadline: Late April. Rules for SASE.

HOUGHTON MIFFLIN LITERARY FELLOWSHIP, Houghton Mifflin Co., 2 Park St., Boston MA 02107. Awards $2,500 grant and $7,500 as an advance against royalties to help authors complete projects of outstanding literary merit. Candidates should submit at least 50 pages of the actual project (fiction or nonfiction), an informal description of its theme and intention, and a brief biography. A finished ms, as well as works in progress will be eligible for an award.

THE HUMANITAS PRIZE, Executive Director, The Human Family Institute, Box 861, Pacific Palisades CA 90272. (213)454-8769. Awards $10,000 for the 30-minute teleplay, $15,000 for the 60-minute teleplay, and $25,000 for the teleplay of 90-minutes or longer previously produced on national network commercial television, aired during prime time hours. "To promote a greater appreciation of the dignity of the human person, to deepen the human family's understanding of themselves, of their relationship with the human community, and to their Creator, to aid individuals in their search for meaning, freedom and love; to liberate, enrich and unify the human family. Submission should be made by someone other than the writer of the produced play (for example, the program producer)." Write for details and entry form.

INGAA-UNIVERSITY OF MISSOURI BUSINESS JOURNALISM AWARDS, University University of Missouri, School of Journalism, 100 Neff Hall, Columbia MO 65211. (314)882-7862. Director: William McPhatter. Estab. 1965. Offered annually.
Purpose: "To honor excellence in business and economics reporting."
Requirements: Topic of previously published work must concern some aspect of business or business government relationship and be of broad reader interest in following categories: I, staff member or team of a daily or weekly newspaper—circulation less than 100,000; II, same as I with circulation of more than 100,000, or syndicated columnist, wire service member or newspaper distributed magazine; III, staff member or team or outside contributor to a general circulation magazine; IV, staff member or team or outside contributor to a publication with either controlled or paid circulation. Awards $1,000 and a silver trophy for winners in each of four; $150 and a plaque for runners-up in each category; plaque for each winning publication. Deadline: Entries must be postmarked by June 10. Rules for SASE.

INTERNATIONAL READING ASSOCIATION PRINT MEDIA AWARD, Public Information Office, International Reading Association, 800 Barksdale Rd., Box 8139, Newark DE 19711. Entries must focus on the field of reading and are judged on the basis of journalistic quality which includes clear and imaginative writing that lifts the material out of the routine category. In-depth studies of reading activities, accounts of outstanding reading practices, relevant reading research reportage, and/or day-to-day coverage of reading programs in the community. Sponsored by the International Reading Association. Awards $500. Deadline: January 15. Estab. in 1960.

JOSEPH HENRY JACKSON/JAMES D. PHELAN LITERARY AWARD, 425 California St., Suite 1602, San Francisco CA 94104. (415)982-1210. Assistant Coordinator: Susan Kelly. Sponsor: The San Francisco Foundation. Annual. Estab. 1935 (Phelan contest); 1957 (Jackson contest). "The two competitions were combined in 1957 and are now administered simultaneously. One can compete for one or both depending on eligibility."
Purpose: To award the author of an unpublished, partly completed book-length work of fiction, nonfictional prose, short story or poetry (Jackson); to award the author of an unpublished, incomplete work of fiction, nonfiction prose, short story, poetry or drama (Phelan). Awards: Both $2,000. Deadline: January 15. Contest rules and entry forms can be obtained by calling the above number.

JACKSONVILLE UNIVERSITY PLAYWRITING CONTEST, Davis Sikes, Director, College of Fine Arts, Jacksonville University, Jacksonville FL 32211. (904)744-3950. Awards prizes up to $5,000 and premiere production of previously unproduced plays (original one-act and full-length). Deadline: January 1. Write for contest rules. SASE.

JEWISH BOOK COUNCIL, FRANK & ETHEL S. COHEN AWARD FOR A BOOK OF JEWISH THOUGHT, 15 E. 26th St., New York NY 10010. Awards $500 and a citation to the author of a published book dealing with some aspect of Jewish thought, past or present, that combines knowledge, clarity of thought and literary merit.

JEWISH BOOK COUNCIL, LEON JOLSON AWARD FOR A BOOK ON THE HOLOCAUST, 15 E. 26th St., New York NY 10010. Awards $500 and a citation to the author of a published nonfiction book dealing with some aspects of the Nazi holocaust period. Books published in English, Yiddish and Hebrew are acceptable.

JEWISH BOOK COUNCIL, HARRY & FLORENCE KOVNER AWARD FOR POETRY, 15 E. 26th St., New York NY 10010. Awards $500 and a citation to the author of a book of poetry of Jewish interest. Books published in English, Yiddish and Hebrew are acceptable.

JEWISH BOOK COUNCIL, CHARLES & BERTIE G. SCHWARTZ JUVENILE AWARD, 15 E. 26th St., New York NY 10010. Awards $500 and a citation to the author of a published Jewish juvenile book.

JEWISH BOOK COUNCIL, WILLIAM AND JANICE EPSTEIN FICTION AWARD, 15 E. 26th St., New York NY 10010. Awards $500 and a citation to the author of a published book of fiction of Jewish interest, either a novel or a collection of short stories, that combines high literary merit with an affirmative expression of Jewish values.

ANSON JONES AWARD, c/o Texas Medical Association, 1801 N. Lamar Blvd., Austin TX 78701. (512)477-6704. $250 cash and engraved plaque in each of eight categories. For excellence in communicating health information to the public through Texas newspapers, magazines, radio and television. Entries are considered between December 1 and November 30. Estab. 1956. Rules and entry forms available from the Communication Department at TMA (address above). Deadline: December 10 of award year.

THE JANET HEIDINGER KAFKA PRIZE, English Department/Writers Workshop, University of Rochester, Rochester NY 14627. (716)275-2340. Dean, University College: Robert G. Koch. Estab. 1975. Offered annually.
Purpose: "The prize shall be awarded to a woman citizen of the US who has written the best book-length published work of prose fiction, whether novel, short stories, or experimental writing. Works primarily written for children and vanity house publications will not be considered." Submissions from publishers must have been published within the previous 12 months; collections of short stories must have been assembled for the first time, or at least 33% must be previously unpublished. Entry deadline: October 31. Contest rules and entry form for SASE.

THE ROBERT F. KENNEDY JOURNALISM AWARDS, Ruth Darmstadter, 1035 30th St. NW, Washington DC 20007. (202)338-7444. The awards ($1,000 first prize in each category, possible additional grand prize of $2,000, honorable mentions and citations) honor journalists, broadcasters and photographers whose work (published or broadcast during 1979) has illuminated the problems of the disadvantaged in the United States. Write in fall for complete details and entry form for the current annual competition.

HAROLD MORTON LANDON TRANSLATION AWARD, The Academy of American Poets, 1078 Madison Ave., New York NY 10028. Awards $1,000 biennially to an American poet for a published translation of poetry from any language into English. Translation may be a book-length poem, collection of poems, or a verse drama translated into verse. Send two copies of published books (no manuscripts) to the academy.

NORMAN LEAR AWARD FOR ACHIEVEMENT IN COMEDY PLAYWRITING, Executive Producer, American College Theatre Festival, John F. Kennedy Center for the Performing Arts, Washington DC 20566. (202)254-3437. Awards $2,800 and a professional assignment to write a complete teleplay for one of the series produced by Norman Lear, a trip to Los Angeles with all expenses paid to participate in story conferences and membership in the Writers Guild of America with the Writers Guild Foundation paying the usual initiation fee of $200, for the best student comedy play produced for the annual American College Theatre Festival.

LEVI'S/I.R.W.A. RODEO PRESS CONTEST, Levi Strauss & Co., in cooperation with the International Rodeo Writers Association, 2 Embarcadero Center, San Francisco CA 94106. (415)544-7217. Director, Corporate Communications: Bud Johns. Estab. 1970. Annual.
Purpose: To recognize each year the best writing and photography published on the subject of rodeo. Award given in categories: Rodeo News Story, Rodeo Feature Story and Rodeo Photography. Submissions must have been published during the previous year. Awards in each category: $100 1st prize, $50 2nd prize and $25 3rd prize; plus a pair of Levi's and a specially designed certificate. Deadline for entry: March. Rules and entry.

JERRY LEWIS/MDA WRITING AWARDS, Horst S. Petzall, Director, Department of Public Health Education, Muscular Dystrophy Association, 810 7th Ave., New York NY 10019. Awards $1,000, $500 and $250, along with award plaques, to those writers whose work fosters better understanding of muscular dystrophy and related neuromuscular diseases and contributes to public support of the effort to conquer these afflictions. Previously published articles, feature stories, editorials or poetry, commentaries, documentaries, dramas, or public-service announcements aired on radio or television are eligible.

ELIAS LIEBERMAN STUDENT POETRY AWARD, Poetry Society of America, 15 Gramercy Park, New York NY 10003. Awards $100 for the "best unpublished poem by a high school or preparatory school student of the US." Deadline: December 31.

DAVID D. LLOYD PRIZE, Harry S. Truman Library Institute (Independence MO), Chairman of the Committee, Professor Thomas C. Blaisdell Jr., Department of Political Science, 210 Barrows Hall, University of California, Berkeley CA 94720. Awards $1,000 biennially for the best published book on the period of the Presidency of Harry S. Truman. Books must deal primarily and substantially with some aspect of the political, economic and social development of the US, principally between April 12, 1945 and January 20, 1953, or of the public career of Harry S. Truman. Publication period: January 1 to December 31.

THE GERALD LOEB AWARDS, UCLA Graduate School of Management, 405 Hilgard Ave., Los Angeles CA 90024. (213)825-7982. Administrator: Bob Nero. Annual. Estab. 1957. Purpose: for distinguished business and financial journalism.
Categories: Single article in a newspaper with daily circulation above 350,000; single article in a newspaper with daily circulation less than 350,000; single article in a national magazine; and syndicated column or editorial. Published submissions only. Award: $1,000 for each category. Deadline: February 15 (for works published from January 1 to December 31). Contest rules and entry forms for SASE.

MADEMOISELLE'S COLLEGE FICTION AND POETRY COMPETITIONS, *Mademoiselle*, 350 Madison Avenue, New York NY 10017. (212)880-8800. Fiction and Poetry Editor: Mary E. McNichols. Offered annually.
Purpose: Fiction and Poetry Competitions for undergraduate students regularly enrolled for a degree in an accredited college or junior college.
Requirements: Midyear graduates must submit their work before graduation. All work submitted must be original; fictitious characters and situations only. Work that has appeared in college publications is acceptable—any other already-published work is not acceptable. In Fiction Competition 1st prize is $700 plus publication of story, 2nd prize is $300 plus option to publish story, Honorable Mentions receive special recognition from *Mademoiselle*. Poetry Competition has two 1st prizes of $100 each plus publication of poems and Honorable Mentions receive special recognition from *Mademoiselle*. Deadline: mid-January. Rules for SASE.

MAN IN HIS ENVIRONMENT BOOK AWARD, E. P. Dutton, 2 Park Ave., New York NY 10016. Offers a guaranteed minimum $10,000 as an advance against earnings for an original single work of adult nonfiction on an ecological theme, dealing with the past, present or future of man in his environment, natural or manmade. Write for details.

HOWARD R. MARRARO PRIZE IN ITALIAN HISTORY, Office of the Executive Directory, American Historical Association, 400 A St. SE, Washington DC 20003. Awards $500 for a book or article which treats Italian history in any epoch of Italian cultural history or of Italian-American relations. Write for submission details.

MELCHER BOOK AWARD, Unitarian Universalist Association, 25 Beacon St., Boston MA 02108. Department Director: Doris Pullen. Estab. 1964. Annual.
Purpose: Given annually to a work published in America during the previous calendar year judged to be the most significant contribution to religious liberalism. Awards $1,000 plus bronze medallion. Publisher submits candidate books to judges.

JIM MERRELL RELIGIOUS LIBERTY MEMORIAL, Merrell Enterprises, 1500 Massachusetts Ave. NW, Washington DC 20005. (202)659-8280. President: Jesse H. Herrell. Estab. 1976. Offered annually.
Purpose: To promote religious freedom as guaranteed by First Amendment.
Requirements: Submissions must have been published during previous calendar year. Awards $1,000 for the news story, column or editorial which best defends, promotes and advances the cause of religious liberty; and $1,000 for the best editorial cartoon on the same theme; and a plaque. Deadline: End of March. Rules for SASE.

MODERN LANGUAGE ASSOCIATION PRIZES, Office of Research Programs, 62 5th Ave., New York NY 10011. Awards the annual James Russell Lowell Prize, $1,000, for an outstanding literary or linguistic study, a critical edition of an important work, or a critical biography written by a member of the Association published in book form. The committee also awards an annual prize for an outstanding article in the *PMLA*, the William Riley Parker Prize.

JAMES MOONEY AWARD, The University of Tennessee Press/The Southern Anthropological Society, Department of Geography and Anthropology, Louisiana State University, Baton Rouge LA 70803. Contact: Miles Richardson.
Purpose: "For the book-length manuscript that best describes and interprets the people or culture of a New World population, which may be prehistoric, historic or contemporary. The purpose of this award is to encourage distinguished writing in anthropology and any student of the cultures and societies of the New World is eligible." Submissions must be previously unpublished. Awards $1,000. Entry deadline: December 31. Contest rules and entry form for SASE.

FRANK LUTHER MOTT-KAPPA TAU ALPHA RESEARCH AWARD IN JOURNALISM, School of Journalism, University of Missouri, Columbia MO 65201. (314)882-4852. Chief, Central Office: William H. Taft. Estab. 1944. Annual.
Purpose: "To recognize outstanding research in journalism. Generally, textbooks are not considered. Books that reflect on journalism considered as well as those that depend heavily on journalism sources, such as Presidential biographies, etc." Submissions must be previously published and copyrighted for year awarded, e.g., in 1979 will consider 1978 books. Awards $250 "plus beautiful hand-lettered scroll. Certificates to top five or so. At times, extra scrolls." Deadline for entry: February. "We have no special forms. We require 5 copies of each book entered. We have 5 judges."

NABW AWARDS FOR DISTINGUISHED JOURNALISM, National Association of Bank Women, Inc., 111 E. Wacker Dr., Chicago IL 60601. (312)565-4100. Contact: Public Relations Dept., Attn: Journalism Awards. Estab. 1974. Offered annually.
Purpose: "To recognize and honor journalists for their interpretative articles about executive women in banking and women's contributions to, and place in, the banking industry.
Requirements: Submissions must have been published June 1 through June 1 of the calendar year preceding award in US newspapers and periodicals or bank-sponsored (in-house) publications and received by June 10 of that year. Awards $300 and recognition plaque for each of above categories. Rules for SASE.

NAEBM DIRECTORS AWARD, National Association of Engine and Boat Manufacturers, Box 5555, Grand Central Station, New York NY 10017. (212)697-1100. Public Relations Manager: Sandy Mills. Estab. 1970. Annual.
Purpose: To recognize an individual within the communications profession who has made outstanding contributions to boating and allied water sports. Submissions must be previously published. Awards $1,000 and certificate and trip to New York in January for presentation during New York National Boat Show. Deadline for entry: October 15. Rules and entry forms for SASE.

NARRATIVE AND DRAMATIC POETRY COMPETITION, World Order of Narrative Poets, Box 2085, Dollar Ranch Station, Walnut Creek CA 94595. President: Mr. Lynne L. Prout. Estab 1975. Offered annually.
Purpose: "To develop a renewed interest in the writing of narrative and dramatic poetry, which has been sadly ignored for many years by clubs, editors and contests.
Requirements: Unpublished submissions only. Awards a minimum of $55 in cash divided in not less than 3 awards, and more if entries deserve same. Deadline: Beginning of September. Rules for SASE.

NATIONAL BOOK AWARDS, sponsored by the Association of American Publishers, 1 Park Ave., New York NY 10016. Awards $1,000 in each of seven categories for literature written or translated by American citizens and published in the US to honor outstanding creative writing. Categories include biography and autobiography, children's literature, contemporary thought, fiction, history, poetry and translation. Deadline: August 15.

THE NATIONAL FOUNDATION FOR HIGHWAY SAFETY AWARDS, Box 3043, Westville Station, New Haven CT 06515. Annual. Estab. 1962. Purpose: to emphasize driving safety. Published submissions only. Award: U.S. Savings Bond and plaques offered to editors, reporters, cartoonists, television and radio directors. $100 US Savings Bond for Letter to the Editor by citizen published in local newspaper. Deadline: January 31 (for works published during the year). Contest rules and entry forms for SASE.

NATIONAL HISTORICAL SOCIETY BOOK PRIZE IN AMERICAN HISTORY, Board of Judges, Box 1831, Harrisburg PA 17105. Awards $1,000 annually for a first book published by an author. Submissions must be nonfiction books published in the preceding calendar year. Three copies of each book bust be submitted by May 31st to the Board of Judges.

NATIONAL MEDIA AWARDS. American Psychological Foundation, 1200 17th St. NW, Washington DC 20036. (202)833-7600. Public Information Aide: Willett K. Vogt. Estab. 1956. Offered annually.
Purpose: "The purpose of the awards is to recognize and encourage outstanding, accurate reporting which increases the public's knowledge and understanding of psychology." Awards are made in 5 categories: TV/Film; Radio; Newspaper Reporting; Magazine Writing; and Books/Monographs. Awards $1,000 and an invitation to attend the annual Convention of the American Psychological Association, expenses paid. Submissions must have been published in the previous calendar year. Entry deadline: May 5. Contest rules and entry form for SASE.

NATIONAL PRESS CLUB AWARD FOR EXCELLENCE IN CONSUMER REPORTING, Dan Moskowitz, Chairman, Consumer Awards, McGraw & Hill Publications, National Press Bldg., Washington DC 20045. Provides the Consumer Reporting Award, and Certificates of Recognition in 11 categories. For members of the working press. Deadline for entries: May 15.

NATIONAL SOCIETY OF PROFESSIONAL ENGINEERS JOURNALISM AWARDS, 2029 K St. NW, Washington DC 20006. (202)331-7020. PR Director: Jack Cox. Annual. Estab. 1966. Purpose: for contributing to public knowledge and understanding of the role of engineering and technology in contemporary life. Published submissions only. Award: Three awards of $500, $300 and $200. Deadline: January 15 (for works published during the previous year). Contest rules and entry forms for SASE.

ALLAN NEVINS PRIZE, Professor Kenneth T. Jackson, Secretary-Treasurer, Society of American Historians, 610 Fayerweather Hall, Columbia University, New York NY 10027. Awards $1,000 and publication of winning manuscript for the best written doctoral dissertation in the field of American history, dealing historically with American arts, literature, and science, as well as biographical studies of Americans in any walk of life.

NEW WORLDS UNLIMITED, Box 556-SM, Saddle Brook NJ 07662. Annual poetry contest sponsored by *New Worlds Unlimited*. Rules for SASE.

NEW WRITERS AWARDS, Great Lakes Colleges Association, c/o English Department, Wabash College, Crawfordsville IN 47933. (317)363-7158, ext. 232. Director: Donald W. Baker. Estab. 1969. Offered annually.
Purpose: To encourage young writers. To make available to the Great Lakes Colleges and Universities young poets and novelists who tour the GLCA.
Requirements: Submission must be a previously published first book in either poetry or fiction, published fall or spring season of year of competition. Invited to tour Great Lakes Colleges and Universities with honorarium and expenses paid by each college visited. Deadline: End of February. Rules for SASE.

NEWCOMEN AWARDS IN BUSINESS HISTORY, c/o *Business History Review*, Harvard University, 215 Baker Library, Soldiers Field, Boston MA 02163. (617)495-6364. Editor: Albro Martin. Offered annually.
Purpose: "To the author of the article judged to be the best published in the *Business History Review* during the preceding year." Awards $300. Special award (in addition to the main award) of $150 to the article judged to be the best published in the *Review* during the year by a non-Ph.D., or a recent (not more than 5 years) Ph.D., and who has not published in book form. "There is no deadline for the prize; any article accepted for publication in the *Business History Review* becomes eligible for the award in the year the publication occurs." Contest rules for SASE; "but they are regularly advertised in the issues of the *Review*."

NEW YORK STATE HISTORICAL ASSOCIATION MANUSCRIPT AWARD, Lake Rd., Cooperstown NY 13326. (607)547-2508. Editorial Associate: Dr. Wendell Tripp. Estab. 1973. Offered annually.
Purpose: "The award is presented to the best unpublished, book-length monograph dealing with the history of New York State. Manuscripts may deal with any aspect of New York history including biographies, literature and the arts, provided that the methodology is historical." Submissions must be previously unpublished. Awards $1,000 and assistance in publication. Entry deadline: February 1. Contest rules and entry form for SASE.

CATHERINE L. O'BRIEN AWARD, c/o Ruder & Finn, Inc., 110 E. 59th St., New York NY 10022. (212)593-6321. Vice President: Jill Totenberg. Sponsor: Stanley Home Products, Inc. Annual. Estab. 1960. Purpose: for achievement in women's interest newspaper reporting. Published submissions only. Award: First prize; $500 and $1,000 journalism scholarship to student of choice; second prize: $300 and $750 journalism scholarship; third prize: $200 and $500 journalism scholarship. Annual deadline: January 31 (for works published from January-December of calendar year). Contest rules and entry forms available on request.

OPEN CIRCLE THEATRE PLAYWRIGHTS AWARD, Goucher College, Towson MD 21204. Director: Barry Knower. Estab. 1976. Offered annually.
Purpose: "To find challenging plays with good roles for women. At least 50% of major roles must be for women." Submissions must be unpublished and unproduced. Awards $200, and production by Open Circle Theatre. Entry deadline: December 31. Contest rules for SASE.

EARL D. OSBORN AWARD, Robert Francis Kane Associates, Inc., Public Relations, 12 E. 41st St., New York NY 10017. Sponsor: EDO Corporation in association with Aviation/Space Writers Association. Annual. Estab. 1970. Purpose: for best writing in any medium (press, magazine, radio or TV) on general aviation. Published submissions only. Award: $500 and trophy. Deadline: February (for works published during the previous calendar year). Contest rules and entry forms for SASE.

OSCARS IN AGRICULTURE, Dekalb AgResearch, Inc., Sycamore Rd., DeKalb IL 60115. (815)758-3461. Director of Public Relations: Ron Scherer. Estab. 1960. Offered annually.
Purpose: "To encourage mass media to develop material that further advances American agriculture. The award recognizes excellence in reporting agricultural news."
Requirements: Submission must have been published June 1 to June 1 of the previous year and should explain and educate to the writer or broadcaster's audience an in-depth story concerning agriculture and related fields. Awards an "Oscar" to winner in each category of newspaper, magazine, television and radio. Plaques are presented to the employers of the four winners. Deadline: Beginning of June. Rules for SASE.

P.E.N. TRANSLATION PRIZE, P.E.N. American Center, 47 5th Ave., New York NY 10003. Contact: Chairman, Translation Committee. Awards $1,000 for the a distinguished book-length translation into English from any language published in the United States. Technical, scientific, or reference works are not eligible. Sponsored by the Book-of-the-Month Club. Deadline: December 31.

FRANCIS PARKMAN PRIZE, Professor Kenneth T. Jackson, Secretary, Society of American Historians, 610 Fayerweather Hall, Columbia University, New York NY 10027. Awards $500 and a bronze medal to recognize the author who best epitomizes the society's purpose—the writing of history with literary distinction as well as sound scholarship. Books must deal with the colonial or national history of the United States. Books submitted by publishers only.

PENNEY-MISSOURI MAGAZINE AWARDS, School of Journalism, University of Missouri, Columbia MO 65211. Awards Director: Ruth D'Arcy. Annual. Estab. 1967. Purpose: for excellence in magazine coverage that enhances lifestyle in today's society.
Categories: Contemporary living; consumerism; health; personal lifestyle; expanding opportunities, and excellence in smaller magazines. Published submissions only. Award: $1,000 in each category. Deadline: May 1 (for works published from January 1-December 31). Write for contest rules and entry forms.

PFIZER AWARD, c/o Isis Editorial Office, University of Pennsylvania, 215 S. 34th St., Philadelphia PA 19104. (215)263-5575. Sponsor: History of Science Society, Inc. Annual. Estab. 1958. Purpose: to recognize and reward the best published work related to the history of science in the preceding year, written by an American or Canadian author. Published submissions only. Award: $1,000 and a medal. Deadline: May 1 (for work published during the previous year).

PIONEER DRAMA PLAYWRITING AWARD, Pioneer Drama Service, 2172 S. Colorado Blvd., Box 22555, Denver CO 80222. (303)759-4297. Publisher: Shubert Fendrich. Estab. 1969. Offered annually.
Purpose: For an outstanding play or plays suitable for educational or community theater.
Requirements: Submissions must be unpublished original scripts or adaptations from literature in the public domain; one-act or full-length; drama, comedy, musical comedy or children's

theater. All entries should be produced prior to submission, and proof of performance (programs, reviews, etc. should be enclosed). Awards First Place $1,000 advance on royalties and publication; five additional awards of $50 advance on royalties and publication. Deadline: March 15th. SASE.

PIONEER EXPOSITION/GREAT PLAINS STORY TELLERS AND POETRY READING CONTEST, Operation Pride of Council Bluffs, Iowa, 106 Navajo, Council Bluffs IA 51501. (712)366-1136. Director: Bob Everhart. Estab. 1976. Offered annually.
Purpose: "The contest is an event to determine how well the writer can present his own material."
Requirements: For writers of short stories and poetry. The writer must be present at the contest. Published and unpublished work accepted. Awards trophies to the top three winners. 1st prize receives $75; 2nd, $50; 3rd, $25; 4th, $15; and 5th, $10. Deadline: Noon on the Saturday of Labor Day weekend. Rules for SASE. Fee: $3 plus gate admission.

EDGAR ALLAN POE AWARDS, Mystery Writers of America, Inc., 105 E. 19th St., New York NY 10003. Awards Edgar Allan Poe statuettes in each of nine categories: best mystery novel published in America, best first mystery novel by an American author, best fact crime book, best juvenile mystery, best paperback mystery, best mystery short story, best mystery motion picture, and best television mystery.

POETRY CONTEST, c/o Arnie Lutz, 32220 Hennepin, Garden City MI 48135. Estab. 1977. Offered annually.
Purpose: To promote poetry in America.
Requirements: All forms of unpublished poetry accepted, but poems should not exceed 40 lines. Awards $75 1st prize, $50 2nd prize and $25 3rd prize. Deadline: Beginning of March.

POETS CLUB OF CHICAGO NATIONAL SHAKESPEAREAN SONNET CONTEST. 3 prizes of $50, $25 and $10. Sponsored by the Poets Club of Chicago. Mail three copies of only one Shakespearean sonnet, typed on 8½x11 paper, to Anne Nolan, c/o Nolan Boiler Co., 8531 S. Vincennes, Chicago IL 60620. Deadline: September 1. Sonnet must be unpublished and must not have won a cash award in this contest previously. No author identification is to appear on the copies. Enclose a separate envelope with the poet's identification on a card inside it. No poems will be returned. SASE.

POETS OF THE VINEYARD ANNUAL POETRY COMPETITION, Poets of the Vineyard, c/o Winnie E. Fitzpatrick, Box 77, Kenwood CA 95452. (707)833-4422. Estab. 1975. Offered annually.
Purpose: "Poets of the Vineyard hopes to see new and experienced poets join us in the enjoyment of sharing competition."
Requirements: "All poems must be original, unpublished and not under consideration for publication or other contest at the time submitted. No previous prizewinning poem will be accepted; Honorable Mention awards are acceptable." Awards first, second, third and Grand Prize money awards ranging from $10 to $25. First and second Honorable Mentions are book awards. Deadline: March 1. SASE or rules and categories. c/o chairperson listed above at 837 Fitch St., Healdsburg CA 95448.

PRIZE IN PHOTOGRAPHIC HISTORY, Prize Committee, Photographic Historical Society of New York, Box 1839, Radio City Station, New York NY 10019. Awards $100 to an individual who has written, edited, or produced an original work dealing with the history of photography. Books, magazine articles and monographs are eligible.

PULITZER PRIZES, Secretary, The Pulitzer Prizes Board, 702 Journalism, Columbia University, New York NY 10027. Awards $1,000 in categories of journalism, letters, and music for distinguished work in United States newspapers, and for distinguished achievement in literature and music by Americans.

PUTNAM AWARDS, G.P. Putnam's Sons, 200 Madison Ave., New York NY 10016. Awards $7,500 advance against royalties for outstanding fiction and nonfiction book manuscripts. Nominations are made by the editors of G.P. Putnam's Sons from mss already under contract to the house.

ERNIE PYLE MEMORIAL AWARD, Scripps-Howard Foundation, 200 Park Ave., New York NY 10017. Awards $1,000 to the winner and medallion plaque to the paper, plus $500 second prize and hand-lettered citation to the paper, for newspaper writing which exemplifies the style, warmth, and craftsmanship of Ernie Pyle. Submissions must have been published in the calendar year previous to the contest closing date. Entry deadline: January 15.

REAL ESTATE JOURNALISM ACHIEVEMENT COMPETITION, National Association of Realtors, 430 N. Michigan Ave., Chicago IL 60611. Public Information Coordinator. Estab. 1965. Offered annually.
Purpose: "To encourage excellence in real estate reporting and writing, and to recognize winners for their accomplishments in the field." Submissions must have been published in the year previous to contest closing date. Awards "plaques and cash awards." Entry deadline: September 1. Contest rules and entry form for SASE.

RECREATION VEHICLE INDUSTRY ASSOCIATION JOURNALISM AWARDS, Recreation Vehicle Industry Assn., 14650 Lee Rd., Chantilly VA 22021. (703)968-7722. Public Relations Administrator: Gary M. LaBella. Estab. 1972. Offered annually.
Purpose: To encourage accurate and well-written articles in consumer and trade press.
Requirements: Submissions must have been published in year prior to deadline. Awards $1,000 first prize and $500 second prize in magazine, newspaper, photo and trade press divisions. Deadline: Last week in October. Query for rules.

REDBOOK'S YOUNG WRITER'S CONTEST III, Box F-3, 230 Park Ave., New York NY 10017.
Purpose: The contest is open to men and women 18-28 years of age at the time of entry, and who have not previously published or had accepted fiction in a magazine with a circulation over 25,000. Awards $500, and *Redbook* will buy publication rights for an additional $1,000 for 1st prize; $300 for second prize; and $100 for 3rd prize. Entry deadline: December 1979. "For a period of 6 months after the deadline, The Redbook Publishing Co. reserves the right to purchase for publication any story entered in the competition that is deemed publishable." Contest rules appear in the October, November and December issues of *Redbook*.

REGINA MEDAL, Catholic Library Association, 461 W. Lancaster Ave., Haverford PA 19041. Awards a silver medal for continued distinguished contribution in literature for children.

RELIGIOUS ARTS GUILD ONE-ACT PLAY COMPETITION, 25 Beacon, Boston MA 02108. (617)742-2100. Chief Judge: Dr. Robert A. Storer. Biannual. Estab. 1950. Unpublished submissions only. Award: $200. Deadline: January 15. Contest rules for SASE.

ST. LAWRENCE AWARD FOR FICTION, *Fiction International*, Department of English, St. Lawrence University, Canton NY 13617. Awards $1,000 to the author of an outstanding first collection of short fiction published by an American publisher during the current year. Editors, writers, agents, readers, and publishers are invited to suggest or submit eligible books. Publisher must submit final nominations. Deadline: January 31.

HENRY SCHUMAN PRIZE, c/o Isis Editorial Office, University of Pennsylvania, 215 S. 34th St., Philadelphia PA 19104. Sponsor: History of Science Society, Inc. Annual. Estab. 1955. Purpose: for original prize essay on the history of science and its cultural influences, open to graduate and undergraduate students in any American or Canadian college. Unpublished submissions only. Papers submitted must be 5,000 words in length, exclusive of footnotes, and thoroughly documented. Award: $500. Deadline: July 1.

ROBERT LIVINGSTON SCHUYLER PRIZE, Committee Chairman, American Historical Association, 400 A St. SE, Washington DC 20003. Awards $500 every five years for recognition of the best work in the field of Modern British, British Imperial, and British Commonwealth history written by an American citizen.

SCIENCE IN SOCIETY JOURNALISM AWARDS, Administrative Secretary, National Association of Science Writers, Box 294, Greenlawn NY 11740. Two awards of $1,000 and engraved medallions to recognize investigative and interpretive reporting about physical sciences and the life sciences and their impact for good and bad. Write for complete details and entry blank.

SCIENCE-WRITING AWARD IN PHYSICS AND ASTRONOMY, Director, Public Information Division, American Institute of Physics, 335 E. 45th St., New York NY 10017. A single prize of $1,500, a certificate and stainless steel Moebius strip is awarded annually to an author whose work has improved public understanding of physics and astronomy. Entries must be the work of physicists, astronomers or members of AIP member and affiliated societies. Co-sponsored by the United States Steel Foundation.

SERGEL DRAMA PRIZE, The Charles H. Sergel Drama Prize, The University of Chicago Theatre, 5706 S. University Ave., Chicago IL 60637. Awards $1,500 biennially for best original play. Write for details and entry blank. Contest deadline is July 1 of the contest year. Please send an SASE for entry blanks which are available by February of the contest year.

ANNE SEXTON POETRY PRIZE, Florida International University, Miami FL 33199. (305)552-2874. Contact: Jim Hall. Estab. 1976. Offered annually.
Purpose: For the best single poem by a woman. Submissions must be unpublished. Awards $250. Entry Deadline: October 1. Rules and entry form for SASE. Beginning in 1979 the Anne Sexton Poetry Prize will be awarded yearly to a book-length manuscript of poems, which will be published by Carnegie-Mellon University Press. A $500 advance will be awarded to the writer. Submissions will be solicited by the judges from promising writers, or manuscripts can be nominated by established writers by writing to Jim Hall.

THE SMOLAR AWARD, Council of Jewish Federations, Inc., 575 Lexington Ave., New York NY 10022. Director of Communications: Frank Strauss. Awards a plaque to recognize outstanding journalists in North America whose work appears in English language newspapers and magazines substantially involved in the coverage of Jewish communal affairs and issues in the United States and Canada. Write for details and required entry form.

SOCIETY OF COLONIAL WARS AWARD, Awards Committee, 122 E. 58th St., New York NY 10022. Awards bronze medallion and citation to recognize contributions of outstanding excellence in the field of literature, drama, music or art relative to colonial Americana (1607-1775).

SPECIAL OLYMPICS AWARDS. For radio and television broadcasters, newspaper and magazine reporters and feature writers, news photographers, athletes, coaches and sports organizations who during the previous calendar year have made the most distinguished contributions to local, national, or international Special Olympics program. The award is presented at an annual luncheon and consists of a specially designed award. Sponsored by Special Olympics, Inc., and The Joseph P. Kennedy Jr. Foundation. For information write: Special Olympics Awards, Joseph P. Kennedy Jr. Foundation, 1701 K St. NW, Suite 205, Washington DC 20006. Estab. in 1973.

THOMAS L. STOKES AWARD, The Washington Journalism Center, 2401 Virginia Ave. NW, Washington DC 20037. Awards $1,000 and a citation for the best analysis, reporting or comment appearing in a daily newspaper on the general subject of development, use and conservation of energy and other natural resources in the public interest, and protection of the environment.

WALKER STONE AWARDS, The Scripps-Howard Foundation, 200 Park Ave., New York NY 10017. President: Jacques A. Caldwell.
Purpose: "To honor outstanding achievement in the field of editorial writing. The yardstick for judging will be for general excellence, which may include quality of writing, forcefulness, and importance to the public interest." Submissions must have been published in the calendar year previous to the contest closing date. Entry deadline: February 1.

JESSE STUART CONTEST, Seven, 115 S. Hudson, Oklahoma City OK 73102. Awards $25, $15, $10 and $5 for the best unpublished poems in the Jesse Stuart tradition; any form or free verse; any length. Write for rules. SASE.

THEATRE ARTS CORPORATION NATIONAL PLAYWRITING CONTEST, Contest Coordinator, Box 5856, Sante Fe NM 87501. (505)982-0252. Four categories, prizes from $200-500. Two children's categories: for child actors and for adult actors for children's audience; prizes $200 each category. Full-length adult entries, prize $500. One act adult, prize $300. All entries must be unproduced originals. SASE for information and forms. Contest supported, in part, by NEA Grant. Final entries: January 31.

THE PAUL TOBENKIN MEMORIAL AWARD, Graduate School of Journalism, Columbia University, New York NY 10027. Awards $250 and a certificate for outstanding achievement in the field of newspaper writing in the fight against racial and religious hatred, intolerance, discrimination and every form of bigotry.

TRA ECLIPSE AWARDS, c/o Thoroughbred Racing Associations, 3000 Marcus Ave., Lake Success NY 11042. Award consists of an Eclipse Trophy. Given for outstanding newspaper writing on thoroughbred racing and outstanding magazine writing on thoroughbred racing. Deadline for entry: November 15, annually. Starting date for entry: January 1, annual entry blank necessary. Submit copy of published article showing date of publication.

TRANSLATION CENTER AWARD, 307-A Math Bldg., Columbia University, New York NY 10027. (212)280-2305. Executive Director: Ms. Dallas Galvin. Estab. 1972. Offered annually.
Purpose: "To assist in the completion of a book of literature (a novel, stories, poems) in translation. The book must be a work in progress and the application must be accompanied by a letter of intent from an interested publisher." Submissions must be unpublished. Awards $500. Entry deadline: February 15. Contest rules and entry form for SASE.

TRANSLATION CENTER FELLOWSHIP, Translation Center, 307-A Math Bldg., Columbia University, New York NY 10027. (212)280-2305. Executive Director: Ms. Dallas Galvin. Estab. 1972. Offered annually.
Purpose: "To encourage literary translators to explore lesser known languages without economic hindrance for 1 year." Submissions may be published or unpublished. Awards $10,000. Entry deadline: January 15. Contest rules and entry form for SASE.

UNITED STATES INDUSTRIAL COUNCIL EDUCATIONAL FOUNDATION EDITORIAL AWARDS COMPETITION, Box 2686, Nashville TN 37219. Awards $100-300 for editorials and editorial cartoons, published in a daily or weekly newspaper, which best interpret the spirit and goals of the free enterprise system in the United States and which describe and analyze the achievements of this one amendment system.

VETERANS' VOICES AWARDS, Hospitalized Veterans' Writing Project, Inc., 5920 Nall, Room 117, Mission KS 66202. "The Hospitalized Veterans' Writing Project, which publishes *Veterans' Voices*, offers cash prizes for original unpublished articles, stories, poems, light verse and patriotic essays by hospitalized veterans of the U.S. Armed Forces, plus poetry prizes, $5; prose, $10; special awards are Joseph Posik Award, $50 each edition; Gladys Feld Helzberg Poetry Award, $25 each edition; two Charlotte Dilling Awards given in June each year for essays on 'Why a Two-Party System' or 'Why the Veterans Should Vote'—$125 first prize—$75 second. Also Beginners' Awards, $5 extra for regular prose or poetry. Manuscripts received all year long. All material must be submitted through a VA facility."

WAGNER MEMORIAL POETRY AWARD. For details, send SASE to Wagner Memorial Award, c/o Secretary, Poetry Society of America, 15 Gramercy Park, New York NY 10003. Awards $250 for the best poem worthy of the tradition of the art, any style or length. Deadline: December 31.

EDWARD LEWIS WALLANT BOOK AWARD, Dr. Lothar Kahn, Central Connecticut College, New Britain CT 06150. Awards $125 and citation for a creative work of fiction published during the current year which has significance for the American Jew.

WATUMULL PRIZE IN THE HISTORY OF INDIA, Committee Chairman, American Historical Association, 400 A St. SE, Washington DC 20003. Awards $1,000 biennially for the best book originally published in the United States on any phase of the history of India.

BERTHA WEISZ MEMORIAL AWARDS, Weiss Philatelic Numismatic Features, 16000 Terrace Rd. (208), Cleveland OH 44112. (216)451-3331. Editor: Julius Weiss. Estab. 1973. Offered biennially in even-numbered years.
Purpose: "To improve on stamp and coin columns and make them newsworthy in newspapers and not a rehash of press releases by governments and commercial interests."
Requirements: Entries must be from newspapers, anywhere in the world, with a circulation of 50,000 or more per issue. Also, entries must come from the writers of the columns and not from readers of the columns. Submissions must be work published between January 1 and December 31 of award year. Categories are Best Stamp Column and Best Coin Column. Awards a $50 U.S. Savings Bond and a plaque for winner in each category. Deadline: End of December. SASE.

WESTERN WRITERS OF AMERICA GOLDEN SPUR AWARD, Rex Bundy, Rt. 1, Box

35H, Victor MT 59875. Annual. Estab. 1952.
Categories: Best western novel; best historical novel; best western nonfiction book; best western juvenile; best western TV show; best western film script; best western short subject (fiction or nonfiction). Published submissions only. Award: Golden Spur Award given at annual convention banquet. Deadline: December 31 (for works published in that year). Contest rules and entry form for SASE.

THE WALT WHITMAN AWARD, Sponsor, The Academy of American Poets, Inc., 1078 Madison Ave., New York NY 10028. Annual. Estab. 1974. Purpose: for a book-length (50-100 pages) manuscript of poetry by an American citizen who has not previously published a book of poems. (The winning poet may have published a chapbook or a small edition of a book of poems, and may have published poems in magazines.) Award: $1,000 cash and publication of winning ms by a major publisher. Deadline: manuscripts received between September 15 and November 15. Send SASE in late summer for contest rules and required entry form.

THOMAS J. WILSON PRIZE, Harvard University Press, 79 Garden St., Cambridge MA 02138. Awards $500 to the author of a first book by a beginning author accepted by Harvard University Press during the calendar year and judged outstanding in content, style and mode of presentation.

AUDREY WOOD AWARD IN PLAYWRITING, Department of Performing Arts, The American University, Massachusetts and Nebraska Aves., Washington DC 20016. (202)686-2315. Director, Theatre Program: Kenneth Baker. Estab. 1970. Annual.
Purpose: To encourage "young" unproduced and unpublished writers with a place and opportunity to have their works given a public showing. Awards $500 and production, or at least a staged reading of play. Deadline for entry: May 15. Rules and entry forms for SASE.

CAPTAIN DONALD T. WRIGHT AWARD, Southern Illinois University, Edwardsville IL 62026. Contact: John A. Regnell. Sponsor: Southern Illinois University Foundation and Department of Mass Communications. Annual. Estab. 1971. Purpose: for distinguished journalism in maritime transportation.
Categories: Newspaper and magazine articles; books; photos and photo essays; tapes; and videotapes and films. Published submissions only. Award: bronze plaque featuring modern and historic forms of river transportation. Deadline: August 1 (for works published within the last two years). Contest rules for SASE.

WRITER'S DIGEST CREATIVE WRITING CONTEST. *Writer's Digest*, 9933 Alliance Rd., Cincinnati OH 45242. Awards 300 prizes worth over $5,000 (in cash value) for the best article, short story and poetry entries. Deadline: midnight, June 30.
Nonfiction, Fiction, and Poetry: All entries must be original, unpublished, and not previously submitted to a *Writer's Digest* contest. Length: short story, 2,000 words maximum; article, 2,500 words maximum; poetry, 16 lines maximum. Entries must be typewritten, double-spaced, on 8½x11 paper with the author's name and address in the upper left corner. An entry form must accompany each entry. Each contestant is entitled to submit one entry in each category. All entries may be submitted elsewhere after they are sent to *Writer's Digest*. No acknowledgment will be made of receipt of mss. Mss will not be returned and enclosure of SASE will disqualify the entry. Announcement of this contest is made yearly in the January through July issues of *Writer's Digest*. The grand prize winner and the top 10 entries in each category will be announced in the October issue. *Writer's Digest* retains one-time publication rights to the 1st, 2nd and 3rd place entries in each category.

WRITERS GUILD OF AMERICA WEST AWARDS. Allen Rivkin, Public Relations, Writers Guild of America West, 8955 Beverly Blvd., Los Angeles CA 90048. Awards plaques in screen, television, and radio categories for best written scripts, to members only.

Writers' Clubs

Cameraderie, instruction, contacts, tips and friendships are a few of the benefits of joining a writers' club. Many clubs have manuscript readings and evaluations, some sponsor workshops, others bring in well-known speakers.

The clubs that are listed here are local or regional groups, and have social and professional functions. National professional groups are listed in the Writers' Organizations section.

Clubs are listed geographically by state, then alphabetically by club name within the state. SASE when querying about membership, meeting times, or any other information.

For information on starting a writers' club, send 50¢ plus SASE for the booklet *How To Start/Run a Writer's Club* (Writer's Digest).

Alabama

CREATIVE WRITERS OF MONTGOMERY, Gary Earl Heath, Secretary, 3816 Governors Dr., #H-233, Montgomery AL 36111.

HUNTSVILLE WRITERS' CLUB, Lorraine Standish, 2216 E. Arbor Dr., Huntsville AL 35811.

Arkansas

ARKANSAS PIONEER BRANCH, NATIONAL LEAGUE OF AMERICAN PEN WOMEN, Ida Rice Rogers, 2409 W. 16th, North Little Rock AR 72114. Estab. 1921. Meets monthly.

AUTHORS, COMPOSERS AND ARTISTS' SOCIETY, Peggy Vining, Publicity Chairman, 6817 Gingerbread Lane, Little Rock AR 72204.

OZARK CREATIVE WRITERS, INC., Lida W. Pyles, President, Box 391, Eureka Springs AR 72632.

OZARK WRITERS AND ARTISTS GUILD, Box 411, Siloam Springs AR 72761. Director: Maggie A. Smith. Estab. 1935. Meets in mid-July.

POETS' ROUNDTABLE OF ARKANSAS, Roberta E. Allen, 6604 Kenwood Rd., Little Rock AR 72207.

SPA WRITERS, 1100 2nd St., Hot Springs AR 71901. (501)321-1174. Secretary: Mildred Wilkinson. Estab. 1976. Meets bimonthly.

California

CALIFORNIA STATE POETRY SOCIETY, Southern California Chapter, 3608 N. San Gabriel, Baldwin Park CA 91706. President: Norma Calderone. Estab. 1974. Meets monthly.

CALIFORNIA WRITERS' CLUB, 2214 Derby St., Berkeley CA 94705. Secretary: Dorothy V. Benson. Estab. 1909. Meets monthly, except July and August. "Membership is open to prize-winning and published writers."

CUPERTINO WRITERS, 10117 N. Portal Ave., Cupertino CA 95014. (408)257-8494. Contact: Phyllis Taylor Pianka. Estab. 1972. Meets semimonthly.

DALY CITY CREATIVE WRITERS' GROUP, Margaret O. Richardson, President, 243 Lakeshire Dr., Daly City CA 94015. Estab. 1965. Meets "by appointment only."

FALLBROOK WRITERS' WORKSHOP, 732 W. College St., Fallbrook CA 92028. President: Helen B. Hicks. Estab. 1977. Meets weekly.

FEMINIST WRITERS' GUILD, Box 9396, Berkeley CA 94709. (405)524-3692. Current Administrator: Laura Tow. Estab. 1977. 1,000 members.
Purpose: To act both as a service and political body for feminist writers. Publishes a newsletter. Referral to agents and to other useful publications; also to local chapters and contact people and to local support groups. Annual dues: $10 ($5 if unemployed), $20 to institutions.

FICTIONAIRES, 10792 Harrogate, Santa Ana CA 92705. Secretary: Armand Hanson. Estab. 1963. Meets semimonthly. Membership limited to 20 members.

FOUNTAIN VALLEY WRITERS WORKSHOP, Clara Schultz, 8815 Hummingbird Ave., Fountain Valley CA 92708. Estab. 1972. Meets monthly.

LITERARY HALL OF FAME, Box 20880, Long Beach CA 90801. (213)436-3132. President: Howard E. Hill. Estab. 1976. Meets monthly.

LOS ESCRIBIENTES, 107 Rancho Alipaz, 32371 Alipaz St., San Juan Capistrano CA 92675. Contact: Nora Collins. Estab. 1971. Meets semimonthly.

MOUNTAIN-VALLEY WRITERS, 18140 Hawthorne, Bloomington CA 92316. Secretary: Pat Wolff. Estab. 1969. Meets semimonthly. Membership limited to published writers.

NORTHERN CALIFORNIA CARTOON & HUMOR ASSOCIATION, Walt Miller, Secretary, 609 29th Ave., San Mateo CA 94403.

PALM SPRINGS WRITERS' GROUP, 677 Dry Falls Rd., Palm Springs CA 92262. Secretary: Shirley Hammer. Estab. 1978. Meets bimonthly.

POMONA VALLEY WRITERS CLUB, Ontario City Library, 215 E. C St., Ontario CA 91761. (714)984-2758. President: Flo Swanson. Estab. 1936. Meets monthly.

PROFESSIONAL WRITERS LEAGUE OF LONG BEACH, Box 20880, Long Beach CA 90801. Director: Howard E. Hill. Estab. 1970. Meets monthly.

SAN DIEGO WRITERS WORKSHOP, Box 19366, San Diego CA 92119. Moderator: Chet Cunningham. Estab. 1962. Meets semimonthly. "Professional writers, shared; selling writers, encouraged; and learning writers, assisted."

SAN FRANCISCO WRITERS WORKSHOP, Dean Lipton, Moderator, Louis Lurie Room, Main Library, McAllister and Larkin Sts., San Francisco CA 94102.

SHOWCASE WRITERS CLUB, Larry Stillman, 7842 Barton Dr., Lemon Grove CA 92045.

SOUTHWEST MANUSCRIPTERS, 560 S. Helberta Ave., Redondo Beach CA 90277. Founding Member: R. E. B. Battles. Estab. 1949. Meets monthly.

SPELLBINDERS LITERARY GUILD, Box 60604, Santa Ana CA 92706. Estab. 1970. Meets monthly. "Prospective members must submit a sample of their work—published or unpublished—to our reading committee. Interested parties may come to one meeting as guests before submitting."

SURFWRITERS, 905 Calle Miramar, Redondo Beach CA 90277. Director: LaVada Weir. Estab. 1958. Meets monthly. Currently there is a waiting list for membership.

WRITER'S CLUB OF PASADENA, 231 S. Hudson, Pasadena CA 91101. Secretary: Willard C. Hyatt. Estab. 1922. Meets monthly.

WRITERS' CLUB OF WHITTIER SEMINAR, 7716 Westman Ave., Whittier CA 90606. (213)699-5935. President: Fern Palmer. Annual. Held in MArch for published and unpublished writers.

WRITERS' WORKSHOP WEST, 17909 San Gabriel Ave., Cerritos CA 90701. President: Bob McGrath. Estab. 1962. Meets semimonthly.

Colorado

ROCKY MOUNTAIN WRITERS GUILD, INC., Box 1635, Boulder CO 80306. President: Dr. James D. Hutchinson. Estab. 1967. Meets biweekly. Professional (publication required) and Associate (patron required) Membership.

WE WRITE OF COLORADO, Box 942, Arvada CO 80001. (303)422-4579. President: Robert C. Walker. Estab. 1967. Meets twice a month.

WEST ROCKIES WRITERS CLUB, 2841 Teller Ave., Sp 10, Grand Junction CO 81501. (303)245-6448. Past President/Founder: Eva Carter. Estab. 1976. Meets monthly.

Connecticut

WOMEN WRITER'S CLUB, 175 Fairview Ave., Bridgeport CT 06606. (203)374-8667. President: Lynn Greenwood. Estab. 1978. Meets monthly.

WRITER'S EXCHANGE, 231 Mile Creek Rd., Old Lyme CT 06371. Moderator: Carolyn Gilbert. Estab. 1975. Meets monthly.

District of Columbia

WASHINGTON AREA WRITERS, 204 Laverne St., Alexandria VA 22305. (703)548-1263. President: Susan Katz. Estab. 1973. Meets monthly.

WRITER'S LEAGUE OF WASHINGTON, 7602 Lynn Dr., Chevy Chase MD 20015. Secretary: Lola Dunn.

Georgia

DIXIE COUNCIL OF AUTHORS AND JOURNALISTS INC., 1212 Lanier Blvd. NE, Atlanta GA 30306. Director: Harold Random. Estab. 1961.

Idaho

CAMAS WRITER'S WORKSHOP, Fairfield ID 83327. (208)764-2536. Director: Penelope Reedy. Estab. 1975. Meets weekly during winter.

Illinois

JUVENILE FORUM, 3403 45th St., Moline IL 61265. (309)762-8985. Host: David R. Collins. Estab. 1975. Meets monthly.

KANKAKEE AREA WRITERS GROUP, 202 Steven Dr., Bourbonnais IL 60914. Secretary: Esther Lunsford. Estab. 1967. Meets semimonthly.

KEY CITY WRITERS' CLUB, 1254 E. Bourbonnais St., Kankakee IL 60901. (815)932-8347. President: Miss Ronne L. Claire. Estab. 1979. Meets biweekly. Writers must have an "avid interest in writing and be willing to help better our club and ourselves." Current membership: 8.

NORTH SHORE CREATIVE WRITERS, Winnetka Library, Winnetka IL (312)752-8377. Workshop Leader: Pierre Long. Estab. 1953. Meets weekly.

OFF CAMPUS WRITERS WORKSHOP, Winnetka Community House, Winnetka IL 60093. Chairman: Rosalyn Goodman. Estab. 1945. Meets weekly.

QUAD CITY WRITERS CLUB, Butterworth Center, Moline IL 61265. President: Melnotte Lindstrom. Estab. 1953. Meets monthly.

SHAGBARK SCRIBES, Ivan Sparling, Box 2400, Illinois Central College, East Peoria IL 61611.

SKOKIE'S CREATIVE WRITERS ASSN., Leo Friedman, 5256 Foster, Skokie IL 60077. Estab. 1974. Meets monthly.

SOUTH SIDE CREATIVE WRITERS, 5744 S. Harper, Chicago IL 60637. (312)752-8377. Workshop Leader: Pierre Long. Estab. 1949. Meets weekly.

WRITERS' STUDIO, 125½ 18th St., Rock Island IL 61201. President: Betty Mowery. Estab. 1967. Meets weekly.

Indiana
CENTRAL INDIANA WRITERS' ASSOCIATION, Norma J. Gardner, Director. 8823 W. Washington St., Indianapolis IN 46231. Estab. 1976. Meets monthly.

POETS' STUDY CLUB OF TERRE HAUTE, Esther Alman, President, 826 S. Center St., Terre Haute IN 47807.

SCHERERVILLE LIBRARY WRITERS' WORKSHOP, 121 E. Joliet St., Schererville IN 46375. Secretary: Barbara Boruff. (219)942-4826. Estab. 1978. Meets twice a month.

SOUTH BEND WRITERS' CLUB, 2419 Riverside Dr., South Bend IN 46616. President: Sonnie Miller. Estab. 1963. Meets biweekly.

THE STRUGGLERS' CLUB, 5024-B Bellemeade Ave., Evansville IN 47715. Contact: M. B. Whittaker.

Kansas
WICHITA LINE WOMEN, Jacquelyn Terral Andrews, 2350 Alameda Pl., Wichita KS 67211. Estab. 1966. Meets monthly.

Kentucky
JACKSON PURCHASE CREATIVE WRITER'S CLUB, Rt. 3, Box 273, Clinton KY 42031. (502)653-6795. Secretary: Diane Hopkins. Estab. 1974. Meets monthly.

LOUISVILLE WRITERS CLUB, Beverly Giammara, 2205 Weber Ave., Louisville KY 40205. Estab. 1952. Meets semimonthly.

Maryland
WORDSMITHS: The Creative Writing Group of the Social Security Administration, 6724 Ransome Dr., Baltimore MD 21207. Chairman: Robert Hale. Estab. 1971. Meets biweekly. "Basically for employees of the Social Security Administration, but we do accept anyone."

Massachusetts
MANUSCRIPT CLUB OF BOSTON, 770 Boylston St., Boston MA 02199. Contact: Dr. Ruth E. Setterberg. Estab. 1911. Meets semimonthly.

NATIONAL LEAGUE OF AMERICAN PEN WOMEN, BOSTON BRANCH, 14 Saxony Dr., Sudbury MA 01776. (617)443-6004. President: Joan Goodstone. Estab. 1927. Meets monthly from October to May. Open to "professional women artists, writers, dramatists, lecturers and composers." Requires "three samples of professional work, with proof of sale in last five years." Current membership: 42.

PIONEER VALLEY SCRIPTORS, Maxine Englehardt, Box 1745, Springfield MA 01101. Estab. 1941. Meets monthly.

SOCIETY OF CHILDREN'S BOOK WRITERS, New England Region, 31 School, Hatfield

MA 01038. Director: Jane Yolen. Estab. 1972. Meets annually.

TWELVE O'CLOCK SCHOLARS, Box 111, West Hyannisport MA 02672. Contact: Mrs. Marion Vuilleumier. Estab. 1952. Meets semimonthly.

Michigan

DETROIT WOMEN WRITERS, 16 Adams Lane, Dearborn MI 48120. Membership chairperson: Elaine Watson. Estab. 1900. Meets semimonthly.

FUSE WRITING LABORATORY, 668 Cherry St., South Haven MI 49090. (616)637-6656. Director: Tim Crawford. Estab. 1976.
Purpose: To help freelance writers locally with materials, encouragement and advice. Collects information, materials and equipment for members use. Fees: Donations.

POETRY SOCIETY OF MICHIGAN, S. Geneva Page, 256 Burr St., Battle Creek MI 49015.

PROJECT BAIT WRITERS WORKSHOP, 13217 Livernois, Detroit MI 48238. (313)834-9729, 931-3427. Director: David Rambeau. Estab. 1977. Meets weekly.

SOCIETY OF MICHIGAN AUTHORS, Box 232, Grayling MI 49738. (517)348-5192. Co-Director: Robert W. Hanson. Estab. 1978. Issues bimonthly publication.

SOUTH OAKLAND WRITERS, 21315 Pembroke, Detroit MI 48219. (313)532-3882. Membership Chairman: Helen Olmstead. Estab. 1968. Meets monthly.

Minnesota

A.A.U.W. WRITER'S WORKSHOP, Minneapolis Branch, American Association of University Women, 2115 Stevens Ave., Minneapolis MN 55427. Estab. 1932. Meets semimonthly.

EASTSIDE FREELANCE WRITERS OF MINNESOTA (EVENING GROUP), 139 Birchwood Ave., Birchwood MN 55110. (612)426-3840. Chairperson: Marlys Oliver. Estab. 1977. Meets semimonthly. Current membership: 8. Membership limited to 15.

EASTSIDE FREELANCE WRITERS OF MINNESOTA (MORNING GROUP), 179 Birchwood Ave., White Bear Lake MN 55110. (612)426-2518. Program Director: Jeannie C. Barnum. Estab. 1965. "Open to all serious writers. If membership is filled, applications for membership may be filled out and interested writers will be notified as soon as there's an opening." Current membership: 40. Membership limited to 50.

LAKE AREA WRITER'S GUILD, 2845 Icerose Lane, Stillwater MN 55082. Coordinator: Karen Melville. Estab. 1978. Meets biweekly. "Applicants need not be published, but must be aiming for publication." Current membership: 11.

MESABI WRITERS CLUB, Mesabi Community College, Virginia MN 55792. Contact: Archie Hill. Estab. 1972. Meets monthly.

MINNEAPOLIS WRITER'S WORKSHOP INC., Contact: Robert J. Schadewald, President. Rt #1, Box 129, Rogers MN 55374.

MINNESOTA AUTHORS GUILD, 2609 Pillsbury Ave. S., Minneapolis MN 55408. President: R. Waterston.

MINNESOTA CHRISTIAN WRITER'S GUILD, 7340 Brunswick Ave. N., Minneapolis MN 55443. Secretary: Dorothy Larson. Estab. 1954. Meets monthly.

PEPIN PEN CLUB, Donna Rosen, Secretary, 615 N. Garden St, Lake City MN 55041. (612)345-4393. Estab. 1975. Meets monthly.

WRITERS BY-LINES, 2936 N. Simpson, Roseville MN 55113. (612)633-6734. Contact: Larry Johns. Meets at Lakewood Community College, White Bear MN.

Missouri

CARTHAGE WRITERS GUILD, 608 W. Highland, Carthage MO 64836. President: Jacqueline Potter. Estab. 1960. Meets monthly.

MISSOURI WRITERS' GUILD, 2501 N. Franklin, Springfield MO 65803. Secretary: Sue McDonald. Estab. 1915. Meets annually, chapters throughout the state meet more frequently for seminars and workshops. Brochure sent on request. "Any Missourian who has met at least one of the following requirements shall be eligible for membership: authorship or co-authorship of a published book; sale of three articles, stories or poems; sale of three briefs, stories, articles, or comparable materials to an educational publisher; sale of one serial or novelette to a periodical; sale of one play; or sale of one motion picture screenplay, radio or TV script."

NATIONAL LEAGUE OF AMERICAN PENWOMEN, ST. LOUIS BRANCH, Bernice Peukertr, President, 117 E. Bodley, B-4, St., St. Louis MO 63122. (314)821-7726. Estab. 1926. Meets monthly.

ST. LOUIS WRITERS' GUILD, 634 Camborne Dr, St. Louis MO 63125. (314)892-0519. President: Mary Gorman. Estab. 1920. Meets monthly except July and August.

WRITER'S GROUP, Communiversity, c/o University of Missouri—Kansas City. For information contact Robert Patrick, Box 2512, Kansas City KS 66110.

Nebraska

CHRISTIAN WRITERS OF OMAHA, Contact: Mary Brite, 11405 Farnam Circle, Omaha NE 68154. Estab. 1975. Classes and critiques available.

NEBRASKA WRITERS GUILD, Box 187, Ogallala NE 69153. Contact: Robert F. Lute.

NORTHEAST NEBRASKA WRITERS, 717 E. Norfolk Ave., Norfolk NE 68701. President: Leatta Stortvedt. Estab. 1974. Meets monthly.

OMAHA WRITERS' CLUB, 517 S. 51st St., Omaha NE 68106. President: Cathy Nelson. Estab. 1945. Meetings announced by mail. Please write.

New Hampshire

NASHUA WRITERS' CLUB, Nashua Public Library, 2 Court St., Hunt Room, Nashua NH 03060. President: Ray Disharoon. Estab. 1964. Meets twice monthly.

New Jersey

NEW JERSEY POETRY SOCIETY, INC., Box 217, Wharton NJ 07885.

New Mexico

FARMINGTON WRITERS ASSOCIATION, Rt. 1, Box 99C, Aztec NM 87410. (505)334-2869. President: Margaret Cheasebro. Estab. 1972. Meets monthly.

ROSWELL WRITERS GUILD, 1104 Avenida Del Sumbre, Roswell NM 88201. Publicity Chairman: Lois Reader. Estab. 1972. Meets monthly. "We also have two workshops on the second Tuesday evening and the second Friday afternoon meeting."

New York

INTERNATIONAL WOMEN'S WRITING GUILD, Box 810, Gracie Station, New York NY 10028. Executive Director: Hannelore Hahn. Estab. 1976. Meets weekly, September through June.

BROOKLYN CONTEST AND FILLER WRITING CLUB, Selma Glasser, 241 Dahill Rd.,

Brooklyn NY 11218. "Please enclude SASE for free details."

NEW YORK POETRY FORUM, Dr. Dorothea Neale, Director, 3064 Albany Crescent, Apt. 54, Bronx NY 10463. Estab. 1958. "We have workshops, public programs and awards. Meets semimonthly.

THE NIAGARA FALLS ASSOCIATION OF PROFESSIONAL WOMEN WRITERS, 147 Chestnut, Youngstown NY 14174. President: Judy Kay. Estab. 1937. Meets monthly. "Full membership is limited to published writers who have been paid for their work. Associate members must be published even though unpaid. Membership is also limited to those in both New York and Canada who are within commuting distance."

North Carolina

CHARLOTTE WRITERS CLUB, 2700 Spring Circle, Matthews NC 28105. Contact: Betty Hill Folts. Estab. 1922. Meets monthly.

Ohio

GREATER CANTON WRITERS' GUILD, Malone College, 515 25th St. NW, Canton OH 44709. President: Judi Bailey. Estab. 1966. Meets monthly.

LUNCH-BUNCH, Norma Sundberg, 1740 Mechanicsville Rd., Rock Creek OH 44084. (216)474-5756.

MANUSCRIPT CLUB OF AKRON, Tom Troyer, 4174 Kent Rd., Stow OH 44224. Estab. 1929. Meets monthly.

MEDINA COUNTY WRITER'S CLUB, Carol J. Wilcox, 3219 Country Club Dr., Medina OH 44256.

QUEEN CITY WRITERS, 6108 Joyce Lane, Cincinnati OH 45237. (513)351-1721. Contact: Rose A. Brook. Estab. 1976. Meets monthly.

SIGMA TAU DELTA, Beta Beta Chapter, 1167 Addison Rd., Cleveland OH 44103. Past President: Bernice Krumhansl. Estab. 1926. Meets monthly October-June. Applicants "must have had the equivalent of one year of college English composition, or special writing workshops. This might be waived for a published author."

TRI-STATE WRITERS, 3386 Robb Ave., Cincinnati OH 45211. (513)481-5409. President: Melba Eydel. Meets monthly.

VERSE WRITERS' GUILD OF OHIO, Jennifer Groce, President, 2384 Hardesty Dr. S., Columbus OH 43204. Estab. 1928. Meets monthly.

WOMAN'S PRESS CLUB, Evelyn P. Johnston, 6350 Salem Rd., Cincinnati, OH 45230. Estab. 1888. Meets monthly, April through December except July, August and September. "Membership is by invitation and requires evidence of written work already published and paid for."

WORD MERCHANTS, The Writer's League of Eastern Cincinnati, Box 312, Milford OH 45150. Contact: Michael A. Banks. Estab. 1978. Meets monthly.

Oklahoma

OKLAHOMA CITY WRITERS, Box 60494, Oklahoma City OK 73146. Affiliate of Oklahoma Writers Federation, Inc. Contact: Kathryn Fanning. Estab. 1914. Meets monthly January to May. Current membership: 200.

SHAWNEE WRITERS ASSOCIATION, 1225 Sherry Lane, Shawnee OK 74801. Director: Ernestine Gravley. Estab. 1968. Meets monthly.

STILLWATER WRITERS, Secretary: Donna Cooper, 1001 Liberty Lane., Stillwater OK 74074. Estab. 1932. Meets monthly. Membership limited to 15-18 members.

WRITERS GROUP OF CUSHING, South Kings Hwy., Cushing OK 74023. President: Mazie Cox Read. Estab. 1968. Meets monthly.

Oregon

GRANTS PASS WRITER'S WORKSHOP, 114 Espey Rd., Grants Pass OR 97526. Director: Dorothy Francis. Estab. 1970. Meets weekly.

WESTERN WORLD HAIKU SOCIETY, 4102 NE 130th Place, Portland OR 97230. Founder: Lorraine Ellis Harr. Estab. 1972. Meets semiannually. Sponsors an annual haiku contest. Anthology of winners available 1976/1977 and 1978 for $3.35. Next contest July 1 to October 1. SASE (legal size) for contest rules.

Pennsylvania

DES SCRIBES, 15 Harbor Rd., Levittown PA 19056. (215)945-7315, from 6-9 p.m. Secretary: Kathryn Kendall Axelson. Estab. 1976. Meets monthly. Current membership: 17. Membership limited to 25.

HOMEWOOD POETRY FORUM, Mary Savage, Inner City Services, Homewood Branch Carnegie Library, 7101 Hamilton Ave., Pittsburgh PA 15206.

LANCASTER AREA CHRISTIAN WRITERS FELLOWSHIP, Mennonite Information Center, 2209 Millstream Rd., Lancaster PA 17603. Contact: John K. Brenneman, 258 Brenneman Rd., Lancaster PA 17603. (717)872-5183. Meets bimonthly.

LEHIGH VALLEY WRITERS' GUILD, Box 74, Springtown PA 18181. President: Theresa S. Hinton. Estab. 1938. Meets biweekly.

THE PITTSBURGH BRANCH OF BOOKFELLOWS, 3461 Harrisburg St., Pittsburgh PA 15204. Contact: Ralph Watson, Carsten Ahrens.

THE SCRIBBLERS, Box 522, Hatboro PA 19040.

SQUIRREL HILL POETRY WORKSHOP, Carnegie Library, Square Hill Branch, Forbes and Murray Aves., Pittsburgh PA 15217. (412)521-1540. Contact: Sue Elkind. Estab. 1976. Meets Biweekly.

WILLIAMSPORT WRITERS FORUM, 2318 Dove St., Williamsport PA 17701. Contact: Cynthia Hoover. Estab. 1959. Meets monthly.

WRITERS WORKSHOP OF DELAWARE VALLEY, c/o Our Lady of Angels College, Aston PA 19014.

Rhode Island

RHODE ISLAND WRITERS' GUILD, 51 Homer St., Providence RI 02905.

South Dakota

SIOUXLAND CREATIVE WRITERS' CLUB, Mrs. Larry Ells, 1905 S. Lake Ave., Sioux Falls SD 57105. Meets twice a month.

Texas

ABILENE WRITERS GUILD, 617 Larkin, Abilene TX 79601. President: Shirley Strawn. Estab. 1967. Meets monthly.

AMERICAN POETRY LEAGUE, Box 253, Junction TX 76849. President: Dr. Stella Woodall. Estab. 1922. Meets annually.

BEAUMONT CHAPTER OF THE POETRY SOCIETY OF TEXAS, Violette Newton, 3230 Ashwood Lane, Beaumont TX 77703.

CHRISTIAN WRITERS' LEAGUE, 1604 E. Taylor, Harlingen TX 78550. Contact: Jean H. Dudley.

CREATIVE WRITING WORKSHOP, Pauline Neff, 10235 Best Dr., Dallas TX 75229.

NATIONAL LEAGUE OF AMERICAN PEN WOMEN, SAN ANTONIO BRANCH, Dr Stella Woodall, Organizer and Charter President, Box 253, Junction TX 76849.

PANHANDLE PEN WOMEN, Box 616, Pampa TX 79065. Director: Evelyn Pierce Nace. Estab. 1920. Meets bimonthly. "Active members must be published writers; associate members are seriously interested in writing, but have not yet been published. Meetings and opportunities are open to both active and associate members."

SOUTH PLAINS WRITERS ASSOCIATION, Box 10114, Lubbock TX 79408. Director: Arline Harris. Estab. 1955. Meets monthly, September-May.

STELLA WOODALL POETRY SOCIETY/INTERNATIONAL, Dr. Stella Woodall, President, Box 253, Junction TX 76849. Sponsors an annual seminar with prizes of more than $100. Dr. Woodall edits and publishes a quarterly magazine with prizes for best poem in each edition.

WRITER'S CLUB OF PASADENA, 2204 Cherry Lane, Pasadena TX 77502. Marketing and Library Chairman: June Caesar. Estab. 1966. Meets monthly.

Utah

GOLDEN SPIKE CHAPTER-UTAH WRITER'S LEAGUE, 528 E. Forest, Box 446, Brigham City UT 84302. (801)723-3667. President: Mrs. Jeanne B. Wilson. Estab. 1976. Meets monthly.

LEAGUE OF UTAH WRITERS, Price Chapter, 625 Washington Ave., Price UT 84501. President: Jeanette McAlpine. Estab. 1976. Meets monthly.

LEAGUE OF UTAH WRITERS, Utah Valley Chapter, 2858 Marrcrest W., Provo UT 84601. (801)377-5019. Secretary: Dorothy Dent. Estab. 1937. Meets monthly.

SEVIER VALLEY CHAPTER OF THE LEAGUE OF UTAH WRITERS, Marilyn A. Henrie, 68 E. 2nd St., South, Richfield UT 84701.

Virginia

THE WRITERS ASSOCIATION OF TIDEWATER, 76 Algonquin Rd., Hampton VA 23661. Chairman: Christine Sparks. Estab. 1976. Meets monthly.

Washington

LEAGUE OF WESTERN WRITERS, President: Drake Harrison Sisley, 5200 16th Ave. NE, Seattle WA 98105. (206)522-1980. Treasurer: Philip Lewis Arena, 5603 239th Place SW, Mountlake Terrace WA 98043. (206)774-3722 (no collect calls). Publishes monthly newsletter.

POETRY LEAGUE OF AMERICA, Philip Lewis Arena, Poetry Manager, 5603 239th Place, SW, Mountlake Terrace WA 98043. Estab. 1972. Publishes monthly newsletter, quarterly poetry magazine, quarterly writing magaine, quarterly haiku and an annual poetry magazine.

TACOMA WRITERS CLUB, Margaret Whitis, 3903 E. 112th St., Tacoma WA 98446. Meets monthly.

WRITERS AND ILLUSTRATORS CO-OP, 2102 Sullivan Dr. NW, Gig Harbor WA 98335. Secretary: Wayne O. Clark. Estab. 1972. Meets monthly.

Wisconsin

SHEBOYGAN COUNTY WRITERS CLUB, Marion Weber, 1929 N. 13th St., Sheboygan WI 53081. Estab. 1958. Meets monthly.

THE UPLAND WRITERS, Mrs. Harry Johns, 213 W. Chapel, Dodgeville WI 53533.

Wyoming

WYOMING WRITERS INC., Stanley Talbott, Box 321, Encompment WY 82325.

Canada

CANADIAN AUTHORS ASSOCIATION, 24 Ryerson Ave., Toronto, Ontario, Canada M5T 2P3.

Canal Zone

CROSSROADS WRITERS, A. Grimm Richardson, Secretary, Box 93, Gatun, Canal Zone.

Writers' Colonies

Some of the best writing of our time has been produced by writers working in writers' or artists' colonies. These institutions offer writers the opportunity to remove themselves from the grind of the day-to-day world, and allow them to work in an atmosphere of comfort and privacy. Interaction with other working artists—another benefit of working in a writers' colony—can greatly enhance the creative process.

The following listings are for artists' colonies that provide facilities for active writers. Listings cover colony capacity, cost, availability of financial aid or grants, and eligibility requirements. Some colonies operate year 'round; others operate only during specific seasons or months.

Send SASE to the colonies that appeal to you for additional information.

Massachusetts

CUMMINGTON COMMUNITY OF THE ARTS, Cummington MA 01026. (403)634-2172. Director: Molly Snyder. Founded 1923. Open to 30 adults and 12 children (summer); 15 adults (winter).
Purpose/Programs: "A place and atmosphere in which artists can work. A retreat in nature and community living (we share some maintenance and housekeeping tasks and eat dinner together). Artists come from various disciplines, age groups, and parts of the country. Aside from some group responsibilities, each artist is free to make his/her own schedule and priorities. Eligibility is based on excellence of work as judged by admissions committees. Fees: $230/month (September-June); $750 for adults, $375 for children in summer session (July-August). "Financial aid is available to some economically disadvantaged writers and artists."

FINE ARTS WORK CENTER, 24 Pearl St., Provincetown MA 02657. (617)487-9960. Contact: Bill Tchakirides, director. Founded 1968. Open to 20 members at one time.
Purpose/Programs: "To give young artists and writers who have finished their formal education time off to work and develop their talents outside an academic situation, but not isolated from their peers as well as older writers and artists. We give grants from $200-250 per month to approximately 20 writers and artists (10 in each discipline). Visual artists receive studios and some writers are given studio apartments. Length of stay is October 1 to May 1. Open during winter only. There is a visiting program of readings and lectures by distinguished writers and artists. Write for application." Deadline, February 1st of year preceding residency. Eligibility is based solely on samples of work. There is an application fee.

New Hampshire

MILDRED I. REID WRITERS' COLONY. Contact: Mildred I. Reid (at the colony), Contoocook NH 03229. (603)746-3625. Established in 1956. Cost: $90-115 weekly includes private room, private conferences, class conferences, food. Fiction, nonfiction, plays, poetry. Length of stay: 1-8 weeks, starting July 2-August 27. No application deadline, but early reservations desirable. Scholarship available for woman acting as hostess halftime or fulltime. No more than 12 writers/week accepted.

New Mexico

HELENE WURLITZER FOUNDATION OF NEW MEXICO. Contact: Henry A. Sauerwein Jr., Executive Director, Box 545, Taos NM 87571. (505)758-2413. Established in 1954. For all creative artists in every field. Free housing; residents supply their own food. No financial assistance available. Length of stay: 3-12 months. Open year-round. Room for 12 persons. No application deadline.

New York

MacDOWELL COLONY. For admissions, contact: The MacDowell Colony, 680 Park Ave., New York NY 10021. Estab: 1907. For writers, sculptors, printmakers, photographers, filmmakers, painters and composers. Cost: $70/week; fellowships available. Length of stay: 1-3 months. Open all year. Accommodates 32 residents, summer; 22, winter. Application deadlines: 6 months in advance, except June through August, when applications must be in by January 15.

MILLAY COLONY FOR THE ARTS, INC. Apply to Ann-Ellen Lesser, Executive Director, Steepletop, Austerlitz NY 12017. (518)392-3103. Established in 1973. For writers, composers and visual artists. Room, board and studio space provided. Length of stay is one month. Open all year. Studio and living facilities for 3-5 residents. This is the former home of the poet Edna St. Vincent Millay. "Admissions committees of professional artists review applications, looking for talent and seriousness of purpose." Applications may be obtained by writing the Admissions Office at the colony, at above address.

YADDO. Contact: Curtis Harnack, Executive Director, Yaddo, Box 395, Saratoga Springs NY 12866. Began operation in 1926. Room and studio space at no cost, but voluntary contributions expected. Length of stay: 1-2 months. Open year-round, but primarily in summer, May through Labor Day. Literary merit, rather than popular appeal, is criterion for admission. Applicants must submit work and 2 letters of recommendation. February 1 is annual deadline for applications. Open to persons of any age and nationality who have already published some work. Visual artists and composers also use Yaddo facilities.

Texas

DOBIE-PAISANO FELLOWSHIP. Contact: Audrey Slate, Dobie-Paisano Project, University of Texas at Austin, Main Bldg. 101, Austin TX 78712. (512)471-7213. Established in 1967. For persons born or living in Texas or those whose work is identified with the region. Free housing in the former Dobie ranch, two $3,000 awards for 6-months each. Length of stay: 6 months. 1980-81 fellowships are for writers. Year begins September 1. Application deadline: March 15.

Virginia

VIRGINIA CENTER FOR THE CREATIVE ARTS AT SWEET BRIAR, Box VCCA, Sweet Briar VA 24595. (804)946-7236. Director: William Smart. Provides room, board and individual studio space for 12 painters, writers, sculptors and composers. Offers 1- to 3-month residencies year-round with longer and shorter periods considered in special circumstances. Fee: $70 weekly with a limited number of abatements available where need is demonstrated. Selective admission: application form, samples of work, curriculum vita, and letters of recommendation required.

Writers' Conferences

Conferences and workshops are sources of two *in's* for writers: inspiration and information. You can learn about trends, market needs and writing techniques. Better yet, you can immerse yourself in a refreshing atmosphere of writers and writing. Attending these events is also a good way of making personal contact with editors.

Select a conference as carefully as you would a publisher. Write for details about staff, workshops, manuscript criticism opportunities, fees, accommo-

dations, and the length and specific dates of the conference. Research the background of speakers—and of the conference itself, if possible. Writer Louise Boggess gives some good tips on selecting and preparing for a conference in "Conference Commandments" in the May 1979 issue of *Writer's Digest*.

Unless otherwise indicated, the conferences listed here are held every year. Check the May issues of *Writer's Digest* and *The Writer* for conference updates.

Alabama

ALABAMA WRITERS' CONCLAVE, Carl Morton, 2221 Woodview Dr., Birmingham AL 35216.

Arkansas

ARKANSAS WRITERS' CONFERENCE, 510 East St., Benton AR 72015. Director: Anna Nash Yarbrough. Held first week-end in June, annually, in Little Rock AR. Large cash awards for the best in prose and poetry. Open to writers in all states. For program and awards, send SASE to the Director.

California

CABRILLO SUSPENSE WRITERS' CONFERENCE, Cabrillo College, 6500 Soquel Dr., Aptos CA 95003. (408)425-6331. Dean, Community Education: Dr. Timothy Welch. Estab. 1976. Annual. Held in September for published and unpublished writers.

CALIFORNIA WRITERS CONFERENCE, Dorothy Benson, 2214 Derby St., Berkeley CA 94705. Held biannually in June or early July.

HOW TO SUCCESSFULLY SELF-PUBLISH YOUR OWN WORK CONFERENCE, Copy Concepts, Inc., Box 9512, San Diego CA 92109. Contact: Marilyn Ross. Biannual. Held each spring and fall for published and unpublished writers. Conferences also held in Arizona, California, District of Columbia, New York, Texas and Washington.

LA JOLLA SUMMER WRITERS' CONFERENCE, University Extension, X-001, University of California, San Diego, La Jolla CA 92093. Director: John Ball. Held each August on UCSD campus for published and unpublished writers.

LITERARY HALL OF FAME WRITERS CONFERENCE, Box 20880, Long Beach CA 90801. (213)436-3132. President: Howard E. Hill. Estab. 1976. Held annually in June for published and unpublished writers.

THE MYSTERY WRITERS' CONFERENCE, University Extension X-001, University of California, San Diego, La Jolla CA 92093. Director: John Ball. Held each August on UCSD campus for published and unpublished writers.

PASADENA CITY COLLEGE ANNUAL WRITER'S FORUM, Sponsored by Pasadena City College Extended Campus Programs, 1570 E. Colorado Blvd., Pasadena CA 91106. Contact: Jerene Hewitt. Held Friday and Saturday of the second week in May.

LYNN ROBERTS AGENCY WRITERS CONFERENCE, Box 23040, San Jose CA 95153.

(408)225-6902. Contact: Lynn Roberts. Estab. 1978. Held in February and September for published and unpublished writers. Emphasis on writing and marketing.

SEMINAR FOR FREELANCE WRITERS, Community Services, Canada College, 4200 Farm Hill Blvd., Redwood City CA 94061. Director: Gladys Cretan. Held each May for published and unpublished writers.

WRITER'S CLUB OF WHITTIER SEMINAR, 7716 Westman Ave., Whittier CA 90606. (213)699-5935. President: Fern Palmer. Annual. Held in March for published and unpublished writers.

WRITERS CONFERENCE IN CHILDREN'S LITERATURE, Box 296, Los Angeles CA 90066. Estab. 1970. Held annually in August for published and unpublished writers.

WRITERS' FORUM, Pasadena City College, Office of Extended Campus Programs, 1570 E. Colorado Blvd., Pasadena CA 91106. Held annually in May.

Colorado
YWCA CO-ED WRITERS WORKSHOP, 1460 Lamar St., Apt. 36, Denver CO 80212. Chairman: Leota Troute. Estab. 1965. Meets weekly except in summer when meetings are monthly.

Connecticut
CONNECTICUT WRITERS' LEAGUE CONFERENCE, Box 78, Farmington CT 06032. Co-chairman: Thomas C. Jonesa and Maryland Linclon. One-day conference held in Hartford CT, for anyone interested in writing.

WESLEYAN-SUFFIELD WRITER-READER CONFERENCE, John W. Paton, Executive Secretary, Wesleyan University, Middletown CT 06457.

District of Columbia
GEORGETOWN UNIVERSITY WRITERS CONFERENCE, Georgetown University School for Summer and Continuing Education, Washington DC 20057. Director: Dr. Riley Hughes. Held on campus each July (abroad, each June) for published and unpublished writers.

Florida
FLORIDA SUNCOAST WRITERS CONFERENCE, University of South Florida, St. Petersburg FL 33701. (813)974-2421. Directors: Marjorie Schunck, Ed Hirshberg. Estab. 1972. Annual. Held in January for published and unpublished writers.

FLORIDA WRITERS' CONFERENCE, Division of Continuing Education, University of Florida, 2012 W. University Ave., Gainsville FL 32603. (904)392-1701. Estab. 1970. Held annually in February for published and unpublished writers.

Georgia
DIXIE COUNCIL OF AUTHORS AND JOURNALISTS CREATIVE WRITING WORKSHOP, Harold R. Random, Director, 1212 Lanier Blvd. NE, Atlanta GA 30306.

Hawaii
HAWAII WRITERS AND ARTISTS CONFERENCE, National League of American Pen Women—Hawaii Branch, 404 Piikoi, Room 218, Honolulu HI 96814. Contact: Carol Hogan. 2-day conference for writers and artists.

Illinois
CHRISTIAN WRITERS INSTITUTE CONFERENCE AND WORKSHOP, Box 513, Glen Ellyor IL. 60137.

ILLINOIS WESLEYAN UNIVERSITY WRITERS' CONFERENCE, Illinois Wesleyan

University, Bloomington IL 61701. Director: Mrs. Bettie W. Story. Held each June or July for published and unpublished writers.

INTERNATIONAL BLACK WRITERS CONFERENCE, INC., 4019 S. Vincennes Ave., Chicago IL 60053. Director: Alice C. Browning. "The first and only ongoing black writers conference in the world. 1980 is our 10th aniversary." Held each June for published and unpublished writers.

McKENDREE WRITERS' CONFERENCE, Helen Church, President, c/o *Lebanon Advertiser,* Lebanon IL 62254.

MISSISSIPPI VALLEY WRITERS' CONFERENCE, 3403 45th St., Moline IL 61265. Director: David R. Collins. Held each June for published and unpublished writers.

WRITING '80, 125½ 18th St., Rock Island IL 61201. Secretary: Kim Ostrom. Held each March for published and unpublished writers.

Indiana
INDIANA UNIVERSITY WRITERS' CONFERENCE, Ballantine 464, Bloomington IN 47401. Director: Roger Mitchell. Estab. 1941. Held each June/July for published and unpublished writers.

MIDWEST WRITERS' WORKSHOP, Ball State University, Muncie IN 47306. Co-Directors: Dwight Hoover, Rita Winters. Held each August for published and unpublished writers. Dates for 1979-August 12-17.

OHIO RIVER WRITERS' CONFERENCE, 16½ SE 2nd St., Evansville IN 47708. (812)422-2111. Executive Director: Jane Moore. Estab. 1976. Held annually first weekend in August for published and unpublished writers. Poetry section with Sandra McPherson and George Hitchock; Children's literature with Madelaine L. Engle; Fiction with Ray Carver; and Nonfiction with Shirley Williams.

Kentucky
CREATIVE WRITING CONFERENCE, Department of English, Eastern Kentucky University, Richmond KY 40475. Director: William Sutton. Held each June for published and unpublished writers.

WRITING WORKSHOP FOR PEOPLE OVER 57, Council on Aging, 4 Frazee Hall, University of Kentucky, Lexington KY 40506. (606)258-2657. Assistant Director: Maude B. Higgs. Estab. 1966. Held in August for published and unpublished writers.

Maine
MAINE WRITERS WORKSHOP, G.F. Bush, Director, Box 82, Stonington ME 04681. (207)367-2484.

SEACOAST WRITERS CONFERENCE, 160 Goodwin Rd., Eliot ME 03903. Registrar: Mrs. Lillian H. Crowell. Held each October for published and unpublished writers.

STATE OF MAINE WRITERS' CONFERENCE, Box 296, Ocean Park ME 04063. Co-Chairman: Richard Burns. Estab. 1941. Held August 21-24.

Massachusetts
CAPE COD WRITERS' CONFERENCE, Box 111, West Hyannisport MA 02622. Executive Secretary: Mrs. Pierre Vuilleumier. Held each August for published and unpublished writers.

SCBW NEW ENGLAND CHILDREN'S LITERATURE CONFERENCE, Box 27, Hatfield MA 01038. Director: Jane Stemple. Held each April for published and unpublished writers.

SCRIPTORS' CONFERENCE, Box 1745, Springfield MA 01101. Secretary: Maxine Englehardt. Held each summer for published and unpublished writers.

Michigan
CLARION SF WRITERS' WORKSHOP. Justin Morrill College, Michigan State University, Olds Hall, Michigan State University, East Lansing MI 48824. Directors: Dr. Leonard N. Isaacs, Dr. R. Glenn Wright. Held each July/August.

CRAFTSMANSHIP OF CREATIVE WRITING CONFERENCE. Conferences and Institutes, Oakland University, Rochester MI 48063. Assistant Director: Douglas Alden Peterson. Held each October for published and unpublished writers.

UNIVERSITY OF MICHIGAN CONFERENCE ON TEACHING TECHNICAL AND PROFESSIONAL COMMUNICATION. Humanities Department, College of Engineering, University of Michigan, Ann Arbor MI 48109.

Minnesota
UPPER MIDWEST WRITERS' CONFERENCE. Sr. Audre Marthaler. Bemidji State University, Bemidji MN 56601. Held 2 weeks in July.

Missouri
MISSOURI PRESS WOMEN. Ann Fair Dodson, 1315 N. Broadway, Springfield MO 65802.

Nebraska
BRITE CHRISTIAN WRITERS CONFERENCE. 11405 Farnam Circle, Omaha NE 68154. Chairman: Mary Brite. Held annually in fall.

OMAHA WRITERS' CLUB SPRING CONFERENCE. 517 S. 51st Ave., Omaha NE 68106. President: Cathy Nelson. Held each May for published and unpublished writers.

New Hampshire
THE STAR ISLAND CONFERENCE FOR CREATIVE WRITERS. 40 Argonne Dr., Kenmore NY 14217. (716)873-6412. Registrar: Sylvia Engen Wilson. Estab. 1949. Held on Star Island in the shoals off Portsmouth NH July-August for two weeks. No publication requirements.

New Jersey
COMEDY AND HUMOR WORKSHOP. 74 Pullman Ave., Elberon NJ 07740. Director: George Q. Lewis. Held each June, July and August in addition to regular spring (February) and fall (September) semesters for published and unpublished writers.

New York
ADIRONDACK-METROLAND WRITERS & EDUCATORS CONFERENCE. Box 189, Clifton Park NY 12065. Director: Dr. Harry Barba. Held each July for published and unpublished writers. SASE for information.

CHAUTAUQUA WRITERS' WORKSHOP. Summer School Office, Box 28, Chautauqua NY 14722.

CORNELL UNIVERSITY CREATIVE WRITING WORKSHOP. 105 Day Hall, Ithaca NY 14853. (607)256-4987. Assistant Dean: Charles W. Jermy Jr. Estab. 1970. Annual. Held June-August for published and unpublished writers.

CREATIVE WRITING WORKSHOP. Niagara County Community College, 3111 Saunders Settlement Rd., Sanborn NY 14132.

FICTION INTERNATIONAL/ST. LAWRENCE UNIVERSITY WRITERS' CON-FERENCE. Joe David Bellamy, St. Lawrence University, Canton NY 13617.

IWWG WOMEN'S WRITING CONFERENCE/RETREAT. Box 810, Gracie Station, New York NY 10028. (212)737-7536. Executive Director, International Women's Writing Guild: Hannelore Hahn. Estab. 1976. Held in February on West Coast and the last weekend in July and the first week in August on the East Coast for published and unpublished writers.

NATIONAL PLAYWRIGHTS CONFERENCE OF THE EUGENE O'NEILL MEMORIAL THEATER CENTER. Suite 1012, 1860 Broadway, New York NY 10023. Artistic Director: Lloyd Richards. Held mid-July to mid-August each year for published and unpublished writers. Submissions for new plays are accepted from September 15th through December 1st. Please write to the above address for submission guides.

NEW YORK HOLIDAY WORKSHOP. 20 Plaza St., Brooklyn NY 11238. Director: Pauline Bloom. Held each October for published and unpublished writers.

NIAGARA FRONTIER CHRISTIAN WRITERS WORKSHOP. 6853 Webster Rd., Orchard Park NY 14157. (716)622-5259. Conference Director: Don Booth. Estab. 1970. Held annually in June for published and unpublished writers.

TECHNICAL WRITERS' INSTITUTE. B.F. Hammet, Director, Rensselaer Polytechnic Institute, Troy NY 12181. Held June 18-22, 1979.

UNIVERSITY OF ROCHESTER WRITERS' WORKSHOP. Dean Robert Koch, Writers' Workshop, Harkness Hall 102, University of Rochester, Rochester NY 14627. Held annually in July for published and unpublished writers.

WRITER-IN-RESIDENCE PROGRAM. Bronx Council on the Arts, 2114 Williamsbridge Road, Bronx NY 10463. (212)931-9500. Writer-in-Residence: Natalie Robins. Estab. 1978. Poetry and fiction workshops held weekly for published and unpublished writers. Individual conferences also arranged.

North Carolina

TAR HEEL WRITERS' ROUNDTABLE. Box 5393, Raleigh NC 27650. Director: Bernadette Hoyle. Held each August for published and unpublished writers.

Ohio

CUYAHOGA WRITERS' CONFERENCE. Cuyahoga Community College Eastern Campus, 25444 Harvard Rd., Cleveland OH 44122. Director: Mrs. Margaret Taylor. Held each April or May for published and unpublished writers.

MIAMI UNIVERSITY CREATIVE WRITING WORKSHOP. Upham Hall, Miami University, Oxford OH 45056. Director: Milton White. Held each May for published and unpublished writers.

MIDWEST WRITERS CONFERENCE. The Barn Campus Center, Malone College, 515 25th St. NW, Canton OH 44709. (216)489-0800 ext. 475. Editors, Agents, Workshops Director: John W. Oliver Jr. Estab. 1969. Annual. Held the 1st weekend in October for published and unpublished writers. Annual workshops in fiction, nonfiction, poetry, inspiration, film and songwriting. Additional workshops on demand.

OHIO POETRY DAY. Evan Lodge, President, 1506 Prospect Rd., Hudson OH 44236.

QUEEN CITY WRITERS WRITING SEMINAR. 3810 Cartwheel Terrace, Cincinnati OH 45239. President: Henry Dorfman. Annual. Held each spring for published and unpublished writers.

WRITER'S WORKSHOP. Gary Mitchner, Director, Sinclair Community College, 444 W. 3rd St., Dayton OH 45402.

Oklahoma

OKLAHOMA WRITERS FEDERATION ANNUAL CONFERENCE. Ernestine Gravley, 1225 Sherry Lane, Shawnee OK 74801. Held annually in May for published and unpublished writers. Send SASE for information.

UNIVERSITY OF OKLAHOMA ANNUAL SHORT COURSE ON PROFESSIONAL WRITING. Leonard Logan, Oklahoma Center for Continuing Education, University of Oklahoma, 1700 Asp Ave., Norman OK 73037.

Oregon

HAYSTACK WRITERS' WORKSHOPS, Dona Beattie, Box 1491, Portland OR 97207.

WILLAMETTE WRITERS CONFERENCE, Mrs. Philip C. Herzog, 3622 SE Lambert, Portland OR 97202.

Pennsylvania

PHILADELPHIA WRITERS CONFERENCE, Box 834, Philadelphia PA 19105. Registrar: Emma S. Wood.

ST. DAVIDS CHRISTIAN WRITERS' CONFERENCE, Rt. 2., Cochranville PA 19330. (215)593-5963. Registrar: Edna Mast. Estab. 1957. Held annually in June for published and unpublished writers, at Eastern College, St. Davids PA.

South Carolina

WINTHROP COLLEGE WRITERS CONFERENCE, Dean of Continuing Education, Joynes Center for Continuing Education, Winthrop College, Rock Hill SC 29733. Held November 15-17, 1979.

Texas

ABLILENE WRITERS GUILD WORKSHOP, Juanita Zachry, 502 E. N. 16th St., Abilene TX 79601.

PANHANDLE PEN WOMEN AND WEST TEXAS STATE UNIVERSITY WRITERS' ROUND-UP, 6209 Adirondack, Amarillo TX 79106. Director: Dolores Spencer. Held October 18-20, 1979. For published and unpublished writers.

PATRIOTIC POETRY SEMINAR, Box 253, Junction TX 76849. President-Director: Dr. Stella Woodall. Held each October for published and unpublished writers. Prizes of more than $100 for best Patriotic Poems submitted by registered poets. The best poems submitted are published in hardback book.

SOUTH TEXAS PRO-AM WRITERS RALLY, 1601 N. Main Ave., San Antonio TX 78284. (512)227-7156. Executive Director: Charles Bradbury. Estab. 1974. Annual. Held in October for published and unpublished writers.

SOUTHWEST WRITERS' CONFERENCE, University of Houston, 4800 Calhoun, Houston TX 77004. Contact: Director of Continuing Education.

Utah

LEAGUE OF UTAH WRITERS ROUNDUP, Box 144, Kaysville UT 84037. (801)376-8537. President: Esther Parks. Estab. 1936. Annual. Held in September for published and unpublished writers.

ROCKY MOUNTAIN WRITERS' CONVENTION, Conferences and Workshops, 124 HRCB, Brigham Young University, Provo UT 84602. Director: Gary R. Bascom. Held each July for published and unpublished writers.

USU MAGAZINE ARTICLE WRITER'S WORKSHOP, Dick Harris, Director, Utah State University, Logan UT 84321. Held every even-numbered year in June.

WESTERN WRITERS' CONFERENCE, Conference and Institute Division, UMC 01, Utah State University, Logan UT 84322. Director: Glenn R. Wilde.

Vermont

GREEN MOUNTAINS WORKSHOP, Johnson State College, Johson VT 05656. (802)635-2356. Director: Roger Rath. Estab. 1973. Held the last two weeks in July for published and unpublished writers.

Virginia

JANUARY WRITERS' CONFERENCE, George Mason University, English Department, Fairfax VA 22030. (703)323-2220. Coordinator, Writing Program: Donald R. Galler. Estab. 1978. Held annually in January for published and unpublished writers.

VIRGINIA HIGHLANDS FESTIVAL CREATIVE WRITING DAY, Brookhill Estates, Abingdon VA 24210. Chairman: Douglas E. Arnold. Held each August for unpublished writers.

Washington

CENTRUM SUMMER SEASON OF THE ARTS, Fort Worden State Park, Port Townsend WA 98368. Poetry symposium and fiction seminar.

FORT WORDEN POETRY SYMPOSIUM, Fort Worden State Park, Port Townsend WA 98368. Coordinator: Jim Heynen.

PACIFIC NORTHWEST WRITERS CONFERENCE, 1811 NE 199th St., Seattle WA 98155. (206)364-1293. Contact: Executive Secretary. Estab. 1956. Annual. Held in July for published and unpublished writers.

PORT TOWNSEND FICTION SEMINAR, Centrum, Fort Worden State Park, Port Townsend WA 98368. (206)385-3102. Program Coordinator: James Heynen. Estab. 1974. Held annually in July for published and unpublished writers.

PORT TOWNSEND POETRY SYMPOSIUM, Centrum, Fort Worden State Park, Port Townsend WA 98368. (206)385-3102. Program Coordinator: James Heynen. Estab. 1974. Held annually in July for published and unpublished writers.

Wisconsin

CHRISTIAN WRITERS' WORKSHOP, American Baptist Assembly, Green Lake WI 54941. (414)294-3323. Director of Programming/Scheduling: Lawrence H. Janssen. Estab. 1953. Held in August for published and unpublished writers.

MIDWEST WRITERS' CONFERENCE, Dr. Wayne Wolfe, University of Wisconsin-River Falls, River Falls WI 54022. Held June 12-14.

OUTDOOR WRITERS ASSOCIATION OF AMERICA ANNUAL CONFERENCE, 4141 W. Bradley Rd., Milwaukee WI 53209. Held each June.

Canada

THE BANFF CENTRE, School of Fine Arts, Box 1020, Banff, Alberta T0L 0C0 Canada. Held annually in May/June for published and unpublished writers.

SUMMER WRITERS WORKSHOP AT NEW COLLEGE, UNIVERSITY OF TORONTO, 165 Spadina Ave., Suite 8, Toronto, Canada M5T 2C4. (416)978-2011. Director: Gerald Lampert. Estab. 1968. Annual. Held the first 2 weeks in August for published and unpublished writers.

Foreign

EUROPEAN HOLIDAY WRITERS' WORKSHOP, 20 Plaza St., Brooklyn NY 11218. Director: Pauline Bloom. Held each September for published and unpublished writers.

COSTA RICA AND GUATEMALA HOLIDAY WRITERS' WORKSHOP, Pauline Bloom, 20 Plaza St., Brooklyn NY 11238.

Writers' Organizations

A major benefit of membership in a professional organization is access to specialized information and publications. Organizations often serve as information clearinghouses, forums for idea exchange among members, and sources of market information. What's more, some organizations sponsor workshops, conferences and seminars.

Association with professional groups sometimes helps build your professional image, as well. In fact, inclusion in a membership directory increases your visibility, and might lead to assignments. Editors sometimes turn to organizations and their memberships when seeking writers with specific talents.

Other financial rewards can result from your association with organizations. For example, some organizations make grants to writers, and others sponsor contests.

An organization can also serve as a liaison between you and some of the people you deal with, and can sometimes act as your representative in certain types of disputes. In these cases, an organization gives you clout by standing behind you or even speaking on your behalf.

Organizations listed here usually require evidence that applicants have attained "professional" status; definitions of "professional" vary from group to group.

Local and regional writers' clubs are listed in the Writers' Clubs section.

ACADEMY OF AMERICAN POETS, 1078 Madison Ave., New York NY 10028. Estab. 1934. President: Mrs. Hugh Bullock. Purpose of the Academy of American Poets is to encourage, stimulate, and foster the production of American poetry. Awards prizes, conducts poetry workshops, readings and other literary events.

AMERICAN ACADEMY AND INSTITUTE OF ARTS AND LETTERS, 633 W. 155th St., New York NY 10032. Executive Director: Margaret M. Mills. Estab. 1898.
Purpose: "To foster, assist, and sustain an interest in literature, music, and the fine arts. The goal is general, but the means are specific, aimed at singling out and encouraging individual artists and their work." Prospective members "must be native or naturalized citizens of the US, qualified by notable achievement in art, music or literature. In order to be eligible, the candidate's work must be essentially creative rather than interpretive. Candidates for membership can only be nominated by members. Candidates must qualify in their own department before their names are submitted for vote to the whole membership."

AMERICAN AUTO RACING WRITERS AND BROADCASTERS ASSOCIATION, 922 N. Pass Ave., Burbank CA 91505. (213)842-7005. Established in 1955. Executive Director: Ms. Dusty Brandel. An organization of writers, broadcasters and photographers who cover auto racing throughout the US. Aims primarily to improve the relationship between the press and the promoters, sanctioning bodies, sponsors and participants in the sport. Dues: $20 annually, full membership: $25 annually, associate membership.

AMERICAN MEDICAL WRITERS ASSOCIATION, 5272 River Rd., 209, Bethesda MD 20016. (301)986-9119. Executive Secretary: Lillian Sablack. Estab. 1945. 1,600 members.
Purpose: "To bring together all those engaged in medical communications and its allied professions, and is dedicated to the advancement and improvement of medical communication." Publishes a membership directory, freelance directory, newsletter and journal; also maintains a job market service. Fees: $35/year.

AMERICAN SOCIETY OF JOURNALISTS AND AUTHORS, INC., 1501 Broadway, Suite 1907, New York NY 10036. Established in 1948. President: Grace W. Weinstein. Initiation fee: $25. Annual dues for residents of New York and environs: $60. Annual dues for those residing 200 or more miles from New York: $45. For further information, contact Holly M. Redell, Executive Director.

AMERICAN TRANSLATORS ASSOCIATION, Box 129, Croton-on-Hudson NY 10520. Executive Secretary: Mrs. Rosemary Malia. Established in 1959 as a national professional society to advance the standards of translation and to promote the intellectual and material interest of translators and interpreters in the United States. Welcomes to membership all those who are interested in the field as well as translators and interpreters active in any branch of knowledge.

ASMP–SOCIETY OF PHOTOGRAPHERS IN COMMUNICATIONS, 60 E. 42nd St., New York NY 10017. (212)661-6450. Established to promote and further the interests of professional photographers in communications media such as journalism, corporate, advertising, fashion, books, etc. Acts as a clearinghouse for photographic information on markets, rates and business practices of magazines, advertising agencies, publishers and electronic media; works for copyright law revision; offers legal advice, through counsel, to members concerning questions or rights, ethics and payment. Membership categories include Sustaining, General, Associate and Student.

ASSOCIATED BUSINESS WRITERS OF AMERICA, 1450 S. Havana, Suite 620, Aurora CO 80012. Associate Director: Donald E. Bower. Members are skilled in one or more facets of business writing (advertising copy, public relations, ghost writing, books, reports, business and technical magazines, etc), and are fulltime writers. Provides directory profiling members to prospective mss buyers (at $10). Dues: $50 annually; $12.50 initiation fee.

THE AUTHORS GUILD, INC., 234 W. 44th St., New York NY 10036. (212)398-0838. Executive Secretary: Peter Heggie. Estab. 1912.
Purpose: "To act and speak with the collective voice of 5,500 writers in matters of joint professional and business concern; to advise members on individual professional and business problems as far as possible. Those eligible for membership include any author who shall have had a book published by an established American publisher within 7 years prior to his application; any author who shall have had 3 works (fiction or nonfiction) published by magazines of general circulation within 18 months prior to application." Dues: $35/year.

AUTHORS LEAGUE OF AMERICA, INC., 234 W. 44th St., New York NY 10036. Estab. 1912. Administrative Assistant: Fay W. Glover. The Authors League membership is restricted to authors and dramatists who are members of the Authors Guild, Inc., and the Dramatists Guild, Inc. Matters of joint concern to authors and dramatists, such as copyright and freedom of expression, are in the province of the league; other matters, such as contract terms and subsidiary rights, are in the province of the guilds.

AVIATION/SPACE WRITERS ASSOCIATION, 22 Pine St., Morristown NJ 07960. (201)538-0050. Executive Secretary: William F. Kaiser. Estab. 1938. Founded to establish and maintain high standards of quality and veracity in gathering, writing, editing and disseminating aeronautical information. The AWA numbers 1,200 members who work for newspapers, press services, TV, radio or other media and specialize in writing about aviation or space. Dues: $35 annually; initiation fee: $10.

CONSTRUCTION WRITERS ASSOCIATION, 202 Homer Bldg., Washington DC 20005. Estab. 1958. CWA offers its members a forum for the interchange of information, ideas and methods for improving the quality of reporting, editing and public relations in the construction field. It also provides contact between the membership and news-making officials in government, contracting firms, equipment manufacturers and distributors, consulting firms, and other construction trade and professional groups. Any person principally engaged in writing or editing material pertaining to the construciton industry for any regularly published periodical of general circulation is eligible for membership. Any public information or public relations specialist who represents an organization or agency the existence of which depends in whole or in part on the construction industry is also eligible. Annual dues: $20.

DOG WRITERS' ASSOCIATION OF AMERICA, INC., 3 Blythewood Rd., Doylestown PA 18901. President: John T. Marvin. Secretary: Sara Futh, Kinney Hill Rd., Washington Depot CT 06794. The association aims to promote and to encourage the exchange of ideas, methods and professional courtesies among its members. Membership is limited to paid dog writers, editors and/or publishers of newpapers, magazines and books dealing with dogs. Annual dues: $12.

FEMINIST WRITERS' GUILD, Box 9396, Berkeley CA 94709. (415)524-3692. Current

Administrator: Laura Tow. Estab. 1977. 1,000 members.
Purpose: To act both as a service and political body for feminist writers. Publishes a national newsletter. Referral to agents, and to other useful publications also to local chapters and contact people, and to local support groups. Fees: $10 ($5 if unemployed), $20 to institutions.

THE FOOTBALL WRITERS ASSOCIATION OF AMERICA, Box 1022, Edmond OK 73034. Secretary-Treasurer: Volney Meece. Membership is mainly sports writers on newspapers and magazines who cover college football, plus those in allied fields, chiefly college sports information directors. Dues: $7.50 annually.

GARDEN WRITERS ASSOCIATION OF AMERICA, INC., 230 Park Ave., New York NY 10017. (212)685-5917. Executive Secretary: Margaret Herbst. Membership Chairman: Gladys Reed Robinson, 680 3rd Ave., Troy NY 12182. Estab. 1944.
Purpose: "Dedicated to improving the standards of horticultural writing, art and photography in printed and broadcast media. GWAA publishes a helpful bulletin quarterly. Members also receive helpful information through Garden Bureau; *Garden News*. Plus material from various seed companies, nurseries and many others associated with the horticultural world." Annual dues: $15.

INTERNATIONAL ASSOCIATION OF BUSINESS COMMUNICATORS, 870 Market St., Suite 928, San Francisco CA 94102. Executive Director: John N. Bailey. Estab. 1970. Dedicated to the advancement of its members and to the advancement of the communication profession. Members are active in the field of business and organizational communication.

INTERNATIONAL WOMEN'S WRITING GUILD, Box 810, Gracie Station, New York 10028. Executive Director: Hannelore Hahn.
Purpose: "Established in 1976 as an alliance open to all women connected to the written word who wish to use writing for personal growth and/or professionally. To facilitate these goals, the IWWG sponsors writing conferences and retreats, as well as regional year-round writing workshops. It also publishes a bimonthly *Network* letter, and refers members to New York literary agents." Dues: $15 annually.

MOTOR SPORTS PRESS ASSOCIATION OF NORTHERN CALIFORNA, c/o Harriet Gittings, Box 484, Fremont CA 94537. Estab. 1963 for the advancement of motor sports and motor sports, journalism in Northern California, for the interchange of ideas and information; to provide a body to authenticate legitimate motor sports journalists, photographers, and radio and TV broadcasters, whether fully employed, part-time employed, or freelancing in northern California. Annual dues: $12.

MYSTERY WRITERS OF AMERICA, INC., 105 E. 19th St., New York NY 10003. Estab. 1945. Executive Secretary: Gloria Amoury. "An organization dedicated to the proposition that the detective story is the noblest sport of man." Membership includes active members who have made at least one sale in mystery, crime, or suspense writing; associate members who are either novices in the mystery writing field or nonwriters allied to the field; editors, publishers and affiliate members who are interested in mysteries. Annual dues: $35 for US members; $10 for Canadian and overseas members.

NATIONAL ASSOCIATION OF EDUCATIONAL BROADCASTERS, 1346 Connecticut Ave. NW, Washington DC 20036. Estab. 1925. President: James A. Fellows. A professional society of individuals in educational telecommunications; composed of men and women who work in public broadcasting, instructional communications and allied fields. Annual dues: $35.

NATIONAL ASSOCIATION OF GAGWRITERS, 74 Pullman Ave., Elberon NJ 07740. (201)229-9472. Contact: George Quipp Lewis. Estab: 1945.
Purpose: "To discover, develop, encourage and showcase future funny men and women; to provide guidance; to coordinate careers in comedy; to promote a national sense of humor and happiness; to maintain a high standard of comedic creativity." Fees: $25/year.

NATIONAL ASSOCIATION OF SCIENCE WRITERS, INC., Box 294, Greenlawn NY 11740. (516)757-5664. Estab. 1934. Administrative Secretary: Diane McGurgan. This organization was established to "foster the dissemination of accurate information regarding science through all media normally devoted to informing the public. In pursuit of this goal, NASW conducts a varied program to increase the flow of news from scientists, to improve the quality of its presentation, and to communicate its meaning and importance to the reading public. Anyone who is actively engaged in the dissemination of science information, and has two years or more experience in this field, is eligible to apply. There are several classes of membership. Active members must be principally engaged in reporting science through media that reach the public directly; newspapers, mass circulation magazines, trade books, radio, television and films. Associate members report science through special media: limited circulation publications and announcements from organizations such as universities, research laboratories, foundations and science-oriented corporations. Lifetime membership is extended to members after they have belonged to NASW for 25 years. Honorary membership is awarded by NASW to outstanding persons who have notably aided the objectives of the association." Annual dues: $35.

NATIONAL LEAGUE OF AMERICAN PEN WOMEN, INC., 1300 17th St. NW, Washington DC 20036. Estab. 1897. "Professionally qualified women engaged in creating and promoting letters, art, and music" are eligible for membership. Women interested in membership must qualify professionally and be presented for membership and endorsed by two active members in good standing in the league. The league holds branch, state and national meetings. Dues: Initiation fee $5. Annual branch dues plus $15 national dues. For further information, write to national president at address given above.

NATIONAL PRESS CLUB, National Press Bldg., 529 14th St. NW, Washington DC 20045. Initiation fee: $25-125. Dues: $40-244 annually, depending on membership.

NATIONAL TURF WRITERS ASSOCIATION, Willco Bldg., Suite 317, 6000 Executive Blvd., Rockville MD 20852. Secretary/Treasurer: Tony Chamblin. Membership limited to newspaper or magazine writers who regularly cover thoroughbred racing, sports editors of newspapers which regularly print thoroughbred racing news and results, and sports columnists who write columns on thoroughbred racing. Dues: $10 annually.

NATIONAL WRITERS CLUB, INC., 1450 S. Havana, Suite 620, Aurora CO 80012. Estab. 1937. Executive Director: Donald E. Bower. "Founded for the purpose of informing, aiding and protecting freelance writers worldwide. Associate membership is available to anyone seriously interested in writing. Qualifications for professional membership are publication of a book by a recognized book publisher; or sales of at least three stories or articles to national or regional magazines; or a television, stage, or motion picture play professionally produced." Annual dues: $25, associate membership; $29.50, professional membership; plus $12.50 initiation fee.

NEWSPAPER FOOD EDITORS AND WRITERS ASSOCIATION, St. Paul Dispatch & Pioneer Press, St. Paul MN 55101. Estab. 1973. President: Donna Morgan. To encourage communication among journalists devoting a substantial portion of their working time to the furthering of public's knowledge of food; to uphold and foster professional ethical standards for such persons; to increase their knowledge about food and to encourage and promote a greater understanding among fellow journalists and those who manage news dissemination organizations. Dues: $25 annually.

OUTDOOR WRITERS ASSOCIATION OF AMERICA, INC., 4141 W. Bradley Rd., Milwaukee WI 53209. (414)354-9690. Estab. 1927. Executive Director: Edwin W. Hanson. A nonprofit professional and educational organization comprised of newspaper and magazine writers, editors, photographers, broadcasters, artists, cinematographers and lecturers engaged in the dissemination of information on outdoor sports such as hunting, boating, fishing, camping, etc., and on the conservation of natural resources. Its objectives are providing a means of cross-communication among specialists in this field, promoting craft improvement, obtaining fair treatment from media, and increasing general public knowledge of the outdoors. Among other subjects, the membership deals extensively in current environmental issues." Requires that each member annually have published a specified quantity of paid material. Sponsorship by an active member of the OWAA is required for membership applicants. Dues: $15 annually; initiation fee: $35.

P.E.N., American Center, 47 5th Ave., New York NY 10003. (212)255-1977. Estab. 1921. Executive Secretary: Karen Kennerly. A world association of poets, playwrights, essayists, editors, and novelists, the purpose of P.E.N. is "to promote and maintain friendship and intellectual cooperation among men and women of letters in all countries, in the interests of literature, the exchange of ideas, freedom of expression, and good will. P.E.N. has more than

80 centers in Europe, Asia, Africa, Australia, and the Americas. Membership is open to all qualified writers, translators and editors who subscribe to the aims of International P.E.N." To qualify for membership, an applicant must have "acknowledged achievement in the literary field, which is generally interpreted as the publication by a recognized publisher of 2 books of literary merit. Membership is by invitation of the Admission Committee after nomination by a P.E.N. member."

PEN AND BRUSH CLUB, 16 E. 10th St., New York NY 10003. Estab. 1893. President: Margaret Sussman. "The Pen and Brush is a club of professional women, writers, painters, graphic artists, sculptors and craftsmen, with a resident membership limited to 350 active members in these fields. Exhibits are held in the galleries of the clubhouse by painters, sculptors, graphic artists, and craftsmen."

POETRY SOCIETY OF AMERICA, 15 Gramercy Park S., New York NY 10003. (212)254-9628. Executive Director: Douglas Blair Turnbaugh. The oldest and largest group working for an appreciation of poetry and for wider recognition of the work of living American poets, the society has a membership of traditionalists and experimentalists. Dues: $18 annually.

POETS & WRITERS, INC., 201 W. 54th St., New York NY 10019. (212)757-1766. Information Coordinator: Elliott Figman. Estab. 1971.
Purpose: "To serve as an information clearinghouse and service organization for the nation's literary community. Anyone who needs help finding the current address of a writer listed with Poets & Writers, Inc., or has a question of a general literary nature should write or call the Information Center." Publishes *Coda: Poets & Writers Newsletter* 5 times/year. Other Publications: *A Directory of American Poets and Fiction Writers, Literary Agents: A Complete Guide, Awards List* and *Sponsors List*. "Anyone with an interest in contemporary literature may use our services, subscribe to our periodicals, or purchase our reference books and pamphlets. Writers who wish to be listed must meet publication requirements: for a poet—10 or more poems in 3 different US literary publications; for a fiction writer—1 book or 3 short works of fiction in 3 US periodicals. Work may be written in English, Spanish or Native American language. Some exceptions are made for performance poets who do not normally publish. No dues or listing fees at all."

ROCKY MOUNTAIN OUTDOOR WRITERS AND PHOTOGRAPHERS, 2163 S. Dudley St., Lakewood CO 80227. Contact: Allen H. Mullen. Founded 1973.
Purpose: "RMOWP is a select regional organization of professional writers, photographers, artists and lecturers residing in the Rocky Mountain states. The organization was founded with the purpose of improving and expanding outdoor writing, photography and other communication forms." Fees: $10 initiation, $10/year (active; $10 initiation fee: $5/year associate; $25 minimum for supporting members).

SCIENCE FICTION WRITERS OF AMERICA, Peter D. Pautz, Executive Secretary, 68 Countryside Apartments, Hackettstown NJ 07840. (201)852-8531. Membership is limited to established science fiction writers in the country. Purposes are to inform writiers of matters of professional benefit, to serve as an intermediary in disputes of a professional nature, and to act as central clearinghouse for information on science fiction and science fiction writers. Dues: $20 annually, with a $12.50 installation fee for new members. Membership is open to anyone with a professional interest or involvement in science fiction and/or fantasy, anywhere in the world. This includes artists, agents, editors, anthologists and publishers.
Dues: $40 annually for active membership; $25 for affiliate. Affiliates also pay an installation fee of $7.50 their first year.

SOCIETY FOR TECHNICAL COMMUNICATION, 815-15th St. NW, Suite 506, Washington DC 20005. (202)737-0035. Estab. 1953. Executive Director: Curtis T. Youngblood. Dedicated to the advancement of the theory and practice of technical communication in all media, the STC aims primarily for the education, improvement, and advancement of its members. Dues: $20 annually. *Technical Communication, Quarterly Journal of the Society* included in membership.

SOCIETY OF AMERICAN SOCIAL SCRIBES, c/o *The Plain Dealer*, 1801 Superior Ave., Cleveland OH 44114. (216)344-4809. Secretary: Mary Strassmeyer. "The Society of American Social Scribes is a nonprofit organization dedicated to serving the interest of the reading public, to promote unbiased, objective reporting of social events and to promote journalistic freedom of movement. It endeavors to upgrade the professional integrity and skill of its members to work to increase the pleasures of the reading public, to support all legitimate efforts toward developing the education of its members, and to help its members offer greater service to their readers. Membership is limited to those regularly engaged as salaried society editors or devoting a substantial or regular part of their time to society coverage and the balance to other strictly editorial work. Society writers on daily newspapers with circulations of 200,000 or more and magazine writers and authors of books on the subject are also eligible for membership." Annual dues: $15.

SOCIETY OF AMERICAN TRAVEL WRITERS, 1120 Connecticut Ave., Suite 940, Washington DC 20036. (202)785-5567. Estab. 1956. Administrative Coordinator: Ken Fischer. Dedicated to serving the interest of the traveling public, to promote international understanding and good will, and to further promote unbiased, objective reporting of information on travel topics. Active membership is limited "to those regularly engaged as salaried travel editors, writers, broadcasters or photographers actively assigned to diversified travel coverage by a recognized medium or devoting a substantial or regular part of their time to such travel coverage to satisfy the Board of Directors; or to those who are employed as freelancers in any of the above areas with a sufficient steady volume of published work about travel to satisfy the board. Associate membership is limited to persons regularly engaged in public relations or publicity within the travel industry to an extent that will satisfy the board of Directors. All applicants must be sponsored by 2 active members with whom they are personally acquainted." Dues: $50 initiation fee for active members, $100 initiation fee for associate members; $54 annual dues for active members, $96 annual dues for associate members.

SOCIETY OF CHILDREN'S BOOK WRITERS, Box 296, Los Angeles CA 90066. President: Stephen Mooser.
Purpose: "The Society of Children's Book Writers is the only national organization designed to offer a variety of service to people who write or share a vital interest in children's literature. The SCBW acts as a network for the exchange of knowledge between children's writers, editors, publishers, illustrators and agents." Fees: $25/year.

SOCIETY OF PROFESSIONAL JOURNALISTS, SIGMA DELTA CHI, 35 E. Wacker Dr., Chicago IL 60601. Estab. 1909. Executive Officer: Russell E. Hurst. Dedicated to the highest ideals in journalism. Membership extends horizontally to include persons engaged in the communication of fact and opinion by all media and vertically to include in its purposes and fellowship all ranks of journalists. Dues: $20 annually.

SOCIETY OF THE SILURIANS, INC., 45 John St., New York NY 10028. (212)233-1897. Secretary: James H. Driscoll. Estab. 1924. Primarily a fraternal organization. Membership totals 700. Men and women are eligible for full membership if their history in the New York City media dates back 25 years, for associate membership after 15 years, whether or not they are still so engaged. Dues: $10 annually.

WASHINGTON AREA WRITERS, 204 Laverne Ave., Alexandria VA 22305. President: Susan Katz. Estab. 1973. Approximately 50 members.
Purpose: "To share information about writing through year-round monthly meetings. Publishes a monthly newsletter and a directory. Offers a library (including cassettes of speakers); monthly meetings on topics of interest to writers; offshoot workshops meet regularly: poetry, fiction, speculative fiction and articles. Fees: $10 plus $5 initiation fee.

WASHINGTON INDEPENDENT WRITERS ASSOCIATION, INC., 1010 Vermont St. NW, Suite 710, Washington DC 20005. Executive Director: Judith Brody Saks. Estab. 1975.
Purpose: "To further the common goals of independent writers and to combat unfair practices that hamper work, and to help establish ethical guidelines for the conduct of the profession. Full membership is open to persons who have written and published for compensation 5,000 words or its equivalent during the previous year or who have authored a book commercially published within the preceeding 5 years. Associate memebership is open to persons with serious interest in the independent writing profession or other independent media professions. "Offers workshops and meetings; an annual directory; a monthly newsletter; legal; contract and tax information; an assignment referral service; group hospitalization; and a major medimedical plan. Its committees work on market information, problems of professional relations and development.

WESTERN WRITERS OF AMERICA, INC., Rt. 1, Box 35H, Victor MT 59875. Contact: Rex Bundy. Writers eligible for membership in this organization are not restricted in their residence, "so long as their work, whether it be fiction, history, adult or juvenile, book-length or short material, movie or TV scripts, has the scene laid west of the Missouri River."

WOMEN IN COMMUNICATIONS, INC., Box 9561, Austin TX 78766. (512)345-8922. Editor/PR Director: Karen Allen. Estab. 1909.
Purpose: "WICI was established to work for a free and responsible press; unite women engaged in all fields of communcation; recognize distinguished achievements of women journalists; maintain high professional standards; and encourage members to greater individual effort." Publishes a monthly newsletter and a quarterly magazine, *Matrix*; prints a twice-monthly job information bulletin for WICI members; conducts a job and salary survey every 5 years; publishes occasional professional papers; and sponsors the Clarion Awards Contest. Dues: $35/year.

WRITERS GUILD OF AMERICA, Writers Guild of America, *East*, 22 W. 48th St., New York NY 10036. Writers Guild of America, *West*, 8955 Beverly Blvd., Los Angeles CA 90048. A labor organization representing all screen, television and radio writers.

Picture Sources

"We believe articles with photos illustrating them are better accepted by readers," says R. Lejeune, editor of *Truck Canada*, a trade journal. Illustrated material is not only accepted more readily by readers, but by editors, as well. A good selection of photos can sell an article or a book, but the writer needn't take those photos himself.

Listed here are photographers, stock photo agencies (clearinghouses of photography that is "on stock") and other commercial sources of illustrations. Most of the firms listed here derive their income from providing illustrations to publications, greeting card publishers, book publishers, advertising agencies, etc. Fees start at about $25 for one-time use of a b&w photo to several hundred dollars for use of a color transparency.

Illustrations can often be obtained more inexpensively from other sources, such as libraries, archives, public relations firms and organizations; check *Writer's Resource Guide* (Writer's Digest Books) for such photo sources. The advantage in going to those sources lies in the price advantage. The advantage in consulting the firms listed here lies in the variety of the selection, the quality of the photos and illustrations, and the fact that public relations photos can be—and most likely have been—used a number of times prior to your use of them. This doesn't mean that the photo supplied by a stock photo agency hasn't been used previously; agencies hope to sell photos again and again, but will be able to supply you with accurate records of exactly when and where the photo has appeared.

Some agencies and photographers indicate that they charge "ASMP rates" for photographs. These are rates recommended by the Society of Photographers in Communications (ASMP). A complete guide to ASMP rate policies, *Business Practices in Photography*, is available from ASMP (60 E. 42nd St., New York City 10017).

ASMP also publishes a directory of its members that supplies name, address and specialties of several hundred professional photographers; this directory is another place to check for photo sources. The Professional Photographers of America (PP of A) also provides a membership list. Write PP of A at 1090 Executive Way, Des Plaines, Illinois 60018.

Other sources of illustrations include *Photographer's Market* (Writer's Digest Books), which lists stock photo agencies, and *Stock Photo and Assignment Source Book* (R.R. Bowker), which covers stock agencies, photographers and a variety of other sources.

AAG PHOTO NEWS, Box 370, Staten Island NY 10314. (212)698-1015. Chief of Photo Service: Wayne T. Parola.
Services: Offers 15,000 b&w and 10,000 color photos. "Our primary focus is news photography in the New York City area. This includes everything from police and fire scenes to sports and politics. We also work on feature news stories."
How to Contact: Offers one-time, editorial, advertising, reproduction and all rights. Charges ASMP rates. Prints made to order. "A writer should inquire by mail with his needs. Many of our photographers have press credentials, and we would be willing to work on assignment with the writer."

AIR PIXIES, 515 Madison Ave., New York NY 10022. (212)486-9828. Contact: Ben Kocivar.
Services: Offers 12,000 b&w and 5,000 color photos. Subjects include how-to, new products, science, sports and travel.
How to Contact: Offers one-time, editorial, advertising, reproduction and all rights. Charges $50-500 for one-time editorial or advertising use; $25 service charge; $25 print fee; $25/print made to order.

ALASKA PICTORIAL SERVICE, Box 6144, Anchorage AK 99502. (907)344-1370. Contact: Steve McCutcheon.
Services: Offers 40,000 b&w and 62,000 color photos. "All subjects pertaining to Alaska, from geomorphology to politics, from scenery to ethnical. We do not ship to individuals; only to recognized business firms, publishing houses, AV productions, governmental bodies, etc."
How to Contact: Reproduction rights offered vary. Charges $50 minimum/b&w photo; $150 minimum/color photo. "We do not charge a service or search fee unless the project has been cancelled, then only a minimum fee ($15-50) depending on the time the search requires and the cost of transportation. We will accept certain types of assignments."

J.C. ALLEN AND SON, Box 2061, West Lafayette IN 47906. (317)463-9614. Managers: John O. Allen, Chester Allen.
Services: Offers 76,000 b&w and 20,000 color photos. "Our file of black and white agricultural illustrations was started by J.C. Allen in 1912. Most of our photos have been produced in the corn belt states, but we have made illustrations in travel from coast to coast. We add many new illustrations of farm crops and farm animals to our collection each year."
How to Contact: Offers one-time, editorial, advertising and reproduction rights. Charges $25-75/b&w one-time editorial or advertising use; $75-250/color. "We take special assignments on request."

ALPINE PHOTOGRAPHY, Box 731, Ephraim UT 84627. (801)283-4526. Contact: Len Miller.
Services: Offers 5,000 photos. Subjects include nature, scenics, scientific, snow crystals, winter recreation, farming, ranching, livestock, outdoor life, avalanches and snowslides.
How to Contact: Offers all rights. Charges $5-500 reproduction fee. Charges $1-35 for prints made to order.

AMERICAN STOCK PHOTOS, 6842 Sunset Blvd., Hollywood CA 90028. (213)469-3908. Contact: Al Greene, Yvonne Binder.
Services: Offers over 2 million b&w and 50,000 color photos. "All subjects: contemporary and historical."
How to Contact: "We offer any rights desired. The only restrictions are limited to previous sales; i.e., one-year calendar exclusive." Charges $35 minimum.

AMWEST PICTURE AGENCY, 1595 S. University Blvd., Denver CO 80210. (303)777-2770. President/Director: Luke Macha.
Services: Offers 50,000 b&w and 75,000 color photos. Subjects include agriculture, business, industry, nature, recreation, sports, travel and the American West.
How to Contact: Offers one-time rights. Charges vary.

ANIMALS ANIMALS ENTERPRISES, 203 W. 81st St., New York NY 10024. (212)580-9595. Contact: Nancy Henderson.
Services: Offers 50,000 b&w and 100,000 color photos. Subjects include "animals from all over the world in their natural habitats: mammals, reptiles, amphibians, fish, birds, invertibrates, horses, dogs, cats, etc."
How to Contact: Offers one-time, world and foreign language rights. Charges $125 minimum for editorial; research fee of $15/hour. "Service fee of $35 is charged if no sale is made—applicable only on lengthy requests. All uses, if unusual, are negotiable. We follow the ASMP guidelines."

BARBARA ANTON, INC., 10 Engle St., Englewood NJ 07631. (201)871-3989. President: Barbara Anton.
Services: Offers photos of jewelry, gemstones in jewelry, and designer Anton wearing her jewelry.
How to Contact: Material is in the public domain. Exclusive photos available on request.

APPEL COLOR PHOTOGRAPHY, Twin Lakes WI 53181. (414)877-2303. Contact: Thomas E. Appel.
Services: Subjects include "outdoor sports, participant and spectator sports, wildlife, children and family activities, young adults, girls, history and points of interest, national parks and monuments, lighthouses, grist mills, bridges, famous houses, churches (including America's oldest), landscapes, farms, gardens, flowers, waterfalls, sunsets, mountains, rivers and lakes, harbors, snow, tourism, industry, food, still life, collectibles, fireworks, boating, and over a score of 12-picture theme sets."

How to Contact: Offers any rights. Return required. Charges vary.

ARIZONA PHOTOGRAPHIC ASSOCIATES, INC., 2350 W. Holly, Phoenix AZ 85009. (602)258-6551. Contact: Dorothy McLaughlin.
Services: Offers 300,000 photos.
How to Contact: Offers one-time, editorial, advertising, reproduction and all rights. Charges ASMP rates.

ART REFERENCE BUREAU, INC., Box 137, Ancram NY 12502. (518)329-0535. Contact: Janet L. Snow.
Services: Offers "over a million subjects in Europe: painting, sculpture, graphics, architecture, archeology and artifacts, principally from European locations."
How to Contact: "B&w glossy photos may be purchased. Color transparencies are supplied on a three-month loan basis only. We clear reproduction rights for most material supplied. Fees vary with the sources that supply material to us."

ASSOCIATED PICTURE SERVICE, Northside Station, Box 52881, Atlanta GA 30355. (404)948-2671. Manager: Buford C. Burch.
Services: Offers 8,000 b&w and 8,000 color photos. Subjects include history, nature, recreation, sports, travel and Georgia.
How to Contact: Write or call. Will send catalog for SASE.

AUTHENTICATED NEWS INTERNATIONAL, 170 5th Ave., New York NY 10010. (212)243-6995, (212)243-6614. Managing Editor: Sidney Polinsky.
Services: Offers approximately 1½ million photos. Photo agency for all types of domestic and foreign news photos and stock photos on all subjects, including politics, pollution, geothermal and solar energy, etc.
How to Contact: Credit line and return of photos required.

BILLY E. BARNES, 313 Severin St., Chapel Hill NC 27514. (919)942-6350.
Services: Offers 50,000 b&w and 15,000 color photos available for one-time use; editorial, advertising and reproduction rights available for some photos. Subjects include "people—especially Southern, urban and rural—working, studying, playing, farming as families: blacks, whites, Indians"; agriculture, business, health/medicine, industry, music, politics, recreation, science, sports and travel.
How to Contact: Will send catalog for SASE. Charges $40 minimum/one-time use b&w; $80 minimum/one-time use color.

BUDDY BASCH FEATURE SYNDICATE, 771 West End Ave., New York NY 10025. (212)749-3775. Publisher: Buddy Basch.
Services: Offers 25,000 b&w photos; 3,000 color. Subjects include celebrities, entertainment, music, recreation, sports and travel. "We specialize mostly travel and show business (old movies, stars, now and then, old and deceased performers, new performers). Travel covers a wide spectrum of the world, locations, people, places, landmarks, fauna and flora, etc. We can get nearly anything needed for photographic illustration, but give us a little time on the more obscure items."
How to Contact: Offers one-time and editorial rights. Charge "depends on circulation, use, etc., and varies widely."

LESTER V. BERGMAN & ASSOCIATES, INC., E. Mountain Rd. S., Cold Spring NY 10516. (914)265-3656. President: Lester Bergman.
Services: Offers 6,000-8,000 b&w photos; 10,000 color photos. Subjects include agriculture, art, health/medicine, nature, science, technical data and travel. "We are very strong in medicine and nature and we will take assignments at stock prices if the subject appeals."
How to Contact: Offers one-time, editorial, advertising, reproduction and all rights. Charges $75-125 for one-time editorial use; $250-1,000 for one-time advertising use. Free catalog on request.

BIOMEDICAL PHOTO LIBRARY, Camera M.D. Studios, Inc., 122 E. 76th St., New York NY 10021. (212)628-4331. Contact: Library Division.
Services: Offers 100,000 biomedical color transparencies and b&w negatives. The biomedical photos illustrate about 30 specialty areas of medicine, such as dermatology, allergy and rheumatology, dentistry, veterinary medicine, botany, entomology and other biological sciences. Also, photos of about 60 sites of normal human anatomy are available of adults and

children, males and females plus matching skeletal views and, where possible, matching normal x-rays.
How to Contact: The 132-page catalog, illustrated in color and b&w, costs $5.75 plus postage.

BLACK STAR, 450 Park Ave. S., New York NY 10016. (212)679-3288. President: Howard Chapnick. Executive Vice President: Benjamin J. Chapnick.
Services: Offers photos. Represents 120 photographers for assignment work. Color and b&w photos of all subjects. Two million photos in collection.
How to Contact: Offers one-time use or negotiations for other extended rights. $75 minimum per b&w, $150 minimum per color. Assignment rates quoted on request.

HARRY BONNER, PHOTOGRAPHER AND WRITER, 5369 Vergara St., San Diego CA 92117. (714)571-0048.
Services: Offers 25,000 b&w photos; 10,000 color of West Coast outdoor subjects: salt and fresh water game fish, most species; seascapes; sunsets; seabirds; boats; fishing, all phases; rivers; scenics; Mexico; whales and other marine animals; sharks and rays; few animals. Extensive fishing coverage and related subjects in Mexico, California, Oregon, Washington, and some Hawaii.
How to Contact: Rights vary with material and use. Reproduction fee: $50 minimum.

PHIL BRODATZ, PHOTOGRAPHER, 100 Edgewater Dr., Coral Gables FL 33133. (305)858-2666 day and 661-5771 evenings. Contact: Phil Brodatz.
Services: Offers 20,000 b&w and 10,000 color photos. Subjects include nature, trees, scenics of USA and Caribbean Islands, clouds, water; textures of many kinds.
How to Contact: Write or call. Offers one-time, editorial, advertising and reproduction rights. "Charges $25 and up depending on use."

BROWN BROTHERS, Box 50, Sterling PA 18463. (717)689-9688. President: Harry B. Collins Jr.
Services: Offers "several million" b&w photos and some color photos. "Our subjects cover almost everything except recent news events. We have a great many original glass plates and films of historical events from 1900 to 1960. Also woodcuts and engravings of events and portraits from beginning of time. Movie stills and religious art."
How to Contact: Write or call. Offers one-time, editorial, advertising and reproduction rights on some photos. Sometimes charges for services.

GUY BURGESS, PHOTOGRAPHER, 202 Old Broadmoor Road, Colorado Springs CO 80906. (303)633-1295. Contact: Guy Burgess.
Services: Offers 1,800 5x7 color transparencies of garden scenes, plant portraits.
How to Contact: Offers one-time use. Charges $100-250. Return required.

CACTUS CLYDE PRODUCTIONS, Box 14876, Baton Rouge LA 70808. (504)387-3704. Photographer: C.C. Lockwood.
Services: Offers 1,500 b&w photos; 10,000 color photos; 16mm educational films on a river basin swamp. Information covers nature, recreation and travel.
How to Contact: Offers one-time, advertising and reproduction rights. Charges $25 for making selection; $125 for one-time editorial or advertising use. Catalog for SASE. "Freelance assignments accepted on natural history subjects only."

CAMERA CLIX, A DIVISION OF GLOBE PHOTOS, INC., 404 Park Ave. S., New York NY 10016. (212)684-3526. Manager: Alix Colow.
Services: Offers 4,000,000 color photos. Subjects include agriculture, art, business, celebrities, economics, entertainment, food, health/medicine, history, how-to, industry, law, music, nature, politics, recreation, science, self-help, sports and travel.
How to Contact: Offers one-time, editorial, advertising, reproduction and all rights. Charges $25 minimum for services; $5/print made to order. $5/catalog.

CAMERA HAWAII, INC., 206 Koula Street, Honolulu HI 96813. (808)536-2302. Contact: Photo Librarian.
Services: Offers over 50,000 color and 20,000 b&w pictures of Hawaii; cross section of all islands, scenics, travel, aerial and general. Also selection of photos from New Zealand, Sydney, Bali, Manila, Taiwan, Hong Kong, Korea, Tokyo and parts of Japan, Guam; minor file of other areas such as Tahiti, West Coast; Washington, New York, Boston area; Quebec, Niagara Falls; spring flowers in Washington DC; New York scenes; and a small selection of London,

Germany, Austria and Switzerland scenes.
How to Contact: Usually offers one-time rights, but subject to negotiation according to needs. Fees dependent upon usage and rights required. Minimum charge generally in line with ASMP standards.

CAMERA M.D. STUDIOS, INC., Library Division, 122 E. 76th St., New York NY 10021. (212)628-4331. Manager: Carroll H. Weiss.
Services: Offers 100,000 photos of the health and biological sciences.
How to Contact: Offers all rights. Credit line, tearsheets and return of prints required. ASMP rates.

CAMERIQUE STOCK PHOTOS, Box 175, Blue Bell PA 19422. (215)272-7649. Contact: Orville Johnson.
Services: Offers photos.
How to Contact: B&w photos and color transparencies on a variety of subject matter. Selection can be sent on 10-day approval. One-time reproduction fee varies with importance of use, media, circulation, etc. Fee quoted on receipt of this information. Return of pictures required in 10 days, unless extended.

WOODFIN CAMP AND ASSOCIATES, 415 Madison Ave., New York NY 10017. Contact: Midge Keator, Woodfin Camp. Washington office: 1816 Jefferson Place NW, Washington DC 20036. (202)466-3830. Manager: Ms. Cathy Sachs.
Services: Offers 100,000 b&w and 300,000 color photos representing general geographic coverage of most countries in the world, with particular emphasis on India, Africa, Russia, Western Europe, South America, Southeast Asia and the US. Subjects include agriculture, art, celebrities, entertainment, food, history, industry, nature, politics, recreation, science, sports and travel. Offers one-time, editorial, advertising, reproduction and all rights.
How to Contact: Charges minimum of $60 for b&w and $125 for color photos, based on space and type of publication and follow ASMP guidelines; $5/print; and $1/photocopy. "We prefer to work directly with publishers and agencies, but are happy to discuss projects with independent writers and art directors." Since most photos were produced from reportage assignments, there are no model releases for the subjects. Requests must be as specific as possible regarding the type of photo needed, its intended use, and rights required.

CANADA WIDE FEATURE SERVICE, LTD., 231 rue St. Jacques, Montreal, Quebec, Canada H2Y 1M6. (514)282-2441. Administrative Manager: Carol Tuck. B&w Photo Editor: Michael Pope. Sales Manager, Image Bank Division: Steve Pigeon.
Services: Offers 1 million b&w photos with access to an additional million; 150,000 color photos with access to an additional million. Subjects include agriculture, art, business, celebrities, economics, entertainment, food, health/medicine, history, industry, law, music, nature, politics, recreation, science, sports, travel, comics and cartoons. "Our material available from b&w and color on almost any subject required."
How to Contact: Offers one-time, editorial, advertising, reproduction and all rights. "Our fees depend entirely on the specific rights granted. We charge service fees and again amount depends on research time required to fulfill request." Free catalog on request.

WILLIAM CARTER, PHOTOGRAPHER AND WRITER, 644 Emerson St., Palo Alto CA 94301. (415)326-1382, 328-3561. Contact: William Carter.
Services: Offers about 30,000 photos on a variety of worldwide subjects, particularly US Middle West, Western ghost towns, children, show horses, Middle East, special subjects.
How to Contact: Write or call. Fees negotiable.

TERENCE W. CASSIDY, 49 Bridge, Berwny PA 19312. (215)644-4858. Proprietor: Terence W. Cassidy.
Services: Offers 4,000 b&w photos; color prints, slides and maps. Subjects include business and history. "Our speciality covers Kansas City urban history, street railway history and transit history."
How to Contact: Charges $25 for one-time editorial or advertising use (no tobacco or liquor); $10/print fee. "We cannot respond to tight deadlines. Our alternate address: Box 7235, Kansas City MO 64113."

WALTER CHANDOHA, PHOTOGRAPHER, 287 Rt. 1, Annandale NJ 08801. (201)782-3666. Owner: Walter Chandoha.

Services: Offers 100,000 color and b&w photos of "cats, dogs, horses and other animals. Information covers nature subjects, weather situations, trees and leaves, flowers (wild, domestic, tropical); growing vegetables and fruits; sunsets, clouds, sky and scenics; water; conservation; gardens and gardening; and the four seasons."
How to Contact: Offers one-time, editorial, advertising, reproduction and all rights. Charges $50 minimum for b&w; $150 minimum for color and up to $3,500, depending on use, $15 minimum for service charge. Free catalog on request. "We do not deal with authors directly; we prefer to work with their publishers."

JOE CLARK, H.B.S.S. PHOTOGRAPHY, 8775 W. 9 Mile Rd., Oak Park MI 48237. (313)399-4480.
Services: Offers 15,000 color and b&w photos on file for sale or loan. Subjects include city and farm subjects, Michigan, Tennessee, Ohio, Kentucky, Detroit, down South, people, pets, children, landscapes.
How to Contact: Rights vary with material and author. Fees vary with material and use.

BRUCE COLEMAN, INC., 381 5th Ave., New York NY 10016. (212)683-5227. Contact: Norman Owen Tomalin.
Services: Offers 300,000 color photos. Subjects include agriculture, art, business, economics, entertainment, food, health/medicine, industry, music, law, recreation, science, sports and travel.
How to Contact: Offers one-time, editorial, advertising, reproduction and all rights. Charges $125 for one-time editorial use; $30 minimum for selection, $30/service charge and $1 minimum holding fee. ASMP reproduction fees.

COLLECTORS BOOK STORE, 6763 Hollywood Blvd., Hollywood CA 90028. (213)467-3296. Contact: Still Department.
Services: Offers 1,000,000 35mm mounted movie slides, movie stills from silent days to present, and some television stills. 2,000,000 b&w and 100,000 color photos available. Subjects include entertainment.
How to Contact: "We have a 50-page catalog ($1) of all the movie and television scripts we have for sale. Scripts extend from the silent days to the present." Charges $1-1.25 for slides and $2.50-5 for stills. "Most are originals."

COLLEGE NEWSPHOTO ALLIANCE, 342 Madison Ave., New York NY 10017. (212)697-1136. Manager: Ted Feder.
Services: Offers 100,000 b&w photos and color transparencies of college life including political activity, people, current economic and social trends, urban and rural subjects, ecology.
How to Contact: Offers one-time to world rights. Fees depend on the reproduction rights and size of reproduction on the page; average $50 for b&w, $125 for color.

CONSOLIDATED NEWS PICTURES, INC., 209 Pennsylvania Ave. SE, Washington DC 20003. (202)543-3203. Contact: Benjamin E. Forte, Arnold Sachs.
Services: Offers 100,000 b&w photos; 50,000 color slides. Subjects include agriculture, business, celebrities, politics, science, sports and news stories.
How to Contact: Offers one-time, editorial, advertising and reproduction rights. Charges $35/print for one-time editorial or advertising use; $35 research fee if no pictures are used, $35 print fee, $2.75/b&w print made to order, $5/b&w copy and $7.50/color copy made, $5/b&w negative and $7.50/color negative made. Price list is available for services such as printing, slide duping and custom services on request. "Consolidated News Pictures and Consolidated Photographic is available for photographic assignments anytime, anywhere. Photographic charges available on request."

CONTACT PRESS IMAGES, INC., 135 Central Park W., New York NY 10023. Contact: Robert Pledge. (212)799-9570.
Services: Offers photos. Subjects include photojournalistic editorial photography (color and b&w) on major personalities, situations, trends, events, countries of the world; political, economics, sociological and cultural points of view.
How to Contact: Photos available on a loan basis for all rights. Service charge: $25. Holding fee: $50. Minimum reproduction fee: $75/b&w and color. Prints made to order: $25 minimum.

CORN'S PHOTO SERVICE, 118 Garrett Dr., Goodlettsville TN 37072. (615)859-5376. Manager: Helen Corn.
Services: Offers 30,000 b&w photos; 9,000 color transparencies. Subjects include agriculture, art/crafts, celebrities, health/medicine, music, nature, politics, recreation, sports, travel and

contemporary photos/persons all ages. "We also have excellent photos for use in religious publications and for textbook publishers."

How to Contact: Offers one-time, editorial, advertising and reproduction rights. Charges $25/b&w or $50/color editorial use; $50/b&w or $100/color advertising use.

COUNTRY LANE PHOTOS, Rt. 3, Box 66, Burlington IA 52601. (319)752-8034. Contact: Jerry A. Hoke.

Services: Offers 5,000 b&w prints and 12,000 35mm and 2¼x2¼ color transparencies. Subjects include Western and Midwestern US—scenics of national parks, the Mississippi River, old and new farms, barns, fences, covered bridges, windmills; seasonal material—spring flowers, fall colors, snow, Christmas lights, garden flowers, trees, leaves; and South America—Bolivian geography, life in Bolivian tribes, farming, building, weaving, homes, fiestas, Bolivian cities, Inca ruins of Peru. Catalog for SASE.

Terms: Usually offers one-time rights, but offers all rights under some circumstances. "Fees vary according to the type of use, the material, and the nature of the publication." Charges $15 minimum. Requires use of credit line and return of the original material.

Tips: Will accept assignments.

CULVER PICTURES, INC., 660 1st Ave., New York NY 10016. (212)684-5054. Associate Director: Tom Logan.

Services: Offers 9,000,000 b&w photos; 750,000 color photos, memoribilia, trade cards, posters, magazine covers and bound magazines of 19th century. "Widely known in historical field, with photos, old prints, engravings, posters, paintings, movie stills covering every imaginable subject, including the Seidman collection. We like to work with writers but cannot send material until acceptance of article or story by magazine or publisher is final. We have found that we cannot tie up pictures on speculative ventures."

How to Contact: Offers one-time, editorial, advertising, reproduction and all rights. Charges $35 minimum for one-time editorial or advertising use; service charge depends on amount of work involved. "All pictures must be returned within 30 days and we do not sell prints for personal use." $2.50/catalog.

CYR COLOR PHOTO AGENCY, Box 2148, Norwalk CT 06852. (203)838-8230. Owner: Mr. E.J. Cyr.

Services: Offers 1,000 b&w photos; 100,000 color transparencies. Subjects include agriculture, art, celebrities, entertainment, food, industry, music, nature, recreation, science, sports, travel, homes, animals, foreign countries, United States, pin-ups, ecology, transportation and scenics.

How to Contact: Offers one-time, editorial, advertising, reproduction and all rights. Charges $100 minimum for one-time editorial or advertising use.

DR. E.R. DEGGINGER, FPSA, Box 186, Convent NJ 07961. President: E.R. Degginger.

Services: Offers 120,000 color transparencies on agriculture, food, industry, nature, recreation, sports, technical data and travel. "We have a very broad base of subject material in natural history including flora, fauna, marine life, geology. Also East Africa, Galapagos Islands, Alaska, Bajo and Sea of Cortey, Ireland, Guateniola, Antarctica, Islands of Indonesia and New Guinea."

How to Contact: Offers one-time, advertising, reproduction and all rights. Charges $125-500 for one-time editorial or advertising use; holding fees for long periods. Free catalog on request.

LISL DENNIS, 135 E. 39th St., New York NY 10016. (212)532-8226. Contact: Lisl Dennis.

Services: Offers 15,000 color photos on travel, people, places and things around the world.

How to Contact: Offers one-time, editorial, advertising and reproduction rights. Charges ASMP rates.

DESIGN PHOTOGRAPHERS INTERNATIONAL, INC., 521 Madison Ave., New York NY 10022. (212)752-3930. President: Alfred W. Forsyth.

Services: Offers over 1 million b&w and color pictures. Comprehensive contemporary collection of worldwide subjects including agriculture, business, food, health/medicine, industry, music, nature, recreation, science, sports and travel.

How to Contact: Offers one-time, editorial, advertising and reproduction rights. "We suggest you let us know your budget limitation when requesting pictures. Be sure to indicate design restrictions, supply detailed information on how pictures will be used, article content, product and brand name where applicable. When you receive pictures please screen and return all unused pictures immediately. The unauthoreized holding of pictures beyond 7-14 days without written permission will incur holding fees." Charges $15-25 service charge depending on work involved.

A. DEVANEY, INC., 415 Lexington Ave., New York NY 10017. (212)682-1017. Contact: George Marzocchi, Alan S. Fernanoez.
Services: Offers 750,000 b&w photos; 250,000 color photos, pen and ink illustrations of wildlife and conservation related subjects. Subjects include agriculture, art, business, economics, entertainment, food, health/medicine, history, industry, law, music, nature, recreation, science, sports and travel.
How to Contact: Offers one-time, editorial, reproduction and all rights. Charges $40-750 for one-time editorial or advertising use. $35 for service charge, $10/print fee. Catalog for SASE.

IRVING DOLIN PHOTOGRAPHY, 124 Ludlow St., New York NY 10002. (212)473-4006. Contact: Irving Dolin.
Services: Offers "several thousand" photos. "All types of auto racing, in b&w and color. Racing drivers. Files date from 1948. Most are 35mm."
How to Contact: Write or call. Prefers to sell one-time rights; depends upon fee paid. Minimum b&w fee is $35 for one-time editorial use.

EARTH SCENES, 203 W. 81st St., New York NY 10024. (212)580-9595. President: Nancy Henderson.
Services: Offers 50,000 b&w photos; 100,000 color photos. Subjects include all domestic and wildlife—mammals, birds, insects, fish, reptiles, etc.; and anything to do with nature—minerals, mushrooms, flowers, trees, etc.
How to Contact: Offers all rights. Charges $125 minimum for editorial use; $35 minimum service charge. Catalog for SASE.

EASTFOTO AGENCY, 25 W. 43rd St., New York NY 10036. (212)279-8846. Manager: Leah Siegel.
Services: Offers 900,000 color and b&w photos on all aspects of life in Eastern Europe, China, Vietnam, etc. Industrial, political, historical, entertainment, news photos.
How to Contact: Offers one-time rights, North American rights, world rights in English, world rights in translation. Fees vary according to usage. Charges $50 minimum for one-time use of b&w photos; $125 for color.

EDITORIAL PHOTOCOLOR ARCHIVES, 342 Madison Ave., New York NY 10017. (212)697-1136. Assistant to the President: Elyse Ellcin.
Services: Offers 1,000,000 b&w photos; 1,000,000 color photos; transparencies: 35mm, 2¼x2¼ formats. Subjects include foreign countries and cultures, ecology, children, works of art, family life, human activities, nature. Fees vary depending on use. Generally charges $50/b&w and $125/color. "We also represent the Scala and Alinari art archives. EPA is a general archive which deals with everyday life and travel."

EKM-NEPENTHE, 7874 Tanglerod Lane, La Mesa CA 92041. (714)463-9513. Vice President: Robert Eckert Jr.
Services: Offers 75,000 b&w photos; 25,000 color photos. Subjects include agriculture, art, business, economics, entertainment, food, health/medicine, industry, law, music, nature, politics, recreation, science, sports, travel and almost all occupations.
How to Contact: Offers one-time, editorial, advertising and reproduction rights. Charges $60 minimum for editorial or advertising use; $5 minimum for prints made to order. Free catalog on request. "When requesting photographs be as specific as possible. As of now, we have only contemporary photographs in the files which go back to the 1960s, there is the possibility of adding older material.

ANTHONY F. ESPOSITO JR., 65 Lynmoor Place, Hamden CT 06517. (203)288-0588. Director: A.F. Esposito.
Services: Offers 5,000 b&w photos; 15,000 color. Subjects include farm subjects; animal husbandry; worldwide scenics and people; children/teenagers; medical/hospital; carnivals; sports; plants and animals (scientific categories); and rural and urban America.
How to Contact: Write or call. Offers one-time, editorial, advertising, reproduction, and all rights (rarely). Charges $15-1,500 for one-time editorial or advertising use; $10 for 8x10 prints. "Query us giving as much information as possible concerning your needs. We will send you a selection on approval. Writer's obligation is to return unused slides via registered mail within 10 days. There is a charge for slides held longer than 10 days. Writers must include information on how slide will be used when querying, in order that we may provide the proper quote. We have a sliding scale based on the use made of the slide."

EUROPEAN ART COLOR SLIDE, Peter Adelberg, Inc., 120 W. 70th St., New York NY 10023. (212)877-9654. Contact: Peter Adelberg.
Services: Offers about 6,000 photos. "Archives of original color transparencies photographed on-the-spot from the original art object in museums, cathedrals, palaces, etc. Prehistoric to contemporary art; all media. Transparencies instantly available from New York office."
How to Contact: Write or call. Charges selection and holding fees. One-time reproduction fee varies from $85 and up for b&w to $150 and up for color. Credit line and return of pictures required.

EXCLUSIVE NEWS PHOTOS, 1248 5th St., Santa Monica CA 90406. (213)451-4312. Editor: Wally Burke.
Services: Offers photos aimed primarily at news, news features, national and international figures in the news.
How to Contact: Offers one-time and advertising rights. Charges $25 for one-time or advertising use; $15 for service charge and $15/print fee. "We will work directly with writers and editors on exclusive pix and layouts."

FLORIDA NEWS BUREAU, 410-C Collins Bldg., Tallahassee FL 32304. (904)488-2494. Contact: Tim Olsson.
Services: Offers photographs on all areas and phases of Florida; b&w available to freelancers, b&w and color transparencies to publications.
How to Contact: "To receive the greatest value for the tax money that supports our operation, we apply the following guidelines in filling photographic requests: 1) requests direct from publications get first priority; 2) requests from freelancers who have established a record of cooperation with us (tearsheets, credit lines and other acknowledgments) receive second priority; and 3) requests from unknown freelancers are handled on a 'time available' basis. A freelancer who has not worked with us previously should allow plenty of time on photo requests." No fees, but credit line and return of transparencies required.

FOCUS ON SPORTS, INC., 222 E. 46th St., New York NY 10017. (212)661-6860. Contact: Robert Tringali, Joyce Mead.
Services: Offers 10,000 b&w photos; 400,000 color photos relating to sports: spectator, leisure, unusual sports and sport personalities.
How to Contact: Offers one-time, editorial, advertising and reproduction rights. Charges $50-1,500 for one-time editorial or advertising use; $35 for service charge. "Call, stating specific request and we will be able to tell you immediately or return your call as to whether or not we can find your request."

FOUR BY FIVE, INC., 485 Madison Ave., New York NY 10022. (212)697-8282. Contact: Joanna Ferrone, Ellyn Skein. California office: 2192 Martin St., Irvine CA 92715. (714)833-2241. Contact: Terry Corlet, Mark Miller.
Services: Offers stock photos of people, scenics, travel and sports.
How to Contact: Charges $150-300 for one-time editorial or advertising use. Full-color catalogs available on subscription. Free sample.

CARL FRANK, 383 E. 17th St., Brooklyn NY 11226. (212)469-9472. Photographer: Carl Frank.
Services: Offers 12,000 b&w photos; 12,000 color photos. Subject include agriculture, business, food, health/medicine, history, industry, nature, recreation, sports and travel.
How to Contact: Offers one-time rights. Charges $45-90 for b&w; $100-250 for color, for one-time editorial or advertising use.

FRANKLIN PHOTO AGENCY, 39 Woodcrest Ave., Hudson NH 03051. (603)889-1289.
Services: Offers photographs of flowers, gardens, trees, plants, wildflowers, etc.; foreign countries; interiors and exteriors of homes; scenics (all seasons), antique cars, insects and small animals, dogs (all breeds), fish pictures, horses (all breeds), fishing and hunting scenes, some sports. Mostly 4x5 color.
How to Contact: Offers one-time reproduction. Fees vary according to use and quantities printed, etc. Charges $50 minimum. Credit line requested and return of pictures required.

FREELANCE PHOTOGRAPHERS GUILD, 251 Park Ave. S., New York NY 10010. (212)777-4210. Research Department Manager: Ann Schneider.
Services: Offers 1 million b&w photos; 2 million color photos. Subjects include agriculture, art, business, celebrities, economics, entertainment, food, health/medicine, history, how-to,

industry, law, mucis, nature, new products, politics, recreation, science, self-help, sports, technical data and travel. "We have a large variety, specializing in large format scenic and human interest, and a large collection of travel-oriented materials."
How to Contact: Offers one-time, editorial, advertising, reproduction and all rights. Charges $60 minimum for b&w; $125-2,000 for color, for one-time editorial or advertising use; $40 for service charge. Free catalog on request. "We will not sign pix out to individuals without the name of a publisher and/or company name that has authorized the work."

LAWRENCE FRIED PHOTOGRAPHY, LTD., 330 E. 49th St., Studio 1A, New York NY 10017. (212)371-3636. Contact: Lawrence Fried.
Services: Offers "500,000 subjects, ranging from travel throughout the world, international and domestic political figures, society, theater (stage and film), sports, editorial and commercial illustration, military, medical, personalities in b&w and color."
How to Contact: Rights offered flexible, "depending on negotiation in each individual case." Fees: minimum b&w, $135; minimum color, $135.

EWING GALLOWAY, 342 Madison Ave., New York NY 10017. Director of Photography: Tom McGeough.
Services: Offers one-time, editorial, advertising, reproduction and all rights. Subjects include "most all situations featuring people."
How to Contact: "Prices are based on how and where a photo will be used." Charges $25 and up for one-time editorial or advertising use. Will send free catalog but "we do screen requests and, in most cases, do not send to individuals. Please send request on company stationery."

GAMMA-LIAISON PHOTO AGENCY, 150 E. 58th St., New York NY 10022. (212)355-7310. Contact: Michael De Wan.
Services: Offers one million b&w and color photos. Subjects include politics, economics, religion, cultural events, newsmakers, politicians, celebrities, human interest, children, animals, nature, sports and fashion.
How to Contact: Offers reproduction, advertising, first, second and editorial rights. Charges $35 selection fee and a $2/day holding fee, after standard holding time. Reproduction fee varies with photo, but generally $75 minimum/b&w photo; $150 minimum/color photo. "We have photographers based in all major capitals of the world available to writers for assignments at $250 per day, plus expenses."

GENERAL PRESS FEATURES, 130 W. 57th St., New York NY 10019. (212)265-6842. Manager: Gabriel D. Hackett.
Services: Offers still photo archives, written and illustrated features. Photos of all subjects; lists available. Over 100,000 photos: historic and documentary, social changes (US and Europe), music, fine arts, artists, Americana; pictorials (US and France, Switzerland). Towns, landscapes, politicians, statesmen, celebrities. Color and b&w.
How to Contact: Rights offered open to negotiation. Charges ASMP minimum code rates. Discount on larger orders.

GLOBE PHOTOS, 404 Park Ave. S., New York NY 10016. (212)689-1340. Executive Vice President: Gary Phillips.
Services: Offers 6,000,000 b&w photos; 4,000,000 color photos. Subjects include agriculture, art, business, celebrities, economics, entertainment, food, health/medicine, history, how-to, industry, law, music, nature, politics, recreation, science, self-help, sports and travel.
How to Contact: Offers one-time, editorial, advertising, reproduction and all rights. Charges $25 minimum for service charge; $5/prints made to order. Catalog $5.

GORNICK FILM PRODUCTIONS/ENVIRONMENTAL MARINE ENTERPRISES, 4200 Camino Real, Los Angeles CA 90065. (213)223-8914. President: Alan Gornick.
Services: Offers 15,000 color photos. Subjects include history, nature, sports, travel, underwater, marine, mountains and deserts. "We have primarily underwater and marine with some coverage of mountains and deserts with emphasis on scenics and coverage of old ghost towns."
How to Contact: Offers one-time, editorial, advertising and reproduction rights. Charges $150-2,500 for one-time editorial or advertising use; $50 selection charge, $10-600/prints made to order.

HAROLD V. GREEN, PHOTOGRAPHER, 570 St. John's Blvd., Pointe Claire, Quebec, Canada. (514)697-4110. Contact: H. Green.

Services: Offers approximately 35,000 photos. "Wide spectrum of natural history and general biology photos, and some botanical, zoological, and crystal photomicrographs. Also places, people, landscapes, seascapes, old farms, etc. Mainly 35mm color."
How to Contact: One-time reproduction rights usually; other rights by agreement. Charges $50-150, color; $25-75, b&w.

ARTHUR GRIFFIN, PHOTOGRAPHER, 22 Euclid Ave., Winchester MA 01890. (617)729-2690. Contact: Arthur Griffin.
Services: Offers 50,000 color photos of New England and other states; Orient, the Scandinavian countries, Canada and South America; mostly scenics. All islands of the West Indies. Majority are 4x5 transparencies.
How to Contact: Offers all rights. Charges ASMP rates.

AL GROTTEL, UNDERWATER PHOTOGRAPHY, 170 Park Row, New York NY 10038. (212)349-3165.
Services: Offers "over 6,000 color transparencies available for reproduction in all media. Subjects include natural history, including underwater scenes, divers, fish corals, sponges, sunken ships, most invertebrates, marine ecology from the Caribbean, Florida Keys and the Bahamas.
How to Contact: "Fees vary with usage."

G.D. HACKETT PHOTOGRAPHY, 130 W 57th St., New York, NY 10019. (212)C05-6842.
Services: Offers photo archives and studio photography. Subjects include history, music, American indians, fine arts, celebrities, social problems, religions, pictoral and Americana.
How to Contact: Write or call. "ASMP Code of Standards, ASMP Stock Picture Code, purchase order requested."

HARPER HORTICULTURAL SLIDE LIBRARY, 219 Robanna Shores, Seaford VA 23696. (804)898-6453. Owner: Pamela Harper.
Services: Offers 15,000 35mm color slides of gardens, trees, shrubs, vines, perennials, alpines, wildflowers, bulbs, and houseplants.
How to Contact: Offers all rights. Charges $35 minimum for one-time editorial or advertising use; $10 selection fee if no photos are used; $2/duplicate slide; $1/catalog.

HEDRICH-BLESSING, LTD., 11 W. Illinois St., Chicago IL 60610. (312)321-1151. Contact: Bob Kincaid.
Services: Offers 20,000 b&w photos; 110,000 color photos of residential interiors and exteriors, commercial and industrial buildings, interiors and exteriors; scenics of mountains, lakes, woods, mostly without people. City views and historic architecture, especially in Chicago.
How to Contact: Offers one-time, editorial, advertising, reproduction and all rights. Charges $25-200 for one-time editorial or advertising use. Credit line frequently required. Return of pictures required for color.

HEILPERN PHOTOGRAPHERS, INC., Box 12266, 151 Homestead Ave., Hartford CT 06112. Contact: George R. Garen.
Services: Offers approximately 35,000 aerial photographs, mostly b&w, "of every type of subject, from close-ups of modern buildings and highway intersections to over-all views of cities."
How to Contact: Offers one-time reproduction rights. Charges $40/7x7 contact print, $10.50 additional for two 8x10 enlargements or one 11x14 enlargement of entire negative or any portion of negative.

HELCERMANAS-BENGE, INC., 1781 W. Georgia St., Vancouver, British Columbia, Canada V6G 2X2. (604)669-0235. Contact President: Cris Helcermanas-Benge.
Services: Offers "general photography from around the world." 175,000 b&w and 230,000 color photos; video and films. "We also have three artists with us." Subjects include agriculture, art, business, celebrities, entertainment, food, health/medicine, how-to, industry, music, nature, new products, politics, recreation, science, self-help, sports, technical material, travel and others by special assignment. Charges as per written agreement.

HERITAGE PRINTS PHOTOGRAPHY, 250 W Center, Suite 106, Continental Plaza, Provo UT 84601. (801)375-7086. Proprietor: Rell G. Francis.
Purpose: "Heritage Prints is a unique western service dedicated to preserve aesthetic and historical values. It offers collectors, historians, decorators and laymen the opportunity to

acquire high-quality photographs from the original glass negatives of George Edward Anderson (1860-1928), pioneer Utah photographer, as well as other stock photographs of Utah, Mexico, and Paris by Rell G. Francis. Our collection also includes the work of Cyrus E. Dallin (American sculptor of Indians) and Arthur C. Pillsbury (innovator of time-lapse photography)." Subjects include agriculture, art, business, entertainment, history, industry, nature, recreation, travel and genealogy.
Services: Offers biographies, brochures/pamphlets, information searches and photos.
How to Contact: Write or call. There is a charge for prints ($5-500).

HISTORICAL PICTURES SERVICE INC., 17 N. State St., Room 1700, Chicago IL 60602. (312)346-0599. Archivist: Jeane Williams.
Services: Offers over 3 million b&w photos and 100,000 color photos, engravings, drawings, photos, paintings, cartoons, caricatures and maps, covering all important persons, places, things and events. Subjects include agriculture, business, celebrities, economics, food, health/medicine, history, industry, music, nature, politics, recreation, science, sports and technical material.
How to Contact: Pictures sent on 60-day approval. Offers one-time, North American, world rights, or multiple use. Charges: one-time editorial or advertising use, $50-300; reproduction fee, $50 when applicable; print fee, $10. Will send free catalog on request. Credit line and return of pictures required.

THE IMAGE BANK, The Penthouse, 88 Vanderbilt Ave., New York NY 10017. (212)371-3636. Sales Managers: Advertising, Lenore Herson; Editorial, Marty Abrams.
Services: Offers 1,000,000 color photos; "all subjects."
How to Contact: Offers all rights. Charges "ASMP minimum as applies" for one-time editorial or advertising use; $40 service charge; $75 print fee. Free catalog. "We have licensed offices in Chicago, Washington DC, San Francisco, Montreal, Toronto, Rio, Sao Paolo, Paris, Hamburg, and Tokyo to expedite the servicing of our clients on an international basis."

IMAGE FINDERS PHOTO AGENCY, INC., 134 Abbott St., Suite 501, Vancouver, British Columbia, Canada V6B 2K4. (604)688-3818. Manager: Dairobi Paul.
Services: Offers 300,000 color photos. Art, architecture, historic sites, North American Indians and their culture; commerce and industry (office buildings, shops, restaurants, hotels, construction, communications, crafts, manufacturing, and people at work); sciences, transportation, foreign countries, people, parks, recreation, sports, cityscapes, cultural events, zoos, aquariums, housing and alternative energy; institutional (military, education, government, law enforcement, medical services, religion, and fire fighting); landscapes, seascapes, plants, animals, agriculture, logging, fishing and mining.
How to Contact: Offers one-time, editorial, advertising, reproduction and all rights. Charges $50-900 for one-time editorial or advertising use; $15 service charge. Charges $5-15/print made to order; $5-10/copy negative.

IMAGE PHOTOS, Main St., Stockbridge MA 01262. (413)298-5500. Director: Clemmens Kalischer.
Services: Offers 500,000 b&w photos; 5,000 color photos of abstractions, arts, architecture, children, crafts, education, ethnic groups, Western Europe, farming, human activities, India, music, nature, New England, personalities, religion, social documentary and theater.
How to Contact: Offers one-time and editorial rights. Charges $50-2,000 for one-time editorial or advertising use; $15-25 selection charge, $10-20 service charge.

INTERCAM, 383 E. 17th St., Brooklyn NY 11226. (212)469-9472. Owner/Photographer: Carl Frank.
Services: Offers 10,000 b&w and 10,000 color photos. "Specializing in Latin America with subject material for textbooks, encyclopedia or advertising use."
How to Contact: Offers "any rights purchaser requires." Charges $40-200 for one-time editorial or advertising use.

INTERPRESS OF LONDON AND NEW YORK, 400 Madison Ave., New York NY 10017. (212)832-2839. Manager: Jeffrey Blyth.
Services: Offers 4,000-5,000 b&w photos of personalities; specializing in photojournalism. British pictures include royalty. Topical or unusual picture stories.
How to Contact: One-time rights available. Fees negotiable; no service charge.

ITALIAN HISTORICAL ARCHIVES, Box 279, Berwyn IL 60402. President: John A. Sisto.

Services: Offers 1 million photos. Subjects include old cars, old advertisements, theater, movies, circus, women's fashions, Italian historical prints, engravings from 12th to 20th centuries, sports, medicine, religious prints, old documents, authors, World Wars I and II, Mussolini, Italian kings, queens, cities, cathedrals, musicians, artists, Popes, autographs, architecture, airplanes, dirigibles, air balloons, World War II posters, and art nouveau of Italy.
How to Contact: Offers one-time, editorial, advertising, reproduction and all rights. Charges $50-150 for one-time advertising or editorial use; $25 selection fee. Catalog for SASE.

LOU JACOBS JR., 13058 Bloomfield St., Studio City CA 91604. Contact: Lou Jacobs Jr.
Services: Offers about 25,000 b&w negatives and 5,000 color slides. "All manner of subjects from animals to industry, human interest to motion picture personalities, action, children, scenic material from national parks and various states."
How to Contact: Offers first rights on previously unpublished material; one-time reproduction rights on the remainder, except for exclusive rights by agreement. Charges minimum $75/b&w photo, $50/photo for five or more; charges $150/color photo, $125/photo for more than five.

ERNST A. JAHN, 18 Blackrock Terrace, Ringwood NJ 07456. (201)962-4114.
Services: Offers 40,000 color transparencies and b&w photos available on purchase or loan basis. Subjects include Alaska, Central and South America, Europe, South Africa, Caribbean Islands, and US coverage ranging from travel, general scenery, cities, new buildings, ships, railways, cattle, festivals and general human interest to special studies on the flying squirrel; local and tropical animals.
How to Contact: Offers reproduction rights, advertising rights, second rights, editorial rights, first rights or all rights. Reproduction fee: $125/color; $35/b&w. Free catalog.

CURT W. KALDOR, 603 Grandview Dr., South San Francisco CA 94080. (415)583-8704.
Services: Offers "several thousand" photos of scenic views and city-suburbs; street scenes, aircraft, people, architectural, railroads, shipping and boating, redwoods and timbering, and others. Offers all types of rights up through complete purchase.
How to Contact: Charges a flat fee for purchase of reproduction rights, based on usage.

JOAN KRAMER AND ASSOCIATES, 5 N. Clover, Great Neck NY 11021. (212)224-1758, (212)246-7600. Contact: Joan Kramer.
Services: Offers over 100,000 photos including abstracts, boats, travel shots from US and other countries, children, ethnic groups, fisheye shots, nature, people shots, scenics, teenagers, winter scenes and zoos. B&w (8x10) and color (35mm).
How to Contact: Rights negotiable. Fees are based on budget available and photo use.

KUSTOM QUALITY, Box 3459, 2416 Montana, El Paso TX 79923. (915)532-3233. President: Steve Steele.
Services: Offers 15,000 photos, 98% of which are b&w. Subjects are historical, emphasizing Old West, Mexican Revolution, nostalgia, early aviation and early post card art of US and Europe. Subjects include celebrities, history and nature.
How to Contact: Offers all rights; some material in the public demain. Charges $5 minimum/print fee; $.50/photocopy; $6.75 minimum/copy negative. "We can assist writers in researching subjects not in our collection."

L.P.I., 1265 S. Cockran, Los Angeles CA 90019. (213)933-7219. Librarian: Tim Long.
Services: Offers 5,000 b&w photos; 200,000 color photos. Subjects include agriculture, celebrities, industry, recreation and sports. "We specialize in sports and people in southwestern United States."
How to Contact: Offers one-time, editorial and advertising rights. Charges $35 minimum one-time editorial or advertising use; $35 service charge.

JAMES W. LA TOURRETTE, PHOTOGRAPHER, 1416 SW 15th Terrace, Fort Lauderdale FL 33312.
Services: Offers about 4,000 b&w and color pictures; "2¼x2¼ and 35mm underwater color transparencies of the waters in the Florida Keys and Bahama Islands. Some 4x5 color scenics. Motor sports events; boat races, sports car races; scenics, eastern US, West Coast, Everglades wildlife and plants." Also scenics of Germany, Austria, Japan and Hong Kong.
How to Contact: Offers one-time rights. Fees: b&w 8x10 prints, $25; color transparencies, $75-250. "Color to be returned after use."

HAROLD M. LAMBERT STUDIOS, INC., Box 27310, Philadelphia PA 19150.

(215)224-1400. Contact: R. W. Lambert.
Services: Offers 1 million b&w photos; 300,000 color transparencies. Subjects include agriculture, art, business, entertainment, food, health/medicine, history, industry, law, music, nature, recreation, sports and travel.
How to Contact: Offers one-time, editorial, advertising and reproduction rights. Charges $35-60 for one-time editorial or advertising use; $6/print fee, $10 minimum for prints made to order. Offers free catalog.

LAS VEGAS NEWS BUREAU, Convention Center, Las Vegas NV 89109. (702)735-3611. Contact: Don Payne, Manager.
Services: Offers 250,000 b&w and 10,000 color photos, both stills and 16mm, available from files or shot on assignment for accredited writers with bonafide assignments. Subjects include entertainment, music, recreation, sports and Las Vegas/southern Nevada scenics.
How to Contact: Offers editorial and reproduction rights. Return of color required.

LATIN AMERICA PHOTOS, 3308 Legation St. NW, Washington DC 20015. (202)686-1609. Contact: Luz Mangurian.
Services: Offers 50,000 color and b&w photos of "a wide variety of subjects from most Latin American countries including agriculture, archaeology, education, energy, folk arts, food, Indians, industry, mining, music, scenics, sports, rural and urban life, and social conditions."
How to Contact: Offers one-time rights. Charges ASMP rates. Free stock list. "All specific queries will be answered, but will not loan pictures for articles being submitted on speculation. Prefer to deal with editors after article has been accepted. Exception: book projects. All requests must be specific to receive attention."

LEVITON/ATLANTA, INC., 1271 Roxbord Dr., Atlanta GA 30324. (404)237-7766. President: Jay B. Leviton.
Services: Offers 20 years of b&w photos. Information covers agriculture, business, celebrities, history, industry, nature, politics, recreation and sports.
How to Contact: Offers one-time rights and editorial rights. Charges $100 for one-time editorial or advertising, $50 selection fee and $3.50 print fee.

FRED LEWIS AGENCY, 390 Ocean Pkwy., Brooklyn NY 11218. (212)282-9219. Owner: Fred Lewis.
Services: Offers 1,000 b&w and 5,000 color photos of "nature, people, experimental and places inside the United States." Offers all rights.
How to Contact: Fees: $75-200 for one-time editorial or advertising use, $5-10 print fee. Free catalog.

FREDERIC LEWIS, INC., 35 E. 35th St., New York, NY 10016. (212)685-0122. President: David Perton.
Services: Offers 700,000 b&w and 300,000 color photos, old engravings and political cartoons. Subjects include agriculture, art, business, celebrities, economics, entertainment, food, health/medicine, history, how-to, industry, law, music, nature, new products, politics, recreation, science, self-help, sports, technical material and travel.
How to Contact: Offers one-time, editorial, advertising, reproduction and all rights. Material is in the public domain.

LIGHTFOOT COLLECTION, Box A-F, Greenport NY 11944. (516)477-2589. Contact: Frederick S. Lightfoot.
Services: Offers 30,000 b&w photos of "Americana—strong coverage of 19th century, representation of 20th century to 1920. City, town, village and country scenes, architecture, transportation, industrial, culture, famous people, wars, agriculture, mining. Also 19th century foreign file, primarily cities and harbors."
How to Contact: Offers all rights. Charges $15 and up for one-time editorial or advertising use; $5 print fee.

THOMAS LOWES, PHOTOGRAPHER, 491 Delaware Ave., Buffalo NY 14202. (716)883-2650. Contact: Liz Mohring.
Services: Offers over 50,000 photos—yachting and boating, tall ships, Americana (people, landscapes, historic objects and landmarks), hot air ballooning, rodeos, ghost towns, Indian crafts and missions. Farming (people and equipment), Canadian provinces. Color transparencies (35mm).
How to Contact: Fees depend on publication.

BURTON McNEELY PHOTOGRAPHY, Box 338, Land o' Lakes FL 33539. (813)996-3025. Contact: Burton McNeely.
Services: Offers "about 10,000 color only: recreation, travel, romance, girls, underwater, and leisure-time activities."
How to Contact: Offers any and all rights. "Fees are based on the use of the photos, such as circulation of magazine or type of book. Minimum one-time rate for any published use is $125."

MEMORY SHOP, 109 E. 12th St., New York NY 10003. (212)473-2404. Owners: Mark or Nancy.
Services: Offers 5,000,000 b&w and 1,000,000 color photos on "all various subjects, but mostly catering to the seven arts: specializing in movies, theater, television, etc. Also categories on almost any subject from animals to zoos; sports, politicians, scenics, westerns, horror, science fiction, classic films, television, music, rock music, and stage."
How to Contact: Offers one-time rights. Fees: charges $10-20 for one-time editorial or advertising use; $10-20 service charge; $15-25 print fee.

LOUIS MERCIER, 342 Madison Ave., New York NY 10017.
Services: Offers stock photographs; color scenics US and worldwide; personalities, fashion, food, industry, the arts, Americana, and 19th century engravings.
How to Contact: Fees: $35 minimum for b&w; $100 for color, depending on use.

MONTGOMERY PICTURES, Box 722, Las Vegas NM 87701. (505)425-3146. Contact: Mrs. C.M. Montgomery.
Services: Offers "6,000 4x5 color transparencies and 10,000 35mm color transparencies of animals, birds, reptiles, flora, scenics, state and national parks, ghost towns, historic, Indian pictographs and petroglyphs."
How to Contact: One-time reproduction rights in one country preferred; all other rights by negotiation. Fees: "ASMP rates, where applicable. Otherwise, the publisher's current rates; but not less than $25 per transparency."

MOVIE STAR NEWS, 212 E. 14th St., New York, NY 10003. (212)777-5564.
Services: Offers "millions of b&w and hundreds of color photos." Subjects include movies.
How to Contact: Charges $25 for one-time editorial or advertising use, $25 service charge, and 50¢ for catalog.

MUNSEY NEWS SERVICE, 41 Union Square W., New York NY 10003. (212)989-7151. Editor: Al LaPresto.
Services: Offers 5,000 b&w photos; 2,000 color. "Photos of spot news events, World Fairs from 1939 to the present, general scenes from New York City, Montreal and most other locations in the US and Canada. We will work on assignment basis anywhere in the world."
How to Contact: Offers all rights. Charges $5-250 for one-time editorial or advertising use. Free catalog.

NATIONAL CATHOLIC NEWS SERVICE, 1312 Massachusetts Ave. NW, Washington DC 20005. Contact: Robert A. Strawn.
Services: Offers 25,000 photos; Catholic-related news and feature and historical material.
How to Contact: Photos offered on on purchase basis only. Rights and fees vary with material and usage.

THE NATIONAL CLEARINGHOUSE FOR COMMERCIAL VEHICLE ACCIDENT PHOTOGRAPHS, 2148 Evans Rd., Flossmoor IL 60422. (312)798-8891. Contact: Director, Charles E. Campbell.
Services: Offers 750 b&w and 100 color photos. Subject: accidents.
How to Contact: Offers one-time, advertising, reproduction and all rights. Charges a minimum of $50 for one-time editorial or advertising, a service charge equal to the cost of the contact sheet and prints made to order at cost. "Write with a full description of the type of photograph required."

NATIONAL FILM BOARD PHOTOTHEQUE, Tunney's Pasture, Ottawa, Ontario, Canada K1A 0M9. (613)593-5826. Photo Librarian: L. Krueger.
Services: Offers about 300,000 b&w photos and color transparencies "illustrating the social, economic and cultural aspects of Canada."
How to Contact: Photos purchased for one-time use only. Pictures can be purchased for

editorial and commercial use. Fees vary according to the purpose for which the photos are required.

NEST PHOTO/VISUAL COMMUNICATION, 7101 Saroni Dr., Oakland CA 94611. (415)339-9733. Contact: Owners, Elaine or Larry Keenan.
Services: Offers 15,000 b&w and 12,000 color photos. Subjects include business, health/medicine, industry, nature, politics, recreation, photo techniques and special effects.
How to Contact: Offers one-time, editorial, advertising and reproduction rights. Charges $50 to $200 for one-time editorial fees and a $24 service charge. Send SASE for free catalog.

NEWSPIX RADIO DISPATCHED NEWS PHOTO SERVICE, 92 S. Lansdowne Ave., Lansdowne PA 19050. (215)622-2200. Contact: Walter M. Faust.
Services: Offers 5,000 b&w and 3,500 color photos. Subjects include historic Philadelphia, soccer, football, personalities (Philadelphia area), greater Delaware Valley views, industrial plants, river scenes, pleasure boating, art, business, economics, health/medicine, nature, recreation, sports, technical material and travel.
How to Contact: Offers all rights. Charges ASMP rates for all uses.

NORTHWOODS STUDIO, 12605 NE 2nd St., Bellevue WA 98005. (206)454-9470. Owner: Ron Arnold.
Services: Offers 800 b&w 12,000 color photos, and graphic layouts on various specific story-related subjects. Subjects include art, business, economics, health/medicine, history, industry, nature, new products, politics, recreation, science, technical material and travel.
How to Contact: Offers one-time, editorial, advertising, reproduction, and all rights (on assignment only). Charges $125 for one-time editorial or advertising use, postage only as service charge, and lab cost only as print fee. "We have great depth in forest/industry/environment/political issues photos of various conflict situations."

OCEANIC PRESS SERVICE, 4717 Laurel Canyon Blvd., North Hollywood CA 91607. (213)980-6600. General Manager: John R. West.
Services: Offers over 10,000 color photos. Subjects include celebrities, food, how-to, cartoons and comic strips.
How to Contact: Offers one-time rights. Fees are negotiable.

OUTDOOR PIX & COPY, 5639 N. 34th Ave., Phoenix AZ 85017. (602)973-9557. Contact: James Tallon.
Services: Offers about 70,000 photos of scenics, education, natural science, agriculture, sports, travel, wildlife, foreign countries (Mexico and Canada), human interest. "Strong on nature, hunting, fishing, camping, recreation. More than 500 selected shots of elk; 2,000 shots of cowboys on cattle drive; thousands of bird shots; lots of plant close-ups including cactus blossoms; national parks and monuments (Western); lots of sealife including fighting elephant seals." 35mm color only.
How to Contact: Rights vary with material and use. Selection on approval. Slides must be returned unless all rights are purchased. Credit line and tearsheets appreciated. Outright purchase price: negotiable. Reproduction fee: $50 minimum. "Selections are mailed to prospective buyers within 48 hours, usually the same day requests come in. List of categories available on request."

PACIFIC AERIAL SURVEYS, 444 Pendleton, Oakland CA 94614. Contact: Jack E. Logan.
Services: Offers 200,000 aerial photographs of Western US only. B&w, color.
How to Contact: Outright purchase price: b&w 8x10, $50; color transparency, $100. One-time reproduction fee: b&w, $30; color, $75. Credit line and return of pictures required.

PACIFIC PRODUCTIONS, Box 2881, Honolulu HI 96802. (808)531-1560.
Services: Offers 25,000 b&w photos; 1,500 color photos. Subjects include agriculture, art, business, celebrities, entertainment, food, history, industry, nature, politics, recreation, sports, technical data and travel.
How to Contact: Offers one-time, editorial, advertising and reproduction rights. Charges $20 for one-time editorial or advertising use; $10 print fee, $10/prints made to order, $2/photocopy and $5/negative copy.

PENQUIN PHOTO COLLECTION AND RESEARCH, 663 5th Ave., New York NY 10022. (212)758-7328. Contact: Mrs. Ena Fielden.
Services: Offers over 50,000 photos in b&w and color. Accent is on the field of entertainment:

film, stage, music, dance, radio and TV. "Photos are for strictly editorial use only." Prevalent current fees. "Photos are on loan from collection."
How to Contact: Offers one-time and editorial rights. Charges one-time editorial or advertising use and service charge. Free catalog. "Request should be as precise as possible and always state deadline."

ROBERT PERRON, PHOTOGRAPHER, 104 E. 40th St., New York NY 10016. (212)661-8796.
Services: Offers 8,000 b&w photos; 12,000 color photos. Subjects include nature, aerials of coastal scenes, architecture, interiors, energy saving houses and travel.
How to Contact: Offers one-time rights. Charges $75/b&w and $250/color one-time editorial use; $6/prints made to order. Free catalog.

PERSONALITY PHOTOS, INC., Box 50, Brooklyn NY 11230. (212)645-9181. Photo Director: Alexander Frank.
Services: Offers 500,00 b&w photos. Subjects include celebrities and entertainment. "We have a lot of movie nostalgia, photos of stars from old movies, 1920-1960 best years and best movies, old TV shows from the start."
How to Contact: Charges $1.50/selection fee; $1/catalog. "Those writing books will be given special attention and help with photos and research for their book upon written request."

PHELPS & THOMPSON, INC., 1375 Peachtree St. NE, Suite 172, Atlanta GA 30309. (404)881-1925. President: Sarah Catherine Phelps.
Services: Offers 5,000 b&w and 10,000 color photos of all subjects. "We supply editorial, advertising, corporate and educational markets."
How to Contact: Offers all rights. Charges ASMP rates for one-time editorial or advertising use: $25 selection fee. Catalog for SASE.

ALLAN A. PHILIBA, 3408 Bertha Dr., Baldwin NY 11510. (212)371-5220, (516)623-7841.
Services: Offers 30,000 photos. Subjects include the Far East, Europe, South America, US, North Africa and the Caribbean.
How to Contact: "Call or mail specific request for photos, giving context and use; we will promptly send only photos which fit the request, if in stock. We will also shoot any reasonable request if contacted." Fees vary with use and material—$150-1,000. One-time rights, editorial rights, advertising rights and reproduction rights available.

THE PHOTO CIRCLE, INC., Box 66288, Houston TX 77006. (713)522-0554. President: Leo Touchet.
Services: Offers 20,000 b&w photos; 100,000 color photos. Subjects include agriculture, business, health/medicine, industry, nature, recreation, science and technical data.
How to Contact: Offers one-time, editorial, advertising and reproduction rights. Charges $50-250 for editorial use and $300 minimum for advertising use. Free catalog.

PHOTO TRENDS, 1328 Broadway, New York NY 10001. (212)279-2130. Contact: R. Eugene Keesee.
Services: Offers 400,000 b&w photos; 100,000 color photos. Subjects include celebrities, children, education, entertainment, food, health/medicine, history, Hollywood candids from circa 1960 to date, industry, music, news photos from England, South Africa, and Spain, politics, recreation, scientific subjects such as photomicrographs, people in places around the world, scenics around the world, wonders and disasters occurring on planet Earth, and travel.
How to Contact: Offers one-time, editorial, advertising, reproduction and all rights. Charges $25 service charge deductable from first reproduction fee; fees: ASMP rates.

PHOTO WORLD, 251 Park Ave. S., New York NY 10010. (212)777-4210. Manager: Selma Brackman.
Services: Offers photos of personalities, history, World War II, and all other subjects; some specialties. Three million photos in collection.
How to Contact: Rights offered negotiable. Fees depend on reproduction rights.

PHOTOGRAPHY BY HARVEY CAPLIN, Box 10393, Alameda NM 87114. (505)898-2020. Contact: Harvey Caplin.
Services: Offers 25,000 b&w and 15,000 color photos of "all southwestern subjects including cattle ranching, sheep, Indians, national parks and monuments, scenery, sports and recreation. Also available for assignment anywhere in the southwest."

How to Contact: Offers all rights. Charges $50 minimum for one-time b&w editorial or advertising use; $100 minimum for color. Free catalog.

PHOTOPHILE, 2311 Kettner Blvd., San Diego CA 92101. (714)234-4431. Director: Frankie Wright.
Services: Offers 500 b&w and 100,000 color photos on national and international subjectrs, with a focus on scenics and human activities of the western US. Offers one-time rights or outright purchase.
How to Contact: "Photophile uses ASMP guidelines for fees charged. Prints, copy negatives and b&w conversions are made from original transparencies." Free catalog.

PHOTOUNIQUE, Suite 340, Bldg. Z, Arrow Press Square, Salt Lake City UT 84101. (801)363-5182.
Services: Offers 5,000 photos for purchase of reproduction rights only; very little material is sold outright. Subjects include Western states (primarily Utah and Idaho): agriculture, industries, outdoor recreation, scenics.
How to Contact: "I follow ASMP guidelines and business practices. I also accept assignment photography." Charges $5/print, plus reproduction fee. Charges holding fee: $1/photo after 21 days.

PHOTOWORLD, 251 Park Ave. S., New York NY 10010. (212)777-4214. Director: Naomi Goldstick.
Services: Offers "several million" b&w photos. "We have a collection of historical photos, drawings and prints, which includes material from the Keystone View Company, the European Picture Service, and both the Paul Thompson and Henry Miller collections. We have coverage of WWI and WWII from both sides of the conflicts and important personalities of the last 100 years, encompassing over 100,000 pictures and more than 10,000 people."
How to Contact: Offers all rights. Charges vary depending on use for one-time editorial or advertising use; $40 service charge. Free catalog.

PHOTRI-PHOTO RESEARCH, Box 971, Alexandria VA 22313. (703)836-4439. Director: Col. Jack Novak.
Services: Offers 100,000 b&w photos; 200,000 color photos. Subjects include agriculture, art, economics, health/medicine, history, industry, nature, politics, science, sports, technical data and travel.
How to Contact: Offers one-time, editorial, advertising, reproduction and all rights. Charges $100-300 for one-time editorial or advertising use; $35 service charge. Catalog for SASE.

PICTUREMAKERS, INC., 1 Paul Dr., Succasunna NJ 07876. (201)584-3000. President: Bill Stahl.
Services: Offers photos of all subjects. "Award-winning features and story-telling pictures." One-time rights, editorial rights, advertising rights and reproduction rights offered.
How to Contact: Write or call. "Our fees are based on how and where the picture is to be used, the number of times and the circulation of the publication."

PIX PHOTO RESEARCH, 3849 S. Main St., Santa Ana CA 92707. (714)957-1749. Manager: Ms. Gerry Wertenberger.
Services: Offers 100,000 35mm color transparencies, 1,000 pieces of b&w artwork and 100 b&w stills made from color transparencies. Subjects include agriculture, art (special effects), food, health/medicine, history, industry, law, nature, recreation, sports and travel.
How to Contact: Offers one-time, editorial, advertising, reproduction and all rights. Charges $35 mimimum one-time editorial use and $50 mimimum one-time advertising use. Free catalog. "We are willing to offer help and suggestions in selections of most appropriate material."

KENNETH C. POERTNER, PHOTOGRAPHER, 613 Hillview Dr., Boise ID 83702. (208)336-0499.
Services: Offers approximately 5,000 b&w and color photos. Western birds and mammals, Western scenes, Idaho's land and people, Western national parks and monuments. Offers one-time, editorial, and advertising rights.
How to Contact: "Fees depend on usage and rights purchased. Credit line requested, return of color originals required. Will accept individual assignments on request."

CARL POST, Box 98 Ambassador Station, Los Angeles CA 90070. (213)383-1083. Contact: Carl Post.

Services: Offers 3,000 b&w photos. Subjects include art, celebrities, entertainment, music, sports and travel. "We have an individual collection of memorabilia of theater, films, music, autographs, manuscripts, posters, stills and material encompassing circus, ballet, sports, art, etc. We also have souvenir programs of films, theater, ballet, music, film one-sheets and travel posters. The entire collection has approximately 10,000 pieces."
How to Contact: Offers editorial and advertising rights. "Any fees are open to minimum negotiation."

RAISNER PHOTOS, Box 298, Nazareth PA 18064. (215)759-5416. Contact: Richard Raisner.
Services: Offers 1,000 b&w photos; more than 10,000 color. Abstracts, children, environment, glamor, nudes, scenic and travel. Offers one-time, editorial, advertising and reproduction rights.
How to Contact: Charges $10 minimum for b&w one-time editorial or advertising use; $25 minimum for color. Charges $2/day for extended holding period over 3 weeks. Credit line requested; return of photos required.

REFLEX PHOTO INTERNATIONAL, INC., 186 5th Ave., New York NY 10010. (212)243-4432. Manager: Lawrence Woods.
Services: Offers 50,000 b&w and 50,000 color photos of foreign countries, animals, armed forces, cities/communities, children, conservation/environment, demonstrations, politics, personalities, parks/monuments, police/firemen, picture stories, photojournalism, recreation, sports, special events, personality journalism, United Nations and peace movements.
How to Contact: Offers all rights. "ASMP minimum standards. All fees are negotiable."

RELIGIOUS NEWS SERVICE (RNS), 43 W. 57th St., New York NY 10019. Photo Editor: Jim Hansen.
Services: Offers over 200,000 items on file. "Religious and secular topics. Largest collection of religious personalities in world. Also fine selection of scenics, human interest, artwork, seasonals, social issues, history, cartoons, etc. RNS can be called on for almost all photo needs, not just religious topics." B&w only.
How to Contact: Offers one-time rights. Fees variable.

REPORTS INTERNATIONALE AGENCY, Box 4574, Denver CO 80204. Manager: R. Johnson.
Services: Offers 20,000 color photos. "Strong 35mm Kodachrome inventory of the Rocky Mountain states, Canada and the Southwest, Florida, New England, Central America, Mexico and France. Scenics, peoples, flowers, nature, the sciences, and mountain sports a specialty."
How to Contact: Offers one-time, editorial, advertising, and reproduction rights. Charges $25 and up for one-time editorial or advertising use.

LEONARD RUE III ENTERPRISES, Rt. 3, Box 31, Blairstown NJ 07825. (201)362-6616.
Services: Offers 45,000 b&w and 50,000 color photos. "We specialize in wildlife, nature, natural history, outdoor subjects, travel, primitive people of the world. Feature North America and Africa. We have one of the largest files on wildlife in the country."
How to Contact: Offers all rights. "All photo rates are according to usage and rights purchased."

SANDAK, INC., 180 Harvard Ave., Stamford CT 06902. (203)348-3721. Art Historian: Armand M. Belmonte.
Services: Offers approximately 18,000 color negatives from which b&w prints and color transparencies are made up on special order. "We specialize in art history slides which are sold primarily to schools and colleges. We can supply publishers with b&w prints or color transparencies for reproduction."
How to Contact: Offers one-time rights. Charges $25 for one-time use. Lab Fees: $10/b&w print; $40/4x5 color, $45/5x7 color and $50/8x10 color print. Free catalog on request.

ERIC SANFORD PHOTOGRAPHY, 219 Turnpike Rd., Manchester NH 03104. Stockfile Manager: Mrs. Gene Tobias Sanford.
Services: Offers over 100,000 photos in collection. "Color (primarily 4x5 transparencies), 35mm, 2¼x2¼, some 8x10 transparencies; color negatives—mostly New England scenics and varied all-occasion type photographs. B&w 8x10 scenics and miscellaneous subjects. Our files in both b&w and color cover a wide range of subjects: flowers, children, animals, houses, industry, pollution, soft focus, some other areas in US and many foreign countries."
How to Contact: Offers one-time, editorial, advertising, reproduction and all rights. Charge for

rights depends on use and size of reproduction; $5 selection fee, $5 service charge and individual quotes on request for prints and copies. "Our rates are based on the schedule of the ASMP." Free catalog.

SEIKA BUNKA PHOTO, 501 5th Ave., New York NY 10017. (212)490-2180. Manager: Al Matano.
Services: Offers over 100,000 color photos of Japan and the Far East for use in New York branch, including modern scenes, historical art treasures, temples/shrines, architecture, costume, manners, etc. Expanding to similar coverage, especially of people and their life styles in the United States and Europe (including calendar pin-ups) for sale in Japan through Tokyo office. B&w are quality 5x7 or larger glossy and color are usually 2¼x2¼, 4x5 or larger.
How to Contact: Offers one-time, editorial, advertising and reproduction rights. Charges $125 minimum one-time editorial use; $25 selection charge, deducted from usage fee, also charges for color conversion for b&w prints. "Allow adequate time for requests both in New York and Tokyo."

ANN ZANE SHANKS, 201 B E. 82nd St., New York NY 10028.
Services: Offers "about 5,000 items. Stock picture file, color and b&w of people—from the very young to the very old. Celebrities, scenes, hospitals, travel, and interracial activities."
How to Contact: Offers first or second rights. Fees: $50 minimum, b&w; $150 minimum, color. Credit line requested.

RAY SHAW, Studio 5B, 255 W. 90th St., New York NY 10024. (212)873-0808.
Services: Offers 100,000 b&w and 45,000 color photos; worldwide editorial features and annual reports. Subjects include animals, ballet, children, inspirational, American Indians, Mennonites; foreign countries: Algeria, Canada, Denmark, Egypt, England, France, Germany, India, Iran, Israel, Jordan, Lebanon, Luxembourg, Mexico, Morocco, Switzerland, Syria, Tunisia, Yugoslavia, etc.
How to Contact: Offers one-time, editorial, reproduction and all rights. Fees negotiable. "It is best to communicate with us and discuss needs in person."

SHOSTAL ASSOCIATES, INC., 60 E. 42nd St., New York NY 10017. (212)687-0696. Contact: David Forbert.
Services: Offers over one million photos available on rental basis. Reproduction rights, advertising rights, first rights, second rights, editorial rights, all rights. All subjects, US and foreign.
How to Contact: Fees vary with material and usage.

SICKLES PHOTO-REPORTING SERVICE, Box 98, 410 Ridgewood Rd., Maplewood NJ 07040. (201)763-6355. Owner: Gus Sickles Jr.
Services: Offers 30,000 b&w photos; 1,000 color photos; "negatives on file, covering a period of about the past 40 years, related to business, industry, agriculture, etc., but we are basically an assignment service, rather than a supplier of stock photos."
How to Contact: Offers one-time, editorial, advertising, reproduction and all rights. Charges ASMP rates "or will quote."

ED SIMPSON STOCK PHOTOGRAPHY, Box 397, South Pasadena CA 91030. (213)682-3131, 799-8979. Owner: Ed Simpson.
Services: Offers over 50,000 color slides. Subjects include agriculture, entertainment, food, industry, nature, recreation, sports and travel. "We sell or rent our slides."
How to Contact: Offers one-time, editorial, advertising and reproduction rights. Charges $750-800 for one-time editorial or advertising use; $25-35 service charge, which is applied to purchase price. Free catalog and price list on request. "I offer a two-year exclusive (longer available) so there would be no danger of the same photo showing up in a competitor's book."

BP SINGER FEATURES, INC., 3164 W. Tyler Ave., Anaheim CA 92801. (714)527-5650. Acting President: Eldon Maynard.
Services: Offers over 10,000 color photos. "Jacket cover art color transparencies is our major subject area. We have cartoons, comic strips, b&w drawings for home repair and How-to books, art, celebrities, entertainment, food, health/medicine, how-to, self-help, sex, glamour, science-fiction, crime, western romance and gothic."
How to Contact: Offers one-time, reproduction and all rights (preferred). "Fees are determined by usage and availability." $1/catalog. "No amateurs, please. We are the parent company of Oceanic Press Service in North Hollywood."

SKYVIEWS SURVEY, INC., 50 Swalm St., Westbury NY 11590. (516)333-3600. President: William J. Fried.
Services: Offers 135,000 b&w negatives and 23,000 color photos. All aerial photography, cross-indexed geographically and by subject.
How to Contact: Offers one-time editorial, advertising and reproduction rights. Fees: $50-500 for one-time editorial or advertising use; $15-20 selection fee.

DICK SMITH PHOTOGRAPHY, Box X, North Conway NH 03860. (603)356-2814.
Services: Offers "10,000 b&w and 5,000 4x5 color transparencies. Scenics, tourist attractions, geologic and geographic features, farming, animals, lakes, mountains, snow scenes, historic sites, churches, covered bridges, flowers and gardens, aerials, Atlantic coast, skiing, fishing, camping, national parks. These are mostly of New England, but I do have some of the South and West."
How to Contact: Offers usually one-time rights for the specific use. Fees: minimum b&w $35, minimum color $100.

GEMINI SMITH, INC., 5858 Desert View Dr., La Jolla CA 92037. (714)454-4321. Contact: Bradley Smith.
Services: Offers 5,000 photos. Reproduction rights, advertising rights, all rights available. B&w and color. Subjects include important paintings and sculptures of the world (all periods, prehistoric to modern); arts, crafts, and historical sites of the US; folkways and scenics (Japan, Spain, Mexico, Europe, United States, West Indies, India); animals in Africa; circus; personalities of the '40s and '50s.
How to Contact: Charges holding fee: $20. Reproduction fee: $80/full-page b&w; $250/full page color.

BILL SNYDER FILMS, INC., Box 2784, Fargo ND 58108. (701)293-3600. President: Bill Snyder.
Services: Offers 30,000 color photos covering agriculture.
How to Contact: Offers one-time and editorial rights. Charges are negotiable for one-time editorial or advertising use; $25 service fee, charge for print fee depend on time and materials.

HOWARD SOCHUREK, INC., 680 5th Ave., New York NY 10019. (212)582-1860. President: Howard Sochurek.
Services: Offers 50,000 b&w; 100,000 color photos. Subjects include economics, health/medicine, industry, new products, science, lasers, electronic micro work and foreign travel.
How to Contact: Offers one-time, advertising, reproduction and all rights. Charges $150-1,000 one-time editorial or advertising use; $50 selection fee, $25 service charge, $10 print fee and for prints made to order, $5 for photocopies and negatives.

SOUTHERN STOCK PHOTOS, Box 693726, Miami FL 33169. Proprietor: Edaward Slater.
Services: Offers 30,000 color photos. Subjects include agriculture, art, business, celebrities, economics, entertainment, food, health/medicine, history, how-to, industry, law, music, nature, new products, politics, recreation, science, self-help, sports, technical data and travel. "We market picture photos and transparencies to advertising agencies, publishers, greeting card companies and periodicals."
How to Contact: Offers one-time, editorial, advertising, reproduction and all rights, and some material is in the public domain. Charges $85-125 one-time editorial or advertising. Free catalog on request.

SOVFOTO/EASTFOTO, 25 W. 43rd St., New York NY 10036. Contact: Leah Siegel.
Services: Offers over 900,000 photos. Photographic coverage from the Soviet Union, China and all East European countries. B&w and color.
How to Contact: Fees vary, depending on use. Minimum charge for b&w photos is $50 for one-time use. Minimum fee for color is $125.

WIDE WORLD PHOTOS, INC., 50 Rockefeller Plaza, New York NY 10020. Contact: On Approval Section.
Services: Offers about 50 million photos. "All subjects in b&w, thousands of them in color. Wide World Photos is a subsidiary of the Associated Press."
How to Contact: Offers all rights; national, North American and world rights. Fees start at $35.

Glossary

All Rights. See "Stand Up for Your Rights."

Alternative culture. The life styles, politics, literature, etc., of those persons with cultural values different from the current "establishment."

Assignment. Editor asks a writer to do a specific article for which he usually names a price for the completed manuscript.

B&W. Abbreviation for black & white photograph.

Beat. A specific subject area regularly covered by a reporter, such as the police department or education or the environment. It can also mean a scoop on some news item.

Bimonthly. Every two months. See also *semimonthly*.

Biweekly. Every two weeks.

Blue-penciling. Editing a manuscript.

Caption. Originally a title or headline over a picture but now a description of the subject matter of a photograph, including names of people where appropriate. Also called cutline.

Chapbook. A small booklet, usually paperback, of poetry, ballads or tales.

Chicago Manual of Style. A format for the typing of manuscripts as established by the University of Chicago Press.

Clean copy. Free of errors, cross-outs, wrinkles, smudges.

Clippings. News items of possible interest to trade magazine editors.

Column inch. All the type contained in one inch of a typeset column.

Contributors' copies. Copies of the issues of a magazine sent to an author in which his/her work appears.

Copy. Manuscript material before it is set in type.

Copy editing. Editing the manuscript for grammar, punctuation and printing style as opposed to subject content.

Copyright. A means to protect an author's work. See "Copyrights and (Copy)Wrongs."

Correspondent. Writer away from the home office of a newspaper or magazine who regularly provides it with copy.

Cutline. See caption.

El-hi. Elementary to high school.

Epigram. A short, witty, sometimes paradoxical saying.

Erotica. Usually fiction that is sexually oriented; although it could be art on the same theme.

Fair use. A provision of the copyright law that says short passages from copyrighted material may be used without infringing on the owner's rights.

Feature. An article giving the reader background information on the news. Also used by magazines to indicate a lead article or distinctive department.

Filler. A short item used by an editor to "fill" out a newspaper column or a page in a magazine. It could be a timeless news item, a joke, an anecdote, some light verse or short humor, a puzzle, etc.

First North American serial rights. See "Stand Up for Your Rights."

Formula story. Familiar theme treated in a predictable plot structure—such as boy meets girl, boy loses girl, boy gets girl.

Gagline. The caption for a cartoon, or the cover teaser line and the punchline on the inside of a studio greeting card.

Ghostwriter. A writer who puts into literary form, an article, speech, story or book based on another person's ideas or knowledge.

Glossy. A black & white photograph with a shiny surface as opposed to one with a non-shiny matte finish.

Gothic novel. One in which the central character is usually a beautiful young girl, the setting is an old mansion or castle; there is a handsome hero and a real menace, either natural or supernatural.

Honorarium. A token payment. It may be a very small amount of money, or simply a byline and copies of the publication in which your material appears.

Illustrations. May be photographs, old engravings, artwork. Usually paid for separately from the manuscript. See also "package sale."

International Postal Reply Coupons. Can be purchased at your local post office and enclosed with your letter or manuscript to a foreign publisher to cover his postage cost when replying.

Invasion of privacy. Cause for suits against some writers who have written about persons (even though truthfully) without their consent.

Kill fee. A portion of the agreed-on price for a complete article that was assigned but which was subsequently cancelled.

Libel. A false accusation; or any published statement or presentation that tends to expose another to public contempt, ridicule, etc. Defenses are truth; fair comment on the matter of public interest; and privileged communication—such as a report of legal proceedings or a client's communication to his lawyer.

Little magazines. Publications of limited circulation, usually on literary or political subject matter.

MLA Handbook. A format for the typing of manuscripts established by the Modern Language Association.

Model release. A paper signed by the subject of a photograph (or his guardian, if a juvenile) giving the photographer permission to use the photograph, editorially or for advertising purposes or for some specific purpose as stated.

Ms. Abbreviation for manuscript.

Mss. Abbreviation for more than one manuscript.

Multiple submissions. Some editors of non-overlapping circulation magazines, such as religious publications, are willing to look at manuscripts which have also been submitted to other editors at the same time. See individual listings for which editors these are. No multiple submissions should be made to larger markets paying good prices for original material, unless it is a query on a highly topical article requiring an immediate response and that fact is so stated in your letter.

Newsbreak. A newsworthy event or item. For example, a clipping about the opening of a new shoe store in a town might be a newsbreak of interest to a trade journal in the shoe industry. Some editors also use the word to mean funny typographical errors.

Novelette. A short novel, or a long short story; 7,000 to 15,000 words approximately.

Offset. Type of printing in which copy and illustrations are photographed and plates made, from which printing is done; as opposed to letterpress printing directly from type metal and engravings of illustrations.

One-time rights. See "Stand Up for Your Rights."

Outline. Of a book is usually a one-page summary of its contents; often in the form of chapter headings with a descriptive sentence or two under each one to show the scope of the book.

Package sale. The editor wants to buy manuscript and photos as a "package" and pay for them in one check.

Page rate. Some magazines pay for material at a fixed rate per published page, rather than so much per word.

Payment on acceptance. The editor sends you a check for your article, story or poem as soon as he reads it and decides to publish it.

Payment on publication. The editor decides to buy your material but doesn't send you a check until he publishes it.

Pen name. The use of a name other than your legal name on articles, stories, or books where you wish to remain anonymous. Simply notify your post office and bank that you are using the name so that you'll receive mail and/or checks in that name.

Photo feature. A feature in which the emphasis is on the photographs rather than any accompanying written material.

Photocopied submissions. Are acceptable to some editors instead of the author's sending his original manuscript. See also multiple submissions.

Plagiarism. Passing off as one's own, the expression of ideas, words to another.

Public domain. Material which was either never copyrighted or whose copyright term has run out.

Publication not copyrighted. Publication of an author's work in such a publication places it in the public domain, and it cannot subsequently be copyrighted. See "Copyrights and (Copy) Wrongs."

Query. A letter of inquiry to an editor eliciting his interest in an article you want to write.

Reporting times. The number of days, weeks, etc., it takes an editor to report back to the author on his query or manuscript.

Reprint rights. See "Stand Up for Your Rights."

Round-up article. Comments from, or interviews with, a number of celebrities or experts on a single theme.

Royalties, standard hardcover book. 10% of the retail price on the first 5,000 copies sold; 12½% on the next 5,000 and 15% thereafter.

Royalties, standard mass paperback book. 4 to 8% of the retail price on the first 150,000 copies sold.

SAE. Self-addressed envelope.

SASE. Self-addressed, stamped envelope.

Second serial rights. See "Stand Up for Your Rights."

Semimonthly. Twice a month.

Semiweekly. Twice a week.

Serial. Published periodically, such as a newspaper or magazine.

Short-short story. Is usually from 500 to 2,000 words.

Simultaneous submissions. Submissions of the same article, story or poem to several publications at the same time.

Slant. The approach of a story or article so as to appeal to the readers of a specific magazine. Does, for example, this magazine always like stories with an upbeat ending? Or does that one like articles aimed only at the blue-collar worker?

Slides. Usually called transparencies by editors looking for color photographs.

Speculation. The editor agrees to look at the author's manuscript but doesn't promise to buy it until he reads it.

Stringer. A writer who submits material to a magazine or newspaper from a specific geographical location.

Style. The way in which something is written—for example, short, punchy sentences of flowing, narrative description or heavy use of quotes of dialogue.

Subsidiary rights. All those rights, other than book publishing rights included in a book contract—such as paperback, book club, movie rights, etc.

Subsidy publisher. A book publisher who charges the author for the cost to typeset and print his book, the jacket, etc., as opposed to a royalty publisher which pays the author.

Syndication rights. A book publisher may sell the rights to a newspaper syndicate to print a book in installments in one or more newspapers.

Tabloids. Newspaper format publication on about half the size of the regular newspaper page, such as as *National Enquirer*.

Tearsheet. Pages from a magazine or newspaper containing your printed story or article or poem.

Think piece. A magazine article that has an intellectual, philosophical, provocative approach to its subject.

Transparencies. Positive color slides; not color prints.

Uncopyrighted publication. Publication of an author's work in such a publication potentially puts it in the public domain.

Unsolicited manuscript. A story, article, poem or book that an editor did not specifically ask to see.

Vanity publisher. See subsidy publisher.

Vignette. A brief scene offering the reader a flash of illumination about a character as opposed to a more formal story with a beginning, middle and end.

I
ndex

H

J

K

N

P